Also by Robert M. Parker, Jr.

BORDEAUX: THE DEFINITIVE GUIDE
FOR THE WINES PRODUCED
SINCE 1961

THE WINES OF THE RHÔNE VALLEY
AND PROVENCE

PARKER'S WINE BUYER'S GUIDE
1987–1988

PARKER'S WINE BUYER'S GUIDE
1989–1990

BURGUNDY: A COMPREHENSIVE GUIDE
TO THE PRODUCERS, APPELLATIONS,
AND WINES

BORDEAUX: A COMPREHENSIVE GUIDE
TO THE WINES PRODUCED
FROM 1961–1990

PARKER'S WINE BUYER'S GUIDE
1993–1994

PARKER'S WINE BUYER'S GUIDE
1994–1995

THE WINES OF THE RHÔNE VALLEY,
REVISED AND EXPANDED EDITION

BORDEAUX: A COMPREHENSIVE GUIDE
TO THE WINES PRODUCED
FROM 1961–1997

PARKER'S WINE BUYER'S GUIDE Fifth Edition

Complete, Easy-to-Use Reference on
Recent Vintages, Prices, and Ratings for More Than
8,000 Wines from All the Major Wine Regions

ROBERT M. PARKER, JR.

A FIRESIDE BOOK
PUBLISHED BY SIMON & SCHUSTER

FIRESIDE
Rockefeller Center
1230 Avenue of the Americas
New York, NY 10020

FIRESIDE and colophon are registered trademarks
of Simon & Schuster, Inc.

Designed by Meryl Sussman Levavi/Digitext, Inc.

Manufactured in the United States of America

1   3   5   7   9   10   8   6   4   2
1   3   5   7   9   10   8   6   4   2   (pbk.)

Library of Congress Cataloging-in-Publication Data

Parker, Robert M.
[Wine buyer's guide]
Parker's wine buyer's guide / Robert M. Parker, Jr.—5th ed.
p.   cm.
"Complete, easy-to-use reference on recent vintages, prices, and ratings
for more than 8,000 wines from all the major wine regions."
Includes index.
1. Wine and wine making.   I. Title: Wine buyer's guide.   II. Title.
TP548.P287 1999
641.2'2—dc21   99-047380

ISBN 0-684-84184-3
ISBN 0-684-80014-4 (pbk.)

Portions of this book were previously published in the
author's bimonthly newsletter, *The Wine Advocate.*

ACKNOWLEDGMENTS

To the following people . . . thanks for your support: Hanna, Johanna and Eric Agostini, Jean-Michel Arcaute, Jim Arseneault, Ruth and the late Bruce Bassin, Jean-Claude Berrouet, Bill Blatch, Jean-Marc Blum, Thomas B. Böhrer, Monique and the late Jean-Eugène Borie, Christopher Cannan, Dick Carretta, Corinne Cesano, Bob Cline, Jean Delmas, Dr. Albert H. Dudley III, Alain Dutournier, Barbara Edelman, Jonathan Edelman, Michael Etzel, Paul Evans, Terry Faughey, Joel Fleischman, Han Cheng Fong, Maryse Fragnaud, Laurence and Bernard Godec, Dan Green, Philippe Guyonnet-Duperat, Josué Harai, Alexandra Harding, Ken-ichi Hori, Dr. David Hutcheon, Brenda Keller, Barbara G. and Steve R. R. Jacoby, Jean-Paul Jauffret, Nathaniel, Archie and Denis Johnston, Ed Jonna, Allen Krasner, Françoise Laboute, Susan and Bob Lescher, Dr. Jay Miller, Bill Molesky, Christian, Jean-François and Jean-Pierre Moueix, Jerry Murphy, Bernard Nicolas, Jill Norman, Les Oenarchs (Bordeaux), Les Oenarchs (Baltimore), Daniel Oliveros, Bob Orenstein, Frank Polk, Bruno Prats, Martha Reddington, Dominique Renard, Dr. Alain Raynaud, Huey Robertson, Helga and Hardy Rodenstock, Dany and Michel Rolland, Yves Rovani, Carlo Russo, Tom Ryder, Ed Sands, Erik Samazeuilh, Bob Schindler, Ernie Singer, Park B. Smith, Jeff Sokolin, Elliott Staren, Daniel Tastet-Lawton, Steven Verlin, Peter Vezan, Robert Vifian, Sona Vogel, Karen and Joseph Weinstock, Larry Wiggins, Jeanyee Wong, Dominique and Gérard Yvernault, Murray Zeligman.

A very special thanks is in order for five people who have done a splendid job in bringing this mass of information to book form: Janice Easton, my editor, and Florence Falkow, my production editor, at Simon & Schuster; Hanna Agostini, my assistant and translator in France, and Joan Passman and Annette Piatek, my assistants stateside. All were immensely helpful, and I am indebted to them.

Lastly, I want to acknowledge the superb information my assistant, Pierre-Antoine Rovani, has provided. This material has undoubtedly improved the quality of this guide.

To Les Oenarques, Roger Bessières,
Henri Boyreau, Pierre Castéja,
Georges Chambarière, Jacques Debayle,
Jean-Bernard Delmas, Bernard Ginestet, and
Jean-François Moueix, who represent the
essence of wine connoisseurship and
generous comradeship.

CONTENTS

INTRODUCTION

HOW TO USE THIS GUIDE

This book is both an educational and a buying manual; it is not an encyclopedic listing of wine producers and growers. It is intended to make the reader a more formidable, more confident wine buyer by providing sufficient insider's information to permit the wisest possible choice when making a wine-buying decision. The finest producers as well as the best known (not necessarily a guarantee of quality) from the world's greatest viticultural regions are evaluated, as well as many of the current and upcoming releases available in the marketplace. If readers cannot find a specific vintage of a highly regarded wine, they still have at their fingertips a wealth of information and evaluations concerning the best producers for each viticultural area. Readers should be confident in knowing that they will rarely make a mistake (unless, of course, the vintage is absolutely dreadful) with a producer rated "outstanding" or "excellent" in this buying manual. These producers are the finest and most consistent in the world. Taste is obviously subjective, but I have done my best to provide an impartial and comprehensive consumer's guide, whose heart, soul, and value are the evaluations (star ratings) of the world's finest producers.

Note: Readers should recognize that my assistant, Pierre-Antoine Rovani, has written the tasting notes and numerical scores for the following chapters: Red Burgundy, White Burgundy, Washington State, Alsace, Oregon, The Loire Valley, Germany, and New Zealand.

ORGANIZATION

Each section on a specific viticultural region covered in this manual is generally organized as follows:
1. An overview of the viticultural region
2. A buying strategy
3. A summary of the quality of recent vintages for the area
4. A quick reference chart to that area's best producers/growers
5. Tasting commentaries, a specific numerical rating for the wine, and a general retail price range for a 750 ml bottle of wine. (See the Wine Price Guide on page 15, which explains the coding system.)

VITICULTURAL AREAS COVERED

This guide covers the world's major viticultural regions. In Western Europe, France and Italy receive the most detailed coverage, followed by Spain, Portugal, and Germany. In North America, California receives significant coverage, reflecting its dominance in the marketplace. The wine regions that are represented most significantly in wine shops are given much more detailed coverage than minor areas whose wines are rarely seen in or exported to the United States. Consequently, the sections dealing with Bordeaux, Burgundy, Champagne, Alsace, and the Rhône Valley in France; Piedmont and Tuscany in Italy; and California receive priority in terms of the amount of coverage because those regions produce the world's greatest wines. In each section there is a thorough analysis of the region's producers, its overachievers and underachievers, as well as the region's greatest wine values.

RATING THE PRODUCERS AND GROWERS

Who's who in the world of wine becomes readily apparent after years of tasting the wines and visiting the vineyards and wine cellars of the world's producers and growers. Great producers are, unfortunately, still quite rare, but certainly more growers and producers today are making better wine, with better technology and more knowledge. The charts that follow rate the best producers on a five-star system, awarding five stars and an "outstanding" to those producers deemed to be the very best, four stars to those producers who are "excellent," three stars to "good" producers, and two stars to those producers rated "average." Since the aim of this book is to provide you with the names of the very best producers, its overall content is dominated by the top producers rather than the less successful ones.

Those few growers/producers who have received five-star ratings are those who make the world's finest wines, and they have been selected for this rating because of the following two reasons: 1) They make the greatest wine of their particular viticultural region, and 2) they are remarkably consistent and reliable even in mediocre and poor vintages. Ratings, whether they be numerical ratings of individual wines or classifications of growers, are always likely to create controversy among not only the growers but among wine tasters themselves. But if done impartially, with a global viewpoint and firsthand, on-the-premises (sur place) knowledge of the wines, the producers, and the type and quality of the winemaking, such ratings can be reliable and powerfully informative. The important thing for readers to remember is that those growers/producers who received either a four-star or five-star rating are producers to search out; I suspect few consumers will ever be disappointed with one of their wines. The three-star-rated growers/producers are less consistent but can be expected to make average to above-average wines in the very good to excellent vintages. Their weaknesses can be either from the fact that their vineyards are not as strategically placed, or because for financial or other reasons they are unable to make the severe selections necessary to make only the finest-quality wine.

The rating of the growers/producers of the world's major viticultural regions is perhaps the most important point in this book. Years of wine tasting have taught me many things, but the more one tastes and assimilates the knowledge of the world's regions, the more one begins to isolate the handful of truly world-class growers and producers who seem to rise above the crowd in great as well as mediocre vintages. I always admonish consumers against blind faith in one grower or producer, or in one specific vintage. But the producers and growers rated "outstanding" and "excellent" are as close to a guarantee of high quality as you are likely to find.

VINTAGE SUMMARIES

Although wine advertisements proclaiming "a great vintage" abound, I have never known more than several viticultural areas of the world to have a great vintage in the same year. The chances of a uniformly great vintage are extremely remote, simply because of significantly different microclimates, soils, and so on in every wine-producing region. It is easy to fall into the trap of thinking that because Bordeaux had great vintages in 1982, 1989, and 1990, every place else in Europe did too. Certainly in 1982 nothing could have been further from the truth. Nevertheless, a Bordeaux vintage's reputation unfortunately seems to dictate what the world thinks about many other wine-producing areas. This obviously creates many problems, since in poor Bordeaux vintages the Rhône or Alsace or Champagne could have an excellent vintage, and in great Bordeaux vintages those same areas could have bad years because of poor climate conditions. For California, many casual observers seem to think every year is a top year, and this image is, of course, promoted by that state's publicity-conscious Wine Institute. It may be true that California rarely has a disastrous vintage, but tasting certainly proves that 1988 and 1989 are different in style and more irregular in quality than either 1994 or 1995. Yet no other viticultural area in the world has enjoyed as many consecutive great vintages as California has in the nineties; 1990, 1991, 1992, 1993, 1994, 1995, 1996, and probably 1997 have all been terrific years for California. In this guide, there are vintage summaries for each viticultural area because the vintages are so very different in both quantity and quality. Never make the mistake of assuming that one particular year is great everywhere or poor everywhere. I know of no year when that has happened.

TASTING NOTES AND RATINGS

When possible, most of my tastings are done in peer-group, single-blind conditions; in other words, the same type of wines are tasted against each other, and the producers' names are not known. The ratings reflect an independent, critical look at the wines. Neither price nor the reputation of the grower/producer affects the rating in any manner. I spend three months of every year tasting in vineyards. During the other nine months, I devote six- and sometimes seven-day workweeks solely to tasting and writing. I do not participate in wine judgings or trade tastings for many reasons, but principal among these are the following: 1) I prefer to taste from an entire bottle of wine, 2) I find it essential to have properly sized and cleaned professional tasting glasses, 3) the temperature of the wine must be correct, and 4) I prefer to determine the amount of time allocated for the number of wines I will critique.

The numerical rating given is a guide to what I think of the wine vis-à-vis its peer group. Certainly, wines rated above 85 are good to excellent, and any wine rated 90 or above will be outstanding for its particular type. While some would suggest that scoring is not well suited to a beverage that has been romantically extolled for centuries, wine is no different from any consumer product. There are specific standards of quality that full-time wine professionals recognize, and there are benchmark wines against which all others can be judged. I know of no one with three or four different glasses of wine in front of him or her, regardless of how good or bad the wines might be, who cannot say "I prefer this one to that one." Scoring wines is simply taking a professional's opinion and applying a numerical system to it on a consistent basis. Moreover, scoring permits rapid communication of information to expert and novice alike.

The score given for a specific wine reflects the quality of the wine at its best. I often tell people that evaluating a wine and assigning a score to a beverage that will change and evolve in many cases for up to ten or more years is analogous to taking a photograph of a marathon runner. Much can be ascertained, but, like a picture of a moving object, the wine will also evolve and change. I try to retaste wines from obviously badly corked or defective bottles, since a wine from such a single bad bottle does not indicate an entirely spoiled batch. If retasting is not possible, I will reserve judgment on that wine. Many of the wines reviewed have been tasted several times, and the score represents a cumulative average of the wine's performance in tastings to date. Scores do not reveal the most important facts about a wine. The written commentary (tasting notes) that accompanies the ratings is a better source of information regarding the wine's style and personality, its relative quality level vis-à-vis its peers, and its relative value and aging potential than any score could ever indicate.

Here, then, is a general guide to interpreting the numerical ratings:

90–100 is equivalent to an A and is given for an outstanding or a special effort. Wines in this category are the very best produced for their type. There is a big difference between a 90 and a 99, but both are top marks. Few wines actually make it into this top category, simply because there are not that many truly great wines.

80–89 is equivalent to a B in school, and such a wine, particularly in the 85–89 range, is very good. Many of the wines that fall into this range are often great values as well. I have many of these wines in my personal cellar.

70–79 represents a C, or an average mark, but obviously 79 is a much more desirable rating than 70. Wines that receive scores between 75 and 79 are generally pleasant, straightforward wines that lack complexity, character, or depth. If inexpensive, they may be ideal for uncritical quaffing.

Below 70 is a D or an F, depending on where you went to school. It is a sign of an unbalanced, flawed, or terribly dull or diluted wine that is of little interest to the discriminating consumer.

Note: A point score in parentheses (75–80) signifies an evaluation made before the wine was bottled.

In terms of awarding points, my scoring system gives a wine 50 points to start with. The wine's general color and appearance merit up to 5 points. Since most wines today have been well made thanks to modern technology and the increased use of professional oenologists, most tend to receive at least 4, often 5 points. The aroma and bouquet merit up to 15 points, depending on the intensity level and dimension of the aroma and bouquet, as well as the wine's cleanliness. The flavor and finish merit up to 20 points, and again, intensity of flavor, balance, cleanliness, and depth and length on the palate are all important considerations when giving out points. Finally, the overall quality level or potential for further evolution and improvement—aging—merits up to 10 points.

Scores are important for the reader to gauge a professional critic's overall qualitative placement of a wine vis-à-vis its peers. However, it is also vital to consider the description of the wine's style, personality, and potential. No scoring system is perfect, but a system that provides for flexibility in scores, if applied by the same experienced taster without prejudice, 1) can quantify different levels of wine quality, and 2) can be a responsible, reliable, uncensored, and highly informative account that provides the reader with one professional's judgment. There can never be any substitute, however, for your own palate nor any better education than tasting the wine yourself.

QUOTED PRICES

For a number of reasons, no one's suggested retail price for a particular wine is valid throughout the country. Take Bordeaux as an example. Bordeaux is often sold as "wine futures" 2 full years before the wine is bottled and shipped to America. This opening or base price can often be the lowest price one will encounter for a Bordeaux wine, particularly if there is a great demand for the wines because the vintage is reputed to be excellent or outstanding. Prices will always vary for Bordeaux, as well as for other imported wines, according to the quality of the vintage, the exchange rate of the dollar against foreign currencies, and the time of purchase by the retailer, wholesaler, or importer. Was the Bordeaux wine purchased at a low futures price in the spring following the vintage, or was the wine purchased when it had peaked in price and was very expensive?

Another consideration in pricing is that, in many states, wine retailers can directly import the wines they sell and can thereby bypass middlemen, such as wholesalers, who usually tack on a 25% markup of their own. The bottom line in all of this is that in any given vintage for Bordeaux, or for any imported wine, there is no standard suggested retail price. Prices can differ by as much as 50% for the same wine in the same city. However, in cities where there is tremendous competition among wine shops, the markup for wines can be as low as 10% or even 5%; this is significantly less than the normal 50%–55% markup. In cities where there is little competition, the prices charged are often full retail price. I always recommend that consumers pay close attention to the wine shop advertisements in major newspapers and wine publications. For example, *The New York Times*'s Living Section and *The Wine Spectator* are filled with wine advertisements that are a barometer for the market price of a given wine. Readers should remember, however, that prices differ considerably, not only within the same state, but also within the same city. The approximate price range that is used reflects the suggested retail price that includes a 40%–60% markup by the retailer in most major metropolitan areas. Therefore, in many states in the Midwest and in other less populated areas where there is little competition among wine merchants, the price may be higher. In major competitive marketplaces where there are frequent discount wars, such as Washington, D.C., New York, San Francisco, Boston, Los Angeles, Chicago, and Dallas, prices are often lower. The key for you as the reader and consumer is to follow the advertisements in a major newspaper and to shop around. Most major wine retailers feature sales in the fall and spring; summer is the slow season and generally the most expensive time to buy wine.

Following is the price guide I have used throughout the book.

WINE PRICE GUIDE

A: Inexpensive—less than $10
B: Moderate—between $10 and $20
C: Expensive—between $20 and $35
D: Very expensive—between $35 and $60
E: Luxury—between $60 and $100
EE: Super luxury—between $100 and $175
EEE: Over $175

THE ROLE OF A WINE CRITIC

"A man must serve his time to every trade save censure—critics all are ready made." Thus wrote Lord Byron.

It has been said often enough that anyone with a pen, notebook, and a few bottles of wine can become a wine critic. And that is exactly the way I started when, in late summer 1978, I sent out a complimentary issue of what was then called the *Baltimore/Washington Wine Advocate*.

There were two principal forces that shaped my view of a wine critic's responsibilities. I was then, and remain today, significantly influenced by the independent philosophy of consumer advocate Ralph Nader. Moreover, I was marked by the indelible impression left by my law school professors, who pounded into their students' heads in the post-Watergate era a broad definition of conflict of interest. These two forces have governed the purpose and soul of my newsletter, *The Wine Advocate*, and my books.

In short, the role of the critic is to render judgments that are reliable. They should be based on extensive experience and on a trained sensibility for whatever is being reviewed. In practical terms, this means the critic should be blessed with the following attributes:

Independence   It is imperative for a wine critic to pay his own way. Gratuitous hospitality in the form of airline tickets, hotel rooms, guest houses, etc., should never be accepted either abroad or in this country. And what about wine samples? I purchase over 75% of the wines I taste, and while I have never requested samples, I do not feel it is unethical to accept unsolicited samples that are shipped to my office. Many wine writers claim that these favors do not influence their opinions. Yet how many people in any profession are prepared to bite the hand that feeds them? Irrefutably, the target audience is the wine consumer, not the wine trade. While it is important to maintain a professional relationship with the trade, I believe the independent stance required of a consumer advocate often, not surprisingly, results in an adversarial relationship with the wine trade. It can be no other way. In order to effectively pursue this independence, it is imperative to keep one's distance from the trade. While this can be misinterpreted as aloofness, such independence guarantees hard-hitting, candid, and uninfluenced commentary.

Courage   Courage manifests itself in what I call the "democratic tasting." Judgments ought to be made solely on the basis of the product in the bottle, and not on the pedigree, the price, the rarity, or one's like or dislike of the producer. The wine critic who is totally candid may be considered dangerous by the trade, but an uncensored, independent point of view is of paramount importance to the consumer. A judgment of wine quality must be based on what is in the bottle. This is wine criticism at its purest, most meaningful. In a tasting, a $10 bottle of petit château Pauillac should have as much of a chance as a $200 bottle of Lafite-Rothschild or Latour. Overachievers should be spotted, praised, and their names highlighted and shared with the consuming public. Underachievers should be singled out for criticism and called to account for their mediocrities. Few friends from the wine commerce are likely to be earned for such outspoken and irreverent commentary, but wine buyers are entitled to such information. When a critic bases his or her judgment on what others think, or on the wine's pedigree, price, or perceived potential, then wine criticism is nothing more than a sham.

Experience   It is essential to taste extensively across the field of play to identify the benchmark reference points and to learn winemaking standards throughout the world. This is the most time-consuming and expensive aspect of wine criticism, as well as the most fulfilling for the critic; yet it is rarely followed. Lamentably, what so often transpires is that a tasting of ten or twelve wines from a specific region or vintage will be held. The writer will then issue a definitive judgment on the vintage based on a microscopic proportion of the wines. This is as irresponsible as it is appalling. It is essential for a wine critic to taste as comprehensibly as is physically possible. This means tasting every significant wine produced in a region or vintage before reaching qualitative conclusions. Wine criticism, if it is ever to be regarded as a serious profession, must be a full-time endeavor, not the habitat of part-timers dabbling in a field that is so complex and requires such time commitment. Wine and vintages, like everything in life, cannot be reduced to black and white answers.

It is also essential to establish memory reference points for the world's greatest wines. There is such a diversity of wine and such a multitude of styles that this may seem impossible. But tasting as many wines as one possibly can in each vintage, and from all of the classic wine regions, helps one memorize benchmark characteristics that form the basis for making comparative judgments between vintages, wine producers, and wine regions.

Individual Accountability   While I have never found anyone's wine-tasting notes compelling reading, notes issued by consensus of a committee are the most insipid, and often the most misleading. Judgments by committees tend to sum up a group's personal preferences. But how do they take into consideration the possibility that each individual may have reached his or her decision using totally different criteria? Did one judge adore the wine because of its typicity while another decried it for such, or was the wine's individuality given greater merit? It is impossible to know. That is never in doubt when an individual authors a tasting critique.

Committees rarely recognize wines of great individuality. A look at the results of tasting competitions sadly reveals that well-made mediocrities garner the top prizes. The misleading consequence is that blandness is elevated to the status of being a virtue. Wines with great individuality and character will never win a committee tasting because at least one taster will find something objectionable about the wine.

I have always sensed that individual tasters, because they are unable to hide behind the collective voice of a committee, hold themselves to a greater degree of accountability. The opinion of a reasonably informed and comprehensive individual taster, despite the taster's prejudices and predilections, is always a far greater guide to the ultimate quality of the wine than the consensus of a committee. At least the reader knows where the individual stands, whereas with a committee, one is never quite sure.

Emphasis on Pleasure and Value Too much wine writing focuses on glamour French wine regions such as Burgundy, Bordeaux, and on California Cabernet Sauvignon and Chardonnay. These are important, and they make up the backbone of most serious wine enthusiasts' cellars. But value and diversity in wine types must always be stressed. The unhealthy legacy of the English wine-writing establishment that a wine has to taste bad young to be great old should be thrown out. Wines that taste great young, such as Chenin Blanc, Dolcetto, Beaujolais, Côtes du Rhône, Merlot, and Zinfandel, are no less serious or compelling because they must be drunk within a few years rather than be cellared for a decade or more before consumption. Wine is, in the final analysis, a beverage of pleasure, and intelligent wine criticism should be a blend of both hedonistic and analytical schools of thought—to the exclusion of neither.

The Focus on Qualitative Issues It is an inescapable fact that too many of the world's renowned growers/producers have intentionally permitted production levels to soar to such extraordinary heights that many wines' personalities, concentration, and character are in jeopardy. While there remain a handful of fanatics who continue, at some financial sacrifice, to reject significant proportions of their harvest to ensure that only the finest-quality wine is sold under their name, they are dwindling in number. For much of the last decade production yields throughout the world have broken records, almost with each new vintage. The results are wines that increasingly lack character, concentration, and staying power. The argument that more carefully and competently managed vineyards result in larger crops is nonsense.

In addition to high yields, advances in technology have provided the savoir faire to produce more correct wines, but the abuse of practices such as acidification and excessive fining and filtration have compromised the final product. These problems are rarely and inadequately addressed by the wine-writing community. Wine prices have never been higher, but is the consumer always getting a better wine? The wine writer has the responsibility to give broad qualitative issues high priority.

Candor No one argues with the incontestable fact that tasting is a subjective endeavor. The measure of an effective wine critic should be his or her timely and useful rendering of an intelligent laundry list of good examples of different styles of winemaking in various price categories. Articulating in an understandable fashion why the critic finds the wines enthralling or objectionable is manifestly important both to the reader and to the producer. The critic must always seek to educate, to provide meaningful guidelines, never failing to emphasize that there can never be any substitute for the consumer's palate, nor any better education than the reader's own tasting of the wine. The critic has the advantage of having access to the world's wine production and must try to minimize bias. Yet the critic should always share with the reader his or her reasoning for bad reviews. For example, I will never be able to overcome my dislike for vegetal-tasting New World Cabernets, overtly herbaceous red Loire Valley wines, or excessively acidified New World whites.

My ultimate goal in writing about wines is to seek out the world's greatest wines and greatest wine values. But in the process of ferreting out those wines, I feel the critic should never shy away from criticizing those producers whose wines are found lacking. Given the fact that the consumer is the true taster of record, the "taste no evil" approach to wine writing serves no one but the wine trade. Constructive and competent criticism has proven that it can benefit producers as well as consumers, since it forces underachievers to improve the quality of their fare, and by lauding overachievers, it encourages them to maintain high standards to the benefit of all who enjoy and appreciate good wine.

About Wine

HOW TO BUY WINE

On the surface, having made your choices in advance, buying wine seems simple enough—you go to your favorite wine merchant and purchase a few bottles. However, there are some subtleties to buying wine that one must be aware of in order to ensure that the wine is in healthy condition and is unspoiled.

To begin with, take a look at the bottle of wine you are about to buy. Wine abuse is revealed by the condition of the bottle in your hand. First of all, if the cork has popped above the rim of the bottle and is pushed out on the lead or plastic capsule that covers the top of the bottle, then look for another bottle. Wines that have been exposed to very high temperatures expand in the bottle, thereby putting pressure on the cork and pushing it upward against the capsule. And it is the highest-quality wines, those that have not been overly filtered or pasteurized, that are the most vulnerable to the ill effects of abusive transportation or storage. A wine that has been frozen in transit or storage will likewise push the cork out, and while the freezing of a wine is less damaging than the heating of it, both are hazardous to its health. Any cork that is protruding above the rim of the bottle is a bad sign, and the bottle should be returned to the shelf and never, ever purchased.

Finally, there is a sign indicating poor storage conditions that can generally be determined only after the wine has been decanted, though sometimes it can be spotted in the neck of the bottle. Wines that have been exposed to very high temperatures, particularly deep, rich, intense, red wines, will often form a heavy coat or film of coloring material on the inside of the glass. With a Bordeaux that is less than 3 years old, a coating such as this generally indicates that the wine has been subjected to very high temperatures and has undoubtedly been damaged. However, one must be careful here, because this type of sediment does not always indicate a poor bottle of wine; vintage port regularly throws it as do the huge, rich Rhône and Piedmontese wines.

On the other hand, there are two conditions consumers frequently think are signs of a flawed wine when nothing could be further from the truth. Many consumers return bottles of wine for the very worst reason—because of a small deposit of sediment in the bottom of the bottle. Ironically, this is actually the healthiest sign one could find in most bottles of wine. Keep in mind, however, that white wines rarely throw a deposit, and it is rare to see a deposit in young wines under 2 to 3 years of age. The tiny particles of sandlike sediment that precipitate to the bottom of a bottle simply indicate that the wine has been naturally made and has not been subjected to a flavor- and character-eviscerating traumatic filtration. Such wine is truly alive and is usually full of all its natural flavors.

Another reason that wine consumers erroneously return bottles to retailers is because of the presence of small crystals called tartrate precipitates. These crystals are found in all types of wines but appear most commonly in white wines from Germany and Alsace. They often shine and resemble little slivers of cut glass, but in fact they are simply indicative of a wine that somewhere along its journey was exposed to temperatures below 40°F in shipment, and the cold has caused some tartaric crystals to precipitate. These are harmless, tasteless, and totally natural in many bottles of wine. They have no effect on the quality and they normally signify that the wine has not been subjected to an abusive, sometimes damaging, cold stabilization treatment by the winery for cosmetic purposes only.

Fortunately, most of the better wine merchants, wholesalers, and importers are more cognizant today of the damage that can be done by shipping wine in unrefrigerated containers, especially in the middle of summer. Far too many wines are still tragically damaged by poor transportation and storage, and it is the consumer who suffers. A general rule is that heat is much more damaging to fine wines than cold. Remember, there are still plenty of wine merchants, wholesalers, and importers who treat wine no differently than they treat beer or liquor, and the wine buyer must therefore be armed with a bit of knowledge before he or she buys a bottle of wine.

HOW TO STORE WINE

Wine has to be stored properly if it is to be served in a healthy condition. All wine enthusiasts know that subterranean wine cellars that are vibration-free, dark, damp, and kept at a constant 55°F are considered perfect for wine. Few of us, however, have our own castles and such perfect accommodations for our beloved wines. While such conditions are ideal, most wines will thrive and develop well under other circumstances. I have tasted many old Bordeaux wines from closets and basements that have reached 65–70 degrees F in summer, and the wines have been perfect. In cellaring wine keep the following rules in mind and you will not be disappointed with a wine that has gone over the hill prematurely.

First of all, in order to safely cellar wines for 10 years or more, keep them at 65°F, perhaps 68 but no higher. If the temperature rises to 70°F, be prepared to drink your red wines within 10 years. Under no circumstances should you store and cellar white wines more than 1 to 2 years at temperatures above 70°F. Wines kept at temperatures above 65°F will age faster, but unless the temperature exceeds 70°F, they will not age badly. If you can somehow get the temperature down to 65°F or below, you will never have to worry about the condition of your wines. At 55°F, the ideal temperature according to the textbooks, the wines actually evolve so slowly that your grandchildren are likely to benefit from the wines more than you. Constancy in temperature is most essential, and any changes in temperature should occur slowly. White wines are much more fragile and much more sensitive to temperature changes and higher temperatures than red wines. Therefore, if you do not have ideal storage conditions, buy only enough white wine to drink over a 1- to 2-year period.

Second, be sure that your storage area is odor-free, vibration-free, and dark. A humidity level above 50% is essential; 70%–75% is ideal. The problem with a humidity level over 75% is that the labels become moldy and deteriorate. A humidity level below 40% will keep the labels in great shape but will cause the corks to become very dry, possibly shortening the potential life expectancy of your wine. Low humidity is believed to be nearly as great a threat to a wine's health as high temperature. There has been no research to prove this, and limited studies I have done are far from conclusive.

Third, always bear in mind that wines from vintages that have produced powerful, rich, concentrated, full-bodied wines travel and age significantly better than wines from vintages that have produced lighter-weight wines. It is often traumatic for a fragile, lighter-styled wine from either Europe or California to be transported transatlantic or cross country, whereas the richer, more intense, bigger wines from the better vintages seem much less travel-worn after their journey.

Fourth, in buying and storing wine I always recommend buying a wine as soon as it appears on the market, assuming of course that you have tasted the wine and like it. The reason for this is that there are still too many American wine merchants, importers, wholesalers, and distributors who are indifferent to the way wine is stored. This attitude still persists, though things have improved dramatically over the last decade. The important thing for you as a consumer to remember, after inspecting the bottle to make sure it appears healthy, is to stock up on wines as quickly as they come on the market and to approach older vintages with a great deal of caution and hesitation unless you have absolute faith in the merchant from whom you have bought the wine. Furthermore, you should be confident that your merchant will stand behind the wine in the event it is flawed from poor storage.

THE QUESTION OF HOW MUCH AGING

The majority of wines made in the world taste best when they are just released or consumed within 1 to 2 years of the vintage. Many wines are drinkable at 5, 10, or even 15 years of age, but based on my experience only a small percentage are more interesting and more enjoyable after extended cellaring than they were when originally released.

It is important to have a working definition of what the aging of wine actually means. I define the process as nothing more than the ability of a wine, over time, (1) to develop more pleasurable nuances, (2) to expand and soften in texture and, in the case of red wines, to exhibit an additional melting away of tannins, and (3) to reveal a more compelling aromatic and flavor profile. In short, the wine must deliver additional complexity, increased pleasure, and more interest as an older wine than it did when released. Only such a performance can justify the purchase of a wine in its youth for the purpose of cellaring it for future drinking. Unfortunately, just a tiny percentage of the world's wines fall within this definition of aging.

It is fundamentally false to believe that a wine cannot be serious or profound if it is drunk young. In France, the finest Bordeaux, the northern Rhône Valley wines (particularly Hermitage and Côte Rôtie), a few red burgundies, some Châteauneuf du Papes, and, surprisingly, many of the sweet white Alsace wines and sweet Loire Valley wines do indeed age well and are frequently much more enjoyable and complex when drunk 5, 10, or even 15 years after the vintage. But virtually all other French wines, from Champagne to Côtes du Rhône, from Beaujolais to the petits châteaux of Bordeaux, to even the vast majority of red and white burgundies, are better in their youth.

The French have long adhered to the wine-drinking strategy that younger is better. Centuries of wine consumption, not to mention gastronomic indulgences, have taught the French something that Americans and Englishmen have failed to grasp: Most wines are more pleasurable and friendly when young than old.

The French know that the aging and cellaring of wines, even those of high pedigree, are often fraught with more disappointments than successes. Nowhere is this more in evidence than in French restaurants, especially in Bordeaux, the region that boasts what the world considers the longest-lived dry red wines. A top vintage of Bordeaux can last for 20 to 30 years, sometimes 40 or more, but look at the wine lists of Bordeaux's best restaurants. The great 1982s have long disappeared down the throats of French men and women. Even the tannic, young, yet potentially very promising 1996 Medocs, which Americans have squirreled away for drinking in the next century, are now hard to find. Why? Because they have already been consumed. Many of the deluxe restaurants, particularly in Paris, have wine lists of historic vintages, but these are largely for rich tourists.

This phenomenon is not limited to France. Similar drinking habits prevail in the restaurants of Florence, Rome, Madrid, and Barcelona. Italians and Spaniards also enjoy their wines young. This is not to suggest that Italy does not make some wines that improve in the bottle. In Tuscany, for example, a handful of Chiantis and some of the finest new-breed Tuscan red wines (e.g., the famed Cabernet Sauvignon called Sassicaia) will handsomely repay extended cellaring, but most never get the opportunity. In the Piedmont section of northern Italy, no one will deny that a fine Barbaresco or Barolo improves after a decade in the bottle. But by and large, all of Italy's other wines are meant to be drunk young, a fact that Italians have long known and that you should observe as well.

With respect to Spain, there is little difference, although a Spaniard's tastes differ considerably from the average Italian's or Frenchman's. In Spain, the intense aroma of smoky vanillin new oak is prized. As a result, the top Spanish wine producers from the most renowned wine region, Rioja, and other viticultural regions as well tend to age their wines in oak barrels so that they can develop this particular aroma. Additionally, unlike French and Italian wine producers, or even their New World counterparts, Spanish wineries are reluctant to release their wines until they are fully mature. As a result, most Spanish wines are smooth and mellow when they arrive on the market. While they may keep for 5 to 10 years, they generally do not improve. This is especially true of Spain's most expensive wines, the Reservas and Gran Reservas from Rioja, which are usually not released until 5 to 8 years after the vintage. The one exception may be the wine long considered Spain's greatest red, the Vega Sicilia Unico. This powerful wine, frequently released when it is already 10 or 20 years old (the immortal 1970 was released in 1995), does appear capable of lasting for 20–35 years after its release. Yet I wonder how much it improves.

All of this impacts on the following notion: Unlike any other wine consumers in the world, most American wine enthusiasts, as well as many English consumers, fret over the perfect moment to drink a wine. There is none. Most modern-day vintages, even age-worthy Bordeaux or Rhône Valley wines, can be drunk when released. Some of them will improve, but many will not. If you enjoy drinking a 1990 Bordeaux now, then who could be so foolish as to suggest that you are making an error because the wine will be appreciably better in 5 to 10 years?

In America and Australia, winemaking is much more dominated by technology. While a handful of producers still adhere to the artisanal, traditional way of making wine as done in Europe, most treat the vineyard as a factory and the winemaking as a manufacturing process. As a result, such techniques as excessive acidification, brutally traumatic centrifugation, and eviscerating sterile filtration are routinely utilized to produce squeaky clean, simplistic, sediment-free, spit-polished, totally stable yet innocuous wines with statistical profiles that fit neatly within strict technical parameters. Yet it is these same techniques that denude wines of their flavors, aromas, and pleasure-giving qualities. Moreover, they reveal a profound lack of respect for the vineyard, the varietal, the vintage, and the wine consumer, who, after all, is seeking pleasure, not blandness.

In both Australia and California, the alarming tendency of most Sauvignon Blancs and Chardonnays to collapse in the bottle and to drop their fruit within 2 to 3 years of the vintage has been well documented. Yet some of California's and Australia's most vocal advocates continue to advise wine consumers to cellar and invest (a deplorable word when it comes to wine) in Chardonnays and Sauvignon Blancs. It is a stupid policy. If the aging of wine is indeed the ability of a wine to become more interesting and pleasurable with time, then the rule of thumb to be applied to American and Australian Sauvignon Blancs and Chardonnays is that they must be drunk within 12 months of their release unless the consumer has an eccentric fetish for fruitless wines with blistering acidity and scorchingly noticeable alcohol levels. Examples of producers whose Chardonnays and Sauvignon Blancs can last for 5 to 10 years and improve during that period can be found, but they are distressingly few.

With respect to red wines, a slightly different picture emerges. Take, for example, the increasingly fashionable wines made from the Pinot Noir grape. No one doubts the immense progress made in both California and Oregon in turning out fragrant, supple Pinot Noirs that are delicious upon release. But I do not know of any American producer who is making Pinot Noir that can actually improve beyond 10 to 12 years in the bottle. Under no circumstances is this a criticism.

Even in Burgundy there are probably no more than a dozen producers who make their wines in such a manner that they improve and last for more than a decade. Many of these wines can withstand the test of time in the sense of being survivors, but they are far less interesting and pleasurable at age 10 than they were at 2 or 3 years old. Of course the producers and retailers who specialize in these wines will argue otherwise, but they are in the business of selling. Do not be bamboozled by the public relations arm of the wine industry or the fallacious notion that red wines all improve with age. If you enjoy them young, and most likely you will, then buy only the quantities needed for near-term consumption.

America's most famous dry red wine, however, is not Pinot Noir but Cabernet Sauvignon, particularly that grown in California and to a lesser extent in Washington State. The idea that most California Cabernet Sauvignons improve in the bottle is a myth. Nonetheless, the belief that all California Cabernet Sauvignons are incapable of lasting in the bottle is equally unfounded. Today no one would be foolish enough to argue that the best California Cabernets cannot tolerate 15 or 20, even 25 or 30 years of cellaring.

I frequently have the opportunity to taste 20- to 30-year-old California Cabernet Sauvignons, and they are delicious. But have they significantly improved because of the aging process? A few of them have, though most still tend to be relatively grapey, somewhat monolithic, earthy, and tannic at age 20. Has the consumer's patience in cellaring these wines for all those years justified both the expense and the wait? Lamentably, the answer will usually be no. Most of these wines are no more complex or mellow than they were when young. Because these wines will not crack up and fall apart, there is little risk associated with stashing the best of them away, but I am afraid the consumer who patiently waits for the proverbial "miracle in the bottle" will find that wine cellaring can all too frequently be an expensive exercise in futility.

If you think it over, the most important issue is why so many of today's wines exhibit scant improvement in the aging process. While most have always been meant to be drunk when young, I am convinced that much of the current winemaking philosophy has led to numerous compromises in the winemaking process. The advent of micropore sterile filters, so much in evidence at every modern winery, may admirably stabilize a wine, but, regrettably, these filters also destroy the potential of a wine to develop a complex aromatic profile. When they are utilized by wine producers who routinely fertilize their vineyards excessively, thus overcropping, the results are wines that reveal an appalling lack of bouquet and flavor.

The prevailing winemaking obsession is to stabilize wine so it can be shipped to the far corners of the world 12 months a year, stand upright in overheated stores indefinitely, and never change or spoil if exposed to extremes of heat and cold or unfriendly storage conditions. For all intents and purposes, the wine is no longer alive. This is fine, even essential, for inexpensive jug wines, but for the fine-wine market, where consumers are asked to pay $30 or more for a bottle of wine, it is a winemaking tragedy. These stabilization and production techniques thus impact on the aging of wine because they preclude the development of the wine's ability to evolve and to become a more complex, tasty, profound, and enjoyable beverage.

HOW TO SERVE WINE

There are really no secrets for proper wine service—all one needs is a good corkscrew, clean, odor-free glasses, a sense of order as to how wines should be served, and whether a wine needs to be aired or allowed to breathe. The major mistakes that most Americans, as well as most restaurants, make are 1) fine white wines are served entirely too cold, 2) fine red wines are served entirely too warm, and 3) too little attention is given to the glass into which the wine is poured. (It might contain a soapy residue or stale aromas picked up in a closed china closet or cardboard box.) All of these things can do much more to damage the impact of a fine wine and its subtle aromas than you might imagine. Most people tend to think that the wine must be opened and allowed to "breathe" well in advance of serving. Some even think a wine must be decanted, a rather elaborate procedure, but essential only if sediment is present in the bottle and the wine is to be poured carefully off. With respect to breathing or airing wine, I am not sure anyone has all the answers. Certainly, no white wine requires any advance opening and pouring. With red wines, 15–30 minutes of being opened and poured into a clean, odor- and soap-free wine decanter is really all that is necessary. There are of course examples that can always be cited where the wine improves for 7 to 8 hours, but these are quite rare.

Although these topics seem to dominate much of the discussion in wine circles, a much more critical aspect for me is the appropriate temperature of the wine and of the glass in which it is to be served. The temperature of red wines is very important, and in America's generously heated dining rooms, temperatures are often 75°–80°F, higher than is good for fine red wines. A red wine served at such a temperature will taste flat and flabby, with its bouquet diffuse and unfocused. The alcohol content will also seem higher than it should be. The ideal temperature for most red wines is 62°–67°F; light red wine such as Beaujolais should be chilled to 55°F. For white wines, 55°–60°F is perfect, since most will show all their complexity and intensity at this temperature, whereas if they are chilled to below 45°F, it will be difficult to tell, for instance, whether the wine is a Riesling or a Chardonnay.

In addition, there is the all-important issue of the glasses in which the wine is to be served. An all-purpose, tulip-shaped glass of 8 to 12 ounces is a good start for just about any type of wine, but think the subject over carefully. If you go to the trouble and expense of finding and storing wine properly, shouldn't you treat the wine to a good glass? The finest glasses for both technical and hedonistic purposes are those made by the Riedel Company of Austria. I have to admit that I was at first skeptical about these glasses. George Riedel, the head of his family's crystal business, claims to have created these glasses specifically to guide (by specially designed rims) the wine to a designated section of the palate. These rims, combined with the general shape of the glass, emphasize and promote the different flavors and aromas of a given varietal.

Over the last six months, I have tasted an assortment of wines in his glasses, including a Riesling glass, Chardonnay glass, Pinot Noir glass, and Cabernet Sauvignon glass, all part of his Sommelier Series. For comparative purposes, I then tasted the same wines in the Impitoyables glass, the INAO tasting glass, and the conventional tulip-shaped glass. The results were consistently in favor of the Riedel glasses. American Pinot Noirs and red burgundies performed far better in his huge 37-ounce, 9½-inch-high Burgundy goblet (model number 400/16) than in the other stemware. Nor could any of the other glassware compete when I was drinking Cabernet- and Merlot-based wines from his Bordeaux goblet (model number 400/00), a 32-ounce, 10½-inch-high, magnificently shaped glass. His Chardonnay glass was a less convincing performer, but I was astounded by how well the Riesling glass (model number 400/1), an 8-ounce glass that is 7¾ inches high, seemed to highlight the personality characteristics of Riesling.

George Riedel realizes that wine enthusiasts go to great lengths to buy wine in sound condition, to store it properly, and to serve it at the correct temperature. But how many connoisseurs invest enough time exploring the perfect glasses for their Pichon-Lalande, Méo-Camuzet, Clos Vougeot, or Maximin-Grunhaus Riesling Kabinett? His mission, he says, is to provide the "finest tools," enabling the taster to capture the full potential of a particular varietal. His glasses have convincingly proven his case time and time again in my tastings. I know of no finer tasting or drinking glasses than the Sommelier Series glasses from Riedel.

I have always found it amazing that most of my wine-loving friends tend to ignore the fact that top stemware is just as important as making the right choice in wine. When using the Riedel glasses, one must keep in mind that every one of these glasses has been engineered to enhance the best characteristic of a particular grape varietal. Riedel believes that regardless of the size of the glass, they work best when they are filled to no more than one-quarter of their capacity. If I were going to buy these glasses (the Sommelier Series tends to run $40–$70 a glass), I would unhesitatingly purchase both the Bordeaux and Burgundy glasses. They outperformed every other glass by a wide margin. The magnificent 37-ounce Burgundy glass, with a slightly flared lip, directs the flow of a burgundy to the tip and the center of the tongue, thus avoiding contact with the sides of the tongue, which deemphasizes the acidity, making the burgundy taste rounder and more supple. This is not just trade puffery on Riedel's part. I have done it enough times to realize these glasses do indeed control the flow, and by doing so, enhance the character of the wine. The large 32-ounce Bordeaux glass, which is nearly the same size as the Burgundy glass, is more conical, and the lip serves to direct the wine toward the tip of the tongue, where the taste sensors are more acutely aware of sweetness. This enhances the rich fruit in a Cabernet/Merlot-based wine before the wine spreads out to the sides and back of the palate, which pick up the more acidic, tannic elements. All of this may sound absurdly highbrow or esoteric, but the effect of these glasses on fine wine is profound. I cannot emphasize enough what a difference they make.

If the Sommelier Series sounds too expensive, Riedel does make less expensive lines that are machine-made rather than hand-blown. The most popular are the Vinum glasses, which sell for about $20 per glass. The Bordeaux Vinum glass is a personal favorite as well as a spectacular glass not only for Bordeaux but also for Rhône wines and white burgundies. There are also numerous other glasses designed for Nebbiolo-based wines, rosé wines, old white wines, and port wines, as well as a specially designed glass for sweet Sauternes-type wines.

For more complete information about prices and models, readers can get in touch with Riedel Crystal of America, P.O. Box 446, 24 Aero Road, Bohemia, NY 11716; telephone number (516) 567-7575. For residents of or visitors to New York City, Riedel has a showroom at 41 Madison Avenue (at Twenty-sixth Street).

Two other good sources for fine wineglasses include St. George Crystal in Jeannette, PA, at (412) 523-6501, and the all-purpose Cristal d'Arques Oenologist glass. I have found the latter glass to work exceptionally well with white wines such as Sauvignon, Chardonnay, Riesling, and Marsanne, and red wines such as Cabernet Sauvignon, Merlot, Malbec, Syrah, Zinfandel, Gamay, Mourvèdre, and Sangiovese. For very fragrant red wines such as those produced from Pinot Noir, Nebbiolo, and Grenache, this glass is acceptable, but I prefer other stemware. Designed by Dany Rolland, the gifted oenologist/wife/partner of Libourne's Michel Rolland, the dimensions are: height 8 inches (4½ inches of that is the stem); circumference 10 inches at the base of the tulip-shaped bowl, narrowing to 8 inches at the rim; capacity 12 ounces, or a half bottle of wine. The cost is $10–$12, depending on the quantity purchased. For more information, readers should contact either Grand Cru Imports, Souderton, PA, at (215) 723-2033, or Portside, Inc., Alexandria, VA, at (703) 683-6220.

And last but not least, remember: No matter how clean the glass appears to be, be sure to rinse the glass or decanter with unchlorinated well or mineral water just before it is used. A decanter or wine glass left sitting for any time is a wonderful trap for room and kitchen odors that are undetectable until the wine is poured and they yield their off-putting smells. That, and soapy residues left in the glasses, has ruined more wines than any defective cork or, I suspect, poor storage from an importer, wholesaler, or retailer. I myself put considerable stress on one friendship simply because I continued to complain at every dinner party about the soapy glasses that interfered with the enjoyment of the wonderful Bordeaux wines being served.

FOOD AND WINE MATCHUPS

The art of serving the right bottle of wine with a specific course or type of food has become one of the most overly legislated areas, all to the detriment of the enjoyment of both wine and food. Newspaper and magazine columns, even books, are filled with precise rules that seemingly make it a sin to be guilty of not having chosen the perfect wine to accompany the meal. The results have been predictable. Instead of enjoying a dining experience, most hosts and hostesses fret, usually needlessly, over their choice of which wine to serve with the meal.

The basic rules of the wine/food matchup game are not difficult to master. These are the tried-and-true, allegedly cardinal principles, such as young wines before old wines, dry wines before sweet wines, white wines before red wines, red wines with meat and white wines with fish. However, these general principles are filled with exceptions, and your choices are a great deal broader than you have been led to expect. One of France's greatest restaurant proprietors once told me that if people would simply pick their favorite wines to go along with their favorite dishes, they would be a great deal happier. Furthermore, he would be pleased not to have to witness so much nervous anxiety and apprehension on their faces. I'm not sure I can go that far, but given my gut feeling that there are more combinations of wine and food that work reasonably well than there are those that do not, let me share some of my basic observations about this whole field. There are several important questions you should consider:

Does the food offer simple or complex flavors? America's, and I suppose the wine world's, two favorite grapes, Chardonnay and Cabernet Sauvignon, can produce majestic wines of exceptional complexity and flavor depth. As food wines, however, they are remarkably one-dimensional. As complex and rewarding as they can be, they work well only with dishes that have relatively straightforward and simple flavors. Cabernet Sauvignon marries beautifully with basic meat and potato dishes: filet mignon, lamb fillets, steaks, etc. Furthermore, as Cabernet Sauvignon- and Merlot-based wines get older and more complex, they require simpler and simpler dishes to complement their complex flavors. Chardonnay goes beautifully with most fish courses, but when one adds different aromas and scents to a straightforward fish dish, either from grilling or from ingredients in an accompanying sauce, Chardonnays are often competitive rather than complementary wines to serve. The basic rule, then, is: simple, uncomplex wines with complex dishes, and complex wines with simple dishes.

What are the primary flavors in both the wine and food? A complementary wine choice can often be made if one knows what to expect from the primary flavors in the food to be eaten. The reason that creamy and buttery sauces with fish, lobster, even chicken or veal, work well with Chardonnay or white burgundies is because of the buttery, vanillin aromas in the fuller, richer, lustier styles of Chardonnay. On the other hand, a mixed salad with an herb dressing and pieces of grilled fish or shellfish beg for an herbaceous, smoky, Sauvignon Blanc or French Sancerre or Pouilly Fumé from the Loire Valley. For the same reason, a steak au poivre in a creamy brown sauce with its intense, pungent aromas and complex flavors requires a big, rich, peppery Rhône wine such as a Châteauneuf du Pape or Gigondas.

Is the texture and flavor intensity of the wine proportional to the texture and flavor intensity of the food? Did you ever wonder why fresh, briny, sea-scented oysters that are light and zesty taste so good with a Muscadet from France or a lighter-styled California Sauvignon Blanc or Italian Pinot Grigio? It is because these wines have the same weight and light texture as the oysters. Why is it that the smoky, sweet, oaky, tangy flavors of a grilled steak or loin of lamb work best with a Zinfandel or Rhône Valley red wine? First, the full-bodied, supple, chewy flavors of these wines complement a steak or loin of lamb cooked over a wood fire. Sauté the same steak or lamb in butter or bake it in the oven and the flavors are less complex; then a well-aged Cabernet Sauvignon- or Merlot-based wine from California, Bordeaux, or Australia is required. Another poignant example of the importance of matching the texture and flavor intensity of the wine with the food is the type of fish you have chosen to eat. Salmon, lobster, shad, and bluefish have intense flavors and a fatty texture, and therefore require a similarly styled, lusty, oaky, buttery Chardonnay to complement them. On the other hand, trout, sole, turbot, and shrimp are leaner, more delicately flavored fish and therefore mandate lighter, less intense wines such as nonoaked examples of Chardonnay from France's Mâconnais region, or Italy's Friuli-Venezia-Guilia area. In addition, a lighter-styled Champagne or German Riesling (a dry Kabinett works ideally) goes extremely well with trout, sole, or turbot, but falls on its face if matched against salmon, shad, or lobster. One further example of texture and flavor matchups is the classic example of drinking a heavy, unctuous, rich, sweet Sauternes with foie gras. The extravagantly rich and flavorful foie gras cannot be served with any other type of wine, as it would overpower a dry red or white wine. The fact that both the Sauternes and the foie gras have intense, concentrated flavors and similar textures is the exact reason why this combination is so decadently delicious.

What is the style of wine produced in the vintage that you have chosen? Several of France's greatest chefs have told me they prefer off years of Bordeaux and Burgundy to great years, and have instructed their sommeliers to buy the wines for the restaurant accordingly. Can this be true? From the chef's perspective, the food should be the focal point of the meal, not the wine. They fear that a great vintage of Burgundy or Bordeaux with wines that are exceptionally rich, powerful, and concentrated not only takes attention away from their cuisine but also makes matching a wine with the food much more troublesome. Thus, chefs prefer a 1987 Bordeaux on the table with their food as opposed to a superconcentrated 1982 or 1990. For the same reasons, they prefer a 1989 red burgundy over a 1990. Thus, the great vintages, while being marvelous wines, are not always the best vintages to choose if the ultimate matchup with food is desired. Lighter-weight yet tasty wines from so-so years can complement delicate and understated cuisine considerably better than the great vintages, which should be reserved for very simple courses of food.

Is the food to be served in a sauce? Fifteen years ago when eating at Michel Guerard's restaurant in Eugénie Les Bains, I ordered a course where the fish was served in a red wine sauce. Guerard recommended a red Graves from Bordeaux, since the sauce was made from a reduction of fish stock and a red Graves. The combination was successful and opened my eyes for the first time to the possibilities of fish with red wine. Since then I have had tuna with a green peppercorn sauce with California Cabernet Sauvignon (the matchup was great) and salmon sautéed in a red wine sauce that did justice to a young vintage of red Bordeaux. A white wine with any of these courses would not have worked. For the very same reason I have enjoyed veal in a creamy morel sauce with a Tokay from Alsace. A corollary to this principle of letting the sauce dictate the type of wine you order is where the actual food is prepared with a specific type of wine. For example, Coq au Vin, an exquisite peasant dish, can be cooked and served in either a white wine or red wine sauce. I have found when I had Coq au Vin au Riesling, the choice of a dry Alsace Riesling to go with it is simply extraordinary. In Burgundy I have often had Coq au Vin in a red wine sauce consisting of a reduced burgundy wine and the choice of a red burgundy makes the dish even more special.

When you travel, do you drink locally produced wines with the local cuisine? It is no coincidence that the regional cuisines of Bordeaux, Burgundy, Provence, and Alsace in France, and Tuscany and Piedmont in Italy seem to enhance and complement the local wines. In fact, most restaurants in these areas rarely offer wines from outside the local region, thus mandating the drinking of the locally produced wines. One always wonders what came first, the cuisine or the wine? Certainly, America is beginning to develop its own regional cuisine, but except for California and the Pacific Northwest few areas promote the local wines as appropriate matchups with the local cuisine. For example, in my backyard a number of small wineries make an excellent white wine called Seyval Blanc that is the perfect foil for both the oysters and blue channel crabs from the Chesapeake Bay. Yet few restaurants in the Baltimore-Washington area promote these local wines, which is a shame. Regional wines with regional foods should not only be a top priority when traveling in Europe but also in America's viticultural areas.

Have you learned the best and worst wine and food matchups? If this entire area of wine and food combinations still seems too cumbersome, then your best strategy is simply to learn some of the greatest combinations as well as some of the worst. I can also add a few pointers I have learned through my own experiences, usually bad ones. Certain wine and food relationships of contrasting flavors can be sublime. Perhaps the best example is a sweet, creamy textured Sauternes wine with a salty, aged stilton or roquefort cheese. The combination of having two opposite sets of flavors and textures is sensational in this particular instance. Another great combination is Alsace Gewurztraminers and Rieslings with ethnic cuisine such as Indian and Chinese. The juxtaposition of sweet and sour combinations in Oriental cuisine and the spiciness of both cuisines seems to work beautifully with these two types of wine from Alsace.

One of the great myths about wine and food matchups is that red wines work well with cheese. The truth of the matter is that they rarely ever work well with cheese. Most cheeses, especially favorite wine cheeses such as brie and double and triple creams have such a high fat content that most red wines suffer incredibly when drunk with them. If you want to shock your guests but also enjoy wine with cheese, it should not be a red wine you serve but rather a white wine made from the sauvignon blanc grape such as a Sancerre or Pouilly Fumé from France. The dynamic personalities of these two wines and their tangy, zesty acidity stand up well to virtually all types of cheese but they especially go well with fresh goat cheeses.

Another myth is that dessert wines go best with desserts. Most people seem to like champagne or a sweet riesling, sweet chenin blanc, or a Sauternes with dessert. Forgetting that chocolate-based desserts are always in conflict with any type of wine, I find dessert wines to be best served as the dessert or after the dessert. Whether it be cake, fruit tarts, ice cream, or candy, I've always enjoyed dessert wines more when they are the centerpiece of attention than when they are accompanying a sweet dessert.

If wine and food matchups still seem too complicated for you, remember that in the final analysis, a good wine served with a good dish to good company is always in good taste. A votre santé.

WHAT'S BEEN ADDED TO YOUR WINE?

Over the last decade people have become much more sensitive to what they put in their bodies. The hazards of excessive smoking, fat consumption, and high blood pressure are taken seriously by increasing numbers of people, not just in America but in Europe as well. While this movement is to be applauded, an extremist group, labeled by observers as "neo-prohibitionists" or "new drys," have tried to exploit an individual's interest in good health by promoting the image that the consumption of any alcoholic beverage is an inherently dangerous abuse that undermines society and family. These extremist groups do not care about moderation; they want the total elimination of wine (one of alcohol's evil spirits) from the marketplace. To do so, they have misrepresented wine and consistently ignored specific data that demonstrates that moderate wine drinking is more beneficial than harmful to individuals. Unfortunately, the law prohibits the wine industry from promoting the proven health benefits of wine.

Wine is the most natural of all beverages, but it is true that additives can be included in a wine (the neo-prohibitionists are taking aim at these as being potentially lethal). Following are those items that can be added to wine.

Acids   Most cool-climate vineyards never have the need to add acidity to wine, but in California and Australia acidity is often added to give balance to the wines, as grapes from these hot-climate areas often lack enough natural acidity. Most serious wineries add tartaric acidity, which is the same type of acidity found naturally in wine. Less quality oriented wineries dump in pure citric acid that results in the wine's tasting like a lemon/lime sorbet.

Clarification Agents   A list of items that are dumped into wine to cause suspended particles to coagulate includes morbid names such as dried ox blood, isinglass, casein (milk powder), kaolin (clay), bentonite (powdered clay), and the traditional egg whites. These fining agents are designed to make the wine brilliant and particle free; they are harmless, and top wineries either don't use them or use them minimally.

Oak   Many top-quality red and white wines spend most of their lives aging in oak barrels. It is expected that wine stored in wood will take on some of the toasty, smoky, vanillin flavors of wood. These aromas and flavors, if not overdone, add flavor complexity to a wine. Cheap wine can also be marginally enhanced by the addition of oak chips that provide a more aggressive, raw flavor of wood.

Sugar   In most of the viticultural regions of Europe except for southern France, Portugal, and Spain, the law permits the addition of sugar to the fermenting grape juice in order to raise the alcohol levels. This practice, called chaptalization, is done in cool years where the grapes do not attain sufficient ripeness. It is never done in the hot climate of California or in most of Australia where low natural acidity, not low sugars, is the problem. Judicious chaptalization raises the alcohol level by 1%–2%.

Sulfates   All wines must now carry a label indicating the wine contains sulfates. Sulfate (also referred to as SO_2 or sulfur dioxide) is a preservative used to kill bacteria and microorganisms. It is sprayed on virtually all fresh vegetables and fruits, but a tiny percentage of the population is allergic to SO_2, especially asthmatics. The fermentation of wine produces some sulfur dioxide naturally, but it is also added to oak barrels by burning a sulfur stick inside the barrel in order to kill any bacteria; it is added again at bottling to prevent the wine from oxidizing. Quality wines should never smell of sulfur (a burning match smell) because serious winemakers keep the sulfur level very low. Some wineries do not employ sulfates. When used properly, sulfates impart no smell or taste to the wine and, except for those who have a known allergy to them, are harmless to the general population. Used excessively, sulfates impart the aforementioned unpleasant smell and a prickly taste sensation. Obviously, people who are allergic to sulfates should not drink wine, just as people who are allergic to fish roe should not eat caviar.

Tannin   Tannin occurs naturally in the skins and stems of grapes, and the content from the crushing of the grape skins and subsequent maceration of the skins and juice is usually more than adequate to provide sufficient natural tannin. Tannin gives a red wine grip and backbone, as well as acting as a preservative. However, on rare occasions tannin is added to a spineless wine.

Yeasts   While many winemakers rely on the indigenous wild yeasts in the vineyard to start the fermentation, it is becoming more common to employ cultured yeasts for this procedure. There is no health hazard here, but the increasing reliance on the same type of yeast for wines from all over the world leads to wines with similar bouquets and flavors.

ORGANIC WINES

Organic wines, those that are produced without fungicides, pesticides, or chemical fertilizers, with no additives or preservatives, continue to gain considerable consumer support. In principle, organic wines should be as excellent as nonorganic. Because most organic wine producers tend to do less manipulation and processing of their wines, the consumer receives a product that is far more natural than those wines that have been manufactured and processed to death.

There is tremendous potential for huge quantities of organic wines, particularly from those viticultural areas that enjoy copious quantities of sunshine and wind, the so-called Mediterranean climate. In France, the Languedoc-Roussillon region, Provence, and the Rhône Valley have the potential to produce organic wines if their proprietors desire. Much of California could do so as well. Parts of Australia and Italy also have weather conditions that encourage the possibility of developing organic vineyards.

THE DARK SIDE OF WINE
The Growing International Standardization of Wine Styles

Although technology allows winemakers to produce better and better quality wine, the continuing obsession with technically perfect wines is unfortunately stripping wines of their identifiable and distinctive character. Whether it is the excessive filtration of wines or the excessive emulation of winemaking styles, it seems to be the tragedy of modern winemaking that it is now increasingly difficult to tell an Italian Chardonnay from one made in France or California or Australia. When the corporate winemakers of the world begin to make wines all in the same way, designing them to offend the least number of people, wine will no doubt lose its fascinating appeal and individualism to become no better than most brands of whiskey, gin, scotch, or vodka. One must not forget that the great appeal of wine is that it is a unique, distinctive, fascinating beverage and different every time one drinks it. Winemakers and the owners of wineries, particularly in America, must learn to take more risks so as to preserve the individual character of their wines, even at the risk that some consumers may find them bizarre or unusual. It is this distinctive quality of wine that will ensure its future.

Destroying the Joy of Wine by Excessive Acidification, Overzealous Fining, and Abrasive Filtration

Since the beginning of my career as a professional wine critic, I have tried to present a strong case against the excessive manipulation of wine. One look at the world's greatest producers and their wines will irrefutably reveal that the following characteristics are shared by all of them—whether they be California, France, Italy, Spain, or Germany. 1) They are driven to preserve the integrity of the vineyard's character, the varietal's identity, and the vintage's personality. 2) They believe in low crop yields. 3) Weather permitting, they harvest only physiologically mature (versus analytically ripe) fruit. 4) Their winemaking and cellar techniques are simplistic in the sense that they are minimal interventionists, preferring to permit the wine to make itself. 5) While they are not opposed to fining or filtration if the wine is unstable or unclear, if the wine is made from healthy, ripe grapes, is stable and clear, they will absolutely refuse to strip it by excessive fining and filtration at bottling.

Producers who care only about making wine as fast as possible and collecting their accounts receivable quickly also have many things in common. While they turn out neutral, vapid, mediocre wines, they are also believers in huge crop yields, with considerable fertilization to promote massive crops, as large as the vineyard can render (6 or more tons per acre, compared to modest yields of 3 tons per acre). Their philosophy is that the vineyard is a manufacturing plant and cost efficiency dictates that production be maximized. They rush their wine into bottle as quickly as possible in order to get paid. They believe in processing wine, such as centrifuging it initially, then practicing multiple fining and filtration procedures, particularly a denuding sterile filtration. This guarantees that the wine is lifeless but stable, a goal where the ability to withstand temperature extremes and stand upright on a grocery store's shelf is given priority over giving the consumer a beverage of pleasure. These wineries harvest earlier than anybody else because they are unwilling to take any risk, delegating all questions regarding wine to their oenologists, who, they know, have as their objectives security and stability, which is at conflict with the consumer's goal of finding joy in wine.

The effect of excessive manipulation of wine, particularly overly aggressive fining and filtration, is dramatic. It destroys a wine's bouquet as well as its ability to express its *terroir* and varietal character. It also mutes the vintage's character. Fining and filtration can be lightly done, causing only minor damage, but most wines produced in the New World (California, Australia, and South America in particular), and most bulk wines produced in Europe are sterile-filtered. This procedure requires numerous pre-filtrations to get the wines clean enough to pass through a micropore membrane filter. This system of wine stability and clarification strips, eviscerates, and denudes a wine of much of its character.

Some wines can suffer such abuse with less damage. Thick, tannic, concentrated, Syrah- and Cabernet Sauvignon-based wines may even survive these wine lobotomies, diminished in aromatic and flavor dimension but still alive. Wines such as Pinot Noir and Chardonnay are destroyed in the process.

Thanks to a new generation of producers, particularly in France, aided by a number of specialist importers from America, there has been a movement against unnecessary fining and filtration. One only has to look at the extraordinary success enjoyed by such American importers as Kermit Lynch and Robert Kacher to realize how much consumer demand exists for producers to bottle a natural, unfiltered, uncompromised wine that is a faithful representation of its vineyard and vintage. Most serious wine consumers do not mind not being able to drink the last half ounce of wine because of sediment. They know this sediment means they are getting a flavorful, authentic, unprocessed wine that is much more representative than one that has been stripped at bottling.

Other small importers who have followed the leads of Lynch and Kacher include Peter Weygandt of Weygandt-Metzler, Unionville, PA; Neal Rosenthal Select Vineyards, New York, NY; Eric Solomon of European Cellars, New York, NY; Don Quattlebaum of New Castle Imports, Myrtle Beach, SC; Fran Kysela of Kysela Père et Fils of Winchester, VA; Martine Saunier of Martine's Wines, San Rafael, CA; North Berkeley Imports, Berkeley, CA; Jorgé Ordonez, Dedham, MA; Leonardo LoCascio, Hohokus, NJ; Dan Phillips, Oxnard, CA; Ted Schrauth, West Australia; John Larchet, Australia; Jeffrey Davies, West Nyack, NY; and Alain Junguenet, Watchung, NJ; to name some of the best known. They often insist that their producers not filter those wines shipped to the United States, resulting in a richer, more age-worthy wine being sold in America than elsewhere in the world. Even some of our country's largest importers, most notably Kobrand, Inc., in New York City, are encouraging producers to move toward more gentle and natural bottling techniques.

I am certain there would have been an even more powerful movement to bottle wines naturally with minimal clarification if the world's wine press had examined the effect of excessive fining and filtration. I find it difficult to criticize many American wine writers since the vast majority of them are part-timers. Few have either the time or resources to taste the same wines before and after bottling. Yet I remain disappointed that many of our most influential writers and publications have remained strangely silent, particularly in view of the profound negative impact filtration can have on the quality of fine wine. The English wine writing corps, which includes many veteran, full-time wine writers, has an appalling record on this issue, especially in view of the fact that many of them make it a practice to taste before and after bottling. For those who care about the quality of wine and the preservation of the character of the vineyard, vintage, and varietal, the reluctance of so many writers to criticize the wine industry undermines the entire notion of wine appreciation.

Even a wine writer of the stature of Hugh Johnson comes out strongly on the side of processed, neutral wines that can be safely shipped 12 months of the year. Readers may want to consider Johnson's and his coauthor, James Halliday's, comments in their book, *The Vintner's Art—How Great Wines Are Made*. Halliday is an Australian wine writer and winery owner and Hugh Johnson may be this century's most widely read wine author. In their book they chastise the American importer Kermit Lynch for his "romantic ideals" which they describe as "increasingly impractical." Johnson and Halliday assert that "The truth is that a good fifty percent of those artisan burgundies and Rhones are bacterial time bombs." Their plea for compromised and standardized wines is supported by the following observation: "The hard reality is that many restaurants and many consumers simply will not accept sediment." This may have been partially true in America 20 years ago, but today, the consumer not only wants but demands a natural wine. Moreover, the wine consumer understands that sediment in a bottle of fine wine is a healthy sign. The fact that both writers argue that modern-day winemaking and commercial necessity require that wines be shipped 12 months a year and be durable enough to withstand months on retailers' shelves in both cold and hot temperature conditions is highly debatable. America now has increasing numbers of responsible merchants, importers, and restaurant sommeliers who go to great lengths to guarantee the client a healthy bottle of wine that has not been abused. Astonishingly, Johnson and Halliday conclude that consumers cannot tell the difference as to whether a wine has been filtered or not! In summarizing their position, they state, ". . . but leave the wine for 1, 2, or 3 months (one cannot tell how long the recovery process will take), and it is usually impossible to tell the filtered from the nonfiltered wine, provided the filtration at bottling was skillfully carried out." After 14 years of conducting such tastings, I find this statement not only unbelievable but also insupportable! Am I to conclude that all of the wonderful wines I have tasted from cask that were subsequently damaged by vigorous fining and filtration were bottled by incompetent people who did not know how to filter? Am I to think that the results of the extensive comparative tastings (usually blind) that I have done of the same wine, filtered versus unfiltered, were bogus? Are the enormous aromatic, flavor, textural, and qualitative differences that are the result of vigorous clarification techniques figments of my imagination? Astoundingly, the wine industry's reluctance to accept responsibility for preserving all that the best vineyards and vintages can achieve is excused rather than condemned.

If excessive fining and filtration are not bad enough, consider the overzealous addition of citric and tartaric acids employed by Australia and California oenologists to perk up their wines. You know the feeling—you open a bottle of Australia or California Chardonnay and not only is there no bouquet (because it was sterile filtered) but tasting the wine is like biting into a fresh lemon or lime. It is not enjoyable. What you are experiencing is the result of the misguided philosophy among New World winemakers to add too much acidity as a cheap but fatal life insurance policy for their wines. Because they are unwilling to reduce their yields, because they are unwilling to assume any risk, and because they see winemaking as nothing more than a processing technique, acidity is generously added. It does serve as an antibacterial, antioxidant agent, thus helping to keep the wine fresh. But those who acidify the most are usually those who harvest appallingly high crop yields. Thus, there is little flavor to protect! After 6–12 months of bottle age, what little fruit is present fades, and the consumer is left with a skeleton of sharp, shrill acid levels, alcohol, wood (if utilized), and no fruit—an utterly reprehensible way of making wine.

I do not object to the use of these techniques for bulk and jug wines, which the consumer is buying for value, or because of brand name recognition. But for any producer to sell a wine as a handcrafted, artisan product at $20 or more a bottle, the adherence to such philosophies as excessive acidification, fining, and filtration is shameful. Anyone who tells you that excessive acidification, fining, and filtration does not damage a wine is either a fool or a liar.

The Inflated Wine Pricing of Restaurants

Given the vast sums of American discretionary income that is being spent eating at restaurants, a strong argument could be made that the cornerstone to increased wine consumption and awareness would be the consumption of wine at restaurants. However, most restaurants treat wine as a luxury item, marking it up an exorbitant 200%–500%, thereby effectively discouraging the consumption of wine. This practice of offering wines at huge markups also serves to reinforce the mistaken notion that wine is only for the elite and the superrich.

The wine industry does little about this practice, being content merely to see its wines placed on a restaurant's list. But the consumer should revolt and avoid those restaurants that charge exorbitant wine prices, no matter how sublime the cuisine. This is nothing more than legitimized mugging of the consumer.

Fortunately, things are slightly better today than they were a decade ago, as some restaurant owners are now regarding wine as an integral part of the meal and not merely as a device used to increase the bill.

Collectors versus Consumers

I have reluctantly come to believe that many of France's greatest wine treasures—the first growths of Bordeaux, including the famous sweet nectar made at Château Yquem; Burgundy's most profound red wines from the Domaine de la Romanée-Conti; and virtually all of the wines from the tiny white wine appellation of Montrachet—are never drunk, or should I say swallowed. Most of us who purchase or cellar wine do so on the theory that eventually every one of our splendid bottles will be swirled, sloshed, sniffed, sipped, and, yes, guzzled with friends. That, of course, is one of the joys of wine, and those of you who partake of this pleasure are true wine lovers. There are, however, other types of wine collectors—the collector-investor, the collector-spitter, and even the nondrinking collector. Needless to say, these people are not avid consumers.

Several years ago I remember being deluged with telephone calls from a man wanting me to have dinner with him and tour his private cellar. After several months of resisting, I finally succumbed. A very prominent businessman, he had constructed an impressive cellar beneath his sprawling home. It was enormous and immaculately kept, with state-of-the-art humidity and temperature controls. I suspect it contained in excess of ten thousand bottles. While there were cases of such thoroughbreds as Pétrus, Lafite-Rothschild, Mouton-Rothschild, and rare vintages of the great red burgundies such as Romanée-Conti and La Tache, to my astonishment there were also hundreds of cases of 10- and 15-year-old Beaujolais, Pouilly-Fuissé, Dolcetto, and California Chardonnays—all wines that should have been drunk during their first 4 or 5 years of life. I diplomatically suggested that he should inventory his cellar as there seemed to be a number of wines that mandated immediate consumption.

About the time I spotted the fifth or sixth case of what was clearly 10-year-old Beaujolais vinegar, I began to doubt the sincerity of my host's enthusiasm for wine. These unthinkable doubts (I was much more naive then than I am now) were amplified at dinner. As we entered the sprawling kitchen and dining room complex, he proudly announced that neither he nor his wife actually drank wine, and then asked if I would care for a glass of mineral water, iced tea, or, if I preferred, a bottle of wine. On my sorrow-filled drive home that evening, I lamented the fact that I had not opted for the mineral water. For when I made the mistake of requesting wine with the meal, my host proceeded to grab a bottle of wine that one of his friends suggested should be consumed immediately. It was a brown-colored, utterly repugnant, senile Bordeaux from perhaps the worst vintage in the last 25 years, 1969. Furthermore, the château chosen was a notorious underachiever from the famous commune of Pauillac. Normally the wine he chose does not merit buying in a good vintage, much less a pathetic one. I shall never forget my host opening the bottle and saying, "Well, Bob, this wine sure smells good."

Regrettably, this Non-Drinking Collector continues to buy large quantities of wine, not for investment and obviously not for drinking. The local wine merchants tell me his type is not rare. To him, a collection of wine is like a collection of crystal, art, sculpture, or china, something to be admired, to be shown off, but never, ever to be consumed.

More ostentatious by far is the collector-spitter, who thrives on gigantic tastings where fifty, sixty, sometimes even seventy or eighty vintages of great wines, often from the same châteaux, can be "tasted." Important members of the wine press are invited (no charge, of course) in the hope that this wine happening will receive a major article in the New York or Los Angeles Times, and the collector's name will become recognized and revered in the land of winedom. These collector-spitters relish rubbing elbows with famous proprietors and telling their friends, "Oh, I'll be at Château Lafite-Rothschild next week to taste all of the château's wines between 1870 and 1987. Sorry you can't be there." I have, I confess, participated in several of these events, and have learned from the exercise of trying to understand them that their primary purpose is to feed the sponsor's enormous ego, and often the château's ego as well.

I am not against academic tastings where a limited number of serious wine enthusiasts sit down to taste twenty or thirty different wines (usually young ones), because that is a manageable number that both neophytes and connoisseurs can generally grasp. But to taste sixty or more rare and monumental vintages at an 8- or 12-hour tasting marathon is carrying excess to its extreme. Most simply, what seems to happen at these tastings is that much of the world's greatest, rarest, and most expensive wines are spit out. No wine taster I have ever met could conceivably remain sober, even if only the greatest wines were swallowed. I can assure you, there is only remorse in spitting out 1929 or 1945 Mouton-Rothschild.

Other recollections of these events have also long troubled me. I vividly remember one tasting held at a very famous restaurant in Los Angeles where a number of compelling bottles from one of France's greatest estates were opened. Many of the wines were exhilarating. Yet, whether it was the otherworldly 1961 or opulent 1947, the reactions I saw on the faces of those forty or so people, who had each paid several thousand dollars to attend, made me wonder whether it was fifty different vintages of France's greatest wines we were tasting or fifty bottles of Pepto-Bismol. Fortunately, the organizer did appear to enjoy the gathering and appreciate the wines, but among the guests I never once saw a smile, or any enthusiasm or happiness in the course of this extraordinary 12-hour tasting.

I remember another marathon tasting held in France by one of Europe's leading collector-spitters, which lasted all day and much of the night. There were more than ninety legendary wines served, and midway through the afternoon I was reasonably certain there was not a sober individual remaining except for the chef and his staff. By the time the magnum of 1929 Mouton-Rothschild was served (one of the century's greatest wines), I do not think there was a guest left who was competent enough to know whether he was drinking claret or Beaujolais, myself included.

I have also noticed at these tastings that many collector-spitters did not even know that a bottle was corked (had the smell of moldy cardboard and was defective) or that a bottle was oxidized and undrinkable, adding truth to the old saying that money does not always buy good taste. Of course, most of these tastings are media happenings designed to stroke the host's vanity. All too frequently they undermine the principle that wine is a beverage of pleasure, and that is my basic regret.

The third type of collector, the investor, is motivated by the possibility of reselling the wines for profit. Eventually, most or all of these wines return to the marketplace, and much of it wends its way into the hands of serious consumers who share it with their spouses or good friends. Of course they often must pay dearly for the privilege, but wine is not the only product that falls prey to such manipulation. I hate to think of wine being thought of primarily as an investment, but the world's finest wines do appreciate significantly in value and it would be foolish to ignore the fact that more and more shrewd investors are looking at wine as a way of making money.

Unspeakable Practices

It is a frightening thought, but I have no doubt that a sizeable percentage (between 10% and 25%) of the wines sold in America has been damaged because of exposure to extremes of heat. Smart consumers have long been aware of the signs of poor storage (see my comments on page 19).

One other sign indicating the wine has been poorly stored is the presence of seepage, or legs, down the rim of the bottle. This is the sometimes sticky, dry residue of a wine that has expanded, seeped around the cork, and dripped onto the rim. Cases of this are almost always due to excessively high temperatures in transit or storage. Few merchants take the trouble to wipe the legs off, and they can often be spotted on wines that are shipped during the heat of the summer, or brought into the United States through the Panama Canal in containers that are not air-conditioned. Consumers should avoid buying wines that show dried seepage legs originating under the capsule and trickling down the sides of the bottle.

You should also be alert for young wines (those less than 4 years old) that have more than one-half inch of air space, or ullage, between the cork and the liquid level in the bottle.

Modern bottling operations generally fill bottles within one-eighth inch of the cork, so more than one-half inch of air space should arouse your suspicion.

The problem, of course, is that too few people in the wine trade take the necessary steps to assure that the wine is not ruined in shipment or storage. The wine business has become so commercial that wines, whether from California, Italy, or France, are shipped 12 months of the year, regardless of weather conditions. Traditionally, wines from Europe were shipped only in the spring or fall when the temperatures encountered in shipment would be moderate, assuming they were not shipped by way of the Panama Canal. The cost of renting an air-conditioned or heated container for shipping wines adds anywhere from twenty to forty cents to the wholesale cost of the bottle, but when buying wines that cost more than $200 a case, I doubt the purchaser would mind paying the extra premium knowing that the wine will not smell or taste cooked when opened.

Many importers claim to ship in reefers (the trade jargon for temperature-controlled containers), but only a handful actually do. America's largest importer of high-quality Bordeaux wine rarely, if ever, uses reefers, and claims to have had no problems with their shipments. Perhaps they would change their minds if they had witnessed the cases of 1986 Rausan-Ségla, 1986 Talbot, 1986 Gruaud-Larose, and 1986 Château Margaux that arrived in the Maryland-Washington, D.C. market with stained labels and pushed-out corks. Somewhere between Bordeaux and Washington, D.C. these wines had been exposed to torridly high temperatures. It may not have been the fault of the importer as the wine passed through a number of intermediaries before reaching its final destination. But pity the poor consumer who buys this wine, puts it in his cellar, and opens it 10 or 15 years in the future. Who will grieve for them?

The problem with temperature extremes is that the naturally made, minimally processed, hand-produced wines are the most vulnerable to this kind of abuse. Therefore, many importers, not wanting to assume any risks, have gone back to their suppliers and demanded "more stable" wines. Translated into real terms this means the wine trade prefers to ship not living wines but vapid, denuded wines that have been "stabilized," subjected to a manufacturing process, and either pasteurized or sterile filtered so they can be shipped 12 months a year. While their corks may still pop out if subjected to enough heat, their taste will not change, because for all intents and purposes these wines are already dead when they are put in the bottle. Unfortunately, only a small segment of the wine trade seems to care.

While there are some wine merchants, wholesalers, and importers who are cognizant of the damage that can be done when wines are not protected and who take great pride in representing hand-made, quality products, the majority of the wine trade continues to ignore the risks. They would prefer that the wine be denuded by pasteurization, cold stabilization, or a sterile filtration. Only then can they be shipped safely under any weather conditions.

Wine Producers' Greed

Are today's wine consumers being hoodwinked by the world's wine producers? Most growers and/or producers have intentionally permitted production yields to soar to such extraordinary levels that the concentration and character of their wines are in jeopardy. There remain a handful of fanatics who continue, at some financial sacrifice, to reject a significant proportion of their harvest so as to ensure that only the finest quality wine is sold under their name. However, they are dwindling in number. Fewer producers are prepared to go into the vineyard and cut bunches of grapes to reduce the yields. Fewer still are willing to cut back prudently on fertilizers. For much of the last decade production yields throughout the world continued to break records with each new vintage. The results are wines that increasingly lack character, concentration, and staying power. In Europe, the most flagrant abuses of overproduction occur in Germany and Burgundy, where yields today are three to almost five times what they were in the fifties. The argument that the vineyards are more carefully and competently managed and that this results in larger crops is misleading. Off the record, many a seriously committed wine producer will tell you that "the smaller the yield, the better the wine."

If one wonders why the Domaine Leroy's burgundies taste richer than those from other domaines, it is due not only to quality winemaking but also to the fact that their yields are one-third those of other Burgundy producers. If one asks why the best Châteauneuf du Papes are generally Rayas, Pegau, Bonneau, and Beaucastel, it is because their yields are one-half those of other producers of the appellation. The same assertion applies to J. J. Prum and Muller-Cattoir in Germany. Not surprisingly, they have conservative crop yields that produce one-third the amount of wine of their neighbors.

While I do not want to suggest there are no longer any great wines and that most of the wines now produced are no better than the plonk peasants drank in the nineteenth century, the point is that overfertilization, modern sprays which prevent rot, the development of highly prolific clonal selections, and the failure to keep production levels modest have all resulted in yields that may well be combining to destroy the reputations of many of the most famous wine regions of the world. Trying to find a flavorful Chardonnay from California today is not much easier than finding a concentrated red burgundy that can age gracefully beyond 10 years. The production yields of Chardonnay in California have often resulted in wines that have only a faint character of the grape and seem almost entirely dominated by acidity and/or the smell of oak barrels. What is appalling is that there is so little intrinsic flavor. Yet Chardonnays remain the most popular white wine in this country, so what incentive is there to lower yields?

Of course, if the public, encouraged by a noncritical, indifferent wine media, is willing to pay top dollar for mediocrity, then little is likely to change. On the other hand, if consumers start insisting that $15 or $20 should at the very minimum fetch a wine that provides far more pleasure, perhaps that message will gradually work its way back to the producers.

Wine Writers' Ethics and Competence

The problems just described have only occasionally been acknowledged by the wine media, which generally has a collective mindset of never having met a wine it doesn't like.

Wine writing in America has rarely been a profitable or promising full-time occupation. Historically, the most interesting work was always done by those people who sold wine. There's no doubting the influence or importance of the books written by Alexis Lichine and Frank Schoonmaker. But both men made their fortunes by selling rather than writing about wine, yet both managed to write about wine objectively, despite their ties to the trade.

There are probably not more than a dozen or so independent wine experts in this country who support themselves entirely by writing. Great Britain has long championed the cause of wine writers and looked upon them as true professionals. But even there, with all their experience and access to the finest European vineyards, most of the successful wine writers have been involved in the sale and distribution of wine. Can anyone name an English wine writer who criticized the performance of Lafite-Rothschild between 1961 and 1974, or Margaux between 1964 and 1977 (periods of time when the consumer was getting screwed)?

It is probably unrealistic to expect writers to develop a professional expertise with wine without access and support from the trade, but such support can compromise their findings. If they are beholden to wine producers for the wines they taste, they are not likely to fault them. If the trips they make to vineyards are the result of the winemaker's largesse, they are unlikely to criticize what they have seen. If they are lodged at the châteaux and their trunks are filled with cases of wine (as, sadly, is often the case), can a consumer expect them to be critical, or even objective?

Putting aside the foolish notion that a wine writer is going to bite the hand that feeds him, there is the problem that many wine writers are lacking the global experience essential to properly evaluate wine. Consequently, what has emerged from such inexperience is a school of wine writing that is primarily trained to look at the wine's structure and acid levels, and it is this philosophy that is too frequently in evidence when judging wines. The level of pleasure that a wine provides, or is capable of providing in the future, would appear to be irrelevant. The results are wine evaluations that read as though one was measuring the industrial strength of different grades of cardboard rather than a beverage that many consider nature's greatest gift to mankind. Balance is everything in wine, and wines that taste too tart or tannic rarely ever age into flavorful, distinctive, charming beverages. While winemaking and wine technology are indeed better, and some of the most compelling wines ever made are being produced today, there are far too many mediocre wines sitting on the shelves that hardly deserve their high praise.

There are, however, some interesting trends. The growth of *The Wine Spectator* with its staff of full-time writers obligated to follow a strict code of conflict of interest, has resulted in better and more professional journalism. It also cannot be discounted that this flashy magazine appears twice a month. This is good news for the wine industry, frequently under siege by the anti-alcohol extremists. Some may protest the inflated ratings that *The Wine Spectator*'s tasting panel tends to bestow, but tasting is, as we all should know, subjective. The only criticism some might have is that their wine evaluations are the result of a committee's vote. Wines of great individuality and character rarely win a committee tasting because there is going to be at least one taster who will find something objectionable about the wines. Therefore, tasting panels, where all grades are averaged, frequently appear to find wines of great individuality unusual. Can anyone name just one of the world's greatest red or white wines that is produced by the consensus of a committee? The wines that too often score the highest are those that are technically correct and designed to please the greatest number of people. Wouldn't most Americans prefer a hamburger from McDonald's than seared salmon served over a bed of lentils at New York City's famed Montrachet restaurant? To *The Wine Spectator*'s credit, more of their tasting reports are authored by one or two people, not an anonymous, secretive committee. The results of the numerous California wine judgings support the same conclusion—that many a truly great, individualistic, and original wine has no chance. The winners are too often fail-safe, technically correct, spit-polished, and clean examples of winemaking—in short, wines for fans of Velveeta cheese, Muzak, and frozen dinners. The opinion of an individual taster, despite that taster's prejudices and predilections, if reasonably informed and comprehensive, is always a far greater guide to the ultimate quality of the wine than that of a committee. At least the reader knows where the individual stands, whereas with a committee, one is never quite sure.

Given the vitality of our nation's best wine guides, it is unlikely that wine writers will have less influence in the future. The thousands and thousands of wines that come on the market, many of them overpriced and vapid, require consumer-oriented reviews from the wine writing community. But until a greater degree of professionalism is attained, until more experience is evidenced by wine writers, until their misinformed emphasis on a wine's high acidity and structure is forever discredited, until most of the English wine media begin to understand and adhere to the basic rules of conflict of interest, until we all remember that this is only a beverage of pleasure to be seriously consumed but not taken too seriously, then and only then will the quality of wine writing and the wines we drink improve. Will all of this happen, or will we be reminded of these words of Marcel Proust:

We do not succeed in changing things according to our desire, but gradually our desire changes. The situation that we hope to change because it was intolerable becomes unimportant. We have not managed to surmount the obstacle as we are absolutely determined to do, but life has taken us round to it, let us pass it, and then if we turn round to gaze at the road past, we can barely catch sight of it, so imperceptible has it become.

WHAT CONSTITUTES A GREAT WINE?

What is a great wine? One of the most controversial subjects of the vinous world, isn't greatness in wine, much like a profound expression of art or music, something very personal and subjective? As much as I agree that the appreciation and enjoyment of art, music, or wine is indeed personal, high quality in wine, as in art and music, does tend to be subject to widespread agreement. Except for the occasional contrarian, greatness in art, music, or wine, if difficult to precisely define, enjoys a broad consensus. I would even argue that the appreciation of fine art and music is even more subjective than the enjoyment of fine wine. However, few art aficionados would disagree with the fact that Picasso, Rembrandt, Bacon, Matisse, Van Gogh, or Michelangelo were extraordinary artists. The same is true with music. Certainly some dissenters can be found regarding the merits of composers such as Chopin, Mozart, Beethoven, or Brahms, or in the more modern era, such musicians/songwriters as Bob Dylan, the Beatles, or the Rolling Stones, but the majority opinion is that exceptional music emanated from them.

It is no different with wine. Many of the most legendary wines of this century—1945 Mouton-Rothschild, 1945 Haut-Brion, 1947 Cheval Blanc, 1947 Pétrus, 1961 Latour, 1982 Mouton-Rothschild, 1982 Le Pin, 1982 Léoville-Las Cases, 1989 Haut-Brion, 1990 Margaux, and 1990 Pétrus, to name some of the most renowned red Bordeaux—are profoundly riveting wines, even though an occasional discordant view about them may surface. Tasting is indeed subjective, but like most of the finest things in life, there is considerable agreement as to what represents high quality, yet no one should feel forced to feign fondness for a work from Picasso or Beethoven, much less a bottle of 1961 Latour.

One issue about the world's finest wines that is subject to little controversy relates to how such wines originate. Frankly, there are no secrets to the origin and production of the world's finest wines. Great wines emanate from well-placed vineyards with microclimates favorable to the specific types of grapes grown. Profound wines, whether they are from France, Italy, Spain, California, or Australia, are also the product of conservative viticultural practices that emphasize low yields and physiologically rather than analytically ripe fruit. In nineteen years spent tasting over 200,000 wines, I have never tasted a superb wine that was made from underripe fruit. Does anyone enjoy the flavors present when biting into an underripe orange, peach, apricot, or cherry? Low yields and ripe fruit are essential for the production of extraordinary wines, yet it is amazing how many wineries never seem to understand this fundamental principle.

In addition to the commonsense approach of harvesting mature (ripe) fruit and discouraging, in a viticultural sense, the vine from overproducing, the philosophy employed by a winery in making wine is of paramount importance. Exceptional wines (whether they be red, white, or sparkling) emerge from a similar philosophy, which includes the following: 1) permit the vineyard's *terroir* (soil, microclimate, distinctiveness) to express itself, 2) allow the purity and characteristics of the grape varietal or blend of varietals to be faithfully represented in the wine, 3) produce a wine without distorting the personality and character of a particular vintage by excessive manipulation, 4) follow an uncompromising, noninterventionalistic winemaking philosophy that eschews the food-processing, industrial mindset of high-tech winemaking—in short, give the wine a chance to make itself naturally without the human element attempting to sculpture or alter the wine's intrinsic character, 5) follow a policy of minimal handling, clarification, and treatment of the wine so that what is placed in the bottle represents as natural an expression of the vineyard, varietal, and vintage as is possible. In keeping with this overall philosophy, winemakers who attempt to reduce such traumatic clarification procedures as fining and filtration, while also lowering sulfur levels (which can dry out a wine's fruit, bleach color from a wine, and exacerbate the tannin's sharpness) produce wines with far more aromatics and flavors, as well as more enthralling textures. In short, these are wines that offer consumers their most compelling and rewarding drinking experiences.

Assuming there is a relatively broad consensus as to how the world's finest wines originate, what follows is my working definition of an exceptional wine. In short—what are the characteristics of a great wine?

THE ABILITY TO PLEASE BOTH THE PALATE AND THE INTELLECT

Great wines offer satisfaction on both a hedonistic level of enjoyment as well as the ability to challenge and satiate the intellect. The world offers many delicious wines that are purely hedonistic but are not complex. The ability to satisfy the intellect is a more subjective issue. Wines that experts call "complex" are those that offer multiple dimensions in both their aromatic and flavor profiles and have more going for them than simply ripe fruit and a satisfying, pleasurable yet one-dimensional quality.

Classic Examples

1990 Dom Perignon Champagne ($125)
1994 Philip Togni Cabernet Sauvignon Napa ($45)
1991 Guigal Côte Rôtie La Mouline ($125)
1995 Müller-Catoir Mussbacher Eselhart Rieslaner ($35)
1997 Turley Cellars Zinfandel Hayne Vineyard ($28)
1995 Clarendon Hills Old Vine Grenache Blewitt Vineyard ($26)

THE ABILITY TO HOLD THE TASTER'S INTEREST

I have often remarked that the greatest wines I have ever tasted could be easily recognized by bouquet alone. They are wines that could never be called monochromatic or simple. Profound wines hold the taster's interest, not only providing the initial tantalizing tease but also possessing a magnetic attraction because of their aromatic intensity and nuance-filled layers of flavors.

Classic Examples

1990 Chapoutier Hermitage Pavillon ($125)
1995 l'Évangile (Pomerol) ($75)
1990 Altesino Brunello di Montalcino ($65)
1997 Peter Michael Chardonnay Clos du Ciel ($35)
1990 Baumard Savennières Clos du Papillon ($30)
1994 Robert Mondavi Cabernet Sauvignon Reserve Napa ($65)

THE ABILITY OF A WINE TO OFFER INTENSE AROMAS AND FLAVORS WITHOUT HEAVINESS

An analogy can be made to eating in the finest restaurants. Extraordinary cooking is characterized by its purity, intensity, balance, texture, and compelling aromas and flavors. What separates exceptional cuisine from merely good cooking, as well as great wines from good wines, is their ability to offer extraordinary intensity of flavor without heaviness. It has been easy in the New World (especially in Australia and California) to produce wines that are oversized, bold, big, rich, but heavy. Europe's finest wineries, with many centuries more experience, have mastered the ability to obtain intense flavors without heaviness. However, New World viticultural areas (particularly in California) are quickly catching up, as evidenced by the succession of remarkable wines produced in Napa, Sonoma, and elsewhere in the Golden State during the decade of the nineties. Many of California's greatest wines of the nineties have sacrificed none of their power and richness, but no longer possess the rustic tannin and oafish feel on the palate that characterized so many of their predecessors of ten and twenty years ago.

Classic Examples

1996 Coche-Dury Corton Charlemagne ($150)
1997 Arrowood Malbec Sonoma ($30)
1996 Bruno Giacosa Barbaresco Santo Stefano ($65)
1998 Yves Cuilleron Condrieu Vieilles Vignes ($50)
1995 Domaine Leflaive Chevalier-Montrachet ($135)
1995 Paul Cotat Sancerre Les Monts Damnes ($30)

THE ABILITY OF A WINE TO TASTE BETTER WITH EACH SIP

Most of the finest wines I have ever drunk were better with the last sip than the first, revealing more nuances and more complex aromas and flavors as the wine unfolded in the glass. Do readers ever wonder why the most interesting and satisfying glass of wine is often the one that finishes the bottle?

Classic Examples

1996 Marcassin Chardonnay Upper Barn Sonoma ($40)
1995 Mouton-Rothschild (Pauillac) ($200)
1994 Fonseca Vintage Port ($75)
1996 Château Léoville-Las Cases (St.-Julien) ($100)
1994 Taylor Vintage Port ($75)
1997 Falesco Montiano ($35)
1995 Château L'Eglise-Clinet (Pomerol) ($65)
1995 Araujo Estate Cabernet Sauvignon Eisele Vineyard Napa ($75)

THE ABILITY OF A WINE TO IMPROVE WITH AGE

This is, for better or worse, an indisputable characteristic of great wines. One of the unhealthy legacies of the European wine writers (who dominated wine writing until the last decade) is the belief that in order for a wine to be exceptional when mature, it had to be nasty when young. My experience has revealed just the opposite—wines that are acidic, astringent, and generally fruitless and charmless when young become even nastier and less drinkable when old. With that being said, new vintages of top wines are often unformed and in need of 10 or 12 years of cellaring (in the case of top California Cabernets, Bordeaux, and Rhône wines), but those wines should always possess a certain accessibility so that even inexperienced wine tasters can tell the wine is—at the minimum—made from very ripe fruit. If a wine does not exhibit ripeness and richness of fruit when young, it will not develop nuances with aging. Great wines unquestionably improve with age. I define "improvement" as the ability of a wine to become significantly more enjoyable and interesting in the bottle, offering more pleasure old than when it was young. Many wineries (especially in the New World) produce wines they claim "will age," but this is nothing more than a public relations ploy. What they should really say is "will survive." They can endure 10–20 years of bottle age, but they were more enjoyable in their exuberant youthfulness.

Classic Examples

1990 Château Latour (Pauillac) ($500)
1997 E. Altare Barolo Arborina ($48)
1998 Haut-Brion (Graves) ($135)
1990 Beaucastel Châteauneuf du Pape ($35)

1990 Château Climens (Barsac/Sauternes) ($85)
1989 Laville-Haut-Brion (Graves) ($135)

THE ABILITY OF A WINE TO OFFER A SINGULAR PERSONALITY
When one considers the greatest wines produced, it is their singular personalities that set
them apart. It is the same with the greatest vintages. The abused usage of a description such
as "classic vintage" has become nothing more than a reference to what a viticultural region
does in a typical (normal) year. Exceptional wines from exceptional vintages stand far above
the norm, and they can always be defined by their singular qualities—both aromatically and
in their flavors and textures. The opulent, sumptuous qualities of the 1982 and 1990 red
Bordeaux, the rugged tannin and immense ageability of the 1986 red Bordeaux, the seamless, perfectly balanced 1994 Napa and Sonoma Cabernet Sauvignons and proprietary
blends, and the plush, sweet fruit, high alcohol and glycerin of the 1990 Barolos and Barbarescos, are all examples of vintage individuality.

Classic Examples
1990 Château Le Tertre-Rôteboeuf (St.-Émilion) ($75)
1990 Sandrone Barolo Boschis ($150)
1989 Château Clinet (Pomerol) ($100)
1994 Bryant Family Vineyard Cabernet Sauvignon Napa ($55)
1994 Colgin Cabernet Sauvignon Napa ($65)
1992 Beringer Cabernet Sauvignon Private Reserve Napa ($45)
1982 Mouton Rothschild (Pauillac) ($750)
1986 Château Margaux (Margaux) ($300)
1996 Lafite-Rothschild (Pauillac) ($300)

THE WINES OF WESTERN EUROPE

France
Alsace
Bordeaux
Burgundy and Beaujolais
Champagne
The Loire Valley
Languedoc-Roussillon
Provence
The Rhône Valley
Bergerac and the Southwest

Italy
Piedmont
Tuscany

Germany and Austria

Spain and Portugal

1. FRANCE

ALSACE

Which viticultural area produces the most versatile white wines to match with food? What region continues to be an underutilized source of amazing values? Where do top wine professionals and true connoisseurs turn for whites of extraordinary aging potential, immediate hedonistic appeal, and affordable daily-drinking bottles?

The answer to all these questions is Alsace, a fairytale viticultural area in northeastern France and one of the most beautiful wine-producing regions on earth.

True connoisseurs of wine must find it appalling that so many importers trip over each other trying to find yet another excessively priced, overcropped, generally insipid Italian white or overacidified Australian Chardonnay that provides little joy, while ignoring the treasures of Alsace. Why then have these wines failed to earn the popularity they so richly deserve?

For consumers who love wine with food, Alsace produces a bevy of dry, surprisingly flavorful, personality-filled wines that generally offer superb value for the dollar. Alsace also makes it easy for the consumer to understand its wines. As is done in California, the wines are named after the grape varietal used to make them. Additionally, one of Alsace's fifty-one grand cru vineyards can be annexed to the name of the varietal. When that occurs, it usually means the wine sells at a price two to three times higher than wines that do not come from grand cru vineyards.

Another remarkable aspect of Alsace wines is how long-lived a top Riesling, Gewurztraminer, and Tokay-Pinot Gris can be. Ten to twenty years of longevity is not out of the question for the totally dry, regular cuvées and grands crus, while the rich, opulent Vendange Tardive and the supersweet, luxuriously priced dessert wines called Sélection de Grains Nobles can survive and benefit from even longer bottle age.

However, uninitiated consumers are typically reluctant to try wines from Alsace. Alsatian bottles are shaped like those from Germany. Therefore many consumers refuse to even taste them because they dislike the stylistically different German wines, or they still have bad memories of the torrents of insipid Liebfraumilchs and Piesporters sold in the United States in the 1960s and 1970s. In European markets, the sales of quality producers are negatively affected by the massive quantities of industrially crafted and tasteless wines made from high-yielding vineyards on the Alsatian plain (fields that are better suited to growing cabbages for sauerkraut, the main ingredient of Alsace's most famous dish: Choucroute Garni). Thankfully, these wines do not reach American shores. Also, Alsatian wines (even those that are completely dry) tend to be fruity and personality-filled, something that shocks consumers accustomed to tasteless or oak-dominated whites. Lastly, and this is a problem Alsatian producers need to resolve (for their own benefit), many wines whose labels would lead a con-

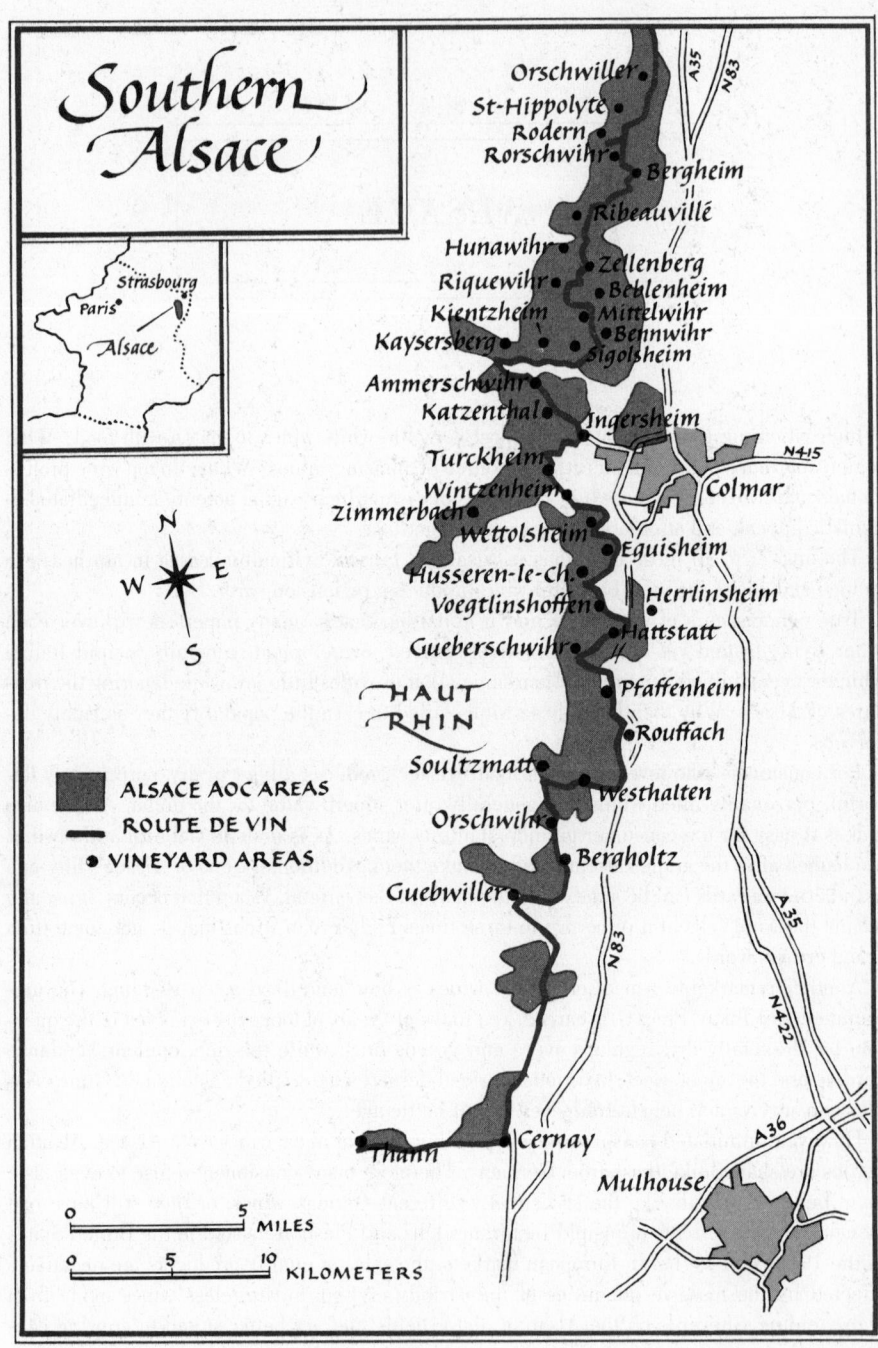

Southern Alsace

Orschwiller
St-Hippolyte
Rodern
Rorschwihr
Bergheim
Ribeauvillé
Hunawihr
Riquewihr   Zellenberg
Kientzheim   Bennwihr
Kaysersberg   Mittelwihr
                   Bennwihr
                   Sigolsheim
Ammerschwihr
Katzenthal   Ingersheim

Strasbourg
Paris
Alsace

Colmar

N415

Turckheim
Wintzenheim
Zimmerbach
Wettolsheim   Eguisheim
Husseren-le-Ch.   Herrlinsheim
Voegtlinshoffen   Hattstatt
Gueberschwihr
                   Pfaffenheim
HAUT   Rouffach
RHIN
Soultzmatt   Westhalten
Orschwihr
                   Bergholtz
Guebwiller

N
W   E
S

■ ALSACE AOC AREAS
— ROUTE DE VIN
• VINEYARD AREAS

Thann   Cernay

Mulhouse

0   5
|————————| MILES

0   5   10
|————|————| KILOMETERS

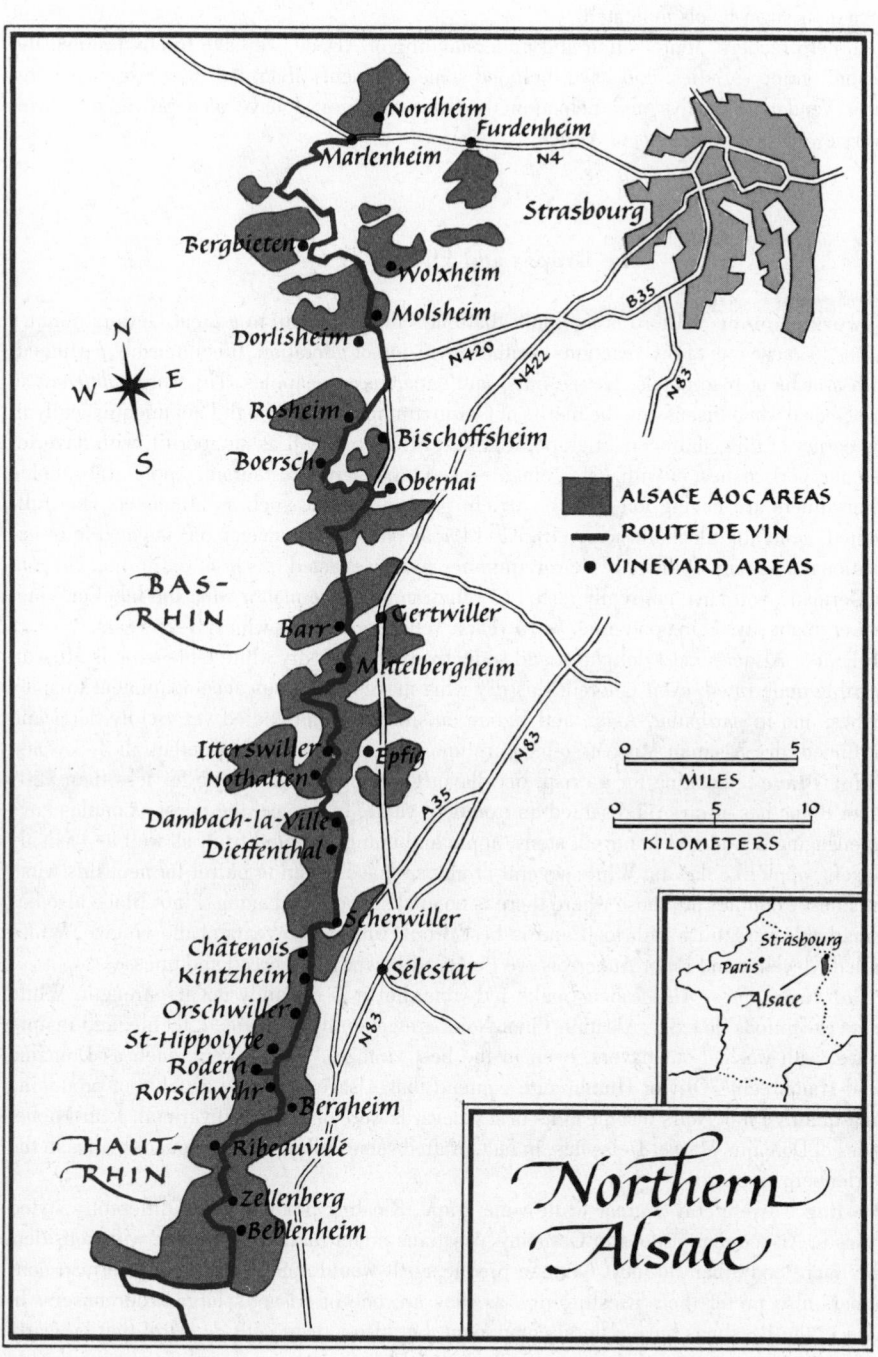

Nordheim
Furdenheim
Marlenheim
N4
Strasbourg
Bergbieten
Wolxheim
B35
Molsheim
Dorlisheim
N420
N422
N83
Rosheim
Bischoffsheim
Boersch
Obernai

ALSACE AOC AREAS
ROUTE DE VIN
VINEYARD AREAS

BAS-
RHIN

Barr
Gertwiller
Mittelbergheim

Itterswiller
Epfig
Nothalten
N83
Dambach-la-Ville
A35
Dieffenthal

Scherwiller
Châtenois
Kintzheim
Sélestat
Orschwiller
St-Hippolyte
Rodern
N83
Rorschwihr
Bergheim
HAUT-
RHIN
Ribeauvillé
Zellenberg
Beblenheim

0   5
MILES
0   5   10
KILOMETERS

Strasbourg
Paris
Alsace

Northern
Alsace

sumer to believe they are dry actually contain significant levels of residual sugar. To reduce consumer confusion, and render the buying process easier, the labels on these wines should have their sugar levels indicated.

To help readers' appreciation and understanding of Alsace, we have briefly profiled the region's grape varieties, and have included some comments about the more expensive and rarer Vendange Tardive and Sélection de Grains Nobles. I have also provided a brief overview of the grands crus of Alsace.

The Grapes and Flavors of Alsace

Gewurztraminer   There is no doubt that one's first exposure to a great Gewurztraminer seems to cause one of two reactions—either revulsion or adoration. It is intensely perfumed, with aromas of rose petals, lychee nuts, and superripe pineapples. The word *subtleness* is rarely used when discussing the merits of Gewurztraminer, and though I am unequivocally in the corner of this controversial grape, it is best drunk by itself as an apéritif, with flavorful fish and pork dishes, or with Asian cuisines. In France, great restaurants applaud its choice when diners are having foie gras or a rich, pungent cheese such as Muenster. This full-bodied, generally alcoholic wine (13.5%–14% alcohol is not uncommon) is capable of exceptional longevity. If the only Gewurztraminer you have tasted was from California, Oregon, or Germany, you have not really tasted Gewurztraminer—no matter what the label or wine-maker might say. Aging potential: 5–15 years; Vendange Tardive wines: 8–25 years.

Muscat   Alsace's most delightful and seductively fragrant dry white table wine is Muscat. Terribly underrated, even ignored, this dry wine makes a glorious accompaniment to spicy dishes, and in particular, Asian and Indian cuisine. Medium bodied yet vividly floral and perfumed, dry Alsatian Muscats offer pure finesse and charm. Aging potential: 3–5 years.

Pinot Blanc   Looking for a crisp, dry, flavorful, complex white wine for less than $20? Pinot Blanc has always represented an excellent value. In Alsace, the finest examples have an engaging bouquet of honeyed, stony, apple and orange-scented fruit, as well as stylishly elegant, applelike flavors. While several producers have begun to barrel-ferment this wine, the finest examples are those where there is no evidence of wood aging. Pinot Blanc also has remarkable versatility with food and is best drunk within 4–5 years of the vintage. Wines called Klevener and Pinot Auxerrois are Pinots with even more breed and finesse.

Pinot Noir   Yes, Alsace does make red wine, but it is certainly not its strength. While some exceptions do exist, Alsatian Pinot Noirs are generally overpriced, feeble, and insipid wines, with washed-out flavors, even in the best vintages. Top growers, such as Domaine Zind-Humbrecht's Olivier Humbrecht, contend that Alsace would be capable of producing high-quality Pinot Noirs if some of its best vineyards were used for that varietal. Jean-Michel Deiss of Domaine Marcel Deiss has, in fact, crafted some delicious reds from old vines in the Burlenberg vineyard.

Riesling   Irrefutably a great white wine grape, Riesling produces very differently styled wines in Alsace than it does in Germany. Alsatians prefer their Riesling dry, with considerably more body than do most German producers. It would appear that some German consumers also prefer their Riesling dry, as they are one of Alsace's largest purchasers. In Alsace, the Rieslings have a floral component, but also a deep *goût de pétrol* that is nearly impossible to articulate. It is an earthy, mineral-like, flinty taste that differs considerably from the slatelike, steely character found in many Rieslings from Germany's Mosel vineyards. Less floral than their German counterparts, with more of a pineapple, honeyed, orange peel character, Alsace Rieslings are medium- to full-bodied wines that can also age remarkably well. Aging potential: 3–15 years; Vendange Tardive wines: 5–25 years.

Sylvaner   This is the least appealing grape of Alsace. The wines often lack an interesting bouquet, tending to be neutral, even vegetal to smell. Because of its high acidity, Sylvaner should frequently be employed as a blending grape rather than be permitted to stand by itself. Aging potential: 1–5 years.

Tokay-Pinot Gris   Capable of producing wines as compelling as the greatest Chardonnays, Tokay-Pinot Gris reaches its height as a dry, full-bodied wine in Alsace. It is a super grape that, when picked late and fermented nearly dry or completely dry, offers a huge perfume of buttery, creamy, smoky fruit, unctuous, intense flavors, and considerable power and palate presence. Its style mandates the same types of food (rich fish dishes, etc.) with which one would normally serve a grand cru white burgundy. The Vendange Tardive Tokay-Pinot Gris wines from Alsace can contain 14%–15% alcohol naturally, and they can age well. Aging potential: 4–10 years; Vendange Tardive wines: 5–20 years.

A Note About Vendange Tardive and Sélection de Grains Nobles Wines

The late-harvested Vendange Tardive wines of Alsace are made from fully ripened (not overripe) fruit, and are powerful, rich, large-scaled wines that range in alcohol content from 14.3% to 16%. The levels of concentration and extract can be majestic. Depending on the wine producer, a Vendange Tardive wine can be fermented completely dry or left with a slight degree of residual sugar. The best of these offerings are superlative expressions of winemaking and can provide thrilling as well as provocative drinking. They also age extremely well. A little-known fact is that they frequently age longer and more gracefully than France's premier and grand cru white burgundies. Any late-harvested wine will have the designation "Vendange Tardive" on the label. The wines called Sélection de Grains Nobles represent the sweet, nectarlike, albeit rare and luxury-priced segment of the Alsatian wine hierarchy. They are often riveting because their sumptuous levels of fruit extract are unencumbered by aromas of new oak. Alsatian winemakers, as a general rule, eschew new wood casks. In effect, these wines are essences of their varietals. A Sélection de Grains Nobles can easily last 15–30 years. Many of these wines now cost more than $100—for a half-bottle!

Recent Vintages

1997—Preliminary tastings reveal that 1997 is a wonderful vintage for Gewurztraminer, and less so for Tokay-Pinot Gris and Riesling. The warmth of the summer led to a drop in natural acidities which accentuates Gewurztraminer's flamboyance, yet renders Rieslings and other varietals less complex and age-worthy. This is an early-drinking vintage, displaying Mother Nature's perfect timing after she produced the superstructured and tightly wound 1996s.

1996—This vintage is uneven in quality. It produced some extraordinary wines as well as many high-acid scorchers. What made the difference? Yields. Cool temperatures and dry winds from the north dominated the weather in August and September, resulting in grapes with abnormally high acidity levels. Those producers who cultivate high yields (in Alsace vignerons have been known to harvest up to 6 or more tons per acre) do not have the fruit to counterbalance the acidity. However, conscientious producers like Olivier Humbrecht (he averaged 2 tons per acre in 1996) crafted wines of extraordinary balance, with loads of concentration and the ability to age remarkably well. This is a vintage where many of the Tokay-Pinot Gris, as well as the majority of Gewurztraminer, lack the opulence and hedonistic appeal generally associated with these varietals because of their high-acid profiles. Riesling performed best in this vintage, with powerful petrol qualities and extraordinary delineation plainly in evidence. The finest Rieslings of 1996 will be extremely age-worthy. Few sweet wines were crafted in 1996 because there was very little botrytis.

1995—The 1995 vintage is uneven in quality. The best producers crafted magnificent Rieslings, Muscats, and Tokay-Pinot Gris while others crafted wines lacking in character, fruit, and concentration. A cold, rainy September was followed by a spectacular October and November. Producers who picked early out of fear harvested unripe grapes with high levels of acidity. Those with the courage and professionalism to wait were rewarded by a long late season with ideal weather conditions. However, 1995 is not a vintage for Gewurztraminer as this varietal requires warm temperatures to express its distinctly flamboyant personality.

1994—The 1994s produced from the finest hillside vineyards, as well as those controlled by growers who crop-thinned and kept yields small, produced massive, extremely concentrated wines. Additionally, while September's weather was fitful, those producers who harvested late were rewarded with an extraordinarily sunny and warm October. Unlike 1993, 1992, and 1991, there are abundant quantities of high-octane, rich, full-bodied Vendange Tardive wines, particularly from the finest vineyards and producers. At the top level, this is a great year.

1993—The 1993s have turned out well, as Alsace escaped the bad weather that battered much of France. The wines are lighter than the 1992s, with better acidity and more structure, as well as clean, ripe fruit. They will not be long-lived. Most 1993s will require consumption in their youth. Very little Vendange Tardive, or the sweet nectar, Sélection de Grains Nobles, was produced in this vintage.

1992—Alsace fared far better than most of southern France in this vintage. The harvest was the earliest since 1976, and the producers reported very high yields, with a lot of ripeness and richness but wines that are extremely low in acidity. There are a lot of near-term drinking wines that are forward, juicy, and user-friendly.

1991—This is Alsace's toughest vintage since 1987. Nevertheless, some producers, such as Domaines Weinbach and Zind-Humbrecht, made wines that are hard to believe came from a mediocre to below average quality year. Most wines are relatively light, overly acidic, and slightly green, in complete contrast to the soft, fruity 1992s.

1990—Amazingly, this vintage is even more consistent in quality than 1989. There were fewer Vendange Tardive and Sélection de Grains Nobles wines produced, which should be good news for consumers looking for the drier Alsatian wines. I was impressed with the quality of all the varietals, but top marks must go to the glorious Rieslings, which are even superior to the 1989s. The Gewurztraminers, which were so stunningly perfumed and rich in 1989, are slightly less intense in 1990, but perhaps better balanced and less overwhelming. All things considered, this is a top-notch vintage that looks to be every bit as good as such previous great vintages as 1989, 1985, and 1983.

1989—The 1989 most resembles 1983 in that the wines are superripe, strong, forceful, and heady, with exceptional perfume, and, at times, mind-boggling richness. The vintage produced amazing quantities of Vendange Tardive and Sélection de Grains Nobles wines. In fact, at the sweeter end of the spectrum, 1989 is probably unequaled by any recent Alsace vintage. Even the totally dry wines tend to be massive. There is plenty of great wine from which to pick, although most wines' aging potential will have to be monitored, given the relatively low acidity.

1988—This is a very good vintage that suffers only when compared with 1989 and 1990. The very dry, stylish wines may lack the concentration and sheer drama of the 1989s and 1990s; they are, nevertheless, elegant, suave, and graceful. Most of the top Rieslings, Gewurztraminers, and grands crus will easily last for a decade or more.

Older Vintages

The 1987 is surprisingly good, particularly in view of its so-so reputation. Some producers, such as Domaine Zind-Humbrecht, made superb wines in 1987. Overall, the quality is at least good, and in many cases excellent. Hardly any Vendange Tardive or Sélection de Grains Nobles were made in this vintage because of fall rains. The 1986 was a patchy vintage, but as is expected from the finest producers, Domaines Zind-Humbrecht and Weinbach made many glorious wines even in this difficult year. To the extent one can still find any of the 1985s, it is one of the four or five best vintages for Alsace in the last 15 years. The wines are rich, with decent acidity, and are evolving gracefully in the bottle. They should provide delicious drinking and, in the case of the better Tokay-Pinot Gris, Rieslings, and Gewurztraminers, are capable of lasting for at least another decade. The 1984 and 1982 vintages get my vote as the two worst of the decade, and are of no interest. However, 1983 was another great vintage for Alsace. I bought nearly twenty cases of the 1983s and have drunk them with immense pleasure since their release. Despite their low acidity and relatively intense, concentrated style, they have displayed no signs of cracking up. Many of the bigger-styled Rieslings and Gewurztraminers are still improving. To the extent that anyone is lucky enough to find well-stored bottles of 1976s, 1971s, or 1967s, these wines can provide remarkable evidence of the aging potential of Alsace's top wines. I suspect the only places they may appear are at auctions, and probably at alluring prices.

THE SIGNIFICANCE OF ALSACE'S GRAND CRU SYSTEM

Alsace, like Burgundy, has developed a complicated grand cru system that is still the subject of considerable controversy. There is no doubt that many of the best hillside vineyards in Alsace have been included in the grand cru classification. However, there is no qualitative justification for excluding the *monopole* (single-proprietor) vineyards from being considered grands crus. For this reason, irrefutably superb sites such as the Clos Sainte Hune, Clos Windsbuhl, and Clos des Capucins are deprived of such status (Clos Sainte Hune is part of a grand cru that the Trimbach's are entitled to list on the label; however, if they were to do so, they would be prevented from listing the famous Clos' name). Moreover, some of the region's top producers—Hugel, Beyer, and Trimbach—have refused to indicate any grand cru designation on their top cuvées, despite the fact that the bulk of their *réserve* wines are made from grand cru vineyards. Add to these problems the fact that the politicians of each wine village in Alsace have effectively persuaded authorities to give them their "own" grand cru. The political concessions have already resulted in over 50 grands crus, which is nearly 20 more than what is permitted in Burgundy's Côte d'Or. Moreover, some of these vineyards have not yet had their boundaries defined by the authorities. In spite of its weaknesses, the grand cru system is an incentive for producers to achieve the best from the most privileged hillside vineyards.

To help readers understand the grands crus, which will, for better or worse, become of increasing significance, we have listed the major grands crus in alphabetical order, along with the best producers from each grand cru. Additionally, we have attempted to summarize some of the more relevant characteristics of each vineyard from information provided by the Alsace Wine Information Bureau.

THE PRINCIPAL GRANDS CRUS OF ALSACE

Altenberg de Bergbieten   SIZE: 67.3 acres; RELEVANT FACTS: hillside vineyard with a full southeast exposure and gypsum, clay, and gravelly soils; PRIVILEGED VARIETALS: Riesling and Gewurztraminer are considered superb, but Tokay-Pinot Gris and Muscat are also grown on these slopes; BEST PRODUCER: Frédérick Mochel

Altenberg de Bergheim   SIZE: 80.6 acres; RELEVANT FACTS: limestone and marl dominate the soil of this hillside vineyard, which is renowned for its superb Riesling, and to a lesser extent, for its Gewurztraminer; PRIVILEGED VARIETALS: Riesling and Gewurztraminer; BEST PRODUCERS: Marcel Deiss, Charles Koehly, Gustave Lorentz

Brand   SIZE: 140 acres; RELEVANT FACTS: This gorgeous hillside vineyard behind the village of Turckheim has a south-southeast exposure. The soil is deep granite, laced with black mica. PRIVILEGED VARIETALS: Riesling, Tokay-Pinot Gris, and Gewurztraminer; BEST PRODUCERS: Zind-Humbrecht, Dopff "Au Moulin," Pierre Sparr, Albert Boxler

Eichberg   SIZE: 142.3 acres; RELEVANT FACTS: Not far from Colmar, Eichberg is renowned for its Gewurztraminers, followed by Tokay-Pinot Gris and Riesling. With its limestone/marl soil and gentle southeast slope, this area can produce powerful wines in hot, sunny years. PRIVILEGED VARIETALS: Gewurztraminer, Riesling, and Tokay-Pinot Gris; BEST PRODUCERS: Leon Beyer's Comtes d'Eguisheim (100% from the Eichberg vineyard), Kuentz-Bas Gewurztraminer

Engelberg   SIZE: 27 acres; RELEVANT FACTS: a limestone/marl soil that drains exceptionally well; PRIVILEGED VARIETALS: Gewurztraminer and Riesling

Florimont   SIZE: 27 acres; RELEVANT FACTS: This steep, south- and east-facing, limestone vineyard is located outside the village of Ingersheim. PRIVILEGED VARIETAL: Gewurztraminer

Frankstein   SIZE: 131 acres; RELEVANT FACTS: Actually four separate parcels, this is a steep, southeast-facing vineyard with superb drainage. PRIVILEGED VARIETALS: Riesling and Gewurztraminer; BEST PRODUCERS: Louis Gisselbrecht, Willi Gisselbrecht

Froehn   SIZE: 32 acres; RELEVANT FACTS: Located outside the village of Zellenberg, this small grand cru has a reputation for long-lived wines. PRIVILEGED VARIETALS: Gewurztraminer, Tokay-Pinot Gris, and Muscat; BEST PRODUCER: Jean Becker

Furstenturm   SIZE: 68 acres; RELEVANT FACTS: This superbly situated, steep, hillside vineyard not far from Kaysersberg has a warm microclimate, producing full-bodied, rich wines. PRIVILEGED VARIETALS: Gewurztraminer, Riesling, and Tokay-Pinot Gris; BEST PRODUCERS: Domaine Weinbach, Paul Blanck

Geisberg   SIZE: 21 acres; RELEVANT FACTS: A steep, terraced vineyard overlooking the charming village of Ribeauvillé, Geisberg is known for its very gravelly and limestone-mixed soils, and its powerful, elegant wines. PRIVILEGED VARIETAL: Riesling; BEST PRODUCER: Trimbach (Cuvée Frédéric Emile)

Gloeckelberg   SIZE: 57.8 acres; RELEVANT FACTS: Located near the villages of Saint-Hippolyte and Rodern, this moderate-sized vineyard has a south and southeast exposure with round, relatively acidic soil composed of sand, gypsum, and gravel. PRIVILEGED VARIETALS: Tokay-Pinot Gris, followed by Gewurztraminer; BEST PRODUCER: Charles Koehly

Goldert   SIZE: 111.9 acres; RELEVANT FACTS: One of the more striking vineyards in Alsace, located north of the village of Gueberschwihr, Goldert is situated at a relatively high altitude with deep calcareous soil and an east-southeasterly exposure. It is particularly renowned for its well-drained soils that produce superb Gewurztraminer and Muscat. PRIVILEGED VARIETALS: Gewurztraminer, followed by Muscat; BEST PRODUCERS: Ernest Burn, Zind-Humbrecht

Hatschbourg   SIZE: 116.8 acres; RELEVANT FACTS: Located south of Colmar, near the village of Voegtlinshoffen, this hillside vineyard has a calcareous, marl-like soil that provides excellent drainage, and a south-southeast exposure. PRIVILEGED VARIETALS: Gewurztraminer, followed by Tokay-Pinot Gris and Riesling; BEST PRODUCERS: Joseph Cattin, Gerard Hartmann

Hengst   SIZE: 187.2 acres; RELEVANT FACTS: This relatively large vineyard, south of the village of Wintzenheim, has a south-southeast exposure. The combined calcareous and marl soils tend to produce rich, full-bodied wines. PRIVILEGED VARIETALS: Gewurztraminer, followed by Tokay-Pinot Gris and Riesling; BEST PRODUCERS: Josmeyer, Zind-Humbrecht, Albert Mann, Barmes-Bucher

Kanzlerberg   SIZE: 8.1 acres; RELEVANT FACTS: This tiny vineyard near the village of Bergheim, just west of the grand cru Altenberg, has a very heavy clay/limestone soil intermixed with gypsum and marl. Powerful wines emerge from this gem of a vineyard. PRIVILEGED VARIETALS: Tokay-Pinot Gris and Gewurztraminer; BEST PRODUCER: Gustave Lorentz

Kastelberg   SIZE: 14.3 acres; RELEVANT FACTS: This steeply terraced vineyard in the very northern part of Alsace's viticultural region, near Andlau, is composed of deep layers of schist and quartz, the perfect soil base for Riesling. PRIVILEGED VARIETAL: Riesling; BEST PRODUCERS: Marc Kreydenweiss, Klipfel

Kessler   SIZE: 70.4 acres; RELEVANT FACTS: Steep, terraced vineyards composed of red sandstone, clay, and sand are situated in the very southern part of Alsace's viticultural region, with a stunning southeast exposure. PRIVILEGED VARIETALS: Gewurztraminer and Tokay-Pinot Gris, followed by Riesling; BEST PRODUCERS: Schlumberger, Dirler

Kirchberg de Barr   SIZE: 92 acres; RELEVANT FACTS: Located in the northern section of Alsace's viticultural region, behind the village of Barr, this vineyard has a southeast exposure and a soil base of calcareous marl with underlying beds of limestone and gravel. PRIVILEGED VARIETALS: Gewurztraminer, Riesling, and Tokay-Pinot Gris; BEST PRODUCERS: Emile Boeckel, A. Willm

Kirchberg de Ribeauvillé   SIZE: 28.2 acres; RELEVANT FACTS: The stony, claylike soil, with a south-southwest exposure, produces relatively full-bodied wines that require some time in the bottle to develop their bouquets. PRIVILEGED VARIETALS: Riesling and Muscat, followed by Gewurztraminer; BEST PRODUCER: Trimbach

Kitterlé   SIZE: 63.7 acres; RELEVANT FACTS: Perhaps the most striking terraced vineyard in Alsace, Kitterlé, which sits on the photogenic, steep slopes overlooking the town of Guebwiller, has three different exposures: south, southeast, and southwest. The soils consist of red sandstone, with plenty of quartz intermixed with lighter, sandier, gravelly soil that produces wines of extraordinary richness and aging potential. PRIVILEGED VARIETALS: Gewurztraminer, Riesling, and Tokay-Pinot Gris; BEST PRODUCER: Schlumberger (astonishing wines from this vineyard)

Mambourg   SIZE: 161 acres; RELEVANT FACTS: Mambourg, a hillside vineyard overlooking the village of Sigolsheim, has a calcareous and marl-like soil that produces very low yields. This heavy soil base is ideal for Gewurztraminer. PRIVILEGED VARIETALS: Gewurztraminer, followed by Tokay-Pinot Gris, Muscat, and Riesling; BEST PRODUCER: Sparr

Mandelberg   SIZE: 29.7 acres; RELEVANT FACTS: Located near the village of Mittelwihr, this hillside vineyard has a marl and limestone soil base. PRIVILEGED VARIETALS: Gewurztraminer, followed by Riesling

Marckrain   SIZE: 111.7 acres; RELEVANT FACTS: Calcareous marl soil with clay makes up this vineyard, located just south of the village of Bennwihr. The heavy soil produces relatively rich, fragrant, full-bodied wines. PRIVILEGED VARIETALS: Gewurztraminer and Tokay-Pinot Gris

Moenchberg   SIZE: 29.5 acres; RELEVANT FACTS: Light, red sandstone intermixed with limestone makes up the soil of this hillside vineyard in northern Alsace, between the villages of Andlau and Eichhoffen. PRIVILEGED VARIETAL: Riesling; BEST PRODUCERS: Ostertag, Kreydenweiss

Muenchberg   SIZE: 62 acres; RELEVANT FACTS: Light gravelly, sandy, nutrient-poor soil is ideal for producing closed but highly concentrated wines. PRIVILEGED VARIETAL: Riesling; BEST PRODUCERS: Julien Meyer, André Gresser

Ollwiller   SIZE: 86.5 acres; RELEVANT FACTS: Located in the most southern sector of Alsace's viticultural region, near the village of Wuenheim (situated midway between Guebwiller and Thann), this hillside vineyard with a southeast exposure has soils made up of red sandstone and clay. PRIVILEGED VARIETALS: Riesling and Gewurztraminer

Osterberg   SIZE: 59.3 acres; RELEVANT FACTS: With stony, claylike soils, the Osterberg vineyard is located near the village of Ribeauvillé. PRIVILEGED VARIETALS: Riesling, Gewurztraminer, and Tokay-Pinot Gris; BEST PRODUCER: Trimbach

Pfersigberg   SIZE: 138 acres; RELEVANT FACTS: Gravelly soils with rich deposits of magnesium make up this vineyard, located near the village of Eguisheim within view of the three ruined towers that dominate the hillside above Husseren-les-Châteaux. PRIVILEGED VARIETALS: Gewurztraminer, Tokay-Pinot Gris, Riesling, and Muscat; BEST PRODUCERS: Kuentz-Bas, Scherer

Pfingstberg   SIZE: 69 acres; RELEVANT FACTS: With its southeast exposure and location in the southern part of Alsace's viticultural region, just to the north of Guebwiller, the red sandstone and mica-based soils produce classic, long-lived wines. PRIVILEGED VARIETALS: Gewurztraminer, Tokay-Pinot Gris, and Riesling; BEST PRODUCER: Albrecht

Praelatenberg   SIZE: 29.6 acres; RELEVANT FACTS: This hillside vineyard, located beneath the formidable mountaintop château of Haut-Koenigsbourg, possesses a heavy but well-drained soil consisting of gravel and quartz. PRIVILEGED VARIETALS: Riesling, followed by Gewurztraminer and Muscat

Rangen   SIZE: 46.4 acres; RELEVANT FACTS: One of the greatest of the grands crus, this vineyard, located at the very southern end of the viticultural region of Alsace, on steeply terraced hillsides with a full southerly exposure, has a soil base composed of volcanic rocks, schist, and numerous outcroppings of rocks. PRIVILEGED VARIETALS: Tokay-Pinot Gris, Gewurztraminer, and Riesling; BEST PRODUCERS: Zind-Humbrecht, Bernard Schoffit, Bruno Hertz, Meyer-Fonne

Rosacker   SIZE: 67.2 acres; RELEVANT FACTS: Located north of the village of Hunawihr, near the Clos Windsbuhl (one of the finest enclosed vineyards, called "clos"), this hillside vineyard with its east-southeast exposure is planted on calcareous, magnesium-enriched, heavy soil, with some sandstone. The greatest enclosed vineyard of Alsace, the Trimbach's Clos Sainte-Hune is located within Rosacker but is not labelled as such (by law, the Trimbachs must choose whether to label it by its grand cru or by its significantly more famous name). PRIVILEGED VARIETALS: Riesling, followed by Gewurztraminer; BEST PRODUCER: Mittnacht-Klack

Saering   SIZE: 66 acres; RELEVANT FACTS: The Saering vineyards, with their east-southeasterly exposure, form part of the same striking hillside that contains the famous Kitterlé vineyard. Both overlook the bustling town of Guebwiller. The soil at Saering is heavy, sandy, mixed gravel and chalk, which is perfect for Riesling. PRIVILEGED VARIETAL: Riesling; BEST PRODUCERS: Schlumberger, Jean-Pierre Dirler

Schlossberg   SIZE: 197 acres; RELEVANT FACTS: Steep, terraced, sandy, gravelly, mineral-rich soils dominate this vineyard, located behind the charming village of Kaysersberg in the direction of Kientzheim. This is one of the largest grands crus, so quality varies enormously. PRIVILEGED VARIETAL: Riesling; BEST PRODUCERS: Domaine Weinbach, Pierre Sparr, Albert Mann

Schoenenbourg   SIZE: 99 acres; RELEVANT FACTS: This outstanding, as well as scenically beautiful, steep vineyard behind the walled village of Riquewihr is rich in marl, gypsum, sandstone, and fine gravelly soil. PRIVILEGED VARIETALS: Riesling, followed by Muscat and some Tokay-Pinot Gris; BEST PRODUCERS: Hugel (their top cuvées usually contain high percentages of Riesling from the Schoenenbourg vineyard), Deiss, Beyer, Mittnacht-Klack

Sommerberg   SIZE: 66.7 acres; RELEVANT FACTS: One of the steepest hillside vineyards in Alsace, Sommerberg is composed of hard granite and black mica, and has a full southerly orientation. The vineyard is located behind the village of Niedermorschwihr. PRIVILEGED VARIETAL: Riesling; BEST PRODUCERS: Albert Boxler, Jean Geiler

Sonnenglanz   SIZE: 81.5 acres; RELEVANT FACTS: The southeasterly exposure and sloping hillside location, with vines planted on relatively heavy soil in a particularly dry microclimate, make Sonnenglanz one of the most favorable vineyard sites for Tokay-Pinot Gris and Gewurztraminer. PRIVILEGED VARIETALS: Tokay-Pinot Gris and Gewurztraminer; BEST PRODUCER: Bott-Geyl

Spiegel   SIZE: 45.2 acres; RELEVANT FACTS: Located between Guebwiller and Bergholtz in the southern area of Alsace, the Spiegel vineyards are on sandy soils with a full easterly exposure. PRIVILEGED VARIETALS: Tokay-Pinot Gris and Gewurztraminer; BEST PRODUCER: Dirler

Sporen   SIZE: 54.3 acres; RELEVANT FACTS: This great vineyard for Gewurztraminer, planted on deep, rich soils with a great deal of phosphoric acid, overlooks the splendid, pretty-as-a-postcard village of Riquewihr. The wines that emerge are among the richest and longest-lived in the region, although they need time in the bottle to develop. PRIVILEGED VARIETALS: Gewurztraminer, followed by Tokay-Pinot Gris; BEST PRODUCERS: Hugel (their top cuvées of Gewurztraminer are almost entirely made from the Sporen vineyard), Mittnacht-Klack, Dopff "Au Moulin"

Steinert   SIZE: 93.8 acres; RELEVANT FACTS: The stony limestone soils of this vineyard, located on a sloping hillside in a particularly dry area of Alsace, produce very aromatic wines. PRIVILEGED VARIETALS: Gewurztraminer, followed by Tokay-Pinot Gris and Riesling

Steingrubler   SIZE: 47 acres; RELEVANT FACTS: Another hillside vineyard with a sandy soil at the top slopes, and richer, less well drained soils at the bottom of the slopes, Steingrubler has a reputation for producing wines of great longevity. PRIVILEGED VARIETALS: Riesling and Gewurztraminer

Steinklotz   SIZE: 59.3 acres; RELEVANT FACTS: This most northerly grand cru Alsace vineyard, located near the village of Marlenheim, has a south-southeasterly orientation and very gravelly calcareous soils. PRIVILEGED VARIETALS: Tokay-Pinot Gris, followed by Riesling and Gewurztraminer

Vorbourg   SIZE: 178 acres; RELEVANT FACTS: This vineyard, located near the village of Rouffach in the southern sector of Alsace's viticultural region, is composed of limestone- and marl-enriched soils spread over the hillside, with a south-southeast exposure. Ideal ripening conditions exist in this relatively hot, dry microclimate. PRIVILEGED VARIETALS: Riesling, Gewurztraminer, Tokay-Pinot Gris, and Muscat; BEST PRODUCER: Muré

Wiebelsberg   SIZE: 25.5 acres; RELEVANT FACTS: This spectacularly situated hillside vineyard, overlooking the village of Andlau, is planted on well-drained sandstone, sandy soils. PRIVILEGED VARIETAL: Riesling; BEST PRODUCERS: Marc Kreydenweiss, Boeckel

Wineck-Schlossberg   SIZE: 59.2 acres; RELEVANT FACTS: Located west of the city of Colmar in the foothills of the Vosges Mountains, near the village of Katzenthal, this relatively obscure grand cru vineyard is planted on deep granite soils, producing very long-lived, subtle wines. PRIVILEGED VARIETALS: Riesling, followed by Gewurztraminer

Winzenberg   SIZE: 123 acres; RELEVANT FACTS: Located in the northern Bas-Rhin sector of Alsace, with a south-southeast exposure, and a granite, mica-infused soil base, Winzenberg is one of the least-known Alsace grands crus. PRIVILEGED VARIETALS: Riesling, followed by Gewurztraminer

Zinnkoepflé   SIZE: 153 acres; RELEVANT FACTS: This stunningly beautiful, steep, hillside vineyard, oriented toward the south-southeast, and planted on deep beds of sandstone in the southern part of Alsace's viticultural region near Soultzmatt, produces very powerful, spicy, rich wines. PRIVILEGED VARIETALS: Gewurztraminer, followed by Riesling and Tokay-Pinot Gris

Zotzenberg   SIZE: 84 acres; RELEVANT FACTS: This vineyard, located north of Epfig just south of Barr, has an easterly and southerly exposure, and is planted on marl- and limestone-based soils. The gradual sloping hillside is best known for its Gewurztraminer and Riesling. PRIVILEGED VARIETALS: Gewurztraminer and Riesling.

THE MOST FAMOUS CLOS OF ALSACE

Some of Alsace's greatest wines come not from grand cru vineyards, but from vineyards entitled to be called "clos" (meaning enclosed or walled vineyards). The most famous of these clos include the spectacular Clos des Capucins (12.6 acres), just outside the village of Kaysersberg, which is owned by the remarkable Madame Faller of Domaine Weinbach. Extraordinary Riesling, Gewurztraminer, and Tokay-Pinot Gris that are often far superior to most grands crus emerge from this vineyard. The Clos Gaensbroennel (14.8 acres), located near the northerly village of Barr, has provided me with some of the most remarkable and long-lived Gewurztraminers I have had the pleasure to taste. Clos Gaensbroennel is owned by Willm. Perhaps the best-known clos in all of Alsace is Clos Sainte Hune (3.08 acres), which is owned by the famous firm of Trimbach in Ribeauvillé. It is planted entirely with Riesling. Rieslings that emerge from this vineyard, often referred to as the Romanée-Conti of Alsace, generally require 5 years of cellaring to attain their peak and can easily last and evolve in a graceful manner for 15–20 or more years.

Other exceptional clos include the Clos Saint Imer (12.5 acres), owned by Ernest Burn. As the tasting notes evidence, the Riesling, Gewurztraminer, and Tokay-Pinot Gris that come from this spectacularly placed clos near the village of Gueberschwihr rank among the very finest in all of Alsace.

Near Rouffach is one of the largest enclosed Alsace vineyards, the Clos Saint Landelin (39.5 acres), owned by the firm of Muré. Rich, full bodied, opulent Gewurztraminer, Riesling, Tokay-Pinot Gris, and even a splendid dry Muscat are made from this enclosed hillside vineyard's grapes.

The Domaine Zind-Humbrecht also owns two well-known vineyards entitled to the designation clos. Their most famous is the Clos Saint Urbain (12.5 acres). This sensationally located, steeply terraced vineyard, planted on granite soils, with a full southeasterly exposure near the village of Thann, makes astonishingly rich, long-lived Gewurztraminer, Riesling, and Tokay-Pinot Gris. The latter wine, for my money, is the Montrachet of Alsace. The other great clos owned by Zind-Humbrecht is the Clos Windsbuhl (11.1 acres). Located on a steep hillside behind the magnificent church of Hunawihr, and near the renowned Trimbach vineyard of Clos Sainte Hune Clos Windsbuhl is planted on a limestone and stony soil, with an east-southeast exposure. Majestic Gewurztraminer is produced, as well as small quantities of Tokay-Pinot Gris and Riesling.

Though I am less familiar with the following vineyards, I have been impressed with the Clos Zisser (12.5 acres), owned by the Domaine Klipfel and planted entirely with Gewurztraminer. Other well-known clos with which I have less experience include proprietor Jean Sipp's Clos du Schlossberg (3 acres) outside the village of Ribeauvillé. Lastly, Marc Kreydenweiss has consistently made some of the finest dry Muscat from the Clos Rebgarten (0.5 acre), which is planted on sandy, gravelly soil just outside the village of Andlau.

The wines from these clos are very bit as sensational as, and in many cases greatly superior to, many of the grands crus. *In vino politiques?*

BUYING STRATEGY:
Readers searching out wines for immediate consumption will tremendously enjoy the 1997s, while those wanting Rieslings structured for the long haul should concentrate on the 1996s.

IN SEARCH OF THE BEST

(Alsace's greatest wines, on par with the world's finest)

Bott-Geyl Gewurztraminer Furstentum
Bott-Geyl Gewurztraminer Sonnenglanz
Vieilles Vignes
Bott-Geyl Muscat Schoenenbourg
Bott-Geyl Tokay-Pinot Gris Sonnenglanz
Ernest or J. et F. Burn Gewurztraminer
Clos Saint Imer Goldert
Ernest or J. et F. Burn Gewurztraminer
Clos Saint Imer Goldert Cuvée La
Chapelle
Ernest or J. et F. Burn Riesling Clos Saint
Imer Goldert
Ernest or J. et F. Burn Tokay-Pinot Gris
Clos Saint Imer Goldert
Ernest or J. et F. Burn Tokay-Pinot Gris
Clos Saint Imer Goldert Cuvée La
Chapelle
Marcel Deiss Gewurztraminer Altenberg
Marcel Deiss Riesling Altenberg
Marcel Deiss Riesling Engelgarten Vieilles
Vignes
Marcel Deiss Riesling Grasberg
Marcel Deiss Riesling Schoenenbourg
Kuentz-Bas Gewurztraminer Eichberg
Kuentz-Bas Gewurztraminer Pfersigberg
Kuentz-Bas Riesling Pfersigberg
Kuentz-Bas Tokay-Pinot Gris Réserve
Personnelle Cuvée Caroline
Gustave Lorentz Gewurztraminer Altenberg
Albert Mann Gewurztraminer Furstentum
Albert Mann Gewurztraminer Hengst
Albert Mann Gewurztraminer Steingrubler
Albert Mann Riesling Schlossberg
Albert Mann Tokay-Pinot Gris Hengst
Domaine Schoffit Gewurztraminer Rangen
Clos Saint Théobald
Domaine Schoffit Riesling Rangen Clos
Saint Théobald
Domaine Schoffit Tokay-Pinot Gris Rangen
Clos Saint Théobald

Domaine Trimbach Gewurztraminer
Seigneurs de Ribeaupierre
Domaine Trimbach Riesling Clos Saint
Hune
Domaine Trimbach Riesling Cuvée
Frédéric Emile
Domaine Weinbach Gewurztraminer Cuvée
Laurence Altenbourg
Domaine Weinbach Gewurztraminer Cuvée
Laurence Furstentum
Domaine Weinbach Riesling Schlossberg
Domaine Weinbach Tokay-Pinot Gris
Sainte Catherine
Willm Gewurztraminer Clos Gaensbroennel
Zind-Humbrecht Gewurztraminer Clos
Windsbuhl
Zind-Humbrecht Gewurztraminer Goldert
Zind-Humbrecht Gewurztraminer
Heimbourg
Zind-Humbrecht Gewurztraminer Hengst
Zind-Humbrecht Gewurztraminer Rangen
Clos Saint Urbain
Zind-Humbrecht Gewurztraminer
Wintzenheim
Zind-Humbrecht Riesling Brand
Zind-Humbrecht Riesling Clos Hauserer
Zind-Humbrecht Riesling Clos Windsbuhl
Zind-Humbrecht Riesling Gueberschwihr
Zind-Humbrecht Riesling Herrenweg
Zind-Humbrecht Riesling Rangen Clos
Saint Urbain
Zind-Humbrecht Riesling Turckheim
Zind-Humbrecht Riesling Wintzenheim
Zind-Humbrecht Tokay-Pinot Gris Clos
Jebsal
Zind-Humbrecht Tokay-Pinot Gris
Heimbourg
Zind-Humbrecht Tokay-Pinot Gris Vieilles
Vignes

RATING ALSACE'S BEST PRODUCERS

***** *(OUTSTANDING)*

Albert Boxler
Ernest and J. et F. Burn
Marcel Deiss
Jean-Pierre Dirler

Hugel (Cuvée Jubilee)
Josmeyer (single-vineyard cuvées)
Marc Kreydenweiss
Albert Mann

Mittnacht-Klack

Charles Schleret

Bernard and Robert Schoffit

Domaine Trimbach (top cuvées)

Domaine Weinbach

Zind-Humbrecht

* * * * (EXCELLENT)

J. B. Adam

Lucien Albrecht

Bott-Geyl

Dopff "Au Moulin" (single-vineyard
  cuvées)

Sick Dreyer

Pierre Frick

Hugel (Cuvée Tradition)

Josmeyer (regular cuvées)

Kuehn

Kuentz-Bas

Julien Meyer

Meyer-Fonne

Muré-Clos Saint Landelin

Domaine Ostertag

Rolly-Gassmann

Jean Schaetzel

Schlumberger

Pierre Sparr (single-vineyard cuvées)

Jeane-Martin Spielmann

Marc Tempé

* * * (GOOD)

Barmes-Buecher

J. M. Baumann

Jean-Claude Beck

Jean-Pierre Becker

Leon Beyer

Emile Boeckel

Bott Frères

Joseph Cattin

Cave de Pfaffenheim

Cave Vinicole Turckheim

Dopff "Au Moulin" (regular cuvées)

Dopff et Irion

Jean Geiler

Gérard et Serge Hartmann

Charles Koehly et Fils

Seppi Landmann

Gustave Lorentz

Muré-Clos Saint Landelin (regular cuvées)

Preiss-Henny

André Scherer

Maurice Schoech

Pierre Sparr (regular cuvées)

Domaine Trimbach (regular cuvées)

Willm

* * (AVERAGE PRODUCERS)

Cave Vinicole de Bennwihr

Cave Vinicole de Hunawihr

Cave Vinicole Kientzheim

Cave Vinicole d'Obernai

Robert Faller

Hubert Hartmann

Bruno Hertz

Jean-Pierre Klein

Preiss Zimmer

Albert Seltz

Louis Sipp

Bernard Weber

Wolfberger

Wunsch et Mann

J. B. ADAM (AMMERSCHWIHR)

1995 Gewurztraminer Cuvée Jean-Baptiste Kaefferkopf	D	88
1997 Gewurztraminer Réserve	C	88
1995 Gewurztraminer Réserve	D	87
1995 Muscat Réserve	C	87
1997 Pinot Blanc d'Alsace Réserve	B	86
1996 Pinot Blanc d'Alsace Réserve	B	86

1996 Riesling d'Alsace Réserve	B	87+
1995 Riesling Cuvée Jean-Baptiste Kaefferkopf	D	87
1995 Riesling Réserve	C	85
1995 Tokay-Pinot Gris Cuvée Jean-Baptiste	D	87
1997 Tokay-Pinot Gris Réserve	C	87

Jean-Baptiste Adam, a charming and engaging man, produces wines from the 37 acres of vineyards he owns and from purchased grapes. Two vintages of his wines currently readily available in the U.S. are the high-acid, focused, and sometimes strident 1996s and the fruit-driven and often opulent 1997s.

The 1996 Pinot Blanc d'Alsace Réserve (on an Adam label "Réserve" indicates the wine was produced from purchased grapes, "Cuvée J-B Adam" indicates it was produced from estate-grown grapes) offers a tangy nose of minerals, citrus fruits, and nuts. This fresh, well-made, lively, floral, and light- to medium-bodied wine exhibits good richness and focus. It should be drunk over the next 1–2 years. The honeysuckle and petrol-scented 1996 Riesling d'Alsace Réserve (Adam calls 1996 "the year of Riesling") displays liquid minerals, chalk, and lemon/lime flavors in its silky, dry, crisp, and medium-bodied character. This appealingly long wine will be loved by those readers who shy away from opulent, thick, fruit-driven wines and prefer superfocused, bright, and vibrant offerings. Anticipated maturity: now–2003.

The 1997 is 1996's opposite. While J-B Adam's 1996 Pinot Blanc's appeal results from its crisp freshness, his 1997 Pinot Blanc d'Alsace Réserve pleases because of its ripe, fat fruit. This wine displays an earthy, stony, and pear-imbued nose as well as a thickly textured, medium-bodied, dense, sweet flower and white fruit-filled personality. Drink it over the next 1–2 years. The 1997 Tokay-Pinot Gris d'Alsace Réserve reveals excellent ripeness and a medium-bodied, extracted, concentrated, and rich core of pears, earth, and sweet white fruits. Anticipated maturity: now–2002. Adam adores the Gewurztraminers produced in 1997, calling them an "all-world Gewurz year." His 1997 Gewurztraminer Réserve displays loads of rose water-drenched lychee nuts on the nose. Its spicy, seductive, and medium-bodied character is packed with white peaches, lychee nuts, roses, and traces of ripe bananas. Readers who appreciate the in-your-face qualities of a warm vintage Gewurz will love what this wine delivers for the price. Drink it over the next 2 years.

Adam's crisp, refreshing, dry-styled wines are among the better values in high-quality Alsatian whites. Adam, whose cellars are in the charming village of Ammerschwihr, has released some of his 1995s, all of which are high-quality, cleanly made, mineral- and fruit-driven wines. Among the Rieslings, the 1995 Réserve offers attractive apple, mineral, and orange skinlike notes, accompanied by medium body, excellent purity, and a crisp, dry, austere finish. The 1995 Riesling Cuvée Jean-Baptiste Kaefferkopf is more intense and longer on the palate, as well as more closed. It exhibits a floral, mineral, and peach-scented nose, medium body, good underlying acidity, and an attractive, long finish with liquefied minerals for added attraction. For a delectable, fruit cocktail-like wine, check out Adam's 1995 Muscat Réserve. The wine possesses an exotic but more restrained nose than offered by many Muscats, giving it finesse and elegance. The wine is medium bodied, dry, and impeccably made. While the Rieslings will drink well for 2–4 years, the Muscat needs to be drunk over the next 12–18 months to take advantage of its enticing aromatics.

The 1995 Tokay-Pinot Gris Cuvée Jean-Baptiste displays an attractive citrusy, lemon custard-scented nose with buttery fruit, medium body, excellent depth, and a dry, fleshy, crisp finish. It is a rich, polished, well-balanced Tokay-Pinot Gris that should drink well for 4–5 years. The 1995 Gewurztraminer Réserve reveals a honeyed grapefruit-scented nose, medium body, surprising elegance for a Gewurztraminer, and a crisp, dry finish. It should be drunk over the next several years. The 1995 Gewurztraminer Cuvée Jean-Baptiste Kaefferkopf is a broader, richer, more expansive wine, but still surprisingly restrained for this varietal. The nose offers up honeyed lychee nuts, pineapple, and grapefruit scents. This medium- to full-bodied, dry, long wine should drink well for 3–4 years.

LUCIEN ALBRECHT (ORSCHWIHR)

1997 Gewurztraminer	B	87
1997 Riesling	B	86

Two early-bottled 1997s that offer very good value for classy whites from Alsace, the 1997 Riesling exhibits a crisp, pear/apple, floral, and mineral-scented nose, dry, light- to medium-bodied, elegant flavors, and a stony, mineral-laden finish. Drink it over the next 1–2 years. The 1997 Gewurztraminer reveals textbook lychee nut, rose petal, and spice aromas and flavors. This medium-bodied, pure, crisp example should be drunk over the next year.

BOTT-GEYL (BEBLENHEIM)

1995 Gewurztraminer Furstentum	D	92
1995 Gewurztraminer Sonnenglanz Vieilles Vignes	D	91+
1995 Muscat Riquewihr	C	90
1995 Pinot Blanc Beblenheim	B	89
1995 Riesling Grafenreben	C	90+
1995 Riesling Mandelberg	D	90
1995 Riesling Riquewihr	C	89
1995 Sylvaner Beblenheim	B	85
1995 Tokay-Pinot Gris Sonnenglanz	D	91

Bott-Geyl has become one of Alsace's most fashionable young wine producers. Three consistent characteristics of these wines are 1) purity and concentration, 2) multilayered textures—the result of extended lees contact for 10–12 months, and 3) faithful interpretation of each varietal's characteristics. The following lineup of wines performed exceptionally well and, for their quality, are reasonably priced.

As longtime readers know, I am not a fan of Sylvaner, but I must admit I would enjoy drinking Bott-Geyl's 1995 Sylvaner Beblenheim. It offers plenty of fruit, more personality and character than most neutral tasting Sylvaners, a citrusy, floral, spicy note, elegance, medium body, and plenty of flavor, concentration, and length. Drink it over the next 1–2 years. The nearly outstanding 1995 Pinot Blanc Beblenheim reveals a gorgeously fresh, tangerine, lemonlike nose, medium-bodied flavors crammed with lively fruit, wonderful purity, and a dry, crisp, authoritatively flavored finish. Drink it over the next 2 years. This beautiful Pinot Blanc is selling for a song. I have long had a weakness for Alsace's dry Muscat. Bott-Geyl's 1995 Muscat Riquewihr is an explosive fruit cocktail-scented and -flavored wine with medium body, crisp, dry, concentrated flavors, a glorious perfume, and a dry, refreshing finish. This wine should drink well for 1–2 years.

I tasted three Rieslings from Bott-Geyl, all top-notch efforts. The 1995 Riesling Riquewihr displays a big, spicy, citrusy, floral, apple, and mineral-scented nose, outstanding ripeness, medium body, and a dry, crisp, vibrant finish. While it is the most developed of this trio, it will last for 5–8 more years. The more backward 1995 Riesling Grafenreben exhibits a crisp, stony nose, followed by seductive, ripe, medium-bodied, dry flavors, excellent flavor definition, and a long, harmonious finish. It is a beautiful, young, unevolved Riesling that should drink well for a decade. The 1995 Riesling Mandelberg offers a fruity, flowery, white peach-scented nose, with liquefied stones in the background. Medium bodied, concentrated, and well made, with a telltale attractive, fleshy texture, this quintessentially elegant yet flavorful wine should drink well for a decade.

One of the strengths of 1995 is Tokay-Pinot Gris. Certainly Bott-Geyl's 1995 Tokay-Pinot Gris Sonnenglanz appears to be an amazing effort. I noted that in two separate tastings I wrote "explosive" in my notes. The wine exhibits a light to medium straw color, as well as a buttery popcorn, honeyed grapefruit, waxy nose that soars from the glass. Unctuous, thick, and rich, but not weighty, this full-bodied, powerful wine changes rapidly in the glass, offering numerous aromatic nuances. It is a rich, large-scaled Tokay-Pinot Gris that has managed to retain its elegance. Drink it over the next 7–10 years.

It was hard to pick a favorite between Bott-Geyl's two Gewurztraminers. The 1995 Gewurztraminer Furstentum is the most hedonistic and luxuriant, offering a knockout nose of lychee nuts, liquefied rose petals, and honeyed grapefruit. The wine is loaded with fruit, is full bodied, with adequate acidity, and has a thick, juicy, blockbuster finish. Gewurztraminer lovers will go bonkers over it; those who do not care for this varietal will be appalled by its ostentatious personality. In contrast, the 1995 Gewurztraminer Sonnenglanz Vieilles Vignes may ultimately turn out better than the Furstentum, but it is less evolved, representing a more restrained yet still powerful style of Gewurztraminer. The wine possesses terrific richness and body, all of which is held in place by a tight corset. It has crisper acidity, as well as a more mineral-dominated character. The rose petal, lychee nut, exotic incense and grapefruit character of Gewurztraminer is also well displayed. The wine's texture should open to reveal considerable intensity. It is a big, dry Gewurztraminer for drinking over the next decade.

BURN (GUEBERSCHWIHR)

1995 Gewurztraminer Goldert Clos Saint Imer Cuvée La Chapelle	D 93
1995 Gewurztraminer V.T. Clos Saint Imer Cuvée La Chapelle	E 96
1995 Riesling Clos Saint Imer Cuvée La Chapelle	D 94

The Burn family domaine produces some of Alsace's greatest wines. Yet other than from knowledgeable insiders who closely follow Alsatian wines, this estate rarely receives the attention it deserves. I was only able to taste these three cuvées from Burn's portfolio, and all of them are sublime wines. Riesling does not get much better than Burn's 1995 Riesling Clos Saint Imer Cuvée La Chapelle. The wine is sensational, offering a stunning display of liquefied minerals, honeyed apples and other tropical fruits, medium to full body, extraordinary precision, and fabulous purity. If Riesling can come close to attaining the texture, richness, and palate-stinging intensity of a great Montrachet, this is it. Expect this wine to age effortlessly for 10–15 years, although few will have the discipline to resist its allure. In a vintage where Gewurztraminer was less successful than other varietals, Burn excelled. The 1995 Gewurztraminer Goldert Clos Saint Imer Cuvée La Chapelle is an off-dry, blockbuster, flamboyantly styled Gewurztraminer with a medium straw color, extraordinary rich, honeyed, lychee nut, and pineapplelike fruit, superfocus, outstanding overall balance, and amazing length and intensity. It is an unctuously thick, rich, chewy wine. One of the most successful and perhaps surprising food/wine combinations is Gewurztraminer with a smoky, ripe, authentic Muenster cheese from Alsace. It should last for 10–12 years. Burn's 1995 Gewurztraminer Vendange Tardive Clos Saint Imer Cuvée La Chapelle is even richer. Only 75 cases were produced of this exceptionally powerful and rich wine. The essence of Gewurztraminer, it possesses layers of flavor presented in a full-bodied, viscous, opulently textured style. Wow! Gewurztraminer does not get much more explosively rich than this. It should age well for 10–15 years, becoming even more delineated and civilized during its time in the bottle.

MARCEL DEISS (BERGHEIM)

1995 Gewurztraminer Saint Hippolyte	C	88
1995 Pinot Blanc Bergheim	B	87
1995 Tokay-Pinot Gris Beblenheim	C	89

These are the first 1995s to be released by the quintessential *"terroirist"* Marcel Deiss. The 1995 Pinot Blanc Bergheim displays an elegant, dry, pear/tangerine-scented fruitiness, medium body, excellent purity, and a crisp, austere, lovely finish. Drink it over the next 2–3 years. The 1995 Tokay-Pinot Gris Beblenheim is a more honeyed style of wine, with Pinot Gris' waxy, fleshy personality well displayed. Medium bodied, with excellent purity, and plenty of rich fruit, this dry, complex, yet still unevolved and youthful Pinot Gris should drink well for 5–6 years. Ironically, Deiss, no admirer of Gewurztraminer, has fashioned one of the more appealing wines in a so-so vintage for this varietal. The 1995 Gewurztraminer Saint Hippolyte possesses a textbook honeyed grapefruit, lychee nut, and spicy-scented nose, medium body, that ostentatiousness that makes Gewurztraminer so popular (or painful, depending on your point of view), and a crisp, dry, luscious finish. It should drink well for 5–6 years.

DIETRICH

1995 Muscat Cuvée Exceptionnelle	C	90
1995 Pinot Blanc Cuvée Exceptionnelle	B	89

Here we have two terrific wine values from Alsace. The 1995 Pinot Blanc Cuvée Exceptionnelle offers a mineral, steely, crisp, tangerine-scented nose, fresh, ripe, medium-bodied flavors, excellent acidity, and admirable flesh and depth. This dry, medium- to full-bodied, purely made Pinot Blanc should drink well for 2–3 years. I am a sucker for a dry Alsatian Muscat, and Dietrich's 1995 Muscat Cuvée Exceptionnelle (almost all of it from the well-known Hatchbourg vineyard) is a dry, medium- to full-bodied, superperfumed (aromas of honeysuckle and tropical fruits galore) wine that can be drunk as an aperitif, or served with asparagus and *foie gras*. The wine is fresh, lively, and intensely flavored. Because of Muscat's delicacy, as well as its tendency to quickly drop its aromatics, this wine needs to be drunk over the next year.

JOSMEYER (WINTZENHEIM)
SINGLE-VINEYARD CUVÉES, REGULAR CUVÉES

1996 Alsace l'Isabelle	B	86

Named after Jean Meyer's (the current director and winemaker at this old estate) daughter, the Alsace l'Isabelle is a rarity in today's varietal-designated Alsatian wine scene as it is produced from a blend of three varietals (Gewurztraminer is the predominant one). Its fresh, lively, and spicy nose is followed by an expansive, rich, medium-bodied, and white fruit-filled character. On the finish traces of fresh lychees can be discerned. This wine will make a delicious apéritif and should be drunk over the next year.

ALBERT MANN (WETTOLSHEIM)

1995 Gewurztraminer	B	85?
1995 Gewurztraminer Furstentum	D	86?
1995 Gewurztraminer Steingrubler	D	89
1996 Pinot Auxerrois Vieilles Vignes	B	87
1995 Pinot Auxerrois Vieilles Vignes	B	88
1995 Riesling Altenbourg	C	88

1995 Riesling Furstentum	D	95
1995 Riesling Schlossberg	C	90+
1995 Tokay-Pinot Gris Furstentum	D	92+
1995 Tokay-Pinot Gris Hengst	D	?
1995 Tokay-Pinot Gris Vieilles Vignes	C	89

I do not think anyone who follows the underrated white wines of Alsace would argue that Albert Mann is one of that beautiful region's brightest stars. His 1995s are exceptionally successful, especially his cuvées of Pinot Blanc, Riesling, and Tokay-Pinot Gris. The 1995 Pinot Auxerrois Vieilles Vignes reveals an alluring white peach and tangerine-scented nose, medium to full body, and stylish, pure, medium-bodied flavors with crisp, underlying, tangy acidity. The wine is dry and lusciously fruity, yet exceptionally well balanced. Drink it over the next 2–3 years.

The three cuvées of Mann's Riesling I tasted were impressive. The 1995 Riesling Altenbourg achieved 13% natural alcohol. With a spring garden/tropical fruit-scented nose, this elegant, dry, medium-bodied wine reveals evidence of minerals, but it emphasizes the more fruity aspects of the Riesling grape. Refreshing acidity gives it a crisp, nearly tart personality. This wine should drink well for 5–6 years. In contrast, the 1995 Riesling Schlossberg (13% alcohol) is a focused, backward, steely, mineral-dominated wine that only hints at its ultimate potential. Made from yields of 2 tons of fruit per acre, this crisp, stony-scented and -flavored, medium-bodied wine requires another 1–2 years of cellaring. It should last for a decade. Mann's 1995 Riesling Furstentum is the most ostentatious of this trio. Copious quantities of tropical fruit, licorice, and minerals burst from this exotic wine's aromatics. Made from extremely tiny yields, with 14.5% alcohol, this full-bodied, terrifically well endowed, dry, refined Riesling is a real head turner. The nose refuses to fade no matter how much aeration the wine receives. This wine represents a dazzling example of the heights Riesling can achieve in such top Alsatian vineyards. Sadly, a minuscule ten cases were imported to the United States. Anticipated maturity: now–2007.

Alsatians think 1995 is a super year for Tokay-Pinot Gris. Certainly Mann's cuvées are strong efforts, yet relatively backward, with surprisingly high acidity, as well as intense, concentrated personalities. For example, the 1995 Tokay-Pinot Gris Vieilles Vignes achieved 13.7% natural alcohol, possesses zinging acidity, and requires 1–2 more years of cellaring to reveal its full array of charms. Suppressed aromatically, it is a dense, fat, and full-bodied wine on the palate, with copious amounts of glycerin, and admirable power and richness. Give it another 1–2 years of cellaring, and drink it over the following decade. The 1995 Tokay-Pinot Gris Furstentum is a slightly off-dry (most readers would consider it dry), exuberantly full-bodied wine with a honeyed, cherry, waxy component. Dense, yet young, this backward, large-scaled wine needs another 2–3 years of cellaring. It should keep for 15 or more years. The 1995 Tokay-Pinot Gris Hengst (25 cases available for America) is made from extremely old vines. It has lofty alcohol (13.8%) as well as high residual sugar (30 grams per liter), and an equally impressive acid level. The Hengst may be the most controversial of Mann's 1995s. A pronounced vegetable, honeyed richness caught me off guard. This slightly bizarre wine is totally unformed, and nearly impossible to evaluate, but there is no doubting its huge richness, high glycerin, and massive extract, all buttressed by amazingly tart acid levels. This wine will unquestionably last for 15–20 years, but whether all its components mesh together remains unanswered. It is potentially outstanding, yet somewhat kinky and unconventional.

The 1995 Gewurztraminer offers spice, lychee nut, and grapefruitlike aromas and flavors in a medium-bodied format. Some bitterness in the finish (an annoying characteristic of many 1995 Gewurztraminers) kept my score low. Drink it over the next 3–4 years. The 1995

Gewurztraminer Furstentum (13.9% alcohol) is a high alcohol, spicy, lychee nut-scented and -flavored wine with excellent ripeness, plenty of power, and some sharpness. The wine develops nicely in the glass, but the finish is pungent and spiky. It should last for 5–6 years. Undoubtedly, the finest of Mann's three Gewurztraminers is the 1995 Gewurztraminer Steingrubler. It exhibits a fragrant, penetrating lychee nut and cherry-scented aromatics, dense, medium- to full-bodied, powerful flavors, plenty of muscle, a slight degree of residual sugar, and a long, heady, alcoholic finish. This wine should drink well for 7–8 years.

Mineral, orange blossom, and white flower aromas are present in the bouquet of the crisp, dry, fresh, medium-bodied 1996 Pinot Auxerrois Vieilles Vignes. It is another fine Pinot from Alsace, but no matter how many times I recommend them, readers do not seem to realize how good these wines are. This offering should drink well over the next 1–2 years.

DOMAINE ANDRE OSTERTAG (EPFIG)

1995 Gewurztraminer Fronholz	C	87
1995 Muscat Fronholz	C	86
1995 Riesling Heisenberg V.T.	D	90
1995 Riesling Muenchberg	D	88
1995 Riesling Muenchberg Vieilles Vignes V.T.	E	90

I was unimpressed with Domaine Ostertag's Pinot Gris, Pinot Blanc Barrique, and some of the lower level Rieslings, particularly the 1995 d'Epfig and Fronholz, but the following wines performed well. Readers should recognize that the Ostertag wines are the antithesis of the Domaine Zind-Humbrecht wines. The 1995 Riesling Muenchberg exhibits a crisp, orange rind, mineral, and floral-scented nose, elegant, tart, light- to medium-bodied flavors, and a dry, mineral-dominated, beautiful finish. It is a classy Riesling that should drink well for 5–6 years. The floral-scented, reserved, bone dry 1995 Muscat Fronholz offers fresh cotton candylike fruit aromas, light body, and a clean, powdered stone-flavored finish. Drink it over the next year.

Ostertag reminds me of Marcel Deiss in the sense that he rarely accords sufficient respect to Gewurztraminer. However, the three Gewurztraminers I tasted were excellent to outstanding. The 1995 Gewurztraminer Fronholz is an elegant, understated style of Gewurztraminer with subtle pineapple and lychee nut components intermixed with minerals. Light to medium bodied, dry, and restrained, it will be enjoyed by those readers who prefer Gewurztraminer to be less intense and flamboyant.

The excellent 1995 Riesling Muenchberg Vieilles Vignes V.T. is a medium-bodied, gorgeously fruity, poised, stylish Riesling with honeyed apple and peachlike fruit. Rich, subtle, and cerebral, this is an austere but well-endowed Riesling that should age well for 7–8 years. The 1995 Riesling Heissenberg V.T. is an off-dry, delicately built Riesling that offers copious quantities of floral, ripe apple, orange rind-scented and -flavored fruit, good acidity, plenty of liquefied stone and rocklike fruit, a cold steel character to its personality, and a long finish. It should drink well for a decade.

CHARLES SCHLERET (TURCKHEIM)

1995 Gewurztraminer Herrenweg	C	90
1995 Gewurztraminer Herrenweg Cuvée Exceptionnelle	E (500 ml)	91
1995 Gewurztraminer Herrenweg Cuvée Speciale	D	91
1995 Muscat d'Alsace Vieilles Vignes	C	90
1995 Riesling Herrenweg	C	87+?

1995 Riesling Herrenweg Cuvée Prestige	D	94
1995 Tokay-Pinot Gris Herrenweg Cuvée Exceptionnelle	E (500 ml)	96

Much like the Domaine Burn, Charles Schleret rarely receives the recognition he deserves, inexplicable in view of the extraordinary wine quality that routinely emerges from this estate. Current releases include two cuvées of Riesling Herrenweg. The 1995 Riesling Herrenweg is a dry, high-acid, high-extract, medium-bodied wine with mouth-searing tartness, intense, mineral, citrusylike flavors, and a dry, austere finish. This young, fresh wine promises to drink well for a decade. The 1995 Riesling Herrenweg Cuvée Prestige (15 grams of residual sugar) is made in a Vendange Tardive style. It is a fabulous, powerful Riesling with pineapple and rich peachlike aromas intertwined with wet steel and mineral-like scents. Deep and concentrated, with a finish that lasts for over 30 seconds, this is a terrific off-dry Riesling that should age well for 10–15 years.

The 1995 Muscat d'Alsace should be drunk over the next year or so to take full advantage of its exotic floral and fruit-scented nose. This dry, refreshing wine offers a knockout bouquet that is hard to resist. For me, this is the perfect apéritif wine.

The three Gewurztraminer cuvées begin with a dry 1995 Herrenweg, move up to the off-dry Herrenweg Cuvée Speciale, and finish with the off-dry, fuller-bodied, and more concentrated Herrenweg Cuvée Exceptionnelle. The regular bottling of 1995 Gewurztraminer Herrenweg displays terrific rose petal, honeyed grapefruit, and pineapplelike fruit in both its aromatics and flavors. Powerful, rich, and dry, it should drink well for 5–8+ years. The 1995 Gewurztraminer Herrenweg Cuvée Speciale (45 grams of residual sugar) reveals a liquefied rose petal-scented nose, ripe, lychee nutlike flavors, massive body, super purity, and an off-dry finish. This is a large-scaled, in-your-face style of Gewurztraminer that fanciers of this varietal will adore. It should drink well for a decade. The limited production (100 cases) 1995 Gewurztraminer Herrenweg Cuvée Exceptionnelle does not taste any sweeter than the Cuvée Speciale, but it does possess higher residual sugar (65 grams). Totally unformed, this monstrous-sized wine boasts huge density and ripeness, in addition to rich flavors that coat the palate with a viscous texture and high extraction. This formidable Gewurztraminer displays the textbook flamboyant characteristics that define this varietal. It will become more civilized with 2–3 more years of bottle age and should last for 10–12 years.

Lastly, the medium gold-colored 1995 Tokay-Pinot Gris Herrenweg Cuvée Exceptionnelle (60 grams residual sugar) exhibits a huge, smoky, waxy, roasted honey, herbal-scented nose that jumps from the glass. The wine is staggeringly concentrated and unctuously textured, yet it is relatively well balanced. The wine's off-dry, fleshy, superconcentrated style make it the perfect match with rich fish and poultry dishes. It should age well for 15 or more years. These are gorgeous wines that unquestionably deserve more attention.

DOMAINE SCHOFFIT (COLMAR)

1995 Chasselas Vieilles Vignes	B	88
1996 Chasselas Vieilles Vignes Cuvée Prestige	C	87
1995 Gewurztraminer Harth Cuvée Caroline	C	90
1995 Gewurztraminer Rangen de Thann V.T.	E	92
1995 Muscat Cuvée Alexandre	D	93
1995 Muscat Rangen de Thann Clos Saint Théobald	D	90
1996 Pinot Blanc Cuvée Caroline	C	88
1995 Pinot Blanc (Auxerrois) Cuvée Caroline	B	90
1995 Riesling Harth Cuvée Alexandre	D	91

1995 Riesling Harth Cuvée Prestige	C	90
1995 Riesling Rangen de Thann Clos Saint Théobald	D	95
1995 Riesling Rangen de Thann Clos Saint Théobald V.T.	E	?
1995 Tokay-Pinot Gris Cuvée Alexandre Vieilles Vignes	D	94+
1995 Tokay-Pinot Gris Rangen de Thann Clos Saint Théobald	E	95
1995 Tokay-Pinot Gris Rangen de Thann S.G.N.	EE (500 ml)	98+

Schoffit might be considered a protégé of Leonard and Olivier Humbrecht as the wines produced at this exceptional domaine share a similar style—very ripe, concentrated, powerful,
and intense! Schoffit's best value is consistently his Chasselas Vieilles Vignes, a wine made
from 65-year-old vines. The fragrant, dry, deliciously fruity 1995 is ripe, medium bodied, and
loaded with fruit and charm. Drink it over the next 1–2 years. The 1996 Chasselas Vieilles
Vignes reveals an exotic, honeyed, incense, spicy-scented nose, medium body, outstanding
ripeness, and a spicy, clove, mineral, and orangelike flavor profile with excellent acidity and
length. Exceptionally spicy and intense for a Chasselas, it should drink well for 1–2 years.
    The 1996 Pinot Blanc Cuvée Caroline, made from 40-year-old vines, exhibits a distinctive
tangerine, tropical fruit-scented nose and flavors, excellent ripeness, tangy underlying acidity, some minerality, and a medium-bodied, lovely, harmonious, dry finish. This wine should
continue to drink well for several years. Schoffit's 1995 Pinot Blanc Cuvée Caroline possesses nearly 14% natural alcohol. An outstanding example of Pinot Blanc, it offers a cherry,
tangerine, honeyed, citruslike nose, medium to full body, gorgeous layers of fruit, outstanding purity, and a long, dry, intense finish. Drink it over the next 2–3 years.
    Schoffit has fashioned two outstanding examples of dry Muscat. I adore these wines and
have had considerable success getting friends to try them, but they still remain relatively unknown. Because so much of Muscat's appeal is its extraordinary spring flower garden, fruit
cocktail-like perfume, these wines require consumption within 1–3 years of the vintage.
Schoffit's 1995 Muscat Rangen de Thann Clos Saint Théobald (from yields of under 2 tons
per acre) is a dry, full-bodied, austerely styled Muscat with a hauntingly intense perfume,
fabulous precision, remarkable depth and richness, and a dry, stony finish. This wine should
be drunk over the next 2–3 years, but I would not be surprised to see it last longer. The terrific (my notes begin with the words "great stuff") 1995 Muscat Cuvée Alexandre demonstrates what heights Muscat can achieve. With 13% alcohol, and made from yields of 25
hectoliters per hectare (under 2 tons per acre), this extraordinarily perfumed (explosive floral
and tropical fruit aromas) wine possesses amazing ripeness, purity, and length. With outstanding acidity buttressing the wine's gorgeous ripeness, richness, and extract, this is a
winemaking tour de force. Drink it over the next 2–3 years.
    I tasted three Riesling cuvées from Schoffit, all of them outstanding. The 1995 Riesling
Harth Cuvée Prestige (12.5% alcohol) is a textbook introduction to a dry Riesling, revealing
moderately intense apple and mineral-scented aromatics. Medium bodied, elegant, dense,
ripe, and concentrated, this outstanding Riesling possesses plenty of character as well as
enough structure to support 5–6 years of cellaring. The 1995 Riesling Harth Cuvée Alexandre is an ultraripe yet remarkably focused wine with the overripe Riesling character normally found in a Vendange Tardive cuvée. The huge nose of honeyed tropical fruits, flowers,
and minerals is followed by a wine with considerable power and richness, yet it still possesses a mineral-like austerity and restraint. This medium- to full-bodied, off-dry, extremely
pure wine should drink well for 10+ years. Speaking of extraordinary wines, the 1995 Riesling Rangen de Thann Clos Saint Théobald, while expensive, is a sensational Riesling. The
light gold color is followed by measured aromatic quantities of honey, baked apples, and wet

stones. On the palate, this is a huge, full-bodied, massively sized wine. Totally dry, this high-impact, layered, superconcentrated wine requires 3–5 years of cellaring, but it should keep for 2 decades. It is packed and stacked (professional jargon for an intense wine) with extraordinary richness, ripeness, and balance. It is a huge Riesling, yet patience is required because this wine is still an infant in terms of development.

Sadly, only 50 cases of Domaine Schoffit's 1995 Tokay-Pinot Gris Cuvée Prestige made it to America's shores. Another baby in need of 3–4 years of cellaring, the wine offers copious amounts of honeyed, ripe fruit reminiscent of cherries and butter. Full bodied and dense, with a slightly sweet Vendange Tardive style, this layered, unctuously textured, thick wine should take on more precision and focus with cellaring. It is capable of lasting for 15–20 years. The 1995 Gewurztraminer Harth Cuvée Caroline, made from yields of 2 tons per acre, and harvested in mid-October, 1995, is an unctuous, oily Gewurztraminer. Its off-dry personality, explosive petrol-like, lychee, and honeyed grapefruit-scented nose and flavors will provide provocative as well as controversial drinking. Full bodied and huge, with only 1.5% residual sugar, this is a large-scaled, viscous style of Gewurztraminer that should drink well for a decade or more.

In 1995, Schoffit produced a bevy of late-harvest Vendange Tardive-styled wines that are extremely powerful and intense. Although they possess considerable levels of residual sugar, much of their sweetness is concealed behind the tangy acidity these late-harvest wines contain. Schoffit's 1995 Riesling Rangen de Thann Clos Saint Théobald V.T. was made from 2 tons of fruit per acre, and possessed all the right technical statistics. However, it was green, tart, backward, and excessively vegetal and mineral-tasting. I could not find the expected fruit, volume, texture, or length in this wine—no matter how hard I tried. Judgment reserved. I had no such difficulty with the other extraordinary late-harvest cuvées. The 1995 Gewurztraminer Rangen de Thann Clos Saint Théobald V.T. was made from grapes harvested in mid-October (yields were well under 2 tons per acre). According to the importer, at a large tasting of 100 Alsatian wines held in Germany, it tied for first place with Zind-Humbrecht's Gewurztraminer Clos Windsbuhl. Schoffit's offering exhibits a fabulous lychee, rose petal, orange, and tangerine-scented nose with abundant spice. The high acid gives this weighty wine plenty of delineation. This large-scaled, expressive Gewurztraminer is extremely rich and full bodied, with exaggerated quantities of fruit, glycerin, alcohol, and extract. It promises to last for 10–15 years. The 1995 Tokay-Pinot Gris Cuvée Alexandre Vieilles Vignes needs another 3–4 years of cellaring. The wine's moderately intense nose only hints at the waxy, buttery, spicy, honeyed richness that will emerge with additional bottle age. Phenomenally dense, high-extract, full-bodied flavors coat the palate with a viscously textured richness. Fortunately, all of this is buttressed by good acidity. Although the wine possesses 4 grams per liter of residual sugar, most tasters will consider it dry. It should keep for 20–25 years. Another profound wine from Schoffit is the 1995 Tokay-Pinot Gris Rangen de Thann Clos Saint Théobald. This wine, which achieved 13% natural alcohol, is another mind-boggling, rich, honeyed, huge, thick, and fleshy wine. Like the Cuvée Alexandre, it requires 3–4 years of cellaring, tasting more akin to a youthful barrel sample than a finished wine. There is good delineation, an unctuous texture, and huge quantities of fruit that ooze over the palate. The wine somehow retains its balance without coming across as ponderous. It will last for 2 decades. Lastly, Schoffit's 1995 Tokay-Pinot Gris Rangen de Thann Sélection de Grains Nobles (S.G.N.) possesses 150 grams per liter of residual sugar, as well as extremely high acidity. This wine should prove to be one of the most fascinating sweet dessert-styled wines produced in Alsace in 1995. Thick and rich, it is still an infant in terms of its aromatic and flavor development. Believe me, my score is conservative in view of the potential this wine possesses. However, prospective purchasers should be prepared to cellar it for a minimum of 7–8 years.

DOMAINE WEINBACH (KAYSERSBERG)

1995 Gewurztraminer Altenbourg Cuvée Laurence	D	90
1995 Gewurztraminer Cuvée Théo	D	87?
1995 Gewurztraminer Furstentum Cuvée Laurence	E	89
1995 Gewurztraminer Réserve Personnelle	C	76
1995 Muscat Réserve Personnelle	D	91
1995 Pinot Blanc Réserve	C	88
1995 Riesling Cuvée Sainte Catherine	D	94+
1995 Riesling Cuvée Sainte Catherine Schlossberg	D	94+
1995 Riesling Cuvée Théo	D	90
1995 Riesling Schlossberg	D	92+
1995 Sylvaner Réserve	C	77
1995 Tokay-Pinot Gris Cuvée Laurence	E	95
1995 Tokay-Pinot Gris Cuvée Sainte Catherine	D	93+

Alsace wine enthusiasts will no doubt argue for decades as to whether Domaine Zind-Humbrecht or Domaine Weinbach produces this fairytale region's most profound wines. The Z-H wines tend to be slightly sweeter, with higher alcohol. Since Laurence Weinbach began making the wines, Domaine Weinbach's wines are drier, although still authoritatively powerful, rich, and concentrated.

Weinbach's unimpressive 1995 Sylvaner Réserve reveals annoyingly aggressive high acidity, as well as a severe, tart, green style. Domaine Weinbach can produce one of Alsace's finest Sylvaners (a varietal I generally do not admire), but the 1995 is disappointing. While the 1995 Pinot Blanc Réserve possesses higher than normal acidity, it has so much richness, fruit, and fresh apple and orangelike flavors, medium body, and superdepth that the acidity serves to give the wine structure and vibrancy. It should drink well for 3–4 years.

All four dry Riesling offerings display high flavor extraction, as well as mouth-searing levels of acidity. The 1995 Riesling Cuvée Théo exhibits extraordinary precision and purity. Despite its high acidity, the wine offers a gorgeous display of steely, mineral-dominated, apple and underripe apricotlike fruit. The wine is medium bodied, dry, and impeccably well balanced, with a finish that lasts for 25–30 seconds. The medium-bodied 1995 Riesling Schlossberg reveals a fabulous nose of steel and minerals. Orange and passion fruitlike aromas make their appearance on the palate of this medium- to full-bodied, highly extracted, dry yet backward Riesling. This superb, superconcentrated wine needs 1–2 years of cellaring; it should keep for 10–15+ years. The 1995 Riesling Cuvée Sainte-Catherine exhibits an intriguing nose of quinine, red currants, and minerals. A darker straw/gold color is followed by a zesty, full-bodied, dry, floral-scented and -flavored wine that is exceptionally long and rich with plenty of white peachlike flavors. This is an impressive, youthful yet compelling example of a large-scaled, elegant Riesling that admirably combines power and finesse. The light golden-colored 1995 Riesling Cuvée Sainte-Catherine Schlossberg offers a closed set of aromatics (with airing some apricot, peach, and mineral-like scents emerge), fabulous purity and ripeness, but extremely high acidity, and a backward, austere, medium- to full-bodied style. This wine improves immensely in the glass, but prospective purchasers should be prepared to wait 2–4 years for it to evolve. It is capable of lasting 15 or more years.

A delicious dry Muscat from Alsace, Domaine Weinbach's 1995 Muscat Réserve Personnelle boasts a glorious perfume of spring flowers and tropical fruits, delicate yet impressively intense flavors, and a dry, medium-bodied, extremely long, subtle finish. This is an exquisite dry Muscat to drink over the next 1–2 years.

The two 1995 Tokay-Pinot Gris offerings I tasted both possessed high extraction of flavor, stunning backbone and grip, and the vintage's telltale lofty acidity. Initially, the 1995 Tokay-Pinot Gris Cuvée Ste.-Catherine revealed few aromatics, but after ten minutes in the glass it began to display waxy, honeyed, incenselike smells, along with buttery, curranty fruit. The wine has considerable presence and intensity on the palate, as well as high acidity, full body, and a multilayered, explosively rich finish. It is so tight and backward that it will not be close to drinkability until the turn of the century. This large-scaled, high-acid Tokay should last for 2 decades, and deliver Montrachet-like portions of flavor and complexity when mature. Even more compelling is the 1995 Tokay-Pinot Gris Cuvée Laurence. This off-dry wine tastes like a Vendange Tardive. The wine has some residual sugar, but the acidity is so high that most readers would consider it to be dry. The intriguing nose of lemon grass, honeyed apricots, white peaches, and marmalade offers a dramatic introduction to this full-bodied, remarkably fresh wine that offers massive doses of power and extract—all allied to unreal elegance and finesse. It is a winemaking tour de force. Drink it between 2000 and 2015.

It is an undisputable fact that Gewurztraminer was the least favored varietal for the 1995 vintage in Alsace. I do not think I have ever tasted as unusual a Gewurztraminer as Domaine Weinbach's 1995 Gewurztraminer Réserve Personnelle. While some spice was present, there was no real varietal character in this medium- to full-bodied, butterscotchlike, disjointed wine. The 1995 Gewurztraminer Cuvée Théo presented an advanced deep golden color, spicy, sweet and sourlike aromas, and full body, but the alcohol, high acidity (hence the sweet and sour impression), and lack of rose petal/lychee nut/honeyed pineapple characteristics are atypical. Nevertheless, this is a mouth-filling, forward-styled Gewurztraminer to drink over the next 4–5 years. The 1995 Gewurztraminer Altenbourg Cuvée Laurence is a dry, floral, exotic, decadently styled wine with medium to full body, and gobs of honeyed, cherry fruit intermixed with intriguing spice and earthy scents. The wine is powerful and rich, with a dry finish. It should drink well for a decade. The medium gold-colored 1995 Gewurztraminer Furstentum Cuvée Laurence exhibits a vanillin, petroleumlike nose, rich, unctuously textured flavors with high acidity, some residual sugar, and a full-bodied, explosively rich finish. The wine possesses the best equilibrium of Weinbach's Gewurztraminers, as well as a spicy, rich finish. It is an outstanding wine, but neither it nor any other of these 1995 Gewurztraminers are comparable to the compelling Gewurztraminers produced at this estate in 1989, 1990, and 1994. Anticipated maturity: now–2007.

DOMAINE ZIND-HUMBRECHT (TURCKHEIM)

1996 Gewurztraminer Clos Windsbuhl	E	91
1995 Gewurztraminer Clos Windsbuhl	EE	91+
1996 Gewurztraminer Goldert	E	89
1995 Gewurztraminer Goldert	E	87
1996 Gewurztraminer Gueberschwihr	D	90
1995 Gewurztraminer Heimbourg	E	90?
1996 Gewurztraminer Hengst	E	91
1995 Gewurztraminer Hengst	E	90
1996 Gewurztraminer Herrenweg Turckheim	D	88
1995 Gewurztraminer Herrenweg Turckheim V.T.	E	91+
1996 Gewurztraminer Rangen Clos Saint Urbain	EE	95

1995	Gewurztraminer Rangen Clos Saint Urbain	EE	96
1996	Gewurztraminer Turckheim	C	86
1996	Gewurztraminer V.T. Heimbourg	E	94
1996	Gewurztraminer Wintzenheim	C	87
1995	Gewurztraminer Wintzenheim	D	88
1996	Muscat Goldert	E	90
1995	Muscat Goldert V.T.	EE	94
1996	Muscat Herrenweg Turckheim	D	88
1995	Muscat Herrenweg Turckheim V.T.	E	93
1996	Pinot d'Alsace	C	87
1995	Pinot d'Alsace	D	91
1996	Riesling Brand	E	95
1995	Riesling Brand V.T.	EE	94+
1996	Riesling Clos Hauserer	D	90
1995	Riesling Clos Hauserer	D	92
1996	Riesling Clos Windsbuhl	E	91
1995	Riesling Clos Windsbuhl	E	94+
1996	Riesling Gueberschwihr	C	88
1995	Riesling Gueberschwihr	D	91
1996	Riesling Herrenweg Turckheim	D	87
1995	Riesling Herrenweg Turckheim V.T.	EE	94
1996	Riesling Rangen Clos Saint Urbain	EE	95
1995	Riesling Rangen Clos Saint Urbain	EE	93+
1996	Riesling Turckheim	C	87
1996	Riesling Wintzenheim	C	84
1996	Tokay-Pinot Gris	D	88
1996	Tokay-Pinot Gris Clos Jebsal	D	91
1995	Tokay-Pinot Gris Clos Jebsal	EE	96
1996	Tokay-Pinot Gris Clos Windsbuhl	D	95+
1995	Tokay-Pinot Gris Clos Windsbuhl	EE	95
1996	Tokay-Pinot Gris Heimbourg	D	92
1995	Tokay-Pinot Gris Heimbourg	E	90
1996	Tokay-Pinot Gris Herrenweg Turckheim	D	86
1996	Tokay-Pinot Gris Rangen Clos Saint Urbain	EE	95+
1995	Tokay-Pinot Gris Rangen Clos Saint Urbain	EE	97
1995	Tokay-Pinot Gris Rotenberg	E	94+

1996 Tokay-Pinot Gris Rotenberg V.T.	E	95
1995 Tokay-Pinot Gris Rotenberg V.T.	EE	92+
1996 Tokay-Pinot Gris Vieille Vigne	D	89
1995 Tokay-Pinot Gris Vieille Vigne	E	94

I have tasted many of Alsace's finest producers' 1996s, and it is a tricky vintage. The most consistent level of high quality I tasted was no surprise—it originated from the wines of Zind-Humbrecht. When I met with Olivier Humbrecht, he said the summer was normal until the end of July, but August was cool and September even cooler but dry. The hallmark of the grapes in September was the extremely high level of acidity that remained, even by the end of September. At Zind-Humbrecht, the harvest occurred in October, under Indian Summer-like conditions. The grapes were healthy, the acid levels high, and there was little evidence of botrytis. Consequently, little sweet wine was produced. Olivier Humbrecht stated that yields in 1996 were huge throughout Alsace, averaging between 82 and 100 hectoliters per hectare (5$^1/_2$–6$^1/_2$ tons per acre). At Zind-Humbrecht, yields for their estate wines averaged 1 ton per acre. As I have written time and time again, there is no secret to great wines—low yields.

As the following tasting notes exhibit, these were highly successful wines with alcohol levels well below 1994, or such great vintages as 1989 and 1990. In general, the alcohol levels range between 11.5% and 13.6%. The wines are characterized by higher than normal acidity levels, which should serve them well as they age. They give the impression of being drier wines than normal, perhaps due to their higher acidity, which tends to effectively buffer or counterbalance any impression of residual sweetness.

After tasting these offerings, I tried to think of another Zind-Humbrecht vintage with similar characteristics, but I was unable to find a legitimate comparison. The wines possess lively acidity, good aromatics, and are long in the mouth, but they are more delicate than some of the blockbuster, powerful vintages previously produced at Z-H (that is, 1994, 1990, and 1989). The 1996s may turn out to be long agers, but my philosophy, for myself and readers, is that if you like the way a wine tastes young, you should not hesitate to drink it. Remember— no one has ever blundered by drinking a delicious wine too soon. However, opening a bottle of wine after its aromatics and fruit have faded is indeed a sorrowful experience!

The 1996 Pinot d'Alsace (12.5% natural alcohol) contains considerable Pinot Auxerrois. The wine is dry, zesty, and elegant, with a tangy, Mandarin orange aroma, medium body, and a crisp finish. Lighter than usual but refreshing, it should drink well for 3–4 years. Zind-Humbrecht produces two Muscats, both reference points for how complex and beautiful wines from this varietal can be. The 1996 Muscat Herrenweg Turckheim reveals a lovely nose of spring flowers intermixed with tropical fruit. Honeyed, medium to full bodied, and fresh, it is ideal for drinking over the next 1–2 years. The 1996 Muscat Goldert is made in a riper, softer style, with a slight degree of residual sugar. It offers up an intriguing spicy, quince, curranty-scented nose reminiscent of a red wine. On the palate, orange blossoms, tropical fruit, petrol, and honeyedlike flavors suggest Muscat. This wine is round, fleshy, and a treat to drink, but consumption over the next 1–2 years is recommended.

In 1996 there are eight dry and off-dry Rieslings. Beginning at the lower level of intensity, the 1996 Riesling Wintzenheim is a crisp, light straw-colored wine with extremely high acidity, candied, berry, and applelike fruit, some mineral notes, and a tart, austere finish. This dry wine should be consumed over the next 2–4 years. With fuller body and slightly more texture, the 1996 Riesling Gueberschwihr emphasizes the tropical fruit side of the Riesling flavor spectrum. It displays good underlying acidity, and a fresh, lively, more forthcoming style. Consume it over the next 3–4 years. The delicate, backward 1996 Riesling Turckheim is one of the lighter-bodied wines in the Z-H portfolio. Subtle, restrained aromas of orange peel, lemon blossom, and apple are followed by a wine with tart acidity, and a compact finish. While the wine's statistics indicate it has 1.2% residual sugar, it tastes dry. Drink it over the next 2–3 years. The pretty, floral and gravelly scented 1996 Riesling Herrenweg Turckheim is medium bodied, angular and austere, but pure, bone dry, and ideal for consuming over the next 2–4 years. Readers who love the minerality in addition to the sometimes searing acidity of a grand cru Chablis will get a thrill from the 1996 Riesling Clos Hauserer. This outstanding Riesling represents the essence of minerals. With its petroleum-like nose and flavors, this wine is like drinking liquid stones. Unevolved but intense, dry, and "serious," this is a wine for passionate connoisseurs as it will take several years to mature. An exceptional effort for the vintage, it is a candidate for 10–12+ years of aging.

The Humbrechts' outstanding talents are displayed in the three other Rieslings, all among the finest wines of the vintage. The 1996 Riesling Clos Windsbuhl exhibits a deeper straw/light golden color and a totally dry personality, with a natural alcohol level of just over 13.5%. The wine offers an explosive nose of honeyed fruits, sweet corn, flowers, and wet stones. Powerful, concentrated, full bodied, and extremely dry, this wine also reveals remarkable balance and a seamless quality to its personality. This is an exceptional dry Riesling that should age effortlessly for a decade. The 1996 Riesling Brand is also completely dry. Made from 45-year-old vines, this wine possesses a medium gold color, and an exotic, maltlike nose intermixed with Asian spices, honeyed fruit, and underbrush. In the mouth, there is Montrachet-like richness, fabulous concentration, a multilayered personality, and an exceptionally long finish that lingers for 40+ seconds. This stunning, dry Riesling was made from modest yields of under 2 tons per acre. The 1996 Riesling Rangen Clos Saint-Urbain (13.5% natural alcohol) was closed, but it is another completely dry, formidably endowed, exceptionally rich, medium- to full-bodied Riesling that symbolizes the essence of this varietal. The color is medium gold. The wine reveals no evidence of botrytis, exhibiting ripe fruit, a profound minerality, and a full-bodied, blockbuster finish. It may turn out to be better than the Brand, but it is more closed and in need of 1–3 years of cellaring. It should keep for 15 or more years.

One of the undisputed success stories of the 1996 vintage in Alsace is Pinot Gris, but only for those who waited until October to harvest. Olivier Humbrecht told me the 1996 Pinot Gris wines are even richer than his 1995s. Of the following Tokay-Pinot Gris, four are enormously endowed, relatively sweet, unctuously textured wines with fabulous purity and length. Viscous, they could be drunk with a spoon and, for that reason, are best served alongside decadently fat foie gras, a killer combination . . . literally! The 1996 Tokay-Pinot Gris (1.5% residual sugar in addition to a touch of botrytis) is a dense, medium- to full-bodied, opulently textured, thick, seductively styled, evolved wine. Its off-dry character, outstanding purity, and gobs of honeyed fruit will make it a crowd pleaser if consumed over the next 4–6 years. The 1996 Tokay-Pinot Gris Herrenweg Turckheim was closed and tight when I tasted it. Made from 35 hectoliters per hectare (2¹/₃ tons per acre), and clearly a dry, medium- to full-bodied Pinot Gris, this wine is dominated by its earthy, loamy soil, sandy-textured *terroir.* There is good fruit, but the earthiness is pronounced. When I questioned Olivier Humbrecht about the wine, he acknowledged that it was made from 7-year-old vines, and perhaps that is why it is one-dimensional when compared to its peers. The 1996 Tokay-Pinot Gris Vieille Vigne (made from 50-year-old vines in Herrenweg) offers a knockout nose of butter, honey, overripe melons, and Cointreau. Extremely fresh, lively acidity holds this medium- to full-bodied, powerful wine together. The high acidity carries through on the palate and in the finish, giving the wine more freshness and uplift than previous vintages have exhibited. It should age well for a decade or more.

The following four Tokay-Pinot Gris were harvested primarily in mid-October, with the Rangen harvested the first week of November. All were produced from exceptionally small yields—a little over 1 ton per acre for the Rangen, to as high as just under 2 tons per acre for the Heimbourg. These are awesomely rich, thick, unctuously textured, moderately sweet Pinot Gris that may be too much of a good thing for many tasters, but impressive wines they are! The 1996 Tokay-Pinot Gris Heimbourg exhibits a butterscotch, honeyed, exotic nose, glycerin-endowed, cherrylike flavors that ooze over the palate with layers of flavor. This thick, full-bodied wine possesses 1.5% residual sugar, yet tastes sweeter. It should continue to evolve and gain more complexity over the next 7–8 years, and last for 15 or more. The 1996 Pinot Gris Clos Jebsal possesses the lowest acidity of these blockbuster efforts and also appears more austere. While that sounds like a contradiction, that's the way the wine tasted. It is thick and rich, but more monolithic than these other monsters. Made from slightly less than 2 tons per acre, it achieved 13.5% alcohol naturally. If my instincts are correct, this wine needs at least 2–3 years of bottle age, and it should keep for 15+ years. Like the Clos Jebsal, the 1996 Tokay-Pinot Gris Clos Windsbuhl also achieved 13.5% natural alcohol. It requires 2–3 years of cellaring, yet will easily keep for 15–20 years. It is a spectacularly full bodied, moderately sweet, pure, seamless effort with copious quantities of honeyed cherry fruit intermixed with scents of butter, smoke, and minerals. Pure and viscous, it is a tour de force in winemaking. The deep gold-colored 1996 Tokay-Pinot Gris Rangen Clos Saint Urbain brought back memories of my childhood, when my mother would bake mincemeat pies. The wine's bouquet, an exotic concoction of spices, pie dough, *jus de viande,* and honey soared from the glass of this awesomely endowed Pinot Gris. In the mouth, it tasted of white truffle oil, something I have only rarely experienced (on occasion, I have had white Hermitage as well as Hermitage Vin de Paille exhibit similar characteristics). Extremely full bodied and thick, moderately sweet, and mammothly endowed, this is another winemaking monument. This wine will evolve gracefully for 2 decades or more.

Never a winery to keep things simple, Zind-Humbrecht produced eight Gewurztraminers in the 1996 vintage. Two of the lighter (although that is a misnomer at this winery) examples are the Turckheim and Wintzenheim. The 1996 Gewurztraminer Turckheim is essentially dry but reveals a textbook rose petal, lychee nut, spicy nose, medium-bodied, slightly oily flavor with crisp acidity, and a short finish. It is a good to very good Gewurztraminer to consume over the next 2–3 years. The totally dry 1996 Gewurztraminer Wintzenheim displays an exotic bacon fat and lychee nut-scented nose, a medium- to full-bodied personality, bitter tannin in the finish, and a spicy, plump, mouth-filling character. While it is undoubtedly a very good wine, the astringent finish kept my score low.

I found the 1996 Gewurztraminer Gueberschwihr to be outstanding. With 15% natural alcohol, and 1.5% residual sugar, it comes across as off-dry, displaying a superb nose of rose petal liqueur intermixed with honeyed, overripe grapefruit and lychee nuts. Full bodied, dense, exotic, and intensely spicy, this classic Gewurztraminer has just enough acidity to permit another 4–6 years of cellaring. I was less impressed with the 1996 Gewurztraminer Herrenweg Turckheim. While it is totally dry and "only" 14% alcohol, it came across as very good but essentially closed in addition to being more monolithic. However, it exhibits Gewurztraminer's telltale spice box, lychee nut, and rose petal characteristics. It should age well for 4–6 years, but it is more restrained than its siblings.

The following four wines were all outstanding. The light gold-colored 1996 Gewurztraminer Hengst was made from 20 hectoliters per hectare (1 1/3 ton per acre), achieved 14.5% natural alcohol, and was bottled with 1.2% residual sugar. While it tasted somewhat closed, it will make a spectacular Gewurztraminer for those willing to wait 1–2 years. It offers a rosewater, intensely spicy, pineapple and grapefruit-scented nose, followed by powerful, thick, juicy flavors, and a large-scaled, massive, off-dry finish. It should last for 10–15 years. The 1996 Gewurztraminer Goldert was revealing some unresolved CO_2, which I suspect suppressed its aromatic and flavor dimensions. A sweeter style (2.5% residual sugar), made from a tiny crop of slightly over 1 ton per acre, the wine was not expressive when I tasted it, but it did remind me of grapefruit and honey. Sweet, with high acidity buffering the sugar, this wine was one of the most backward in the Z-H portfolio. It requires a minimum of 1–2 years of cellaring, and it should keep for 12–15 years. I was superimpressed with the

1996 Gewurztraminer Clos Windsbuhl. I recently opened one of my last bottles of the 1989 Gewurztraminer Clos Windsbuhl, and it remains a perfect wine. The 1996 Clos Windsbuhl, made from just over 1 ton of fruit per acre, possesses less of a Gewurztraminer character than the others, but it displays an extremely dense, full-bodied personality with great purity, an intense minerality, and a striking orange and tangerine-scented nose with similar flavors on the palate. A full-scaled, large-framed, powerful wine, it needs 2–3 years of cellaring and should age well for 15+ years. The driest of these four offerings is the 1996 Gewurztraminer Rangen Clos Saint-Urbain. It possesses nearly 17% alcohol and 2% residual sugar. The grapes were harvested during the first week of November. Its fermentation lasted 12 months! How do I describe such an intriguing, provocative, and multidimensional wine? Its medium gold color is followed by aromas of honeyed grapefruit, roasted coffee, white truffles, lychee nuts, and musty smells. Oily and viscous, with a honeyed tealike character, this powerful, rich, exceptionally pure wine is extremely unevolved and in need of at least 2–3 years of cellaring. It will develop at a glacial pace over the next 15–25 years. This is a wine to consume by the spoonful, with only the richest of dishes—an indulgent but sumptuous combination.

I tasted only two 1996 Vendanges Tardives from Zind-Humbrecht, both of which are brilliant wines. The oily 1996 Tokay-Pinot Gris Rotenberg Vendange Tardive is dense, powerful, fat, and unctuously textured. An infant in terms of development, I would not expect any complexity to emerge for at least another 5–6 years. It should only get better and last for 20–25 years. The more evolved 1996 Gewurztraminer Vendange Tardive possesses a honeyed grapefruit, pineapple, and rose petal-scented nose, full-bodied flavors, and hefty alcohol levels. Both of these wines are moderately sweet efforts that need to be paired with the right foods.

The production from Domaine Zind-Humbrecht in 1995 totaled 9,700 cases, which is just over half of what this estate produced in 1992. Since 1992, the production has dwindled because of (1) stricter selection, and (2) more conservative viticultural practices designed to produce tiny crops. From what are probably the smallest yields of any notable Alsatian estate, Zind-Humbrecht's average production in 1995 was 23 hectoliters per hectare (under 2 tons of fruit per acre). According to Olivier Humbrecht (France's only Master of Wine), the 1995 vintage was saved by a spectacular month of October, and growers who had higher yields and noticed the formation of rot after the rainy, cold period during the end of September, often picked grapes that were not physiologically ripe. However, growers who waited until October to harvest (Domaine Zind-Humbrecht's harvest lasted 4–5 weeks, beginning on October 5 and finishing in early November) had the potential to produce high-quality wines, particularly from Riesling, Tokay-Pinot Gris, and Muscat.

The Zind-Humbrecht 1995s possess approximately 10% higher acidity than the crisp, high-acid 1994s, largely because September was a very cool month. There was no need to chaptalize any of the Z-H wines, and extremely long fermentations resulted in high alcohol.

When tasting through the Z-H wines I am always struck by the fact that other than Guigal and Domaine Leroy, France has no other producers who consistently make so many brilliant wines. As readers will note, prices for the 1995s are higher, reflecting both their quality and the significantly smaller production. Readers should be prepared to lay away many of the finest offerings, as the Rieslings and Tokay-Pinot Gris are extremely high in acidity, although marvelously concentrated and intense. While this estate did produce several exceptional Gewurztraminers, this varietal produced the weakest wines in 1995. I am a fan of this flamboyant varietal, and what it lacks in 1995 is the intense liquefied, rose petal, fresh lychee nut, honeyed pineapple aromatics and flavors. Those readers who find Gewurztraminer too ostentatious, might prefer the 1995s since they are so obviously "less Gewurztraminer-like." In any event, the following reviews are from a memorable tasting held in April 1997.

The 1995 Pinot d'Alsace, from such vineyards as Herrenweg, Rotenberg, and Clos Windsbuhl, is made from primarily Pinot Auxerrois. It is a terrific success. The light gold color, ripe, intense, old-vine richness, gorgeous texture, dry, crisp, mineral and tangerine-flavored finish make for a pure, dry white that should drink well for 4–5 years.

I tasted seven 1995 Rieslings from Z-H, five of them dry and two entitled to the Vendange Tardive (late harvest) designation. The 1995 Riesling Gueberschwihr offers a citrusy, pineapple, steely nose. Of the Rieslings, it is the most open-knit, flattering, and delicious to drink. There are powerful, concentrated, mineral-like flavors, medium to full body, and a dry, long, citrusy finish. The wine is exotic with more honeyed pineapplelike flavors than other offerings. It is a super, showy Riesling to drink over the next 5–8 years. The 1995 Riesling Herrenweg Turckheim is not as open-knit as the Gueberschwihr. It tastes lighter bodied and more tightly knit, with an even higher acid profile. However, wine roars across the back of the palate, displaying power, as well as the textbook elegance and telltale steely, citrusy, apple and orangelike fruit of the Riesling grape. This medium-bodied, dry Riesling will benefit from another 1–2 years of cellaring and will keep for 10–12 years. The 1995 Riesling Clos Hauserer (made from grapes harvested in mid-October) exhibits a deeper medium gold color, no evidence of botrytis, but a very honeyed orange marmalade, full-bodied, layered texture and a massive personality. Concentrated and powerful, with amazing length, this huge, highly extracted Riesling should be cellared for 1–2 years and drunk over the following 10–12. The 1995 Riesling Clos Windsbuhl (made from yields of 1½ tons of fruit per acre) represents the essence of the Riesling grape. Extremely powerful liquid steel and mineral-like aromas intermixed with those of citrus and ripe apples emerge from this awesomely endowed, dry, full-bodied Riesling. Ripe, with extremely high acidity, this is a classic Riesling that should age effortlessly for 10–15+ years. The last of the drier-styled Rieslings, the 1995 Riesling Rangen Clos St.-Urbain (made from just over 1 ton per acre) does not possess the weight or volume offered by the Clos Windsbuhl. Nevertheless, it is an impressive, unevolved, tightly knit Riesling that is still in its infancy. According to Olivier Humbrecht, it took 10 months for this wine to ferment. The intriguing nose of roasted nuts, ginger, and spice hints at an exotic future. Rich and medium bodied, with high acidity and a spicy, earthy personality, this wine needs 1–3 years of cellaring; it should keep for 10–15+ years.

The two 1995 Vendange Tardive Rieslings I tasted were both medium sweet and thus more open knit and approachable. The 1995 Riesling Herrenweg Turckheim V.T. is an exotic, honeyed, stunningly rich wine with medium sweetness, great purity, and a hefty amount of alcohol and extract. It is clearly a wine that must be matched with intensely flavored foods. It should last for 15–20 years. The 1995 Riesling Brand V.T. (13% residual sugar and a whopping 12.5% total acidity) is a medium sweet, orange and tangerine-scented and -flavored, spicy, full-bodied, highly extracted wine with superb richness, mouth-searing acidity, and a backward, unevolved, potentially profound style. This wine should be cellared for 1–3 years and drunk over the following 2 decades.

I tasted six dry 1995 Tokay-Pinot Gris offerings from Zind-Humbrecht and one Vendange Tardive. As the enthusiastic notes that follow reveal, it is a tossup as to whether Riesling or Pinot Gris was the more successful varietal in 1995. For followers of the Z-H Tokay-Pinot Gris Vieille Vigne the good news is that the 1995's quality is spectacular; the bad news is that the price is now at the level of top premier cru white Burgundies. The price is not unjustified in view of the quality, but it is a blow to the sensitivities of those of us who remember buying this wine for $16–$20 a bottle a decade ago. The 1995 Tokay-Pinot Gris Vieille Vigne (made from a vineyard planted in 1946) exhibits an explosive nose of honeyed, buttery popcorn, incense, and jammy fruit aromas. This off-dry, spectacularly concentrated, slightly botrytised wine is loaded with fruit, has an unctuous texture, and a massive, thick finish oozing with glycerin, fruit, and alcohol. This wine must tip the scales at 14.5% alcohol. I would opt for drinking it over the next decade. The 1995 Tokay-Pinot Gris Rotenberg (produced from minuscule yields of 14 hectoliters per hectare—less than 1 ton of fruit per acre), is a backward, dense, potentially compelling example of Pinot Gris; it needs 1–4 years of cellaring. Made from a vineyard planted in pure limestone, the wine is totally dry, with no evidence of botrytis. While it displays massive body, glycerin, and concentration, it is closed and unevolved. This wine has unlimited potential, but patience will be required. Purchasers of the handful of cases that will make it to the United States will need to cellar it for 2–4 years—at the minimum. It should keep and evolve for 2 decades. It will not be easy finding any of the 1995 Tokay-Pinot Gris Heimbourg as only six cases were exported to the United States. The most exotic of Z-H's Pinot Gris offerings, it reveals a Gewurztraminer-like honeyed peach and apricot character. Full bodied, with a mélange of tropical fruit flavors that soar from the glass and cascade over the palate, this surprisingly well defined, rich, slightly sweet, flashy Pinot Gris should drink well for 12–15 years. I found the 1995 Tokay-Pinot Gris Clos Windsbuhl to be classic. Totally dry, this medium gold-colored wine exhibits an intriguing nose of minerals, vanilla (not from new oak), subtle floral scents, and plenty of steely, buttery fruit. Fabulous on the palate, this full-bodied, intensely concentrated, brilliantly delineated wine should be cellared for 2–4 years. It possesses remarkable length (approximately 40+ seconds). The slightly sweet 1995 Tokay-Pinot Gris Clos Jebsal reveals a honeyed botrytis character. The wine is massive, with full body, unreal extract and fruit, as well as exceptional purity and equilibrium. The extract levels of Z-H's Pinot Gris are high, yet the harmony among the wines' elements is impeccable. This wine would do wonders with such duck or goose liver dishes as foie gras. It should drink well for 2 decades.

The only 1995 Vendange Tardive Tokay-Pinot Gris I tasted was the Rotenberg, a wine with 9.5% total acidity and 14.5% alcohol. It is nearly too intense, yet who could not admire its amazing display of powerful, highly extracted, buttery, slightly botrytised flavors, remarkably high acidity for such intensity, and marvelous purity of flavor and length. The wine coats the palate with viscous fruit, yet the acidity gives it vibrancy and freshness. It possesses a remarkable sweet and sour flavor combination. The wine should drink well for 20+ years.

Over the years, I have expressed my fondness for Alsatian Muscat. In 1995, Z-H produced two Vendange Tardive Muscats, both riveting examples of this underrated varietal. The 1995 Muscat Herrenweg Turckheim V.T. offers abundant tropical fruit cocktail aromas, off-dry, gorgeously floral, honeyedlike flavors, wonderful freshness and vibrancy, and a long, lusty finish. This wine must carry a minimum of 14% alcohol in its medium- to full-bodied personality. Because Muscat is more delicate and fragile than Riesling, Tokay-Pinot Gris, or Gewurztraminer, it must be drunk during its first several years of life. The 1995 Muscat Goldert V.T. is a mineral-dominated, dry wine with an intriguing, mushroomy and floral-scented nose, high acidity (to the point of tartness), and intense, concentrated flavors. This backward albeit ageworthy wine is perplexing to evaluate because of its tightness. Muscats rarely age well past 2–3 years, but my instincts suggest this offering will last for 7–8 years.

After tasting through all the top Alsatian estates, it was obvious that Gewurztraminer was less consistent than Pinot Gris or Riesling. As several producers told me, the uneven crop set, which seemed to afflict Gewurztraminer more than other varietals, led to a smaller production, as well as uneven ripening. As Olivier Humbrecht stated, he had to be extremely careful with Gewurztraminer because it is a varietal that requires a considerable amount of heat to reach physiological ripeness, and September was an extremely cold month in Alsace. Many producers picked too early, fearing the grapes would rot. As it turned out, October was a splendid month weather-wise, and those who waited produced better Gewurztraminer.

Among the drier-styled Zind-Humbrecht Gewurztraminers, the 1995 Gewurztraminer Wintzenheim reveals good spice and ripeness, plenty of power and richly fruity flavors, but not enough of the varietal character to merit higher marks. Although dense, alcoholic, and off-dry, it lacks the telltale rose petal and lychee nut fragrance that Gewurztraminer admirers appreciate. It should drink well for 3–4 years. The light golden color of the 1995 Gewurztraminer Goldert was more evolved. This wine did not display a true Gewurztraminer character. Somewhat diffuse, it offers copious quantities of fruit, medium to full body, and a mouth-filling, gutsy, floral, richly fruity character. This off-dry wine is satisfying, yet it lacks the finesse, complexity, and ostentatiousness that typifies this varietal. Anticipated maturity: now–2002. Four of the finest Gewurztraminers of the vintage are the 1995 Hengst, 1995 Clos Windsbuhl, 1995 Heimbourg, and 1995 Rangen Clos Saint-Urbain. The 1995 Gewurztraminer Hengst exhibits a light golden color, followed by butterscotchlike, honeyed-orange aromatics, sweet and sourlike flavors, high extract, a dry, full-bodied personality, and considerable alcoholic clout. It is a forceful, powerful, impressively built wine for drinking over the next 7–8 years. The 1995 Gewurztraminer Clos Windsbuhl displays a much lighter color (there was no botrytis in this vineyard), as well as a pure, mineral, richly fruity-scented nose, layers of extract, full body, and a massive, powerful, heady, dry finish. This may turn out to be one of the most classic and longest-lived Gewurztraminers of the vintage. Drink it between now and 2012. The 1995 Gewurztraminer Heimbourg offers a spicy, sweet nose, full body, and copious amounts of concentrated, powerful fruit flavors but not much complexity or Gewurztraminer's telltale characteristics. The wine is hugely extracted, but it lacks equilibrium and focus, normally a hallmark of a Z-H wine. I would opt for drinking this slightly disjointed, but impressively large scaled Gewurztraminer over the next 5–7 years. I suspect the 1995 Gewurztraminer Rangen Clos Saint-Urbain will be controversial. Few readers will ever get a chance to taste it as only 450 bottles were produced. The wine exhibits an advanced deep golden color, an explosive, sweet, honeyed nose, monstrous extract, and a remarkably dry, full-bodied, superintense finish that is nearly fatiguing to taste and analyze. Harvested at S.G.N. (Sélection des Grains Nobles) sugar levels, and made from a microscopic 9.5 hectoliters per hectare (slightly more than 1/2 ton of fruit per acre), this Gewurztraminer took nearly a year to complete fermentation. It is a dry, staggeringly concentrated, yet controversial wine. I suspect it could actually be classified as food—it's that rich! It will keep for 20+ years.

The 1995 Gewurztraminer Herrenweg Turckheim V.T. boasts an advanced deep golden color, extremely botrytised, honeyed, spicy, jammy fruit aromas, and sweet and sour flavors. The telltale Gewurztraminer lychee nut/rose petal/pineapplelike character is nowhere to be found in this enormous, long, and moderately sweet wine. Drink it over the next 10–15 years.

BORDEAUX

The Basics

TYPES OF WINE

Bordeaux is the world's largest supplier of high-quality, ageworthy table wine, from properties usually called châteaux. The production in the eighties and the nineties has varied between 25 and 60 million cases of wine a year, of which 75% is red.

Red Wine   Much of Bordeaux's fame rests on its production of dry red table wine, yet only a tiny percentage of Bordeaux's most prestigious wine comes from famous appellations such as Margaux, St.-Julien, Pauillac, and St.-Estèphe, all located in an area called the Médoc,

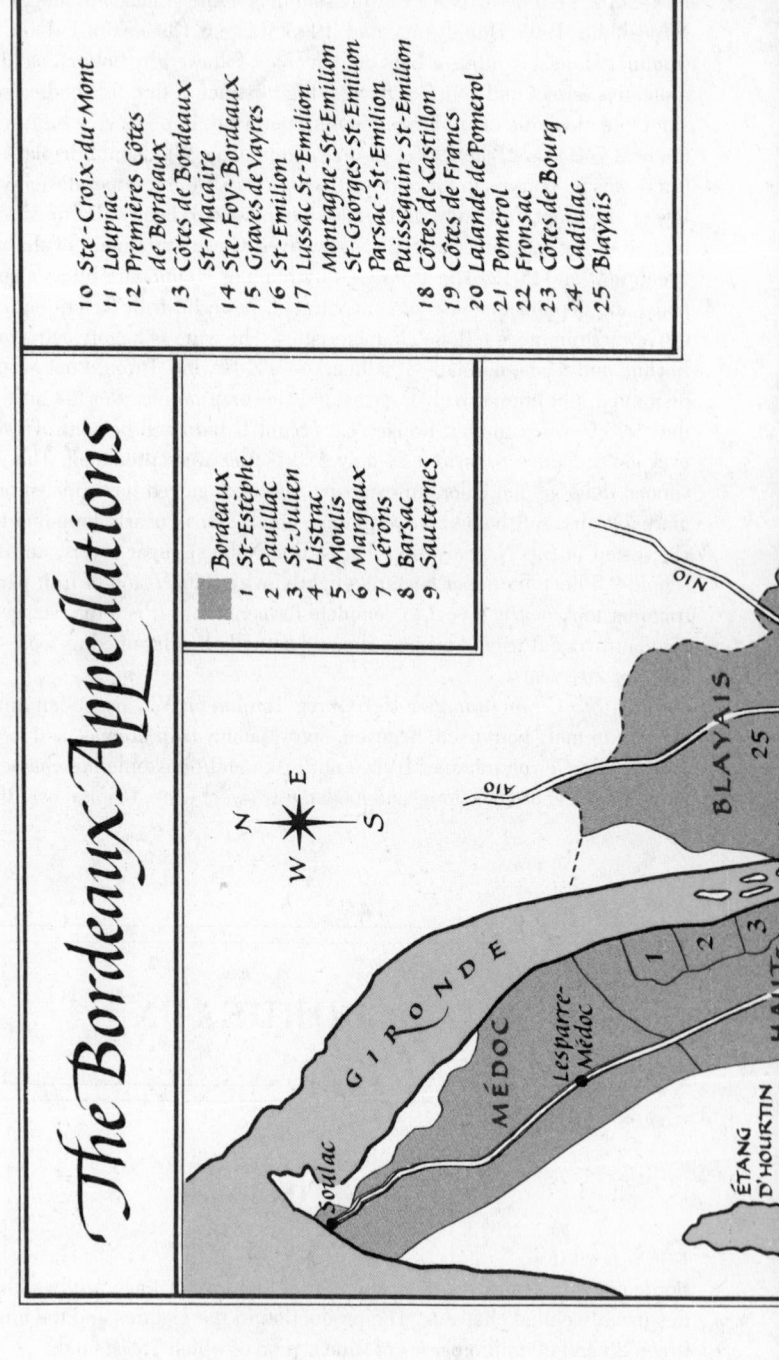

The Bordeaux Appellations

N
W · E
S

Bordeaux
1 St-Estèphe
2 Pauillac
3 St-Julien
4 Listrac
5 Moulis
6 Margaux
7 Cérons
8 Barsac
9 Sauternes

10 Ste-Croix-du-Mont
11 Loupiac
12 Premières Côtes
    de Bordeaux
13 Côtes de Bordeaux
14 Ste-Macaire
15 Ste-Foy-Bordeaux
16 Graves de Vayres
17 St-Emilion
    Lussac St-Emilion
    Montagne-St-Emilion
    St-Georges-St-Emilion
    Parsac-St-Emilion
    Puisseguin-St-Emilion
18 Côtes de Castillon
19 Côtes de Francs
20 Lalande de Pomerol
21 Pomerol
22 Fronsac
23 Côtes de Bourg
24 Cadillac
25 Blayais

GIRONDE

MÉDOC

Soulac

Lesparre-
Médoc

ÉTANG
D'HOURTIN

HAUT-

BLAYAIS

25

1
2
3

OIN

A10

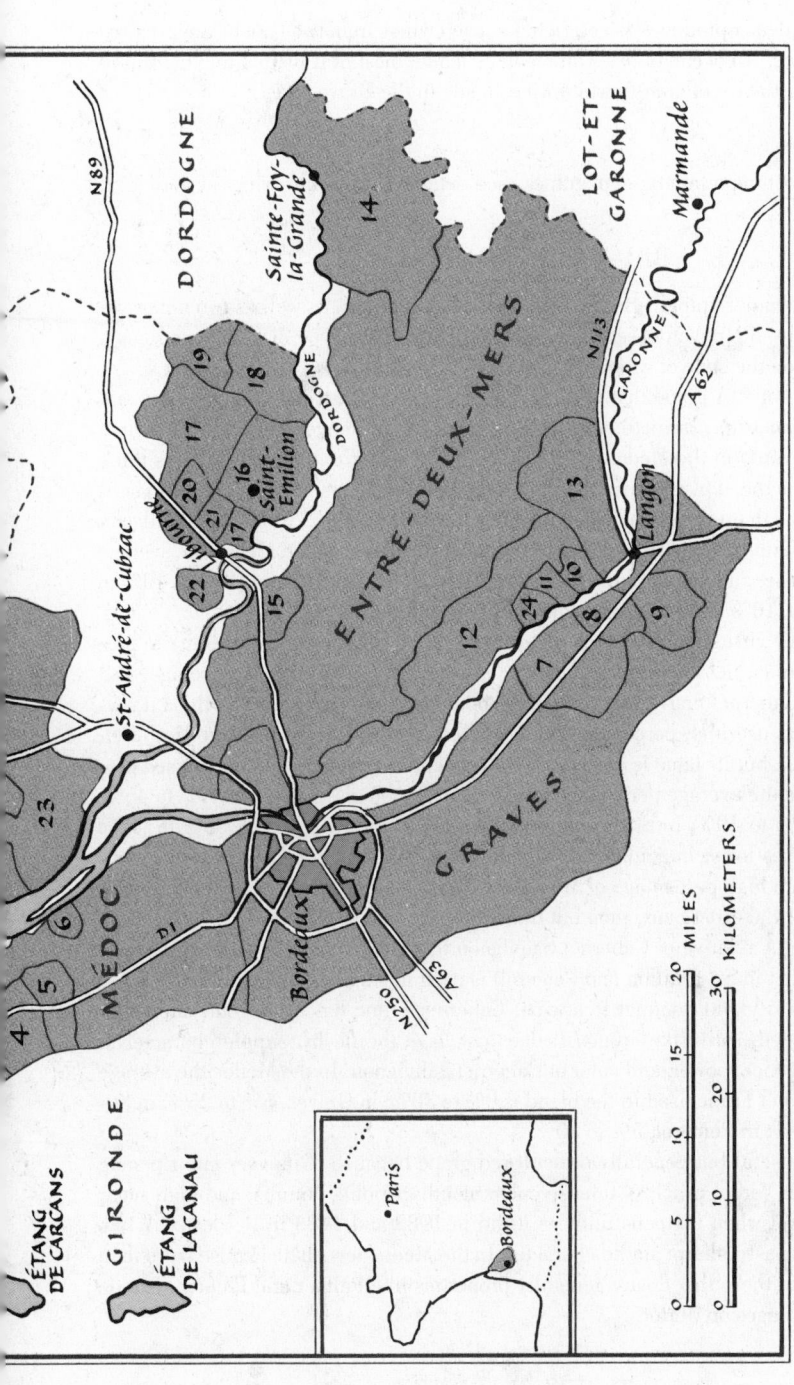

ÉTANG
DE CARCANS

GIRONDE

ÉTANG
DE LACANAU

N89

DORDOGNE

Sainte-Foy-
la-Grande

LOT-ET-
GARONNE

Marmande

14

19
18
17
16 Saint-
Emilion
20
21
17
22
15

ENTRE-DEUX-MERS

DORDOGNE

Libourne

St-André-de-Cubzac

23

MÉDOC

D1

Bordeaux

N250

A63

6

5

4

GARONNE

N113

Langon

A62

13

24 11
10

12

7

8

9

GRAVES

MILES

KILOMETERS

20   15   10   5   0

30   20   10   0

Paris

Bordeaux

and Graves, Pomerol, and St.-Émilion. From these areas the wine is expensive yet consistently high in quality.

White Wine   Bordeaux produces sweet, rich, honeyed wines from two famous areas called Sauternes and Barsac. An ocean of dry white wine is made, most of it insipid and neutral in character, except for the excellent dry white wines made in the Graves area.

GRAPE VARIETIES

Following are the most important types of grapes used in the red and white wines of Bordeaux.

RED WINE VARIETIES

For red wines, three major grape varieties are planted in Bordeaux, as well as two minor varieties, one of which—Petit Verdot—will be discussed here. The type of grape used has a profound influence on the style of wine that is ultimately produced.

Cabernet Sauvignon   A grape that is highly pigmented, very astringent, and tannic and that provides the framework, strength, dark color, character, and longevity for the wines in a majority of the vineyards in the Médoc. It ripens late, is resistant to rot because of its thick skin, and has a pronounced black currant aroma, which is sometimes intermingled with subtle herbaceous scents that take on the smell of cedarwood with aging. Virtually all Bordeaux châteaux blend Cabernet Sauvignon with other red grape varieties. In the Médoc the average percentage of Cabernet Sauvignon in the blend ranges from 40% to 85%; in Graves, 40% to 60%; in St.-Émilion, 10% to 50%; and in Pomerol, 0% to 20%.

Merlot   Utilized by virtually every wine château in Bordeaux because of its ability to provide a round, generous, fleshy, supple, alcoholic wine, Merlot ripens, on an average, 1–2 weeks earlier than Cabernet Sauvignon. In the Médoc this grape reaches its zenith, and several Médoc châteaux use high percentages of it (Palmer, Cos d'Estournel, Haut-Marbuzet, and Pichon-Lalande), but its fame is in the wines it renders in Pomerol, where it is used profusely. In the Médoc the average percentage of Merlot in the blend ranges from 5% to 45%; in Graves, from 20% to 40%; in St.-Émilion, 25% to 60%; and in Pomerol, 35% to 98%. Merlot produces wines lower in acidity and tannin than Cabernet Sauvignon, and as a general rule wines with a high percentage of Merlot are drinkable much earlier than wines with a high percentage of Cabernet Sauvignon but frequently age just as well.

Cabernet Franc   A relative of Cabernet Sauvignon that ripens slightly earlier, Cabernet Franc (called Bouchet in St.-Émilion and Pomerol) is used in small to modest proportions in order to add complexity and bouquet to a wine. Cabernet Franc has a pungent, often very spicy, sometimes weedy, olivelike aroma. It does not have the fleshy, supple character of Merlot or the astringence, power, and color of Cabernet Sauvignon. In the Médoc the average percentage of Cabernet Franc used in the blend is 0% to 30%; in Graves, 5% to 25%; in St.-Émilion, 25% to 66%; in Pomerol, 5% to 50%.

Petit Verdot   A useful but generally difficult red grape because of its very late ripening characteristics, Petit Verdot provides intense color, mouth-gripping tannins, and high sugar and thus high alcohol when it ripens fully, as it did in 1982 and 1983 in Bordeaux. When unripe it provides a nasty, sharp, acidic character. In the Médoc few châteaux use more than 5% in the blend, and those that do are generally properties like Palmer and Pichon Lalande that use high percentages of Merlot.

WHITE WINE VARIETIES

Bordeaux produces both dry and sweet white wine. Usually only three grape varieties are used: Sauvignon Blanc and Semillon, for dry and sweet wine, and Muscadelle, which is used sparingly for the sweet wines.

Sauvignon Blanc Used for making both the dry white wines of Graves and the sweet white wines of the Barsac/Sauternes region, Sauvignon Blanc renders a very distinctive wine with a pungent, somewhat herbaceous aroma and crisp, austere flavors. Among the dry white Graves, a few châteaux employ 100% Sauvignon Blanc, but most blend it with Semillon. Less Sauvignon Blanc is used in the winemaking blends in the Sauternes region than in Graves.

Semillon Very susceptible to the famous noble rot called botrytis, which is essential to the production of excellent, sweet wines, Semillon is used to provide a rich, creamy, intense texture to both the dry wines of Graves and the rich, sweet wines of Sauternes. Semillon is quite fruity when young, and wines with a high percentage of Semillon seem to take on weight and viscosity as they age. For these reasons higher percentages of Semillon are used in making the sweet wines of the Barsac/Sauternes region than in producing the white wines of Graves.

Muscadelle The rarest of the white wine grapes planted in Bordeaux, Muscadelle is a very fragile grape that is quite susceptible to disease but, when healthy and mature, produces a wine with an intense flowery, perfumed character. It is used only in tiny proportions by châteaux in the Barsac/Sauternes region. It is not used at all by the white wine producers of Graves.

Major Appellations

Following are the general flavor characteristics of Bordeaux's most notable types of wines.

St.-Estèphe While the wines of St.-Estèphe are known for their hardness because of the heavier, thicker soil in this area, the châteaux have more Merlot planted in their vineyards than elsewhere in the Médoc. Although generalizations can be dangerous, most St.-Estèphe wines possess less expressive and flattering bouquets, have a tougher character, and are more stern, tannic wines than those found elsewhere in the Médoc. They are usually full bodied, with considerable aging potential.

Pauillac A classic Pauillac seems to define what most people think of as Bordeaux—a rich black currant, cedary bouquet, followed by medium- to full-bodied flavors with a great deal of richness and tannin. The fame of this area equates with high prices.

St.-Julien St.-Juliens are frequently indistinguishable from the wines of Pauillac. The wines of St.-Julien are filled with rich curranty fruit and smell of cedar and spices. The overall quality of this appellation's winemaking is superb, so consumers take note!

Margaux Margaux are the lightest wines of the Médoc, but in great vintages they are perhaps the most seductive. Although the overall quality of the winemaking in this appellation is lower than any other appellation in the Médoc, in a top vintage a great Margaux has an undeniable floral, berry-scented bouquet backed up by the smell of new oak. In body and tannin, Margaux wines, despite elevated percentages of Cabernet Sauvignon, tend to mature more quickly than a St.-Julien, Pauillac, or St.-Estèphe. For bouquet lovers, the best wines of Margaux can be compelling.

Graves Red Textbook Graves (including the sub-appellation of Pessac-Léognan) wines are the easiest of all Bordeaux wines to pick out in blind tastings, as they have a distinctive mineral smell as well as the scent and taste of tobacco and cedar. Graves are generally the lightest wines made in Bordeaux.

St.-Émilion It is difficult to generalize about the taste of St.-Émilions, given the divergent styles, but most St.-Émilions tend to be softer and fleshier wines than Médocs, but not as succulent and lush as Pomerols. Because of the elevated percentages of Cabernet Franc planted in this appellation, St.-Émilions often have a distinctive herbaceous, cedary bouquet.

Pomerol   Pomerols are often called the burgundies of Bordeaux because of their rich, supple, more monolithic personalities, but they age extremely well and are undeniable choices for hedonists, as they provide oodles of rich black currant, black cherry, sometimes blackberry fruit. In the great vintages one can find an exquisite opulence in these wines.

Graves White   The top-notch white Graves are aged in oak and made from the Sauvignon Blanc and Semillon grapes. They start off life often excessively oaky but fill out beautifully with age and develop creamy, rich flavors that marry beautifully with the oak. Other white wines of Bordeaux are often totally neutral and insipid in character and simply taste of acidity and water.

Barsac/Sauternes   Depending on the vintage and the degree of the noble rot (botrytis) that affects the grapes, the wines can either taste fat, ripe, and characterless in those years when there is little botrytis or wonderfully exotic with a bouquet of honeyed tropical fruits, buttered nuts, and crème brûlée in those great vintages where there has been plenty of the noble rot.

Satellite Appellations   Very large quantities of wine are produced in a bevy of other lesser-known appellations of Bordeaux. Most of these wines are widely commercialized in France but have met with little success in America because of this country's obsession with luxury names and prestigious appellations. For the true connoisseur, the wines of Bordeaux's satellite appellations can in fact represent outstanding bargains, particularly in top vintages such as 1982, 1985, 1989, 1990, and 1998, where excellent climatic conditions, the dominance of the merlot grape, and the improved use of modern technology by many of these estates resulted in a vast selection of fine wines at modest prices. Following are the most important satellite appellations.

Fronsac and Canon-Fronsac—In the eighteenth and nineteenth centuries the vineyards sprinkled over the hillsides and hollows of Fronsac and Canon-Fronsac—only several miles west of Libourne—were better known than the wines of Pomerol and sold for higher prices than the wines of St.-Émilion. But because access to Pomerol was easier and because most of the brokers had their offices in Libourne, the vineyards of Pomerol and St.-Émilion were exploited more than those of Fronsac and Canon-Fronsac. Consequently this area fell into a long period of obscurity from which it has just recently begun to rebound.

Lalande-de-Pomerol—Lalande-de-Pomerol is a satellite commune of nearly 2,250 acres of vineyards located just north of Pomerol and Néac. The vineyards, which produce only red wine, are planted on relatively light, gravelly, sandy soils with the meandering river, Barbanne, as the appellation's northern boundary. The very top level of good Lalande-de-Pomerol is easily the equivalent of a midlevel Pomerol, with certain wines, such as Belles-Graves, La Croix-St.-André, and du Chapelain, very good, even by Pomerol's standards. The only downside to the wines of Lalande-de-Pomerol is that they generally need to be consumed within 5–6 years of the vintage. Sadly, the only recent vintage that can be recommended is 1990.

Côtes de Bourg—The Côtes de Bourg, a surprisingly vast appellation of nearly 10,000 acres, is located on the right bank of the Gironde River, just a 5-minute boat ride from the more famous appellation of Margaux. The vineyards here are actually older than those in the Médoc, as this attractively hilly area was once the center of the strategic forts built during the Plantagenet period of France's history. The views from the hillside vineyards adjacent to the river are magnificent. The local chamber of commerce has attempted to draw the public's attention to this area by calling Bourg "the Switzerland of the Gironde." They should instead stress the appeal of the best wines from the Côtes de Bourg, which are made in an uncomplicated but fruity, round, appealing style, and talk up the lovely port village of the area, the ancient hillside town of Bourg-Sur-Gironde.

Blaye—There are just over 6,700 acres of vines in the Blaye region, located directly north of Bourg. The best vineyard areas are entitled to the appellation called Premières Côtes de

Blaye. While quantities of white wine are produced in the Blaye region, most of the Premières Côtes de Blaye are dedicated to the production of red wine, which is very similar to the red wine of Bourg. At its best, it is forward, round, richly fruity, soft, and immensely satisfying in a low-key manner.

Loupiac and Ste.-Croix-de-Mont—With the wine prices of Barsac and Sauternes soaring, I predict a more important role for the producers of the sweet white wines of Loupiac and Ste.-Croix-de-Mont. These two appellations, 24 miles south of Bordeaux on the right bank of the Garonne, facing Barsac and Sauternes across the river, have an ideal southern exposure. These areas received appellation status in 1930, and many observers believe the excellent exposure of the top vineyards and the clay/limestone soil base is favorable for producing sweet wines, particularly in view of the fact that the morning mists—so essential for the formation of the noble rot, *Botrytis cinerea*—are a common occurrence in this area. The entire appellation of Loupiac consists of 1,359 acres. Although the sweet wines are receiving increasing attention from wine lovers, dry white wines, as well as a moderate quantity of dry red wines, are also produced.

AGING POTENTIAL

St.-Estèphe: 8–35 years

Pauillac: 8–40 years

St.-Julien: 8–35 years

Margaux: 8–30 years

Graves Red: 8–30 years

St.-Émilion: 8–25 years

Pomerol: 5–30 years

Graves White: 5–20 years

Barsac/Sauternes: 10–50+ years

Fronsac/Canon-Fronsac: 5–20 years

Lalande-de-Pomerol: 3–6 years

Bourg: 3–10 years

Blaye: 2–4 years

Loupiac: 5–15 years

Ste.-Croix-de-Mont: 4–12 years

OVERALL QUALITY LEVEL

Of all the great viticultural regions of the world, Bordeaux consistently produces wine of the highest level of quality. Although one-dimensional, innocuous wines can be found, bad wine is rare. For the world's top producers of Cabernet Sauvignon, Merlot, and Cabernet Franc, Bordeaux remains the point of reference.

THE MOST IMPORTANT INFORMATION TO LEARN

For the wine consumer trying to develop a degree of expertise when buying the wines of Bordeaux, the most important information to learn is which wine-producing estates (called châteaux) are producing the best wines today. A review of the top categories of châteaux in Bordeaux is a quick way to learn of those producers with high commitments to quality. However, consumers should also familiarize themselves generally with the styles of the wines from the different appellations. Some tasters will prefer the austere, sterner style of Bordeaux represented by St.-Estèphe or Pauillac, whereas others will love the lavish lushness and opulence of a Pomerol. It has been my experience that the Graves wines with their distinctive mineral scent and tobacco bouquet are often the least-favored wines for neophytes, but with more experience this character becomes one that is admired by connoisseurs. As far as the famous official classifications of wine quality in Bordeaux, they are all out of date and should be of only academic interest to the consumer. These historic classifications of wine quality were employed both to promote more wines and to establish well-delineated, quality benchmarks. But because of negligence, incompetence, or just plain greed, some of these châteaux produce mediocre and poor wines that hardly reflect their placement in these classifications. A more valid guideline to the quality of Bordeaux wines is the rating of producers starting on page 145; these ratings reflect the overall quality of the wines produced rather than their historical pedigree.

BORDEAUX VINTAGE SUMMARIES: 1945–1998

This is a general assessment and profile of the Bordeaux vintages 1945 through 1997. While the top wines for each acceptable vintage are itemized, the perception of a vintage is a general view of that particular viticultural region. In mediocre and poor vintages, good wines can often be made by skillful vintners willing to make a careful selection of only the best grapes and cuvées of finished wine. In good, even great, years thin, diluted, characterless wines can be made by incompetent and greedy producers. For wine consumers, a vintage summary is important as a general guide to the level of potential excellence that could have been attained in a particular year by a conscientious grower or producer of wine.

1998—A Quick Study (9-15-98)

St.-Estèphe**	Graves Red****
Pauillac***	Graves White****
St.-Julien***	Pomerol*****
Margaux***	St.-Émilion****
Médoc/Haut-Médoc Crus Bourgeois**	Barsac/Sauternes****

Size: A slightly smaller crop than in 1996 and 1995.

Important information: A year that favored the Merlot grape, but the finest other wines are powerful and tannic.

Maturity status: Most wines will require considerable cellaring, as they possess elevated tannin.

Price: The Médoc prices fell 20%–25% below the 1997 prices. Elsewhere the prices are very high.

In 20 years of tasting young Bordeaux, I have always found there to be vintages where one appellation or a certain sector produces more complete and interesting wines. Never before have I tasted a vintage where the differences between regions have been so extreme. There may be some historical references among ancient vintages, but so much has changed today that I question the legitimacy of such analogies. Certainly 1975 turned out a bevy of exceptionally powerful, tannic Pomerols and a handful of stunning wines from Graves, but elsewhere, relatively hard, charmless wines were produced. In Bordeaux it is not uncommon to hear 1964 being compared with 1998, especially by successful producers. The former French minister of agriculture declared 1964 "the vintage of the century" before any grapes were picked. Early harvesters, particularly those in the precocious *terroirs* of Pomerol and to a lesser extent St.-Émilion and Graves, turned in very good to superlative performances (for example, Cheval Blanc, Pétrus, Lafleur, La Mission-Haut-Brion, Trotanoy, and Figeac), but the Médoc's Cabernet Sauvignon had not been harvested by the time the deluge arrived. The result was a dreadful vintage for the Médoc, with only a handful of surprising exceptions (such as Latour and Montrose).

However, 1998 is different. Viticulture is better, vineyards are healthier, the serious châteaux practice strict selections for their *grand vin*, and modern-day technology offers temperature-controlled fermentation tanks and, for the wealthiest, concentration machines that incorporate reverse osmosis and the removal of water by vacuum. For those reasons alone, 1998 is superior to both 1975 and 1964.

March 1998 was an exceptionally hot month in Bordeaux, which propelled the vineyards off to a roaring and precocious start. However, April was generally cold and wet. May also began unseasonably cold and damp, but by the second week a high-pressure system settled over much of southwestern France, and the remainder of the month was warm and dry. The number crunchers predicted the harvest would begin in mid-September if the summer turned out to be normal. In spite of erratic weather in June, the flowering in most regions took place with none of the dreaded problems such as *coulure*. The end of June was spectacularly warm and sunny, causing optimism to rise throughout Bordeaux.

Is any weather normal today? July was a bizarre month by Bordeaux standards. High temperatures, with occasional thunderstorms serving to irrigate the vineyards, traditionally defines this month in the Aquitaine. Yet July 1998 was unseasonably cool, overcast, and, as Bill Blatch said in his *Vintage Report*, "drab." The hours of sunshine during the month were particularly deficient, even though the average temperatures fell within the normal parameters. In short, there had been only 3 days of extremely hot weather. One weather phenomenon that might explain some of the superconcentrated, massive Pomerols was a hailstorm that damaged some of the vineyards in Pomerol's tenderloin district—the so-called plateau—which forced the vignerons to do an early *vendange verte* (green harvest and/or crop thinning). Unquestionably this accounts for the fact that yields in Pomerol were extremely low by modern-day standards (30–35 hectoliters per hectare on average).

French vignerons believe in the axiom "June makes the quantity, September makes the quality, and August makes the style." August was also destined to put its imprint on the 1998 Bordeaux. The boring, overcast conditions of July were replaced by an intense high-pressure system that produced one of the most torrid heat waves Bordeaux has ever had to suffer. For more than half the month temperatures were in excess of 95 degrees Fahrenheit, and between August 7 and 11 the mercury soared over 100 degrees (not unusual in northern Napa Valley, but rare in Bordeaux). Because of qualitative advances in viticulture such as leaf pulling and culling out excess bunches, this intense heat wave had the effect of roasting/sunburning many grapes, a common problem in hotter climates, such as southern France and California, but rarely encountered in Bordeaux. In addition to the punishing heat, August brought on drought conditions. By the end of the month the vines had begun to exhibit extraordinary stress. Leaves turned yellow, and the malnourished vines began to curtail photosynthesis (blockage of maturity). As many producers have said, this huge heat wave, accompanied by the excessive drought, largely determined the style of many 1998s. The grapes shriveled up, with their skins becoming extremely thick, resulting in the powerful, tannic constitution of the 1998s.

By the beginning of September growers were hoping for rain to reignite the maturity process. Their wishes came true. On September 2, 3, and 4, the area received a series of light showers, which were beneficial for the rain-starved vineyards. The weather cleared on September 5, and ideal conditions ensued through September 11. During this period, much of the white wine crop, not only in the high-rent district of Pessac-Léognan, but also in the generic Bordeaux appellations as well as Entre-Deux-Mers, was harvested under textbook conditions. Beginning on September 11 much of Bordeaux experienced 3 days of relatively heavy rainfall. If August had been wet, this would have undoubtedly been deleterious, but the water-depleted soil and vines thrived with the additional rainfall. To the surprise of most observers, the analyses of the vineyards after these rains showed little difference in sugars, acids, and dry extract. In short, the heavy rains of September and lighter showers of the following days had no serious effect on quality. September 15–27 was a period of exceptional weather. It was during this period that most of the Merlot in Pomerol, the Médoc, and St.-Émilion was harvested—under superb conditions. By the time the weather began to disintegrate, during the weekend of September 26 and 27, Pomerol had virtually finished the harvest, and much of the Merlot in St.-Émilion and the Médoc had been picked. It takes no genius to realize that this beneficial period of weather undoubtedly explains why Pomerol is 1998's most favored appellation.

Between September 26 and October 1 a whopping 70 millimeters of rain (nearly 3 inches) fell throughout Bordeaux. The late Jean-Eugène Borie, proprietor of Ducru-Beaucaillou, was buried on October 1, and more than a dozen people told me that driving to his funeral was nearly impossible because the Médoc's Route du Vin was inundated by the soaking rains. The Médoc's Cabernet Sauvignon was not yet ripe, but how much water could it take? By the end of September the amount of rainfall in the Médoc was virtually the same as had fallen in 1994, an interesting statistic to remember as readers peruse my tasting notes. The Cabernet Franc harvest was completed after the heavy rainfall of late September and October 1. In the Médoc the Cabernet Sauvignon harvest continued until mid-October. Another important statistic to remember is that except for October 3, 6, and 7, rain, sometimes heavy, fell every day between October 1 and October 12. By the time the weather cleared on October 13, little unharvested Cabernet Sauvignon was left in the Médoc.

Yields in Pomerol were relatively small (between $1^2/_3$ and $2^2/_3$ tons per acre), and in the Médoc yields averaged $3^1/_2$ tons per acre. All things considered, this would appear to be a year in which the top appellations have produced less wine than in 1997, 1996, 1995, or, for that matter, 1994.

The northern Médoc (St.-Julien, Pauillac, and St.-Estèphe) has so many superstar estates that it is usually the source for a bevy of terrific wines, even in difficult vintages. Certainly there are good Médocs in 1998, but these areas represent the most uninspiring appellations of the vintage. If readers were to buy on color alone, they would invest huge sums in the 1998 northern Médocs, since they are all well-colored wines (the influence of modern technology and the grapes' thick skins). However, the wines lack fat and charm and are often exceedingly tannic with pinched/compressed personalities. They possess plenty of grip and a boatload of tannin but are irrefutably inferior to the Médocs of 1995 and 1996. Moreover most of them lack the charm of the finest 1997s. This is not to say that some fine wines won't emerge, but the Médoc is the least impressive region of 1998.

In the southern Médoc, particularly the appellation of Margaux (usually the most disappointing area for high-quality wines), the wines are more complete, with sweeter tannin and riper fruit. There are few great wines, but there are many good ones. Many châteaux that have been beaten up by my critical prose over recent years have turned in competent performances. Overall, it appears that the area's finer drainage served these vineyards well.

South of Bordeaux, in Pessac-Léognan, 1998 is a very good vintage. Some of the most elegant, complete wines of the vintage were produced in Pessac-Léognan, and the appellation's most precocious *terroirs* (Haut-Brion, La Mission-Haut-Brion, Pape-Clément) were favored by the early-ripening Merlot and the excellent weather during the first 3 weeks of September. The dry white wines of Graves and Pessac-Léognan are also very good, but, paradoxically, only a handful have proven to be exceptional.

The excitement in this vintage is primarily focused in St.-Émilion and Pomerol. It does not take a great palate to recognize wines that are often black in color, extremely ripe, thick, and rich, yet also ferociously tannic. This is not a vintage in the style of 1989 and 1990, but, rather, one that recalls the massive Pomerols of 1975. In St.-Émilion, Bordeaux's most exciting appellation given the extraordinary number of sexy wines being produced, there are few disappointments and many excellent wines, although a shortage of true superstars. Even in St.-Émilion there are few supple, flashy wines such as were produced in 1989 and 1990; rather, the region produced broad, muscular, concentrated, tannic examples.

One of the silver linings of this vintage is how many tasty "little" wines I found in Bordeaux's generic and satellite appellations. In addition to the excitement in St.-Émilion, the fever of quality and competition has spread to the surrounding satellites, and a number of delicious Merlot-based wines are being produced from these lesser appellations. Additionally, because of the high concentration of Merlot (which was ripe and succulent in 1998) in many of these vineyards, numerous attractive wines have been produced. Retailers, restaurants, and consumers looking for values will be pleased to learn there will be some tasty, early-to-drink Merlot-based wines from the least prestigious (and least expensive) Bordeaux vineyards.

THE BEST WINES

St.-Estèphe: None

Pauillac: Lafite-Rothschild, Latour, Mouton-Rothschild

St.-Julien: Léoville-Barton, Léoville-Las Cases

Margaux: Château Margaux, Palmer

Médoc/Haut-Médoc: None

Graves Red: Haut-Brion, La Mission-Haut-Brion, Pape-Clément, Smith-Haut-Lafitte

Graves White: Couhins-Lurton, Haut-Brion, Laville-Haut-Brion, Pape-Clément, Smith-Haut-Lafitte

Pomerol: Bon Pasteur, Bourgneuf, Certan-de-May, Clinet, Clos l'Église, l'Église-Clinet, l'Évangile, La Fleur de Gay

Gazin: La Fleur-Petrus, Lafleur, Latour à Pomerol, Le Moulin, Nénin, Pétrus, Le Pin, Trotanoy, Vieux Château-Certan

St.-Émilion: Angélus, Ausone, Beau-Séjour-Bécot, Beauséjour-Duffau, Canon La Gaffelière, Clos Dubreuil, Clos de l'Oratoire, La Clusière, La Couspaude, Croix de Cabrie, La Gomerie, Gracia, Magdelaine, Monbousquet, La Mondotte, Pavie, Pavie-Decesse, Pavie-Macquin, Quinault l'Enclos, Rol-Valentin, Le Tertre-Rôteboeuf, Valandraud

Barsac/Sauternes: Not yet evaluated

1997—A Quick Study (9-5-97)

St.-Estèphe***	Graves Red***
Pauillac***	Graves White**
St.-Julien***	Pomerol****
Margaux***	St.-Émilion****
Médoc/Haut-Médoc Crus Bourgeois**	Barsac/Sauternes***

Size: An exceptionally abundant vintage, but slightly less than in 1996 and 1995.

Important information: A seductive, user-friendly, soft (low acidity/high pHs) vintage that will have exceptionally broad appeal because of the wines' precociousness and evolved personalities. Most wines will have to be drunk during their first decade of life.

Maturity status: A quickly evolving vintage that, except for the most concentrated wines, will be over the hill in 10–12 years.

Price: Prices for 1997 Bordeaux are high. However, in March 1998, despite talk of dropping prices in view of the fact that the vintage was less successful than the very high-priced vintages of 1996 and 1995, most producers increased prices, largely because of the unprecedented ruthless selections they made in order to put good wine in the bottle. This has proven to be a stupid decision because consumers have not purchased the wines.

After 2 weeks spent intensively tasting all of the major, and many of the minor, wines of Bordeaux (often four separate times), there can be no doubt that this is a good vintage. Stylistically the wines, whether Merlot or Cabernet Sauvignon based, are characterized by very good ripeness (often an element of overripeness is present), extremely low acidity, high pHs, and juicy, succulent personalities with sweet tannin and an easily appreciated, friendly style. While exceptions exist, and some profoundly concentrated, long-lived wines were produced, this is a vintage that will require consumption at a relatively early age. Almost all the best petits châteaux, cru bourgeois, and lesser cru classé wines already offer delicious drinking, even though they are only 6 months old. Since they will not be bottled for another year, I fully expect these wines to be delicious upon release and best drunk within their first 2–6 years of life. The top classified growths, particularly those estates that produced bigger, more dense wines, will be capable of lasting 10–15 years, but all of them will have appeal and charm when released.

In contrast with 1996, where the Cabernet Sauvignon–dominated wines were clearly superior to the Merlot-based wines, 1997 did not favor any one appellation over another. The Pomerols are superior to their 1996 counterparts, and there is a bevy of exciting 1997 St.-Émilions, but soft, open-knit, supple-textured, somewhat diffuse wines are commonplace in every appellation. After considerable reflection over which vintage 1997 could be compared with, I found it impossible to find a similar vintage in my 20 years of tasting Bordeaux. There were other vintages (1985) that were easy to taste from barrel and possessed a similar smoothness and tenderness, but 1997 differs considerably from 1985. Most 1997s are not "big," muscular wines; rather, they are graceful and seductive, full of charm and elegance, yet somewhat fragile. I believe this vintage will be ideal for restaurants and consumers looking for immediate gratification. Because of that, there is no intelligent reason for speculators to "invest" in this vintage and drive up the prices. However, the market has become increasingly complicated, and the demand for top-quality Bordeaux remains insatiable.

I think everyone who enjoys a good glass of wine will find the 1997s attractive. Consumers are unlikely to be knocked out by their depth or flavor intensity, but they are well-made, soft, user-friendly wines that are highly complementary to such vintages as 1996, 1995, and 1994, all tannic years that require significant bottle age.

The 1997 vintage began auspiciously. For the last 18 years I have spent the final 2 weeks of March in Bordeaux, and March 1997 was the hottest I have ever experienced. Temperatures were in the mid-80s, and even hit 90 degrees on occasion, making me think it was late June rather than March. This hot weather jump-started the vineyards, causing a roaring vegetative cycle. The flowering occurred at the earliest dates on record, leading many châteaux to conclude that the harvest would be well under way by mid-August.

The flowering hit a few glitches and tended to drag on for nearly a month. The irregular flowering, which led to uneven ripening of the grapes, was exacerbated by the unusual pattern of summer weather. The weather was hot at the beginning of June, but it cooled off and became very wet later in the month. July was abnormal. Usually a torridly hot month in Bordeaux, in 1997 it was cool yet humid. By the end of July high pressure had settled in and the weather became sultry. July was followed by unusual tropical-like weather in August, with record-breaking levels of humidity as well as high temperatures. Despite extensive crop-thinning and leaf-pulling efforts by well-run châteaux, the prolonged flowering, unusual end of June, and tropical August (growers said it felt more like Bangkok than Bordeaux) created severe uneven ripening within each grape bunch. The most heard complaint was that within each bunch of grapes there were red grapes, green grapes, and rosé-colored grapes—a nightmare scenario for growers.

The incredibly early spring, bud break, and flowering did prompt some Pessac-Léognan properties to harvest (in full view of the nation's television cameras) their white wine grapes as early as August 18. This made 1997 an "earlier" vintage than the legendary year of 1893. Just after the beginning harvest for the whites, the hot tropical weather deteriorated, and a succession of weather depressions buffeted Bordeaux. From August 25 through September 1, sizable quantities of rain fell throughout the region. The fact that so many 1997s are soft, with low acidity but without the great concentration and density found in the finest 1996s and 1995s, is no doubt attributable to these heavy rains. One need not be a nuclear physicist to understand the taste of wines made from bloated grapes. Producers who panicked and began picking in early September, fearing the onset of rot and further weather deterioration, made the vintage's least successful wines. However, those who had the intestinal fortitude and discipline to wait were rewarded with a fabulous month of September. Aside from a few scattered rain showers on September 12 and 13, it was one of the driest, sunniest Septembers this century. The later a producer was able to wait, the more the vines, and subsequently the wine, benefited.

Virtually all of the Merlot was picked between September 2 and 23. The Cabernet Franc was harvested between mid-September and early October. The Cabernet Sauvignon harvest began slowly in mid-September but lasted even longer, with some producers waiting until mid-October to harvest their last Cabernet Sauvignon parcels.

One of the more intriguing statistics about this unusual weather pattern is the extraordinary "hang time" the grapes enjoyed between the date of flowering and the harvest date. In Bordeaux the general rule is that if the producer can get 110 days between flowering and harvest, he will harvest mature grapes. In 1997 it was not bizarre for the Merlot vineyards to be harvested 115–125 days after flowering. For the Cabernet Sauvignon, a whopping 140 days was not an unusual hang time. Normally this would be a sign of extraordinary flavor concentration, but the weather at the end of August destroyed all hopes for a great vintage.

Yields were relatively modest, and when the overall production for Bordeaux was tabulated, the region's harvest was slightly smaller than either 1996 or 1995. More important, and the obvious explanation for the quality at the classified growth level, is the unprecedented selection that took place. It was not unusual to learn that 50%–30% of a château's total crop was all that was deemed acceptable for the estate's *grand vin*.

The Bordeaux marketplace has become almost impossible to predict. Last year I was positive that prices would come out at the same level as the 1995s, and although I anticipated active futures buying for many of the great Médocs, I was not prepared for the buying hysteria that would ensue or the high prices demanded by the châteaux. It seems to me that the 1997s should be priced below the 1996s and 1995s, but I can fully understand the predicament of the top producers who made rigorous selections and thus produced far less wine under the *grand vin* label than usual. Since all the top wines sell out so quickly, why shouldn't they take advantage of what is obviously an overheated marketplace? Nevertheless, are the 1997s worth buying as futures? Certainly for some of the limited-production wines, as well as the first-growths and super-seconds (always the most difficult wines to procure), purchasing futures may continue to make sense, if only to guarantee getting such wines. However, this is a vintage not for speculators, but for true wine drinkers. I do not see prices for 1997s escalating significantly, as have the top 1995s and 1996s. However, since I totally underestimated the worldwide demand for Bordeaux over the last few years, who knows what will happen? In November the feeling in Bordeaux was that prices would drop, but by March the hotels were full of buyers from around the world, all clamoring (despite complaints about the prices) to buy as much as they could, desperate to ensure they will be guaranteed their allocations when the 1998s and 1999s—and, God forbid, the 2000s!—become available. At the time of publication nobody knows what prices will emerge for the 1997s.

There is one thing I do know. No one has ever gone wrong buying the finest Bordeaux from a profoundly great vintage, or even superb Bordeaux wines from an excellent vintage. As the tasting notes that follow indicate, 1997 is not a great vintage, nor are there that many great wines, but there are many consumer-friendly, satisfying efforts that will, hopefully, be reasonably priced.

THE BEST WINES

St.-Estèphe: Cos d'Estournel, Montrose
Pauillac: Lafite-Rothschild, Latour, Lynch-Bages, Mouton-Rothschild, Pichon-Longueville
  Baron

St.-Julien: Branaire, Gloria, Gruaud-Larose, Lagrange, Léoville-Barton, Léoville-Las Cases, Léoville-Poyferré, Talbot
Margaux: D'Angludet, Château Margaux
Médoc/Haut-Médoc Crus Bourgeois: Sociando-Mallet
Graves Red: Les Carmes-Haut-Brion, Domaine de Chevalier, Haut-Brion, Pape-Clément, Smith-Haut-Lafitte
Graves White: Domaine de Chevalier, Fieuzal, Haut-Brion, Laville-Haut-Brion, Smith-Haut-Lafitte
Pomerol: Clinet, Clos l'Église, l'Église-Clinet, l'Évangile, La Fleur-Pétrus, Lafleur, Pétrus, Le Pin, Trotanoy
St.-Émilion: Angélus, Ausone, Cheval Blanc, Clos de l'Oratoire, Faugères, Gracia, Grandes-Murailles, l'Hermitage, Monbousquet, La Mondotte, Moulin St.-Georges, Pavie-Decesse, Pavie-Macquin, Troplong-Mondot, Valandraud
Barsac/Sauternes: I do not believe in commenting on these sweet wines until they are at least 1 year old, so judgment is reserved. It should be at least a 3-star vintage based on the wines tasted.

1996—A Quick Study (9-16-96)

St.-Estèphe*****	Graves Red****
Pauillac*****	Graves White***
St.-Julien*****	Pomerol***
Margaux****	St.-Émilion****
Médoc/Haut-Médoc Crus Bourgeois***	Barsac/Sauternes****

Size: An exceptionally large crop, just behind the superabundant 1995 and 1986 vintages.
Important information: In addition to being the most expensive young Bordeaux vintage in history, with opening prices 50%–100% above the opening future prices of the 1995s, this is a great vintage for the Médoc- and Cabernet Sauvignon–based wines.
Maturity status: The powerful Cabernet Sauvignon–based wines of the Médoc will be more accessible than the vintage 1996 most closely resembles, 1986, but in general the wines will require 10–15 years of cellaring following bottling. The wines from Graves and the right bank will be more accessible at a younger age and should be drinkable by 7–10 years of age.
Price: As indicated, this is a very expensive vintage with record-breaking prices.

    For over 20 years I have followed (in considerable detail) the weather patterns during Bordeaux's spring, summer, and early fall. I have also studied available information on the weather patterns for virtually every significant Bordeaux vintage this century. Several conclusions can be readily gleaned from such weather statistics. Most of Bordeaux's greatest years have been the product of exceptionally hot, dry summers, with below average rainfall and above average temperatures. While a number of this century's celebrated vintages have had moderate amounts of rain in September, unless a significant quantity falls, the effect on quality has usually been minor. In every viticultural region of France, vignerons sing the same tune: "June makes the quantity, and September makes the quality." Some go even further, saying, "August makes the style."

    Given the number of high-quality wines produced in 1996, Bordeaux's weather from March through mid-October was decidedly unusual. The winter of 1996 was wet and mild. When I arrived in Bordeaux on March 19, 1996, I thought it was mid-June rather than March, thanks to the blast of heat the region was experiencing. This heat wave lasted the entire 12 days I was there. Many growers predicted an early flowering and, consequently, an early harvest. The heat wave broke in early April, with a cold period followed by another burst of surprisingly high temperatures in mid-April. Atypically, the month of May was relatively cool.

When I returned to France for 17 days in mid-June, the country was experiencing blazingly torrid temperatures in the 90+-degree range. This made for a quick and generally uniform flowering. In Bordeaux most estates were thrilled with the flowering, which took only 3–4 days rather than the usual 7–10. The cold spell that hit during the end of May and beginning of June caused severe *millerandange* (the failure of a vine to fully set its entire bunch, thus reducing yields) for the warmer *terroirs* on the plateau of Pomerol. By the end of June a large, precocious crop was anticipated. Except for the reduced crop size in Pomerol, viticulturally speaking, things could not have looked better. But then the weather turned unusually bizarre.

While the period between July 11 and August 19 was relatively normal (statistically it was slightly cooler and wetter than usual), the first 11 days of July and the period between August 25 and 30 received abnormally huge quantities of rainfall, in addition to below normal temperatures. Statistics can be misleading, as evidenced by the fact that while the normal amount of rainfall for Bordeaux during the month of August is just over 2 inches (53 millimeters), in 1996 the quantity of rainfall was a whopping 6 inches (144 millimeters). Yet the heaviest rainfall was localized, with over 4 inches falling on Entre-deux-Mers and St.-Émilion, 2 inches on Margaux, 1.75 inches on St.-Julien, 1.5 inches on Pauillac, and under 1 inch in St.-Estèphe and the northern Médoc. I remember telephoning several friends in Bordeaux around America's Labor Day weekend and receiving conflicting viewpoints about the prospects for the 1996 vintage. Those in the southern Graves and on the right bank were obviously distressed, expressing concern that the vintage was going to be a disaster along the lines of 1974. They hoped that a miraculous September would turn it into a 1988 or 1978. In contrast, those in the Médoc, especially from St.-Julien north, were optimistic, sensing that a good September would result in a terrific vintage. The large quantities of rain that had bloated the grapes to the south and east had largely missed the Médoc. The below average quantity of rain the Médoc did receive kept the vines flourishing, as opposed to shutting down photosynthesis as a result of excessive heat and drought, as had occurred in 1995 and 1989.

Large quantities of early September rain had been a pernicious problem in 1991, 1992, 1993, 1994, and to a lesser extent 1995, but this climatic pattern would not repeat itself in 1996. Between August 31 and September 18 there was a remarkable string of 18 sunny days, followed by light showers throughout the region on September 18 and 19. There were several days of clear weather, then drizzle on September 21, and, finally, the arrival of heavy rains the evening of September 24 that lasted through September 25.

Another important characteristic of this period between August 31 and September 24 was the omnipresent gusty, dry, easterly and northeasterly winds that played a paramount role in drying the vineyards after the late August rains. Moreover, these winds were consistently cited by producers as the reason sugar accumulated at rates that seemed impossible at the end of August. Another beneficial aspect to this windy period was that any potential for rot was minimalized by Mother Nature's antibiotic.

The Merlot harvest took place during the last 2 weeks of September. The Cabernet Franc was harvested during late September and the first 4–5 days of October. The later-ripening, thicker-skinned Cabernet Sauvignon grapes were harvested between the end of September and October 12. Except for a good-size rainfall throughout the region on October 4, the weather in October was sunny and dry, offering textbook conditions for harvesting Cabernet Sauvignon. In fact, most Médoc producers saw a distinct parallel between the Cabernet Sauvignon harvest in 1996 and that of 1986. While rain had marred the 1986 harvest for the early-ripening varietals (such as Merlot and Cabernet Franc), it stopped, to be followed by a nearly perfect 4 weeks of dry, windy, sunny weather, during which the Cabernet Sauvignon harvest took place under ideal conditions.

Given this weather pattern, it is not surprising that most of 1996's finest wines emerged from the Médoc, which harvested Cabernet 10–18 days later than vineyards having high proportions of Merlot.

As was expected from the highly successful flowering during the torrid month of June, the 1996 Bordeaux harvest produced an abundant crop (6.5 million hectoliters), which is marginally below the 1995 crop size (which produced a crop of 6.89 million hectoliters). However, readers should recognize that the production of some of the top Pomerol estates, especially those on the plateau, was off by 30%–50%. In St.-Émilion many estates produced 10%–15% less wine than normal. Most of the top Médoc estates produced between 45 and 55 hectoliters per hectare, about 20%–30% less than their 1986 yields.

In conclusion, there are eight things to know about the 1996 vintage:

1. This is the most expensive young Bordeaux vintage in the history of the region, with opening prices 50%–100% above the opening prices for the 1995s.

2. In contrast with 1995, which had a fabulous summer marred by a rainy September, 1996 experienced a most unusual weather pattern. It started off as one of the earliest vintages of the century, with blazingly hot weather in early spring, followed by a cold period, and then torrid temperatures in June. The summer was relatively normal, except for several abnormally cold periods. Late August, usually hot and dry, witnessed freakish quantities of rain, in addition to below normal temperatures. September was a relatively dry and, most important, windy month. The gusty northern winds played a paramount role in drying out the vineyards after the late August rains. In addition, these winds (along with the dry, sunny days) were the primary reason for the extraordinary accumulation of sugar in the grapes, particularly the Cabernet Sauvignon, which was harvested very late.

3. A giant crop was produced with quantities slightly below the 1995 crop.

4. This is an irregular vintage without the quality consistency of 1995. The great strength of 1996 is the Cabernet Sauvignon–dominated wines of the Médoc.

5. I spent several weeks in November 1997 tasting through all the wines again, and in the 20 years I have been visiting the area and tasting young Bordeaux vintages, I have never tasted Cabernet Sauvignon as rich, ripe, pure, and intense as the finest 1996 Médocs exhibit. I believe some Cabernet Sauvignon–based wines of the Médoc may turn out to be among the greatest red wines Bordeaux has produced in the last 50 years.

6. The 1996 vintage is most comparable to the 1986 because of the weather pattern and the fact that the late-picked Cabernet Sauvignon was so successful for both vintages. When I first tasted the 1996s it was easy to see the comparison, as it was in November 1997. However, the finest 1996 Cabernet-based wines of the Médoc have a sweetness, completeness, and aromatic and flavor dimensions that exceed the greatest 1986s.

7. The lofty prices fetched by the 1996s in the overheated Bordeaux marketplace of 1997 ensured that many 1996s, particularly wines below the first-growth and super-second levels, have not sold through to the consumer. There have been reports of canceled orders, in addition to merchants unable to make their payments on the 1996s. Much of this has been verified with colleagues in Bordeaux, but other markets have stepped in to absorb any returned stock that was unsold by the American wine trade. Undoubtedly there are 1996s that remain overpriced vis-à-vis their quality. Yet once consumers have a chance to taste the 1996 Cabernet Sauvignon–dominated wines, it will become evident that many Médoc estates have produced a profoundly great vintage of classic, long-lived wines that will rival such heralded vintages as 1990, 1989, 1982, 1961, and 1959. That being said, readers should not make the mistake of thinking that the finest 1996s will be flamboyant, delicious, and opulently textured in their youth. The vintage's most compelling wines will require patience.

8. It is no secret that Pomerol, St.-Émilion, and Graves (including the northern tier with the appellation of Pessac-Léognan) were less successful, but there were still some extraordi-

nary wines produced in these appellations. However, readers should be aware that none of these appellations is as consistent in quality as 1995.

THE BEST WINES

St.-Estèphe: Calon-Ségur, Cos d'Estournel, Haut-Marbuzet, Lafon-Rochet, Montrose

Pauillac: d'Armailhac, Batailley, Clerc-Milon, Duhart-Milon, Grand-Puy-Lacoste, Haut-Batailley, Lafite-Rothschild, Latour, Lynch-Bages, Lynch-Moussas, Mouton-Rothschild, Pichon-Longueville Baron, Pichon-Longueville-Comtesse de Lalande, Pontet-Canet

St.-Julien: Branaire (Duluc Ducru), Ducru Beaucaillou, Gloria, Gruaud-Larose, Hortevie, Lagrange, Léoville-Barton, Léoville-Las Cases, Léoville-Poyferré, Talbot

Margaux: d'Angludet, d'Issan, Kirwan, Malescot-St.-Exupéry, Château Margaux, Palmer, Rauzan-Ségla, Du Tertre

Médoc/Haut-Médoc Crus Bourgeois: Cantemerle, Charmail, Domaine de Chiroulet Réserve, Les Grandes Chênes Cuvée Prestige, La Lagune, Lanessan, Reignac Cuvée Spéciale, Roc des Cambes, Sociando-Mallet

Graves Red: Les Carmes-Haut-Brion, Haut-Bailly, Haut-Brion, La Mission-Haut-Brion, Pape-Clément, Smith-Haut-Lafitte, La Tour-Haut-Brion

Graves White: de Fieuzal, Haut-Brion, Laville-Haut-Brion, Pape-Clément, Smith-Haut-Lafitte

Pomerol: Beau-Soleil, Bon Pasteur, Clinet, La Conseillante, La Croix-du-Casse, l'Église-Clinet, l'Évangile, La Fleur de Gay, La Fleur-Pétrus, Gazin, Grand-Puy-Lacoste, Lafleur, Latour à Pomerol, Pétrus, Le Pin, Trotanoy, Vieux-Château-Certan

St.-Émilion: Angélus, l'Arrosée, Ausone, Beau-Séjour-Bécot, Beauséjour-Duffau, Canon-La-Gaffelière, Cheval Blanc, Clos Fourtet, Clos de l'Oratoire, La Couspaude, La Dominique, Ferrand-Lartigue, La Gaffelière, La Gomerie, Grand-Mayne, Grand-Pontet, Larmande, Monbousquet, La Mondotte, Moulin St.-Georges, Pavie-Macquin, Rol Valentin, Le Tertre-Rôteboeuf, Troplong-Mondot, Trotte Vieille, Valandraud

Barsac/Sauternes: This is a promising, potentially 4-star vintage, but at the time of writing it was too early to effectively evaluate the wines.

1995—A Quick Study (9-20-96)

St.-Estèphe****	Graves Red****/*****
Pauillac****/*****	Graves White***
St.-Julien****/*****	Pomerol*****
Margaux****	St.-Émilion****
Médoc/Haut-Médoc Crus Bourgeois***	Barsac/Sauternes**

Size: Another huge harvest, just short of the record-setting crop of 1986. However, most major châteaux crop-thinned, and yields were more modest. In addition to crop thinning, the selection process of the top first-growths, super-seconds, and quality-oriented châteaux was severe, resulting in far less wine being produced under their grand vin label than in such abundant vintages as 1989 and 1990.

Important information: The most consistently top-notch vintage since 1990. Almost all the major appellations turned in exceptional wines of uniform quality.

Maturity status: While it has been reported that the highly successful 1995 Merlot crop resulted in precocious wines meant to be consumed immediately, all of my tastings have revealed that while the Merlot is undoubtedly successful, the Merlot, Cabernet Sauvignon, and Cabernet Franc produced wines with considerable weight, tannin, and structure. Although there are obvious exceptions, most of the finest 1995 Bordeaux are classic *vin de garde* wines with considerable tannin that, while accessible, require bottle age. I do not see the big wines being close to full maturity before 2003–2005.

Price: The second most expensive young Bordeaux vintage, both as futures and in the bottle . . . ever.

June, July, and August made the 1995 vintage, as they were among the driest and hottest months in the last 40 years. However, like most vintages since 1991, the Bordelais could not get past the first week of September without the deterioration of weather conditions. The showery weather lasted only between September 7 and 19, rather than the entire month, as it had in 1992, 1993, 1994, and, to a lesser extent, 1991. Unlike the record rainfall of 275 millimeters in September 1992, and 175 millimeters in September 1994, the rainfall in September 1995 was only 145 millimeters. In the northern Médoc communes of St.-Julien, Pauillac, and Pomerol, the amount of rain ranged from 91 millimeters to 134 millimeters.

While it was a huge harvest, the key to the most successful 1995s appears to have been a severe selection once the wines had finished alcoholic and malolactic fermentations. The Merlot was certainly ripe, but this was the first vintage since 1990 where the Cabernet Sauvignon (at least the late-harvested Cabernet) was extremely ripe. Most châteaux that delayed their harvest until late September were rewarded with physiologically mature Cabernet Sauvignon.

In short, there are seven things to remember about the 1995 vintage, a year that should be considered both exceptional and uniform:

1. This was the second most expensive young Bordeaux vintage this century.

2. In spite of a rainy September, the outstanding success enjoyed by many châteaux in the 1995 vintage was the result of splendid weather in June, July, and August, a period that was among the driest and hottest in the last 40 years.

3. A huge crop of wine was produced, but the ruthless selection process employed by many top châteaux has resulted in more modest quantities of top classified-growths than in such abundant vintages as 1989 and 1990.

4. This vintage has turned out to be consistently uniform throughout all appellations. From cask, the vintage looked particularly strong in St.-Julien, Pauillac, and Pomerol, but since bottling, it does not appear to have any regional weaknesses except for the dry whites of Graves and the sweet whites of Barsac/Sauternes, which are pleasant but generally of average quality.

5. Readers who purchased the 1995s early, before prices began to soar, will be thrilled to know that after bottling, the 1995s, for the most part, are exhibiting more promise than they did from cask. At the minimum, 1995 is an excellent vintage, yet given the high percentage of outstanding wines, a strong argument can be made that 1995 comes close to rivaling such great vintages as 1990 and 1982.

6. It is hard to generalize about the overall style of a vintage, but readers should not assume that the highly successful 1995 Merlot crop resulted in precocious wines meant to be consumed immediately. My tastings revealed that while the Merlot and Cabernet Sauvignon had taken on flesh, weight, and fat during their time in barrel (*élevage*), they had also taken on more delineation and tannin. While there are obviously exceptions, most of the finest 1995 Bordeaux are classic *vin de garde* wines with considerable tannin and, while accessible, require bottle age.

7. In summary, 1995 is an excellent to outstanding vintage of consistently top-notch red wines across all appellations. As I have stated from the beginning, the 1995 vintage may represent a modern-day clone of 1970. However, given today's winemaking, selection process, and the fact that the overall commitment to quality is far higher, there are undoubtedly more outstanding wines in 1995 than in 1970. Prices of the bottled 1995s are extremely

high, but from an overall perspective, 1995 has produced the most consistently high-quality wines since 1990.

THE BEST WINES

St.-Estèphe: Calon-Ségur, Cos d'Estournel, Cos Labory, Lafon-Rochet, Montrose

Pauillac: D'Armailhac, Clerc-Milon, Grand-Puy-Lacoste, Haut-Batailley, Lafite-Rothschild, Latour, Lynch-Bages, Mouton-Rothschild, Pichon-Longueville Baron, Pichon-Longueville-Comtesse de Lalande, Pontet-Canet

St.-Julien: Branaire (Duluc Ducru), Ducru Beaucaillou, Gloria, Gruaud-Larose, Lagrange, Léoville-Barton, Léoville-Las Cases, Léoville-Poyferré, Talbot

Margaux: d'Angludet, Malescot-St.-Exupéry, Château Margaux, Palmer, Rauzan-Ségla

Médoc/Haut-Médoc Crus Bourgeois: Charmail, La Lagune, Roc des Cambes, Sociando-Mallet

Graves Red: de Fieuzal, Haut-Bailly, Haut-Brion, La Mission-Haut-Brion, Pape-Clément, Smith-Haut-Lafitte, La Tour-Haut-Brion

Graves White: de Fieuzal, Haut-Brion, Laville-Haut-Brion, Pape-Clément, Smith-Haut-Lafitte

Pomerol: Bon Pasteur, Bourgneuf, Certan de May, Clinet, La Conseillante, La Croix-du-Casse, l'Église-Clinet, l'Évangile, La Fleur-de-Gay, La Fleur-Pétrus, Gazin, Grand-Puy-Lacoste, La Grave à Pomerol, Lafleur, Latour à Pomerol, Pétrus, Le Pin, Trotanoy, Vieux-Château-Certan

St.-Émilion: Angélus, l'Arrosée, Ausone, Beau-Séjour-Bécot, Canon-La-Gaffelière, Cheval Blanc, Clos Fourtet, Clos de l'Oratoire, Corbin-Michotte, La Couspaude, La Dominique, Ferrand-Lartigue, Figeac, La Fleur-de-Jaugue, La Gomerie, Grand Mayne, Grand Pontet, Larmande, Magdelaine, Monbousquet, Moulin-St.-Georges, Pavie-Macquin, Le Tertre-Rôteboeuf, Troplong-Mondot, Valandraud

Barsac/Sauternes: none

1994—A Quick Study (9-24-94)

St.-Estèphe***	Graves Red****
Pauillac***/****	Graves White*****
St.-Julien***/****	Pomerol****
Margaux***	St.-Émilion***
Médoc/Haut-Médoc Crus Bourgeois**	Barsac/Sauternes*

Size: Another exceptionally large Bordeaux crop; however, the top properties had to be exceptionally severe in their selection process in order to bottle under the grand vin label only the finest cuvées. Consequently production of the top estates is relatively modest.

Important information: A hot, dry summer provided the potential for a great vintage, but the weather deteriorated in September, and a whopping 175 millimeters of rain fell between September 7 and September 29. Producers who were unwilling to declassify 30%–50% of their harvest were incapable of making top-quality wines. Those who did enjoyed considerable success in this vintage, the finest year after 1990 and before 1995. Merlot was the most successful grape in this inconsistent vintage. Even the most successful Médocs employed a higher percentage of Merlot than Cabernet Sauvignon, which had a tendency to be austere and herbaceous, with very high tannin. Another key to understanding 1994 is that the best drained vineyards (those lying next to the Gironde in the Médoc and Graves) tended to produce very good wines, assuming they made a strict selection.

Maturity status: Most 1994s will be slow to evolve given their relatively high tannin levels. This is a classic, *vin de garde* vintage, with the top wines being well colored and quite structured and powerful. They require additional bottle age.

Price: Initially reasonably priced, the 1994s have benefited from the international interest and, at times, speculation in all good-quality Bordeaux vintages. Prices appear to be high for the vintage's potential.

At the top level, 1994 has produced some excellent, even outstanding, wines, with far higher peaks of quality than 1993. However, too many wines have not fared well since bottling, with the fragile fruit stripped out by excessive fining and filtration. As a result, the wines' more negative characteristics, a hollowness and high levels of harsh tannin, are well displayed. The 1994 could have been an exceptional vintage had it not rained, at times heavily, for 13 days between September 7 and September 29. As is so often the case with a vintage that enjoyed 3 months of superb weather during the summer, only to be negatively impacted by excessive rain before and during the harvest, the willingness of the producer to declassify 30%–50% of the harvest was often the difference between producing a high-quality wine and one that is out of balance.

The overall characteristic of the 1994s is a backwardness, caused in large part by the high tannin levels. Yet the vintage's great successes possess the fruit and extract necessary to balance out the tannin. Those who failed to make a strict selection, or had too little Merlot to flesh out and counterbalance the more austere Cabernet Sauvignon, have turned out dry, hard, lean, and attenuated wines. The 1994 is unquestionably an irregular vintage and is more frustrating to taste through than 1993, but some outstanding wines were produced. Shrewd buyers will find a number of smashing wines, but this is a vintage where cautious selection is mandatory.

In 1994, much as in 1993, the most favored appellations were those that either had a high percentage of Merlot planted or had exceptionally well-drained soils. As in 1993, Pomerol appears once again to have been the most favored region. However, that is not a blanket endorsement of all Pomerols, as there are disappointments. The Graves and Médoc estates close to the Gironde, with gravelly, deep, stony, exceptionally well-drained soils, also had the potential to produce rich, well-balanced wines. However, it was essential in 1994, particularly in the Médoc, to eliminate a considerable quantity of the crop (the top estates eliminated 30%–50% or more) and to utilize a higher percentage of Merlot in the final blend. Moreover, the wines had to be bottled "softly," without excessive fining and filtering, which will eviscerate flavors and body.

THE BEST WINES

St.-Estèphe: Cos d'Estournel, Lafon-Rochet, Montrose

Pauillac: Clerc-Milon, Grand-Puy-Lacoste, Lafite-Rothschild, Latour, Lynch-Bages, Mouton-Rothschild, Pichon-Longueville Baron, Pichon-Longueville-Comtesse de Lalande, Pontet-Canet

St.-Julien: Branaire-Ducru, Clos du Marquis, Ducru-Beaucaillou, Hortevie, Lagrange, Léoville-Barton, Léoville-Las Cases, Léoville-Poyferré

Margaux: Malescot-St.-Exupéry, Château Margaux

Médoc/Haut-Médoc Crus Bourgeois: Roc des Cambes, Sociando-Mallet

Graves Red: Bahans-Haut-Brion, Haut-Bailly, Haut-Brion, La Mission-Haut-Brion, Pape-Clément, Smith-Haut-Lafitte

Graves White: Domaine de Chevalier, de Fieuzal, Haut-Brion, Laville-Haut-Brion, Pape-Clément, Smith-Haut-Lafitte, La Tour-Martillac

Pomerol: Beaurégard, Bon Pasteur, Certan de May, Clinet, La Conseillante, La Croix du Casse, La Croix de Gay, l'Église-Clinet, l'Évangile, La Fleur de Gay, La Fleur-Pétrus, Gazin, Lafleur, Latour à Pomerol, Pétrus, Le Pin

St.-Émilion: Angélus, l'Arrosée, Beau-Séjour-Bécot, Beauséjour-Duffau, Canon La
    Gaffelière, Cheval Blanc, Clos Fourtet, La Dominique, Ferrand-Lartigue, Forts de Latour,
    Grand-Pontet, Larcis-Ducasse, Magdelaine, Monbousquet, Pavie-Macquin, Le Tertre-
    Rôteboeuf, Troplong-Mondot, Valandraud
Barsac/Sauternes: none

1993—A Quick Study (9-26-93)

St.-Estèphe**	Graves Red***
Pauillac**	Graves White***
St.-Julien**	Pomerol***
Margaux*	St.-Émilion**
Médoc/Haut-Médoc Crus Bourgeois*	Barsac/Sauternes*

Size: A very large crop.

Important information: Another vintage conceived under deplorable weather conditions.
However, this one offers a number of pleasant surprises. It has produced more attractive
clarets than either 1992 or 1991.

Maturity status: The finest wines should continue to drink well through the first 5–6 years of
the next century.

Price: The last reasonably priced vintage of the nineties still available in the marketplace,
the 1993s came out at low prices and have remained essentially reasonably priced.

In some quarters 1993 has been written off as a terrible vintage due to the enormous
amount of rainfall in September. The amount of rainfall that fell in 1991 and 1992 was
frightfully high, but what fell in and around Bordeaux in September 1993 broke a 30-year
average rainfall record by an astonishing 303%! For this reason it was easy to conclude that
no one could have possibly made good wine. Moreover, the spring weather was equally atro-
cious, with significant rainfall in both April and June.

However, July was warmer than normal, and August was exceptionally hot and sunny. In
fact, before the weather deteriorated on September 6, the proprietors were beginning to think
that an exceptional vintage was attainable. The September rain destroyed this optimism, but
because of exceptionally cold, dry weather between the deluges, the rot that growers feared
the most did not occur. Most châteaux harvested when they could, finishing around mid-
October.

The better wines of 1993 suggest it is a deeply colored, richer, potentially better vintage
than either 1991 or 1992. The wines can be characterized as deeply colored, with an unripe
Cabernet Sauvignon character, good structure, more depth and length than expected, and
some evidence of dilution.

THE BEST WINES

St.-Estèphe: Cos d'Estournel, Montrose
Pauillac: Clerc-Milon, Grand-Puy-Ducasse, Grand-Puy-Lacoste, Latour, Mouton-Rothschild
St.-Julien: Clos du Marquis, Hortevie, Lagrange, Léoville-Barton, Léoville-Las Cases,
    Léoville-Poyferré
Margaux: Château Margaux
Médoc/Haut-Médoc Crus Bourgeois: Sociando-Mallet
Graves Red: Bahans-Haut-Brion, de Fieuzal, Haut-Bailly, Haut-Brion, La Mission-Haut-
    Brion, Smith-Haut-Lafitte, La Tour-Haut-Brion
Graves White: Haut-Brion, Laville-Haut-Brion, Smith-Haut-Lafitte

Pomerol: Beauregard, Bon Pasteur, Clinet, La Conseillante, La Croix de Gay, l'Église-Clinet, l'Évangile, La Fleur de Gay, Gazin, Lafleur, Latour à Pomerol, Pétrus, Le Pin, Trotanoy

St.-Émilion: Angélus, l'Arrosée, Beau-Séjour-Bécot, Beauséjour-Duffau, Canon-La-Gaffelière, Cheval Blanc, La Dominique, Ferrand-Lartigue, Grand-Pontet, Magdelaine, Monbousquet, Pavie-Macquin, Le Tertre-Rôteboeuf, Troplong-Mondot, Valandraud

Barsac/Sauternes: none

1992—A Quick Study (9-29-92)

St.-Estèphe**	Graves Red**
Pauillac**	Graves White***
St.-Julien**	Pomerol***
Margaux*	St.-Émilion**
Médoc/Haut-Médoc Crus Bourgeois*	Barsac/Sauternes*

Size: A large crop was harvested, but the top properties implemented a ruthless selection. Consequently quantities of the top wines were modest.

Important information: At the top level, the 1992s are pleasantly soft, yet even the finest wines had trouble avoiding the taste of dilution and herbaceousness from the excessive amounts of rain that fell before and during the harvest.

Maturity status: Most 1992s should be drunk during their first 10–12 years of life.

Price: Because of the vintage's poor to mediocre reputation, prices are very low. The real value of this vintage is that many of the first-growths could be purchased for $35–$40, and the second- through fifth-growths for $15–$25 . . . remarkably low prices in the overheated Bordeaux wine market.

The 1992 vintage was marked not by a tragic frost, as in 1991, but rather by excessive rainfall at the worst possible time. Following a precocious spring, with an abundance of humidity and warm weather, the flowering of the vines occurred 8 days earlier than the 30-year average, raising hopes of an early harvest. The summer was exceptionally hot, with June wet and warm, July slightly above normal in temperature, and August well above normal. However, unlike such classic hot, dry years as 1982, 1989, and 1990, 1992 saw significant rainfall (more than three times the normal amount) in August. For example, 193 millimeters of rain were reported in the Bordeaux area in August 1992 (most of it falling during several violent storms the last 2 days of the month), compared with 22 millimeters in 1990 and 63 millimeters in 1989.

By mid-August it was evident that the harvest would be enormous. For the serious estates, it was imperative that crop thinning be employed to reduce the crop size. Properties that crop-thinned produced wines with more richness than the light, diluted offerings of those that did not.

The first 2 weeks of September were dry, although abnormally cool. During this period the Sauvignon and Semillon were harvested under ideal conditions, which explains the excellent and sometimes outstanding success (despite high yields) of the 1992 white Graves.

From September 20 through most of October the weather was unfavorable, with considerable rain interspersed with short periods of clear weather. The harvest for the majority of estates took place over a long period of time, although most of the Merlot crop from both sides of the Gironde was harvested during 3 days of clear, dry weather on September 29, 30, and October 1. Between October 2 and October 6 more violent rainstorms lashed the region, and the châteaux, realizing nothing could be gained from waiting, harvested under miserable weather conditions. To make good wine it was essential to hand-pick the grapes, leaving the damaged, diseased fruit on the vine. An even stricter selection was necessary in the cellars.

Overall, 1992 is a more successful vintage than 1991 because no appellation produced a high percentage of poor wines, such as happened in Pomerol and St.-Émilion in 1991. The 1992s are the modern-day equivalents of the 1973s. But with better vinification techniques, stricter selection, better equipment, and more attention to yields, the top properties produced 1992s that are more concentrated, richer, and overall better wines than the best 1973s or, for that matter, the 1987s. All the 1992s tend to be soft, fruity, and low in acidity, with light to moderate tannin levels and moderate to good concentration.

The appellation that appears to have fared best is Pomerol. Certainly the top properties of the firm of Jean-Pierre Moueix crop-thinned severely. In the case of their two flagship estates, Trotanoy and Pétrus, Christian Moueix boldly employed an innovative technique, covering these two vineyards with black plastic at the beginning of September. The heavy rains that subsequently fell accumulated on the plastic and ran off instead of saturating the soil. I have seen photographs of this elaborate, costly endeavor, and after tasting the wines I can say that Moueix's daring and brilliance paid off. Trotanoy and Pétrus are two of the three most concentrated wines of the vintage, confirming that the incredible amount of labor required to cover the 21-acre Trotanoy vineyard and 28-acre Pétrus vineyard with black plastic was well worth the effort.

Elsewhere there are successes and failures in every appellation, with no real consistency to be found. Those properties that were attentive to the enormous crop size and crop-thinned, who were lucky enough to complete part of their harvest before the deluge of October 2–6 and discarded any questionable grapes, have turned out fruity, soft, charming wines that, like the 1991s, will have to be drunk in their first 10–12 years of life.

THE BEST WINES

St.-Estèphe: Haut-Marbuzet, Montrose
Pauillac: Lafite-Rothschild, Latour, Pichon-Longueville Baron
St.-Julien: Ducru-Beaucaillou, Gruaud-Larose, Léoville-Barton, Léoville-Las Cases
Margaux: Giscours, Château Margaux, Palmer, Rauzan-Ségla
Médoc/Haut-Médoc Crus Bourgeois:none
Graves Red: Carbonnieux, Haut-Bailly, Haut-Brion, La Louvière, La Mission-Haut-Brion, Smith-Haut-Lafitte
Graves White: Domaine de Chevalier, de Fieuzal, Haut-Brion, Laville-Haut-Brion, Smith-Haut-Lafitte
Pomerol: Bon Pasteur, Certan de May, Clinet, La Conseillante, l'Église-Clinet, l'Évangile, La Fleur de Gay, La Fleur-Pétrus, Gazin, Lafleur, Pétrus
St.-Émilion: Angélus, l'Arrosée, Beauséjour-Duffau, Canon, Fonroque, Magdelaine, Troplong-Mondot, Valandraud
Barsac/Sauternes: none

1991—A Quick Study (9-30-91)

St.-Estèphe**	Graves Red**
Pauillac**	Graves White 0
St.-Julien**	Pomerol 0
Margaux*	St.-Émilion 0
Médoc/Haut-Médoc Crus Bourgeois 0	Barsac/Sauternes**

Size: A very small crop, largely because the killer freeze during the weekend of April 20–21 destroyed most of the crop in Pomerol and St.-Émilion.

Important information: A disaster in the right bank appellations of Pomerol and St.-Émilion, but as one proceeds north in the Médoc, the quality improves. Some surprisingly pleasant, even good, wines were produced in Pauillac and St.-Estèphe.

Maturity status: The wines are maturing quickly and should be drunk within their first 10–12 years of life.

Price: Because of its terrible reputation, this has always been an easily affordable, low-priced vintage.

The year 1991 is remembered for the big freeze. During the weekend of April 20–21 temperatures dropped as low as minus 9 degrees centigrade, destroying most vineyards' first-generation buds. The worst destruction occurred in Pomerol and St.-Émilion, east of the Gironde. Less damage occurred in the northern Médoc, especially in the northeastern sector of Pauillac and the southern half of St.-Estèphe. The spring that followed the devastating freeze did see the development of new buds, called "second-generation fruit" by viticulturists.

Because the crop size was expected to be small, optimists began to suggest that 1991 could resemble 1961 (a great year shaped by a spring killer frost that reduced the crop size). Of course, this hope was based on the assumption that the weather would remain sunny and dry during the growing season. By the time September arrived, most estates realized that the Merlot harvest could not begin until late September and the Cabernet Sauvignon harvest in mid-October. The second-generation fruit had retarded most vineyards' harvest schedules, yet sunny skies in late September gave hope for another 1978-ish "miracle year." Then, on September 25, an Atlantic storm dumped 116 millimeters of rain, precisely twice the average rainfall for the entire month!

Between September 30 and October 12 the weather was generally dry. Most of the Merlot vineyards on the right bank (Pomerol and St.-Émilion) were harvested during this period as quickly as possible. In Pomerol and St.-Émilion there was significant dilution, some rot, and unripe grapes. In the Médoc much of the Cabernet Sauvignon was not yet fully ripe, but many estates recognized that it was too risky to wait any longer. Those estates that harvested between October 13 and 19, before the outbreak of 6 consecutive days of heavy rain (another 120 millimeters), picked unripe but surprisingly healthy and low-acid Cabernet Sauvignon. Those properties that had not harvested by the time the second deluge arrived were unable to make quality wine.

The 1991 vintage is a poor, frequently disastrous year for most estates in Pomerol and St.-Émilion. I find it inferior to 1984, making it the worst vintage for these two appellations since the appalling 1969s. Many well-known estates in Pomerol and St.-Émilion completely declassified their wines, including such renowned St.-Émilion estates as l'Arrosée, Ausone, Canon, Cheval Blanc, La Dominique, and Magdelaine. In Pomerol several good wines were somehow made, but overall it was a catastrophe for this tiny appellation. Among the better-known Pomerol châteaux that declassified their entire crop are Beauregard, Bon Pasteur, l'Évangile, Le Gay, La Grave à Pomerol, Lafleur, Latour à Pomerol, Pétrus, Trotanoy, and Vieux-Château-Certan.

Despite all this bad news, some soft, pleasant, light- to medium-bodied wines did emerge from Graves and those Médoc vineyards adjacent to the Gironde. Consumers will be surprised by the quality of many of these wines, particularly from St.-Julien, Pauillac, and St.-Estèphe. In these northern Médoc appellations, much of the first-generation fruit was not destroyed by the frost, resulting in diluted but physiologically riper fruit than second-generation fruit produced. However, the good wines must be priced low or no consumer interest will be justified.

The appellations that stand out for consistently good wines in 1991 are St.-Julien, Pauillac, and St.-Estèphe. These areas suffered less frost damage to the first-generation grapes.

Virtually all of the better-run estates in these appellations made above average, sometimes excellent, wine.

Because the intelligent properties in the Médoc utilized more Merlot in the blend rather than the unripe Cabernet Sauvignon, the 1991s are soft, forward wines that will need to be drunk in their first decade of life.

THE BEST WINES

St.-Estèphe: Cos d'Estournel, Lafon-Rochet, Montrose

Pauillac: Forts de Latour, Grand-Puy-Lacoste, Lafite-Rothschild, Latour, Lynch-Bages, Mouton-Rothschild, Pichon-Longueville Baron, Pichon-Longueville-Comtesse de Lalande, Réserve de la Comtesse

St.-Julien: Beychevelle, Branaire-Ducru, Clos du Marquis, Ducru-Beaucaillou, Langoa-Barton, Léoville-Barton, Léoville-Las Cases

Margaux: Giscours, Château Margaux, Palmer, Rauzan-Ségla

Médoc/Haut-Médoc Crus Bourgeois: Citran

Graves Red: Carbonnieux, Domaine de Chevalier, Haut-Brion, La Mission-Haut-Brion, Pape-Clément, Smith-Haut-Lafitte, La Tour-Haut-Brion

Graves White: none

Pomerol: Clinet

St.-Émilion: Angélus, Troplong-Mondot

Barsac/Sauternes: none

1990—A Quick Study (9-12-90)

St.-Estèphe*****	Graves Red****
Pauillac*****	Graves White***
St.-Julien*****	Pomerol*****
Margaux****	St.-Émilion*****
Médoc/Haut-Médoc Crus Bourgeois****	Barsac/Sauternes***

Size: Enormous; one of the largest crops ever harvested in Bordeaux.

Important information: The hottest year since 1947 and the sunniest year since 1949 caused extraordinary stress in some of the best vineyards in the Graves and Médoc. Consequently the heavier soils from such appellations as St.-Estèphe, the limestone hillsides and plateau areas of St.-Émilion, and the Fronsacs excelled, as did those top châteaux that made a severe selection.

Maturity status: Exceptionally low-acid wines, but high tannins have consistently suggested early accessibility. The most complete wines have another 20–25 years of longevity, but there is not a wine from this vintage that cannot be drunk with a great deal of pleasure in the late nineties.

Price: Opening future prices were down 15%–20% below 1989, but no modern-day Bordeaux vintage, with the exception of 1982, has appreciated more in price than 1990.

Most of the great Bordeaux vintages of this century are the result of relatively hot, dry years. For that reason alone, 1990 should elicit considerable attention. The most revealing fact about the 1990 vintage is that it is the second-hottest vintage of the century, barely surpassed by 1947. It is also the second-sunniest vintage, eclipsed only by 1949 in the post–World War II era. The amount of sunshine and the extraordinarily hot summers Bordeaux has enjoyed during the eighties are frequently attributed to the so-called greenhouse effect and consequent global warming about which such ominous warnings have been issued by the scientific community. Yet consider the Bordeaux weather for the period between 1945 and 1949. Amazingly, that era was even more torrid than 1989–1990. (One wonders if there was concern then about the glaciers of the North and South Poles melting.)

The weather of 1990 was auspicious because of its potential to produce great wines, but weather is only one part of the equation. The summer months of July and August were the driest since 1961, and August was the hottest since 1928, the year records were first kept. September (the month that most producers claim "makes the quality") was not, weather-wise, a particularly exceptional month, and 1990 was the second wettest year among the great hot-year vintages, surpassed only by 1989. As in 1989, the rain fell at periods that were cause for concern. For example, on September 15 a particularly violent series of thunderstorms swept across Bordeaux, inundating much of the Graves region. On September 22–23 there was modest rainfall over the entire region. On October 7 and October 15 light showers were reported throughout the region. Most producers have been quick to state that the rain in September was beneficial. They argue that the Cabernet Sauvignon grapes were still too small and their skins too thick. Many Cabernet vines had shut down, and the grapes refused to mature because of the excessive heat and drought. The rain, the producers suggest, promoted further ripening and alleviated the blocked state of maturity. This is an appealing argument that has merit. While some panicked and harvested too soon after these rainstorms, the majority of the top estates got the harvest dates covered.

When tasting the wines from 1990, the most striking characteristic is their roasted quality, no doubt the result of the extremely hot summer. The September rains may have partially alleviated the stress from which those vineyards planted with Cabernet in the lighter, better-drained soils were suffering, but they also swelled many of the grape bunches and no doubt contributed to another prolifically abundant crop size.

There is no doubt that the great vintages have all been relatively hot, dry years. But was 1990 too torrid? Were the yields so high that in spite of the exceptional weather there were just too many grapes to make profound wines? The weather in 1990 put even more stress on the Bordeaux vineyards than the heat and drought of 1989. One of the keys to understanding this vintage is that the finest wines of 1990 have emerged from 1) those vineyards planted on the heavier, less well-drained, less desirable vineyard soil; and 2) those top châteaux that employed a particularly ruthless selection process. For example, in my tasting notes, heavier soils from such appellations as St.-Estèphe, Fronsac, and the hillside and plateau vineyards of St.-Émilion produced richer, more concentrated, and more complete wines than many of the top vineyards planted on the fine, well-drained, gravel-based soils of Margaux and the Graves.

The crop size was enormous in 1990, approximately equivalent to the quantity of wine produced in 1989. In reality, more wine was actually made, but because the French authorities intervened and required significant declassifications, the actual declared limit matches that for 1989, which means that for both vintages the production is 30% more than in 1982. Officially, however, many châteaux (especially the first-growths and super-seconds) made even stricter selections in 1990 than in 1989, and the actual quantity of wine declared by many producers under the grand vin label is less than in 1989.

Across almost every appellation, the overall impression one gets of the dry red wines is that of extremely low acidity (as low as and in some cases even lower than in 1989), high tannins (in most cases higher than in 1989), but an overall impression of softness and forward, precocious, extremely ripe, sometimes roasted flavors. Because the tannins are so soft (as in 1982, 1985, and 1989), these wines will provide considerable enjoyment when they are young, yet they possess decades or more of longevity.

The second consecutive year of great heat, sunshine, and drought apparently caused even more stress for those vineyards planted in light, gravelly soil than in 1989. Many proprietors in the Graves and Margaux regions suggested that they were almost forced to harvest their

Cabernet too soon because it was drying up on the vine. This, combined with extremely high yields, no doubt explains why the Graves and Margaux appellations, much as in 1989 and 1982 (two other hot, dry years), were less successful. Yet each appellation produced some brilliant wines.

Some surprising strengths in this vintage include most of the Médoc first-growths (Mouton-Rothschild being the exception). It can be said that they have made richer, fuller, more complete wines in 1990 than in 1989. Elsewhere in the Médoc, particularly in St.-Julien and Pauillac, a bevy of relatively soft, round, forward, fruity wines with high alcohol, high, soft tannin, and extremely low acidity have been made. For me, the most intriguing aspect of the 1990 vintage is that as the wines aged in cask and continued their evolution in bottle, the vintage took on additional weight and structure, much like 1982 (but not 1989). I clearly underestimated some of the St.-Juliens and Pauillacs early on, as it was apparent at the time of bottling that these appellations had generally produced many profoundly rich, concentrated wines that were to be the greatest young Bordeaux since 1982. The fly in the ointment when attempting to comprehend this vintage early on was that two of Bordeaux's superstars, Mouton-Rothschild and Pichon-Lalande, produced wines that were far less complete than their 1989s. Their wines were somewhat disappointing for the vintage and well below the quality of their peers. The puzzling performances of these two châteaux continues to be confirmed by my tastings in the late nineties. However, the other top wines in the Médoc have gained considerable stature and richness. They are the most exciting wines produced in Bordeaux between 1982 and 1995–1996.

On the right bank, it first appeared that Pomerol enjoyed a less successful vintage than 1989, with the exception of those estates situated on the St.-Émilion border—l'Évangile, La Conseillante, and Bon Pasteur—which from the beginning had obviously produced wines that were richer than their 1989 counterparts. However, as the Pomerols evolved in cask, the vintage, while never quite approaching 1989 in terms of greatness, did seem to strengthen from an overall perspective, with the wines gaining weight, definition, and complexity. As the end of the century approaches, 1990 is a vintage that produced some profoundly great Pomerols, but overall the vintage is less harmonious than 1989.

St.-Émilion, never a consistent appellation, has produced perhaps its most homogeneous and greatest vintage of the last 50 years for all three sectors of the appellation—the plateau, the vineyards at the foot of the hillsides, and the vineyards on sandy, gravelly soil. It is interesting to note that Cheval Blanc, Figeac, Pavie, l'Arrosée, Ausone, and Beauséjour-Duffau produced far greater 1990s than 1989s. In particular, both Cheval Blanc and Beauséjour-Duffau look to be wines of legendary quality. Figeac is not far behind, with the 1990 being the finest wine made at this estate since its 1982 and 1964.

The dry white wines of Graves, as well as generic white Bordeaux, have enjoyed a very good vintage that is largely superior to 1989, with two principal exceptions, Haut-Brion-Blanc and Laville-Haut-Brion. There is no doubt that the 1989 Haut-Brion-Blanc and 1989 Laville-Haut-Brion are two of the greatest white Graves ever produced. Both are far richer and more complete than their 1990s. Poor judgment in picking the 1989s too soon was not repeated with the 1990s, which have more richness and depth than most 1989s.

As for the sweet white wines of the Barsac/Sauternes region, this vintage was historic in the sense that most of the sweet white wine producers finished their harvest before the red wine producers, something that had not happened since 1949. While powerful, sweet, and sugary in cask and early in bottling, the wines have slowly begun to take on more complexity and focus. It really comes down to personal preference as to whether readers prefer 1990, 1989, or 1988 Barsacs and Sauternes, but there is no question this is the third and last vintage of a glorious trilogy, with the most powerful and concentrated Barsacs and Sauternes produced in many years. The wines, which boast some of the most impressive statistical credentials I have ever seen, are monster sized in their richness and intensity. They possess

30–40 years of longevity. Will they turn out to be more complex and elegant than the 1988s? My instincts suggest they will not, but they are immensely impressive, blockbuster wines.

In summary, readers should consider the following points with respect to the 1990 vintage:

1. I have consistently written that 1990 is a greater vintage overall than 1989. I have also stated that, in my opinion, 1990 is an even greater vintage than 1982—particularly in view of the fact that a number of estates making superb wine today were not especially well managed or motivated in 1982. For examples of this, readers need look no further than such châteaux as Angélus, Beauséjour-Duffau, Canon-La-Gaffelière, Clinet, Clos Fourtet, l'Église-Clinet, La Fleur de Gay, Gazin, Lafon-Rochet, Lagrange (St.-Julien), Monbousquet, Pape-Clément, Phélan-Ségur, Pichon-Longueville Baron, Smith-Haut-Lafitte, Le Tertre-Rôteboeuf, Troplong-Mondot, and Valandraud, all estates trying to produce superlative wine in the nineties that were indifferently administered (or nonexistent, in the case of Valandraud) in 1982. It is undoubtedly one of the greatest young Bordeaux vintages of modern times, with a style not dissimilar from 1982, but with more consistency from top to bottom than 1982. Yet the extraordinary concentration and opulence of the most profound 1982s still exceed that of the best 1990s.

2. With the exception of Pomerol, and the two splendid performances by La Mission-Haut-Brion and Haut-Brion in 1989, 1990 usually triumphs in side-by-side tastings of the two vintages. There are several other exceptions, but in general the 1990s are more concentrated, complex, and richer than their 1989 counterparts, except, of course, for the Pomerols and 1989 La Mission-Haut-Brion and Haut-Brion, which are undoubtedly legendary wines.

3. Prices for the 1990s are even higher than the 1982s. Sadly, I do not see any direction but upward for the prices of the 1990s or, for that matter, the 1982s. There are too many wealthy people in the world who insist on having the best of the best at any cost. The wine market today is considerably more diversified and broader than it was 5 or 10 years ago. Furthermore, a depressed economy in one country is not likely to cause a decline in prices for the greatest wines from the greatest vintages—a sad, but inescapable conclusion based on today's international wine market.

4. In looking at the finest Bordeaux vintages this century, I believe it is apparent that there are two types of great vintages. There are torridly hot, dry years that produce low-acid wines with explosive levels of fruit and what the French call *sur-maturité* (overripeness). Wines from these types of vintages tend to be delicious young because of their ripe tannin and low acidity. It is easy to think such vintages will not keep, but based on some ancient vintages that possessed these characteristics, the wines have proven ageworthy for a remarkably long time. Great vintages that fall in this category include 1900, 1921, 1929, 1947, 1949, 1959, 1961, 1982, 1989, and 1990.

The other type of great Bordeaux vintage produces extremely concentrated but formidably tannic wines that taste more dominated by Cabernet Sauvignon. These wines are almost impenetrable when young and, as a result, test their purchasers' patience for decades. This type of great vintage is often a more questionable purchase, since 10–20 years of cellaring is generally required for the wine to shed sufficient tannin to be enjoyable. The twentieth century's greatest vintages for wines of this style include 1926, 1928, 1945, 1948, 1955 (for the Médoc and Graves), 1975 (for the Pomerols and a selected handful of other estates), and 1986, as well as 1995, 1996 (but only for the Médoc), and 1998 (but only for the Pomerols).

THE BEST WINES

St.-Estèphe: Calon-Ségur, Cos d'Estournel, Cos Labory, Haut-Marbuzet, Montrose, Phélan-Ségur

Pauillac: Les Forts-de-Latour, Grand-Puy-Lacoste, Lafite-Rothschild, Latour, Lynch-Bages, Pichon-Longueville Baron

St.-Julien: Branaire-Ducru, Gloria, Gruaud-Larose, Lagrange, Léoville-Barton, Léoville-Las Cases, Léoville-Poyferré

Margaux: Malescot-St.-Exupèry, Margaux, Palmer, Rausan-Ségla

Médoc/Haut-Médoc/Moulis/Listrac/Crus Bourgeois: Lanessan, La Tour-St. Bonnet, Moulin-Rouge, Sociando-Mallet, Tour Haut-Caussan, Tour du Haut-Moulin

Graves Red: Haut-Bailly, Haut-Brion, La Louvière, La Mission-Haut-Brion, Pape-Clément

Graves White: Domaine de Chevalier, Clos Floridene, de Fieuzal, La Tour-Martillac

Pomerol: Bon Pasteur, Certan de May, Clinet, La Conseillante, l'Église-Clinet, l'Évangile, La Fleur de Gay, Gazin, Lafleur, Petit-Village, Pétrus, Le Pin, Trotanoy, Vieux-Château-Certan

Fronsac/Canon Fronsac: Canon-de-Brem, de Carles, Cassagne-Haut-Canon-La-Truffière, Fontenil, Pez-Labrie, La Vieille-Cure

St.-Émilion: Angélus, l'Arrosée, Ausone, Beauséjour-Duffau, Canon, Canon-La-Gaffelière, Cheval Blanc, La Dominique, Figeac, Grand-Mayne, Pavie, Pavie-Macquin, Le Tertre-Rôteboeuf, Troplong-Mondot

Barsac/Sauternes: Climens, Coutet, Coutet Cuvée Madame, Doisy-Daëne, Lafaurie-Peyraguey, Rabaud-Promis, Raymond-Lafon, Rieussec, Sigalas-Rabaud, Suduiraut, La Tour Blanche, Y'Quem

1989—A Quick Study (8-31-89)

St.-Estèphe****	Graves Red***
Pauillac****	Graves White**
St.-Julien****	Pomerol*****
Margaux***	St.-Émilion****
Médoc/Haut-Médoc Crus Bourgeois****	Barsac/Sauternes****

Size: Mammoth; along with 1990 and 1986, the largest declared crop in the history of Bordeaux.

Important information: Excessively hyped vintage by virtually everyone but the Bordeaux proprietors. American, French, even English writers were all set to declare it the vintage of the century until serious tasters began to question the extract levels, phenomenally low acid levels, and puzzling quality of some wines. However, plenty of rich, dramatic, fleshy wines have been produced that should age reasonably well.

Maturity status: High tannins and extremely low acidity, much as with 1990, suggest early drinkability, with only the most concentrated wines capable of lasting 20–30 or more years.

Price: The most expensive opening prices of any vintage, until 1995 and 1996.

The general news media, primarily ABC television and *The New York Times,* first carried the news that several châteaux began their harvest during the last days of August, making 1989 the earliest vintage since 1893. An early harvest generally signifies a torrid growing season and below average rainfall—almost always evidence that a top-notch vintage is achievable. In his annual *Vintage and Market Report,* Peter Sichel reported that between 1893 and 1989 only 1947, 1949, 1970, and 1982 were years with a similar weather pattern, but none of these years were as hot as 1989.

Perhaps the most revealing and critical decision (at least from a qualitative perspective) was the choice of picking dates. Never has Bordeaux enjoyed such a vast span of time (August 28–October 15) over which to complete the harvest. Some châteaux, most notably Haut-Brion and the Christian Moueix–managed properties in Pomerol and St.-Émilion, harvested during the first week of September. Other estates waited and did not finish their harvesting until mid-October. During the second week of September, one major problem developed. Much of the Cabernet Sauvignon, while analytically mature and having enough sugar to potentially produce wines with 13% alcohol, was actually not ripe physiologically. Many châteaux, never having experienced such growing conditions, became indecisive. Far too many deferred to their oenologists, who saw technically mature grapes that were quickly losing acidity. The oenologists, never ones to take risks, advised immediate picking. As more than one proprietor and *négociant* said, by harvesting the Cabernet too early, a number of châteaux lost their chance to produce one of the greatest wines of a lifetime. This, plus the enormously large crop size, probably explains the good yet uninspired performance of so many wines from the Graves and Margaux appellations.

There was clearly no problem with the early-picked Merlot, as much of it came in between 13.5% and a whopping 15% alcohol level—unprecedented in Bordeaux. Those properties that crop-thinned—Pétrus and Haut-Brion—had yields of 45–55 hectoliters per hectare (3–3 1/2 tons of fruit per acre) and super concentration. Those that did not crop-thin had yields as preposterously high as 80 hectoliters per hectare.

Contrary to the reports of a totally "dry harvest," there were rain showers on September 10, 13, 18, and 22 that did little damage unless the property panicked and harvested the day after the rain. Some of the lighter-style wines may very well be the result of jittery châteaux owners who unwisely picked after the showers.

The overall production was, once again, staggeringly high.

In general, the wines are the most alcoholic Bordeaux I have ever tasted, ranging from 12.8% to over 14.5% for some Pomerols. Acidities are extremely low and tannin levels surprisingly high. Consequently, in looking at the structural profile of the 1989s, one sees wines 1%–2% higher in alcohol than the 1982s or 1961s, with much lower acidity levels than the 1982s, 1961s, and 1959s, yet high tannin levels. Fortunately the tannins are generally ripe and soft, à la 1982, rather than dry and astringent as in 1988. This gives the wines a big, rich, fleshy feel in the mouth, similar to the 1982s. The top 1989s have very high glycerin levels, but are they as concentrated as the finest 1982s, 1990s, 1995s, and 1996s? In Margaux the answer is a resounding "No," as this is clearly the least-favored appellation, much as it was in 1982. In Graves, except for Haut-Brion, La Mission-Haut-Brion, Haut-Bailly, and de Fieuzal, the wines are relatively light and undistinguished. In St.-Émilion the 1982s and 1990s are more consistent as well as more deeply concentrated. Some marvelously rich, enormously fruity, fat wines were made in St.-Émilion in 1989, but there is wide irregularity in quality. However, in the northern Médoc, primarily St.-Julien, Pauillac, and St.-Estèphe, as well as in Pomerol, many exciting, full-bodied, very alcoholic, and tannic wines have been made. The best of these seem to combine the splendidly rich, opulent, fleshy texture of the finest 1982s with the power and tannin of the 1990s yet curiously taste less concentrated than these two vintages.

Like the 1982s, this vintage will probably be enjoyable to drink over a broad span of years. Despite the high tannin levels, the low acidities combined with the high glycerin and alcohol levels give the wines a fascinatingly fleshy, full-bodied texture. While there is considerable variation in quality, the finest 1989s from Pomerol, St.-Julien, Pauillac, and St.-Estèphe will, in specific cases, rival some of the greatest wines of the last 20 years.

THE BEST WINES

St.-Estèphe: Cos d'Estournel, Haut-Marbuzet, Meyney, Montrose, Phélan-Ségur
Pauillac: Clerc-Milon, Grand-Puy-Lacoste, Lafite-Rothschild, Lynch-Bages, Mouton-
   Rothschild, Pichon-Longueville Baron, Pichon-Longueville-Comtesse de Lalande

St.-Julien: Beychevelle, Branaire-Ducru, Ducru-Beaucaillou, Gruaud-Larose, Lagrange,
   Léoville-Barton, Léoville-Las Cases, Talbot
Margaux: Cantemerle, Margaux, Palmer, Rauzan-Ségla
Médoc/Haut-Médoc/Moulis/Listrac/Crus Bourgeois: Beaumont, Le Boscq, Chasse-Spleen,
   Gressier Grand-Poujeaux, Lanessan, Maucaillou, Moulin-Rouge, Potensac, Poujeaux,
   Sociando-Mallet, La Tour de By, Tour Haut-Caussan, Tour du Haut-Moulin, La Tour-St.
   Bonnet, Vieux-Robin
Graves Red: Bahans-Haut-Brion, Haut-Bailly, Haut-Brion, La Louvière, La Mission-Haut-
   Brion
Graves White: Clos Floridene, Haut-Brion, Laville-Haut-Brion
Pomerol: Bon Pasteur, Clinet, La Conseillante, Domaine de l'Église, l'Église-Clinet,
   l'Évangile, Lafleur, Lafleur de Gay, La Fleur-Pétrus, Le Gay, Les Pensées de Lafleur,
   Pétrus, Le Pin, Trotanoy, Vieux-Château-Certan
Fronsac/Canon Fronsac: Canon, Canon-de-Brem, Canon-Moueix, Cassagne-Haut-Canon-
   La-Truffière, Dalem, La Dauphine, Fontenil, Mazeris, Moulin-Haut-Laroque, Moulin-
   Pey-Labrie
St.-Émilion: Angélus, Ausone, Cheval Blanc, La Dominique, La Gaffelière, Grand-Mayne,
   Magdelaine, Pavie, Pavie-Macquin, Soutard, Le Tertre-Rôteboeuf, Troplong-Mondot,
   Trottevieille
Barsac/Sauternes: Climens, Coutet, Coutet-Cuvée Madame, Doisy-Védrines, Guiraud,
   Lafaurie-Peyraguey, Rabaud-Promis, Raymond-Lafon, Rieussec, Suduiraut, Suduiraut-
   Cuvée Madame, La Tour Blanche, Yquem

1988—A Quick Study (9-20-88)

St.-Estèphe***	Graves Red*****
Pauillac****	Graves White***
St.-Julien****	Pomerol****
Margaux***	St.-Émilion***
Médoc/Haut-Médoc Crus Bourgeois**	Barsac/Sauternes*****

Size: A large crop equivalent in size to 1982, meaning 30% less wine than was produced in
1989 and 1990.
Important information: Fearing a repeat of the rains that destroyed the potential for a great
year in 1987, many producers once again pulled the trigger on their harvesting teams too
soon. Unfortunately, copious quantities of Médoc Cabernet Sauvignon were picked too
early.
Maturity status: Because of good acid levels and relatively high, more astringent tannins,
there is no denying the potential of the 1988s to last for 20 or 30 years. How many of these
wines will retain enough fruit to stand up to the tannin remains to be seen.
Price: Ranges 20%–50% below more glamorous vintages, so the best wines offer considerable value.
   The year 1988 is a good but rarely thrilling vintage of red wines and one of the greatest
vintages of this century for the sweet wines of Barsac and Sauternes.
   The problem with the red wines is that there is a lack of superstar performances on the
part of the top châteaux. This will no doubt ensure that 1988 will always be regarded as a
very good rather than excellent year. While the 1988 crop size was large, it was exceeded in
size by the two vintages that followed it, 1989 and 1990. The average yield in 1988 was between 3 and 3¹/₃ tons of fruit per acre, which was approximately equivalent to the quantity
of wine produced in 1982. The wines tend to be well colored, tannic, and firmly structured.

The less successful wines exhibit a slight lack of depth and finish short, with noticeably green, astringent tannins. Yet Graves and the northern Médoc enjoyed a fine, rather deliciously styled vintage.

These characteristics are especially evident in the Médoc, where it was all too apparent that many châteaux, apprehensive about the onset of rot and further rain (as in 1987), panicked and harvested their Cabernet Sauvignon too early. Consequently they brought in Cabernet that often achieved only 8%–9% sugar readings. Those properties that waited, or made a severe selection, produced the best wines.

In Pomerol and St.-Émilion the Merlot was harvested under ripe conditions, but because of the severe drought in 1988 the skins of the grapes were thicker and the resulting wines were surprisingly tannic and hard.

In St.-Émilion many properties reported bringing in Cabernet Franc at full maturity and obtaining sugar levels that were reportedly higher than ever before. However, despite such optimistic reports much of the Cabernet Franc tasted fluid and diluted in quality. Therefore St.-Émilion, despite reports of a very successful harvest, exhibits great irregularity in quality.

The appellation of Graves probably produced the best red wines of Bordeaux in 1988.

While there is no doubt that the richer, more dramatic, fleshier 1989s have taken much of the public's attention away from the 1988s, an objective look at the 1988 vintage will reveal some surprisingly strong performances in appellations such as Margaux, Pomerol, and Graves and in properties in the northern Médoc that eliminated their early-picked Cabernet Sauvignon or harvested much later. The year 1988 is not a particularly good one for the crus bourgeois because many harvested too soon. The lower prices they receive for their wines do not permit the crus bourgeois producers to make the strict selection that is necessary in years such as 1988.

The appellations that did have a superstar vintage were Barsac and Sauternes. With a harvest that lasted until the end of November and textbook weather conditions for the formation of the noble rot, *Botrytis cinerea*, 1988 is considered by some authorities to be one of the finest vintages since 1937. Almost across the board, including the smaller estates, the wines have an intense smell of honey, coconut, oranges, and other tropical fruits. It is a remarkably rich vintage, with wines of extraordinary levels of botrytis, great concentration of flavor; yet the rich, unctuous, opulent textures are balanced beautifully by zesty, crisp acidity. It is this latter component that makes these wines so special.

THE BEST WINES

St.-Estèphe: Calon-Ségur, Haut-Marbuzet, Meyney, Phélan-Ségur

Pauillac: Clerc-Milon, Lafite-Rothschild, Latour, Lynch-Bages, Mouton-Rothschild, Pichon-Longueville Baron, Pichon-Longueville-Comtesse de Lalande

St.-Julien: Gruaud-Larose, Léoville-Barton, Léoville-Las Cases, Talbot

Margaux: Monbrison, Rausan-Ségla

Médoc/Haut-Médoc/Moulis/Listrac/Crus Bourgeois: Fourcas-Loubaney, Gressier Grand-Poujeaux, Poujeaux, Sociando-Mallet, Tour du Haut-Moulin

Graves Red: Les Carmes Haut-Brion, Domaine de Chevalier, Haut-Bailly, Haut-Brion, La Louvière, La Mission-Haut-Brion, Pape-Clément

Graves White: Domaine de Chevalier, Clos Floridene, Couhins-Lurton, de Fieuzal, Laville-Haut-Brion, La Louvière, La Tour-Martillac

Pomerol: Bon Pasteur, Certan de May, Clinet, l'Église-Clinet, La Fleur de Gay, Gombaude-Guillot-Cuvée Speciale, Lafleur, Petit-Village, Pétrus, Le Pin, Vieux-Château-Certan

St.-Émilion: Angélus, Ausone, Canon-la-Gaffelière, Clos des Jacobins, Larmande, Le Tertre-Rôteboeuf, Troplong-Mondot

Barsac/Sauternes: d'Arche, Broustet, Climens, Coutet, Coutet-Cuvée Madame, Doisy-

Daëne, Doisy-Dubroca, Guiraud, Lafaurie-Peyraguey, Lamothe-Guignard, Rabaud-Promis, Rayne-Vigneau, Rieussec, Sigalas Rabaud, Suduiraut, La Tour Blanche

1987—A Quick Study (10-3-87)

St.-Estèphe**	Graves Red***
Pauillac**	Graves White****
St.-Julien**	Pomerol***
Margaux**	St.-Émilion**
Médoc/Haut-Médoc Crus Bourgeois*	Barsac/Sauternes*

Size: A moderately sized crop that looks almost tiny in the scheme of the gigantic yields during the decade of the eighties.

Important information: The most underrated vintage of the 1980s, producing a surprising number of ripe, round, tasty wines, particularly from Pomerol, Graves, and the most seriously run estates in the northern Médoc.

Maturity status: The best examples are deliciously drinkable and should be consumed before 2000.

Price: Low prices are the rule rather than the exception for this sometimes attractive, low-priced vintage.

More than one Bordelais has said that if the rain had not arrived during the first 2 weeks of October 1987, ravaging the quality of the unharvested Cabernet Sauvignon and Petit Verdot, the 1987—not 1989 or 1982—would be the most extraordinary vintage of the decade of the 1980s. Wasn't it true that August and September had been the hottest 2 months in Bordeaux since 1976? But the rain did fall, plenty of it, and it dashed the hopes for a top vintage. Yet much of the Merlot was primarily harvested before the rain. The early-picked Cabernet Sauvignon was adequate, but that picked after the rains began was in very poor condition. Thanks in part to the two gigantic-size crops of 1985 and 1986, both record years at the time, most Bordeaux châteaux had full cellars and were mentally prepared to eliminate the vats of watery Cabernet Sauvignon harvested in the rains that fell for 14 straight days in October. The results for the top estates are wines that are light to medium bodied, ripe, fruity, round, even fat, with low tannins, low acidity, and lush, captivating, charming personalities.

While there is a tendency to look at 1987 as a poor year and to compare it with such other recent uninspiring vintages as 1977, 1980, and 1984, the truth is that the wines could not be more different. In the 1977, 1980, and 1984 vintages the problem was immaturity because of cold, wet weather leading up to the harvest. In 1987 the problem was not a lack of maturity, as the Merlot and Cabernet were ripe. In 1987 the rains diluted fully mature, ripe grapes.

The year 1987 is the most underrated vintage of the decade for those estates where a strict selection was made and/or the Merlot was harvested in sound condition. The wines are deliciously fruity, forward, clean, fat, and soft, without any degree of rot. Prices remain a bargain, even though the quantities produced were relatively small. This is a vintage that I search out on restaurant wine lists. I have bought a number of the wines for my cellar because I regard 1987, much like 1976, to be a very soft, forward vintage that produced wines for drinking in their first decade of life.

THE BEST WINES

St.-Estèphe: Cos d'Estournel
Pauillac: Lafite-Rothschild, Latour, Mouton-Rothschild, Pichon-Longueville Baron, Pichon-Longueville-Comtesse de Lalande
St.-Julien: Gruaud-Larose, Léoville-Barton, Léoville-Las Cases, Talbot

Margaux: d'Angludet, Margaux, Palmer

Médoc/Haut-Médoc/Moulis/Listrac/Crus Bourgeois: none

Graves Red: Bahans-Haut-Brion, Domaine de Chevalier, Haut-Brion, La Mission-Haut-
Brion, Pape-Clément

Graves White: Domaine de Chevalier, Couhins-Lurton, de Fieuzal, Laville-Haut-Brion, La
Tour-Martillac

Pomerol: Certan de May, Clinet, La Conseillante, l'Évangile, La Fleur de Gay, Petit-Village,
Pétrus, Le Pin

St.-Émilion: Ausone, Cheval Blanc, Clos des Jacobins, Clos Saint-Martin, Grand-Mayne,
Magdelaine, Le Tertre-Rôteboeuf, Trottevieille

Barsac/Sauternes: Coutet, Lafaurie-Peyraguey

1986—A Quick Study (9-23-86)

St.-Estèphe****	Graves Red***
Pauillac*****	Graves White**
St.-Julien*****	Pomerol***
Margaux****	St.-Émilion***
Médoc/Haut-Médoc/Crus Bourgeois***	Barsac/Sauternes*****

Size: Colossal; one of the largest crops ever produced in Bordeaux.

Important information: An irrefutably great year for the Cabernet Sauvignon grape in the northern Médoc, St.-Julien, Pauillac, and St.-Estèphe. The top 1986s beg for more cellaring, and one wonders how many purchasers of these wines will lose their patience before the wines have reached full maturity.

Maturity status: The wines from the crus bourgeois, Graves, and the right bank can be drunk now, but the impeccably structured Médocs will not become accessible until 2005.

Price: Still realistic except for a handful of the superstar wines.

The year 1986 is without doubt a great vintage for the northern Médoc, particularly for St.-Julien, Pauillac, and St.-Estèphe, where many châteaux produced wines that are their deepest and most concentrated since 1982, and with 20–30 plus years of longevity. Yet it should be made very clear to readers that unlike the great vintage of 1982, or very good vintages of 1983 and 1985, the 1986s are not flattering wines to drink young. Most of the top wines of the Médoc will require a minimum of a decade of cellaring to shed their tannins, which are the highest ever measured for a Bordeaux vintage. If you are not prepared to wait for the 1986s to mature, this is not a vintage that makes sense to buy. If you can defer your gratification, then many wines will prove to be the most exhilarating Bordeaux wines produced since 1982.

Why did 1986 turn out to be such an exceptional year for many Médocs as well as Graves wines and produce Cabernet Sauvignon grapes of uncommon richness and power? The weather during the summer of 1986 was very dry and hot. In fact, by the beginning of September Bordeaux was in the midst of a severe drought that began to threaten the final maturity process of the grapes. Rain did come, first on September 14 and 15, which enhanced the maturity process and mitigated the drought conditions. This rain was welcome, but on September 23 a ferocious, quick-moving storm thrashed the city of Bordeaux, the Graves region, and the major right bank appellations of Pomerol and St.-Émilion.

The curious aspect of this major storm, which caused widespread flooding in Bordeaux, was that it barely sideswiped the northern Médoc appellations of St.-Julien, Pauillac, and St.-Estèphe. Those pickers who started their harvest around the end of September found bloated Merlot grapes and unripe Cabernets. Consequently the top wines of 1986 came from those châteaux that 1) did most of their harvesting after October 5; or 2) eliminated from their final blend the early-picked Merlot, as well as the Cabernet Franc and Cabernet Sauvignon harvested between September 23 and October 4. After September 23 there were an extraordinary 23 days of hot, windy, sunny weather that turned the vintage into an exceptional one for those who delayed picking. It is, therefore, no surprise that the late-harvested Cabernet Sauvignon in the northern Médoc that was picked after October 6, but primarily between October 9 and 16, produced wines of extraordinary intensity and depth. To no one's surprise, Château Margaux and Château Mouton-Rothschild, which produced the vintage's two greatest wines, took in the great majority of their Cabernet Sauvignon between October 11 and 16.

In Pomerol and St.-Émilion, those châteaux that harvested soon after the September 23 deluge got predictably much less intense wines. Those that waited (for example, Vieux-Château-Certan, Lafleur, and Le Pin) made much more concentrated, complete wines. As in most vintages, the harvest date in 1986 was critical, and without question the late pickers made the finest wines. Perhaps the most perplexing paradox to emerge from the 1986 vintage is the generally high quality of the Graves wines, particularly in spite of the fact that this area was ravaged by the September 23 rainstorm. The answer in part may be that the top Graves châteaux eliminated more Merlot from the final blend than usual, therefore producing wines with a much higher percentage of Cabernet Sauvignon.

Last, the size of the 1986 crop established another record, as the harvest exceeded the bumper crop of 1985 by 15% and was 30% larger than the 1982 harvest. This overall production figure, equaled in both 1989 and 1990, is somewhat deceiving, as most of the classified Médoc châteaux made significantly less wine in 1986 than in 1985. It is for that reason, as well as the super maturity and tannin levels of the Cabernet Sauvignon grape, that most Médocs are noticeably more concentrated, more powerful, and more tannic in 1986 than they were in 1985. All things considered, 1986 offers numerous exciting, as well as exhilarating, wines of profound depth and exceptional potential for longevity. Yet I continue to ask myself, How many readers are willing to defer their gratification until the turn of the century, when these wines will be ready to drink?

THE BEST WINES

St.-Estèphe: Cos d'Estournel, Montrose
Pauillac: Clerc-Milon, Grand-Puy-Lacoste, Haut-Bages-Libéral, Lafite-Rothschild, Latour, Lynch-Bages, Mouton-Rothschild, Pichon-Longueville Baron, Pichon-Longueville-Comtesse de Lalande
St.-Julien: Beychevelle, Ducru-Beaucaillou, Gruaud-Larose, Lagrange, Léoville-Barton, Léoville-Las Cases, Talbot
Margaux: Margaux, Palmer, Rausan-Ségla
Médoc/Haut Médoc/Moulis/Listrac/Crus Bourgeois: Chasse-Spleen, Fourcas-Loubaney, Gressier Grand-Poujeaux, Lanessan, Maucaillou, Poujeaux, Sociando-Mallet
Graves Red: Domaine de Chevalier, Haut-Brion, La Mission-Haut-Brion, Pape-Clément
Graves White: none
Pomerol: Certan de May, Clinet, l'Église-Clinet, La Fleur de Gay, Lafleur, Pétrus, Le Pin, Vieux-Château-Certan
St.-Émilion: l'Arrosée, Canon, Cheval Blanc, Figeac, Pavie, Le Tertre-Rôteboeuf
Barsac/Sauternes: Climens, Coutet-Cuvée Madame, de Fargues, Guiraud, Lafaurie-Peyraguey, Raymond-Lafon, Rieussec, Yquem

1985—A Quick Study (9-29-85)

St.-Estèphe***
Pauillac****
St.-Julien****

Margaux***
Médoc/Haut-Médoc Crus Bourgeois***
Graves Red****

Graves White****   St.-Émilion***

Pomerol****   Barsac/Sauternes**

Size: A very large crop (a record at the time) that was subsequently surpassed by harvest sizes in 1986, 1989, and 1990.

Important information: The top Médocs may turn out to represent clones of the gorgeously seductive, charming 1953 vintage. Most of the top wines are surprisingly well developed, displaying fine richness, a round, feminine character, and exceptional aromatic purity and complexity. It is one of the most delicious vintages to drink in 1998.

Maturity status: Seemingly drinkable from their release, the 1985s continue to develop quickly yet should last in the top cases for another 10–15 years. The top Crus Bourgeois are delicious and should be consumed before the end of the nineties.

Price: Released at outrageously high prices, the 1985s have not appreciated in value to the extent of other top vintages.

Any vintage, whether in Bordeaux or elsewhere, is shaped by the weather pattern. The 1985 Bordeaux vintage was conceived in a period of apprehension. January 1985 was the coldest since 1956. (I was there on January 16 when the temperature hit a record low minus 14.5 degrees centigrade.) However, fear of damage to the vineyard was greatly exaggerated by the Bordelais. One wonders about the sincerity of such fears and whether they were designed to push up prices for the 1983s and create some demand for the overpriced 1984s. In any event, the spring and early summer were normal, if somewhat more rainy and cooler than usual in April, May, and June. July was slightly hotter and wetter than normal; August was colder than normal but extremely dry. The September weather set a meteorological record—it was the sunniest, hottest, and driest September ever measured. The three most recent top vintages—1961, 1982, and 1989—could not claim such phenomenal weather conditions in September.

The harvest commenced at the end of September, and three things became very apparent in that period between September 23 and September 30. First, the Merlot was fully mature and excellent in quality. Second, the Cabernet Sauvignon grapes were not as ripe as expected and barely reached 11% natural alcohol. Third, the enormous size of the crop caught everyone off guard. The drought of August and September had overly stressed the many Cabernet vineyards planted in gravelly soil and actually retarded the ripening process. The smart growers stopped picking Cabernet, risking foul weather but hoping for higher sugar levels. The less adventurous settled for good rather than very good Cabernet Sauvignon. The pickers who waited and picked their Cabernet Sauvignon in mid-October clearly made the best wines, as the weather held up throughout the month of October. Because of the drought, there was little botrytis in the Barsac and Sauternes regions. Those wines have turned out to be monolithic, straightforward, and fruity but lacking complexity and depth.

In general, 1985 is an immensely seductive and attractive vintage that has produced numerous well-balanced, rich, very perfumed yet tender wines. The 1985s are destined to be consumed over the next 15 years while waiting for the tannins of the 1986s to melt away and for richer, fuller, more massive wines from vintages such as 1982, 1989, 1990, and 1996 to reach full maturity. The year 1985 was a year of great sunshine, heat, and drought, so much so that many of the vineyards planted on lighter, more gravelly soil were stressed.

In the Médoc, 1985 produced an enormous crop. Where the châteaux made a strict selection, the results are undeniably charming, round, precocious, opulent wines with low acidity and an overall elegant, almost feminine quality. The tannins are soft and mellow. Interestingly, in the Médoc it is one of those years, much as in 1989, where the so-called superseconds, such as Cos d'Estournel, Lynch-Bages, Léoville-Las Cases, Ducru-Beaucaillou, Pichon-Longueville-Comtesse de Lalande, and Léoville-Barton, made wines that rival and in some cases even surpass the more illustrious first-growths. In many vintages (1986, for example) the first-growths soar qualitatively above the rest. That is not the case in 1985.

In the best-case scenario, the top 1985s may well evolve along the lines of the beautiful, charming 1953 vintage.

Most of the Médoc growers, who were glowing in their opinion of the 1985s, called the vintage a blend in style between 1982 and 1983. Others compared the 1985s with the 1976s. Both of these positions seem far off the mark. The 1985s are certainly lighter, without nearly the texture, weight, or concentration of the finest 1982s or 1986s, but at the same time most 1985s are far richer and fuller than the 1976s.

On Bordeaux's right bank, in Pomerol and St.-Émilion, the Merlot was brought in at excellent maturity levels, although many châteaux had a tendency to pick too soon (such as Pétrus and Trotanoy). While the vintage is not another 1982 or 1989, it certainly is a fine year in Pomerol. It is less consistent in St.-Émilion because too many producers harvested their Cabernet before it was physiologically fully mature. Interestingly, many of the Libournais producers compared 1985 stylistically with 1971.

The vintage, which is one of seductive appeal, was priced almost too high when first released. The wines have not appreciated to the extent that many deserve and now look more reasonably priced than at any time in the past.

THE BEST WINES

St.-Estèphe: Cos d'Estournel, Haut-Marbuzet
Pauillac: Lafite-Rothschild, Lynch-Bages, Mouton-Rothschild, Pichon-Longueville-
  Comtesse de Lalande
St.-Julien: Ducru-Beaucaillou, Gruaud-Larose, Léoville-Barton, Léoville-Las Cases, Talbot
Margaux: d'Angludet, Lascombes, Margaux, Palmer, Rausan-Ségla
Graves Red: Haut-Brion, La Mission-Haut-Brion
Graves White: Domaine de Chevalier, Haut-Brion, Laville-Haut-Brion
Pomerol: Certan de May, La Conseillante, l'Église-Clinet, l'Évangile, Lafleur, Le Pin, Pétrus
St.-Émilion: Canon, Cheval Blanc, de Ferrand, Soutard, Le Tertre-Rôteboeuf
Barsac/Sauternes: Yquem

1984—A Quick Study (10-5-84)

St.-Estèphe*	Graves Red**
Pauillac*	Graves White*
St.-Julien*	Pomerol*
Margaux*	St.-Émilion**
Médoc/Haut-Médoc Crus Bourgeois*	Barsac/Sauternes*

Size: A small to medium-size crop of primarily Cabernet-based wine.

Important information: The least attractive current vintage for drinking today, the 1984s, because of the failure of the Merlot crop, are essentially Cabernet-based wines that remain well colored, but compact, stern, and forbiddingly backward and tannic.

Maturity status: These wines need to be consumed.

Price: Virtually any 1984 can be had for a song, as most retailers who bought this vintage are stuck with the wines, even in 1998.

After three abundant vintages, 1981, 1982, and 1983, the climatic conditions during the summer and autumn of 1984 hardly caused euphoria among the Bordelais. First, the vegetative cycle began rapidly, thanks to a magnificently hot, sunny April. However, that was followed by a relatively cool and wet May, which wreaked havoc in the flowering of the quick-to-bud Merlot grape. The result was that much of the 1984 Merlot crop was destroyed long before the summer weather actually arrived. The terrible late spring and early summer conditions made headlines in much of the world's press, which began to paint the vintage as an impending disaster. However, July was dry and hot, and by the end of August some overly enthusiastic producers were talking about the potential for superripe, tiny quantities of Cabernet Sauvignon. There were even several reporters who were calling 1984 similar to the 1961 vintage. Their intentions could only be considered sinister, as 1984 could never be compared with 1961.

Following the relatively decent beginning in September, the period between September 21 and October 4 was one of unexpected weather difficulties climaxed by the first cyclone (named Hortense) ever to hit the area, tearing roofs off buildings and giving the jitters to winemakers. However, after October 4 the weather cleared up and producers began to harvest their Cabernet Sauvignon. Those who waited picked relatively ripe Cabernet, although the Cabernet's skin was somewhat thick and the acid levels extremely high, particularly by the standards of more recent vintages.

The problem that existed early on with the 1984s and that continues to present difficulties today is that the wines lack an important percentage of Merlot to counterbalance their narrow, compact, high-acid, austere, and tannic character. Consequently there is a lack of fat and charm, but these herbaceous wines are deep in color, as they were made from Cabernet Sauvignon.

Unquestionably the late pickers made the best wines, and most of the more interesting wines have emerged from the Médoc and Graves. They will be longer lived but probably less enjoyable than the wines from the other two difficult vintages of that decade, 1980 and 1987.

In St.-Émilion and Pomerol, the vintage, if not quite an unqualified disaster, is disappointing. Many top properties—Ausone, Canon, Magdelaine, Belair, La Dominique, Couvent-des-Jacobins, and Tertre-Daugay—declassified their entire crop. It was the first vintage since 1968 or 1972 where many of these estates made no wine under their label. Even at Pétrus only 800 cases were made, as opposed to the 4,500 cases produced in both 1985 and 1986.

In 1998 the better 1984s remain relatively narrowly constructed, tightly knit wines still displaying a healthy color but lacking fat, ampleness, and charm. It is unlikely they will ever develop any charm, but there is no doubt that the better-endowed examples will keep for another decade.

THE BEST WINES

St.-Estèphe: Cos d'Estournel
Pauillac: Latour, Lynch-Bages, Mouton-Rothschild, Pichon-Longueville-Comtesse de Lalande
St.-Julien: Gruaud-Larose, Léoville-Las Cases
Margaux: Margaux
Graves Red: Domaine de Chevalier, Haut-Brion, La Mission-Haut-Brion
Graves White: none
Pomerol: Pétrus, Trotanoy
St.-Émilion: Figeac
Barsac/Sauternes: Yquem

1983—A Quick Study (9-26-83)

St.-Estèphe**	Margaux*****
Pauillac***	Médoc/Haut-Médoc Crus Bourgeois**
St.-Julien***	Graves Red****

Graves White****   St.-Émilion****

Pomerol***   Barsac/Sauternes****

Size: A large crop, with overall production slightly inferior to 1982, but in the Médoc most properties produced more wine than they did in 1982.

Important information: Bordeaux, as well as all of France, suffered from an atypically tropical heat and humidity attack during the month of August. This caused considerable over-ripening as well as the advent of rot in certain *terroirs,* particularly in St.-Estèphe, Pauillac, Pomerol, and the sandier plateau sections of St.-Émilion.

Maturity status: At first the vintage was called more classic (or typical) than 1982, with greater aging potential. Fifteen years later the 1983s are far more evolved and, in most cases, fully mature—unlike the 1982s. In fact, this is a vintage that attained full maturity at an accelerated pace.

Price: Prices for the best 1983s remain fair.

The year 1983 was one of the most bizarre growing seasons in recent history. The flowering in June went well for the third straight year, ensuring a large crop. The weather in July was so torrid that it turned out to be the hottest July on record. August was extremely hot, rainy, and humid, and as a result, many vineyards began to have significant problems with mildew and rot. It was essential to spray almost weekly in August of 1983 to protect the vineyards. Those properties that did not spray diligently had serious problems with mildew-infected grapes. By the end of August, a dreadful month climatically, many pessimistic producers were talking apprehensively about a disastrous vintage like 1968 or 1965. September brought dry weather, plenty of heat, and no excessive rain. October provided exceptional weather as well, so the grapes harvested late were able to attain maximum ripeness under sunny, dry skies. Not since 1961 had the entire Bordeaux crop, white grapes and red grapes, been harvested in completely dry, fair weather.

The successes that have emerged from 1983 are first and foremost from the appellation of Margaux, which enjoyed its greatest vintage of the decade. In fact, this perennial under-achieving appellation produced many top wines, with magnificent efforts from Margaux, Palmer, and Rausan-Ségla (the vintage of resurrection for this famous name), as well as d'Issan and Brane-Cantenac. These wines remain some of the best-kept secrets of the decade.

The other appellations had numerous difficulties, and the wines have not matured as evenly or as gracefully as some prognosticators had suggested. The northern Médoc, particularly the St.-Estèphes, are disappointing. The Pauillacs range from relatively light, overly oaky, roasted wines that are hollow in the middle, to some exceptional successes, most notably from Pichon-Longueville-Comtesse de Lalande, Mouton-Rothschild, and Lafite-Rothschild.

The St.-Juliens will not be remembered for their greatness, with the exception of a superb Léoville-Poyferré. In 1983 Léoville-Poyferré is amazingly as good as the other two Léovilles, Léoville-Las Cases and Léoville-Barton. During the eighties there is not another vintage where such a statement could be made. The Cordier siblings, Gruaud-Larose and Talbot, made good wines, but overall 1983 is not a memorable year for St.-Julien.

In Graves the irregularity continues, with wonderful wines from those Graves châteaux in the Pessac-Léognan area (Haut-Brion, La Mission-Haut-Brion, Haut-Bailly, Domaine de Chevalier, and de Fieuzal), but with disappointments elsewhere.

On the right bank, in Pomerol and St.-Émilion, inconsistency is again the rule of thumb. Most of the hillside vineyards in St.-Émilion performed well, but the vintage was mixed on the plateau and in the sandier soils, although Cheval Blanc made one of its greatest wines of the decade. In Pomerol it is hard to say who made the best wine, but the house of Jean-Pierre Moueix did not fare well in this vintage. Other top properties, such as La Conseillante, l'Évangile, Lafleur, Certan de May, and Le Pin, all made wines that are not far off the quality of their great 1982s.

THE BEST WINES

St.-Estèphe: none

Pauillac: Lafite-Rothschild, Mouton-Rothschild, Pichon-Longueville-Comtesse de Lalande

St.-Julien: Gruaud-Larose, Léoville-Las Cases, Léoville-Poyferré, Talbot

Margaux: d'Angludet, Brane-Cantenac, Cantemerle (southern Médoc), d'Issan, Margaux, Palmer, Prieuré-Lichine, Rausan-Ségla

Médoc/Haut Médoc/Moulis/Listrac/Crus Bourgeois: none

Graves Red: Domaine de Chevalier, Haut-Bailly, Haut-Brion, La Louvière, La Mission-Haut-Brion

Graves White: Domaine de Chevalier, Laville-Haut-Brion

Pomerol: Certan de May, l'Évangile, Lafleur, Pétrus, Le Pin

St.-Émilion: l'Arrosée, Ausone, Belair, Canon, Cheval Blanc, Figeac, Larmande

Barsac/Sauternes: Climens, Doisy-Daëne, de Fargues, Guiraud, Lafaurie-Peyraguey, Raymond-Lafon, Rieussec, Yquem

1982–A Quick Study (9-13-82)

St.-Estèphe*****	Graves Red***
Pauillac*****	Graves White**
St.-Julien*****	Pomerol*****
Margaux***	St.-Émilion*****
Médoc/Haut-Médoc Crus Bourgeois****	Barsac/Sauternes***

Size: An extremely abundant crop, which at the time was a record year but has since been equaled in size by 1988 and surpassed in volume by 1985, 1986, 1989, and 1990.

Important information: The most concentrated and potentially complex and profound wines between 1961 and 1990 were produced in virtually every appellation except for Graves and Margaux.

Maturity status: Most crus bourgeois should have been drunk by 1995, and the lesser wines in St.-Émilion, Pomerol, Graves, and Margaux are fully mature. For the bigger-style Pomerols, St.-Émilions, and the northern Médocs—St.-Julien, Pauillac, and St.-Estèphe—the wines are evolving at a glacial pace. They have lost much of their baby fat and gone into a much more tightly knit, massive, yet much more structured, tannic state.

Price: With the exception of 1990, no modern-day Bordeaux vintage since 1961 has accelerated as much in price and yet continues to appreciate in value. Prices are now so frightfully high, consumers who did not purchase these wines as futures can only look back with envy at those who bought the 1982s when they were first offered at what now appear to be bargain-basement prices. Who can remember a great vintage being sold at such enticing opening case prices for châteaux like Pichon-Lalande ($110), Léoville-Las Cases ($160), Ducru-Beaucaillou ($150), Pétrus ($600), Cheval Blanc ($550), Margaux ($550), Certan de May ($180), La Lagune ($75), Grand-Puy-Lacoste ($85), Cos d'Estournel ($145), and Canon ($105)? These were the average prices for which the 1982s were sold during the spring, summer, and fall of 1983! Yet potential buyers should be careful, as many fraudulent 1982s have shown up in the marketplace, particularly Pétrus, Lafleur, Le Pin, Cheval Blanc, and the Médoc first-growths.

When I issued my report on the 1982 vintage in the April 1983 *Wine Advocate,* I remember feeling that I had never tasted richer, more concentrated, more promising wines than the

1982s. Sixteen years later, despite some wonderfully successful years such as 1985, 1986, 1989, 1990, 1995, and 1996, 1982 remains the modern-day point of reference for the greatness Bordeaux can achieve.

The finest wines of the vintage have emerged from the northern Médoc appellations of St.-Julien, Pauillac, and St.-Estèphe, as well as from Pomerol and St.-Émilion. They have hardly changed since their early days in barrel, and while displaying a degree of richness, opulence, and intensity I have rarely seen, as they approach their sixteenth birthdays, the vintage's top wines remain relatively unevolved and backward.

The wines from other appellations have matured much more quickly, particularly those from Graves and Margaux and the lighter, lesser wines from Pomerol, St.-Émilion, and the crus bourgeois.

Today no one could intelligently deny the greatness of the 1982 vintage. However, in 1983 this vintage was received among America's wine press with a great deal of skepticism. There was no shortage of outcries about these wines' lack of acidity and "California" style after the vintage's conception. It was suggested by some writers that 1981 and 1979 were "finer vintages" and that the 1982s, "fully mature," should have been "consumed by 1990." Curiously, these writers fail to include specific tasting notes. Of course, wine tasting is subjective, but such statements are nonsense, and it is impossible to justify such criticism of this vintage, particularly in view of how well the top 1982s taste in 1998 and how rich as well as slowly the first-growths, super-seconds, and great wines of the northern Médoc, Pomerol, and St.-Émilion are evolving. Even in Bordeaux the 1982s are now placed on a pedestal and spoken of in the same terms as 1961, 1949, 1945, and 1929. Moreover, the marketplace and auction rooms, perhaps the only true measure of a vintage's value, continue to push prices for the top 1982s to stratospheric levels.

The reason why so many 1982s were so remarkable was because of the outstanding weather conditions. The flowering occurred in hot, sunny, dry, ideal June weather that served to ensure a large crop. July was extremely hot and August slightly cooler than normal. By the beginning of September the Bordeaux producers were expecting a large crop of excellent quality. However, a September burst of intense heat that lasted for nearly 3 weeks sent the grape sugars soaring, and what was considered originally to be a very good to excellent vintage was transformed into a great vintage for every appellation except Margaux and the Graves, whose very thin, light, gravelly soils suffered during the torrid September heat. For the first time many producers had to vinify their wines under unusually hot conditions. Many lessons were learned that were employed again in subsequent hot vinification years such as 1985, 1989, and 1990. Rumors of disasters from overheated or stuck fermentations proved to be without validity, as were reports that rain showers near the end of the harvest caught some properties with Cabernet Sauvignon still on the vine.

When analyzed, the 1982s are the most concentrated, high-extract wines since 1961, with acid levels that, while low, are no lower than in years of exceptional ripeness such as 1949, 1953, 1959, 1961, and, surprisingly, 1975. Though some skeptics pointed to the low acidity, many of those same skeptics fell in love with the 1985s, 1989s, and 1990s, all Bordeaux vintages that produced wines with significantly lower acids and higher pHs than the 1982s. Tannin levels were extremely high, but subsequent vintages, particularly 1986, 1988, 1989, and 1990, produced wines with even higher tannin levels than the 1982s.

Recent tastings of the 1982s continue to suggest that the top wines of the northern Médoc need another 5–10 years of cellaring. Most of the best wines seem largely unevolved since their early days in cask. They have fully recovered from the bottling and display the extraordinary expansive, rich, glycerin- and extract-laden palates that should serve these wines well over the next 10–20 years. If the 1982 vintage remains sensational for the majority of St.-Émilions, Pomerols, St.-Juliens, Pauillacs, and St.-Estèphes, the weakness of the vintage becomes increasingly more apparent with the Margaux and Graves wines. Only Château

Margaux seems to have survived the problems of overproduction, loosely knit, flabby Cabernet Sauvignon wines from which so many other Margaux properties suffered. The same can be said for the Graves, which are light and disjointed when compared with the lovely 1983s Graves produced. Only La Mission-Haut-Brion and Haut-Brion produced better 1982s than 1983s.

On the negative side are the prices one must now pay for a top wine from the 1982 vintage. Is this a reason why the vintage still receives cheap shots from a handful of American writers? Those who bought them as futures made the wine buys of the century. For today's generation of wine enthusiasts, 1982 is what 1945, 1947, and 1949 were for an earlier generation of wine lovers.

Last, the sweet wines of Barsac and Sauternes in 1982, while maligned originally for their lack of botrytis and richness, are not that bad. In fact, Yquem and the Cuvée Madame of Château Suduiraut are two remarkably powerful, rich wines that can stand up to the best of the 1983s, 1986s, and 1988s.

THE BEST WINES

St.-Estèphe: Calon-Ségur, Cos d'Estournel, Haut-Marbuzet, Montrose

Pauillac: Les Forts de Latour, Grand-Puy-Lacoste, Haut-Batailley, Lafite-Rothschild, Latour, Lynch-Bages, Mouton-Rothschild, Pichon-Longueville Baron, Pichon-Longueville-Comtesse de Lalande

St.-Julien: Beychevelle, Branaire-Ducru, Ducru-Beaucaillou, Gruaud-Larose, Léoville-Barton, Léoville-Las Cases, Léoville-Poyferré, Talbot

Margaux: Margaux, La Lagune (southern Médoc)

Médoc/Haut Médoc/Moulis/Listrac/Crus Bourgeois: Tour Haut-Caussan, Maucaillou, Potensac, Poujeaux, Sociando-Mallet, La Tour-St. Bonnet

Graves Red: Haut-Brion, La Mission-Haut-Brion, La Tour-Haut-Brion

Graves White: none

Pomerol: Bon Pasteur, Certan de May, La Conseillante, l'Enclos, l'Évangile, Le Gay, Lafleur, Latour à Pomerol, Petit-Village, Pétrus, Le Pin, Trotanoy, Vieux-Château-Certan

St.-Émilion: l'Arrosée, Ausone, Canon, Cheval Blanc, La Dominique, Figeac, Pavie

Barsac/Sauternes: Raymond-Lafon, Suduiraut-Cuvée Madame, Yquem

1981—A Quick Study (9-28-81)

St.-Estèphe**	Graves Red**
Pauillac***	Graves White**
St.-Julien***	Pomerol***
Margaux**	St.-Émilion**
Médoc/Haut-Médoc Crus Bourgeois*	Barsac/Sauternes*

Size: A moderately large crop that in retrospect now looks modest.

Important information: The first vintage in a succession of hot, dry years that would continue nearly uninterrupted through 1990. The year 1981 would have been a top vintage had the rain not fallen immediately prior to the harvest.

Maturity status: Most 1981s are close to full maturity, yet the best examples are capable of lasting for another 5–10 years.

Price: A largely ignored and overlooked vintage, 1981 remains a reasonably good value.

This vintage has been labeled more "classic" than either 1983 or 1982. What classic means to those who call 1981 a classic vintage is that this year is a typically good Bordeaux vintage of medium-weight, well-balanced, graceful wines. Despite a dozen or so excellent wines, 1981 is in reality only a good vintage, surpassed in quality by both 1982 and 1983 and also by 1978 and 1979.

The year 1981 could have been an outstanding vintage had it not been for the heavy rains that fell just as the harvest was about to start. There was a dilution of the intensity of flavor in the grapes as heavy rains drenched the vineyards between October 1 and 5 and again between October 9 and 15. Until then the summer had been perfect. The flowering occurred under excellent conditions; July was cool, but August and September were hot and dry. One can only speculate that had it not rained, 1981 might well have also turned out to be one of the greatest vintages in the post–World War II era.

The year 1981 did produce a large crop of generally well-colored wines of medium weight and moderate tannin. The dry white wines have turned out well but should have been consumed by now. Both Barsacs and Sauternes suffered as a result of the rains, and no truly compelling wines have emerged from these appellations.

There are a number of successful wines in 1981, particularly from such appellations as Pomerol, St.-Julien, and Pauillac. Seventeen years after the vintage, the 1981s have generally reached their plateau of maturity, and only the best will keep for another 5–7 years. The wines' shortcomings are their lack of richness, flesh, and intensity, qualities that more recent vintages have possessed. Most red wine producers had to chaptalize significantly because the Cabernets were harvested under 11% natural alcohol and the Merlot under 12%, no doubt because of the rain.

THE BEST WINES

St.-Estèphe: none
Pauillac: Lafite-Rothschild, Latour, Pichon-Longueville-Comtesse de Lalande
St.-Julien: Ducru-Beaucaillou, Gruaud-Larose, Léoville-Las Cases, St.-Pierre
Margaux: Giscours, Margaux
Médoc/Haut-Médoc Crus Bourgeois: none
Graves Red: La Mission-Haut-Brion
Graves White: none
Pomerol: Certan de May, La Conseillante, Pétrus, Le Pin, Vieux-Château-Certan
St.-Émilion: Cheval Blanc
Barsac/Sauternes: Climens, de Fargues, Yquem

1980—A Quick Study (10-14-80)

St.-Estèphe*	Graves Red**
Pauillac**	Graves White*
St.-Julien**	Pomerol**
Margaux**	St.-Émilion*
Médoc/Haut-Médoc Crus Bourgeois*	Barsac/Sauternes****

Size: A moderately sized crop was harvested.

Important information: Nothing very noteworthy can be said about this mediocre vintage.

Maturity status: With the exception of Château Margaux and Pétrus, virtually every 1980 should have been consumed.

Price: Low.

For a decade that became known as the golden age of Bordeaux, or the decade of the century, the eighties certainly did not begin in an auspicious fashion. The summer of 1980 was cool and wet, the flowering was unexciting because of a disappointing June, and by early September the producers were looking at a return of the two most dreadful vintages of the last 30 years, 1963 and 1968. However, modern-day antirot sprays did a great deal to protect the grapes from the dreaded *pourriture*. For that reason, the growers were able to delay their harvest until the weather began to improve at the end of September. The weather in early October was favorable until rains began in the middle of the month, just as many producers began to harvest. The results have been light, diluted, frequently disappointing wines that have an unmistakable vegetal and herbaceous taste and are often marred by excessive acidity as well as tannin. Those producers who made a strict selection and who picked exceptionally late, such as the Mentzelopoulos family at Château Margaux (the wine of the vintage), made softer, rounder, more interesting wines that began to drink well in the late eighties and should continue to drink well until the turn of the century. However, the number of properties that could be said to have made wines of good quality are few.

As always in wet, cool years, those vineyards planted on lighter, gravelly, well-drained soils, such as some of the Margaux and Graves properties, tend to get better maturity and ripeness. Not surprisingly, the top successes generally come from these areas, although several Pauillacs, because of a very strict selection, also have turned out well.

As disappointing as the 1980 vintage was for the red wine producers, it was an excellent year for the producers of Barsac and Sauternes. The ripening and harvesting continued into late November, generally under ideal conditions. This permitted some rich, intense, high-class Barsac and Sauternes to be produced. Unfortunately, their commercial viability suffered from the reputation of the red wine vintage. Anyone who comes across a bottle of 1980 Climens, Yquem, or Raymond-Lafon will immediately realize that this is an astonishingly good year.

THE BEST WINES

St.-Estèphe: none
Pauillac: Latour, Pichon-Longueville-Comtesse de Lalande
St.-Julien: Talbot
Margaux: Margaux
Médoc/Haut-Médoc/Moulis/Listrac/Crus Bourgeois: none
Graves Red: Domaine de Chevalier, La Mission-Haut-Brion
Graves White: none
Pomerol: Certan de May, Pétrus
St.-Émilion: Cheval Blanc
Barsac/Sauternes: Climens, de Fargues, Raymond-Lafon, Yquem

1979—A Quick Study (10-3-79)

St.-Estèphe**	Graves Red****
Pauillac***	Graves White**
St.-Julien***	Pomerol***
Margaux****	St.-Émilion**
Médoc/Haut-Médoc Crus Bourgeois**	Barsac/Sauternes*

Size: A huge crop that established a record at that time.
Important information: In the last 2 decades this is one of the only cool years that turned out to be a reasonably good vintage.

Maturity status: Contrary to earlier reports, the 1979s have matured very slowly, largely because the wines have relatively hard tannins and good acidity, two characteristics that most of the top vintages during the decade of the eighties have not possessed.

Price: Because of the lack of demand, and the vintage's average to good reputation, prices remain low except for a handful of the limited-production, glamour wines of Pomerol.

The year 1979 has become the forgotten vintage in Bordeaux. A record-setting crop that produced relatively healthy, medium-bodied wines that displayed firm tannins and good acidity closed out the decade of the seventies. Over the next decade this vintage was rarely mentioned in the wine press. No doubt most of the wines were consumed long before they reached their respective apogees. Considered inferior to 1978 when conceived, the 1979 vintage will prove superior—at least in terms of aging potential. Yet aging potential alone is hardly sufficient to evaluate a vintage, and many 1979s remain relatively skinny, malnourished, lean, compact wines that naive commentators have called classic rather than thin.

Despite the inconsistency from appellation to appellation, a number of strikingly good, surprisingly flavorful, rich wines have emerged from appellations such as Margaux, Graves, and Pomerol.

With few exceptions, there is no hurry to drink the top 1979s, since their relatively high acid levels (compared with those from more recent hot-year vintages), good tannin levels, and sturdy framework should ensure that the top 1979s age well for at least another 10–15 years.

This was not a good vintage for the dry white wines of Graves or sweet white wines of Barsac and Sauternes. The dry whites did not achieve full maturity, and there was never enough botrytis for the Barsac and Sauternes to give the wines the honeyed complexity that is fundamental to their success.

Prices for 1979s, where they can still be found, are the lowest of any good recent Bordeaux vintage, reflecting the general lack of excitement for most 1979s.

THE BEST WINES

St.-Estèphe: Cos d'Estournel
Pauillac: Lafite-Rothschild, Latour, Pichon-Longueville-Comtesse de Lalande
St.-Julien: Gruaud-Larose, Léoville-Las Cases
Margaux: Giscours, Margaux, Palmer, du Tertre
Graves Red: Les Carmes Haut-Brion, Domaine de Chevalier, Haut-Bailly, Haut-Brion, La
    Mission-Haut-Brion
Pomerol: Certan de May, l'Enclos, l'Évangile, Lafleur, Pétrus
St.-Émilion: Ausone
Barsac/Sauternes: none

1978—A Quick Study (10-7-78)

St.-Estèphe**	Graves Red****
Pauillac***	Graves White****
St.-Julien***	Pomerol**
Margaux***	St.-Émilion***
Médoc/Haut-Médoc Crus Bourgeois**	Barsac/Sauternes**

Size: A moderately sized crop was harvested.
Important information: The year Harry Waugh, England's gentlemanly wine commentator, dubbed "the miracle year."
Maturity status: Most wines are fully mature.

Price: Overpriced for years, the 1978s are fairly priced 20 years after the vintage.

The year 1978 turned out to be an outstanding vintage for the red wines of Graves and a good vintage for the red wines from the Médoc, Pomerol, and St.-Émilion. There was a lack of botrytis for the sweet white wines of Barsac and Sauternes, and the results were monolithic, straightforward wines of no great character. The dry white Graves, much like the red wines of that appellation, turned out exceedingly well.

The weather profile for 1978 was hardly encouraging. The spring was cold and wet, and poor weather continued to plague the region through June, July, and early August, causing many growers to begin thinking of such dreadful years as 1963, 1965, 1968, and 1977. However, in mid-August a huge anticyclone, high-pressure system settled over southwestern France and northern Spain, and for the next 9 weeks the weather was sunny, hot, and dry, except for an occasional light rain shower that had negligible effects.

Because the grapes were so behind in their maturation (contrast that scenario with the more recent advanced maturity years such as 1989 and 1990), the harvest began extremely late, on October 7. It continued under excellent weather conditions, which seemed, as Harry Waugh put it, miraculous in view of the miserable weather throughout much of the spring and summer.

The general view of this vintage is that it is a very good to excellent year. The two best appellations are Graves and Margaux, which have the lighter, better-drained soils that support cooler weather years. In fact, Graves (except for the disappointing Pape-Clément) probably enjoyed its greatest vintage after 1961. The wines, which at first appeared intensely fruity, deeply colored, moderately tannic, and medium bodied, have aged much faster than the higher-acid, more firmly tannic 1979s, which were the product of an even cooler, drier year. Most 1978s had reached full maturity 12 years after the vintage, and some commentators were expressing their disappointment that the wines were not better than they had believed.

The problem is that, much as in 1979, 1981, and 1988, there is a shortage of truly superstar wines. There are a number of good wines, but the lack of excitement in the majority of wines has tempered the postvintage enthusiasm. Moreover, the lesser wines in 1978 have an annoyingly vegetal, herbaceous taste because those vineyards not planted on the best soils never fully ripened despite the impressively hot, dry *fin de saison*. Another important consideration is that the selection process, so much a fundamental principle in the decade of the eighties, was employed less during the seventies, as many properties simply bottled everything under the grand vin label. Many proprietors today feel that 1978 could have lived up to its early promise had a stricter selection been in effect when the wines were made.

This was a very difficult vintage for properties in the Barsac/Sauternes region because very little botrytis formed owing to the hot, dry autumn. The wines, much like the 1979s, are chunky and full of glycerin and sugar, but they lack grip, focus, and complexity.

THE BEST WINES

St.-Estèphe: none

Pauillac: Les Forts de Latour, Grand-Puy-Lacoste, Latour, Pichon-Longueville-Comtesse de Lalande

St.-Julien: Ducru-Beaucaillou, Gruaud-Larose, Léoville-Las Cases, Talbot

Margaux: Giscours, La Lagune (southern Médoc), Margaux, Palmer, Prieuré-Lichine, du Tertre

Médoc/Haut-Médoc/Moulis/Listrac/Crus Bourgeois: none

Graves Red: Les Carmes Haut-Brion, Domaine de Chevalier, Haut-Bailly, Haut-Brion, La Mission-Haut-Brion, La Tour-Haut-Brion

Graves White: Domaine de Chevalier, Haut-Brion, Laville-Haut-Brion

Pomerol: Lafleur
St.-Émilion: l'Arrosée, Cheval Blanc
Barsac/Sauternes: none

1977—A Quick Study (10-3-77)

St.-Estèphe 0	Graves Red*
Pauillac 0	Graves White*
St.-Julien 0	Pomerol 0
Margaux 0	St.-Émilion 0
Médoc/Haut-Médoc Crus Bourgeois 0	Barsac/Sauternes*

Size: A small crop was produced.

Important information: A dreadful vintage, clearly the worst since 1972; it remains, in a pejorative sense, unequaled since.

Maturity status: The wines, even the handful that were drinkable, should have been consumed by the mid-eighties.

Price: Despite distress sale prices, there are no values to be found.

This is the worst vintage for Bordeaux during the decade of the seventies. Even the 2 mediocre years of the eighties, 1980 and 1984, are far superior to 1977. Much of the Merlot crop was devastated by a late spring frost. The summer was cold and wet. When warm, dry weather finally arrived just prior to the harvest, there was just too little time left to save the vintage. The harvest resulted in grapes that were both analytically and physiologically immature and far from ripe.

The wines, which were relatively acidic and overtly herbaceous to the point of being vegetal, should have been consumed years ago. Some of the more successful wines included a decent Figeac, Giscours, Gruaud-Larose, Pichon-Lalande, Latour, and the three Graves estates of Haut-Brion, La Mission-Haut-Brion, and Domaine de Chevalier. However, I have never been able to recommend any of these wines. They have no value from either a monetary or a pleasure standpoint.

1976—A Quick Study (9-13-76)

St.-Estèphe***	Graves Red*
Pauillac***	Graves White***
St.-Julien***	Pomerol***
Margaux**	St.-Émilion***
Médoc/Haut-Médoc Crus Bourgeois*	Barsac/Sauternes****

Size: A huge crop, the second largest of the decade, was harvested.

Important information: This hot, droughtlike vintage could have proved to be the vintage of the decade had it not been for preharvest rains.

Maturity status: The 1976s tasted fully mature and delicious when released in 1979. Yet the best examples continue to offer delightful, sometimes delicious drinking. It is one of a handful of vintages where the wines have never closed up and been unappealing. Yet virtually every 1976 (with the exception of Ausone) should be consumed prior to 2000.

Price: The 1976s have always been reasonably priced because they have never received accolades from the wine pundits.

A very highly publicized vintage, 1976 has never quite lived up to its reputation. All the ingredients were present for a superb vintage. The harvest date of September 13 was the earliest harvest since 1945. The weather during the summer had been torridly hot, with the average temperatures for the months of June through September exceeded only by the hot summers of 1949 and 1947. However, with many vignerons predicting a "vintage of the century," very heavy rains fell between September 11 and 15, bloating the grapes.

The crop that was harvested was large, the grapes were ripe, and while the wines had good tannin levels, the acidity levels were low and their pHs dangerously high. The top wines of 1976 have offered wonderfully soft, supple, deliciously fruity drinking since they were released in 1979. I had fully expected that these wines would have to be consumed before the end of the decade of the eighties. However, the top 1976s appear to have stayed at their peak of maturity without fading or losing their fruit. I wish I had bought more of this vintage given how delicious the best wines have been over such an extended period of time. They will not make "old bones," and one must be very careful with the weaker 1976s, which have lacked intensity and depth from the beginning. These wines were extremely fragile and have increasingly taken on a brown cast to their color as well as losing their fruit. Nevertheless, the top wines continue to offer delicious drinking and persuasive evidence that even in a relatively diluted, extremely soft-style vintage, with dangerously low acid levels, Bordeaux wines, where well stored, can last 15 or more years.

The 1976 vintage was at its strongest in the northern Médoc appellations of St.-Julien, Pauillac, and St.-Estèphe, weakest in Graves and Margaux, and mixed in the Libournais appellations of Pomerol and St.-Émilion. The wine of the vintage is Ausone.

For those who admire decadently rich, honeyed, sweet wines, this is one of the two best vintages of the seventies, given the abundant quantities of botrytis that formed in the vineyards and the lavish richness and opulent style of the wines of Barsac/Sauternes.

THE BEST WINES

St.-Estèphe: Cos d'Estournel, Montrose
Pauillac: Haut-Bages-Libéral, Lafite-Rothschild, Pichon-Longueville-Comtesse de Lalande
St.-Julien: Beychevelle, Branaire-Ducru, Ducru-Beaucaillou, Léoville-Las Cases, Talbot
Margaux: Giscours, La Lagune (southern Médoc)
Médoc/Haut Médoc/Moulis/Listrac/Crus Bourgeois: Sociando-Mallet
Graves Red: Haut-Brion
Graves White: Domaine de Chevalier, Laville-Haut-Brion
Pomerol: Pétrus
St.-Émilion: Ausone, Cheval Blanc, Figeac
Barsac/Sauternes: Climens, Coutet, de Fargues, Guiraud, Rieussec, Suduiraut, Yquem

1975—A Quick Study (9-22-75)

St.-Estèphe**	Graves Red**
Pauillac***	Graves White***
St.-Julien***	Pomerol*****
Margaux**	St.-Émilion***
Médoc/Haut-Médoc Crus Bourgeois***	Barsac/Sauternes****

Size: After the abundant vintages of 1973 and 1974, 1975 was a moderately sized crop.
Important information: After 3 consecutive poor to mediocre years, the Bordelais were ready to praise to the heavens the 1975 vintage.
Maturity status: The slowest-evolving vintage in the last 30 years.

Price: Trade and consumer uneasiness concerning the falling reputation of this vintage, as well as the style of even the top wines (which remain hard, closed, and nearly impenetrable), makes this an attractively priced year for those with the knowledge to select the gems and the patience to wait for them to mature.

Is this the year of the great deception or the year where some irrefutably classic wines were produced? Along with 1964 and 1983, this is perhaps the most tricky vintage with which to come to grips. There are some undeniably great wines in the 1975 vintage, but the overall quality level is distressingly uneven, and the number of failures is too numerous to ignore.

Because of the three previous large crops and the international financial crisis brought on by high oil prices, the producers, knowing that their 1972, 1973, and 1974 vintages were already backed up in the marketplace, pruned their vineyards to guard against a large crop. The weather cooperated; July, August, and September were all hot months. However, in August and September several large thunderstorms dumped enormous quantities of rain on the area. It was localized, and most of it did little damage except to frazzle the nerves of winemakers. However, several hailstorms did ravage the central Médoc communes, particularly Moulis, Lamarque, and some isolated hailstorms damaged the southern Léognan-Pessac-Arcins region.

The harvest began during the third week of September and continued under generally good weather conditions through mid-October. Immediately after the harvest, the producers were talking of a top-notch vintage, perhaps the best since 1961. So what happened?

Looking back after having had numerous opportunities to taste and discuss the style of this vintage with many proprietors and winemakers, I am convinced that the majority of growers should have harvested their Cabernet Sauvignon later. Many feel it was picked too soon, and the fact that at that time many were not totally destemming exacerbated the relatively hard, astringent tannins in the 1975s.

This is one of the first vintages I tasted (although on a much more limited basis) from cask, visiting Bordeaux as a tourist rather than a professional. In 1975, many of the young wines exhibited great color, intensely ripe, fragrant noses, and immense potential. Other wines appeared to have an excess of tannin. The wines immediately closed up 2–3 years after bottling and in most cases still remain stubbornly hard and backward. There are a number of badly made, excessively tannic wines where the fruit has already dried out and the color has become brown. Many of them were aged in old oak barrels (new oak was not nearly as prevalent as it is now), and the sanitary conditions in many cellars were less than ideal. However, even allowing for these variations, I have always been struck by the tremendous difference in the quality of wines in this vintage. To this day the wide swings in quality remain far greater than in any other recent year. For example, how could La Mission-Haut-Brion, Pétrus, l'Évangile, and Lafleur produce such profoundly great wines yet many of their neighbors fail completely? This remains one of the vintage's mysteries.

This is a vintage for true Bordeaux connoisseurs who have the patience to wait the wines out. The top examples, which usually come from Pomerol, St.-Julien, and Pauillac (the extraordinary success of La Mission-Haut-Brion and La Tour-Haut-Brion and, to a lesser extent, Haut-Brion, is an exception to the sad level of quality in Graves), are wines that have still not reached their apogees. Could the great 1975s turn out to resemble wines from a vintage such as 1928, which took 30-plus years to reach full maturity? The great successes of this vintage are capable of lasting and lasting because they have the richness and concentration of ripe fruit to balance out their tannins. However, many wines are too dry, too astringent, or too tannic to develop gracefully.

I purchased this vintage as futures, and I remember thinking I secured great deals on the first-growths at $350 a case. But I have invested in 23 years of patience, and the wait for the top wines will be at least another 10 years. This is the vintage for delayed gratification.

THE BEST WINES

St.-Estèphe: Haut-Marbuzet, Meyney, Montrose

Pauillac: Lafite-Rothschild, Latour, Mouton-Rothschild, Pichon-Longueville-Comtesse de Lalande

St.-Julien: Branaire-Ducru, Gloria, Gruaud-Larose, Léoville-Barton, Léoville-Las Cases

Margaux: Giscours, Palmer

Médoc/Haut-Médoc/Moulis/Listrac/Crus Bourgeois: Greysac, Sociando-Mallet, La Tour-St. Bonnet

Graves Red: Haut-Brion, La Mission-Haut-Brion, Pape-Clément, La Tour-Haut-Brion

Pomerol: l'Église-Clinet, l'Enclos, l'Évangile, La Fleur-Pétrus, Le Gay, Lafleur, Nenin, Pétrus, Trotanoy, Vieux-Château-Certan

St.-Émilion: Cheval Blanc, Figeac, Magdelaine, Soutard

Barsac/Sauternes: Climens, Coutet, de Fargues, Raymond-Lafon, Rieussec, Yquem

1974—A Quick Study (9-20-74)

St.-Estèphe*	Graves Red**
Pauillac*	Graves White*
St.-Julien*	Pomerol*
Margaux*	St.-Émilion*
Médoc/Haut-Médoc Crus Bourgeois*	Barsac/Sauternes*

Size: An enormous crop was harvested.

Important information: Should you still have stocks of the 1974s, it is best to consume them over the next several years or donate them.

Maturity status: A handful of the top wines of the vintage are still alive and well, but aging them any further will prove fruitless.

Price: These wines were always inexpensive, and I can never imagine them fetching a decent price unless you find someone in need of this year to celebrate a birthday.

As a result of a good flowering and a dry, sunny May and June, the crop size was large in 1974. The weather from mid-August through October was cold, windy, and rainy. Despite the persistent soggy conditions, the appellation of choice in 1974 turned out to be Graves. While most 1974s remain hard, tannic, hollow wines lacking ripeness, flesh, and character, a number of the Graves estates did produce surprisingly spicy, interesting wines. Though somewhat compact and attenuated, they are still enjoyable to drink 24 years after the vintage. The two stars are La Mission-Haut-Brion and Domaine de Chevalier, followed by Latour in Pauillac and Trotanoy in Pomerol. Should you have remaining stocks of these wines in your cellar, it would be foolish to push your luck. In spite of their well-preserved status, my instincts suggest drinking them soon. The vintage was equally bad in the Barsac/Sauternes region. I have never seen a bottle to taste. It is debatable as to which was the worst vintage during the decade of the seventies—1972, 1974, or 1977.

1973—A Quick Study (9-20-73)

St.-Estèphe**	Graves Red*
Pauillac*	Graves White**
St.-Julien**	Pomerol**
Margaux*	St.-Émilion*
Médoc/Haut-Médoc Crus Bourgeois*	Barsac/Sauternes*

Size: Enormous; one of the largest crops of the seventies.

Important information: A sadly rain-bloated, swollen crop of grapes in poor to mediocre condition was harvested.

Maturity status: The odds are stacked against finding a 1973 that is still in good condition, at least from a regular-size bottle.

Price: Distressed sale prices, even for those born in this year.

In the mid-1970s, the best 1973s had some value as agreeably light, round, soft, somewhat diluted, yet pleasant Bordeaux wines. With the exception of Domaine de Chevalier, Pétrus, and the great sweet classic, Yquem, all of the 1973s have faded into oblivion.

So often the Bordelais are on the verge of a top-notch vintage when the rains arrive. The rains that came during the harvest bloated what would have been a healthy, enormous grape crop. Modern-day sprays and techniques such as *saigner* were inadequately utilized in the early seventies, and the result in 1973 was a group of wines that lacked color, extract, acidity, and backbone. The wines were totally drinkable when released in 1976. By the beginning of the eighties, they were in complete decline, save for Pétrus.

THE BEST WINES

St.-Estèphe: de Pez
Pauillac: Latour
St.-Julien: Ducru-Beaucaillou
Margaux: none
Médoc/Haut-Médoc/Moulis/Listrac/Crus Bourgeois: none
Graves Red: Domaine de Chevalier, La Tour-Haut-Brion
Graves White: none
Pomerol: Pétrus
St.-Émilion: none
Barsac/Sauternes: Yquem

1972—A Quick Study (10-7-72)

St.-Estèphe 0	Graves Red*
Pauillac 0	Graves White 0
St.-Julien 0	Pomerol 0
Margaux*	St.-Émilion*
Médoc/Haut-Médoc Crus Bourgeois 0	Barsac/Sauternes 0

Size: A moderately sized crop was harvested.

Important information: Rivals 1977 as the worst vintage of the decade.

Maturity status: Most wines have long been over the hill.

Price: Extremely low.

The weather pattern of 1972 was one of unusually cool, cloudy summer months with an abnormally rainy month of August. While September brought dry, warm weather, it was too late to save the crop. The 1972 wines turned out to be the worst of the decade—acidic, green, raw, and vegetal tasting. The high acidity did manage to keep many of them alive for 10–15 years, but their deficiencies in fruit, charm, and flavor concentration were far too great even for age to overcome.

As in any poor vintage, some châteaux managed to produce decent wines, with the well-drained soils of Margaux and Graves turning out slightly better wines than elsewhere.

There are no longer any wines from 1972 that would be of any interest to consumers.

THE BEST WINES*

St.-Estèphe: none
Pauillac: Latour
St.-Julien: Branaire-Ducru, Léoville-Las Cases
Margaux: Giscours, Rausan-Ségla
Médoc/Haut-Médoc/Moulis/Listrac/Crus Bourgeois: none
Graves Red: La Mission-Haut-Brion, La Tour-Haut-Brion
Graves White: none
Pomerol: Trotanoy
St.-Émilion: Cheval Blanc, Figeac
Barsac/Sauternes: Climens

1971—A Quick Study (9-25-71)

St.-Estèphe**	Graves Red***
Pauillac***	Graves White**
St.-Julien***	Pomerol****
Margaux***	St.-Émilion***
Médoc/Haut-Médoc Crus Bourgeois**	Barsac/Sauternes****

Size: Small to moderate crop size.

Important information: A good to very good, stylish vintage, with the strongest efforts emerging from Pomerol and the sweet wines of Barsac/Sauternes.

Maturity status: Every 1971 has been fully mature for nearly a decade, with only the best cuvées capable of lasting another decade.

Price: The small crop size kept prices high, but most 1971s, compared with other good vintages of the last 30 years, are slightly undervalued.

Unlike 1970, 1971 was a small vintage because of a poor flowering in June that caused a significant reduction in the Merlot crop. By the end of the harvest the crop size was a good 40% less than the huge crop of 1970.

Early reports of the vintage have proven to be overly enthusiastic. Some experts (particularly Bordeaux's Peter Sichel), relying on the small production yields when compared with those of 1970, even claimed that the vintage was better than 1970. This has proved to be totally false. Certainly the 1971s were forward and delicious, as were the 1970s when first released, but unlike the 1970s, the 1971s lacked the great depth of color, concentration, and tannic backbone. The vintage was mixed in the Médoc, but it was a fine year for Pomerol, St.-Émilion, and Graves.

Buying 1971s now could prove dangerous unless the wines have been exceptionally well stored. Twenty-five years after the vintage there are a handful of wines that have just reached full maturity—Pétrus, Latour, Trotanoy, La Mission-Haut-Brion. Well-stored examples of these wines will continue to drink well for at least another 10–15 years. Elsewhere, storage is everything. This could be a vintage at which to take a serious look provided one can find reasonably priced, well-preserved bottles.

The sweet wines of Barsac and Sauternes were successful and are in full maturity. The best of them have at least 1–2 decades of aging potential and will certainly outlive all of the red wines produced in 1971.

*This list is for informational purposes only, as I suspect all of the above wines, with the possible exception of Pétrus, are in serious decline unless found in larger-format bottlings that have been perfectly stored.

THE BEST WINES

St.-Estèphe: Montrose
Pauillac: Latour, Mouton-Rothschild
St.-Julien: Beychevelle, Gloria, Gruaud-Larose, Talbot
Margaux: Palmer
Médoc/Haut-Médoc/Moulis/Listrac/Crus Bourgeois: none
Graves Red: Haut-Brion, La Mission-Haut-Brion, La Tour-Haut-Brion
Graves White: none
Pomerol: Petit-Village, Pétrus, Trotanoy
St.-Émilion: Cheval Blanc, La Dominique, Magdelaine
Barsac/Sauternes: Climens, Coutet, de Fargues, Yquem

1970—A Quick Study (9-27-70)

St.-Estèphe***	Graves Red****
Pauillac***	Graves White***
St.-Julien***	Pomerol****
Margaux***	St.-Émilion***
Médoc/Haut-Médoc Crus Bourgeois***	Barsac/Sauternes***

Size: An enormous crop that was a record setter at the time.

Important information: The first modern-day abundant crop that combined high quality with large quantity.

Maturity status: Initially the 1970s were called precocious and early maturing. Most of the big 1970s have aged very slowly and are now in full maturity, with only a handful of exceptions. The smaller wines, crus bourgeois, and lighter-weight Pomerols and St.-Émilions should have been drunk by 1980.

Price: Expensive, no doubt because this is the most popular vintage between 1961 and 1982.

Between the two great vintages 1961 and 1982, 1970 has proved to be the best year, producing wines that were attractively rich and full of charm and complexity. They have aged more gracefully than many of the austere 1966s and seem fuller, richer, more evenly balanced, and more consistent than the hard, tannic, large-framed, but often hollow and tough 1975s. The year 1970 proved to be the first modern-day vintage that combined high production with good quality. Moreover, it was a uniform and consistent vintage throughout Bordeaux, with every appellation able to claim its share of top-quality wines.

The weather conditions during the summer and early fall were perfect. There was no hail, no weeks of drenching downpours, no frost, and no spirit-crushing inundation at harvesttime. It was one of those rare vintages where everything went well, and the Bordelais harvested one of the largest and healthiest crops they had ever seen.

The year 1970 was the first vintage that I tasted out of cask, visiting a number of châteaux with my wife as tourists on my way to the cheap beaches of Spain and North Africa during summer vacations in 1971 and 1972. Even from their early days I remember the wines exhibiting dark color, an intense richness of fruit, fragrant, ripe perfume, full body, and high tannin. Yet when compared with the finest vintages of the eighties and nineties, 1970 seems to suffer. Undoubtedly, the number of top wines from vintages such as 1982, 1985, 1986, 1988, 1989, 1990, 1994, 1995, and 1996 exceed those produced in 1970.

As for the sweet wines, they have had to take a backseat to the 1971s because there was less botrytis. Although the wines are impressively big and full, they lack the complexity, delicacy, and finesse of the best 1971s.

In conclusion, 1970 will no doubt continue to sell at high prices for decades to come, because this is the most consistent, and in some cases outstanding, vintage between 1961 and 1982.

THE BEST WINES

St.-Estèphe: Cos d'Estournel, Haut-Marbuzet, Lafon-Rochet, Montrose, Les-Ormes-de-Pez, de Pez

Pauillac: Grand-Puy-Lacoste, Haut-Batailley, Latour, Lynch-Bages, Mouton-Rothschild, Pichon-Longueville-Comtesse de Lalande

St.-Julien: Ducru-Beaucaillou, Gloria, Gruaud-Larose, Léoville-Barton, St.-Pierre

Margaux: Giscours, Lascombes, Palmer

Médoc/Haut-Médoc/Moulis/Listrac/Crus Bourgeois: Sociando-Mallet

Graves Red: Domaine de Chevalier, de Fieuzal, Haut-Bailly, La Mission-Haut-Brion, La Tour-Haut-Brion

Graves White: Domaine de Chevalier, Laville-Haut-Brion

Pomerol: La Conseillante, La Fleur-Pétrus, Lafleur, Latour à Pomerol, Pétrus, Trotanoy

St.-Émilion: l'Arrosée, Cheval Blanc, La Dominique, Figeac, Magdelaine

Barsac/Sauternes: Yquem

1969—A Quick Study (10-6-69)

St.-Estèphe 0	Graves Red*
Pauillac 0	Graves White 0
St.-Julien 0	Pomerol*
Margaux 0	St.-Émilion 0
Médoc/Haut-Médoc Crus Bourgeois 0	Barsac/Sauternes*

Size: Small.

Important information: My candidate for the most undesirable wines produced in Bordeaux in the last 30 years.

Maturity status: I never tasted a 1969, except for Pétrus, that could have been said to have had any richness or fruit. I have not seen any of these wines except for Pétrus for a number of years, but they must be unpalatable.

Price: Amazingly, the vintage was offered at a relatively high price, but almost all the wines except for a handful of the big names are totally worthless.

Whenever Bordeaux has suffered through a disastrous vintage (like that of 1968), there has always been a tendency to lavish false praise on the following year. No doubt Bordeaux, after their horrible experience in 1968, badly wanted a fine vintage in 1969, but despite some overly optimistic proclamations by some leading Bordeaux experts at the time, 1969 has turned out to be one of the least attractive vintages for Bordeaux wines in the last 3 decades.

The crop was small, and while the summer was sufficiently hot and dry to ensure a decent maturity, torrential September rains dashed everyone's hopes for a good vintage, except some investors who irrationally moved in to buy these insipid, nasty, acidic, sharp wines. Consequently the 1969s, along with being extremely unattractive wines, were quite expensive when they first appeared on the market.

I can honestly say I have never tasted a red wine in 1969 I did not dislike. The only exception would be a relatively decent bottle of Pétrus (rated in the upper 70s) that I had 20 years after the vintage. Most wines are harsh and hollow, with no flesh, fruit, or charm, and it is hard to imagine that any of these wines are today any more palatable than they were during the seventies.

In the Barsac and Sauternes region a few proprietors managed to produce acceptable wines, particularly d'Arche.

1968—A Quick Study (9-20-68)

St.-Estèphe 0	Graves Red*
Pauillac 0	Graves White 0
St.-Julien 0	Pomerol 0
Margaux 0	St.-Émilion 0
Médoc/Haut-Médoc Crus Bourgeois 0	Barsac/Sauternes 0

Size: A small, disastrous crop in terms of both quality and quantity.

Important information: A great year for California Cabernet Sauvignon, but not for Bordeaux.

Maturity status: All of these wines must be passé.

Price: Another worthless vintage.

The year 1968 was another of the very poor vintages the Bordelais had to suffer through in the sixties. The culprit, as usual, was heavy rain (it was the wettest year since 1951) that bloated the grapes. However, there have been some 1968s that I found much better than anything produced in 1969, a vintage with a "better" (I am not sure that is the right word to use) reputation.

At one time wines such as Figeac, Gruaud-Larose, Cantemerle, La Mission-Haut-Brion, Haut-Brion, and Latour were palatable. Should anyone run across these wines today, the rule of caveat emptor would seemingly be applicable, as I doubt that any of them would have much left to enjoy.

1967—A Quick Study (9-25-67)

St.-Estèphe**	Graves Red***
Pauillac**	Graves White**
St.-Julien**	Pomerol***
Margaux**	St.-Émilion***
Médoc/Haut-Médoc Crus Bourgeois*	Barsac/Sauternes****

Size: An abundant crop was harvested.

Important information: A Graves, Pomerol, St.-Émilion year that favored the early-harvested Merlot.

Maturity status: Most 1967s were drinkable when released in 1970 and should have been consumed by 1980. Only a handful of wines (Pétrus and Latour, for example), where well stored, will keep for another few years, but they are unlikely to improve.

Price: Moderate.

The year 1967 was a large, useful vintage in the sense that it produced an abundant quantity of round, quick-maturing wines. Most should have been drunk before 1980, but a handful of wines continue to display remarkable staying power and are still in the full bloom of their maturity. This is a vintage that clearly favored Pomerol and, to a lesser extent, Graves. Holding on to these wines any longer seems foolish, but I have no doubt that some of the biggest wines, such as Latour, Pétrus, Trotanoy, and perhaps even Palmer, will last for another 5–10 years. Should one find any of the top wines listed below in a large-format bottle (magnums, double magnums, and so forth) at a reasonable price, my advice would be to take the gamble.

As unexciting as most red wines turned out in 1967, the sweet wines of Barsac and Sauternes were rich and honeyed, with gobs of botrytis present. However, readers must remember that only a handful of estates were truly up to the challenge of making great wines during this very depressed period for the wine production of Barsac/Sauternes.

THE BEST WINES

St.-Estèphe: Calon-Ségur, Montrose
Pauillac: Latour
St.-Julien: none
Margaux: Giscours, La Lagune (southern Médoc), Palmer
Médoc/Haut-Médoc/Moulis/Listrac/Crus Bourgeois: none
Graves Red: Haut-Brion, La Mission-Haut-Brion
Graves White: none
Pomerol: Pétrus, Trotanoy, La Violette
St.-Émilion: Cheval Blanc, Magdelaine, Pavie
Barsac/Sauternes: Suduiraut, Yquem

1966—A Quick Study (9-26-66)

St.-Estèphe***   Graves Red****
Pauillac***   Graves White***
St.-Julien***   Pomerol***
Margaux***   St.-Émilion**
Médoc/Haut-Médoc Crus Bourgeois** Barsac/Sauternes**

Size: An abundant crop was harvested.
Important information: The most overrated "top" vintage of the last 25 years.
Maturity status: The best wines are in their prime, but most wines are losing their fruit before their tannins.
Price: Expensive and overpriced.

While the majority opinion is that 1966 is the best vintage of the decade after 1961, I would certainly argue that for Graves, Pomerol, and St.-Émilion, 1964 is clearly the second-best vintage of the decade. And I am beginning to think that even 1962, that grossly under-rated vintage, is, on overall merit, a better year than 1966. Conceived in somewhat the same spirit as 1975 (overhyped after several unexciting years, particularly in the Médoc), 1966 never developed as well as many of its proponents would have liked. The wines, now 37 years of age, for the most part have remained austere, lean, unyielding, and tannic, losing their fruit before their tannin melts away. Some notable exceptions do exist. Who could deny the exceptional wine made at Latour (the wine of the vintage) or the great Palmer?

All the disappointments that emerged from this vintage were unexpected in view of the early reports that the wines were relatively precocious, charming, and early maturing. If the vintage is not as consistent as first believed, there are an adequate number of medium-weight, classically styled wines. However, they are all overpriced, as this vintage has always been fashionable and has had no shortage of supporters, particularly from the English wine-writing community.

The sweet wines of Barsac and Sauternes are also mediocre. Favorable conditions for the development of the noble rot, *Botrytis cinerea,* never occurred.

The climatic conditions that shaped this vintage started with a slow flowering in June, intermittently hot and cold weather in July and August, and a dry and sunny September. The crop size was large, and the vintage was harvested under sound weather conditions.

I would be skeptical about buying most 1966s except for one of the unqualified successes of the vintage.

THE BEST WINES

St.-Estèphe: none

Pauillac: Grand-Puy-Lacoste, Latour, Mouton-Rothschild, Pichon-Longueville-Comtesse de
Lalande

St.-Julien: Branaire-Ducru, Ducru-Beaucaillou, Gruaud-Larose, Léoville-Las Cases

Margaux: Lascombes, Palmer

Médoc/Haut-Médoc/Moulis/Listrac/Crus Bourgeois: none

Graves Red: Haut-Brion, La Mission-Haut-Brion, Pape-Clément

Pomerol: Lafleur, Trotanoy

St.-Émilion: Canon

Barsac/Sauternes: none

1965—A Quick Study (10-2-65)

St.-Estèphe 0	Graves Red 0
Pauillac 0	Graves White 0
St.-Julien 0	Pomerol 0
Margaux 0	St.-Émilion 0
Médoc/Haut-Médoc Crus Bourgeois 0	Barsac/Sauternes 0

Size: A tiny vintage.

Important information: The quintessential vintage of rot and rain.

Maturity status: The wines tasted terrible from the start and must be totally reprehensible today.

Price: Worthless.

   The vintage of rot and rain. I have had little experience tasting the 1965s. It is considered by most experts to be one of the worst vintages in the post–World War II era. A wet summer was bad enough, but the undoing of this vintage was an incredibly wet and humid September that caused rot to voraciously devour the vineyards. Antirot sprays had not yet been developed. It should be obvious that these wines are to be avoided.

1964—A Quick Study (9-22-64)

St.-Estèphe***	Graves Red*****
Pauillac*	Graves White***
St.-Julien*	Pomerol*****
Margaux**	St.-Émilion****
Médoc/Haut-Médoc Crus Bourgeois*	Barsac/Sauternes*

Size: A large crop was harvested.

Important information: The classic example of a vintage where the early-picked Merlot and Cabernet Franc produced great wine, and the late-harvested Cabernet Sauvignon, particularly in the Médoc, was inundated. The results included numerous big-name failures in the Médoc.

Maturity status: The Médocs are past their prime, but the larger-scale wines of Graves, Pomerol, and St.-Émilion can last for another 5–10 years.

Price: Smart Bordeaux enthusiasts have always recognized the greatness of this vintage in Graves, Pomerol, and St.-Émilion, and consequently prices have remained high. Nevertheless, compared with such glamour years as 1959 and 1961, the top right bank and Graves 1964s are not only underrated, but in some cases underpriced as well.

One of the most intriguing vintages of Bordeaux, 1964 produced a number of splendid, generally underrated and underpriced wines in Pomerol, St.-Émilion, and Graves where many proprietors had the good fortune to have harvested their crops before the rainy deluge began on October 8. Because of this downpour, which caught many Médoc châteaux with un-harvested vineyards, 1964 has never been regarded as a top Bordeaux vintage. While the vintage can be notoriously bad for some of the properties of the Médoc and the late-harvesting Barsac and Sauternes estates, it is excellent to outstanding for the three appella-tions of Pomerol, St.-Émilion, and Graves.

The summer had been so hot and dry that the French minister of agriculture announced at the beginning of September that the "vintage of the century was about to commence." Since the Merlot grape ripens first, the harvest began in the areas where it is planted in abundance. St.-Émilion and Pomerol harvested at the end of September and finished their picking before the inundation began on October 8. Most of the Graves properties had also finished harvest-ing. When the rains came, most of the Médoc estates had just begun to harvest their Caber-net Sauvignon and were unable to successfully complete the harvest because of torrential rainfall. It was a Médoc vintage noted for some extraordinary and famous failures. Pity the buyer who purchased Lafite-Rothschild, Mouton-Rothschild, Lynch-Bages, Calon-Ségur, or Margaux! Yet not everyone made disappointing wine. Montrose in St.-Estèphe and Latour in Pauillac made the two greatest wines of the Médoc.

Because of the very damaging reports about the rainfall, many wine enthusiasts ap-proached the 1964 vintage with a great deal of apprehension.

The top wines from Graves, St.-Émilion, and Pomerol are exceptionally rich, full-bodied, opulent, and concentrated wines, with high alcohol, an opaque color, super length, and un-bridled power. Amazingly, they are far richer, more interesting, and more complete wines than the 1966s and, in many cases, compete with the finest wines of the 1961 vintage. Be-cause of low acidity, all of the wines reached full maturity by the mid-1980s. The best exam-ples exhibit no sign of decline and can easily last for another 5–10 or more years.

THE BEST WINES

St.-Estèphe: Montrose
Pauillac: Latour
St.-Julien: Gruaud-Larose
Margaux: none
Médoc/Haut-Médoc/Moulis/Listrac/Crus Bourgeois: none
Graves Red: Domaine de Chevalier, Haut-Bailly, Haut-Brion, La Mission-Haut-Brion
Pomerol: La Conseillante, La Fleur-Pétrus, Lafleur, Pétrus, Trotanoy, Vieux-Château-Certan
St.-Émilion: l'Arrosée, Cheval Blanc, Figeac, Soutard
Barsac/Sauternes: none

1963—A Quick Study (10-7-63)

St.-Estèphe 0	Graves Red 0
Pauillac 0	Graves White 0
St.-Julien 0	Pomerol 0
Margaux 0	St.-Émilion 0
Médoc/Haut-Médoc Crus Bourgeois 0	Barsac/Sauternes 0

Size: A small to moderate-size crop was harvested.

Important information: A dreadfully poor year that rivals 1965 for the feebleness of its wines.

Maturity status: The wines must now be awful.

Price: Worthless.

The Bordelais have never been able to decide whether 1963 or 1965 was the worst vintage of the sixties. Rain and rot, as in 1965, were the ruination of this vintage. I have not seen a bottle of 1963 for over 20 years.

1962—A Quick Study (10-1-62)

St.-Estèphe****	Graves Red***
Pauillac****	Graves White****
St.-Julien****	Pomerol***
Margaux***	St.-Émilion***
Médoc/Haut-Médoc Crus Bourgeois***	Barsac/Sauternes****

Size: An abundant crop size—in fact, one of the largest of the decade of the sixties.

Important information: A terribly underrated vintage that had the misfortune of following one of the greatest vintages of the century.

Maturity status: The Bordeaux old-timers claim the 1962s drank beautifully by the late sixties and continued to fill out and display considerable character, fruit, and charm in the seventies. As the decade of the nineties ends, the top 1962s are still lovely, rich, round wines full of finesse and elegance.

Price: Undervalued, particularly when one considers the prices of its predecessor, 1961, and the overpriced 1966s.

Coming after the great vintage of 1961, it was not totally unexpected that 1962 would be underestimated. This vintage appears to be the most undervalued year for Bordeaux in the post–World War II era. Elegant, supple, very fruity, round, and charming wines that were neither too tannic nor too massive were produced in virtually every appellation. Because of their precociousness, many assumed the wines would not last, but they have kept longer than anyone would have ever imagined. Most 1962s do require consumption, but they continue to surprise me, and well-preserved examples of the vintage can easily be kept through the turn of the century.

The weather was acceptable but not stunning. There was a good flowering because of a sunny, dry May, a relatively hot summer with some impressive thunderstorms, and a good *fin de saison*, as the French say, with a hot, sunny September. The harvest was not rain free, but the inundations that could have created serious problems never occurred.

Not only was the vintage very successful in most appellations, but it was a top year for the dry white wines of Graves as well as the sweet nectars from Barsac/Sauternes.

THE BEST WINES

St.-Estèphe: Cos d'Estournel, Montrose

Pauillac: Batailley, Lafite-Rothschild, Latour, Lynch-Bages, Mouton-Rothschild, Pichon-Longueville-Comtesse de Lalande

St.-Julien: Ducru-Beaucaillou, Gruaud-Larose

Margaux: Margaux, Palmer

Médoc/Haut-Médoc/Moulis/Listrac/Crus Bourgeois: none

Graves Red: Haut-Brion, Pape-Clément

Graves White: Domaine de Chevalier, Laville-Haut-Brion

Pomerol: Lafleur, Pétrus, Trotanoy, La Violette

St.-Émilion: Magdelaine
Barsac/Sauternes: Yquem

1961—A Quick Study (9-22-61)

St.-Estèphe*****	Graves Red*****
Pauillac*****	Graves White***
St.-Julien*****	Pomerol*****
Margaux*****	St.-Émilion***
Médoc/Haut-Médoc Crus Bourgeois***	Barsac/Sauternes**

Size: An exceptionally tiny crop was produced; in fact, this is the last vintage where a minuscule crop resulted in high quality.

Important information: One of the legendary vintages of the century.

Maturity status: The wines, drinkable young, have, with only a handful of exceptions, reached maturity and were all at their apogee by 1990. Most of the prestige examples will keep for at least another 5–10 years, but many 1961s have begun to fade.

Price: The tiny quantities plus exceptional quality have made the 1961s the most dearly priced, mature vintage of great Bordeaux in the marketplace. Moreover, prices will only increase, given the microscopic qualities that remain—an auctioneer's dream vintage. But buyers beware: many 1961s have been poorly stored or traded frequently. Moreover, some fraudulent 1961s show up in the marketplace.

The year 1961 is one of nine great vintages produced in the post–World War II era. The others—1945, 1947, 1949, 1953, 1959, 1982, 1989, 1990—all have their proponents, but none is as revered as 1961. The wines have always been prized for their sensational concentration and magnificent penetrating bouquets of superripe fruit and rich, deep, sumptuous flavors. Delicious when young, these wines, which have all reached full maturity except for a handful of the most intensely concentrated examples, are marvelous to drink. However, I see no problem in holding the best-stored bottles for at least another 10 years.

The weather pattern was nearly perfect in 1961, with spring frosts reducing the crop size and then sunny, hot weather throughout the summer and the harvest, resulting in splendid maturity levels. The small harvest guaranteed high prices for these wines, and today's prices for 1961s make them the equivalent of liquid gold.

The vintage was excellent throughout all appellations of Bordeaux except for the Barsac/Sauternes. This region benefited greatly from the vintage's reputation, but a tasting of the 1961 sweet wines will reveal that even Yquem is mediocre. The incredibly dry weather conditions resulted in very little botrytis, and the results are large scaled, but essentially monolithic sweet wines that have never merited the interest they have enjoyed. The only other appellation that did not appear to be up to the overall level of quality was St.-Émilion, where many vineyards had still not fully recovered from the killer freeze of 1956.

After tasting the 1961s, I am convinced that only two vintages are somewhat similar in richness and style: 1959 and 1982. The 1959s tend to be lower in acidity but have actually aged more slowly than the 1961s, whereas the 1982s would appear to have the same physical profile of the 1961s but less tannin.

THE BEST WINES

St.-Estèphe: Cos d'Estournel, Haut-Marbuzet, Montrose
Pauillac: Grand-Puy-Lacoste, Latour, Lynch-Bages, Mouton-Rothschild, Pichon-
    Longueville-Comtesse de Lalande, Pontet-Canet
St.-Julien: Beychevelle, Ducru-Beaucaillou, Gruaud-Larose, Léoville-Barton

Margaux: Malescot St.-Exupéry, Margaux, Palmer
Médoc/Haut-Médoc/Moulis/Listrac/Crus Bourgeois: none
Graves Red: Haut-Bailly, Haut-Brion, La Mission-Haut-Brion, La Tour-Haut-Brion, Pape-
   Clément
Graves White: Domaine de Chevalier, Laville-Haut-Brion
Pomerol: l'Église-Clinet, l'Évangile, Lafleur, Latour à Pomerol, Pétrus, Trotanoy
St.-Émilion: l'Arrosée, Canon, Cheval Blanc, Figeac, Magdelaine
Barsac/Sauternes: none

1960—A Quick Study (9-9-60)

St.-Estèphe**	Graves Red**
Pauillac**	Graves White*
St.-Julien**	Pomerol*
Margaux*	St.-Émilion*
Médoc/Haut-Médoc Crus Bourgeois 0	Barsac/Sauternes*

Size: A copious crop was harvested.
Important information: The two rainy months of August and September were this vintage's undoing.
Maturity status: Most 1960s should have been consumed within their first 10–15 years of life.
Price: Low.

I remember drinking several delicious magnums of 1960 Latour, as well as having found good examples of 1960 Montrose, La Mission-Haut-Brion, and Gruaud-Larose in Bordeaux. However, the last 1960 I consumed, a magnum of Latour, was drunk over 15 years ago. I would guess that even that wine, which was the most concentrated wine of the vintage according to the Bordeaux cognoscenti, is now in decline.

1959—A Quick Study (9-20-59)

St.-Estèphe*****	Graves Red*****
Pauillac*****	Graves White****
St.-Julien****	Pomerol***
Margaux****	St.-Émilion**
Médoc/Haut-Médoc Crus Bourgeois***	Barsac/Sauternes*****

Size: Average.
Important information: The first of the modern-day years to be designated "vintage of the century."
Maturity status: The wines, maligned in their early years for having low acidity and lacking backbone (reminiscent of the 1982s), have aged more slowly than the more highly touted 1961s. In fact, comparisons between the top wines of the two vintages often reveal the 1959s to be less evolved, with deeper color and more richness and aging potential.
Price: Never inexpensive, the 1959s have become increasingly more expensive as serious connoisseurs have begun to realize that this vintage not only rivals 1961, but in specific cases surpasses it.

This is an irrefutably great vintage. The wines, which are especially strong in the northern Médoc and Graves and less so on the right bank (Pomerol and St.-Émilion were still recovering from the devastating deep freeze of 1956), are among the most massive and richest ever made in Bordeaux. In fact, the two modern-day vintages that are frequently compared with 1959 are the 1982 and 1989. Those comparisons may have merit.

The 1959s have evolved at a glacial pace and are often in better condition (especially the first-growths Lafite-Rothschild and Mouton-Rothschild) than their 1961 counterparts, which are even more highly touted. The wines do display the effects of having been made in a classic, hot, dry year, with just enough rain to keep the vineyards from being stressed. They are full bodied, extremely alcoholic, and opulent, with high degrees of tannin and extract. Their colors have remained impressively opaque and dark and display less brown and orange than the 1961s. If there is one nagging doubt about many of the 1959s, it is whether they will ever develop the sensational perfume and fragrance that is so much a part of the greatest Bordeaux vintages. Perhaps the great heat during the summer of 1959 did compromise this aspect of the wines, but it is still too soon to know.

THE BEST WINES

St.-Estèphe: Cos d'Estournel, Montrose, Les-Ormes-de-Pez
Pauillac: Lafite-Rothschild, Latour, Lynch-Bages, Mouton-Rothschild, Pichon-Longueville Baron
St.-Julien: Ducru-Beaucaillou, Langoa-Barton, Léoville-Barton, Léoville-Las Cases
Margaux: Lascombes, Malescot-St.-Exupéry, Margaux, Palmer
Graves Red: Haut-Brion, La Mission-Haut-Brion, Pape-Clément, La Tour-Haut-Brion
Pomerol: l'Évangile, Lafleur, Latour à Pomerol, Pétrus, Trotanoy, Vieux-Château-Certan
St.-Émilion: Cheval Blanc, Figeac
Barsac/Sauternes: Climens, Suduiraut, Yquem

1958—A Quick Study (10-7-58)

St.-Estèphe*	Graves Red***
Pauillac*	Graves White**
St.-Julien*	Pomerol*
Margaux*	St.-Émilion**
Médoc/Haut-Médoc Crus Bourgeois*	Barsac/Sauternes*

Size: A small crop was harvested.
Important information: An unfairly maligned vintage.
Maturity status: The wines are now fading badly. The best examples almost always emerge from the Graves appellation.
Price: Inexpensive.

I have fewer than two dozen tasting notes of 1958s, but several that do stand out are all from the Graves appellation. Haut-Brion, La Mission-Haut-Brion, and Pape-Clément all made very good wines. They probably would have provided excellent drinking if consumed during the sixties or early seventies. I most recently had the 1958 Haut-Brion in January 1996. It was still a relatively tasty, round, soft, fleshy, tobacco- and mineral-scented and -flavored wine, but one could see that it would have been much better if it had been consumed 10–15 years ago. Even richer was the 1958 La Mission-Haut-Brion, which should still be excellent if well-preserved bottles can be found.

1957—A Quick Study (10-4-57)

St.-Estèphe**	Graves Red***
Pauillac***	Graves White**
St.-Julien**	Pomerol*
Margaux*	St.-Émilion*
Médoc/Haut-Médoc Crus Bourgeois*	Barsac/Sauternes***

Size: A small crop.

Important information: A brutally cold, wet summer.

Maturity status: Because the summer was so cool, the red wines were extremely high in acidity, which has helped them stand the test of time. Where well-kept examples of 1957 can be found, this could be a vintage to purchase, provided the price is right.

Price: The wines should be realistically and inexpensively priced given the fact that 1957 does not enjoy a good reputation.

For a vintage that has never been received very favorably, I have been surprised by how many respectable and enjoyable wines I have tasted, particularly from Pauillac and Graves. In fact, I would be pleased to serve my most finicky friends the 1957 La Mission-Haut-Brion or 1957 Haut-Brion. And I would certainly be pleased to drink the 1957 Lafite-Rothschild. I had two excellent bottles of Lafite in the early eighties but have not seen the wine since.

It was an extremely difficult year weather-wise, with very wet periods from April through August that delayed the harvest until early October. The wines had good acidity, and in the better-drained soils there was surprising ripeness given the lack of sunshine and excessive moisture. The 1957 Bordeaux, much like their Burgundy counterparts, have held up relatively well given the high acid and green tannins these wines have always possessed.

1956—A Quick Study (10-14-56)

St.-Estèphe 0	Graves Red 0
Pauillac 0	Graves White 0
St.-Julien 0	Pomerol 0
Margaux 0	St.-Émilion 0
Médoc/Haut-Médoc Crus Bourgeois 0	Barsac/Sauternes 0

Size: Minuscule quantities of pathetically weak wine were produced.

Important information: The coldest winter in Bordeaux since 1709 did unprecedented damage to the vineyards, particularly those in Pomerol and St.-Émilion.

Maturity status: I have not seen a 1956 in over 15 years and have a total of only five notes on wines from this vintage.

Price: A worthless vintage produced worthless wines.

The year 1956 stands out as the worst vintage in modern-day Bordeaux, even surpassing such unspeakably bad years as 1963, 1965, 1968, 1969, and 1972. The winter and unbelievably cold months of February and March killed many of the vines in Pomerol and St.-Émilion and retarded the budding of those in the Médoc. The harvest was late, the crop was small, and the wines were virtually undrinkable.

1955—A Quick Study (9-21-55)

St.-Estèphe****	Graves Red****
Pauillac****	Graves White***
St.-Julien****	Pomerol***
Margaux***	St.-Émilion****
Médoc/Haut-Médoc Crus Bourgeois**	Barsac/Sauternes****

Size: A large, healthy crop was harvested.

Important information: For a vintage that is now almost 40 years old, this tends to be an underrated, undervalued year, although it is not comparable to 1953 or 1959. Yet the wines have generally held up and are firmer and more solidly made than the once glorious 1953s.

Maturity status: After a long period of sleep, the top wines appear to finally be fully mature. They exhibit no signs of decline.

Price: Undervalued, except for La Mission-Haut-Brion, the wine of the vintage, if not the decade.

For the most part, the 1955s have always come across as relatively stern, slightly tough textured, yet impressively deep, full wines with fine color and excellent aging potential. What they lack, as a general rule, is fat, charm, and opulence.

The weather conditions were generally ideal, with hot, sunny days in June, July, and August. Although some rain fell in September, its effect was positive rather than negative.

For whatever reason, the relatively large 1955 crop has never generated the excitement that other vintages in the fifties, such as 1953 and 1959, elicited. Perhaps it was the lack of many superstar wines that kept enthusiasm muted. Among more recent years, could 1988 be a rerun of 1955?

THE BEST WINES

St.-Estèphe: Calon-Ségur, Cos d'Estournel, Montrose, Les-Ormes-de-Pez
Pauillac: Latour, Lynch-Bages, Mouton-Rothschild
St.-Julien: Léoville-Las Cases, Talbot
Margaux: Palmer
Graves Red: Haut-Brion, La Mission-Haut-Brion, Pape-Clément
Pomerol: l'Évangile, Lafleur, Latour à Pomerol, Pétrus, Vieux-Château-Certan
St.-Émilion: Cheval Blanc, La Dominique, Soutard
Barsac/Sauternes: Yquem

1954—A Quick Study (10-10-54)

St.-Estèphe 0	Graves Red*
Pauillac*	Graves White 0
St.-Julien*	Pomerol 0
Margaux 0	St.-Émilion 0
Médoc/Haut-Médoc Crus Bourgeois 0	Barsac/Sauternes 0

Size: A small crop was harvested.

Important information: A terrible late-harvest vintage conducted under appalling weather conditions.

Maturity status: It is hard to believe anything from this vintage would still be worth drinking.

Price: The wines have no value.

The year 1954 was a miserable vintage throughout France, but especially in Bordeaux, where the producers continued to wait for full maturity after an exceptionally cool, wet August. While the weather did improve in September, the skies opened toward the end of the month and for nearly 4 weeks one low-pressure system after another passed through the area, dumping enormous quantities of water that served to destroy any chance for a moderately successful vintage.

It is highly unlikely any wine from this vintage could still be drinkable today.

1953—A Quick Study (9-28-53)

St.-Estèphe*****	Graves Red****
Pauillac*****	Graves White***
St.-Julien*****	Pomerol***
Margaux****	St.-Émilion***
Médoc/Haut-Médoc Crus Bourgeois***	Barsac/Sauternes***

Size: An average-size crop was harvested.

Important information: One of the most seductive and hedonistic Bordeaux vintages ever produced.

Maturity status: According to Bordeaux old-timers, the wines were absolutely delicious during the fifties, even more glorious in the sixties, and sublime during the seventies. Charm, roundness, fragrance, and a velvety texture were the hallmarks of this vintage, which now must be approached with some degree of caution unless the wines have been impeccably stored and/or are available in larger-format bottlings.

Price: No vintage with such appeal will ever sell at a reasonable price. Consequently the 1953s remain luxury-priced wines.

The year 1953 must be the only Bordeaux vintage where it is impossible to find a dissenting voice about the quality of the wines. Bordeaux old-timers and some of our senior wine commentators (particularly Edmund Penning-Rowsell and Michael Broadbent) talk of 1953 with adulation. Apparently the vintage never went through an unflattering stage. They were delicious from cask and even more so from bottle. For that reason, much of the vintage was consumed before its tenth birthday. Those who waited have seen the wines develop even greater character during the sixties and seventies. Many wines, especially on this side of the Atlantic, began displaying signs of age (brown color, dried-out fruit flavors) during the eighties. In Bordeaux, when a château pulls out a 1953 it is usually in mint condition, and these are some of the most beautifully sumptuous, rich, charming clarets anyone could ever desire. A more modern-day reference point for 1953 may be the very best 1985s, perhaps even some of the lighter 1982s, although my instincts tell me the 1982s are more alcoholic, richer, fuller, heavier wines.

If you have the discretionary income necessary to buy this highly prized vintage, prudence should dictate that the wines be from cold cellars and/or in larger-format bottles.

THE BEST WINES

St.-Estèphe: Calon-Ségur, Cos d'Estournel, Montrose
Pauillac: Grand-Puy-Lacoste, Lafite-Rothschild, Lynch-Bages, Mouton-Rothschild
St.-Julien: Beychevelle, Ducru-Beaucaillou, Gruaud-Larose, Langoa-Barton, Léoville-
    Barton, Léoville-Las Cases, Talbot
Margaux: Cantemerle (southern Médoc), Margaux, Palmer
Graves Red: Haut-Brion, La Mission-Haut-Brion
Pomerol: La Conseillante
St.-Émilion: Cheval Blanc, Figeac, Magdelaine, Pavie
Barsac/Sauternes: Climens, Yquem

1952—A Quick Study (9-17-52)

St.-Estèphe**	Graves Red***
Pauillac***	Graves White***
St.-Julien***	Pomerol****
Margaux**	St.-Émilion***
Médoc/Haut-Médoc Crus Bourgeois**	Barsac/Sauternes**

Size: A small crop was harvested.

Important information: The 1952 vintage was at its best in Pomerol, which largely completed its harvest prior to the rains.

Maturity status: Most wines have always tasted hard and too astringent, lacking fat, charm, and ripeness. The best bottles could provide surprises.

Price: Expensive, but well-chosen Pomerols may represent relative values.

An excellent spring and summer of relatively hot, dry weather with just enough rain was spoiled by stormy, unstable, cold weather before and during the harvest. Much of the Merlot and some of the Cabernet Franc in Pomerol and St.-Émilion was harvested before the weather turned foul; consequently the best wines tended to come from these appellations. The Graves can also be successful because of the superb drainage of the soil in that appellation, particularly in the Pessac/Léognan area. The Médocs have always tended to be relatively hard and disappointing, even the first-growths.

THE BEST WINES

St.-Estèphe: Calon-Ségur, Montrose
Pauillac: Latour, Lynch-Bages
St.-Julien: none
Margaux: Margaux, Palmer
Graves Red: Haut-Brion, La Mission-Haut-Brion, Pape-Clément
Pomerol: La Fleur-Pétrus, Lafleur, Pétrus, Trotanoy
St.-Émilion: Cheval Blanc, Magdelaine
Barsac/Sauternes: none

1951—A Quick Study (10-9-51)

St.-Estèphe 0	Graves Red 0
Pauillac 0	Graves White 0
St.-Julien 0	Pomerol 0
Margaux 0	St.-Émilion 0
Médoc/Haut-Médoc Crus Bourgeois 0	Barsac/Sauternes 0

Size: A tiny crop was harvested.
Important information: Even today 1951 is considered one of the all-time worst vintages for dry white, dry red, and sweet wines from Bordeaux.
Maturity status: Undrinkable young, undrinkable old.
Price: Another worthless vintage.

Frightfully bad weather in the spring, summer, and both before and during the harvest (rain and unseasonably cold temperatures) was the complete undoing of this vintage, which has the ignominious pleasure of having one of the worst reputations of any vintage in the post–World War II era.

1950—A Quick Study (9-17-50)

St.-Estèphe**	Graves Red***
Pauillac***	Graves White***
St.-Julien***	Pomerol*****
Margaux***	St.-Émilion****
Médoc/Haut-Médoc Crus Bourgeois*	Barsac/Sauternes****

Size: An abundant crop was harvested.
Important information: Many of the Pomerols are great, yet they have been totally ignored by the chroniclers of the Bordeaux region.
Maturity status: Most Médocs and Graves are now in decline. The top heavyweight Pomerols can be splendid, with years of life still left.
Price: The quality of the Pomerols is no longer a secret.

The year 1950 is another example where the Médoc formed the general impression of the Bordeaux vintage. This relatively abundant year was the result of good flowering, a hot, dry summer, and a difficult early September complicated by large amounts of rain.

The Médocs, all of which are in decline, were soft, forward, medium-bodied wines that probably had a kinship to more recent vintages such as 1971 and 1981. The Graves were slightly better, but even they are probably passé. The two best appellations were St.-Émilion, which produced a number of rich, full, intense wines that aged quickly, and Pomerol, which had its fourth superb vintage in succession—unprecedented in the history of that area. The wines are unbelievably rich, unctuous, and concentrated and in many cases are capable of rivaling the greatest Pomerols of such more highly renowned vintages as 1947 and 1949.

The other appellation that prospered in 1950 was Barsac/Sauternes. Fanciers of these wines still claim 1950 is one of the greatest of the post–World War II vintages for sweet wines.

THE BEST WINES

St.-Estèphe: none
Pauillac: Latour
St.-Julien: none
Margaux: Margaux
Médoc/Haut-Médoc/Moulis/Listrac/Crus Bourgeois: none
Graves Red: Haut-Brion, La Mission-Haut-Brion
Pomerol: l'Église-Clinet, l'Évangile, La Fleur-Pétrus, Le Gay, Lafleur, Latour à Pomerol, Pétrus, Vieux-Château-Certan
St.-Émilion: Cheval Blanc, Figeac, Soutard
Barsac/Sauternes: Climens, Coutet, Suduiraut, Yquem

1949—A Quick Study (9-27-49)

St.-Estèphe*****	Graves Red*****
Pauillac*****	Graves White***
St.-Julien*****	Pomerol****
Margaux****	St.-Émilion****
Médoc/Haut-Médoc Crus Bourgeois***	Barsac/Sauternes*****

Size: A small crop was harvested.
Important information: The driest and sunniest vintage since 1893 and rivaled (weather-wise, not qualitatively) in more recent years only by 1990.
Maturity status: The finest wines are still in full blossom, displaying remarkable richness and concentration, but their provenance and history of storage are critical factors when contemplating a purchase.
Price: Frightfully expensive.

Among the four extraordinary vintages of the late forties—1945, 1947, 1948, and 1949—this has always been my favorite. The wines, slightly less massive and alcoholic than the 1947s, also appear to possess greater balance, harmony, and fruit than the 1945s and more complexity than the 1948s. In short, the top wines are magnificent. This is certainly one of the most exceptional vintages of the twentieth century. Only the right bank wines (except for Cheval Blanc) appear inferior to the quality of their 1947s. In the Médoc and Graves it is a terrific vintage, with nearly everyone making wines of astounding ripeness, richness, opulence, power, and length.

The vintage was marked by the extraordinary heat and sunny conditions that Bordeaux enjoyed throughout the summer. Those consumers who have been worried that 1989 and 1990 were too hot to make great wine only need to look at the weather statistics for 1949. It was one of the two hottest vintages (the other being 1947) since 1893, as well as the sunniest vintage since 1893. It was not a totally dry harvest, but the amount of rainfall was virtually identical to that in a year such as 1982. Some of the rain fell before the harvest, which, given the dry, parched condition of the soil, was actually beneficial.

Even the sweet wines of Barsac and Sauternes were exciting. Buying 1949s today will cost an arm and a leg, as these are among the most expensive and sought-after wines of the twentieth century.

THE BEST WINES

St.-Estèphe: Calon-Ségur, Cos d'Estournel, Montrose
Pauillac: Grand-Puy-Lacoste, Latour, Mouton-Rothschild
St.-Julien: Gruaud-Larose, Léoville-Barton, Talbot
Margaux: Palmer
Graves Red: Haut-Brion, La Mission-Haut-Brion, Pape-Clément
Pomerol: La Conseillante, l'Église-Clinet, l'Évangile, Le Gay, Lafleur, Latour à Pomerol,
    Pétrus, Trotanoy, Vieux-Château-Certan
St.-Émilion: Cheval Blanc
Barsac/Sauternes: Climens, Coutet, Yquem

1948–A Quick Study (9-22-48)

St.-Estèphe***	Graves Red****
Pauillac****	Graves White***
St.-Julien****	Pomerol***
Margaux****	St.-Émilion***
Médoc/Haut-Médoc Crus Bourgeois***	Barsac/Sauternes**

Size: An average to below average crop size was harvested.
Important information: A largely ignored, but good to excellent vintage overshadowed by both its predecessor and successor.
Maturity status: The hard and backward characteristics of these wines have served them well during their evolution. Most of the larger, more concentrated 1948s are still attractive wines.
Price: Undervalued given their age and quality.

When Bordeaux has three top vintages in a row it is often the case that one is totally forgotten, and that has certainly proven correct with respect to 1948. It was a very good year that had the misfortune to fall between two legendary vintages.

Because of a difficult flowering due to wet, windy, cool weather in June, the crop size was smaller than in 1947 and 1949. However, July and August were fine months weather-wise, with September exceptionally warm and dry.

Despite the high quality of the wines, they never caught on with claret enthusiasts. And who can fault the wine buyers? The 1947s were more flashy, opulent, alcoholic, and fuller bodied and the 1949s more precocious and richer than the harder, tougher, more tannic, and unforthcoming 1948s.

This is a vintage that in many cases has matured more gracefully than the massive 1947s. The top wines tend to still be in excellent condition. Prices remain reasonable, if only in comparison with what one has to pay for 1947 and 1949.

THE BEST WINES

St.-Estèphe: Cos d'Estournel
Pauillac: Grand-Puy-Lacoste, Latour, Lynch-Bages, Mouton-Rothschild
St.-Julien: Langoa-Barton, Léoville-Barton (the wine of the Médoc)
Margaux: Cantemerle (southern Médoc), Margaux, Palmer
Graves Red: La Mission-Haut-Brion, Pape-Clément
Pomerol: l'Église-Clinet, Le Gay, Lafleur, Latour à Pomerol, Petit-Village, Pétrus, Vieux-Château-Certan
St.-Émilion: Cheval Blanc
Barsac/Sauternes: none

1947—A Quick Study (9-15-47)

St.-Estèphe***	Graves Red****
Pauillac***	Graves White***
St.-Julien***	Pomerol*****
Margaux**	St.-Émilion*****
Médoc/Haut-Médoc Crus Bourgeois*	Barsac/Sauternes***

Size: An abundant crop was harvested.

Important information: A year of extraordinary extremes in quality, with some of the most portlike, concentrated wines ever produced in Bordeaux. This is also a vintage of unexpected failures (such as the Lafite-Rothschild).

Maturity status: Except for the most concentrated and powerful Pomerols and St.-Émilions, this is a vintage that requires immediate consumption, as many wines have gone over the top and are now exhibiting excessive volatile acidity and dried-out fruit.

Price: Preposterously high given the fact that this was another "vintage of the century."

This quintessentially hot-year vintage produced many wines that are among the most enormously concentrated, portlike, intense wines I have ever tasted. Most of the real heavyweights in this vintage have emerged from Pomerol and St.-Émilion. In the Médoc it was a vintage of remarkable irregularity. Properties such as Calon-Ségur and Mouton-Rothschild made great wines, but certain top growths, such as Lafite-Rothschild and Latour, as well as super-seconds such as Léoville-Barton, produced wines with excessive acidity.

The top wines are something to behold if only because of their excessively rich, sweet style, which comes closest in modern-day terms to the 1982s. Yet I know of no 1982 that has the level of extract and intensity of the greatest 1947s.

The reasons for such intensity were the exceptionally hot months of July and August, which were followed (much like in 1982) by a torridly hot, almost tropical heat wave in mid-September just as the harvest began. Those properties that were unable to control the temperatures of hot grapes had stuck fermentations, residual sugar in the wines, and in many cases levels of volatile acidity that would horrify modern-day oenologists. Those who were able to master the tricky vinification made the richest, most opulent red wines Bordeaux has produced during the twentieth century.

THE BEST WINES

St.-Estèphe: Calon-Ségur
Pauillac: Grand-Puy-Lacoste, Mouton-Rothschild
St.-Julien: Ducru-Beaucaillou, Léoville-Las Cases

Margaux: Margaux
Graves Red: Haut-Brion, La Mission-Haut-Brion, La Tour-Haut-Brion
Pomerol: Clinet, La Conseillante, l'Église-Clinet, l'Enclos, l'Évangile, La Fleur-Pétrus,
    Le Gay, Lafleur, Latour à Pomerol, Nenin, Pétrus, Rouget, Vieux-Château-Certan
St.-Émilion: Canon, Cheval Blanc, Figeac, La Gaffelière-Naudes
Barsac/Sauternes: Climens, Suduiraut

1946—A Quick Study (9-30-46)

St.-Estèphe**	Graves Red*
Pauillac**	Graves White 0
St.-Julien**	Pomerol 0
Margaux*	St.-Émilion 0
Médoc/Haut-Médoc Crus Bourgeois 0	Barsac/Sauternes 0

Size: A small crop was harvested.
Important information: The only year in the post–World War II era where the Bordeaux vine-yards were invaded by locusts.
Maturity status: The wines must certainly be over the hill.
Price: Except for the rare bottle of Mouton-Rothschild (needed by billionaires to complete their collections), most of these wines have little value.

A fine, hot summer, particularly in July and August, was spoiled by an unusually wet, windy, cold September that delayed the harvest and caused rampant rot in the vineyards. The 1946s are rarely seen in the marketplace. I have only eleven tasting notes for the entire vintage. I do not know of any top wines, although Edmund Penning-Rowsell claims the 1946 Latour was excellent. I have never seen a bottle.

1945—A Quick Study (9-13-45)

St.-Estèphe****	Graves Red*****
Pauillac*****	Graves White*****
St.-Julien*****	Pomerol*****
Margaux****	St.-Émilion*****
Médoc/Haut-Médoc Crus Bourgeois****	Barsac/Sauternes*****

Size: A tiny crop was harvested.
Important information: The most acclaimed vintage of the century.
Maturity status: Certain wines from this vintage (only those that have been stored impecca-bly) are still not fully mature.
Price: The most expensive clarets of the century.

No vintage in the post–World War II era, not even 1990, 1989, 1982, 1961, 1959, or 1953, enjoys the reputation of the 1945. The celebration of the end of an appallingly destructive war, combined with the fact that the weather was remarkable, produced one of the smallest, most concentrated crops of grapes ever seen. In the late eighties I was fortunate to have had the first-growths on two separate occasions, and there seems to be no doubt that this is in-deed a remarkable vintage that has taken almost 45 years to reach its peak. The great wines, and they are numerous, could well last for another 20–30 years, making a mockery of most of the more recent great vintages, which must be consumed within 25–30 years of the vintage.

The vintage is not without critics, some of whom have said that the wines are excessively tannic and many are drying out. There are wines that match these descriptions, but if one judges a vintage on the performance of the top properties, such as the first-growths, super-seconds, and leading domaines in Pomerol and St.-Émilion, 1945 remains in a class by itself.

The reason for the tiny crop was the notoriously frigid spell during the month of May (*la gelée noire*), which was followed by a summer of exceptional heat and drought. An early harvest began on September 13, the same day that the harvest began in both 1976 and 1982.

THE BEST WINES

St.-Estèphe: Calon-Ségur, Montrose, Les-Ormes-de-Pez

Pauillac: Latour, Mouton-Rothschild, Pichon-Longueville-Comtesse de Lalande, Pontet-Canet

St.-Julien: Gruaud-Larose, Léoville-Barton, Talbot

Margaux: Margaux, Palmer

Graves Red: Haut-Brion, La Mission-Haut-Brion, La Tour-Haut-Brion

Graves White: Laville-Haut-Brion

Pomerol: l'Église-Clinet, La Fleur-Pétrus, Gazin, Lafleur, Latour à Pomerol, Pétrus, Rouget, Trotanoy, Vieux-Château-Certan

St.-Émilion: Canon, Cheval Blanc, Figeac, La Gaffelière-Naudes, Larcis-Ducasse, Magdelaine

Barsac/Sauternes: Suduiraut, Yquem

RATING BORDEAUX'S BEST PRODUCERS OF DRY RED WINES

Note: Where a producer has been assigned a range of stars, * * */* * * * for example, the lower rating has been used for placement in this hierarchy.

* * * * * (OUTSTANDING)

l'Angélus (St.-Émilion)

Ausone (St.-Émilion)

Canon-La-Gaffelière (St.-Émilion)

Cheval Blanc (St.-Émilion)

Clinet (Pomerol)

La Conseillante (Pomerol)

Cos d'Estournel (St.-Estèphe)

Ducru-Beaucaillou (St.-Julien)

l'Église-Clinet (Pomerol)

l'Évangile (Pomerol)

La Fleur de Gay (Pomerol)

La Fleur-Pétrus (Pomerol) (since 1995)

La Gomerie (St.-Émilion)

Grand-Puy-Lacoste (Pauillac)

Gruaud-Larose (St.-Julien)

Haut-Brion (Graves)

Lafite-Rothschild (Pauillac)

Lafleur (Pomerol)

Lagrange (St.-Julien)

Latour (Pauillac)

Léoville-Barton (St. Julien)

Léoville-Las Cases (St.-Julien)

Léoville-Poyferré (St.-Julien)

Lynch-Bages (Pauillac)

Château Margaux (Margaux)

La Mission-Haut-Brion (Graves)

La Mondotte (St.-Émilion)

Montrose (St.-Estèphe)

Mouton-Rothschild (Pauillac)

Palmer (Margaux)

Pétrus (Pomerol)

Pichon-Longueville Baron (Pauillac)

Pichon-Longueville-Comtesse de Lalande (Pauillac)

Le Pin (Pomerol)

Le Tertre-Rôteboeuf (St.-Émilion)

Troplong-Mondot (St.-Émilion)

Trotanoy (Pomerol)

Valandraud (St.-Émilion)

* * * * (EXCELLENT)

l'Arrosée (St.-Émilion)

Barde-Haut (St.-Émilion)

Beau Séjour-Bécot (St.-Émilion)

Beauséjour-Duffau (St.-Émilion)

Bon Pasteur (Pomerol)

Calon-Ségur (St.-Estèphe)

Les Carmes-Haut-Brion (Graves)

Certan de May (Pomerol)

Domaine de Chevalier (Graves)

Clerc-Milon (Pauillac)

Clos l'Église (Pomerol)
Clos de l'Oratoire (St.-Émilion)
La Couspaude (St.-Émilion)
La Dominique (St.-Émilion)
Duhart-Milon-Rothschild (Pauillac)
Faugères (St.-Émilion)
Ferrand-Lartique (St.-Émilion)
de Fieuzal (Graves)
Figeac (St.-Émilion)
Gazin (Pomerol)
Gracia (St.-Émilion)
Grand-Corbin (St.-Émilion)
Grand-Mayne (St.-Émilion)
Haut-Bailly (Graves)
Haut-Marbuzet (St.-Estèphe)
Lafon-Rochet (St.-Estèphe)
La Lagune (Ludon)

Larmande (St.-Émilion)
Latour à Pomerol (Pomerol)
La Louvière (Graves)
Monbousquet (St.-Émilion)
Le Moulin (Pomerol)
Moulin St. Georges (St-Émilion)
Pape-Clément (Graves)
Pavie-Macquin (St.-Émilion)
Pontet-Canet (Pauillac)
Quinault L'Enclos (St.-Émilion)
Rausan-Ségla (Margaux)
Rol Valentin (St.-Émilion)
St. Pierre (St.-Julien)
Smith-Haut-Lafitte (Graves)
Sociando-Mallet (Haut-Médoc)
Talbot (St.-Julien)
Vieux-Château-Certan (Pomerol)

* * * (GOOD)

d'Angludet (Margaux)
d'Armailhac (Pauillac)
Bahans-Haut-Brion (Graves)
Balestard-La-Tonnelle (St.-Émilion)
Batailley (Pauillac)
Beauregard (Pomerol)
Bel-Air (Lalande-de-Pomerol)
Belles-Graves (Lalande-de-Pomerol)
Bertineau St.-Vincent (Lalande-de-
    Pomerol)
Beychevelle (St.-Julien)
Bonalgue (Pomerol)
Le Boscq (Médoc)
Bourgneuf (Pomerol)
Branaire-Ducru (St.-Julien)
Cadet-Piola (St.-Émilion)
Canon (Canon-Fronsac)
Canon (St.-Émilion)
Canon de Brem (Canon-Fronsac)
Canon-Moueix (Canon-Fronsac)
Cantemerle (Macau)
Cantenac-Brown (Margaux)
Cap de Mourlin (St.-Émilion)
Carbonnieux (Graves)
de Carles (Fronsac)
Carruades de Lafite (Pauillac)
Cassagne-Haut-Canon-La Truffière (Canon-
    Fronsac)
Certan-Giraud (Pomerol)
Chantegrive (Graves)
La Chapelle de la Mission (Graves)

Chasse-Spleen (Moulis) ***/****
Chauvin (St.-Émilion)
Citran (Haut-Médoc)
Clos du Clocher (Pomerol)
Clos Dubreuil (St.-Émilion) ***/****
Clos Fourtet (St.-Émilion)
Clos des Jacobins (St.-Émilion)
Clos du Marquis (St.-Julien)
Clos René (Pomerol)
Clos St.-Martin (St.-Émilion) ***/****
La Clotte (St.-Émilion)
Corbin (St.-Émilion)
Corbin-Michotte (St.-Émilion)
Cormeil-Figeac (St.-Émilion)
Cos Labory (St.-Estèphe)
Côte de Baleau (St.-Émilion) ***/****
Coufran (Haut-Médoc)
Château Courrière Rongieras (Lussac-
    St.-Émilion)
Coutelin-Merville (St.-Estèphe)
Couvent des Jacobins (St.-Émilion)
La Croix du Casse (Pomerol)
La Croix de Gay (Pomerol)
La Croix de Cabrie (St.-Émilion)
Croque Michotte (St.-Émilion)
Dalem (Fronsac)
La Dame de Montrose (St.-Estèphe)
Dassault (St.-Émilion)
Daugay (St.-Émilion)
La Dauphine (Fronsac)
Dauzac (Margaux)

Durfort-Vivens (Margaux)

Domaine de l'Église (Pomerol)

l'Enclos (Pomerol)

de Ferrand (St.-Émilion)

La Fleur (St.-Émilion)

La Fleur de Jaugue (St.-Émilion) ***/****

Fongaban (Puisseguin-St.-Émilion)

Fonplégade (St.-Émilion)

Fontenil (Fronsac)

Les Forts de Latour (Pauillac) ***/****

Fourcas-Loubaney (Listrac)

La Gaffelière (St.-Émilion)

La Garde Réserve du Château (Graves)

Le Gay (Pomerol)

Giscours (Margaux)

Gloria (St.-Julien)

Gombaude-Guillot (Pomerol)

Grand-Pontet (St.-Émilion)

Grand-Puy-Ducasse (Pauillac)

Les Grandes Chênes (Médoc)

Grandes-Murailles (St.-Émilion)***/****

La Grave à Pomerol (Trigant de Boisset)
    (Pomerol)

Guillot-Clauzel (Pomerol)

La Gurgue (Margaux)

Haut-Bages-Libéral (Pauillac)

Haut-Batailley (Pauillac)

Haut-Corbin (St.-Émilion)

Haut-Faugères (St.-Émilion)

Haut-Sociondo (Blaye)

L'Hermitage (St.-Émilion) ***/****

Hortevie (St.-Julien)

Château Hostens-Picant (Sainte-Foy)

d'Issan (Margaux) ***/****

Jonqueyrès (Bordeaux Supérieur)

Kirwan (Margaux)

Labégorce-Zédé (Margaux)

Laplagnotte-Bellevue (St.-Émilion)

Lalande-Borie (St.-Julien)

Lanessan (Haut-Médoc)

Langoa-Barton (St.-Julien)

Larrivet-Haut-Brion (Graves)

Lascombes (Margaux)

Lucie (St.-Émilion)

Lusseau (St.-Émilion) ***/****

Magdelaine (St.-Émilion)

Magneau (Graves)

Malescot-St.-Exupéry (Margaux) ***/****

Marquis de Terme (Margaux)

Maucaillou (Moulis)

Mazeris (Canon-Fronsac)

Meyney (St.-Estèphe)

Monbrison (Margaux)

Moulin-Haut-Laroque (Fronsac)

Moulin-Pey-Labrie (Canon-Fronsac)

Moulin Rouge (Haut-Médoc)

Nénin (Pomerol) ***/****

Olivier (Graves)

Les-Ormes-de-Pez (St.-Estèphe)

Les Ormes-Sorbet (Médoc)

Parenchère (Bordeaux Supérieur)

Patache d'Aux (Medoc)

Pavie (St.-Émilion)

Pavie-Decesse (St.-Émilion)

du Pavillon (Canon-Fronsac)

Pavillon Rouge de Margaux (Margaux)

Les Pensées de Lafleur (Pomerol)

Petit-Village (Pomerol)

Pey Labrie (Canon-Fronsac)

Peyredon-Lagravette (Listrac)

de Pez (St.-Estèphe)

Phélan-Ségur (St.-Estèphe)

Picque-Caillou (Graves)

de Pitray (Côtes de Castignon)

Plaisance (Premières Côtes de Bordeaux)

Potensac (Médoc) ***/****

Poujeaux (Moulis)

Prieuré-Lichine (Margaux)

Réserve de la Comtesse (Pauillac)

Roc des Cambes (Côtes de Bourg)

Rochebelle (St.-Émilion)

Rouet (Fronsac)

St.-Pierre (St.-Julien)

La Serre (St.-Émilion)

Siran (Margaux)

Soudars (Haut-Médoc)

Soutard (St.-Émilion)

Tayac (Côtes de Bourg)

Tertre-Daugay (St.-Émilion)

La Tonnelle (Blaye)

La Tour de By (Médoc) ·

La Tour Figeac (St.-Émilion)

La Tour-Haut-Brion (Graves)

Tour Haut-Caussan (Médoc)

Tour du Haut-Moulin (Haut-Médoc)

La Tour du Pin Figeac Moueix (St.-
    Émilion)

La Tour-St. Bonnet (Médoc)

La Tour Seguy (Bourg)

La Tourelles de Longueville (Pauillac)

Trotte Vieille (St.-Émilion)
Veyry (Côtes de Castillon)
La Vieille-Cure (Fronsac)

Vieux Fortin (St.-Émilion)
La Violette (Pomerol)

* * (AVERAGE)

Beaumont (Haut-Médoc)
Bel Air (St.-Émilion)
Belgrave (Haut-Médoc)
Bellegrave (Pomerol)
Boyd-Cantenac (Margaux)
Brane-Cantenac (Margaux)
La Cabanne (Pomerol)
Cadet-Bon (St.-Émilion)
Chambert-Marbuzet (St.-Estèphe)
Clarke (Listrac)
Clos La Madeleine (St.-Émilion)
La Clusière (St.-Émilion)
Cordeillan-Bages (Pauillac)
La Croix (Pomerol)
Croizet-Bages (Pauillac)
Curé-Bon (St.-Émilion)
Destieux (St.-Émilion)
Faurie de Souchard (St.-Émilion)
Ferrière (Margaux)
Feytit-Clinet (Pomerol)
La Fleur Gazin (Pomerol)
La Fleur Pourret (St.-Émilion)
La Fleur St.-Georges (Lalande-de-Pomerol)
Fonbadet (Pauillac)
Fonreaud (Listrac)
Fonroque (St.-Émilion)
Fourcas-Dupré (Listrac)
Fourcas-Hosten (Listrac)
Franc-Mayne (St.-Émilion)
de France (Graves)
Château Gassies (Premières Côtes de
   Bordeaux)
Gressier Grand Poujeaux (Moulis)
Haut-Bages-Averous (Pauillac)
Haut-Bergey (Graves)

Haut-Sarpe (St.-Émilion)
Le Jurat (St.-Émilion)
Lagrange (Pomerol)
Lamarque (Haut-Médoc)
Larcis-Ducasse (St.-Émilion)
Larose-Trintaudon (Haut-Médoc)
Laroze (St.-Émilion)
Larruau (Margaux)
Liversan (Haut-Médoc)
Lynch-Moussas (Pauillac)
Malartic-Lagravière (Graves)
Malescasse (Haut-Médoc)
Marbuzet (St.-Estèphe)
Marjosse (Bordeaux)
Martinens (Margaux)
Mazeyres (Pomerol)
Montviel (Pomerol)
Moulin du Cadet (St.-Émilion)
Pedesclaux (Pauillac)
Petit-Faurie-Soutard (St.-Émilion)
Petit-Figeac (St.-Émilion)
Pibran (Pauillac)
Plince (Pomerol)
Pouget (Margaux)
Puy-Blanquet (St.-Émilion)
Rahoul (Graves)
Rauzan-Gassies (Margaux)
Rocher-Bellevue-Figeac (St.-Émilion)
Rolland-Maillet (St.-Émilion)
de Sales (Pomerol)
Taillefer (Pomerol)
La Tour-Martillac (Graves)
La Tour de Mons (Margaux)
Vieux Clos St.-Émilion (St.-Émilion)
Villemaurine (St.-Émilion)

RATING BORDEAUX'S BEST PRODUCERS OF DRY WHITE WINES

* * * * * (OUTSTANDING)

Domaine de Chevalier (Graves)
de Fieuzal (Graves)
Haut-Brion (Graves)

Laville-Haut-Brion (Graves)
La Louvière (Graves)

* * * * (EXCELLENT)

Carbonnieux (Graves)
Clos Floridene (Graves)
Couhins-Lurton (Graves)
Pape-Clément (Graves)

Pavillon Blanc de Château Margaux
 (Bordeaux)
Smith-Haut-Lafitte (Graves)
La Tour-Martillac (Graves)

* * * (GOOD)

d'Archambeau (Graves)
Bauduc Les Trois Hectares (Bordeaux)
Blanc de Lynch-Bages (Pauillac)
Bouscaut (Graves)
Caillou Blanc de Talbot (Bordeaux)
Carsin (Bordeaux)
Domaine Challon (Bordeaux)
Chantegrive (Graves)
La Closière (Bordeaux)
Château Coucheroy (Pessac-Léognan)
Doisy-Daëne (Bordeaux)
Château Ferbos (Graves)
Ferrande (Graves)
G de Château Guiraud (Bordeaux)
La Garde-Réserve du Château (Graves)
Château Graville-Lacoste (Graves)
Haut-Gardère (Graves)

Larrivet-Haut-Brion (Graves)
Loudenne (Bordeaux)
Malartic-Lagravière (Graves)
Château de Malle (Graves)
Château Millet (Graves)
Numéro 1 (Bordeaux)
Pirou (Graves)
Plaisance (Bordeaux)
Pontac Monplaisir (Graves)
R de Rieussec (Graves)
Rahoul (Graves)
Respide (Graves)
Reynon (Bordeaux)***/****
Château de Rochemorin (Pessac-Léognan)
Roquefort (Bordeaux)
Thieuley (Bordeaux)

* * (AVERAGE)

Aile d'Argent (Bordeaux)
de France (Graves)

Olivier (Graves)

RATING BORDEAUX'S BEST PRODUCERS OF BARSACS/SAUTERNES

* * * * * (OUTSTANDING)

Climens (Barsac)
Coutet-Cuvée Madame (Barsac)
Doisy-Daëne L'Extravagance (Barsac)
Gilette (Sauternes)

Lafaurie-Peyraguey (Sauternes)
Rieussec (Sauternes)
Suduiraut-Cuvée Madame (Sauternes)
d'Yquem (Sauternes)

* * * * (EXCELLENT)

d'Arche-Pugneau (Sauternes)
Coutet (regular cuvée) (Barsac)
Doisy-Dubroca (Barsac)
de Fargues (Sauternes)
Guiraud (Sauternes)

Rabaud-Promis (Sauternes)
Raymond-Lafon (Sauternes)
Suduiraut (Sauternes)****/*****
La Tour Blanche (Sauternes)

* * * (GOOD)

d'Arche (Sauternes)
Bastor-Lamontagne (Sauternes)
Broustet (Barsac)
Caillou (Barsac)

Clos Haut-Peyraguey (Sauternes)
Doisy-Daëne (Barsac)
Doisy-Dubroca (Barsac)
Doisy-Védrines (Barsac)

Filhot (Sauternes)

Haut-Claverie (Sauternes)

Les Justices (Sauternes)

Lamothe (Sauternes)

Lamothe-Despujols (Sauternes)

Lamothe-Guignard (Sauternes)***/****

Liot (Sauternes)

de Malle (Sauternes)

Nairac (Barsac)

Piada (Barsac)

Rabaud-Promis (Sauternes)

Rayne-Vigneau (Sauternes)

Romer du Hayot (Sauternes)

Roumieu-Lacoste (Barsac)

Sigalas Rabaud (Sauternes)

** *(AVERAGE)*

Suau (Barsac)

Myrat (Sauternes)

GETTING A HANDLE ON SECONDARY LABELS

Secondary wines with secondary labels are not a recent development. Léoville-Las Cases first made a second wine (Clos du Marquis) in 1904, and in 1908 Château Margaux produced its first Le Pavillon Rouge du Château Margaux.

Yet a decade ago about the only second labels most Bordeaux wine enthusiasts encountered were those from Latour (Les Forts de Latour), Margaux (Le Pavillon Rouge du Château Margaux), and perhaps that of Lafite-Rothschild (Moulin des Carruades). Today virtually every classified growth, as well as many crus bourgeois and numerous estates in Pomerol and St.-Émilion, has second labels for those batches of wine deemed not sufficiently rich, concentrated, or complete enough to go into their top wine, or grand vin. This has been one of the major developments of the eighties, fostered no doubt by the enormous crop sizes in most of the vintages. A handful of cynics have claimed it is largely done to keep prices high, but such charges are nonsense. The result has generally been far higher quality for a château's best wine. It allows a château to declassify the production from young vines, from vines that overproduce, and from parcels harvested too soon or too late, into a second or perhaps even a third wine that still has some of the quality and character of the château's grand vin.

The gentleman who encouraged most châteaux to develop second wines was the famed oenologist Professor Emile Peynaud. Over the last decade the number of second wines has increased more than tenfold. Some properties, such as Léoville-Las Cases, have even begun to utilize a third label for wines deemed not good enough for the second label!

Of course all this complicates buying decisions for consumers. The wine trade has exacerbated matters by seizing on the opportunity to advertise wine that "tastes like the grand vin" for one-half to one-third the price. In most cases there is little truth to such proclamations. I find that most second wines bear only a vague resemblance to their more esteemed siblings. Most are the product of throwing everything that would normally have been discarded into another label for commercial purposes. Some second wines, such as those of the first-growths, particularly Les Forts de Latour and Bahans-Haut-Brion, are indeed excellent, occasionally outstanding (taste the 1982 Les Forts de Latour or 1989 Bahans-Haut-Brion), and can even resemble the style and character of the grand vin. But the words "caveat emptor" should be etched strongly in the minds of consumers who routinely purchase the second labels of Bordeaux châteaux thinking they are getting something reminiscent of the property's top wine.

In an effort to clarify the situation of second labels, the following chart rates the secondary wines on a 1- to 5-star basis. While I think it is important to underscore the significance that the stricter the selection, the better the top wine, it is also important to remember that most second wines are rarely worth the price asked.

Note: Where a second wine merits purchasing, the vintage is listed.

EXPLANATION OF THE STARS

*****—The finest second wines

****—Very good second wines

***—Pleasant second wines

**—Average-quality second wines

*—Of little interest

SECONDARY LABELS

GRAND VIN SECOND VIN

Andron-Blanquet

St.-Roch**

l'Angélus

Carillon de L'Angélus**

d'Angludet

Domaine Baury**

d'Arche

d'Arche-Lafaurie**

l'Arrosée

Les Côteaux du Château L'Arrosée**

Balestard-La-Tonnelle

Les Tourelles de Balestard**

Bastor-Lamontagne

Les Remparts du Bastor**

Beau Séjour-Bécot

Tournelle des Moines**

Beaumont

Moulin-d'Arvigny*

Beauséjour-Duffau

La Croix de Mazerat**

Belair

Roc-Blanquant*

Beychevelle

Amiral de Beychevelle***

Réserve de l'Amiral***

Bonalgue

Burgrave*

Bouscaut

Valoux**

Branaire-Ducru

Duluc**

Brane-Cantenac

Château Notton**

Domaine de Fontarney**

Broustet

Château de Ségur**

La Cabanne

Compostelle**

Cadet-Piola

Chevaliers de Malta**

Caillou

Petit-Mayne*

Calon-Ségur

Marquis de Ségur**

Canon

Clos J. Kanon**

Canon-La-Gaffelière

Côte Migon-La-Gaffelière**

Cantemerle

Villeneuve de Cantemerle**

Cantenac-Brown

Canuet**

Lamartine**

Carbonnieux

La Tour-Léognan**

Certan-Giraud

Clos du Roy**

Chambert-Marbuzet

MacCarthy**

Chasse-Spleen

L'Ermitage de Chasse-Spleen**

Chauvin

Chauvin Variation*

Cheval Blanc

Le Petit Cheval**

Climens

Les Cyprès de Climens**

Clos Fourtet

Domaine de Martialis**

Clos Haut-Peyraguey

Haut-Bommes**

Clos René

Moulinet-Lasserre**

Columbier-Monpelou

Grand Canyon**

Corbin-Michotte

Les Abeilles**

Cos d'Estournel

Pagodes de Cos***

Couvent-des-Jacobins

Beau-Mayne***

La Croix

Le Gabachot**

Croizet-Bages
Enclos de Moncabon*
Dauzac
Laborde**
Doisy-Védrines
La Tour-Védrines**
La Dominique
Saint-Paul de la Dominique**
Ducru-Beaucaillou
La Croix**
Duhart-Milon-Rothschild
Moulin de Duhart**
Durfort-Vivens
Domaine de Curé-Bourse*
l'Église-Clinet
La Petite l'Église**
de Fieuzal
L'Abeille de Fieuzal**
Figeac
Grangeneuve**
Fonplégade
Château Côtes Trois Moulins**
La Gaffelière
Clos la Gaffelière**
Château de Roquefort**
Giscours
Cantelaude**
Gloria
Haut-Beychevelle Gloria**
Peymartin**
Grand-Mayne
Les Plantes du Mayne**
Grand-Puy-Ducasse
Artigues-Arnaud**
Grand-Puy-Lacoste
Lacoste-Borie**
Gruaud-Larose
Sarget de Gruaud-Larose***
Guiraud
Le Dauphin**
Haut-Bailly
La Parde de Haut-Bailly***
Haut-Batailley
La Tour d'Aspic**
Haut-Brion
Bahans-Haut-Brion***** (1998, 1995,
    1990, 1989, 1988, 1987)
Haut-Marbuzet
Tour de Marbuzet**
d'Issan
Candel**

Labegorcé-Zédé
Château de l'Amiral**
Lafite-Rothschild
Carruades de Lafite**** (1996, 1995,
    1990, 1989)
Lafleur
Les Pensées de Lafleur***** (1990, 1989,
    1988)
Lafon-Rochet
Le Numero 2 de Lafon-Rochet***
Lagrange
Les Fiefs de Lagrange***
La Lagune
Ludon-Pomiès-Agassac**
Lanessan
Domaine de Sainte-Gemme**
Langoa-Barton
Lady Langoa****
Larmande
Château des Templiers**
Lascombes
Segonnes**
La Gombaude**
Latour
Les Forts de Latour***** (1996, 1995,
    1990, 1989, 1982, 1978)
Léoville-Barton
Lady Langoa**** (1989)
Léoville-Las Cases
Clos du Marquis***** (1996, 1995, 1994,
    1990, 1989, 1988, 1986, 1982)
Grand Parc***
Léoville-Poyferré
Moulin-Riche**
La Louvière
L de Louvière****
Coucheray**
Clos du Roi**
Lynch-Bages
Haut-Bages-Averous****
Malescot-St.-Exupéry
de Loyac*
Domaine du Balardin*
de Malle
Château de Sainte-Hélène**
Château Margaux
Pavillon Rouge du Château Margaux****
    (1996, 1995, 1990)
Marquis de Terme
Domaine des Gondats**
Maucaillou

Cap de Haut**
Franc-Caillou**
Meyney
Prieuré de Meyney***
Monbrison
Cordat***
Montrose
La Dame de Montrose**** (1991, 1990)
Palmer
Réserve du Général***
Pape-Clément
Le Clémentin du Pape-Clément***
Phélan-Ségur
Franck Phélan***
Pichon-Longueville Baron
Les Tourelles de Pichon***
Pichon-Longueville-Comtesse de Lalande
Réserve de la Comtesse**** (1997, 1996, 1995)
Pontet-Canet
Les Hauts de Pontet**
Potensac
Gallais-Bellevue**
Lassalle**
Goudy-la-Cardonne**
Poujeaux
La Salle de Poujeaux**
Le Prieuré
Château L'Olivier**
Prieuré-Lichine
Clairefont**
Rabaud-Promis
Domaine de L'Estremade**
Rahoul
Petit Rahoul**
Rausan-Ségla

Lamouroux**
Rieussec
Clos Labère***
St.-Pierre
Clos de Uza**
St.-Louis-le-Bosq**
de Sales
Chantalouette**
Siran
Bellegarde**
St.-Jacques**
Smith-Haut-Lafitte
Les Hauts de Smith-Haut-Lafitte*
Sociando-Mallet
Lartigue de Brochon**
Soutard
Clos de la Tonnelle**
Talbot
Connétable de Talbot***
Tertre-Daugay
Château de Roquefort***
La Tour-Blanche
Mademoiselle de Saint-Marc***
La Tour de By
Moulin de la Roque*
La Roque de By*
Tour Haut-Caussan
La Landotte**
La Tour-Martillac
La Grave-Martillac**
Troplong-Mondot
Mondot***
Valandraud
Virginie de Valandraud***
Vieux Château Certan
Clos de la Gravette***

THE BEST WINE VALUES IN BORDEAUX

(The top estates for under $25 a bottle)

St.-Estèphe   Marbuzet, Meyney, Les-Ormes-de-Pez, Phélan-Ségur, Tronquoy-Lalande
Pauillac   Fonbadet, Grand-Puy-Ducasse, Pibran
St.-Julien   Clos du Marquis, Gloria, Hortevie
Margaux and the Southern Médoc   d'Angludet, La Gurgue, Labégorcé-Zédé
Graves   Bahans-Haut-Brion, La Louvière, Picque-Caillou
Moulis and Listrac   Fourcas-Loubaney, Gressier Grand Poujeaux, Maucaillou, Poujeaux
Médoc and Haut-Médoc   Beaumont, Le Boscq, Lanessan, La Tour-St. Bonnet, Moulin-Rouge, Potensac, Sociando-Mallet, La Tour de By, Tour Haut-Caussan, Tour du Haut-Moulin, Vieux-Robin
Pomerol   Bonalgue, l'Enclos
St.-Émilion   Grand-Mayne, Grand-Pontet, Haut-Corbin, Pavie-Macquin

Fronsac and Canon-Fronsac   Canon de Brem, Canon-Moueix, Cassagne-Haut-Canon-La-Truffière, Dalem, La Dauphine, Fontenil, La Grave, Mazeris, Moulin-Haut-Laroque, Moulin-Pey-Labrie, du Pavillon, Pez-Labrie, Rouet, La Vieille-Cure

Lalande-de-Pomerol   Bel-Air, Bertineau-St.-Vincent, du Chapelain, Grand-Ormeau, Les Hauts-Conseillants, Siaurac

Côtes de Bourg   Brûléscailles, Guerry, Haut-Maco, Mercier, Roc des Cambes, Tayac-Cuvée Prestige

Côtes de Blaye   Bertinerie, Pérenne, La Rose-Bellevue, La Tonnelle

Bordeaux Premières Côtes and Supérieurs   La Croix de Roche, Dudon-Cuvée Jean-Baptiste, Fontenil, Haux Frère, Jonqueyrès, Plaisance, de Plassan, Prieuré-Ste.-Anne, Recougne, Reynon

Côtes de Castillon   Pitray

Barsac/Sauternes   Bastor-Lamontagne, Doisy-Dubroca, Haut-Claverie, de Malle

Loupiac   Bourdon-Loupiac, Clos-Jean, Loupiac-Gaudiet, Ricaud

Entre-Deux-Mers (dry white wines)   Bonnet, Bonnet-Cuvée Réserve, Tertre-Launay, Turcaud

Bordeaux Premières Côtes and Generic Bordeaux (dry white wines)   Alpha, Bauduc-Les Trois-Hectares, Blanc de Lynch-Bages, Caillou Blanc de Talbot, Cayla-Le Grand Vent, Clos-Jean, De La Cloisère du Carpia, Numéro 1-Dourthe, Reynon-Vieilles Vignes, Roquefort-Cuvée Spéciale, Sec de Doisy-Daëne, Thieuley

Buying Bordeaux Wine Futures: The Pitfalls and Pleasures

The purchase of wine, already fraught with pitfalls for consumers, becomes immensely more complex and risky when one enters the wine futures sweepstakes.

On the surface, buying wine futures is nothing more than investing money in a case or cases of wine at a predetermined "future price" long before the wine is bottled and shipped to this country. You invest your money in wine futures on the assumption that the wine will appreciate significantly in price between the time you purchase the future and the time the wine has been bottled and imported to America. Purchasing the right wine, from the right vintage, in the right international financial climate, can represent significant savings. On the other hand, it can be quite disappointing to invest heavily in a wine future only to witness the wine's arrival 12 to 18 months later at a price equal to or below the future price and to discover that the wine is inferior in quality as well.

For years, future offerings have been largely limited to Bordeaux wines, although they are seen occasionally from other regions. In Bordeaux, during the spring following the harvest, the estates or châteaux offer for sale a portion of their crops. The first offering, or *première tranche*, usually offers a good indication of the trade's enthusiasm for the new wine, the prevailing market conditions, and the ultimate price the public will have to spend.

Those brokers and *négociants* who take an early position on a vintage frequently offer portions of their purchases to importers/wholesalers/retailers to make available publicly as a "wine future." These offerings are usually made to the retail shopper during the first spring after the vintage. For example, the 1990 Bordeaux vintage was being offered for sale as a wine future in April 1991. Purchasing wine at this time is not without numerous risks. While 90% of the quality of the wine and the style of the vintage can be ascertained by professionals tasting the wine in its infancy, the increased interest in buying Bordeaux wine futures has led to a soaring number of journalists, some qualified, some not, to judge young Bordeaux wines. The results have been predictable. Many writers serve no purpose other than to hype the vintage as great and have written more glowing accounts of a vintage than the publicity firms doing promotion for the Bordeaux wine industry. Consumers should read numerous points of view from trusted professionals and ask the following questions: 1) Is the professional taster experienced in tasting young as well as old Bordeaux vintages? 2) How much time does the taster actually spend tasting Bordeaux during the year, visiting the properties, and thinking about the vintage? 3) Does the professional taster express his or her viewpoint in an independent, unbiased form, free of trade advertising? 4) Has the professional looked deeply at the weather conditions, harvesting conditions, grape-variety-ripening profiles, and soil types that respond differently depending on the weather scenario?

When wine futures are offered for sale there is generally a great deal of enthusiasm for the newest vintage from both the proprietors and the wine trade. The saying in France that "the greatest wines ever made are the ones that are available for sale" are the words many wine producers and merchants live by. The business of the wine trade is to sell wine, and consumers should be aware that they will no doubt be inundated with claims of "great wines from a great vintage at great prices." This has been used time and time again for good vintages and, in essence, has undermined the credibility of many otherwise responsible retailers, as well as a number of journalists. In contrast, those writers who fail to admit or to recognize greatness where warranted are no less inept and irresponsible.

In short, there are only four valid reasons to buy Bordeaux wine futures:

1. Are you buying top-quality, preferably superb, wine from an excellent, or better yet a great, vintage?

No vintage can be reviewed in black-and-white terms. Even in the greatest vintages there are disappointing appellations as well as mediocre wines. At the same time, vintages that are merely good to very good can produce some superb wines. Knowing who are the underachievers and overachievers is paramount in making a good buying decision. Certainly when one looks at the last 20 years the only irrefutably great vintages have been 1982 for Pomerol, St.-Émilion, St.-Julien, Pauillac, and St.-Estèphe; 1983 for selected St.-Émilions and Pomerols, as well as the wines from Margaux; 1985 for the wines of Graves; 1986 for the northern Médocs from St.-Julien, Pauillac, St.-Estèphe, and the sweet wines from Barsac/Sauternes; 1989 for selected Pomerols, St.-Émilions, St.-Juliens, Pauillacs, and St.-Estèphes; and 1990 for the first-growths and a handful of Pomerols and St.-Émilions. There is no reason to buy wines as futures except for the top performers in a given vintage, because prices generally will not appreciate in the period between the release of the future prices and when the wines are bottled. The exceptions are always the same—top wines and great vintages. If the financial climate is such that the wine will not be at least 25% to 30% more expensive when it arrives in the marketplace, then most purchasers are better off investing their money elsewhere.

Recent history of the 1975 and 1978 Bordeaux future offerings provides a revealing prospectus to futures buyers. Purchasers of 1975 futures have done extremely well. When offered in 1977, the 1975 future prices included $140 to $160 per case for such illustrious wines as Lafite-Rothschild and Latour, and $64 to $80 for second-growths, including such proven thoroughbreds as Léoville-Las Cases, La Lagune, and Ducru-Beaucaillou. By the time these wines had arrived on the market in 1978, the vintage's outstanding and potentially classic quality was an accepted fact, and the first-growths were retailing for $325 to $375 per case; the lesser growths, $112 to $150 per case. Buyers of 1975 futures have continued to prosper, as this vintage is now very scarce and its prices have continued to escalate from $900 to $1,200 a case for first-growths and $350 to $550 for second- through fifth-growths. In 1995 the 1975 prices have come to a standstill because of doubts about how gracefully many of the wines are evolving. I would not be surprised to see some prices even drop—another pitfall that must always be considered.

The 1978 Bordeaux futures, offered in 1980, present a different picture; 1978 was another very good vintage year, with wines similar in style but perhaps less intense than the excellent 1970 vintage. Opening prices for the 1978 Bordeaux were very high and were inflated because of a weak dollar abroad and an excessive demand for the finest French wines. Prices for first-growths were offered at $429 to $499, prices for second- through fifth-growths at $165 to $230. Consumers who invested heavily in Bordeaux have purchased good wine, but when the wines arrived on the market in spring 1981, the retail prices for these wines were virtually the same as future price offerings. Thus consumers who purchased 1978 futures and invested their money to the tune of 100% of the case price could have easily obtained a better return simply by investing in any interest-bearing account.

With respect to the vintages 1979, 1980, 1981, 1982, 1983, and 1985, the only year that has represented a great buy from a futures perspective was 1982. Because it was of mediocre quality, 1980 was not offered to the consumer as a wine future. As for the 1979 and 1981, the enthusiast who purchased these wines on a future basis no doubt was able, within 2 years of putting up his or her money, to buy the wines when they arrived in America at approximately the same price. While this was not true for some of the highly rated 1981s, it was true for the 1979s. As for the 1982s, they have jumped in price at an unbelievable pace, outdistancing any vintage in the last 20 years. The first-growths of 1982 were offered to consumers in late spring 1983 at prices of $350 to $450 for wines like Lafite-Rothschild, Latour, Mouton-Rothschild, Haut-Brion, and Cheval Blanc. By March 1985 the Cheval Blanc had jumped to $650–$800, the Mouton to $800–$1,000, and the rest to $700. Today, prices for 1982 first-growths range from a low of $2,000 a case for Haut-Brion to $3,000–$5,000 a case for any of the three Pauillac first-growths.

This is a significant price increase for wines so young, but it reflects the insatiable world-wide demand for a great vintage. Rare, limited-production wines like the Pomerols have sky-rocketed in price. Pétrus has clearly been the top performer in terms of increasing in price; it jumped from an April 1983 future price of $600 to a 1991 price of $10,000. This is absurd given the fact that the wines will not be close to maturity for a decade. Other top 1982 Pomerols such as Trotanoy, Certan de May, and l'Évangile have quadrupled in price. Trotanoy, originally available for $280, now sells (when you can find it) for at least $3,000. Certan de May has jumped from $180 to $3,000, and l'Évangile from $180 to $3,000.

The huge demand for 1982 Bordeaux futures and the tremendous publicity surrounding this vintage have led many to assume that subsequent years would similarly escalate in price. That has not happened, largely because Bordeaux has had too many high-quality, abundant vintages in the decade of the eighties. The only exceptions have been the 1986 first-growths, which continue to accelerate because it is a great, long-lived, so-called clas-sic year.

2. Do the prices you must pay look good enough that you will ultimately save money by paying less for the wine as a future than for the wine when it is released in 2 to 3 years?

Many factors must be taken into consideration to make this determination. In certain years Bordeaux may release its wines at lower prices than it did the previous year (the most recent examples are 1986 and 1990). There is also the question of the international marketplace. In 1995 the American dollar is weak. Other significant Bordeaux-buying countries, such as England, have unsettled and troublesome financial problems as well. France's economy is stable but fragile. Newer marketplaces, such as Japan, are experiencing financial apprehen-sion and increasing banking problems. Even Germany, which has become such a major Bor-deaux player, has experienced an economic downspin because of the financial ramifications of trying to revitalize the moribund economy of East Germany. Three countries that appear to have sound economies and are in a healthy enough economic position to afford top-class Bordeaux are Belgium, Denmark, and Switzerland. These factors change, but the interna-tional marketplace, the perceived reputation of a given vintage, and the rarity of a particular estate all must be considered in determining whether the wine will become much more ex-pensive when released than its price when offered as a wine future. There are not likely to be many American wine buyers of 1994 Bordeaux futures, even though this is a successful year.

3. Do you want a guarantee of getting top, hard-to-find wine from a producer with a great reputation who makes only small quantities of wine?

Even if the vintage is not irrefutably great, or you cannot be assured that prices will increase, there are always a handful of small estates, particularly in Pomerol and St.-Émilion, that produce such limited quantities of wine, and who have worldwide followers, that their wines warrant buying as a future if only to reserve your case from an estate whose wines have pleased you in the past. In Pomerol, limited-production wines such as Le Pin, Clinet, La Conseillante, l'Évangile, Le Fleur de Gay, Lafleur, Gombaud-Guillot, and Bon Pasteur have produced many popular wines during the decade of the eighties yet are very hard to find in the marketplace. In St.-Émilion some of the less renowned yet modestly sized estates such as l'Angélus, l'Arrosée, Canon, Grand-Mayne, Pavie-Macquin, La Dominique, Le Tertre-Rôteboeuf, and Troplong-Mondot produce wines that are not easy to find after bottling. Consequently their admirers throughout the world frequently reserve and pay for these wines as futures. Limited-production wines from high-quality estates merit buying futures even in good to very good years.

4. Do you want to buy wine in half-bottles, magnums, double magnums, jeroboams, or imperials? Frequently overlooked as one of the advantages of buying wine futures is the fact that you can request that your merchant have the wines bottled to your specifications. There is always a surcharge for such bottlings, but if you have children born in a certain year, or you want the luxury of buying half-bottles (a size that makes sense for daily drinking), the only time to do this is when buying the wine as a future.

Last, should you decide to enter the futures market, be sure you know the other risks involved. The merchant you deal with could go bankrupt, and your unsecured sales slip would make you one of probably hundreds of unsecured creditors of the bankrupt wine merchant hoping for a few cents on your investment. Another risk is that the supplier the merchant deals with could go bankrupt or be fraudulent. You may get a refund from the wine merchant, but you will not get your wine. Therefore be sure to deal only with a wine merchant who has dealt in selling wine futures before and one who is financially solvent. Finally, buy wine futures only from a wine merchant who has received confirmed commitments as to the quantities of wine he or she will receive. Some merchants sell Bordeaux futures to consumers before they have received commitments from suppliers. Be sure to ask for proof of the merchant's allocations. If you do not, then the words "caveat emptor" could have special significance to you.

For many Bordeaux wine enthusiasts, buying wine futures of the right wine, in the right vintage, at the right time, guarantees that they have liquid gems worth four or five times the price they paid. However, as history has proven, only a handful of vintages over the last 20 years have appreciated that significantly in their first 2 or 3 years (for example, 1982, 1989, and 1990). The fact that Bordeaux has had four consecutive vintages that have been plagued by rain at the harvest (1991, 1992, 1993, and 1994) for the first time since the early seventies has eliminated the need to buy wine futures, although the finest 1994s merit interest. The 1990s merited considerable attention from serious Bordeaux collectors, since many of the wines are extraordinary. However, prices for the top wines had more than doubled at the time of writing in summer 1995, with demand seemingly insatiable.

For the next several years consumers should be looking back to bargains that exist from inventories of already bottled Bordeaux, rather than investing their money in wine futures, which, at the time of writing, makes no sense except for a rare case where a parent may desire to buy a child's birth-year wine in large-format bottles such as magnums or double magnums.

L'ANGÉLUS (ST.-ÉMILION)

1998	EE	(90–92)
1997	EE	(88–91)

1996		EE	91+
1995		EE	95

Now that Angélus is a premier grand cru classé, I detect a subtle shift in style to a more civilized, graceful wine without the power and intensity of vintages such as 1988, 1989, and 1990. If so, the 1998 is an excellent prototype for the new-breed Angélus. The color is a saturated dark purple, and the bouquet reveals telltale aromas of minerals, black cherries, cassis, dried herbs, new saddle leather, and vanillin. Medium bodied and rich, with excellent concentration, superb purity, and a structured, spicy, moderately oaked finish, this beautifully made Angélus combines richness with elegance. This wine will require 4–5 years of cellaring because of the aggressive tannin in the finish. Anticipated maturity: 2005–2018.

Since 1988 a persuasive argument can be made that no other St.-Émilion has been as consistently brilliant as Angélus. Even in such difficult vintages as 1992 and 1993 Angélus produced wines of significant merit. In 1997 this estate's harvest began on September 12 and finished on October 10. The final blend is 60% Merlot and 40% Cabernet Franc. The 1997 Angélus reveals a saturated purple/black color. The nose offers up aromas of sweet blackberry and truffle-scented fruit with a notion of Provençal olives and toasty, smoky oak. Surprisingly powerful for the vintage, with moderate tannin, medium to full body, and excellent depth, this wine should merit an outstanding score after bottling (no fining or filtration is performed at this estate). Anticipated maturity: 2002–2016.

A massive, powerful Angélus, the 1996 exhibits a saturated black/ruby/purple color as well as an impressively endowed nose of dried herbs, roasted meats, new saddle leather, plum liqueur, and cassis. In the mouth, olive notes make an impression. This sweet, full-bodied, exceptionally concentrated wine is atypically backward and ferociously tannic. It was revealing more sweetness and forwardness immediately prior to bottling, but I would now recommend 7–8 years of cellaring. Anticipated maturity: 2007–2025.

A superb effort in this vintage, Angélus's opaque purple-colored 1995 is a massive, powerful, rich offering with plenty of ripe, sweet tannin. The wine's aromatics include scents of Provençal olives, jammy black cherries, blackberries, truffles, and toast. A very full-bodied wine, it is layered, thick, and pure. This is the most concentrated of the 1995 St.-Émilion premiers grands crus. Anticipated maturity: 2002–2025.

Past Glories: 1994 (92), 1993 (92), 1990 (96), 1989 (96), 1988 (91).

D'ANGLUDET (MARGAUX)

1997		C	(87–89)
1996		C	88
1995		C	88

In the 20 years I have been writing about wine, I do not remember a 12-month period like 1998, where so many prominent people in the world of wine passed away. Sadly, Peter Sichel, the highly competent proprietor of d'Angludet, must be added to the long list of well-known winemakers/proprietors who died in 1998. Sichel's last vintage, 1997, promises to be exciting, as he fashioned one of the finest wines of the vintage. The 1997 performed freakishly well in my tastings. It reveals a deep purple color and gobs of chewy, fat, blackberry and mocha-tinged cherry fruit. An opulent 1997, it possesses superb fruit purity, medium to full body, low acidity, and a seductive, fleshy personality. Anticipated maturity: now–2012.

D'Angludet's 1996 is as fine from bottle as it was from cask. The wine is deeply colored, with a ripe, cassis-and-blackberry-scented nose, with subtle notions of licorice and melted road tar. There is excellent richness, medium body, and moderate tannin in the jammy, rich finish. It should age nicely. Anticipated maturity: 2002–2015. Both the 1997 and 1996 are sleepers of the vintage.

In contrast with the powerful, tannic 1996, the 1995 is a silky, supple, charming, forthcoming wine that is well above its cru bourgeois classification. The color is a healthy saturated deep ruby/purple, and the wine offers up gobs of jammy black fruits intermixed with subtle herbs, spice, and toast. In the mouth, the wine displays excellent richness, a layered, medium-bodied personality, well-disguised tannin and acidity, and a hedonistic mouth-feel. Anticipated maturity: now–2010. A sleeper of the vintage.

D'ARMAILHAC (PAUILLAC)

1997	D	(87–89)
1996	D	87
1995	D	89

The 1997 is a blend of 58% Cabernet Sauvignon, 23% Merlot, and 19% Cabernet Franc. This excellent, dense purple-colored wine offers moderate tannin, plenty of juicy cassis fruit, low acidity, and a plump, silky-textured finish. An opulent wine, it should be a real crowd pleaser upon its release later this year. Anticipated maturity: now–2010.

Both the 1995 and 1996 showed exceptionally well, with the 1995 possibly the finest d'Armailhac I have yet tasted. The 1996 is just as successful as the seductive 1995. The 1996's saturated ruby color is followed by sweet, roasted herb, and black currant aromas with lush toasty oak notes. A blend of 45% Cabernet Sauvignon, 30% Merlot, and 25% Cabernet Franc, this medium-weight, elegant, yet richly fruity wine possesses enough tannin to last 2 decades, but it will be one 1996 Médoc that will be drinkable at an early age. Anticipated maturity: 2004–2018.

To reiterate, the 1995 may be the best d'Armailhac ever produced. The blend was 50% Cabernet Sauvignon, 18% Cabernet Franc, and 32% Merlot. This deep ruby/purple-colored wine possesses low acidity, plenty of sweet tannin, and, in both its aromatics and flavors, gobs of ripe cassis fruit nicely framed by the judicious use of toasty oak. Flavorful, round, generous, and hedonistic, this is a crowd pleaser! Anticipated maturity: now–2012.

L'ARROSÉE (ST.-ÉMILION)

1998	E	(87–89)
1997	E	(86–87)
1996	E	87+?
1995	E	90

An understated, dark ruby-colored wine with aromas of framboise, black cherries, and high-quality toasty new oak, the 1998 l'Arrosée is not a massive St.-Émilion. Restrained and harmonious, this medium-bodied, nuanced, rich, yet backward wine should turn out to be impressive, but patience will be required. There is good sweetness on the attack and mid-palate, but the wine becomes compressed. Anticipated maturity: 2003–2015.

The 1997 l'Arrosée offers sweet plum, cherry fruit in addition to high-quality *pain grillé* scents. This elegant, soft, medium-bodied wine has a sweet entry but finishes with dry tannin. There is also an abrupt finish. It should turn out to be a good to very good l'Arrosée, albeit slightly angular. Anticipated maturity: 2001–2010.

A tightly knit, closed wine, the 1996 l'Arrosée has not yet begun to put on weight or reveal its true character. It possesses a medium dark ruby color and muted aromatics, which, with airing, offer notes of dusty minerals mixed with black cherries and raspberries. Subtle high-quality toasty oak makes an appearance along with black raspberry and cherry fruit. This firmly knit, sinewy, austere, elegant wine displays some positive potential, but I would appear to have overrated it based on cask tastings. Anticipated maturity: 2004–2016.

With a medium dark ruby color and a complex, kirsch, *pain grillé*, smoky, deliciously complex and fruity nose, the fragrant 1995 offers a wealth of raspberry, currant, and cherry-like fruit. It is not a blockbuster but, rather, an elegant, multidimensional, round, velvety-textured wine with a lushness and sweetness of fruit that makes it irresistible. This is one of the more seductive wines of the vintage. Anticipated maturity: now–2012.

Past Glories: 1990 (93), 1986 (92), 1985 (93), 1982 (93), 1961 (94).

AUSONE (ST.-ÉMILION)

1998	EEE	(91–93+)
1997	EEE	(91–92+)
1996	EEE	93+
1995	EEE	93

You should not contemplate purchasing the 1998 Ausone unless you are willing to cellar it for at least 10–15 years. An extremely saturated black/purple color is followed by aromas of minerals, black fruits, and flowers. It is ferociously tannic but gorgeously extracted, with outstanding purity and an old-vine intensity that kicks in on the midpalate and continues through the wine's finish. Backward, rich, and massive for Ausone, it requires considerable bottle age. Anticipated maturity: 2012–2040. To be purchased for your children and/or grandchildren!

An impressively extracted wine, the 1997 was revealing copious black currant fruit in addition to floral and toasty smells. The color is a saturated dark ruby/purple, and the wine is ripe with low acidity as well as high tannin. Very rich for the vintage, with a pronounced sweet midpalate, it appears to have considerable promise. Anticipated maturity: 2007–2025.

Proprietor Alain Vauthier continues to build on the quality of Ausone, since he is now in sole control of this famous property strategically situated on the limestone hillsides of the village of St.-Émilion. Vauthier has reduced yields, begun to harvest more mature fruit, and believes malolactic fermentation should be done in small barrels as opposed to tank. The results are wines that are even more expressive of this extraordinary *terroir*, yet richer and more intriguing aromatically. Those who have suggested that Ausone has lost its soul seem to be ignoring the taste of the 1995 and 1996, serving instead as the obedient parrots of the old guard in St.-Émilion who prefer to turn back the clock half a century, when this property was producing far too many dried-out, fruitless, hollow wines.

I do not understand the critics of Alain Vauthier, who is taking the estate's quality to a higher level. Moreover, the wine is much more consistent, with greater depth and richness on the midpalate, without sacrificing Ausone's 40–50+ years of longevity. As I suspected, the 1996 is beginning to shut down. I left it in the glass for nearly 30 minutes and was impressed with the nuances that developed. The color is a dense ruby/black/purple. Reluctant aromas of blueberries, blackberries, minerals, flowers, truffles, and subtle new oak eventually emerge. Elegant on the attack, with sweet ripeness and a delicate, concentrated richness, this wine offers subtlety rather than flamboyance. A sweet midpalate sets it apart from many of the uninspiring Ausones of the eighties and seventies. The wine is stylish and presently understated, with tremendous aging potential. Anticipated maturity: 2008–2040.

The 1995 will be remembered as a historic vintage for Ausone. It is the first year where, after more than a decade of infighting among the owners, Alain Vauthier emerged as the sole proprietor and thus had complete control of the wine's viticulture, vinification, and upbringing. Ausone's extraordinary minerality is present in the 1995, yet there are more aromatics, a richer, more multidimensional palate impression, and a fuller texture—all with the *terroir* brilliantly expressed. The wine boasts a dense ruby/purple color and an emerging but tightly knit nose of spring flowers, minerals, earth, and black fruits. Rich, with an opulent texture and surprising sexiness for a young vintage of Ausone, the medium-bodied 1995 displays exquisite balance among its acid, tannin, alcohol, and fruit. Although it is not yet seamless, all the elements are present for an extraordinary evolution in the bottle. Given its backward style, this wine will require 5–7 years of cellaring and will age at a glacial pace for 30–40 years. Anticipated maturity: 2003–2045.

Past Glories: 1990 (92+), 1988 (91), 1983 (94), 1982 (95+), 1929 (96), 1921 (92), 1900 (94), 1874 (96).

BAHANS-HAUT-BRION (PESSAC LÉOGNAN)

1997	D	(86–87)
1996	D	88
1995	D	89

One of the finest second wines being made in Bordeaux is Haut-Brion's Bahans-Haut-Brion. I have drunk several cases of the remarkable 1989, and I believe the 1995 and 1996 both merit consumer interest. The 1996 Bahans-Haut-Brion showed every bit as well as it did prior to bottling, which makes me think my score for its bigger sister is going to move up considerably after the wine has had a year or so of bottle age. The 1996 Bahans-Haut-Brion is an atypically powerful, rich, tobacco- and black fruit-scented wine that is much less forward than normal, but rich, with a nose that is unmistakably Haut-Brion-like. It reveals roasted herbs, scorched earth, and sweet black fruits in both its aromas and flavors. This tannic, structured Bahans will be at its finest between 2002 and 2012. The 1995 is an aromatic, round, complex, elegant wine that possesses all the characteristics of its bigger, richer sibling, but less depth and more immediate appeal. Very "Graves" with its smoky, roasted nose and sweet, smoke-infused black cherry and currant fruit, it should drink well for a decade.

The 1997 Bahans-Haut-Brion exhibits a dark ruby color as well as a subtle mineral, tobacco, earthy, black plum-and-currant-scented nose. Light tannin is present in the finish, but this is an up-front, hedonistic wine to drink during its first 7–8 years of life.

Past Glories: 1989 (90).

BALESTARD (BORDEAUX)

1997	B	(86–87)

An excellent generic Bordeaux made with the help of Valandraud's Jean-Luc Thunevin, this smoky, surprisingly rich, creamy-textured wine displays intense notes of cherry jam, plum-like fruit, and spicy new oak. It is a tasty example of Bordeaux to enjoy over the next 3–4 years.

BALESTARD-LA-TONNELLE (ST.-ÉMILION)

1997	C	(79–82)
1996	C	83

The 1997 reveals tannin in addition to a compressed, one-dimensional personality, without enough sweetness, glycerin, or fruit to stand up to the wine's structure.

The 1996 exhibits an evolved ruby/garnet color, a spicy, earthy, dried herb-scented nose, medium body, and a nearly mature personality with sweet cherry fruit in the finish. Drink it over the next 5–6 years.

BARDE-HAUT (ST.-ÉMILION)

1998	E	(86–87)
1997	E	(90–92)

Barde-Haut's marvelous 1997 is more complete and better balanced than the 1998. On the three occasions I tasted the 1998, the tannins were aggressive and the finish shorter than expected. The wine is at least very good and may be even better with further evolution. The impressive ruby/purple color is followed by an elegant wine revealing sweet black cherry fruit, spice, and oaky characteristics. This finesse-style Barde-Haut possesses less fat and succulence than the 1997. Anticipated maturity: now–2010.

The impressive 1997, made by Dominique Philippe, emerges from a vineyard close to Troplong-Mondot. In 1997 Michel Rolland, Bordeaux's most influential oenologist, was brought in to push the level of quality even higher. The result is a splendidly rich, sexy St.-Émilion that deserves considerable attention. As it begins its last months in barrel before being bottled, it is a sleeper of the vintage and a stunning new name in the St.-Émilion firmament. The wine boasts a saturated black/purple color in addition to a sumptuous bouquet of blackberries, cassis, licorice, and *pain grillé*. It is fleshy, medium to full bodied, with low acidity, gorgeously pure fruit, and a silky, long finish. What an impressive debut performance from this up-and-coming star. Anticipated maturity: 2001–2012. An amazing wine!

BATAILLEY (PAUILLAC)

1997	C	(83–85)
1996	C	87
1995	C	87

This estate has been fashioning better wines over recent years—consumers take note.

The 1997 reveals black currant fruit as well as a touch of cedar, tobacco, and earth in the nose. There is some structure, but this wine is more evolved and softer than the 1996. This medium-bodied effort should drink well during its first decade of life.

Batailley's 1996 is a well-structured, old-style Pauillac with a dense ruby/purple color, earthy, cedar-tinged, black currant fruit in the aromatics and flavors, medium body, an excellent midpalate, good depth, and a moderately tannic, firm, but pure finish. This very good to excellent Batailley will keep for 2 decades. Anticipated maturity: 2003–2020.

The 1995 has turned out well, displaying a dark ruby/purple color and aromas of minerals, black currants, and smoky new oak. In the mouth, it is a medium-weight, backward, well-delineated Pauillac with plenty of tannin and a true *vin de garde* style. Anticipated maturity: 2002–2015.

BEAU-SÉJOUR BÉCOT (ST.-ÉMILION)

1998	D	(91–93)
1997	D	(87–88)
1996	D	89
1995	D	89

The 1998's ostentatious, nearly over-the-top style will have its detractors, but if wine is a beverage of pleasure, Beau-Séjour Bécot delivers the goods. The color is a saturated ruby/purple. The wine is lavishly oaked, jammy, and rich, with oodles of glycerin and extract, medium to full body, and moderately aggressive tannin in the blockbuster finish. This concentrated, rich offering will become more civilized with 3–5 years of cellaring. Anticipated maturity: 2003–2017.

Although similarly styled to the 1996, Beau-Séjour Bécot's 1997 is lower in acidity, with a more evolved dark ruby color and a big, fleshy, toasty nose with scents of cherry jam and smoky oak. Medium bodied, lush, and easy to drink and understand, this wine will need to be consumed during its first 8–9 years of life.

The lavishly oaked, hedonistically styled 1996 exhibits a dark plum/purple color. The nose offers up sweet jammy fruit (primarily black currants and cherries) intermixed with toasty new oak. Medium bodied, with excellent, nearly outstanding, richness, a nicely layered midpalate, and sweet tannin in the long finish, it needs 2–3 years of bottle age and should last for 15+ years.

Beau-Séjour Bécot's sexy 1995 offers a dark plum color, followed by a sweet, vanillin, spicy, black cherry, and curranty nose that jumps from the glass. In the mouth, this is a supple, round, hedonistically styled claret with copious quantities of palate-pleasing plushness, no hard edges, and an impressively endowed, rich finish. Although the wine is accessible, I recommend another 1–2 years in the bottle. Anticipated maturity: 2000–2014.

BEAUSOLEIL (POMEROL)

1998	D	(85–87)
1997	D	(86–87)
1996	D	(85–86?)
1995	D	87

Lavish new oak, jammy black cherries, smoke, roasted herbs, and licorice notes are followed by a lovely, ripe, medium-bodied 1998 Beausoleil. It is slightly disjointed but well made and impressively extracted. Anticipated maturity: 2002–2012.

The 1997 Beausoleil reveals a dense ruby/plum color and a sweet, ripe nose of black raspberries, cherries, and spice. Attractive on the attack, with layers of fruit, medium body, low acidity, and light to moderate tannin in the oaky finish, this wine should turn out to be very good. Anticipated maturity: 2001–2010.

The 1996 appears to be at an awkward stage, with the oak dominating its personality. Additionally, the tannin is dry. However, there is a healthy, saturated ruby/purple color, good weight, and plenty of structure and richness. The wood must become better integrated if this wine is to achieve harmony among its diverse component parts. Judgment reserved.

The 1995 is a deep ruby/purple-colored wine with a cassis liqueur nose that soars from the glass. This deep, medium- to full-bodied, richly fruity, dense, concentrated Pomerol is a sleeper of the vintage. Anticipated maturity: now–2007.

BEAUREGARD (POMEROL)

1998	D	(86–88)
1997	D	(85–86)
1996	D	87
1995	D	87

A powerful but rough-hewn wine, the deep ruby/purple-colored 1998 Beauregard reveals copious quantities of toasty oak, medium body, fine ripeness, and some elegance. However, it possesses a jagged texture, and the oak and tannin are not as well integrated as in other wines from this appellation. Nevertheless, there is plenty to like—depth, intensity, and size. If it all comes together, this effort will merit a score in the upper 80s. Anticipated maturity: 2002–2015.

The 1997 exhibits a dark ruby color, toasty new oak, fine ripeness, attractive spicy aromatics, and lovely fruit. Although not complex, it is a medium-bodied, satisfying Pomerol with 6–7 years of aging potential.

Beauregard's deep ruby-colored 1996 reveals a sweet, jammy cherry-scented nose with noticeable strawberry notes. The wine is medium bodied, soft, elegant, and moderately weighty, with hints of toasty new oak. It should drink well for 6–8 years.

An excellent wine, the 1995 offers an alluring deep ruby color with a smoky, vanillin, berry, chocolatey nose. Medium bodied and ripe, with sweet fruit, moderate tannin, and low acidity, this is a fine example of Beauregard. Anticipated maturity: now–2010.

BEAUSÉJOUR-DUFFAU (ST.-ÉMILION)

1998	E	(91–93)
1997	E	(87–89)
1996	E	87?
1995	E	?

The finest wine made at this estate since the perfect 1990, Beauséjour-Duffau's black/purple-colored 1998 exhibits a gorgeous concoction of blackberry, violet, and blueberry aromas with notes of minerals and sweet oak. It has power and depth, but remarkable symmetry, an impressive sweet midpalate, and an old-vine intensity in the finish. This beauty is impressively nuanced and textured. Anticipated maturity: 2002–2020.

The dark purple-colored 1997 exhibits mineral and black raspberry notes intermixed with earth and licorice. Long and rich, with nobility and class to its fruit, this *vin de garde* has plenty of substance and high tannin, but the tannin is sweet and better integrated than in the 1996. Anticipated maturity: 2008–2018.

It appears that I overestimated the quality of the 1996 Beauséjour-Duffau. I was able to taste it only once out of bottle, but it seemed to have very little of the multidimensional concentration and intensity I had indicated from cask. The wine is dark ruby colored, with the telltale attractive black raspberry, pronounced mineral characteristics this small vineyard produces. The wine was lighter and more angular than in cask tastings, with dry, astringent tannin in the moderately long finish. This wine is very good, but it is not outstanding, as I had expected it to be. Moreover, the 1996 Beauséjour-Duffau will have a tendency to dry out given the way the tannin is behaving. Anticipated maturity: 2005–2015.

On numerous occasions the 1995 was gorgeous from cask, exhibiting a saturated dark purple color and a sweet kirsch, black cherry, mineral, and trufflelike character not dissimilar from the old-vine intensity found in the great Pomerol, Lafleur. However, the wine was totally closed, with earth, minerals, and black fruits emerging after extended airing. In the mouth, the wine was completely shut down, with extremely high levels of tannin. I was able to taste it only once, so I am reserving judgment until it can be retasted.
Past Glories: 1990 (100).

BEL-AIR-LA-ROYÈRE (CÔTES DE BLAYE)

1997	B	(85–86)

A serious "little" wine made with the consulting assistance of Valandraud's Jean-Luc Thunevin, this 1997 boasts an opaque ruby/purple color, excellent ripeness, a straightforward character, good fruit, and fine length. Drink it over the next 4–5 years.

BEL AIR (ST.-ÉMILION)

1997	D	(86–87)
1996	D	83?
1995	D	85

Winemaker Pascal Delbeck appears to have produced an atypically soft, forward, appealing 1997 that will not take long to come around. A dark ruby color is followed by aromas of sweet, mineral-infused, black cherry fruit, medium body, and light tannin in the round, attractive finish. This wine requires 2–3 years of cellaring and should keep for 10–12 years.

Tasted on three separate occasions, the 1996 did not perform well. An angular, light-bodied, mineral-scented wine came across as austere and spartan, lacking fruit, glycerin, and flesh. Perhaps I caught it in an awkward stage, since it performed far better earlier in the year. Anticipated maturity: 2003–2012.

The 1995 is a low-key claret with red and black currants competing with distinctive wet stone and mineral-like components. New oak is present in this medium-bodied, hard, austere, yet extraordinarily subtle and restrained St.-Émilion. It may be too polite for its own good. Anticipated maturity: 2002–2015.

BELLEFONT-BELCIER (CÔTES DE CASTILLON)

1997	C	(78–80)
1996	C	87

The excellent 1996, made by François Mitjaville's son, is a potential sleeper of the vintage. The wine offers a dark ruby color and sweet black cherry fruit intermixed with smoke, dried herbs, and toast. This round, generous, medium- to full-bodied wine is already delicious; enjoy it over the next 7–8 years. The lighter-bodied 1997 is less complex and concentrated. What could have happened between these two vintages?

BELLEGRAVE (POMEROL)

1998	D	(85–87)
1997	D	(80–83)
1996	D	84

The saturated dense ruby color of the 1998 Bellegrave is followed by aromas of high-class toasty oak and fat, concentrated flavors. While this wine does not yet reveal much complexity, it is concentrated, with excellent purity, a savory mouth-feel, and moderate tannin. Anticipated maturity: 2000–2010.

The 1997 exhibits a dark ruby color, spicy new oak, a fresh, lively bouquet, medium body, and soft tannin in the short, diluted finish. Drink it over the next 4–5 years.

An open-knit, soft, smoky, black cherry-scented wine with spicy oak in the background, the pure, pleasant, light-bodied 1996 is ideal for drinking over the next 2–5 years.

BERLIQUET (ST.-ÉMILION)

1998	D	(87–88)
1997	D	(87–89)

Patrick Valette has resurrected this once moribund estate. The 1997 was one of the vintage's sleepers and, to my taste, slightly richer and better balanced than the more tannic 1998. However, the 1998 is very fine, exhibiting a saturated dark ruby/purple color and a sweet nose of jammy blackberries/cherries, grilled meats, and dried herbs. Medium bodied, moderately tannic, stylish, and well made, this is an attractive St.-Émilion. Anticipated maturity: 2002–2012.

The finest Berliquet I have ever tasted, the saturated dark purple-colored 1997 offers a sweet black currant-and-cherry-scented nose, medium to full body, excellent purity, a layered, multidimensional personality, and a fine finish with no hard edges. A sleeper of the vintage, it will drink well between now and 2012.

LA BERNADOTTE (HAUT-MÉDOC)

1997	C	(85–87)
1996	C	85?

This property was acquired by Madame de Lenquesaing, and beginning in 1997, the wine is being vinified by the team from Pichon-Lalande. Both vintages are blends of 60% Cabernet Sauvignon and 40% Merlot. The interesting 1997 exhibits a Pauillac-like cedary, leafy tobacco, black currant fruitiness. Soft and round, with low acidity, elegance, and fine length, it should be consumed over the next 6–7 years.

The 1996 was not vinified but was bottled by the staff of Pichon-Lalande. It possesses a medium ruby color, plum, black currant, and dried herb scents and flavors, with dry tannin in the finish. Nevertheless, this is a well-made, delicate Bordeaux that should drink well for 5–6 years.

BERTINEAU ST. VINCENT (LALANDE DE POMEROL)

1997	B	(85–86)

An attractive, open-knit, luscious, moderately ruby-colored wine, this 1997 offers plenty of jammy cherry fruit. An uncomplicated, savory, supple-textured wine, it will offer ideal drinking for 3–5 years after its release.

BEYCHEVELLE (ST.-JULIEN)

1998	D	(87–89)
1997	D	(78–79)
1996	D	86
1995	D	85

The 1998 Beychevelle is a charming, medium-bodied wine from one of St.-Julien's only underachievers. It is good to see the effort put forth by Beychevelle, as this wine exhibits a deep ruby/purple color, in addition to a sweet, floral, black currant, dried herb, toasty-scented bouquet. There is excellent richness, an overall sense of elegance and symmetry, and a graceful, moderately long finish. Anticipated maturity: 2000–2012.

Beychevelle's 1997 is herbaceous, austere, tannic, and lacking fruit, glycerin, and extract. The angular, austere finish further complicates its future. Anticipated maturity: now–2009.

The 1996 reveals an evolved, dark plum color. The nose offers toasty new oak in an open, charming style with berry fruit intermixed with spice. It is an uninspiring example, particularly for such a top-notch *terroir,* but the wine is medium bodied and cleanly made, with moderate longevity. Anticipated maturity: 2001–2012.

The 1995 displays a medium ruby color and a distinctive nose of underbrush, damp earth, and loamy-tinged black currant fruit. Moderately tannic, with medium body and some angularity, the 1995 possesses good extract but not much soul or character. Anticipated maturity: 2001–2012.

Past Glories: 1986 (92), 1982 (91), 1953 (92), 1928 (97).

BON PASTEUR (POMEROL)

1998	E	(91–93)
1997	E	(86–89)
1996	E	88
1995	E	89

The exquisite 1998 Bon Pasteur is the most compelling wine produced at this estate since Michel and Dany Rolland's sumptuous 1982. With an opaque black/purple color, it has an exquisite nose of blackberries, subtle toasty oak, minerals, and floral scents. The wine is medium to full bodied and gorgeously concentrated with low acidity, high tannin, and sensational extract and purity. A profound Bon Pasteur, it will age effortlessly for 15 or more years. Anticipated maturity: 2004–2015. Bravo!

The 1997 is a soft, charming wine, with a dark ruby/purple color and copious quantities of smoky, chocolatey, berry-tinged fruit intermixed with subtle new oak. Medium to full bodied, with more flesh than the 1996, and a longer finish, this offering should be at its finest between 2001 and 2013.

Bon Pasteur's 1996 is lighter than I thought from cask. The wine reveals dry, slightly gritty tannin in the finish, which kept my score more conservative. It exhibits spicy new oak, medium body, abundant smoky, black cherry, mocha-tinged fruit, good weight, excellent purity, and a firm, structured, muscular finish. This wine should evolve nicely for 10–12 years.

The 1995 may turn out to be outstanding. It offers a dark plum color and high-quality aromatics consisting of *pain grillé*, lead pencil, smoke, and black cherry and currant fruit. In the mouth, this is a sweet, medium-bodied, round, spicy, succulently textured Bon Pasteur with a plump, fleshy finish. Anticipated maturity: 2001–2012.

Past Glories: 1990 (91), 1989 (90), 1982 (96).

BONALGUE (POMEROL)

1998	C	(87–88)
1997	C	(85–86)
1996	C	86
1995	C	86

A sleeper of the vintage, the succulent, dense ruby/purple-colored, well-made 1998 Bonalgue displays extra layers of fat and richness. Opaque purple colored, with oodles of blackberry, plum, and cherry fruit, it is a low-acid, hedonistic fruit bomb that should drink well for a decade.

The 1997 is also well made, exhibiting a dark ruby color and a distinctive nose of cherry/kirsch liqueur, dried herbs, and Chinese tea. Medium bodied and rich, with light tannin and a spicy finish, it should drink well for 5–6 years.

The 1996 is another example of this consistently well-made wine. It offers up a sweet nose of plum fruit intertwined with cherries. Sweet fruit, good fat, and a touch of oak give the wine a plump, savory mouth-feel. This is a charming, bistro-style red with more depth and ripeness than many wines costing twice as much. Drink it over the next 5–6 years.

A dark ruby-colored wine with sweet, spicy, berry fruit and a roasted peanut-scented nose, the 1995 Bonalgue is soft, round, and velvety textured, with low acidity and moderate weight. It is an attractive wine for near-term drinking. Anticipated maturity: now–2004.

LE BOSCQ (MÉDOC)

1997	C	(85–86)
1997 Vieilles Vignes	C	(85–86)
1996 Vieilles Vignes	C	86
1995 Vieilles Vignes	C	85

An exuberantly fruity, sweet black currant- and spice box-scented and -flavored wine, the 1997 Le Boscq possesses good purity, well-integrated tannin, and a fleshy finish. It should drink well for 5–7 years.

A dark ruby-colored wine, with a straightforward, attractive, sweet berry-scented nose infused with minerals and spice, the medium-bodied, round, supple-textured 1997 Vieilles Vignes should drink well for 4–5 years.

A delicious, richly fruity wine, the 1996 Vieilles Vignes offers a deep color, a good mid-palate, and a moderately long, medium-bodied, spicy, rich finish. Anticipated maturity: now–2008.

A spicy, black currant-scented and -flavored offering with fine depth, the attractive, medium-bodied, cleanly made 1995 Vieilles Vignes offers good value and immediate drinkability. It will keep for 3–4 years.

BOURGNEUF (POMEROL)

1998	D	(90–92)
1997	D	(87–89+)
1996	D	87+?
1995	D	89

The past few vintages have demonstrated Bourgneuf's newfound predilection for turning out high-quality Pomerol. This estate has again hit the bull's-eye with a blockbuster, monster 1998. My rating is deliberately conservative because I have never tasted a Bourgneuf this rich and intense. The wine looks like vintage port, with a saturated black/purple color, huge extraction (from low yields), and a viscous, full-bodied personality. The nose offers aromas of roasted coffee, grilled meats, jammy black cherries, and licorice. Unctuous and superconcentrated, with a 45-second finish, this is one of the sleepers of the vintage. Anticipated maturity: 2005–2020.

This estate has been producing fine, robust, concentrated wines. While they may ultimately lack complexity, the exuberant display of density, muscle, and richness is impressive. The potentially outstanding 1997 Bourgneuf exhibits a saturated black/purple color, as well as sweet blackberry and cherry liqueur aromas with notes of licorice and truffles. Powerful, with excellent depth, but not yet revealing the complexity or finesse that wines from Pomerol's finest *terroirs* exhibit, this ponderous wine is impressive for its size, richness, and purity. For now, I am giving it the benefit of the doubt. Anticipated maturity: 2002–2015.

The 1996 has turned out well, although it is somewhat monolithic. The color is saturated ruby/plum. The wine offers earthy, black cherry, licorice, and dried herb scents, medium to full body, and muscular, concentrated flavors with moderately high tannin. If more complexity emerges, this Bourgneuf will score in the high 80s. It is a mouth-filling, robust Pomerol to drink between 2000 and 2012.

A sleeper of the vintage, Bourgneuf's 1995 may be the finest wine I have tasted from this estate. The color is an opaque purple, and the wine offers a closed but promising nose of black cherries, raspberries, and coffee-tinged fruit. Packed and stacked, as they say in the vernacular, this medium- to full-bodied, powerful, mouth-filling Pomerol is big, bold, and boisterous. If additional complexity develops in this excellent, decadently rich wine, it will merit an outstanding rating. Anticipated maturity: 2000–2014.

BOYD CANTENAC (MARGAUX)

1998	C	(86–87)
1997	C	(82–85)

It has been a long time since I have written a positive tasting note about this estate. The 1998 Boyd Cantenac is a dark ruby-colored wine with mature ripe fruit, a sweet entry, supple tannin, and a medium-bodied, well-balanced finish. Not a blockbuster, it is a well-made, medium-weight Margaux with class and style. Anticipated maturity: 2002–2010.

Although there is some density in the 1997, it comes across as somewhat savage and rustic, with an excessive amount of tannin for its delicate fruit. The color is a healthy dark ruby, and the wine reveals attractive aromatics, but there is a ferocious tannin level and none of the charm or opulence found in the top 1997s.

BRANAIRE (DULUC-DUCRU) (ST.-JULIEN)

1998	D	(87–89)
1997	D	(86–87)
1996	D	89
1995	D	90

The dark ruby-colored 1998 Branaire's expressive aromatics offer mineral, floral, and sweet jammy cherry/strawberry fruit. It also appears to possess some lead pencil characteristics. Made in a stylish, elegant, medium-bodied manner, with soft tannin for the vintage and ripe fruit, it will be ready to drink upon release and will last for 10–15 years.

The 1997 Branaire comes across as a soft, open-knit, attractive, round, fruity wine without good depth and length. If it continues to perform in this manner, it will merit consumption in its first 7–8 years of life. I was charmed by its forward aromatics and round texture.

My concerns about the 1996 Branaire turning out too tannic were unfounded. Tasted three times out of bottle, it is a textbook Branaire, with a telltale floral, raspberry-and-black currant-scented nose intermixed with minerals and floral nuances. Elegant and pure, with surprising lushness and sweet, well-integrated tannin, this medium-bodied, finesse-style wine should be at its finest between 2005 and 2018.

A beauty in the elegant, restrained, finesse school of winemaking, the dark ruby/purple-colored 1995 Branaire exhibits a floral, cranberry, cherry, and black currant nose intermixed with high-quality toasty new oak. Medium bodied, with excellent definition, supple tannin, and an attractive, alluring personality, this pleasant, measured, yet complex wine should drink well young and keep for 2 decades.

Past Glories: 1989 (92), 1982 (90), 1975 (91).

BRANE CANTENAC (MARGAUX)

1998	C	(86–87)

Brane-Cantenac appears to have recognized the potential problems of overextraction, producing a charming, supple wine with excellent fruit as well as sweet blackberry and cassis aromas with notes of dried herbs and earth. It is a lighter-style, well-balanced, alluring Margaux that should drink well upon release and keep for 10–12 years.

CALON-SÉGUR (ST.-ESTÈPHE)

1997	E	(80–83)
1996	E	92
1995	EE	92+

Wouldn't you know it? After naming proprietor Madame Gasqueton as one of my heroines of 1997, and having praised to the heavens Calon-Ségur's brilliant 1995 and 1996, I was let down by the rather unsubstantial, closed, tannic, and evolved 1997. This wine was disappointing on three separate occasions, exhibiting light to medium body and a diluted personality, with notes of grilled vegetables, old leather, and cherry fruit but little intensity or length. It will require consumption during its first 7–8 years of life.

Prior to bottling, I thought the 1996 Calon-Ségur would be a match for the spectacular 1995, but the two vintages tasted blind, side by side, on two occasions in January 1998, and once in March, convinced me that the 1995 has the edge because of its element of *surmaturité* and more accessible, richer midpalate. The 1996 may not be as profound as I had predicted from cask, but it is an exceptional wine. Dark ruby colored, with a complex nose of dried herbs, Asian spices, and black cherry jam intermixed with cassis, it possesses outstanding purity and considerable tannin in the finish. This classic, medium- to full-bodied, traditionally made wine improves dramatically with airing, suggesting it will have a very long life. Anticipated maturity: 2009–2028.

As I have said many times since I first tasted this wine, the 1995 Calon-Ségur is one of the great sleepers of the vintage (I bought the wine as a future for a mere $250 a case). The wine has closed down completely since bottling, but it is a sensational effort that may ultimately merit an even higher score. The wine is opaque purple colored. With coaxing, the tight aromatics reveal some weedy cassis intertwined with truffles, chocolate, and beef blood-like aromas. On the palate, there is an element of *sur-maturité* (1995 was an extremely late harvest at Calon-Ségur), fabulous density and purity, and a boatload of tannin. This deep, broodingly backward, classic Bordeaux will require a decade of cellaring. Anticipated maturity: 2005–2035.

Kudos to Calon-Ségur, as both the 1995 and 1996 have a strong buy recommendation from me, but only for readers who have the patience to wait them out.

Past Glories: 1990 (90), 1988 (91), 1982 (94).

CANON (ST.-ÉMILION)

1998	D	(86–87)
1997	D	(82–85)
1996	D	80
1995	E	74

The new owners have been struggling to get this beautifully placed vineyard back on track, and the 1998 is a reassuring effort. While not profound, it is very good with a dark ruby color, sweet mineral and black cherry aromas, medium body, excellent purity, and a fresh, vibrant, elegant style. Anticipated maturity: 2002–2012.

Although the 1997 possesses some ripe fruit and charm, it also reveals abrasive, grittylike tannin that is worrisome. This astringency gives the wine an uncharacteristic hardness in the finish, but overall it exhibits more fruit, ripeness, and purity than the 1996. Anticipated maturity: 2003–2010.

The 1996 Canon is a lean, austere, delicate wine with a dark ruby color and medium body, but little intensity or length. Angular and compressed, it is likely to dry out over the next decade. Anticipated maturity: 2002–2015.

I could not find any redeeming qualities in the sinewy, thin, austere, high-acid, ferociously tannic 1995. As hard as I tried, I could not see any positive side to the manner in which this wine is going to develop. Anticipated maturity: 2000–2008.

Past Glories: 1989 (92), 1982 (94), 1959 (95).

CANON DE BREM (CANON-FRONSAC)

1998	C	(88–90)
1997	C	(85–86)
1996	C	78
1995	C	86

The 1998 Canon de Brem's amazingly rich, sweet midpalate knocked me out. It tastes like a combination of raspberry and blackberry liqueur. Tannic, but medium to full bodied, with amazing purity and richness, this Canon-Fronsac may merit an outstanding score if it turns out to be as good as the sample I tasted. Anticipated maturity: 2002–2012.

The 1997 exhibits a dark color, medium body, sweetness in the nose and flavors, a dominant dried herb, mineral, and black cherry component, and moderate tannin in the finish. It will age well for 5–6 years.

The 1996 is a dark ruby-colored, stylish, medium-bodied, structured, elegant wine without much depth or fruit. Drink it over the next 3–7 years.

The dark plum/ruby color of the 1995 is followed by a wine with plenty of spice and a distinctive mineral *terroir* characteristic intermingled with sweet plum and cherry fruit. Medium bodied and dense, this muscular claret will be approachable young but should age nicely for 10–12 years.

CANON-LA-GAFFELIÈRE (ST.-ÉMILION)

1998	E	(90–93)
1997	E	(89–92)
1996	E	90
1995	E	91+

One of Bordeaux's most exotic wines, the 1998 Canon-La-Gaffelière is a blockbuster effort, with a thick purple color and an exotic nose of roasted herbs, jammy black fruits, incense, *pain grillé*, violets, and coffee. It is an explosive, superconcentrated, highly extracted St.-Émilion with plenty of soft tannin. Rich and full bodied, with a 40+-second finish, this multidimensional, flamboyant/ostentatiously styled wine will have many admirers and will no doubt provoke controversy among those looking for subtlety and restraint. Anticipated maturity: 2002–2017.

The sensational 1997 exhibits an opaque black/purple color in addition to an exotic nose of cappuccino and black fruits intermixed with licorice and toasty new oak. It offers an opulent, sexy, full-bodied palate, terrific fruit intensity, low acidity, and hedonistic levels of glycerin. This succulent, massive 1997 will be drinkable young yet keep for 15 or more years. A gorgeous wine for the vintage! Anticipated maturity: 2001–2014.

The 1996 is one of St.-Émilion's most impressively constituted and expressive wines. From its saturated purple color to its soaring aromatics (*pain grillé*, jammy black fruits, chocolate, roasted coffee, and smoke), this full-bodied, meaty, chewy, powerful wine is loaded with extract and sweet tannin for the vintage and possesses a layered, multidimensional finish. It should continue to improve for a decade and drink well for 15–20 years. Anticipated maturity: 2007–2020.

A massive wine, with a cigar box, chocolatey, thick, black currant and cherry nose, the full-bodied 1995 is crammed with layers of fruit, extract, glycerin, and alcohol. Spicy yet rich, with high tannin, the 1995 Canon-La-Gaffelière will need a minimum of 5–6 years of cellaring. The finish is long and rich and the tannin sweet rather than astringent. Anticipated maturity: 2004–2020.

Past Glories: 1994 (90), 1990 (92).

CANON-MOUEIX (CANON-FRONSAC)

1998	C	(88–91)
1997	C	(86–88)
1996	C	86

A prodigious example from Canon-Fronsac, the opaque purple-colored 1998 Canon-Moueix possesses sumptuous aromas of superconcentrated, layered, black cherries intermixed with cassis, minerals, and earth. Gorgeously balanced, concentrated, and full bodied, this massive wine requires 4–5 years of cellaring; it should keep for 2 decades. This is one of the finest Canon-Fronsacs I have ever tasted. Let's hope it turns out this good in bottle.

The 1997 appears to be a better example of Canon-Fronsac than the 1996, with sweeter fruit, lower acidity, a combination of black cherry and currant fruit intertwined with minerals, and an elegant, medium-bodied, nicely concentrated style. Drink it over the next decade.

The dark ruby-colored 1996 possesses fine depth, a spicy, sweet nose of berry fruit, pepper, and dried herbs, medium body, and fine ripeness. Although well made, it is slightly short in the finish. Drink this sound Canon-Fronsac over the next 5–6 years.

CANTEMERLE (MACAU)

1998	D	(86–88)
1997	D	(85–86)
1996	D	87
1995	C	86

The 1998 Cantemerle is a fine effort from the southern Médoc. Although not powerful, its dark ruby/purple color and sweet nose of cassis, flowers, and truffles is captivating. Medium bodied, with no hard edges and a lush midpalate, this low-acid, moderately tannic wine should be drinkable between 2003 and 2014.

The tasty 1997 is a light- to medium-bodied, round, richly fruity wine with lower acidity and less structure and tannin than its more muscular older sibling. Offering an attractive display of red fruits, minerals, and spice, it should drink well during its first decade of life.

I had hoped the 1996 would turn out closer to outstanding, but it is an excellent Cantemerle, if not quite as stunning as I had expected. The wine offers a dark ruby color and a sweet nose of black raspberries, subtle new oak, and acacia smells. There is fine sweetness and solid tannin in this elegant, symmetrical wine. It is more forward and lighter than it was from cask, but it is a stylish example of Cantemerle. Anticipated maturity: 2003–2015.

The 1995 does not possess the depth of the 1996 and reveals a more evolved medium ruby color that is already lightening at the edge. Peppery, herb-tinged red currant fruit aromas are pleasant but uninspiring. This medium-bodied, straightforward wine lacks the depth, dimension, and power of a topflight classified growth. It will be at its best between 2001 and 2010. *Past Glories:* 1989 (91), 1983 (91), 1961 (92), 1953 (94).

CANTENAC-BROWN (MARGAUX)

1998	D	(86–87?)
1997	D	(85–87)
1996	D	86
1995	D	78

The question mark for the 1998 relates to the abrupt, tannic finish. Otherwise this is a dark, saturated ruby/purple-colored 1998 with sweet fruit in the aromatics and on the attack, medium body, and fine purity. If the tannin becomes more integrated and the wine expands in texture, it will merit a very good to excellent score. Anticipated maturity: 2003–2015.

I liked Cantenac Brown's 1997, a blend of 65% Cabernet Sauvignon, 25% Merlot, and 10% Cabernet Franc. Whether it is the estate's *terroir* or the winemaking style, Cantenac Brown tends to be a stern, tannic wine, but the softness of the 1997 vintage has given this effort plenty of charm and precociousness. The color is a dark ruby/purple, and the wine offers up sweet black raspberry/cassis fruit intermixed with licorice, underbrush, and oaky aromas. The wine is medium bodied, with a supple texture, good purity, and a low-acid, plump finish. It could turn out to be one of the better Cantenac Browns from recent vintages, as well as a candidate for an upper-80-point rating if it continues to develop well. Anticipated maturity: 2000–2014.

I know AXA, the huge umbrella corporation that owns many Bordeaux châteaux, particularly Jean-Michel Cazes, has not been happy with my reviews of Cantenac-Brown, but I find the wine too tough textured, tannic, and dry. Therefore I am happy to say the 1996, while tannic, looks to be one of the better-balanced efforts to emerge under the AXA administration. The color is a deep ruby/purple. The wine offers simple but pleasing aromas of black currants, licorice, and vanillin. In the mouth, it is medium to full bodied, powerful, muscular, somewhat foursquare, but mouth-filling, rich, and with the potential to move up in score if more complexity develops. Anticipated maturity: 2004–2015.

Although the 1995 reveals a good color, it has been consistently angular, austere, and too tannic. This is a lean, spartan style of claret that is likely to dry out before enough tannin melts away to reach a balance with the wine's fruit. Anticipated maturity: 2000–2010.

CARBONNIEUX (GRAVES)

1998	D	(85–86)
1997	D	(82–84)
1996	D	86
1995	D	87

Burgundian-like in its open-knit, strawberry/cherry fruitiness, the medium-bodied, smoky, elegant, fruity 1998 Carbonnieux is round, forward, and ideal for drinking over the next 7–10 years.

The 1997 Carbonnieux is a light-bodied, diluted wine, but it possesses charm and sweet fruit in the aromas and flavors. Drink this picnic-style wine over the next 4–7 years.

The 1996 is a stylish, medium-bodied, dark ruby-colored wine with attractive cherry and raspberry fruit intermixed with *pain grillé* notes in both the aromatics and flavors. This elegant wine reveals a Volnay-like personality. It should drink well young yet keep for a decade.

An attractive, sexy effort from Carbonnieux, the medium-bodied, deep ruby-colored 1995 reveals subtle aromas of smoky oak intertwined with tobacco, kirsch, and black currant fruit. In the mouth, elegance, balance, suppleness, finesse, and an overall allure characterize this round, lightly tannic, lush, and captivating claret. Anticipated maturity: now–2011.

LES CARMES-HAUT-BRION (GRAVES)

1998	D	(88–90)
1997	D	(86–87)
1996	D	87
1995	D	87

This little treasure of a vineyard near Haut-Brion consistently produces fine wines. The 1998 may ultimately be outstanding and is unquestionably a sleeper of the vintage. The opaque purple color is accompanied by an enticing aromatic concoction of smoky, grilled herb, and black currant/cherry-scented fruit. Medium bodied, with excellent to outstanding concentration and purity, a sweet midpalate, and ripe tannin, this beauty is well worth searching out. Anticipated maturity: 2002–2013.

The 1997 is similar to the 1996, with less structure and lower acidity, giving it a sweet, forward, succulent personality with smoky tobacco-tinged cherry and currant fruit well displayed. Pure, complex, and impeccably well made, it should be consumed over the next 7–8 years.

A medium ruby-colored, sexy, seductive Graves, with loads of tobacco-tinged jammy cherry fruit intermixed with smoke and earth, the spicy, round, generous 1996 reveals no hard edges. It continues to be one of the most stylish, underrated wines from the Pessac-Léognan region. Although it will not be long-lived, this wine offers plenty of appeal for drinking over the next decade.

This small jewel of an estate (not far from Haut-Brion and Pape-Clément) has produced a medium-bodied, sweet, round, berry, complex, elegant, savory 1995 with no hard edges. Low acidity and a luscious, ripe Merlot component dominate the wine, giving it immediate appeal. A classic example of Graves's smoky, tobacco-tinged, berry fruit, this is a plump, delicious wine for consuming over the next decade.

Past Glories: 1959 (93).

CARONNE STE.-GEMME (MÉDOC)

1996	C	86

A well-made cru bourgeois, this dark ruby/purple-colored wine offers a soft, plump entry, with sweet cherry fruit intermixed with spicy oak and earth. The wine is low in acidity, surprisingly open knit for a 1996, and medium bodied. Drink it over the next 5–6 years.

CARRUADES DE LAFITE (PAUILLAC)

1997	D	(87–88)
1996	D	89
1995	D	87

The 1997 Carruades de Lafite (a blend of 32% Merlot, with the rest mainly Cabernet Sauvignon and a small portion of Cabernet Franc) maintains its reputation as one of Bordeaux's better second wines. The color is dark ruby with purple nuances. The wine is soft, fleshy, and round, with more up-front fat than Lafite but not nearly the length or perfume. Supple, with low acidity and an easygoing, silky finish, it will drink well between now and 2006. The 1996 Carruades de Lafite, a blend of 63% Cabernet Sauvignon and 37% Merlot, may turn out to be the finest Carruades I have ever tasted. It possesses as much power, ripeness, and fleshy fruit (because of the high percentage of Merlot) as I have ever detected in this offering. While it does not quite have the characteristics of Lafite, being fleshier and more accessible, it is a beautifully made wine with a subtle dosage of toasty new oak, an appealing texture, and excellent length. Given its power, this second wine will need 2–4 years of cellaring and keep for 15+ years (I would not be surprised to see it last for 2 decades). The 1995 is a 40% Merlot/60% Cabernet Sauvignon blend. It exhibits more of the trademark characteristics of its bigger sibling. Elegant, with spicy new oak, lead pencil, and creamy black currant fruit, this is a medium-bodied, finesse-style wine with excellent purity and overall equilibrium. It is much more accessible than the 1996 and should drink well between now and 2010.

DU CAUZE (ST.-ÉMILION)

1998	C	(87–88)

This wine may turn out to be a sleeper of the vintage. It exhibits sweet toasty oak along with copious quantities of jammy black cherry fruit intermixed with floral, licorice, and roasted herb scents. Deep, medium to full bodied, and rich, with good fat on the midpalate, this is a hedonistic, gloriously exuberant, fruity wine to drink during its first 10–12 years of life.

CERTAN-GIRAUD (POMEROL)

1997	D	(78–82)
1996	D	84
1995	D	87

The midweight, medium ruby-colored 1997 displays sweet earth and subtle earth aromas as well as a short finish. Pleasant, round, and easy to understand, but lacking concentration, depth, and length, it requires consumption over the next 4–5 years.

I suspect a far richer, more complex wine could emerge from this outstanding Pomerol *terroir*. The 1996 possesses a medium ruby color and an evolved, complex nose of cedar, kirsch, roasted herbs, and spice. Good fruit combines with moderate levels of glycerin in this medium-bodied, richly fruity, yet essentially one-dimensional, straightforward Pomerol. Drink it over the next 5–6 years.

Typical for this property, the 1995 has turned out to be a very good Pomerol with sweet, jammy flavors that border on overripeness. The wine displays a deep ruby color with a flamboyant nose of smoke and black fruits. There is noticeable glycerin on the palate, medium to full body, low acidity, and plenty of power, intensity, and richness in this big, fleshy, mouth-filling, savory, hedonistic Pomerol. Anticipated maturity: now–2009.

CERTAN DE MAY (POMEROL)

1998	EE	(91–93+)
1997	EE	(87–89)
1996	EE	87?
1995	EEE	90+

A huge, powerfully tannic, backward wine that will require considerable patience, Certan de May's 1998 is a worthy rival to the still youthful, unevolved 1982. The color is a dense purple. This wine was not easy to evaluate, but as it sat in the glass, its thickness and impressive credentials became obvious. Sweet cherry liqueur, kirsch, cassis, dried herbs, cedar, and toasty oak gradually emerge from the wine's restrained aromatics. The palate is inundated with exceptional concentration, ferocious tannin, and high levels of extract. This is one of the most backward wines of the vintage, but it appears to possess the intense concentration needed to match its tannin. Anticipated maturity: 2008–2025.

The 1997 Certan de May reveals less color saturation than other top Pomerols, but it is extremely evolved aromatically, with a gorgeous nose of jammy plum fruits intermixed with dried Provençal herbs and spicy oak. It offers a creamy, medium- to full-bodied texture with excellent ripeness, a full, fleshy, succulent personality, and a heady, spicy finish. Although it will not make old bones, for drinking over the next 10–12 years this is a seductive, cleanly made, well-balanced wine. Anticipated maturity: now–2012.

The 1996 reveals an intensely aromatic cedary, dried herb, and black cherry nose, but its abrasive tannin level is troublesome. Although well made, it displays a gritty texture, medium body, and an angular, rustic character to the tannin. If that softens (which I doubt), this wine will merit its 87-point score. Anticipated maturity: 2004–2015.

An impressive Certan de May, the 1995 exhibits a dense ruby/purple color and a moderately intense nose of black olives, cedar, raspberries, and cherry fruit intermixed with toasty new oak. In the mouth, the new oak is noticeable, as is an elevated level of tannin. Notwithstanding the aggressive vanillin flavors and powerful tannin, this wine has outstanding depth and a layered, concentrated style with considerable muscle and power. It is a big, backward, formidably endowed Certan de May that may turn out to be the finest wine made at this estate since the 1988, but patience is most definitely required. Anticipated maturity: 2006–2020.

Past Glories: 1990 (91), 1988 (92+), 1986 (90), 1985 (94), 1982 (96+), 1981 (90), 1979 (93), 1945 (96).

DE CHAMBRUN (LALANDE DE POMEROL)

1997	C	(86–88)
1996	C	87

Another impressive effort from this well-run estate that turns out about 800 cases of top-notch Lalande de Pomerol, the dark ruby/purple-colored 1997 offers powerful aromas of blackberries, toasty oak, and earth. This deep, tannic, big-framed effort reveals moderate tannin in the long finish. It will require 1–2 years of cellaring and will last for a decade or more.

One of the finest Lalande de Pomerols, the 1996 is well worth seeking out. This excellent wine exhibits a deep ruby/purple color and sweet, blackberry and jammy cherry aromas and flavors. Medium bodied, with impressive glycerin, sweet tannin, and a long, lush, concentrated finish, it may be the finest Lalande de Pomerol from this vintage. Anticipated maturity: now–2010.

CHAPELLE-HAUT-BRION (PESSAC LÉOGNAN)

1997	D	(83–85)
1996	D	86
1995	D	90

The new second wine of La Mission-Haut-Brion, Chapelle-Haut-Brion is a worthy addition to the Dillon family's portfolio. The soft, round, herb-tinged 1997 Chapelle-Haut-Brion (made from the youngest vines) is up front, easy to understand, fruity, straightforward, and simple. I would opt for drinking it during the first 4–5 years after release. The 1996 is a soft, round, lovely, cedary, smoky, complex wine with medium body and luscious sweet fruit. It will not make old bones, but for a textbook Graves to drink over the next 7–8 years, this wine has considerable merit. The 1995 is a sleeper and one of the better second wines of this vintage. It comes across as more extracted than the 1996 but offers a lovely, rich, medium-bodied, well-endowed personality. The wine reveals much of the character of La Mission-Haut-Brion in its sweet berry fruit intertwined with smoke, tobacco, and roasted herbs. Round, spicy, and generous, with no hard edges, it will provide ideal drinking over the next 7–8 years.

CHARMAIL (HAUT MÉDOC)

1997	D	(87–89)
1996	D	89

The intriguingly made 1996 Charmail (it enjoys a 2 week prefermentation cold maceration) exhibits an opaque black/purple color, sweet black berry, raspberry and cassis fruit, medium to full body, luxuriant, hedonistic, smoky, jammy fruit flavors, and copious quantities of sweet tannin. A severe selection has resulted in a Merlot-dominated wine that includes 30% Cabernet Sauvignon and 20% Cabernet Franc. Anticipated maturity: now–2010.

A fat, low-acid, hedonistic offering, the black/purple-colored 1997 Charmail offers sweet, jammy black fruit aromas, an expansive, chewy, smoky palate, and long, intense, velvety-textured flavors. It should drink well for 10–12 years.

CHASSE-SPLEEN (MOULIS)

1997	D	(86–87+)
1995	D	86

Dark ruby/purple colored, with aromas of spice, black currants, vanillin, and berries, the medium-bodied 1997 reveals very good to excellent depth, fine overall balance, ripe tannin, and not a great deal of acidity. It should drink well for 8–10 years.

The 1995 has everything in its aromatics and attack and very little at the back of the mouth—not a good sign for long-term aging. It possesses a dark ruby/purple color and black currant fruit intermixed with smoke and weediness. Drink it over the next 5–7 years.

Past Glories: 1989 (91), 1986 (90), 1985 (90), 1975 (90), 1970 (90), 1949 (94).

CHAUVIN (ST.-ÉMILION)

1997	C	(86–88)
1996	C	88

Another St.-Émilion to watch, Chauvin has been impressive in recent vintages. The 1996 exhibits a dark ruby color as well as an excellent bouquet of *pain grillé* intermixed with jammy cherry fruit. There is good glycerin, medium body, an overall sense of elegance, fine equilibrium, and a tasty, richly fruity finish. Some tannin is present, but this is a stylish, finesse-driven wine that should drink nicely for 10–12 years.

The 1997 is less complex and elegant, but fatter, lusher, and more obvious. It possesses an attractive deep ruby color and a sweet, black cherry-scented nose intermixed with smoke, *pain grillé*, and dried herbs. Medium bodied, round, and open knit, this precociously styled wine should be drunk over the next 7–9 years.

CHEVAL BLANC (ST.-ÉMILION)

1998	EEE	(90–93)
1997	EEE	(88–89)
1996	EEE	90
1995	EEE	90

For the 1998, Cheval Blanc harvested its Merlot in mid- to late September and the Cabernet Franc after the rains of September 27 and 28. Yields were a modest just over 2 tons of fruit per acre, and approximately 72% of the production went into the *grand vin*. The 1998's final blend was 52% Merlot and 48% Cabernet Franc. A beautifully made Cheval, it may be the finest effort since 1990, although it does not possess that vintage's overripeness and opulence. Nevertheless, it is an impressive, sweet, distinctive wine with a deep dark ruby/purple color and aromas of blackberry liqueur, vanillin, coconut, and a touch of coffee. The 1998 is elegant and sweet, with surprisingly good fatness, medium body, and well-integrated, velvety tannin. This wine can be difficult to taste young (because of the high percentage of Cabernet Franc) and often puts on considerable weight, meriting an even higher score after several years. That being said, the 1998 performed extremely well for such a young Cheval Blanc. Anticipated maturity: 2002–2016.

Cheval Blanc's 1997 (70% Merlot and 30% Cabernet Franc) exhibits sweet cherry jam intermixed with Asian spices and this estate's telltale coconut note. Ripe and medium bodied, with low acidity, this charming wine possesses good length for the vintage but is destined to be drunk during its first decade of life because of its undeniable seductiveness. Anticipated maturity: now–2012.

The elegant, moderately weighted 1996 Cheval Blanc reveals a deep garnet/plum, evolved color. Quintessentially elegant, with a complex nose of black fruits, coconut, smoke, and *pain grillé*, this medium-bodied wine exhibits sweet fruit on the attack, substantial complexity, and a lush, velvety-textured finish. It is very soft and evolved for a 1996. Anticipated maturity: 2000–2015.

A pretty, attractive Cheval Blanc, the 1995 contains a higher percentage of Merlot in the final blend than usual (50% Merlot/50% Cabernet Franc). This wine has not developed as much fat or weight as its younger sibling, the 1996, but it appears to be an outstanding Cheval Blanc, with an enthralling smoky, black currant, coffee, and exotic bouquet. Complex, rich, medium- to full-bodied flavors are well endowed and pure, with surprisingly firm tannin in the finish. Unlike the sweeter, riper 1996, the 1995 may be more structured and potentially longer lived. Anticipated maturity: 2002–2020.

Past Glories: 1990 (90), 1986 (92), 1985 (93), 1983 (95), 1982 (100), 1981 (90), 1975 (90), 1964 (95), 1961 (93), 1959 (92), 1955 (90), 1953 (95), 1949 (96), 1948 (96), 1947 (100), 1921 (98).

DOMAINE DE CHEVALIER (GRAVES)

1998	E	(87–89)
1997	E	(86–87)
1996	E	88

Domaine de Chevalier appears to have reduced the overt oakiness found in recent vintages and is consequently producing more complex wines without intrusive wood. The dark ruby/purple-colored 1998 boasts an elegant, floral, earthy-scented nose with notes of black cherry and berry fruit. The wine is medium bodied, with sweet tannin, pure, lush flavors, and a nicely layered, nuanced finish. This is a complete Domaine de Chevalier that may turn out to be outstanding. Anticipated maturity: 2003–2015.

The 1997 is also well made, with low acidity, ripe, dried herb-tinged cherry fruit, medium body, nicely integrated wood, and a plush, succulent texture. It should drink well during its first 10–12 years of life.

The 1996 has turned out beautifully from the bottle. It is an exceptionally elegant wine, with well-integrated oak and tobacco-tinged, cherry and cassis fruit. It appears to be a return to the style of the seventies and early eighties. Lush, with excellent concentration, a beautiful texture, and a flattering, potentially complex aromatic profile, this medium-bodied wine should be at its finest between 2003 and 2016.

Past Glories (red): 1988 (90), 1983 (91), 1978 (92), 1970 (90), 1964 (90), 1953 (92).

Past Glories (white): 1994 (91+), 1992 (90), 1988 (90), 1985 (93), 1983 (93), 1970 (93), 1962 (93).

CITRAN (HAUT-MÉDOC)

1996	C	(86–87)
1995	C	86

Opaque ruby/purple, with plenty of intensity, fruit, body, glycerin, and tannin, the 1996 is a forceful, muscular, broad-shouldered claret for drinking between 2003 and 2015. Softer than the 1996, the deep ruby/purple-colored 1995 reveals licorice, vanillin, and ripe black currant fruit presented in a straightforward but savory, mouth-filling style. Drink it over the next 7–8 years.

CLERC-MILON (PAUILLAC)

1997	E	(89–90)
1996	E	90
1995	E	89

Clerc-Milon appears to be on a hot streak lately, turning out excellent, sometimes outstanding, wines that remain reasonably priced among Bordeaux's classified growths. A blend of

53% Cabernet Sauvignon, 34% Merlot, 9% Cabernet Franc, and 4% Petit Verdot, the 1997 is a soft, cedary, smoky, toasty wine with lush berry fruit, an open-knit, easy-to-understand, accessible personality, and a silky-textured finish. Very opulent, even flamboyant, this wine offers intense chocolate espresso flavors that are deep and accessible. This is a Pauillac fruit bomb. Anticipated maturity: now–2012.

The 1996 is among the finest wines I have ever tasted from this estate. Lavishly oaked, with gobs of *pain grillé* and rich fruit, it is more massive and concentrated than previous vintages. The color is dense ruby/purple. The bouquet offers notes of roasted coffee, tobacco, and jammy cassis. Although surprisingly soft and opulent on the attack, the wine possesses a midsection and finish that reveal its full body, high flavor extraction, and moderate tannin. This complete, large-scale Clerc-Milon will be at its finest between 2005 and 2018.

The 1995 Clerc-Milon, a 56% Cabernet Sauvignon, 30% Merlot, 14% Cabernet Franc blend, reveals more tannin and grip than the 1996 (ironically, the 1995 has more of a 1996 vintage character, and vice versa for the 1996). This attractive dark ruby/purple-colored wine has impressive credentials and may merit an outstanding score with another 1–2 years in the bottle. It offers a gorgeous nose of roasted herbs, meats, cedar, cassis, spice, and vanillin. This dense, medium- to full-bodied wine possesses outstanding levels of extract, plenty of glycerin, and a plush, layered, hedonistic finish. A luscious, complex wine, it reveals enough tannin and depth to warrant 15 or more years of cellaring. Anticipated maturity: 2002–2015. A sleeper.

Past Glories: 1989 (90), 1986 (90).

CLINET (POMEROL)

1998	EE	(90–92?)
1997	EE	(86–88)
1996	EE	91+?
1995	EEE	96

Clinet is a challenging wine to evaluate at a young age, as it often seems disjointed, tannic, and marked by lavish quantities of new oak. After its sojourn in cask and a year or so in bottle, it begins to strut its potential. The 1998 Clinet is a broodingly backward, oaky, full-bodied wine that was completely closed when I tasted it. It reveals admirable richness, a concentrated, full-bodied personality, high tannin, and intense extract. The color is opaque ruby/purple, and the nose offers scents of earth, truffles, oyster shells, *pain grillé*, and jammy black fruits. In the mouth, the tannin dominates, but the wine's finish exhibits sweet glycerin and intensity. Anticipated maturity: 2005–2022.

Clinet's 1997 appears to be going through a lighter stage than I remember from my earlier tasting. The wine exhibits a dark ruby/purple color, good fat and ripeness in the mouth, blackberry, truffle, and Asian spice characteristics, an expansive, open-knit style, but a short finish. My instincts suggest I caught this wine at an awkward stage of development, since it did not reveal its earlier depth and intensity. Anticipated maturity: 2003–2016.

The 1996 is a backward, muscular, highly extracted wine with a boatload of tannin; thus the question mark. The saturated plum/purple color is followed by an aggressively oaky nose with scents of roasted coffee, blackberries, and prunes. It is somewhat of a freak for a 1996 Pomerol given its richness, intensity, and overripe style. Medium bodied and powerful, but extremely closed and in need of 5–7 years of cellaring, it will be an interesting wine to follow, to determine if, over time, the tannin fully integrates itself into the wine's concentrated style. If not, it will have a slight rusticity to its tannin and structure. Anticipated maturity: 2007–2020. I sense this wine will be much more controversial than I had anticipated.

Another extraordinary wine made in a backward *vin de garde* style, the 1995 Clinet represents the essence of Pomerol. The blackberry, cassis liqueur-like fruit of this wine is awesome. The color is saturated black/purple, and the wine extremely full bodied and powerful, with layers of glycerin-imbued fruit, massive richness, plenty of licorice, blackberry, and cassis flavors, full body, and a thick, unctuous texture. This is a dense, impressive offering from administrator Jean-Michel Arcaute. This wine should continue to improve for another 10–25 years. Anticipated maturity: 2006–2025.

Past Glories: 1994 (92), 1993 (90), 1990 (95), 1989 (100), 1988 (90), 1987 (90), 1947 (96).

CLOS DU CLOCHER (POMEROL)

1998	D	(87–89)
1997	D	(83–85)
1996	D	86
1995	D	86

Another impressively saturated dark ruby/purple-colored wine, the 1998 possesses excellent ripeness, low acidity, and high tannin. This forceful, powerful, large-scale wine requires 2–3 years of cellaring. Anticipated maturity: 2002–2015.

The 1997 has a touch of prunes and raisiny fruit with an element of overripeness. The wine is dark ruby colored, medium bodied, spicy, and medium weight. Its low acidity and forward, fragile style suggest drinking it over the next 5–6 years.

The 1996 displays a distinctive note of Chinese tea, cherry jam, and dried herbs. Open knit, with low acidity and a plump, savory, seductive style, this medium-bodied wine should drink well for 4–6 years.

A soft, well-made, attractive Pomerol, the 1995 offers smoky, dried herb, black cherry aromas intermixed with earth and spicy oak. Round and fruity, with moderate tannin in the finish, this is a medium-bodied, straightforward, yet pleasing Pomerol. Anticipated maturity: 2001–2010.

CLOS DUBREUIL (ST.-ÉMILION)

1998	D	(91–93)
1997	D	(87–88)

Before readers get too excited about the fabulous 1998, I should note that there are only 250 cases from this tiny, 100% Merlot vineyard. Made by François Mitjavile's son, Louis, this black/purple-colored wine displays an unctuous texture and thick, juicy, black cherry aromas and flavors that compete with smoke, minerals, incense, and high levels of glycerin. This is a mouth-filling, multilayered wine of considerable potential. Anticipated maturity: 2004–2016. A sleeper.

This tiny 3.5-acre property has produced a sleeper in 1997. The wine possesses a dense, dark ruby/purple color, sweet, jammy, ripe blackberry and cherry fruit, an excellent texture with low acidity, and plenty of mocha, chocolate, coffee, and berry flavors with a hint of roasted herbs. Unfortunately the quantity produced was minuscule. Drink it over the next 5–7 years.

CLOS L'ÉGLISE (POMEROL)

1998	E	(92–95)
1997	E	(90–92)

A breakthrough effort for Clos l'Église, the 1997 is the greatest wine I have ever tasted from this estate. The new owners, the Garcins, have done everything right—harvesting ripe fruit, mandating a strict selection, and eschewing fining and filtration at bottling. The 1997 is a sumptuous, extremely concentrated, multidimensional wine that will make believers out of tasters. In total contrast with the thin, vegetal wines previously produced at this property, this is an exotic effort with a dense ruby/purple color and a fascinating nose of plum liqueur intermixed with blackberries, coffee, mocha, and chocolate. Sumptuously textured, with full body, great fruit purity, and a long, layered, velvety finish, this exquisite wine can be drunk after bottling or cellared for 15–18 years. Bravo!

The 1998's raw materials were even richer and more concentrated than the 1997's. The wine is extremely low in acidity, but that should not bother those who want to drink the wine in their lifetime. The color is an opaque black/purple, and the nose offers extraordinary notes of black cherry liqueur intermixed with blackberries, roasted coffee, cold steel, toasty new oak, and truffles. There is fabulous concentration, full body, and a wonderful midpalate with explosive richness and sweetness. The finish lasts for over 40 seconds. The wine's low acidity, sweet tannin, and massive feel in the mouth promise a dazzling Pomerol and the finest Clos l'Église has ever produced. Awesome! Anticipated maturity: 2002–2020.

CLOS FOURTET (ST.-ÉMILION)

1998	D	(88–90)
1997	D	(87–89)
1996	D	89
1995	D	88

An obvious, richly fruity style of St.-Émilion, Clos Fourtet is impeccably well made. The ruby-colored 1998 is fruit driven, medium bodied, corpulent, and exuberant. Glorious fruit, sweet oak, and stony mineral scents make for an attractive wine that can be drunk immediately after bottling, as well as over the next 10–15 years.

Under the leadership of proprietor André Lurton, this property has been producing fine wines. The 1997 Clos Fourtet exhibits a saturated purple color in addition to a sweet, pure, blackberry-scented nose that has not yet taken on additional nuances. The wine is medium bodied, low in acidity, ripe, hedonistic, and seductive. This is one more example of how delicious many 1997s are. Sadly, the problem is their extremely high prices. Anticipated maturity: now–2010.

On one of the three occasions I tasted the 1996 Clos Fourtet from bottle, I rated it outstanding (90 points). The color is a saturated dark ruby. The nose offers up sweet black raspberry and blackberry fruit intermixed with toasty oak and floral scents. It is fleshy and surprisingly expansive and forward for a 1996, with low acidity and a long, multilayered, fruit-driven finish. The tannin is ripe; thus the fruit comes forward and the wine is seductive and charming. This 1996 possesses the weight, richness, and extract to last for 15–20 years, but it should be drinkable early. I would not be surprised for readers to feel my score is too conservative based on how well this wine is showing. Anticipated maturity: 2003–2018.

A very fine effort from Clos Fourtet, the 1995 exhibits a medium dark plum color, followed by sweet black cherry and kirsch fruit intertwined with minerals and toasty oak. Tightly wound on the palate, with medium body, excellent delineation and purity, and a spicy finish with plenty of grip, this example has closed down considerably since bottling, but it does possess excellent sweetness and depth. However, the tannin is more elevated, so this 1995 will require patience. Anticipated maturity: 2004–2018.

Past Glories: 1990 (90).

CLOS DES JACOBINS (ST.-ÉMILION)

1997	D	(83–85)
1996	D	82

The straightforward, pleasant, soft, fruity 1996 exhibits a licorice- and Provençal herb-scented nose and medium-bodied, open-knit, cherrylike flavors. It is meant to be drunk over the next 4–5 years. The 1997 reveals more cassis in its sweet, jammy nose, lower acidity, a riper, plusher texture, and more volume and length. It, too, will require consumption during its first 4–5 years of life.

CLOS DU MARQUIS (ST.-JULIEN)

1998	D	(87–89)
1997	D	(86–87)
1996	D	90
1995	D	90

The second wine of Léoville-Las Cases is one of the finer St.-Juliens, as well as one of the best second wines being produced in Bordeaux. Displaying much of its bigger sibling's character, the 1998 is an elegant, finesse-style offering with medium body and fresh, pure black cherry fruit flavors combined with earth and spicy wood. Exhibiting a saturated color as well as sweet tannin, this will be a 1998 to consume during its first 10–12 years of life.

Already evolved and tasting relatively mature, the dark ruby/purple-colored 1997 offers an excellent berry-scented nose intermixed with dried herbs, earth, and sweet oak. It possesses medium body, low acidity, excellent concentration, and a nicely layered and nuanced finish. Anticipated maturity: now–2012.

A terrific Clos du Marquis, and clearly of second- or third-growth quality, the dark purple-colored 1996 reveals much of its bigger sibling's structure, brooding backwardness and rich, expansive character. The wine is less massive than Léoville-Las Cases but exhibits plenty of sweet kirsch black currant fruit intermixed with high-quality, subtle new oak and steely, mineral characteristics. Rich and medium to full bodied, with ripe tannin, this is a dazzling Clos du Marquis. Anticipated maturity: 2002–2018.

In contrast, the 1995 is the quintessentially elegant style of Las Cases, with copious quantities of sweet fruit, outstanding depth, ripeness, and overall equilibrium, but no sense of heaviness. Like so many of this estate's great wines, everything is in proper proportion, with the acidity, alcohol, and tannin well integrated. The 1996 should hit its peak at the turn of the century and last for 15 or more years. The 1995 is slightly more up front and precocious; it can be drunk now as well as over the next 15 years.

CLOS DE L'ORATOIRE (ST.-ÉMILION)

1998	D	(89–92)
1997	D	(89–91)
1996	D	90
1995	D	89

The 1998 is an explosively rich, weighty, multitextured wine with high tannin. This blockbuster effort needs to integrate some of its aggressive wood and tannin, but it has impressive concentration, richness, and palate presence. This estate has come of age since the young Count de Neipperg took charge. Black/purple colored, with stunning aromatics of roasted herbs, *jus de viande*, licorice, and black fruits, this monster, massive 1998 should merit an outstanding score. Anticipated maturity: 2003–2015.

The 1997 exhibits a gorgeously impressive black/ruby/purple color, as well as exotic aromas of smoky oak intermixed with jammy black fruits, licorice, toast, and Asian spices. The wine possesses superb fruit, an unctuous texture for a 1997, low acidity, and excellent

ripeness. It is another beautiful 1997 that will have immediate appeal upon release. Anticipated maturity: now–2012.

The 1996 is even better out of bottle than it was from cask. The wine boasts an opaque
plum/purple color. Intense aromas of Asian spices, espresso, roasted meats, and sweet, exotic cedar and blackberry fruit soar from the glass of this exotic, ostentatiously styled St.-
Émilion. It is medium to full bodied, with moderate tannin, a sweet midpalate (always a good
sign), and a dense, concentrated, long, powerful finish. This muscular, impressively endowed
offering should drink well between 2002–2017.

An impressive, possibly outstanding wine, the 1995 Clos de l'Oratoire is a sleeper of the
vintage. This dense ruby/purple-colored offering possesses attractive, meaty, sweet cherry
fruit in the nose, intertwined with smoky, toasty oak. Medium to full bodied, spicy, and layered on the palate, the wine reveals fine delineation, grip, and tannin in the long, heady, impressively endowed finish. Some bottle age is warranted. Anticipated maturity: 2001–2015.

CLOS ST.-MARTIN (ST.-ÉMILION)

1998	D	(90–92)
1997	D	(88–89)

Undeniably a sleeper of the vintage, Clos St.-Martin has fashioned a rich, multidimensional
1998, but sadly, only 600 cases were produced. My tasting notes begin with a persuasive
"wow." It boasts a saturated black/purple color, in addition to thick, juicy, black fruit flavors
with notes of minerals, smoky new oak, and dried herbs. Full bodied and rich, with moderately high tannin, most of which is buried within its glycerin and extract level, this is an impressively rich, pure, intense wine that requires 4–5 years of cellaring. Anticipated maturity:
2004–2016.

The 1997 is a potential sleeper of the vintage. This excellent property has produced a
deep, richly fruity wine with admirable concentration and delineation, big, chewy flavors,
and excellent blackberry and cherry fruit presented in a medium-bodied, ripe style. There is
some tannin in the finish. Anticipated maturity: 2001–2012.

LA CLOTTE (ST.-ÉMILION)

1997	D	(85–86)

This straightforward, chunky, low-acid, uncomplex wine offers immediate appeal and reasonably abundant quantities of fruit, glycerin, and alcohol. Its spicy cherry fruit and easygoing style will have many admirers. Drink it over the next 4–5 years.

LA CLUSIÈRE (ST.-ÉMILION)

1998	E	(90–92)

The first vintage produced under the administration of its new owner, Gérard Perse, the 1998
is the finest La Clusière I have ever tasted. Formerly it was a dried-out, hollow, insipid wine.
Under Perse, La Clusière, much like its siblings on the hillsides of St.-Émilion (Pavie and
Pavie-Decesse) has become impressive. The 1998 (made from 100% Merlot that yielded
only 15 hectoliters per hectare) offers a saturated ruby/purple color, as well as an elegant,
sweet black raspberry-and-currant-scented nose, medium body, and stylish, pure, nicely
textured, ripe, layered, fruit-driven, smoky flavors. There is sweet tannin in addition to
considerable elegance and personality. Production was 300 cases. Anticipated maturity:
2002–2015.

LA CONSEILLANTE (POMEROL)

1998	EE	(88–90)
1997	EE	(85–86?)

1996	EE	88
1995	EE	89

While the positive attributes of the 1998 La Conseillante include its openness, undeniably sexy voluptuousness, and forwardness, I wonder if it could not be even better with slightly more intensity and concentration? The medium-bodied 1998 is a candidate for the finest La Conseillante since the 1989 and 1990, particularly if it puts on some weight. The color is dark ruby (much less saturated than other top Pomerols), and the wine offers fragrant peppery, raspberry jam, and cherry notes along with toasty oak and licorice scents. In the mouth, it reveals a noteworthy finesse, elegance, and velvety texture. Because of its low acidity and forward, open-knit style, this wine will be drinkable upon release and keep for 12–15 years.

The 1997 La Conseillante performed inconsistently in three separate tastings in January 1999. It exhibits a medium ruby color, a soft, open-knit personality, fragrant cherry/raspberry fruit and new oak aromas and flavors, and a straightforward, one-dimensional finish. It will be interesting to taste this wine from bottle; it could be charming or slightly diluted, depending on how the bottling is handled. In any event, it will be a wine to drink during its first 7–8 years of life.

La Conseillante, a quintessentially elegant, plump, fruit-driven wine (it can even have a Burgundian character in vintages such as 1989 and 1990), has turned out an open-knit, seductive wine in the generally tough-textured, tannic year of 1996. The color is a deep ruby. The wine possesses medium body and a sweet, open-knit nose of black raspberries intermixed with *pain grillé*, licorice, and smoke. Soft, round, and charming, this offering provides a fine example of the *terroir*'s raspberry fruit. This 1996 can be drunk now but should keep nicely for 12–15 years. Anticipated maturity: now–2014.

It is tempting to give the 1995 an outstanding score because of its seductiveness. However, I do not think it possesses quite the level of extract and concentration to merit an exceptional rating. Nevertheless, it is an extremely pleasing style of claret. The deep ruby color is followed by an open-knit, black cherry, raspberry, and smoky, roasted herb-scented nose. There is round, lush, ripe fruit, medium body, exceptional elegance and purity, and a soft, velvety-textured finish. Think of it as liquid charm and silk. Anticipated maturity: 2000–2014.

Past Glories: 1990 (97), 1989 (97), 1985 (94), 1982 (95?), 1970 (93), 1959 (95), 1949 (97), 1947 (92).

CORBIN MICHOTTE (ST.-ÉMILION)

1998	D	(86–87)
1997	D	(86–87)
1996	D	86
1995	D	89

The fruity, succulent, juicy, easygoing 1998 St.-Émilion offers an intriguing nose of dried herbs, seaweed, and black cherries. Soft, medium bodied, and velvety textured, it is a candidate for early consumption—over the next 7–8 years.

The 1996 follows in the style of most Corbin-Michottes, even though the vintage had a tendency to produce tannic, hard wines. However, Corbin-Michotte seems always to aim for ripeness and a seductive, forward fruity style with no hard edges. The dark ruby-colored 1996 is round and soft, with plenty of herb-tinged berry fruit intermixed with smoke and earth. Ripe and medium bodied, it is ideal for drinking over the next 7–8 years.

The 1997 is a jammier-style wine, with elements of *sur-maturité* and good, fat, cherry/berry fruit intermixed with smoke, earth, and spice scents. It is a medium-bodied, potentially excellent wine for the vintage with low acidity and a seductive, hedonistic appeal. Drink it over the next 5–6 years.

A hedonistic effort from Corbin-Michotte, the 1995 reveals a deep ruby color, a jammy plum, cherry, spice box nose, and medium-bodied, lush, low-acid, juicy, opulently textured, fruity flavors. This is an exuberantly fruity, tasty St.-Émilion that should be reasonably priced. On a pure scale of pleasure, it merits even higher marks. Anticipated maturity: now–2007.

COS D'ESTOURNEL (ST.-ESTÈPHE)

1997	EE	(88–89+)
1996	EE	93+
1995	EE	95

Jean-Guillaume Prats, the administrator, claims that for most of the Cos d'Estournel vineyard, there was a minimum of 120 days between flowering and harvest in 1997. In normal years 105–110 days are usual. The 1997 is surprisingly structured for the vintage. It boasts a deep color in addition to a sweet black currant- and pepper-scented nose with toast in the background. The wine reveals medium body, moderate tannin, and excellent depth and length. About 45% of the crop made it into this cuvée. Anticipated maturity: 2003–2014.

Made from 65% Cabernet Sauvignon and 35% Merlot, the 1996 is a huge, backward wine reminiscent of the 1986 Cos d'Estournel. At the château, they claim the three vintages I love, 1982, 1985, and 1990, are less "classic" than years such as 1986, 1988, 1996, and 1998. The 1996 possesses an opaque purple color, as well as pure aromatics consisting of cassis, grilled herbs, coffee, and toasty new oak. Massive in the mouth, and one of the most structured and concentrated young Cos d'Estournels I have ever tasted, this thick, structured, tannic wine has closed down significantly since bottling. It requires 7–8 years of cellaring and should last for 30–35 years. It is a fabulous Cos, but patience is required. Anticipated maturity: 2006–2030.

A wine of extraordinary intensity and accessibility, the 1995 Cos d'Estournel is a sexier, more hedonistic offering than the muscular, backward 1996. Opulent, with forward aromatics (gobs of black fruits intermixed with toasty *pain grillé* scents and a boatload of spice), this terrific Cos possesses remarkable intensity, full body, and layers of jammy fruit nicely framed by the wine's new oak. Because of low acidity and sweet tannin, the 1995 will be difficult to resist young, although it will age for 2–3 decades. Anticipated maturity: 2001–2025. *Past Glories:* 1994 (91), 1990 (95), 1986 (95), 1985 (93), 1982 (96), 1961 (92), 1959 (92), 1953 (93).

COS LABORY (ST.-ESTÈPHE)

1997	D	(78–82)
1996	D	88
1995	D	88+?

The 1997 is medium bodied and diluted, with a watery rim and black cherry fruit in the nose and flavors. Round and soft, with low acidity, it will need to be drunk over the next 5–7 years.

My concerns about the 1996's tannic ferocity were alleviated by its performance out of bottle. It has turned out to be a classic, dark ruby/purple-colored St.-Estèphe with earthy black currant fruit, medium to full body, moderate tannin, and excellent purity. As the wine sits in the glass, blackberry jam and mineral notes emerge. This well-made, reasonably priced wine should drink well between 2005 and 2018.

Although the dark ruby/purple-colored 1995 Cos Labory is more charming since bottling, aromatically it is closed, with red and black fruits just beginning to emerge. In the mouth, dusty tannin appears elevated, giving the wine a hard, dry, rough-textured finish. However, there is medium to full body and plenty of sweet, ripe fruit on the attack, and my instincts suggest there is good extract behind the wall of tannin. This is not a wine for readers seeking immediate gratification. Anticipated maturity: 2003–2015.

CÔTE DE BALEAU (ST.-ÉMILION)

| 1998 | C (86–88) |

Côte de Baleau is an up-and-coming St.-Émilion estate owned by the Reiffer family, who also own Clos St.-Martin and Grandes-Murailles. The largest of these three estates, Côte de Baleau produces just under 3,000 cases of wine, whereas Grandes-Murailles produces 700 cases and Clos St.-Martin, 600 cases. These wines' upbringings are overseen by the famed, omnipresent oenologist Michel Rolland. The 1998 Côte de Baleau exhibits a saturated purple color, thick, juicy, jammy cherry and spicy new oak aromas, an impressive texture, admirable layers of fruit and glycerin, and moderate tannin. This impressive, pure, excellent offering deserves attention. Anticipated maturity: 2003–2012.

COUFRAN (HAUT-MÉDOC)

| 1996 | C 86 |

This well-made, succulently textured 1996 exhibits a deep ruby color, spicy oak, black cherry/mocha-tinged fruit, and a moderately long finish. It should drink well for 5–7 years.

LA COUSPAUDE (ST.-ÉMILION)

1998	D (90–92)
1997	D (88–91)
1996	D 89
1995	D 90

One of the new-breed St.-Émilions that has caused attention to be focused on this appellation, La Couspaude has hit the bull's-eye in 1998. The opaque purple color is accompanied by knockout aromatics of roasted nuts, smoky toasty oak, and jammy black currant and kirsch. Medium to full bodied, moderately tannic, and more structured and muscular than usual, this Merlot-based wine is not only a sleeper of the vintage, but an outstanding St.-Émilion. It is a candidate for 15 or more years of cellaring. Anticipated maturity: 2003–2015.

The 1997 displays a saturated ruby/purple color in addition to thick, jammy black cherry scents intermixed with smoke, minerals, and coffee notes. Spicy, with low acidity and an open-knit, plump, fleshy, medium- to full-bodied personality, this alluring, flamboyantly styled wine will be delicious following bottling and will keep for 10–12+ years. Anticipated maturity: now–2012.

La Couspaude's 1996 has turned out well. This wine, made from 70% Merlot and 30% Cabernet Franc (3,000 cases), is given 100% new oak malolactic fermentation. Following malolactic fermentation, 25% of the new oak is replaced with additional new oak barrels; thus that portion of the cuvée is entitled to the so-called 200% new oak *élevage*. This is a richly fruity, sexy, medium-bodied, surprisingly soft, fragrant 1996. Its open-knit aromatics consisting of *pain grillé*, cherry liqueur, smoke, and black currants are followed by a luscious, soft, lightly tannic wine. It is destined to be drunk during its first 10–12 years of life.

The 1995 is another offering from the exotic Le Pin-school of St.-Émilions that are made from extremely ripe fruit, aged in 100% new oak (the malolactic fermentation is also done in new oak), and bottled without filtration. The 1995 La Couspaude exhibits ripe, jammy kirsch, black currant, licorice scents with plenty of smoky, *pain grillé* notes. Full bodied, with low acidity and a flamboyant personality, this wine will unquestionably cause heads to turn. Traditionalists may argue that it is too obvious and sexy, but this is a fun wine to taste, and no one can argue that it does not provide pleasure . . . and isn't that the ultimate objective of drinking this stuff? Moreover, it will age well and become even more civilized with cellaring. Anticipated maturity: 2000–2015.

LA CROIX-CANON (CANON-FRONSAC)

1998	C	(89–91)
1997	C	(86–88)
1996	C	86

An unctuous texture and a raspberry, *eau de vie*–like scented nose and flavors result in an astonishing 1998 Canon-Fronsac. Rich and multifaceted, with gorgeous purity, full body, and oodles of concentrated black raspberry and cassis fruit, this is a mind-blowing effort. Anticipated maturity: 2003–2016.

The 1997 La Croix-Canon may be the finest Canon-Fronsac I tasted in this vintage. Its dark ruby color is followed by expressive aromas of cherries, plums, and cassis, excellent purity, medium body, and surprising length. The wine's low acidity gives it more expansiveness and richness in the mouth. Drink it over the next decade.

This splendid *terroir* has produced a deep ruby-colored 1996 with a stylish, complex, elegant nose of sweet cherry jam meshed with floral scents and spice. It presents light fruit on the attack, medium body, light to moderate tannin, and a fine texture and finish. Drink it over the next 6–7 years.

LA CROIX DU CASSE (POMEROL)

1998	D	(87–89+?)
1997	D	(86–88)
1996	D	88
1995	D	90

The opaque black/purple-colored, highly extracted, ferociously tannic 1998 La Croix du Casse is reminiscent of a 1975 Pomerol. There are tons of new oak, as well as power, high tannin, and a rustic earthiness and aggressiveness. If the tannin becomes better integrated and the wood more subtle, this wine will merit an outstanding score. If not, look for it to be controversial. Anticipated maturity: 2003–2015.

La Croix du Casse's 1997 displays an overripe, raisiny, pruny character intermixed with copious quantities of black cherries and blackberries. There is also plenty of toasty new oak. The wine does possess some tannin, but it is forward, with fine depth, ripeness, and expansiveness. Anticipated maturity: 2000–2012.

An impressive Pomerol from proprietor Jean-Michel Arcaute, the 1996 possesses a saturated plum/purple color and a pure nose of spicy, sweet oak, minerals, black fruits, and prunes. The wine is surprisingly open knit for a 1996, with an expansive, medium- to full-bodied, succulent texture. There is tannin in the finish, but it is nearly obscured by the wine's glycerin, fruit extraction, and ripeness. Drink this attractive, silky Pomerol now and over the next 10–12 years.

An outstanding wine, the dense ruby/purple-colored 1995 offers up a knockout nose of blackberries, cassis, minerals, and spicy new oak. Medium to full bodied, with plenty of *pain grillé*–like flavors and abundantly sweet fruit imbued with glycerin and tannin, this wine possesses a long midpalate as well as a finish that builds in the mouth. It is an impressively built, pure, rich Pomerol that merits considerable attention. Anticipated maturity: 2000–2015.

LA CROIX DE GAY (POMEROL)

1998	D	(87–90)
1997	D	(85–87)
1996	D	‹85
1995	D	87

The finest wine from this estate in many years, the multilayered, beautifully textured 1998 exhibits black cherry fruit, cassis, and subtle new oak aromas. Its low acidity, excellent richness, medium to full body, and concentrated, long finish suggest a wine that will evolve gracefully yet keep for 12–15 years. Impressive!

The 1997 exhibits a cherry, strawberry jam component in its spicy aromatics. The wine is elegant, with good ripeness, sweetness, and medium body. It may be slightly more concentrated and longer than the light 1996. Drink it over the next 5–7 years.

The medium ruby-colored 1996 displays a moderately intense nose of roasted herbs intermixed with cherry jam. Seductive, easygoing, open knit, and light, it offers low acidity and an accessible style that suggest consuming it over the next 5–6 years.

The 1995 is a seductive, elegant, attractive Pomerol with a deep ruby color and plenty of sweet, plum, cherry and berry fruit intermixed with subtle toasty new oak. The wine is round and lush, with copious fruit and enough glycerin to provide a nicely layered texture in a stylish format. Anticipated maturity: now–2006.

Past Glories: 1964 (90), 1947 (92).

CROIX DE LABRIE (ST.-ÉMILION)

1998	D	(90–94)

Made by Jean-Luc Thunevin (of Valandraud fame), this wine, from a microscopic estate, will be nearly impossible to find, but those lucky enough to procure a bottle are in for one of the vintage's great tasting experiences. A saturated, viscous black/purple color suggests unbelievable texture and richness. Tasters' palates will get lost in the thick, rich, intense concentration of this full-bodied St.-Émilion. It possesses oodles of jammy blackberry and currant fruit nicely buttressed by moderate tannin and toasty oak. Thick, full bodied, and spectacularly long, this fabulous effort should age effortlessly for 15–20 years. It is an unqualified sleeper of the vintage, but who will be able to find it?

CROIZET-BAGES (PAUILLAC)

1997	C	(78–83)
1996	C	87
1995	C	85

The soft, round, elegant 1997 Croizet-Bages is not concentrated, but it does possess moderately sweet jammy cassis and red currant fruit intermixed with spicy, smoky oak. Already soft, it is ideal for consuming during its first decade of life. Anticipated maturity: now–2010.

The 1996 has turned out even better than I had expected, continuing this estate's progression in quality that began several years ago. The dark ruby color is followed by sweet, elegant notes of black currants, cherries, spicy oak, and cedar. The wine is medium bodied, with sweet tannin and a moderately long finish. Purely made, with good depth, it represents one of the more forward Pauillacs of the vintage. Anticipated maturity: 2003–2014.

Based on its performance from cask, I had hoped the 1995 would be slightly better. Nevertheless, it has turned out to be a good claret, made in a lighter style. The medium ruby color is followed by straightforward, soft, berry, and black currant aromatics. In the mouth, the wine reveals an attractive, spicy, fleshy feel, not much weight or depth, but a superficial charm and fruitiness. This wine can be drunk young and should last for 10–12 years. Anticipated maturity: 2000–2009.

CROQUE MICHOTTE (ST.-ÉMILION)

1998	C	(85–87)

A ripe, fruit-driven, dark ruby-colored wine, this stylish, easygoing effort possesses blackberry and cherry fruit, fine purity, and a medium-bodied, clean, slightly tannic finish. Drink it over the next 7–8 years.

CRUZEAU (PESSAC-LÉOGNAN)

1998	C	(85–87)

Deep ruby/purple colored, with moderately intense aromatics consisting of ripe, berry scents and spicy, weedy notes, elegant, moderately concentrated flavors, and sweet tannin in the finish, this 1998 Cruzeau should drink well during its first 7–10 years of life.

CUVÉE POMONE (ST.-ÉMILION)

1998	D	(87–88)

The luxury cuvée of Château Haut-Villet, this wine has a lamentable tendency to be too oaky, but the 1998 appears to be better balanced than previous vintages. It possesses huge extraction, medium to full body, aggressive tannin, and excellent purity. The wine's structure is not totally integrated into its rich fruit, but there is plenty of potential to this backward, impressively endowed St.-Émilion. Anticipated maturity: 2004–2012.

DALEM (FRONSAC)

1998	C	(85–87)
1997	C	(85–86)
1995	C	85

A delicious, fruit-driven Fronsac, the 1998 Dalem exhibits excellent ripeness, abundant jammy cassis fruit, spice, and a medium-bodied structure. It should drink well for a decade.

The saturated dark purple color of the 1997 is followed by a masculine, structured, well-delineated Fronsac with plenty of sweet berry fruit, as well as the telltale minerality displayed by many wines from this beautiful appellation. A slight hardness kept my score down, but I suspect the tannin will melt away to reveal a charming, concentrated, well-made wine that will drink well in 2–3 years and last for a decade.

A good, solid wine, the ruby-colored 1995 Dalem displays minerals, berry fruit, and weediness in the scents and flavors, as well as a soft underbelly and mild tannin in the moderately long finish. It should drink well for 5–8 years.

DASSAULT (ST.-ÉMILION)

1997	C	(85–86)
1996	C	76?

The very good, dark ruby-colored 1997 Dassault offers crushed black cherry and raspberry fruit and a low-acid, lush, medium-bodied personality. It is an easygoing, pleasant wine destined for near-term consumption. Anticipated maturity: now–2006.

The 1996 was suspicious in cask samples because of a distinctive mustiness. Dassault has corrected this problem with the 1997. The 1996 is one-dimensional and sterile. It is nowhere near the quality of some of Dassault's older vintages or the delicious, fruit-driven 1997.

DAUGAY (ST.-ÉMILION)

1996	C	(85–86)
1995	C	85

Daugay's 1996 is a spicy, medium-bodied, Cabernet Franc–dominated wine with weedy, red and black currant, and tobacco notes, good depth, and more softness than many wines from this sector of St.-Émilion. Drink it over the next 7–8 years. The 1995 is meaty and ripe, with a deep ruby color, a sense of elegance, herb-tinged black fruit, good ripeness, and a lush palate feel.

LA DAUPHINE (FRONSAC)

1998	C	(87–88)
1997	C	(85–86)
1996	C	86
1995	C	87

One of the most sumptuous La Dauphines I have ever tasted, the 1998 is reminiscent of black cherry liqueur. The deep ruby/purple color is followed by a wine with good fat and succulence, medium to full body, low acidity, and an exuberant personality. It is well worth seeking out. Anticipated maturity: now–2008.

The rich, fruity 1997 Dauphine is similarly styled to the 1996 but displays more fat and plumpness. Aromas and flavors of cherries are present in this medium-bodied, pure wine with a soft, satisfying finish.

The 1996 possesses a dark ruby color and soft, pleasant, straightforward flavors of cherries, ripe plums, dried herbs, and minerals. Smoothly textured and light to medium bodied, it is a fruity, cleanly made wine to enjoy over the next 4–5 years.

A fine effort from La Dauphine, the 1995 reveals more fat, fruit, and lushness than its 1996 sibling. The color is a healthy dark ruby, and the nose offers aromas of cinnamon, black cherries, currants, and spice. Revealing a lovely combination of fruit and spice, this round, medium-bodied wine possesses excellent concentration, low acidity, and a precocious appeal. Anticipated maturity: now–2003.

DAUZAC (MARGAUX)

1998	D	(86–88)
1997	D	(78–82)
1996	D	86
1995	C	86+

An opaque purple-colored wine, Dauzac's 1998 exhibits copious quantities of black fruits intermixed with toasty new oak, tar, and licorice. Deep, rich, and medium bodied, with moderate tannin, this well-made, complete wine should age gracefully. Anticipated maturity: 2004–2015.

The 1997 possesses a hollow middle and a washed-out, clipped/compressed finish. It lacks fruit concentration and comes across as diluted. Anticipated maturity: now–2007.

The 1996 offers sweet black currant fruit intertwined with smoke, herbs, and new oak. Medium bodied, with good extract, moderate depth and tannin, and a ripe finish, it will drink well between 2002 and 2015. It is a good, middle-weight Margaux.

A broodingly backward, tannic, dark ruby-colored wine, Dauzac's 1995 borders on being too austere, but there is enough sweet black currant fruit, as well as medium body and a fleshy midpalate, to elicit enthusiasm. While this will never be a great claret, it is a well-made, competent Margaux that will age nicely. Anticipated maturity: 2003–2015.

DESTIEUX (ST.-ÉMILION)

1997	C	(86–87)
1996	C	86+
1995	C	85

This reasonably priced, underrated St.-Émilion estate turns out rustic, muscular, mouth-filling wines with hefty extract. What they lack in complexity, they make up in richness and intensity. The black/purple-colored 1997 Destieux exhibits sweet blackberry fruit inter-mixed with truffle and licorice notes. On the palate, herbs and earthy flavors make an ap-pearance, along with copious tannin. However, the acidity is low, and the wine possesses an expressive, succulent texture. It should drink well for 10–12 years.

The dark ruby/purple-colored 1996 displays sweet blackberry and cherry fruit, medium body, aggressive tannin, and a savory character. It will benefit from 1–3 years of cellaring and keep for a decade or more. Anticipated maturity: 2002–2012.

Well made, with a deep ruby/purple color and sweet, earthy, black currant aromas, the medium-bodied, moderately tannic 1995 reveals good fruit on the attack, spice, leather, and iron in the flavors, and good depth but some hardness in the finish. Anticipated maturity: 2001–2010.

LA DOMINIQUE (ST.-ÉMILION)

1998	D	(87–88)
1997	D	(86–87)
1996	D	88
1995	D	89

An open-knit, surprisingly soft wine, La Dominique's 1998 exhibits a dark ruby color. In ad-dition, it offers copious aromas of vanillin and black currant fruit, excellent ripeness, medium body, and sweet tannin. It is a St.-Émilion to consume during its first 10–12 years of life.

The 1997 La Dominique displays a notion of overripeness in its prunelike, blackberry-scented nose. New oak and black raspberry fruit emerge in the mouth. This soft, sexy, medium-bodied, low-acid St.-Émilion possesses sweet tannin and loads of lush, jammy fruit. Drink it over the next 7–8 years.

The smoky, lavishly oaked 1996 reveals an impressive dark ruby/purple color. The nose offers up plenty of *pain grillé* along with black cherries, raspberries, and dried herbs and smoke. The wine provides sweet fruit on the attack, low acidity, medium body, and a nicely textured finish with fat/glycerin in evidence. Prior to bottling, I noted some astringency and awkward tannin, but neither was noticeable on the three separate occasions I had the wine out of bottle. Anticipated maturity: 2001–2012.

While 1995 is also a tannic vintage for La Dominique, there is sweeter fruit as well as more ripeness and intensity (at least at present) in the wine's moderately intense nose of vanillin, blackberry and raspberry fruit. In the mouth, there is good sweetness, medium to full body, moderate tannin, and a layered, rich, classic-tasting profile. Anticipated maturity: 2003–2016.

Past Glories: 1990 (92), 1989 (92), 1982 (91).

DUBOIS-GRIMON (CÔTES DE CASTILLON)

1997		C	(85–87)

Dubois-Grimon is an impressive newcomer from this satellite appellation east of St.-Émilion. The 1997 Dubois-Grimon exhibits a deep ruby/purple color as well as pure berry fruit aromas, medium body, a low-acid, pure, well-endowed personality, and a nicely layered texture. Elegant, richly fruity, and soft, it will provide ideal drinking for 3–4 years.

DUCRU-BEAUCAILLOU (ST.-JULIEN)

1998	EE	(88–90)
1997	EE	(87–89+)
1996	EE	96
1995	EE	94

Sixty-eight percent of Ducru's harvest for the 1998 made it into the grand vin, which is a blend of 70% Cabernet Sauvignon and 30% Merlot. An excellent wine, possibly meriting an outstanding score depending on how it develops, the 1998 Ducru is more evolved than usual, but it reveals the vintage's telltale tannic hardness in its finish. Classically proportioned with plenty of plum and cassis fruit intermixed with toasty oak as well as minerals, it possesses good power, medium body, excellent richness, and a concentrated, firm, angular finish. Although not of the same quality as the 1995 or 1996, it has been well made.

The 1997 Ducru-Beaucaillou is a potential sleeper of the vintage in the sense that it could merit an outstanding score, no small achievement for a second-growth in the 1997 vintage. The wine possesses Ducru's elegance allied with structure, power, and concentration. It should keep for 14–15 years. There is plenty of mineral-tinged black currant fruit intermixed with spicy new oak. Medium bodied, elegant, ripe, and impeccably well made, it will be fully mature between 2001 and 2014.

I tasted the 1996 Ducru-Beaucaillou on four separate occasions from bottle in January 1999 and was twice able to taste it blind against the fabulous 1995. It is a marginal call, but the 1996 appears slightly longer, with a deeper midpalate. It also reveals more tannin in the finish. Both the 1995 and 1996 are remarkable. Many readers may see them as identical twins, but I suspect the 1995, with its slightly higher percentage of Merlot, will drink well at an earlier age. If the 1995 is more charming, the 1996 is more muscular, concentrated, and classic. Bottled in late June 1998, the 1996 exhibits a saturated ruby/purple color as well as a knockout nose of minerals, licorice, cassis, and an unmistakable lead pencil smell that I often associate with top vintages of Lafite-Rothschild. It is sweet and full bodied yet unbelievably rich, with no sense of heaviness or flabbiness. The wine possesses high tannin, but it is extremely ripe, and the sweetness of the black currant, spice-tinged Cabernet Sauvignon fruit is pronounced. This profound, backward Ducru-Beaucaillou is a must-purchase. It will be fascinating for readers who own both the 1995 and 1996 to follow the evolution of these two exceptional vintages. Anticipated maturity: 2008–2035.

Once again, the 1995 is of first-growth quality, not only from an intellectual perspective, but in its hedonistic characteristics. More open knit and accessible than the 1996, Ducru's 1995 exhibits a saturated ruby/purple color followed by a knockout nose of blueberry and black raspberry/cassis fruit intertwined with minerals, flowers, and subtle toasty new oak. Like its younger sibling, the wine possesses a sweet, rich midpalate (from extract and ripeness, not sugar), layers of flavor, good delineation and grip, but generally unobtrusive tannin and acidity. It is a classic, compelling example of Ducru-Beaucaillou that should not be missed. Anticipated maturity: 2003–2025.

Past Glories: 1994 (90), 1986 (92), 1985 (92), 1982 (94), 1978 (90), 1970 (92), 1961 (96), 1959 (90), 1953 (93), 1947 (93).

DUHART MILON (PAUILLAC)

1997	D	(86–88)
1996	D	90
1995	D	87

A soft, low-acid, ripe, seductive wine, the dark ruby-colored 1997 Duhart reveals cassis fruit, a plump, corpulent texture, and a nice finish. This is a user-friendly, easy-to-understand offering. Anticipated maturity: now–2010.

A strong case can be made that the 1996 is the finest Duhart produced since the 1982. The color is a saturated dark ruby/purple. The bouquet offers aromas of blackberry fruit intermixed with licorice, minerals, and dried herbs. Rich and intense, with considerable finesse, medium to full body, and outstanding concentration and purity, this should be a reasonably priced wine. It reflects the increased attention Lafite's administrator, Charles Chevalier, has been giving this nearby estate. Anticipated maturity: 2005–2020.

Made from a blend of 80% Cabernet Sauvignon/20% Merlot, the 1995 is slightly sweeter, more supple, and slenderer than the broader-shouldered 1996. The wine's bouquet offers aromas of ripe berry fruit intermixed with minerals, toasty oak, and spice. Medium bodied, with fine extract, it is a finesse-style Pauillac (in the best sense of the word). Anticipated maturity: 2002–2014.

Past Glories: 1982 (93).

DOMAINE DE L'ÉGLISE (POMEROL)

1997	D	(85–86)

Intriguing roasted coffee, berry, chocolate, and toast aromas emerge from this medium dark ruby-colored wine. Round, plump, and succulent, with moderately good concentration, and a short finish, this is a cleanly made, competent Pomerol to drink over its first 4–7 years of life.

Past Glories: 1989 (90).

L'ÉGLISE-CLINET (POMEROL)

1998	EEE	(92–95)
1997	EEE	(89–92)
1996	EEE	93
1995	EEE	96

One of the vintage's stars, l'Église-Clinet's 1998, while unlikely to be superior to the glorious 1995 or 1985, is a blockbuster within the standards set by Pomerol in this vintage. The color is an intense saturated ruby/purple. The nose offers up licorice, spice, sweet blackberry and cherry liqueur-like scents. Layer after layer of concentrated fruit cascade over the palate with exceptional purity and medium to full body. Unlike its neighbor, Clinet, this wine has successfully integrated its tannin and new oak. The 1998 possesses low acidity, high extract, and impressive tannin, but it is more forward than Clinet. Anticipated maturity: 2002–2020.

The forward 1997 l'Église-Clinet exhibits low acidity, a saturated ruby/purple color, medium body, and gobs of jammy black cherry fruit intermixed with cassis, truffles, raspberries, and smoke. Fruit driven, with plenty of glycerin, and fine length, this seductive, soft, velvety-textured wine should drink well for 10–15 years.

One of the few profound Pomerols in 1996, l'Église-Clinet turned out an uncommonly rich, concentrated wine that is performing well from bottle, even though it is displaying a more tightly knit structure than it did from cask. The dark ruby/purple color is followed by notes of charcoal, jammy cassis, raspberries, and a touch of *sur-maturité*. Spicy oak emerges as the wine sits in the glass. It is fat, concentrated, and medium to full bodied, with a layered, multidimensional, highly nuanced personality. This muscular Pomerol will require 3–5 years of bottle age. Anticipated maturity: 2004–2020.

One of the vintage's most awesome wines, l'Église-Clinet's 1995 has been fabulous from both cask and bottle. The color is opaque purple. The wine is closed aromatically, but it does offer a concoction of black raspberries, kirsch, smoke, cherries, and truffles. Full bodied and rich, with high tannin but profound levels of fruit and richness, this dense, exceptionally well-delineated, layered, multidimensional l'Église-Clinet only hints at its ultimate potential. This looks to be a legend in the making. I could not get over the extraordinary texture of this wine in the mouth. Intensity and richness without heaviness—a tour de force in wine-making! Anticipated maturity: 2008–2030.

Past Glories: 1994 (90), 1990 (92), 1989 (90?), 1986 (92), 1985 (95), 1975 (92), 1971 (92), 1961 (92), 1959 (96), 1950 (95), 1949 (99), 1947 (100), 1945 (98), 1921 (100).

L'ENCLOS (POMEROL)

1997		C	(85–86)

An easygoing, low-acid, plump claret, l'Enclos's 1997 displays moderately rich, chocolate, and mocha-tinged black cherry fruit, medium body, a supple texture, and a short finish. It is ideal for drinking over the next 5–6 years.

L'ÉVANGILE (POMEROL)

1998	EEE	(90–92)
1997	EEE	(89–91)
1996	EEE	90?
1995	EEE	92+

Based on the accolades I was hearing around Bordeaux about how profound 1998 l'Évangile was, I expected to be impressed. Admittedly, I was not bowled over to the extent some of my acquaintances were. The color of the 1998 is a saturated dark ruby, and the nose offers up telltale black raspberry scents along with dried herbs, licorice, and earth. Elegant and medium bodied, with exceptional purity, outstanding concentration, and moderate tannin in the finish, the 1998 is neither as soft and succulent as the 1995, 1990, and 1989, nor as structured and concentrated as the 1985. Given the propensity of many Pomerols to behave like modern-day versions of their 1975 counterparts, I cannot suggest that this offering is as profound as that great vintage of l'Évangile. Anticipated maturity: 2003–2020.

The 1997 reveals elements of *sur-maturité*, as well as blackberry and raspberry fruit, a touch of tea and raisins, medium to full body, and a low-acid, fat, jammy finish. It should be more hedonistic and accessible at an earlier age than the 1996. Anticipated maturity: 2001–2015.

Much like its neighbor, Clinet, the 1996 l'Évangile will undoubtedly be controversial. The wine gives the impression of being overextracted in its dark ruby/purple color and notes of prunes, raisins, Chinese black tea, blackberries, and cherry liqueur. It is rich and powerful, as well as tannic and disjointed, but medium to full bodied, with excellent richness and a long, overripe finish. It may take a few years to round into shape, but this could turn out to be an outstanding wine. Anticipated maturity: 2003–2016.

Tasted three times, the 1995 is closed, backward, and marginally less impressive after bottling than it was from cask. It is still an outstanding l'Évangile that may prove to be longer lived than the sumptuous 1990, but perhaps not as opulently styled. It remains one of the year's top efforts. The dense ruby/purple color is accompanied by aromas of minerals, black raspberries, earth, and spice. The bottled wine seems toned down (too much fining and filtration?) compared with the prebottling samples, which had multiple layers of flesh and flavor dimension. High tannin in the finish and plenty of sweet fruit on the palate suggest this wine will turn out to be extra special. Could it have been even better if the filters had been junked in favor of a natural bottling? I think so, yet that being said, the wine's ferocious tannin level cannot conceal its outstanding ripeness, purity, and depth. However, do not expect this Pomerol to be drinkable for another 5–8 years, which is longer than I initially expected. Anticipated maturity: 2005–2020.

Past Glories: 1994 (92), 1990 (96), 1989 (90), 1985 (95), 1983 (90), 1982 (96), 1975 (96), 1961 (99), 1947 (97).

FAUGÈRES (ST.-ÉMILION)

1998	D	(88–89)
1997	D	(87–90)
1996	D	87
1995	C	87

I remember visiting this superb St.-Émilion estate several years ago and being impressed by the commitment to quality evidenced by the owners, Peby and Corinne Guisez. They have breathed new life into this well-placed property with its striking eighteenth-century château. Sadly, Peby died tragically at age 52, but his widow, Corinne, seems fully committed to running this estate and turning out high-quality wines.

Madame Guisez has turned out another convincing sleeper of the 1998 vintage. The color is an impressively saturated purple. The gorgeous nose offers up notes of smoke, licorice, black raspberries, and cassis. The wine is dense, sweet, and rich, with a creamy texture, moderately high tannin, and a medium-bodied, layered, yet well-delineated finish. Anticipated maturity: 2002–2015.

Another sleeper, the 1997 Faugères reveals sweeter fruit than the 1996, more volume and glycerin in the mouth, low acidity, a fleshy, black raspberry-scented and -flavored personality, and lavish quantities of toasty new oak. This is an excellent, possibly outstanding, wine that should drink well when released and evolve nicely for 10–14 years.

This property has turned out a dense ruby/purple-colored 1996 offering aromas of toasty new oak, black fruits, and spice. Rich and medium to full bodied, with moderate tannin, this sleeper of the vintage can probably still be purchased for a reasonable price. Anticipated maturity: 2001–2012.

Dark ruby/purple colored with a smoky, sexy nose of black cherry fruit, licorice, vanillin, and spice, the medium-bodied, elegant, yet flavorful, mouth-filling 1995 St.-Émilion possesses excellent depth and fine overall balance. The long finish exhibits some tannin, but in general this is an accessible, up-front claret to consume over the next 7–8 years. It is also a reasonably good value. A sleeper.

FERRAND-LARTIGUE (ST.-ÉMILION)

1998	D	(91–93)
1997	D	(86–88)
1996	D	90
1995	D	89

Louis Mitjavile, François's son, has taken over the vinification of this microestate dedicated to producing world-class wines. The 1998 (a blend of 95% Merlot and 5% Cabernet Franc) is his first vintage. Whether because of Mitjavile's influence or the vintage's raw materials, this is the finest Ferrand-Lartigue in its short history. The color is saturated black/purple. The dazzlingly, exquisite aromatics offer up Asian spices, toasty *pain grillé*, cherry liqueur, chocolate, licorice, and smoke. It is more powerful than usual, extremely rich and concentrated, with the intense Merlot character well presented. A large-scale, massive effort, it will require 2–3 years of cellaring before it reaches full maturity. It should drink well for 15–16 years. Bravo!

The 1997 is an open-knit, toasty, medium-bodied wine with a lush, hedonistic personality, plenty of jammy cherry fruit, low acidity, and an attractive finish. It will be delicious after bottling and should last for 5–6 years.

The 1996 is one of St.-Émilion's stars. Even though it is not a premier grand cru or even a grand cru classé, it is superior to many wines with those higher pedigrees. The dense purple-colored 1996 reveals lavish toasty new oak in the nose intermixed with framboise, kirsch, and black currant fruit. In the mouth, it displays a sweet midpalate, gorgeous purity, moderate tannin, and a round, impressively long finish. This wine is accessible, but readers who have tasted previous vintages of Ferrand-Lartigue will want to cellar it for 1–2 years and drink it over the following 12–15. It will be atypically long-lived for a wine from this estate. Anticipated maturity: 2001–2013.

A sexy, open-knit wine, the 1995 Ferrand-Lartigue exhibits a dark ruby/purple color, a jammy, candied fruit and toasty-scented nose, ripe, velvety-textured, complex, generous black cherry and cassis flavors, and low acidity. This medium-bodied, already delicious wine is ideal for drinking now and over the next decade. A sleeper of the vintage.

FERRIÈRE (MARGAUX)

1997	D	(81–83)
1996	D	86
1995	D	86+

The 1997 is a soft, red currant/cassis-scented wine with good fruit on the attack but a compressed, short finish. Drink it over the next 5–6 years.

The 1996 exhibits a dark ruby color and a stern, unevolved, backward personality with hard tannin in the finish. Nevertheless there is fine ripeness, good purity, and a medium-bodied, traditional style. Anticipated maturity: 2004–2014.

If it were not for the 1996, the 1995 would be the best Ferrière I have ever tasted. The wine exhibits an impressively saturated ruby/purple color and an attractive nose of sweet toasty oak, licorice, and jammy black fruits. In the mouth, the attack begins well, with good ripeness, purity, and fruit, but it narrows out with an uninspiring midpalate and gobs of tannin in an astringent, tough-textured finish. The tannin should become better integrated with another 4–5 years of bottle age. This is a well-made Ferrière, with a firm, angular personality and plenty of aging potential. How good it is to see this château finally get back on its feet after a prolonged period of mediocrity. Anticipated maturity: 2004–2015.

FEYTIT-CLINET (POMEROL)

1998	D	(87–89)

This 1998 is the finest Feytit-Clinet I have tasted. Dark purple colored, with a deep, intense, extracted feel, the 1998 is a moderately closed, yet promising, medium- to full-bodied wine with excellent richness and earthy, licorice, and black cherry/cranberry-like fruit flavors. There is plenty of glycerin, moderately high tannin, and a mouth-filling personality to this large-scale effort from one of Pomerol's perennial underachievers. Anticipated maturity: 2002–2016.

DE FIEUZAL (PESSAC LÉOGNAN)

1998	D	(85–86+?)
1997	D	(86–88)
1996	D	88+
1995	D	90

Dark ruby/purple colored, with plenty of wood and minerals in the aromatics, the 1998 Fieuzal reveals astringency and greenness in its tannin as well as an abrupt finish. This wine could turn out better than I have indicated, but the tannin is worrisome. Anticipated maturity: 2003–2012.

The dark ruby/purple-colored 1997 de Fieuzal offers jammy black fruit aromas intermixed with lavish quantities of toasty new oak. The wine is low in acidity, without the volume and power of the 1996, but it is a well-made, forward effort. Anticipated maturity: 2000–2012.

As I had optimistically hoped, de Fieuzal's 1996 has fleshed out its midpalate. It exhibits a saturated purple color in addition to intense charcoal, smoky, mineral, and black fruit aromatics. Highly extracted and rich, with a sweet, concentrated midpalate and plenty of muscle and tannin in the moderately long finish, this backward yet promising Fieuzal should last for 2 decades. Anticipated maturity: 2006–2020.

The quintessentially elegant 1995 reveals a deep ruby/purple color and an attractive smoky, black currant, mineral, floral-scented nose. There are sweet, ripe, lush flavors, medium body, ripe tannin, and a velvety texture that borders on opulence. There is no heaviness to the wine. Moreover, neither the tannin, the acidity, nor the alcohol are intrusive. This seamless, extremely well-made claret is a candidate for early drinking, yet it possesses excellent aging potential. Anticipated maturity: 2003–2020.

Past Glories (white): 1994 (92), 1993 (92), 1992 (91), 1989 (90), 1988 (92), 1985 (93).

FIGEAC (ST.-ÉMILION)

1998	EE	(88–91)
1997	EE	(86–87)
1996	EE	82
1995	E	89

Undoubtedly the 1998 is the finest Figeac produced since the gorgeously rich, complex 1990. This perennial underachiever has turned out a sexy, complex, elegant wine with a dark ruby color, cedar, cigar box, spice, and black currant scents, and a medium-bodied, supple, round, velvety-textured personality. With beautiful fruit and nicely integrated tannin, it is not a blockbuster, but a Figeac that combines richness with a stylish yet intense perfume. Anticipated maturity: 2001–2015.

The 1997 Figeac is very good, possibly excellent. Charming and delicious, with dried herb, black cherry, licorice, and fruitcake aromas, it possesses soft, lush, currancy flavors, but not a great deal of body or depth. It is beautifully harmonious and cleanly made. Drink it over the next 7–8 years.

I know the proprietors of Figeac think I am unduly tough on their wines, but I am a huge fan of Figeac. When it is exceptional, as it certainly was in 1964, 1982, and 1990, I purchase and drink it with great pleasure. However, too many Figeacs lack concentration and evolve too quickly. Such is the case with the 1996. Medium ruby colored, with a mature nose of cedar, tobacco, fruitcake, and cherry fruit, it is a light, medium-bodied wine with evidence of dilution. The finish is abrupt with light tannin. Drink it over the next 7–8 years.

The fiftieth anniversary release of the proprietors, the Manoncourt family, the 1995 Figeac is a gorgeously complex, dark ruby-colored wine that is all delicacy and complexity. The multidimensional, alluring, smoky, toasty, Asian spice, menthol, and cherry nose is followed by soft, round, rich, kirschlike flavors intermixed with black currants, herbs, and weedy tobacco. While it is less impressive in the mouth, the nose is outstanding. This is a soft, forward style of Figeac that can be drunk young or cellared. Anticipated maturity: now–2010.

Past Glories: 1990 (94), 1982 (93), 1970 (90), 1964 (94), 1961 (94?), 1959 (91), 1955 (95), 1953 (93), 1949 (94).

LA FLEUR (ST.-ÉMILION)

1998	C	(86–88)
1997	C	(85–86)
1996	C	86
1995	C	87

The typically fruity, soft, consumer-friendly 1998 exhibits more structure and tannin than normal, as well as a denser, more saturated color and an extra dimension of muscle and richness. It offers a sweet, black cherry-scented nose with earth and oak in the background. Medium bodied, with more delineation than in past efforts, this should turn out to be a good wine but, atypically, in need of 2–4 years of cellaring. Anticipated maturity: 2002–2010.

Although similarly styled to the 1996, the 1997 possesses more body and structure. It has a deep ruby color, in addition to a rich, jammy nose, low acidity, good volume and weight in the mouth, and an attractive, clean finish. Anticipated maturity: now–2009.

The excellent 1996 La Fleur is a good choice for restaurants and consumers looking for a wine with immediate drinkability. Over recent years the style of this wine has offered straightforward, open-knit, ripe fruit presented in an easy-to-understand manner. The medium ruby-colored 1996 reveals a gorgeous nose of overripe cherries intermixed with framboise and currants. In the mouth, the wine is medium bodied, with a velvety texture, fine purity, and gobs of fruit. This satiny-textured claret will continue to drink well for 5–6 years.

Consumers and restaurants looking for soft, seductive, richly fruity Bordeaux wines that are not priced like Tiffany jewelry should check out this seductive, medium- to full-bodied, round, velvety-textured 1995 St.-Émilion. It is medium deep ruby colored, with an evolved, lovely nose of jammy black cherries, strawberries, and spice. The supple palate is all finesse, fruit, and succulence. Drink this delicious 1995 La Fleur now and over the next 7–8 years.

LA FLEUR DE GAY (POMEROL)

1998	EE	(91–93)
1997	EE	(85–86)
1996	EE	85
1995	EE	90+

Unquestionably the finest wine produced at this microestate since the 1989, the 1998 displays a gorgeously saturated black/purple color followed by aromas of blackberries/blueberries, flowers, minerals, and sweet vanillin. It is a wine of exceptional intensity yet is beautifully seamless, medium to full bodied, and superbly concentrated. The tannin is sweet, but high. This rich, layered, multidimensional La Fleur de Gay should be at its finest between 2003 and 2020.

The medium-bodied, pleasant 1997 La Fleur de Gay is a wine of undeniable finesse and elegance, but it lacks concentration in its midpalate and finish. Moderate quantities of sweet black currant fruit intermixed with new oak and minerals are present in the nose and finish. This medium-bodied, stylish wine will drink well for 6–7 years.

Given this vineyard's *terroir*, the 1996 La Fleur de Gay is a light, disappointing effort. Its nose of new oak, dried herbs, and red fruits is followed by an elegant, compressed wine that is correctly made but uninspiring. There is dry, astringent tannin in the finish. I do not believe this wine will soften and fatten up, so consume it over the next 7–8 years.

The 1995 La Fleur de Gay has begun to shut down following bottling. The color is a healthy dense ruby/purple. The nose displays aromas of minerals, *pain grillé,* a touch of prunes, and gobs of black cherries and cassis intertwined with vanillin from new oak casks. This medium-bodied wine exhibits fennel-like black currant flavors, high tannin, and impressive purity, depth, and length. However, patience will be required. Anticipated maturity: 2003–2018.

Past Glories: 1990 (92), 1989 (94+), 1988 (93), 1987 (90).

LA FLEUR GAZIN (POMEROL)

1997	D	(86–87)
1996	D	86

The medium-bodied, well-made, elegant 1996 La Fleur Gazin offers attractive coffee and tobacco-tinged berry fruit, surprising softness for the vintage, and good overall equilibrium. Drink it over the next 8–10 years. The 1997 reveals more herbaceousness, in addition to plum/cherry flavors intermixed with truffle and earthy notes. Surprisingly, there is more body and tannin than in the 1996, but at the same time a more vegetal characteristic. Anticipated maturity: 2000–2010.

LA FLEUR DE JAUGUE (ST.-ÉMILION)

1998	C	(88–89)
1997	C	(86–87)
1996	C	87
1995	C	89

Readers take note: This consistently well-made St.-Émilion remains undervalued relative to the high prices fetched by many of its peers. The dense ruby/purple-colored 1998 displays big, juicy, succulent, black cherry-dominated aromatics with hints of dried herbs, earth, and wood. Medium to full bodied, with a heady, fleshy mouth-feel as well as a long, richly fruity finish, this wine will be accessible upon release and drink well for 10–12 years.

One of the best-run properties in St.-Émilion, La Fleur de Jaugue (a second wine called Jaugue Blanc is also produced) has produced a very fine 1997. The wine is soft, with lovely fruit, good ripeness, and a more evolved personality than the 1996. It is all flesh and fruit, offering a nice display of cherries and spice. Drink it over the next 5–6 years.

The 1996 is similarly styled, deep ruby colored, with plenty of sweet cherry and plumlike fruit intermixed with dried herbs, smoke, and a touch of earth and new oak. Fleshy, with excellent texture, and ripe fruit, it is a tasty St.-Émilion to enjoy over the next 5–6 years.

Unquestionably a sleeper of the vintage, the delicious, dark plum/purple-colored 1995 reveals flashy, jammy red and black fruits (primarily cherries and cassis) in the nose, sweet vanillin, medium to full body, excellent, nearly outstanding ripeness and depth, and a low-acid, sumptuous, opulent personality. This is a delicious, plump, juicy St.-Émilion to consume over the next 8–10 years.

LA FLEUR-PÉTRUS (POMEROL)

1998	E	(91–94)
1997	E	(90–92)
1996	E	89+
1995	E	93

La Fleur-Pétrus is finally living up to its name. Obviously the acquisition of the finest parcel of old vines from Le Gay has given this wine added richness and power. The splendid 1998 is not only a true *vin de garde,* but also a sumptuous, concentrated, intense Pomerol that marries elegance with exceptional concentration and muscle. The color is a dense black/ruby and the wine more fruit driven than some of Christian Moueix's other Pomerols. It is full bodied, with luscious purity, layers of sweet black cherry-and-cassis-scented fruit nicely touched by subtle, toasty oak, admirable length, sweet tannin, low acidity, and high concentration. The overall impression is one of structured opulence. Anticipated maturity: 2005–2020.

The 1997 La Fleur-Pétrus is an outstanding example from this vintage. The wine offers up a gorgeously sweet nose of black raspberry and blueberry fruit intertwined with spicy oak and minerals. In the mouth, it is all finesse and fruit, with medium body, no hard edges, and an excellent, surprisingly long finish. Not a huge, blockbuster style of Pomerol, it emphasizes harmony and richness without the accompanying muscle and tannin. Given the wine's overall balance and depth, it will drink beautifully young yet have the ability to age for 12–15+ years.

This property has come of age with the acquisition of Le Gay's old-vine parcel. It is now consistently one of the finest wines of the appellation and clearly merits its famous name. The 1996 may deserve an outstanding score with 1–2 years of bottle age. It boasts an impressively saturated ruby/purple color, as well as a pure, sweet nose of cherries, plum liqueur, spicy oak, and floral scents. The wine possesses excellent depth, medium body, superb purity, and an overall elegant personality offering a combination of power and finesse. Anticipated maturity: now–2015.

Dazzling since birth, the 1995 has not lost a thing since bottling. A saturated dark purple color suggests a wine of considerable depth and concentration. The nose offers up gorgeous aromas of sweet kirsch intermixed with black raspberry, mineral, and smoky notes. Full bodied, with superb richness and purity, loads of tannin, and a layered, multidimensional personality, this terrific La Fleur-Pétrus is the finest wine I have tasted at this property in the 20 years I have been visiting Bordeaux. A 10-acre old-vine sector of Le Gay was sold to La Fleur-Pétrus, increasing the latter's vineyard to 33 acres. I believe this 10-acre acquisition has beefed up La Fleur-Pétrus, a fact particularly evident in this 1995. It is a splendid effort! Anticipated maturity: 2005–2025.

Past Glories: 1989 (91), 1982 (90?), 1975 (90), 1961 (92), 1952 (91), 1950 (95), 1947 (90).

FONROQUE (ST.-ÉMILION)

1997	D	(78–82)
1996	D	76
1995	C	87

The dark ruby-colored 1997 Fonroque reveals earthy, mineral characteristics, medium body, and an austere personality. It is likely to dry out over the next 5–6 years.

A lean, hard, rustic wine, the 1996 Fonroque reveals animal scents, gritty tannin, and a lack of fruit and intensity.

The dark ruby-colored, spicy, medium- to full-bodied 1995 exhibits a firm but promising nose of iron, earth, jammy kirsch, and currant fruit, excellent richness, a distinctive earth/truffle component throughout its flavors, and moderate tannin in the solid finish. Muscular but fleshy, this is a fine effort from Fonroque. Anticipated maturity: 2000–2012.

FONTENIL (FRONSAC)

1998	C	(86–87)
1997	C	(85–87)
1996	C	(85–86)
1995	C	87

The residence of Dany and Michel Rolland, this estate has produced consistently reliable, impeccably well-made Fronsacs. The deep ruby/purple-colored 1998 offers an expressive nose of smoky, toasty new oak, black cherry and cassis fruit as well as licorice. Good depth, soft tannin, and a plush texture result in a forward-style wine that will have broad popular appeal. Drink it over the next 7–8 years.

Fontenil usually turns out one of the most concentrated and intense wines of the appellation. The 1997 is undoubtedly a success. Exhibiting blueberry and blackberry fruit, with spicy oak in the background, this medium-bodied wine displays an elegant, suave, supple texture, very good concentration and purity, and a ripe, lightly tannic finish. It stood out as one of the most concentrated Fronsacs in my tastings. Anticipated maturity: 2000–2009.

Fontenil's 1996 is very good for the vintage, with cigar box, cedar, and berry fruit, medium body, moderate tannin, and good structure. It is more austere than the plump 1995. The latter wine is a delicious, soft, sweet example with plum, black cherry, mineral, licorice, and vanillin scents, medium body, good to excellent depth, and well-integrated tannin, acidity, and alcohol. It should drink well for a decade. A sleeper.

LES FORTS DE LATOUR (PAUILLAC)

1997	D	(87–88)
1996	D	90
1995	D	88

Latour's second wine, Forts de Latour, is now one of the two or three finest second wines of Bordeaux (Bahans-Haut-Brion and the Clos du Marquis of Léoville-Las Cases are two other personal favorites).

The 1997 Les Forts de Latour reveals a rich, blackberry, jammy (the French call it *confituré*) nose nicely intermingled with spice and earth. Soft, with low acidity, medium body, and good length, this plump, precocious-tasting Les Forts de Latour should drink well during its first decade of life.

The dense ruby/purple-colored 1996 Les Forts de Latour is exceedingly tannic, with cassis and mushroomlike notes in the aromatics. This full-bodied wine is impressively constituted and one of the finest Forts de Latours of the last 2 decades. Anticipated maturity: 2005–2018.

The dark ruby/purple-colored 1995 Forts de Latour possesses a sweet, jammy black fruit-scented nose intertwined with smoky minerals, earth, and spicy oak. The wine is surprisingly thick and rich in the mouth, with its glycerin and concentration of fruit largely concealing the moderate tannin. This excellent, sweet wine is less powerful but more accessible than the 1996. Anticipated maturity: 2001–2015.

Past Glories: 1990 (90), 1982 (92).

FOURCAS-DUPRÉ (LISTRAC)

1997	B	(85–86)
1996	B	(84–86)
1995	B	84

An attractive wine with plenty of black currant fruit, this 1997 provides a ripe entry on the palate, good purity, medium body, and nice length. It should drink well for 5–7 years.

The 1996 reveals spicy, berry fruit intermixed with minerals, herbs, and earth. This attractive, soft claret is ideal for drinking over the next 3–4 years.

The 1995 is more elegant and less deep than the 1996, but cleanly made and spicy, with berry/cherry fruit. Drink it over the next 3–4 years.

FOURCAS LOUBANEY (LISTRAC)

1997	C	(86–87)

Consistently one of the finest examples from Listrac, Fourcas Loubaney's current offering is forward, with excellent, smoky, toasty, black currant fruit. On the palate, the wine is round, low in acidity, with easy-to-understand and -appreciate fruit, glycerin, and sweet tannin. This velvety-textured wine will drink well for 6–7 years.

FRANC-MAYNE (ST.-ÉMILION)

1998	D	(86–87)

A distinctive minty/vanillin/black currant-scented nose suggests a Médoc or California Cabernet more than a right bank St.-Émilion. The dark ruby/purple color is followed by an elegant wine with excellent fruit, medium body, and nicely integrated oak and acidity. It should drink well for 10–12 years.

DE FRANCE (PESSAC LÉOGNAN)

1996	C	80
1995	C	78

De France's 1996 displays an herbal, smoky, weedy, red fruit-scented nose and flavors. There is good spice, medium body, ripeness, and moderate tannin, but overall this is a linear, lighter-style effort. Drink it over the next decade.

The 1995 is clean, soft, pleasant, elegant, and fruity, but one-dimensional.

LA GAFFELIÈRE (ST.-ÉMILION)

1998	D	(88–90)
1997	D	(86–88)
1996	D	87
1995	D	87

Consistently among the most elegant, stylish wines of St.-Émilion, La Gaffelière has beefed up its midpalate, which is now more concentrated and sweeter than vintages produced 10–15 years ago. The stylish, savory 1998 exhibits a dark ruby color with purple nuances. The complex nose of berry fruit, dried herbs, new saddle leather, and toast is followed by a medium-bodied wine with a sweet midpalate, excellent concentration and purity, and a classically balanced, finesse-style finish. Anticipated maturity: 2003–2014.

The 1997 is lusher and sweeter than previous vintages, with low acidity and less noticeable tannin. It is a medium-weight, stylish wine with plentiful floral, red cherry, and currant notes, excellent texture and purity, and a silky finish. It should drink well for 7–10 years.

The 1996 La Gaffelière is a quintessentially elegant wine, with charm, sweet fruit, and a velvety texture. Tannin in the finish suggests it will last longer than expected. The color is a deep ruby, and the nose offers up sweet black cherries intermixed with a peppery, mineral character, subtle new oak, and well-integrated acidity and tannin. The finish is long and pure. Anticipated maturity: 2002–2012.

The dark ruby-colored 1995 offers spicy, smoky oak and soft, ripe, cherry and red currant flavors presented in a compressed but alluring, medium-bodied, finesse-filled format. Some tannin is present, but the overall impression is one of pretty fruit and a dry, crisp finish. Anticipated maturity: 2000–2010.

Past Glories: 1990 (90).

LE GAY (POMEROL)

1998	D	(85–88)
1997	D	(85–87)
1996	D	74
1995	D	82

Since the finest old-vine parcel of Le Gay was sold to La Fleur-Pétrus, this estate has not produced any exceptional wines. The 1998 may be the best wine made since that plot was sold, but it is less exciting than other top Pomerols. This dark ruby-colored, medium-bodied, firmly structured, earthy effort reveals scents of meat, black fruits, and dried herbs in its aromatics, as well as a juicy midcore. This Pomerol will be ready to drink in 5–6 years and will last for 15.

In January 1999 I had the pleasure of tasting the 1945, 1947, 1948, and 1950 Le Gays from magnum. All of them remain superlative wines, with the 1950, 1947, and 1945 flirting with perfection. It is the second time I have bestowed a perfect rating on a magnum of 1947 Le Gay. Several years ago the tenderloin section of Le Gay vineyard (a parcel of old-vine Merlot) was sold to La Fleur-Pétrus in an effort to propel that property to a higher-quality level. Not surprisingly, I have been disappointed with recent vintages of Le Gay. For example, there is no midpalate in the dark ruby-colored, hollow, tannic 1996, nor does it exhibit much depth, charm, or fat. Anticipated maturity: 2001–2008.

The 1997 has improved since I tasted it last year. Christian Moueix told me the château made a severe selection, producing only 900 cases in order to produce the finest cuvée possible. It is a very good wine, with much more fat than recent vintages have possessed. The wine displays a dark ruby/purple color and a structured, moderately tannic palate with good sweetness and purity. This is unquestionably the finest wine produced at Le Gay since the best vineyard parcel was sold to La Fleur-Pétrus. Anticipated maturity: 2003–2015.

Lacking the depth, flesh, fruit, and charm that one expects in most Pomerols, the dark ruby-colored 1995 exhibits an excess of tannin, body, and structure for the amount of fruit it possesses. It will not provide near-term consumption given its severe personality. Anticipated maturity: 2005–2015.

Past Glories: 1989 (90), 1950 (98), 1949 (96), 1947 (100), 1945 (94).

GAZIN (POMEROL)

1998	E	(89–92)
1997	E	(90–91)

1996	E	89
1995	E	90+

Gazin has been one of the most impressive Pomerols over the last decade. That's good news for consumers, since it is a large estate, with the potential to produce 10,000 cases.

Huge extract and power should result in an outstanding rating for the 1998, but this blockbuster's ferocious tannin and lavish new oak are not totally integrated. Aromas of smoke, camphor, charcoal, blackberry liqueur, truffles, and *pain grillé* soar from the glass of this saturated, plum-colored wine. It is medium- to full-bodied, highly extracted, layered, and impressive, but patience will be required. Anticipated maturity: 2005–2020.

The gorgeous densely colored 1997 Gazin exhibits lavishly wooded aromatics intermixed with Asian spices, licorice, black cherries, and smoky-tinged, dried herbs and plumlike fruit. Deep and medium to full bodied, with sweet tannin and excellent concentration, this hedonistic wine needs 2–4 years of cellaring; it will keep for 12–15 years.

The 1996 is an atypically tannic, serious Gazin with a dense ruby/purple color and lavish quantities of toasty new oak in the nose intermixed with licorice, black cherries, and mocha/coffee notes. The wine displays excellent concentration but is backward, with medium to full body and moderately high tannin. Give it 5–6 years of cellaring, as it will be potentially long-lived. It is unquestionably an impressive effort for a 1996 Pomerol. Anticipated maturity: 2005–2018.

The deep ruby/purple-colored 1995 has shut down following bottling, and while it hints at some of its exotic grilled herb and meatlike character, the reluctant nose reveals primarily new oak, smoke, spice, and background jammy fruit. On the palate, the wine is deep, medium to full bodied, refined, and, except for some noticeably hard tannin in the finish, relatively seamless. This expansively flavored wine offers plenty of spice, new oak, fruit, and depth. Anticipated maturity: 2002–2018.

Past Glories: 1994 (90), 1990 (93), 1961 (93).

GISCOURS (MARGAUX)

1998	D	(86–88)
1997	D	(85–86)
1996	D	84
1995	D	85

Giscours handled the 1998 vinification well, producing a charming, round, lush, open-knit, fruity wine. Intelligently, they did not try to overextract and thus avoided the problems with excessive as well as astringent tannin. The wine possesses a dark ruby/purple color, low acidity, and rich, ripe, herb-tinged black cherry and plumlike fruit. Supple and medium bodied, it is already delicious to drink. Anticipated maturity: 2001–2012.

The 1997 is a charming wine, with deep color saturation, dense fruit, and more volume and length than the 1996. It possesses low acidity and smoky, dried herb, black currant fruit with notes of smoke and tobacco. Drink it during its first decade of life.

Giscours's 1996 is atypical for the vintage, being soft, forward, and open knit, with an absence of tannin. The wine exhibits a dark ruby color and attractive berry fruit, but it is straightforward and easygoing. It, too, should be consumed during its first decade of life.

An easygoing claret with plenty of crowd appeal, the dark ruby-colored 1995 exhibits roasted herb, meaty, black currant, and cherry fruit scents. Underbrush and herbaceousness are intertwined with ripe fruit on the palate of this medium-bodied, spicy, pleasant, soft wine with some tannin in the finish. It will be ready for prime-time drinking after another 1–3 years of bottle age. Anticipated maturity: 2000–2010.

Past Glories: 1978 (90), 1975 (92).

GLORIA (ST.-JULIEN)

1998	C	(85–86)
1997	C	(87–88)

The 1998 Gloria is an attractively fat, commercially styled, surprisingly soft wine. It displays herb-tinged berry fruit, notes of saddle leather, and a medium-bodied, round finish. It should drink well for 7–8 years.

The cunningly made 1997 offers mouth-filling levels of black cherry, herb-tinged, cassis fruit. There is plenty of glycerin in this velvety-textured, medium-bodied Gloria. Pure, plump, and succulent, it is all a young, exuberant claret should be. However, do not expect it to age long; this is a wine to drink during its first decade of life. A sleeper of the vintage.

LA GOMERIE (ST.-ÉMILION)

1998	EE	(91–94)
1997	EE	(89–91)
1996	EE	92
1995	EE	93

A Le Pin look-alike from St.-Émilion, La Gomerie is a microvinification of approximately 750 cases made from a 6.2-acre parcel planted with 35-year-old Merlot vines. The wine is made from extremely ripe fruit and low yields, with malolactic fermentation in barrel. To the owner's credit, it is bottled with no fining or filtration. Not surprisingly, the consulting oenologist is Michel Rolland.

Pardon me, but the 1998 is about as hedonistic a Bordeaux as can be produced. Fat, succulent, and oozing with glycerin and extract, it is a sultry tease. The saturated ruby/purple color is accompanied by a lavishly oaked wine with a portlike viscosity and richness. As with previous vintages, the 1998 managed to avoid the vintage's structure and tannin, resulting in an uncommonly open, fat, and expansively flavored effort oozing with fruit. A sensual, full-bodied wine for hedonists only, La Gomerie's 1998 takes voluptuousness to new heights. Anticipated maturity: 2002–2015.

The color of the 1997 is a dark saturated purple, and the wine offers up plenty of sweet *pain grillé* notes intermixed with roasted coffee, blackberry jam, cherry liqueur, and gobs of smoke and toasty oak. Rich, with lower acidity than the 1996, it possesses sweet tannin, a viscous texture, and a heady, plump, layered finish. It should drink better at an earlier age than the 1996, but does it possess as much longevity? Anticipated maturity: 2000–2013.

The spectacular 1996 La Gomerie exhibits a dark ruby color and explosive aromatics of *pain grillé,* roasted nuts, kirsch liqueur, and assorted black fruits. It is full bodied, with sweet tannin and a ripe, intensely concentrated finish with high levels of glycerin and extract. This flamboyant, full-bodied wine should be at its finest between 2001 and 2018.

The debut vintage for La Gomerie, the 1995 Le Pin look-alike is showing fabulously well after bottling. The color is dense ruby/purple, and the nose offers up exotic aromas of Asian spices, soy, coffee, and ripe berry/cherry fruit. This full-bodied, thick, unctuously textured wine is marvelously concentrated, with plenty of sweet, well-integrated tannin. The acidity is low, which only adds to the voluptuous personality of this strikingly rich, head-turning effort. Anticipated maturity: now–2012.

GRACIA (ST.-ÉMILION)

1998	D	(90–93)
1997	D	(88–90)

A spectacular wine, the 1998 Gracia was produced from yields of 22 hectoliters per hectare. After being hand-harvested and destemmed, the wine was given full malolactic fermentation in 100% new oak barrels (all from the coopers Sylvain, Taransaud, Demptos, and Berger). The wine boasts a black/purple color as well as a sweet, chocolatey, cherry liqueur-scented nose with licorice and Asian spice notes. Full bodied, with great opulence, viscosity, and richness, this wine will be bottled with neither fining nor filtration. Full bodied and remarkably concentrated, it possesses all the hallmarks of a potentially profound drinking experience. Production in 1998 was only 325 cases. Anticipated maturity: 2001–2012.

The sexy, hedonistically styled 1997 Gracia exhibits a dark ruby/purple color, lavish quantities of smoky new oak, low acidity, a lush, layered texture, and deep, soft, kirsch liqueur and black currant fruit in the flavors and finish. Anticipated maturity: now–2010.

GRAND-CORBIN DESPAGNE (ST.-ÉMILION)

1998	C	(88–89+)

This is a breakthrough vintage for this property, which is trying to increase its level of quality. The color is a black/purple. The wine is thick and intense, with a viscous texture, gobs of black cherry and cassis fruit, toasty new oak, licorice, and earth, and a medium- to full-bodied, moderately tannic finish. Anticipated maturity: 2003–2014.

GRAND-MAYNE (ST.-ÉMILION)

1998	D	(86–88)
1997	D	(87–89)
1996	D	88
1995	D	90

Displaying less weight and richness than I normally expect, the 1998 Grand-Mayne is restrained, stylish, and understated. The saturated dark ruby/purple color is followed by sweet blueberry and cassis aromas, along with scents of new oak and steel. This lacy wine is medium bodied and graceful, with sweet fruit, an easy, open-knit texture, and subtle fruit flavors. It should drink well for 10–12 years.

The saturated dark ruby/purple-colored 1997 Grand-Mayne offers up sweet, jammy black fruits (particularly cassis) intermixed with licorice, lead pencil, and a floral note. Ripe, with enough potential to merit an outstanding score, this chewy wine possesses lovely texture and nicely integrated, smoky, toasty oak. The wine's low acidity and riper style auger well for its future. Anticipated maturity: 2001–2014.

I had the 1996 Grand-Mayne three times from bottle, rating it 88 once and 89 twice. I decided to go with the more conservative rating given the wine's backward style. Grand-Mayne is one of St.-Émilion's best-run properties. Aside from a couple of hiccups in the early nineties, the quality has been consistently excellent, often outstanding. The 1996 Grand-Mayne exhibits a dense purple color and an attractive nose of white flowers, sweet blackberries, cherries, minerals, and *pain grillé*. It is medium to full bodied, with excellent depth, an elegant personality, and a clean, mineral-like finish with moderate tannin. New oak is noticeable in the flavors. Anticipated maturity: 2003–2014.

An unqualified sleeper of the vintage, the opaque purple-colored 1995 Grand-Mayne displays a sweet, creamy, black raspberry-scented nose with subtle notes of smoky, toasty oak. Both powerful and elegant, this wine exhibits layers of richness, nicely integrated acidity and tannin, and an impressive full-bodied, long finish. This offering should be drinkable early and keep for over a decade. Anticipated maturity: 2000–2013.

Past Glories: 1990 (90), 1989 (92).

GRAND-PONTET (ST.-ÉMILION)

1998	D	(87–88)
1997	D	(87–88)
1996	D	89
1995	D	88

This up-and-coming St.-Émilion is somewhat underrated given the consistently high quality of recent vintages. Dried herbs, sweet toasty oak, coffee, and black currant aromas soar from the glass of the dark purple-colored 1998. Chunky and medium bodied, it may merit a higher score if the wood and tannin become better integrated. Anticipated maturity: 2002–2014.

The dark ruby/purple-colored 1997 is a wine for hedonists. Completely fruit driven, it offers jammy notes of prunes intertwined with kirsch, toasty new oak, and smoky notes. This lush, medium- to full-bodied, soft, tasty wine will be drinkable after bottling and should keep for a decade. Anticipated maturity: now–2009.

The 1996 is a flamboyant, dark ruby/purple-colored wine with a soaring bouquet of plum liqueur, toasty new oak, black cherries, smoke, and dried herbs. In the mouth, evidence of *sur-maturité* jamminess and richness emerge from this medium-bodied, rich, spicy, impressively endowed wine. There is tannin in the medium- to full-bodied finish. Anticipated maturity: 2003–2014.

Dark ruby/purple colored with a forward, evolved nose of spice, black cherries, and toast, the supple, round, generous, medium- to full-bodied 1995 possesses low acidity and some tannin in the finish. There is good delineation to this plump, succulently styled wine that can be drunk now as well as over the next dozen years.

GRAND-PUY-DUCASSE (PAUILLAC)

1997	D	(80–83)
1996	D	87
1995	D	87

The 1997 Grand-Puy-Ducasse is dark ruby colored, with a sweet black fruit-scented nose intermixed with weedy scents, vanilla, and earth. The midpalate is plump and round, but the wine displays an abrupt finish with a certain austerity and angularity. This offering requires more flesh and concentration to merit a higher score. Anticipated maturity: now–2010.

This estate, which tends to turn out forward, soft Pauillacs, has made a firmer, more structured wine in 1996. The color is a healthy dark ruby with purple nuances. The nose offers up aromas of cassis, dusty, earthy notes, tobacco leaf, cedar, and spice. Medium bodied, with excellent depth and ripeness and the Cabernet Sauvignon component dominating its personality, this is a fine Grand-Puy-Ducasse that should be reasonably priced. Anticipated maturity: 2002–2015.

Dark ruby colored with purple nuances, the supple, lush, fruity 1995 Pauillac possesses medium body, light intensity new oak, soft tannin, and low acidity. Made in a clean, medium-bodied, user-friendly, accessible style, this wine will have many fans. Anticipated maturity: now–2010.

GRAND-PUY-LACOSTE (PAUILLAC)

1997	EE	(86–87)
1996	EE	93+
1995	EE	95

A very good effort, the 1997 Grand-Puy-Lacoste exhibits a youthful, evolved nose of cassis fruit. In the mouth, there is good fatness on the attack, light tannin, medium body, and a round, gentle, concentrated finish. No, it is not a large-scale Grand-Puy-Lacoste, but it is one of charm and elegance. It should drink well for 7–8 years.

What extraordinary wines Grand-Puy-Lacoste produced in both 1995 and 1996. At present I have a marginal preference for the blockbuster 1996, but I am not about to argue with anybody who prefers the 1995! Both are compelling wines.

The 1996 is unquestionably a profound Grand-Puy-Lacoste, but it is excruciatingly backward. It reveals an essence of crème de cassis character that sets it apart from other Pauillacs. The wine is displaying plenty of tannin, huge body, and sweet black currant fruit intermixed with minerals and subtle oak. Massive, extremely structured, and with 25–30 or more years of longevity, this immensely styled Grand-Puy-Lacoste will require 7–8 years of patience, perhaps longer. A superb, classic Pauillac. Anticipated maturity: 2007–2030.

Another unbelievably rich, multidimensional, broad-shouldered wine, with slightly more elegance and less weight than the powerhouse 1996, the gorgeously proportioned, medium- to full-bodied, fabulously ripe, rich, cassis-scented and -flavored 1995 Grand-Puy-Lacoste is another beauty. It should be drinkable within 4–5 years and keep for 25–30. This classic Pauillac is a worthy rival to the otherworldly 1996. Anticipated maturity: 2002–2025.

Past Glories: 1994 (90), 1990 (95), 1986 (91), 1982 (95), 1970 (91), 1959 (92), 1949 (96), 1947 (94).

GRANDES-MURAILLES (ST.-ÉMILION)

1998	C	(87–89+)
1997	C	(87–89)

There are 700 cases of the 1998, a blend of 90% Merlot and 10% Cabernet Franc produced by the Reiffers, the owners of Clos St.-Martin and Côte de Baleau, two other properties that are enjoying a renaissance under their administration. The saturated ruby/purple-colored 1998 Grandes-Murailles exhibits a sweet, perfumed nose of jammy blackberry and cherry fruit intermixed with mineral and smoke notes. Sweet, pure, ripe, and medium bodied, with a portlike essence to the fruit, this rich, multilayered wine may merit an outstanding score if it is not excessively processed at bottling. It is a sleeper of the vintage. Anticipated maturity: 2003–2014.

This property is making a major effort to improve the quality of its wines, and that is evident with the 1997, the finest wine to emerge from Grandes-Murailles in many years. The color is dark ruby/purple with garnet at the edge. The smashing nose of blueberry jam, raspberries, damp earth, and toasty oak is followed by a medium-bodied, pure, elegant wine full of fruit and finesse. Not a blockbuster, it is deliciously well balanced and fruit dominated. Anticipated maturity: 2000–2010.

LES GRANDS CHÊNES (MÉDOC)

1996 Grands Chênes	C	86
1996 Cuvée Prestige	C	87

One of the finest Médoc Crus Bourgeois, the 1996 Les Grands Chênes is an excellent, richly fruity wine with subtle new oak, plenty of black currant fruit, and notes of tobacco, minerals, and spice. It should drink well for 5–6 years. The 1996 Cuvée Prestige reveals more new oak, greater depth, and a riper, more concentrated, longer finish. This impressively endowed wine should be taken seriously. Anticipated maturity: now–2010.

GRAULET (CÔTES DE BLAYE)

1997 Cuvée Prestige	B	87

This special cuvée of 100% old-vine, hand-harvested Merlot that has been aged in 100% new oak is one of the best Blaye wines I have tasted. It boasts excellent color saturation, some tannin, and gobs of black currant fruit nicely buttressed by toasty oak. Drink it over the next 2–4 years.

LA GRAVE À POMEROL (POMEROL)

1998	D	(88–90)
1997	D	(86–88)
1996	D	86+
1995	D	88

This 1998 must be the most powerful La Grave I have tasted. The wine displays huge, gritty tannin, surprising body, and a robust constitution. Normally an elegant, savory wine, La Grave's 1998 will probably take on a more stylish, feminine character with aging, but at present it exhibits an inky dark ruby color, sweet black fruit, earth, and dried herb aromas, admirable richness, full body, and the potential for an outstanding rating. Anticipated maturity: 2003–2012.

The sexy cherry, berry, coffee, roasted herb, and cedary nose of the 1997 is followed by a seductive, charming wine. There are no hard edges to this round, medium-bodied, nicely concentrated, pure, silky-textured Pomerol. Drink it within 7–8 years of its release.

A well-made wine with a smoky, coffee, and cherry aromatic profile, the 1996 La Grave à Pomerol exhibits good concentration, nicely integrated acidity and tannin, and a round, attractive softness that makes it an ideal candidate for consuming in its youth. Anticipated maturity: now–2007.

One of the strongest efforts from this property (previously called La Grave-Trigant-de-Boisset) over recent years, this lovely, charming 1995 reveals a deep ruby color and plenty of sweet cherry fruit intertwined with high-quality, spicy new oak. Medium bodied, with excellent concentration and a nicely layered, sexy personality, this is a textbook midweight Pomerol for drinking over the next 10–12 years.

GRUAUD-LAROSE (ST.-JULIEN)

1998	E	(87–88+?)
1997	E	(86–88)
1996	E	89
1995	E	89

The question mark for the 1998 denotes the presence of elevated, astringent tannin in this wine's finish. Otherwise it is well made, exhibiting a deep ruby/purple color, sweet, pure, black currant fruit, medium body, and an angular midpalate. Four to five years of cellaring may be beneficial, but this wine will have to be watched carefully in case it begins to lose its fruit.

The 1997 Gruaud-Larose is a charming, elegant, fleshy, dark ruby-colored wine with copious amounts of sweet black fruits intermixed with roasted herbs, smoke, and earthy overtones. This delicious 1997 will drink well for a decade. Anticipated maturity: now–2011.

Gruaud-Larose was purchased in 1997 by Jacques Merlaut, the well-known proprietor of many other châteaux, including Chasse-Spleen. Merlaut was not responsible for making the 1996 or 1995, but he is responsible for their *élevage* and bottling.

In the bottle, the 1996 Gruaud Larose appears to have returned to the form it possessed when I first tasted it from cask—a stylish, surprisingly civilized, medium-bodied wine without the muscle and power expected from both this *terroir* and vintage. It still possesses excellent density, as well as roasted herb, licorice, and black currant flavors intermixed with incenselike smells. The wine is medium to full bodied, pure, rich, and forward, especially for the vintage. Anticipated maturity: 2004–2018.

Revealing more grip and tannin since bottling, the 1995 Gruaud-Larose exhibits a dark ruby color and a nose of sweet black cherries, licorice, earth, and spice. Rich, with medium to full body, high tannin, and subtle oak in the background, the 1995 is nearly as structured and tannic as the 1996. The two vintages are more similar than dissimilar. Anticipated maturity: 2005–2020.

Past Glories: 1990 (93), 1986 (94+), 1985 (90), 1983 (90), 1982 (96), 1961 (96), 1953 (93), 1945 (96+), 1928 (97).

JEAN DU GUE (LALANDE DE POMEROL)

1997 Cuvée Prestige	C	(85–86)

An impressive new entry from the appellation of Lalande de Pomerol, this property, owned by one of St.-Émilion's best-known families, the Auberts, fashioned a lush, medium-bodied, dark ruby/purple-colored 1997 with copious quantities of kirsch/cherry fruit complemented by glycerin, a plush, textural softness, low acidity, and a plump finish. It is a hedonistic, juicy wine to drink during its first 3–4 years of life.

HAUT-BAGES-LIBÉRAL (PAUILLAC)

1997	D	(81–83)
1996	D	87+
1995	D	85

The light-bodied, soft, fruity 1997 from Haut-Bages-Libéral is essentially one-dimensional, even though it is pleasant and charming. It requires consumption during its first 8–10 years of life.

The very good 1996 reveals an element of jammy black currant fruit intermixed with dried roasted herbs, sweet earthy smells, and new oak. It offers excellent definition, moderate tannin, medium to full body, and a long finish. As the wine sits in the glass, elements of the Cabernet Sauvignon's *sur-maturité* become noticeable. It is a potential sleeper of the vintage and possibly a realistic value, because Haut-Bages-Libéral rarely sells for an excessive price. Anticipated maturity: 2004–2017.

The 1995 possesses a bit more depth and intensity than its younger sibling, but it is also lean and austere. The attractive saturated ruby/purple color suggests plenty of intensity, which is evident on the attack, but, again, the midpalate is deficient in fruit, glycerin, and concentration, and the finish is dry, with a high level of tannin. This wine may soften with more bottle age and become better than my rating suggests. Let's hope so. Anticipated maturity: 2003–2012.

Past Glories: 1986 (90), 1982 (91).

HAUT-BAILLY (PESSAC LÉOGNAN)

1998	D	(86–87)
1997	D	(86–88)
1996	D	87
1995	D	90

This delicate, subtle wine is often difficult to evaluate young. However, Haut-Bailly's 1998 is a fruit-driven, soft, black currant-and-cherry-scented and -flavored wine with undeniable elegance, but not much volume, depth, or length. If more richness emerges with barrel aging, this well-balanced and symmetrical 1998 will deserve a higher rating. Anticipated maturity: now–2010.

The 1997 is a charming and flattering wine to drink now. The medium deep ruby color is accompanied by sweet berry fruit, dried herbs, tobacco leaf, and spicy oak aromas. There is a plump, opulent texture, low acidity, and a disarming roundness. Drink it over the next 10–12 years.

Haut-Bailly's 1996 displays less charm than usual, but it does offer moderately intense red currant/cherry fruit combined with earth, smoke, and new oak. An elegant, medium-bodied wine with dry tannin in the finish, it will never be a heavyweight, but it possesses considerable personality and potential complexity. Anticipated maturity: 2003–2015.

A beauty, the deep ruby-colored 1995 offers a classic, smoky, cherry, red and black currant nose, sweet, lush, forward fruit, medium body, true delicacy and elegance (as opposed to thinness and dilution), perfect balance, and a lovely, long, supple, velvety-textured finish. This is a ballerina of a claret, with beautiful aromatics, lovely flavors, and impeccable equilibrium. Anticipated maturity: 2000–2018.

Past Glories: 1990 (92), 1961 (93), 1928 (90).

HAUT-BATAILLEY (PAUILLAC)

1997	D	(86–87)
1996	D	81
1995	D	89

This seductive, low-acid, soft 1997 Pauillac reveals a dark ruby color, roasted herb- and black currant-scented aromas, round, medium-bodied, plush flavors, no aggressiveness to its tannin, and a flat, easy finish. It should be drunk during its first 7–8 years of life.

Both the 1996 and 1995 may merit outstanding ratings after a few years of bottle age. These are sleeper selections in both vintages. The 1996 exhibits a dense purple color as well as a wonderfully sweet, classic Pauillac nose of black currants and cigar box notes. Powerful for Haut-Batailley (normally a light, elegant, supple Pauillac), the 1996 possesses intense fruit, medium to full body, ripe tannin, and a surprisingly long, layered finish. This appears to be a classic and may merit an outstanding score. Anticipated maturity: 2003–2015.

Silky, sexy, supple, and altogether a gorgeous effort from Haut-Batailley, the 1995 is a medium-bodied, seamless, beautifully pure Pauillac with gobs of black currant fruit intermixed with smoke, vanilla, and lead pencil. Already approachable, it promises to become even better over the next 10–12 years. A very hedonistic wine.

HAUT-BRION (PESSAC LÉOGNAN)

1998	EEE	(94–96)
1997	EEE	(89–90)
1996	EEE	92+
1995	EEE	96

Jean Delmas is thrilled with what he achieved at Haut-Brion and La Mission-Haut-Brion in 1998. Statistically, the cuvées that went into Haut-Brion indicate that the 1998 has more to it than either 1995 or 1996 and comes close (in numbers) to equaling 1989 and 1990. It is one of the great successes of the vintage. Moreover, it is the paradigm for elegance allied to power. The color is an opaque purple. The nose offers up sweet black fruits intermixed with roasted herbs, *pain grillé,* and minerals. There is a sensational, plush texture, yet the wine comes across as medium bodied, with multiple levels of flavor as well as gorgeous ripeness and purity. It possesses fine density, but there is no sense of heaviness or imbalance. While it may never achieve the opulence and extravagant richness of the 1989, it is a brilliant classic. Lovers of this estate's distinctive, highly individualized, complex wines should not miss it. Anticipated maturity: 2004–2025.

The 1997 Haut-Brion displays a deep, saturated ruby/purple color as well as an excellent, evolved nose of black fruits, minerals, earth, and *pain grillé.* It is a wine of finesse and rich fruit rather than one of power, structure, and volume. Medium bodied, lush, and remarkably easy to drink (particularly when tasted next to the 1996), this wine should evolve quickly and keep for 15+ years. Anticipated maturity: 2001–2015.

The backward 1996 Haut-Brion was bottled in July 1998. Even administrator Jean Delmas was surprised by how closed it was when I tasted it in January 1999. Only 60% of the crop was utilized in the final blend, which was 50% Merlot, 39% Cabernet Sauvignon, and 11% Cabernet Franc. Out of barrel, this wine exhibited far more forthcoming aromatics as well as a sweeter midpalate than it revealed from bottle. I had expected it to be more forward and thus slightly downgraded the wine, although I am thrilled to own it and follow what appears to be a slow evolution. It will be a potentially long-lived wine, but I suspect it is slightly less successful than the extraordinary 1995. The 1996 exhibits a deep ruby/purple color and a surprisingly tight bouquet. With aeration, notes of fresh tobacco, dried herbs, smoke, asphalt, and black fruits emerge . . . but reluctantly. It is tannic and medium bodied, with outstanding purity and a layered, multidimensional style. However, the finish contains abundant tannin, suggesting that this wine needs 5–8 years of cellaring. Anticipated maturity: 2008–2030.

The 1995 has been brilliant on every occasion I have tasted it. More accessible and forward than the 1996, it possesses a saturated ruby/purple color as well as a beautiful, knockout set of aromatics, consisting of black fruits, vanillin, spice, and wood-fire smoke. Multidimensional and rich, with layers of ripe fruit and beautifully integrated tannin and acidity, this medium- to full-bodied wine is a graceful, seamless, exceptional Haut-Brion that should drink surprisingly well young. Anticipated maturity: 2000–2030.

Past Glories: 1994 (93), 1993 (92), 1992 (90), 1990 (96), 1989 (100), 1988 (91), 1986 (96), 1985 (94), 1982 (94), 1979 (93), 1978 (90?), 1975 (93+), 1964 (90), 1961 (100), 1959 (99), 1957 (90), 1955 (97), 1953 (95), 1949 (91), 1945 (100), 1928 (97), 1926 (97).

HAUT CARLES (FRONSAC)

1998	C (87–88)

A dense black/purple color is followed by aromas of black cherries, cassis, and damp forests. This 1998 is an intense, medium-bodied, powerful Fronsac that should drink well for 10–15 years.

HAUT GRAVET (ST.-ÉMILION)

1998	D (87–89)

This appears to be another potential sleeper of the vintage. It is an abundantly fruity, glycerin-imbued, medium-bodied wine with surprising elegance for its fruit-driven personality. There is plenty of black raspberry and jammy cherry fruit intermixed with subtle new oak. It possesses low acidity, well-integrated moderate tannin, a seamless personality, and a surprisingly fine, concentrated finish. This effort performed well in my tastings and looks to be an impressive newcomer to the growing list of well-made St.-Émilions. Anticipated maturity: 2002–2010.

HAUT-MAILLET (POMEROL)

1997	**C**	**(75–80)**
1996	**C**	**80**

The 1997 exhibits more tannin than the 1996, in addition to an austere, tight personality. If the tannin melts away and the fruit comes forward, the wine will merit a slightly above average rating. If not, look for this offering to be attenuated and compressed. Anticipated maturity: 2000–2007.

The light- to medium-bodied, pleasant, straightforward, simple 1996 Pomerol displays an evolved plum/garnet color, moderate levels of cranberry and cherry fruit, a sweet attack, and a soft, straightforward personality. Drink it over the next 4–5 years.

HAUT-MARBUZET (ST.-ESTÈPHE)

1997	**D**	**(84–86)**
1996	**D**	**87–88**
1995	**D**	**87**

I had the 1997 on three occasions and was surprised that it did not possess more stuffing and intensity. While good, it is not up to this château's usual standards. The aggressively woody 1997 Haut-Marbuzet reveals a hollow midsection, but it does offer soft, ripe, coffee, earthy, black cherry fruit presented in a pleasant, medium-bodied format. A bit more concentration, extract, and length would have been preferable. Drink this wine during its first 4–5 years of life.

Telltale, lavish, toasty new oak aromas jump from the glass of the dark ruby/purple-colored 1996. Well made, attractive, and boldly wooded, the wine possesses plenty of rich fruit to easily compensate for all the oak. Neither the 1996 nor the 1995 offers the depth found in the 1990, 1989, and 1982, but they are excellent wines. This medium-bodied, spicy, lush, open-knit 1996 will be better with 2–3 years of cellaring and will keep for 10–15.

The 1995 reveals gobs of kirsch and coffee in its nose, along with smoky, toasty, oaky notes. Medium bodied, with smoky, black currant fruit, low acidity, good lushness, and a layered palate, this is a hedonistic, accessible Haut-Marbuzet to consume over the next decade. *Past Glories:* 1990 (93), 1986 (90), 1982 (94), 1975 (90), 1970 (90), 1961 (90).

L'HERMITAGE (ST.-ÉMILION)

1998	**D**	**(88–90)**
1997	**D**	**(87–90)**

One of the microestates turning out fine St.-Émilions, the 1998 l'Hermitage (70% Merlot and 30% Cabernet Franc) is a richly fruity, opulently textured, medium- to full-bodied wine with a saturated purple color as well as outstanding purity and potential. It cuts a broad swath in the mouth and reveals moderate tannin in the long finish. Impressive and well made, it is a sleeper of the vintage. Anticipated maturity: 2002–2015.

A potential sleeper of the vintage, the richly fruity 1997 offers a complex nose of dried herbs, spicy oak, and black cherries. Medium bodied and ripe, with excellent purity and a lush, low-acid finish, this will be a hedonistic, velvety-textured wine to drink during its first 7–10 years of life.

HORTEVIE (ST.-JULIEN)

1997	C	(86–87)
1996	C	88
1995	C	87

Proprietor Pradère makes fine wine from this estate, which consists essentially of old-vine parcels that are vinified and aged separately from Pradère's other St.-Julien estate, Terrey-Gros-Cailloux.

This consistently attractive, plump, juicy, succulent wine is made in a very approachable style. Consequently 1997 is an ideal vintage for this plump, precocious winemaking style. The deep ruby/purple-colored 1997 Hortevie offers gobs of juicy black currant fruit intertwined with herbs and earth. Lush, low-acid flavors exhibit fine ripeness as well as a layered feel on the palate. There is no aggressiveness, harshness, or sharp edges to any component in the wine's pliant personality. Drink it over the next 5–6 years.

Performing well, the deep opaque purple-colored 1996 offers sweet, ripe, jammy cassis and cherry fruit, and fleshy, full-bodied flavors with moderate tannin in the finish. The tannin is sweet, ripe, and mature, so this wine will not require an inordinate amount of patience. It is a potential sleeper of the vintage. Anticipated maturity: 2001–2012.

The dense purple-colored 1995 displays a delicious personality, from its no-holds-barred, uncomplicated, but intense, creamy, black currant, cedar, smoky nose to its deep, chewy, spicy, fleshy flavors. Fruit, glycerin, body, and tannin are the major components of this St.-Julien, which can be drunk young or cellared. Anticipated maturity: 2000–2012. It is another sleeper of the vintage.

D'ISSAN (MARGAUX)

1997	D	(85–87)
1996	D	88
1995	D	87

This property continues to reassert itself, with a renewed commitment to quality. The 1997 performed well, revealing sweet fruit, a velvety texture, a deep ruby color, and abundant fat and succulence in the long finish. A hedonistic, seductive offering, it should drink well for a decade. Anticipated maturity: now–2010.

The 1996 d'Issan has turned out beautifully in bottle. It exhibits a dark ruby/purple color as well as elegant, floral, blackberry, smoky aromas. The wine is medium bodied and complex in the mouth, with subtle new oak, gorgeously ripe, sweet black currant fruit, and well-integrated tannin and acidity. This quintessential Margaux-style wine is elegant and rich. Anticipated maturity: 2004–2020.

An excellent d'Issan, with more noticeable tannin than the 1996, the 1995 possesses a deep ruby color, an excellent spicy, weedy, licorice, and black currant nose, sweet fruit on the attack, and very good purity, ripeness, and overall balance. The wine is well made and more backward than the 1996, even though I suspect the latter wine has more tannin. Anticipated maturity: 2003–2014.

KIRWAN (MARGAUX)

1998	D	(87–89+)
1997	D	(87–89)
1996	D	88
1995	D	85

Readers should note that this property has significantly improved the quality of its wines and now deserves a serious look in nearly every vintage.

One of the sleepers of the vintage, the 1998 Kirwan displays an opaque purple color and a concentrated, powerful style with moderately high tannin, intense extract, and copious new oak. It is an excellent, possibly outstanding, wine. If the tannin becomes better integrated, this medium- to full-bodied powerhouse may be one of the finest values of the vintage, but it will require patience. Anticipated maturity: 2005–2018.

The 1997 Kirwan possesses one of the most saturated purple colors of any Médoc I saw. The wine reveals an element of *sur-maturité,* along with lavish blackberry fruit, new oak, and cassis aromas and flavors. This could turn out to be a sleeper! Anticipated maturity: 2003–2016.

The 1996 Kirwan is a highly extracted, rich, medium-bodied wine with a deep ruby/purple color and ripe cassis fruit intermixed with a touch of new oak, prunes, and spice. The wine has come together nicely since I first tasted it from cask. It appears to be an excellent, nearly outstanding, effort. There is moderate tannin in the finish, so give this beefy, rich, muscular wine 6–7 years of cellaring. Anticipated maturity: 2006–2025.

I downgraded the 1995 because of the aggressive new oak and vanillin that dominate the wine's personality. This dark ruby/purple-colored wine displays sweet cranberry and jammy black currant fruit on the attack but narrows in the mouth with a compressed personality. Nevertheless there is fine purity, medium body, and plenty of tannin. This 1995 will merit a higher score if it turns out the fruit is deep enough to absorb the wood. Anticipated maturity: 2002–2018.

LABÉGORCE-ZÉDÉ (MARGAUX)

1998	C	(85–86+)
1997	C	(86–87)
1996	C	(85–86)
1995	C	85

Round, attractive, sweet tannin gives the 1998 Labégorce-Zédé an up-front, expansive appeal. The fruit is ripe and redolent with black cherries and berries. The wine is velvety textured, medium bodied, and ideal for drinking over the next 7–8 years.

A lovely, well-made cru bourgeois Margaux, the 1997 Labégorce-Zédé possesses good ripeness, sweet licorice, Asian spice, cherry, and black currant fruit, medium body, and light tannin in the supple finish. Drink it over the next 7–8 years.

The 1996 is dense, peppery, and smoky, with some austerity but rich, medium-bodied flavors, as well as fine power, depth, and ripeness. The wine will need 3–4 years of cellaring and will keep for 10–15 years.

The dark ruby-colored 1995 exhibits tarry, licorice, plum, earthy scents, medium-bodied, soft, round flavors, and immediate appeal. It should drink well for 5–6 years.

LILIAN LADOUYS (ST.-ESTÈPHE)

1997	C	?
1996	C	86
1995	C	81

Tasted three times with similar notes, the 1997 reveals a musty, damp cardboard smell that is offputting.

Performing better than its older sibling, the 1995, Lilian Ladouys's 1996 reveals a deep ruby color and earthy, mineral, cherry, and black currant aromas with oaky notes in the background. This medium-bodied, tannic wine comes across as well balanced, monolithic, and generally well made and ageworthy. Anticipated maturity: 2001–2012.

Austere, tightly knit, and excessively tannic and structured for the amount of fruit, the dark ruby-colored 1995 is muted aromatically. It appears to be all structure and grip in the mouth. Additional fruit and charm may be there, but neither was poking its head through the wine's hardness when I tasted it in November 1997.

LAFITE-ROTHSCHILD (PAUILLAC)

1997	EEE	(90–92)
1996	EEE	100
1995	EEE	95

Tasted three times since bottling, the 1996 Lafite-Rothschild is unquestionably this renowned estate's greatest wine since the 1986 and 1982. As I indicated last year, only 38% of the crop was deemed grand enough to be put into the final blend, which is atypically high in Cabernet Sauvignon (83% Cabernet Sauvignon, 7% Cabernet Franc, 7% Merlot, and 3% Petit Verdot). This massive wine may be the biggest, largest-scale Lafite I have ever tasted. It will require many years to come around, so I suspect all of us past the age of 50 might want to give serious consideration as to whether we should be laying away multiple cases of this wine. It is also the first Lafite-Rothschild to be put into a new engraved bottle (designed to prevent fraudulent imitations). The wine exhibits a thick-looking, ruby/purple color and a knockout nose of lead pencil, minerals, flowers, and black currant scents. Extremely powerful and full bodied, with remarkable complexity for such a young wine, this huge Lafite is oozing with extract and richness yet has managed to preserve its quintessentially elegant personality. This wine is even richer than it was prior to bottling. It should unquestionably last for 40–50 years. Anticipated maturity: 2012–2050.

I thought the 1997 Lafite-Rothschild to be one of the vintage's stars. Made in a more precocious style, much less massive and concentrated than the 1996, it possesses aromas of lead pencil, minerals, plums, and black currant fruit. Exhibiting surprising richness, a supple texture, medium body, and delicious purity and ripeness, this lighter-style but beautiful Lafite-Rothschild should be ready to drink in 3–5 years. Anticipated maturity: 2004–2018.

The 1995 Lafite-Rothschild (only one-third of the harvest made it into the final blend) is a blend of 75% Cabernet Sauvignon, 17% Merlot, and 8% Cabernet Franc. The wine was showing spectacularly well when I tasted it in November 1997. It exhibits a dark ruby purple color and a sweet, powdered mineral, smoky, weedy, cassis nose. Beautiful sweetness of fruit is present in this medium-bodied, tightly knit, but gloriously pure, well-delineated Lafite. The 1995 is not as powerful or as massive as the 1996, but it is beautifully made, with outstanding credentials in addition to remarkable promise. Anticipated maturity: 2008–2028.

Past Glories: 1994 (90+?), 1990 (92+), 1989 (90+), 1988 (94), 1986 (100), 1983 (93), 1982 (100), 1981 (91), 1976 (93), 1975 (92?), 1959 (99), 1934 (90), 1921 (93), 1870 (96), 1864 (92), 1848 (96).

LAFLEUR (POMEROL)

1998	EEE	(91–93)
1997	EEE	(89–91)
1996	EEE	90+?
1995	EEE	93+

Given how profound some of the 1998 Pomerols are, and my adoration of this estate's wines, I had expected to be astonished by the 1998 Lafleur. Perhaps it was the fact that I tasted it sandwiched between Trotanoy and Pétrus, although I am usually able to compartmentalize and forget about what's on either side of a particular wine. In any event, this appears to be an outstanding effort, but less massive and more civilized than I would have expected given the vintage character of many Pomerols. The wine exhibits a saturated purple color and a sweet nose of kirsch and spice. In the mouth, it is medium bodied, tannic, and concentrated, with a restrained, surprisingly elegant personality. It is impressively pure, with outstanding length, but I cannot see it turning out to be profound. Anticipated maturity: 2008–2025.

Lafleur's 1997 is easier to assess than the 1996. The color is dark ruby with purple nuances. Medium bodied, with striking kirsch liqueur and black raspberry scents, moderate tannin, excellent purity and ripeness, it displays more sweetness and glycerin than the closed 1996. It should be ready to drink early, and I expect it to be one of the longer-lived wines from the 1997 vintage. Anticipated maturity: 2004–2018.

As I suspected, the 1996 Lafleur is a painfully backward, austere wine that represents a modern-day clone of this estate's 1966. It possesses a backward, tannic, Médoc-like character, with none of Pomerol's hallmark generosity. The wine exhibits a saturated dark purple color as well as a distinctive mineral, black raspberry, and berry nose with the steely, mineral Lafleur character well displayed. Powerful, long, and rich, but excruciatingly tannic, this wine may or may not resolve all of its tannin. In short, it is an impressively constituted wine that is no sure thing. Anticipated maturity: 2012–2025.

The 1995 is another awesome Lafleur, but it is also an amazingly backward, tannic monster that will need more cellaring than any Médoc in this vintage. The wine boasts an opaque black/purple color as well as a closed but promising nose that represents the essence of blackberry, raspberry, and cherry fruit. Intertwined with those aromas is the telltale mineral *terroir* of Lafleur, full body, blistering dry, astringent tannin, and a layered, weighty feel on the palate. This is the kind of young claret that I couldn't wait to rush out and buy 2 decades ago, but now I have to be content to admire it and wish I were 20 years younger. It is formidable, prodigious, and oh, so promising, but I cannot see it being ready to drink before the end of the second decade of the next century! Anticipated maturity: 2020–2050.

Past Glories: 1994 (93+), 1993 (90+), 1992 (91), 1990 (97), 1989 (95+), 1988 (94), 1986 (94+), 1985 (96), 1983 (93), 1982 (97), 1979 (98+), 1978 (93), 1975 (100), 1966 (96), 1962 (91), 1961 (98), 1955 (92), 1950 (100), 1949 (96+), 1947 (100), 1945 (100).

LAFON-ROCHET (ST.-ESTÈPHE)

1997	D	(86–88)
1996	D	90
1995	D	89+

The 1997 exhibits the fat, charm, and forward fruit possessed by many wines of this vintage. A fleshy, medium-bodied offering, it looks to be an excellent effort from this vintage, as well as a decent value. Anticipated maturity: now–2012.

One of the sleepers of the 1996 vintage, Lafon-Rochet has turned out an atypically powerful, rich, and concentrated wine bursting with black currant fruit. The opaque purple color gives way to a medium- to full-bodied, tannic, backward wine with terrific purity, a sweet, concentrated midpalate, and a long, blockbuster finish. This wine remains one of the finest values from the luxury-priced 1996 vintage and is well worth purchasing by readers who are willing to invest 5–6 years of patience; it should keep for 2 decades. Anticipated maturity: 2005–2020.

The 1995 may merit an outstanding score after several more years in the bottle. Although it has closed down since bottling, it is an impressively endowed, rich, sweet cassis-smelling and -tasting Lafon-Rochet. The wine's impressively saturated deep ruby/purple color is accompanied by vanillin, earth, and spicy scents, medium to full body, excellent to outstanding richness, and moderate tannin in the powerful, well-delineated finish. Anticipated maturity: 2003–2018.

LAGRANGE (POMEROL)

1998	D	(88–89+)
1997	D	(85–87)
1996	D	76

A candidate for one of the finest efforts this estate has produced, the rich, opaque ruby/purple-colored 1998 Lagrange displays excellent purity, abundant quantities of black cherry liqueur-like flavors, a thick, glycerin-imbued texture, and a long, lusty finish. It is unevolved and backward, but impressively rich and extracted. Anticipated maturity: 2003–2016.

The 1997 Lagrange reveals new oak notes and riper berry fruit intermixed with dried herbs and earth. Medium to full bodied, with a sweet ripeness, it is a very good midlevel Pomerol for drinking during its first decade of life. Anticipated maturity: now–2010.

The average-quality 1996 displays an herbaceous, saddle leather-scented nose that lacks fruit. It is medium bodied, with decent concentration and a rustic, earthy finish. This wine also possesses entirely too much tannin for the amount of fruit. Anticipated maturity: 2001–2007.

LAGRANGE (ST.-JULIEN)

1998	E	(86–88)
1997	E	(86–87)
1996	E	90
1995	E	90

The 1998 Lagrange is deep ruby/purple colored with copious amounts of spicy oak in the moderately jammy nose of black currants and earth. This effort is lighter than previous vintages, with medium body and a soft midpalate, but hard tannin in the compact, compressed finish. It should turn out to be very good, but the tannin needs to be watched. Anticipated maturity: 2003–2016.

The dense ruby/purple-colored 1997 Lagrange is a soft, ripe, medium-bodied wine with herbaceous, weedy, black currant fruit, low acidity, and smoky, toasty oak. Round, ripe, and charming, it will drink well between now and 2008.

This impeccably run, Japanese-owned property has fashioned a superb 1996. Opaque purple colored, with a backward yet promising nose of classically pure cassis intermixed with *pain grillé* and spice, this medium- to full-bodied, powerful yet stylish wine possesses superb purity, a nicely layered feel in the mouth, and plenty of structure. It will not be an early-drinking St.-Julien, but one to lay away and enjoy over the next 2–3 decades. Anticipated maturity: 2006–2022.

The 1995 Lagrange is similar to the 1996, but the fruit is sweeter, the acidity lower, and the wine less marked by Cabernet Sauvignon. The color is a deep ruby/purple. The wine boasts roasted herb, charcoal, black currant, mineral, and new oak scents. Medium to full bodied and ripe, with copious quantities of jammy black cherry and cassis flavors presented in a medium-bodied, low-acid, moderately tannic style, this well-endowed, purely made wine requires cellaring. Anticipated maturity: 2003–2020.

Past Glories: 1990 (93), 1989 (90), 1986 (92).

LA LAGUNE (LUDON)

1997	D	(85–86)
1996	D	86
1995	D	88

The dark garnet/plum-colored 1997 offers up notes of roasted nuts, smoky new oak, and sweet cherry fruit. The wine is medium bodied, open knit, expansive, and more charming and approachable than the 1996 and is more evolved. Anticipated maturity: 2000–2012.

The 1996 La Lagune is another tannic, austere 1996, but it is well endowed. Copious aromas of spicy new oak are present in the moderately intense bouquet, as well as cherry notes intertwined with dried herbs. The wine is medium bodied and well made, with good spice, a slight austerity, and moderate tannin in the long finish. In many vintages La Lagune can be drunk at an early age, but this effort will require 5–6 years of patience. Anticipated maturity: 2006–2018.

La Lagune's seductively styled 1995 displays a dark ruby color, as well as copious amounts of black cherry, kirsch, and plumlike fruit nicely dosed with high-quality smoky, toasty oak. This medium-bodied, elegant, round, generous, charming wine can be drunk young or cellared for a decade or more. Anticipated maturity: 2000–2012.

Past Glories: 1990 (90), 1989 (90), 1982 (92).

LANESSAN (HAUT-MÉDOC)

1997	C	(85–87)
1996	C	88
1995	C	87

An insider's wine, Lanessan often makes wines of classified-growth quality that can keep for decades. Readers should consider them as hypothetical crosses between a St.-Julien and Pauillac.

The sweet black currant-and-cherry-scented nose of the 1997 Lanessan exhibits fine purity and maturity. This is a savory, medium-bodied, fleshy, mouth-filling, satisfying wine that should drink well for 7–8 years.

A sleeper of the vintage, Lanessan's 1996 boasts an impressively saturated dark ruby/purple color, and knockout aromatics of melted chocolate, asphalt, and cassis. Deep, rich, and medium bodied, with excellent concentration and purity, this impressively endowed, flavorful, well-structured wine should be at its finest between 2004 and 2016.

The 1995 reveals less power and muscle, but more elegance and fleshy, weedy, tobacco-tinged red and black currant fruit than the 1996, presented in a soft, supple, alluring, medium-bodied format. Anticipated maturity: now–2008.

LANGOA-BARTON (ST.-JULIEN)

1998	D	(87–89)
1997	D	(78–81)
1996	D	86+?
1995	D	86+?

The well-made 1998 Langoa-Barton exhibits a softer style than its big sister, Léoville-Barton. It reveals a deep ruby/purple color, excellent fruit, a juicy midpalate, and sweet tannin in the finish. Anticipated maturity: 2003–2014.

The 1997 Langoa-Barton did not perform well on several occasions. It is a medium-bodied, diluted, straightforward, simple wine without enough charm or character to merit interest. Anticipated maturity: now–2009.

I consistently found the 1996 to be a hard wine. Despite its deep ruby/purple color, it is monolithic, with notes of earth and black currant fruit submerged beneath a tannic structure. Although medium bodied, with some weight and extract, the wine is ferociously hard and backward. Give it 3–5 years of cellaring and hope for the best. Anticipated maturity: 2008–2020.

The 1995 Langoa-Barton has been perplexing to evaluate. It is woody, monolithic, and exceptionally tannic without the fruit and flesh necessary to provide equilibrium. There are some positive components—a saturated dark ruby/purple color, hints of ripe fruit, and pure, clean flavors—but the wine's angularity/austerity is troublesome. It will probably be a good but old-style claret that will never resolve all of its tannic bite. Anticipated maturity: 2003–2016.

Past Glories: 1959 (90), 1953 (90), 1948 (93).

LANIOTE (ST.-ÉMILION)

1997	D	(85–87)
1996	D	?

The 1996 Laniote is aggressively tannic without the balancing fruit, glycerin, and intensity. The wine is sharp and lean in the mouth, with its austerity dominating its personality. Judgment reserved. The 1997 is a sexier, more seductive wine with more fruit, medium body, good purity, and obvious aromas of black cherry jam intermixed with herbs, spice, and smoke. It should drink well for 6–7 years.

LAPLAGNOTTE BELLEVUE (ST.-ÉMILION)

1998	C	(85–87)
1997	C	(85–86)
1996	C	86

The 1998 is a beguiling, dark ruby-colored wine with black cherry aromas. Undeniably elegant, it reveals a feminine style and sweet raspberry fruit. It is medium bodied, soft, succulent, and ideal for drinking over the next 7–8 years.

The charming, open-knit, richly fruity 1997 is light to medium bodied and soft, with no hard edges. Drink it over the next 5–6 years.

A soft, richly fruity wine, the 1996 exhibits medium dark ruby color and an elegant, sweet nose of black cherry fruit intermixed with floral scents, earth, and spice, and dry tannin in the finish. This is an elegant, finesse-style, fruit-driven wine for enjoying over the next 5–6 years.

LARCIS-DUCASSE (ST.-ÉMILION)

1997	D	(75–77)
1996	D	81

This property possesses a magnificent *terroir*, but the wines are not inspirational. The medium ruby-colored 1997 reveals sweet fruit in the aromatics, but little else. Anticipated maturity: 2000–2009.

The medium ruby-colored 1996 displays an intriguing herbaceously scented black cherry nose with dusty, crushed seashell scents. A spicy, straightforward, monolithic, foursquare offering, it will drink well between 2000 and 2008.

Past Glories: 1945 (90).

LARMANDE (ST.-ÉMILION)

1998	D	(88–89+)
1997	D	(86–87)
1996	D	88
1995	D	88

If the 1998 were not so massively tannic, I would have been tempted to pull the trigger and give it an outstanding score. It reveals toasty new oak as well as impressive levels of cassis and black cherry fruit. Consistently well made, seemingly regardless of vintage conditions, Larmande's 1998 is more powerful and structured than usual, with excellent depth and richness and an impressively nuanced finish. It should be at its finest between 2003 and 2014.

The dark ruby-colored 1997 Larmande is a seductive, sexy wine with low acidity, soft, velvety-textured, licorice, dried herb, black cherry, and currant aromas and flavors, and a plush, satiny-textured, ripe finish. Anticipated maturity: now–2010.

One of the most impeccably run properties of St.-Émilion, Larmande's 1996 is a big, rich wine offering up scents and flavors of toast, licorice, Asian spice, fruitcake, and smoky black cherries. It reveals medium body, good richness, moderate tannin, and a long, concentrated finish. The 1996 will benefit from 2–4 years of cellaring and keep for 15 or more years.

The 1995 is cut from the same mold as the 1996, except the 1995 possesses more accessible glycerin and fruit, as well as lower acidity. It offers a dense ruby/purple color and an intense herb, *pain grillé*, jammy blackberry-and-cassis-scented nose intertwined with wood-fire-like aromas. The wine is soft, round, and medium to full bodied, with a sexy combination of glycerin, fruit, sweet tannin and heady alcohol. It should drink well for 10–12 years.
Past Glories: 1988 (90).

LAROSE-TRINTAUDON (HAUT-MÉDOC)

1996 Larose Trintaudon	C	86
1996 Larose Perganson	C	86

Two excellent wines, the deep ruby-colored 1996 Larose Trintaudon offers sweet jammy black cherry and currant fruit, spicy oak, surprising depth and richness, and a convincing midpalate and length. This seriously made, fruit-driven 1996 will drink well for 7–8 years. The 1996 Larose Perganson exhibits more new oak in its aromatics and flavors, with excellent, fleshy fruit, medium body, and good purity. It, too, should drink well for 7–8 years.

LAROZE (ST.-ÉMILION)

1998	C	(86–88)
1997	C	(85–87)
1996	C	86

Another excellent St.-Émilion, the deep ruby-colored 1998 Laroze exhibits plenty of spicy, herb-tinged, blackberry and cherry fruit, sweet, moderate tannin, and good grip and length. This powerful offering is less evolved than usual. Anticipated maturity: 2003–2012.

Medium bodied, lighter, and less evolved than the 1996, the ruby-colored 1997 Laroze offers good purity and a spicy, well-delineated finish. Anticipated maturity: now–2006.

The 1996 Laroze reveals evidence of *sur-maturité* in its pruny, overripe cherry nose. Its dark ruby/garnet color is followed by sweet, expansive flavors, a forward, plush texture, and a fine finish. It will not make old bones, but its distinctive, evolved style will provide pleasure over the next 5–6 years.

LARRIVET-HAUT-BRION (PESSAC-LÉOGNAN)

1998	D	(87–88)
1997	D	(86–88)
1996	D	87

Another surprising sleeper of the vintage, this estate seems to be getting things right after a long period of mediocrity. The 1998 Larrivet-Haut-Brion possesses a dense ruby/purple color in addition to a gorgeous nose of smoked herbs, meats, and jammy black cherries. Long, ripe, and succulent, with good fat, sweet tannin, and excellent depth, this beautifully etched wine should develop the complex aromatics of a top-notch Pessac-Léognan. Anticipated maturity: 2002–2014.

The 1997 may turn out to be slightly denser after bottling. The wine possesses a dark saturated ruby/plum color and a sweet, earthy, smoky-scented nose with aromas of dried herbs, black fruits, and incense. Medium bodied and impressively ripe, with low acidity and a plush texture, this wine may merit a score in the upper-80s. It is also evolved and disarming. Anticipated maturity: 2001–2012.

I was seduced by the 1996 Larrivet-Haut-Brion, one of the better wines this estate has produced over recent years. Although not a powerhouse, it is medium bodied, with expressive tobacco-tinged black currant fruit, a succulent, velvety texture, and smoky, expressive aromatics and flavors. This stylish, evolved 1996 can be drunk now and over the next decade.

LASCOMBES (MARGAUX)

1997	D	(76–78)
1996	D	80
1995	D	79?

The 1997 Lascombes is made in an up-front, light- to medium-bodied, soft style, but at present the oak seems excessive for the moderate quantities of fruit. It will need to be drunk during its first 7–8 years of life.

The 1996 is a mainstream, oaky, soft, fruity wine without much depth or length. It is open knit, with dried herb and black currant fruit in its moderately intense aromatics. The short finish reveals no hard edges. Drink it over the next 7–8 years.

Far less impressive after bottling than it was from cask, the 1995 is now a candidate for drying out given its hollow middle and hard, austere, angular finish. The color is medium ruby, the wine has moderate weight and sweet fruit in the nose and on the attack, but it closes down to reveal a tart, spartan personality. Anticipated maturity: 2000–2008.

Past Glories: 1959 (90).

LATOUR (PAUILLAC)

1997	EEE	(90–91)
1996	EEE	97
1995	EEE	96+

I cannot say enough good things about the exceptional administration of Latour under the joint helmsmanship of Christian Le Sommer and Frederic Engerer, both of whom have been given considerable latitude by Latour's proprietor, François Pinault.

The 1997 Latour will be a surprisingly fine wine, as well as one of the longest-lived offerings of the vintage. It possesses more tannin and depth than most 1997s, along with medium to full body and a textured, multidimensional personality. Sweet, jammy fruit is intertwined with dried herbs, coffee, and earth in this saturated ruby/purple-colored wine. The finish lasts for 20 seconds, a positive sign for a 1997. Anticipated maturity: 2006–2018.

Fifty-six percent of the 1996 production made it into the grand vin, a blend of 78% Cabernet Sauvignon, 17% Merlot, 4% Cabernet Franc, and 1% Petit Verdot. It is a massive, backward wine that comes close to being a monster. The 1996 appears to be a modern-day version of the 1966 or 1970, rather than the sweeter, more sumptuous, fatter styles of the 1982 or 1990. The wine reveals an opaque ruby/purple color, as well as reticent but emerging aromas of roasted nuts, blackberry fruit, tobacco, and coffee, with hints of *pain grillé* in the background. Massive and full bodied in the mouth, it possesses extremely high tannin, fabulous concentration and purity, and an impeccably long finish. This wine, bottled in July 1998, will require at least a decade of cellaring. Anticipated maturity: 2012–2040.

I have been blown away by the 1995 on recent occasions, and all of my hopes for it being a prodigious example of Latour after bottling have proven to be correct. The wine is a more unctuously textured, sweeter, more accessible Latour than the 1996. What a fabulous, profound wine this has turned out to be. It is unquestionably one of the great wines of the vintage and will probably need 10–12 years of cellaring before it can be approached. The wine reveals an opaque purple color and a knockout nose of chocolate, walnuts, minerals, spice, and blackberry and cassis fruit. Exceptionally full bodied, with exhilarating levels of glycerin, richness, and personality, this wine, despite its low acidity, possesses extremely high levels of tannin to go along with its equally gargantuan proportions of fruit. It is a fabulous Latour that should age effortlessly for 40–50 years.

Past Glories: 1994 (94), 1993 (90+), 1990 (98+), 1986 (90), 1982 (100), 1978 (94), 1975 (93+), 1971 (93), 1970 (98+), 1966 (96), 1964 (90), 1962 (94), 1961 (100), 1959 (98+), 1949 (100), 1948 (94), 1945 (96), 1928 (100), 1926 (93), 1924 (94), 1921 (90).

LATOUR À POMEROL (POMEROL)

1998	E	(90–93)
1997	E	(87–89)
1996	E	88
1995	E	89+

The 1998 Latour à Pomerol is the finest wine made at this estate since the 1982 and 1970. Sweet toasty new oak adds to the complex combination of blackberry, cassis, and cherry fruit. Minerals, floral scents, and caramel add to the wine's complexity. Full bodied, with moderate tannin and a layered, multitextured feel, this outstandingly pure wine will get Pomerol enthusiasts excited. Anticipated maturity: 2002–2017.

The 1997's dark ruby color is followed by scents of cappuccino intermixed with blackberries and cassis. Open, expansive, and elegant, it offers a lovely texture and a medium-bodied, silky finish. Anticipated maturity: now–2012.

The 1996 has turned out well after bottling, revealing a saturated dark ruby color and excellent blackberry and cherry aromas intermixed with toast, roasted nuts, and vanilla. Medium bodied, with admirable concentration, moderate levels of spicy oak, and sweet tannin, this dense wine is already delicious. Anticipated maturity: 2000–2014.

The 1995 Latour à Pomerol should develop into an outstanding wine, but it was revealing considerable grip and structure following bottling. It possesses a dark ruby/purple color as well as a distinctive nose of smoked herbs, black fruits, iron, mulberries, and spice. The wine is generous, ripe, and mouth filling, with medium to full body and excellent richness and purity, but the wine's tannic clout and slight bitterness kept it from receiving an outstanding score. Several years in the bottle could result in an excellent, perhaps outstanding, Latour à Pomerol. Anticipated maturity: 2004–2020.

Past Glories: 1982 (94), 1970 (93), 1961 (100), 1959 (98), 1950 (98), 1948 (96), 1947 (100).

LÉOVILLE-BARTON (ST.-JULIEN)

1998	E	(90–92)
1997	E	(85–87)
1996	E	92
1995	E	91

Along with Léoville-Las Cases, this appears to be one of the two finest 1998 St.-Juliens. Impressive, it exhibits an opaque ruby/purple color and a sweet nose of blackberry and cassis fruit intermixed with licorice, earth, and wood. Extremely high in tannin, but with the concentration and muscle to support its brawny structure, this is a big, dense, old-fashioned wine that will require 7–10 years to round into shape. Full bodied and impressively endowed, as well as harmonious, Léoville-Barton has turned in an exemplary performance. Anticipated maturity: 2008–2025.

A successful wine, Léoville-Barton's dark ruby-colored 1997 is soft and fruity, with medium body and good roundness, charm, and character. It will drink well after bottling and should evolve nicely for a decade or more. Anticipated maturity: 2001–2012.

The impressive 1996 is a classic for the vintage. Although backward, it exhibits a dense ruby/purple color in addition to abundant black currant fruit intertwined with spicy oak and trufflelike scents. The wine is brilliantly made, full bodied, and tightly structured, with plenty of muscle and outstanding concentration and purity. It should turn out to be a long-lived Léoville-Barton (almost all this estate's recent top vintages have shared that characteristic) and something of a sleeper of the vintage. However, patience will be required. Anticipated maturity: 2007–2030.

Somewhat closed and reticent after bottling, but still impressive, the 1995 possesses a dark ruby/purple color as well as an oaky nose with classic scents of cassis, vanillin, cedar, and spice. Dense and medium to full bodied, with softer tannin and more accessibility than the 1996, but not quite the packed and stacked effect on the palate, the 1995 is an outstanding textbook St.-Julien that will handsomely repay extended cellaring. Anticipated maturity: 2004–2025.

Past Glories: 1994 (90+), 1990 (92+), 1989 (90), 1986 (92), 1985 (92), 1982 (93+), 1975 (90), 1961 (92), 1959 (94), 1953 (95), 1949 (95), 1948 (96), 1945 (98).

LÉOVILLE-LAS CASES (ST.-JULIEN)

1998	EEE	(90–93)
1997	EEE	(90–92)
1996	EEE	98+
1995	EE	95

The 1998 Léoville-Las Cases is one of the few St.-Juliens that comes close to matching the high quality of its 1995. The 1998 appears to be a less complex wine, but Michel Delon and his son, Jean-Hubert, have turned in another superlative performance. It is a saturated purple-colored Las Cases with a classic nose of vanillin, black currants, cherries, and spice. Medium bodied, with ripe, well-integrated tannin and impressive length, this layered, concentrated, moderately tannic effort should be at its finest between 2002 and 2018.

The 1997 Léoville-Las Cases is unquestionably one of the stars of the vintage. The color is a saturated ruby purple, and the wine offers up plenty of blackberry and cherry fruit intermixed with smoke, cedar, and herbs. It possesses outstanding richness, low acidity, and a sweetly tannic, nicely textured, surprisingly long finish. The 1997 is clearly better than the 1993, 1992, 1991, and 1997 and may be close to the quality of vintages such as 1988, 1989, and 1994. Anticipated maturity: 2000–2014.

Having previously rated it nearly perfect, I was apprehensive of a letdown about tasting the 1996 Léoville-Las Cases once it had been bottled, but that concern was quickly dismissed once I put my nose in the glass. A profound Léoville-Las Cases, it is one of the great modern-day wines of Bordeaux, rivaling what proprietors Michel and Jean-Hubert Delon have done in vintages such as 1990, 1986, and 1982. The 1996's hallmark remains a *surmaturité* (overripeness) of the Cabernet Sauvignon grape. Yet the wine has retained its intrinsic classicism, symmetry, and profound potential for complexity and elegance. The black/purple color is followed by a spectacular nose of cassis, cherry liqueur, *pain grillé*, and minerals. It is powerful and rich on the attack, with beautifully integrated tannin and massive concentration, yet no hint of heaviness or disjointedness. As this wine sits in the glass it grows in stature and richness. It is a remarkable, seamless, palate-staining, and extraordinarily elegant wine—the quintessential St.-Julien made in the shadow of its next-door neighbor, Latour. Despite the sweetness of the tannin, I would recommend cellaring this wine for 7–8 years. Anticipated maturity: 2007–2035.

If it were not for the prodigious 1996, everyone would be concentrating on getting their hands on a few bottles of the fabulous 1995 Léoville-Las Cases, which is one of the vintage's great success stories. The wine boasts an opaque ruby/purple color and exceptionally pure, beautifully knit aromas of black fruits, minerals, vanillin, and spice. On the attack, it is staggeringly rich yet displays more noticeable tannin than its younger sibling. Exceptionally ripe cassis fruit, the judicious use of toasty new oak, and a thrilling mineral character intertwined with the high quality of fruit routinely obtained by Las Cases make this a compelling effort. There is probably nearly as much tannin as in the 1996, but it is not as perfectly sweet as in the 1996. The finish is incredibly long in this classic. Only 35% of the harvest was of sufficient quality for the 1995 Léoville-Las Cases. Anticipated maturity: 2005–2025.

Past Glories: 1994 (93), 1993 (90), 1992 (90), 1990 (96), 1989 (91), 1988 (92), 1986 (98+), 1985 (93), 1983 (91), 1982 (100), 1978 (90), 1975 (92+).

LÉOVILLE-POYFERRÉ (ST.-JULIEN)

1998	E	(87–89+)
1997	E	(85–87)
1996	E	93
1995	E	90+

The 1998 Léoville-Poyferré has turned out well, although it does not possess the depth of the 1996 or 1995. The color is an attractive dark ruby/purple. The modest aromatics reveal toasty new oak, lead pencil, and jammy black currant fruit. The wine is medium bodied, with good ripeness as well as a nice follow-through to the midpalate. On a cautionary note, hard tannin makes an appearance in the abrupt finish. There are fine raw materials here, and if the wine puts on a bit of weight and integrates the tannin, it could merit a higher score. Anticipated maturity: 2004–2018.

The medium-bodied 1997 is a light wine with a soft, open-knit personality, weedy, cedary, black currant fruit, a touch of earth, and a short but charming finish. Anticipated maturity: 2001–2011.

The fabulous 1996 Léoville-Poyferré was tasted three times from bottle, and it is unquestionably the finest wine produced by this estate since their blockbuster 1990. Medium to full bodied, with a saturated black/purple color, the wine offers a nose that reveals notes of cedar, jammy black fruits, smoke, truffles, and subtle new oak. In the mouth, there is impressive fruit extraction, a tannic, full-bodied structure, and a classic display of power and finesse. The longer it sat in the glass, the more impressive the wine became. Backward, and massive in terms of its extract and richness, this should prove to be a sensational Léoville-Poyferré for drinking over the next 3 decades. Anticipated maturity: 2007–2028.

While not as backward as the 1996, the opaque purple-colored 1995 is a tannic, unevolved, dense, concentrated wine that will require 8–10 years of cellaring. The 1995 exhibits *pain grillé*, black currant, mineral, and subtle tobacco in its complex yet youthful aromatics. Powerful, dense, concentrated cassis and blueberry flavors might be marginally softer than in the 1996, but there is still plenty of grip and structure to this big wine. Anticipated maturity: 2005–2030.

Past Glories: 1990 (96), 1983 (90), 1982 (93+), 1900 (93).

LA LOUVIÈRE (PESSAC LÉOGNAN)

1998	D	(87–88)
1997	D	(85–87)
1996	D	87
1995	D	87

Consistently well made, La Louvière's 1998 boasts a deep purple color in addition to an excellent nose of smoked herbs and cassis fruit. The wine is medium bodied, with a nicely layered richness, admirable purity, moderate tannin, and a long finish. Not a blockbuster, it is elegant and nicely concentrated with sweet tannin and an attractive texture. Anticipated maturity: 2001–2014.

The 1997 La Louvière is more evolved than the 1996, with low acidity as well as intense black cherry and cassis fruit intertwined with smoky, toasty new oak scents. Fleshy and forward, with medium body and rich fruitiness, it should drink well for 10–12 years.

La Louvière's dark ruby/purple-colored, ripe 1996 exhibits an excellent combination of sweet black currant fruit meshed with notes of Provençal olives, licorice, smoke, and toasty new oak. With medium to full body, excellent sweetness, and a layered, concentrated finish, this wine should be at its finest between 2003–2015.

Exceptionally seductive and open knit La Louvière's 1995 reveals telltale tobacco, smoky, leafy, herb-tinged red and black currant fruit that jumps from the glass of this aromatic wine. Exhibiting excellent ripeness, a supple texture, medium body, and a delicious, roasted fruitiness, this textbook Graves can be drunk now or over the next 10–12 years.

Past Glories (red): 1990 (90).

Past Glories (white): 1994 (90), 1993 (90).

LUCIE (ST.-ÉMILION)

1997	D	(84–85)
1996	D	86
1995	C	87

The medium ruby-colored 1997 possesses attractive up-front fruit, but dry tannin in the finish is cause for concern.

The well-made, structured 1996 possesses medium body, moderate weight, and sweet berry fruit intermixed with spice and toast. Some of the fleshy opulence it was displaying in the spring of 1997 has fallen away to reveal more tannin, but this will be an accessible, quick-to-mature wine requiring consumption during its first 5–7 years of life. It is attractive and a fine value.

Deep ruby colored, with an herbaceous, jammy cherry-and-berry-scented nose, the soft, round, fruity, open-knit 1995 St.-Émilion displays a user-friendly personality and a supple finish. It will provide ideal drinking over the next 3–5 years. A sleeper.

LUSSEAU (ST.-ÉMILION)

1998	D	(87–88)
1997	D	(87–88)
1996	D	86

Crafted by the cellar master of Monbousquet, the 1998 Lusseau is a sexy, smoky, hedonistically styled wine with jammy black cherry fruit infused with *pain grillé* notes. Medium bodied, soft, and with copious quantities of fruit, this low-acid, lusty St.-Émilion will be admired for its open-knit, consumer-friendly style. Anticipated maturity: now–2010.

The 1997 exhibits a dense, saturated color, along with a jammy, black raspberry-and-berry-scented nose intertwined with earth and spice aromas. With copious quantities of fruit, medium to full body, and excellent purity, it is a sexy, low-acid St.-Émilion to drink now and over the next decade. A sleeper of the vintage.

The medium-bodied 1996 offers black cherry fruit and currants in both the aromatics and flavors. Attractive and soft, with a plump richness, this friendly-style wine should drink well for 5–7 years.

LYNCH-BAGES (PAUILLAC)

1997	E	(87–98)
1996	E	91+
1995	E	90

The elegant, seductive, medium-bodied 1997 Lynch-Bages is what the French call *un vin de plaisir*. Soft, with copious quantities of sweet black currant fruit intermixed with scents of smoky oak, roasted nuts, and weedy tobacco, it possesses a dark color, creamy texture, and no hard edges. It should drink well for a decade. This is another example of a delicious 1997, but, sadly, this vintage was preposterously priced by nearly every Bordeaux château.

Lynch-Bages has turned out an outstanding 1996 that is less forward than the 1990 or 1995 and built along the lines of the tannic, blockbuster 1989. It offers an opaque purple color and outstanding aromatics consisting of dried herbs, tobacco, cassis, and smoky oak. Full bodied and classic in its proportions, this dense, chewy, pure Lynch-Bages will have considerable longevity. Anticipated maturity: 2005–2025.

On the three occasions I tasted the 1995 out of bottle it came across in an elegant, restrained, 1985/1953 Lynch-Bages style. While attractive and soft, with obvious tannin in the background, the 1995 is not made in the blockbuster style of the 1996, 1990, 1989, or 1986. Deep ruby colored, with an evolved nose of sweet, smoky, earthy, black currant fruit, this fleshy, round, seductive, fat and fruity Lynch-Bages should drink well young yet age for 2 decades. Anticipated maturity: 2000–2015.

Past Glories: 1990 (93), 1989 (95+), 1988 (90), 1986 (90), 1985 (91), 1982 (93), 1970 (93), 1961 (94), 1959 (94), 1955 (92), 1953 (90), 1952 (91), 1945 (92).

LYNCH-MOUSSAS (PAUILLAC)

1997	D	(78–80)
1996	D	86
1995	D	86

The 1997 Lynch-Moussas is a lean, elegant, light-bodied, short wine with some sweet fruit. It appears it will always remain a foursquare, monolithic wine with barely sufficient depth. Anticipated maturity: now–2007.

A very good example of this underachieving estate, the 1996 displays a saturated dark ruby/plum color that is accompanied by textbook aromas of black currants, smoky new oak, minerals, and tobacco. Well made, with moderate tannin, excellent purity, and a medium-bodied, ripe, melted asphalt-flavored finish, this seductive Lynch-Moussas should drink well at a young age. Anticipated maturity: 2004–2012.

After bottling, the 1995 Lynch-Moussas is a very good wine, with a dark ruby color, spicy, cedary, cassis fruit in its moderately endowed nose, good ripeness and flesh on the attack, and a dry, clean, moderately tannic finish with grip and delineation. Anticipated maturity: 2002–2016.

MAGDELAINE (ST.-ÉMILION)

1998	E	(90–93)
1997	E	(87–89)
1996	E	88
1995	E	91

An impressively saturated black/ruby color makes the 1998 the deepest-colored Magdelaine I have ever seen. Pure and layered, with a black cherry liqueur-like fragrance, this is a well-balanced, intense, elegant, medium-bodied wine with more stuffing and tannin than usual. Never a blockbuster, this is a model of symmetry, purity, and fruit. Anticipated maturity: 2003–2015.

The 1997 is fatter, richer, and more impressively extracted than the 1996, with a more saturated dark ruby/purple color. The fruit possesses more sweetness, and the wine contains more glycerin and length, in addition to a sweet, fat midpalate. Once again the overall fruit character is one of kirsch liqueur/cherry jam, a hallmark of this property. Look for the 1997 Magdelaine to drink well within 2–3 years and last for 15. It is a very successful wine for the vintage.

I am pleased with how the 1996 Magdelaine has turned out after bottling, as the wine appears to have more to it than I suspected. Its dark ruby color is accompanied by a telltale nose of kirsch and cherry jam intermixed with spicy new oak. Medium bodied, elegant, and harmonious, this wine will undoubtedly close down but should open nicely, offering a stylish, classic St.-Émilion for drinking between 2003 and 2015.

A terrific effort from Magdelaine, the 1995 possesses a saturated ruby/purple color and a sweet, kirsch, and black cherry-scented nose with notes of sexy toast and vanillin. The wine is ripe, rich, and full bodied, with outstanding intensity, purity, and equilibrium. It is a beautiful, harmonious, long, surprisingly seductive, and accessible Magdelaine that will have many admirers. Anticipated maturity: 2000–2020.

Past Glories: 1990 (92), 1989 (90), 1961 (92), 1959 (90).

MALARTIC-LAGRAVIÈRE (PESSAC LÉOGNAN)

1998	D	(86–88)
1997	D	(85–87)
1996	D	76
1995	D	76

Improvements have been made at this estate, and the result is one of the finest red Malartics I have ever tasted. The elegant, soft, stylish 1998 does not possess much power or weight, but it offers attractive, ripe, smoky, black cherry, and cassis flavors welded to a supple, round, symmetrical, medium-bodied format. The wine offers good sweetness as well as a captivating, charming appeal. Drink it over the next 10–12 years.

The 1997 is a competent effort from this perennial underachiever. The medium-deep saturated ruby color is followed by sweet black cherry and cassis fruit and subtle oak aromas. On the palate, it displays good purity, excellent extract, and a nicely layered, rich, medium-bodied, surprisingly long finish. Anticipated maturity: 2002–2014.

The insubstantial 1996 reveals a feeble light ruby color. It offers plenty of new oak and moderate cherry fruit in the nose, medium body, and a pleasant, straightforward, one-dimensional finish. The wine possesses tannin and structure, but not much extract or richness. Anticipated maturity: 2001–2010.

There is excessive toasty new oak in the medium-bodied, straightforward, monolithic 1995. Soft plum and cherry fruit are present, but the wine is too woody and tannic.

MALESCOT-ST.-EXUPÉRY (MARGAUX)

1998	D	(88–90)
1997	D	(78–82)
1996	D	90
1995	D	90

This is a beautifully made 1998 Malescot, with an opaque ruby color and rich, complex, floral notes intertwined with cassis, berry fruit, toasty oak, and cedar. It is rich in the mouth, with nicely integrated tannin, acidity, and wood. The overall effect is one of elegance allied with richness and a suave, savory, lush mouth-feel. This impeccably made wine reveals no hard edges. Anticipated maturity: 2003–2016.

I was less impressed with the 1997, which is pleasant, but medium bodied and straightforward, with strawberry and dried herb-tinged cherry fruit presented in a foursquare format. It will be interesting to see if this wine puts on more weight and exhibits more character after bottling, since Malescot-St.-Exupéry has been especially consistent over recent years. Anticipated maturity: 2000–2007.

The impressively constructed 1996 Malescot offers a saturated deep ruby/purple color, followed by elegant aromas of berry fruit intermixed with tobacco, flowers, and vanillin scents. It is layered and medium to full bodied, with outstanding purity and fruit extraction. Although deep, rich, and powerful for a wine from this estate, it has not lost any of its elegance or potential complexity. Anticipated maturity: 2006–2025.

The 1995 may merit an outstanding rating. It offers a classic Margaux combination of elegance and richness. Medium bodied, with delicate, beautifully ripe, black currant, floral aromas that compete with subtle new oak, the 1995 Malescot hits the palate with a lovely concoction of fruit, nicely integrated tannin and acidity, and a stylish, graceful feel. This quintessentially elegant Bordeaux should continue to improve in the bottle. A beauty! Anticipated maturity: 2002–2018.

Past Glories: 1990 (90), 1961 (92), 1959 (90).

CHÂTEAU MARGAUX (MARGAUX)

1998	EEE	(90–92)
1997	EEE	(90–91)
1996	EEE	99
1995	EEE	95

Forty-five percent of Château Margaux's 1998 crop made it into the grand vin, a blend of 75% Cabernet Sauvignon, 17% Merlot, 5% Petit Verdot, and 3% Cabernet Franc. The harvest began on September 28 and continued under mixed conditions until October 9. It is a classy Margaux, with a dark ruby/purple color, sweet tannin, medium weight, and excellent floral and black currant fruit intermixed with toasty new oak. The wine is concentrated, with a velvety texture and a nicely layered finish. A quintessentially elegant wine, it does not possess the power and concentration of the 1995 and 1996, but it is captivating and charming. Anticipated maturity: 2004–2022.

The 1997 Château Margaux is an immensely charming, open-knit, beautifully made wine offering soft, lush blackberry/cassis fruit intermixed with toasty oak. The wine exhibits excellent concentration, a seductive personality, and an easygoing, round, expansive finish. It should be drinkable after bottling in June and last for 15 or more years. I would not be surprised to see this wine's rating rise; I just wish it were less expensive. Anticipated maturity: 2000–2015.

The 1996 Château Margaux, which was bottled in September 1998, is undoubtedly one of the great classics produced under the Mentzelopoulos regime. In many respects it is the quintessential Château Margaux, as well as the paradigm for this estate, combining measured power, extraordinary elegance, and admirable complexity. I tasted the wine on three separate occasions in January, and in short, it's a beauty! The color is opaque purple. The wine offers extraordinarily pure notes of blackberries, cassis, *pain grillé*, and flowers, gorgeous sweetness, a seamless personality, and full body, with nothing out of place. The final blend (85% Cabernet Sauvignon, 10% Merlot, and the rest Petit Verdot and Cabernet Franc) contains the highest percentage of Cabernet Sauvignon since the 1986. Both Corinne Mentzelopoulos and administrator Paul Pontallier claim they prefer it to 1995, which is saying something given how fabulous that wine has turned out. When tasted side by side, the 1996 does taste more complete and longer, although just as backward. My instincts suggest this wine will shut down, but at present it is open-knit, tasting like a recently bottled wine. The fruit is exceptionally sweet and pure, and there are layers of flavor in the mouth. I posed the question last year as to whether it was capable of surpassing the quality of the 1995, 1990, 1986, 1983, and 1982. Time will tell. Personally, I prefer the opulence and viscosity of the 1990 from a purely hedonistic standpoint, but I do believe this wine will develop an extraordinary perfume and possess the same level of richness as the most concentrated vintages Margaux has produced. It is one of the strongest candidates for the wine of the vintage. Anticipated maturity: 2005–2040.

Bottled very late (November 1997), the 1995 has continued to flesh out, developing into one of the great classics made under the Mentzelopoulos regime. The color is opaque ruby/purple. The nose offers aromas of licorice and sweet smoky new oak intermixed with jammy black fruits, licorice, and minerals. The wine is medium to full bodied, with extraordinary richness, fabulous equilibrium, and hefty tannin in the finish. In spite of its large size and youthfulness, this wine is user-friendly and accessible. This is a thrilling Margaux that will always be softer and more evolved than its broader-shouldered sibling, the 1996. How fascinating it will be to follow the evolution of both of these vintages over the next half century. Anticipated maturity: 2005–2040.

By the way, the 1998 may be the finest Pavillon Blanc (100% Sauvignon Blanc made from yields of 1²/₃ tons per acre) produced at Château Margaux. It is a superbly elegant, concentrated wine, with copious fruit and glycerin and a full-bodied finish. Lovers of intense, honeyed, dry Sauvignon Blanc will love this delicious effort. It unquestionably merits an outstanding rating.

Past Glories: 1994 (92), 1990 (100), 1986 (96+), 1985 (94), 1983 (96), 1982 (98+), 1981 (91), 1979 (93), 1978 (92), 1961 (93), 1953 (98), 1947 (92), 1928 (98), 1900 (100).

MAZERIS (CANON-FRONSAC)

1998	C	(86–88)
1997	C	(85–86+)
1996	C	84

This Canon-Fronsac always reveals a distinctive black raspberry, earthy, *terroir*-driven character. Loaded with gritty tannin, the 1998 displays a dusty, rich, backward personality, an opaque purple color, and admirable structure and power. Give it 3–4 years of bottle age, and drink it over the following decade.

The 1997 offers excellent fruit, medium body, good ripeness, and a dark ruby/purple color. It should drink well for 8–10 years.

Mazeris is normally backward with considerable structure, meant for long-term aging. In 1996 this gives the wine more leanness and aggressive tannin than usual. Potentially it could dry out, but it is above average and well made in a medium-bodied, muscular, tannic style. Anticipated maturity: 2001–2007.

MAZEYRES (POMEROL)

1997	C	(74–76)
1996	C	74

Light bodied, but surprisingly tannic, the herbaceous, vegetal-tasting 1997 is short and uninteresting. Overt aromas of green pepper combined with herbaceousness in the mouth are the undoing of the lean, diluted, medium ruby-colored 1996. Drink it over the next 4–5 years.

MEYNEY (ST.-ESTÈPHE)

1997	C	(78–80)
1996	C	85

I tasted the 1997 Meyney only once, but it was extremely diluted, light, and soft, with little character or depth. It appears to be a commercial, one-dimensional effort designed to be consumed in its first 5–7 years of life.

A soft, easygoing, ripe, dried herb- and red currant-scented wine, the 1996 is surprisingly open and evolved. It is made in a mainstream, consumer-friendly style that will have wide appeal, although it is neither concentrated nor complex. Drink it over the next decade.
Past Glories: 1989 (90), 1986 (90), 1982 (90), 1975 (90).

LA MISSION-HAUT-BRION (PESSAC LÉOGNAN)

1998	EE	(91–94)
1997	EE	(86–87)
1996	EE	89+?
1995	EEE	91

It is always interesting to compare La Mission-Haut-Brion to Haut-Brion. In 1998 both are outstanding wines, but La Mission is a plumper, more viscous, fuller-bodied wine with less nobility and complexity than the highly nuanced, quintessentially elegant Haut-Brion. La Mission's dense saturated purple color is followed by a ripe, expansive, chewy wine with moderately high, ripe, sweet tannin. This full-bodied, multidimensional La Mission is the finest wine produced since the dynamic duo of 1989 and 1990. Anticipated maturity: 2003–2025.

The 1997 La Mission-Haut-Brion is an easy-to-drink, medium-bodied wine with soft, ripe black currants intermixed with tobacco and notes of hot stones and spice. Charming, with low acidity, good fruit, but not much body or length, this open-knit, tasty La Mission should prove to be seductive if consumed over the next 10–12 years.

Much like its sibling, Haut-Brion, the 1996 La Mission-Haut-Brion was closed and backward when I tasted it in January 1999. The wine was bottled in summer 1998 and should have had sufficient time to overcome any suppression from going from wood to glass. It possesses considerable potential, and I would not be surprised to see it merit an outstanding score after 2–4 years of cellaring. The color is a healthy plum/purple, and the wine exhibits some of the black fruit, smoky mineral character of La Mission, but it is medium bodied and moderately high in tannin, with notes of cedar. The finish was totally closed, with the tannin in danger of dominating the wine's fruit. This muscular, structured La Mission will take longer to come around than I originally predicted. Anticipated maturity: 2007–2020.

The 1995 La Mission-Haut-Brion was tight and closed when I tasted it, not revealing as much fragrance or forwardness as it did on the multiple occasions I tasted it from cask. But don't worry, the wine is obviously high-class, exhibiting a dense ruby/purple color and a reticent but promising nose of roasted herbs, sweet, peppery, spicy fruit, medium to full body, and admirable power, depth, and richness. As outstanding as it is, readers should not expect the 1995 to tower qualitatively over vintages such as 1994. Anticipated maturity: 2003–2020.

Past Glories: 1994 (91), 1993 (90), 1990 (94+), 1989 (100), 1988 (90), 1986 (91), 1985 (92), 1982 (98), 1981 (90), 1979 (91), 1978 (96), 1975 (100), 1964 (91), 1961 (100), 1959 (100), 1955 (100), 1953 (93), 1952 (93), 1950 (95), 1949 (100), 1948 (93), 1947 (95), 1945 (94), 1929 (97).

MONBOUSQUET (ST.-ÉMILION)

1998	E	(90–93)
1997	E	(89–92)
1996	E	90
1995	E	92

Since Gérard Perse took over this estate, Monbousquet has become one of the most opulently textured, sexiest, and popular St.-Émilions. The 1998 is no exception, and Perse believes it is the finest wine he has yet made. The color is a deep saturated black/purple. Stunning aromatics of blackberries, raspberries, and smoky new oak explode from the glass. A textured, open-knit, full-bodied wine with abundant glycerin, concentration, and ripe fruit, this hedonistic, consumer-friendly effort will be immensely popular when released. It should drink reasonably well young, even though it possesses more structure than previous vintages, yet keep for 12–15+ years. In 1998 yields were a little under 2 tons per acre, and the final blend was 60% Merlot, 30% Cabernet Franc, and 10% Cabernet Sauvignon.

The dark purple-colored 1997 is undeniably sexy juice, with a deep purple color and a pronounced smoky nose exhibiting gobs of blackberry fruit intermixed with cherries and minerals. Full bodied, with low acidity and a plush, velvety-textured finish, this is a Bordeaux made expressly for lovers of hedonistic wines. Anticipated maturity: now–2012.

I extend my congratulations and accolades to the relatively young new proprietor of Monbousquet, Gérard Perse. With his acquisition of Pavie, Pavie-Decesse, and La Clusière, he has quickly become the most powerful player in St.-Émilion. This is good news for consumers, since Perse is obsessed with quality. For example, he has reduced yields to under 2 tons per acre and is doing everything to ensure a natural expression of his vineyards' *terroirs*. At a blind tasting in New York City, Monbousquet, inserted as one of the sleeper picks in a tasting of the top 1995s, was selected as the finest wine by a majority of the more than 125 people in attendance! I have heard grumblings from some of St.-Émilion's old-timers about Perse's aggressive acquisitions, but no one can criticize the man's commitment to quality. The 1996 Monbousquet is another outstanding effort. The wine is more tannic than the 1995, but it exhibits an exotic nose of kirsch liqueur, cassis, roasted herbs, espresso, and mocha. It possesses excellent texture, impressive depth and richness, and sweet toasty oak. The saturated dark ruby/purple color suggests a dense wine. The finish is both long and well delineated, with moderate tannin. This beautifully etched Monbousquet will take several years longer to come around than the flamboyant, open-knit 1995. Anticipated maturity: 2002–2017.

Although similar to the 1996, the 1995 offers more accessible fruit, and while the tannin is elevated, it is buffered by lower acidity as well as more glycerin and fat. The 1995 displays opaque purple color and a glorious nose of new oak, spice, and abundant black fruits. This full-bodied, superextracted, multilayered wine must be tasted to be believed—especially for readers who remember Monbousquet as the soft, innocuous, commercially styled St.-Émilion it was for many decades. The 1995 has more accessibility than its blockbuster younger sibling, but it still requires 4–5 years of cellaring. Anticipated maturity: 2003–2022.

Readers should also be aware that Gérard Perse is producing approximately 3,000 bottles of a delicious white Monbousquet made primarily from Sauvignon Blanc, with additions of Semillon and Muscadelle. The 1998 (13.8% alcohol) is a surprisingly rich, concentrated wine of impeccably high quality.

Past Glories: 1994 (90).

MONBRISON (MARGAUX)

1998	**D**	**(85–87)**

After some disappointing efforts, Monbrison's 1998 is an elegant, stylish wine with a dark ruby color, ripe strawberry/cherry fruit, and notes of minerals and oak. It is a restrained, civilized wine that should be drunk during its first decade of life.

Past Glories: 1988 (90).

LA MONDOTTE (ST.-ÉMILION)

1998	**EEE**	**(94–98)**
1997	**EEE**	**(93–95)**
1996	**EEE**	**97+**

Okay, let's deal with the criticisms of La Mondotte first. Too little of it is produced (under 1,000 cases), it is too rich, too concentrated, too extracted, too massive, and, sadly, too damn flavorful. That being said, La Mondotte continues to be one of the most profound wines made anywhere in the world. Proprietor Count de Neipperg should be encouraged for pushing quality this high. In essence, La Mondotte sends the following message to every underachiever in Bordeaux: "Make profound wine, and the world will support it." The 1998 comes across as dry vintage port. It is a staggering wine with great complexity, which will be proven time and time again as this vintage and its predecessors, the 1997 and 1996, evolve in the bottle. Is the black/inky purple-colored 1998 better than the 1997 and 1996? I don't really know, but it is massive and highly extracted, with knockout aromatics of roasted coffee, smoke, blackberries, and cherry liqueur. It is huge, as well as unbelievably harmonious, with the tannin, alcohol, and glycerin in balance. Stunning, profound, and provocative, this is about as impressive a young wine as money can buy. Anticipated maturity: 2008–2025.

The 1997 La Mondotte is similar to the 1996, except it is less delineated, with overall lower acidity, but in terms of ripeness, extraction, glycerin levels, and richness, it is cut from the same mold. The wine is massive and unctuously textured and has an awesomely long finish, with gobs of sweet blackberry-, blueberry-, and kirsch-flavored fruit. It oozes across the palate with remarkable concentration and potential complexity. For their immense size, these wines are neither heavy nor overdone. Anticipated maturity: 2002–2020. Kudos to proprietor Comte de Neippberg!

An amazing wine, the 1996 La Mondotte (approximately 800 cases made from a 30-year-old parcel of 100% Merlot planted on a hillside between Le Tertre-Roteboeuf and Canon-La-Gaffelière) is one of Bordeaux's new superstars. If readers cannot get excited by tasting the 1996, they should change beverages. It is amazing for both its appellation and the vintage, revealing a remarkable level of richness, profound concentration, and integrated tannin. The thick purple color suggests a wine of extraordinary extract and richness. This superconcentrated wine offers a spectacular nose of roasted coffee, licorice, blueberries, and black currants intermixed with smoky new oak. It possesses full body, a multidimensional, layered personality with extraordinary depth of fruit, a seamless texture, amazing viscosity, and a long, 45-second finish. The tannin is sweet and well integrated. This blockbuster St.-Émilion should be at its best between 2006 and 2025. A dry, vintage port Fonseca!

MONTROSE (ST.-ESTÈPHE)

1997	E	(85–87)
1996	E	91+
1995	E	93

An elegant, soft, fruity wine without much body or length, the 1997 Montrose is well made and clean, with copious amounts of black cherries and currants and subtle oak in the background. Drink it over the next 7–10 years.

The 1996 Montrose reveals outstanding potential. It boasts a saturated dark ruby/purple color and aromas of new oak, jammy black currants, smoke, minerals, and new saddle leather. This multilayered wine is rich and medium to full bodied, with sweet tannin, a nicely textured, concentrated midpalate, and an impressively long finish. Anticipated maturity: 2009–2025.

An explosively rich, exotic, fruity Montrose, the 1995 displays even more fat and extract than the 1996. There is less Cabernet Sauvignon in the 1995 blend, resulting in a fuller-bodied, more accessible, friendlier style. The wine exhibits an opaque black/ruby/purple color as well as a ripe nose of black fruits, vanillin, and licorice. Powerful yet surprisingly accessible (the tannin is velvety and the acidity low), this terrific example of Montrose should be drinkable at a young age. Anticipated maturity: 2003–2028.
Past Glories: 1994 (91), 1990 (100), 1989 (96), 1986 (91), 1982 (91), 1970 (92+), 1964 (92), 1961 (95), 1959 (95), 1955 (94), 1953 (96).

MONTVIEL (POMEROL)

1998	C	(86–88)

If the 1998 Montviel continues to perform as it did in March of 1999, it will be a candidate for a sleeper of the vintage. Dark ruby/purple colored, with a sweet blackberry and cherry liqueur-scented nose with licorice and toast in the background, this is a long, deep, medium- to full-bodied Pomerol with moderately aggressive tannin. Large scaled and powerful, it will age well for 10–15 years.

LE MOULIN (POMEROL)

1998	E	(89–91)

One of Pomerol's resurrected estates, Le Moulin's 1998 could turn out to be an outstanding wine, as well as one of the vintage's sleepers. The color is an opaque black/purple. The bouquet offers gorgeously sweet black raspberry and berry aromas along with smoke and truffle scents. This is a luxurious wine, with a voluptuous texture, admirable fat and concentration, and a sweet, long, impressively pure, highly extracted finish. It is one 1998 Pomerol with the sweet tannin to encourage at least 15 years of longevity. Anticipated maturity: 2002–2016.

MOULIN-PEY-LABRIE (CANON-FRONSAC)

1998	C	(86–87)
1997	C	(85–87)
1995	C	85+

The deep purple-colored, fruit-driven, rich, medium- to full-bodied 1998 possesses excellent ripeness, copious quantities of sweet blackberry and cherry fruit, a touch of minerals, and a surprisingly long, layered finish. It should drink well for 10–15 years.

One of the better Fronsacs of the vintage, this 1997 exhibits a dark saturated ruby/purple color and a chewy, impressive attack consisting of sweet, mineral-infused black currant fruit and spice. In the mouth, there is good fatness, medium body, and moderate chalky tannin in the impressive finish. This wine needs 2–3 years of cellaring and should keep for 12–15 years.

A well-made, nicely structured, cleanly etched wine, the 1995 offers a deep ruby color, sweet cherry and mineral fruit, some spicy, loamy, earthy notes, and moderate tannin in the long finish. This wine may improve in the bottle and will easily evolve for a decade or more.

MOULIN-ROUGE (HAUT-MÉDOC)

1996	C	85

An old favorite, Moulin-Rouge has again turned in a workmanlike effort, with deep color, spicy, earthy fruit (primarily red currants and cherries), excellent purity, and a moderately long, persuasive finish. Drink it over the next 5–7 years.

MOULIN ST.-GEORGES (ST.-ÉMILION)

1998	D	(87–88)
1997	D	(87–88)
1996	D	89
1995	D	90

This small estate located at the bottom of the Ausone vineyard has the same proprietor and winemaker as Ausone, Alain Vauthier. Over the last several years it has consistently been one of the sleeper wines of the vintage.

The 1998 is a fine effort, although not as complete and concentrated as the 1996. The 1998 Moulin St.-Georges exhibits a deep purple color, admirable intensity (primarily blackberries and minerals), high tannin, medium body, and a backward, eloquent personality. This wine requires 2–3 years of cellaring. Anticipated maturity: 2003–2014.

The 1997 exhibits a fruit-driven nose of raspberries and cherries, followed by sweet jammy flavors, medium body, low acidity, and a soft, plump finish. It should drink well for 5–6 years.

The dark ruby/purple-colored 1996 offers a complex nose of plums and other black fruits, steely mineral notes, and subtle new oak. A classic, elegant, rich, medium-bodied wine with outstanding purity, readers should think of it as the frugal buyer's Ausone. Anticipated maturity: 2001–2015.

A gorgeous wine, and another sleeper of the vintage, Moulin St.-Georges's 1995 exhibits a dense purple color and a sweet, black raspberry and currant nose intertwined with high-quality toasty oak and minerals. Deep, rich, impressively pure, ripe, elegant, and harmonious, this gorgeous, persuasive St.-Émilion has a bright future. Anticipated maturity: 2001–2016.

MOUTON-ROTHSCHILD (PAUILLAC)

1997	EEE	(91–93)
1996	EEE	94
1995	EEE	95+

The superb 1997 Mouton-Rothschild is composed of 82% Cabernet Sauvignon, 13% Merlot, 3% Cabernet Franc, and 2% Petit Verdot. This wine reveals a sensationally flamboyant nose of black fruits, coffee, licorice, and crème de cassis. Medium bodied, with sweet tannin and more layers of flavor than most 1997s, it possesses good spice, an opulent texture, and remarkable length. This is a very hedonistic, open-knit Mouton that has put on considerable weight. Only 55% of the crop made it into the 1997 Mouton. Anticipated maturity: 2000–2022.

This estate's staff believes that the 1996 Mouton-Rothschild is far more complex than the 1995 but less massive. I agree that among the first-growths, this wine is showing surprising forwardness and complexity in its aromatics. It possesses an exuberant, flamboyant bouquet of roasted coffee, cassis, smoky oak, and soy sauce. The impressive 1996 Mouton-Rothschild offers impressive aromas of black currants, framboise, coffee, and new saddle leather. This full-bodied, ripe, rich, concentrated, superbly balanced wine is paradoxical in the sense that the aromatics suggest a far more evolved wine than the flavors reveal. Anticipated maturity: 2007–2030. By the way, the 1996 blend was identical to the 1995—72% Cabernet Sauvignon, 20% Merlot, and 8% Cabernet Franc.

Bottled in June 1997, the profound 1995 Mouton is more accessible than the more muscular 1996. It reveals an opaque purple color and reluctant aromas of cassis, truffles, coffee, licorice, and spice. In the mouth, the wine is "great stuff," with superb density, a full-bodied personality, a rich midpalate, and a layered, profound finish that lasts for 40+ seconds. There is outstanding purity and high tannin, but my instincts suggest this wine is lower in acidity and slightly fleshier than the brawnier, bigger 1996. Both are great efforts from Mouton-Rothschild. Anticipated maturity: 2004–2030.

Past Glories: 1994 (91+), 1993 (90), 1989 (90), 1986 (100), 1985 (90+), 1983 (90), 1982 (100), 1970 (93?), 1966 (90), 1962 (92), 1961 (98?), 1959 (100), 1955 (97), 1953 (95), 1949 (94), 1947 (97), 1945 (100).

NÉNIN (POMEROL)

1998	D	(90–92)
1997	D	(87–89)
1996	D	85

The 1998 is a breakthrough effort for Jean-Hubert Delon and the newly resurrected estate of Nénin. Sixty percent of the production made it into this dense purple-colored 1998. Sumptuous, fat, and rich, this wine has gobs of black cherry fruit backed up by glycerin, full body, and sweet tannin. It is not showing as much complexity as may yet emerge, but there is outstanding purity (as one might expect from the Delons) and a layered, concentrated, long finish. Anticipated maturity: 2005–2015.

The 1997 was the first vintage of Nénin produced under the new owners, the powerful father-and-son team of Michel and Jean-Hubert Delon. They are investing a significant fortune in resurrecting this famed vineyard from the throes of mediocrity. An entire drainage system is being installed in the vineyard, in addition to other large-scale expenditures, all designed to take Nénin to the top of Pomerol's qualitative hierarchy. I do not doubt the Delons' ability to do just that. One-third of the harvest was relegated to the second wine, which will be called Fugue de Nénin. The 1997 Nénin is the finest wine from this estate over recent vintages, but I suspect it offers only a glimpse of the quality level that will ultimately emerge.

The 1997 is a bigger, more complete, concentrated wine than the 1996, with riper fruit, more texture, and a longer finish. It displays a deep ruby/purple color, medium to full body, attractive plum and black cherry fruit intermixed with toast, excellent depth, fine equilibrium, and good spice and sweetness of fruit. This wine possesses some tannin but should drink well for 10–12 years. This is another example of why 1997 is a far better vintage in Pomerol than 1996.

The 1996 was not an easy vintage in Pomerol. Although the 1996 Nénin exhibits lean, rustic tannin in the finish, it offers pleasant plum and chocolatey fruit, medium body, and clean winemaking. Given the balance between fruit and tannin, I would recommend consuming it over the next 5–6 years.

OLIVIER (PESSAC LÉOGNAN)

1997	D	(86–87)
1996	D	86

After years of uninspiring performances, Olivier's vineyards, crowned by one of the region's most gorgeous medieval moated châteaux, are beginning to fashion elegant, stylish, richly fruity wines. The 1996 is a soft, medium-bodied wine with a moderate display of red and black currants, adequate acidity, and sweet tannin. Although not a big wine, it is well constructed and harmonious. Anticipated maturity: 2000–2012. The 1997 reveals a more saturated purple color, in addition to a jammy black fruit character with roasted herbs and leafy tobacco notes. There is excellent sweetness on the attack, a good midpalate, and a fine finish. This fruit-driven example should develop as much complexity as the 1996 with several more years of cellaring. Anticipated maturity: 2002–2012.

LES-ORMES-DE-PEZ (ST.-ESTÈPHE)

1997	C	(81–83)
1996	C	86
1995	C	86

The 1997 is round and easygoing, with low acidity and a nose of vanilla, dried herbs, and red currant fruit. Much lighter than the 1996, it is best drunk over the next 5–6 years.

A potential sleeper of the vintage, the 1996 exhibits a saturated dark ruby color and an excellent blackberry-and-cassis-scented nose with smoky oak in the background. It is sweet, opulently textured, and surprisingly accessible and round, with an excellent finish. This is one of the finest wines from Les-Ormes-de-Pez over recent years. Anticipated maturity: 2000–2014.

I am tempted to say the 1995 is too obviously commercial, but it is still an attractive, soft, round, medium to dark ruby-colored claret with herb, black cherry, and currant fruit notes. Lush, with some elegance, medium body, soft tannin, and an easygoing finish, this wine should be drunk during its first 7–8 years of life.

LES ORMES-SORBET (MÉDOC)

1996	C	86

A consistent performer among the crus bourgeois, this excellent wine offers an elegant, moderately scented nose of black fruits, spicy oak, and minerals. Rich in flavor, harmonious, and with sweet tannin in the finish, it should be drunk over the next 5–7 years.

LES PAGODES DE COS (ST.-ESTÈPHE)

1997	EE	(85–86)

The 1997 vintage of Cos d'Estournel's second wine, now called Les Pagodes de Cos, exhibits a medium ruby color and easygoing, soft, perfumed aromatics, with charming berry fruit, light tannin, and low acidity. It should be drunk over the next 6–7 years.

PALMER (MARGAUX)

1998	E	(90–92)
1997	E	(86–88)
1996	EE	91+
1995	EE	90

An outstanding success for the vintage, Palmer's 1998 (52% of the harvest was included in the final blend) is a blend of 50% Merlot, 45% Cabernet Sauvignon, and 5% Petit Verdot. The Merlot was harvested under ideal conditions on September 25, but the Cabernet Sauvignon harvest was not completed until October 17. The wine reflects the superb Merlot crop with its dense black/purple color, gorgeous nose of cassis, cherry liqueur, and licorice, great fruit, supple tannin, and medium to full body. This is a layered, concentrated, yet surprisingly velvety-textured Palmer that achieved 12.7% natural alcohol. It is one of the stars of both Margaux and the Médoc. Anticipated maturity: 2005–2020.

Palmer's 1997 has put on weight (typical for this estate) since I tasted it a year ago. It is an elegant, medium-bodied, soft, supple wine that will be ready to drink after bottling. A blend of 50% Cabernet Sauvignon, 45% Merlot, and 5% Petit Verdot, it displays a deep ruby color as well as an attractive nose of white flowers and black fruits. Soft, elegant, and seductive, it will drink well after bottling. Anticipated maturity: now–2011.

The 1996, a blend of 55% Cabernet Sauvignon, 40% Merlot, and 5% Petit Verdot, is performing well after its July 1998 bottling. It boasts an impressively saturated purple color, in addition to a backward yet intense nose of black plums, currants, licorice, and smoke. Following terrific fruit on the attack, the wine is taken over by its structure and tannin. This impressively endowed, surprisingly backward Palmer may develop into a modern-day version of the 1966. There is plenty of sweet fruit, and the tannin is well integrated, but the wine requires 7–8 years of cellaring. Anticipated maturity: 2007–2028.

Bottled in July 1997, the 1995 includes an extremely high percentage of Merlot (about 43%). It is a gloriously opulent, low-acid, fleshy Palmer that will be attractive early and keep well. Dark ruby/purple colored, with smoky, toasty new oak intertwined with gobs of jammy cherry fruit, and floral and chocolate nuances, this medium- to full-bodied, plump yet elegant wine is impressive. Anticipated maturity: 2002–2020.

Past Glories: 1989 (95), 1983 (97), 1978 (90), 1975 (90), 1970 (95+), 1966 (96), 1962 (91), 1961 (99), 1945 (97), 1928 (96), 1900 (96).

PAPE-CLÉMENT (PESSAC LÉOGNAN)

1998	E	(89–91)
1997	E	(86–88)

1996	E	90
1995	E	90

One of the quintessentially elegant, complex, and most distinctive wines of Bordeaux, Pape-Clément has been in top form since the 1986 vintage.

Pape-Clément's potentially outstanding 1998 displays a dark ruby/purple color and gorgeously pure, sweet, blackberry and currant fruit, dried herb, earthy, and smoky scents. Ripe, rich, and medium bodied, with moderate tannin and outstanding purity, this is a stylish wine with a layered feel in the mouth. There are no hard edges, as the acidity is low and the tannin is moderate yet sweet. Anticipated maturity: 2003–2015.

The 1997 Pape-Clément displays the scorched earth, tar, mineral character found in certain Graves wines. This vintage has good fruit, low acidity, a sweet midpalate, and a plush finish. It should drink well during its first decade of life. Anticipated maturity: now–2010.

The 1996 is another elegant, complex, distinctive wine that depends on its aromatic complexity and harmonious display of fruit and structure for appeal. It will not knock over tasters with a display of power or muscle. The color is a healthy dark ruby. The wine offers up roasted herb, tobacco, sweet cranberry and black currant fruit aromas. It is medium bodied, with a rich, layered, silky impression, excellent purity, and soft tannin in the finish. Surprisingly forward for a 1996, it appears to be on a rapid evolutionary track, although it will keep for 15 or more years. Anticipated maturity: 2001–2016.

A softer, more accessible version of the more tannic 1996, Pape-Clément's 1995 exhibits a deep ruby/purple color and a lovely nose of spice, lead pencil, minerals, smoke, and tobacco-tinged black currants. Rich and ripe, with medium body, sweet fruit on the attack, and an overall sense of elegance and impeccable equilibrium, this beautifully knit, complex wine is already enjoyable. Anticipated maturity: now–2015.

Past Glories (red): 1990 (91), 1988 (92), 1986 (91), 1961 (92).
Past Glories (white): 1994 (91), 1993 (90).

PATACHE D'AUX (MÉDOC)

1996	B	86

This is one of the most successful wines made by this reliable cru bourgeois since the delicious 1982. Usually dominated by Cabernet Sauvignon (about 70%), the 1996 reveals plenty of new oak. Obviously made from ripe fruit, this dense, chewy, minty, cassis-scented and -flavored wine is a sleeper of the vintage. Drink it over the next 5–7 years.

PAUILLAC (PAUILLAC)

1997	C	(85–86)
1996	C	(86–88)
1995	C	87

Latour's third wine seems to be particularly impressive in 1995 and 1996. It is called simply Pauillac. The 1996 Pauillac is a blend of 50% Merlot and 50% Cabernet Sauvignon. It is a fat wine, with plenty of cassis fruit, excellent purity, and a surprising personality and complexity for its reasonable price, and its potential rating of between 86–88 is high praise indeed. It should drink well for 7–8 years. The 1995 Pauillac exhibits a classic black currant nose with notes of minerals, licorice, and spice. There is good sweetness, medium body, soft tannin, and a classy finish. It should also drink well for 7–8 years. The 1997, a blend of 40% Merlot and 60% Cabernet Sauvignon, is a straightforward, uncomplex, smoky, herbaceous, round, fruity wine with good purity and ripeness. It should be drunk during its first 5–7 years of life.

PAVIE (ST.-ÉMILION)

1998	D	(91–93)
1997	D	(83–85)
1996	D	85
1995	D	78

Gérard Perse, the exceptionally passionate and motivated proprietor of Monbousquet, has become the biggest quality landholder in St.-Émilion. He recently purchased Pavie-Decesse (in time to make a superb 1997) and, following the 1997 vintage, consummated the purchase of Pavie and La Clusière. Anyone who has spent time in the vineyards of St.-Émilion knows that Pavie has one of that appellation's finest *terroirs*, yet it has largely been an underachieving property. Look for that to change.

Making wine in the style of Lafite-Rothschild, Gérard Perse has produced a 1998 that retains its *terroir*'s legendary elegance and complexity, but with more intensity and richness. This is the quintessentially refined Bordeaux that is also immensely flavorful and authoritatively powerful. The color is a dense ruby/purple. Its sweet aromatics reveal red and black fruits intermixed with subtle oak, minerals, and spice. Medium bodied, with layers of fruit, it is gorgeously proportioned and exquisite. Anticipated maturity: 2005–2025.

Monsieur Perse could not do much for the 1997, since it was already made, so this wine is not typical of what will ultimately emerge. The dark ruby-colored 1997 is herbal and earthy, with a lean palate and none of the charm, fat, or richness of the appellation's better wines. Its dry tannin, medium body, and overall size and depth suggest it should be drunk during its first 7–8 years of life.

The dark ruby-colored 1996 Pavie exhibits a pinched, tart personality with moderate quantities of red currant fruit in the nose, along with earth and spice. Although it exhibits good, clean winemaking, this understated, lean, angular wine does not possess much stuffing, flesh, or length. It should keep for 10–15 years. Anticipated maturity: 2000–2012.

Medium plum/ruby in color, with a distinctive peppery, leafy, spicy nose with vague hints of red cherry and currant fruit, the 1995 is a rigid, austere wine with an angular personality and severe tannin. There is some ripe fruit on the attack, but that is quickly dominated by the wine's structural components. This may turn out to be a pleasant wine, but my best guess is that it will dry out. Anticipated maturity: 2000–2010.

Past Glories: 1990 (92), 1986 (90), 1961 (90).

PAVIE-DECESSE (ST.-ÉMILION)

1998	D	(90–92+)
1997	D	(87–89)
1996	D	77?
1995	D	82?

The layered, black/ruby/purple-colored 1998 displays sweet black cherry and cassis fruit as well as subtle toasty oak. It is layered, with gorgeous symmetry, plenty of glycerin and extract, moderate tannin, and a long, persuasively rich finish that lasts for 30+ seconds. The oak is subtle and restrained in contrast with the smoky, flamboyant style of the owner's other St.-Émilion estate, Monbousquet. Anticipated maturity: 2002–2020.

Even though the 1997 was not made by the team of Perse/Rolland, it is the result of a severe selection of only the finest cuvées. It is completely different from its 1996 sibling. The color is a dense ruby/purple, and the bouquet offers up plenty of sweet, black cherry and cassis fruit intermixed with *pain grillé*. Medium to full bodied, with copious quantities of blackberry and raspberry fruit, low acidity, and sweet tannin in the long finish, this is an elegant, stylish wine that should be at its finest between 2001–2012.

New proprietor Gérard Perse had the unenviable task of trying to sell the 1996 Pavie-Decesse, the last vintage made under the old regime. The wine is pleasant, but there is very little to it. Moreover, the dry tannin in the finish suggests that graceful aging will be almost impossible. The overall impression is one of leanness, high tannin, and not enough fruit or concentration. This wine has no place to go but down. Anticipated maturity: 2000–2007.

I may have badly misled readers when I first rated the 1995, giving it an (86–88) range of score. Now that it has been bottled, the 1995 Pavie-Decesse is extraordinarily austere, with elevated tannin levels, some sweet black currant, cranberry, and cherry fruit, but a hollow midpalate and a dry, sharp finish with noticeable astringent tannin. I liked this wine much better from three separate cask tastings, but two tastings from bottle have made me question my earlier reviews. Anticipated maturity: 2002–2010.

Past Glories: 1990 (90).

PAVIE-MACQUIN (ST.-ÉMILION)

1998	D	(91–94+)
1997	D	(91–93)
1996	D	89+?
1995	D	89+?

I adored the 1998 Pavie-Macquin. The estate's old vines have produced a wine with none of the razzle-dazzle ostentatiousness found in some of the new-breed St.-Émilions. Fabulously concentrated, it possesses a nobility and grandeur that must be tasted to be believed. In short, this wine represents the essence of its vineyard. The 1998 may be the finest Pavie-Macquin yet produced (and there have been some impressive ones over recent vintages). It manifests a saturated black/purple color as well as astounding aromatics of blackberry, blueberry, and cassis fruit with whiffs of minerals and steel. A 1998 of extraordinary purity and great symmetry, it offers a medium- to full-bodied personality that oozes with fruit and extract. This 1998 will require 4–6 years of cellaring, possibly longer depending on which direction the tannin goes. One of the vintage's stars. Anticipated maturity: 2005–2020.

The fabulous 1997 Pavie-Macquin is one of the sleepers of the vintage. It represents the essence of old-vine intensity. The color is an opaque black/purple. The nose offers up copious quantities of *pain grillé* intermixed with minerals, blackberry jam, and raspberry liqueur. It is medium to full bodied, rich, intense, and layered with fruit. The finish lasts for more than 30 seconds. The tannin is sweet but present. This terrific example of the 1997 vintage will be uncommonly long-lived. Anticipated maturity: 2002–2018.

I don't think you have to be a gambler to purchase the 1996 or 1995, but the question marks do suggest a level of aggressive tannin that makes forecasting fraught with peril. These are both exceptionally powerful, uncompromising, classic, old-style Bordeaux that should age for 3 decades or more. The only questions are 1) To what degree will the tannin melt away? and 2) How much fruit will remain? No one can doubt the seriousness or concentration of these wines, but their tannin levels are cause for concern.

The 1996 Pavie Macquin could be served next to the 1996 Lafleur. They appear to be cut from the same old-vine, superconcentrated, yet backward, ferociously tannic style. It is an uncompromising wine with a *vieilles vignes* intensity, as well as an abrasively high tannin level. Some of the *terroir*'s telltale mineral and blueberry fruit comes through in the nose and flavors, but this medium-bodied, structured, muscular wine will require 8–10 years of cellaring. Anticipated maturity: 2010–2020.

Made in a style similar to the 1996, the 1995 reveals copious quantities of black fruits and

obvious old-vine intensity (note the minerals and deep midpalate), but its mouth-searing levels of tannin will be enjoyed only by masochists. There are many good things about this wine, but the elevated tannin level is cause for concern. If the tannin melts away and the fruit holds, this will be an outstanding effort. Anticipated maturity: 2008–2025.
Past Glories: 1990 (91), 1989 (90).

PAVILLON DU CHÂTEAU MARGAUX (MARGAUX)

1997	D	(86–87)
1995	D	89

Château Margaux's second wine, Pavillon du Château Margaux, has come of age over recent vintages. The 1997, a 40% Merlot/60% Cabernet Sauvignon blend, is a slightly herbal, upfront, lushly styled wine with plenty of pure fruit, medium body, and no harshness or aggressiveness in the finish. Look for it to drink well during its first 10–12 years of life.

The 1995 Pavillon du Château Margaux may turn out to be one of the most delicious examples the property has made. The wine is forward, sexy, round, and generous, with gobs of black fruit and a subtle dosage of new oak. It should drink well for 10–15 years.

PETIT-BOCQ (ST.-ESTÈPHE)

1996	B	86+
1995	B	86

This is a seriously run, small estate of 17+ acres planted with 70% Merlot, 25% Cabernet Sauvignon, and 5% Cabernet Franc. Both of the following vintages merit interest, particularly for those seeking value in Bordeaux.

A potential sleeper of the vintage, the reasonably priced, well-made 1996 St.-Estèphe displays a dense ruby/purple color as well as plenty of cassis and fruit in its straightforward but satisfying nose. Ripe, with dense, sweet flavors on the attack and chewy levels of glycerin, this foursquare yet plump, attractive wine should drink well for a decade.

The 1995 Petit-Bocq exhibits a deep ruby color, attractive sweet, rich fruit, nice spice, good purity, and a medium-bodied, seamless personality. This is a stylish, supple St.-Estèphe to consume over the next 7–8 years.

PETIT-VILLAGE (POMEROL)

1998	E	(88–90)
1997	E	(86–87)
1996	E	86
1995	E	86

The finest Petit-Village since the 1982, the rich, concentrated 1998 boasts an opaque ruby/purple color and a sweet, perfumed, blackberry-and-cherry-scented nose with hints of toasty new oak and chocolate. Intense and medium to full bodied, with moderately high tannin, low acidity, impressive extract, and a savory, silky finish, this offering should be drinkable young yet keep for 15 years.

The 1997 is another forward, plump, fat Pomerol with chewy blackberry and cherry fruit. The color is more saturated than the 1996, and the wine reveals copious quantities of smoky new oak, low acidity, medium to full body, and a succulent finish. Drink it over the next decade.

The 1996 Petit-Village exhibits an intriguing, intense bouquet of smoked herbs, grilled meats, and cherry jam. In the mouth, black currants make an appearance, along with lavish quantities of wood. Medium bodied, with low acidity, this sexy, accessible, luscious, hedonistic Pomerol will drink well between now and 2007. Hedonists will undoubtedly rate both the 1997 and 1996 even higher.

The 1995 is exhibiting more structure and definition that it did in cask. The wine has an evolved dark garnet/ruby color, sweet, smoky, herb, and cherry perfume, and fat, round, generously endowed, straightforward but satisfying flavors. This is a seductive, hedonistic, plump style of Pomerol that will offer uncritical drinking for the next 5–8 years.

Past Glories: 1990 (90), 1988 (92), 1982 (93).

PÉTRUS (POMEROL)

1998	EEE	(96–98+)
1997	EEE	(90–94)
1996	EEE	92
1995	EEE	96+

Pétrus, the undisputed king of Pomerol, was an inconsistent performer between 1976 and 1988, but since 1989 there have been few Bordeaux wines that match this property for its extraordinary combination of power, richness, complexity, and elegance. The following wines are all noteworthy efforts.

At this early juncture, Pétrus appears to be the unchallenged wine of the 1998 vintage, when 2,500 cases were produced of this monster. I have rarely tasted a Pétrus as powerful, concentrated, and tannic as the 1998. Readers expecting another 1990, 1989, or 1982 will be disappointed, because this wine has much more in common with the 1975 and 1964 (I never tasted the 1964 in its youth). This is a burly, massive, portlike Pétrus, with ferocious levels of tannin yet surreal levels of concentration and intensity. The Pétrus character—thick, mocha, fudge, black cherry liqueur, and sweet jammy fruit flavors—is presented in an enormously concentrated, massively endowed style. This fabulous wine will need at least 8–15 years of cellaring upon release. Anticipated maturity: 2012–2040.

The 1997 Pétrus may ultimately turn out to be a superior wine, but something of an insider's secret. The color is a saturated ruby/purple. The wine offers up copious quantities of sweet coffee, mocha, and blackberry fruit intermixed with cherry and subtle new oak notes. This medium- to full-bodied wine is not a blockbuster, but it is gorgeously rich, with layers of glycerin, extract, and richness coating the palate. Dense and ripe, with moderate tannin in the surprisingly long finish, it should be at its peak between 2007–2025.

Proprietor Christian Moueix's 1996s have turned out well in the bottle. However, I do agree with him that 1997 is a superior vintage for his portfolio, and he has hit the proverbial home run in 1998. The 1996 Pétrus is a big, monolithic, foursquare wine with an impressively opaque purple color and sweet berry fruit intermixed with earth, *pain grillé*, and coffee scents. Full bodied and muscular, with high levels of tannin and a backward style, this wine (less than 50% of the production was bottled as Pétrus) will require patience. It is a mammoth example, but without the sweetness of the 1997 or the pure, exceptional richness and layers of the multidimensional 1995. Anticipated maturity: 2010–2035.

It is interesting how the 1995 continues to evolve. Unquestionably one of the vintage's superstars, the 1995 Pétrus is taking on a personality similar to the extraordinarily backward, muscular 1975. This is not a Pétrus that can be approached in its youth (as with the perfect duo of 1989 and 1990). The wine exhibits an opaque ruby/purple color, followed by a knockout nose of *pain grillé*, jammy black fruits, and roasted coffee. On the palate, it possesses teeth-staining extract levels, massive body, and rich, sweet black fruits buttressed by powerful, noticeable tannin. A formidably endowed wine with layers of extract, this is a huge, tannic, monstrous-size Pétrus that will require a minimum of 10 years of cellaring. Forget all the nonsense about Merlot producing sweet, soft, ready-to-drink wines, because low-yielding, old Merlot vines made in the way of Pétrus and other top Pomerols frequently possess as much aging potential as any great Cabernet Sauvignon–based wine in the world. Look for the 1995 Pétrus to last for 50+ years. Anticipated maturity: 2007–2050.

Past Glories: 1994 (93+), 1993 (92+), 1992 (90+), 1990 (100), 1989 (100), 1988 (91), 1982 (98?), 1975 (98+), 1971 (95), 1970 (98+), 1967 (92), 1964 (97), 1962 (91), 1961 (100), 1959 (93), 1950 (99), 1949 (95), 1948 (95), 1947 (100), 1945 (98+), 1929 (100), 1921 (100), 1900 (89).

PHÉLAN-SÉGUR (ST.-ESTÈPHE)

1997	D	(82–84)
1996	D	86
1995	D	84

The 1997 is a light-bodied, slightly herbaceous, and diluted wine with a straightforward, pleasant feel, but not much depth or length. It should drink well for 3–4 years.

The well-made 1996 Cru Bourgeois exhibits a dark ruby color and a round, attractive nose of black currants, raspberries, and earth. Medium bodied, with sweet tannin and good purity, this wine should drink well for a decade.

Consistently open knit, soft, and pleasant, but essentially one-dimensional and monochromatic, the 1995 Phélan-Ségur offers enjoyable fruit in the nose, but it lacks the depth and richness of other top vintages of this well-placed St.-Estèphe crus bourgeois. Anticipated maturity: now–2005.

PIBRAN (PAUILLAC)

1997	C	(74–76)
1996	C	89

In contrast with the 1996 Pibran, the 1997 is a disappointment. It displays distinctive herbaceous aromas, a short, compressed personality, and no depth or intensity. I was surprised to see such a mediocre wine following the strong performance in 1996.

The 1996 Pibran has turned out to be a sleeper of the vintage. A big, muscular wine, it boasts a saturated purple color and sweet cassis fruit intermeshed with cedar and spice. In the mouth, it is medium to full bodied, with ripe, well-integrated tannin, adequate acidity, and a long, well-delineated finish. This large-scale, reasonably-priced Pauillac should drink well between 2004 and 2016. It is a blend of 70% Cabernet Sauvignon and the balance mostly Merlot, with a small dollop of Cabernet Franc.

PICHON-LONGUEVILLE BARON (PAUILLAC)

1997	E	(85–87)
1996	E	91
1995	E	90

The 1997 Pichon-Longueville Baron is a fruit-driven wine with good quantities of black currant fruit, medium body, and a nicely saturated color, but no weight and a soft, diffuse finish. It should firm up with more cask aging and be delicious when released later this year. Anticipated maturity: now–2010.

Pichon-Longueville Baron's 1996 has turned out to be even better than I thought from cask. The high percentage of Cabernet Sauvignon in the blend (about 80%) resulted in a wine that has put on weight in the bottle. An opaque purple color is accompanied by beautiful aromas of tobacco, new saddle leather, roasted coffee, and cassis. It is dense, medium to full bodied, and backward, with moderately high tannin but plenty of sweet fruit, glycerin, and extract to balance out the wine's structure. This well-endowed, classic Pauillac should be at its finest between 2006 and 2022.

A stylish, elegant, more restrained style of Pichon Baron, with less obvious new oak than usual, the deep ruby/purple-colored 1995 offers a pure black currant-scented nose with subtle aromas of coffee and smoky toasty oak. In the mouth, the wine displays less weight and muscle than the 1996, but it offers suave, elegant, rich fruit presented in a medium- to full-bodied, surprisingly lush style. Anticipated maturity: 2001–2016.

Past Glories: 1990 (96), 1989 (95+), 1988 (90), 1982 (92).

PICHON-LONGUEVILLE-COMTESSE DE LALANDE (PAUILLAC)

1997	EE	(87–89)
1996	EE	96
1995	EEE	96

Readers will enjoy the 1997 Pichon-Lalande, but I am not sure it is better than the 1996 Réserve de Comtesse. Its dark ruby color is accompanied by luscious, black cherry and currant fruit intermixed with notes of mocha, smoke, and toast. The wine displays excellent richness, a sweet, expansive midpalate, medium body, and a supple finish. It will provide ideal drinking during its first 10–12 years of life. Restaurants and readers who are unable to defer their gratification, take notice!

The 1996 Pichon-Lalande is just as awesome from bottle as it was from multiple cask tastings. For Pichon-Lalande, the percentage of Cabernet Sauvignon is atypically high. This wine normally contains 35%–50% Merlot in the blend, but the 1996 is a blend of 75% Cabernet Sauvignon, 15% Merlot, 5% Cabernet Franc, and 5% Petit Verdot. Only 50% of the estate's production made it into the grand vin. The color is a saturated ruby/purple. The nose suggests sweet, nearly overripe Cabernet Sauvignon, with its blueberry/blackberry/cassis scents intermixed with high-quality, subtle, toasty new oak. Deep and full bodied, with fabulous concentration and a sweet, opulent texture, this wine was singing in full harmony when I tasted it in January. Given the wine's abnormally high percentage of Cabernet Sauvignon, I would suspect it will close down. It possesses plenty of tannin, but the wine's overwhelming fruit richness dominates its personality. Could the 1996 turn out to be as extraordinary as the 1982? Anticipated maturity: 2004–2025.

What sumptuous pleasures await those who purchase either the 1996 or 1995 Pichon-Lalande. It is hard to choose a favorite, although the 1995 is a smoother, more immediately sexy and accessible wine. It is an exquisite example of Pichon-Lalande, with the Merlot component giving the wine a coffee/chocolatey/cherry component to go along with the Cabernet Sauvignon's and Cabernet Franc's complex blackberry/cassis fruit. The wine possesses an opaque black/ruby/purple color and sexy, flamboyant aromatics of *pain grillé*, black fruits, and cedar. Exquisite on the palate, this full-bodied, layered, multidimensional wine should prove to be one of the vintage's most extraordinary success stories. Anticipated maturity: 2001–2020.

Past Glories: 1994 (91), 1989 (92), 1988 (90), 1986 (94), 1985 (90), 1983 (94), 1982 (99), 1979 (90), 1978 (92), 1975 (90), 1961 (95), 1945 (96).

LE PIN (POMEROL)

1998	EEE	(94–96)
1997	EEE	(90–92)
1996	EEE	91
1995	EEE	93+

The 1998 is one of the most impressive Le Pins I have ever tasted at this early stage of its development. This wine normally puts on weight and becomes more delineated and complex after several years, so this is a profound performance for such a young Le Pin. A great wine, the dark purple-colored 1998 offers wonderful sweet aromas of *sur-maturité*, blackberry-and-chocolate-infused cherry jam, phenomenal purity, and a sensationally, unctuous, layered palate without a hard edge to be found. Unlike some other Pomerols of the vintage, there is tannin and structure, but it is more silky and integrated. This full-bodied, impressive effort is the quintessential Le Pin—pure opulence and velvety sexiness. Anticipated maturity: 2002–2018.

Le Pin's evolved 1997 displays complex aromatics consisting of roasted coffee, smoke, Provençal herbs, sweet kirsch liqueur, and black cherry fruit. In the mouth, the wine is round, with a velvety texture, low acidity, and excellent concentration and length. It is a succulent, juicy, captivating style of wine to consume during its first 10–11 years of life.

The 1996 Le Pin has softened since I first tasted it. In January 1999 it was extremely open knit, with a dark ruby color and evolved notes of roasted coffee, melted chocolate, exotic coconut scents, and jammy black cherry fruit. Round, soft, supple textured, and medium bodied, this is one of the most flamboyant yet evolved wines of the vintage. Will it firm up now that it has been bottled? There is very little production of the 1996 Le Pin, since only one-third of the harvest made it into the final blend. Anticipated maturity: now–2012.

A dense ruby-colored Le Pin, the 1995 offers up aromas of lead pencil, roasted nuts, smoke, spice, fruitcake, and black cherries intermixed with white chocolate. Luscious and full bodied, with low acidity but plenty of grip and tannin in the finish, this wine, with its abundant cola, kirsch, and black raspberry flavors, is revealing far more structure since bottling than it did in cask. It appears to be every bit as structured and tannic as the 1996. The 1995 Le Pin will take a few years to come around. Anticipated maturity: 2002–2018.

Past Glories: 1994 (91+), 1993 (90), 1990 (98), 1989 (96), 1988 (92), 1986 (91), 1985 (93), 1983 (98), 1982 (100).

LA POINTE (POMEROL)

1998	D	(87–90)

Another perennial underachiever, La Pointe appears to have produced the finest wine I have ever tasted from this property. The color is an opaque black/purple. The wine exhibits ripe, jammy blackberry and cherry aromas intermixed with licorice and oak. Opulent and full bodied, with layers of flavor, this is terrific stuff, albeit atypical for La Pointe. Anticipated maturity: 2002–2015.

PONTET-CANET (PAUILLAC)

1997	E	(87–89)
1996	E	92+
1995	E	92

The deep ruby-colored 1997 reveals abundant quantities of mature fruit in a medium-bodied, charming format. The wine exhibits good depth, lower acidity, and less tannin than its powerful older sibling. Anticipated maturity: 2003–2014.

I was shocked by how backward the 1996 Pontet-Canet was on the three occasions I tasted it in January 1999. This wine possesses superb potential, but it appears a decade's worth of patience will be necessary. The color is a saturated dark purple. With coaxing, the wine offers aromas of black currant jam intertwined with minerals, sweet oak, and spice. A full-bodied wine, it possesses layered, concentrated, sweet fruit, with an elevated level of ripe tannin. Anticipated maturity: 2010–2035.

An old-style Pauillac, yet made with far more purity and richness than the estate's ancient vintages, the broad-shouldered, muscular, classic 1995 exhibits a saturated purple color and sensationally dense, rich, concentrated, cassis flavors that roll over the palate with impressive purity and depth. The wine is tannic and closed, but powerful and rich. It appears to possess length and intensity similar to the 1996. This is a great young Pauillac. Anticipated maturity: 2005–2025.

The extraordinary effort that Alfred Tesseron is making at this property is reconfirmed with each new tasting note I write on Pontet-Canet. Having recently had the exceptionally impressive 1994 in several tastings, it is a pleasure to see this historic estate turning out wines that behave like super-seconds rather than fifth-growths.

Past Glories: 1994 (93), 1961 (94?), 1945 (93), 1929 (90).

POTENSAC (MÉDOC)

1997	C	(86–87)
1996	C	89
1995	C	87

The 1997 Potensac has turned out well, with a sweet, round, berry-scented nose, an open-knit, ripe, supple-textured midpalate and finish, and good length. It is a charming, forward, less massive style of Potensac to drink over the next 6–7 years. Credit is due Jean-Hubert and Michel Delon and their staff for turning out one of Bordeaux's most impressive cru bourgeois wines.

The 1996 Potensac is the most amazing wine this estate has ever produced. It rivals the 1982, being even richer and potentially longer lived. It boasts a dark purple color, as well as a sweet, earthy, black currant and cherry liqueur-scented nose. There is terrific fruit intensity and purity, as well as moderate tannin in the medium-bodied, impressively rich finish. This wine should drink well between 2002 and 2014. A sleeper of the vintage.

Elegant, complex, and evolved, the saturated dark ruby-colored 1995 exhibits herb-tinged, black currant/weedy cassislike flavors that are supple, round, generous, and appealing. This wine does not possess the power and density of fruit found in the 1996, but it is a delicious, reasonably priced claret that should have broad crowd appeal for a decade or more. A sleeper.

POUJEAUX (MOULIS)

1997	D	(89–91)
1996	D	87
1995	C	87

One of the big-time sleepers of the vintage, the 1997 is one of the finest Poujeauxs I have ever tasted. It stands out in the vintage for its opulence, wonderfully sweet, ripe, jammy black currant and cherry fruit, in addition to copious quantities of glycerin, extract, fat, and lusciousness. Unctuously textured, thick, and juicy, with low acidity, exceptional purity, and gobs of fruit, this knockout Poujeaux will be drinkable when released yet age well for 12–15 years. Kudos to the Theil family.

Opaque purple colored, with moderately high tannin yet excellent sweet black currant fruit, the medium-bodied, well-structured, muscular, densely packed 1996 Poujeaux will require 7–8 years of cellaring. Anticipated maturity: 2006–2015.

A very good wine, with grip, tannin, medium to full body, and excellent ripeness, the unevolved, backward, yet promising 1995 Poujeaux needs cellaring. There is some mineral-tinged, sweet black currant fruit in both the aromatics and flavors. Anticipated maturity: 2003–2015.

PRIEURÉ-LICHINE (MARGAUX)

1998	D	(85–87)
1997	D	(79–82)
1996	D	86
1995	D	85

Prieuré-Lichine, which tends to be lighter bodied and elegant, exhibits a dark ruby/purple color, sweet fruit, and attractive levels of black currants and raspberrylike flavors in 1998. Medium bodied, with spice and Provençal herbs in the background, this well-structured effort is a success for the vintage. Anticipated maturity: 2002–2012.

The 1997 possesses a dark ruby color, sweet fruit in the nose and attack, a light personality, and a dry, fruitless finish. It will need to be drunk during its first 7–8 years of life.

Medium ruby colored with a leafy, dried tobacco, red currant, and berry nose, the 1996 displays good ripeness, spicy new oak, and a forward, juicy style. It is not a powerful, backward 1996, but rather a stylish, open-knit claret for consuming over the next 10–12 years.

I expected the 1995 to turn out better than it has. Hard tannin in the finish and a slight hollowness in the midpalate kept my score down. The wine reveals a dark ruby color, light to medium body, good aromatics (earth, underbrush, sweet cherries, and vanillin), and pleasing ripe fruit on the attack. The severe finish is dry and austere. Anticipated maturity: 2000–2008.

QUINAULT-L'ENCLOS (ST.-ÉMILION)

1998	E	(92–95)
1997	E	(87–89)

This property, the jewel of Dr. Alain Raynaud and his wife, Françoise, is an enclosed vineyard within the city limits of Libourne. Walking through the vineyard makes me think this could easily be called the Haut-Brion of the right bank, given its gravelly soil and location within the city. Every effort is made to produce a great wine, with two tables for sorting, Burgundian-style *pigeage* in the style of Burgundy, the implementation of such modern techniques for extracting fruit as reverse osmosis, *microbullage,* and lees stirring. The wines are bottled with neither fining nor filtration.

The 1998 is a breakthrough for this small vineyard owned by Dr. Raynaud. The harvest, completed by September 27, produced a wine of exceptional richness and complexity. It exhibits a saturated blue/purple color and a compelling bouquet of blackberries, blueberries, cassis, minerals, and beautifully integrated subtle oak. The 1998 is rich in the mouth yet is neither heavy nor excessively extracted. The tannin is sweet and the wine long, medium to full bodied, and gorgeously seamless. This striking, symmetrical effort is a star of both St.-Émilion and the vintage. Anticipated maturity: 2001–2018.

The 1997, which was scheduled to be bottled in March 1999, is a beautifully elegant, seductive wine with a dark ruby/purple color and a gorgeous nose of black raspberries intermixed with minerals and floral scents. Medium bodied and ripe, with low acidity and excellent purity, it is a stylish, seductive wine for consuming during its first 10–12 years of life.

RAHOUL (GRAVES)

1996	C	80
1995	C	83

Medium dark ruby colored, with an earthy, smoky nose intermixed with weedy tobacco, the lean, austere 1996's personality is dominated by tannin. Perhaps more flesh and charm will emerge with further cask aging. Anticipated maturity: 2001–2007.

Basically a soft, innocuous, light-bodied wine, the 1995 Rahoul possesses some elegance, but there is not much depth or fruit. It exhibits medium body and some pleasant cherry fruit. Drink it over the next 7–8 years.

RAUZAN-GASSIES (MARGAUX)

1997	D	(85–86)
1996	D	75

The shallow, medium ruby-colored 1996 reveals earthy overtones, little depth, an attenuated, compressed personality, and an herbaceous finish. It will not improve. Anticipated maturity: now–2006. The 1997 is an improvement for this underachieving estate. Made in a completely different style from that of its predecessor, it offers a dark ruby color, sweet, ripe black currant fruit, medium body, low acidity, and excellent purity and depth. It should turn out to be a good, mainstream wine with more character and personality than other recent vintages. Anticipated maturity: 2002–2010.

RAUZAN-SÉGLA (MARGAUX)

1998	E	(86–87+?)
1997	E	(84–85)
1996	E	88
1995	E	90

Although the 1998 Rauzan-Ségla is well made, the austere finish and dry, hard tannin are troublesome. The wine's dark ruby/purple color is accompanied by sweet black currant fruit aromas. There is a good attack and a medium-bodied, concentrated midpalate, but the wine is angular and rustic. Only time will reveal the direction in which this wine is going. Anticipated maturity: 2004–2015.

The well-made 1997 Rauzan-Ségla is lean in the context of the vintage but possesses good berry fruit, medium body, light tannin, and a medium-weight style. Anticipated maturity: 2002–2010.

The dense, ruby/purple-colored, unfriendly-style 1996 is tannic, backward, and in need of 8–10 years of cellaring. The wine does seem to possess the requisite fruit and extract, however, to stand up to its powerful structure. Although pure and rich, this wine should not be touched for at least a decade. The sweet cassis aromas of this Cabernet Sauvignon–dominated wine are combined with floral and mineral notes. Anticipated maturity: 2010–2025.

The 1995 was consistently outstanding from cask, and I suspect it may eventually merit an even higher score, but it was totally closed when I saw it in November of 1997. Unfortunately it was one of the few wines that I was able to taste only once after bottling. Nevertheless, it is a classic *vin de garde*, with a saturated ruby/purple color and a tight but promising nose of sweet plum and cassis fruit intertwined with underbrush, vanillin, and licorice scents. The wine is ripe, medium to full bodied, and rich, as well as unyielding, ferociously tannic, pure, and layered. The finish is extremely dry (*sec*, as the French would say), with a brooding angularity and toughness. In spite of this, my instincts suggest the requisite depth is present to balance out the structure. This effort will also require a decade of cellaring. Anticipated maturity: 2007–2025.

Past Glories: 1990 (93+), 1988 (91), 1986 (96), 1983 (90), 1868 (96), 1865 (99+), 1858 (92).

REIGNAC (BORDEAUX)

1997	C	(86–88)
1996	C	88

One of the finest generic Bordeaux estates, Reignac is producing wine of classified-growth quality owing to a committed proprietor and strict selection. The 1997 offers a saturated ruby/purple color and a sweet, jammy nose of black fruits intermixed with spice, minerals, and toasty oak. In the mouth, it is open knit, expansive, and chewy, with a good texture and an excellent finish. It should drink well for a decade.

The excellent 1996 exhibits a deep ruby color as well as a sweet nose of black currants intermixed with minerals and toast. The wine possesses a fine texture, excellent purity, well-integrated acidity and tannin, and a surprisingly long finish. It is hard to believe this is only a generic Bordeaux. Drink it over the next decade.

RÉSERVE DE LA COMTESSE (PAUILLAC)

1996	C	89+

The 1996 Réserve de la Comtesse is the finest second wine Pichon-Lalande has produced. A blend of 69% Merlot, 30% Cabernet Sauvignon, and 1% Cabernet Franc, this wine may merit a 90-point rating. Production was over 10,000 cases, so it should be easily available. It is a fat, sumptuously textured, rich, hedonistically styled wine that will surprise many consumers with its high quality. It should drink well for a decade.

ROC DE CAMBES (CÔTES DE BOURG)

1997	C	(87–88)
1996	C	88
1995	C	89

The undisputed leader from the Côtes de Bourg appellation, Roc de Cambes continues to turn out delicious, chocolate-scented and -flavored wines. I had a magnum of 1989 at my favorite Hong Kong–style Chinese restaurant in Washington, D.C., in mid-February 1999, and it continues to sing.

Cut from the same mold as the 1996 Roc de Cambes, although slightly riper, with low acidity and less tannin, the 1997 reveals seductive smoky, berry, chocolate/coffee scents and flavors. It should drink well for 7–8 years.

The dark ruby-colored 1996 offers up a sweet, mocha, chocolatey nose with ripe berry fruit in the background. Although not complex, it is soft, velvety textured, medium to full bodied, and a delicious, hedonistically styled wine that should continue to drink well for 5–6 years.

The 1995 offers up a telltale Merlot nose of smoky, roasted coffee, sweet chocolate, mocha, and berry scents. Amazingly deep and rich, this is among the finest wines I have ever tasted from the Côtes de Bourg. There is low acidity, good fat, glycerin, and extract, and a layered, chunky, fleshy finish. It should drink well for 7–8 years.

Past Glories: 1990 (90).

ROCHEBELLE (ST. ÉMILION)

1997	D	(86–88)
1996	D	87

This well-placed property (next to Troplong-Mondot) produces fine wines that remain reasonably priced for their quality level. The dark purple-colored 1997 reveals aromas of black raspberry jam and toasty new oak. Medium bodied and richly fruity, with excellent purity and low acidity, it should drink well during its first 10–12 years of life.

The impressive 1996 Rochebelle displays a deep, saturated, ruby/purple color and a sweet nose of black currants, cherries, incense, and smoky oak. The wine possesses a sweet, fleshy texture, elements of *sur-maturité*, surprisingly low acidity for a 1996, and an expansive, nicely layered finish. If this wine were slightly more complex, it would have merited an even higher score. Anticipated maturity: 2001–2010.

ROCHEMORIN (PESSAC-LÉOGNAN)

1998	C	(86–87)

Dark ruby/purple colored with a tobacco, cedary, black cherry-scented nose, delicate, medium-bodied flavors, elegance, and a soft, sweetly tannic finish, the 1998 Rochemorin can be drunk now and over the next decade.

ROCHER-BELLEVUE-FIGEAC (ST.-ÉMILION)

1997	C	(85–86)
1996	C	85

These two wines are more similar than dissimilar given the vintages. The 1996 is soft, open knit, dark ruby colored, evolved, fruity, and easy to understand and drink. It should be consumed over the next 5–6 years. The 1997 could pass for its older sibling, although it is slightly fatter, with lower acidity and an element of jammy fruit. Both are commercial, well-made, straightforward offerings.

ROL VALENTIN (ST. ÉMILION)

1998	D	(90–93)
1997	D	(90–91)
1996	D	90

A superb 1998 continues the successful string of vintages produced by this up-and-coming St.-Émilion star. The vineyard, not far from La Dominique, on the plateau near Pomerol, is composed of 90% Merlot, 7% Cabernet Franc, and 3% Cabernet Sauvignon. The saturated black/purple-colored 1998 displays an extravagant nose of crème de cassis, sweet new oak, and licorice. Deep, powerful, and full bodied, with the high extract and glycerin level concealing rugged tannin, this is a blockbuster. Anticipated maturity: 2003–2014.

The saturated purple-colored 1997 offers impressive extract as well as ripe, blackberry and vanillin notes in the restrained but promising aromatics. Deep and medium to full bodied, with noticeable tannin and lavish oak, this chewy, fleshy, full-bodied St.-Émilion will require several years of bottle age. Anticipated maturity: 2003–2016.

This vineyard near both Cheval Blanc and La Dominique has turned in an exemplary performance in 1996. A blend of 90% Merlot, 7% Cabernet Franc, and 3% Cabernet Sauvignon, it boasts a dark ruby/purple color as well as a sweet nose of black currants intermixed with licorice, toasty new barrel aromas, and smoked herbs. Medium bodied, rich, ripe, and hedonistically styled, this wine was made from low yields, enjoyed an impeccable *élevage*, and was bottled without filtration. Anticipated maturity: 2001–2014.

ROLLAND-MAILLET (ST.-ÉMILION)

1996	C	85

From one of Michel Rolland's estates, this wine is a well-made, bistro-style St.-Émilion. The color is dark ruby, and the nose offers up seductive, earthy, black cherry fruit, medium body, no hard edges, and a ripe, fruity, savory style. Drink it over the next 5–6 years.

ROUGET (POMEROL)

1998	D	(87–89)
1997	D	(84–87)
1996	D	85

This estate appears to be making an effort to produce higher-quality wines. The finest Rouget since the 1982, the 1998 is undoubtedly a sleeper of the vintage. It offers an impressively saturated dark ruby/purple color and excellent blackberry fruit intertwined with licorice, toast, and smoke. This backward Pomerol's low acidity and high extract tend to hide the wine's sizable tannin. There is plenty of fat and excellent length in this wine, which should be a reasonably good value for the vintage. Anticipated maturity: 2001–2014.

I would not be surprised to see the 1997 turn out to be more serious and merit a higher score than the 1996. The saturated ruby color reveals purple hues. The wine possesses a jammy, black cherry-and-berry-scented nose along with earth and spicy oak. In the mouth, it is elegant and medium bodied, with lovely fruit and a straightforward, ripe, concentrated finish. Drink it over the next 6–7 years.

The 1996 reveals a deceptively light ruby color, along with ripe fruit (cherries) and toasty new oak in the nose. It is a pretty, elegant wine with medium body and an unmistakable cherry flavor component. Readers should think of this as a Pomerol modeled along the lines of De Sales. Drink it over the next 5–6 years.

ROYLLAND (ST.-ÉMILION)

1997	C	(83–85)
1996	C	86

The dark ruby-colored 1997 Roylland displays sweet fruit on the attack, but it narrows in the mouth. It should drink well for 5–6 years.

The 1996 exhibits a dark ruby color and sweet berry fruit, dried herb, leafy tobacco, and sweet oak aromas. The wine's ripeness and lushness make it a successful effort for the vintage. It should drink well young yet age for 8–10 years.

ST.-PIERRE (ST.-JULIEN)

1998	D	(87–88)
1997	D	(87–89)

The underrated estate of St.-Pierre deserves more attention. While the wines do not quite hit the heights of Léoville-Las Cases, Léoville-Barton, or Léoville-Poyferré, they are remarkably consistent, chunky, husky Bordeaux with considerable character.

Several samples of the 1998 revealed a mustiness and were unjudgeable. The healthy sample I tasted was deep ruby/purple colored, with juicy, black currant fruit intermixed with smoke, dried herbs, and spice. Extremely tannic, but fat and succulent in the midpalate, this medium-bodied, ripe, angular wine should turn out to be very good. Anticipated maturity: 2004–2014.

The 1997 reveals a nicely saturated ruby/purple color and an earthy, spicy, fruit-driven bouquet (primarily jammy black currants) with subtle new oak in the background. Dense on the palate, and slightly backward, this fleshy, expansive, but moderately tannic wine will be one of the few 1997s that will not be ready to drink upon release. However, it is approachable. Anticipated maturity: 2002–2013.

Past Glories: 1990 (90), 1986 (90).

DE SALES (POMEROL)

1998	C	(86–88)
1997	C	(85–86)
1996	C	79
1995	C	87

De Sales is on a comeback trail, which is good news for readers looking for a more reasonably priced Pomerol.

Unquestionably the finest De Sales since the 1982, the medium- to full-bodied, ripe, sweet, cherry- and toasted nut-scented 1998 offers succulent fruit, admirable acidity, and sweet tannin. There is good glycerin and an easygoing, open-knit texture, but not without some structure. This large-scale De Sales should age nicely for 10–12 years.

The 1997 has much more to it than the 1996, with sweeter fruit, lower acidity, and a clean, pure, black cherry, fruit-driven style. It should drink well for 7–8 years.

Although it is a pleasant, medium ruby-colored wine, the 1996 De Sales is dry in the finish. It reveals ripe cherry fruit intermixed with dusty, earthy elements as well as a suggestion of roasted nuts. Drink it over the next 3–4 years.

The 1995 may turn out to be the best De Sales since the 1982. The wine displays a deep ruby color and a seductive nose of jammy cherries, earth, kirsch, and an intriguing balsam wood note. In the mouth, this supple wine possesses very good concentration, a round, velvety texture, plenty of crowd appeal, and a clean, lush, berry-infused finish. Already drinking well, this 1995 Pomerol should keep for 7–8+ years. A sleeper.

SIRAN (MARGAUX)

1998	D	(87–88)
1997	D	(78–81)
1996	D	83
1995	D	87

An impressive effort, the blue/black-colored 1998 Siran displays a thick-looking appearance in addition to powerful licorice, incense, and mineral notes combined with cherry jam and cassis. The wine is deep and medium bodied, with moderate tannin in the long, layered finish. Anticipated maturity: 2003–2018.

The 1997 lacks fruit and richness in the midpalate but does exhibit attractive cherry/currant aromas intermixed with minerals and smoky oak. The finish is attenuated. Anticipated maturity: 2000–2007.

Siran's 1996 is a compressed, hard-textured, lean, austere wine with a medium ruby color and an angular personality. Anticipated maturity: 2003–2012.

A very good effort from Siran, the dark ruby-colored 1995 offers attractive aromas of vanillin, spicy new oak, and sweet, creamy cassis fruit interspersed with subtle fennel and spice box notes. Medium bodied and ripe, with savory richness, sweet tannin, and low acidity, this excellent, elegant Margaux is already accessible. Anticipated maturity: 2000–2014.

SMITH-HAUT-LAFITTE (PESSAC LÉOGNAN)

1998	E	(90–92)
1997	E	(86–88)
1996	E	90
1995	E	90

Since the acquisition of this estate by the Cathiard family, this property has become one of Bordeaux's success stories, producing elegant, flavorful, complex, very complete wines. This winery continues to move from strength to strength under the committed leadership of Florence and Daniel Cathiard. Never a heavyweight or blockbuster, Smith-Haut-Lafitte tends to produce the quintessentially elegant style of Bordeaux, offering an impressive marriage of intense flavors, finesse, and complexity.

The 1998 Smith-Haut-Lafitte is potentially the finest wine made under the administration of the Cathiards. The deep ruby/purple color is followed by an elegant mélange of floral scents, black cherry liqueur, cassis, minerals, and subtle new oak. The wine hits the palate in layers, with little sense of weight and nicely integrated sweet tannin. A hallmark of purity, symmetry, and complexity, this beautifully etched, expansively flavored wine should age well. Anticipated maturity: 2004–2022.

The dark ruby-colored 1997 exhibits medium body, excellent ripeness, and loads of charm and finesse. The black fruit character is well displayed along with toasty oak and low acidity. Its hallmark is elegance and finesse as opposed to power and structure. Nevertheless it possesses such good balance that I suspect it will drink well for 12–15 years.

The 1996 Smith-Haut-Lafitte is the quintessentially elegant Bordeaux. With a dark ruby/purple color, it displays a beautiful presentation of blackberry and cassis fruit nicely dosed with subtle new oak. On the attack, the wine is sweet and pure, with striking symmetry and a compellingly balanced midpalate and finish. Although not as big as some blockbusters from this vintage, it is extremely complex (both aromatically and flavor-wise) and impressive for its restraint, subtlety, and impeccable balance. Anticipated maturity: 2003–2016.

The 1995 is already showing exceptionally well, even though it is not close to its plateau of maturity. The deep ruby/purple color is followed by scents of roasted herbs intermixed with sweet black currant fruit, truffles, vanillin, and minerals. Lush, with ripe cassis fruit on the attack, outstanding balance, medium body, and layers of intensity, this is an elegant, graceful, smoothly textured, beautifully made Bordeaux. Anticipated maturity: 2001–2018. *Past Glories (white):* 1994 (91).

SOCIANDO-MALLET (HAUT-MÉDOC)

1997	D	(89–91)
1996	D	90
1995	D	90

I think I like the 1997 even more than the 1996. First of all, it is one of the most forward, upfront Sociando-Mallets produced in the last decade. The color is a saturated opaque purple and the wine extremely low in acidity, but oh, so captivating. There are gorgeous layers of sweet cassis liqueur-like fruit intermixed with vanillin, lead pencil, and mineral aromas. Medium bodied, with outstanding concentration and as smooth a texture as will ever be found in such a young Sociando-Mallet, this wine will drink beautifully young and last for 12–15 years. Very impressive. Anticipated maturity: 2000–2014.

A classic Sociando-Mallet, with a style not dissimilar from that of the 1986, the 1996 boasts a saturated purple color as well as an intense nose of cassis liqueur, chocolate, and minerals. Dense and medium bodied, with outstanding purity and high tannin, this beautifully made wine is better than many classified growths. Anticipated maturity: 2007–2020.

The accessible yet tannic 1995 example of Sociando-Mallet possesses a deep ruby/purple color and excellent aromatics consisting of jammy black cherries, blackberries, and cassis, as well as subtle notes of minerals, earth, and new oak. This is a deep, long, muscular, tannic wine that is structurally similar to the 1996. Patience will be required from purchasers of this high-class wine. Anticipated maturity: 2006–2025.
Past Glories: 1990 (92), 1989 (90), 1986 (90), 1985 (90), 1982 (92).

SOUDARS (HAUT-MÉDOC)

1997	D	(83–84)
1995	B	85

Dark ruby colored, with an earthy, soft, lighter style than usual, the 1997 should be drunk over the next 2–3 years.

A soft, fruity, oaky wine with a medium dark garnet/ruby color, the spicy, peppery, herb-tinged, plum-and-currant-scented and -flavored 1995 is round, tasty, and alluring. Drink it over the next 3–4 years. This consistently well-made wine also offers very good value.

TALBOT (ST.-JULIEN)

1998	D	(86–87)
1997	D	(85–86)
1996	D	89
1995	D	88

I enjoyed the elegant, medium-weight 1998 Talbot because of its ripe, open-knit style. It does not possess significant volume or concentration, but it exhibits a dark ruby color with purple nuances. Smoked olive and cassis fruit aromas and flavors characterize this soft, medium-bodied 1998 with a round, generous finish. A supple wine, it was made without excessive extraction, thus avoiding the problem of astringent tannin. Drink it over the next 10–12 years.

The 1997 Talbot is soft, medium bodied, and herbaceous, with red currant fruit intertwined with smoke and herbs. The wine is clean, light bodied, and ideal for drinking over the next 5–6 years. Restaurants should take note of this offering.

I tasted the 1996 three times in January 1999, rating it 88, 89, and 90 with similar tasting notes. The wine is close to being outstanding, exhibiting a saturated dark ruby color and excellent aromatics consisting of black fruits intermixed with licorice, dried herbs, and roasted meat smells. It is full, with impressive extract, a fleshy texture, low acidity, excellent purity, and a long, deep, chewy finish. This 1996 will be drinkable at a young age yet keep for 15–20 years. Anticipated maturity: 2003–2017.

The 1995 has turned out to be more impressive from bottle than it was in cask. It is a charming, intensely scented wine with a telltale olive, earth, grilled beef, and black currant-scented bouquet soaring from the glass. Medium to full bodied, with low acidity and round, luscious, richly fruity flavors, this is a meaty, fleshy, delicious Talbot that can be drunk now. Anticipated maturity: now–2012.

Past Glories: 1986 (96), 1983 (91), 1982 (96), 1953 (90), 1945 (94).

DU TERTRE (MARGAUX)

1998	D	(87–88)
1997	D	(86–88)
1996	D	89
1995	C	86

Readers should be aware that this property was recently sold by Madame Gasqueton (the proprietor of Calon-Ségur) to a Dutchman named Eric Jelgersma, also the new proprietor of Château Giscours.

A potential sleeper of the vintage, Du Tertre's 1998 exhibits a dense ruby/purple color in addition to a sweet black cherry-and-cassis-scented nose, soft, velvety-textured tannin, medium body, and a surprisingly succulent, fat midpalate. The wine reveals good length and a charming, up-front, expansive appeal. This is another estate that did not overextract, thus producing a wine of charm, ripe fruit, and harmony. Anticipated maturity: 2002–2012.

The 1997 performed admirably well on the several occasions I tasted it. Du Tertre's dark ruby/purple-colored 1997 offers copious quantities of sweet blackberry and currant fruit in the evolved nose. Soft, lush, and low in acidity, this medium-bodied wine was tasting akin to a succulent fruit bomb. Anticipated maturity: 2000–2007.

A sleeper, Du Tertre's 1996 exhibits a black ruby/purple color, a sweet black fruit-scented nose, medium to full body, well-integrated tannin, and fine purity and depth. This wine should age very nicely yet have a degree of accessibility young. Anticipated maturity: 2004–2018.

A chocolatey, berry-scented nose with weedy cassis, licorice, and earth aromas is followed by a medium-bodied 1995 with fine concentration. Although monolith, the 1995 is well made, mouth filling, and moderately tannic. Anticipated maturity: 2003–2015.

LE TERTRE-RÔTEBOEUF (ST.-ÉMILION)

1998	EE (92–95)
1997	EE (87–88)
1996	EE 90
1995	EE 95

If wines were whores, Le Tertre-Rôteboeuf would certainly be a potential candidate. These lavishly rich, sumptuously textured, hedonistic wines hit all the sweet spots on the palate.

An explosive, sensual, mind-boggling effort from the garrulous François Mitjavile, the 1998 offers a telltale melted chocolate, licorice, and cherry jam nose that explodes upward from the glass. The saturated plum/purple color is followed by fabulous concentration, terrific extract, great purity and ripeness, and a full-bodied, low-acid, unctuously textured finish. Undoubtedly the finest Le Tertre-Rôteboeuf produced since the blockbuster, hedonistic 1990, this voluptuous 1998 will be delicious upon release and keep for 12–15+ years. Fabulous stuff!

The 1997 Le Tertre-Rôteboeuf possesses an intense chocolatey character intermixed with Asian spice, smoky, toasty oak, and black cherry fruit. It is a very good, luscious, low-acid, richly fruity wine for enjoying during its first 7–8 years of life.

The 1996 Le Tertre-Rôteboeuf is less sumptuous out of bottle than it was from cask. Nevertheless this is an outstanding wine produced in the telltale style of this well-placed hillside vineyard. The color is a deep ruby, and the nose offers up hedonistic notes of smoky, crème brûlée, roasted coffee, and chocolate-covered cherries. This medium-bodied wine is exhibiting more structure, muscle, and tannin than I remember from cask. In fact, after the sweet aromatics and initial blast of fruit on the attack, the wine seems to close down, revealing moderate tannin in the very good finish. Unlike most vintages of Le Tertre-Rôteboeuf, which can be drunk immediately, the 1996 requires 2–3 years of cellaring and should keep for 15–16 years.

The 1995 is the third vintage (1989 and 1990 were the other two) where Le Tertre-Rôteboeuf exhibits a Le Pin-like exotic richness and opulence. The wine exhibits a dense ruby/purple color and a compelling set of aromatics consisting of *pain grillé* and ripe black cherry and cassis fruit intermixed with truffles, mocha, and toffee. Dense and full bodied, with layers of intensely ripe fruit, this plump, gorgeously pure, expansively flavored, multi-dimensional wine is even better out of bottle than it was in cask. Anticipated maturity: 2001–2018.

Past Glories: 1994 (90), 1993 (90), 1990 (98), 1989 (95), 1988 (91), 1986 (91), 1985 (90).

LA TOUR-FIGEAC (ST.-ÉMILION)

1998	D	(86–88)
1996	D	86
1995	D	87

This estate is on the qualitative rebound after some uninspiring efforts. I recently drank my last bottle of the 1982, which was still in fine shape.

A corpulent, juicy, succulently styled wine, La Tour-Figeac's dark ruby-colored 1998 displays plenty of black cherry and cassis fruit, not much complexity, but depth, richness, and symmetry. If it takes on more nuances, it should merit a score in the upper 80s. Anticipated maturity: 2000–2012.

The dark plum/ruby color of the 1996 is accompanied by dusty, earthy, sweet cherry, currant, smoke, and vanillin scents. A medium-bodied wine with moderate levels of tannin, admirable extract, and a linear personality, this 1996 possesses fine raw materials and good ripeness but may turn out to be angular and austere given the elevated tannin level. Anticipated maturity: 2001–2012.

In contrast with the more spartan 1996, the 1995 is a sexy, deep ruby-colored wine with gobs of herb-tinged, spicy, berry fruit in the nose and flavors. Medium bodied, soft, friendly, and juicy, this is an appealing style of St.-Émilion for consuming over the next 7–8 years. A sleeper.

LA TOUR-HAUT-BRION (PESSAC LÉOGNAN)

1998	D	(87–88)
1997	D	(84–86)
1996	D	87
1995	D	89+

Deep ruby colored, with a pronounced cedary, herb-tinged, black currant-scented nose, the medium-bodied, elegant 1998 exhibits fine ripeness, sweet tannin, and a moderately long finish. Already complex and evolved, it should drink well for a decade or more.

The 1997 is a lighter-style, elegant, soft, cedary, smoky Cabernet-dominated wine with no hard edges and an easygoing, straightforward personality. Drink it over the next 7–8 years.

La Tour-Haut-Brion's 1996 is an aromatic, surprisingly evolved wine for the vintage with a dark plum color and a pronounced, smoky, cassis, weedy, dried herb-scented bouquet. A medium-bodied, classic, midweight Bordeaux with plenty of spice, sweet fruit, elegance, and complexity, it is a blend of 50% Cabernet Sauvignon and 50% Cabernet Franc. It should provide delicious drinking early and last for a decade.

One of the finest La Tour-Haut-Brions over the last 15 years, the 1995 offers a heady perfume of coffee beans, tobacco, spice, smoke, grilled herbs, and sweet red and black fruits. It is long and round, with copious quantities of red currants as well as good underlying acid, which gives the wine definition, and a spicy, lush, sweet finish with light but noticeable tannin. Anticipated maturity: 2001–2015.

Past Glories: 1982 (95), 1978 (95), 1975 (96), 1961 (95), 1959 (92), 1955 (94), 1947 (95).

LA TOUR-MARTILLAC (PESSAC LÉOGNAN)

1998	D	(87–88)
1997	D	(86–87)
1996	D	83
1995	D	86

A concentrated effort for this estate, the 1998 La Tour-Martillac exhibits sweet, toasty, black currant fruit intertwined with tar and earth scents. With ripe tannin, medium body, and fine balance, this excellent wine should drink well between 2003 and 2016.

The 1997 is a richer, sweeter wine than the 1996, with more color, extract, and length. It offers smoky toasty oak in the nose, attractive black currant fruit, and notes of licorice. It should drink well for 10–12 years.

La Tour-Martillac's 1996 is a medium-bodied, straightforward wine with good spice, moderate fruit, and a simple personality. There is some tannin, but the wine is light. Anticipated maturity: 2002–2008.

The olive, tobacco, smoky, red currant-and-cherry-scented nose of the 1995 is followed by an elegant, medium-bodied, soft, smoothly textured wine that can be drunk now or over the next decade.

Past Glories (white): 1994 (90), 1992 (90), 1988 (90).

TROPLONG-MONDOT (ST.-ÉMILION)

1998	E	(88–90)
1997	E	(88–90)
1996	E	89
1995	E	92

I am a huge fan of this property run by Christine Valette and have been an avid purchaser of many of her wines, particularly the 1988, 1989, and 1990. I tasted all three of these vintages in a minivertical in January 1998, and they were sensationally good.

On three separate tastings of the 1998 Troplong-Mondot, the wine came across as surprisingly elegant and less powerful and intense than in vintages such as 1995, 1990, and 1989. It boasts an impressively saturated purple color, as well as a beautifully etched bouquet of cassis, blackberries, and subtle new oak. The wine is medium bodied and stylish, with excellent concentration, dry tannin in the finish, and a floral, finesse-style personality. With moderate tannin it will benefit from 4–5 years of cellaring and keep for 15–17 years. Do I detect a slight shift from the powerhouse style of recent vintages?

While the 1997 is backward for the vintage, it does reveal soft tannin and accessibility because of its sweet fruit. The deep ruby/purple color is followed by a medium-bodied, stylish, charming wine with nicely integrated toasty oak, and copious quantities of blackberry and cassis fruit intermixed with licorice, Asian spices, and new oak. Anticipated maturity: 2002–2015.

I am pleased with the way the 1996 has turned out. The ferocious tannin has been slightly tamed now that the wine is in bottle. Still a backward style of Troplong-Mondot, it will require 6–7 years of cellaring. The wine exhibits a deep ruby/purple color and a powerful nose of licorice, black currants, and spicy new oak. There is sweet fruit on the attack and medium body, but the firm tannin gives the wine grip and delineation, as well as a certain austerity. This wine does possess the requisite depth to support its tannic clout, but patience is required. Anticipated maturity: 2007–2019.

Closed but immensely promising, the dark purple-colored 1995 exhibits a reticent but intriguing nose of underbrush, jammy black fruits, minerals, and vanillin. Deep, rich, and medium to full bodied, with outstanding extract and purity, the wine possesses a seamless personality with sweeter, more integrated tannin than in the 1996. This is a *vin de garde* to cellar for another 7–8 years. It is not far off the splendid level of quality achieved in both 1989 and 1990. Anticipated maturity: 2005–2020.

Past Glories: 1994 (90), 1990 (98), 1989 (96).

TROTANOY (POMEROL)

1998	EE	(94–98)
1997	EE	(90–91)
1996	EE	89+
1995	EE	93+

Let me make it crystal clear: Readers have to go back to 1961 to find a Trotanoy of such exhilarating power, richness, and potential complexity as the 1998. There are 2,800 cases of this black beauty. Harvested at the perfect time, Trotanoy's 1998 boasts a saturated black/purple color as well as a gorgeous nose of truffles, licorice, black currants, overripe cherries, cedar, and coffee. Amazingly full bodied, with fabulous concentration and firm yet sweet tannin, this massive wine will require 8–10 years of cellaring. Those seeking a Trotanoy made in a forward 1995 or 1990 style will need to recalibrate their palates when tasting this blockbuster. Anticipated maturity: 2008–2025.

The 1997 Trotanoy outperforms the 1996 when tasted side by side. This wine boasts a dense ruby/purple color and outstanding aromatics of black raspberries, cherries, minerals, and toast. In the mouth, it exhibits a fat midpalate, medium to full body, good power, sweet tannin, low acidity, and excellent to outstanding ripeness. The finish goes on for over 30 seconds. Will this wine close down as the 1996 has done? Anticipated maturity: 2003–2020.

I would not be surprised to see the 1996 Trotanoy merit an outstanding score. When I saw it in January 1999, it had begun to tighten up and close down. The wine possesses a dense, medium plum color, tight but promising aromatics, a sweet, pure core of mineral-tinged blackberry and cherry fruit, plenty of power and richness, a chewy texture, and muscle and firm tannin in the finish. Anticipated maturity: 2006–2017.

A fabulous success for Trotanoy, the 1995 has considerable potential and may ultimately merit a higher score than I have bestowed upon it. The 1995 boasts a saturated deep purple color followed by a knockout nose of black truffles, cherries, raspberries, and kirsch fruit intermixed with spicy oak and beef blood-like scents. Full bodied, dense, and as powerful and backward as its rival, Lafleur, this broad-shouldered, superextracted Trotanoy is superb, but don't make the mistake of thinking it will provide easygoing drinking over the near term. While splendid, this wine possesses extremely high tannin and needs at least 7–8 years of cellaring. Anticipated maturity: 2005–2025. Bravo!

Past Glories: 1993 (90), 1990 (91), 1982 (94), 1975 (95), 1971 (93), 1970 (96+), 1967 (91), 1964 (90), 1961 (98).

TROTTE VIEILLE (ST.-ÉMILION)

1997	D	(86–87)
1996	D	87
1995	D	?

Well made, the deep ruby-colored 1997 Trotte Vieille offers aromas of smoky new oak intertwined with licorice and black raspberry fruit. The wine displays a lovely texture, low acidity, and a fleshy, easy-to-understand finish. Anticipated maturity: now–2010.

The 1996 Trotte Vieille appears to be a step up for this St.-Émilion premier grand cru. Soft and elegant, it possesses nicely integrated smoky new oak along with blackberry and cherry fruit. It is medium bodied, with excellent purity and a nicely textured, stylish finish. This will be a 1996 to enjoy at an early age. Anticipated maturity: 2002–2012.

I have very good tasting notes of the 1995 before bottling, but when I tasted it twice after bottling, the wine revealed an evolved medium ruby color already displaying amber at the edge. Additionally, the wine came across as austere, hard, tannic, and out of balance. This is completely at odds with prebottling samples, so I prefer to reserve judgment until I can taste the wine after it has had a chance to calm down in the bottle.

Past Glories: 1989 (90).

VALANDRAUD (ST.-ÉMILION)

1998	EEE	(90–92)
1997	EEE	(89–91)
1996	EEE	91
1995	EEE	95

Proprietor Jean-Luc Thunevin deserves credit for serving as an inspiration for other St.-Émilion producers. The success he has enjoyed with Valandraud has undoubtedly fueled many of the qualitative efforts going on elsewhere. The opaque ruby/purple-colored 1998 Valandraud offers a gorgeous nose of black cherries, earth, and vanillin. It is supple, velvety textured, and voluptuous, with high, but sweet tannin. As the 1998 sits in the mouth, flavors of dried herbs, new saddle leather, and meat emerge. This rich, beautifully textured, long, concentrated wine will not rival the exquisite 1995, but it is a top-notch effort. Anticipated maturity: 2001–2015.

The 1997 Valandraud exhibits an impressively saturated plum/purple color and sweet black cherry fruit, toasty new oak, spice, and chocolate aromas. It is seamless, with a velvety texture, medium to full body, moderate tannin, and a long finish. The wine's low acidity and forward, charming style suggest it should be consumed during its first 12–15 years of life.

The 1996 has firmed up significantly since bottling. Unfined and unfiltered, this viscous wine displays the telltale thickness of color (saturated dark ruby/plum/purple). The wine's exotic bouquet is just beginning to form, offering up notes of iodine, roasted coffee, jammy black fruits, and *pain grillé*. In the mouth, it is medium to full bodied, with sweet tannin, terrific texture, and outstanding purity and length. Anticipated maturity: 2003–2018.

The splendid 1995 Valandraud ranks with the finest wines proprietor Jean-Luc Thunevin has produced since his debut 1991 vintage. The wine exhibits an opaque purple color and a sensational nose of roasted herbs, black fruits (cherries, currants, and blackberries), and high-class toasty oak (the latter component is more of a nuance than a dominant characteristic). Very concentrated, with layers of fruit, glycerin, and extract, yet seamlessly constructed, this wine contains the stuff of greatness and appears to be the finest Valandraud yet produced. The finish lasts for over 30 seconds. The wine's high tannin is barely noticeable because of the ripeness and richness of fruit. Anticipated maturity: 2003–2020.

Past Glories: 1994 (94+), 1993 (93).

VEYRY (CÔTES DE CASTILLON)

1997	C	(86–87)

Made with the assistance of Valandraud's Jean-Luc Thunevin, this multidimensional, intense, richly fruity, smoky, black currant-scented and -flavored wine possesses excellent richness, a lush texture, and a surprisingly long finish. Readers looking for good value should check out this delicious wine. Drink it over the next 4–5 years.

LA VIEILLE-CURE (FRONSAC)

1998	C	(86–88)
1997	C	(84–85)

1996	C (86–87)
1995	C 87

The 1998 La Vieille-Cure is surprisingly structured and tannic for this estate (which has a high percentage of Merlot). It also reveals lavish quantities of new oak. However, the fruit quality is excellent, with plenty of blackberry and jammy cherry fruit allied to a medium-bodied, structured, well-delineated wine. This is a consistently well-made Fronsac, and the 1998 is one of their more muscular, ageworthy efforts. Anticipated maturity: 2001–2010.

Seemingly lighter and less well-endowed than previous vintages, but cleanly made, with plenty of uncomplicated Merlot fruit, the 1997 is a soft, medium dark ruby-colored wine with a sense of elegance as well as good overall equilibrium. It will drink well for 5–6 years.

The 1996 performed admirably in what is a more mixed Fronsac vintage. Deep ruby colored, with plenty of sweet blackberry and cherry fruit in both its aromatics and flavors, this medium-bodied wine reveals *pain grillé* notes, moderate tannin, and 5–12 years of aging potential. It is quite well made.

A delicious, attractive, Merlot-dominated wine, the 1995 La Vieille-Cure presents a deep ruby color, attractively sweet, ripe, black cherry, kirsch, and cedar-tinged aromatics, round, ripe, medium-bodied flavors with some grip and tannin, excellent purity, and a nicely layered finish. This wine can be drunk now as well as over the next 7–8 years. A sleeper of the vintage.

VIEUX-CHÂTEAU-CERTAN (POMEROL)

1998	EE (94–96)
1997	EE (85–87)
1996	EE 87
1995	EE 88?

An "atypical wine," according to proprietor Thienpont, the 1998 used no Cabernet Franc; it is instead a 90% Merlot, 10% Cabernet Sauvignon blend. The wine was harvested at the optimum time in Pomerol (September 21–26), and the vineyard produced a measly 34 hectoliters per hectare. In short, the 1998 is the most profound Vieux-Château-Certan produced since this estate's great historic period, when it made profound wines in 1945, 1947, 1948, 1949, and 1950. It is a massive, black/purple-colored wine with a viscous texture, formidable richness, and high tannin. This powerhouse/blockbuster will require a minimum of 8–10 years of cellaring. It is a mammoth, superconcentrated, compelling effort that will need to be purchased as a future. Bravo! P.S. It seems to me Vieux-Château-Certan should produce more "atypical" wines. Anticipated maturity: 2010–2035.

Vieux-Château-Certan's dark ruby-colored 1997 displays an elegant, charming personality with low acidity, evidence of moderate new oak, and a medium-bodied, weedy, fruit-driven finish. It will drink well young and keep for 10–12 years. It is good but uninspiring.

Tasted three times from bottle in January 1999, the 1996 merited a slightly higher score on one occasion, but my policy is to go with the more conservative rating. The wine exhibits a dark plum color and a complex nose of roasted herbs, Asian spices, earth, and sweet black cherry fruit. A refined claret, with excellent concentration, a sweet midpalate, and moderate tannin in the finish, it is a finesse-style Pomerol. Anticipated maturity: 2003–2016.

Frightful bottle variation left me perplexed about just where this 1995 fits in Bordeaux's qualitative hierarchy. I tasted the wine three times since bottling, all within a 14-day period. Twice the wine was extremely closed and firm, with an evolved plum/garnet color, high levels of tannin, sweet black currant, prune, and olive-tinged fruit, and astringent tannin in the medium-bodied finish. Those two bottles suggested the wine was in need of at least 5–7 years of cellaring and would keep for 2 decades. The third bottle was atypically evolved, with a similar color, but it was far more open knit, displaying Provençal herbs and black cherry and cassis fruit in a medium-bodied, jammy, lush style. I expect marginal bottle variation, but while the quality was relatively the same in all three bottles, the forward, open-knit example left me puzzled.

Past Glories: 1990 (91), 1988 (91), 1986 (92), 1975 (90), 1964 (90), 1952 (94), 1950 (97), 1948 (98), 1947 (97), 1945 (98–100), 1928 (96).

VIEUX FORTIN (ST.-ÉMILION)

1998	C	(87–89)
1997	C	(83–85)
1996	C	86
1995	C	86

This consistently well-made St.-Émilion has fashioned its finest effort to date with the 1998. The vineyard, not far from Figeac and Cheval Blanc, has produced a powerful wine that is undoubtedly a sleeper of the vintage. Its heady, intoxicating combination of black fruits, earth, and toast, and easy, open-knit, ebulliently fruity style make for a hedonistic drinking experience. There is more tannin than usual, but it is soft and well integrated. Drink this fleshy, well-made 1998 over the next 7–8 years.

Not as successful as either the 1995 or 1996, the medium-bodied 1997 is slightly austere, with hard tannin. It does reveal attractive black cherry fruit as well as good clean winemaking. Perhaps more charm will emerge.

Impressive for a wine in this price category, the deep ruby-colored 1996 St.-Émilion reveals a tobacco-tinged, black cherry-scented nose and spicy, medium-bodied flavors with excellent purity and ripeness. Forward and soft for a 1996, without much structure or tannin, it should be consumed over the next 5–7 years. This is a very good value.

The medium deep ruby-colored 1995 Vieux-Fortin offers a moderately intense, herb-tinged, berry, spicy, chocolatey-scented nose and a creamy texture. There is a tannic overlay, but the wine's primary appeal is its up-front fruit, plumpness, and easygoing, open-knit character. Anticipated maturity: now–2006. This wine is an excellent value.

VRAY CROIX DE GAY (POMEROL)

1998	E	(89–91+?)

Another hulking behemoth, with a personality similar to some 1975 Pomerols, this black/ruby/purple-colored, powerful, dense, and massive wine reveals mouth-searing levels of tannin (hence the question mark). The bouquet displays scents of roasted herbs, cappuccino, and sweet black cherry fruit. Oozing with extract and exhibiting some astringency, this full-bodied, superconcentrated effort appears to be the biggest, brawniest wine I have ever tasted from Vray Croix de Gay. I will wait another year to see if everything comes together, as it is still somewhat angular and disjointed but loaded with potential. Anticipated maturity: 2006–2020.

The Sweet White Wines of Bordeaux: 1996 and 1997 Barsac/Sauternes

The Barsac and Sauternes wine-producing region is located a short 40-minute drive south from downtown Bordeaux. Labor intensive and expensive to produce, the sweet wines of Barsac and Sauternes have long had huge climatic and manpower problems to overcome almost every year. Additionally, for most of this century the producers have had to confront a dwindling demand for these luscious, sweet, sometimes decadently rich and exotic wines because of the consumer's growing demand for drier wines. Given the fact that it is rare for a particular decade to produce more than three excellent vintages for these wines, the producers in this charming and rural viticultural region have become increasingly pessimistic that their time has passed. Château owners have changed at a number of properties, and more and more vineyards are also producing a dry white wine to help ease cash-flow problems.

Yet surprisingly, many growers continue. They know they make one of the most remarkable wines in the world, and they hope that Mother Nature, good luck, and an increasing consumer awareness of their products will result in accelerated demand and appreciation of these white wines, which until recently were France's most undervalued and underappreciated great wines.

Perhaps their persistence has finally paid off. The second half of the eighties may well be viewed by future historians as the beginning of the renaissance for Barsac and Sauternes. There are many reasons for this turnaround in fortune. The fact that Mother Nature produced three superb, perhaps even legendary, vintages—1986, 1988, and 1989—helped focus attention on the region's producers and their wines. Moreover, the decade of the nineties started auspiciously, with 1990 producing sumptuous and powerful wines.

Second, a number of estates that had been in the doldrums for a while began to turn out wine that merited significant interest. In particular, the resurrection of the French Ministry of Agriculture's famed Château La Tour Blanche, with profound wines in 1988, 1989, and 1990, served as a sign that even the French government was interested in vindicating the great reputation of this famous estate.

Another premier grand cru classé, Rabaud-Promis, also began to make topflight wines, culminating in sensational efforts in 1988, 1989, and 1990. Furthermore, the acquisition of one of the flagship estates of the region, Château Rieussec, by the Domaines Rothschild in 1984 suggested that the great red wine–making empire of the Rothschilds would now be expanded to include lavishly rich, sweet white wines. That promise has been fulfilled with compelling efforts in 1988, 1989, and 1990.

At the same time, the continued revival of Château Guiraud, under Canadian ownership, went on with a succession of fine vintages.

All of this appeared to culminate with the 1988 and 1990 vintages, which are being called the greatest Sauternes vintages since 1937. Futures of these vintages became difficult to find, and a renewed confidence emerged. After all the difficulties they had experienced, the sweet wines of Barsac and Sauternes appeared poised to once again become fashionable on the world's best tables.

While Mother Nature can be exceptionally kind to the region's producers (1986–1990, for example), the period between 1991 and 1995 produced few inspirational wines from this area. Yet modern-day technology has helped producers combat nature with a radical new winemaking procedure called cryoextraction. This technique could be employed in less successful vintages to freeze the grapes and transform many so-so wines into something much richer and more interesting. Whether or not this will gain favor with the top estates, and whether or not it produces weaknesses in the wines when they are 10–25 years old cannot be measured until after the turn of the century. But there is no question that it has helped raise the current quality of many wines from this appellation.

No one doubts that the winemakers of Barsac and Sauternes face the most forbidding odds for producing successful wines. The hopes and fears regarding the outcome of a vintage normally begin at the time most of the red wine–producing appellations to the north have commenced or even finished their harvests. During the latter half of September Mother Nature begins to unfold the climatic conditions that will be important for the vintages of this region. The climate in Barsac and Sauternes is normally misty, mild, and humid at this time of year. The foggy, damp mornings (created by the Ciron River, which runs through the heart of Sauternes) and sunny, dry afternoons encourage the growth of a mold called *Botrytis cinerea*.

This mold—commonly called "noble rot"—attacks each ripe, mature grape individually, devouring the grape skin and causing the grape to die and become dehydrated. Of course, only grapes that are undamaged and have been attacked by the noble botrytis rot are selected. Botrytis causes a profound change particularly in the Semillon grape. It shrivels the skin, consumes up to 50% of the sugar content, forms glycerol, and decomposes the tartaric acids. The result is a grape capable of rendering only one-fourth of its volume of juice prior to the botrytis attack—an unctuous, concentrated, aromatic, sweet nectar. Curiously, the reaction causes a superconcentration of the grape's juice, which becomes considerably higher in sugar than normal. This happens without any loss of acidity.

This process is erratic and time-consuming. It can often take as long as 1 or 2 months for a significant portion of the white grapes to become infected by the botrytis mold. In some years (for example, 1978, 1979, and 1985) very little botrytis develops, and the wines lack flavor dimension and complexity. When the noble rot does form, its growth is painfully slow and uneven. Therefore the great wines of this region can be made only by an arduous, time-consuming, labor-intensive process of sending teams of pickers into the vineyard to pick the afflicted grapes one at a time rather than bunch by bunch. The best estates have their pickers descend on the vineyard up to half a dozen times over this period, which usually occurs throughout October and November. The famous Château d'Yquem often sends pickers through the vineyard ten separate times. As expensive and time-consuming as picking is, the most hazardous risk of all is the weather. Heavy rains, hailstorms, or frost, all common meteorological developments for Bordeaux in late fall, can instantly transform a promising vintage into a disaster.

Since the conditions for making great wine are so different for Barsac and Sauternes, it is not surprising that what can be a great vintage for the red wines of Bordeaux can be mediocre for the sweet white wines from this area. The years 1982 and 1961 are two vintages in point. Both are undeniably great years for the red wines, but for the sweet wines of Barsac and Sauternes the vintages are at best average. In contrast, 1988, 1980, 1967, and 1962 are four vintages for Barsac and Sauternes that most observers would consider very fine to superb. With the exception of 1988 and 1962, these vintages were less successful for most of the red wines of Bordeaux. Like the red wines of the Médoc, the wines of Barsac and Sauternes were considered important enough to be classified into quality groupings in 1855. The hierarchy established Yquem as the best of the region, and it was called a premier grand cru classé. Following Yquem were premiers crus classés (now 11 as a result of several vineyards' being partitioned) and 14 deuxièmes crus classés (now 12 because one has ceased to exist and two others have merged).

From a consumer's perspective, three unclassified cru bourgeois estates, Raymond-Lafon, de Fargues, and Gilette, are making exquisite wines that rival all of the best estates' wines except for Yquem. However, they were not included in the 1855 classification. Additionally, there are a number of first-growths and second-growths that simply cannot afford to make wine the traditional way—using numerous crews of pickers working sporadically over a 4- to 8-week period. Several do not merit their current status and have been downgraded in my evaluations of the châteaux of this region.

As for Château d'Yquem, it towers (both literally and figuratively) above the other estates here, producing a splendidly rich, distinctive, unique wine. In my opinion, it is Bordeaux's single greatest wine. The official first-growths of the Médoc have worthy challengers every year who produce wine often as impressive, and the right bank trio of Cheval Blanc, Ausone, and Pétrus can in some vintages be not only matched, but surpassed by the brilliance of other estates in their respective appellations. Yquem, however, rarely has a challenger (except perhaps the rarely seen microscopic luxury cuvées of Coutet and Suduiraut called Cuvée Madame). This is not because top Barsac and Sauternes properties such as Climens, Rieussec, or Suduiraut cannot produce superlative wine, but rather because Yquem pro-

duces a wine at such an extravagantly expensive level of quality that it is commercial mad-
ness for any other property to even attempt to emulate it.

Since 1991 the entire region has been transformed by the great success of the vintages
from the mid-1980s on. Most producers are now enjoying a degree of financial prosperity
(perhaps even security) that they had only dreamed of in the early eighties. These wines,
even with such revolutionary techniques as cryoextraction, will always be the most difficult
wines in the world to produce, and a few bad vintages in a row or overreliance on new technology would no doubt dampen much of the appellation's enthusiasm, but for now, optimism
reigns supreme in what once was a most distressingly sad region of Bordeaux.

Recent Vintages

1997—A very good, possibly excellent, year for Barsac/Sauternes, the 1997 vintage witnessed a slow formation of botrytis. The wines possess excellent complexity, copious
amounts of honeyed fruit, and more evolved personalities than the 1996s, another very fine
vintage. Even though the 1997s taste riper and lower in acidity than their 1996 counterparts,
an analysis of most of the top wines indicates they are actually higher in acidity, leading me
to believe they possess more raw materials and richness. The 1997 vintage favored Semillon
more than Sauvignon, which accounts for the fat, honeyed style exhibited by so many 1997s.
It is hard to compare vintages, but it appears the 1997s will have a quick evolution but
should age quite well. I cannot say they are as terrific as the 1990s, 1989s, or 1988s, but
1997 is unquestionably the finest overall vintage since that spectacular trio. Perhaps the
most interesting statistic about this vintage, particularly when compared with 1996, is that
production was 30% less in 1997 than 1996.

1996—In this vintage, Sauvignon was the favored varietal used in making the sweet wines
of Barsac/Sauternes. At least that is what many proprietors suggested, although it was not
necessarily borne out in my tastings. The 1996s reveal a slightly greener tint than the more
golden-colored 1997s. While they possess high levels of botrytis, it is less noticeable in the
1996s than in the 1997s. To a grower, the producers claim that the botrytis formed rapidly in
1996. In contrast, the botrytis was slow to infiltrate the grapes in 1997 and happened over a
far longer period of time.

As has been my policy over recent years, I prefer to wait until these sweet wines have had
at least a year in cask before making any judgments. Because these wines tend to be full of
sugar, in addition to having huge quantities of sulfur, they can be notoriously difficult to
judge at 5–7 months of age. Certainly 1997 and 1996 are the finest back-to-back vintages
since the 1988, 1989, and 1990, but my early instincts suggest neither year is as profound as
those three historical vintages. Moreover, shrewd consumers can often find wines from these
three vintages at prices below those demanded for the 1996s and 1997s. *C'est la vie!*

BARSAC AND SAUTERNES—AN OVERVIEW

Location: Southeast of Bordeaux, about 26 miles from the center of the city
Acres Under Vine: 4,940 acres; Sauternes—3,952 acres; Barsac—998 acres
Communes: Barsac, Bommes, Fargues, Preignac, and Sauternes
Average Annual Production: Sauternes—325,000 cases; Barsac—145,000 cases
Classified Growths: 26 classified growths and 1 premier cru superior—Château d'Yquem;
  11 first-growths; and 14 second-growths
Principal Grape Varieties: Semillon and Sauvignon Blanc, with tiny quantities of
  Muscadelle

BARSAC AND SAUTERNES—AN INSIDER'S VIEW

Overall Appellation Potential: Good to superb

The Most Potential for Aging: Climens, Coutet-Cuvée Madame, Gilette, Rieussec, Suduiraut, Yquem

The Most Elegant: Climens, Coutet, Doisy-Vedrines, Rieussec, La Tour-Blanche

The Most Concentrated: D'Arche-Pugneau, Coutet-Cuvée Madame, Lafaurie-Peyraguey, Raymond Lafon, Suduiraut, Yquem

The Best Value: D'Arche-Pugneau, Bastor-Lamontagne, Haut-Claverie, Les Justices, Rabaud-Promis, La Tour-Blanche

The Most Exotic: D'Arche-Pugneau, Raymond Lafon

The Most Difficult to Understand (when young): Until these wines are 4–6 years old, they rarely reveal much delineation or true personalities

The Most Underrated: Rabaud-Promis, La Tour-Blanche

The Most Difficult to Appreciate Young: All of them, at least until they are 4–6 years old

Up-and-Coming Estates: D'Arche-Pugneau, Rabaud-Promis, La Tour-Blanche

Greatest Recent Vintages: 1990, 1989, 1988, 1986, 1983, 1976, 1975, 1967, 1962, 1959.

D'ARCHE (SAUTERNES)

1997	D	(86–87)
1996	D	85

This is an estate where the younger vintage possesses more botrytis, complexity, potential ripeness, and longevity. The 1997 is an excellent, elegant, medium- to full-bodied Sauternes with noteworthy smoky, pineapple, and orange notes. Ripe and creamy textured, with moderate sweetness, this cleanly made wine should evolve nicely for 12–15+ years.

The lighter-style, well-delineated, fruit-driven 1996 is simple and straightforward, with medium sweetness. Anticipated maturity: now–2010.

BASTOR-LAMONTAGNE (SAUTERNES)

1997	C	(87–89)
1996	C	87

Excellent tropical fruit (primarily pineapples) intermixed with scents of lanolin are attractive in the medium- to full-bodied, fresh, concentrated 1997. Good underlying acidity nicely buttresses the wine's weighty feel in the mouth. An excellent lower-level Sauternes, it should drink well during its first 2 decades of life. Anticipated maturity: 2003–2020.

Compared with the 1997, the 1996 is made in a lighter style, with less fat as well as the telltale apricot/pineapple and lanolin characteristics of Semillon (which dominates the blend). Medium bodied and refreshing, this midweight Sauternes is easily appreciated. Anticipated maturity: 2000–2012.

BROUSTET (BARSAC)

1997	D	(78–82)
1996	D	84

The diluted, light-bodied, undistinguished 1997 Broustet offers fruit cocktail notes in the nose, light to moderate sweetness, medium body, and a clean finish. It should drink well young and keep for a decade. Anticipated maturity: now–2011.

The 1996 is another monolithic example, with more fruit, elegance, and potential complexity than the 1997. It is straightforward and foursquare, with some botrytis and honeyed orange and pineapple fruit. Drink it over the next 10–15 years.

CAILLOU (BARSAC)

1997	C	(86–87)
1996	C	85

The 1997 Caillou possesses low acidity, an unctuous texture, plenty of honeyed tropical fruit, medium to full body, and a cloying, fat, extremely sweet style. It needs to firm up and exhibit more focus. It will last for 10–15 years.

The 1996 is a foursquare, fruit-driven, clean, medium-bodied wine with a moderately sweet finish. Anticipated maturity: now–2012.

CLIMENS (BARSAC)

1997	E	(90–94)
1996	E	(88–90)

Consistently one of the most profound wines of Barsac/Sauternes, this wine, made from 100% Semillon, is one of the most ravishing examples of just how much elegance can be built into a powerful racehorse style of wine. The classic 1997 Climens boasts gorgeously pure pineapple, citrus, butter, mineral, and floral scents in its soaring aromatics. While it is not a blockbuster, it is medium to full bodied, with extraordinary precision, elegance, and purity. This slightly sweet Climens should drink well young but evolve nicely for 15–30 years. My early feeling is that it does not match the sumptuousness of the 1990 or the complexity of the 1988 and 1986. Nevertheless it is unquestionably a high-class Barsac. Anticipated maturity: 2003–2025.

The 1996 is a lighter wine, offering a lemony, citrusy, white fruit-scented nose with notes of minerals and spice. Medium bodied, with good acidity, lively fruit, some sweetness, and a youthful finish, this wine should be at its finest between 2003 and 2015.

Past Glories: 1990 (95), 1989 (90), 1988 (96), 1986 (96), 1983 (92), 1980 (90), 1971 (94), 1959 (90), 1949 (94), 1947 (94), 1937 (90), 1929 (92).

CLOS-HAUT-PEYRAGUEY (SAUTERNES)

1997	D	(85–87)
1996	D	85

While it was less concentrated than many of its peers, I enjoyed the 1997 Clos-Haut-Peyraguey, a honeyed orange/citrusy-style wine with elegance, medium body, and a fresh, lively personality. Exhibiting good botrytis and moderate sweetness, it should drink well for 10–12 years.

The 1996 is off-dry, with apricot and fruit cocktail scents and flavors, medium body, fine purity, unobtrusive oak, and a spicy, stylish finish. It will require consumption during its first 10–12 years of life, although I am sure it will live longer. Anticipated maturity: now–2016.

Past Glories: 1990 (90).

COUTET (BARSAC)

1997	E	(90–91)
1996	E	(87–88)

Another classic example of elegance allied to richness and intensity, Coutet's 1997 exhibits an expressive, floral, citrusy, honeyed nose, with notes of orange, Chinese black tea, pineapple, and spicy oak. It is all finesse, with honey, medium to full body, gorgeous delineation, and refreshing underlying acidity. It should drink well young. Anticipated maturity: 2002–2020.

A cooler, lighter-bodied wine with a greenish hue to its light gold color, the ripe, medium-bodied 1996 Barsac reveals *pain grillé* notes along with fresh, citrusy tropical fruit, medium body, some sweetness, and a clean, pure finish. It is a good all-purpose Barsac to drink as an aperitif, with food, or after dinner with dessert. Anticipated maturity: 2001–2018.

Past Glories—Cuvée Madame: 1990 (98), 1989 (95), 1988 (99), 1986 (96), 1981 (96), 1971 (98).

DOISY-DAËNE (BARSAC)

1997	D	(88–90)
1996	D	86
1997 l'Extravagance	EE	(96–99)
1996 l'Extravagance	EE	98

The impressive 1997 regular bottling offers a moderately intense nose of coconuts intermixed with smoke, cherries, and honeyed lemons and pineapples. There is outstanding purity, gorgeous fruit, seemingly low acidity, and an excellent fat, fleshy finish. This wine may merit an outstanding score if it develops more complexity.

The 1996 is a more stylish, mineral-laden, moderately sweet wine with midweight, honeyed complexity, and a fresh, lively finish. Drink it over the next 10–12 years.

The limited-production cuvée l'Extravagance (produced only in the greatest vintages, such as 1990, 1996, and 1997) is spectacular in both 1996 and 1997. The 1997 (100% Semillon) contains 20% residual sugar and a well-hidden 14.5% alcohol. The wine is mammoth in the mouth, with layers of unctuously textured, honeyed tropical fruits, beautifully integrated toasty new oak, plenty of botrytis, and considerable sweetness. It is a triumph in winemaking and will undoubtedly last 50–100 years. Anticipated maturity: 2007–2050+.

The 1996 l'Extravagance is pure Sauvignon Blanc. It boasts a deep gold color, in addition to an unctuous texture, fabulous freshness, and notes of grapefruit and subtle oak (the 200% new oak treatment is utilized for the whopping 100–125 cases produced). A huge wine, with more acidity and less mass and volume than the 1997, this tour de force in winemaking should drink well for 50+ years. Readers should note that these two offerings are available only in 1-bottle wood cases! Anticipated maturity: 2007–2050+.

Past Glories—regular cuvée: 1990 (91), 1983 (90).

Past Glories—l'Extravagance: 1990 (95).

FILHOT (SAUTERNES)

1996	D	87

An elegant, medium-bodied wine with scents of quince, orange marmalade, and pineapple presented in a moderately endowed aromatic profile, this Sauternes displays moderate sweetness, excellent ripeness and purity, and a tasty, harmonious personality. Drink it over the next 10–15 years.

Past Glories: 1990 (90).

GUIRAUD (SAUTERNES)

1997	E	(88–90)
1996	E	91

The medium gold-colored 1997 Guiraud exhibits a fat, foursquare personality with copious quantities of orange marmalade, melted butter, and lychee nut notes. Buttered white corn flavors make an appearance in this corpulent, full-bodied, unctuously textured wine. It does not possess the complexity, delineation, and freshness of the 1996, but it is a mouth-filling, well-endowed, hefty style of Sauternes. Anticipated maturity: 2002–2025.

One of the stars of the vintage for Sauternes, the 1996 Guiraud offers a sumptuous nose of tangerine fruit intermixed with caramel and buttered corn. The wine displays a deep golden color and striking flavors of Chinese black tea, marmalade, honey, and citrus. The powerful yet elegant flavors remain in the mouth for a significant period of time. Keep in mind that the quality of Sauvignon Blanc was excellent in 1996, and while this wine is traditionally a blend of 65% Semillon and 35% Sauvignon, Xavier Plantey, the estate's manager, told me that there is nearly 45% Sauvignon Blanc in the final blend of the 1996. Anticipated maturity: 2000–2025.

Past Glories: 1990 (91), 1986 (92).

LAFAURIE-PEYRAGUEY (SAUTERNES)

1997	E	(90–92)
1996	E	90

This 1997 displays gorgeous aromas of coconut, honeyed oranges, tangerines, pineapples, mangoes, and other tropical fruits. The wine is medium to full bodied and superrich, but not a blockbuster in the mold of such years as 1990 and 1988. It possesses low acidity (in flavor, but not in terms of analyses) and a long, 40-second finish. This superb 1997 exhibits considerable botrytis as well as a thick, unctuously textured style. Anticipated maturity: 2002–2025.

Also outstanding, the 1996 offers aromas of Grand Marnier orange liqueur intertwined with *pain grillé,* coconut, and other exotic fruits. It is dense and medium to full bodied, with layers of fruit, more structure than the 1997, and a pure, viscous finish. Anticipated maturity: 2004–2025.

Past Glories: 1990 (92), 1988 (95), 1986 (92).

LAMOTHE (SAUTERNES)

1997	D	(?)
1996	D	86

Two samples of the 1997 revealed a moldy/mushroomy note in its unexpressive aromatics. I attempted to extrapolate what this wine might taste like without the mold, and it does appear to possess medium body, underlying minerality, and honeyed fruit, but it is straightforward and one-dimensional. Anticipated maturity: now–2012.

A lean, light-style Sauternes with tropical fruit notes in its medium-bodied personality, the 1996 is a pleasant, straightforward, good wine for picnics and the like. Drink it over the next 10–12 years.

LAMOTHE-GUIGNARD (SAUTERNES)

1997	D	(84–86?)
1996	D	87

The 1997 reveals considerable botrytis and a monolithic, fat, somewhat disjointed personality. It does offer currant, coconut, and honeyed fruit and medium to full body, but no focal point or potential complexity. It needs more time to reveal its true identity.

Less botrytis and a Sauvignon Blanc–dominated personality characterize the melony, herb-tinged, honeyed nose of the medium-weight 1996. Relying on elegance, purity, and finesse as opposed to power and blockbuster strength, this medium-bodied Sauternes should be drinkable young yet keep for 15 years.

Past Glories: 1990 (91), 1989 (91).

DE MALLE (SAUTERNES)

1997	D	(88–90)
1996	D	87

An exotic, flamboyant bouquet of orange marmalade, honeyed citrus, caramel, coconut, and *pain grillé* soars from the glass of this well-bodied, potentially outstanding 1997. In the mouth, it reveals an unctuous texture with tangy underlying acidity, medium to full body, and gobs of fruit. Anticipated maturity: 2004–2020.

The 1996 tastes high in acidity, with the Sauvignon Blanc more dominant (normally three-quarters of this wine is Semillon). It is medium bodied, slightly off-dry as opposed to the sweeter, more viscous 1997, with evidence of pineapple, medium body, and a clean, moderately long finish. Anticipated maturity: 2002–2016.
Past Glories: 1990 (90), 1988 (91).

MYRAT (SAUTERNES)

1997	D	(82–84)
1996	D	?

The 1997 Myrat (a blend of 88% Semillon, 8% Sauvignon Blanc, and 4% Muscadelle) is a citrusy, bright, lighter-bodied style with less sweetness than many 1997s, as well as significantly less evidence of botrytis. This is an aperitif style of Sauternes to be quaffed casually without introspection. Drink it over the next decade.

I was turned off by the bizarre diesel fuel aromas of the 1996. I like the scent of petroleum in some wines, particularly Alsatian Riesling, but this wine carries that component too far. I will wait until I see another bottle to render an evaluation.

NAIRAC (BARSAC)

1997	D	(88–90)

With 90% Semillon in the blend, in a year that favored this varietal, Nairac's 1997 is an impressively endowed, full-bodied, intensely sweet wine with layers of flavor, considerable glycerin, a chewy, cherry liqueur-like, honeyed, smoky new oak-scented bouquet, and a long, intense, thick finish. It exhibits plenty of botrytis, seemingly low acidity, and the potential for an outstanding rating. Anticipated maturity: 2005–2020.

RAYNE-VIGNEAU (SAUTERNES)

1997	E	(86–88)
1996	E	87

Both of these wines are uninspiring, mainstream, blatantly commercial examples of Sauternes. The 1997 exhibits a syrupy pineapple-scented nose, medium body, moderate sweetness, and a fruit-driven personality with little complexity. Anticipated maturity: 2003–2017.

More complex, the 1996 reveals a honeyed melon-and-pineapple-scented nose, medium body, and fine purity and ripeness. Drink it over the next 10–15 years.
Past Glories: 1988 (91), 1986 (90).

RIEUSSEC (SAUTERNES)

1997	EE	(90–92)
1996	EE	89

This wine contains an extremely high percentage of Semillon (usually about 90%), which was to its benefit in 1997. The 1997 is light medium gold colored, with a blockbuster nose of Grand Marnier liqueur intertwined with flower blossoms, smoky new oak, and coconut. Well-integrated wood has resulted in a seamless, full-bodied, unctuously textured wine with considerable sweetness. This stunningly proportioned, beautifully pure wine may be one of the few 1997s that can compete with the top wines from 1990, 1989, and 1988. Anticipated maturity: 2002–2025.

The 1996 Rieussec is neither as fat nor as flamboyant as its younger sibling. Revealing less botrytis, it offers an orange, caramel, and honeyed nose with intriguing quince/kumquat fruit flavors, a complex personality, and a lower level of glycerin in the mouth. This medium-to full-bodied, long wine will be at its peak between 2000 and 2020.

Past Glories: 1990 (90), 1989 (92), 1988 (93+), 1986 (91), 1983 (92), 1976 (90), 1975 (90).

ROMER DU HAYOT (BARSAC)

1997	D	(86–87+)
1996	D	89

I would not be surprised to see this medium- to full-bodied 1997 turn out to be a better wine than my note suggests. It possesses attractive pear liqueur, pineapple, and apricot fruit in its moderate aromatics, plenty of botrytis, and a sweet, long, unctuously textured, thick finish. However, the wine comes across as disjointed and in need of delineation. It should keep and evolve for 15 or more years.

The 1996 is a classic, pure wine with well-integrated toasty oak, smoky, honeyed pineapple, mineral and fruit cocktail-like notes, a firm underpinning of acidity, round, smoky richness, medium to full body, and outstanding purity. Anticipated maturity: now–2015.

SIGALAS RABAUD (SAUTERNES)

1997	E	(87–89)
1996	E	87

The 1997 is a honeyed, luscious, forward style of Sauternes, with low acidity and copious quantities of orange, pineapple, and mangolike fruit. In fact, the fruit almost hides the bouquet's other nuances. Full bodied and rich, with a viscous texture, this lusty, unrestrained wine will be appreciated by tasters looking for immediate gratification. Anticipated maturity: now–2015.

The 1996 Sigalas Rabaud is a cooler climate–style wine with more quince, kiwi, and honeyed pineapplelike fruit. It is medium bodied, with less viscosity than the 1997, as well as zesty underlying acidity and an austere yet clean, crisp, mineral-like finish. Drink it over the next 10–15 years.

Past Glories: 1990 (91), 1986 (90).

SUAU (BARSAC)

1997	C	(86–87)
1996	C	85

My first impression of the 1997 Suau's aromas was of apricots that had been macerating in cognac. There is not much finesse in the nose, but in the mouth, this medium- to full-bodied, somewhat clumsy wine is rustic, pure, rich, and substantial with plenty of botrytis. Perhaps it just needs more time to find its form.

In contrast, the 1996 is a lighter-style, well-made Barsac with citrusy, white corn, apple, and white peach-like fruit. It is a moderately sweet, lightweight wine to enjoy over the next decade.

SUDUIRAUT (SAUTERNES)

1997	**EE**	**(89–90)**
1996	**EE**	**86**

The 1997 Suduiraut reveals surprisingly crisp acidity for its weight, as well as excellent richness. An intense, weighty, moderately sweet feel in the mouth, copious quantities of buttery, honeyed fruit, impressive power, and a corpulent style characterize this well-delineated wine. It should develop more complexity and may merit an outstanding score after bottling. Anticipated maturity: 2004–2022.

The 1996 is a greener, leaner, more tart style of Suduiraut with spicy oak dominating its otherwise indifferent aromatics. Anticipated maturity: 2001–2014.

Past Glories—regular cuvée: 1976 (92), 1959 (93), 1947 (93), 1945 (90).

Past Glories—Cuvée Madame: 1989 (96), 1982 (90).

LA TOUR BLANCHE (SAUTERNES)

1997	**E**	**(90–92)**
1996	**E**	**89**

The gorgeously perfumed and layered 1997 La Tour Blanche displays a medium golden color as well as a honeyed, kinky nose of buttered roasted fruit, quince, oranges, and minerals. Dense and full bodied, with terrific fruit extraction, this unctuously textured, sweet, full-bodied wine is one of the stars of the vintage. Anticipated maturity: 2003–2025.

The lighter-style 1996 possesses a light golden color, moderate sweetness, and a flinty, citrusy, buttery nose with evidence of coconut, pears, oranges, and pineapples. In the mouth, it is medium bodied and stylish with considerable elegance. Anticipated maturity: now–2015.

Past Glories: 1990 (92), 1989 (90), 1988 (92).

CHÂTEAU D'YQUEM (SAUTERNES)

1991	**EEE**	**91**
1990	**EEE**	**99**

Yquem's 1991 is a beautifully made, medium gold-colored wine with a gorgeous nose of crème brûlée, roasted coffee, and sweet, honeyed pineapple and other assorted fruits. Full bodied, unctuously textured, and rich, but not yet revealing the complexity or enormous weight of such vintages as 1990, 1989, and 1988, this classic, outstanding Yquem will always have to live in the shadow of its three predecessors. Anticipated maturity: 2005–2040.

An extraordinary effort in this powerful, blockbuster vintage, Yquem's 1990 is the richest of the fabulous trilogy of superb sweet wine vintages in Bordeaux—1988, 1989, 1990. This wine also possesses more elegance and finesse than many 1990s, at least at this early stage of their development. The wine's medium gold color is accompanied by an exceptionally sweet nose of honeyed tropical fruits, peaches, coconut, and apricots. High-quality, subtle toasty oak is well integrated. The wine is massive on the palate, with layers of intensely ripe botrytis tinged, exceptionally sweet fruit. Surprisingly well-integrated acidity and a seamless, full-bodied power and richness have created a wine of remarkable harmony and purity. It is tempting to compare this wine with such Yquem behemoths as the 1989 and 1983. Certainly it is one of the richest Yquems I have ever tasted, with 50–100 years of potential longevity. It may mature at a quicker pace than the 1989, 1988, or 1986, but all of these wines will easily pass their half-century birthdays in splendid condition. An awesome Yquem! Anticipated maturity: 2003–2050+.

Past Glories: 1989 (97+), 1988 (99), 1986 (98), 1983 (96), 1982 (92), 1981 (90), 1980 (93),

1976 (96), 1975 (99), 1971 (91), 1970 (90), 1967 (96), 1962 (90), 1959 (95), 1950 (94), 1945 (91), 1937 (97), 1929 (97), 1928 (97), 1921 (100), 1847 (100), 1811 (100).

BURGUNDY AND BEAUJOLAIS

The Complex Côte d'Or

Even the most enthusiastic burgundy connoisseurs admit that the wines of Burgundy are expensive, variable in quality, and often quick to fall apart, as well as difficult and troublesome to find. Why, then, are they so cherished?

While it is tempting for those who have neither the financial resources nor the enthusiasm for these wines to conclude that burgundies are purchased only by wealthy masochists, the point is that Burgundy produces the world's most majestic, glorious, and hedonistic Pinot Noir and Chardonnay. Burgundy has somehow defied definition, systemization, or even standardization. No matter how much research and money is spent trying to taste and understand the complexity of the wines of Burgundy and Burgundy's myriad vineyards, to a large extent they remain a mystery. Perhaps this is best shown in the analogy between several famous Bordeaux vineyards and a handful of renowned Burgundy vineyards. Take the famous St.-Julien vineyard of Ducru-Beaucaillou in the heart of the Médoc. It is 124 acres in size. Compare it with its famous neighbor about 10 miles to the south, Château Palmer in Margaux, with a vineyard of 111 acres in size. Any consumer who buys a bottle of a specific vintage of Ducru-Beaucaillou or Palmer will be getting exactly the same wine. Of course it may have been handled differently or subjected to abuse in transportation or storage, but the wine that left the property was made by one winemaking team, from one blend, and the taste, texture, and aromatic profile of a specific vintage should not be any different whether drunk in Paris, Vienna, Tokyo, New York, or Los Angeles. Compare that situation with the famous grand cru from Burgundy's Côte de Nuits, Clos de Vougeot. Clos de Vougeot has 124 acres, making it approximately the same size as Ducru-Beaucaillou. Yet while there is only one proprietor of the latter vineyard, Clos de Vougeot is divided among more than eighty different proprietors. Many of these growers sell their production to *négociants,* but in any given vintage there are at least three dozen or more Clos de Vougeots in the marketplace. All of them are entitled to grand cru status, they vary in price from $70 to $500+ a bottle, but fewer than a half dozen are likely to be compelling wines. The remainder range in quality from very good to dismal and insipid. Clos de Vougeot is the most cited as a microcosm of Burgundy—infinitely confusing, distressingly frustrating. Yet majestic wines do indeed come out of Clos de Vougeot from a few top producers.

Also consider the most renowned Burgundy vineyard—Chambertin. This 32-acre vineyard is 3 acres larger than Château Pétrus, maker of one of Bordeaux's most expensive red wines. Pétrus has only one producer, and there is only one wine from a given vintage, all of which has been blended prior to bottling and all of it equal in quality. But among Chambertin's 32 acres, there are 23 different proprietors, with only a handful of them committed to

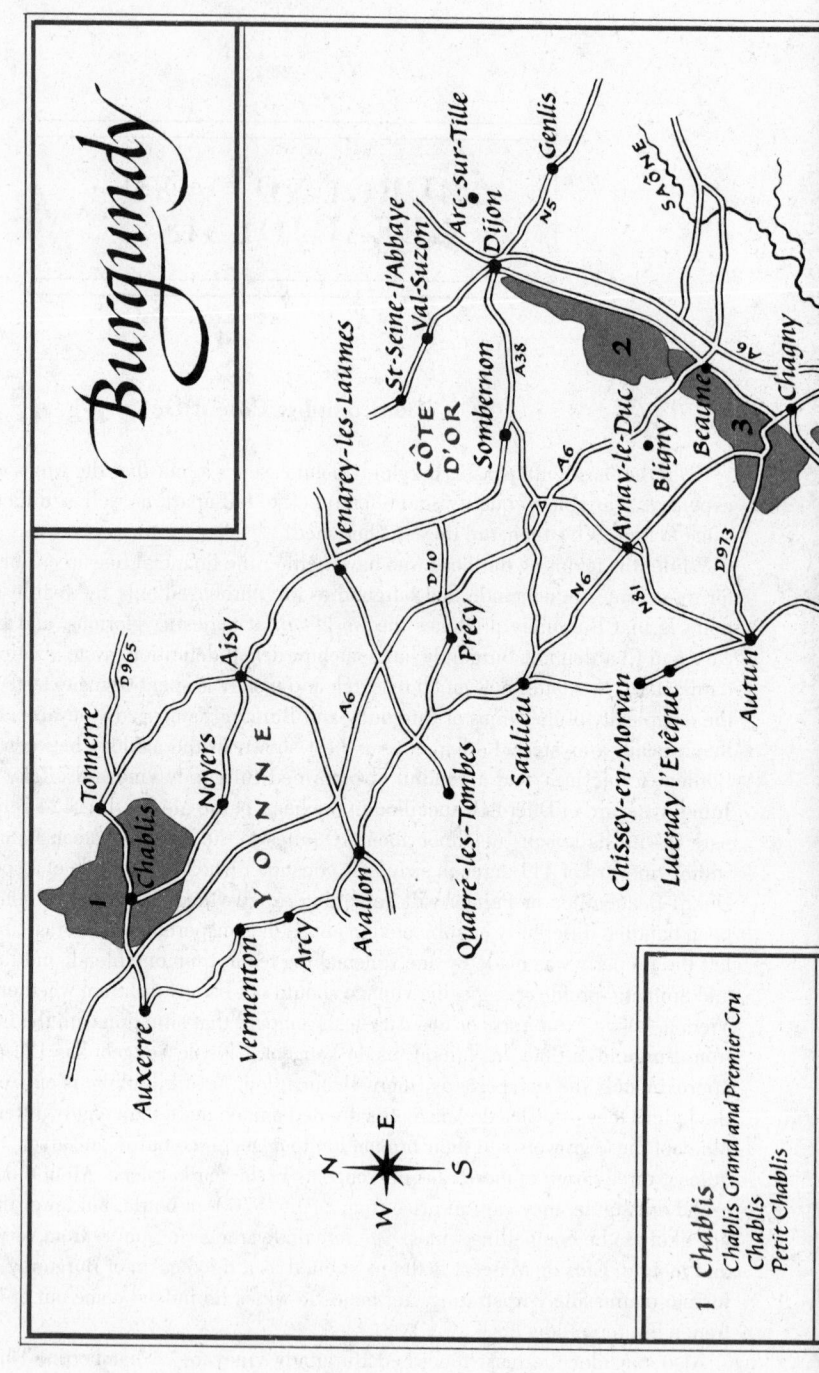

Burgundy

1 **Chablis**
   Chablis Grand and Premier Cru
   Chablis
   Petit Chablis

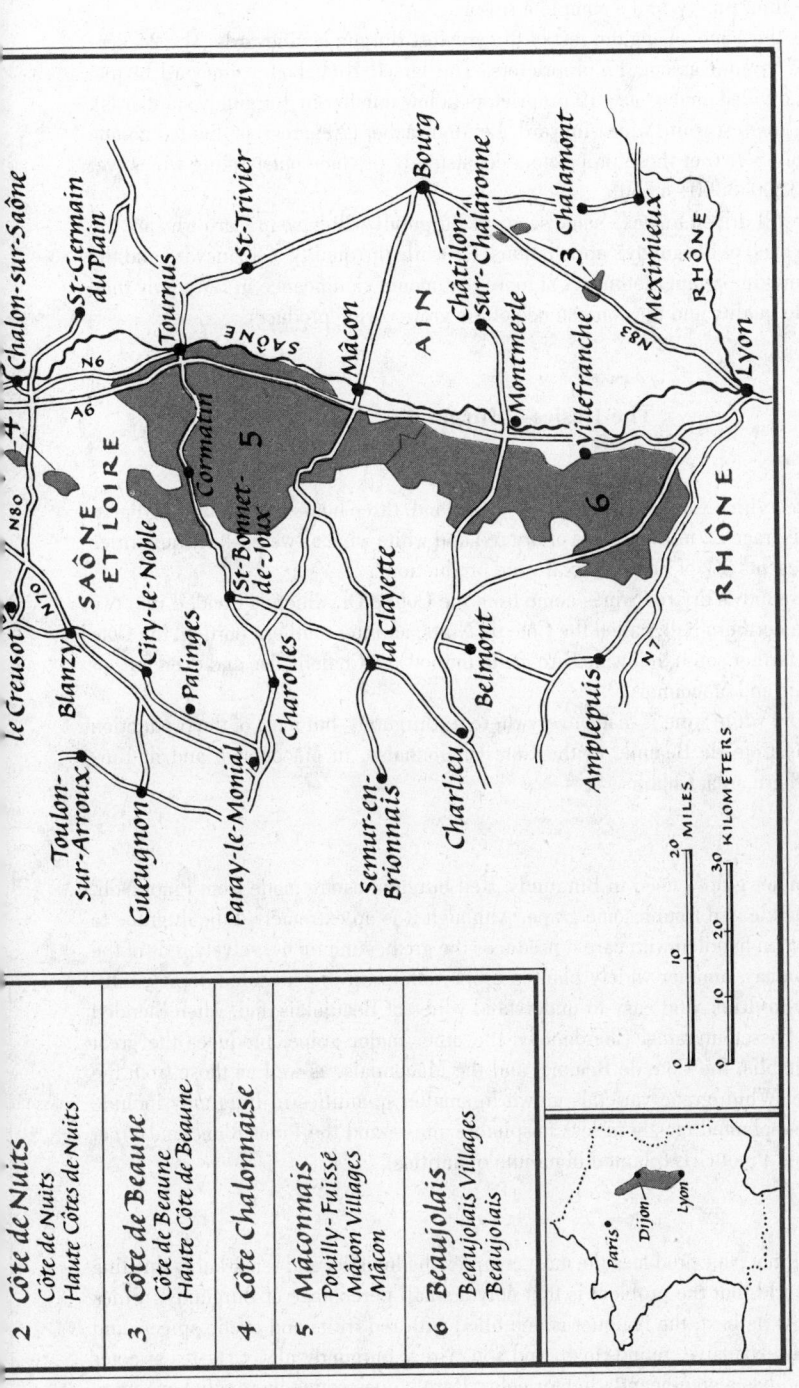

2 Côte de Nuits
Côte de Nuits
Haute Côtes de Nuits

3 Côte de Beaune
Côte de Beaune
Haute Côte de Beaune

4 Côte Chalonnaise

5 Mâconnais
Pouilly-Fuissé
Mâcon Villages
Mâcon

6 Beaujolais
Beaujolais Villages
Beaujolais

le Creusot
Toulon-
sur-Arroux
Gueugnon
Paray-le-Monial
Blanzy
Ciry-le-Noble
Palinges
Charolles
Semur-en-
Brionnais
St-Bonnet-
de-Joux
Cormatin
La Clayette
Belmont
Charlieu
Amplepuis

SAÔNE ET LOIRE

N70
N80
A6
N6
Chalon-sur-Saône
St-Germain
du Plain
St-Trivier
Tournus
Mâcon
SAÔNE

AIN
Bourg
Châtillon-
sur-Chalaronne
Montmerle
Villefranche
Chalamont
Meximieux
RHÔNE
Lyon
N83
N7

RHÔNE

MILES
KILOMETERS

Paris
Dijon
Lyon

producing extraordinary wine. Most Chambertins sell for well in excess of $150 a bottle. Many of them are thin, watery, and a complete rip-off.

The situation is the same among the rest of the greatest Burgundy vineyards. The 24-acre Musigny vineyard is split among 17 proprietors. The famed Richebourg vineyard of just under 20 acres is divided among *only* 12 proprietors (a low number by Burgundy standards). Even Burgundy's greatest white wine vineyard, Le Montrachet (20 acres), is divided among 15 producers. Only 5 or 6 of these proprietors consistently produce outstanding wines, yet all of them fetch $200–$300+ a bottle.

Any consumer still driven to make some sense of Burgundy will have to learn who are the best producers in each of Burgundy's appellations, for while the quality of a vineyard and the vintage are certainly important, nothing is of more paramount significance in Burgundy than the commitment to quality and the competence of the grower/wine producer.

The Basics—Burgundy

TYPES OF WINE

This modestly sized viticultural area in France's heartland, three hours by car south of Paris, produces on the average 22 million cases of dry red and white wine as well as tiny quantities of rosé. This represents 3% of France's total wine production.

Red Wine   Burgundy's dry red wines come from the Côte d'Or, which is divided into two distinct areas: the northern half, called the Côte de Nuits, and the southern portion, the Côte de Beaune. A bit farther south, red wines are made in the Côte Chalonnaise and even farther south in Beaujolais and Mâconnais.

White Wine   Dry white wine is made everywhere in Burgundy, but most of the production is centered in the Côte de Beaune, in the Côte Chalonnaise, in Mâconnais, and in Burgundy's most northern area, Chablis.

GRAPE VARIETIES

There are three major grapes used in Burgundy. Red burgundies are made from Pinot Noir, the world's most fickle and troublesome grape. Although it is an extremely difficult grape to make into wine, when handled with care it produces the great, sumptuous, velvety reds of the Côte d'Or. The Gamay, another widely planted grape, offers up the succulent, spicy, effusively fruity, easy-to-drink, and easy-to-understand wines of Beaujolais and, when blended with Pinot Noir, Passetoutgrains. Chardonnay, the other major grape, produces the great white wines of Chablis, the Côte de Beaune, and the Mâconnais, as well as those from the Côte Chalonnaise. White grape varietals grown in smaller quantities in Burgundy include the Aligoté grape—planted mostly in less hospitable sites—and the Pinot Blanc and Pinot Beurrot, also called Pinot Gris (planted in minute quantities).

FLAVORS

When it is great, Pinot Noir produces the most complex, hedonistic, and remarkably thrilling red wine in the world, but the problem is that only a small percentage of Burgundy's wines attain this level. At its best, the bouquet is one filled with red fruits and exotic spices, and the taste is broad, expansive, round, lush, and soft. Great burgundy always tastes sweeter than Bordeaux and has a significantly lighter color. Rarely does young burgundy have more than a medium cherry color. Gamay is drunk not for its complexity, but rather for its heady, direct, ripe, soft, fleshy, exuberant fruitiness and easygoing texture. Chardonnay can range from stony and mineral-scented with high acidity in Chablis, to buttery, smoky, creamy, decadently rich, and tasting of sautéed almonds and hazelnuts in a great Côte de Beaune white burgundy, to beautifully rich, chalk-infused, and lemony gems of the top Mâconnais producers.

AGING POTENTIAL

Seemingly nowhere in the wine world is ageworthiness as much an issue as it is in Burgundy. Each individual vintage, producer, and vineyard of origin have an enormous effect on a wine's capacity for aging. Furthermore, adequate transportation and storage conditions (important for all wines) are vital if one wishes to age a red or white burgundy.

RED WINES

Côte de Nuits: 2–15+ years
Côte de Beaune: 2–15 years
Beaujolais: 1–5+ years

WHITE WINES

Chablis: 1–10+ years
Côte de Beaune: 4–10+ years
Mâconnais: 1–8+ years

OVERALL QUALITY LEVEL

No matter which appellation one looks at in Burgundy, the range in quality from watery, poorly made, incompetent wines to majestic wines of great flavor and dimension is enormous. There are more great wines being crafted by more topflight producers in Burgundy than ever before; however, this region continues to be filled with precarious pitfalls for the uninformed consumer. The number of poor and mediocre wines, while significantly less than in years past, still greatly outnumbers the amount of fine wines made.

THE MOST IMPORTANT INFORMATION TO LEARN

Knowing the names of the finest domaines and *négociants* is vital (consult the guide to Burgundy's best producers on pages 285 and 309), and to a lesser degree but still of paramount importance is having a grasp of the quality of the vintages (consult the vintage guide on pages 279–84). The greatest mistake a consumer can make when buying a Burgundy is to select it based on the appellation. Uninformed consumers are playing right into the hands of the plonk pushers if they seek a *Grand Cru* (Chambertin, Clos de Vougeot, Bâtard-Montrachet, and so on) or a *Premier Cru* without paying attention to the name of the producer.

BURGUNDY'S RENAISSANCE

The nineties have witnessed a renaissance in Burgundy. The wines emanating from this region are, on the whole, far better than they were in the past. Today there are more high-quality producers crafting first-rate wines than ever before. Why? Consider the following:

1. *Négociant*-suppliers to estates: Even though this is an extremely old winemaking region, estate-bottled wines are a relatively new phenomenon. In fact, some of the first Burgundians to have begun this practice are still working today (Gevrey-Chambertin's Charles Rousseau and Volnay's Marquis d'Angerville, for example). In the past, Burgundian vignerons would harvest their grapes, ferment them, and then sell the wine to *négociants*, who would take them through their *élevage* and bottle them. Over the past 50+ years, however, hundreds of vignerons—both good and bad—have switched from being *négociant*-suppliers to bottling their own wines. While in some cases this trend has been a real positive for consumers (the great vignerons' wines were no longer being mixed with lesser ones to fashion *négociant* cuvées), it has also led to large quantities of expensive yet poor-quality

wines being made by producers with little to no training or knowledge about *élevage* and bottling techniques.

Furthermore, the amount of money a *négociant* pays for a wine is determined by its appellation, not its quality. A bad Chambertin sells for the same price as a great one. This system benefits growers whose vineyard practices produce high yields, not those who are quality conscious. This lesson was one that took many years to be unlearned by producers who switched from being *négociant*-suppliers to being estate bottlers.

2. Appellation buying: For years uninformed or ill-informed consumers based their buying decisions on the appellation instead of the quality of the wine. This practice, perpetuated by the Burgundian obsession of ascribing all positive wine traits to *terroir*, provided ready markets for mediocre offerings from heralded vineyards or villages.

3. Insularity: In the past, Burgundy was extremely parochial. Growers drank wines only they themselves had made, so they had nothing to compare their work against. Some of the more adventurous might have tasted those wines produced in the same village. A famous producer from Chablis once told me that he had never tasted a wine that was not from Burgundy. Another well-known vigneron, this one from Gevrey-Chambertin, admitted that Chambolle-Musigny (only a few miles away) was like a foreign country to him; he knew none of the growers there and had never tasted their wines.

Vineyard and cellar work was learned from one's father, so deficiencies in winemaking were carried over from generation to generation under the guise of tradition. The few new techniques that were adopted over the years generally were those that tended to lower the quality of the wines (excessive fertilization, fining and filtration, and so forth) instead of improving them. Because of this insularity, Burgundy has not experienced the revolutionizing and modernizing effects of high-quality-oriented consultants who have encouraged and served as a catalyst for better and better wines (Bordeaux's Professor Emile Peynaud and Michel Rolland, and in California Tony Soter and Helen Turley, to name but a few). Starting in the mid- to late seventies, Guy Accad attempted to fulfill that role. His techniques (which included tight spacing of the vines, harvesting very ripe fruit, extended prefermentation macerations with extremely high doses of sulfur), although controversial, were adopted by a number of domaines. Yet the results were mixed. Accad was buried by a barrage of criticism that his wines were not "typical" or "traditional," and today Accad has few clients and his influence is insignificant—at least when it comes to winemaking.

Renaissance: A younger generation, men and women in their twenties, thirties, and early forties, have taken over the estates of their parents and have brought much needed changes to Burgundy. These vignerons, led by the likes of Christophe Roumier, Dominique Lafon, Jean-François Coche, and others, are well traveled, have tasted the finest wines produced throughout the world, exchange winemaking ideas, and competitively strive to produce the best wines they can. Throughout Burgundy new viticultural and vinification techniques are being tested, fining and filtering is being eschewed, and the fertilizers once used to produce huge yields are being abandoned. This generation, educated in winemaking schools and trained in the finest wineries the world over, is taking Burgundy to a level of quality never before achieved.

American consumers should be especially proud of the activist role small specialty burgundy importers in this country have played in Burgundy's renaissance. Special recognition should be given to David Hinkle (North Berkeley Wine Imports), Robert Kacher Selections, Kobrand, Inc., Patrick Lesec (a Paris broker), Louis/Dressner, Kermit Lynch Wine Merchant, Martine's Wines (Martine Saunier), Select Vineyards (Neal Rosenthal), Peter Vezan Selections (a Paris broker), Vineyard Brands (Robert Haas), and Weygandt-Metzler (Peter Weygandt). All of these importers have aggressively persuaded their growers to halt unnecessary fining and filtration if the wines are otherwise stable and clear. For many wines, Americans are getting far better burgundy cuvées than any other consumers in the world because some growers bottle only unfined and unfiltered wines for sale in America. These

American specialists have seen what damage can be done to wines by excessive crop yields, overmanipulation, and aggressive fining and filtration.

RECENT VINTAGES

1997—The 1997 white burgundies are, in general, fat, ripe wines, yet sometimes perplexingly oxidative and alcoholic. In addition, excessive oak and sulfur aromas and flavors were not uncommon, and many wines had relatively abrupt finishes. Collectors searching for long-lived wines with admirable complexity and concentration are well advised to search the market for the remaining 1996s. However, readers who wish to purchase wines for near-term consumption will be quite pleased with what the 1997 vintage offers.

There is no doubt that 1997 is a very good vintage for whites from the Côte d'Or. While the finest 1996s were crafted from vineyards generally known for their power (situated lower on the slopes, such as Bâtard-Montrachet), the best 1997s are from sites higher on the slopes (Corton-Charlemagne, Chevalier-Montrachet, and so forth). The 1997 vintage does not compete with such outstanding years as 1996 or 1989 but is certainly better than 1994, 1993, and 1991. To paraphrase Jean-Marie Guffens of Maison Verget, if 1996 could be compared to a brilliant, intellectual Ingmar Bergman film, then 1997 could be compared to a Hollywood blockbuster such as *Titanic*—easy to understand and enormously pleasing. While that vintage's overall quality of wines is high, it cannot approach the long-lived classics of 1996 and 1995.

The Mâconnais, however, enjoyed an outstanding vintage and is responsible for many of 1997's most successful wines. Estates such as Daniel Barraud, Bongran, Guffens-Heynen, and Robert-Denogent crafted stellar Pouilly-Fuissés and Mâcons. In Chablis no one attained the level of quality achieved in 1995 or 1996, but, like the Côte d'Or, this region had a very good 1997. As the 1997 vintage approached harvesttime, reports out of Burgundy glowed with optimism. Grapes were healthy, as the late summer had been hot and dry, and vignerons were ecstatic. The air was filled with statements like "The reds will be like the 1947s, and the whites like the 1989s, but better!"

Excessive heat in September brought an end to the growers' general ebullience. When the Côte de Beaune's *ban de vendange* (the first day the harvest can legally begin) was set for September 13, many vignerons came to the realization that their grape sugars were high yet full physiological ripeness had not been attained. More than one grower suggested that the stressed vines had stopped the maturation process because of the high temperatures and lack of rain. The vast majority of vignerons I spoke with said they waited at least a week after the *ban de vendange* to begin harvesting. This strategy worked wonders in the cooler 1996 vintage because the north wind and sunny days accelerated maturity without causing a loss of natural acidity in the grapes. In 1997, however, the days and evenings were warm, occasionally hot. Vignerons watched as phenolic ripeness inched its way forward and acidity levels dropped (many growers picked their reds *before* their whites).

At harvest, the high temperatures were troublesome. Some producers acknowledged that they were unable to prevent fermentations from starting earlier than desired. Flash alcoholic fermentations, immediately followed by rapid malolactic fermentations, believed by many growers to decrease complexity, were reported throughout the Côte d'Or.

Across the board, acidity levels were lower than average, but not dangerously so. Since malic acid made up only a small portion of the overall acidity level (the opposite was true in the 1996 vintage), malolactic fermentations were quick, in total contrast with 1996, where some malolactic fermentations took over a year to complete.

The 1997 vintage for reds is extremely heterogeneous. Some producers, who were able to harness the year's qualities while avoiding its pitfalls, crafted spectacular wines. However, the majority of 1997 red burgundies are beautifully ripe, dense, and fruit-driven wines that lack the complexity, depth, structure, and concentration for greatness. Were it not for their frightfully high prices, these would have been ideal wines for restaurants and consumers searching out delicious near-term drinking offerings.

Stylistically reminiscent of the 1989s, the 1997 red burgundies generally exhibit loads of ripe fruit characteristics in an easygoing, low-acid, and simple manner. Like most of the 1989s, the 1997s will be ready to drink upon release and should, for the most part, be drunk within the next 7 years. However, a few 1997s, notably wines produced by Domaine Leroy, Bertrand Ambroise, the Marquis d'Angerville, and the domaine wines from Maison Louis Jadot (to name but a few), should age remarkably well, as they appear to have extraordinary structure.

1996—1996 is an outstanding vintage for white burgundies. The best examples offer a combination of magnificent structure, ripeness, and aging potential. It is difficult to compare this vintage with previous ones, as no Burgundian I spoke with had ever witnessed one with similar weather. The vintage's finest wines have high acidity, total purity of flavors (rot or mildew were not a problem), excellent fruit ripeness (without any overripe or stewed-fruit problems), and impressive extract.

In the Côte d'Or, an exceedingly dry spring led to a late bud break for the vines' leaves in April. Rain in May (from then on the vintage qualifies as a drought year) provided the vines with necessary nourishment prior to June's dry, sunny warmth. It was during this ideal period that the flowering occurred rapidly (some vignerons say it lasted just four days) and evenly. Unlike the 1995 vintage, 1996 would experience little *coulure* (damaged flowering due to inclement weather) or *millerandage* (stunted fruit embryos) to concentrate the fruit. Numerous healthy grape bunches formed on each vine. Cool, sunny days (as in the Loire, Burgundians noted the *luminosite*, or brightness, of the vintage) and cold nights combined with minimal precipitation, and a persistent dry wind from the north lasted throughout the summer and into the first days of November. This combination of light (photosynthesis) and cool evening temperatures promoted the ripening of the grapes without a significant loss of acidity (heat is blamed for reducing acid in grapes), while the gusty, unusually persistent north winds dehydrated (concentrated) the grapes. Chablis endured a small harvest, caused largely by hail prior to flowering in May, a violent storm on June 8, and the dehydrating effects of the gusty dry northeasterly wind.

Qualitatively, the top whites from 1996 are on par with 1989, but stylistically they are completely different. These are fresher and livelier wines that can be cellared longer than the 1989s; however, they do not exhibit the thick textures and extraordinary ripeness of the latter vintage. This is not a vintage for those who love fat, unctuous, tropical, hedonistic, and luscious white burgundies. In contrast with a vintage such as 1989, 1996's strength is its purity, balance, crystalline acidity, and ageworthiness. Whereas the 1995s exhibited red berry fruit and oily textures from more massive concentration and extract than the 1996s, the latter vintage exhibits enormous minerality and crisp, well-delineated, elegant, and citrusy personalities. Some examples, most probably owing to the vintage's acidity and lack of rain, exhibit ground rock dust flavors—appearing somewhat like a caricature of minerality.

The 1996 is an outstanding vintage for red burgundies, even better than 1995, particularly in the Côte de Beaune. As with Chardonnay, the Pinot Noir vines had a rapid and even flowering that led to numerous grape bunches on each vine. Many vignerons were concerned that the grapes would not fully ripen because each vine was so heavily loaded. The potentially large crop was even more worrisome because the weather was not particularly hot or sunny during the summer months. By late August an extremely bright sun emerged, promoting ripeness through photosynthesis, and a persistent cool and dry wind blew from the north, maintaining acidity levels and preventing the onset of any rot or mildew. The resulting harvest was copious, ripe, and healthy.

Stylistically, this vintage can best be characterized as "juicy." The wines appear to burst in the taster's mouth, as would a juicy, ripe berry. These are lively, fresh, pleasure-giving wines that are fruit-driven and, to their credit, remarkably pure. In addition to the cherry, raspberry, and blackberry flavors that are common in top Burgundy vintages, 1996 offered copious amounts of blueberries and juicy black currants. The vintage's tannins are soft (I very rarely encountered wines with problematic tannins), which helped such appellations as Chassagne-Montrachet, Santenay, Nuits-St.-Georges, Fixin, and others that sometimes have difficulty coping with their tannins. Comparisons with previous vintages are never easy, and this is particularly true with 1996. Maybe the best analogy would be to imagine 1990 with less lushness and structure yet more freshness and vibrancy. There are no baked, stewed, or jammy fruit characteristics in the flavor profiles of the 1996s (as opposed to some 1990s).

I have one nagging reservation about all the accolades 1996 has been bestowed—the wines' level of acidity. Wines produced by growers who harvested excessive yields will not have enough fruit to handle the vintage's acidity levels. These wines will dry out and become unpleasant to drink relatively quickly. However, in 1996 quality-conscious producers crafted extraordinary wines capable of aging for a decade or more.

1995—This is the finest vintage for white burgundies since 1989. From this hallowed region's most conscientious producers, the 1995 vintage frequently combines the ripeness, richness, and concentration of 1989 with the delineation, complexity, and volume of 1986. While I doubt this vintage is as superlative as either 1989 or 1986, I do believe it will provide fabulous wines for both near- and long-term cellaring—depending upon selection. Thick, oily textures and flavors of superripe fruits (in some instances reminiscent of red berries!) are characteristics of many top 1995s. Several highly respected producers shared the view that their 1995s lacked the balancing acidity for long-term cellaring, but that deficiency only adds to their flattering, up-front appeal. Depending on what stage of the growing cycle the wines were in, snow in May severely damaged the flowering (*coulure*) and/or stunted the development of the fruit embryos (*millerandage*). With *coulure*, fewer grape bunches are formed as the damaged flowers fall off the vine. In the case of *millerandage*, the undeveloped grape clusters remain on the vine with tiny, undersize berries. At harvest these berries (known in French as *millerands*) contain small quantities of hugely concentrated juice. In both instances the result is the same—nature has forced the hand of the vignerons by imposing lower yields, thus producing concentrated and oily-textured wines. A long, hot, and dry summer further concentrated the juice in the grapes. Warm, sunny days provided the vine with the necessary sunshine to ripen the grapes. Moreover, a deficiency of rain in 1995 prevented the absorption of juice-diluting rainwater, which could have been a problem, as rain did fall at harvest (though much too late to seriously dilute the wine). Additionally, much as in 1986, botrytis (a beneficial, up to a point, fungus that forms on the grape, imparting a honeyed component to the wine's flavors) did affect certain producers' vineyards. However, I did not find any wines that exhibited negative botrytis flavors such as existed in a few 1986s, in particular the extremely botrytised style of Comte Lafon's 1986s. The ageworthiness of the 1995 white burgundies is dependent upon the presence of botrytis. Those wines that were affected with this noble rot will need to be drunk over the next 5–7 years, and the others should prove to be extremely ageworthy.

The 1995 vintage is excellent for red burgundies, certainly the finest since the great 1990s set modern-day standards for lush, ageworthy Pinot Noirs. Going back, it is a finer vintage than the 1989s, 1988s, 1987s, and 1986s and will be more ageworthy than the 1985s. Some vignerons described the 1995 vintage as being a hypothetical blend of 1985 and 1988, with the forward fruit of the 1985s yet the aging ability of the 1988s. Others felt it was more like 1990, but not as lush. Finally, several others defined it as similar to 1993, but with lusher fruit and less acid and tannin.

It is a year where certain producers produced stellar, mind-blowing wines and others crafted excellent and outstanding offerings. A number of vignerons and importers told me that what separated the great wines from the good to excellent wines in this vintage was the sorting table. Those producers who mercilessly sorted out grapes with evidence of rot or unripened fruit were assured of having fabulous raw materials to work with.

As with the whites, *coulure* and *millerandage* in the spring assured low yields, and a long, hot, and dry summer concentrated the fruit flavors in the grapes. Some rainfall at harvesttime did cause some rot, but elimination of these grapes on the sorting tables prevented the potential problem of stale mushroom flavors in the wines. Few wines I have tasted had any off aromas or flavors.

Overall, the 1995 red burgundies are dark, thick, and dense wines packed with concentrated fruit flavors and the necessary structure for aging. Some wines in this vintage are tannic (though less severe than 1988 and 1993). These will require extended cellaring.

1994—This was the fourth consecutive vintage where rain fell immediately before and during the harvest. Much of the Chardonnay crop was brought in with minimal dilution and produced relatively low-acid, rich, high-alcohol, ripe wines that lack the charm and hedonistic pleasures associated with the 1992s. The vast majority of 1994 white burgundies will need to be consumed by 2004. As for the red wines, the Pinot Noir vineyards were hit hard by the heavy rains Mother Nature hurled at France during September. The wines do not have the color, body, or intensity of the very good 1993s. The majority have the plummy fruit characteristics of the 1992s but tend to finish on dry, dusty tannins.

1993—The 1993 Chardonnay crop was abundant and sadly diluted by heavy rain immediately prior to the harvest. Many of the white wines are monolithic, lack interior flavor, and are simply shells of acidity and alcohol with light fruit and concentration. Those growers/producers who crop-thinned and had very low yields have produced wines with more depth and concentration, but overall this is an average-quality year for white burgundy. The 1993 vintage will have to be carried by the reputation of the very good reds. The red wines are unbelievably dark-colored, rich, and tannic, rather astonishing given the heavy rainstorms that pummeled the Côte d'Or in early September. The crop size was not large, and the Pinot skins were surprisingly resistant to the formation of rot as the temperatures remained cool during the harvest. While there is impressive color (as deep in most cases as the 1990s), the wines do not reveal the fat and richness possessed by the finest 1990s. There is plenty of tannin, and the wines have fine structure. The 1993 burgundies will be more appreciated by readers with a Bordeaux mind-set than by those who prefer the traditional style of succulent, expansively rich, velvety-textured red burgundies. The 1993s will require patience, but the top wines should turn out to be very good, with some exceptional, because of tiny yields and highly concentrated and extracted flavors. The 1993 vintage is unlikely to be one of precocious wines, but, rather, one where some aging will be required. However, caveat emptor! The majority of 1993 red burgundies do not have enough fruit to outlast the tannins. All too many 1993s will dry out like their 1988 counterparts.

1992—A glorious year of big, ripe, juicy, succulent white burgundies and, at the top-quality level, remarkably charming, round, delicious, low-acid, moderately concentrated red burgundies. The white wines have moved through to the marketplace with considerable speed, notwithstanding what are frightfully high prices. For the most part, 1992 white burgundies will need to be consumed over the next 5 years. The red wines have been bashed by many wine-writing professionals, but the fact remains that there are plenty of top-quality, supple red wines from both the Côte de Beaune and Côte de Nuits that were offered at the lowest prices consumers had seen in more than a decade. Careful selection of the best wines is imperative, but treasures can be found in this vintage. The 1992s need to be consumed over the next 3–5 years.

1991—The stars of this vintage are usually from the Côte de Nuits. Because of abnormally low yields (1–2⅓ tons per acre), the top wines display excellent concentration and richness. The finest 1991s are close in quality to the 1990s and are richer, fuller, more complete wines than the finest 1988s, 1987s, and 1986s. These wines, which are often priced 25%–40% below the 1990s, are worthy additions to any burgundy connoisseur's cellar. Because the yields were so low, quantities of the top wines are small. Many producers made 50% less wine than they turned out in 1990. If the vintage has a dark side, it is the tannin level in many wines. Consumers must be careful, because balance is everything. Many 1991s possess tannin levels that may never melt away.

In the Côte de Beaune the vintage is much more difficult to peg, but there are numerous disappointments—wines that are excessively light and/or frightfully tannic and out of balance. This being said, the best producers (notably Volnay's Michel Lafarge) crafted gorgeous 1991s that will age remarkably well.

1990—This is a very good vintage for white burgundies, but only a handful of producers achieved greatness, because the yields were entirely too high to obtain the requisite concentration. Those growers who meticulously pruned back to restrict their yields and who picked physiologically mature fruit have made stunning wines. There are some high-class wines in Chablis, above-average-quality wines in Meursault, and good to excellent wines in Puligny-Montrachet and Chassagne-Montrachet. One appellation that enjoyed considerable success is Corton-Charlemagne, where the wines are superior to the 1989s! At the top levels, the red wines are the finest red burgundies of the last five decades. They are darkly colored, with sumptuous, rich, thick fruit. Moreover, many of the wines possess excellent structure and moderate levels of sweet tannins. The 1990 vintage is one of those rare red burgundy vintages that will offer an exceptionally broad window of drinkability. Qualitatively, it towers above such vintages as 1988 and 1985.

1989—It is a spectacular vintage for white burgundy that may ultimately prove to be the best year for the white wines of Corton-Charlemagne, Meursault, Puligny-Montrachet, and Chassagne-Montrachet in more than 20 years. The 1989 red burgundies are delicious, forward, ripe wines that are flattering at present and in many cases better balanced and more complex than the 1988s. Not surprisingly, most growers prefer their 1989s to the 1988s. I would opt for drinking them sooner (over the next 2–5 years) than later.

1988—The question about this vintage is why so many wine writers, above all the English press (who judge burgundy as if it is Bordeaux), rated this vintage so highly. A handful of great wines have been produced that can be compared with the superb red burgundies of 1969. But what about the high yields and astringent level of tannins of the 1988s? It will be an aging race between the fruit and the tannin. In Pinot Noir, highly tannic wines usually age poorly. Burgundy enthusiasts who have stashed away quantities of 1988s are likely to be more disappointed than pleased by what they are finding. Most Burgundy growers are presently expressing concern about the high level of tannins, which are astringent, green, and dry rather than soft, sweet, and mature, as in 1985 and 1990. Recent tastings of the 1988s have shown many to be excessively austere and hard. The lean, austere 1988 white burgundies recall the 1981s. If they develop along similar lines, they will be more acidic and alcoholic than fruity in 2–4 years.

1987—From the top estates, delicious, supple red wines were made, which is amazing given the fact that most producers had to harvest under heavy rain. Recent tastings of 1987 red burgundies indicate that the vast majority of them are past their plateau of maturity. Only the very finest wines from the top estates will survive cellaring past 2000. This is a mediocre year for white wines.

1986—This is a great year for white burgundy and an unexciting one for red burgundy. Most of the red wines possess structure and tannin but are hollow on the midpalate. Their lack of succulence and chewiness, found in top years such as 1985 and 1990, makes them dubious choices. With very few exceptions, 1986 red burgundies should have been consumed by 1996. In 1999, 1986 white burgundies are either reaching their peak or are at full maturity. Having recently had the opportunity to taste the 1986s from Domaine Niellon,

Louis Jadot, Domaine Ramonet, and Domaine Coche-Dury, I can unequivocally state that these wines demonstrate the extraordinary heights Burgundian Chardonnays can attain.

1985—Initially proclaimed as Burgundy's vintage of the century, the white wines continue to merit the accolades they received, providing rich, sumptuous drinking. The top whites should last for another 5–7 years. Presently the reds offer a mixed bag of impressions. Some of the larger-scale red wines appear muted, monolithic, and one-dimensional. The best of them continue to exhibit a healthy deep ruby color and good depth and weight. The lighter reds have taken on some amber at the edge, are soft and fruity, but have not developed the aromatic complexity initially expected. The 1985 vintage has produced some outstanding wines, but as the 1985s have matured, the overall quality is mixed.

1984—All of us remember 1984. This year, like 1980, was declared by several wine writers to be a major catastrophe long before they ever tasted the wines. In 1980 the source for information was the *négociant* Louis Latour, who had all sorts of problems with the vintage and indeed made poor wine that year. As all burgundy lovers know, 1980 has turned out some of the most delicious and best balanced wines of the 1980s, and some of the wines from the Côte de Nuits are superb. Well, 1984 is not likely to be as good as 1980, but many of the finest growers made wines that turned out better than anyone expected. The vintage was late, yields were low because of a poor flowering, and everyone had to employ *chaptalisation* because the natural alcohol levels were only 9%–10%. However, the resulting red wines were often quite elegant, very cleanly made, fruity, soft, and agreeable. The good 1984s should already have been consumed, as they were not long-lived wines, and are dubious choices today.

1983—The red burgundies of 1983 were plagued by rampant rot. While natural sugar levels were abnormally high, far too many wines smell and taste of rot and/or are unbelievably tannic and astringent. However, this being said, the great 1983s, from producers such as Roumier, the Domaine de la Romanée-Conti, Henri Jayer, Hubert Lignier, Mongeard-Mugneret, and Ponsot, should provide some of the longest-lived wines of the last three decades. Yet this is a vintage to approach with the greatest of caution.

BURGUNDY'S GREATEST RED WINES

Bertrand Ambroise Corton Le Rognet
Bertrand Ambroise Nuits-St.-Georges Les
 Vaucrains
Marquis d'Angerville Volnay Clos des Ducs
Robert Arnoux Romanée-St.-Vivant
Robert Arnoux Vosne-Romanée Les
 Suchots
d'Auvenay Bonnes-Mares
d'Auvenay Mazis-Chambertin
Bouchard Père et Fils La Romanée (since
 1995)
Chopin-Groffier Clos de Vougeot
Bruno Clair Chambertin-Clos de Bèze
J. J. Confuron Romanée St.-Vivant
Claude Dugat Charmes-Chambertin
Claude Dugat Gevrey-Chambertin Lavaux
 St.-Jacques
Claude Dugat Griottes-Chambertin
Dugat-Py Charmes-Chambertin
Dugat-Py Gevrey-Chambertin Lavaux
 St.-Jacques

Dugat-Py Mazis-Chambertin Vieilles
 Vignes
Dujac Bonnes Mares
Dujac Clos de la Roche
Dujac Clos St.-Denis
René Engel Grands-Echézeaux
Jean Grivot Clos Vougeot
Jean Grivot Richebourg
Robert Groffier Bonnes-Mares
Robert Groffier Chambertin-Clos de Bèze
Anne Gros Clos de Vougeot Le Grand
 Maupertiu
Anne Gros Richebourg
Haegelen-Jayer Clos de Vougeot Vieilles
 Vignes
Louis Jadot Bonnes Mares
Louis Jadot Chambertin-Clos de Bèze
Louis Jadot Gevrey-Chambertin Clos
 St.-Jacques
Louis Jadot Musigny
Jayer-Gilles Echézeaux

Michel Lafarge Volnay Clos des Chênes
Michel Lafarge Volnay Clos du Château
des Ducs
Comte Lafon Volnay Champans
Comte Lafon Volnay Santenots
Lecheneaut Clos de la Roche
Lecheneaut Nuits-St.-Georges Les Cailles
René Leclerc Griotte-Chambertin
Domaine Leroy Chambertin
Domaine Leroy Chambolle-Musigny Les
Charmes
Domaine Leroy Clos de la Roche
Domaine Leroy Clos de Vougeot
Domaine Leroy Corton Les Rénardes
Domaine Leroy Gevrey-Chambertin Les
Combottes
Domaine Leroy Latricières-Chambertin
Domaine Leroy Musigny
Domaine Leroy Nuits-St.-Georges Aux
Boudots
Domaine Leroy Nuits-St.-Georges Les
Vignes Rondes
Domaine Leroy Richebourg
Domaine Leroy Romanée St.-Vivant
Domaine Leroy Vosne-Romanée Les Beaux
Monts
Domaine Leroy Vosne-Romanée Les
Brûlées
Hubert Lignier Charmes-Chambertin
Hubert Lignier Clos de la Roche
Hubert Lignier Morey-St.-Denis Premier
Cru Vieilles Vignes
Méo-Camuzet Clos de Vougeot
Méo-Camuzet Richebourg
Méo-Camuzet Vosne-Romanée Les Brûlées

Mongeard-Mugneret Richebourg
Jacques-Frédéric Mugnier Musigny
Jacques Prieur Musigny (since 1995)
Jean Raphet Chambertin-Clos de Bèze
Jean Raphet Charmes-Chambertin
Domaine de la Romanée-Conti Grands-
Echézeaux
Domaine de la Romanée-Conti Richebourg
Domaine de la Romanée-Conti Romanée-
Conti
Domaine de la Romanée-Conti La Tâche
Joseph Roty Charmes-Chambertin
Joseph Roty Griotte-Chambertin
Joseph Roty Mazis-Chambertin
Emmanuel Rouget Echézeaux
Emmanuel Rouget Vosne-Romanée Cros
Parantoux
Georges et Christophe Roumier Bonnes
Mares
Georges et Christophe Roumier
Chambolle-Musigny Les Amoureuses
Georges et Christophe Roumier Ruchottes-
Chambertin
Armand Rousseau Chambertin
Armand Rousseau Chambertin Clos de
Bèze
Armand Rousseau Gevrey-Chambertin
Clos St.-Jacques
Christian Serafin Charmes-Chambertin
Christian Serafin Gevrey-Chambertin Les
Cazetiers
Comte de Vogüé Bonnes-Mares (prior to
1973 and after 1989)
Comte de Vogüé Musigny Vieilles Vignes
(prior to 1973 and after 1989)

RATING THE RED BURGUNDY GROWERS, PRODUCERS, AND *NÉGOCIANTS*

No one will ever have a great deal of success selecting a burgundy without a thorough knowledge of the finest growers and *négociants*. The most meticulous producers often make better wine in mediocre vintages than many less dedicated growers and producers make in great vintages. Knowing the finest producers in Burgundy is unquestionably the most important factor in your success in finding the best wines.

The following is a guide to the best red and white burgundy producers. Consistency from year to year and among the producers' total range of wines were the most important considerations. One should be cognizant of the fact that many lower-rated producers may make specific wines that are qualitatively above their placement.

Note: These ranks provided for these estates are based on their special cuvées crafted for North Berkeley Wine Imports. Many other Burgundy estates have special bottlings for their

U.S. importers, yet the differences between the "house cuvées" and the U.S. bottlings are not as marked as those crafted for North Berkeley. They are therefore not indicated.

Where a producer has been assigned a range of stars—***/****, for example—the lower rating has been used for placement in this hierarchy.

RATING BURGUNDY'S RED WINE PRODUCERS

* * * * * (OUTSTANDING)

Domaine Marquis d'Angerville (Volnay)

Domaine d'Auvenay (St. Romain)§

Domaine Daniel Chopin-Groffier (Prémeaux-Prissey)

Domaine Jean-Jacques Confuron (Prémeaux-Prissey)

Domaine Claude Dugat (Gevrey-Chambertin)§

Domaine Dugat-Py (Gevrey-Chambertin)§

Domaine Jayer-Gilles (Magny-Lès-Villers)

Domaine Michel Lafarge (Volnay)

Domaine des Comtes Lafon (Meursault)

Domaine Lécheneaut (Nuits-St.-Georges)

Domaine Leroy (Vosne-Romanée)§

Domaine Hubert Lignier (Morey-St.-Denis)

Domaine de la Romanée-Conti (Vosne-Romanée)

Domaine Christian Serafin (Gevrey-Chambertin)

Domaine du Comte de Vogüé (Chambolle-Musigny)§

* * * * (EXCELLENT)

Bertrand Ambroise (Prémeaux-Prissey)****/*****

Domaine Amiot-Servelle (Chambolle-Musigny)

Domaine de l'Arlot (Prémeaux-Prissey)

Domaine Robert Arnoux (Vosne-Romanée)****/*****

Domaine Ghislaine Barthod-Noellat (Chambolle-Musigny)

Bouchard Père et Fils (Beaune) (since 1995)

Domaine Jacques Cacheux et Fils (Vosne-Romanée)

Domaine Robert Chevillon (Nuits-St.-Georges)

Domaine Bruno Clair (Marsannay)

Domaine Marius Delarche (Pernand-Vergelesses)

Domaine Dujac (Morey-St.-Denis)

Domaine Maurice Ecard et Fils (Savigny-Lès-Beaune)

Domaine René Engel (Vosne-Romanée)

Domaine Geantet-Pansiot (Gevrey-Chambertin)

Vincent Girardin (Santenay)

Domaine Jean Grivot (Vosne-Romanée) (since 1993)****/*****

Domaine Robert Groffier (Morey-St.-Denis) (since 1995)****/*****

Domaine Anne Gros (Vosne-Romanée)****/*****

Domaine Haegelen-Jayer (Vosne-Romanée)

Louis Jadot (Beaune)****/*****

Domaine Joblot (Givry)

Dominique Laurent (Nuits-St.-Georges)

Domaine Philippe Leclerc (Gevrey-Chambertin)

Domaine René Leclerc (Gevrey-Chambertin)

Frédéric Magnien (Morey-St.-Denis)

Domaine Michel Magnien (Morey-St.-Denis)

Domaine Méo-Camuzet (Vosne-Romanée)****/*****

Domaine Mongeard-Mugneret (Vosne-Romanée)

Domaine Albert Morot (Beaune)

Domaine Denis Mortet (Gevrey-Chambertin) (since 1995)****/*****

Domaine Mugneret-Gibourg/Georges

§: These five superstar estates deserve special recognition for the spectacular wines they have crafted in the 1993, 1994, 1995, 1996, and 1997 vintages. Every wine at each of these domaines in those vintages can be highly recommended. This remarkable feat would not be possible without brilliant vineyard and cellar work.

Mugneret (Vosne-Romanée) (since 1995)****/*****

Domaine Jacques-Frédéric Mugnier/Ch. de Chambolle-Musigny (Chambolle-Musigny)

Domaine des Perdrix (Prémeaux-Prissey) (since 1995)

Domaine Henri Perrot-Minot (Morey-St.-Denis) (since 1995)

Domaine Jacques Prieur (Meursault) (since 1995)

Domaine Jean Raphet (Morey-St.-Denis)

Domaine Daniel Rion (Nuits-St.-Georges)

Antonin Rodet (Mercurey) (since 1995 on Cave Privée wines)

Domaine Joseph Roty (Gevrey-Chambertin)

Domaine Emmanuel Rouget (Flagey-Echézeaux)****/*****

Domaine Georges et Christophe Roumier (Chambolle-Musigny)****/*****

Domaine Armand Rousseau (Gevrey-Chambertin)

Domaine Tollot-Beaut et Fils (Chorey-Lès-Beaune)

Domaine Jean et J. L. Trapet (Gevrey-Chambertin) (since 1995)

* * * (GOOD)

Domaine Pierre Amiot et Fils (Morey-St.-Denis)

Domaine Arlaud Père et Fils (Nuits-St.-Georges)***/****

Domaine Comte Armand (Pommard)***/****

Domaine Charles Audoin (Marsannay)

Domaine Jean-Claude Belland (Santenay)

Domaine Xavier Besson (Givry)

Domaine Bitouzet-Prieur (Volnay)

Domaine Simon Bize et Fils (Savigny-Lès-Beaune)***/****

Domaine Jean-Yves Bizot (Vosne-Romanée)***/****

Domaine Daniel Bocquenet (Nuits-St.-Georges)***/****

Domaine Jean Boillot (Volnay)***/****

Domaine Jean-Marc Boillot (Pommard)***/****

Domaine Reyanne et Pascal Bouley (Volnay)

Domaine Alain Burguet (Gevrey-Chambertin)***/****

Domaine du Château de Chamirey (Mercurey)

Domaine Chandon de Briailles (Savigny-Lès-Beaune)

Domaine Jean Chauvenet (Nuits-St.-Georges)

Domaine Chauvenet-Chopin (Nuits-St.-Georges)***/****

Domaine Pascal Chevigny (Nuits-St.-Georges)***/****

Colin-Deléger (Chassagne-Montrachet)

Domaine Edmond Cornu (Ladoix-Serrigny)

Joseph Drouhin (Beaune)***/****

Domaine Jean-Luc Dubois (Chorey-Lès-Beaune)

Domaine Dureuil-Janthial (Rully)***/****

Domaine Arnauld Ente (Meursault)

Fery-Meunier (Nuits-St.-Georges)

Domaine Jean-Noël Gagnard (Chassagne-Montrachet)

Domaine Jean Garaudet (Pommard)***/****

Domaine Philippe Gavignet (Nuits-St.-Georges)

Domaine Henri Gouges (Nuits-St.-Georges) (since 1995)***/****

Domaine Pierre Guillemot (Savigny-Lès-Beaune)

Domaine Antonin Guyon (Savigny-Lès-Beaune)

Domaine Henri Jouan (Morey-St.-Denis)

Domaine des Lambrays (Morey-St.-Denis) (since 1995)***/****

Domaine Latour-Giraud (Meursault)

Domaine Philippe Livera/Dom. des Tilleuils (Gevrey-Chambertin)***/****

Domaine du Château de la Maltroye (Chassagne-Montrachet)

Domaine Joseph Matrot (Meursault)

Domaine Maume (Gevrey-Chambertin)

Domaine du Château de Mercey (Mercurey)

Domaine Jean-Marc Millot (Comblanchien)

Domaine Monthélie-Douhairet (Monthélie) (since 1995)

Bernard Morey et Fils (Chassagne-Montrachet)***/****

Domaine Philippe Naddef
(Couchey)***/****
Domaine Ponsot (Morey-St.-Denis)***/****
Domaine de la Pousse d'Or (Volnay) (until
1995)***/****
Domaine Ramonet (Chassagne-Montrachet)
Domaine Henri Remoriquet (Nuits-
St.-Georges)
Domaine Armelle et Bernard Rion (Vosne-
Romanée)

Domaine du Château de Rully (Rully)
Domaine Jean Tardy (Vosne-Romanée)
Domaine du Clos de Tart (Morey-
St.-Denis)***/****
Domaine A. & P. de Villaine (Bouzeron)
Domaine Christophe Violot-Guillemard
(Pommard)
Domaine Thierry Violot-Guillemard
(Pommard)
Domaine Joseph Voillot (Volnay)

* * (AVERAGE)

Domaine Guy Amiot et Fils (Chassagne-
Montrachet)**/***
Domaine Bertagna (Vougeot)**/***
Domaine Lucien Boillot et Fils (Gevrey-
Chambertin)
Domaine Bonneau du Martray (Pernand-
Vergelesses)**/***
Domaine Borgeot (Remigny)**/***
Domaine Jean-Marc Bouley
(Volnay)**/***
Bourée Père et Fils (Gevrey-Chambertin)
Domaine Philippe Brenot
(Santenay)**/***
Domaine du Manoir de la Bressandière
(Pommard)
Domaine Lucien Camus-Brochon (Savigny-
Lès-Beaune)**/***
Chartron et Trébuchet (Puligny-
Montrachet)
Alain Corcia Selections (Savigny-Lès-
Beaune)
Domaine du Château de Cray*/**
Domaine Henri Delagrange et Fils (Volnay)
Domaine Bruno Desaunay-Bissey (Flagey-
Echézeaux)**/***
Domaine de la Ferté (Givry)**/***
Domaine Jean-Philippe Fichet
(Meursault)**/***
Domaine Forey Père et Fils (Vosne-
Romanée)
Domaine Génot-Boulanger
(Meursault)**/***
Machard de Gramont (Nuits-
St.-Georges)**/***
Domaine Rémi Jobard (Meursault)
/*
Labouré-Roi (Nuits-St.-Georges)

Domaine René Lamy-Pillot (Chassagne-
Montrachet)
Louis Latour (Beaune)**/***
Domaine Aleth Leroyer-Girardin
(Pommard)
Domaine Georges Lignier (Morey-
St.-Denis)**/***
Domaine Prince Florent de Mérode
(Ladoix-Serrigny)**/***
Domaine du Château de Monthélie
(Monthélie)**/***
Domaine Jean-Marc Morey (Chassagne-
Montrachet)
Domaine Pierre Morey (Meursault)
Domaine Lucien Muzard et Fils (Santenay)
Domaine Fernand et Laurent Pillot
(Chassagne-Montrachet)
Jean Pillot (Chassagne-Montrachet)
Domaine de la Poulette (Corgoloin)
Domaine du Château de Prémeaux
(Prémeaux-Prissey)
Domaine Roland Rapet (Pernand-
Vergelesses)**/***
Domaine Jean-Claude Rateau
(Beaune)**/***
Domaine Philippe Rossignol (Gevrey-
Chambertin)
Domaine Rossignol-Trapet (Gevrey-
Chambertin)**/***
Domaine Laurent Roumier (Chambolle-
Musigny)**/***
Domaine Saint Martin**/***
Domaine Jacky Truchot (Morey-
St.-Denis)**/***
Domaine des Varoilles (Gevrey-
Chambertin)**/***
Domaine Virot (Mercurey)*/**

Where Are Burgundy's Red Wine Values?

The glamour appellations of the Côte de Nuits and the Côte de Beaune offer high prices as well as irregular quality. As in the world's other best-known wine-growing regions, values are few and far between in Burgundy. However, if values are to be found, consumers must look beyond the most prestigious names and most renowned appellations, searching out some of the less highly acclaimed appellations. Following are some wines to check out in the Côte de Nuits, Côte de Beaune, and possibly the best source of red and white burgundies, the Côte Chalonnaise, located just south of the Côte d'Or.

Aloxe-Corton Appellation (Côte de Beaune)   The highly sought after red and white grand crus from the famed Corton hillside lie mostly within Aloxe-Corton's appellation, yet this village's premier cru and village wines attract little consumer attention. While the majority of Aloxe-Cortons tend to be hard and lacking in charm, some excellent wines are produced in this appellation.

The best wines include Jean-Claude Belland—Aloxe-Corton; Simon Bize—Aloxe-Corton Le Suchot; Edmond et Pierre Cornu—Aloxe-Corton Les Moutottes, Aloxe-Corton Les Valozières, Aloxe-Corton Vieilles Vignes; Jean-Luc Dubois—Aloxe-Corton Les Brunettes Réserve; Génot-Boulanger—Aloxe-Corton Clos du Chapître; Antonin Guyon—Aloxe-Corton Les Vercots, Antonin-Rodet—Aloxe-Corton Les Valozières Cave Privée; Tollot-Beaut—Aloxe-Corton, Aloxe-Corton Les Fournières, Aloxe-Corton Les Vercots.

Auxey-Duresses Appellation (Côte de Beaune)   Auxey-Duresses has often been described as the poor person's Volnay. Such comments are pejorative and tend to irritate the local vignerons, who are proud of their spicy, robust, black cherry-scented and -flavored wine that often possesses surprising aging potential. The key is ripe fruit. If the fruit is not ripe when picked, the tannins tend to be green and the acids can reach shrill levels.

The best wines include Comte Armand—Auxey-Duresses, Auxey-Duresses Premier Cru.

Bourgogne Appellation   Wines bearing this "regional" appellation can emanate from poor vineyard sites or can be the result of a "declassification" from a more acclaimed appellation. Many Bourgognes produced by *négociants* contain wines from Beaujolais and the Mâconnais. While most wines from this appellation are insipid, tart, and not worthy of consumers' attention, those produced by Burgundy's most conscientious producers are often, in the best vintages, excellent values for near-term drinking.

Ghislaine Barthod-Noellat—Bourgogne; Alain Burguet—Bourgogne; Dugat-Py—Bourgogne; Robert Groffier—Bourgogne; Anne Gros—Bourgogne Pinot Noir; Michel Lafarge—Bourgogne; Philippe Leclerc—Bourgogne Les Bons Batons; Hubert Lignier—Bourgogne; Denis Mortet—Bourgogne; Georges Mugneret—Bourgogne; Emmanuel Rouget—Bourgogne.

Bourgogne Passetoutgrain Appellation   These wines, crafted from an assemblage of Pinot Noir and Gamay, are very rarely good. More often than not, even the finest producers treat their Passetoutgrain with disdain, bringing in extremely high yields and paying little attention to their vinification and *élevage*. However, the following two growers consistently produce Bourgogne Passetoutgrains meriting consumer attention.

Michel Lafarge—Bourgogne Passetoutgrain; Emmanuel Rouget—Bourgogne Passetoutgrain.

Chassagne-Montrachet (Côte de Beaune)   The downside of Chassagne-Montrachet's fame as one of Burgundy's great white wine villages is that few people pay attention to the tasty red wines with their Bing cherry, almond, earthy fruitiness. There are premiers crus that can be bought for $25–$30 a bottle, making this an interesting market. Most red Chassagnes also have the virtue of lasting for 10 years in a top vintage.

The best wines include Guy Amiot et Fils—Chassagne-Montrachet Clos St.-Jean, Chassagne-Montrachet La Maltroie; Borgeot—Chassagne-Montrachet Clos St.-Jean; Colin-Deléger—Chassagne-Montrachet Morgeot, Chassagne-Montrachet Vieilles Vignes; Jean-Noël Gagnard—Chassagne-Montrachet, Chassagne-Montrachet Morgeot, Chassagne-Montrachet Clos St.-Jean; Vincent Girardin—Chassagne-Montrachet Clos de la Boudriotte Vieilles Vignes, Chassagne-Montrachet Morgeot Duc de Magenta (Louis Jadot)—Chassagne-Montrachet Morgeot; Château de la Maltroye—Chassagne-Montrachet Clos du Château de la Maltroye, Chassagne-Montrachet Clos St.-Jean; Bernard Morey—Chassagne-Montrachet Vieilles Vignes; Domaine Ramonet—Chassagne-Montrachet Clos de la Boudriotte.

Chorey-Lès-Beaune Appellation (Côte de Beaune)   From its best producers, this relatively unknown appellation just north of Beaune can make lovely early-drinking wines. The flat vineyards of Chorey are responsible for a multitude of poorly made, insipid, hollow, and watery wines crafted from huge yields. However, conscientious growers produce wines in the $16–$25 range that merit consumer attention.

The best wines include Jean-Luc Dubois—Chorey-Lès-Beaune Clos du Margot Vieilles Vignes Réserve; Tollot-Beaut—Chorey-Lès-Beaune.

Côte de Nuits-Villages Appellation (Côte de Nuits)   Wines bearing this appellation are produced from vineyards located in Corgoloin, Comblanchien, and Prissey (all three are located south of Nuits-St.-Georges), as well as from Brochon and Fixin (two villages north of Gevrey-Chambertin). From the finest producers these wines reflect the dark fruit characteristics of the Côte de Nuits and can often be complex and ageworthy wines.

The best wines include Chauvenet-Chopin—Côte de Nuits-Villages; Chopin-Groffier—Côte de Nuits-Villages; Jean-Jacques Confuron—Côte de Nuits-Villages Les Vignottes; Edmond et Pierre Cornu—Côte de Nuits-Villages; Philippe Gavignet—Côte de Nuits-Villages Les Vignottes Réserve; Louis Jadot—Côte de Nuits-Villages; Robert Jayer-Gilles—Côte de Nuits-Villages.

Fixin Appellation (Côte de Nuits)   It may be situated next to the famed appellation Gevrey-Chambertin, but Fixin has never overcome its reputation of producing exceptionally robust, sturdy, muscular wines that are short on finesse. However, some producers excel in crafting wines with serious flavor and balance.

The best wines include Philippe Livera—Fixin en Olivier Vieilles Vignes Réserve; Mongeard-Mugneret—Fixin; Philippe Naddef—Fixin; St. Martin—Fixin Hervelets.

Givry Appellation (Côte Chalonnaise)   Givry has one of the finest winemakers in all of Burgundy, Jean-Marc Joblot, who crafts wines that compete with some of the finest of the Côte d'Or.

The best wines include Xavier Besson—Givry Le Petit Pretan Réserve; Domaine de la Ferté—Givry; Joblot—Givry Clos du Bois Chevaux, Givry Clos du Cellier aux Moines, Givry Clos de la Servoisine.

Ladoix Appellation (Côte de Beaune)   Ladoix is Burgundy's least-known appellation, making it one of the more attractive places to shop, but you must know the right addresses. Amazingly, the best Pinot Noirs here cost less than Pinot Noirs from California and Oregon. This is not an appellation to buy blindly, as the wines can be dusty and earthy, with too little fruit.

The best wines include Edmond Cornu—Ladoix, Ladoix Les Carrières, Ladoix Les Corvées, Ladoix Vieilles Vignes.

Marsannay Appellation (Côte de Nuits)   You are not likely to find great wines from this appellation, but good producers can make wines that are far above the normal quality level, which means something better than the compact, straightforward, hard, charmless Pinot Noirs that often emanate from Marsannay.

The best wines include Bruno Clair—Marsannay Les Grasses Têtes, Marsannay Les Longeroies, Marsannay Vaudenelles; Louis Jadot—Marsannay; Denis Mortet—Marsannay

Les Longeroies; Philippe Naddef—Marsannay; Joseph Roty—Marsannay, Marsannay Champs St.-Etiennes, Marsannay Ouzeloy, Marsannay Sampagny.

Mercurey Appellation (Côte Chalonnaise)   Mercurey prices have risen to $25 a bottle as the world has begun to discover the progress Mercurey producers have made. This is an up-and-coming source of good wines.

The best producers include Château de Chamirey—Mercurey; Vincent Dureuil-Janthial—Mercurey Le Bois de Lalier Réserve; Génot-Boulanger—Mercurey Les Sazenay; Château de Mercey—Mercurey En Sazenay; Domaine de Suremain—Mercurey Clos l'Eveque, Mercurey Clos Voyen; A. & P. de Villaine—Mercurey Les Montots.

Monthélie Appellation (Côte de Beaune)   The vineyards of Monthélie are adjacent to Volnay, yet the wines could not be more different. The old-style Monthélies are plagued by excessive tannin and body, but a younger generation of winemakers is bringing out the wines' fruit and character, hoping that consumers will make the one- to two-minute trek from the neighboring villages of Volnay and Pommard to take a look at this hilltop village where most red burgundies can still be bought for under $20–$30 a bottle.

The best wines include Bouchard Père et Fils—Monthélie Les Champs Fulliots; J. F. Coche-Dury—Monthélie; Jean Garaudet—Monthélie; Paul Garaudet—Monthélie, Monthélie Les Duresses, Monthélie Clos Gauthey; Comte Lafon—Monthélie Les Duresses; Monthélie-Douhairet—Monthélie Duresses, Monthélie Le Meix Bataille; Eric de Suremain/ Château de Monthélie—Monthélie Château de Monthélie, Monthélie Sur La Velle.

Pernand-Vergelesses Appellation (Côte de Beaune)   This small village, nestled on the western side of the Corton hill, is little known and yet can produce—particularly in warm, dry years—high-quality wines. In the best vintages, Pernand's finest producers craft muscular, full-bodied, dark fruit-packed, and ageworthy wines.

The best wines include Chandon de Briailles—Pernand-Vergelesses Ile de Vergelesses, Pernand-Vergelesses Les Vergelesses; Marius Delarche—Pernand-Vergelesses Les Boutieres Vieilles Vignes Réserve, Pernand-Vergelesses Ile de Vergelesses Réserve, Pernand-Vergelesses Les Vergelesses Réserve; Antonin Guyon—Pernand-Vergelesses Les Vergelesses; Louis Jadot—Pernand-Vergelesses Clos de la Croix de Pierre; Roland Rapet—Pernand-Vergelesses Ile de Vergelesses.

Rully Appellation (Côte Chalonnaise)   As with any appellation, one has to be well informed, but the spicy, cherry, strawberry, dusty aromas and flavors of a good Rully can be purchased for prices in the mid-teens to mid-twenties.

The best wines include Vincent Dureuil-Janthial—Rully En Guesnes Réserve, Rully Rosey Réserve; Château de Rully—Rully.

Santenay Appellation (Côte de Beaune)   It is amazing that Santenay continues to have problems overcoming its image as the last of the Côte d'Or appellations. Over 99% of its wine is red, all of it made from the Pinot Noir grape. The wine trade still bristles when reminded of a quotation from one of Britain's leading wine merchants, who said, "Life is too short to drink Santenay." Thanks largely to the efforts of Vincent Girardin, this village's top producer and one of the Côte d'Or's finest *negociants*, Santenay has become more fashionable. Thrifty consumers looking for a solid, frequently delicious bottle of Pinot Noir for $18–$30 should search out this village's top wines. While many Santenays can be excessively tannic, hollow, and pleasureless, the good producers make a wine that is medium weight by burgundy standards, with a pronounced bouquet of strawberry and cherry fruit allied to a mineral, almost almondlike smell.

The best wines include Jean-Claude Belland—Santenay Les Gravières; Borgeot—Santenay Beauregard; Bouchard Père et Fils—Santenay; Colin-Deléger—Santenay Les Gravières; Jean-Noël Gagnard—Santenay Clos de Tavannes; Vincent Girardin—Santenay Clos de la Confrerie, Santenay Les Gravières, Santenay La Maladière; Louis Jadot—Santenay Clos de

Malte; Bernard Morey—Santenay Grand Clos Rousseau; Santenay Passetemps, Santenay Vieilles Vignes; Jean-Marc Morey—Santenay Grand Clos Rousseau.

Savigny-Lès-Beaune Appellation (Côte de Beaune) Savigny-Lès-Beaune has a good reputation for light, berry-scented (primarily cherry) wines that at their worst can have an overwhelming rusty, earthy undertone. The vineyards on the northern hillsides overlooking the Rhoin River, which cuts this appellation in half, produce the finest wine. Most sell for prices between $18 and $30 a bottle. They are not as inexpensive as Marsannay or Ladoix, but at their best they exhibit considerably more complexity as well as a compelling Pinot Noir perfume.

The best wines include Simon Bize—Savigny-Lès-Beaune Les Bourgeots, Savigny-Lès-Beaune Les Fourneaux, Savigny-Lès-Beaune Les Grands Liards, Savigny-Lès-Beaune Les Guettes, Savigny-Lès-Beaune Les Marconnets, Savigny-Lès-Beaune Les Serpentières, Savigny-Lès-Beaune Les Vergelesses; Jean Boillot—Savigny-Lès-Beaune Les Lavières; Bouchard Père et Fils—Savigny-Lès-Beaune, Savigny-Lès-Beaune Les Lavières; Lucien Camus-Brochon—Savigny-Lès-Beaune Les Grands Liards, Savigny-Lès-Beaune Les Lavières, Savigny-Lès-Beaune Les Narbantons, Savigny-Lès-Beaune Les Vieilles Vignes; Chandon de Briailles—Savigny-Lès-Beaune Les Lavières; Edmond et Pierre Cornu—Savigny-Lès-Beaune; Jean-Luc Dubois—Savigny-Lès-Beaune Les Picotins Vieilles Vignes Réserve; Maurice Ecard—Savigny-Lès-Beaune Les Jarrons, Savigny-Lès-Beaune Les Narbantons, Savigny-Lès-Beaune Les Peuillets, Savigny-Lès-Beaune Les Serpentières; Pierre Guillemot—Savigny-Lès-Beaune Les Jarrons, Savigny-Lès-Beaune Les Serpentières; Louis Jadot—Savigny-Lès-Beaune La Dominode, Savigny-Lès-Beaune Clos des Guettes, Savigny-Lès-Beaune Les Lavières, Savigny-Lès-Beaune Les Vergelesses; Albert Morot—Savigny-Lès-Beaune Les Vergelesses Clos la Bataillière; Tollot-Beaut—Savigny-Lès-Beaune Champs Chevreys, Savigny-Lès-Beaune Les Lavières.

Beaujolais

What is the most successful and lucrative wine produced in Burgundy? The answer is Beaujolais. This wine is made from vineyards strung across a number of enchanted mountainsides that mark the beginning of what is known as France's "Massif Central." The region of Beaujolais is 34 miles long from north to south, and 7 to 9 miles wide. The granite mountainsides range in height from 2,300 feet to more than 3,400 feet and provide a backdrop for what is one of France's two most beautiful viticultural regions (the other being Alsace). Nearly 4,000 growers make a living in this idyllic area. Some of them sell tiny portions of their crops locally, but most prefer to sell to one of the large firms that dominate the business.

The only grape permitted by law to be used in making Beaujolais is the Gamay, or Gamay Noir à jus Blanc, its official name. It seems to thrive in the stony, schistose soils of the region. Most red wine grapes have trouble producing high-quality crops in granite-based soils, but Gamay seems to be a natural. The compelling characteristic of Gamay is its youthful, fresh, exuberant, crunchy fruit, which the vignerons of Beaujolais have learned to maximize by producing it in an unusual method called "carbonic maceration." In this style of vinification, the grapes are not pressed but are simply dumped unceremoniously into a vat in full bunches. Grapes at the very bottom of the vat burst because of the weight on top of them. That juice begins to ferment, warming up the vat and causing fermentation in the unbroken grapes to actually begin inside their skins. The advantage of this technique is that a wine's perfume and fruity intensity is largely related to what is inside the grape skin. The acid and tannin are largely extracted from the breaking and pressing of the skins. This interesting fermentation method results in fruity, exuberant, intensely perfumed wines that are ideal when chilled and drunk in the so-called nouveau style. Today this nouveau style is a phenomenon in the export markets, but it started only in the late seventies. Beaujolais Nouveau, which can be released only on the third Thursday in November, accounts for nearly half of the enormous production of this region. It is one of France's most successful export items, since the insatiable thirst for this wine results in hundreds of thousands of cases being air-freighted to such far-flung locations as Sydney, Tokyo, Hong Kong, Seoul, San Francisco, New York, Stockholm, London, and, of course, Paris.

The nouveau hysteria and incredible profits taken by the wine trade from the sales of nouveau have resulted in a school of thought that has attempted to disparage not only the wine, but those who consume it. This is all nonsense, because there is no doubting that in vintages such as 1994, delicious, zesty, exuberant, fresh, vibrantly fruity Beaujolais Nouveau is made. The only limitation is that it should be drunk within 3–4 months of its release. Beaujolais Nouveau has become a useful wine for introducing people to the glories of red wine. It has also weaned people off some of the sugary, sweet, white Zinfandels and cloying Liebfraumilchs that dominate the marketplace. A few arrogant wine snobs would have you believe it is not fashionable, but that is ludicrous. However, to think of Beaujolais only in terms of Beaujolais Nouveau is to do this fascinating region a great injustice. In addition to Beaujolais Nouveau, there is Beaujolais Supérieur, which generally comes on the market about a month after Beaujolais Nouveau. There is also Beaujolais-Villages, which is an appellation unto itself, spread out over most of the entire Beaujolais appellation, where 39 communes have been selected by the legislature for producing some of the better wines of the region. Many of the top producers produce a Beaujolais-Villages Nouveau because it has a firmer, more robust character and can last 3 to 4 months longer than the straight Beaujolais Nouveau. If you are drinking Nouveau for its up-front, exuberant, fresh, unabashed fruitiness, then a good Beaujolais Nouveau will often be more pleasing than a Beaujolais-Villages Nouveau.

The glories of Beaujolais, aside from its narrow, winding roads, sleepy valleys, photogenic hillsides, and quaint old villages, are the 10 Beaujolais crus. These wines all come from a village or group of villages in the northern end of the Beaujolais region; each cru is believed to have its own individual style.

A NOTE ON RECENT VINTAGES AND GENERAL CHARACTERISTICS OF THE 10 BEAUJOLAIS CRUS
While examples of old bottles of Beaujolais that have retained their fruit can be found (in 1991 Robert Parker drank a bottle of 1929 Moulin-à-Vent at New York's superb restaurant Le Montrachet, with its sommelier, Daniel Johnnes, that was marvelously intact), most Beaujolais should be consumed within several years of the vintage. If you are going to take a gamble on aging Beaujolais, it should be Moulin-à-Vent. It comes down to a matter of personal taste, but if you are buying these wines for their vibrant, up-front, exuberant, unabashed fruitiness, then drink them young!

With respect to a quick overview of the different crus and what you might expect, the top Beaujolais crus, from north to south, begin with Saint-Amour.

Saint-Amour is a wine known for its good color, but it is often lacking in body and length, as the vineyards usually fail to achieve maximum ripeness except in exceptionally hot, dry years such as 1989. When good, the wines exhibit a blackberry, raspberry fruitiness, medium body, and soft textures.

Juliénas is one of the larger appellations for top Beaujolais. There are many fine producers from Juliénas, so the competition for top-quality wine is intense. The finest examples display the exuberant, rich, fresh fruitiness of Beaujolais, backed up by plenty of body, intensity, and relatively high alcohol.

The smallest Beaujolais cru, Chénas, produces wines with a kinship to the full-bodied wines of its neighbor, Moulin-à-Vent. A top Chénas displays a deep, robust, intense color and a muscular, rich, concentrated style. It is a fuller, more chunky style of Beaujolais that occasionally lacks perfume and elegance. Given its rusticity, many wines of Chénas can age for 4–5 years. Moulin-à-Vent is often referred to as "the King of Beaujolais," and it is certainly the most expensive. Moulin-à-Vent costs $3–$5 more than other Beaujolais. Moulin-à-Vent produces the most powerful, concentrated, and ageworthy Beaujolais. While it is highly prized, in many ways it is atypical, resembling a medium-weight red burgundy from the Côte d'Or rather than an effusively fruity Beaujolais. The wines can easily last for more than 10 years, particularly those from the best producers.

The same people who call Moulin-à-Vent King of Beaujolais refer to Fleurie as its Queen. With one of the bigger vineyard acreages, Fleurie may be the quintessential example of Beaujolais—heady, perfumed, and rich, without the weight, body, or tannin of the bigger wines from Moulin-à-Vent or Chénas. At its best it is a pure, lush, silky, fruity wine that is undeniably seductive and disarming.

Chiroubles's vineyards sit at the highest altitude of Beaujolais. The wines are considered the most ethereal and fragrant of all the Beaujolais crus. Chiroubles derives much of its character from its penetrating, pervasive fragrance. The downside is that it can lack body, can mature very quickly, and almost always must be drunk within 1–2 years of the vintage for its freshness.

Morgon has a reputation of being among the more robust and ageworthy of the Beaujolais crus. There is considerable variation in style, given the large size of this cru. Many wines are quite full and rich, while others are dull and hollow. A great Morgon will have exotic flavors of overripe cherries, peaches, and apricots as well as a taste of kirsch.

The newest of the Beaujolais crus, Régnié offers many different styles. Most of the local cognoscenti claim a classic Régnié possesses an intense smell of cassis and raspberries. It is a relatively light- to medium-bodied wine that needs to be drunk within 3 years of the vintage.

Brouilly, another large Beaujolais cru, produces relatively light, aromatic, fruity wines that are often no better than a Beaujolais-Villages. However, in the hands of the best producers, the wines have an additional degree of charm and fruit, making them ideal Beaujolais.

In contrast, the Côte de Brouilly is composed of vineyards on better-drained and -exposed slopes. The wines tend to be more alcoholic than those from Brouilly, with more body and glycerin. As for the generic Beaujolais and Beaujolais-Villages, again, the producer is most important. One of the best values in the marketplace is a top-quality Beaujolais or Beaujolais-Villages.

With respect to vintages, 1997 offers fat, round, wines filled with lush sweet fruit. An extremely hot August was followed by a September of warm days and cool nights ("it was the finest September of my career," said Georges Dubœuf, this region's most famous *négociant*), fashioning fruit-driven wines that have relatively low acidity levels—particularly when compared with the 1996s. The 1997s are wines that will be at their best early, and the majority will need to be consumed by 2003.

As elsewhere in central and northern France, rain was a concern in Beaujolais during the 1998 harvest. After an extremely hot and sunny month of August, harvesting began in the first days of September and was interrupted by showers every three days or so. Preliminary tastings reveal that conscientious growers were able to avoid the diluting effects of rain by harvesting each parcel at the optimal time. Those who crop thin and have reasonable yields saw their grapes attain full maturity while their neighbors had to wait through the rains. Overall, 1998 appears to be a good vintage for Beaujolais, with appealingly forward fruit (yet not as lush as the 1997s) and nice balance. Most of them should be consumed between now and 2004.

THE "REAL" REALITIES OF BURGUNDY

What is the most important information to know in order to purchase top-quality red and white burgundy? The French frequently utilize the following expression when they discuss Burgundy: *L'homme fait la différence,* meaning it is the man who makes the difference. This simplistic and male-chauvinistic viewpoint (it is a woman, Lalou Bize-Leroy, who produces Burgundy's greatest wines) reflects the cardinal rule when it comes to buying red or white burgundy. While the quality of the vintage is an important fact to know when buying burgundy, it is essential to recognize the quality of the producer. This is important because a superb grower or *négociant* will make a better wine in an off year than a mediocre or incompetent producer or *négociant* will make in a great year. If readers desire to have the odds in their favor when purchasing burgundy, it is imperative that they learn the names of the finest producers for each of the Burgundy appellations. Of course, their styles of wine may not always be to your liking, but at least you should be aware of the names of the most committed and highly motivated winemakers. Simply memorizing a top vintage year in Burgundy and then buying blindly is a practice fraught with the potential for disaster.

What's all this about terroir, *and does it really exist only in Burgundy?* Consumers who have had the opportunity to visit Burgundy, meet with one of its vignerons, or talk with someone enthralled by this hallowed region's wines has certainly heard that *terroir* is the be-all and end-all of Burgundy's wines. Burgundians will tell you that their wines are good because of *terroir,* that their primary duty as vignerons is to allow *terroir* to express itself, and, from time to time, they will comment on a wine's *goût de terroir* (taste of *terroir*). So what does it all mean, and what is *terroir,* anyway?

Terroir is a French word that encompasses all of the nonhuman effects on a wine's character. Geology, subsoil, topsoil, drainage, exposure to the sun, climate, microclimate, slope, and so forth are all considered to be components of *terroir.* Using this definition, it is plain to see that any parcel of vines, whether in France, Chile, Australia, or the United States, has a *terroir.* The quality of the *terroir* and the characteristics it will impart on a wine will be different, but *terroirs* are everywhere. In fact, California winemakers, once the first to claim that all notions of *terroir* were bunk, have embraced the notion for their own wines. Over the course of the last decade a multitude of single-vineyard wines have come out of California, and the Bureau of Alcohol Tobacco and Firearms (BATF) has overseen the creation and enforcement of American Viticultural Areas (AVAs) since the early eighties. Australia, seemingly the last bastion of anti-*terroir* winemakers, is now the source of numerous single-vineyard wines.

The fact, and it is undoubtedly a fact, that *terroir* plays a role in a given wine's aromatic and flavor profile is a given. Pinot Noir vines grown in clay-based soils are different from those grown in solid limestone. However, what Burgundian vignerons and the pseudointelligentsia (so-called *terroir*-ists) will have you believe is that *terroir* is the most important factor governing a wine's quality and character. Simply put, this is nonsense.

Soil, exposition, and microclimate (*terroir*) most certainly impart an influence on a wine's character, but the men and women who select which rootstocks to plant and who make all the key viticultural, harvesting, vinification, and *élevage* decisions also impart a huge influence. Consider the following:

1. rootstock—Is it designed to produce prolific or small crop levels?

2. yeasts—Does the winemaker use the vineyard's and winery's wild yeasts, or are commercial yeasts employed? Every yeast, wild or commercial, will give a wine a different set of aromatics, flavor, and texture.

3. yields and vine age—High yields from perennial overcroppers result in diluted wine. Low yields, usually less than 3 tons per acre or 35–40 hectoliters per hectare, result in wines with much more concentration and personality. Additionally, young vines have a tendency to

overproduce, whereas old vines produce small berries and less wine. Crop thinning is often employed with younger vineyards to increase the level of concentration.

4. harvest philosophy—Is the fruit picked underripe to preserve more acidity, or fully ripe to emphasize the lushness and opulence of a given varietal?

5. vinification techniques and equipment—There are an amazing number of techniques that can change the wine's aromas and flavors. Moreover, equipment choice (different presses, destemmers, and the like) can have a profound influence on the final wine.

6. *élevage* (or the wine's upbringing)—Is the wine brought up in oak barrels, concrete vats, stainless steel, or large wood vats (which the French call *foudres*)? What is the percentage of new oak? All of these elements exert a strong influence on the wine's character. Additionally, transferring wine (racking) from one container to another has an immense impact on a wine's bouquet and flavor. Is the wine allowed to remain in long contact with its lees (believed to give the wine more aromatic complexity and fullness)? Or is it racked frequently for fear of picking up an undesirable lees smell?

7. fining and filtration—Even the most concentrated and profound wines that *terroir*-ists consider quintessential examples of the soil can be eviscerated and stripped of their personality and richness by excessive fining and filtering. Does the winemaker treat the wine with kid gloves, or is the winemaker a manufacturer/processor bent on sculpturing the wine?

8. bottling date—Does the winemaker bottle early to preserve as much fruit as possible, or does he or she bottle later to give the wine a more mellow, aged character? Undoubtedly the philosophy of when to bottle can radically alter the character of a wine.

9. cellar temperature and sanitary conditions—Some wine cellars are cold, and others are warm. Different wines emerge from cold cellars (development is slower, and the wines are less prone to oxidation) than from warm cellars (the maturation of aromas and flavors is more rapid, and the wines are quicker to oxidize). Additionally, are the wine cellars clean or dirty?

These are just a handful of factors that can have extraordinary impact on the style, quality, and personality of a wine. The choices that men and women make, even when they are unquestionably in pursuit of the highest quality, can contribute far more to a wine's character than the vineyard's *terroir*.

Terroir, as used by many of its proponents, is often a convenient excuse for upholding the status quo. If one accepts the fact that *terroir* is everything, and is essential to legitimize a wine, how should consumers evaluate the wines from Burgundy's most famous grand cru vineyard, Chambertin? This 32-acre vineyard boasts 23 different proprietors. But only a handful of them appear committed to producing an extraordinary wine. Everyone agrees this is a hallowed piece of ground, but only a few producers craft wines that merit the stratospheric reputation of this vineyard. Yet the Chambertins of three of these producers, Leroy, Ponsot, and Rousseau, are completely different in style. The Ponsot wine is the most elegant, supple, and round, Leroy's is the most tannic, backward, concentrated, and meaty, and Rousseau's is the darkest-colored, most dominated by new oak, and most modern in style, taste, and texture. Among the other 18 or 20 producers (not counting the various *négociant* offerings), what Burgundy wine enthusiasts are likely to encounter on retailers' shelves ranges from mediocre to appallingly thin and insipid. What wine speaks for the soil of Chambertin? Is it the wine of Leroy, the wine of Ponsot, the wine of Rousseau?

Arguments such as this can be made with virtually any significant Burgundy vineyard. Consider Corton-Charlemagne and the products of four of its most celebrated producers. The firm of Faiveley may own the most prized parcel atop this famous hill, and they make an elegant Corton-Charlemagne. Stylistically it is the antithesis of the superconcentrated, lavishly oaky, broadly flavored, alcoholic Corton-Charlemagne made by Louis Latour. Again, Domaine Leroy makes a backward, hard, tough Corton-Charlemagne that resembles a tannic red more than a white wine. Domaine Coche-Dury makes a wine with extraordinary mineral components, as well as remarkable richness, unctuousness, and opulence where the oak takes a backseat to the wine's fruit and texture. Which of these Corton-Charlemagnes has that notion of "somewhereness" that is raised by the *terroir*-ists to validate the quality of a vineyard?

For example, if in a blind tasting one serves the five premier cru Beaunes of Domaine Albert Morot and one of Louis Jadot's and another from Tollot-Beaut, the Jadot and Tollot-Beaut wines will stand out as being completely different from the Morots. This same exercise can be attempted with any appellation of Burgundy, and the results will be the same: *L'homme fait la différence.* However, for those looking for a fascinating tasting that truly delineates *terroir* differences, Bruno Clair has two neighboring Gevrey-Chambertins (Cazetiers and Clos St. Jacques) that were 1) planted the same year, 2) planted with the same rootstock, and 3) handled identically in the vineyard and winery. There are profound differences between the two wines: the Cazetiers is generally more polished, elegant, and crisp, whereas the Clos St. Jacques tends to be an in-your-face, powerful, explosive wine.

In conclusion, consumers should understand that a vineyard's *terroir* is a factor in a wine's character; however, the preeminent factor is the quality of the producer who crafted it. All too often the hyperventilation and hyperbole over *terroir* obscures the most important issue of all—identifying and discovering those producers who make wines worth drinking and savoring!

Are the wines of Burgundy as good today as they were 20 or 40 years ago? The wines of Burgundy are better today than they were in the past. First, there is no longer any evidence of adulterating red burgundies. The illegal practice of blending inferior, more alcoholic, and more deeply colored wine from southern France and northern Africa, a wide practice until the early seventies, appears to have been discontinued.

Second, many producers recognized the folly of planting clones of Pinot Noir (such as the Pinot Droit, which emphasized prolific yields rather than quality) and have begun, encouraged and supported by the oenology departments of the leading universities, to replant with lower-yielding Pinot Noir clones, such as the Pinot Fin called 115.

A third, and possibly even more important, quality factor has been the strong movement, started in the mid-eighties, to move away from the excessive fining and filtration of Pinot Noir and Chardonnay for fear of eviscerating the wine and removing its flavor. With the advent of modern technology, many growers learned how to bottle their wines as quickly as possible, aided immeasurably by German micropore filters and centrifuges that could clarify (and eviscerate) a wine with a push of a button. This eliminated the need for the cumbersome and labor-intensive racking. It also allowed the growers to be paid for their wines more quickly, since the wines could be rushed into the bottle. The results, all too often, were wonderfully brilliant, polished, attractive-looking wines that had little character or flavor. The excessive fining and filtration of wines continues to be a major problem in Burgundy. Yet more and more producers are assessing the need to fine on a vintage-by-vintage basis and have stopped filtering in response to increasing demands from some of America's finest burgundy importers for natural, unprocessed, and unmanipulated wines. Even Professor Feuillat, the head of the Department of Oenology at the University of Dijon, has recommended not filtering premiers crus and grands crus of Burgundy if the wine was otherwise biologically stable and clear. However, too many of those brokers and importers responsible for purchasing burgundy have encouraged their producers to excessively fine and filter, rather than to assume responsibility for shipping the wine in temperature-controlled containers and guaranteeing that the wine be distributed in a healthy condition. The growing number of American burgundy importers who not only insist that their wines be minimally fined and filtered, but who also ship their wines in temperature-controlled containers, is to be applauded. Joe Dressner of Louis/Dressner Selections in New York City; David Hinkle of North Berkeley Wines in Berkeley, California; Daniel Johnnes of Jeroboam Imports in New York City; Robert Kacher of Robert Kacher Selections in Washington, D.C.; Fran Kysela of Kysela Père et Fils in Winchester, Virginia; Kermit Lynch in Berkeley, California; Martine Saunier of Martine's Wines in San Rafael, California; Peter Weygandt of Weygandt-Metzler in Uniontown, Pennsylvania; and the transplanted American Peter Vezan, who has immersed himself in Burgundy in search of natural unmanipulated wines, are the most prominent importers of high-quality burgundy who do indeed care.

These factors, combined with lower yields, the use of higher-quality barrels, and improved sanitary conditions in the cellars, have resulted in more complete and aromatically complex as well as more flavorful wines. In addition, there is a new generation of highly motivated winemakers who are taking quality more seriously than ever. Such people as André Porcheret, Lalou Bize-Leroy, Dominique Laurent, Jean-Nicolas Méo, Christophe Roumier, Dominique Lafon, Jean-François Coche-Dury, Laurent Ponsot, Jacques Lardière, and Jean-Pierre de Smet are pushing themselves as well as their peers to produce the highest-quality burgundies possible. In addition, more and more producers and *négociants* are branding the corks used in the bottle with both the vintage and the vineyard name, packaging the wines in wooden cases, and using heavier and better bottles for their wines. In the last decade, the use of excessive fertilization and other chemical soil enhancers, as well as herbicides, fungicides, and pesticides has continued to be a dangerous practice, but some producers, such as Lalou-Bize at her Domaine Leroy, have decided to produce wines under the severe organic doctrine known as "biodynamic farming." Despite these positive trends, I do not want to suggest that all is well. There remain many underachievers, some with historically revered names, who are turning out wines that are thin, vapid, denuded, and pleasureless. There remain too many producers who present buyers and writers with barrel samples of wine that are not representative of what later appears in the bottle—misrepresentation at the minimum, fraud at the worst.

What are the significant differences in the wines of the Côte de Beaune and Côte de Nuits? The Côte d'Or, or Burgundy's Golden Slope, as it is sometimes called, is where the most profound wines from all of Burgundy are produced. However, there are significant differences between the two hillsides that make up the Côte d'Or. The Côte de Nuits, which starts just south of Dijon and runs south of Nuits-St.-Georges, produces essentially all red wine, while the Côte de Beaune, which starts just north of Beaune and extends to Santenay south of Beaune, produces both superlative red and white wines.

The red wines of the Côte de Nuits tend to be fuller and slightly more tannic and are characterized by a more earthy, black fruit (black currants, black cherries, and plums) and exotic character than those from the Côte de Beaune. Of course, these are generalizations, but the red wines from the Côte de Beaune tend to offer slightly less body, as well as less tannin (Pommards being a notable exception), and seem to be filled with aromas and flavors of red fruits (strawberries, cherries, and red currants). In addition, they seem less earthy, less exotic, and in most cases less ageworthy, although there are exceptions. One might also argue that a big, rich, generous, virile Pommard from the Côte de Beaune is a larger-scale, fuller wine than anything produced from Chambolle-Musigny in the Côte de Nuits.

While the Côte de Nuits produces only a handful of white wines, of which a few are superlative, the Côte de Beaune produces the world's greatest white wines from the Chardonnay grape. Whether it is the extraordinarily long-lived, rich, precisely defined white wines of Corton-Charlemagne; the nutty, luscious, lusty, easy-to-drink Meursaults; the elegant, steely Puligny-Montrachets; or the opulent, fleshy Chassagne-Montrachets, the Côte de Beaune is known for both elegant, stylish reds and extraordinary whites.

Does burgundy have to be handled or served differently from Bordeaux? The most striking thing to anyone who has eaten in a restaurant in Burgundy, or in the home of a Burgundy producer, is the revelation that rarely does a Burgundian decant a bottle of red burgundy, even an old one with a great deal of sediment. In contrast with Bordeaux, where even young vintages are routinely decanted, in Burgundy the practice is simply to pull the cork and serve the wine directly from the bottle. Why is there such a dramatic difference in wine service between these two regions? Is it based on the fact that Bordeaux actually improved with decantation and burgundy did not? Or are there other reasons, based more on history?

Some Burgundians have suggested that Burgundy, being principally a land of farmers and small growers, never tolerated the sort of haute service and rigidity experienced in Bordeaux, which for centuries was dominated by the British, long known for their emphasis on formality. This is apparent in the way of life of both these regions today. It is quite unusual to find anyone in the wine trade or any professional taster traveling around Bordeaux without a suit and tie. On the other hand, growers in Burgundy are never seen in a suit and tie. Casual dress is not only tolerated, it is accepted form when visiting the growers. Does this extend also to the table, where a decanter clearly seems to imply a more pompous sort of service? Certainly the large English glassworks built in the eighteenth and nineteenth centuries promoted the use of decanters for claret, which has always seemed to have a heavier sediment than the lighter, finer sediment often found in burgundies. Is this why it became routine to decant Bordeaux and not burgundy? Perhaps, but many growers in Burgundy have said that decanters were looked upon as an extravagance and were therefore to be eschewed.

Much of a great burgundy's character comes from its immense aromatic complexity. Bottle bouquet, particularly a highly nuanced one, can be very ephemeral and begin to break apart if exposed to air. Decanting a tight, young, austere Bordeaux can often make it seem more open after 5 or 10 minutes in a decanter. However, with only a handful of exceptions, excessive airing of burgundy by decanting often causes it to totally lose its bouquet and become flaccid and formless. No doubt there are exceptions. Many of the *négociants* who have old stocks claim that certain ancient wines require a good 1 to 2 hours of breathing as well as decantation prior to being consumed. However, experience suggests the contrary to be true.

White burgundies, on the other hand (particularly when young), improve significantly with 20 to 25 minutes of airing. Superrich Montrachets from producers such as Ramonet or the Domaine de la Romanée-Conti are best served at room temperature (cool, not cold) and decanted, as aeration of 20 to 25 minutes tends to enhance these particular wines.

Another major difference between burgundy and Bordeaux is the stemware in which burgundy is often served. In Bordeaux the standard tulip-shaped glass or the famous INAO glass is preferred. In Burgundy a balloon-shaped, cognac-style, fat, squat glass with a short stem can be found not only in the growers' cellars and *négociants'* offices, but even in Burgundy's restaurants. It is believed that these broader glasses tend to accentuate the intense, heady burgundian perfume. Some restaurants carry this to the extreme and offer their clients an oversize, 24-ounce glass. This glass is so large that the wine can actually get lost, and the bouquet disappears so quickly that the patron never has a chance to smell it. The small balloon-shaped, cognac-style glasses are excellent for burgundy, but the INAO and tulip-shaped glasses should be used only for Bordeaux. It is extremely important that red burgundy be served cooler than Bordeaux, preferably at 58 to 62 degrees Fahrenheit, no warmer. Red burgundy, given its relatively high alcohol content and perfume, is best served at a slightly chilled temperature, where the precision of its flavors and the purity and delineation of all the complex nuances in its bouquet can be deciphered. To prove the point, all you have to do is serve the same wine at 65 to 70 degrees and see how soupy, muddled, and alcoholic it tastes. Beaujolais should be served even colder, 53 to 56 degrees Fahrenheit, and good white burgundy at 58 to 60 degrees Fahrenheit. A great Montrachet or Meursault should be served slightly warmer, at 60 to 65 degrees Fahrenheit, or at room temperature, assuming it is not over 68 degrees. It is foolish to spend the money for a compelling, complex white burgundy and then overchill it, ushering its bouquet and flavors into hibernation.

In conclusion, there are two things to remember when serving and handling burgundy as opposed to Bordeaux. First, burgundy can be damaged severely by excessive aeration, whereas Bordeaux is rarely hurt, although it is debatable as to how much it improves with decanting. Second, burgundy must be served slightly chilled to be at its very best, but Bordeaux can be served at 64 to 66 degrees Fahrenheit, a good 4 to 6 degrees warmer than burgundy.

What is the optimum age at which to drink red and white burgundy? To try to predict when most burgundies will reach maturity is a particularly dangerous game to play, given the variation in winemaking techniques and philosophies employed by the growers and *négociants* in Burgundy.

However, the majority of the wines of Chablis should be consumed in their first 5 or 6 years of life, as only a handful of Chablis producers (such as Raveneau) make wines that last or improve after 6 years in the bottle.

In terms of the wines of Beaujolais and Mâconnais, while one can always point to a 10-year-old Beaujolais or an extraordinary Pouilly-Fuissé that lasted 10 or 20 years, these are indeed rare wines. Ninety-five percent of the wines of Beaujolais and Mâconnais should be drunk before they attain 3 years of age. Once past 3 years, the odds are stacked against the consumer.

As for the big red and white wines of Burgundy's Côte d'Or, while it is a matter of taste, if readers are buying burgundy and not drinking it within its first 10 years of life, I am convinced they will be disappointed by most bottles opened after that time. Even the most rugged, concentrated, intense red and white Burgundies seem to shed their tannins surprisingly fast and reach a plateau of maturity 5 to 6 years after the vintage. At that point they begin to lose their freshness, and decay sets in after 10 to 12 years. Obviously the vintage itself can make a great deal of difference. Those who purchased 1982 red burgundies should have consumed them well before they reached the age of 10. Those who purchased 1983s and felt that time would make these brawny, tannic, often rot-afflicted, controversial wines better are going to be disappointed. The once sensational 1985 red burgundies were fully mature and excellent wines in 1995, but most are losing their fruit and pleasurable qualities over the last few years. A good rule of thumb is to drink your red burgundy within 10 years of the vintage, realizing there are certain vintages, such as 1996, 1995, 1993, 1990, 1988, 1978, 1976, and 1972 for red burgundy, that may, for a handful of the finest examples, take more than 10 years to reach full maturity. But these are the exceptions, even for wines from those vintages.

The window of opportunity for drinking red and white burgundy is also one of the smallest of any great wine in the world. One of the great attributes of Bordeaux, and a reason, no doubt, why it commands the prices and international following it does, is the broad span of years over which it can be drunk. When a bottle of Bordeaux reaches its plateau of maturity, it can frequently remain there for 10, 15, sometimes 20 years before it begins a very slow process of decline. Burgundies can reach their plateau of maturity in 5 years and unceremoniously begin to fade after another 6 or 7 months. The optimum drinking window for most red and white burgundies is small and closes quickly. This is not an unusual phenomenon. Collectors who have cellared and drunk burgundy relate similar experiences, many of them sad. While Bordeaux has a broad, generous period over which it can be consumed, connoisseurs of burgundy should pay fastidious attention to the development of their wines or suffer the unsavory consequences. Most burgundies can literally peak and begin their decline, which is often frightfully rapid, within 6 to 9 months after having attained full maturity. This is distressing, but it is a reality of buying and cellaring both red and white burgundies. Put another way, a reliable tasting evaluation of a top Bordeaux can be accurate for a 10- to 15-year period. A tasting note on a top burgundy may have meaning and reliability for only 6 months or less. Consequently readers should attach significantly less importance to burgundy tasting notes and devote more attention to the producer, the quality of his or her wines, and the producer's finest vineyards or offerings.

What should a great red burgundy taste like when fully mature? It is easier to agree upon those key factors that frequently result in great red burgundy. In order of importance they are 1) the soil and exposition of the vineyard; 2) low yields; 3) physiologically ripe grapes, and 4) superior winemaking, which includes exacting sanitary conditions as well as vigilant concern over the wine's upbringing, with minimal intervention save for the occasional racking (transfer of the wine from one barrel to another barrel). All the greatest red burgundies, at the very least, are the product of these factors. But red burgundy at its most sublime is the most difficult wine to describe, as it matures quickly, goes through numerous stages of evolution, and can fade at an alarming pace. Truly profound red burgundy is rarely encountered, because the Pinot Noir grape possesses an unfathomable mystery that yields no telltale, discernible signature such as Cabernet Sauvignon or Chardonnay.

The greatest examples of mature red burgundy all share the following characteristics. First, they have penetrating and compelling bouquets that exhibit a decadent, even raunchy, almost decaying or aged-beef sort of smell, combined with an intense and exhilarating aroma of Asian spices and dried herbs. Second, they have layers and layers of black and red fruits that virtually explode on the palate with a cascade of increasingly expanding textural sensations. They are relatively high in alcohol, possess adequate acidity rather than tannin for structural delineation, and texturally finish with a lusciousness and a silky quality that lasts several minutes. Drinking the finest mature red burgundies is an experience akin to eating candy because of the extraordinary sweetness they convey.

What constitutes the aromatic and flavor profiles of great white burgundy? Everyone who drinks wine no doubt has a strong idea of what the finest Chardonnays, particularly those from the New World, offer in terms of smell and taste. But how many of you have drunk truly profound white burgundy? Certainly the frightfully high prices of $100–$600 a bottle for grands crus limits their market to less than 1% of the wine-consuming public. Actually, comparing a great white burgundy with a New World Chardonnay is almost unfair. The preponderant number of New World Chardonnays must be consumed within 2 to 3 years after the vintage. As enjoyable as they are, they often have all their components playing against one another rather than in complete harmony. Perhaps because most New World Chardonnays must be acidified, when one tastes them, the overall perception is one of separate but equal building blocks of acid, structure, fruit, and wood. On the other hand, great white burgundies incorporate all these components, resulting in a blend where no one element has the upper hand. The greatest examples combine an extraordinary perfume of apples, honey, vanilla, wet stones, and sometimes oranges, lemons, and tangerines with flavors that range from a smoky, buttery, and nutty taste to occasionally peaches and, in the more opulent, ripe examples, to tropical fruits such as bananas, mangoes, and pineapples. Of course, what makes them so compelling is their precision and balance, with all of these marvelously complex components unfolding in the glass and on the palate. It should also be noted that some white burgundies have the added advantage that in certain vintages a small percentage can last for as many as 10 to 20 years in the bottle, improving and developing more nuances as they age; but the number of them that truly improve beyond 7 to 8 years is minuscule. The greatest producers of white burgundy, such as Niellon, Colin-Deléger, Bernard Morey, and Ramonet in Chassagne-Montrachet; Sauzet and Leflaive in Puligny-Montrachet; Jean-Marie Raveneau and René et Vincent Dauvissat in Chablis; Guffens-Heynen and Daniel Barraud in the Mâconnais; the fabled Domaine de la Romanée-Conti Montrachet; the exquisite Corton-Charlemagnes of the Maison Louis Latour and Louis Jadot in Corton-Charlemagne; and the unfiltered, compelling Meursaults of Jean-Francalois Coche-Dury and Comte Lafon, all seem to share these characteristics in various proportions, depending on the quality of the vintage.

Is burgundy as good a candidate for cellaring and aging as a top Bordeaux, Hermitage, California Cabernet, or Italian Barolo or Barbaresco? The answer to this question is a resounding "No." While some old-timers lament that burgundy is not made the way it once was, they seem to have forgotten that most burgundy has never aged extremely well. There is no doubt that one can point to a handful of rare examples of truly exciting burgundies that lasted two, three, sometimes four or more decades, retaining their fruit and developing greater nuances and subtleties, but those cases are a distinct minority. This applies equally to both red and white burgundy.

It is an uncontestable truism that anyone who advises readers to lay away most burgundies for a decade clearly does not have the consumer's best interests at heart. To reiterate, most modern-day red burgundies, even from the finest vintages (such as 1990), should be consumed within 10 to 12 years of the vintage. This rule is even more restrictive for white burgundies. The window of drinking opportunity is normally within 7 to 8 years of the vintage for white burgundies. The reasons for this are simple. Red burgundies, made from the Pinot Noir grape, simply do not have the tannin level or extraction of flavor to sustain them for more than 10 to 12 years. Additionally, the Pinot Noir grape's most distinct pleasures are its bouquet and its sweet, ripe, velvety fruitiness, both of which tend to be the first characteristics of a Pinot Noir to crack up and dissipate. Even the finest red burgundies, while they may last two or more decades, are generally more enjoyable to drink in their first decade of life. Even the rare, long-lived, powerful vintages such as 1959, 1964, 1969, and 1978 were best drunk during their first 10 to 15 years of life, although the finest examples of the top producers can still be wondrous today. Anyone who loves great red burgundy should buy only enough to drink within the immediate future. Red burgundy's suspect aging capabilities have always been a problem and are not due to any modern-day winemaking techniques, although high yields and addictive reliance on chemical fertilizers as well as fungicides, herbicides, and pesticides have further exacerbated red burgundy's ability to age gracefully beyond a decade.

If you are buying burgundy for drinking in 15 or 20 years, you should be restricting your purchases to the wines from no more than a half dozen or so producers. In particular, Domaine Leroy, Domaine du Comte de Vogüé, and small producers such as Comte Lafon still produce wines that are compelling and sumptuous at 10 years of age and, in some cases, 20 years. Even burgundy's most expensive and frequently greatest wines, those of such superlative producers as the Domaine de la Romanée-Conti, Domaine Méo-Camuzet, Domaine Dujac, and Philippe Leclerc, are usually at their best between 8 and 15 years of age, rarely improving or holding well beyond that.

Are the best wines of burgundy viable candidates for investment? While investment in wine has become more popular given the luxury prices demanded for the top châteaux of Bordeaux, burgundy has never represented as good an investment as Bordeaux. The practice of investing in wine for financial profit is abhorrent. It is done regularly, at least with the first-growths and supersecond châteaux of Bordeaux, as well as a handful of the limited-production Pomerols and St.-Émilions. But there is a great deal of difference between buying Bordeaux and buying burgundy. For starters, in the spring following the vintage, Bordeaux is offered as a wine future at what is called an "opening" or entry-level price. If the vintage is widely acclaimed and of great quality, the price is propelled in only one direction—upward. Burgundy is not sold as a wine future, although specialist merchants regrettably offer to sell burgundy to their customers on a "prearrival" basis. This often requires the consumer to put up considerable monetary sums 6 to 12 months prior to arrival. In essence, consumers are financing the merchant's burgundy purchases. Today, most burgundies from current vintages sell at prices higher than do the older vintages of the same wine. A review of any of the auction results from Christie's, Sotheby's, the Chicago Wine Company, or the numerous New York and California auctions illustrates this. Some of the greatest burgundies from vintages from the forties, fifties, and sixties sell at prices that are significantly less than those from 1990, 1993, and 1995, three of the most recent highly regarded vintages. The reasons for this are 1) consumers lack confidence in burgundy; 2) smart buyers recognize burgundy's fragility and dubious aging potential; and 3) unlike the situation with Bordeaux, due to scarcity there is virtually no information available to potential auction buyers on the evolution of older burgundies. Rarely do these same wines appreciate in value after release. In fact, in most cases their value collapses. There are exceptions, such as some limited-production Montrachets and Romanée-Conti and La Tâche of the Domaine de la Romanée-Conti, as well as Comte de Vogüé's Musigny. All in all, burgundy is a notoriously bad investment.

Why are the best burgundies so expensive? The pricing of burgundy can be explained entirely by the rules of supply and demand. Historically, burgundy has had the unique and enviable situation of having far more admirers and prospective purchasers than available wine. This is particularly true at the premier and grand cru levels, which are usually the only burgundies that merit purchasing, given the feeble qualities of most village and generic burgundies. In addition, great burgundy alone among the finest French wines has no competition from within the borders of France or in most of the wine world. The problem at the premier cru and grand cru levels is exacerbated by the truly microscopic quantities of wine offered by the best producers. Some specific case production figures demonstrate the point dramatically. For example, the most expensive red burgundies are those of the Domaine de la Romanée-Conti. In an abundant year, the production of their Romanée-Conti ranges from 300 to 500 cases. Their exclusively owned *monopole* vineyard, La Tâche, produces between 900 and 1,800 cases a year. One of Burgundy's most sought-after winemakers, Claude Dugat, usually produces, in a prolific year, 50 cases of Griotte-Chambertin and 100 cases of Charmes-Chambertin. Lalou Bize-Leroy, whose Domaine Leroy in Vosne-Romanée since 1988 has consistently produced Burgundy's most sublime and ageworthy wines, usually makes only 25 cases of her two grands crus of Musigny and Chambertin. The Domaine Roumier is one of the most revered names in Burgundy, and their Bonnes Mares is considered to be a heroic wine, but only 100 cases were made in the plentiful vintage of 1988. Everyone who loves great burgundy considers Hubert Lignier's Clos de la Roche to be one of the top dozen or so red wines made in Burgundy, yet he rarely makes more than 300 cases.

By no means are these isolated examples. Louis Jadot's production of the excellent Beaune-Clos des Ursules is considered massive by burgundy standards, but only 1,100 cases are made in a hugely abundant year, about one-fourth the amount of a very limited-production Pomerol such as Pétrus! Jadot sells his wines to every civilized country in the world. How much of this lovely wine will make it to the shelves of the finest wine merchants in Omaha, Nebraska, or Edinburgh, Scotland? Perhaps a case or two? In Bordeaux a production of 1,000 cases is considered minuscule. A favorite Bordeaux of wine consumers is the muscular and flavorful Lynch-Bages, and a popular California Cabernet Sauvignon is Robert Mondavi's exquisite Reserve. There are 35,000–45,000 cases of Lynch-Bages and 15,000–20,000 cases of Mondavi Reserve Cabernet produced!

This frustrating situation (at least for buyers) is similar for white burgundies. Usually, no more than 50 cases are made of J. F. Coche-Dury's ethereal Corton-Charlemagne. Louis Jadot, who makes sublime Corton-Charlemagne, can, in an abundant year, produce 1,200 cases, but that must be spread around not only to the restaurants of France, but to Jadot's clients throughout the world. Even worse is the situation with the Domaine Ramonet's celestial Montrachet. A whopping 50 cases are made in an abundant vintage!

Most of the finest grand cru and premier cru red and white burgundies could be sold exclusively to a few of Europe's top restaurants, should the producers so desire. Of course, that is not their intention, and they try to ensure an equitable distribution to their suppliers throughout the world. But it is because of these tiny quantities that the prices for burgundy are so astronomically high. As more and more wine connoisseurs from a growing number of countries demand fine wine, the pressure on suppliers will only create more and more exorbitant prices for the new vintages.

Why are the finest burgundies so difficult to find in the American marketplace? The answer again relates to the tiny quantities of top wines that are produced. America is an extremely important purchaser of top-quality burgundies, both red and white. In fact, consumers in other countries continually complain that the United States gets more than its fair share of Burgundy's finest wines. So how does the system work?

Each estate in Burgundy allocates wines to the importers that represent them around the world. The U.S. importers then allocate small quantities to the ten or twelve best wine mar-

kets in the United States. Therefore a top merchant may end up with only a case or two of
Leflaive Chevalier-Montrachet and six bottles of a Domaine de la Romanée-Conti Montrachet. However, since demand in the United States for the finest wines from the best vintages
is huge, secondary channels (known as the "gray market") provide additional supply by selling to U.S. merchants allocations meant for other nation's markets. Nevertheless, overall production of the most highly sought after burgundies is so small that supply will never match
demand. For example, Robert Kacher, Claude Dugat's official U.S. importer, is allocated 10
cases of Griotte-Chambertin per year. The gray market may supply the U.S. market with an
additional 3 or 4 cases, certainly not enough to satisfy demand. These are the realities when
dealing with burgundy and seemingly only add to its mystique.

Are estate-bottled burgundies superior to those from the négociants? *Négociant* is the
French word for a wine broker. *Négociants* include firms that do not own any vineyards. They
rely totally on purchases of finished wines from growers, which they then sell under their
own names. *Négociants* can also be firms that own vineyards. Several—for example, Faiveley
and Bouchard Père et Fils—are among the largest vineyard owners in Burgundy. *Négociants*
have long controlled the burgundy wine business, as the movement of growers to estate-
bottle their wines has been a relatively recent phenomenon. The fact that many of the most
insipid and vapid burgundies have consistently been produced by several of the largest and
most prominent *négociants* has been the principal reason for the negative image many consumers have of a burgundy *négociant*. *Négociants* have also been maligned by growers and
importers, who argue that the most authentic and individualistic burgundies can emerge only
from individual domaines. The better *négociants* have responded in a positive manner to this
criticism. Since the mid-1980s Louis Jadot has been a reference point for high-quality *négociant* wine, as has Louis Latour for their white wines. Other firms, particularly Bouchard
Père et Fils, have significantly upgraded the quality of their wines.

The trend of estate-bottled burgundies, started by the late founder of the *Revue du Vin de
France*, Raymond Baudoin, and subsequently encouraged by the late Frank Schoonmaker,
an American importer, has still not reached its zenith. The *négociants*, faced with losing
many of their sources for wine thanks to growers who decided to become freelancers and to
estate-bottle their own production, not only tried to sign up certain growers to exclusivity
contracts, but recognized the need to improve the quality of their wines.

There are, however, *négociants* that continue to lag behind in quality. Among the most notable of these is the huge firm of Jean-Claude Boisset, the firms of Patriarche, Albert Bichot,
and the highly promoted wines of La Reine-Pédauque. Today you are likely to get, not a bad
wine from these firms, but rather a sound, commercial one with no soul or personality. Admittedly there must be a vast market for such wines, as these firms are among the wealthiest
and most successful in France.

One argument frequently offered is that the wines of the *négociants* have the same taste.
To me that seems irrelevant. The top *négociants*, while they respect the individual vineyard's
terroir (Jadot's winemaker, Jacques Lardière, is one of Burgundy's most fervent *terroir*-ists),
obviously employ the same philosophy in making all of their wines and try to keep the identity of the vineyard and appellation unto itself. The wines of Louis Jadot or Bourée all share
a similar signature, but then so do the wines of domaines such as Roumier, Ponsot, Roty,
Claude Dugat, or the Domaine de la Romanée-Conti. At the most meticulously run estate-
bottled operation the same philosophy is employed for making each wine. The wines from
the well-known domaine of Armand Rousseau in Gevrey-Chambertin will have a certain
similarity because the winemaking, the *élevage*, and the overall philosophy is precisely the
same for each wine. Nevertheless, Rousseau's Chambertin will taste different from a Gevrey-
Chambertin Clos St.-Jacques or Clos de la Roche from neighboring Morey-St.-Denis. The
signature is just as prominent in a grower's cellar as it is in a *négociant*'s.

How is great red burgundy made? Most burgundy growers will tell you only so much, but the three most important components that contribute to great red burgundy are 1) the excellence of the vineyard; 2) low yields; and 3) the competence of the winemaker. If all three of these exist, the end result is likely to be quite compelling and exciting.

How all the different growers and *négociants* vinify and handle their wines differs far more in Burgundy than it does in Bordeaux. In Bordeaux, the basic winemaking and upbringing of the wine are essentially the same at all the major properties. In Burgundy, there are many different ways of making top-class red wine.

One of the most popular techniques today at the top level is partial or total destemming of the grapes. Destemming is the process whereby the stems are removed from the grape bunches. Many producers feel the stems impart a vegetal flavor to the wine, decrease the color, and add astringent tannin. For these reasons many producers routinely destem 100% of the grapes. Other producers believe a certain percentage of stems adds structure and more character to the wine. Most of the finest producers tend to use between 50% and 100% new oak for their top premiers and grands crus. Many burgundies taste excessively woody, but new oak is ideal for Pinot Noir and is the most sanitary vessel in which to make wine. However, high yields combined with the lavish use of new oak is a formula for thin, woody wines. As the controversial Belgian Jean-Marie Guffens (of Domaine Guffens-Heynen and Maison Verget fame) says, "No wine is overoaked, merely underwined."

Today many Burgundy producers follow the methods of Burgundy's most influential winemaker, the recently retired Henri Jayer, who employs a 5- to 7-day cold prefermentation maceration of his Pinot Noir. Proponents of this practice believe this "cold soak" adds color, richness, aromatics, and fat to a wine.

But even these talented winemakers disagree on certain principles. Henri Jayer, the Domaine de la Romanée-Conti, and the Domaine Ponsot believe that 90% of the wine is made in the vineyard and that "winemaking" in the cellars can destroy, but cannot contribute more than another 10% to, the final quality. They feel the search for high quality obligates the grower to prune back the vineyard, if conditions warrant, by cutting off grape bunches—in essence doing a "green harvest" in summer to reduce yields. To these producers high yields are the undoing of the wine, regardless of how talented the winemaker is or what wizardry can be accomplished within the cellar. On the other hand, some producers, most notably Jacques Seysses, argue that large yields are acceptable and that concentration can still be obtained by the process of bleeding off the excess juice (which the French call *saigner*). This technique increases the proportion of skins and stems to the remaining juice and therefore, according to its proponents, increases the concentration. Henri Jayer claims this is nothing but a gimmick whose shortcomings become apparent after the wine spends 5 or 6 years in the bottle.

Another area where these irrefutably great winemakers disagree concerns the percentage of new oak used. Henri Jayer believes in 100% new oak, the firms of Bourée and Jadot significantly less, and the Domaine Ponsot abhors it altogether. However, it should be noted that the trend for premiers and grands crus in Burgundy is toward increased percentages of new oak. Great wines have emerged more from an elevated use of new oak than from the absence of it.

Another school of winemaking embraces an extremely long period of cold maceration (with loads of sulfur) prior to fermentation, a technique that lasts well beyond the 5 to 7 days employed by the Jayer-ists. It is practiced by a group of winemakers who have employed controversial Nuits-St.-Georges oenologist Guy Accad to look after their winemaking. This practice has been condemned by many in Burgundy for producing wines that have more in common with Côte Rôtie than Pinot Noir. Accad does not believe in destemming and allows the grape bunches to macerate chilled for 10 days or more before any fermentation starts. To his credit, he does not believe in rushing anything into the bottle. He counsels his clients against fining and filtration and advises them not to bottle their wines until they are fully ready. Former clients, such as Jacky Confuron in Vosne-Romanée, Etienne Grivot in Vosne-Romanée, Georges Chicotot in Nuits-St.-Georges, Daniel Senard in Aloxe-Corton, and the Château de la Clos Vougeot in Vougeot, to name a few of the most prominent, all seem to produce intensely colored, rich, aromatic, concentrated wines that are impressive young. In recent tastings, Domaine Jean Grivot's (an Accad-ist at the time) grand crus from the 1989 vintage were significantly more evolved than would be expected for wines of their stature. However, conclusions cannot, and should not, be drawn from one estate's wines in one vintage. More comprehensive comparative tastings will have to be conducted in the years to come to determine the ageworthiness of the Accad methods.

The other schools of thought for making top-quality red burgundy basically eschew any of the cold maceration prior to fermentation. They believe in crushing and fermenting at warm temperatures in order to extract color, body, and tannin via a more traditional method. They disagree with those who argue that great aromatic Pinot Noir can be obtained only by a cool fermentation or cold maceration prior to fermentation. Some of the best examples of this school of thought include the Maison Louis Jadot, whose red wines are macerated for a long time, fermented at extremely high temperatures, yet still retain their aromatic purity and last and last in the bottle. Philippe Leclerc, the Domaine Ponsot, and the Domaine Georges Mugneret are three other top producers who think cold maceration prior to fermentation is nonsense.

Of course, the big question is, what does the Domaine Leroy do? Unquestionably these are the most consistently brilliant, as well as among the most expensive, wines of Burgundy. Leroy's yields are half, sometimes one-third, that of the other domaines. That in itself is probably the reason why these wines attain such great concentration. The Domaine Leroy averages $1^1/_3$–$1^2/_3$ tons per acre, as opposed to the $2^2/_3$–$3^1/_3$ obtained elsewhere. There is usually no destemming. A cold maceration of 5 to 6 days prior to fermentation, a long fermentation, and maceration using only wild yeasts are employed. The wines spend 15 to 18 months in 100% new Allier oak casks and are bottled unfined and unfiltered.

As all of this indicates, there are a multitude of methods employed that can result in great wines. All of the producers I have mentioned are capable of producing some of the finest wines in Burgundy. Those people who tend to turn out neutral, vapid, mediocre red burgundies seem also to possess the following in common: 1) their crop sizes are excessive; 2) they bottle either too early or too late; 3) they are processors and manufacturers of wine, practicing traumatic fining and filtering; and 4) they take no risks, as their goal is complete stability and/or sterility of the product. As a result, most of the wines are pale imitations of what red burgundy should be.

How is great white burgundy made? As with red burgundy, there are myriad decisions a winemaker must make when crafting a white burgundy. Reasonably low Chardonnay yields, while important, are not as vital as with Pinot Noir. Many of the best estates of the Côte de Beaune, producers of some of the most sought-after white burgundies, are known to harvest relatively high yields and yet are able to craft superlative wines. The talented Henri Boillot refuses to purchase Pinot Noir fruit for his Volnay-based *négociant* business because he knows that its quality was determined in the vineyard. With Chardonnay, he says, "the quality is mostly produced in the cellars."

Compared with red burgundy producers, this region's white wine vignerons are extremely tight-lipped concerning pressing, vinification, and *élevage* techniques. Trying to obtain specific information from Michel Niellon or Jean-François Coche generally results in a shrugging of the shoulders, a smile, and a "the wines make themselves" statement.

There are a multitude of winemaking philosophies concerning white burgundies. Producers such as François Jobard in Meursault never decants his must off its gross lees (*débourbage*), has never stirred the fine lees (*bâtonnage*) while the wines were in the barrel, and allows the *élevage* to last up to 18 months. Conversely, his nephew Rémi Jobard (who recently took over the estate from his father, Charles) generally performs a *débourbage*, employs regular *bâtonnages,* and bottles the wines within 11 months. Most Côte de Beaune winemakers ferment their whites in oak barrels, yet Colin-Deléger (a top Chassagne-Montrachet producer) begins the process in stainless-steel tanks. At Puligny-Montrachet's famed Domaine Leflaive, the reverse is true. Leflaive ferments its whites and begins their *élevage* in barrel, then transfers them to large stainless-steel vats for an extended upbringing period.

Countless conversations with top white burgundy producers has shown, however, that the most important factors in crafting a superlative wine are 1) harvesting late in order to obtain full physiological ripeness (rot is significantly less of a concern with Chardonnay than with Pinot Noir); 2) sorting out unripe or unhealthy grapes; 3) a long and soft pressing; 4) quality clean barrels; 5) as few rackings as possible; 6) allowing the wines to "nourish" themselves on their fine lees; and 7) not stripping the wine of its richness and fruit by excessive fining and filtration prior to bottling. Furthermore, most high-quality white burgundies at the premier cru and grand cru levels see about 50% to 100% new oak casks, usually Allier, but it can be a blend of different oaks.

Will the prices for burgundy wines ever moderate? Unfortunately, the answer to this question is "No." There is always the chance that an international financial crisis could precipitate a worldwide depression that would affect a luxury item such as fine wine. For example, prices for 1991 and 1992 red burgundies dropped by 35% to 50% compared with the prices of 1989s and 1990s. But prices for 1993s, 1994s, 1995s, 1996s, and 1997s soared ever higher. Given growing international demand for the top-quality wines of this region, the general trend for prices in burgundy can only be upward. While the huge quantities of wines produced in Mâconnais, Beaujolais, and Chablis may show more variation in prices, the economic prognosis for the premiers and grands crus from Burgundy's famed Côte d'Or is for frighteningly higher prices. When one considers the fact that there are only 30 grands crus, producing barely 1% of the total wine of Burgundy, the unmistakable message conveyed is that prices can only escalate. Currently there are more purchasers of fine wine throughout the world than ever before.

The wine market has become even more competitive in the last 5 years with the aggressive purchasing by the Japanese, Swiss, Germans, and Pacific Rim countries, especially Singapore. Japan, a relative newcomer to the world of fine wine, in 1998 overtook Switzerland as the world's largest consumer of red burgundies in both volume *and* value. In 1998's first quarter Japan increased its purchases of red and white burgundies by 100% (they have tripled their share of the market since early 1997).

The same can be said for the awakening interest in great wines in France itself. While France has traditionally consumed oceans of wine, it has never developed much of an appreciation for its own great wines. Increasing interest from Switzerland, Germany, Belgium, Sweden, and Denmark, all with strong economies and a thirst for fine wine, has further strained the supplies of good burgundies. The traditional markets of England and America will have to adjust to higher and higher prices or be isolated from the burgundy marketplace. Eastern Europe, now that the walls of communism have been torn down, offers an entirely new market. Its countries have rich traditions that frequently involve the consumption of fine wine. For nearly four decades their hedonistic desires have been suppressed. When their economies strengthen and a middle class arises, what additional pressures will they put on the available supplies of red and white burgundy?

As for the generic appellation wines, they certainly will not appreciate to the extent that the premiers crus and grands crus will. However, burgundy, much like Bordeaux, has become somewhat of a caste system for wine producers. The greatest wines from the greatest producers are able to fetch astronomical prices because there is no shortage of wealthy clients prepared to buy them. While the prices exclude most consumers and students of wine, it does encourage them to look for values in the more obscure appellations, such as Santenay, Savigny-Lès-Beaune, and, of course, the up-and-coming appellations of the Côte Chalonnaise. While none of these wines will ever approach the magnificent qualities of a grand cru such as Musigny or Chambertin Clos de Bèze, they still have enough burgundy character to satisfy a great majority of even the most demanding palates.

The situation with the great white burgundies is even more exacerbated by excessive demand. When one considers that such great grands crus as Montrachet and Chevalier-Montrachet consist of only 19.7 and 18.1 acres, respectively, it seems inevitable that prices will double or even triple over the next decade.

Today's connoisseur of burgundy must be prepared either to pay a high price or to search elsewhere for great Pinot Noir and Chardonnay.

The growth of estate-bottled burgundies is a relatively recent phenomenon. Who was responsible for that development? Raymond Baudoin was the man responsible for encouraging some of Burgundy's best small growers, such as Ponsot in Morey-St.-Denis, Rousseau in Gevrey-Chambertin, Roumier in Chambolle-Musigny, Gouges in Nuits-St.-Georges, and d'Angerville in Volnay, to estate-bottle their wines. In the 1920s Baudoin founded *Revue du Vin de France,* which to this day remains the leading French wine publication. Baudoin had lamented the fact that the great burgundies of the Côte d'Or would be sold to *négociants* and then would lose their individual identities by being blended with a large quantity of inferior wine. He began to purchase barrels of wine directly from the growers, who would estate-bottle them for him. In turn, he would sell them privately to clients and restaurants in Paris. Baudoin, who died in 1953, is the father of the estate-bottling movement in Burgundy.

However, it was Frank Schoonmaker, the American importer, who deserves the recognition for being the first to see the potential and quality of these estate-bottled burgundies and to expose the American market to them. Frank Schoonmaker died in 1976, and most wine neophytes, unfortunately, are probably not familiar with the significance of his contributions. For these wine consumers, *The Frank Schoonmaker Encyclopedia of Wine,* a classic that was first published in 1964 and most recently updated by the well-known New York wine writer Alex Bespaloff, in 1988, is highly recommended. This encyclopedia is only one of the legacies Frank Schoonmaker left wine enthusiasts. Schoonmaker, a Renaissance man born in the town of Spearfish, South Dakota, came from a family that stressed education and enlightenment. His father taught at Columbia University, and his mother was a leading feminist of her time. After graduating from college in the mid-1920s, Schoonmaker went to Europe. There he had his first exposure to wine. In 1927, at age twenty-one, he authored the book *Through Europe on $2 a Day.* Although it appeared just before the Depression, the book was a success and led to Schoonmaker's collaboration with Lowell Thomas on two additional travel books: *Come with Me through France* and *Come with Me through Spain.* These in turn resulted in several magazine articles about wine in *The New Yorker,* commissioned by shrewd editors who realized the potential for interest in wine when Prohibition ended in 1933.

In 1935 Schoonmaker and some other investors formed the importing firm of Bates and Schoonmaker. At the same time, men like Frederick Wildman and Julian Street were starting merchant businesses dedicated to the sale of fine French wine and estate-bottled burgundies. The Marquis d'Angerville shared with Robert Parker a copy of his first wine order from Bates and Schoonmaker. It came on April 30, 1935, when Schoonmaker ordered 10 cases of Volnay Clos des Fremiets 1929, costing a total of 1,680 francs. Other producers, such as the Tollots in Chorey-Les-Beaune as well as Rousseau and Gouges, remember selling wine directly to Schoonmaker's firm in New York City at about the same time.

Schoonmaker's heir apparents include Robert Haas, who founded one of America's leading companies dedicated to estate-bottled burgundies, and the late Alexis Lichine, who in the 1960s developed the idea of purchasing wine directly from the growers, commercializing it under his own name but also indicating the name of the grower on the label.

These gentlemen were the cornerstones of the estate-bottled burgundy movement. The Schoonmaker selections are represented today by Château and Estate. Frederick Wildman and Company is still an import firm in New York City, as is Vineyard Brands, the company started by Robert Haas in Chester, Vermont. Alexis Lichine sold his wine company to the English firm of Bass-Charrington and concentrated on his beloved Château Prieuré-Lichine, which he purchased in 1951.

As more and more growers begin to domaine-bottle their wines, the recognition and promotion of estate-bottled burgundies has never been stronger. In addition to Château and Estate, Frederick Wildman and Company, and Robert Haas, the American importers of estate-bottled burgundy include the idiosyncratic, outspoken Berkeley importer Kermit Lynch; Robert Kacher Selections in Washington, D.C.; Martine Saunier Selections in San Rafael, California; Kysela Père et Fils in Winchester, Virginia; North Berkeley Wines in Berkeley, California; Louis/Dressner Selections in New York City; Weygandt-Metzler in Uniontown, Pennsylvania; Kobrand, Inc., a leading importer that also owns the excellent house of Louis Jadot; and a handful of American and French specialists living and working in France. These include the Paris-based Peter Vezan, a transplanted American who is one of the world's most knowledgeable people on the subject of burgundy. Patrick Lesec is another broker in search of handcrafted great burgundies. He has ferreted out many top growers, whose wine he sells to importers in America, the United Kingdom, and Europe.

Red Burgundy

THE INSIDE SCOOP

A CONSUMER'S PROFILE OF THE BEST-KNOWN BURGUNDY PRODUCERS

DOMAINE BERTRAND AMBROISE (PRÉMEAUX-PRISSEY)* * * */* * * * *
Ambroise, a youthful, robust, exuberant individual, makes wines similar to his own physical profile. These are powerful, muscular, full-bodied, highly concentrated burgundies. They often require aging, as they are among the more backward, concentrated, tannic reds being made in Nuits-St.-Georges. Ambroise has been successful in so-called difficult years like 1991, 1992, and 1994.
Best Wines: Clos Vougeot, Corton Le Rognet, Nuits-St.-Georges Rue du Chaux, Nuits-St.-Georges Les Vaucrains

PIERRE AMIOT ET FILS (MOREY-ST.-DENIS)* * * †
This estate has significantly improved the quality of its wines recently. Pierre Amiot is retiring, and his sons, Jean-Louis and Didier, have apparently made the commitment to lower the yields and practice noninterventionist winemaking. They are working closely with Paris-based broker Patrick Lesec, whose cuvées are neither fined nor filtered and are bottled by hand.
Best Wines: Clos de la Roche, Gevrey-Chambertin Les Combottes

DOMAINE MARQUIS D'ANGERVILLE (VOLNAY)* * * * *
Jacques, Marquis d'Angerville, is certainly one of the finest producers of the Côte de Beaune. His wines, when properly shipped and stored, have proven to be extremely well

---

†This estate's ranking is based on tastings of the Lesec cuvées, available throughout the world (however, there are non-Lesec bottlings as well that have not been tasted).

structured, rich, crammed with fruit, and quite ageworthy. While most 1989 burgundies in my cellar are at their peak of maturity or fading fast, d'Angerville's are still youthful and vibrant. In top vintages these are wines that can be cellared for 12–15 years.

Best Wines: Volnay Les Caillerets, Volnay Champans, Volnay Clos des Ducs, Volnay Taillepieds

DOMAINE ARLAUD PÈRE ET FILS (NUITS-ST.-GEORGES)* * */* * * * †

Arlaud crafts seductive, hedonistic, supple, and spicy wines crammed with luscious fruit. While they are not immensely complex or intellectually gratifying, they are some of the most delicious produced in Burgundy. Arlaud's top wines are meant to be drunk within the first 10 years after their release and his lesser appellations within the first 5 years.

Best Wines: Charmes-Chambertin Réserve, Clos de la Roche Réserve, Clos St.-Denis Réserve, Morey-St.-Denis Les Ruchots Réserve

DOMAINE DE L'ARLOT (PRÉMEAUX)* * * *

Jean-Pierre de Smet, a former apprentice of Jacques Seysses of the Domaine Dujac, fashions wines in the image of Domaine Dujac. They are elegant, sweet, juicy, and filled with pure Pinot Noir fruit. If readers want to see how much flavor can be crammed into a light ruby-colored wine, they should take a look at this estate's wines. Smet has been especially consistent, even in tough years. The wines are aged in oak casks, at least half of which are new, and there is no question that the smoky vanillin character adds considerable seductiveness to the sweet berry fruit. These are wines to drink within their first 6–8 years of life.

Best Wines: Nuits-St.-Georges Clos de l'Arlot, Nuits-St.-Georges Clos des Forêts St.-Georges, Romanée-St.-Vivant

DOMAINE DU COMTE ARMAND (POMMARD)* * */* * * *

Burgundy's resident Canadian, Pascal Marchand, loves big, robust, muscular, and ageworthy reds and therefore fashions the famed Pommard Clos des Epeneaux to reflect his tastes. His wines are concentrated, well extracted, and densely packed with dark fruits. They are very "Pommard," foursquare, broad-shouldered, and often tannic. Comte Armand's wines require cellaring and in the top vintages should be consumed between 6 and 10 years after their release.

Best Wine: Pommard Clos des Epeneaux

DOMAINE ROBERT ARNOUX (VOSNE-ROMANÉE)* * * */* * * * *

Since 1993 this famous estate has been in the hands of Pascal Lachaux, the deceased Robert Arnoux's son-in-law. A former pharmacist, Lachaux methodically studied all of the domaine's practices and made the decisions necessary to increase quality. Yields were lowered, chemical fertilizers are rarely used, the percentage of new oak barrels has been increased, rackings have been reduced, and fining and filtration have been abandoned. This estate, once dependent on the intervention of Mother Nature to keep yields moderate enough to make outstanding and ageworthy wines, is presently a source of consistently first-rate burgundies.

Best Wines: Clos de Vougeot, Echézeaux, Romanée St.-Vivant, Vosne-Romanée Les Chaumes, Vosne-Romanée Les Suchots

DOMAINE D'AUVENAY (ST. ROMAIN)* * * * *

This domaine, located in a spectacularly beautiful fortified farmhouse on the plateau above St. Romain, is Mme. Lalou Bize-Leroy's personal estate (Domaine Leroy is a joint-venture

† This rank is based on the estate's special cuvées crafted for North Berkeley Wine Imports.

with Japanese investors). Its vineyard parcels in Bonnes Mares and Mazis-Chambertin are farmed with the same biodynamic methods used at Domaine Leroy, and the wines are also vinified in the same meticulous manner. Bize-Leroy crafts, year in and year out, some of the finest—and most expensive—wines in the world.
Best Wines: Bonnes Mares, Mazis-Chambertin

DOMAINE GHISLAINE BARTHOD-NOELLAT (CHAMBOLLE-MUSIGNY)* * * *
Ghislaine Barthod, the daughter of Gaston Barthod, manages the cellar of this impeccably run, underrated Chambolle-Musigny producer. Firm but elegant wines are produced. Although never the richest or flashiest, they are consistently stylish and ageworthy. There is not much qualitative difference between the bevy of premiers crus offered, but Les Charmes is generally the most precocious and elegant. Despite their lack of muscle, these wines have the uncanny ability to age well for 10–12 years.
Best Wines: Chambolle-Musigny Les Beaux Bruns, Chambolle-Musigny Les Charmes, Chambolle-Musigny Les Cras, Chambolle-Musigny Les Varoilles

DOMAINE JEAN-CLAUDE BELLAND (SANTENAY)* * *
Jean-Claude Belland, who recently took over this estate from his retired father, Adrien, crafts a wide range of reds from the Côte de Beaune and Côte de Nuits. The wines are well made and structured and, in top vintages, offer considerable value.
Best Wines: Chambertin, Corton-Grèves

DOMAINE BERTAGNA (VOUGEOT)* */* * *
This good-sized domaine, situated just off the main road through the Côte d'Or in the village of Vougeot, is increasing the quality of their once average wines. Efforts have been made to lower yields, chemical fertilizers were eschewed a decade ago, rackings have been reduced, and in recent vintages (1995 and 1996) the wines have not been subjected to fining and filtration. The young couple who manage the domaine, Eva Reh and Mark Siddle, have the willingness and financial resources necessary to take the estate to the next level of quality.
Best Wines: Clos de Vougeot, Clos-St.-Denis

DOMAINE BITOUZET-PRIEUR (VOLNAY)* * *
Bitouzet is better known for his white than his red wines, but the reds, especially the Volnay Clos des Chênes, Volnay Pitures, and Volnay Taillepieds, are attractive, well-made wines. They rarely hit the highest peaks, but they are consistently authentic examples of Volnay. They can last for 5–10 years.
Best Wines: Volnay Clos des Chênes, Volnay Pitures, Volnay Taillepieds

DOMAINE SIMON BIZE ET FILS (SAVIGNY-LES-BEAUNE)* * */* * * *
Patrick Bize, who once dreamed of spending his life on the high seas and touring the world with the French navy, was compelled to return to the family estate when his father was ill in 1972. He took charge of the domaine in 1977 and has been making very good to excellent wines since. Recent vintages have shown an upswing in quality, with denser fruit and softer tannins than in the past. They are classic, light- to medium-bodied wines from the unheralded appellations of Savigny-Lès-Beaune. Clean, fruity, and surprisingly ageworthy, this is one of the rare Burgundy estates where there is a good quality/price rapport.
Best Wines: Savigny-Lès-Beaune Fourneaux, Savigny-Lès-Beaune Les Guettes, Savigny-Lès-Beaune Les Marconnets, Savigny-Lés-Beaune Les Vergelesses

DOMAINE JEAN-MARC BOILLOT (POMMARD)* * */* * * *
Boillot crafts wines in his image: broad-shouldered and muscular. Known more for his thick, dense, and immensely flavorful whites, Boillot is building a reputation as an excellent red

wine producer. His Bourgogne and *villages* offerings are accessible immediately upon release, but his tannic premier cru Volnays and Pommards require cellaring.

Best Wines: Pommard Jarolières, Pommard Rugiens

DOMAINE BOUCHARD PÈRE ET FILS (BEAUNE)* * * *

This firm has significantly increased the quality of its wines since the late eighties, and particularly so since being purchased by Joseph Henriot in 1994. Bouchard's estate-bottled wines from vintages such as 1989, 1990, 1995, and 1996 are good enough to compete with the finest wines of Burgundy. This is encouraging news for burgundy lovers, because Bouchard possesses the largest and most impressive vineyard holdings in the entire Côte d'Or and Chablis. The red wines are now handled more gently in their state-of-the-art facilities in Beaune. There are a number of luscious, rich, impressively endowed reds emerging from Bouchard Père et Fils. Their unequivocal successes in 1990 were followed by good but uninspiring 1991s, very attractive, soft, forward 1992s, intense and concentrated 1995s, and an outstanding array of 1996s that were well above the standard level of quality for the vintage.

Best Wines: Beaune Les Grèves Vignes de L'Enfant Jesus, La Romanée

DOMAINE JEAN-MARC BOULEY (VOLNAY)* */* * *

Bouley's wines have been more impressive in the past. This is an important estate with many fine vineyards, but often the wines taste overly oaked or underwined, depending on your point of view. There have been some successful vintages, but it appears Bouley should be lowering his crop yields and going for more concentration, especially in view of his love of lavish doses of toasty oak.

Best Wines: Pommard Les Rugiens, Volnay Clos des Chênes

ALAIN BURGUET (GEVREY-CHAMBERTIN)* * * */* * * *

This tiny, seriously run domaine owns a bevy of vineyard parcels in Gevrey and crafts some of the finest *villages* wines from this often overrated appellation. Recent vintages such as 1995 and 1996 have demonstrated that Burguet is back in the swing of things after his less than stellar 1991s and 1992s.

Best Wine: Gevrey-Chambertin Vieilles Vignes

DOMAINE JACQUES CACHEUX ET FILS (VOSNE-ROMANÉE)* * * *

Beautifully rendered burgundies that are rich, elegant, and aromatically compelling are the rule of thumb from this underrated Vosne-Romanée estate. Moreover, the Cacheux's wines age well for 12–15 years. Cacheux produced brilliant wines in 1985, 1987, 1988, 1989, 1990, 1992, 1995, and 1996.

Best Wines: Echézeaux, Vosne-Romanée Les Suchots

DOMAINE CHANDON DE BRIAILLES (SAVIGNY-LES-BEAUNE)* * *

This is a beautifully run domaine with impeccable cellars and stellar vineyard holdings. The excellent raw materials present in cask are the results of moderate yields and the estate's philosophy of "protecting the fruit at all costs" (they assert that no pumping or filtration ever takes place). However, the estate's policy of fining with two to three egg whites per barrel has the effect of stripping away some of the fruit prior to bottling, so the wines appear austere, firm, and ungiving for the first few years after release.

Best Wines: Corton Clos du Roi, Corton Les Bressandes

DOMAINE JEAN CHAUVENET (NUITS-ST.-GEORGES)* * *

This underrated producer makes pure, well-delineated Pinot Noirs from fine holdings in Nuits-St.-Georges. While approachable in their youth, these wines age beautifully. Christo-

pher Drag (the retired Jean Chauvenet's son-in-law) neither fines nor filters his wines, resulting in Pinot Noirs in the top vintages that are loaded with red and black fruits.
Best Wines: Nuits-St.-Georges Les Perrières, Nuits-St.-Georges Les Vaucrains

ROBERT CHEVILLON (NUITS-ST.-GEORGES)* * * *

Chevillon is a man of the earth; finding a vigneron in Burgundy that spends more time in his vineyards is all but impossible. He produces darkly colored, fruit-filled, spicy wines that are flattering to taste from cask but, in certain vintages (1985, 1987, 1988), have taken on a toughness with age and never fully blossomed. However, in other vintages (1989, 1990, and 1993, for example) the wines have softened and developed marvelously.
Best Wines: Nuits-St.-Georges Les Cailles, Nuits-St.-Georges Les St.-Georges, Nuits-St.-Georges Les Vaucrains

DOMAINE DANIEL CHOPIN-GROFFIER (PRÉMEAUX-PRISSEY)* * * * *

Exceedingly few red burgundies are purer, riper, and more seductive than those crafted by Daniel Chopin. Regrettably, like the great Henri Jayer, Chopin has recently retired (1996 was his last vintage). His vineyard holdings are now in the highly capable hands of Hubert Chauvenet, his son-in-law. Chopin's wines have been remarkably consistent. The downside is that Chopin-Groffier's wines require drinking early—in their first 10–12 years of life.
Best Wines: Clos de Vougeot, Nuits-St.-Georges Les Chaignots, Vougeot

DOMAINE BRUNO CLAIR (MARSANNAY)* * * *

Bruno Clair and his highly talented winemaker, Philippe Brun, craft a vast array of quality wines from Savigny-Lès-Beaune in the south to their bevy of value-priced Marsannays in the north. Clair's 1995s and 1996s were extremely impressive wines, and the 1997s were quite good but not among the finest of the Côte.
Best Wines: Chambertin Clos de Bèze, Gevrey-Chambertin Les Cazetiers, Gevrey-Chambertin Clos St.-Jacques, Savigny-Les-Beaune Les Dominaudes

DOMAINE JEAN-JACQUES "JJ" CONFURON (PRÉMEAUX-PRISSEY)* * * * *

It is no secret why this estate's wines are superb. The domaine practices extensive crop thinning, with average yields of under 30 hectoliters per hectare. These are powerful, rich, and yet elegant wines that are bottled early to protect their rich, concentrated fruit. Confuron enjoyed stunning success in 1991, 1992, 1993, 1995, and 1996. The 1997s, while quite good, are not to this estate's standard. Winemaker Alain Meunier and his wife, Sophie (the late Jean-Jacques Confuron's daughter), deserve kudos for this estate's magnificent array of wines.
Best Wines: Clos de Vougeot, Nuits-St.-Georges Les Boudots, Nuits-St.-Georges Les Chaboeufs, Romanée-St.-Vivant, Vosne-Romanée Les Beaux Monts

DOMAINE EDMOND ET PIERRE CORNU (LADOIX-SERRIGNY)* * *

Except for Cornu's Corton Les Bressandes, this estate's vineyard holdings are in the lesser-known and more modest appellations of Chorey-Lès-Beaune and Aloxe-Corton. As has recently occurred at many Burgundian domaines, there has been a generational transition at this estate, with Edmond Cornu passing the baton to his bright, dedicated, and talented son, Pierre. Significant changes (destemming, a sorting of the grapes at harvest, and the abandonment of *foudres* in favor of oak barrels) have raised the level of this already good estate's wines.
Best Wines: Aloxe-Corton Les Moutottes, Aloxe-Corton Les Valozières, Corton Les Bressandes

DOMAINE MARIUS DELARCHE (PERNAND-VERGELESSES)* * * * †

Delarche is one of the Côte de Beaune's top producers, at least for his special North Berkeley bottlings. Low yields and high-quality, non-interventionist winemaking are the rule of thumb at this little-known estate in the backwater village of Pernand-Vergelesses. This domaine's wines offer considerable value.

Best Wine: Corton-Renardes Réserve, Corton Réserve, Pernand-Vergelesses Ile de Vergelesses Réserve

DOMAINE JOSEPH DROUHIN (BEAUNE)* * */* * * *

Fifty-one percent of this well-known *négociant* house was sold in 1995 to a Japanese company, although Robert Drouhin remains in charge of this firm. Drouhin wants his reds to be highly defined, elegant burgundies and guides his talented winemaker (Laurence Jobard) to craft them in such a style. They are consistently good to excellent, but rarely inspirational, and are at their best in concentrated, fruit-packed vintages like 1989, 1990, and 1995, whose characteristics complement (or combat, depending on your viewpoint) the house style. Drouhin's son Frédéric, who is responsible for the firm's vineyard holdings, has an excellent and growing reputation among Burgundy's vignerons as a serious man of the earth. His dedication to organic farming, intensive vineyard work, and experimentations with biodynamic methods augur a bright future for this firm's estate bottlings.

Best Wines: Beaune Clos des Mouches, Bonnes Mares, Chambolle-Musigny Les Amoureuses, Grands Echézeaux, Musigny

DOMAINE CLAUDE DUGAT (GEVREY-CHAMBERTIN)* * * * *

One of Burgundy's greatest wine producers, this estate is making sensationally sumptuous wines. Tiny yields, physiologically ripe grapes, and a noninterventionist winemaking philosophy (fining or filtering is rarely done) result in enormously rich, aromatically complex, spectacular wines. Even in difficult vintages such as 1991, 1992, and 1994 Claude Dugat produced superb wines, proving once again that the producer makes all the difference. Lamentably, only 50 cases of Griotte-Chambertin and 100 cases of Charmes-Chambertin are produced in a prolific vintage. This is one of the rare estates in Burgundy where all the wines, from top to bottom, are seemingly always super.

Best Wines: Charmes-Chambertin, Gevrey-Chambertin, Gevrey-Chambertin Lavaux St.-Jacques, Gevrey-Chambertin Premier Cru, Griottes-Chambertin

DOMAINE BERNARD DUGAT-PY (GEVREY-CHAMBERTIN)* * * * *

This estate, formerly known simply as Domaine Bernard Dugat and prior to that as Domaine Pierre Dugat, is one of Burgundy's greatest turnaround stories. Bernard Dugat and his lovely wife, Jocelyne, have, since the 1993 vintage, crafted some of Burgundy's finest wines. Every offering crafted at this domaine in the 1993, 1994, 1995, 1996, and 1997 vintages are highly recommended. Blessed with the same small berry-producing old vines that Claude Dugat farms (both inherited them from their grandfather), Bernard Dugat fashions supple, powerful, seductive, and sweet fruit-packed gems. These wines are superb to drink young, yet the top ones can age for 10–15+ years. Regrettably, as is all too often the case in Burgundy, these wines are produced in microscopic quantities.

Best Wines: Charmes-Chambertin, Gevrey-Chambertin Le Fonteny, Gevrey-Chambertin Lavaux St.-Jacques, Gevrey-Chambertin Petite Chapelle, Mazis-Chambertin Vieilles Vignes

DOMAINE DUJAC (MOREY-ST.-DENIS)* * * *

This is an extremely well-run estate managed with an intelligent, open-minded view of winemaking by proprietor Jacques Seysses. Seysses is a member of the new generation of Bur-

†This rank is based on the estate's special cuvées crafted for North Berkeley Wine Imports.

gundy winemakers who have traveled extensively and who recognize that if Burgundy is going to make a viable product, it must be devoted to producing extremely high-quality wines that justify the high prices asked, as well as the expectations of consumers. The style of wine Seysses aims for is one of elegant, soft, sweet, fragrant, velvety-textured Pinot fruit. The wines are light colored and aromatically superb, with rarely more than medium body, and earthy, juicy, Pinot flavors. Experience suggests that these wines are at their peak of maturity relatively early and should be consumed within the first 10 years after their release.
Best Wines: Bonnes Mares, Charmes-Chambertin, Clos de la Roche, Clos St.-Denis

DOMAINE MAURICE ECARD ET FILS (SAVIGNY-LÈS-BEAUNE)* * * *

It is a shame there are not more red burgundies like Ecard's premiers crus from Savigny-Lès-Beaune. His wines go from strength to strength, offering vivid, ripe, elegant Pinot Noirs that are full of fruit, wonderfully pure, representative of their different *terroirs,* and sold at reasonable prices. Ecard's wines drink well young yet can age for 10–12 years. This is an estate to seek out for modestly priced Pinot Noir that delivers the goods.
Best Wines: Savigny-Lès-Beaune Les Jarrons, Savigny-Lès-Beaune Les Narbantons, Savigny-Lès-Beaune Les Peuillets, Savigny-Lès-Beaune Les Serpentières

DOMAINE RENÉ ENGEL (VOSNE-ROMANÉE)* * * *

Philippe Engel produces wines that continue to exhibit his strengths as a winemaker. The first vintages I tasted were above average but hardly inspiring. Today his wines are close to five-star quality. Engel owns some wonderful vineyards, including a plot of Clos de Vougeot composed mostly of vines planted in 1922. The wines are authoritatively rich, well-colored, medium- to full-bodied red burgundies with well-integrated tannin as well as excellent purity, richness, and complexity. Just about everything produced by Engel is noteworthy. The wines can be drunk young or cellared for 10–15 years. Engel has enjoyed considerable success both in top years and in off years.
Best Wines: Clos de Vougeot, Echézeaux, Grands Echézeaux, Vosne-Romanée Les Brûlées

DOMAINE JEAN GARAUDET (POMMARD)* * */* * * *

This is a reliable source for attractively rich, medium- to full-bodied red burgundies. Garaudet's Pommard Les Charmots from a vineyard planted in 1902 is a five-star wine in top vintages. My only reservation concerning Garaudet's red wines is that they are sometimes monolithic and rustic. However, they are cleanly made, rich, and satisfying, with Les Charmots a cut above the rest.
Best Wines: Pommard Les Charmots, Pommard Noizons

DOMAINE HENRI GOUGES (NUITS-ST.-GEORGES)* * */* * * *

This estate, responsible for an array of remarkable burgundies through the 1960s, dropped significantly in quality in the seventies and eighties. The early nineties witnessed slight improvements, but in recent years Domaine Henri Gouges appears to be returning to the quality levels of its glorious past. Cousins Pierre and Christian Gouges have been emphasizing organic vineyard practices, moderate yields, fining only rarely, and no filtration. The results of their efforts can be tasted in their dark, concentrated, well-structured, and simply delicious wines.
Best Wines: Nuits-St.-Georges Les St.-Georges, Nuits-St.-Georges Les Vaucrains

DOMAINE JEAN GRIVOT (VOSNE-ROMANÉE)* * * */* * * * *

Etienne Grivot, a bright, thoughtful, and contemplative man, is one of the leaders of the new generation of Burgundians who are crafting wines in line with this hallowed region's glorious reputation. After having worked with the controversial Guy Accad for a number of years,

Grivot has finally settled on viticultural and cellar techniques of his own. While Grivot's wines used to be delicious young and then faded rather rapidly, they are presently some of the finest made in Burgundy. This estate is certainly in the running for a five-star ranking. *Best Wines:* Clos de Vougeot, Echézeaux, Nuits-St.-Georges Les Boudots, Nuits-St.-Georges Les Pruliers, Richebourg, Vosne-Romanée Les Brûlées, Vosne-Romanée Les Suchots

DOMAINE ROBERT GROFFIER (MOREY-ST.-DENIS)* * * */* * * * *
In the last edition of this book, Robert Parker wrote that "this domaine's irritating inconsistency is largely a result of overcropping." Enter Serge Groffier, Robert's son. His meticulous vineyard work (rival Burgundian vignerons are in awe of his vines) combined with Robert Groffier's experienced and immensely talented winemaking have elevated this estate's quality to dizzying heights. Domaine Robert Groffier in 1996 and 1997 produced some of the finest wines in the Côte d'Or, from their benchmark setting Bourgogne Rouge to their out-of-this-world Chambertin Clos de Bèze and Bonnes Mares. This estate is presently on the verge of meriting a five-star ranking.
Best Wines: Bonnes Mares, Chambertin Clos de Bèze, Chambolle-Musigny Les Amoureuses

DOMAINE ANNE GROS (VOSNE-ROMANÉE)* * * */* * * * *
Formerly known as Domaine Anne et François Gros, this estate is crafting incredibly concentrated and extracted wines. In the 1995 and 1996 vintages the wines were so dense, inky, structured, and backward that I immensely respected their sheer size but questioned what cellaring would bring. There simply is no precedent to this style of wine. However, in 1997 the gracious, intelligent, and charming Anne Gros crafted much more ingratiating, accessible, and supple wines while maintaining her trademark fruit-packed style. I have enormous confidence in Madame Gros and believe this domaine's future is tremendously bright.
Best Wine: Clos Vougeot Le Grand Maupertui, Richebourg

DOMAINE HAEGELEN-JAYER (VOSNE-ROMANÉE)* * * *
Alfred Haegelen, owing to his marriage to Robert Jayer's sister (Henri Jayer's cousin), has remarkable vineyard parcels to work with. This estate's old-vine Clos Vougeot is generally one of the finest wines crafted from that famous yet overrated grand cru vineyard. The Echézeaux, from a parcel contiguous with Jayer-Gilles's and Emmanuel Rouget's, while rarely at the quality level attained by those two superstar estates, is often outstanding. I have been surprised, however, by the inconsistency of his other wines. The *villages* and premier cru offerings are not at the level I expect from a domaine that is capable of fashioning such delectable grands crus.
Best Wines: Clos de Vougeot Vieilles Vignes, Echézeaux

LOUIS JADOT (BEAUNE)* * * */* * * * *
This firm, a *négociant* as well as a vineyard owner, remains the reference point for how a Burgundy *négociant* should make wine. Pierre-Henri Gagey, the firm's director, is supported by one of the Côte d'Or's finest oenologist/winemakers, Jacques Lardière. Just about everything produced by Jadot, from their generic Bourgogne Rouge to their top-of-the-line Chambertin Clos de Bèze or Bonnes Mares, is of high, often superb, quality. Lardière's wines are typically extremely gorgeously made, crammed with fruit, and rich and have the necessary structure for extended cellaring.
Best Wines: All of Jadot's Beaune premiers crus, Bonnes Mares, Chambertin Clos de Bèze, Chambolle-Musigny Les Amoureuses, Chapelle-Chambertin, Clos de Vougeot, Gevrey-Chambertin Clos St.-Jacques, Gevrey-Chambertin Estournelles St.-Jacques, Ruchottes-Chambertin

DOMAINE ROBERT JAYER-GILLES (MAGNY-LES-VILLERS)* * * * *

In the past few years numerous Burgundian estates have undergone major changes as a new generation has taken charge. While Robert Jayer has recently retired, this domaine's wine-making remains the same, as Gilles Jayer, Robert's son and the estate's new director, has been crafting its wines since 1990. All the wines are aged in 100% new oak in one of the most beautiful cellars in Burgundy. He produces seductive, rich wines that are tightly wound and backward young yet age magnificently well for 10–15 years. The best value in Jayer-Gilles's portfolio is the Côte de Nuits-Villages, which is often better than many producers' premiers or grands crus.

Best Wines: Côte de Nuits-Villages, Echézeaux, Nuits-St.-Georges Les Damodes, Nuits-St.-Georges Les Hautes Poirets

DOMAINE JOBLOT (GIVRY)* * * *

It is a shame there are not more producers as dedicated and talented as Jean-Marc Joblot. Working in Givry, one of the lesser-known appellations of the Côte Chalonnaise, he fashions rich, concentrated, chewy, pure red burgundies that can be drunk young yet are capable of lasting over a decade. They embarrass many premiers and grands crus from the more prestigious Côte d'Or. Burgundy fanatics have been gobbling up Joblot's wines since he burst on the scene with gorgeous 1985s. His wines have continued to demonstrate a progression in quality. In a recent tasting of three 1988s, Joblot's Givry Cellier aux Moines and a Chambertin and Clos Vougeot from two well-known Côte de Nuits producers, this estate's wine was notably better than the Chambertin and gave the Clos Vougeot serious competition—once again demonstrating that the appellation does not make the wine.

Best Wines: Givry Clos du Cellier aux Moines, Givry Clos de la Servoisine

DOMAINE MICHEL LAFARGE (VOLNAY)* * * * *

Michel Lafarge and his son Frédéric craft Volnays as seductive and classic as any made in the village. Moreover they have been extremely consistent, even in tough years such as 1981 and 1994. In top years the Lafarge team is capable of hitting home runs, particularly with their top cuvées. These are rich, concentrated, seductive, elegant, yet authoritatively flavored Volnays that can age well for 10–15 years.

Best Wines: Volnay Clos des Chênes, Volnay Clos du Château des Ducs

DOMAINE DES COMTES LAFON (MEURSAULT)* * * * *

This producer is renowned the world over for its spectacular white burgundies. Proprietor Dominique Lafon makes equally riveting red wines. Since quantities are tiny, the extraordinary quality of these red wines goes largely unnoticed. Lafon's Volnay Champans, Volnay Clos des Chênes, and Volnay Santenots are some of the finest wines of the Volnay appellation. Rich, extremely concentrated, gorgeously pure, yet never heavy or tannic, these are wines that can last and evolve for decades, even in years such as 1987. Unfortunately they are extremely difficult to find.

Best Wines: Volnay Champans, Volnay Clos des Chênes, Volnay Santenots

DOMAINE DES LAMBRAYS (MOREY-ST.-DENIS)* * */* * * *

In December 1996 this perennially underachieving estate was purchased by Gunther Freund, a seventy-four-year-old German businessman. His stated goal was to produce some of Burgundy's finest reds by the turn of the millennium. The Clos des Lambrays was elevated to grand cru status in 1981, presumably because of its superb *terroir* rather than the quality of the wines. Older vintages, dating back to the thirties, were wonderful, yet more recently it has a dismal track record of disappointing vintages, including a terrible 1983, a now senile 1985, a frightfully light, diluted 1986, 1987, and 1988, and a fruitier but undistinctive 1990 and 1991. The 1994, 1995, 1996, and 1997 Clos des Lambrays have shown marked improvement over the wines of the 1980s. However, significantly more efforts need to be made for Freund's goal to be achieved.

DOMAINE LOUIS LATOUR (BEAUNE)* */* * *

Much has been made of the flash pasteurization process that Louis Latour utilizes for this firm's red wines. Opinion is divided as to whether it is significant. Latour maintains that the wines require less processing and the procedure is less brutal than sterile filtration. This firm is, justifiably, widely renowned for their bevy of rich, full-bodied white wines. While the lower-level red wines tend to taste alike, this is a good source for sturdy, medium-bodied, tannic Corton-Grancey. Other red wines, especially the selections from Beaune, Pernand-Vergelesses, and Savigny can be meager. The 1996 and, especially, 1997 were quite successful vintages for Louis Latour's reds.

Best Wines: Corton Clos de la Vigne au Saint, Corton-Grancey, Romanée St.-Vivant

DOMINIQUE LAURENT (NUITS-ST.-GEORGES)* * * *

Laurent, an ex-pastry chef, launched this *négociant* firm with the 1989 vintage. He purchases wines from growers, ages them in 100% new oak, enormously works their lees, and then bottles them by hand without fining or filtration. He is known in Burgundy and elsewhere as the "200% new oak man" because he sometimes racks wines from one new barrel to another after their malolactic fermentations. In barrel these are among the most seductive and sumptuous wines found in Burgundy. However, postbottling tastings have revealed that Laurent's *élevage* techniques can produce uneven results. Some wines that were magnificent in barrel have appeared dried out, overly oaked, and lean, while others have been as good as or better than when first tasted. Nevertheless, Dominique Laurent is serious about establishing himself as one of the few guardians of rich, high-quality burgundies and appears to be aware of his problems and is taking steps to correct them. This is a name to follow.

Best Wines: There are sure to be variations, depending on what Laurent is able to purchase. To date his finest wines have included the Bonnes Mares, Charmes-Chambertin, Clos de la Roche, and Mazis-Chambertin.

DOMAINE LÉCHENEAUT (NUITS-ST.-GEORGES)* * * * *

Based on what Lécheneaut has achieved in 1990, 1991, 1992, 1995, 1996, and 1997, it is easy to conclude that this must be the new superstar of Nuits-St.-Georges. Philippe and Vincent Lécheneaut are making far greater wines than some of the village's more illustrious *négociants* and growers. Their successes in tough years such as 1991 and 1992 suggest this could be a five-star producer. The wines are deeply colored, rich, framed by significant toasty new oak, succulent, expansive, structured, and well balanced. This is a fabulous source for great red burgundies that drink well young yet possess the requisite harmony to age for 10–15 years.

Best Wines: Clos de la Roche, Nuits-St.-Georges Les Cailles, Nuits-St.-Georges Les Damodes

PHILIPPE LECLERC (GEVREY-CHAMBERTIN)* * * *

Rarely in Burgundy does one encounter such intense, backward, muscular, extracted, and concentrated wines as those of Philippe Leclerc's. They have the color, structure, flavor, tannin, and mouth-feel, when young, more reminiscent of oak-infused northen Rhône Syrahs than of red burgundy. One of Gevrey's three latest harvesters, Leclerc ages his wines for up to 3 years in 100% new oak barrels and neither fines nor filters them. I have been a fan of Philippe Leclerc's wines for some time and have extolled their qualities. Recently, however, I am increasingly uncertain about my original stand. I have been patiently cellaring his 1985

Gevrey-Chambertin Combe aux Moines, tasting it every few years in the hope that it would shed its oak and tannins while displaying its dense and luscious fruit. Regrettably, the latest bottle I tasted was still dominated by oak and tannin and revealed a loss of fruit. The 1990 Bourgogne Les Bons Batons (also out of my cold cellar) hit its plateau of maturity in mid-1997 and was past it by 1998. I hope these two examples are not indicative of how all of Leclerc's wines will evolve, but I do have concerns. Time will tell.

Best Wines: Gevrey-Chambertin Les Cazetiers, Gevrey-Chambertin Combe aux Moines

RENÉ LECLERC (GEVREY-CHAMBERTIN)* * * *

René Leclerc is the brother of Philippe Leclerc. I have had glorious bottles of wine from this estate in the past; however I've also tasted many that appeared thin, dried out, and lacking in freshness. Recently, however, René Leclerc has changed some of his long-standing practices, notably reducing the length of his *élevage* and increasing the percentage of new oak, to offset past deficiencies. His 1995s, 1996s, and 1997s reveal that this estate is crafting first-rate burgundies that can be drunk when released but have the capacity to age well for more than 10 years.

Best Wines: Gevrey-Chambertin Clos Prieur, Gevrey-Chambertin Combe aux Moines, Gevrey-Chambertin Lavaux St.-Jacques, Griotte-Chambertin

DOMAINE LEROY (VOSNE-ROMANÉE)* * * * *

Lalou Bize-Leroy stands alone at the top of Burgundy's quality hierarchy. Because she is a perfectionist, and because she has had the courage to produce wines from extraordinarily low yields and to bottle them naturally, without fining or filtration, she has been scorned by many Burgundy *négociants* and even by the proprietors of other top domaines. Their envy and jealousy is appalling.

Since she launched her wines from the Domaine Leroy, Lalou Bize-Leroy has made the highest percentage of Burgundy's greatest wines in virtually every vintage. Just about everything in Leroy's portfolio is profound, as well as astronomically expensive. Moreover, these wines are a sure bet when it comes to buying red burgundy for aging more than 15–20 years. They often require 5–10 years just to open. Leroy offers an education in what great burgundy is all about.

Best Wines: Chambertin, Chambolle-Musigny Les Charmes, Clos de la Roche, Clos de Vougeot, Gevrey-Chambertin Les Combottes, Latricières-Chambertin, Musigny, Nuits-St.-Georges Les Boudots, Nuits-St.-Georges Les Vignes Rondes, Pommard Les Vignots, Richebourg, Romanée St.-Vivant, Savigny-Les-Beaune Les Narbantons, Volnay Santenots, Vosne-Romanée Les Beaux Monts, Vosne-Romanée Les Brûlées

DOMAINE GEORGES LIGNIER (MOREY-ST.-DENIS)* */* * *

Georges Lignier's wines are mystifying. Lignier is enthusiastic and possesses great vineyards, yet often the wines turn out light and diluted. It seems that if Lignier lowered his yields and threw away his filter, and perhaps bottled his wines before they went through a second winter in cask, he would be a consistent four-star producer. At present his wines rarely stand above the crowd.

Best Wines: Clos de la Roche, Clos St.-Denis, Gevrey-Chambertin Les Combottes, Morey-St.-Denis Clos des Ormes

DOMAINE HUBERT LIGNIER (MOREY-ST.-DENIS)* * * * *

The fact that Domaine Hubert Lignier is a source for fabulous wines is no longer a secret. They are as difficult for consumers to find as any producer's in Burgundy, including those from the microscopic estate of Claude Dugat. Yet the European wine press has continued to ignore this domaine or, worse yet, have failed to notice the outstanding quality of its wines.

This is burgundy at its finest—rich, aromatic, medium to full bodied, concentrated, and velvety textured, with a stunning bouquet of black raspberries and black cherries intertwined with scents of new oak. The wines also age well, as a taste of Lignier's 1978s will prove. Magnificent wines emerge from holdings in Clos de la Roche and Charmes-Chambertin. As at many Burgundian estates, winemaking and management responsibilities were recently passed from father to son. But consumers need not worry. As hard as this may be to believe, Roman Lignier may be an even more talented winemaker than his father.

Best Wines: Chambolle-Musigny Premier Cru, Charmes-Chambertin, Clos de la Roche, Morey-St.-Denis Premier Cru Vieilles Vignes

CHÂTEAU DE LA MALTROYE (CHASSAGNE-MONTRACHET)* * *

This gorgeous Chassagne-Montrachet estate turns out spicy, rustic, medium-bodied red wines that offer reasonably good value. They are a good introduction to the underrated, modestly priced red wines of Chassagne-Montrachet.

Best Wine: Chassagne-Montrachet Clos St.-Jean

DOMAINE MÉO-CAMUZET (VOSNE-ROMANÉE)* * * */* * * * *

This superb domaine, which only began estate bottling in 1983, possesses some of Burgundy's finest vineyards and often fashions spectacular wines. The famed Henri Jayer, formerly one of the domaine's *métayers* (sharecroppers), taught the talented and brilliant Jean-Nicolas Méo and Christian Faurois (Méo's assistant) his winemaking, *élevage*, and bottling philosophies. Jayer's basic tenets are still employed at this impeccably run estate even though Méo is constantly experimenting with new techniques. He is presently performing *bâtonnage* on his reds, for example. Méo-Camuzet can generally be counted on to produce fabulous red burgundies. The few lapses I've encountered prevented me from giving the estate a five-star rating, yet I would not be surprised if the Méo and Faurois team ultimately make this one of the five or six top Burgundian estates in the near future. These thrilling red burgundies are made from yields of under 2 tons of fruit per acre, aged in primarily new oak casks, and bottled without filtration and in some cases without fining. There are riveting expressions both aromatically and on the palate—rich, authoritative, velvety textured, and concentrated, as well as complex, elegant, and exceptionally well balanced.

Best Wines: Clos de Vougeot, Corton, Nuits-St.-Georges Les Boudots, Nuits-St.-Georges aux Murgers, Richebourg, Vosne-Romanée Les Brûlées, Vosne-Romanée Cros Parantoux

DOMAINE MONGEARD-MUGNERET (VOSNE-ROMANÉE)* * * *

I learned with surprise from Vincent Mongeard that he—not his father—had been responsible for this estate's winemaking since the late eighties. This large domaine with vineyards spread throughout the Côte d'Or produces bold, authoritative, rich, and concentrated wines that are typically at their best within the first 10 years after their release. My experience with older bottles suggests that they become hard and dry out with long-term cellaring.

Best Wines: Clos de Vougeot, Echézeaux Vieilles Vignes, Grands Echézeaux, Nuits-St.-Georges Les Boudots, Richebourg, Vosne-Romanée Les Suchots

DOMAINE ALBERT MOROT (BEAUNE)* * * *

Albert Morot, both a *négociant* and a vineyard owner, has always fashioned classic wines from its Côte de Beaune holdings. However, in the early nineties Mademoiselle Choppin began to do severe crop thinnings and increased the percentage of new oak casks to 60%. Perhaps even more important, she returned to bottling all of her wines without fining or filtration. The results have been beautiful expressions of savory, succulent, yet structured Pinot Noir that are both modestly priced and ageworthy. This is one of the rare estates (it no longer does any *négociant* work but maintains its license) of Burgundy crafting outstanding wines that sell for less than $45 a bottle.

Best Wines: Beaune Les Bressandes, Beaune Les Cent Vignes, Beaune Les Teurons, Beaune Les Toussaints, Savigny Vergelesses Clos la Bataillière

DOMAINE DENIS MORTET (GEVREY-CHAMBERTIN)* * * */* * * * *

In the last edition of this book, Robert Parker wrote that Denis Mortet "had the potential to be one of the stars of Gevrey-Chambertin." The potential is finally bearing fruit. Mortet has abandoned chemical fertilizers, works his vineyard's soils incessantly, and has significantly reduced yields. Furthermore, Mortet has installed a sorting table, increased the percentage of new oak barrels in his cellar, and neither sulfurs nor racks his wines during their 18-month *élevage*. The result? One of Burgundy's greatest turnaround stories. Mortet's wines are lush, fruitpacked, supple, and exuberant. Some cuvées have been somewhat dominated by new oak flavors, and they may not be Burgundy's most ageworthy wines, but they are hedonistic, deeply ripe, and a pure delight to drink.

Best Wines: Chambertin, Chambolle-Musigny Les Beaux Bruns, Gevrey-Chambertin Les Champeaux, Gevrey-Chambertin Lavaux St. Jacques

DOMAINE MUGNERET-GIBOURG/GEORGES MUGNERET (VOSNE-ROMANÉE)* * * */* * * * *

These two estates (Mugneret-Gibourg is composed of the vineyards purchased by Dr. Mugneret's mother in the 1930s, and Domaine Georges Mugneret is composed of the parcels he purchased), which often turn out five-star wines, particularly their Ruchottes-Chambertin, Clos de Vougeot, and Echézeaux, are run by the late Dr. Georges Mugneret's widow and their two daughters. Recent efforts taken by Mme. Mugneret and her daughters (Christine and Marie-Andrée) to increase quality are paying dividends. Current vintages, notably the 1996s and 1997s, appear to indicate that these two estates have corrected whatever deficiencies caused their wines in the 1980s to be less than stellar. These are high-quality, high-class, excellent to outstanding red burgundies that generally can be consumed young or aged for 10 years or more.

Best Wines: Chambolle-Musigny Les Feusselottes, Clos de Vougeot, Echézeaux, Nuits-St.-Georges Les Chaignots, Ruchottes-Chambertin

PHILIPPE NADDEF (COUCHEY)* * * */* * * *

Naddef's Mazis-Chambertin and Gevrey-Chambertin Les Cazetiers can be stunning, especially in top vintages. Unfortunately there is not much of it. The other wines are less enticing, but they are always soundly made. The Mazis is a 10- to 15-year wine in top years, and Les Cazetiers can age gracefully for nearly as long. Naddef is close to entering the top hierarchy of Burgundy wine producers.

Best Wines: Gevrey-Chambertin Les Cazetiers, Mazis-Chambertin

DOMAINE PONSOT (MOREY-ST.-DENIS)* * * */* * * *

In vintages such as 1947, 1949, 1972, 1980, 1985, 1990, 1991, and 1993, this fascinating domaine produced some of the greatest wines of Burgundy. However, there has also been a frustrating lack of consistency, with deplorable wines being produced in 1984, 1986, 1987, 1994, and 1995 and less than thrilling 1988s, 1989s, and 1996s. Laurent Ponsot is a notoriously late harvester and utilizes traditional winemaking methods. No new oak is employed (the barrels range from 5 to 40 years old), and the wines are fined with egg whites, but never filtered. Moreover, no sulfur has been used in the winemaking since 1988—a rarity in wine-dom. At their worst, this estate's wines have the color of a rosé, reveal off odors, and have no fruit to speak of. At their finest, Ponsot's wines are classic examples of great red burgundy, rich and accessible enough to be drunk young yet capable of lasting 20–30 years. How does one rank an estate that goes from stunning successes in one vintage (1993) to utter failures in the following year (1994)?

Best Wines: Clos de la Roche Vieilles Vignes, Clos St.-Denis, Griotte-Chambertin

DOMAINE DE LA POUSSE D'OR (VOLNAY)* * */* * * *

Gérard Potel, this estate's director and winemaker, regrettably passed away in fall 1997. This estate used to be one of Robert Parker's reference points for great burgundy, since he loved its 1964s, 1966s, 1976s, and 1978s. I loved the estate's Volnay Clos de la Bousee d'Or in the 1985 and 1990 vintages, finding that they seemingly put on weight and heft with cellaring. The estate is now owned by Patrick Landanger, a highly successful French businessman, and the winemaking responsibilities are overseen by Bernard Canonica (who had worked at Labouré-Roi from 1980 to 1987 and subsequently at the Château de Bligny). The ranking attributed this estate is for Potel's tenure, as I have not tasted any wines crafted by this new regime.

Best Wines: Pommard Les Jarolières, Volnay Les Caillerets, Volnay Les Caillerets Clos des 60 Ouvrées, Volnay Clos de la Bousse d'Or

DOMAINE JACQUES PRIEUR (MEURSAULT)* * * *

Since this property was acquired by the firm of Antonin Rodet the quality has increased significantly. The hugely talented hand of Rodet's winemaking genius, Nadine Goublin, can be experienced in each taste of these deeply ripe, large-size, lavishly oaked, and solidly colored red burgundies. They are capable of 10–15 years of aging.

Best Wines: Chambertin Clos de Bèze, Clos de Vougeot, Musigny, Volnay-Champans, Volnay Clos des Santenots

DOMAINE DANIEL RION (NUITS ST.-GEORGES)* * * *

This is one of the few Burgundy domaines from the Côte de Nuits that has a popular following in the United States. Made in a forward, seductive, easy-to-understand style, these wines exhibit ripe fruit and the generous use of toasty new oak. Patrice Rion, who oversees this estate's winemaking, wants his wines to be lush, soft, and crammed with thick, sweet fruit the day they are released—and they are.

Best Wines: Chambolle-Musigny Les Charmes, Nuits-St.-Georges Clos des Argillières, Nuits-St.-Georges Les Vignes Rondes, Vosne-Romanée Les Beaux Monts, Vosne-Romanée Les Chaumes

ANTONIN RODET (MERCUREY)* * * * †

I am extremely impressed by the quality of Rodet's red wines from its "Cave Privée" portfolio. These supple, intensely fruity, fleshy, nicely oaked burgundies stand as testimony to Nadine Goublin's highly talented winemaking and director Bertrand Devillard's quality-conscious philosophies.

Best Wines: Charmes-Chambertin Cave Privée, Gevrey-Chambertin Estournelles St.-Jacques Cave Privée, Richebourg Cave Privée

†This ranking is for Antonin Rodet's "Cave Privée" series of wines.

DOMAINE DE LA ROMANÉE-CONTI (VOSNE-ROMANÉE)* * * * *

The most famous estate in Burgundy, if not in all of France, the Domaine de la Romanée-Conti (DRC) has always been a target for criticism given its exquisite *monopole* vineyards of La Tâche and Romanée-Conti and the staggeringly high prices fetched for these wines. While there have been some disappointments (1992 and 1994 most recently), there have been enough great wines, particularly in 1978, 1980, 1990, 1995, and 1996, to keep the domaine's mythical reputation intact. Small yields and late harvests result in some of the most fragrant, spicy, and opulent wines of Burgundy. All the wines are aged in 100% new oak and, according to the domaine, undergo only one racking and are neither fined nor filtered.

Best Wines: Grands-Echézeaux, Richebourg, Romanée-Conti, Romanée-St.-Vivant, La Tâche

DOMAINE JOSEPH ROTY (GEVREY-CHAMBERTIN)* * * *

This idiosyncratic domaine, run by the loquacious, chain-smoking Roty, has made extraordinary wines in a number of vintages, particularly 1978, 1980, 1985, 1988, and 1990. In less concentrated years the wines can turn out frightfully woody and out of balance. The finest vintages reveal wines crammed with concentrated, ripe fruit and tannin. These are forceful, rich, beautifully oaked wines that require 5–7 years of cellaring. Roty is capable of producing five-star red burgundies, but the inconsistency in years such as 1983, 1986, 1987, and 1992 remains a problem.

Best Wines: Charmes-Chambertin, Gevrey-Chambertin Les Fontenys, Griotte-Chambertin, Mazis-Chambertin

DOMAINE EMANUEL ROUGET (FLAGEY-ECHÉZEAUX)* * * */* * * * *

Henri Jayer's nephew Emanuel Rouget continues to turn out classy, rich, Jayeresque wines that are well colored, with sweet aromatic profiles and wonderfully ripe, opulent, medium-to full-bodied personalities. This estate's wines combine power with elegance and depth with suppleness and are some of the classiest to be found in Burgundy. Rouget is certainly one of the finest winemakers of the new generation that has provided Burgundy its renaissance.

Best Wines: Echézeaux, Vosne-Romanée Les Beaux Monts, Vosne-Romanée Cros Parentoux

DOMAINE GEORGES ET CHRISTOPHE ROUMIER
(CHAMBOLLE-MUSIGNY)* * * */* * * * *

Many great wines have emerged from this 40-acre domaine. The late American importer Frank Schoonmaker discovered these wines, which were estate-bottled long before that was a common practice in Burgundy. The domaine is run by Christophe Roumier, one of the leaders of Burgundy's younger generation of winemakers. This estate has been remarkably consistent in difficult years such as 1982, 1983, 1986, and 1988, yet it slipped a bit in 1985, 1990, and 1991. Recent vintages, such as 1995 and 1996 have been spectacular, and the domaine's 1997s are delicious. Roumier's Bonnes Mares, Musigny, and Chambolle-Musigny Les Amoureuses are often reference points for these renowned vineyards and can age well for 20 years.

Best Wines: Bonnes Mares, Chambolle-Musigny Les Amoureuses, Musigny, Ruchottes-Chambertin

DOMAINE ARMAND ROUSSEAU (GEVREY-CHAMBERTIN)* * * *

This historic estate, which began to estate-bottle in the thirties, could easily be a five-star producer if Charles Rousseau would apply his magic touch to all of his wines. The consistently spectacular Chambertin, Chambertin Clos de Bèze, and Gevrey-Chambertin Clos St.-Jacques are far better than the Gevrey-Chambertin Les Cazetieres, Mazis-Chambertin, Clos de la Roche, and Charmes-Chambertin. I have no idea why. Rousseau's top wines are delicious young but can be cellared for 10–15 years in the finest vintages.

Best Wines: Chambertin, Chambertin Clos de Bèze, Gevrey-Chambertin Clos St.-Jacques, Ruchottes-Chambertin Clos des Ruchottes

DOMAINE CHRISTIAN SERAFIN (GEVREY-CHAMBERTIN)* * * * *

In a village populated by many underachievers, Christian Serafin stands out as one of its sure-handed winemakers. His wines have been remarkably consistent from vintage to vintage (the 1988s are some of the best to emerge from Gevrey-Chambertin in that difficult year). He is a perfectionist in the vineyards and the cellars, taking great care not to manipulate his wines and never to fine or filter them. Serafin's wines are rich and medium to full bodied, with a huge depth of fruit, considerable complexity, and unquestionable aging potential. To date, his top two wines, Gevrey-Chambertin Les Cazetiers and Charmes-Chambertin, are capable of lasting 10–15+ years. Serafin has recently added two vineyards to his holdings (Morey-St.-Denis Les Millandes and Chambolle-Musigny Les Baudes), fabulous news for lovers of great burgundies!

Best Wines: Charmes-Chambertin, Gevrey-Chambertin Les Cazetiers, Gevrey-Chambertin Le Fonteny, Gevrey-Chambertin Vieilles Vignes

DOMAINE JEAN TARDY (VOSNE-ROMANÉE)* * *

Tardy is capable of producing four- or five-star-quality wines, particularly from the small parcels in Clos de Vougeot and Nuits-St.-Georges Les Boudots he works under *métayage* (sharecropping) arrangements. In some vintages his wines have lacked concentration and fruit and have appeared overoaked; nevertheless, this is a producer who can fashion top-notch wines.

Best Wines: Clos de Vougeot, Nuits-St.-Georges Les Boudots

DOMAINE TOLLOT-BEAUT ET FILS (CHOREY-LES-BEAUNE)* * * *

Although this historic estate should throw away its filters, their top wines (such as Corton Les Bressandes, Corton, Beaune Clos du Roi, and Beaune Grèves) are filled with red and black cherry fruit judiciously touched by toasty oak. The domaine's wines are delicious young and should be consumed within the first 10 years after their release. This is an excellent source of fairly priced red burgundies.

Best Wines: Beaune Clos du Roi, Beaune Les Grèves, Corton, Corton Les Bressandes

DOMAINE JEAN ET JEAN-LOUIS TRAPET (GEVREY-CHAMBERTIN)* * * *

Jean-Louis Trapet has taken over the responsibility of this domaine from his father and has made some significant changes in its operation. Thanks to lowered yields, high-quality non-interventionist winemaking, and the abandonment of fining and filtering, this estate is finally crafting superlative wines from its extraordinary array of vineyards. The disasters of the past are now all but forgotten, and Jean-Louis Trapet is well on his way to being one of Gevrey's top producers. The wines have excellent intensity, superb ripeness, depth of fruit, and, in 1996 and 1997, fabulously soft tannins.

Best Wines: Chambertin, Chapelle-Chambertin, Latricières-Chambertin

DOMAINE DU COMTE DE VOGÜÉ (CHAMBOLLE-MUSIGNY)* * * * *

This is Chambolle-Musigny's most significant and famous estate, largely because it owns 18 acres, or 70%, of the grand cru, Musigny. It also has important holdings in Bonnes Mares and Chambolle-Musigny Les Amoureuses. In the forties, fifties, and sixties it was hard to find a greater burgundy than this estate's Musigny Vieilles Vignes (magnums of the 1949 and 1959 tasted in 1996 were truly ethereal). Between 1973 and 1988 the quality slipped badly. Since then the estate's winemaker, François Millet, has resurrected this famed domaine's quality. Comte de Vogüé has produced splendidly rich, impressively concentrated, full-bodied, powerful wines in 1990, 1991, 1993, 1995, 1996, and 1997 and very good wines in 1992 and 1994. These wines are now among the most concentrated, deeply colored, and respected burgundies. Moreover, they possess the requisite richness and intensity to age well for 20–30 years. The Domaine du Comte de Vogüé is unquestionably one of Burgundy's five best estates (with Domaines d'Auvenay, Leroy, Claude Dugat, and Bernard Dugat-Py).

Best Wines: Bonnes Mares, Chambolle-Musigny, Chambolle-Musigny Les Amoureuses, Musigny Vieilles Vignes

SELECTED TASTING NOTES

DOMAINE BERTRAND AMBROISE (NUITS-ST.-GEORGES)

1996	Bourgogne Pinot Noir Cuvée Vieilles Vignes	C	87
1996	Clos Vougeot	EE	(90–92+)
1995	Clos Vougeot	EE	91
1996	Corton Le Rognet	EE	(93–95)
1995	Corton Le Rognet	EE	93
1996	Côtes de Nuits-Villages	D	87+
1995	Côtes de Nuits-Villages	C	86
1995	Nuits-St.-Georges	D	88
1996	Nuits-St.-Georges Rue de Chaux	D	(90–92?)
1995	Nuits-St.-Georges Rue de Chaux	D	89
1996	Nuits-St.-Georges Les Vaucrains	E	(92–94)
1995	Nuits-St.-Georges Les Vaucrains	E	91
1996	Nuits-St.-Georges Vieilles Vignes	D	(89–91)
1996	Vougeot Les Cras	E	(88–90+)

My friends that live for California Cabernets and the reds of Bordeaux consistently adore the wines of Bertrand Ambroise. These are not subtle, elegant, cherry-and-strawberry-filled wines but, rather, are dark, boisterous bruisers that make their presence felt through their power and intensity. Ambroise does not filter his whites and neither fines nor filters his reds. Both are left on their lees for a year and see 100% new oak.

Made from 40-year-old vines located in Corgoloin, which yielded 35 hectoliters/hectare, the medium to dark 1995 Côte de Nuits-Villages reveals strawberry bubble-gum aromas and a beautifully concentrated, medium-bodied, strawberry cola-packed mouth. Drink it between now and 2005. Aged in 75% new oak, the dark, medium-bodied 1995 Nuits-St.-Georges displays mocha and dark spices on the nose and an intense, muscular, rugged, thick-textured mouth crammed with chewy, spicy black fruits, yet surprisingly it has a certain elegance. Drink it between 2002 and 2009.

The next four wines (none of which are for the faint-hearted) were all aged in 100% new oak and are intense, tannic, robust wines that demand a few years of cellaring before being consumed. The dark, nearly black 1995 Nuits-St.-Georges Rue de Chaux reveals an austere, almost brooding nose of burnt wood and black fruits (similar to unsweetened licorice) and a masculine, chewy, tannic, dark berry-filled mouth. Full bodied and thick, this wine requires

5–7 years of cellaring before being enjoyed over the subsequent 7–9 years. The black-colored 1995 Nuits-St.-Georges Les Vaucrains exhibits a deep, somber, intense nose of dark fruits and a mouthful of powerful, rustic, tannic, blackberries, minerals, and stones. Long, complex, and almost overpowering, this monster demands to be cellared for 7 years. It is probably capable of lasting until 2013. Made from 45–50-year-old vines that yielded 2 tons of fruit per acre in 1995, Ambroise's dark Clos Vougeot possesses a brooding nose of struc-tured, roasted dark fruits and a fat, full-bodied, chunky, thick-textured mouthful of oak-imbued fruit. Masculine and backward, this concentrated, massive behemoth will be at its peak between 2004 and 2014. Based on my tastings, 1995 may be as dazzling a year for Cor-ton. The 1995 Corton Le Rognet is dark colored and boasts a nose of candied black cherries, sweet oak, café au lait, and butterscotch(!). This massive, powerful, thick, velvety-textured, vibrant, and full-bodied blockbuster is crammed with supersweet red and black fruit, blueberries, and mocha. Its intensely long finish reveals loads of supple tannins and strong toasted-oak flavors. Out of barrel this was a hugely tannic wine; now it is elegant and focused—yet still muscular and fruit-driven.

I had the pleasure of seeing fun-filled Bertrand Ambroise twice in Burgundy to taste his 1996s. When I visited him in November of 1997, many of the 1996s were unapproachable (the Corton Le Rognet had completed only 5% of its malolactic fermentation!). Subsequently the wines have softened and become much more expressive. All of Ambroise's wines are bot-tled unfined and unfiltered. As I lifted my glass to taste his first red in November 1997, Am-broise flashed a big smile and said, "Remember, now, my wines are not for kids!" With that comment began yet another tasting of intensely flavored and structured Domaine Bertrand Ambroise wines. Some people like to say that masters resemble their dogs. In this instance, the wines resemble the vigneron.

The medium to dark ruby-colored 1996 Bourgogne Pinot Noir Cuvée Vieilles Vignes (it was aged in 100% new oak barrels and bottled in December 1997) has rich and sweet red cherry aromas and a fat, silky-textured, concentrated, extracted, and medium- to full-bodied core of layered, and chewy red fruits. This is a topflight Bourgogne! Sweet, luscious, packed with fruit, and with a delightful, oaky finish, it should be drunk over the next 3–4 years. The slightly darker colored 1996 Côtes de Nuits-Villages (bottled on December 29, 1997) was showing some reduction when I tasted it. This should have dissipated by now, and it may therefore be better than my initial impression. Behind the meaty and gamey aromas of re-duction I perceived sweet black raspberries and traces of freshly laid asphalt. This medium-to full-bodied, velvety-textured, fresh, and somewhat backward wine offers a flavor profile composed of blackberries and dark cherries. Anticipated maturity: 2000–2003.

Exhibiting a dark ruby color and intense aromatics of blackberries, minerals, and metal shavings, the 1996 Nuits-St.-Georges Vieilles Vignes is a broad-shouldered, massively chewy, full-bodied, powerful, concentrated, and meaty wine. It is dense, a little rough around the edges, and boisterous and offers intense flavors of cassis, blackberries, and road tar. Cel-laring will easily round out this wine's ripe tannins, resulting in a flavorful mouthful of dark fruits. This impressive wine should be at its peak between 2001 and 2006. The 1996 Vougeot Les Cras is dark colored and reveals intense blackberry, tobacco, mocha, and toasted-oak aromatics. It possesses immense breadth and an appealing juiciness, as well as a velvety texture and full body. This wine does not have the punch of the previous wine, yet its flavor profile (cassis, coffee, and tangy red berries) is dense, extracted, and persistent. Anticipated maturity: 2001–2006. The saturated, dark-colored 1996 Nuits-St.-Georges Rue de Chaux has expressive aromas of lively black currants and licorice. This wine's character is so dense, chewy, and structured that a knife and fork may be required to taste it. It is foursquare, backward, intense, and redolent in cassis, blackberry, and road tar-like flavors. This was a difficult wine to taste, as it assaulted my palate. It will either ultimately merit an outstanding rating in the range I ascribed to it (maybe higher) or succumb to its elevated tannins. I would suggest trying it in 5 years. There is no doubting the quality of the dark, almost black 1996 Nuits-St.-Georges Les Vaucrains. Its lively and enthralling nose of cassis, violets, roses, and black raspberries is followed by an intense, oily-textured, massively powerful, and full-bodied core of superripe black cherries and blackberries. This expansive, plump, structured, sweet, and highly concentrated wine rolls across the tongue in viscous waves that refuse to relinquish their hold on the palate. Anticipated maturity: 2003–2009.

The medium to dark ruby-colored 1996 Clos Vougeot (produced from yields averaging $2^2/_3$ tons per acre) reveals scents of spicy red currants and cherries and hints of tar. This huge, full-bodied, masculine, chewy-textured, and backward wine is crammed with ripe black fruits, kirsch, Asian spices, and earth. Impressively dense, concentrated, and extracted, it also possesses a long finish. This brooding giant will require cellaring patience. Anticipated maturity: 2003–2008. Produced from yields averaging just under 2 tons per acre (5 bunches per vine according to Ambroise), the dark-as-night 1996 Corton Le Rognet is spectacular. Aromas of Peking duck laced with plum sauce, black fruits, spices, and roasted oak are followed by a massively ripe, mouth-coating, full-bodied, and broad-shouldered personality. This monster is hugely extracted, concentrated, juicy, fresh, chewy textured, and densely packed with dried cherries, blackberries, cassis, raw meat, stones, and minerals. Its awesomely long finish reveals loads of supple, well-integrated tannins wrapped in even more sweet fruits and vanilla-imbued oak. Wow! Anticipated maturity: 2003–2009.

DOMAINE GUY AMIOT ET FILS (CHASSAGNE-MONTRACHET)

1996 Chassagne-Montrachet Clos St.-Jean	D	(87–88+)
1996 Chassagne-Montrachet La Maltroie	D	(86–88)
1996 Santenay La Comme Dessus	D	(85–87)

Produced from 30-year-old vines, the 1996 Santenay La Comme Dessus exhibits a spicy nose of raspberries and red currants, followed by a lush, expressive, sweet red cherry-packed, and medium-bodied character. This straightforward, pleasurable, soft wine should be drunk over the next 3 years. Aromatically revealing fresh herbs and Asian spices intermingled with minerals, the medium to dark ruby-colored 1996 Chassagne-Montrachet La Maltroie offers excellent concentration of brambleberries and blackberries, a medium-bodied and silky-textured personality, and loads of supple tannins. This well-crafted wine is delicious to drink yet will easily hold through 2002. The 1996 Chassagne-Montrachet Clos St.-Jean displays a medium to dark ruby/purple color and a lovely nose of perfumed violets and blueberries. On the palate, sweet red and black berries come on full bore in this masculine, medium- to full-bodied, velvety-textured, and intense wine. Its appealing finish reveals blackberries, minerals, and traces of earthlike flavors and well-rounded tannins. Anticipated maturity: now–2003.

DOMAINE PIERRE AMIOT (MOREY-ST.-DENIS)

1996 Clos de la Roche	E	(90–92)
1996 Gevrey-Chambertin Les Combottes	D	(90–92+)
1996 Morey-St.-Denis Les Millandes	D	(88–90+)
1996 Morey-St.-Denis Les Ruchots	D	(86–88+)

Note: The wines I tasted from Domaine Pierre Amiot are special 100% new oak cuvées that are neither fined nor filtered and are bottled by hand for Patrick Lesec, this estate's broker. My understanding is that they are available throughout the world but that other, non-Lesec cuvées, are also available.

Readers should take note of this estate's name. As with many Burgundian domaines, this one is undergoing a generational change since Pierre Amiot is relinquishing the reins to sons Jean-Louis and Didier (another son, the highly talented Christian Amiot, is responsible for the wines of Domaine Amiot-Servelle in Chambolle-Musigny). The estate has old vines—the Morey premiers crus are 50 years old, and half of the Clos de la Roche parcel is 50, with the balance having been planted in 1981. The first-rate quality of their 1996s appear to indicate that low yields as well as conscientious and noninterventionist winemaking are finally gaining the upper hand at this address. These wines are certainly values given their appellations and excellent to outstanding quality.

The ruby-colored 1996 Morey-St.-Denis Les Ruchots reveals sweet cherry and toasty oak aromas that give way to a medium-bodied, juicy, silky-textured, and fresh personality. Its beautifully ripe flavor profile is filled with layers of raspberries, black cherries, and stonelike flavors. The sample I was given to taste still contained a great deal of carbon dioxide (a natural by-product of malolactic fermentations as well as extended lees contact), which has the effect of "tightening" a wine's body, texture, and fruit. If that has taken place with this wine—and I assume it has—my score will appear conservative after aeration and bottling. Drink it between now and 2005. Amiot's medium to dark ruby-colored 1996 Morey-St.-Denis Les Millandes is a wonderful wine. It has candied black cherry aromatics that give way to a deeply ripe, medium- to full-bodied, harmonious, and concentrated personality. Sweet raspberries, chocolate-covered cherries, and vanilla-imbued oak can be found in this intense, velvety, refined, and rich wine. It is masculine, ample, and has a long and supple finish. Anticipated maturity: now–2006.

Most growers from Morey believe that the only reason the Gevrey-Chambertin Les Combottes vineyard is not a grand cru is that Morey producers own more of it than growers from Gevrey (one of the steps required for the elevation of an appellation's status is a vote of vignerons from the commune in which the vineyard is located). The reason this is important is that growers treat grands crus, and vineyards they think should have that status, with more respect and care than others. Witness the attention owners of Chambolle-Musigny Les Amoureuses, Meursault Perrières, and Gevrey-Chambertin Clos St.-Jacques lavish on their parcels and the resulting wines. Domaine Pierre Amiot's medium to dark ruby-colored 1996 Gevrey-Chambertin Les Combottes appears to continue this trend. Exhibiting a rich, pure, and spicy nose of dark cherries and raspberries, this is a medium- to full-bodied, well-proportioned, velvety-textured, and powerful wine. It is focused yet opulent, juicy yet dense, and offers delicious layers of black raspberries, cassis, and minerals in its flavor profile as well as in its admirably long finish. It should be at its peak of maturity between 2002 and 2008.

The bright, medium to dark ruby-colored 1996 Clos de la Roche displays red berry fruit drenched in charred-oak scents and a medium- to full-bodied, broad-shouldered, and oily-textured character. This thick and concentrated wine possesses seductive cassis, blackberry, earth, stone, and juniper-smoked bacon flavors in its tightly wound and austere personality. Anticipated maturity: 2003–2009.

DOMAINE AMIOT-SERVELLE (CHAMBOLLE-MUSIGNY)

1996 Bourgogne	C	(85–86)
1996 Chambolle-Musigny	D	(86–87)
1995 Chambolle-Musigny	D	87
1996 Chambolle-Musigny Les Amoureuses	EE	(91–93)
1995 Chambolle-Musigny Les Amoureuses	EE	93
1996 Chambolle-Musigny Les Charmes	E	(88–90)
1995 Chambolle-Musigny Les Charmes	E	89+
1996 Chambolle-Musigny Derrière La Grange	E	(90–92+)

1995 Chambolle-Musigny Derrière La Grange	EE	92
1996 Clos Vougeot	EE	(90–92+)
1995 Clos Vougeot	E	92

Christian Amiot has been responsible for this estate's wines since 1990, and the quality of his wines has progressed admirably with each vintage. As Robert Parker has stated, the wines of the Domaine Amiot-Servelle "go from strength to strength." I was quite taken by the opulent yet structured nature of these graceful, juicy, beautifully ripe and extracted wines. Amiot is a star in the making.

The medium to dark ruby-colored 1995 Chambolle-Musigny offers a refined, feminine nose of roses and red fruits whose flavors are intermingled with notes of coffee, cassis, and blueberries for additional complexity. It has a gorgeously balanced, silky-textured, opulent, and medium- to full-bodied flavor profile. I wish all of Burgundy's village wines were this delicious! Anticipated maturity: now–2004. Amiot's slightly darker-colored 1995 Chambolle-Musigny Les Charmes (aged in 10% new oak) bursts with dried flowers as well as cassis-laden aromas and possesses a beautifully delineated core of tangy blueberries, black cherries, and violets in its highly structured, oily-textured medium- to full-bodied character. It is delicious now, and its structure and ripe tannins will allow it to age marvelously. Anticipated maturity: now–2009. Aged in 30% new oak, the deep ruby-colored 1995 Chambolle-Musigny Derrière La Grange (the vineyard's name means "behind the barn" in French) reveals a lively, fresh blueberry-and-cherry-scented nose with intermingled notes of vanilla. This superb wine possesses a silky texture and explodes with flavors of blackberries, red fruits, and touches of underbrush and roasted meats on its exceptionally long finish. Drink this gem between 2000 and 2009.

Produced from vines planted in 1942, the bright ruby-colored 1995 Clos Vougeot exhibits roses, violets, and Asian spices aromatically as well as a concentrated, highly structured, powerful, full-bodied, and vivacious mouthful of sweet red berries and cinnamon and, surprisingly, distinct notes of fresh ginger. This outstanding offering possesses a ripe tannic backbone that will require cellaring. Depressingly, upon returning to the United States, I learned that Christian's wife accidentally broke 400 bottles while moving them in the cellar. Anticipated maturity: 2004–2012. Amiot's finest wine is his blockbuster 1995 Chambolle-Musigny Les Amoureuses. Revealing a dark ruby color and intense aromas of blackberries, wild blueberries, cassis, earth, and sweet sautéed mushrooms, it bursts with tangy, concentrated, admirably extracted and layered red and black berry fruit. Refined, elegant, and stupendously long (it finishes on sweet notes of cinnamon candy), this full-bodied beauty will be at its best between 2004 and 2012. Bravo!

The light to medium ruby-colored 1996 Bourgogne has floral, crisp, and sweet red cherry aromas and a lively, medium-bodied, and refreshing character filled with strawberries and black cherries. My sense is that this wine needs to be drunk up in the near term. Anticipated maturity: now. Revealing a ruby color and a nose of mineral-laced red and black berries, the 1996 Chambolle-Musigny has a delicate yet intense palate presence composed of stones and blackberries. This appealing wine should be drunk over the next 2–3 years.

Displaying a ruby color as well as aromatics reminiscent of plums, blueberries, and minerals, the 1996 Chambolle-Musigny Les Charmes is medium-bodied, silky-textured, feminine, fat, and refined. This well-crafted, detailed, and supple wine will be at its best between now and 2003. Produced from a parcel whose oldest vines were planted in 1936, the medium to dark ruby-colored 1996 Chambolle-Musigny Derrière La Grange is a fragrant wine that reveals scents of smoked pork, crisp black fruits, and allspice. This medium- to full-bodied, expressive, vivacious, mouth-coating, and sweet (but not cloying) offering is expansive and soft and possesses blackberry and cassis flavors. Anticipated maturity: now–2004.

The slightly darker-colored 1996 Clos Vougeot has an extremely spicy nose of candied red fruits. It is medium to full bodied, broad, superbly balanced and fresh and offers ripe blackberry and Asian spice flavors. Its long and focused finish reveals loads of supple tannins. Since this wine had been racked and sulfured 10 days prior to my visit, it is possible that its color, fruit, and density had been temporarily compressed by the SO_2 (hence the "+"). Anticipated maturity: 2000–2005. Christian Amiot's 1996 Chambolle-Musigny Les Amoureuses has a bright, medium to dark ruby color and a delightfully elegant and fresh nose of violets, roses, blueberries, and cherries. It explodes on the palate with layered and deeply ripe black cherries, mocha, and toasted-oak flavors. This feminine, refined, medium- to full-bodied, and silky wine also possesses a formidably long and supple finish. Drink it between 2002 and 2008.

DOMAINE DU MARQUIS D'ANGERVILLE (VOLNAY)

1996	Volnay Premier Cru	D	(87–89)
1995	Volnay Premier Cru	D	(87–89)
1996	Volnay Champans	D	(89–92)
1995	Volnay Champans	D	91
1996	Volnay Clos des Ducs	E	(92–94+)
1995	Volnay Clos des Ducs	E	(91–93+)
1996	Volnay Taillepieds	D	(91–93)
1995	Volnay Taillepieds	D	(90–93)

Jacques, Marquis d'Angerville, is without a doubt one of the finest producers in Burgundy. However, prior to working in the retail wine trade I firmly believed that he did not deserve his reputation as such. I rapidly came to realize that the wines I had been purchasing in the United States had been damaged by careless shipping or storage. Wines purchased in shops in France are often substantially better than those found in the United States.

Charming, sensitive, and extremely intelligent, the Marquis produces beautifully concentrated and superbly elegant wines. Furthermore, when properly shipped and cellared, they can age gracefully for well over a decade.

For every "great truth" in the wine world there are numerous exceptions. For example, while it is generally true that clean and antiseptic cellars are desired by many winemakers (it provides them with more control over their wines), enormous quantities of world-class wines are produced in wineries that are anything but sterile. The fauna growing in Henri Bonneau's (Châteauneuf-du-Pape) cellar is mind-blowing, as are the multicolored mosses in Gérard and Jean-Louis Chave's (Hermitage). The Marquis d'Angerville's *caves* are the birthplace of some of Burgundy's finest bottles, yet, while not comparable to the two I have mentioned, it could never be confused with a hospital ward. There are winemaking theories that fauna indigenous to cellars has an enormous impact on the style and quality of the resulting wines. Yeasts and bacteria that live and breed in these cool and dank environments can affect fermentations (both alcoholic and malolactic) and perhaps other important steps in the winemaking process. For whatever reasons, whether they include his cellars or not, the Marquis wines can be extraordinary.

Produced from his youngest vines, d'Angerville's ruby-colored 1995 Volnay Premier Cru reveals superripe cherries and mocha aromatically and a thick-textured, medium- to full-bodied core of sweet and luscious strawberries and blueberries. Beautifully balanced and admirably delineated, it lacks the necessary length for an outstanding rating. Drink it between now and 2002. The medium to dark ruby-colored 1995 Volnay Champans displays highly expressive cherry and mineral aromas as well as superb flavors reminiscent of unctuous blueberries, strawberries, and Asian spices. Concentrated and well balanced, this full-bodied and charmingly refined wine was shockingly good immediately after bottling and will remain so through 2006.

As is obvious from the scores, I absolutely adored d'Angerville's two top wines. The dark ruby/purple-colored 1995 Volnay Taillepieds possesses beguiling aromas of deeply spicy blackberries and cherries and a massively thick, highly structured, hugely extracted, and sweet flavor profile oozing with tangy and lively dark cherries, cassis, and wild blueberries. Notes of vanilla and Asian spices are found in this wine's exemplary finish. Anticipated maturity: now–2009. Offering a gorgeous, saturated black/purple color, the 1995 Volnay Clos des Ducs has a sublime nose of violets, roses, and superripe plums, cherries, and blueberries. Full bodied, oily textured, and massively concentrated, this wine has a mouthwatering core of Asian spices, fresh herbs, and deeply sweet red and black fruits. Its purity, precision, and elegance are simply mind-boggling. Bravo! Anticipated maturity: now–2010.

The 1996 Volnay Premier Cru, fashioned from vines located in the En L'Ormeau and Pitures vineyards and from the youngest vines from d'Angerville's more famous sites, reveals a bright ruby color and a candied red cherry-and-violet-infused nose. This wine's succulent character is composed of fat, plump, and sweet cherries encased in an elegant, medium-bodied, and silky texture. It will be delicious to drink from its release to 2003. The medium ruby-colored 1996 Volnay Champans has a creamy cherry-scented nose and an outstanding, sweet, medium-bodied, and supple character packed with ripe black cherries and minerals. This lovely and well-focused wine should be at its peak from its release to 2003. Produced from yields below 2²/₃ tons per acre (admirable for 1996), the 1996 Volnay Taillepieds exhibits beguiling aromas of black cherries, blackberries, and spices. On the palate, this complex, concentrated, and extracted wine is beautifully refined, sumptuous, yet structured. It is expansive, broad, medium to full bodied, and packed with juicy cassis and blueberries. This well-balanced and fruit-driven wine has an admirably persistent finish that displays loads of ripe tannins. Anticipated maturity: 2000–2006. I flipped over the Marquis d'Angerville's 1996 Volnay Clos des Ducs. Sporting a medium to dark ruby color, this wine offers mouthwatering aromas of cream-covered black cherries and the inviting scents of a deep-dish cherry pie. Powerful and explosive layers of sweet red and black fruits greet the palate in this profound, broad, concentrated, and complex wine. It is slightly more structured, intense, and extracted than the previous wine. It will also require more patience. Anticipated maturity: 2002–2008.

DOMAINE ARLAUD PÈRE ET FILS (NUITS-ST.-GEORGES)

1996	Bourgogne Roncevie Cuvée Unique Réserve	C	87
1996	Chambolle-Musigny Vieilles Vignes Cuvée Unique Réserve	D	89
1996	Charmes-Chambertin Cuvée Unique Réserve	EE	91
1996	Clos de la Roche Cuvée Unique Réserve	EE	90+
1996	Clos St.-Denis Cuvée Unique Réserve	EE	94
1995	Clos St.-Denis Cuvée Unique Réserve	E	(91–93)
1996	Gevrey-Chambertin Les Combottes Cuvée Unique Réserve	E	91
1996	Morey-St.-Denis Les Cheseaux Cuvée Unique Réserve	D	89
1995	Morey-St.-Denis Les Cheseaux Cuvée Unique Réserve	D	(87–89)
1995	Morey-St.-Denis Les Millandes Cuvée Unique Réserve	D	(88–90)

1996 Morey-St.-Denis Les Ruchots Cuvée Unique Réserve	E	92
1995 Morey-St.-Denis Les Ruchots Cuvée Unique Réserve	D	(89–92)

The Domaine Arlaud rarely receives much attention from the wine press, in large part because the wines can be uninspiring and blatantly commercial. However, thanks to the efforts of Peter Vezan and David Hinkle of North Berkeley Imports, this estate is now producing splendid wines. But readers should be very careful when acquiring them. *These ratings are for the special cuvées made specifically for North Berkeley; other bottlings from different importers will not be the same wines.* As Hervé Arlaud candidly pointed out, "The North Berkeley cuvées are 100 times better than mine." What are the differences in winemaking? Arlaud's regular bottlings are fined and filtered and see a maximum of only 10% new oak. North Berkeley's cuvées are neither fined nor filtered, are aged in lavish quantities of new oak, and are bottled by hand using a small contraption that looks as if it were borrowed from a museum of vigneron's artifacts. Kudos to Arlaud for having 1) the courage to try the Vezan and Hinkle-inspired techniques, and 2) the honesty to recognize the vast difference in quality between his regular bottling and these cuvées.

Displaying a dark ruby color and deep, intense aromas of wild fruit and spices, the 1995 Morey-St.-Denis Les Millandes is a massively chewy, silky-textured, concentrated gem packed with wild, dark berries and a clean, attractive earthy component. Medium to full bodied, this wine should be cellared for 4–5 years and drunk over the following 6 years. Not as explosive and intense as the preceding wine, but impressive, the 1995 Morey-St.-Denis Les Cheseaux reveals a dark ruby color, a nose of red and black fruits with intriguing sweet candle wax and mineral notes and an elegant, polished mouth with flavors of dark cherries, stones, and earth. Medium bodied and long, it should be drunk between 2001 and 2007. Dark colored, the 1995 Morey-St.-Denis Les Ruchots possesses a super nose of dark flowers and berries with a touch of candle wax and a huge mouthful of chewy, perfumed, floral dark cherries. Beautifully velvety textured and creamy, this awesome example of a Morey premier cru should be enjoyed between 2002 and 2010. For me, nothing beats tasting a spectacular wine from a winery largely unfamiliar to me. The thrilling, dark-colored 1995 Clos St.-Denis offers a luxurious black berry-filled nose and gorgeously spicy mouth jam-packed with milk chocolate, floral red fruits, candied orange peel, earthiness, and wax. Armed with an awesomely thick texture, this full-bodied, fabulously explosive beauty requires 7 years of cellaring and will hold its peak for 8–9+ years.

"Pure unadulterated pleasure. Liquid hedonism. Great drinking! Great mouth-feel! Sexy. Total seduction. Why even cellar? Must buy." These are some of the words that adorned the margins of my notebook after my tasting of Hervé Arlaud's 1996s. With the exception of the Clos St.-Denis, these are not wines a taster will spend much time contemplating or intellectually analyzing; rather, these are drinking wines that provide enormous pleasure and huge satisfaction and are guaranteed to induce smiles. If I had let myself get even more seduced by them, I could have forgotten that complexity is a significant factor in scoring. Yet while we all want a brilliant conversationalist as a spouse, is that what we dreamt of as 16-year-olds?

Produced from a parcel just below the Gevrey-Chambertin En Etelois vineyard and bordering the RN74, the 1996 Bourgogne Roncevie Cuvée Unique Réserve was aged in 3-year-old oak barrels. It has a bright ruby color and a lovely nose of rich sweet red fruits, as well as a big, fat, oily-textured, medium-bodied, spicy, and dense core of candied red cherries. If there had been a trace of complexity to this straightforward and luscious offering, I would have jumped at the opportunity to give it an excellent rating. This delicious wine, a fabulous example of the heights a "regional" appellation burgundy can achieve if given some attention, should be enjoyed over the next 3 years.

The 1996 Chambolle-Musigny Vieilles Vignes Cuvée Unique Réserve (a blend of premier cru Les Sentiers and old-vine village wines) is dark ruby colored and reveals violet, blue-berry, and black cherry scents. This rich, velvety, broad, concentrated, seductive, and im-peccably balanced wine regales with its loads of spicy, rose-petal-imbued, red cherry flavors. It is a medium- to full-bodied and sexy offering with some of the most supple and soft tan-nins I have yet experienced. It should be consumed over the next 4–5 years. Produced from a parcel that abuts the grand cru Latricières-Chambertin vineyard, the 1996 Gevrey-Chambertin Les Combottes Cuvée Unique Réserve has a floral-and-cassis-laden nose as well as a medium- to full-bodied, expansive, broad, and juicy core of wild blueberries and red cherries. Soft, opulent, and luscious, this offering reveals tannins so imbued with fruit as to be almost unnoticeable. Drink this beauty over the next 5 years.

I've always been perplexed by the fact that Morey-St.-Denis does not get the respect it de-serves. When wine lovers consider the Côte de Nuits they tend to think of Vosne-Romanée, Gevrey-Chambertin, Chambolle-Musigny, and Nuits-St.-Georges, and only rarely do they consider this village nestled between Gevrey and Chambolle. It is home to a number of grand cru vineyards (including the famed Clos de la Roche and Clos St. Denis), some of which are *monopoles* (Clos de Tart and Clos des Lambrays), and some extraordinary premiers crus. I was surprised to hear from a number of Morey vignerons that Americans seem to be more aware of them and their work than the French!

The medium- to dark-colored 1996 Morey-St.-Denis Les Cheseaux Cuvée Unique Réserve offers blackberry and stone aromas as well as an enticing, velvety, medium-bodied, and truly delicious core of gorgeously ripe blueberries and minerals. A longer finish and more com-plexity would have earned this lovely wine an outstanding score. Drink it over the next 4–5 years. Produced from what is quickly becoming my favorite Morey premier cru vineyard (it is just below Bonnes Mares and the Clos de Tart and borders the premier cru Chambolle-Musigny Les Sentiers vineyard to the south), the 1996 Morey-St.-Denis Les Ruchots Cuvée Unique Réserve (tasted both in Burgundy and the United States) displays lovely blueberry, black cherry, and stonelike scents. On the palate, this lively, focused, refined wine is redo-lent with sweet plums, blackberries, and wild blueberries that seemingly burst open on the palate, liberating their tangy and vibrant juices. This offering is medium to full bodied, pow-erful, filled with supple (almost melted) tannins, and armed with a detailed and sweet/spicy finish. This beauty should be drunk over the next 5 years.

Arlaud's 1996 Charmes-Chambertin Cuvée Unique Réserve exhibits a medium to dark ruby color, perfumed floral aromas, and a charming (the name fits!), feminine, luscious, and medium- to full-bodied character with flavors reminiscent of deep-dish blueberry pie. This juicy and long-finishing wine has more noticeable tannins than any of the previous offerings, yet they are silky and soft. Anticipated maturity: 2000–2007. When I tasted the medium to dark ruby-colored 1996 Clos de la Roche Cuvée Unique Réserve for the first time in Bur-gundy, I scored it slightly higher than I did at a blind tasting stateside a few months later (the quoted score is the most recent). Smoked bacon blows off after a few minutes, revealing blackberries, cassis, stones, and a dusting of mocha powder. This highly pleasing, expan-sive, and expressive wine is filled with blueberries, spices, plums, brambleberries, iron, and traces of underbrush. Medium to full bodied and oily textured (yet lively), it appeared to have more complexity and a longer finish when I first tasted it. Will that return? Anticipated maturity: now–2005. The spectacular 1996 Clos St.-Denis Cuvée Unique Réserve is medium to dark ruby colored and exhibits deeply ripe black fruit aromas that give way to an explo-sive, fat, velvety-textured, lush, and opulent personality. This offering does not lack com-plexity, yet it has the same seductive qualities as Arlaud's other wines. Violets, black cherries, freshly ground white pepper, pork fat, juicy blueberries, and loads of North African spices tantalize the palate. Its admirably long and soft finish reveals loads of supple tannins. Drink this gem between 2000 and 2007. Bravo!

DOMAINE DE L'ARLOT (PRÉMEAUX-PRISSEY)

1996	Cote de Nuits-Villages Clos du Chapeau	D	86
1996	Nuits-St.-Georges	D	(86–87)
1996	Nuits-St.-Georges Clos de l'Arlot	E	(88–91)
1996	Nuits-St.-Georges Clos des Forêts St.-Georges	E	(89–92)
1996	Romanée-St.-Vivant	EEE	(89–91)
1996	Vosne-Romanée Les Suchots	EE	(86–88?)

AXA, the French-owned international insurance conglomerate, created this estate in 1987 by purchasing the former Domaine Jules Belin and adding to it other acquired vineyards. I've always wondered why AXA (which also owns famous châteaux in Bordeaux) and other French insurance companies fixated on owning wine-producing properties. Jean-Pierre de Smet, the estate's director and winemaker, explained to me that French law mandates that a percentage of an insurance company's holdings be in land or agriculture. He also noted that many of France's large tracts of forests—highly conservative investments—are owned by these firms.

After selling his Paris-based accounting and management consulting firm to Coopers & Lybrand, de Smet traveled around the world on his yacht before deciding to follow another passion—wine. He worked with Jacques Seysses (Domaine Dujac) for a number of years before going to Beaune's oenology school in 1986 and organizing the purchase and creation of Domaine de l'Arlot in 1987.

A close friend and admirer of Seysses, de Smet vinifies in much the same way. No cold maceration is forced upon the whole clusters. Fermentations are allowed to begin on their own (with the indigenous yeasts), so typically a 3-to-5-day maceration occurs. As at Dujac, the fermentation temperatures are closely monitored and never allowed to surpass 30–32 degrees Celsius. Sulfur is used sparingly, and the wines sometimes undergo fining but are never filtered. In general, bottling takes place between January 15 and early March.

Dark colors are not what de Smet (or Seysses, for that matter) searches out, as the light ruby-colored 1996 Côte de Nuits-Villages demonstrates. This wine reveals a flower-infused and perfumed nose as well as a powerful burst of blackberries and black cherries. This medium-bodied, elegant, and well-balanced wine should be drunk over the next 4 years. The ruby-colored 1996 Vosne-Romanée Les Suchots has lovely blueberry and cherry aromas and a structured, medium-bodied, blackberry, herbal, and cassis-laden personality. It is presently slightly rough (which prevented it from meriting a higher score), but its long finish and persistent fruit may well gain supremacy over its stemmy tannins. Anticipated maturity: now–2003.

The 1996 Nuits-St.-Georges Clos de l'Arlot is ruby/purple colored and has blueberries, blackberries, and mocha in its nose. This silky-textured, medium-bodied, refined, juicy, and rich wine has licorice, black cherries, and stones in its flavor profile. It is well concentrated and harmonious and does not suffer from the dry tannins I found in the Beaune Grèves and Vosne. Its long and drawn-out finish exhibits densely ripe fruits and supple tannins. Drink it between 2000 and 2006.

Because a 1985 freeze severely damaged the Nuits-St.-Georges Clos des Forêts St.-Georges vineyard, large sections were replanted in 1987 and 1989. De Smet declassifies the wines produced from the younger vines to craft a village Nuits-St.-Georges. The 1996 is ruby colored, with aromas of black raspberries and stones, and is chewy textured, foursquare, and well structured. Flavors of cassis and blackberries intermingled with minerals can be found in this tannic and masculine wine. Produced from vines ranging from 20 to 45 years old, the 1996 Nuits-St.-Georges Clos des Forêts is a splendid Nuits. Its deep cherry scents are intertwined with cookie dough aromas. Its character explodes on the palate with sumptuously ripe cherries, raspberries, and traces of minerals. This expressive, medium- to full-bodied, and gorgeously pure wine has loads of supple tannins in its long and persistent finish. Anticipated maturity: 2001–2007+.

The medium to dark ruby-colored 1996 Romanée-St.-Vivant (1991 was the estate's first vintage) exhibits delightful floral, perfumed, violet, and blueberry aromas. This elegant, lace-like, medium-bodied, feminine wine offers flavors of raspberries, red currants, sugar-coated strawberries, and earth. It does not have the density or palate presence of the Clos des Forêts but remains extremely appealing for its precision and purity. Drink it between 2000 and 2007.

DOMAINE DU COMTE ARMAND (POMMARD)

1996	Auxey Duresses	D	(87–88)
1996	Auxey Duresses Premier Cru	D	(87–89)
1995	Auxey Duresses Premier Cru	D	(85–87)
1996	Pommard Clos des Epeneaux	EE	(91–93+)
1995	Pommard Clos des Epeneaux	EE	(88–91)
1996	Volnay Fremiets	E	(88–90)
1995	Volnay Fremiets	E	(87–89+)

Pascal Marchand, who runs this estate for the Paris-based Comte Armand, is the only Canadian ex–merchant marine who is a vigneron in Burgundy. Instead of becoming an officer by attending the Canadian merchant marine academy, Marchand decided to follow his passion for wine by going to Burgundy in 1983, thereby seeing vineyards for the first time. One thing led to another, and by the 1985 vintage (talk about luck!) he was managing the Comte Armand's domaine. Gregarious, intelligent, straightforward, full of life, and armed with a fabulous sense of humor and a contagious smile, Pascal Marchand is one of Burgundy's most engaging personalities . . . and an excellent winemaker to boot!

Produced from yields averaging $1^2/_3$ tons per acre, the medium to dark ruby-colored 1995 Volnay Fremiets offers beautifully refined aromas of sweet cherries and a medium- to full-bodied, lush, and silky-textured flavor profile jam-packed with gorgeously ripe strawberries and tangy currants. Its floral, soft tannin-filled, and exceptionally long finish serves as testimony to Marchand's skills as a winemaker. Anticipated maturity: 1999–2005. The ruby-colored 1995 Auxey-Duresses Premier Cru (from a total of $2^1/_2$ acres rented in both the Les Duresses and Les Bréterins vineyards) possesses a ripe cherry, flint, and mineral-scented nose and a crisp red currant-and-raspberry-flavored, soft, and medium-bodied personality that ends on a long and supple finish. It will be at its best between now and 2000.

Comte Armand's famed Clos des Epeneaux vineyard generally yields 2 tons per acre, but the 1995 harvest (owing primarily to Marchand's draconian sorting) produced yields of less than $1^2/_3$ tons. This *monopole* (solely owned) vineyard is composed of vines ranging from 10 to 65 years of age that Marchand harvests and vinifies in three lots: the first is made up of the 10–14- and 18-year-old vines, the second is from vines averaging 25 to 45 years of age, and the third is composed of the oldest vines, ranging from 50 to 65 years old. Prior to bottling, Marchand practices a distinctly un-Burgundian technique: he performs an *assemblage*—the art of taking distinctly different lots and blending them to produce a wine better than the sum of its individual components. I tasted all three of Marchand's lots and found the final blend to be superior to each component, seemingly taking the positive aspects of each while doing away with the flaws.

The dark ruby-colored 1995 Pommard Clos des Epeneaux offers deep black cherries, Asian spices, and roasted herbs aromatically and a refined, well-balanced, thick-textured, full-bodied, highly concentrated and extracted core of intensely powerful blackberries, cherries, and boysenberries, with notes of coffee and smoke for additional complexity. Its exemplary finish ends on a backbone of ripe, round tannins that provide it with the necessary structure for years of cellaring. Anticipated maturity: 2000–2007.

Produced from 30-year-old vines located in a vineyard with a southern exposure, the 1996 Auxey-Duresses is medium to dark ruby colored and offers mouthwatering aromas of sweet red berries and raspberries. This medium-bodied, supple, well-crafted, and admirably balanced wine is filled with delicious layers of ripe red cherries, strawberries, and traces of blackberries. Anticipated maturity: now–2001. The 1996 Auxey-Duresses Premier Cru, an assemblage of grapes from the Les Duresses and Les Bréterins vineyards, is medium to dark ruby colored and exhibits cassis and blackberry aromas. Its medium-bodied and oily-textured character reveals blueberries, sweet cherries, and minerals that linger on its long and oak-imbued finish. Projected maturity: now–2003. Medium to dark ruby colored, the 1996 Volnay Fremiets has refined cherry scents that give way to its medium- to full-bodied, soft, supple, and juicy character. Flavors of black cherries, blueberries, violets, and traces of tar can be discerned in this lovely, feminine wine.

The famed Clos des Epeneaux vineyard yielded 2²/₃ tons per acre in 1996, compared with 1²/₃ tons in 1995 and a 10-year average of a little over 2 tons per acre. As always, Marchand divided the harvest into separate cuvées determined by the age of the vines. In 1995, because of the abnormally low yields, he crafted three cuvées; in 1996 he fashioned four. The first is made up of vines planted 11, 15, and 19 years ago, the second from vines between the ages of 30 and 35, the third with vines averaging 40 to 45 years of age, and the fourth from the estate's oldest vines, between 50 and 65 years old. Two-thirds of the cuvée made from the youngest vines will be declassified to village status and sold under the Pommard label (it should merit a score in the 85–87 range). The wine is aged in 45% new oak (with the balance being 1-year-old barrels) until the following year's harvest. At that time it is racked into second-, third-, and fourth-year barrels in which the wine will end its *élevage*.

Marchand allowed me to taste each separate cuvée and then fashioned what he believes to be the final *assemblage* in a beaker. The 1996 Pommard Clos des Epeneaux will be outstanding when it is finally assembled, with three out of the four cuvées meriting scores whose upper reaches were 90 or above. Medium to dark ruby colored, it exhibits rich black cherries, crisp ripe currants, and blackberries on the nose. Its medium- to full-bodied, refined, yet powerful core is packed with assorted sweet red and black fruits, stones, candied cassis, and traces of leather and underbrush. This complex, intense, and elegant wine has a sumptuous velvety texture and loads of soft, ripe tannins in its long and persistent finish. It is the finest Clos des Epeneaux I have had in years and should age admirably well. Bravo! Anticipated maturity: 2002–2010.

DOMAINE ROBERT ARNOUX (VOSNE-ROMANÉE)

1996 Bourgogne	C	(86–87)
1996 Clos Vougeot	EE	(89–92)
1996 Echézeaux	EE	(90–92+)
1996 Nuits-St.-Georges	D	(86–88)
1996 Nuits-St.-Georges Les Corvées Pagets	E	(88–90+)
1996 Nuits-St.-Georges Les Poisets	E	(88–90)
1996 Nuits-St.-Georges Les Procès	E	(87–89)
1996 Romanée-St.-Vivant	EEE	(93–96)
1996 Vosne-Romanée	D	(86–88+)

1996 Vosne-Romanée Les Chaumes	E	(89–91)
1996 Vosne-Romanée Les Hautes Maizières	D	(87–89)
1996 Vosne-Romanée aux Reignots	E	(88–91)
1996 Vosne-Romanée Les Suchots	EE	(91–93+)

As I was about to leave the Domaine de la Romanée-Conti after having tasted through their spectacular wines, Aubert de Villaine asked me where my next visit was. When I said Domaine Robert Arnoux he smiled and replied that I would be tasting some wonderful wines. He was not kidding.

Pascal Lachaux, an extremely bright, meticulous, and serious man, has been solely responsible for the wines of Domaine Robert Arnoux since 1993. Lachaux studied to be a pharmacist and after graduating spent three months working as one before being called up to serve his military service. Immediately thereafter, in 1985, the father of his girlfriend (and later wife), Arnoux, asked him to come and work at the estate. His scientific background and love of wine led Lachaux to methodically study what actions could be taken to improve the domaine's wine.

He is a firm believer in working the earth, follows *lutte raisonnée* ("reasoned struggle"— meaning he uses as few chemical fertilizers as possible) practices, and performs serious prunings that have dramatically lowered this estate's formerly high yields. Bunches are 100% destemmed and fermentation temperatures are closely monitored and kept low, and Lachaux has increased the use of new oak barrels (the percentage ranges from a low of 15% on the Bourgogne to 70% on the Vosne-Romanée Les Suchots, Clos Vougeot, and Echézeaux and 100% on the Romanée-St.-Vivant). Lachaux, who says his duty as a Burgundian winemaker is "to search for fruit, elegance, and soft tannins," now limits rackings to two a year and has discontinued the estate's fining and filtering practices.

The results of Lachaux's changes speak for themselves. This estate has always had one of the finest "portfolios" of the Côte d'Or, and now it produces some of its best wines.

The ruby-colored 1996 Bourgogne reveals a nose of flowers, cherries, and blackberries that is followed by a medium-bodied, velvety-textured, red and black currant-flavored character. This extremely well-crafted and balanced wine can be drunk over the next 3–4 years. The similarly colored 1996 Nuits-St.-Georges has pure red cherry aromas that give way to a medium-bodied, rich, silky-textured, and candied red fruit-filled core. This soft, seductive, and supple wine is crafted to deliver loads of pleasure in its youth yet has the necessary structure to withstand a few years of cellaring. Drink it over the next 5–6 years. Displaying a bright ruby color and fragrances of violet-infused blackberries, the 1996 Vosne-Romanée has excellent richness, a medium body, and tightly wound sweet cherries and red currants in its harmonious character. This wine has a more powerful palate presence than the Nuits. Its long finish, admirable for a village appellation offering, possesses fine, ripe tannins. Anticipated maturity: now–2004. Produced from 45-year-old vines in a vineyard located on the eastern flank of the premier cru Les Suchots, the medium- to dark ruby-colored 1996 Vosne-Romanée Les Hautes Maizières aromatically offers black raspberry fruit spiced with toasty oak and freshly brewed coffee. This is a more intense wine than the previous ones, exhibiting a broad, ample, and medium- to full-bodied character replete with blackberries, dark cherries, earth, and hints of tar. It is structured, somewhat masculine, firm, and offers a long and focused finish. Anticipated maturity: 2000–2006. Crafted from vines that are over 60 years old in a vineyard wedged between the RN74 and the premier cru Les Cailles, the slightly darker-colored 1996 Nuits-St.-Georges Les Poisets (also known as Les Poirets) reveals brooding black fruit aromas. This concentrated, extracted, highly structured, and medium- to full-bodied wine raises the flavor intensity level one more notch. It is a well-proportioned, powerful, balanced, firm, and velvety offering that is crammed with blueberries and cassis flavors. Loads of well-ripened tannins are evident in its long finish. This wine should evolve wonderfully with cellaring. Anticipated maturity: 2001–2006.

Legends state that the Nuits-St.-Georges Les Procès vineyard earned its name because trials (Procès means trial in French) were held in this field before it was planted with vines. Lachaux's 1996 has a medium to dark ruby color, plummy and cassis aromas, and a medium-bodied, austere, juicy, and masculine character. Flavors of dry minerals, stones, earth, and black currants are present in this aristocratic, foursquare, nonexuberant wine. Readers looking for wines with charm, expressiveness, and seductive qualities should select another of Lachaux's offerings, as this severe yet excellent wine has none of those qualities. Drink it between 2001 and 2007. Produced from a premier cru vineyard in the Prémeaux sector of Nuits (the southernmost), the bright, medium to dark ruby-colored 1996 Nuits-St.-Georges Les Corvées-Pagets displays blackberry, cassis, fresh herb, and mineral-laden aromas. This medium- to full-bodied, masculine, chewy-textured, and complex wine is densely packed with beautifully ripe black fruit. It is refined, expressive, and extremely well balanced and has the necessary stuffing and structure for cellaring. Anticipated maturity: 2001–2007.

Exhibiting a medium to dark ruby color and complex cherry, blackberry, and earthy aromatics, the 1996 Vosne-Romanée Les Chaumes is a sweet, delicious, medium- to full-bodied, and oily-textured wine. It offers a mouthful of gorgeously ripe and supple red and black fruits, hints of toasty oak, and copious quantities of suave tannins in its refined and pure personality. Drink this seductive wine between 2000 and 2007. Produced from a parcel located 3 meters (slightly less than 10 feet) from the Domaine de la Romanée-Conti's Richebourg vines, the bright, medium to dark ruby-colored 1996 Vosne-Romanée aux Reignots (prior to the 1994 vintage Domaine Robert Arnoux sold wines produced from this vineyard as Vosne-Romanée Premier Cru) has enthralling aromas of morels, porcinis, violets, and raspberries. It is an elegant, delineated, medium- to full-bodied, velvety-textured, and concentrated wine. Layers of sweet red berries, Asian spices, and vanilla-imbued oak are found in its complex and persistent flavor profile. Anticipated maturity: 2001–2007. Possessing a deep, brilliant, and dark ruby color, the 1996 Vosne-Romanée Les Suchots is of grand cru quality (this is not particularly surprising for *terroir*-ists since its vineyard is bordered to the south by Romanée-St.-Vivant and Richebourg and to the north by Echézeaux). Awesomely sweet cherry and raspberry aromas give way to its massively ripe, profound, rich, and intense character. Layer upon layer of refined yet powerful black cherries, tangy currants, cassis, and toasty oak flavors grace this opulent yet refined and structured wine. Its formidably long finish is packed with even more waves of fruit and loads of supple tannins. This Vosne should be at its peak between 2002 and 2010.

Produced from a parcel located to the left of the château, near the entrance to the Grands Echézeaux vineyard, Lachaux's dark ruby-colored 1996 Clos Vougeot reveals a nose reminiscent of roasted spices and café au lait. This soft, supple, medium- to full-bodied, and silky-textured wine is seductive and filled with complex blackberry, cassis, coffee, mocha, and spice flavors. Its long finish is firmer than the Suchots yet should easily melt into this offering's glorious fruit. Anticipated maturity: 2001–2008. The similarly colored 1996 Echézeaux displays rich, earthy, and mocha cream scents as well as a full-bodied, ample, lively, structured, juicy, and extremely well-balanced personality. Its complex flavor profile is composed of red and black cherries, minerals, toast, and beef blood whose flavors linger throughout its long and refined finish. Anticipated maturity: 2002–2009.

Displaying a brilliant, dark ruby with traces of purple color and an enthralling violet, cherry, raspberry, cassis, rose blossom, and grilled oak-scented nose, Domaine Robert Arnoux's 1996 Romanée-St.-Vivant is a stunner. This velvety-textured, full-bodied, superbly balanced, refined, powerful, and intense wine is filled with highly detailed—yet explosive—plump cherries, blackberries, and plums. It is one of those magnificent red burgundies that seemingly combine the muscle and strength of a body-builder with the grace and elegance of a ballerina. It possesses enormous depth of fat, sumptuous, and deeply ripe fruits that drench its substantial yet supple tannins. This prodigiously long wine offers red currants, raspberries, Asian spices, and new wood flavors in its spectacular finish. It should be at its peak between 2004 and 2012+. Bravo!

DOMAINE D'AUVENAY (ST. ROMAIN)

1996	Bonnes Mares	EEE	95
1995	Bonnes Mares	EEE	93+
1996	Mazis-Chambertin	EEE	97+
1995	Mazis-Chambertin	EEE	95

This domaine is solely owned by Mme. Lalou-Bize Leroy, of Domaine Leroy fame. Mme. Leroy has many detractors, in large part, I suspect, because she has no equals. If there is one thing I have learned, it is that Burgundians love to criticize but hate to be criticized. The vast majority of them are envious of the financial and critical success Mme. Leroy has enjoyed. Instead of accepting or learning from her well-deserved fame (trying to emulate her meticulous attention to detail might be useful), her critics seem content to snipe away at her and her methods. Maybe Madame Leroy should encourage more of her neighbors to visit and taste her wines (admittedly, few can afford to buy them) in an effort to stop these shameful attacks, which serve no useful purpose.

Made from yields averaging 1 ton of fruit per acre, Domaine d'Auvenay's superb 1995 Bonnes Mares displays a fabulously perfumed, elegant nose of roses in addition to red and dark fruits. In the mouth, this explosive, intensely powerful and structured wine offers deeply roasted, lush, dark fruits. Full bodied, it has a brilliant combination of elegance and power (a hallmark of great wines). It should be cellared for 8+ years and enjoyed over the subsequent decade. Amazingly, the 1995 Mazis-Chambertin was made from even lower yields (a little over ½ ton)! Possessing a very dark, almost black color and an engulfing, deeply intense, brooding nose, this wine, with its oily texture, wild berries, and spices intertwined with minerals and rocks, must be tasted to be believed. Highly structured, full bodied and powerful, this superconcentrated offering needs 7–9 years of cellaring. I suspect it will be at its best over the subsequent 10–14 years.

Lalou Bize-Leroy bottled her Domaine d'Auvenay 1996s before harvesting the 1997s because "they were so good, I did not think they could get better." She compared them to the 1959s, saying they had the same richness, fruit, and body at this stage of their evolution. Not having been born yet, I did not taste the 1959s young, but I have been fortunate enough to drink a number of them in recent years. If Mme. Bize-Leroy is correct, and the 1996s evolve along the same lines, they will be mind-boggling in 40 years.

The dark-colored 1996 Bonnes Mares has a violet and cookie dough-laced nose that gives way to a velvety-textured, massively concentrated, masculine, broad-shouldered, and powerful character. This full-bodied, thick, highly structured, intense, and extraordinarily proportioned wine is crammed with candied blackberries, cassis liqueur, beef blood, and loads of supple tannins. Its immensely long finish tails off after 40 seconds on notes of sweet blueberries and vanilla-imbued oak. Anticipated maturity: 2005–2015+. Revealing a black color with bright purple tints, the 1996 Mazis-Chambertin has a brooding nose of jammy blackberries and stones. This thick (almost syrupy), massively powerful, muscular, and backward wine is even bigger, denser, and more concentrated than the Bonnes Mares. Layers of black cherries, cassis, minerals, iron shavings, and plums can be found in this blockbuster's superbly focused and extraordinarily delicious personality. Its prodigiously long and persistent finish makes the previous wine's almost seem short! Anticipated maturity: 2006–2020. Bravo!

DOMAINE GHISLAINE BARTHOD-NOELLAT
(CHAMBOLLE-MUSIGNY)

1996 Bourgogne	C	(86–87)
1995 Bourgogne	D	(85–87)
1996 Chambolle-Musigny	D	(86–88)
1995 Chambolle-Musigny	D	(87–89)
1996 Chambolle-Musigny Les Baudes	D	(87–89)
1995 Chambolle-Musigny Les Baudes	D	(?)
1996 Chambolle-Musigny Les Beaux Bruns	D	(88–91)
1995 Chambolle-Musigny Les Beaux Bruns	D	(88–91+)
1996 Chambolle-Musigny Les Charmes	E	(91–93)
1995 Chambolle-Musigny Les Charmes	E	(89–92)
1996 Chambolle-Musigny Les Chatelots	D	(87–89)
1996 Chambolle-Musigny Les Cras	D	(89–91+)
1995 Chambolle-Musigny Les Cras	D	(88–91)
1996 Chambolle-Musigny Les Fuées	E	(88–91+)
1995 Chambolle-Musigny Les Fuées	D	(88–90)
1996 Chambolle-Musigny Les Véroilles	D	(90–92)

The vivacious Ghislaine Barthod makes elegant Chambolle-Musignys with a noticeable wild mushroom/earthy component that I find very attractive. Her wines age well and have good structure. Qualitatively, Barthod's premiers crus do not differ that much, but the flavors and styles change with the *terroir*. Barthod's yields in 1995 (similar to those of other producers) were much lower than average (just under 2 tons to just over 2 tons versus 2²/₃ tons of fruit per acre).

One of the best generic Bourgognes I tasted, the 1995 offering is medium ruby colored with an appealing nose of deep, sweet cherries. Silky smooth, with refined flavors of red fruits, this is a delicious wine for near-term consumption (now–2001). The medium ruby 1995 Chambolle-Musigny possesses enticing and elegant scents of sweet red cherries and crisp red berry flavors combined with a lively spice. This delineated, medium-bodied wine will provide excellent drinking over the next 5 years. From a vineyard near Morey-St.-Denis, the 1995 Chambolle-Musigny Les Baudes troubled me because of its overabundance of mushroomy, earthy scents and flavors. I hope this problem is not due to rot and resolves itself before bottling. Medium to dark ruby colored, the super 1995 Chambolle-Musigny Les Beaux Bruns exhibits an elegant nose of deep, dark cherries and violets. Silky textured and packed with lush fruit, this medium-bodied wine has a lovely wild earthy component that makes it stand out. Structured, refined, and long, it will be at its best between 2001 and 2008. Lighter in color, the medium ruby 1995 Chambolle-Musigny Les Fuées displays an extremely floral nose of roses and sweet red fruits and flavors of dark cherries in its velvety-textured, medium-bodied, highly structured palate. Because of its tannic backbone, I suggest drinking this masculine wine between 2003 and 2010. Barthod's most tannic wine, the 1995 Chambolle-Musigny Les Cras, displays a medium to dark ruby robe and spectacular aromatics of wild blueberries. In the mouth, floral notes of violets and dark fruits are inter-mingled with clean earthy flavors in this silky-textured yet tannic and structured wine. I be-lieve the tannins will soften over the next 3–5 years. Stylistically meriting its name, the Chambolle-Musigny Les Charmes is Barthod's finest 1995: dark ruby colored, with a super-refined nose of roses, violets, and sweet fruits, this velvety textured, medium- to full-bodied wine is packed with concentrated ripe sweet cherries. Extremely elegant, yet flavor filled, this long and complex wine will be at its best between 2002 and 2010.

As for her 1996s, Ghislaine Barthod was "charmed by this vintage; it has purity of fruit, raspberries mostly, and elegance." She informed me that she had dropped grapes a month or so before the harvest to reduce yields to a little under 3 tons per acre. Barthod has enlarged her formerly cramped cellar and installed an elevator to assist her in making her delicious Chambolles. Since her wines are all produced with the same techniques, including 25% new oak, tasting at this domaine represents a lesson in this village's *terroirs*.

Her 1996 Bourgogne (mostly produced from the Bons Batons vineyard) is a little jewel. It reveals a ruby color and floral, perfumed, and black cherry-laced aromas. This medium-bodied, well-crafted, and silky wine has excellent depth of fruit, flavors reminiscent of stones and blackberries, and a supple finish. Drink it over the next 4 years.

The ruby-colored 1996 Chambolle-Musigny displays candied blueberries and violets on the nose and a bright, crisp, refreshing, and medium-bodied character with red and black cherry flavors intermingled with stones and traces of oak. This vibrant wine should be con-sumed over the next 3 years. Exhibiting a shiny, ruby color and ripe raspberry aromas, the 1996 Chambolle-Musigny Les Chatelots has aromas reminiscent of black raspberry and metal shavings as well as a medium-bodied, rich, and well-focused character with plum, mineral, stone, and raspberry flavors. It should be drunk between now and 2004.

Revealing a medium to dark ruby color, the 1996 Chambolle-Musigny Les Baudes has lively black cherry aromas and an earth, wild mushroom, blackberry, mineral, stone, and tangy currant-laced flavor profile. This medium-bodied, masculine, foursquare, austere wine will require patience. Anticipated maturity: 2001–2005. Somewhat dark colored, with traces of purple on the rim, the 1996 Chambolle-Musigny Les Beaux Bruns has a dense nose of beautifully ripe blackberries. Medium to full bodied, broad, and rich, its mouth-coating character is packed with candied blueberries, black raspberries, and Asian spices. It possesses an admirably long finish that reveals soft tannins. Anticipated maturity: 2001–2007. The bright and medium to dark ruby-colored 1996 Chambolle-Musigny Les Fuées offers vivacious aromas of black cherries intermingled with roasting spices and fresh herbs. This medium- to full-bodied, silky-textured, and well-delineated wine has a complex character composed of ripe blackberries, Asian spices, and freshly cracked black pepper. If it develops more body and loses none of its fruit as it completes its *élevage*, it will ultimately merit a higher score. Drink it between 2001 and 2007. The same can be said about the slightly darker-colored 1996 Chambolle-Musigny Les Cras. It has an expressive nose of vio-lets, black raspberries, stones, and toasted oak, followed by a rich, wide, medium- to full-bodied, and velvety-textured core of red currants, minerals, and blackberries. This masculine, foursquare, structured offering will require cellaring. Anticipated maturity: 2003–2007.

The dark-colored, highly expressive 1996 Chambolle-Musigny Les Véroilles has gorgeous floral, black raspberry, and cherry aromatics that lead to its masculine, dense, medium- to full-bodied, and crunchy (*croquant*, the French would say) personality. This fresh, wild blue-berry, and candied cherry-filled wine has a long and focused finish. Projected maturity: 2002–2007. My favorite of Barthod's 1996s is her dark-colored Chambolle-Musigny Les Charmes. Superripe and jammy black fruits, road tar, and rose blossoms can be found in this outstanding wine's aromas. It is intensely sweet, thick, refined, full bodied, and reserved.

This beauty saturates the palate and aftertaste with loads of candied blackberries, cassis liqueur, and sugar-coated blueberries. Drink it between 2003 and 2008.

DOMAINE JEAN-CLAUDE BELLAND (SANTENAY)
(formerly Domaine Adrien Belland)

1996 Aloxe-Corton	D	(85–88)
1996 Chambertin	E	(91–93)
1996 Corton Clos de la Vigne au Saint	D	(88–90)
1996 Corton-Grèves	D	(90–92)
1996 Corton-Perrières	D	(87–89)
1996 Santenay Les Gravières	C	(86–88)

Note: Selections exported to the United States are bottled unfiltered.

Everywhere in Burgundy fathers are passing the baton to their children. Adrien Belland, whose marriage to a member of the Latour family added Chambertin, Corton Clos de la Vigne au Saint, Corton Perrières, and some Aloxe-Corton to the estate's holdings, has handed over the domaine to his son Jean-Claude, who has worked with him for nearly two decades.

This estate's winemaking practices are a blend of old and modern. Such techniques as *pigeage* (breaking and submerging of the cap), the avoidance of cold maceration, the use of indigenous yeasts, and the eschewal of acidification are combined with modern-day practices such as destemming, extended fermentations, and malolactics in barrel. Additionally, Adrien Belland has abandoned *Guyon* pruning (very prevalent in Santenay) in favor of *Royat* in order to lower yields. Normally the reds are left in barrel (never more than 25% of which are new) for 18 to 24 months, but in 1996 the Bellands decided to bottle earlier.

Belland's wines are made to last yet deliver enormous amounts of fruit. This is an excellent source of high-quality and reasonably priced burgundies.

The medium to dark ruby-colored 1996 Santenay Les Gravières offers a deep cherry and herbal-spiced nose followed by a rich, expansive, and masculine personality. Loads of red and black fruits intermingled with metallic and mineral-like flavors can be found in this beautifully ripe and structured wine. Anticipated maturity: now–2004. Produced from 41-year-old vines, the black-colored 1996 Aloxe-Corton reveals a mouthwatering nose of licorice and jammy blueberries. This broad, medium- to full-bodied, foursquare wine's character is filled with juicy black currants and steel-like flavors. Its ultimate quality will be determined by how Belland copes with the dry dusty tannins. Drink it between 2000 and 2004.

The medium to dark ruby/purple-colored 1996 Corton-Perrières exhibits violet, plum, and stone scents that give way to a large, powerful, masculine structure and medium- to full-bodied wine. Layers of blackberries, fruit pits, warm rocks, and minerals are discernible in this austere yet delicious wine. Anticipated maturity: 2000–2005. The dark ruby-colored 1996 Corton-Grèves is a step up in quality. It offers a mouthwatering cookie dough, perfumed, floral, and profound nose that is followed by a ripe, full-bodied, fat, juicy, and expansive personality. Concentrated and vibrant red/black fruits as well as minerals are found in this wine. Anticipated maturity: 2001–2006. The medium to dark ruby-colored 1996 Corton Clos de la Vigne au Saint displays lilies and Provençal herbs on the nose and a complex, refined, feminine, and medium- to full-bodied character. I found this wine (Adrien Belland's favorite Corton) difficult. Hints of fresh herbs, mint, licorice, and stones are intertwined with juicy blackberries and blueberries in its austere and highly structured core. It should be at its peak between 2002 and 2006.

Offering a saturated, dark ruby color and a wonderful nose of black fruits and coffee beans, this estate's 1996 Chambertin is a superexpansive, rich, mouth-coating, and gorgeously layered wine with enormous depth of fruit. Waves of ripe red and black cherries are intermingled with earth and toasty oak flavors in this well-made, scrumptious wine. Its long finish reveals soft tannins. Ironically, if Belland were based in Gevrey-Chambertin, not Santenay, this wine would sell for considerably more. Anticipated maturity: 2002–2008.

DOMAINE BERTAGNA (VOUGEOT)

1996	Chambertin	EE	(86–88)
1995	Chambertin	EE	92
1996	Clos St.-Denis	EE	(86–87)
1995	Clos St.-Denis	EE	89+
1996	Clos de Vougeot	EE	(87–89)
1995	Vosne-Romanée Les Beaux Monts	E	89
1996	Vougeot Clos de la Perrière	E	(86–88)
1995	Vougeot Clos de la Perrière	E	88

Domaine Bertagna is recognized for producing average to good wines. Under the direction of a German (Eva Reh, who owns the estate with her family) and her English husband, Mark Siddle, they stated, "We made the decision in 1989 not to make 'okay' wines, but to dedicate ourselves to quality."

The vineyards have not been fertilized in 10 years and are usually green-harvested to lower yields (2 tons of fruit per acre in 1995, 2²/₃ tons in 1996, and 2 tons in 1997). In addition, canopy management is employed to increase air circulation around the bunches and to promote consistent ripeness. A sorting table is used twice to ensure that only the healthiest grapes are fermented. After a light *foulage* (breaking of the grape's skins) of a portion of the grapes, they undergo a 5–6-day cold maceration (10–12 degrees Celsius). The whites are 100% fermented in wood (50% new barrels), and the reds are submitted to a 24–48-hour *débourbage* (settling of the gross lees followed by a decanting off of them). Between 50% and 60% new oak is employed across the board on the reds (some grands crus see 100% new barrels), and they are subjected to only two rackings. The 1995s and 1996s were neither fined nor filtered. Bottling is done at the domaine using an ultramodern vacuum machine (so that no oxygen comes in contact with the wines).

Eva Reh and Mark Siddle have the dedication and financial backing necessary to upgrade this estate's reputation. The wines I tasted (a revisit of the 1995s and the 1996s) are excellent.

Exhibiting a ruby color and ripe cherry aromas, the *monopole* (or solely owned vineyard) 1996 Vougeot Clos de la Perrière is a structured, masculine, medium-bodied, and silky-textured wine with minerals, stones, and blackberries in its flavor profile. Anticipated maturity: now–2003. The 1996 Chambertin is ruby colored and displays floral, cassis, and earthy scents. This oily-textured, medium-bodied, and focused offering is filled with stones, black raspberries, and blackberries. A slight dryness to the finish lowered my evaluation. Projected maturity: 2000–2004. Medium to dark ruby colored, and revealing aromas reminiscent of sweet red fruits spiced with new oak, the 1996 Clos Vougeot is a stylish, nicely concentrated, and medium-bodied wine with blackberry and Asian spice flavors. It should be consumed between now and 2004. The slightly darker-colored 1996 Clos St.-Denis has warm and embracing aromas of boysenberries and cassis that are followed by a proportioned, currant-and-stone-flavored core. Revealing good concentration and a soft texture, this wine suffers from a trace of alcoholic heat and dryness in the finish. Drink it between now and 2004.

The estate's 1995s are better than the 1996s. Revealing a touch of brick in its otherwise ruby color, the 1995 Vougeot Clos de la Perrière (originally rated an 88) has a strawberry, raspberry, stone, and gravel-laden nose as well as a chewy, pretty, fresh, and pure character filled with black cherries and cassis flavors. It will be at its best between 2000 and 2004.

The 1995 Clos St.-Denis (originally rated a 90) is medium to dark ruby colored and offers a nose of blackberries, stones, and cracked white pepper. This dense, rich, and extracted wine displays superb ripeness to its layered and black fruit-flavored personality. When I originally tasted this wine a year ago, new oak flavors played a much more dominant role. As its tightly wound core blossoms with cellaring, I am relatively sure it will again merit an outstanding rating. Anticipated maturity: 2002–2008.

Slightly darker colored than the Vougeot Clos de la Perrière, the 1995 Vosne-Romanée Les Beaux Monts' aromas suggest sweet cherries and roses. This wine displays a velvety, extracted, elegant, and feminine flavor profile filled with creamy black raspberries and plums. In its long finish it possesses flavors of toast and vanilla. It will be at its best between 2000–2006.

A superb wine, the dark ruby/purple-colored 1995 Chambertin reveals sweet cassis and floral aromas as well as a lavish, silky-textured, full-bodied, harmonious, and elegant personality with flavors reminiscent of jammy cherries and blackberries intermingled with toasty oak and touches of earth. Powerful and highly structured, it has the requisite components to age gracefully and should be at its best between 2004 and 2012.

DOMAINE XAVIER BESSON (GIVRY)

1996 Givry Le Petit Prétan Réserve		C	88

Note: This "Réserve" bottling is produced exclusively for the United States market and specifically for North Berkeley Imports. It is neither fined nor filtered and is bottled by hand.

The medium to dark ruby-colored 1996 Givry Le Petit Prétan Réserve reveals gorgeously pure Pinot Noir aromas of red berries followed by a rich, medium-bodied, and silky core filled with black cherries, boysenberries, and metals. This ripe, chewy, and pleasure-giving wine should be consumed over the next 4 years.

DOMAINE VINCENT BITOUZET-PRIEUR (VOLNAY)

1996 Beaune Cent Vignes	D	(85–88)
1995 Beaune Cent Vignes	D	(86–89)
1996 Volnay	D	(86–88)
1995 Volnay	D	(84–87)
1996 Volnay Aussy	D	(86–88)
1995 Volnay Aussy	D	(85–87)
1996 Volnay Caillerets	D	(90–92)
1995 Volnay Caillerets	D	(87–89)
1996 Volnay Clos des Chênes	D	(88–90)
1995 Volnay Clos des Chênes	D	(87–90)
1996 Volnay Pitures	D	(90–92)
1995 Volnay Pitures	D	(88–90+)
1996 Volnay Taillepieds	D	(89–91)
1995 Volnay Taillepieds	D	(88–91)

Vincent Bitouzet produces a wide range of wines from Volnay, each one quite different from the other, well representing their respective *terroirs*. He crafted marvelous 1996s, capturing this vintage's succulent fruit. Unlike most vignerons with whom I spoke, Bitouzet reported that his wines' malos took place normally and were not retarded. He did not heat the cellars or use malo-inducing artificial yeasts, attributing the rapid malolactic fermentation to the fact that little sulfur was used during vinification.

The ruby/purple-colored 1996 Volnay offers jammy red cherry aromas and a thick, medium- to full-bodied, oily-textured, and chewy character packed with cherries and candied raspberries. This soft and straightforward wine will offer generously fruity and immensely pleasurable drinking. Anticipated maturity: now–2001. The medium to dark ruby-colored 1996 Beaune Cents Vignes has a sweet raspberry and black cherry-scented nose as well as a well-crafted, refined, and medium-bodied character. This wine is more structured and tannic and is redolent with strawberry and raspberry fruit. I suggest drinking it between now and 2003. The rare 1996 Volnay Aussy (Génot-Boulanger also produces one) is medium to dark ruby colored and offers black cherry, raspberry, and violet-laden aromatics. Tasting this supple and ingratiating wine is akin to drinking a glass of thick, sweet cherry juice. Medium bodied and lively, this is not a structured or complex wine; rather, it is seductive, opulent, and lovely. Drink it over the next 3–4 years.

The ruby/purple-colored 1996 Volnay Taillepieds reveals a dark berry and black cherry-infused nose as well as a medium- to full-bodied, broad, structured, and masculine character with generous fruit. This meaty, chewy-textured, and gorgeously ripe wine is densely packed with red cherries, blackberries, minerals, and fresh herbs. While not as concentrated as the 1995 Taillepieds, it is more seductive and inviting. It should be at its best between now and 2005. Displaying a dark purple color and superripe plummy aromas, the 1996 Volnay Clos des Chênes is full bodied, lively, rich, thickly textured, and filled with blackberries, cassis, and earth tones. This wine is broad yet vivacious, with high acidity yet dense fruit. Its persistent and cherry-laced finish reveals plenty of supple and ripe tannins. Drink this wine over the near term while the acidity provides freshness and the admirable fruit compensates for it. With extended cellaring the acid may overpower the fruit. Anticipated maturity: now–2003. Medium to dark ruby colored and exhibiting a rich, floral, and refined nose, the 1996 Volnay Caillerets has a tangy, mouth-coating, full-bodied, complex, and rich core of cassis, cherries, and stonelike flavors. This broad-shouldered and focused wine is elegant, beautifully ripe and velvety textured and possesses an impressively long and supple finish. Well crafted and harmonious, it should be at its best between now and 2005. The healthy, ruby/purple-colored 1996 Volnay Pitures has an elegant, tangy, sweet-and-sour red currant and cherry-infused nose preceded by a thick, full-bodied personality. This refined, fat, supple, chewy, and superripe wine is ample, round, and filled with sweet red fruits. Of all of Bitouzet's offerings, the Pitures is the most tannic. Anticipated maturity: 2000–2006.

The light to medium ruby-colored 1995 Volnay possesses a sweet and tangy cherry nose as well as a beautifully ripe, well-structured, medium-bodied, and soft personality with flavors of strawberries, crisp red berries, and fresh herbs. Drink it between now and 2000. The 1995 Beaune Cents Vignes offers a ruby color, intense aromas of mocha and jammy red fruits, and a thick-textured, cherry pie filling and chocolate-flavored, medium-bodied character. This powerful offering (particularly considering it is from a vineyard that generally produces rather light wines) succeeds in marrying its big jammy flavors with an attractive finesse. Anticipated maturity: now–2002.

Ruby colored and exhibiting smoky blackberry aromas, the 1995 Volnay Aussy is a well-structured, medium-bodied, refined wine packed with cassis and blueberries. Anticipated maturity: now-2001. A big step up in quality, the potentially outstanding medium to dark ruby-colored 1995 Volnay Taillepieds explodes from the glass with gorgeously sweet red cherries aromatically and a viscous, velvety, medium- to full-bodied, superripe, and chewy flavor profile filled with red currants, strawberries, raspberries, and a delightful touch of Asian spices. Admirably long and possessing a backbone of soft, round tannins, this wine should be at its best between now and 2005. The ruby-colored 1995 Volnay Clos des Chênes reveals enticing earthy, spicy, cherry, and herbal aromatics and a crisp, powerful, medium- to full-bodied and deeply concentrated palate with boysenberry and currant flavors. Its tannins are slightly harder than the previous wine's, so I recommend drinking it between 2001 and 2005. The 1995 Volnay Caillerets is medium ruby colored and displays mineral and blueberry aromas as well as a refined, medium-bodied character with cassis, blackberry, and stonelike flavors. A touch of dryness in its finish prevents this wine from meriting a higher rating. Drink it between now and 2004. Produced from a parcel at the very top of the Pitures vineyard, bordering the village appellation, Bitouzet's ruby-colored 1995 Volnay Pitures possesses blackberry, mineral, and deep roasting spice aromas and a powerful, superripe, highly structured flavor profile filled with cassis, black raspberries, and stones. At present it is brooding and backward, but it will evolve into a glorious wine.

DOMAINE SIMON BIZE (SAVIGNY-LÈS-BEAUNE)

1996	Aloxe-Corton Le Suchot	D	(87–88)
1996	Bourgogne	C	(85–87)
1996	Latricières-Chambertin	EE	(88–90)
1996	Savigny-Lès-Beaune Les Bourgeots	D	(87–88)
1996	Savigny-Lès-Beaune Les Fourneaux	D	(89–91)
1996	Savigny-Lès-Beaune Les Grands Liards	D	(87–89)
1996	Savigny-Lès-Beaune Les Guettes	D	(89–91)
1996	Savigny-Lès-Beaune Les Marconnets	D	(88–90+)
1996	Savigny-Lès-Beaune Les Serpentières	D	(88–90)
1996	Savigny-Lès-Beaune Les Vergelesses	D	(90–92)

Patrick Bize, the 46-year-old director of this estate, said the following about 1996: "The 1996 vintage is Burgundy's finest since 1990, and at the same quality level as that great year. After those two I would list, in order, 1995, 1993, 1991, 1992, and lastly 1994—but none can be characterized as a bad year. What makes 1996 so wonderful is its silkiness, purity, and class. It has better acidity than any vintage of the 1990s, and a firm structure."

In contrast with many of his colleagues, Bize (pronounced just like the plural of "bee") participates in many tastings, visiting numerous domaines throughout the Côte to observe the work of his peers. Bize is a *terroir*-ist, producing seven different Savignys from the village's hillside vineyards.

In May 1996 Bize and his employees did an enormous amount of pruning ("I sensed a heavy vintage"), which resulted in low yields, ranging from $1^1/_3$ to $2^1/_3$ tons per acre. A traditionalist, Bize does not destem any of the grapes produced from his $54^1/_3$-acre estate.

The day of my visit, a typically cold and humid January afternoon, Bize was racking his 1996 Bourgogne. It had already been drained from its barrels and was in a large, baby-pool-size vessel. We dipped our glasses into the ruby-colored liquid and the tasting began. It reveals loads of fresh red fruit aromatics and a medium-bodied, beautifully rich, plump, black cherry and stone-filled character. This seductive, simple, and focused wine will be at its best if drunk over the next 3 years.

The bright ruby-colored 1996 Savigny-Lès-Beaune Les Bourgeots has delightfully sweet red fruit aromas that give way to a refined, pleasure-giving, rich, silky-textured, nicely concentrated style. It displays its focused, medium-bodied, and well-ripened red and black cherry flavors in an expressive, simple, and delightful manner. Anticipated maturity: now–2002. Produced from vines that average 46 years old (the youngest are 17 and the oldest 57), the ruby-colored 1996 Savigny-Lès-Beaune Les Grands Liards has black cherry, earth, and wild mushroom scents that lead to a masculine, medium-bodied, structured, and well-balanced personality. Minerals, stones, blackberries, and fresh herbs can be found in its delineated flavor profile. Drink it between now and 2004. Exhibiting a medium to dark ruby color, the 1996 Savigny-Lès-Beaune Les Serpentières was crafted from vines planted in 1959. Richly aromatic, it offers minerals, black cherries, and blackberries on the nose and a lush, fat, rich, and silky-textured medium to full body. This well-delineated, structured, and concentrated wine is extracted, concentrated, and flavorful. Cassis, blueberries, and brambleberries intermingled with iron and gravel are found in its flavor profile and long, supple finish. Anticipated maturity: now–2005.

Patrick Bize has been producing the *monopole* (solely owned) 1996 Aloxe-Corton Le Suchot *en métayage* (sharecropping) since 1991. It displays a medium to dark ruby color and a black fruit-scented nose. This ample, plump, and juicy offering is medium to full bodied, structured, harmonious, and masculine. It offers complex flavors of metal, gravel, and minerals drenched in blackberries. It should be at its best between now and 2004.

Aged in 50% new oak (the most Bize believes he should use), the medium to dark ruby-colored 1996 Savigny-Lès-Beaune Les Fourneaux (this word means "kitchen range" or "industrial oven") displays deep, earthy, and blackberry aromas as well as a medium- to full-bodied, silky, undeniably gorgeous personality. This tangy, lively (verging on crisp), and medium- to full-bodied wine is ripe and plump yet elegant. Asian spice drenched in cherry syrup with a dusting of minerals can be found in this flavorful wine. As long as Bize does not lose any of the copious fruit following bottling, its high acidity will remain a focus-giving and refreshing asset, not a liability. Anticipated maturity: 2000–2006. The medium to dark ruby colored 1996 Savigny-Lès-Beaune Les Guettes has fresh black raspberry aromas and a fat, powerful, intense, concentrated, oily-textured, structured, and mouth-coating core of brambleberries, blackberries, and minerals. This medium- to full-bodied wine also possesses a long and silky finish. At present it lacks the refinement of the Fourneaux but impresses through its sheer power and palate presence. Anticipated maturity: 2000–2006. A significantly more feminine wine, described by Bize as "more Beaune than Savigny in style," the medium to dark ruby-colored 1996 Savigny-Lès-Beaune Les Marconnets has a perfumed, floral, stony, and candied cherry-filled nose. This medium-bodied, silky-textured, chewy, and harmonious wine is extremely well balanced and proportioned. It reveals flavors reminiscent of black cherries, cassis liqueur, and gravel. Drink it between now and 2006. The ruby-colored 1996 Savigny-Lès-Beaune Les Vergelesses possesses sweet black cherry and cassis aromatics followed by an oily-textured burst of powerful sugar-coated grape and candied cherry flavors. Medium to full bodied, it is a ripe, rich, intense, and elegant wine. According to Bize, wines from this vineyard formerly sold at prices identical to red Corton. It is balanced and extremely flavorful and boasts a long, supple, and focused finish. Anticipated maturity: 2000–2007.

The 1996 Latricières-Chambertin, aged in 50% new oak, is a medium ruby-colored wine with blackberry, black cherry, fresh herb, and briery aromas. Medium to full bodied, velvety textured, and mouth-coating, it has powerful and ripe earthy flavors of cassis liqueur, blueberries, and black raspberries, as well as hints of Asian spices. Drink it between 2001 and 2007.

DOMAINE JEAN-YVES BIZOT (VOSNE-ROMANÉE)

1996 Echézeaux	E	(91–93)
1995 Echézeaux	E	91
1996 Vosne-Romanée Premier Cru	D	(88–91?)
1995 Vosne-Romanée Premier Cru	D	89+
1996 Vosne-Romanée Les Jachères	D	(88–90)

1996 Vosne-Romanée Les Réas	D	(89–91+)
1995 Vosne-Romanée Les Réas	D	88
1996 Vosne-Romanée Vieilles Vignes	D	(88–90)

"I learned more tasting with Henri Jayer than I did in oenology school," stated Jean-Yves Bizot, the famed Jayer's 32-year-old next-door neighbor. In a region where most vignerons have scarred muscular hands (from pruning) and sun-baked skin and wear jean overalls and tattered sweaters, Bizot stands out with his tall, lanky, pale figure and toothy smile. He looks more like a college senior majoring in mathematics than a man of the soil and cellars.

The son of a doctor who had placed his vines *en métayage*, Bizot reacquired control of his vines in 1993 to form an estate; "however, 1994 is my first vintage from vine to glass," he is quick to point out.

His minimalist winemaking philosophy is based significantly more on Jayer than on the lessons he learned in oenology school. He uses whole clusters, does a cold maceration, uses only indigenous yeasts, never pumps over, and performs several *pigéages* in order to extract color and flavor. Bizot fears the drying-out effects of sulfur and oxygen on his wines and therefore uses as little SO_2 as possible and has never racked a wine (he informed me that this was not a "religion" for him and that if a wine ever required a racking, he would do it). His offerings are aged in new and 1-year-old oak barrels and are bottled by hand, without ever having been fined or filtered. This admirable technique insures minimal contact with air but does pose a problem for consumers, since we cannot know whether we are purchasing wine that was in new oak or not. Furthermore, since each barrel is bottled separately it assures significant bottle variation, as each barrel's pores, toast, and grain are distinct. To assist consumers, Bizot will in the future be indicating on each bottle's label a number that will correspond to the barrel it was aged in (a technique borrowed from the German AP number system).

Produced from vines planted in 1927 and 1933, the ruby-colored 1996 Vosne-Romanée Vieilles Vignes has profound aromas of black cherries imbued in violets. This thickly textured, medium- to full-bodied, expansive, and elegant wine is extremely well crafted and offers intense flavors of cassis, blackberries, fresh herbs, and Asian spices. Drink it between 2000 and 2005. The similarly colored 1996 Vosne-Romanée Les Jachères (from a 50+-year-old parcel near Bizot's home and cellar) reveals a pure, floral, and fresh nose of cassis liqueur and boysenberries. It is a deeply ripe, refined, meaty, and rich offering with medium to full body and a silky texture. Sweet candied cherries, raspberries, and oak spices can be found in its palate-saturating character. Anticipated maturity: now–2005. Revealing a dark ruby/purple color and a violet, rose, and black raspberry-scented fragrance, the 1996 Vosne-Romanée Les Réas is similar to the Jachères yet more expansive, chewier, and longer in the finish. This rich, sweet, broad, and ample wine has black raspberries, Asian spices, and hints of licorice in its medium- to full-bodied and thick personality. Its tannic backbone (ripe and supple) will require cellaring patience. Anticipated maturity: 2003–2009.

A sure sign of Bizot's commitment to quality is the fact that he declassifies one of his two parcels in the grand cru Echézeaux vineyard because he feels it does not produce wine meriting that lofty appellation. Produced from vines located in the Les Treux sector of Echézeaux (on the southern end of this large grand cru), the Vosne-Romanée Premier Cru is medium to dark ruby/purple colored and displays enthrallingly refined blackberry, cherry, and violet aromas. This broad, masculine, silky-textured, and medium- to full-bodied offering is filled with red cherries, raspberries, and strawberries laced with new oak flavors. Its firm, long finish is a little warm and has dryish, oaky tannins. Cellaring may or may not resolve this problem, as this wine has copious quantities of dense fruit. Readers should try it in 2003 and reevaluate its ageworthiness at that time.

Produced from Echézeaux's most northern sector (En Orveaux), this medium to dark ruby/purple-colored 1996 has a delightfully elegant and feminine nose of candied cherries, raspberries, smoke, and Asian spices. This deeply ripe, dense, broad, medium- to full-bodied, and expansive wine is intense, powerful, and muscular yet is completely refined and focused. Its chewy-textured and cassis-and-blackberry-flavored personality needed air to blossom the day of my tasting (remember, these wines have never been racked). Its admirably long and pure finish is crammed with ripe tannins and new oak flavors. It will require several years of cellaring. Anticipated maturity: 2005–2010+. Bravo!

The unfined, unfiltered, and hand-bottled 1995 offerings were crafted with only minimal doses of sulfur. All three 1995s are first-rate wines. This was the first time I tasted anything from Bizot, so I was ecstatic to see the high level of quality achieved by this small estate. The medium to dark ruby-colored 1995 Vosne-Romanée Les Réas reveals invitingly ripe, candied red cherries and raspberries on the nose and a silky-textured, soft, elegant, and well-made medium-bodied palate replete with flavors of red berries and bacon. Drink it between now and 2005. Even better, and potentially outstanding with some bottle age, the dark ruby-colored 1995 Vosne-Romanée Premier Cru displays fresh, lively cherries aromatically and a delicious, chewy, velvety, medium- to full-bodied personality packed with red and black currants, stones, and a touch of earthiness. It will be at its best between 2001 and 2008. The dark ruby-colored 1995 Echézeaux possesses marvelously concentrated and deep aromas of black cherries and toasty oak. This wine is extremely chewy and full bodied and has copious quantities of thick, superripe red and black fruits, mocha, and a beguiling underbrush characteristic. I recommend holding it for 5 years and enjoying it through 2008.

DOMAINE DANIEL BOCQUENET (NUITS-ST.-GEORGES)

1995 Echézeaux	E	93
1995 Nuits-St.-Georges	D	(88–90+)
1996 Nuits-St.-Georges aux Saints Juliens	D	89+
1996 Vosne-Romanée La Croix Blanche	D	88

Note: I tasted the 1996 Echézeaux prior to its malos having started and do not feel it would be appropriate to comment on a wine in such an embryonic stage of its evolution. Interestingly, a number of producers of wines from this vineyard had stubbornly slow malolactic fermentations.

Readers should be forewarned that if they visit Daniel Bocquenet's estate, they will most assuredly leave it having tasted first-rate and reasonably priced wines but will have a sore right hand. Mr. Bocquenet, after years of using clippers, the vigneron's primary tool, has immensely powerful hands and forearms. Hence shaking his hand is a memorable (and painful) experience. This is an excellent yet little-known source for very well-crafted wines.

The medium to dark ruby-colored 1996 Vosne-Romanée La Croix Blanche (the southeasternmost vineyard of Vosne, bordering Nuits) displays floral, blackberry, and salt pork aromas. This juicy, medium- to full-bodied, broad, and silky wine has excellent concentration as well as a delightful flavor profile composed of raspberries and cherries. It should be at its best between now and 2004. Revealing a medium to dark ruby color and a mouthwatering nose of flowers, raspberries, strawberries, and cherries, the 1996 Nuits-St.-Georges aux Saints Juliens is wonderful. Silky textured, rich, concentrated, medium to full bodied, and supple, it delights with its loads of black cherries that seem almost to burst open on the palate. If this wine develops more complexity, it will certainly merit an outstanding score. Anticipated maturity: now–2004.

Readers who were able to secure some bottles of Bocquenet's 1995 Echézeaux should be pleased. It has a bright, medium to dark ruby color and fabulous aromatics of roses, violets, red and black currants, and cherries. It is chewy, oily textured, extremely concentrated and firm and exhibits highly extracted blackberries intermingled with stones and sun-dried herbs. I am convinced that this beauty will age gracefully for at least another dozen years. Drink it between 2005 and 2012+.

Medium to dark ruby colored and displaying deeply spicy dark fruit on the nose, the 1995 Nuits-St.-Georges has an excellent silky textured personality, with flavors of black fruits, minerals, and stones. Intense and hugely concentrated, this masculine wine needs 5–6 years of cellaring before it will be at its best.

DOMAINE JEAN BOILLOT (VOLNAY)

1996	Beaune Clos du Roi	D	(88–90)
1996	Beaune Epenottes	D	(89–90+)
1996	Nuits-St.-Georges Les Cailles	E	(90–92)
1996	Savigny-Lès-Beaune Les Lavières	D	(87–88)
1996	Volnay Caillerets	E	(90–92)
1996	Volnay Chevrets	E	(89–91)
1996	Volnay Frémiets	E	(90–92)

Henri Boillot, the director of this estate (which bears his father's name), is the brother of Jean-Marc Boillot (Pommard) and the brother-in-law of Gérard Boudot (Domaine/Maison Etienne Sauzet in Puligny-Montrachet). Half the domaine's 34¹/₂ acres of vines produce red wine and the rest white wine from vineyards in Puligny-Montrachet, Meursault Genevrières, and Savigny-Lès-Beaune Les Vergelesses. The Boillot *négoce* business (Maison Henri Boillot) does not produce red wines, as he believes that a Pinot Noir's quality is preponderantly determined in the vineyard, not the cellars.

Many red wine producers in Burgundy told me that sorting tables were useless in 1996, yet Boillot felt his were essential. Boillot informed me that rot and mildew were not the concern, as there was none. What his sorters were looking for were unevenly ripened grapes. According to him, the fact that the bunches had been dependent upon sunlight (photosynthesis) for ripening meant that the bunches on the north-facing side were unripe and those on the south-facing side were perfect. Boillot told me that 40% of the harvest had to be discarded. Relative to his neighbors, Domaine Jean Boillot's 2 tons per acre yields are low for the vintage.

The ruby-colored, vibrant 1996 Savigny-Lès-Beaune Les Lavières offers a metallic and blackberry-scented nose. Medium bodied, with a silky texture, it is filled with cassis, blueberries, and ironlike flavors, with a long, soft finish. Drink this beauty between now and 2003. Exhibiting a medium to dark ruby color and an immensely appealing nose of black cherries and metals, the 1996 Beaune Clos du Roi is a medium-bodied, satiny-textured, gorgeously ripe, and delineated wine. I was impressed with the depth and complexity of this delicious Beaune. It should be at its best between now and 2004. Whereas the previous wine hails from the northern border of Beaune (touching Savigny-Lès-Beaune), the 1996 Beaune Epenottes is the southernmost of Beaune's premier cru vineyards, touching Pommard. This dark ruby-colored wine displays loads of sweet red fruit aromatics as well as a powerful, deep, luscious, velvety, and structured core of ripe black cherries, stones, and earth. This delicious, seductive, and muscular wine should be drunk between now and 2005.

If the wines I tasted out of the assembling tanks reflect what ultimately is bottled (I have no tasting experience comparing both pre- and postbottling wines from Domaine Jean Boillot), then Henri Boillot will most certainly have crafted three outstanding Volnays. Produced from a little-known vineyard located below Volnay Caillerets and bordering the Clos de Santenots (Santenots de Milieu), the medium to dark ruby-colored 1996 Volnay Chevrets reveals sweet violets and black cherries. This wine is velvety textured, medium to full bodied, deep, beautifully ripe, and packed with cherries, plums, and well-defined metallic flavors. Let's hope this tangy and vibrant offering does not suffer from heavy-handed bottling, excessive SO_2 additions, or flavor-eviscerating fining and filtering. It should be a scrumptious drink between now and 2004. The medium to dark ruby-colored 1996 Volnay Frémiets (a vineyard located on the northern edge of Volnay, touching Pommard) displays mineral, metal, flower, and blueberry-infused aromas. It is very ripe (jammy but focused), medium to full bodied, chewy textured, and packed with grapes, plums, cherries, and boysenberries. This well-defined wine should be at its best between now and 2006. The 1996 Volnay Caillerets is medium to dark ruby/purple colored and offers a stone, violet, and blackberry-laced nose. This masculine, foursquare, highly structured, and full-bodied wine behaves like a Nuits-St.-Georges. Its flavor profile is reminiscent of dark fruits intermingled with metal shavings and traces of Asian spices. It is delicious and impressive but will require patience. Anticipated maturity: 2003–2007.

The 1996 is the last vintage Domaine Jean Boillot will offer a Nuits-St.-Georges Les Cailles, because Henri Boillot traded this parcel to Bouchard Père et Fils for a plot of Volnay Frémiets. He is particularly pleased with his final vintage. It is dark ruby colored and exhibits a rich, profound, and intense nose of sweet blackberries. On the palate, this medium-to full-bodied wine is silky textured, foursquare, and focused. Exhibiting superb depth, it reveals layer upon layer of cherries awash in stones, minerals, and traces of earth. Anticipated maturity: 2003–2008.

DOMAINE JEAN-MARC BOILLOT (POMMARD)

1996	Beaune Les Montrevenots	D	(87–88)
1995	Beaune Les Montrevenots	D	86?
1996	Bourgogne	C	(85–86)
1995	Bourgogne	C	85?
1996	Pommard	D	(87–88)
1996	Pommard Les Jarollières	E	(88–90)
1995	Pommard Les Jarollières	E	91
1996	Pommard Les Rugiens	EE	(91–93+)
1995	Pommard Les Rugiens	EE	92+
1996	Volnay	D	(86–87)
1995	Volnay	D	86
1996	Volnay La Carelle Sous La Chapelle	D	(87–89)
1995	Volnay La Carelle Sous La Chapelle	D	88
1996	Volnay Les Pitures	D	(?)
1995	Volnay Les Pitures	D	89
1996	Volnay Roncerets	D	(88–90)

When I visited Jean-Marc Boillot's Pommard estate to taste his 1996 reds, he had just finished assembling them in preparation for bottling.

The ruby-colored 1996 Bourgogne has ripe red fruit aromas and a tangy, sweet cherry-laced, medium-bodied, lively character. Simple, pleasurable, and thirst-quenching, it should be quaffed over the next 2–3 years. The ruby/purple-colored 1996 Volnay exhibits very ripe black cherries on the nose and a crisp, pure, and focused medium body filled with deliciously sweet black cherry fruit and ever-so-soft tannins. Owing to its high acidity, I believe it would be foolhardy to cellar this wine for an extended period, but it will deliver pleasure over the next few years. Qualitatively, the ruby-colored 1996 Pommard is slightly better than the Volnay. It displays lovely aromas of sweet red cherries, perfume, and raw meat. Medium to full bodied, fat, chewy textured, structured, and rich, this wine has ripe raspberries, cassis, and cherries in its delicious flavor profile. Anticipated maturity: now–2003. The 1996 Beaune Les Montrevenots offers a healthy ruby/purple color and a nose of raspberries, cherries, and spicy sweet oak. It is rich, ripe, medium bodied, and silky textured. Revealing deep red and black berry flavors, it will be at its best between now and 2002.

Displaying a medium to dark ruby color as well as blackberry and cassis scents, the 1996 Volnay La Carelle Sous La Chapelle is a medium- to full-bodied, fruit-driven, juicy, and velvety-textured wine. Layers of ripe blueberries, black currants, and earthlike flavors can be found in its expressive personality. Anticipated maturity: now–2005. The classy 1996 Volnay Roncerets has a medium to dark ruby color in addition to delightful aromas of violets, perfume, and dark chocolate-covered cherries. This masculine, concentrated, medium- to full-bodied, and extracted wine is replete with licorice, blackberry, and metallic flavors. With its excellent depth of fruit and an admirable balance, it finishes with a structured and tannic backbone. Anticipated maturity: 2001–2007. The ruby/purple-colored 1996 Volnay Les Pitures is a difficult wine to evaluate. On one hand it reveals an outstanding nose of candied cherries and freshly cut flowers in addition to an oily-textured, palate-saturating, rich, medium- to full-bodied personality. On the other hand, this masculine wine's structure and tannin nearly obliterates the fruit. Judgment reserved.

I had no similar trouble analyzing Jean-Marc Boillot's medium to dark ruby/purple-colored 1996 Pommard Les Jarollières. Spicy cherries and raspberries can be discerned in its lovely aromatics. Its medium- to full-bodied, concentrated, and silky-textured core of blackberries, assorted red fruits, and meatlike flavors is harmonious, seductive, and well structured. Anticipated maturity: 2000–2005. The 1996 Pommard Les Rugiens, produced from vines that are over 80 years old, is consistently my favorite red wine Chez Boillot. While the 1996 exhibited signs of *sur-maturité*, it did not possess the Banyuls-like character of his 1995. Black/purple colored and bursting with superripe red fruits and plums, this is a thick, massive, full-bodied, and lavishly rich wine. Its velvety-textured and structured core is crammed with layers of sweet cherries, blackberries, and cassis, as well as loads of magnificently supple tannins. Formidably long and pure in its finish, this Pommard is undoubtedly of superb quality. Anticipated maturity: 2002–2009.

Jean-Marc Boillot's 1995 reds were produced from yields in the $1^1/_3$–2 tons per acre range. The 100% destemmed grapes are put through a 1-week cold maceration and then a high-temperature fermentation (between 32 and 35 degrees centigrade), followed by another maceration at 26–27 degrees centigrade. The vinification lasts three weeks. The wines are then placed in 20%–30% new oak barrels (the remaining barrels are first- and second-year oak) for aging. Boillot believes his reds should be fined only in tannic vintages such as 1993 and 1990. He did not fine his 1995s, but they were subjected to a Kieselguhr (diatomaceous earth) filtration.

While this domaine's 1995s exhibit an excellent concentration of ripe fruit, they also have a level of dry tannin that is worrisome (hence the question marks). Will the fruit outlive the tannin?

The medium to dark ruby-colored 1995 Bourgogne reveals an intense floral and ripe cherry nose as well as a medium-bodied, chewy, blackberry, and tangy cassis flavor profile. Regrettably, this delicious wine finishes with some rugged dry tannin that may not soften before the fruit dissipates. Time will tell. Similarly colored, the 1995 Beaune Les Montrevenots displays ripe banana and earth aromatics. This thick-textured, concentrated, and medium-bodied wine is jam-packed with sweet dark fruits and minerals in addition to a dry tannic finish. The medium to dark ruby-colored 1995 Volnay exhibits violet and perfume-infused aromas, flavors of sweet plums, grapes, tangy blueberries, and traces of roses and chocolate. This medium-bodied, oily wine also possesses troublesome tannin, but the depth of concentrated fruit suggests that they will not pose a problem to its evolution. Anticipated maturity: now–2004.

Medium to dark ruby colored, the 1995 Volnay La Carelle Sous La Chapelle offers aromas of bananas, roses, and violets and a thick-textured, medium- to full-bodied palate packed with ripe blackberries and dark cherries. Drink it between now and 2005. A step up, the dark ruby-colored 1995 Volnay Les Pitures reveals a floral-and-raspberry-scented nose as well as an oily-textured, powerful, full-bodied, chewy personality with flavors of blackberries, cassis, and coffee. Its admirably long finish ends on a strong tannic backbone that will require a few years of cellaring. Drink it between 2000 and 2006. Produced from 60-year-old vines, the 1995 Pommard Les Jarollières is dark ruby colored and displays an intensely superripe, almost grapey nose. This wine possesses a thick-textured, deeply flavorful, complex, highly structured, and extracted palate packed with blackberries and cassis. Extremely well made and long, it will be at its best between 2000 and 2007. Boillot's black-colored 1995 Pommard Les Rugiens is extraordinarily impressive and atypical. Produced from vines that are over 80 years old, it reveals a nose of almost overripe, amazingly concentrated sweet black fruits that is more reminiscent of a Banyuls from Dr. Parcé. Flavors of prunes, plums, sweetened coffee, and black cherry jam are found in this thick, full-bodied, and massively endowed wine. A raw, rugged backbone of tannin is present in this offering's stupendously long finish. Akin to a late-harvest Pinot Noir, without the residual sugar, this thrilling wine may ultimately merit a higher score when it settles down and develops more civility. Anticipated maturity: 2002–2010+.

DOMAINE LUCIEN BOILLOT (GEVREY-CHAMBERTIN)

1995 Beaune Epenottes	C	(85–87)
1995 Bourgogne	C	(84–86)
1995 Côte de Nuits-Villages	C	(85–87)
1995 Fixin	C	(85–87)
1995 Gevrey-Chambertin	D	(84–86?)
1995 Gevrey-Chambertin Les Champonnets	D	(87–90)
1995 Gevrey-Chambertin Les Cherbaudes	D	(89–91+)
1995 Gevrey-Chambertin Les Corbeaux	D	(87–90)
1995 Gevrey-Chambertin Les Evocelles	D	(87–89)
1995 Nuits-St.-Georges Les Pruliers	D	(91–93)
1995 Pommard	D	(85–87)
1995 Pommard Les Croix Noires	D	(88–90+)
1995 Pommard Les Fremiets	D	(85–88)
1995 Volnay	D	(84–87?)
1995 Volnay Les Angles	D	(86–89)

| 1995 Volnay Les Brouillards | D   (85–88) |
| 1995 Volnay Les Caillerets | D   (88–90+) |

The two Boillot brothers, Louis and Pierre, who run this estate equally share the vineyard and vinification responsibilities. A large domaine (34.6 acres) by Burgundy standards, the domaine's vineyards are spread out from the village of Volnay in the south to Fixin in the north. A cold maceration (5–10 days) is employed to encourage dark colors and riper fruit, and the wines are aged in 30% new oak. Wines destined for this estate's U.S. importer, Kermit Lynch, are not filtered but do undergo a light fining. Those sold to other markets are filtered.

I was surprised by the uniformity of flavors and personality of these offerings: they all shared a black color, exhibiting dark, robust fruit flavors and hard, tannic finishes. Stylistically they are reminiscent of Philippe Leclerc's wines, but without as much oak and depth of fruit. For most Burgundian domaines 1995 is a wonderful year for noting *terroir* differences, yet Boillot's wines share similar flavor profiles, often submerging as well as masking the wine's *terroir* nuances. As my ratings suggest, I did not factor this characteristic into my judgment on the wine's quality.

Produced from vineyards located in the communes of Gevrey-Chambertin and Brochon (a tiny village just north of Gevrey), the medium to dark ruby-colored 1995 Bourgogne displays dark, sweet fruits on the nose and robust flavors of ripe cherries, spices, and earth in its medium-bodied, slightly tannic, and surprisingly powerful (for a regional appellation) personality. Drink it from now to 2003. The 1995 Côte de Nuits-Villages is slightly darker colored and exhibits tarry as well as Asian spice aromas and sweet berry flavors. Medium bodied and tannic, this structured wine will require 2–4 years of cellaring and will drink well for 4 years. Produced from a vineyard just below the famed Clos du Chapître, the dark-colored 1995 Fixin reveals black, roasted berries, followed by a very sweet but muscular and tannic flavor profile filled with black fruits. It has the ability to age, but will the wine's hard backbone mellow with age? It should be at its best between 2000 and 2006.

The dark ruby-colored 1995 Gevrey-Chambertin village offering reveals a dark, brooding, roasted nose and sweet, virile black fruit flavors. Currently backward, this wine offers hard tannins that may outlive its fruit. Time will tell. This should not be a problem for the equally tannic yet fruit-packed 1995 Gevrey-Chambertin Les Evocelles (from a little-known village appellation vineyard in the northwest corner of Gevrey). Dark colored and bursting with deep aromas of spices, roasted black fruits, and a mouth of dense grilled berries, this is an impressively powerful and deep wine, especially considering the fact that it is not a premier or grand cru. It should drink well between 2002 and 2007. Exhibiting a black color and aromas of spicy red fruits and cinnamon, the feminine and supple 1995 Gevrey-Chambertin Les Champonnets offers sweet and dark, crisp, roasted fruits with touches of underbrush. Well structured, medium to full bodied, and chewy, it should be aged for 4+ years and drunk over the following 7 years. Medium to dark ruby colored, the aromatically tight and muted (at least on the day of my tasting) 1995 Gevrey-Chambertin Les Corbeaux is an intensely spicy, thick, juicy, cassis-and-blueberry-packed medium- to full-bodied wine. It will make delicious robust drinking between 2002 and 2007. Made from a vineyard bordered to the west by Mazis-Chambertin and to the south by Chapelle-Chambertin, the star of Boillot's Gevrey lineup is his 1995 Gevrey-Chambertin Les Cherbaudes, produced from vines averaging 80 years of age. Displaying a dark ruby color and robust aromas of sweet black cherries and underbrush, this wine reveals numerous complex flavors including sweet berries, raw and grilled meats, a touch of chocolate, and a distinct prune/cherry component. Full bodied, thick, and dense, it should be at its peak between 2004 and 2010.

My favorite Boillot offering is the fabulous 1995 Nuits-St.-Georges Les Pruliers. A spectacularly intense nose of deep, sweet, spicy fruit, minerals, and earth gives way to an equally impressive palate impression that exploded with stones, iron, toast, and massive quantities of red berries. Full bodied, thick, and dense, this powerful, deeply flavorful wine will require 7–8 years of cellaring before attaining its full maturity. It will then easily last 9+ years.

The medium ruby-colored 1995 Beaune Epenottes reveals a perfumed, strawberry-and-raspberry-scented nose and a feminine, medium-bodied, creamy personality filled with sweet red cherries. It is beautifully made and is Boillot's most supple wine. Drink it between now and 2002. Produced from the Les Poisots vineyard (the first Volnay appellation vineyard encountered after Pommard as you drive south from Beaune on the RN74), the medium to dark ruby-colored 1995 Volnay displays blueberry and blackberry aromas and a big, chewy, rugged, yet refined, medium-bodied flavor profile packed with dark fruit and coffee flavors. Its intensity is impressive, but its hard tannins are worrisome—will they outlive the fruit? The slightly darker-colored 1995 Volnay Les Brouillards (a premier cru vineyard that borders Pommard) possesses an elegant and floral nose with hints of roasting spices in the background. This medium- to full-bodied wine reveals thick cherry and blueberry flavors as well as a long, tannic finish. Anticipated maturity: now–2005. Medium to dark purple colored, the aromatically tight and muted (at least on the day of my tasting) 1995 Volnay Les Angles is a silky-textured, complex, extremely ripe wine with tangy red currants, cherries, and blueberries in its big, chewy, medium- to full-bodied and long character. It will be at its best between now and 2006. Produced from yields of less than 2 tons per acre, the dark ruby-colored 1995 Volnay Les Caillerets offers deep aromas of minerals, violets, blackberries, and roasting spices. Highly extracted and powerful cherries, currants, and ripe cassis are found in its thick, oily-textured, full-bodied palate. Built to last, it will be at its best between now and 2009.

Produced from the Les Poisots and the premier cru Les Combes vineyards, the medium to dark ruby-colored 1995 Pommard exhibits powerful aromas of blackberries and cherries. Its medium- to full-bodied, thick, and intense flavor profile is packed with ripe dark fruits yet is a well-structured, elegant wine with a long finish. Impressive for a village offering, it will provide delicious drinking between now and 2004. The ruby-colored 1995 Pommard Les Fremiets reveals a spicy, sweet blueberry-and-cherry-scented nose as well as an oily-textured, herb-infused, medium- to full-bodied core of beautifully ripe red and black fruits. Possessing a long, tannic finish, it needs 4–5 years of cellaring before reaching its peak. Drink it between 2000 and 2005. Potentially the Boillot brothers' most complete 1995 Côte de Beaune, the dark ruby-colored Pommard Les Croix Noires was produced from 70-year-old vines. It offers aromas of superripe raspberries and cherries. On the palate, it has an intense, thick, layered, full-bodied personality filled with flavors of sweet blueberries and red fruits. Concentrated and powerful, it possesses the necessary structure and fruit to easily outlive its tannic backbone. Anticipated maturity: now–2009.

DOMAINE BONNEAU DU MARTRAY (PERNAND-VERGELESSES)

1995 Corton   **E 88?**

Unquestionably this estate's attention is focused on its Corton-Charlemagne, not its red wine. Once Jean-Charles de la Morinière, the estate's director and winemaker, feels that he has attained a level of comfort in his white wine-making, I hope he will dedicate more of his talent, intelligence, and passion to his grand cru red. The 1995 Corton (yields were between less than 1²/₃ to 2 tons per acre) is medium to dark ruby colored and offers aromas of black raspberries and cherries. On the palate, this medium-bodied and somewhat raw wine reveals good concentration and flavors of brambleberries, blackberries, metals, and stones. I am not convinced that this wine's hard tannins will soften with cellaring; hence the question mark. I would suggest trying this wine around 2003.

DOMAINE BORGEOT (REMIGNY)

1996 Chassagne-Montrachet Clos St.-Jean	D	88+
1996 Santenay Beauregard	C	(86–88)
1996 Santenay	C	86

This 47-acre estate used to sell its wines to *négociants,* but the young Borgeot brothers have recently begun bottling their wines (without subjecting them to fining or filtering). Readers may want to keep an eye out for these offerings, as they provide considerable bang for the buck.

The medium to dark ruby-colored 1996 Santenay Beauregard offers a dark fruit, metal, and stone-scented nose. This is an expansive, broad, well-made, and beautifully ripe, silky-textured, medium- to full-bodied wine filled with cherries, strawberries, and raspberries. It will be at its best if drunk before 2002. The slightly lighter-colored, medium-bodied 1996 Santenay (produced from vines planted in 1922 and 1937) exhibits sweet cookie dough aromas and a smile-inducing burst of red cherries. Its glorious fruit makes up for some dry tannins. Quaff this wine over the next 2–3 years. My favorite of Borgeot's reds is the dark ruby-colored 1996 Chassagne-Montrachet Clos St.-Jean. Produced from 1²/₃ tons-per-acre yields (dramatically low for the vintage) and aged in 33% new oak, this offering reveals strong cherry and raspberry aromas that give way to a powerful, intense, and full-bodied personality. Layers of deeply ripe blackberries, cassis, and metals are found in this well-crafted and persistent wine. Anticipated maturity: 2000–2004.

BOUCHARD PÈRE ET FILS (BEAUNE)

1996 Beaune Grèves Vignes de L'Enfant Jesus	E	89+
1995 Beaune Grèves Vignes de L'Enfant Jesus	D	(86–88)
1996 Beaune Clos de la Mousse	D	88
1995 Bonnes Mares	E	(89–92)
1996 Bourgogne Hautes Côte de Beaune	C	86
1996 Chambertin	EEE	92+
1996 Chambertin Clos de Bèze	EEE	91?
1996 Chambolle-Musigny	D	88+
1995 Chambolle-Musigny	D	(86–88+)
1996 Clos Vougeot	EE	(90–92)
1995 Clos Vougeot	E	(88–91)
1996 Corton	E	90
1995 Corton	E	(87–89+)
1996 Côte de Beaune-Villages	C	86
1996 Echézeaux	EE	91
1995 Echézeaux	E	(88–90)
1996 Gevrey-Chambertin	D	(86–87)
1995 Gevrey-Chambertin	D	(84–87)
1996 Gevrey-Chambertin Les Cazetiers	EE	90

1995	Gevrey-Chambertin Les Cazetiers	D	(85–87)
1996	Maranges	C	86+
1996	Monthélie Les Champs Fulliots	D	88
1996	Nuits-St.-Georges	D	88
1996	Nuits-St.-Georges Clos des Argillières	E	(87–89)
1996	Nuits-St.-Georges Clos St.-Marc	E	(89–91+)
1995	Nuits-St.-Georges Clos St.-Marc	D	(87–89)
1996	Pommard	D	87
1996	Pommard Premier Cru	D	89
1995	Pommard Premier Cru	D	(84–87)
1996	La Romanée	EEE	(93–95)
1995	La Romanée	EEE	(90–93)
1996	Santenay	C	88
1996	Savigny-Lès-Beaune	C	88
1996	Savigny-Lès-Beaune Les Lavières	D	88+
1996	Volnay Caillerets Ancienne Cuvée Carnot	D	89+
1995	Volnay Caillerets Ancienne Cuvée Carnot	D	(86–88)
1996	Volnay Frémiets Clos de la Rougeotte	D	88
1996	Volnay Taillepieds	D	90
1996	Vosne-Romanée Aux Reignots	E	(88–91)
1995	Vosne-Romanée Aux Reignots	E	(85–88)

Bouchard is making considerable strides in improving the quality of its wines. The efforts of Joseph Henriot, this *négociant*'s new owner, and those of Bernard Hervet (its director) and Philippe Prost (its winemaker), are to be commended. Bouchard has consistently dropped yields over the past 4 years and has been making other changes in its viticulture that will produce higher-quality grapes. This, combined with a newfound commitment to new oak barrels and lighter filtration techniques, is making Bouchard a source for excellent to outstanding burgundies.

Overall, the 1995s are clean, cherry-filled, spicy wines exhibiting good extraction of ripe fruit. The medium ruby-colored 1995 Gevrey-Chambertin displays spice aromas and a mouth filled with sweet, roasted red cherries and dark fruits. Medium bodied and well structured, it will be at its best within the first 6 years of release. I was extremely pleased by the quality of the 1995 Chambolle-Musigny (162 cases produced from 2¹/₂ acres). Medium to dark ruby colored, it reveals a nose of sweet, spicy cinnamon and dark fruits and a gorgeously silky-textured mouth of deep, concentrated cherry fruit and violets. Medium to full bodied, it stands out among the other Bouchard village offerings. Anticipated maturity: now–2007. Exhibiting a ruby/purple color and a deep, dark nose of cinnamon, spice, and red apples, the 1995 Gevrey-Chambertin Les Cazetiers has ripe red fruits and sweet touches of oak in the mouth. Easy to drink and supple, this medium-bodied wine should be drunk from now to 2004. Extremely reminiscent of its village's style of wine (*terroir*), the medium to dark ruby-colored 1995 Nuits-St.-Georges Clos St.-Marc offers a dark, minerally nose and a foursquare, highly structured, concentrated mouthful of deeply roasted dark fruits, stones, and iron. Medium to full bodied, it should be consumed between 2000 and 2007. Slightly lighter in color, the 1995 Vosne-Romanée Aux Reignots displays a deep, sweet, feminine nose of violets and red fruits and a fresh, lively mouth filled with ripe, crisp cherries. Medium bodied and well balanced, it will be at its best from release to 2005.

Revealing refined, spicy red and dark fruit aromas, the medium to dark ruby-colored 1995 Echézeaux is a beautifully structured, feminine (almost dainty) wine with cherries, touches of cinnamon, and supple tannins. Well delineated and balanced, this medium-bodied, silky-textured wine will provide excellent drinking between 2001 and 2007. Also quite elegant, the darker-colored and more aromatically intense 1995 Clos Vougeot possesses a thick texture, medium to full body, and well-defined flavors of Asian spices, minerals, and red and black fruits. It should be at its best between 2002 and 2009. Even better, the superripe, highly concentrated, darkly colored 1995 Bonnes Mares displays an explosive nose packed with sweet red fruits and a judiciously oaked, velvety-textured mouth crammed with dark berries, minerals, and violets. This excellent, full-bodied wine needs to be cellared for 3–4 years; it will easily last for 8 more. The *monopole* (solely owned) La Romanée is, along with La Grande Rue, the least known of Vosne-Romanée's grand cru vineyards. It has an extraordinary location, nestled between Richebourg, Romanée St.-Vivant, La Romanée Conti, La Grande Rue, and the premier cru vineyards of Aux Reignots, Les Petits Monts, and Cros Parantoux. The wines, in the past uninspiring, have benefited from Bouchard's progress. Their 1995 is dark ruby/purple colored, with elegant, sweet aromas of spices, mocha, toffee, and red fruits (reminiscent of Romanée St.-Vivant) and refined, delineated, and fabulously deep flavors of cherries, candied grapes, Asian spices, and cocoa. Luxurious and full bodied, this gem is velvety textured and extremely long. Projected maturity: 2004–2012.

Medium to dark ruby colored and revealing a restrained but spicy, minerally nose, the 1995 Beaune Grèves Vignes de L'Enfant Jesus has a structured, thick, medium- to full-bodied character filled with the flavors of black cherries, Asian spices, stones, and herbs that continue through its long finish. I've had the opportunity to taste older vintages of this wine and am amazed at how it consistently gathers flesh and depth with time. Anticipated maturity: now–2004+. The slightly darker-colored 1995 Volnay Caillerets Ancienne Cuvée Carnot displays blackberries and deeply roasted coffee aromas and a highly structured, medium- to full-bodied, thick core of cherries and blueberries. Presently tight-fisted and unyielding, it should be at its best between now and 2004. Exhibiting blackberries and cassis aromatically, the ruby/purple-colored 1995 Pommard Premier Cru offers deeply sweet currants, black raspberries, and jammy cherries in its foursquare, medium- to full-bodied, oily-textured flavor profile. Drink it between now and 2004. The dark ruby-colored 1995 Corton, which has the potential to be outstanding, has blackberry and coffee scents, a ripe, full-bodied, and tightly structured personality, and layers of thick black cherries, cassis, and herbs. Its concentrated core of fruit and admirable length lead me to believe this wine may have more to it than my tasting revealed. Anticipated maturity: 2000–2006.

The medium to dark ruby-colored 1996 Bourgogne Hautes Côtes de Beaune offers a floral and red berry-filled nose as well as a crisp, vibrant, and refreshing core of red currants, violets, and strawberries. This medium-bodied wine should be drunk over the next 2–3 years. The slightly lighter-colored 1996 Côtes de Beaune-Villages reveals a metal, mineral, and blueberry-scented nose and a medium-bodied freshness filled with juicy red and black cherries. Anticipated maturity: now–2001. Displaying a medium to dark ruby color and blackberry and mineral aromas, the 1996 Maranges has flavors reminiscent of tangy berries, metal shavings, and stones. Its depth of fruit, grip, and length lead me to believe this wine may merit a higher score. Anticipated maturity: now–2001. I was impressed with Bouchard's bright medium to dark ruby-colored 1996 Santenay. It exhibits a sweet black cherry and violet-infused nose as well as a medium-bodied and juicy character filled with gorgeously ripe red and black cherries that linger in the finish. It will be at its best if drunk over the next 3–4 years. The similarly colored 1996 Savigny-Lès-Beaune offers a black cherry and sugar-coated raspberry nose as well as a lovely, medium- to full-bodied, and silky personality. Cherries, currants, and strawberries are intertwined in this soft, well-made wine. Drink it between now and 2002.

Produced from a vineyard that abuts Volnay's famous Clos des Chênes, the medium to dark ruby-colored 1996 Monthélie Les Champs Fulliots reveals a beguiling nose of fresh herbs, minerals, and perfume. It also possesses a medium- to full-bodied, fresh, and lively character loaded with ripe and juicy blackberries and traces of *garrigue* (the sun-roasted wild herbs of Provence) flavors. Its long finish reveals supple tannins that should provide excellent structure for midterm aging. Anticipated maturity: now–2004. The 1996 Savigny-Lès-Beaune Les Lavières is medium to dark ruby colored and ripe dark berry and iron scented and offers a delightful, medium- to full-bodied, extremely juicy, silky personality loaded with assorted red and black berries. This attractive wine should drink well through 2003. Displaying a medium to dark ruby color and an appealing nose composed of flowers, perfumes, and sweet red fruits, the 1996 Beaune Clos de la Mousse is a light- to medium-bodied, feminine, joyful wine with red currant, raspberry, and strawberry flavors. My notes read, "Fabulous for quaffing!" It has the fruit, balance, and supple tannins required for successful aging, but my instincts suggest drinking this beauty between now and 2002. Stylistically different, the medium to dark ruby-colored 1996 Beaune Grèves Vignes de L'Enfant Jesus (translated, this vineyard's name means "the vines of the child Jesus") offers a nose of violets, minerals, stones, and cassis. On the palate, this masculine, expansive, and broad-shouldered wine is jam-packed with sweet blackberries, black cherries, and cassis. Medium to full bodied, structured, and velvety textured, it possesses an impressively long and soft finish. Anticipated maturity: 2000–2006.

The 1996 Volnay Frémiets Clos de la Rougeotte exhibits a medium to dark ruby color, an attractive nose of sweet red cherries, and a medium-bodied, juicy character with raspberry, red cherry, mineral, stone, and currantlike flavors. This refined, feminine wine should be drunk over the next 4 years. The medium to dark ruby-colored 1996 Volnay Caillerets Ancienne Cuvée Carnot displays a profound, blackberry-scented nose. This medium- to full-bodied, masculine, structured, and explosive wine has superb depth, lovely, dark fruit and mineral flavors, and excellent length. Anticipated maturity: 2002–2006. The 1996 Volnay Taillepieds reveals a slightly darker color and a hugely ripe, dense, and sweet nose of plums, candied cherries, and violets. On the palate, this thick, wide, superripe, and full-bodied offering is packed with loads of red and black fruits and minerals. It should be at its best between 2001 and 2006.

The ruby/purple-colored 1996 Pommard has a red fruit and floral-infused nose that gives way to a well-made, masculine, juicy, and medium- to full-bodied core of blueberries and fresh herbs. It should be drunk over the next 3–4 years. Aromatically, the medium to dark ruby-colored 1996 Pommard Premier Cru (produced from the Combes, Rugiens, and Pézerolles vineyards) offers violet and blackberry aromas. This is an intense, explosive, medium- to full-bodied, and velvety-textured wine. With its ripe red and black fruits, excellent depth, and soft tannins, this wine should drink well between 2000 and 2005.

The massive, broad-shouldered, full-bodied, ripe 1996 Corton is medium to dark ruby colored and exhibits a blackberry and toasty oak-laden nose. This structured, masculine, and tannic wine is filled with juicy cassis, cherries, blackberries, and dark raspberries that linger in its long finish. Anticipated maturity: 2002–2007.

The impressive 1996 Nuits-St.-Georges is a medium to dark ruby-colored, profoundly sweet, blackberry-and-licorice-scented, medium- to full-bodied, foursquare, and thickly textured wine. Candied cassis, black raspberries, licorice, minerals, and stones are found in this powerful offering. Anticipated maturity: 2001–2005. Similarly colored, the 1996 Gevrey-Chambertin has gamey, meaty, and black fruit-laced aromas that give way to a medium- to full-bodied, juicy, and sweet character filled with black raspberries, cassis, and porcini. It doesn't have the power or *sur-maturité* of the previous wine but pleases as a result of its fresh and intricate flavors. Drink it between now and 2003. The slightly darker-colored 1996 Chambolle-Musigny reveals smoked pork fat and blackberries on the nose and a well-crafted, medium- to full-bodied, refined, and chewy personality with black currant, plum, and stonelike flavors. Its long finish reveals plenty of supple, round tannins. It should be at its best between now and 2004.

Medium to dark ruby colored and exhibiting a nose of violets, blackberries, and stones, the 1996 Nuits-St.-Georges Clos des Argillières is a foursquare, tannic, masculine, broad-shouldered, medium- to full-bodied wine. Cassis, minerals, and black raspberries can be found in this austere and brooding offering's flavor profile. Anticipated maturity: 2001–2005. I was quite impressed with the dark ruby-colored, flower, stone, and black cherry-scented 1996 Nuits-St.-Georges Clos St.-Marc. Its powerful and expressive character comes on full bore with juicy and mouthwatering layers of blackberries, cassis, and cherries that are inter-mingled with strong mineral flavors. This thick and chewy wine's density and depth are matched by its highly structured, masculine, and typically Nuits tannic backbone. Antici-pated maturity: 2001–2006. The dark ruby-colored 1996 Gevrey-Chambertin Les Cazetiers reveals spice cake, cassis, and coffee aromas as well as a beautifully ripe explosion of red and black berries, raw meat, and gamelike flavors. It is a well-made, exciting, complex, dense, scrumptious, medium- to full-bodied, and thickly textured wine. It should be at its peak be-tween 2001 and 2006. The 1996 Vosne-Romanée Aux Reignots (produced from the vineyard located just above the grand cru La Romanée) is medium to dark ruby colored and displays a floral, perfumed, and red cherry-infused nose. This delicious, elegant, and rich wine is medium to full bodied, silky textured, and immensely juicy. I suggest drinking it by 2004.

The medium to dark ruby-colored 1996 Echézeaux is produced from a parcel in the En Orveaux sector (bordering Chambolle-Musigny). It exhibits floral (violets and lilies) and red berry aromas as well as a medium- to full-bodied, elegant, structured, silky-textured, and fruit-filled personality. This feminine yet broad and muscular wine offers flavors reminiscent of ripe red cherries and candied raspberries dusted with freshly cracked black pepper. An-ticipated maturity: 2001–2006. The 1996 Clos Vougeot from a parcel located near the top of the vineyard, to the left of the castle, offers a similar color and a plummy, superripe, toasty nose. Flowers, sweet red cherries, blueberries, and currants can be found in this medium- to full-bodied, well-crafted, and immensely juicy wine. It may lack the depth and complexity of the Echézeaux but makes up for it with its hedonistic qualities. Anticipated maturity: 2000–2005. Regrettably, only 50 cases (2 barrels) of Bouchard's fabulous 1996 Chambertin were produced. This dark-colored offering has an enthralling nose of sweet blackberries and lilacs, followed by a massive explosion of cassis, black cherries, minerals, stones, and plums. This full-bodied, concentrated, thick wine (it merited a double underlined "big" in my notes) also possesses an admirably long, well-defined, and focused finish. It should be at its peak between 2002 and 2007. The equally dark-colored 1996 Chambertin Clos de Bèze has a brooding, backward nose of black berries and roasted spices. On the palate, this mas-culine, extracted, full-bodied, dense, and thickly textured wine reveals dark fruits, toasted oak, and herbal flavors. Its extremely long and oak-dominated finish displays considerable tannin. If the fruit outlives the tannin and oak, this wine may ultimately merit a higher rat-ing. Anticipated maturity: 2003–2008.

The magnificent 1996 La Romanée offers a medium to dark ruby color and an extraordi-nary nose of perfume, violets, and myriad red fruits. I was blown away by this wine's combi-nation of precision, femininity, focus, and jammy, candied cherries. Traces of sweet, vanilla-infused oak grace this wine's complex and concentrated yet lacelike flavor profile. Medium to full bodied and silky textured, this wine also possesses a long, soft, gorgeous finish that leaves the taster yearning for more. Finally, a La Romanée worthy of its name! Bravo to Henriot, Hervet, and Prost for bringing Bouchard to such a high level of quality.

DOMAINE JEAN-MARC BOULEY (VOLNAY)

1996 Beaune Reversées	C	(85–86)
1996 Pommard Fremiers	D	(87–89)
1996 Pommard Pézerolles	D	(86–87)
1996 Pommard Rugiens	D	(88–90)
1996 Volnay	C	(86–87)
1996 Volnay Caillerets	D	(87–89)
1996 Volnay Clos de la Cave	D	(86–87)
1996 Volnay Clos des Chênes	D	(86–88)
1996 Volnay Roncerets	D	(86–87)

Jean-Marc Bouley is one of Burgundy's rare self-starters. He put together his entire estate (29½ acres) through hard work, intelligent purchases, and perseverance. He started bottling his own wines 10 years ago but continues to sell a percentage of his production to *négociants*.

Yields were high in 1996, on average 3 tons of fruit per acre or more according to Bouley. The wines are fined and filtered (though exceptions are made for the premiers crus that don't "need" filtration). My impression is that these wines should be drunk early.

The ruby-colored 1996 Beaune Reversées offers strawberry and raspberry aromas followed by a silky-textured, light- to medium-bodied, cherry- and sweet strawberry-filled, and easy-going character. Its tannins are supple and soft, so it will make lovely quaffing wine over the next 3 years. Similarly colored, the 1996 Volnay reveals violet and cherry scents and a more concentrated, richer personality. It is medium bodied, lively, and possesses appealing red and black cherry fruit. This well-made wine should be at its best over the next 3–4 years. The ruby-colored 1996 Volnay Clos de la Cave displays a strawberry-and-cherry-scented nose as well as a silky, light- to medium-bodied, elegant core of raspberries, currants, and minerals. It should also be drunk over the next 4 years. Exhibiting a light to medium ruby color, and sweet cherry aromatics, the 1996 Volnay Roncerets is slightly deeper. It is light to medium bodied and has red and black cherries and strawberries in its flavor profile. Anticipated maturity: now–2002. The light to medium ruby-colored 1996 Volnay Clos des Chênes may ultimately be a better wine than the Roncerets. It offers a nose of sweet cherries and a light- to medium-bodied and silky palate with complex herbal, stone, mineral, and black cherry flavors. Anticipated maturity: now–2003. Revealing a ruby color and spicy, sweet black cherry, and mineral aromas, the 1996 Volnay Caillerets is the thickest, sweetest, most concentrated and complete of Bouley's Volnays. This rich and medium-bodied wine's flavors are reminiscent of raspberries, cherries, herbs, and minerals. Drink it between now and 2003.

Light to medium ruby colored, the cherry-scented 1996 Pommard Pézerolles has a beautifully ripe, medium-bodied, chewy-textured character. This supple and uncomplicated wine will provide delicious drinking over the next 3–4 years. The ruby-colored and more substantial medium-bodied 1996 Pommard Fremiers displays a refined nose of red and black cherries. This velvety wine has excellent depth, breadth, and ripeness in its red fruit-filled personality. Its finish, though not long or complex enough to warrant an outstanding score, has wonderfully soft tannins. Drink this wine over the next 5 years. Bouley's best 1996 is his ruby/purple-colored, meaty 1996 Pommard Rugiens. Earthy and sweet red cherry aromas give way to a medium- to full-bodied, broad wine packed with blackberries and dark cherries. This is an excellent and potentially outstanding wine that has the required depth, balance, fruit, and structure. Anticipated maturity: now–2005.

DOMAINE REYANNE ET PASCAL BOULEY (VOLNAY)

1996 Beaune	D	(85–87)
1995 Beaune	D	(85–88)
1996 Pommard	D	(87–88)
1995 Pommard	D	(86–89)
1996 Volnay	D	(85–87)
1995 Volnay	D	(86–89)
1996 Volnay Premier Cru	D	(87–89)
1995 Volnay Premier Cru	D	(87–90)
1996 Volnay Champans	D	(88–91)
1995 Volnay Champans	D	(90–92+)
1996 Volnay Clos des Chênes	D	(88–91)
1995 Volnay Clos des Chênes	D	(89–91)
1996 Volnay Santenots	D	(88–91)

Located opposite Volnay's church, this domaine is an excellent if little-known source for Côte de Beaunes. Pascal Bouley and his wife, Reyanne, are up-and-coming stars. Robert Parker was extremely impressed by their 1993s, writing that the wines "merit serious interest from burgundy wine lovers." The Bouleys' wines are packed with intense and concentrated fruit. After a 2-day cold maceration, their alcoholic fermentations are induced. Pascal Bouley is not a believer in large quantities of new oak (he never uses more than 25%), preferring to have the wines dominated by fruit. Only two wines are filtered (using a Kieselguhr)—the Beaune and Volnay.

Produced from a rented parcel in the Prèvoles vineyard, the light to medium ruby-colored 1996 Beaune displays a brambleberry, herb, and mineral-laden nose. This supple, straightforward, light- to medium-bodied, and delicious quaffing wine is replete with blackberries, cherries, and currants. It should be drunk over the next 3 years. The ruby-colored 1996 Volnay offers a nose of flowers and sweet cherries. Light to medium bodied, soft, with red cherry and currant flavors, it is a well-made, simple wine for near-term drinking. Anticipated maturity: now–2001. Produced from vines averaging between 35 and 40 years old located in Chanlins, the 1996 Pommard reveals a beautiful medium to dark ruby color and ripe, red and black berry fruit aromas. It is an oily-textured, medium-bodied, dense, and red fruit-driven wine with excellent length. It will be at its best if drunk over the next 4 years.

The medium to dark ruby-colored, structured, and ripe 1996 Volnay Premier Cru is produced from vines located in Ronceret and Robardelle. Deep aromas of black cherries give way to a rich, medium- to full-bodied, oily-textured, elegant wine flavored with red cherries and raspberries. Anticipated maturity: now–2003. The 1996 Volnay Clos des Chênes has a medium to dark ruby color and lovely violet and black berry fruit scents. On the palate, this medium- to full-bodied, refined, broad, and silky wine is resplendent with black cherries, cassis, and flowers. The complex flavors persist throughout the long, detailed finish. Anticipated maturity: 2000–2005. Regrettably, only 300–450 bottles of 1996 Volnay Santenots (from a parcel located just above Dominique Lafon's) were produced. None of them are being sold to this estate's U.S. importer. Exhibiting a healthy ruby/purple color and sweet red cherry aromatics, this medium- to full-bodied, chewy-textured, lively, and elegant wine is concentrated and packed with juicy red fruits. Anticipated maturity: now–2003. The medium to dark ruby-colored 1996 Volnay Champans displays beautifully ripe red cherry aromas and a candied, well-extracted, powerful, and medium- to full-bodied core of concentrated black and red fruits. This velvety, complex, and persistent wine is more tannic and will require patience by readers. Anticipated maturity: 2001–2006.

The medium to dark ruby-colored 1995 Beaune displays an enticingly sweet nose of cherries and cinnamon as well as a beautifully crafted, medium-bodied, silky-textured, and supple personality crammed with spicy and jammy red cherries. Succulent to drink now, it will age gracefully through 2001. Slightly darker colored, the superb village 1995 Volnay exhibits a gorgeously ripe nose of blueberries and strawberries as well as a magnificently sweet, oily-textured, and medium- to full-bodied character with blackberry, red currant, and herb flavors. This is a concentrated, complex, admirably long, and well-crafted wine. It will be at its best between 1998 and 2003. Equally good, the dark ruby-colored 1995 Pommard offers deep cherry fruit aromas and a highly structured, almost foursquare flavor profile with smoky strawberries and boysenberries in its thick-textured, full body. Anticipated maturity: now–2004. These are three first-rate village wines!

Dark colored and revealing intense blackberry, cassis, and coffee aromatics, the 1995 Volnay Premier Cru is an extremely well-structured, full-bodied, and thick wine jam-packed with layers of strawberries, cherries, and roasted wood notes. Its gorgeously long finish ends on a backbone of supple tannins. It will be at its peak between now and 2005. The 1995 Volnay Clos des Chênes possesses a saturated dark ruby color and an intensely ripe cherry-and-anise-scented nose. This wine has a thick, massively endowed, and full-bodied personality replete with huge quantities of sweet red cherries and sugar-coated raspberries. Beautifully integrated and superbly ripe tannins are found in its outstanding finish. Anticipated maturity: now–2007+. Even better, and exhibiting a saturated black/purple color, the 1995 Volnay Champans bursts from the glass with black cherry and sweet new oak aromas. This impressive, full-bodied, oily-textured, and hugely concentrated wine overflows with blackberries, candied blueberries, and mouthwatering toasted oak notes. The balance between oak flavors and fruit in this wine is absolutely brilliant. An exceptionally long finish reveals perfectly ripe and round tannins. It will be at its best between 2000 and 2009. Bravo!

DOMAINE ALAIN BURGUET (GEVREY-CHAMBERTIN)

1996 Bourgogne	C	(86–87)
1995 Bourgogne	C	(85–87)
1996 Gevrey-Chambertin en Billiard	D	(87–88)
1995 Gevrey-Chambertin en Billiard	D	(86–89)
1996 Gevrey-Chambertin Les Champeaux	E	(89–91?)
1995 Gevrey-Chambertin Les Champeaux	D	(91–93)
1996 Gevrey-Chambertin en Reniard	D	(88–90)
1995 Gevrey-Chambertin en Reniard	D	(87–90)
1996 Gevrey-Chambertin Vieilles Vignes	E	(90–93)
1995 Gevrey-Chambertin Vieilles Vignes	D	(89–92)

Alain Burguet is a hunter. This is true in the normal sense of the word, but also when it comes to his approach to life and winemaking. In addition to stalking wild boar and caribou, Burguet also seeks old-vine Gevrey vineyards he can afford. This last endeavor is even more difficult since vineyard prices have become preposterously high. To date, Burguet, who dreams of owning a grand cru site, must be content with producing some of Burgundy's finest village wines. Jean Troisgros, one of France's most influential and talented chefs, and one of the few people in this world to intimately understand wine's role with cuisine, discovered Burguet in the early eighties. Today Burguet's wines still occupy places of honor at the three-star Michelin guide Troisgros Restaurant.

Burguet, without compromise, strives to make the highest-quality wines he can. No herbicides are ever used on the vines, yields are kept low, and a severe sorting of the grapes is conducted on tables placed in the vineyards at harvesttime. In the cellars, Burguet never fines or uses sulfur, nor has he ever added tartaric acid to give his wines structure (a common but illegal practice in Burgundy—U.S. wineries are allowed to acidify and do it regularly). Burguet subjects his wine to a light Kieselguhr filtration. He suggests that his wines be decanted prior to drinking because his winemaking techniques minimize air contact.

Attractive and well made, the 1995 Bourgogne reveals a fat, thick, cherry core of fruit and spices in its medium-bodied, oily-textured mouth. Delicious to drink right out of the barrel, it should be enjoyed within 4 years of its release. Aged in 45% new oak barrels, the medium to dark ruby-colored 1995 Gevrey-Chambertin en Billiard exhibits enticingly deep and elegant aromas of sweet cherries and dark spices. The fat, thick, velvety-textured flavors are packed with crisp berries, dried cherries, Asian spices, and earth tones. Structured and delineated, it will be at its best between 2001 and 2006. Produced from 35-year-old vines, the ruby/purple-colored 1995 Gevrey-Chambertin en Reniard has beautiful depth to its brooding, dark-roasted, spice-filled nose. Flavors of black cherries, tangy berries, rocks, and the forest floor are found in this full-bodied, long, wonderfully thick-textured wine. Tannic and structured, it is built to last (2004–2010). One of Burgundy's finest village wines in 1995 is Burguet's Gevrey-Chambertin Vieilles Vignes. Exhibiting the concentration, extract, power, and thick body of a grand cru, this darkly colored, intensely spicy, chewy, tangy, highly structured wine is a testimony to Burguet's uncompromising winemaking. Velvety textured, supple, yet tannic, it requires 6+ years of cellaring and will last 9+ years.

Given the fact that Burguet can make an outstanding wine from unheralded village vineyards, it will come as no surprise to readers that his only premier cru offering is first-rate. The dark-colored 1995 Gevrey-Chambertin Les Champeaux possesses a beguiling nose of deep, sweet dark berries, cherries, and a touch of milk chocolate. Its mouth explodes with lively black and red fruits, Asian spices, and stones all embedded in a chewy, fabulously thick texture. This formidably long, powerful, highly structured beauty has big, ripe, round tannins. It will be held in my cellar for 8+ years and consumed with a broad smile over the following 8 years . . . if I can find any. Bravo!

According to the burly Alain Burguet, "1996 is a great vintage that will age admirably; it has richness, finesse, structure, fruit, and marvelous equilibrium. At harvest the grapes were black, not pink, red, or purple." He went on to tell me that while he loves 1995's "richness, concentration, and equilibrium," 1996 is a better year.

Burguet produced fine 1996s, from his Bourgogne to the superb Gevrey-Chambertin Vieilles Vignes.

The ruby-colored 1996 Bourgogne has a rich nose crammed with cherries that gives way to a silky-textured, medium-bodied, well-crafted, dense, and sweet black cherry-filled personality. This delicious, if not complex, wine should be drunk over the next 3–4 years. Crafted from 12-year-old vines, the 1996 Gevrey-Chambertin en Billiard is slightly darker colored and has fresh black cherry scents. This concentrated, dense, pure, medium- to full-bodied, and forceful wine is crammed with black fruits and supple tannins. Regrettably, this otherwise succulent wine tails off abruptly. Drink it between now and 2003. The 1996 Gevrey-Chambertin en Reniard, produced from older vines, is a darker-colored, more intense, concentrated, longer wine. It displays a spicy, wild blueberry-scented nose and bursts on the palate with a highly expressive flavor profile composed of cassis liqueur, candied blueberries, and fresh herbs. Anticipated maturity: 2000–2005. Burguet crafted his 1996 Gevrey-Chambertin Vieilles Vignes from vines averaging 60 years old (consisting of 15 different parcels), it is dark colored and has profound aromas of blackberries, underbrush, Asian spices, and earth. This velvety-textured and medium- to full-bodied wine explodes on the palate with powerful layers of black cherries and blackberries. It is a muscular yet refined offering that has immensely impressive richness, concentration, and palate presence. Its admirably long finish reveals satiny tannins, delineation, and sweet-and-spicy oak flavors. Anticipated maturity: 2002–2008. The 1996 Gevrey-Chambertin Les Champeaux (only 3 barrels—or 75 cases—produced) displays a dark ruby color and a candied cassis nose of gorgeous aromatic purity. This powerfully concentrated, rich, thickly textured, and full-bodied offering is crammed with sweet blueberry and black cherry flavors but is dominated at present by its lavish oak. If it resolves its oakiness, this wine will certainly merit a score in the range I have given it. Anticipated maturity: 2003–2009.

DOMAINE JACQUES CACHEUX ET FILS (VOSNE-ROMANÉE)

1996	Echézeaux	E	(91–93+)
1995	Echézeaux	E	92
1996	Nuits-St.-Georges au Bas de Combe	D	(86–89)
1996	Vosne-Romanée	D	(85–87)
1995	Vosne-Romanée	D	(84–86)
1996	Vosne-Romanée La Croix Rameau	E	(89–92)
1995	Vosne-Romanée La Croix Rameau	D	(88–91)
1996	Vosne-Romanée Les Suchots	E	(89–92)
1995	Vosne-Romanée Les Suchots	E	(88–90)

Located on the main road that separates the vaunted vineyards of the Côte d'Or (Route Nationale 74) from the plain, Domaine Jacques Cacheux is one of the few Burgundy estates that produces high-quality wines yet remains relatively unknown in the United States. A quiet man, Cacheux uses 100% new oak in his premiers and grands crus and once used oak on his village appellations. Fining and filtering was abandoned in 1987.

Quite tight and muted on the nose, the medium ruby-colored 1995 Vosne-Romanée exhibits an appealing silky texture, dark cherry fruit, and a fresh, tangy finish. Anticipated maturity: now–2000. Slightly darker, the 1995 Vosne-Romanée Les Suchots reveals a beautiful, deep, sweet cherry fruit-filled nose with notes of rose petals and an exciting, supple mouth with fat red and dark fruit flavors. Elegant and well structured, it should be drunk between 2000 and 2008. Medium to dark ruby colored, the 1995 Vosne-Romanée La Croix Rameau (located just below the grand cru Romanée-St.-Vivant) displays an intense perfume of dark and red fruits and an enticing mouth of fat, jammy red fruits. Silky, delineated, and chewy, this medium- to full-bodied complex wine can be enjoyed in 4–5 years yet will keep another 6–8 more. One of the best sources in Burgundy for Echézeaux, Cacheux's is made from vines planted in 1934, 1952, and 1990, which makes the vines, on average, 36 years old. However, the old-vine intensity of the 1934 and 1952 plantings make up for the youth of the 1990 vineyard. Medium to dark ruby colored, this outstanding 1995 exhibits a mouthwatering nose of smoky bacon intermingled with red and black fruits. The silky-textured palate is packed with fat, chewy, lively wild berries and an extraordinary juniper-smoked bacon component (reminiscent of the best bacon to be found in the United States, produced in a small smokehouse in northwest Connecticut: Nodine's, 1-800-222-2059). Medium to full bodied, and beautifully proportioned, it should be cellared for 6–7 years and drunk over the following 7–8 years.

Why this estate has not attracted more attention from lovers of red burgundy escapes me. Readers are well advised to make an effort to find these fairly priced, delicious wines.

Jacques Cacheux, a gracious, quiet, reserved man, officially retired in 1993, handing over the direction of the estate to his 40-year-old son, Pascal. The father is so reserved, in fact, that Pascal Cacheux, who was responsible for the 1995s, had no idea that I had visited the estate and tasted the wines in 1997.

The medium to dark ruby-colored, sweet cherry-and-violet-scented 1996 Vosne-Romanée has powerful flavors of ripe cherries in its thick, creamy, medium-bodied, and soft character. This delicious wine should be drunk over the next 5 years. Similarly colored, the 1996 Nuits-St.-Georges au Bas de Combe has candied raspberry aromas and a rich, refined, medium- to full-bodied, extremely well-crafted core of intense red currant, cherry, and raw meat-like flavors. This supple (yet structured), deep, and focused wine will be at its peak between 2000 and 2005.

Slightly darker colored, and displaying candied red fruits drenched in bacon fat aromas, the 1996 Vosne-Romanée Les Suchots has a mouthwatering flavor profile of smoked pork and gorgeously ripe and juicy cherries. This medium- to full-bodied, velvety-textured, and well-balanced wine has a long finish that reveals its satin-laced tannins. Anticipated maturity: 2000–2006. The 1996 Vosne-Romanée La Croix Rameau is medium to dark ruby colored and exhibits a nose composed of violets and candied black cherries and raspberries. On the palate, this powerful, masculine, highly structured, and intense wine offers loads of blackberries, brambleberries, fresh herbs, and toasted oak. Presently quite firm, this wine offers copious (yet soft) tannins that should melt with cellaring. Anticipated maturity: 2002–2007.

Revealing a dark ruby color and, interestingly, the same juniper-smoked bacon and juicy red and black fruit aromas I had smelled in the 1995 (it has to be the oak), Cacheux's 1996 Echézeaux is, once again, a great wine. Its superelegant, feminine, medium- to full-bodied, and profound character offers delightful layers of cherries, raspberries, and currants intermingled with toasted and grilled oak. This beautifully ripe, highly detailed, and focused wine is harmonious, admirably long, and extremely well crafted. Drink it between 2003 and 2010.

Pascal Cacheux was kind enough to allow me to retaste the estate's dark ruby-colored 1995 Echézeaux at the end of my most recent visit. The saliva-inducing scents of bacon had dissipated and were now laced with toast-infused, blackberry, and cassis aromas. It is a concentrated, mouth-coating, full-bodied, powerful, and deeply ripe wine with densely packed red and black cherries, plums, and grilled oak notes. This silky-textured and extremely refined beauty should hit its stride in 2005 yet hold through 2012.

DOMAINE LUCIEN CAMUS-BROCHON (SAVIGNY-LÈS-BEAUNE)

1996 Savigny-Lès-Beaune Les Grands Liards Vieilles Vignes	D	(88–89)
1996 Savigny-Lès-Beaune Les Lavières	D	(88–89)
1996 Savigny-Lès-Beaune Les Narbantons	D	(89–91)
1996 Savigny-Lès-Beaune Vieilles Vignes	D	(87–88)

Note: The following wines are Patrick Lesec Selections, which are neither fined nor filtered. The first three wines were aged in 100% new oak barrels (the fourth in half new and half 1-year-old barrels); I am unaware of the cellaring and bottling procedures employed for Camus-Brochon's cuvées not represented by Lesec.

The medium to dark ruby-colored and blackberry-and-metal-scented 1996 Savigny-Lès-

Beaune Vieilles Vignes exhibits a tangy, well-crafted, medium-bodied, and cassis- and red currant-filled character with excellent breadth. Its concentrated fruit and silky texture suggest lovely drinking if its structured backbone melts away. Drink it between 2000 and 2004. Produced from a vineyard located just below Les Lavières, the 1996 Savigny-Lès-Beaune Les Grands Liards Vieilles Vignes has a bright, medium to dark ruby color and a spicy, cassis-laden nose. This chewy-textured, densely packed, and medium- to full-bodied wine offers blackberry and ironlike flavors. Broad shouldered, fruit driven, and refined, this offering also possesses an admirably long finish. Anticipated maturity: 2000–2005. Equally excellent, the similarly colored 1996 Savigny-Lès-Beaune Les Lavières offers an intense nose of black currants intermingled with mineral-like scents. This is a plump, medium- to full-bodied, juicy, velvety-textured, and deep wine filled with loads of blackberries and dark cherries. Anticipated maturity: 2000–2005. Revealing a bright, medium to dark ruby color and a beguiling nose of violets, cassis, and black cherries, the 1996 Savigny-Lès-Beaune Les Narbantons is concentrated, complex, and medium to full-bodied. Its intense and silky-textured core is layered with succulent black currants, fresh herbs, blackberries, and cherries, all intertwined with distinctive stone and mineral flavors. This burgundy combines power and strength with elegance and refinement. Anticipated maturity: 2000–2006.

CHÂTEAU DE CHAMIREY

1996 Mercurey	C	(86–88)

This delicious Mercurey has a medium to dark ruby color and a charming nose of violets, roses, and sweet cherries. On the palate it boasts beautiful ripeness, medium to full body, a silky texture, and loads of red cherries and blueberries. Some rusticity can be discerned in the wine's finish. Anticipated maturity: now–2001. The Château de Chamirey is owned by the Antonin Rodet *négociant* house.

DOMAINE CHANDON DE BRIAILLES (SAVIGNY-LÈS-BEAUNE)

1996 Aloxe-Corton (Les Valozières)	D	(85–87)
1996 Corton-Bressandes	E	(88–90+)
1996 Corton Clos du Roi	E	(89–92)
1996 Corton Les Maréchaudes	D	(87–89)
1996 Pernand-Vergelesses Ile de Vergelesses	D	(87–89)
1996 Pernand-Vergelesses Les Vergelesses	C	(86–88)
1996 Savigny-Lès-Beaune Les Fourneaux	D	(85–87)
1996 Savigny-Lès-Beaune Les Lavières	D	(86–88)

This estate is one of the most beautiful properties in Burgundy. Situated in Savigny-Lès-Beaune, the count and countess de Nicolay's home, nestled at the back of a gravel courtyard, is a gem.

Mme. de Nicolay and her winemaker, Jean-Claude Bouveret (or Kojak, as he prefers to be called), practice what the French call *lutte raisonnée*. In short, no chemical products are used in the vineyards unless essential. Yields are kept moderately low, averaging about 2¹/₂ tons of fruit per acre for most vineyards and 2 tons per acre for grands crus. Neither Mme. de Nicolay nor Kojak are enchanted by new oak, as the barrels (some over 20 years old) on display in the cellars proved. Every precaution is taken to safeguard the wine's fruit—there are no pumps or filters. "As little manipulation as possible; we need to be soft with our wines," claims Bouveret. The wines are fined, using two or three egg whites per barrel.

Mme. de Nicolay said, "We make severe wines," and she's right. These are not dark-colored, luscious, seductive, and hedonistic offerings, nor are they powerful, muscular, and highly extracted. They are elegant, structured, and well proportioned.

The ruby-colored and earth-, blackberry-, and mineral-scented Savigny-Lès-Beaune Les Fourneaux was produced from 40-year-old vines. Its medium-bodied, sweet, and rich character offers silky-textured cherry and stonelike flavors. It will be at its best if drunk between now and 2003. From 40-year-old vines, the ruby-colored Savigny-Lès-Beaune Les Lavières has lively blackberry and smoky aromas. On the palate, it offers a precise, well-balanced, medium-bodied, red fruit and mineral-laced personality with excellent depth and oily texture. It would have received higher praise had it not had an abrupt finish. Anticipated maturity: now–2004.

Revealing a bright ruby color and a nose of deeply rich dark fruits, earth, minerals, and mushrooms, the Pernand-Vergelesses Les Vergelesses is a medium-bodied, creamy-textured, and succulent wine filled with beautifully ripe red cherries. This expressive wine will provide delicious near-term drinking, but it lacks the necessary structure for extended cellaring. Drink it over the next 3–4 years. The Pernand-Vergelesses Ile de Vergelesses displays a healthy ruby/purple color and earthy black fruit aromas. This medium- to full-bodied, rich, intense, focused, chewy-textured, yet vibrant wine is packed with flavors suggestive of ripe black cherries and sautéed porcini mushrooms. Ile de Vergelesses may very well be my favorite vineyard from this appellation. This offering, as with many of this terroir's best examples, has extremely appealing depth and layered fruit. Anticipated maturity: now–2005.

Produced from vines planted a decade ago, the Aloxe-Corton is entitled to premier cru status, as it hails from Les Valozières. In recent years, however, Mme. de Nicolay, a proud and quality-conscious woman, has refused to label it as such because the wines, in her opinion, lacked premier cru quality. Whether the 1996 will be labeled as a village wine or as an Aloxe-Corton Les Valozières will be determined at the time of bottling. This ruby-colored, violet-and-blueberry-scented wine offers a medium-bodied, structured, and tannic core of red grapes, stones, and earthlike flavors. Its lack of density and short finish suggest it will be labeled only as an Aloxe-Corton. Drink it between now and 2003.

Domaine Chandon de Briailles offers three grands crus from Corton. Maréchaudes is the simplest of the three, immensely satisfying yet not intensely complex or long. Bressandes is the most seductive, more complex than the Maréchaudes but still dependent on its opulent fruit. Clos du Roi is the most intricate and complex, more refined, structured, and classier, but it lacks the expressive and succulent fruit that make the Maréchaudes and Bressandes so appealing.

Medium to dark ruby/purple colored and exhibiting black raspberry and cassis aromas, the 1996 Corton Les Maréchaudes is a supple, fat, feminine, medium-bodied, velvety-textured wine. Sweet, juicy cherries are intermingled with minerals and stones in this pleasing, expressive, and long wine. Anticipated maturity: now–2004. The ruby-colored 1996 Corton-Bressandes offers a beguiling nose of sweet red fruits, wild mushrooms, and underbrushlike scents. This rich, oily-textured, dense, powerful, medium- to full-bodied, and deep wine is jam-packed with layers of candied blackberries, cassis, stones, and minerals. I tasted this wine from two barrels; the younger cask revealed traces of Asian spices and the older barrique touches of chalk and dried smoky minerals. Both casks contain a wine of admirable depth, purity, and length. Anticipated maturity: 2000–2006. Medium to dark ruby colored, and displaying stony, metallic, and blackberry aromatics, the 1996 Corton Clos du Roi is a medium- to full-bodied, structured, masculine, ripe wine that is packed with cassis, brambleberries, and stones. Somewhat austere and foursquare, this complex and aristocratic wine is well concentrated and possesses a persistent, well-defined finish. Anticipated maturity: 2002–2008.

CHARTRON ET TREBUCHET (PULIGNY-MONTRACHET)

1996 Chassagne-Montrachet Les Morgeots	D	85?
1996 Puligny-Montrachet Clos du Cailleret	D	86?

I had no experience with this *négociant* house's reds prior to my visit in November 1997. Both had worrisome dry and chalky tannins, even though 1996 is *not* a vintage where I found tannins to be problematic. Two can be recommended, with reservations. The medium ruby-colored 1996 Chassagne-Montrachet Les Morgeots reveals a violet, stone, and red berry-filled nose and a medium-bodied, lively, tangy core of minerals and red currants. Dry and slightly rustic tannins are found on its otherwise long and elegant finish. Anticipated maturity: now–2003. The 1996 Puligny-Montrachet Clos du Cailleret has beautiful floral and stone aromas and a sweet red cherry, black raspberry, and mineral-laden, medium-bodied, racy, and refined personality. Again, the dry tannins take away from this otherwise stylish and delicious wine. It should be consumed between now and 2003.

DOMAINE JEAN CHAUVENET (NUITS-ST.-GEORGES)

1995 Nuits-St.-Georges	D	(83–86?)
1995 Nuits-St.-Georges Les Bousselots	D	(84–87?)
1995 Nuits-St.-Georges Les Damodes	D	(85–88)
1995 Nuits-St.-Georges Les Perrières	D	(88–91)
1995 Nuits-St.-Georges en Rue de Chaux	D	(86–89)
1995 Nuits-St.-Georges Les Vaucrains	E	(87–90)

Jean Chauvenet is retiring, and thanks to his daughter's selection of an intelligent, inquisitive, and driven husband (Christopher Drag), this estate is in good hands. No defoliants are used in the vineyards (with the exception of Vaucrains), and organic viticulture is employed whenever Drag deems it possible. Grape bunches have been fully destemmed since the 1990 vintage (inclusive), and a long maceration (15–21 days) is generally practiced. New oak is not used in large quantities at this estate (10%–25%), with wines aging in barrels up to 5 years old. As the rating (and the following notes) suggests, this is an excellent, if little-known, source of burgundies. More than a third of this domaine's wines are sold to *négociants*, but this may change: the combination of Jean Chauvenet's experience and Christopher Drag's desire and abilities will more than likely result in more of the wine being estate-bottled.

Displaying a medium ruby color and aromas of red and black currants, the 1995 Nuits-St.-Georges offers supple, elegant fruit, a thick texture, and a medium-bodied, long finish. My palate was pasty sweet after having tasted it, suggesting an overabundance of unfermented sugar. The same can be said for the darker-colored 1995 Nuits-St.-Georges Les Bousselots, which reveals a sweet, minerally nose and an oily texture, with fat superripe cherries, a medium body, and good persistence on the palate. Both these wines should be consumed within the first 6 years after their release.

Displaying some spice in its closed nose, the 1995 Nuits-St.-Georges en Rue de Chaux is packed with flavors reminiscent of red Delicious apples, Asian spices, and sweet, luscious cherries. Beautifully concentrated and medium to full bodied, this wine has a good finish and possesses all the components for a better rating except one—complexity. Anticipated maturity: now–2004. A step up, the medium to dark-colored 1995 Nuits-St.-Georges Les Vaucrains offers tightly wound aromas of minerals and spice, an oily texture, and gorgeous, concentrated layers of ripe and spicy cherries and wild berries, a medium to full body, and good length. It will be at its best between 2001 and 2007. The 1995 Nuits-St.-Georges Les

Damodes reveals a ruby/purple color, a tight, reticent nose of currants, and a spicy, ripe cherry-filled, silky-textured, medium- to full-bodied personality. This wine will benefit from 3–4 years of cellaring and hold for 5–7 additional years. Chauvenet's dark-colored 1995 Nuits-St.-Georges Les Perrières possesses intense, deep, sweet, lavender and cinnamon aromas and an excellent, explosive attack filled with wild berries, flint, and minerals. Powerful, concentrated, and complex, this thick, full-bodied wine needs to be held for 5–6 years and will drink beautifully over the subsequent 8–9 years.

DOMAINE CHAUVENET-CHOPIN (NUITS-ST.-GEORGES)

1996	Chambolle-Musigny	D	(88–89)
1996	Cote de Nuits-Villages	D	88
1996	Nuits-St.-Georges aux Argillats	E	(89–92)
1995	Nuits-St.-Georges aux Argillats	E	(87–89?)
1996	Nuits-St.-Georges Les Murgers	E	(90–92+)
1995	Nuits-St.-Georges Les Murgers	E	(89–92)
1996	Nuits-St.-Georges Vieilles Vignes	D	(88–90?)
1995	Nuits-St.-Georges Vieilles Vignes	D	(86–89)

With the retirement of Daniel Chopin (Domaine Chopin Groffier), this estate, run by his son-in-law, Hubert Chauvenet, is going to become significantly more important. In 1996 one-third of this domaine's holdings were under *métayage* agreements with Chopin. Starting with the 1997s, Chauvenet will take over Chopin's holdings.

These wines are stylistically very reminiscent of Daniel Chopin's. They are fruit driven, supple, and immensely pleasurable, no doubt because Chauvenet has been Chopin's pupil for years.

The ruby-colored 1996 Côtes de Nuits-Villages (bottled in mid-October 1997) has perfumed aromas of violets and blackberries. This thickly textured, soft, medium-bodied, and deeply ripe wine is redolent with cassis and floral flavors that linger in its long and supple finish. Drink it over the next 4 years. The 1996 Chambolle-Musigny is darker colored than the previous offering and reveals mineral, earth, and dark fruit scents. This broad, plump, velvety-textured, bright, rich, juicy, and cherry-laced wine is seductive, and oh, so enjoyable. It will be at its best if drunk over the next 5 years. Produced from vines planted in 1927 and 1966 in the Les Charmottes vineyard, the 1996 Nuits-St.-Georges Vieilles Vignes is medium to dark ruby colored and displays intense dark berry aromas. This broad, masculine, highly structured, and concentrated wine is crammed with rich and ripe blackberries, cassis, and stones. This wine is surprisingly tannic, considering the suppleness of the estate's other offerings; how Chauvenet copes with the rough character and finish of this wine will determine its ultimate quality. Anticipated maturity: 2002–2006?

The slightly darker-colored 1996 Nuits-St.-Georges aux Argillats (from 15- to 40-year-old vines) has powerful aromas of freshly brewed coffee laced with mocha cream. This thick, intense, mouth-coating, profound, and rich wine is medium to full bodied, concentrated, and expressive. Its jammy cassis, black cherry, and blackberry flavors are intermingled with chalk and minerals. This offering's impressive finish reveals loads of superbly ripened tannins enveloped in sweet dark fruits. Anticipated maturity: 2001–2006. Potentially even better, the medium to dark ruby-colored 1996 Nuits-St.-Georges Les Murgers has an expressive nose of cassis, cherries, Asian spices, and minerals. This massive, chewy-textured, full-bodied, and plump wine is rich, concentrated, muscular, and crammed with superripe blackberries awash in toasty oak. It should be at its best between 2002 and 2007.

Hubert Chauvenet's 1995 Nuits-St.-Georges Les Murgers was 100% destemmed and aged in 40% new oak barrels. As I noted when I reviewed it originally (it rated an 89–92), this is a wine for those who prefer Vosne's elegance over Nuits' structure. Medium to dark ruby colored, it reveals a delightful nose of beautifully ripened blueberries and blackberries intermingled with Asian spices. This soft, oily-textured, seductive, medium- to full-bodied and elegant wine offers plums, blueberries, and stonelike flavors in its supple yet structured character. It is one of the rare first-rate wines I have tasted from this backward vintage that is forward enough to be drunk in the near term (it should be noted, however, that the bottle I tasted had been open for 3 hours prior to my trying it). Anticipated maturity: now–2006.

With a deep nose of café au lait, the medium to dark ruby-colored 1995 Nuits-St.-Georges Vieilles Vignes has silky-textured, intense mocha and superdark cherry flavors. It can be drunk now or over the subsequent 5–7 years. Dark ruby colored, the 1995 Nuits-St.-Georges aux Argillats exhibits strong roasted fruit aromatics and a distinct stinkiness in the nose (this offputting odor will most probably blow off prior to bottling, but . . . hence the question mark) and a highly structured, masculine, chewy, and slightly tannic mouth of superdark fruits. Built to last, this wine should be cellared for 4+ years. It will keep for another 6–8.

DOMAINE PASCAL CHEVIGNY (NUITS-ST.-GEORGES)

1996 Hautes Côtes de Nuits Réserve	C	87
1996 Nuits-St.-Georges Les Hauts Pruliers	E	90
1996 Vosne-Romanée Les Champs Perdrix	D	92
1996 Vosne-Romanée La Combe Brûlée	E	90
1996 Vosne-Romanée Les Petits Monts	EE	91
1996 Vosne-Romanée Vieilles Vignes Réserve	D	89+

Note: Those wines that carry the "Réserve" designation are crafted exclusively for North Berkeley Imports and are bottled unfined and unfiltered.

Pascal Chevigny is a tall, soft-spoken, intense, and handsome man who has a tendency to "disappear." He is happiest when alone in the wilderness, fending for himself, or alone with his thoughts. His sense of duty forces him to fulfill his family responsibility by running this estate, however. Most people, knowing they would rather be elsewhere, would cut corners and not make all the necessary efforts for success. That is not the case with Chevigny, a dedicated vigneron who dragged me through his parcel of Vosne-Romanée Les Champs Perdrix, proudly proving his viticultural prowess.

Since Champs Perdrix is a steep vineyard (directly above the grands crus of La Grande Rue and La Tâche), much of its topsoil is washed away each time it rains. Chevigny regularly collects the earth that amasses along the wall at the base of the vineyard and redistributes it around the vines. Thanks to his plowing (an arduous task on a vineyard this steep), his vines have deep roots that firmly hold the vines on the hillside. In contrast, neighbors' plants, treated with herbicides and fertilizers, have extremely shallow roots, some of which can be spotted aboveground.

Pascal Chevigny crafts older-style burgundies. Firm, structured, and broad shouldered, his wines are not hedonistic or luscious. His stated wish is to craft hard wines, vinified with all their stems intact, the way he says his grandfather Lucien Rousseau made them (a batch of 1996s were made in this way to celebrate the birth of his daughter). To demonstrate this style of wine's ability to age, Chevigny pulled the original cork on a half bottle of 1947 Vosne-Romanée Les Champs Perdrix his grandfather had produced and let it sit for 2 hours before allowing me to have a taste. It was stunning—unbelievably fresh, focused, and packed with dense yet elegant and delicate fruit. While I don't believe that one bottle of wine from one of this century's greatest vintages can be used to prove a point, there is no doubting the fact that it has remained youthfully magnificent.

The ruby-colored 1996 Hautes Côtes de Nuits Réserve displays mineral and blackberry aromatics that are followed by a precise, lively, and medium-bodied personality. This black-berry, spice, underbrush, and mineral-flavored wine has excellent depth and richness. It should be at its best between now and 2003.

Produced from parcels in three vineyards (Damaudes, Chalandins, and Ormes), the 1996 Vosne-Romanée Vieilles Vignes Réserve has a medium to dark ruby color and fabulous aro-mas of sweet black cherries and fresh herbs. This medium- to full-bodied, concentrated, chewy, rich, and plump wine is crammed with cinnamon and Asian spice-imbued black fruits. Its admirably long finish is loaded with supple and ripe tannins. Drink this beauty be-tween 2000 and 2006. The slightly darker 1996 Vosne-Romanée La Combe Brûlée exhibits warm, embracing dark fruit and hot stone aromas that give way to a massively concentrated, oily-textured, structured, and powerful personality. Spicy and sweet blackberries can be found in this delicious, complex, and impressively persistent wine's flavor profile. Antici-pated maturity: 2000–2006. The dark-colored 1996 Nuits-St.-Georges Les Hauts Pruliers reveals profound cassis scents enveloped in Asian spices. This hugely structured, foursquare, robust, masculine, and powerful wine is an archetypical Nuits. Intense black fruits intermingled with stones, minerals, and traces of sagebrush are found in this full-bodied and slightly rustic offering. If its tannic backbone softens more quickly, my score will seem conservative. Anticipated maturity: 2002–2007.

The 1996 Vosne-Romanée Les Champs Perdrix (this vineyard's name translates as "the partridges' fields") is dark colored and offers a superb nose of violets, candied raspberries, and spices. This rich, broad, concentrated, full-bodied, well-balanced, and massively struc-tured wine is packed with harmonious layers of brambleberries, blackberries, stones, and minerals. Its long finish displays copious quantities of ripe and supple tannins, suggesting a long and successful evolution. Anticipated maturity: 2003–2009. Equally outstanding, the dark-colored 1996 Vosne-Romanée Les Petits Monts (the vineyard overlooking Richebourg) has an austere nose reminiscent of brambleberries and rocks. It is full bodied, masculine, broad shouldered, hugely endowed, and powerful. Flavors of ripe black fruits, metals, and minerals cover its firmly structured backbone. My instincts suggest that this wine will shut down for a few years before roaring back to life, rerevealing its glorious and intense fruit. Drink it between 2003 and 2008.

DOMAINE ROBERT CHEVILLON (NUITS-ST.-GEORGES)

1996	Nuits-St.-Georges	D	(86–88)
1995	Nuits-St.-Georges	D	(86–88)
1996	Nuits-St.-Georges Les Bousselots	D	(88–90)
1995	Nuits-St.-Georges Les Bousselots	D	(87–89)
1996	Nuits-St.-Georges Les Cailles	E	(91–94)
1995	Nuits-St.-Georges Les Cailles	E	(91–93)
1996	Nuits-St.-Georges Les Chaignots	D	(89–91)
1995	Nuits-St.-Georges Les Chaignots	D	(89–91)
1996	Nuits-St.-Georges Les Perrières	D	(89–92)
1995	Nuits-St.-Georges Les Perrières	D	(90–92)
1996	Nuits-St.-Georges Les Pruliers	D	(90–92+)
1995	Nuits-St.-Georges Les Pruliers	D	(90–92)
1996	Nuits-St.-Georges Les Roncières	D	(88–90)

1995	Nuits-St.-Georges Les Roncières	D	(90–92)
1996	Nuits-St.-Georges Les St. Georges	E	(92–94+)
1995	Nuits-St.-Georges Les St. Georges	E	(90–92+)
1996	Nuits-St.-Georges Les Vaucrains	E	(91–94)
1995	Nuits-St.-Georges Les Vaucrains	D	(91–93)

All hail the king of Nuits-St.-Georges! When I think of this village, known for its highly structured, foursquare, masculine reds, I cannot help but recall the wonderful Chevillon bottles I've tasted over the years. He makes remarkably pure burgundies, powerful and extremely well delineated. Tasting through Chevillon's cellars is a lesson in the *terroirs* of Nuits, each wine beautifully demonstrating its vineyard of origin. With the exception of his village offering, all his reds have a bright, healthy dark ruby color, a precursor of their intensity of fruit. Wines sold to Domaine Robert Chevillon's U.S. importer (Kermit Lynch) are not subjected to filtration but undergo a fining with egg whites. Wines sold to other markets are subjected to a light filtration.

Medium to dark ruby colored, the 1995 Nuits-St.-Georges reveals a jammy raspberry bouquet with beautiful depth and an explosively fresh and exciting red berry-filled, medium-bodied personality with a good finish. Anticipated maturity: now–2002. From a vineyard located near Vosne-Romanée, the dark-colored 1995 Nuits-St.-Georges Les Bousselots exhibits concentrated dark cherries with an attractive midpalate in its medium- to full-bodied, elegant, silky-textured, and persistent personality. It will be at its best within 7 years of its release. A step up, the 1995 Nuits-St.-Georges Les Chaignots reluctantly displays its brooding, austere nose after considerable coaxing. Scents of roses and beautifully ripe cherries emerge from this velvety-textured wine. With airing it offers an explosion of gorgeously elegant cherries and red berries, a medium to full body, and a complex, long finish. It needs to be held for 2–3 years and will easily hold for 7–8 more.

Displaying toasted spices, dark berries, and cinnamon on the nose, the chewy, austere, minerally and well-structured 1995 Nuits-St.-Georges Les Perrières is an intense, concentrated, pure wine with a very long finish; it screams out for a grilled steak. Full bodied and extremely well defined, it will be at its best between 2002 and 2009+. The 1995 Nuits-St.-Georges Les Roncières offers an earthy, black truffle-laden, sweet nose with touches of mocha and an austere, foursquare, powerful, and concentrated attack that opens up gradually to reveal spicy chocolate-covered cherries in addition to huge amounts of ripe, soft tannins. Built to last, it should be held for 5–6 years and consumed over the following 8–9 years. Displaying a spicy, minerally, and stony bouquet, the 1995 Nuits-St.-Georges Les Pruliers is packed with crisp cherries and iron rocklike flavors ensconced in a highly structured, intense, full-bodied, and admirably endowed personality. Masculine and broad shouldered, it will require 5–6 years of cellaring to reach its peak and will hold for another 7+ years.

Produced from a parcel of 75-year-old vines, the 1995 Nuits-St.-Georges Les Cailles is a stupendous wine. Possessing an intensely deep nose of superripe red berries and spices, this powerful, elegant, full-bodied wine is jam-packed with sweet cherries, crisp stones, and steel flavors. It also has an extremely long and complex finish. Drink from 2003 to 2012. From the southernmost of Nuits' litany of premier cru vineyards, the 1995 Nuits-St.-Georges Les St. Georges is an austere, foursquare wine with flavors of minerals, stones, and dark berries. Oily textured and chewy, this highly concentrated wine possesses an extremely long finish and a superstructured core. It will be at its best between 2002 and 2010. Along with the Cailles, my favorite Chevillon 1995 is the fabulous Nuits-St.-Georges Les Vaucrains. In spite of my coaxing, this behemoth refused to reveal its aromatic profile, but the mouth was convincing enough. The intensity and depth of fruit, packed with thick, chewy chocolate and cherries embedded in an amazingly structured wine, was buttressed by massive (but ripe and round) tannins. Lively yet restrained, it was delicious to drink from the barrel, but my experience with prior vintages suggests that it will shut down after bottling and require at least 6 years of patience. It will then hold for a decade.

Robert Chevillon is a man of extremely few words (he lets the wines do the talking), so I was tremendously surprised when he blurted out about his 1996s, "I adore this vintage. It has perfect color, aromas, acidity, and amplitude." I tried to pursue the issue but found that the conversation was over and it was time to taste.

The medium to dark ruby-colored 1996 Nuits-St.-Georges has lovely sweet black fruit aromas and a medium-bodied, rich, tangy, and silky-textured core of beautifully ripe blackberries, plums, cassis, stones, and minerals. Drink it over the next 5 years.

The 1996 Nuits-St.-Georges Les Bousselots may be the finest wine Chevillon has crafted from this little-known premier cru vineyard. It reveals a medium to dark ruby color and rich scents of plump red fruits. This feminine, supple, focused, medium- to full-bodied offering has dense layers of ripe red and black berries that last throughout its admirable finish. Anticipated maturity: now–2006. The slightly darker-colored 1996 Nuits-St.-Georges Les Chaignots has red and black currant aromatics and a sweet, ripe, broad core of spicy red cherries, raspberries, stones, and minerals. It is more structured but also richer, denser, broader, and longer in the finish than the Bousselots. Anticipated maturity: 2000–2006. Displaying a medium to dark ruby color and mineral-dusted cassis and blackberry scents, the 1996 Nuits-St.-Georges Les Perrières is a full-bodied, juicy, powerful, and velvety-textured wine that is crammed with plump blueberries and blackberries. This concentrated, structured (yet lush), and expressive wine possesses an admirable and supple finish. The similarly colored 1996 Nuits-St.-Georges Les Roncières has black raspberry and powerful toasted-oak aromas that give way to an expressive, medium- to full-bodied, rich, and mineral-dominated flavor profile. This impressive offering's persistent finish is at present dominated by oak, but it should melt away with cellaring. Drink it between 2000 and 2006. Revealing a dark ruby color, the 1996 Nuits-St.-Georges Les Pruliers has a nose of blackberry and brambleberry scents that leads to a fat (the French would say *gras*), concentrated, broad, mouth-coating, and austere character. This dense, foursquare, muscular, and powerful wine is a quintessential Nuits. Firm, with deeply ripe black fruits, stones, and mineral flavors as well as a highly structured personality, this offering does not seduce as much as it impresses. As this wine's enormous depth of fruit blossoms out of its shell with cellaring, I would not be surprised to see it surpass the high point in the range I have given it. Anticipated maturity: 2002–2008+.

Chevillon's last three 1996 Nuits offerings are fabulous! The dark ruby/black-colored 1996 Nuits-St.-Georges Les Cailles has intensely ripe red and black fruit aromas that are followed by a palate-staining, full-bodied, and massively concentrated wine with enormous richness and depth. This powerful, harmonious, and extremely well-balanced and focused Nuits possesses layers of sweet red and black fruits that dominate its flavor profile and admirably long finish. Its satiny tannins should have melted by 2003. It can be drunk until 2010. Potentially Chevillon's finest 1996, the dark-colored 1996 Nuits-St.-Georges Les Saints Georges (if Nuits were ever to have a vineyard elevated to grand cru status, this would be the one) had an unyielding yet floral nose the day of my tasting. It is a full-bodied, richly fruited, complex, concentrated, intense, and profound wine. Dense and yet focused waves of blackberries, brambleberries, cherries, and boysenberries are intricately laced with Asian spices, minerals, and stones. Anticipated maturity: 2003–2010+. The similarly colored 1996 Nuits-St.-Georges Les Vaucrains aromatically displays cassis liqueur, road tar, blackberries, and dried prunes. This backward, austere, muscular, broad-shouldered behemoth is velvety textured (but don't be fooled by this youthful trait—it will demand patience!), gorgeously focused, full bodied, and packed to the gills with black fruits, metal shavings, minerals, and stones. Its exceedingly long finish reveals more dense fruit and copious quantities of tannins that will shut this wine down for half a dozen years or more. With cellaring, however, its personality should blossom magnificently. Anticipated maturity: 2005–2012.

DOMAINE CHOPIN-GROFFIER (COMBLANCHIEN)

1996 Clos Vougeot	EE	(92–95)
1995 Clos Vougeot	EE	92+
1996 Cote de Nuits-Villages	D	(87–88)
1996 Nuits-St.-Georges Les Chaignots	E	(90–92)
1995 Nuits-St.-Georges Les Chaignots	E	(89–91)
1996 Vougeot	D	(88–90)
1995 Vougeot	D	(87–89)

All good things must end, as 1996 marks Daniel Chopin's last vintage. Burgundy, and wine lovers, are losing a man who for years crafted luscious, friendly, and smile-inducing wines. Always supple, opulent, seductive, and fruit driven, Chopin's offerings will continue to bring joy to those who have squirreled them away. Starting with the 1997 vintage, his son-in-law and pupil, Hubert Chauvenet (Domaine Chauvenet-Chopin), will take over this estate's vineyards. May Daniel Chopin enjoy retirement as much as I have enjoyed his wines. Naturally he chose to go out with a bang, crafting an impressive lineup of 1996s.

The dark ruby-colored 1996 Côtes de Nuits-Villages (from Comblanchien) offers a fresh, perfumed, deeply ripe blackberry-scented nose as well as a fat, plump, supple, medium- to full-bodied, and rich personality. This velvety wine is filled with chocolate-covered cherries, blueberries, and spices. Its finish reveals Chopin's trademark—silky tannins enveloped in succulent fruits. Drink this beauty over the next 4 years. The slightly lighter-colored 1996 Vougeot reveals smoked pork and chocolate aromas that give way to its gorgeously ripe, medium- to full-bodied, and silky-textured core of thick cherries, bacon, juniper berries, mocha, and hints of brambleberries. This complex and immensely satisfying wine will be at its best if drunk over the next 5–6 years. Displaying a medium to dark ruby color, the 1996 Nuits-St.-Georges Les Chaignots has a sweet, spicy, red cherry-laced nose and an extremely feminine, elegant, and opulent character. This medium- to full-bodied, superripe, velvety-textured, and chewy wine is thick, wide, and well focused and offers layer upon layer of candied raspberries, cherries, and strawberries. It is seductive, fruit driven, long, and absolutely delicious. Anticipated maturity: now–2005.

Daniel Chopin produces his consistently outstanding Clos Vougeot from a parcel located directly below that famed vineyard's château. The bright, medium to dark ruby-colored 1996's spicy red and black cherry-infused nose precedes its expressive, rich, sultry (yet serious), full-bodied, and concentrated core of violets, plump cherries, plums, and blackberries. This broad, feminine, expansive, hedonistic (yet structured), and seductive wine combines flavorful, sweet, and supple fruits with a firm, softly tannic backbone. Surprisingly, given the vintage's forward nature, this may ultimately be one of Chopin's longest-lived wines. Anticipated maturity: 2002–2010+.

The dark-colored 1995 Clos Vougeot (originally rated 89–92) displays mouthwatering aromas of *saucisson* (the French answer to salami), violets, roses, black cherries, and Asian spices. This gorgeous, medium- to full-bodied, thick, opulent, and silky-textured wine is even better and more seductive than I remembered it. Armed with a wonderful depth of dark fruit (plums, blackberries, and blueberries), this luscious and refined wine is also admirably focused, expressive, and fresh. A delight! Anticipated maturity: 2002–2009.

Made from declassified premier cru Vougeot Les Petits Vougeots juice, the medium to dark ruby 1995 Vougeot is an excellent wine. Aromatically it reveals creamy mocha, chocolate, and dark fruits as well as similar flavors intertwined with a roasted fruit characteristic and a touch of sweet oak. This medium-bodied, slightly chewy wine should be at its peak from now to 2004. Also medium to dark ruby colored, the fabulous 1995 Nuits-St.-Georges Les Chaignots reveals an austere, minerally nose with reticent dark fruits and an elegant, delicious mouth of roasted, spicy black cherries. Thick textured and medium bodied, with enormous depth, this potentially outstanding wine should be drunk between now and 2006.

DOMAINE BRUNO CLAIR (MARSANNAY-LA-CÔTE)

1996	Chambertin-Clos de Bèze	EEE	(92–95)
1995	Chambertin-Clos de Bèze	EE	(91–93)
1996	Chambolle-Musigny Les Véroilles	D	(86–88)
1995	Chambolle-Musigny Les Véroilles	D	(83–86)
1996	Gevrey-Chambertin	D	(87–89)
1996	Gevrey-Chambertin Les Cazetiers	E	(91–93)
1995	Gevrey-Chambertin Les Cazetiers	E	91+
1996	Gevrey-Chambertin Clos du Fonteny	E	(88–90)
1995	Gevrey-Chambertin Clos du Fonteny	E	(88–91)
1996	Gevrey-Chambertin Clos St. Jacques	EE	(91–93)
1995	Gevrey-Chambertin Clos St. Jacques	EE	93
1996	Gevrey-Chambertin Petite Chapelle	E	(89–91)
1996	Marsannay Les Grasses Têtes	D	(87–89)
1995	Marsannay Les Grasses Têtes	C	(86–88)
1996	Marsannay Les Longeroies	D	(87–89)
1995	Marsannay Les Longeroies	D	(86–88+)
1996	Marsannay Les Vaudenelles	D	(86–88)
1995	Marsannay Les Vaudenelles	C	(85–87)
1996	Morey-St.-Denis en la Rue Vergy	E	(87–89)
1995	Morey-St.-Denis en la Rue Vergy	D	87
1996	Savigny-Lès-Beaune Les Dominodes	E	(90–92)
1995	Savigny-Lès-Beaune Les Dominodes	D	(90–92)
1996	Vosne-Romanée Les Champs Perdrix	E	(88–90)
1995	Vosne-Romanée Les Champs Perdrix	D	(88–91)

Bruno Clair and his winemaker, Philippe Brun, run this estate with its vineyards sprinkled throughout the Côte d'Or, from Savigny in the Côte de Beaune to Marsannay in the Côte de Nuits. In 1995 it took them 13 days to complete the harvest, an extremely long time considering the anxiety and stress such events can cause. Clair and Brun, both straight-shooting and honest, spoke at length with me about the problems facing Burgundy today. They believe that overall, the 1970s were a "horror and a catastrophe" for Burgundy, with estates making terrible wines in large quantities. Burgundy's credibility with consumers, severely damaged during this era, has yet to be corrected. They also feel that consumers make the mistake of buying burgundy "by appellation instead of by producer." As they see it, why does someone pay five times the price of one of their Marsannays for a bad grand cru? The Marsannay appellation, the northernmost of the Côte d'Or, in reality a suburb of Dijon, is known only to the Burgundy cognoscenti, but on these hillsides Clair makes some of Burgundy's finest values. In 1995, a hailstorm on July 23 damaged Clair's grapes in Marsannay, popping some berries open and threatening the onset of rot. However, subsequent rainstorms washed the broken berries from the vines, leaving only the healthy ones. His yields were significantly reduced because of this occurrence (a mere 1^1/$_2$ tons of fruit per acre), but Clair's wines are clean.

From a vineyard high on the Marsannay hill planted between 1965 and 1970, the medium to dark ruby-colored 1995 Marsannay Les Vaudenelles bursts from the glass with a bright explosion of cherry and strawberry fruit intermingled with slate and mineral scents. Thick textured and slightly tannic, the fresh fruit flavors have a wild component that is quite appealing. Anticipated maturity: now–2003. The medium ruby-colored 1995 Marsannay Les Grasses Têtes, from a vineyard halfway up the hill, exhibits a deeply sweet cherry nose and ripe, chewy, structured, lively, red fruit-filled flavors. The finish is slightly dry and tannic, so I recommend drinking this wine between now and 2003. Displaying scents of smoked pork and black cherries, with a touch of earthiness, the delicious 1995 Marsannay Les Longeroies has a layered, silky-textured, medium-bodied personality with smoked fruit flavors and an excellent finish. Anticipated maturity: now–2005. All three Marsannays offer good values . . . for burgundies. From very young vines (7 years old), the medium ruby-colored 1995 Chambolle-Musigny Les Véroilles reveals an attractive floral nose with scents of roses, violets, and strawberries and a silky-textured, sweet, and elegant personality. Short in the finish and lacking complexity (probably owing to the age of the vines), this wine should be consumed between its release and 2003. The medium to dark ruby-colored 1995 Morey-St.-Denis en la Rue Vergy's nose was totally muted when I tasted it, but it revealed thick, velvety-textured dark fruits with earthy and minerally notes ensconced in a highly structured, masculine, medium body. Big and slightly tannic, this wine will be at its best between 2002 and 2006.

From a 60-year-old parcel, the medium ruby-colored 1995 Vosne-Romanée Les Champs Perdrix exhibits an extremely elegant floral nose (lilies and violets) and silky-textured, medium-bodied flavors reminiscent of tangy cherries and flowers. Possessing exceptional length and structure, this delicious offering should be drunk between 2000 and 2005. Consistently one of the benchmark wines of its village, the very dark-colored 1995 Savigny-Lès-Beaune Les Dominodes, made from 94-year-old vines, displays an intensely deep nose packed with nuts and dark berries. Its gorgeous, concentrated, powerful, full-bodied flavors display dark fruits, wild berries, and minerals. Structured, complex, and long, this wine should be cellared for 5 years and drunk over the following 8. The medium- to dark-colored 1995 Gevrey-Chambertin Clos du Fonteny possesses a deep cherry- and berry-filled nose and dense, high-class flavors of layered and concentrated ripe, dark fruits. Well made and medium to full bodied, this wine will be at its best between 2002 and 2010.

For those looking for a fascinating study of what the French call *terroir* (the aromatic and taste profile derived from a particular site's microclimate and geology), Bruno Clair has two neighboring Gevrey-Chambertins (Cazetiers and Clos St. Jacques) that were 1) planted the same year, and 2) handled identically in the vineyard and winery. There are profound differences between the two wines: the Cazetiers is polished, elegant, and crisp, whereas the Clos St. Jacques is an in-your-face, powerful, explosive wine. The terrific medium to dark ruby-colored 1995 Gevrey-Chambertin Les Cazetiers displays an intense, deep nose of spicy dark fruits and a dense, pure, silky-textured, medium- to full-bodied mouth packed with wild berries. This excellent offering should reach its peak in 7 years and hold for 8 more. Similarly colored, the 1995 Gevrey-Chambertin Clos St. Jacques exhibits a deep, dark nose of sweet black fruits and a fat, thick-textured, chewy, full-bodied mouth filled with black, almost plummy fruit, minerals, and earth. Outstanding, this wine should be drunk between 2003 and 2012. Very dark in color, the 1995 Chambertin-Clos de Bèze is superb, displaying a profoundly intense nose of dark berry fruit and minerals. In the mouth, its awesome silky texture and powerful attack give way to layers of fat, sweet, chewy black fruits. Complex and long, this full-bodied wine will be at its best between 2005 and 2015.

Bruno Clair described the 1996 vintage as abundant (he says his Marsannays averaged $2^2/_3$–3 tons of fruit per acre and his other vineyards averaged yields in the $2^1/_3$–$2^2/_3$ tons per acre range) and perfectly healthy, as not a trace of rot was spotted. He went on to say that his 1996s have as much as 4 grams per liter of acid, the highest level he has ever seen in Burgundy. Only one of Clair's 1995s was fined (the Marsannay Les Grasses Têtes), and he did not anticipate needing to fine any of his 1996s when I visited the estate (Clair does not filter his wines).

The 1996 Marsannay Les Vaudenelles is medium ruby colored and offers a beautifully perfumed nose of red berries. This attractive, medium-bodied, and silky-textured wine reveals crisp currants and ripe raspberries in its flavor profile. Anticipated maturity: now–2002. A more intense and expressive wine, the 1996 Marsannay Les Grasses Têtes displays a ruby color as well as bacon fat and blackberry aromas. It is juicy, seductive, medium bodied, oily textured, and resplendent with roast pork, sweet plum, red currant, and ripe cherry flavors. Delicious to drink now, it should easily hold through 2002. The medium ruby-colored 1996 Marsannay Les Longeroies exhibits toasty oak scents and a medium-bodied, full-flavored, velvety-textured, and tangy core of cassis, succulent black cherries, and blueberries. This tightly knit and well-crafted wine will require a year of cellaring. Anticipated maturity: now–2003.

Produced from 8-year-old vines, the ruby-colored 1996 Chambolle-Musigny Les Véroilles displays aromas of violets, stones, and dark fruits that give way to a refined, easygoing, tangy, medium-bodied, and fresh herb-tinged core of sweet cherries, raspberries, and currants. It will be at its best if consumed before 2001. The slightly darker-colored 1996 Morey-St.-Denis en la Rue Vergy offers a nose reminiscent of intensely sweet cherries imbued with smoke and earth tones. On the palate, this medium-bodied, thick, well-defined, and expressive wine reveals loads of black cherries and soft, round tannins. Anticipated maturity: now–2003. Clair's first vintage of Gevrey-Chambertin (from rented vines) displays floral and black fruit scents as well as a masculine, medium-bodied, and focused personality. Its silky flavor profile is composed of beautifully sweet blackberries and cassis. It should be at its peak between now and 2003.

The medium to dark ruby-colored 1996 Vosne-Romanée Les Champs Perdrix is produced from an old-vine parcel on the steep hill that overlooks Vosne's world-famous grands crus. It offers a mouthwatering nose of violets and black cherries drenched in bacon fat and a velvety, medium- to full-bodied, fresh, and beautifully balanced character filled with salt pork, juniper berry, and blackberry flavors. Anticipated maturity: now–2004. Crafted from one of Burgundy's oldest parcels of vines (over 70% of them were planted in 1902), the 1996 Savigny-Lès-Beaune Les Dominodes is a dark ruby-colored wine with fabulous aromas of blackberries, dark cherries, earth, and perfumed violets. Its profound, full-bodied, intense, thickly textured, and complex character is packed with gorgeously ripe black fruits intermingled with stone, earth, and mineral flavors. Anticipated maturity: 2001–2006.

The 1996 Gevrey-Chambertin Clos du Fonteny is medium to dark ruby colored and offers floral, sweet blackberry, and perfume aromas as well as a chewy and medium- to full-bodied mouthful of dark plums and black cherries that linger on its admirable finish. This wine should be at its peak between 2000 and 2004. The darker-colored 1996 Gevrey-Chambertin Petite Chapelle reveals beguiling black cherry, mineral, stone, and earth aromas. This muscular yet elegant wine explodes on the palate with a powerful fistful of ripe and lively blackberries, plums, and cherries. Its prodigious finish reveals traces of *sur-maturité* and loads of supple tannins. Anticipated maturity: 2000–2005. Displaying a dark ruby color, the outstanding 1996 Gevrey-Chambertin Les Cazetiers has a gorgeously refined floral, perfumed, and red cherry-laden nose. On the palate, this full-bodied, thick, dense, concentrated, and satiny-textured offering is jam-packed with intensely ripe red cherries, sweet cassis, and blackberries (Clair said it has the lowest acidity of his 1996s). Its superb structure, balance, and loads of fruit should allow it to evolve beautifully for a decade or more. Anticipated maturity: 2001–2006. As with the previous wine, the 1996 Gevrey-Chambertin Clos St. Jacques is produced from a parcel planted in 1957. It is medium to dark ruby colored and boasts a highly defined nose of black fruits, minerals, and stones. This massive, masculine, expansive, and deep wine is full bodied, strictly structured, and drenched in immensely ripe black cherries, plums, and blackberries. It will be at its peak between 2001 and 2006. The magnificent, dark ruby-colored 1996 Chambertin-Clos de Bèze possesses awesome aromas reminiscent of cookie dough covered with blackberry syrup, violets, and roses. This powerful and masculine, yet elegant and refined gem has a complex, concentrated, and deep character that displays layer upon layer of ripe red and black fruits intermingled with stones, earth, and minerals. Loads of soft, ripe tannins can be discerned in its prodigiously long finish. It may very well be the finest red I've yet tasted from Bruno Clair. Anticipated maturity: 2003–2008.

Clair invited me to retaste two of his 1995s, and I am pleased to report that his opposition to fining and filtering combined with his gentle touch at bottling produced two gorgeous wines that fulfilled all of my original expectations. The 1995 Gevrey-Chambertin Les Cazetiers is medium to dark ruby colored and offers a nose of toasty red and black fruits as well as an immensely concentrated and medium- to full-bodied character filled with roasted herbs, spices, and blackberries. Anticipated maturity: 2003–2010. The slightly lighter-colored 1995 Gevrey-Chambertin Clos St. Jacques is a spectacular wine. It displays a profound nose of ripe dark fruits, earth, and touches of wild mushrooms. On the palate, this masculine, powerful, highly extracted, and complex wine is thickly textured, massively concentrated, full bodied, and jam-packed with seductively sweet blackberries and cassis. Anticipated maturity: 2004–2010. Bravo!

DOMAINE COLIN-DELÉGER (CHASSAGNE-MONTRACHET)

1996	Chassagne-Montrachet Morgeot	D	(85–87)
1995	Chassagne-Montrachet Morgeot	D	(87–89)
1995	Chassagne-Montrachet Vieilles Vignes	D	(85–88)
1995	Maranges La Fussière	C	(85–87)
1996	Santenay Les Gravières	D	(85–86)
1995	Santenay Les Gravières	D	(85–87)

Note: Those wines destined for Kermit Lynch are bottled unfined and unfiltered, while those sold elsewhere are subjected to a light filtration (using either a #5 or #7 filter pad). The following notes are from unfined cask samples.

Michel Colin is known for being one of Burgundy's top white wine producers, but he also makes very good to excellent red wines from vineyards in Chassagne-Montrachet, Maranges, and Santenay. Like most reds from these appellations, Colin's wines have a predilection for being too structured, but in 1995 and 1996 he succeeded in attaining soft, ripe tannins.

The ruby-colored 1996 Santenay Les Gravières displays ripe and rich cookie dough aromas awash in juicy red berries. It is a medium-bodied, fat, fruit-driven, and silky wine that finishes with traces of rusticity. Drink it between now and 2002. The 1996 Chassagne-Montrachet Morgeot has blackberry and cassis scents and a medium- to full-bodied, broad, ripe, and highly structured core of blueberries, metals, and minerals. It is slightly rough around the edges and somewhat tannic, but its gorgeous ripeness and depth of fruit compensate. Anticipated maturity: 2000–2003.

The medium ruby-colored 1995 Santenay Les Gravières displays a fresh, sweet nose of crisp red fruits and a spicy, explosive attack of lively cherries with touches of cracked pepper. Soft and with a nice follow-through in the finish, it is supple enough to drink now and should easily last until 2002. The slightly darker-colored 1995 Maranges La Fussière reveals deep and fresh blackberry aromas as well as a medium-bodied, highly structured lively core of spicy wild blueberries and minerals. Drink it now to 2003. Produced from vines ranging in age from 30 to 60 years old, the 1995 Chassagne-Montrachet Vieilles Vignes is medium to dark ruby colored and possesses a fabulous aromatic intensity of superripe blackberries and stones. This medium- to full-bodied, masculine, and chewy wine offers tightly wound cherry and dark fruits in its flavor profile. Highly structured and built to last, it should be at its peak between now and 2005. Colin's top red wine in 1995, the Chassagne-Montrachet Morgeot exhibits a beautifully floral nose packed with cherries and violets. Highly structured and tannic, this medium- to full-bodied, masculine, and thick offering has powerful, concentrated, and candied blackberries as well as wild blueberries in its flavor profile. Anticipated maturity: now–2006.

DOMAINE JEAN-JACQUES ("JJ") CONFURON (PRÉMEAUX-PRISSEY)

1996	Chambolle-Musigny	D	(88–89+)
1995	Chambolle-Musigny	D	(85–88)
1996	Chambolle-Musigny Premier Cru	E	(90–92)
1996	Clos Vougeot	EE	(91–93)
1995	Clos Vougeot	EE	(90–92)
1995	Côte de Nuits-Villages	C	87
1996	Côte de Nuits-Villages Les Vignottes	D	(87–88)
1996	Nuits-St.-Georges aux Boudots	E	(91–93+)
1995	Nuits-St.-Georges aux Boudots	E	(89–92)
1996	Nuits-St.-Georges Les Chaboeufs	E	(89–91+)
1995	Nuits-St.-Georges Les Chaboeufs	E	(88–90)
1996	Nuits-St.-Georges Les Fleurières	D	(87–89)
1996	Romanée-St.-Vivant	EEE	(94–96+)
1995	Romanée-St.-Vivant	EEE	(92–94)
1996	Vosne-Romanée Les Beaux Monts	E	(91–93)
1995	Vosne-Romanée Les Beaux Monts	E	(89–92)

In wine circles, the politically correct thing for those who do more pontificating than tasting is to bash those burgundies imported by Bobby Kacher as being overoaked wines that taste the same. Such remarks are completely inane and obviously made by people who have not tasted through his portfolio. Claude Dugat's sweet luscious cherry fruit has nothing to do with Jayer-Gilles's dark berries; Ambroise's boisterous, powerful wines have little in common with Confuron's elegant, feminine beauties. What Kacher's growers do have in common is a desire to make the finest wines their *terroirs* can. With the exception of Jayer and Albert Morot, they were, prior to Kacher's representation, an unknown band of vineyard owners who had the desire to progress. Today each one is known for making fabulous wines in separate, distinctive, and individual styles. Moreover, some of Kacher's growers have become the benchmark producers for their specific appellations.

Alain Meunier, a former mechanic, runs this estate with his wife, Sophie Confuron. Their vineyards are organically grown, and at harvesttime unworthy grapes are sorted out (15% of the 1995 was discarded!). The grapes are all destemmed, and as Meunier stated, "Total respect is given the fruit; we try to reduce all manipulation as much as possible." Meunier and his wife make superb wines in an elegant, forward style.

With many vignerons, I take their answers to my questions with a grain of salt. In the split second before the response is spoken, it is obvious that their minds are racing ahead, not formulating the generally easily answered words but, instead, determining what responses are most beneficial. With Meunier things are very different. Answers are blurted out honestly and forthrightly. "My yields were very high in this vineyard; I tried to keep them low and failed," he said when referring to his 1996 Côtes de Nuits-Villages. Because I knew that I would get a truthful, bare-boned answer, I asked him the question I believe many burgundy wine lovers in the United States would want to ask: "Since you make two cuvées of many of your wines, one for Robert Kacher [the estate's U.S. importer] and one for the rest of the world, which do you prefer, and why?" His immediate response was that within the first 3 of so years after bottling, he finds the Kacher cuvées to be too oaky, but later they are the fresher, better wines.

Meunier has started a small *négociant* business (Maison Fery-Meunier) with a friend who is a lawyer from Lyon.

Medium ruby colored, the 1995 Côte de Nuits-Villages (made from 25-year-old vines in 30% new oak) reveals a cherry cola and cinnamon-laced nose and a medium- to light-bodied, easily quaffable, red currant, mineral, and spice-laden mouth. It is made for drinking over the near term. The 1995 Chambolle-Musigny (note: Kacher's bottling of this wine receives 100% new oak, but all other bottlings are aged in only 40% new oak) reveals aromas of sweet perfume and ripe cherries and a light- to medium-bodied, elegant, fresh, and lively mouth filled with crisp cherries and strawberries. Drink it from now to 2003. Aromatically nutty and minerally, the medium ruby-colored 1995 Nuits-St.-Georges Les Chaboeufs exhibits a silky-textured, elegant, direct, clean, lively, and fresh personality filled with tangy cherries. Anticipated maturity: now–2005. Made from 45-year-old vines, the delicious 1995 Nuits-St.-Georges aux Boudots displays dark fruits and mocha on the nose and a fat, elegant, creamy-textured personality with quantities of deep, sweet, lively, cherry fruit. Already enticing to drink, this beauty will be at its best between 2002 and 2008. Equally impressive, the medium ruby-colored 1995 Vosne-Romanée Les Beaux Monts reveals scents of rose petals and red cherries. Lively ripe red berries are embedded in a silky-textured and medium-bodied, elegant, and lively crafted wine. Delicious to drink, this wine will be better between 2000 and 2007. Medium to dark ruby colored, the 1995 Clos Vougeot is a winner! Aromatically packed with dark and powerful roasted fruits, this refined, thick-textured, full-bodied, extremely elegant wine has fabulous flavors of dark cherries and spices. Drink it from 2002 to 2010. One of the most memorable wines of my trip, Meunier's dark-colored 1995 Romanée-St.-Vivant rocked my olfactory senses with its sublimely elegant nose of mocha and cinnamon-covered berries. Full bodied, it possesses a silky texture, gorgeous sweetness, and a superrefined combination of cherries, flowers, and spice in the long and enticing finish. Anticipated maturity: 2003–2015.

Produced from yields of 3 tons of fruit per acre and aged in 30% new oak, the ruby-colored 1996 Côtes de Nuits-Villages displays a ripe blackberry-and-cassis-scented nose. This lively, medium-bodied, rich, silky-textured, and intensely flavored wine is filled with black fruits, brambleberries, and fresh herbs. As is generally the rule with Meunier's offerings, it is elegant, well balanced, and beautifully proportioned. Drink it over the next 4 years. Meunier is a man of the earth, seemingly happiest when he is in his vineyards, who prides himself on knowing the distinctive characteristics of each of his parcels. As he poured the ruby/purple-colored 1996 Nuits-St.-Georges Les Fleurières (a vineyard wedged between the RN74 and the premier cru Les Pruliers) into my glass, he informed me that this parcel desperately wants to produce 5 tons per acre and that it takes draconian pruning and vigilance to maintain it at 3 tons of fruit per acre. Its red berry and sweet oak aromas give way to a medium- to full-bodied, thick, rich velvety, and layered core of plums, black cherries, and vanilla-laced oak. This lovely, graceful wine offers beautifully ripe fruit and supple tannins. It should be drunk between now and 2003. Meunier informed me that vintage in and vintage out, his parcel of Chambolle-Musigny always produces 2½ tons per acre. The 1996 offers an extremely appealing nose of violets and blackberries drenched in mocha that gives way to a ripe, dense, feminine, medium- to full-bodied, and refined character filled with sweet blueberries and raspberries. It also possesses a thick texture, excellent concentration, and lovely soft tannins. Anticipated maturity: now–2004.

Produced from vines located in the Chatelots and Feusselottes vineyards, the medium to dark ruby-colored 1996 Chambolle-Musigny Premier Cru exhibits smoke, roses, minerals, and blueberries on the nose. This medium- to full-bodied, elegant, extremely well-balanced, silky-textured, and seductive wine is rich, dense, and focused. Spiced apples, cherries, black raspberries, and hints of new oak can be found in its enthralling flavor profile and in its admirably long finish. Anticipated maturity: now–2006. The 1996 Nuits-St.-Georges Les Chaboeufs is ruby/purple colored and reveals aromas of freshly cut flowers, blackberries, and hints of road tar. Its chewy-textured, medium- to full-bodied, and structured personality is layered with black fruits, cherries, and traces of raw meat. I preferred the concentration of the Chambolle Premier Cru but admired this wine's power and depth of fruit. It should evolve beautifully. Anticipated maturity: 2001–2006. The medium to dark ruby-colored 1996 Vosne-Romanée Les Beaux Monts has delightful aromatics of red cherries, violets, and blackberries. This harmonious, elegant, feminine, medium- to full-bodied, and velvety-textured offering is luscious, structured, plump and sweet and has complex flavors of deeply ripe red and black fruits, flowers, and hints of prunes. Anticipated maturity: 2001–2007. Displaying a medium to dark ruby/purple color, the 1996 Nuits-St.-Georges aux Boudots has precise floral, stone, and blackberry aromatics. It is a masculine, expansive, broad-shouldered, yet refined wine. Readers should note the copious candied and juicy dark fruits, minerals, and licorice flavors. This extremely elegant wine has depth, harmony, and purity of fruit. Drink this superb Nuits between 2003 and 2009.

Produced from a parcel located behind the vineyard's famous château, the 1996 Clos Vougeot is medium to dark ruby colored and reveals, spicy, rich, and candied red fruit aromas. This dense, powerful, thickly textured, and full-bodied wine is crammed with chocolate-covered black cherries, blackberries, cassis, fresh herbs, and notes of earth. It is concentrated, backward, dense and mouth-filling and possesses an extremely long and supple tannin-packed finish. Anticipated maturity: 2003–2010. Domaine Jean-Jacques Confuron's 1996 Romanée-St.-Vivant is a stunning wine. This dark ruby-colored beauty displays a beguiling nose of roses, violets, perfume, and candied red fruits that is followed by a superripe (*sur-maturité!*), unbelievably classy, and splendidly balanced character. Its mouth-coating, powerful (yet elegant), rich, and plump flavor profile is jam-packed with red and black fruits, flowers, and silky tannins that persist throughout its defined and amazingly long finish. This magnificent wine is a testimony to Meunier's dedication, work ethic, and huge talent. Anticipated maturity: 2004–2012+. Bravo!

ALAIN CORCIA SELECTIONS (SAVIGNY-LÈS-BEAUNE)

1996 Côte de Beaune-Villages	A	86
1996 Mazis-Chambertin Cuvée Madeleine Collignon (Hospices de Beaune)	EEE	(94–96+)

Alain Corcia speaks faster than I can write. This would normally not be a problem, except that my "information" notes on this blockbuster are jumbled. What I am certain of is that four parties, Corcia, Chef Pierre Troisgros (of the stellar Restaurant Troisgros in Roanne—one of my all-time favorites), and two others (one of whom is a cheese specialist in Roanne), acquired this Hospices de Beaune cuvée with the intention of using it to commemorate the 30 years that Restaurant Troisgros has had three Michelin stars. I also know that 6 barrels of unfinished wine were purchased (out of a total of 18 produced) and that each cost 40,000 French francs (roughly equivalent to $6,600). At this point my notes become difficult to sort out, including the information on the number of "eyes" per vine (2) and the fact that a sorting table was used. Since the viticulture and vinification are conducted by the Hospices under the supervision of André Porcheret—and not Corcia—I didn't pay close attention to his mile-a-minute explanations.

However, one thing is certain: This wine is spectacular. I tasted it twice, once alone with Corcia and once in the presence of Jean Tardy of Vosne-Romanée, and both times came away utterly surprised by the fact that it was a Mazis (it tastes significantly more like a Charmes- or Griotte-Chambertin) and also at how closely it mirrored the style of Claude Dugat. This black/purple-colored wine reveals massively ripe aromas of black raspberries, blackberries, and dark cherries that are followed by a sumptuous, immensely rich, full-bodied, and velvety-textured character. Its wide, awesomely chewy, and concentrated flavor profile is densely packed with candied red fruits and hints of sweet new oak that coat the palate for minutes. While its power and intensity are truly outstanding in their own right, what makes this wine even more special (and Claude Dugat–like) is its awesome purity, precision, harmony, and elegance as well as its virtually perfect and supple tannins.

As with all Hospices wines, it was transferred to its new owners after having been purchased at the annual November auction. I have no experience with wines of this stature being finished by Alain Corcia. If he succeeds in getting this into bottle uncompromised (he assured me that it would be neither fined nor filtered), this will be a sublime Mazis to be drunk between 2005 and 2015. Revealing a bright ruby color and dark berry fruit aromas, the 1996 Côte de Beaune-Villages is a well-made, blackberry, blueberry, and metal-flavored, silky, and medium-bodied wine. It is simple, not particularly complex or concentrated, but flawless and pleasing. This is the only under $10 1996 red burgundy I tasted that I can recommend. Alain Corcia once again delivers a delicious wine at a reasonable price.

DOMAINE EDMOND ET PIERRE CORNU (LADOIX)

1996	Aloxe-Corton Les Moutottes	D	(88–90)
1996	Aloxe-Corton Les Valozières	D	(89–91)
1996	Aloxe-Corton Vieilles Vignes	D	(86–88)
1996	Chorey-Lès-Beaune Les Bons Ores	C	(85–87)
1996	Corton-Bressandes	E	(91–93)
1996	Côte de Nuits-Villages	C	(85–88)
1996	Ladoix Bois Roussot	C	(85–87)
1996	Ladoix Les Carrières	C	(86–88)
1996	Ladoix Les Corvées	D	(88–90+)
1996	Ladoix Vieilles Vignes	C	(87–89+)
1996	Savigny-Lès-Beaune	C	(85–88)

Edmond Cornu, one of the venerable mainstays of Burgundy, is passing the baton to his son, Pierre, a highly talented, dedicated, and focused young man. Having sold Edmond Cornu's wines as a retailer, I had a good sense of what I was going to taste—delicious, well-made, traditional-style burgundies. Instead I encountered fresh, lively, youthful, expressive, fruit-driven, modern-style wines. The changes instituted by Pierre Cornu include a destemmer (he believes the stems produced a vegetal character, harshness, and excessive tannin), sorting tables, and more barrels (*foudres* have been discontinued). Even malolactic fermentation is now done in barrel.

After the grapes are sorted, a cold maceration that lasts several days (in 1997 fermentations started immediately owing to the high temperature of the harvest) takes place in large cement vats. The fermentation is dragged out as long as possible before the wines are aged in barrels (5%–15% new oak is used except for the grand cru Corton-Bressandes) for 18 months. Wines sold in the United States were unfiltered, but Pierre Cornu claims that blind comparative tastings conducted with their American importer revealed "no consistent difference." And guess what . . . the estate's wines are now subjected to a Kieselguhr filtration. I find this regrettable, as *every* comparative blind tasting I have done, with both young and older red burgundies, has strongly favored the unfiltered wines. These are *excellent values,* but remember, my tasting notes are for wines that had not yet been pressed through filter pads.

The bright ruby/purple-colored 1996 Chorey-Lès-Beaune Les Bons Ores exhibits a blackberry and metallic nose followed by a medium-bodied, silky-textured, and spicy core of freshly cracked white pepper-laced sweet red and black fruits. This well-made wine should be drunk over the next 3 years. The similarly colored 1996 Savigny-Lès-Beaune offers delightful aromas of wild strawberries, blueberries, and traces of minerals. This is followed by a medium-bodied, velvety wine. This soft and lovely yet structured offering is packed with lively red and black cherries. It will be at its best if drunk over the next 4 years. Produced from vines located in Corgoloin (the southernmost village of the Côte de Nuits), the ruby-colored 1996 Côte de Nuits-Villages reveals an enticing nose of deep black cherry fruit intermingled with violet petals. On the palate, this medium-bodied, expansive, and silky wine is loaded with plums and blueberries that linger. Anticipated maturity: now–2002+.

Produced from vines planted in 1951 and 1926, the medium to dark ruby-colored 1996 Ladoix Vieilles Vignes displays an expansive nose of blackberries and black raspberries. This medium- to full-bodied, intense, and silky-textured wine offers copious quantities of ripe black cherries and other assorted dark fruits. It is a scrumptious wine. Drink this beauty between now and 2003. I was also impressed with Cornu's ruby-colored 1996 Ladoix Bois Roussot, particularly given the fact that it emanates from 5-year-old vines. Aromatically it reveals cassis and black cherries. In the mouth, this medium-bodied, elegant, and focused wine is redolent with juicy blueberries, blackberries, and cherries. It won't make old bones, but it is delicious now. Drink it over the next 2–3 years. Produced from 9-year-old vines, the medium to dark ruby-colored 1996 Ladoix Les Carrières (the vineyard borders the grand cru Corton-Rognets) has a metal shaving and blackberry-laced nose as well as a powerful, intense, and expressive core of black fruits and minerals in its medium-bodied, silky-textured, and vibrant personality. It will be at its best if drunk over the next 3–4 years. My favorite of Cornu's Ladoix offerings, and certainly a candidate for an outstanding rating (assuming it manages to survive the Kieselguhr unharmed), is the 1996 Ladoix Les Corvées. This bright and medium to dark ruby/purple-colored wine exhibits a complex nose of blackberries, warm gravel, raw meat, and cassis. This expressive, lively, and broad wine is medium to full bodied and velvety textured and coats the palate with gorgeously ripe flavors reminiscent of grapes, plums, cherries, earth, and stones. It is fresh and focused and should be at its peak between 2000 and 2005.

Cornu has fashioned three impressive Aloxe-Cortons. The bright ruby-colored 1996 Aloxe-Corton Vieilles Vignes offers dark cherry and flower-infused aromatics as well as a juicy explosion of sweet and perfumed red fruits. This medium-bodied wine is masculine, refined and supple and possesses a long finish that reveals mineral and metal flavors that cover its copious quantities of ripe tannins. Anticipated maturity: now–2003. The impressive 1996 Aloxe-

Corton Les Moutottes is medium to dark ruby colored and displays beguiling black cherries awash in mochalike scents. This medium- to full-bodied wine explodes on the palate with red cherries that saturate the taster's palate, suggesting tangy juice intermingled with mineral flavors. Anticipated maturity: now–2004. Produced from vines over 35 years old located just below Corton-Bressandes, the slightly darker-colored 1996 Aloxe-Corton Les Valozières (Cornu described this vineyard as being a *terre de chien,* meaning that only a dog should have to enter its rocky, inhospitable terrain) is better. Its lively nose is reminiscent of gorgeously ripe red cherries, lilies, and violets. This wine offers layer upon layer of sweet red fruits, wild herbs, freshly cracked black pepper, and spices. In addition to the wine's impressive depth, it has a delicious and complex personality. Anticipated maturity: now–2004+.

Cornu's medium to dark ruby-colored 1996 Corton-Bressandes is a winner. Its oak-laced and gorgeously perfumed nose is followed by an explosion of juicy, profound, and luscious red and black cherries intertwined with fresh meat and earth flavors. This medium- to full-bodied, velvety-textured, and refined wine is complex, powerful, and concentrated and possesses a long finish. Anticipated maturity: 2000–2006.

DOMAINE HENRI DELAGRANGE ET FILS (VOLNAY)

1996 Volnay Clos des Chênes Cuvée Selectionée	D	86

The ruby-colored 1996 Volnay Clos des Chênes Cuvée Selectionée offers blackberry aromas and a medium-bodied, silky, and almost sticky-sweet core of deliciously ripe black fruits. It lacks the density and concentration to be a very good or excellent wine but will provide pleasure to those who drink it over the next 2–3 years.

DOMAINE MARIUS DELARCHE (PERNAND-VERGELESSES)

1996 Corton Réserve	E	93
1995 Corton Réserve	E	93
1996 Corton Renardes Réserve	E	91
1995 Corton Renardes Réserve	E	92
1996 Pernand-Vergelesses Les Boutières Réserve	C	89+
1995 Pernand-Vergelesses Les Boutières Réserve	B	88
1996 Pernand-Vergelesses Ile de Vergelesses Réserve	D	92
1995 Pernand-Vergelesses Ile de Vergelesses Réserve	D	90
1996 Pernand-Vergelesses Les Vergelesses Réserve	D	90

Note: These "Réserve" bottlings are produced exclusively for the United States market and specifically for North Berkeley Imports. They are neither fined nor filtered and are bottled by hand. Other offerings are fined and filtered.

Delarche's bottlings for North Berkeley Imports are rapidly elevating this domaine to the forefront of Côte de Beaune producers. The quality-to-price ratio found in these wines is astounding for Burgundy and even embarrasses some of the great Bordeaux châteaux. This is a particularly meritorious feat, as Burgundy estates generally produce hundreds of cases, not the 20,000+ case quantities of Bordeaux.

The ruby-colored 1995 Pernand-Vergelesses Les Boutières Réserve reveals a deep minerality and spicy blackberry fruit aromatically, as well as a silky-textured, lush, medium-bodied flavor profile jam-packed with lively red cherries. This is one of the finest values I have encountered in a red burgundy in quite a while, and I highly recommend purchasing it for drinking over the next 5 years. Aged in 100% new oak barrels, the ruby-colored 1995 Pernand-Vergelesses Ile de Vergelesses Réserve is also a fine value. Displaying intense aromas of cassis and blackberries intertwined with mineral components, this wine bursts on the palate with notes of coffee, blueberries, dark fruits, and stones. It is well structured, medium to full bodied, and concentrated and possesses an admirable length. Drink it between now and 2005.

Delarche's two offerings from the Corton hillside are absolutely fabulous examples of what excellent vineyard work and uncompromising winemaking will produce in an excellent vintage. The medium to dark ruby-colored 1995 Corton Renardes Réserve possesses a beguiling nose filled with candied cherries and plums with slight notes of wild game. This thick, chewy, full-bodied wine explodes with flavors of layered blueberries, blackberries, and black cherries as well as notes of sautéed wild mushrooms, coffee, minerals, and Asian spices. Its admirably long finish ends on soft, ripe tannins, boding well for its future. Anticipated maturity: 2000–2007. I was absolutely bowled over by Delarche's dark-colored 1995 Corton Réserve. It exhibits chocolate-covered and kirsch-filled cherries aromatically whose intense flavors are again found in its massive, highly expressive personality. This full-bodied wine is so thick with chewy, superripe fruits that it is amazing how bright, fresh, refined, and elegant it remains. Bravo!

Sometimes, regrettably, we can benefit from the misery of others. According to Peter Vezan and David Hinkle, this estate's representatives, during the 1996 growing season three new vineyard workers were fired by Philippe Delarche when he realized just how draconian their pruning was. The results are mind-blowingly concentrated and intense wines. These are *excellent values.*

The 1996 Pernand-Vergelesses Les Boutières Réserve will certainly merit an outstanding score if it can develop more nuances and complexity with time. It reveals a black color with traces of deep purple on the rim of the glass and an unbelievable depth of black cherry, sweet candy, and perfume on the nose. This massive, chewy, medium- to full-bodied, and hyperconcentrated wine is packed to the gills with pure and superripe blackberries, boysenberries, metals, and stones. Stylistically it is what I would imagine Lalou Bize-Leroy would craft if she were to own any Pernand-Vergelesses village vineyards. Anticipated maturity: now–2004. The dark-colored 1996 Pernand-Vergelesses Les Vergelesses Réserve offers cassis aromas followed by a medium to full-bodied, rich, masculine, intense, and concentrated core of red cherries, blackberries, and black currants. Slightly more complex than the previous wine, it also possesses a long and admirable finish. Anticipated maturity: now–2004. Produced in what I believe to be Pernand's finest premier cru vineyard, the 1996 Pernand-Vergelesses Ile de Vergelesses Réserve exhibits an incredible nose of blueberry muffins, stones, shingles, and cassis liqueur. Its massive intensity on the palate, combined with its extraordinary concentration, power, refinement, and purity of fruit, makes this the finest Pernand I have tasted. Layer upon layer of deep black cherries, wild blueberries, and juicy, sugar-coated blackberries are interspersed with flavors of underbrush, minerals, and metals in this captivating offering. It is structured yet seductive, firm yet supple, and an all-around delight. Wow! Drink this beauty between 2000 and 2006.

After tasting the three previous wines, I had the impression walking papers had been drawn up prior to the pruning of the 1996 Corton Renardes Réserve vineyard. There is no denying that it is an outstanding wine; however; it lacks the unbridled power, intensity, and concentration of this estate's other 1996s. It offers a medium to dark ruby color and scents reminiscent of red and black cherries as well as Asian spices. On the palate, this wine is medium to full bodied, fresh, feminine, pure, beautifully ripe, and armed with precise and perfumed cherry flavors. It is elegant, detail-oriented, and impressively long. It should be at its peak between now and 2004. The black and purple-colored 1996 Corton Réserve is spectacular. It reveals a nose that draws up thoughts of cocoa powder and confectioners' sugar-coated blackberries and a flavor profile composed of plump, juicy blueberries, stones, minerals, and oak spices. This wine is intensely powerful (almost like a punch to the mouth

of fruit!), concentrated, and extracted, yet delineated, pure, and bordering on refined. Its incredibly long finish reveals copious supple tannins buried in plums, cassis liqueur, and
cherry juice. Anticipated maturity: 2000–2007. Kudos to Delarche, Vezan, and Hinkle! (Re-
hire the vineyard workers!)

DOMAINE BRUNO DESAUNAY-BISSEY (FLAGEY-ECHÉZEAUX)

1996 Chambolle-Musigny	D	(85–86)
1996 Echézeaux	E	(90–92+)
1996 Gevrey-Chambertin	D	(85–87)
1996 Grands-Echézeaux	?	(92–94+)
1996 Vosne-Romanée	D	(85–87)
1996 Vosne-Romanée Les Beaumonts	E	(90–92)
1996 Vosne-Romanée Les Rouges	D	(86–88)

Well, there is something more in Flagey than Domaine Emmanuel Rouget and one of my favorite restaurants! Domaine Bruno Desaunay-Bissey, while difficult to locate (there is another domaine in this tiny town called Desaunay-Bissey), is well worth the effort.

Bruno Desaunay quietly produces very good to outstanding wines (including a great
Grands Echézeaux) in this sleepy little town located on the wrong side of the RN74. Desaunay's wines are racked only twice (once after malos and once for the *assemblage*) and are
all bottled unfined and unfiltered (he says he threw out the filters in 1990).

The ruby-colored 1996 Chambolle-Musigny has floral red cherry fruit aromas and a nicely
concentrated, light- to medium-bodied, silky-textured character flavored with delectable
blueberries and violets. A delicious quaffing wine, it should be drunk over the next 2–3
years. Revealing a ruby/purple color, the 1996 Gevrey-Chambertin has a powerful (especially when compared to the color) nose of sweet black cherries that gives way to a medium-
bodied, well-crafted, and soft personality. Blackberries, cassis, and stones can be found in
its flavor profile as well as in its long, supple finish. Drink it over the next 4 years. The ruby-
colored 1996 Vosne-Romanée has elegant red cherry aromas as well as a refined, medium-
bodied, tangy, harmonious, and supple character dominated by floral red berry flavors.
Anticipated maturity: now–2001.

Produced from a vineyard located on the hillside adjacent to Echézeaux, the ruby-colored
1996 Vosne-Romanée Les Rouges has bright red cherry aromatics and a structured, medium-
bodied, soft, and stone-laced black cherry flavor profile. It is a more serious wine. Drink it
over the next 4 years. The medium to dark ruby-colored 1996 Vosne-Romanée Les Beaumonts has immensely appealing aromas of earth soaked in sweet black cherry juice. This
rich, dense, concentrated, highly detailed, and absolutely delicious wine is packed with ripe
red cherries, hints of minerals, and traces of toasty oak. Anticipated maturity: 2000–2006.

Desaunay's medium to dark ruby-colored 1996 Echézeaux has an earthy, red cherry-laced
nose and a medium- to full-bodied, highly defined, expressive, seductive, opulent, and concentrated personality that also possesses great depth and purity of fruit. While its sweet
cherry-filled character is similar to the Beaumonts', this offering is slightly more refined and
longer. Anticipated maturity: 2000–2007. I am not the first to discover the splendor of Bruno
Desaunay-Bissey's Grands-Echézeaux, which is produced from vines planted in 1928. Of
the 4 barrels he produced from the 1996 vintage, 3 were sold to *négociants* in Nuits-St.-
Georges, 1 to Labouré-Roi, and 2 to Dominique Laurent. The remaining barrel is being divided among this estate's regular customers, including its U.S. importer, Peter Weygandt.
When consulting a map of Burgundy's vineyards, notice that Grands Echézeaux has the
shape of a triangle, with its northern point aimed toward Musigny, its eastern flank bordered

by the Clos Vougeot, and its western flank bordered by Echézeaux. Desaunay's old-vine parcel is the actual point of the triangle. The wine is dark ruby colored and offers profound aromas of cassis drenched in smoke and earth. On the palate, it explodes with juniper and
clove-spiced blackberries and black cherries. In addition, it reveals a highly delineated and
refined medium- to full-bodied character. This delicate yet powerful wine is feminine
and muscular and has enormous depth. No wonder Michel Bettane has raved about
Desaunay's Grands-Echézeauxs in the *Revue des Vins de France* and Dominique Laurent
shops here! Drink it between 2003 and 2010.

MAISON JOSEPH DROUHIN (BEAUNE)

1996	Beaune Clos des Mouches	D	(86–88)
1995	Beaune Clos des Mouches	D	91
1995	Beaune Grèves	D	(87–90)
1996	Bonnes Mares	EE	(89–91)
1995	Bonnes Mares	EE	(90–92)
1996	Chambertin Clos de Bèze	EEE	(91–94)
1995	Chambertin Clos de Bèze	EE	(90–92+)
1996	Chambolle-Musigny	D	(85–87)
1995	Chambolle-Musigny	D	85
1996	Chambolle-Musigny Les Amoureuses	EE	(90–92)
1995	Chambolle-Musigny Les Amoureuses	EE	(90–92)
1996	Chambolle-Musigny Les Baudes	D	(87–89)
1996	Charmes-Chambertin	EE	(89–92)
1995	Charmes-Chambertin	EE	92
1995	Clos de la Roche	EE	(90–92)
1995	Clos Vougeot	E	(89–91)
1996	Côte de Beaune	C	(85–87)
1995	Côte de Beaune	C	87
1996	Côte de Nuits-Villages	C	86
1995	Côte de Nuits-Villages	C	85
1995	Gevrey-Chambertin	D	86
1996	Grands Echézeaux	EEE	(88–91)
1995	Grands Echézeaux	EE	91
1995	Griotte-Chambertin	EE	(90–93)
1996	Morey-St.-Denis	D	(86–87)
1996	Musigny	EEE	(91–93)
1995	Musigny	EEE	(90–92)
1995	Nuits-St.-Georges	D	86?
1996	Nuits-St.-Georges Les Procès	E	(86–88)

1995 Pommard	D	(85–88)
1996 Romanée-St.-Vivant	EEE	(91–93)
1995 Romanée-St.-Vivant	EEE	(89–91)
1996 Savigny-Lès-Beaune	D	(85–87)
1995 Volnay	D	(84–87)
1995 Volnay Chevret	D	(85–88+)
1996 Volnay Clos des Chênes	D	(86–87+)
1995 Volnay Clos des Chênes	D	(87–90)
1996 Vosne-Romanée Petits Monts	E	(88–91)

As I tasted through Drouhin's offerings of 1995 red burgundies, I was struck by just how differently each *terroir* expressed itself. Generally, in truly great vintages (1985 and 1990 in Burgundy and 1982 and 1990 in Bordeaux), young reds, at least when young, tend to express vintage characteristics more than individual *terroirs*. The 1995 is an outstanding vintage, just below the quality of 1985 and 1990. However, the *terroir* characteristics of the 1995s are very evident, especially at Maison Joseph Drouhin. Perhaps the tight, concentrated fruit that characterizes 1995 allows more room for the *terroir* to show itself (as opposed to 1985 and 1990's lush forward, expressive fruit).

Produced entirely from premier cru vineyards in the Beaune appellation (including a high percentage from the youngest vines of the Beaune Clos des Mouches) the delicious, ruby-colored 1995 Côte de Beaune reveals a deeply spicy, cherry-scented nose. It has a luscious, silky, soft, medium-bodied, and extremely ripe personality packed with lively yet jammy red fruits. Readers who have not experienced the pleasures derived from drinking an excellent, sweet, young red burgundy should search for a bottle of this fairly priced wine. Drink it between now and 2000. Similarly colored and possessing tightly wound red and dark berry aromatics, the 1995 Volnay is a much more structured and unyielding wine. Cassis, blackberries, and minerals are found in its medium-bodied, slightly rough-textured character. Anticipated maturity: now–2002. A step up, the ruby-colored 1995 Pommard displays a deeply sweet and perfumed nose of ripe red cherries and a silky-textured, medium-bodied, lively, floral, raspberry, cinnamon-and-spice-flavored palate. Vivacious and well crafted, it will be at its best between now and 2003.

The slightly darker-colored 1995 Volnay Clos des Chênes offers cloves, violets, and cherries aromatically, as well as a powerful, elegant, oily-textured, medium- to full-bodied core of concentrated and complex layers of roses and spicy red and black fruits. Armed with a long finish and an admirable balance, it should evolve beautifully with cellaring. Anticipated maturity: now–2005. The medium to dark ruby-colored 1995 Volnay Chevret reveals floral and raspberry-scented aromas and a delicate, feminine, supple, medium-bodied personality with refined flavors of crisp cherries and strawberries. If wines can be compared to people, this offering would have to be thought of as a graceful young ballerina. Drink it between now and 2004.

The 1995 Beaune Grèves displays mineral and roasting spice-laden aromatics and a well-structured, cherry-and-strawberry-flavored core of fruit. This is an excellent, medium-bodied, oily-textured wine packed with dark cherries and touches of underbrush. It will be at its best between now and 2004.

The medium ruby-colored 1995 Côte de Nuits-Villages reveals expressive spicy dark fruit aromas and is fat textured, chewy, roasted black cherry filled, and medium bodied on the palate. Drink it between now and 2002. Austere and brooding aromatically, the medium to dark-colored 1995 Nuits-St.-Georges exhibits a highly structured, foursquare, tannic, spicy, minerally, medium-bodied personality. While it is not particularly concentrated or long, it is a well-made, extremely *terroir*-expressive wine. Owing to its slightly hard tannins, it requires 2 years of cellaring. Anticipated maturity: now–2003. Displaying dark cherry and spice aromas, the ruby-colored 1995 Gevrey-Chambertin is packed with Asian spice, cherry, and strawberry flavors. Medium bodied and well balanced, it is a silky-textured, slightly chewy wine. Anticipated maturity: now–2004.

Drouhin's medium to dark ruby-colored 1995 Clos Vougeot explodes from the glass with inviting aromas of Asian spices and blackberries. On the palate, this deep, thick, velvety-textured wine is jam-packed with cherries and currants. It should be at its best between 2002 and 2009. Darker colored, and exhibiting black cherries, stones, and bacon in the nose, the 1995 Clos de la Roche is a superstructured, full-bodied, intense, chewy, minerally floral (roses and violets), and very long wine. Fabulously well balanced and defined, it will be at its best between 2004 and 2012.

Possessing a dark color and an enticing nose filled with aromas of Asian spices and sweet cherries, the 1995 Charmes-Chambertin is gorgeous. Elegant and—yes, I have to say it—charming, this wine has awesome purity of fruit (cherries and red currants), a velvety texture, soft and supple tannins, a full body, and beautiful length. Drink it between 2002 and 2010. Even better, the spectacular Griotte-Chambertin is my favorite of Drouhin's offerings in 1995. Darkly colored and revealing a sublime nose of bacon and luscious, jammy cherries, it explodes with intensely ripe red fruits, mocha, and the flavors of a well-reduced veal stock (a dark, sweet, meat savor). It is silky smooth, full bodied, and powerful, and its flavors go on and on. It needs to be cellared for 6–7 years and will drink admirably for 8+ years. Displaying toasty, smoky black fruits aromatically, the dark ruby-colored 1995 Chambertin Clos de Bèze possesses a concentrated, full-bodied, highly structured personality packed with layers of roasted berries. Well made and delineated, this masculine, densely built wine will be at its best between 2003 and 2012.

Revealing mocha and toffee on the nose, the medium to dark ruby-colored 1995 Grands Echézeaux is an extremely elegant, structured, masculine, spicy, medium- to full-bodied wine. Already delicious to drink, it will be at its best between 2000 and 2007. Typical of its appellation, Drouhin's 1995 Romanée-St.-Vivant is significantly better aromatically than on the palate. Its enthralling nose is absolutely sublime—elegant flowers and spices intermingled with crisp red fruits. Medium bodied and smooth, it possesses a cherry-and-berry-flavored mouth that does not carry through on the excitement caused by the aromas. Drink it between now and 2005.

Surprisingly, the spectacular 1995 Chambolle-Musigny Les Amoureuses is produced from 15-year-old vines. . . . I look forward to tasting the quality wines made from this parcel in 20+ years! Aromatically it displays fabulously elegant waves of violets and small red berries. On the palate, this awesome wine possesses a deep, powerful, and refined personality jam-packed with lush cherries, cassis, and touches of mocha. Begging to be drunk right now, it will hit its peak between 2002 and 2010. Significantly more masculine, the dark-colored 1995 Bonnes Mares is loaded with stones, iron, and lavender aromas. It also displays Asian spices and tangy yet thick cherries in the mouth. This wine is full bodied, harmonious, and long. Drink it between 2002 and 2010. The day I tasted the dark-colored 1995 Musigny, it was extremely muted aromatically. On the palate, it revealed tightly wound, superdelineated, and polished fresh cherries, cassis, and violets. Medium to full bodied, supple, and very long, it is obviously an outstanding wine, but it is closed. Anticipated maturity: 2002–2010.

Mme. Laurence Jobard, this *négociant* house's charming, intelligent, and highly talented winemaker, works hand in hand with Robert Drouhin, the firm's director and one of Burgundy's gentlemen, in the crafting of the wines. They both informed me that Maison Drouhin no longer feels all its wines should be fined or filtered—the question is raised on a case-by-case basis prior to bottling. Jobard (no relation to the Jobards of Meursault), not one to mince words, informed me she "had been totally against the affording of PLCs" allowing growers to harvest up to 30% more than normal in 1996. When an old, established, and highly respected *négociant* house voices its dismay over the loosening of yield restrictions and softens its stance on fining and filtration, it speaks volumes for the bright future of this region.

Interestingly, certain house styles are better suited to certain vintage characteristics. The forward, juicy, and plump fruit of 1996, as well as its high levels of acidity and soft tannins, brought out the best in estates that generally tend toward rough, rustic wines. The 1995, a highly concentrated, muscular, and structured vintage, worked extremely well with producers whose style often emphasizes elegance and refinement. Such was the case at Maison Joseph Drouhin.

With 1996, however, I feel the Drouhin style did not marry with the vintage as well as it did the previous year.

Produced primarily from younger vines in Beaune premier cru vineyards (including the famous Beaune Clos des Mouches), the 1996 Côte de Beaune is bright ruby colored and has expressive aromas of black raspberries. This pleasing, light- to medium-bodied, and vibrant wine offers crunchy cherry flavors intermingled with zesty orange peels. It should be consumed over the next 2 years. The 1996 Savigny-Lès-Beaune has a medium to dark ruby color and a sweet red cherry-infused nose. It is silky textured, medium bodied, and filled with pure, refined, and precise black cherries and minerals. Anticipated maturity: now–2001. The slightly darker-colored 1996 Volnay Clos des Chênes exhibits a perfumed nose of violets immersed in dark fruits and a medium-bodied, slightly rough personality packed with ripe blackberries, minerals, and boysenberries. The "+" next to the rating indicates that I believe Mme. Jobard will find a way to soften this wine (most likely through fining) and that it may ultimately merit a higher rating.

The medium to dark ruby-colored 1996 Beaune Clos des Mouches offers an austere nose of minerals and stones that gives way to a medium- to full-bodied, strict, and structured character. Blackberries, gravel, and notes of underbrush can be discerned in this masculine wine. It does not have the joyful, plump, juicy, and bursting fruit characteristics of the vintage, yet it is well crafted, balanced, and appealing in a severe sort of way. The 1995 Beaune Clos des Mouches, tasted for the third time (once out of barrel, once out of bottle in the United States, and again at the firm's headquarters in Beaune), is truly delicious. Medium to dark ruby colored (hints of purple are still present on the rim), this wine displays roses, violets, black raspberries, and cherries on the nose and a medium- to full-bodied, silky, complex, and gorgeously balanced personality. Its flavor profile is packed with intense cherries, strawberries, and minerals that linger in its prodigious finish. Anticipated maturity: 2000–2009.

Maison Joseph Drouhin's 1996 Côtes de Nuits-Villages reveals a medium to dark ruby color and rich, sweet red cherry aromas. This fat, juicy, lively, medium-bodied, and silky wine has wonderful flavors of cinnamon-and-clove-spiced black cherries. Drink this appealing wine over the next 3 years.

The ruby-colored 1996 Chambolle-Musigny has a perfumed, violet, and rose-infused nose that gives way to its medium-bodied, silky, well-made, and refined core of supple and sweet red and black cherry fruit. It is a delicious wine to drink over the next 3–4 years. The slightly darker-colored 1996 Morey-St.-Denis offers superripe plummy scents and a prune, spice cake, mineral, and earth-flavored character. This seductive, succulent, and corporeally pleasing wine suffers a bit from its relatively short finish. Drink it over the next 3–4 years.

Only 3 or 4 barrels of the medium to dark ruby-colored 1996 Nuits-St.-Georges Les Procès are produced, and Robert Drouhin told me that "no one knows just how old the vines are, but this is truly *vieilles vignes*." It has a nose of fresh herbs and coarse black cherries that is followed by a medium-bodied, foursquare, slightly rustic, and intense character. Its flavor profile reveals minerals, stones, blackberries, and hints of tart orange peels. Anticipated maturity: now–2004. The 1996 Chambolle-Musigny Les Baudes is medium to dark ruby colored and displays expressive and plump blackberry scents. This medium-bodied, classy, and somewhat chewy wine has lovely black cherry, metal, and cassis flavors in its well-crafted, focused personality. Anticipated maturity: now–2005. Revealing a bright and medium to dark ruby color, the 1996 Vosne-Romanée Petits Monts has delicate floral red fruit aromas. Concentrated, beautifully ripe, and velvety textured, this wine has candied spiced cherries and violets in its flattering flavor profile. Additionally, its admirably long finish reveals silky tannins that are soaked in sweet red fruits. Drink it between 2001 and 2006.

The medium to dark ruby-colored 1996 Charmes-Chambertin has a fine nose of deeply ripe blackberry and cassis. On the palate, this well-concentrated, thick, complex, and harmonious wine is replete with loads of black cherries and spices. As with the previous offering, it has extremely ripe and supple tannins in its long finish. Anticipated maturity: 2002–2007. Similarly colored, the blueberry, mineral, and earth-scented 1996 Grands Echézeaux has an intense, concentrated, masculine, medium- to full-bodied character packed with stones, juicy blackberries, and oak spices. It is complex and moderately powerful but lacks the length of the last two wines. Anticipated maturity: 2002–2007.

The 1996 Chambolle-Musigny Les Amoureuses has a medium to dark ruby color and mouthwatering aromas of cookie dough, candied red cherries, and violets. This masculine, medium- to full-bodied, highly structured, elegant, and silky-textured wine has minerals, stones, and ripe black cherries in its flavor profile. This complex and highly detailed wine will require cellaring. It should be at its best between 2003 and 2008. Exhibiting a bright and medium to dark ruby/purple color as well as oak-imbued blackberries, the 1996 Bonnes Mares is a medium- to full-bodied, tangy, concentrated, tightly wound, and lively wine. Cherries, red and black currants, earth, stones, and new oak flavors can be discerned in this well-crafted and proportioned offering. Anticipated maturity: 2002–2007.

The next three wines are more concentrated and extracted than what I am used to at Maison Joseph Drouhin. The medium to dark ruby-colored 1996 Romanée-St.-Vivant exhibits lovely aromas of freshly cut flowers and perfumed red fruit. This full-bodied, powerful, fresh, highly concentrated, and extracted wine is packed with blackberries, cassis, and oak flavors that linger throughout its refined and admirably long finish. Anticipated maturity: 2004–2010. The slightly darker-colored 1996 Musigny has malty black cherry scents and a broad-shouldered, masculine, highly structured (verging on tannic) character. Its chewy texture offers loads of sweetened and creamed blackberries, violets, and earth. This wine coats the mouth with copious quantities of fine tannins that, in time, will easily be overcome by this impressive offering's dense fruit. Drink it between 2005 and 2010+. Displaying a deep ruby/purple color as well as floral, fresh herb, earth, and cassis aromas, Drouhin's 1996 Chambertin Clos de Bèze is the biggest, broadest, most powerful, extracted, and concentrated wine I tasted from this *négociant*. This harmonious, silky-textured, and refined, yet muscular and brooding behemoth is extremely well crafted and proportioned. Cassis liqueur, minerals, underbrush, black cherries, and licorice are found in this gem's flavor profile and superb finish. Anticipated maturity: 2005–2010+.

Robert Drouhin allowed me to retaste two of his 1995s Côte de Nuits wines when I returned to taste his 1996s. The 1995 Chambolle-Musigny maintains its 85-point rating. Surprisingly, it was more advanced aromatically and gustatorily than I would have believed possible, possessing some brick to its otherwise light to medium ruby color and a mature nose of floral and candied red fruits intermingled with mature Pinot aromas of caramelized leaves. Its appealingly elegant character is losing a bit of its fruit, so readers who purchased this wine should drink up. The 1995 Grands Echézeaux (originally rated 90–92 after bottling merits a 91) has a healthy medium to dark ruby/purple color and a spicy, fresh, and black cherry-laced nose. This medium to full-bodied, refined, and well-concentrated wine has an expansive character that reveals blackberry, cassis, and stonelike flavors that can be found throughout its extremely long and precise finish. It can be drunk now or held through 2006.

DOMAINE JEAN-LUC DUBOIS (CHOREY-LÈS-BEAUNE)

1996 Aloxe-Corton Les Brunettes Réserve*	D	89
1995 Aloxe-Corton Les Brunettes Réserve*	D	88
1996 Beaune Bressandes Réserve	D	90
1995 Beaune Bressandes Réserve	D	89+
1995 Chorey-Lès-Beaune Clos du Margot Réserve	C	87
1996 Chorey-Lès-Beaune Clos du Margot Vieilles Vignes Réserve	C	88
1996 Côte de Beaune Villages Les Beaumonts Vieilles Vignes Réserve	C	87
1996 Savigny-Lès-Beaune Les Picotins Vieilles Vignes Réserve	D	90

Note: Jean-Luc Dubois fashions many different cuvées from the same vineyard parcels. The wines that are described in the following notes are produced exclusively for North Berkeley Imports (which means no fining and filtration) for the U.S. market.

Jean-Luc Dubois is an intelligent, dynamic young vigneron located in the town of Chorey-Lès-Beaune, a village northeast of Beaune at the frontier of what Burgundians derisively refer to as the Plain (the cereal-producing flatland between the Côte d'Or and the mountains to the east). Dubois has been working for a few years with David Hinkle (of North Berkeley Imports) and Peter Vezan (a Paris-based wine broker), providing them with the opportunity to select the barrels they wish to purchase. The wines are then produced according to their specifications, eschewing any fining or filtration.

Mrs. Yasuko Goda, a Japanese importer who works closely with the Vezan/Hinkle team, tasted with me at this estate. She informed me that some wine merchants in Japan have special sections dedicated to unfined and unfiltered wines because Japanese consumers search them out, as they realize they are of superior quality. Regrettably, Dubois continues to filter those wines that are sold in Europe. He told me that he was "totally convinced" that the unfiltered wines are better than those subjected to "a loss of concentration and body" through filtration. However, he noted that European consumers and restaurants "demanded" filtered wines.

The medium to dark ruby-colored 1996 Côte de Beaune Villages Les Beaumonts Vieilles Vignes Réserve reveals aromas reminiscent of ripe grapes laced with finely ground white pepper and an oily-textured, rich, broad, and spicy core of blueberries, cherries, and spices. This delicious, medium-bodied, and well-made wine should be drunk over the next 4 years. Displaying a slightly darker color, the 1996 Chorey-Lès-Beaune Clos du Margot Vieilles Vignes Réserve offers an intensely aromatic nose of blackberries and brambleberries. This medium- to full-bodied, delineated, and silky wine is packed with layers of black currants, plums, and metallic flavors. Anticipated maturity: now–2002. The dark ruby-colored 1996 Aloxe-Corton Les Brunettes Réserve possesses enticing aromas of jammy black cherries intermingled with traces of mocha. On the palate, readers will find a chewy, medium- to full-bodied, plump, and exciting wine packed with gorgeously ripe blackberries, cassis, metals, and stones. Its admirable finish reveals supple tannins. It is already fabulous to drink yet should easily hold through 2004. Produced from vines planted over 70 years ago, the dark ruby-colored 1996 Savigny-Lès-Beaune Les Picotins Vieilles Vignes Réserve offers ripe red fruit aromas and a broad, rich, concentrated, powerful, medium- to full-bodied, and tangy core of red and black currants, brambleberries, and red cherries intermingled with mineral-

*The Aloxe-Corton Les Brunettes Réserve is sold under the Paul Dubois label.

and metal-like flavors. The old-vine intensity of this offering is confirmed by the wine's excellent depth and persistent finish. Anticipated maturity: now–2004. The equally dark-colored 1996 Beaune Bressandes Réserve exhibits beautifully ripe and candied red fruit aromas that are followed by a lusciously seductive, medium- to full-bodied, sexy, and chewy-textured personality brimming with black cherries, cassis, and blackberries. Drink this beauty between now and 2003.

The medium ruby-colored 1995 Chorey-Lès-Beaune Clos du Margot Réserve reveals deep aromatics composed of fresh and spicy cherries. This medium-bodied wine possesses a lively personality jam-packed with crisp, sweet and delicious red berry fruit. Its soft texture and supple tannins make this a wonderful offering to drink over the next 3–4 years—and an excellent value for burgundy! Slightly lighter in color, the 1995 Aloxe-Corton Les Brunettes Réserve displays a sweet strawberry-and-red-fruit-filled nose as well as a medium-bodied and silky-textured palate filled with lush, sweet, spicy, candied, and mouth-coating cherries. Drink it between now and 2003. Dubois's top wine is his potentially outstanding 1995 Beaune Bressandes Réserve. It is medium to dark ruby colored and offers tightly wound aromas of blueberries and cherries intermingled with roasting spices. In its fabulous oily-textured and medium- to full-bodied flavor profile, loads of fat, ripe blackberries and dark cherries are intertwined with minerals and stones for added complexity. Anticipated maturity: now–2005.

DOMAINE CLAUDE DUGAT (GEVREY-CHAMBERTIN)

1996	Charmes-Chambertin	EE	(97–99)
1995	Charmes-Chambertin	EE	(93–95)
1996	Gevrey-Chambertin	E	(89–91)
1995	Gevrey-Chambertin	D	(87–89)
1996	Gevrey-Chambertin Premier Cru	E	(90–92)
1995	Gevrey-Chambertin Premier Cru	E	(88–91)
1996	Gevrey-Chambertin Lavaux St. Jacques	EE	(93–95)
1995	Gevrey-Chambertin Lavaux St. Jacques	E	(90–92+)
1996	Griotte-Chambertin	EEE	(98–100)
1995	Griotte-Chambertin	EEE	99

Claude Dugat is one of the finest winemakers in the world. His wines have a richness and purity of sweet fruit that is rare. But what characterizes Dugat's wines is a suppleness that is unusual in young red wines. These wines are scrumptious to drink—even from the barrel. While there is no reason to believe these wines cannot age, they provide such opulent and flattering drinking early on, it is hard to recommend extended cellaring.

At my tasting of the Robert Kacher portfolio, where all the Burgundy winemakers he represents were present, a hush fell over the room when Dugat's wines were poured. A self-effacing, modest man, Dugat smiled uncomfortably as each of the winemakers, all stars in their own right, came to congratulate him on the spectacular quality of his wines. Importer Kacher feels Dugat's 1995s are slightly better than his 1993s, including the otherwordly Griotte-Chambertin. I believe they are stunning, benchmark wines. Sadly, only the luckiest burgundy wine consumers will be able to taste a bottle of the 1995 Griotte next to a 1993, as only 100 cases (4 barrels) were produced. Overall, Dugat has only 7.4 acres of vines on which to work his magic.

In 1995 Dugat fashioned one of the finest village wines produced in the Côte d'Or. Deep ruby/purple colored, the 1995 Gevrey-Chambertin reveals a sweet, enticing nose of perfumed flowers and red fruits. In the mouth, this medium-bodied, concentrated, silky-textured wine is packed with ripe, fresh, lively, crisp, clean, and pure cherries. This gorgeous offering will be delicious from release to 2002+. Made from the Les Craipillots and La Perrière vineyards, the medium to dark ruby-colored 1995 Gevrey-Chambertin Premier Cru displays an enthralling nose of roses as well as ripe red and black fruits. The flavors are reminiscent of the village offering but are more extracted and substantial. Velvety textured and medium bodied, this sultry wine should be drunk between now and 2004. More complex and explosive aromatically, the 1995 Gevrey-Chambertin Lavaux St. Jacques bursts with scents of minerals, mocha, wild berries, and sweet toasty oak notes. Velvety textured, rich, and chewy, with flavors suggestive of ripe red and black fruits, mocha, stones, and spices, this beautifully concentrated wine has the structure to last for 8–12 years. While many offerings from Charmes-Chambertin are disappointingly weak, Claude Dugat's consistently outstanding offerings reinforce the point that the vineyard deserves its Grand Cru status. In 1995 Dugat produced another spectacular Charmes. Medium to dark ruby colored with touches of purple, this elegant gem's thick texture and cascade of fat, chewy black fruits are divine. Spiced with toasty oak, long and refined, this wine should be cellared for 4 years and then enjoyed over the ensuing 6+ years. One of the most profound young wines I have tasted, Dugat's 1995 Griotte-Chambertin is a candidate for the red burgundy of the vintage. Deep ruby and purple colored, this wine explodes from the glass with incredible sweetness of fruit, perfume, and flowers. Each time I put my nose in the glass I was mesmerized by its stunningly complex aromatics. Unbelievably, the mouth was even better than the nose! Astonishingly deep, intense, and superripe, this velvety-textured, virtually perfect wine flooded my mouth with concentrated red and black cherries, spices, and roasted fruits. The 30+-second finish was also immensely impressive. Robert Parker once described Dugat's 1993 Griotte as "a religious experience." Let it be known that the out-of-this-world 1995 will also convert anyone to the glories of red burgundy!

What remains to be said about the wines crafted by the shy, self-effacing, and ever-smiling Claude Dugat? Well, they might be getting even better.

While still having the opulence of fruit and suppleness that have made his wines renowned throughout the world, they appear to have more structure. My instincts have, in the past, been that Dugat's wines were best drunk young, but the 1995s and 1996s display the necessary balance among fruit, acidity, and backbone for extended cellaring.

Dugat is a kind man, soft-spoken and modest (he attributes his success to the grafting work his father and grandfather did to the vines that now produce his fruit). Three years ago, as I was speeding (actually flying) to an appointment, I almost ran him and his bicycle off the road. His reaction? A smile and a handshake.

This tiny estate was recently enlarged to 3.5 hectares (8.65 acres) with the purchase of an old-vine parcel of Gevrey.

Perhaps Jean-Marc Joblot, the extremely talented Givry producer, said it best: "Claude Dugat's 1996s are the most beautiful expression of Pinot Noir I've ever had." A taster would have to be dead not to fall in love with these wines.

The 1996 Gevrey-Chambertin has a deep ruby/purple color and displays a mouthwatering nose of lush red and black cherries that gives way to an awesomely supple, concentrated, extremely rich, and broad character. This satiny wine is loaded with deeply ripe and seductive cherries that linger in its impressively soft finish. Anticipated maturity: now–2004. Revealing a medium to dark ruby color and aromas of sugar-encrusted red cherries, the 1996 Gevrey-Chambertin Premier Cru lavishes the palate with unending waves of sumptuously sweet cherries. This rich, pure, elegant, feminine, concentrated, and velvety offering is more profound, complex, and structured than the previous wine. Anticipated maturity: now–2006. Dugat's 1996 Gevrey-Chambertin Lavaux St. Jacques is significantly better than most grands crus I have tasted. It has a medium to dark ruby color, an incredibly dense nose of superripe red and black fruits, and a sublime full-bodied character. As with the previous offerings, this wine is redolent with luxurious, deeply ripe, and seamless red and black cherry fruit. However, it is more concentrated, powerful, broad, rich, dense, structured, and complex than either of the two outstanding wines that preceded it. Anticipated maturity: 2000–2008.

I have no argument with anyone who states that both of Dugat's grands crus merit perfect scores. The dark ruby/purple-colored 1996 Charmes-Chambertin regales the olfactory senses with sweet and perfumed red and black cherry scents that are lively, profound, and verging on jammy—reminiscent of the filling of a deep-dish cherry pie. On the palate, this wondrous wine's combination of superripe candied red fruits and violets with virtually perfect precision and purity of flavors is mind-boggling. This complex, velvety-textured, chewy, and delineated wine is utterly extraordinary and otherworldly. Had it not been followed by an even better wine, I might have been convinced it was perfect.

It would take a writer of Shakespeare's eloquence to do justice to Dugat's 1996 Griotte-Chambertin. It has a deep ruby/purple color and spiritual aromas of raspberry and cherry jam, violets, perfume, and Asian spices. Its aromatic purity, definition, and depth were so captivating that I feared the palate could not match up. Wrong! An explosion of satin-laced fruit greeted my tongue. Layer upon layer of perfectly ripened, sweet and jammy cherries, candied violets, roses, and blueberries provided a levitating experience. For minutes I could neither see nor feel my surroundings—nor did I care to—as this wine took my senses hostage. It is velvety, supple, powerful, stylish, refined, and concentrated and possesses the backbone (as silky as can be imagined!) to allow this heavenly offering to evolve magnificently. Its awesomely long finish has loads of fruit-drowned, soft, and round tannins. As I looked across the room (he had gone off to stand with some friends), my eyes met Claude Dugat's—he smiled.

One of the extraordinary benefits of my job is that generous wine lovers open stunning wines for me just to see if I still like them as much as I originally did. I've tasted Dugat's 1995 Griotte-Chambertin on five (!) separate occasions since my original review was published (it was rated 96–99+ from a barrel sample).

This is a mesmerizing wine. It is dark ruby colored, almost inky black, with bright streaks of purple on the edges. Aromatically it reveals an unreal depth of intense black fruits that give way to an explosion of black cherries, plums, blackberries, blueberries, violets, mocha, café au lait, sweet oak, and Asian spices. Wave upon wave of luscious fruit unfold on the palate in this opulent and hedonistic offering's velvety-textured core. Perfectly balanced and harmonious, intense yet soft, structured yet supple, it is a tour de force. Wow! Anticipated maturity: 2002–2010. Bravo!

DOMAINE BERNARD DUGAT-PY (GEVREY-CHAMBERTIN)

1995	Bourgogne	C	(85–88)
1996	Charmes-Chambertin	EE	(92–95)
1995	Charmes-Chambertin	EE	(92–94)
1996	Gevrey-Chambertin Coeur du Roi Vieilles Vignes	E	(88–90)
1995	Gevrey-Chambertin Coeur du Roi Vieilles Vignes	D	(90–92)
1996	Gevrey-Chambertin Evocelles	E	(90–92+)
1996	Gevrey-Chambertin Le Fonteny	E	(91–93+)
1996	Gevrey-Chambertin Lavaux St. Jacques	EE	(92–94)
1995	Gevrey-Chambertin Lavaux St. Jacques	E	(91–93)
1996	Gevrey-Chambertin Petite Chapelle	EE	(90–92)

1996	Gevrey-Chambertin Vieilles Vignes	D	(87–88)
1995	Gevrey-Chambertin Vieilles Vignes	D	(87–90)
1996	Mazis-Chambertin Vieilles Vignes	EEE	(94–97)
1995	Mazis-Chambertin Vieilles Vignes	EE	(94–97)

Formerly known simply as Domaine Bernard Dugat, the Domaine Dugat-Py has been quietly producing some of Burgundy's finest wines in recent years. Saddled with the same last name as that of his megastar cousin Claude, Bernard's wines have not received the attention they so richly deserve. In 1993 and 1994, both difficult vintages that many topflight growers were unable to harness, Dugat produced some of the Côte d'Or's best wines. The 1995 is no different. Rich and concentrated and offering layers of perfectly ripened fruit, these offerings firmly ensconce Bernard Dugat in the top echelon of the world's best Pinot Noir producers.

Dugat is blessed with old-vine parcels, and he puts them to excellent use. The entire family (son, daughter, and Bernard's charming wife) works the vines, unmercifully cutting them back to lower yields. New oak is used judiciously (50%–100% depending on the wine), and all the offerings exported to the United States are never fined or filtered (the Bourgogne is filtered for France and the European market).

Medium dark colored, the delicious 1995 Bourgogne undergoes its malolactic fermentation in stainless-steel tanks and is then transferred to 1-year-old oak barrels. Revealing a sweet, enticing nose and a supple, deep, medium-bodied palate packed with red berries and spices, this beautifully thick-textured wine is made to provide tons of pleasure during its first 5 years. Produced from vines averaging 40 years of age (wines from his younger vines are sold to *négociants*), the medium to dark ruby-colored 1995 Gevrey-Chambertin Vieilles Vignes is a super village offering (superior to many a producer's grands crus). Exhibiting a deeply spicy, meaty nose, the wine has awesomely concentrated sweet cherries, deep spices, and a roasted berry element. Thick, chewy, and full-bodied, it will be at its peak of maturity between 2000 and 2007. The dark ruby/purple-colored 1995 Gevrey-Chambertin Coeur du Roi Vieilles Vignes (produced from the Petite Chapelle, Evocelles, and Coeur de Lion vineyards) displays gorgeously deep aromas of spicy blackberries and an extraordinarily intense palate of dark fruits, spices, chocolate, and sweet toasty oak. Full bodied, dense, and admirably concentrated, it should be cellared for 6 years and will last for 8 more.

Regrettably, only 50 cases of the 1995 Gevrey-Chambertin Lavaux St. Jacques were produced. A stunning wine, it possesses fabulous dark berries on the nose and a superconcentrated personality packed with layers of chewy and spicy currants, black cherries, and sweet oak. Full bodied, complex, long, and just outrageously delicious, this beauty will repay 5 years of cellaring yet keep for another decade. As the vines in Dugat's Charmes-Chambertin parcel mature (at present they are only 17 years old), I predict this vineyard site will produce one of the most sought-after red burgundies. His style of winemaking seems perfectly suited to Charmes. Displaying deep, sweet spices, dark fruit, and meat aromas, the 1995's oily, silky, complex, and elegant personality is crammed with tangy berries and milk chocolate. Thick and supple, it will be at its best between 2000 and 2008. The world's burgundy lovers will have to have both exceptional contacts or the riches of a professional athlete to acquire Dugat's otherworldly 1995 Mazis-Chambertin Vieilles Vignes. Only 37 cases were produced. Made from 55-year-old vines, this intensely black-colored wine possesses a massively dark, spicy, and meaty nose, a mind-boggling flavor profile of powerful Asian spices, and layers of sweet black fruits that go on and on. Amazingly deep and seductive, the wine offers ripe, round tannins that provide plenty of backbone and delineation. Anticipated maturity: 2005–2020. Bravo!

Bernard Dugat, with the assistance of his charming wife, son, and daughter, has fashioned extraordinary 1996s, nothing new for this family which, since the 1993 vintage, has been crafting some of Burgundy's finest wines.

As I left Dugat-Py's cellars (her maiden name is Py, and they added it to the estate's name to differentiate themselves from Bernard's famous cousin Claude), I felt that while his 1996s were superb, his 1995s were even better. With reflection, and with my notes from both tastings in hand, I realize that it comes down to the specific wines. Certain *terroirs* performed better in 1995 and others in 1996, most probably owing to the weather, which dramatically cut back yields in 1995.

Produced from vines ranging in age from 30 to 50 years old, the medium to dark ruby-colored 1996 Gevrey-Chambertin Vieilles Vignes was crafted using 20% new oak barrels. It displays roses, minerals, and cherries on the nose and offers a juicy, silky-textured, medium-bodied, and gorgeously sweet core of black cherries. Its slightly dry finish prevented this wine from reaching the heights it had a year ago (it is also not as concentrated or dense as its older sibling). Drink it between 2000 and 2005. The 1996 Gevrey-Chambertin Coeur du Roi Vieilles Vignes (from 50–86-year-old vines and aged in 80% new oak) is darker colored and has aromas reminiscent of candied red and black berries awash in spicy oak. Its profound, expansive, medium- to full-bodied, and silky-textured character is replete with plump, juicy cherries and toasted-oak flavors that last throughout its supple finish. It should be at its best between 2000 and 2006. Bernard Dugat works the 70–75-year-old vines in the Gevrey-Chambertin Evocelles vineyard with an *en métayage* (sharecropping) arrangement. This parcel had drastically low 1.2 tons of fruit per acre yields in 1996. It displays a dark ruby color with complex aromas of boysenberries. With its brambleberries strongly spiced with freshly cracked black pepper, this wine has an unbelievably deep, intense, and concentrated personality, as well as superb precision to its candied blackberry, cassis liqueur, and blueberry-crammed flavor profile and extremely long finish. This behemoth will require patience given its firm and highly structured backbone. Anticipated maturity: 2003–2008.

Only 1 barrel (25 cases) of the dark-colored Gevrey-Chambertin Petite Chapelle was produced in 1996. However, a year earlier there was so little of it that Dugat found it necessary to blend it with his Coeur du Roi cuvée. Its precise aromas are composed of cassis liqueur, candied blackberries, beef blood, fresh herbs, perfume, and spicy oak. This feminine, juicy, plump, ample, and concentrated wine drenches the palate with black cherries, tar, wild dark berries, and toasted-oak flavors. Anticipated maturity: 2002–2007. Dugat had a special, 350-liter barrel (traditional Burgundian barrels are 228 liters) made for his newly purchased Gevrey-Chambertin Le Fonteny (Dugat-Py's parcel is the last one before entering Ruchottes-Chambertin). The 1996 reveals a dark ruby/purple color and intense aromatics of black raspberries, cassis, and oak spices. This hugely sweet, velvety-textured, harmonious, thick, muscular, and powerful wine is a spectacular example of a Gevrey premier cru. Elegant and graceful yet highly concentrated and brutally strong, it also possesses a formidably long finish filled with supple tannins drowned in plump fruits. Drink it between 2003 and 2010. The 1996 Gevrey-Chambertin Lavaux St. Jacques has similar color and a nose of candied wild berries, briar patch, and grilled oak. This gorgeously expansive, hedonistic, lush, full-bodied, and velvety-textured wine is liquid candy. "Pure adulterous pleasure!" says my notes. Cookie dough soaked in cherry syrup and topped with sugar-coated blueberries can be found in this awesome offering's flavor profile and exceedingly long as well as silky-smooth finish. Wow! Anticipated maturity: 2002–2009.

Produced from a blend of two-thirds Charmes-Chambertin and one-third Mazoyères-Chambertin (all Mazoyères are entitled to the Charmes appellation, but not vice-versa) and aged in 80% new oak barrels, Dugat's 1996 Charmes-Chambertin is stunning. It is dark ruby colored and has a mouthwatering nose of deep-dish cherry pie, cookie dough, perfume, licorice, and vanilla bean. This liquid silk, decadent, sexy, corporeally exciting, and hedonistic wine is full bodied and deeply satisfying and has the sweetest, most supple tannins imaginable. Jammy and candied cherries and raspberries dance across the taster's palate, taking possession of it and refusing to relinquish their hold. An intensely long wine on the finish, does it have enough brains to go with its sensuality? Drink it between 2002 and 2009. Produced from 51–56-year-old vines and aged in 3 new barrels (2 Tronçais, 1 Allier), the 1996 Mazis-Chambertin is even better. It displays a black color and amazingly expressive aromas of syrupy blackberries, Asian spices, stones, briars, rosemary, and hoisin sauce. This blockbuster is more serious and intellectual than the Charmes yet maintains a great deal of that wine's sensual nature. Velvety black fruits, metals, and juicy cherries can be found in this sublimely delineated yet thick wine. Powerful, graceful, muscular, elegant, concentrated, perfectly balanced, and intensely flavorful, this magnificent wine should age extraordinarily well. Anticipated maturity: 2005–2014+. Bravo!

DOMAINE DUJAC (MOREY-ST.-DENIS)

1996	Bonnes Mares	EEE	(91–93)
1995	Bonnes Mares	E	91+
1996	Chambolle-Musigny	E	(87–89)
1996	Charmes-Chambertin	EE	(89–91)
1995	Charmes-Chambertin	E	89+
1996	Clos de la Roche	EEE	(90–92)
1995	Clos de la Roche	EE	92
1996	Clos St. Denis	EEE	(90–92)
1995	Clos St. Denis	EE	90+
1996	Echézeaux	EEE	(88–91)
1995	Echézeaux	E	91
1996	Gevrey-Chambertin aux Combottes	EE	(89–91)
1995	Gevrey-Chambertin aux Combottes	E	88
1996	Morey-St.-Denis	E	(87–89+)

A charming man with an articulate command of the English language (his wife is from San Francisco, and one of his sons is a student at England's Oxford University), Jacques Seysses makes beautifully refined wines. A Pinot Noir's color can often mislead a taster. In 1997 I conducted a tasting of grand cru burgundies from 1987. Seysses' Dujac wines were by far the lightest in the group, yet when tasted blind, they were found to be the best. Surrounded by dark wines from the likes of Ponsot and Jadot, Dujac's had the most fruit and depth.

Seysses never uses press wine (the result of a second, more pressure-filled pressing of the grapes, producing more tannic juice), has never filtered his wines, abandoned fining in 1991, and uses rackings to rid the wine of flavors he doesn't like (he hates meat and game flavors and will rack the wine if he senses those flavors appearing). Seysses also believes in low yields. In 1995 his yields averaged just under 2 tons of fruit per acre.

Made from a Burgundy premier cru totally surrounded by grand cru vineyards (the vignerons from Morey say that the Gevrey producers have not asked for it to be upgraded, as most of the vineyard belongs to proprietors from Morey), the light ruby-colored 1995 Gevrey-Chambertin aux Combottes displays a sweet perfumed cherry-and-raspberry-filled nose with a touch of spice. There are red fruits and cinnamon in this silky-textured, light- to medium-bodied, slightly tannic wine. Drink it between now and 2005. Seysses told me that his goal for Charmes-Chambertin is to make a complex and elegant wine rather than an extracted one. While I am convinced the two are not mutually exclusive, his 1995 is a delicious, light ruby-colored wine. Aromatically possessing refined notes of sweet perfume and an attractive, silky texture, this spicy, cherry-and-strawberry-flavored offering has adequate length and a light to medium body. It should be cellared for 4–5 years and drunk over the subsequent 6–8 years. Slightly darker, the excellent 1995 Clos St. Denis exhibits aromas of creamy blueberries. This oily-textured, light- to medium-bodied, beautifully ripe wine is filled with cherry, earth, and mineral flavors. It is slightly tannic, and I recommend holding it for 5 years before drinking it over the next 8 years. Domaine Dujac's finest wine in 1995 is the Clos de la Roche. It appears to be a touch lighter in color than the preceding wine but possesses powerful aromas of sweet black fruits. In the mouth, the wine explodes with dark berries, rocks, iron, and roasted spice, all embedded in this chewy, velvety-textured, medium-bodied wine. Possessing copious amounts of soft, ripe tannins, this feminine wine should be cellared for 8 years before enjoying it over the subsequent 7+. Dujac's light-colored wines are a testament to how much punch a deceptively shallow-looking Pinot Noir can deliver. The medium ruby-colored 1995 Echézeaux displays sweet, plummy fruits in the nose and an extremely refined, silky-textured, violet- and-cherry-filled, beautifully intense flavor profile. This delicate gem should be at its best between 2004 and 2012. Bursting with expressive superripe berry fruits on the nose, the 1995 Bonnes Mares is both elegant and powerful (for Domaine Dujac). An oily-textured, medium-bodied wine packed with cherries, blackberries, minerals, and a touch of cassis, it is well delineated and built to last. It should be at its peak between 2004 and 2012.

My most recent visit to the Domaine Dujac was perplexing. Jacques Seysses, the estate's owner and director, informed me that the 1996 vintage was defined by its low acidity. This statement was shocking to hear, as I had already been tasting the vintage's wines for a few weeks (I had started at the southern extremity of the Côte d'Or and was working my way north) and everybody I had visited had expressed the contrary.

Upon tasting Dujac's wines, I understood his position. While 1996 reds at virtually every estate of the Côte are packed with crisp, juicy, and lively berry fruit, Dujac's are jammy, supple, and sultry—more reminiscent of 1985s or 1990s than 1996s. The hundreds of 1996s I tasted indicate that the Seysses are wrong in their assessment of the vintage as a whole, but are simply reflecting the character of their estate's wines.

Seysses believes, and I concur, that his 1995s are more concentrated and structured—and will therefore require more cellaring—than his 1996s. The estate's yields were high in 1996 (almost 50% higher than in 1995), ranging from 3.2 tons of fruit per acre in the village appellations to 2.7 tons for the grands crus, yet sugar levels were slightly higher than in 1995.

The ruby-colored 1996 Chambolle-Musigny has enticing cherry and violet aromas followed by superb blueberry and red fruit flavors in its medium-bodied, soft, inviting, supple, broad, rich, and delicious character. There are no hard edges to this feminine, straightforward, and sexy wine. It should be consumed by 2002. Produced from a blend of village wines, some premiers crus, and the youngest vines of the Clos de la Roche, the medium ruby-colored 1996 Morey-St.-Denis possesses a blueberry custard, perfume, and flower-infused nose. On the palate, this medium-bodied, somewhat structured, yet supple wine is oily textured, expansive, and filled with sweet jammy red and black fruits. Anticipated maturity: now–2004.

The slightly darker-colored 1996 Gevrey-Chambertin aux Combottes reveals ripe red fruit and perfumed aromas as well as a rich, medium- to full-bodied, masculine, black fruit, stone, and earth-laced flavor profile. It is more concentrated, firmer, and longer than the two village offerings yet does not possess their sultriness. It should be at its best between now and 2005. The medium to dark ruby-colored 1996 Charmes-Chambertin offers spicy red fruit aromatics and a pure, sexy, plump, red and black cherry-packed personality. Medium to full bodied and soft, it possesses a long finish that reveals layered fruits intermingled with smoky and toasty oak notes. Anticipated maturity: now–2004.

The bright ruby-colored 1996 Clos St. Denis exhibits raspberries, violets, porcini mushrooms, and black cherries on the nose. This extremely well-balanced wine is oily textured, rich, and medium to full bodied and offers a gorgeous mouthful of sweet cherries, earth, and metallic flavors that linger on the finish amid traces of lightly charred oak. Anticipated maturity: 2000–2006. The slightly dark-colored 1996 Clos de la Roche displays cherry-laced cookie dough aromas and a medium- to full-bodied, refined, yet intense core of tangy berries, cherries, earth, minerals, and metals. This broad, rich, chewy, and well-crafted wine has many admirable components but lacks the power and "punch" that would have emanated from lower yields. Anticipated maturity: 2000–2006. The ruby-colored 1996 Echézeaux offers aromas of red and black fruits and Asian spices. On the palate, this feminine, straightforward, medium-bodied, velvety-textured, and ripe wine reveals sweet red berries and toasty oak flavors. Its tannic finish leads me to believe this offering will require more cellaring than Dujac's other 1996s. I would suggest drinking it between 2002 and 2006.

Dujac's medium to dark ruby-colored 1996 Bonnes Mares reveals dark cherries, perfume, and violets. This masculine yet gorgeously elegant wine has outstanding breadth and concentration as well as a medium to full body with floral, mineral, stone, blackberry, and red cherry flavors. It possesses more "stuffing" than the estate's other 1996s. Anticipated maturity: 2001–2007.

DOMAINE VINCENT DUREUIL-JANTHIAL (RULLY)

1996 Mercurey Le Bois de Lalier Réserve	D	88
1995 Rully En Guesnes Vieilles Vignes	D	90
1996 Rully En Guesnes Vieilles Vignes Réserve	D	89
1996 Rully Rosey Réserve	D	89+

Note: The wines that are described in the following notes are produced exclusively for North Berkeley Imports for the U.S. market. They are neither fined nor filtered.

The 1996 Mercurey Le Bois de Lalier Réserve is medium to dark ruby colored and reveals an intense and fresh nose of blueberries, a floral bouquet, minerals, and steel. On the palate, this medium- to full-bodied, powerful, well-balanced, and harmonious wine bursts with black cherries, stones, and brambleberries. Drink this tasty Mercurey over the next 4 years. Dark ruby colored and offering black cherry-laced aromas, the 1996 Rully En Guesnes Réserve possesses a thick, chewy, medium- to full-bodied, spicy, tangy, earthy, and red cherry-filled personality. This is an intense, fruit-driven wine with excellent depth, soft tannins, and a long, focused finish. It will be at its best if drunk between now and 2002. Produced from 45-year-old vines, the super 1996 Rully Rosey Réserve is a potentially outstanding wine. Dark colored and exhibiting sweet oak-infused hyperripe black fruit aromas, this massive, broad-shouldered, intense, concentrated, and powerful offering is full bodied and chewy textured. Loads of cassis and blackberries can be found in this palate-staining and muscular wine. The only thing that kept it from meriting an outstanding score was some rustic tannins. Anticipated maturity: now–2004.

As with his white offerings, this 25-year-old vigneron from the unheralded village of Rully merits accolades for his fabulous 1995 Rully En Guesnes Vieilles Vignes. Produced from 55-year-old vines, it displays a dark ruby color and a deep nose of Rhône-like toasted fruit intermingled with stones and minerals. On the palate this wine explodes with flavors reminiscent of Peking duck smothered in hoisin sauce, with notes of leather. Full bodied, thick, and highly extracted, it possesses a ripe, plummy flavor intensity that makes it the antithesis of the light, tangy cherry-and-strawberry-flavored burgundies many consumers search out.

DOMAINE MAURICE ECARD ET FILS (SAVIGNY-LÈS-BEAUNE)

1996 Savigny-Lès-Beaune Les Jarrons	D	92
1995 Savigny-Lès-Beaune Les Jarrons	D	89
1996 Savigny-Lès-Beaune Les Narbantons	D	90+
1995 Savigny-Lès-Beaune Les Narbantons	D	91
1996 Savigny-Lès-Beaune Les Peuillets	D	90
1995 Savigny-Lès-Beaune Les Peuillets	D	89
1996 Savigny-Lès-Beaune Les Serpentières	D	90
1995 Savigny-Lès-Beaune Les Serpentières	D	90

The name Maurice Ecard is synonymous with quality winemaking in the town of Savigny-Lès-Beaune. Of the three producers who make the best wines from the vineyards surrounding this little village just west of Beaune, Ecard is the only one who lives and works in Savigny (the other two are Bruno Clair with his La Dominode and Mme. Lalou Bize-Leroy with her Les Narbantons). Ecard's red 1995s are highly structured and tannic wines that will require a few years of cellaring before being at their peak. They were fined but not filtered.

The ruby-colored 1995 Savigny-Lès-Beaune Les Serpentières displays blackberries, stones, and minerals aromatically and an oily-textured, lush, medium-bodied, and elegant flavor profile jam-packed with ripe dark berry fruit and Asian spices. Its beautifully long finish ends on a strong tannic backbone. Anticipated maturity: now–2006. The slightly darker-colored 1995 Savigny-Lès-Beaune Les Peuillets offers an intensely spicy nose intermingled with scents of creamy mocha and a sweet, silky-textured, and supple character crammed with blueberries, black cherries, and café au lait flavors. Much more accessible in its youth than the previous wine, it can be drunk between now and 2005. Ecard's top wine in 1995 is his medium to dark ruby-colored 1995 Savigny-Lès-Beaune Les Narbantons. It possesses deep aromas of wild blueberries, coffee, and minerals as well as a thick, chewy, full-bodied, meaty, superripe personality filled with the flavors of stones, black cherries, and mocha. This wine's superb finish is buttressed with a massive dose of ripe tannins. Drink it between now and 2008. The ruby-colored 1995 Savigny-Lès-Beaune Les Jarrons exhibits powerful aromas of sweet cherries and a highly structured, tannic, full-bodied personality filled with the flavors of minerals, mocha, and blackberries. The most tannic and backward of Ecard's 1995 offerings, it needs to be cellared for a few years before being approachable. Drink it between 2000 and 2008.

Maurice Ecard bottled (fined but unfiltered) all his 1996s in September 1997, just barely 12 months after the harvest. He describes the vintage as "supple and aromatic, perfect to drink while waiting for the 1995s."

Ecard aged his reds in 15% new oak barrels; he stated that any additional amount "taints Savigny's *terroir;* now, if I were dealing with grands crus from Vosne-Romanée, I might be singing a different tune." He recently acquired another 2¹/₂ acres of 1996 Savigny-Lès-Beaune Les Serpentières from a family member, bringing the estate's total acreage in this vineyard to almost 10 acres. It is bright ruby colored and offers aromas of sweet red cherries. Gorgeous and sumptuous layers of succulent red fruits can be found in this medium- to full-bodied, velvety, delineated, and broad wine. It has the structure for aging, but who will be able to keep their hands off this beauty? Anticipated maturity: now–2005. The medium ruby-colored 1996 Savigny-Lès-Beaune Les Peuillets displays earth, mineral, and ripe cherry fruit scents. This delicious, rich, well-crafted, silky, and medium- to full-bodied wine is firmer than the previous one. Metals, stones, and wild red berries can be found its flavor profile and in its lingering, supple tannin-packed finish. Anticipated maturity: now–2005. Possessing a medium to dark ruby color and intense blackberry aromas, the 1996 Savigny-Lès-Beaune Les Narbantons exhibits powerful, highly expressive red and black cherries as well as earth, truffles, and stones in its complex and medium to full body. This concentrated, focused, and extracted wine should be at its peak between 2000 and 2006. As an aside, I've recently tasted superb bottles of the 1993 Narbantons and Serpentières, one in the United States and one at a Beaune restaurant. These delicious wines are now entering their plateau of maturity.

Produced from vines planted in 1945, the medium to dark ruby-colored 1996 Savigny-Lès-Beaune Les Jarrons (this is the original name of the vineyard that is sometimes referred to as La Dominode) has a profound and rich nose of candied red fruits intermingled with cookie dough aromas. Its personality reveals great ripeness, an oily texture, and a broad, mouth-coating, medium to full body. Blackberries, minerals, metals, and oaky spices saturate the palate in this fabulous Savigny, and its long, drawn-out finish reveals copious quantities of supple tannins. Anticipated maturity: 2001–2007. Bravo!

DOMAINE RENÉ ENGEL (VOSNE-ROMANÉE)

1996	Clos Vougeot	EE	(90–93)
1995	Clos Vougeot	E	93
1996	Echézeaux	EE	(?)
1995	Echézeaux	E	91+
1996	Grands Echézeaux	EE	(91–94)
1995	Grands Echézeaux	EE	93
1996	Vosne-Romanée	D	88
1995	Vosne-Romanée	D	87+
1996	Vosne-Romanée Les Brûlées	E	(89–92)
1995	Vosne-Romanée Les Brûlées	D	90

The motorcycle-loving, blue-jeans-and-baseball-cap-wearing Philippe Engel is one vigneron who would go unnoticed in downtown Nashville, Tennessee. With his unmistakable joie de vivre, Engel truly enjoys opening bottles of wine for visitors as much as for friends. In off vintages and great vintages alike, the Domaine René Engel can be counted on for excellent wines. While in the trade, I sold large quantities of his 1987s, delicious and well-balanced wines that did not suffer from the high-acid, low-fruit profile of so many others from this vintage. His 1991s, 1992s, 1993s, and 1994s all must be included in the top tier of wines made in those difficult years. As for his 1995s, these are unfined and unfiltered wines of quality that will stand up to years of cellaring.

Medium ruby colored, the 1995 Vosne-Romanée displays a deep, sweet cherry fruit-filled nose and long, well-structured, ripe, dark berry-filled flavors. Medium bodied and vivacious, this wine should be drunk by 2004. Exhibiting enticing aromas of dark and toasted berries, the ruby-colored, silky 1995 Vosne-Romanée Les Brûlées has a spicy, soft-textured, delineated, full-bodied style. Delicious now, it will age beautifully for a decade. Medium to dark ruby colored, the 1995 Echézeaux's aromatics define the word *finesse:* violets, roses, and small berries. It displays powerful and roasted, fat, dark cherries and a touch of cassis. Rather bulky for its appellation (Echézeaux offerings can be overcropped and thus weak and watery), this medium- to full-bodied wine should be aged for 5 years. It will last for another 7 years. I often prefer Engel's Grands Echézeaux over his Clos Vougeot, but in 1995 I found them to be equally spectacular. Dark colored and with a brooding, tight, muted nose, the massively endowed Grands Echézeaux explodes on the palate with powerful, huge, black, roasted fruits. Rugged and dark, this full-bodied, muscular, rich, and spicy behemoth demands to be held for 8 or more years before being drunk over the following decade. Aromatically offering roasted cherries, plums, and other purple fruits, the Clos Vougeot's mouth is intensely spiced and minerally. Toasted fruit flavors and wet, hot stones vied for my attention with the plummy, Asian spices. Powerful and full bodied, this delicious wine should drink well between 2002 and 2009.

Philippe Engel crafted superb 1996s, but what else is new? This estate can be consistently depended upon to produce first-rate wine.

When I visited Engel at the end of January 1998 he had recently bottled the Vosne-Romanée and had performed the final racking on the Vosne-Romanée Les Brûlées.

The ruby-colored 1996 Vosne-Romanée displays a spicy, rich, and red cherry-scented nose that gives way to a fat, ample, lively, and elegant core of fresh raspberries, cherries, and Asian spices. This delicious and succulent wine also possesses an admirably long finish. Drink it between now and 2004. Revealing a medium to dark ruby color and aromas reminiscent of stones and spices drenched in raspberry juice, the 1996 Vosne-Romanée Les Brûlées has superb density on the palate as well as a silky texture and medium to full body. This complex, gorgeously ripe, and harmonious wine is filled with cherries, blueberries, earth tones, Asian spices, and a dash of freshly cracked pepper. Anticipated maturity: now–2007.

The 1996 Echézeaux exhibits a medium to dark ruby color and fabulously rich and deep aromas of black cherries and spices. The day of my tasting, this wine's austere palate was impossible to judge, as it was in need of the racking Engel was about to perform. Dark fruits, stones, and minerals were in evidence, but its character was lifeless and not showing its true texture and body. Judgment reserved. Engel's medium to dark ruby-colored 1996 Clos Vougeot, however, was outstanding. Profound aromas of deeply ripe red cherries, blueberries, and blackberries steeped in hoisin sauce are followed by a medium- to full-bodied, beautifully ripened, and silky-textured core of black fruits, beef blood, porcini mushrooms, and hints of earth. This wine's outstanding finish reveals loads of supple tannins complemented by blackberry flavors. Anticipated maturity: 2003–2009. The 1996 Grands Echézeaux is slightly darker colored and releases aromas of perfectly ripened red fruits spiced with toasty oak. This ample, rich, velvety-textured, and full-bodied offering is crammed with blackberries, gamey meats (this characteristic will most likely disappear with racking), cinnamon, juniper berries, and metallic shavings. Its immensely long and satiny finish offers flavors of cloves, cassis, and black cherries intermingled with traces of new oak spiciness for additional complexity. Anticipated maturity: 2003–2010.

DOMAINE ARNAULD ENTE (MEURSAULT)

1996 Volnay Santenots (du Milieu)	D	(87–89+)

The young and talented Arnauld Ente produces excellent red wines in addition to his first-rate whites. When I visited him he allowed me to taste two reds, a delicious Bourgogne Grand Ordinaire made from 100% Gamay and a wonderful Volnay Santenots (du Milieu). The latter wine is bright ruby colored and offers an expressive nose of deeply ripe cassis and black cherries. It is medium to full bodied, thickly textured, and filled with layer after layer of sweet red cherries, together with traces of minerals and stones. Drink this beauty between now and 2004.

DOMAINE DE LA FERTÉ (GIVRY)

1996 Givry	C	(85–87)

This Givry has a medium to dark ruby color and a beautifully floral, violet-infused nose. It is a refined, powerful, silky-textured, and medium-bodied wine that would have merited a higher rating if its finish had been softer and longer. However, readers willing to overlook that transgression will appreciate its seductive black and red fruits intertwined with mineral and metal-like flavors. Drink it by 2001. The Domaine de la Ferté is owned by the Antonin Rodet *négociant* house.

MAISON FERY-MEUNIER (NUITS-ST.-GEORGES)

1996 Chambertin	EE	(88–90+?)
1996 Charmes Chambertin	EE	(87–88)
1996 Clos Vougeot	EE	(89–91)
1996 Pommard Epenots	D	(87–89)

Alain Meunier of Domaine Jean-Jacques Confuron, in partnership with a lawyer friend from Lyon, has created this new *négociant* house. Maison Fery-Meunier's goal is to purchase first-rate grapes (not must or wine) from conscientious growers. Meunier informed me that he was "pushing the vignerons to reduce yields, but I've had to reject grapes already." The wine-making is pure Meunier, beautifully highlighting the wines' elegance and fruit. However, years of drinking J.-J. Confuron's wines, coupled with the fact that I had just moments before tasted that estate's 1996s, stressed the differences of viticultural techniques. The Charmes Chambertin in particular lacked the depth of fruit and length of finish I have come to expect from Meunier.

The ruby-colored 1996 Pommard Epenots offers sweet perfume and red berry aromas that give way to a medium-bodied, silky-textured, juicy, and extracted character. Flavors of red cherries, minerals, and hints of toasty oak can be found in this elegant offering. Drink it between 2000 and 2005. Produced from 100% destemmed grapes, the ruby-colored 1996 Charmes Chambertin reveals roses, violets, cherries, and loads of raspberries in its aromatics. This medium-bodied, velvety, cherry-flavored, and soft wine is extremely well made, refined, and delicious, yet it lacks the depth, hold, complexity, and length I expect from an Alain Meunier–crafted grand cru. The medium to dark ruby-colored 1996 Chambertin was crafted from older vines and was only 50% destemmed. Its exquisitely perfumed nose is laced with black fruits, stones, and earthlike tones. On the palate, this medium- to full-bodied, rich, thick, and powerful wine offers a mouthful of blackberries, cassis, and minerals. I was impressed by the depth and flavor intensity of this wine; however, its ultimate quality will be determined by how well Meunier deals with its rough and tannic finish. Anticipated maturity: 2003–2007. This firm's finest 1996 is the Clos Vougeot. Produced from a parcel just below the Grands Echézeaux vineyard, this medium to dark ruby-colored wine has aromas of cassis, blackberries, Asian spices, and mocha. It is an extremely refined, medium- to full-bodied, juicy, and thickly textured wine full of deeply ripe dark fruits and roasted herbs. If this crisp, well-delineated wine had had a longer finish, it would have certainly merited a higher score. Anticipated maturity: 2002–2007.

DOMAINE JEAN-PHILIPPE FICHET (MEURSAULT)

1996 Bourgogne	B	86
1996 Chassagne-Montrachet	C	(86–88)
1996 Côte de Beaune	C	(86–87)
1996 Monthélie	C	(86–87)

The light to medium ruby-colored Bourgogne displays enticing red cherry aromas and a lively, medium-bodied, silky-textured character filled with ripe red fruits and traces of ground white pepper. This one-dimensional yet delicious wine is an excellent value for Pinot Noir and an extraordinary one for burgundy! Drink it over the next 2 years. The ruby-colored Chassagne-Montrachet reveals gorgeously perfumed aromas and a plump, medium-bodied, and delightful character brimming with sweet, juicy cherries, soft tannins, and a long finish.

It will be at its best if drunk over the next 3 years. Produced from vineyards in Auxey-Duresses, the medium to dark ruby-colored Côte de Beaune offers a cassis and metal-laced nose followed by a medium-bodied, well-crafted, and black cherry-and-mineral-packed flavor profile. Anticipated maturity: now–2002. The Monthélie is light to medium ruby colored and exhibits aromas reminiscent of freshly cut flowers, perfume, and cassis. This medium-bodied, silky-textured, focused wine offers stonelike flavors intermingled with violets, minerals, and blueberries. Anticipated maturity: now–2002.

DOMAINE FOREY PÈRE ET FILS (VOSNE-ROMANÉE)

1995 Echézeaux	E	(86–88)
1995 Nuits-St.-Georges	D	(83–86)
1995 Nuits-St.-Georges Les Perrières	D	(85–87)
1995 Vosne-Romanée	D	(83–86)
1995 Vosne-Romanée Les Petits Monts	D	(85–87)

Unlike most Burgundians who maintain their cellars under their homes, Régis Forey, who lives on the same street as the Domaine de la Romanée Conti, makes his wines in two off-site cellars. One cellar is located under the stately old Château de Vosne-Romanée, a quasi-abandoned building in the center of the village. He is planning on building or acquiring a new cellar, because moving barrels up and down steps is exceedingly inconvenient, not to mention backbreaking. Forey makes austere, highly structured wines that require cellaring for a few years to round out. However, these are not massively deep, extracted, and concentrated wines that will hold their peak for an extended period.

The medium ruby-colored 1995 Vosne-Romanée offering reveals tangy cherries on the nose and a silky-textured, creamy mouth with flavors of sweet red berries. Drink it between now and 2001. Exhibiting dark and roasted fruits on the nose, the 1995 Nuits-St.-Georges has an attractive velvety texture, black cherries, and good length. It should be at its apogee in 3 years. Offering a nose of jammy red fruits, the 1995 Nuits-St.-Georges Les Perrières has a structured, minerally, and earthy personality. Medium bodied and austere, it should be at its peak between 2001 and 2005. Surprisingly, the 1995 Vosne-Romanée Les Petits Monts is just as structured as the Nuits Perrières offering. Tight and brooding on the nose, it has a foursquare dark roasted fruit-filled character. Medium bodied, it will be at its best between 2002 and 2005. Forey's best offering, the medium to dark ruby-colored 1995 Echézeaux reveals a deeply floral, ripe, and sweet nose and a structured, fresh, lively chewy, red and black fruit-filled flavor profile. Velvety textured and medium bodied, it will drink well between 2002 and 2006.

DOMAINE JEAN-NOËL GAGNARD (CHASSAGNE-MONTRACHET)

1996 Chassagne-Montrachet	C	(86–88)
1995 Chassagne-Montrachet Clos St. Jean	D	87
1995 Chassagne-Montrachet Morgeot	D	88
1996 Chassagne-Montrachet Morgeot	D	(88–90+)
1995 Santenay Clos de Tavannes	D	88

Even though she is located in a village known for its whites, Caroline Lestimé (Jean-Noël Gagnard's daughter) loves red wines, and it is in their quality that her participation in the estate's vinification practices is most felt. Mme. Lestimé introduced the use of new oak barrels (25%) and abandoned the use of filters, much to the concern of her father. Having tasted the resulting qualitative improvement, Gagnard now fully supports his daughter's efforts.

The ruby-colored and herbal, blueberry, strawberry, and metallic-scented 1996 Chassagne-Montrachet is a fabulous quaffing wine. It is neither complex nor superconcentrated but is filled with scrumptious and tender red currants and cherries. This feminine, beautifully ripe, and soft wine should be drunk over the next 3 years. The slightly darker-colored 1996 Chassagne-Montrachet Morgeot is a more serious and profound wine. It displays deeply sweet red cherries on the nose and has a rich, well-crafted, medium-bodied, and velvety-textured character. Raspberries, candied strawberries, cherries, and traces of toasty oak can be found in its flavor profile. Anticipated maturity: now–2004.

The ruby-colored 1995 Chassagne-Montrachet Clos St. Jean reveals raspberry and mineral aromas and an elegant, well-balanced, softly textured, medium-bodied, and crisp personality with flavors of stones and red currants. Anticipated maturity: now–2001. Displaying a medium ruby color and an intriguing nose of sweet cherries, orange rinds, and touches of Asian spices, the 1995 Chassagne-Montrachet Morgeot has a fabulous oily texture, great delineation, and delicious boysenberries, blueberries, and spices in its medium to full body. Lestimé's judicious use of oak is noticeable in this wine's subtle vanilla and smoke flavors. Drink it between now and 2002. The slightly lighter in color 1995 Santenay Clos de Tavannes possesses raspberry and stone-infused aromatics as well as a rich, silky-textured, well-balanced, and medium- to full-bodied core of chewy ripe cherries, minerals, and cinnamon. Delicious to drink now, it will maintain its peak until 2002.

DOMAINE JEAN GARAUDET (POMMARD)

1996	Beaune Belissand	D	86
1995	Beaune Belissand	D	(86–87)
1996	Beaune Clos des Mouches	D	88
1995	Beaune Clos des Mouches	D	(87–89)
1996	Hautes Côtes de Beaune	C	87
1995	Hautes Côtes de Beaune	C	(84–86)
1996	Monthélie	C	88
1995	Monthélie	C	(85–88)
1996	Pommard Charmots	D	92
1995	Pommard Charmots	D	(90–93)
1996	Pommard Noizons	D	89
1995	Pommard Noizons	D	(88–91)

Tucked away on a back street in the village of Pommard, Jean Garaudet produces beautifully extracted and concentrated wines and is an excellent source of Côte de Beaune red burgundies. This quiet, shy man was pleased with his 1996s and bottled them early to preserve their vibrant fruit. Like other vignerons I visited, Garaudet commented on the unusual length of the vintage's malolactic fermentations. He also remarked that his pHs changed significantly during this secondary fermentation, having moved from a frightfully low 3.1 to a reasonable yet low 3.4. Two rackings are performed at this estate, one immediately after the malos are completed and the next for the *assemblage*. Garaudet does not fine his wines, but he does subject them to a light filtration.

The ruby-colored 1996 Hautes Côtes de Beaune, bottled at the end of October 1997 (all the other wines were bottled before Christmas), offers an intense nose of red and black cherries infused with violet aromas. On the palate, this medium-bodied, tangy, lively, and well-crafted wine reveals raspberry and blackberry flavors in its vibrant character. Drink it over the next

2–3 years. Produced from 39-year-old vines, the 1996 Beaune Belissand is ruby colored and displays dark fruit, stone, and mineral scents. This medium-bodied, slightly rough wine has brambleberry, black currant, and metallic flavors. While I was impressed with this wine's lovely fruit, I could not overlook its dry tannins and unyielding personality. It should be at its best over the next 3 years. Garaudet's ruby-colored 1996 Monthélie is produced with a high percentage of premier cru Les Riottes. It exhibits a gorgeous nose of candied blueberries and lilies as well as a medium-bodied, ripe, and structured character filled with blackberries, brambleberries, and stonelike flavors. Anticipated maturity: now–2003. Equally good, the medium to dark ruby-colored 1996 Beaune Clos des Mouches has a rose petal and cookie dough-laden nose that is followed by a medium-bodied, powerful, masculine, foursquare, and blackberry, mineral, and stone-laced flavor profile. Anticipated maturity: now–2004.

The medium to dark ruby-colored 1996 Pommard Noizons has deep black cherry aromas and an explosive, intense, thickly textured, medium- to full-bodied, and chewy core of blackberries, cassis, and stones. Its layered and extremely ripe fruit lingers in this excellent offering's impressive finish. It should be at its peak between 1999 and 2004. Produced from vines planted in 1902 and 1922, the dark-colored 1996 Pommard Charmots has penetrating sweet cookie dough aromas in addition to a highly concentrated, extracted, masculine, and broad-shouldered personality that saturates the palate with its blackberry, leather, and mocha-laced fruit. This massive, full-bodied wine is immensely impressive for its girth and power as well as for its extraordinarily ripe fruit. It will require patience. I wonder which will be better 7–8 years from now, the 1995 or the 1996? Anticipated maturity: 2002–2008.

The medium to dark ruby-colored 1995 Hautes Côtes de Beaune offers blackberry and raw meat aromas as well as an elegant, tangy, chewy, thick-textured personality with blueberry and cassis flavors. Drink it now. The dark ruby-colored 1995 Monthélie displays a blackberry-and-chocolate-laden nose and an oily-textured, medium- to full-bodied and deep mouthful of black cherries, minerals, and mocha. This is a beautifully structured Monthélie that will not suffer from being cellared. Anticipated maturity: now–2001. The 1995 Beaune Belissand possesses a medium to dark ruby color as well as a sweet, floral, and dark cherry-filled nose. Its medium-bodied, blackberry, and mocha-flavored palate is buttressed by a firm (and slightly rugged) tannic backbone. Drink it between now and 2003.

The dark ruby-colored 1995 Beaune Clos des Mouches exhibits minerals and blackberries in its nose and a thick, chewy, deeply concentrated, and cherry-laden palate. Elegant, well structured, and admirable long, it should be at its peak between now and 2004. Produced from 60-year-old vines, the dark purple-colored 1995 Pommard Noizons reveals ripe black fruits with earthy undertones in its aromatics and a beautiful cherry, blackberry, and cassis-packed personality. Hugely concentrated and thick, this fabulous full-bodied offering should be drunk between now and 2005. Garaudet's Pommard Charmots (from 70-year-old vines) stands out as one of the finest Pommards produced in the 1995 vintage. Black colored and bursting with ripe cassis aromas, this full-bodied and thick wine explodes on the palate with layers of massively concentrated cassis, blackberries, and plums, with notes of leather, chocolate, and minerals for additional complexity. The power and assertiveness of the fruit flavors in this wine reminded me of the dried-fruit rolls sold in grocery stores when I was a kid. Fabulous! Drink it between 2000 and 2009.

DOMAINE PHILIPPE GAVIGNET (NUITS-ST.-GEORGES)
1996 Côte de Nuits-Villages Les Vignottes Vieilles Vignes Réserve   C 88

Note: The wine described in the following notes is produced exclusively for North Berkeley Imports for the U.S. market.

The ruby-colored 1996 Côte de Nuits-Villages Les Vignottes Vieilles Vignes Réserve has a beautiful nose of mineral-laced black raspberries. This broad, rich, expansive, silky-textured, and medium-bodied offering is packed with ripe and juicy blackberries, assorted dark fruit, and Asian spices. Anticipated maturity: now–2002.

DOMAINE GEANTET-PANSIOT (GEVREY-CHAMBERTIN)

1996 Bourgogne Pinot Fin	C	86
1996 Chambolle-Musigny Premier Cru	E	90
1996 Chambolle-Musigny Vieilles Vignes	D	88
1996 Charmes-Chambertin	EE	93
1996 Gevrey-Chambertin Les Jeunes Rois	D	88
1996 Gevrey-Chambertin Le Poissenot	D	91
1996 Gevrey-Chambertin Vieilles Vignes	D	90
1996 Marsannay Champs Perdrix	C	87

Vincent Geantet, a young man who appears to be in his mid-30s, produces seductive, supple, flavorful, and immensely pleasurable wines. Each and every offering I tasted (out of bottle) was filled with exuberant and lush fruit and was seemingly ready to drink. All of his wines are aged in one-third new oak (from a multitude of sources), with a heavy reliance on first-year barrels, and are neither fined nor filtered. Geantet informed me that they had all been bottled on January 7 by an itinerant bottling truck.

The 1996 Bourgogne Pinot Fin is medium ruby colored and offers sweet aromas of cassis and cherries. It is delicious, silky, and medium bodied and offers a delightful core of ripe strawberries and raspberries. This easy-to-drink and joyful wine should be consumed over the next 3 years. Offering a ruby/purple color and a nose of blackberries and black currants, the 1996 Marsannay Champs Perdrix has a rich, supple, velvety-textured character filled with candied black raspberries and traces of minerals. I was disappointed to find a slight hollowness in the midpalate of this otherwise delicious and well-crafted wine. Drink it over the next 4 years.

Produced from 50-year-old vines, the medium to dark ruby-colored 1996 Chambolle-Musigny Vieilles Vignes displays perfumed blackberry and blueberry aromas as well as a thick, dense, and structured personality. Cassis liqueur, black cherries, and stones are found in this luscious yet muscular and masculine wine. Its long, firm finish offers a glimpse at its well-ripened and satin-textured tannins. Crafted from 40–48-year-old vines from equal-size parcels in three vineyards (Les Baudes, Feusselottes, and Plantes), the dark purple-colored 1996 Chambolle-Musigny Premier Cru has lovely violet, perfumed, and blueberry-infused scents. This masculine, highly structured, chewy-textured, concentrated, and extracted offering is crammed with candied blueberries, blackberries, and minerals. This outstanding wine should be at its peak between 2000 and 2006.

Produced from 40-year-old vines, the 1996 Gevrey-Chambertin Les Jeunes Rois is medium to dark ruby colored and has powerful cassis aromas on the nose. This oily-textured, decadently supple wine has an excellent mouth-feel, a medium to full body, and layers of sweet black fruit flavors. While not complex, it has a long, well focused, and sumptuous finish. It should be at its peak between now and 2004. Geantet crafts his dark-colored 1996 Gevrey-Chambertin Vieilles Vignes from 45–93-year-old vines spread out over 17 parcels throughout the Gevrey commune.

Harvested at a meager 1 ton of fruit per acre, this outstanding offering had a reticent nose. After some cajoling it reluctantly revealed scents of superripe blackberries and touches of leather. Loads of concentrated and dense (almost viscous) cassis, boysenberries, and blackberries can be found in this full-bodied, fat, and lively wine. Anticipated maturity:

2001–2007. The Gevrey-Chambertin Le Poissenot hails from a little-known premier cru vineyard located west of Estournelles St. Jacques and just above Les Verroilles in the Combe de Lavaux sector. According to Geantet, this site is particularly cool and windy because the Combe acts as a funnel, guiding brisk air into the valley. He informed me that in 1996 the vines suffered from *coulure* and *millerandage* (damaged flowering and stunted fruit embryos, respectively) that severely lowered yields. This black-colored wine has licorice and cassis liqueur aromas that are followed by a huge, massively concentrated, broad-shouldered, intense personality. It is chewy textured yet admirably focused, with well-integrated and refreshing acidity. Even though this is a powerful and structured wine, its copious tannins are supple and silky. It can be drunk young but should evolve marvelously. Anticipated maturity: 2001–2008.

The dark ruby-colored 1996 Charmes-Chambertin has a delightful nose of both sugar-coated blueberries and blackberries that gives way to a huge burst of candied red, purple, and black fruits. This harmonious and refined, yet concentrated and full-bodied wine is plump, velvety textured, and complex. Flavors of soft milk chocolate and cassis liqueur are found in its seductive, succulent, and silky-smooth finish. Drink this gem between 2002 and 2009. Bravo!

DOMAINE GÉNOT-BOULANGER (MEURSAULT)

1996	Aloxe-Corton Clos du Chapitre	D	(87–90)
1996	Beaune Grèves	C	(89–91+)
1996	Beaune Montrevenots	C	(87–89)
1996	Clos Vougeot	E	(88–91)
1996	Corton	E	(87–89)
1996	Mercury Les Saumonts	B	(85–87)
1996	Mercurey Les Sazenay	C	(86–88)
1996	Pommard	D	(87–89)
1996	Volnay	C	(87–89)
1996	Volnay Les Aussy	D	(87–89)

Guillaume de Castelnau is as enthusiastic about his red 1996s as he is about his whites. Moderate yields in the 2²/₃ tons of fruit per acre range were harvested by hand and transported to the winery in small boxes to prevent bruising of the grapes. Damaged and unhealthy bunches are then sorted out prior to be being 75%–95% destalked. Castelnau then cools the must prior to fermentation (he is a big proponent of temperature control) and allows it to proceed with a 10–13-day fermentation, slowly raising the temperature to 30–33 degrees Celsius. No SO_2 is added to the wines until their first rackings after the malolactic fermentations are completed.

Castelnau, like many military officers, loves traditions. Each year on Christmas Day he and his assistants return to the winery to give each barrel a vigorous *bâtonnage* (stirring the lees on red burgundies is becoming increasingly fashionable). Prior to bottling, the wines are assembled unfined and a decision is made concerning filtration on a wine-by-wine basis.

Domaine Génot-Boulanger's reds can best be described as "full-throttle," "in your face" wines. They cannot be defined as being elegant or refined; rather, these offerings are full-flavored, dark fruit-filled, and intense wines. In effect, lovers of Châteauneuf-du-Pape will find them immensely appealing. Many of these offerings are *excellent values*.

The ruby-colored 1996 Mercurey Les Saumonts (whose *terroir* is being considered for elevation to premier cru status) offers ripe berry and orange peel aromatics followed by a delicious, well-crafted, medium-bodied, silky core of blackberries and plums. This wine should be consumed over the next 3 years. The 1996 Mercurey Les Sazenay is dark ruby colored and blackberry scented and offers an intense, concentrated, masculine, and medium- to full-bodied character. Boysenberries, blueberries, and minerals can be found in this highly structured (particularly for a 1996) and persistent wine. It should be at its peak between now and 2002.

Produced from an assemblage of three separate parcels, the 1996 Volnay exhibits ripe black fruit aromas and a medium- to full-bodied, silky-textured, boysenberry- and fresh herb-imbued personality. This seductive and expansive wine should be drunk between now and 2003. The 1996 Volnay Les Aussy has blueberries and violets on the nose and a broad, masculine, medium- to full-bodied, chewy, and full-flavored character filled with wild game, cracked black pepper, cassis, metals, and blackberries. It is intense, deeply ripe, and powerful. Anticipated maturity: 2000–2004.

Castelnau fashioned two impressive Beaunes in 1996. Displaying a dark ruby color and a violet-and-plum-scented nose, the 1996 Beaune Montrevenots is an explosive, broad-shouldered, expansive, buttery-textured, medium- to full-bodied wine packed with minerals, metals, and roses, and black cherries. This concentrated and expressive wine should be at its peak between now and 2003. Even better, and one of the finest Beaunes I tasted out of barrel from the 1996 vintage, the black-colored 1996 Beaune Grèves reveals hyperripe aromas of bananas, plums, and dried red fruits. It is a massively concentrated and extracted wine, with a powerful, chewy, and medium- to full-bodied personality. Layer upon layer of blackberries, cherries, minerals, metals, and traces of black truffles can be found in its extraordinarily ripe yet balanced flavor profile. Its long finish offers loads of soft and supple tannins. Anticipated maturity: 2001–2005.

The 1996 Pommard was vinified in two separate cuvées that will be assembled prior to bottling—one from grapes that were 100% destalked and the other from nondestalked bunches. Surprisingly, the destalked cuvée appeared to be slightly dryer and more tannic than the darker-colored and herbal-scented nondestalked cuvée. The assembled wine reveals a bright dark ruby color and intense black raspberry, cherry, and violet aromatics. It offers cassis, boysenberry, metal, and stone flavors in its attractive, medium- to full-bodied, tangy, and lively flavor profile. Anticipated maturity: now–2003. Displaying a medium to dark ruby color and a rich, deep, and metallic nose, the 1996 Aloxe-Corton Clos du Chapitre is a highly expressive, profound, lively, beautifully crafted, and medium- to full-bodied wine. Ripe, juicy black currants and blueberries are intermingled with metals and mineral in its structured yet broad and seductive personality.

Génot-Boulanger's 1996 Corton is produced from vines located in Les Combes, the southernmost grand cru vineyard on the Corton hillside. Exhibiting a medium to dark ruby color and aromas reminiscent of minerals, violets, and roses, this wine is broad shouldered, masculine, medium to full bodied, and highly structured. To my palate, it lacks the intensity and power of the best Cortons yet possesses a complex flavor profile of blackberries, minerals, and stones. It should be at its peak between 2000 and 2005. There is no lack of intensity in this estate's only Côte de Nuits wine, however. The purple/black-colored 1996 Clos Vougeot boasts a floral, black cherry, and Asian spice-laced nose as well as a hugely powerful, massively expressive, and masculine character. Soy sauce, blackberries, truffles, iron, and traces of underbrush can be discerned in this brooding monster. As much as its power, concentration, and extraordinary extract were impressive, I did not find equivalent levels of complexity in this offering. It is one of the most tannic 1996s I tasted and will require considerable patience. Anticipated maturity: 2003–2008.

How these wines are dealt with at bottling will determine the ultimate quality of this, only Castelnau's second vintage as a winemaker.

VINCENT GIRARDIN (SANTENAY)

1996	Beaune Clos des Vignes Franches	D	89*
1995	Beaune Clos des Vignes Franches	D	90*
1996	Chassagne-Montrachet Clos de La Boudriotte Vieilles Vignes	D	(89–91)
1995	Chassagne-Montrachet Clos de La Boudriotte Vieilles Vignes	D	90
1996	Chassagne-Montrachet Morgeot	D	(89–92)
1995	Chassagne-Montrachet Morgeot	D	88
1996	Corton Perrières Vieilles Vignes	E	(92–94)*
1995	Corton Perrières Vieilles Vignes	E	93+*
1996	Corton Renardes	EE	(91–94)
1996	Maranges Clos des Loyères Vieilles Vignes	C	(86–88)*
1995	Maranges Clos des Loyères Vieilles Vignes	C	88+*
1996	Pommard Les Chanlins Vieilles Vignes	E	(89–91+)
1995	Pommard Les Chanlins Vieilles Vignes	D	93
1996	Pommard Les Epenots	E	(90–92)*
1996	Pommard Clos de Lambots Vieilles Vignes	D	(88–91)*
1995	Pommard Clos de Lambots Vieilles Vignes	D	91*
1996	Pommard Les Rugiens Vieilles Vignes	E	(90–92+)*
1995	Pommard Les Rugiens Vieilles Vignes	E	93+*
1995	Pommard Les Vignots	D	92
1996	Santenay Clos de La Confrèrie	D	(86–88)
1995	Santenay Clos de La Confrèrie	D	86
1996	Santenay Les Gravières	D	87*
1995	Santenay Les Gravières	D	89+
1996	Santenay La Maladière	D	(87–89)
1995	Santenay La Maladière	D	89
1996	Volnay Champans	D	(88–90)*
1995	Volnay Champans	D	92+*
1996	Volnay Clos des Chênes	E	(90–93)
1995	Volnay Clos des Chênes	E	94+
1996	Volnay Santenots	D	(88–91)
1995	Volnay Santenots	D	92

Note: Wines marked with an asterisk, as well as a Maranges Clos Roussot and a Pommard Vignots (I tasted neither), are also sold under the Baron de la Charrière label.

I was absolutely blown away by the quality of Vincent Girardin's red 1995 Côte de Beaunes at my April 1997 tasting in Washington. Whereas there is always an element of doubt concerning the end product when tasting out of barrel, what I saw from Girardin was already bottled and in retail stores throughout the United States (all of them were tasted with their American importer, and many were later retasted blind with other '95 burgundies). These are superlative red burgundies with a superb rapport in quality and price.

Vincent Girardin produces wines from vineyards he owns and, as a *négociant*, purchases grapes (not juice, must, or wine as many other *négociants* do) from old-vine parcels throughout the Côte de Beaune. He requires that his growers reduce their yields and use a bare minimum of chemical fertilizers and herbicides. As might be expected from such a dedicated producer, Girardin neither fines nor filters.

This estate's wines exhibit superb ripeness, outstanding balance, beautiful purity of fruit, and extraordinarily well-integrated oak and tannin. In the top cuvées there is unsurpassed length. I know of no other producer/*négociant* in Burgundy who can deliver as broad a range of outstanding wines at such reasonable prices. Furthermore, Girardin, like Bernard Dugat in Gevrey-Chambertin, has worked hard to improve the quality of his wines. To top it all off, we can look forward to many more years of sublime wines from this estate/*négociant*, as Girardin and his wife, Véronique, are quite young.

If readers love Burgundian reds, run, don't walk, to your wine merchant and purchase these dazzling wines.

Produced from a *monopole* (solely owned vineyard), the ruby-colored 1995 Santenay Clos de La Confrèrie offers black currant and sweet cherry aromas as well as a light- to medium-bodied, well-defined, slightly rustic, cassis, and mineral-infused personality. While very good, it is Girardin's weakest wine and should be drunk before 1999. The medium to dark ruby-colored 1995 Maranges Clos des Loyères Vieilles Vignes (produced from vines over 70 years old) displays a superripe nose of candied strawberries, roses, and toffee as well as a gorgeously explosive, concentrated, deep, beautifully balanced, medium- to full-bodied, and velvety character jam-packed with fresh Bing cherries. This supple and sultry wine offers a superb value. Drink it from now to 2002. The ruby-colored 1995 Santenay La Maladière reveals crisp and defined cherry and violet aromas as well as a highly structured, well-delineated, masculine-style, medium- to full-bodied and silky core filled with complex and concentrated flavors of blackberries, minerals, roasted herbs, earth, and iron. It will be at its best between now and 2002. Medium to dark ruby colored and possessing an intensely expressive nose of cherries and boysenberries, the 1995 Santenay Les Gravières is the finest wine I have tasted from this little-known appelation. It has an extraordinarily velvety texture, perfect structure, and intensely powerful layers of stewed cherries, cassis, and traces of flint in its dense, chewy, rich, and full-bodied personality. At present it is tightly wound and backward, so it requires a few years of patience. Anticipated maturity: 2000–2005.

Both Chassagne-Montrachet offerings are produced from purchased grapes. The 1995 Chassagne-Montrachet Morgeot is dark ruby colored and reveals ripe blackberries and iron aromatically as well as a deeply intense, rugged, masculine, medium- to full-bodied character with black cherry and embedded mineral flavors. Structured and tannic, it needs to be cellared for 4–5 years. Drink it between 2001 and 2005. The black/ruby-colored 1995 Chassagne-Montrachet Clos de La Boudriotte Vieilles Vignes is one of the finest red Chassagnes I have ever tasted. Possessing a black currant, mineral, and iodine-scented nose, this viscous, medium- to full-bodied, robust, sweet, and delicious wine is packed with cherries, iron, blueberries, and flint. The admirably long finish boasts the silkiest tannins I have experienced in a Chassagne. Anticipated maturity: 2000–2007. The ruby-colored 1995 Beaune Clos des Vignes Franches offers cinnamon, gingerbread, and raspberry aromas as well as a silky-textured, medium- to full-bodied, well-delineated, and driven character filled with cherries, strawberries, and traces of cookie dough. The marvelous flavors of this wine reminded me of a multi-red fruit cobbler sprinkled with cinnamon-sugar I used to eat at a diner in Nashville. Anticipated maturity: now–2004.

Produced from vines over 60 years old, the medium to dark ruby-colored 1995 Pommard Clos de Lambots Vieilles Vignes reveals beguiling aromas of blueberries, black currants, and traces of freshly dug earth. This is a thick, medium- to full-bodied, powerful, highly structured, and intense wine with an exemplary depth of cassis and blackberry fruit. Rich, superripe, admirably well balanced, exceptionally long, and possessing supple tannins, this gem will be at its peak between now and 2005. When tasting the darker-colored 1995 Pommard Les Vignots, one finds it hard to believe that this is a village appelation wine. Readers who prefer Cabernets to what they perceive as the lightly flavored Pinot Noir varietal should try this bruiser. Displaying metallic, earthy, and blackberry aromas, this is a full-bodied, robust, viscous, chewy, tightly wound, and backward wine layered with concentrated and intense cassis, boysenberry, and underbrush flavors. Its huge backbone of tannins will require cellaring patience. Anticipated maturity: 2000–2006.

Girardin offers three absolutely superb Volnays from purchased fruit. The dark ruby-colored 1995 Volnay Santenots possesses a fresh, lively, and elegantly floral and perfumed nose as well as a fabulously explosive, sweet, deep, delineated, full-bodied, and luscious core of black cherries, cassis, roses, and boysenberries. Exhibiting extraordinary ripeness of fruit and tannin, this amazingly long wine will offer years of superb drinking. Anticipated maturity: 2000–2007. Purple/ruby colored and revealing enticingly ripe aromas of black cherries and violets, the 1995 Volnay Champans is a more austere but slightly more complex wine than the preceding one. It offers a sublime core of currants, blueberries, blackberries, and earth and distinct notes of black truffles in its robust, awesomely concentrated, extracted, and thick full body. This refined yet muscular wine has highly present and firm tannins in its exceedingly long finish. Drink it between 2001 and 2008. My favorite of Girardin's 1995s, the black-colored Volnay Clos des Chênes is a show-stopping and mind-blowing wine. It reveals a deeply ripe nose of coffee, toffee, and gorgeous black currants as well as a velvety textured, full-bodied, highly structured, rich, and sublime flavor profile crammed with extraordinarily sweet layered cassis, cherries, and blackberries. Its driven, pure, floral, and supple finish seemingly goes on forever. This magnificent wine will be at its best between 2000 and 2008.

Another extraordinary wine produced from 47-year-old vines in a vineyard bordering the Volnay appellation, the dark ruby-colored 1995 Pommard Les Chanlins Vieilles Vignes offers elegant aromas of sweet roses, violets, strawberries, and blackberries. This delectable beauty has a full-bodied, exotic, amazingly viscous, lively, succulent, and sultry personality jam-packed with superconcentrated raspberries, cherries, plums, and flowers. It possesses a formidably long and lush finish with perfectly ripe supple tannins in evidence. Anticipated maturity: 2000–2006. The slightly lighter-colored 1995 Pommard Les Rugiens Vieilles Vignes is produced from purchased fruit. It reveals enticingly intense aromatics of red currants and cassis as well as a perfectly balanced, highly structured, superconcentrated, and awe-inspiring depth of cherries, blackberries, and stones. Full bodied, thick and spectacularly long, this may well be the Pommard of the vintage. Anticipated maturity: 2001–2009.

The superb, dark-colored 1995 Corton Perrières Vieilles Vignes offers deep aromas of fabulously ripe dark fruits, Asian spices, and new oak as well as a gloriously viscous, awesomely powerful, and full-bodied core of concentrated, extracted, and intense blackberries, candied plums, and metallic flavors. This unbelievably long, rich, and succulent wine will be at its best between 2000 and 2007. Bravo!

Vincent Girardin's 1996s are generally fresher and more supple than his 1995s but are not as concentrated or structured. Since he personally prefers softer-style wines, Girardin favors the 1996 vintage. My feeling is that many of his 1995s will develop better over time than these delicious midterm drinking wines.

The 1996 Maranges Clos des Loyères Vieilles Vignes has a ruby color and a blackberry-scented nose as well as a medium body, beautiful ripeness, and a silky texture. Tangy black currants, raspberries, and metallic flavors can be found in this charming offering. Drink it before 2002. Similarly colored, the 1996 Santenay Clos de La Confrèrie offers violet and cherry aromas as well as a medium-bodied, highly structured, and powerful mineral and blackberry-flavored palate. The barrel sample I tasted appeared a touch tannic on the finish, but I suspect this will be resolved before bottling. Anticipated maturity: now–2000. The medium to dark ruby-colored 1996 Santenay La Maladière reveals sweet blackberry scents and a beautifully ripe, medium-bodied, bright, and deep core of metallic, stone, mineral, and luscious cherry flavors. Its long, soft finish ends on traces of oak spice and black raspberries. Anticipated maturity: now–2001. The 1996 Santenay Les Gravières is ruby colored and offers a steel and black cherry-infused nose. Its silky textured and rich medium body is awash in deliciously tangy red berry fruits, minerals, and ironlike flavors. I tasted this wine immediately after its bottling and found its finish to be a tad short and slightly dry. It should be drunk by 2000. The medium to dark ruby-colored 1996 Beaune Clos des Vignes Franches aromatically displays loads of sweet red and black cherries. On the palate, this medium-bodied, velvety-textured wine is superripe, expansive, expressive, and densely packed with candied red fruits and traces of minerals. It should be at its peak between now and 2003.

In the majority of vintages, red Chassagnes suffer from hard, rustic tannins. However, in 1996 I found a number of truly first-rate wines offered from this village renowned primarily for its whites. Girardin's 1996 Chassagne-Montrachet Clos de La Boudriotte Vieilles Vignes is a wonderful wine, exhibiting a ruby color and floral, violet aromas. Its personality is medium to full bodied, thickly textured, intense, and filled with ripe and succulent black cherries. This bright and lively, yet soft and supple wine should be consumed over the next 4 years. The slightly darker-colored 1996 Chassagne-Montrachet Morgeot is highly impressive. Blackberry and mineral scents give way to a luscious and awesomely oily-textured character loaded with sweet red and black cherries. This wine also possesses a long and glycerin-filled finish that reveals soft, ripe tannins. Anticipated maturity: now–2004.

The dark ruby-colored 1996 Volnay Santenots offers an intense nose of ripe black fruits and hints of tar. Its character is marked by a medium to full body, a velvety texture, great depth, and layered sweet plums, blackberries, and minerals. Anticipated maturity: now–2004. Revealing mineral and boysenberry aromatics, the 1996 Volnay Champans exhibits a quite structured, almost foursquare, medium- to full-bodied, firm personality packed with stone and black fruit flavors. It should be at its peak between 2000 and 2005. The outstanding and dark ruby-colored 1996 Volnay Clos des Chênes offers a wonderfully intriguing nose of mocha-covered black raspberries as well as a deep, intense, full-bodied, concentrated, and extracted core of dark cherries, plums, blueberries, and traces of earth. This wine is neither opulent nor seductive; rather, it is serious, structured, powerful, and extremely well proportioned. Anticipated maturity: 2000–2005.

Exhibiting a dark ruby color and huge quantities of ripe black fruits on the nose, the 1996 Pommard Clos de Lambots Vieilles Vignes is a thick-textured, full-bodied, juicy, elegant, and rich wine packed with sweet cherries, blackberries, blueberries, and traces of fresh herbs. This succulent wine should be drunk between now and 2004. Equally dark colored, the 1996 Pommard Les Chanlins Vieilles Vignes boasts a lively nose of roses, sweet black cherries, and traces of underbrush. Its full-bodied personality is chewy textured, mineral and blackberry laced, and somewhat backward for a 1996. This intensely concentrated and well-balanced wine may merit a higher rating when it reaches its peak between 2002 and 2005. Sporting a dark ruby-colored robe, the 1996 Pommard Les Epenots beguiles with its sultry wild blueberry, spice, and intense aromatics. On the palate, this rich, profound, dense, and powerful wine is full bodied, thick, and packed with black fruits, sweet plums, and earth tones. Anticipated maturity: 2002–2006. I look forward to serving the 1996 Pommard Les Rugiens Vieilles Vignes side by side with the 1995 in about 6 or 7 years. My feeling is that the more muscular 1995 will stand out, but I'm convinced the 1996 will be superb. It is dark ruby colored and possesses a deep, dense, black fruit-scented nose as well as a strong, focused, full-bodied, and oily-textured character. Sweet cherries, traces of licorice, cassis, and

Asian spices can be found in this structured and delicious wine. Anticipated maturity: 2002–2006.

The magnificent 1996 Corton Perrières Vieilles Vignes is dark colored and reveals deep aromas of black fruits, earth, and toasted oak. This wine is highly concentrated, velvety, broad shouldered, muscular, profound, and intensely powerful. Layers of beautifully ripe cassis, black cherries, and prunes are intermingled with iron, violets, and minerals in this complex offering. It should be at its peak between 2002 and 2007. This is the first vintage in which Vincent Girardin is offering a Corton Renardes, and judging from its quality, I hope there are many more to come. Medium to dark ruby colored, this wine exhibits massive ripeness on the nose, displaying scents of raisins, prunes, and chocolate-covered cherries. The palate is no less ripe, offering loads of ripe black cherries, dark raspberries, and cassis, as well as a silky texture and a full body. It does not have quite the depth or concentration of the Perrières but is so opulent, fruit packed, and persistent in the finish as to deserve an equal rating. Anticipated maturity: 2000–2006. Importer: Vineyard Brands, Birmingham, Alabama; phone (205) 980-8802.

DOMAINE HENRI GOUGES (NUITS-ST.-GEORGES)

1996 Nuits-St.-Georges	D	(86–88)
1995 Nuits-St.-Georges	D	(85–87)
1996 Nuits-St.-Georges Les Chaignots	E	(86–88)
1995 Nuits-St.-Georges Les Chaignots	D	(86–88)
1996 Nuits-St.-Georges Clos des Porrets St. Georges	E	(87–89)
1995 Nuits-St.-Georges Clos des Porrets St. Georges	E	(87–90)
1996 Nuits-St.-Georges Les Pruliers	E	(88–90)
1995 Nuits-St.-Georges Les Pruliers	D	(87–90)
1996 Nuits-St.-Georges Les St. Georges	E	(91–93+)
1995 Nuits-St.-Georges Les St. Georges	E	(88–91)
1996 Nuits-St.-Georges Les Vaucrains	E	(90–92+)
1995 Nuits-St.-Georges Les Vaucrains	E	(88–91)

Pierre Gouges, who has the responsibility of the vineyards, rarely if ever uses herbicides, fungicides, and pesticides, preferring organic composts. Grass grows freely between the rows of vines because he feels that it prevents erosion and adds stress to the plants, therefore promoting *terroir* typicity. Christian Gouges (Pierre's cousin), responsible for all the cellar work, threw away the estate's filters in 1991. The 1995s are the finest wines from this estate I have tasted, and I hope the progress continues.

Produced from vineyards located throughout the Nuits appellation, the ruby-colored 1995 Nuits-St.-Georges reveals a fresh blackberry aroma and a silky-textured, medium-bodied personality with attractive traces of wild game, dark cherries, and minerals to complement its highly structured core. It requires 2–3 years cellaring and will be at its best for the subsequent 3–4 years. The slightly darker-colored 1995 Nuits-St.-Georges Les Chaignots (produced from young vines) offers a smoky, meaty nose and a rugged, foursquare, medium-bodied, masculine, toasty palate drenched in jammy black fruits with a touch of game. Drink it between now and 2003. Possessing a dark color and a tight, reticent nose offering only a dark, spicy sweetness, the 1995 Nuits-St.-Georges Clos des Porrets St. Georges bursts forth on the palate with black currants, dark cherries, smoky oak notes, a velvety texture, a medium to full body, and a long finish. Rich and concentrated, it will be at its best between 2001 and 2009.

Dark ruby colored, the 1995 Nuits-St.-Georges Les Pruliers offers red currants and blackberries on the nose and a mouthful of rich, concentrated, medium-bodied, delineated but chewy dark fruits and raspberries, ripe, round tannins, and a long, complex finish. Drink it between 2002 and 2009. Slightly lighter colored, the 1995 Nuits-St.-Georges Les Vaucrains displays spicy black cherries aromatically and a chewy, thick, slightly rustic, medium- to full-bodied personality with a persistent finish. Anticipated maturity: 2002–2009. Equally good, the medium to dark ruby-colored 1995 Nuits-St.-Georges Les St. Georges possesses a muted nose but an explosive, intensely chewy mouth jam-packed with huge black fruits (cassis, blackberries, and so on), loads of sun-baked thyme and rosemary, a full body, and a slightly rugged but long finish. It will be at its best between 2002 and 2010.

I am happy to report that progress at Domaine Henri Gouges continues. Run by Pierre and Christian Gouges, responsible respectively for the viticulture and winemaking, the estate is charging forward to reclaim its spot as one of Nuits's most highly respected domaines. As with every estate in Burgundy—most were reluctant to admit it—the 1996 yields were much higher than normal, averaging 3 tons of fruit per acre (as opposed to 2$\frac{1}{3}$ tons in 1995 and 2 tons in 1997). However, the wines are rich and dense and have lovely ripe fruit characteristics. The Gougeses threw out their filters in 1991 and fine only if they feel the tannins require softening. The 1996 wines I tasted were still on their lees (except for the white, which had been bottled in September, 1997) and were going to be racked in February and then bottled a month later (earlier than normal). Christian Gouges felt as though they would not require fining.

The medium to dark ruby-colored 1996 Nuits-St.-Georges has sweet cassis and blackberry aromatics that are followed by a big, lush, supple, and medium- to full-bodied personality. This delicious wine, filled with plump black berry, mineral, and metallic flavors, was a delight to drink from barrel. Anticipated maturity: now–2004. Christian Gouges described the 1996 Nuits-St.-Georges Les Chaignots as being "our young-vine wine," even though I've seen other estates call wines made from vines this old (22 years) *cuvée vieilles vignes.* Everything is relative. This medium to dark ruby-colored wine offers pure aromas of black cherries and licorice and has an earth, stone-laced, minerally, and sweet cherry-flavored profile. This is a masculine, medium- to full-bodied, and detailed offering. Drink it over the next 5–6 years. Similarly colored, the 1996 Nuits-St.-Georges Clos des Porrets St. Georges reveals rich, spicy, and sweet black cherry aromas. It is a feminine-style Nuits, with lush red and black fruits and minerals in its medium- to full-bodied, forward, chewy-textured, and seductive flavor profile. Interestingly, this wine's finish is firmer and more Nuits than its attack or midpalate suggested. However, readers should not be concerned, as the tannins are well ripened and supple. Anticipated maturity: now–2005. The bright, medium to dark ruby-colored 1996 Nuits-St.-Georges Les Pruliers is produced from 60-year-old vines. It displays blueberries and black and purple fruits dusted with minerals, cracked black pepper, and spices, as well as a medium- to full-bodied, juicy, broad, and masculine personality. This foursquare and oily-textured wine has iron, steel, earth, and blackberry flavors and a firm finish. It is a structured and tannic (again, not problematic) Nuits that will require cellaring. Anticipated maturity: 2003–2008.

Both of the Gougeses' final wines are outstanding. Revealing a color verging on dark ruby, the 1996 Nuits-St.-Georges Les Vaucrains (also from 60-year-old vines) has expressive aromas of blackberries, cassis, minerals, and porcini mushrooms. It has intense, mouth-coating, and rich layers of sweet black fruit-drenched stones and earthlike flavors, as well as a rich, broad, and deeply ripe full body. In addition, this very impressive wine offers an extremely long finish loaded with fat and round tannins. Drink it between 2004 and

2009. The 1996 Nuits-St.-Georges Les St. Georges was reserved, yet it will most assuredly have a glorious future. Time, air, and cajoling offered a glimpse at its cassis liqueur, tar, and spicy aromatics. This tightly wound, backward, and firm wine is oily textured, rich, full bodied, and immensely powerful. Behind its broad yet austere, masculine character, I was able to notice superripe blackberries, minerals, and hints of smoked bacon. Its tannins, on display in its formidably long finish, are dense yet supple. Anticipated maturity: 2005–2010+.

DOMAINE MACHARD DE GRAMONT (PRÉMEAUX-PRISSEY)

1996 Vosne-Romanée Les Gaudichots		D	(85–87)

This inconsistent estate is now in the hands of the intelligent Alban de Gramont, a 26-year-old with the flair, potential, brains, and desire to take it to new heights. With the exception of one wine, however, the wines I tasted cannot be recommended for a host of reasons. Some were too high in acid and others too dry and tannic.

The medium to dark ruby-colored 1996 Vosne-Romanée Les Gaudichots offers intense aromas of red and black fruits that give way to a medium-bodied, rich, well-crafted, and defined character. Spicy cherries and blackberries can be found in this silky-textured, elegant wine. Drink it between now and 2004.

DOMAINE JEAN GRIVOT (VOSNE-ROMANÉE)

1996 Bourgogne		C	(85–86)
1996 Clos Vougeot		E	(89–92)
1995 Clos Vougeot		E	93+
1996 Echézeaux		E	(92–94+)
1995 Echézeaux		E	91
1996 Nuits-St.-Georges Les Boudots		D	(90–93)
1995 Nuits-St.-Georges Les Boudots		D	89+
1996 Nuits-St.-Georges Les Charmois		D	(86–88)
1996 Richebourg		EEE	(94–97*)
1995 Richebourg		EEE	95+
1996 Vosne-Romanée		D	(87–89)
1995 Vosne-Romanée		D	87
1996 Vosne-Romanée Beaumonts		D	(90–92+)
1995 Vosne-Romanée Beaumonts		D	89

The Domaine Jean Grivot is brilliantly run by Jean's son Etienne Grivot. He is one of the young vignerons who are driving up the quality of Burgundy's wines. His 1995s are some of the best I tasted in the Côte d'Or, bringing together superb balance with thick, concentrated, and elegant fruit.

The light to medium ruby-colored 1995 Vosne-Romanée reveals enticing aromas of violets and roses and a beautifully balanced, medium-bodied personality packed with black currants, blueberries, and floral notes. Drink it between 2000 and 2007. Slightly darker, the 1995 Vosne-Romanée Beaumonts has a nose reminiscent of the village Vosne but with the added dimension of candied cassis for additional complexity. This oily-textured and medium- to full-bodied wine displays blackberries and dark cherries in its structured and elegant flavor profile. Powerful and armed with an exceptionally long finish, it will be at its peak between 2001 and 2008. Potentially outstanding, the ruby-colored 1995 Nuits-St.-Georges Les Boudots offers a mineral-and-blueberry-filled nose as well as a highly structured, masculine, medium- to full-bodied, and oily-textured palate packed with concentrated and delineated sweet cherries. Anticipated maturity: 2001–2009.

Medium to dark ruby colored and with a blackberry, mineral, and underbrush-infused nose, the beautifully elegant yet powerful 1995 Echézeaux displays an oily, chewy, medium-to full-bodied character packed with red and black cherries. Exceedingly long and possessing big, ripe tannins, this delicious wine should be at its peak between 2002 and 2010. One of the finest Clos Vougeots produced in 1995, Grivot's exhibits a bright, medium to dark ruby color and sublime aromatics of Asian spices, cinnamon, violets, and ripe red fruits. This full-bodied wine offers a thick texture and an amazingly refined yet powerful burst of sweet cherries, spices, and minerals as well as a spectacularly long, well-defined and pure finish. It will be at its best between 2004 and 2012. Even better, and one of the best burgundies I tasted in June 1997, the dark ruby-colored 1995 Richebourg floored me with its highly complex nose of superripe cassis, plums, and black cherries. Its awesomely concentrated and massively endowed, thick-textured personality is jam-packed with chewy and fabulously extracted cherry flavors intermingled with Asian spices, cinnamon, and notes of underbrush. Gorgeously structured and amazingly long, it will be at its peak between 2004 and 2012+.

Note: The following wines had finished their malolactic fermentations in September 1997 and had been racked and sulfured two weeks before my visit (the sole exception to this is the Richebourg, which was racked, not sulfured, and was just finishing its malos). This process can have the effect of temporarily drying out the fruit and decreasing the intensity of color in wines. Some of these wines were difficult to taste the day of my visit. If anything, they will become darker, have more body, and be lusher than my notes would suggest.

"The most important thing for me is harmony. I don't want hard and tannic wines. Those that are too tannic will never be good." So stated Etienne Grivot, the tall, intelligent, basset hound–eyed, youngish man in charge of the domaine that bears his father's name. This estate produces some of Burgundy's finest wines, and consumers need to search them out before their prices reflect their quality.

The ruby/purple-colored 1996 Bourgogne offers spicy black currant aromas and a medium-bodied, tangy, silky, and lively core of red currants and blueberries. This delicious and refreshing wine should be consumed over the next 2–3 years.

The darker-colored 1996 Nuits-St.-Georges Les Charmois reveals a nose of perfume, violets, and black currants as well as a delightfully supple, medium-bodied, red currant, and cassis-flavored character. This is a simple yet immensely pleasing wine that will provide early drinking. Anticipated maturity: now–2004. Displaying a medium to dark ruby color and scents of roses, lilies, and red currants, the 1996 Vosne-Romanée is a medium-bodied, attractively packed wine with dark fruits and violets. Although it has a velvety texture, this offering finishes on a dryish, oaky note that I attribute to its recent racking and sulfuring. I am confident the final wine will merit an excellent rating. Anticipated maturity: now–2005.

Exhibiting a medium to dark ruby color and fabulous aromas of black cherries, flowers, Asian spices, and toasty oak, the 1996 Vosne-Romanée Les Beaumonts has extraordinary richness, depth, and refinement. This medium- to full-bodied, silky, complex, focused, and fat wine is filled with tangy red currants, cherries, candied orange peels, and a firm structure. This admirably long wine should be at its peak between 2002 and 2008. The darker-colored 1996 Nuits-St.-Georges Les Boudots has a rich, fragrant, toasted-oak-scented nose as well as a marvelously concentrated, full-bodied, superripe, elegant, deeply rich, and velvety character. This wine has layers of intense and sweet black cherries, Asian spices, and hints of minerals and grilled oak flavors that coat the palate throughout its long and persistent finish. Anticipated maturity: 2003–2009.

Grivot's deep ruby/purple-colored 1996 Clos Vougeot offers aromas of strongly spiced black cherries dusted with earth. This rich, concentrated, dense, full-bodied, and thick wine is crammed with blackberries, cherries, cassis, stones, Asian spices, and toasted oak. It lacks the elegance of the two previous wines but is more expressive and powerful. Anticipated maturity: 2003–2009. The 1996 Echézeaux is a stunning example of this all too often weak grand cru. It possesses enthralling aromas of black raspberries, dark cherries, beef blood, and Asian spices that give way to an oily-textured, magnificently concentrated, highly refined, and very focused personality. This superbly sweet and lush offering is feminine, opulent, well structured, and powerful. Its prodigiously long finish reveals loads of soft tannins. Drink it between 2003 and 2010.

Even though I have a stated policy of reviewing only wines that have completed their malolactic fermentations, I decided to make an exception for Grivot's spectacular 1996 Richebourg. First, its malos were virtually finished, and second, readers deserve to know about this wine's sublime qualities. It offers a gorgeously bright medium to dark ruby color and extraordinary fragrances of superripe plums, cherries, and morel mushrooms. This brooding, powerful, full-bodied, mouth-coating, and refined blockbuster is crammed with awesomely sweet black raspberries, cherries, candied strawberries, cassis, stones, and raw meat flavors that last throughout its unending finish. Wow! Bravo!

DOMAINE ROBERT GROFFIER (MOREY-ST.-DENIS)

1996 Bonnes Mares	EE	95+
1995 Bonnes Mares	EE	92
1996 Bourgogne	C	88
1996 Chambertin Clos de Bèze	EE	95
1995 Chambertin Clos de Bèze	EE	(91–92+)
1996 Chambolle-Musigny Les Amoureuses	EE	93+
1995 Chambolle-Musigny Les Amoureuses	E	91
1996 Chambolle-Musigny Les Hauts Doigts	E	89
1995 Chambolle-Musigny Les Hauts Doigts	D	88
1996 Chambolle-Musigny Les Sentiers	E	91
1995 Chambolle-Musigny Les Sentiers	D	89
1996 Gevrey-Chambertin	D	89
1995 Gevrey-Chambertin	D	86

I was impressed with Robert Groffier's 1995s. They displayed good ripeness, concentration, and structure. It is the first vintage where his wines will not be subjected to either a fining or a filtration. I have purchased, drunk, and cellared some of his previous vintages (and sold them when I worked in retail) and have seen the heights this domaine is capable of achieving.

Medium to dark ruby colored, the 1995 Gevrey-Chambertin reveals dark cherry and spice aromas and an attractive burst of crisp berry fruit that tailed off quickly. Drink it within 4 years of its release. A step up, the delicious 1995 Chambolle-Musigny Les Hauts Doigts offers fat, chewy, black cherries, dark berries, red apple, and spice flavors to complement its good length and structure. Enjoyable now, it will age well for 8 years. Displaying dark cherries on the nose, the dark ruby-colored 1995 Chambolle-Musigny Les Sentiers is an elegant, thick, sweet, chewy floral wine with excellent concentration and length. Structured and medium to full bodied, it will be at its best between 2000 and 2006.

A superb wine, the dark-colored 1995 Chambolle-Musigny Les Amoureuses reveals an attractive nose composed of black cherries and violets and a fabulously chewy, thick, and velvety mouth densely packed with flowers, berries, and a touch of earth. Full bodied, this outstanding offering can be drunk in 5 years or cellared until 2010. Even better, the masculine, highly concentrated, dark purple-colored 1995 Bonnes Mares aromatically displays mocha, chocolate scents to go along with its superb underlying sweetness. Jammy overripe fruits cascade over the palate; this is a huge, thick, and chewy wine. What a delight! Powerful, intense, complex, and full bodied, it will drink splendidly between 2001 and 2010. Potentially a spectacular wine, the Chambertin Clos de Bèze was the only 1995 Groffier offering that had not been bottled. Behind its dark, floral aromas a dense, brooding ripe sweetness of black fruits can be discerned with coaxing. On the palate, this intensely concentrated, extracted, chewy, thick, and full-bodied monster reveals copious amounts of baked fruits, mocha, stones, minerals, and dark, roasted spices in its flavor profile. Long and built to last, it should be at its peak between 2005 and 2015.

Each and every 1996 at Domaine Robert Groffier was a first-rate example of its *terroir*, from the Bourgogne to the grands crus. The meticulous work of Serge Groffier (Robert's son) in the vineyards is evidenced by each glassful of nectar from this well-known and certainly soon-to-be-famous domaine.

All the following wines were bottled unfined and unfiltered between December 1, 1997, and mid-January 1998.

The medium to dark ruby-colored 1996 Bourgogne reveals intense, sweet, and expressive aromas of raspberries drenched in cream and dusted with confectioners' sugar. This excellent, silky-textured, plump, and medium-bodied wine is filled with luscious layers of fat, deeply ripe black cherries. If it had been complex, I would have ecstatically given this superior regional appellation wine an outstanding score. Drink it over the next 3–4 years. The 1996 Gevrey-Chambertin displays a spicy, grilled oak, and dark cherry-scented nose. This delicious wine (note the boisterous red and black fruit and stone-filled character) is harmonious, lively, medium bodied, and velvety textured and has brilliant intensity and power. It is more complex and structured than the previous offering and possesses a long, well-focused finish. Anticipated maturity: now–2004.

Produced from a vineyard that serves as Les Amoureuses's northeastern border, the ruby-colored 1996 Chambolle-Musigny Les Hauts Doigts has smoky, grilled meat, and sweet cherry aromas. On the palate, this offering has excellent power, structure, and density and is crammed with blueberries, boysenberries, stones, and metallic shavings. It is medium to full bodied, firm, and somewhat foursquare (I would have guessed Nuits-St.-Georges in a blind tasting). Anticipated maturity: 2000–2006. The first-rate 1996 Chambolle-Musigny Les Sentiers has a medium to dark ruby color and lovely violet, rose blossom, and blackberry fragrances. This powerful, oily-textured, dense, and medium- to full-bodied wine has expansiveness on the palate and layers of black cherries, rocks, brambleberries, and fresh herbs. Its impressively long and drawn-out finish reveals a soft and supple backbone. It should be at its best between 2000 and 2008.

Groffier's medium to dark ruby-colored 1996 Chambolle-Musigny Les Amoureuses is a grand cru in quality, if not officially. Its perfumed nose of roses, sweet red fruits, blackberries, and hints of freshly laid asphalt leads to a stunning, medium- to full-bodied, and silky-textured personality. Readers will be enthralled by this wine's richness, purity, and precision, as well as by its extraction and depth of fruit. It offers intense layers of black cherries, Asian spices, and just a hint of new oak toastiness. This refined yet muscular and formidably long Amoureuses is a formidable wine. Drink it between 2003 and 2010. The extraordinary 1996 Bonnes Mares (it may ultimately be better than the superb Chambertin Clos de Bèze) is dark ruby colored and displays awesome aromas of deeply ripe cassis, blackberries, and violets. It is oily textured, superextracted, rich, ample, broad, and concentrated. This masculine, structured, and muscular wine is also refined, delineated, and lively.

Waves of candied plums, blueberries, and cherries are intermingled with oak, spices, and mineral flavors in this immensely long and admirable Bonnes Mares. Anticipated maturity: 2003–2012+. Incredible as it may seem after the previous description, the dark ruby-colored 1996 Chambertin Clos de Bèze is even bigger, denser, and more muscular. Produced from 55-year-old vines, it displays smoke, blackberry, cassis, stones, beef blood, and Asian spices on the nose. This brooding, fat, broad-shouldered, massively deep, intense, and chewy-textured wine has a highly concentrated and extracted full body. It possesses a tannic (soft, round tannins that will most assuredly melt with cellaring) structure and loads of superripe black fruits. This is a stellar example of its highly reputed *terroir*. My instincts suggest that the Bonnes Mares may become even more complex in time, but there is no doubting the sublime quality of this Bèze. Bravo to Robert and Serge Groffier!

DOMAINE ANNE GROS (VOSNE-ROMANÉE)
(Formerly Known as Domaine Anne et François Gros)

1996	Bourgogne "Pinot Noir"	D	88
1996	Chambolle-Musigny La Combe d'Orveaux	E	89?
1995	Clos Vougeot	EEE	(91–93)
1996	Clos Vougeot Le Grand Maupertui	EE	92+
1996	Richebourg	EEE	93+
1995	Richebourg	EEE	(92–94)
1996	Vosne-Romanée Les Barreaux	D	90
1995	Vosne-Romanée Les Barreaux	D	(89–91)

Anne Gros has bought out her father François's interest in this estate and is making superextracted, black, deeply layered, intense wines. The two grands crus are lightly filtered but not fined, and she uses between 80% and 90% new oak on both. I consider it impossible to produce an inkier wine from Pinot Noir than she did in 1995. Readers who search out Pinot Noir with refined notes of strawberries, raspberries, and tangy cherries should be aware that these wines are the antithesis.

Very dark colored, the 1995 Vosne-Romanée Les Barreaux displays penetrating aromas of superripe black fruits and berries and a flavor profile packed with chewy, hyperconcentrated, floral blackberries and cassis. Deep and rich, this powerful wine should be consumed between 2000 and 2007. Even darker, aromatically the fragrant 1995 Clos Vougeot explodes with highly concentrated cassis and blueberries. In the inky, almost impenetrable mouth, abundant quantities of toasted dark fruits, oak, and Asian spices are found in this full-bodied hunk of a wine. Long and powerful, it will require considerable patience. Anticipated maturity: 2004–2014. Just as dark as the Clos Vougeot, but even more prodigiously concentrated, the 1995 Richebourg is among the blackest and inkiest (both in color and taste) Pinot Noirs I have tasted. Exhibiting sweet Asian spices and grilled black fruits on the nose, this behemoth is a rich, chewy, rugged, silky-textured wine packed with superripe, highly concentrated ripe berries. Possessing impressive depth and structure, this wine may well deserve a higher rating when it has had time to soften out. Drink it between 2005 and 2015+.

Readers looking for ruby-colored, delicate, refined, elegant wines to drink over the next decade are well advised to shop elsewhere. Domaine Anne Gros's offerings are highly extracted monsters. Anne Gros is pushing the extraction and concentration envelope of these wines to uncharted limits. These inky, hugely dense, and highly structured wines may, in time, evolve into stellar burgundies, meriting significantly higher ratings than the ones I've provided, but wines of such sheer size and weight do not always age gracefully. Time will tell.

The medium to dark ruby-colored 1996 Bourgogne "Pinot Noir" reveals candied blackberry and blueberry aromas as well as a powerful, lively, dense, concentrated, and thick core of black cherries and hints of tar. It also possesses a long finish that reveals supple tannins and additional layers of deeply ripe fruit. Drink it over the next 5 years.

The 1996 Chambolle-Musigny La Combe d'Orveaux has a dark ruby color and an elegant, dense, violet-imbued nose. This full-bodied, chewy-textured, extracted, and hugely powerful wine shovels superripe blackberries, cassis, and candied grapefruits (!) across the taster's palate. I am concerned about the hard, dry tannins its finish revealed. If they soften over the course of the next 3 or 4 years, this wine will certainly be excellent and potentially outstanding. The dark ruby/black-colored 1996 Vosne-Romanée Les Barreaux conveys an impression of cookie dough soaked in cherry syrup and covered with Peking duck skins. This is a massively structured, muscular, highly concentrated, creamy-textured, and extracted wine. Its flavor profile is densely packed with black cherries, blackberries, cinnamon sticks, and Asian spices, particularly the condiment called hoisin. Anticipated maturity: 2002–2008.

Anne Gros's black-colored 1996 Clos Vougeot Le Grand Maupertui offers aromas of creamy red cherries and Asian spices imbued with charred oak. An explosion of superextracted and massively powerful cassis, blackberries, and brambleberries assault the palate in this full-bodied, chewy-textured, and unbelievably dense wine. It is inconceivable to imagine a more concentrated and intensely packed wine. Its formidably long finish displays satiny yet firm tannins. In 10 or more years, if this wine has evolved, my score may appear pathetically low. Anticipated maturity: 2004–2012+. The 1996 Richebourg is also inky black colored, but its tightly wound blackberry, cassis, and mint scents are quite different from the Clos Vougeot's. Superripe cherries, black raspberries, and cassis are drenched in copious quantities of fat and round tannins in this blockbuster's flavor profile. This is an expansive, thickly textured, full-bodied, highly extracted, and awesomely powerful wine that impresses by its size, balance, density of fruit, and sublime length. Anticipated maturity: 2005–2012+.

DOMAINE PIERRE GUILLEMOT (SAVIGNY-LÈS-BEAUNE)

1995 Savigny-Lès-Beaune Les Jarrons	C	88
1995 Savigny-Lès-Beaune Les Serpentières	C	89

The medium to dark ruby-colored 1995 Savigny-Lès-Beaune Les Serpentières reveals a masculine nose of wet stones and blackberries and a delicious, silky-textured medium- to full-bodied personality jam-packed with black cherries, slate, cracked black pepper, and minerals. This highly structured wine is complex, concentrated, and a delight to drink. Anticipated maturity: now–2005. I was extremely taken by the medium to dark ruby-colored 1995 Savigny-Lès-Beaune Les Jarrons. It offers black raspberry, stone, and roasting spice aromas as well as a fabulously oily-textured, well-delineated, medium- to full-bodied, and structured mouthful of dark cherries and minerals. This fabulous offering is superby concentrated and has an extremely long finish. A real winner and an excellent value!

DOMAINE ANTONIN ET DOMINIQUE GUYON (SAVIGNY-LÈS-BEAUNE)

1996 Aloxe-Corton Les Vercots	D	(87–88)
1996 Chambolle-Musigny	D	(88–89)
1996 Corton-Bressandes	D	(90–92)
1996 Gevrey-Chambertin	D	(86–88)
1996 Hautes Côtes de Nuits	C	86
1996 Pernand-Vergelesses Les Vergelesses	D	(87–89)
1996 Volnay Clos des Chênes	D	(88–91)

At first glance, Domaine Antonin et Dominique Guyon in Savigny-Lès-Beaune appears to be an old-style winery, steeped in tradition. However, as I listened to the winemaking techniques employed by this large estate (118½ acres that stretch from one end of the Côte d'Or to the other), I realized how modern and avant-garde Guyon has become.

For the past 10 years no commercial fertilizers have been added to the vineyards, as Guyon believes they rob the *terroir* of its natural balance. At harvest the grapes are placed in small stackable boxes to ensure that they will not be harmed during movement to the winery. Once there, each bunch is inspected on sorting tables for imperfections (rot, mildew, unripe berries). The bunches that pass inspection are destemmed and undergo a cold maceration that lasts 5–6 days (this "cold soak" has been stretched to 12 days when deemed necessary). Alcoholic fermentations (at 28 degrees Celsius) are long, most often between 10 and 20 days, and are followed by a 3-day soak at 32 degrees. Each day during this process a vigorous *pigéage* is performed. Following a 48-hour *débourbage* (the decanting of the wine off its gross lees), the wines are transferred to oak barrels. Each 228-liter barrel (the traditional Burgundian size) is filled with 218 liters of wine, 10 liters of fine lees, and no sulfur. The malos take place generally in April or May, but the wines are not racked. If it is deemed necessary, the lees are sulfured using a long, intravenouslike needle. According to Guyon, this process ensures that the wine does not come into unwanted contact with air and treats the problem (the theory being that any potential problem remedied by the addition of sulfur is caused by the lees, so why risk drying out the wine if the lees can be treated independently).

In July all the barrels are racked, separating the lees from the wine, and sulfured (the lees receive 10 centiliters of sulfur, the wine 5 centiliters). The lees are then placed back into the bottom of the barrels, followed by the wine. In January, at bottling, there are no more lees left in the barrels. According to the Guyon team, the wines have completely consumed them, adding depth and richness to their flavor profiles.

The results of all these efforts speak for themselves. Domaine Guyon's wines are excellent, displaying plenty of ripe, concentrated fruit.

The medium to dark ruby-colored 1996 Pernand-Vergelesses Les Vergelesses was aged in 20% new oak barrels. Offering a blackberry, stone, and toasty nose, it is a large, chewy-textured, medium- to full-bodied, and expansive wine with excellent depth and loads of tangy black cherry fruit. It should be at its best between now and 2004. Similarly colored, the 1996 Volnay Clos des Chênes reveals floral (roses and violets) and red berry aromatics complemented by a concentrated, fat, deeply extracted, and structured core of dense blackberries, cherries, and raspberries. This admirably long and masculine wine should be at its peak of maturity between 2000 and 2005. The ruby/purple-colored 1996 Aloxe-Corton Les Vercots, aged in 30% new oak barrels, displays stone, gravel, and blueberrylike scents followed by a plum, brambleberry, and metallic character. It is medium to full bodied, chewy, and velvety textured, yet its finish possesses rustic tannins that prevent it from receiving a higher rating. Anticipated maturity: 2000–2004.

The superb, ruby/purple-colored 1996 Corton-Bressandes has a fabulous nose of flowers, cherries, minerals, and oak spices. On the palate, layer after layer of expansive and candied red cherries can be found in this broad, superripe, oily-textured, and supple wine. I would suggest cellaring it for 2–3 years. Anticipated maturity: 2001–2006.

The ruby purple-colored 1996 Hautes Côtes de Nuits was vinified in both barrels (15%) and *foudres* (85%). It is a delicious, pleasurable, well-crafted, and creamy-textured wine offering Bing cherries and sweet raspberries. Quaff this reasonably priced burgundy over the next 2–3 years. The 1996 Chambolle-Musigny is ruby colored and offers lovely aromatics reminiscent of violets and perfumed red cherries. This lively, beautifully concentrated and extracted wine is elegant, medium to full bodied, silky textured, and packed with sweet and floral red fruits. Its persistent finish reveals additional layers of raspberries and cherries as well as soft and supple tannins. Anticipated maturity: now–2003. The darker-colored 1996 Gevrey-Chambertin has an appealing nose of blueberries intermingled with cherries and a foursquare, highly structured, and chewy-textured core of blackberries and stones. This austere, medium- to full-bodied, and backward wine will require cellaring. Anticipated maturity: 2000–2004.

DOMAINE HAEGELEN-JAYER (VOSNE-ROMANÉE)

1996	Chambolle-Musigny Combe d'Orveaux	D	(86–88?)
1995	Chambolle-Musigny Combe d'Orveaux	E	(87–89)
1996	Clos Vougeot Vieilles Vignes	EE	(92–95)
1995	Clos Vougeot Vieilles Vignes	EE	(93–95)
1996	Echézeaux	EE	(89–91+)
1995	Echézeaux	EE	(90–92)
1995	Nuits-St.-Georges	D	(84–86)
1996	Nuits-St.-Georges Les Damodes	D	(86–88)
1995	Nuits-St.-Georges Les Damodes	E	(86–88)
1996	Vosne-Romanée	D	(85–87)

A former high school physical education teacher who is originally from Alsace, Alfred Haegelen (married to a Jayer, hence the domaine's name) produces one of Burgundy's finest Clos Vougeots. A charming, intelligent man, Haegelen fashions concentrated, rich, and exciting wines. If he were to apply the magic touch he uses on the Clos Vougeot to his other offerings, he would qualify as one of Burgundy's handful of top growers. Haegelen never filters, but he does fine his wines.

Medium to dark ruby colored, the 1995 Nuits-St.-Georges displays red and black berries on the nose and a supple, silky-textured, structured, sweet, tobacco, and mineral-tinged flavor profile. Medium bodied, this 1995 will be at its best between now and 2003. Revealing a beautiful ruby/purple color, the 1995 Nuits-St.-Georges Les Damodes exhibited a tight, floral nose and an oily-textured, violet, deep berry, mineral, spicy personality. Showing good ripeness and underlying power, this medium- to full-bodied wine should be drunk between 2001 and 2007. Produced from 40-year-old vines, the medium to dark ruby-colored 1995 Chambolle-Musigny La Combe d'Orveau possesses super, deep, floral, and dark cherry aromas and a delicious, elegant sweet dark berry-flavored character. Medium bodied and long, it will provide considerable enjoyment between 2000 and 2006.

Originally part of the Jayer holding of Echézeaux, Haegelen's lovely 1995 is dark ruby colored and displays a massive explosion of violets, black and red cherries, and Asian spices. Concentrated and supple, it possesses excellent structure and length. Delicious already, it will be even better between 2002 and 2010. The star of the show, the dark-colored 1995 Clos Vougeot Vieilles Vignes exhibits a sweet, gorgeous nose containing myriad spices, perfume, flowers, and superripe, sweet red fruits. Bursting with unctuously textured flavors of lightly roasted cherries in its elegant yet chewy mouth, this fabulous, full-bodied wine possesses precision, beauty, and admirable length. Spectacular to drink, it will improve over the next 12 years.

The dark-colored 1996 Vosne-Romanée (harvested at a little under 3 tons of fruit per acre) has red cherry and blackberry aromas that are followed by a well-defined, soft, precise, broad, and medium-bodied core of black cherries. Drink it over the next 4 years. The similarly colored 1996 Nuits-St.-Georges Les Damodes reveals a nose of blackberries and fresh herbs as well as a rich, sweet, tangy, medium-bodied, and fat character with mineral, stone, iron, cassis, and orange peel flavors. Anticipated maturity: now–2005. Displaying a medium to dark ruby color and scents reminiscent of violets and blackberries soaked in vanilla-imbued oak, the 1996 Chambolle-Musigny Combe d'Orveaux is a rich, chewy-textured, broad, medium-bodied, and sweet cherry-laced wine. Its finish reveals a high level of acidity, which gives me some concern.

Exhibiting a dark ruby color and superripe plummy fruit aromas, the 1996 Echézeaux (it, as well as the Clos Vougeot, was harvested at 2¹/₃ tons of fruit per acre) is a powerful, concentrated, fat, broad, full-bodied, and chewy wine that somehow manages to also be subtle and feminine. Layers of red and black cherries intermingled with hints of earth and minerals grace this wine's character and its long, firm finish. Anticipated maturity: 2003–2008. As is usually the case, the star is the estate's superb 1996 Clos Vougeot. Dark ruby colored and offering candied black fruit scents interspersed with floral and red currant fragrances, this hugely concentrated, extracted, and expansive wine is densely packed with seamless layers of blackberries, cassis liqueur, Asian spices, and stones. It is broad shouldered, full bodied, and elegant and possesses an incredibly long and fabulously precise finish. It will be fascinating to taste it side by side with the magnificent 1995 in a decade or so. Anticipated maturity: 2004–2012.

MAISON LOUIS JADOT (BEAUNE)

1995	Auxey-Duresses	C	(84–86)
1995	Beaune Boucherottes	D	(85–87)
1996	Beaune Bressandes	D	(88–90)
1996	Beaune Les Chouacheux	D	(88–90)
1996	Beaune Clos des Couchereaux	D	(88–91)
1995	Beaune Clos des Couchereaux	D	(86–88)
1996	Beaune Theurons	D	(89–91+)
1995	Beaune Theurons	D	(87–89+)
1996	Beaune Clos des Ursules	D	(88–91+)
1996	Bonnes Mares	EE	(94–96+)
1995	Bonnes Mares	EE	(91–94)
1996	Chambertin	EE	(90–92+)
1996	Chambertin Clos de Bèze	EE	(92–95)
1995	Chambertin Clos de Bèze	EE	(91–94)
1996	Chambolle-Musigny	D	(87–89)
1995	Chambolle-Musigny	D	(85–87)
1996	Chambolle-Musigny Les Amoureuses	EE	(91–93)
1995	Chambolle-Musigny Les Amoureuses	EE	(89–92+)
1995	Chambolle-Musigny Les Baudes	E	(86–89)
1996	Chambolle-Musigny Les Feusselottes	E	(88–91)
1996	Chambolle-Musigny Les Fuées	D	(90–92+)
1996	Chapelle Chambertin	EE	(92–94)
1995	Chapelle Chambertin	EE	(89–91+)

1996	Charmes Chambertin	EE	(88–90)
1995	Charmes Chambertin	EE	(88–91)
1995	Chassagne-Montrachet Morgeot	D	(86–89)
1996	Chassagne-Montrachet Morgeot Duc de Magenta	D	(89–91)
1996	Clos de la Roche	E	(89–91)
1996	Clos St. Denis	EE	(89–92)
1995	Clos St. Denis	EE	(89–92)
1996	Clos Vougeot	E	(93–95+)
1995	Clos Vougeot	E	(88–91+)
1996	Corton Grèves	E	(92–94)
1996	Corton Pougets	E	(88–90)
1995	Corton Pougets	E	(88–90+)
1996	Côtes de Beaune-Villages	B	(85–87)
1996	Côtes de Nuits-Villages	D	(86–88)
1996	Echézeaux	EE	(89–91)
1995	Echézeaux	EE	(88–90)
1996	Gevrey-Chambertin	D	(85–87)
1995	Gevrey-Chambertin	D	(85–88)
1996	Gevrey-Chambertin Clos St. Jacques	E	(91–93+)
1995	Gevrey-Chambertin Clos St. Jacques	E	(91–94)
1996	Gevrey-Chambertin Estournelles St. Jacques	D	(90–92)
1995	Gevrey-Chambertin Estournelles St. Jacques	E	(90–93)
1996	Grands-Echézeaux	EE	(91–93)
1995	Marsannay	C	(84–87)
1996	Mazis-Chambertin	EE	(90–93)
1996	Monthélie	C	(85–87)
1995	Monthélie	C	(84–86)
1996	Musigny	EEE	(93–95+)
1995	Musigny	EEE	(90–93)
1996	Nuits-St.-Georges	D	(84–87)
1996	Nuits-St.-Georges Les Boudots	E	(89–92)
1995	Nuits-St.-Georges Les Boudots	E	(88–91)
1996	Nuits-St.-Georges Les Porrets	D	(87–90)
1996	Pernand-Vergelesses Clos de la Croix de Pierre	C	(86–88)
1996	Pommard	D	(86–88)
1995	Pommard	D	(84–86)

1996	Pommard Grands Epenots	D	(88–91)
1995	Pommard Grands Epenots	D	(87–89+)
1996	Richebourg	EEE	(92–94+)
1996	Romanée-St.-Vivant	EEE	(91–93)
1996	Ruchottes-Chambertin	EE	(91–93+)
1996	Santenay Clos de Malte	C	(86–88)
1995	Santenay Clos de Malte	C	(84–87)
1996	Savigny-Lès-Beaune La Dominode	C	(88–90+)
1995	Savigny-Lès-Beaune La Dominode	C	(85–88)
1996	Savigny-Lès-Beaune Clos des Guettes	C	(87–89)
1996	Savigny-Lès-Beaune Les Lavières	C	(87–89)
1995	Savigny-Lès-Beaune Les Vergelesses	C	(85–88)
1996	Volnay Clos de La Barre	D	(89–92)
1995	Volnay Clos de La Barre	D	(86–89)
1996	Volnay Les Santenots	D	(85–87+)
1996	Vosne-Romanée	D	(86–88)
1995	Vosne-Romanée	D	(85–87)
1996	Vosne-Romanée Les Petits Monts	E	(87–89)
1996	Vosne-Romanée Les Suchots	E	(89–92)
1995	Vosne-Romanée Les Suchots	E	(87–89)

Pierre-Henri Gagey, the director of this well-respected *négociant* house, echoed the sentiments of many Burgundians when he stated that the greatest impediment to Burgundy's reputation is that "appellations sell wines, regardless of quality." By this he means that too many consumers purchase burgundies based on the reputation of their vineyard of origin and not on the merits of the wine or its producer. He shares my sentiment that better-educated consumers and a quality-driven younger group of vignerons and *négociants* have changed the overall quality of the region's wines for the better. He singled out Etienne Grivot (Domaine Jean Grivot), Christophe Roumier, Bruno Clair, Dominique Lafon, Gerard Boudot (Domaine Etienne Sauzet), and Jean-Marc Boillot as being some of the pioneers of this younger generation.

Jacques Lardière, this firm's extremely talented winemaker, employs what he describes as a "hands off" winemaking philosophy. Jadot's reds do not undergo temperature-controlled fermentation or pumping-over (*remontage*) of the juice onto the cap. Only traditional *pigéage* techniques are employed. The malolactic fermentations generally take place in the spring (the malos of the 1995s continued until September 1996!) following the harvest, and only one racking (at bottling) is performed. The wines are rarely filtered, and no enzymes are added in order to "consume" suspended proteins.

Overall, 1995 is another in a string of successful vintages for Jadot. If there is one *négociant* house consumers can feel comfortable buying blindly, vintage to vintage, it is Jadot.

Beautifully bright and ruby/purple colored, the 1995 Vosne-Romanée reveals penetrating aromas of sweet cherries and vanilla as well as silky-textured, thick, and elegant red berry flavors. Well delineated and structured, this wine will be at its best between now and 2002. Equally good, the purple-colored 1995 Chambolle-Musigny possesses deep blueberry and violet aromas and an intense, tangy, blackberry-filled palate with traces of toasty oak in its long finish. Anticipated maturity: now–2004. Medium ruby colored, the 1995 Gevrey-Chambertin exhibits minerals and Asian spices in its bouquet. The wine's deliciously savory, blackberry-packed palate seems to increase in power on the finish. This medium-bodied, concentrated wine requires 3 years of cellaring yet should be drunk before 2005. From the northern extremity of the Côte d'Or, the ruby-colored 1995 Marsannay possesses a sulking, austere, yet sweet nose and flavors suggesting steel, stones, coffee, herbs, and blackberries. Medium bodied and chewy, it should be drunk between now and 2003.

Aromatically, the medium to dark ruby-colored 1995 Nuits-St.-Georges Les Boudots reveals lively and spicy scents. This superb medium- to full-bodied, concentrated, and thick wine explodes on the palate with layers of powerful dark cherry, roasted coffee, vanilla, and mineral flavors. Anticipated maturity: 2000–2008. The medium to dark-colored 1995 Vosne-Romanée Les Suchots displays candied, cherry/plummy, *garrigue* (the sun-roasted wild herbs of the south of France, which include thyme and rosemary) scents. It exhibits chewy, chocolate-covered cherries and superripe, almost prunelike, flavors in its thick, medium- to full-bodied personality. Drink it between 2000 and 2007. Similarly colored, the 1995 Chambolle-Musigny Les Baudes reveals well-defined red currant and blackberry aromas as well as a precise, highly delineated, medium-bodied personality filled with tangy red berries and violets. Anticipated maturity: 2000–2007.

The splendid medium to dark ruby-colored 1995 Gevrey-Chambertin Estournelles St. Jacques displays gorgeously ripe red cherries, blackberries, stones, and a touch of tar on the nose. This full-bodied, viscous, yet delineated wine boasts harmonious flavors of sweet, tangy cherries, cinnamon, coffee, and herbs with well-integrated oak. Anticipated maturity: 2002–2010. Slightly better, the spectacular 1995 Gevrey-Chambertin Clos St. Jacques (one of the best premier cru vineyards) reveals aromatics and flavors that are reminiscent of Château Rayas. Dark ruby colored, it exhibits intense scents of spicy, superripe black cherries, plums, and cassis fruit as well as exceptionally powerful sweet blackberry and mocha flavors. This full-bodied, zesty wine will be at its best between 2002 and 2012.

Dark ruby colored, the 1995 Clos Vougeot displays Asian spices and oak-imbued aromas and a highly extracted, deeply concentrated, full-bodied, tannic, chewy flavor profile packed with layers of dark fruits. Drink it between 2002 and 2010. Much more feminine stylistically, the medium to dark ruby-colored 1995 Echézeaux reveals floral perfumed scents and a medium-bodied, delineated, velvety personality with smoke, mocha, and dark cherry flavors. Anticipated maturity: now–2007. Slightly darker colored, the 1995 Clos St. Denis offers a sweet, waxy, minerally, and floral nose and a viscous yet precise palate filled with blackberry, cassis, and earth flavors. Full bodied and rich, it should be at its best between 2000 and 2009.

The medium to dark ruby-colored 1995 Chambolle-Musigny Les Amoureuses reveals sublime scents of tangy, earthy black currants, cherries, and violets. Gorgeously feminine and elegant, this silky-textured, medium- to full-bodied wine is highly delineated, precise, and packed with ripe blackberries. Possessing the necessary structure for extended cellaring, it will be at its best between 2002 and 2012. Darker colored, the spectacular 1995 Bonnes Mares jumps from the glass with aromas of blackberries, cherries, flowers, and minerals. It is a massively concentrated, powerful, full-bodied wine packed with stones, wild cherries, red currants, and touches of iron, tar, and chocolate for additional complexity. Highly structured and with an exceptionally long finish, it should be cellared for 7–9 years and will hold through 2012. Also quite dark colored, Jadot's 1995 Musigny reveals touches of cinnamon and blackberries in its intensely floral nose. On the palate, this full-bodied, velvety-textured, powerful wine explodes with copious quantities of roasted herbs, coffee, blackberries, and violets and has an admirable finish. Anticipated maturity: 2002–2012.

The dark-colored 1995 Charmes Chambertin displays intensely ripe cherries, plums, and touches of earth on the nose and a well-structured, powerful, full-bodied, character filled with the flavors of Asian spices, cassis, and boysenberries. It will be at its best between 2000 and 2008. Revealing enticing aromas of cherries and raspberries, the dark ruby-colored 1995 Chapelle Chambertin possesses a fabulous, medium- to full-bodied, well-delineated, silky personality crammed with exceptionally ripe red berry fruit. Deliciously supple, it should be drunk between 2000 and 2009. Jadot's opaque, black-colored 1995 Chambertin Clos de Bèze reveals superripe cherries and prunes intertwined with roasted notes of coffee, herbs, and stones. This wine's immense, full-bodied personality is packed with massive, thick, viscous, highly extracted, and concentrated black fruits. Unapproachable, this behemoth will be at its peak between 2005 and 2015.

The light to medium ruby/purple-colored 1995 Monthélie offers fresh and tangy aromas of minerals, blueberries, and plums as well as a lively, medium-bodied, well-concentrated, oily-textured, and driven mouthful of black cherries, stones, and a touch of raw meat for additional complexity. Its finish ends on slightly rugged tannins. Drink it now. Possessing a slightly darker color and an expressive nose of jammy strawberries and black cherries, the 1995 Auxey-Duresses is a structured, chewy, rugged, medium-bodied wine with flavors reminiscent of red currants, flint, minerals, and stones. Anticipated maturity: now. The ruby-colored 1995 Pommard reveals beautiful aromas of violets, perfume, cherries, and freshly cut flowers. This well-structured wine has a velvety texture, medium body, and flavors of toast, cola, and cassis. It will be at its best between now and 2000.

The ruby-colored and impressive 1995 Chassagne-Montrachet Morgeot displays a concentrated, flinty, and blackberry-infused nose as well as a highly extracted, rugged, medium- to full-bodied, rustic core of black cherries, stones, metals, and a distinct rubber/eraser flavor. Masculine and brooding, it will be at its peak between now and 2003. In a significantly more feminine style, the ruby/purple-colored 1995 Santenay Clos de Malte exhibits sweet cherry aromas and a supple, velvety-textured, highly extracted, and medium-bodied personality with blackberry, chalk, flint, toasty oak, and mineral flavors. Drink it between now and 2000. Even better, the medium ruby-colored 1995 Savigny-Lès-Beaune La Dominode offers pure, precise, and crisp strawberries aromatically and a silky-textured, concentrated, medium- to full-bodied, beautifully ripe, and harmonious character with deep cherry flavors and a soft, long finish. It is so delicious to drink now, I would not risk losing its purity and freshness by cellaring it beyond 1999. From the same village but radically different stylistically, the medium to dark ruby-colored 1995 Savigny-Lès-Beaune Les Vergelesses possesses a tight, dense, and brooding nose with scents of black currants and stones. This rugged, backward, medium- to full-bodied, masculine wine is jam-packed with blackberries, cassis, and raw meat and iodine flavors. Highly structured and with a strong tannic backbone, it will require a few years of cellaring to soften. Anticipated maturity: now–2003.

The medium to dark ruby-colored 1995 Volnay Clos de La Barre offers sweet blueberries, violets, and touches of underbrush aromatically as well as a fresh, lively, medium- to full-bodied, oily-textured character with grape, dried raisin, and plum flavors. Its wonderfully long finish tails off on touches of minerals and stones. Anticipated maturity: now–2004. The delicious, extremely well-made, and bright ruby-colored 1995 Pommard Grands Epenots reveals sublime scents of red cherries, blackberries, and earth. This slightly rugged, full-bodied, and thick wine is crammed with intensely ripe plums, prunes, and cassis, with notes of tar, coffee, and roasted herbs for additional complexity. Well structured and built to last, it will be at its best between now and 2006.

The Maison Louis Jadot is justifiably known for its excellent lineup of offerings from the vineyards overlooking the town of Beaune. The medium ruby-colored 1995 Beaune Boucherottes offers a dense, beautifully ripe nose with scents of cherries and strawberries, as well as a medium-bodied, silky-textured personality bursting with sweet black currants and blueberries. This wine is not particularly long or intense, but its soft and supple style is quite enjoyable. Drink it between now and 2000. Darker colored and more intense, the 1995

Beaune Clos des Couchereaux exhibits ripe cassis and flint aromas and a powerful, medium- to full-bodied, oily-textured, and complex mouthful of blackberries, meat, metal, stones, and vanilla. Well made and beautifully balanced, it has the necessary structure and core of fruit for cellaring. Anticipated maturity: now–2004. The ruby/purple-colored 1995 Beaune Theurons displays deep strawberries, black currants, and candle wax aromas and a gorgeously supple, medium- to full-bodied, thickly textured, metallic, and stony core of chewy blackberries, roasted herbs, and cassis. This fresh and lively wine is fabulously balanced, well structured, and beautifully ripe and extracted. Anticipated maturity: now–2005.

The medium to dark ruby-colored 1995 Corton Pougets offers gorgeously perfumed and sweet aromas of violets, roses, and currants. Admirable, ripe, and refined, this medium- to full-bodied wine has an oily texture crammed with superripe black currants, blueberries, and dark cherries. It is a highly structured, tightly wound, yet well-extracted wine; this Corton will benefit from a few years of cellaring. Drink it between 2000 and 2006.

"I am in love with 1996's purity and its touch of tension," said Pierre-Henri Gagey, Maison Louis Jadot's director. Jacques Lardière, this *négociant* house's talented winemaker, shares Gagey's enthusiasm for the 1996s, feeling they beautifully reflect their respective *terroirs*. He has crafted a stunning lineup of wines from the 1996 vintage. I believe winemaking styles cope with a vintage's intrinsic qualities. A vigneron who generally produces highly structured and tannic wines will have problems in a backward and hard vintage, while one who crafts light and lacelike offerings will have difficulties in a delicately fruited year. Lardière bled (a technique of removing the watery juice of a light pressing to increase concentration) many of the 1996s, "but never more than 10%," and performed a 28–35-day *cuvaison* in order to extract a maximum amount of flavor, color, and aromas while softening the tannins. These wines will be neither fined nor filtered prior to bottling.

The 1996 vintage boasts lively fruit with relatively high acidity levels, yet paradoxically it is a forward, not particularly structured year. Lardière's winemaking, which stresses fruit as well as structure, seems to be a perfect match for the vintage. His wines always seem to evolve slowly, holding back their fruit with their strong (sometimes strict) but soft tannic backbones. Lardière has captured the fruit, given it structure and some firmness, and has brilliantly averted the potential pitfalls of high acidity (final pHs are neither high nor low— between 3.4 and 3.7 across the board). The vintage complements Lardière, and vice-versa.

Revealing a medium ruby color and aromas of black cherries and orange peels, the 1996 Côte de Beaune-Villages is a well-structured, delineated, medium-bodied, and delicious wine filled with juicy blackberries and minerals. It should be drunk over the next 3 years. Similarly colored, the 1996 Monthélie offers a talcum (baby) powder and dark fruit-scented nose as well as a medium-bodied, silky, and delicious core of blueberry, metal, mineral, and stone flavors. Anticipated maturity: now–2001. The medium to dark ruby-colored 1996 Pernand-Vergelesses Clos de la Croix de Pierre has grapey and toasted-oak scents that give way to a black currant- and stone-flavored, medium-bodied, velvety-textured, and beautifully ripe character. If it were not for a touch of rusticity to this wine's finish, it would have merited a slightly higher rating. Anticipated maturity: now–2002. The 1996 Santenay Clos de Malte is medium to dark ruby colored and offers aromas reminiscent of roses, violets, stones, and cherries. This silky-textured, structured, and medium-bodied offering is richer and more full flavored than I remember the 1995 being at the same stage. Blackberries, stones, and minerals are found in this firm and delicious wine. It should be drunk between now and 2002.

The seductive 1996 Savigny-Lès-Beaune Les Lavières is medium to dark ruby colored and has a perfumed, violet-infused nose. On the palate, this expressive, well-crafted, medium- to full-bodied, and silky-textured wine is filled with juicy cherries, blackberries, blueberries, and minerals. Anticipated maturity: now–2003. Produced from a vineyard recently purchased by Pierre-Henri Gagey (as opposed to the Maison Jadot itself), the bright ruby-colored 1996 Savigny-Lès-Beaune Clos des Guettes reveals roses and red fruit aromatics as well as a blackberry, blueberry, and boysenberry-flavored, medium-bodied, and structured personality. Unlike the previous wine's forward, lush, and fruit-driven character, this offering bases its appeal on its finesse, femininity, delineation, and elegance. It should be at its peak between now and 2003. Of the three Jadot wines I tasted from this village, the darkest, richest, and most powerful is the 1996 Savigny-Lès-Beaune La Dominode. Exhibiting a dark ruby color and profound aromatic richness, this wine offers a fabulous explosion of ripe red and black berries that saturate the palate with their juices. Broad, masculine, and structured, this highly concentrated and somewhat foursquare offering also possesses a long, sweet oak-infused finish. Anticipated maturity: now–2004.

The 1996 is a particularly successful vintage for red from Chassagne-Montrachet, and Lardière took full advantage of that fact in crafting a sensational 1996 Chassagne-Montrachet Morgeot Duc De Magenta. This bright and dark ruby-colored wine has a perfumed, floral nose and a fat, luscious, supple, gorgeously sweet, and ripe personality. Thick, juicy layers of red cherries, powdered sugar-coated strawberries, and traces of Asian spices can be found in this medium- to full-bodied and velvety-textured wine. It should be at its best between now and 2005.

Produced from purchased wine, the ruby-colored 1996 Volnay Les Santenots exhibits an earth-and-cherry-scented nose followed by a medium-bodied, lively, and vibrant character with plump, beautifully ripe, and juicy berry fruit encased in a rather tannic and rough structure. My score may appear conservative if Lardière applies some of his magic on this wine before bottling. Anticipated maturity: now–2003. The darker-colored 1996 Volnay Clos de La Barre offers a mouthwatering nose of malt balls and deeply ripe blackberries. This creamy-textured, medium- to full-bodied, sweet black cherry-packed, fat, and seductive wine has immense richness. It also possesses an impressively long finish that reveals additional layers of opulent fruit and oak spices. Anticipated maturity: now–2006.

Medium to dark ruby colored and boasting dark cherry, blueberry, and toasty oak aromas, the 1996 Pommard is a masculine, structured, robust, and medium- to full-bodied wine. Ripe red fruits and Asian spices can be found in this delicious offering's flavor profile. Drink it over the next 4 years. The dark-colored 1996 Pommard Grands Epenots is armed with an austere, foursquare nose filled with gamey meats, black fruits, and leather. It is broad shouldered, fat, powerful, chewy, full bodied, and muscular. Delicious layers of boysenberries, blackberries, stones, and earth can be discerned in this wine. If some wines can be compared (as I have done in the past) to graceful ballerinas, then this one must be described as a massive scar-covered rugby player. Anticipated maturity: 2000–2004.

Wine lovers have come to expect first-rate Beaunes from the Gagey-Lardière team at Maison Jadot, and that's exactly what they delivered in 1996. The bright sunny days of September allowed the vines on these hillside vineyards to attain full physiological ripeness, which is not an annual occurrence in these cool sites. The 1996 Beaune Les Bressandes has a bright ruby color, a sweet red cherry and Asian spice-laden nose, and an expressive, velvety, refined, rich, succulent, and candied red fruit-filled personality. This delightful wine should be at its peak between now and 2004. Slightly darker colored, the 1996 Beaune Les Chouacheux aromatically reveals sweet red fruits and spices. It possesses an opulent, silky-textured, and medium- to full-bodied mouth resplendent with crunchy and juicy red cherries. Anticipated maturity: now–2004. The medium to dark ruby-colored 1996 Beaune Les Theurons offers profound cherry and raspberry aromas followed by a structured, foursquare, thickly textured, and chewy core of blackberries and blueberries. Its impressively long finish exhibits loads of soft and supple tannins buried in plenty of sweet fruit. It should be at its peak between 2000 and 2005. I flipped for the cookie dough and sugar-coated raspberry aromatics of the 1996 Beaune Clos des Couchereaux. On the palate, it offers plump, sweet cherries (reminiscent of a deep-dish pie) encased in a firmly structured and medium to full body. This superb Beaune will require 2–3 years of cellaring after its release. Drink it between

2001 and 2005. Equally good, but potentially better, the dark ruby/purple-colored 1996 Beaune Clos des Ursules has a delightful violet, blackberry, blueberry, stone, and earth-infused nose. This wine's medium to full body and silky and deeply sweet personality is replete with candied red fruits and possesses a firm structure. It is less lush or dense than the superb 1990 but is the finest Clos des Ursules since that great wine was crafted by Lardière. Anticipated maturity: 2001–2006.

The medium to dark ruby-colored 1996 Corton-Pougets has pure raspberry pie-filling aromas and an expansive, wild strawberry, mineral, and earth-filled character. This medium-bodied, lively, and feminine wine lacks the fat and opulence of the vintage's better Cortons but is extremely well crafted, delineated, and delightful. Anticipated maturity: now–2004. The 1996 Corton-Grèves, however, is spectacular. Dark ruby/purple colored, it exhibits an awesomely ripe nose awash in sweet cherries and oak spice. A massive explosion of juice-packed chocolate-covered cherries greets the palate and is followed by waves of kirsch-soaked blackberries, boysenberries, blueberries, and stones in this powerful, hugely concentrated, and masculine wine. This velvety-textured, full-bodied, and seductive offering possesses an impressive lingering finish that reveals load of ripe, round tannins. It should be at its best between 2002 and 2008. Bravo!

Produced from a vineyard bordering the premier cru Nuits-St.-Georges Clos de la Maréchale, the ruby-colored 1996 Côte de Nuits-Villages reveals ripe blackberry scents and a refined, well-structured, medium-bodied, and silky-textured core dominated by delicious cherries, blueberries, stones, and metal-like flavors. This delightful wine should be consumed between now and 2003. Medium to dark ruby colored and offering black raspberry and gravel aromas, the 1996 Nuits-St.-Georges is a medium-bodied, foursquare, and firm wine that exhibits perfumed cherries, stones, and raspberries in its somewhat short flavor profile. The 1996 Vosne-Romanée is similarly colored and reveals sweet black cherries in its earthy and malt-laced aromatics. This creamy-textured, medium-bodied, well-crafted, and red fruit-filled offering will be delightful to drink upon release and will easily hold through 2003. The finest of Jadot's village wines is the marvelous 1996 Chambolle-Musigny. It possesses a medium to dark ruby color and a nose of lovely raspberries and cherries basking in traces of spicy and toasty oak. This focused, medium-bodied, velvety-textured, and seductive wine displays a flavor profile reminiscent of a red and black cherry deep-dish pie. This persistent and mouth-filling beauty is a delight! Drink it between now and 2003. The medium to dark ruby-colored 1996 Gevrey-Chambertin exhibits earthy and spicy cassis aromas. This wine may be slightly more complex than the Chambolle, but it lacks that wine's presence and hedonistic qualities. The Gevrey is medium to full bodied, firm, masculine, and filled with stones, blackberries, and underbrushlike flavors. Anticipated maturity: now–2004.

The 1996 Nuits-St.-Georges Les Porrets is medium to dark ruby colored and has an intricate nose of small red and black berry fruits and minerals. On the palate, beautifully ripe black raspberries, stones, and fresh herbs can be found in this chewy-textured, structured, medium- to full-bodied, and rich wine. Anticipated maturity: 2000–2006. The slightly darker-colored 1996 Nuits-St.-Georges Les Boudots has a perfumed and floral nose that gives way to an expansive, profound, and firm core of intensely sweet red cherries, leather, and plums. Velvety textured, medium to full bodied, and well built, this wine also possesses outstanding richness and length. Anticipated maturity: 2002–2008.

From a vineyard just above the grand cru Richebourg, the medium to dark ruby-colored 1996 Vosne-Romanée Les Petits Monts offers blackberry, wheat, and spicy oak aromas. This is a highly structured wine (a Nuits framework but with a Vosne's softness), medium to full bodied, slightly austere and restrained, yet delicious. Black fruits, stones, and minerals can be found in this tightly wound and excellent wine. Anticipated maturity: 2001–2006. The dark ruby-colored 1996 Vosne-Romanée Les Suchots has beguiling aromas of fresh tobacco, sweet cherries, flowers, and toasty oak. It is medium to full bodied, silky textured, broad, profound, and deeply ripe and offers layers of black cherries, blackberries, stones, and a touch of gaminess. Its admirably long finish reveals a strong tannic backbone that will require some cellaring. Anticipated maturity: 2003–2008.

The 1996 Echézeaux (*note:* this is the domaine bottling; there may also be a *négociant* bottling) is produced from a parcel in the Rouges sector (the westernmost) of this large grand cru vineyard. It is medium to dark ruby colored and exhibits dense and earthy red cherry aromatics. This full-bodied, thickly textured, chewy, and structured wine is packed with powerful freshly laid asphalt, blackberry, and charred oak flavors. Its long and well-defined finish reveals loads of powerful yet ripe tannins. Anticipated maturity: 2002–2008. The dark-colored 1996 Grands-Echézeaux is fabulous. An extremely elegant nose of black fruits, flowers, leather, and sweet vanilla is followed by a profoundly rich, broad, dense, and expansive medium- to full-bodied wine. Refined, powerful, gorgeously ripe, fresh, and packed with cherries, blackberries, and toasty oak, this is a well-proportioned, focused, and immensely long wine. Anticipated maturity: 2002–2009. Pierre-Henri Gagey and Jacques Lardière were ecstatic to offer a 1996 Richebourg, the first since 1979. Dark colored and aromatically displaying deep and sweet red cherries and blackberries sprinkled with perfume, this is a magnificent, expansive, expressive, and exquisite wine. It is full bodied, elegant, powerful, velvety textured, and jam-packed with candied red and black cherries, cassis, and minerals. Its long, defined, and classy finish displays soft, luxurious, and extraordinarily supple tannins. Anticipated maturity: 2003–2009. The medium to dark ruby-colored 1996 Romanée-St.-Vivant exhibits lacelike, delicate, and refined aromas of sweet red fruits, flowers, and perfume. This is a medium-bodied, feminine, intricately detailed, and elegant wine with tightly wound red berry fruit. It is obvious to me that with cellaring this wine will develop more body and power as its fruit blossoms and expands. Its persistent finish offers loads of perfectly ripened soft tannins. It should be at its best between 2003 and 2009.

I believe 1996 will be remembered at Maison Louis Jadot as particularly successful in Chambolle-Musigny. From the village wine through the grands crus, each offering was excellent to outstanding. Medium to dark ruby colored and offering violet, coffee, and perfumed aromas, the 1996 Chambolle-Musigny Les Feusselottes is a broad, expressive, expansive, and medium- to full-bodied wine. Its powerful, velvety-textured core offers copious quantities of blackberries, minerals, and sweet black cherries that linger throughout its focused and persistent finish. Anticipated maturity: 2000–2006. I tasted two gorgeous 1996 Chambolle-Musigny Les Fuées (a vineyard that lies on the southwestern border of the grand cru Bonnes Mares), Domaine Henri Perrot-Minot's and Maison Louis Jadot's. Medium to dark ruby colored and offering tightly wound blueberry scents, this powerful, masculine, broad-shouldered, and superb wine saturates the palate with mouth-coating blackberries, earth, and minerals. Its long, seductive, defined, and supple tannins carry the fruit forth for 30 or more seconds. When this offering's nose unwinds and blossoms, my score may seem conservative. Anticipated maturity: 2002–2007+. The medium to dark ruby-colored 1996 Chambolle-Musigny Les Amoureuses reveals perfumed violet, black fruit, and stone aromatics. The day of my tasting, this stunning wine's character was in a broodingly backward state. It is concentrated, masculine, broad, complex, and medium to full bodied and has a blueberry, violet, and stone-packed core that lingers in the tannic yet suave finish. It should be at its peak between 2003 and 2008. The dark ruby-colored 1996 Bonnes Mares is unbelievable and potentially will be Jadot's finest 1996. An awesome nose of deep black cherries intermingled with sautéed mushrooms, underbrush, stones, and minerals is followed by an amazingly powerful yet tense personality. Complex layers of intense, precise, pure, and earthy fruit cascade over the palate in this full-bodied, thickly textured, muscular, masculine, and well-delineated wine. The harmonious juxtaposition between this offering's outstanding depth and richness and its elegant focus is mind-blowing. A tour de force! Anticipated maturity: 2004–2010+. The 1996 Musigny, also dark ruby colored, does its best to compete with its cross-village rival, the Bonnes Mares. It offers sublime aromas of violets, roses, and blackberries dusted with baby powder and has a full-bodied, thickly textured, powerful, yet controlled personality. Its flavor profile is tense and tightly wound, but extraordinary layers of chocolate-covered cherries, sweetly charred oak, and coffee are discernible. It has the elegant femininity of a ballerina and the muscle of a body-builder. Its seemingly unending finish is buttressed by loads of ripe tannins. Drink it between 2003 and 2010.

Jacques Lardière consistently produces two of Gevrey's finest premiers crus. The medium to dark ruby-colored 1996 Gevrey-Chambertin Estournelles St. Jacques exhibits a spicy, cinnamon-laced, floral, and black cherry-scented nose as well as a marvelously expressive, broad, silky-textured, and powerful core of candied raspberries and cherries. This extroverted, full-bodied, seductive, and complex offering also possesses a soft, supple, and long finish. Anticipated maturity: 2001–2006. Jadot's 1996 Gevrey-Chambertin Clos St. Jacques, similar to Domaine Armand Rousseau's, is often of grand cru quality. Medium to dark ruby colored and offering lovely aromas of roses, currants, and raspberries, this wine is admirably expressive yet more introverted than the Estournelles St. Jacques. While the previous wine appears to have been crafted to ensure early drinking, this one is made for the long haul. It is a feminine, highly structured, and vibrant wine filled with supersweet red and black fruits. This focused, defined, and classy offering also possesses an extraordinarily long finish. Anticipated maturity: 2004–2010.

Revealing roses and persimmons on the nose, the medium to dark ruby-colored 1996 Charmes Chambertin offers a medium- to full-bodied, silky-textured, and elegant character with sweet and tangy cherry flavors. This well-defined and harmonious wine lacks the depth and power of Jadot's other grands crus. However, it is a delicious, well-crafted, and excellent offering that will provide immensely pleasurable drinking over the near term. Anticipated maturity: now–2005. The bright, medium to dark ruby/purple-colored 1996 Chapelle Chambertin is extraordinary. Intense aromas of cassis, blackberries, and fresh herbs all covered in luscious milk chocolate give way to this wine's full-bodied, rich, and dense personality. Expressive layers of sweet dark fruits, earth, and spices as well as roasted and grilled herbs can be found in this complex, structured, and broad wine. Its formidably long and expansive finish also possesses copious yet supple tannins. Wow! Readers who have never had a glorious Chapelle are well advised to scour their favorite wine shops for this gem. Anticipated maturity: 2004–2010+. The dark ruby-colored and cassis, tangy black berry, leather, and grilled oak-scented 1996 Mazis-Chambertin is a brooding, masculine, foursquare, and broadshouldered wine. This highly concentrated and extracted offering is packed with sweet blackberries, assorted dark fruits, and traces of licorice and underbrush flavors that linger in its impressively long, tannic, yet soft finish. As it will require cellaring patience, I would suggest drinking it between 2005 and 2012. The similarly colored 1996 Ruchottes-Chambertin is a step up in quality. Displaying a nose of deeply ripe blackberries, flowers, and hints of minerals, this full-bodied, foursquare, velvety-textured, thick, and chewy offering is redolent with sweet black raspberries, brambleberries, and roasted herbs. With its tender tannins, it is more refined and harmonious than the Mazis-Chambertin, but, while still being quite concentrated, it doesn't have the previous wine's power. Anticipated maturity: 2004–2012. Given Jadot's track record with Chambertin (the 1990, tasted recently, is stupendous), I found the 1996 to be tight and reserved. Dark ruby colored and offering a delightful nose of roses, perfume, and chocolate-covered cherries, it is a silky-textured, rich, lively, and wonderfully dense wine jam-packed with deeply ripe red and black fruits as well as hints of underbrush. What I tasted was certainly an outstanding wine, but my instincts and experience with past vintages of this wine suggest there is more to it. Anticipated maturity: 2004–2010+. Fortunately, the 1996 Chambertin Clos de Bèze was extroverted and boastful when I encountered it. This magnificent offering has a saturated black/ruby color and an enthralling nose of candied cherries, roses, blackberries, stones, earth, and toasty oak. It is full bodied, velvety textured, and unbelievably dense, yet superbly focused. Fresh and lively layers of red cherries, clay, currants, and Asian spices can be found in this powerful, intense, classy, and persistent wine. It should hit its peak around 2006 and be cellared through 2014. Wow!

The medium to dark ruby-colored 1996 Clos de la Roche offers rich and plump red fruits intermingled with fresh herbs and stones on the nose. Gorgeous layers of sweet black cherries, violets, and cassis are wed to flavors of chocolate-chip cookie dough in this seductive, medium- to full-bodied, luscious, and delicious wine. Regrettably, it lacks the concentration, power, and length of Jadot's best 1996s. Drink it between 2002 and 2007. I was slightly more inspired by the medium to dark ruby-colored 1996 Clos St. Denis. Revealing a sublime, almost spiritual, nose of flowers, perfume, plums, and spices, this medium- to full-bodied wine has great refinement and elegance. Candied red and black fruits as well as stones are found in its pure, delightful, and lingering flavor profile. Anticipated maturity: 2002–2007.

The saturated and dark-colored 1996 Clos Vougeot, with its extraordinarily spicy nose of sweet red and black fruits, sent me soaring. This massive, intense, broad-shouldered, masculine, structured, and chewy wine is crammed with superripe, rich, and layered blackberries, cassis, licorice, earth, and Asian spices. As if that were not enough, its dense fruit comes roaring back after expectoration, lingering on the palate for nearly a minute. This is an extraordinary Clos Vougeot! Anticipated maturity: 2006–2014. Bravo to Jacques Lardière and Pierre-Henri Gagey!

DOMAINE JAYER-GILLES (MAGNY-LES-VILLERS)

1996	Côte de Nuits-Villages	D	(88–90)
1995	Côte de Nuits-Villages	D	(87–89+)
1996	Echézeaux	EEE	(93–95)
1995	Echézeaux	EEE	94
1996	Hautes Côtes de Beaune	D	(87–88)
1995	Hautes Côtes de Beaune	D	88
1996	Hautes Côtes de Nuits	D	(87–89)
1995	Hautes Côtes de Nuits	D	(87–89)
1996	Nuits-St.-Georges Les Damodes	EE	(90–92+)
1995	Nuits-St.-Georges Les Damodes	EE	(90–92)
1996	Nuits-St.-Georges Les Hauts Poirets	EE	(90–92)
1995	Nuits-St.-Georges Les Hauts Poirets	E	(89–91)

Robert Jayer, one of the deans of Burgundy winemaking, produces dark, highly concentrated and extracted wines. Stoic, square jawed, and sporting a large handlebar mustache, this tough, muscular man with the look of a Scottish drill sergeant makes excellent wines.

In 1995 Jayer fashioned three wines that are good values. Possessing a dark color and roasted aromatics, the 1995 Hautes Côtes de Beaune is a structured, slightly rugged, well-balanced, dark toasty fruit and spice-packed medium- to full-bodied wine. It should be at its peak of maturity between 2001 and 2006. The 1995 Hautes Côtes de Nuits also exhibits Jayer's trademark roasted fruit nose. It reveals deep, sweet, cherry-and-mineral-filled, concentrated flavors. Often better than many producers' premiers and grands crus, Jayer's dark-colored 1995 Côte de Nuits-Villages displays minerally, stony, and ripe fruits on the nose and dark, intense, oaky, robust fruit flavors. Highly structured, this medium- to full-bodied wine requires 4 years of cellaring. It will easily last 5–7 years.

The newest addition to Domaine Jayer-Gilles's vineyards, the dark-colored 1995 Nuits-

St.-Georges Les Hauts Poirets reveals explosive aromatics of roasted cassis fruit and delicious, thick-textured, superripe, deep, dark, layered, intense cassis flavors. Tannic, but possessing the requisite fruit and structure for balance, this beauty will be at its peak between 2001 and 2009. Consistently one of the finest Nuits made, Jayer's large-scaled, dark-colored 1995 Nuits-St.-Georges Les Damodes exhibits deep, floral, sweet, red berry fruit aromatics and flavors in its explosive personality that is also crammed with highly extracted red fruit flavors. Viscous and full bodied, it will repay 6 years of cellaring by providing superb drinking for up to a decade. The dark ruby-colored 1995 Echézeaux displays an elegant and refined, yet dark and brooding, intense nose of blackberries and perfume. Its dense texture and full-bodied, chewy flavors provide an enthralling combination of lively, intense red and black fruits. Powerful, balanced, and gorgeously well delineated, this gem should be at its peak of maturity between 2005 and 2012.

I retasted the 1995 Echézeaux in the United States after bottling. This dark ruby-colored wine is a behemoth! Its brooding aromas of blackberries, tar, mocha, and roasted oak is followed by a full-bodied, superstructured, foursquare, yet velvety-textured character. This immensely concentrated and well-balanced wine is filled with lively cassis, blackberries, brambleberries, and stonelike flavors. Those readers lucky enough to have purchased a few bottles, and patient enough to allow them to soften out with cellaring, are in for a treat. Drink it between 2006 and 2015.

Gilles Jayer took charge of this domaine with the 1996 vintage upon the retirement of his father.

Jayer-Gilles's 1996 Echézeaux and Nuits-St.-Georges Les Hauts Poirets have been quarantined by the French government pending the results of a trial that will take place in December 1998. The government claims that the estate, at that point still under the direction of Robert Jayer, chaptalized both wines over the limit set by the European Commission. According to the domaine's U.S. importer, the Jayers claim that the wines were chaptalized within permissible ranges set by the INAO (the national body that governs winemaking for wines with appellation status). Both of the wines targeted are outstanding. As Jayer defends himself in court (an expensive proposition), the ultimate fate of the wines in question is uncertain. There are three potential results. They could be released for sale with their proper labels, they could be declassified to vin de table status, or they could be distilled into alcohol. Readers who have preordered these offerings will have to await the outcome of the trial to know whether they will receive their wines.

The medium to dark ruby-colored 1996 Hautes Côtes de Beaune has an appealing nose of ripe dark fruits and fresh herbs. It is a medium-bodied, dense, lively, and silky wine with sweet cassis, vibrant red currants, and traces of toasty oak. It should be at its peak between now and 2003. Similarly colored, the 1996 Hautes Côtes de Nuits reveals blackberry and cassis aromas that give way to its medium- to full-bodied, silky-textured, and black cherry-laced personality. This wine is more intense and concentrated than the Beaune. Its persistent finish reveals powerful grilled oak characteristics. Drink it between now and 2004. The 1996 Côte de Nuits-Villages is medium to dark ruby colored and offers an expressive nose of sweet black currants, cherries, spices, and vanilla-imbued oak. This intense, deep, medium- to full-bodied, richly textured, and lively wine is packed with powerful black cherry fruit, herbs, blackberries, and hints of minerals. Its long finish displays roasted oak flavors and copious quantities of supple tannins. Domaine Jayer-Gilles consistently produces one of Burgundy's finest Côte de Nuits-Villages. Anticipated maturity: 2000–2005.

The medium to dark ruby-colored 1996 Nuits-St.-Georges Les Hauts Poirets displays a gorgeous nose of deep and spicy red berries. This delightful, velvety-textured, medium- to full-bodied, refreshing, and chewy wine offers loads of candied cherries in its seductive flavor profile. Its opulence is buttressed by a firm backbone composed of tons of soft and superbly ripened tannins that reappear in its admirably long finish. Anticipated maturity:

2001–2006. I generally have a preference for Jayer-Gilles's Nuits-St.-Georges Les Damodes over the Hauts Poirets, but in 1996 I found them to be qualitative equals (the Damodes received a "+" because I have a sense that it may get better). Its expressive blackberry-and-cassis-infused nose gives way to a foursquare, highly structured, and expansive core of plump black fruits and stones. This backward wine is broad and concentrated and has an impressively long finish. It should be at its best between 2003 and 2008.

The dark-colored, complex 1996 Echézeaux has a refined nose of violets, cassis, blackberries, freshly laid asphalt, and toasted oak. Its expressive, full-bodied, powerful, and fat personality is fresh and lively. This concentrated wine is packed with Bing cherries, tangy cassis, hints of leather, and traces of toasted oak that linger in its impressively long finish. Anticipated maturity: 2005–2012+.

OMAINE REMI JOBARD (MEURSAULT)

1996 Monthélie Les Vignes Rondes	D	87

Domaine Rémi Jobard, known primarily for its delicious Meursaults, also produces red wines. The delicious, medium ruby-colored 1996 Monthélie Les Vignes Rondes demonstrates that Rémi Jobard is also a skilled red wine maker. Revealing rich red currant aromas, this juicy, dense, beautifully ripe, and medium-bodied wine is packed with plump blackberries, minerals, stones, metals, and just the right amount of oak spice. I suggest drinking it by 2001.

DOMAINE JOBLOT (GIVRY)

1996 Givry Clos Des Bois Chevaux	D	89+
1995 Givry Clos de Cellier aux Moines	D	(89–91)
1996 Givry Clos de Cellier aux Moines	D	(89–92)
1996 Givry Clos de la Servoisine	D	(89–91+)

Justifiably recognized as one of the great producers in Burgundy, the Joblot family consistently craft Givrys that are as good as or better than most grands crus from the Côte d'Or. Their work proves that the tiered appellation system used in the Côte is but a reflection of the potential a vineyard offers, not representative of the actual quality of its wines.

Jean-Marc Joblot, who runs this family estate with his wife and brother, is one of the most highly regarded winemakers in Burgundy. Readers who have not heeded this publication's repeated recommendations of Joblot's wines are missing out on grand cru Côte d'Or quality at Côte Chalonnaise prices. Snobs, more impressed by renowned labels than impressive wines, will continue to refuse even to taste these offerings.

Joblot vinifies with a minimal contact to air in order to maintain freshness of fruit. As a result, his wines tend to be extremely tight and compact after bottling. If they are to be drunk young, Joblot recommends that consumers allow the wines to breathe in a decanter for 2–3 hours.

The medium to dark ruby-colored 1995 Givry Clos de Cellier aux Moines displays dark cherries, black currants, and Asian spices aromatically. Medium to full bodied, highly structured, concentrated, intense, and extremely well delineated, this wine is packed with black fruits, minerals, and smoky/leathery flavors. Built to last, this impressive wine will be at its peak between now and 2007.

Produced from a vineyard with a completely southern exposure, the 1996 Givry Clos de la Servoisine displays a medium to dark ruby color as well as expressive mineral and black raspberry aromas. It boasts layer upon layer of sweet red and black cherries, raspberries, and red currants in its medium- to full-bodied, velvety-textured, powerful, and intense character. Its impressively long finish reveals loads of soft, supple tannins buried in sweet, luscious fruit. Anticipated maturity: now–2006. This is the first time I have tasted Joblot's 1996 Givry Clos Des Bois Chevaux, which is produced from an east-facing vineyard. Medium to dark ruby colored, it exhibits a perfumed, blackberry, metal, and mineral-laced nose. On the palate, this delicious wine is medium to full bodied, silky, feminine, elegant, and filled with juicy red and black cherries. It is more seductive and less structured than the Servoisine. Anticipated maturity: now–2004. The immensely impressive and dark ruby-colored 1996 Givry Clos de Cellier aux Moines is, like the Servoisine, from a vineyard with a southern exposure. It offers beguiling aromas of chocolate-covered cherries, truffles, stones, and Asian spices. This wine's medium- to full-bodied personality is concentrated, extracted, rich, and chewy. It saturates the palate with intensely ripe black cherries, leather, candied blood oranges, and cassis whose flavors linger on its impressively long finish. Bravo!

DOMAINE HENRI JOUAN (MOREY-ST.-DENIS)

1996 Clos St. Denis	E	(88–90)
1996 Gevrey-Chambertin aux Echézeaux	D	88+
1996 Morey-St.-Denis	D	87

According to Patrick Lesec, this estate's broker, Henri Jouan is a true traditionalist. He believes in tightly pruning his vines, never uses pumps on the wines, and bottles them unfined and unfiltered. I found his wines to have plump and juicy fruit in addition to excellent flavor intensity on the palate. The Morey-St.-Denis and the Morey-St.-Denis Clos Sorbé were both reduced the day of my tasting. (The opposite of oxidized, reduced is a state wines can be in when they have had little or no contact with air. It is recognizable by aromas of meat, rubber, and game and can generally be quickly eliminated by aerating the wine either in the glass or by performing a racking if it is in barrel.) With some air and by decanting them repeatedly, the Morey-St.-Denis came around, but I was unable to get a taster's bead on the Clos Sorbé.

The ruby-colored 1996 Morey-St.-Denis has sweet red and black berry fruit aromas and a silky-textured, intense, medium-bodied, and ample core of plump black cherries. This well-proportioned wine may well require some air time if opened in the next year because it is somewhat reduced. Drink it between now and 2004. Revealing a similar color and dense black fruit fragrances, the 1996 Gevrey-Chambertin aux Echézeaux is a beautifully ripe, thickly textured, medium-bodied, and delicious wine with layers of juicy cherries and raspberries. It should be drunk over the next 5–6 years. Medium to dark ruby colored and displaying a clean, pure, rich, and blackberry-imbued nose, Jouan's 1996 Clos St. Denis is a concentrated, extracted, oily-textured, juicy, fat, and sweet wine. Its flavor profile is composed of cassis, blackberries, red cherries, and candied raspberries, all of which are spiced with grilled new oak. This excellent and potentially outstanding offering would have received a higher score had it been longer in the finish. Anticipated maturity: 2002–2008.

MAISON LABOURÉ-ROI (NUITS-ST.-GEORGES)

1996 Charmes-Chambertin	EE	87
1996 Echézeaux	EE	87+

This négociant house's 1996 Charmes-Chambertin has a healthy dark ruby/purple color, a nose of perfumed cherries and traces of cookie dough, and a medium-bodied, oily-textured, and rich core of plump red fruits. It would have merited a higher score if its tannins had not appeared to be pasty and the finish had been longer. Anticipated maturity: now–2003. The similarly colored 1996 Echézeaux has elegant, floral, raspberry-laced, and spicy aromas that give way to its medium- to full-bodied, soft, and tangy character. Its flavor profile is composed of vibrant red and black cherries, and it exhibits a touch of dryness and heat in the finish. Anticipated maturity: now–2004.

DOMAINE MICHEL LAFARGE (VOLNAY)

1996 Beaune Grèves	EE	(88–91)
1995 Beaune Grèves	EE	(87–90)
1996 Bourgogne	D	(86–88)
1995 Bourgogne	D	(85–88)
1996 Bourgogne Passe-Tout-Grain	C	(86–88)
1995 Bourgogne Passe-Tout-Grain	C	87
1996 Pommard Pezerolles	EE	(90–92+)
1995 Pommard Pezerolles	EE	(88–91+)
1996 Volnay	D	(87–89)
1995 Volnay	D	(86–88)
1996 Volnay Premier Cru	E	(88–91)
1996 Volnay Clos du Château des Ducs	EE	(90–92+)
1995 Volnay Clos du Château des Ducs	EE	(90–92)
1996 Volnay Clos des Chênes	EE	(92–94+)
1995 Volnay Clos des Chênes	EE	(90–93+)
1996 Volnay Vendanges Selectionées	E	(88–91)
1995 Volnay Vendanges Selectionées	E	(87–89)

Year after year, Michel Lafarge and his son Frédéric produce some of Burgundy's most supple, precise, and succulent wines. Whether in barrel or after years of cellaring, they are always ready to drink, seemingly never going through the "dumb periods" other red burgundies often suffer from. The father-and-son team is exactly that: a team. There is no jealousy, rancor, or overly dominant figure between the two of them. From the simplest Bourgogne-Passe-Tout-Grain to the sublime Volnay Clos des Chênes, these are wines all burgundy wine lovers should search out.

Michel and Frédéric Lafarge told me that they spend as much time and effort on their two generic bottlings as on the village and premiers crus—and it shows! When asked by a friend to assist him in putting together a great burgundy cellar, Dominique Lafon of the Domaine des Contes Lafon headed straight for the Lafarge estate to purchase the 1995 Bourgogne, as it is consistently one of the finest generic burgundies produced. Ruby colored and displaying deep, sweet cherry aromatics, it is a gorgeously ripe, defined, medium-bodied, chewy wine with succulent and luscious spicy red fruits and a supple finish. Produced from vines over 50 years old (half Pinot Noir and half Gamay), the medium ruby-colored 1995 Bourgogne Passe-Tout-Grain is, with Emmanuel Rouget's, Burgundy's best. It reveals spicy blackberries and currants aromatically and an oily-textured, medium-bodied, earthy, and sweet cherry-filled character. These are both excellent values and should be drunk between now and 2000.

It is only appropriate that a producer who crafts the top generic bottlings in Burgundy should also be responsible for some of its finest village wines. The medium ruby-colored 1995 Volnay offers a deeply ripe nose with cherry and earth scents and a silky-textured, medium-bodied core of raspberry and boysenberry fruit with touches of underbrush for additional complexity. Anticipated maturity: now–2002. The Lafarges also make a Volnay Vendanges Selectionées from their best parcels in the village appellation. Medium to dark ruby colored, the 1995 possesses a cherry-and-blackberry-scented nose and a medium- to full-bodied, thick-textured, and intense flavor profile composed of cassis, blueberries, and porcini mushrooms. Admirably long, elegant, and supple, it should be at its best between now and 2004.

The medium to dark ruby-colored 1995 Beaune Grèves displays lively aromatics reminiscent of red currants and raspberries as well as superbly precise flavors of tangy cherries, strawberries, and mineral notes in its medium-bodied, oily-textured, and exceptionally long palate. This gem should be consumed between now and 2004. The *monopole* (solely owned) 1995 Volnay Clos du Château des Ducs possesses a ruby color, aromas of crisp black currants, and a charmingly elegant, medium- to full-bodied, and silky character jam-packed with cherries, blackberries, and earth tones. Gorgeously long and perfectly delineated, it is a superb example of the combination of power and elegance Volnays can achieve. Drink it between now and 2006. My favorite Lafarge offering is the dark ruby-colored 1995 Volnay Clos des Chênes. It possesses an enticing nose of dark fruits, roasted herbs, hazelnuts, and fresh blood, as well as a sublimely elegant, concentrated, full-bodied, and oily-textured flavor profile drenched in cherries, blackberries, currants, and notes of underbrush. A judicious use of oak provides additional complexity with subtle flavors of smoky herbs that are discernible in its prodigiously long finish. Awesomely delicious right out of the barrel, it will be at its best between 2000 and 2008. The dark ruby-colored 1995 Pommard Pezerolles reveals roses, deep red cherries, earth, and coffee aromatically and an explosive, thick-textured, medium- to full-bodied character with gorgeously delineated and powerful flavors of superripe black cherries and boysenberries. An admirable finish of round, ripe tannins guarantees that this wine will age effortlessly. Anticipated maturity: now–2006. Bravo!

In the 1996 vintage, Michel Lafarge and his son Frédéric have produced, once again, a fabulous lineup of wines. My only regret, and one that I know is shared by many readers, is that these wines are extremely difficult to locate. My local wine shop, staffed by admirers of Lafarge's wines, sold out of the 1996s the date they bought them as futures (no, no one thought of calling me).

Whereas Volnay producers averaged 3 tons of fruit per acre in 1996, the Lafarges (who finish each other's sentences only the way two people who have lived and worked together for decades could) say their yields were $2^1/_3$ tons per acre for village wines, and 2 tons for premiers crus. Even so (low yields promote earlier ripening), they waited "for a few days after the *ban de vendange*" (the first day that vignerons are allowed to harvest) before sending out their harvesting teams. The 1996s took a great deal of time to finish their malolactic fermentations, but according to the Lafarges, the malos "were calm; they did not tire the wines." These offerings will be bottled unfiltered in April/May 1998 (with the exception of the Passe-Tout-Grain and Bourgogne, which were already assembled for bottling when I visited the estate in November 1997).

The Lafarge style is supple, precise, and succulent, all three also characteristics of the 1996 vintage. Michel and Frédéric Lafarge's magical touch, combined with the pure and juicy 1996 vintage, created a cellar full of beauties.

Lafarge's 1996 Bourgogne Passe-Tout-Grain, consistently one of Burgundy's finest, is produced from a 50-50 blend of Pinot Noir and Gamay grapes from vines that are over 50 years old. If the old adage that a cellar should be judged on its lowliest wine is true, then Domaine Michel Lafarge is a very fine estate indeed. Because old vines produce less then younger ones, most vignerons would not have 50-year-old vines in regional appellation vineyards. Furthermore, they would not blend grapes from those elderly vines with Gamay to produce a Passe-Tout-Grain. And, last, in a region where most regional appellation Bourgognes are raised tanks, few vignerons would perform the *élevage* of their Passe-Tout-Grains in oak barrels as this father-and-son team does. Their commitment to quality is remarkable. Bright ruby colored and redolent with spicy, cracked black pepper-covered blackberries, the Bourgogne Passe-Tout-Grain is a medium-bodied, fresh, lively, silky-textured, and expressive wine. Soft and supple on the finish, this beauty should be consumed over the next 4 years. Revealing a medium ruby color and gorgeous aromas of ripe red cherries, the 1996 Bourgogne seduces the taster with bursting, juicy, and sweet raspberries and cherries as well as floral and perfumed notes. This medium-bodied wine admirably accomplishes its goal—it gives pleasure. It is almost impossible not to smile as the succulent fruits pop on your tongue in this plump, fat, and soft offering. The Lafarges maintain that their Bourgognes age well, but I suggest drinking this wine in its youth, as its primary fruit is so enjoyable. Anticipated maturity: now–2002.

The medium to dark ruby-colored 1996 Volnay offers refined violet, rose, and cherry aromatics as well as a medium-bodied, tangy, lively, delicious, and black cherry-and-currant-packed character. It has excellent richness, balance, and a long and opulent finish that reveals plenty of ripe tannins. Anticipated maturity: now–2004. The 1996 Volnay Vendanges Selectionées (a selection of their best village appellation parcels) has a bright medium to dark ruby color and a complex and deep nose of red fruits intermingled with traces of mocha and violets. On the palate, this medium- to full-bodied, rich, broad, and gorgeously expansive wine is packed with spicy black cherries. It is more structured than the previous wine, with firmer, more evident tannins, but it also possesses deeper, richer fruit. It should be at its best between 2001 and 2007.

Produced from a blend of the premier cru Chanlins and Mitans vineyards, the 1996 Volnay Premier Cru is slightly darker colored than the previous wine and exhibits deep aromas reminiscent of black cherries and cassis. This full-bodied and vibrant wine comes on at full bore, with loads of minerals, blackberries, and cherries. It is more masculine, firmer, tighter, and more tannic than any of the previous wines, yet it reveals impressive richness, dense fruit, and a certain refinement. Anticipated maturity: 2002–2007. The bright ruby-colored 1996 Beaune Grèves displays a sweet red cherry, spice, and mineral-laden nose as well as a silky-textured, medium- to full-bodied, concentrated, pure, precise, and opulent personality. It is loaded with scrumptious, juicy red and black fruits, Asian spices, and traces of wild game. This delicious wine also possesses a long, detailed, and spicy finish. Anticipated maturity: 2001–2006.

The 1996 Volnay Clos du Château des Ducs is medium to dark ruby colored and offers a delightful nose of plums, roses, violets, and red cherries. It is oily textured, medium to full bodied, elegant, hedonistically plump and fat (what the French call *gras*), and filled with layers of creamy cherries. This wine is an amalgamation of sultriness and refinement, almost as if it were a vinous cross of Raquel Welch and Audrey Hepburn. Its persistent finish coats the mouth with loads of sweet fruits and supersupple tannins. It should be at its peak between 2002 and 2007. Even better, the dark ruby/purple-colored 1996 Volnay Clos des Chênes bowled me over with its highly expressive, profound, and complex aromas of plums, violets, blackberries, dark cherries, and Asian spices. This powerful, intense, muscular (yet refined!), deeply rich, and enthralling offering captivates the palate. I had the distinct feeling that this wine was showing me only what it wanted to display—more was in reserve and would be be revealed only when it chose to. It is compelling, concentrated, intricate, broad shouldered, and packed with blueberries, blackberries, red cherries, hints of new oak, and traces of wild game. This outstanding wine has a spectacularly long and lingering finish in which can be discerned copious quantities of ripe tannins drenched in fat and juicy fruits. Wow! Anticipated maturity: 2003–2010.

The bright purple/ruby-colored 1996 Pommard Pezerolles has a superripe (almost port-like, but without the heat) nose of red cherries, plums, dried fruits, and traces of tar. Its thick, wide, juicy, well-balanced, and medium- to full-bodied character is overflowing with sumptuous red cherries, sugar-coated strawberries, and Asian spices. This concentrated, precisely focused, and admirably long wine has huge quantities of supple tannins buried in fruit. It should age remarkably well. Anticipated maturity: 2002–2008.

Many 1989s I have recently drunk out of my cellar have been disappointing, including some heralded wines from top producers. They are aging prematurely and are losing their fruit. However, there are notable exceptions to this trend. I recently tasted two 1989s from Lafarge, the Clos des Ducs and Clos des Chênes, and found them to be vibrant, youthful, densely packed with succulent fruit, and in need of time. My parents, my guest, and the accompanying roasted chicken were all enthralled by this outstanding duo. Kudos to Michel and Frédéric Lafarge for crafting such extraordinary wines!

DOMAINE DES COMTES LAFON (MEURSAULT)

1996	Monthélie Les Duresses	D	(86–88)
1995	Monthélie Les Duresses	D	(85–88)
1996	Volnay Champans	E	(90–92+)
1995	Volnay Champans	E	(88–90)
1996	Volnay Clos des Chênes	E	(89–92)
1995	Volnay Clos des Chênes	E	(89–91)
1995	Volnay Santenots	E	(90–93)
1996	Volnay Santenots du Milieu	E	(92–94)

Dominique Lafon is one of the rare winemakers in Burgundy—indeed, in the world—whose talents seem to be equally suited to producing first-rate red wines and first-rate white wines. A thoughtful, intense, and intelligent person, Lafon is one of the young Burgundians who serves as a locomotive by pulling the region's vignerons to produce better and better-quality wines.

Lafon harvested his 1996 reds at 2²/₃ tons of fruit per acre, his highest yields since the 1990 vintage. He described 1996 as "the year of the fruit," commenting on how pure it was, with strong, solid skins that resulted in "the juice having trouble flowing." The grapes came in at 13% potential natural alcohol, and Lafon chaptalized them in order to extend the length of the fermentations—they are currently at 13.1% or 13.2% alcohol (in contrast, the 1997s were harvested at 13.5% potential natural alcohol and were not chaptalized). Malolactic fermentations were slow and long lasting and did not finish until August 1997. Lafon does not filter his reds and had no intention of fining them.

Lafon's 1996s are the finest red wines I have tasted from this first-rate and highly reliable estate to date.

The ruby-colored 1996 Monthélie Les Duresses displays a mouthwatering nose of violets and candied blueberries, followed by a deep, well-crafted, medium-bodied, and magnificently sweet core of cassis, blackberries, minerals, and metals. This fabulous Monthélie possesses a luscious and long finish with none of the harshness/astringency often associated with this village's wines. It should be drunk between now and 2003.

Ever since Dominique Lafon assumed control of the domaine in 1987, he has been reclaiming its vineyards, many of which had been leased in long-term *métayage* agreements (whereby the vigneron provides a percentage of the wine produced to the vineyard owner as payment). In 1993 he was able to reclaim the estate's 1996 Volnay Clos des Chênes. Offering a medium to dark ruby color and a well-defined, elegant, black cherry-and-mineral-scented nose, this is a lovely, refined, harmonious, velvety-textured, and medium- to full-bodied wine. Sweet and juicy black cherries intermingled with minerals and earth tones can be found in its complex flavor profile. This is one of those red burgundies that will be fabulous upon release. I suggest drinking it between now and 2005. Lafon says the slightly darker-colored 1996 Volnay Champans reminds him of the 1990. Its brooding nose exhibits blackberry and cassis fruit. On the palate, its masculine, big, broad-shouldered, and muscular full body is densely packed with black cherries, blueberries, stones, and blackberries. Even though it is from the same village as the previous wine, it is hard to imagine two burgundies so dissimilar. This is a huge and expansive wine. Anticipated maturity: 2002–2007. Consistently Lafon's finest red wine, the dark ruby-colored 1996 Volnay Santenots du Milieu is magnificent. Intense and profound blackberry aromas are followed by a massive explosion of red and black cherries. It possesses amazing richness, freshness, juiciness, and depth, as well as admirable concentration, complexity, harmony, and balance. Its persistent finish reveals fresh herbs, candied raspberries, cherries, and supple tannins. Drink this gem between 2002 and 2007. Bravo!

The medium ruby-colored 1995 Monthélie Les Duresses (aged in 10% new oak) reveals minerals and blackberries aromatically as well as a medium- to full-bodied, powerful, and masculine personality jam-packed with stones, cassis, and black cherries whose flavors linger on this wine's long finish. Drink it between now and 2003. Produced from 75-year-old vines and aged in 30% new oak, the medium to dark ruby-colored 1995 Volnay Champans exhibits refined currants and cassis aromas intermingled with violets and roses. This medium- to full-bodied wine possesses an explosive cherry, blackberry, spice, and fresh herb-flavored character in its elegant, silky core. Supple enough to drink now, it will evolve beautifully for a decade. The dark ruby-colored 1995 Volnay Clos des Chênes (also aged in 30% new oak) refused to display its aromatics the day of my tasting—regardless of how much I coaxed it. However, its lively, full-bodied, thick, Asian spice, wild blueberry-and-blackberry-packed palate was enough to grasp this wine's greatness. Its exceptionally long finish ends on notes of sweet red fruits and cracked black pepper. Anticipated maturity: now–2009. Lafon's finest 1995 red burgundy is his spectacular Volnay Santenots. Extremely dark in color, and with a totally unyielding nose, it offers a spectacular flavor profile that is immensely concentrated and deep. Revealing powerful layers of chewy black fruits (berries, plums, and cassis) and notes of fresh tar, this amazingly extracted, thick, and full-bodied behemoth is armed with an amazingly long finish. I highly recommend allowing this wine to age for a number of years. Anticipated maturity 2003–2010.

DOMAINE DES LAMBRAYS (MOREY-ST.-DENIS)

1996	Clos des Lambrays	EE	(90–92+)
1995	Clos des Lambrays	E	92
1994	Clos des Lambrays	D	88
1996	Morey-St.-Denis Premier Cru	D	(87–89)
1995	Morey-St.-Denis Premier Cru	D	89

This estate (which also owns some premier cru Puligny-Montrachet) was purchased (for nearly $9 million) in December 1996 by Gunther Freund, a 74-year-old German businessman. His goal is to produce first-class wine within 4 years.

The Clos des Lambrays is a grand cru (it was upgraded in 1981) vineyard located on the hill overlooking the village of Morey-St.-Denis. It is not a *monopole* (or solely owned vineyard), as three other families are proprietors of tiny sections (two of them cultivate it as gardens, and the third, Jean Taupenot, simply blends the wine into his village cuvée). The 21.24 acres (8.6 hectares) of Clos des Lambrays is the largest grand cru parcel in Burgundy under one proprietor.

Winemaking has continued in the hands of Thierry Brouin, who has been at the estate since 1979. When he first arrived, the vineyard was in such a deplorable state that the cognoscenti of Morey had decided it was better for hunting than grape growing! In the cellars he found that the 1973 vintage was still in barrel! He undertook a severe replanting campaign (today a third of the vines are 17 years old, and the remaining vines average 43 years in age), brought in new barrels (33%–40% new oak is used), decided to destem (grape bunches are 20%–100% destemmed depending on the vintage), and abandoned such blatantly commercial techniques as fining and filtering.

Because of financial difficulties, Brouin was unable to reduce yields and declassify wines from the younger vineyards under the previous regime. Yet Gunther Freund's insistence that this estate be at the forefront of Burgundy winemaking should lead to quick results.

Displaying a medium ruby color, the 1994 Clos des Lambrays has deep aromas of earthy dark fruits and a silky-textured, creamy, medium-bodied personality. Filled with flavors of creamy blackberries, mocha, milk chocolate, and sweet red fruits, this delicious wine is made for the near term. It does not have the dry, dusty tannins so common in the 1994s. Drink it over the next 6 years.

Exhibiting a medium to dark ruby color and deep aromas of cassis, rosemary, freshly cracked black pepper, and stones, the 1995 Morey-St.-Denis Premier Cru is medium to full bodied and silky textured and offers intense flavors of cracked pepper, juniper berries, blood oranges, and blackberries. It possesses a strong backbone of copious but ripe tannins that will require some cellaring to melt away. Anticipated maturity: 2003–2008. The slightly deeper-colored 1995 Clos des Lambrays has a darker-scented nose than its sibling's and reveals the same pepper and black fruit scents, yet it does not have the herbal component. Very spicy, it is a thickly textured, full-bodied, dense, and expansive wine redolent with a massive juniper berry, clove, cinnamon, meaty, wild game, brambleberry, mineral, stone, and cassis liqueur-flavored core. This complex, tightly wound, and firmly structured wine demands cellaring. Drink it between 2005 and 2015.

The medium to dark ruby-colored 1996 Clos des Lambrays displays aromas of red cherries, currants, candied orange peels, and smoky bacon. This medium- to full-bodied, expansive, broad, and oily-textured wine has admirable concentration, focus, and intensity. Its complex flavor profile is composed of hot stones, minerals, sweet red fruits, and fresh herbs. I was also impressed with this offering's admirable finish and soft, fat tannins. Anticipated maturity: 2001–2008. Produced from a blend of 80% declassified Clos des Lambrays and 20% Morey-St.-Denis La Riotte, the 1996 Morey-St.-Denis Premier Cru is ruby colored and reveals a nose of candied raspberries, strawberries, and cherries intermingled with rosemary, stones, and minerals. On the palate, this wine is reminiscent of the grand cru yet lacks the flavor intensity, breadth, power, mineral characteristics, or length. It is in its own right, however, an excellent wine. Soft, seductive, and medium bodied, it has elegant and lively red fruit flavors that linger in its long finish. It will be at its best between now and 2004.

LOUIS LATOUR (BEAUNE)

1996	Corton	E	(86–88)
1995	Corton-Grancey	E	(84–86)
1996	Romanée-St.-Vivant	EEE	(88–91)
1995	Romanée-St.-Vivant	EEE	(86–88)

Light to medium ruby colored, the 1995 Corton-Grancey displays sweet strawberries in the nose as well as in its silky-textured character. A lovely raspberry soda-flavored and light- to medium-bodied wine to quaff, it is simple, beautifully textured, and made for near-term drinking. The slightly darker 1995 Romanée-St.-Vivant reveals crisp strawberry and spice aromas and flavors of sweet cherries. Elegant and long, this well-structured, light- to medium-bodied wine should be drunk within the first 6 years of its release.

I have rarely been enthusiastic about Maison Latour's reds, vastly preferring their whites, but I found myself quite impressed with their efforts in 1996. The bright ruby/purple-colored 1996 Corton, produced from vineyards owned by this old, Beaune-based *négociant* house, offers blackberries and blueberries in the nose and a beautifully ripe, medium-bodied, and silky core of black cherries and cassis. This well-crafted wine should be at its peak between now and 2004. The excellent and potentially outstanding 1996 Romanée-St.-Vivant is medium to dark ruby colored and reveals profound aromas of black raspberries, violets, and cherries. Its medium- to full-bodied, elegant, and velvety-textured personality has delicious red and black berries intermingled with roses and fresh herbs. Its long finish reveals plenty of soft and supple tannins. Anticipated maturity: now–2005.

DOMAINE LATOUR-GIRAUD (MEURSAULT)

1996	Maranges La Fussière	C	(85–86)
1996	Meursault Caillerets Cuvées Selectionées	D	(87–89)
1996	Pommard La Refène Cuvées Selectionées	D	(88–90)
1996	Volnay Clos des Chênes Cuvées Selectionées	D	(90–92+)

Note: Wines marked "Cuvées Selectionées" are crafted and hand-bottled for Patrick Lesec, a Paris-based broker, who sells them throughout the world.

The qualitative resurgence at Domaine Latour-Giraud is dramatically evident with their 1996 red burgundy offerings. All four wines were impressive.

The medium to dark ruby-colored 1996 Maranges La Fussière offers an intense nose of dark fruits and a broad, ripe, medium-bodied, and tangy core of blackberries, cassis, minerals, and metal shavinglike flavors. It possesses excellent depth but suffers from rustic tannins and a dry finish. Drink it between now and 2002. One of the rare red wines from Meursault, the 1996 Meursault Caillerets Cuvées Selectionées is dark ruby colored with a gorgeous nose of brambleberries, blackberries, and assorted dark fruits. This medium- to full-bodied, masculine, structured, and fruit-driven wine was vinified in 100% new oak but reveals no wood or toast flavors. Plummy black raspberries, metals, and dark cherries are found in this delicious yet tannic offering. Anticipated maturity: 2000–2004+. The 1996 Pommard La Refène Cuvées Selectionées is dark ruby colored and exhibits an expressive nose of blackberries, and minerals, with traces of licorice. This expansive, broad, superripe, medium- to full-bodied, and dense wine is filled with extremely sweet red and black cherries, raspberries, and cassis. Its long, focused finish displays supple tannins. It is a delicious Pommard that should be at its peak between now and 2005. The dark ruby/black/purple-colored 1996 Volnay Clos des Chênes Cuvées Selectionées had just finished its malolactic fermentation. Sweet violets, smoked pork fat, and intensely aromatic blackberries are found in this fabulous wine's nose. It is a full-bodied, highly extracted, rich, and massive offering that is packed with plump blackberries and red cherries. Its superb finish possesses magnificently round and ripe tannins as well as traces of fresh herbs, stones, and fruit. Anticipated maturity: 2000–2006. Bravo!

DOMINIQUE LAURENT (NUITS-ST.-GEORGES)

1996	Auxey-Duresses Cuvée Boillot (Hospices de Beaune)	E	(88–89)
1996	Beaune Premier Cru	E	(88–90+)
1996	Beaune Clos des Mouches	EE	(90–93)
1996	Beaune Grèves	EE	(89–92)
1995	Bonnes Mares	EEE	(95–98)
1995	Chambertin	EEE	(93–96+)
1995	Chambertin Clos de Bèze	EEE	(95–97+)
1995	Chambolle-Musigny Les Amoureuses	EE	(89–92?)

1995	Chambolle-Musigny Les Cras	E	(90–93)
1995	Charmes-Chambertin	EE	(91–94)
1996	Chorey-Lès-Beaune	D	(86–88)
1995	Clos Vougeot	EE	(92–95)
1996	Corton Cuvée Docteur Peste (Hospices de Beaune)	EE	(89–91+)
1995	Echézeaux	EE	(89–92)
1995	Gevrey-Chambertin Les Champeaux	E	(89–92)
1995	Gevrey-Chambertin Clos St. Jacques	E	(89–92?)
1995	Gevrey-Chambertin Combe aux Moines	E	(89–92?)
1995	Gevrey-Chambertin Lavaux St. Jacques	E	(91–94)
1995	Gevrey-Chambertin Vieilles Vignes	D	(90–93)
1995	Grands-Echézeaux	EE	(93–96)
1995	Mazis-Chambertin Cuvée A	EE	(92–95)
1995	Mazis-Chambertin Cuvée B	EE	(94–97)
1995	Musigny	EEE	(94–97)
1995	Nuits-St.-Georges Les Argillières	E	(90–93)
1995	Nuits-St.-Georges Les Cailles	E	(92–95)
1995	Nuits-St.-Georges Les Pruliers	E	(90–93?)
1995	Nuits-St.-Georges La Richemone	E	(90–93)
1995	Nuits-St.-Georges Les St. Georges	E	(92–95)
1995	Nuits-St.-Georges Les Vaucrains	E	(91–94)
1996	Pommard Charmots	EE	(90–92+)
1995	Pommard Charmots	E	(90–92)
1996	Pommard Cuvée Dames de la Charité (Hospices de Beaune)	EE	(89–91)
1996	Pommard Epenots	EE	(91–93)
1995	Pommard Epenots	E	(91–93)
1996	Pommard Rugiens	EE	(92–94)
1995	Pommard Rugiens	E	(91–94)
1996	Pommard Vieilles Vignes	E	(88–89+)
1995	Pommard Vieilles Vignes	D	(88–90+)
1996	Savigny-Lès-Beaune	D	(87–88)
1996	Volnay	E	(87–90)
1995	Volnay	D	(87–89)
1996	Volnay Clos des Chênes	E	(87–89)
1995	Volnay Clos des Chênes	E	(90–92+)

1995 Volnay Santenots	E	(89–92)
1995 Vosne-Romanée Cuvée Royale	EE	(88–91?)
1995 Vosne-Romanée Les Beaux Monts	E	(89–92?)
1995 Vosne-Romanée Les Champs Perdrix	EE	(90–93)
1995 Vosne-Romanée La Croix Blanche	EE	(90–93)
1995 Vosne-Romanée La Croix Rameau	EE	(89–92)
1995 Vosne-Romanée Les Petits Monts	EE	(91–94)
1995 Vosne-Romanée Les Suchots	E	(89–92)

Dominique Laurent is producing some of Burgundy's finest red wines. An assistant pastry chef by training, Laurent has created, in a few short years (his first vintage was 1989), a *négociant* firm whose spectacular wines sell out on a prearrival basis . . . before any reviews can be published!

He works closely with a number of growers whom he encourages to employ organic or even biodynamic viticultural practices. The grapes are crushed and the resulting juice fermented into wine by the individual vignerons. Laurent then assembles a group of tasters he trusts (including Michel Bettane, a highly respected French wine critic) to assist him in selecting the finest wines. Financed by a wealthy Belgium consortium, Laurent is capable of paying exorbitant prices for wines coming from some of Burgundy's oldest parcels. Once purchased, the wines are transferred to one of Laurent's three or four cellars in the town of Nuits for their *élevage* (literally the upbringing of the wines; this consists of everything that takes place after the fermentation, including bottling).

He is not willing to spell out his *élevage* techniques, largely because he does not want people to know his "secrets." He told me that he uses the earth's and moon's gravitational pulls in his winemaking and spoke of assisting the "biological development" of the wines, performing "sulfur optimization techniques," never topping off barrels during the summer months, and "precipitating volatile acidity out of the wines." Laurent is obsessed with lees, which he feels nourish and enrich his wines, providing them with their immense depth and dimension. What is understood about his *élevage* techniques is that he never adds sulfur to a wine located in a new oak barrel and that he often racks his wines from one barrel to another (sometimes from one new oak cask to another new one, thereby earning his wines the 200% new oak moniker).

My tasting history with Dominique Laurent's wines is limited. I have had a few of his 1992s, 1993s, and 1994s, as well as the 1995s, 1996s, and 1997s tasted from barrel. They are rich, concentrated, tight wines with well-integrated oak and structured, balanced personalities, with excellent aging potential.

The medium to dark ruby-colored 1996 Chorey-Lès-Beaune reveals lovely aromas of violet-laced blueberries. This elegant, refined, light- to medium-bodied, creamy-textured wine offers cherries and blackberries in its pure, pleasing, and easy-to-drink character. It is neither complex, powerful, nor long, but it is absolutely delicious. Drink it over the next 3–4 years. Similarly colored, the 1996 Savigny-Lès-Beaune displays blackberries awash in toast-infused mineral and ironlike scents. This silky-textured, medium-bodied, and harmonious wine is filled with sexy layers of red and black fruits as well as spicy oak notes. Anticipated maturity: now–2004. The dark ruby/purple-colored 1996 Volnay has ripe blackberries blended with floral, mineral, and earthlike aromas. What follows is concentrated, chewy textured, yet elegant. Gorgeous layers of plums, cassis, licorice, and black cherries make up this wine's complex flavor profile. Anticipated maturity: now–2004.

Lovers of new oak will be seduced by Laurent's Hospices de Beaune offerings. However, I would have prefered it to be less obtrusive. It is unfair to fault Laurent, as the Hospices is required to use 100% new oak. Nevertheless, the dark-colored 1996 Auxey-Duresses Cuvée Boillot exhibits sweet blackberries laced with vanilla and toastlike flavors and a medium- to full-bodied, thickly textured, chewy personality. This concentrated and extracted wine is densely packed with licorice, superripe blackberries, and copious oak. Drink it between 2000 and 2005.

Produced from 60-year-old vines located in the Noizons vineyard (just above the premier cru Charmots), the medium to dark ruby-colored 1996 Pommard Vieilles Vignes has profound red and black fruit aromas. This gorgeously delineated wine is replete with black cherries, cassis, and violets in its velvety-textured, opulent, and medium- to full-bodied flavor profile. Anticipated maturity: now–2004. From even older vines (nearly 100 years old!), the black/purple-colored 1996 Pommard Charmots reveals supersweet black fruit aromas infused with violets, roses, and Asian spices. This fabulously ripe and extraordinarily layered wine is full bodied, creamy textured, seductive, and oh, so hedonistic! Intense waves of jammy (yet focused) blueberries, cherries, and raspberries overpower the senses in this formidably long wine. If this sensual Pommard takes on additional complexity, my score will appear conservative. Anticipated maturity: now–2006. Produced from vines planted in 1899, the dark-colored 1996 Pommard Epenots has deep black cherry, Asian spice, and gamey scents. This oily-textured, full-bodied, refined wine is more complex and profound than the Charmots and nearly as seductive. Dense and rich, it is crammed with blackberries, plums, blueberries, red cherries, and earth. This muscular yet elegant offering should reach its peak of maturity by 2002 and can easily be cellared through 2007. Even better, and produced from 60-year-old vines, the black/ruby-colored 1996 Pommard Rugiens has overripe cassis and blackberry aromas infused with violets and traces of toasted oak. A massive blockbuster, it is full bodied and silky textured and saturates the palate with layers of black currants, cherries, licorice, dried plums, and leather. The incredibly long finish allows a glimpse of this formidable wine's copious yet supple tannins. Anticipated maturity: 2002–2009. The 1996 Pommard Cuvée Dames de la Charité (Hospices de Beaune) has a dark ruby color and a gorgeous bouquet of plummy ripe fruit. This fat, oily-textured, and medium- to full-bodied wine is intense and fresh and has a massively sweet core of cherries, black raspberries, and raspberries intermingled with abundant spicy oak. While well crafted, it lacks the punch of Laurent's three previous wines and finishes on an excessively oaky and slightly rough (tannic) note. Anticipated maturity: 2001–2006.

Produced from four vineyards, Montrevenots, Tuvilains, Sizies, and Reversées (the highest percentage being from Montrevenots), the bright, medium to dark ruby-colored 1996 Beaune Premier Cru has an intricate black fruit, mineral, and stone-scented nose. On the palate, it offers thick, silky-textured, and medium- to full-bodied layers of blackberries, raspberries, and cherries as well as traces of gravel, chalk, and mocha. This first-rate Beaune should be at its peak of maturity between 2000 and 2006. Whole-cluster fermentation was employed to craft the fabulous and medium to dark ruby-colored 1996 Beaune Grèves. Lovely aromas of candied orange peels, raspberries, cherries, and strawberries give way to this medium- to full-bodied, intense, seductive (yet structured and firm), vibrant wine. Its floral, red fruit-filled flavor profile lingers for at least 30 seconds. This impressive wine will provide near-term drinking yet should evolve effortlessly for up to 10 years. Anticipated maturity: now–2008. The dark ruby/purple-colored 1996 Beaune Clos des Mouches should turn out to be awesome. Profound aromas of blueberries, violets, and roses are intermingled with raw meat, stones, and traces of leather in this rich, powerful, and medium- to full-bodied wine. Silky textured and mouth coating, it possesses an impressive hold on the palate, saturating it with perfumed blackberries, minerals, and cassis liqueur-like flavors. While this wine is seductive, it is also structured and firm. Last, its persistent finish reveals copious quantities of supple tannins. Anticipated maturity: 2000–2008.

When Laurent filled my glass with the 1996 Volnay Clos des Chênes my expectations were high because I had been enthralled with the 1995. However, this medium to dark ruby-colored and well-made wine did not inspire me. It offers beautiful black cherry and floral aromas as well as a medium- to full-bodied, well-balanced, and silky-textured personality. Blackberries, cherries, and black raspberries are found in this toasty and spicy wine. Where is the concentration, power, and depth I found in the 1995? Laurent informed me that the wine was produced from the same old-vine source as the previous vintage. Could it be that the yields were too high? Anticipated maturity: now–2004.

According to Laurent, the Hospices de Beaune employed whole-cluster fermentation when it crafted the dark ruby-colored 1996 Corton Cuvée Docteur Peste. Intense aromas of ripe red fruits and toasty oak are followed by a massive and powerful explosion of cherries, candied raspberries, and strawberries in this full-bodied, concentrated, rich, and well-proportioned wine. This wine is well made and offers wonderful fruit but finishes with a pre-ponderance of oak flavors, a characteristic shared by all of the Hospices' wines. However, I have no doubt about this wine's quality, as it will almost assuredly be an outstanding offering after it is bottled, particularly given Laurent's soft, hand-bottling methods. Anticipated maturity: 2000–2007.

Produced from 50-year-old vines, the dark ruby-colored 1995 Vosne-Romanée Les Beaux Monts reveals elegant, refined, and intense aromatics of deep black cherries and a magnificently velvety-textured, full-bodied, cassis and white pepper-laden, oak-imbued flavor profile. The abundant oak was not integrated when I tasted this wine (hence the question mark), but Laurent assures me that it will "precipitate out." Anticipated maturity: 2002–2012. Similarly dark colored, the 1995 Vosne-Romanée Les Suchots exhibits coffee, herb, cassis, and roasted aromas, extremely thick, blackberry and blueberry flavors, and full body. Concentrated and intense, the wine has a distinct wild game animalistic side that Laurent claims will not be present in the bottled wine. It will be at its best between 2002 and 2011.

Aromatically, the dark ruby-colored 1995 Chambolle-Musigny Les Cras reveals elegant cherry, crisp currant, and mineral scents. Superripe plummy and black cherry flavors are found in its highly structured, masculine, full-bodied, intense flavor profile. Anticipated maturity: 2001–2009. Ruby colored, the 1995 Chambolle-Musigny Les Amoureuses possesses lovely, sweet, refined aromatics of red currants and violets and a thick, massively endowed, slightly gamey, blueberry-and-cassis-packed personality intertwined with touches of raw meat. This wine's oak was not well integrated when I tasted it. Will it be resolved at the time of bottling? It will be at its best between 2000 and 2009.

The dark ruby-colored 1995 Gevrey-Chambertin Combe aux Moines (whole-cluster fermentation was employed on this wine) reveals a deep and amazingly concentrated nose of raspberries and superripe cherries. Extraordinarily extracted flavors of blackberries, cassis, cola, and Asian spices together with an admirably long finish characterize this full-bodied, husky wine. Anticipated maturity: 2004–2012. The spectacular 1995 Gevrey-Chambertin Lavaux St. Jacques possesses a black color as well as intense and complex aromatics of coffee, roasted herbs, cassis, cherries, stones, and flowers. Produced in equal parts from 90- and 50+-year-old vineyards, this wine offers an amazingly deep, silky, sultry, yet elegant flavor profile packed with tangy, sweet cherries. Highly structured and full bodied, this wine (which Laurent referred to as a "reactionary Gevrey") will be at its best between 2002 and 2012. Laurent employed his "200%" new oak treatment on the medium to dark ruby-colored 1995 Gevrey-Chambertin Clos St. Jacques. It reveals deeply spicy red berry aromatics and superbly silky, supple plums and strawberries in its chewy yet elegant, medium- to full-bodied, extremely oaky flavor profile. Laurent, who says the excessive oak flavors will melt away during his élevage, does not feel this wine will age well. Anticipated maturity: 2000–2007. Whole-cluster fermentation was again used on the dark ruby-colored 1995

Gevrey-Chambertin Les Champeaux. It offers sweet red and black berry aromatics and an intensely ripe, jammy, viscous, full-bodied flavor profile packed with plummy concentrated fruit. Well delineated and structured, it possesses ripe, round tannins in its admirable finish. Anticipated maturity: 2002–2009. I tasted the fabulous, ruby/purple-colored 1995 Gevrey-Chambertin Vieilles Vignes prior to its being transferred from a previously used barrel into a new one. Revealing superbly well-defined aromatics of sweet cherries and herbs, this exceptionally well-made wine possesses a full-bodied, thick, concentrated, and lively core of red berry fruit. The outstanding score I have given this wine may appear overly conservative after it has acquired additional complexity and nuanced flavors from aging in the new oak barrels. Anticipated maturity: 2002–2010.

In the 1995 vintage, Dominique Laurent acquired two separate Mazis-Chambertins, which he did not blend because he believed they were so different. Aromatically, the medium to dark ruby-colored 1995 Mazis-Chambertin Cuvée A reveals roasted herb and mocha scents. This full-bodied, thick wine is highly structured and possesses attractive flavors of raspberries, and black cherries. Copious quantities of tannin can be discerned in its remarkably long, well-defined finish. Anticipated maturity: 2003–2012. Produced from a vineyard planted in 1904, the dark ruby-colored 1995 Mazis-Chambertin Cuvée B is an extraordinary wine. It displays mind-blowingly expansive aromas of cherry cola, Asian spices, and violets. Enormously concentrated, it explodes with flavors of blackberries, cherries, and cassis intertwined with stones, herbs, and superbly integrated oak notes for added complexity. It is full bodied, powerful, and gorgeously balanced and structured for the long haul. Anticipated maturity: 2003–2015+.

The medium ruby-colored 1995 Nuits-St.-Georges Les Argillières possessed a muted, unyielding nose the day of my tasting, but on its medium- to full-bodied and velvety palate, it revealed beautifully ripe, sweet cherries intermingled with crisp currants and an elegant yet tannic and oaky finish. Its copious quantities of lush fruit will outlive the tannins. Anticipated maturity: 2003–2008. Exceedingly different stylistically, the ruby/purple-colored 1995 Nuits-St.-Georges Les Pruliers (produced from an old-vine parcel of an uncertain age) exhibits deep blackberry and roasted coffee aromas and a foursquare, highly structured, earthy, cassis-laden, and extremely oaky flavor profile. If the oak is well integrated into this wine prior to bottling, it will easily merit its rating. Anticipated maturity: 2002–2009. Laurent's dark-colored, almost black, 1995 Nuits-St.-Georges Les Vaucrains reveals a brooding, masculine nose of tangy cherries and an exquisite, superconcentrated, thick-textured, lively yet highly structured flavor profile packed with stones, minerals, and red berries. This superb wine will be at its best between 2002 and 2012. Harvested at 13% natural sugar levels (almost unheard of in Burgundy!), the dark ruby-colored 1995 Nuits-St.-Georges La Richemone displays hugely concentrated, ripe red and black fruit aromas with a touch of volatile acidity and a sublimely sweet and lively, deep cherry, and currant flavor profile. This is a delicious, medium- to full bodied, polished, feminine-style Nuits. It will be at its peak between 2001 and 2008. Laurent jokingly refers to his out-of-this world 1995 Nuits-St.-Georges Les St. Georges as his "Michel Bettane cuvée" because it possesses all the components he believes Bettane wants to see in a wine. Medium to dark ruby colored, it reveals raspberries and Bing cherries in its lively, perfumed nose and a sublime, medium- to full-bodied flavor profile composed of superripe, chewy red fruits, violets, and Asian spices. With an admirable finish as well as exceptional length and focus, it will be at its best between 2002 and 2012. His "Robert Parker cuvée," the dark ruby-colored 1995 Nuits-St.-Georges Les Cailles, is crafted from 75-year-old tiny cluster-producing vines harvested at a ton of fruit per acre. Revealing unheard-of quantities of Asian spices, roasted herbs, and superconcentrated cassislike aromas, it is an intensely thick, full-bodied, powerful, immense wine packed with chocolate-covered cherries. Highly structured and built for the long haul, it possesses an amazingly long finish. Anticipated maturity: 2002–2012+.

Dominique Laurent has created what he refers to as his "Rare Series." The following five wines (in addition to the Vosne-Romanée Cuvée Royale) will be offered only in 6-bottle cases, containing 1 bottle from each vineyard. The medium to dark ruby-colored 1995 Vosne-Romanée Champs Perdrix possesses a superripe concentrated nose of red berry fruit as well as a mocha, chocolate, and cherry-laced, elegant flavor profile. Medium to full bodied and supple, this exceptionally delicious wine will be at its best between 2000 and 2008. The darker-colored 1995 Vosne-Romanée La Croix Blanche reveals sweet, minerally, and stony aromas and a concentrated, complex, medium- to full-bodied, oily-textured personality packed with sultry flavors of wild cherry bubble gum, leather, and earth. Anticipated maturity: 2001–2009. Ruby/purple colored, the 1995 Vosne-Romanée La Croix Rameau displays an elegant, feminine nose of blackberries, stones, and touches of salty sea breeze. Flavors of iodine are intertwined with sweet black cherries and raspberries in this medium- to full-bodied, thick, and delicious wine. It will be at its best between 2001 and 2008. The ruby/purple-colored 1995 Vosne-Romanée Les Petits Monts is an extraordinary Vosne, better than many producers' grands crus. It displays intensely ripe, luscious red fruit aromas and an exquisite velvety, sultry, amazingly intense, full-bodied flavor profile packed with thick, almost unctuous cherries. Laurent's "200%" new oak treatment was employed on this magnificent wine, yet the oak is so well integrated that it quasi-impossible to detect. Anticipated maturity: 2002–2010+.

The ruby-colored 1995 Echézeaux surprised me with its almost Pauillac-style nose composed of oil, salt, and what Dominique Laurent referred to as pencil lead. It is an elegant, medium-bodied, sweet, and beautifully concentrated wine packed with crisp berries and violets. Anticipated maturity: 2000–2008. Truly extraordinary, Laurent's medium to dark ruby-colored 1995 Grands-Echézeaux (produced from vines planted in 1926) reveals mouthwatering superripe black cherry, perfumed aromas of amazing depth. Awesomely sweet, this violet and red berry-laden, spicy, full-bodied, harmonious wine is elegant and perfectly structured and possesses an intensely long finish. It will be at its best between 2002 and 2012. Medium to dark ruby colored, Laurent's 1995 Clos Vougeot displays a beautifully elegant Asian spice and blackberry-scented nose and an extraordinarily velvety-textured, full-bodied, candied fruit-packed flavor profile. Exceedingly well made and concentrated, it has a superbly long and supple finish. Anticipated maturity: 2002–2012.

Produced from old wines, the dark-colored 1995 Musigny has an enticingly gorgeous nose of Asian spices, violets, and sweet plums. Earthy, minerally, and floral on the palate, this is a full-bodied, stupendous wine—powerful yet refined, muscular yet elegant. Highly structured and harmonious, it will age gracefully. Drink it between 2004 and 2014. Extremely dark colored, Laurent's Bonnes Mares is one of the finest burgundies produced in the 1995 vintage. It displays amazingly concentrated aromas of cassis, violets, and blackberries. This wine possesses extraordinary depth of flavor, exhibiting thick cherry and earth tones intertwined with a mineral component. Full bodied, incredibly intense, and armed with a prodigious finish, it is highly structured and capable of extended cellaring. Anticipated maturity: 2003–2015+.

Produced from vines over 80 years old, the dark ruby-colored 1995 Chambertin Clos de Bèze has incredibly floral (orange blossoms, violets, and vine flowers) and blackberry scents that jump from the glass. This wine's explosive attack is packed with cassis and blueberries as well as earth tones for additional complexity. A precise, dense, full-bodied blockbuster, it possesses great depth as well as an exemplary finish. Anticipated maturity: 2005–2015. Also very dark colored, the regal 1995 Chambertin reveals enveloping aromas of coffee, herbs, and black cherries as well as a viscous, full-bodied, massively endowed, rich, blackberry-and-cassis-laden flavor profile. It exhibits a touch of volatile acidity, which will likely disappear prior to bottling. Anticipated maturity: 2003–2014. Laurent's dark-ruby colored 1995

Charmes-Chambertin reveals a portlike nose of superripe fruits and white pepper. It is a beautifully crafted, elegant, sweet cherry-packed, supple wine with touches of vanilla, Asian spices, and violets for additional complexity. It will be at its best between 2002 and 2010.

Produced from 70-year-old vines, the medium to dark ruby-colored 1995 Pommard Vieilles Vignes is one of the finest village wines I have tasted. It reveals explosive and intense aromas of cherries and blackberries as well as a lively, thick, full-bodied character jam-packed with highly extracted and crisp black cherries and blueberries. A fabulously long finish ends on copious quantities of soft tannins and touches of new oak. Anticipated maturity: 2000–2006. Potentially Laurent's weakest wine (and still meriting an excellent rating!), the medium to dark ruby-colored 1995 Volnay is produced from 30–40-year-old vines and is 100% destemmed prior to vinification. It offers elegant red and black berry aromas and a silky-textured, medium- to full-bodied, and chewy personality with plum, blueberry, and floral flavors. Anticipated maturity: now–2005. The ruby-colored 1995 Volnay Santenots possesses a superripe concentrated nose of Bing cherry jam and plums as well as an explosive yet structured and elegant, prune, violet, and currant-laced flavor profile. Medium to full bodied and thickly textured, this superb wine will be at its best between 2001 and 2007. The sublime 1995 Volnay Clos des Chênes possesses a dark ruby/purple color as well as intense aromatics of black cherries, flowers, and coffee. This full-bodied and viscous wine offers an amazingly deep, highly extracted, and concentrated mouthful of cassis, blackberries, and violets. Its exceptionally long finish with soft, ripe tannins tapers off after 45 seconds. Drink it between 2003 and 2009.

In 1995 Dominique Laurent crafted three reference-point Pommards. Produced from vines that are almost 100 years old, the medium to dark ruby-colored 1995 Pommard Charmots displays gorgeous and elegant aromas of raspberries, crisp cherries, and touches of mocha. This superbly concentrated wine has complex, powerful, and extracted flavors of blackberries, red currants, Asian spices, coffee, and herbs in its oily-textured, full-bodied, and exquisite character. Anticipated maturity: 2002–2009. Even better, the dark ruby-colored 1995 Pommard Epenots (from vines planted in 1898!) exhibits mouthwatering, superripe blackberries, violets, roses, and roasting spices aromatically. Amazingly deep and beautifully delineated flavors of black cherries, cassis, and stones are found in this full-bodied, awesomely sweet, superbly balanced, and thick wine. Its superb structure and amazingly long and persistent finish guarantee its longevity. Anticipated maturity: 2003–2011+. Laurent's black/purple-colored extraordinary 1995 Pommard Rugiens roars out of the glass with hugely sweet cherry and perfumed aromas. It possesses mind-blowing, superconcentrated flavors of candied cherries, blackberries, and red currants intermingled with dried plums and raisins in its massively endowed, thick-textured, and incredibly long flavor profile. This extraordinary Pommard has all the components for long-term cellaring—perfect structure, superb balance, copious but supple tannins, huge quantities of fruit, and an awesome ripeness. It amazes me that this wine, subjected to Laurent's "200% new oak" technique, has perfectly integrated wood flavors! Amazing! Anticipated maturity: 2002–2015.

DOMAINE LÉCHENEAUT (NUITS-ST.-GEORGES)

1996 Chambolle-Musigny	D	(87–89)
1995 Chambolle-Musigny	D	(86–88)
1996 Chambolle-Musigny Premier Cru	E	(89–91)
1995 Chambolle-Musigny Premier Cru	E	(88–90)
1996 Clos de la Roche	EE	(96–98)
1995 Clos de la Roche	EE	(91–94)

1996	Morey-St.-Denis	D	(86–88)
1995	Morey-St.-Denis Pierre Vivant	D	(86–88)
1996	Nuits-St.-Georges	D	(87–89)
1996	Nuits-St.-Georges Les Cailles	E	(92–94+)
1995	Nuits-St.-Georges Les Cailles	E	(90–93)
1996	Nuits-St.-Georges Les Damodes	E	(90–93)
1995	Nuits-St.-Georges Les Damodes	E	(89–92)
1996	Vosne-Romanée	D	(87–89+)

Note: The Lécheneaut brothers produce 100% new oak cuvées of their village appellation wines for their U.S. importer. Other markets receive wines aged in 70% new oak. When asked which they prefer they said that in the near term they like their own cuvées, but with bottle aging they "may" prefer the Kacher cuvées.

The two Lécheneaut brothers, Philippe and Vincent, run this 22.23-acre (9-hectare) estate employing a conservative philosophy of cutting back the vines for low yields. Additionally, all the unworthy grapes are discarded, the remaining ones are all destemmed, and a cold prefermentation maceration is practiced, followed by a warm fermentation. A high percentage of new oak casks are used during the *élevage,* and the wines are bottled without any fining or filtering. The results speak for themselves. These wines are lush and sweet but capable of aging well, as the 1990s I have in my cellar continue to prove.

Medium to dark ruby colored, the 1995 Morey-St.-Denis Pierre Vivant ("living stone" in French), displays an enticing nose of sweet cherries with an intense floral spice and flavors of ripe red berries with a touch of earth and mineral. Silky textured and medium bodied, this delicious, yet not complex wine will offer excellent drinking from now to 2004. The 1995 Chambolle-Musigny reveals a charming spicy and floral nose and an elegant mouth packed with dark cherries and rose petals. Slightly tannic on the finish, this medium-bodied wine should be cellared for 3–4 years before 2005. Regrettably, only 75 cases of the medium to dark ruby-colored 1995 Chambolle-Musigny Premier Cru (made from 53-year-old vines in the Les Borniques 75% and Les Plantes 25% vineyards) were produced. Perfumed with roses and minerals, this structured, medium- to full-bodied, thickly textured wine is packed with fat, ripe red fruits and should be at its best between 2000 and 2005. From a 40-year-old parcel bordering Vosne-Romanée, the dark ruby-colored 1995 Nuits-St.-Georges Les Damodes reveals a fabulously perfumed, spicy sweet nose and an extremely elegant, structured, delineated, thick-textured, tangy fruit-packed personality. A real winner! Drink it between 2002 and 2008. Domaine Lécheneaut's top Nuits have consistently been their Nuits-St.-Georges Les Cailles. The 1995 is no different: dark ruby colored, it possesses an intense, complex, but tight nose, with spectacular, explosive ripe black fruits intermingled with minerals, spices, and stones. Remarkably, this wine continues to build in intensity on the palate after expectoration. Thick textured, full bodied, long (30 seconds), and beautifully delineated, it will be at its peak between 2002 and 2012. Last, the dark-colored 1995 Clos de la Roche offers powerful blackberry and cassis fruit with clean earthy aromas. Chewy flavors of sweet and lush stones, minerals, mocha, and earth are ensconced in superripe black cherries. This is a powerful, full-bodied, huge, yet feminine, highly structured wine with an extremely long finish. Anticipated maturity: 2003–2015. Bravo!

Philippe and Vincent Lécheneaut produce wines that resemble them—strong, muscular, and expressive. In the past I have described certain wines as being like ballerinas, well-known actresses, football players, and so on. These wines are rugby players, strong, rough (at first), but explosive, with considerable stamina (staying power). I tasted their 1996s twice, once in November 1997 and then again in late January 1998. At my first tasting the wines were quite backward, oaky, and tannic, but 2¹/₂ months later they had softened while still displaying loads of fruit. Some of these wines are worth making every effort to locate.

The medium to dark ruby-colored 1996 Morey-St.-Denis is produced from this estate's youngest vines, planted in 1977. It offers a sweet, red and black fruit-laced nose that is followed by a character of excellent depth, intensity, and ripeness. This is a medium- to full-bodied, expressive, thick, lively, and fat wine with plump cherries, blackberries, spices, and toasty oak flavors. Drink it over the next 5 years. The 1996 Chambolle-Musigny is also medium to dark ruby colored and reveals a floral nose of violets, black cherries, and spicy oak. This silky-textured, medium- to full-bodied, bright, and fresh wine has jammy raspberries, roses, and minerals in its highly appealing flavor profile. Its long finish offers loads of soft tannins. Anticipated maturity: now–2004. Displaying a bright, medium to dark ruby color and aromas reminiscent of minerals soaked in cassis liqueur and violets, the 1996 Nuits-St.-Georges is a tangy, rich, broad, and medium- to full-bodied wine. Layers of juicy and intense black cherries, blackberries, and stones can be found in this structured, thick, and powerful offering. Stylistically, I preferred the more charming and elegant Chambolle, but this offering's palate-saturating presence is impressive. Anticipated maturity: 2000–2005. This estate's 1996 Vosne-Romanée may prove to be their finest village wine. Medium to dark ruby colored and revealing sweet blackberries, roses, violets, and Asian spices on the nose, this intense, fat, broad-shouldered, full-bodied offering is crammed with superripe fruits. Layers of candied raspberries, cassis, cherries, and stones are discernible in this mouth-coating, highly structured, and firm beauty. It is presently lacking harmony, but I am confident its components will come together. It should be at its peak between 2001 and 2006.

Produced from the Les Borniques and Les Plantes vineyards, the dark-colored 1996 Chambolle-Musigny Premier Cru exhibits an extroverted nose of black cherries, blueberries, violets, and toast. This offering is more powerful, intense, and profound. Its full-bodied, thick, and muscular core of inky dark fruits, minerals, and flowers is juicy, plump, and broad yet has an appealing refinement. It is an extremely well-made wine, proportioned, balanced, and flavorful and possessing a long, supple finish. It should evolve beautifully with cellaring. Anticipated maturity: 2002–2008. The 1996 Nuits-St.-Georges Les Damodes is dark ruby colored and has an expressive nose of blackberries, cassis liqueur, and black cherries. This chewy-textured, masculine, powerful, fat, and muscular offering is crammed with red and black cherries, minerals, and toasty oak. It is juicy, fresh, highly structured, and filled with satiny tannins and has a persistent, focused, and marvelously delineated finish. Consumers lucky enough to acquire this wine are advised to cellar it for a few years. Anticipated maturity: 2002–2008. Lécheneaut's extraordinary 1996 Nuits-St.-Georges Les Cailles is better than many grands crus I tasted. Dark ruby colored, it offers an enticing nose of black cherries, violets, licorice, and toasty oak scents. This massive, harmonious, superripe, rich, juicy, full-bodied, and almost overpowering wine has loads of blackberries, cassis, black raspberries, minerals, and mocha in its complex flavor profile. This broad, expansive, concentrated, refined, and extremely long offering is truly special. Anticipated maturity: 2002–2008+.

How do you top the Lécheneaut brothers' 1996 Les Cailles? With their 1996 Clos de la Roche! When I tasted this stunning wine in November 1997, I was blown away by its density of hugely ripe fruit, yet it took a few minutes of tasting for me to be convinced that its powerful oak flavors and boatloads of tannin would not present a problem. When I retasted it at the end of January, the oak and tannins were substantially more integrated. This dark ruby/purple-colored blockbuster reveals intense aromas of cassis, blackberries, Asian spices, hoisin sauce, earth, and toasty oak. Its awesome full-bodied, velvety-textured, and mouth-coating personality is so densely packed with superripe black fruits that a knife and fork seem re-

quired to taste it effectively. This wine's power, depth, concentration, and immense length
are given glorious focus by its fresh acidity. Wow! Anticipated maturity: 2004–2012+.

DOMAINE PHILIPPE LECLERC (GEVREY-CHAMBERTIN)

1995 Bourgogne Les Bons Batons	C	(86–87+)
1995 Chambolle-Musigny Les Babillères	D	(87–89)
1995 Gevrey-Chambertin Les Cazetiers	E	(90–92?)
1995 Gevrey-Chambertin Les Champeaux	E	(89–91)
1995 Gevrey-Chambertin en Champs	D	(88–90)
1995 Gevrey-Chambertin Combe aux Moines	E	(90–94)
1995 Gevrey-Chambertin Les Platières	D	(88–90)

Dressed in black, with long hair, tattoos, and leather "accessories," Philippe Leclerc looks
more like a guitar player out of a 1970s rock band than a vigneron from a small village in
France. Everyone seems to have a favorite Leclerc anecdote. Mine involves the black coffin
draped with a nude female mannequin he used to have in his living room.

Philippe Leclerc's wines are not for the faint-hearted! Readers must be forewarned—these
are dense, black, superconcentrated, *tannic*, backward, rugged wines that demand to be cellared. Generally they tend to be preferred by lovers of big Cabernets than by those wanting
elegant, supple Pinot Noirs. Their "packaging," as people in the business refer to it, involves
strangely shaped bottles with labels depicting jousting knights. The labels Leclerc had originally designed were deemed so outlandish by his importers and distributors that he was
forced to scale them back . . . a bit!

Along with his brother, René, and Christian Serafin, Philippe Leclerc is the latest picker
in Gevrey. Always aged in 100% new oak, sometimes for upward of 3 years, Leclerc's wines
are never fined or filtered. Expect these wines to be long-lived and to throw a substantial
sediment.

In years where the fruit ripens enough to withstand the onslaught of new oak (such as
1990 and 1995), Leclerc produces a Bourgogne Les Bons Batons, which is one of the rare
values to be found in Burgundy. Revealing a deep, enticing nose of roasted dark fruits and a
silky-textured, powerful, blackberry-filled, medium- to full-bodied mouth, it is a wine that
needs 5–7 years to soften its tannins, not unlike the 1990 offering, which is drinking beautifully out of my cellar now. The ruby-colored 1995 Chambolle-Musigny Les Babillères has an
elegant nose of violets and dark fruits with touches of sweet oak and a huge, tannic mouth
packed with floral flavors and chewy black cherries. It will be at its best between 2003 and
2009. Exhibiting a deep nose of mocha and sweet, dark berries, the 1995 Gevrey-
Chambertin Les Platières offers a velvety texture on the entry followed by a massively structured, tannic core of ripe black berries and oak. Full bodied and long, it requires 7–9 years
of cellaring and will keep for 8+ years. Equally good but with flavors leaning more toward
chocolate, stones, and minerals, the 1995 Gevrey-Chambertin en Champs should also be
drunk between 2003 and 2012+. A step up, the dark-colored 1995 Gevrey-Chambertin Les
Champeaux displays deeply roasted fruits, coffee, and chocolate on the nose and an awesomely sweet and powerful mouth packed with bacon, blackberries, and cassis. Concentrated, full bodied, tannic, and long, it will be at its peak between 2005 and 2013. The one
1995 Leclerc offering that has me questioning whether the fruit has a chance to outlive the
massive, aggressive tannin is the Gevrey-Chambertin Les Cazetiers. Possessing a black
color and an oaky, grilled fruit nose, this highly extracted and concentrated wine has a
dense, ripe core of dark fruits ensconced in huge, mean tannins. If this wine's fruit has out-
lasted its tannins after 12+ years of cellaring, it will be a spectacular wine.

A few wine writers have recently written that some producers in Burgundy are making Pinot Noir that resembles Syrah. My impression is that highly extracted, late-picked, and lavishly oaked Pinot Noir does in fact show traits of Syrah in its youth. Both varietals have a tendency to contain high acid levels (relative to Merlot and Cabernet) and often exhibit berry fruit characteristics. Philippe Leclerc's dynamite 1995 Gevrey-Chambertin Combe aux Moines certainly could be confused with a northern Rhône wine during its early stage of development. Readers who love Côte Rôtie and Hermitage will adore it. Dark colored, almost black, and revealing an awesomely dense, ripe, deep, nose of cassis, mocha, spices, and oak, this monster of a wine explodes in the mouth with rich, layered, roasted black fruits. Full bodied and thick, with a hard tannic backbone, it indeed reminds me more of a young Syrah (but without the typical raspberry and red currant notes) than what I generally taste in Burgundy.

DOMAINE RENÉ LECLERC (GEVREY-CHAMBERTIN)

1996	Gevrey-Chambertin Clos Prieur	D	(87–88)
1995	Gevrey-Chambertin Clos Prieur	D	(86–88)
1996	Gevrey-Chambertin Combe aux Moines	E	(90–93)
1995	Gevrey-Chambertin Combe aux Moines	D	(90–92)
1996	Gevrey-Chambertin Lavaux St. Jacques	E	(88–91+)
1995	Gevrey-Chambertin Lavaux St. Jacques	D	(87–90)
1996	Griotte-Chambertin	EE	(91–94)
1995	Griotte-Chambertin	EE	(91–93+)

Tall, bearded, curly haired, and bespectacled, René Leclerc does not look like a typical Burgundian vigneron (not to speak of his brother, Philippe Leclerc!). Headquartered on the Route Nationale 74, the main Côte d'Or highway that serves as the eastern border to Burgundy's most renowned hillside vineyards, Leclerc has been making concentrated, extracted, elegant, ageworthy burgundies for years. For the first time, he is experimenting with new oak barrels—a positive influence.

The ruby/purple-colored 1995 Gevrey-Chambertin Clos Prieur reveals cassis, black cherries, and a touch of chocolate in the nose, good ripeness, structure, and a medium to full body. Even better, the 1995 Gevrey-Chambertin Lavaux St. Jacques displays attractive spicy and cracked black pepper aromas, lively red fruit flavors, and a chewy, oily, medium-bodied personality. Capable of aging for a minimum of 10 years, both these wines can be drunk much earlier because of their ripe, round tannins. Produced from extremely old vines (ranging from 40 to 80 years old), the dark ruby-colored 1995 Gevrey-Chambertin Combe aux Moines possesses a fabulously deep nose of sweet, dark spices with a touch of mocha. On the palate, this silky-textured, thick, and highly concentrated wine offers flavors of huge ripe black fruits intertwined with a touch of milk chocolate. Built to last, it should be at its best between 2002 and 2014.

Starting with the 1995 vintage, René Leclerc is responsible for producing (en fermage— an arrangement where Leclerc does the vineyard and cellar work and gets to keep two-thirds of the production, with the balance going to the proprietor) some Griotte-Chambertin. This is the first opportunity he has had to produce a grand cru. Dark ruby colored, it reveals an enticing and elegant crisp cherry nose with touches of sweet spice. In the mouth, the wine displays an impressive explosion of dark berries, cherries, and Asian spices. Chewy, fat, silky textured, full bodied, and quite long, this superb wine will repay 6 years of cellaring and keep for at least a decade.

René Leclerc's wines are improving. They are less manipulated than they used to be and are now aged in some new oak (25%–30% according to Leclerc). Additionally, he has reduced the time they spend in the barrel by 6 months. Begrudgingly, Leclerc admits that his former policy of 24 months in barrel resulted in some wines drying out.

The ruby-colored 1996 Gevrey-Chambertin Clos Prieur has a delightfully spicy cookie dough-scented nose that gives way to a well-crafted, medium-bodied, and silky-textured character. This beautifully ripe, tangy, and rich wine is filled with sweet red cherry flavors. Drink it between now and 2003. The 1996 Gevrey-Chambertin Lavaux St. Jacques displays a medium to dark ruby color and aromas of blackberries, cassis, black cherries, and creamy wood spices. It is a delicious, velvety-textured, medium- to full-bodied, and very well-proportioned offering that is redolent in ripe cherries and hints of earth. In addition, its long, focused finish reveals supple tannins. Anticipated maturity: 2001–2007. Exhibiting a darker color, the 1996 Gevrey-Chambertin Combe aux Moines has black raspberries, dark cherries, and freshly ground white pepper in its brooding and austere nose. This sweet, rich, ample, full-bodied, and silk-textured wine has superb breadth, and power. Red cherries, candied apples, loads of Asian spices, and ground black pepper can be found in its flavor profile and long finish. Anticipated maturity: 2003–2010.

Reportedly, the owner of the Domaine des Chézeaux has been reconsidering which vignerons will be tending his vines and crafting his wines in *fermage* and *métayage* agreements. The first evidence of this is the fact that he provided René Leclerc with a parcel of Griotte-Chambertin to work with. It displays a medium to dark ruby color and an enthrallingly expressive nose of sweet red cherries, fresh herbs, and Asian spices. The 1996 is an impressively extracted, powerful, concentrated, and fabulously balanced wine packed with harmonious layers of red and black fruits. Its formidably long finish reveals spicy new oak flavors and plenty of soft tannins. It should be at its peak between 2002 and 2008.

DOMAINE LEROY (VOSNE-ROMANÉE)

1996	Chambertin	EEE	99+
1995	Chambertin	EEE	(95–98)
1996	Chambolle-Musigny Les Charmes	EEE	95
1995	Chambolle-Musigny Les Charmes	EEE	(92–95)
1996	Chambolle-Musigny Les Fremières	EEE	92
1995	Chambolle-Musigny Les Fremières	EEE	(90–92+)
1996	Clos de la Roche	EEE	98+
1995	Clos de la Roche	EEE	(96–98+)
1996	Clos de Vougeot	EEE	98
1995	Clos de Vougeot	EEE	(94–96)
1996	Corton Renardes	EEE	94+
1995	Corton Renardes	EEE	(96–98+)
1995	Gevrey-Chambertin	EE	(89–91)
1996	Gevrey-Chambertin Les Combottes	EEE	93+
1995	Gevrey-Chambertin Les Combottes	EEE	(92–94)
1996	Latricières-Chambertin	EEE	97+
1995	Latricières-Chambertin	EEE	(97–99+)
1996	Musigny	EEE	99+
1995	Musigny	EEE	(96–98+)

1996	Nuits-St.-Georges aux Allots	EE	93
1995	Nuits-St.-Georges aux Allots	EE	(90–93)
1996	Nuits-St.-Georges au Bas de Combe	EE	90
1995	Nuits-St.-Georges au Bas de Combe	EE	(90–93)
1996	Nuits-St.-Georges aux Boudots	EEE	96+
1995	Nuits-St.-Georges aux Boudots	EEE	(94–97)
1996	Nuits-St.-Georges Les Lavières	EE	93
1995	Nuits-St.-Georges Les Lavières	EE	(91–94)
1996	Nuits-St.-Georges Les Vignes Rondes	EEE	95
1995	Nuits-St.-Georges Les Vignes Rondes	EEE	(91–94)
1996	Pommard Les Trois Follots	EE	91
1996	Pommard Les Vignots	EE	92
1995	Pommard Les Vignots	EE	(92–94)
1996	Richebourg	EEE	98+
1995	Richebourg	EEE	(97–99+)
1996	Romanée-St.-Vivant	EEE	97
1995	Romanée-St.-Vivant	EEE	98+
1993	Romanée-St.-Vivant	EEE	100
1996	Savigny-Lès-Beaune Les Narbantons	EE	91+
1995	Savigny-Lès-Beaune Les Narbantons	EE	(90–93+)
1996	Volnay Santenots	EEE	90+
1995	Volnay Santenots	EEE	(91–93+)
1996	Vosne-Romanée Les Beaux Monts	EEE	96
1995	Vosne-Romanée Les Beaux Monts	EEE	(93–96+)
1996	Vosne-Romanée Les Brûlées	EEE	93+
1995	Vosne-Romanée Les Brûlées	EEE	(92–95+)
1996	Vosne-Romanée Les Genevrières	EE	91
1995	Vosne-Romanée Les Genevrières	EE	(89–92)

Robert Parker and I have previously extolled the fact that Mme. Lalou Bize-Leroy makes her wines from incredibly low yields. Why is this point so important that it has to be repeated? Vines, like all fruit-bearing plants, will concentrate their energy in the fruit. This energy is split among all the grape clusters and each individual grape found on a plant. The more this energy is divided among the clusters and grapes, the less each receives. The fewer clusters and grapes a plant possesses, the higher the ratio of energy—and the riper and more concentrated the grape becomes. Call it commonsense agriculture. By keeping her yields so low, Mme. Leroy is able to produce superdark, intense, concentrated, highly extracted, and, to my palate, spectacular wines. In 1995 Domaine Leroy's vineyards averaged 1 ton of fruit per acre (15 hectoliters/hectare). Such yields are the lowest in Burgundy.

Prices for Leroy's wines are astronomical. I recognize that the vast majority of readers cannot afford these wines—assuming they can ever find a bottle. Yet Leroy's wines sell out quickly because she enjoys worldwide demand. My hope is that more vignerons will try to emulate her success and provide burgundy enthusiasts with a greater supply of such stunning wines. Will she serve as a locomotive, pulling the rest of burgundy to a new level of quality?

I have included the cases production for each wine in order for readers to appreciate the rarity of these wines.

Dark ruby colored, the 1995 Volnay Santenots (50 cases) displays dark roasted berries, perfume, and spices on the nose as well as a beautifully elegant, extremely well-balanced, velvety-textured personality packed with black fruits. The finish in this full-bodied wine is impressively long. Drink it between 2004 and 2014. Aromatically, the black-colored 1995 Pommard Les Vignots (200 cases) reveals dark, superripe, and toasty fruits and an intense attack of massively chewy red and black fruits in its powerful, highly structured, and delineated, very long flavor profile. Anticipated maturity: 2003–2012. Ruby/black colored, the 1995 Savigny-Lès-Beaune Les Narbantons (125 cases) exhibits a gorgeous, raspberry, stone, and mineral-packed nose with well-delineated flavors of wild red and black berries and spices in its powerful and full-bodied, thick personality. It should be at its best between 2002 and 2010. Lalou Bize-Leroy told me she felt she had been particularly successful with her 1995 Corton Renardes (125 cases). I thought that it was the single greatest Corton I have ever tasted. Displaying a dark, almost black color and aromas of gamey wild berries, this stupendous wine explodes on the palate with powerful flavors of awesomely ripe cherries, sweet black fruits, and animal notes all embedded in a thick, superstructured, velvety texture. Intense and incredibly long, this wine should be cellared for 10 years before drinking it over the following decade.

The handful of critics that whine about Mme. Leroy's wines all tasting the same should go to the trouble of acquiring and tasting her wines rather than repeating some of Burgundy's most appalling and vicious rumors. The proof is in the pudding, as this intense lineup of distinctly different Nuits demonstrates: the 1995 Nuits-St.-Georges au Bas de Combe (25 cases) reveals an earthy, spicy, dark nose and a highly structured, powerful, masculine, stony, and minerally taste. Medium to full bodied, this chewy, highly extracted wine should be at its peak between 2000 and 2008. Very different, the 1995 Nuits-St.-Georges Les Lavières (125 cases) displays elegant aromas of mocha, stones, and minerals and an awesomely beautiful, powerful, sweet, perfumed, refined, silky texture with rose-packed flavors. Full bodied yet quite feminine, this fabulous Nuits will delight those fortunate enough to acquire any. Drink it between 2003 and 2012. Aromatically spicy and flinty, the dark-colored 1995 Nuits-St.-Georges aux Allots is a superb, masculine, foursquare, minerally, cassis-and-blueberry-filled, medium- to full-bodied, powerful hunk of a wine. Anticipated maturity: 2000–2007. Another super wine, the 1995 Nuits-St.-Georges Les Vignes Rondes (75 cases) is a synthesis in style between the Au Bas de Combe and the Les Lavières; it has the former's spices and earth aromas, masculine structure, yet the latter's elegance and power. Full bodied and packed with baking spices, it will be at its best between 2002 and 2012. Leroy's most profound Nuits is the benchmark-setting opaque and black-colored 1995 Nuits-St.-Georges aux Boudots (250 cases). This extraordinary wine possesses an enthralling nose of wild berries, iron, stones, and some intriguing saltiness. Explosive, powerful, and elegant as well as velvety textured, and packed with copious amounts of sweet red and black fruits, this is a wine of intense depth. It will be at its peak between 2005 and 2018.

Displaying a medium to dark ruby color and a lovely, feminine nose of sweet cherries and roses, the 1995 Vosne-Romanée Les Genevrières (100 cases) is a well-made and structured example of an early-drinking (for Leroy!) Vosne. Medium to full bodied, it will be at its best from now to 2006. From a vineyard I adore for its forward, sultry style, the 1995 Vosne-Romanée Les Brûlées (25 cases) reveals an enticing and exotic nose of spices and berries and a beautifully silky-textured palate crammed with lush red fruits and Asian spices. Attractive, opulent, and sensual, this medium- to full-bodied wine should be at its peak between 2000 and 2010. Mme. Leroy's top Vosne premier cru offering, the dark-colored 1995 Vosne-Romanée Les Beaux Monts (350 cases) exhibits invitingly spicy, deep red and black fruit aromas. The flavors are packed with fat, ripe cherries and touches of earth and cinnamon. Full bodied, velvety textured, incredibly long, and stunningly elegant, this gem will require 7–8 years of cellaring, and hold for 12–15 more years.

A consummate perfectionist, Mme. Leroy feels that with the 1995 vintage she has finally understood how to make a stunning Romanée-St.-Vivant. When all the 1995s have reached their respective peaks, Domaine Leroy's 1995 Romanée-St.-Vivant (175 cases) will most probably be considered as her greatest wine and one of the best burgundies ever produced. Tears filled my eyes as I returned, time and again, to my glass. This vineyard is known by the burgundy cognoscenti as having the most remarkable aromatics to be found but often lacking volume and texture. Its stunning nose was matched with equally marvelous flavors. Dark ruby/purple colored with engulfing aromas of Asian spices, roses, violets, cassis, and red cherries (intermingled with touches of sweet oak), this medium- to full-bodied wine provided a spiritual, nearly levitating experience. Flavors of chewy dark berries, sweet sautéed mushrooms, and a touch of tar unfolded in this sublimely elegant, complex, deeply concentrated wine. A compelling effort, this classic should be at its best between 2005 and 2020.

Exhibiting a black color and deep, powerful cassis and mineral aromas, the otherworldly 1995 Richebourg (100 cases) is a rugged, mammoth wine. Broad shouldered, thick textured, full bodied, and intensely lively, it is packed with sweet toasty red and black currants. Long and stunningly structured, this refined and highly extracted mind-boggling wine needs 10 years of cellaring and will last for 15+. Displaying a luxurious nose of cinnamon, dark cherries, and Asian spices, the 1995 Clos de Vougeot (350 cases made from 5 acres!) has a beautifully spicy entry and deeply structured, stony, highly extracted, dark berry-filled flavors. Velvety textured and medium to full bodied, it requires cellaring for 8–9 years. Anticipated maturity: 2005–2017.

Revealing attractive aromatics of blackberries and violets in addition to flavors of stones, mocha, and superripe purple fruits, the silky-textured, medium- to full-bodied 1995 Chambolle-Musigny Les Fremières (50 cases) will be at its peak from 2002 to 2010. Seductive and gorgeously elegant, the 1995 Chambolle-Musigny Les Charmes (50 cases) exhibits fragrant aromas of sweet, floral red fruits and awesome flavors of luscious cherries with a touch of earth. Medium to full bodied, velvety textured, intensely concentrated, this gem should be drunk between 2004 and 2015. Truly extraordinary, Leroy's 1995 Musigny (50 cases made from 1.24 acres!) displays a spectacularly powerful nose of floral scents and mocha cream. This sublime wine is highly structured, intense, with flavors suggestive of fat, red and black fruits as well as violets. Thick textured, full bodied, and amazingly long, this wine requires 8–10 years of cellaring. It will be at its best after 2006. The 1995 Clos de la Roche (50 cases) offers extravagant aromas of black truffles, nuts, stones, and dark fruits, a delineated thick yet chewy texture, and layers of ripe dark fruits, leather, and earth tonelike flavors. Highly extracted, complex, and intense, this full-bodied behemoth must be cellared for a dozen years. Anticipated maturity: 2009–2024.

Leroy's 1995 Gevrey-Chambertin (25 cases) is superior to some of Burgundy's premiers crus and grands crus. Displaying sweet, roasted, spicy fruits, this medium- to full-bodied, velvety-textured wine has mocha and dark fruit flavors and good structure and length. Drink it between now and 2007. A step up, the exciting 1995 Gevrey-Chambertin Les Combottes (50 cases) reveals aromas of cinnamon and deeply roasted and spicy fruits and a huge, velvety-textured palate that offers fabulously ripe chewy red fruits and Asian spices. Rich and full bodied, this super wine should be drunk between 2004 and 2012. Simply put, Leroy's 1995 Latricières-Chambertin (75 cases) is the finest offering from that vineyard I have tasted. Mouthwatering aromas of sizzling bacon and black fruits wafted from my glass. There is unbelievably great depth of dark cherry fruit and raspberries with roasted, wild game notes in this full-bodied, thick, and incredibly well delineated, lively wine. This stunningly profound wine should not be touched for at least 10 years. Anticipated maturity: 2007–2022. The 1995 Chambertin displays deep aromas of black fruits, stones, and Asian spices. In the mouth this thick, full-bodied, robust wine bursts with layers of toasty, jammy cassis, earth tones and an attractive wild game component. Powerful but tight and tannic, this huge wine will repay extended cellaring; drink it between 2010 and 2020+.

Mme. Bize-Leroy's yields were under 1²/₃ tons of fruit per acre in 1996, dramatically low for the vintage but high for this estate. When I visited her in mid-1997 to taste the 1995s (1 ton per acre), the cellars had a morose look to them—everywhere I looked there were large gaps between the barrels. The two-thirds increase in production drastically changed the appearance of the cellar. When I stopped by in November 1997 for a quick visit and tasting (these notes are from a postbottling tasting done at a later time), gone were the gaps, barrels were stacked on top of each other, and the cellar had taken on a joyful vibrancy. The character of the two vintages reflected this as well. The 1995s were immensely impressive because of their massive concentration. They were not happy or smile-inducing wines; rather, they were brooding and backward. The 1996s, in contrast, were bursting with loads of extroverted, almost effervescent fruit that leads to smiles and laughter.

"There is never any bleeding in my cellars," said Mme. Bize-Leroy just before I gouged myself with my corkscrew, proving her wrong. Of course, she was referring to the winemaking technique of increasing concentration by "bleeding off" the watery juice of a light pressing prior to fermentation, not the results of my battles with her recently bottled 1996s.

As wine lovers have come to expect with every new vintage from this domaine, the 1996 Leroys are extraordinary, benchmark-setting wines. This is the only estate I visited whose 1996s were as concentrated as the 1995s, obviously owing to the fact that Mme. Bize-Leroy kept her yields exceedingly low. These wines will reach their respective peaks sooner than their 1995 counterparts, however, thanks to their softer tannins and brighter, more forward fruit.

Would I be surprised if a few of these wines ultimately merited perfect scores? Absolutely not! To quote Mme. Bize-Leroy, "The 1996s have the best fruit ever!"

The dark ruby-colored 1996 Savigny-Lès-Beaune Les Narbantons reveals a deep, black raspberry-and-cherry-scented nose. On the palate, this gorgeously precise, thick, chewy, intensely concentrated, and extracted wine is medium to full bodied and packed with black cherries, minerals, and currants. This superb Savigny's finish is exceptionally long. Anticipated maturity: 2001–2009. Somewhat lighter colored, the 1996 Pommard Les Trois Follots offers an earth and toasty oak-infused nose followed by a masculine, foursquare, broad-shouldered, and muscular character. This offering is medium to full bodied and structured and boasts blackberries, blueberries, and grilled oak flavors. It should be at its best between 2001 and 2007. The medium to dark ruby-colored 1996 Pommard Les Vignots possesses feminine and refined aromas of violets intertwined with sweet red cherries. This seductive, silky-textured, powerful, and opulent wine enthralls with its dried and fresh red fruit flavors as well as its long, luscious, supple tannin-filled finish. Anticipated maturity: 2000–2009. The 1996 Corton Renardes color appeared to be a touch lighter than the previous wine's. It reveals mouthwatering aromas of superripe cherries, plums, bacon, and sweet rose blossoms. This massive, powerful, superbly balanced, delineated, and velvety-textured wine explodes on the palate with juicy black and red berries, prunes, and wild game flavors. Its mind-boggling finish exhibits loads of dried fruits and soft, supple tannins. I envy the wealthy collectors who will be able to serve it alongside the equally extraordinary 1995! Anticipated maturity: 2003–2012.

The medium to dark ruby-colored 1996 Nuits-St.-Georges au Bas de Combe has a feminine, floral, and blackberry-infused nose as well as a medium- to full-bodied, structured, foursquare, and refined character. It is powerful and velvety textured yet highly detailed. Deeply sweet black fruits and minerals are found in its precise and persistent flavor profile. Drink it between 2002 and 2007. Displaying a saturated, medium to dark ruby color and delightful aromas of fresh blueberries and violets, the 1996 Nuits-St.-Georges Les Lavières is a silky-textured, thick, full-bodied, and magnificently complex wine. This offering's black cherries, cassis, and blackberries explode on the palate, coating it with sweet juices. Its extremely long finish offers minerals, stones, and tons of superripe but well-focused dark fruits. Anticipated maturity: 2002–2008. The medium to dark ruby-colored 1996 Nuits-St.-Georges aux Allots exhibits scents of cassis bathed in mocha and chocolate. Its full-bodied, velvety-textured, and bright character is awash in blueberries dusted with confectioner's sugar, fresh herbs, candied red cherries, stones, and myriad oaky spices. This gem also possesses a long, supple, and soft finish. Anticipated maturity: 2002–2008. The 1996 Nuits-St.-Georges Les Vignes Rondes has a bright, dark ruby color and an enthralling nose of roses, sweet black cherries, and stones. This extraordinary offering is full bodied, silky textured, opulent, and packed with fat, intensely ripe red cherries, candied raspberries, minerals, and toasty oak flavors. What makes it even better than the three previous Nuits is its stunning depth, complexity, sensuality, and refinement. Drink it between 2003 and 2010. The slightly lighter-colored 1996 Nuits-St.-Georges aux Boudots is among the finest Nuits to have graced my palate. An amazingly elegant, floral, and blueberry, cherry, stone, chocolate, and rose-filled nose warns the palate of the impending pleasures to follow. This full-bodied, velvety-textured, and sublimely proportioned wine offers layer upon layer of candied blackberries, cherries, and assorted dried fruits, as well as a seductively supple and lively personality. Even though it comes across as luscious and forward, it has a firm structure that is difficult to perceive through the loads of superripe fruit. It should be at its peak between 2004 and 2012.

If the medium to dark ruby-colored 1996 Vosne-Romanée Les Genevrières were solely to be judged on its aromatics, it would merit a substantially higher score. Its deeply spicy, floral, perfumed, and coffee-infused nose is marvelous. This hedonistic, medium- to full-bodied, silky-textured, and seductive offering is opulently packed with candied blueberries, cherries, and freshly cut flowers. It is brilliantly crafted and has the fruit necessary for a higher rating but lacks the complexity and structure for greatness. Anticipated maturity: 2000–2006. The darker-colored 1996 Vosne-Romanée Les Brûlées offers fresh and sweet berries, dried fruits, and intense grilled oak aromas. This highly concentrated, extracted, fresh, juicy, medium- to full-bodied, and extremely elegant wine offers ripe cherries that seemingly burst on the palate. This extremely complex, harmonious, and persistent wine is gorgeously supple, silky, and sexy. It should be at its best between 2003 and 2010. The dark-colored 1996 Vosne-Romanée Les Beaux Monts is, like the Nuits-St.-Georges aux Boudots was vis-à-vis its village neighbors, a cut above. Profound aromas of intensely sweet cherries, raspberries, stones, and earth give way to a full-bodied, extremely feminine, and massively ripe and vibrant core of roses, cherries, and candied blueberries. This silky-textured, hedonistic (yet wonderfully structured), and focused wine ends on an incredibly long and detailed finish. Anticipated maturity: 2004–2010+.

The dark-colored 1996 Romanée-St.-Vivant offers a mind-blowing nose of dried roses, small wild berry fruit, and Asian spices. This is liquid silk! It is soft and supple, yet powerful, concentrated, and massively complex. Red currants, flowers, cherries, blood oranges, and viscous blueberry juice can be found in this intricate, show-stopping wine. It is supremely elegant, remarkably long, and stunning. Drink this gem between 2004 and 2010+. The saturated, dark-colored 1996 Richebourg displays an expressive nose of massively sweet and intense cherries that is followed by an oily-textured, mouth-coating, profound, and powerful character. Layer upon layer of black cherries, Asian spices, dried (almost stewed) prunes, cassis, and blackberries can be found in this majestic and masculine wine's flavor profile, as well as in its magnificently long finish. This offering's huge fruit flavors come across as almost jammy yet precisely focused, an extraordinary combination! Its firm and muscular structure will require some cellaring patience. Anticipated maturity: 2006–2014.

Lalou Bize-Leroy's dark-colored 1996 Clos de Vougeot is a stupendous wine from this famed yet often disappointing grand cru. Its intensely spicy and black cherry-laced nose gives way to a massive, profound, hugely concentrated, beautifully extracted, and explosive character. Viscous layers of densely packed blackberries, cassis, and cherries are intermingled with loads of Asian spices and sweet, vanilla-infused oak in this blockbuster's flavor profile. This full-bodied and velvety-textured wine's superripe, seductive, and luscious fruit dominate its firm structure, making it appear ready to drink. However, readers wealthy enough to purchase this gem, and patient enough to allow it to evolve, will be treated to a profoundly moving drinking experience. Anticipated maturity: 2005–2012+.

The medium to dark blue/ruby-colored 1996 Chambolle-Musigny Les Fremières offers an intense nose of violets, sweet cherries, and minerals. On the palate, this succulent, thick, velvety-textured, medium- to full-bodied, and seductive wine is crammed with candied raspberries, sugar-coated cherries, and stones. Well focused and pure, it hides its structured character under wave after wave of rich fruit. It should be at its best between 2001 and 2006. The 1996 Chambolle-Musigny Les Charmes is darker colored, reveals a violet, raspberry, and blueberry-scented nose, and is more complex and concentrated than the Fremières. Tasting this plump, round, medium- to full-bodied, and harmonious wine is akin to having liquid silk drenched in candied cherries, blueberries, plums, and raspberry liqueur poured across the palate. If it were not for this gem's focus and delineation, I would be hard-pressed not to describe it as overripe. Its layered and supersweet fruit covers its copious quantities of marvelously supple tannins. Anticipated maturity: 2002–2008+. It is all but impossible to imagine a better wine than the dark ruby/purple-colored 1996 Musigny. Incredibly complex and dense aromas of sugar-coated blackberries, blueberries, and cassis are intertwined with stones, minerals, and chocolate. This sublime and supremely elegant offering boggles the mind with its seemingly self-controlled core. As I was tasting it I felt as though it were judging me, selectively showing me what it chose to share. Its thick and velvety texture is soft, focused, and refined, yet hedonistically opulent. This gloriously concentrated wine is full bodied, powerful (yet graceful), vibrant (yet muscular), expressive and forward (yet tightly wound and with plenty in reserve), and precise (yet intricate). Layer upon layer of minerals, earth, and violets are drenched in plums and blueberry liqueur that saturate the palate's aftertaste. Anticipated maturity: 2005–2015.

The black/purple-colored 1996 Clos de la Roche offers superripe blackberry and earthy aromatics that are followed by a full-bodied, dense, and thick-as-paint personality. Verging on overripe, this muscular, powerful, masculine, and intensely rich wine coats the palate with almost stewed plums, prunes, blackberries, cassis, and cherries that are intermingled with distinct gravel and underbrush flavors. It is amazing that Mme. Bize-Leroy was able to maintain this offering's freshness and vibrancy while attaining the levels of ripeness and extract characteristic of this blockbuster. As I have come to expect from her top wines, the Clos de la Roche's unbelievably long finish refused to relinquish its grasp on my palate, drenching it with layers of dark fruits. Anticipated maturity: 2005–2012.

The only 1996 Domaine Leroy wine that could possibly be described as tannic is the saturated, medium- to dark-colored Gevrey-Chambertin Les Combottes. Aromatically revealing blackberries, cassis, violets, and Asian spices dusted with cinnamon, this backward, tightly wound, and introverted wine is a bruiser. It is powerful, highly structured, massively concentrated, foursquare, full bodied, masculine, and packed with stewed blackberries, plums, earth, and rocklike flavors. It should be at its peak between 2004 and 2010. The dark ruby-colored 1996 Latricières-Chambertin exhibits intensely sweet and lively blueberry and floral aromas. This seductively silky, full-bodied, opulent, and luscious wine has extraordinary candied cassis and blackberry flavors intermingled with hints of earth, and minerals. Its oily-textured character combines delicacy and refinement with power and muscle. Much more feminine and forward than my recollection of the 1995 at the same stage of evolution, this offering shares its older sibling's extraordinary structure, balance, and concentration, but it is not likely to be as long-lived. Anticipated maturity: 2004–2010. Lalou Bize-Leroy's black-colored 1996 Chambertin offers powerful aromas of Asian spices, cloves, juniper berries, and licorice soaked in blackberry and blueberry syrups. A huge, chewy, and formidably extracted wine, it possesses the unlikely combination of freshness, delicacy, and definition, with *sur-maturité*, viscosity, and massive concentration. Obviously a strong candidate for a perfect rating, this stunning wine regales with its cascade of cassis, red currants, cherries, and plums, as well as compelling depth and length. Wow!

After having had the privilege of tasting through her 1996s, Mme. Bize-Leroy generously served me three vintages of Romanée-St.-Vivant: the 1993, 1995, and 1996. The latter was by far the most opulent and forward of the three, the 1995 the most concentrated, and the 1993 the best.

Displaying a dark ruby-colored center with traces of blood orange tints on the edge, the 1993 Romanée-St.-Vivant is the quintessential Pinot Noir. Candied red fruits are intermingled with violets, roses, and hints of caramel-covered autumn leaves in this wine's enthralling aromas. Its supremely elegant, complex, full-bodied, broad, concentrated, and highly defined character is richly textured, dense, and perfectly focused. Black cherries, flowers, earth, minerals, and perfumelike flavors last for well over a minute, tantalizing the palate. Having tasted numerous wines from the 1993 vintage, I am amazed by how supple this wine's tannins are—no astringency, rusticity, or rough edges. Pure ecstasy! This opulent yet structured wine is built for the long haul (up to 25 years) but is already drinkable. The dark ruby/purple-colored 1995 Romanée-St.-Vivant displayed earthy underbrush scents upon being uncorked, and then its aromas quickly took on a floral, violet, spice, and red berry-infused freshness. This hugely powerful, velvety-textured, and feminine wine is precise and gloriously focused and has an even broader body than I remember. Its flavors explode on the palate, coating it with sweet black cherries, Asian spices, roses, blueberries, and traces of chocolate. This supremely elegant yet immensely concentrated wine requires patience—a difficult proposition given how grand it is! Anticipated maturity: 2005–2020. Bravo!

DOMAINE GEORGES LIGNIER (MOREY-ST.-DENIS)

1995	Bonnes Mares	EE	(86–89)
1995	Clos de la Roche	EE	(85–88?)
1995	Clos St. Denis	EE	(85–88?)
1995	Gevrey-Chambertin Les Combottes	D	(85–88?)
1995	Morey-St.-Denis Clos des Ormes	D	(83–86?)

Georges Lignier is a bright, gracious, and thoughtful man who, if he lowered his yields, could significantly raise the overall quality of his wines.

In 1991 an attempt to produce unfiltered wines was made, but Lignier succumbed to the complaints about the presence of deposit from some of his more ignorant European customers and in 1993 returned to his old ways. He ages his wines for 18 months in 50% new oak casks for the grands crus and less for other appellations. My question marks relate to the high level of dry tannins I detected in these wines.

Medium/dark ruby colored and displaying a nose of berry and mineral scents and an earthy, minerally, and sweet cherry-flavored palate, the 1995 Morey-St.-Denis Clos des Ormes is an appealing wine marred by the presence of dry, dusty tannins. Surprisingly, the

1995 Clos St.-Denis appeared lighter in color than the preceding wine but exhibited attractive tangy, dark and red berry, mocha, underbrush, and mineral flavors. It is medium bodied and well structured, and if its slightly dry tannins resolve themselves, this wine will provide enjoyable drinking for 6 years after its release. Revealing baked, reductive fruit aromas, the medium to dark ruby-colored 1995 Clos de la Roche possesses delicious sweet berry, milk chocolate, spice, mineral, and earth flavors in its chewy, medium-bodied mouth. It should drink well between now and 2004. Georges Lignier's finest 1995, the violet-and-cherry-scented ruby/purple-colored Bonnes Mares, displays a silky texture and thick, chewy flavors of violets, ripe berries, and stones. Full bodied and possessing a zippy power as well as good length, it should be at its best from 2000 to 2006. Lighter colored, the medium to dark ruby 1995 Gevrey-Chambertin Les Combottes had a tight and muted nose when I tasted it. On the palate, however, it exhibited deep, attractive, chewy dark spicy fruit, earth tones, and a mineral component. A big, medium- to full-bodied wine, it should age gracefully for up to 7 years if its tannins round out prior to bottling. But beware: the filtering of this wine may strip out the fruit and texture yet leave the tannins.

DOMAINE HUBERT LIGNIER (MOREY-ST.-DENIS)

1996 Bourgogne	C	(85–86)
1995 Bourgogne	C	(85–87)
1996 Chambolle-Musigny	D	(87–89)
1995 Chambolle-Musigny	D	(86–89)
1996 Chambolle-Musigny Les Baudes	E	(90–93)
1995 Chambolle-Musigny Les Baudes	E	(90–92)
1996 Charmes-Chambertin	EE	(90–93)
1995 Charmes-Chambertin	EE	(91–93)
1996 Clos de la Roche	EE	(94–96+)
1995 Clos de la Roche	EE	97
1996 Gevrey-Chambertin	D	(86–88)
1995 Gevrey-Chambertin	D	(86–88+)
1996 Gevrey-Chambertin Les Combottes	EE	(92–94)
1995 Gevrey-Chambertin Les Combottes	EE	(90–92)
1996 Morey-St.-Denis	D	(87–88)
1995 Morey-St.-Denis	D	(86–88)
1996 Morey-St.-Denis Premier Cru Vieilles Vignes	E	(91–93)
1995 Morey-St.-Denis Premier Cru Vieilles Vignes	E	93
1996 Morey-St.-Denis Les Chaffots	E	(88–90)
1995 Morey-St.-Denis Les Chaffots	E	(88–90)
1996 Morey-St.-Denis La Riotte	E	(89–91)
1995 Morey-St.-Denis La Riotte	E	(87–90)

Hubert Lignier and his son, Roman, an avid bicycle racer and trumpeter (who can often be heard serenading the vines!), run this topflight estate. A bundle of energy, the 26-year-old

Roman is an important member of the younger Burgundian generation who are attempting to rejuvenate the region.

Like most of Burgundy's small growers, Hubert Lignier for years sold the majority of his wine to *négociants*. In 1989 this estate bottled only 40% of its production. Today all of its wines are bottled at the domaine. As an aside, Roman attributes this fact to the readers of *The Wine Advocate* because, as he puts it, "Robert Parker discovered our wines."

Hubert and Roman (who is particularly interested in vineyard work) use as few chemicals as possible on their vines and age their wines in 10%–60% new oak, depending on the appellation. This domaine's offerings are first-rate, possessing the combination of beautifully aromatic lively cherry fruit and concentrated, rich flavors that makes burgundies irresistible.

Delicious to drink right out of barrel, the light ruby-colored 1995 Bourgogne exhibits aromas of crisp, sweet cherries and flavors of fresh, wild raspberries and red fruits. Light to medium bodied and supple, this well-made, easy-to-drink Pinot will deliver delicious near-term drinking. Medium ruby colored, the 1995 Morey-St.-Denis displays an appealing nose of dark berries, earth tones, and well-delineated, medium-bodied flavors packed with lively, tangy berries, minerals, and a touch of mocha. Possessing a beguiling nose of berries, violets, and roses, this rich wine has floral, ripe cherry, and milk chocolate flavors. This silky-textured and well-balanced 1995 Chambolle-Musigny is an excellent example of its appellation. Denser and darker, the ruby/purple-colored, structured 1995 Gevrey-Chambertin offers smoky, spicy, dark fruit aromas and flavors of perfumed berries in its medium-bodied, chewy personality. These excellent village wines will be at their peak between now and 2006.

The 1995 is the first vintage for Roman's Morey-St.-Denis La Riotte, a vineyard he purchased in conjunction with a friend. Made from 32-year-old vines (total production is 75 cases), this delicious, ruby/purple-colored wine offers fresh, lively, deep cherry scents and a powerful, cleanly made, medium-bodied, berry-and-spice-filled character. It will benefit from 3–4 years of cellaring and last for 7 years. I tasted 4 barrels of the 1995 Morey-St.-Denis Les Chaffots, each barrel having been made by a different *tonnelier* (or barrel maker). The results were fascinating: While the overall quality of the wine did not change, the non-fruit components (bacon, earth, mocha, coffee, and other various oak nuances) in the nose and mouth certainly did. This is an excellent, probably outstanding, wine. Packed with ripe, tangy, berry fruits embedded in a creamy, silky-textured style, this medium-bodied, complex beauty needs 4–5 years of cellaring; it will hold for up to 8 years. A blend of Lignier's oldest premier cru Morey vines, the 1995 Morey-St.-Denis Premier Cru Vieilles Vignes is one of the finest premier cru wines from the Côte d'Or: medium to dark ruby colored, it possesses intense dark berry, stone, and spice aromas. A fat, rich, ripe, extracted, powerful, velvety-textured cleanly made wine, it has incredible depth of flavor and excellent length. Hold it for 6 years and drink it over the subsequent 8+ years.

Fabulously aromatic, the 1995 Chambolle-Musigny Les Baudes displays deep scents of violets, ripe cherries, and sweet oak. Full bodied, elegant, and truly delicious, this chewy, floral, sweet currant-packed, complex, and intense wine will benefit from 5 years of cellaring and hold for 8+ years. Medium to dark ruby colored, the 1995 Gevrey-Chambertin Les Combottes is packed with intense spice, cinnamon, and black currant aromas. It possesses layers of beautiful, ripe, deep berry fruit. Complex, extracted, and thickly textured, this fabulous wine will drink well between 2002 and 2010. Possessing enthralling aromas of deeply spicy cherries, Lignier's multidimensional 1995 Charmes-Chambertin is a fabulously concentrated, elegant, powerful, medium- to full-bodied, berry-and-cherry-filled wine touched by some sweet oak. It is spectacular, yet it will be better with 4 years of cellaring. Anticipated maturity: 2001–2010. The profound, dark-colored 1995 Clos de la Roche is splendid—obviously one of the wines of the vintage. It explodes aromatically with scents of nuts, dark spices, black fruits, and raw and grilled meats. Exhibiting intense richness, an oily texture, and complex flavors of minerals, spices, earth, and red and black berries, this chewy, full-bodied wine is built to last. It requires 7 years of cellaring, but it will hold for a dozen or more years. Bravo!

Whereas at many estates in Burgundy the passing of the domaine from father to son is a welcome change, here at Domaine Hubert Lignier it is going to bring more of the same. And we should be thankful for that! Roman Lignier is a brilliant winemaker, as is his father. At a recent tasting of 1990 Clos de la Roches, Lignier's was spectacular, better than any of the other wines from more famed properties. Roman's wondrous 1995s (two of which were re-tasted out of bottle and merited better ratings than the high ones I originally gave them from cask) and this fabulous lineup of 1996s speak volumes for this 27-year-old's immense talents.

What's even better is that Roman Lignier is a kind, modest, ever-smiling, honest, and intelligent man. What better attributes for one of the men who will lead Burgundy into the next century?

The ruby-colored 1996 Bourgogne offers strawberry and cherry aromas that give way to a light- to medium-bodied, and silky-textured wine with cherry and red currant flavors. This simple but delicious wine should be drunk over the next 3 years.

Revealing a medium to dark ruby color and deeply ripe blackberries and violets on the nose, the 1996 Chambolle-Musigny is a medium-bodied, well-balanced, refined, and velvety-textured wine with excellent intensity of black raspberry and blackberry flavors. Its admirable, supple finish offers traces of minerals drenched in more dark fruits. Drink it between now and 2004. The similarly colored 1996 Morey-St.-Denis displays blackberry aromatics and a lush, cherry, and earth-flavored, medium-bodied, and seductive character. This well-made, satiny, and easygoing wine will make for excellent near-term drinking (I wanted to drink it right out of the barrel!). Anticipated maturity: now–2003. Exhibiting a bright, medium to dark ruby color and black cherry, blueberry, and stonelike scents, the 1996 Gevrey-Chambertin has a medium-bodied, well-focused, sweet perfumed cherry-flavored personality. It is more structured than either of the two previous village wines, but its tannins are ripe and refined. Anticipated maturity: now–2003.

The medium to dark ruby-colored 1996 Morey-St.-Denis Les Chaffots displays rich, toast-imbued aromas of jammy blueberries. This medium- to full-bodied, silky-textured, and extremely elegant wine (generally not one of Morey's strengths) has gorgeous floral and perfumed black cherry flavors. It is very pleasurable, with a long finish. Drink it between now and 2005. The darker-colored 1996 Morey-St.-Denis La Riotte is a more serious, intense, and concentrated wine. Aromas of cherries, minerals, fresh herbs, stones, and Asian spices give way to a bold, wide, and thick, medium- to full-bodied personality. Profound and juicy layers of fat blackberries, cassis, and toasted oak are found in this structured and powerful offering. Its admirable finish is loaded with beautifully ripe fruit and supple and tannins. Anticipated maturity: 2001–2008. Hubert and Roman Lignier craft their Morey-St.-Denis Premier Cru Vieilles Vignes from a contiguous 50-year-old parcel that sits astride two vineyards, Les Façonnières and Les Chenevery. The 1996 is fabulous. Verging on dark ruby colored, it reveals rich blackberry, blueberry, earth, fresh herb, and stone aromas that are followed by a thick, dense, velvety-textured, chewy, and juicy personality. This concentrated, plump, firm (yet generous), deep, delineated, and full-bodied wine is surprisingly refined for a wine this structured and fat. Intense layers of black cherries, blackberries, minerals and superbly ripe tannins saturate the palate and finish. From a quality/price ratio, experience has taught me to search out this wine in every vintage, as it is always first-rate. Anticipated maturity: 2002–2010.

The similarly colored 1996 Chambolle-Musigny Les Baudes possesses complex aromas of delicate flowers immersed in blackberries, cassis, earth, minerals, and smoky oak. If readers expect all Chambolles to be delicate, lacelike wines, they are in for a surprise with this powerful, extracted, concentrated, and intense offering. This black fruit, mineral, gravel-flavored, and medium- to full-bodied beauty is impressive because of its focused, exuberant character, and it is not without finesse. Drink it between 2002 and 2010. The 1996 Gevrey-Chambertin Les Combottes has a bright, medium to dark ruby color and a profound nose of jammy black cherries immersed in a spicy veal *demi-glace*. It explodes on the palate with copious ripe red and black fruit, Asian spices, perfume, and toasted oak. This superb wine is oily textured, full bodied, muscular, chewy, and yet highly defined and sublimely elegant. Its prodigiously long finish reveals a firm backbone tightly packed with supple and round tannins. Anticipated maturity: 2004–2010. Exhibiting a medium to dark ruby color and sweet red cherry and Asian spice aromas, the 1996 Charmes-Chambertin is less powerful, intense, and structured than the Combottes, yet it is an outstanding wine in its own right. It offers a silky-textured, charming (no pun intended), feminine, extremely well-balanced, and harmonious medium to full body filled with raspberries, strawberries, cherries, and toasted oak flavors. While it has the requisite structure for extended cellaring, this gem will also offer superb early drinking. Anticipated maturity: 2000–2010.

I am ecstatic to announce that the Ligniers' holdings in the Clos de la Roche have increased by 25%. A recent purchase of "a very good parcel" rounded out their ownership to an even 1 hectare (2.471 acres) of vines ranging from 32 to 40 years old. The 1996 is dark ruby colored and offers a nose of extraordinary purity, depth, and richness. Scents of gravel, earth, violets, perfume, jammy blueberries, cassis liqueur, and black cherries and a hint of road tar are followed by a velvety-textured, full-bodied, and magnificently concentrated wine. Candied cherries, stones, rosemary, spicy oak, Asian spices, and hints of chocolate can be found in this blockbuster's powerful yet graceful flavor profile and substantial finish. Armed with virtually perfect balance and harmony, an amazing depth of fruit, and copious quantities of seamless, satin-textured tannins, this marvel should prove to be one of the vintage's most ageworthy wines. Anticipated maturity: 2005–2018.

Roman Lignier felt as though I had underappreciated some of his 1995s from barrel, and he generously offered to allow me to retaste them. He was right: I had underrated them.

The medium to dark ruby-colored 1995 Morey-St.-Denis Premier Cru Vieilles Vignes (originally rated 90–92) reveals superb aromas of caramelized blackberries, cassis liqueur, underbrush, and Asian spices. This marvelously rich, pure, silky-textured, and expansive wine has enormous breadth, depth of fruit, and impressive precision to its fresh blueberry and cedar flavors. It is a medium- to full-bodied, refined, powerful, and gorgeously ripe wine that also possesses formidable length. Anticipated maturity: 2003–2010+. Lignier's dark ruby-colored 1995 Clos de la Roche (originally rated 93–95) displays enthralling scents of candied hazelnuts, stones, fresh herbs, blackberries, blueberries, plums, and wet gravel basking in the sun. It is just as extraordinary and complex on the palate as it is aromatically, offering an awesomely intense, broad, and expansive character. This full-bodied, mouth-coating, oily-textured, and juicy yet immensely rich wine is redolent with blackberry, cassis, cedar, stone, and briary flavors. Its stunningly long finish offers copious quantities of fruit complemented by supple tannins. Drink it between 2006 and 2020+. Bravo!

DOMAINE PHILIPPE LIVERA (DOM. DES TILLEULS) (GEVREY-CHAMBERTIN)

1996	Chapelle-Chambertin Réserve	E	92+
1996	Fixin En Olivier Vieilles Vignes Réserve	D	89
1996	Gevrey-Chambertin Les Champs Perriers Vieilles Vignes Réserve	D	90
1995	Gevrey-Chambertin En Etelois	D	90
1996	Gevrey-Chambertin en Vosne Vieilles Vignes Réserve	D	89

Note: The following wines are crafted exclusively for North Berkeley Imports and are bottled unfined and unfiltered.

I had never heard of this estate when I tasted the superb 1995 Gevrey-Chambertin En Etelois. I understand Livera produces wines from other, more highly vaunted vineyards, but they were not made available to taste. This wine was outstanding . . . and it comes from only a village appellation vineyard! For those readers interested in the geographical layouts of vineyards, Etelois is located just below Griotte-Chambertin, between that touted grand cru and the Route Nationale 74, with the exception of one small parcel that juts out between Charmes-Chambertin (Mazoyères sector) and Griotte-Chambertin. Not surprisingly, Livera produces this wine from this parcel. Dark ruby colored, with aromas of blackberries, cassis, and roasted spices, this huge wine boasts an oily-textured mouthful of grilled red and black fruits, cherries, and touches of cinnamon. Backward and highly structured, it should be held for 4 years before drinking it over the subsequent 5 years.

Fixin, a quaint village north of Gevrey-Chambertin (rarely visited by tourists because it is bypassed by the highly traveled RN74), generally produces backward, meaty, and hearty red wines. Livera produced a fine 1996 Fixin En Olivier Vieilles Vignes Réserve. It possesses a dark color and a nose of baked plums, cherry compote, and intense Asian spices as well as a thick, medium- to full-bodied, and powerful core of *garrigue*-laced blackberries, leather, and black olives. Surprisingly (I generally find Fixins to be a little rough when young), this wine's copious tannins are supple and round. To get a sense of this wine's personality, readers should imagine concocting a blend of 40% Châteauneuf-du-Pape, 40% Gevrey-Chambertin, and 20% Côte-Rôtie. Anticipated maturity: now–2004.

The medium to dark-colored 1996 Gevrey-Chambertin en Vosne Vieilles Vignes Réserve exhibits intensely ripe blackberry, mocha, spice, and cinnamon aromas. This is a rich, muscular, broad-shouldered, juicy, and medium- to full-bodied wine with myrtle, cassis, and black cherry flavors. Its tangy and powerful profile lingers in its long finish and reveals blood oranges and loads of soft tannins. It should be at its best between 2000 and 2005. The 1996 Gevrey-Chambertin Les Champs Perriers Vieilles Vignes Réserve is medium to dark ruby colored and displays a nose reminiscent of a cinnamon roll covered with blueberry jam, then saturated with blackberry liqueur. This explosive, muscle-bound, cassis-laden, and thick wine is intensely concentrated, superripe, and admirably persistent in the finish. Anticipated maturity: 2000–2005. I did not taste Livera's 1996 Gevrey-Chambertin En Etelois, which is regrettable given the fact that this was his last vintage.

One of the rarest Gevrey-Chambertin grands crus, the Chapelle-Chambertin vineyard is located just below Chambertin Clos de Bèze (across the Route des Grands Crus and abutting Griotte-Chambertin's northern border). Philippe Livera's dark-colored 1996 Chapelle-Chambertin Réserve exhibits a complex nose of black fruits, stones, and underbrushlike scents. On the palate, this chewy, medium- to full-bodied, juicy, tangy, and silky-textured offering is packed with blackberries, black cherries, minerals, and grilled oak. This refined yet powerful wine is harmonious, classy, and deeply ripe and possesses an outstanding intensity of flavors. Anticipated maturity: 2001–2006+.

FREDERIC MAGNIEN (MOREY-ST.-DENIS)

1996 Chambolle-Musigny Les Sentiers Réserve	D	91
1995 Charmes-Chambertin	E	91
1996 Charmes-Chambertin Réserve	EE	93
1996 Gevrey-Chambertin Les Seuvrées Réserve	D	88?
1996 Morey-St.-Denis Réserve	D	89
1995 Morey-St.-Denis Les Ruchots	D	90
1996 Morey-St.-Denis Les Ruchots Réserve	E	92

Note: These ratings and notes are for the special North Berkeley cuvées; I did not taste the regular commercial bottlings. They are bottled unfined and unfiltered.

I was impressed by the young Frédéric Magnien's commitment to quality winemaking and his experimental, inquisitive mind. Readers should watch for this young man's wines. The son of Michel Magnien, he believes in destemming all his grapes by hand and doing a thorough and severe sorting of the grapes. The results speak for themselves. Frédéric Magnien has the capacity and drive to be a future star.

Displaying a fabulous nose of beautifully floral and spicy, superripe fruit, the splendid 1995 Morey-St.-Denis Les Ruchots has a thick texture, sweet, fresh, red cherry fruit, and a beguiling tangy-spice component. Medium to full bodied, this outstanding bottle can be enjoyed in its youth or held for up to 9 years. The tight and muted nose of the 1995 Charmes-Chambertin revealed attractive perfumed and floral aromas after some coaxing, but the explosive, spectacularly silky, wild and dark fruit-filled, sublimely elegant mouth was enough to ascertain this wine's prodigious quality. Medium to full bodied, beautifully extracted, and exhibiting great length, this gem should be drunk between 2004 and 2012.

Vezan and Hinkle are convinced that "bottle shock" is in reality "filter shock." Since none of their offerings are fined or filtered, they felt the wines would show as well as, if not better than (because of the obligatory aeration at hand bottling) in the barrel. They were willing to gamble that "bottle shock" would be proven to be the myth that it is. They were right.

As readers peruse this article they should be aware that virtually all of North Berkeley Imports special cuvées were bottled over a 2-month span prior to my tasting them. A cursory glance at the reviews should prove that none of them suffered from having been tasted soon after bottling. On the contrary, I found North Berkeley's wines more often than not to be vivacious, lively, and expressive. The following notes are from wines that were bottled 48 hours before being tasted.

Produced from vines over 40 years old located in a vineyard on the far side of the RN74 from the grand cru Mazoyères-Chambertin, the medium to dark ruby-colored 1996 Gevrey-Chambertin Les Seuvrées Réserve offers blackberry and roasted herb aromatics. This super-extracted, tannic, somewhat rough, medium- to full-bodied, and dense wine has ripe black fruit and stonelike flavors. Its power and concentration are impressive, but I am worried about its ability to soften its hard backbone before the fruit begins to dissipate. Anticipated maturity: 2002–2006. The medium to dark ruby-colored 1996 Morey-St.-Denis Réserve was produced from 50-year-old vines in the Herbuottes vineyard (this is not indicated on the label). It reveals deep candied cassis aromas and a medium- to full-bodied, chewy, thickly textured, and massively ripe personality packed with cherries and plums. Even though this wine is presently on the rugged side, I have no doubts that its copious fruit will outlast this characteristic. Anticipated maturity: 2000–2005.

The dark ruby-colored 1996 Chambolle-Musigny Les Sentiers Réserve (a vineyard located below Bonnes Mares and just south of Morey-St.-Denis Les Ruchots) was produced from vines averaging 40 years of age. Aromas of superripe red and black fruits enveloped in licorice are followed by a profound, medium- to full-bodied, chewy-textured, and massive core of candied blackberries, black cherries, plums, stones, and tar. Again, this wine displays somewhat rugged tannins in its long and palate-saturating finish, but its extraordinary density of fruit is more than a match for the tannins. Drink it between 2002 and 2007. The black-colored 1996 Morey-St.-Denis Les Ruchots Réserve has an extraordinary nose of perfumed and floral black cherries and violets. This expansive, full-bodied, concentrated, and extracted wine is replete with sugar-coated blackberries, stones, minerals, and hints of freshly laid asphalt. While I would have preferred its tannins to be more supple, this powerful wine is outstanding. Anticipated maturity: 2003–2008.

The slightly light-colored 1996 Charmes-Chambertin Réserve exhibits superripe plum aromas and a chewy-textured, thick, and full-bodied core of cooked and baked fruits. While

I generally find the latter characteristic to be a negative, Magnien (and the vintage's high acidity) somehow harmoniously married it with structure, freshness, and focus. Layers of stewed cherries, figs, plums, minerals, and stones can be found in this exceedingly long and admirable wine. Anticipated maturity: 2002–2008.

DOMAINE MICHEL MAGNIEN (MOREY-ST.-DENIS)

1996	Bourgogne Réserve	C	86
1996	Charmes-Chambertin Réserve	EE	92
1996	Clos de la Roche Réserve	EE	93
1996	Clos St. Denis Réserve	EE	95
1996	Gevrey-Chambertin Les Cazetiers Réserve	E	90?
1995	Gevrey-Chambertin Les Cazetiers	E	89
1996	Morey-St.-Denis Les Chaffots Réserve	E	92
1995	Morey-St.-Denis Les Chaffots	E	88+
1996	Morey-St.-Denis Les Millandes Réserve	E	90+
1996	Morey-St.-Denis Les Monts Luisants Réserve	D	89
1996	Morey-St.-Denis Le Très Girard Réserve	D	88+

Note: These ratings and notes are for the special North Berkeley cuvées; I did not taste the regular commercial bottlings.

Michel Magnien is a serious and thoughtful man. Responsible for the vineyard management of the Maison Louis Latour, he is an excellent winemaker in his own right. The following wines are neither fined nor filtered.

Medium to dark ruby colored, the 1995 Morey-St.-Denis Les Chaffots displays an intriguing nose of mocha and butterscotch (yes, it is a red!) and a wonderfully silky-textured, medium-bodied mouth resplendent with flavors of soft and lush supersweet cherries and an earthy component. This wine's soft tannins and supple style allow it to be drunk now or cellared for up to 8 years. Revealing milk chocolate and mocha on the nose, the 1995 Gevrey-Chambertin Les Cazetiers is a thick, chewy, medium- to full-bodied, oily-textured, dark cherry, and porcini-packed wine. Delicious now, it can be enjoyed over the next 7+ years.

Note: The following wines are crafted exclusively for North Berkeley Imports and are bottled unfined and unfiltered. Only 25 cases (one barrel) of each of these special cuvées were produced.

Michel Magnien, like his son Frédéric, has produced a stunning lineup of 1996 red burgundies. Certain of these offerings are among the more tannic 1996s I tasted and will require more cellaring than most of this vintage's wines.

The 1996 Bourgogne Réserve offers a sweet blackberry-scented nose and a fresh, well-crafted, lively, medium-bodied, and delicious character filled with black cherries and blackberries. It should be drunk over the next 3 years.

The black/purple-colored 1996 Morey-St.-Denis Le Très Girard Réserve reveals a smoky, black fruit, and mocha-dusted nose that gives way to a masculine, thick, chewy, powerful, tannic, and structured personality. This concentrated wine's flavor profile is composed of blackberries, minerals, and cracked black pepper. It should be at its best between 2001 and 2005. Medium to dark ruby/purple colored and exhibiting bright and rich dark fruit aromatics, the 1996 Morey-St.-Denis Les Millandes Réserve is a massive, firm, highly structured, masculine, and full-bodied wine. Violets, brambleberries, myrtle, black cherries, stones, and minerals are found in this tannic monster. This fruit-packed offering will require some cellaring, but it will certainly be worth the wait. Anticipated maturity: 2003–2007. Produced from a vineyard located just above the grand cru Clos St. Denis, the 1996 Morey-St.-Denis Les Chaffots Réserve has intense aromas of blackberries, earth, and cherries. On the palate there is a massive explosion of superripe and layered candied black fruits intermingled with stones. This highly extracted, concentrated, chewy, oily-textured, powerful, and profound wine also possesses a long, flavorful finish. Anticipated maturity: 2001–2007. The dark ruby-colored 1996 Gevrey-Chambertin Les Cazetiers Réserve offers a fabulous nose reminiscent of a chocolate malt shake dosed with cherry syrup. Abundant quantities of deeply ripe black fruits struggle to fight through this massively structured wine's tannic shell. This powerful, masculine, thick, and full-bodied monster should soften enough to let the fruit dominate. I would suggest waiting until 2003 before opening the first bottle and recalibrating its life expectancy at that time.

Dark ruby colored and exhibiting an enticing nose of Asian spices covered with sweet black cherries, the 1996 Charmes-Chambertin Réserve is a muscular, velvety-textured, full-bodied, and highly extracted wine verging on *sur-maturité*. Superripe layers of red and black berry fruit stain the palate in this structured offering. I was blown away by this wine's extraordinarily long, fruit and tannic finish. Anticipated maturity: 2003–2007. The 1996 Clos de la Roche Réserve displays a black/purple color and fresh and lively aromas of violets and blueberries. This classy, muscle-bound behemoth bursts forth on the palate with lavish quantities of blackberries, cassis, black raspberries, stones, spices, and earthlike flavors. This is not a wine for the weak of heart, as its fruit and tannin are present in substantial portions. It should be at its best between 2003 and 2007+. The 1996 Clos St. Denis Réserve is even more complete. Dark ruby/black/purple colored, it possesses a profound nose of rich red and black fruits, meat, and earth tones. Massively chewy, thick, deep, and expansive, it offers a structured shell that contains dense layers of juicy blackberries and cassis intertwined with stones and minerals. This masculine, concentrated, and extracted wine also possesses a long finish. Yes, it's tannic, but its fruit is dominant. Anticipated maturity: 2003–2008.

DOMAINE DU CHÂTEAU DE LA MALTROYE
(CHASSAGNE-MONTRACHET)

1996 Chassagne-Montrachet Clos du Château de la Maltroye	D	(87–88+)
1996 Chassagne-Montrachet Clos St. Jean	D	(86–88)
1996 Santenay La Comme	C	(85–87)
1996 Santenay Les Gravières	C	(85–87)

The ruby-colored 1996 Santenay Les Gravières has an expressive nose of crisp red berries and cherries as well as a medium-bodied, oily-textured character with red fruit and mineral flavors. It will be at its best if drunk over the next 2–3 years. Revealing a light to medium ruby color with aromas reminiscent of minerals and strawberries, the 1996 Santenay La Comme is a medium-bodied, silky, refined, and lively wine with cherry and fresh herb flavors. Drink it over the next 2–3 years. Similarly colored, the 1996 Chassagne-Montrachet Clos St. Jean offers sweet black raspberry and herbal aromatics as well as a medium-bodied, well-crafted, and soft personality with red cherry, mineral, and blueberrylike flavors. Anticipated maturity: now–2003. Displaying a light to medium ruby color and a lovely nose of ripe black cherries, the 1996 Chassagne-Montrachet Clos du Château de la Maltroye has a softly textured, concentrated, mineral, metal, and dark fruit-filled personality, a medium body, and excellent length. It will be at its best if drunk between now and 2003.

DOMAINE JOSEPH MATROT (MEURSAULT)

1995 Blagny La Pièce Sous Le Bois	D	89+
1995 Volnay Santenots	D	90

Thierry Matrot runs this domaine that bears his grandfather's name. His delicious and succulent reds are aged in 20% new oak.

Blagny is a tiny hamlet and appellation within the Meursault boundaries near the wooded crest of the slope on the Puligny-Montrachet side of Meursault. Whites from Blagny bear either the name "Meursault-Blagny" or simply "Meursault," and reds must be under the Blagny label. I have been a big fan of Matrot's Blagny La Pièce Sous Le Bois (which translates to "the parcel under the woods"), since I tasted it a number of years ago after Jean-Marc Roulot (of the Domaine Guy Roulot) told me it was one of the best red Côte de Beaunes. The 1989, 1990, and 1992 are extremely well-made, sultry, sweet, thick, and juicy examples of intensely cherry-flavored Pinot Noir. Matrot's 1995 Blagny La Pièce Sous Le Bois is another superb offering. Possessing a bright ruby color and gorgeously expressive raspberry and black cherry aromas, this succulent, beautifully ripe, medium- to full-bodied and oily-textured wine explodes on the palate with layered cherry and candied strawberry flavors. Its long and intense finish ends on a solid backbone of tannin. Anticipated maturity: now–2004. The outstanding 1995 Volnay Santenots is medium to dark ruby colored and reveals a wonderfully elegant nose of roses, black cherries, currants, and soy sauce. This exceptionally well-made wine offers a thickly textured, medium- to full-bodied, and intensely deep flavor profile of blackberries, cassis, and touches of earth and underbrush for additional complexity. It is magnificently balanced and is armed with ripe, round tannins in its exquisite finish. Anticipated maturity: now–2006.

DOMAINE BERNARD MAUME (GEVREY-CHAMBERTIN)

1995 Charmes-Chambertin	E	(89–92)
1995 Gevrey-Chambertin Premier Cru	D	(86–89)
1995 Gevrey-Chambertin Les Champeaux	D	(85–88)
1995 Gevrey-Chambertin Lavaux St. Jacques	D	(87–90)
1995 Gevrey-Chambertin en Pallud	D	(85–87)
1995 Mazis-Chambertin	E	(89–92)

Bernard Maume and his son, Bertrand, who is taking over daily control of this estate, make old-style, robust, ageworthy, very tannic burgundies at their estate located on the Route National 74 in Gevrey. These are wines that demand several years of aging because of their tannin level. Subsequently they develop flavors of burnt and caramelized leaves and fruits that many burgundy lovers admire. However, impatient readers searching out easy-to-drink, supple wines should be forewarned to steer clear of these wines.

Produced from 55-year-old vines, the purple/ruby-colored 1995 Gevrey-Chambertin en Pallud reveals a violet-filled, floral nose and a thick-textured, rugged, chewy mouth packed with minerals, stones, spices, and an appealing sweet cigar flavor. Built to last, this robust, medium- to full-bodied wine should be drunk between 2001 and 2007. The medium to dark ruby/purple-colored 1995 Gevrey-Chambertin Les Champeaux is produced from 17-year-old vines located in the northwest corner of the Gevrey commune. Aromatically showing spices, flowers, and dark fruits, this medium- to full-bodied wine exhibits sweet caramelized grapes, violets, and an intriguing underbrush quality. Not quite as tannic as the en Pallud, it will provide enjoyable drinking between 2000 and 2006. Hiding behind a tight floral nose, the 1995 Gevrey-Chambertin Premier Cru (from the Cherbaudes and Perrières vineyards) displays beautifully ripe, rugged dark fruits, earth, and rocks in its rich, chewy, thick mouth. Structured and tannic, it requires 6–7 years of cellaring and will last 5–6 more. Ruby/purple colored and exhibiting superripe, purple fruit-filled, deep, dark aromas, the 1995 Gevrey-Chambertin Lavaux St. Jacques is a massive, hard wine with dark berry, stones, and a touch of licorice flavors. Full bodied and intense, it should be enjoyed between 2004 and 2012.

The 1995 Charmes-Chambertin displays a dark ruby color and an elegant, beautifully ripe, floral nose. Its feminine, silky, full-bodied flavors revealed tangy crisp cherries, minerals, and spices that go on and on. The least tannic wine of the Maume lineup, it should be drunk between 2003 and 2011. An impressive display of extract and power, the 1995 Mazis-Chambertin would have merited a higher rating if its tannins had been better kept in check. Nevertheless, this black-colored wine possesses an incredibly deep nose of dark, spicy, extremely ripe fruits and a velvety-textured, sweet black fruit, mineral, earth, and mushroom-filled mouth. Broad shouldered, full bodied, and masculine, it is at present an austere, brooding, and tannic giant. I hope the tannins will soften by 2008 and that this wine will hold for 10–14 years more.

DOMAINE MÉO-CAMUZET (VOSNE-ROMANÉE)

1996 Clos Vougeot	EE	(92–94+)
1996 Corton	EE	(91–93)
1996 Nuits-St.-Georges	D	(87–88)
1996 Nuits-St.-Georges Les Boudots	EE	(91–93)
1996 Nuits-St.-Georges Les Murgers	EE	(88–90)
1996 Richebourg	EEE	(93–95+)
1996 Vosne-Romanée	D	(84–86?)
1996 Vosne-Romanée Les Brulées	EE	(91–93)
1996 Vosne-Romanée Les Chaumes	E	(88–89+)
1996 Vosne-Romanée Cros Parentoux	EEE	(?)

Jean-Nicolas Méo administers this famed estate with the able assistance of Christian Faurois. Although he is only 34 years old, his serious demeanor and cosmopolitan appearance make him appear older. Having learned winemaking from the legendary Henri Jayer, who for years was one of this estate's *métayers*, or sharecroppers (the Faurois family was also a *métayer*, and Jean Tardy still is), Jean-Nicolas Méo has set out to terminate the *métayage* arrangements since taking over 10 years ago. The basic tenets of the Henri Jayer wine making philosophies are still practiced even though Méo, an intellectually curious sort, continues to experiment. In conjunction with Patrice Rion, he has been doing *bâtonnage* (stirring of the lees) trials on his wines.

"Le 1996 est trés beau, c'est un grand millésime." With those words Méo asserted the grandeur of the vintage. He went on to explain why he felt this way: "It has a great deal of equilibrium, with body, ripeness, and acidity. Some wines can be drunk early, yet all of them will age admirably. Some, however will require cellaring—for example, the Vosne-Romanée—because of their high acidity."

The village appellation offerings from Vosne and Nuits have the lowest pHs (3.35) of Méo's wines (the rest are between 3.45 and 3.5). The ruby-colored 1996 Vosne-Romanée has creamy cherry aromas and a velvety (almost pasty) texture, a medium body, and lively blueberries and cherries on the palate. I am concerned about this wine's high acidity level. Méo believes it just needs time for the body to build, but my instincts suggest consuming it before the fruit dissipates and all that is left is acidic harshness. Interestingly, the 1996 Nuits-St.-Georges has the same pH yet appears deeper and richer and is, in my view, a substantially safer bet for cellaring. It reveals a ruby/purple color and a lovely nose of blueberries and black cherries. This expressive, rich, medium- to full-bodied, and refined wine has the structure of a Nuits and the opulent, spicy red and black fruit flavors of a Vosne. Anticipated maturity: now–2004.

Medium ruby colored, and offering delightfully floral and perfumed red cherry scents, the 1996 Vosne-Romanée Les Chaumes is an excellent and potentially outstanding wine. This medium- to full-bodied, silky-textured, fresh, and gorgeously ripe wine has candied blueberries, blackberries, cherries, and traces of minerals in its flavor profile. Drink this lovely wine between now and 2004. Similarly colored, the 1996 Nuits-St.-Georges Les Murgers has a deep and sweet nose of red and black cherries. What follows is a lively, creamy-textured, medium-bodied, and plump personality. This well-balanced and juicy wine displays refined flavors of jammy blueberries, cherries, and hints of gravel. Its long and supple finish reveals beautifully ripened tannins. Anticipated maturity: 2001–2006. Revealing a medium to dark ruby color and enticing aromas of blueberries, blackberries, and stones, the 1996 Nuits-St.-Georges Les Boudots is a first-rate example of this famed vineyard. Its expressive, powerful, refined, and plump, medium to fat body is replete with fat, juicy black cherries and notes of spicy oak. In addition, this offering has a long, rich, and complex finish that displays loads of supple tannins. It should be at its best between 2003 and 2008.

Domaine Méo-Camuzet's 1996 Corton is medium to dark ruby colored and exhibits a cherry and stone-laced nose. This full-bodied, explosive, velvety-textured, and highly structured wine has an impressive balance between its superripe fruit, copious quantities of soft tannins, and its zesty acidity. Layers of red cherries, roses, boysenberries, and spicy oak can be found in this broad and extremely persistent wine. Anticipated maturity: 2003–2010. The famed 1996 Clos Vougeot is produced from a relatively large (7.4 acres, almost as large as Claude Dugat's entire estate), old-vine parcel located near the top of the *clos*. This medium to dark ruby/purple-colored offering has a magnificent nose of deeply ripe dark fruits intermingled with traces of underbrush and Asian spices. This fat, expressive, rich, expansive, and full-bodied wine has an awesome texture (pure velvet), gorgeous balance, and loads of showy and opulent fruit. Plump black cherries, plums, blueberries, and cassis are intertwined with minerals, earth, and hints of porcini mushrooms in this elegant, muscular wine's flavor profile. Anticipated maturity: 2003–2010+.

The bright, dark ruby-colored 1996 Vosne-Romanée Les Brûlées offers lovely fragrances of perfume, candied cherries, and stones. On the palate this wine's full-bodied, thickly textured, and silky character reveals massively sweet layers of cherries awash in vanilla-imbued oak. Well structured yet succulent, this refined offering is complex, harmonious, extremely well proportioned, and seductive. It should be at its peak between 2002 and 2009. I am perplexed by this estate's 1996 Vosne-Romanée Cros Parentoux. This vineyard is consistently the source of some of my favorite Vosne premiers crus; however, I would be hard-pressed to tell you if that was because of its *terroir* or because its producers are some of Burgundy's finest (Henri Jayer, Emmanuel Rouget, and Méo-Camuzet). Méo's 1996 has a bright, dark ruby color, an enticing cherry and toasty oak-scented nose, and a hard, dryish, high-acid, yet paradoxically rich and broad personality. It was disjointed, with well-ripened and spicy fruit in conflict with its crisp acidity. Its aromas would suggest a 90+-point score, its fruit an excellent to outstanding rating, and its balance a distressingly low score. Will it harmonize or remain awkward?

I have no such concerns about Méo's spectacular 1996 Richebourg. It is medium to dark ruby colored and displays a flattering nose of deeply intensely red and black fruits and hints of mint-laced chocolate. Its magnificent personality has gorgeous definition, a full body, and spectacularly rich and fat cherry fruit. This highly concentrated, profound, harmonious, exceedingly classy, and superbly balanced wine has a formidably long and supple finish that reveals loads of oak-imbued, juicy, and popping (the French would say *croquant*) red and black fruits. Wow! Drink this gem between 2004 and 2012.

CHÂTEAU DE MERCEY

1996 Bourgogne Hautes-Côtes de Beaune	C	(85–87)
1996 Mercurey En Sazenay	C	(86–87)

The medium ruby-colored 1996 Bourgogne Hautes-Côtes de Beaune offers rich aromas of cherries and blackberries that give way to a warm, embracing, medium-bodied, superripe (almost jammy), and chewy character filled with cherries and raspberries. It will be at its best if drunk over the next 2 years. Displaying a ruby color and a violet-infused nose, the 1996 Mercurey En Sazenay is a fresh, masculine, foursquare wine with a medium body and flavors reminiscent of metals, blueberries, and traces of wild game. While it is not as seductive, it does appear to be more complex. Drink it over the next 2 years. The Château de Mercey is owned by the Antonin Rodet *négociant* house.

DOMAINE DU PRINCE DE MÉRODE (LADOIX)

1995 Corton Bressandes	D	(85–88)
1995 Corton Clos du Roi	D	(87–90)
1995 Corton Maréchaudes	D	(85–87)
1995 Corton Renardes	D	(86–89)
1995 Pommard Clos de la Platière	D	(84–87)

Readers who tour Burgundy should take the time to visit this domaine. The quality of the wines has been progressing slowly over the past decade, but what makes this estate worthy of a detour is the magnificent turreted château surrounded by a moat—one of the rare true châteaux of the Côte d'Or.

According to Didier Burelle, the domaine's winemaker, wines destined for the U.S. market have not been filtered since the 1989 vintage, and the 1995s are the first not to have been fined (wines bottled for markets other than the United States continue to be subjected to filtration). New oak is used sparingly. The grands crus are aged in 25% new oak, and the others see none. Floral, perfumed aromatics and tangy Pinot Noir fruit with the structure for medium-term aging characterize this domaine's wines.

Light to medium ruby colored, the 1995 Pommard Clos de la Platière reveals an inviting violet-infused and perfumed nose and a silky-textured, supple, medium-bodied personality filled with deep cherry flavors. Drink it between now and 2001. A touch darker, the 1995 Corton Maréchaudes displays floral and red berry-scented aromas and a crisp, well-structured, softly textured, medium-bodied flavor profile packed with tangy red currants and sweet and sour cherries. Anticipated maturity: now–2002. The medium ruby-colored 1995 Corton Bressandes exhibits elegant aromatics reminiscent of roses and cherry pie filling as well as a well-delineated, highly structured, silky-textured, medium-bodied, and masculine personality packed with layered cherries and strawberries. Its tannic finish requires 3–4 years of cellaring, and it will then hold its peak for 5 years. A step up, the slightly darker-colored 1995 Corton Renardes displays sweet blackberry and dark cherry aromas and an oily-textured, beautifully delineated cassis and wild strawberry-filled palate. This medium-bodied wine is supple enough for near-term drinking but has the structure to last for 7 or more years. Mérode's best 1995 is the potentially outstanding Corton Clos du Roi. Ruby colored and possessing an expressive nose of black cherries and wild strawberries, it exhibits a well-structured, medium- to full-bodied character filled with the flavors of chewy sweet red fruits, and its long finish ends on soft, round, ripe tannins. Anticipated maturity: now–2004.

DOMAINE JEAN-MARC MILLOT (COMBLANCHIEN)

1995	Clos Vougeot	E	(87–90)
1996	Côte de Nuits-Villages	C	87+
1995	Côte de Nuits-Villages	C	(84–87)
1996	Echézeaux	E	(88–91)
1995	Echézeaux	E	(88–91)
1996	Savigny-Lès-Beaune	C	87

Note: The wines I tasted from Jean-Marc Millot are special cuvées that are neither fined nor filtered and are bottled by hand for Patrick Lesec, this estate's broker. My understanding is that they are available throughout the world but that other, non-Lesec cuvées, are also available.

This estate's wines are produced in a natural way, with as little intervention as possible. Minimal doses of sulfur are used, and the wines are hand-bottled unfined and unfiltered. The medium to dark ruby-colored 1995 Côte de Nuits-Villages displays a black currant and spice-filled nose and a beautifully delineated, red and black cherry-packed, well-crafted, medium-bodied personality. Drink it between now and 2003. Revealing scents of Asian spices and red cherries, the darker-colored 1995 Clos Vougeot is a fabulously thick yet elegant, medium- to full-bodied wine with delicious flavors of red and black fruits and café au lait and a long finish. Anticipated maturity: 2000–2006. The dark ruby-colored 1995 Echézeaux offers aromas of mocha, cassis, and minerals and a viscous, layered, concentrated, polished, full-bodied personality packed with red berries and chocolate. It will be at its peak between 2002 and 2009.

With the possible exception of the Clos Vougeot (which concerns me, as it appears to be dominated by oak and tannin), I was impressed by the 1996s from this little-known property.

The medium ruby-colored 1996 Savigny-Lès-Beaune has a malty, rich, and blackberry-infused nose with hints of minerals and metallic shavings. It has an appealing chewy texture, a medium to full body, and lovely flavors of plums, raspberries, and cherries. This well-made and fruit-driven wine should be drunk over the next 4–5 years. The 1996 Côtes de Nuits-Villages reveals a slightly darker color and aromas of blackberries, violets, and minerals. This medium- to full-bodied, concentrated, cassis liqueur and metal-flavored offering has a foursquare character and firm structure. Anticipated maturity: now–2004. Exhibiting ripe and spicy cherries awash in new oak, the medium to dark-colored 1996 Echézeaux has a sweet, chewy-textured, medium- to full-bodied, thick personality. This concentrated, extracted, and gorgeously ripe wine has dense layers of cassis that are at present buried in powerful oak flavors throughout its flavor profile and finish. I believe this wine has the necessary fruit to balance out the new wood. Anticipated maturity: 2003–2008.

DOMAINE MONGEARD-MUGNERET (VOSNE-ROMANÉE)

1995	Clos Vougeot	EE	?
1995	Echézeaux	E	(87–90)
1996	Echézeaux Vieilles Vignes	E	(91–93)
1995	Echézeaux Vieilles Vignes	E	(88–92)
1996	Fixin	C	(86–88)
1996	Grands-Echézeaux	EE	(90–92)
1995	Grands-Echézeaux	EE	(91–94)

1996	Richebourg	EEE	(91–94)
1995	Richebourg	EEE	(91–94)
1996	Vosne-Romanée	D	(86–88)
1995	Vosne-Romanée	D	(85–87)
1996	Vosne-Romanée Les Orveaux	D	(87–89)
1995	Vosne-Romanée Les Orveaux	E	(86–89?)

I was surprised to learn from Vincent Mongeard that he had taken over all the winemaking duties at this famous domaine in 1985. I, like Robert Parker and the rest of the world's wine press, was under the impression that Vincent's father, Jean, was still very much in control (Parker wrote in the past that "Jean Mongeard has made many superb burgundies. The quality may have dipped slightly in the late eighties, but Mongeard rebounded with gorgeous 1990s and 1991s"). Interestingly, the late 1980s was just when Vincent Mongeard was learning the ropes. He started by being responsible for the vineyards, performing what he says were Burgundy's first green harvests in 1982 and also, according to him, turning the Domaine Mongeard-Mugneret into the region's first organic estate that same year. Mongeard believes the 1995 vintage is better than 1990 and said it reminded him of 1985 but with more structure.

The medium ruby colored, slightly rugged 1995 Vosne-Romanée reveals an appealing bouquet of wild berries, smoke, a touch of underbrush, and a thick, chewy, medium-bodied palate packed with dark cherries and notes of earthiness. Drink it between now and 2002. Slightly darker colored, the 1995 Vosne-Romanée Les Orveaux displays black currants and toasty oak on the nose and intensely explosive flavors of dark fruits and smoke in its medium- to full-bodied, rustic mouth. At this stage it is a severe wine, with hard tannins buttressing the fruit. If the fruit outlives the tannin, it will merit an excellent rating. Anticipated maturity: 2003–2009.

Mongeard-Mugneret's medium ruby-colored 1995 Echézeaux reveals, with coaxing, an elegant, floral nose and a silky-textured, feminine palate bursting with cherries and strawberries. Well crafted, harmonious, and possessing excellent structure, it lacks, however, the complexity of a great grand cru. The medium ruby-colored 1995 Clos Vougeot was extremely tannic and oaky the day I tasted it. I'm worried that the copious quantities of elegant blackberries and currants I detected will not be able to outlive the aggressive, rough tannins or the oak.

Mongeard's 1995 Echézeaux Vieilles Vignes is produced from two old-vine parcels, one planted in 1927 and the other in 1929. Medium to dark ruby colored, the old-vine intensity can easily be discerned in its deeply powerful, black cherry-filled aromas and thick-textured, chewy personality. Packed with flavors of black raspberries and ripe red cherries, this wine has superb structure and length. It will be at its best between 2003 and 2012. Amazingly enough (for Burgundy!) the dark ruby-colored 1995 Richebourg was harvested at 12.9% sugar and not chaptalized according to Mongeard. Displaying fabulous toasty wild berries and hints of game and earth, it possesses loads of dark cherries and crisp berries and ripe, soft tannins in its thick, full-bodied, well-balanced personality. This wine has all the component parts to age gracefully. Drink it between 2004 and 2020. The dark ruby-colored 1995 Grands-Echézeaux exhibits deep, sensual, spicy berry fruit aromas and an intense, concentrated, chewy, blackberry, dark cherry, currant, and Asian spice-packed, velvety-textured palate leading to a long, rich, and sweet finish. Combining elegance and power, in-your-face fruit, yet delineation, this outstanding wine should provide years of immense satisfaction. Anticipated maturity: 2003–2014.

All of Vincent Mongeard's 1996s appeared a little strange to me when taken in the context of the vintage. In general the vintage offers bright fruit, whereas at Domaine Mongeard-Mugneret it was less vibrant, fatter perhaps, and ever-so-slightly pasty.

After having found the 1995 Fixin tannic and backward, I was surprised to find the medium to dark-colored 1996 to be the contrary. Its aromas of intensely ripe cassis and red cherries leads to a supple, soft, well-crafted, medium-bodied, and rich wine with easygoing and delicious flavors of blackberries and licorice. Drink it over the next 4–5 years. The similarly colored 1996 Vosne-Romanée (I tasted from a new barrel, but the final blend will only contain 30% new oak) has an oak spice, raspberry, and cherry-scented nose that gives way to a medium-bodied, and creamy-textured character. Candied cherries, spicy oak, and floral tones can be found in this well-balanced and delicious wine. Anticipated maturity: now–2004.

Vosne's answer to Nuits, Mongeard's 1996 Vosne-Romanée Les Orveaux is medium to dark ruby colored and possesses a blackberry, smoke, and toasty oak-laden nose. This foursquare, austere, and tannic wine is full bodied, backward, chewy textured, and densely packed with metallic, minerally, briary, gamey, and cassislike flavors. Additionally this wine has a long, firm, and tannin-strewn, slightly rustic finish. Anticipated maturity: 2002–2006.

The dark ruby/purple-colored 1996 Echézeaux Vieilles Vignes has cassis liqueur and bacon fat aromas as well as a concentrated, jammy, powerful, oily-textured, full-bodied, and rich personality. Intense layers of cherries, black currants, and herbs are found in its flavor profile as well as in its extremely long finish. It has the power, concentration, depth, and length of the finest Echézeauxs of the vintage but lacks their elegance, precision, and purity. Anticipated maturity: 2003–2010. Mongeard's dark-colored 1996 Grands-Echézeaux has a nose reminiscent of stony blackberries, brambleberries, and smoke. This rich, powerful, expansive, pasty, and concentrated wine offers loads of cassis and black cherries in its flavor profile. It is more elegant yet does not match the Echézeaux's flavor intensity, sheer power, or length. Anticipated maturity: 2003–2008. The 1996 Richebourg has a sheeny, medium to dark ruby color and candied red cherries, minerals, and perfumed flowers on the nose. This complex, velvety-textured (slightly pasty), full-bodied, and jammy wine is packed with supersweet black cherries and raspberries intermingled with stones, fresh herbs, and Asian spices. It is more focused and refined than any of the previous wines, and it possesses an extremely long and fruit-dominated finish. Drink it between 2003 and 2008.

DOMAINE MONTHÉLIE-DOUHAIRET (MONTHÉLIE)

1996 Monthélie	D	(85–87)
1996 Monthélie Les Duresses	D	(86–89)
1996 Monthélie Le Meix Bataille	D	(87–89+)
1996 Monthélie Clos Le Meix Garnier	D	(85–87+)
1996 Pommard Les Chanlins	E	(89–92)
1996 Pommard Les Fremiers	E	(88–91)
1996 Volnay en Champans	D	(90–92+)

A nonagenarian and one of the *grandes dames* of Burgundy, Mme. Armande Douhairet owns and continues to manage this seventeenth-century estate, with the assistance of Françis Lechauve. Since 1989 André Porcheret also partakes in viticultural, vinification, and *élevage* issues while being employed at the Domaine Leroy and, later (as today), at the Hospices de Beaune. The estate's holdings total 14.8 acres in the communes of Monthélie, Pommard, and Volnay. From 1980 to 1993 (inclusive) the wines of this domaine were often irregular in quality, rustic, and with offputting aromas. Enormous progress has taken place here since 1993; the wines are now cleaner and more intense, their tannins rounder and softer. Yields are moderate, averaging $2^2/3$ tons of fruit per acre for the village wines and $2–2^1/3+$ for the premiers crus. The domaine's finest offerings, the Volnay en Champans and Pommard Les Chanlins, are first-rate examples of their appellations and appear quite age-worthy.

The wines, whose malos had ended in November, were still on their lees when I visited the domaine in late January. The estate's whites, which I was not offered to taste, were bottled prior to the harvest, as is the case each year according to Lechauve.

The medium ruby purple-colored 1996 Monthélie reveals a rich grapey nose and a ripe, fat, sweet, medium-bodied, and silky character. This lovely wine is filled with supple cherries, plums, and traces of metallic flavors. It should be drunk over the next 3 years. The slightly darker-colored 1996 Monthélie Clos Le Meix Garnier has a more complex nose of minerals and blackberries. On the palate, this wine offers a structured, black cherry, metal, and stone-flavored personality. Its tannins, while quite present, are ripe and will not pose a problem if the fruit is not stripped by excessive filtering. Anticipated maturity: now–2003. Displaying a medium to dark ruby color, the 1996 Monthélie Les Duresses is an excellent wine. Blackberry, metallic, and mineral scents give way to a deep, concentrated, and extracted core of black cherries, steel, and stones. This medium-bodied, complex, and persistent offering should be drunk between 2000 and 2004. Monthélie-Douhairet's 1996 Monthélie Le Meix Bataille is one of the finest wines I have tasted from this little-known village. Produced from 20-year-old vines, it reveals a perfumed and black fruit-scented nose followed by a delightfully rich, extracted, medium-bodied, and complex character. This offering's seductive flavor profile is made up of violets, dark raspberries, blueberries, cherries, and traces of metallic flavors. Anticipated maturity: now–2004.

Produced from 60- and 30-year-old vines in the estate's 2.47-acre parcel, the 1996 Volnay Champans is an outstanding wine. Revealing powerful and profound blackberry aromas, it is a medium- to full-bodied, beautifully ripe, and concentrated wine jam-packed with cherries, freshly ground black pepper, violets, and minerals. This structured, well-balanced, and concentrated wine will require some cellaring patience. Anticipated maturity: 2002–2009. Both of Mme. Douhairet's parcels of Pommard are in premier cru vineyards that border Volnay. The 1996 Pommard Les Fremiers (100 cases in 1996 from .74 acre, or 2 tons of fruit per acre) is medium to dark ruby colored and offers a cherry-and-blackberry-imbued nose. This masculine, thick, medium- to full-bodied, and beautifully ripe wine is filled with black cherries, raspberries, and metallic flavors. It should be at its best between 2000 and 2005. Exhibiting a medium to dark ruby color and intense cherry aromatics, the 1996 Pommard Les Chanlins is a sweet, powerful, broad-shouldered, and concentrated he-man of a wine. Characterized by Lechauve as "not a lady's wine" (which every woman I know would disagree with), this brooding monster is packed with deeply ripe and highly extracted red cherries, minerals, and blackberries. Its long and muscular finish reveals loads of supple tannins. Anticipated maturity: 2002–2007.

BERNARD MOREY ET FILS (CHASSAGNE-MONTRACHET)

1996	Beaune Grèves	D	90
1995	Beaune Grèves	D	87+
1996	Chassagne-Montrachet	C	86
1996	Chassagne-Montrachet Vieilles Vignes	D	89+
1995	Chassagne-Montrachet Vieilles Vignes	C	87
1996	Maranges La Fussière	C	87
1995	Maranges La Fussière	C	86

1996 Santenay Grand Clos Rousseau	D	89+
1995 Santenay Grand Clos Rousseau	D	88
1996 Santenay Passetemps	D	89
1995 Santenay Passetemps	D	87
1996 Santenay Vieilles Vignes	C	88

Bernard Morey's reds offer excellent concentration, sweet fruit, and dark colors. He and his sons crafted seven lovely 1996 red burgundies, many from old vines. Moreover, all of them are reasonably priced.

Produced from 10–20-year-old vines, the 1996 Chassagne-Montrachet displays a bright ruby color and a lovely nose of sweet black cherries. This is a medium-bodied, silky, lively, and fruit-driven offering filled with juicy blackberries. Supple, it should be drunk over the next 3 years. Ruby colored and revealing a nose reminiscent of Peking duck (complete with plum sauce), the 1996 Maranges La Fussière is an extremely well-made, vibrant, supple, and medium-bodied wine with cassis, blackberries and stonelike flavors. All too often, wines from the Maranges villages appear backward when young and lose their fruit before softening out. This offering from Morey is delicious and ready to drink. The 1996 Santenay Vieilles Vignes exhibits a ruby/purple color expressive aromas of blackberries, violets, and stones and a thick, glycerin-packed, plump, and medium-bodied core of ripe blackberries and gooseberries. This oily-textured wine should be drunk over the next 4 years.

Bernard Morey's 1996 Chassagne-Montrachet Vieilles Vignes is produced from vines that average 50 years in age. It is medium to dark ruby colored and intense. Iron, mineral, and sweet blackberry aromas give way to its extracted, concentrated, structured, medium- to full-bodied, rich, and deep character. This Chassagne offers scrumptious red and black fruits intermingled with stones. Aditionally, it has the power and backbone to evolve gracefully. Anticipated maturity: now–2004+. Crafted from vines planted in 1952, the medium to dark ruby-colored 1996 Santenay Passetemps reveals candied black raspberry scents and a layered core of cassis, red currants, raspberries, and black cherries. This delicate wine has a medium to full body, a silky texture, and admirable length with soft tannins. It should be at its best between now and 2004. In a vintage where high yields were the norm, Bernard Morey harvested the 1996 Santenay Grand Clos Rousseau at 2+ tons of fruit per acre. This impressive wine reveals a medium to dark ruby color and aromas of perfumed and floral black cherries. On the palate, this medium- to full-bodied, ripe, succulent, and oily-textured wine offers copious quantities of sweet cherries and black raspberries. It is harmonious, intense, expansive, and extremely well balanced. Anticipated maturity: now–2004. My favorite of Morey's 1996s is the medium to dark ruby-colored 1996 Beaune Grèves. It reveals an enthralling nose of perfume-soaked black cherries and a refined, velvety, rich, complex, and medium- to full-bodied personality bathed in candied grapes, sweet red cherries, stones, and metals. Its long finish displays even more layers of fruit, ranging from raspberries to plums. Given the wine's supple tannins, it will be tempting to drink this gem immediately upon release, but I would suggest 1–2 years of cellaring. Anticipated maturity: 2000–2006.

The bottling line was churning away when I visited this estate in January of 1997, and many of the 1995s I tasted had been bottled but were not yet corked. The ruby-colored 1995 Maranges La Fussière exhibits blackberry aromas and a concentrated, medium-bodied, thick, and tangy flavor profile packed with cassis, cherries, and minerals. It will be at its best between now and 2000. Possessing a medium to dark ruby color and a deeply sweet cherry and blackberry-scented nose, the 1995 Santenay Passetemps is an oily-textured, chewy, medium- to full-bodied and lively wine with well-extracted cassis, raspberry, and Asian spice flavors. Drink it between now and 2002. Produced from 35–70-year-old vines, the dark ruby-colored 1995 Chassagne-Montrachet Vieilles Vignes displays intense mineral and sweet red berry aromas and a well-concentrated, highly structured, rustic, medium- to full-bodied personality with cherries and roasted herb flavors. Its admirable length ends on a slightly hard tannic finish (rather typical for red Chassagnes). Anticipated maturity: now–2004. The medium to dark ruby-colored 1995 Beaune Grèves reveals blackberry, Asian spices, and coffee aromas and a silky-textured, medium- to full-bodied, highly extracted, and well-endowed character filled with crisp yet chewy cassis, raspberries, and black cherries. It will be at its best between now and 2003. Morey's best red is the dark ruby/purple-colored 1995 Santenay Grand Clos Rousseau. It offers a highly expressive nose of roasting spices and blueberries as well as a highly structured and intense, silky-textured, full-bodied core of minerals, herbs, blackberries, and red cherries. Anticipated maturity: now–2004.

DOMAINE JEAN-MARC MOREY (CHASSAGNE-MONTRACHET)

1996	Beaune Grèves	C	(86–87)
1995	Beaune Grèves	D	87
1996	Chassagne-Montrachet Champs Gains	C	(85–87)
1996	Chassagne-Montrachet Clos St. Jean	C	(85–87)
1996	Santenay Grand Clos Rousseau	D	(86–87)
1995	Santenay Grand Clos Rousseau	C	88

Note: Jean-Marc Morey had added a fining solution to his reds 3 days prior to my tasting his 1996s. This process can certainly have an effect on a wine's ability to express itself.

One of the most joyfully exuberant vignerons I have ever met, Jean-Marc Morey (Bernard Morey's brother) informed me that he believed 1996 "may be better in red than in white." While I do not agree, I do understand why a vigneron from Chassagne would have this opinion. This village, famous for its whites, actually produces more red wine. While its whites are easy to sell, the rustic reds do not command the same respect and are difficult to sell. When was the last time you thought "tonight a red Chassagne-Montrachet would be perfect"? Since many 1996s from this village are juicy, fresh, fruity, and soft, maybe the reds will be an easier sell.

The medium ruby-colored 1996 Chassagne-Montrachet Champs Gains has deep mineral and dark berry aromas that give way to a medium-bodied, highly structured, metal-and-blackberry-filled wine. The wine's tannins are a touch rustic, so it will require a year or more of cellaring. It should taste best between 2000 and 2003. The medium to dark ruby-colored 1996 Chassagne-Montrachet Clos St. Jean (this vineyard often produces superlative red Chassagnes) reveals red cherry and raspberry aromas. On the palate, this medium-bodied, seductive, and charming wine offers an assortment of ripe red fruits in its feminine and supple personality. Anticipated maturity: now–2004. The 1996 Santenay Grand Clos Rousseau has a medium to dark ruby color and a wild herb (almost *garrigue*), metal, and blackberry-infused nose. This medium-bodied and structured wine is packed with black cherries and blackberries but has a touch of rusticity to its long finish. It should be at its best between now and 2004. The ruby-colored 1996 Beaune Grèves reveals nice depth to its red fruit-laced aromatics. It is medium bodied and silky textured and has flavors reminiscent of sun-dried herbs, metals, minerals, blackberries, and cassis. Anticipated maturity: now–2003.

Jean-Marc Morey's ruby-colored 1995 Beaune Grèves reveals dark cherries, minerals, and roasted herbs aromatically and a beautifully oily-textured, and medium-bodied personality filled with strawberries and sweet red cherries. A delightfully delicious wine to drink now, it will easily last until 2001. Even better, the medium to dark ruby-colored 1995 Santenay Grand Clos Rousseau displays sweet boysenberry, slate, and Asian spice aromas as well as a thick, superripe, medium-bodied core of cherries, minerals, and rustic stone flavors. Anticipated maturity: now–2002.

DOMAINE PIERRE MOREY (MEURSAULT)

1995 Pommard Les Grands Epenots	D	(86–88)

The amiable Pierre Morey, internationally known for the delicious whites he produces at this estate, at his *négociant* house (Morey-Blanc), and at the Domaine Leflaive (where he works hand in hand with Anne-Claude Leflaive), also produces small quantities of a delicious Pommard Les Grands Epenots. The 1995 is medium ruby colored and offers sweet aromas of wild blackberries and blueberries as well as a medium-bodied, silky-textured black cherry-filled flavor profile. Its long finish ends on awkward but ripe and soft tannins. Drink it between now and 2004.

DOMAINE ALBERT MOROT (BEAUNE)

1996 Beaune Bressandes	D	(90–92)
1995 Beaune Bressandes	D	(88–91)
1996 Beaune Cent Vignes	D	(87–89)
1995 Beaune Cent Vignes	D	(85–87)
1995 Beaune Grèves	D	(87–90)
1996 Beaune Marconnets	D	(89–91)
1996 Beaune Teurons	D	(91–93)
1995 Beaune Teurons	D	(89–92)
1996 Beaune Toussaints	D	(89–91)
1995 Beaune Toussaints	D	(86–89)
1996 Savigny-Lès-Beaune La Bataillière	D	(87–89)
1995 Savigny-Lès-Beaune La Bataillière	D	(86–89)

When I first met Mademoiselle Choppin, this estate's owner and director, my initial (and incorrect) impression of frailty was immediately squashed by her self-assured look, her rapid step, and her high level of energy. Young women in Burgundy owe a great deal to the efforts of this lady, who has made superb Beaunes in the cold and damp cellars of her beautiful old home. There was a time when winemaking was considered a man's job (ignorants and a few old-timers stuck in their ways still believe that a woman's presence in a cellar will "turn" their wines), yet Mlle. Choppin's track record over the years—in many vintages crafting the finest wines from Beaune's hillsides—has proved that a woman's place can be the cellar.

Visiting the Domaine Albert Morot is like taking a step back in time. Mlle. Choppin likes to do things the way she has for decades. "Why change when I have good results?" she demands. Choppin believes low yields are the key to success. The wines ferment in large open wooden vats and are emptied via gravity into the spacious barrel room one flight down. Aged in new and 1-year oak barrels, they are neither fined nor filtered prior to bottling. Albert Morot at one time did a good deal of *négociant* work, so the facilities are quite large. Mlle. Choppin has since decided to concentrate on her vineyards and rarely purchases grapes, must, or wine. However, she maintains her *négociant* license.

Burgundy aficionados and neophytes alike who are shocked at the high prices demanded by this region's top wines should search out these offerings. They are delicious, supple yet structured, powerful yet elegant expressions of Pinot Noir and their respective *terroirs*—and great values! These wines can be drunk young and can also age quite well, as was demonstrated by two superb 1983s (Beaune Bressandes and Beaune Cent Vignes) I recently tasted.

This domaine's 1995s were tasted twice, first in January 1997 and then at the end of June, both times from barrel. My notes were consistent.

Produced from a *monopole* (solely owned) vineyard, the ruby-colored 1995 Savigny-Lès-Beaune La Bataillière reveals a gorgeous purity of sweet dark cherries and blackberries aromatically and a pretty, silky, supple, medium-bodied mouthful of blueberries and red fruits. Its long finish ends on beautifully ripe tannins. Drink it between now and 2005. The medium ruby-colored 1995 Beaune Cent Vignes displays bright cherry and blueberry aromas and a soft, tangy, lively, medium-bodied mouthful of blackberries, red currants, and strawberries. This wine is always the first of Morot's offerings to reach its peak. Drink it between now and 2002. Slightly darker colored, the 1995 Beaune Toussaints possesses a gorgeous nose of blackberries, Asian spices, and cinnamon as well as a thick, concentrated, elegant, medium- to full-bodied personality packed with candied black cherries. Anticipated maturity: 2001–2008. The Beaune Grèves (only 50 cases were produced in 1995) is medium to dark ruby colored and exhibits a perfumed cherry-and-blueberry-scented nose as well as a tangy, minerally, medium-bodied, highly structured, dark berry-flavored personality. Its tannins will require a few years of cellaring to soften. Drink it between 2001 and 2008. Often my favorite Albert Morot offering (a recently tasted 1990 from my cellar was outstanding!), the Beaune Bressandes is again a huge success in 1995. Ruby colored and offering a superb nose of wild blueberries and red currants, this thick, silky-textured, and medium-bodied wine has a gorgeously spicy and deep cherry-filled character. Elegant and packed with layered fruit, it will offer delicious drinking from now to 2007. The bright, dark ruby-colored 1995 Beaune Teurons is a spectacular example of what the hillside overlooking the town of Beaune is capable of producing. Revealing minerals, blackberries, and dark cherries aromatically, it displays a powerful, oily-textured, and full-bodied personality that explodes with concentrated flavors of blueberries, plums, earth, and stones. Serious, masculine, and built to last, it will be at its best between 2002 and 2009. These are the best wines produced at this estate since the 1990s.

Mademoiselle Choppin has fashioned (with her young and able assistant, Joel) a first-rate lineup of 1996s from her hillside vineyards overlooking the town of Beaune. Owing to her severe pruning and green harvesting, Mlle. Choppin's vineyards yielded between 2 and 2¹/₃ tons of fruit per acre—admirable figures in any vintage, and superb in this one. She laughed and said, "After tasting the wines, I wished I had not dropped as much fruit in green harvesting. I think I could have done just as well and made more." My impression, having tasted hundreds upon hundreds of 1996s harvested at higher yields, is that her fabulous, concentrated, and deep wines are partially due to her draconian pruning and fruit dropping.

Mlle. Choppin's *monopole* 1996 Savigny-Lès-Beaune La Bataillière has a bright ruby color as well as fresh and lively aromas of blackberries, cherries, and perfume. Its medium-bodied, masculine, and structured character is packed with vibrant and ripe black fruits as well as metallic flavors. Anticipated maturity: now–2003. The darker-colored 1996 Beaune Cent Vignes reveals fresh brambleberry aromatics and lively, crunchy, and juicy red fruits on the palate. This medium-bodied wine is well structured, silky textured, precise, and lively. It should be at its best between now and 2002.

When I tasted these wines in mid-November, the 1996 Beaune Toussaints had just finished its malolactic fermentation (14 months after the harvest!). Produced from vines planted in 1959, it offers a dark ruby color and sweet cherries bathing in mocha on the nose. Its concentrated, medium- to full-bodied, and gorgeously ripe character is packed with chocolate-covered cherries and black currants. This well-balanced wine's long finish reveals plenty of soft, supple tannins. Anticipated maturity: now–2005. Even better, and often my favorite wine from Domaine Albert Morot, the medium to dark ruby-colored 1996 Beaune Bressandes was produced from old vines as well (three-quarters of them are over 45 years old). Beguiling aromas of rich and deep black cherries awash in toasty oak are followed by a seductive, juicy, and hedonistic personality. This velvety wine's flavor profile is awash in thick layers of red cherries, sugar-coated raspberries, and candied currants. Its backbone is firmer and more structured than the Toussaints, which may be a blessing, because without it consumers would want to suck down this beauty before it reached its peak. Anticipated maturity: 2000–2006. The clear, bright, and dark red ruby-colored 1996 Beaune Marconnets has minerals, earth, metals, and blackberries in its nose. This masculine, medium- to full-bodied, and thick wine is densely filled with wild mushroom and black cherry flavors that linger in its long and ripe tannic-packed finish. It should be at its peak between 2000 and 2006. The 1996 Beaune Teurons is a blockbuster. It is dark ruby colored and offers a super-ripe, intense, and complex nose of black cherries, earth, leather, violets, and perfume. Prodigious quantities of sweet, ripe, juicy, and powerful black cherries captivate the palate in this thick (where's my knife and fork?), profound, and chewy wine. As the French would say, *"Quelle mâche!"* Its fabulously long finish reveals loads of soft and round tannins drowned in copious quantities of fruit. Bravo!

DOMAINE DENIS MORTET (GEVREY-CHAMBERTIN)

1996	Bourgogne Rouge	C	(87–88)
1996	Chambertin	EEE	(92–95)
1996	Chambolle-Musigny Les Beaux-Bruns	E	(88–89?)
1996	Clos de Vougeot	EE	(91–94)
1996	Gevrey-Chambertin	D	(87–88+)
1996	Gevrey-Chambertin Les Champeaux	E	(91–94)
1996	Gevrey-Chambertin En Champs	E	(89–91)
1996	Gevrey-Chambertin Lavaux-St.-Jacques	E	(90–92+)
1996	Gevrey-Chambertin En Motrot	D	(88–89?)
1996	Gevrey-Chambertin au Velle	D	(88–91)
1996	Marsannay Les Longeroies	D	(87–89)

This estate, which had been drifting for years, is now run by Denis Mortet, an extremely proud man who has undertaken the enormous task of turning it around. His father retired in 1991, but, according to Mortet, he started instituting viticultural changes in 1990, such as 1) abandoning the use of fertilizers; 2) working the soils to force the roots to dig deeper; and 3) reducing yields. Mortet says the secret to properly reducing yields is to go vine by vine, not parcel by parcel. His philosophy is that each vine has an optimum number of bunches it should produce and that the secret is to prune it to exactly that number. Furthermore, Mortet "feeds" only those parcels that require nutrition with organic composts; others are left to fend for themselves.

Having "total confidence in the fruit," Mortet instituted new winemaking philosophies in 1993. A sorting table was installed to guarantee the quality of the grapes, and Mortet began crafting wines with absolutely no sulfur or rackings, letting them sit on their lees for 18 months. He informed me that since he put this new philosophy into effect the only problem he has encountered is high levels of carbon dioxide (a by-product of fermentations) that are easily eliminated with aeration at bottling. His filters were discarded in 1991.

But what do the wines taste like? Well, they are dark colored, delicious, deeply ripe (flavors of cassis liqueur and jammy black cherries were recurrent themes), sweet, and intensely concentrated. Time will tell if these are wines to cellar for extended periods. My instincts suggest drinking them while they are still so exuberant, fleshy, and hedonistic. Two offerings, recognizable by the question marks beside their ratings, may prove to have problems with oaky tannins, but overall Mortet is crafting some extraordinary burgundies out of his newly refurbished cellars.

The dark ruby/purple-colored 1996 Bourgogne was aged for 6 months in large cement vats and then transferred to 1-year-old barrels. It reveals aromas of cassis liqueur that give way to a rich, silky-textured, medium- to full-bodied, concentrated, and fresh character packed with candied black currants. Drink it over the next 4 years. The 1996 Marsannay Les Longerois is also dark ruby colored and offers sweet black fruits spiced with new oak (it was aged in 80% new barrels). This thick, candied, medium- to full-bodied, concentrated, well-balanced, velvety-textured, and blackberry- as well as licorice-flavored wine has a long, soft, and supple finish. Drink it over the next 5 years.

Revealing a dark ruby/purple color as well as candied cherry and Asian spice aromatics, the 1996 Gevrey-Chambertin is chewy textured, medium to full bodied, juicy, sweet, and redolent with jammy red and black cherries. Anticipated maturity: now–2004. The black-colored 1996 Gevrey-Chambertin En Motrot has complex aromas of earth, cassis liqueur, and beef blood. This big, broad, ample, medium- to full-bodied, and expressive wine displays layer upon layer of candied black cherries, cassis, and spiced oak in its flavor profile. However, I am concerned because of the preponderance of dry, oaky tannins in this potentially outstanding wine's finish.

Produced from five parcels Mortet owns in Gevrey-Chambertin Lavaux St. Jacques, the bright dark ruby-colored 1996 has an awesome nose reminiscent of blueberry compote. On the palate, this highly concentrated, chewy-textured, medium- to full-bodied, extracted, and profound wine offers candied cherries drenched in Asian spices. This delicious, seductive, and sexy wine also possesses a long finish. Drink it between 2000 and 2006. Even better, the dark ruby/purple-colored 1996 Gevrey-Chambertin Les Champeaux displays gorgeously fresh aromas of candied cherries, cassis, and blackberries that lead to an explosive flavor profile densely packed with jammy blueberries. This full-bodied, highly concentrated, oily-textured, powerful, and sweet wine has one of the longest and most fruit-filled finishes I've experienced in Burgundy. Anticipated maturity: 2001–2007. The 1996 Chambolle-Musigny Les Beaux-Bruns exhibits a nose of violets and sugar-coated blueberries, followed by a structured, masculine, full-bodied, firm, and muscular personality. This rich, fruit-packed wine appears to have the same oaky tannin problem I encountered in the 1996 Gevrey-Chambertin En Motrot. My instincts suggest that with cellaring it may or may not be absorbed by this offering's dense fruit. Time will tell. Try it in 2002.

The bright, medium to dark ruby/purple-colored 1996 Clos de Vougeot has sweet-and-spicy plums intermingled with Asian spices. This awesomely fresh, full-bodied, explosive, powerful, and velvety-textured gem reveals layer upon layer of black cherries, cassis liqueur, and new oak. Well balanced, and focused, it also possesses enormous depth, concentration, and a spectacularly long finish. Anticipated maturity: 2002–2008. Mortet's extraordinary 1996 Chambertin is black/purple colored and displays intense aromas of candied black fruits, cinnamon, Asian spices, and fresh herbs. This massively large, broad, magnificently balanced, proportioned, and deeply ripe behemoth coats the palate with supersweet black cherries and blueberries whose flavors seemingly last forever. Its firm structure and huge oak flavors are drowned in fruit, as are its copious quantities of fine tannins. It should be drunk between 2002 and 2010.

The 1996 Gevrey-Chambertin au Velle is dark ruby/purple and displays scents of sweet and juicy cherries and black currants. This oily, fat, broad, plump, firmly structured, foursquare, and masculine wine is crammed with brambleberries, iron, and stones. This tannic, brooding, and austere offering will require patience, but I am confident it will evolve beautifully—much like a similarly constructed Nuits. Anticipated maturity: 2003–2008+.

The similarly colored 1996 Gevrey-Chambertin En Champs exhibits sweet and pungent aromas of cassis liqueur. This is a very concentrated, intense, extracted, chewy, full-bodied, and powerful wine that buries the palate in shovels full of black cherries, cassis, and spices. It is extraordinarily long and not particularly elegant (sometimes a nose tackle is more useful than a ballerina) and will require patience to allow its tannic personality to subside. Anticipated maturity: 2003–2009.

DOMAINE GEORGES MUGNERET/MUGNERET-GIBOURG
(VOSNE-ROMANÉE)

1996 Bourgogne	D	(87–88)
1996 Chambolle-Musigny Les Feusselottes	E	(89–91+)
1996 Clos Vougeot	EE	(90–93)
1996 Echézeaux	EE	(89–92)
1996 Nuits-St.-Georges Les Chaignots	E	(88–90)
1996 Ruchottes-Chambertin	EE	(92–94+)
1996 Vosne-Romanée	D	(88–90)

If there is a more charming woman in Burgundy than Mme. Mugneret, I have yet to meet her. The widow of Dr. Georges Mugneret, the ophthalmologist who created this estate, she and her two daughters (Christine and Marie-Andrée) manage the domaine. There are, in effect, two estates—Mugneret-Gibourg is composed of vineyards purchased by the doctor's mother in the 1930s, and Domaine Georges Mugneret is composed of the parcels purchased by the doctor. Since he passed away in 1988 many changes have taken place.

A sorting table purchased by Marie-Andrée (an oenologist) is credited with significantly increasing the quality of the 1996s. According to her, there was no rot or mildew to sort out, but unripened or irregularly ripened bunches had to be culled. Having an inquisitive mind, she kept the grapes that had been sorted out and vinified them. The natural alcohol levels of these (not to be released) wines were a whopping 2 degrees below the sorted cuvées. Another significant change took place in 1993 with the purchase of a mechanical *pigéage* machine. Marie-Andrée informed me that she has much better control of the *pigéages* and is no longer dependent upon getting an employee to come to the estate during off hours and risk his life (a number of people have died asphyxiated by the fermentation fumes or drowned after passing out) in the cuvées.

Often, when children take over an estate from a successful parent, they have a tendency to fear change. This obviously did not happen at Domaines Georges Mugneret and Mugneret-Gibourg. Marie-Andrée is bright, open-minded, outgoing, delightful, and charming. Together with her sister, Christine (whom I have yet to meet), who has a Ph.D. in pharmacology, she has made sure that these estates are in excellent hands.

The day of my visit, Mme. Mugneret was in the dining room entertaining a Japanese couple who spoke no French and barely a hint of English. She tried to communicate using hand signals and smiles, but what truly got the message across was a corkscrew, some glasses, and delicious wine: the universal language of wine enthusiasts.

As the above-listed scores suggest, I was impressed with the entire portfolio. They are all pure, ripe, well structured, and have supple tannins. Village wines are aged in 30% new oak, the premiers crus in 40%, and the grands crus range from 60%–80% new barrels. These wines will be fined prior to bottling, but the Mugnerets have never used filters according to Marie-Andrée and Peter Vezan (the estate's broker).

The ruby-colored 1996 Bourgogne is a first-rate example of this regional appellation. Its gorgeous creamed cherry scents give way to a truly delicious, well-balanced, medium-bodied, and concentrated core of sweet red cherries. This lovely wine should be drunk between now and 2003. The 1996 Vosne-Romanée is slightly darker colored and offers aromas reminiscent of candied cherries wrapped in smoky bacon. This is an expressive, deep, intense, rich, harmonious, and extremely well-proportioned wine. Its medium- to full-bodied character is redolent with plump black cherries that last throughout its persistent and silky finish. Anticipated maturity: now–2004.

Displaying a medium to dark ruby color and violet, rose, blackberry, and blueberry-infused aromatics, the 1996 Nuits-St.-Georges Les Chaignots is highly expressive and medium to full bodied. It is more structured and dense than the Vosne but exhibits less opulent fruit. However, don't be fooled: this is a rich, beautifully ripe, and concentrated wine that is filled with raspberry, cherry, and stonelike flavors that linger in its long and oak-imbued finish. Anticipated maturity: 2000–2006. The 1996 Chambolle-Musigny Les Feusselottes has a bright, medium to dark ruby color, and fabulously floral aromas of violets, lilies, blackberry juice, and earth notes. This extracted, broad, deeply ripe, marvelously balanced, and medium- to full-bodied wine is silky textured, powerful, and crammed with blueberries, cassis, and hints of minerals. It should be at its best between 2000 and 2007.

The 1996 Echézeaux is dark ruby colored and displays earth-dusted scents of violets and red currants. This highly elegant wine is medium to full bodied and velvety textured and has a tightly wound character that with aeration blossomed, displaying immense power, concentration, and ripeness of fruit. Its flavor profile is filled with cherries, blackberries, and blueberries that linger throughout its admirable finish. Anticipated maturity: 2000–2007.

In 1977 Charles Rousseau of Domaine Armand Rousseau in Gevrey-Chambertin approached his friend Dr. Georges Mugneret with a brilliant idea: A large parcel of Ruchottes-Chambertin, including the Clos des Ruchottes, was being offered for sale. Rousseau's idea was that he, Mugneret, and a wealthy wine lover from Reims (in Champagne) named Michel Bonnefond purchase the parcel and divide it into three smaller ones. The three parcels are located in different sectors of the vineyard, with the Mugneret's being in the lower Ruchottes du Bas and Rousseau having the Clos des Ruchottes at the top of the vineyard (I am not certain where Bonnefond's is located). Bonnefond's parcel is vinified by Christophe Roumier of Domaine Georges et Christophe Roumier in Chambolle Musigny by a *métayage* arrangement (interested readers should know that Ruchottes's labeled Roumier and Bonnefond are virtually identical wines).

Domaine Georges Mugneret's parcel of Ruchottes-Chambertin is composed of sickly 50–55-year-old vines that produce low yields (in 1996, a vintage that saw huge crops, it produced a meager under 2 tons of fruit per acre). The 1996 is spectacular. This medium to dark ruby-colored offering has beguiling aromas reminiscent of spiced and sweetened cherries and assorted flowers dusted with freshly cracked white pepper. This medium- to full-bodied, creamy-textured, concentrated, and magnificently refined wine has flavors of raspberries, cherries, strawberries, minerals, and Asian spices in its delightfully harmonious core. Even though this wine is intensely ripe and plump, it has outstanding balance and focus as well as a prodigiously long finish. I would not be surprised if my score seemed overly conservative in a few years. Anticipated maturity: 2004–2012+. Wow!

The medium to dark ruby-colored 1996 Clos Vougeot is also an impressive wine with an intensely spicy nose of black cherry syrup laced with mocha. This medium- to full-bodied, fat, broad, expressive, and thickly textured offering is jam-packed with candied cherries, blackberries, flower blossoms, earth, and minerals. This is a firmer, less opulent and seductive wine than the Ruchottes, yet its huge depth of fruit, density, and structure are all immensely impressive. Anticipated maturity: 2004–2010. Bravo to the three ladies of these two estates!

DOMAINE JACQUES-FRÉDÉRIC MUGNIER (CHAMBOLLE-MUSIGNY)
(Also Known as the Château de Chambolle-Musigny)

1995 Chambolle-Musigny Les Amoureuses	EE	91
1995 Musigny	EEE	93

Frédéric Mugnier had just recently bottled his 1995s when I visited him in June of 1997, and he was reluctant to allow me to taste them (wines often shut down after bottling). Two of the wines were showing admirably well and deserve to be mentioned.

The ruby-colored 1995 Chambolle-Musigny Les Amoureuses exhibits delightful aromas of wild strawberries and touches of underbrush as well as an extremely elegant, silky-textured, medium- to full-bodied personality jam-packed with lively cherries, violets, minerals, and spices. This superb wine possesses plenty of ripe, round tannins for structure and a beautifully long finish. Drink it between 2001 and 2009. Surprisingly, Mugnier's 1995 Musigny seemed slightly lighter in color, but its highly expressive nose of ripe cassis, wild blueberries, blackberries, and a bouquet of freshly cut flowers served as an omen to the power I would find in its flavors. An explosive burst of layered red and black cherries as well as notes of violets, stones, and sweet mushrooms are found in this superb wine's oily-textured, full-bodied, and sublimely long flavor profile. Anticipated maturity: 2001–2009.

DOMAINE PHILIPPE NADDEF (COUCHEY)

1996 Fixin	C	(85–88)
1996 Gevrey-Chambertin Les Cazetiers	D	(89–91)
1996 Gevrey-Chambertin Les Champeaux	D	(88–90)
1996 Gevrey-Chambertin Vieilles Vignes	C	(87–89)
1996 Marsannay	C	(85–87)
1996 Marsannay Blanc	C	87+
1996 Mazis-Chambertin	E	(90–92)

Philippe Naddef, clad in a warm-up suit, T-shirt, and sneakers, and with tousled hair, looks like an 18-year-old ready to go play soccer with his buddies—not at all like a 39-year-old vigneron. He is so youthful looking that when he informed me that he had worked at the Domaine du Comte de Vogüé from 1979 to 1984, I had trouble believing he had yet been born.

Naddef started creating this estate, located in the small town of Couchey (between Fixin and Marsannay-la-Côte), in 1983 with rented parcels from his mother and others. He informed me that he had been criticized in the past for producing wines that were excessively tannic and that in 1995 he began using techniques designed to craft more supple wines.

Like a number of other young vignerons, Naddef is concentrating his efforts on reducing rackings, using as little sulfur as possible, and making sure his wines feed on large quantities of fine lees while aging in barrels. After fermentation, the wines are transferred to barrels in which he has already placed 5 liters of lees. After the secondary fermentation (malolactic) is complete, he racks his wines, adding a minute quantity of sulfur to the lees (but none in the wine itself) and then returns the lees and wines back to the barrels. Furthermore, Naddef performs his *ouillage* (the topping off of barrels) with additional lees.

Naddef sells a significant portion of his wines to *négociants* (for example, 50% of his Gevrey-Chambertin in 1996), some of which are purchased by Maison Dominique Laurent. Like many Burgundians, Naddef believes Laurent is a first-rate winemaker but that his 200% new oak approach "denatures the wines."

Produced from equal proportions of 6-year-old and over 40-year-old vines, the ruby-colored 1996 Marsannay (the yields averaged between 2²/₃ and 3 tons of fruit per acre) displays sweet black raspberry and cassis aromas. On the palate, the wine is juicy, well delineated, and medium bodied, with a rich core of blueberries and black cherries. Naddef's judicious use of first-year oak barrels provided just a trace of spiciness to this appealing, silky wine. It will provide delicious drinking over the next 3–4 years. The impressive and bright, medium to dark ruby-colored 1996 Fixin (2²/₃ per acre) was aged in 40% new oak barrels. It offers an extremely spicy nose of dark cherries and black currants as well as a sweet (almost leesy), medium- to full-bodied character of candied cherries, raspberries, and toasty oak. Naddef's efforts to reduce the tannic edge of his wines is reflected in this offering's supple and soft finish (rare for a wine from this generally tannic appellation). Anticipated maturity: now–2004.

Produced from 5 parcels interspersed between Brochon and the border of Morey-St.-Denis that yielded an average of 2 tons of fruit per acre (low for the vintage), the 1996 Gevrey-Chambertin Vieilles Vignes has a perfumed, black cherry and cassis-scented nose. This well-concentrated, powerful, balanced, juicy, medium- to full-bodied, and flavorful wine exhibits expressive blackberry, beef blood, and toasty oak flavors. It will be at its best between now and 2004. Naddef's grandfather planted the vines that crafted the 1996 Gevrey-Chambertin Les Champeaux 45 years ago. Displaying black cherry and candied tangerine orange peel aromas, this refined wine is thick, chewy, and medium to full bodied and offers an excellent—potentially outstanding—flavor profile of intense blackberries and assorted dark fruits. Anticipated maturity: 2001–2006. The 1996 Gevrey-Chambertin Les Cazetiers, also from 45-year-old vines, has lovely aromatics reminiscent of violets, roses, perfume, and cherries. This concentrated, silky-textured, broad, and mouth-coating wine reveals broad and rich flavors of raspberries, tangy currants, and cherries. It is an extroverted, harmonious, medium- to full-bodied, and feminine offering with an admirably long and suave finish. Anticipated maturity: 2000–2006.

Like many producers in Burgundy, Naddef receives only about 10% of the Tronçais oak barrels he orders (demand is much greater than what that forest can supply), yet he ages his 1996 Mazis-Chambertin in 100% new Tronçais oak barrels. Produced from vines averaging 60 years old (the oldest are 80), this wine displays a medium to dark ruby color and a fragrant nose composed of violets, sweet cassis, blackberries, and perfume. This concentrated, extracted, powerful, and structured offering is full bodied, rich, and densely packed with blackberries, stones, and tangy raspberries. Anticipated maturity: 2003–2010.

DOMAINE DES PERDRIX (NUITS-ST.-GEORGES)

1996 Echézeaux	EE	(93–95+)
1996 Nuits-St.-Georges	D	(88–89)
1996 Nuits-St.-Georges Aux Perdrix	E	(89–91)
1996 Vosne-Romanée	D	(88–90)

The Domaine des Perdrix, recently purchased by Bertrand Devillard (the director of Maison Antonin Rodet) and his wife, markets its wines through Rodet's sales network. I was impressed with the estate's 1996s. The dazzling Echézeaux is one of the finest examples I have tasted from that grand cru vineyard.

The medium to dark ruby-colored 1996 Nuits-St.-Georges (produced from Bas de Combe, just below Aux Boudots and bordering Vosne's Les Chaumes and Aux Réas to the north and east) offers a perfume- and violet-laden nose as well as an extracted, concentrated, gorgeously ripe, and lip-smackingly delicious character filled with candied red fruits. Its long finish reveals loads of soft, round tannins that should easily melt away with cellaring. Drink this beautiful example of a Nuits "village" wine between 2000 and 2004. The 1996 Vosne-Romanée sports a bright medium to dark ruby/purple color and has sweet, floral, and cherry-infused aromas. This feminine, elegant, and deep wine regales with its loads of candied cherries, plums, traces of *sur-maturité*, and great depth. It is medium to full bodied, enticing, and extremely well proportioned. Anticipated maturity: now–2005. The dark ruby-colored 1996 Nuits-St.-Georges Aux Perdrix underwent a 15%–20% *saignée* and was aged in 80% new oak barrels. Aromatically displaying violets, perfume (these two olfactory characteristics seem to be present in most of the wines made by or associated with the Maison Antonin Rodet in 1996), and blueberries, this wine has excellent intensity and concentration to its medium- to full-bodied, highly structured, and foursquare personality. Layers of blackberries, cassis, plums, black raspberries, and other dark fruits can be found in this superbly ripe offering. Anticipated maturity: 2002–2006+.

Recently a subscriber to *The Wine Advocate* called and expressed disappointment that there were never any new names among the producers of stupendous red burgundies. I pointed out to him that new stars could be found in almost every issue of *The Wine Advocate*, most notably Claude Dugat, Bernard Dugat, Hubert Lignier, Chopin-Groffier, Ambroise, and Cacheux, and that Burgundy is filled with young winemakers yearning to become known as the best producer in their village. I was thinking specifically of Domaine des Perdrix's 1996 Echézeaux. If the wine I tasted out of barrel is bottled without losing its extraordinary fruit and precision (that is, with little fining or filtration), it will be a blockbuster. Dark ruby colored and exhibiting copious quantities of sweet dark fruits, violets, and traces of minerals, this wine is magnificently defined, elegant, and feminine. An intense, juicy, and fabulously pure core of candied cherries, plums, blueberries, and flowers can be found in this full-bodied, velvety, and admirably long wine. Anticipated maturity: 2003–2009+. Bravo!

DOMAINE HENRI PERROT-MINOT (MOREY-ST.-DENIS)

1996 Chambolle-Musigny La Combe d'Orveaux	EE	(90–93)
1996 Chambolle-Musigny Les Fuées	EE	(92–94+)
1996 Chambolle-Musigny Vieilles Vignes	D	(89–91+)
1996 Charmes-Chambertin	E	(92–94)
1996 Gevrey-Chambertin	D	(87–88)
1996 Mazoyères-Chambertin	EE	(91–93)
1996 Morey-St.-Denis La Riotte	E	(88–90)
1996 Morey-St.-Denis En La Rue de Vergy	D	(87–89)

Speaking of potential future superstars . . . Christophe Perrot-Minot (Henri's son) is a name that may become as famous as Lignier, Dugat, Lafon, Roumier, and the like. I was as excited when I left this domaine as I was when I walked out of Arnauld Ente's in Meursault. There is nothing more gratifying and invigorating than tasting a young person's wines for the first time and finding them to be superb.

Christophe Perrot-Minot was a *courtier* (brokers who serve as middlemen between growers and *négociants*) before joining his father at the domaine. Three years later his father retired, leaving the young Christophe on his own. Changes were fast and furious. Chemical fertilizers are eschewed (replaced with organic compost), vines are cut back severely, the *verjus* (the secondary crop that never ripens in time for the harvest) is systematically removed, leaves are pulled to promote air flow and ripening, and a green harvest is performed to ensure that each vine produces only 6–7 bunches. A sorting table is used to weed out all unwanted grapes (in 1994, 14 tons of harvested grapes were thrown out).

A long cold maceration (at 10–12 degrees Celsius and lasting 10 days for village wines and 15 days for the premiers and grand crus) is performed in a closed tank with daily *pigéages*. Subsequently, an 8–12-day fermentation (the 1996s were chaptalized to drag out this process; the 1997s were not chaptalized) takes place, followed by a 2–3-day warm maceration at 33 degrees Celsius. The wines are then quickly dropped to 6 degrees Celsius before being placed in barrels (a minimum of 30% new oak for village wines and 45%–50% for premiers and grands crus). Perrot-Minot's preference in *tonneliers* is the Rémond firm, who crafted 95% of the estate's barrels in 1996. His wines are never racked before bottling and receive only 3 centiliters of sulfur per barrel after the malolactic fermentation is completed (using a long hypodermic needle, Perrot-Minot injects the sulfur directly into the lees). As would be expected of someone as dedicated to quality and noninterventionist winemaking as this young man is, he neither fines nor filters. Prior to 1993, 30%–40% of the domaine's wines were sold to *négociants*. Today all of it is estate-bottled.

The domaine's village appellation wines had yields averaging 3 tons of fruit per acre, the Morey-St.-Denis La Riotte 2+ tons per acre, the Chambolle-Musigny Combe d'Orveaux just under 2 tons, the Chambolle-Musigny Les Fuées 1²/₃ tons per acre, the Mazoyères-Chambertin 2 tons per acre, and the Charmes-Chambertin just over 2 tons. Perrot-Minot's style of winemaking is exactly what I love. It brings concentration and extraction together with elegance, refinement, and focus. Too many producers seem to search out either power or finesse (not both) and in the process produce wines that are caricatures of what they were trying to accomplish. What this young man has achieved in such a short time is truly remarkable.

Revealing a medium to dark ruby color and rich aromas of dark cherries, stones, and minerals, the 1996 Morey-St.-Denis En La Rue de Vergy is a broad, ample, medium- to full-bodied, velvety-textured, and gorgeously ripe wine. Its dense yet highly focused flavor profile is composed of blackberries, smoked bacon, and black cherries, and it possesses a long and supple finish. Drink it between now and 2005. The 1996 Gevrey-Chambertin is medium to dark ruby/purple colored with a brooding nose of blackberries and a highly structured, firm, masculine, and tangy character. Flavors of an assortment of fruits, baked into a compote (yet without the negative jammy texture baked fruits call to mind), and then dusted with minerals and crushed gravel, can be found in this foursquare, harder-edged wine. Anticipated maturity: 2000–2004. Produced from old vines (75%–80% are over 100 years old!) in the La Bussière vineyard, the slightly darker-colored 1996 Chambolle-Musigny Vieilles Vignes (*vieilles vignes* may or may not appear on the label) has violets, roses, lilies, candied blueberries, raspberries, and minerals on the nose. This magnificent wine has extraordinary breadth, a medium to full body, a silky texture, and a hugely complex core of wild blueberries, brambleberries, cassis, stones, and gravel that last throughout its long and soft finish. It is better than the majority of premiers crus produced in Burgundy! Drink it between 2001 and 2007. The 1996 Morey-St.-Denis La Riotte (it had nearly finished its malo) is medium to dark ruby colored. Aromatically, it exhibits black fruits and roasted coffee. This medium- to full-bodied, plump, silky-textured, and concentrated wine has intense flavors of blueberries and earth as well as a well-defined, long, and supple finish. Anticipated maturity: now–2006.

Revealing a slightly darker color and a deep, floral, gamey, and kirsch-infused nose, the 1996 Chambolle-Musigny La Combe d'Orveaux is special. This offering's medium- to full-bodied, velvety-textured, powerful, and highly structured personality has mouth-coating wild blueberries, brambleberries, blackberries, earth, sautéed mushrooms, roasted herbs, and Asian spices. The firm but beautifully ripe tannins found in its extremely long finish will require patience. Anticipated maturity: 2003–2009. I was blown away by Perrot-Minot's medium to dark ruby/purple-colored 1996 Chambolle-Musigny Les Fuées. Produced from a newly purchased parcel of vines planted in 1945, it reveals intricate aromas of blueberries, cassis, blackberries, minerals, gravel, thyme, and Asian spices. On the palate, it is lively, bright, profoundly complex, masculine yet elegant, powerful yet detailed. This magnificent offering has a full-bodied silky texture, and exciting flavors of juicy black currant, berries, candied oranges, and toast. Wow! Anticipated maturity: 2002–2008.

Both of Domaine Perrot-Minot's grands crus are produced from 55-year-old *sélection massale* vines (propagated by selecting the healthiest and best-producing plants in a vineyard and taking cuttings from them—as opposed to clonal selections). Because of the quirky rules and regulations that govern Burgundy, Perrot-Minot is entitled to blend both his Mazoyères and Charmes and call the assemblage Charmes-Chambertin, as do most Burgundians (which is why Mazoyères is so rare). However, he told me that since they were produced from vines selected the same way and planted the same year and were vinified identically, they truly defined their differences in *terroir*.

Revealing a dark ruby color and aromas reminiscent of gravel soaked with sweet blackberry juice with a light dusting of earth for additional complexity, the full-bodied 1996 Mazoyères-Chambertin is a compelling wine. This extremely rich and penetrating wine has a chewy texture and extraordinary flavors of underbrush, sautéed mushrooms, stones, and candied cherries. Its admirably long finish offers loads of ripe tannins. Anticipated maturity: 2002–2008. The dark ruby-colored 1996 Charmes-Chambertin has a mulberry, black raspberry, blueberry, earth, briar, and roasted oak-laden nose. This is a soft, sweet, supple, full-bodied, powerful, thickly textured, gorgeously concentrated, and seductive offering. Crammed with candied cherries, mushrooms, and fresh herbs, and refined, it has extraordinary richness and a superbly long, suave, and focused finish. Anticipated maturity: 2002–2009. These are 1996s not to be missed! Bravo to Christophe Perrot-Minot!

MAISON/DOMAINE JEAN PILLOT ET FILS (CHASSAGNE-MONTRACHET)

1996 Santenay Les Champs-Claude	C	87

The 1996 Santenay Les Champs-Claude is a medium ruby-colored wine that reveals ripe raspberries and cherries on the nose and a medium-bodied, juicy, sweet, silky-textured core of red berries and fresh herbs. Drink it before 2002.

DOMAINE PONSOT (MOREY-ST.-DENIS)

1996 Chapelle-Chambertin	EEE	87
1996 Clos de la Roche Vieilles Vignes	EEE	87?
1995 Clos de la Roche Vieilles Vignes	EEE	85?
1996 Gevrey-Chambertin Cuvée de l'Abeille	D	81?
1995 Gevrey-Chambertin Cuvée de l'Abeille	D	67?
1996 Griotte-Chambertin	EEE	86?
1995 Griotte-Chambertin	EEE	87?
1996 Morey-St.-Denis Cuvée des Alouettes	E	86?

As longtime readers of *The Wine Advocate* know, Robert Parker and I purchase enormous quantities of wine each year to taste for upcoming issues of the journal and *The Wine Buyer's Guide,* to track their evolution, and to see if what we tasted in barrel corresponds to what consumers find on the retailers' shelves.

In this job, there is nothing more heartbreaking than to revisit a wine that was spectacular as a cask sample and find it anemic and feeble in the bottle. In response to distressing reports concerning Domaine Ponsot's 1995s out of Burgundy as well as from friends and subscribers who tasted them immediately upon their release in the United States, I acquired a number of them from stateside retailers. Furthermore, upon my visit to Domaine Ponsot in late January 1999, I asked Laurent Ponsot, the estate's director and winemaker, to allow me to taste with him his bottled 1995s and 1996s prior to visiting the 1997s from barrel. Ponsot generously opened a few 1996s. I was unable to taste any 1995s with him, however, as he informed me that all of his 1995s were located in another cellar in the village and were not accessible within the short time I had (Domaine Ponsot's cellars are spread out throughout the village).

The following notes are based on tastings I conducted in Washington, D.C. (one was blind), in which Domaine Ponsot's 1995s and 1996s were served alongside wines from other highly regarded Burgundian estates. Additionally, these notes include the results of my tasting with Laurent Ponsot of a few of his 1996s.

The 1995 Gevrey-Chambertin Cuvée de l'Abeille is a major disappointment (this was my first tasting of this wine, as Laurent Ponsot had not offered me a barrel sample when I visited his estate in 1997). It reveals an orangish/pink color marked with amber on the edge of the glass. To my great surprise, this wine offers little aroma or flavor, even after considerable efforts to coax something out of it. I was unable to discern any positive or negative traits, or much fruit. After considerable airing, this Gevrey remained in the same anemic state. I cannot imagine its getting any better with cellaring. In *The Wine Advocate*'s Issue #111, I rated the 1995 Griotte-Chambertin a 91–94 and described it as "dark ruby colored . . . with aromas of deep, dark berries and touches of underbrush, this is a powerful, large-scaled wine that offers layer upon layer of thick, chewy, and grilled fruits . . . tannic, full bodied, and backward, it requires 6–7 years of cellaring and should age well for another 12–15 years." At my recent encounter with this Griotte out of bottle, it had a brick/ruby color and revealed the amber edge of an older wine. Exhibiting the aromas of an already well-evolved Pinot (roses, raspberries, and earth), this wine possesses an elegant, light- to medium-bodied core of tea leaves, cherries, and strawberries. It appears already to be drying out; however, it offers a long and fruit-flavored finish. Readers who own this wine should consider drinking it up. In my article on Ponsot's 1995s out of barrel, I heaped conderable praise on the Clos de la Roche Vieilles Vignes, describing it as "prodigious" and going so far as to say that "I would not be surprised if it deserved a perfect rating!" At my recent tasting I found it to be light to medium ruby colored, with an ambered edge. Its slightly alcoholic nose is reminiscent of cherry-flavored Bubble-Yum bubble gum mixed with white pepper and grapefruit. On the palate, this wine is a pale shadow of its former self. Amid an earthy, stony, red pit fruit-flavored, and medium-bodied core, there remains a ghostlike trace of the richness and ripeness I originally had seen in this wine. After it had been opened for 48 hours, I revisited it. To its credit, this Clos de la Roche had not deteriorated, yet it had not gotten any better, either. I will not be drinking my remaining bottles in the near term, as I want to see if Laurent Ponsot's assertion that these wines will regain their fruit in time is correct. However, I cannot recommend the same course of action to readers, as I see no reason to believe that cellaring will help this wine or any of the other 1995 and 1996 Domaine Ponsot offerings I have recently tasted.

The 1996s I have revisited in the past few months fared better than the 1995s. I do not know, however, if it is because they are actually finer wines or because their shorter time in bottle has not dried the fruit out as much (Ponsot's 1996s were all bottled in September 1998). The 1996 Gevrey-Chambertin Cuvée de l'Abeille (originally rated 85–87 in Issue #118) has a ruby color as well as an orange rind-and-clay-scented nose with hints of black cherries. It is light to medium bodied, has briary flavors, is lacking in fruit, and is drying out in the finish. If readers own this wine, they are well advised to drink it up as soon as possible. The 1996 Morey-St.-Denis Cuvée des Alouettes (original score 87–88) is ruby colored and offers earth, wax, and black cherry aromas. On the palate, this medium-bodied, bright, perfumed, and tangy wine reveals floral flavors of roses intermingled with a trace of licorice.

Some fruit is present, but it is not dominant, something I expect in such a youthful wine. My suggestion to readers who own this wine? Drink up. I had loved the 1996 Griotte-Chambertin out of barrel, bestowing upon it a 90–93-point rating. However, in bottle it too is extremely disappointing. It is ruby colored and displays scents of blood oranges and smoke with faint hints of red fruits in the background. This wine reveals tangy berries, stones, a light to medium body, and the telltale finish of a wine that is drying out. Ponsot's 1996 Chapelle-Chambertin, tasted three times since its bottling, is ruby colored and offers cinnamon-infused aromas of spices and sweet red fruits. This Chapelle has 1996's vibrance, a medium body, and excellent balance and focus. It has significantly more fruit than any of the 1995 and 1996 Ponsots I have recently tasted, its flavors being dominated by red currants, tangy cherries, and berries. However, it does not approach the 89–91 rating I originally gave it in Issue #118. Anticipated maturity: now–2002. The 1996 Clos de la Roche Vieilles Vignes, originally rated a whopping 92–95, was also a disheartening wine to revisit after bottling. It exhibits a somewhat darker color than the Griotte and has a muted nose that revealed some strawberry scents only after considerable coaxing. This is an oily-textured, medium-bodied, well-balanced, and persistent wine, yet its flavors are dominated by earth, gravel, and under-brush. I have no idea what happened to the "layers of blackberries, cherries, cassis, mocha, and fresh herbs" I had tasted 12 months before.

Robert Parker and I have reported on this famed domaine's inconsistency numerous times. Glorious wines were crafted here in 1947, 1949, 1972, 1980, 1985, 1990, 1991, and 1993; less than thrilling wines were produced in 1988, 1989, and now 1996; disappointing wines were made in 1984, 1986, 1987, 1994, and now 1995. What gives? In *The Wine Advocate*'s Issue #111 I reiterated this point. Upon arriving at Ponsot's estate in 1998 to taste the 1996s out of barrel, I asked him about this inconsistency. He answered that he was proud of it because it proved that his wines reflected the vintages and that he was not doctoring his wines like many other producers.

DOMAINE DE LA POUSSE D'OR (VOLNAY)

1995 Pommard Les Jarollières	E	(87–90)
1995 Santenay Clos des Tavannes	D	(85–88)
1995 Volnay Caillerets	E	(86–89)
1995 Volnay Clos d'Audignac	D	(84–87)
1995 Volnay Clos des 60 Ouvrées	E	(90–93)
1995 Volnay Clos de la Bousse d'Or	E	(90–93)

Gérard Potel has produced some of the purest and most elegant Volnays I have tasted. His 1985 Clos de la Bousse d'Or is graceful, sweet, silky, and simply magnificent today, as well as one of the few 1985s that is putting on body as it evolves. Potel, historically an interventionist winemaker, lectured me on his belief that fining and filtering do not damage a wine's quality, later informing me that he was not subjecting his wines to either procedure in 1995 because they were so clear and healthy.

According to Potel, when he and his partners originally purchased the estate it was called "Domaine de la Bousse d'Or," bearing the name of its most famous vineyard. Shortly thereafter, a little-known law stating that estates can bear the name of a vineyard only if it is the only vineyard the domaine owns was pointed out to the authorities by a rival (the Domaine de la Romanée Conti has been given an exemption from this law for historical reasons). Potel, forced to rename the estate, created the name "Pousse d'Or."

The medium ruby-colored 1995 Santenay Clos des Tavannes had finished its malolactic fermentation just prior to my tasting. It displays beautiful aromas of sweet cherries and a silky-textured, medium-bodied, and soft personality with beguiling flavors of fresh herbs, ripe currants, and creamy Earl Grey tea. Drink it between now and 2002. Darker colored and possessing gorgeous red berry aromas and a supple, light- to medium-bodied character, the 1995 Volnay Clos d'Audignac is a well-made and delicate wine with sweet cherry fruit and distant spice flavors. Anticipated maturity: now–2002. The ruby-colored 1995 Volnay Caillerets reveals beautifully ripe raspberries and boysenberries aromatically and a delicious medium-bodied, soft-textured, luscious, cherry, and Asian spice-filled palate. It is an elegant and well-defined wine that should be at its best between now and 2003.

The dark ruby-colored 1995 Volnay Clos des 60 Ouvrées (from an enclosed parcel within the Caillerets vineyard) offers magnificent aromas of deeply sweet and superspicy (reminiscent of thyme, sage, and tarragon) blackberries and raspberries. Its fabulously oily texture and superbly elegant medium to full body is filled with beautifully ripe red fruits, and its admirably long finish ends on round and supple tannins. This outstanding wine will age gracefully and should be at its peak between 2000 and 2008. Slightly lighter colored, the 1995 Pommard Les Jarollières reveals dark berry aromas intermingled with roasting spices and a thick-textured, medium- to full-bodied character filled with copious quantities of concentrated and extracted black cherries with notes of herbal spices for additional complexity. Potentially Potel's finest 1995 (the 60 Ouvrées will certainly be in the running for this honor), the dark ruby-colored Volnay Clos de la Bousse d'Or exhibits delightful aromas of ripe blackberries, fresh rosemary, and Asian spices. It possesses a deeply sweet, medium- to full-bodied, and oily-textured core with layers of cherries, raspberries, earth, mocha, and spices. This highly structured and awesomely elegant wine is tightly wound and built to last. With proper shipping and cellaring it will evolve gracefully for well over a decade. Anticipated maturity: 2000–2010.

DOMAINE DU CHÂTEAUX DE PRÉMEAUX (PRÉMEAUX-PRISSEY)

1996 Côte de Nuits-Village	C	(84–87)
1996 Nuits-St.-Georges	D	(85–87)
1996 Nuits-St.-Georges Les Argillières	D	(87–88)

The original Château de Prémeaux was plundered and destroyed prior to the French Revolution. The building that now bears its name, while attractive, does not conjure up images of a French castle. M. Pelletier, this 29.6-acre estate's owner and director, explained to me that the château is, in effect, a working farm. His brother is responsible for all the non-wine-related agriculture. Viticulture and winemaking are controlled by M. Pelletier. After the passing away of his father, who was asphyxiated from a cuvée's fermentation fumes, Pelletier dedicated himself to trying to increase the quality of the estate's wine. Since 1990 he says he has lowered yields and has begun to bottle all his wines without subjecting them to fining or filtration. A close friend to Alain Meunier (Domaine Jean-Jacques Confuron) and Bertrand Ambroise, both of Prémeaux, Pelletier gives them credit for helping raise the quality level. While these are not outstanding wines, they offer attractive fruit and reasonable values.

I tasted two cuvées (prior to assemblage) of the ruby/purple-colored 1996 Côtes de Nuits-Villages. The first (rated 85–87+) was better than the second (84–86), which was slightly drier and a touch hollow. The final blend should offer lively aromas of ripe grapes and cherries and have a fresh, well-ripened core of red fruits, a silky texture, and a medium body. My suggestion would be to drink it over the next 3 years. The slightly darker-colored 1996 Nuits-St.-Georges reveals blackberry and stonelike aromatics as well as a well-crafted, vibrant, medium-bodied, and tangy character with crisp cherry flavors. Anticipated maturity: now–2002. Displaying a medium to dark ruby color and a lovely nose of bacon fat-drenched cherries, the 1996 Nuits-St.-Georges Les Argillières is a silky-textured, medium-bodied, well-proportioned wine with a delightful black raspberry and cherry-filled flavor profile. Drink it between now and 2004.

DOMAINE JACQUES PRIEUR (MEURSAULT)

1996	Beaune Champs Pimont	D	(87–88)
1996	Beaune Clos de la Féguine	E	(87–89)
1996	Beaune Grèves	D	(86–87)
1996	Chambertin	EEE	(89–91)
1996	Clos Vougeot	EE	(89–91+)
1996	Corton-Bressandes	E	(90–92)
1996	Echézeaux	EE	(92–95)
1996	Meursault Clos de Mazeray	D	(86–88)
1996	Musigny	EEE	(94–96)
1996	Volnay Champans	E	(88–91)
1996	Volnay Clos des Santenots	E	(90–92)
1996	Volnay Santenots	E	(88–90)

The Domaine Jacques Prieur is no longer an independent, family-owned estate but rather a part of the larger Rodet umbrella (which, in turn, is owned by the Worms group). This being said, Martin Prieur, the domaine's amiable and talented director, is responsible for the estate's wines and independently vinifies them (albeit with the assistance of Rodet's chief winemaker, the gifted Nadine Goublin). As my scores and the following tasting notes indicate, I am tremendously impressed with the quality of Prieur's wines. Two vineyards in Beaune (Grèves and Champs Pimont) were added (through long-term *en fermage*—or rental—contracts) to the domaine's already impressive lineup. What had been an average to good estate has rapidly become one of the Burgundy's finest domaines.

Martin Prieur and his team took control of its parcel of 1996 Beaune Grèves only 21 days prior to the 1996 harvest. They therefore had to cope with the results of the previous tenant's viticultural work. According to Prieur, a severe 20% *saignée* (bleeding of the tanks) was required to give the wine some depth. It is medium to dark ruby colored, offers a nose of violets and perfume, and has very masculine character with tangy, metallic black fruit flavors. This medium-bodied and structured wine will be at its best if drunk over the next 3–4 years. Produced from an enclosed parcel of vines nestled between Au Coucherias and Aux Cras, the 1996 Beaune Clos de la Féguine reveals a saturated ruby color and aromas of freshly cut flowers and smoke. A deeply ripe, explosive, medium-bodied, silky, and feminine wine, it also has traces of *sur-maturité*, evident in this delicious offering's cherry, raspberry, and floral flavor profile. It is a wine that will provide considerable pleasure in the near term. Drink it by 2001. The floral, violet-infused scents of the medium to dark ruby-colored 1996 Beaune Champs Pimont were seductive. All of Prieur's wines, as well as those produced by the rest of the Antonin Rodet group, share this trait. This well-crafted wine has a structured and medium-bodied core of blackberries, metals, stones, and minerals. Anticipated maturity: now–2002.

I was impressed by the quality of Prieur's Volnays because they easily competed with the finest wines of the village. The medium to dark ruby-colored 1996 Volnay Santenots (this vineyard is officially in Meursault, but its red wines always carry Volnay's name) was aged in 50% new oak barrels and displays a nose of violets, roses, and perfume. On the palate, this powerful, medium- to full-bodied, concentrated, and well-extracted wine offers abundant black cherries and tangy blackberries. Traces of oak can be discerned in its long, soft finish. Anticipated maturity: 2000–2004. The similarly colored 1996 Volnay Champans (aged in 50% new oak) exhibits a delightfully intense, deep nose of violets and black cherries. This expansive, broad, well-structured yet seductive wine is medium to full bodied, velvety textured, and filled with sweet dark fruits, metals, and minerals. It is elegant yet powerful and possesses an impressive finish. It should be at its best between 2000 and 2005. The 1996 Volnay Clos des Santenots (produced from an enclosed vineyard located on the Volnay side of the Santenots du Milieu) is fabulous! Slightly darker colored than the previous wine, this offering was subjected to a 10% *saignée* and aged in 80% new oak barrels. It offers a sweet red cherry and spicy oak-laden nose as well as an explosive, superbly ripe, medium- to full-bodied, oily-textured, and opulent personality crammed with cherries (red and black), raspberries, and traces of plums. This defined, structured, expressive, and gorgeously fruit-driven wine delivers undeniable pleasure. Anticipated maturity: 2001–2006.

It is unquestionable that 1996 is a year in which many first-rate Cortons were produced (in both red and white), and Prieur's 1996 Corton-Bressandes is no exception. Dark ruby colored and with a nose redolent with sweet dark fruits, this feminine wine explodes on the palate with superripe fat black cherries. It is full bodied, velvety textured (no hard edges), and multilayered, with opulence and splendidly concentrated fruit. Anticipated maturity: 2001–2006.

One of the rare red wines to carry Meursault's name, the *monopole* (solely owned) 1996 Meursault Clos de Mazeray has a medium to dark ruby color, a floral, metallic nose, and a deliciously juicy character filled with red and black cherries as well as stonelike flavors. This impressive Meursault should be drunk over the next 3–4 years.

The medium to dark ruby-colored 1996 Chambertin offers beautifully ripe red and black fruits on the nose and fat, dense, chewy, and thick layers of delicious cherries, black currants, and raspberries. It is powerful and full bodied and possesses a formidably long finish. On reflection, I would have expected more concentration and complexity from a wine bearing such an illustrious name and vineyard. Anticipated maturity: 2001–2007. In contrast, the 1996 Echézeaux is fabulous. Dark ruby colored and possessing an intense nose of superripe black fruits, this wine is highly extracted, massively concentrated, powerful, full bodied, and densely packed with plums, cassis, blackberries, minerals, and stones. This masculine, structured, and muscular Echézeaux offers a fascinating contrast to the Domaine des Perdrix's more feminine elegant style (they were served to me side by side). Anticipated maturity: 2002–2008. Prieur's dark ruby-colored 1996 Musigny exhibits gorgeous aromatics of violets, perfume, blackberries, and earth tones. It is a powerful, extraordinary ripe and layered wine jam-packed with juicy black cherries, cassis, and plums bordering on overripeness. This full-bodied, velvety-textured, and muscular wine has an absolutely awesome finish that lingers seemingly for minutes. Revealing layers of sweet fruit infused with toasty oak, it exhibits impressive fruit and power, but its lack of refinement and soul precluded a score in the "extraordinary" range. Anticipated maturity: 2003–2008. The medium to dark ruby-colored 1996 Clos Vougeot reveals an intriguing nose of Asian spices and sweet red fruits. It is medium to full bodied, supple, round, seductive, and filled with blackberries, dark raspberries, and cherries as well as beautifully ripe tannins. It should be at its best between 2000 and 2005.

DOMAINE ROLAND RAPET (PERNAND-VERGELESSES)

1996 Beaune Clos du Roi	C	87
1996 Corton	D	(88–90)

1996 Corton-Pougets	D	(89–91)
1996 Pernand-Vergelesses Ile de Vergelesses	D	89+

Roland Rapet, a forceful, expressive, and extroverted man, is stepping aside and leaving the estate in his son Vincent's capable hands. Somewhat shy and demure, particularly when compared with his father, Vincent Rapet is quietly producing excellent wines that should be searched out.

The medium to dark ruby-colored 1996 Beaune Clos du Roi reveals black cherry aromas and a broad, medium-bodied, rich, deep personality filled with beautifully ripe red fruits, iron, and minerals. Its slightly rustic and angular finish prevented this wine from meriting a higher score. Anticipated maturity: 2000–2004. Medium to dark ruby colored and potentially outstanding, the 1996 Pernand-Vergelesses Ile de Vergelesses is an excellent value. It exhibits admirable aromas of plums, cherries, and dark fruits as well as a medium- to full-bodied core of intensely ripe blackberry, cassis, and cherry flavors that linger in the finish. This first-rate offering will provide delicious near-term drinking yet should evolve nicely because of its excellent structure. Anticipated maturity: now–2007.

The 1996 Corton displays a medium to dark ruby color, cassis and blackberry aromas, and a thick, chewy, ripe, and medium- to full-bodied personality. Sweet cherries, minerals, stones, and toasty oak flavors are ensconced in this wine's foursquare and tannic structure. Anticipated maturity: 2002–2007. The 1996 Corton-Pougets exhibits mouthwatering aromas of dark berries and ripe red fruits. This wine is dense, medium to full bodied, plump, and satiny textured. Loads of cherries, black raspberries, brambleberries, candied strawberries, metals, and minerals can be found in its flavor profile. It is rich, well balanced, and fruit packed and has a long finish that reveals ripe, round tannins. It should be at its best between 2001 and 2007.

DOMAINE JEAN RAPHET ET FILS (MOREY-ST.-DENIS)

1995 Chambertin Clos de Bèze	EE	(91–94)
1996 Charmes-Chambertin	EE	95
1995 Clos Vougeot	E	(88–91+)
1995 Gevrey-Chambertin Les Combottes	E	(88–91)
1996 Gevrey-Chambertin Les Combottes Réserve	E	92
1996 Gevrey-Chambertin Lavaux St. Jacques Réserve	E	92
1996 Morey-St.-Denis Les Millandes Réserve	E	91
1996 Morey-St.-Denis Vieilles Vignes Réserve	D	89

A bundle of energy, Jean Raphet is always on the go. Dedicated to quality, he is one of the rare Burgundians to have never used a filter. Contrast that with many Burgundy estates that informed me (with pride) that they have recently abandoned filtration.

Note: The Combottes and Clos Vougeot listed are North Berkeley cuvées, aged in 100% new oak. I did not taste the regular bottlings for these wines. Only one cuvée of the Chambertin Clos de Bèze is made, so all bottlings are the same.

Aged in 100% new oak, the medium to dark ruby-colored 1995 Gevrey-Chambertin Les Combottes displays a spicy, dark cherry-filled nose and silky-textured, fat, concentrated flavors of cassis and Asian spices. Medium to full bodied, this extracted, exceptional wine should be drunk between 2001 and 2007. Aromatically spicy, with notes of toasty oak, the 1995 Clos Vougeot exhibits a velvety texture and flavors of crisp, deep cherries and sweet oak. Full bodied and long, this admirably extracted Pinot should be at its peak between 2003 and 2010. Jean Raphet is known in France as being one of the very best sources of

Chambertin Clos de Bèze. Made from 80-year-old vines, and aged in 75% new oak, the 1995 is an absolutely stunning wine! Masculine, slightly austere, but beautifully aromatic on the nose, with touches of roses, spices, and violets, this well-endowed, full-bodied, spectacularly balanced gem is packed with red and black berries and Asian spices. Tight and somewhat backward, I recommend drinking this noble work of art between 2004 and 2012.

Note: The following wines, with the exception of the Charmes-Chambertin, are crafted exclusively for North Berkeley Imports and are bottled unfined and unfiltered. Only 25 cases of each of these special cuvées were produced.

The medium to dark ruby-colored 1996 Morey-St.-Denis Vieilles Vignes Réserve (100% from the Clos des Ormes, but this does not appear on the label) was produced from 70-year-old vines. It displays a mouthwatering nose of mocha-covered blueberries. On the palate, this is a full-bodied, broad, juicy, and velvety wine offering chocolate-enveloped candied red cherries, blackberries, and cassis complemented by sweet new oak. This ripe and impressively long wine will be at its best if drunk between now and 2004. On the nose, the dark ruby/purple 1996 Morey-St.-Denis Les Millandes Réserve exhibits profoundly ripe red cherries dusted with cinnamon and a broad, complex, luscious, chewy, full-bodied, and exciting personality bursting with overripe cherries. This tremendously hedonistic wine can be enjoyed immediately or cellared for up to 5 years.

The opaque, dark ruby-colored 1996 Gevrey-Chambertin Les Combottes Réserve displays an intense blackberry and cracked black pepper-scented nose. A massive explosion of black cherries, minerals, sweet oak, and Asian spices greets the palate in this full-bodied, classy, silky-textured, and muscular wine. Its impressively persistent finish reveals roasted herb flavors intermingled with traces of gamey meats and loads of soft, perfectly ripe tannins. Anticipated maturity: 2000–2006. The 1996 Gevrey-Chambertin Lavaux St. Jacques Réserve has a bright dark ruby color, a fabulous nose of violets, black cherries, and cinnamon candy, and a beautifully ripe, delineated, defined, medium- to full-bodied core of juicy red cherries that seemingly explode on the palate. This broad, expansive, and velvety wine has ripe tannins. Anticipated maturity: 2000–2006.

Raphet's 1996 Charmes-Chambertin is extraordinary. Medium to dark ruby colored, it reveals awesome aromatics of fruit cake, cinnamon, spicy chutney, and assorted red fruits. This is a sexy, intense, decadent, and full-bodied gem crammed with loads of sweet cherries, perfume, flowers, and spices. Imagine covering a basket of fresh cherries with chutney, then throwing in some freshly cut flowers, a touch of raspberry jam, and a sprinkling of grenadine liqueur. The mouthwatering flavors continue to coat the palate for what seems like minutes. Anticipated maturity: 2000–2007. Bravo!

DOMAINE JEAN-CLAUDE RATEAU (BEAUNE)

1996 Beaune Les Bressandes	D	(85–87)
1995 Beaune Les Bressandes	D	(86–88)
1996 Beaune Les Reversées	D	(86–88)
1995 Beaune Les Reversées	D	(86–88?)

Note: The following notes are of the Patrick Lesec Selections that were neither fined nor filtered in addition to being bottled by hand. I did not taste the non-Lesec cuvées.

Jean-Claude Rateau is one of Burgundy's early pioneers in biodynamic viticultural viticulture, having farmed his Les Reversées in this manner for 10 years. This vineyard and soil management philosophy gains converts each year among France's vignerons, even though some of its precepts appear unusual. It is clear, however, that "biodynamists" (as they call themselves) generally produced top-quality wines. But the question remains: Is it biodynamics that makes great wines, or is it that the tiny yields that emerge from this labor-intensive, quasi-intellectual, and costly method attract only those vignerons whose dedication to quality would be translated into top wines no matter which viticultural practice they followed? Regardless of the answer to this question, consumers are the beneficiaries. Rateau's wines have excellent fruit and reveal this vigneron's potential. If he finds a way to soften the tannins without compromising the fruit, this domaine will merit significant attention.

The ruby-colored 1996 Beaune Les Bressandes displays ripe blackberry and dark cherry aromas. Its expansive, medium-bodied, mineral-laden personality is complemented by powerful cassis and black raspberry flavors. It is an austere wine with a strong tannic backbone. It should be at its best between now and 2003. The 1996 Beaune Les Reversées has a medium to dark ruby color and a concentrated, fruit-packed, dense personality encased in a highly structured, medium- to full-bodied, tannic format. Its flavor profile is reminiscent of juicy black raspberries, gravel (similar to a Graves), cassis, and minerals. Anticipated maturity: 2000–2004.

The medium to dark ruby-colored 1995 Beaune Les Bressandes possesses an enticing nose of black cherries, mocha, and smoky bacon as well as an extraordinary and unbelievably silky texture. It is a supple, medium- to full-bodied, cassis-and-blackberry-infused wine with notes of smoked pork for additional complexity. This sultry gem should be at its best between now and 2001. The ruby/purple-colored 1995 Beaune Les Reversées is extremely different in style. It reveals roasted herbs and coarse red berries aromatically as well as a backward, tannic, and medium- to full-bodied character filled with copious amounts of ripe strawberries, raspberries, and a wild, spicy streak to its long finish. I question whether this wine's hard tannins will soften before the fruit dissipates. Fortunately, Rateau neither fines nor filters, so the fruit that was in the barrel sample I tasted will not have been denuded prior to bottling, giving it an opportunity to compete with the tannins.

DOMAINE DANIEL RION (PRÉMEAUX-PRISSEY)

1996	Bourgogne	C	87
1995	Chambolle-Musigny	D	(86–89)
1996	Chambolle-Musigny Les Beaux-Bruns	D	(89–91+)
1996	Chambolle-Musigny Les Charmes	EE	(90–93)
1995	Chambolle-Musigny Les Charmes	E	(88–91)
1995	Clos Vougeot	EE	(89–92)
1996	Côte de Nuits-Villages	C	86
1996	Nuits-St.-Georges Clos des Argillières	D	(88–90)
1995	Nuits-St.-Georges Clos des Argillières	D	(88–91+)
1996	Nuits-St.-Georges Les Grandes Vignes	D	(86–88)
1995	Nuits-St.-Georges Les Hauts Pruliers	D	(87–89)
1996	Nuits-St.-Georges Les Vignes-Rondes	D	(89–92)
1995	Nuits-St.-Georges Les Vignes-Rondes	D	(88–91)
1996	Vosne-Romanée	D	(86–88)
1995	Vosne-Romanée	D	(85–87)
1996	Vosne-Romanée Les Beaux-Monts	E	(89–92)
1995	Vosne-Romanée Les Beaux-Monts	D	(88–91)
1996	Vosne-Romanée Les Chaumes	E	(89–92)

Patrice Rion, a dynamic, inquisitive, and intelligent man, runs this domaine with his brothers, Christophe and Olivier. As with many estates managed by siblings, there is a clear-cut division of labor at Domaine Patrice Rion. Patrice is responsible for the winemaking, Olivier the viticulture, and Christophe the production of the estate's own organic compost (no chemical fertilizers have been used in 20 years). Spread out over 18 appellations in the Côte de Nuits, the estate covers 49.4 acres.

Rion's goal, it seems, is to make soft, unctuous, luscious burgundies that are at their peak the day they get released. I found no hard tannins or tightly wound fruit in any of his offerings, just thick, sweet fruit. As time has proven that tannins are not needed in Pinot Noir to allow it to age (as is the case in Bordeaux and Cabernets), Rion may truly be on to something.

Rion employs organic viticulture in the care of his vineyards, natural compost replacing the herbicides, pesticides, fungicides, and chemical fertilizers used by so many others. Grape bunches are 100% destemmed, and the villages, premiers crus, and grands crus age in 50%–100% new oak barrels.

Medium to dark ruby colored, the 1995 Nuits-St.-Georges Les Hauts Pruliers reveals blackberries and touches of chocolate and orange peel aromas and an oily-textured, extremely spicy, red and black fruit-filled, long personality. Anticipated maturity: now-2006. The darker-colored 1995 Nuits-St.-Georges Les Vignes-Rondes offers spices and sweet oak aromatically and an intense explosion of silky-textured, soft, chewy, thick, concentrated, ripe cherries, a medium to full body, and a good length. It will be at its best from release to 2006. My favorite of Rion's Nuits offering is his 1995 Nuits-St.-Georges Clos des Argillières, which reveals a dark ruby color and a fabulous nose of herbs, dried spices, minerals, and sea breeze. The wine is explosively powerful on the attack, and layers of ripe cherries, mocha, and lavender are found in this medium- to full-bodied, persistent blockbuster. Drink it between now and 2010.

Medium to dark ruby colored, the 1995 Vosne-Romanée displays an elegant spicy and red berry-filled nose and a classy, silky, well-structured, candied cherry personality. Exuberant and supple, it begs to be drunk now but will hold for 5+ years. Darker colored, the 1995 Vosne-Romanée Les Beaux-Monts reveals a fresh, clean, nose of crisp red currants and cherries, an elegant and lively mouthful of creamy, cherry pie filling, and a long finish. Superb to drink now, it will age well for 8+ years.

Rion's 1995 Chambolle-Musigny Les Charmes offers a medium to dark ruby color, sweet aromas of chocolate and mocha, and an enticingly seductive, yet big and powerful personality packed with explosive black currants, violets, and luscious dark cherries. This wine satisfies the hedonistic desires, not the intellectual ones. Patrice Rion is not a man to act without thinking things through carefully, so when he offered me his 1995 Chambolle-Musigny after the premier cru Charmes, I knew he was quite proud of it. And justifiably so: it is one of the best 1995 village wines I tasted! Medium to dark ruby colored, and possessing beautifully elegant aromas of delineated but creamy cherries and a truly pretty, refined palate with violets, roses, and assorted red berry fruit, this seductive and lush charmer should prove to be an excellent value. Drink it over the next 5–6 years.

Patrice Rion informed me that 1995 will be the last vintage for his Clos Vougeot (produced from a parcel of 55-year-old vines) because his lease is up. It is quite sad to see a talented vigneron losing access to great vineyard sites. It is the only one of Rion's offering to have been aged in 100% new oak barrels. The wine displays a dark ruby/purple color and a tight, reticent nose of spicy cherries, a velvety texture, and plenty of dark berry flavors that are judiciously oaked. Admirably structured, yet with some unctuousness, this is an extremely well-made wine that possesses excellent length. Drink it between now and 2010.

Not a believer in recipe winemaking, Patrice Rion is constantly experimenting with new ideas. Used only once, a huge stainless-steel tank, equipped with an intricate system of gas nozzles, stands by the front door of the *cuverie,* serving as a constant reminder of this man's penchant for experimentation. Rion's latest idea is to stir the lees of his red wines. On the 1996s he performed between 2 and 6 *bâtonnages* prior to the onset of malolactic fermentations. He told me that there was a direct correlation between the number of *bâtonnages* and the amount of lees "consumed" by the wines. Those that had undergone the process twice had significantly less lees at bottling than his nonstirred "control" barrels, and the wines that had undergone 6 *bâtonnages* had practically no lees left.

From a tasting standpoint, this process gives the wines a lush, almost pasty mouth-feel when tried out of barrel. Rion says that by the time the wines are bottled the pastiness will have subsided and been replaced with a rich, velvety texture.

Rion did not employ his *bâtonnage* technique on his ruby-colored 1996 Côte de Nuits-Villages. It offers an unyielding nose of dark berry fruit, followed by a lively, medium-bodied, and crisp character with blackberries and plum flavors. It should be consumed over the next 2–3 years. Conversely, Rion performed his maximum number of premalo *bâtonnages* (6) on the darker-colored and jammy red fruit-scented 1996 Bourgogne. This wine, bottled 2 months prior to my visit, appeared to validate Rion's statement that the pastiness I witnessed in the barrel samples would disappear at bottling. It reveals a lush, rich, medium-bodied, and velvety-textured core of ripe red cherries intermingled with tangy candied orange peels. Drink it by 2001.

The dark ruby-colored 1996 Nuits-St.-Georges Les Grandes Vignes has a zesty black currant-infused nose and a thick, somewhat pasty mouth-feel. This well-crafted, medium-bodied, and dense wine offers loads of sweet blueberry flavors. Anticipated maturity: now–2002. The 1996 Nuits-St.-Georges Les Lavières is slightly lighter colored and displays aromas of black cherries and blueberries. It is broad, velvety textured, intense, well delineated, medium to full bodied, and filled with rich and supple blackberries and plums. Anticipated maturity: now–2003. Medium to dark ruby colored and offering delightful scents of cassis liqueur, the 1996 Nuits-St.-Georges Clos des Argillières is a thicker, denser, and more concentrated wine. This well-focused, tangy, lush, medium- to full-bodied, and silky-textured offering is packed with blackberries and sweet blueberries. It will be at its best if consumed between now and 2005. Produced from a vineyard located on the Vosne side of Nuits, the 1996 Nuits-St.-Georges Les Vignes-Rondes is medium to dark ruby colored and exhibits sweet red and black berry aromas intermingled with hints of toasty oak. This powerful, ample, concentrated, medium- to full-bodied, velvety-textured, and impressive wine is crammed with layers of ripe black cherries that linger throughout its long and supple finish. Anticipated maturity: 2000–2007.

The medium to dark ruby-colored 1996 Vosne-Romanée has sweet cherry aromas intertwined with violets and lilies. This delightfully lush, medium-bodied, and silky-textured offering has a personality loaded with well-ripened red cherry flavors. Drink it between now and 2002. The 1996 Vosne-Romanée Les Beaux-Monts has beguiling aromas of raspberries, cherries, violets, and Asian spices. It is an extremely well-proportioned, seductive, concentrated, medium- to full-bodied, and velvety-textured beauty. Sweet red cherries and currants can be found in its delicious flavor profile as well as in its long finish. Anticipated maturity: now–2006. Medium to dark ruby colored and revealing a blueberry and cherry-scented nose, the 1996 Vosne-Romanée Les Chaumes is opulent, silky textured, medium to full bodied, and profoundly rich. Its succulent personality offers mineral-like flavors intermingled with sweet red cherries that last throughout an admirable finish. Anticipated maturity: 2000–2006.

The bright ruby-colored 1996 Chambolle-Musigny Les Beaux-Bruns aromatically displays cherries, raspberries, and blackberries. On the palate, this medium- to full-bodied, silky-textured, soft, and structured wine offers loads of stones, minerals, and sweet dark fruits. It is impressively concentrated and intensely flavored and should evolve beautifully with cellaring. Drink it between 2001 and 2007. The 1996 Chambolle-Musigny Les Charmes has a floral, blackberry, cherry, and cassis-scented nose. This outstanding wine is oily textured, profoundly rich, and packed with chewy layers of red cherries, blueberries, Asian spices, and hints of minerals. More structured and firm than any of Rion's other wines, this gem will require cellaring. Anticipated maturity: 2003–2008.

ANTONIN RODET (MERCUREY)

1996 Aloxe-Corton Les Valozières Cave Privée	D	(87–89)
1996 Bourgogne Les Vignes Rouges Cave Privée	C	(85–87)
1996 Chambolle-Musigny Cave Privée	D	(87–89)
1996 Charmes-Chambertin Cave Privée	EE	(91–93)
1996 Clos Vougeot Cave Privée	E	(89–91)
1996 Gevrey-Chambertin Cave Privée	D	(86–87)
1996 Gevrey-Chambertin Les Cazetiers Cave Privée	E	(88–90?)
1996 Gevrey-Chambertin Estournelles St. Jacques Cave Privée	E	(91–93)
1996 Gevrey-Chambertin Lavaux St. Jacques Cave Privée	E	(89–91)
1996 Nuits-St.-Georges Cave Privée	D	(87–89)
1996 Nuits-St.-Georges Les St. Georges Cave Privée	E	(90–92)
1996 Richebourg Cave Privée	EEE	(92–94+)
1996 Savigny-Lès-Beaune Les Gravains Cave Privée	D	(86–88)

At the end of May 1997 Antonin Rodet and all of its holdings were purchased by Worms (a major international conglomerate involved in shipping, paper manufacturing, insurance, and sugar, to name but a few) from the Laurent Perrier Champagne house. Over the past few years Rodet has acquired a number of Burgundy estates, including Château de Chamirey, Château de Mercey, Château de Rully, and the famed Domaine Jacques Prieur.

The Antonin Rodet "Cave Privée" label is given to their luxury cuvées, all of which are purchased as grape musts.

Burgundy lovers who wish to have a head start on this region's wine cognoscenti should memorize the name of Nadine Goublin. She has the focus, energy, passion, palate, and intelligence to become as famous as Maison Jadot's Jacques Lardière. She is the highly talented winemaker for Maison Antonin Rodet in addition to its affiliated properties. In a short time she has succeeded in making this house a top-notch source of *négociant* bottlings (particularly the Cave Privée cuvées).

Madame Goublin does not use "recipe" winemaking. Each cuvée is treated differently. For example, the three 1996 "village" Côte de Nuits I tasted were aged in different percentages of new oak barrels (Gevrey 80%, Chambolle 60%, and Nuits 50%).

The 1996 Bourgogne Les Vignes Rouge Cave Privée is ruby colored and offers a jammy nose of sweet red cherries laced with candied orange peels. This medium-bodied, well-crafted, and delightful wine has strawberries, raspberries, cherries, and plums in its easygoing, noncomplex, yet pleasurable personality. Drink it before 2000. Medium to dark ruby colored, the 1996 Savigny-Lès-Beaune Les Gravains Cave Privée reveals deep violet and blueberry aromas as well as a medium- to full-bodied and lively core of tangy currants, plums, metals, and stones. This silky-textured wine should be at its peak between now and 2003. Aged in 50% new oak barrels, the medium to dark ruby-colored 1996 Aloxe-Corton Les Valozières Cave Privée has an expressive nose of roses, violets, and sweet red and dark fruits. It offers blackberries, black cherries, and cassis intermingled with metallic flavors in its medium- to full-bodied and velvety character. This wine's long, persistent finish reveals loads of supple tannins buried in lush fruit and spicy oak. Anticipated maturity: 2000–2004.

The medium to dark ruby-colored 1996 Gevrey-Chambertin Cave Privée reveals a sweet cherry and violet-infused nose as well as a well-proportioned, medium-bodied, silky-textured, and dark fruit-filled personality. This offering lacks the grip and power of an excellent or outstanding wine, yet it is delicious to drink. Anticipated maturity: now–2003. The 1996 Chambolle-Musigny Cave Privée (it was just finishing its malo when I tasted it) offers a slightly darker color and a floral and blackberry-laced nose. This wine exhibits cassis, black raspberries, plums, and black cherries in its medium- to full-bodied and intense character. It will be at its peak if drunk between 2000 and 2005. Rodet's dark ruby/purple-colored 1996 Nuits-St.-Georges Cave Privée has a deep nose of violets, stones, and blackberries. On the palate, it offers a foursquare, perfumed, minerally, medium- to full-bodied, and structured core of black fruits. It is the most complex of the three village wines and should be at its best between 2000 and 2005.

The medium to dark ruby-colored 1996 Nuits-St.-Georges Les St. Georges Cave Privée has an expressive nose of sweet blackberries and cassis followed by an intense, concentrated, and powerful character of plums, black raspberries, and cherries. This oily-textured, medium- to full-bodied, and dense wine is seductive for a Nuits. Anticipated maturity: 2000–2007. The 1996 Gevrey-Chambertin Lavaux St. Jacques Cave Privée is similarly colored and offers a nose of deeply ripe fruit awash in a vanilla cream sauce. On the palate, it exhibits superb depth and power, candied red and black fruits, a medium to full body, and a soft, feminine structure. This oily-textured, opulent, and admirably long wine is slightly less concentrated but is just as seductive and fruit driven. Anticipated maturity: 2000–2006. The dark ruby-colored 1996 Gevrey-Chambertin Estournelles St. Jacques Cave Privée reveals dark fruit aromas intermingled with minerals and stones. This spectacular Gevrey premier cru offers immense power, structure, a chewy texture, and loads of blackberries, cassis, and black cherries while maintaining gorgeous refinement. It is full bodied and expressive and possesses a long, juicy, and soft finish. It should be at its peak between 2002 and 2007. I am confused by the 1996 Gevrey-Chambertin Les Cazetiers Cave Privée. Aromatically, its display of grapefruits and tangy berries set off warning bells, suggesting I was about to taste a wine lacking in ripeness and most probably the result of excessively high yields. Its flavor profile, however, was outstanding. Layers of beautifully ripe plums, blackberries, and floral perfume can be found in this medium- to full-bodied, masculine, structured, and silky-textured wine. Its drawn-out finish offers cassis and mineral-like flavors and loads of ripe, round tannins. In general, my instincts lead me to trust a wine's nose at this stage of its evolution, but I must confess that this offering was more impressive on the palate. Anticipated maturity: 2000–2005.

The dark ruby-colored 1996 Clos Vougeot Cave Privée reveals violet, spice, and sweet red fruit scents and a juicy, expressive, medium- to full-bodied, and velvety-textured character. Traces of *sur-maturité* can be discerned in its cherry, plum, and sweet prune-packed core. It should be at its apogee between 2001 and 2006. The 1996 Charmes-Chambertin Cave Privée is medium to dark ruby colored and offers a mouthwatering nose of profoundly sweet red cherries basking in smoky bacon fat. This elegant yet powerful, expressive yet defined, juicy yet fat, and intensely ripe wine has copious quantities of cherries, plums, and raspberries in its soft, silky, and medium- to full-bodied flavor profile. Its impressive finish reveals loads of soft and sweet tannins, which will assure a beautiful evolution. Anticipated maturity: 2002–2008. Rodet's dark ruby/purple-colored 1996 Richebourg Cave Privée may prove to be even better than the huge score I've bestowed it. Rich and candied layers of smoky red and black fruit aromas give way to a dense, powerful, deep, full-bodied, and awesomely textured personality. This magnificent wine's oily waves of red and black cherries, cassis, and raspberries intermingled with earth and sweet porcini flavors explode on the palate. It is elegant, muscular, structured, and opulent and possesses a formidable finish. Anticipated maturity: 2000–2012.

DOMAINE DE LA ROMANÉE-CONTI (VOSNE-ROMANÉE)

1996	Echézeaux	EEE	(90–92)
1995	Echézeaux	EEE	91
1996	Grands Echézeaux	EEE	(91–93+)
1995	Grands Echézeaux	EEE	92+
1996	Richebourg	EEE	(93–96)
1995	Richebourg	EEE	94
1996	Romanée-Conti	EEE	(96–98+)
1995	Romanée-Conti	EEE	95+
1996	Romanée-St.-Vivant	EEE	(91–93)
1995	Romanée-St.-Vivant	EEE	91
1996	La Tâche	EEE	(94–97)
1995	La Tâche	EEE	95+

Aubert de Villaine presides over the Domaine de la Romanée-Conti, possibly the most famous winemaking estate in the world. Lalou-Bize Leroy's forced departure from the domaine in 1991 created a shroud of controversy that lingers to this day. M. de Villaine feels the estate's wines have not received the praise they deserve from wine writers too enamored with Domaine Leroy's offerings. His implication is that there is a Leroy camp and a DRC camp, something that holds no merit with this publication.

Over the years I have heard all sorts of theories about why the estate's wines have a distinct spiciness to them, and most of these center around the barrels: the DRC uses lightly toasted François Frères barrels (the preferred source for most of the great estates of the Côte d'Or), which are air-dried for 3 years prior to use. Bernard Noblet, the cellar master, assured me that they are neither steam-cleaned nor rubbed with any special ointments, as speculation has suggested.

Organic viticulture is employed, with no chemical fertilizers or pesticides being used; only an estate-made compost is applied to the vineyards. The wines are not subjected to any filtration or fining and undergo only one racking.

Medium ruby colored, the 1995 Echézeaux displays a deep nose of berries and spice and an elegant, floral (roses), cherry-filled, perfumed, medium-bodied personality. Delicious and easy to drink, this wine should be held for 4 years and consumed over the following 6–8 years. Slightly darker, the 1995 Grands-Echézeaux offers spicy wild berry aromas intermingled with smoky oak and a concentrated, oily-textured, medium- to full-bodied inner core with an intense depth of floral, dark cherry-packed fruit. Drink this gem from 2002 to 2008. Why is it that I can be so thrilled with the bouquet of many Romanée-St.-Vivants and then disappointed with their flavor profile? The DRC's 1995 offering exhibits gorgeously elegant aromas of flowers, spice, herbs, and berries and deliciously chewy flavors of minerals, cherries, and roses embedded in its silky texture. The wine's aromatics suggest one of the best wines of the vintage. When tasted, it revealed itself to be an excellent to outstanding wine without the necessary inner core to reach the heights of greatness. It should be cellared for 4–5 years yet will hold until 2010.

Medium to dark ruby colored and possessing aromas of jammy red and black fruits, mocha, and sweet oak, the 1995 Richebourg explodes with a full-bodied, thick-textured mouthful of fabulously ripe dark berries, wild cherries, blueberries, round tannins, and persistent length. Anticipated maturity: 2003–2014. Equally impressive, the dark ruby-colored 1995 La Tâche displays a black cherry and superspicy bouquet with touches of buttery toast from the new oak and a concentrated, enveloping, minerally, red and black fruit-filled, Asian spice-packed personality. Full bodied, intense, with excellent length, this is certainly the finest La Tâche produced since the out-of-this-world 1990. Drink between 2003 and 2012+. Whereas most estates had much lower yields than usual because of the damage done during the flowering by a May cold spell, the DRC produced as much Romanée-Conti as it usually does according to Noblet. So much the better, because the 1995 is a spectacular wine: possessing a dark ruby color and a tight but sweet and velvety nose made up of mocha, toast, perfume, and dark berries, this wine bowled me over with its incredible depth of chewy, spiced chocolate-covered cherries, violets, unctuous texture, and incredibly persistent length. Admirably structured, it is built to last. I recommend holding it for 10 years and drinking it over the following 10–15 years.

Aubert de Villaine, this famed domaine's *gérant* (manager) and part owner, and Bernard Noblet, its cellar master, appeared justifiably proud of their 1996s. After having produced a fabulous lineup of 1995s, they repeated that stellar performance in this radically different vintage. Yields were moderate for the Domaine de la Romanée-Conti (an average of a little over 2 tons of fruit per acre), and the wines' richness, depth, and body are all the better for it. Surprisingly, I found two wines, the Echézeaux and Romanée-St.-Vivant, to be denser and richer than their 1995 counterparts.

The medium to dark ruby-colored 1996 Echézeaux has gorgeous floral, perfumed, spicy, and refined aromatics. Its medium-bodied and silky-textured palate offers a fabulous burst of sweet cherries, candied strawberries, and violets. This lively, highly defined wine also possesses a firm, supple-tannined structure that should allow it to age gracefully for years. Anticipated maturity: now–2008. The darker-colored 1996 Grands Echézeaux displays a magnificently elegant nose of cassis, black cherries, and roses. This is an austere yet expansive, complex, medium- to full-bodied, ripe, and masculine wine. It is denser and more powerful than the Echézeaux yet maintains a refined combination of muscle and class. Its tightly wound core offers red and black currants, cherries, minerals, and toasted oak flavors, all of which linger in its admirably focused and firm finish. Anticipated maturity: 2003–2012. The bright ruby-colored 1996 Romanée-St.-Vivant's nose is magnificent. Its complex fragrances of perfume, roses, violets, crisp cherries, and cassis are intermingled with Asian spices, mocha, and faint hints of earth. Wow! Its aromas merit a score in the upper 90s! As often happens with wines from this vineyard, it is more appealing aromatically than gustatorily. That being said, the 1996 Romanée-St.-Vivant has a denser, riper, and more expressive character than the outstanding 1995. It is a delicious, medium- to full-bodied, refined, highly delineated, and toasty cherry-flavored offering. Drink (and smell!) it between 2002 and 2012.

As is often the case with youthful 1996 Richebourgs, the nose was extremely reticent. After considerable coaxing, I had a peek at this offering's deeply ripe dark fruit aromatics. But what a flavor profile! A massive explosion of profound and intense cherries, raspberries, boysenberries, and strawberries coated my palate. It is a medium- to full-bodied, densely fruited, and powerful wine that is perfectly balanced and delineated. Anticipated maturity: 2005–2018. When I originally described the 1995 La Tâche, I wrote that it was the finest wine produced from that *monopole* vineyard since the 1990. Well, it may be surpassed by the dark ruby/purple-colored, blockbuster 1996 La Tâche. Its profound nose exhibits awesomely ripe red and black fruits, raw meat, and Asian spices, all of which are encased in sweet toasty oak. This full-bodied, wide, thick, focused, harmonious, and intense wine releases amazingly powerful layers of candied black cherries and blackberries. It is structured, totally precise, and pure and possesses an exceptionally long finish loaded with abundant sweet tannins. It will require patience. Anticipated maturity: 2005–2020. Among the world's most expensive wines (as far as I know, only certain late-harvest wines from Germany are more expensive) is the Domaine de la Romanée-Conti's Romanée-Conti. The 1996 has a gorgeously bright dark ruby/purple color and extremely complex aromatics of fresh herbs, Asian spices, creamy cherries, superripe blackberries, and vanilla-imbued oak. This superb wine offers a mouthful of silky-textured cherries, blueberries, plums, boysenberries, earth, minerals, and spiced oak. This masterpiece is full bodied, dense (yet extremely elegant and defined), thickly textured, and immensely concentrated. Moreover, I sensed this wine was holding a significant amount in reserve!

I retasted the 1995s when I visited the domaine. Space constraints prevent me from including detailed notes, but readers may find the following notes of interest:

The 1995 Echézeaux is a gorgeously elegant, complex, feminine, highly detailed, and rich wine. I was surprised by how well it showed and feel it can be drunk over the course of the next 10 years. The 1995 Grands Echézeaux is more austere, masculine, dense, and backward. It offers superb black fruit flavors and a firm tannic backbone. Drink it between 2003 and 2012+. The aromatics of the 1995 Romanée-St.-Vivant are enthralling. Its medium-bodied character is richer than I remembered. This sublimely elegant wine lacks the density and length for a higher rating. It should be at its best between 2002 and 2010. The 1995 Richebourg is spectacular. Powerful, dense, meaty, and thick, it is exceedingly long and possesses a firm tannic backbone that requires cellaring. Anticipated maturity: 2005–2018. The 1995 La Tâche and the 1995 Romanée-Conti are both mind-boggling and have gathered even more body, power, and density than they displayed from barrel. The La Tâche is the more powerful of the two, intensely profound, and superripe yet harmonious. Its extraordinarily long finish (it tails off with a sweet kirsch kiss) flabbergasted me. I could not help but think of the finishes of two wines I love—Château Rayas and Château Lafleur. The Romanée-Conti is the more complex of the two, with distinctive flavors of morel and porcini mushrooms intermingled with cassis and black cherries. Both of these stupendous wines appeared to be holding an enormous amount in reserve and may ultimately merit higher ratings. They should both be held at least 10 years and will easily last through 2020 given proper cellar conditions. Bravo!

DOMAINE JOSEPH ROTY (GEVREY-CHAMBERTIN)

1996 Bourgogne Les Pressoniers	C	(85–87)
1996 Charmes-Chambertin	EE	(92–95)
1996 Gevrey-Chambertin Champs-Chenys	D	(89–92)
1996 Gevrey-Chambertin Clos de la Brunelle	D	(88–91+)
1996 Gevrey-Chambertin Clos Prieur	D	(88–91)
1996 Gevrey-Chambertin Fonteny	E	(89–92)
1996 Griotte-Chambertin	EEE	(92–94+)
1996 Marsannay	D	(86–88)
1996 Marsannay Les Champs St. Etienne	D	(87–89+)
1996 Marsannay Ouzeloy	D	(88–90)
1996 Marsannay Rosé	B	(85–87)
1996 Marsannay Sampagny	D	(86–88+)
1996 Mazis-Chambertin	EE	(92–95)

Note: The Marsannay Les Champs St. Etienne's label indicates Domaine Philippe Roty, Joseph Roty's son.

"Your boss has publicly humiliated me and my family, and I have been meaning to yell at him. Since you are here, you will hear what I have to say." So began my visit to Joseph Roty's estate. Fortunately, a glint in his eye and a smile on his face allowed me to realize that he was only half-serious. Apparently Robert Parker's book on the wines of Burgundy contained an error concerning Roty's relationship with Philippe Rossignol, another Gevrey-Chambertin producer. To set the record straight, Philippe Rossignol is the brother of Roty's wife, and Mr. and Mrs. Roty's daughter remains unmarried.

Tasting at Domaine Joseph Roty is an experience I will not forget. The ailing Roty, smoking incessantly, spoke with passion about the Burgundy he loves ("I want to serve Burgundy, not have Burgundy serve me"), the tricks employed by neighbors to produce wines that appear to be super young but will self-destruct in time ("The future will humiliate them!"), the blasphemy of a well-known Beaune *négociant* blasting away large rocks in the Griotte-Chambertin vineyard ("And they dare speak of *terroir!*"), and countless other topics. Roty likes to talk, smile, and laugh, yet he is deadly serious about two things: his stamp collecting and winemaking.

I have never found Roty's wines to be seductive or hedonistic. He consistently crafts tannic, often backward, wines that are well proportioned and impressive for their power, flavor intensity, and structure. These old-style burgundies take years to reach their peaks (the 1985 Charmes-Chambertin is still an infant) but can, in ripe years, be some of the finest and most ageworthy wines produced in Gevrey-Chambertin.

This estate consistently produces one of my favorite rosés in Burgundy. The pale pink-colored 1996 Marsannay Rosé offers fresh strawberry aromas and has a lively, rich, silky-textured, and medium-bodied personality balanced by a core of tangy red fruits. It is a fruity yet dry wine ideal for quaffing over the next 2 years. Produced from a vineyard that was entitled to Gevrey-Chambertin status until 1964, the medium to dark ruby-colored 1996 Bourgogne Les Pressoniers has a rich black cherry-scented nose and a well-crafted, structured, and medium- to full-bodied character. This powerful and intense wine is crammed with earthy red and black fruits. Anticipated maturity: now–2003.

Produced from a number of parcels sprinkled throughout the appellation (including Rosey and Echézeaux), the 1996 Marsannay displays a medium to dark ruby/purple color and an expressive nose of blackberries and black cherries. This rich, medium-bodied, velvety-textured, harmonious, focused, and flavorful wine offers delicious cassis, blackberry, and mineral flavors. It should be drunk between now and 2004. Equally good, the medium to dark ruby-colored 1996 Marsannay Sampagny has ripe dark fruit aromas and a powerful, extremely well-made, structured, and medium- to full-bodied character. Its firm, tightly wound, and bordering on the austere flavor profile offers fresh black fruits. With cellaring it may well merit a slightly higher rating. Anticipated maturity: 2000–2005. The black-colored 1996 Marsannay Ouzeloy is a powerful and intense wine. Cassis liqueur, blackberries, and earth can be detected in its spicy aromas. This tightly wound, backward, masculine, and muscular offering reveals dense black fruits, traces of licorice, and stonelike flavors that are enveloped in tannins. This wine's lack of charm and refinement is made up by its old-vine viscosity, full body, and impressive power. It will require cellaring patience. Anticipated maturity: 2002–2007. Stylistically different, the medium- to dark-colored 1996 Marsannay Les Champs St. Etienne has a nose reminiscent of black currants, game, and licorice ("I always add licorice sticks to the cuvées," joked Roty), as well as a pure, powerful, dense, broad-shouldered, yet feminine personality. Juicy blackberries, earth, and black cherries can be found in this full-bodied, thick, and well-delineated wine. Tannic at present, this wine is more elegant and less intense. Drink it between 2001 and 2007.

The medium to dark ruby-colored 1996 Gevrey-Chambertin Clos Prieur has blueberries and cherries on the nose in addition to an expansive, deeply ripe, and plump character packed with boysenberries, red cherries, and spices. This medium- to full-bodied, expressive, and silky-textured wine has a firm (almost foursquare) backbone and a long, fruit-and-tannin-filled finish. Anticipated maturity: 2001–2006. Exhibiting a darker color and intense aromas of jammy blackberries and cassis, the 1996 Gevrey-Chambertin Clos de la Brunelle is an impressively endowed, powerful, superripe, full-bodied, and mouth-coating wine. It saturates the palate with its concentrated, dense, and delicious blackberry liqueur, licorice, and lingering black cherry flavors. Anticipated maturity: 2002–2007. The black/purple-colored 1996 Gevrey-Chambertin Champs-Chenys (a vineyard located between the RN74 and the grand cru Charmes-Chambertin) has awesomely ripe black raspberry aromas intermingled with violets and rosemary. This full-bodied, thickly textured, profound, and complex wine has loads of jammy raspberry, blackberry, and cassis in its oily, feminine, yet structured personality. This extremely well-proportioned wine is more expressive than his other Gevreys. Drink it between 2002 and 2007. Roty's dark-colored 1996 Gevrey-Chambertin Fonteny, displays black cherry, violet, earth, and Asian spicelike scents. This thick, juicy, full-bodied, velvety-textured, and enormously appealing offering is jam-packed with plums, cherries, cassis, and minerals. It is concentrated, complex, well extracted, and fat and possesses a long and satin-tannined finish. This outstanding wine should be at its peak between 2003 and 2010.

Roty is blessed with some of the oldest-vine grands crus of the Côte d'Or (the Mazis and Griotte were planted in 1919 and the Charmes-Chambertin in 1881). The dark ruby-colored 1996 Mazis-Chambertin has sweet, perfumed, and spicy cherry aromas followed by an intense, highly concentrated, powerful, and pure core of plums, cassis, stones, earth, and fresh herbs. This full-bodied, well-proportioned wine offers briary notes of underbrush and a fine finish. Anticipated maturity: 2005–2012+. The 1996 Griotte-Chambertin has a bright black color and a profound nose of sweet cherries laced with toasty oak. This elegant, velvety-textured, medium- to full-bodied, and concentrated wine reveals smoked bacon, black cherries, cassis, minerals, and grilled oak. While seemingly not as dense and intense as the Mazis, this offering appears to be holding a great deal in reserve. Roty told me that the Griotte-Chambertin vineyard was formed by a meteorite that crashed to earth thousands of years ago. He claims this explains the large deposits of iron that render it so distinct from the Chapelle-Chambertin, Charmes-Chambertin, and Chambertin Clos de Bèze vineyards that border it. The 1996 should be consumed between 2005 and 2010.

Roty's 1996 Charmes-Chambertin displays a deep black/ruby color and extraordinary aromas of sweet red fruits intertwined with violets and roses. This awesomely deep and ripe wine is dense, velvety textured, and highly concentrated and extracted and has a full body crammed with cassis, black cherries, bacon, minerals, and hints of cinnamon. Its powerful and profound flavors linger in its long and supple finish. It will require patience from consumers lucky enough to acquire it. Anticipated maturity: 2006–2015. Bravo!

DOMAINE EMMANUEL ROUGET (FLAGEY-ECHÉZEAUX)

1995	Bourgogne	C	(85–87)
1995	Bourgogne Passe-Tout-Grain	C	(85–87)
1996	Echézeaux	EE	(92–94)
1995	Echézeaux	EE	(90–93)
1996	Nuits-St.-Georges	E	(87–89)
1995	Nuits-St.-Georges	D	(86–88)
1996	Savigny-Lès-Beaune	D	(86–88)

1995 Savigny-Lès-Beaune	D	(85–87)
1996 Vosne-Romanée	E	(87–89)
1995 Vosne-Romanée	D	(86–89)
1996 Vosne-Romanée Les Beaux Monts	EE	(90–92)
1995 Vosne-Romanée Les Beaux Monts	E	(89–91+)
1996 Vosne-Romanée Cros Parantoux	EE	(93–95)
1995 Vosne-Romanée Cros Parantoux	EE	(92–94+)

Emmanuel Rouget lives on the eastern side of Flagey. I remember a comment Rouget made to me on my first visit. When I remarked that his home was hard to find because there is no nameplate or street address, he said, "Pierre-Antoine, always remember, the bigger the sign in front of a cave, the worse the wine." A mechanic by training, Rouget learned winemaking under the watchful eye of his uncle, the inestimable Henri Jayer. His wines combine suppleness with power, and elegance with depth. They represent some of the finest Pinot Noirs made in Burgundy. He served me blind his 1991 Bourgogne Passe-Tout-Grain, and it could have easily been a premier cru! Tall, strong, and quiet (until he knows you), Rouget is one of the young vignerons who are rejuvenating Burgundy.

Yes, a wine from the lowly Bourgogne Passe-Tout-Grain appellation deserves the rating I've given. Medium to dark ruby colored, the 1995 possesses a deep, sweet, mocha cream nose and palate packed with spicy berries and cherries. This elegant and seductive wine should be drunk over the near term. Revealing sweet lively berry aromas, the superripe 1995 Bourgogne is packed with crisp cherry fruit. Chewy and medium bodied, the wine is difficult to resist. Much more structured and austere, the 1995 Savigny-Lès-Beaune displays a nose of dark, minerally fruit and Asian spices. Velvety-textured, medium-bodied, chewy, and slightly tannic flavors suggest a masculine and foursquare wine. It needs 3–4 years of cellaring. Aromatically deep, superripe fruits and mocha emerge from the 1995 Nuits-St.-Georges, which also has a gorgeous silky texture and flavors of plums and minerals in its medium-bodied, structured, and slightly tannic finish. Drink it between 2000 and 2006. Feminine and elegant, the 1995 Vosne-Romanée has aromas of sweet red cherries, perfume, and roses. I thought the flavors reminded me of beautifully ripe red fruits and violets. Velvety textured, and enticing, this delicious wine will drink well from now to 2006. Very reminiscent of the preceding wine, but with more aromatics and substance, the medium ruby-colored 1995 Vosne-Romanée Les Beaux Monts is a gorgeous medium- to full-bodied wine with elegant candied, delineated fruit and spices. Lively, and with excellent depth and length, it should be at its peak between 2001 and 2009.

Medium to dark ruby colored, the silky 1995 Echézeaux (175 cases for the world) is an intensely refined and delineated wine. Revealing cinnamon and red currants in its aromas, this is a thick, awesomely textured, jammy, yet well-defined wine. I believe it should be consumed between 2002 and 2010. The seductive 1995 Vosne-Romanée Cros Parantoux (one of my favorites) is an extremely spicy, exotic, and sublimely elegant wine. It displays roasted, sweet Asian spices, minerals, and superripe berries in addition to superb levels of red and black fruits. A touch of tar and hot, wet stones adds additional complexity. Refined and delineated, this wine serves as testimony to the winemaking skills of Emmanuel Rouget. Bravo!

The medium to dark ruby-colored 1996 Savigny-Lès-Beaune has mocha-imbued blackberry scents and a deliciously rich, ripe, medium- to full-bodied character replete with loads of black cherries, minerals, and metal shavings. This extremely well-made wine has a silky texture and a long finish. It should be consumed between now and 2004. Exhibiting a darker color and deep aromas of red cherries, the 1996 Nuits-St.-Georges offers superb ripeness, refinement, purity, and an awesomely rich, seductive personality. Its persistent finish reveals perfectly supple and fat tannins. Drink this beauty between now and 2005. Rouget's dark ruby-colored 1996 Vosne-Romanée displays spicy red cherry and raspberry scents and an unbelievably elegant, oily, fresh, and flavorful core of cherry and strawberry fruit. This medium- to full-bodied, dense, and fleshy wine is structured yet seductive and opulent. Anticipated maturity: 2000–2006. The 1996 Vosne-Romanée Les Beaux Monts, with its dark color and deep spicy red cherry aromas, is reminiscent of the village Vosne. However, it has even more depth, weight, and complexity. Medium to full bodied, this wine offers layer after layer of sweet cherries and jammy raspberries in addition to a fine finish. Anticipated maturity: 2001–2008.

The bright, dark ruby-colored 1996 Echézeaux is superb. Rose, violet, lily, perfume, cherry, blackberry, and earth aromas lead to a full-bodied, velvety-textured, and immensely refined wine. This feminine yet powerful beauty is magnificently proportioned and balanced and reveals creamy blackberries, candied cherries, and hints of chocolate in its complex, concentrated, and pure personality. Its immensely long finish reveals a firm backbone. Drink this great wine between 2003 and 2010+. The dark-colored 1996 Vosne-Romanée Cros Parantoux possesses an intensely spicy nose filled with ripe red berries and minerals. This unbelievably broad, rich, powerful, and compellingly deep wine is also elegant and complex. Its flavor profile is composed of stones soaked in cherry juice, Asian spices, licorice, flowers, and hints of freshly laid asphalt. It is more backward than the Echézeaux, seemingly keeping more in reserve, but shares that superb offering's amazing finish. Anticipated maturity: 2005–2012. Bravo!

DOMAINE GEORGES ET CHRISTOPHE ROUMIER
(CHAMBOLLE-MUSIGNY)

1996 Bonnes Mares	EE	(93–95+)
1995 Bonnes Mares	EE	(93–95)
1996 Bourgogne	C	(86–87)
1995 Bourgogne	C	(85–87)
1996 Chambolle-Musigny	D	(88–89)
1995 Chambolle-Musigny	D	(87–89)
1996 Chambolle-Musigny Les Amoureuses	E	(91–93)
1995 Chambolle-Musigny Les Amoureuses	EE	(93–95)
1996 Chambolle-Musigny Les Cras	D	(89–92)
1995 Chambolle-Musigny Les Cras	E	(88–91)
1996 Charmes-Chambertin	EE	(90–93)
1995 Charmes-Chambertin	EE	(92–94)
1996 Clos Vougeot	EE	(89–91+)
1995 Clos Vougeot	EE	(90–93)
1996 Morey-St.-Denis Clos de la Bussière	D	(88–90)
1995 Morey-St.-Denis Clos de la Bussière	E	(88–90)
1996 Musigny	EEE	(94–97)
1995 Musigny	EEE	(95–98+)

1996 Ruchottes-Chambertin	EE	(92–94)
1995 Ruchottes-Chambertin	EE	(92–94)

When I visited his estate to taste through the 1995s, Christophe Roumier was sailing with friends in the Caribbean (where everyone suffering through a frigid and damp Burgundian January wanted to be), so I tasted with Delphine, his sister. She told me the secret to making top wines in 1995 was simple—a severe selection of the grapes was mandatory (Roumier does this on sorting tables in the vineyard itself, not wanting poor or rotten grapes to be commingled in the same baskets with healthy). Delphine, a young woman, told me the grapes in 1995 were the smallest she had ever seen. More often than not, small grapes mean intensely flavored wines. The sorters had to be careful to cull out all the *verjus*. This is a French term for the second crop of grapes that do not fully ripen. If they are not sorted out or cut off the vine prior to the harvest, the resulting wine can have a green, acidic taste. The term is probably derived from the French *vert jus,* meaning "green juice." The harvest took place here between October 2 and 9 for the reds. Yields averaged a little under 2 tons of fruit per acre.

Overall, Roumier's 1995s are stunning wines. They have breathtaking ripeness of fruit, elegance, power, and texture. Bravo!

The medium-bodied generic 1995 Bourgogne displays a medium ruby color and appealing flavors of dark, sweet cherries that are ensconced in a silky texture. Possessing some length for a regional wine, it will be at its best over the next 3–4 years. Exhibiting a fabulous nose of supersweet spicy red cherry fruit and violets, the ruby/purple-colored 1995 Chambolle-Musigny is a terrific example of how good village wines could be if more Burgundian vignerons cared as much as Roumier about vineyard work and winemaking. Earthy, floral, and perfumed red fruit flavors, excellent balance, a medium body, and an appropriately long finish make this supple wine a lovely bottle to drink over the next 5–7 years. Medium ruby colored, the 1995 Morey-St.-Denis Clos de la Bussière offers a dazzling nose of deep wild berries, a beautiful velvety texture, and spicy, earthy red fruit flavors. Medium bodied and well delineated, it should be at its best between 2000 and 2005. The medium- to full-bodied 1995 Chambolle-Musigny Les Cras reveals a spectacular nose of refined violets and dark cherries; it is an elegant as well as extremely well-structured, concentrated, cassis-and-blackberry-filled (if a touch tannic) wine. Drink it between 2000 and 2008.

This estate's 1995 Clos Vougeot displays a medium ruby/purple color and scents and flavors of elegant, fat, ripe, stuffed dark fruits. Medium to full bodied, this thick-textured, complex, and powerful wine has a tannic backbone that will require 5 years of cellaring; it should last for 10+ years subsequently. In 1995 the Charmes-Chambertin (generally not one of Roumier's strongest offerings) is fabulous! Medium to dark ruby colored with touches of purple, this wine's fragrant nose offers floral-scented sweet fruit. Medium to full bodied and thick textured, the Charmes covers the palate with superripe fresh red and purple berries. Slightly tannic, I suggest drinking this wine between 2002 and 2012. I am hardly alone in believing that the Chambolle-Musigny Les Amoureuses deserves to be upgraded to a grand cru. Roumier's 1995 offering is a persuasive example of this vineyard's potential. Dark ruby colored, it explodes from the glass with powerful scents of dark berries. A spectacular wine, it is packed with blueberry flavor. Long and intensely elegant, this full-bodied gem should be cellared for 5–8 years and consumed over the following 10–15 years—a true *vin de garde.* From a grand cru vineyard that rarely produces exciting wines, the 1995 Ruchottes-Chambertin is breathtaking: dark ruby colored and with a penetrating nose of sweet/slightly sour cherries and baskets of freshly cut violets, this flattering, immensely seductive wine is powerful, yet defined, lively, and elegant. Thick textured and full bodied, it should provide memorable drinking between 2002 and 2012. Roumier's Bonnes Mares is consistently one of the benchmarks of the appellation. The 1995 offering is spectacular: dark ruby colored with touches of blue and purple, the wine offers a masculine but elegant nose of deep, sweet, spicy dark fruits. This burgundy has an enthralling silky texture and finishes with a huge burst of powerful dark berries and a touch of earthiness. Structured for the long haul, this superb bottle should be drunk between 2003 and 2015. Red burgundy enthusiasts will have to fight, cajole, beg, and plead to get some of Roumier's 1995 Musigny (with a total production of only 400 bottles, 180 will be imported to the United States through normal channels). This is an utterly mind-blowing wine! The robe is superdark with touches of purple (similar to a high-class northern Rhône.). When I raised the glass to my nose I felt as though I had fallen into a blueberry-filled well lined with sweet, dark violets. I've rarely experienced such sublime aromatics. This hyperstructured and extraordinarily balanced wine is jam-packed with gorgeously concentrated and floral ripe dark berries. The finish is as long as any burgundy I've had (including those from Leroy!). Full bodied, powerful, thick textured, and stunningly elegant, this is a show-stopping sumptuous burgundy that should be cellared for at least 8 years. Anticipated maturity: 2005–2020.

Roumier informed me he was planning to bottle his 1996s earlier than usual to "trap the fruit." He is of the opinion that they will not be exuberant, charming, and seductive following bottling. Virtually every vigneron agreed that the 1996s have been a delight to drink from the moment the grapes were pressed. Yet Roumier thinks they will need years to be expressive. Those 1996s that I have tasted stateside have maintained their forward, fruity character, but time will tell.

The deep ruby-colored 1996 Bourgogne reveals a super nose of sweet and creamed cherries leading to a tangy, medium-bodied, and vibrant core of raspberries and red currants. This delicious wine should be consumed over the next 2–3 years. Displaying a medium to dark ruby color and mouthwatering aromas of cookie dough and candied red cherries, the 1996 Chambolle-Musigny had been assembled and was ready for bottling. It is a rich, sweet, silky-textured, and medium-bodied wine that offers delightfully floral black cherry flavors and hints of toast. Drink this gem between now and 2005. The ruby-colored 1996 Morey-St.-Denis Clos de la Bussière reveals candied red cherry, rosemary, and stone aromatics that lead to a medium-bodied, beautifully ripe, well-delineated, and fresh personality. Complex flavors of earth, minerals, assorted sweet red fruits, and fresh herbs can be found in its flavor profile and supple finish. Anticipated maturity: now–2005.

Exhibiting a medium to dark ruby color as well as candied red fruit and violet aromatics, the 1996 Chambolle-Musigny Les Cras is a firm, masculine, medium- to full-bodied, velvety-textured, tangy, and complex wine. It has outstanding density, concentration, and flavors of earth, sautéed mushrooms, cassis, and blackberries that linger in its well-focused finish. Anticipated maturity: 2002–2007. Christophe Roumier described his 1996 Chambolle-Musigny Les Amoureuses as having "serenity and calm." This ruby-colored wine offers aromas of sweet cherries, fresh herbs, blackberries, violets, and blueberries that give way to its oily-textured, rich, broad, lively, and highly detailed personality. Morels soaked in blackberry juice and dusted with minerals can be found in this expansive and concentrated beauty's flavor profile as well as in its oaky, satiny finish. Drink it between 2003 and 2008.

The 1996 is the last Clos Vougeot this estate will produce. Christophe Roumier's cousin Laurent has reclaimed the parcel for his newly founded domaine (see Domaine Laurent Roumier). This medium to dark ruby-colored offering has sweet cherry aromas immersed in Asian spices. It is a broad, ripe, austere, highly structured, and concentrated wine crammed with cassis liqueur, road tar, game, and roasted spices. Somewhat backward and unyielding, it will require cellaring. Anticipated maturity: 2004–2009. I tasted the medium to dark ruby-colored 1996 Charmes-Chambertin as it was being racked. It exhibits a gorgeous nose of deeply ripe black raspberries and a voluptuous, refined, graceful ("jovial," said Roumier), and delicious character. This seductive wine has layered red and black cherries, boysenberries, and Asian spices that are present throughout its flavor profile and supple finish. Anticipated maturity: 2002–2008. The similarly colored 1996 Ruchottes-Chambertin has seductive aromas of red currants, black cherries, fresh herbs, tar, smoke, and vanillin. This is an immensely complex, masculine, and structured wine that possesses formidable density and richness. Blackberries, cassis, minerals, stones, and hints of gaminess make up this wine's delectable flavor profile. Its admirably long finish reveals copious quantities of firm yet well-ripened tannins. Drink it between 2004 and 2010+. Displaying a dark ruby color and a fabulous nose of candied red fruits and cookie dough, Roumier's 1996 Bonnes Mares is an immensely rich, multidimensional masterpiece. This broad-shouldered, ample, oily-textured, masculine, structured, and medium- to full-bodied wine is formidably concentrated and complex. Highly focused blackberries, violets, lilies, stones, earth, and cassis flavors are intermingled with grilled and spiced new oak. Its prodigiously long finish is expansive, rendering its copious and supple tannins invisible. Anticipated maturity: 2005–2017. The dark-colored 1996 Musigny's aromas burst from the glass, inundating the nasal passages with loads of candied black currants, cherries, rose blossoms, lilies, and rosemary. This huge, velvety-textured, mouth-coating, and full-bodied wine is another in a long string of spectacular Musignys crafted by Christophe Roumier. Its palate is not as expressive as the previous wine's, but it is potentially more complex, revealing black cherries, stones, cassis liqueur, sautéed morels, porcini mushrooms, and violets. Its awesomely long finish presents a new spectrum of flavors, including black raspberries and roses. I did not have the opportunity to retaste Roumier's 1995 Musigny, but my memory suggests it was even more concentrated and profound. Readers lucky enough to acquire this 1996 should cellar it through 2006 and drink it through 2018. Bravo!

DOMAINE LAURENT ROUMIER (CHAMBOLLE-MUSIGNY)

1996 Bonnes Mares	E	(89–91+)
1996 Clos Vougeot	E	(88–90)

In 1994 Laurent Roumier, Christophe's cousin, started a winery just up the road from the famed Domaine Georges et Christophe Roumier, a modern hangarlike building with a U.S. Army four-wheel-drive parked out front. The estate, less than 10 acres, includes Clos Vougeot vines that cousin Christophe had been renting (1997 will be Laurent Roumier's first vintage with that parcel).

The medium to dark ruby-colored 1996 Clos Vougeot (harvested at 2⅓ tons of fruit per acre) has spicy, earthy aromas and a rich, sweet, medium-bodied, and well-balanced personality. Its flavor profile offers black cherries enveloped in Asian spices and hints of toasty oak. Sadly, Laurent Roumier told me he was ripping up and replanting all his Clos Vougeot vines that were over 50 years old. Anticipated maturity: now–2006. Produced from vines planted prior to World War II, the medium to dark ruby-colored 1996 Bonnes Mares (Roumier claims he harvested this at 1⅓ tons of fruit per acre) reveals a perfumed black raspberry-laced nose and a sweet, medium-bodied, rich, lush, and seductive character with flavors of plummy fruit, minerals, candied orange peels, and metal. Drink it between now and 2006.

DOMAINE ARMAND ROUSSEAU (GEVREY-CHAMBERTIN)

1996 Chambertin	EEE	(94–96+)
1995 Chambertin	EEE	(92–95)
1996 Chambertin Clos de Bèze	EEE	(92–94)
1995 Chambertin Clos de Bèze	EEE	(91–94+)
1996 Charmes-Chambertin	EE	(88–90)
1995 Charmes-Chambertin	EE	(87–89)
1996 Clos de la Roche	EE	(88–90)

1995 Clos de la Roche	EE	(88–91)
1996 Gevrey-Chambertin	D	(85–86)
1995 Gevrey-Chambertin	D	(85–87)
1996 Gevrey-Chambertin Les Cazetiers	E	(86–87)
1995 Gevrey-Chambertin Les Cazetiers	E	(87–88)
1996 Gevrey-Chambertin Clos St. Jacques	EE	(92–94)
1995 Gevrey-Chambertin Clos St. Jacques	EE	(91–94)
1996 Mazis-Chambertin	EE	(87–88)
1995 Mazis-Chambertin	EE	(87–89)
1996 Ruchottes-Chambertin Clos des Ruchottes	EE	(90–92)
1995 Ruchottes-Chambertin Clos des Ruchottes	EE	(89–91)

Charles Rousseau, the charming and convivial owner of Domaine Armand Rousseau, has been making this estate's wines since 1959. He shared with me how ecstatic he is that his village is regaining the stature it once had because of the numerous young men who are increasing the quality of wines produced at their estates. "I would be even happier if I did not see bottling trucks outside many of these noninterventionist and minimalist estates. I won't name them, but it seems strange to call oneself a noninterventionist and then pump wines through long tubes to a truck in the courtyard. Oh, well, that's how it is."

Lovers of red burgundy may be as surprised as I was to learn that he rarely drinks his own wines. "My personal cellar is a Bordeaux cellar." When whites are called for he drinks white burgundies, other Chardonnays, and occasional Sancerres and Pouilly-Fumés.

I am a big admirer of Charles Rousseau's wines and am proud to have a collection of them cellared. The wines I have bought, and will continue buying until I'm carted off to debtor's prison, are the glorious trilogy of Chambertin, Chambertin Clos de Bèze, and Gevrey-Chambertin Clos St. Jacques. Why the other wines (all from acclaimed vineyards) are rarely, if ever, at the same quality level is puzzling. The vines in the Ruchottes and Gevrey Cazetiers parcels owned by Rousseau are, on average, 50 years old. Where is the concentrated and complex fruit? They are fine wines, ones that I would be glad to find at most other estates, but Rousseau knows how to make great wine.

Charles Rousseau is a gracious, kind, intelligent man who seems always to have a smile on his face. He believes in having the malolactic fermentation take place immediately after the alcoholic fermentation. Pumps are never used here to move wines, fining is done with egg whites in the April following the vintage, and the wines are subjected to filtration. Rousseau defended his filtration philosophy by saying that the filters he uses are so big, they catch only "flies and stones, nothing else."

The medium ruby-colored 1995 Gevrey-Chambertin has an attractive dark, sweet cherry aroma with hints of cinnamon. In the mouth it is a pretty, elegant, well-made, light- to medium-bodied wine made for drinking over the next 5–6 years. Slightly darker colored, the 1995 Gevrey-Chambertin Les Cazetiers (aged in 1-year-old oak) reveals dark fruit and spices in the nose and an attractive, sweet, spicy, minerally, and dark cherry-filled mouth. Silky with nice length, this delicious wine will be at its best between 1999 and 2006. Also aged in 1-year-old oak casks, the dark-colored 1995 Charmes-Chambertin exhibits ripe cherry fruits, a touch of spiciness in the nose, and an extremely elegant dark berry, chewy palate. Slightly more austere than other Rousseau Charmes I've tasted over the years, it is a medium-bodied, velvety-textured wine. For those readers who prefer more masculine wines, the 1995 Mazis-Chambertin reveals a dark ruby color, aromas of minerals and smoky, black fruits, and a chewy, medium-bodied wine containing flavors of currants, underbrush, and berries. Better yet, the medium to dark ruby-colored 1995 Clos de la Roche displays a deep nose of dark berries and meat and an explosive personality filled with cherries and blueberries. Surprisingly feminine for this vineyard, this chewy, medium-bodied, silky-textured wine will be at its best between 2000 and 2007. The 1995 Ruchottes-Chambertin Clos des Ruchottes possesses an appealing nose of dark berries, cherries, and Asian spices. It is a medium- to full-bodied wine bursting with currants, minerals, earth, and cinnamon. Complex, long, and velvety textured, this delicious wine should be held 5–6 years and enjoyed over the following 7+ years.

Consistently of grand cru quality, the 1995 Gevrey-Chambertin Clos St. Jacques is a breathtakingly great wine. Aromas of juniper berries, smoked bacon, spices, and dark berries and gorgeously delineated flavors of fresh herbs, roasted duck, and crips cherries are found in this complex, full-bodied wine. Structured and tannic, it requires 7 years of cellaring and will then provide outstanding drinking for 8+ years. Dark ruby colored, the killer 1995 Chambertin Clos de Bèze floored me with its nose of roses, violets, black cherries, and Asian spices. Its sublimely elegant palate impression is intense, complex, chewy, austere, minerally, stony, full bodied, and long. It possesses considerable tannin behind the rich fruit, so it should be at its best between 2006 and 2016. Displaying a bright, dark color and huge aromas of Pinot fruit, smoky oak, and rocks, the 1995 Chambertin has a massive, deeply spicy, sweet, very thick, supercomplex palate with sautéed bacon notes. Tannic, extremely tight, and stunning, this backward wine will reach its peak between 2007 and 2020.

As far as the 1996 vintage is concerned, Rousseau's comments were bluntly candid: "The North wind is concentration. It saves a harvest, prevents rot, concentrates color and sugar, concentrates everything we want. The 1996 is better than 1990; it may be too early to say, but there, I said it."

With that, Rousseau picked up one of the *tastevins* hanging on the wall (these are the small, wide, shallow, and traditional silver utensils used for tasting. As far as I know, he is the only Burgundian who continues to use them on a regular basis), and the tasting began.

The ruby-colored 1996 Gevrey-Chambertin has fresh, spicy, and candied strawberry aromas that lead to an oily-textured, glycerine-feeling, medium-bodied, and appealing core of black raspberries and cherries. It is a well-made, simple, and delightful wine for drinking over the next 3 years. Revealing a similar color, but more intense aromatics of blackberries and minerals, the 1996 Gevrey-Chambertin Les Cazetiers is a soft, supple, oily, and medium-bodied offering with black raspberry and briary flavors. It is well balanced—if a trace warm—and more complex than the previous wine, but it lacks the depth necessary for a more exalted score. Drink it over the next 5 years.

Rousseau's ruby-colored 1996 Mazis-Chambertin displays a tight nose of kirsch, black cherries, and rosemary, followed by a medium- to full-bodied, masculine, structured, and unyielding personality. Flavors of blackberries, minerals, and stones are found in this firm, velvety-textured, and persistent wine. Anticipated maturity: now–2006. The slightly darker-colored 1996 Charmes-Chambertin may earn a score at the top of the range, if it gathers some more depth during its *élevage*. It displays a deep nose of supersweet black cherries and a pleasing, seductive, and medium- to full-bodied character filled with delineated and pure flavors of candied raspberries and cherries. This spicy, silky-textured, expressive, and elegant wine concludes with a long, satiny finish. Anticipated maturity: now–2005. Exhibiting a medium to dark ruby color and lovely floral aromas of cherries, cassis, leather, and blackberries, the 1996 Clos de la Roche has excellent intensity and concentration of black fruits as well as earthy and stony flavors. This medium- to full-bodied, harmonious, introverted (particularly after the previous offering), and oily-textured wine also possesses a long and firm finish. Drink it between 2001 and 2007.

Qualitatively, I generally find Rousseau's Ruchottes-Chambertin Clos des Ruchottes to be in the same class as the three previous grands crus. His 1996 is an improvement. The Clos was purchased in 1977 from Thomas Bassot and is composed of old vines, of which one-sixth are 37 years old and the remaining are between 75 and 80. The medium to dark ruby-colored 1996 has profound aromas of violets, roses, earth, rocks, blood, sweet red grapes, and toasty oak. It is more powerful, concentrated, intense, structured, and complex than the previous wines. This medium- to full-bodied, firm, foursquare, and oily-textured offering has floral and perfumed flavors of grapes, red/black currants, and brambleberries. The focused finish is long and tannic. Drink it between 2003 and 2009.

The following wine trilogy sets the standard by which this domaine has built its reputation. The slightly darker-colored 1996 Gevrey-Chambertin Clos St. Jacques is produced from vines that were planted in 1920 and 1921. Profound aromas of red cherries, blackberries covered in chocolate, morel and porcini mushrooms, road tar, and toasty oak lead to an awesome explosion of densely packed fruit on the palate. Layers of juicy and plump cherries, minerals, stones, and fresh herbs are intertwined with vanilla-imbued oak in this expressive and feminine beauty. It possesses extraordinary depth, concentration, and structure. This full-bodied, velvety-textured, refined, and focused wine also possesses an extremely long and delineated finish. It should be at its best between 2003 and 2010. The dark ruby-colored 1996 Chambertin Clos de Bèze exhibits a nose of charred oak encrusted with blackberries, cassis, and stones. It has a full-bodied, expansive, highly defined, complex, and silky-textured personality that possesses black cherries, iron, minerals, gravel, and cassis. This firm and highly structured wine will require cellaring. Anticipated maturity: 2005–2012. The 1996 Chambertin reveals a dark ruby color and mouthwatering aromas of smoked pork, bacon, juicy blackberries, road tar, raw meat, and a hint of eucalyptus. This blockbuster is bigger, broader, denser, and more concentrated and complete than the Clos de Bèze. It is oily textured and full bodied and offers sublime layers of candied black raspberries, blueberries, violets, lilies, fresh herbs, Asian spices, leather, stones, smoke, and toast. This formidably structured and profound wine demands patience. Anticipated maturity: 2005–2018. Bravo!

CHÂTEAU DE RULLY (RULLY)

1996 Rully	C	(85–87)

The medium to dark ruby-colored 1996 Rully reveals steely black fruit aromas as well as a medium-bodied, silky-textured, and structured character with blueberry, blackberry, and stone flavors. It will be at its best if consumed over the next 3 years. The Château de Rully is owned by the Antonin Rodet *négociant* house.

DOMAINE ST. MARTIN (MARSANNAY)

1996 Bonnes Mares	E	(89–91+)
1996 Fixin Hervelets	C	(86–88)

The ruby-colored 1996 Fixin Hervelets offers blackberry and stone aromas. On the palate, it has a silky-textured, concentrated, extracted, thick, and delicious character filled with black cherries. Its long finish reveals loads of juicy black fruits and soft tannins. It should be drunk between now and 2005. The day of my tasting, the medium to dark ruby-colored 1996 Bonnes Mares had a reticent nose revealing sweet blueberries. However, it is expressive, harmonious, and refined. This velvety-textured, well-crafted, and concentrated wine, packed with dark cherries, cassis, and violets, is an impressive offering from a little-known estate.

DOMAINE SERAFIN (GEVREY-CHAMBERTIN)

1996 Chambolle-Musigny Les Baudes	E	(88–90)
1996 Charmes-Chambertin	EE	(93–95+)

1995 Charmes-Chambertin	EE	94
1996 Gevrey-Chambertin Les Cazetiers	EE	(91–93)
1995 Gevrey-Chambertin Les Cazetiers	E	(89–92)
1996 Gevrey-Chambertin Les Corbeaux	E	(89–91)
1995 Gevrey-Chambertin Les Corbeaux	E	(88–90)
1996 Gevrey-Chambertin Le Fonteny	E	(90–92+)
1995 Gevrey-Chambertin Le Fonteny	E	(89–91)
1996 Gevrey-Chambertin Vieilles Vignes	E	(88–90)
1995 Gevrey-Chambertin Vieilles Vignes	D	(87–89+)
1996 Morey-St.-Denis Les Millandes	E	(88–90)

Recent tastings of 1988 burgundies have led me to believe that the fruit in a high percentage of them will not outlive the tannin. In short, most of the wines are drying out. One notable exception are the 1988s from Christian Serafin. They are beautifully made wines with intense fruit and well-integrated tannins—even in 1988.

An extremely hardworking man, Serafin pledges a commitment to quality that is evidenced by his low yields (he severely cuts back the yields for his vines), late harvests (he and the Leclerc brothers are consistently the last pickers of Gevrey), the fact that he destems his grapes (90%), and his belief in abundant use of new oak. Dark in color and flavor, Serafin's wines exhibit a deep spiciness and are ageworthy. He is one of the few true stars of Gevrey-Chambertin, and his success has allowed him to acquire some new vineyard sites.

From vineyards spread out over the appellation, Serafin's medium- to dark-colored 1995 Gevrey-Chambertin Vieilles Vignes reveals a deep, sweet, dark nose of black cherries and spices. Explosive on the attack, this medium-bodied wine bursts with cinnamon and red and black berries. Drink it between now and 2003. From a vineyard recently upgraded to premier cru status, the deep ruby-colored 1995 Gevrey-Chambertin Les Corbeaux possesses cinnamon and dark fruit aromas and some of the spiciest wild berry flavors I have encountered. Medium bodied and thick textured, this gorgeous bottle should be drunk between now and 2003. Generally one of the best values to be found in premier cru red burgundies is the 1995 Gevrey-Chambertin Le Fonteny. Displaying a dark ruby color and a fresh, spice-laden candied nose, this velvety-textured beauty is packed with pure and fabulous sweet/sour and wild cherry and berry flavors. Long on the finish, and well structured, this wine should be drunk between 2001 and 2008. Made from 40-year-old vines yielding 2½ tons of fruit per acre, the dark-colored 1995 Gevrey-Chambertin Les Cazetiers displays aromas of creamy spices and dark fruits. In the velvety-textured mouth, powerful and zesty blackberries and cherries vied for my attention along with dark roasted spices. Long and concentrated, this wine requires 5–7 years of cellaring; it will hold its peak for 8+ years.

With a recent purchase of old vines, Serafin has increased the production of his consistently stellar Charmes-Chambertin (the vines now average 54 years in age) to 100 cases (4 barrels). I previously underrated Serafin's medium to dark ruby/purple-colored 1995 Charmes-Chambertin (91–93 in my first rating). This wine's lively nose presents candied orange peels, black cherries, and Asian spices. It is powerful, layered, intensely complex, full bodied, and ripe. Densely packed blackberries, cherries, and cassis are intertwined with minerals and hints of earth in this highly impressive offering. As is spelled out in the margin of my notebook, "Super!" Anticipated maturity: 2004–2012+. Bravo!

Produced from vines averaging 45 years old, the 1996 Gevrey-Chambertin Vieilles Vignes is medium to dark ruby colored and reveals lovely aromas of flowers, perfume, and black fruits. This rich, medium- to full-bodied, silky-textured, and expansive wine is filled with candied black raspberries, violets, and sweet oak notes. Fruit-drenched satiny tannins can be found in its long finish. Drink this beauty between now and 2005.

Beginning with the 1996 vintage, Serafin has two new wines in his lineup: the Morey-St.-Denis Les Millandes and Chambolle-Musigny Les Baudes. The former is produced 75% from 19-year-old vines, 25% from 60-year-old vines. It is medium to dark ruby colored, with candied cherry aromatics followed by a beautifully ripe, harmonious, medium- to full-bodied, and velvety character. Sweet raspberries and cherries laced with vanilla bean can be discerned in this intense, elegant, and well-proportioned wine. Anticipated maturity: now–2005. The similarly colored 1996 Chambolle-Musigny Les Baudes exhibits scents of tangy and sweet red currants, as well as a medium- to full-bodied, deep, and powerful core of blueberries and minerals. This expansive wine has a chewy texture and excellent concentration and focus. It should be at its best between now and 2005.

Produced from 30-year-old vines, the 1996 Gevrey-Chambertin Les Corbeaux has an intense nose of brambleberries and metal shavings, in addition to a broad, juicy, masculine, and plump personality. This structured wine's flavor profile is packed with cassis, blackberries, minerals, and iron. It is medium to full bodied, velvety textured, and persistent. Anticipated maturity: 2000–2006. Crafted from 40-year-old vines, the 1996 Gevrey-Chambertin Le Fonteny is slightly darker colored and possesses an expressive nose of violets, cassis, and blueberries. This broad, concentrated, extracted, and exceptional wine is crammed with layer after layer of fresh, splendidly ripe cassis and black cherries. Its long, supple finish is intermingled with stones and minerals. Anticipated maturity: 2001–2008. Serafin's Gevrey-Chambertin Les Cazetiers (a vineyard wedged between Clos St. Jacques and Combe au Moine) has been consistently outstanding. Profoundly complex aromas of sweet blackberries and cassis, intertwined with the scents of minerals and wet stones, are followed by a broad, huge, very ripe wine. Reminiscent of the Fonteny, it is even more powerful, intense, deeper, and thicker. Brambleberries, cassis, blueberries, juniper berries, cloves, blood, and toasted oak can be found in this full-bodied, chewy offering. Readers should cellar it until at least 2003. It will easily hold through 2009.

Produced from 55-year-old vines, Serafin's dark ruby/purple-colored 1996 Charmes-Chambertin is stunning. Explosive aromas of sweet blackberries and raspberries as well as a massive mouthful of chewy, dense, and seductive red currants and plump cherries tantalize the palate. This full-bodied, refined, velvety-textured, thick wine is complex and concentrated. Its long finish reveals myriad spices, loads of red and black fruits, and ripe tannins. Drink this gem between 2002 and 2010.

DOMAINE JEAN TARDY (VOSNE-ROMANÉE)

1996	Chambolle-Musigny	D	(87–89)
1996	Clos Vougeot	E	(91–93)
1996	Nuits-St.-Georges aux Bas de Combe	D	(87–89)
1996	Nuits-St.-Georges Les Boudots	D	(90–92)
1996	Vosne-Romanée Les Chaumes	D	(88–90)

Jean Tardy loves to laugh. This short, muscular, good-natured man is so ebullient and gracious that a former colleague of mine (from my retail days) and his wife named their black Labrador retriever "Tardy" after visiting him. When I told Tardy this story, he burst out laughing and demanded a photograph of the dog.

Both of Tardy's top wines are from *métayage* arrangements that will expire over the next decade. My hope is that this highly talented winemaker finds other worthy parcels.

The ruby-colored 1996 Chambolle-Musigny Les Athées offers aromas reminiscent of smoked pork roast and caramelized onions, as well as a profound, delicious, concentrated, rich, velvety-textured, and medium- to full-bodied core of sweet red and black cherries and oak flavors. Drink it between 2001 and 2006. The slightly darker-colored 1996 Nuits-St.-Georges aux Bas de Combe is produced from 35–40-year-old vines. It is medium to full bodied, tangy, silky, and redolent with ample red and black fruits, minerals, and toasty oak. This seductive yet structured Nuits will be at its peak between 2001 and 2006. Revealing a deep ruby color as well as blackberries laced with violets and roses, the 1996 Vosne-Romanée Les Chaumes is a juicy, wide, and medium- to full-bodied wine. More intensely flavored and powerful than either of the two previous wines (and neither of them was subtle!), this thick, elegant offering is filled with plump red and black fruits. Anticipated maturity: 2001–2007.

Produced from 50–70-year-old vines, the medium to dark ruby-colored 1996 Nuits-St.-Georges Les Boudots has cassis liqueur and blackberry aromas. This intense, full-bodied, thick, and concentrated offering is crammed with beautifully ripe black fruits, fresh herbs, minerals, and toasted oak. Denser, more powerful, and more profound, this rich and well-balanced wine also possesses a persistent and focused finish. Anticipated maturity: 2002–2008. The dark ruby-colored 1996 Clos Vougeot has an intensely spicy nose filled with superripe red and black fruits. This superb wine attacks the palate with powerful waves of cherries, cassis, blackberries, Asian spices, and powerful smoked oak flavors. It is concentrated, dense, profound, extremely expressive, and formidably long. Layers of oak juice-soaked fruits drench loads of fine tannins in its highly impressive finish. Drink this beauty between 2004 and 2010+.

DOMAINE DU CLOS DE TART (MOREY-ST.-DENIS)

1996 Clos de Tart	EE	(91–94)
1995 Clos de Tart	EE	92

Sylvain Pithiot, known for having produced with Pierre Poupon, his father-in-law, the exceptional topographical maps of Burgundy's intricate vineyards, administers Clos de Tart. He officially took over the direction of the estate in March 1996 but worked with the former director for the 1995 vintage.

This 7.5-hectare (18.5-acre) grand cru *monopole* (under sole ownership) has remained intact since its creation and has had only three owners in its 850-year history (Benedictine monks, the Marey-Monge family, and, since 1932, the Mommessins). Located directly above the village of Morey, the Clos de Tart (bordered to the north by the Clos des Lambrays and to the south by Bonnes Mares) is easily recognizable because its vines are planted horizontally along the hillside. Virtually all Burgundian vineyards are set in vertical rows.

Pithiot has instituted a number of changes in the estate's policies to increase the wine's quality. He is converting all the vines' training into the *Cordon de Royat* (a horizontal stem from which the fruiting canes grow) that has been used for years in Santenay to reduce yields; uses no fertilizers (only organic compost); performs a green harvest if necessary; and has installed a sorting table. His aim is to produce a moderate 2 tons of fruit per acre each year (1996 had a little more than 2 per acre yields, and 1997 had 1¹/₂ tons). A second wine (the Morey-St.-Denis Premier Cru "La Forge") was created in 1987 by his predecessor and is produced from vines under 15 years old (the grand cru is crafted from vines averaging between 45 and 50 years old).

After having been sorted, the Clos's bunches are 80% destemmed and undergo a 5-day cold (12 degrees Celsius) maceration. The temperature is then raised to 20 degrees for the indigenous yeast fermentations to begin. It is dragged out as long as possible by chaptalizing in small doses over the course of a few days. Once the sugars have been converted, the wine undergoes a warm, 2-day postfermentation maceration and is pressed, given a 1-hour *débourbage* (dropping of the gross lees), and then transferred to 100% new oak barrels. Pithiot is committed to not filtering the domaine's wines and, unless he deems it absolutely necessary, will not fine them.

The medium to dark ruby-colored 1996 Clos de Tart has rich aromas of deeply ripe dark fruits that give way to a broad, full-bodied, silky-textured, and concentrated wine. It is richer and more intense than any wine I have tasted from this estate and reveals earthy, stone-laced, black cherry, and blackberry flavors. This wine is harmonious, seductive (yet structured), focused, and well balanced. Its extremely long and soft finish is replete with magnificently soft tannins. Anticipated maturity: 2002–2009. Displaying a medium to dark ruby color and a lovely nose of spicy red berries, cracked black pepper, Asian spices, and distinctive notes of cedar, the 1995 Clos de Tart is a medium- to full-bodied, velvety-textured, and complex wine. Its enthralling flavor profile offers layers of rich black pepper-laced blueberries and blackberries that are intensely spiced with cinnamon, juniper berries, and hints of eucalyptus. Drink it between 2001 and 2008.

DOMAINE TOLLOT-BEAUT (CHOREY-LÈS-BEAUNE)

1996	Aloxe-Corton	D	(85–88)
1996	Aloxe-Corton Les Fournières	D	(87–89)
1996	Aloxe-Corton Les Vercots	D	(87–89)
1996	Beaune Clos du Roi	D	(87–88)
1996	Beaune Grèves	D	(87–89)
1995	Chorey-Lès-Beaune*	C	(84–86)
1996	Chorey-Lès-Beaune*	C	(85–87)
1996	Le Corton	E	(88–91)
1996	Corton Bressandes	E	(91–93)
1996	Côte de Beaune*	C	(85–87)
1996	Savigny-Lès-Beaune Les Champs Chevreys	C	(85–88)
1995	Savigny-Lès-Beaune Les Lavières	D	(86–88)
1996	Savigny-Lès-Beaune Les Lavières	C	(86–88+)

Note: The Chorey-Lès-Beaune and the Côte de Beaune are the same wines sold under different labels. This domaine's U.S. representative imports this wine only under the Côte de Beaune label.

Regrettably, I was not permitted to taste this domaine's 1995 Aloxe-Cortons, Beaunes, Corton Le Corton, or Corton Bressandes in January of 1997 because they were being filtered and bottled. However, I was given the opportunity to taste two delicious reds. The light to medium ruby-colored 1995 Chorey-Lès-Beaune displays delightful aromas reminiscent of wild cherries and a forest's underbrush as well as an attractive, straightforward, light- to medium-bodied, softly textured, and well-balanced character with crisp strawberry and cherry flavors. Drink it between now and 2000. Possessing a ruby color and blackberry, mineral, and earth-infused aromatics, the 1995 Savigny-Lès-Beaune Les Lavières is a medium-bodied, silky-textured wine with deeply sweet wild cherry, pickling spice, and mineral flavors. Its long finish ends on soft, round tannins. Delicious to drink now, it will last at least until 2002 given proper shipping and storage.

The 1996 Chorey-Lès-Beaune/Côte de Beaune is medium ruby colored and reveals a spicy blackberry nose. This well-crafted and medium-bodied wine is filled with sweet and tangy black cherries and minerals. It should be drunk over the next 3 years. Displaying a ruby color and an austere nose of stones, minerals, and black fruits, the 1996 Savigny-Lès-Beaune Les Lavières is an excellent wine. On the palate, this medium-bodied, juicy, masculine, and well-balanced offering has deep cherry, blackberry, and mineral flavors. Anticipated maturity: now–2003. The 1996 Savigny-Lès-Beaune Les Champs Chevreys (a Tollot-Beaut exclusive, or *monopole*) is a floral, violet-scented offering with a medium-bodied, earthy, and minerally core of black fruits. It is more structured and forward than the previous wine but does not have quite as much intensity or complexity. Anticipated maturity: now–2002.

Revealing a medium ruby color, the 1996 Beaune Clos du Roi has a red currant, raspberry, and flower blossom-infused nose. This wine is medium to full bodied, thick, beautifully ripe, and filled with loads of sweet red and black cherries. It is supple, seductive, and a delight to drink now. I suggest consuming it before 2002. The 1996 Beaune Grèves is slightly darker colored and displays a blackberry and mineral-laced nose. Its medium- to full-bodied and thickly textured personality is densely packed with ripe black fruits, and its long finish reveals loads of ripe tannins. This well-structured wine will be at its best between 2000 and 2004.

The 1996 Aloxe-Corton is medium ruby colored and offers earth, minerals, and dark fruits on the nose. This softly textured wine's medium body is composed of spicy and tangy black cherries. It should be drunk within 3 years. Revealing black cherry and Asian spice aromas, the 1996 Aloxe-Corton Les Fournières has great depth of fruit, a medium body, and a silky texture. Its flavor profile is filled with ripe blackberries, minerals, and iron. This structured wine will require some cellaring before it reaches its peak. Anticipated maturity: 2000–2003. Equally good, but quite different stylistically, the 1996 Aloxe-Corton Les Vercots displays a smoky, spicy, and lavender-infused nose. This feminine, concentrated, supple, and medium-bodied wine is filled with plums, minerals, and raspberries. It will be at its best if drunk over the next 4 years.

Produced from vines in the southernmost sector of the grand cru Corton vineyard (Les Combes), near the base of the hill, the medium to dark ruby-colored 1996 Le Corton reveals an herbal and black fruit-scented nose. This complex, rich, and deep wine is medium to full bodied, silky, and well made. Layers of dark cherries, blackberries, and roasting spices can be found in its delicious flavor profile. Anticipated maturity: 2000–2005. This estate's 1996 Corton-Bressandes is a wine I search out in vintages with good ripeness. It is never huge, muscular, or a blockbuster but can often be sultry, seductive, detailed, and simply lovely. A recently tasted 1990, while at least 3 years from maturity, was fabulous. The 1996 displays sweet red cherry and Asian spice aromatics as well as a gorgeously refined character filled with candied and delineated cherries. This elegant, sexy, and feminine offering is medium to full bodied and silky textured and possesses a long and refreshing finish. Anticipated maturity: 2002–2007.

DOMAINE JEAN et JEAN-LOUIS TRAPET (GEVREY-CHAMBERTIN)

1996	Chambertin	EE	(92–94+)
1995	Chambertin	EE	(89–91+)
1996	Chapelle-Chambertin	E	(91–93)
1995	Chapelle-Chambertin	EE	(89–92)
1996	Gevrey-Chambertin Clos Prieur	D	89
1995	Gevrey-Chambertin La Petite Chapelle	D	(87–90)
1996	Gevrey-Chambertin Vieilles Vignes	D	88
1995	Gevrey-Chambertin Vieilles Vignes	D	(85–88)

1996 Latricières-Chambertin	E	(90–92)
1995 Latricières-Chambertin	EE	(88–91)

Jean-Louis Trapet, with the help of his Paris-based wine broker (Patrick Lesec), is attempting to return this estate back to its glory years of 4 decades ago. Efforts are being made in the vineyards (lower yields and later-harvested fruit) and in the winery (fining and filtration have been abandoned). Aromatically, the dark ruby-colored 1995 Gevrey-Chambertin Vieilles Vignes reveals intense scents of perfume, cinnamon, and cassis. It possesses Asian spices, cherries, earth, and wild game flavors in its medium- to full-bodied, well-extracted, dense palate. Delicious now, it should be drunk between 1999 and 2005. The equally opaque 1995 Gevrey-Chambertin La Petite Chapelle displays an appealingly sweet nose of red and black cherries and tangy currants on the nose. It has a beautifully supple, velvety-textured, medium- to full-bodied personality packed with blueberries and raspberries. This potentially outstanding wine has gorgeously ripe, round tannins that will allow it to age gracefully. Anticipated maturity: 2002–2009.

Displaying mouthwatering aromas of grilled meats, smoke, blackberries, and red currants, the 1995 Chapelle-Chambertin possesses a dense, silky, full-bodied palate replete with red cherries, herbs, and admirably well-integrated oat notes of vanilla and bacon. Concentrated and powerful, yet delineated, feminine, and elegant, this exceptional wine has the requisite tannins for extended cellaring yet also possesses the luscious forward fruit desired for early drinking. Drink it between 2000 and 2012. The dark ruby-colored 1995 Latricières-Chambertin reveals aromas of blackberries, cherries, coffee, earth, and minerals, and superb flavors reminiscent of game, berries, Asian spices, and a touch of underbrush for added complexity. Concentrated and highly extracted, this elegant yet masculine, full-bodied wine is extremely well made and structured. Anticipated maturity: 2004–2012. The dark-colored 1995 Chambertin's bouquet of black cherries, roasted spices, and mocha jumps from the glass. This fabulously ripe and intense wine is packed with flavors suggesting stones, minerals, and blackberries in its regal, full-bodied, and thick personality. Slightly rugged and backward, it will require extended cellaring before it is ready to drink. Anticipated maturity: 2004–2015.

The medium to dark ruby-colored 1996 Gevrey-Chambertin Vieilles Vignes has spicy black fruit aromas and an immensely appealing core of licorice-laced blackberries, cassis, and black cherries. This ripe, dense, medium-bodied, and powerful wine has a velvety texture, ripe tannins, and a precise and flavorful finish. Drink it between 2000 and 2005. Displaying a similar color and a cinnamon-and-cassis-scented nose, the 1996 Gevrey-Chambertin Clos Prieur is a medium-bodied, thick (pasty?), juicy, harmonious, and elegant offering. I was quite impressed by its ripe, black cherry-and-blackberry-flavored character, as well as by its long, well-delineated finish. Anticipated maturity: 2000–2006.

The dark ruby-colored 1996 Chapelle-Chambertin has a nose that is crammed with ripe black fruits and traces of toasted oak. This full-bodied, silky-textured, concentrated, and immensely complex wine offers flavors of red and black cherries, earth, rosemary, juniper berries, and cloves that are persistent. Anticipated maturity: 2003–2010. Displaying a similar color and aromas reminiscent of fresh black cherries intermingled with scents of leather and candied orange peels, the 1996 Latricières-Chambertin is a full-bodied, thick, and chewy wine. More masculine and structured than the Chapelle, it offers cassis, Asian spices, and morel and porcini mushroom flavors in its intricate and concentrated character. Drink it between 2003 and 2009. The spectacular 1996 Chambertin exhibits a dark ruby/purple color and offers a nose that calls to mind a chocolate milk shake in which cherry syrup has been poured. This is a massive, superthick, hugely concentrated, and extracted wine. It is powerfully flavored (plums, prunes, and cherries drenched in chocolate), intense, dense, and prodigiously long. I am ecstatic about this domaine's progress. Bravo!

DOMAINE A. & P. DE VILLAINE (BOUZERON)

1995 Bourgogne Côte Chalonnaise La Digoine	C	86
1995 Mercurey Les Montots	C	88

Known primarily for producing the finest Aligoté in Burgundy, Aubert de Villaine's family estate also crafts well-made reds. The medium to dark ruby-colored 1995 Bourgogne Côte Chalonnaise La Digoine possesses an assertive nose of tangy black cherries and a fresh, lively, silky-textured, medium-bodied, red fruit, and spice-flavored personality. Well delineated and delicious on the attack and in the midpalate, this wine may merit a higher rating if its tannins soften over the coming year. Drink it between now and 2000. Similarly colored, the 1995 Mercurey Les Montots displays beautiful cranberry, cassis, mineral, and Asian spice-laden aromatics. Soft, oily textured and supple, this scrumptious wine is packed with blackberries, dark cherries, and mineral notes. Drink it from now to 2003.

DOMAINE CHRISTOPHE VIOLOT-GUILLEMARD (POMMARD)

1996 Beaune Clos des Mouches	D	(86–87)
1995 Pommard Clos Orgelot	D	(86–88)
1996 Pommard Clos Orgelot	D	(87–89)
1995 Pommard Les Epenots	D	(87–89+)
1996 Pommard Les Epenots	D	(88–89+)
1996 St. Romain Sous Le Château	C	(85–87)

Christophe Violot-Guillemard's red burgundies are vinified without any pumping of the wine and are bottled by hand unfined and unfiltered. With the exception of his parcels in St. Romain, all of Christophe Violot-Guillemard's vines were planted between 1930 and 1945.

The ruby-colored 1995 Pommard Clos Orgelot reveals intense blackberry, cassis, and vanilla aromas and a highly structured, well-concentrated, and tightly wound core of black cherries, roasted herbs, and coffee flavors. This medium-bodied and crisp wine has a rustic, old-style feel to it while having modern burgundy's highly extracted and ripe fruit. Anticipated maturity: now–2004. The slightly darker-colored 1995 Pommard Les Epenots had an unyielding nose the day of my tasting, but its thick, velvety, medium- to full-bodied core of extremely ripe, dense black cherries, cassis, and blueberries are testimony to its greatness. This full-flavored and intense wine's finish ends on notes of vanilla and delightful flavors of sweet sauteed porcini mushrooms. Anticipated maturity: now–2005.

The ruby-colored 1996 St. Romain Sous Le Château offers a sweet dark fruit-filled nose and a medium-bodied, foursquare, and broad character with flavors reminiscent of metals, minerals, stones, and black raspberries. It should be drunk by 2001. The 1996 Beaune Clos des Mouches has a ruby color and tangy currant and herbal aromas. Expressive cherries and minerals can be found in this medium-bodied, silky, and refreshing wine. While it is more welcoming, joyful, and rich than the St. Romain, it lacks the length, density, and complexity of an excellent wine. Drink it before 2001.

Medium to dark ruby colored and exhibiting an intriguing nose of blackberries, underbrush, and grilled oak, the 1996 Pommard Clos Orgelot is a medium- to full-bodied, well-crafted, beautifully ripe, and broad wine. Its silky-textured core reveals excellent richness and loads of juicy black cherries, oak spices, and minerals that linger on its long and supple tannin-filled finish. Anticipated maturity: now–2004. Similarly colored, the 1996 Pommard Les Epenots offers red currants, sweet strawberries, underbrush, and fresh herbs on the nose and a concentrated, medium- to full-bodied, and rich core of fruit. Flavors reminiscent of blackberries, red cherries, cassis, herbes de Provence, and boysenberries can be found in this delicious wine. It may ultimately merit an outstanding rating if Christophe Violot-Guillemard can soften the slightly rustic tannins in this wine's long finish without stripping the fruit. Anticipated maturity: 2000–2006.

DOMAINE THIERRY VIOLOT-GUILLEMARD (POMMARD)

1996	Beaune Clos des Mouches	D	(87–89)
1995	Beaune Clos des Mouches	D	(86–88)
1996	Pommard La Platière Vieilles Vignes	D	(88–90)
1995	Pommard La Platière	D	(87–89)
1996	Pommard Rugiens	D	(89–91+)
1995	Pommard Rugiens	D	(88–90)

Thierry Violot-Guillemard harvests slightly earlier than his brother Christophe but performs more *pigéage* (the technique of punching down the cap) in order to extract additional color, flavor, and aromas from his grapes.

The medium to dark ruby-colored 1995 Beaune Clos des Mouches offers beguiling aromas of sweet cherries and Asian spices as well as an oily-textured, medium-bodied character with flavors reminiscent of rosemary, candied raspberries, and stones. Delicious to drink now, it can be cellared until 2002. The extremely attractive ruby/purple-colored 1995 Pommard La Platière has a gorgeous nose of wild flowers, ripe cherries, and touches of vanilla. This wine possesses a medium- to full-bodied and velvety core of intense strawberries, Bing cherries, minerals, and a mouthwatering bacon flavor. Its beautifully long finish ends on a nice backbone of ripe tannins, ensuring its ability to age gracefully. Anticipated maturity: now–2003. My favorite of Thierry Violot-Guillemard's offerings is his fabulous, and potentially outstanding, 1995 Pommard Rugiens. It possesses a brooding nose of blackberries, stones, mocha, and embedded minerals, as well as a highly concentrated, powerful, rugged, thickly textured, and full-bodied personality jam-packed with superripe plums, blueberries, and cassis. Intensely long and persistent, this extremely well-structured and driven wine has big ripe tannins in its finish. It will be at its best between 2000 and 2006.

The light to medium ruby-colored 1996 Beaune Clos des Mouches offers aromas of violets intermingled with red and black cherries. This is a delicious, medium-bodied, expressive, lively, and plump wine filled with strawberries and candied cherries. It is well crafted and well balanced and possesses a long and lingering finish. Anticipated maturity: now–2002. The bright ruby-colored 1996 Pommard La Platière Vieilles Vignes displays a red cherry and mocha-imbued nose as well as a gorgeously ripe, masculine, concentrated, and highly expressive medium to full body. This wine's firm structure is packed with sweet cherries, spices, and minerals. Its tannins, while quite evident, are ripe and sound. I suggest cellaring it for 3 years and drinking it between 2001 and 2005. The ruby-colored 1996 Pommard Les Rugiens exhibits deep and intense scents of blackberries drenched in mocha. On the palate, its medium to full body is thick, chewy, broad shouldered, and masculine. Richly layered flavors reminiscent of cassis, black fruits, stones, leather, and tar can be found in this concentrated and powerful wine. It is another example of a Pinot Noir whose palate presence cannot be judged by its color. Anticipated maturity: 2001–2007.

DOMAINE DU COMTE DE VOGÜÉ (CHAMBOLLE-MUSIGNY)

1996	Bonnes Mares	EEE	(92–95)
1995	Bonnes Mares	EEE	(91–94)
1996	Chambolle-Musigny	EE	(88–90)

1995 Chambolle-Musigny	EE	(86–88)
1996 Chambolle-Musigny Les Amoureuses	EEE	(90–93)
1995 Chambolle-Musigny Les Amoureuses	EEE	(90–92+)
1996 Musigny	EEE	(94–97+)
1995 Musigny Vieilles Vignes	EEE	(93–96+)

Owned by the Baronne Bertrand de Ladoucette, the Domaine du Comte Georges de Vogüé is the crown jewel of Chambolle-Musigny, not only because of its large holdings (including 70% of the Musigny vineyard), but also because of the spectacular quality of its wines. In 1996 I had the immense honor of tasting its Musignys from 1949 and 1959, experiences I will never forget. As Robert Parker has reported, the quality of the estate's wines suffered dramatically from 1973 to 1988 (even the 1985, tasted in early April, was disappointing) but came roaring back in the late eighties with the arrival of its present winemaker, François Millet. In 1990 and 1991 Vogüé's Musignys are "wine of the vintage" material. Quality at any expense is the philosophy at this estate: in order to produce the fabulous 1991, Millet had an army of pickers using tweezers to remove any rotten grapes from the bunches.

Millet and Jean-Luc Pépin (the domaine's administrative director) informed me that the estate has very few, if any, older bottles of its wines cellared and that their tasting experience was due to the generosity of collectors throughout the world.

Medium ruby colored, the 1995 Chambolle-Musigny displays a crisp nose of raspberries and cherries and a silky-textured, elegant, well-balanced rose and black cherry-filled personality, described by Millet as having "good vibrations." It will be at its best for the first 5 years after its release. Slightly darker, the 1995 Chambolle-Musigny Les Amoureuses (the domaine owns 12.5% of the vineyard) possesses an enticingly elegant bouquet of violets, roses, and crisp berries and an extremely tightly wound, concentrated, dark berry-filled mouth. Chewy, deep, and with plenty of ripe tannins in its backbone, this gem should be held for 6–7 years and drunk over the subsequent decade.

Medium to dark ruby colored, the spectacularly aromatic 1995 Bonnes Mares explodes out of the glass with spiced apples, dark cherries, and cola scents. Chewy, powerful, polished, and intensely structured, this full-bodied wine is packed with wild berries, plums, and red fruits. Drink it between 2003 and 2012+. One of the greatest wines of the vintage, Vogüé's 1995 Musigny Vieilles Vignes reminded me of Château Margaux at its best: an iron fist in a velvet glove. How can anything be this massive, powerful, and robust and yet be strikingly elegant and refined? Possessing a dark ruby color and an amazingly spicy, floral (roses), and black fruit-filled nose, this stupendous burgundy has a thick, almost viscous, velvety texture, with copious quantities of fat, chewy, red berries. Surprisingly, the fruit almost tastes stewed yet is perfectly and clearly delineated. Complex, intensely deep, and buttressed with huge but ripe tannins, this wine should be at its plateau of maturity between 2006 and 2016. Bravo!

When I visited the estate in February 1998, all the 1996s were about to be fined. Millet, a conscientious, soft-spoken, serious, and intelligent man, answers questions in an extremely thoughtful and deliberate way. Each word seems to have been measured and considered before being uttered. He feels that "1996 is a sensual and structured vintage with generous fruit, lots of personality, and great potential. The structure is discreet, however." As the scores listed here suggest, I found 1996 to be another stellar vintage for this benchmark-setting estate.

The 1996 Chambolle-Musigny is bright ruby colored and reveals delightful black raspberry aromatics. This juicy, perfectly balanced, feminine, and harmonious wine is silky textured, medium bodied, and exceedingly refined. It offers fabulous flavors of sweet and juicy red cherries and violets. Its admirably long, precise, and pure finish displays supple tannins. This gem should be consumed between now and 2005. Exhibiting a slightly dark color and fragrant scents of freshly cut flowers and blueberries, the dense, well-proportioned 1996 Chambolle-Musigny Les Amoureuses is a highly detailed, elegant, medium- to full-bodied, and velvety wine. Traces of chocolate can be discerned in the abundant raspberry and blueberry fruit that saturate the palate. Anticipated maturity: 2001–2008.

I loved this estate's medium to dark ruby-colored 1996 Bonnes Mares. Earthy aromas of stones, minerals, blood, and blueberries can be found in this medium- to full-bodied, tightly wound, sensual, and seductive wine. Seemingly unending layers of black raspberries, cherries, wild blueberries, tangy red currants, and fresh herbs can be found in this complex, rich, silky-textured, and profound wine. Its sublime finish, which provides the taster with yet another opportunity to witness this offering's gorgeous purity of fruit, has a firm yet supple backbone. An extraordinary Bonnes Mares! Anticipated maturity: 2003–2010+.

The bright, dark ruby-colored 1996 Musigny is exceptional. It is a feminine version of the 1995. Its enticing nose reveals extraordinarily refined aromas of myriad flowers soaked in cherries, blueberries, and traces of sweet mocha. This oily-textured, full-bodied, perfectly harmonious, and compellingly delineated wine could not be any more elegant. It possesses awesome depth, concentration, and purity in its violet and cherry cream pie-flavored personality. Moreover, its formidably long finish displays a strong yet satiny backbone. I predict it will evolve magnificently. Anticipated maturity: 2004–2014+.

White Burgundy

BURGUNDY'S GREATEST WHITE WINES

Guy Amiot et Fils Chassagne-Montrachet Les Caillerets

Guy Amiot et Fils Le Montrachet

Guy Amiot et Fils Puligny-Montrachet Les Demoiselles

d'Auvenay Auxey-Duresses Les Bouttoniers

d'Auvenay Chevalier-Montrachet

d'Auvenay Criots-Bâtard-Montrachet

d'Auvenay Meursault Goutte d'Or

d'Auvenay Meursault Narvaux

d'Auvenay Puligny Montrachet Les Folatières

Daniel Barraud Pouilly-Fuissé En Buland Vieilles Vignes Réserve

Daniel Barraud Pouilly-Fuissé Les Crays Vieilles Vignes Réserve

Jean-Marc Boillot Puligny-Montrachet Les Combettes

Jean-Marc Boillot Puligny-Montrachet La Truffière

Domaine de la Bongran (Jean Thevenet) Mâcon-Clessé Quintaine

Bouchard Père et Fils Le Montrachet

Louis Carillon Bienvenue-Bâtard-Montrachet

Jean-François Coche-Dury Corton-Charlemagne

Jean-François Coche-Dury Meursault Les Perrières

Jean-François Coche-Dury Meursault Rougeot

Marc Colin Le Montrachet

Colin-Deléger Chassagne-Montrachet Les Chevenottes

Colin-Deléger Chevalier-Montrachet

Colin-Deléger Puligny-Montrachet Les Demoiselles

Colin-Deléger Puligny-Montrachet La Truffière

René et Vincent Dauvissat Chablis Les Clos

Marius Delarche Corton-Charlemagne

Joseph Drouhin Beaune Clos des Mouches

Joseph Drouhin Montrachet Marquis de Laguiche

Jean-Noël Gagnard Bâtard-Montrachet

Jean-Noël Gagnard Chassagne-Montrachet Les Caillerets

Guffens-Heynen Pouilly-Fuissé Clos des Petits Croux

Guffens-Heynen Pouilly-Fuissé Les Croux

Guffens-Heynen Pouilly-Fuissé La Roche

Louis Jadot Chevalier-Montrachet Les Demoiselles

Louis Jadot Corton-Charlemagne

Louis Jadot Le Montrachet

Patrick Javillier Meursault Les Narvaux "Mise Spéciale"

Patrick Javillier Meursault Cuvée Tête de Murger "Mise Spéciale"

François Jobard Meursault Les Charmes

François Jobard Meursault Les Genevrières

Rémi Jobard Meursault Les Charmes

Rémi Jobard Meursault Les Genevrières

Comte Lafon Meursault Les Charmes

Comte Lafon Meursault Les Genevrières

Comte Lafon Meursault Les Perrières

Comte Lafon Le Montrachet

Laroche Chablis Blanchots Réserve de l'Obédiencerie

Louis Latour Bâtard-Montrachet

Louis Latour Chevalier-Montrachet

Louis Latour Corton-Charlemagne

Louis Latour Le Montrachet

Domaine Leflaive Bâtard-Montrachet

Domaine Leflaive Chevalier-Montrachet

Domaine Leflaive Le Montrachet

Domaine Leflaive Puligny-Montrachet Les Combettes

Domaine Leflaive Puligny-Montrachet Les Folatières

Domaine Leflaive Puligny-Montrachet Les Pucelles

Domaine Leroy Corton-Charlemagne

Louis Michel et Fils Chablis Les Clos

Louis Michel et Fils Chablis Les Grenouilles

Louis Michel et Fils Chablis Vaudesir

François Mikulski Meursault Les Charmes

François Mikulski Meursault Les Genevrières

Bernard Morey Chassagne-Montrachet Les Caillerets

Bernard Morey Chassagne-Montrachet Les Embrazées

Bernard Morey Puligny-Montrachet La Truffière

Marc Morey Bâtard-Montrachet

Marc Morey Puligny-Montrachet Les Pucelles

Michel Niellon Bâtard-Montrachet

Michel Niellon Chassagne-Montrachet Les Champs Gains

Michel Niellon Chassagne-Montrachet Les Chaumées

Michel Niellon Chassagne-Montrachet Clos de la Maltroie

Michel Niellon Chassagne-Montrachet Les Vergers

Michel Niellon Chassagne-Montrachet Clos St. Jean

Michel Niellon Chevalier-Montrachet

Jacques Prieur Chevalier-Montrachet

Jacques Prieur Corton-Charlemagne

Jacques Prieur Le Montrachet

Château de Puligny-Montrachet Chevalier-Montrachet

Château de Puligny-Montrachet Le Montrachet

Ramonet Bâtard-Montrachet

Ramonet Le Montrachet

François et Jean-Marie Raveneau Chablis Les Blanchots

François et Jean-Marie Raveneau Chablis Les Clos

François et Jean-Marie Raveneau Chablis Montée de Tonnerre

François et Jean-Marie Raveneau Chablis Vaillons

François et Jean-Marie Raveneau Chablis Valmur

Domaine de la Romanée-Conti Le Montrachet

Guy Roulot Meursault Perrières

Etienne Sauzet Bâtard-Montrachet

Etienne Sauzet Bienvenue-Bâtard-Montrachet

Etienne Sauzet Le Montrachet

Etienne Sauzet Puligny-Montrachet Les Champs Canet

Etienne Sauzet Puligny-Montrachet Les Combettes

Tollot-Beaut Corton-Charlemagne

Valette Pouilly-Fuissé Clos de Monsieur Noly Vieilles Vignes

Verget Chablis Bougros

Verget Chablis Fourchaume Vieilles Vignes

Verget Chablis Valmur

Verget Chassagne-Montrachet Morgeot
   Vieilles Vignes
Verget Chassagne-Montrachet La Remilly

Verget Chassagne-Montrachet La Romanée
Verget Corton-Charlemagne
Verget Meursault Charmes Vieilles Vignes

RATING BURGUNDY'S WHITE WINE PRODUCERS
(Including Côte de Beaune, Mâconnais, and Chablis Wine Producers)

***** (OUTSTANDING)

d'Auvenay (St. Romain)
Daniel Barraud (Vergisson)
Bongran/Jean Thevenet (Quintaine)
Jean-François Coche-Dury (Meursault)
Colin-Deléger (Chassagne-Montrachet)
René et Vincent Dauvissat (Chablis)
Guffens-Heynen (Vergisson)
Comte Lafon (Meursault)
Domaine Leflaive (Puligny-Montrachet)

Domaine Leroy (Vosne-Romanée)
Bernard Morey (Chassagne-Montrachet)
Michel Niellon (Chassagne-Montrachet)
François et Jean-Marie Raveneau (Chablis)
Domaine de la Romanée-Conti (Vosne-
   Romanée)
Etienne Sauzet (Puligny-Montrachet)
Verget (Sologny)

**** (EXCELLENT)

Bertrand Ambroise (Prémeaux-Prissey)
Guy Amiot et Fils (Chassagne-Montrachet)
Billaud-Simon (Chablis)
Blain-Gagnard (Chassagne-Montrachet)
Jean Boillot/Henri Boillot (Volnay)
Jean-Marc Boillot (Pommard)
Bouchard Père et Fils (Beaune) (since
   1995)
Boyer-Martenot (Meursault)
Louis Carillon (Puligny-
   Montrachet)****/*****
Bruno Clair (Marsannay)
Marc Colin (Gamay-St. Aubin)
Cordier et Fils (Fuissé)****/*****
Marius Delarche (Pernand-Vergelesses)
Jean-Paul Droin (Chablis)
Joseph Drouhin (Beaune)
Vincent Dureuil-Janthial (Rully)
Arnauld Ente (Meursault)****/*****
Fontaine-Gagnard (Chassagne-Montrachet)
Jean-Noël Gagnard (Chassagne-
   Montrachet)
Vincent Girardin (Santenay)
Guillemot-Michel (Quintaine)****/*****
Louis Jadot (Beaune)
Patrick Javillier (Meursault)****/*****

François Jobard (Meursault)
Rémi Jobard (Meursault)****/*****
Joblot (Givry)
Roger Lassarat (Vergisson)
Louis Latour (Beaune)
Duc de Magenta (Louis Jadot) (Chassagne-
   Montrachet)
Louis Michel et Fils (Chablis)
François Mikulski (Meursault)
Albert Morey (Chassagne-Montrachet)
Marc Morey (Chassagne-Montrachet)
Jacques Prieur (Meursault) (since 1995)
Château de Puligny-Montrachet (Puligny-
   Montrachet)****/*****
Ramonet (Chassagne-Montrachet)
Robert-Denogent (Fuissé)
Antonin Rodet (Cave Privée Cuvées
   (Mercurey)
Antonin Rodet (Mercurey) (since 1995 on
   Cave Privée wines)
Guy Roulot (Meursault)
Georges et Christophe Roumier
   (Chambolle-Musigny)
Tollot-Beaut (Chorey-Lès-Beaune)
Valette (Vinzelles)****/*****

*** (GOOD)

Domaine de l'Arlot (Prémeaux-
   Prissey)***/****
Comte Armand (Pommard)

Barat (Chablis)
Jean-Claude Belland (Santenay)
Bitouzet-Prieur (Volnay)

Simon Bize (Savigny-Lès-Beaune)

Etienne Boileau/Domaine du Chardonnay (Chablis)***/****

Bonneau du Martray (Pernand-Vergelesses)***/****

Brintet (Mercurey)

Caillot (Meursault)

Château de Chamirey (Mercurey)

Chandon de Briailles (Savigny-Lès-Beaune)

Chartron et Trébuchet (Puligny-Montrachet)***/****

Alain Coche-Bizouard (Meursault)***/****

Bernard Defaix (Milly-Chablis)

Domaine des Deux Roches (St. Véran)

Druid (Morey-St.-Denis)

Georges Dubœuf (Romanèche-Thorins)

Maurice Ecard (Savigny-Lès-Beaune)

Jean-Philippe Fichet (Meursault)***/****

Château Génot-Boulanger (Meursault)***/****

Emilien Gillet/Jean Thevenet (Quintaine)***/****

Henri Gouges (Nuits-St.-Georges)***/****

Antonin Guyon (Savigny-Lès-Beaune)

Thierry Hamelin (Lignorelles-Chablis)

Jayer-Gilles (Magny-Lès-Villers)***/****

Laroche (Chablis)***/****

Latour-Giraud (Meursault)***/****

Olivier Leflaive Frères (Puligny-Montrachet)***/****

Château de la Maltroye (Chassagne-Montrachet)

Manciat-Poncet (Charnay-Les-Mâcon)

Joseph/Pierre Matrot (Meursault)***/****

Château de Mercey (Mercurey)

Alice et Olivier de Moor (Chablis)***/****

Bernard Moreau (Chassagne-Montrachet)

Jean-Marc Morey (Chassagne-Montrachet)

Pierre Morey (Meursault)***/****

Morey-Blanc (Meursault)

Domaine de Perraud (St. Véran)***/****

Jean Pillot (Chassagne-Montrachet)

Paul Pillot (Chassagne-Montrachet)

Denis Pommier (Poinchy-Chablis)

Rapet Père et Fils (Pernand-Vergelesses)

Château de Rully (Rully)

Francine et Olivier Savary (Maligny-Chablis)

Domaine de Vauroux (Chablis)

Domaine des Vieilles Pierres (St. Véran)

A. P. de Villaine (Bouzeron)

Robert Vocoret et Fils (Chablis)

* * (AVERAGE)

Bachelet-Ramonet (Chassagne-Montrachet)**/***

Bertagna**/***

Borgeot (Remigny)**/***

Philippe Brenot (Santenay)**/***

Sylvain Bzikot (Puligny-Montrachet)**/***

Pascal Chevigny (Nuits-St.-Georges)**/***

Condemine (Mâconnais)**/***

Alain Corcia Selections (Savigny-Lès-Beaune)**/***

Jean-Luc Dubois (Chorey-Lès-Beaune)**/***

Michel Dupont-Fahn (Meursault)

René Fleurot-Larose (Santenay)

Philippe Gavignet (Nuits-St.-Georges)**/***

Ghislaine et Jean-Hughes Goisot (St. Bris Le Vineux)**/***

Labouré-Roi (Nuits-St.-Georges)

Lamy-Pillot (Santenay)

Domaine de Legères (Mâconnais)**/***

Méo-Camuzet (Vosne-Romanée)**/***

Mestre Père et Fils (Santenay)**/***

Château de Meursault (Meursault)

Michelot (Meursault)**/***

Ponsot (Morey-St.-Denis)**/***

Jean Claude Rateau (Beaune)**/***

Château de Rontets (Fuissé)**/***

Philippe Rossignol (Nuits-St.-Georges)**/***

Domaine Thomas (Prissé)**/***

Christophe Viollot-Guillemard (Pommard)**/***

WHERE ARE BURGUNDY'S WHITE WINE VALUES?

Bertrand Ambroise Ladoix Les Grechons
Bertrand Ambroise St. Romain Chardonnay
Barat Chablis
Daniel Barraud Mâcon-Vergisson La Roche
   Réserve
Caillot Bourgogne Les Herbeux
Château de Chamirey Mercurey
Chartron et Trébuchet Bourgogne Cuvée
   Jean Chartron
Chartron et Trébuchet Rully La Chaume
Alain Corcia Selections Montagny Premier
   Cru Vieilles Vignes
Alain Corcia Selections St. Véran Vieilles
   Vignes Domaine Jobert
Cordier Bourgogne Blanc
Cordier Mâcon Chardonnay
Domaine des Deux Roches St. Véran
Domaine des Deux Roches St. Véran Les
   Terres Noires
Jean-Paul Droin Chablis Tête de Cuvée
Joseph Drouhin Rully
Georges Duboeuf Mâcon-Villages (flower
   label)
Georges Duboeuf Pouilly-Fuissé Domaine
   Béranger
Georges Duboeuf Pouilly-Fuissé Clos
   Reissier
Georges Duboeuf St. Véran (flower label)
Georges Duboeuf St. Véran Domaine de la
   Batie

Vincent Dureuil-Janthial Bourgogne
   Aligoté
Emilien Gillet/Jean Thevenet Mâcon-Viré
Vincent Girardin Rully Les Clous
Guillemot-Michel Mâcon-Clessé Quintaine
Thierry Hamelin Chablis Vieilles Vignes
Louis Jadot Rully
Patrick Javillier Bourgogne Cuvée des
   Forgets Mise Spéciale
Rémi Jobard Bourgogne Aligoté
Louis Latour Mâcon Lugny
Louis Latour Montagny Premier Cru
Louis Latour Saint-Véran
Château de Mercey Bourgogne Hautes
   Côtes de Beaune
Perraud Mâcon-Villages Les Roches
   Anciennes
Perraud St. Véran Les Crays Roses
Robert-Denogent Mâcon-Solutré
   Bertillones
Château de Rully Rully
Valette Mâcon-Chaintré Jeunes Vignes
Valette Mâcon-Chaintré Vieilles Vignes
Verget Bourgogne Blanc
Verget Ladoix
Verget Mâcon-Villages Tête de Cuvée
Aubert de Villaine Aligoté de Bouzeron
Aubert de Villaine Bourgogne Le Clous

Consumers should note that the majority of wines in the previous list of white burgundy values come from the Mâconnais (Mâcons, Pouilly-Fuissés, St. Vérans, and so on), a picturesque region south of the more famous and costlier Côte d'Or. It cannot be stressed enough that the top Mâconnais producers deserve considerable consumer attention because of the high quality of their Chardonnay-based whites and their reasonable prices. Furthermore, consumers should also notice the high number of Côte Chalonaise wines (Rully, Mercurey, and so forth) listed. This little-known region immediately south of the Côte de Beaune can be the source of delicious, mineral-laden whites and are often considerable values.

DOMAINE BERTRAND AMBROISE (PRÉMEAUX-PRISSEY)

1996	Bourgogne Chardonnay	C	87
1996	Chassagne-Montrachet La Maltroie	E	91
1996	Corton-Charlemagne	EE	(94–96)
1995	Corton-Charlemagne	E	90+

1996 Ladoix Les Gréchons	D	88
1996 St. Romain Chardonnay	C	88+

The ever-smiling Bertrand Ambroise is one of the rare winemakers who produces high-quality white and red burgundies. Gregarious, intelligent, and always armed with a new joke or witty remark, Ambroise gets serious when talk turns to winemaking. In 1996 he crafted his whites 100% in barrel, with twice weekly *bâtonnages* until the malolactic fermentations began. He stopped stirring the lees at this stage "because the lees did not taste good."

The 1996 Bourgogne Chardonnay, aged in 50% new oak (as with the two following wines), reveals extremely ripe fruit aromas intermingled with minerals and baking spices. On the palate, this medium-bodied, rich, and silky-textured wine has powerful Earl Grey tea, tangy pears, and stone flavors. It should be at its best if drunk before 2002. Displaying white flower and anise scents, the 1996 Ladoix Les Gréchons is an intense, medium-bodied, and lively wine packed with candied citrus fruits, pears, and minerals. Anticipated maturity: now–2002. The 1996 St. Romain Chardonnay has a smoky and minerally nose as well as a delicious, medium- to full-bodied, and oily-textured core packed with loads of sweet orange peels, and flint. Like most of Ambroise's wines, this offering is intensely flavored and powerful. Its persistent finish reveals excellent purity and delineation. Anticipated maturity: now–2003.

The outstanding 1996 Chassagne-Montrachet La Maltroie (75% new oak) exhibits strong mineral aromas and a powerful, intense, and deep personality filled with lively almonds, pears, and spices. This expressive, rich, medium- to full-bodied, and silky-textured wine is concentrated, complex, and admirably long. It should be at its peak between 2000 and 2006.

The 1996 vintage was particularly successful in Corton-Charlemagne; Ambroise has fashioned a stunning wine. Aged in 100% new oak, this offering reveals mouthwatering tropical fruits, spices, and anise aromas. On the palate, this full-bodied, hyperrich, massive, powerful, and intense wine is jam-packed with layers of roasted peaches, minerals, red berries, honeysuckle blossoms, toast, and anise. This profound, broad, concentrated, focused, and amazingly persistent wine is simply extraordinary.

Exhibiting a nose of green apples and red berries, the thick-textured and powerful 1995 Corton-Charlemagne offers flavors of star anise, spicy oak, and tropical fruits. This concentrated, full-flavored, and very well-structured wine needs 5–6 years to cope with its lavish use of oak, but then it will be wonderful for 7+ years.

DOMAINE GUY AMIOT ET FILS (CHASSAGNE MONTRACHET)
(Formerly Known as Domaine Amiot-Bonfils)

1996 Chassagne-Montrachet	D	86
1996 Chassagne-Montrachet Les Baudines	E	87
1996 Chassagne-Montrachet Les Caillerets	E	93
1995 Chassagne-Montrachet Les Caillerets	E	92
1996 Chassagne-Montrachet Les Champs Gains	E	90
1995 Chassagne-Montrachet Les Champs Gains	E	89
1996 Chassagne-Montrachet Clos St. Jean	E	88+
1995 Chassagne-Montrachet Clos St. Jean	E	90
1996 Chassagne-Montrachet Les Macherelles	D	89
1996 Chassagne-Montrachet Les Vergers	E	90
1995 Chassagne-Montrachet Les Vergers	E	90+

1996 Montrachet	EEE	96
1995 Montrachet	EEE	93+
1996 Puligny-Montrachet Les Demoiselles	EE	93
1995 Puligny-Montrachet Les Demoiselles	EE	91
1996 St. Aubin En Remilly	D	88

Amiot made his 1995s in the new cellars he built under his home and courtyard. With pre-fabricated vaulted and insulated ceilings, he now has the most modern and beautiful cellar for miles around. His 1995s, while not blockbusters like his 1992s, have the concentrated fruit of this vintage. In particular, they should be noted for good balancing acidity, something not everyone was able to achieve.

The 1995 Chassagne-Montrachet Les Champs Gains shows a floral and minerally nose with smoky fruit flavors and zippy acid. This medium-bodied wine has good length and structure and should be drunk between 1998 and 2004. The 1995 Chassagne-Montrachet Les Vergers has aromas of wet stones in the sunlight and a great minerally depth. In the mouth, its velvety texture is appealing, as is its long, stony finish. Drink this wine between 2000 and 2006. With more mineral flavors, but without quite the intensity of the Vergers, the 1995 Chassagne-Montrachet Clos St. Jean has a thick, oily texture and is full bodied. This well-balanced wine needs 3–4 years of cellaring and will drink well for the subsequent 5–7 years. From over 70-year-old vines, the full-bodied 1995 Chassagne-Montrachet Les Caillerets has a beautiful silky and intense texture and powerful mineral and floral flavors in the mouth. Slight nuances of black truffles are found on the back end of this long wine. Roasted tropical fruit aromas are discernible in the distance on the tight nose of the 1995 Puligny-Montrachet Les Demoiselles. This full-bodied wine displays an elegant minerality and great velvety texture; it should be drunk between 2000 and 2008. Amiot's delicious 1995 Montrachet exhibits a floral nose and thrilling flavors of powerful roasted fruits inter-mingled with deeply toasted minerals and slight notes of seawater. A full-bodied, tightly wound white burgundy that is built to last, this wine should be held for 6–8 years and then enjoyed until 2015.

The 1996 Chassagne-Montrachet has a sweet floral nose and a lively, soft, and light- to medium-bodied core of tangy minerals. This well-made wine bases its appeal on its refreshing nature, not on complexity, depth, or richness. I suggest drinking it within 2–3 years. Reveal-ing spicy, floral aromas, the 1996 Chassagne-Montrachet Les Baudines has a ripe, rich, and medium-bodied character with anise, minerals, and leesy flavors. Well balanced and silky textured, this wine will provide delicious drinking until 2002. The 1996 St. Aubin En Remilly is a sweet mineral and white peach-scented wine with fat, oily, and dense layers of stones and candied pears in its medium-bodied flavor profile. Anticipated maturity: now–2002.

Displaying good richness and mineral aromas, the 1996 Chassagne-Montrachet Clos St. Jean possesses a medium-bodied, masculine, chewy, and focused personality with earthy, toasty, and stonelike flavors. This wine's structure and mouth-coating fruit lead me to believe that it may ultimately be even better than my score suggests. It should be consumed between 2001 and 2004. The 1996 Chassagne-Montrachet Les Vergers had a completely reticent nose the day I visited the estate. On the palate, however, this outstanding wine offers a ripe, rich, medium- to full-bodied, and oily-textured personality stacked with loads of minerals, stones, and metals. Well balanced and crafted, it should attain its peak by 2001 and hold it through 2005. The equally impressive 1996 Chassagne-Montrachet Les Champs Gains is an earth-and-licorice-scented, expressive, intensely ripe, and highly structured wine. Dense layers of minerals, sweet pears, and toast can be discerned in its medium- to full-bodied, thick, and expressive character. Anticipated maturity: 2001–2005. Produced from a vine-yard located on the northeastern edge of the village's cemetery and immediately below Les

Vergers, Amiot's 1996 Chassagne-Montrachet Les Macherelles is crafted from 13-year-old vines. Its rich and spicy nose is followed by a complex, highly defined, silky-textured, and medium- to full-bodied personality. Delicious anise, licorice, flowers, and white peaches are found in this well-crafted but not particularly concentrated wine. Anticipated maturity: 2000–2004. The superb 1996 Chassagne-Montrachet Les Caillerets' sweet toast and gravel aromas give way to a deep, intricately laced, extracted, and powerful mouth. Layers upon layers of minerals, pears, and white peaches are imbued with grilled oak notes in this medium- to full-bodied, concentrated, and gorgeously balanced wine. Consume this gem between 2003 and 2008.

Intense richness could be discerned on Amiot's 1996 Puligny-Montrachet Les Demoiselles' tightly wound nose the day of my tasting (it was too muted to reveal specific aromas). Its full-bodied flavor profile explodes on the palate with awesome depth, power, elegance, minerals, flowers, pears, and stones. This wine's velvety-textured and perfectly balanced character lingers on the palate for at least 30 seconds. Anticipated maturity: 2003–2010. This estate's 1996 Montrachet is an extraordinary wine. Complex aromas of minerals, stones, flowers, and sweet toast are followed by a massively powerful and refined personality. Mouth coating and intense, with saturating waves of roasted peaches, anise, liquid minerals, and rocks, this is an oily-textured, broad, and elegant blockbuster of a wine! Gorgeously balanced and focused, it should age admirably well. Anticipated maturity: 2006–2015+.

DOMAINE DE L'ARLOT (PRÉMEAUX-PRISSEY)

1996 Nuits-St.-Georges	D	86
1996 Nuits-St.-Georges Clos de l'Arlot	EE	90

Consistent with most Burgundian estates, Jean-Pierre de Smet, Domaine de l'Arlot's director and winemaker, has visitors taste his whites after the reds. Produced from 4-year-old vines in the Clos de l'Arlot, the 1996 Nuits-St.-Georges (white) reveals mineral, floral, and chestnut aromas that give way to a short burst of rich and broad mineral flavors. This lively and cleanly made wine lacks the hold and follow-through required for a higher rating, but it is an attractive quaffing wine. Drink it over the next 3 years. The outstanding 1996 Nuits-St.-Georges Clos de l'Arlot (white) was aged in 20% new oak and displays an expressive nose of minerals, earth, and honeysuckle blossoms. This silky-textured, dense, mouth-coating, and medium- to full-bodied wine is packed with minerals and smokelike flavors and has traces of white and red currants. This extremely well-delineated, complex, and refined wine is significantly more than a curiosity (a white from the Côte de Nuits). Anticipated maturity: 2000–2007.

DOMAINE DU COMTE ARMAND (POMMARD)

1996 Auxey-Duresses	D	(85–88)
1995 Auxey Duresses	D	(85–87)
1996 Meursault Les Meix Chavaux	D	(88–90)
1995 Meursault Les Meix Chavaux	D	(86–88)

The Comte Armand purchased a parcel of Volnay Fremiets prior to the 1994 vintage (which was declassified and/or sold to a *négociant*) and is now renting some parcels in Auxey-Duresses and Meursault. The 1995 was Pascal Marchand's first vintage as a white wine producer. Philosophically Marchand is a noninterventionist. He does not use herbicides and rarely fines or filters (he plans on using a Kieselguhr filter on his white 1995s but will discontinue the practice in the future).

Produced from a total of 9 parcels with vines averaging 30 years of age, the 1995 Auxey-Duresses was aged in 10% new oak (Marchand says he will double the amount of new oak in future vintages) and reveals an excellent ripeness of fruit as well as minerally and spicy components aromatically. This crisp, medium-bodied wine has papaya, mango, and citrus fruit flavors in its leesy, deep, and malty character. Drink it between now and 2000. The 1995 Meursault Les Meix Chavaux (two-thirds produced from 60-year-old vines, with the balance having been planted in 1986) displays a deep floral and nut-infused nose and a medium- to full-bodied, oily-textured, hazelnut, white flower, and pear-flavored character, as well as an admirable finish. Anticipated maturity: now–2002. I was pleasantly surprised by the quality of both these wines given that they are the first whites ever produced by the domaine.

Pascal Marchand's second vintage as a white wine producer is also impressive. The 1996 Auxey-Duresses reveals minerals and tangy citrus aromas and has a medium- to full-bodied, oily-textured, and deep personality filled with smoke, nut, and toast flavors. It should be at its peak between 1999 and 2002. The superimpressive 1996 Meursault Les Meix Chavaux displays sweet, rich, and ripe white fruit aromas followed by an intense, medium- to full-bodied, and dense character. Its flavor profile is composed of nuts, anise, minerals, and honeysuckle blossoms. This wine's opulent fruit works wonder with 1996's hallmark zesty acidity.

DOMAINE D'AUVENAY (AUXEY-DURESSES)

1997	Auxey-Duresses Les Boutonniers	E	92
1996	Auxey-Duresses Les Boutonniers	E	92
1995	Auxey-Duresses Les Boutonniers	E	93
1995	Auxey-Duresses Les Clous	E	91+
1996	Bourgogne Aligoté Sous Chatelet	D	89
1997	Chevalier-Montrachet	EEE	96
1996	Chevalier-Montrachet	EEE	98
1997	Criots-Bâtard-Montrachet	EEE	93?
1996	Criots-Bâtard-Montrachet	EEE	96
1997	Meursault Goutte d'Or	EEE	93
1996	Meursault Goutte d'Or	EEE	94
1997	Meursault Narvaux	EE	92+
1996	Meursault Narvaux	EE	96+
1995	Meursault Narvaux	EE	94
1997	Puligny-Montrachet Les Folatières	EEE	91
1996	Puligny-Montrachet Les Folatières	EEE	95
1995	Puligny-Montrachet Les Folatières	EEE	94

Note: Lalou Bize-Leroy is the sole proprietor of Domaine d'Auvenay, in contrast with Maison Leroy (the Leroy *négociant* arm) and Domaine Leroy, which is owned by a consortium that includes Mme. Leroy and Japanese investors. Readers should note that retailers commonly list Domaine d'Auvenay, Domaine Leroy, and Maison Leroy wines simply under the Leroy name. This has been a cause for confusion, as Maison Leroy has sold wine from the same appellations as some held by Domaine d'Auvenay.

The style of these wines resembles those made at the Domaine Leroy, as the same methods, both in biodynamic viticulture and in winemaking, are employed. Moreover, Leroy's yields are just as amazingly low. Leroy's many critics suggest that her yields sound lower than they actually are, as up to one-third of the vines are either missing or nonproducing. As their argument goes, yields based on the amount produced from a given area will appear exceedingly low, while the per vine yields are actually much higher. Yet consider the following: If readers take Leroy's stated fruit per acre yields and add 33% to make up for the supposed lack of productive vines in the vineyards, she still has the lowest yields in Burgundy! Furthermore, the argument that per-vine yields should be used at Domaine Leroy may have some merit, as vines are in fact missing there, but at Domaine d'Auvenay the vineyards are fully planted (with the exception of a few missing vines in Mazis-Chambertin) and her 1995 yields are stunningly low: on average little more than half a ton of fruit per acre for the whites and 1 ton of fruit per acre on very densely planted vines for the reds.

A light gold hue in the robe of the 1995 Auxey-Duresses Les Clous makes me question this wine's long-term aging ability, but the extremely complex floral and spicy nose and the delicious ensuing flavors make this an outstanding wine. Full bodied, with a thick oily texture and a mouth filled with deep minerals (iron) and spicy oak, this long-finishing wine should be consumed over the next 5 years. From vines planted in 1924, the 1995 Auxey-Duresses Les Boutonniers has superconcentrated aromas of minerals and anise. The mouth is incredibly deep and complex, with silky rolling fruits filled with minerals. This long and full-bodied wine is as intense a white Auxey-Duresses as I could imagine; it should be drunk between 2000 and 2008. The attention-getting 1995 Meursault Narvaux has an awesome sweet and spicy component on the nose and an incredibly viscous and oily-textured mouth. Powerful flowers and nuts float through the taster's mouth with flavors that easily last 30 seconds. Drink it between 2002 and 2010. Equally great, and with an intense nose of bakery spices and floral notes reminiscent of a spring meadow, the 1995 Puligny-Montrachet Les Folatières has the same oily texture as the Meursault Narvaux. This wine has a very floral, medium- to full-bodied mouth and great length; it should be at its peak between 2002 and 2012.

If I were still in college, I would visit my professor of ethics to debate the wisdom of spending hundreds of dollars for a bottle of wine that may not be at its peak for 15 years after the vintage. My sense is that after an hour or so of spirited discussion we would come to the banal conclusion that rather than taste, discipline, and passion, one's discretionary income was the critical factor. These wines are astronomically expensive and will require considerable age before attaining their respective peaks. Ideally, enormously wealthy wine lovers will acquire them for their children to enjoy. (Mme. Bize-Leroy boldly said, "I fully expect my white 1996s to remain youthful for 50 years.")

I mentioned to Mme. Leroy how depressed I would be if one of my few d'Auvenay and Domaine Leroy bottles were to be corked. She commiserated with me and said that she has taken every precaution possible in this regard. As with many of the top producers in the world, Leroy purchases the longest and finest-quality corks available. None of her corks are exposed to chlorine baths or are bleached or waxed. She claims to take an additional step, paying her cork producer for an extra employee to go through the corks one at a time, sorting out any potentially marred ones (however, this should have little effect on "corked" corks, as the responsible bacteria are invisible). According to her, she "has never had a corked wine from Domaine d'Auvenay and only two over the years from Domaine Leroy." Robert Parker claims to have experienced a disproportionate number of corked 1985 Leroys, including two bottles of the legendary 1985 Mazis Chambertin Cuvée Madeleine Collignon (Hospices de Beaune).

Whereas other producers covered me with explanations as to why high yields were acceptable in 1996, Lalou Bize-Leroy averaged a ton of fruit per acre on her whites, less than one-third the yields she could have taken. A self-proclaimed noninterventionist, she told me that "all the oenologists told me to deacidify my wines in 1996. To me it is a crime, akin to deboning a man. Wine is life." Leroy, who says she always harvests late in order to gain additional ripeness, chaptalized only one of her 1996s, the Chevalier-Montrachet (2 kilograms—almost 4$\frac{1}{2}$ pounds—of sugar per barrel). None of these offerings were fined or filtered. Consequently they are already throwing a deposit.

The most "reasonably" priced of these wines is the 1996 Bourgogne Aligoté Sous Chatelet. Produced from vines located on the steep hill behind the estate, it has a magnificently expressive nose of butterscotch, anise, candied white fruits, and spices. On the palate, it is medium bodied, silky, and loaded with orange rinds, red currants, baking spices, minerals, and smokelike flavors. This is the only one of Lalou Bize-Leroy's whites that will reach its peak in this millenium. Anticipated maturity: now–2003. The 1996 Auxey-Duresses Les Boutonniers has a smoky and oak spice-imbued nose that gives way to an explosion of intense and bracing minerals, gravel, white grapes, sweet berries, and stones on the palate. This medium- to full-bodied, velvety-textured, and admirably balanced wine is hugely concentrated and unbelievably long on the finish. It should hit its peak around 2004 and last at least until 2010.

Domaine d'Auvenay's 1996 Meursault Narvaux is a masterpiece. Extraordinarily complex aromas of freshly cut flowers, hazelnuts, and minerals are followed by a thick, full-bodied, profound, hyperconcentrated personality. Layer upon layer of highly extracted white peaches, poached and spiced pears, anise, and liquid minerals coat the palate in this magnificently balanced and focused wine. This offering's mind-blowing finish is at least a minute long. Its massive ripeness and powerful, expressive flavors are married with bright and lively acidity, rendering this a wine that will easily age for decades given proper storage. Anticipated maturity: 2006–2020+. The 1996 Puligny-Montrachet Les Folatières possesses a floral and mineral-laden nose as well as a highly refined, feminine, superbly focused, oily-textured, medium to full body. This pure, muscular, and expansive wine is packed with flavors reminiscent of fresh hazelnut butter, white flowers, anise, and candied pears. It is a concentrated, elegant, and extremely persistent wine that expresses both power and lacelike delicacy. It should be at its best between 2005 and 2015+. Revealing grilled nut, minerals, and lemon drops on the nose, the 1996 Meursault Goutte d'Or explodes on the palate with massive waves of flower blossoms, ripe white peaches, metals, and poached pears. This beautifully refined and extraordinarily delineated wine has great depth, a full body, and a silky texture. As with all of Lalou Bize-Leroy's 1996 white burgundy offerings, the Goutte d'Or is intensely concentrated and powerful. Anticipated maturity: 2005–2014.

An amazingly complex and profound minerality is evident on the nose of the 1996 Criots-Bâtard-Montrachet. Its character is tightly wound, defined, medium to full bodied, and racy. Stones, gravel, metals, and white flowers are found in this vibrant, yet dense and oily-textured wine. Its awesomely long finish holds the palate captive for at least 45 seconds, revealing precise mineral and chalk flavors. It will be at its peak between 2007 and 2018. The 1996 Chevalier-Montrachet from Domaine d'Auvenay is mind-boggling. Fresh, lively, and perfumed aromas of minerals, spicy oak, and touches of candied orange rinds give way to a velvety, full-bodied, massively ripe, and hugely concentrated personality. This wine's purity, precision, delineation, and focus render its citrus fruit-infused minerality almost lacelike. At present a touch austere, it possesses unbridled power, intensity, and concentration of fruit. It should hit its stride around 2010 and last until well past 2020.

A number of subscribers and retailers contacted me to voice their displeasure concerning the fact that there were two 1996 Meursault Narvaux produced by Mme. Bize-Leroy. The problem stems from the existence of a 1996 Meursault Narvaux from Maison Leroy (I purchased this wine and rated it an 88) and 1996 Meursault Narvaux from Domaine d'Auvenay (rated a 96+). Consumers, retailers, importers, and gray marketers who persist in calling any wine "Leroy," whether it is from Domaine d'Auvenay (owned privately by her and an estate), Domaine Leroy (owned by a consortium and an estate), or Maison Leroy (a *négociant* firm that typically purchases wines and resells them with the firm's label), are exacerbating an already confusing situation. When I asked Mme. Bize to clarify the situation, she stated that she was furious at "greedy" gray marketers and retailers for creating this confusion. She also assured me that from now on there would no longer be any wines sold with the same vineyard sites on the labels from the three wineries she controls.

Mme. Lalou Bize-Leroy loves the 1997 vintage for both red and white wines. "These are distinguished and intellectual wines," she insisted. In fact, she feels her reds are more complex than her 1996s. While I disagree with her assessment of the 1997 vintage, particularly considering the hundreds of wines I tasted at her colleagues' estates, there is no doubting that Mme. Bize has done it yet again. These are magnificent wines, impeccably balanced (she ferociously maintains that she does not acidify her wines—rumors to the contrary are omnipresent), and immensely rich. Their colors reflect traces of straw and gold, unlike the pale, virtually crystal-clear 1996s.

Produced from a parcel planted in 1922, the powerful 1997 Auxey-Duresses Les Boutonniers has a chalk and rock dust-scented nose. Its explodes on the palate with intense liquid mineral flavors intermingled with juicy squirts of lemon juice. This medium- to full-bodied, dense, and magnificently defined wine has huge concentration, depth, and complexity. Drink it between 2001 and 2008. The 1997 Meursault Narvaux displays an oak-imbued and rich white fruit-laden nose. This massive, thick, chewy, and medium- to full-bodied offering is crammed with expansive metal, mineral, and hazelnut flavors. When I asked Mme. Bize how she had been able to obtain this level of unbelievable ripeness and superb balance, she said, "There are no secrets: yields and respecting the vine as well as nature." This beauty should be at its peak between 2001 and 2008. Revealing fresh aromas of superripe fruits, the 1997 Meursault Goutte d'Or is oily textured and exuberant yet focused. This powerful, muscular, and full-bodied wine coats the palate with sweet pears, caramelized apples, candied oranges, minerals, hazelnut cream, and hints of quince. Anticipated maturity: 2002–2008. The 1997 Puligny-Montrachet Les Folatières' nose is less boisterous than those of the previous wines. It expresses sweet floral and earthy aromas, followed by a fat, almost unctuously textured personality. This superb wine is redolent with layers of earth, acacia blossom, white truffles, and peaches. It does not appear to be as extraordinarily well balanced as her other offerings. It should be consumed between 2000 and 2005.

Mme. Bize-Leroy's 1997 Criots-Bâtard-Montrachet, produced from a parcel on the vineyard's eastern extremity, has baked pear and apple aromas intermingled with spices. This is a profound, well-focused, and deeply ripe wine with flavors of marzipan, minerals, peanuts, and white flowers. It is medium to full bodied, forward, and superexpressive yet possibly reveals faint traces of oxidation. Nonetheless, it is so extraordinarily flavorful and muscular that I highly recommend it. Try it in 2002 to see how it is evolving. The 1997 Chevalier-Montrachet is certainly one of the stars of the vintage. Aromatically, it reveals rocks, stones, and salty seashells. This magnificent masterpiece has a personality of unheard-of intensity, ripeness, and focus. Its overpowering minerality is gorgeously precise, revealing traces of anise, pears, and oak spices that last throughout the stupendous finish. Drink it between 2004 and 2012.

Other recently tasted wines: 1997 Auxey Duresses (91), 1997 Auxey-Duresses Les Clous (91), 1997 Bourgogne Aligoté Sous Chatelet (88).

DOMAINE BACHELET-RAMONET (CHASSAGNE-MONTRACHET)

1996 Bâtard-Montrachet	EE	(90–92+)
1995 Bâtard-Montrachet	EE	(88–90?)
1995 Bienvenue-Bâtard-Montrachet	E	(88–90)

1995	Chassagne-Montrachet	D	(84–86)
1996	Chassagne-Montrachet Les Caillerets	D	(87–90)
1995	Chassagne-Montrachet Les Caillerets	E	(86–88)
1996	Chassagne-Montrachet La Grande Montagne	D	(88–91)
1995	Chassagne-Montrachet La Grande Montagne	D	(87–89)
1996	Chassagne-Montrachet Les Grandes Ruchottes	D	(89–92)
1995	Chassagne-Montrachet Les Grandes Ruchottes	E	(87–89?)
1995	Chassagne-Montrachet Morgeot	D	(86–88)
1996	Chassagne-Montrachet La Romanée	D	(88–91)
1995	Chassagne-Montrachet La Romanée	E	(88–90)

Note: Unlike many of the wines represented by Patrick Lesec, there are no separate "Patrick Lesec Selection" cuvées at this estate. Also, I was unable to taste this estate's 1996 Bienvenue-Bâtard-Montrachet, often one of its better wines.

Alain Bonnefoy, the winemaker at Domaine Bachelet-Ramonet, committed himself to bottling his 1995s without filtration. As my scores indicate, some of these wines fall just short of being outstanding. There is reason to believe, however, that I may be extolling the virtues of these wines in the near future. Why? The domaine is working closely with Patrick Lesec, a Paris-based wine broker who prods those estates he represents to adopt noninterventionist winemaking, lower yields, and later harvests.

Displaying minerally, flinty, and stony aromas, the 1995 Chassagne-Montrachet has deep sweetness of fruit in the mouth and a slightly tangy finish. This nice, medium-bodied wine should be drunk upon release. Better yet, the medium-bodied 1995 Chassagne-Montrachet Les Caillerets reveals attractive sweet minerals and stone on the nose and flavors of ripe, salty, and smoky fruits. Drink it between now and 2002. Equally good, the 1995 Chassagne-Montrachet Morgeot exhibits aromas of sweet pink grapefruits that get carried over to the light- to medium-bodied mouth. On the back end a nutty and tangy minerality becomes apparent. It should be drunk within 3–4 years of release. The 1995 Chassagne-Montrachet La Grande Montagne displays stones and minerals in the nose and a rather angular and sharp mouth filled with steely citrus fruit. This medium-bodied wine needs 2–4 years of cellaring and will drink well for 4–5 years after that. A touch better, the 1995 Chassagne-Montrachet La Romanée has a beautiful floral nose. With candied and spicy red berry fruit flavors and a nice minerality, this medium-bodied wine will drink well between now and 2004. Revealing a slight offputting stinkiness in the nose that should blow off before bottling, the 1995 Chassagne-Montrachet Les Grandes Ruchottes has delicious floral and minerally flavors coupled with good structure. This medium-bodied wine should be drunk between now and 2003. Potentially Bachelet-Ramonet's best 1995, the Bienvenue-Bâtard-Montrachet displays a sweet, spicy nose and flavors of anise and other spices in a sweet, medium-bodied wine. This well-structured wine will age gracefully for up to 10 years. With a completely muted nose and a fabulous entry and midpalate, the 1995 Bâtard-Montrachet is an extremely hard wine to evaluate because of its back end: after a burst of buttered and roasted fruits with notes of candied berries, the wine drops off and leaves a bitterness in the mouth. Will this be resolved before bottling?

Surprisingly, Alain Bonnefoy, who was moving toward noninterventionist winemaking in 1997, decided in 1998 that he would subject his 1996s to fining and filtering. The purity of this vintage's wines would lead me to ponder about why such "corrective" or "purifying" measures would be necessary.

This being said, the 1996s are the finest wines I have tasted from Domaine Bachelet-Ramonet. There is a richness and density of fruit in these offerings that I have not previously experienced from this estate. If Bonnefoy continues to progress in his winemaking as he has over the last 2 or 3 years, Chassagne's small group of stars will have to make room for another member.

Aromatically, the 1996 Chassagne-Montrachet La Grande Montagne has rich, deep mineral scents. On the palate, its medium- to full-bodied and oily-textured character is packed with liquid minerals, anise, spices, and ripe pears. This concentrated, highly expressive, and broad wine should age quite well. Anticipated maturity: 2000–2006. The 1996 Chassagne-Montrachet Les Caillerets possesses an extremely refined, mineral-laden nose. This wine is medium to full bodied, velvety textured, bright, and extremely rich. Layers of stones and gravel covered in honey can be found in this vibrant wine's core, as well as in its long, persistent finish. It should be at its best between 2000 and 2007. Exhibiting floral and red berry aromas, the 1996 Chassagne-Montrachet Les Grandes Ruchottes is a wide, dense, mouth-coating, medium- to full-bodied, and thickly textured offering. Seductive flavors of poached pears, perfume, tangy peaches, stones, and minerals can all be found in this well-made, exciting, and delicious wine. Anticipated maturity: 2000–2006. The 1996 Chassagne-Montrachet La Romanée has an extremely spicy, smoky, floral, and elegant nose. On the palate, this medium-bodied, refined, and silky-textured wine has minerals, oak, spices, and honeysuckle flavors. It should be at its peak between 2000 and 2005.

The 1996 Bâtard-Montrachet reveals a powerfully rich, spicy, and floral nose followed by a deep, dense, mouth-coating, medium- to full-bodied, and velvety-textured personality. Candied peaches, poached and spiced pears, liquid minerals, and honeysuckle blossoms are found in this well-crafted and complex wine. Its long finish dissipates with notes of grilled oak. Anticipated maturity: 2002–2008.

DOMAINE BARAT (CHABLIS)

1996 Chablis	B	88
1996 Chablis Côte de Lechet	C	90
1996 Chablis Vaillons	C	91

Barat's delicious Chablis reveals lively and pure flint aromas and possesses a medium-bodied, silky, yet tightly wound and crisp personality with citrus and metallic flavors. Drink it between now and 2001. The 1996 Chablis Côte de Lechet, from what is obviously an excellent *terroir*, is an outstanding wine. Aromatically revealing tightly wound fruit, this offering displays loads of flint, stones, minerals, and lively citrus fruits in its crisp, medium- to full-bodied core. Anticipated maturity: now–2005. Even better, the Chablis Vaillons exhibits stony, crispy, flinty aromas and a well-focused, medium- to full-bodied personality with steel, metallic, floral, lemon, and chalk flavors. It should be at its best after 3–4 years of cellaring and will maintain its peak well past 2005.

DOMAINE DANIEL BARRAUD (VERGISSON)

1997 Mâcon-Vergisson La Roche Réserve	C	87
1996 Mâcon-Vergisson La Roche Réserve	C	88
1995 Mâcon-Vergisson La Roche Réserve	C	88+
1997 Pouilly-Fuissé En Bulands Vieilles Vignes Réserve	D	94+
1996 Pouilly-Fuissé En Bulands Vieilles Vignes Réserve	D	92+
1995 Pouilly-Fuissé En Bulands Vieilles Vignes Réserve	D	91
1997 Pouilly-Fuissé Les Crays Vieilles Vignes Réserve	D	94

1996 Pouilly-Fuissé Les Crays Vieilles Vignes Réserve	D	92
1997 Pouilly-Fuissé La Roche	D	91+
1996 Pouilly-Fuissé La Roche	D	91
1997 Pouilly-Fuissé La Verchère Vieilles Vignes Réserve	D	91
1996 Pouilly-Fuissé La Verchère Vieilles Vignes Réserve	D	91
1995 Pouilly-Fuissé La Verchère Vieilles Vignes Réserve	D	90+
1997 Pouilly-Fuissé Cuvée Vieilles Vignes	D	90
1996 Pouilly-Fuissé Cuvée Vieilles Vignes	D	92
1997 St. Véran En Crèches	D	89+
1996 St. Véran En Crèches	C	88
1997 St. Véran Les Pommards Réserve	D	91
1996 St. Véran Les Pommards Réserve	C	90

Daniel Barraud can step out of his home each day, look at the neighboring hill, and see the residence of his good friend and fellow winemaking genius: Jean-Marie Guffens. Both these men—with the crucial assistance of their wives—are crafting superlative wines that equal or surpass the finest offerings of the Côte de Beaune's grand cru vineyards.

After harvesting extremely ripe grapes, Daniel Barraud neither fines nor filters his wines and leaves them on their lees for 15 months. They are full-flavored blockbusters and will be considered steals when their prices are compared with those of other white burgundies.

With a nose reminiscent of Puligny-Montrachet because of its roasted fruits, the 1995 Mâcon-Vergisson La Roche Réserve is an excellent example of the heights this unheralded region can attain. It exhibits a toasty, buttery mouth filled with minerals, stones, and candied fruits. This medium- to full-bodied wine finishes with an attractive lemony tang and should be drunk young. The 1995 Pouilly-Fuissé La Verchère Vieilles Vignes Réserve exhibits a steely, lemony nose, a very good, thick texture, and great flavors of powerful and very ripe candied fruits. This medium- to full-bodied gem is quite long and finishes on notes of buttered toast. Drink it between now and 2003. The estate's top wine is the rarest, as only 50 cases were produced. Made from 60–70-year-old vines, the 1995 Pouilly-Fuissé En Bulands Vieilles Vignes Réserve displays an enticing *sur-maturité* (overripeness) in the nose and an intense and complex mouth of lemons, minerals, flint, and toasty roasted fruit. A thick-textured wine, this beauty has excellent length and should be drunk between its release and 2005.

Daniel Barraud, a hardworking, intelligent, and dedicated man, is one of the Mâconnais's finest producers. He believes that his 1996s are "more powerful, both in acidity and in ripeness" than his 1995s and are "magnificently precise and clean." I was blown away by Barraud's 1995s, finding both his En Buland and La Verchère to be outstanding, but his 1996s are even better. Moreover, these wines are excellent values.

Barraud is not a believer in *bâtonnage;* his wines obtain their richness from late harvests and extended lees contact in barrel (as opposed to the traditional Mâconnais vats). He neither fines nor filters his offerings.

The 1996 Mâcon-Vergisson La Roche was aged in one-third new oak and two-thirds 3-year-old oak barrels. It reveals crisp mineral and stone aromas and has a beautifully concentrated, medium-bodied, and racy character packed with fresh and lively citrus fruits. This excellent wine will be at its peak between now and 2002. Equally delicious, the 1996 St. Véran En Crèches displays floral and smoke scents as well as a balanced and medium- to full-bodied core of rich, complex, and precise flavors of minerals, metals, and flowers. Anticipated maturity: now–2002. I tasted the 1996 St. Véran Les Pommards in November of 1997, 2 weeks after its bottling. Produced from a vineyard that borders the Pouilly-Fuissé appellation, this wine exhibits fabulous toasty oak and mineral aromas. On the palate, this silky-textured, medium- to full-bodied, highly defined, and deeply extracted offering regales with loads of citrus fruits, stones, and fresh herbs and spices. Its powerful flavors linger on the palate for at least 25 seconds. Anticipated maturity: now–2003+.

Crafted from vines ranging from 45 to 60 years old, the 1996 Pouilly-Fuissé La Verchère Vieilles Vignes Réserve displays smoky mineral aromas and an impressive, medium- to full-bodied, and complex personality. Superbly balanced and precise, this broad and velvety-textured wine is packed with stones, red currants, and flowers. Spicy oak notes can be discerned in its admirable finish. It should be at its best between now and 2004. The outstanding 1996 Pouilly-Fuissé En Buland Vieilles Vignes Réserve (only 50 cases produced) has toasted oak touches intermingled with strong mineral aromas. This wine explodes on the palate with incredibly concentrated and awesomely precise flavors of smoke, minerals, and currants. It is a highly expressive, medium- to full-bodied, oily-textured, and profound wine. Anticipated maturity: 1999–2004+. Exhibiting gravel, ripe white fruit, spice, and smoke scents, the 1996 Pouilly-Fuissé Les Crays Vieilles Vignes Réserve is a more austere but no less outstanding wine than the En Buland. Its thickly textured character coats the palate with minerals, chalk, stone, and tangy citrus flavors. This massively expansive, focused, and full-bodied gem also possesses an incredibly long and pure finish. Anticipated maturity: 2001–2006. The 1996 Pouilly-Fuissé La Roche reveals racy mineral and stone aromas and a broad, rich, and expressive medium- to full-bodied character. This steely, crisp, and lively wine offers powerful stone and mineral flavors. It should be at its best between now and 2003. Produced from old vines located in various vineyards (including En Buland and Les Crays), the 1996 Pouilly-Fuissé Cuvée Vieilles Vignes is a flint and smoke-scented beauty. Creamy textured and medium to full bodied, this delicious offering has citrus fruits, minerals, stones, and chalk in its concentrated and intense flavor profile. I would suggest drinking it between now and 2004. Bravo!

Barraud feels 1997 was his greatest harvest. The huge heat of August actually slowed maturation as the vines shut down in self-defense. Malic acid levels dropped, yet overall acidity levels were maintained. "Certain wines actually have the same acidity levels as the 1996s," said Barraud. He stretched the harvest for almost 3 weeks, starting on September 12 and ending on September 30. "The heat was intense, but we were not worried because we studied the parcels. We took our time, and I believe we harvested each parcel at the optimal moment. It was a wonderful Indian summer!"

The 1997 Mâcon-Vergisson La Roche Réserve has earth and mineral aromas that lead to its medium-bodied, pear, butter, anise, and sweet apple-flavored core. This delicious wine would have merited a higher rating if its finish had been less angular. Drink it over the next 3–4 years. The 1997 St. Véran En Crêches is aromatically reminiscent of buttered lobster and minerals. This rich, creamy, and medium- to full-bodied wine is loaded with mouthwatering white flowers, spices, rocks, apples, minerals, and white currants. Its complex and harmonious personality is such a delight, I was tempted to swallow. Drink this beauty over the next 4–5 years. I loved the 1997 Pouilly-Fuissé La Roche. It reveals stone, quinine, flint, and toasted oak aromas. On the palate, this medium- to full-bodied, oily-textured, impeccably focused, and hugely expressive wine is filled with crisp peach, pear, and liquid mineral flavors. This boldly ripe yet superbly balanced wine has the capacity to age marvelously. Anticipated maturity: 2000–2007. Produced from 45–65-year-old vines located in the En Bulands, Les Crays, and Les Vignes Dessus vineyards, the 1997 Pouilly-Fuissé Cuvée Vieilles Vignes has a creamy, salty nose and an intensely ripe, concentrated, candied lemon, and chalk-flavored character. This medium- to full-bodied wine was aged in 50%–60% new oak barrels, yet the wood is barely noticeable. Anticipated maturity: now–2005. The 1997 St.

Véran Les Pommards Réserve is certainly one of the finest wines I have tasted from this picturesque village. Its fresh nose of minerals and earth leads to an awesomely ripe character replete with peaches, pears, quince, and stones. This medium- to full-bodied offering's opulently thick texture and *sur-maturité* flavors do not prevent this wine from being bone dry, as evidenced by the long and mineral-laden finish. It should be at its peak between 2000 and 2006. Displaying aromas reminiscent of buttered toast, smoke, and chalk, the 1997 Pouilly-Fuissé La Verchère Vieilles Vignes Réserve is an elegant, precise, yet dense wine. It is velvety textured and medium to full bodied, with a concentrated core of white fruits and flint. Offering admirable balance, purity, and structure, it doesn't possess the previous wine's density or power but, rather, has refinement and crystalline flavors. Anticipated maturity: 2000–2006.

To reiterate, Pouilly-Fuissé enjoyed a tremendous 1997. Daniel Barraud, Cordier, Guffens-Heynen, and others crafted benchmark-setting wines that equal or surpass the extraordinary ones they produced in 1996. The 1997 Pouilly-Fuissé Les Crays Vieilles Vignes Réserve, crafted from a vineyard with a southern exposure, has a pineapple, mango, kumquat, and candied orange rind-infused nose. This immensely powerful yet impeccably balanced wine is full bodied, oily textured, and exceedingly expressive. While its 1996 counterpart was somewhat austere, this expansive offering saturates the palate with white peaches, spiced pears, red and white currants, stones, and an almost overpowering minerality that lingers in its stunningly long finish. Anticipated maturity: 2000–2007. The equally stellar (and potentially better) 1997 Pouilly-Fuissé En Bulands Vieilles Vignes Réserve has a more restrained yet no less beguiling nose. It reveals pure aromas of chalk, smoky flint, fruit pits, and rock dust followed by a superconcentrated and tightly wound personality. This velvety-textured, vibrant wine is crammed with mouth-coating layers of liquid minerals, melted stones, and earth. While the Les Crays conquered with fruit, the En Bulands does so with flavors of the earth and rocks. It is impeccably well made and mind-numbingly precise and possesses an amazingly long (40 seconds!) finish. I would not be surprised to see this wine gain more complexity. Anticipated maturity: 2002–2009. Bravo!

DOMAINE JEAN-CLAUDE BELLAND (SANTENAY)

1996 Corton-Charlemagne	E	(90–92+)
1996 Puligny-Montrachet La Rue aux Vaches	D	(85–88)

Note: This estate was formerly called Domaine Adrien Belland.

Produced from 50-year-old vines, the Puligny-Montrachet La Rue aux Vaches ("the cows' road" in French) reveals minerals and earth on the nose and an attractive, medium-boded, and beautifully ripe character. Flowers, anise, and stones can be discerned in this classy, refined, and admirably persistent wine. It should be at its best between now and 2002. Displaying deep richness in its white flower and buttered toast-scented nose, the Corton-Charlemagne is an outstanding, silky, medium- to full-bodied, and complex wine. It possesses tangy white peach, chalk, pear, red currant, and toasted oak flavors in its gorgeously balanced, elegant, feminine, and long personality. I have no doubt that this wine will age effortlessly, taking on additional complexity with time. Anticipated maturity: 2002–2010.

DOMAINE BERTAGNA (VOUGEOT)

1996 Vougeot Blanc Premier Cru	E	(87–88)
1995 Vougeot Blanc Premier Cru	E	89

The 1996 Vougeot Blank Premier Cru offers a rich nose of minerals and smoky oak that gives way to an oily-textured, concentrated, and plump character with almond and toasted hazelnut flavors. It lacks the vintage's brightness and focus (where's the acidity?) but is balanced and well crafted. Drink it between now and 2003.

The 1995 Vougeot Blanc Premier Cru was even better than I remembered it (originally rated an 88). Its rich, mineral, earth, gravel, and almond aromas are followed by an oily-textured, concentrated, and medium- to full-bodied wine filled with stones, flowers, and ripe white fruits. Over the course of the past year it appears to have gained in power and density, as have many other 1995 whites. Anticipated maturity: now–2006.

DOMAINE VINCENT BITOUZET-PRIEUR (VOLNAY)

1996 Meursault	D	87
1996 Meursault Charmes	D	(90–92)
1995 Meursault Charmes	E	(88–90)
1996 Meursault Clos du Cromin	D	(87–89)
1995 Meursault Clos du Cromin	D	(86–89)
1996 Meursault Les Corbins	D	88+
1995 Meursault Corbins	D	(86–89)
1996 Meursault Perrières	D	(91–93)
1995 Meursault Perrières	E	(90–93)
1996 Meursault Santenots	D	(88–91)
1995 Meursault Santenots	D	(87–89+)

Note: The 1995 wines were all tasted prior to being fined.

Vincent Bitouzet is one of those rare winemakers in Burgundy who makes both red and white wines equally well (Dominique Lafon, Lalou Bize-Leroy, Jacques Lardière of Jadot, and Vincent Girardin also come to mind). His whites are all fermented in wood and tend to be leesy and buttery, not sharply defined but fat and luscious. All the white wines have been produced from vineyards added to the domaine through his marriage to a daughter from the Prieur family. Interestingly, Bitouzet still considers himself a red wine producer who dabbles in whites. He believes his whites are long-term wines; however, I am not convinced of this (except for the Perrières). Time will tell.

The 1995 Meursault Corbins, like the Santenots and the Clos du Cromin, is from a vine-yard on the Volnay side of Meursault. It shows deep minerality in the nose and mouth, has good length, and exhibits Bitouzet's trademark leesy touch. Drink it between now and 2001. More buttery and citrusy, the 1995 Meursault Clos du Cromin also has a mineral aspect to the nose and is well balanced. An excellent wine with the potential to be outstanding, the 1995 Meursault Santenots has an earthy, buttery nose, a fat, oily-textured mouth, and flavors of spiced apples, cassis, and red currants. Its structure should allow it to age gracefully for 6 or so years. The 1995 Meursault Charmes is quite fat, round, and leesy yet has an innate el-egance. Flavors of stones and minerals are present, with a touch of freshly cut flowers. The real winner is the fabulous 1995 Meursault Perrières. It offers an excellent nose of stony hazelnuts, a leesy, buttery palate, admirable structure, and a distinctly steely aspect to its long finish.

Vincent Bitouzet has produced wonderful 1996s. Whereas his white 1995s were luscious and opulent (ideal for near-term drinking), Bitouzet crafted refined and elegant 1996s built for the long haul.

The 1996 Meursault offers fresh hazelnut aromas (reminiscent of when I would eat them right off the tree at my grandmother's home), as well as a medium-bodied, well-focused, structured, and austere character packed with roasted nuts. Drink it between now and 2002.

Revealing toasted almonds and white flower aromatics, the 1996 Meursault Les Corbins is a seductive, dense, silky, and medium-bodied wine. While not particularly complex, this truly delicious wine's supple candied almond, mineral, earth, buttered toast, and lemon zestlike flavors are enthralling. With time it may merit a higher score. Anticipated maturity: now–2004.

Displaying rich aromas of marzipan, the 1996 Meursault Clos du Cromin has a well-delineated, focused, and gorgeously balanced personality filled with minerals and rock dust. This medium-bodied and elegant wine should be at its peak between now and 2004. The 1996 Meursault Santenots, aged in 25% new oak, is a first-rate wine. Pear, white flower, and mineral scents are followed by a juicy, refined, medium- to full-bodied, and silky-textured flavor profile packed with concentrated red currants, orange rinds, and toasty wood. Anticipated maturity: 2000–2005.

Bitouzet has two parcels of Meursault Charmes, one in the lower half of the vineyard (du bas), with very old vines; and the other in the upper half (du haut), where the vines are 10 years old. The Burgundian cognoscenti generally believe that the better terroir is the Charmes du haut (also known as du dessus), which appeared to coincide with my tasting of the component parts. Whereas the wine from older du bas vines seemed to have additional concentration, the du haut wine was rounder, more refined, and more persistent. The final blend is an outstanding wine, revealing orange rinds and almonds on the nose and a beautifully extracted, medium- to full-bodied, and silky-textured character filled with candied red currants, flowers, minerals, and traces of vanilla. This elegant, well-crafted, and wonderfully long wine should be at its peak between 2002 and 2007. Potentially even better, the 1995 Meursault Perrières reveals aromas of minerals and stones as well as a magnificently defined and focused core of gravel, spices, pears, and loads of minerals. This refined and elegant wine's precision, purity, and delineation are something to behold. It is medium to full bodied, lively, and silky textured and possesses a persistent finish that seems to go on forever.

DOMAINE SIMON BIZE (SAVIGNY-LÈS-BEAUNE)

1996 Bourgogne Blanc Les Champlains Pinot Beurot	C	87
1996 Savigny-Lès-Beaune	D	(85–87)

Patrick Bize, with his chiseled good looks (he appears to be 30 but is actually 46), lean, athletic frame, dark hair, cigarette, and quiet, measured speech, resembles a romantic French movie star more than he does a vigneron. After 3 years in the navy, he returned home for a 3-week visit in 1972 to see his father, who was ill, and to help with the vinification. He stayed, and by 1977 he had taken over the operations of this old 55-acre estate.

While this estate's focus is on its red wine production, it does produce some interesting whites, in particular a rare Pinot Beurot (in Alsace this varietal is called Pinot Gris). Also, I tasted a 1997 Corton-Charlemagne that promises to be quite good. Patrick Bize's close friend Jean-Marie Raveneau (of Chablis fame) regularly assists Bize with his white wine-making.

The 1996 Savigny-Lès-Beaune has earth, gravel, and flowers on the nose as well as a lively, tangy, and floral, medium-bodied, and racy character. It is a refreshing, delicious, and thirst-quenching wine to drink over the next 2 or 3 years. The 1996 Bourgogne Blanc Les Champlains Pinot Beurot has intense smoke aromas and a medium-bodied, vibrant, spice-and-mineral-packed personality. Anticipated maturity: now–2003. (Bize served me a 1991 Pinot Beurot from Raveneau "private stash" that was truly excellent, revealing fat, rich sweet anise, spices, and smoky flavors.)

DOMAINE ETIENNE BOILEAU/DOMAINE DU CHARDONNAY (CHABLIS)

1996 Chablis	C	86
1996 Chablis Montmains	C	89

1996 Chablis Vaillons	C	91
1996 Chablis Vaugiraut	C	89
1996 Chablis Vieilles Vignes	C	88

Note: With the exception of the American market, this estate is known as Domaine du Chardonnay. The wines remain the same, only the estate name is different.

The 1996 Chablis reveals stone and lime aromatics and possesses a medium-bodied, vibrant character with flint, citrus, and liquid mineral flavors. This refreshing and crisp wine should be consumed over the next 3 years. Exhibiting aromas of toasty oak, the 100% barrel-fermented 1996 Chablis Vieilles Vignes is a concentrated, rich, medium- to full-bodied, silky, and fruit-driven wine. Oak-infused flint and minerals can be found in its complex flavor profile. Anticipated maturity: now–2003. The 1996 Chablis Vaugiraut displays crisp citrus fruits, white flowers, and minerals on the nose as well as a beautifully ripe, concentrated, and extracted character. It has a medium body, a steely texture, and loads of flinty and citrusy flavors that linger in its long finish. Anticipated maturity: 2000–2004.

Revealing a floral, iron, and steel-scented nose, the 1996 Chablis Montmains is a strident, highly focused, beautifully extracted, well-crafted, and medium-bodied wine. Its flavor profile is filled with minerals, gravel, traces of earth, and juicy citrus fruits. It should be at its peak between 2000 and 2004. Produced from 55-year-old vines, the 1996 Chablis Vaillons is an outstanding wine. Hints of minerals, limes, and lemon zests can be discerned in its tight aromatics. This offering's medium- to full-bodied, racy, and refined core is packed with seashells, salt, flint, a deep minerality, and succulent layers of candied lemons. It is an elegant yet powerful, concentrated, and highly extracted wine. Anticipated maturity: 2001–2006.

DOMAINE JEAN BOILLOT—MAISON HENRI BOILLOT (VOLNAY)

1996 Bourgogne Blanc	C	88*
1996 Chevalier-Montrachet	EEE	94*
1996 Meursault	D	87*
1996 Meursault Charmes	E	89*
1996 Meursault Genevrières	E	92
1996 Meursault Perrières	E	90*
1996 Puligny-Montrachet	E	88
1996 Puligny-Montrachet Clos de la Mouchère	E	93
1996 Puligny-Montrachet Les Perrières	E	92
1996 Puligny-Montrachet Les Pucelles	E	93
1996 Savigny-Lès-Beaune Les Vergelesses	D	88

Henri Boillot, the brother of Jean-Marc Boillot and brother-in-law of Gérard Boudot (of Maison Etienne Sauzet fame) is responsible for the family estate (Domaine Jean Boillot) that bears his father's name, as well as for a small *négociant* business he has recently created. To assist readers in differentiating the two, I have placed an asterisk (*) beside the *négociant* bottlings.

The estate owns 35 acres of vines, divided equally among red and white vineyards. Henri Boillot, an excellent red wine maker, decided that his new *négociant* business would not produce reds because he is convinced that their quality is determined predominantly in the vineyard, not in the winery. Whites, on the other hand, are much more dependent upon skillful winemaking. All his *négociant* wines were purchased as grapes or must (the pressed but not fermented grapes). All his whites are aged in 350-liter oak barrels (the norm is 225 liters), are subjected to a *bâtonnage* (stirring the lees at the bottom of the barrel) twice a week, are never racked, and are fined and lightly filtered prior to bottling. Stylistically, Henri Boillot's wines are reminiscent of his brother Jean-Marc's. In short, they appear to have slightly less body but more definition than Jean-Marc's.

Produced from grapes purchased from Alain Gras, St. Romain's most famous vigneron, the Bourgogne Blanc is as good as any regional "Bourgogne appellation" wine I have tasted. Ripe, leesy, and deep aromas give way to a broad, expansive, concentrated, focused, and medium-bodied core of buttery white fruits. Drink this beauty between now and 2002. As with the previous wine, the delicious Savigny-Lès-Beaune Les Vergelesses was aged in 1- and 2-year-old oak barrels. Revealing toasted fruit scents, this wine exhibits a medium- to full-bodied and thick but precise personality packed with peach, pear, mineral, and vanilla flavors. Anticipated maturity: now–2003.

The Meursault, while very good to excellent, is not as interesting as the two previous wines. Toasted hazelnut aromas are followed by a well-focused, medium-bodied, and appealing tangy lemon and nut-filled flavor profile. It should be consumed before 2002. Displaying an elegant nose of walnuts, the Meursault Charmes is a medium- to full-bodied, lively, well-delineated, and rich wine with leesy, tangy citrus, and stonelike flavors. Anticipated maturity: 2001–2005. Exhibiting toasted hazelnuts and stones on the nose, the Meursault Perrières possesses a refined, silky-textured, ripe, well-focused, and defined, medium to full body with leesy and smoky components. Anticipated maturity: 2001–2007. The Meursault Genevrières' floral, perfume, and peach jam aromas are followed by extremely ripe (yet beautifully focused), thick, and concentrated layers of white peaches, apple compote, butter, and traces of honey. It should be at its best between 2002 and 2008.

The estate's Puligny-Montrachet has a mineral, stone, and white fruit-laced nose as well as an oily, well-focused, and defined, medium body filled with liquid minerals. Drink it between now and 2002. Revealing stone and slate scents, the Puligny-Montrachet Les Perrières has superb delineation and focus, as well as a thick, medium- to full-bodied, chewy core of minerals. Anticipated maturity: 2001–2006. The *monopole* (solely owned) Puligny-Montrachet Clos de la Mouchère was a cow pasture for 70 years before Henri Boillot's family replanted it with vines in 1939. Since the vineyard has not undergone any replantings since 1939, it is now uniformly 58 years old. Located under the Clos de La Garenne, it is bordered by Clavoillon to the south and Les Perrières to the east. Boillot's 1996 reveals a smoky minerality on the nose and a medium- to full-bodied, silky, and fabulously focused, concentrated personality. This Clos de la Mouchère is packed with beautifully ripe and rich white peaches, pears, and stones that are seemingly driven across the palate by this wine's strident acidity. Anticipated maturity: 2003–2010. Aromatically, the Puligny-Montrachet Les Pucelles displays smoke, stones, and the sweet kiss of overripeness. On the palate, it has awesome presence, delineation, balance, great depth, and a medium to full body redolent with baked peaches, white flowers, and slate. Exhibiting a minerally, buttered toast, and floral nose, the Chevalier-Montrachet is a full-bodied, supremely elegant wine with loads of stones, rock dust, and pear flavors. Refined, complex, deep, and almost ethereal, this superb wine has all the stuffing, concentration, and balance for it to evolve magnificently with extended cellaring. Anticipated maturity: 2003–2010+.

DOMAINE JEAN-MARC BOILLOT (POMMARD)

1995 Bâtard-Montrachet	EEE	93+
1995 Givry	C	87+

1995 Montagny Premier Cru	C	87
1996 Puligny-Montrachet	D	87
1995 Puligny-Montrachet	D	86
1996 Puligny-Montrachet Les Champs-Canet	E	91
1995 Puligny-Montrachet Les Champs-Canet	E	89+
1996 Puligny-Montrachet Les Combettes	E	93
1995 Puligny-Montrachet Les Combettes	E	92
1995 Puligny-Montrachet Les Folatières	E	88+
1996 Puligny-Montrachet Les Réferts	E	90
1995 Puligny-Montrachet Les Réferts	E	89
1996 Puligny-Montrachet La Truffière	E	92
1995 Puligny-Montrachet La Truffière	E	92
1995 Rully Grésigny	C	88

Jean-Marc Boillot looks as if he's been in training at Gold's Gym for most of his life. Broad shouldered, thick chested, and with a rugby player's muscular neck, he moves at full speed through the cellars, darting from place to place and returning every once in a while with new bottles to open. His effervescent smile may be due to the fact that his wines have become, in just a few years, some of Burgundy's most sought after. Boillot inherited most of his white wine vineyards from the Etienne Sauzet estate (his sister is married to Gérard Boudot, that domaine's director), and 1993 was his first vintage.

For the most part, the domaine's wines are fat, rich, full of fruit, and sometimes verging on off-dry. Yields are kept low. In 1995 the premiers crus averaged 1¹/₃ tons of fruit per acre. Boillot stirs the lees once a week (every Monday, he says) in most vintages and more often in others (1996, for example). Furthermore, he doesn't rack his wines, preferring to do a serious stirring of the lees prior to transferring his wines to large vats for fining and filtering before bottling. There is no track record regarding the aging potential of his white wines, 1995 and 1996 being only Jean-Marc Boillot's third and fourth vintages with his inherited Puligny vineyards. An overly sweet characteristic found in many of these wines makes me believe that most should be consumed over the short term.

I was unable to taste all of Jean-Marc Boillot's offerings when I visited him in November of 1997 because he had "nothing left." According to him, demand had been so high for his wines that he was unable to put a few bottles aside for himself, let alone visitors.

This estate's wines push the residual sugar envelope more than any other domaine I can think of in Burgundy. In massively concentrated and extracted vintages like 1995, this method tends to give the wines a sticky-sweet characteristic on the palate. In Boillot's 1996s, however, this sweetness is much more harmonious. I was surprised that these wines revealed so little of the vintage's telltale tangy acidity.

Throughout Burgundy vignerons are debating the advantages and disadvantages of *bâtonnage*. Boillot stands firmly in the corner of those convinced that stirring the lees benefits a wine's aromatics, body, texture, and flavor profile. To counter 1996's vibrant acidity and sharp personalities, Jean-Marc Boillot performed a *bâtonnage* 3–4 times a week until February, rendering them fat, leesy, and rich.

Revealing rich, tropical fruit, and floral aromas, the 1996 Puligny-Montrachet is a thick, medium-bodied, leesy, and mandarin orange-flavored wine. It should be consumed before 2001. The 1996 Puligny-Montrachet Les Réferts has sweet buttery aromas and a medium- to full-bodied, oily-textured, and dense personality. Layers of citrus peels, mangoes, bananas, and minerals are found in this powerful and rich wine. Anticipated maturity: now–2003. The smoky, grilled oak, and peach-scented 1996 Puligny-Montrachet Les Champs-Canet has a viscous, full-bodied, stone-and-mineral-flavored character. This intense, concentrated, and muscular wine possesses an impressive and lingering finish. Anticipated maturity: now–2003. The 1996 Puligny-Montrachet La Truffière displays an earthy, floral, and mineral-infused nose and a thick, oily, and full-bodied personality. Complex layers of mushroom, lees, stones, poached pears, and anise are found in this concentrated and dense wine. It will be at its best between 1999 and 2004. Offering sweet, white flower, and candied orange aromatics, the 1996 Puligny-Montrachet Les Combettes is a superripe, deep, powerful, extracted, and complex wine. Layer upon layer of peaches, honeysuckle, earth, buttery oak, and red currants can be discerned in this full-bodied, viscous, yet somewhat elegant wine. In its long, mouth-coating finish, traces of quince and minerals linger for at least 25 seconds. Anticipated maturity: now–2006.

With a deep green herbal spice on the nose, the 1995 Montagny Premier Cru displays sweet, creamy, spicy, and minerally fruit on the mouth. This medium-bodied wine is made to provide immediate enjoyment and should be consumed within 3–4 years of its release. Aged in 20% new oak, the delicious 1995 Rully Grésigny shows thick, buttery spices on the nose and flavors of minerals ensconced in a silky texture. Surprisingly, this wine, which is *almost* sticky sweet on the palate, has very good structure and can be cellared for 5–6 years. An unyielding nose on the Givry gives way to a sweet, spicy, and candied mouth full of spices. Drink this thick-textured and medium-bodied wine between now and 2001. Minerally on the nose, the 1995 Puligny-Montrachet village offering displays wonderfully ripe roasted fruit flavors and would have merited a better score were it not for a sticky-sweet aspect on the palate and a lack of structure-giving acidity. Less sticky than the preceding wine, the 1995 Puligny-Montrachet Les Folatières has floral and spicy roasted fruit aromas and a fresh, silky texture intertwined with sweet toasted fruits. This medium- to full-bodied wine has good length and should be drunk between now and 2003. An extremely minerally nose on the 1995 Puligny-Montrachet Les Réferts gives way to ripe baked sweet fruits. This wine has better structure and would have been outstanding were it not for the sugary stickiness it left behind on my palate. Exhibiting aromas of minerals and sea breezes on the nose, the 1995 Puligny-Montrachet Les Champs-Canet has a thick, deep, and sweet texture infused with roasted fruits and stones. Medium to full bodied, this wine should be drunk between now and 2004. An outstanding offering, the 1995 Puligny-Montrachet La Truffière displays a stony-and-mineral-scented nose in addition to a personality bursting with spicy apricots, bananas, and tropical fruits. For added complexity, flint and stone flavors vie with the fruit for attention. This long and powerful, full-bodied wine can be drunk now or held for 5–7 years. Even better, the 1995 Puligny-Montrachet Les Combettes (tasted both in the cellars and blind in the United States) has an elegant and refined nose of minerals and steel with rich, floral fruits in the background. A thick, silky texture rolls very ripe, roasted and steely fruits over the tongue, and the finish lasts for 20 seconds or more. Ever so slightly sticky sweet on the back end, this wine should be drunk within the first 7 years after its release. With a profoundly sweet nose, the 1995 Bâtard-Montrachet has an almost off-dry, viscous, and chewy personality filled with rich roasted fruits. It is nearly impossible to imagine a wine as densely packed as this thick and long bruiser. What it lacks in refinement and complexity it makes up for in sheer size. Drink it between now and 2005.

DOMAINE DE LA BONGRAN/DOMAINE EMILIAN GILLET
(CLESSE-QUINTAINE)

1997 Mâcon-Viré	C	91
1997 Mâcon-Clessé Quintaine	D	93+

Jean Thevenet, who looks more like a college professor than a vigneron from a minuscule village in the Mâconnais, is an extremely controversial figure. In a region where abundant use of chemical fertilizers produces huge yields of unripened grapes frequently machine-harvested and bolstered with large amounts of sugar (chaptalization) to attain reasonable alcohol levels, Thevenet's practices are anything but typical. His vineyards are farmed organically, worked to assure moderate yields, and harvested by hand at full maturity.

None of Thevenet's actions should cause controversy—assuming he did them quietly and didn't rock the establishment. However, because of the overwhelmingly positive press he has received from this journal and others, as well as his outspoken criticism of his neighbors' practices, he has become a target. From the conference rooms of Beaune *négociants* to the meeting halls of the Mâconnais's growers syndicates, Thevenet's wines are under scrutiny and attack. Why?

Thevenet crafts wines of unbelievable depth, complexity, and concentration. In warm, botrytized vintages they often have traces of residual sugar. In certain years they can be considered off-dry or even sweet. He maintains that these wines are but a continuation of his region's historical tradition. An avid researcher, Thevenet possesses countless wine reviews, some from the turn of the century, to support his argument. Furthermore, he has organized vertical tastings going back to 1929 for the region's authorities to prove that his wines are not atypical.

Why does Thevenet have to prove anything? Why can't he simply craft his wines the way he has done throughout his career and continue to earn adulation throughout the world? Because in France regional appellation laws are governed democratically. Since Thevenet is making highly acclaimed wines that are out of the ordinary, he represents a threat to the cooperatives and mediocre producers who overwhelmingly control the votes in the syndicates. The large *négociant* houses have their say in the drafting and enforcement of appellation laws, of course, since they sell untold quantities of the region's wines as Mâcons and Bourgogne Blancs (over 70% of Bourgogne Blancs are from Mâconnais vineyards). Yet the *négociants'* interests are linked to those of the syndicates who produce the wines they sell.

"Typicity," a word I have come to loathe, is the battle cry of mediocrity. A "typical" Mâcon, made from high yields and machine-harvested unripened grapes, has grassy, smoky aromas, hollow metallic flavors, and a short, high-acid finish. The prevailing mentality is that these wines are the norm, are "typical." Wines crafted from ripe grapes are atypical and must be banned. New rules drafted with this purpose in mind have recently been approved and are awaiting the signature that will make them law. Unless a last minute change takes place, it appears that Jean Thevenet, far and away Clessé's top producer, will no longer be entitled to label his wines with the region's appellation. In short, Thevenet and a handful of other quality-conscious producers will be forced to use the unrespected *vin de table* designation.

The cooperatives, growers syndicates, INAO (the French governing body that enforces appellation laws), and *négociants* may believe that delegating Thevenet to *vin de table* status will make him disappear. However, experience, particularly in Italy, shows the contrary. Consumers make a market, not bureaucracies. In Tuscany, where wines crafted outside the region's antiquated laws are now known as "Super Tuscans," *vino da tavola* wines command much higher prices than those with the region's appellation designation. Soon this may become true in the Mâconnais.

This being said, Thevenet fashioned two extraordinary wines in 1997. The 1997 Mâcon-

Viré, sold under the Domaine Emilian Gillet label, reveals superb ripeness in its aromatics. Ripe pears intermingled with cold steel, lemon, and stones make up this beauty's nose. On the palate, this medium- to full-bodied, soft, and superbly focused offering is crammed with liquid minerals, chalk, and traces of lime juice. It is concentrated, lively, and possesses an admirably long and precise finish. Anticipated maturity: now–2004. The Domaine de la Bongran's 1997 Mâcon-Clessé Quintaine is a stunner. Its fresh and pure aromatics are composed of ripe apples, honeysuckle blossoms, and touches of spicy anise. This massively intense wine is medium to full bodied and hugely ripe and possesses a sweet minerally backbone to its layered chalk and spiced pear flavor profile. Its personality has an awe-inspiring precision of flavors, enormous complexity, a mouthwatering oily texture, and an unbelievably long finish. This is an amazing Mâcon, one that should set a benchmark for others to emulate for decades to come. Anticipated maturity: 2000–2010.

DOMAINE BONNEAU DU MARTRAY (PERNAND-VERGELESSES)

1996	Corton-Charlemagne	EE	(92–94)
1995	Corton-Charlemagne	EE	93+
1994	Corton-Charlemagne	EE	90
1993	Corton-Charlemagne	EE	88

Jean-Charles de la Morinière, a Paris-based architect specializing in the restoration of historical buildings, acceded to his father's call to return to the family's Pernand-Vergelesses estate in 1994. A gregarious, introspective, charming, tall, slender, and self-assured man, de la Morinière tackled this large responsibility with an almost academic analysis of the domaine's vineyard management and winemaking practices. Unlike his father, the Count Jean de la Morinière, he decided that he had to live in Pernand-Vergelesses itself and abandoned his thriving architectural practice. His wife still lives in Paris, where Jean-Charles de la Morinière spends his weekends, with the couple's sons during the school year.

Unusual for Burgundy, this domaine's vineyards are all in one contiguous holding, 23 acres of 50-year-old Corton-Charlemagne vines straddling the communes of Pernand-Vergelesses and Aloxe-Corton, and $3^3/_4$ acres of 48-year-old red Corton vines in Aloxe-Corton.

De la Morinière's stated goal is to raise quality without changing the house style. To achieve this end, he has reduced yields, instructing his vineyard team to train, prune, and green harvest to guarantee $2^2/_3$ tons of fruit per acre each year for its only white wine, the estate's flagship Corton-Charlemagne. Since taking over the estate's management in 1994, de la Morinière has restricted yields to $2^1/_2$ tons in 1994, 2 tons in 1995, 3 tons in 1996, and $2^1/_2$ tons in 1997.

For the purposes of vinification, de la Morinière has divided the Corton-Charlemagne into 16 parcels, which he keeps separated until the final *assemblage*. The harvest is done by 40 *vendangeurs* who return to the estate each year. No destemming is performed, and the wine undergoes a *débourbage* (dropping of the gross lees) for 2–8 hours, depending on the health of the lees.

De la Morinière is a firm believer in controlling the wines. The must is placed in a multitude of stainless-steel tanks of various sizes—each one dedicated to one of the "parcels"—until the fermentation starts. They are then immediately transferred via gravity to barrels (33% of which are new and the balance being 1 and 2 years old), from three separate coopers (*tonneliers*), to undergo alcoholic as well as malolactic fermentation and for 12 months of aging. The wines are then transferred (again using gravity) for the *assemblage* to large tanks before bottling.

The 1993 Corton-Charlemagne reveals appealing honeysuckle and butterscotch aromas and a medium-bodied, softly textured personality. Caramel, nut cream, and anise flavors are interrupted by a lack of breadth in the midpalate in this otherwise flavorful, long, and delicious wine. Anticipated maturity: now–2003. The outstanding 1994 Corton-Charlemagne has a pure (difficult to achieve in this rot-plagued vintage) mineral, nut, cream, and almond-laden nose. On the palate, this medium-bodied and velvety-textured wine offers mouth-coating, precise, and crisp stonelike flavors intermingled with ripe white fruits. Well structured and focused, it is one of the rare 1994s I have tasted that should age well. Anticipated maturity: 2000–2006. I was bowled over by the quality of the 1995 Corton-Charlemagne; it is certainly the finest wine I have tasted from this famous estate. Beguiling aromas of red berries, vanilla, and traces of coconut are followed by a powerful punch of concentrated, extracted, and intense flavors. This gorgeous medium- to full-bodied wine has a tightly wound "nugget" of red currants, almonds, hazelnuts, pears, and minerals in its silky-textured, extremely well-balanced, and admirably long character. It should be at its peak between 2002 and 2010. The 1996 Corton-Charlemagne promises to be a spectacular wine as well. Floral, mineral, and hazelnut scents give way to a powerful, concentrated, medium- to full-bodied, silky-textured, and extracted personality. Highly focused and delineated flavors of minerals, stones, gravel, and traces of tangy candied lemons are found in this lovely offering. Anticipated maturity: 2003–2010.

Bravo to Jean-Charles de la Morinière for the three outstanding Corton-Charlemagnes he has crafted since taking over this estate!

DOMAINE BORGEOT (REMIGNY)

1996 Chassagne-Montrachet	D	86
1996 Chassagne-Montrachet Morgeot	D	88
1996 Santenay Les Gravières	C	88

The Borgeot brothers took over their father's estate when they were respectively 16 and 24 years old. Today, 8 years later, they are suppliers to several notable *négociants* and have begun to export wines to the United States. The younger of the two brothers is building a large and modern home over the new winery he recently completed—he is doing all the construction, from the masonry to the plumbing, by hand, with the help of an employee. According to him, he and his brother are dedicated to bottling their wines without subjecting them to fining or filtration. I found the whites to be good to very good and hope the brothers continue to strive for progress, as they seem to have the potential to become an important address wine lovers will want to flock to.

The delicious 1996 Santenay Les Gravières has mineral and toasty aromas as well as a thick, medium- to full-bodied, and silky core of stones, metals, and traces of lemon peel. Well balanced and rich, it will be at its best if consumed before 2002. Revealing minerals and stones on the nose, the 1996 Chassagne-Montrachet is a medium-bodied, focused, bone-dry, and lively wine with chalk-dust flavors. It should be drunk by 2000. The 1996 Chassagne-Montrachet Morgeot was aged in 33% new oak barrels. It has stone, flint, and powerful mineral aromas as well as a beautifully ripe, firm, and medium-bodied personality packed with tangy lemons. Anticipated maturity: now–2003.

BOUCHARD PÈRE ET FILS (BEAUNE)

1997 Bâtard-Montrachet	EEE	(88–90+)
1996 Bâtard-Montrachet	EE	90
1996 Beaune Premier Cru	D	88
1995 Beaune Premier Cru	D	87

1997	Beaune Clos St. Landry	E	(85–86)
1996	Beaune Clos St. Landry	E	89+
1995	Beaune Clos St. Landry	E	89
1997	Chablis Beauroy	D	86
1997	Chablis Bougros	E	(88–90)
1997	Chablis Côte de Lèchet	D	87
1997	Chablis Fourchaume	E	88+
1996	Chablis Fourchaume	E	88
1997	Chablis Vaillons	E	87
1997	Chassagne-Montrachet	E	(86–87)
1996	Chassagne-Montrachet	D	87
1995	Chassagne-Montrachet	D	86+
1997	Chevalier-Montrachet	EEE	(90–92+)
1997	Chevalier-Montrachet La Cabotte	EEE	(93–95)
1996	Chevalier-Montrachet	EEE	93
1995	Chevalier Montrachet	EEE	92
1997	Corton-Charlemagne	EE	(89–91)
1996	Corton-Charlemagne	EE	91+
1995	Corton-Charlemagne	EE	91+
1997	Meursault	D	(85–86)
1996	Meursault	D	87+
1995	Meursault	D	87
1997	Meursault Charmes	EE	(87–89)
1996	Meursault Charmes	E	88
1995	Meursault Charmes	E	88+
1997	Meursault Domaine Bouchard	E	(87–89)
1997	Meursault Clos des Corvées de Cîteaux	D	(85–87)
1997	Meursault Genevrières	EE	(88–90)
1996	Meursault Genevrières	E	90+
1995	Meursault Genevrières	E	90
1997	Meursault Goutte d'Or	EE	(89–91)
1997	Meursault Perrières	EE	(91–92+)
1997	Montrachet	EEE	(94–96+)
1996	Montrachet	EEE	94
1995	Montrachet	EEE	93
1997	Puligny-Montrachet	E	(85–86)

1996 Puligny-Montrachet	D	87+
1995 Puligny-Montrachet	D	87
1997 Puligny-Montrachet Les Folatières	EE	(88–90+)
1996 Puligny-Montrachet Les Folatières	E	89
1995 Puligny-Montrachet Les Folatières	E	89
1997 Puligny-Montrachet Les Pucelles	EE	(88–90)
1996 Puligny-Montrachet Les Pucelles	E	92+
1995 Puligny-Montrachet Les Pucelles	E	90
1996 Rully	C	87
1996 St. Aubin Premier Cru	D	88
1997 St. Aubin Les Murgers des Dents de Chiens	D	(87–88)

I am ecstatic to see the progress this old *négociant* house is making vintage to vintage. The qualitative resurgence at Bouchard began in 1987 with earnest efforts to increase the overall quality of their wines, yet both financial and legal difficulties contributed to the sale of the firm to Joseph Henriot (former president of Veuve Clicquot and also a member of the Henriot champagne house) in 1994. Henriot has both the desire and the financial means necessary to take Bouchard, the largest vineyard owner in the Côte d'Or, to the next level of quality. For example, recent changes such as the aging of their whites in oak casks, lower yields, and fewer traumatic filtrations have brought immediate progress.

Bernard Hervet and Philippe Prost, respectively the director and chief winemaker of Maison Bouchard, produced a large and delicious lineup of 1997 white burgundies. According to the pair, none of these wines were acidified, as they believe that process harms white wines (a few 1997 reds had their acidity "adjusted"). Prost and Hervet believe that well-ripened fruit is the key to crafting first-rate-Chardonnays, and they claim to have been the last to harvest in many villages. Since they found the lees to be less than ideal (the opposite of 1996), the 1997s were racked soon after fermentation to maintain purity of fruit. Interestingly, Jean-Marie Guffens (Maison Verget) and Laurence Jobard (Maison Drouhin) echoed this sentiment, yet virtually all the other vignerons I spoke with claimed to have had perfectly healthy lees.

I learned something new from Prost during my visit to the firm's Beaune cellars. He informed me that Maison Bouchard had stopped using corks from Portugal, preferring the quality of those from Spain's Catalonia region. According to him, the corks are not as aesthetically appealing, yet they have a lower incidence of corkiness and produce a better seal.

The flint-scented 1997 Chablis Beauroy reveals good richness in its expressive, medium-bodied character. This sea salt-and-mineral-flavored wine is harmonious and well crafted and possesses a firm and structured finish. Drink it by 2002. I was impressed with the 1997 Chablis Côte de Lèchet. It offers aromas of marzipan and iron as well as a thick, medium- to full-bodied, and broad core of candied nuts and minerals. This concentrated and dense offering should be drunk by 2003. The perfume-and-white-fruit-scented 1997 Chablis Vaillons is more structured and focused than the previous wine yet lacks its opulence. This mineral-and-stone-flavored offering is pure, firm, and masculine and has a tightly wound, rather serious personality. Anticipated maturity: now–2003. The impressive 1997 Chablis Fourchaume has red berry, mineral, and toast aromas. This excellent wine is oily textured, rich, gorgeously balanced, and filled with metallic and stonelike flavors. I would not be surprised if this wine garnered additional complexity with aging. Anticipated maturity: 2000–2004. The 1997 Chablis Bougros reveals sweet pear and perfume scents intermingled with toasted oak. It has a deep, medium- to full-bodied, opulent personality with mineral, baked apple, and freshly cut wood flavors. This complex, concentrated, and persistent wine will require 2–3 years of cellaring to absorb its oak. Drink it between 2002 and 2006.

The mineral-and-earth-scented 1997 Chassagne-Montrachet is well focused yet ripe, broad, and silky textured. It is an expressive wine, offering delicious layers of stones and nuts as well as a toasty, oak-spiced finish. It should be consumed over the next 3–4 years. The 1997 Meursault exhibits aromas reminiscent of freshly dug earth. It is a harmonious yet uninspiring wine with a medium body, an appealingly velvety texture, and a mineral-laden character. Drink it over the next 2–3 years. Named after an abbey that celebrated its nine hundredth anniversary in 1998, the 1997 Meursault Clos des Corvées de Cîteaux is produced from a vineyard that was originally planted in 1116. An extremely ripe wine, it offers aromas of candied nuts and a forward, easygoing personality crammed with oily-textured spiced pears and hazelnuts. It is medium bodied, somewhat flabby, yet delicious. It will require consumption over the next 2–3 years, as it does not have the requisite balance for cellaring. The 1997 Meursault Domaine Bouchard is a first-rate village wine. Produced from vineyards owned and farmed by this firm (80% of the wine comes from Les Clous), it displays a beguiling nose of ripe pears and acacia blossoms. This medium-bodied wine reveals superb ripeness, excellent balance, and a deft use of oak in its hazelnut, mineral, and flower-packed personality. It is well concentrated, harmonious, and expressive and possesses a long and complex finish. Anticipated maturity: 2000–2005. Seventy percent of Bouchard's 1997 Puligny-Montrachet was purchased as finished wine from a host of different producers, with the balance vinified by Philippe Prost at the firm's new white wine–making facility in Meursault. Appealing aromas of candied nuts, minerals, and white flowers leads to a well-made yet not complex personality. This plump, medium-bodied, and simple wine has delicious earthy pear flavors, a creamy texture, and a soft finish. It should be consumed over the next 2–3 years. The 1997 Beaune Clos St. Landry offers a mineral-and-stone-scented nose and, like the previous offering, an uncomplicated, simple, yet flawless character. This floral, well-balanced, and medium-bodied wine should be consumed over the next 2–3 years.

The 1997 St. Aubin Les Murgers des Dents de Chiens reveals sweet grilled oak aromas and a dense, flavorful, and fruit-packed character. This medium- to full-bodied, gorgeously ripe, and concentrated wine is silky textured, rich, and well focused. Tangy minerals, honeysuckle, and spiced pears can be found in its expressive flavor profile. Anticipated maturity: now–2003. Displaying a mouthwatering hazelnut cream-scented nose, the 1997 Meursault Charmes is an extremely ripe yet balanced offering. This medium-bodied, marzipan-and-mineral-flavored wine displays excellent concentration, a velvety texture, and lovely persistence. While it lacks the complexity of an outstanding wine, it is immensely pleasurable. Anticipated maturity: now–2004. The 1997 Meursault Genevrières offers crisp pear and stone aromatics. It is medium to full bodied, broad shouldered, silky textured, and crammed with sweet nuts, baked apples, and toasty oak spices. This thick, chewy, and powerful wine has good delineation of its flavors as well as a sultry personality. Drink it over the next 5–6 years. The 1997 Meursault Goutte d'Or exhibits a floral, perfumed, hazelnut, and anise-infused nose. It is deeply ripe, dense, and very concentrated and offers rich layers of candied pears and apple compote. This hedonistic offering is expansive and mouth filling and has an admirably long, palate-coating finish. Anticipated maturity: now–2005. The 1997 Meursault Perrières satisfies my cravings for both corporal and intellectual gratification. It has a somewhat austere nose of roasted nuts, rocks, and wet stones that leads to a magnificently rich yet superbly focused character. This medium- to full-bodied beauty is profoundly ripe and complex, and enormously concentrated, yet it possesses lacelike precision to its mineral, earth, and crisp pear flavors. Its combination of superb balance and depth of fruit guarantees that it will be one of the more ageworthy 1997 white burgundies. Anticipated maturity: 2001–2008.

The 1997 Puligny-Montrachet Les Folatières reveals sweet, toasty aromas of honeysuckle blossoms. This medium- to full-bodied wine offers loads of toasted hazelnuts and ripe pears in its fat, rich, and tangy character. Stylistically more reminiscent of a Meursault than a Puligny, it is a thick, dense, and opulently textured wine. Drink it over the next 5 years. Over 75% of Bouchard's Puligny-Montrachet Les Pucelles is sold in the United States. The 1997 displays a fresh, candied orange-infused nose. It is a medium- to full-bodied wine with chlorophyll, white flower, and toasted mineral flavors as well as excellent focus and richness. This silky-textured and well-crafted wine is harmonious, forward, and simply delicious, yet it lacks some persistence and complexity. Anticipated maturity: now–2005.

To ensure optimum ripeness, the Bouchard team harvested its parcel of Corton-Charlemagne three different times. The grapes, which averaged 13.3% natural alcohol, did not require chaptalization. It reveals a sweet baby powder (talcum) and toasted oak nose as well as an intensely ripe yet beautifully balanced character. Apples, metals, minerals, and flowerlike flavors can be found in this serious and tightly wound wine. Anticipated maturity: 2000–2007. The Bâtard-Montrachet, like so many 1997s from this vineyard, appealed to my hedonistic side yet wasn't complex, focused, or elegant enough to merit a rave review. Its nose, which initially was reminiscent of wet wool, revealed sweet pear and floral aromas with a few minutes of air. This is a broad, medium- to full-bodied, and immensely rich wine crammed with ripe and spicy white fruits. Its mouth-coating, unctuously textured personality lacks delineation yet delivers loads of pleasure. Drink it over the next 5 years.

Beginning with the 1997 vintage, Maison Bouchard is offering two separate Chevalier-Montrachets, both from parcels owned and farmed by the firm. The first, which will have Bouchard's traditional 1997 Chevalier-Montrachet label, has a profound nose of minerals, chalk, and flowers. It is an outstanding wine, with magnificent richness of fruit, ripeness, and balance. Thick layers of stones and crisp white peaches can be found in its bright, vibrant, and floral flavor profile. With an admirably long and precise finish, it should be at its peak between 2002 and 2007. The second 1997 Chevalier-Montrachet, which will be given an as-yet-undetermined name, was crafted from a tiny parcel of less than half an acre that the Bouchard team contends merits the Montrachet appellation. It is an absolutely stunning wine, with profound aromas of baked white fruits and stones. On the palate, this awesome offering combines 1997's telltale richness of fruit with impeccable balance and focus. Rich waves of deeply ripe pears, apples, nuts, and traces of peach pits are found in this dense, complex, and velvety-textured gem. Lucky tasters will also find that the blockbuster finish reveals layers of minerals. Anticipated maturity: 2002–2009+.

One of the finest wines of the vintage, Bouchard's 1997 Montrachet has an unbelievably refined and penetrating nose of candied nuts, flowers, and liquid minerals. This extraordinarily elegant offering has awesome balance, richness, and a profound depth to its tightly wound personality. Vibrant minerals, crisp pears, and stones are intermingled with flavors reminiscent of pineapple Life Savers in this medium- to full-bodied and velvety beauty. It is spiritual, superbly focused, and magnificently precise. The vast majority of 1997 white burgundies will have long passed into oblivion when this great wine reaches its peak of maturity. Anticipated maturity: 2005–2012+. Bravo!

Bouchard, the largest owner of premier and grand cru Côte d'Or vineyards (321 acres), had already bottled a large percentage of their red wines when I visited their cellars in November 1997 to taste the 1996 whites, yet their five most prestigious whites were still in cask. This struck me as strange because in burgundy white wines are always bottled and sold before the reds. Misters Hervet and Prost, respectively Bouchard's director and winemaker, told me that this was further evidence of their *négociant* house's commitment to quality. Instead of following market demand or tradition, they did what they perceived was best. The whites having perfectly healthy lees and high natural acidity could ameliorate themselves with more time in cask on their lees. The reds, on the other hand, needed to have their fresh, plump fruit sealed in a bottle quickly. Other estates and brokers (notably Peter Vezan) shared the Bouchard team's worry that extended *élevage* for the 1996 reds might lead to their acidity, assuming a dominant role as the fruit dried out.

The 1996 Chablis Fourchaume displays salt and flint aromas and an excellent, bracingly racy, medium body. On the palate, deep, lively, citrusy, and minerally fruit are found in this tangy, crisp, complex, and persistent wine. It should be consumed between 1999 and 2003. Revealing metallic and mineral scents, the 1996 Rully is a juicy, medium-bodied, well-balanced and -crafted, refreshing wine filled with red currants, lemon peels, and stones. It should be drunk by 2001. Aromatically, the 1996 Chassagne-Montrachet exhibits this vintage's trademark smoke and mineral aromas. In its rich, ripe, medium-bodied, and tangy character can be found stones, rocks, and flowers. Anticipated maturity: now–2001. The 1996 Meursault is a more expressive wine, displaying nuts and excellent ripeness on the nose, followed by a sweet pear- and red currant-laced, lively, medium-bodied, and silky-textured personality. I suggest drinking this wine before 2002. With a sweet nose of oak and coconut scents, the medium-bodied 1996 Puligny-Montrachet possesses fresh, ripe, rich, broad, and expressive white peach and floral notes. Anticipated maturity: now–2002.

Bouchard's delicious 1996 Beaune Premier Cru is a smoke, toast, mineral, metal, and white pepper-scented, medium-bodied, and rich wine. Flavors of orange peel, tangy cherry, and stones are found in this silky, ripe, and focused offering. Drink it between 1999 and 2002. Displaying minerals, white grapes, and rocks on the nose, the 1996 Beaune Clos St. Landry is medium bodied, oily textured, well balanced, and rich. Layers of cookie dough, sweet oak, almonds, and minerals can be discerned in its complex and persistent personality. It may ultimately be outstanding with cellaring. Anticipated maturity: 2000–2005. The 1996 St. Aubin Premier Cru offers a minerally nose and an expressive, ripe, tangy, and medium- to full-bodied character. Packed with stonelike flavors, this rich and well-focused offering should be at its peak between 1999 and 2003. Revealing nuts and minerals on the nose, the 1996 Meursault Charmes offers slate, wild mushroom, and earth flavors in its tangy, medium-bodied, and silky flavor profile. I expected more from this wine, as it is from a vineyard that produced some extraordinary 1996s. Anticipated maturity: 1999–2003. The 1996 Meursault Genevrières fulfilled my expectations. It combines this vineyard's trademark rich, broad, tropical fruit with the purity, focus, and precision provided by the vintage's racy acidity. Powerful layers of ripe peaches, minerals, lemons, and candied hazelnuts are found in this outstanding wine's expressive, fat, medium- to full-bodied personality. It should be at its best between 2000 and 2005. Displaying earth and floral scents, the 1996 Puligny-Montrachet Les Folatières is a well-constituted, medium-bodied, silky-textured, and concentrated offering. Wild mushrooms, minerals, and honeysuckle nuances are present in this focused and long wine. Anticipated maturity: 2000–2004.

The phenomenal 1996 Puligny-Montrachet Les Pucelles exhibits deep, smoky, and minerally aromatics followed by a powerful, elegant, exciting, and fresh core of layered pears, flowers, and stones. Medium to full bodied, rich, and ripe, this complex, concentrated, and refined wine is extraordinarily focused, balanced, and long. It's a keeper! Anticipated maturity: 2002–2009. Surprisingly, Bouchard's 1996 Bâtard-Montrachet (only 37 cases produced) was not in the same league as the Pucelles, though it is an excellent and potentially outstanding wine in its own right. Its ripe and rich nose gives way to an extremely thick, oily, full-bodied, and sweet personality filled with toasty pears and peaches. It should be drunk between 2000 and 2005. The 1996 Chevalier-Montrachet is a superb wine. Detailed and intricate aromas of minerals, stones, and smoke are followed by a complex, lively, and medium to full body. Its powerful, vibrant, elegant, and refined flavor profile is composed of layer upon layer of minerals, intertwined with lemon notes that seemingly last forever in its admirable finish. Anticipated maturity: 2002–2010. Displaying a dense and rich nose of minerals and toast, the 1996 Montrachet has an intense, multilayered, superripe, yet magnificently detailed character. Pure and precise stones, flowers, honeysuckle, nuts, and anise are found in this classy, noble wine. Its elegant, tightly wound, racy character carries through to its exquisitely long and delicately laced, full-bodied finish. Wow! This stupendous wine will require cellaring patience. I recommend waiting until at least 2004 before opening it; it will easily last through 2012.

Revealing a healthy green-hued color, the rich, ripe, dense, and butter-scented 1996 Corton-Charlemagne is also a first-rate offering. Intensely deep and concentrated, this wine possesses a highly focused and velvety-textured full body replete with flavors of chalk and buttered lemons. Anticipated maturity: 2002–2007.

The 1995 Chassagne-Montrachet has an attractive nose of enticing white flowers. A fat-textured wine with good extracted fruit and spicy oak flavors, it should drink well for the next 5 years. Bouchard is responsible for 15% of Meursault wine sales (excluding those made directly by vignerons from the estate), and their 1995 is a successful effort. It has a beautiful nose of toasted hazelnuts, is well structured, and has floral flavors. Displaying roasted fruit in the nose, the 1995 Puligny-Montrachet has a mouth of toasted candied nuts and tropical fruits. This is a reasonably priced burgundy for people who prefer California Chardonnays but want a slight change of pace. With its greenish, floral aromas and masculine, minerally mouth, the 1995 Beaune Premier Cru has a slight lemon-custard finish. Viewed by Bouchard as the commercial equivalent to Drouhin's highly successful Beaune Clos des Mouches, the 1995 Beaune Clos St. Landry has an appealing floral nose and a deep, structured, minerally mouth. With its austere and tight nose and elegant nutty flavors, the 1995 Meursault Charmes is built for aging and will easily last 10 years. Fruity and floral aromatically, the 1995 Meursault Genevrières has a very good oily texture, chewy tropical fruit, and a deep, distant spice in the mouth. A comment was made by one of Bouchard's employees that the grapes for this wine may have been harvested too late, but I disagree. It has the concentration of fruit and texture of a wine harvested at the optimal moment. With scents of roasted sweet fruits, the 1995 Puligny-Montrachet Les Folatières is an extremely structured Puligny. It has big, up-front fruit and roasted nut flavors with a floral aspect on the finish. Surprisingly, this wine resembled a Meursault more than a Puligny because its hazelnut flavors dominated the floral and fruit components. A real winner, the 1995 Puligny-Montrachet Les Pucelles boasts a floral, roasted nose with rolls of fruit and nuts on the palate. This nicely made wine should age well for at least 10 years. Very representative of its *terroir*, the 1995 Corton-Charlemagne has a deep, superripe nose and a mouth full of enticingly ripe tropical fruits. It will age well for the next dozen years. An outstanding wine, the 1995 Chevalier-Montrachet has abundant stony, flinty, minerally flavors, excellent length, and a fat texture, attributable to the wine's excellent ripeness and low yields. Potentially better than the Chevalier, the unbottled 1995 Montrachet has an extremely expressive, layered nose of attractive fruit. Judicious use of oak has been employed to produce a delicately toasty, nutty, and tropical fruit-laden wine that is full-bodied, complex, and very long. Anticipated maturity: 2004–2012.

Other wines recently tasted: 1997 Beaune Premier Cru (84–86), 1997 Bourgogne Aligoté (84), 1997 Bourgogne Ancien Domaine Carnot (82), 1997 Bourgogne Chardonnay (85), 1997 Chablis (84–86), 1997 Montagny Premier Cru (85), 1997 Petit Chablis (85), 1997 Rully (85).

DOMAINE BOYER-MARTENOT (MEURSAULT)

1996 Bourgogne Blanc Chardonnay Réserve	C	88
1995 Bourgogne Blanc Chardonnay Réserve	C	85
1997 Meursault Charmes Réserve	E	90
1996 Meursault Charmes Réserve	E	92+
1995 Meursault Charmes Réserve	E	90

1997 Meursault Les Narvaux Réserve	E	90
1996 Meursault Les Narvaux Réserve	E	92
1995 Meursault Les Narvaux Réserve	D	88+*
1997 Meursault L'Ormeau Réserve	D	88
1996 Meursault L'Ormeau Réserve	D	89
1995 Meursault L'Ormeau Réserve	D	87
1997 Meursault Perrières Réserve	EE	92
1996 Meursault Perrières Réserve	E	94
1995 Meursault Perrières Réserve	E	91
1997 Meursault Le Pré de Manche Réserve	D	87
1996 Meursault Le Pré de Manche Réserve	D	90
1997 Meursault Les Tillets Réserve	E	90+
1996 Meursault Les Tillets Réserve	E	92
1997 Puligny-Montrachet Les Caillerets Réserve	EE	91+

Yves Boyer works closely with David Hinkle and Peter Vezan for the wines he sells to North Berkeley Imports. Readers need to be aware that bottles imported by North Berkeley are decidedly different from those imported by others. Hinkle and Vezan select specific barrels and request that their selections be bottled with minimal fining and no filtration. Also, they demand that the wines be bottled when they determine the wine has attained its peak in barrel. As might be expected, this practice annoys producers who prefer to have their year planned out, but Hinkle and Vezan believe extended aging in barrel is not always an advantage and that there are times when a wine's freshness in the bottle can be compromised if it is not bottled in time. Some readers may wonder, as I did, why all importers don't exercise such hands-on, quality-conscious philosophies as North Berkeley. I posed this question to a number of top importers and was told that what Hinkle and Vezan do is impossible, unless it's done for microscopic quantities of wines . . . precisely what is taking place. I was impressed with the wines produced by Mr. Boyer and was excited that a heretofore unknown name (to me) was producing wines of such quality.

The 1995 Bourgogne Blanc (75 cases) exhibits an up-front, tangy nose with nice Chardonnay roasted fruit. The mouth explodes with buttery crisp apples. This medium-bodied and nicely balanced, refreshing wine should be consumed in the near term. From time to time wines have noses that reflect the wine's texture, as the 1995 Meursault L'Ormeau (50 cases) does with its thick, oily, and nutty nose. Although this well-balanced wine, made from 71-year-old vines, lacks the complexity of a premier cru, it is a delicious village wine, displaying beautiful buttered nut flavors and having nice length. The asterisk next to the 1995 Meursault Les Narvaux (50 cases) is due to the fact that this unfiltered wine is quite cloudy. The day I tasted this wine the nose was totally unyielding, but the mouth revealed intense ripeness of fruit and a tangy, zippy acid. This well-balanced and medium- to full-bodied wine can be drunk upon its release and will hold for 5–8 years thereafter. With an elegant nose of flowers and ripe fruits, the 1995 Meursault Charmes bursts on the scene with a powerful floral and green apple explosion in the mouth. Silky textured, this beautiful wine has excellent balance and length and should be drunk between 2002 and 2008. Boyer's best wine, the 1995 Meursault Perrières, has an intriguing roasted and minerally nose, a silky texture, and intense flavors of toasted nuts buttressed by tangy acidity. This outstanding wine has excellent length and will be at its peak between 2003 and 2010.

Domaine Boyer-Martenot's 1996 North Berkeley Imports bottlings are at a quality level generally attained only by a handful of Meursault's finest producers. Yves Boyer's efforts combined with David Hinkle and Peter Vezan's constant attention to detail and noninterventionist philosophies have led some of this estate's wines to the top.

The 1996 Bourgogne Blanc Chardonnay Réserve is smoke and nut scented and has a delicious, lively, and medium- to full-bodied character filled with red currants, flowers, spices, and anise. This beautifully balanced, concentrated, and well-made wine should be drunk between now and 2002. Produced from 80-year-old vines, the 1996 Meursault L'Ormeau Réserve (only 75 cases made) reveals toasty oak and white fruit aromas as well as a medium- to full-bodied, highly concentrated, and superbly focused character filled with ripe pears and white grapes. This excellent wine is fresh and lively and its powerful fruit flavors linger in its long and persistent finish. Anticipated maturity: 1999–2003. In contrast with the previous wine's fruit-based appeal, Boyer's 1996 Meursault Le Pré de Manche Réserve (75 cases) offers aromas reminiscent of gravel and nuts as well as a powerful minerality on the palate. This full-flavored, medium- to full-bodied, and beautifully ripe wine has awesome breadth, superb delineation, and an admirable finish. Boyer used two extremely old barrels and one new one to craft this offering. It should be at its peak between 1999 and 2004. Displaying deep, ripe aromas of candied almonds, the opulent 1996 Meursault Les Narvaux Réserve is a full-bodied, mouth-coating, buttery, oily-textured, and hedonistic wine. It possesses layered flavors of yellow peaches, hazelnut butter-cream, and anise that linger on the palate for at least 25 seconds. Anticipated maturity: 1999–2005. Equally outstanding, but completely different stylistically, the 1996 Meursault Les Tillets Réserve reveals bracing aromas reminiscent of a rock that has been basking in the hot sun. On the palate, this silky-textured, lacy, precise, superrefined, and medium- to full-bodied wine has focused and tangy flavors of liquid minerals, crisp pears, and stones. This elegant and highly delineated offering exhibits traces of spicy oak in its formidable finish. It should be at its peak between 2000 and 2006.

Revealing beguiling scents of stones, flowers, and gravel, the 1996 Meursault Charmes Réserve is a medium- to full-bodied, refined, precise, and highly focused wine with spice, liquid mineral, and white pepper flavors. This outstanding, fresh, lively, and feminine wine will be at its best between 2000 and 2006. The 1996 Meursault Perrières Réserve's nose blew me away with its noble aromas of stones, gravel, minerals, and salted butter. This silky-textured, full-bodied, and stunning wine possesses an expansive personality jam-packed with seashell, smoke, and liquid mineral-like flavors. Its combination of breadth, superb balance, purity, power, and elegance makes this an extraordinary offering. Anticipated maturity: 2002–2007.

Domaine Boyer-Martenot is continuing to produce first-rate Meursaults, and in 1997 Yves Boyer and his wife have added an outstanding Puligny-Montrachet Les Caillerets to their impressive portfolio. All of the estate's special North Berkeley cuvées were bottled between September 10 and September 18, 1998, 1 year after the harvest. Boyer-Martenot's 1997s are livelier than the norm for the vintage. Both Yves Boyer and Peter Vezan assured me that none of the wines had been acidified and appeared perplexed as to why they were so vibrant and well delineated (an anomaly for 1997s). They informed me that unlike the majority of 1997s produced in Burgundian cellars, Boyer's had undergone their malolactic fermentations rather late because their natural acidity levels had been normal.

The 1997 Meursault Le Pré de Manche Réserve has a nose dominated by charred oak. It is a medium-bodied wine with a tangy, well-focused, and bright character filled with toasty and smoky hazelnut flavors that will require 1–2 years of cellaring to soften. Drink it between 2000 and 2004. Produced from vines planted in 1924, the 1997 Meursault L'Ormeau Réserve reveals nuts and grilled oak aromas. This medium-bodied, gorgeously ripe, and extremely well-crafted wine is packed with minerals, almonds, and sweet oak flavors. It is extremely well delineated and possesses a long and focused finish. Anticipated maturity: 2000–2004. Displaying a mineral-and-stone-laden nose, the 1997 Meursault Les Narvaux Réserve has superb richness in its medium- to full-bodied personality. This delicious wine coats the palate with delectable hazelnut cream, mineral, and golden fruit flavors that linger for nearly 30 seconds. While it appears to have the required balance for aging, my inclination would be to consume this wine over the next 5 years. Potentially better, the 1997 Meursault Les Tillets Réserve appears to combine the qualities of the 1996 and 1997 vintages. From 1996 it draws a dried mineral- and rock dust-dominated nose, as well as a highly structured, superelegant, and delineated character. From 1997 it acquired a fat richness, velvety texture, and superb ripeness of fruit. Anticipated maturity: 2001–2006.

The 1997 Meursault Charmes Réserve reveals toasty mineral and lemon-infused spice scents. It is a medium- to full-bodied, thickly textured, broad, and complex wine crammed with smoked nuts and grilled oak flavors. I was highly impressed by its concentration, depth of well-ripened fruit, and persistence. Readers should be aware that the oak is very dominant. It is nonetheless an outstanding effort. Drink it between 2000 and 2006. Crafted from a parcel located near the summit of Meursault Perrières, Boyer-Martenot's 1997 Réserve bottling is first rate. A stone-and-gravel-packed nose is followed by a tangy, highly focused, and extremely rich flavor profile. Layer upon layer of minerals, rocks, and crisp pears can be found in this medium- to full-bodied, silky-textured, extremely persistent wine. It should age remarkably well, particularly considering it was made in a vintage that generally produced wines that warrant early consumption. Anticipated maturity: 2001–2007. Yves Boyer and his wife purchased a small parcel of 25–30-year-old vines in Puligny-Montrachet Les Caillerets. The 1997 Réserve, their first vintage, is superb, suggesting that consumers have another first-rate source from this heralded *terroir*. It displays dusty rock and mineral aromas as well as a medium- to full-bodied and dense core of pears, apples, stones, earth, spices, and white pepper. Similar to the Meursault Les Tillets described earlier, this wine also appears to be a synthesis of 1996's telltale focus and liveliness with 1997's characteristic richness and forward fruit. Anticipated maturity: 2001–2007.

Other wines recently tasted: 1997 Bourgogne Blanc Chardonnay Réserve (84).

DOMAINE PHILIPPE BRENOT (SANTENAY)

1996 Chassagne-Montrachet En L'Ormeau	D	(86–88)
1996 Puligny-Montrachet Les Enseignères	D	(88–91+)
1996 Santenay Clos Genet	D	(87–89)

Philippe Brenot is an extremely bright, high-strung, inquisitive, and dedicated man. He is the fourth generation of Brenots to run a wine-related enterprise out of the family's mid–nineteenth century winery and cellars. In his opinion, he is the family's first true vigneron. A trained oenologist, Brenot was "making the vines piss" to pump out the largest quantity of "technically correct" wines as possible when he was embarrassed by Michel Bettane's (France's most respected and controversial wine writer) remarks at a tasting.

Not one to take negative comments lightly, he telephoned Bettane to complain. The next thing he knew, he was accompanying the French critic to Burgundy's finest estates, tasting extraordinary wines and learning techniques never taught in oenology schools. He swore off being an oenologist and dedicated himself to becoming a vigneron.

Gone are the herbicides, fertilizers, artificial yeasts, and filters less quality-conscious winemakers depend on. Yields have dropped from an average of 4 tons of fruit per acre to $2^1/_3$ tons. Brenot does not use any new oak and no longer filters his wines. The whites are subjected to a light fining. According to Brenot, his 1996 yields did not surpass 2^1/$_3$ tons on a single one of his wines, and one was harvested at a measly 1^1/$_3$ tons per acre. This is particularly impressive considering some of the most famous estates of Puligny-Montrachet had yields over 3^1/$_3$ tons per acre!

Brenot's dedication to quality has paid off—he is a supplier to Verget for two of its best wines, the Bâtard-Montrachet (one of two suppliers) and the Puligny-Montrachet Les Enseignères (Brenot is responsible for about 10% of Verget's final blend). In addition, he now has a highly reputable U.S. importer.

The delicious 1996 Santenay Clos Genet reveals rich floral aromas and an excellent, gorgeously ripe, lively, concentrated, and medium-bodied character. Its silky and complex flavor profile is filled with candied pears, dollops of sweet butter, and honeysuckle. Brenot says all his attempts at aging white Santenays have failed. After 5–7 years the wines may still be holding on, but they have lost their appeal. He recommends drinking them in their youth while they are still expressing lively fruit—I could not agree more. Drink it between now and 2000. Produced from young vines, the 1996 Chassagne-Montrachet En L'Ormeau displays mineral, floral, and deeply ripe white fruit aromas. On the palate, its medium- to full-bodied, oily, and well-balanced character has honey, lemon drop, and mineral flavors. Anticipated maturity: now–2001. I tasted the 1996 Puligny-Montrachet Les Enseignères while it still had a small percentage of its malo to finish. I have a sixth sense that my score may be conservative. Exhibiting a luxurious nose of dried white raisins, anise, and poached pears, this superb wine is jam-packed with tangy red currants, cherries, raspberries, and minerals. This wine is medium to full bodied, deep, concentrated, and oily textured and has a lovely persistence. Anticipated maturity: now–2004+.

DOMAINE BRINTET (MERCUREY)

1995 Mercurey Vieilles Vignes	C	87

The Mercurey Vieilles Vignes from the Domaine Brintet is an excellent example of white Mercurey. It displays an attractive nose of spices and star anise and a mouth filled with spices intermingled with touches of coconut and oak. This silky textured, medium- to full-bodied wine has a nice long finish and will last for 4–5 years, but it won't improve with cellaring.

DOMAINE SYLVAIN BZIKOT (PULIGNY-MONTRACHET)

1996 Bourgogne	C	86
1996 Puligny-Montrachet	D	88
1996 Puligny-Montrachet Les Folatières	D	90

Sylvain Bzikot, the grandson of Polish immigrants, is a huge man. Broad shouldered, cauliflower eared, muscle-bound, and reeking power, he was getting ready for a rugby match when I visited him. The wines resemble the man. Readers desiring ageworthy, lacelike, refined, delicate, and elegant Pulignys are advised to look elsewhere. These are rich, full-bodied, expansive, broad, and mouth-coating wines made for near-term drinking.

The 1996 Bourgogne reveals a ripe, stone-and-mineral-filled nose, excellent richness, a thick, medium to full body, and sweet pear flavors. It should be consumed by 2000. Produced from yields in the 3^1/$_3$ to 4 tons of fruit per acre range and aged in 40% new oak, the 1996 Puligny-Montrachet reveals deep buttered toast aromas. On the palate, this oily-textured, full-bodied, superbly ripe, and rich wine is packed with sweet, fat, and rich white fruits. Its high levels of glycerin continued to coat my mouth after I had spat out the wine. I recommend consuming it by 2001. Bzikot crafted an outstanding 1996 Puligny-Montrachet

Les Folatières from 3⅓-ton yields. I cannot help but wonder what this wine might have been if he had practiced draconian vine pruning. This being said, it is a stone-and-mineral-scented, fabulously rich, full-bodied, thick, and mouth-coating wine. Layers of cookie dough, poached pears, ripe peaches, and minerals are found in its expansive, rich, and deep personality. An excellent value. Anticipated maturity: now–2003.

DOMAINE CAILLOT (MEURSAULT)

1997	Bâtard-Montrachet	EEE	(89–92)
1996	Bâtard-Montrachet	EE	(*)
1995	Bâtard-Montrachet	EE	90
1997	Bourgogne Les Herbeux	B	(85–87)
1995	Bourgogne Les Herbeux	B	84+
1995	Meursault En La Barre Clos Marguerite	D	85
1996	Meursault Le Limozin	D	87
1997	Meursault Les Tessons	D	(87–89)
1995	Meursault Les Tessons	D	87+
1995	Monthelie Les Toisières	C	68?
1996	Puligny-Montrachet Les Folatières	D	88
1995	Puligny-Montrachet Les Folatières	E	87+
1997	Puligny-Montrachet Les Pucelles	EEE	(88–89)
1995	Puligny-Montrachet Les Pucelles	EE	89
1995	Santenay	C	83

Note: The wines reviewed here can bear labels with a variety of Caillot family members' names. Look for Domaine Caillot, Roger Caillot, R. Caillot-Moreu, Michel Caillot, or Dominique Caillot. The labels look the same: old-style burgundy labels in an orange brown color with a drawing of a Burgundian wedding cup on the top of the label.

Currently, Domaine Caillot, like many Burgundian estates, is undergoing a generational change in leadership. Slowly Roger Caillot is relinquishing the reins to Michel, his son, who, I was told, is committed to noninterventionist winemaking. Already he has made the decision to discontinue filtration and to utilize indigenous yeasts as often as possible. I shall look forward to seeing how this estate progresses over the years.

If history repeats itself, retailers who acquire large amounts of the 1995 Bourgogne Les Herbeux will be able to offer it to their customers at much better prices than that quoted. This wine has an herbal nose and attractive flavors of crisp red berries and some green apples wrapped up in a thick texture. Offputting smells and flavors of cardboard, chocolate, and dirt make me think I was either given an unrepresentative sample of the 1995 Monthelie Les Toisières or that the wine is flawed. The 1995 Santenay offers minerals and earth tones on the nose and crisp red currants and green apples in the mouth. This light- to medium-bodied wine is made for immediate consumption. Thicker textured, the 1995 Meursault En La Barre Clos Marguerite displays toasted nuts in both the nose and mouth and an applelike tanginess on the back end. This is an enjoyable wine, but it lacks the complexity, intensity, and length of a great wine. A step up is the 1995 Meursault Les Tessons, which exhibits spices and freshly cut grass in the nose (aromas reminiscent of Sauvignon Blanc) and a thick, spicy, chewy mouthful of herbs and nuts. Equally good, the 1995 Puligny-Montrachet

Les Folatières had a muted nose but pleasing flavors of chewy and spicy roasted fruit. This wine, like the previous three, should be drunk within the first 3 years after its release. Verging on outstanding, the 1995 Puligny-Montrachet Les Pucelles reveals an elegant nose of perfume and red currants followed by an oily-textured, floral, and berry-filled mouth. This well-made wine has good length and will improve with cellaring over the next 5–7 years. With beautiful ripeness, the 1995 Bâtard-Montrachet displays deep mineral, toasted fruit, and spice aromas and a thick-textured mouth packed with apples and roasted apricots. Well made and with good length, this wine should be drunk between now and 2006.

As with many of Patrick Lesec's clients, Domaine Caillot appears to be experiencing a qualitative resurgence. According to Lesec, the youngish Michel Caillot is perfecting his pressing techniques (considered by many to be the key component of white wine–making) and is using more new oak. While Caillot is committed to abandoning artificial yeasts, he felt compelled to employ them with the 1996 vintage in order to better cope with the high acidities.

The nut- and white flower-scented 1996 Meursault Le Limozin is a light- to medium-bodied, silky-textured, and extracted wine packed with anise, pears, and juniper berries. This well-crafted, balanced, and delicious wine should be at its peak between 1999 and 2005. Also impressive, the 1996 Puligny-Montrachet Les Folatières possesses a rich and flower blossom-laden nose and an attractive, medium-bodied, broad, lively, and gorgeously balanced personality. Honeysuckle, minerals, crisp pears, and nuts are found in its flavor profile. Anticipated maturity: 2000–2006.

This estate's flagship wine is its Bâtard-Montrachet, which is produced from 40–50-year-old vines located in the heart of this grand cru on the Puligny-Montrachet side. The 1996 still had to complete approximately 15% of its malolactic fermentation when I tasted it in late January 1998; hence the asterisk. Its admirable density, ripeness, balance, concentration, and persistence assure that this wine will ultimately be outstanding.

Michel Caillot, a shy yet determined 34-year-old, has recently modernized his winery, ensuring that he will be able to perform all his rackings and *assemblages* using gravity instead of pumps.

The Bourgogne Les Herbeux is crafted using 10% new oak. This consistently excellent value is produced in large enough quantities for consumers to have a good chance of locating it—a combination of value and availability that is a rarity in Burgundy! The 1997 reveals a smoky white fruit-scented nose and a beautifully ripened yet balanced core of pears, minerals, and toasty oak nuances. This delicious, medium-bodied wine should be drunk over the next 3 years. The 1997 Meursault Les Tessons offers aromas of fresh herbs and citrus fruits. This elegant, medium-bodied, silky, and well-focused wine exhibits a sweet mineral and ripe apple-flavored character. It is extremely well focused and boasts a long and precise finish. Anticipated maturity: now–2004. The 1997 Puligny-Montrachet Les Pucelles, a mineral-and-stone-scented wine, has loads of fat, ripe, dense white fruits in its tangy, refined, precise, and well-concentrated personality. It is medium to full bodied and velvety textured. Drink it between now and 2004. Caillot's finest wine is Bâtard-Montrachet, crafted from 40–50-year-old vines located in the very middle of the vineyard. The 1997 has a resplendent nose filled with rich and ripe white fruits, minerals, and fresh earth. This medium- to full-bodied, extremely thick, and chewy offering is surprisingly well balanced. It possesses over-ripe pear and apple compote flavors, an intense minerality, and mind-boggling focus for such an opulent wine. Anticipated maturity: 2000–2006.

Other recently tasted wines: 1996 Bourgogne Les Herbeux (85), 1996 Santenay (87), 1997 Meursault En la Barre (87–89), 1997 Meursault Clos du Cromin (86–88), 1997 Meursault Le Limozin (87–88), 1997 Puligny-Montrachet Les Folatières (86–87), 1997 Santenay (86–87).

DOMAINE LOUIS CARILLON ET FILS (PULIGNY-MONTRACHET)

1997	Bienvenue-Bâtard-Montrachet	EEE	(92–94+)
1996	Bienvenue-Bâtard-Montrachet	EEE	95
1995	Bienvenue-Bâtard-Montrachet	EEE	93
1997	Puligny-Montrachet	D	(87–88)
1996	Puligny-Montrachet	D	88+
1995	Puligny-Montrachet	D	87
1997	Puligny-Montrachet Champs Canet	E	(88–89+)
1996	Puligny-Montrachet Champs Canet	E	90
1995	Puligny-Montrachet Champs Canet	E	89
1997	Puligny-Montrachet Les Combettes	E	(87–89)
1996	Puligny-Montrachet Les Combettes	E	90
1997	Puligny-Montrachet Les Perrières	E	(89–91)
1996	Puligny-Montrachet Les Perrières	E	92
1995	Puligny-Montrachet Les Perrières	E	91
1997	Puligny-Montrachet Les Réferts	E	(89–91)
1996	Puligny-Montrachet Les Réferts	E	93+
1995	Puligny-Montrachet Les Réferts	E	91

I've often felt that Domaine Louis Carillon made some of the most delicate Puligny-Montrachets around. These are not fat, superripe wines like those of Etienne Sauzet but are refined, elegant, and feminine. Wines from this estate generally need a few years for the fruit to emerge, so I recommend cellaring the village offerings 3–4 years and the crus at least 5 years.

A visit to Domaine Louis Carillon et Fils also includes a tour of the village. Unlike neighboring Chassagne-Montrachet, where cranes busily expanding cellars litter the skyline, in Puligny-Montrachet the water table is only a few feet below street level—so deep underground cellars, such as Comte Lafon's in Meursault, are impossible. Wines are produced aboveground or, as is the case at Domaine Leflaive, for example, in cellars where the floor is only 3–4 feet below street level (in the Leflaive cellars a grate can be removed, revealing the water table just inches below). Over the years the Carillons have collected a number of houses throughout the village and converted their ground floors into winemaking facilities. A refrigeration system, copious insulation—and presto! a cellar is built. To taste all of Carillon's wines, I am taken from the main office, near the post office, by car to another building. There I taste and then follow Jacques Carillon through a barnlike building filled with a winemaker's tools, across a medieval courtyard, and into another building for more tasting, all the time scribbling in my notebook and trying to keep up with his fast-paced jaunt.

Jacques Carillon, a congenial man, has been responsible for winemaking at this old family estate since 1985. He told me that he hopes consumers will drink their 1997s while waiting for the 1996s to age. "The 1996 is a great vintage, one that will return the investment of patience. The 1997s won't age as well as the 1989s have, but they will be delicious young."

The Carillons harvested their 1997s at an average of 13% natural alcohol, a high figure for Burgundy. Moreover, no wines were artificially acidified. Jacques Carillon noted that acid levels were low but that the relative percentage of tartaric to malic acid was high. He was correct in assuming that the malolactic fermentations would have no significant effect on his wines. Carillon pointed out an interesting fact concerning the 1997s—while wines from the 1996 vintage began their painstakingly slow malolactic fermentations in the month of March following their harvest, the 1997s had finished malolactics by March 1998!

The 1997 Puligny-Montrachet has an immensely expressive nose (something quite rare for a young wine from this producer) of tropical fruits, spices, and anise. This super village offering is densely packed with fat and rich white fruits and spices yet is well balanced. This medium-bodied wine isn't particularly complex and won't make old bones, but it does deliver an enormous amount of pleasure. Drink it over the next 4 years. Revealing a nose composed of spices, minerals, and metals, the 1997 Puligny-Montrachet Champs Canet is slightly richer, riper, and longer. It offers layers of spiced pears, fruit cake, anise, and fresh earth in its medium-bodied and velvety personality. Anticipated maturity: now–2004. Produced from a vineyard replanted in 1992, the 1997 Puligny-Montrachet Les Combettes has a less forthcoming nose than either of the two previous wines. It offers subtle aromas of minerals and flowers followed by a broad, silky, and expansive core of sultry and sweet white fruits. This opulent and dense Puligny should be drunk over the next 3–4 years.

The gravel-and-perfume-scented 1997 Puligny-Montrachet Les Perrières delivers an extremely flavorful mouthful of minerals and hazelnuts. This medium- to full-bodied, dense, oily, and rich wine is better focused and balanced yet boisterous. Anticipated maturity: now–2005. The 1997 Puligny-Montrachet Les Réferts exhibits chalk and ripe white fruit aromas. It is a thickly textured wine with huge density, admirable palate presence, and an excellent structure for the vintage. Its expressive and persistent flavor profile is composed of stones, earth, and white flowers. Drink it over the next 5–6 years. The Carillons consistently craft one of the finest Bienvenue-Bâtard-Montrachets. Only 580 bottles of the outstanding 1997 were produced (average production is usually 600–750 bottles). This beauty offers up scents of talcum powder, tropical fruit, stone, and chalk within a framework of admirable richness and balance. It is tightly wound and austere, yet powerful, packed with dense layers of minerals and faint hints of candied lemons that linger throughout its extensive finish. I was blown away by its combination of precision and superripe qualities. Anticipated maturity: 2000–2006+.

A slender, serious, and obviously dedicated man, Jacques Carillon loves the structure and ageworthiness of his family's 1996s. He compared the aging of a wine to a wave, saying the optimum time to drink it is during its crests. He feels his 1996s will be in the trough of the wave between 2000 and 2001 and should hit their first crest between 2003 and 2005. I tend to agree with his assessment and will add what this modest man did not: These are absolutely fabulous examples of elegant, mineral-packed Pulignys that will offer years of enjoyment to those lucky enough to acquire them.

. Domaine Carillon produced 30,000 bottles of 1996 Puligny-Montrachet from the 11 parcels totaling 12¹/₃ acres they own (which computes to 3 tons of fruit per acre). Most of Carillon's famous neighbors had 20%–30% higher yields. It reveals a lively, deep, smoke-and-mineral-infused nose as well as a polished, rich, and crisp medium body. Combining oily, fat richness (what the French call *gras*) with precise, pure, and delineated mineral and lemon flavors, this excellent village offering may, in time, deserve an outstanding score. Carillon says it reminds him of the 1990 but is significantly richer in style. Anticipated maturity: 2002–2005. The 1996 Puligny-Montrachet Champs Canet displays rich, toasty honeysuckle aromas and a vibrant, thick, medium-bodied, highly focused core of lemon, steel, and stone flavors. Fat and oily on the attack, it quickly transforms itself into a feminine, lively, and crisp wine that lingers on the palate with floral and mineral notes. This superbly balanced wine will be at its peak between 2003 and 2007. The 1996 vintage marks the return of Puligny-Montrachet Les Combettes to the Domaine Louis Carillon lineup. Jacques Carillon explained that his family had torn out all of their Les Combettes vineyard (from pre–World War II plantings) after the 1986 vintage, let it stand fallow for 6 years to "give it back life," and replanted it in 1992. So for 10 years this estate paid massive property taxes on a non-revenue-producing and highly sought-after premier cru vineyard, a testimony to this domaine's dedication to quality. Exhibiting rich, earthy, and wild mushroom aromatics, this medium- to full-bodied gem has an expressive, white pepper, spice cake, and anise-laden flavor profile. While it lacks the vibrant acidity, deep minerality, and ageworthiness of Carillon's other offerings, this is a broad, expansive, and delicious wine. Anticipated maturity: now–2005.

The magnificent 1996 Puligny-Montrachet Les Perrières possesses a complex, honeysuckle, and grilled oak-laced nose and a powerful, precise, pure, and refined attack. Layer upon layer of flint, minerals, and stones are found in its intricate, highly focused, medium- to full-bodied, masculine, and elegant personality. This wine requires patience, as its formidable acidity and structure demand cellaring. It should be at its best between 2004 and 2010. Aromatically displaying very defined flint, stones, and smoke, the superb 1996 Puligny-Montrachet Les Réferts is an austere, strict, yet expressive beauty. This wine has great richness, broad shoulders, a medium to full body, and unbelievable focus. Its highly detailed flavor profile is packed with minerals, orange rinds, flowers, and sautéed mushrooms that seem to last forever on its exceedingly long and pure finish. Readers searching for leesy, oaky, and fruit-packed wines for near-term drinking are well advised to stay away from this brooding monster. Anticipated maturity: 2005–2010. The Carillons' 1996 Bienvenue-Bâtard-Montrachet is one of the finest wines I have tasted from this grand cru vineyard. Regrettably, as is so often the case with stunning wines, it is exceedingly rare. The domaine produced only 67 cases, a whopping 2 of which were sold to their largest U.S. importer (Vineyard Brands). After a year in 50% new oak, it was transferred to 4-year-old barrels, as the Carillons do not want the wine to be overly marked by wood. It displays rich, deep, expansive, and toasty aromas and a stunningly clear, bright, and ripe personality. This wine possesses an oily texture and full body yet is superbly focused by its vibrant acidity. Jampacked with minerals, cardamon, candied lemons, earth, and honeysuckle, this extraordinary Bienvenue-Bâtard-Montrachet has mind-boggling depth, richness, and length. Bravo!

The 1995 Puligny-Montrachet is made in large quantities (for Burgundy), generally around 2,500–3,000 cases, but the quality is impressive. With an attractively fresh, floral, spicy nose and flavors of minerals and citrus fruits, this elegantly wrought style of wine is a lively alternative to heavier Chardonnays. With a nose full of white flowers, the 1995 Puligny-Montrachet Champs Canet possesses a delightfully thick texture full of lively, racy, and subtle floral tones. More flavorful, the 1995 Puligny-Montrachet Les Perrières reveals a stony, minerally, and floral concentration of fruit and a slight touch of nut in the background. It will age well for 10 or so years. With an austere nose of flint and stones, the medium- to full-bodied 1995 Puligny-Montrachet Les Réferts possesses complexity, direction, and floral, apple, and slight candied flavors. Drink it between 2000 and 2008. The top Louis Carillon offering is the Bienvenue Bâtard-Montrachet. The 1995 is a terrific effort, exhibiting a deep, elegant, and minerally nose. In the mouth, a racy, citrusy explosion of concentrated flavors of nuts and minerals cascades over the palate. This wine needs half a dozen or more years to attain full maturity; it will last up to 10 years.

CHATEAU DE CHAMIREY (MERCUREY)
1996 Mercurey Blanc   **C 87**

The Château de Chamirey's 1996 Mercurey Blanc has powerful maltlike scents intermingled with traces of milk chocolate on the nose. This butter-and-metal-flavored wine has a creamy texture, a medium body, and excellent balancing acidity to go along with its delightfully fat and ripe character. It will be at its best if drunk by 2001. The Château de Chamirey is owned by the Antonin Rodet *négociant* house.

CHANDON DE BRIAILLES (SAVIGNY-LÈS-BEAUNE)

1996	Corton	EE	(87–89)
1996	Corton-Charlemagne	EE	(90–92)
1996	Pernand-Vergelesses Ile de Vergelesses	D	(85–87)

"We are a red wine estate." With those words, the countess de Nicolay had "Kojak" hand me a glass of the estate's white Pernand. Mme. de Nicolay, an energetic, determined, self-assured, and proud woman, manages this estate, which her husband (Count Aymar-Claude de Nicolay) inherited from his grandmother, Countess Chandon de Briailles.

Kojak, as he himself likes to be called, is actually Jean-Claude Bouveret, the estate's winemaker. Bald as a cue ball, smiling, and with an intelligent glint in his eye, he needs only a lollipop, 6 more inches in height, and a fat Greek sidekick to make you believe you were dealing with the fictional New York City detective. Kojak told me the alcoholic fermentations lasted through February for the 1996 whites and that he performed a weekly *bâtonnage* to give them additional body.

Lively white flower aromas are followed by a tangy, smoky, leesy (sweet?), mineral-and-toast-flavored character in the 1996 Pernand-Vergelesses Ile de Vergelesses. Medium bodied and racy, it will offer delicious near-term drinking. Drink it between now and 2001. As Kojak handed me a glass of the 1996 Corton, Mme. de Nicolay interjected that she "hates wood flavors," which succinctly explained the old barrels that surrounded us as we tasted. It displays fresh and rich smoke scents and an attractive, deep, precise, and medium-bodied personality with white peach, anise, mineral, and stonelike flavors. Its long finish possesses traces of honeysuckle and gravel. Anticipated maturity: now–2005. The 1996 Corton-Charlemagne (tasted just after racking, post-*assemblage*) is an outstanding wine and the best white I have tasted from this estate. A rich, leesy, and smoky nose gives way to an extremely rich, thick, dense, medium- to full-bodied core of buttered minerals, pears, lees, roasted white fruits, anise, and stones. This wine has great depth of fruit and balance, as well as an admirably long and pure finish. Anticipated maturity: 2002–2009.

CHARTRON ET TRÉBUCHET (PULIGNY-MONTRACHET)

1996	Bâtard-Montrachet	EEE	93
1995	Bâtard-Montrachet	EEE	91
1995	Bourgogne Aligoté	B	85
1995	Bourgogne Blanc	B	84
1997	Bourgogne Cuvée Jean Chartron	C	86
1997	Chassagne-Montrachet	E	87+
1997	Chassagne-Montrachet Les Morgeots	E	88
1996	Chassagne-Montrachet Les Morgeots	D	90
1997	Chevalier-Montrachet Clos des Chevaliers	EEE	92
1996	Chevalier-Montrachet Clos des Chevaliers	EEE	94
1995	Chevalier-Montrachet Clos des Chevaliers	EEE	93
1996	Corton-Charlemagne	E	93
1996	Mercurey	C	86
1995	Mercurey	C	86+

1997 Meursault	D	86
1996 Meursault	D	87
1995 Meursault	D	87
1996 Montagny Les Grandes Vignes	C	86
1997 Montrachet	C	92
1996 Pernand-Vergelesses	C	87
1995 Pernand-Vergelesses	C	87
1997 Puligny-Montrachet	D	87
1996 Puligny-Montrachet	D	87
1995 Puligny-Montrachet	D	88
1997 Puligny-Montrachet Clos du Cailleret	EE	91+
1996 Puligny-Montrachet Clos du Cailleret	E	92
1995 Puligny-Montrachet Clos du Cailleret	E	93
1996 Puligny-Montrachet Les Folatières	E	91
1995 Puligny-Montrachet Les Folatières	E	89+
1997 Puligny-Montrachet Clos de la Pucelle	EE	89+
1996 Puligny-Montrachet Clos de la Pucelle	E	90+
1995 Puligny-Montrachet Clos de la Pucelle	E	92
1996 Puligny-Montrachet Les Réferts	E	89+
1995 Puligny-Montrachet Les Réferts	D	90
1997 Rully La Chaume	C	86
1996 Rully La Chaume	C	88
1995 Rully La Chaume	C	86
1997 St. Aubin La Chatenière	D	86?
1996 St. Aubin La Chatenière	D	87
1995 St. Aubin La Chatenière	D	88
1997 St. Aubin Les Murgers des Dents de Chien	D	88
1996 St. Aubin Les Murgers des Dents de Chien	D	88+
1996 St. Romain	C	87
1996 Santenay	D	86

Chartron et Trébuchet is a partnership between Jean Chartron and Louis Trébuchet. Chartron is head of the Domaine Jean Chartron and proprietor of some fabulous vineyards, including the two *monopoles* (solely owned vineyards) Puligny-Montrachet Clos du Cailleret and the Puligny-Montrachet Clos de la Pucelle. Trébuchet, a graduate of one of France's elite schools (Polytechnique), is originally from what was French Morocco and came to Burgundy because of his passion for wine. His technical and academic background is evident in the firm's constant research for ways to improve their wines. For example, they are conducting studies on the aromas, flavors, and character that a wide range of different types of oak barrels impart to wines. Following the death of Jean Chartron's father in 1983, huge inheritance taxes were levied by the French government. In order to pay these taxes, Chartron was forced to sell his Puligny-Montrachet Les Caillerets, some of his Puligny-Montrachet Les Folatières, and a parcel of his Chevalier Montrachet (to Lalou Bize-Leroy's Domaine d'Auvenay). Trébuchet believes young white wines, especially his, deserve to be afforded the same right to breathe as red wines before being consumed. He recommends decanting them a half hour or more before they are served. Olivier Humbrecht of the Domaine Zind-Humbrecht in Alsace shares a similar belief, convincing me a number of years ago of the beneficial characteristics breathing can add to his wines. The goal of this firm is to produce firm, elegant wines that are made for the long haul. These are not big leesy, flamboyant wines because Jean Chartron and Louis Trébuchet do not believe that style of white will age well. Trébuchet stated that "overly stirring the lees covers a wine's finesse and typicity more than oak ever could."

The 1997 Bourgogne Cuvée Jean Chartron, produced from older vines than those used for the regular cuvée and vinified in cask, is a delicious, highly expressive, and fun wine. Revealing well-ripened white fruit aromas, this rich, medium-bodied, and silky offering bursts on the palate with pear, white peach, and mineral flavors. Drink this simple yet delightful wine over the next 2 years. Offering floral and nutty scents, the 1997 Rully La Chaume has a tangy mineral and apple-laced character. This light- to medium-bodied wine is lively yet has nice density. It should be consumed before 2002. The 1997 St. Aubin La Chatenière has an oak-dominated nose and a thick, medium- to full-bodied core of sweet white fruit, anise, and spice flavors. I was concerned about oxidative traits I found in it and the St. Romain. Both need to be drunk over the next 2 years. The 1997 St. Aubin Les Murgers des Dents de Chien exhibits gorgeous aromas of flowers, minerals, and nuts. This ripe, dense, concentrated, and rich offering is crammed with candied nuts and honeysuckle blossoms. It will make for great drinking over the next 3–4 years. The talcum powder- and nut-scented 1997 Meursault has good balance, a light to medium body, and lovely flavors of sweet white fruit candies. This is a soft, simple, and easygoing wine that should be drunk over the next 3–4 years. The excellent 1997 Chassagne-Montrachet has an almond cookie- and anise-infused nose. This thickly textured, medium- to full-bodied, rich, and densely packed wine has earth and candied hazelnut flavors. Anticipated maturity: now–2003. The 1997 Puligny-Montrachet was aromatically muted the day of my tasting. However, on the palate, this fat, opulent, and medium-bodied offering was extremely expressive. It displays intense flavors of pear and anise in its oily-textured and well-crafted character. Drink it over the next 3–4 years.

The 1997 Chassagne-Montrachet Les Morgeots has a rich, floral, and perfumed nose. This thick-textured, tangy, medium-bodied, and sultry wine is filled with ripe white berry fruit, earth, and hints of toasty new oak. Anticipated maturity: now–2004. Revealing a beguiling nose of sweet anise and spiced/poached pears, the 1997 Puligny-Montrachet Clos de la Pucelle has the potential to be an outstanding wine. It displays a gorgeous core of thickly textured white fruit immersed in spicy oak. This opulent offering is dense and immensely rich. Anticipated maturity: now–2004. The 1997 Puligny-Montrachet Clos du Cailleret has dusty chalk and mineral aromas. This fat, intense, and deep wine is more concentrated, refined, and elegant than the Clos de la Pucelle. It explodes on the palate with flavors reminiscent of pears, white peaches, apples, and toasty minerals. Drink it between now and 2005.

The impressive 1997 Chevalier-Montrachet Clos des Chevaliers has an elegant nose made up of minerals, lemons, and stones. This well-focused, delineated, and structured wine is rich, thick, and ripe. Its gravel-, pear-, and apple-laced flavor profile is medium to full bodied, concentrated, and undeniably persistent. Anticipated maturity: 2000–2005. A showstopper, the 1997 Montrachet reveals tantalizing crème brûlée, vanilla, and mineral aromatics. Immensely ripe, extremely elegant, and well structured, this medium- to full-bodied wine offers powerful mineral and spiced pear flavors as well as an oily texture and a long finish. It is rich, deeply flavorful, and forward. Anticipated maturity: 2001–2006.

The 1996 Montagny Les Grandes Vignes is a toast-and-smoke-scented, rich, medium-bodied, well-crafted, and bone-dry wine filled with pears and buttery notes. It should be drunk by 2000. Revealing tantalizing aromas of anise, white flowers, minerals, and almonds, the 1996 Rully La Chaume is one of the finest values in white burgundy. Ripe, rich, medium bodied, and with fresh stone and toasty oak flavors, this beauty has an excellent silky texture and finish. Anticipated maturity: now–2001. The 1996 Mercurey exhibits fresh herb and stone aromatics and an appealing, focused, light- to medium-bodied, floral, and chalky character. It should be consumed by 2001. Displaying an oaky and smoky nose, the delicious 1996 St. Romain offers an oily-textured and expansive medium body with metallic and sweet new oak notes. Anticipated maturity: now–2000. Aromatically, the 1996 Santenay reveals tropical white fruits and minerals. On the palate, this new oak- and stone-flavored wine has an attractively rich and silky medium body. It should be drunk by 2001. The 1996 Pernand-Vergelesses possesses a metallic and mineral nose as well as a delightfully deep, ripe, and silky medium body filled with steel, chalk, and stones. Well balanced and crafted, it will provide refreshing drinking until 2001. The equally good, floral, and perfumed 1996 St. Aubin La Chatenière is rich, oily textured, medium bodied, and filled with minerals, stones, chalk, and traces of honeysuckle. Anticipated maturity: now–2001. Revealing deep, malty, mineral, and flower aromas, the 1996 St. Aubin Les Murgers des Dents de Chiens has a thick, oily-textured, expansive, and ripe character with lovely, tangy, mineral, metal, and toasty flavors. It will be at its best if drunk by 2002. Rich nuts can be found lurking in the tightly wound nose of the 1996 Meursault. This well-crafted, mineral-and-nut-laced, silky-textured, medium-bodied, and focused wine should be consumed by 2001. The 1996 Puligny-Montrachet displays floral, perfumed, and almond aromas followed by a medium-bodied, velvety, well-crafted, butter cookie-flavored, and rich personality. Well balanced and delineated, it should be at its best between now and 2003.

Displaying mouthwatering mineral, marzipan, and cake icing aromas, the 1996 Chassagne-Montrachet Les Morgeots is a precise, highly focused, medium- to full-bodied wine. Its thick, silky-textured, and expansive personality is filled with candied almonds, stones, and vanilla beans. This impressive wine should be at its peak between 2000 and 2004. The 1996 Puligny-Montrachet Les Réferts has stones, earth, flowers, and lovely purity to its bouquet. On the palate, minerals, anise, and honeysuckle can be found in its rich, oily, medium to full body. Anticipated maturity: now–2004. Aromatically, the 1996 Puligny-Montrachet Les Folatières is reminiscent of a bouquet of freshly cut flowers. This mouth-coating and full-bodied offering regales with its expansiveness, great richness, and pear, peach, and new oak-laced flavors. Its long and precise finish reveals intricate mineral and stone nuances. Anticipated maturity: 2000–2006. The 1996 Puligny-Montrachet Clos de la Pucelle has powerful stony, earthy, and sautéed mushroom aromas. While I have no doubt this is an outstanding wine, the day of my tasting I found the preceding Folatiéres to be more intricate and lively. This is a wide, rich, thick, full-bodied, and velvety wine packed with layer upon layer of minerals, earth, and wood notes. It should be at its best between 2000 and 2005. Exhibiting complex and well-defined aromas of stones and minerals, the 1996 Puligny-Montrachet Clos du Cailleret is a superb wine. Medium to full bodied, magnificently focused, and packed with seashells, rock dust, and flowers, this silky gem also has a formidably long, mineral-laced finish. This impressive Chevalier-Montrachet-style wine should be at its peak between 2002 and 2009.

The first-rate 1996 Bâtard-Montrachet possesses a deep, rich, almond, and honeyed nose and a wide, expansive, full-bodied, and superripe personality. This full-bodied wine has marzipan, honeysuckle, sweet peach, and pear flavors as well as magnificent depth. It is also well delineated, focused, and beautifully structured. Long and complex, it should be consumed between 2003 and 2008. It is another example of a Bâtard that is elevated to new heights by 1996's telltale acidity. Displaying loads of minerals and traces of earthiness on the nose, the 1996 Chevalier-Montrachet Clos du Chevalier is fabulous and, once again, is Chartron et Trébuchet's standard-bearer. A powerful explosion of minerals, highly defined pears, stones, and white flowers are found in this extraordinarily refined, elegant, and superbly focused wine. If a fluid nobility exists, this full-bodied, silky-textured, and classy gem is certainly a member. Anticipated maturity: 2003–2010.

Louis Trébuchet, like many of his Burgundian brethren, feels compelled to place his Corton-Charlemagne last in tastings because, as he says, "it is so stylistically different, it does not fit elsewhere." Revealing ripe tropical fruits and minerals, the 1996 possesses an intensely explosive, rich, and full-bodied character filled with sweet peaches, pears, red currants, and spicy oak. As with the Bâtard, the Corton-Charlemagne has benefited from the vintage's precision, focus, and balance-giving acidity. It is full bodied, oily textured, and superripe, all buttressed by its vibrant, tangy acid. Anticipated maturity: 2001–2008.

The 1995 Bourgogne Blanc is a nice wine with slight buttery aromas and a crisp lemony, medium-bodied mouth. It is the only white wine at Chartron et Trébuchet not to be vinified entirely in wood barrels. The 15% new oak used for the 1995 Rully La Chaume has given an appealing roasted, spicy element to its fresh, lively fruit. Displaying a distant, austere, stony nose, the 1995 Mercurey possesses a mouth of concentrated and well-structured minerally and flinty fruit. Reminiscent of the Mercurey, but with a touch more austerity, flintiness, and focus, is the 1995 Pernand-Vergelesses. As a retailer, I frequently recommended Chartron et Trébuchet's St. Aubin La Chateniére to provide customers a good white burgundy value. The 1995 again merits attention. It exhibits fat, extracted, and concentrated roasted fruit with excellent structure and mineral undertones. The 1995 Meursault offers a fresh nose of flowers along with vague nuances of nuts. In the mouth an oily texture brings forth flavors of toasted hazelnuts. From Chartron et Trébuchet's home turf, the 1995 Puligny-Montrachet is an excellent example of what a village wine should be. It reveals a floral nose with flavors of sweet, deeply roasted fruits. This wine has good length and will hold well for the next 5+ years. The 1995 Puligny-Montrachet Les Réferts is a step up. A concentrated nose of white flowers and roasted, toasted fruits leads to an equally concentrated palate with good intensity, length, and refinement. It will be at its peak between 2004 and 2008. An elegant wine, the 1995 Puligny-Montrachet Les Folatiéres doesn't attain the qualitative level of the Réferts. In both the nose and mouth, it displays good minerality and floral components, and has fine length, but it lacks the burst of fruit displayed by the previous wine. Hold it for 6 years and enjoy it over the subsequent 6+. Possessing deep, sweet, almost candied fruit aromas, and waves of rolling, spicy, plump-textured fruit, the 1995 Puligny-Montrachet Clos de la Pucelle is a fabulous wine. Its medium- to full-bodied core of concentrated thick fruit is more reminiscent of a grand cru Bâtard than a premier cru. Drink it between 2004 and 2010. The 1995 Puligny-Montrachet Clos du Cailleret is truly of grand cru quality. It explodes from the glass with ginger, star anise, and profound underlying mineral components. This beautifully extracted, delineated, and concentrated wine serves up spices, almonds, and a long finish. It should be cellared for 5 years and drunk over the following 10–15. Sadly, the 1995 Bâtard-Montrachet was a letdown, but an outstanding effort nonetheless. It has floral, spicy, and candied aromatics and flavors combined with an oily mouth-feel and good concentration. While it did not excite me the way the previous wine did, it will provide delicious drinking between 2002 and 2008. The 1995 Chevalier Montrachet Clos du Chevalier is a superb wine. Displaying a stony, precise, and refined nose, it is an extremely well structured, elegant, and delineated wine with a lively, superspicy, and mineral-filled mouth. This medium-bodied gem should age effortlessly for 15–20 years—where stored properly.

Other 1997s recently tasted: Auxey-Duresses (86), Bâtard-Montrachet (88), Bourgogne Blanc (84), Puligny-Montrachet Les Folatiéres (88), St. Romain (85?), Santenay (86), Savigny-Lés-Beaune (86).

DOMAINE PASCAL CHEVIGNY (NUITS-ST.-GEORGES)

1996 Hautes Côtes de Nuits	C	86

The 1996 Hautes Côtes de Nuits is produced from Chardonnay vines ranging from 35 to 70 years old. It offers a smoke- and spice-laden nose and a mineral-laced, beautifully ripe, well-crafted, medium-bodied, and vibrant character. It should be drunk over the next 4–5 years.

DOMAINE BRUNO CLAIR (MARSANNAY-LA-CÔTE)

1996 Marsannay	D	87
1995 Marsannay	D	87
1996 Morey-St. Denis En La Rue Vergy	D	89
1995 Morey-St. Denis En La Rue Vergy	D	89
1996 Corton-Charlemagne	EE	(92–94)
1995 Corton-Charlemagne	EE	(91–93+)

An engaging pair, Bruno Clair and his winemaker, Philippe Brun, run this domaine in Marsannay la Côte, the northernmost appellation of the Côte d'Or. Each year at harvesttime they coordinate the harvesters, who must work from one end of the Côte to the other, as the domaine has vineyards sprinkled throughout the area, from Savigny to Marsannay. Known for their red wines, this domaine also makes one of Burgundy's finest rosés and, in general, good to very good whites. I was pleasantly surprised by the overall quality of the three 1995 whites I tasted on my visit in January 1997. All are extremely well made, displaying nice structure and excellent ripeness.

Aged in 10% new oak, the 1995 Marsannay jumps from the glass with enticing white flower, nutty, minerally, and honeysuckle aromas. In the mouth, this wine displays very good richness, flowers, red berries, and an appealing tanginess on the finish. Drink it between now and 1999. One of the rare whites from the Cote de Nuits, the 100% Chardonnay 1995 Morey St. Denis En La Rue Vergy reveals an earthy, minerally nose followed by a minerally, stony, and fruity mouth. Exhibiting a beautiful thick body, this wine can be enjoyed in the near term or held for 6–8 years. It evolved into an excellent wine in the year between my first and second tastings. Mouthwatering aromas of *cèpes* sautéed in butter are followed by an oily-textured, gorgeously balanced, ripe, pear compote, juniper berry, mushroom, and mineral-laden character.

The best white wine I've had from Bruno Clair, the 1995 Corton-Charlemagne, is a delicious example of that renowned vineyard. Clair and Brun both assured me this wine, which took 3 months to ferment, would be neither fined nor filtered prior to its bottling. (Clair wants readers to be aware that it may throw a deposit.) With airing, the slightly muted nose began to reveal roasted sweet fruits and buttered toast. Abundant flavors of tropical fruits and minerals, with a skillful touch of oak, can be found in this viscous-textured and extremely well-balanced wine. Drink it between 2002 and 2010.

Produced from a blend of 25% Pinot Blanc and 75% Chardonnay, Bruno Clair's 1996 Marsannay has rich, deep white fruit aromas and a ripe, light- to medium-bodied, and racy core of flowers and crisp pears. This refreshing and palate tingling wine should be consumed by the turn of the millennium. Aromatically, the delicious 1996 Morey-St.-Denis En La Rue Vergy reveals earth, mineral, and toasty oak aromas. On the palate, this medium- to full-bodied, oily-textured, bright, and lively wine regales with sweet anise, sautéed mushroom, and stone flavors. Anticipated maturity: now–2005. Clair's spectacular 1996 Corton-Charlemagne, from a tiny under an acre parcel, is redolent with intense white flower and anise aromas. It possesses an awesome concentration of ripe and layered pears, bananas, honeysuckle, and buttered toast in its medium- to full-bodied, silky-textured, and beautifully focused personality. It should be at its best between 2002 and 2010.

DOMAINE ALAIN COCHE-BIZOUARD (MEURSAULT)

1996	Auxey-Duresses	D	(85–87)
1996	Meursault	D	(87–88)*
1996	Meursault Charmes	D	(91–93)
1996	Meursault Chevalières	D	(88–90)
1996	Meursault Goutte d'Or	D	(89–91)
1996	Meursault Le Limouzin	D	(88–90)
1996	Meursault en L'Ormeau	D	(87–88)

Alain Coche, a cousin of Domaine Coche-Dury's Jean-François Coche, is a hardworking, dedicated, and contemplative man. This is one of the rare self-made domaines in a region where estates are inherited by vignerons or purchased by *négociant* houses, banks, insurance companies, or industry magnates. Over the course of the last 50 years, Coche and his now deceased father saved whatever money they had to buy vineyards. Today the estate covers 21 acres (12¹⁄₃ in white), and Coche is justifiably proud of each and every vine he owns. I had the impression that these vines are more cherished than most because of the backbreaking work, sweat, and years of saving money that went into their purchase.

Coche believes in being the last to harvest and the last to bottle, two philosophies that paid dividends in 1996. "The Coches prune short," was the proud reply to my question about yields. The wines were subjected to a regular *bâtonnage* every 8 days until January, and then once a month.

Overall, these offerings have excellent richness and depth as well as vibrant and piercing acidity. If they are patiently cellared, I am convinced these beauties will blossom into delicious, complex, and highly nuanced wines.

The 1996 Auxey-Duresses reveals minerals and stones on the nose and a lively, light- to medium-bodied, metallic, and tangy citrus juice-flavored personality. It should be at its best from now to 2002. Produced from 35–40-year-old vines, 90% of which are from the Les Luchets vineyard, the 1996 Meursault is a delicious hazelnut- and mineral-scented wine. Medium bodied, rich, and vibrant, it offers a complex flavor profile filled with toasted nuts, wild mushrooms, and lemon. Anticipated maturity: 2001–2004. The Meursault en L'Ormeau's vineyard produced some very impressive wines in 1996, which Coche attributes to its excellent drainage (oddly enough, when I visited this "all gravel" vineyard, I was able to get totally covered with mud). This offering has flowers, earth, and orange peel aromatics and a very structured, medium-bodied, broad, wild mushroom- and stone-flavored character with excellent underlying richness. Anticipated maturity: 2001–2004. Crafted from 55–60-year-old vines, the 1996 Meursault Le Limouzin has sweet mineral and white flower aromas as well as a racy, ripe, deep, oily-rich, concentrated, and medium-bodied core of mouth-staining lemony fruit. This superb "village" wine is better than many premiers crus I have tasted. It should be at its peak from 2002 to 2006. The 1996 Meursault Chevalières, produced from 38-year-old vines, exhibits deep aromas of minerals and almonds, and on the palate, this is a rich, medium-bodied, mouth-coating, strident, and toasty wine. Structured and backward, this wine will require cellaring before blossoming. Anticipated maturity: 2002–2006.

*The Meursault reviewed is the special cuvée produced for Robert Kacher, this estate's U.S. importer.

Coche's 1996 Meursault Goutte d'Or has rich, leesy scents and an intense, broad, mineral-laced, medium-bodied, and persistent personality. Much more focused, bracing, and vibrant than expected for a wine from this vineyard, it should be at its peak by 2003 and can be held through 2007. My favorite 1996 from Domaine Coche-Bizouard is the outstanding Meursault Charmes. Elegant aromas of white flowers and delicately laced minerals are followed by a superdeep, refined, ripe, bright, concentrated, complex, and medium- to full-bodied character. Layers of liquid minerals and citrus zests can be found in this marvelous offering's flavor profile and also in its admirably long finish. Anticipated maturity: 2003–2008.

DOMAINE COCHE-DURY (MEURSAULT)

1997	Bourgogne Chardonnay	D	(86–88)
1996	Bourgogne Chardonnay	D	88
1997	Corton-Charlemagne	EEE	(91–93+)
1996	Corton-Charlemagne	EEE	98
1995	Meursault	E	91
1997	Meursault Narvaux	E	(89–90+)
1996	Meursault Narvaux	E	90
1996	Meursault Vireuils	E	90
1997	Meursault Caillerets	EE	(90–92)
1996	Meursault Caillerets	EE	91
1997	Meursault Les Chevalières	EE	(89–90)
1996	Meursault Les Chevalières	EE	91
1997	Meursault Perrières	EEE	(91–93)
1996	Meursault Perrières	EEE	99
1995	Meursault Perrières	EEE	98+
1997	Meursault Rougeots	EE	(89–90+)
1996	Meursault Rougeots	EE	92
1997	Puligny-Montrachet Les Enseignères	EE	(89–90)
1996	Puligny-Montrachet Les Enseignères	EE	92

Tall, slender, and modest, Jean-François Coche rules over the village of Meursault the way one imagines Einstein would have reigned over his highly esteemed and brilliant colleagues. While speaking to other growers, I learned that Coche has an impeccable reputation for his vineyard work and that he consistently sells up to one-third of his wines to *négociants.* This blew my mind. Many vignerons use lesser *négociants* to dispose of wines below their normal quality level, but I have never heard of a top producer providing such quantities of first-rate wine, year in and year out. What other vigneron, capable of easily selling ten times over his annual production, would provide a large amount to merchants for a fraction of their potential value? Furthermore, in this day and age, where people in all walks of life search out the spotlight, why is it that Coche would have superb wines blended with other producers' and then labeled anonymously by a *négociant?* I asked him, and the men he sells to (Louis-Fabrice Latour of Maison Louis Latour and Pierre-Henri Gagey of Maison Louis Jadot), and received the same answer—loyalty. They were there for him when he was unknown, and he feels it is only right to reciprocate today (this is quite a different story from the myriad "mail order" wineries on our own shores who have forgotten the retailers and distributors who supported them when they were unknown).

Domaine Coche-Dury's 1997s are candidly described by the forthright Jean-François Coche: "The white 1997s are easy wines; we will not have to wait for them. They have very good ripeness, but they lack complexity and depth for greatness." He's right, with the exception of the Corton-Charlemagne and Meursault Perrières, both outstanding efforts.

For comparison, he served me a glass of the 1996 Meursault Perrières. It is a monumental work of art and one of the finest wines I have ever put to my lips.

I was pleasantly surprised to learn that Coche, certainly one of the finest producers of white burgundies, "adores" California Chardonnays. Asked to list some he had recently tasted, he quickly replied that Kistler, Marcassin, and Newton Unfiltered were his favorites because they are *"très, très mûr mais avec une belle structure. Ce sont des vins de plaisir"* (very, very ripe but with a good structure. They are wines of pleasure).

A helicopter spraying chemicals on a neighbor's plot crashed into Jean-François Coche's Corton-Charlemagne vines on July 23, 1998. Ten rows were damaged (46 vines planted in 1959 were completely destroyed), yet Coche was primarily relieved that none of the chemicals or the aircraft's fuel had leaked into the precious soil.

The 1997 Bourgogne Chardonnay has ripe pear aromas and a delicious, mineral-dominated core of fruit. This pure, austere, soft, and medium-bodied wine has all the components to be considered excellent yet finishes abruptly. Drink it over the next 3–4 years. Coche bottles 3 *villages* wines with the same exact label (it plainly states "Meursault" without a vineyard being designated), the Vireuils du Dessus, Vireuils du Milieu, and Narvaux. Both 1997 Vireuils have rather austere finishes. The Du Dessus is more explosive and richer and has delightful white plum flavors. The Du Milieu's silky character is made up of chalk, stone, and oak spices. However, my favorite of his three "Meursault" bottlings is the 1997 Meursault Narvaux. Kermit Lynch, the estate's official U.S. importer, purchases 600 of the 2,000 bottles produced. Fashioned from a parcel that touches Genevrières, this offering exhibits aromas reminiscent of golden fruits, red berries, and sweet oak spices. It is an ample, broad, and spicy wine filled with flavors suggesting roasted pears, apples, and nuts. This medium- to full-bodied, well-balanced, velvety, and sexy wine also possesses a beautifully long finish. Anticipated maturity: now–2004+.

Revealing candied almonds, marzipan, and overripe pear aromas, the 1997 Puligny-Montrachet Enseignères is just as opulent as the Narvaux. Spiced apples, caramel, poached white fruits, and grilled oak can be found in this thick and medium- to full-bodied offering. Its finish, rather austere and chalky, prevented it from meriting a higher rating. Drink it between now and 2004. The 1997 Meursault Les Chevalières has bright, rather rich mineral and honeysuckle aromas that give way to its citrusy, earthy, and floral character. This expansive wine is dense, thickly textured, and medium to full bodied. Its finish, similar to the previous offering's, prevented me from getting overly excited. Nonetheless, it is opulent, delicious, and concentrated, meriting serious attention. Drink it over the next 6 years. Revealing leesy and sweet vanilla bean scents, the 1997 Meursault Rougeots is silky textured and thick. This sultry, ample, medium- to full-bodied wine is both extraordinarily spicy and filled with candied nuts and acacia blossoms. If its oak-dominated finish is absorbed by its copious fruit, this complex and concentrated wine may merit a higher score. I was enthralled by the 1997 Meursault Caillerets' sweet butter-and-cinnamon-infused nose. Its flavor profile, crammed with apples, peach pits, minerals, and stones, also reveals traces of citrus fruits. This medium- to full-bodied and velvety wine has admirable breadth of flavors, superb focus, and a fine finish. Anticipated maturity: 2000–2006+.

The 1997 Meursault Perrières displays lovely aromas of candied limes, lemons, minerals, rocks, and smoke. This is a hugely rich, medium- to full-bodied, viscously textured wine. It has great class and enormous elegance to its peach, stone, earth, clay, and red berry-filled flavor profile. Were it not for an austere and lightly dusty finish, I would have been even more enamored by this offering's rich panoply of flavors and exquisite texture. Anticipated maturity: 2001–2007+. The 1997 Corton-Charlemagne exhibits superripe buttery pears, apples, and traces of tropical fruits in its nose. This is a huge wine, packed with layers of grilled nuts, peaches, almonds, and sweet white fruits that saturate the palate. It is full bodied, expansive, and immensely opulent. Like many wines from the 1997 vintage, however, it appears to have trouble fully integrating its alcohol and finishes on a warm and slightly austere note. I loved this offering, but it does not rival Coche's legendary Cortons from 1986, 1990, 1995, and 1996. Drink it between 2001 and 2008.

As I wrote earlier, Coche served me his 1996 Meursault Perrières in order to put the 1997s in perspective. Believe me, tasting this wine is an out-of-this-world experience! This masterpiece adds perfect balance, focus, and delineation to the 1997's richness, density, and weight. It is vibrant, spiritual, and as complex a wine as I can imagine. It attacks the palate with waves of candied lemons, marzipan, creamed hazelnuts, pears, grilled oak, curry, red berries, and loads of minerals. It is truly mind-blowing!

Many people in Burgundy and elsewhere, myself included, felt as though Coche's wines were not made for long-term cellaring. They were so good young, we were all convinced they would not get any better with time. We were wrong. Recent tastings of some of his older offerings have demonstrated that Domaine Coche-Dury's wines are spectacular young and even better with time. The 1996s, in his opinion, "are wines that will age immensely; they are not meant for restaurants."

Coche feels that 1996 is similar to 1978, but better, especially for the top wines. He is tremendously impressed with the "great acidity and great density" of the 1996s and was surprised by how long it took for malos to complete (a number of his barrels were still in the throws of malolactic fermentation in late November 1997).

The following tastings notes are given in the order in which the wines were presented. Coche started with wines that were still progressing through their malos (selecting barrels that were almost 100% finished with their malolactics), then proceeding to the Corton-Charlemagne that had finished its malolactic but had yet to be racked, and ending with the three wines that had terminated their malolactic fermentations and had been racked.

The 1996 Bourgogne reveals a lovely nose of smoke and grilled toast, followed by a deep, ripe, dense, medium-bodied, and thick core with great richness of fruit. Harvested at a whopping (for Burgundy) 13% potential alcohol, yet with vibrant and bracing acidity, this well-balanced wine is filled with oily nuts, minerals, and toast. Anticipated maturity: now–2004.

Coche allowed me to taste two of his "village" Meursaults, one from the Vireuils vineyard and the other from Les Narvaux. Both will be bottled separately, but neither vineyard name will appear on the label—there will be no visual way to differentiate between the two. The medium- to full-bodied 1996 Meursault (Vireuils) displays rich toast and hazelnut aromas and a juicy, superripe, deep, elegant, and superbly balanced personality. Mouth-coating layers of extracted minerals and hazelnut butter-cream are found in this gem. Anticipated maturity: 2000–2006. Aromatically, the 1996 Meursault (Narvaux) exhibits toasted almonds and honeysuckle. On the palate, this exceedingly rich, medium- to full-bodied, oily-textured, and superripe wine has excellent balance and tons of sweet white peaches, pears, minerals, and lemon zest. As with the previous wine, it should be at its best between 2000 and 2006. Revealing enticingly deep floral aromas, the 1996 Meursault Les Chevalières has an expansive, broad, and medium- to full-bodied core of crisp, complex, and highly focused minerally and toasty fruit. Extraordinary well balanced and delineated, this wine should be at its peak between 2000 and 2007. The outstanding 1996 Meursault Rougeots possesses awesome mineral depth on the nose and a superconcentrated, luscious, broad-shouldered, yet defined, focused, and highly delineated personality. Medium to full bodied, refined, and precise, this wine is filled with oily minerals intertwined with zest citrus peels. Anticipated maturity: 2001–2008.

Displaying unbelievable depth to its spicy pear, white peach, and floral aromas, the full-bodied 1996 Corton-Charlemagne is an awesomely rich as well as perfectly delineated and balanced wine. This oily-textured tour de force has an embracing, almost enveloping, flavor profile crammed with intense stones, minerals, superripe pears, waves of nuts and minerals, and touches of grilled toast. The taster's palate is held prisoner by the interminable layers and layers of concentrated, highly extracted, and powerful fruit that roll across it, each sublimely defined and focused by this wine's racy acidity. This show-stopper should reach its peak by 2003 and hold it through 2010.

The 1996 Puligny-Montrachet Les Enseignères has a deeply ripe, floral- and white peach-infused nose. On the palate, this fat, luscious, broad-shouldered, and full-bodied wine offers mouth-coating layers of velvety white fruits, hazelnuts, and candied orange peels. While not as precise or balanced as Coche's other wines, this gem has an admirable finish that reveals traces of minerals and stones. Anticipated maturity: 2000–2005. In 1996, Domaine Coche-Dury introduced a new wine to his lineup: the Meursault Caillerets. This is the first wine produced (only 1,000 bottles) from these recently planted vines. Exhibiting a refined nose of chalk and minerals, it has breathtaking finesse and precision as well as a full-bodied, wild mushroom, stone, juniper berry, clove, and poached pear flavor profile. I recommend drinking this beauty between 2000 and 2004.

The 1995 Meursault is an extraordinary "village" appellation wine and an absolutely fabulous offering in its own right. Coche told me that virtually every grape that went into making this gem was a *millerand* (a stunted fruit embryo packed with concentrated juice), which partially explains its grandeur. Produced from a blend of the Les Luchets and Aux Moulin Landin vineyards, it displays a ripe, deep, and vanilla-infused nose. On the palate, it is unbelievably rich, broad, expansive, concentrated, and jam-packed with lively candied pears, toast, minerals, and hazelnut cream. Anticipated maturity: 2001–2007. Jean-François Coche produced a total of 900 bottles (at over a ton of fruit per acre) of his otherworldly 1995 Meursault Perrières. This quintessentially elegant wine reveals liquid minerals intertwined with flowers, spices, and stones. The French would say it is *aerien,* meaning it is spiritual. On the palate, this highly defined and hyperconcentrated, thick, full-bodied, yet perfectly delineated Meursault Perrières exhibits waves of toasted almonds, hazelnuts, and wet stones and an unbelievably long finish. Literally minutes after I had tasted it, my palate remained permeated with its sumptuous flavors. When I visited the domaine in January 1997 to taste the 1995s, Coche did not allow me to try them, saying they were being subjected to a severe fining. He then smiled, almost winked, and said, "But when they are ready you will not find them to be too bad." Those few people lucky enough to secure a few bottles of this gem should consume it between 2005 and 2014. Bravo!

Other wines recently tasted: 1997 Meursault Vireuils du Dessus (88–90), 1997 Meursault Vireuils du Milieu (88–89).

DOMAINE MARC COLIN ET FILS (GAMAY-ST. AUBIN)

1996 Bâtard-Montrachet (Domaine Pierre Colin)	EEE	92
1996 Chassagne-Montrachet	D	88
1996 Chassagne-Montrachet Les Caillerets	E	92
1996 Chassagne-Montrachet Les Champs-Gain	E	91
1996 Chassagne-Montrachet Vide Bourse	E	89
1996 Montrachet	EEE	96

1996 Puligny-Montrachet La Garenne	E	92
1996 Puligny-Montrachet Le Trézin	D	87
1996 St. Aubin Le Charmois	D	89
1996 St. Aubin La Chatenière	D	88
1996 St. Aubin En Remilly	D	87

The 56-year-old Marc Colin (a cousin of Chassagne's Michel Colin of Domaine Colin-Deleger fame) is now in semiretirement—1994 was the last vintage he harvested and vinified alone—and his two sons, Pierre-Yves and Joseph, have taken over the domaine's day-to-day. The estate is located in the hamlet of Gamay, almost directly behind the hillside that produces Montrachet, Chevalier-Montrachet, and so on.

Pierre-Yves Colin, the tall, self-assured, and intelligent elder son, is responsible for all cellar work, whereas Joseph is responsible for the vineyards. Due to the fact that the cellars tend to be warmer than most of Burgundy's, malolactic fermentations take place relatively quickly, and the *élevages* are kept short (all the 1996s were in bottle by the first week of September 1997). *Bâtonnage* is employed extensively, at least 3 times a week until Christmas, or when the malos start, and new oak is used judiciously, with the St. Aubins seeing 25% new barrels, the Chassagnes and Puligny-Montrachet Le Trézin 30%, the Puligny-Montrachet La Garenne 40%, and the Bâtard and Montrachet 50%. Pierre-Yves Colin, who trained at California's famous Chalk Hill winery, believes in using barrels from a large number of coopers because he doesn't want one *tonnelier*'s style to "mark" his wines.

Domaine Marc Colin's wines do not impress with sheer size. These are not wines for those searching out full-bodied monsters, as these are generally elegant, refined, and defined. They have excellent to outstanding concentration, richness, and ripeness and can often be quite expressive.

Revealing stone and mineral aromas, the 1996 St. Aubin En Remilly is a rich, pear- and gravel-laden, medium-bodied, silky, and well-crafted wine. Balanced, ripe, and with attractive purity in its long finish, this delicious wine should be at its peak between 1999 and 2002. The 1996 St. Aubin La Chatenière is anise, flower, and fresh cream scented and possesses a concentrated, well-structured, and medium-bodied core of pears and minerals. It is more powerful and expressive than the previous wine yet is also stylistically more austere. Anticipated maturity: now–2003. Produced from one of my favorite St. Aubin vineyards, abutting the northern border of Chassagne-Montrachet Les Chaumées, the 1996 St. Aubin Le Charmois is truly excellent and verging on outstanding. It exhibits a creamy, spicy nose and a deep, refined, medium- to full-bodied, and velvety-textured character packed with anise, malt, stones, and oaky spices. This well-balanced, seductive, and long wine should be at its peak of maturity between now and 2003.

The 1996 Puligny-Montrachet Le Trézin's nose was so tight the day I visited the domaine that I was unable to discover any of its aromas. However, on the palate, it reveals a silky texture, a medium to full body, and an appealingly powerful minerality. I recommend drinking this wine by 2001.

Ninety percent of the grapes that went into the 1996 Chassagne-Montrachet are from the well-placed Encégnières vineyard—it borders Bâtard-Montrachet to the north and west, Puligny-Montrachet Les Enseignères to the northeast, and the premier cru Chassagne-Montrachet Vide Bourse to the southwest. It displays a fresh and pure nose composed of minerals and nuts as well as a very dry yet ripe, medium-bodied, delineated, and well-crafted character. White flowers and gravel can be discerned in its flavor profile as well as in its long and precise finish. Anticipated maturity: now–2003. Marc Colin always blended his 1996 Chassagne-Montrachet Vide Bourse into his village offering, but since 1994 his sons have bottled it separately. Its floral and perfumed nose is followed by a mouth-coatingly rich, oily-textured, yet medium-bodied core of complex flavors of rock dust, chalk, and minerals. This excellent wine should be at its peak between 2000 and 2004. The 1996 Chassagne-Montrachet Les Champs-Gain exhibits a gorgeous purity to its stone and gravel aromatic profile. On the palate, this medium-bodied, silky-textured, refined, concentrated, and complex wine offers minerals and spicy oak flavors. Its long, intricate, and precise finish is a delight. Anticipated maturity: 2002–2007. Forty percent of the vines in Colin's 1996 Chassagne-Montrachet Les Caillerets parcel are 90 years old, with the balance split evenly among 40- and 15-year-old vines. It reveals rock dust aromas and a bone-dry, medium-bodied, and beguiling core of slate, stones, and gravel. Medium bodied and rich, this vibrant wine has dazzling concentration, power, and extraction. It should age effortlessly. Anticipated maturity: 2004–2010+.

Produced from 70-year-old vines, the outstanding 1996 Puligny-Montrachet La Garenne has an expressive nose laden with candied almonds and honeysuckle blossoms. This fat, medium- to full-bodied, rich, and mouth-coating wine is concentrated and powerful, yet refined and detailed. Poached pear, nuts, and lees can be found in its flavor profile in addition to its lingering finish. It should be at its best between 2002 and 2007.

The 1996 Bâtard-Montrachet (from 18-year-old vines) carries the same label as the rest of Marc Colin's wines except that it lists Domaine Pierre Colin (a family member) as the proprietor. Aromatically, it reveals deep richness and powerful honeysuckle blossoms. Its medium- to full-bodied, mouth-coating, oily-textured, profound, and well-focused character is lively and packed with minerals. It should be at its peak between 2002 and 2006. Produced from vines that are at least 70 years old, Colin's 1996 Montrachet is truly stunning. In 1996, 2 barrels (50 cases) were produced from the estate's tiny parcel of vines (slightly less than one-third of an acre). The harvest came in at 13.9% natural potential alcohol, practically unheard of in Burgundy. Aromatically, this wine displays a deep richness, stones, and nuts. This superbly balanced and defined wine saturates the palate with almond paste, white flowers, minerals, honeysuckle blossoms, anise, and fresh, sweet butter flavors. Complex, concentrated, powerful, yet magnificently refined and elegant, this spectacular offering should age effortlessly. As the wine sat in the glass its flavor profile and aromas gathered more strength and expressiveness, and its body appeared to grow even thicker. Readers who have never had the opportunity to try a bottle of this estate's Montrachets should know that the Colins are planning to uproot their parcel and replant in the not-so-distant future. Anticipated maturity: 2004–2015.

DOMAINE COLIN-DELÉGER (CHASSAGNE-MONTRACHET)

Year	Wine		
1997	Bâtard-Montrachet	EEE	88
1996	Bâtard-Montrachet	EE	95
1995	Bâtard-Montrachet	EEE	93+
1997	Chassagne-Montrachet	D	86
1996	Chassagne-Montrachet	D	88
1995	Chassagne-Montrachet	D	87
1996	Chassagne-Montrachet Les Chaumées	D	89
1995	Chassagne-Montrachet Les Chaumées	D	90
1997	Chassagne-Montrachet Les Chenevottes	E	88
1996	Chassagne-Montrachet Les Chenevottes	D	91+
1995	Chassagne-Montrachet Les Chenevottes	D	92+

1997 Chassagne-Montrachet La Maltroie	E	88+
1996 Chassagne-Montrachet La Maltroie	D	90
1995 Chassagne-Montrachet La Maltroie	D	89
1997 Chassagne-Montrachet Morgeot	E	89+
1996 Chassagne-Montrachet Morgeot	D	92
1995 Chassagne-Montrachet Morgeot	D	90?
1997 Chassagne-Montrachet En Remilly	E	88
1996 Chassagne-Montrachet En Remilly	D	92
1995 Chassagne-Montrachet En Remilly	D	91
1997 Chassagne-Montrachet Les Vergers	E	90
1996 Chassagne-Montrachet Les Vergers	D	93+
1995 Chassagne-Montrachet Les Vergers	D	91+
1997 Chevalier-Montrachet	EEE	91
1995 Chevalier-Montrachet	EEE	?
1997 Puligny-Montrachet La Truffière	EE	90+
1996 Puligny-Montrachet La Truffière	E	93
1995 Puligny-Montrachet La Truffière	EE	92
1997 Puligny-Montrachet Les Demoiselles	EE	92
1996 Puligny-Montrachet Les Demoiselles	EE	94
1995 Puligny-Montrachet Les Demoiselles	EE	93
1997 St. Aubin En Charmois	D	87
1996 St. Aubin En Charmois	D	86
1996 St. Aubin Les Combes	D	88
1995 St. Aubin Les Combes	C	88+

Michel Colin, the extremely talented owner of this estate, consistently bottles his white wines early, generally during the month of August. Domaine Colin-Deléger works 47 acres of vines, over half of which is *en fermage*, a relatively large spread by Burgundy standards.

Colin, a gifted winemaker, performed less *bâtonnage* than usual on his 1997 white burgundies. While he felt compelled to "rectify" the acid levels of his reds, he did not touch the whites. These are fat, slightly flabby wines, yet they are expressive, full of fruit, and delicious and will require near-term to midterm consumption.

Unlike most of his Burgundian colleagues, Colin begins the vinifications of his white wines in stainless-steel tanks before transferring them to oak barrels. He believes this technique provides his wines with more elegance, freshness, and purity of fruit. The vast majority of high-quality producers perform the entire vinification and *élevage* of their wines in barrel. Another notable exception to this is Puligny's famous Domaine Leflaive, where the wines are transferred from barrels to tanks to finish the aging process.

Revealing talcum powder aromas, the 1997 St. Aubin En Charmois is an ample, generous, and flavorful offering. Its concentrated and dense character reveals sweet pears and minerals, as well as a slight pastiness to its texture. Drink it over the next 3–4 years. The 1997 Chassagne-Montrachet offers an earthy, mineral-laden nose. This medium-bodied, fat, and thick wine has flint and stone flavors in its heavy and expressive personality. Anticipated maturity: now–2002. The quartz- and chalk-scented 1997 Chassagne-Montrachet La Maltroie is ample, medium to full bodied, and powerful. It has a velvety texture, excellent concentration, loads of earth and clay flavors, and a warm, slightly alcoholic finish. Drink it over the next 4+ years. Displaying floral and perfumed aromas, the 1997 Chassagne-Montrachet En Remilly is another rich, dense, and thick offering. It is medium to full bodied, broad, and crammed with fresh earth, almond paste, and ripe white fruits. Its somewhat pasty finish reveals a warm and alcoholic trait that can be found in numerous 1997s. Anticipated maturity: now–2003. The 1997 Chassagne-Montrachet Les Chenevottes has a bright mineral and flower-laden nose. This wine has a firm structure and a long, pure finish. It is well crafted, silky textured, and elegant and offers subtle flavors reminiscent of stones and crisp pears. Drink it over the next 5 years. I loved the tangy mineral and stone aromatics of the 1997 Chassagne-Montrachet Les Vergers. This is a well-focused wine. It offers a medium to full body, citrus juice-covered minerals, and an oily texture. Its admirable finish is long, precise, and devoid of the pastiness and the alcoholic warmth I found in some of Colin-Deléger's 1997s. Anticipated maturity: now–2004. The vanilla- and poached pear-scented 1997 Chassagne-Montrachet Morgeot is an unbelievably thick and rich wine. Its full-bodied and opulent personality offers honeyed and buttered earth flavors that are surprisingly well defined given this monster's weight. It will not make old bones but will certainly deliver loads of pleasure over the next 5 years.

Revealing aromas of freshly sautéed wild mushrooms and lemons, the layered 1997 Puligny-Montrachet La Truffière is a dense, medium- to full-bodied wine. I tremendously enjoyed its well-focused, fat, and flavorful character (filled with powerful earth, marzipan, and floral tones) yet was less enthralled by its pasty mouth-feel. If time changes that characteristic, my score will appear to have been conservative. Nonetheless, this is an outstanding wine. It is powerful and medium to full bodied and possesses an admirably long finish. Anticipated maturity: now–2005. Colin's Puligny-Montrachet Les Demoiselles is his most complete 1997. It exhibits floral, perfumed mineral scents as well as a medium- to full-bodied and beautifully focused personality. Layers of earth, tangy white fruits, stones, and oak spices can be found in its complex and silky flavor profile. This elegant, well-delineated wine also boasts the longest and purest finish of any of Colin's 1997s. Drink it between 2001 and 2007+.

The Colin-Deléger 1997 Bâtard-Montrachet is more a syrup of Chardonnay than white burgundy. Rich aromas of talcum powder, superripe pears, anise, and oak spices lead to its overpoweringly thick and dense personality. It is full bodied and crammed with oily layers of spiced fruits, honey, molasses, citrus candies, wet wool, and roasted apples. This wine is impressive for its size yet less pleasurable to drink. Anticipated maturity: now–2003. I much preferred the 1997 Chevalier-Montrachet. It reveals a nose of fresh minerals and buttered toast, as well as a richly textured core of powerful peach pit, stone, and petrol flavors (reminiscent of a dry Alsatian Riesling). This medium- to full-bodied, fat, and broad wine has beautiful focus and elegance. It would have merited an even more enthusiastic review were it not for a slight pastiness in its otherwise long and complex finish. Drink it between 2001 and 2007.

In my first tasting of Michel Colin's 1996s, I was compelled to give the St. Aubin Les Combes a question mark instead of a numerical because it was in an undecipherable state when I visited the estate. Retasted a few months ago, the wine had sorted itself out, offering a lovely nose of toasted oak and sweet minerals as well as a candied white fruit, leesy, stony, and spicy character. It is an exceedingly well-made wine. Drink it between now and 2003.

Always among the first of the major white burgundy producers to bottle, Michel Colin makes forward wines that can be enjoyed the moment they are released. This estate's 1995s were some of the best wines produced to date, combining first-rate extraction of fruit with excellent balance. The 1996 vintage has proven to be a spectacular one for Colin's wines. The bright, bracing, focus-providing acidity that characterizes the vintage married magnificently well with his trademark plump, ripe, rich, and concentrated wine style.

Revealing an expressive mineral-and-stone-scented nose, the 1996 St. Aubin En Charmois is a rich, balanced, medium-bodied, and floral wine. Drink it before the millennium. The 1996 Chassagne-Montrachet exhibits buttered popcorn aromatics and a mouth-coating, oily, medium-bodied, superripe, and almost unctuous character. Poached pears, juniper berries, peaches, and spicy oak can be found in its concentrated flavor profile. This first-rate village offering will be at its best from now to 2001. Aromatically, the outstanding 1996 Chassagne-Montrachet La Maltroie displays flowers and almond butter. On the palate, this expansive, medium- to full-bodied, thick, very ripe, and concentrated wine has wonderful cookie dough, marzipan, and mineral flavors. While it has the necessary components for midterm cellaring, I recommend drinking this opulent wine in its youth. Anticipated maturity: now–2002. Colin's 1996 Chassagne-Montrachet Les Chaumées has minerals, stones, and steel on its nose and an explosive, rich, broad, and ample mouth revealing some Earl Grey tea and pear flavors. It appeared a bit warm and alcoholic when I tasted it, but this trait will most probably be resolved by the time it reaches our shores. Drink it between now and 2002.

The impressive 1996 Chassagne-Montrachet En Remilly possesses fabulous licorice and butter cookie aromas and an expansive, rich, medium- to full-bodied, and hyperripe but wonderfully balanced core of baked peaches, poached pears, and honeysuckle. This elegant yet powerful beauty should be at its best between now and 2004. Produced from vines planted in 1929, the 1996 Chassagne-Montrachet Les Chenevottes reveals stones, minerals, and sweetened tea on the nose, followed by a lively, exciting, silky, medium-bodied, and well-focused core of concentrated chalk, rock dust, and earthy flavors. It is the only one of Colin's 1996 offerings where I preferred the 1995 version. Anticipated maturity: now–2004. The 1996 Chassagne-Montrachet Morgeot had an unyielding nose the day of my visit but displayed a marvelously ripe, wide, masculine, and chewy medium to full body jam-packed with highly focused liquid minerals and stones. It has the mouth-feel of a red wine yet the crispness and delineation found in racy whites. Anticipated maturity: 2001–2006. I was blown away by Colin's 1996 Chassagne-Montrachet Les Vergers, undoubtedly the finest and most ageworthy of his 1996 Chassagnes. Displaying a deep, rich, and spicy nose, this magnificent wine combines stellar ripeness with classy refinement. Exotic and juicy white fruits, minerals, and steel are found in its expansive, medium- to full-bodied, and oily-textured personality. Complex, elegant, powerful, and gloriously persistent, it will provide superb pleasure in the short and mid- to long term. Anticipated maturity: 2001–2010.

Both of Colin's Puligny-Montrachet premiers crus are stunning wines. Revealing a highly expressive floral nose, the 1996 Puligny-Montrachet La Truffiére offers wonderful cake icing, honeysuckle, poached pear, and toasted mineral flavors in its classy and refined character. In addition, this wine has extraordinary depth and richness to its highly defined, feminine, supremely elegant, and full body. It will be at its best between 2001 and 2010. Earth, wild mushrooms, citrus fruits, flowers, minerals, and traces of honey are found in the 1996 Puligny-Montrachet Les Demoiselles' complex and beguiling aromatics. This enthralling Chevalier-Montrachet look-alike has enormous class and refinement. It offers a rich, ripe, highly concentrated, and extremely detailed flavor profile filled with walnuts, stones, and sweet but crisp pears. In its admirable finish anise and juniper berries can be discerned. Drink this magnificent wine between 2002 and 2010.

The 1996 Bâtard-Montrachet reveals a superripe yet lively nose and an expansive, broad-shouldered, and full-bodied personality. Almond paste, deeply imbedded minerals, stones, white flowers, and sweet oak spices are found in this powerful, superthick, and mouth-coating yet racy and well-balanced wine. I was so struck by this tour de force's mouth-feel that I unknowingly wrote the words "superrich," "unreal richness," "deep richness," and, finally, "*rich!*" one after the other in my notepad. This luxurious offering should be at its best between 2002 and 2010.

Offering scents of minerals, nuts, and fresh spices, the 1995 Chassagne-Montrachet is beautifully floral, with good balance and length. This medium-bodied wine should be enjoyed in its youth but will last for 4–5 years. With mineral-scented aromatics, the 1995 St. Aubin Les Combes is, for Burgundy, an excellent value. Medium bodied and thick textured, this steely, flinty wine exhibits good length and the capacity to age well for 5+ years. The day I tasted the 1995 Chassagne-Montrachet La Maltroie its nose was completely unyielding, but its delicious, silky-textured mouth convinced me of its quality. Powerful flavors of minerals, white flowers, and crisp red currants make this an excellent, medium-bodied wine to drink over the next 5–7 years. Even though its robe has a touch of gold, which tends to worry me in whites this young, the thick and luscious deep fat fruits and lovely floral touches the 1995 Chassagne-Montrachet Les Chaumées exhibits merit an outstanding score. Medium to full bodied, it can be drunk from now to 2005. Also with a slight gold hue to its color, the roasted fruit- and nut-scented 1995 Chassagne-Montrachet En Remilly displays a robust and powerful, oil-textured mouth filled with toasted apricots and peaches. Concentrated and long, this delicious offering should be enjoyed over the next decade. Not coincidentally, the 1995 Chassagne-Montrachet Les Chenevottes, Colin-Deléger's finest value, is also made from his oldest vines. Combining excellent length with powerful explosive flavors as well as elegance, this is a dazzling white burgundy for under $50 a bottle. Revealing deep aromas of minerals, flowers, and crisp peaches, this gem offers a thick core of steel, iron, minerals, and wild mushrooms in the mouth. Drink it between now and 2008. Unyielding on the nose, the 1995 Chassagne-Montrachet Les Vergers exhibits an extremely floral mouth with touches of flint, stones, and honeysuckle. Very refined, rich, and with excellent persistence, this medium- to full-bodied and structured beauty will provide delightful drinking from its release to 2008. Difficult to assess the day I tasted it, the 1995 Chassagne-Montrachet Morgeot shows a stony, minerally, and almondy core and superb balance. This medium-bodied offering may ultimately be better than the score suggests. Both of Michel Colin's 1995 Pulignys are marvelous: deep sweet fruits can be discerned lurking in the tightly wound nose of the Puligny-Montrachet La Truffière. Gorgeously ripe, and with notes of refined roasted fruits, this silky beauty has the stuffing and structure needed for 10–12 years of cellaring, if those lucky enough to own some can resist its charms. Sublimely elegant, the Puligny-Montrachet Les Demoiselles displays a superb spicy and almondy nose and silky-textured flavors bursting with superripe, sweet roasted and toasted fruits. Beautifully long on the finish, this medium- to full-bodied wine can be consumed upon release or held for a decade or more. Possibly a touch better, the 1995 Bâtard-Montrachet exhibits a superripe nose of candied fruits and white chocolate and a floral, spicy, smoky, oily-textured mouth filled with ripe peaches. Well delineated and impressively long, this fabulous wine can be drunk between now and 2010. Colin's 1995 Chevalier-Montrachet was impossible to assess, as it appeared quite sulfured the day of my visit. Earth tones, wild mushrooms, and slight floral scents could be discerned, as well as a tangy and superminerally component in the mouth.

Other wines recently tasted: 1997 Bourgogne Chardonnay (85), 1997 Chassagne-Montrachet Les Chaumées (88?), 1997 Puligny-Montrachet (86), 1997 St. Aubin Les Combes (86).

DOMAINE DE LA CONDEMINE (MÂCONNAIS)

1997 Mâcon Peronne	B	86

This very good to excellent, lemony, citrusy Chardonnay exhibits a creamy texture, low acidity, fine ripeness, and good length. It is a fruit-driven wine that has never spent any time in oak. Drink it over the next 1–2 years.

ALAIN CORCIA SELECTIONS (SAVIGNY-LÈS-BEAUNE)

1997 Chablis	B	86
1996 Meursault Charmes Vieilles Vignes Cuvée Albert Grivault (Hospices de Beaune)	E	?
1996 Meursault Narvaux	D	88
1996 Meursault Premier Cru	D	89
1996 Meursault Tillets	D	88
1996 Meursault Les Vireuils—Domaine Bernerd Vaudoisey-Mutin*	D	87
1996 Montagny Premier Cru Crème de La Crème Domaine Daventure Frères	B	87?
1997 Montagny Premier Cru Vieilles Vignes	B	86
1996 Montagny Premier Cru Vieilles Vignes Domaine Daventure Frères	B	87
1996 Pouilly-Fuissé Cuvée Françoise Poisard (Hospices de Beaune)	D	88?
1996 St. Véran Domaine des Vieilles Pierres	A	87
1997 St. Véran Patricia Vieilles Vignes Aged in Oak	B	86
1996 St. Véran Vieilles Vignes Domaine Jobert	B	87

Alain Corcia continues to be a fine source of fairly priced whites from the Mâconnais and the Côte de Beaune. Few brokers or importers offer such outstanding values.

The 1997 Chablis offers ripe pear and herbal aromas as well as a medium-bodied and silky-textured personality. This delicious wine reveals a flinty and white fruit-dominated flavor profile that has appealing richness, density, and grip. Drink it over the next 3–4 years. Interestingly, the 1997 St. Véran Patricia Vieilles Vignes was crafted using significantly more new oak barrels (70%) than the "Julie" cuvée (30%) yet coped with it much better. This sweet pear-and-apple-scented offering has an attractive core of minerals, almonds, and well-ripened white fruits. It is a medium-bodied, silky-textured, well-concentrated and -crafted wine with a spicy, oaky finish. It should be consumed over the next 4 years. Corcia's dependable 1997 Montagny Premier Cru is once again delicious. It displays sweet and spicy oak aromas intermingled with hints of poached pears. This broad, rich, medium-bodied, and thick wine offers flavors reminiscent of baked apples and smoky wood. Anticipated maturity: now–2002.

The results of Alain Corcia's later efforts to locate additional reasonably priced whites from the 1996 vintage were mixed. However, the Domaine Bernard Vaudoisey-Mutin's 1996 Meursault Les Vireuils (Corcia's name does not appear on the label) was a find. It offers mineral, nut, and citrus-laced aromas as well as a beautifully balanced, well-crafted, medium body. This fresh, focused, and vivacious wine has sweet pear, candied hazelnut, and spicy oak flavors in its crisp yet rich personality. Anticipated maturity: now–2004+.

*Corcia's name does not appear on the label.

Produced from an old-vine vineyard near the village of Vergisson and aged in 10% new oak, the 1996 St. Véran Domaine des Vieilles Pierres has a rich smoky nose and a dense, ripe, mineral and nut-laden palate. Medium bodied, silky textured, and well balanced, this wine will provide delicious drinking over the next 3 years. The 1996 St. Véran Vieilles Vignes Domaine Jobert was aged in 75% new oak. It reveals toasted and spiced oak scents and a dense, medium-bodied, and thickly textured core of minerals and metals drenched in vanilla. This wine should be consumed over the next 3 years as well. Domaine Daventure Frères' 1996 Montagny Premier Cru Vieilles Vignes was crafted from 20-year-old vines (young for the vieilles vignes designation, in my opinion) and aged in 30% new oak barrels. Smoke, minerals, and earth aromas are followed by a medium-bodied, well-balanced, and vibrant character filled with citrus fruits. The Domaine Daventure Fréres 1996 Montagny Premier Cru Crème de la Crème has a rich, tropical fruit-packed nose. On the palate, it exhibits a medium body and tangy, crisp—almost strident—lemons. I'm not convinced this wine's fruit can withstand its massive levels of citrusy acidity, hence the question mark.

The 1996 Pouilly-Fuissé Cuvée Françoise Poisard (Hospices de Beaune) possesses smoke, stone, and oak aromas as well as a dense, ripe, and medium- to full-bodied personality. Its flavor profile reveals lemon and minerals awash in sweet, grilled, and toasty oak. This wine has the potential to be excellent if its beautifully extracted core of fruit can overcome the (overly?) lavish use of oak. Anticipated maturity: now–2003. Aromatically revealing loads of minerals, the 1996 Meursault Narvaux is a rich, medium- to full-bodied, and thick beauty filled with gorgeous layers of candied hazelnuts and almonds. This well-proportioned and balanced wine also offers a long and persistent finish. It should be at its best between now and 2003. Displaying powerful mineral aromas and traces of honey on the nose, the 1996 Meursault Tillets has a delightfully velvety texture, a medium to full body, and well-delineated flavors of flint, honeysuckle, and lemon in its character. Anticipated maturity: now–2004. Produced from vines located in the Poruzots and Charmes vineyards, the 1996 Meursault Premier Cru offers wild mushroom and white flower scents as well as a medium-to full-bodied, well-balanced, and oily-textured personality. Its flavor profile is composed of pears, minerals, anise, and honeysuckle. This concentrated and extremely well-crafted wine should age quite well. Drink it between 2000 and 2006. The 1996 Meursault Charmes Vieilles Vignes Cuvée Albert Grivault (Hospices de Beaune) displayed outstanding ripeness and richness but seemed to be completely dominated by its overpowering oak aromas and flavors. Alain Corcia was planning to have the wine removed from the new oak barrels provided by the Hospices to allow it to mellow for some time in older vessels.

Other wines recently tasted: 1997 Bourgogne Chardonnay (83), 1996 Chassagne-Montrachet (82?), 1997 Chassagne-Montrachet (70?), 1996 Meursault (84), 1997 Montagny (84), 1997 Pouilly-Fuissé (85), 1996 Puligny-Montrachet (80?), 1997 Puligny-Montrachet (85), 1997 St. Aubin (85), St. Véran Domaine Jobert (84), St. Véran Julie Vieilles Vignes Aged in Oak (80).

DOMAINE CORDIER ET FILS (FUISSÉ)

1997 Bourgogne Blanc	B	87
1997 Mâcon Chardonnay	B	87
1996 Mâcon Chardonnay	B	87
1997 Mâcon-Fuissé	B	88
1997 Pouilly-Fuissé Champs-Murgers	D	(89–91)
1996 Pouilly-Fuissé Juliette La Grande	E	93*
1997 Pouilly-Fuissé Metertière	D	(90–92)

1997	Pouilly-Fuissé Vers-Cras	D	(91–93)
1997	Pouilly-Fuissé Vieilles Vignes	D	(89–91)
1997	Pouilly-Fuissé Vigne Blanche	D	(90–92)
1997	Pouilly-Loché	C	88
1997	St. Véran	C	(88–90)

Christophe Cordier, the intense, thoughtful, bright, and cheery young man who runs this estate (his father, Roger, recently retired) is dedicated to producing high-quality wines. I was tremendously impressed with his 1996s and was ecstatic to see that his 1997s confirmed this future star's potential.

When I visited him in late October 1998 I learned he had finished his 1998 harvest just a week earlier. Constantly tinkering with new approaches and techniques, Cordier had decided to cut the number of harvesters by half, employing 15 skilled hands instead of the normal 30. "I thought it would be easier to explain to 15 people exactly what I wanted them to do instead of to 30. I was also able to do a better job of supervising the quality of their work." His 1998 harvest, spread out over a month, resulted in extremely low yields due to frost and hail damage. Some of his vineyards, such as Pouilly-Loché and Mâcon-Fuissé, had yields of $2/3$ of a ton of fruit per acre. In his St. Véran parcels, he produced one-third of what he was legally entitled. For example, Cordier is permitted to make 12 barrels of St. Véran, yet he produced only 4 in 1998 and 5 in 1997.

There are two cuvées of 1997 Mâcon Chardonnay, both qualitatively equal yet stylistically different. For the English market, Cordier vinified the wine in stainless steel and used *microbullage* (a system of releasing small quantities of air inside tanks or barrels). It reveals a sweet tea, quince-infused nose as well as an oily-textured and medium-bodied character with bright mineral flavors. The cuvée crafted for the U.S. and French markets was aged in large wooden *foudres* and has smoky, toasty aromas. It is slightly less oily textured than the English cuvée but more vibrant and lemony. This delicious, vibrant, and crisp offering is wonderfully thirst-quenching and will be a terrific match for subtle seafood dishes. Both cuvées should be consumed over the next 3 years. The 1997 Mâcon-Fuissé initially displayed smoky pine scents that mutated into candied lemon aromas. This rich, medium- to full-bodied, and layered wine is filled with delightful nutty and sweetened Earl Grey tea flavors. Concentrated and thickly textured, it admirably displays the density and power associated with moderate yields and well-ripened fruit. Drink it over the next 4 years.

Cordier's Bourgogne Blanc is entitled to the Mâcon-Villages appellation; however, according to him, the market is more responsive if he declassifies it. This sad state of affairs reflects the fact that the vast majority of wines bearing the Mâcon moniker are mediocre, produced from machine-harvested high-yielding vineyards. When producers start declassifying wines in order to sell them, it should serve as a wake-up call to the bureaucrats who set the standards for the appellation. That being said, the 1997 offering has a lovely nose composed of stone and chalk aromas and a soft, well-extracted, balanced, and rich character. Its dried white fruit, nut, and mineral flavors could have elevated this wine to a higher rating if it had a longer finish. Drink it over the next 3 years. The flint-and-mineral-scented 1997 Pouilly-Loché has a rock dust and lemon-laced flavor profile. This medium-bodied, vibrant wine has extremely good grip as well as excellent depth and focus. It will be at its best if drunk over the next 4 years.

Christophe Cordier aged the 1997 St. Véran in one second-year and four third-year oak barrels, performing regular and numerous *bâtonnages* throughout its *élevage*. Revealing a freshly cut hay and charred oak-infused nose, it possesses a medium- to full-bodied, well-crafted, and structured core of minerals and earth. It is dense, silky textured, and extremely flavorful and has a long, drawn-out finish. Anticipated maturity: now–2004. The 1997

Pouilly-Fuissé Champs-Murgers (a blend of recently purchased 15-year-old parcels in the Champs and Murgers vineyards) was harvested at 14% natural alcohol. It displays a rich, creamy nose of white flowers, nuts, and stones. On the palate, this medium- to full-bodied, gorgeously ripe, and velvety wine is crammed with sweet pears, marzipan, and anise flavors. While I suspect that it has a very modest amount of residual sweetness, it would certainly qualify as a dry wine. Anticipated maturity: now–2005. The 1997 Pouilly-Fuissé Vieilles Vignes, harvested at the same ripeness level as the previous wine, offers a dramatically different character. Spiced pear and earthy scents lead to an intense, tangy, almost Chablis-like personality. It offers great concentration, flavors reminiscent of two chalk-caked erasers slammed against each other, and an excellent hold. Drink it between 2000 and 2005.

The impressive 1997 Pouilly-Fuissé Metertière reveals a deep nose crammed with earth and minerals. Wave upon wave of white chocolate-covered minerals coat the palate in this powerful and well-delineated wine. It is medium to full bodied, expansive, boldly flavored, yet still unevolved. Anticipated maturity: 2001–2006. Cordier's most complete wine in 1997 is his super Pouilly-Fuissé Vers-Cras. It displays a wet wool, sweat, and liquid mineral nose as well as a gorgeously elegant, medium- to full-bodied, and impeccably balanced character. Almond extract, acacia blossoms, and myriad spices can be found in this beautifully harmonious, silky-textured, medium- to full-bodied, and tightly wound offering. Anticipated maturity: 2001–2007. The 1997 Pouilly-Fuissé Vigne Blanche was harvested at a huge 14.7% natural alcohol. It is Cordier's most intense 1997, exhibiting aromas verging on tropical notes and a bracing personality. A mouthful, this full-bodied, dense wine assaults the palate with successive waves of powerful flavors of spiced pears, baked apples, honeysuckle, minerals, and flint. If it develops more harmony and elegance, it may merit a higher rating. Anticipated maturity: 2001–2007.

In 1997, when I first visited the estate, Christophe Cordier served me the components of the 1996 Pouilly-Fuissé Juliette La Grande, named after his young daughter. Crafted from overripe, late-harvested grapes, this is an atypical Pouilly-Fuissé, hence the asterisk (*) next to its score. "I know it is a great wine," said Cordier, "but what is its purpose, and what dishes will it go with? I just don't know." Its aromas are reminiscent of an older semisweet Chenin Blanc from the Loire, with roasted nuts, chocolate milk, sweetened tea, and quince notes. It is a superbly concentrated, massively powerful, medium- to full-bodied, and intense wine with liquid mineral, spiced pear, and apple compote flavors. Its high alcohol gives it a warm, almost spiritlike finish that may well be absorbed by the abundant fruit in time. My inclination is that this outstanding wine will work wonders with pungent cheeses and spicy Asian dishes. Readers should approach it the way they would a first-rate Alsatian Vendange Tardive. Drink it over the next 10+ years.

Cordier's 1996 Mâcon Chardonnay is made from 100% Chardonnay. It is an elegant, stylish wine with an attractive mouth-feel, a layered texture, crisp, flowery, and mineral-laden fruit, medium body, good acidity, and outstanding purity. Drink this beautiful Mâcon over the next 2–3 years.

DOMAINE RENÉ AND VINCENT DAUVISSAT (CHABLIS)

1996	Chablis	D	(87–89)
1996	Chablis Les Clos	E	(94–96+)
1996	Chablis Forest	D	(91–93)
1996	Chablis Preuses	E	(91–93)
1996	Chablis Sechet	D	(88–90)

1996 Chablis Vaillons	D (90–92+)
1996 Petit Chablis	C (85–87)

Vincent Dauvissat said he had never seen a vintage with grapes as concentrated, mature, healthy, and high in acidity as 1996, calling it "a 200% Chablis vintage." His father, René Dauvissat, reportedly believes it is comparable to 1949. A hailstorm in May struck the village and premier cru vineyards, but fortunately the grands crus were spared. The younger Dauvissat believes that the dry wind from the northeast that blew constantly during the months of August and September is responsible for dropping yields 25% through dehydration and the thickening of skins and that the spring hail was responsible for another 25% drop in yields. He deduced this from the fact that yields in his village and premier cru vineyards were 50% off the norm, while yields in Les Clos were only 25% below average.

The estate is extending its normal *élevage* time to allow the wines to build body and complexity in the barrels and to take advantage of this winter's drop in temperatures to help reduce the acidity levels (cold precipitates tartaric acid).

Dauvissat's Petit Chablis, produced from 2-year old vines, reveals fresh earth and mineral scents and a medium-bodied, lively, chalk- and lemon-laced personality. This refreshing wine should be consumed before the turn of the millennium. The austere but delicious Chablis displays smoke and limestone aromas, as well as chalk, grapefruit, and mineral flavors in its concentrated, medium-bodied, and racy personality. It will be at its best between now and 2003.

Aromatically, the Chablis Sechet displays stones and flint. On the palate, tangy lemons and touches of honey can be found in its crisp, deep, highly concentrated, medium- to full-bodied character. This wine will require 2–3 years of cellaring and should be at its peak between 2002 and 2006. The Chablis Vaillons exhibits strong mineral, honeysuckle, and flint aromas as well as a rich, masculine, medium- to full-bodied, complex, highly focused, and oily-textured flavor profile packed with layers of flint, white fruits, and flowers. Superbly balanced, structured, and ripe, it should age effortlessly. Anticipated maturity: 2002–2008. Dauvissat's Chablis Forest reveals austere smoke and flint scents, fabulous structure, immense concentration, a full body, and mouthwatering flint, cardamom, anise (almost licorice!), and spices in its flavor profile. Super! Anticipated maturity: 2002–2008. Possessing an expressive toasty oak and mineral-laced nose, the Chablis Preuses is an exciting, broad, full-bodied, extremely ripe, but superdefined and fresh wine. It has layers of resin, menthol, and licorice flavors intertwined with touches of new oak that can be discerned in its exceedingly long finish. When I commented to Dauvissat about the wood aromas and flavors, he flashed a wry smile and informed me, to my surprise, that wood is a *terroir* characteristic of his Preuses when young. Moreover, very little new oak is used during its *élevage*. Drink this gem between 2003 and 2008.

Revealing powerful and expansive aromas of liquid minerals, spices, and cloves, the massive, oily, and full-bodied Chablis Les Clos is a he-man of a wine. Its complex and layered core is tightly packed with minerals, juniper berries, citrus fruit, and apples. This extraordinary Chablis offers superb definition and delineation as well as an exemplary finish. As it finishes its *élevage* in Dauvissat's cellar, I would not be surprised if this elegant monster becomes even better than when I tasted it in November 1997. Anticipated maturity: 2003–2010. Bravo!

DOMAINE BERNARD DEFAIX (MILLY-CHABLIS)

1997 Chablis Côte de Lechet	D 89
1997 Petit Chablis	B 86

The 1997 Petit Chablis offers aromas reminiscent of a chestnut cutting board topped with a freshly cut slice of honeydew melon. On the palate, this rich, velvety, medium- to full-bodied, and flavorful wine has uncomplicated creamy white fruit flavors, a trace of minerals, and a dry—albeit short—finish. This food-friendly offering should be consumed over the next 2–3 years. The sea breeze- and lemon-scented 1997 Chablis Côte de Lechet is a fat, ripe, medium- to full-bodied wine with richly strewn layers of pears, stones, and flintlike flavors. This lively wine was aged in 15% new oak barrels, yet there are no traces of wood in either its aromas or its character. Anticipated maturity: now.

DOMAINE MARIUS DELARCHE (PERNAND-VERGELESSES)

1997 Corton-Charlemagne Réserve	EE	93
1996 Corton-Charlemagne Réserve	EE	94
1995 Corton-Charlemagne Réserve	E	92+
1997 Pernand-Vergelesses Les Quartiers Réserve	D	89
1996 Pernand-Vergelesses Les Quartiers Réserve	D	90
1995 Pernand-Vergelesses Les Quartiers Réserve	C	88

The energetic Philippe Delarche started running this estate, which is named after his father, in 1987. Delarche is a believer in noninterventionist winemaking and doesn't fine or filter his reds *or* whites. Burgundy enthusiasts have a penchant for looking only for great wines from those estates located in the most famous villages. In the backwater, one-horse village of Pernand-Vergelesses, Delarche has been largely ignored. Having tasted Delarche's 1995s (as well as some older vintages out of my cellar), I can assure readers that this is one estate worthy of a detour, for both the reds and the whites! Delarche owns or works 22$^1/_4$ acres of vines, 7$^1/_3$ planted with white varietals and almost 15 with red.

Clear and bright, but with a slight golden hue, the 1995 Pernand-Vergelesses Les Quartiers Réserve possesses robust minerally aromas. In the mouth, this fresh and lively wine bursts forth with minerals, honeysuckle, spices, and candied nuts wrapped up in a silky texture. This well-balanced wine will keep for a few years but should be drunk over the near term to fully exploit its freshness of fruit. The 1995 Corton-Charlemagne Réserve has a muted nose, but the wine is truly fabulous. Awesomely textured, with deep, silky candied fruits and beautiful minerality, this wine may merit a better score when its nose comes out of hiding. Drink it between 2002 and 2008+.

Note: the 1996 wines tasted are special North Berkeley Imports bottlings, which are neither fined nor filtered.

Delarche's North Berkeley Imports cuvées are fabulous! Produced from a south-facing vineyard that may soon be upgraded to premier cru status, the 1996 Pernand-Vergelesses Les Quartiers Réserve reveals intense floral and stone aromas as well as an oily-textured, richly structured, and expansive character. This muscular, medium- to full-bodied, and thick wine is densely packed with minerals, white fruits, and spices. Anticipated maturity: now–2003. I was floored by the 1996 Corton-Charlemagne Réserve. Its rich and ripe nose is followed by a massively powerful, superbly balanced, and explosive personality filled with concentrated flavors reminiscent of candied pears, minerals, warm gravel, and lemon drops. This exquisite wine's seductive, thick, and layered mouth-feel is magnificently focused by its racy acidity. Its admirable finish is long, precise, and wonderfully delineated. I would suggest drinking this gem between 2002 and 2007.

Readers who have not been able to secure bottles of recent offerings from Domaine Marius Delarche are missing out on some of Burgundy's real gems. I have been extremely impressed with the results of Philippe Delarche's work with Peter Vezan and David Hinkle. The 1997 Pernand-Vergelesses Les Quartiers Réserve is produced from a south-facing vineyard geologically similar to Corton-Charlemagne. This *terroir* may be upgraded to premier cru status. The 1997 explodes from the glass with superripe white fruit and mineral aromas. It offers a dense, fat, luscious, and medium- to full-bodied mouthful of spiced pears and candied apples without losing the elegance and delineation that make white burgundies so special. Anticipated maturity: now–2003. The spectacular 1997 Corton-Charlemagne Réserve will rival the wondrous 1996. Crafted from two southwest-facing parcels, one high on the Corton hill and one near the base, Delarche's 1997 is more reminiscent of a first-rate Meursault Perrières than the typical Corton-Charlemagne because of its intense minerality, found in abundance both aromatically and in its flavor profile. Elegant, powerful, highly concentrated, this great wine reveals superb ripeness of fruit (mostly pears and apples) and is medium to full bodied, thick, yet extremely fresh and delineated. It currently displays loads of charred oak scents and flavors that should easily be integrated into its dense core of fruit with cellaring. Drink it between 2002 and 2008. Bravo!

DOMAINE DES DEUX ROCHES (ST. VÉRAN)

1996 St. Véran	C	87
1996 St. Véran Les Terres Noires	C	89

Exhibiting an earthy and peanut oil-scented nose, the 1996 St. Véran is a medium-bodied, well-balanced, and velvety-textured wine with mouth-coating minerals and citrus fruits. Its high-glycerin mouth-feel, lively flavors, and long finish make this a delicious wine to drink over the next 3 years. Sporting a healthy green hue in its otherwise pale straw color, the 1996 St. Véran Les Terres Noires has intense, rich, and floral aromas. This medium- to full-bodied, highly concentrated, and extracted wine is oily textured and packed with minerals, chalk, and what appear to be faint traces of oak. It is a well-crafted and sturdily built, full-flavored wine. Anticipated maturity: now–2003. Both of these offer excellent values.

DOMAINE J-P DROIN (CHABLIS)

1996 Chablis Les Clos	D	93+
1996 Chablis Montée de Tonnerre	C	90
1996 Chablis Montmain	C	90+
1996 Chablis Tête de Cuvée	C	87
1996 Chablis Vaillons	C	88
1996 Chablis Valmur	D	92
1996 Chablis Vaudesir	D	92+
1996 Chablis Vosgros	C	89

Domaine Droin has been imported to the United States for decades. In the early fifties, thanks to the efforts of the legendary Frank Schoonmaker, 95% of the estate's production came to our shores. The present-day owner, Jean-Paul Droin remembers, as a child, joining the family to label each and every bottle by hand and placing, at the appropriate angle, Schoonmaker's strip label—for thousands of bottles. Since those days Chablis has lost much of its interest in the United States. Many producers in Chablis attribute America's abandonment of Chablis from the 1970s to the late 1980s to the low-quality, mass-produced wines bearing the Chablis name that were produced in California. I believe it may also be due to the fact that the Chablisiens dramatically lowered the quality of their wines in the sixties, seventies, and eighties through high yields, mechanized harvesting, cold stabilizing, and overfiltration.

The Chablis Tête de Cuvée (only 300 cases) is produced solely for the estate's U.S. importer (Eric Solomon's European Cellars). Aromatically displaying stones and intense smoke scents, this medium-bodied, silky textured wine reveals expressive flint, mineral, and tangy citrus flavors with just a hint of toasty new oak appearing in the finish. Anticipated maturity: now–2002. The Chablis Vaillons reveals an attractive lemon drop and liquid mineral-infused nose and a bone-dry, crisp, beautifully ripe, medium-bodied, and lively personality packed with chalk, lime, and grapefruit flavors. Drink it between now and 2003.

Droin, who loves to try new techniques in the cellar, regularly stirred the lees on his Chablis Vosgros. Working the lees, or *bâtonnage* in French, is common in the Côte d'Or, California, Australia, and just about any other place that has Chardonnay—except Chablis. Typically, a cellar worker will insert a long and narrow steel tool that resembles a rake (sometimes with chains attached) into a barrel and literally stir the lees that have been deposited on the bottom of the barrel. Frequent *bâtonnage* significantly increases the body of white wines, giving them a thick and, in extreme cases, unctuous texture. Flavors tend toward sweet, leesy, buttery, and even malty characteristics. Traditionally, Chablisiens have not stirred the lees in their wines because 1) it leads to textures and flavors that are the antithesis of "typical" Chablis, and 2) their wines are normally aged in massive *foudres*, or stainless-steel vats, that make it extremely difficult to do a proper *bâtonnage*. "Typicity hunters" (who like to refer to themselves as purists) will not appreciate the result of Droin's efforts. Those whose only criteria is quality will be quite pleased. This wine offers ripe pear and leesy aromas as well as a bone-dry, highly concentrated, medium- to full-bodied core of roasted stones, minerals, and, surprisingly, a delicious flavor reminiscent of the Italian Cynar liqueur (produced from artichokes). Anticipated maturity: now–2003.

Constantly experimenting, Droin aged his Chablis Montmain in first-, second-, and third-year oak barrels for 5 months before putting them in stainless steel for the remainder of their *élevage*. The result is outstanding. Toasty oak and citrus aromas are followed by lively lemon and flint flavors in this strident, superfocused, medium-bodied, and dry-as-the-Sahara wine. Anticipated maturity: 2000–2005. With the Chablis Montée de Tonnerre, Droin experimented with different types of new oak and found that he "despised the effects of American and Russian oak," so he felt compelled to sell off those barrels. The final *assemblage* is 20% from wine aged in new oak with the balance having been in stainless-steel cuvées. It displays stones, toasty oak, and traces of vanilla aromas as well as a medium- to full-bodied, silky, and intensely powerful core of smoky liquid minerals. This well-crafted and focused wine should be at its peak between 2000 and 2005.

All three of Droin's grands crus were fermented and aged in a blend of old and new barrels. The Chablis Valmur, accurately described by Droin as *la classe*, displays smoke, stones, and a touch of honey on the nose. It is a silky, massively intense, medium- to full-bodied, and extremely refined wine packed with liquid minerals, honeysuckle, chalk dust, and traces of sweet oak. It should be at its best between 2000 and 2008. The Chablis Vaudésir exhibits floral and cardamom spice scents and a masculine, medium- to full-bodied, lively, highly concentrated, and intense, crisp, and white flower, mineral, and flint-filled flavor profile. Anticipated maturity: 2000–2008. The 1996 was a fabulous vintage for the Chablis Les Clos appellation for the same reasons I found it to be a particularly successful year for Bâtard-Montrachet—its power and intensity is given additional focus by the vintage's high acidity levels. Droin's reveals a rich, spice cake and butter-laced nose as well as a massively powerful, magnificently balanced, full-bodied, and layered core of smoky minerals, lemon zests, pears, flint, and touches of sweet oak. The flavors seemingly go on forever in this superb wine's stunning finish.

DOMAINE JOSEPH DROUHIN (BEAUNE)

1997 Bâtard-Montrachet	EEE	88+
1996 Bâtard-Montrachet	EEE	94
1995 Bâtard-Montrachet	EEE	92

1997	Beaune Clos des Mouches	EE	88
1996	Beaune Clos des Mouches	EE	92
1995	Beaune Clos des Mouches	E	92
1996	Chablis Les Clos	E	?
1997	Chablis Secher	D	87
1996	Chablis Vaillons	D	89
1997	Chablis Vaudésir	D	89+
1997	Chablis Domaine de Vaudon	C	86+
1996	Chablis Domaine de Vaudon	D	88
1996	Chassagne-Montrachet	D	88
1995	Chassagne-Montrachet	D	87
1997	Chassagne-Montrachet Marquis de Laguiche	EE	86+
1995	Chassagne-Montrachet Marquis de Laguiche	E	90+
1996	Corton-Charlemagne	EE	92
1995	Corton-Charlemagne	EE	92
1996	Meursault	D	87
1995	Meursault	D	88
1997	Meursault Perrières	E	88
1996	Meursault Perrières	E	90
1995	Meursault Perrières	E	92
1996	Montagny	C	86
1997	Montrachet Marquis de Laguiche	EEE	(90–92+)
1996	Montrachet Marquis de Laguiche	EEE	95
1995	Montrachet Marquis de Laguiche	EEE	94
1996	Pouilly-Fuissé	D	88
1996	Puligny-Montrachet	E	88+
1995	Puligny-Montrachet	D	88+
1997	Puligny-Montrachet Les Folatières	E	87
1996	Puligny-Montrachet Les Folatières	E	91
1995	Puligny-Montrachet Les Folatières	E	91
1997	Rully	C	86
1996	Rully	C	87
1995	Rully	C	85+
1996	St. Aubin	D	87
1995	St. Aubin Premier Cru	D	87
1996	St. Véran	D	87

The tall, elegant, and regal Robert Drouhin runs this old Burgundy *négociant* house with the help of his beautiful daughter, Véronique (who is responsible for Domaine Drouhin in Oregon as well), and two sons, Philippe and Frédéric. After having tasted through the 1995s and 1996s, I suspect that Drouhin is making strides to better what was already a fine source for red and white burgundies. Could it be Philippe's attention to vineyard work? Having already moved toward organic farming, he is interested in biodynamic viticulture but hasn't yet gotten the go-ahead from his father to implement this philosophy. The talented Laurence Jobard (no relation to the Jobards of Meursault fame) is responsible for the firm's winemaking. What is Robert Drouhin's definition of a successful Chardonnay and Pinot Noir? His wines must exhibit elegance and finesse and reflect their *terroirs*. Adamantly against the large-scale, rugged, very oaky wines made by some producers in Burgundy, he asserts that the Drouhin style will not change.

Laurence Jobard, Maison Drouhin's straightforward and talented winemaker, told me that 1997's *bourbes* (gross lees) and fine lees were of poor quality (this sentiment was echoed by a few other forthright winemakers). She believes this contributed to the wines being reductive during fermentation and later, during *élevage*, somewhat oxidative. All of Maison Drouhin's 1997s were bottled in July 1998 (except for the Montrachet), 2–3 months earlier than for the 1996s.

As is true throughout most of the Côte d'Or, Maison Drouhin's 1997 white burgundies are of high quality yet do not reach the heights attained by the 1996s.

Produced from purchased grapes and must, the 1997 Rully reveals floral, mineral, and chalklike aromatics. This light- to medium-bodied and well-crafted offering has mineral-dominated flavors with traces of tangy peaches and chlorophyll. It is a fresh, interesting, and delicious wine. Drink it over the next 3 years. The 1997 Chablis Domaine de Vaudon has an expressive, flinty nose, which is surprising given its austere character. It is a light- to medium-bodied and silky-textured wine with tightly wound minerals and stones in its flavor profile. Anticipated maturity: now–2002. Maison Drouhin crafts its 1997 Chablis Secher entirely in tanks, leading me to believe that the toasty oak characteristics found in its aromatics are due to its *terroir*. This is an excellent wine, well balanced, possessing loads of forward white fruits, chalk, and minerals in its medium-bodied, soft personality. Anticipated maturity: now–2003. Drouhin's impressive 1997 Chablis Vaudésir's beguiling nose serves up aromas reminiscent of gravel, fresh herbs, and hints of spicy oak (a small amount of new oak was used in its vinification). On the palate, this concentrated, medium- to full-bodied, and intense wine has vivacious mineral and flint flavors. It possesses an excellent grip and an admirably long finish. Anticipated maturity: 2001–2005+.

The 1997 Meursault Perrières, harvested at 13.6% natural alcohol, has rich aromas of minerals and grilled oak. This thick, broad, medium- to full-bodied wine is crammed with crisp pears, stones, and gravel. Were it not for a slightly warm and alcoholic aspect to its character (a common trait of 1997s), it would have merited additional praise. Drink it before 2004. The mineral-and-earth-scented 1997 Puligny-Montrachet Les Folatières exhibits a well-balanced, medium-bodied, silky character. Its flavor profile, dominated by an intense minerality, also offers touches of white fruits and grilled oak notes. It will require 1–2 years of cellaring in order to harmonize its currently somewhat discombobulated character and should be at its peak between 2001 and 2004. The 1997 Chassagne-Montrachet Marquis de Laguiche has an appealing nose and flavor profile yet is lacking in complexity, depth, and length. It displays spicy, mineral, floral, and earth aromas. This medium-bodied wine has attractively tangy white currant flavors that drop off quickly to reveal a slightly hot finish. Drink it over the next 3 years.

The delicious 1997 Beaune Clos des Mouches displays an earthy, minerally, toasty nose. This well-made, medium-bodied, silky wine has scrumptious woody, stone flavors. It is balanced and reveals excellent ripeness and depth. Anticipated maturity: now–2005. Aromatically muted the day of my tasting, the 1997 Bâtard-Montrachet has mouth-coating richness, a medium to full body, and excellent depth of fruit. Flavors of pears, apples, and a judicious amount of oak spices make up this well-crafted wine's flavor profile. Anticipated maturity: 2000–2005. The 1997 Montrachet Marquis de Laguiche was bottled in December 1998, 15 months after the harvest. The 1996, in contrast, was not bottled until April 7, 1998, 19 months after its harvest! The 1997 Montrachet has splendid aromatics. Profound scents of minerals, earth, flowers, pears, and toasty oak lead to a broad, ample, concentrated, and rich character. This medium- to full-bodied wine has layers of minerals, stones, and white fruits in its core as well as its persistent finish.

All of Drouhin's 1996 whites, with the sole exception of the Montrachet, were bottled between early September and the end of October 1997.

The 1996 St. Véran reveals a ripe, flinty, fruit-filled nose and a vibrant, silky, and medium-bodied wine with mouth-coating richness. Well crafted and tangy, this refreshing wine should be consumed before 2001. The 1996 is a particularly successful vintage in the Mâconnais, as Drouhin's delicious Pouilly-Fuissé demonstrates. Its expressive, chalk-scented aromas are followed by an oily, wide, beautifully delineated, balanced, medium-bodied, and lively character. Drink it before 2002. Revealing citrus and floral scents, the 1996 Chablis Domaine de Vaudon is a racy, medium-bodied, and crisp wine with flavors reminiscent of stones and juicy grapefruit wedges. Anticipated maturity: now–2004. The 1996 Chablis Vaillons has a lovely nose composed of slate, minerals, and lemon drops, as well as a flinty, chalky, and citrus zest-packed flavor profile. This is a medium- to full-bodied, bright, lively, well-balanced, and rich wine. Anticipated maturity: 2000–2004. Displaying toasty oak and smoke aromas, the tightly wound 1996 Chablis Les Clos has excellent ripeness of fruit, a medium to full body, and bracing acidity in its personality. Layers of sweet oak and mouth-puckering lemons were discernible the day of my tasting, but the wine was too reticent to judge. My experience with Drouhin's wines from Chablis and this vintage suggests that this wine will evolve beautifully over time and be an excellent to outstanding offering, but I am not confident enough to assign a score at present.

Deep, malty aromas appear on the nose of the 1996 Montagny. As with many *négociant* wines from this village, this is a well-crafted wine seemingly in search of an identity. Loads of minerals, stones, and a creamy texture are found in this medium- to full-bodied offering. Drink it before 2001. The 1996 Rully reveals a smoky, toasty nose as well as excellent richness, expansiveness, and a metal, mineral, and red berry-laden character. This lively, medium- to full-bodied, and delicious wine should be at its best between now and 2003. Aromatically, the 1996 St. Aubin offers tropical fruits and orange zests. On the palate, this is a medium-bodied, ample, well-crafted, and silky wine with flavors reminiscent of nuts, stones, and ripe pears. Anticipated maturity: now–2002.

Drouhin's 1996 Meursault had an unyielding nose the day of my tasting. It reveals hints of hazelnuts, smoke, and minerals in its well-balanced, medium-bodied, racy, and tightly wound flavor profile. Anticipated maturity: 1999–2003. The 1996 Chassagne-Montrachet was much more expressive, displaying stone and mineral aromatics as well as a medium-bodied, well-focused, gravelly and lemon-filled, refined core of fruit. It should be at its best between now and 2003. Exhibiting a rich, almond paste- and anise-scented nose, the 1996 Puligny-Montrachet has deep ripeness, impressive breadth, delineation, and a full to medium body. This pear- and white peach-flavored wine should be at its peak between now and 2003.

The Beaune Clos des Mouches is Drouhin's flagship white, and the 1996 is superb. Revealing deep, austere mineral aromas, it possesses a gorgeously ripe, juicy, medium- to full-bodied, and superbly balanced personality. Almond paste, honeysuckle blossoms, and gravel flavors can be found in this silky wine. Its long, drawn-out, and precise finish is admirable. Anticipated maturity: 2003–2009. Revealing a complex nose of minerals and flowers, the

1996 Puligny-Montrachet Les Folatières is a feminine, well-defined, elegant, medium- to full-bodied, and persistent wine. Its intricate and delightful flavor profile is composed of stone, anise, and floral elements. Anticipated maturity: 2002–2008. The 1996 Meursault Perrières has wonderful stone, mineral, and white flower aromatics as well as a broad-shouldered and superbly delineated character. Liquid minerals, gravel, and traces of honeysuckle can be found in its highly focused, refined, and racy medium to full body. It will require at least 5 years of cellaring and should hold its peak until 2010.

Displaying a ripe, rich, and honeysuckle-infused nose, the 1996 Corton-Charlemagne has superb depth of sweet white fruit, a distinct minerality, and a medium- to full-bodied personality. Its racy, extracted, and powerful core is buttressed by structure-giving acidity. Moreover, it exhibits an impressively long and pure finish. It should be consumed between 2003 and 2009. The 1996 Bâtard-Montrachet possesses fabulously intense anise and honeysuckle aromas as well as an expansive, full-bodied, and elegant character. Layers of minerals, white peaches, buttered toast, and sweet pears are found in this lively, highly focused, and superbly persistent wine. Anticipated maturity: 2003–2010. As is always the case with this *négociant* house, the Montrachet Marquis de Laguiche is given a longer *élevage* than any of the other white wines. The 1996 promises to be a stunner! Massively rich but precisely defined minerals, grilled hazelnuts, and toast engulf the nose. The impressive aromatics are followed by an awesomely complex, wide, broad-shouldered, tart, tightly wound style of wine. As its minerals, toasted almonds, and notes of tropical fruits saturate the palate, they appear to grow in power and focus with each passing second. Intense, superconcentrated, highly extracted, yet pure and steely, this Montrachet demands patience. I recommend holding it at least until 2005, and it should certainly evolve magnificently through 2015 given proper cellaring conditions.

The 1995 Rully is a well-made wine with a sweet, enticing, tropical fruit-filled nose and a faint touch of toastiness (oak?). In the mouth, it is medium bodied and has nice balancing acidity and a slight citrus flavor. It is in complete contrast with the 1995 St. Aubin Premier Cru, which has an austere, mineral, and stony mouth that finishes with a distinct lemon-custard parting shot. A very nice effort for a village wine, the 1995 Meursault offers freshly cut flowers in the nose and toasted hazelnut, spice, and applelike flavors. It is medium bodied and has a good follow-though. The 1995 Chassagne-Montrachet has austere floral aromas in the nose. In the mouth, the wine tastes of baked spiced apples and is well balanced, with well-integrated acidity. Explosive flavors of toasted and roasted ripe fruits are evident in the 1995 Puligny-Montrachet, which would be an outstanding wine if it were more complex and longer. From a vineyard that was recently considered for grand cru status, the 1995 Meursault Perrières boasts a gorgeous nose of liquid rocks and flowers. Explosive in the mouth, this wine's cascade of sweet, ripe, structured, stony, minerally fruits is followed by fine length. In my mind, Perrières should be upgraded to a grand cru. The Chassagne-Montrachet Marquis de Laguiche is produced from the Premier Cru Morgeot vineyard yet is not permitted to carry a premier cru designation because the Drouhins want it to bear the Laguiche name. The 1995 exhibits an unyielding but fresh and austere nose as well as deep minerally flavors complemented by anise and other spices, an oily texture, and a substantial finish. The 1995 Puligny-Montrachet Les Folatières has extremely expressive, toasty, sweet, and floral aromatics with an attractive underlying spice component. Unctuously textured, this wine displays waves of rich, buttery, and smoky tropical fruits, along with a citrusy finish. Most of Burgundy's *négociants* are envious of Drouhin's highly successful Beaune Clos des Mouches, frequently the appellation's best and most popular white wine. The outstanding 1995 is an unqualified success. The well-delineated aromas are enticing and attractive (copious quantities of honeysuckle, anise, and minerals). In the mouth, the wine offers a fabulous array of white flowers and deliciously roasted fruits. This full-bodied, refined wine is well crafted, has excellent length, and should be drunk between 2000 and 2005. With its provocative, earthy, anise nose, the Corton-Charlemagne is more floral than the minerally Beaune. The most elegant and structured 1995 Corton-Charlemagne I tasted, it may lack the sweet explosion of oaky fruit and ostentatiousness one associates with such Cortons as Latour or Coche-Dury, yet it is typified by a refined precision and restraint. Drink it between 1998 and 2005. With an intriguing nose of spiced fruits, Drouhin's 1995 Bâtard-Montrachet is ideal for readers in search of viscous, full-bodied, fat, rich, and oily white burgundy packed and stacked with ripe fruit. Anticipated maturity: 2002–2010. To no one's surprise, the Montrachet Marquis de Laguiche is Drouhin's finest 1995. Made entirely in first-year oak (oak barrels that have been used once, not new oak), the wine explodes with rich honeysuckle aromas and hints of honeyed spice, all bursting from the glass. This beauty is extremely viscous and fat (my notes say: "Wouldn't legally be considered a liquid") and has very ripe flavors of rich, toasted and roasted, lively fruits. This full-bodied, beautifully delineated wine exemplifies Montrachet, as it combines Bâtard's forward, sultry fruit and Chevalier's elegance and precision. Drink it between 2005 and 2012.

Other wines recently tasted: 1997 Montagny (85), 1997 Puligny-Montrachet (86), 1997 St. Véran (85).

MAISON DRUID (MOREY-ST.-DENIS)

1996	Meursault Les Cloux	D	87
1996	Meursault Le Limozin	D	88
1996	Puligny-Montrachet	E	88

Druid is an American company that vinifies its wines in Burgundy from purchased grapes and then exports its entire production (800–900 cases a year) to the United States. This arrangement was conceived to permit the company to produce and commercialize wines without all the administrative and fiscal regulations French wineries must face. Jacques Seysses, of Domaine Dujac fame, says he is "obsessed by the search for harmony" in his white wine–making. To assure that the growers he buys from maintain moderate yields, Dujac pays the *vignerons* in advance a sum based on what their revenues would be if they had high yields and then demands short pruning. This method ensures low yields while permitting the growers to make as much money as if they were selling huge quantities of wine to other *négociants.* Seysses plans to increase Druid's production when his sons join the family business.

The 1996 Meursault Les Cloux reveals toasted nut aromatics and a fat, minerally, and silky-textured medium body. It has charred oak nuances in its finish. Drink it before 2002. Displaying a flower-infused nose, the 1996 Meursault Le Limozin offers a rich, medium-bodied, well-balanced, and delicious core of minerals, hazelnuts, and touches of lemon zests thrown in for additional complexity. Anticipated maturity: now–2003. The 1996 Puligny-Montrachet exhibits deep leesy aromas and medium- to full-bodied, well-focused, and delineated character. Its flavor profile is filled with tangy candied lemons, stones, and white flowers. It should be at its best between now and 2003.

MAISON GEORGES DUBŒUF (ROMANÈCHE-THORINS)

1997	Mâcon-Villages (Flower label)	A	86
1997	Pouilly-Fuissé Domaine Béranger	C	?
1997	Pouilly-Fuissé Clos Reissier	C	89
1997	St. Véran (Flower label)	A	87
1997	St. Véran Domaine de la Bâtie	A	87

| 1997 Viognier (Flower label) Vin de Pays de l'Ardèche | A | 87 |
| 1997 Viognier Or Blanc | B | 87 |

Yes, "Le Roi du Beaujolais" also produces white wines. In fact, Dubœuf, famous throughout the world for his red Beaujolais bottles, is a native of Chaintré, a small village in the Mâconnais well regarded for its whites, where his father was a vigneron and his brother, Roger Dubœuf, continues the family tradition. Close inspection of Georges Dubœuf's wine labels reveals that his Pouilly-Fuissé Clos Reissier is different from all the other wines. The label indicates that the wine was *récolté* (harvested) by Georges Dubœuf *propriétaire à Chaintré* (owner in Chaintré) because it is an estate bottling, produced from his 4.4 acres. Every other wine's label states that the wine was bottled (*mise en bouteille*) by him and then lists the town where his *négociant* business is located (Romanèche-Thorins).

You can take the vigneron out of his native rural surroundings, but you cannot take the small village vigneron out of the man. I recently met with Georges Dubœuf in his suite at a posh New York hotel to taste through his 1997s. As always, he was dressed to the nines, wearing a beautifully tailored sport coat and slacks, well-shined shoes, a fashionable checkered shirt, and a delightful Hermès tie. He looked the part of a dapper, wealthy, and cosmopolitan Frenchman. However, when he knelt on a couch by the window to peer out at the vastness of the city and the beauty of Central Park in the springtime, his expressions and the wonder in his eyes revealed that he's still just a small-town boy, awestruck at the sight of this great city.

The 1997 Mâcon-Villages (Flower label) reveals minerals, mangoes, and traces of honey on the nose and a medium-bodied and well-balanced character filled with honeysuckle and tropical fruit flavors. It is refreshing and delicious and will make for an excellent aperitif wine. It should be consumed over the next year. Dubœuf produced the 1997 St. Véran (Flower label) entirely in large stainless-steel tanks but devised a method to constantly stir the lees to provide it with richness. It exhibits aromas reminiscent of bananas and acacia blossoms as well as a medium-bodied, plump, and extremely ripe core of tropical white and yellow fruits and honeysuckle. Even though it appears almost overripe and fat, it is well delineated and quite balanced (Dubœuf flatly stated that he does not acidify his wines). As with the previous wine, it should be drunk before 2000. Stylistically, I prefer the equally good 1997 St. Véran Domaine de la Bâtie. Dubœuf explained that to maintain its mineral-driven character he had vinified it at low temperatures. A malt-scented nose is followed by a medium-bodied, well-ripened, elegant, fresh, lively, floral, mineral, and stone-flavored personality. Anticipated maturity: now–2000. The 1997 Pouilly-Fuissé Domaine Béranger offers oak- and vanilla-infused aromas followed by an extracted, concentrated, and well-delineated character. At present its flavor profile is dominated by sweet coconuts and vanilla beans, reflecting a possibly too heavy dose of new oak. If this wine's fruit can absorb the overwhelming oak characteristics, it will be an excellent wine, as its has all the necessary components. Displaying a deep minerality intermingled with traces of toasty oak, the 1997 Pouilly-Fuissé Clos Reissier is an impressive wine. It boasts a powerful concentration and intensity in its mineral-imbued and well-crafted personality. While oak was evident in its nose it was indistinguishable in its deep and structured flavor profile. Anticipated maturity: now–2003.

I am a big proponent of Viognier. As an aperitif wine it has few equals, and a chilled bottle served on a warm summer day can deliver unbridled happiness to those present. Drawing on the recent resurgence of Condrieu (a Viognier-based Rhône), Dubœuf fashions two delicious Viogniers. Revealing fresh floral, apricot, and peach aromas, the 1997 Viognier (Flower label) Vin de Pays de l'Ardèche (harvested at slightly more than 2 tons of fruit per acre) is a lively, refreshing, light- to medium-bodied wine filled with refreshing honeysuckle and crunchy apricot flavors. The 1997 Viognier Or Blanc has a similar nose, offers more concentration, intensity, and complexity on the palate, but is less "gay" and refreshing than the previous wine. Both of these well-made Viogniers should be consumed over the next year while they are vibrant and fresh.

DOMAINE JEAN-LUC DUBOIS (CHOREY-LÈS-BEAUNE)

1996 Chorey-Lès-Beaune Vieux Pressoir Réserve	D 88

Note: Jean-Luc Dubois fashions many different cuvées from the same vineyard parcels. The wine that is described in the following notes is produced exclusively for North Berkeley Imports (which means it undergoes no fining or filtration) for the U.S. market.

The 1996 Chorey-Lès-Beaune Vieux Pressoir Réserve takes its name from the ancient vertical press that Dubois uses for this particular wine. Dubois feels the vertical press provides him with more lees, a key factor when vinifying white wines. This offering exhibits rich white fruits and spices on the nose and a medium-bodied, silky, deep, intense flavor profile packed with minerals and metals. Drink it over the next 2 years.

DOMAINE DUPONT-FAHN (MEURSAULT)

1995 Meursault Vireuils	D 87+
1995 Puligny-Montrachet Les Grands Champs	D 85

The 1995 Puligny-Montrachet Les Grands Champs (aged in 30% new oak) has an elegant mineral nose and an attractive floral, perfumed, and stony mouth. This medium- to full-bodied wine would have received higher praise were it not for a slight green woody flavor on the back end. Made from vines planted in 1929, the 1995 Meursault Vireuils possesses an intense spicy nose with touches of star anise. Its mouth exhibits very good intensity and flavors of minerals and spices. This well-made, medium- to full-bodied wine should be drunk within 4 years of release.

DOMAINE VINCENT DUREUIL-JANTHIAL (RULLY)

1997 Bourgogne Aligoté Réserve	B	87
1996 Bourgogne Aligoté Réserve	B	87
1997 Bourgogne Blanc Les Chaillots Réserve	C	87
1997 Rully La Bergerie	D	(87–89)
1996 Rully La Bergerie	D	89
1997 Rully La Crée Réserve*	D	89+
1997 Rully Le Meix Cadot	D	(88–90+)
1996 Rully Le Meix Cadot	D	90+
1995 Rully Le Meix Cadot	D	91+
1997 Rully La Martelle Réserve*	D	(88–89+)
1996 Rully La Martelle Réserve*	D	90

No, the score of the 1995 is not a typo! The fabulous 1995 Rully Le Meix Cadot was made from 80-year-old vines by a youthful 28-year-old vigneron who doesn't believe in fining and filtering—the asterisk is because this is the cloudiest, most deposit-filled white I have ever seen. (David Hinkle likes to refer to it as a white wine blizzard.) This is not for the faint-hearted! There is a possibility that over time the thick deposits will give this wine off flavors,

*The La Martelle and La Crée labels indicate Raymond Dureuil-Janthial as the owner of the vineyard, but the younger Vincent Dureuil is responsible for the winemaking.

but when I tasted it, it was clean, fresh, and bright. I am convinced that this wine would not have had the power, depth, intensity, and texture that make it outstanding if its core had been stripped by excessive fining and filtration. Anyone who questions this fact should taste wines from growers who make superb natural wines (in this case for an American importer) for certain markets and denuded ones (that is, those that are excessively fined and filtered) from the same vineyard sites for other markets!

A superripe and deeply roasted nose with minerally fruits in the background made me check the label, because it certainly didn't smell like any Rully I have ever tasted. In the mouth, a huge explosion of extremely ripe fruit, intermingled with toasty, roasted, nuts, minerals, and steel. This fat-textured, long, and full-bodied wine needs to be stood up a few hours before being decanted so as to allow the deposit to settle. I have tasted this wine five times and feel cellaring is only enhancing it. Anticipated maturity: now–2004. Many Burgundians believe that "lesser" vineyards or areas (like Rully in their eyes) cannot handle new oak, which should be reserved solely for the more "noble" areas. Mr Dureuil used 40% new oak for this wine, and it has the fruit and structure to easily absorb it. Bravo!

The 1996 Bourgogne Aligoté reveals sweet creamed corn aromas and a spicy, smoky, and mineral-laced core. This rich, well-focused, medium-bodied, and delicious wine should be drunk over the next 3 years. Exhibiting toasty oak scents, the 1996 Rully La Martelle Réserve (the label lists Vincent's father, Raymond Dureuil, as the proprietor) is a deep, concentrated, and medium- to full-bodied wine densely packed with metal, mineral, and lemon flavors that linger on the palate in its first-rate finish. It will be at its best if drunk before 2003. The 1996 Rully La Bergerie has an austere, stone-infused nose yet an expansive and expressive character that possesses a powerful and deep minerality. This excellent medium-bodied and silky-textured wine should be at its peak between now and 2003. While I preferred the 1995, the 1996 Rully Le Meix Cadot is certainly an outstanding wine. Its tightly wound nose reveals steel and gravel-like scents. On the palate, this medium- to full-bodied wine has superb refinement, precision, purity, and focus. Layers of minerals, citrus fruits, and traces of smoke can be discerned in its intense and persistent flavor profile. Anticipated maturity: now–2005.

Produced from over 60-year-old vines planted on slopes within the Rully appellation, the 1997 Bourgogne Aligoté Réserve is a top-class example of its varietal. Concentrated aromas of spicy white fruits give way to a fresh, smoky, tangy, and peppery mouthful of spices and intensely ripe apples. This fabulous Aligoté is thirst-quenching yet interesting, complex yet fun, and—equally important—an excellent value. Drink it over the next 3 years. The Bourgogne Blanc Les Chaillots Réserve is produced from a vineyard in Prémeaux-Prissey Vincent Dureuil obtained through his recent marriage. Three barrels are produced (1 comes to the United States, another is sold to a Japanese importer, and the third is sold in Europe). The 1997 reveals a mocha cream and mineral-infused nose, as well as a rich, well-balanced, and lively character. This medium-bodied, spiced pear-packed, silky-textured, and layered wine should be consumed over the next 3 years.

The 1997 Rully La Bergerie, crafted from 60-year-old vines, has a mineral- and buttered toast-scented nose. A medium- to full-bodied, rich, and oily-textured wine, it is extremely well focused, dense, and filled with flavors suggesting white peaches, apples, and honeysuckle blossoms. Anticipated maturity: now–2004. The 1997 Rully La Martelle Réserve's label indicates Raymond Dureuil-Janthial (Vincent's father) as the owner of the vineyard, but the younger Dureuil was responsible for the winemaking. Aromatically dominated by toasted oak, this deep, mouth-coating, and immensely ripe wine is medium to full bodied, thick, and expansive. Graves-like flavors of stones are intermingled with ripe pears and white flowers in this intense yet balanced offering. Anticipated maturity: now–2004. Displaying a very ripe, white fruit- and earth-dominated nose, the 1997 Rully Le Meix Cadot Réserve is a superb and potentially outstanding wine. It combines the vintage's telltale fat with surprising balance and focus. Sweet, nearly overripe white fruits interspersed with minerals and nuts, it has a long, bone dry finish. This medium- to full-bodied wine is extremely well made, with hints of new oak barely discernible behind its powerful and expressive core of fruit. Drink it between 2000 and 2006. Only 2 barrels (1 new and the other 1 year old) of Rully La Crée Réserve were produced in 1997. This wine's label also indicates Raymond Dureuil-Janthial as the vineyard owner. It sports a deep, earthy, and spice-laden nose as well as a medium- to full-bodied, concentrated, intense, and broad personality. This gorgeously ripe, white pear-flavored, and thick wine is complex, powerful, and impressively long in the finish. Anticipated maturity: now–2001.

DOMAINE MAURICE ECARD ET FILS (SAVIGNY-LÈS-BEAUNE)

1996	Savigny-Lès-Beaune Les Hauts-Jarrons	D	88
1995	Savigny-Lès-Beaune Les Hauts Jarrons	D	87

Produced from albino Pinot Noir (also known as the Henri Gouges Pinot), the 1995 Savigny-Lès-Beaune Les Hauts Jarrons reveals ripe and toasty red currant aromas and a thick-textured, medium- to full-bodied, mineral- and tangy berry-filled personality. The 1996 Savigny-Lès-Beaune Les Hauts-Jarrons was fermented and aged in previously used oak barrels. It reveals wild mushroom aromas as well as a concentrated, bright, lively, and medium-bodied core of stones and tangy citrus fruits. Delicious to drink now, it will remain so until 2001.

DOMAINE ARNAUD ENTE (MEURSAULT)

1996	Bourgogne Aligoté	C	(86–88)
1996	Bourgogne Blanc	C	(86–88)
1996	Meursault Goutte d'Or	E	(88–90)
1996	Meursault en L'Ormeau	D	(88–90)
1996	Meursault Vieilles Vignes	D	(90–92+)
1996	Puligny-Montrachet Les Réferts	E	(92–94+)

Robert Parker, in Châteauneuf du Pape's La Mirande restaurant, was told by the sommelier that he had to taste a Meursault Goutte d'Or by a young vigneron named Arnauld Ente. Later, as I was planning my November tasting trip to Burgundy, Parker told me that Ente was a required visit. Jean-François Coche of Domaine Coche-Dury fame informed me that Meursault had two first-rate young stars on the rise, Rémi Jobard and Ente. He explained that Ente had come to see him for advice and the very busy Coche had turned him away. As he tells the story, he later saw Ente's vineyards ("he works the vines very well") and decided the kid was worth making some time for.

Arnauld Ente, virtually unknown in the wine world, will make his mark. I am positive of it. Young, dynamic, and very intelligent, this slim, crew-cut-sporting, bright-eyed 31-year-old has the desire, dedication, work ethic, smarts, and palate to be one of the best. Ente began his career as a vigneron in 1992, at the ripe old age of 26, selling his entire production to *négociants*. By 1994 he was bottling wines himself, and today his French customers purchase his entire production prior to bottling.

Ente is a believer in working the vineyard's soils, hoeing often to force the roots deep into the bedrock, providing oxygen to the earth, and feeding the ground with the uprooted grasses. One cold, dreary, and rainy November morning I saw him hard at work aboard his tractor in the middle of the En L'Ormeau vineyard. While many famous estates had premier cru vineyards producing $3^2/_3$ tons of fruit per acre in 1996, Ente's Bourgogne Blanc was harvested at just under 3 tons per acre. After an 18-month *élevage*, Ente does not filter his

604

PARKER'S WINE BUYER'S GUIDE

wines and subjects them to a light fining only if absolutely necessary. Later, each wine is bottled by hand.

The smoke- and spice-scented 1996 Bourgogne Aligoté is produced solely from Aligoté grapes (other producers will often blend in a little Chardonnay for body). This is an extremely rich and palate-tingling example of this often bland varietal. Sweet flowers, tangy citrus fruits, and minerals are found in its silky-textured medium body. Drink it before 2000. Produced from 45-year-old vines, the 1996 Meursault en L'Ormeau reveals deep ripeness and candied nuts on the nose. This is a rich, awesomely deep, medium- to full-bodied, balanced, and velvety wine packed with white fruits, smoke, toast, and grilled hazelnuts. Anticipated maturity: now–2003. The 1996 Meursault Goutte d'Or (6-year-old vines) has intense, golden fruit, anise, and floral aromas and an intense, broad, medium- to full-bodied, and candied almond-laden flavor profile. It is a more refined and detailed wine than one would expect from this vineyard (generally characterized by its power). It will be at its best if consumed before 2002. I was floored by Ente's 1996 Meursault Vieilles Vignes, produced from vines over 100 years old located in the center of the En L'Ormeau vineyard. In November 1997 Ente had not yet decided whether he was going to bottle this cuvée separately or blend it into the Meursault en L'Ormeau (it would then account for one third of that *assemblage*). Displaying extraordinary richness and concentrated honey on the nose, it is an awesomely extracted, full-bodied, dense, and massive wine. Layers of mouth-coating and oily white peaches, sweet toast, and almond/butter cookies make up this blockbuster's flavor profile. Anticipated maturity: now–2004. Ente produced 3 barrels (75 cases) of a show-stopping 1996 Puligny-Montrachet Les Réferts. Offering an elegant floral nose, this unbelievably rich and intense wine has massive depth of fruit. Loads of poached pears spiked with cloves and juniper berries, honeysuckle, and minerals are found in its complex, oily-textured, full-bodied, and refined character. Brilliantly balanced and focused, this gem should be drunk between 2000 and 2006. Bravo!

DOMAINE JEAN-PHILIPPE FICHET (MEURSAULT)

1996 **Bourgogne**	B	86
1996 **Bourgogne Vieilles Vignes**	C	88
1996 **Meursault Les Gruyaches**	D	(87–89)
1996 **Meursault Le Meix Sous Le Château**	D	(87–89)
1996 **Meursault Le Tesson**	D	(88–90)

Note: I also tasted Fichet's Auxey-Duresses and Meursault Les Chevalières but will not comment or rate them because they were still in malo and I do not believe accurate reviewing can be performed at this stage of a wine's evolution. This being said, neither wine is flawed and both have excellent potential.

Jean-Philippe Fichet is a young and dynamic vigneron with enormous potential. Currently his estate consists of almost 20 acres of vines, mostly in *métayage* and *fermage* arrangements, but Fichet expects to acquire some additional parcels from his family this year. Readers are well advised to remember Fichet's name, as he has star potential.

The 1996 Bourgogne reveals rich almond paste and Earl Grey tea aromas followed by a fat, superripe, medium-bodied, and full-flavored core reminiscent of hazelnut cream. What this wine lacks in finesse, class, and definition, it makes up for with hedonism. It should be drunk by 2001. Produced from 30-year-old vines, the 1996 Bourgogne Vieilles Vignes displays ripe pears and peaches on the nose, as well as a more concentrated, balanced, and complex character than its younger vine counterpart. Filled with minerals, spices, and candied nuts, it has a fresh, lively, and excellent medium to full body. Anticipated maturity: now–2002.

Fichet's 1996 Meursault Le Meix Sous Le Château (Meix in the old Burgundian dialect means "house" or "barn," much like Mas in Provence) exhibits a nutty, earthy nose and a racy, medium- to full-bodied, rich yet tangy core of white currants and minerals. Anticipated maturity: now–2004. Produced from a vineyard planted in 1928 and located directly below Meursault Charmes, the 1996 Meursault Les Gruyaches reveals massively ripe, nut, and pear aromas. This is a deeply rich, medium- to full-bodied, and oily heavyweight wine that has no pretense for refinement but delivers concentrated layers of sweet white fruits and nuts. It should be drunk by 2002. The 1996 Meursault Le Tesson possesses a delightful nose of minerals, orange rinds, and hazelnuts. On the palate, this ripe, dense, fresh, silky, precise, and medium- to full-bodied wine is layered with candied nuts and flowers. If it had had a longer finish, it would have merited a better score.

DOMAINE DU CHÂTEAU DE FUISSÉ (FUISSÉ)

1997	Mâcon-Fuissé	C	87
1997	Mâcon-Villages	B	86
1997	Pouilly-Fuissé	C	85
1997	Château Fuissé Pouilly-Fuissé	D	91+
1997	Château Fuissé Pouilly-Fuissé Les Brûlées	D	90
1997	Château Fuissé Pouilly-Fuissé Le Clos	D	91+
1997	Château Fuissé Pouilly-Fuissé Les Combettes	D	88+
1997	Château Fuissé Pouilly-Fuissé Vieilles Vignes	E	(91–92+)
1997	St. Véran	C	88

The 1997 Mâcon-Villages, crafted from vineyards in the villages of Devayé and Solutré, has smoky, flinty, acacia-scented aromas. It is a soft, nicely layered, and well-ripened wine with a silky texture, mouth-coating flavors of white flowers and minerals, and an easygoing, silky texture. Drink it over the next 2–3 years. The 1997 Mâcon-Fuissé, produced from parcels located high on the hill overlooking the village, has a pine- and smoke-infused nose. This medium-bodied, brightly focused, and well-crafted offering is fresh, vivacious, and reveals lemon and stonelike flavors. It is thirst-quenching and possesses excellent grip. Anticipated maturity: now–2001. Displaying toasty mineral scents, the 1997 St. Véran has a beautiful silky texture, a splendid balance, and a more substantial palate presence than either of the two previous wines. This honeysuckle, peanut, and mineral-flavored offering is medium-bodied and harmonious and reveals excellent purity and precision. It will be at its best if drunk over the next 3–4 years. I had expected more from this famed estate's 1997 Pouilly-Fuissé, particularly given the fact that the vintage was so generous to the region. It has an expressive pine-laden nose and a soft, light- to medium-bodied, rather short personality. It is well balanced, offers delicious lemon and mineral flavors, but dissipates quickly. Anticipated maturity: now–2001.

Readers need to be on the lookout for this domaine's special bottlings, recognizable by the moniker "Château Fuissé" indicated in large bold letters across the label. They are delicious, complex, and concentrated wines that tend to be a significant step up in quality from the other offerings. The "Château Fuissé" wines, known at the domaine as the *crus*, are made in 3,500–5,000-bottle lots. There are three single vineyard offerings and two *assemblages*. The 1997 Château Fuissé Pouilly-Fuissé Les Combettes has a deep nose that reveals earth and stony aromas. It is a boldly expressive, acacia blossom- and toasted nut-flavored wine with excellent grip, complexity, and definition. This medium-bodied offering should be at its best between now and 2003. Interestingly, because no new barrels are ever used at this domaine, the 1997 Château Fuissé Pouilly-Fuissé Les Brûlées exhibits oak-infused honey-suckle and white flower aromas. This massive, medium- to full-bodied, broad-shouldered, and mouth-coating wine has a thick and masculine personality. Stylistically more reminiscent of a Chassagne-Montrachet Morgeot than a wine from Fuissé, it has powerful earth and mineral flavors that last throughout its extended finish. Anticipated maturity: 2000–2005. The 1997 Château Fuissé Pouilly-Fuissé Le Clos combines the best qualities of the two previous *crus*. Its piney, mineral-laced nose leads to a stony, nutty, smoky, and floral character filled with orchard fruits and dried white raisins. It has the focus, freshness, and precision of Les Combettes and nearly as much power, density, and length as Les Brûlées. This complex and well-extracted wine should age well. Drink it between 2001 and 2007.

The 1997 Château Fuissé Pouilly-Fuissé (consumers should not confuse it with the regular Pouilly-Fuissé offering) is an *assemblage* crafted from 13 parcels. It displays wood, mineral, and floral aromas as well as a vibrant, superbly focused, and medium- to full-bodied personality. This exceedingly refined wine offers a fruit-pit, stone, flint, citrus, and cold steel flavor profile. Anticipated maturity: 2002–2007+. With Elvis Presley singing "Hound Dog" in the background, I tasted from the two tanks containing the assembled final blend of the 1997 Château Fuissé Pouilly-Fuissé Vieilles Vignes. To my surprise, as well as to the consternation of the owners, each tank contained a distinctly different wine (previously these cuvées were blended before being placed in the cement tanks to await bottling). Both wines were qualitative equals but had different textures and flavor profiles. The first revealed a somewhat muted stony nose as well as a magnificently focused, vibrant, and intense core of salty minerals. The second, significantly oilier, offered flavors reminiscent of a hazelnut-cream cake brushed with touches of lime juice. The owners were not sure if they should re-blend the two, fine or filter them again, or bottle them as is. Anticipated maturity: 2002–2008.

DOMAINE JEAN-NOËL GAGNARD (CHASSAGNE-MONTRACHET)

1996	Bâtard-Montrachet	EEE	(93–95)
1995	Bâtard-Montrachet	EEE	(91–94)
1996	Chassagne-Montrachet Les Caillerets	E	(91–93+)
1995	Chassagne-Montrachet Les Caillerets	E	(91–93)
1996	Chassagne-Montrachet Les Champs Gain	E	(89–92)
1995	Chassagne-Montrachet Les Champs Gain	E	(89–92)
1996	Chassagne-Montrachet Les Chenevottes	E	(88–91)
1995	Chassagne-Montrachet Les Chenevottes	D	(88–91)
1996	Chassagne-Montrachet Clos de la Maltroie	D	(89–92)
1995	Chassagne-Montrachet Clos de la Maltroie	D	(87–88+)
1996	Chassagne-Montrachet Les Mazures	D	(86–88+)
1995	Chassagne-Montrachet Les Mazures	D	(86–89)
1996	Chassagne-Montrachet Morgeot	E	(90–92)
1995	Chassagne-Montrachet Morgeot	E	(88–91?)

In 1997, on my first visit to the Domaine Jean-Noël Gagnard, after spending 15 minutes driving around the small village of Chassagne-Montrachet trying to find the winery, I finally gave up and called to have Gagnard's daughter (Caroline Lestimé) come and find me. It seems most growers in Chassagne desperately want to protect their privacy, as almost none of them have their names on their wineries or mailboxes. I am quite pleased Mrs. Lestimé came to my rescue, however, as I liked her wines very much and feel that this domaine is making the strides necessary to break into the next level. Mrs. Lestimé has been working with her father for a few years and seems ready to take over the domaine when he decides to retire.

Caroline Lestimé is justifiably proud of the new cellars that have been added to the cramped ones she and her father have utilized for years. Chassagne-Montrachet can be easily recognized from a distance because of its crane-strewn skyline. Many vignerons are investing their profits into the construction of much needed additional cellar space. Many estates are currently bottling earlier than they would like in order to make room for the following vintage.

In 1995 yields here were down one-third from the norm because inclement weather in the spring damaged the flowering. Jean-Noël Gagnard's brilliant 1996s will require patience, as they have bracing acidity. These are rich, ripe, and extremely well-made wines that, with time, will provide remarkable complexity, minerality, and, most important, pleasure.

The 1996 Chassagne-Montrachet Les Mazures reveals a floral nose and a superfocused, light- to medium-bodied, crisp, and tangy core of minerals, lemon peels, and steel. Anticipated maturity: 2001–2004. Displaying concentrated red currant and grapefruit zest aromas, the 1996 Chassagne-Montrachet Les Chenevottes is a ripe, medium-bodied, and highly delineated wine filled with slate, minerals, and flint. This extremely concentrated offering possesses superb richness as well as strident balancing acidity and an admirable persistence on the finish. It will require cellaring. Anticipated maturity: 2002–2007. The 1996 Chassagne-Montrachet Clos de la Maltroie has enthralling aromas of candied red fruits and smoke. On the palate, this medium- to full bodied, extracted, bright, and rich wine reveals layers of minerals, meaty earth tones, and delectable poached pears. Armed with deeply concentrated fruit and superb grip, this wine should evolve magnificently with cellaring. Drink this beauty between 2001 and 2006. Exhibiting orange peel, charred toast, and floral aromatics, the 1996 Chassagne-Montrachet Les Champs Gains is a broad-shouldered, expansive, yet highly focused and racy, medium- to full-bodied wine. Stones, sautéed mushrooms, lemon drops, and citrus fruit zests are intermingled with a deep minerality in this crisply textured gem. Anticipated maturity: 2002–2007. Boasting fresh, steely red berry aromas, the outstanding 1996 Chassagne-Montrachet Morgeot is lively, somewhat tart, complex, and highly defined. Lemons, butter, cardamom, nuts, and white flowers are found in its medium- to full-bodied, rich, yet racy core. It should be consumed between 2002 and 2008.

Gagnard's 1996 Chassagne-Montrachet Les Caillerets is a phenomenal wine. Aromatically revealing loads of sweet/sour cherries, it exhibits penetrating aromas of highly defined stones, minerals, sweet nuts, flowers, and gorgeously ripe yet crisp pears. Racy, gripping, and rich, this medium- to full-bodied, refined, and extremely elegant wine has a persistent, razor-sharp, complex finish. Anticipated maturity: 2003–2010. The 1996 Bâtard-Montrachet has replaced the 1995 as the finest wine I have ever tasted from this estate. Displaying deep, floral, white peach, and mineral aromas, its amazingly rich, full-bodied, and oily-textured core explodes as waves of candied citrus fruits, minerals, metals, pears, honeysuckle, and sweet toasty oak are unleashed across the palate by vibrant and bright acidity. Hugely structured yet fat and chewy, this expansive, broad, and highly delineated wine possesses an exceedingly long and intricate finish.

The 1995 Chassagne-Montrachet Les Mazures (a village appellation located just below the premier cru Champs Gain) reveals an elegant and buttery nose filled with deep mineral tones. In the mouth, it displays vibrant tones of crisp apples. Medium bodied, it should be drunk between now and 2003. Another very lively wine is the 1995 Chassagne-Montrachet Les Chenevottes. It boasts steely, fresh aromas and flavors with a touch of citrus fruits and a deep minerally core. Silky textured and medium bodied, it has an anticipated maturity of now–2005. Exhibiting an attractive nose of steel and minerals, the rich and concentrated 1995 Chassagne-Montrachet Les Champs Gain is a masculine, full-bodied, powerful, and spicy wine. Drink it between 2001 and 2007. Possessing a floral and flinty nose, the 1995 Chassagne-Montrachet Clos de la Maltroie shows all the signs of a wine wanting to be outstanding and just missing because the vines are too young (planted in 1989). It starts off fat, with beautiful minerally fruit and star anise, then suddenly drops off. It is a very good to excellent wine but lacks the follow-through necessary for greatness. I was confused by divergent tastes of 2 barrels of 1995 Chassagne-Montrachet Morgeot, which differed in taste but not in quality. The first barrel revealed spicy red berries in the nose and a thickly textured mouth of red currants with a nice length. The second barrel was equally good, but with robust, nutty, minerally flavors and floral aromas. The quality is present, but what will it be like in the bottle? No reservations exist about the 1995 Chassagne-Montrachet Les Caillerets, a deep earthy, minerally, and spicy wine. The mouth possesses an excellent explosion of profoundly spicy, steely, and concentrated fruit. Perfectly balanced and long, this wine should be consumed between 2002 and 2010. The 1995 Bâtard-Montrachet displays a very deep and enticingly sultry nose of sweet roasted fruits. On the palate, red fruits such as currants and wild raspberries are exhibited in this rich, full-bodied, extremely spicy wine. Possessing excellent length, this is the one of the finest bottles of wine I have tasted from this domaine.

DOMAINE PHILIPPE GAVIGNET (NUITS-ST.-GEORGES)
1996 Bourgogne Blanc Les Maladières Réserve   **C 87**

Note: The wine described in the following notes is produced exclusively for North Berkeley Imports for the U.S. market.

Only 75 cases of the 1996 Bourgogne Blanc Les Maladières Réserve were produced. This wine hails from a 100% Chardonnay parcel that borders the Nuits-St.-Georges Maladières vineyard, and it was completely vinified in used oak barrels. It reveals a mineral, chalk, and flint nose as well as a well-crafted, medium-bodied, fresh, and lively core of tangy white fruits, minerals, and traces of earth. Drink this vibrant and appealing wine over the next 3 years.

DOMAINE GÉNOT-BOULANGER (MEURSAULT)

1996 Chassagne-Montrachet Les Chenevottes	D	(88–90+)
1996 Chassagne-Montrachet Les Vergers	D	(88–90+)
1996 Corton-Charlemagne	E	(91–94)
1996 Mercurey Les Bacs	B	(85–87)
1996 Meursault Clos du Cromin	D	(88–90)
1996 Meursault Les Vireuils	D	(86–88)
1996 Savigny-Lès-Beaune	C	(86–88)

Many readers who have traveled to Burgundy have certainly noticed the magnificent manor house located below the Comtes Lafon property and wondered, as I have, what took place within its gates. Charles Henri Génot, a Parisian who built a considerable wealth in the pharmaceutical industry, purchased the estate in 1974. The small vineyard holdings were cultivated by outsiders for Génot, an absentee owner, until his death in 1988. During this period the wines were all sold to *négociants* except for a small percentage held back for M. Génot's private cellar. His widow gave the estate to their daughter, Mme. Marie Delaby-Génot, who in 1993 hired an outside consultant to analyze why the estate was losing money.

The consultant, Guillaume de Castelnau, is a tall, handsome, and retired major in the French calvary (tank corps). He did what any consultant would do (I know, I was one): he recommended spending more money. The result of his analysis was that Domaine Génot-Boulanger needed to sell all their wines in bottle—no more *négociants* as customers—and had to greatly expand their vineyard holdings to generate a profit. Massive outlays of cash were spent on vineyards (today the estate owns almost 57 acres across 43 parcels in 22 appellations—from Mercurey in the south to the Clos Vougeot in the north—25% white and 75% red). The construction of an ultramodern (an eyesore) winery on the opposite side of the interstate that runs parallel to the Côte was also accomplished. Also, Castelnau recommended that the estate dedicate itself to the production of high-quality wines and that he be installed as director of the domaine. When I asked him why he had retired from the army, as he appears to have been chiseled for that profession, he responded that he had gotten to a point in his life where he "preferred to kick asses than to have my own kicked."

With his military discipline and obvious intelligence, Castelnau set out to learn his new occupation. He stresses moderate yields (in 1996 his whites were harvested at 3 tons of fruit per acre, within Meursault's limits and below those of other villages), and a harvesting date is selected by scientific analysis, not the *ban de vendange* that is set by bureaucrats. Grapes are hand-harvested and placed into small boxes that travel back to the winery in an enclosed truck to protect them from the sun or rain. Sorting tables are placed between the arriving grapes and the pneumatic presses, and each bunch is inspected. After the pressing and a 1-night *débourbage*, the must is divided into three parts, the juice, the fine lees, and the gross lees, or *bourbes*. As alcoholic fermentation starts, the fine lees are reincorporated into the juice, as well as the *bourbes* if they are healthy, as in 1995 and 1996. The wines are then placed in oak barrels (10%–15% new oak for Mercurey, 25% for all the others except the Corton, which is aged in 30%–35% new oak), and the lees are stirred once every 7–10 days, led toward an oxidative state, and then brought back into a reductive state prior to malos. After the malolactic fermentation is completed, all the whites (except the Corton-Charlemagne) are assembled in large stainless-steel vats "to gain body," says Castelnau (as the timing coincides with the new harvest, I presume space and the opportunity to reuse barrels are also considerations). All the whites are then fined and filtered prior to bottling in January or February with "the rising moon."

The wines I tasted were delicious, in both white and red, with a few being outstanding. If Castelnau can get these quality wines into bottles without stripping them with excessive fining and filtering, then consumers will certainly have a new source for first-rate burgundies.

The 1996 Mercurey Les Bacs has a smoky, minerally, and metallic nose followed by a fresh, lively, rich, and medium-bodied core. His superb example of its appellation is filled with white flowers, stones, and spices. It will be at its best if consumed over the next 3 years. Produced from three parcels spread throughout the commune, the 1996 Savigny-Lès-Beaune offers wonderful deep, toasty, and minerally aromas as well as an excellent racy, extracted, and well-balanced personality with flavors reminiscent of stones and minerals. Anticipated maturity: now–2002. Revealing nuts, spicy oak, and gravel scents, the 1996 Meursault Les Vireuils is a well-crafted, silky, and medium-bodied wine with complex flavors of wild mushrooms, anise, hazelnuts, and charred oak. Anticipated maturity: now–2003. The potentially outstanding 1996 Meursault Clos du Cromin possesses an earth-and-mineral-infused nose as well as a fabulous, medium- to full-bodied, oily, and broad personality. Delicious layers of concentrated sweet sautéed mushrooms, gravel, pears, and white flowers are found in its complex flavor profile. It should be at its best between now and 2004.

Displaying liquid minerals and stones, the 1996 Chassagne-Montrachet Les Vergers is a well-proportioned, velvety, and medium- to full-bodied wine with tons of chalk dust, gravel, earth, smoke, and grilled toast. Its powerful and concentrated flavors extend into its long and pure finish. Anticipated maturity: 2001–2005. The equally good 1996 Chassagne-Montrachet Les Chenevottes has white flowers and anise aromas as well as pears, stones, citrus zests, and spicy oak in its medium to full body. This offering is much more feminine than the preceding one, with delicate floral elements in its concentrated, tangy, and silky character. Drink it between 2001 and 2005. According to Castelnau, the estate's Corton-Charlemagne parcel is located in the very center of the vineyard, and the 1996 was produced from grapes harvested at 13.7 natural potential alcohol, quite high by Burgundian standards. An intense, powerful, and superripe nose reminiscent of creamy, malty vanilla with oak spices is followed by a massively deep, rich, broad, and expansive full-bodied personality. This potentially awesome wine comes on full bore with layer upon layer of oily fruit, yet it has outstanding delineation and focus. Anticipated maturity: 2001–2006. I am extremely impressed with Castelnau's efforts, particularly considering it is only his second vintage. Now comes the tricky part—bottling.

DOMAINE VINCENT GIRARDIN (SANTENAY)

1996 Bourgogne Blanc	C	86
1995 Bourgogne Cuvée St. Vincent	C	87
1996 Chassagne-Montrachet Les Caillerets*	D	92
1995 Chassagne-Montrachet Les Caillerets	D	91+
1995 Chassagne-Montrachet Clos de la Truffière Vieilles Vignes*	D	91+
1996 Chassagne-Montrachet Morgeot Vieilles Vignes*	D	92+
1995 Chassagne-Montrachet Morgeot Vieilles Vignes*	D	92+
1996 Corton-Charlemagne*	E	93+
1996 Meursault Charmes*	E	91+
1995 Meursault Les Genevrières	E	91
1996 Meursault Les Narvaux	D	90
1995 Meursault Les Narvaux	D	90
1996 Meursault Perrières*	E	92
1995 Puligny-Montrachet Le Cailleret	E	91+
1995 Puligny-Montrachet Les Combettes*	?	92
1996 Puligny-Montrachet Les Perrières	E	92
1995 Puligny-Montrachet Les Perrières	E	90
1996 Puligny-Montrachet Les Pucelles	E	92
1995 Puligny-Montrachet Les Pucelles	E	90+
1996 Puligny-Montrachet Les Réferts	E	90
1996 Rully Les Clous	C	87
1995 Rully Les Clous	C	88
1996 St. Aubin Les Murgers des Dents de Chiens	D	89
1996 Santenay Clos du Beauregard	D	88+
1995 Santenay Clos du Beauregard	D	89+
1996 Santenay Beaurepaire	D	88
1995 Santenay Beaurepaire	D	89
1996 Santenay Les Gravières	D	89

1996 Santenay Le St. Jean	**D**	**87**
1995 Santenay Le St. Jean	**D**	**88**
1996 Savigny-Lès-Beaune Les Vergelesses	**D**	**89**
1995 Savigny-Lès-Beaune Les Vergelesses	**D**	**89**
1995 Savigny-Lès-Beaune Les Vermots*	**D**	**87+**
1996 Savigny-Lès-Beaune Les Vermots-Dessus*	**C**	**88+**

Note: Wines marked with an asterisk are also produced under the Baron de la Charrière label.

Vincent Girardin and his Swiss wife, Véronique, do not live in one of the more famed villages of the Côte d'Or, but this young couple are well on their way to making Santenay famous. Having recently started a *négociant* firm, they have increased the breadth of their offerings to include some of the more famous vineyards of the Côte de Beaune. Girardin believes that the trick to a successful *négociant* business is to have as much control as possible. Whereas most *négociants* are satisfied with purchasing wine or must (the grape juice prior to fermentation), Girardin concentrates on buying grapes. He demands that his growers cut back on yields and use a bare minimum of chemical fertilizers. This philosophy costs more, but the results are superior.

Vincent Girardin continues to impress with his wide range of delicious wines and is almost single-handedly responsible for the attention other *négociants* and consumers are giving to the wines of Santenay.

Most growers of the Côte d'Or do not particularly like admitting that they sell part of their production to *négociants*, and they rarely tell me to whom their wines are sold. Yet numerous growers have proudly informed me that they are suppliers to Verget's Jean-Marie Guffens, Dominique Laurent, and Vincent Girardin. These three men are described as nitpicking, difficult, and demanding by their growers. However, these same vignerons gladly admit that they have great esteem and respect for Girardin and his two *négoce* colleagues.

The restaurant world has discovered the quality and outstanding value of Girardin's wines. The chef of Le Sévigné (a restaurant in Cosne-Sur-Loire that made my list of most memorable meals in the last issue) jokingly castigated me for broadcasting what he believed was his little secret. Jean-Luc Le Du, the first-rate sommelier at Restaurant Daniel in New York City, called to tell me he loved Girardin's wines and found the Baron de la Charrière labels to provide particularly excellent values. This positive quality-to-price ratio will not continue. Prices in Burgundy are rising across the board, and the increased demand for these particular wines will certainly lead Girardin and/or his U.S. importer to desire higher profits. In 1996 Girardin produced 27,500 cases of wine. He told me demand was so high, he could have sold three times that amount.

The 1996 Bourgogne Blanc reveals minerals on the nose and appealing richness and focus in its light- to medium-bodied, silky, well-balanced, stone-filled character. Drink it between now and 2001. Displaying toasty mineral aromas, the 1996 Rully Les Clous is a beautifully ripe, well-made, crisp, medium-bodied, and metallic-flavored wine. It should be drunk by 2001. Girardin's 1996 Santenay Le St. Jean has a fresh and lively nose. It is a silky-textured, light- to medium-bodied, ripe, well-structured, and white pepper- and mineral-infused wine. It will be at its best between now and 2001.

Exhibiting an expressive nose of minerals, the 1996 Santenay Beaurepaire has a concentrated, stone- and lemon-flavored, rich, medium-bodied, and oily-textured personality. The 1996 Santenay Clos du Beauregard reveals stone and flower aromas as well as a delineated, rich, and medium-bodied core of slate, iodine, and white pepper flavors. Both these wines should be drunk between now and 2003. Displaying a beautifully ripe bouquet filled with white peaches and stones, the 1996 Santenay Les Gravières has a concentrated, masculine, oily, medium-bodied, and ample personality with loads of minerals and marly flavors. Anticipated maturity: now–2003.

The 1996 Savigny-Lès-Beaune Les Vermots-Dessus has a perfumed, floral nose and an excellent, well-focused and defined, medium-bodied core of minerals and lemon zests. It should be consumed before 2002. Revealing a stone- and white pepper-laced nose, the 1996 Savigny-Lès-Beaune Les Vergelesses has a beautifully ripe, complex, highly delineated, and medium-bodied personality filled with flavors of cold steel and flowers. Drink it between now and 2004. The 1996 St. Aubin Les Murgers des Dents de Chiens has tangy lemon, butter, and stone aromas as well as a rich, silky, defined, ample, and medium bodied character with smoky mineral flavors. It should be consumed before 2003.

The delicious 1996 Meursault Les Narvaux reveals stony, nut and liquid smoke scents and has a tightly wound, medium- to full-bodied, oily-textured, concentrated, and well-extracted core of minerals and ripe white fruits. Anticipated maturity: 2000–2006. Elegant white flowers and pears can be found in the lovely nose of the 1996 Meursault Charmes. This is a complex, layered, beautifully defined, medium- to full-bodied and rich wine filled with minerals and honeysuckle. It will be delicious young but should age effortlessly through 2005. The 1996 Meursault Perrières has oil, mineral, and wood-fired aromas as well as a superb, medium- to full-bodied, highly delineated, elegant, and complex character with exciting and lively gravelly flavors. This wonderfully refined wine possesses a remarkably focused and long finish. Anticipated maturity: 2002–2010.

Aromatically, the 1996 Chassagne-Montrachet Les Caillerets displays fabulous ripeness, liquid stones, and anise. On the palate, this complex and deep wine has layers of sweet and delicious minerals, buttery pears, and a touch of honey. Medium to full bodied, refined, and powerful, this beauty's extraordinary focus and concentration may, in time, make my score appear stingy. Anticipated maturity: 2003–2009. Girardin's Chassagne-Montrachet Morgeot Vieilles Vignes is consistently one of his finest wines. The 1996 reveals an austere, stone-and-flint-infused nose as well as a broad-shouldered, massively ripe, mouth-coating, oily-textured, chewy, full-bodied, and masculine personality filled with minerals and rock dust. It should be at its best between 2001 and 2007.

Revealing peach and pear aromas, the 1996 Puligny-Montrachet Les Réferts is a beautifully ripe, silky, complex, and concentrated medium- to full-bodied wine. Its layered flavor profile is packed with white fruits, flowers, and traces of anise. Anticipated maturity: 2001–2006. The outstanding 1996 Puligny-Montrachet Les Perrières has stone and mineral aromas as well as an intense, ripe, concentrated, medium to full body with great depth of fruit. Layers of chalk and pears are intermingled with traces of candied citrus fruits in this impressively endowed and well-crafted wine. Anticipated maturity: 2001–2006. The 1996 Puligny-Montrachet Les Pucelles is undoubtedly a first-rate wine. Aromatically, it reveals a soft, feminine, and smoky nose. On the palate, this medium-bodied, supple, and elegant wine has complex flavors of metals, toasty oak, and white flowers. I love this wine's refinement and delineation but am not convinced it has the power or concentration for extended cellaring. I recommend drinking it between 2000 and 2004. Displaying lively, rich, pear compote and mineral aromatics, the 1996 Corton-Charlemagne soars with terrific richness, amazing focus, class, and exquisite balance. This full-bodied, highly intricate, and oily-textured wine is filled with peaches, minerals, and white flowers that seem to last forever in this gem's exceedingly long finish. Girardin's only white grand cru, it combines the depth of ripe fruit expected from a first-rate Corton-Charlemagne from a ripe year with the precision and focus that is 1996's trademark. Anticipated maturity: 2002–2010+.

The 1995 Rully Les Clous, vinified in 25% new oak and 75% stainless steel, offers a deep, superripe nose followed by a steely, flinty, mouth-filling, lively wine. Crisp and citrusy, this medium-bodied offering is not made for aging; it should be drunk by the turn of the century. Displaying a buttery and leesy nose, the 1995 Bourgogne Cuvée St. Vincent (named after the patron saint of wine growers) exhibits ripe smoky fruits, a thick oily texture, and excellent balance. Revealing a flinty, stony nose, the 1995 Savigny-Lès-Beaune Les Vermots has a vibrant metallic minerality to its mouth. This delicious medium-bodied wine should be consumed over the next 5 years. The mineral-scented 1995 Savigny-Lès-Beaune Les Vergelesses, produced from 20-year-old vines, is even more impressive. Displaying a silky texture, admirable minerality, toastiness, and good length, this is an excellent wine to enjoy between its release and 2005. Girardin is one of the few believers in white Santenays, having noticed that the strip of *terroir* possessing premier cru vineyards of neighboring Chassagne-Montrachet continues through his commune. While others are planting Pinot Noir, Vincent pushes forward with Chardonnay. Revealing stony and rocky aromas, the 1995 Santenay Le St. Jean exhibits the same silky texture as the previous wine, in addition to flavors of freshly ground white pepper, minerals, and toast. This is a refreshing wine made for near-term drinking. Elegant and refined, the 1995 Santenay Beaurepaire offers a floral and flinty nose followed by some boldly stated, steely, ripe fruit. Its oily texture and long finish possess staying power. Equally good is the floral- and stony-scented 1995 Santenay Clos du Beauregard. This well-balanced wine exhibits an intense mineral quality with a white pepper streak. It will be drinkable young, but it has the necessary backbone for 7 years of aging. The 1995 Meursault Les Narvaux possesses a floral, nutty component to its fresh nose. In the mouth, this medium- to full-bodied wine reveals Girardin's trademark silkiness and a long, hazelnut finish. Displaying nuts and wild flower aromas, the 1995 Meursault Les Genevrières is reminiscent of the Narvaux yet possesses more stuffing. Thick textured, this wine is densely packed with roasted nuts. Drink it between now and 2005. Produced from 60-year-old vines in an enclosed parcel of Les Chaumées vineyard, the 1995 Chassagne-Montrachet Clos de la Truffière Vieilles. Vignes possesses an awesome floral nose filled with sweet fruits and slight earthy tones. In the mouth, a powerful explosion of ripe and vivacious fruit with complex flavors of nuts and minerals makes this an outstanding medium- to full-bodied wine for drinking between now and 2009. Also fabulous is the mineral- and smoky nut-scented 1995 Chassagne-Montrachet Les Caillerets. It displays flavors of warm stones and pecans ensconced in a velvety, thick texture. Delicious to drink now, it should be consumed over the next 8 years. The most impressive wine I encountered at this domaine, and maybe the finest wine Girardin has ever made, is the 1995 Chassagne-Montrachet Morgeot Vieilles Vignes (at least 50-year-old vines). Revealing an elegant and explosive nose of white flowers and sweet honeysuckle, and a mouth exhibiting great minerality, nuttiness, and a touch of white pepper, this superbly delineated and full-bodied wine should age well for up to 10 years. Possessing a sweet roasted fruit- and nut-scented nose, the 1995 Puligny-Montrachet Les Perrières has concentrated, smoky, toasted ripe peach fruit well meshed in its silky texture. Well defined and complex, it would have received higher praise if it had possessed the length of a great wine. Maybe a touch better, the lively, floral-scented 1995 Puligny-Montrachet Les Pucelles shares the same thick texture as the Perrières. Powerful and zippy, this wine possesses candied nut and mineral flavors, a medium to full body, and good length. Drink it between now and 2007. Revealing aromas of freshly cut flowers, the 1995 Puligny-Montrachet Le Cailleret blossoms on the palate with rich, sweet, toasted fruits and touches of fresh earth. It is extremely well made, exhibiting power, delineation, length, and concentration. This full-bodied wine should age well for 10+ years. Almost as good as the Chassagne Morgeot V.V. is the superb 1995 Puligny-Montrachet Les Combettes. An aromatic explosion of flowers and steely minerals gives way in the mouth to major league sweetness of fruit studded with star anise and other spices. This wine offers an exciting mouthful of roasted peaches, flowers, and a nice mineral component carried forth on an oily texture. Long and concentrated, this full-bodied beauty will give unbridled joy for 10–12 years.

DOMAINE GHISLAINE ET JEAN-HUGUES GOISOT (ST. BRIS LE VINEUX)

1996 Bourgogne Côtes d'Auxerre	B	86
1996 Bourgogne Côtes d'Auxerre Corps de Garde	C	87

Revealing an earth-and-stone-imbued nose, the 1996 Bourgogne Côtes d'Auxerre is a medium-bodied, lively, and well-made wine with rich doses of citrus fruit flavors. It should be drunk over the next 2–3 years. The 1996 Bourgogne Côtes d'Auxerre Corps de Garde offers perfumed and fresh aromas reminiscent of talcum powder. This wine is a touch austere (like many wines from this northern Burgundy region) and displays good ripeness, a medium body, and sweet layers of minerals, flowers, chalk, and earth. Anticipated maturity: now–2001.

DOMAINE HENRI GOUGES (NUITS-ST.-GEORGES)

1995 Nuits-St.-Georges Clos des Porrets	E	89
1996 Nuits-St.-Georges Les Perrières	E	90
1995 Nuits-St.-Georges Les Perrières	E	89+

The Gouges cousins produce two whites from the famous "Henri Gouges Albino Pinot Noir" plants. The story has it that in the late 1940s Gouges discovered that some of his Pinot Noir vines were producing both red and white grapes. He took cuttings from the plants and propagated them. Today the Gouges are not the only producers of wines from these mutant vines, as they have generously provided cuttings to other interested vignerons. Generally, according to the Gouges, these mutant Pinot Noir vines produce their best wines in years better suited for reds than whites. Moreover, they state that they age well and should be served at the same temperature as for a red wine. I have tasted every vintage going back to 1985 and agree that they age well but believe they are at their best when served cooler than reds but warmer than is the norm for whites. The Gouges said it best when they described their whites as "fascinating curiosities."

If served the 1995 Nuits-St.-Georges Les Perrières blind, I would have picked it out for a lighter-style red. Crisp and ripe raspberry aromas are followed by a well-structured wine (it even has soft but noticeable tannins!) with medium body. This lively and fresh cherry-filled wine is delicious but will improve over the next 8–9 years. If readers want to have some fun at tastings, they should put the 1995 Nuits-St.-Georges Clos des Porrets in black-colored glasses (so no one can see the color). With its deep aromas of minerals and stones and a red currant, raspberry, and crisp cherry-filled, medium-bodied personality, this wine will fool many a taster. Drink it between now and 2008.

The 1996 Nuits-St.-Georges Les Perrières is, as they so aptly described it a year ago, a fascinating curiosity. It is a strange wine, revealing characteristics of Pinot Noir yet being as white as any Meursault, that evolves wonderfully well. The 1996, produced from 50-year-old vines, offers rich aromas of pears, candied raspberries, strawberries, and notes of vanilla bean. Its palate provided me with flashbacks of going to Mme. Scanviou's *épicerie* (market) in my mother's native village in Brittany and talking with the proprietress until she gave me sweet raspberry- or strawberry-flavored lollipops—this wine tasted like those treats! This spicy, medium- to full-bodied, and exceedingly well-balanced wine can be drunk in its youth or held for up to 15 years.

DOMAINE GUFFENS-HEYNEN (VERGISSON)

1997 Mâcon-Pierreclos	D	(88–90)
1996 Mâcon-Pierreclos	C	89+

1997	Mâcon-Pierreclos Le Chavigne	D	(90–92)
1996	Mâcon-Pierreclos Le Chavigne	D	92
1995	Mâcon-Pierreclos en Chavigne Cuvée Vieilles Vignes	D	90
1995	Pouilly-Fuisse Premier Jus	E	91+
1997	Pouilly-Fuissé Clos des Petits Croux	EE	(92–93+)
1997	Pouilly-Fuissé Les Croux	E	(89–90)
1996	Pouilly-Fuissé Les Croux	D	92+
1997	Pouilly-Fuissé La Roche	E	(93–95)
1996	Pouilly-Fuissé Vintans	E	94

A few years after Jean-Marie Guffens and his wife came to Burgundy in 1976 to learn wine-making, they purchased a couple of vineyards in the Mâconnais with some money inherited from a relative. It is here that Guffens experimented with different concepts of vinification and came up with the multiple cuvée system he uses today (this is described more fully in the Verget section). Using a seventeenth-century vertical press located under his home, and with his wife responsible for all the vineyard work, Guffens makes intense wines from unheralded appellations. Guffens told me that winemaking at Guffens-Heynen is done "with passion, experience, intuition, and no oenological analysis whatsoever." Winemaking decisions are made by taste alone. He feels the knowledge and intelligence used at Verget are the results of the experience and intuition used at Guffens-Heynen. This estate never chaptalizes, fines, or filters, and the bottling takes place a year after the harvest. In 1995 Guffens and his wife started the harvest after everyone else had ended and then dragged it out over a 1-month period; in 1996 he did a 45-day harvest, picking almost grape by grape!

Displaying a stony and sweet fruit-filled nose, the 1995 Mâcon-Pierreclos en Chavigne Cuvée Vieilles Vignes has superripe and unbelievably deep (especially for a Mâcon!) fruit with slight touches of minerals and herbal spices in the mouth. Thick textured, this medium- to full-bodied wine is beautifully balanced and has excellent length. Drink it between now and 2003. The 1995 Pouilly-Fuisse Premier Jus, which was aged in 90% new oak, reveals superrich spices and flint aromas, as well as a flavor intensity found in late-harvest wines. With gorgeous balancing acidity and delicious touches of fresh herbs, steel, and flint, this medium- to full-bodied wine possesses excellent length; it will age beautifully for up to 10 years.

"Traditionalists" enjoy criticizing Jean-Marie Guffens's Verget wines as being manipulated. And they are. Guffens will employ any technique he can devise at Verget to produce quality wines. At their private domaine, however, he and his delightful wife practice "traditional" winemaking, going so far as to use a seventeenth-century vertical press. According to Guffens, no modern-day vinification tools such as chemical analyses, chaptalization, acidification, fining agents, filters, or bottling machines are employed at this estate. Located below his small but beautiful, charming, and well-situated home (the view of the vineyards is breathtaking), the "winery" is but a press and a few barrels.

Jean-Marie Guffens is a controversial figure. This Belgian émigré's influence in Burgundy is increasing vintage to vintage. Vineyards he has been particularly successful with (Meursault Poruzots and Chassagne-Montrachet La Romanée, for example) have seen their bulk grape prices soar as other *négociants* attempt to get in on the action. Estates that sell (or have sold) grapes to Verget now advertise their own estate-bottled wines as being "the same grapes used by Guffens at Verget." Numerous vignerons are trying to "work the lees" in an attempt to achieve the same results as Verget.

The 1996 Guffens-Heynen wines are spectacular. Guffens and his wife harvested over a

45-day period, from September 19 to November 2 (a minuscule amount of wine was produced for their personal consumption from grapes harvested on November 11). Over the course of his 20 years in France, Guffens says he never saw a vintage with such perfect harvesting weather as 1996. As the harvest dragged on grape sugars kept rising, yet the health and vibrant acidity levels of the grapes were maintained (the grapes he harvested on November 11 had a natural potential alcohol of 17.85%—mind-blowingly high in any region of the world—yet their acidity is quite present). While these may be the most expensive wines of the Mâconnais, they are worth it.

The 1996 Mâcon-Pierreclos (it no longer carries the "jeunes vignes" moniker, as the vines have aged) reveals bright mineral aromas and possesses a fresh, lively, expressive, medium-bodied core of rich, dense, and deep citrus fruits, stones, and gravel. This precise, highly focused, and gorgeously ripe wine has extraordinary balance. Anticipated maturity: now–2004. Produced from grapes harvested at 13.5% natural potential alcohol, the 1996 Mâcon-Pierreclos Le Chavigne has an amazingly ripe and intense white fruit-filled nose. On the palate, this expansive, powerful, elegant, and concentrated wine displays layers of minerals, stones, gravel, pears, and buttered white raisins. It is vibrant, muscular, extracted, and magnificently harmonious. My experience with previous vintages of this wine, including a recently tasted 1985 and 1986, indicate that it will evolve beautifully with cellaring. Anticipated maturity: 2000–2007+.

Exhibiting flinty and smoky aromas, the 1996 Pouilly-Fuissé Les Croux is a supple, feminine, fat, opulent, and intensely powerful wine. It is full bodied and velvety textured and has seductive mineral, spice, floral, and anise flavors as well as a formidably long and persistent finish. It should be at its peak from 1999 to 2007. Domaine Guffens-Heynen's 1996 Pouilly-Fuissé Vintans is a mind-boggling wine. Harvested at 14.4% natural potential alcohol, with a whopping 5.4 grams of acidity, it stands as a testimony to Guffens's boundless dedication to quality winemaking. It offers a nose composed of spices, fresh herbs, smoke, and ripe pears that gives way to an oily-textured, magnificently rich, and brilliantly balanced character. It reveals dense layers of sweet and candied white fruits, rocks, chalk, earth, and minerals along with a finely integrated (but still bracing) acidity. Intensely rich yet focused, sweet yet dry, high in alcohol but unnoticeably so, this is a stupendous Pouilly-Fuissé. Anticipated maturity: 2002–2012. Bravo!

In 1997, once again, Jean-Marie Guffens and his wife crafted spectacular wines in the tiny winery located under their home. The 1997 Mâcon-Pierreclos was difficult to assess the day of my tasting because it was in a reductive state (the opposite of oxidized; wines in this state reveal leather, rubber, and gamey aromas and flavors that can be corrected with aeration). After considerable aeration it revealed an intensely sweet and floral bouquet. On the palate, this medium-bodied, fresh, tangy, silky, and expressive wine is crammed with candied lemons, liquid minerals, and a trace of quinine. Anticipated maturity: now–2004. The outstanding 1997 Mâcon-Pierreclos Le Chavigne offers vibrant aromas of acacia and honeysuckle blossoms. This velvety-textured, highly focused, and gorgeously ripe wine is broad, powerful, and structured. Its intense minerality is seemingly coated with candied nuts and myriad citrus fruits that last throughout its prolonged finish. It is a stunning Mâcon! Drink it between 2000 and 2006.

The chalk-and-earth-scented 1997 Pouilly-Fuissé Les Croux has a layered medium- to full-bodied personality crammed with sweet white pears, spices, and stonelike flavors. It is a well-delineated, delicious, and creamy-textured wine that may ultimately merit a higher rating if it takes on more complexity with cellaring. Anticipated maturity: now–2005. Domaine Guffens-Heynen's 1997 Pouilly-Fuissé La Roche is unbelievably great! Readers who have yet to taste a wine from the Mâconnais that can compete with the finest grands crus of the Côte de Beaune should experience this masterpiece. Its deeply ripe nose offers liquid mineral, rock, gravel, and almond paste aromas. It possesses a spiritual quality (the French say *aerien*) that can sometimes be found in the finest Chevalier-Montrachets and Montrachets. It has magnificent focus, bold and deep flint and white fruit flavors, impeccable balance, and intense concentration. This medium- to full-bodied, oily-textured (yet bright and vivacious) offering also has a mind-bogglingly long, crisp, and pure finish. Wow! Anticipated maturity: 2001–2008+. Exhibiting an earthy, stone-laden nose, the 1997 Pouilly-Fuissé Clos des Petits Croux, an even larger wine, is extraordinarily impressive because of its size, density, and beguiling—almost superripe—flavors. This full-bodied monster is viscous yet not ponderous or flabby. Its waves of poached/spiced pears, minerals, and earth flavors coat the palate in successive layers. Anticipated maturity: 2001–2008. Bravo!

DOMAINE GUILLEMOT-MICHEL (QUINTAINE)

1997 Mâcon-Clessé Quintaine	C	90
1996 Mâcon-Clessé Quintaine	C	90+
1995 Mâcon-Clessé Quintaine	C	90
1992 Mâcon-Clessé Quintaine Selection des Grains Cendres	D (375 ml)	91

Pierrette Guillemot, Jean Thévenet's (of Domaine Bongran fame) cousin and goddaugther, and her husband, Marc, are young, dedicated, and talented vignerons. They have employed biodynamic viticulture on their almost 15-acre estate since 1991. Previously the vineyards had been farmed organically for well over a decade. To lower yields and produce better-quality fruit, the Guillemots prune their vines to have only one fruit-bearing stick, abandoning the two-stick method prevalent throughout the Mâconnais.

The Guillemots are late harvesters. For example, in 1997 they brought in the crop $3^1/2$ weeks after their neighbors. Avid tandem cyclists, they enjoy leisurely rides through the countryside, watching their neighbors coordinating the harvesting machines. Guillemot-Michel's yields generally average $2^2/3$ tons of fruit per acre (lower than many famed estates of the Côte de Beaune), with the hand-collected grapes placed in small boxes for the short drive to the winery. Whole clusters are pressed in a pneumatic press and, following a *débourbage*, are fermented with their indigenous yeasts below 21 degrees Celsius.

The wines are left on their lees in large enamel-lined vats throughout their *élevage*. Malolactic fermentations take place naturally, and the wines are never acidified or chaptalized; only minute doses of sulfur, a natural product, are added. Prior to bottling, the wines are subjected to a light bentonite fining and a Kieselguhr (diatomaceous earth) filtration.

An overwhelming majority of Domaine Guillemot-Michel's wines are sold in the United States and Japan, with the French market curiously all but nonexistent. According to Mme. Guillemot, many French consumers are so used to insipid Mâcons that they are unwilling to try the more expensive, higher-quality offerings.

Marc and Pierrette Guillemot hand-harvested their 1997 Mâcon-Clessé Quintaine almost a month after their neighbors had garaged their machine harvesters. Thirty thousand bottles of this sweet mineral- and acacia blossom-scented wine were produced. It is a thick, oily, profoundly rich wine that is immensely expressive and full flavored. Much more ample and fat than the 1996, this medium- to full-bodied, superripe, and dense wine offers layers of liquid minerals, almond cakes, and traces of quince in its delightful flavor profile. Drink it over the next 5 years; I will!

I purchased 2 cases of Guillemot-Michel's 1996 Mâcon-Clessé Quintaine and have been ecstatic, even though the wine is not yet at its peak. Readers who own it should do what I've been incapable of doing and wait; it will only get better over the next 5 years. Revealing honeyed liquid mineral aromas, the 1996 Mâcon-Clessé Quintaine is an outstanding, rich, medium- to full-bodied, and silky-textured wine. Its expressive personality is packed with candied lemons as well as gravel-like flavors and is buttressed by a bracing acidity. Anticipated maturity: 2000–2005. The 1995 Mâcon-Clessé Quintaine's nose is reminiscent of smoke-imbued honeydew melons. On the palate, this oily-textured, medium- to full-bodied, beautifully balanced, and mineral-flavored offering displays profound richness and a long, bone-dry finish. Anticipated maturity: now–2005.

According to Pierrette Guillemot and Jean Thévenet, there was a time when the villages of Clessé and Quintaine were known for their sweet wines. In an effort to maintain this tradition, Domaine Guillemot-Michel crafts late-harvest, botrytis-rich wines. In vintages where noble rot is present on some bunches, the Guillemots will leave those grapes on the vine for later harvesting (in 1996 it took place in mid-November). Prevented by law from using the name "Selections de Grain Noble" (the Alsatians have the name copyrighted), the Guillemots created the term "Selection de Grains Cendrés" (literally "ashed" grapes, so-called because of their appearance). The 1992 displays a light straw color and a mineral, melon, and botrytis-laden nose. This concentrated, well-balanced, elegant, velvety-textured, and medium-bodied wine has verbena, stone, lemon drop, and mineral flavors. It has outstanding focus (particularly for a sweet Chardonnay-based offering) as well as a long, complex finish. It should be drunk between now and 2005.

DOMAINE ANTONIN AND DOMINIQUE GUYON
(SAVIGNY-LÈS-BEAUNE)

1996	Corton-Charlemagne	EE	(?)
1995	Corton-Charlemagne	EE	94
1996	Meursault Charmes du Dessus	D	(89–92)
1996	Pernand-Vergelesses	D	88

This extremely large estate (by Burgundian standards) works 118.5 acres of vines spread out throughout the Côte d'Or. Known more for its red wines, it produces excellent to outstanding white wines as well.

The delicious 1996 Pernand-Vergelesses is produced (2–2¹/₃ tons of fruit per acre in 1996) from a vineyard (Sous La Vierge) that is being seriously considered for premier cru status. It reveals ripe aromas of metals, minerals, and flower blossoms. On the palate, this medium-bodied and concentrated wine has sweet, floral, and anise flavors. Well crafted and focused, it should be drunk before 2002. The Domaine Guyon owns 2¹/₂ acres of Meursault Charmes du Dessus, from which they crafted a marvelous 1996. Exhibiting toasty oak and honeysuckle aromas, this wine has impressive richness, a medium to full body, a thick texture, and deeply ripe concentrated fruit. Layered minerals, pears, and spicy oak are found in this lively, tangy, and extremely well-made wine. Anticipated maturity: 2000–2005. The 1996 Corton-Charlemagne was in an extremely difficult stage of its evolution to judge; hence the question mark. Aromatically revealing charred oak spices, this wine has an exceedingly tight core of extremely concentrated and tangy white currants and superb depth. It appears to have the definition, power, ripeness, and extraction of an outstanding wine, but I will reserve judgment until I have the opportunity to retaste it.

The 1995 Corton-Charlemagne is spectacular. Profound aromas of almond paste, ripe pears, white flowers, and anise are followed by a broad, medium- to full-bodied, powerful, magnificently concentrated, and extracted core of honeysuckle blossoms, red berries, minerals, and spicy oak. This superb offering should be at its peak between 2002 and 2009.

DOMAINE THIERRY HAMELIN (CHABLIS)

1996	Chablis	C	88
1995	Chablis Vau Ligneau	C	90

1997 Chablis Vieilles Vignes	C	88
1996 Petit Chablis	B	87

Crafted from 70-year-old vines, the hand-harvested (a rarity in this sector) 1997 Chablis Vieilles Vignes was produced entirely in stainless-steel tanks. Chestnut aromas are intermingled with almond cookies and seashells in this medium-bodied, well-delineated, earthy wine. It finishes with a complex display of lemon, melon, and pear flavors that transform into minerals and flint. Anticipated maturity: now–2004.

Thierry Hamelin's 1996 Petit Chablis offering is one of the finest I have tasted. A dry, smoky nose is followed by a well-focused, light- to medium-bodied, crisp, stony, and structured core of minerally fruit with hints of lemon to give it a tangy zest. Refreshing and mouth cleansing, this delicious wine will provide 2–3 years of excellent drinking. Displaying fresh and lively aromas of grapefruit and minerals, the 1996 Chablis is a smoke-and-flint-laden wine with good concentration of fruit, medium body, and a razorlike, strident finish. This excellent wine should be consumed before 2002. I also had the opportunity to taste one of Hamelin's 1995s, the Chablis Vau Ligneau. Revealing aromas of flowers, stones, flint, earth, and lime zests, this outstanding offering possesses an exceedingly well-balanced and medium- to full-bodied core of minerals, chalk, wet rocks, and layered citrus fruit flavors. It will be at its best between now and 2004. This is an excellent value.

LOUIS JADOT (BEAUNE)

1996 Auxey-Duresses	C	86
1995 Auxey-Duresses	C	86
1997 Bâtard-Montrachet	EEE	(91–93)
1996 Bâtard-Montrachet	EEE	94
1995 Bâtard-Montrachet	EEE	92+
1996 Beaune Grèves	D	88
1995 Beaune Grèves	D	89+
1996 Bienvenue-Bâtard-Montrachet	EEE	92+
1995 Bienvenue-Bâtard-Montrachet	EEE	91
1996 En Charlemagne	EE	90
1995 En Charlemagne	EE	89+
1996 Chassagne-Montrachet	D	87
1995 Chassagne-Montrachet	D	87
1996 Chassagne-Montrachet Caillerets	E	91
1995 Chassagne-Montrachet Caillerets	D	91
1997 Chassagne-Montrachet Les Grandes Ruchottes	E	(89–90)
1997 Chassagne-Montrachet Morgeot	E	(90–91)
1996 Chassagne-Montrachet Morgeot	E	90+
1995 Chassagne-Montrachet Morgeot	D	90
1997 Chassagne-Montrachet Morgeot Duc de Magenta	E	(89–90+)
1996 Chassagne-Montrachet Morgeot Duc de Magenta	D	90
1997 Chassagne-Montrachet La Romanée	E	(89–91)

1996	Chassagne-Montrachet La Romanée	E	92
1995	Chassagne-Montrachet La Romanée	E	90
1997	Chevalier-Montrachet	EEE	(91–93)
1996	Chevalier-Montrachet	EEE	94
1997	Chevalier-Montrachet Les Demoiselles	EEE	(93–94+)
1996	Chevalier-Montrachet Les Demoiselles	EEE	96
1995	Chevalier-Montrachet Les Demoiselles	EEE	95
1997	Corton-Charlemagne	EEE	(89–90)
1996	Corton-Charlemagne	EE	92
1995	Corton-Charlemagne	EE	91+
1996	Corton-Vergennes	EE	91
1995	Corton-Vergennes	EE	90
1997	Criots-Bâtard-Montrachet	EEE	(90–91)
1996	Criots-Bâtard-Montrachet	EEE	92+
1995	Criots-Bâtard-Montrachet	EEE	90
1995	Marsannay	C	85
1997	Meursault	D	(87–88)
1996	Meursault	D	88
1995	Meursault	D	85
1995	Meursault Bouchères	D	88
1997	Meursault Charmes	E	(89–90)
1996	Meursault Charmes	E	89
1995	Meursault Charmes	D	90
1996	Meursault Genevrières	E	90
1995	Meursault Genevrières	E	91
1997	Meursault Goutte d'Or	E	(88–89)
1995	Meursault Goutte d'Or	D	90
1995	Meursault Perrières	E	91
1996	Montrachet	EEE	96
1995	Montrachet	EEE	95
1996	Pernand-Vergelesses	C	87
1995	Pernand-Vergelesses	C	86
1997	Pouilly-Fuissé	C	87
1997	Pouilly-Fuissé Réserve*	C	87
1997	Puligny-Montrachet	D	(87–88)

*This wine is sold in every market except the United States as Pouilly-Fuissé Mont de Pouilly.

1995	Puligny-Montrachet	D	86
1996	Puligny-Montrachet Les Champs Gain	E	89
1995	Puligny-Montrachet Les Champs Gain	D	89
1997	Puligny-Montrachet Clos de la Garenne Duc de Magenta	E	(91–92+)
1996	Puligny-Montrachet Clos de la Garenne Duc de Magenta	E	92+
1995	Puligny-Montrachet Clos de la Garenne Duc de Magenta	E	91+
1997	Puligny-Montrachet Les Folatières	E	(89–91)
1996	Puligny-Montrachet Les Folatières	E	92
1995	Puligny-Montrachet Les Folatières	E	91+
1996	Puligny-Montrachet Perrières	E	90
1995	Puligny-Montrachet Perrières	D	90
1997	Puligny-Montrachet Les Réferts	E	(91–92)
1996	Puligny-Montrachet Les Réferts	E	92
1996	Rully	C	87
1995	Rully	C	84
1997	St. Aubin	D	(86–87)
1995	St. Aubin	C	85
1996	St. Romain	C	86
1995	St. Romain	C	86
1996	Santenay Clos de Malte	C	86
1995	Santenay Clos de Malte	C	88
1995	Savigny	C	84
1997	Savigny-Lès-Beaune	D	(87–88)
1996	Savigny-Lès-Beaune	C	86
1996	Savigny-Lès-Beaune Clos des Guettes	D	87+

Jacques Lardière, the ever-smiling, intense, philosophizing, warm, and engaging winemaker at Maison Louis Jadot, now works his magic in a "wine temple." Located in Beaune on the road to Savigny-Lès-Beaune, it has a classical exterior that does not hint at the modernity of the interior. The central *cuverie* (or vat room) is a large circular space with a three-story-high ceiling, filled with stainless-steel and wooden vats arranged in concentric circles. In the middle of the room is a raised wooden platform resembling a temple's altar. On this altar stands Jacques Lardière, overseeing the fermentations of Jadot's wines.

Pierre-Henri Gagey, the boyish-looking director of this *négociant* house, is an astute businessman with a passionate love of his product and his region. From its modest status just 2 decades ago, he has seen Jadot grow into a large (between 6 and 7 million bottles annually) and internationally respected purveyor of fine wine. Realizing that the old winery was no longer capable of expanding its production while maintaining this firm's high standards, he chose to build a new one in which Lardière's prodigious talents could be fully exploited.

Everywhere I went throughout Burgundy in October and November 1998, vignerons chanted the same song—the 1997 whites are forward, low-acid wines that had rapid malolactic fermentations. The exception—Maison Jadot. I thought I was getting used to Jacques

Lardière going against the grain, but he still surprises me. The fact that some of his white burgundies were still in full malolactic was baffling, but what truly shocked me was a statement he made at the end of our white wine tasting: "The whites are delicious," Lardière said, "but the reds may be the greatest wines of my life. They are my 1947s or 1959s. I will probably never see anything like this vintage again." I looked at him with such disbelief that he walked me over to a few barrels and had me taste some profound wines. Stay tuned, as I will taste the entire range on my scheduled mid-January visit to Maison Jadot.

How does he do it? Why are things so different for Lardière than for others? As I've mentioned before, asking the right questions does not guarantee an understandable answer. For example, on my last visit I asked Lardière if he had blocked the malolactic fermentations on some of his 1997 white burgundies, a practice this firm frequently does in low-acid vintages (1983 and 1989 are two prominent examples). His response? "At Maison Jadot we do not block malos. We perturb the bacterias that cause it. They are much easier to perturb than humans, you know." I got no further, no matter how much I pressed for information.

Jadot's 1997 white burgundies are super, among the finest of the vintage. Lardière's magical touch (he firmly stated that he does not acidify white wines) allowed these wines to have the vintage's telltale fat and richness, yet for the most part they retained focus, balance, and structure.

The 1997 Pouilly-Fuissé offers flint and tealike aromas. This beautifully focused, medium-bodied, and fresh wine offers a vibrant personality with pure mineral flavors. Drink it over the next 4–5 years. The 1997 Pouilly-Fuissé Réserve (this wine is sold in every market except the United States as Pouilly-Fuissé Mont de Pouilly) reveals sweet white fruit and wet wool scents. A more commercially made wine, it adds a strong oak influence to the flavor profile but should be able to absorb it given a year or so of cellaring. It is silky textured, medium bodied, and ripe. Anticipated maturity: 2001–2004.

Jadot's 1997 St. Aubin offers ripe white fruit and mineral aromas interspersed with traces of spicy new oak. This medium-bodied, fat, and luscious wine is oily textured and filled with superripe pears and apples. Drink it over the next 4 years. Produced from a high percentage of Pinot Blanc, the 1997 Savigny-Lès-Beaune is an extremely expressive and super wine. It reveals aromas of candied orange peels and flowers that lead to a bright and boisterous personality filled with sweet minerals and white fruits. This medium-bodied and silky textured beauty should be drunk in its youth in order to adequately enjoy its vibrant flavors. Anticipated maturity: now–2001. The 1997 Meursault has an elegant nose of toasted hazelnuts and sweet oak spices. This lively, expansive, medium-bodied wine offers an intense mouthful of assorted nuts and pears. It is well crafted and balanced and has an appealingly velvety texture. Drink it over the next 4 years. The 1997 Puligny-Montrachet is equally good and displays an acacia blossom and almond-laced nose. This layered, broad, and rich offering exhibits delicious apple, white raisin, and stone flavors in its medium body. Anticipated maturity: now–2003.

The deeply ripe nose of the 1997 Meursault Goutte d'Or consists of almonds and hazelnuts. This medium- to full-bodied, explosive, full-flavored wine is crammed with white and yellow fruits and toasty oak. It is richly textured, powerful, and mouth coating. Drink it over the next 5 years. Revealing beguiling aromas of crushed red berries, flowers, and nuts, the flavorful 1997 Meursault Charmes is gorgeously focused. Waves of pears, honeysuckle, hazelnuts, and minerals can be found in its medium- to full-bodied, silky-textured, and forward personality. Anticipated maturity: now–2005.

I loved both of Jadot's 1997 wines from Chassagne-Montrachet's Morgeot vineyard. The 1997 Duc de Magenta's offering has a mineral-and-earth-laden nose and a superripe, medium- to full-bodied, and dense character. Its flavor profile is packed with clay, poached pears, and baked apples. A concentrated, thick wine, it will be at its best if drunk over the next 5–6 years. The 1997 Chassagne-Montrachet Morgeot (domaine bottling) displays aromas of fresh earth, rocks, and grilled oak. It is a powerful, complex, and profound wine with a gorgeous array of clay, pear, baked apple, and spicy wood flavors that last throughout its long finish. This medium- to full-bodied and fabulously expressive wine has excellent structure. Anticipated maturity: 2000–2006. Revealing a bold and mineral-dominated nose, the lovely 1997 Chassagne-Montrachet La Romanée is powerful and concentrated. Its broad, thickly textured, and well-extracted flavor profile is loaded with red fruits, earth, and oak spices. In a vintage that fashioned heavy wines verging on flabbiness, it is amazing how fresh and focused this offering is. Anticipated maturity: 2000–2006. The 1997 Chassagne-Montrachet Les Grandes Ruchottes has more subtle aromatics, displaying hints of berries dusted with minerals. It is beautifully harmonious, with layers of well-ripened pears and red currants beautifully intermingled with earth and oak spices. This medium- to full-bodied wine has a silky texture, excellent concentration, and a long finish. Drink it over the next 6 years.

The 1997 Puligny-Montrachet Les Réferts has a mouthwatering nose of superripe pears and apples. This dense, oily-textured, and fat wine has traces of *sur-maturité* in its otherwise bright, spicy, and almond cookie-flavored character. It is medium to full bodied, thick, and surprisingly well balanced and offers an impressive finish. Anticipated maturity: now–2004. Displaying floral and anise aromas, the 1997 Puligny-Montrachet Les Folatières is broad and powerful, yet feminine. A medium-bodied, velvety-textured, forward wine, it is filled with flavors reminiscent of pears, minerals, apples, and honeysuckle. Drink it over the next 6 years. The outstanding 1997 Puligny-Montrachet Clos de la Garenne Duc de Magenta has a fresh earth-and-stone-scented nose. This full-bodied, mouth-filling, and explosive wine is dense yet refined. Candle wax, white peaches, and clay can be found in its powerful, harmonious, and concentrated flavor profile. It may ultimately merit a more glowing review if it resolves the slight warmth (alcohol) I detected in its finish. Drink it between 2001 and 2006.

Produced from purchased grape must, the 1997 Criots-Bâtard-Montrachet reveals a spicy, anise, and mineral-infused nose. This expressive and forward offering is deep, intense, focused, and crammed with nutty pear flavors. It is extremely well crafted and medium to full bodied and has outstanding extraction, density, and power. It will be at its best between 2001 and 2006. Jadot's Bâtard-Montrachet may be this vineyard's finest wine in 1997, as it aptly reflects the vintage's huge richness and density yet has remained in balance. It offers overripe aromas of tropical fruits intermingled with scents of clay and tangerines. On the palate, it is massively broad and thickly textured yet has superb delineation to its candied pear and apple flavors. Concentrated and powerful, it appears to have the ability to age. Anticipated maturity: 2001–2008. The 1997 Chevalier-Montrachet has an enthralling nose of minerals, gravel, and crisp white pears. This impeccably delineated and focused wine has outstanding depth, medium to full body, and a richly layered personality. Its flavor profile offers an intense minerality that coats the palate throughout its long finish. Anticipated maturity: 2002–2008. Jadot's 1997 Chevalier-Montrachet Les Demoiselles is a fabulous wine. Its nose was slightly reticent the day of my tasting, reluctantly revealing nuts, minerals, and stones. However, its spectacular presence on the palate more than demonstrated its greatness. This is an offering of outstanding richness and density. It is crammed with candied hazelnuts, almonds, and spicy minerals. It also has an ethereal quality that I sometimes find in the best Chevaliers. This is one of the rare 1997s from the Côte de Beaune that will age for at least a decade. Drink it between 2003 and 2012.

The 1997 Corton-Charlemagne exhibits aromas of anise, white flowers, and oak spices. This is a lovely, medium- to full-bodied, and intense wine. It has superb richness, an expressive and powerful minerality, and a delightfully silky texture. While this wine ultimately deserves an excellent score, I was disappointed in its somewhat short finish. Drink it between 2000 and 2006.

Jacques Lardière told me that 1996 was not a vintage in which to stir the lees. This was in complete contradiction with what most other white wine producers told me. His reasoning, which I freely admit is beyond my understanding, involved the "breaking of molecular strings" and a "molecular explosion" (*éclatement moléculaire*), a risky proposition in 1996 according to Lardière. It does not surprise me that I was unable to understand this explanation, since I have yet to grasp his theory on what makes white burgundies stand out— "Chardonnay is but a vehicle to express the vibratory center of the *terroir.*"

The mineral-scented 1996 Rully reveals a vibrant, medium-bodied, ripe, well-crafted, and deep core of buttery gravel-like flavors. The 1996 St. Romain displays toasty mineral aromas and a medium-bodied, tangy, crisp, nut, and lemon/lime-filled character. Both of these wines should be drunk for their lively fruit over the next 2–3 years. Exhibiting a flint-and-metal-infused nose, the 1996 Auxey-Duresses is a fresh, medium-bodied, bright wine with candied anise and mineral flavors. Anticipated maturity: now–2001. The 1996 Santenay Clos de Malte has a perfumed and mineral-laden nose as well as a rich, crisp, medium-bodied character. This wine's wide and deep flavor profile is composed of minerals and lemon zests. It will at its best if drunk before 2002. Revealing white flower aromas, the 1996 Pernand-Vergelesses has excellent richness of fruit, a medium body, and a racy personality filled with flavors of sweet anise and white currants. Anticipated maturity: now–2002. Produced from 60% Pinot Blanc and 40% Chardonnay, the 1996 Savigny-Lès-Beaune has freshly cut flower aromas. This wine has a juicy, silky-textured, medium-bodied, zesty, floral, anise, and mineral-flavored character. The 1996 Savigny-Lès-Beaune Clos des Guettes, from a vineyard owned by Pierre-Henri Gagey, displays attractive nutty and mineral scents. It is a medium- to full-bodied, rich, deep, and somewhat powerful wine filled with metals, gravel, and white flowers. It should be at its best between now and 2003. Produced from the Narvaux and Tillets vineyards, Jadot's 1996 Meursault has lovely hazelnut and mineral aromas as well as a deep, rich, thick, and delicious character. It is medium bodied, creamy, and packed with nuts and lemon zests. Anticipated maturity: now–2003. The delicious 1996 Chassagne-Montrachet reveals sweet floral and citrus aromas followed by a medium- to full-bodied, tangy, rich, racy, and mineral-packed personality. Drink this wine before 2002.

The 1996 Beaune Grèves reveals deep mineral aromatics as well as intense richness and a medium to full body. This silky, masculine, and well-crafted wine is filled with gravel, toast, and stonelike flavors. Anticipated maturity: now–2003. Even though the 1996 Meursault Charmes had a tight, muted nose the day of my tasting, its broad, medium- to full-bodied, rich, and supple-textured character was evidence enough of its quality. Layers of minerals, flowers, and anise can be found in this well-delineated wine. It should be at its best from 2000 to 2006. The 1996 Meursault Genevrières reveals candied nut and mineral aromas as well as an oily-textured, rich, superripe, yet highly delineated personality. Poached pears, white peaches, and tangy lemons can be found in this concentrated and complex wine. Anticipated maturity: 2001–2007.

Displaying a lovely and refined nose of minerals, the 1996 Chassagne-Montrachet Caillerets is a powerful, pure, broad-shouldered, wide, medium- to full-bodied, velvety-textured wine. Its profound character is packed with gravel, citrus, and floral flavors. It should be at its best between 2001 and 2006. The 1996 Chassagne-Montrachet Morgeot has attractive stony, anise, and white flower aromas as well as a medium- to full-bodied, structured, masculine, well-delineated, and stylish palate. It possesses a deep, earth, mineral, and citrus zest-flavored personality and a long and precise finish. I suggest consuming it from 2001 to 2006. Lardière has fashioned a fabulous 1996 Chassagne-Montrachet Morgeot Duc de Magenta. It reveals an elegant, stone-infused nose and a medium- to full-bodied, thick, concentrated, complex, and deeply rich personality. Its expansive and muscular flavor profile is packed with sweet nuts, minerals, and smoke. The finish is impressively long and detailed. Anticipated maturity: 2002–2008. Exhibiting mouthwatering smoked pork fat and stony scents, the 1996 Chassagne-Montrachet La Romanée is a beautifully ripe, complex, smoothly textured, and powerful wine. It is highly extracted, precise, well defined, and packed with deep layers of red currants and minerals. I recommend consuming it between 2003 and 2009.

The 1996 Puligny-Montrachet Les Champs Gain reveals flowers and crisp red berry aromas and a medium-bodied, feminine, delineated, and well-balanced character. This elegant and focused wine is filled with pears, spices, and anise. It should be at its peak between now and 2004. The delicious 1996 Puligny-Montrachet Perrières has a white flower-laden nose and a medium- to full-bodied, refined, and gorgeously precise and focused personality. Its flavor profile is composed of candied lemons, baking spices, cloves, and minerals. Anticipated maturity: 2000–2006. Displaying beguiling smoke and stone aromas, the 1996 Puligny-Montrachet Les Réferts is another well-defined, powerful, medium- to full-bodied, and mouth-coatingly rich offering. This silky-textured, broad, fat, and complex wine has superb grip and a tantalizingly pure finish. Anticipated maturity: 2003–2009. The 1996 Puligny-Montrachet Clos de la Garenne Duc de Magenta bursts from the glass with an anise- and white flower-scented nose. It is a magnificently ripe, concentrated, superrich, full-bodied, and powerful wine. Earth, minerals, and a springtime bouquet can be found in its oily-textured and intense character. It should be cellared until at least 2003 and can be drunk through 2009. Produced from a vineyard planted in 1970, the 1996 Puligny-Montrachet Les Folatières has delicate, feminine, floral, and perfumed aromas. While this wine is not particularly concentrated or powerful, it possesses considerable refinement and lacelike qualities. An elegant, precise, and highly delineated wine, it reveals spiced pears, flowers, and tangy lemons in its flavors. It will be at its peak from 2002 to 2008.

Exhibiting smoky mineral scents, Jadot's 1996 Criots-Bâtard-Montrachet has superb mineral richness, powerful chalk flavors, and an extremely well-crafted and balanced charac-ter. Silky textured and medium to full bodied, it is one of the finest examples I have tasted from this grand cru vineyard. Anticipated maturity: 2003–2010. Revealing a rich, pear-and-mineral-infused nose, the 1996 Bienvenue-Bâtard-Montrachet is an intense, powerful, deeply ripe, yet austere wine. Superbly defined and softly textured layers of stones, gravel, earth, and anise are found in this medium- to full-bodied and highly structured wine. Anticipated maturity: 2003–2010. Maison Louis Jadot's 1996 Bâtard-Montrachet has a superripe, intensely floral nose and a massive, muscular, dense, oily-textured, and full-bodied core of sweet fruit. White peaches, poached pears, juniper berries, and oak nuances can be discerned in this opulent yet focused wine. It should be at its peak from 2003 to 2010. The 1996 Chevalier-Montrachet has a piercing, mineral-filled nose and a powerfully rich, full-bodied, extracted, crystalline, and silky character. This beautifully refined wine has layers of stones, gravel, and flowerlike flavors. Its long and detailed finish reveals traces of sweet oak. Anticipated maturity: 2003–2012. One of Burgundy's perennial stars, Jadot's 1996 Chevalier-Montrachet Les Demoiselles is a stunner. Its aromatic purity and precision is something to behold, displaying extraordinary depth and ripeness as well as loads of liquid minerals. On the palate, it has unbridled power, a full body, an oily texture, and exquisite anise, spice, pear, and floral flavors. This highly delineated and wonderfully structured wine will require patience. I suggest holding it until 2005 and consuming it before 2015. The 1996 Montrachet exhibits earth, wild mushroom, smoke, and mineral aromas as well as a hugely concentrated, extracted, and intensely complex personality. Copious quantities of Brazil nuts, gravel, spiced pears, buttered toast, and flowers saturate the palate in this velvety-textured, magnificently balanced, and full-bodied blockbuster. Its admirably long finish appears to last close to 40 seconds. Anticipated maturity: 2006–2015.

The 1996 is the last vintage in which Maison Jadot will offer an En Charlemagne, which is a shame. I always found it to be a fascinating *terroir* tasting to compare it with this firm's other two wines from the same grand cru vineyard. The En Charlemagne is from vines located near Pernand-Vergelesses (facing north and west), the Corton-Vergennes is from the other extremity of this large hill, near Ladoix (east-facing), and the Corton-Charlemagne is from the center, facing south.

The 1996 En Charlemagne has a perfumed, floral nose and a medium-bodied, silky-textured, and warmly embracing character. This well-balanced and delineated wine reveals flavors of white flowers, traces of anise, and touches of clay on its persistent finish. It should be consumed between 2000 and 2005. The 1996 Corton-Charlemagne has a deep, rich, and ripe nose packed with white fruits. On the palate, it is an oily-textured, medium- to full-bodied, and dense wine with metal, mineral, sweet candied nut, buttered popcorn, and poached pear flavors. Anticipated maturity: 2002–2008. Revealing a warm yet fresh nose filled with white flowers, the 1996 Corton-Vergennes is a silky, rich, masculine, structured, and densely packed offering. Its flavor profile is composed of red currants, salty nuts, earth, and crisp white peaches. Anticipated maturity: 2001–2007.

Pierre-Henri Gagey and Jacques Lardière were excited about their 1995s. Like everybody else in the Côte, they saw the flowering on their whites get seriously damaged by the May snowfall. This resulted in a 30% reduction of their overall production, with some vineyards having yields more than 50% below the norm (Montrachet, for example). The resulting grapes were very small and packed with concentrated juice, thereby providing fabulous raw material for Lardière to display his considerable talent.

Jadot is owned by Kobrand, an American wine and liquor distribution company, and therefore its wines are generally widely distributed throughout the United States. This does not mean, however, that all these wines are easy to find. As with most burgundies, the production of individual wines is often quite small. For example, there are only 50 cases of the 1995 Chassagne-Montrachet La Romanée for the world!

A well-made wine, the 1995 Rully has a toasty, floral (ever so slightly green) bouquet and a nice oily-textured, nutty flavor. This light- to medium-bodied wine, like all of Jadot's 1995s, has good balance and structure. An excellent value, the 1995 St. Romain exhibits a deep, nutty, stony, extracted, and concentrated nose with touches of almond paste. Medium bodied, this wine has a flinty flavor married nicely with an oaky spice. St. Romains are generally very flinty (some winemakers like to stress that aspect), yet Lardière prefers to soften it with a touch of wood. One of the few white burgundies not made from Chardonnay or Aligoté, the 1995 Marsannay is made from Chardonnay Rosé, whose grapes are dark pink (darker than Pinot Gris). It displays an enticing and exotic red berry and floral nose and tightly structured stony flavors. Made in a different style, the masculine, medium-bodied 1995 Auxey-Duresses exhibits a smoky, stony aspect to its aromas. On the palate, the flavors are reminiscent of iodine and sea air. This wine, as well as the preceding offerings, are meant for near-term drinking—within 3 years of their release.

Revealing white flowerlike scents in the nose, the 1995 Pernand-Vergelesses offers elegantly feminine, crisp red berries and mineral flavors, medium body, and admirable structure. It is a very good value. Drink it between now and 2000. Made from 60% Pinot Blac and 40% Chardonnay, the 1995 Savigny exhibits an extremely tight nose with notes of smoke and toasted bread. Well delineated and floral, it possesses a strong acid component that a German wine fanatic would appreciate. Drink this light- to medium-bodied wine over the next 2–3 years. Another wine whose acid stands out is the 1995 St. Aubin. Here the acid is reminiscent of a crisp green apple. This medium-bodied wine displays flavors of candied fruits and minerals. A step up is the 1995 Santenay Clos de Malte (it gets its name from the fact that the Knights of Malta once owned this 17¹/₃-acre vineyard). It reveals a fabulous nose of dried white raisins and oaky spices, followed by a fat, oily texture and distinct stony flavors. Consume this medium-bodied wine between now and 2002. Possessing the characteristic toasted hazelnuts aromas of its appellation, the medium-bodied 1995 Meursault displays sweet fruit and nuts in the mouth, as well as fine structure, but it lacks complexity. Drink it between now and 2000. A more interesting wine, the 1995 Puligny-Montrachet had an un-yielding nose (it was undergoing fining) but a mouth of ripe, sweet, roasted apples and tropi-cal fruits and a long, dry finish. This medium-bodied, well-balanced wine should be enjoyed between now and 2003. The best of the village wines from the holy trilogy of white burgundy villages, Puligny, Meursault, and Chassagne, is certainly the 1995 Chassagne-Montrachet. It displays a beautifully elegant, floral-scented nose, and the mouth exhibits well-structured flavors of stones and flowers with a touch of spicy oak. Medium bodied, it has an anticipated maturity of now–2004.

None of the following wines had undergone fining when I tasted them in early January 1997. Produced from 10-year-old vines, the 1995 Beaune Grèves is Jadot's attempt at un-seating Drouhin as the producer of the most commercially successful white Beaune. While Jadot won't succeed with the 1995, this is the kind of competition that benefits consumers. The wine reveals a deep, sweet, enticing nose and candied, almondy flavors in the mouth, with a stony, long finish. This excellent, medium-bodied wine should be consumed between now and 2006. The 1995 Meursault Bouchères's unyielding nose is followed by ripe fruit and intense stony, minerally flavors. Drink this medium-bodied wine between now and 2003. Re-vealing aromas of sweet nuts and flowers, the 1995 Meursault Charmes has an elegant mouth full of sweetened Earl Gray tea, flowers, and toasty fruits. This medium- to full-bodied wine should age well for 10+ years. From the same village, but radically different, the sultry 1995 Meursault Goutte d'Or has tropical fruits and distant licorice aromas jumping from the glass. Well structured and displaying a judicious use of oak, this long, luscious, medium- to full-bodied wine will drink beautifully from now to 2004. Jadot's two best 1995 Meursault offer-ings are the Meursault Perrières and the Meursault Genevrières. The former reveals toasted hazelnuts in its tightly wound nose. In the mouth, it possesses awesome structure and persis-tence, with well-delineated flavors of minerals, stones, nuts, and a light tropical fruit touch. The Genevrières has an enticingly spicy and sweet nose, as well as a fat, spicy, oily texture, with touches of star anise and candied nuts. Both of these full-bodied wines will age grace-fully for 10–15+ years.

Exhibiting a beautifully floral nose, the 1995 Chassagne-Montrachet Caillerets has deeply imbedded sweet fruit and a long finish of smoke and stones on the mouth. This elegant, medium- to full-bodied wine has excellent structure and can easily be cellared for 10+ years given good storage. Revealing beautiful ripeness on the nose, the 1995 Chassagne-Montrachet La Romanée has an oily texture, which Jacques Lardière likened to the estate's 1979. Surprisingly, it is more minerally than the Caillerets, but it doesn't have the structure. The ripe fruit reveals an appealing smoky component. Possessing a tight, citrusy nose, the unchaptalized, crisp 1995 Chassagne-Montrachet Morgeot exhibits a stony, superripe mouth redolent with flavors of white peaches. Thick textured and medium to full bodied, this wine should be drunk between now and 2005. The Puligny-Montrachet Les Champs Gain, which yielded only half its normal crop in 1995, has a deep and enticing fruit-filled nose. The mouth is very Puligny-ish with mocha, almonds, sweet roasted fruit, and a powerful floral character. This full-bodied wine isn't highly structured, so I recommend drinking it over the next 7 years. Revealing a perfumed nose of flowers and minerals, the 1995 Puligny-Montrachet Perrières is much more structured than the Champs Gain, with sweet, driven fruit and stony components to the mouth. This refined and medium-bodied wine needs 3–4 years of cellaring; it will drink beautifully over the subsequent 8. Displaying a steely and floral perfumed nose, the 1995 Puligny-Montrachet Folatières has a gorgeous lemon-custard, floral, and spicy flavor profile with good length, structure, and great driving acidity. This outstanding medium- to full-bodied wine should be held for 4–5 years; it will age gracefully for 10+. Gagey described the Folatières vineyard as "rock dust covering rock."

From 72-year-old vines, the 1995 Puligny-Montrachet Clos de la Garenne shocked me with a nose that reminded me of the Bazooka bubble gum I sometimes chewed as a kid: sweet, perfumed, and slightly floral. The mouth exhibits the effect of old vines with deeply concentrated fruit and great length. Thick textured, this fabulous wine should be consumed between 2002 and 2012.

Displaying reduced or cooked fruits on the nose, the 1995 Bienvenue-Bâtard-Montrachet starts out the grand cru lineup here with waves of superripe or dried fruits and spices in the mouth. This full-bodied and oily-textured wine has good length and structure. Jadot's 1995 Criots-Bâtard-Montrachet's nose conjures up scents of green apples. The wine's flavors come through in the mouth along with touches of minerals and spice. Silky textured and medium to full bodied, this wine should be consumed between 2002 and 2010. Following a superripe, concentrated nose of tropical fruits, the 1995 Bâtard-Montrachet serves up layers of spice-laden tropical fruit. With great staying power, this intense, long, full-bodied wine is a true grand cru. Drink it between 2000 and 2010. According to Lardière, the Bâtard had 13.7% natural sugar, eclipsing the 1995 Chevalier-Montrachet Les Demoiselles' 13.5%. I've been lucky enough to drink the 1985 and 1986 Chevaliers recently, and I can attest to the fact that these wines age admirably. The 1995's nose displays butter, minerals, stones, and spice. The flavors present fabulous harnessed fruit with well-integrated acidity. This high-class wine possesses formidable structure and impressive persistence; it will drink well for 15–20 years, but it begs for another 6 years of cellaring to open up. Regrettably, only 100 cases were produced of this sublime Chevalier. Possessing a harnessed, supertightly wound nose of sweet fruit and steely components, the 1995 Montrachet is a compelling wine. Its powerful racy mouth, jam-packed with dense underlying fruit and minerals, is just waiting to explode to the surface. Lardière's touch can be seen in the brilliant use of oak, which provides a gorgeous spiciness to the wine. Full bodied, complex, intense, and long, this wine *needs* 7–9 years to blossom; it will age effortlessly for 20+ years. At this point the wine is like a Thoroughbred caged in at the starting gates, waiting impatiently for the race to begin, its muscles trembling in anticipation of what is to come.

Made from purchased fruit on the western slope of the Corton vineyard near Pernand Vergelesses, the 1995 En Charlemagne is made for people who prefer an early-drinking, low-acid, superripe Chardonnay. This wine displays an extravagantly rich nose packed with buttery tropical fruits, followed by flavors that explode with candied, highly extracted fruit. This wine does not have the best structure or delineation, but it will provide hedonistic pleasure over the near term (now–2002). It was given the name En Charlemagne so as to not confuse consumers used to Jadot's Corton-Charlemagne and Corton-Vergennes. The latter wine is completely different from the Charlemagne, as it reveals a stony, flinty nose and a well-structured and delineated body packed with tightly wound minerally fruit. This medium- to full-bodied wine has good length and will age well for 10+ years. The 1995 Corton-Charlemagne is one of those rare Cortons with class and finesse, in contrast with the majority of Cortons, which are big, powerful, and brawny wines that rely on their strength, not finesse, to awe the drinker. With reticent, nearly concealed ripe fruit aromas, this tightly knit wine offers great richness (green apple essence) and long, persistent flavor. Thick textured and medium to full bodied, it will age for 10–15 years.

Other 1997s recently tasted: Auxey-Duresses (86–87), Beaujolais Blanc Château des Jacques (85), Beaune Grèves (87–88+), Bienvenue-Bâtard-Montrachet (88–89?), Bourgogne Blanc (85), Chassagne-Montrachet (86–88), Corton Vergennes (88–89), Côte de Nuits-Villages (86–87), Fixin (86–87), Mâcon-Villages Grand Clos Loyse Château des Jacques (86), Marsannay (87–88), Meursault Bouchères (87–89), Puligny-Montrachet Les Champs Gains (88–89+), Rully (85–86), St. Romain (85–86), Santenay Clos de Malte (82–84+?), Savigny-Lès-Beaune Clos des Guettes (87–89).

DOMAINE PATRICK JAVILLIER (MEURSAULT)

1996	Bourgogne Aligoté	C	87
1995	Bourgogne Aligoté	C	86
1997	Bourgogne Blanc Cuvée des Forgets	C	86
1996	Bourgogne Blanc Cuvée des Forgets	C	87
1995	Bourgogne Blanc Cuvée des Forgets	C	87
1997	Bourgogne Blanc Cuvée des Forgets "Mise Spéciale"	C	(87–89)
1996	Bourgogne Blanc Cuvée des Forgets "Mise Spéciale"	C	88
1997	Bourgogne Blanc Cuvée Oligocène	D	87
1995	Bourgogne Blanc Cuvée Oligocène	D	88
1997	Bourgogne Blanc Cuvée Oligocène "Mise Spéciale"	D	(88–90+)
1996	Bourgogne Blanc Cuvée Oligocène "Mise Spéciale"	D	89
1995	Meursault Casse Têtes	D	87+
1997	Meursault Les Clous	D	89
1996	Meursault Les Clous	D	88+
1995	Meursault Les Clous	D	92
1997	Meursault Clos du Cromin	D	88
1996	Meursault Clos du Cromin	D	89+
1995	Meursault Clos du Cromin	D	90
1997	Meursault Cuvée Tête de Murger	E	90+
1996	Meursault Cuvée Tête de Murger	E	92+
1996	Meursault Cuvée Tête de Murger "Mise Spéciale"	E	94
1995	Meursault au Murger	D	91
1996	Meursault Les Narvaux	E	91+
1995	Meursault Les Narvaux	D	93+
1997	Meursault Les Narvaux "Mise Spéciale"	E	(89–91+)
1996	Meursault Les Narvaux "Mise Spéciale"	E	93
1997	Meursault Les Tillets	D	88
1996	Meursault Les Tillets	D	90
1995	Meursault Les Tillets	D	89
1997	Meursault Les Tillets "Mise Spéciale"	D	(88–90)
1997	Puligny-Montrachet Les Levrons	E	88
1996	Puligny-Montrachet Les Levrons	D	87
1995	Savigny-Lès-Beaune Les Montchenevoy	D	89

Note: Javillier fashions two bottlings: a "Mise Spéciale" (indicated on the label, it means late bottling) and a regular bottling (no special marking on the label). The Mise Spéciale, more complex, broader, and fuller bodied than the standard cuvées, is bottled 18 months after the harvest, while the regular bottling, destined primarily for the European market (which supposedly prefers leaner wines), is done only after 11–14 months. The "Mise Spéciale" is bottled unfiltered whenever possible.

Some friends have described Javillier's wines as being the poor man's Coche-Dury. I understand the connection, as both Meursault producers make full-flavored, superripe wines—but a look at the prices will convince anyone that these wines won't be consumed by any indigents.

Patrick Javillier is an extremely bright, thoughtful, and detail-oriented man who looks as though he would be more comfortable in a boardroom than a cellar. An electrical engineer by training, he later became an oenologist. Javillier uses his winemaking knowledge, constant experimentation, passion, and impressive palate to craft extraordinary regional and village appellation wines. While talking with Javillier, I had the feeling that this man must wake up in the middle of the night with new ideas on how to improve his already first-rate wines.

Javillier is justifiably proud of his 1997s. He approaches each vintage differently, analyzing the grapes at harvest and tasting continuously throughout their *élevage* to determine how to proceed. Like all Burgundians, Javillier noted that the overall acidity levels were somewhat low following the alcoholic fermentations. However, his analyses indicated that the percentage of acidity that was malic was exceedingly low. Therefore he knew that the effect of the malolactic fermentation on the structure of the wines would be minimal (pHs averaged 3.2 premalo and 3.25 postmalo), so acidification was unnecessary. Furthermore, the 1997 vintage's abnormally low acid levels led Javillier to leave as much gas in the wines as possible (CO_2 is a natural by-product of fermentation) until bottling. This technique permitted him to maintain freshness in his whites (acidity and gas protect wines from oxidation during their *élevages*).

Aged in 10% new oak barrels, the 1997 Bourgogne Blanc Cuvée des Forgets offers up soft scents of anise and white flowers. This light- to medium-bodied wine is packed with sweet white fruit and leesy flavors intermingled with traces of oak. Well crafted (if somewhat short in the finish), it should be drunk over the next 3 years. The 1997 Bourgogne Cuvée Oligocène, perennially one of Burgundy's best regional wines, reveals smoky and spicy oak aromas. This rich, mouth-coating, medium-bodied, and thick offering is crammed with ripe pears, buttered toast, and stones. Its dry, mineral-ridden finish reveals the vintage's telltale alcoholic clout. Anticipated maturity: now–2002.

The 1997 Meursault Les Tillets exhibits pear, banana, and honeysuckle aromas. It is medium bodied and well focused and has an appealingly oak-infused minerality. While undeniably excellent, this fresh and toasty wine is significantly shorter in the finish than the 1996. It should be consumed over the next 4 years. After crafting the first "Mise Spéciale" of the Meursault Clos du Cromin in 1996, Javillier has returned to his habit of bottling the entire production in the September following the vintage. He believes this wine's *terroir* does not produce wines with enough natural acidity to withstand long barrel aging. The 1997 was harvested at 12.9% natural alcohol and was not chaptalized. It offers superripe white fruit and honeyed aromas that give way to its fat and almost unctuous character. This thick, medium-bodied, and fruitcake-flavored wine is destined to be an early drinker, as opulence clearly has the upper hand over balance. Anticipated maturity: now–2002. The 1997 Meursault Les Clous is a more elegant and refined wine. It has a toasty, smoky, and pear-infused nose as well as an apple-and-nut-dominated flavor profile. This silky-textured medium-bodied offering is complex and layered, with a well-defined long finish. Drink it over the next 5–6 years. The "house blends" of Meursault Casse Têtes and Meursault au Murger are outstanding. Javillier decided to bottle his entire production of 1997 Meursault Cuvée Tête de Murger in September, foregoing the production of a *"Mise Spéciale,"* as he felt the wine would not improve with extended barrel aging. It displays intense ripe pear and lees aromas, as well as a rich, oily-textured, and medium- to full-bodied character. Its flavor profile offers dense layers of sweet white fruits, flint, smoke, and loads of spices that linger in its exceedingly long finish. Anticipated maturity: 2000–2005. The day of my tasting, Javillier's most expressive 1997 was the Puligny-Montrachet Les Levrons. It revealed a white fruit and earth-packed nose and an elegant, beautifully ripe, mineral-laced personality. If it develops some complexity and length, my rating will appear conservative. Drink it over the next 4 years.

I preferred Javillier's "Mise Spéciale" bottlings to the regular cuvées. Not all of his wines would benefit from longer *élevages* (such as the 1997 Clos du Cromin), but I am perplexed as to why Javillier persists in producing two cuvées of Forgets, Oligocène, and Tillets when the "Mise Spéciale" tastes superior to the earlier bottling. That being said, the 1997 Bourgogne Blanc Cuvée des Forgets "Mise Spéciale" (tasted out of tank) had explosive aromas reminiscent of honeysuckle blossoms, pears, and apples. This delicious, lively, yet thick offering is medium bodied, densely packed with fruit, and velvety textured. Anticipated maturity: now–2004. Aromatically revealing lemon curd and lees, the 1997 Meursault Les Tillets "Mise Spéciale" has flavors suggesting banana, sweet pear, flowers, and candied fruits. Surprisingly well balanced for such a dense wine, it possesses a well-integrated acidity that buttresses the complex flavors. Drink it between now and 2005. Javillier's 1997 Bourgogne Blanc Cuvée Oligocène "Mise Spéciale" should be tremendous. Lightly toasted white fruit scents are followed by a rich, creamy, hazelnut paste- and pear-flavored core. This complex, hedonistically as well as intellectually satisfying wine is medium to full bodied, extremely well balanced, and armed with a long, mineral-laced finish. Why can't more Bourgogne appellation wines be of such quality? Drink it between 2000 and 2006. Javillier fashioned two cuvées of the 1997 Meursault Narvaux, but I was allowed to taste only the Mise Spéciale. Behind a touch of reduction, dense nuts and minerals could be discerned in this wine's nose. On the palate, it is layered, crammed with sweet white fruit, medium to full bodied, and intensely rich yet balanced. It is a highly impressive offering that finishes strongly with impressions of spiced and baked pears. Anticipated maturity: 2000–2006.

What's Javillier's spin on the 1996 vintage? "It has the most perfect balance between body, acid, fruit, extract, and purity in my lifetime."

All the "regular cuvées" were bottled in September 1997. The bone-dry 1996 Bourgogne Aligoté reveals spicy candied fruit aromas as well as a medium-bodied, explosive, rich, silky-textured core of tangy red berries, orange rind, and minerals. This excellent wine will provide refreshing drinking between now and 2000. Equally delicious, the 1996 Bourgogne Blanc Cuvée des Forgets (regular bottling) has red currant and smoky scents and a medium-bodied, crisp, and precise personality filled with tangy red fruits and minerals. It should be consumed by 2001. Displaying a lovely nose of stones and toasted hazelnuts, the 1996 Meursault Les Clous possesses an excellent, medium-bodied and superfocused flavor profile filled with tantalizing anise and stonelike flavors. Complex and magnificently balanced, this wine may ultimately deserve a higher rating. Anticipated maturity: now–2004. The lively 1996 Puligny-Montrachet Les Levrons offers floral, mineral, and honeysuckle aromas. A medium-bodied, rich, and well-crafted wine, it reveals flavors dominated by pears, stones, and buttered toast. It should be consumed by 2001. The outstanding 1996 Meursault Les Narvaux's nose revealed deep richness and ripeness, but it was tight and muted the day I tasted it. Much more expressive on the palate, this ample, broad, expansive, gorgeously ripe, medium- to full-bodied, and silky-textured beauty reveals liquid minerals, nuts, tangy lemons, and red berries. Complex and armed with an admirable finish, it should be at its peak between 2000 and 2005. The 1996 Meursault Cuvée Tête de Murger, a one-third blend of Meursault Casse Tête and two-thirds Meursault Les Murgers, is an extraordinary "village" offering, on par with first-rate premiers crus. After revealing cake batter aromas, this wine offers an explosive attack followed by an awesome hold and length. This harmonious, intricate, medium- to full-bodied, and oily wine is jam-packed with ripe pears and salty almond cookies whose flavors linger on through its long and intense finish. Javillier stated that he had always been baffled by the east-facing Casse Tête vineyard. Wines from this site had an excellent attack yet lacked hold and persistence. To rectify this, he blended Casse Tête with Les Murgers, which in his opinion produces wines with magnificent body and length but has a "boring front end." The blend is remarkable! Anticipated maturity: 2000–2005.

The 1996 Bourgogne Cuvée des Forgets "Mise Spéciale" has rich toasty aromas and a broad, medium- to full-bodied, and oily core of leesy, buttery, and lemony fruit. While it lacks the precision of the "regular cuvée," it makes up for it with additional complexity and body. Drink it between now and 2001. Possibly the finest regional appellation white I have tasted from Burgundy, the 1996 Bourgogne Blanc Cuvée Oligocène "Mise Spéciale" reveals earth and minerals in its admirable aromatic depth. On the palate, the wine is wide, rich, ample, and medium to full bodied, with an oily personality. Layers of minerals, seashells, hazelnuts, and candied lemons are found in this expressive and superb wine. I recommend drinking it by 2002. Chalk, stone, and nut aromas are found in the well-balanced, expansive, complex, and ripe 1996 Meursault Les Tillets "Mise Spéciale." Vibrant, bright, and rich, this medium- to full-bodied wine is filled with minerals, earth, and touches of lemon peel. Anticipated maturity: now–2003. Generally, Javillier offers the Meursault Clos du Cromin only as a regular cuvée because it rarely possesses the natural acidity he feels is necessary for extended *élevage*. The 1996's bright and lively high acidity levels forced him to revise his plans and produce it as a Mise Spéciale. Unexpectedly I discerned ripe olive oil aromas intermingled with more typical toasted hazelnuts. On the palate, this vivacious, racy, and medium-bodied wine has a mouth-coating oily texture and flavors reminiscent of black olives (!), stones, and tangy and salty candied lemons and nuts. Anticipated maturity: now–2003. The 1996 Meursault Les Narvaux "Mise Spéciale" is a lusher, more luxurious, and deeper version of its regular cuvée. Elegant and complex aromas of white flowers, earth, nuts, and stones give way to an extraordinary combination of fat, ripe, oily-textured, and supple fruit within a racy and refined personality. Expansive, soft, and mouth coating, this tangy red cherry and mineral-flavored wine is also focused, crisp, and vivacious. To top it all off, its finish is exceedingly long, pure, and defined. It should be at its peak between 2000 and 2006. Revealing spice, stones, butter cookie, and earth tones in its aromatics, the 1996 Meursault Cuvée Tête de Murger "Mise Spéciale" has all the superb characteristics of the earlier bottling yet possesses additional complexity and elegance. Its broad, powerful, full-bodied, and hugely ripe flavor profile is redolent with red fruits, earth, minerals, apricots, and candied almonds. This refined yet fat and hedonistic wine has impressive finesse and length. It should be at its best between 2000 and 2007. Bravo!

Displaying a toasty and spicy nose, the 1995 Bourgogne Aligoté is a well-made medium-bodied wine with flavors of buttered spices and sweet fruit. It has good length and will make for nice refreshing drinking in the near term. Irreverently described to me by one of its importers as "a wine made for American palates," the hazelnut-scented 1995 Meursault Casse Têtes' mouth is silky textured, full of toasted nuts and fat ripe roasted fruits. This medium- to full-bodied wine is quite soft and lacking balancing acidity (which explains the importer's comment), so it should be drunk within the first 3 years after its release. Javillier makes two distinct cuvées of generic white burgundy: the first is the Bourgogne Blanc Cuvée des Forgets, which has an appealing nose of lightly roasted fruits and soft, sweet spices. A silky texture and leesy, buttery toasted spices are found in this delicious wine made for near-term drinking. Revealing aromas of fresh spices and slate, the Bourgogne Blanc Cuvée Oligocène, named after the subsoil the vineyard is planted over, is flinty, minerally, and dry. This medium-bodied wine can be drunk now or held for 2–3 years. Possessing fresh herbs and spices on the nose, the 1995 Meursault Clos du Cromin has an oily texture, crisp red berries, and a clean, well-balanced finish. This beautiful medium-bodied wine should be drunk between now and 2004. Javillier's wine that sees the most new oak is the 1995 Meursault Les Tillets (30%, whereas the other nongeneric wines see only 25%). Earthy and spicy on the nose, this wine displays fat, leesy, buttery hazelnut flavors within a thick texture. Minerals come to the fore on the backend. Drink it between now and 2004. A very minerally wine on the nose, the 1995 Savigny-Lès-Beaune Les Montchenevoy has a silky texture, tangy crisp white berries, and good toasted mineral flavors. This well-balanced wine can keep for 5–8 years, but I recommend drinking it over the near term because I don't see it improving with age. An outstanding wine, the 1995 Meursault Les Clous exhibits earthy, hazelnut, and anise aromas. On the palate, the wine is fat, buttery and spicy. Powerful, with zippy acid and very good length, this beautifully structured, medium- to full-bodied offering should be drunk between 2000 and 2010. Produced from a north-facing vineyard, the 1995 Meursault au Murger exhibits a muted nose, silky texture, powerful fruit intermingled with stones and minerals and excellent length. Qualitatively, this medium- to full-bodied offering is nearly the equal of Les Clous, but it lacks complexity. Drink it between now and 2006. Javillier's finest 1995 is the Meursault Les Narvaux, which displays a fabulous nose of flowers and spices. In the mouth, a thick and silky texture offers explosively rich tropical fruits (including bananas!), hazelnuts, and crisp red berries. This powerful, beautiful, full-bodied wine can be drunk over the near term or cellared for 10–12 years. (Javillier also makes a Meursault Charmes, but I did not have the opportunity to taste it.)

Other wines recently tasted: 1997 Bourgogne Aligoté (84).

DOMAINE JAYER-GILLES (MAGNY-LES-VILLERS)

1996 Bourgogne Hautes Côtes de Beaune	D	88
1995 Bourgogne Hautes Côtes de Beaune	D	88+
1996 Bourgogne Hautes Côtes de Nuits	D	89
1995 Bourgogne Hautes Côtes de Nuits	D	88

As I have reported, sweeping changes have taken place in Burgundy over the past few years. A new generation has taken charge of family domaines, bringing (in most cases) needed change. Whereas a generational change in the management of this well-respected estate is also taking place, I was surprised to learn from Robert Kacher, Domaine Jayer-Gilles's U.S. importer, that the winemaker would remain the same.

Apparently, Gilles Jayer, Robert Jayer's son, has been crafting the estate's wines since 1990! Robert Jayer, one of Burgundy's most respected vignerons, was the "front man," while his son was ultimately responsible for the quality of the wines. Recently the elder Jayer officially retired from the estate and moved to a smaller home across the street in Magny-Les-Villers. Gilles Jayer, viewed for all these years as somewhat of a bon vivant in Beaune circles, is beginning to receive the accolades he had manifestly been due for years. The domaine's name, buildings, vineyards, and equipment are being sold and/or rented to Gilles Jayer by his father for astronomical sums of money—a sign of the times. . . .

Known primarily for his red wines, Jayer has split his production evenly between red and white. For the whites, his Hautes Côtes de Beaune vineyard is planted with 30% Chardonnay and 70% Pinot Noir Albino (also known as the Henri Gouges Pinot), and the Hautes Côtes de Nuits is planted in reverse proportions of the two varietals. Aged in 50% new oak barrels, his white wines are extremely well balanced, age well, and are very good values for consumers searching out affordable white burgundies.

Displaying a concentrated nose of deeply roasted fruit, the 1995 Bourgogne Hautes Côtes de Beaune reveals an attractive floral note and good ripeness in its medium-bodied mouth. With excellent balance and structure, this wine can be enjoyed now, but it will evolve for 6–8 years. Different in style, the aromatically steely and minerally 1995 Bourgogne Hautes

Côtes de Nuits is packed with stones, flint, and metallic flavors with a slight floral touch. Drink this medium-bodied, delicious wine over the next 6 years.

The delicious 1996 Bourgogne Haute Côtes de Beaune reveals a ripe peach and toast-infused nose as well as a smoke and pear flavor profile. Medium bodied, this wine has great richness, depth, and ripeness while remaining bright and lively. It should be drunk over the next 5 years. Displaying expressive aromas of minerals and spicy oak, the 1996 Bourgogne Hautes Côtes de Nuits is slightly more complex and powerful than the previous wine. This offering's rich and medium- to full-bodied personality is packed with stones, gravel, honeysuckle, and anise. Its long and flavorful finish exhibits floral and chalk notes. Anticipated maturity: now–2005.

DOMAINE FRANÇOIS JOBARD (MEURSAULT)

1996	Bourgogne Blanc	D	(86–87)
1995	Bourgogne Blanc	D	?
1996	Meursault	D	(87–88)
1995	Meursault	D	(86–88)
1996	Meursault Blagny	E	(88–90)
1995	Meursault Blagny	E	(87–90)
1996	Meursault Charmes	EE	(91–94)
1995	Meursault Charmes	EE	(90–93)
1996	Meursault Genevrières	E	(90–93)
1995	Meursault Genevrières	E	(89–91+)
1996	Meursault Poruzots	E	(89–91)
1995	Meursault Poruzots	E	(88–91)
1995	Puligny-Montrachet Le Trézin	E	(86–89)

Note: The 1996 Puligny-Montrachet Le Trézin had not completed its malo when I visited the estate in November 1997.

A man of few words, François Jobard makes some of Meursault's tightest and longest-lived wines. Readers in search of lush, decadent, leesy, buttery Chardonnays are well advised to look elsewhere. However, those looking for elegant, crisp, precise, and defined Meursaults to cellar will love this domaines's offerings.

The soft-spoken François Jobard feels the 1996 vintage is "like 1985, but riper and with better concentration," it has "great richness in sugar and acidity" in his opinion. Jobard never performs a *débourbage* and ages his wines in 10%–12% new oak for village wines and 15%–20% for the premiers crus.

While most vignerons in the Côte d'Or now perform extensive *bâtonnage*, Jobard does none. He told me his experience with wines whose lees were stirred often have "a faster evolution in the bottle" because of their loss of CO_2. Interestingly enough, virtually every vigneron in Meursault I spoke with said Jobard's wines age better than anyone else's in the village. Maybe he's on to something? Carbon dioxide is a by-product of fermentation. It is trapped in the barrel and serves as a preservative, protecting the wine from oxygen. The *bâtonnage* technique involves removing the barrel's bung, inserting a rakelike steel rod, and briskly stirring the lees that have deposited to the bottom. Jobard theorizes that each time this technique is employed, CO_2 escapes the wine and oxygen enters, thereby promoting premature aging.

There is no doubt that wines produced by vignerons who stir the lees often taste mature at an early stage, while Jobard's take years to open. Some older bottles from *bâtonneurs* I have tasted tend to bear out his theory, but I am not yet comfortable making a sweeping statement about their ageworthiness. This being said, only masochists will open Jobard's 1996s upon release. These are bracing wines that have extraordinary underlying richness, but they require patience.

The 1996 Bourgogne Blanc reveals appealing rich and smoky aromas as well as a light- to medium-bodied, ripe, broad, and defined core of freshly baked bread flavors. It should be at its peak between 2000 and 2002. Jobard's 1996 Meursault has a bright, earth and wild mushroom-infused nose and a crisp, clean, light- to medium-bodied, and beautifully delineated personality. In its youth it will appear shrill and lean but should blossom between 2000 and 2003. Displaying ripe roasted peach aromatics, the 1996 Meursault Blagny is a rich, wide, medium-bodied, and racy offering with pear and mineral flavors. It lacks the refinement found in Jobard's other premiers crus but has a chewy, meaty characteristic they do not share. Anticipated maturity: 2002–2005. The 1996 Meursault Poruzots offers minerals and stones on the nose and a layered, rich, ripe, focused, medium-bodied, masculine, and complex flavor profile packed with minerals, grilled toast, and earth. This is a well-made, concentrated, and deep wine that should be at its best from 2003 to 2008.

If I can locate any of Jobard's two top Meursault cuvées, I will be sure to save them for my nephew Lucas, who was born in 1996. They should still be holding their peak by the time he is old enough to appreciate them. The 1996 Meursault Genevrières offers a rich nose of nuts and stones as well as a perfectly balanced, medium-bodied, and concentrated character. This is not your typical Genevrières, jam-packed with ripe white or tropical fruits, but an elegant, mineral-filled wine. Its tightly wound but expansive and layered flavor profile reveals terrific richness and extraction buttressed by powerful acidity. Drink it between 2005 and 2013. Produced from vines planted in 1963, the 1996 Meursault Charmes has floral, nut, and mineral aromas and a wide, expansive, rich, and dense core of precisely defined stones, white flowers, and gravel. Powerful, ripe, and with enormous depth of fruit, this wine has phenomenal acidity and an admirable persistence. Anticipated maturity: 2005–2013+.

Jobard normally has yields around 3 tons of fruit per acre, but in 1995 his yields were dropped to an average of $2^1/_2$ tons per acre by the effects of the spring freeze on the flowering. He ages his wines in 20%–30% new oak.

Surprisingly, the 1995 Bourgogne Blanc displays off smells of old chestnuts yet has a pleasing and structured toasty, mineral core. . . . Time will tell. Made primarily from the De La Barre vineyard, the 1995 Meursault exhibits a lovely, fresh nutty nose and a light- to medium-bodied, highly structured, tight mouth. Needing at least 3 years to come around, this wine can be enjoyed over the subsequent 6. Extremely muted in the nose (it had just been racked), the 1995 Puligny-Montrachet Le Trézin offers a lively mouth of toasty sweet fruits ending with a tangy and toasty finish. Drink this medium-bodied wine between now and 2005. With rich, sweet, toasted hazelnut scents, the 1995 Meursault Blagny displays an oily texture, tangy, nutty fruit, and a lively freshness. Enjoy this medium-bodied wine from 2001 to 2009. A touch better, the oily-textured 1995 Meursault Poruzots displays concentrated and ripe candied fruit in the nose and mouth, along with good length. Anticipated maturity: 2004–2012. Similar to the Meursault Poruzots except with aromas and flavors of fresh spices added to the mélange, the 1995 Meursault Genevrières is built for the long haul and will require patience (8–9 years) from its purchasers in order for the fruit to come to the fore. Looking for a (somewhat) affordable wine to purchase for a child born in 1995 to drink on his or her twenty-first birthday? If so, Jobard's 1995 Meursault Charmes is the wine for you. Honeysuckle and ripe fruits on the nose, and a highly concentrated mouth of white flowers combined with a tight but powerful core of sweet fruit, make this a fabulous example of ageworthy Chardonnay. Drink it between 2005 and 2017.

DOMAINE RÉMI JOBARD (MEURSAULT)
(Formerly Known as Domaine Charles et Rémi Jobard)

1996 Bourgogne Aligoté	B	86
1996 Bourgogne Blanc	C	87
1995 Bourgogne Blanc	C	86
1996 Meursault en Luraule	D	89
1995 Meursault en Luraule	D	88+
1996 Meursault Sous La Velle	D	88+
1995 Meursault Sous La Velle	D	87+
1996 Meursault Les Charmes	E	93+
1995 Meursault Les Charmes	D	91
1996 Meursault Les Chevaliers	D	89+
1995 Meursault Les Chevaliers	D	89
1996 Meursault Les Genevrières	E	93
1995 Meursault Les Genevrières	D	90+
1996 Meursault Poruzots-Dessus	E	92
1995 Meursault Poruzots-Dessus	D	90

Charles Jobard, the brother of François and Jean-Pierre (winemaker at Louis Latour), has retired, and this domaine is now completely in the highly capable hands of his son Rémi. Described by Domaine Coche-Dury's Jean-François Coche as one of Meursault's future stars, Rémi Jobard is bright, shy, inquisitive, dedicated, and hardworking. After having tasted Jobard's wines, I am convinced that Coche is wrong. Jobard is a present-day star.

When Rémi's grandfather divided the estate among his sons, his uncle François Jobard kept the family home high in the village with its large, deep, and cold cellar. Charles Jobard purchased a house at the bottom of the Meursault hillside, and therefore his cellar is smaller and warmer. This has a tremendous impact on the winemaking.

Rémi Jobard has neither the space nor the consistently cold cellar needed for an extended *élevage*. All his 1996s were therefore bottled in September 1997. François Jobard never performs a *débourbage* (allowing the larger, gross less—or *bourbes*—to settle so that the must can be separated from them) and permits his wines to feed off the fine and gross lees, gathering richness, for well over a year, rarely if ever stirring the lees (*bâtonnage*). Constrained by his smaller and warmer cellar, Rémi performs a *débourbage* in years when he is worried about the *bourbes'* health and consistently stirs the lees to gather as much richness as possible during the relatively short *élevage*. No *débourbage* was performed in 1995, and in 1996 the *bourbes* were so healthy that he reincorporated them back into the wines.

Rémi Jobard commented on the incredibly long and stable fermentations of the 1996s, saying that he felt it was due to the high levels of acidity. Furthermore, he stressed that ever since the domaine abandoned fertilizers the fermentations had become longer and more steady. This is a theme I heard throughout Burgundy this past November. The theory is that by not providing any ground-level nourishment to the vines, and by hoeing around them, the roots are forced deeper into the high-acid limestone that lies beneath Burgundy's vineyards. High, natural acidity levels extend and stabilize fermentations, allowing for more complex wines.

In Jobard's opinion, the key to producing great white burgundies in 1996 was to harvest late, allowing the grapes to produce higher natural sugar levels than were present at the *ban de vendange.*

A wonderful aperitif wine, the 1996 Bourgogne Aligoté reveals a smoky nose and a deeply spicy, medium-bodied, rich, and velvety core of fruit. This thirst-quenching and lively offering should be drunk within the next 18 months. Jobard's 1996 Bourgogne Blanc has rich minerals and smoke aromas and a well-crafted and focused medium body filled with nuts, tangy lemons, and flowers. Drink it by 2000. Displaying intense hazelnut and floral aromatics, the 1996 Meursault Sous La Velle offers dazzling sweetness of fruit in its medium- to full-bodied, rich, ripe, and thick character. Layers of minerals, stones, and racy currants are infused with lemon drops in this lively wine. Anticipated maturity: now–2004. Even more expressive aromatically, the 1996 Meursault en Luraule exhibits a ripe and rich nose. Jobard commented that he found the Luraule's lively nose atypical because it has a tendency to be restrained and austere. On the palate, this broad, oily-textured, medium- to full-bodied, and expansive wine has luxurious mineral, pear, and stonelike flavors beautifully delineated by crisp acidity. Anticipated maturity: 2000–2005. The potentially outstanding 1996 Meursault Les Chevaliers possesses a mouthwatering bouquet of hazelnut butter-cream. Medium to full bodied, velvety, wide, and refined, this wine has beautifully defined floral and citrus fruit flavors. It should be at its best between 2000 and 2005.

Revealing a powerful nose infused with liquid minerals, the 1996 Meursault Poruzots-Dessus explodes on the palate with superripe pears, candied fruits, minerals, and spice. This is a full-bodied, oily-textured, yet gorgeously balanced wine armed with massive extract, brilliant, racy acidity, and an admirably long finish. It should age effortlessly. Anticipated maturity: 2001–2008. The next two wines are extremely representative of their respective *terroirs* and would make for a fascinating (and decadent!) evening for readers lucky enough to acquire both. The 1996 Meursault Les Genevrières has profound richness and ripeness in its almond cream-scented nose. This intensely concentrated, superripe, and powerful gem saturates the palate with pear compote, cardamom, peaches, and copious quantities of sweet spices. Full bodied, oily textured, and magnificently balanced, it is a muscular masterpiece. I recommend consuming it between 2001 and 2008. Produced from a parcel located just below Perrières, Jobard's 1996 Meursault Les Charmes plays the role of an elegant sibling to the power and intensity of his Genevrières. Orange rind, nut, and mineral aromas are found in this medium- to full-bodied, silky, and concentrated wine. Mouth-coating layers of creamy nuts, stones, and gravel are woven in lacelike fashion throughout this beauty's superrefined and extraordinarily long personality. Anticipated maturity: 2002–2009+. Bravo!

This small domaine is truly a family-run operation, with Mrs. Jobard, Rémi's mother, doing all the bottling by hand. Rémi believes that the 1995 vintage is better than 1992 because of its balance and structure. The fact that the estate's yields in 1995 are 40% below the average contributed greatly to the vintage's overall quality. My impression after speaking with the Jobards and tasting through their wines is that this is an up-and-coming estate. Rémi is definitely part of the new generation of Burgundians who are improving the overall quality of the region's wines.

The 1995 Bourgogne Blanc saw 10%–15% new oak, which gave this delicious and easy-to-drink wine buttery tones to complement its explosive nose and concentrated, oily-textured mouth. The 1995 Meursault Sous La Velle and 1995 Meursault en Luraule are both first-rate village wines, better than some highly touted premiers crus. Exhibiting a hazelnut-scented nose, the 1995 Sous La Velle exhibits an oily texture, excellent balance, and thick, fat, concentrated fruit interspersed with buttery tones. Drink it between now and 2001. From a parcel located 5 meters from the premier cru Goutte d'Or vineyard, the aromatically nutty 1995 En Luraule is produced from young wines that Rémi severely cuts back to decrease yields and increase concentration. His hard work and obvious dedication to quality are apparent in this forward, highly extracted wine. It explodes in the mouth with a burst of ripe and toasted hazelnuts. When the vines are older, if Rémi continues to keep yields down, this parcel has the potential to produce outstanding wine. Anticipated maturity: now–2003. From 55-year-old vines, the 1995 Meursault Les Chevaliers (muted on the nose) is superripe, bordering on off-dry, with deep, sweet, toasted, lively fruit and an oily texture. Medium to full bodied, it should be consumed over the next 5 years. Displaying an expressive nose of deep, sweet fruit, the excellent 1995 Meursault Poruzots-Dessus offers a mouth of concentrated, powerful, superripe roasted fruits. This medium- to full-bodied wine is more reminiscent of a Puligny-Montrachet than a Meursault because of the dominating sweet and smoky fruits. Drink it over the next 7–8 years. An excellent combination of power and elegance, the 1995 Meursault Les Charmes reveals a superb flinty, minerally nose, followed by a thick-textured mouth of sweet smoky fruits intertwined with a deep minerality. Medium to full bodied, this delicious wine should be drunk between 2000 and 2007. Exhibiting sweet nut and ripe citrus fruit aromas, the 1995 Meursault Les Genevrières provides a big burst of candied, star anise-laden fruits on the palate. This sultry, medium- to full-bodied wine possesses the intensity and precociousness of the Poruzots but a more elegant and delineated style. Anticipated maturity: 2000–2007.

DOMAINE JOBLOT (GIVRY)

1995 Givry Clos de la Servoisine	C	(87–89)
1996 Givry Clos de la Servoisine	C	88

Produced from a vineyard with a completely southern exposure, the 1995 Givry Clos de la Servoisine possesses an intense nose of minerals, white flowers, and grilled apricots as well as a powerful, medium- to full-bodied, silky-textured personality with layers of ripe white fruits and hints of toasty new oak. It is reminiscent of a Puligny-Montrachet but more minerally and masculine in style. Drink it between now and 2001. Produced in 50% new oak, 30% 1-year-old barrels, and the balance in stainless-steel tanks, the 1996 Givry Clos de la Servoisine has a mineral-and-smoke-scented nose and a rich, juicy, fresh, medium-bodied, and concentrated core of white flowers, minerals, tangy and candied grapefruits, and traces of white raisins. Well crafted and refreshing, this wine will be at its peak if drunk between now and 2003.

MAISON LABOURÉ-ROI (NUITS-ST.-GEORGES)

1996 Corton-Charlemagne	E	88
1996 Meursault Bouches Chères Domaine René Manuel	D	88
1996 Meursault Clos de La Baronne Domaine René Manuel	D	86

Owned by the two Cottin brothers (Cottin Frères), the Labouré-Roi *négociant* house does not own any vineyards. This firm has spent the last 20 years investing in its buildings and winemaking equipment. Today Labouré-Roi's headquarters (near the interstate's Nuits-St.-Georges exit) is a ultramodern and robot-laden winemaking facility.

The Cottins have established what they refer to as "partnerships" with the (approximately) 60 vignerons that provide Labouré-Roi with its wines. The firm interferes very little in the vineyard work of its growers but organizes seminars on vinification for them and also sends oenologists to the domaines to assist in the winemaking.

Over the past 30 years an increasing number of growers have converted from *négociant* suppliers to bottling their own production. Remember, with the exception of the Domaine de la Romanée-Conti and a handful of others, most burgundies were bottled by *négociants* 40 years ago. Henri Jayer, Charles Rousseau, Henri Gouges, Domaine du Comte de Vogüé, and the Marquis d'Angerville (Rousseau and d'Angerville still run their respective estates, and

Jayer is recently retired) are the forefathers of estate-bottled burgundies. For *négociants* like Labouré-Roi who do not own any vineyards this translates to a dependence on a shrinking pool of quality wines.

To counter this trend, which Cottin states is cyclical in nature, Labouré-Roi has created a new corporation of sorts with seven of its growers (known as SICA in France) to lock them into being suppliers and to assist them in their production. Also, Labouré-Roi works in exclusive arrangements with some domaines, including Domaine René Manuel in Meursault, to bottle their wines as luxury "estate" bottlings, indicating the estate on the label in much the same way Maison Joseph Drouhin does with the wines of the Marquis de Laguiche. By having a "luxury" line that garners attention, Labouré-Roi may be hoping to affect its "regular" wine sales, which I believe is also the thinking behind Maison Antonin Rodet's "Cave Privée" collection.

The 1996 Meursault Clos de la Baronne Domaine René Manuel reveals grilled oak and hazelnut aromas followed by an oily-textured, glycerin-packed, and medium-bodied core of tangy nuts and minerals. It should be drunk over the next 3 years. Exhibiting a golden hue to its color, the 1996 Meursault Bouches Chères Domaine René Manuel (another spelling for the premier cru Bouchères vineyard) has ripe peach and anise scents and a medium- to full-bodied, oily, and expansive character (as with the preceding wine, I was struck by the high glycerin levels in this offering). Extremely spicy poached pear, nut, and mineral flavors can be found in this broadly structured and persistent wine. Anticipated maturity: now–2003. The 1996 Corton-Charlemagne displays a smoke-and-mineral-laden nose as well as a medium- to full-bodied, silky-textured, and intensely smoky (almost bacon) flavor profile. Anticipated maturity: now–2003.

DOMAINE DES COMTES LAFON (MEURSAULT)

1997 Meursault	E	(88–90)
1996 Meursault	E	88
1995 Meursault	E	88
1997 Meursault Les Charmes	EE	(91–93)
1996 Meursault Les Charmes	EE	93
1995 Meursault Les Charmes	EE	93
1997 Meursault Clos de la Barre	E	(90–92)
1996 Meursault Clos de la Barre	E	91+
1995 Meursault Clos de la Barre	E	91
1997 Meursault Désirée	E	(89–91)
1996 Meursault Désirée	E?	90
1995 Meursault Désirée	E	90
1997 Meursault Les Genevrières	E	(93–95)
1996 Meursault Les Genevrières	EE	93
1995 Meursault Les Genevrières	EE	91
1997 Meursault Goutte d'Or	E	(90–92)
1996 Meursault Goutte d'Or	E	88+
1995 Meursault Goutte d'Or	E	91+
1997 Meursault Les Perrières	EE	(93–95)

1996 **Meursault Les Perrières**	EE	95
1995 **Meursault Les Perrières**	EE	93
1997 **Montrachet**	EEE	(95–97+)
1996 **Montrachet**	EEE	98
1995 **Montrachet**	EEE	94+
1997 **Puligny-Montrachet Champs Gain**	EE	(91–93)
1996 **Puligny-Montrachet Champs Gain**	EE?	92
1995 **Puligny-Montrachet Champs Gain**	EE?	91

Not only do I believe the 1997s are some of the finest wines ever produced by Dominique Lafon, they may be the finest array of 1997 white burgundies from the Côte de Beaune. Lafon, whose wines are increasingly difficult to purchase (only 15%–18% of his production is sold in the United States), is red hot. I have always enjoyed his wines, particularly in their youth, but sense that Lafon has raised his winemaking to new heights. Whereas I used to believe that Dominique Lafon was striving to merit his reputation, now I feel he is surpassing it.

In contrast with 1996, where Lafon strived to lengthen the fermentations of his whites, 1997 received the opposite treatment. "The key to success in 1997 was to have short fermentations, very little *bâtonnage* [lees stirring], and retain as much CO_2 [a natural by-product of fermentation] as possible during the *élevage*."

The 1997 Meursault was crafted from vines located in En Luraule, En La Barre, and Charmes. It is a fabulous *villages* wine, and better than many premiers crus. It offers bold aromas of pears, white flowers, hazelnuts, and buttered toast, followed by a satiny and concentrated personality. It is medium bodied, bright, and densely layered with ripe fruits, spices, and nuts. Drink it over the next 5 years. The 1997 Meursault Désirée is slightly more opulent and has a longer finish. It displays apricot, acacia blossom, and grilled wood scents as well as a seductively rich character. White peaches, currants, and minerals can be found in its forward, rich, yet structured medium- to full-bodied personality. Anticipated maturity: 2000–2006. Harvested at 13.3% natural potential alcohol, the 1997 Meursault Clos de la Barre reveals sweet aromas of candied pears, apples, and honeysuckle. This vibrant, medium- to full-bodied, and deeply rich wine is crammed with peaches, minerals, and clay. It is velvety textured, thick, and exquisitely dense and possesses an admirably long finish. Drink it between 2001 and 2007.

I was immensely impressed with Lafon's extremely spicy, toasty, white/yellow fruit-scented 1997 Puligny-Montrachet Champs Gains. This boisterous, medium- to full-bodied, opulently textured, yet gorgeously refined wine is broad, rich, and impressively concentrated. Its harmonious, complex, and layered flavor profile reveals white peaches, flowers, stones, and hints of tropical fruits. It will be at its best between 2002 and 2007. The delightful 1997 Meursault Goutte d'Or, harvested at a whopping 13.5% natural potential alcohol, has a nose composed of minerals, honeysuckle blossoms, stones, and citrus fruits. This creamy-textured, masculine, and dense wine explodes on the palate with a dizzying array of tropical fruits, hazelnut butter, candied lemons, and spicy oak. It is full bodied, hedonistic, and powerful. It would have merited a more glowing review if its finish had not betrayed its high level of alcohol. Drink it between 2001 and 2006. The 1997 Meursault Les Genevrières is spectacular! As he poured it, Lafon said enthusiastically, "It is the best wine of my life. I'm very proud of it." Sweet almond cookies intermingled with juicy citrus fruits can be found in this beauty's aromas. It explodes on the palate with richly textured and expansive flavors reminiscent of spiced apples, earth, minerals, and mangoes. This is a medium- to full-bodied, intensely flavored, and opulent wine that is amazingly refined. Its exceptionally long finish lasted for at least 40 seconds. Impressive! Anticipated maturity: 2002–2008+. The 1997 Meursault Les Charmes offers an extraordinary elegant nose of earth, minerals, nuts, and flowers. This vivacious, medium- to full-bodied, and harmonious wine has sweet mineral, chalk, citrus, and floral flavors. It is rich, gorgeously refined, and velvety textured. Drink it between 2002 and 2008. The magnificent 1997 Meursault Les Perrières displays profound aromas of stones, limes, flowers, and crisp pears. This thick, dense, and satin-textured wine offers loads of caramel-covered apples, fresh butter, minerals, and oak spices in its explosive yet elegant personality. It is full bodied, fat, and impeccably balanced and possesses a stupendously long finish. Anticipated maturity: 2002–2009+.

The 1997 Montrachet is a candidate for the wine of the vintage. Lafon believes it is one of the two best (1992 being the other) he has ever crafted. I prefer the 1996, but at this level of quality it is splitting hairs. It exhibits deep aromas of stones, minerals, honeysuckle blossoms, candied hazelnuts, and sweet oak spices. It is extraordinary expansive, pure, richly textured, and superbly delineated. Akin to liquid silk, it has enormously ripe yet fresh flavors of red currants, raspberries, minerals, peaches, apricots, and poached pears that persist in the finish. It is a levitating experience to taste, one I have not yet forgotten. Bravo!

Dominique Lafon performed more *bâtonnage* than usual on his 1996s, "to give them more richness," he said. However, unlike some other vignerons, Lafon abandons the practice when the malos start because he wants his wines to be protected by the carbon dioxide gas that is a by-product of a wine's malolactic fermentation. Lafon's yields were between 2 and 3 tons of fruit per acre, demonstrating his dedication to quality in this potentially high-yielding vintage.

Produced from vines located in En La Barre, En Luraule, and Charmes, the 1996 Meursault reveals mouthwatering hazelnut, toast, and mineral aromatics. On the palate, this medium-bodied, rich, lively, bright, and silky wine has ripe apple, stone, nut, and tangy citrus flavors. It should be at its best between now and 2003. The 1996 Meursault Désirée has toasted almond and mineral scents as well as an extremely refined, ripe, ample, delineated, and medium-bodied core of stones and spicy poached pears. Well balanced and vibrant, this wine should peak around 2001 and continue to evolve beautifully through 2005. Displaying candied nuts on the nose, the 1996 Meursault Clos de la Barre is an absolutely delicious, expansive, rich, elegant, and well-defined wine. Sweet layers of toasty and buttered brioches, hazelnuts, poached pears, spices, and traces of anise are found in this medium- to full-bodied, velvety-textured, and superbly balanced wine. Anticipated maturity: 2001–2006. Dominique Lafon was not pleased with his 1996 Meursault Goutte D'Or when I visited him in November and was considering blending it in with his regular Meursault cuvée if it did not evolve properly. While it is excellent, and potentially outstanding, I can understand Lafon's concern, as it does not appear to be at the level of his other premiers crus. A tightly wound, buttered popcorn-scented nose gives way to a wide, broad, expressive, creamy, and medium- to full-bodied personality with toasty minerals and white peaches. At the time of my tasting this wine's personality seemed to tail off abruptly. Anticipated maturity: 2000–2004.

Aromatically exhibiting beautiful richness as well as deep minerality, the 1996 Puligny-Montrachet Champs Gains is exquisitely dense, lively, and complex. This smoky wine appears to have derived its flavors from having been immersed in a bed of minerals and flowers. Its medium to full body and silky personality are gorgeously defined by a racy acid streak. I recommend drinking this gem, only Lafon's second vintage with this *en fermage* vineyard, between 2001 and 2006. Surprisingly, the 1996 Meursault Les Genevrières finished its malolactic fermentation prior to completing its alcoholic fermentation, a rarity in this vintage. Golden aromas of ripe pears, dry flowers, and white peaches complement the wine's immense concentration, intensity of flavor, and superb definition on the palate. This wine's massive yet elegant, full-bodied, opulent, and oily character is jam-packed with spicy poached pears, cloves, juniper berries, fresh herbs, and cardamon. Anticipated maturity: 2002–2009. Lafon segregates the grapes from his Meursault Les Charmes' youngest vines, blending them with his village Meursault cuvée. The most intense and concentrated berries are earmarked for his premier cru bottling. His dedication to quality is evidenced by the 1996s tantalizing floral, white peach, and toast aromas. Medium to full bodied, thick, yet feminine and gracious, this superb offering combines power with lace like definition. Ripe white peaches, flower blossoms, and traces of anise are found in this precise, pure, and age-worthy beauty. Anticipated maturity: 2003–2010. The breathtaking 1996 Meursault Les Perrières has an extraordinary defined and elegant nose of stones, earth, and minerals. As Lafon tasted it he smiled and said, "Yes, it is classic, like the Charmes." Classic to me means representative of the norm, and this wine is more than that: it is an exquisite example of the heights this vineyard can attain. Harmonious, lively, gorgeously delineated, silky textured, rich, medium to full bodied, and profoundly deep, this wine's stone and mineral flavors seems to linger on the palate indefinitely. Wow! This magnificent wine should be consumed between 2004 and 2012.

Harvested at a whopping 14% potential natural alcohol, Lafon's mind-blowing 1996 Montrachet is brilliant. Sublime mineral, stone, smoke, and toasted nut aromatics are followed by a wondrous, concentrated, extracted, and sublimely classy personality. Oily layers of liquid minerals, red berries, anise, hazelnuts, and white flowers can be found in this massive, full-bodied, mouth-coating, and palate-saturating wine. Incredibly, just when the taster believes the palate has realized the brunt of this explosive gem's assault on the senses, it expands to even greater heights. The wine has a compellingly long finish. This is a tour de force!

I have not had a chance to retaste the Domaine des Comtes Lafon's 1995s, but I am told they are even better than my early laudatory reviews suggested. Lafon says that "their problem is they are too good today; few people will age them to their peak."

Generally, Lafon blends declassified premiers crus into his village Meursault. In 1995 the yields were so low and the quality of fruit so high that he decided against it. Revealing a deep nutty nose filled with roasted peaches and toasted notes, this medium-bodied wine will be delicious upon release and will drink well for at least 6 years. More flattering, the 1995 Meursault Désirée has a lively floral nose, with notes of honeysuckle. There are hints of fresh peach blossoms in the explosive, flavor-filled, medium- to full-bodied mouth. It should drink well from release to 2005. Lafon says that wine lovers who visit him either love the Désirée or the 1995 Meursault Clos de la Barre, but never both. The latter wine has an unyielding nose but explosive flavors of hazelnuts and minerals. This forward, full-bodied wine with good length should be drunk between 2000 and 2008. This was my first opportunity to taste Lafon's 1995 Puligny-Montrachet Champs Gain. He recently took on this vineyard in what is known in Burgundy parlance as *fermage*. In short, Lafon cares for the vineyards and makes the wine, providing the vineyard owner with half of the finished product. In 1995 only 50 cases were made, and Lafon does not intend to sell any of his 25 cases to his U.S. importer (therefore any bottles readers find in the United States will have entered through the gray market). This is a delicious bottle of Puligny. A nose of perfume and honeysuckle complemented by roasted fruits is followed by a full-bodied, candied mouth of explosive and elegant, ripe fruits. Medium to full bodied, it will be delicious upon release yet age well for 8–10 years. Displaying a nose reminiscent of a vine's flower in the springtime (beautifully sweet with hints of cream and spice), the silky-textured 1995 Meursault Goutte d'Or exhibits an explosive flavor profile packed with flavors of spices and sweet fruit. This full-bodied wine will age gracefully for 10 years. Lafon's 1995 Meursault Les Genevrières offers beautiful roasted fruit aromas, a fat, oily texture, sweet, salty nut flavors, and excellent balance. This full-bodied wine should be drunk between 2000 and 2007. More complex, the 1995 Meursault Les Charmes exhibits piercing and refined floral aromas, as well as a great saturation of powerful mineral and flint flavors. This full-bodied wine needs 3–4 years of cellaring;

it will offer delicious drinking over the following 8 years. Equally superb, the 1995 Meursault Les Perrières has deep mineral and earth tones in the nose and toasty, nutty, iron flavors in the mouth. Powerful and full bodied, it possesses great length and balance. Drink it between 2000 and 2010. Dominique Lafon was faced with an interesting problem after the 1995 harvest. The low yields provided him with enough Montrachet to fill only 2½ casks. He considered using 1 half cask and 2 regular ones but decided against it because he feels wines do not age well in small casks. His solution was to have a new cask built that would hold the equivalent of 1½ regular ones. To offset the new oak flavors of this large vessel, the second cask he is using has been used previously to make 5 vintages of wine. Possessing a supertight and unyielding nose, this full-bodied 1995 Montrachet displays intense minerally fruit, and striking elegance. While not as forward or sultry as I expected, it has a superb structure. This tight wine will need 6–7 years to blossom and will drink admirably for another 15–20.

DOMAINE LAMY-PILLOT (CHASSAGNE-MONTRACHET)

1996 Chassagne-Montrachet Clos St. Jean	D	88

Unlike other 1996s I tasted from Lamy-Pillot, which all shared a wet cardboard, mildewy smell that could also be discerned on the palate, the Chassagne-Montrachet Clos St. Jean does not exhibit any offputting aromas. This wine offers a rich, floral, minerally, and almond-scented nose. On the palate, it reveals a beautifully ripe, medium-bodied, thick, and well-crafted character packed with candied nuts, stones, and white fruits. Anticipated maturity: now–2005.

DOMAINE LAROCHE (CHABLIS)

1996 Chablis Blanchots	E	(88–90)
1996 Chablis Blanchots Réserve de L'Obédiencerie	EE	(91–93+)
1996 Chablis Les Clos	E	(90–92)
1996 Chablis Les Fourchaumes	D	88
1996 Chablis St. Martin	C	86

Michel Laroche, the dapper director of this large Chablis producer, stated he had not witnessed a vintage comparable to 1996 in the 30 years he has been crafting wines. Laroche sighted the bright sun (*luminosité*) that drove up sugar levels through photosynthesis while cool temperatures (22 degrees Celsius daytime and 4 degrees Celsius evening) maintained high acidity levels. He went on to say that 1996 is 10% richer in sugar and 10% higher in acidity than 1995, another excellent Chablis vintage. Furthermore, he said that in 1997 his wines attained high sugar levels from heat, not sun, and therefore had low acidity levels.

Laroche produces 15,000 cases of the Chablis St. Martin, the only one of his wines that is made exclusively in stainless steel. As is regrettably the case with the vast majority of Chablis, this wine is the result of mechanically harvested grapes and a blend of commercial (75%) and indigenous yeasts. That being said, the 1996 is a lovely wine. It reveals mineral scents and nice aromatic richness, as well as an oily-textured, medium-bodied, and glycerin-laden personality with strident acidity and lemon/lime flavors. Drink it between now and 2000.

According to Michel Laroche, the estate harvests its grands crus and "almost all" its premiers crus by hand. Produced from 30-year-old vines, one-third of the Chablis Les Fourchaumes is made in stainless steel, one-third in 5,000 liter *foudres,* and the balance in small oak barrels (10% of the assembled wine was aged in new oak). Displaying minerals, stones, flowers, and smoke on the nose, it has a medium body, crisp texture, and well-delineated steel and flint flavors. It should be at its best between now and 2003. The 1996 Chablis Blanchots (2,000-case production from 11½ acres—2⅔ tons of fruit per acre) is 100% barrel fermented, 20% of which are new. It exhibits spicy oak, minerals, and smoky hickory aromas and an oily, thick, luscious, extremely ripe, yet highly focused personality packed with citrus and oak flavors. This wine is so concentrated and ripe that, with bottle age, the wood flavors will be absorbed by the fruit. Anticipated maturity: 2000–2006. Frequently the most massive of Chablis's grands crus, the 1996 Chablis Les Clos has huge amounts of glycerin, as its legs appear to be in suspended animation on the sides of the glass. It reveals a superrich and deep nose with toast and wet stone scents and a hugely powerful, thick, luscious, full-bodied, bone-dry, and tight-fisted core of citrus fruits, minerals, flint, and ever so slight touches of spicy oak (even though it was aged in 30% new oak). Its brawn, impeccable balance and extremely long finish are all outstanding. Anticipated maturity: 2000–2008. Laroche's luxury cuvée, the Chablis Blanchots Réserve de l'Obédiencerie (200 cases), is crafted from a selection of the finest barrels of Chablis Blanchots. Interestingly, it has none of the strong oak scents and flavors found in the firm's regular Chablis Blanchots, even though the same percentage of new oak (20%) went into its *assemblage*. This fabulous wine displays a floral, mineral, and pear-scented nose as well as a tangy, highly delineated and focused personality. Concentrated, silky textured, and full bodied, it has beautiful purity and elegance to its steel and flintlike flavors that seem to go on forever in its interminable finish. It should be at its peak between 2002 and 2010. (*Note:* In 1995 Laroche bottled the entire production of the Obédiencerie in magnums but had not decided whether to continue that policy with the 1996 when I met with him. The price code listed is for a 750-milliliter bottle.)

DOMAINE ROGER LASSARAT (MÂCON-VERGISSON)

1997	Pouilly-Fuissé Très Vieilles Vignes Réserve	D	90
1996	Pouilly-Fuissé Très Vieilles Vignes Réserve	D	91+

Roger Lassarat's old-vine cuvée, produced from vines over 100 years old (some predating phylloxera), is consistently one of the finest wines produced in the Mâconnais. The 1997 has a concentrated nose of deeply rich spices and minerals. This superb Pouilly-Fuissé is dense, medium to full bodied, and fabulously focused, offering seemingly unending layers of liquid stones, nuts, and flowers. The power and refinement of this wine needs to be tasted to be believed!

The 1996 Pouilly-Fuissé Très Vieilles Vignes Réserve is a superb wine. It displays mouthwatering mineral, toasted nut, and floral aromas as well as a highly detailed, yet rich and concentrated core of candied almonds, gravel, and minerals. This is one of those rare wines to combine refinement and elegance with power and extract. Bravo!

LOUIS LATOUR (BEAUNE)

1996	Bâtard-Montrachet	EEE	(92–94)
1995	Beaune	D	87
1996	Bienvenue-Bâtard-Montrachet	EE	(91–93)
1995	Bourgogne Blanc	B	84+
1995	Chablis	D	87+
1996	Chassagne-Montrachet	D	(87–89)
1995	Chassagne-Montrachet	D	88
1996	Chassagne-Montrachet Morgeot	D	(89–92)
1995	Chassagne-Montrachet Morgeot	D	(89–91+)
1996	Chevalier-Montrachet	EEE	(92–94)

Year	Wine	Rating	Score
1996	Corton-Charlemagne	EE	(93–95)
1995	Corton-Charlemagne	EE	(93–95)
1995	Mâcon Lugny Les Genevrières	B	85
1996	Meursault	D	(86–88)
1995	Meursault	D	87
1996	Meursault Blagny	D	(88–90)
1995	Meursault Blagny	D	(86–87+)
1996	Meursault Charmes	E	(89–92)
1995	Meursault Goutte d'Or	D	(87–89)
1996	Montagny Premier Cru	C	87+
1995	Montagny Premier Cru	C	87+
1996	Montrachet	EEE	(94–96)
1995	Montrachet	EEE	(94–96)
1996	Puligny-Montrachet	D	(85–87)
1995	Puligny-Montrachet	D	88
1996	Puligny-Montrachet Les Folatières	E	(89–92)
1995	Puligny-Montrachet Les Folatières	D	(90–92)
1995	Puligny-Montrachet La Garenne	D	(89–91)
1996	Puligny-Montrachet Les Réferts	E	(89–92)
1996	St. Véran	C	86
1995	Savigny-Lès-Beaune	C	86?

Louis Latour celebrated its bicentennial in 1997, having been founded in 1797. A walk-through the lobby of the Beaune headquarters on my visit in 1997 revealed photographs, paintings, and drawings chronicling this famed *négociant*'s first 200 years. Amid this my eyes were attracted to the price lists of past years. Even after taking inflation into consideration, the prices were more reasonable a hundred years ago than today, a reality confronted by all modern-day consumers of fine Burgundy.

Louis-Fabrice Latour, this *négociant*'s young director, was concerned about the rise in bulk wine prices when I visited the firm's cellars in Aloxe-Corton's Château de Grancey in November 1997. Well traveled, bright, and inquisitive, Latour realizes that Burgundy must compete on a price-to-quality level with the rest of the world's wines and cannot depend on rhetoric about *terroir* and history to sell its offerings.

Latour's 1996s do not exhibit the vibrant and sometimes sharp acidity found in other firms' or domaines' wine. These are rich, glycerin-filled, ripe, and silky wines. The 1996 St. Véran reveals smoky, flinty aromas and a glycerin-filled, oily-textured, medium-bodied, and mineral character. This appealing wine should be drunk over the next 2–3 years. Exhibiting tropical fruit and toasty oak on the nose, the 1996 Montagny Premier Cru has a concentrated, orange peel, and red berry-filled personality. Well crafted, medium bodied, silky, and beautifully ripe, this wine should provide delicious drinking until 2001. The 1996 Meursault offers toasted nut and mineral scents as well as a medium-bodied, round, beautifully ripe, oily-textured, rich, and gravel-flavored character. Anticipated maturity: now–2001. Displaying floral and stone aromatics, the 1996 Puligny-Montrachet is a silky, medium-bodied, mineral-rich, and fat wine. Anticipated maturity: now–2001. The 1996 Chassagne-Montrachet shows candied citrus fruit on the nose as well as a liquid mineral and lemon zest-infused, medium-bodied, rich, ripe, and persistent personality. It will be at its best if consumed by 2001.

Revealing nuts and flowers on the nose, the 1996 Meursault Blagny is a focused, silky, broad, and medium-bodied wine filled with flavors reminiscent of stones, gravel, and minerals. It will be at its peak from now to 2002. The 1996 Meursault Charmes exhibits sweet white flower and grilled nut aromas as well as an elegant, well-balanced, rich, oily-textured, and medium- to full-bodied character. Layers of gravel, flowers, smoke, and minerals are found in this complex and beautifully persistent wine. Anticipated maturity: 2000–2005. Displaying highly detailed metallic and mineral scents, the 1996 Puligny-Montrachet Les Réferts is a thick-textured, wide, powerful, delineated, medium- to full-bodied, and refined wine packed with earth, stones, and sweet aniselike flavors. Anticipated maturity: 2000–2005. The white flower- and chalk-scented 1996 Puligny-Montrachet Les Folatières is a broad, medium- to full-bodied, silky, and extremely elegant wine. Crisp red currants, apple blossoms, and minerals can be found in this highly delineated and focused offering. It should be at its best between 2001 and 2006. The 1996 is particularly successful in *terroirs* that generally produce powerful, rich, and ripe wines that often lack focus. Such is the case with Latour's Chassagne-Montrachet Morgeot. A rich, mineral-infused nose gives way to a full-bodied, wide, oily-textured, yet bright personality packed with tangy metal, mineral, and earthlike flavors. Well delineated and surprisingly refined for a Morgeot (they tend to be meaty wines, in my opinion), it offers a long, pure, and well-defined finish. Anticipated maturity: 2000–2006.

Bienvenue-Bâtard-Montrachet is a flat vineyard bordered by Bâtard-Montrachet to the west, Puligny-Montrachet Les Pucelles to the northeast, and two village wines (Rue Rousseau and Les Enseignères) to the east and south. It greatly benefited from this vintage's telltale acidity. Latour's full-bodied 1996 has mineral and floral aromas and a precise, magnificently focused, highly delineated personality. Its rich, oily, and powerful core is packed with chalk, liquid minerals, and lemon twists. Anticipated maturity: 2005–2009. The 1996 Bâtard-Montrachet reveals intense anise, cake icing, candied white fruit, and raspberry aromas. On the palate, this highly expressive, dense, intense, mouth-coating, thick, broad, and full-bodied wine is filled with red currants, buttered toast, and minerals. It should be at its peak from 2005 to 2010. Displaying rich smoky and rock dust aromas, the 1996 Chevalier-Montrachet is a tightly wound, medium- to full-bodied, rich, and multidimensional wine. Liquid minerals, pears, flowers, and red berries can be found in its delicious, focused, and silky personality. Its exceedingly long finish reveals delightful nuances of sweet oak and candied lemons. Anticipated maturity: 2004–2011. The 1996 Montrachet exhibits expressive liquid mineral, stone, and floral scents as well as an oily, superrich, dense, and muscular character jam-packed with earth, anise, citrus zests, and a superb minerality. This seductive, elegant, powerful, and awesomely balanced wine has the potential to age magnificently for 2 decades or more with good cellaring. Anticipated maturity: 2006–2018.

Louis Latour's 1996 Corton-Charlemagne is fabulous. Its deeply ripe nose reveals minerals, pears, nuts, and roasted peach smells. On the palate, it explodes with massive, mouth-coating, and superfocused layers of gravel, stones, sweet white fruits, and honeysuckle blossoms. Full bodied, oily textured, and dense, this wine has exquisite balance as well as a precise, pure, highly defined, and formidably long finish. It should be at its peak from 2004 to 2010.

At Louis Latour the winemaking is entrusted to Jean-Pierre Jobard, the brother of François and Charles Jobard, two well-known names in Meursault. Jobard commented that the acid in 1995 reminded him of the 1988.

The 1995 Bourgogne reveals aromas of deep, sweet Chardonnay fruit, and in the mouth, it is lively and fresh, with nice buttery flavors. Another good value, the vibrant 1995 Mâcon

Lugny Les Genevrières is slightly buttery, with flavors of ripe apples and aromas of freshly cut flowers. Perennially one of Burgundy's best values, the medium-bodied, well-balanced Montagny Premier Cru exhibits a fresh, lively, floral nose and flavors suggestive of green apples and buttery tones. Louis-Fabrice commented that as his Montagny gains in popularity, his costs for purchasing wine in that relatively unknown village increase as more and more *négociants* are scurrying there with the intent of exploiting Latour's success with this wine. He intimated that Latour may not be making the wine in a few years because the costs will be driven beyond what he perceives as Montagny's quality-to-price threshold. The 1995 vintage was an outstanding one in Chablis, and Latour's village offering serves up lemony apples on the nose. This citrusy aspect is displayed in the flavors, resulting in a fresh, crisp, lively, medium-bodied wine for near-term drinking. Undergoing fining when I tasted it, the 1995 Savigny-Lès-Beaune was suffering from that process and was difficult to assess. This masculine wine is slightly austere and minerally. Displaying aromas of stones, red currants, and cassis, the 1995 Beaune is also a muscular wine. Crisp red berry flavors are intermingled with a minerally, slightly steely aspect. Medium bodied, it should be consumed within 4 years of its release. With an impressive structure, the 1995 Meursault offers up aromas of roasted and toasted hazelnuts with oaky nuances. In the mouth, this medium-bodied wine has nicely delineated hazelnuts and good length for a village offering. Drink it between now and 2002. A step up, the 1995 Puligny-Montrachet exhibits a sweet, roasted apricot nose followed by an explosion of toasted, spiced apples in the mouth. This medium-bodied wine should be drunk between its release and 2002. In a more structured vein, the 1995 Chassagne-Montrachet displays stony, slightly flinty aromas with a delicious mouth of minerals and steel. This long, medium-bodied wine should be consumed between now and 2003. For those who don't know the aroma and flavor signatures of the three main white Côte d'Or villages, I recommend trying the 1995 Latour Meursault, Puligny, and Chassagne offerings side by side, as they are representative of their respective *terroirs*.

The 1995 Meursault Blagny did not perform well, as it was being fined when it was tasted. (I've tasted many previous vintages of this wine and know it well.) It offered moderate quantities of red berries in the mouth as well as a sweet, fruity nose, yet not much structure. Also being fined but in fine tasting form, the 1995 Meursault Goutte d'Or possesses aromas of sweet red currants and a flavor profile packed with crisp berries intermingled with toasted nuts. This forward, medium- to full-bodied wine is not made for long-term aging, but it will drink well for 7 or so years. Another wine in its fining stage that was showing well is the 1995 Puligny-Montrachet La Garenne. Full bodied, with admirable length, this wine explodes out of the glass with aromas of ripe fruit. It offers a mouthful of tropical and citrus fruits, finishing with a touch of apple flavors. With slightly more potential, the 1995 Puligny-Montrachet Les Folatières displays a bouquet of sweet white flowers, followed by deep, luscious, beautifully delineated ripe fruits. This excellent, full-bodied wine has superb concentration and finesse and will age well for 10 or so years. Another winner, but in a completely different style, is the 1995 Chassagne-Montrachet Morgeot. Its aromatics offer minerals and flowers, with a slight hint of almond paste (a characteristic for me of optimum ripeness in Chardonnay, Chenin Blanc, and even sometimes Riesling). With exquisite direction, the mouth guides you through flavors of flowers and stony, minerally fruits. Medium to full bodied, this beauty should be consumed between 2001 and 2008.

Corton-Charlemagne is Latour's flagship wine, as the Griotte Chambertin is to Claude Dugat and the Musigny Vieilles Vignes is to the Comte de Vogüé. True to form, the 1995 is an outstanding effort. An extremely tight but superripe nose of sweet fruits is followed by a massive cascade of deep, sweet, intense, tropical fruits mixed with candied apples and red currants. This full-bodied, excellently structured wine has enormous depth and concentration, as well as a long finish (flavors of cassis, apples, and a touch of lemon linger for 30 seconds or more). Hold it for 5 years and drink it over the subsequent 8. Displaying a deep, sweet, but unyielding nose, the 1995 Montrachet possesses a superstructured, buttery, hyperripe (not overripe) mouth. A textbook Montrachet, it combines the elegant, minerally aspects of a Chevalier and the fat, lush, almost tropical tones of a Bâtard in a full-bodied wine with great length. Made for the long haul, it will age beautifully for 20+ years.

DOMAINE LATOUR-GIRAUD (MEURSAULT)

1995	Bourgogne Chardonnay	C	80
1996	Meursault Cuvée Charles Maxime	D	87
1996	Meursault Charmes	D	91
1996	Meursault Clos du Cromin	D	85+
1995	Meursault Clos du Cromin	D	84
1997	Meursault Genevrières	E	(87–89)
1996	Meursault Genevrières	D	90
1995	Meursault Genevrières	D	86+
1997	Meursault Genevrières Cuvée des Pierres	EE	(90–92)
1996	Meursault Genevrières Cuvée des Pierres	E	91
1996	Meursault Limozin	D	87
1995	Meursault Limozin	D	86
1997	Meursault Narvaux	D	(87–89)
1996	Meursault Narvaux	D	88
1995	Meursault Narvaux	D	85
1997	Meursault Perrières	E	(88–90)
1996	Meursault Perrières	D	91
1995	Meursault Perrières	D	87+
1996	Meursault Poruzots	D	89
1995	Meursault Poruzots	D	86
1996	Puligny-Montrachet Champs Canet	D	89
1995	Puligny-Montrachet Champs Canet	D	85

This large domaine is obviously making huge efforts to increase the wine quality. Working closely with Patrick Lesec, its Paris-based wine broker, Latour-Giraud has committed itself to a noninterventionist style of winemaking. Jean-Pierre Latour, the estate's director, has reduced yields, jettisoned his filters, pledged to eschew tartaric acid additions, abandoned chaptalizing (at least in 1995), and last, is trying to utilize more wild yeasts for fermentation. This new winemaking philosophy is ripe with risks, but if producing great wines is the objective, it is their only avenue. At first Latour was hesitant, but Lesec's insistence that he taste wines from Burgundy's finest producers convinced him. He realizes the qualitative progress made by his wines and is doubling his efforts. The good to very good 1995s exhibit attractive ripeness but lack the necessary complexity and length to be outstanding wines. However, they are a sign of what is to come if Jean-Pierre Latour sticks to this winemaking philosophy.

An offputting nose of cheese rinds and sweat mar the otherwise delicious 1995 Bourgogne Chardonnay. Deep, almondy (almost marzipan), and superripe, this medium-bodied and tangy wine should be drunk within the first 2 years of its release. With its muted nose just barely revealing dusty nuts, the 1995 Meursault Clos du Cromin is a thick-textured wine full of candied nuts and a tangy, stony finish. Drink this medium-bodied wine within 4–5 years of release. The 1995 Meursault Narvaux has a candied, spicy nose and an attractive spicy, nutty quality in its oily-textured mouth. This lively, medium- to full-bodied wine should be drunk before 2003. A step up, the 1995 Meursault Limozin exhibits almonds, hazelnuts, and anise in the nose. Rugged and austere, it has flavors of sharp citrus fruits and minerals. This medium-bodied wine will drink well until 2001. The medium-bodied 1995 Puligny-Montrachet Champs Canet possesses a nose of deep spices and freshly ground white pepper, which is followed by an explosive burst of minerally fruit. This wine should not be cellared for more than 5 years. Muted on the nose, the 1995 Meursault Poruzots displays superripe candied apples and tropical fruit with touches of toasted nuts in its medium-bodied personality. Drink it between now and 2002. Latour-Giraud is the largest proprietor of Meursault Genevrières. The 1995 displays an herbal, stony nose in addition to an attractive nutty and minerally quality on the palate. Tangy and sharp on the back end, this wine is not made for extended cellaring; drink it before 2003. The domaine's best wine, the 1995 Meursault Perrières, reveals deeply embedded spice on the nose, a thick texture, and flavors of nuts, spices, and stony minerals. This delicious, medium- to full-bodied wine should be held for 2 years after release and enjoyed over the following 3–4.

Thanks to the efforts of Jean-Pierre Latour and Patrick Lesec, the estate's broker, Domaine Latour-Giraud is a turnaround story. The qualitative leap this domaine has achieved in the last 3 years is nothing short of remarkable. In 1995, an outstanding vintage for white burgundies, my ratings for these wines ranged from a low of 80 for the Bourgogne Chardonnay to a high of 87+ for the Meursault Perrières. A glance at the scores listed here will reveal that this estate's 1996s are, across the board, up to 4 points better than the 1995s—and the vintage, while also outstanding, is no better than 1995. Jean-Pierre Latour's dedication to reducing yields and noninterventionist winemaking is paying off with a dramatic increase in the quality of this large domaine's wines. Readers need to search out these offerings, as they offer superb values for outstanding white burgundies.

The 1996 Meursault Cuvée Charles Maxime displays an expressive nose of almond and hazelnut cream followed by a dense, medium-bodied, ripe, well-balanced, and rich personality. It should be drunk over the next 3–4 years. Exhibiting nut-infused aromas of minerals, the 1996 Meursault Clos du Cromin is a light- to medium-bodied, well-crafted, tangy, and silky-textured wine. This offering's delicious gravel, hazelnut, spicy oak, and crisp pear flavors are somewhat marred by a slight hollowness in the midpalate. Drink it by 2001. The 1996 Meursault Limozin displays toasted hazelnut aromas and a precise, focused, broad, medium-bodied, and smoky mineral-filled character. Anticipated maturity: now–2002. Latour used only indigenous yeasts when crafting his excellent 1996 Meursault Narvaux (cultured yeasts were employed for all his other wines). It exhibits a rich, expansive, and mineral-laced nose followed by a well-focused, ripe, medium-bodied, and velvety textured core of minerals, nuts, pears, and oak spices. Anticipated maturity: now–2004.

Revealing flower and mineral scents, the 1996 Meursault Poruzots possesses deep richness and ripeness in its medium- to full-bodied and silky-textured personality. This structured wine has white flowers, nuts, and tangy peaches in its well-proportioned and balanced flavor profile. It should be at its peak between now and 2005. Domaine Latour-Giraud's almost 6 acres of Meursault Genevrières make them that famed vineyard's largest proprietor. Jean-Pierre Latour, in the 1996 vintage, decided to bottle two separate cuvées of Genevrières, his traditional one and a luxury bottling. Aged in 40% new oak, the 1996 Meursault Genevrières has a tropical fruit- and nut-scented nose as well as an expansive, mouth-coating, medium- to full-bodied core of honey-covered nuts and spicy minerals. This broad-shouldered, seductive, and dense wine also possesses a long and supple finish. Anticipated maturity: 2000–2006. The 50 cases of Latour's luxury cuvée, the 1996 Meursault

Genevrières Cuvée des Pierres, were produced from a parcel of vines that abut the Meursault Perrières vineyard and were aged in 100% new oak barrels. Aromatically, this cuvée displays more minerals, and on the palate, it is richer, denser, and appears more extracted. This deeply ripe, full-bodied, velvety-textured, and opulent wine is packed with ripe pears, oak spices, stones, and honeysuckle. Anticipated maturity: 2000–2006. The 1996 Meursault Charmes has a liquid mineral- and orange rind-infused nose. This refined, elegant, silky-textured, highly defined, yet deeply ripe wine has perfumed and floral flavors in its medium- to full-bodied character. Its long and delineated finish reveals honeysuckle blossoms for additional complexity. It should be at its best between 2000 and 2005. The 1996 Meursault Perrières was aged in 100% new oak and exhibits stones and minerals on the nose as well as an explosive gravel, stone, earth, oak spice, and rock dust flavor profile. This complex, well-balanced, and persistent wine should age quite well. Anticipated maturity: 2000–2007.

The 1996 Puligny-Montrachet Champs Canet has a rich floral and honeyed nose as well as a wide, ripe, medium- to full-bodied, and mouth-coating personality. Flavors of orange peel, white flowers, stones, and poached pears can be found in this long and delicious wine. Drink it between now and 2004.

Jean-Pierre Latour used his new, state-of-the-art press for the first time in 1997. Even though he felt compelled to "rectify" the acidity on a few of his whites, he credits this new press with having allowed him to draw as much natural acidity as possible from the grapes. Latour's 1997s are excellent, and his luxury cuvée of Meursault Genevrières outstanding. They all beautifully display the vintage's telltale ripe and dense fruit.

The pear- and flower-scented 1997 Meursault Narvaux reveals excellent ripeness and focus in its medium-bodied character. This silky-textured and thick wine has delightful toasted nut and mineral flavors as well as a long, well-delineated finish. Anticipated maturity: now–2003. Latour, the largest single owner of Meursault Genevrières with 2.4 hectares (5.9 acres), crafted a delightful 1997. It exhibits aromas reminiscent of toasted white fruits and hazelnuts. This medium- to full-bodied, intensely ripe, yet well-balanced offering is crammed with peanut, almond, and fruit pit-like flavors. Drink it over the next 4–5 years. I loved the aromas of the 1997 Meursault Perrières, as they reminded me of a sweet green apple-flavored gum. This well-crafted offering reveals deep ripeness and excellent focus in its fresh, earthy, and mineral core. Over the last few years I've noticed Latour's use of new barrels become increasingly deft. This wine's gentle oak spice gorgeously permeates its flavor profile and persistent finish. Anticipated maturity: now–2005. Domaine Latour-Giraud's most complex and complete 1997 is its Meursault Genevrières Cuvée des Pierres (75 cases were produced). Intensely ripe white fruit and candied orange rind aromas lead to an awesomely sweet, dense wine. This full-bodied, concentrated, and complex offering is crammed with caramelized apples, spiced and poached pears, and traces of grilled oak. It has admirable balance for a wine of this richness. With its long, mouth-coating finish, this opulent beauty should be drunk between 2000 and 2006.

Other recently tasted wines: 1997 Meursault Charmes (87–88), 1997 Meursault Cuvée Charles Maxime (83–85), 1997 Meursault Limozin (86–88), 1997 Meursault Poruzots (86–88), 1997 Puligny-Montrachet Champs Canet (87–89).

DOMAINE VINCENT LEFLAIVE (PULIGNY-MONTRACHET)

1996 Bâtard-Montrachet	EEE	(95–97+)
1995 Bâtard-Montrachet	EE	(91–94)
1995 Bienvenue Bâtard-Montrachet	EE	(91–93)
1996 Bourgogne Blanc	D	(85–88)
1995 Bourgogne Blanc	D	(84–87)

1996	Chevalier Montrachet	EEE	(95–97)
1995	Chevalier Montrachet	EEE	(94–97)
1996	Montrachet	EEE	(97–99+)
1995	Montrachet	EEE	(96–98+)
1996	Puligny-Montrachet	E	(87–89)
1995	Puligny-Montrachet	D	(85–89)
1996	Puligny-Montrachet Clavoillon	EE	(88–91)
1995	Puligny-Montrachet Clavoillon	D	(88–91)
1995	Puligny-Montrachet Les Combettes	EE	(91–94)
1996	Puligny-Montrachet Les Folatières	EE	(89–92)
1995	Puligny-Montrachet Les Folatières	E	(89–92)
1995	Puligny-Montrachet Les Pucelles	EE	(92–95)

Domaine Leflaive, now completely managed by Anne-Claude Leflaive, is renowned through-out the world for consistently offering some of the finest white burgundies. What struck me on my visit here is Madame Leflaive's obsession with improving an already admirable pro-duction. A few years ago she decided to shift the domaine's vineyards to organic viticulture because she noticed the damage caused by years of chemical treatments. A short time later she again shifted the viticulture, this time to the more radical biodynamic system utilized by Lalou Bize-Leroy, Michel Chapoutier, and Nicolas Joly (of Coulée de Serrant), among others. Biodynamic viticulture is beyond organic, with such issues as the phases of the moon play-ing significant roles. Those who think biodynamic farming is rubbish poke fun at the nettle teas that are blended in grounded "dynamizers" and dismiss as cultist the decision to es-chew chemical pesticides and fertilizers. I understand that the moon moves oceans and therefore may have an effect on the sap in a vine, but I have trouble with some of the more farfetched theories behind this practice. However, I am certain of the quality of the products emanating from several of the domaines practicing biodynamic viticulture. I also know that when Madame Leflaive served me blind two samples of the 1995 Bâtard (vinified identically and from the same parcels), one from biodynamic viticulture and the other from organic farming, I easily gravitated to the biodynamic one. It tasted more precise and possessed more fruit and length.

The wines at the domaine are made by Meursault's Pierre Morey. I was impressed with the relationship he has with Madame Leflaive. The two share their thoughts openly, respecting each other's opinions completely. In most cellars there is an obviously dominant player, but at Domaine Leflaive it is a team effort. The wines spend on average 11 months in oak before being placed in stainless-steel tanks for another 7–9 months (the Montrachet is never re-moved from oak. The domaine averaged 25 hectoliters/hectare in 1995—less than 2 tons of fruit per acre.

Displaying a fresh herbal and floral greenish nose, the 1995 Bourgogne Blanc offers tangy acid, a nice texture, and ripe fruits. Light to medium bodied, this wine is made for near-term consumption. The 1995 Puligny-Montrachet has a nose of deep roasted fruits and possesses good concentration of fruit and fine length. Medium bodied, this delicious wine can be drunk over the near term, but it will evolve for 6+ years. With intense star anise and fat ripe fruit in the nose, the 1995 Puligny-Montrachet Clavoillon makes a noteworthy first impression. Thick, concentrated fruit coats the palate, as this wine possesses beautiful depth and bal-ance with a touch of sweet spicy oak. The Clavoillon needs 2–3 years of cellaring before being drunk; it will last for 6–8 years. Possessing a deep but unyielding nose, the 1995

Puligny-Montrachet Les Folatières has a fabulous texture and nicely roasted fruit and nut flavors. Concentrated but not as structured, this wine requires relatively early drinking—say, between now and 2003. Displaying a sublime explosion of intense candied white flower aromas, the Puligny-Montrachet Les Combettes (1995 produced 175 cases and 1996 a whopping 400 cases!) has a silky texture and a huge burst of sweet floral fruits complemented by a judicious use of oak. This superb and refined, medium- to full-bodied wine should drink well young yet age for 10+ years. A stunning wine, the 1995 Puligny-Montrachet Les Pucelles displays an intensely spicy and floral nose, followed by a complex flavor profile of deeply roasted peaches, apricots, and minerals. This medium- to full-bodied wine has a driving raciness that reminded me of Jadot's 1995 Montrachet. I recommend waiting 4–5 years before opening your first bottle, then drinking it over the following 10 years. These last two wines are some of the most profound Pulignys I have tasted.

Displaying candied spices on the nose, the 1995 Bienvenue Bâtard-Montrachet possesses a fat, oily, powerful mouth densely packed with intense toasted fruits and minerals. This extremely well-balanced, full-bodied wine should be held for a minimum of 4 years and consumed enthusiastically over the subsequent decade. Intense but unyielding on the nose, the Bâtard-Montrachet isn't quite as exciting as the Pucelles, but it has enormous power and concentration. Displaying fat, candied fruit (ever so slightly flabby) with flavors of tangy minerals, spices, and flowers, this thick-textured, full-bodied wine should be drunk early, as I'm not convinced it possesses the backbone for serious aging. Drink it between 2002 and 2007. The 1995 Chevalier Montrachet is spectacular. Racy, floral, fresh, and engaging on the nose, this wine possesses an awesome entry filled with intense flavors of minerals and toasted apricots. Silky textured, full bodied, classy, and refined, this wine should not be touched for 6 years; enjoy it over the following 10–15 years. A stunning wine, the 1995 Montrachet may ultimately merit a higher score. Regrettably, few wine lovers will ever have the opportunity to taste this rare gem, as only 25 cases were produced. White flowers and deeply imbedded honeysuckle and minerals provided a gustatory overload. The mouth possesses amazingly elegant yet intense, gorgeous candied fruit notes revealing an awesome minerally sweetness as well as a judicious touch of oak. This oily-textured, floral, powerful, full-bodied wine displays the stuffing and structure to age admirably. Hold it for 6–8 years and drink it over the subsequent 10–18.

Anne-Claude Leflaive, this famed estate's director, and Pierre Morey, its winemaker, are justifiably excited about their 1996s. Some of their lots had 14% natural alcohol potential yet huge acidity levels. Morey said that the malic and tartaric acid levels were even at harvest, an unprecedented occurrence in a ripe vintage in Burgundy. Like his colleagues at other domaines, he attributes the high levels of malic acid to the cool temperatures that were present in late summer and early fall. Madame Leflaive added that the estate's policy of hoeing the vineyards to force the vine's roots deep into the soil also increases acidity levels.

The 1996 Bienvenue Bâtard-Montrachet, 1996 Puligny-Montrachet Les Combettes, and 1996 Puligny-Montrachet Les Pucelles had begun their malos but were not in a condition to be accurately judged. When I contacted Madame Leflaive in January 1998 to see if their *élevages* had advanced enough for them to be retasted, I learned that the winter's cool temperatures had arrested any further development. My November 1997 tastings convinced me that all three wines would turn out to be extraordinary, but professionally it is unfair to evaluate wines at such an embryonic stage of their development.

The delicious 1996 Bourgogne Blanc, one of the finest I've tasted from this "regional" appellation, reveals fresh and ripe white fruits on the nose and a bracing, light- to medium-bodied, lively core of stones, minerals, and toast. Drink it between now and 2002. Aromatically, the 1996 Puligny-Montrachet displays huge ripeness, deep minerality, and honeysuckle. On the palate, this rich, medium- to full-bodied, structured, focused, and crisp wine has hazelnut, mineral, and stone flavors. It will be at its best between 2000 and 2004. The 1996 Puligny-Montrachet Clavoillon, tasted from a new oak barrel (only 30% of the assembled wine will be from new oak, but the other barrels were still in early stages of malo), exhibits toasted hazelnut aromas and a bone-dry, deep, rich, elegant, medium- to full-bodied, and tightly wound personality jam-packed with minerals. This wine will require patience. Anticipated maturity: 2003–2010.

Leflaive's 1996 Puligny-Montrachet Les Folatières possesses a magnificently rich, deep, and minerally nose as well as a beautifully defined, medium- to full-bodied, and bright personality. Outstanding depth of fruit—pears, lemons, and white peaches—and buttery notes are found in this wine's core and its fabulous finish. Anticipated maturity: 2002–2010.

The 1996 is a particularly successful year for Bâtard-Montrachet. It explodes from the glass with highly expressive mineral, hazelnut, and toasty oak aromas. On the palate, this full-bodied, silky, and awesomely rich wine has highly delineated yet fat and layered waves of white fruits, stones, and spices. Brawny yet feminine, powerful yet elegant, this gem is a tour de force! Anticipated maturity: 2002–2010. The 1996 Chevalier-Montrachet is not as rich and expressive as the Bâtard but is even more elegant and refined. Displaying defined rock, mineral, and flower aromas, this medium- to full-bodied and perfectly balanced wine's precision is mind-blowing. Chalk, rock dust, stones, and crisp pears are found in its superbly focused flavor profile. Drink it between 2002 and 2010.

Ultimately the show-stopping 1996 Montrachet may merit a perfect score. Ethereal mineral, floral, and spicy oak aromas are followed by an incredibly rich, awesomely deep, elegant, and full-bodied personality. Layers of oily-textured honeysuckle, white pears, concentrated liquid minerals, and buttery oak roll over the palate; the intensely long finish reveals traces of rock and limestone dust. This magnificent, benchmark wine has all the components to age effortlessly. Anticipated maturity: 2004–2015+.

MAISON OLIVIER LEFLAIVE (PULIGNY-MONTRACHET)

1997	Auxey-Duresses	D	86
1997	Bâtard-Montrachet	EEE	(89–91)
1997	Bienvenue Bâtard-Montrachet	EEE	(88–90)
1997	Chassagne-Montrachet Abbaye de Morgeot	E	(86–87)
1997	Chassagne-Montrachet Les Chaumées	E	(87–89)
1997	Chassagne-Montrachet Les Ruchottes	E	(87–89)
1997	Chevalier-Montrachet	EEE	(89–91)
1997	Meursault Charmes	E	(87–89)
1997	Meursault Perrières	EE	(88–89)
1997	Meursault Tillets	D	(87–88)
1997	Montrachet	EEE	(90–92)
1997	Puligny-Montrachet	E	(85–86)
1997	Puligny-Montrachet Champs Gains	E	(88–89)
1997	Puligny-Montrachet Les Folatières	EE	(87–88)
1997	St. Aubin Les Dents de Chiens	D	87
1997	St. Aubin Remilly	D	86

This Puligny-based *négociant* is run by Olivier Leflaive, the cousin of Anne-Claude Leflaive (of Domaine Vincent Leflaive). Maison Leflaive, located just down the street from Domaine Vincent Leflaive, is also owned by 32 of the same shareholders who make up part of the 36-person consortium that owns the Domaine Leflaive. Until this year, the two producers worked with the same U.S. importer. The gregarious Olivier Leflaive, whose handsome features and dapper clothing bring to mind Hollywood's characterization of the archetypical romantic Frenchman, is first and foremost a businessman. With the assistance of his now deceased uncle Vincent, Leflaive set up this firm with the plan to sell all of its wines as futures. Today 70% of its production is sold in this manner, with the balance sold prior to the *élevage* being completed. The United States and England, the firm's largest markets, each purchase 15,000 cases of their 70,000 cases.

Started in 1984, the firm's first winemaker was Jean-Marc Boillot, who left in 1989 to manage his own estate. The talented Franc Grux, who previously ran Domaine Guy Roulot in Meursault, is at the reins, and he is crafting a delicious array of offerings from 65 different appellations. For quality control, Olivier Leflaive insists on purchasing only grapes or must (98% of the 1997s were acquired this way). Stylistically Leflaive's goal is to produce elegant wines reminiscent of those crafted at the domaine. While I found that this philosophy did not work wonders in the 1996 vintage, it did quite well with the fat and dense 1997s.

Franc Grux believes that the 1997 vintage "will not be fascinating for collectors and professionals, but it is certainly a very good year." He went on to explain that the weather, not the producers, "directed" the vintage. A good flowering was followed by an extremely hot and dry summer. The maturation of the grapes was blocked by the drought conditions, and when the *ban de vendange* (the first day growers can legally harvest) was announced, Grux realized many vineyards were not mature. Acids were low, and Grux "saved" about 20% of the firm's production by acidifying them. "I was not looking to attain a specific pH the way they teach in school; all I wanted was for the wine to have enough acidity to survive."

Maison Olivier Leflaive's wines are not powerhouses. They are well crafted, sometimes understated, and often refined. As Grux said, "We want elegance, not richness or power."

The 1997 Auxey-Duresses, bottled in August 1998, reveals a mineral- and cold steel-laden nose. This fat, well-crafted, medium-bodied, and lively wine has ripe white fruit and mineral flavors. It should be consumed over the next 2–3 years. This firm produces a delicious range of wines from St. Aubin. My favorite of Leflaive's 1997s from this village is the St. Aubin Les Dents de Chiens. It displays beautiful ripeness in its peach and apricot aromas. On the palate, this expressive, thick, and medium-bodied wine is filled with lusciously ripe fruits and minerals. It is neither complex nor particularly concentrated, but, oh, what a drink! Anticipated maturity: now–2002. Leflaive produced 2,000 cases of the 1997 St. Aubin Remilly. Exhibiting smoky and toasty ripe fruit scents, this is a silky-textured, elegantly styled, and easygoing offering. Medium bodied and filled with stones, crisp pears, and minerals, this wine should be drunk over the next 3 years.

I tasted two separate 1997 Puligny-Montrachet cuvées. The first had a slightly more interesting nose, revealing apples, flowers, and toasty oak. Its medium-bodied character offered an appealingly rich, marzipan-flavored attack that dissipated quickly. The second cuvée is creamed nut scented and exhibits a tangy, grilled almond character. Both cuvées are delicious and well made yet would have needed to have more depth, palate presence, and length for a loftier review.

The 1997 Meursault Tillets is the finest of Leflaive's single-vineyard wines from Meursault. It offers rich aromas of stones and minerals that lead to its fresh and vibrant character. This medium-bodied, beautifully refined, and focused wine is filled with gravel and nuts. Drink it over the next 4–5 years. The 1997 Meursault Charmes, a pear- and stone-scented offering, reveals an elegant, harmonious, and intense personality. This excellent wine is feminine, precise, and has a mineral-laden personality that finishes on a toasty note. Anticipated maturity: now–2004. The 1997 Meursault Perrières is more forward but no less refined. It displays stone and earth aromas as well as a delicious, medium-bodied, and silky character. Flavors of wet gravel and minerals are found in this well-focused and bone-dry wine. It lacks the requisite balance for extended cellaring and should be consumed over the next 4–5 years.

The 1997 Puligny-Montrachet Champs Gains exhibits aromas of white flowers, anise, acacia blossoms, and toasty berries. This lovely offering is fat and rich and possesses excellent grip to its almond and earth-filled flavor profile. Anticipated maturity: now–2004. Maison Leflaive has sold its entire production of 1997 Puligny-Montrachet Les Folatières to its U.S. importer. Its earth and honeyed nose is followed by a well-crafted medium body. This honey-suckle-flavored wine has traces of *sur-maturité* in its dense, velvety, and rich core of fruit. Drink it over the next 4 years.

I loved the 1997 Chassagne-Montrachet Les Chaumées' ripe apricot, peach, and anise-infused nose. On the palate, this medium- to full-bodied, layered, and oily-textured wine is filled with lemony minerals. Delicious to drink now, it should easily hold for another 4–5 years. This firm began purchasing vineyards in 1990, and one of its first acquisitions was a parcel of Chassagne-Montrachet Abbaye de Morgeot. This wine offers up aromas of earth, clay, flowers, and spice, followed by an attractive medium body filled with pears, seashells, and minerals. Like many 1997s, it lacks some concentration, complexity, and length but is delicious. Drink it over the next 4 years. Produced from purchased grape must, the 1997 Chassagne-Montrachet Les Ruchottes has an intensely spicy nose filled with fruitcakelike aromas. This medium- to full-bodied expansive wine is soft and inviting, beautifully expressing its pear, mineral, and buttered toast flavors. Anticipated maturity: now–2004.

The 1997 Bienvenue-Bâtard-Montrachet has on loads of makeup and is all dressed up and waiting to be picked up for the prom. Its huge, ripe, and opulent nose gives way to a spicy, sultry, and leesy core of fat fruit. This is a medium- to full-bodied, oily-textured, and dense wine that excites all the senses and then goes home early for the night. Drink it over the next 4–5 years. The toasty pear-scented 1997 Bâtard-Montrachet is more fun and extravagant and will offer even more satisfaction to hedonists. This plump, smile-inducing, and opulent wine is medium to full bodied, with intense flavors of ripe white fruits, spices, and anise. Anticipated maturity: now–2005. The 1997 Chevalier-Montrachet reveals red currant and violet aromas. Harvested at 12.7% natural alcohol, and chaptalized to 13.2%, this fresh, concentrated, and thick wine is medium bodied and velvety textured. Its flavor profile, filled with minerals and pears, offers excellent grip and flavor intensity. Drink it between 2000 and 2005. Maison Leflaive purchased three barrels of Montrachet as grape must. The day of my tasting it was in an oxidative state, displaying some gold to its color. It exhibits a rich, spicy, butterscotch, and mineral-laden nose as well as an intense and densely packed personality. Flavors of almond cookies, stones, clay, and baked apples can be found in this sensual and thick offering. Grux was planning to add sulfur to the barrels after my tasting to take the Montrachet out of its oxidative condition. Anticipated maturity: 2000–2006.

Other 1997s recently tasted: Bourgogne Les Sétilles (83), Chassagne-Montrachet (85–86), Chassagne-Montrachet Caillerets (87–88), Chassagne-Montrachet La Romanée (86–87), Chassagne-Montrachet Vergers (87–89), Corton-Charlemagne (88–89), Criots-Bâtard-Montrachet (88–89), Meursault (85–86), Meursault Casse Tête (86–87), Meursault Narvaux (86–87+), Puligny-Montrachet Champs Canet (87–88), Rully Premier Cru (84), Rully Les Clous (85), St. Aubin La Châtenière (86), St. Aubin Sur Gamay (86), St. Romain (85).

DOMAINE DE LEGÈRES (MÂCONNAIS)
1996 Mâcon Péronne   **B 87**

This delicious tank-fermented and aged Chardonnay is from the well-known producer Pierre Janny. The wine exhibits a lemony custard- and mineral-scented nose and crisp, lively, pure flavors that admirably express the naked qualities of Chardonnay fruit. With attractive texture, fine ripeness, and medium body, this example should drink well for another year.

DOMAINE LEROY (VOSNE-ROMANÉE)

1995 Corton-Charlemagne	EEE	93

Known throughout the wine-loving world for her reds, Mme. Leroy also fashions first-class whites, usually tight and unapproachable in their youth but very long-lived. However, the 1995 Corton-Charlemagne is atypically delicious now yet can be held for a dozen years: slightly gold colored and exhibiting aromas of superripe, toasty and spicy fruit, this fat, thick-textured, and structured wine possesses buttery, tropical fruit flavors.

DOMAINE DU CHÂTEAU DE LA MALTROYE
(CHASSAGNE-MONTRACHET)

1996 Bâtard-Montrachet	EE	93
1996 Chassagne-Montrachet Les Chenevottes	D	87
1996 Chassagne-Montrachet Clos du Château de la Maltroye	D	88
1996 Chassagne-Montrachet La Dent de Chiens	E	91+
1996 Chassagne-Montrachet Les Grandes Ruchottes	E	90+
1996 Chassagne-Montrachet La Vigne Blanche	D	89

On November 20, 1997, a ship carrying hundreds of containers packed with cases of wine broke in half off the Azores, dumping a large percentage of its cargo into the ocean. After its crew had been rescued, salvagers attempted to tow the two hulls to safety. As camera crews recorded their efforts for French television, a container could be seen slowly slipping away from its moorings. When it finally broke free, those behind it fell like dominoes into the frigid North Atlantic. On board were hundreds of cases of burgundies, including most of Haegelen-Jayer's incredible 1995 Clos Vougeot (I hope my case will be consumed by a worthy shark) and large quantities of this estate's 1996 production. Jeanne-Marie de Champs, the Château de la Maltroye's broker, informed me that most of the production of the 1996 Chassagne-Montrachet La Romanée's special unfiltered cuvée, produced exclusively for New York City's Burgundy Wine Co., was lost in this disaster. Incredibly, subsequent shipment of this outstanding wine, including *every* bottle that had not been placed on the first container, was lost at sea by another distressed ship.

The Chassagne-Montrachet Les Chenevottes reveals sweet toast, vanilla, and anise aromas followed by a silky, medium-bodied, refined, and mineral-laced character. A hollowness in the midpalate prevents me from giving this otherwise excellent wine a better rating. Anticipated maturity: now–2003. Displaying beautifully ripe fruit and minerals on the nose, the Chassagne-Montrachet Clos du Château has wonderful depth to its medium-bodied and racy character. Stones, spices, and gravel-like flavors can be found in this well-crafted wine. It should be at its peak between 2000 and 2004. Aromatically, the Chassagne-Montrachet La Vigne Blanche exhibits enticing floral and mineral scents. On the palate, this beautifully ripe, oily yet lively, and medium- to full-bodied wine is richly layered with stones and honeysuckle blossoms. Anticipated maturity: 2000–2005. Produced from vines only 12 years of age, the outstanding Chassagne-Montrachet Les Grandes Ruchottes reveals a nose of spicy minerals, toasty almonds, and traces of honey. Medium to full bodied, elegant, broad, and with great ripeness, this velvety wine offers crisp pears, sweet peaches, stones, and a long, complex finish. Drink this beauty between 2001 and 2006. Jean-Pierre Cornut, this estate's owner and winemaker, told me that he is trying to have his Chassagne-Montrachet La Dent de Chiens reclassified as part of the Montrachet appellation (it was removed in 1936). Sadly, according to Mme. De Champs, 25–35 cases of the 75 cases produced of this lovely wine were lost in the aforementioned shipping disaster. Its tight but mineral and floral nose gives way to an extremely well-defined, balanced, and delineated personality. Stylistically it is more reminiscent of a Chevalier than a Montrachet because of its superelegant, gravel-and-mineral-laced core of fruit. This medium- to full-bodied and silky wine should be at its peak between 2002 and 2007.

Slightly less than half of the Bâtard-Montrachet's total production is currently located at the bottom of the Atlantic Ocean. This is heart-wrenching, as Cornut has fashioned a fabulous, rich, sweet, white flower, and anise-scented beauty. Superb ripeness, lively minerals, and lemons, as well as razor-sharp precision, depth, and complexity, are found in its oily and powerful character. This Bâtard-Montrachet's admirable finish reveals wonderful purity and traces of seashells, toasty oak, and candied almonds. Anticipated maturity: 2002–2007.

DOMAINE JOSEPH/PIERRE MATROT (MEURSAULT)

1996	Meursault	D	86
1995	Meursault	D	87
1996	Meursault Blagny	D	88
1995	Meursault Blagny	D	89
1996	Meursault Chevalière	D	88+
1996	Meursault Charmes	D	91
1996	Meursault Perrières	E	93
1996	Puligny-Montrachet Les Chalumeaux	E	89+
1995	Puligny-Montrachet Les Chalumeaux	D	89
1996	Puligny-Montrachet Les Combettes	E	92+

Note: This estate officially has two names, Domaine Joseph Matrot and Domaine Pierre Matrot. "Joseph" is used for wines sold to Vineyard Brands (these include the Meursault, Meursault Les Chevalières, Meursault Blagny, Meursault Charmes, Puligny-Montrachet Les Chalumeaux). The Seagram Château & Estate Wines Company imports Domaine Pierre Matrot's wines, which include the Meursault, Puligny-Montrachet Les Combettes, Meursault Perrières, Puligny-Montrachet Les Chalumeaux, and the Volnay Santenots.

As Daniel Haas, this estate's U.S. importer, put it so succinctly, "Thierry hates new oak in white wine." Thierry Matrot, the gentleman in question, runs this domaine that bears his grandfather's name. In 1995 both his red and white offerings show perfectly ripe fruit, which in the case of the whites is particularly important, as no new oak flavors are present to mask any flaws in the fruit.

The 1995 Meursault reveals grapefruit and honeyed aromas more reminiscent of a superripe Sauvignon Blanc than a Chardonnay. This delicious, silky-textured, medium-bodied, and tangy wine explodes on the palate with sweet nuts and touches of pear jelly and orange marmalade. Drink it between now and 2000. Even better, the 1995 Meursault Blagny displays deep and intense ripeness on the nose with scents of hazelnuts and white peaches as well as a well-structured, medium- to full-bodied, thickly textured, and expressive personality filled with citrus and honeylike flavors. Anticipated maturity: now–2003. The straw and slightly golden-hued 1995 Puligny-Montrachet Les Chalumeaux (harvested at over 14% natural sugar—extraordinary for Burgundy) exhibits superripe tropical fruit and floral aromas with notes of beeswax in the background. This thick, extraordinarily well-balanced, and full-bodied wine is densely packed with sweet, candied citrus fruits and has an admirably long and driven finish. Built to last, it will be at its best between now and 2005.

Thierry Matrot is ever-smiling, bright, and most important, a gourmet. Throughout our tasting he spoke of dishes he had prepared or eaten in restaurants over the years, resulting in my being terribly hungry and detesting the fact that he is so slender. He says he produces "wines made to go with food, not to win shows" and proudly asserts that "oak is not my thing." A longtime customer of Matrot's requested that he make a cuvée using a high percentage of new oak, which he reluctantly agreed to do, but only after stating that his name would not appear on the label. He believes that new oak "hides primary Chardonnay aromas" and overly oxidizes wines. To prove this last point, Matrot cites the fact that many 1992s attained or passed their peaks "without ever developing evolutionary notes." In a Beaune restaurant in January 1998 I tasted a 1992 Meursault Blagny from this estate. It was so youthful and tight that it required a half hour or more of air time to start opening, and by the end of the meal it had blossomed into an excellent wine.

In their youth, Matrot's whites often appear to be lean, but, like François Jobard's Meursaults, it is because they are wound as tightly as a spring. If they must be drunk young, readers should decant them prior to the meal.

The mineral- and walnut-scented 1996 Meursault is a medium-bodied, crisp, racy, and ripe wine with tangy and pure lemon and stonelike flavors. It should be drunk between 2001 and 2004. The 1996 Meursault Chevalière was aged in more new oak (25%) than any other Matrot wine. It possesses an expressive nose of minerals, chalk, and toast. A medium- to full-bodied, well-defined, broad-shouldered, rich wine, it has a vibrant personality marked by gravel, minerals, and citrus zests. Anticipated maturity: 2001–2005. Displaying spicy smoke aromas, the 1996 Meursault Blagny has anise, flint, white grapes, stones, and grapefruits in its bright, medium-bodied, and gripping flavor profile. Matrot laughed and said it was rude, like the inhabitants of Blagny, a hamlet inhabited mostly by members of his family, and should be served with spicy foods. Anticipated maturity: 2002–2006. Revealing beguiling stone, flower, and almond scents, the 1996 Puligny-Montrachet Les Chalumeaux is a rich, broad, medium- to full-bodied, and dense wine loaded with nut-laced candy, chalk, and floral elements. Vibrant, well balanced, and elegant, this offering should be at its peak from 2001 to 2005.

The 1996 Meursault Charmes has a refined, hazelnut, flower-filled nose and an extremely deep, lively, exciting, bright, and medium-bodied personality. Minerals, anise, flint, and toast can be found in this rich, racy, and tightly wound wine. Anticipated maturity: 2002–2006. Exhibiting creamy mineral, honeysuckle, and malt aromas, the 1996 Puligny-Montrachet Les Combettes has a wonderfully thick, defined, elegant, oily, and mouth-coating medium- to full-bodied personality. Layers of cake icing, nuts, flowers, and ripe pears are buttressed by bright acidity in this superripe, complex, and extremely long wine. Anticipated maturity: 2003–2008. Matrot's aversion to new oak is evidenced by the fact that the 1996 Meursault Perrières was aged in previously used barrels, only 20% of which were 1 year old. Its mineral-laced, creamy, yet tightly wound nose is followed by a medium- to full-bodied, broad, powerful, extracted, and gorgeously elegant wine. Abundant quantities of minerals, grilled almonds, stones, anise, steel, and traces of oak spice are found in this complex, ample, yet racy, and exceedingly long wine. It may well be the finest wine I have tasted from Thierry Matrot. I recommend cellaring this offering until at least 2004. It should easily hold its peak through 2010 with good cellar conditions.

DOMAINE MÉO-CAMUZET (VOSNE-ROMANÉE)

1996 Hautes-Côtes de Nuits	C	(85–87)

Jean-Nicolas Méo is producing a white burgundy in the hills that overlook this part of the Côte d'Or. Located within the commune of Flagey, and at an altitude of 380 meters, Méo's 8.6 acres of Hautes Côtes de Nuits were planted on an extremely rocky vineyard between 1990 and 1992. Harvested at almost 2 tons of fruit per acre (and Méo asserts that even at that moderate level he still had unripened grapes to eliminate), the 1996 offers an expressive nose of minerals, stones, and orange peels. This bright, floral, tangy, and medium-bodied wine has tangerine, anise, apple, and spicy oak flavors in its vibrant core. It should be drunk over the next 3 years.

CHÂTEAU DE MERCEY (MERCUREY)

1996 Bourgogne Hautes Côtes de Beaune	B	87

The delicious 1996 Bourgogne Hautes Côtes de Beaune reveals ripe malty aromas and a light- to medium-bodied, creamy-textured, yet lively core of mandarin orange infused white fruits, flowers, and currants. It should be drunk before 2002. The Château de Mercey is owned by the Antonin Rodet *négociant* house.

DOMAINE MESTRE PÈRE ET FILS (SANTENAY)

1996 Chassagne-Montrachet Tonton Marcel "Monopole"	D	87+

The 1996 Chassagne-Montrachet Tonton Marcel, from a little known *monopole* premier cru vineyard (located over and adjacent to Chassagne's Les Caillerets vineyard), reveals almond paste and lime aromas and a medium-bodied, rich, minerally, lemon zest-infused core of well-focused and balanced fruit.

DOMAINE LOUIS MICHEL (CHABLIS)

1996 Chablis	C	87
1996 Chablis Les Clos	D	93+
1996 Chablis Les Grenouilles	D	94
1996 Chablis Montée de Tonnerre	D	91
1996 Chablis Montmain	D	90
1996 Chablis Vaillons	D	90
1996 Chablis Vaudesir	D	92

Oak barrels are nowhere to be seen at Domaine Louis Michel, and it will stay that way as long as Jean-Loup Michel, the estate's director, has a say in the matter—stainless steel is his weapon of choice. Inexplicably, this domaine is often forgotten when wine lovers consider the top growers of this region. Some time ago I attended a blind tasting of aged Chablis at a friend's home. All the big names and the best vintages were present, and Louis Michel carried the day, to the surprise of many. Often austere and tightly wound young, these wines blossom with time and reveal enormous richness and complexity.

Michel was so impressed with the health and acidity levels of his grapes that he decided, for the first time, to age his Chablis on their fine lees. He feels this technique brought additional richness and body to the wines. Even though he is (justifiably) quite proud of his 1996s, he feels he might have been able to produce better wines if he could have extended their *élevage* beyond the scheduled shipping date imposed by his U.S. importer.

The Chablis reveals fresh, spicy scents and a lively, silky, medium-bodied, concentrated, and ripe character filled with minerals and touches of lemon zests. Drink it between now and 2001. Displaying aromas reminiscent of "liquid smoke" but without the saltiness, the Chablis Vaillons is an extremely rich, medium- to full-bodied, and oily-textured wine with exceptional structure and leesy, mineral, floral, honeyed, and stonelike flavors. In its long, crystalline finish, traces of anise can be discerned. Anticipated maturity: 2000–2006. As with the previous wine, the Chablis Montmain exhibits strong smoky scents and a beautifully ripe, concentrated, highly structured, yet thick and rich medium to full body. Complex layers of chalk dust, minerals, and traces of honey are found in this wine's exciting flavor profile. Anticipated maturity: 2000–2006. Michel's Chablis Montée de Tonnerre had a tight, muted nose the day of my tasting. On the palate, however, it exploded with liquid mineral, chalk, flint, lemon, and honeysuckle flavors. This highly concentrated, complex, medium- to full-bodied wine combines Chablis's austerity with fabulous richness. It should be at its peak between 2000 and 2007.

The magnificent Chablis Les Clos displays tons of flint and scents reminiscent of wet rocks baking in the sun. Its austere yet expansive personality is massive, full bodied, super-extracted, mouth coating, and packed with stones, honeysuckle, minerals, flowers, and traces of butterscotch. This superb wine should age gloriously and effortlessly. Anticipated maturity: 2002–2010. Produced from the smallest of Chablis's grand cru vineyards, the Chablis Les Grenouilles reveals a complex nose of liquid minerals, Earl Grey tea, and smoke. This full-bodied, rich, complex, focused, precise, superripe, but bone-dry wine has an extraordinary depth of flint, chalk, and mineral flavors. I was blown away by its awesomely long and defined finish. Bravo!

DOMAINE MICHELOT (MEURSAULT)

1996 Meursault Charmes	E	87
1996 Meursault Genevrières	E	86?
1996 Meursault Narvaux	D	86
1996 Meursault Perrières	E	86
1996 Puligny-Montrachet Les Folatières	D	88

This large (56.8 acres, 14.8 of which are regional appellations) and old estate lies on the southern border of the village of Meursault, on the road to Puligny-Montrachet. One of my first vinous memories is emptying the adults' glasses of Michelot's 1966 Meursaults in my mother's family home in Brittany. In my mind I can still taste those extraordinary nectars.

Today the estate is in the hands of Jean-François Mestre, the husband of one of Bernard Michelot's daughters. Under their unassuming house, Domaine Michelot has stockpiled vast quantities of wine. Tunnel after tunnel, and subterranean room after subterranean room is stacked with bottles from numerous vintages, from floor to ceiling, sometimes 6–10 bottles deep. As Mestre put it, "We use the squirrel's philosophy, we like to have tons of stock." He went on to explain that the estate likes to sell wines at least 1 year behind their colleagues in the village, "so the wine can open."

The 1996 vintage is an outstanding one for white burgundies, and Domaine Michelot owns large parcels of some of Meursault's finest vineyards, yet none of the wines I tasted were worthy of an outstanding rating.

The 1996 Meursault Narvaux reveals mineral and citrus aromas and a medium-bodied and racy personality with flavors reminiscent of stones and flint. It should be drunk between 2001 and 2004. The Michelots own 3.7 acres of Meursault Charmes and, according to Mestre, use only the oldest vines (averaging 40 years of age) for the premier cru cuvée. The youngest vines are declassified to the regular village cuvée. It displays an appealing floral and mineral-laced nose as well as a well-crafted, medium-bodied, and ripe character filled with gravel and stones. Anticipated maturity: 2001–2005. The 1996 Meursault Genevrières (Michelot also owns 3.7 acres of this renowned vineyard) had a reticent nose the day of my tasting. On the palate, it is wide, well structured, medium bodied, deep, and minerally and possesses a sharp acid streak. It is possible that with time this wine will build some richness to combat its strident nature, but I am not convinced of it. Those who wish to find out should wait at least until 2002 to taste it. Produced from 14-year-old vines, the 1996 Meursault Perrières has attractive mineral aromas and a medium-bodied, spicy, flinty, and racy personality. It lacks the depth, concentration, complexity, intensity, and, for lack of a better word, interest I expect from this topflight premier cru vineyard. Anticipated maturity: 2001–2004. The finest wine I tasted at this estate is the 1996 Puligny-Montrachet Les Folatières, but as luck would have it, it is not imported to the United States. Produced from 40-year-old vines, this wine has floral, anise, and almond aromas and a delicious, medium-bodied, silky, smoky, toasty, minerally, and candied nut-flavored character. It should be at its best between 2001 and 2006.

DOMAINE FRANÇOIS MIKULSKI (MEURSAULT)

1996 Meursault	D	(87–89)
1996 Meursault Charmes	E	(93–95)
1995 Meursault Genevrières	E	93+
1996 Meursault Genevrières	E	(92–94+)
1996 Meursault Poruzots	D	(89–91)

François Mikulski, a young and little-known vigneron in Meursault, has the potential to become one of that village's stars. He is the son of a Pole who fought the Germans in World War II as a member of the Polish contingent of the Allied forces. To start a new domaine in 1992, Mikulski obtained some vines from his uncle (Pierre Boillot), with the others *en métayage*. Three years later Mikulski hit a home run with his spectacular 1995 Meursault Genevrières. Produced from 30–40-year-old vines, this golden straw-colored offering reveals pears, hazelnut cream, and roasted wood scents as well as a full-bodied, massive, thick, oily-textured, and overripe (yet well-balanced!) character packed with sweet pear, toasted nut, and floral flavors. Spicy oak flavors are apparent in its admirably long finish, even though no new oak was used (only first- and second-year barrels). Robert Kacher, this estate's importer, summed it up well when he said that it was like "syrup of Meursault." Anticipated maturity: now–2003.

With the 1996 vintage Mikulski has catapulted himself into the top echelon of Meursault's producers. The 1996 Meursault exhibits a fresh minerally, nut-infused nose as well as a rich, lively, medium-bodied personality filled with white fruits, stones, and touches of lemon. Drink it between now and 2003. Displaying elegant flowers and minerals on the nose, the 1996 Meursault Poruzots has outstanding intensity and richness in its superbly well-focused, silky, medium- to full-bodied, pear- and white plum-laden flavor profile. This impressive Poruzots should be at its peak between now and 2006. Mikulski's 1996 Meursault Genevrières has gorgeous floral and sweet fruit scents followed by intensely rich, ripe, and densely layered flavors of roasted peaches, candied white grapes, honey, and poached pears in this full-bodied, broad, powerful, highly concentrated, and oily-textured wine. Verging on being overripe, this wine has excellent focus and brightness due to the vintage's acidity. Anticipated maturity: now–2005. The stunning 1996 Meursault Charmes is completely different in style. While the Genevrières has explosive levels of muscle and waves of sweet fruit, the Charmes enthralls the taster with its femininity, elegance, class, refinement, and definition. Revealing floral, mineral, and perfumed aromas, this deep, complex, highly focused, broad, and medium- to full-bodied wine offers sweet white flowers, crisp pears, and intense minerality in its flavor profile. The exceedingly long finish maintains its complexity and definition of flavors for nearly 45 seconds. Bravo!

DOMAINE ALICE ET OLIVIER DE MOOR (CHABLIS)

1996 Bourgogne Aligoté Réserve Vieilles Vignes	B	88
1996 Chablis Bel Air Réserve	C	92
1996 Chablis La Rosette Réserve	C	90
1996 Sauvignon-de-Saint-Bris Vieilles Vignes Réserve	C	89

The overwhelming majority of wine-producing estates in France have been handed down from generation to generation. A few established ones have been purchased relatively recently either by the wealthy or by corporations with a passion for wine or as an investment. It is exceedingly rare to hear about a domaine started from nothing but a desire to produce great wines. Domaine Alice et Olivier De Moor is just such an estate. All of this domaine's wines are bottled without being subjected to fining or filtration and are excellent values.

Produced from vines that are over 95 years old, the 1996 Bourgogne Aligoté Réserve Vieilles Vignes has a hugely expressive nose of smoke, toast (even though it is 100% tank fermented), minerals, perfume, and spices. On the palate, this enticing, silky-textured, and medium-bodied wine is packed with bright flavors of tangy lemons, currants, and steel. This refreshing Aligoté is juicy, pleasure giving, and thirst-quenching. A great picnic wine! Drink it over the next 2 years.

Readers who have tasted Sauvignon-de-Saint-Bris before will understand my reluctance when I was served a sample of De Moor's 1996. I had never tasted a good wine from this appellation, the only white burgundy that is Sauvignon Blanc based, and therefore braced myself for another insipid, unripe, and acidic wine. Boy, was I wrong! De Moor's 1996 Sauvignon-de-Saint-Bris Vieilles Vignes Réserve is a scrumptious, exciting, and fun wine. Mouthwatering aromas of blueberries and violets are followed by a rich, medium-bodied, intense, juicy, and tangy core of crisp red currants, minerals, and lively citrus fruits. David Hinkle, this offering's U.S. importer, told me that it was one of the house wines at Spago's of Beverly Hills, a testimony to that famous restaurant's wine staff.

Both of this domaine's Chablis (there are only 75 cases of each of these two "reserve" bottlings) were aged in previously used oak barrels in order to maximize lees contact (as opposed to the more traditional massive tanks) and not impart unwanted oak flavors. Produced from a steep vineyard composed of crushed shells left behind by receding seas, the 1996 Chablis La Rosette Réserve reveals deep and fresh mineral and floral aromas. On the palate, this wine is broad, rich, bright, and medium to full bodied. Its concentrated core possesses flavors reminiscent of raspberries, seashells, minerals, smoke, and white flowers. This lacy yet powerful wine will provide fabulous drinking between now and 2004. The 1996 Chablis Bel Air Réserve displays ethereal smoke, chalk dust, and gravel aromas as well as a flattering, expressive, and rich core of fruit. Layers of liquid minerals, apple compotes, and candied pears are found in this silky, medium- to full-bodied, racy wine. Anticipated maturity: now–2004. Bravo!

DOMAINE ALBERT MOREY (CHASSAGNE-MONTRACHET)

1996 Bâtard-Montrachet	EEE	?

The semi-retired Albert Morey, Bernard and Jean-Marc Morey's father, continues to produce his Bâtard-Montrachet from a parcel of old and ailing vines (4 barrels—100 cases in 1996). I was stunned by this wine, as I have never tasted anything quite like it. Aromas of candied grapefruits are followed by hyperconcentrated, bright, yet viscous layers of tangy and sugar-coated citrus fruits. This offering's ripeness, power, extraction, and balance denote an outstanding wine, but it appeared so monolithic and was so lacking in harmony and complexity when I tasted it that I found myself perplexed as to its actual quality. Will its enormous concentration and ripeness evolve into a masterpiece, or will it remain disjointed and single faceted?

MAISON/DOMAINE BERNARD MOREY ET FILS
(CHASSAGNE-MONTRACHET)

1996 Bâtard-Montrachet	EEE	95
1995 Bourgogne Blanc	C	85+
1996 Bourgogne Chardonnay	C	86
1996 Chassagne-Montrachet Vieilles Vignes	D	87
1995 Chassagne-Montrachet Vieilles Vignes	D	87
1996 Chassagne-Montrachet Les Baudines	D	90
1995 Chassagne-Montrachet Les Baudines	D	87
1996 Chassagne-Montrachet Les Caillerets	D	94
1995 Chassagne-Montrachet Les Caillerets	D	92+
1996 Chassagne-Montrachet Les Embrazées	D	93
1995 Chassagne-Montrachet Les Embrazées	D	89
1996 Chassagne-Montrachet La Maltroie	D	93
1996 Chassagne-Montrachet Morgeot	D	92
1995 Chassagne-Montrachet Morgeot	D	89
1996 Chassagne-Montrachet Vide Bourse	D	92+
1995 Chassagne-Montrachet Vide Bourse	D	91
1996 Meursault Genevrières Cuvée Baudot (Hospices de Beaune)	E	?
1996 Puligny-Montrachet	D	87
1995 Puligny-Montrachet	D	87+
1996 Puligny-Montrachet Le Truffière	EE	94
1995 Puligny-Montrachet Le Truffière	E	92
1996 St. Aubin Les Charmois	D	90
1995 St. Aubin Les Charmois	D	88
1996 St. Aubin En Remilly	D	88+
1996 Santenay Passetemps	D	88
1995 Santenay Passetemps	D	86+

While many producers mentioned *millerandage* (stunted growth of the fruit embryos) as the cause of their small yields in 1995, for Bernard Morey it was due to *coulure* (the dropping of flowers because of bad weather conditions). Whatever the reason for their occurrence, low yields can benefit consumers because the result is greater concentration of fruit. Morey and his two sons had bottled the whites during the end of August and the beginning of September and were bottling the reds when I visited in January. Wines from this estate are generally full bodied and thick, with excellent ripeness.

The 1995 Bourgogne Blanc is a textbook example of this generic appellation. With grapes coming from Santenay, Chassagne-Montrachet, and Puligny-Montrachet, this wine exhibits a fresh, nutty nose and a toasty, minerally mouth with good balance and a nice hazelnut-laced finish. Revealing fresh floral and stony aromas, the 1995 Chassagne-Montrachet Vieilles Vignes possesses a fat, concentrated, minerally, and nutty fruit personality. Drink this silky-textured, medium- to full-bodied wine between now and 2002. A step up is the 1995 Puligny-Montrachet, which displays toasted and roasted notes on the nose followed by flavors of ripe, sweet fruits. Oily textured and somewhat dense, this medium- to full-bodied offering should be consumed over the near term. Displaying a slight golden hue to its robe, the 1995 Santenay Passetemps (which means "to pass the time") has rocky, metallic aromas and flavors of minerals and stones. Medium bodied, this wine can age for 6+ years but won't get better with time. From old vines (the vineyard was planted in 1957), the 1995 St. Aubin Les Charmois is a very muscular wine offering a nose of rocks and steel. The mouth is full of flint, stones, minerals, and nicely roasted fruits. Medium to full bodied, this appealingly rich wine should age well for 5 or 6 years. The 1995 Chassagne-Montrachet Les Baudines (planted in 1970–73) has a floral and minerally nose followed by light-bodied yet charming flavors of flowers and clean earth. It lacks the depth of fruit and concentration I would expect to see in a premier cru Chassagne from such a highly respected grower. Drink it over the next 4–5 years. Displaying deeply roasted fruits with nuts and minerals on the nose, the medium- to full-bodied 1995 Chassagne-Montrachet Les Embrazées has a well-crafted, tightly wound, toasted, smoky personality. Both Les Embrazées and the Chassagne-Montrachet Morgeot lack the length and complexity to be outstanding wines. The 1995 Chassagne-Montrachet Morgeot exhibits fresh, floral, and minerally aromas accompanied by superripe, slightly stony flavors. Medium to full bodied, it should be enjoyed over the next 6 years. In contrast, the 1995 Chassagne-Montrachet Vide Bourse is outstanding. Deriving its name from French for "empty change purse," this wine offers good value, especially for a burgundy. It reveals a stony and minerally nose, admirably extracted fruit, and concentrated flavors of stones and flint. This long and impressive, medium- to full-bodied offering should age well for 7–8 years. Morey's most impressive wine is the 1995 Chassagne-Montrachet Les Caillerets. It displays deeply embedded steely and minerally aromas, as well as floral, flinty flavors. This beautifully concentrated, well-structured, full-bodied, delicious wine will age effortlessly for 10 years. Almost as impressive, the 1995 Puligny-Montrachet Le Truffière (a beautiful but little-known vineyard nestled high on the hill near Blagny) offers an enticing nose of earth tones and stones, followed by fat, beautifully ripe, concentrated, densely packed tropical and roasted fruit flavors. Impeccably balanced and long, this full-bodied wine should be drunk between 2000 and 2007.

I was tremendously impressed with the quality of Morey's 1996s. While I generally had a slight preference for most vignerons' 1995s because of that vintage's extraordinary concentration, I feel that 1996's crisp, focused, and vibrant profile married admirably well with Morey's rich, plump, and ripe winemaking style. These are some of the finest wines I have tasted from this consistently first-rate estate.

Bernard Morey, one of Burgundy's star white wine producers, is not above changing his winemaking techniques if he thinks it will ameliorate his wines. Over the course of the last few years Morey has 1) reduced the amount of *bâtonnage* he performs, 2) elongated his *élevages,* and 3) has delayed his first racking by 3 months (previously done in April, the wines are now racked in July). He believes longer *élevages* allow the wines to obtain the "richness and fat" he used to get from extensive *bâtonnage* without the "overpowering lees flavors." Interestingly, I detected distinct lees flavors in only two of his wines, the Chassagne-Montrachet Vieilles Vignes and the Puligny-Montrachet.

Morey has been a vigneron-*négociant* since 1989.

The 1996 Bourgogne Chardonnay is smoke and toast scented. It has a buttery, creamy, and light- to medium-bodied character with white berry flavors. Lovely to drink—or quaff!—today, it will maintain its peak for another 2 years. Displaying mineral and charred oak aromas, the 1996 Chassagne-Montrachet Vieilles Vignes is a delicious, lively, medium-bodied, and well-balanced wine. Leesy and tangy berry flavors can be discerned in this well-crafted and fun (yes, some wines just make me smile because they're fun to taste or drink) offering. Anticipated maturity: now–2003. The 1996 Puligny-Montrachet has a sweet honeysuckle blossom-imbued nose and a medium-bodied, oily-textured, and fat personality. Flowers, candied white fruits and leesy flavors are found in this surprisingly plump (where's 1996's acidity?) offering. I suggest drinking it before 2002. Produced from vines planted in 1952, the 1996 Santenay Passetemps has a minerally and toasted oak-laced nose. On the palate, it is rich, layered, medium-bodied, thickly textured, and filled with complex, ripe, and concentrated white pear, chalk, and oak flavors. It should hold its peak through 2002.

Both of Bernard Morey's St. Aubins are impressive and offer very good values. The 1996 St. Aubin En Remilly has almond and floral aromas as well as a focused, medium-bodied, silky-textured, and concentrated character. Tangy berries, nuts, stones, and fresh butter can be found in its flavor profile. Anticipated maturity: now–2003. Aromatically, the 1996 St. Aubin Les Charmois displays ripe white fruits and toasty oak. On the palate, this outstanding wine is medium to full bodied, oily textured, extremely well balanced, and filled with minerals, pears, vanilla beans, and spices. It should be at its peak between 2001 and 2005.

The delicious 1996 Chassagne-Montrachet Les Baudines has an earth- and mushroom-scented nose as well as a tangy, thick, and medium to full body filled with concentrated flavors of pears, underbrush, and lees. This wine is well balanced and armed with an admirably long finish and will evolve beautifully with cellaring. Anticipated maturity: 2000–2005. The 1996 Chassagne-Montrachet Les Embrazées is one of the finest Embrazées I've tasted from Bernard Morey. It combines the depth and power generally associated with this vineyard with this vintage's trademark acidity, creating a profound wine with outstanding ripeness, elegance, refinement, and focus. Aromatically, it reveals earthy floral scents, and its medium- to full-bodied flavor profile is packed with minerals, white flowers, pears, and anise. This silky-textured, complex, and concentrated wine has great balance and a pure, delineated finish. Anticipated maturity: 2001–2006. Another vineyard that greatly benefited from 1996's telltale acidity is the Chassagne-Montrachet La Maltroie. Exhibiting a nose reminiscent of ripe white berries soaked in fresh cream, this wine offers a medium- to full-bodied, bright, and exciting character. Flavors of pear compote, white flowers, and toasty oak are found in this deep, layered, sweet, and vibrant wine. It should be at its best between 2001 and 2006. As with the preceding Chassagnes, the 1996 Chassagne-Montrachet Morgeot was aged in 30% new oak barrels. It displays earth and underbrush notes on the nose and a deep, tangy, mineral laden, and thickly textured (almost milklike) core. This wine, like many from this *terroir,* has a red wine mouth-feel. Concentrated, complex, and persistent, it will develop gorgeously with cellaring. Anticipated maturity: 2001–2006. Produced from extremely old vines, the 1996 Chassagne-Montrachet Vide Bourse reveals a maltball-scented nose and a tangy, vibrant, highly defined, and concentrated personality packed with pears, minerals, and toasty oak spices from the 40% new oak barrels it was aged in. This medium- to full-bodied and silky-textured wine may ultimately deserve a higher score. It should be at its peak of maturity between 2002 and 2008. The 1996 Chassagne-Montrachet Les Caillerets is an exquisite wine. Oak, mineral, pear, flower blossom, and smokelike aromas give way to a precise, pure, defined, complex, and refined character. This concentrated and extraordinarily balanced wine beguiles with its lively minerals, stones, and white fruit flavors, which appear to linger on the palate indefinitely. This superb offering will be at its peak between 2003 and 2008.

The fabulous 1996 Puligny-Montrachet Le Truffière displays earth, underbrush, and truffle aromas as well as an awesomely precise, balanced, and elegant personality. This feminine wine is highly concentrated, bright, and refined and has magnificent definition of mineral, stone, and spiced pear flavors intermingled with tangy lemon notes for additional complexity. Anticipated maturity: 2003–2010. I am concerned about the preponderance of oak aromas and flavors in the 1996 Meursault Genevrières Cuvée Baudot (Hospice de Beaune). On the palate, it reveals huge concentration of fruit, layers of nuts and flowers, and a fat, full-bodied, and thick character that currently lacks definition. While I believe it will develop a more harmonious personality with time, I am not convinced it will ever integrate the over-powering oak.

Bernard Morey fashioned an extraordinary Bâtard-Montrachet in 1996. Perfumed, floral, and candied almond aromas are followed by a mouth-coatingly rich, thick, and expansive personality jam-packed with hazelnut cream, poached and spiced pears, anise, and white peaches. This powerful, full-bodied, and broad-shouldered offering is explosive and extremely well focused and possesses an impressive persistence on the finish. Wow! Anticipated maturity: 2002–2010. Bravo!

DOMAINE JEAN-MARC MOREY (CHASSAGNE-MONTRACHET)

1996	Chassagne-Montrachet	D	86
1995	Chassagne-Montrachet	D	86
1996	Chassagne-Montrachet Les Caillerets	E	89
1995	Chassagne-Montrachet Les Caillerets	E	91
1995	Chassagne-Montrachet Les Champs Gains	E	90+
1996	Chassagne-Montrachet Les Chaumées	?	88+
1995	Chassagne-Montrachet Les Chaumées	E	90+
1996	Chassagne-Montrachet Les Chenevottes	E	88+
1995	Chassagne-Montrachet Les Chenevottes	E	88
1996	St. Aubin Les Charmois	?	88
1995	St. Aubin Les Charmois	D	87
1995	Santenay Les Cornières	D	85

An extremely jovial and engaging fellow, Jean-Marc Morey was leaving a week after my tasting to visit Bali. Not the kind of trip one typically expects from someone living in a small rural farming village! His wines are close in style to his brother Bernard's, but less powerful, with slightly higher acidity. Yields were down by a third for Jean-Marc Morey's 1995s.

Revealing mineral and honeysuckle aromas, the 1996 Chassagne-Montrachet has an attractive, light- to medium-bodied, well-defined, and mineral-flavored character. It will be at its best if consumed before 2001. The aromatically floral 1996 St. Aubin Les Charmois is a rich, medium- to full-bodied, focused, and feminine wine with supple layers of tangy minerals and buttery fruits. It should be drunk by 2002. The 1996 Chassagne-Montrachet Les Chaumées displays deep mineral aromas and an impressive richness in its silky, medium- to full-bodied, and ample personality. Honeyed and stonelike flavors are found in this feminine, round, and well-focused wine. Anticipated maturity: now–2003. Unyielding and closed the day I tasted it, the 1996 Chassagne-Montrachet Les Chenevottes exhibits excellent richness, a medium- to full-bodied, oily, liquid mineral- and stone-filled core, and great focus. Anticipated maturity: now–2005. The 1996 Chassagne-Montrachet Les Caillerets reveals rich, deep mineral aromas and a ripe, silky, mouth-coating, well-crafted, medium to full body. Its flavor profile is composed of stones and chalk. Drink it between now and 2006.

Revealing steely and minerally aromas, the 1995 Santenay Les Cornières reveals notes of crisp green apples with citrus fruits in the finish. This light- to medium-bodied wine is not made for cellaring, and I recommend drinking it before the turn of the century. Reminiscent of the Santenay, but with an oily texture and more earthy flavors, the stone-scented 1995 St.

Aubin Les Charmois is a well-made, medium-bodied wine that will age, but why wait? The 1995 Chassagne-Montrachet village offering displays aromas of citrus fruits and minerals, buttery, stony flavors, and an appealing silky texture. I would have liked the wine more if it did not have a tangy acid kick toward the end (blocked malo?). Drink it over the next 2–3 years. A big step up is the 1995 Chassagne-Montrachet Les Chaumées. Toasted and roasted sweet fruit aromas vie for attention. In the mouth, there is good extract, as well as concentrated, powerful, thick fruit. Medium to full bodied, this long wine should be consumed between now and 2004. After that offering, the 1995 Chassagne-Montrachet Les Chenevottes was a bit of a letdown. The nose, a beautiful combination of nuts, stones, and salty minerals, is followed by excellent delineation of steely fruit, and then everything comes to a halt. What started out as an outstanding wine ended so abruptly that I was caught by surprise. Drink it between now and 2003. The 1995 Chassagne-Montrachet Les Champs Gains did not share the same problem. Aromatically spicy, it reveals a fabulous oily texture with well-extracted, minerally, stony, and sweet fruits and a long, spicy finish. As with his brother Bernard, this estate's best wine is the Chassagne-Montrachet Les Caillerets. With beautiful direction, the 1995 comes on the scene like gangbusters. It explodes out of the glass with structured steeliness, minerals, and stones. In the mouth, it is more of the same, but with a roasted spice component that is appealing. This is a wine whose sound delineation will repay good storage by evolving beautifully. Cellar it for at least 5 years and drink it over the following 6–8.

DOMAINE MARC MOREY (CHASSAGNE-MONTRACHET)

1996	Bâtard-Montrachet	EEE	94
1995	Bâtard-Montrachet	EE	93
1996	Chassagne-Montrachet	D	88
1996	Chassagne-Montrachet Les Caillerets	E	88+
1995	Chassagne-Montrachet Les Caillerets	E	87+
1996	Chassagne-Montrachet Les Chenevottes	D	89
1995	Chassagne-Montrachet Les Chenevottes	D	89
1996	Chassagne-Montrachet Morgeot	E	92
1995	Chassagne-Montrachet Morgeot	E	92
1996	Chassagne-Montrachet Les Vergers	E	90
1995	Chassagne-Montrachet Les Vergers	D	90
1996	Chassagne-Montrachet Les Virondots	D	92+
1995	Chassagne-Montrachet Les Virondots	D	91
1996	Puligny-Montrachet Les Pucelles	EE	93+
1995	Puligny-Montrachet Les Pucelles	EE	91

Due to the efforts of Bernard Mollard, Marc Morey's son-in-law and this domaine's director, this estate has made more progress than any other in Chassagne-Montrachet. I first noticed the changes taking place with the 1992 vintage, and I am ecstatic to report that the overall quality continues to increase. Mollard is convinced that low yields are the key to making great wines; therefore he prunes his vines remorselessly throughout the year. Mollard ages his wines in only 30% new oak . . . and they handle it beautifully.

The 1996 vintage is no exception to this trend, as Bernard Mollard crafted his finest wines to date. Mollard's malos started late (normal for this vintage), but only after he heated the cellar. With the 1996 vintage he stirred the lees once a week until the malos started because he felt the high levels of acidity needed the additional body provided by this *bâtonnage*. All of Mollard's wines were bottled in September 1997.

The 1996 Chassagne-Montrachet possesses an extremely minerally, earthy, and smoky nose and reveals excellent richness, focus, and toasted almond flavors in its light- to medium-bodied, silky-textured core. Drink it over the next 5 years. As with all his premiers crus, Mollard ages his Chassagne-Montrachet Les Chenevottes in 25%–30% new oak barrels. It displays an elegant sautéed mushroom- and mineral-infused nose as well as a refined, medium-bodied, crisply textured, well-defined, stone, flower, and earth-flavored palate. Anticipated maturity: now–2004. The 1996 Chassagne-Montrachet Les Vergers reveals stone, white flower, and ripe fruit scents as well as a broad, expansive, medium-bodied, structured core filled with liquid mineral and floral flavors. This delicious wine has exemplary focus and balance. It should be at its best between now and 2006. Produced from 7-year-old vines, the 1996 Chassagne-Montrachet Les Caillerets displays fresh aromas of stone and citrus fruit. Moreover, it offers refined, bright, and well-delineated mineral, pear, and earth flavors in its medium-bodied, focused, and lively mouth. This delicious wine lacks the depth, breadth, and hold to be outstanding (most probably because the vines are so young) but is certainly excellent. Anticipated maturity: now–2004.

Mollard's outstanding 1996 Chassagne-Montrachet Morgeot is crafted from 40-year-old vines. It reveals deep and intense earth scents and an oily, thick, rich, chewy, medium- to full-bodied, liquid mineral-filled core that is sustained throughout its admirably long finish. Its exquisite depth and broad, almost mouth-coating flavor profile is given focus by its superb balance. Anticipated maturity: 2001–2008. While the 1996 Chassagne-Montrachet Les Virondots was the qualitative equal to the Morgeot when I tasted it, I feel it has the potential to evolve into a more complete wine. Its bouquet offers white flowers and perfume. The wine is silky textured, harmonious, medium to full bodied, and feminine with mineral flavors. It should be cellared for 4–5 years and consumed before 2010. I was impressed by Domaine Marc Morey's 1996 Puligny-Montrachet Les Pucelles' floral, orange peel, and perfume-laced aromas. On the palate, it soars with intense precision and definition of flavors (stones, ripe white fruits, and anise) yet enthralls with its richness, depth, medium to full body, and thick personality as well as its awesome length. If wines were to be compared to people, this Pucelles would be a ballerina because of its combination of power and sublime elegance. Anticipated maturity: 2002–2010. The 1996 Bâtard-Montrachet, like many wines from this fabulous vineyard, benefited from the purity and delineation the vintage's hallmark zesty acidity provided. Its nose exhibits outstanding richness and admirable depth of ripe fruit and perfumed flowers. It has full body, an oily texture, and an intensely refined yet powerful and broad core of earthy, floral, and minerally flavors. This wine's exemplary finish reveals crystal-clear purity and appears to last at least 40 seconds. It should be at its best between 2002 and 2010.

Surprisingly, the delicious 1995 Chassagne-Montrachet Les Caillerets is made from 6-year-old vines. Elegant floral aromas are followed by nutty, minerally, and stony flavors. This silky-textured wine will give pleasure from its release to 2002. In 20 years, when these vines have taken on some age, this will be an even more outstanding source for Caillerets. The 1995 Chassagne-Montrachet Les Chenevottes displays a buttery and minerally nose followed by a thick, oily-textured mouth possessing good intensity and structure. This medium- to full-bodied wine will age gracefully for 7–9 years. Produced from 40-year-old vines, and exhibiting scents of white flowers and minerals, the outstanding 1995 Chassagne-Montrachet Les Vergers is a fat, ripe, elegant wine. With intense, concentrated red berries, star anise, and buttery touches, this rich wine should be drunk between its release and 2003. Even better, the deeply layered, white flower-scented 1995 Chassagne-Montrachet Les Virondots exhibits a fabulous silky texture, great structure, and a deft touch of oak. Spicy and floral in the mouth, this wine should be held for 3–4 years and consumed over the subsequent 5–7. A textbook example of its *terroir*, the 1995 Chassagne-Montrachet Morgeot displays an intensely stony and minerally nose with an elegant, superminerally personality. This truly outstanding wine needs 3–4 years of cellaring and can be enjoyed over the following 6–8 years. With a nose of toasty, buttery fruit, the 1995 Puligny-Montrachet Les Pucelles exhibits gorgeously concentrated, roasted and baked sweet fruits. This oily-textured, medium- to full-bodied wine provides immediate pleasure, and it can be held for 5+ years. One of the most elegant 1995 Bâtard-Montrachets I tasted, Marc Morey's offering bursts from the glass with deep, forward, sweet, roasted and toasted fruits. Intense and concentrated, this huge, richly textured wine rolls across the palate with gobs of thick toasty fruit. Full bodied and long, this gem can be enjoyed in the near term or held for 10+ years.

DOMAINE PIERRE MOREY (MEURSAULT)

1996	Bâtard-Montrachet	EEE	(93–95+)
1995	Bâtard-Montrachet	EEE	(89–92+)
1996	Bourgogne Aligoté	B	86
1995	Bourgogne Aligoté	C	73
1996	Bourgogne Blanc	D	(86–87)
1995	Bourgogne Blanc	D	(83–86)
1996	Meursault	D	(87–88+)
1995	Meursault	E	(85–88)
1996	Meursault Perrières	EE	(91–93)
1995	Meursault Perrières	EE	(88–91)
1996	Meursault Tessons	E	(88–91)
1995	Meursault Tessons	E	(86–89)

Pierre Morey is a pensive, quiet man. It is obvious a few minutes after you meet him that he is not given to making rash decisions. He likes to ponder the pros and cons. After a few years of implementing Anne-Claude Leflaive's decision to switch to biodynamic viticulture at the Domaine Leflaive, Morey is still considering whether to do it at his estate. Currently he employs organic farming methods, but he is reluctant to go further because of the high cost.

Produced from 47-year-old vines, Morey's 1996 Bourgogne Aligoté has smoky spice aromas and a tangy, well-balanced, nicely ripened, and medium-bodied character. This well-crafted wine should be drunk within the next 3 years. The 1996 Bourgogne Blanc reveals a lively nut- and anise-scented nose followed by a juicy white peach and mineral-filled medium body. This wine is tangy, rich, focused, and racy and should provide delicious drinking between now and 2002.

Exhibiting dry mineral and stone aromas, the 1996 Meursault is a rich, fresh, structured, beautifully balanced, and medium-bodied offering filled with toasted hazelnuts. This is one of the rare village wines that will handsomely repay cellaring. It should be at its best between 2001 and 2004. The 1996 Meursault Tessons has deep almond and smoky aromatics. Rich, broad, deep, medium to full bodied, and highly delineated, this wine has lively stones, minerals, and rock dust in its bone-dry flavor profile. Anticipated maturity: 2002–2006. Revealing an intense nose of minerals and stones, the fabulous 1996 Meursault Perrières has awesome depth, richness, and delineation. This elegant wine is packed with gravel, smoke, and toasted nuts and possesses a medium- to full-bodied, silky-textured, and highly concentrated personality. It should be consumed between 2004 and 2010.

Pierre Morey's *en métayage* Bâtard-Montrachet is produced from a parcel that runs parallel

to the small road that separates Bâtard-Montrachet from Montrachet. All its vines are between 15 and 35 meters from Montrachet, within the Puligny-Montrachet commune but on
the Chassagne end of the vineyard. The 1996 displays an extravagant nose of stones and
gravel as well as a powerful, exquisitely rich, and broad character. This full-bodied, amazingly deep, ripe, complex, and concentrated wine is filled with candied peaches, minerals,
hazelnuts, anise, and toasty oak nuances. Its thick and oily flavor profile is perfectly balanced
by a lively and slightly tangy acidity. This stunner will be at its best from 2004 to 2012.

The 1995 Bourgogne Aligoté reveals a surprising cheesy and sweaty nose. Pleasing flavors
of herbs with a tangy and sharp citrus aspect cannot make up for its offputting bouquet. The
1995 Bourgogne Blanc is a medium-bodied wine with nice Chardonnay fruit, good structure,
and decent length. I was impressed with the 1995 Meursault's staying power and length. Flavors of tangy, nutty fruits are found in this medium-bodied wine. These first three wines are
made for early drinking and will not repay years of cellaring. Full bodied and well balanced,
the 1995 Meursault Tessons exhibits a fat, oily texture. It will drink well early but will improve over the course of 5–6 years. The medium- to full-bodied 1995 Meursault Perrières
possesses the necessary structure and fullness of fruit for aging, as well as an attractive minerality and nuttiness. Drink it between now and 2008. Made from yields of 18
hectoliters/hectare (just over 1 ton per acre), the 1995 Bâtard-Montrachet offers a thick, oily
texture and chewy, roasted fruits with a nice touch of minerals. It needs 4 years of cellaring
and will last for 10.

DOMAINE MOREY-BLANC (MEURSAULT)

1996	Meursault	D	(87–89)
1995	Meursault	D	(85–87)
1996	Meursault Les Bouchères	E	(88–90+)
1996	Meursault Les Charmes	EE	(90–92)
1995	Meursault Les Charmes	E	(87–89+)
1996	Meursault Les Genevrières	EE	(90–92)
1995	Meursault Les Genevrières	E	(89–92)
1996	Meursault Les Narvaux	E	(88–90)
1995	Meursault Les Narvaux	E	(86–89)
1996	Montrachet	EEE	(93–96)
1996	St. Aubin Les Combes	D	(86–88)
1995	St. Aubin Les Combes	D	(84–87)

Morey-Blanc is the name of Pierre Morey's *négociant* firm (Blanc being his wife's maiden
name). For fiscal and legal reasons, Morey had to separate his wines from those he purchased from the outside as a *négociant*. He is assisted by the young and dynamic Christophe
Chauvel, who seems to be very eager to learn whatever Pierre Morey will teach him. They
have fashioned a first-rate lineup of 1996 whites, including an outstanding Montrachet.

The 1996 St. Aubin Les Combes has a white fruit-filled nose and a tangy, impressively
ripe, medium-bodied, and thick personality packed with minerals and candied lemons.
Drink it over the next 4 years. Morey-Blanc's excellent 1996 Meursault possesses super aromas of sweet white fruits and minerals as well as a broad, creamy, medium to full body. Its
admirable depth, ripeness, and zesty flavor profile reveals hazelnuts, mandarin peels, and almonds. Anticipated maturity: now–2003. Displaying smoky nut scents and excellent richness, the 1996 Meursault Narvaux is a wide, medium- to full-bodied, oily, yet refined and

precise wine jam-packed with lemons, minerals, and sweet pears. Its powerful flavors linger on the palate for close to 30 seconds. Anticipated maturity: 2000–2005. The first-rate 1996 Meursault Les Bouchères is a much more feminine wine. Aromatically, it offers minerals and nuts, and on its complex, silky, and medium- to full-bodied palate there are layers of flowers, wild mushrooms, lemons, and toast. This well-balanced and elegant wine should be at its peak from 2001 to 2005. Exhibiting a delightful and deep nose of flowers, nuts, and minerals, the 1996 Meursault Les Charmes has great breadth and depth to its character. This is a medium- to full-bodied, refined, silky, and complex wine with tons of ripe honeysuckle blossoms, liquid minerals, and pears. Anticipated maturity: 2003–2007. Equally outstanding, the 1996 Meursault Les Genevrières reveals beguiling aromas of minerals and sweet white fruits. It is a powerful, full-bodied, large, deep, and oily wine with toasted hazelnut, stone, candied almond, and white peach flavors. This beautifully balanced and complex offering should be at its peak from 2003 to 2007.

Pierre Morey was heartbroken that he was unable to offer a Montrachet in 1995—he said no Montrachets were available for sale that were up to his standards and that therefore it was the first vintage in which his *négociant* house did not produce one. In 1996, however, Morey secured quality juice on which to apply his winemaking magic. Exhibiting a stunning nose of smoked pork, liquid minerals, and honeysuckle, Morey-Blanc's 1996 Montrachet has awesome richness, layered depth and exquisite ripeness to its personality. Loads of stones, gravel, honeysuckle, and spicy oak can be found in this opulent, full-bodied, powerful, intricate, superbly refined, and extraordinarily long wine. This gem's harmony, grace, and muscle assure that it will age admirably well. Anticipated maturity: 2005–2015.

The 1995 St. Aubin Les Combes has floral (green), earthy, and minerally aromas, a fine texture, and crisp flavors of steel and flint. Light to medium bodied, this wine is made for near-term drinking. Revealing a nose of nuts and minerals, and fat-textured, tangy, nutty flavors, the clean, fresh, medium-bodied village 1995 Meursault can be drunk immediately upon release or held for up to 5 years. The 1995 Meursault Les Narvaux's appealing blossoming honeysuckle aromas are followed by a silky-textured, nutty-flavored wine with a tangy, floral finish. This medium-bodied Meursault possesses the structure to last for up to 10 years. Displaying an extremely elegant nose filled with white flowers and honeysuckle blossoms, the 1995 Meursault Les Charmes' corpulently textured mouth is pierced by floral and nutty fruits. Medium to full bodied, this wine has a long finish and a structure that will support cellaring for up to a decade. The 1995 Meursault Les Genevrières had a muted nose, but its extremely spicy and lively palate feel, with a faint touch of minerals, demonstrated this medium- to full-bodied wine's quality. Hold it for 4–5 years and then drink it over the following 6–8.

DOMAINE MICHEL NIELLON (CHASSAGNE-MONTRACHET)

1997	Bâtard-Montrachet	EEE	93
1996	Bâtard-Montrachet	EEE	99
1995	Bâtard-Montrachet	EE	93
1996	Chassagne-Montrachet	D	89+
1995	Chassagne-Montrachet	D	89+
1997	Chassagne-Montrachet Les Champs Gain	E	90
1996	Chassagne-Montrachet Les Champs Gain	E	92
1995	Chassagne-Montrachet Les Champs Gain	D	92
1996	Chassagne-Montrachet Les Chaumées	E	95

1997 Chassagne-Montrachet Les Chenevottes	E	91+
1996 Chassagne-Montrachet Clos St. Jean	E	94
1997 Chassagne-Montrachet Clos de la Maltroie	E	89
1996 Chassagne-Montrachet Clos de la Maltroie	E	95
1997 Chassagne-Montrachet Les Vergers	E	88+?
1996 Chassagne-Montrachet Les Vergers	E	96
1995 Chassagne-Montrachet Les Vergers	E	95+
1997 Chevalier Montrachet	EEE	92+
1996 Chevalier Montrachet	EEE	99
1995 Chevalier Montrachet	EE	96+

How good is Michel Niellon? An extraordinary winemaker, he is, in my opinion, the finest in Chassagne-Montrachet and one of the world's five best producers of Chardonnay. My heart temporarily stopped beating when he announced that he was "retired." It started functioning again only because he went on to say that he intended to continue working indefinitely (with his two sons-in-law), irrespective of his official classification vis-à-vis the French government.

Obtaining winemaking information from Niellon is exceedingly difficult. His response to questions is, more often than not, a shrug of the shoulders and a smile (a disarming technique he shares with Jean-François Coche, also one of the world's finest makers of Chardonnay). The sum total of what I have been able to learn from Niellon is that he rarely stirs the lees, uses 20% new oak barrels on his wines, and has never acidified. His wines are always bottled early—in the August following the vintage.

Niellon, like many of his forthright colleagues, described the 1997 whites as "delicious and easy to drink." No hyperbole at this address.

In the corner of Michel Niellon's cellar stands a barrel on which he places the bottles he serves visitors. When I arrived for my annual tasting, Niellon did what he always does—he moved those bottles to the floor and pulled new, unopened ones from the stacks awaiting shipping. To my shock they were painfully closed and reeked of sulfur. After some prodding, Niellon acquiesced and allowed me to taste from the wines that had been opened for a few hours. Readers take note: these comments are from bottled wines that have been opened and had benefited from exposure to air (with the exception of the Vergers).

The 1997 Chassagne-Montrachet Clos de la Maltroye offers vibrant aromas of minerals, stones, flowers, and citrus fruits. This is a well-focused, silky-textured wine with lemony minerals, traces of superripe white fruit flavors, and a long finish. Drink it over the next 5+ years. Offering tangy lemon and mineral aromas, the 1997 Chassagne-Montrachet Les Champs Gain is well balanced and medium to full bodied. This wine is beautifully delineated and has precise clay, earth, stone, and anise flavors and a velvety-textured personality. It is rich and dense, yet Niellon somehow maintained its outstanding balance. Anticipated maturity: now–2005. There were no previously opened bottles of the 1997 Chassagne-Montrachet Les Vergers, so I had to taste one that was overpowered by sulfur. After a good deal of cajoling, the wine revealed aromas of stones, gravel, minerals, and crisp pears. The sulfur had tightened up the palate, yet candied lemon peels, poached pears, and a richly thick texture could be discerned. My inclination is that (with air, if readers intend to open this wine in the next year) this wine will certainly merit a rating in the upper range of excellence. Drink it over the next 5 years. The 1997 Chassagne-Montrachet Les Chenevottes has floral red berry aromas and a deeply rich yet balanced personality. This offering is filled with delightful waves of minerals, flint, chalk, lemons, and crisp pears. Its medium body is beautifully delineated and concentrated and has admirable persistence. Anticipated maturity: now–2006+.

Both of Niellon's grands crus are oustanding in 1997. The Chevalier-Montrachet reveals superb ripeness in its expressive, mineral, and chalk-packed nose. This fabulous offering is medium bodied, rich, concentrated, and beautifully focused and has mouthwatering mineral flavors that last throughout its extended and bone-dry finish. Anticipated maturity: 2002–2009. Sadly, Niellon plans to rip out his parcel of Bâtard-Montrachet after the 2000 harvest. Planted in 1928, these old vines have produced numerous stunning wines. The 1997 is certainly one of the finest Bâtards of the vintage. It offers hyperripe pear and apple aromas, as well as a highly concentrated and extracted core of fruit. This is an extremely profound wine, with intense honeyed fruitcake flavors as well as an opulent, viscous, and almost flabby texture. If it had better balance, there is no telling how high my score could have gone. Drink it over the next 5–6 years.

Niellon is reluctant to pass judgment on a vintage until the wine has been in the bottle for several years. However, he commented that the 1996s are "very lively without being disagreeable" and are similar to his 1993s, "but with fruit and more body." Malos were slow to start (a story heard throughout the Côte) and lasted an abnormally long time.

With the exception of my visit to Domaine Coche-Dury, I cannot recall having ever tasted such an extraordinary lineup of young white burgundies. I left Niellon's cellar yearning for more.

The potentially outstanding 1996 Chassagne-Montrachet has smoke, mineral, and honeysuckle aromas. Its intense attack is followed by a deep, powerful, liquid mineral, and flowerfilled, silky, yet tangy medium body. Anticipated maturity: now–2004. The 1996 Chassagne-Montrachet Les Champs Gains displays loads of stones and white flowers. On the palate, this concentrated, highly extracted, ample, and medium- to full-bodied wine delivers waves of liquid minerals and traces of oak nuances that linger in its admirable finish. It will be at its best between 2000 and 2006. I found sweet red cherries, smoke, and violets in the 1996 Chassagne-Montrachet Clos St. Jean's nose. It is one of those rare 1996 whites to have red fruit aromas, a characteristic I associate most frequently with the 1995 vintage. This wine has enormous intensity and an awesomely focused, powerful full body. Tons of flint, minerals, and seashells can be found in its broad and oily-textured character. Anticipated maturity: 2000–2008.

Satisfying both the intellect and hedonistic senses, the 1996 Chassagne-Montrachet Les Vergers has expressive floral, mineral, quince, and honeyed aromas. This oily-textured and incredibly powerful wine devours the taster with its liveliness, complexity, and superb depth. Stones, flint, tangy berries, Earl Grey tea, orange peels, and exciting touches of oak spice are found in the wine's full-bodied and highly focused character. Wow! Anticipated maturity: 2001–2010. Niellon's 1996 Chassagne-Montrachet Clos de la Maltroie displays a floral, honeysuckle-packed nose that leads to a massively intense attack filled with minerals, stones, gooseberries, lemon drops, and white flowers. This is a full-bodied, thickly textured, concentrated, racy, and tightly wound wine that should age effortlessly through 2009. In 1996 Niellon produced a Chassagne-Montrachet Les Chaumées (from a parcel he has taken on *en métayage*). Its elegant, feminine, white peach, and floral nose is followed by an explosive, fat, full-bodied, and fruit-filled personality. Thick layers of spiced pears, lychee nuts, minerals, gooseberries, and sweet new oak are found in this immensely rich wine. Anticipated maturity: 2000–2009.

Both of Niellon's grands crus are unbelievable, possessing everything I could hope for in a white wine. Are they candidates to merit perfect scores? Produced from vines planted in 1968 and 1972, the profound 1996 Chevalier Montrachet offers a mind-blowingly intricate, precise, and refined nose of minerals, chalk, rock dust, and flowers. On the palate, this breathtaking wine enthralls with its superbly defined and harmonious medium to full body.

Each time I raised the glass to my lips I found new flavors. Minerals, stones, gooseberry, plums, seashells, toast, raspberries, peaches, pears, honeysuckle blossoms, "champagne" currants, and flint can all be discerned in this silky, lovely, refined, and ethereal wine. Words simply cannot do it justice. Anticipated maturity: 2003–2012. The equally compelling 1996 Bâtard-Montrachet is produced from 49-year-old vines. This benchmark-setting wine has such deep richness on the nose, it almost instills awe in both the taster's heart and palate. Superripe fruits, white flowers, mulling spices, and sweet toast soar from the glass. A massive wine, this powerful, broad-shouldered, expansive, and mouth-coating monster managed to retain extraordinary elegance and delineation—a rare combination to achieve. Full bodied, it offers layers of hazelnuts, roasted peaches, liquid minerals, and candied pears as well as a seemingly unending finish. It is a grand-slam home run! Anticipated maturity: 2003–2012.

These are some of the most difficult Burgundy wines to purchase, as they are made in minuscule quantities. And not surprisingly, they boast an insatiable fan club. Although a quiet man, Niellon is passionate about his work and wines in general (his face lit up when he and his Alsatian wife spoke to me about a Tokay Pinot Gris they had recently tasted). He feels 1995 is a very good, rather than stellar, vintage. Niellon harvested early, starting on September 20, but the wines show surprisingly great ripeness and balance.

As one would expect from such a winemaking star, the 1995 Chassagne-Montrachet is a real winner. Deeply toasted aromas with sweet underlying fruit coated with butter waft from the glass. In the mouth, I found a fat, super oily-textured, ripe wine with waves of toasted and roasted fruit. If Niellon can make a village wine this good, why can't everybody else? The 1995 Chassagne-Montrachet Les Champs Gain, unlike the village Chassagne, needs time to reveal all it has to offer. Layers of buttered popcorn try to hide the toasty, smoky fruit. Fat and minerally, with superb balance, this beautifully structured, medium- to full-bodied wine should be held for 4–5 years.

I have retasted Niellon's 1995 Chassagne-Montrachet Les Vergers four times and have been blown away by this stunning wine from the king of Chassagne. It reveals intense liquid mineral, spice, and floral aromas and a fabulous, oily-textured, medium- to full-bodied, muscular, yet elegant personality of layered white fruits, stones, and nuts. In its core, it possesses the red berry sweetness that I attribute to the huge extract caused by high levels of *coulure* and *millerandage* in 1995. It should reach its peak in 2003 and hold it through 2008. Kudos!

The 1995 Bâtard-Montrachet sports a superb warm, enveloping spiciness on the nose, with faint touches of citrus fruit. Superdeep rolls of roasted fruits bathed in mulling spices can be found in this velvety-textured, full-bodied wine. The only thing that prevents the Bâtard from receiving even higher praise is a lack of balancing acidity. That is certainly not a problem in Niellon's Chevalier Montrachet, one of my trip's most profound bottles. An enticing, floral, superspicy nose with touches of stones and minerals compels the taster to raise the glass to his lips. In the mouth, an engulfing sweetness of spicy fruits married judiciously with new oak nearly blew my mind. This full-bodied wine combines refinement and elegance with power and brawn. Although remarkable, this is not a 15- or 20-year wine. It should be held for 3–4 years and enjoyed over the ensuing 8 years.

DOMAINE PERRAUD (ST. VÉRAN)

1997 Mâcon-Villages Les Roches Anciennes Vieilles Vignes Réserve	B	87
1997 St. Véran Les Crays Roses Réserve	C	89
1996 St. Véran Les Crays Roses Réserve	C	89
1995 St. Véran Les Crays Roses Réserve	D	89

Note: David Hinkle of North Berkeley Imports and Peter Vezan (an American wine broker based in Paris) had me taste both their cuvée and the one sold through the Cave Cooperative de Prissé. There was no comparison. Bottles labeled with the North Berkeley markings are a minimum of 2–3 points better than those without.

Made from grapes 75% barrel-fermented and the balance done in stainless steel, the 1995 St. Véran Les Crays Roses Réserve displays a buttery nose with crisp red berries and floral tones. In the mouth, this wine exhibits great ripeness and concentration, a deep, silky texture, and toasted, buttered red berries. Perraud's 1995 Les Crays Roses Réserve offers a pleasing mouthful of wine, as well as excellent value. Drink it between now and 2004.

Revealing aromas of minerals, white flowers, and smoke, the 1996 St. Véran Les Crays Roses Réserve is a delicious, medium- to full-bodied, silky-textured, and well-balanced offering. Its richly layered and concentrated character displays anise, spices, and gravel-like flavors. This is one of those wines that is so soft and appealing, I have to remind myself that I'm working so that I don't go into quaffing mode. An excellent value.

The 1997 Mâcon-Villages Les Roches Anciennes Vieilles Vignes Réserve has a delightfully ripe nose of white flowers and spiced pears. Medium bodied, mineral laden, fresh, and lively, this Mâcon will provide delicious drinking over the next 3 years. Revealing aromas reminiscent of stones and earth, the medium- to full-bodied 1997 St. Véran Les Crays Roses Réserve has excellent concentration, focus, and depth. Flavors of flint, chalk, and minerals can be discerned in this extremely well-crafted and intense wine. Anticipated maturity: now–2003+.

MAISON/DOMAINE JEAN PILLOT ET FILS (CHASSAGNE-MONTRACHET)

1995	Bourgogne Aligoté	B	86
1996	Chassagne-Montrachet Les Caillerets	D	91
1995	Chassagne-Montrachet Les Caillerets	E	91
1995	Chassagne-Montrachet Les Champs Gains	D	89
1996	Chassagne-Montrachet Les Chenevottes	D	87
1995	Chassagne-Montrachet Les Chenevottes	D	88+
1996	Chassagne-Montrachet Morgeot	D	89
1995	Chassagne-Montrachet Morgeot	D	90+
1996	Chassagne-Montrachet Les Vergers	D	88
1995	Chassagne-Montrachet Les Vergers	D	90
1995	Puligny-Montrachet	D	88
1996	Puligny-Montrachet Les Caillerets	EE	88

Sometimes these wines appear under the name of Jean Pillot's son, Jean-Marc Pillot, who is now responsible for the domaine. The wines are exactly the same as those listed. My first encounter with Pillot's wines was with the 1992 vintage. I remember a colleague of mine serving Pillot's 1992 Caillerets blind in the midst of other 1992 Chassagnes from the deities of this appellation. While it was not considered to be the best wine in the tasting, it certainly held its own and was by far the best value. The 1995s are better-made wines than the 1992s, which bodes well for the future.

Fresh and lively, the 1995 Bourgogne Aligoté possesses aromas of herbs and spice. This well-balanced, thick-textured, spicy wine will provide enjoyable drinking for 2–3 years after its release. A strong effort for a village wine, the light-bodied 1995 Puligny-Montrachet exhibits an earthy and stony nose. On the entry, this wine starts out slowly, then comes on strong with rolling, roasted fruits. Drink it over the next 5–6 years. Slightly better, the 1995 Chassagne-Montrachet Les Chenevottes reveals salty minerals on the nose, a silky texture, and a well-balanced, leesy, and lightly smoked mouth. Drink this medium-bodied wine between now and 2003. At this stage, the 1995 Chassagne-Montrachet Les Champs Gains has a totally muted nose, but in the mouth, it is fat textured and expressive, exhibiting deep flinty and salty minerals. This wine should be cellared for 4 years and drunk over the subsequent 5. An outstanding wine, the aromatically austere and minerally 1995 Chassagne-Montrachet Morgeot possesses a silky texture, powerful flavors of toasted nuts, and a long finish displaying sweet orange peels and stones. This medium- to full-bodied wine should be drunk between now and 2007. The full-bodied 1995 Chassagne-Montrachet Les Vergers reveals an appealing streak of mushrooms intermingled with citrus fruit in the nose, as well as a long, oaky, velvety mouth filled with minty fruits. Drink it between now and 2005. Pillot's top wine in 1995, the Chassagne-Montrachet Les Caillerets is aromatically unyielding, barely revealing an attractive stony component. This full-bodied, chewy-textured, minerally, flinty, spicy wine is complex and long. It should be drunk between 2000 and 2007.

Like many other growers (particularly I find in Chassagne-Montrachet), the Pillots are both an estate and a *négociant*. All of the domaine's 1996s were bottled prior to the 1997 harvest, and unlike many estates represented by Patrick Lesec, there are no special bottlings of these wines. Pillot's village wines, while well made, suffer from appearing overly commercial. This estate seems to be experimenting with a variety of winemaking techniques. For example, the Chassagne Chenevottes was fermented solely with indigenous yeasts, and the Puligny Caillerets was bottled unfiltered.

The 1996 Chassagne-Montrachet Les Chenevottes reveals almond, nut, and mineral aromas as well as a medium- to full-bodied, rich, broad, and expressive core of stones and assorted nut flavors. This wine would have merited a higher rating if its finish had not ended so abruptly. Drink it over the next 3 years. The same could be said about the 1996 Chassagne-Montrachet Les Vergers, whose mineral- and smoke-laced nose as well as its deep, tangy, dense, and medium- to full-bodied personality are fabulous. Mouthwatering flavors of liquid minerals, earth, and honeysuckle blossoms are cut short in this wine by a somewhat precipitous finish. Anticipated maturity: now–2003. Displaying earthy mineral scents, the 1996 Chassagne-Montrachet Morgeot is a creamy-textured and medium- to full-bodied offering filled with ripe pears, toasted hazelnuts, and stones. This excellent wine lingers on the palate, revealing appealing layers of crisp white peaches and minerals. Anticipated maturity: now–2004. This estate's top wine is the 1996 Chassagne-Montrachet Les Caillerets. Beguilingly rich, floral, and stone-laced aromas are followed by a concentrated, oily-textured, well-crafted, and expressive core of minerals, honeysuckle, candied lemons, and anise. Well structured yet seductive, this outstanding wine should be at its peak between 2001 and 2007.

The 1996 Puligny-Montrachet Les Caillerets has an extraordinarily complex nose of flowers, almonds, minerals, and oak spices. This wine's charmless flavor profile was unable to match the sensory pleasures I experienced from its aromatics. It possesses good ripeness, a medium to full body, and a velvety texture as well as loads of primary and sweet white fruit flavors. As much as its nose is intricate and compelling, its character is not. Anticipated maturity: now–2002.

DOMAINE PAUL PILLOT (CHASSAGNE-MONTRACHET)

1995	Bourgogne Blanc	C	83
1996	Chassagne-Montrachet Les Caillerets	E	89
1995	Chassagne-Montrachet Les Caillerets	D	91
1996	Chassagne-Montrachet Clos St. Jean	E	88

1995	Chassagne-Montrachet Clos St. Jean	D	89
1996	Chassagne-Montrachet La Grande Montagne	E	88
1995	Chassagne-Montrachet La Grande Montagne	D	89+
1996	Chassagne-Montrachet Les Grandes Ruchottes	E	89+
1995	Chassagne-Montrachet Les Grandes Ruchottes	D	90
1995	Chassagne-Montrachet Les Masures	D	87
1996	Chassagne-Montrachet La Romanée	EE	91+
1995	Chassagne-Montrachet La Romanée	E	91+
1995	St. Aubin Les Charmois	C	87+

The delicious 1996 Chassagne-Montrachet Clos St. Jean reveals a mineral-infused nose and a deep, medium-bodied, silky, lively, rich, and powerful character filled with stones, white flowers, and rock dust. Anticipated maturity: now–2005. Displaying sweet pear and white peach aromas, the 1996 Chassagne-Montrachet La Grande Montagne offers a thick and medium- to full-bodied personality. This wine has excellent richness and depth, with lovely lemon drop and mineral flavors, and would have certainly received an outstanding score if it were not for a marked dropoff in its midpalate. Is this a result of the vintage's propensity for high yields? It should be drunk between now and 2005. The 1996 Chassagne-Montrachet Les Grandes Ruchottes possesses earth, mineral, and red currant aromas. Its tightly wound, medium- to full-bodied core reveals impressive richness, ripe white fruits, tangy lemon zests, and metallic nuances. Complex and well balanced, it may ultimately deserve an outstanding score. Anticipated maturity: 2001–2007. Exhibiting a beautifully ripe and floral nose, Pillot's 1996 Chassagne-Montrachet Les Caillerets has all the attributes of an outstanding wine except for its continuity on the palate. As with the La Grande Montagne, this wine has a slight hollowness on the midpalate. This being said, I was impressed by its thick, ripe, highly focused, and complex medium to full body and its layers of stone, cardamom, and minerals. It should be consumed between now and 2004. The 1996 Chassagne-Montrachet La Romanée is a wonderful wine. Smoke and minerals can be discerned on its nose, followed by a wide, fat, medium- to full-bodied core of buttery stones, currants, sweet oak, and pears. Complex, concentrated, extremely well balanced, and defined, this wine possesses a midpalate as rich and full flavored as its attack and finish. Anticipated maturity: 2001–2008.

Revealing a lively, sweet, fruity nose, toasty, smoky tones in the mouth and good balance, the 1995 Bourgogne Blanc would have received a better score were it not for a slight bitterness to the back end. Muted on the nose, the austere 1995 St. Aubin Les Charmois offers flavors of minerals and stones and a good midpalate, structure, and length. Medium bodied and well delineated, this wine should be drunk within 4 years of its release. Equally good, the floral-scented 1995 Chassagne-Montrachet Les Masures is a medium-bodied wine filled with elegant flowers and flinty touches amid a silky texture. Drink it between now and 2003. Vinified in 50% wood and the balance in enamel tanks, the 1995 Chassagne-Montrachet Clos St. Jean has a good minerally sweetness and nice floral qualities to its nose. In the mouth, there are appealing red berry and toasty fruits as well as a liquid stonelike component, fine structure, and balance. Medium bodied, this wine should be consumed between now and 2005. With slightly muted aromas of minerals and flowers, the 1995 Chassagne-Montrachet La Grande Montagne possesses a silky texture and an explosion of ripe fruits and minerals. This medium- to full-bodied, well-balanced wine should age effortlessly for a decade or more. Aromatically floral and stony, the 1995 Chassagne-Montrachet Les Grandes Ruchottes displays candied red berries and well-defined floral qualities in the mouth. This medium- to full-bodied wine exhibits fine ripeness, good structure, and attractive length. Drink it between 2002 and 2009. The excellent, metallic-and-rock-scented 1995 Chassagne-Montrachet Les Caillerets is extremely oily and silky. It bursts from the glass with sweet toasty fruit, stones, and minerals. This medium-bodied, elegant wine will age beautifully for a decade. Pillot's top wine is the splendid 1995 Chassagne-Montrachet La Romanée, which exhibits an extremely deep minerality and smokiness in the nose. An explosion of sweet flowers, stones, and red currants greets the palate. This well-made, thick-textured, medium- to full-bodied wine needs to be cellared 2–3 years; it will drink well for 6–7.

DOMAINE DENIS POMMIER (POINCHY-CHABLIS)

1997 Chablis Beauroy	D	89

This small estate of 15 acres (6 hectares) has produced an excellent 1997 Chablis Beauroy. Its kinky nose—creamy, salty aromas reminiscent of smells found on a fishing boat—is followed by a medium-bodied personality filled with allspice, anise, minerals, and touches of oak. It is gorgeously ripe, well balanced, complex, and extremely spicy. Drink it over the next 5–6 years.

DOMAINE PONSOT (MOREY-ST.-DENIS)

1996 Morey-St.-Denis Clos des Monts Luisants	E	(86–88)

Ponsot has ripped out all the albino Pinot Noir (also known as Pinot Gouges) vines in favor of Chardonnay so that the 1996 Morey-St.-Denis Clos des Monts Luisants is produced from 30% Chardonnay and 70% from 75-year-old Aligoté vines. The 1996 stopped its fermentation with 30 grams of residual sugar and did not restart it until the 1997s were fermenting. When I visited, it had 1 gram of sugar left. Its sweet, white flower-laced, and slightly citrusy nose is followed by a tangy, medium- to full-bodied, and crisp core of candied almonds and minerals. It should be drunk between 2000 and 2006.

DOMAINE JACQUES PRIEUR (MEURSAULT)

1996 Beaune Clos de la Feguine	E	86
1995 Beaune Clos de la Feguine	D	86
1996 Chevalier-Montrachet	EEE	(91–93)
1995 Chevalier-Montrachet	EEE	95
1996 Corton-Charlemagne	EE	(93–95)
1995 Corton-Charlemagne	EE	93
1996 Meursault Clos de Mazeray	D	87
1995 Meursault Clos de Mazeray	D	88
1996 Meursault Perrières	EE	(92–94)
1995 Meursault Perrières	EE	91?
1996 Montrachet	EEE	(93–96)
1995 Montrachet	EEE	97+
1996 Puligny-Montrachet Les Combettes	E	(89–92)
1995 Puligny Montrachet Les Combettes	E	89+

Martin Prieur, this domaine's director, with the assistance of Nadine Goublin, Antonin Rodet's winemaker, has greatly raised the quality of this famed estate's wines. I was extremely impressed with Prieur's three top wines, the Meursault Perrières, Corton-

Charlemagne, and Montrachet, which are at a level attained only by the very best Burgundian estates. The gregarious, handsome, and ever-smiling Martin Prieur has reason to be proud of his work.

Produced from 6-year-old vines, the 1996 Beaune Clos de la Feguine reveals a ripe, sweet herbal tea-scented nose and a rich, plump, well-balanced, and medium-bodied character filled with ripe pear flavors. It will provide very good drinking over the next 3 years. The *monopole* (solely owned) 1996 Meursault Clos de Mazeray has a toasty oak-imbued nose and a delicious, masculine, medium- to full-bodied, and silky-textured core of earthy minerals, smoke, and stones. Anticipated maturity: now–2003.

The 1996 Puligny-Montrachet Les Combettes (aged in 50% new oak) displays a gorgeously perfumed and floral nose followed by an oily-textured, full-bodied, well-balanced, and feminine personality. This graceful yet powerful wine offers anise, pear, and spicy oak flavors that linger on its persistent finish. It should be at its best between 2000 and 2005. Prieur's superb 1996 Meursault Perrières exhibits floral and honeyed pear aromas and possesses a full-bodied, complex, rich, and velvety-textured character. Layers of rock dust, white flowers, gravel, and scrumptious oak notes (from 100% new oak barrels) can be discerned in its delicious, broad, and focused flavor profile. This fresh, profound, and magnificently crafted wine will be at its best between 2002 and 2007.

According to Jacques Prieur, the yields on the 1996 Corton-Charlemagne were lower than average because its south-facing vines had a successful early first flowering, but subsequent flowers were aborted by cool weather. Its mouthwatering, rich, and deep nose reveals marvelous ripeness (Prieur stated that the 1996 is the ripest Corton he has produced since he started with the 1992 vintage), sweet pears, white peaches, and minerals. On the palate, this massive, full-bodied, and thick wine boasts waves of superripe white fruits, earth, mineral, and toast flavors. It is an awesomely powerful yet focused offering that should age effortlessly. Anticipated maturity: 2002–2010. Prieur's small parcel (only 2 barrels—50 cases—produced in 1996) of Chevalier-Montrachet is located just over the Montrachet vineyard. Aged in 100% new oak, the 1996 exhibits tightly wound honeysuckle and rock dust aromas followed by a full-bodied, fresh, refined, powerful, and medium- to full-bodied core. Gravel, honey, and a deep minerality can be found in this well-crafted and outstanding wine. Anticipated maturity: 2002–2007. The 1996 Montrachet, while not quite at the level of this estate's 1995, is a spectacular wine. Its refined, ripe, and beguiling nose of flowers and minerals is followed by an intricate, highly delineated, silky-textured, and full-bodied personality. Complex and concentrated flavors of gravel, minerals, red currants, earth, chalk, and honeysuckle are found in this defined yet broadly structured offering. Its admirably long and focused finish revealed traces of sweet oak spice. It should be at its plateau of maturity between 2003 and 2012. Bravo!

Produced from extremely young vines (averaging 5 years old), the 1995 Beaune Clos de la Feguine reveals a smoke- and mineral-scented nose and a tangy, lively, medium-bodied personality with flavors of stones and candied citrus fruits. While the freshness and flavors of this wine are excellent, it does not have the length and staying power to merit a higher rating. I have no doubt that this steeply sloped and well-placed vineyard will produce first-rate white Beaunes after the vines mature. Drink it from now to 2000. The 1995 Meursault Clos de Mazeray (as with the previous wine, this is produced from a *monopole*, or solely owned, vineyard) displays aromas of fresh hazelnuts and sweet pears as well as a silky-textured, medium-bodied palate. This wine is packed with beautifully ripe, concentrated white fruits, nuts, and tangy smoke flavors and has an impressive length. Anticipated maturity: now–2003. Exhibiting fresh white peaches aromatically, the 1995 Puligny-Montrachet Les Combettes (harvested at a little over 1 ton of fruit per acre) possesses a lively, medium- to full-bodied, rich, well-balanced, and oily-textured character filled with concentrated red currants, flowers, and poached pears. This impressive offering should be at its best between now and 2005. Aged in

100% new oak barrels, the 1995 Meursault Perrières had a tight and muted nose the day of my tasting. However, it offers a fabulously deep and complex core of oak, minerals, grilled nuts, and ripe white fruits in its thick-textured, highly extracted full body. At this stage oak flavors dominate the wine's personality; hence the question mark. Anticipated maturity: now–2005.

From a parcel adjacent to Lalou Bize-Leroy's near the top of the Corton hillside (over Ladoix), Prieur's 1995 Corton-Charlemagne reveals highly expressive aromatics of deeply ripe fruits, vanilla, and toasty oak. Its extraordinary ripeness is again found in its driven, powerful, superbly extracted, and gorgeously balanced, red berry, floral, and peach flavor profile. This massive yet elegant wine has the necessary structure for years of cellaring but will also be fabulous young. Anticipated maturity: now–2010. Regrettably, only 50 cases of the magnificent Chevalier-Montrachet were produced in 1995. A tight but floral and minerally nose gives way to a magnificently delineated, silky-textured, full-bodied, and refined character with complex, layered minerals, stones, flowers, white pepper, baking spices, and touches of gingerbread for added complexity. This spectacular wine's amazingly long finish seems to be unending. It will be at its peak between 2002 and 2015. For those who can spend astronomical amounts of money, the sublime 1995 Montrachet (from a 1.5-acre parcel harvested at $1^1/_2$ tons of fruit per acre) is available in larger quantities, as 150 cases were produced. Aged in 100% new oak barrels and possessing extraordinarily rich aromatics of minerals, white peaches, flowers, and notes of vanilla, this massively endowed yet precisely refined powerhouse explodes on the palate with layered flavors of honeysuckle, stones, ripe peaches, spices, and sweet smoke. Full bodied, intense, and oily, this wine offers amazing richness, a virtually perfect balance, and a breathtaking length. It will provide prodigious drinking between 2005 and 2020. Bravo!

CHÂTEAU DE PULIGNY-MONTRACHET (PULIGNY-MONTRACHET)

1997	Bâtard-Montrachet	EEE	(88–92)
1996	Bâtard-Montrachet	EE	94
1997	Chassagne-Montrachet	D	(87–88)
1997	Chevalier-Montrachet	EEE	(93–94)
1996	Chevalier-Montrachet	EE	92
1995	Chevalier-Montrachet	EE	92
1997	Meursault	D	(86–88)
1997	Meursault Perrières	E	(89–91)
1996	Meursault Perrières	D	91+
1995	Meursault Perrières	D	91
1997	Meursault Poruzots	E	(87–88)
1996	Meursault Poruzots	D	90
1995	Meursault Poruzots	D	88
1997	Montrachet	EEE	(93–95)
1996	Montrachet	EEE	93+
1997	Puligny-Montrachet	D	(87–88)
1995	Puligny-Montrachet	D	87
1997	Puligny-Montrachet Les Chalumeaux	E	(88–90)
1997	Puligny-Montrachet Les Folatières	E	(89–91)

1996 Puligny-Montrachet Les Folatières	E	92
1995 Puligny-Montrachet Les Folatières	D	89+
1997 Puligny-Montrachet La Garenne	E	(89–91)
1996 Puligny-Montrachet La Garenne	D	91
1995 Puligny-Montrachet La Garenne	D	91
1997 St. Aubin En Remilly	D	(88–89)
1996 St. Aubin En Remilly	C	88
1995 St. Aubin En Remilly	C	87

This 20-hectare (50-acre) estate has vines (both red and white) spread out over 21 appellations. Purchased a few years ago by a major French bank, the Crédit Foncier de France, the Château de Puligny-Montrachet has undergone major renovations, including the construction of a modern, temperature-controlled winery. Winemaker Jacques Montagnon, a young and dynamic man, is dedicated to making this estate one of Puligny's best. He believes in dropping yields, working the lees to extract as much flavor and sweetness as he can, using new oak barrels whenever possible (40%–50% depending on the wine), and bottling as late as the wine allows. For the 1995 vintage, he planned on bottling in February, while most other producers bottled in August or early September of the preceding year. Although the Crédit Foncier is undergoing difficulties at present, I hope their financial commitment to restoring this domaine to prominence will continue.

Montagnon, Château de Puligny-Montrachet's highly talented winemaker, captured the 1997 vintage's best qualities while avoiding any of this year's potential weaknesses. Montagnon joins a select group of winemakers, including Jadot's Jacques Lardière, Domaine d'Auvenay's Lalou Bize-Leroy, and Dominique Lafon, all of whom admirably succeeded in 1997.

Montagnon did not acidify his 1997s. "Why would I have resorted to that? I knew what the acidity levels were and was aware that they would not change after the malolactic fermentations," he stated confidently.

The spicy oak, almond, and bacon-scented 1997 Chassagne-Montrachet offers a medium-bodied and softly textured character. It is a rich, broad, and flavorful wine with layers of well-ripened pear, apples, and hazelnuts. Drink it between now and 2004. Produced from the vineyards located directly in front of the château, the 1997 Meursault reveals nutty and floral aromas filled with spicy anise. This medium- to full-bodied wine, though not as complex as the Chassagne, delights the palate with its well-crafted and powerful personality. Its flavor profile, filled with roasted salty nuts and minerals, has impressive richness. It should be consumed over the next 3–4 years. The super 1997 St. Aubin En Remilly benefited from 40% new oak. It exhibits mouthwatering aromas of ripe white fruits interspersed with fresh earth, lemons, oak spices, and anise. Its impressive personality is jam-packed with sur-maturité-tinged white fruits whose oily consistency saturates the palate. This medium- to full-bodied, relatively thick wine will certainly be a crowd pleaser! Anticipated maturity: now–2003+.

Revealing a mineral and floral nose, the 1997 Meursault Poruzots has a broad, expansive, and expressive personality. Earth, clay, tangy fruits, and minerals can be found in its medium-bodied, silky core. Drink it over the next 4–5 years. The 1997 Meursault Perrières displays enthralling almond butter aromas as well as a fat, creamy character. This is a bold, deeply ripe offering with a dried honey, mineral, and hazelnut extract flavor profile and fine length. An exceptionally well-balanced wine for the vintage, it should evolve well with cellaring. Anticipated maturity: 2000–2006+.

Produced from vines located in Chalumeaux and Petits Charons, the 1997 Puligny-

Montrachet reveals subtle aromas of ripe white fruits, minerals, and toasty oak. Medium bodied and dense, this thick wine is filled with poached pears, flowers, and earthy nuances. It will be at its best if drunk over the next 4–5 years. The 1997 Puligny-Montrachet Les Chalumeaux has a pungent nose of bright minerals, vanilla ice cream, hazelnuts, and oak spices. This well-focused wine has a rich texture, excellent weight, balance, and a freshness that is rare in 1997. Anticipated maturity: now–2005. The 1997 Puligny-Montrachet La Garenne was slightly reduced, yet with air, its profound nose of minerals, lemons, and honeysuckle emerged. A well-concentrated and medium- to full-bodied wine with copious layers of clay, citrus fruits, and toasted oak, it also had a persistent finish. Anticipated maturity: 2000–2006+. The 1997 Puligny-Montrachet Les Folatières is more elegant. Its aromas exhibit acacia blossoms, grilled nuts, and wood spices. On the palate, this medium- to full-bodied, flavorful wine offers well-defined mineral and hazelnut flavors. While not as dense as the La Garenne, it appears to be more harmonious. The 1997's telltale alcoholic warmth was detectable in its otherwise deliciously oak-imbued finish, lowering my score. Drink it over the next 5–6 years.

The 1997 Chevalier-Montrachet was harvested at 14% natural potential alcohol. It has an extraordinary nose of minerals, cardamom, peanuts, acacia blossoms, and anise. This impeccably focused, precise, and concentrated wine has enormous complexity, a medium to full body, and a magnificently long finish. Its flavor profile is composed of chalk, flint, crisp pears, boisterous minerals, and sweet spicy oak. Anticipated maturity: 2001–2008+. The 1997 Bâtard-Montrachet displays passion fruit, mangoes, and overripe pear aromas. Reminiscent of Chardonnay jelly, this is a hugely thick, hyperdense, and full-bodied wine revealing an extraordinary panoply of cherries, raspberries, and tropical fruits. Its power, texture, and weight are extremely impressive. Might it be too intense and/or over the top? Drink it over the next 4–6 years. The 1997 Montrachet reveals dusty mineral, peach, and earth aromas. This powerful, medium- to full-bodied, opulent, viscous wine recalls the enormous Bâtard, but it is substantially better balanced and delineated. Buttered toast, stones, chalk, minerals, poached pears, apricots, and red currants can be discerned in its complex, explosive, and highly concentrated personality. Anticipated maturity: 2001–2009. Bravo!

The Château's yields averaged 2⅔ of fruit per acre in the 1996 vintage, while many of Montagnon's more esteemed, and more expensive, neighbors harvested 40% more. Not one to mince words, Montagnon described the 30% increase in permissible yields Puligny's vignerons obtained from the INAO to be a "total aberration and heresy."

Robert Kacher, this estate's U.S. importer, is given the permission to select the barrels he would like, as are other nations' importers. In 1996 Kacher's "cuvées" have been subjected to a longer *élevage* than England's and the rest of Europe's. For the Chevalier-Montrachet, Kacher's selection of barrels tended to be slightly more oaky and less minerally than others. The following notes reflect the wines shipped to the United States.

Montagnon's 1996s have the ripe, rich, and lively qualities I associate with this outstanding vintage yet seem to have avoided its potential pitfalls, namely hollowness from high yields and teeth-clenching acidity.

The 1996 Meursault Poruzots exhibits mouthwatering almond candy aromas and a rich, fat, floral, and grilled nut-packed flavor profile. It is medium to full bodied, silky, flavorful, complex, and surprisingly complete for a wine crafted from only 13-year-old vines. I recommend consuming it between 2000 and 2005. Tasted from barrel on two separate occasions (as with the Perrières), the 1996 St. Aubin En Remilly is a white flower-scented, ripe, dense, medium- to full-bodied, and velvety-textured wine with broad, tangy, sweet, and delicious peach, anise, and stonelike flavors. Anticipated maturity: 2000–2004. Revealing an attractive gravel, rock dust, and nut-filled nose, the 1996 Meursault Perrières is a medium- to full-bodied, oily-textured, concentrated, extracted, and rich offering. Broad layers of spiced pears, minerals, and sweet toasty oak are found in its deep, well-balanced, and persistent personality. It should be at its peak from 2002 to 2007. Produced from a 35-year-old vine parcel purchased by the estate in 1992, the 1996 Puligny-Montrachet La Garenne has lively, sweet, floral, and oaky aromas as well as a medium- to full-bodied, mouth-coating, precise, feminine, candied lemon, and anise-filled flavor profile. This focused, pure, and tangy offering should be consumed between 2000 and 2004. Montagnon's superb 1996 Puligny-Montrachet Les Folatières reveals liquid minerals, stones, and chalk on the nose as well as a smoky, toasty, flinty, leesy, buttery, and citrusy core of ripe fruit. This well-crafted, medium- to full-bodied, delineated, and silky wine possesses first-rate concentration, depth, extraction, and a delightfully long and pear-infused finish. Anticipated maturity: 2002–2006.

The Château de Puligny-Montrachet's 1996 Chevalier-Montrachet displays tantalizing and spicy marzipan aromatics and a superripe, broad, concentrated, complex, buttery, leesy, and full-bodied personality. This gorgeously focused, precise, and persistent wine has the intricacy and purity of an outstanding wine, but not enough intensity and power for greatness. Anticipated maturity: 2002–2007. The sublime 1996 Bâtard-Montrachet is the finest wine I have ever tasted from this estate. Massively ripe, rich, and toasty aromas are followed by an extraordinarily broad, expansive, structured, delineated, chewy, oily, and full-bodied character. This powerful and massive, yet finely detailed offering is jam-packed with buttery minerals, toast, poached pears, and anise. Layers of focused and sweet fruit saturate the palate and seem to linger for 30 seconds or more on the admirable finish. This is a great wine! I suggest drinking it from 2002 to 2008. Produced from grapes harvested at 14.3% natural potential alcohol, the 1996 Montrachet has deeply rich, floral, anise, and toast aromas. Velvety textured, full bodied, and magnificently concentrated, this beauty possesses a mouth-coating mineral, rock dust, white peach, and candied fruit flavor profile. I tended to prefer the Bâtard-Montrachet for its extraordinary juxtaposition of power and refinement, but this dense, tightly wound offering may yet prove to be its equal. Anticipated maturity: 2004–2010.

With scents of white flowers and honeysuckle, the 1995 St. Aubin En Remilly is a big and thickly textured wine loaded with huge, concentrated, sweet fruit. It has nice balance and should be consumed within 3–4 years of its release. From only 13-year-old vines, the 1995 Meursault Poruzots displays a sweet nose and a leesy, honeysuckle-filled mouth. This medium- to thick-bodied wine reveals an appealing midpalate return and good length. Drink it between now and 2003. Slightly toasty aromatically, the 1995 Puligny-Montrachet exhibits spicy, floral, and lightly roasted fruit flavors. Drink it over the next 3–4 years. Deeply floral, honeyed, and with touches of red berries on the nose, the fat, silky-textured 1995 Puligny-Montrachet Les Folatières may merit a better score if it develops more structure prior to bottling. Certainly outstanding, the 1995 Puligny-Montrachet La Garenne displays deep, sweet fruit scents, and flavors of white flowers, roasted fruits and honey. This fat, sweet, thick, medium- to full-bodied, leesy wine should be drunk between now and 2005. Made from yields of 1½ tons of fruit per acre, the outstanding 1995 Chevalier-Montrachet boasts deep minerals and floral perfume notes on the nose. An appealing floral, red berry, and minerally mouth combines with good length to make this medium- to full-bodied wine a real success. Consume it over the next decade.

Other wines recently tasted: 1997 Bourgogne Chardonnay (84), 1997 Monthélie (85).

DOMAINE RAMONET (CHASSAGNE-MONTRACHET)

1995	Bâtard-Montrachet	EEE	(89–92)
1995	Bienvenue Bâtard-Montrachet	EEE	(88–91?)
1995	Bourgogne Aligoté	C	85
1995	Chassagne-Montrachet	D	86

1996	Chassagne-Montrachet Les Boudriottes	D	87
1995	Chassagne-Montrachet Les Boudriottes	E	88
1996	Chassagne-Montrachet Les Caillerets	E	88
1995	Chassagne-Montrachet Les Caillerets	E	89
1995	Chassagne-Montrachet Les Chaumées	E	88+
1996	Chassagne-Montrachet Morgeot	E	86
1995	Chassagne-Montrachet Morgeot	E	87+
1995	Chassagne-Montrachet Les Ruchottes	E	(88–91)
1996	Chassagne-Montrachet Les Vergers	E	87+
1995	Chassagne-Montrachet Les Vergers	E	89
1995	Montrachet	EEE	94
1995	Puligny-Montrachet Champs Canet	E	(86–89?)
1995	St. Aubin Les Charmois	D	86?

My expectations were high when I arrived for my tasting of the 1995s at this world-renowned cellar. I had drunk the 1978 and 1992 Chassagne-Montrachet Les Ruchottes with a good friend over dinner a few nights before and I was reminded of the beautiful wines Ramonet is capable of making. While the 1995s were excellent, I found them to be disappointing for an estate of Ramonet's stature. (The few 1994 Ramonets I have tasted were also a letdown, lacking fruit and revealing signs of oxidation.)

Displaying an herbal nose, the 1995 Bourgogne Aligoté has spicy, fresh, lively, concentrated fruit, and good structure. Like most aligotés, it needs to be drunk sooner rather than later. The lively and mineral-scented village offering from 1995 Chassagne-Montrachet is just a tad better, offering tightly wound and structured floral fruit as well as striking acid. This light- to medium-bodied wine should be drunk early. Another good offering is the aromatically fresh and minerally 1995 St. Aubin Les Charmois, which also possesses a sharp acid streak. Will this wine flesh out to cover its pronounced acidity? Revealing stones and minerals on its tightly wound nose, the 1995 Chassagne-Montrachet Morgeot is an improvement (the domaine owns almost 10 acres of this vineyard, which is a very large parcel by Burgundy standards). In the mouth, a nice minerally and stony component comes through this tight wine. With time, it will blossom into an appealing medium-bodied wine. Drink it between 2001 and 2005. Exhibiting an interesting earthy and minerally nose, the 1995 Chassagne-Montrachet Les Boudriottes has flavors of red berries and flint. Light to medium bodied, this wine should be consumed between 2002 and 2008. The 1995 Chassagne-Montrachet Les Chaumées displays deep ripe fruit aromas and an attractive minerally and floral sweetness. This medium-bodied wine may, with time, be better than my initial impressions. Drink it between 2003 and 2010. Aromatically floral, the 1995 Chassagne-Montrachet Les Vergers exhibits deep, nutty, floral mineral flavors, but it does not provide the excitement I had anticipated. Medium bodied and superstructured, it should be consumed between 2003 and 2010. The same holds true for the aromatically muted 1995 Chassagne-Montrachet Les Caillerets. With a good texture, deep minerality, and a nice spicy touch, this medium-bodied wine has the capacity to age for up to 10 years. Interestingly, the 1995 Puligny-Montrachet Champs Canet tastes more like a Chassagne. This medium-bodied wine displays a sharp acid streak that worries me, but the underlying deep roasted fruits may blossom in time to overtake it. Drink it between 2003 and 2010. Among my favorites, the 1995 Chassagne-Montrachet Les Ruchottes reveals a deep minerality on the nose and has fatter fruit than the previous wines. However, it possesses a lean side that prevents it from attaining the heights attained by other vintages of Ramonet's Ruchottes. Medium to full bodied, this potentially outstanding offering should be drunk between 2003 and 2012. Exhibiting beautifully ripe fruit aromas, the 1995 Bienvenue Bâtard-Montrachet offers abundant spicy, minerally flavors. All the components are present for this wine to be outstanding, except for a slight bitterness in the finish. I look forward to tasting this medium- to full-bodied wine after it is bottled. Anticipated maturity: 2004–2012. Revealing a beautiful deep sweetness in the nose, the 1995 Bâtard-Montrachet displays interesting roasted and toasted smoky fruit flavors. This medium- to full-bodied wine exhibits admirable staying power and balance. It should age well for 10 or more years (give it 3–4 years before opening it).

I had the opportunity to retaste Ramonet's 1995 Montrachet in December 1997. It is displaying lively, fresh aromas of minerals, pears, spice, and, with time, spearmint. On the palate, this wine has superb concentration, extraction, breadth, and powerful toasty oak, poached pears spiced with cloves and juniper berries, and stones. At this stage in its evolution it is rather disjointed, its flavor profile dominated by alcohol and oak, but all the elements are there for future greatness. The Montrachet possesses all the ingredients necessary to become a stunning wine. A tightly wound nose of sweet roasted fruits is followed by beautifully ripe, toasty, mineral, earthy fruit buried in an acid sheath. This is not a wine for those who want immediate gratification, as it demands 7–8 years for the fruit to fight its way through the wine's acidity. However, the striking acid in this wine may allow it to outlive most people who are contemplating purchasing it. Although it requires a minimum of 7–8 years for its core of fruit to evolve, it will easily last until 2025. Drink it between 2005 and 2025+.

I became persona non grata at Domaine Ramonet after my comments on the 1995 vintage were published, so I set out to purchase bottles to taste the 1996s. Upon seeing my name on my credit card, a wine shop in Chassagne-Montrachet declined the sale, the clerk stating that the Ramonets had warned them never to sell to journalists. I sent a friend to purchase them.

The 1996 Chassagne-Montrachet Morgeot reveals grassy, floral aromas and a light- to medium-bodied, crisp, earth, grapefruit, and lemon flavor profile. Anticipated maturity: 2000–2005. Displaying mineral scents, the 1996 Chassagne-Montrachet Les Boudriottes' medium-bodied and racy flavor profile has attractive mineral undertones. With approximately 2 hours of air time, traces of lemon drops and earth appeared on the palate. Anticipated maturity: 2001–2006. The 1996 Chassagne-Montrachet Les Vergers has liquid minerals, seashells, and citrus juice on the nose and a medium-bodied, vibrant, stone-and-gravel-flavored mouth. With time, traces of candied lemons could be discerned in this tightly wound wine's character. I recommend drinking it between 2001 and 2006. Exhibiting steel, rock dust, and traces of orange peel aromas, the 1996 Chassagne-Montrachet Les Caillerets possesses a medium-bodied, racy, tangy, and concentrated core of liquid minerals, wet stones, and sweet lemons. Anticipated maturity: 2002–2008. As a longtime Ramonet fan, I find it lamentable that these 1996 premiers crus fall short of the high standards set by many of Burgundy's other top producers.

DOMAINE RAPET PÈRE ET FILS (PERNAND-VERGELESSES)
1996 Corton-Charlemagne   E   92

Rapet's 1996 Corton-Charlemagne reveals a tight, nut- and flower-infused nose as well as a rich, bright, medium- to full-bodied core of tangy citrus fruits, hazelnuts, and powerful mineral flavors. This deep, concentrated, and complex wine also offers a beautifully focused and persistent finish. It should be at its best between 2003 and 2008.

DOMAINE JEAN-CLAUDE RATEAU (BEAUNE)

1996 Beaune Les Coucherias	D	(85–86)

Produced from 5-year-old vines planted in this stone-and-gravel-laden vineyard, the 1996 Beaune Les Coucherias offers a ripe, rich, and smoky nose as well as a medium-bodied, broad, silky-textured, deeply mineral, delicious, and toasty character that finishes (rather short) with traces of dried honey and oak. It should be drunk over the next 3 years.

DOMAINE FRANÇOIS ET JEAN-MARIE RAVENEAU (CHABLIS)

1996 Chablis Blanchots	EE	(93–95)
1996 Chablis Les Clos	EE	(94–96+)
1996 Chablis Montée de Tonnerre	EE	(90–93)
1996 Chablis Montmain	E	(89–91)
1996 Chablis Vaillons	E	(90–93)
1996 Chablis Valmur	EE	(92–94)

Bernard Raveneau feels that the 1996s he and his brother Jean-Marie crafted will require 10 years of cellaring before being approachable because of their tightly wound, high-acid structures. His father, François Raveneau, has reportedly compared them to his 1969s. I have not tasted any 1969 Domaine Raveneau bottlings, so I cannot comment on the comparison but found his remark interesting because most other vignerons I met in Chablis and the Côte d'Or were unable to recall a similar vintage (the only exception to this being Dauvissat's father who reportedly compared the 1996 vintage to 1949).

This estate's cellars, like those of René & Vincent Dauvissat, resemble the cellars of the Côte d'Or. Why? Instead of the massive *foudres* and stainless-steel *cuves* found in other Chablis cellars, the Raveneaus and Dauvissats use oak barrels to ferment and age their wines.

The Raveneaus lived up to their reputation with the 1996 vintage, crafting stunningly complex, beautifully ripe, highly delineated, crystalline, and exceedingly long wines. Readers who wish to taste benchmark Chablis are advised to locate some of these gems.

Revealing a healthy pale green color and rich, minerally, and vanilla-toast aromas, the Chablis Montmain offers an intense, medium- to full-bodied, oily textured, and highly focused core of flint, citrus fruits, and oak spice. Anticipated maturity: 2002–2007. The smoke and charred oak-scented Chablis Vaillons possesses unreal definition of tangy, flinty, and minerally flavors in its medium- to full-bodied, and crisp personality. Powerful, strident, and superbly balanced, it needs to be cellared until at least 2003 and will easily hold its peak through 2009. The Chablis Montée de Tonnerre has smoke, steel, and rock aromas as well as a beautifully complex, expressive, ample, muscular, and broad flavor profile filled with stones, lemon zests, and toast. Anticipated maturity: 2003–2008.

Raveneau's superb Chablis Blanchots displays a gorgeously ripe, floral, and honeyed nose. On the palate, this amazingly concentrated, full-bodied, structured, powerful, yet elegant and feminine wine boasts layers of mineral and flint and traces of butterscotch flavors that linger in the finish. Anticipated maturity: 2004–2010. Revealing earth and mushroom scents, the Chablis Valmur is a tightly wound, crisp, full-bodied, highly expressive, refined, and intense wine packed with lemon, minerals, and stones. Superbly balanced and delineated, this stunning Chablis should still be at its peak in 15 years. Drink it between 2004 and 2010+. Raveneau's Chablis Les Clos is a blockbuster! Liquid mineral, spice, and honeysuckle aromas are followed by a mouth-coating, hugely powerful, broad-shouldered, oily-textured, well-focused, and masculine wine. Layer upon layer of intense minerals, flowers, butterscotch, alluvial, and chalk flavors roll across the palate and are held in suspended animation in the finish for at least 40 seconds. It is an awesome Chablis! Anticipated maturity: 2004–2010+. Bravo!

DOMAINE ROBERT-DENOGENT (FUISSÉ)

1997	Mâcon-Solutré Clos des Bertillones	C	88
1995	Mâcon-Solutré Clos des Bertillones	C	89+
1997	Pouilly-Fuissé Les Carrons Vieilles Vignes	D	94
1996	Pouilly-Fuissé Les Carrons Vieilles Vignes	D	91
1997	Pouilly-Fuissé La Croix Vieilles Vignes	D	(88–89)
1996	Pouilly-Fuissé La Croix Vieilles Vignes	C	90
1997	Pouilly-Fuissé Cuvée Claude Denogent Vieilles Vignes	D	92+
1996	Pouilly-Fuissé Cuvée Claude Denogent Vieilles Vignes	D	92
1995	Pouilly-Fuissé Cuvée Claude Denogent Vieilles Vignes	D	92+
1997	Pouilly-Fuissé Les Reisses Vieilles Vignes	D	91+
1996	Pouilly-Fuissé Les Reisses Vieilles Vignes	C	90
1995	Pouilly-Fuissé Les Reisses Vieilles Vignes	D	91

A firm believer in low yields and late harvesting, Jean-Jacques Robert's 1995s are a testament to his uncompromising devotion to quality winemaking. He attributes this vintage's high concentration to three factors: 1) all of the estate's vines range from over 40 to 82 years old; 2) he fervently cuts back his vines each year to further lower yields; and 3) *coulure* (the damage caused to the flowering by adverse weather conditions) reduced the number of bunches per vine. Normally, over a 10-year period, the domaine's yields average 2²/₃ tons of fruit per acre, but in 1995 overall yields were just over 2 tons—astonishingly low for wines from the Mâconnais. Robert ferments and ages his wines in wood and uses a high percentage of new oak. The domaine's offerings can be enjoyed young but will improve with bottle age because they are highly concentrated, tightly wound wines.

With a rich, sweet, floral and almond nose, the 1995 Mâcon-Solutré Clos des Bertillones displays highly concentrated, superripe, red berry, and floral fruit in its thick-textured personality. Beautifully balanced and medium bodied, this slightly tangy, nearly outstanding wine should be enjoyed between now and 2003. From 58-year-old vines aged in 70% new oak (evenly split between Allier and Vosges) and 30% 1-year-old oak, the super 1995 Pouilly-Fuissé Les Reisses Vieilles Vignes exhibits a gorgeously rich nose composed of candied almonds and minerals. Explosive on entry, and with thick rolls of rich mineral and metallic flavors, this long, medium- to full-bodied wine will prove uncommonly long-lived. Anticipated maturity: 2000–2007. Made from 73-year-old vines planted by Robert's grandfather (after whom the wine is named) in the limestone-laden Les Chaillots vineyard, the 1995 Pouilly-Fuissé Cuvée Claude Denogent Vieilles Vignes is better than many Côte d'Or grands crus. Possessing an incredibly deep, superfloral-and-honeysuckle-filled nose and a hyperrich, ripe mouth of candied nuts and flint, this perfectly balanced full-bodied wine ends with a beautifully dry, long finish. A rhetorical question for sure, but think about it: Why spend five times more for lesser wines from more heralded sites?

Committed to low yields and late harvesting, Jean-Jacques Robert, one of the Mâconnais's finest winemakers, has crafted four outstanding 1996s.

Revealing intense aromatic depth to its mineral, nut, and citrus fruit nose, the 1996 Pouilly-Fuissé Les Reisses Vieilles Vignes is a tightly wound, medium-bodied, bracing, crisp, and pure offering filled with racy, concentrated minerals and limes. It will reward consumers patient enough to cellar it by rounding out its vibrant personality. Anticipated maturity: 2000–2005. The 1996 Pouilly-Fuissé La Croix Vieilles Vignes has mouthwatering aromas of honeysuckle blossoms and sugar-coated minerals. On the palate, this medium- to full-bodied wine is rich, expressive, and broad. Much more approachable at this stage than the previous offering, the La Croix's silky-textured flavor profile is composed of stones and traces of butterscotch and tangerines. It should be at its peak between now and 2005. Robert's vines all qualify for the "vieilles vignes" moniker, ranging in age from 43 to 90 years old. His oldest parcel produces the Pouilly-Fuissé Les Carrons Vieilles Vignes. The 1996 exhibits an herbal, creamy, and honeyed nose as well as a superbly balanced, medium- to full-bodied core of liquid minerals, acacia blossoms, gravel, and notes of citrus fruits. This concentrated and thick wine also possesses a wonderfully long and persistent finish. Anticipated maturity: 2000–2006. Robert named the Pouilly-Fuissé Cuvée Claude Denogent Vieilles Vignes after his grandfather, who planted the 74-year-old vines that produce this wine. A muted but obviously intensely rich and deep nose gives way to powerful layers of creamy minerals, candied almonds, stones, and touches of lime juice. This awesomely balanced, rich, medium- to full-bodied, profound, and dense wine has an extraordinarily long, dry, and oily finish filled with smoke, tangy citrus, and honey flavors. It should be at its best between 2001 and 2007.

Jean-Jacques Robert defined 1997 as "a school vintage," explaining that "the analyses were extraordinary. We had great maturity and magnificent acidity." He feels as though the 1995s are possibly too rich and that the 1996s "are magnificently pure, have high acidity levels, and will age exceptionally well." The 1997s will not last as long as the 1996s, in his opinion, but have excellent aging potential.

Robert's 1997 Mâcon-Solutré has a Riesling-like petrol-infused minerality in its bright and vibrant nose. Because of its structure, this wine is more reminiscent of a 1996. It is a vivacious, lemon-packed wine with superb balance, brisk acidity, and well-ripened fruit. It will make excellent drinking over the next 3–4 years.

The 1997 Pouilly-Fuissé La Croix Vieilles Vignes, with scents of flint, rock, mineral, and peach pits, is crammed with flavors reminiscent of well-salted roasted nuts sprinkled with lemon juice. This is a delicious, medium-bodied, silky-textured, gorgeously focused offering. Anticipated maturity: now–2004. Produced from over-60-year-old vines, the 1997 Pouilly-Fuissé Les Reisses' nose reveals peanuts, hazelnuts, and white flowers. This medium-bodied, complex, and structured wine offers loads of acacia blossoms, chalk, and pears in its tightly wound and concentrated core of fruit. Drink it between 2000 and 2006. Like the previous wine, the 1997 Pouilly-Fuissé Cuvée Claude Denogent Vieilles Vignes was vinified in 60% new oak, with the balance being 1 year old. Produced from 77-year-old vines, this fabulous offering displays admirable ripeness in its concentrated aromatics. It has a clenched, intense, and powerful personality with mineral, chalk, and citrus flavors. Traces of oak spices can be discerned in the impressively long and pure finish. Anticipated maturity: 2002–2007+. Robert describes his 1997 Pouilly-Fuissé Les Carrons Vieilles Vignes as "very Zen-like." Crafted from 82-year-old vines and aged in 100% new oak barrels, this stunning wine reveals a profound nose composed of acacia blossoms, smoke, and sun-drenched gravel. Explosive, jam-packed with flavors that saturate the palate (liquid minerals, chalk, crisp pears, and earth), it also boasts exceptional purity, precision, ripeness, and balance. This massively concentrated and complex wine should age remarkably well. Drink it between 2003 and 2009. Bravo!

MAISON ANTONIN RODET CAVE PRIVÉE CUVÉES (MERCUREY)

1996 Bourgogne Chardonnay Les Vignes Blanches Cave Privée	C	86?
1996 Chassagne-Montrachet Cave Privée	D	(85–88)

1996 Chassagne-Montrachet La Grande Montagne Cave Privée	E	(89–92)
1995 Chevalier Montrachet Cave Privée	EEE	92
1995 Corton-Charlemagne Cave Privée	E	91
1995 Meursault Goutte d'Or Cave Privée	E	88
1996 Meursault Perrières Cave Privée	E	(90–93)
1995 Meursault Perrières Cave Privée	E	90
1996 Pouilly-Fuissé Cave Privée	D	89+
1996 Puligny-Montrachet Le Cailleret Cave Privée	E	(90–93)
1995 Puligny-Montrachet Hameau de Blagny Cave Privée	E	88
1996 Savigny-Lès-Beaune Les Gravains Cave Privée	D	(86–89)

Under the stewardship of Bertrand Devillard, this *négociant* house's director, and the talents of winemaker Nadine Goublin, Maison Antonin Rodet has created an impressive lineup of luxury cuvées, known as "Cave Privée." I have not had the opportunity to taste the "regular" Rodet bottlings.

The 1996 Bourgogne Chardonnay Les Vignes Blanches Cave Privée is Rodet's first offering of a Bourgogne appellation wine in the Cave Privée line. Produced from purchased must and wine, it is 100% barrel-fermented, 30% of which was aged in new oak. It reveals toasty wood aromas intermingled with hints of red berries and a medium-bodied, silky-textured, ripe character filled with sweet white fruit and oak flavors. The question mark accompanying the score reflects my uncertainty as to whether the fruit will ultimately gain the upper hand on the oak. I would suggest drinking this wine before 2002. The potentially outstanding 1996 Pouilly-Fuissé Cave Privée was purchased as must from one of the Mâconnais's most respected and renowned estates. It displays flint and slate aromas and a medium-bodied, bright, and concentrated personality. This exciting wine's tightly wound flavors are reminiscent of dried apricots, minerals, and crisp pears. Anticipated maturity: now–2004. As with the previous wine, the must that produced the 1996 Savigny-Lès-Beaune Les Gravains Cave Privée was purchased from only one estate. It displays a fresh, floral nose and a highly delineated light to medium body packed with concentrated and extracted mineral and red currant flavors. This elegant, well-balanced, and well-crafted offering should be at its peak of maturity between now and 2003. Like the three preceding wines, the 1996 Chassagne-Montrachet Cave Privée was aged in 30% new oak, with the balance being first- and second-year barrels. Its rich, fresh cream-scented nose is followed by a medium-bodied, velvety-textured character with malt, mineral, earth and new oak flavors. This wine is lush and forward—particularly for a 1996—and should be consumed within the next 3 years.

Rodet's 1996 Meursault Perrières Cave Privée reveals an appealing gravel, rock dust, and sweet oak-laden nose as well as an outstanding, medium- to full-bodied, and silky-textured character. This wine has superb concentration and an intensely powerful flavor profile packed with liquid minerals and stones. Gorgeously balanced and focused, it also offers a long, precise, and complex finish. It should be at its peak of maturity between 2000 and 2007. The 1996 Chassagne-Montrachet La Grande Montagne Cave Privée was purchased as must from one estate, and then fermented and aged in 100% new oak. Its nose displays stones, minerals, earth, and crisp red currants. On the palate, this medium- to full-bodied and highly delineated wine has pure and precise flavors of tangy white berries gorgeously spiced with sweet oak notes. Anticipated maturity: now–2005. Bertrand Devillard was able to purchase from one source 6 barrels (the equivalent of 150 cases) of must of the 1996 Puligny-Montrachet Le Cailleret. It exhibits delightful aromas of sweet flowers, stones, and minerals. This wine offers a medium- to full-bodied, velvety-textured, and well-balanced personality. Flavors of red and white berries are intermingled with honeysuckle blossoms, spicy oak, and a powerful minerality. Its impressively long finish tails off on notes of clove-spiked candied pears. Anticipated maturity: 2000–2007.

Aged in 50% oak barrels (the balance were one year casks), the 1995 Meursault Goutte d'Or Cave Privée reveals a rich, sweet floral nose and a tangy, thick-textured, concentrated, and extracted full body with flavors of toasted hazelnuts, white peaches, and touches of mouth-watering smokiness. Drink it between now and 2004. The 1995 Meursault Perrières Cave Privée (aged in 100% new oak) possesses a refined nose of flowers, stones, and defined white fruits as well as a hugely dense, full-bodied, gorgeously ripe palate made up of highly extracted and concentrated roses, minerals, and white "Champagne" currants. This wine has a beautifully persistent finish. Anticipated maturity: now–2005+. Offering scents of ripe fruits, vanilla, and sweet, grilled/toasty oak notes, the 1995 Puligny-Montrachet Hameau de Blagny Cave Privée is a rich, oily-textured, dense, beautifully balanced, concentrated wine jam-packed with layers of spicy white fruits reminiscent of pears poached with junipers and cloves. Anticipated maturity: now–2004.

Produced on the Ladoix side of the Corton hillside, the 1995 Corton-Charlemagne Cave Privée exhibits deep ripe fruit and powerful toasty oak scents as well as an unctuous, full-bodied mouthful of white peaches, red currants, pears, vanilla, and a touch of coconut. This wine's intensity and thick fruit is so impressive that it makes up for its monochromatic nature. Drink it between 2000 and 2007. Not surprisingly, Rodet's top 1995 is the Chevalier Montrachet Cave Privée. It reveals liquid minerals and flowers aromatically and a gorgeously rich, elegant full-bodied core of stones, flint, toasty, and defined white fruits, tangy berries, and a prodigious use of new oak (100%) whose flavors are barely discernible. Complex and extracted, this wine would have merited a higher score if it had been more intense in the finish. It will be at its best between 2001 and 2010.

DOMAINE DE LA ROMANÉE-CONTI (VOSNE ROMANÉE)

1996 Montrachet	EEE	(95–98)
1995 Montrachet	EEE	99
1994 Montrachet	EEE	93

The few men and women that have the contacts and resources to acquire the world's most esteemed white wine from one of this planet's most famous estates are very fortunate. Aubert de Villaine, the domaine's director, has fashioned extraordinary Montrachets that will be talked about, compared, fawned over, and hopefully drunk over the next few decades by those worthy and deserving enough. Tasting these wines is an unforgettable experience.

The 1996 Montrachet has extraordinary aromatic depth and richness, revealing complex and nuanced spices, minerals, and toast. A full-bodied flavor profile of citrus fruit, dried hazelnuts, minerals, toasted almonds, wet stones, and flowers is present in this dense, fabulously delineated, rich, superbly focused, and precise wine. It is not as lush or extracted as the 1995 but has levels of concentration few other wines can dream of approaching. Anticipated maturity: 2008–2025.

Simply put, the 1995 Montrachet is a mind-boggling, virtually perfect wine. It displays breathtaking aromas of liquid minerals, creamed hazelnuts, candied chestnuts (*marrons glacés*), white flowers, anise, and buttered toast that seem to gain in expressiveness and intensity with time. On its utterly extraordinary palate, layer upon layer of stones, straw, minerals, grilled bread, and sweet white flowers can be found. Oily, full bodied, magnificently concentrated and extracted, this is as complex a wine as I have ever had the honor to pour over my lips and palate. Perfectly balanced and structured for the long haul, this wine also possesses one of the longest and purist finishes I have ever encountered. A winemaking tour de force! Anticipated maturity: 2008–2025.

The 1994 Montrachet, from 1²/₃ tons per acre yields, has a deep mineral spice on the nose with touches of star anise and orange blossoms. In the mouth, it displays an awesome silky texture and good length, with touches of nuts and spices. This full-bodied wine has the components to be a great Montrachet, but it lacks the necessary drive to carry the fruit through to its summit. My impression is that this wine will age gracefully for 10+ years.

CHÂTEAU DE RONTETS (FUISSÉ)

1996 Pouilly-Fuissé	C	86
1996 Pouilly-Fuissé Vieilles Vignes	C	87+

Claire Gazeau and her Italian husband are among the young vignerons who are putting the Mâconnais back on the list of wine-growing regions consumers should give serious attention to. Neither of the two wines I tasted had been deacidified, a rarity in this high-acid vintage.

The 1996 Pouilly-Fuissé reveals a rich, smoky, lemon-infused nose as well as a flinty, stony, and grapefruit-flavored character. Light to medium bodied, vibrant, and yet somewhat velvety textured, this crisp and bracing wine should be consumed over the next 3 years. Produced from 60–70-year-old vines that were grown organically, the 1996 Pouilly-Fuissé Vieilles Vignes may ultimately merit a higher rating. Aromatically displaying a ripe and profound minerality, this wine is medium bodied, strident, and concentrated and has more depth of fruit than the preceding one. Its flavor profile is composed of stones, flint, and citrus zests. Anticipated maturity: now–2003.

DOMAINE PHILIPPE ROSSIGNOL (GEVREY-CHAMBERTIN)

1995 Côte de Nuits-Villages	C	86

Revealing spices and minerals in the nose, the silky-textured Côte de Nuits-Villages is an attractive, well-balanced, and structured minerally wine for near-term consumption.

DOMAINE GUY ROULOT (MEURSAULT)

1996 Bourgogne Chardonnay	C	86
1995 Bourgogne Chardonnay	D	85+
1996 Meursault Bouchères	EE	(90–93)
1996 Meursault Charmes	EE	(90–93)
1996 Meursault Les Luchets	D	(88–90)
1995 Meursault Les Luchets	E	87+
1996 Meursault Les Meix-Chavaux	D	(87–89)
1996 Meursault Perrières	EE	(92–95)
1996 Meursault Les Tessons	E	(89–91)
1996 Meursault Les Vireuils	D	(87–89)
1996 Monthélie Les Champs-Fulliots	D	(86–88)

This relatively large (by Meursault standards) domaine is run by the bright and multitalented Jean-Marc Roulot (accomplished actor, screenwriter, and winemaker), his sister Michele, and their mother (Guy Roulot's widow). The estate owns many highly regarded vineyard sites (including Perrières and an old-vine parcel of Charmes). Roulot's wines are characterized by a combination of purity and richness, in short a synthesis in style between the wines of François Jobard (tightly wound) and those of Coche-Dury (opulence).

Since taking over the estate in 1989 (I can almost still taste the stunning 1989 Meursault Perrières I drank with dinner in Beaune in November of 1997), Roulot has tinkered with different winemaking techniques in an effort to raise the quality of his wines. Following a short *débourbage* (less than 1 day), a 6–7-day cold maceration is the norm. Roulot allows fermentations to begin on their own. A *terroir*-ist at heart, Roulot uses only indigenous yeasts to promote each vineyard's individual *terroir*. He looks for a long, steady fermentation and keeps as many lees as possible—even after racking. *Bâtonnage* is sparingly employed because Roulot wishes to maintain finesse and feels that overly stirring the lees can have a negative impact on a wine's delicacy, refinement, and intricacy of flavors. New oak is used in small amounts, 33% for the premiers crus and 20%–30% for the others.

The delicious 1996 Bourgogne Chardonnay has stone, flint, and spicy aromas followed by an appealing, medium-bodied, silky-textured, focused, and lively character marked by minerals and lemons. It should be drunk by 2002. Roulot's excellent 1996 Monthélie Les Champs-Fulliots displays a metallic and floral nose as well as an elegant, structured, lively, and delineated medium body filled with mineral and steel flavors. Drink this wine by 2003.

Revealing smoke and toasted hazelnuts on the nose, the 1996 Meursault Les Vireuils is a masculine, rich, racy, deep, medium- to full-bodied, and nut-infused wine. The 1996 Meursault Les Meix-Chavaux is less rich but more refined than the Vireuils. An elegant nose of creamy nuts and toast is followed by a delicious, extremely lively, medium-bodied core of mineral and metallic flavors. Both these first-rate village wines should be consumed between now and 2004. Roulot's 1996 Meursault Les Luchets has a smoke- and mineral-infused nose as well as a lemon drop, metallic, and crisp pear-flavored, medium-bodied, rich, and ample personality. Its impressive ripeness, refinement, and length go a long way to prove that "village appellation" wines can attain excellence. Anticipated maturity: 2001–2006. My favorite of Jean-Marc Roulot's village Meursaults is the outstanding 1996 Meursault Les Tessons. Almost ethereal mineral, earth, and *cèpe* mushroom aromas are followed by a beautifully elegant, powerful, medium-bodied, racy, and quite deep character filled with stone and pearlike flavors. Anticipated maturity: 2001–2006.

Produced from the lower portion (what the Burgundians call *du dessous*) of the Meursault Charmes vineyard, this is an earthy-scented wine with enormous depth, richness, and elegance. This highly defined, mineral, flower, and lemon-infused wine possesses an admirably long and precise finish. It should be at its peak between 2002 and 2007. Roulot recently purchased a parcel of Meursault Bouchères, located between the Poruzots and Goutte d'Or vineyards. This estate's first vintage of Bouchères is a resounding success. Displaying ripe, minerally aromas, this is an outstanding, magnificently polished, pure, and well-delineated wine filled with flavors of stones, poached pears, and spices. Anticipated maturity: 2002–2007. The spectacular 1996 Meursault Perrières will repay consumers with the patience to cellar it. Revealing a complex nose of gravel, sautéed mushrooms, and flowers, this awesomely rich and deep wine has superb concentration, delineation, and definition to its thick-textured and medium- to full-bodied personality. Layers of minerals, white fruits, and traces of honeysuckle can be found in this powerful and broad, yet totally elegant Perrières. Bravo!

Exhibiting toasted hazelnuts on the nose, Roulot's 1995 Bourgogne Chardonnay possesses a thick, oily texture, attractive flavors of roasted nuts, medium body, and good length for a generic bottling. It should be drunk within the first 3–4 years after its release. The 1995 Meursault Les Luchets displays piercing toasted nuts on the nose, followed by a mouth made up of roasted nutty fruits and green apples. This medium-bodied, well-balanced village offering should be consumed between now and 2002.

DOMAINE GEORGES ET CHRISTOPHE ROUMIER (CHAMBOLLE-MUSIGNY)
1995 Corton-Charlemagne   EE 93

Roumier made a gorgeous Corton-Charlemagne in 1995 that displays a fabulous nose of sweet vanillin, toasted oak, and superripe fruits. The explosive palate bursts with tropical fruits (somewhat reminiscent of a top-of-the-line California Chardonnay in style) and is full bodied, thick textured, and with excellent length. Normal production for this wine runs between 1,200 and 1,400 bottles per year. In 1995 only 882 were produced. Drink it between now and 2006.

CHÂTEAU DE RULLY (RULLY)

1996 Rully	C	(85–87)

Revealing smoke and toasted oak aromas, the 1996 Rully is a bright, racy, yet oily-textured wine. Sweet metallic flavors are intertwined with candied pears, crisp currants, and traces of vanilla bean in its character. It should be drunk by 2002. The Château de Rully is owned by the Antonin Rodet *négociant* house.

DOMAINE ETIENNE SAUZET (PULIGNY-MONTRACHET)

1996 Bâtard-Montrachet*	EEE	95
1995 Bâtard-Montrachet*	EEE	94
1996 Bienvenue-Bâtard-Montrachet*	EEE	93+
1995 Bienvenue-Bâtard-Montrachet*	EEE	93
1995 Bourgogne Blanc*	D	85+
1996 Bourgogne "Chardonnay"	D	87
1996 Chassagne-Montrachet*	D	88
1995 Chassagne-Montrachet*	E	87
1996 Chevalier-Montrachet	EEE	92+
1995 Chevalier-Montrachet	EEE	93
1996 Montrachet	EEE	96
1995 Montrachet	EEE	95+
1996 Puligny-Montrachet	E	87
1995 Puligny-Montrachet*	E	87
1996 Puligny-Montrachet Les Champs Canet*	EE	93
1995 Puligny-Montrachet Les Champs Canet*	EE	92
1996 Puligny-Montrachet Les Combettes*	EE	94
1995 Puligny-Montrachet Les Combettes*	EE	93
1996 Puligny-Montrachet La Garenne	EE	89
1995 Puligny-Montrachet La Garenne	EE	88
1996 Puligny-Montrachet Les Folatières	EE	91
1995 Puligny-Montrachet Les Folatières	EE	90+
1996 Puligny-Montrachet Les Perrières*	EE	90
1995 Puligny-Montrachet Les Perrières*	EE	89
1996 Puligny-Montrachet Les Réferts*	EE	92+
1995 Puligny-Montrachet Les Réferts*	EE	90+

A former rugby player, Gérard Boudot married Etienne Sauzet's granddaughter Jeanine and took over the reins of one of Puligny-Montrachet's most famous estates. Jean-Marc Boillot, Jeanine's brother, took his share of the inherited vines a few years ago, dramatically cutting back this domaine's production. Boudot's answer was to start a small *négociant* house to off-set the losses. Due to a loophole in French labeling laws, it is impossible to discern whether a particular bottle was produced from the domaine's vines or from purchased fruit, must, or wine. This is because a *négociant* who makes a wine from the appellation he is based in doesn't have to indicate that it is a *négociant* bottling. To assist readers in understanding which of the following offerings are produced from vineyards owned by this domaine, I have put an asterisk (*) by its name.

Gérard Boudot, this firm's director, bottled the following wines between September and November 1997. The 1996 Bourgogne "Chardonnay," two-thirds of which is produced from estate-grown grapes, is bottled at three different times, each lot being essentially the same according to Boudot. Half of the wine is vinified in oak, the balance being in stainless steel, and 10% of the overall cuvée is aged in new oak barrels. It reveals a ripe pear-scented nose and a broad, rich, sweet, medium-bodied, and silky core of leesy, tangy, spicy, and buttery white fruits. It will be at its best if consumed by 2002. Interestingly, Boudot was compelled to include quotation marks around the word Chardonnay on this wine's label. Apparently, vignerons from the town of Chardonnay, following France's trend toward becoming as litigious a society as the U.S., are suing producers who label their wines in a way that could be inferred as originating from their town.

The 1996 Chassagne-Montrachet is produced from a vineyard located just below Bâtard-Montrachet. It displays sweet maltball aromatics as well as a lively, medium-bodied, and thick character. Powerful mineral, toasty oak, and white peach flavors are found in this well-balanced and focused wine. Anticipated maturity: now–2003. Exhibiting bright, citrusy scents, the 1996 Puligny-Montrachet is a light- to medium-bodied, delineated, floral, and gravel-infused wine. It is feminine, delicate, and almost lacelike in nature. Anticipated maturity: now–2002. Produced from 26-year-old vines and having spent 12 months on its lees, the 1996 Puligny-Montrachet La Garenne has an exceedingly minerally nose (almost like rock dust, a smell I associate with having been around machines that pulverize rocks). On the palate, this medium-bodied, highly structured, and vibrant wine has dusty stone and gravel-like flavors. Its long finish delivers traces of spicy oak nuances from the 30% new barrels that were used in its *élevage*. The fabulous 1996 Puligny-Montrachet Les Réferts offers earth and mineral aromas as well as a powerful, deeply rich, complex, and medium- to full-bodied personality. Highly defined and pure, this wine also has loads of fat (*gras* as the French would say) to satisfy a taster's hedonistic cravings. Layers of gravel, pears, anise, and sweet oak are found in this well-crafted gem. I suggest drinking it between 2001 and 2006. Produced from 14-year-old vines, the 1996 Puligny-Montrachet Les Perrières has a liquid mineral-scented nose and a fresh, racy, feminine, and medium-bodied core of slate, floral, stone, and lemonlike flavors. It is well balanced and delineated and should be at its peak from 2000 to 2005. The 1996 Puligny-Montrachet Les Folatières has superripe cookie dough aromas intermingled with dry rock dust scents. Its highly focused, bright, and almost striking medium-bodied character is packed with buttered almonds, minerals, and white flowers. Anticipated maturity: 2002–2006.

The following wines had been bottled 1 week prior to my visit, having spent 14 months on their lees. The 1996 Puligny-Montrachet Les Champs Canet possesses an intense, deeply rich, broad, and white peach-scented nose. It displays a lacelike, elegant, and highly defined, yet expansive and powerful medium- to full-bodied character. Leesy notes, together with minerals, pears, and sweet oak, are found in this exciting and seductive wine. I suggest drinking it between 2002 and 2007. Produced from 45-year-old vines and aged in 40% new oak barrels, the 1996 Puligny-Montrachet Les Combettes is a stunning wine. While less expressive aromatically than the Champs Canet, it exhibits tantalizing floral scents. On the palate, this offering explodes with concentrated, lively, complex, and gorgeously defined honeysuckle, candied almonds, roasted hazelnuts, pears, anise, and white flowers. Medium to full bodied and velvety textured, this bright yet fat wine beautifully combines Boudot's rich winemaking style with this vintage's bright acidity. Anticipated maturity: 2002–2007. Wow!

Produced entirely from purchased wine (as opposed to grapes or must), the 1996 Chevalier-Montrachet was aged in 50% new oak. It reveals floral and mineral aromas and has a bone-dry, medium- to full-bodied, highly delineated, and focused personality. Flint, slate, chalk, and dusty flavors are found in this precise and persistent wine. Anticipated maturity: 2002–2006. Gérard Boudot informed me that his 62-year-old parcel of 1996 Bienvenue-Bâtard-Montrachet has consistently produced 2 tons of fruit per acre since 1990 (63 cases), regardless of the vagaries of weather. It offers a precise, mineral- and earth-infused nose as well as a highly concentrated, extracted, powerful, full-bodied, superbly balanced, and focused character. Its flavor profile is jam-packed with crisp red berries, pears, minerals, and stones. It should be at its peak from 2003 to 2010. Crafted from 29-year-old vines, Sauzet's spectacular 1996 Bâtard-Montrachet offers intense mineral aromatics and a powerful, expansive, full-bodied, and profound personality. Layers of poached pears, stones, gravel, juniper berries, and spicy oak are found in this magnificently structured and focused, yet fat and oily masculine wine. Anticipated maturity: 2003–2010+. Surprisingly, the 1996 Montrachet's nose revealed intense aromas of petrol, a characteristic I generally associate with Alsatian and German Rieslings. I view this as a sort of extreme minerality. On the palate, this extraordinary wine displays a hugely concentrated, muscular, highly expressive, expansive, silky-textured, and massive body. It is packed with loads of buttered hazelnuts, seashells, gravel, and white peaches. Even though it is decadently fat and rich, this Montrachet has superb delineation and focus. Its mouth-coating flavors persist for at least 45 seconds in its admirably long finish. Bravo!

Boudot believes that what characterizes his lower- and medium-level wines in the 1995 vintage is abundant concentrated, dry extract fruit—without great balancing acid. I agree. He is extremely excited about the 1996s, saying they "exhibit phenomenally concentrated fruit and great balancing acid."

Produced from 12-year-old vines and vinified completely in wood (15% new), the toast-scented 1995 Bourgogne Blanc suffers from a deficiency of structure-giving acidity. Yet this concentrated, precocious wine offers up roasted fruit with a nice touch of sweet and toasty new oak. Made from 40-year-old vines in the Enseignières vineyard, the aromatic, mineral-scented 1995 Chassagne-Montrachet has good concentration, deep flinty and toasty flavors, and a slight leesy characteristic. This medium-bodied wine was aged in 25% new oak, noticeably revealed in the vanilla flavor on the midpalate. Produced primarily from vineyards bordering Chassagne, the medium-bodied, austere 1995 Puligny-Montrachet possesses a flinty, dusty nose, with a mineral component and a tight but concentrated core of fruit. Both the Puligny- and Chassagne-Montrachet will be at their drinking peak over the next 3–5 years. Made from purchased fruit, the 1995 Puligny-Montrachet La Garenne has a beautiful floral nose of honeysuckle and white flowers. This thick-textured, well-delineated wine displays a great deal of sweet, fat, floral fruit. Medium to full bodied, with fine precision, this wine has an anticipated maturity of now to 2005. Displaying an elegant and charming minerality ensconced amid a sweet, richly fruity nose, the 1995 Puligny-Montrachet Les Perrières has good concentration and extracted fruit in its oily-textured, medium- to full-bodied personality. Drink it between now and 2002. Boudot's Perrières vines are young (11–14 years old), which explains the partial absence of complexity and length. I predict this vineyard will, in time, produce outstanding wines. With an expressive, toasty nose of star anise and other spices, the 1995 Puligny-Montrachet Les Réferts is the dividing line in Boudot's lineup between the wines that are lacking in acidity and those that are balanced enough to warrant cellaring. A large, muscular, structured wine with a deep stoniness as well as good length, this delicious medium- to full-bodied wine should drink well for 8 or more years. Equally good, but distinctly different, the 1995 Puligny-Montrachet Les Folatières has a very expressive floral- and mineral-scented nose with a striking midpalate of candied fruits and minerals. Long and concentrated, this medium- to full-bodied wine will age gracefully for up to 10 years. Revealing fabulous aromas of deep candied fruit with a distinct spicy and slightly oaky feature, the 1995 Puligny-Montrachet Les Champs Canet possesses a thick-textured mouth packed with concentrated and slightly leesy, fat fruits, and toasted hazelnuts. My tendency would be to drink this wine within 8 years or so to enjoy its decadent sultry aspects.

The next five wines were bottled 3 days prior to my visit. My favorite of the Sauzet Puligny portfolio was the spectacular 1995 Puligny-Montrachet Les Combettes. Because of high levels of *millerandage* (fruit embryos that were prevented from maturing because of the cold spell in May), Boudot attained yields of only 27 hectoliters per hectare (less than 2 tons per acre). The result is a beautifully concentrated, spicy explosion of floral fruit that lingers on the palate. Aged in 40% new oak for 13½ months, this powerful, complex, extracted, and full-bodied wine will provide enormous pleasure between now and 2010. Offering an elegant floral and buttery nose, the 1995 Bienvenue-Bâtard-Montrachet, made from 60-year-old vines, is more precocious. This fat, viscous, oily-textured wine is packed with dense, candied and spicy fruit and exhibits the necessary structure to age well. Drink it between 1999 and 2010. Sometimes I think Domaine Sauzet is the reference point for Bâtard-Montrachet. Top vintages of Sauzet's Bâtard exhibit a trademark deep, dense, almost sultry fruitiness. The 1995 is no exception. A muted (from the recent bottling) but superdeep nose precedes a monster wine with huge, concentrated, and extracted roasted fruit, buttressed by fabulous flavors of toasted nuts and very good length. Produced from 30+-year-old vines and aged in 50% new oak, this full-bodied blockbuster should have no trouble aging for 15+ years. Displaying flinty and floral aromas on the nose, the 1995 Chevalier Montrachet exhibits a fat-textured (not as thick as the Bâtard), stony and minerally personality. It is more elegant than the previous wine, but it does not possess the intense power. Drink this medium- to full-bodied beauty between 2002 and 2012. A stunning wine, the 1995 Montrachet (only the third vintage produced at Sauzet) offers formidable waves of spicy, ripe, concentrated fruit aromas. On the palate, an awesome, nearly overpowering explosion of hugely extracted, roasted and toasted fruits guided by impressive balancing acidity is mind-boggling. Made from low yields (1⅓ tons of fruit per acre), this full-bodied, superdelineated wine has great length. Hold it for 7 years and drink it over the next 10–12.

DOMAINE FRANCINE ET OLIVIER SAVARY (MALIGNY-CHABLIS)

1997 Chablis	C	88

This delicious wine exhibits milklike scents spiced with anise and cardamom. Well made, with a pear compote, nutmeg, allspice, and mineral-laden personality, this is a fat, beautifully ripe, and medium-bodied offering. It will make for excellent drinking over the next 4–5 years.

DOMAINE THOMAS (PRISSÉ)

1997 St. Véran	C	85
1997 St. Véran Vieilles Vignes	C	87

The 1997 St. Véran reveals earth and minerals in both its aromas and its flavor profile. It is a well-made, light- to medium-bodied tangy wine with a fresh and velvety-textured personality. It should be drunk over the next 3 years. Displaying a more impressive nose of white peaches, flowers, and stones, the 1997 St. Véran Vieilles Vignes is more concentrated and complex. This medium-bodied and well-ripened offering has minerals, slate, clay, and pearlike flavors in its oily-textured character. Drink it over the next 4 years.

DOMAINE TOLLOT-BEAUT (CHOREY-LÈS-BEAUNE)

1996	Bourgogne Blanc	D	86
1996	Corton-Charlemagne	EE	(91–94)
1995	Corton-Charlemagne	EE	(90–93)

The toast- and flower-scented 1996 Bourgogne Blanc is a medium-bodied, well-defined wine with a ripe, crisp, floral, pear, and anise flavor profile. Drink it between now and the new millennium. Tollot-Beaut's superb 1996 Corton-Charlemagne reveals fabulous ripeness of fruit and buttery oak tones on the nose. On the palate, this medium- to full-bodied, highly focused, and balanced wine has all the elegance I've come to expect from this estate's Corton-Charlemagnes. Layers of tangy, ripe, and rich white peaches, pears, minerals, and spices remain well defined for over 30 seconds on its admirable finish.

The wonderful 1995 Corton-Charlemagne reveals an inviting and intense nose of melted butter, ripe white peaches, and toasted nuts as well as a powerful, gorgeously ripe, medium to full bodied, oily-textured, and highly concentrated core of buttered popcorn and poached pears. Its admirably long finish ends on notes of creamy caramel. My experience with Tollot-Beaut's consistently elegant Corton-Charlemagne suggests that this wine will age gracefully. Anticipated maturity: now–2007.

DOMAINE VALETTE (VINZELLES)

1997	Mâcon-Chaintré Jeunes Vignes	C	87
1996	Mâcon-Chaintré Jeunes Vignes	B	87
1997	Mâcon-Chaintré Vieilles Vignes	C	(88–90)
1996	Mâcon-Chaintré Vieilles Vignes	C	89
1997	Pouilly-Fuissé Clos de Monsieur Noly Réserve Vieilles Vignes	E	(92–94)
1996	Pouilly-Fuissé Clos de Monsieur Noly Réserve Vieilles Vignes	E	91
1995	Pouilly-Fuissé Clos de Monsieur Noly Réserve Vieilles Vignes	E	92
1997	Pouilly-Fuissé Clos Reyssie Réserve Particulière	E	(90–92)
1996	Pouilly-Fuissé Clos Reyssie Réserve Particulière	E	90
1995	Pouilly-Fuissé Clos Reyssie Réserve Particulière	E	90+*
1997	Pouilly-Fuissé Tradition	D	(88–90)
1996	Pouilly-Fuissé Tradition	D	88
1997	Pouilly-Vinzelles	D	(88–89)
1996	Pouilly-Vinzelles Vieilles Vignes	D	90
1995	Pouilly-Vinzelles Vieilles Vignes	D	92

Located near the crest of a steep hill outside the town of Vinzelles, Domaine Valette is setting new standards for superripe, lush, and hedonistic wines in the Mâconnais. It has been the subject of much debate and discussion since its 1994 Pouilly-Fuissé Clos de Monsieur

*There are two cuvées of the 1995 Clos Reyssié Réserve Particulière. According to Valette, his estate's U.S. importer prompted him to bottle part of the 1995 prior to its sugars having been completely converted to alcohol (it has over 5 grams of residual sugar per liter) to satisfy U.S. market demand. The cuvée I tasted is the final (dry) product. It will be sold throughout the world and will also be available in the United States. As the two cuvées have the same labels, readers in the United States will not be able to visually differentiate between the two.

Noly Réserve Vieilles Vignes outperformed 14 1994 Montrachets in a blind tasting held in Paris in January 1997.

Mr. Valette and his son Philippe broke their 30-acre estate away from the local coop in the early 1980s. They had grown disenchanted with the fact that their wines were blended with lower-quality products from neighbors. Moreover, as with virtually all coops, vignerons were paid on quantity, not quality—high-yield producers earned more than their conscientious colleagues.

Since 1991, in order to reduce yields and raise the overall maturity of its grapes, Domaine Valette's vines have been trained and pruned using the single-stick Guyot method. No herbicides or chemical fertilizers are ever used; the earth is hoed regularly, and compost is spread sporadically throughout the vineyards. The estate does not green-harvest "because I've done all the pruning beforehand; it is not necessary." The harvest generally takes place 1 week to 10 days after the neighboring vignerons have finished. Mr. Valette says that by lowering yields and harvesting later, he is able to achieve sufficient ripeness levels of his grapes to forgo chaptalizing.

Valette loves Champagne. He told me his winemaking philosophy was "to try to combine the purity of Champagne [which he says is attained at the pressing of the grapes] with the breadth of sweet wines but without residual sugar." The wines are left on their lees for 12–24 months and are subjected to regular *bâtonnage* prior to malos, with only a sporadic stirring of the lees after the malolactic fermentation is completed. Prior to bottling, the wines are fined only if they have high protein levels and are subjected to a Kieselguhr filtration.

Mr. Valette, like other top producers in the Mâconnais, is concerned about the possibility of losing the right to appellation-designate his wines. The authorities, democratically governed by the region's vignerons (the vast majority produce mediocre wines), use "typicity" as one of the most important criteria for label approval. Valette's wines, like those of other Mâconnais stars, are significantly better than the norm and are therefore atypical. If this trend continues, the Mâconnais will become like Tuscany, where the most sought-after wines are only permitted to carry the designation of "table wine."

Beginning with the 1997 vintage, all of his wines are being bottled at the estate using a new state-of-the-art bottling machine.

The 1997 Mâcon-Chaintré Jeunes Vignes has an Earl Grey tea and mineral-scented nose in addition to an immensely flavorful, explosive personality. This medium-bodied, highly expressive offering is neither complex nor particularly concentrated, but its silky texture and mineral, quincelike flavors deliver plenty of hedonistic pleasure. Drink this gem over the next 3 years. The 1997 Mâcon-Chaintré Vieilles Vignes, tasted from tank, is more serious, with concentrated aromas of minerals, stones, and lemons. It is a denser, thicker, and more intricate version of the previous wine. Medium to full bodied and velvety textured, this chalk-, flint-, pear-flavored wine has gorgeous balance in addition to a long, complex finish. Anticipated maturity: now–2004.

Valette's 1997 Pouilly-Vinzelles was aged both in barrels and in stainless-steel tanks. It is a plump, expressive wine for near-term drinking. The bouquet reveals earth and sweet white fruits. Medium bodied, with acacia blossom, almond, and chalk flavors, this offering has a forceful personality and an oily texture. Its rich, sweet, and deeply ripe flavors are belied by a bone-dry finish. Anticipated maturity: now–2002. The 1997 Pouilly-Fuissé Tradition has a vibrant (particularly for the vintage), lemon-tinged minerally nose. This medium-bodied, chalk-flavored, concentrated wine has a medium body, superb depth of fruit, and excellent grip. Even though its silky texture and flavorful character are already delicious, I suspect this wine has sufficient balance for short-term cellaring. Anticipated maturity: now–2004.

The 1997 Pouilly-Fuissé Clos Reyssié Réserve Particulière was vinified in oak barrels, two-thirds of which were new. It reveals smoke, pears, apples, honeysuckle, and grilled wood aromas. On the palate, this medium- to full-bodied, dense, and powerful wine has admirable purity of fruit (primarily white peaches and apples) and a mouth-coating oily texture. With no hard edges, this wine offers pure, unadulterated pleasure. I must confess that it took considerable self-discipline not to swallow at my tasting. Anticipated maturity: now–2004. Valette's most complete wine is the 1997 Pouilly-Fuissé Clos de Monsieur Noly Réserve Vieilles Vignes. Its superconcentrated aromatics reveal evidence of *sur-maturité* as well as scents reminiscent of almond and acacia flower extracts. Its muscular, powerful, medium- to full-bodied, and surprisingly vibrant personality saturates the palate with layers of peach pit, mineral, peanut oil, anise, and poached pear flavors. This hedonistic, thick, unctuously textured gem is particularly stunning because of its brilliant balance and well-delineated finish. Anticipated maturity: 2000–2008.

The ubiquitous "vieilles vignes" moniker seems to have lost some of its luster because of its preponderance on wine shop shelves. Kudos to Valette for his honesty in the naming of his 1996 Mâcon-Chaintré Jeunes Vignes. Produced from 10-year-old vines (in prior vintages this wine was sold to the *négoce*), it offers smoke and mineral aromas as well as a medium-bodied, oily-textured, and well-balanced core of tangy citrus fruit. Drink it by 2001. Revealing expressive stone and mineral aromas, the 1996 Mâcon-Chaintré Vieilles Vignes is an intense, concentrated, thickly textured, and powerful wine. Layers of tightly wound lemons and liquid minerals are found in this impressive wine's flavor profile. Anticipated maturity: now–2003.

The 1996 Pouilly-Fuissé Tradition offers flint and smoke scents and an oily, rich, medium-bodied, well-balanced, and bone-dry personality. Flavors reminiscent of wet stones, anise, and citrus fruits can be discerned in this well-crafted offering. Anticipated maturity: now–2003. Aged in equal proportions of new, first-, and second-year oak barrels, the 1996 Pouilly-Fuissé Clos Reyssié Réserve Particulière has deep vanilla and mineral aromas. This oily-textured, medium- to full-bodied, lively, and broadly structured wine has loads of minerals and flint in its flavor profile. It is gorgeously ripe and yet possesses the 1996 vintage's trademark tangy acidity. It should be at its best between 2000 and 2005. Produced from vines planted before World War II, the 1996 Pouilly-Vinzelles Vieilles Vignes displays mandarin orange and white flowers aromas. Fat, voluptuous fruit, minerals, and chalklike flavors are found in this medium- to full-bodied, well-balanced, velvety-textured, and persistent wine. Anticipated maturity: now–2004. The 1996 Pouilly-Fuissé Clos de Monsieur Noly Réserve Vieilles Vignes reveals tropical fruit aromas intertwined with vanilla aromas. This is a richly textured, broad, deep, and medium- to full-bodied offering. Beautifully ripe white peaches and apricots compete with smoke and minerals for the palate's attention in this concentrated and persistent wine. It should be at its peak between 2000 and 2005. The outstanding 1995 Pouilly-Fuissé Clos Reyssié Réserve Particulière offers sweet scents of bananas and jellied white fruits. It is silky textured, medium to full bodied, and opulently crafted. Layers of mango, passion fruit, mineral, and chalk flavors are found in its highly extracted and concentrated core. Anticipated maturity: now–2005. Displaying mouthwatering aromas of caramel, vanilla, and candied pears, the 1995 Pouilly-Fuissé Clos de Monsieur Noly Réserve Vieilles Vignes is an oily-textured, full-bodied, and mouth-coating wine. It combines flavors associated with sweet wines (butterscotch, white fruit compotes, candied apples) with liquid minerals and stones to create a dry, complex, and profound offering. Anticipated maturity: 2000–2006.

Valette harvested his 1995 Pouilly-Vinzelles Vieilles Vignes at such high levels of ripeness that he was unable to make a dry wine. Its botrytis scents and flavors (50% of the grapes were affected by noble rot) are more reminiscent of an Alsatian Vendanges Tardive than a wine from the Mâconnais. Sweet aromas of Earl Grey tea are followed by a gorgeously balanced (the acidity is so high that it compensates for the 20 grams of residual sugar), hugely concentrated, and full-bodied character packed with crisp mangoes, flint, and chalk. Readers who enjoy powerful and pungent ripe cheeses (Epoisses, Munster, and so on) will find this wine to be a great accompaniment.

DOMAINE DE VAUROUX (CHABLIS)

1996	Chablis Montmains	C	88

This wine displays a ripe and earthy nose followed by an extremely well-made, oily-textured, medium-bodied, and rich character. It is beautifully balanced, concentrated, and dense with a powerful flavor profile of minerals and candied grapefruit. Anticipated maturity: 2000–2005.

VERGET (SOLOGNY)

1997	Bâtard-Montrachet	EEE	(89–91)
1996	Bâtard-Montrachet	EEE	99
1995	Bâtard-Montrachet	EEE	98+
1997	Bourgogne Blanc	C	87
1996	Bourgogne Blanc	C	88
1995	Bourgogne Blanc	C	86+
1997	Chablis	C	87
1996	Chablis	C	89
1997	Chablis Bougros	EE	(91–93)
1996	Chablis Bougros	E	97
1997	Chablis Fourchaume	D	90
1996	Chablis Fourchaume	D	90
1995	Chablis Fourchaume	D	88+
1997	Chablis Fourchaume Vieilles Vignes	E	(90–92)
1996	Chablis Fourchaume Vieilles Vignes	D	95
1996	Chablis Montée de Tonnerre	D	92+
1995	Chablis Montée de Tonnerre	D	92
1997	Chablis Vaillons	D	90+
1996	Chablis Vaillons	D	91+
1997	Chablis Valmur	EE	(92–94)
1996	Chablis Valmur	E	95+
1995	Chablis Valmur	E	98+
1996	Chablis Vaudesir	E	92+
1997	Chassagne-Montrachet	D	88+
1996	Chassagne-Montrachet	D	89
1995	Chassagne-Montrachet	D	88
1997	Chassagne-Montrachet Les Chaumées	E	(88–90+)
1996	Chassagne-Montrachet Les Chaumées	D	91+
1996	Chassagne-Montrachet La Maltroye Vieilles Vignes	E	93
1995	Chassagne-Montrachet La Maltroye Vieilles Vignes	D	94
1997	Chassagne-Montrachet Morgeot Vieilles Vignes	EE	(91–93+)

1996	Chassagne-Montrachet Morgeot Vieilles Vignes	E	94
1995	Chassagne-Montrachet Morgeot Vieilles Vignes	D	91+
1997	Chassagne-Montrachet La Romanée	EE	(91–93)
1996	Chassagne-Montrachet La Romanée	E	96+
1995	Chassagne-Montrachet La Romanée	E	95+
1997	Chassagne-Montrachet En Remilly	EE	(89–91)
1996	Chassagne-Montrachet En Remilly	E	95
1995	Chassagne-Montrachet En Remilly	E	95+
1997	Corton-Charlemagne	EEE	(92–94)
1996	Corton-Charlemagne	EE	97
1995	Corton-Charlemagne	EE	94
1997	Ladoix	C	88
1996	Ladoix	C	87
1995	Ladoix	C	88
1997	Mâcon-Villages Tête de Cuvèe	C	88
1996	Mâcon-Villages Tête de Cuvèe	B	88
1995	Mâcon-Villages Tête de Cuvèe	B	88
1997	Meursault	E	87
1995	Meursault	D	86+
1997	Meursault Les Casses Têtes	E	(88–91)
1996	Meursault Les Casses Têtes	D	92
1995	Meursault Les Casses Têtes	D	91+
1997	Meursault Charmes	EE	(89–90)
1996	Meursault Charmes	E	92+
1996	Meursault Charmes Cuvée Bahèzre de Launlay (Hospices de Beaune)	E	91?
1997	Meursault Charmes Vieilles Vignes	EE	(92–93+)
1996	Meursault Charmes Vieilles Vignes	E	96
1995	Meursault Charmes Vieilles Vignes	E	96
1997	Meursault Les Poruzots	EE	(92–94+)
1995	Meursault Les Poruzots	E	92
1997	Meursault Rougeots	D	(88–89)
1996	Meursault Rougeots	D	91
1995	Meursault Rougeots	D	90
1997	Meursault Les Tillets	E	(89–91+)
1996	Meursault Les Tillets	D	92

1997	Pouilly-Fuissé	C	87
1996	Pouilly-Fuissé	C	88
1995	Pouilly-Fuissé	D	88
1997	Pouilly-Fuissé Tête de Cuvée	D	90+
1996	Pouilly-Fuissé Tête de Cuvée	D	90
1997	Puligny-Montrachet Les Enseignères	E	(88–91)
1996	Puligny-Montrachet Les Enseignères	D	92+
1995	Puligny-Montrachet Les Enseignères	D	91
1997	Puligny-Montrachet Sous Les Puits	EE	(90–93)
1996	Puligny-Montrachet Sous Les Puits	D	91
1995	Puligny-Montrachet Sous Les Puits	D	91
1996	St. Aubin Premier Cru	D	89
1995	St. Aubin En Montceau	D	88
1995	St. Aubin Murgers des Dents de Chiens	D	86
1996	St. Romain	C	87
1995	St. Romain	C	87
1997	St. Véran	C	86
1997	St. Véran Tête de Cuvée	D	88
1996	St. Véran Tête de Cuvée	C	88
1996	Santenay	C	86

The Belgian Jean-Marie Guffens has built a cutting-edge winery in the sleepy little village of Sologny in the Mâconnais. Guffens has all the tools and gadgets his heart can dream of and his brain can devise—from the special stainless-steel tanks that allow him to adjust the amount of gross lees as he transfers the wines (via gravity, of course) to casks, to the grape crusher perched atop a two-story cargo belt on wheels devised to gently hoist the whole grape clusters to the crusher/destemmer, which then immediately drops the resulting juice and grapes into the horizontal pneumatic presses below. Guffens does something unusual: he separates the results of the pressing into four distinct cuvées, which get fermented and vinified separately. Later, these four cuvées of the same wine (the free-run juice, the second pressing, wine heavy in gross lees, and a fourth one) may or may not be brought together into a final *assemblage*. Some wineries find it difficult to keep track of three or four wines at a time. Guffens has wines from 32 appellations spread over hundreds of miles (Mâcon to Chablis) and vinifies each wine with four separate cuvées! This means he is keeping track of 128 "different" wines at one time! So much for traditional wine making!

Guffens is a mad genius. As you speak with him you notice that his mind tends to operate faster than his mouth, as he has trouble expressing his many thoughts as quickly as he wants. He also has no shortage of critics. In Burgundy there is a direct corollary between the amount of negative things people say about others and the quality of their work. The more impressive the work product, the more vicious the criticism. Take, for example, the appalling jealousy most Burgundians have of Madame Leroy. I don't know what upsets Burgundians the most with Guffens. Is it that a foreigner (and for Burgundians a guy from the next town is a foreigner!) came to Burgundy and is doing so well? Is it that he has the audacity to take grapes from the most noble Côte d'Or and Chablis vineyards and truck them to his winery in the lowly esteemed Mâconnais? Is it his reputation for having a violent temper and not suffering fools in his negotiations with growers? My advice: Ignore his critics and taste the wines!

Critics say that Verget wines will not age. His wines have good fruit, balance, and acid structure, all the components necessary for cellaring. Guffens also makes every effort to prevent oxygen from entering into contact with the wines because this can either cause them to oxidize or stunt their ability to evolve in the bottle. When I asked Guffens about these comments on the aging ability of his wines, he scoffed and replied that some people believe that if a wine is good young, it can't age well, "so maybe they should buy bad wine and age it," he said. Another criticism is that the wines all taste the same. After having tasted all of the 1995s, 1996s, and 1997s, as well as having had a number of Verget wines from previous vintages the following is clear: Guffens pushes for silky textures and long finishes, and his wines are generally thick and often full bodied. The only other similarity (and I was looking!) is an herbal spiciness that can be found on the nose of many of the wines. Most important, each wine reflects its *terroir*. Moreover, each wine is one of the finest examples of its appellation.

The Verget *négociant* house is fast becoming a large operation. For example, the 1996 vintage produced 350,000 bottles. As readers might already suspect, Guffens is a hands-on manager and winemaker, taking time to visit his growers and inspect their vines throughout the year. He is directly involved in every decision they make. He believes the best way to assure quality is to buy only fruit (not must or finished wines, as *négociants* do). He will often oversee the harvest. I was told that his harvesting teams, with their green Verget T-shirts, are bussed throughout the Côte d'Or and Chablis. To say Guffens is obsessed with details and quality would be an understatement.

My annual visit to Jean-Marie Guffens's *négociant* firm is one of the year's highlights. In addition to the consistently high quality of his wines, Guffens is a forcefully candid man who suffers no fools. In short, a tasting Chez Guffens is an educational experience. Concerning 1997, Guffens said, "Some may believe 1997 is a better vintage than 1996. Last year I compared 1996 to an Ingmar Bergman movie. You have to understand it to appreciate it. It can be very intellectual. And 1997 is like the movie *Titanic*, much more Hollywood. It is a very good vintage." Guffens believes that 1997 is superior to 1996 in the Mâconnais because yields tended to be lower.

The 1997 St. Véran has baby powder (talc), floral, and chalky aromas. It is a delicious, focused, well-crafted, if simple, wine. Medium bodied, fresh, and dominated by mineral flavors, it will provide pleasurable drinking over the next 3 years. Consistently one of the finest values to emerge out of Burgundy, Verget's 1997 Mâcon-Villages Tête de Cuvée (81,000 bottles were produced in 1997) is an excellent wine. It reveals a sweet hazelnut cream, white flower, and spice-infused nose, as well as a medium-bodied, delineated, silky character. Readers searching for affordable bone-dry white burgundies with the region's distinctive mineral flavor profile are well advised to search for this wine. Anticipated maturity: now–2003. The 1997 St. Véran Tête de Cuvée displays dusty mineral and ripe pear aromas. It is a fresh, lively, and focused wine with stone and gravel flavors intermingled with traces of sweet white fruits. Medium bodied and extremely well made, this offering will be at its best if drunk over the next 4–5 years. Packed with aromas of superripe pears and apples as well as leesy almond notes, the 1997 Bourgogne Blanc is a resounding success. This medium-bodied, silky-textured, and flavorful wine is rich, immensely pleasurable, and filled with nuts and honeysucklelike flavors. Drink it over the next 3 years. I was also impressed with Verget's 1997 Ladoix. Crafted from 50% Pinot Blanc, with the balance Chardonnay, it is reminiscent of an Alsatian Pinot aged in oak (Domaine Ostertag's offerings come to mind). Soft floral aromas with traces of new oak nuances are followed by a rich, buttery, chalky, and mineral-laden core of ripe fruit. This wine, one of the best white Ladoixes I have tasted, is a delight to drink. Anticipated maturity: now–2002.

Crafted with fruit predominantly originating from the village of Vergisson, Verget's 1997 Pouilly-Fuissé exhibits toasted oak and wet rock scents. An intensely rich wine crammed with ripe white fruits, it is oily textured and medium bodied. What it lacks in complexity and depth it makes up for in lushness. It should be consumed before 2003. One of Guffens's undeniable successes in 1997 is the Pouilly-Fuissé Tête de Cuvée. Produced in equal parts from fruit purchased in the villages of Fuissé and Vergisson, and aged in 30% new oak barrels, it offers aromas of white chocolate-covered pears. It is medium to full bodied and packed with white fruits, flint, stones, and flower blossoms. Densely layered, fat, and profoundly ripe, this intense wine has enormous sweetness of fruit in addition to a long, bone-dry finish. My instincts suggest that it may become even better with cellaring. Anticipated maturity: now–2007+.

Last year I found Verget's 1996 Meursault to be inferior to the firm's other offerings. Guffens revealed to me that he had been experimenting with new oak *foudres* (large wooden vessels) but had abandoned that practice. "When you buy a sapphire," he added, "it's important to mount it in gold, not steel. Lesson learned." The 1997 Meursault is excellent. It reveals minerals, fruit pits, and traces of charred oak on the nose. With an explosive, tropical fruit-dominated character, this medium-bodied, intensely ripe, minerally wine will be at its best if drunk over the next 4–5 years. The 1997 Chassagne-Montrachet (from young vines in premier cru Morgeot vineyard) offers tangy red berry (*groseille*), cherry aromas and flavors. This beautifully concentrated wine has excellent density and fruit ripeness, hints of earthiness and spiciness for complexity, and a long, lush finish. Anticipated maturity: now–2004.

Verget's 1997 Chablis has a flint- and wet stone-scented nose as well as an oily-textured, apple- and mineral-laced character. Medium bodied and well balanced, this thick wine revealed a trace of reduction that blew off with a few minutes of air. Drink it over the next 3–4 years. The immensely impressive 1997 Chablis Vaillons exhibits a crystalline, pure nose of pears, minerals, and chalk. Medium bodied, hugely flavorful, it is a rich, admirably delineated wine crammed with ripe mineral and fresh seawater flavors that linger throughout its exceedingly long finish. Anticipated maturity: 2000–2007. The 1997 Chablis Fourchaume reveals sweet mineral, seashell, and spicy oak aromas. With a flamboyant pear, honeysuckle, and acacia blossom flavor profile, this is a concentrated, full-flavored, and medium- to full-bodied wine. In contrast with the Vaillons, it is a larger, more powerful offering that may develop additional complexity with cellaring. Drink it between now and 2006.

Displaying mocha, toast, and sweet mineral aromas, the 1997 Chablis Fourchaume Vieilles Vignes is a sweet, intense, and powerful wine. Its flavor profile is loaded with liquid minerals, candied pears, steel, and flint. This complex, medium- to full-bodied, and expressive Chablis is the result of exquisitely ripe fruit, evidenced by the wine's unending layers of oily-textured, flavor-packed waves. Anticipated maturity: 2001–2006+. The 1997 Chablis Bougros, displaying aromas of salt, mineral, and chalk, is fatter, denser, and richer, yet not as intense or full flavored as the Fourchaume Vieilles Vignes. It is a complex, concentrated, pristine wine with extraordinary balance (particularly for the vintage). Sweet oak spices, stones, and a salty sea breeze can be found in this superb offering's flavor profile and long finish. Anticipated maturity: 2001–2007. The 1997 Chablis Valmur has toasted hazelnut, eucalyptus, lemon, and stonelike aromas. The biggest as well as most delineated of Verget's 1997 Chablis, it has a velvety-textured, precise, and complex core of white/red berries intermingled with spiced pears and anise. It lasts longer on the palate than even the Bougros. This blockbuster does not compare in quality with the heroic 1995 yet is an extraordinary wine, in addition to offering further evidence of Guffens's brilliant winemaking skills. Drink it between 2001 and 2007+.

The 1997 Chassagne-Montrachet Les Chaumées has a talcum powder, toasted oak, and red berry nose. On the palate, this medium- to full-bodied, oily-textured, intensely flavorful wine offers red currants, nuts, and traces of earth. If it garners more complexity, my rating may look conservative. Drink it between 2000 and 2006. I adored the velvety-textured 1997 Chassagne-Montrachet Morgeot Vieilles Vignes! Its nose smells like a shovelful of fresh earth, and it possesses an enthralling richness. This thick, powerful, immensely ripe wine is jam-packed with minerals, red cherries, poached pears, oak spices, and earth. It is magnificently concentrated, revealing wave upon wave of dense yet expressive fruit. The pure finish is mind-bogglingly long. Anticipated maturity: 2000–2008. The 1997 Chassagne-Montrachet En Remilly has a spiced oak and toasted almond nose as well as a thick, fat, and sweet personality. While it lacks the Morgeot Vieilles Vignes' intensity, it is immensely pleasing because of its forward display of fruit. Displaying a pear, peach, and anise flavor profile, this wine does not have the equilibrium of Verget's finest 1997s. A broad, ample, and dense offering, it will provide super near-term to midterm drinking. Anticipated maturity: now–2005. The 1997 Chassagne-Montrachet La Romanée exhibits fruit cake, acacia flower, and anise aromas. On the palate, its acidity and fruit appeared to be slightly disjointed, but there was no mistaking this wine's outstanding potential. Its full-bodied, concentrated, complex, oily-textured flavor profile is loaded with hazelnut cream, spices, minerals, and hints of red berries. As it finishes its *élevage,* I am certain that this superb wine will integrate all its components. Drink it between 2001 and 2008.

The 1997 Puligny-Montrachet Les Enseignères is a sweet white fruit- and buttered toast-scented wine that will certainly be excellent. If its medium- to full-bodied, powerful, focused, and superripe core of pears and apples is able to integrate its acidity better, it will merit an outstanding rating. Drink it between 2000 and 2005. I have no doubts about the compelling 1997 Puligny-Montrachet Sous Les Puits. It possesses a magnificent nose of red currants, rocks, and candied apples. On the palate, this complex, magnificently delineated, and precise wine is medium to full bodied, harmonious, and packed with gorgeously ripe pears and cherries. Its impressively long finish offers an elegant mineral and stone component that is more reminiscent of a zesty, well-delineated 1996 than a low-acid, somewhat flabby 1997. Anticipated maturity: 2000–2007.

The 1997 Meursault Rougeots has sweet toast and hazelnut aromas. With an intense, medium-bodied, white fruit-dominated personality, it is rich and dense yet has excellent balancing acidity and copious poached pear and apple flavors. Anticipated maturity: now–2006. The 1997 Meursault Les Casse Têtes was aromatically reduced, but its certain quality showed through on the palate. It is a medium- to full-bodied, gorgeously ripe, dense, and beautifully balanced wine with a delightful hazelnut-and-almond-flavored core. Drink it between 2000 and 2006. The 1997 Meursault Les Tillets (a *terroir* that performed impressively well for a number of estates) has a beguiling nose reminiscent of a nutty cream sauce. It has a fresh, well delineated, and medium to full-bodied personality laced with flavors of citrus fruits, spiced apples, and red currants. This penetrating, powerful, elegant, and extremely well-crafted offering is a first-rate village wine. Readers should note that Les Tillets, a vineyard located high on the hill overlooking Poruzots (a premier cru), produced numerous successes in 1997. This offering should be at its peak between 2001 and 2007.

The excellent 1997 Meursault Charmes is potentially outstanding. This offering reveals oak-infused talcum and floral aromas, as well as a sweet cookie dough, new wood spice, and mineral-laced flavor profile. It is an impeccably crafted wine, with each component in place. Yet it lacks the personality and soul required for a more exalted review. Drink it between 2000 and 2006. In contrast, the magnificent 1997 Meursault Charmes Vieilles Vignes will provide consumers with years of pleasure. Its extremely expressive aromatics reveal earthy red fruit scents interspersed with new oak spices. On the palate, this full-bodied, broad, powerful, highly concentrated, and magnificently focused wine offers multiple dimensions of minerals, nuts, superripe apples, and grilled oak flavors. This huge yet refined Meursault pleases the intellect with its purity and complexity yet will also satisfy hedonists with its thick, chewy, and sultry depth of fruit. Anticipated maturity: 2001–2008. Verget's 1997 Meursault Les Poruzots is a work of art. Its drool-inducing nose of candied hazelnuts and lemons leads to a full-flavored and humongous personality densely packed with tropical fruits and nuts. This wine is amazingly ripe yet has impeccable precision and balance, an anomaly given its oily, almost viscous texture. Many wines, tasted at this stage of their *élevage*, appear to be holding some of their components in reserve. This offering flaunts everything it has in an unabashedly sexy and voluptuous manner. Anticipated maturity: 2000–2007.

I tasted Verget's 1997 Bâtard-Montrachet with the greatness of the 1996 still vivid in my memory. While 1996 was truly a Bâtard year, 1997 was not. I don't want to take anything away from this wine; it is excellent and may ultimately merit an outstanding score. However, it lacks the focus, elegance, concentration, and complexity necessary for greatness. It reveals mango, papaya, and candied orange rind aromas that lead to an enormously fat (verging on flabby) core of tropical fruit flavors. Full bodied and very flavorful, it is hedonistically appealing and will provide enormous pleasure over the next 5–6 years. Displaying fresh butter, minerals, and candied lemon scents, the 1997 Corton-Charlemagne has many of the qualities the Bâtard lacks. This profoundly rich yet structured wine is intense, highly concentrated, powerful, full bodied, refined, and beautifully delineated. Baked apples, kiwis, stones, and hints of mango are found in this beauty's flavor profile and throughout its impressively long finish. While it is a delight to drink now, this is one of those rare 1997s that is likely to be better with a few years of cellaring. Anticipated maturity: 2002–2008+.

In early 1997 Jean-Marie Guffens told me that 1996 was the greatest vintage of his lifetime. While he did not repeat that comment when I visited him the following November, Guffens was bursting with pride as I tasted the wines.

Verget's 1996 Mâcon-Villages Tête de Cuvée (over 50,000 bottles were produced) reveals expressive honeysuckle aromas and a rich, oily, medium- to full-bodied, beautifully balanced personality packed with powerful liquid mineral and lemon zest flavors. This Mâcon is an excellent value and is a superb introductory wine, very reflective of Verget's style of winemaking. The 1996 St. Véran Tête de Cuvée is equally good but quite different. Displaying earthy, steel, and almond scents, this wine may not have quite the balancing acidity of the Mâcon, but it is denser and riper. Its flavor profile offers hazelnuts, touches of toast, minerals, and an attractive mushroom component. (Both these wines were tasted from bottles purchased in the United States.) These should be drunk between now and 2003. Fully 90% of Verget's brilliant 1996 Bourgogne Blanc (81,300 bottles) is produced from grapes or must entitled to Puligny-Montrachet and Meursault appellations. The remaining 10% were also entitled to village status, as they were from vines grown within the boundaries of St. Véran, Pouilly-Fuissé, and Santenay. It reveals a precise, fresh, nut- and mineral-infused nose, a medium body, and superb richness and ripeness of fruit. Well balanced, lively, and crisp, it is packed with minerals, traces of citrus zests, and sweet oak. As surprising as it may seem to readers familiar with regional burgundies, this wine should age well. Anticipated maturity: now–2003. The 1996 St. Romain possesses a deeply rich and buttery nose as well as a racy, mineral- and chalk-flavored, light- to medium-bodied character.

Both of Guffens's 1996 Pouilly-Fuissés are first rate. How does he do it? He starts by reserving as much topflight grapes as he can from growers. Then he vinifies the wine and sorts out cuvées he does not like, selling them to other *négociants* (in 1997 Guffens sold 28,000 liters of Pouilly-Fuissé to other merchants, enough to make 37,300 bottles, or more than 3,100 cases). The 1996 Pouilly-Fuissé displays flint, metal, and stone aromas as well as a silky-textured, focused, medium-bodied, and bright personality filled with powerful and persistent flavors of gravel and lemon peel. It should be at its best between now and 2003. Even better, the 1996 Pouilly-Fuissé Tête de Cuvée's bouquet is reminiscent of a fresh bar of sweet butter embedded with minerals and oak spices. Medium to full bodied and beautifully balanced, this elegant, steely, and spicy wine is rich and complex and possesses an extremely long finish. Anticipated maturity: 2000–2005.

Guffens's Chablis offerings continue to enthrall me. Displaying fresh, lively, flint and floral aromas, the 1996 Chablis is a rich, crisp, and medium-bodied wine bursting with white "champagne" currants, lemon drops, and a superb minerality. Anticipated maturity: now–2004. The 1996 Chablis Vaillons is an outstanding wine at an affordable price. Revealing liquid stones, smoke, and traces of oak on the nose, this is an expressive, rich, broad, bright, concentrated, and extremely ripe wine packed with flint, flowers, dried herbs, and spicy oak. Its impressively long and pure finish is nuanced by metallic lemon flavors. It should be at its best between 2002 and 2008. What do you have when you combine superb richness, exquisite ripeness, and enough acidity to bore through the Sixth Fleet? Verget's 1996 Chablis Fourchaume. Malty vanilla scents are followed by a superripe, rich, medium-bodied, concentrated, and sharply acidic character. Highly focused flavors of crisp red berries, spicy oak, lemons, and steel are found in this teeth-clenchingly bright offering. As I tasted this bracing Fourchaume I remembered a comment Guffens once made to me: "The best way to deacidify a wine is to make it richer." Anticipated maturity: 2002–2009. The fabulous 1996 Chablis Montée de Tonnerre reveals mineral and earth aromas as well as a medium- to full-bodied, highly delineated, rich, velvety, yet crisp core of stones, flint, lemon, and note of sweet oak. Refined, highly extracted, and bright, this wine will require cellaring patience. Anticipated maturity: 2003–2010.

Produced from 50% Pinot Blanc and the balance Chardonnay, the 1996 Ladoix has white flower and metallic aromas. On the palate, its well-crafted, fresh, austere, and medium-bodied character has stone and wood flavors. It should be drunk over the next 2–3 years. The 1996 Santenay has floral, stone, and gravel aromas and a rich, medium-bodied, focused personality with chalk and white currant flavors. Drink it before 2001. The excellent 1996 Chassagne-Montrachet (made entirely from premier cru vineyards, two-thirds of which is declassified young-vine Morgeot) was fermented in *foudres* (large wooden vessels) and raised in barrels. It exhibits deep minerality and red currants on the nose. Moreover, this bright, medium-bodied wine is superbly focused, with a rich core of stones, gravel, and raspberries. Anticipated maturity: now–2001. The 1996 St. Aubin Premier Cru is a blend of such vineyards as Dents de Chiens, Montceau, and Remilly. It possesses an earthy, wild mushroom, and honeysuckle-laced nose, as well as a bright, medium- to full-bodied, deeply rich, and broad personality. Layers of minerals, white flowers, steel, and anise can be found in its crystalline flavor profile. Its admirable finish reveals traces of sweet citrus fruit and flint. Anticipated maturity: now–2004.

The following wines were tasted from the barrel after they had been racked. The outstanding 1996 Meursault Les Tillets has rich hazelnut and red berry aromas. A medium- to full-bodied, creamy, gorgeously focused, and elegant wine, it reveals powerful flavors of cookie dough, lees, and nut butter in its thick, concentrated, dense personality. Anticipated maturity: 2000–2006. Revealing sweet oak, pear compote, and caramel aromas, the 1996 Meursault Les Rougeots is an oily-textured, expansive, medium- to full-bodied, extracted, and rich offering. It is packed with minerals, nut extract, and juicy white fruits. It should be at its best between 2000 and 2005. The 1996 Meursault Les Casses Têtes is more restrained aromatically than the two previous wines, revealing only traces of white flowers and nuts. On the palate, however, it bursts forth with a medium- to full-bodied, rich, concentrated core of deep and toasty mineral flavors. This velvety, complex, and powerful wine possesses a long and delineated finish. Anticipated maturity: 2000–2006. Displaying rich floral- and berry-infused aromas, the 1996 Puligny-Montrachet Les Enseignères is lively and refined—a truly delicious wine. It explodes on the palate with flavors reminiscent of juicy white currants, flowers, anise, and minerals. Pure, precise, wonderfully delineated, and balanced, it brilliantly combines the richness associated with this vineyard's *terroir* and the vintage's zesty, high acidity. Anticipated maturity: 2001–2007.

Why is Guffens, a Belgian winemaker with a *négoce* in the Mâconnais, producing some of the finest Chablis? Because he is buying the best grapes he can find, harvesting them by hand with his own teams (most of Chablis is mechanically harvested), sorting out unwanted grapes (even the finest estates in Chablis do not sort; one "star" told me with pride that "sorting is not a Chablis tradition"), and, last, vinifying and raising the wines with the same care and techniques that he uses for his finest Côte d'Or whites. Knowledgeable wine lovers have complained to me that Guffens's Chablis are not "typical" because of his *élevage*, and they are right. His wines are profound, while "typical" or classic Chablis is usually mediocre—abused and manipulated products of extraordinary *terroirs*. "Typicity" in Chablis means high yields, low ripeness, stainless-steel fermentation and *élevage*, no contact with lees, deacidification, and cold stabilization. The 1996 Chablis Vaudesir (harvested at a whopping 14.4% natural potential alcohol) reveals superripe grape aromas and an oily, rich, and full-bodied core of anise, smoke, and candied lemons. Bright and vibrant, while almost syrupy thick, this extraordinary wine should develop magnificently with cellaring. Drink it between 2002 and 2009+. Readers who purchased the 1995 Chablis Valmur are in for a real treat. I have retasted it on a few occasions and have loved it each time. I apologize to readers for not having included a maturity date in my notes; it seems I was so taken by the wine that I skipped that all-important fact. It requires cellaring patience because it is so tightly wound and concentrated. I suggest drinking it between 2004 and 2012. The 1996 Chablis Valmur, while not quite as mind-blowing as the 1995, is a stunning wine. Rich aromas of liquid minerals, white flowers, red berries, and sweet oak notes are followed by a broad, full-bodied, and supremely complex character. Silky textured, deep, and broad, this steely offering is filled with flint, metals, minerals, and dried herbs. As with its older brother, the 1995, this Valmur has an unbelievably long, precise, and pure finish. Anticipated maturity: 2003–2012. Displaying stone and gravel aromas, the 1996 Chablis Fourchaume Vieilles Vignes has an explosive, powerful, thick, mouth-coating personality filled with layers of lemon drops, flowers, anise, flint, and spicy new oak. It is a massively concentrated and extracted, yet racy and bright wine. Its awesome finish appears to last for a full minute, revealing traces of nuts, white fruits, and smoky flint. Guffens's most stunning Chablis in 1996 is the Chablis Bougros, a testimony to the greatness of the vintage and to his brilliant winemaking. It exhibits sublime lemon, mineral, flower, and wet stone aromatics as well as a feminine, silky, refined, classy, and medium- to full-bodied personality. Raspberries, currants, roses, flint, and flavors reminiscent of a massive bouquet of freshly cut spring flowers are found in this complex and detailed beauty. Guffens put it best: "I decided to throw away the Chardonnay and keep the flowers." I suggest cellaring this gem until 2003 at the earliest and drinking it over the subsequent 12 years.

The following wines were tasted from barrel prior to racking. The profound 1996 Chassagne-Montrachet La Maltroye Vieilles Vignes has a deeply spicy nose and a thick, rich, broad, full-bodied character. This offering's mouth-feel is more reminiscent of a red wine's than a white's. Layered minerals and gravel can be found in its concentrated, extracted, and deep flavor profile. Its long and delineated finish reveals smoky nuts and traces of oak spice. Anticipated maturity: 2002–2009. Displaying flower, mineral, and wet stone aromas, the 1996 Chassagne-Montrachet Les Chaumées is a silky, medium- to full-bodied, well-defined, and concentrated wine. Its earthy and floral flavors linger in its admirable finish. Anticipated maturity: 2001–2006. The spectacular 1996 Chassagne-Montrachet Morgeot Vieilles Vignes reveals an elegant floral nose with heavenly mineral components (what the French call *aerien*). Its immensely concentrated, bright, full-bodied, dense core is packed with red currants, white flowers, and gravel-like flavors. This wine is gorgeously refined (especially surprising for a Morgeot!) and possesses an unbelievably long finish. It should be at its best between 2002 and 2010. The 1996 Chassagne-Montrachet En Remilly has expressive raspberry, red currant, and strawberry aromas (yes, it is a white) and a sublime, perfectly balanced, focused, silky-textured, medium- to full-bodied, and expansive personality. Magnificently defined yet dense, it reveals flavors of minerals, candied orange rinds, and spicy oak. Underneath the surface, this wine appears to have a core of highly extracted fruit that is as tightly wound as a clenched fist. I suggest drinking it between 2003 and 2010+. Guffens's 1996 Chassagne-Montrachet La Romanée is a winemaking tour de force. Its refined and feminine nose reveals an unreal depth of candied red berries and an awesome purity. On the palate, layer upon layer of flowers, liquid minerals, anise, sweet citrus fruits, and oak spices can be found in this full-bodied, oily-textured, complex, and profound offering. After literally a minute, I still could feel and taste this wine's presence in my mouth. Wow! Anticipated maturity: 2003–2012.

The 1996 Meursault Les Poruzots had completed only two-thirds of its malolactic fermentation when I tasted it in November 1997. Its bright nutty aromas and dense, thick core of minerals lead me to believe this will be an outstanding wine. Displaying elegant floral aromatics, the 1996 Meursault Charmes is a handsomely delineated, medium- to full-bodied, silky, and feminine offering. On the palate, the taster encounters loads of freshly cut flowers, nuts, and minerals. Anticipated maturity: 2000–2006. Referring to his hugely powerful and superripe, yet highly acidic 1996 Meursault Charmes Vieilles Vignes, Guffens said, "Like with an Ingmar Bergman film, you must like its style to like it." It offers a tightly wound yet deeply rich nose of minerals and vanillalike scents, followed by an intense, racy, thick, and full-bodied character. Unending layers of liquid minerals and almond paste streak across the palate of this immensely rich, well-delineated wine. Harvested at over 14% natural potential alcohol and possessing more than 5 grams of acidity per liter, it achieves nearly perfect balance—rare for such an extreme style of wine. I suggest waiting until at least 2004 before approaching a bottle. It should easily last until 2014.

I was disappointed by most of the Hospices de Beaune whites I tasted in November 1997, and later in January 1998, including Verget's 1996 Meursault Charmes Cuvée Bahèzre de Launlay. The Hospices are under strict guidelines to use 100% new oak barrels because of past problems with used casks. While André Porcheret is certainly a highly skilled winemaker, not all grapes can handle such an onslaught of oak. This being said, if the cuvée purchased by Verget can absorb its massive oak aromas and scents, it will be an outstanding wine. Revealing floral, vanilla, and coconut aromas, it has a silky-textured, full-bodied, and concentrated core of candied white fruits, minerals, anise, and an avalanche of oak flavors. Anticipated maturity: 2003–2008.

The 1996 Puligny-Montrachet Sous Le Puits displays mineral and white flowers in its aromatics. A powerful, highly focused, racy, medium- to full-bodied wine, it has a concentrated and rich core of fruit packed with powerful mineral flavors. Anticipated maturity: 2001–2006. Guffens claims his 1996 Corton-Charlemagne was harvested with 13.8% natural potential alcohol. Moreover, not one single rotten grape was found on the sorting tables! The wine's bouquet bursts from the glass with intensely sweet tropical fruit aromas. On the palate, this compelling offering reveals massively powerful and rich layers of metals, nuts, liquid minerals, hazelnut butter, and traces of almond candies. This wine is full bodied, thick, and magnificently rich, yet it is also refined, delineated and precise. Drink this extraordinary Corton between 2004 and 2012+.

I feel that 1996 will be a vintage cherished for the heights it achieved in vineyards that generally produce wines appreciated for their sheer size, weight, and ripeness. The vintage has imparted to Bâtard-Montrachet a freshness, elegance, and focus that is extraordinary, particularly when combined with this vineyard's power and richness. Jean-Marie Guffens's 1996 Bâtard-Montrachet is mind-boggling. Displaying superripe and candied tropical fruits on the nose, this is a full-bodied, mouth-coating, thick, complex, and complete wine. Its unbelievable breadth and depth is awesomely focused by its high levels of fresh, lively acidity. It combines decadence and hedonism with precision and delineation in an unprecedented manner. There is a breathtaking purity to its sweet anise, liquid mineral, pear, and white peach flavors as well as in its profoundly long, spicy oak-infused finish. In short, it is awesome! I recommend drinking this stupendous wine between 2006 and 2015. Bravo!

The 1995 Mâcon-Villages Tête de Cuvée is made from grapes that come from nine villages in the Mâconnais. It is left on its lees for 1 year to give it fullness and flavor (most Mâcons have neither). An herbal spiciness in the nose with just a touch of smoke leads to an explosion of minerals, roasted fruit, and spices in the silky-smooth mouth. Drink it between now and 2000. Made from grapes originating mostly in the area of Puligny-Montrachet but also including some declassified St. Aubin Premier Cru and other press wines, the citrus-scented 1995 Bourgogne Blanc (50,000 bottles) is certainly one of the best examples of this generic appellation. With Verget's trademark silky mouth-feel, this fresh, clean, medium-bodied wine is a delicious value. Drink it between now and 2001. Displaying nuts and minerals on the nose, the 1995 Ladoix (produced from 50% old-vine Pinot Blanc and 50% Chardonnay purchased from a vineyard that borders the grand cru Corton) is a surprisingly rich and lush wine for Ladoix, especially considering the high percentage of Pinot Blanc in the blend. Flavors of red berries, slightly roasted fruits, and minerals make up this delicious wine. Drink it between now and 2003. Revealing clean and fresh floral tones, and with flavors of green apples, slate, and steel, the 1995 St. Romain is a beautifully made wine with a nice length. Medium bodied and not particularly complex, it should be drunk between now and 2003. Displaying a fresh herbal nose with touches of slate, the 1995 Pouilly-Fuissé has an explosively rich mouth with lively floral fruit and flinty direction. Medium bodied and bordering on crisp, this wine should be enjoyed over the next 5 years.

The remaining wines are vinified in wood and aged in oak casks (depending on the wine, the casks can be new or up to 4 years old). Exhibiting a rich, herbal nose of stones, the 1995 St. Aubin Murgers des Dents de Chiens, from 10-year-old vines, has a thick-textured personality with toasty and stony flavors. This medium- to full-bodied wine lacks delineation, but it is delicious. Drink it between now and 2003. Displaying herbal minerals on the nose, the 1995 St. Aubin En Montceau has richness with an explosion of spice. Thick textured and medium to full bodied, this offering should be drunk between now and 2005. The 1995 Chassagne-Montrachet is not made from any Chassagne village appellation vineyards. According to Guffens and Ryckaert, it is a blend of young vines from the premier cru Morgeot and Chaumes vineyards, as well as the press wines from other Chassagne premier crus. Revealing herbal and stony aromas, this wine is explosively rich, with stony, earthy minerals abundantly displayed. This fat-textured, structured, medium- to full-bodied wine will age well for 7+ years. The nut- and mineral-scented 1995 Meursault doesn't have the drive and freshness of the Chassagne, but it exhibits appealing flavors of fresh hazelnuts. Drink it between now and 2002. The 1995 Chablis Fourchaume, with the exception of a slight flinty characteristic, doesn't resemble most Chablis. A touch overoaked, this delicious, superripe medium- to full-bodied wine is fat, rich, and filled with herbal spices. Anticipated maturity: now–2004. With a combination of rich Chardonnay fruit and steely acid, the 1995 Chablis Montée de Tonnerre roars across the palate with clean notes of flint and slate, tailing off to reveal an excellent length. This is a textbook Chablis, in contrast with the watered-down, green-tasting, light, and acidic wines that are sold by irresponsible *négociants*. Medium to full bodied, this wine can age gracefully for 9+ years. Displaying a superspicy nose, the 1995 Meursault Les Casses Têtes offers deep, rich, nutty flavors. This thick-textured and medium- to full-bodied wine lingers on the palate, offering notes of hazelnuts, spices, and toast. The finish lasts for 20 seconds. Drink it between now and 2005. In an even richer style, but not as delineated, is the aromatically muted 1995 Meursault Rougeots. With touches of vanilla, some red berries, and a distinct hazelnut note, this ripe, oily-textured wine has excellent balance and structure. Medium to full bodied, it should drink well for 8+ years. Revealing roasted herbs and fruit on the nose, the 1995 Puligny-Montrachet Les Enseignères is bursting with sweet smoky spice and peach scents. This full-bodied wine reveals dazzling length, balance, and structure; it will reward cellaring for 10+ years. All of the above wines were submitted to a light filtration and fining.

The following wines were not filtered but were fined, as Guffens says that tiny particles of bacteria that can create off flavors need to be removed from white wines. (The reality may be that Verget is a large commercial operation that cannot afford to have its clients rejecting bottles because of sediment. It is telling that Guffens neither filters nor fines the wines he makes at his private estate.)

Displaying a fat, rich, deep nose, the 1995 Puligny-Montrachet Sous Les Puits is a slightly richer and stonier version of the Enseignères. With excellent structure and full body, it will age beautifully for 10+ years. An extremely elegant wine, the 1995 Chassagne-Montrachet Morgeot Vieilles Vignes reveals a subtle nose of spices and minerals, as well as a clean, rich, silky mouth full of floral fruit. Full bodied, with beautiful delineation and structure, this concentrated wine will age gracefully for 10+ years. From yields as low as 1 ton of fruit per acre, the aromatically spicy and minerally 1995 Chassagne-Montrachet La Maltroye Vieilles Vignes is a great wine. Fabulously complex and beautifully precise, this deep, thickly textured wine, with intertwined flavors of star anise, spices, minerals, and stones, is truly outstanding. The awesome 1995 Chassagne-Montrachet En Remilly explodes on the nose and mouth with refined, smoky stones and a huge, thick texture. Picture this: It has the flavors and class of Chevalier Montrachet with the core of fruit and full-bodied mass of a Bâtard-Montrachet. Silky, yet possessing mind-boggling length (over 30 seconds), this profound wine can age for 12+ years. Equally splendid, the 1995 Chassagne-Montrachet La Romanée exhibits sweet red currants on the nose that made my spine tingle. Beautifully made, and with the same extraordinary length as the Remilly, this fat, silky, and complex wine contains layers of sweet floral and perfumed fruits. It will provide immediate pleasure and last for 12+ years. This wine is full bodied, powerful, and stunning. I have never encountered a lineup of Chassagne-Montrachets of this quality from a single producer and vintage.

Displaying herbal spices on the nose, the 1995 Meursault Les Poruzots is a beautifully made wine, with ripe fruits and roasted nuts and stones on the mouth. Complex, long, and full bodied, this wine needs 2–3 years of cellaring and can be enjoyed over the subsequent 8+. The star of Meursault at Verget, and the finest example of this great appellation I tasted, is the 1995 Meursault Charmes Vieilles Vignes. Made with 100% new oak (which doesn't show), this stunning wine is a lesson to those Burgundians who believe that thick fruit extraction compromises a wine's elegance. Revealing a rich, deep nutty nose, this refined and complex wine offers flavors of hazelnuts and dense berry fruits that cascade over the palate. Full bodied and viscous, this wine possesses an intensity and power that is mind-boggling. Anticipated maturity: 2000–2010. The wine's finish lasted for over 30 seconds. With scents of licorice and spices, the 1995 Corton-Charlemagne is an explosive wine. A massive burst of spicy vanilla oak, followed by ripe tangy red currants and roasted peaches, leads to an unbelievably long finish. This monstrous, full-bodied wine is spectacular yet is capable of aging splendidly for 12+ years. Quite possibly the most powerful dry white wine I've ever put in my mouth, the 1995 Bâtard-Montrachet is so long that it should be used in Timex commercials (over 40 seconds!). A sultry, ripe, enticing nose is compelling. Sweet, chewy, red berry fruits and roasted peaches build in the mouth to reveal unreal levels of power and intensity. Only 850 bottles of this nectar were produced from yields of 15 hectoliters/hectare (1 ton of fruit per acre). Drink it between now and 2015.

Knowing that Verget didn't make a Montrachet in 1995, I was surprised that Guffens still had a wine to serve after the intensely powerful Bâtard-Montrachet. Monster wines are not followed by lighter ones at tastings, so I thought Guffens had made an error. Consider the unbelievable. The 1995 Chablis Valmur is the most impressive Chablis I have ever tasted. I had no idea Chablis could be this incredible. The nose was so compelling in its combination of ripe fruits and steely flint that I was afraid to taste the wine: if it wasn't as good as the nose, I'd be terribly disappointed. When the time came to taste this wine, I was blown away by the utterly remarkable flinty, steely, almost petrolly, superripe fruit it contained, and contained, and contained. After (literally) a minute I still had the flavors in my mouth. Explosions of unreal minerality and superrich fruits took over. I soon realized that I had tears rolling down my cheeks. Looking up, I saw the other tasters were also stunned by this wine's exceptional stature and presence on the palate. This wine has a melancholic, steely power that drives emotions to the fore. It shares with the greatest German and Alsatian Rieslings a strong acid component that gives the wine remarkable clarity for its amazing extract and length. Terry Theise, the well known American importer of German and Austrian wines, told me he thought Chablis was the "true home" of Chardonnay. In this tasting, Guffens told me he hoped he never received a perfect score, as he'd have to live up to it his entire life. It "would be like a slap to my face," he said. Sorry, Jean-Marie, but the Chablis Valmur may one day deserve it.

Other wines recently tasted: 1997 Bourgogne Aligoté (85).

DOMAINE DES VIEILLES PIERRES (ST. VÉRAN)

1996 St. Véran	B	87

Proprietor Jean-Jacques Litaud has produced an attractive ripe pear-, pineapple-, and honey-scented 100% Chardonnay from this village in the Mâconnais. Fleshy, with succulently textured fruit, and less acidity than I would expect in a 1996, it can be drunk over the next year.

DOMAINE A. & P. DE VILLAINE (BOUZERON)

1995 Bourgogne Aligoté de Bouzeron	C	87
1995 Bourgogne Les Clous	C	86
1995 Rully Les Saint Jacques	D	87+

This domaine is owned by Aubert de Villaine (one of the owners of the Domaine de la Romanée-Conti) and his wife and is located in Bouzeron. This sleepy village south of the Côte d'Or is so renowned for its Aligotés that it was granted its own appellation. Some may find it strange that one of the principals of such a highly regarded estate as the DRC, which produces only grands crus, would also own an estate that specializes in the unrespected Aligoté varietal (known primarily for its use as the wine used to blend with liqueur de cassis to make a kir). It is only fitting, however, that this domaine be considered by the cognoscenti to make the finest Aligoté in Burgundy.

From the Côte Chalonnaise, the Bourgogne Les Clous has an attractive nose of flowers and star anise; in the mouth a nice thick texture carries forth flavors of minerals. This fresh and lively wine should be drunk within 2–3 years of its release. Displaying an explosive smoky nose filled with herbs and spices, the Bourgogne Aligoté de Bouzeron has flavors of minerals and spices. It is an excellent benchmark example of its varietal and will provide its drinkers with a refreshing mouthful, but the question remains: Can an Aligoté be worth this much? The Rully Les Saint Jacques has a toasty, minerally nose and crisp flavors of red currants and green apples. This medium-bodied wine's driving fresh acidity suggests that this wine should be drunk sooner rather than later.

DOMAINE CHRISTOPHE VIOLOT-GUILLEMARD (POMMARD)
1996 St. Romain Sous Le Château   **C 86**

Offering almond and mineral-laced aromas, the 1996 St. Romain Sous Le Château is a vibrant, medium-bodied, racy, and rich wine with citrus floral, and gravel flavors. Drink it before 2000.

CHAMPAGNE

Not too long ago champagne buyers never had it so good. The strong dollar, bumper crops of solid-quality wine in Champagne, and intense price competition by importers, wholesalers, and retailers all combined to drive prices down. It was a wonderful buyer's market. A small, mediocre crop in 1984, a top-quality but tiny crop in 1985, and a sagging American dollar caused champagne prices to soar. This was evident in the nineties as prices rose 30%–75%. But the international recession, the downsizing of the consumer's appetite for expensive products, including champagne, and a bevy of abundant crops have caused most champagne houses to slice prices, except for their luxury cuvées. Champagne remains the quintessential luxury product, superexpensive, and likely to stay that way with the turn of the century just a few deep breaths away.

The Basics

TYPES OF WINE

Only sparkling wine (more than 200 million bottles a year) is produced in Champagne, a viticultural area 90 miles northeast of Paris. Champagne is usually made from a blend of three grapes—Chardonnay, Pinot Noir, and Pinot Meunier. A champagne called Blanc de Blancs must be 100% Chardonnay. Blanc de Noirs means that the wine has been made from red wine grapes, and the term *crémant* signifies that the wine has slightly less effervescence than typical champagne.

GRAPE VARIETIES

Chardonnay: Surprisingly, only 25% of Champagne's vineyards are planted in Chardonnay.
Pinot Meunier: The most popular grape in Champagne, Pinot Meunier accounts for 40% of the appellation's vineyards.
Pinot Noir: This grape accounts for 35% of the vineyard acreage in Champagne.

FLAVORS

Most people drink champagne young, often within hours of purchasing it. However, some observers would argue that high-quality, vintage champagne should not be drunk until it is at least 10 years old. French law requires that nonvintage champagne be aged at least 1 year in the bottle before it is released, and vintage champagne 3 years. As a general rule, most top

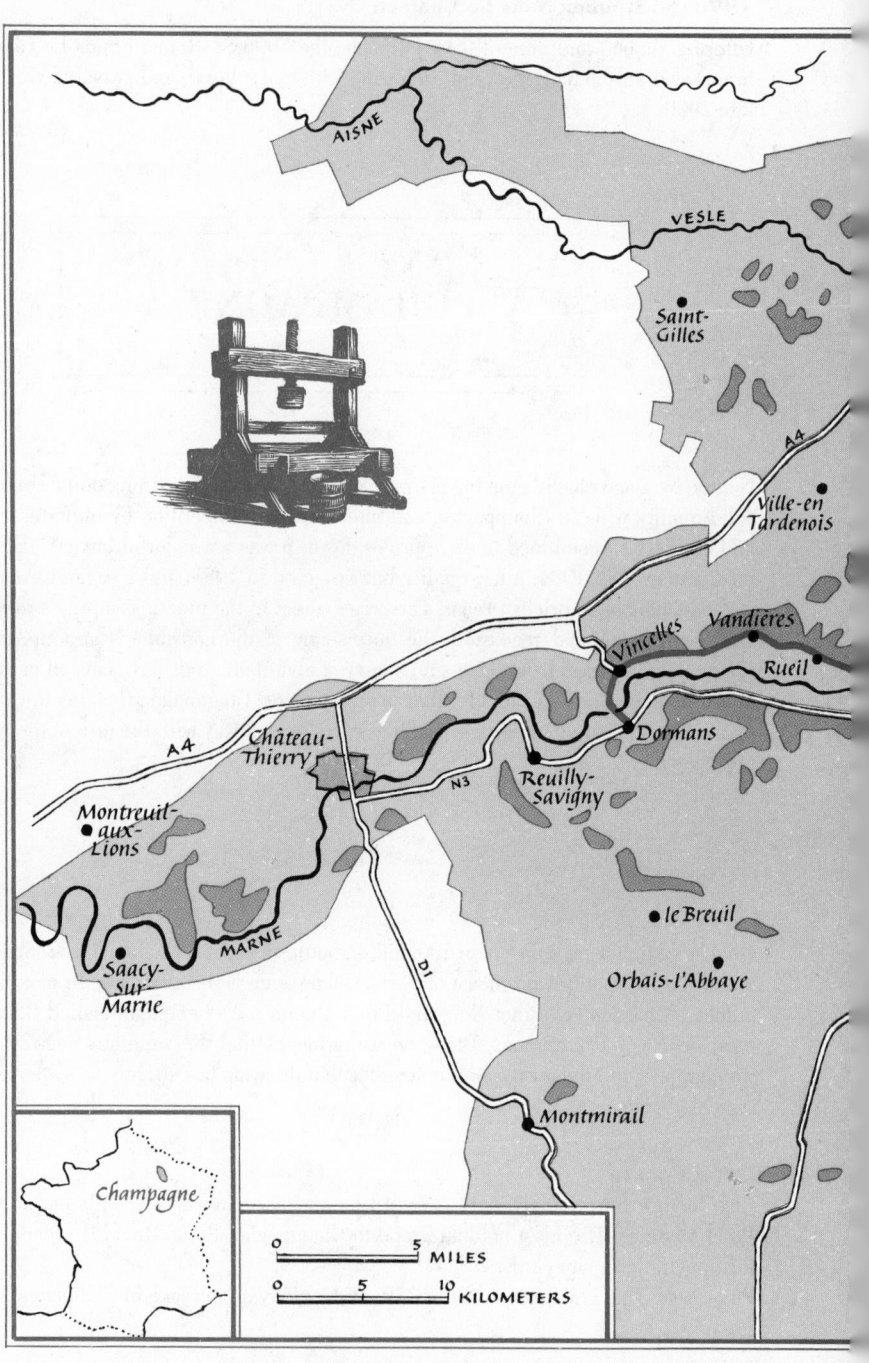

AISNE

VESLE

Saint-Gilles

A4

Ville-en-Tardenois

Vincelles   Vandières

Rueil

Château-Thierry

Dormans

A4

Reuilly-Savigny

N3

Montreuil-aux-Lions

le Breuil

MARNE

Orbais-l'Abbaye

D1

Saacy-sur-Marne

Montmirail

Champagne

0 ⊢——————⊣ 5 MILES

0 ⊢————⊣————⊣ 10 KILOMETERS

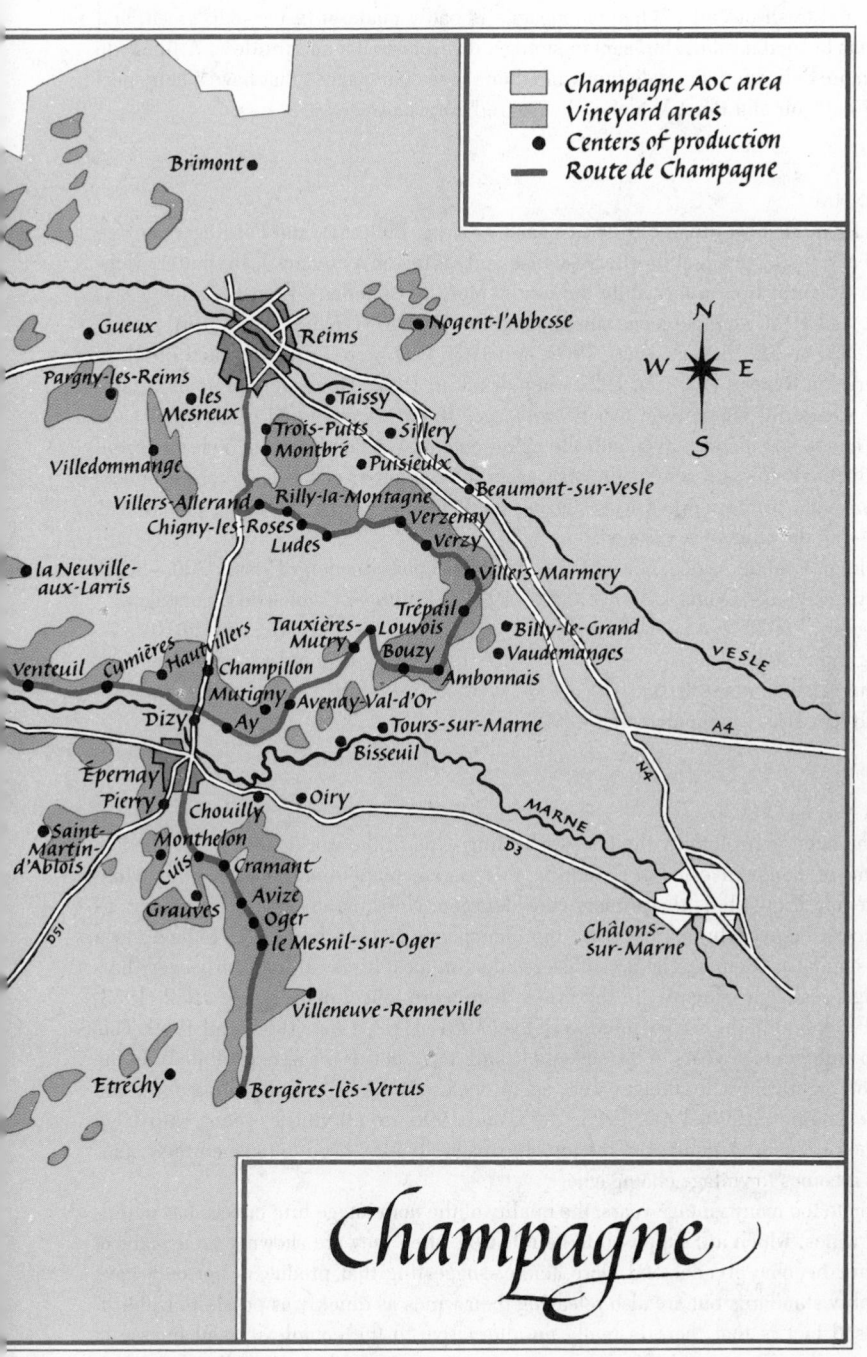

Champagne

producers are just releasing their 1990s in 1999/2000. The reason for this is that good champagne not only should taste fresh but should also have flavors akin to buttered wheat toast, ripe apples, and fresh biscuits. When champagne is badly made, it tastes sour, green, and musty. If it has been abused in shipment or storage, it will taste flat and fruitless. A Blanc de Blancs is a more delicate, refined, lighter wine than those champagnes that have a hefty percentage of Pinot Noir and Pinot Meunier, the two red grapes utilized.

AGING POTENTIAL

Champagne from the most illustrious houses such as Krug, Bollinger, and Pol Roger can age for 25–30 years, losing much of its effervescence and taking on a creamy, lush, buttery richness not too different from a top white burgundy. Moët & Chandon's Dom Pérignon 1947, 1964, 1969, and 1971 were gorgeous when tasted in 1994. Also, Krug's 1947, 1961, 1962, 1964, and 1971; and Bollinger's 1966, 1969, and 1975 R.D. were exquisite when drunk in 1994, as were Pol Roger's 1928 and 1929 when drunk in 1992. These were profound examples of how wonderful champagne can be with age. But readers should realize that each champagne house has its own style, and the aging potential depends on the style preferred by that producer. Below are some aging estimates for a number of the best-known brands currently available in the market. The starting point for measuring the aging potential is 1999/2000—not the vintage mentioned.

1990	Bollinger Grande Année: now–2015		1990	Louis Roederer Cristal: 2003–2020
1990	Bollinger Vieilles Vignes: 2002–2020		1990	Taittinger Comtes de Champagne
1989	Krug: now–2020			Blancs de Blanc: now–2010
1985	Krug: now–2020		1990	Veuve Clicquot La Grande Dame:
1990	Dom Pérignon: now–2010			now–2015
1990	Pol Roger Brut Chardonnay: now–2008			

OVERALL QUALITY LEVEL

French champagne is irrefutably the finest sparkling wine in the world. Despite the hoopla and vast sums of money invested in California, there is no competition from any other wine-producing region if quality is the primary consideration. Nevertheless, the extraordinary financial success enjoyed by many of the big champagne houses has led, I believe, to a lowering of standards. Commercial greed has resulted in most firms calling nearly every harvest a vintage year. For example, in the fifties there were four vintage years, 1952, 1953, 1955, and 1959, and in the sixties there were five, 1961, 1962, 1964, 1966, and 1969. This increased to eight vintage years in the seventies (only 1972 and 1977 were excluded). In the decade of the eighties, eight vintages were again declared, the exceptions being 1984 and 1987. In the nineties, 1990, 1992, 1993, 1995, and 1996 are all vintage years, with 1990 and 1996 the two stars. A number of the top champagne houses need to toughen their standards when it comes to vintage champagne.

In addition to too many vintage years, the quality of the nonvintage brut cuvées has deteriorated. The wines, which are supposed to be released when they are showing some signs of maturity, have become greener and more acidic, suggesting that producers not only have lowered quality standards but are also releasing their wines as quickly as possible. Unfortunately, the sad fact is that there is really no alternative to the complexity and finesse of French champagne. There are less-expensive alternatives, particularly sparkling Loire Valley wines, some *crémants* from Alsace and Burgundy, and the sparkling wines from California, Spain, and Italy. Save for a few exceptions, however, none of the bubblies from these sources remotely approaches the quality of French champagne.

MOST IMPORTANT INFORMATION TO KNOW

First, you have to do some serious tasting to see which styles of champagne appeal to you. Additionally, consider the following guidelines:

1. The luxury or prestige cuvées of the champagne houses are always expensive (all sell for $125–$300 a bottle). The pricing plays on the consumer's belief that a lavish price signifies a higher level of quality. In many cases it does not. Moreover, too many luxury cuvées have become pawns in an ego contest among Champagne's top houses as to who can produce the most expensive wine in the most outrageous, dramatic bottle. Consumers often pay just for the hand-blown bottle and expensive, hand-painted, labor-intensive label.

2. Purchase your champagne from a merchant who has a quick turnover in inventory. More than any other wine, champagne is a fragile, very delicate wine that is extremely vulnerable to poor storage and bright shop lighting. Buying bottles that have been languishing on retailers' shelves for 6–12 months can indeed be a risky business. If your just-purchased bottle of champagne tastes flat, has a deep golden color, and few bubbles, it is either too old, or dead from bad storage.

3. Don't hesitate to try some of the best nonvintage champagnes I have recommended. The best of them are not that far behind the quality of the best luxury cuvées, yet they sell for a quarter to a fifth of the price.

4. There has been a tremendous influx of high-quality champagnes from small firms in Champagne. Most of these wines may be difficult to find outside of major metropolitan markets, but some of these small houses produce splendid wine worthy of a search of the marketplace. Look for some of the estate-bottled champagne from the following producers: Baptiste-Pertois, Paul Bara, Bonnaire, Cattier, Delamotte, Drappier, Duvay-Leroy, Egly-Ouriet, Michel Gonet, Lancelot-Royer, Guy Larmandier, Lassalle, Legras, Mailly, Serge Mathieu, Joseph Perrier, and Ployez-Jacquemart, Alain Robert, and Tarlant.

5. Several technical terms that appear on the label of a producer's champagne can tell you additional things about the wine. Brut champagnes are dry but legally can have up to 0.2% sugar added (called dosage). Extra-dry champagnes are those that have between 1.2% and 2% sugar added. Most tasters would call these champagnes dry, but they tend to be rounder and seemingly fruitier than brut champagnes. The term *ultra brut, brut absolu,* or *dosage zéro* signifies that the champagne has had no sugar added and is bone dry. These champagnes are rarely seen but can be quite impressive as well as austere and lean tasting.

6. Below is a guide to champagne bottle sizes:

Nebuchadnezzar = 20 bottles = 16 liters	Jeroboam = 4 bottles = 3.2 liters
Balthazar = 16 bottles = 12.8 liters	Magnum = 2 bottles = 1.6 liters
Salmanazar = 12 bottles = 9.6 liters	Bottle = 75 centiliters
Methuselah = 8 bottles = 6.4 liters	Half-bottle = 37.5 centiliters
Rehoboam = 6 bottles = 4.8 liters	Quarter-bottle = 20 centiliters

BUYING STRATEGY

There is one lesson in terms of a buying strategy for Champagne as we head to the end of the century—buy all the 1990 vintage Champagnes you can afford. This is the greatest Champagne vintage I have ever tasted, and it is the finest overall year since 1959. The next great vintage appears to be 1996, and most of those wines will not be released for 3–4 years.

VINTAGE GUIDE

1996—Reported to be a superb vintage with fresh acidity and considerable flavor authority. It is the finest vintage after 1990, but most top cuvées will not be released until 2002–2005.

1995—A good to very good vintage, but not exceptional.

1994—Very difficult weather conditions (considerable rain fell between August 20 and September 14) have resulted in a small crop of average quality. Because of this, pressure to increase prices significantly is likely.

1993—With a large crop of mostly average-quality juice, 1993 is unlikely to be a highly desirable vintage year.

1992—This hugely abundant yet potentially good-quality vintage escaped most of the bad weather that plagued the southern half of France. The quality is above average and the quantity is enormous. A vintage year, but I don't anticipate many inspiring wines.

1991—A small, exceptionally difficult vintage that is unlikely to be declared a vintage year except by the greediest of producers. It rivals 1987 and 1984 as one of the three worst vintages for champagne in the last 15 years.

1990—A gigantic crop of splendidly rich, opulently textured, full-bodied, gorgeously proportioned Champagnes were produced. This is unquestionably the finest Champagne vintage I have ever tasted. I have not tasted anything less than an excellent wine. In particular, the Blancs de Blanc cuvées are surreal in terms of their elegance allied to richness.

1989—Another high-quality, abundant year should produce wines similar to the ripe, rich, creamy style of the 1982 champagnes, with a very ripe, fat style of fizz.

1988—Not much champagne was made because of the small harvest, but this is undoubtedly a vintage year. The 1988s are leaner, more austere, and higher in acidity than the flamboyant 1989s and 1990s.

1987—A terrible year, the worst of the decade, 1987 is not a vintage year.

1986—This is a vintage year, producing an abundant quantity of soft, ripe, fruity wines.

1985—Along with 1982 and 1989, 1985 is the finest vintage of the eighties thanks to excellent ripeness and a good-sized crop. A superb champagne vintage!

1984—A lousy year, but there were vintage champagnes from 1984 in the market. Remember what P. T. Barnum once said?

1983—A gigantic crop of good-quality champagne was produced. Although the wines may lack the opulence and creamy richness of the 1982s, they are hardly undersized wines. Most 1983s have matured quickly and are delicious now. They should be drunk up.

1982—A great vintage of ripe, rich, creamy, intense wines. If they were to be criticized, it would be for their very forward, lower than normal acids that suggest they will age quickly. No one should miss the top champagnes from 1982; they are marvelously rounded, ripe, generously flavored wines.

1981—The champagnes from 1981 are rather lean and austere, but that has not prevented many top houses from declaring this a vintage year.

OLDER VINTAGES

The 1980 vintage is mediocre; 1979 is excellent; 1978 is tiring; 1976, once top-notch, is now fading; 1975 is superb, as are well-cellared examples of 1971, 1969, and 1964. When buying champagne, whether it is 3 years old or 20, pay the utmost care to the manner in which it was treated before you bought it. Champagne is the most fragile wine in the marketplace, and it cannot tolerate poor storage.

RATING CHAMPAGNE'S BEST PRODUCERS

* * * * * (OUTSTANDING)

Bollinger (full bodied)	Henriot (full bodied)
Egly-Ouriet (full bodied)	Krug (full bodied)
Gosset (full bodied)	J. Lassalle (light bodied)

Laurent-Perrier (medium bodied)
Alain Robert (full bodied)
Pol Roger (medium bodied)
Louis Roederer (full bodied)

Salon (medium bodied)
Taittinger (light bodied)
Veuve Clicquot (full bodied)

* * * *(EXCELLENT)

Baptiste-Pertois (light bodied)
Paul Bara (full bodied)
Billecart-Salmon (light bodied)
Bonnaire (light bodied)
de Castellane (light bodied)
Cattier (light bodied)
Charbaut (light bodied)
Delamotte (medium bodied)
Diebolt-Vallois (medium bodied)
Drappier (medium bodied), since 1985
Alfred Gratien (full bodied)
Grimonnet (medium bodied)
Heidsieck Monopole (medium bodied)
Jacquart (medium bodied)
Jacquesson (light bodied)
Lancelot-Royer (medium bodied)

Guy Larmandier (full bodied)
Lechère (light bodied)
R. & L. Legras (light bodied)
Mailly (medium bodied)
Serge Mathieu (medium bodied)
Moët & Chandon (medium bodied)****/*****
Bruno Paillard (light bodied)
Joseph Perrier (medium bodied)
Perrier-Jouët (light bodied)
Ployez-Jacquemart (medium bodied)
Pommery (medium bodied)
Dom Ruinart (light bodied)
Jacques Selosse (light bodied)
Taillevent (medium bodied)
Tarlant****/*****

* * * (GOOD)

Ayala (medium bodied)
Barancourt (full bodied)
Bricout (light bodied)
Canard Ducheafne (medium bodied)
Deutz (medium bodied)
Duval-Leroy (medium bodied)
Nicolas Feuillatte (light bodied)
H. Germain (light bodied)
Michel Gonet (medium bodied)

Georges Goulet (medium bodied)
Charles Heidsieck (medium bodied)
Lanson (light bodied)
Launois Père (light bodied)
Mercier (medium bodied)
Mumm (medium bodied)
Philipponnat (medium bodied)
Piper Heidsieck (light bodied)

* * (AVERAGE)

Beaumet-Chaurey (light bodied)
Besserat de Bellefon (light bodied)
Boizel (light bodied)
Goldschmidt-Rothschild (light bodied)
Jestin (light bodied)

Oudinot (medium bodied)
Rapeneau (medium bodied)
Alfred Rothschild (light bodied)
Marie Stuart (light bodied)

FINDING THE BEST CHAMPAGNE: THE BEST PRODUCERS OF NONVINTAGE BRUT

Billecart-Salmon	Alfred Gratieu
Bollinger Special Cuvée	Gosset Grand Réserve
Cattier	Krug
Charbaut	Larmandier
Delamotte	Lechère Orient Express
Drappier Maurice Chevalier	Bruno Paillard Première Cuvée
Egly-Ouriet	Perrier-Jouët

Ployez-Jacquemart
Pol Roger
Louis Roederer Brut Premier

Tarlant Cuvée Louis
Veuve Clicquot Yellow Label

THE BEST PRODUCERS OF ROSÉ CHAMPAGNE

Billecart-Salmon N.V.
Billecart-Salmon Cuvée Elizabeth Salmon
  1990
Bollinger Grande Année 1985, 1988, 1990
Nicholas Feuillatte 1994
Gosset 1985, 1988, 1990
Heidsieck Monopole Diamant Bleu 1985,
  1988, 1990
Krug N.V.
Laurent-Perrier Grand Siècle Cuvée
  Alexandra 1985, 1988, 1990
Moët & Chandon Brut Impérial 1988,
  1989, 1990

Moët & Chandon Dom Pérignon 1980,
  1982, 1985, 1986, 1988, 1990
Perrier-Jouët Blason de France N.V.
Perrier-Jouët Fleur de Champagne 1986,
  1988, 1990
Pol Roger 1985, 1986, 1988, 1990
Dom Ruinart 1985, 1988, 1990
Taittinger Comtes de Champagne 1985,
  1988, 1990
Veuve Clicquot La Grande Dame 1985,
  1988, 1990

THE BEST PRODUCERS OF 100% CHARDONNAY BLANC DE BLANCS

Ayala 1988, 1990
Baptiste-Pertois Cuvée Réservée N.V.
Billecart-Salmon 1990
Charbaut N.V.
Delamotte 1985, 1988, 1990, 1992
Jacquesson 1990
Krug Clos de Mesnil 1983, 1985. 1989,
  1990
Lassalle 1985, 1990
Lancelot-Royer
Guy Larmandier Cramant 1992

Guy Larmandier Cramant N.V.
Lechère 1990
R. & L. Legras
Bruno Paillard
Joseph Perrier Cuvée Royale
Alain Robert
Pol Roger Brut Chardonnay 1985, 1986,
  1988, 1990
Salon 1982, 1983, 1985, 1990
Taittinger Comtes de Champagne 1990

THE BEST PRODUCERS OF LUXURY CUVÉES

Billecart-Salmon Cuvée Nicolas François
  Billecart 1990
Bollinger R.D. 1975, 1982, 1985
Bollinger Grande Année 1985, 1988, 1990
Bollinger Vieilles Vignes 1985, 1990
Cattier Clos du Moulin 1985, 1990
Drappier Grand Sendrée 1985, 1990
Nicolas Feuillatte Cuvée Palmes d'Or 1990
Gosset Celebris Brut 1990
Heidsieck Monopole Diamant Bleu 1985,
  1988, 1990
Henriot Cuvée des Enchanteleurs 1985
Krug 1982, 1985, 1989, 1990
Lassalle Cuvée Angeline 1985, 1990
Laurent-Perrier Grand Siècle 1985, 1988,
  1990

Moët & Chandon Dom Pérignon 1982,
  1985, 1988, 1990
Mumm René Lalou 1985, 1990
Joseph Perrier Cuvée Josephine 1985, 1990
Perrier-Jouët Fleur de Champagne 1990
Philipponnat Clos des Goisses 1988, 1990
Pommery Cuvée Louise 1990
Alain Robert Le Mesnil Séléction 1979
Pol Roger Cuvée Winston Churchill 1985,
  1988, 1990
Louis Roederer Cristal 1985, 1988, 1990
Jacques Selosse Origine N.V.
Taittinger Comtes de Champagne 1985,
  1988, 1990
Veuve Clicquot La Grande Dame 1985,
  1988, 1990

THE LOIRE VALLEY

The Basics

The Loire Valley is by far France's largest wine-producing area, stretching 635 miles from the warm foothills of the Massif Central (a short drive west from Lyon and the vineyards of the Rhône Valley) to the windswept shores of the Atlantic Ocean in Brittany. Most wine drinkers can name more historic Loire Valley châteaux than Loire Valley wines. That is a pity, because the Loire Valley wine-producing areas offer France's most remarkable array of wines. Its wines are produced from a wide range of varietals, the best known being Sauvignon Blanc, Chenin Blanc, Pinot Noir, and Cabernet Franc. Its vineyards are some of the world's oldest, yet Loire Valley wines remain relatively inexpensive. Stylistically, the whites range from the bone dry to the amazingly sweet. Similarly, the Loire's reds can also be found in a wide variety of styles, from carbonic maceration (Beaujolais-like) wines meant for immediate consumption to ageworthy, austere, yet serious Cabernets. In short, this region produces an astonishing array of lovely wines. Over the last few years consumers have experienced soaring wine prices from the world's best-known regions, with California, Italy, and Bordeaux leading the way. The Loire Valley, a little-known and underappreciated region, produces wines that have the combination of quality and value that merits considerable attention from consumers.

WHY ARE THE LOIRE'S WINES SO LITTLE-KNOWN?
The vast majority of wine lovers have only a passing knowledge of the Loire's wines. Why? Consider the following:

1. The Loire Valley is confusing. Its ever-growing number of appellations (well over 60), thousands of vigneron names, numerous varietals, and countless vineyards of varying quality make grasping Burgundy in comparison seem like child's play.

2. The overall quality of wines is average at best. Consumers who blindly purchase wines from this region have the odds stacked against them, because the majority of the Loire's wines are mediocre (well over 50% of the wines tasted from the excellent 1995, 1996, and 1997 vintages cannot be recommended).

3. Vintage quality is highly erratic, largely because much of the Loire is in northern Europe, where the climate is marginal and unpredictable. In great vintages this region's offerings combine ripeness with high acidity, resulting in wines as outstanding as any in the world. In vintages characterized by cold, damp summers, the wines will have searing acidity and insufficient fruit.

4. Finally, the Loire is, in large measure, ignored. With few exceptions, importers have approached the Loire as a secondary wine-growing region, spending extremely little time and energy ferreting out good producers or working closely to improve the quality with those they do represent. The efforts of hands-on, quality-driven importers whose positive influence is strongly felt in Burgundy, the Rhône, and the south of France do surprisingly little in the Loire. While it is all but impossible to visit Burgundy without tripping over famous Ameri-

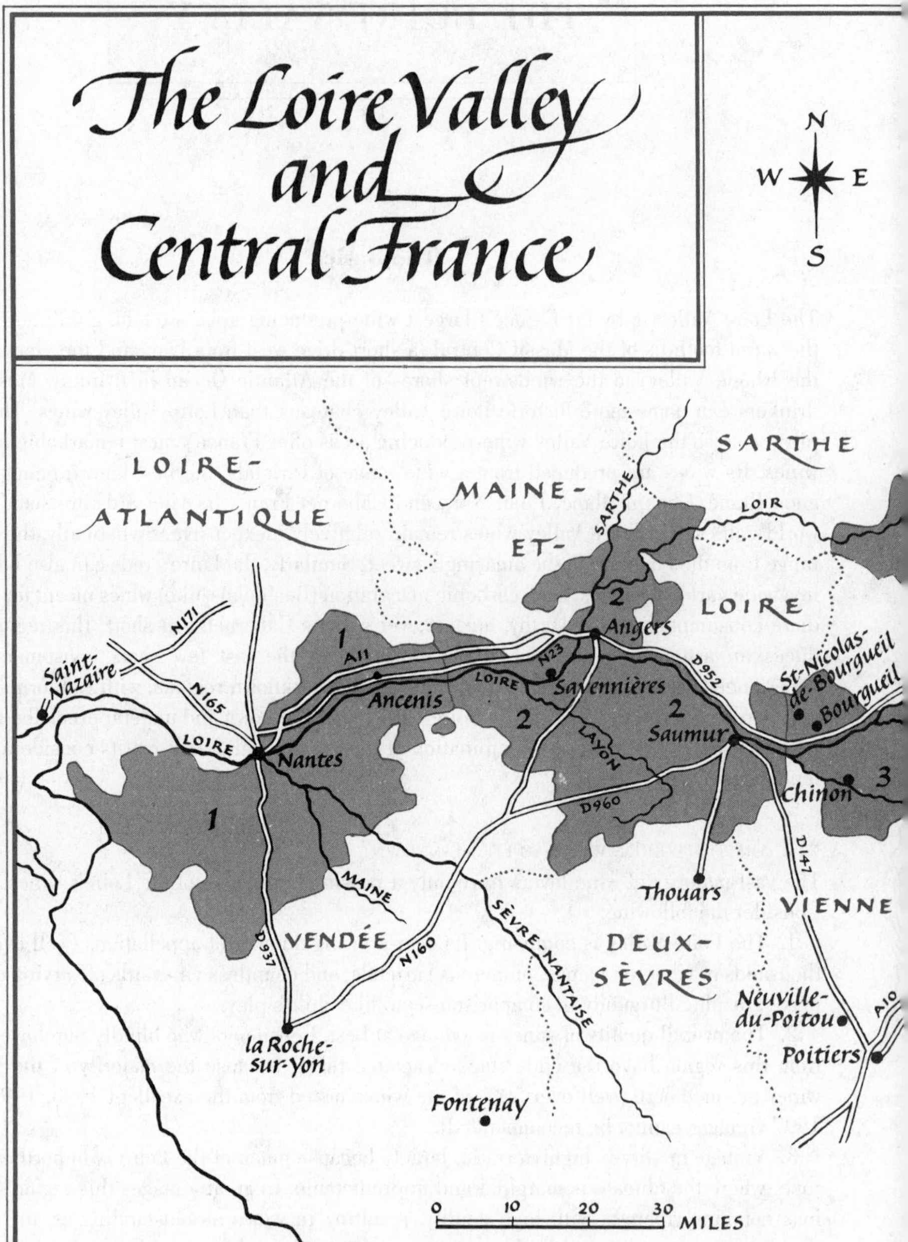

The Loire Valley and Central France

LOIRE-ATLANTIQUE

MAINE-ET-LOIRE

SARTHE

SARTHE

LOIR

Saint-Nazaire

N171

N165

LOIRE

Nantes

Ancenis

A11

LOIRE

N23

2 Angers

Savennières

LAYON

2

2 Saumur

St-Nicolas-de-Bourgueil

Bourgueil

3

Chinon

D952

D147

1

D960

MAINE

D937

VENDÉE

N160

Thouars

SÈVRE-NANTAISE

DEUX-SÈVRES

VIENNE

Neuville-du-Poitou

A10

Poitiers

la Roche-sur-Yon

Fontenay

0   10   20   30 MILES

0   20   40 KILOMETERS

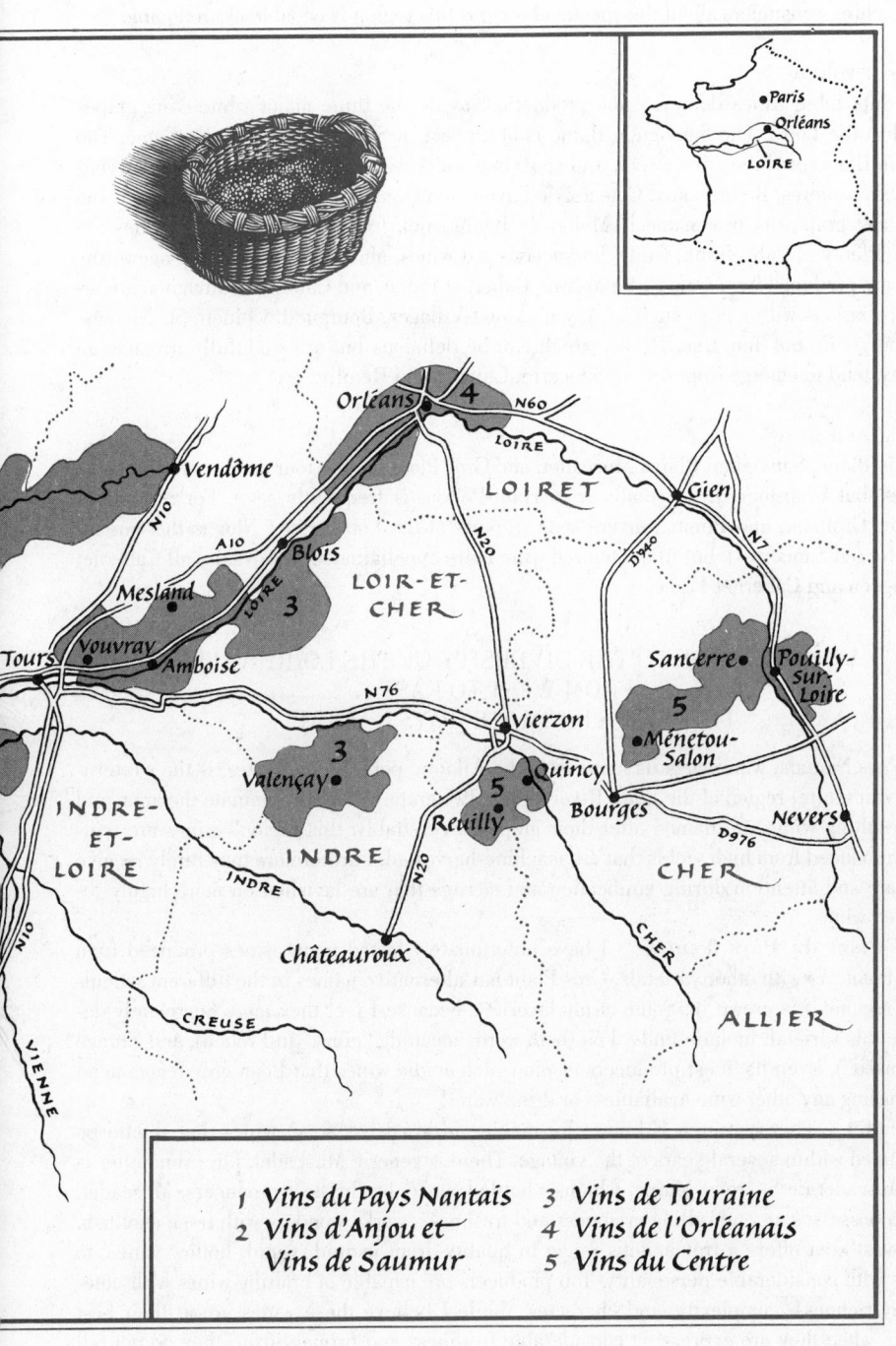

Paris
Orléans
LOIRE

Orléans
N60
LOIRE
LOIRET
Gien
Vendôme
N10
A10
LOIRE
Blois
LOIR-ET-
CHER
N20
D940
N7
Mesland
Vouvray
Tours
Amboise
N76
Vierzon
Sancerre
Pouilly-
sur-
Loire
5
Ménetou-
Salon
INDRE-
ET-
LOIRE
Valençay
3
Quincy
Reuilly
5
Bourges
D976
Nevers
N20
INDRE
CHER
N10
INDRE
Châteauroux
CHER
VIENNE
CREUSE
ALLIER

1 Vins du Pays Nantais   3 Vins de Touraine
2 Vins d'Anjou et   4 Vins de l'Orléanais
  Vins de Saumur   5 Vins du Centre

can importers, in the Loire there are numerous quality producers that have never sold a bottle in the United States. Furthermore, wine merchants and writers have not done an adequate job teaching consumers about the spectacular gems this region is capable of producing.

TYPES OF WINE

Dry white table wines dominate the production, as do the three major white wine grapes found in the Loire. The Sauvignon Blanc is at its best in Sancerre and Pouilly-Fumé. The Chenin Blanc produces dry, sweet, and sparkling white wines. It reaches its zenith in Vouvray, Savennières, Bonnezeaux, Coteaux du Layon, and Quarts de Chaume. Last, there is the Muscadet grape (its true name is Melon de Bourgogne), from which Muscadet wines are made. Plenty of light, frank, fruity, herbaceous red wines, and a few serious and ageworthy ones, are produced from Gamay, Pinot Noir, Cabernet Franc, and Cabernet Sauvignon grapes in appellations with names such as Anjou, Anjou-Villages, Bourgueil, Chinon, St.-Nicolas-de-Bourgueil, and Touraine. Rosés, which can be delicious but are frightfully irregular in quality, tend to emerge from Anjou, Sancerre, Chinon, and Reuilly.

GRAPE VARIETIES

Chenin Blanc, Sauvignon Blanc, Muscadet, and Gros Plant are the four dominant white wine grapes, but Chardonnay, especially from Haut-Poitou, is frequently seen. For red wines, Gamay, Grolleau, and Pinot Noir are seen in parts of the Loire (Pinot Noir is the varietal used for red Sancerres), but in the top red wine Loire appellations it is virtually all Cabernet Sauvignon and Cabernet Franc.

A QUICK GUIDE TO THE DIVERSITY OF THE LOIRE VALLEY FROM WEST TO EAST THE WINES FROM THE PAYS NANTAIS

The Pays Nantais, which gets its name from the Atlantic port city of Nantes, is the westernmost viticultural region of the Loire River valley. Two grape varietals dominate the area, and the resulting wines are named after their grapes. Regrettably, this region's wines are typically produced from high yields that are machine-harvested. Furthermore they rarely receive the care and attention during vinification and *élevage* that are lavished on more highly respected wines.

Gros Plant du Pays Nantais   I have unfortunately tasted many wines produced from Gros Plant. As with other varietals, Gros Plant has alternative names in the different viticultural regions it is grown in. Some of my favorites, because I feel they more adequately describe this varietal, include Folle, Fou (both words meaning "crazy" in French), and Enragé ("enraged"). Even its finest producers fashion such acidic wines that I can only recommend purchasing any other wine available—or drink water!

Muscadet   This vast area is known for making inexpensive, fresh wines that should be consumed within several years of the vintage. There is generic Muscadet, but even better is the Muscadet de Sèvre et Maine, which is bottled *sur-lie* by the best producers. Muscadet, which possesses an enthralling crispness and freshness, works wonders with fresh shellfish. This vast area offers a tremendous range in quality, from insipid, vapid, hollow wines, to wines with considerable personality. Top producers are capable of crafting wines with noteworthy richness, complexity, and character. While I believe these wines are at their best young, when they are expressing considerable freshness and primary fruit, they do not fall apart with aging. Topflight older Muscadets take on some Chenin-like nuances of almonds and herbs with cellaring. The best recent vintages for Muscadet have been 1997 and 1996.

Muscadet's finest producers include Château de Chasseloir, Chéreau-Carré (particularly their "Château l'Oiseliniere de la Ramée"), Domaine des Dorices, Domaine de l'Ecu, Domaine le Fief Dubois (particularly their "Le Fief du Breil"), Domaine de la Haie Trois Sols, Louis Métaireau, Domaine du Moulin de la Minière (particularly their "Cuvée Prestige"), Domaine La Quilla, and the Vignerons de la Noëlle (particularly their "Les Follies Siffait").

THE WINES FROM ANJOU AND THE SAUMUROIS

Angers (the region around it is called Anjou) and Saumur (its region is the Saumurois) are towns located on the Loire River in western France. As the crow flies, Angers is approximately 100 miles from the Atlantic Ocean and Saumur slightly less than 200. The vineyards around Angers and Saumur are all located quite close to the Loire and its many tributaries, which serve to moderate vineyard temperatures. In fact, freezing temperatures in winter and early spring prevent vines from growing just a few miles north of the Loire. The geology of each region differs, with Anjou's being composed primarily of schist, volcanic rocks, sedimentary deposits, sandstone, and slate and the Saumurois's having mostly chalk and sedimentary deposits.

Whites   What both regions' whites have in common is their reliance on Chenin Blanc. All the whites produced in the appellations of Anjou and the Saumurois are made either entirely from Chenin Blanc or, in the case of the regional appellations, from a preponderance of Chenin. Whites from these neighboring areas can be either dry, off-dry, or sweet.

Sweet Whites   One of the best-kept secrets in the wine world are the sweet wines produced in Anjou. These are, without a doubt, the finest values to be found in French sweet wines. Produced from Chenin Blanc, a varietal that, like Riesling, can produce world-class sweet *and* dry wines, many of these offerings have prodigious cellaring capacity. Anyone who has ever tasted a top Quarts de Chaume, Coteaux du Layon, or Bonnezeaux knows the amazing heights that can be attained by these wines in top vintages. Whereas young Sauternes and New World sweet wines can often be heavy (sometimes even flabby) and oak laden, sweet Anjou Chenin Blancs can be amazingly delicate, lacelike, supremely nuanced wines. In their youth they are often more accessible than German sweet offerings because their acidity, while quite high, is generally more integrated and the fruit more dominant. In time, like all sweet wines, those from Anjou take on an added dimension as their sweetness and fruit melt into their mineral-laden cores. Some of the most extraordinary wines I have ever tasted have been mature Chenins from Anjou (including René Renou's 1947 Bonnezeaux and Baumard's 1945 Quarts de Chaume).

Off-Dry Whites   The off-dry wines of Anjou and Saumur, in addition to being virtually unknown, suffer from the same fate as most of the world's off-dry wines—they are ignored by consumers who seem to want wines to be either dry *or* sweet. In my view, this is a mistake. Anjou and the Saumurois's off-dry wines can often provide the best of both worlds. They have a trace of residual sugar that excites the palate and matches well with spicy and intensely flavored foods, yet they do not possess the overpowering weight of fully sweet wines.

Dry Whites   Dry Chenin Blanc has many faces, best exemplified by the extremely ageworthy, mineral-laden Savennières and the crisp lemon/lime Saumurs that require immediate consumption. They often possess bracing acidity, providing a lively and refreshing alternative to the thick and often dry, flabby whites routinely encountered on the market.

Red and Rosé Wines   Anjou is (wrongly) acclaimed for its rosé wines, which can range from dry to medium sweet. In the 1980s Anjou and Saumur reds produced from Cabernet Franc, Cabernet Sauvignon, Gamay, and Grolleau began to receive considerable attention from bargain hunters looking for inexpensive, light-bodied, fruity red wines. In particular, Gamay has done well in Anjou, producing richly fruity wines. Cabernet Franc and Cabernet Sauvignon have made considerable progress in the nineties as some producers realized that ripeness matters. Currently a handful of producers craft wines with intense dark fruit aromatics and rich Cabernet personalities packed with blackberries and fresh herbs. Hard tannins in this northern region continue to be a problem, yet considerable progress has been made. While there is still much work to be done, Anjou, Anjou-Villages, Saumur, and Saumur-Champigny do offer a few delicious (very reasonably priced) alternatives to frightfully expensive Bordeaux for Cabernet lovers.

A FEW NOTEWORTHY APPELLATIONS

Anjou Whites (Dry)　Wines from this regional appellation (similar to the generic "Bourgogne" and "Bordeaux" appellations) must be produced from a minimum of 80% Chenin Blanc, with Chardonnay and Sauvignon Blanc providing the balance. Recent tastings have confirmed that Anjou is making enormous progress in the quality of its wines. Yields are being reduced, and innovative vignerons are doing their best to provide consumers with a viable option to the omnipresent Chardonnay. In the past few years, the vignerons of Anjou (and a few other appellations like Bonnezeaux) have taken steps to ensure this qualitative resurgence. In order to be entitled to appellation status, each grower must now submit his or her vineyards to three inspections during the growing season by experts who check to make sure proper viticultural practices are employed to remain within the legal yield limits.

The finest recent vintages include 1997 (rich) and 1996 (vibrant and lemony). Consumers searching out great values in lemony, minerally whites should consider some offerings from the Domaine de la Bergerie, Château du Breuil, Château de Fesles ("F" de Fesles), Domaine Vincent Ogereau, or Domaine Richou.

Cabernet d'Anjou (Sweet Rosé)　The name suggests a red wine, but in essence this is a rosé that tends to be herbaceous and sweet. It is a style of wine that does not particularly appeal to me, but in superripe vintages like 1997 some producers crafted supple, sweet, cherry-flavored rosés that some consumers may enjoy. Domaine Vincent Ogereau and Château de Passavant are Cabernet d'Anjou producers of merit.

Coteaux de l'Aubance (Off-Dry or Sweet)　This appellation is all but unknown in the United States (and even in France!). Its wines are generally off-dry or sweet, delicate, floral, with touches of honeysuckle, almond extract, and flavors reminiscent of cool Earl Grey tea with cream and sugar. They are not as long-lived as some others from the region and should be drunk over their first 10 years of life. They can easily accompany food, as their sweetness is not overpowering (except in very ripe years like 1997). Several of my favorite matches are with fish or lightly spiced chicken dishes. I use them when a full-bodied Alsatian VT would be too much for a dish or meal or when a dry wine would be overpowered by a food's intense flavors. The finest recent vintages include 1997, 1996, 1995, 1990, and 1989. Some of the better producers to search out include Domaine des Charbotières, Domaine de Montgilet, Moulin des Besneries, and Domaine Richou.

Coteaux du Layon (Sweet)　Truly one of the world's most undervalued sweet wines, a Coteaux du Layon can sport the names of seven recognized villages (including Faye, St. Aubin, St. Lambert, Rablay, Beaulieu, Rochefort, and Chaume). The local cognoscenti consider Chaume the best (at present, Chaume producers are attempting to have their appellation upgraded to grand cru status). Bonnezeaux and Quarts de Chaume are "crus" of Coteaux du Layon. They must be produced from vines in specifically delimited areas and, in addition, must attain certain minimum sugar levels in order to legally be called Bonnezeaux and Quarts de Chaume. If they cannot meet these requirements, they are entitled only to Coteaux du Layon status. The finest recent vintages include 1997, 1996, 1995, 1990, and 1989.

Coteaux du Layons are sweet wines that are not generally as powerful as the Bonnezeaux and Quarts de Chaume but tend to be significantly richer than wines from Coteaux de l'Aubance. The flavors of Coteaux du Layon are very much like those of Coteaux de l'Aubance, but with more density and an added mineral dimension. These are often elegant wines with a refined blend of fruit, sweetness, and acid. In France, wines from Coteaux du Layon, Bonnezeaux, and Quarts de Chaume are often consumed as the ideal apéritif or to accompany foie gras, but I enjoy them as a substitute for dessert. These wines age remarkably well, with bottle age revealing flavors of spiced apples, minerals, traces of honey, caramel, butterscotch, and loads of honeysuckle.

Some of the finest Coteaux du Layon producers are Patrick Baudoin, Domaine des Baumards, Domaine de la Bergerie, Château du Breuil, Philippe Delesvaux, Domaine Gaudard, Château de la Genaiserie, Domaine des Grandes Vignes, Château de la Guimonière, Domaine Vincent Ogereau, Domaine du Petit Val, Jo Pithon, Château de Plaisance, Château de la Roulerie, Domaine des Sablonnettes, Domaine Sauveroy, and Château Soucherie.

Some of the finest Bonnezeaux producers include Château de Fesles, Domaine des Grandes Vignes, Domaine du Petit Val, Domaine des Petits Quarts, and Domaine René Renou. Some of the finest Quarts de Chaume producers include Domaine des Baumards, Château de Plaisance, and Château de Suronde.

Coteaux de Saumur (Off-Dry)   These 100% Chenin Blanc–based wines can be delicate, lacelike beauties with superb delineation. Lively herbal tea, mineral, and citrus flavors are softened by small amounts of residual sugar. I recommend drinking them as an aperitif or with cream-based, grilled, or spicy foods. The 1997s are excellent yet richer than the norm, and the 1996s are bright, lemony, and vibrant. Both vintages are highly recommended. Some of the best producers of Coteaux de Saumur include Domaine des Champs Fleuris and Domaine de Nerleux.

Saumur (Reds)   Lower yields, less manipulation, and good vintages have produced some excellent wines in this historically underachieving appellation. These reasonably priced, Cabernet Franc- and Cabernet Sauvignon-dominated wines can be delicious near-term drinking wines from the region's best producers.

Some Saumur producers of merit include Domaine Langlois-Château and Domaine des Raynières.

Saumur (Whites: dry)   Saumur, a town to the east of Angers on the Loire River, is best known for its red wines, yet its refreshing, crisp, lively, and citrus-flavored whites merit attention. As with "Anjou" whites, this regional appellation's wines must be produced from a minimum of 80% Chenin Blanc (Sauvignon Blanc and Chardonnay can be added to the blend). The finest recent vintages include 1997 (rich) and 1996 (vibrant and lemony). The best producers include Domaine des Nerleux and Domaine de Saint Jean.

Saumur-Champigny (Reds)   Produced primarily from Cabernet Franc (known as "Breton" in this region), Saumur-Champignys may also include up to 20% Cabernet Sauvignon or Pineau d'Aunis in their blends (this last varietal is slowly disappearing). Just a few years ago this appellation's reputation for producing first-rate reds was unjustified. The wines were often hollow, revealing evidence of unripe fruit, and finished on hard, astringent tannins. Recently, however, the efforts of a handful of producers have paid enormous dividends. While topflight Saumur-Champignys are far from inexpensive, they are noteworthy values when compared with Bordeaux's absurdly high prices. Young, the finest Saumur-Champignys display dark ruby colors, cassis and fresh herb aromas, and rich personalities crammed with blackberries and dark cherries. Hard tannins remain a concern in some vintages. With aging these wines develop considerable complexity, with slate, earth, and mineral notes intertwined with strawberries, raspberries, and black currants. Consumers take note: This appellation has a few producers crafting truly outstanding wines! The finest recent vintages include 1997 (the ripest and most supple), 1996 (bright and in need of cellaring), 1990, and 1989 (these last two vintages are at their peaks).

Saumur-Champigny's finest producers include Domaine des Champs Fleuris, Château de Hureau, Domaine René Noël Legrand (particularly the "Les Rogelins"), Château de Parnay, Domaine des Roches Neuves (particularly the "Cuvée Marginale"), Clos Rougeard (the famed Foucault brothers), Domaine de Saint-Just (particularly the "Clos Moleton").

Savennières (Generally Dry, but Can Be Off-Dry or Sweet)   Located on the northern bank of the Loire River just west of Angers and directly across the river from the vineyards of Coteaux du Layon and Coteaux de l'Aubance, Savennières's vineyards benefit from the moderating climatic influence of the river. These are not lush, oaky wines, but rather austere, steely, crisp, highly delineated, and amazingly long-lived whites that exhibit mineral, stone, floral, and earth flavors. Prior to World War I, Savennières were so prized by wine aficionados that bottles often sold for more than a Montrachet! Today they are largely forgotten, so extraordinary, complex, and ageworthy wines can be purchased for little more than a song. These wines are delicious within the first 4 years of their release, when they are expressing primary fruit flavors, then shut down and become awkward for 5–6 years. Ten years or so of cellaring reveals wines of considerable complexity and magnificent minerality.

The best producers of Savennières include Domaine des Baumards, Château de Chamboureau, Domaine du Closel, Château d'Epiré, Domaine de la Monnaie, Château Soucherie, and Clos des Varennes.

THE RED AND WHITE WINES OF TOURAINE

Touraine, as the regions around the city of Tours are known, is responsible for some of the Loire's most famous red and white wines. Names like Vouvray and Chinon are not unknown to the majority of the world's wine lovers. Interestingly, however, while the names are known, the wines themselves are not. This bucolic region stretches from Bourgeuil, St. Nicolas de Bourgeuil, and Chinon in the west (about a 45-minute drive from Tours), to the regional Touraine appellation vineyards that stretch across vast plains and rolling hills to the east and southeast of Tours.

The glorious Chenin Blanc is the predominant varietal (Vouvray, Montlouis, and the whites of Chinon are 100% Chenin) for whites; Cabernet Franc is the driving force behind Chinon, Bourgeuil, and St. Nicolas de Bourgeuil; and a host of different grape types are found in the regional appellation wines (Sauvignon Blanc, Gamay, Cabernet Franc, and Cabernet Sauvignon dominate).

Bourgueil   If you ask a Parisian about Bourgueil, chances are it is one of his or her favorites. More popular in France than in America, Bourgueil makes a fruity, raspberry-scented and -flavored wine that should be drunk in its first 5–6 years of life. The problem is that unless the vintage is exceptionally ripe, as it was in 1989, 1990, 1996, and 1997, these wines are strikingly vegetal. The finest producers include Jean-Yves Billet (for his Vieilles Vignes and Cuvée les Bezards), Domaine de la Chanteleuserie (Thierry Boucard), Domaine des Chesnaies, Domaine de la Chevalerie (Pierre Caslot), and all the cuvées of the supertalented Pierre-Jacques Druet (including his scrumptious and moderately priced Bourgueil Rosé).

Chinon   This appellation is considered by many to produce the best red wines of the Loire Valley. Made from Cabernet Franc, in exceptionally ripe years such as 1997, 1996, 1990, and 1989 it possesses abundant herb-tinged raspberry fruit. In less ripe years Chinon wines are intensely acidic and vegetal. Several minimal interventionists turn out handcrafted wines that deserve to be tasted; however, the vast majority of Chinons are harvested phenologically unripe, a problem that plagues the Loire's reds. Grape sugars can attain adequate levels (and are invariably boosted via chaptalization), yet if the skins, pits, and stems (for those who don't destem) have not had sufficient time to ripen, the resulting wines have hard, astringent, and rustic finishes. The best recent vintages have been 1997, 1996, 1990, and 1989.

Chinon's finest producers include Philippe Alliet, Bernard Baudry, Couly-Dutheil (particularly the "Clos de l'Echo"), Pierre-Jacques Druet, Château de la Grille, Charles Joguet, Wilfred Rousse (particularly the "Vieilles Vignes"), and Gérard Spelty (particularly the "Clos de Neuilly").

Jasnières   This 47-acre appellation north of Tours produces very dry, often excellent white wines from Chenin Blanc. These powerfully minerally wines are not easy to find, but if you come across any, you are well advised to try them for their delicacy, as well as rarity.

Montlouis   Montlouis is often regarded as the stepchild of its more famous northern neighbor, Vouvray. Its wines can be dry, medium sweet, or sweet and are generally less expensive than those from Vouvray. Given the greatness of Chenin Blanc as a varietal, and the excellent *terroirs* at their disposal, it is a travesty that Montlouis's producers do not craft better wines. This appellation's finest producers include Olivier Delétang and François Chidaine.

St.-Nicolas-de-Bourgueil   This may well be the most overrated red wine–producing appellation of the Loire. Parisians, enamored by this appellation's name, have led its once reasonable prices to skyrocket. When they are good, they are either light, early drinkers, with delightful perfumes of raspberry and currant fruit flavors followed by a soft, round, supple texture; or dark fruit filled, highly structured, and deserving of cellaring. Regrettably, however, the majority of St.-Nicolas-de-Bourgueils are harvested unripe and chaptalized to an "acceptable" alcohol level and have rustic, tannic finishes—perfect for the Parisian bistros that serve them as cold as their whites!

Touraine   This general appellation covers considerable acreage, so it is important to know who are the best producers, as generalizations about the wines cannot be made. Certainly the Sauvignon Blanc and Chenin Blanc range from plonk to delicious fruity, vibrant wines. The red wines can also range from disgustingly vegetal to richly fruity, aromatic offerings. One constant is that any Touraine white or red wine should be consumed within 2–3 years of the vintage. The best recent vintage has been 1997 and 1996. The region's finest winemaker, the Domaine de la Charmoise's Henri Marionet, produces one of France's and the world's greatest Sauvignon Blancs (the "M de Marionet") in top vintages. His reds are meticulously crafted and fruit packed and offer superb value. Touraine's finest producers include Domaine de la Charmoise and Maurice Barbou's Domaine des Corbillières (Sauvignon Blanc is a perennial "best buy").

Vouvray   Vouvray vies with Sancerre for the best-known appellation of the Loire Valley. Unlike Sancerre, no rosé or red wine is produced in Vouvray. It is all white and all from the Chenin Blanc grape, which can reach spectacular levels of acidity in the limestone and chalky/clay soils of these charming vineyards located a short distance east of Tours. A huge appellation (over 3,800 acres), Vouvray produces tasty, sparkling wines, wonderfully crisp, delicious, bone-dry wines, medium sweet wines that are superb as an aperitif or with spicy foods, and some of the most spectacularly honeyed sweet wines one will ever taste.

Regrettably, the majority of this appellation's producers live off of its reputation in England and France and generally produce diluted, rot-infested, and oversulfured wines. Pinot Noir may be the most fragile and fickle grape, but Chenin Blanc is possibly the world's most unforgiving varietal; any and all flaws in these wines appeared magnified. From a good producer, Vouvrays can be as great as any wine made on earth. From a mediocre or bad producer, they are simply awful. The sweet wines, sometimes indicated by the words *moëlleux* or *liqoureux* on the label (or a proprietary name or a variation of *réserve*), are the result of the noble rot and can last for 40–50 or more years. The finest sweet wines produced in the 1997, 1996, 1995, 1990, and 1989 vintages are show-stoppers, mind numbing and awe inspiring. The 1996 vintage is a particularly great year, as it forced even mediocre producers to make stellar wines, while only the best were able to harness the potential greatness of 1995 and 1997. The finest wines from these recent vintages are modern-day equivalents of the 1959s and 1947s (both vintages are still delicious today), and consumers are well advised to stock up.

The following paragraph lists Vouvray's top producers, but two deserve special mention. Domaine Gaston Huet's Noël Pinguet and Domaine du Clos Naudin's Philippe Foreau are two of the best producers of white wines in the world. Pinguet, a biodynamic farmer, crafted stellar, world-class dry, demi-sec (medium-sweet), and sweet wines in 1989, 1995, and 1997. Foreau, one of the finest tasters I have had the honor to meet, made out-of-this-world wines in 1990 and 1996. Both producers craft sparkling wines (Domaine Huet's Pinguet a "Pétillant" and Foreau a "Brut Traditionel") that are superb and compete qualitatively with top-notch Champagnes at a fraction of the price. Regrettably, this appellation's two locomotives (Pinguet and Foreau) are pulling very few wagons behind them. Of the 200–300 vignerons and *négociants* who fashion wines from Vouvray's great *terroirs*, only a handful can be recommended. Vouvray's finest producers include Domaine Huet—Noël Pinguet and Domaine du Clos Naudin—Philippe Foreau (both of these are five-star estates), followed (alphabetically) by Domaine des Aubuisières (Bernard Fouquet), Domaine de la Biche (Christophe et Jean-Claude Pichot), Domaine Bourillon-Dorléans, Domaine Champalou, Domaine de la Fontainerie (Catherine Dhoye-Deruet), Château Gaudrelle, Thierry Nérisson, Domaine des Orfeuilles (Bernard Hérivault), Domaine François Pinon, Domaine de la Saboterie, Vigneau-Chevreau, Vignobles Brisebarre, and Domaine du Viking.

THE RED AND WHITE WINES OF THE SANCERROIS

Ménétou-Salon　Ménétou-Salon, a relatively small appellation of 250 acres, produces excellent white wines from Sauvignon Blanc and some herbal, spicy, light-bodied rosé and red wines from Pinot Noir. In my opinion, the wines to buy are the Sauvignons, which exhibit a pungent, herbaceous, earthy, currant nose and crisp, rich, grassy flavors. The best recent vintage has been 1997 and 1996. Ménétou-Salon's finest producer is Henri Pellé.

Pouilly-Fumé　Pouilly is the name of the village, and *fumé* means smoke. This appellation, renowned the world over for its richly scented, flinty (some say smoky), earthy, herbaceous, melony white wines that can range from medium bodied to full and intense, does indeed produce some of the world's most exciting wines from Sauvignon. The best recent vintages include spectacular 1990s that should drink well for another 2–3 years, 1996s that will be excellent over the next 5–7 years, and 1997s that should be drunk over the next 2–3 years. By the way, a food that is heavenly with Pouilly-Fumé is goat cheese.

One producer, Didier Dagueneau, is clearly this appellation's finest. His wines have purity, richness, depth, complexity, concentration, and significant aging potential. Is it any wonder that he is one of the rare vignerons of the appellation to have moderate yields and to eschew machine harvesters? After Didier Dagueneau, the finest producers of Pouilly-Fumé are Francis Blanchet, Domaine A. Cailbourdin, Jean-Claude Châtelain, Domaine La Croix Canat (F. Tinel-Blondelet), Domaine Serge Dagueneau et Filles, Charles Dupuy (particularly the "Vieilles Vignes"), Domaine des Fines Caillottes (Jean Pabiot), Masson-Blondelet, Château de Nozet / de Ladoucette, Régis Minet, La Moynerie (particularly the "Cuvée Majorum"), and Hervé Seguin.

Pouilly-sur-Loire　This tiny yet interesting appellation relies on the Chasselas grape, a lowly regarded varietal that can make fruity, floral, soft wines when yields are restricted. Wines from this appellation should be inexpensive and can be an ideal aperitif if consumed within 1 year of the vintage. The finest Pouilly-sur-Loires I have tasted have come from Domaine Serge Dagueneau et Filles.

Quincy　Another appellation dedicated to Sauvignon Blanc, Quincy, which is near the historic city of Bourges, takes Sauvignon to its most herbaceous (some would say vegetal) limit. This can be an almost appallingly asparagus-scented and -flavored wine in underripe years, but in top years, such as 1997, that character is subdued. Quincy wines are bone dry and, even though their ageworthiness is touted, should be drunk within 4 years of their release.

Sancerre　Sancerre and Vouvray are probably the best-known appellations of the vast Loire Valley viticultural region. A highly fashionable wine for over 2 decades, white Sancerre's success is based on its crisp acidity allied with rich, zesty, Sauvignon fruitiness.

A small amount of red and rosé, which are rarely recommendable, is made from Pinot Noir. Sancerre's success with whites is justifiable in view of the number of high-quality producers in this region. The steep slopes of chalk and flint that surround Sancerre's best villages—Bué, Chavignol, and Verdigny—are undoubtedly responsible for the flinty, subtle, earthy character evident in so many of the top wines.

Consumers should note that two of this appellation's finest vignerons, Edmond Vatan and Paul Cotat (whose wines also appear with the names Francis and François Cotat), produce old-style Sancerres, quite different from the norm found today. Cotat's and Vatan's wines are rich, full flavored, thick, and sometimes not bone dry. They are also some of the finest Sauvignon Blancs I have ever put to my lips.

The finest recent vintages have been 1997, 1996, 1995, and 1990. White Sancerre and the limited quantities of rosés should be drunk within 2–3 years of the vintage, although some can last longer. Red Sancerre can last for 4–5 years.

A small group of standouts clearly produce this appellation's best wines. They are Paul Cotat, Lucien Crochet (Gilles Crochet), André Neveu, Vincent Pinard, and Edmond Vatan. Sancerre has many topflight producers, including Franck et Jean-François Bailly, Henri Bourgeois, Domaine le Colombier (Roger Neveu), Vincent Delaporte, Charles Dupuy ("Vieilles Vignes" cuvée), Comte Lafond, Domaine de Montigny (Henri Natter), Domaine de la Moussière (Alphonse Mellot), Domaine Henri Pellé (from Ménétou-Salon), Hippolyte Reverdy, Etienne Riffault, Domaine Jean-Max Roger, Domaine de la Rossignole (Pierre Cherrier et Fils), Domaine de St. Pierre (Pierre Prieur et Fils), Domaine de St. Romble (Paul Vattan), and Domaine Lucien Thomas (Jean and Ginette Thomas).

1999–2000 BUYING STRATEGY

To the extent you can still find any of the great 1989s, 1990s, 1995s, and 1996s from Vouvray, Savennières, Bonnezeaux, Coteaux de l'Aubance, Coteaux du Layon, and Quarts de Chaume, you should move quickly to purchase them. A few magnificent white 1997s were produced in the Loire, yet the majority of wines are heavy and ponderous. However, the 1997s do offer exceptional early drinking (particularly when compared with the 1998s, which were plagued by rot and rain).

VINTAGE GUIDE

1998—Preliminary tastings and conversations with vignerons leads me to believe that 1998 will not be remembered as a good vintage, at least for dry whites and reds. However, some sweet wine producers in Anjou and Vouvray were able to craft excellent, if not outstanding, wines in this vintage.

1997—The heat that plagued Europe during 1997's summer and early fall, combined with untimely rains in certain areas of the Loire, fashioned this vintage. High temperatures are responsible for the ripest, most approachable, and most succulent Loire reds in memory. Thick, supple, and fruit-packed reds were produced by the best estates in all of the Loire's red wine appellations. Given the absurdly high prices of the more famous red wine–producing regions, consumers should certainly look to the Loire's 1997s for a reprieve. In general, the Loire's whites, from Sancerre in the east to Muscadet in the west, are ripe, dense, and often plodding wines (for the Loire!). Some sweet wine producers, notably Domaine des Baumard's Florent Baumard (Quarts de Chaume), Domaine Gaston Huet's Noël Pinguet (Vouvray), and René Renou in Bonnezeaux, were able to maintain freshness and vibrancy in this hugely rich and superripe vintage.

1996—Throughout the Loire, 1996 was a superb vintage. A warm and sunny summer was followed by an equally fine late summer and fall (many vignerons commented that they had never seen such a bright autumn, stressing its "luminosity") that saw moderate daytime temperatures and cool evenings in addition to a persistent dry wind from the north. This combination of light (photosynthesis) and relatively cool temperatures promoted the ripening of the grapes without a significant loss of acidity (heat is blamed for reducing acid in grapes), while the north winds dehydrated (concentrated) the grapes. The resulting wines, in both red and white, have exceptional ripeness (including well-ripened tannins in the reds), vibrancy, and exceptional ageworthiness. For the Loire, 1996 is certainly one of the finest vintages of the century.

1995—The 1995 vintage, as in many parts of France, is a year of intense concentration. Warm and dry summer months led to great ripeness in the grapes' sugars, yet sporadic rains prior to the harvests promoted rot in many of the region's vineyards. Sorting was a necessity. The red wines of the Loire are densely crammed with black fruits (because of the heat), yet all share one thing in common: astringent tannins (because of the rains, they were harvested without having attained full phenolic ripeness). From the reds of Anjou, through the famous red appellations of Touraine, to the reds of Sancerre, all of the Loire's 1995s are impressive for their colors, aromatics, attacks, and midpalates yet are aggressive and harsh in the finish. The 1995 vintage in whites, however, was a great success in the Sancerrois, with the top producers of Vouvray Domaine Huet (Pinguet), Domaine du Clos Naudin (Foreau), and Domaine François Pinon, and with many top vignerons of Anjou (Domaine Baumard, for example).

1994—A stormy, hot summer had most producers hoping for a repeat of 1989 and 1990. September's 3 weeks of intermittent rain and storms prevented 1994 from being a great vintage. Nevertheless, the top producers have fashioned very good dry white wines, if the rot-tinged grapes were left in the vineyard. Production is smaller than normal for the finest estates that practiced serious selection. Consequently pressure to raise prices is a strong possibility. Sauvignon Blanc is the most successful varietal in 1994. With respect to the red wine grapes, Gamay was the least affected by the rains. The Chenin Blancs were more mixed.

1993—Another rain-plagued harvest, 1993 has turned out to be a good to very good vintage for the dry whites, an average-quality vintage for the reds, and an irregular vintage for the sweet white wines. The 1993 dry Sauvignons are crisp, lively, medium-bodied wines, with more pleasing aromas than the soft, diffuse 1992s or the lean, high-acid 1991s. All things considered, 1993 is a far more successful vintage than was expected following the miserable, wet, cold month of September.

1992—The Loire Valley escaped most of the horrific downpours that plagued southern France, but the crop size was appallingly large. Reports of excessive yields from virtually every appellation were numerous. Growers had a chance to pick relatively ripe fruit that produced a good vintage, but only those who kept their yields low produced good wines. This is a vintage of pleasant, straightforward, fruity, soft wines that should be drunk up by 1996. The most successful appellations for white wines are Muscadet, Sancerre, and Pouilly-Fumé. Chinon was the most successful for red wines.

1991—This is a difficult vintage throughout the Loire Valley, with relatively acidic, lean, light-bodied wines that lack ripeness and flavor authority. Successes can be found, but overall, a small crop combined with inadequate ripeness produced ungenerous wines lacking fruit and charm.

1990—This is one of the all-time greatest vintages for just about every region of the Loire Valley, especially the sweet wine appellations and the great dry white wines of Savennières, Pouilly-Fumé, and Sancerre. The levels of richness and intensity of the 1990s are mind-boggling. Consumers lucky enough to be able to find and afford the top cuvées of the decadently sweet wines from Bonnezeaux, Coteaux du Layon, Quarts de Chaume, and Vouvray, as well as some of the spectacularly full-bodied, awesomely rich, dry Savennières, will have treasures that will last in their cellars for 25–30 or more years. Most Muscadet should have been drunk by the beginning of 1993, but the top cuvées of dry Sancerre and Pouilly-Fumé will last (where well stored) through 2000.

The red wines are also surprisingly good; because of the drought and superripeness they are less herbaceous than usual and offer copious quantities of red and black fruits.

1989—Somewhat similar to 1990, although yields were higher and there was less botrytis in the sweet wine vineyards, 1989 is an excellent, in many cases a superb, vintage for Vouvray, Quarts de Chaume, Coteaux du Layon, and Bonnezeaux. It is also a super vintage for Savennières. All the drier wines from Sancerre, Pouilly-Fumé, Touraine, and Muscadet should have been consumed by now, as they were exceptionally low in acidity.

1988—A good but unexciting vintage produced pleasant, textbook wines that admirably represent their appellation or region but lack the huge perfumes, richness, and depth of the finest 1989s and 1990s.

1987—A mediocre to poor year.

OLDER VINTAGES

The decadently rich dessert wines of the Coteaux du Layon, Bonnezeaux, Quarts de Chaume, and Vouvray from 1983, 1976, 1971, 1962, 1959, 1949, and 1947 can be spectacular wines. These wines are still modestly priced and are undoubtedly the greatest bargains in rich dessert wines in the world. While it is not easy to find these older vintages, consumers should put this information to good use by stocking up on the 1989s, 1990s, 1995s, 1996s, and the best 1997s.

Savennières is probably the world's greatest buy in dry, full-bodied white wines. Older Savennières vintages to look for are 1986, 1985, 1978, 1976, 1971, 1969, 1962, and 1959. Occasionally, small quantities of these wines come up for auction. They are well worth the low prices being asked.

Consumers who may have the opportunity to travel to the bucolic Loire Valley should be aware of one of the wine world's great secrets. No other viticultural region I know of has better natural cellars than those found in Vouvray. The cold and humid caves, dug deep into the tufa hillsides, offer extraordinary wine storage conditions. Vouvray producers have seemingly always known this, so their caves are stocked with large quantities of older vintages (including wines going back to the nineteenth century) . . . and many are still for sale. . . .

LANGUEDOC-ROUSSILLON

Great Wine Values

Among all the French viticultural regions, none has made more progress than the vast region referred to as the Languedoc-Roussillon area. Bounded on the northeast by the Rhône Valley, on the east by the Mediterranean Sea, on the west by the hilly terrain known as the "massif central," and on the south by the Pyrenees Mountains of Spain, this sun-drenched

region produces more than half of France's red table wine. Once known for its barely palatable, acidic, thick, alcoholic wines from huge industrial-oriented cooperatives that placed
quantity before quality, the Languedoc-Roussillon region has undergone an amazing trans-
formation since the mid-eighties. Moreover, some of America's most innovative importers are
flocking to the region in search of delicious, bargain-priced white, red, and rosé wines.

There is no shortage of wine from which to choose, because the Languedoc-Roussillon
area, with its 72,000 acres of vines, annually produces an ocean of 310 million cases. The
finest vineyard sites generally tend to be planted on hillsides, with heavy soils that provide
outstanding drainage. Excluding Corsica, Languedoc-Roussillon is the hottest viticultural
region of France. Torrential rainstorms are common during the summer, but the total amount
of rainfall is small and the area, much like the southern Rhône, is buffeted by winds from
both inland and the Mediterranean, thus creating an ideal climate for the sanitary cultivation
of vineyards, with minimal need for fungicides, herbicides, and insecticides.

Most of the progress that has been made is attributable to two major developments. The
advent of temperature-controlled stainless-steel fermentation tanks (an absolute necessity in
this torridly hot region) has greatly enhanced the aromatic purity and fruit in the wines. Even
more important, many of the indigenous grape varieties of this area, Carignan, Cinsault, and
Terret Noir for red and rosé wines, and Clairette, Ugni Blanc, Picpoul, and Maccabeo for
white wines, are used decreasingly in favor of widely renowned, superstar grapes such as
Syrah, Mourvèdre, Cabernet Sauvignon, Merlot, and Grenache. White wine varietals making
significant inroads include Chardonnay, Sauvignon Blanc, and Chenin Blanc. Since the mid-
eighties, thousands of acres of these varietals have been planted.

Across this vast area, stretching from southwest of Avignon, where the appellations of
Châteauneuf du Pape and Tavel end, to the Spanish border, are well over 20 different viticultural regions producing an enormous array of dry white, rosé, and red table wine, as well as
the famed *vins doux naturels,* those sweet dessert wines that are slightly fortified. Much of the
wine from the region has either just recently achieved *appellation contrôlée* status, or remains
entitled to VDQS status, or nothing more than a *vin de pays* designation. As the following
tasting notes indicate, some of the very finest wines can legally be called only *vins de pays.*

Following is a quick rundown of the major viticultural areas.

Costières de Nîmes   This area, which received *appellation contrôlée* status in 1986, produces white, red, and rosé wines. The area takes its name from the extraordinary Roman city
of Nîmes. This is one of the up and coming appellations of France. The vineyard area consists of a group of pebble-strewn slopes and a plateau region that lie in the Rhône delta.
Much of the area could well be called Châteauneuf du Pape south. The production is 75% in
red wine, 20% in rosé, and the remainder in white. There are a number of superb, still relatively unknown estates making terrific wines. The red wines are permitted to be made from a
maximum of 50% Carignan. Other allowable grape varieties include Cinsault, Counoise
Grenache, Mourvèdre, Syrah, Terret Noir, and two obscure red varietals called Aspiran Noir
and Oeillade. The finest estates are turning out delicious cuvées based on blends of Syrah,
Grenache, and Cinsault. White varietals are dominated by Clairette and Grenache Blanc,
with small amounts of Picpoul, Roussanne, Terret Blanc, Ugni Blanc, Malvoisie, Marsanne,
and Maccabeo also present. Readers should search out the following estates: Grande Cassagne, Mas Carlot, Saint-Antoine, Mas des Bressades, Valcombe, Mourgues du Grès, and
Château Tuillerie.

Coteaux du Languedoc   This vast area (given *appellation contrôlée* status in 1985) includes vineyards in three French departments, Aude, Garde, and Herault. It runs from
Nîmes in the north to Narbonne in the south. Consumers will find wines labeled merely with
the appellation of Coteaux du Languedoc, as well as those where the individual village
names are affixed. Two of the finest villages, Saint-Chinian and Faugères, were elevated to
their own *appellation contrôlée* status in 1982. The grape varieties are essentially the same

as in the Costières de Nimes, although the more serious estates use higher percentages of Syrah, Mourvèdre, Grenache, and Counoise in their red wines, generally at the expense of Carignan and Cinsault. The best wines of Faugères have consistently come from Haut-Fabrègues and Gilbert Alquier. Among the best wines of Saint-Chinian are those from Domaine des Jougla, Mas Jullien, Cascaux, Saint-Martin de la Garrigue, and Cazal Viel. Perhaps the greatest wines of the entire appellation of Coteaux du Languedoc (as well as the most expensive) are the Prieuré de Saint-Jean-de-Bebian and Peyre Rose. This wine, and the Mas-de-Daumas Gassac, a *vin de pays*, are irrefutably the two reference-point red wines of the Languedoc-Roussillon region.

Minervois   Minervois may have the best long-range potential of the appellations in the Languedoc-Roussillon area. To say that there are still many underachievers would not be unjust. This area of nearly 14,000 acres of vineyards is bounded on the west by the extraordinary fortified fortress city of Carcassonne and on the east by Saint-Chinian. Minervois flourished under Roman rule but never recovered from the phylloxera epidemic that devastated France's vineyards in the late 19th century. The vineyards, the best of which tend to be located on gently sloping, south-facing, limestone hillsides sheltered from the cold north winds, endure the hottest microclimate of the region. Virtually all of the wine production is red, although it is not surprising to see microquantities of a surprisingly tasty rosé emerge. The amount of white wine produced makes up less than 2% of the total production. Some of the best estates represented in America include Clos l'Escandil, Piccinini, Borie de Maurel, Château de Paraza, Château de Gourgazaud, Daniel Domergue, Tour-Saint-Martin, and Domaine Sainte-Eulalie. Readers should also look for the splendid wines of Minervois produced by the Rhone Valley *négociant* Tardieu-Laurent.

Corbières   Corbières, which is located further down the coast, south of Minervois, was recently elevated to *appellation contrôlée* status. It boasts the largest production area (over 57,000 acres) of the entire Languedoc-Roussillon region. Red wine accounts for 90% of the production, and the predominant varietal is the omnipresent Carignan, although the more serious estates have begun to employ increasing percentages of Syrah and Mourvèdre. The outstanding estates in Corbières include the brilliant Château Le Palais, Château Etang des Colombes, Domaine Saint-Paul, Domaine de Villemajou, La Voulte Gasparets, Maylandie, Serres-Mazard, and the various cuvées from Tardieu-Laurent.

Fitou   Fitou, the oldest of the *appellation contrôlée* regions of the Languedoc-Roussillon area (its *appellation contrôlée* status was bestowed in 1948), represents two separate areas bounded on the north by Corbières. One region, representing low-lying vineyards near the coast, is planted on shallow, gravelly soil atop limestone beds. No one I have ever talked with believes top-quality wines can emerge from this particular sector. On the hillsides farther inland, the best vineyards are planted on sloping, well-drained, sandstone-and-limestone-mixed soils. The ripest, fattest, fruitiest wines from Fitou generally emanate from this area. The grape varieties for Fitou are the same as for the other regions of Languedoc, with Carignan once again the dominant varietal, but the more serious producers are utilizing more Mourvèdre, Syrah, and Grenache. Some rosé wines are made in Fitou, but I have never seen a bottle of white. I do not believe any is permitted under the *appellation contrôlée* laws. Several of the finest estates in Fitou are Lerys, La Rochelière, and Roudène.

Côtes de Roussillon and Côtes de Roussillon-Villages   The Roussillon vineyards, all of which run from the Mediterranean Sea inland, surrounding Perpignan, France's last urban bastion before the Spanish border, are known to have produced wines since the 7th century B.C. There is immense potential, not only for dry red table wines but also for the sweet, fortified wines that often excel in this windy, sun-drenched region. The best vineyards, which are entitled to the Côtes de Roussillon or Côtes de Roussillon-Villages appellation, stretch out over a semicircle of hills facing the Mediterranean Sea. These hillside vineyards, planted on expanses of limestone and granite, enjoy a phenomenally sunny, hot summer. Virtually all of the rainfall results from thunderstorms. It has always amazed me that these wines are still so reasonably priced given the amount of labor necessary to cultivate so many of the terraced vineyards of this region. The tiny amount of white wine produced is generally from such obscure varietals as Malvoise de Roussillon and Maccabeo. The red wines are generally produced from the ubiquitous Carignan, as well as Grenache, Syrah, and Mourvèdre. These are full-bodied, relatively rich wines, with a big, fleshy, peppery character. Despite their softness and easy drinkability when young, several properties make wines that can last for up to a decade. The best estates in the Côtes de Roussillon and Côtes de Roussillon-Villages are Pierre d'Aspres, Cazes Frères, Château de Jau, Domaine Sarda-Malet, Domaine Salvat, and Domaine Saint-Luc. There are also a bevy of cooperatives, none of which I have visited, but several have received high praise, particularly the cooperative of Maury.

Collioure   This tiny appellation, the smallest in the Languedoc-Roussillon region for dry red wine, is located just to the south of the Côtes de Roussillon on an expanse of terraced, hillside vineyards called the Côtes Vermeille. Virtually all of the Collioure vineyards are located on these steeply terraced slopes, and the red wine is produced largely from a blend of Grenache, Carignan, Mourvèdre, Syrah, and Cinsault. Tiny yields are commonplace in Collioure, and as a result the wines tend to be relatively rich and full. They have never been discovered by American wine enthusiasts. The best Collioures come from the great Domaine du Mas Blanc of the late Dr. Parcé, also renowned for his fabulous fortified, portlike Banyuls. There are generally two cuvées of Collioure, one called Les Piloums and the other, Cosprons Levants. Other interesting producers include Thierry Parcé at the Domaine de la Rictorie, and the Celliers des Templiers.

Pic-Saint-Loup and Montpeyroux   These two viticultural areas are relatively small, but some of the most complete and complex wines from the Languedoc-Roussillon have emerged from these *terroirs*. Readers should look for wines from Clos Marie, Domaine Mas Mortiès, and Domaine d'Aupilhac.

Vins Doux Naturels   The Languedoc-Roussillon area abounds with some of the greatest values in sweet and fortified sweet dessert wines in Europe. The most famous are those from Banyul (located on the coastline south of Perpignan) and Maury (located in the hillsides north of Perpignan). Both appellations require that these decadently rich, fortified wines be made from at least 50% Grenache. In the case of those wines entitled to the Banyul Grand Cru designation, they must be composed of at least 75% Grenache.

Other areas producing sweet wines include Muscat de Rivesaltes, Muscat de Lunel, Muscat de Frontignan, and the two smaller appellations of Muscat de Mireval and Saint-Jean-de-Minervois. Both the Muscat de Frontignan and Muscat de Mireval are located near Herault. Muscat de Lunel is produced east of Nimes in the northern sector of the Languedoc-Roussillon.

The most famous of these wines are the great Banyuls from Dr. Parcé. They have a legendary reputation in France, but remain, to my surprise, largely unknown in the United States. Almost all of these wines can handle considerable aging and are remarkable for their value, particularly when compared with the soaring prices for vintage and tawny ports.

The Basics

TYPES OF WINE

The appellations, the wines, the estates, and the areas here are not well known to wine consumers; consequently there are some great wine values. The range in wines is enormous. There is sound sparkling wine such as Blanquette de Limoux; gorgeously fragrant, sweet muscats like Muscat de Frontignan; oceans of soft, fruity red wines, the best of which are from Minervois, Faugères, Côtes du Roussillon, Costières du Gard, and Corbières; and even

France's version of vintage port, Banyuls. These areas have not yet proven the ability to make interesting white wines, except for sweet muscats.

GRAPE VARIETIES

Grenache, Carignan, Cinsault, Mourvèdre, and Syrah are the major red wine grapes planted in this hot region. Small vineyards of Cabernet Sauvignon and Merlot are becoming more common.

With respect to white wine varietals, Chardonnay, Sauvignon Blanc, and Chenin Blanc can now be found in this area, but the older white wine vineyards generally consist of such workhorse varietals as Ugni Blanc, Picpoul, Maccabeo, and two of the better traditional varietals, Marsanne and Roussanne.

FLAVORS

Until the late eighties, this hot, frequently torrid part of France produced wines that never lacked ripeness, but rather suffered from overripeness. However, the advent of a new generation of young, enthusiastic, and better-equipped winemakers, significant investment in temperature-controlled stainless-steel fermentation tanks, and more attention to harvesting the fruit before it becomes raisiny have resulted in soaring quantities of inexpensive, gorgeously ripe, perfumed, fruity wines. There are remarkable variations in style—from serious, relatively long-lived reds to those made by the carbonic maceration method and designed to be drunk within several years of the vintage. Top producers have begun to offer luxury cuvées (for now, still modestly priced) that have been aged in new oak barrels. Some of these cuvées are highly successful, while others are overwhelmingly woody.

AGING POTENTIAL

The dry red wines of Mas de Daumas Gassac, Saint-Jean de Bebian, Grange des Pères, and a few other top producers can age for 10–15 years. The longest-lived wines of the region are the portlike wines of Banyuls, which can last for up to 30 years when made by a great producer such as the late Dr. Parcé. Other red wines should be drunk within 5–7 years of the vintage. The white wines should be drunk within several years of the vintage.

OVERALL QUALITY LEVEL

Long known for monotonous mediocrity, quality levels have increased significantly as wine market insiders have realized the potential for well-made, inexpensive wines from this area. America's small specialist importers now make annual pilgrimages to this area looking for up-and-coming producers.

MOST IMPORTANT INFORMATION TO KNOW

Most consumers, as well as retailers, probably cannot name more than two or three Languedoc-Roussillon producers. However, if you are going to take advantage of some of the best-made wines that sell at low prices, it is important to learn the names of the finest producers, as well as their American importers.

BUYING STRATEGY

The finest vintage in the Languedoc-Roussillon this decade is 1998. These are the wines to buy. Prices will be higher given the small crop size in many areas in 1998, but the quality is splendid. The years 1997, 1996, and 1995 are all irregular vintages.

SUPER SPARKLING WINE VALUES

It is probably the least-known, well-made sparkling wine of France, at least to the Anglo-Saxon world. From an appellation called Blanquette de Limoux, hidden in the Languedoc-

Roussillon area just north of Spain's border, comes France's oldest sparkling wine, made a century before a monk named Dom Pérignon was credited with discovering the process of producing champagne. Made primarily from the Chardonnay, Chenin Blanc, and Mauzac grapes, the wines are qualitatively close to a high-quality, nonvintage champagne at one-third the price—most dry brut vintage sparkling wines from this appellation retail for $10 a bottle. The best are the Saint-Hilaire Blanc de Blancs, the Maison Guinot, and the two top wines from the Cooperative Aiméry, the Cuvée Alderic and Cuvée Sieur d'Arques.

THE WORLD'S GREATEST WINES WITH CHOCOLATE

Some of the most unique wines in the world are the late-harvested wines from Banyuls made by the Parcé family's Domaine du Mas Blanc. One Banyuls labeled *dry* is an explosively rich, full-bodied, Grenache-based wine that should be drunk with hearty fare on cool fall and winter evenings. Another, a dry red wine called Collioure, is a complex table wine, impeccably made from a blend of 40% Syrah, 40% Mourvèdre, and 20% Grenache. And then there are Parcé's famous portlike sweet Banyuls made from very ripe Grenache. Complex, decadent, and the only wine I have found to work well with chocolate desserts, this is a spectacular wine that can age well for 20–25 years. The alcohol content averages 16%–18%. Parcé also makes a special cuvée of Vieilles Vignes (old vines) that is even more stunning. Parcé's sweet Banyuls usually sell for under $25 a bottle, making them a moderately priced alternative to vintage port. The other decadent wine to serve with chocolate is from the Domaine Mas Amiel, a superlative producer from the obscure appellation of Maury. The French equivalent of a vintage port, Mas Amiel's wines are stunning in quality and remarkably low in price. Don't miss them.

MARVELOUS MUSCATS

Looking for a sweet, ripe, honeyed, aromatic, reasonably priced wine to serve with fresh fruit or fruit tarts? Then be sure to try the Muscat de Frontignan from the Château de la Peyrade or the Muscat de Lunel from Clos Bellevue, both sell for about $15 a bottle. They represent a heady drink, but the Muscat's seductive charm and power is very evident in this excellent wine. Another terrific sweet wine comes from Domaine Cazes. They produce a splendid Muscat de Rivesaltes that sells for about $20.

FINDING THE WINES OF LANGUEDOC-ROUSSILLON

Unlike most other wines, the wines of Languedoc-Roussillon remain a specialized item. It will assist readers to list the importers who have done most of the exploration of this area. Some of these importers are regional, and others are national. These include:

Jeffrey Davies Selections, West Nyack, NY; (914) 353-8767 (Jeffrey Davies has made a major contribution to the quality of wines we enjoy from the Languedoc-Roussillon. He works closely with a number of producers to secure hand-crafted wines of considerable intensity.)

European Cellars, New York, NY; (212) 924-4949 (The enthusiastic Eric Solomon, a top specialist for the wines of southern France, sells his wines nationally.)

Hand Picked Selections, Warrenton, VA; (703) 347-9400 (Perhaps the top importer in the country for specializing in wines that sell for under $10, owner Dan Kravitz represents a considerable number of wines from this region.)

Ideal Wines, Medford, MA; (617) 395-3300

Robert Kacher Selections, Washington, D.C.; (202) 832-9083 (One of the first to exploit this region's potential, Robert Kacher brings in some of the finest wines from the Languedoc-Roussillon region. He dominates the sale of wines from Costières de Nîmes.)

Langdon-Shiverick, Chagrin Falls, OH; (216) 861-6800

Kermit Lynch Selections, Berkeley, CA; (510) 524-1524 (This trailblazer, who has long represented many of France's small artisan producers, has plunged into Languedoc-Roussillon with considerable enthusiasm.)

North Berkeley Wines, Berkeley, CA; (510) 848-8910 (This California importer specializes in limited production unfined/unfiltered cuvées that can be sumptuous. Readers need to get on their mailing list to be assured of having a chance to buy some of their gems.)

Martin Sinkoff, Dallas, TX; (214) 528-8467 (In addition to representing the wines of the Val d'Orbieu, this importer also has a fine portfolio of small estate wines.)

Weygandt-Metzler, Unionville, PA; (610) 932-2745 (Peter Weygandt has an impeccable selection of small estates—all of which offer superb value.)

Wines of France, Mountainside, NJ; (908) 654-6173 (Frenchman Alain Junguenet, the first to see Languedoc-Roussillon's potential, has one of the most extensive portfolio of wines from this region, as well as some of its top estates.)

RATING LANGUEDOC-ROUSSILLON'S BEST PRODUCERS

* * * * *(OUTSTANDING)

Domaine l'Aiguelière-Montpeyroux (Coteaux du Languedoc)

Domaine Borie de Maurel Cuvée Sylla (Minervois)

Canet Valette Cuvée Maghani (Saint-Chinian)

Clos Marie (Pic Saint-Loup)

Grande Cassagne (Costières des Nimes)

La Grange des Pères (Vin de Pays-Herault)

Domaine de l'Hortus (Coteaux du Languedoc)

Mas de Aveylans (Vin de Pays du Gard)*

Mas de Clavel Cuvée Copa Santa (Coteaux du Languedoc)

Mas de Guiot Prestige (Vin de Pays du Gard)*

Château de la Negly (La Porte du Ciel)

Dr. Parcé Mas Blanc (Banyuls)

Domaine Peyre Rose Clos des Sistes (Coteaux du Languedoc)

Domaine Peyre Rose Clos Syrah (Coteaux du Languedoc)

Tardieu-Laurent (various cuvées in Corbières)

* * * *(EXCELLENT)

Domaine des Aires-Hautes (Minervois)

Gilbert Alquier-Cuvée Les Bastides (Faugères)

Domaine d'Aupilhac (Vin de Pays)

Domaine de Barroubio Muscat de Saint-Jean (Minervois)

Domaine de Baruel VDP (Cevennes)

Château Bastide-Durand (Corbières)

Domaine Bois Monsieur (Coteaux du Languedoc)

Borie de Maurel Syrah (Minervois)

Château de Campuget Cuvée Prestige (Costières de Nimes)

Canet-Valette (Saint-Chinian)

Domaine Capion (Vin de Pays)

Domaine Capion Merlot (Vin de Pays)

Château de Casenove (Côtes du Roussillon)

Château de Cazeneuve (Pic Saint-Loup)

Château de Cazeneuve Grand Cuvée (Pic Saint-Loup)

Chapoutier Banyuls (Banyuls)

Chapoutier Muscat de Rivesaltes (Rivesaltes)

Chapoutier Muscat Sec VDP (Côtes Catalans)

Domaine des Chênes-Truffiers (Coteaux du Languedoc) ****/*****

Clos de l'Escandil (Minervois)

Clos de Paulilles (Collioure)

Domaine La Colombette (Vin de Pays)

Domaine de la Combe-Blanche (Minervois)

Domaine Coussergues Sauvignon Blanc (Coteaux du Languedoc)

Domaine Couthiat Cuvée de la Couthiat Syrah VDP

Daniel Domergue (Minervois)

*(Included here although an argument can be made that they are Rhone wines.)

Château Donjon Cuvée Prestige
(Minervois)
Château des Estanilles (Faugères)
Château des Estanilles Cuvée Syrah
(Faugères)
Domaine Gauby Cuvée Muntada (Cotes du
Roussillon Villages)
Château Hélène Cuvée Hélène de Troie
(Vin de Pays)
Domaine Lacoste Muscat de Lunel
Château Lascaux Les Nobles Pierres
(Coteaux du Languedoc)
Château Mansenoble (Corbières)
Château Mansenoble Réserve de Château
(Corbières)
Domaine Maris (Minervois)
Mas Amiel (Maury)
Mas des Bressades Cabernet Sauvignon
Mas des Bressades Syrah
Mas des Bressades VDP
Mas Bruguière (Pic Saint-Loup)
Mas Cal Demoura (Coteaux du Languedoc)
Mas de Clavel Cuvée Garrigue (Coteaux du
Languedoc)
Mas de Clavel Cuvée Mejanelle (Coteaux
du Languedoc)
Mas de Daumas Gassac (L'Hérault)
****/*****
Mas Jullien Les Cailloutis (Coteaux du
Languedoc)
Mas Jullien Les Dedierre (Coteaux du
Languedoc)
Mas Jullien Les Vignes Oubliés (Coteaux
du Languedoc)
Mas Morties (Pic Saint-Loup) ****/*****
Mourgues du Gres Cuvée Terre (Costières
de Nimes) ****/*****
Marquise des Mures (Saint-Chinian)

Château de Nages (Costières de Nimes)
Château d'Oupia Cuvée des Barons
(Minervois)
Château Les Palais (Corbières)
Château Les Palais Cuvée Randolin
(Corbières)
Château de Paraza Cuvée Speciale
(Minervois)
Château de la Peyrade (Muscat-Frontignan)
Domaine Piccinini (Minervois)
Domaine Piquemal (Côte du Roussillon)
Domaine La Pleiade (Maury)
Prieuré de Saint-Jean de Bebian (Vin de
Pays)
Puech-Haut-Saint-Drezery (Coteaux du
Languedoc)
La Rochelière (Fitou)
Roudène (Fitou)
Catherine de Saint-Juery (Coteaux du
Languedoc)
Saint-Martin de la Garrigue Cuvée Saint-
Martin (VDP)
Château Sancho (Pech de la Lune)
****/*****
Château La Sauvagéonne (Coteaux du
Languedoc)
Château Le Thou (Vin de Pays d'Oc)
Domaine La Tour Boisée Cuvée Marie-
Claude (Minervois)
Domaine des Tourelles (Coteaux du
Languedoc)
Château de la Tuilierie Cuvée Ecole
(Costières de Nimes)
Val d'Orbieu La Cuvée Mythique (VDP)
Château de Valcome Cuvée Prestige
(Costières de Nimes)
La Voulte Gasparets (Corbières)

* * * (GOOD)

Abbaye de Valmagne (Coteaux du
Languedoc)
Gilbert Alquier (Faugères)
Domaine de L'Arjolle (Côtes de Thongue)
Pierre d'Aspres (Côtes du Roussillon)
Domaine des Astruc (Vin de Pays)
Château La Baronne (Corbières)
Château Belle-Coste (Vin de Pays)
Château de Blomac Cuvée Tradition
(Minervois)

Château de Calage (Coteaux du
Languedoc)
Château du Campuget (Costières de Nimes)
Domaine Capion Syrah (L'Hérault)
Château Capitoul (Coteaux de Languedoc)
Cazal-Viel (Saint-Chinian)
Cazal-Viel Cuvée Georges A. Aoust (Saint-
Chinian)
Cazes Frères (Côtes du Roussillon)
Celliers des Tempières (Vin de Pays)

Les Chemins de Bassac Pierre Elie (Vin de Pays)

Guy Chevalier La Coste (Corbières)

Guy Chevalier La Coste-Cabernet/Syrah (L'Aude)

Guy Chevalier L'Église-Grenache Noir (Corbières)

Guy Chevalier Le Texas-Syrah (Corbières)

Domaine Dona Baissas (Côtes du Roussillon)

Château Etang des Colombes Cuvée du Bicentenaire (Corbières)

Château Fabas Cuvée Alexandre (Minervois)

Domaine des Gautier (Fitou)

Château de Gourgazaud (Minervois)

Domaine de Gournier (Vin de Pays)

Château Haut-Fabrègues (Faugères)

/*

Le Jaja de Jau (Vin de Pays)

Les Jamelles (Vin de Pays)

Château de Jau (Côtes du Roussillon)

Domaine Lalande (Vin de Pays d'Oc)

Château des Lanes (Corbières)

Laville-Bertrou (Minervois)

Château de Luc (Corbières)

Mas Champart (Coteaux du Languedoc)

Mas de Ray Cuvée Caladoc (Bouches du Rhône)

Mas de Ray Cuvée Camargue (Bouches du Rhône)

Château Maurel Fonsalade (Saint-Chinian)

Domaine La Noble (Vin de Pays)

Château d'Oupia (Minervois)

Prieuré Château Les Palais (Corbières)

Dr. Parcé Mas Blanc Collioure-Cosprons Levants (Banyuls)

Dr. Parcé Mas Blanc Collioure-Les Piloums (Banyuls)

Château de Pena Côtes du Roussillon-Villages (Côtes du Roussillon)

Domaine Piccinini (Minervois)

Domaine de Pilou (Fitou)

Domaine de Pomaredes Merlot (Vin de Pays)

Château La Roque (Coteaux du Languedoc)

Château La Roque (Pic Saint-Loup)

Château Rouquette sur Mer (Coteaux du Languedoc)

Château Routas Agrippa (Coteaux Varois)

Château Routas Infernet (Coteaux Varois)

Château Routas Traditionnel (Coteaux Varois)

Château Routas Truffière (Coteaux Varois)

Domaine du Sacre Coeur (Saint-Chinian)

Domaine Salvat (Côtes du Roussillon)

Domaine Sarda-Malet Black Label (Côtes du Roussillon)

Tour Saint-Martin (Minervois)

Château de la Tuilerie (Costières de Nimes)

Bernard-Claude Vidal (Faugères)

Les Vignerons d'Octaviana Grand Chariot (Corbières)

* * (AVERAGE)

Domaine des Bories (Corbières)

Domaine du Bosc (L'Hérault)

Domaine du Bosccaute (L'Hérault)

Château de Cabriac (Corbières)

Domaine de Capion (L'Hérault)

Domaine de Coujan (Vin de Pays)

Château L'Espigne (Fitou)

Château Etang des Colombes Cuvée Tradition (Corbières)

Domaine de Fontsainte (Corbières)

Château de Grezan (Faugères)

Château Hélène (Vin de Pays)

Domaine des Jougla Cuvée Tradition (Saint-Chinian)

Domaine des Jougla Cuvée White Label (Saint-Chinian)

Château de Lascaux (Coteaux du Languedoc)

Domaine de la Lecugne (Minervois)

Domaine de Mayranne (Minervois)

Château Milhau-Lacugue (Saint-Chinian)

Château La Mission Le Vignon (Côtes du Roussillon)

Caves de Mont Tauch (Fitou)

Domaine de Montmarin (Côtes de Thongue)

Château de Nouvelles (Fitou)

Château de Paraza (Minervois)

Cuvée Claude Parmentier (Fitou)

Château Pech-Rédon (Coteaux du Languedoc)

Domaine Perrière-Les Amandiers (Corbières)

Qrmand de Villeneuve (Côtes du
    Roussillon)
Château de Queribus (Corbières)
Domaine de la Rictorie (Banyuls)
Domaine de la Roque (Coteaux du
    Languedoc)
Château de Roquecourbe (Minervois)
Saint-André (L'Hérault)
Château Saint-Auriol (Corbières)

Château Saint-Laurent (Corbières)
Domaine Sainte-Eulalie (Minervois)
Sarda-Malet (Côtes du Roussillon)
Domaine du Tauch (Fitou)
Domaine de Villemajou (Corbières)
Château de Villerambert-Julien (Minervois)
Caves de Vins de Roquebrun (Saint-
    Chinian)

PROVENCE

It is easy to regard Provence as just the dramatic playground for the world's rich and famous, for few wine lovers seem to realize that this vast viticultural region in southern France is at least 2,600 years old. For centuries, tourists traveling through Provence have been seduced by the aromatic and flavorful thirst-quenching rosés that seem to complement the distinctive cuisine of the region so well. Yet today, Provence is an exciting and diverse viticultural region that is turning out not only extremely satisfying rosés but also immensely promising red wines and a few encouraging whites. It remains largely uncharted territory for wine consumers, however. Provence is a mammoth-sized region that has seven specific viticultural areas. The best way to get a grasp on the region is to learn what each of these viticultural areas has to offer and which properties constitute the leading wine-producing estates. While Provence is blessed with ideal weather for grape growing, not all the vintages are of equal merit. Certainly for the white and rosé wines of Provence, which require consumption in their youth, only 1999 and 1998 ought to be drunk today. The super vintages for all of Provence are 1998, 1995, 1989, and 1985, followed by 1983 and 1982. As a general rule, the top red wines of Provence can handle aging for up to a decade in the aforementioned vintages.

Following is a brief synopsis of the seven major wine-producing areas in Provence, along with a list of the top wines from each area that merit trying. While the wines of Provence are not overpriced, these wines are less attractively priced than they were several years ago. Yet when the top wines are compared with wines of similar quality from France's more famous areas such as Burgundy and Bordeaux, their relative value as French wines is obvious.

Bandol   In France, Bandol is often called the most privileged appellation of France. Certainly, the scenic beauty of this storybook area offers unsurpassed views of the azure-colored Mediterranean Sea with the vineyards spread out over the hillsides overlooking the water. Bandol produces red, rosé, and white wines. It is most famous for its rosé wine, which some people consider the best made in France, and its long-lived, intense, tannic red wine, which is unique in France in that it is made from at least 50% of the little-known Mourvèdre grape. If anyone has any doubts about the quality of Mourvèdre, Pradeaux's 1989 and 1990

Mourvèdre Vieilles Vignes are monumental wines. Prices for Bandol have never been cheap, largely because of the never-ending flow of tourists to the area who buy up most of the wine made by the local producers.

There seems to be no doubt among connoisseurs that the best red wines come from such producers as the Domaine Pradeaux, Domaine Tempier, Domaine de Pibarnon, Ott's Château Romassan, Château Vannières, and two properties called Moulin des Coste and Mas des Rouvière. While most of these producers also make a white wine, it is not a wine I can recommend with a great deal of enthusiasm, as it always seems to taste dull and heavy. However, the red wines as well as the fresh, personality-filled rosés from these estates are well worth seeking out and are available in most of the major markets in America. Prices for the rosés now average $15–$20 a bottle with the red wines costing $20–$30 a bottle. While I have had the good fortune to taste red wines of Bandol as old as 15–20 years, most of the wines seem to hit their peak after 6–10 years in the bottle. Bandol, one of the most strictly regulated appellations in France, is certainly the leading candidate of all the Provence appellations for producer of the longest-lived and best-known red wines.

Bellet   Like all of the Provence appellations, the tiny appellation of Bellet, tucked in the hillside behind the international seaside resort of Nice, produces red, white, and rosé wines. The history of Bellet is rich, as its vineyards were originally cultivated by the Phoenician Greeks in 500 B.C. But unless one actually spends time on the Riviera, one is unlikely ever to know how a fine Bellet tastes. Most of the wine produced in this microappellation of only 100-plus acres never makes it outside of France, as the local restaurant demand is insatiable. There are only a handful of producers making wine here, and the very best is the Château de Crémat, owned by the Bagnis family, a splendid estate of 50 acres that produces nearly 6,000 cases of wine. It is imported to the United States, but its high price of $20–$25 a bottle has ensured that few consumers know how it really tastes. Château de Crémat is a unique estate in Provence in that the white wine is of extremely high quality, and the local connoisseurs claim the rosé and red wines are the best made in this part of the French Riviera. The best recent vintages have been the 1998 and 1995, but I have tasted the red wines from Château de Crémat back through 1978, and they have shown no signs of decline. However, the wines of Bellet remain esoteric, enjoyed by only a handful of people, with prices that seem steep for the quality.

Cassis   The tiny village of Cassis, located on the western end of France's famous Côte d'Azur, is one of the most charming fishing villages on the Riviera. Located on a secluded bay, it is dwarfed by the surrounding steep limestone cliffs. The hordes of tourists that frequent the area ensure that most of the wine made here is consumed at the local bistros along with the area's ubiquitous *soupe de poisson*. While this appellation makes red wine as well as rosé, it is white wine that has made Cassis famous. The red wine tends to be heavy and uninteresting, and while the rosé can be good, it never seems to approach the quality level of its nearby neighbor Bandol. The white wine, which is often a blend of little-known grapes such as Ugni Blanc, Clairette, and Bourboulenc, is a spicy, fleshy wine that often seems unattractive by itself, but when served with the rich, aromatic seafood dishes of the region, it takes on a character of its own. The estates of Cassis producing the best white wines include Clos Sainte-Magdelaine, La Ferme Blanche, and Domaine du Bagnol. Prices average $20 or more for these white wines, which, even in 1999, make them bad values. They have a distinct character that requires fairly rich, spicy fish courses to complement their unique personality.

Coteaux d'Aix-en-Provence   This gigantic viticultural region, which extends primarily north and west of Aix-en-Provence, has numerous small estates making acceptable but generally overpriced wines that require drinking within the first 7–8 years of their lives. However, two of the very finest red wines produced in Provence are produced here: Domaine Trevallon and Chapoutier's Terra d'Or. Both producers specialize in red wine, capable of

Provence

KILOMETERS
MILES

St-Rémy-de-Provence
Plan d'Orgon
les Baux
Eygalières
1
Arles
2
DURANCE
Salon-de-Provence
Lambesc
N113
Meyrargues
2
Rians
RHÔNE
Eguilles
Vauvenargues
N568
Istres
La Fare-les-Oliviers
2
Aix-en-Provence
N7
4
BOUCHES-DU-RHÔNE
ÉTANG DE BERRE
Rognac
Vitrolles
Palette
3
A52
Trets
Martigues
A55
A51
4
St-Zacharie
A8
Allauch
A52
Marseille
7
4
A50
Cassis
La Ciotat
Bandol

MEDITERRANEAN

Paris

Provence
Marseille

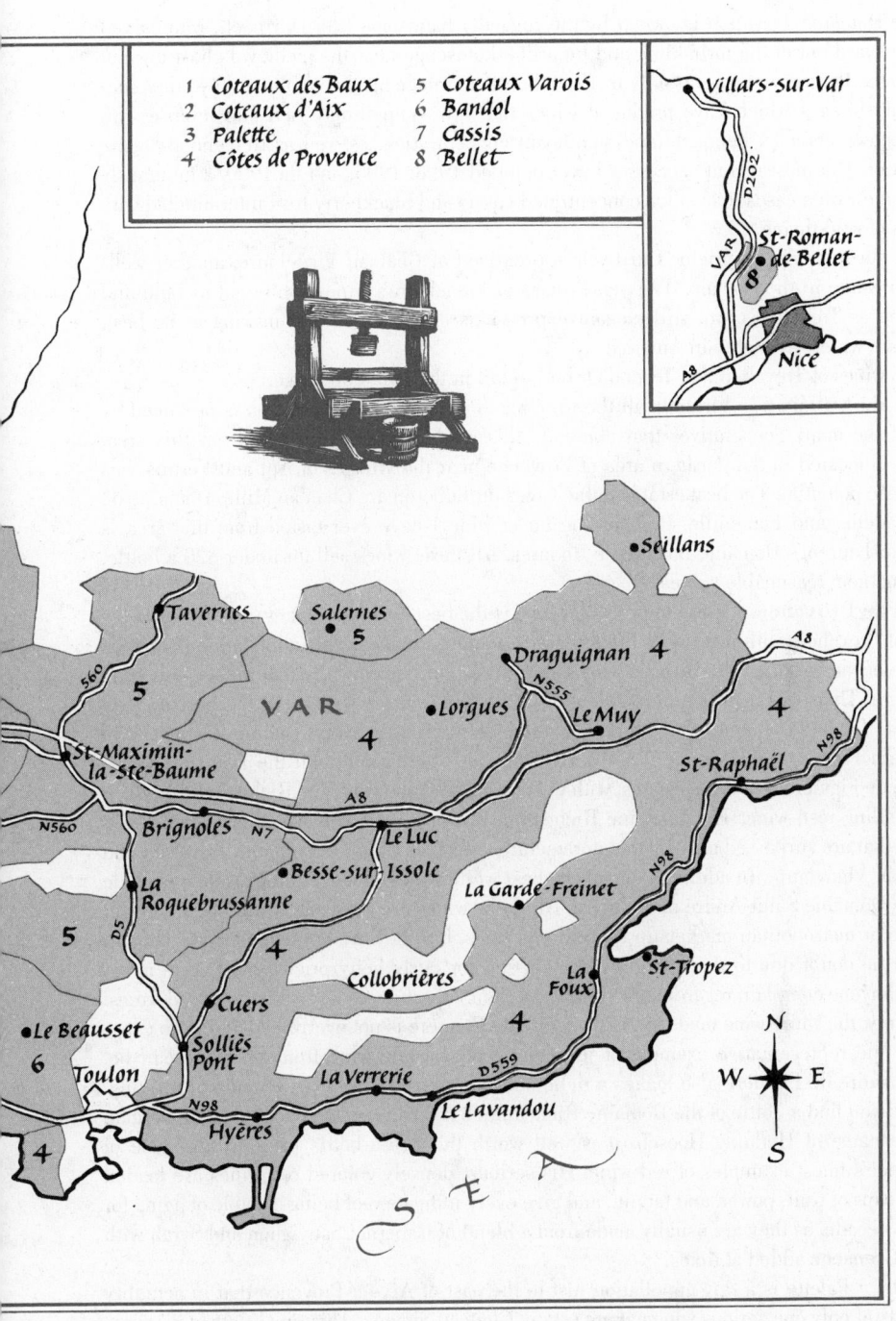

1 Coteaux des Baux   5 Coteaux Varois
2 Coteaux d'Aix   6 Bandol
3 Palette   7 Cassis
4 Côtes de Provence   8 Bellet

Villars-sur-Var

D 202

VAR

St-Roman-
de-Bellet

8

Nice

A 8

Seillans

Tavernes   Salernes

5

A 8

560

5

Draguignan   4

VAR

N 555

Lorgues   Le Muy

4

4

St-Maximin-
la-Ste-Baume

N 98

A 8

St-Raphaël

N 560

Brignoles   N 7

Le Luc

La
Roquebrussanne

Besse-sur-Issole

La Garde-Freinet

N 98

5

D 5

4

Collobrières

La
Foux   St-Tropez

Le Beausset

Cuers

4

6

Solliès
Pont

Toulon

La Verrerie

D 559

N

Hyères

N 98

Le Lavandou

W   E

4

S

SEA

aging 15–20 years, made from a blend of two great red wine grapes, the Cabernet Sauvignon and the Syrah.

The Domaine Trevallon is owned by the ruggedly handsome Eloi Durrbach, who carved his vineyard out of the forbidding and lunarlike landscape near the medieval ghost town of Les Baux. Its first vintage was only in 1978, but that vintage has been followed by other successful vintages which have produced wines that are compellingly rich and intense with enormously complex bouquets and significant concentration, as well as tremendous aging potential. The most recent successes have included 1998, 1995, and the1990, a fabulously rich wine with a cascade of silky, concentrated cassis and blackberry fruit intermingled with scents of wild thyme.

Not surprisingly, proprietor Durrbach apprenticed at Château Vignelaure, another well-known estate in the Coteaux d'Aix-en-Provence. Vignelaure's wines, while not as bold and striking as Trevallon's, are still elegant expressions of Provençal winemaking at its best. They are widely available in America.

The wines of Trevallon and Terra d'Or both retail in the $30–$50 range.

Côtes du Lubéron   Virtually all the wine made in the Côtes du Lubéron is produced by one of the many cooperatives that dominate this region's production. However, this area, which is located in the northern area of Provence near the villages of Apt and Pertuis, has immense potential. The best estates in the Côtes du Lubéron are Château Mille, Domaine de la Citadelle, and Fontenille. Perhaps the finest wine I have ever tasted from this area is Tardieu-Laurent's Domaine Bastide de Rodares. All these wines sell for under $20 a bottle, making them reasonable values.

Côtes de Provence   The Côtes de Provence is the best-known and largest viticultural region of Provence, with just under 50,000 acres planted in vines. This appellation is famous for the oceans of dry, flavorful rosé wine that tourists gulp down with great thirst-quenching pleasure. There are many fine producers of Côtes de Provence wines, but the best include the very famous Domaines Ott, which is available on virtually every restaurant wine list in southern France, the Domaine Gavoty, the Domaine Richeaume, and the Domaine Saint-André de Figuière. All these estates, with the exception of the Domaine Richeaume, produce outstanding rosé wine. The Domaine Richeaume specializes in intense, rich, complex red wines that are surpassed only by the aforementioned wines from the Domaine Trevallon and Château Vignelaure. In addition, one of the best white wines produced in Provence is made by the Domaine Saint-André de Figuière. All these wines are currently available in most of the major metropolitan markets in the United States, but they are not inexpensive. The Ott wines, no doubt due to their fame in France, sell for fairly hefty prices, but I have never heard anyone complain regarding the quality of their superb rosés and underrated red wines. Certainly, the white wine made by Saint-André de Figuière is not overpriced and is an especially fine representative example of just how good a white wine from Provence can be. Saint-André de Figuière also makes a delicious, supple red wine that is well worth trying. Should you find a bottle of the Domaine Richeaume's red wine, made by a fanatical German by the name of Henning Hoesch, it is well worth the $15-a-bottle price to taste one of Provence's finest examples of red wine. His serious, densely colored red wines are loaded with heaps of fruit, power, and tannin, and give every indication of being capable of aging for over a decade, as they are usually made from a blend of Cabernet Sauvignon and Syrah with some Grenache added at times.

Palette   Palette is a tiny appellation just to the east of Aix-en-Provence that in actuality consists of only one serious winemaking estate, Château Simone. This tiny estate of 37 acres produces a surprisingly long-lived and complex red wine, a fairly oaky, old-style rosé wine, and a muscular, full-bodied white wine that behaves as if it were from the northern Rhône Valley. Simone's wines are not inexpensive, but they do age extremely well, and have always had a loyal following in France.

The Basics

TYPES OF WINE
A huge quantity of bone-dry, fragrant, crisp rosés is made as well as rather neutral but fleshy white wines and higher-and-higher-quality red wines.

GRAPE VARIETIES
For red wines, the traditional grape varieties have always been Grenache, Carignan, Syrah, Mourvèdre, and Cinsault. Recently, however, a great deal of Cabernet Sauvignon has been planted in the Côtes de Provence and Coteaux d'Aix-en-Provence. The most interesting red wines are generally those with elevated levels of either Syrah, Mourvèdre, or Cabernet Sauvignon. For white wines, Ugni Blanc, Clairette, Marsanne, Bourboulenc, and to a lesser extent Semillon, Sauvignon Blanc, and Chardonnay are used.

FLAVORS
There is immense variation due to the number of microclimates and different grapes used. Most red wines have vivid red fruit bouquets that are more intense in the Coteaux des Baux than elsewhere. In Bandol the smells of tree bark, leather, and currants dominate. The white wines seem neutral and clumsy when served without food, but when drunk with the spicy Provençal cuisine, they take on life.

AGING POTENTIAL
Rosés: 1–3 years
White wines: 1–3 years, except for that of Château Simone, which can last for 5–10 years
Red wines: 5–12 years, often longer for the red wines of Bandol and specific wines such as Domaine Trevallon that can age well for 15+ years

OVERALL QUALITY LEVEL
The level of quality has increased and in general is well above average, but consumers must remember to buy and drink the rosé and white wines only when they are less than 3 years old.

MOST IMPORTANT INFORMATION TO KNOW
Master the types of wine of each appellation of Provence, as well as the names of the top producers.

BUYING STRATEGY
The vintage of choice for the wines of this region is 1998.

RATING PROVENCE'S BEST PRODUCERS

*****(OUTSTANDING)

Domaine des Béates Terra d'Or (Coteaux d'Aix-en-Provence)
Luigi-Clos Nicrosi (Corsica)
Château Pradeaux (Bandol)
Château Pradeaux Mourvèdre Vieilles Vignes (Bandol)
Tardieu-Laurent–Domaine Bastide de Rodares (Côtes du Lubéron)

Domaine Tempier Cabasseau (Bandol)
Domaine Tempier Cuvée Spéciale (Bandol)
Domaine Tempier La Migoua (Bandol)
Domaine Tempier La Tourtine (Bandol)
Domaine de Trevallon (Coteaux d'Aix-en Provence-Les Baux)

* * * *(EXCELLENT)

Domaine Canorgue (Côtes du Lubéron)
Commanderie de Peyrassol (Côtes de
    Provence)
Château de Crémat (Bellet)
Domaine de Féraud (Côtes de Provence)
Domaine Le Gallantin (Bandol)
Domaine de la Garnaude Cuvée Santane
    (Côtes de Provence)
Domaines Gavoty (Côtes de Provence)
Domaine Hauvette (Coteaux des Baux)
Domaine de l'Hermitage (Bandol)
Mas de la Dame (Coteaux d'Aix-en-
    Provence-Les Baux)
Mas de Gourgonnier (Coteaux d'Aix-en-
    Provence-Les Baux)
Mas de la Rouvière (Bandol)

Château de Mille (Côtes du Lubéron)
Moulin des Costes (Bandol)
Domaines Ott—all cuvées (Bandol and
    Côtes de Provence)
Domaine de Pibarnon (Bandol)
Domaine Richeaume (Côtes de Provence)
Domaine de Rimauresq (Côtes de
    Provence)
Saint-André de Figuière (Côtes de
    Provence)
Domaine Saint-Jean de Villecroze (Coteaux
    Varois)
Domaine Tempier Rosé (Bandol)
Domaine Torraccia (Corsica)
Château Vannières (Bandol)

* * *(GOOD)

Domaine du Bagnol (Cassis)
Château Barbeyrolles (Côtes de Provence)
Commanderie de Bargemone (Côtes de
    Provence)
Château Bas (Coteaux d'Aix-en-Provence)
La Bastide Blanche (Bandol)
Domaine de Beaupré (Coteaux d'Aix-en-
    Provence)
Domaine La Bernarde (Côtes de Provence)
Domaine Caguelouf (Bandol)
Château de Calissanne (Coteaux d'Aix-en-
    Provence)
Castel Roubine (Côtes de Provence)
Cave Cooperative d'Aleria Réserve du
    Président (Corsica)
Chapoutier Matines Béats (Coteaux d'Aix-
    en-Provence)
Clos Catitoro (Corsica)
Clos Sainte-Magdelaine (Cassis)
Domaine de Curebreasse (Côtes de
    Provence)
Château Ferry-Lacombe (Côtes de
    Provence)
Domaine Fiumicicoli (Corsica)
Château de Fonscolombe (Coteaux d'Aix-
    en-Provence)
Domaine du Fontenille (Côtes du
    Lubéron)***/****
Domaine Frégate (Bandol)
Hervé Goudard (Côtes de Provence)
Château de l'Isolette (Côtes du Lubéron)

Domaine de Lafran-Veyrolles (Bandol)
Domaine La Laidière (Bandol)
Domaine Lecci (Corsica)
Domaine du Loou (Coteaux Varois)
Château Maravenne (Côtes de Provence)
Mas de Cadenet (Côtes de Provence)
Mas Sainte-Berthe (Coteaux d'Aix-en-
    Provence)
Domaine de la Noblesse (Bandol)
Domaine Orenga (Corsica)
Domaine de Paradis (Coteaux d'Aix-en-
    Provence)
Domaine Peraldi (Corsica)
Château de Rasque (Côtes de Provence)
Domaine Ray-Jane (Bandol)
Château Real-Martin (Côtes de Provence)
Château Saint-Esteve (Côtes de Provence)
Château Saint-Jean Cuvée Natasha (Côtes
    de Provence)
Château Sainte-Anne (Bandol)
Château Sainte-Roseline (Côtes de
    Provence)
Domaine des Salettes (Bandol)
Domaine de la Sanglière (Côtes de
    Provence)
Château Simone (Palette)
Domaine de Terrebrune (Bandol)
Toussaint Luigi-Muscatella (Corsica)
Château Val-Joanis (Côtes du Lubéron)
Château Val-Joanis Cuvée Les Griottes
    (Côtes du Lubéron)

Domaine de la Vallongue (Coteaux des Baux)

La Vieille Ferme (Côtes du Lubéron)

Château Vignelaure (Coteaux d'Aix-en-Provence-Les Baux)

THE RHÔNE VALLEY

Grape Varieties

RED WINE VARIETALS

Cinsault All the growers seem to use a small amount of Cinsault. It ripens very early, gives good yields, and produces wines that offer a great deal of fruit. It seems to offset the high alcohol of the Grenache and the tannins of the Syrah and Mourvèdre. Despite its value, it seems to have lost some appeal in favor of Syrah or Mourvèdre, but it is a valuable asset to the blend of a southern Rhône wine.

Counoise Very little of this grape exists in the south because of its capricious growing habits. However, I have tasted it separately at Château Beaucastel in Châteauneuf du Pape, where the Perrin family is augmenting its use. It had great finesse and provided deep, richly fruity flavors and a complex perfume of smoked meat, flowers, and berry fruit. The Perrins feel Counoise has as much potential as Mourvèdre, a high-quality ingredient in their blend.

Grenache A classic hot-climate grape varietal, Grenache is, for better or worse, the dominant grape of the southern Rhône. The quality of the wines it produces ranges from hot, alcoholic, unbalanced, coarse wines to rich, majestic, very long-lived, sumptuous wines. The differences are caused largely by the yield of juice per vine. Where Grenache is pruned back and not overly fertilized, it can do wondrous things. The sensational Châteauneuf du Pape, Château Rayas, is an example of what majestic heights Grenache can achieve. At its best, it offers aromas of kirsch, black currants, pepper, licorice, and roasted peanuts.

Mourvèdre Everyone seems to agree on the virtues of Mourvèdre, but few people want to take the risk and grow it. It flourishes in the Mediterranean appellation of Bandol, but only Château Beaucastel in Châteauneuf du Pape has made it an important part (one-third or more) of their blend. It gives great color, a complex, woodsy, leathery aroma, and superb structure, and is resistant to oxidation. However, it ripens very late and, unlike other grape varietals, has no value until it is perfectly mature. When it lacks maturity, the growers say it gives them nothing, for it is colorless and acidic. Given the eccentricities of this grape, it is unlikely that anyone other than the adventurous or passionately obsessed growers will make use of this grape. Its telltale aromas are those of leather, truffles, fresh mushrooms, and tree bark.

Muscardin More common than Terret Noir, Muscardin provides wine with a great deal of perfume as well as a solid measure of alcohol and strength. Beaucastel uses Muscardin, but by far the most important plantings of Muscardin at a serious winemaking estate are at

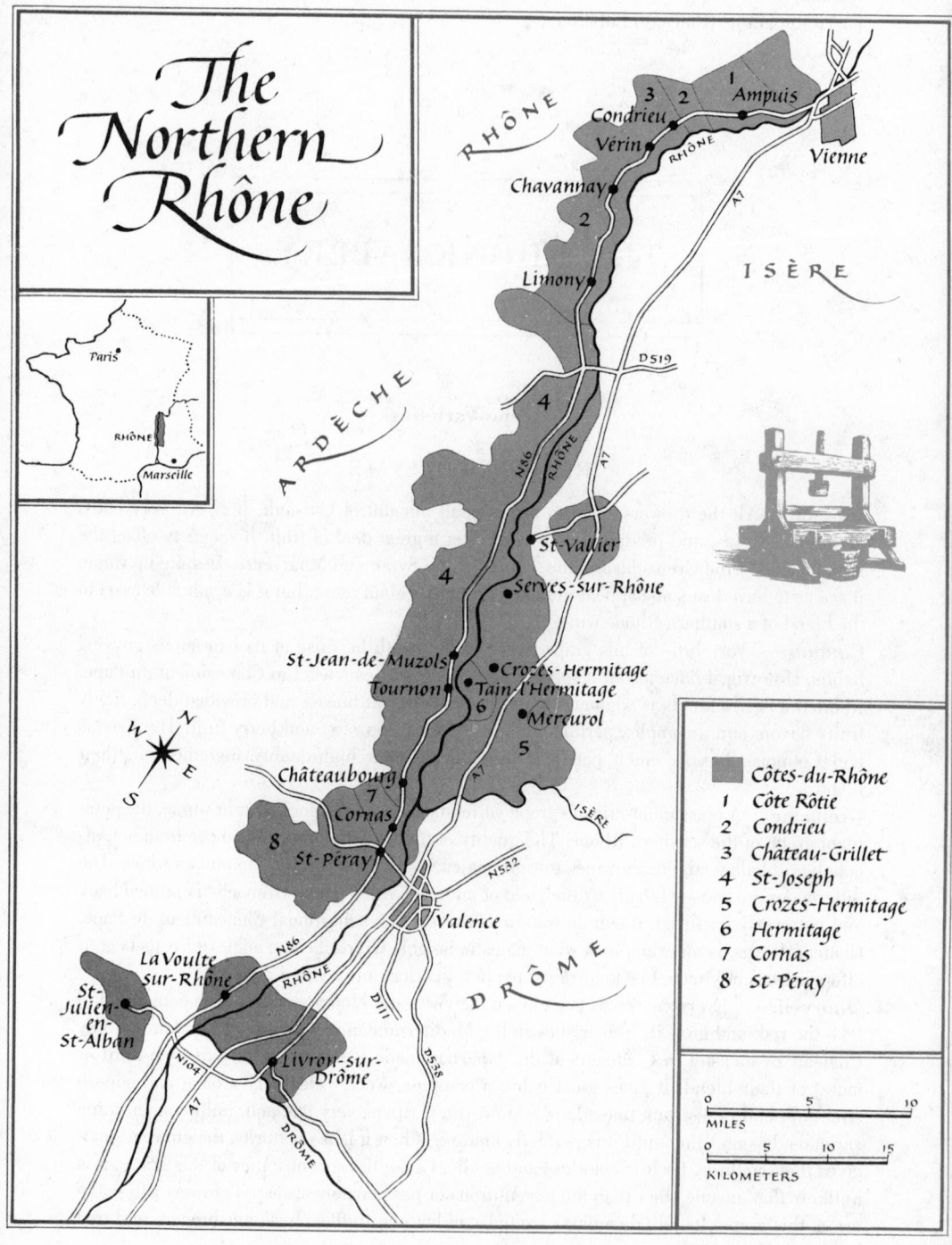

The Northern Rhône

Paris

RHÔNE

Marseille

RHÔNE

ISÈRE

ARDÈCHE

3
1 Ampuis
2
Condrieu
Vérin
Vienne
Chavannay
2
Limony
D 519
4

N86
RHÔNE
A7

St-Vallier
Serves-sur-Rhône
4
St-Jean-de-Muzols
Crozes-Hermitage
Tournon
Tain-l'Hermitage
6
Mereurol
5
Châteaubourg
7
Cornas
ISÈRE
8
St-Péray

N W E S

Valence
La Voulte
sur-Rhône
N86
RHÔNE
N532
St-Julien-en-St-Alban
Livron-sur-Drôme
DRÔME
A7
DRÔME

Côtes-du-Rhône
1 Côte Rôtie
2 Condrieu
3 Château-Grillet
4 St-Joseph
5 Crozes-Hermitage
6 Hermitage
7 Cornas
8 St-Péray

0   5   10
MILES

0   5   10   15
KILOMETERS

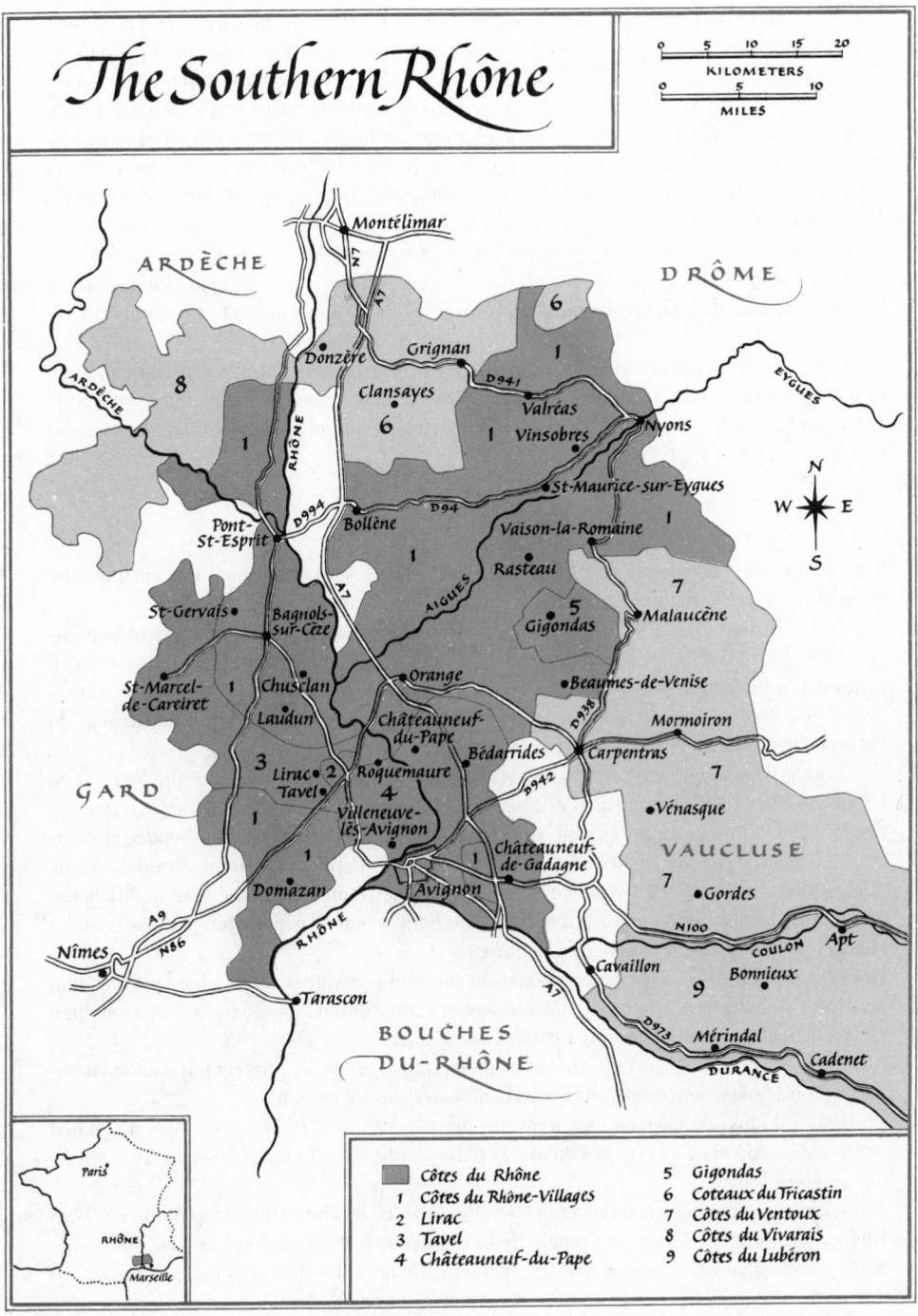

The Southern Rhône

KILOMETERS
0 5 10 15 20

MILES
0 5 10

ARDÈCHE

DRÔME

Montélimar

6

Grignan

Donzère

1

Clansayes

D941

Valréas

6

Vinsobres

Nyons

1

EYGUES

St-Maurice-sur-Eygues

Vaison-la-Romaine

1

Pont-St-Esprit

Bollène

D94

Rasteau

N

W   E

S

St-Gervais

Bagnols-sur-Cèze

Gigondas

5

Malaucène

7

St-Marcel-de-Careiret

Chusclan

1

Orange

Beaumes-de-Venise

Mormoiron

Laudun

Châteauneuf-du-Pape

Bédarrides

Carpentras

3

Lirac

2

Roquemaure

4

Vénasque

7

Tavel

VAUCLUSE

1

Villeneuve-lès-Avignon

1

Châteauneuf-de-Gadagne

7

Gordes

GARD

Domazan

Avignon

N100

Apt

COULON

Nîmes

Cavaillon

Bonnieux

Tarascon

9

Mérindal

Cadenet

DURANCE

BOUCHES-DU-RHÔNE

Paris

RHÔNE

Marseille

	Côtes du Rhône		5	Gigondas
1	Côtes du Rhône-Villages		6	Coteaux du Tricastin
2	Lirac		7	Côtes du Ventoux
3	Tavel		8	Côtes du Vivarais
4	Châteauneuf-du-Pape		9	Côtes du Lubéron

Chante Perdrix in Châteauneuf du Pape. The Nicolet family uses 20% in their excellent Châteauneuf du Pape.

Syrah   The only game in town in the northern Rhône, Syrah is relegated to an accessory role in the south. However, its role in providing needed structure, backbone, and tannin to the fleshy Grenache is incontestable. Some growers believe it ripens too fast in the hotter south, but it is, in my opinion, a very strong addition to many southern Rhône wines. More and more of the Côtes du Rhône estates are producing special bottlings of 100% Syrah wines that show immense potential. The finest Syrahs made in the southern Rhône are the cuvées of Syrah from the Château de Fonsalette and Domaine Gramenon. Both wines can last and evolve for 15–25 years. Their aromas are those of berry fruit, coffee, smoky tar, and hickory wood.

Terret Noir   Little of this grape is now found in the southern Rhône, although it remains one of the permitted varieties. It was used to give acidity to a wine and to mollify the strong character provided by Grenache and Syrah. None of the best estates care to employ it anymore.

Vaccarese   It was again at Beaucastel where I tasted the wine produced from this grape, which the Perrins vinify separately. It is not as powerful and deep as Syrah, nor as alcoholic as Grenache, but has its own unique character, giving aromas of pepper, hot tar, tobacco, and licorice.

WHITE WINE VARIETALS

Bourboulenc   This grape offers plenty of body. The local cognoscenti also attribute the scent of roses to Bourboulenc, although I cannot as yet claim the same experience.

Clairette Blanc   Until the advent of cold fermentations and modern equipment to minimize the risk of oxidation, Clairette produced heavy, alcoholic, often deep yellow-colored wines that were thick and ponderous. Given the benefit of state-of-the-art technology, it produces soft, floral, fruity wine that must be drunk young. The superb white Châteauneuf du Pape of Vieux Télégraphe has 35% Clairette in it.

Grenache Blanc   Deeply fruity, highly alcoholic yet low-acid wines are produced from Grenache Blanc. When fermented at cool temperatures and when the malolactic fermentation is blocked, they can be vibrant, delicious wines capable of providing wonderful near-term pleasure. The exquisite white Châteauneuf du Pape from Henri Brunier, Vieux Télégraphe, contains 25% Grenache Blanc; that of the Gonnet Brothers' Font de Michelle, 50%. In a few examples such as this, I find the floral scent of paper-white narcissus and a character vaguely resembling that of Condrieu.

Marsanne   The Marsanne grape planted in the south produces rather chunky wines that must receive help from other varieties because it cannot stand alone. Jancis Robinson often claims it smells "not unpleasantly reminiscent of glue."

Picardin   This grape has fallen out of favor, largely because the growers felt it added nothing to their blends. Apparently, its neutral character was its undoing.

Picpoul   Frankly, I have no idea what this grape tastes like. I have never seen it isolated or represented in such a hefty percentage as to be identifiable. Today, it is seen very rarely in the southern Rhône.

Roussanne   For centuries, this grape was the essence of white Hermitage in the northern Rhône, but its small yields and proclivity to disease saw it largely replaced by Marsanne. Making somewhat of a comeback in the southern Rhône, it has the most character of any of the white wine varietals—aromas of honey, coffee, flowers, and nuts—and produces a wine that can be very long-lived, an anomaly for a white wine in the southern Rhône. The famous Châteauneuf du Pape estate, Beaucastel, uses 80% Roussanne in their white wine, which, not surprisingly, is the longest-lived white wine of the appellation. Since 1986, they have also produced a 100% old-vine Roussanne that can be profound.

Viognier   Viognier produces a great and unique white wine that is synonymous with Condrieu and Château Grillet, both in the northern Rhône. In the south, there is little of it, but the experimental plantings that have been made have exhibited immense potential. The finest example in the southern Rhône is the Domaine Ste.-Anne in the Côtes du Rhône village of Gervais. St.-Estève is another domaine in the Côtes du Rhône that produces a good Viognier. Beaucastel began to utilize it in their white Coudoulet in 1991. Unfortunately, Viognier is not a permitted varietal in Châteauneuf du Pape, where it could immensely enhance the neutral character of so many of that village's white wines. Viognier is increasingly an important component of white Côtes du Rhône and in large measure, the most significant reason why these wines have increased in quality.

Appellations

NORTHERN RHÔNE

Condrieu   This exotic, often overwhelmingly fragrant wine is low in acidity and must be drunk young, but offers hedonistic aromas and flavors of peaches, apricots, and honey, and an unbelievably decadent, opulent finish.

Cornas   The impenetrable black/ruby color, the brutal, even savage tannins in its youth, the massive structure, and the muddy sediment in the bottle are all characteristics of a wine that tastes as if it were made in the nineteenth century. But Cornas wines are among the most virile, robust wines in the world, with a powerful aroma of cassis and raspberries that develops into chestnuts, truffles, licorice, and black currants as it ages. These wines are among the most underrated great red wines of the world but one must have patience with them.

Côte Rôtie   This is an immense, fleshy, rich, fragrant, smoky, full-bodied, stunning wine with gobs of cassis fruit frequently intertwined with the smell of frying bacon. It is one of France's greatest wines and can last for up to 25 years where well stored.

Crozes-Hermitage   Despite this appellation's proximity to the more famous appellation of Hermitage, the red wines tend to be soft, spicy, fruity, chunky, vegetal, and rather one-dimensional, instead of distinguished. The white wines vary enormously in quality and can be pleasant but are often mediocre and too acidic.

Hermitage   At its best, Hermitage is a rich, almost portlike, viscous, very full bodied, tannic red wine that can seemingly last forever. It is characterized by intense, even pungent smells of pepper and cassis, intertwined at times with aromas of Provençal herbs. The white Hermitage can be neutral, but the finest examples display a bouquet of herbs, minerals, nuts, acacia flowers, peaches, and a stony, wet slatelike component.

St.-Joseph   This is the northern Rhône's most underrated appellation for red and white wine. The reds and whites are juicy and best drunk young.

St.-Péray   Tiny quantities of still and sparkling white wines are made from this forgotten appellation of the Rhône Valley. Neither merits consumer interest, as the wines often are dull, heavy, and diffuse.

SOUTHERN RHÔNE

Châteauneuf du Pape   There is an enormous diversity in the styles of Châteauneuf du Pape produced. It can be made to resemble Beaujolais, in which case it offers jammy, soft, fruity flavors and must be drunk quite young. If the wine is vinified in a classic manner, it can be very dense in color, quite rich, and full bodied, and can last 15–20 years. It is often characterized by the smell of saddle leather, fennel, licorice, black truffles, pepper, nutmeg, and smoked meats. Wines made by both these methods and then blended together, and dominated by the Grenache grape, often smell of roasted peanuts and overripe Bing cherries. White Châteauneuf du Papes are usually neutral and uninteresting, but a few examples have a floral and tropical fruit-scented bouquet. However, they must be drunk extremely young.

Côtes du Rhône   The best Côtes du Rhônes offer uncomplicated but deliciously succulent, crunchy, peppery, blackberry and raspberry fruit in a supple, full-bodied style that is meant to be consumed within 5–6 years of the vintage.

Gigondas   Gigondas offers up a robust, chewy, full-bodied, rich, generous red wine that has a heady bouquet and supple, rich, spicy flavors. A tiny quantity of a very underrated rosé wine is often made and should be tried by consumers looking for something special.

Muscat de Beaumes de Venise   This sweet, alcoholic, but extraordinarily perfumed, exotic wine offers up smells of peaches, apricots, coconut, and lychee nuts. It must be drunk in its youth to be fully appreciated.

AGING POTENTIAL

Condrieu: 2–5 years

Châteauneuf du Pape (red): 5–20 years

Cornas: 5–15 years

Châteauneuf du Pape (white): 1–2 years

Côtes du Rhône: 4–8 years

Côte Rôtie: 5–25 years

Crozes-Hermitage: 3–8 years

Gigondas: 5–12 years

Hermitage (red): 5–30 years

Hermitage (white): 3–15 years

Muscat de Beaumes de Venise: 1–3 years

St.-Joseph: 3–8 years

Tavel: 1–2 years

OVERALL QUALITY LEVEL

In the northern Rhône appellations of Côte Rôtie, Hermitage, Condrieu, and Cornas, the general level of winemaking is excellent. In the other appellations, it is irregular. In the southern Rhône, Châteauneuf du Pape has the broadest range in quality, from superb to irresponsible and inept producers. Gigondas has the highest level of quality winemakers.

MOST IMPORTANT THINGS TO KNOW

NORTHERN RHÔNE

Côte Rôtie at a Glance

Appellation creation:	October 18, 1940
Type of wine produced:	Red wine only
Grape varieties authorized:	Syrah and Viognier (up to 20% can be added, but as a rule, few producers utilize more than 5% in their wines)
Total surface area:	497 acres
Quality level:	At least good; at best exceptional; among the finest red wines in the world
Aging potential:	The finest age 5–30 years
General characteristics:	Fleshy, rich, very fragrant, smoky, full-bodied, stunning wines
Greatest recent vintages:	1998, 1997, 1995, 1991, 1990, 1989, 1988, 1985, 1983, 1978, 1976, 1969
Price range:	$40–$75, except for Guigal's and Chapoutier's single vineyard and/or luxury cuvées, which cost $150 or more
Aromatic profile:	These intensely fragrant wines offer compelling bouquets showcasing scents and flavors of cassis, black raspberries, smoke, bacon fat, violets, olives, and grilled meats. For wines where a healthy dosage of new oak casks are employed, add vanillin, toast, and *pain grillé* aromas.

Textural profile:	These are elegant yet authoritatively powerful wines that are often chewy and deep. They are usually medium to full bodied, with surprisingly good acid levels for such ripeness and power. Tannin levels are usually moderate.

The Côte Rôtie appellation's most profound wines:

Chapoutier La Mordorée
Domaine Clusel-Roch Les Grandes Places
Delas La Landonne
Gentaz-Dervieux*
Jean-Michel Gérin Les Grandes Places
Guigal Château D'Ampuis
Guigal La Landonne
Guigal La Mouline

Guigal La Turque
Jean-Paul et Jean-Luc Jamet
Michel Ogier Belle-Hélène
René Rostaing Côte Blonde
René Rostaing Côte Brune La Landonne
Tardieu-Laurent (Côte Brune)
L. de Vallouit Les Roziers
Vidal-Fleury La Chatillonne

RATING THE CÔTE RÔTIE PRODUCERS

* * * * * (OUTSTANDING)

Chapoutier (La Mordorée)
Clusel-Roch (Les Grandes Places)
Delas (La Landonne)
Marius Gentaz-Dervieux
Guigal (Château D'Ampuis)
Guigal (La Landonne)
Guigal (La Mouline)

Guigal (La Turque)
Jean-Paul et Jean-Luc Jamet
Michel Ogier Belle-Hélène
René Rostaing (Côte Blonde)
René Rostaing (Côte Brune La Landonne)
Tardieu-Laurent (Côte Brune)
L. de Vallouit (Les Roziers)

* * * * (EXCELLENT)

Bernard Burgaud
Domaine Clusel-Roch (other cuvées)
Henri Gallet
Yves Gangloff
Jean-Michel Gérin (Les Grandes Places)
Guigal (Côtes Brune et Blonde)
Laffoy et Gasse

Michel Ogier
René Rostaing (regular cuvée)
René Rostaing (Côte Brune La Viaillère)
  (since 1991)
Vidal-Fleury (La Chatillonne)
Vidal-Fleury (Côtes Brune et Blonde)

* * * (GOOD)

Gilles Barge (including Pierre Barge)
Guy et Frédéric Bernard
Gérard Bonnefond
Domaine de Bonserine (Domaine de la
  Rousse)
Emile Champet
Joel Champet (La Viaillère)
Chapoutier (regular cuvée)

Domaine Clusel-Roch (regular cuvée)
Delas Frères (Les Seigneurs de Maugiron)
Albert Dervieux-Thaize†
Jean-Michel Gérin (Champin de Seigneur)
Paul Jaboulet-Ainé (Les Jumelles)
Robert Jasmin (***/****)
Lyliane Saugère

Condrieu at a Glance

Appellation creation:	April 27, 1940
Type of wine produced:	White wine only

*Gentaz retired following the 1992 vintage and his vineyard holdings are now farmed by René Rostaing, a 5-star producer.
†Dervieux-Thaize, retired since 1991, leases his vineyards to René Rostaing.

Grape varieties authorized: Viognier
Acres currently under vine: Condrieu: 250, Château Grillet: 7.6
Quality level: The top wines are exceptional, as this is one of the rarest and
                                most unique wines in the world, but quality is increasingly
                                irregular.
Aging potential: 1-4 years; Château Grillet will keep 4-8 years.
General characteristics: An exotic, often overwhelming apricot/peach/honeysuckle
                                fragrance is followed by low-acid, very rich wines that are
                                usually short-lived; ironically, the less successful vintages
                                with higher acidity age longer.
Greatest recent vintages: 1998, 1997, 1994
Price range: $30–$65
Aromatic profile: Honeysuckle, peaches, apricots, and candied tropical fruit
                                aromas should soar from a glass of a top Condrieu.
Textural profile: In ripe vintages, Condrieu tends to be low in acidity, but not
                                flabby. Fleshy, decadent, dry, and gloriously fruity and layered
                                flavors should be intense, but not heavy.

The Condrieu appellation's most profound wines:

Yves Cuilleron Condrieu Les Chaillets
  Vieilles Vignes
Yves Cuilleron Condrieu Les Eguets
  Vendange Tardive
Pierre Dumazet Condrieu Coteau de Côte
  Fournet
Yves Gangloff Condrieu
Guigal Condrieu La Doriane
Lys de Volan Condrieu

Domaine de Monteillet (Antoine Montez)
  Condrieu
André Perret Condrieu Coteau du Chéry
René Rostaing Condrieu
Georges Vernay Condrieu Les Chaillées de
  l'Enfer
Georges Vernay Condrieu Coteaux du
  Vernon
François Villard Condrieu Coteaux de
  Poncin

RATING THE CONDRIEU PRODUCERS

* * * * * (OUTSTANDING)

Yves Cuilleron (Les Chaillets Vieilles
  Vignes)
Yves Cuilleron (Les Eguets)
Pierre Dumazet (Côte Fournet)
Yves Gangloff
Guigal (La Doriane)
Guigal (*négociant* bottling)

Domaine du Monteillet (Antoine Montez)
André Perret (Clos Chanson)
André Perret (Coteau du Chéry)
Georges Vernay (Les Chaillées de l'Enfer)
Georges Vernay (Coteaux du Vernon)
François Villard (Coteaux de Poncin)

* * * * (EXCELLENT)

Patrick et Christophe Bonnefond
Chapoutier
J. L. Chave
Yves Cuilleron (regular cuvée)
Delas Frères (Clos Boucher)
Pierre Dumazet (Rouelle Midi)
Robert Niero

Philippe et Christophe Pichon
Hervé Richard
René Rostaing (****/*****)
Georges Vernay (other cuvées)
François Villard (Les Terrasses du Palat)
Gérard Villano

* * * *(GOOD)*

Gilles Barge

Domaine du Chêne-Marc Rouvière

Domaine Louis Chèze

Domaine Farjon

Philippe Faury

Château Grillet*

Paul Jaboulet-Aîné

Niero-Pinchon (***/****)

Vidal-Fleury

Hermitage at a Glance

Appellation creation:	March 4, 1937
Types of wine produced:	Red, white, and vin de paille, a dessert-styled white wine
Grape varieties planted:	Syrah for the red wine; primarily Marsanne and some Roussanne for the white wine; up to 15% white wine grapes can be blended with the red wine, but as a practical matter, this is widely eschewed.
Acres currently under vine:	321
Quality level:	Prodigious for the finest red wines, good to exceptional for the white wines
Aging potential:	Red wine: 5–40 plus years; white wine: 3–25 years
General characteristics:	Rich, viscous, very full-bodied, tannic red wines. Full-bodied white wines with a unique scent of herbs, minerals, nuts, and peaches.
Greatest recent vintages:	1998, 1997, 1995, 1991, 1990, 1989, 1979, 1978, 1972, 1970, 1966, 1961, 1959
Price range:	$50–$100 will purchase any wine except for Chapoutier's L'Orée and Le Pavillon, and Chave's Cuvée Cathelin, which can cost $150 a bottle
Aromatic profile:	*Red Hermitage*—Cassis, black pepper, tar, and very ripe red and black fruits characterize a fine young vintage of red Hermitage. With a decade of bottle age, cedar, spice, and cassis can (and often do) resemble a first-growth Pauillac. *White Hermitage*—Pineapple aromas intertwine with acacia flowers, peach, and honey scents. With extended age (15 or more years), scents of smoked nuts, fino sherry, and honey can be overpowering.
Textural profile:	*Red Hermitage*—Unusually full bodied, powerful, and tannic, as well as resistant to oxidation, results in a wine that ages at a glacial pace. *White Hermitage*—Fruity, full bodied, and fragrant when young, white Hermitage closes down after 4–5 years of bottle age, only to reemerge 15–25 years later as an unctuous, dry, thick white wine.

The Hermitage appellation's most profound wines:

Chapoutier Ermitage Cuvée de l'Orée
  (white)

Chapoutier Ermitage Le Pavillon (red)

Chapoutier Hermitage L'Ermite

Chapoutier Hermitage Le Méal

J. L. Chave Hermitage (red)

J. L. Chave Hermitage (white)

---

*Prior to 1979 *****; since 1979 ***. Château Grillet is entitled to its own appellation—a very unusual situation in France.

J. L. Chave Hermitage Cuvée Cathelin (red)
Bernard Faurie Hermitage Le Méal (red)
Delas Frères Hermitage Les Bessards (red)

Paul Jaboulet-Aîné Hermitage La Chapelle
(red)
Marc Sorrel Hermitage Gréal (red)
Tardieu-Laurent Hermitage Vieilles Vignes

RATING THE RED HERMITAGE PRODUCERS

* * * * * (OUTSTANDING)

Chapoutier (Le Pavillon)
Chapoutier Hermitage L'Ermite
Chapoutier Hermitage Le Méal
J. L. Chave (Cuvée Cathelin)
J. L. Chave (regular cuvée)

Delas (Les Bessards)
Bernard Faurie (Le Méal)
Paul Jaboulet-Aîné (La Chapelle)
Marc Sorrel (Le Gréal)
Tardieu-Laurent Vieilles Vignes

* * * * (EXCELLENT)

Albert Belle
Chapoutier (La Sizeranne) (since 1989)
Domaine du Colombier

Bernard Faurie (regular cuvée)
Marc Sorrel (Cuvée Classique)
L. De Vallouit (Les Greffières)

* * * (GOOD)

Caves Cottevergne-L. Saugère
Bernard Chave
Dard et Ribo
Delas Frères (Marquise de la Tourette)
Desmeure
Domaine Fayolle

Ferraton Père et Fils (Cuvée Les Miaux)
Alain Graillot
Guigal
Paul Jaboulet-Aîné (Pied La Côte)
Jean-Michel Sorrel
Vidal-Fleury

RATING THE WHITE HERMITAGE PRODUCERS

* * * * * (OUTSTANDING)

Chapoutier (Cuvée de l'Orée)
Chapoutier (Le Méal)

J. L. Chave

* * * * (EXCELLENT)

J. L. Grippat
Guigal

Paul Jaboulet-Aîné (Chevalier de
Stérimberg) (since 1989)
Marc Sorrel (Les Rocoules)

Crozes-Hermitage at a Glance

Appellation creation:	March 3, 1937
Type of wine produced:	Red and white wine
Grape varieties authorized:	Marsanne and Roussanne for the white wine; Syrah for the red wine, which represents 90% of the appellation's production
Acres currently under vine:	2,550
Quality level:	Mediocre to good, occasionally excellent, a few wines are superb
Aging potential:	White wine: 1–4 years; red wine: 3–10 years
General characteristics:	Tremendous variability in the red wines; white wines are fleshy, chunky, solid, and rather undistinguished

Greatest recent vintages:	1998, 1995, 1991, 1990, 1989, 1988, 1978
Price range:	$18–$35
Aromatic profile:	It is not dissimilar to Hermitage, but less intense, and often with more Provençal herb and olive scents. The Crozes-Hermitage *terroirs* are variable, and the Syrah does not achieve the exceptional ripeness found in Hermitage. The top wines are medium to full bodied, with attractive, smoky, peppery, cassis scents and flavors that can resemble a down-sized Hermitage. Textural profile: In addition to its deep ruby/purple color, this wine generally possesses medium to full body, moderate tannin, and fine depth in the best examples. It rarely rewards cellaring for more than a decade, except in vintages such as 1978, 1989, and 1990.

The Crozes-Hermitage appellation's most profound wines:

Albert Belle Cuvée Louis Belle
Chapoutier Les Varonnières
Laurent Combier Clos des Grives
Delas Tour d'Albon
Ferraton Le Grand Courtil
Alain Graillot Les Guiraudes

Paul Jaboulet-Aîné Domaine Raymond
 Roure
Paul Jaboulet-Aîné Domaine de Thalabert
Domaine du Pavillon Vieilles Vignes
 (Stephan Cornu)
Remizières Cuvée Christophe (red and
 white)

RATING THE CROZE-HERMITAGE PRODUCERS

****(EXCELLENT)

Albert Belle (Cuvée Louis Belle)
Chapoutier (Les Varonnières)
Delas (Tour d'Albon)
Domaine du Colombier (Cuvée Gaby)
Domaine du Combier (Clos des Grives)
Ferraton (Le Grand Couitil)
Alain Graillot (Cuvée La Guiraude)

Paul Jaboulet-Aîné (Domaine Raymond
 Roure)
Paul Jaboulet-Aîné (Domaine de Thalabert)
Domaine du Pavillon (G.A.E.C. Cornu)
 (Cuvée Vieilles Vignes)
Remizières (Cuvée Christophe)
Vidal-Fleury

***(GOOD)

Luc Arnavon (Domaine du Veau d'Or)
Albert Bégot
Albert Belle (Cuvée Les Pierrelles)
Chapoutier (Les Meysonnières)
Chapoutier (Petite Ruche)
Bernard Chave
Domaine Collonge
Dard et Ribo/Domaine Blanche Laine
Domaine des Entrefaux (Le Dessus des
 Entrefaux)

Domaine Fayolle (La Grande Séguine)
Domaine Fayolle (Les Voussères)
Michel Ferraton
Alain Graillot (Cuvée Classique)
Jean Marsanne
Domaines Pochon/Château de Courson
Domaine Jacques et Jean-Louis Pradelle
 (Les Hirondelles)
L. de Vallouit (Château du
 Larnage***/****)

St.-Joseph at a Glance

Appellation creation:	June 15, 1956
Type of wine produced:	Red and white wine
Grape varieties planted:	Marsanne and Roussanne for the white wine; Syrah for the red wine
Acres currently under vine:	1,729
Quality level:	Average to excellent
Aging potential:	White wine: 1–5 years; red wine: 3–8 years
General characteristics:	The red wines are the lightest, fruitiest, and most feminine of the northern Rhône. The white wines are perfumed and fleshy with scents of apricots and pears.
Greatest recent vintages:	1998, 1997, 1995, 1990, 1989, 1978
Price range:	$18–$25
Aromatic profile (white wines):	At the top level, the finest white wines are medium-bodied, refreshing, peach/apricot, sometimes pear-scented wines with good citrusy acidity that are delightful to drink within their first 2–3 years of life. Unfortunately, only a small percentage of dry whites meet these criteria. The majority of white St.-Joseph tend to be neutral, monolithic wines lacking charm and personality.
Aromatic profile (red wines):	Syrah can be at its fruitiest, lightest, and most charming in this appellation. A good St.-Joseph red should display a Burgundy-like black cherry, raspberry, and occasionally cassis-scented nose with medium body, light tannin, and zingy acidity. These are the Rhône Valley's lightest reds, and are thus best drunk in their first 5–6 years of life.
Textural profile (white wines):	Light to medium body is the prevailing rule with not much weight. Good freshness, crisp acidity, and uncomplicated fruit give these wines an appealing lightweight character.
Textural profile (red wines):	Good fruit presented in a medium-bodied, zesty format is the hallmark of a fine St.-Joseph red. They should not possess tannin for support, but rather, crisp acidity.

The St.-Joseph appellation's most profound wines:

Chapoutier Les Granits (red and white)
J. L. Chave (red)
Domaine Louis Chèze Cuvée Prestige de Caroline
Domaine Courbis Les Royes
Yves Cuilleron (white)
Yves Cuilleron Prestige l'Amarybelle
Yves Cuilleron les Serines
Delas François de Touron
Delas Ste.-Epine
Paul Jaboulet-Ainé Le Grand Pompée (red)
J. L. Grippat Vignes de l'Hospices (red)

J. L Grippat (white)
Domaine du Monteillet-Antoine Montez Cuvée de Papy (red)
André Perret (white)
André Perret Cuvée Les Grisières (red)
Pascal Perrier Domaine de Gachon (red)
Pascal Perrier Cuvée de Collonjon (red)
Raymond Trollat (red)
L. de Vallouit Les Anges (red)
François Villard Les Côtes du Mairlant (red and white)

RATING THE ST.-JOSEPH PRODUCERS

***** *(OUTSTANDING)*

Chapoutier (Les Granits) (red)
Domaine Courbis (Les Royes)
Yves Cuilleron (Prestige l'Amarybelle)
Yves Cuilleron (Les Serines)

Delas (François de Touron)
Delas (Ste.-Epine)
Pascal Perrier (Domaine de Gachon) (red)

**** *(EXCELLENT)*

Chapoutier (Les Granits) (white)
J. L. Chave (red)
Domaine du Chêne (Cuvée Anaïs) (red)
Domaine Louis Chèze (Cuvée Prestige de
 Caroline) (red)
Yves Cuilleron (white)
Yves Cuilleron (Cuvée Prestige Le Bois
 Lombard) (white)
Bernard Faurie (red)
Alain Graillot (red)
Jean-Louis Grippat (white)

Paul Jaboulet-Aîné (Le Grand Pompée)
 (red)
Domaine du Monteillet-Antoine et
 Monique Montez (Cuvée du Papy) (red)
André Perret (white)
André Perret (Les Grisières) (red)
Pascal Perrier (Cuvée de Collonjon) (red)
Raymond Trollat (red)
L. de Vallouit (Les Anges) (red)
François Villard (Les Côtes du Mairlant)
 (red and white)

*** *(GOOD)*

Clos de l'Arbalestrier (red)
Roger Blachon (red)
Chapoutier (Les Deschants) (red and white)
Domaine du Chêne (red)
Domaine Louis Chèze (red)
Domaine Collonge (red)
Maurice Courbis (red and white)
Pierre Coursodon (Paradis St.-Pierre) (red)
Pierre Coursodon (l'Olivaie) (red)
Bernard Faurie (white)
Philippe Faury (red)
Bernard Grippa (red)
Bernard Grippa (Cuvée Le Berceau) (white
 and red)

J. L. Grippat (red)
Paul Jaboulet-Aîné (white)
Jean Marsanne (red)
Domaine du Monteillet-Antoine et
 Monique Montez (red)
Alain Paret (Chais St.-Pierre l'Arm de
 Père) (red)
Alain Paret (Chais St.-Pierre Domaine de
 la Couthiat) (red)
André Perret (red)
St.-Désirat Cave Coopérative (red and
 white)
Vidal-Fleury (red)

Cornas at a Glance

Appellation creation:	August 5, 1938
Type of wine produced:	Red wine only
Grape varieties authorized:	only Syrah
Total surface area:	1,358 acres, of which 220 acres are planted
Quality level:	Good to exceptional
Aging potential:	5–20 years
General characteristics:	Black/ruby in color, very tannic, full-bodied, virile, robust wines with powerful aromas and rustic personalities
Greatest recent vintages:	1998, 1997, 1991, 1990, 1989, 1985, 1979, 1978, 1976, 1969
Price range:	$30–$60

Aromatic profile: Black fruit, earth, minerals, occasionally truffles, smoked herbs, and meats are common.

Textural profile: Massive, tannic, nearly coarse flavors have full body, intensity, length, and grip, but are often too savage and uncivilized for many tasters.

The Cornas appellation's most profound wines:

Auguste Clape

Jean-Luc Colombo La Louvée

Jean-Luc Colombo Les Ruchets

Paul Jaboulet-Ainé Domaine de St.-Pierre

Tardieu-Laurent (Côteaux)

Tardieu-Laurent (Vieilles Vignes)

Noël Verset Cornas

Alain Voge Les Vieilles Fontaines

Alain Voge Cuvée Vieilles Vignes

RATING THE CORNAS PRODUCERS

* * * * * (OUTSTANDING)

Auguste Clape

Jean-Luc Colombo (Cuvée La Louvée)

Jean-Luc Colombo (Les Ruchets)

Tardieu-Laurent (Côteaux)

Tardieu-Laurent (Vieilles Vignes)

Alain Voge (Les Vieilles Fontaines)

* * * * (EXCELLENT)

Thierry Allemand (Cuvée Les Chaillots)

Thierry Allemand (Cuvée Reynard)

L. et D. Courbis-Domaine des Royes (Champelrose)

L. et D. Courbis-Domaine des Royes (La Sabarotte)

Paul Jaboulet-Ainé (Domaine St.-Pierre)

Marcel Juge (Cuvée Coteaux)

Jacques Lemencier

Robert Michel (Le Geynale)

Noël Verset

* * * (GOOD)

René Balthazar

Cave Coopérative de Tain l'Hermitage

Caves Guy de Barjac

Chapoutier

Jean-Luc Colombo (Terres Brûlées)

L. et D. Courbis (regular cuvée)

Delas Frères (Cuvée Chante-Perdrix)

Cave Dumien-Serette ***/****

Eric et Joel Durand

Domaine de la Haute Fauterie

Paul Jaboulet-Ainé (négociant bottling)

Marcel Juge (regular cuvée)

Jean Lionnet (Cuvée Rochepertuis)

Robert Michel (Cuvée des Coteaux)

Robert Michel (Cuvée le Pied du Coteau)

J. L. Thiers

Domaine du Tunnel

Alain Voge (Cuvée Barriques)

St.-Péray at a Glance

Appellation creation: December 8, 1936

Type of wine produced: Still and sparkling white wines, the latter representing 60% of the production

Grape varieties planted: Marsanne and Roussanne

Acres currently under vine: 160

Quality level: Below average to average

Aging potential: 2–4 years

General characteristics: Dull, somewhat odd, uninteresting wines that are heavy and diffuse

Greatest recent vintages:	None
Price range:	$15–$20
Aromatic profile:	The acceptable examples—sadly, there are too few—offer a vague lemony/peachlike smell, with neutral fruit flavors. The majority of the wines are acidic, heavy, and lacking fruit.
Textural profile:	The sparkling wines are crisp, and at times refreshing, but in a low-brow sense. The still wines can be flabby, full-bodied, chewy wines with no real vibrancy. There are no profound St.-Péray wines.

RATING THE ST.-PÉRAY SPARKLING WINE PRODUCERS

* * * (GOOD)

Jean-François Chaboud   Jean-Marie Teysseire
Pierre et Guy Darona   Jean-Louis Thiers

RATING THE ST.-PÉRAY STILL WINE PRODUCERS

* * * (GOOD)

Auguste Clape   Jean-Marie Teysseire
Jean-René Lionnet   Jean-Louis Thiers

SOUTHERN RHÔNE

Côtes du Rhône at a Glance

Appellation creation:	November 19, 1937
Type of wine produced:	Red, white, and rosé, although over 95% of the production is red wine
Grape varieties planted:	24 grapes are authorized, 14 designated as primary varietals and 10 as accessory, but for all practical purposes, the predominant red wine grape is Grenache, followed by Syrah, Mourvèdre, and Cinsault. For the white wines, Grenache Blanc, Clairette, Bourboulenc, and increasingly Viognier and Roussanne are the principal grapes.
Acres currently under vine:	110,495
Quality level:	At the cooperative level, which accounts for 75%–80% of the entire generic Côtes du Rhône production, quality ranges from insipid and sterile, to very good to excellent; at the estate-bottled level, the quality ranges from below average to exceptional in the case of a half-dozen or so overachievers.
Aging potential:	Over 95% of every bottle of generic Côtes du Rhône, whether red, white, or rosé, should be drunk early; the whites and rosés within 2 years of the vintage, and the reds within 2 to 4 years of the vintage. However, some of the seriously endowed wines from the top estates can age for 20+ years.
General characteristics:	At the top levels, the white wines have made tremendous progress in quality as a result of modern cold fermentation and the introduction of Viognier and Roussanne in the blend. Even with these improvements, these are wines that are fresh,

lively, and meant to be drunk quickly. The red wines vary enormously. A well-made Côtes du Rhône should be bursting with red and black fruits, have a peppery, Provençal herb-scented nose, a supple, velvety texture, and a heady, lusty, spicy finish.

Greatest recent vintages: 1998, 1995, 1990, 1989

Price range: $10–$25, except for the single-vineyard and old-vine cuvées of a handful of estates

The Côtes du Rhône appellation's most profound wines:

Coudoulet de Beaucastel Côtes du Rhône

Domaine de Beaurenard

Domaine de l'Espigouette Plan de Dieu

Château de Fonsalette

Château de Fonsalette Cuvée Syrah

Domaine Gramenon Cuvée des Ceps Centenaires

Domaine Gramenon Cuvée des Laurentides

Domaine du Grand Moulas Côtes du Rhône

Domaine de la Guichard Cuvée Genet

Domaine de la Janasse Les Garrigues

Jean-Marie Lombard Cuvée Eugène de Monicault

Roger Perrin Réserve des Vieilles Vignes

Domaine Réméjeanne Les Genevrières

Château St.-Estève d'Uchaux Grand Réserve

Château St.-Estève d'Uchaux Vieilles Vignes

Tardieu-Laurent Guy Louis

RATING THE CÔTES DU RHÔNE PRODUCERS

* * * * * (OUTSTANDING)

Coudoulet de Beaucastel

Château de Fonsalette

Château de Fonsalette Cuvée Syrah

Domaine Gramenon (Ceps Centenaire)

Domaine Gramenon (Cuvée de Laurentides)

Tardieu-Laurent (Guy Louis)

* * * * (EXCELLENT)

Domaine de la Becassonne

Domaine A. Brunel

Domaine de la Cabasse

De la Canorgue

Domaine de Couroulu

Domaine Gramenon (various cuvées)

Château du Grand Moulas

Château du Grand Prébois

Domaine des Grand Devers

Domaine de la Guichard

Guigal

Paul Jaboulet-Aîné Parallel 45

Domaine de la Janasse

Jean-Marie Lombard

Plan Dei

Rabasse-Charavin

Domaine de la Réméjeanne

Domaine des Richards

Domaine St.-Gayan

Château St.-Maurice

Domaine St.-Apollinaire

Domaine Santa Duc

Domaine de la Solitude

Château des Tours

Domaine des Treilles

Vidal-Fleury

La Vieille Ferme (Perrin Réserve de Vieilles Vignes)

Domaine du Vieux Chêne (various cuvées)

* * * (GOOD)

Domaine des Aires Vieilles

Le Clos du Caillou

Daniel Combe

Cros de la Mure

Château de Domazan

Domaine de l'Espigouette ***/****

Domaine les Goubert

Domaine du Grand Prieur

Domaine de la Millière
Domaine Mireille et Vincent
Domaine Mitan
Domaine de Mont Redon
Domaine des Moulins ***/****
Domaines Mousset
Nero-Pinchon Ste.-Agathe

Domaine de la Présidente
Domaine de la Renjarde
Château St.-Estève d'Uchaux
Domaine St.-Michel
Domaine St.-Pierré
Château de Trignon
La Vieille Ferme (other cuvées)

Châteauneuf-du-Pape at a Glance

Appellation creation:	May 15, 1936
Type of wine produced:	Red, 93%; white, 7%
Grape varieties planted:	13 (actually 14 if the white clone of Grenache is counted) varieties are permitted; for red wines, Grenache, Syrah, Mourvèdre, Cinsault, Muscardin, Counoise, Vaccarèse, and Terret Noir; for white wines, Grenache Blanc, Clairette, Bourboulenc, Roussanne, Picpoul, and Picardin
Acres currently under vine:	8,100
Quality level:	Red wine: at the estate-bottled level, very good to exceptional; at the *négociant* level, mediocre to very good; white wine—mediocre to exceptional
Aging potential:	Red wine: depending on the style, 5–20 years; white wine: 1–3 years, except for Beaucastel and La Nerthe's Beauvenir
General characteristics:	Red wine: considerable diversity in stylistic approach can result in full-bodied, generous, rich, round, alcoholic, and long-lived wines to soft, fruity wines that could be called the Beaujolais of Provence; white wine: floral, fruity, straightforward and fresh if drunk within 2 years of the vintage
Greatest recent vintages:	1998, 1995, 1990, 1989, 1981, 1979, 1978, 1970, 1967, 1961
Price range:	$25–$50, with special old-vine and/or single-vineyard cuvées costing considerably more; $50–$85 is not an unusual price for such rarities
Aromatic profile:	Red wines: Given the enormous diversity of winemaking styles in this appellation, the following is a simplified view. Producers who turn out carbonic maceration wines are aiming for very early bottling, and easy-to-understand red and black fruit aromas that are jammy and appealing. Those producers aiming for fuller-bodied, more classically made Châteauneuf du Pape produce wines with a vast array of aromatics, ranging from black cherries, black currants, and blueberries, to roasted herbs, the noted Provençal *garrigue* smell (an earthy, herbes de Provence aromatic concoction), overripe peaches, and raspberry jam.
Aromatic profile:	White wines: The great majority of Châteauneuf du Pape white wines have their malolactic fermentation blocked, and are made in a style that sees no oak and very early bottling (usually within 3–4 months of the vintage). These wines are meant to be consumed within 1–2 years. They offer floral, tropical fruit aromas in a pleasing, but uncomplicated bouquet.

Textural profile: Red wines: The lighter-styled red wines that have seen partial
                           or full carbonic vinifications can be full bodied, but tend to be
                           soft and fruity, with the appellation's lusty alcohol present, but
                           not the weight and layered, multidimensional personality.
                           More classical offerings vary from muscular, full-bodied,
                           concentrated wines, to those of immense proportions, that are
                           chewy and thick, with high glycerin and alcohol. They saturate
                           the palate, and fall just short of staining the teeth.

Textural profile: White wines: The modern style, nonmalolactic, early bottled
                           whites are surprisingly full bodied and alcoholic, as well as
                           plump and mouth-filling. Their size suggests longevity, but
                           they are meant to be consumed quickly. The few producers
                           who practice full malolactic fermentation and later bottling
                           produce honeyed, unctuously textured, thick, juicy wines that
                           can be special if they are bottled without oxidizing.

The Châteauneuf du Pape appellation's most profound wines:

WHITE WINES

Château Beaucastel Cuvée Classique

Château Beaucastel Roussanne Vieilles
  Vignes

Clos des Papes

Font de Michelle

Domaine de la Janasse

Domaine du Marcoux

Domaine de Nalys

Château de la Nerthe Clos de Beauvenir

Château Rayas

Domaine de Vieux-Télégraphe

RED WINES

Château Beaucastel Cuvée Classique

Château Beaucastel Hommage à Jacques
  Perrin

Domaine de Beaurenard Cuvée Boisrenard

Domaine Henri Bonneau Réserve des
  Céléstins

La Bosquet des Papes Cuvée Chantemerle

Les Cailloux

Les Cailloux Cuvée Centenaire

Chapoutier Barbe Rac

Domaine de la Charbonnière Mourre des
  Perdrix

Domaine de la Charbonnière Vieilles
  Vignes

Gérard Charvin

Clos du Mont Olivet Cuvée Papet

Clos des Papes

Font de Michelle Cuvée Etienne Gonnet

Château Fortia (since 1994)

Château de la Gardine Cuvée des
  Générations

Domaine de la Janasse Cuvée Chaupin

Domaine de la Janasse Cuvée Vieilles
  Vignes

Domaine de Marcoux Cuvée Vieilles
  Vignes

Domaine de la Mordorée Cuvée de la
  Reine des Bois

Château de la Nerthe Cuvée des Cadettes

Domaine du Pegau Cuvée Réservée

Domaine du Pegau Cuvée Laurence

Château Rayas

Domaine Roger Sabon Cuvée Prestige

Domaine St.-Benoît Grande Garde

Domaine St.-Benoît Truffière

Tardieu-Laurent

Pierre Usseglio Grande Serres

Jean-Paul Versino Cuvée des Félix

Domaine de la Vieille Julienne Vieilles
  Vignes

Domaine de la Vieille Julienne Réserve

Le Vieux Donjon

Domaine du Vieux-Télégraphe

RATING THE RED CHÂTEAUNEUF DU PAPE PRODUCERS

* * * * * (OUTSTANDING)

Château Beaucastel

Château Beaucastel (Hommage à Jacques
  Perrin)

Domaine de Beaurenard (Cuvée
  Boisrenard)

Bois de Boursan (Cuvée Félix)

Domaine Henri Bonneau (Réserve des
  Céléstins)

Le Bosquet des Papes (Cuvée
  Chantemerle)

Les Cailloux

Les Cailloux (Cuvée Centenaire)

Domaine Le Clos du Cailloux Réserve

Chapoutier (Barbe Rac)

Clos du Mont Olivet (Cuvée Papet)

Clos des Papes

Cuvée du Vatican Sixtine

Font de Michelle (Cuvée Etienne Gonnet)

Château de la Gardine (Cuvée des
  Générations)

Domaine du Grand Tinel Alexis Establet

Domaine de la Janasse (Cuvée Chaupin)

Domaine de la Janasse (Cuvée Vieilles
  Vignes)

Domaine de Marcoux (Cuvée Vieilles
  Vignes)

Domaine de la Mordorée (Cuvée de la
  Reine des Bois)

Château de la Nerthe (Cuvée des Cadettes)

Domaine du Pégau (Cuvée Réservée)

Domaine du Pégau (Cuvée Laurence)

Château Rayas

Domaine Roger Sabon (Cuvée Prestige)

Tardieu-Laurent

Pierre Usseglio (Mon Aieul)

Domaine de la Vieille Julienne (Vieux
  Vignes)

Domaine de la Vieille Julienne (Réserve)

Le Vieux Donjon

Domaine du Vieux-Télégraphe

* * * * (EXCELLENT)

Pierre André

Paul Autard (Cuvée La Côte Ronde)

Lucien Barrot

Domaine de Beaurenard (Cuvée Classique)

Domaine Bois de Boursan

Henri Bonneau (Cuvée Marie Beurrier)

Le Bosquet des Papes (Cuvée Classique)

Domaine de Chante-Perdrix

Domaine de la Charbonnière

Domaine Les Clefs d'Or

Domaine Clos du Caillou

Clos du Mont Olivet (Cuvée Classique)

Clos St.-Michel

Domaine de la Côte de l'Ange

Henriet Crouzet-Féraud

Cuvée de Boisdauphin

Cuvée du Vatican

Domaine de Ferrand

Font du Loup (Le Puy Rolland)

Font de Michelle (Cuvée Classique)

Château Fortia (since 1994)

Domaine du Galet des Papes

Château de la Gardine

Domaine Haut des Terres Blanches

Domaine les Hautes Brusquières

Domaine de la Janasse (Cuvée Classique)

Domaine de Marcoux (Cuvée Classique)

Mas de Bois Lauzon

Domaine de Montpertuis (Cuvée Tradition)

Domaine de la Mordorée (Cuvée Classique)

Moulin-Tacussel

Domaine de Nalys

Château de la Nerthe (Cuvée Classique)

Père Caboche (Cuvée Elisabeth
  Chambellan)

Domaine du Père Pape

Domaine Roger Perrin (Réserve de Vieilles
  Vignes)

Domaine de la Présidente

Château Rayas Château Pignan

Domaine de la Roquette

Domaine Roger Sabon (Cuvée Réservée)

Domaine St.-Benoît (Grande Garde)

Domaine St.-Benoît (La Truffière)

Domaine de St.-Siffrein

Pierre Usseglio (Cuvée Tradition)

Raymond Usseglio

Domaine de la Vieille Julienne (Cuvée   Domaine de Villeneuve
  Tradition)

* * * (GOOD)

Paul Autard   Château Maucoil (**/***)
Jean Avril   Château Mongin
Domaine de Bois Dauphin   Domaine de Mont Redon
Château Cabrières (Cuvée Prestige)   Domaine de Montpertuis (Cuvée Classique)
Domaine des Chanssaud   Domaine de Palestor
Domaine Chantadu   Père Anselme
Domaine Chante-Cigale   Père Caboche (Cuvée Classique)
Chapoutier (La Bernadine)   Roger Perrin
Clos de l'Oratoire des Papes   Domaine de la Pinède
Clos St.-Jean   Domaine Pontifical (***/****)
Domaine de Cristia   Domaine des Relagnes
Cuvée du Belvedere (***/****)   Domaine Riche
Domaine Durieu   Domaine Roger Sabon (Les Olivets)
Château des Fines Roches   St.-Benoît (Cuvée Elise)
Lou Fréjau   St.-Benoît (Soleil et Festins)
Domaine du Grand Tinel   Domaine des Sénéchaux
Domaine Grand Veneur   Château Simian
Guigal   Domaine de la Solitude
Domaine Haut des Terres Blanches   Domaine Terre Ferme
Paul Jaboulet-Ainé (Les Cèdres)   Domaine Trintignant
  (***** prior to 1970)   Jean-Pierre Usseglio
Domaine de la Jaufrette   Château Vaudieu
Domaine Mathieu   Vidal-Fleury

RATING THE WHITE CHÂTEAUNEUF DU PAPE PRODUCERS

* * * * * (OUTSTANDING)

Château Beaucastel (Roussanne Vieilles   Le Grand Veneur (La Fontaine)
  Vignes)

* * * * (EXCELLENT)

Château Beaucastel (Cuvée Classique)   Domaine de Nalys
Clos des Papes   Domaine de la Nerthe (Cuvée Beauvenir)
Font de Michelle   Château Rayas
Domaine de la Janasse (Cuvée Prestige)   Saint Benoît Vieille Vignes Roussanne
Domaine du Marcoux   Domaine du Vieux-Télégraphe

* * * (GOOD)

Domaine de Beaurenard   Château de la Nerthe
Les Cailloux   Domaine du Père Caboche
Château de la Gardine   Domaine de la Roquette
Domaine de Mont Redon   Domaine Trintignant (La Reviscoulado)

Gigondas at a Glance

Appellation creation:	January 6, 1971
Type of wine produced:	Red wine represents 97% of the production. The only other wine permitted is rosé.
Grape varieties planted:	Grenache, Syrah, Mourvèdre, and Cinsault are the dominant varietals.
Acres currently under vine:	2,569
Quality level:	Average to exceptional
Aging potential:	5–15 years
General characteristics:	A robust, chewy, full-bodied, rich, generous red wine; light, vibrant, fresh, underrated rosé
Greatest recent vintages:	1998, 1995, 1990, 1989, 1985, 1979, 1978
Price range:	$20–$45
Aromatic profile:	Earth, *garrigue*, pepper, sweet black cherry, blueberry, and cassis fruit are evident in top examples of Gigondas.
Textural profile:	Light, fruity, soft, commercially styled wines are produced, but classic Gigondas possesses a full-bodied, muscular, unbridled power that is fine tuned in the best examples, and rustic to the point of being savage in the more uncivilized styles.

The Gigondas appellation's most profound wines:

Domaine La Bouissière La Font de Tonin
Domaine de Cayron
Domaine Font-Sane Cuvée Futée
Domaine les Goubert Cuvée Florence
Les Hauts de Montmirail
Moulin de la Gardette Cuvée Spéciale

Château Redortier
Château de Saint-Cosme Cuvée Valbelle
Domaine Santa Duc Cuvée des Hautes Garrigues
Domaine Santa Duc Cuvée Classique

RATING THE GIGONDAS PRODUCERS

* * * * * *(OUTSTANDING)*

Domaine La Bouissière La Font de Tonin
Domaine de Cayron
Les Hauts Montmirail (Daniel Brusset)
Domaine Raspail (Dominique Ay)

Château de Saint-Cosme Valbelle (since 1995)
Domaine Santa Duc
Tardieu-Laurent

* * * * *(EXCELLENT)*

Clos du Joncuas
Domaine la Bouissière (Cuvée Tradition)
Domaine de Font-Sane
Domaine de la Garrigue
Domaine les Goubert
Domaine de Longue-Toque
Moulin de la Gardette

Domaine les Pallieroudas (Edmonde Burle)
Domaine de Piauger
Château Redortier ****/*****
Château de Saint-Cosme (Cuvée Tradition)
Domaine St.-Gayan
Domaine du Terme
Château du Trignon

* * * *(GOOD)*

La Bastide St.-Vincent
Domaine de Cassan

Caves des Vignerons de Gigondas
Domaine le Clos des Cazaux

Domaine des Espiers

Domaine du Gour de Chaule

Domaine Grand-Romane

Domaine du Grapillon d'Or

Guigal

Paul Jaboulet-Aîné

Domaine de la Mavette

Château de Montmirail

L'Oustau Fouquet

Domaine Les Pallières ***/****

Domaine du Pesquier

Château Raspail (Meffre family)

Domaine Romane-Machotte

Domaine Roucas de St.-Pierre

Domaine Ste.-Anne

Domaine Les Teyssonières

Domaine de la Tourade

Domaine des Tourelles ***/****

Vidal-Fleury

Muscat de Beaumes de Venise at a Glance

Type of wine produced: The appellation is most famous for its sweet vins doux naturels, which are essentially fortified sweet wines made from the Muscat grape, but dry red, white, and rosé are also produced, some of it excellent.

Grape varieties planted: All permitted southern Rhône varietals, as well as the only legal plantations of Muscat à Petits Grains in the Rhône Valley (both the white and black variety)

Acres currently under vine: 1,087

Quality level: Good to exceptional

Aging potential: 2–4 years

General characteristics: The Muscat is a sweet, alcoholic, extraordinarily perfumed and exotic, rich, decadent dessert wine. The best examples of red wine are classic Côtes du Rhône-Villages with plenty of red and black cherry fruit, peppery, Provençal herb-scented noses, and gutsy, lusty flavors.

Greatest recent vintages: 1998

Price range:

(Muscat de Beaumes

de Venise): $15–$30

(Côtes du Rhône-Villages

Beaumes de Venise red): $10–$16

The village's best-kept secret: The excellent dry red wines produced by Domaine de Fenouillet, Domaine les Goubert, and Château Redortier

RATING THE MUSCAT DE BEAUMES DE VENISE PRODUCERS

* * * * * (OUTSTANDING)

Domaine de Baumalric

Domaine de Durban

Paul Jaboulet-Aîné

* * * * (EXCELLENT)

Domaine des Bernardins

Chapoutier

Domaine de Coyeux

Domaine de Fenouillet

Château St.-Sauveur

Vidal-Fleury

*** *(GOOD)*
Cave des Vignerons de Vacqueyras   Vignerons de Beaumes de Venise

Vacqueyras at a Glance

Appellation creation:	August 9, 1990
Type of wine produced:	Red wine represents 95% of the production, with 4% rosé and 1% white
Grape varieties planted:	Grenache, Syrah, Mourvèdre, and Cinsault for the red and rosé wines, and Grenache Blanc, Clairette, and Bourboulenc for the white wines
Acres currently under vine:	3,211
Quality level:	Average to good, but increasing
Aging potential:	4–12 years
General characteristics:	Powerful, rustic, full-bodied red wines that tend to lack the complexity and finesse of Gigondas or Châteauneuf du Pape
Greatest recent vintages:	1998, 1995, 1990, 1989
Price range:	$10–$16
Aromatic profile:	A classic Provençal/Mediterranean nose of herbes de Provence, *garrigue,* red and black fruits, earth, and olives
Textural profile:	Unbridled power, as well as coarse tannin and a fleshy mouthfeel make for a substantial and mouth-filling glass of wine.

RATING THE VACQUEYRAS PRODUCERS

***** *(OUTSTANDING)*
Domaine des Amouriers   Tardieu-Laurent Vieilles Vignes

**** *(EXCELLENT)*

Domaine de la Charbonnière   Domaine La Fourmone
Domaine le Clos des Cazaux   Domaine de la Tourade
Domaine Le Couroulu   Château des Tours

*** *(GOOD)*

La Bastide Saint-Vincent   Château de Montmirail
Domaine de Boissan   Domaine de Montvac
Domaine Chamfort   Château des Roques
Domaine le Clos des Cazaux***/****   Domaine le Sang des Cailloux
Domaine de la Garrigue   Château de la Tour
Paul Jaboulet-Aîné   Domaine de Verquière
Domaine des Lambertins   Vidal-Fleury

Tavel at a Glance

Appellation creation:	May 15, 1936
Type of wine produced:	Dry rosé only—the sole appellation in France to recognize rosé as the only authorized wine
Grape varieties planted:	There are 9 authorized varieties; Grenache and Cinsault

dominate, followed by Clairette, Syrah, Bourboulenc, Mourvèdre, Picpoul, Carignan, and Calitor.

Acres currently under vine:	2,340
Quality level:	Average to very good rosé wines
Aging potential:	1–3 years
General characteristics:	The finest Tavels are dry, full bodied, and boldly flavored.
Greatest recent vintages:	1998
Price range:	$14–$22
Aromatic profile:	Strawberries, cherries, and a vague scent of Provençal *garrigue*.
Textural profile:	Dry, sometimes austere, full-bodied wines can taste surprisingly rugged and shocking to those weaned on semi-sweet, soft, flabby, New World rosés. There are no profound Tavel wines.

RATING THE TAVEL PRODUCERS

* * * (GOOD)

Château d'Acqueria	Guigal
Domaine Canto-Perdrix	Domaine Méjan-Taulier
Domaine de Corne Loup	Domaine de la Mordorée
Domaine de la Forcardière	Domaine de Roc Epine
Domaine de la Genestière	Château de Trinquevedel

Lirac at a Glance

Appellation creation:	October 14, 1947
Type of wine produced:	Red, rosé, and white wines, of which 75% of the production is red, 20% rosé, and 5% white
Grape varieties planted	(red): Grenache Noir, Syrah, Mourvèdre, Cinsault, and Carignan; (white): Grenache Blanc, Clairette, Bourboulenc, Ugni Blanc, Picpoul, Marsanne, Roussanne, and Viognier
Acres currently under vine:	1,037
Quality level:	Mediocre to good, but improving
Aging potential:	2–8 years
General characteristics:	Soft, very fruity, medium-bodied red wines; neutral white wines; exuberantly fresh, fruity rosés (the frugal consumers' Tavel)
Greatest recent vintages:	1998, 1995, 1994, 1990, 1989
Price range:	$10–$15
Aromatic profile:	Similar to a Côtes du Rhône, with scents of red fruits, spices, and herbes de Provence
Textural profile:	Soft, fruity, generally medium-bodied red wines, and relatively innocuous, one-dimensional white wines. The rosés can be excellent, and are not dissimilar from a top Tavel.

The Lirac appellation's most profound wine:
Domaine de la Mordorée

RATING THE LIRAC PRODUCERS

*****(OUTSTANDING)*

Domaine de la Mordorée (Cuvée de la Reine
des Bois)

**** *(EXCELLENT)*

Domaine de Cantegril   Château St.-Roch
Domaine de la Mordorée (Cuvée Tradition)   Domaine de Ségriès
Domaine Roger Sabon

*** *(GOOD)*

Château Boucarut***/****   Domaine de la Forcardière
Domaine Canto-Perdrix   Domaine des Garrigues
Domaine des Causses et de St.-Eymes   Domaine Jean Marchand
Domaine Les Costes   Domaine de Roc Epine

Recent Vintages

1998—This will undoubtedly be a fabulous vintage in the south, particularly in Châteauneuf du Pape, and to a lesser extent Gigondas and Côtes du Rhône-Villages. In Châteauneuf, the wines possess uncommon color saturation, richness, and potential complexity and excitement, but prices for the bulk wine of this AOC rose 25%–40% immediately after the vintage, so 1998 is likely to be expensive. Textbook harvest conditions followed a hot summer with just enough rain to nourish the vineyards. Unlike other areas of France that received rain during the harvest, the southern Rhône was virtually moisture-free. I had the opportunity to taste more than five dozen samples of the 1998s, even though they were only a few months old. They were remarkably consistent in their saturated ruby/purple colors, extraordinary ripeness of fruit, and splendidly concentrated, full-bodied personalities. As more than one Châteauneuf du Pape grower told me, the vintage offers the volume, power, and opulence of 1990, but with the structure, finesse, and potential longevity of 1978. That sounds too good to be true, but 1998 will unquestionably be the greatest vintage in the southern Rhône since 1990.

In the north, everyone was pleased with the harvest, but no one ranks it higher than 1997, a year that stands out as very successful in Condrieu, Côte Rôtie, Hermitage, and to a lesser degree Cornas, Crozes-Hermitage, and St.-Joseph.

1997—This vintage is gorgeous in the north, with wines of low acidity, outstanding ripeness, concentrated styles, and considerable accessibility. It is undoubtedly a superior vintage in the north.

In the southern Rhône, I would currently place the 1997 vintage slightly behind 1996, but that is a difficult judgment to make until the 1997s are in bottle. The 1997s may be slightly more irregular given the difficult harvest conditions, but the wines are ripe, low in acidity, and somewhat diluted. They possess many of the characteristics of the 1996s, being forward, fruity, and charming, but they are not intensely concentrated or capable of significant longevity.

1996—I am pleased with the way the 1996 southern Rhônes have turned out in bottle. They are richly fruity, soft, not terribly concentrated, but user-friendly, low in acidity, and nicely textured, easy-to-drink wines that will be ideal for consumption over the next 5–8 years.

In the north, 1996 produced wines with higher than normal acidity (much like in Burgundy), deep color saturation, a compressed style, and a lean, firm tannic backbone. It is not a style of wine that excites me, but I realize some readers prefer higher-acid, firmer, more compressed wines. Nevertheless, where producers in Côte Rôtie, Hermitage, Cornas, and the other appellations had low yields and made concentrated wines, some exceptional wines were produced that will be unaccessible young but long-lived and potentially profound. However, this vintage needs to be approached with caution as those cooler climate vineyards and vignerons who did not keep their crop yields down produced wines with intensely herbaceous characteristics that are a defect, particularly when allied with higher than normal acidity.

1995—For a handful of producers in Côte Rotie (Guigal, Chapoutier, Jamet, and René Rostaing), 1995 turned out to be an exceptional vintage. Much like 1994, the summer was warm, even hot at times, with just barely enough rain. Like 1991, 1992, 1993, and 1994, September began on a positive note, but on September 9 the rains began. Intermittently showery weather followed for ten consecutive days. Those producers who felt 1995 was a replay of 1994, where the rains continued throughout the entire month of September, tended to harvest too soon, picking Syrah that was not physiologically ripe. Because Syrah possesses naturally high acidity, those producers who did not destem in 1995 have only exacerbated the impression of greenness and tart acidity. Producers who took the risk and delayed their harvests were rewarded with superb weather after September 20. Grapes picked at the end of September and the beginning of October were not only physiologically ripe but had retained surprising levels of acidity. As Marcel Guigal has so correctly said, 1995 can be a great vintage, similar to 1985, but with more acidity. Michel Chapoutier felt that those who waited until early October to harvest, both in Côte Rôtie and Hermitage, have had an exceptionally great year, in the same mold as such legendary Rhône vintages as 1947, 1961, and 1990. The vintage's stars, Guigal, Chapoutier, Jamet, and Rostaing, all agree that yields were extremely low, for their wines, with the average production down by at least 10%. All in all, this will be an inconsistent vintage, with the exceptional wines carrying, and possibly distorting, the vintage's reputation. One thing is certain, the 1995s, because of their refreshing acidity and high extraction, will be very long-lived by Côte Rôtie standards.

This was a more troublesome vintage for Condrieu than initially believed. A handful of great wines were produced by Guigal, Vernay, Villard, and Cuilleron, but too many producers refused to destem and harvested too early, resulting in wines that are too high in acidity, and taste vegetal. This is a vintage in which Condrieu enthusiasts must choose carefully, but the top examples are marvelous. These wines should be consumed by the turn of the century.

The white Hermitage are structured, backward, and elegant, but they are not as powerful or concentrated as the finest 1994s. The wines possess better acidity than the 1994s, so longevity will not be an issue. The top 1995 red wine cuvées are richer, fuller, more complete, and better structured than the 1994s. Jaboulet made his finest La Chapelle since 1990, and the Chaves, who produced a marvelous wine in 1994, made two profoundly great 1995s, a small quantity of their famed Cuvée Cathelin, as well as their Hermitage. Michel Chapoutier believes his two cuvées of Hermitage, La Sizeranne and Le Pavillon, will be reference point wines for his firm, even superior to the great Hermitages he produced in 1991, 1990, and 1989. Hermitage unquestionably enjoyed tremendous success in 1995, but the wines will require many years in bottle to reach full maturity. Optimum maturity: 2005–2040.

On paper, this looked like a very good to excellent vintage for Cornas, despite 2 weeks of unsettled weather and intermittent showers in September. The wines have turned out to be well colored, but high acid levels give them a compact, compressed personality. Some wines taste as if they were made from underripe fruit. Such producers as Clape, Colombo, and Jaboulet turned in strong efforts, but overall Cornas was less successful in 1995 than most other Rhône Valley appellations.

The year 1995 is generally a very good to excellent vintage in Crozes-Hermitage. Alain Graillot said he had never harvested such ripe fruit with such high acidity. The wines should prove to be firm, and while less flattering at an early age than the 1994s, this vintage's best cuvées have the potential to last for 10–15 years. The white wines will need to be drunk up over the next several years. They are more acidic and less concentrated than the 1994s. The year 1995 also marked the debut vintage for Chapoutier's new luxury cuvée of Crozes-Hermitage Les Varonnières, a wine destined to be an instant legend.

This is generally a very good to excellent vintage in St.-Joseph. The wines should prove to be firm, and while less flattering at an early age than the 1994s, this vintage's best cuvées have the potential to last for 10–15 years. The white wines will need to be drunk up over the next several years. They are more acidic and less concentrated than the 1994s.

On paper, the 1995 Châteauneuf du Pape vintage is an irrefutably promising year. In large part, a replay of 1994, 1995 enjoyed a hot summer (less torrid than 1994). At the beginning of September, as in 1994, there was widespread optimism for a great vintage if the September weather was good. Lightning can strike twice in the same place, and on nearly the same date as in 1994, the heavens opened, dumping 2 weeks of heavy showers on the Rhône Valley between September 7 and September 20. But there was one significant difference. In 1994, early harvesters usually had more success because the grape maturity was so advanced at the time of the rains. Delaying the harvest meant potential rot. In 1995, the grapes were 1–2 weeks behind the maturity curve of the 1994s; thus the rain was less of a reason to harvest early. Moreover, there was significantly less rain in September 1995, than in September 1994. Unlike 1994, the rain was finished by the end of the third week of September, and several weeks of clear, dry, warm, windy weather followed, allowing late harvesters to bring in very ripe, healthy fruit that, surprisingly, possessed a high degree of acidity for the degree of physiological ripeness the grapes possessed. While the 1995 vintage can clearly be called exceptional in the south, it is not as profound as 1989 or 1990.

In 1995, Gigondas may turn out to be the most successful appellation in southern France, even surpassing Châteauneuf du Pape. Even those estates and *négociants* that tend to produce lighter-styled wines fashioned black/purple-colored wines with exceptionally ripe fruit, good structure and acidity, and superb concentration. Most Gigondas producers bottle their wine as it is sold, often aging their wine too long in musty old *foudres*. This is hardly conducive to producing the best wine, but that's the way it is. However, the raw materials in 1995 are superb, and I am hoping that most of these wines get into the bottle before the end of 1997. This vintage has the potential to be as good if not superior to 1989 and 1990.

1994—Much like all the Rhone Valley vintages following the great 1990 vintage, 1994 is another complicated year. The torridly hot, sunny summer offered the potential for another 1990 or 1989, but harvest rains caught most northern producers with unharvested grapes. Nevertheless, the better producers who had low crop yields are pleased with the quality, claiming that the 1994s from Côte Rôtie, Hermitage, and Cornas are superior to 1993 and 1992, and possibly as fine as 1991 or 1985.

In the southern Rhone, many producers were able to harvest a significant portion of their vineyards before the heavy rains began. Early assessments of the 1994 vintage suggest that Châteauneuf du Pape, followed by Gigondas and several of the Côtes du Rhone villages have produced their richest, most complete cuvées since the great 1990 vintage. Quantities, however, are small, so look for prices to rise if the quality turns out to be as fine as believed.

1993—1993 is both a confusing and irregular year. The vintage's failures are concentrated in the northern Rhone, especially in Côte Rôtie and Hermitage. Rain and high humidity caused serious problems with mildew and rot in the northern Rhone vineyards, thus devastating producers who were on the verge of having a high-quality vintage. It is possible that an event of historical proportions has emerged from the disastrous 1993 vintage in the northern Rhone. Michel Chapoutier, whose faith in the principles of biodynamic organic farming created such a controversy among his peers, produced brilliant wines in this dreadful year, offering, in the brash Chapoutier's view, uncontroverted evidence of the merits of this philosophy of vineyard farming.

In contrast, the southern Rhone fared well in 1993. Why? Approximately 50%–75% of the crop was harvested before any damaging rain. The 1993 vintage illustrates how different the microclimates are in the northern and southern Rhone, not to mention the *terroirs* and grape varietals. If the northern Rhone's 1993 vintage looks to be the worst that sector of the Rhone has experienced since 1977, 1975, or 1984, the southern Rhone may turn out a vintage that is capable of rivaling 1988, and perhaps even 1985.

As the tasting notes that follow evidence, plenty of fine wines have emerged from the last three vintages. Selection is always critical, but Rhone wines, particularly the reds, remain France's least-known great wines. While the limited-production great red wines of the northern Rhone, especially Côte Rôtie and Hermitage, are rare and expensive, the southern Rhone red wines, such as Châteauneuf du Pape, Gigondas, Vacqueyras, and the top Côtes du Rhones, continue to offer fabulous quality/price rapport.

1992—This year is mediocre in quality, with considerable failures in the Côtes du Rhone villages. Additionally, Gigondas is below average in quality, but Châteauneuf du Pape is surprisingly good, although the wines are lighter and significantly less concentrated than such great years as 1989 and 1990.

In the northern Rhone, the vintage has turned out to be of average quality, with the most meticulous producers turning out surprisingly good, ripe, soft wines that will require early consumption. Chapoutier's 1992s are brilliant wines.

1991—Côte Rôtie enjoyed exceptional success in 1991, and other northern Rhone appellations unquestionably produced very good wines in that vintage. For Côte Rôtie, 1991 has proven to be an exceptional vintage, superior as well as more consistent than 1990. Other northern Rhone appellations that enjoyed success included Cornas, Hermitage, St.-Joseph, and Crozes-Hermitage.

The southern Rhone appellations were devastated by torrential rains in 1991 and the quality of virtually every Gigondas and Châteauneuf du Pape is suspect, although a few worthy wines have emerged.

1990—This is a superlative vintage throughout the Rhone Valley. In the south, the torridly hot, dry summer resulted in superripe grapes packed with sugar. At the top levels the wines are deeply colored, exceptionally powerful, with high levels of soft tannins, and alcohol of 14%–15% plus. The wines have a more roasted, extreme style than the more classic 1989s, but they are sumptuous, as well as loaded with concentrated fruit. It is unquestionably a great vintage in Châteauneuf du Pape, an excellent one in Gigondas, and a topflight year in most of the Côtes du Rhone-Villages. The red wines from both Gigondas and Châteauneuf du Pape, despite higher alcohol than the 1989s, will probably mature more quickly than the 1989s because their acidity levels are lower and because the wines are so opulent and precocious. Nevertheless, the top cuvées of Châteauneuf du Pape should easily last for 15–20 years.

If you are a lover of Hermitage and Crozes-Hermitage, grab your wallet! In Hermitage, 1990 looks to be even better than the great 1978 vintage. Gérard Chave, Michel Chapoutier, and Gérald Jaboulet all believe it is the finest year for this renowned appellation since 1961. The massive wines are almost black in color, with extraordinary extraction of fruit, high tannins, and a textural sweetness and succulence. Jaboulet's La Chapelle, Chave's Hermitage, and Chapoutier's luxury cuvée, Le Pavillon, are likely candidates for perfection, provided those who can both find and afford them wait the 15 or more years they will need to attain maturity. Even the wines of Crozes-Hermitage are superconcentrated. Those from Alain Graillot and Paul Jaboulet-Aîné are especially exciting. Côte Rôtie is a mixed bag, with the top cuvées of Chapoutier, Guigal, and a handful of others looking excellent, sometimes extraordinary. Other wines are merely above average in quality. St.-Joseph and Cornas are at least good.

1989—This is unquestionably a great vintage for Châteauneuf du Pape and gets my nod as the finest vintage for that appellation since 1978. In fact, it is 1978 that comes to mind when looking for a vintage of similar characteristics. The hot, dry weather produced small grapes with more noticeable tannins than the 1990s. However, when analyzed, most 1990s have the same level of tannins as the 1989s, but the 1989s taste more structured and more classically rendered. Given the stunning ripeness and reasonable yields, the 1989 Châteauneuf du Papes are nearly as powerful as the 1990s. They have low acidity, spectacular levels of fruit extraction, and a full-bodied, potentially long-lived style. It is a matter of personal taste whether one prefers the 1990s or the 1989s, but both are dazzling vintages. One really has to look to the individual domaine as to who fared better in one vintage or the other. A more consistent vintage in Gigondas, 1989 is that appellation's best overall year since 1978. For Rhone wine enthusiasts, these two years offer the best opportunities to replenish your cellars since 1978 and 1979.

Less massive, more supple and opulent wines were produced throughout the northern Rhone. The most successful appellations were Hermitage and Côte Rôtie. The least successful was Cornas. While Côte Rôtie producers were ecstatic after the vintage, only the best cuvées of Guigal and a few other wines have the requisite concentration and grip to live up to the initial hyperbole. While the wines are flattering and will make delicious drinking over the next 10–15 years, this is an excellent rather than a great vintage. In Hermitage it would be considered a great vintage except for the fact that 1990 succeeded it. The top cuvées are rich and full bodied, with 20 or more years of longevity. They also have a softness and are less massive on the palate, particularly when tasted next to the 1990s. The vintage is irregular in Cornas. The heat and drought appear to have caused problems for many vineyards in that appellation. As in Hermitage, Crozes-Hermitage enjoyed an excellent year.

DANIEL ET DENIS ALARY

1995	Cairanne Côtes du Rhône-Villages	B	87
1995	Cairanne Côtes du Rhône-Villages La Font d'Estebans	C	91
1995	Cairanne Côtes du Rhône-Villages Réserve de Vigneron	C	90
1996	Côtes du Rhône	A/D	85
1995	Côtes du Rhône	B	86
1996	Côtes du Rhône-Villages Cairanne	A/D	86
1996	Côtes du Rhône-Villages Cairanne La Font d'Estevenas	A/D	88

One of the bright, shining stars in the Côtes du Rhône firmament, the Alarys produce some of the richest, most complex and complete wines in the southern Rhône. Even in the light 1996 vintage their wines are meritorious. The straightforward, monolithic, fruity, unfiltered 1996 Côtes du Rhône displays a dark ruby color, and sweet berry fruit allied with earth, *garrigue*, and spice. Drink it over the next 1–2 years. Slightly more serious, with more crushed seashell, dried herbes de Provence, and cherry fruit is the 1996 unfiltered Côtes du Rhône-Villages Cairanne. It cuts a more structured feel in the mouth, but I do not think that ensures greater longevity, so consume it over the next several years. The excellent 1996 Côtes du Rhône-Villages Cairanne La Font d'Estevenas exhibits a more saturated ruby/purple color, and jammy black cherry and currant fruit intermixed with dried herb and pepper smells. Medium bodied, with a juicy midsection and sweet tannin in the moderately long finish, it should be enjoyed over the next 3–4 years.

Daniel and Denis Alary are superstars of the sun-drenched, wind-swept, Provençal village of Cairanne, a short 30-minute drive northeast of Châteauneuf du Pape. Their talents are well displayed in the following four wines. The 1995 Côtes du Rhône, a blend of Grenache and Syrah, aged both in tank and oak *foudre*, and bottled unfiltered, is a soft, ripe, tarry, peppery, berry-scented and -flavored wine with an unmistakable Provençal herb/peppery personality. The wine is actually more delicious than its point score indicates, but it is not complex or potentially long-lived. However, this is a mouth-filling, generous Côtes du Rhône that scores high on the pleasure quotient. Drink it over the next 2–3 years. The 1995 Cairanne, a blend of 80% Grenache and 20% Mourvèdre, is a more serious wine, exhibiting a deep ruby/garnet color. The Mourvèdre component provides earthy, saddle leather notes, along with kirsch, roasted nuts, and chocolate-covered berry fruits. Sweet on the entry (from extract, not sugar, as this wine is dry), it is a ripe, long, excellent Côtes du Rhône possessing more structure and delineation than its predecessor. It should drink well for 5–6 years.

At the top of the Alary hierarchy are the two cuvées, Réserve de Vigneron and La Font d'Estebans. The 1995 Réserve de Vigneron is a blend of 60% Syrah, 30% Grenache, and 10% Counoise. Made from low yields (approximately 25 hectoliters per hectare, or under 2 tons of fruit per acre), in addition to spending 6 months in oak before bottling, this is an extremely ripe and complex wine. It is a sexy, beautifully made, opaque ruby-colored wine with a knockout nose of chocolate, sweet berry fruit, and spice. Opulently textured, with explosive ripeness, and a creamy, lush richness, this is an outstanding, full-bodied, deep, succulent Côtes du Rhône to consume over the next 5–8 years. As for the 1995 La Font d'Estebans (a 50% Grenache, 40% Syrah, 10% Mourvèdre blend, with some of the Grenache coming from 110-year-old vines), this wine offers a raspberry liqueur-scented nose with spice and pepper in the background. It reveals some of the smoked herb/dried candy fruit of the other bottlings but is richer and fuller, with more structure, power, and extract. It is a terrific Côtes du Rhône, with a knockout midpalate, and a finish that goes on for nearly 35 seconds. Made from yields of 1½ tons of fruit per acre, it, like the other cuvées, was bottled without filtration. Anticipated maturity: now–2005.

DOMAINE DE L'AMEILLAUD

1996 Cairanne Côtes du Rhône-Villages	B	86
1996 Côtes du Rhône	B	85

These two offerings are distinctive because they have been bottled unfiltered, but only for America. The dark ruby-colored 1996 Côtes du Rhône exhibits a smoky, Provençal herb, cherry, and peppery-scented nose, medium body, and elegant, open-knit, straightforward, pleasant flavors. Drink it over the next year. The 1996 Cairanne, from one of the Côtes du Rhône's finest villages, reveals deeper fruit, a denser texture, and more Provençal herbs, pepper, and kirsch fruit. It is a spice/fruit-driven wine to drink over the next 1–2 years.

DOMAINE DES AMOURIERS

1995 Vacqueyras	B	87

From one of the finest Vacqueyras estates, this 1995 offering reveals a kirsch, pepper, Provençal herb, and earthy aromas and flavors, medium body, an attractive texture, mouth-filling richness, and a medium- to full-bodied finish. Sadly, the person responsible for this high-class Vacqueyras, proprietor Jocelyn Chudzikiewicz, died in early 1997.

DOMAINE DES ANGES

1995 Côtes du Ventoux Clos de la Tour Syrah	B	89

I still have some 1990 of this cuvée in my cellar that has continued to drink impressively. This 1995 looks to be as high class as the 1990. The luxury cuvée of Domaine des Anges, the wine offers a dense ruby/purple color, and a smoky, bacon fat, and cassis-scented nose that jumps from the glass. In the mouth, there is outstanding richness, gobs of black fruits, good underlying acidity, and moderate tannin. This is a top-class, 100% Syrah cuvée that should age well for 5–8 years.

PAUL AUTARD

1997	Châteauneuf du Pape Cuvée Classique	D	(85–86)
1995	Châteauneuf du Pape Cuvée Classique	D	86
1997	Châteauneuf du Pape Cuvée La Côte Ronde	D	(86–87)
1996	Châteauneuf du Pape Cuvée La Côte Ronde	D	88
1995	Châteauneuf du Pape Cuvée La Côte Ronde	D	90

There are two Châteauneuf du Pape cuvées produced at this excellent estate situated in the northern section of the appellation, not far from Château Beaucastel. The regular cuvée is a softer, fruitier wine that is meant to be drunk young. The Cuvée La Côte Ronde, made from a 5-acre parcel of 70–95-year-old vines, is given a lengthier fermentation/maceration, and aged for 18 months, with 50% of the production kept in new oak casks for 12 months and then assembled. Autard has produced very fine wines over recent years.

Paul Autard's dark ruby-colored 1996 Châteauneuf du Pape Cuvée La Côte Ronde is a Provençal-styled wine with notes of herbs, crushed seashells, iodine, *garrigue*, pepper, cedar, and black cherry fruit. Fleshy, moderately complex, generous, and round, with light tannin in the medium- to full-bodied finish, it will drink deliciously for 4–5 years. The 1997 Châteauneuf du Pape Cuvée Classique reveals an evolved medium plum color, a sweet, spicy, cherry-scented nose, good fruit, medium body, and a pleasing, pure, elegant, spicy finish. It is ideal for drinking over the next several years. The 1997 Châteauneuf du Pape Cuvée La Côte Ronde offers kirsch, cedar, and spice aromas, and sweet black cherry fruit intermixed with coffee and fruitcake smells. A juicy, pure, expansive, medium- to full-bodied wine, it may turn out to be as good, perhaps better than the 1996. It should be consumed over the next 5–6+ years.

The 1995 Châteauneuf du Pape Cuvée Classique's dark ruby/plum color is followed by a tight but intriguing nose of green peppercorns, herbes de Provence, and black cherries. The wine starts off lean, but blossoms to reveal medium body, ripe fruit, good acidity, and fine grip. Although not one of the stars of the vintage, it is a well-made Châteauneuf du Pape to drink over the next 7–8 years. The 1995 Châteauneuf du Pape Cuvée La Côte Ronde is outstanding. The saturated, dense purple/plum color is accompanied by a closed nose that, with airing, gives up classic aromas of kirsch, cassis, jammy cherries, Provençal herbs, and toasty, smoky oak. The wine is medium to full bodied, thick and rich, with admirable structure and depth. When I tasted it in 1996, I thought there was more to this wine than it was revealing at the time, and indeed there is. However, it needs 2–3 years of cellaring and should keep for 16–18 years. Impressive!

RENÉ BALTHAZAR

1995	Cornas	D 86

Balthazar's elegant, well-vinified 1995 Cornas exhibits a deep ruby/purple color, a soft suppleness, and less acidity than many of this appellation's offerings. It is a finesse-styled Cornas for drinking over the next 6–7 years.

GILLES BARGE

1997	Côte Rôtie Côte Brune	D	(87–89)
1996	Côte Rôtie Côte Brune	D	87
1997	Côte Rôtie Cuvée du Plessy	D	(86–88)
1996	Côte Rôtie Cuvée du Plessy	D	85

Barge was complaining about too many massive Côte Rôties when I saw him in October 1998. His Cuvée du Plessy (made primarily from Côte Blonde fruit, with some Viognier in the blend) is unquestionably one of the more elegant, aromatic expressions of the appellation. Barge calls it his *cuvée du plaisir*. The medium ruby-colored (with some garnet at the edge) 1997 Cuvée du Plessy exhibits an herbaceous, peppery nose with notes of bacon fat, in a soft, round, perfumed style. This evolved, open-knit, soft Côte Rôtie will be drinkable upon release and should be consumed within its first 5–6 years of life. The 1997 Côte Rôtie Côte Brune reveals more structure, a deeper ruby color, earthy, black raspberry, licorice, and truffle notes, medium body, and moderate tannin. This very good, possibly excellent Côte Rôtie should be at its finest between 2000 and 2008.

Barge's 1996s are more aromatic and softer than most wines from this vintage, which tend to be slightly tart and angular. The medium ruby-colored 1996 Côte Rôtie Cuvée du Plessy is supple and round with adequate acidity, and smoky barbecue spice aromas intermixed with cherry and black currant fruit. This attractive example is low key and straightforward. Consume it over the first 3–4 years of life. The 1996 Côte Rôtie Côte Brune is surprisingly seductive and aromatic for a wine from this *terroir*. The color is deep ruby. The wine offers up aromas of roasted herbs, black fruits, toast, and spice. In the mouth, it is medium bodied, with very good to excellent richness, and an easygoing, soft, open-knit texture. Drink it over the next 5–6 years.

LUCIEN BARROT

1997 Châteauneuf du Pape	C	(85–87)
1996 Châteauneuf du Pape	C	87

Over the holidays I drank my last bottle of Barrot's sumptuous 1981 Châteauneuf du Pape, and thought how remarkably consistent his wines have been, yet he rarely gets the accolades he deserves. Readers unhappy with the ever-increasing high prices of wines would be well advised to check out this source for very good Châteauneuf du Pape. I can hardly wait to see what Barrot has done in the fabulous 1998 vintage. As for the 1997 Châteauneuf du Pape, it is undoubtedly a successful wine for this vintage. The color is medium to dark ruby, and the wine offers up iodine, licorice, roasted herb, and black cherry scents intermixed with hints of Provençal herbs. Spicy, fat, and juicy, with low acidity, an element of *sur-maturité*, and a lusty finish, this smooth, silky-textured Châteauneuf du Pape demonstrates what could be achieved if growers did not overextract in this vintage. It should drink well for 3–4 years. The 1996 Châteauneuf du Pape exhibits an evolved ruby/garnet color, as well as a fragrant nose of blackberry/cherry fruit intermixed with scents of cured olives. Ripe and medium bodied, with gobs of juicy fruit, a tasty, fat midsection, and lofty alcohol in the soft finish, this is a pleasing, satisfying red wine for enjoying over the next 3–4 years.

CHÂTEAU BEAUCASTEL

1997 Châteauneuf du Pape	D	(89–91)
1996 Châteauneuf du Pape	D	89+
1995 Châteauneuf du Pape	D	93+
1997 Châteauneuf du Pape Blanc	D	93
1996 Châteauneuf du Pape Blanc	D	89
1995 Châteauneuf du Pape Hommage à Jacques Perrin	EE	96+
1997 Châteauneuf du Pape Roussanne Vieilles Vignes	EE	95

1996 Châteauneuf du Pape Roussanne Vieilles Vignes	EE	92
1995 Châteauneuf du Pape Roussanne Vieilles Vignes	EE	96
1997 Côtes du Luberon La Vieille Ferme Blanc	A	86
1996 Côtes du Luberon La Vieille Ferme	A	81
1997 Côtes du Rhône Coudoulet Blanc	C	89
1997 Côtes du Rhône Coudoulet	C	(86–87)
1996 Côtes du Rhône Coudoulet	C	84?
1997 Côtes du Rhône Grand Prébois	B	86
1996 Côtes du Rhône Grand Prébois	B	86
1997 Côtes du Rhône Perrin Réserve Blanc	B	87
1997 Côtes du Rhône Perrin Réserve	B	83
1996 Côtes du Rhône Perrin Réserve	B	84
1997 Côtes du Ventoux La Vieille Ferme	A	81

François Perrin said 1997 was a difficult vintage in the northern sector of Châteauneuf du Pape. After damaging spring frosts, there was a major hailstorm, which significantly cut yields. August was exceptionally rainy, and the early ripening varietals (Syrah and Cinsault) were affected by *pourriture*. At Beaucastel, the red varietal harvest was finished by October 15, and in spite of the disappointments with Syrah and Cinsault, they were pleased with their later-ripening old-vine Grenache, Mourvèdre, and Counoise. There will be significantly less Beaucastel in 1997, which is a shame as it is a forward style of wine for this estate, which tends to produce classic *vin de garde* wines that often require years of bottle age. Yields for the 1997 Châteauneuf du Pape were tiny, averaging 22 hectoliters per hectare (1½ tons per acre), and the wine is one of the most seductive and forward young Beaucastels I have tasted since the 1985. The blend was 35% Mourvèdre, 30% Grenache, 10% Counoise, 5% Syrah, 5% Cinsault, and the rest other southern Rhône varietals. The deep ruby color is accompanied by forward, attractive aromatics consisting of black raspberries, cherries, licorice, floral, and herb scents. The wine is fruit driven, with less structure than usual, but luscious cassis, licorice, and blackberries inundate the palate with no hard edges. A seductive, supple-textured, medium- to full-bodied Beaucastel, this wine should drink well young and last for 15 or more years. The 1996 Beaucastel is performing better after time in the bottle. With high acidity, this tannic, austere example is reminiscent (at least texturally) of a young Médoc. Blackberry, earthy, leathery, spicy notes can be found in the aromas. In the mouth, the wine exhibits medium body, tangy acidity, plenty of meaty Mourvèdre characteristics, and a structured, austere finish. It should be purchased only by those with the patience to wait for this wine to develop. Anticipated maturity: 2004–2015.

A convincing argument can be offered that the finest white Châteauneuf du Papes are being produced at Beaucastel. There are two cuvées, both heavily dependent on the exotic Roussanne grape. The 1997 Châteauneuf du Pape blanc (now packaged in an attractive heavy antique bottle) is a blend of 80% Roussanne, 15% Grenache Blanc, and 5% diverse white varietals. An excellent vintage for white Châteauneuf du Pape, the 1997 reveals the bold, fleshy, sappy, full-bodied fruit so evident in the vintage. It exhibits plenty of honeyed citrus and floral (rose) scents, an unctuous texture, good glycerin, and heady alcohol in the long, luscious finish. This impressively endowed Châteauneuf is ideal for drinking over the next decade or more. The 1997 Châteauneuf du Pape Roussanne Vieilles Vignes (100% Roussanne from 50-year-old vines) could easily be called the Montrachet or Chevalier-Montrachet of Châteauneuf du Pape. This cuvée has been remarkable in the past, and the 1997 is spectacular. It reveals more definition than the regular bottling, as well as spectacular concentration, a viscous texture, honeyed floral and citrusylike flavors, full body, and a finish that goes on for 40–50 seconds. A quintessential Roussanne, it is a great example of the heights this unheralded varietal can achieve. The 1997 should drink well for 2 decades or more.

The 1996 cuvées of white Châteauneuf du Pape contain more noticeable acidity than the 1997s. Both were closed when I tasted them in late fall 1998. The 1996 Châteauneuf du Pape Blanc (70% Roussanne, 20% Grenache Blanc, and 10% various varietals) offers a citrusy, spicy nose, medium body, tangy acidity (a hallmark of this vintage), and good weight and richness. It has already begun to close down and is in need of 2–3 years of cellaring. It should keep for 15 or more years. The 1996 Châteauneuf du Pape Roussanne Vieilles Vignes was extremely closed, but it is loaded with extract. With coaxing, scents of minerals, mint, honey, acacia flowers, and spice emerge. The wine is medium to full bodied, long, and powerful, with everything buttressed by zesty acidity. It is extremely backward, especially when tasted alongside the flamboyant, ostentatiously styled 1997. Look for this wine to evolve for 2 decades.

The Coudoulet de Beaucastel Côtes du Rhône emerges from a vineyard adjacent to Beaucastel, with virtually the same *terroir*. The excellent 1997 Coudoulet blanc (a blend of 30% Viognier, 30% Bourboulenc, 30% Marsanne, and 10% Clairette) displays the honeyed, rich, medium- to full-bodied style of its bigger sibling. Soft, pure, and creamy textured, with terrific fruit, this fruit-driven wine should be consumed during its first 4–5 years of life. This wine remains somewhat of an insider's buy, so the 1,000 cases tend to disappear quickly. I tasted two vintages of the red Coudoulet. The better offering, the 1997 Coudoulet rouge is a blend of 30% Mourvèdre, 30% Grenache, 20% Syrah, and 20% Cinsault. It displays a deep ruby color, a smoky, roasted herb, licorice, leathery, berry richness, low acidity, and a lush, medium-bodied, heady finish. This advanced, evolved Coudoulet will require drinking over its first 5–6 years of life. The medium ruby-colored 1996 Coudoulet rouge is an attenuated, leaner-styled wine. It gives the impression of being closed, but frankly, I think it just lacks fruit. The wine is dry, austere, and lacking the fat and richness of the 1997. While it is fresh, with good fruit on the attack, it is hollow in the mouth. I doubt that further fruit will emerge with aging.

Brothers François and Jean-Pierre Perrin produce a bevy of good values from the southern Rhône. The very good Côtes du Rhône Grand Prébois can be particularly impressive in top vintages. The 1997 Côtes du Rhône Grand Prébois (65% Grenache, 10% Syrah, 10% Mourvèdre, 10% Counoise, and 5% Carignan) is a delicious Côtes du Rhône to drink over the next 2–3 years. While it reveals dry tannin in the finish, its herbes de Provence, black cherry, chocolatey flavors are attractive. The 1996 Côtes du Rhône Grand Prébois is more acidic but possesses a nicely saturated dark ruby color, ripe, peppery, black currant aromas and flavors, good ripeness, and a medium-bodied, tangy finish. More concentrated than the 1997, with higher acidity, it should drink well for 3–4 years.

The wines of Jean-Pierre Perrin include his value-priced La Vieille Ferme and Perrin Reserve cuvées. These are delicious, well-made, tank-fermented and aged wines that admirably evidence the southern Rhône Valley's fruit. The 1997 La Vieille Ferme Côtes du Luberon blanc is a richly fruity, fat, dry white meant to be drunk during its first year of life. More serious is the 1997 Perrin Reserve Côtes du Rhône blanc. This offering reveals surprising floral/honeyed notes in the nose, good fat and richness, and copious fruit. To its credit, it contains 10% Viognier and 10% Roussanne, but the wine is dominated by Grenache Blanc.

Among the red wines, the 1997 La Vieille Ferme Côtes du Ventoux rouge is a Grenache-based wine with a hefty dollop of Syrah in the blend. The wine is monolithic, fruity, foursquare, and gutsy. Drink it over the next 2–3 years. The 1997 Perrin Reserve Côtes du

Rhône rouge (60% Grenache, 20% Syrah, 10% Mourvèdre, and 10% Cinsault) exhibits more allspice, pepper, and leather in the nose, as well as good ripeness, medium body, and a clean, refreshing finish.

The 1996 La Vieille Ferme Côtes du Ventoux rouge and 1996 Perrin Reserve Côtes du Rhône rouge are leaner, more austere wines, with higher acidity, larger quantities of Grenache, and medium body. Not as charming as the 1997s, the 1996s are best drunk over the next several years before they become more attenuated.

I had an amazing educational opportunity on my visit to Beaucastel in the fall of 1998, as I was able to taste the unblended cuvées of 1998 varietals. After twenty years of tasting young wines, it never ceases to amaze me that when a region has a mediocre vintage, whenever I taste the wine I am always told, "it's too soon." In contrast, when the region has a great vintage, I am inundated with requests to taste the wines, even if they are still fermenting! 1998 looks to be a spectacular vintage in the southern Rhône, particularly in Châteauneuf du Pape. In fact, I saw so many 1998s that had finished primary fermentation but had not begun malolactic that I couldn't wait to return in June 1999, after the wines had time to develop more defined personalities. The 1998 vintage offers extraordinary color saturation, fabulously ripe fruit, and looks to be a vintage with the potential to rival 1990, 1989, and 1978. At Beaucastel, many of the varietals, including Mourvèdre, reached 14.5%–14.8% natural alcohol! The wines were fabulous! Stay tuned.

The bevy of white wine offerings from Château Beaucastel is impressive. The limited production (approximately 10,000 bottles) of Châteauneuf du Pape Roussanne Vieilles Vignes in both 1996 and 1995 ensures that few readers will ever get a chance to taste what is undeniably the greatest dry white wine made in the southern Rhône Valley. These are wines of extraordinary richness, with profound quantities of rose petals, honey, and smoke, as well as luxuriant richness, unctuous textures, and super density. The 1996 possesses more acidity, and may be marginally less concentrated and higher in acidity than the blockbuster 1995, but both of these full-bodied, multidimensional wines are glorious. The jury is still out as to how well they age, but the debut vintage of this wine, 1986, is still relatively young, and even lighter years are proving to be stunning, even better than many people (including me) initially thought. This cuvée is the Montrachet of the southern Rhône, but production is extremely small.

The classic 1995 Châteauneuf du Pape will require discipline. Like most top vintages of Beaucastel, a decade of patience will be warranted before this wine will be enjoyable to drink. Given how tight and closed the 1993 and 1994 are, it is the rare vintage of Beaucastel (1989, 1990, and 1995) that is accessible in its youth, yet they will remain capable of aging for 20–25 years. In some ways, proprietors François and Jean-Pierre Perrin might be accused of trying to make the wine too long-lived, as if this is the primary merit to a great red wine. The 1995 will have 3 decades of longevity, but it will not be approachable before 2006. It exhibits a deep dark ruby/purple color, and a provocative (probably controversial) aromatic profile of animal fur, tar, truffles, black cherries, cassis, licorice, and minerals. A medium- to full-bodied wine, with a boatload of tannin, considerable grip and structure, and a weighty feel in the mouth, this appears to be a classic *vin de garde* made in the style of the 1978 Beaucastel (which is still not close to full maturity). Prospective purchasers over the age of forty should be buying this wine for their children.

The limited cuvée of Châteauneuf du Pape Hommage à Jacques Perrin is spectacular in 1995, but will require 10–15 years of cellaring. Fewer than 300 cases were made in the vintage. The textbook blend of 70% Mourvèdre, 15% Syrah, 10% Grenache, and 5% Counoise was utilized in 1989, 1990, and 1994, but in 1995, the Mourvèdre component was reduced, with the amount of Counoise and Syrah increased significantly. The 1995 reveals more of an aged beef, smoked ducklike component, no doubt because of the higher percentage of Counoise and Muscardin. Although there is less Mourvèdre in this cuvée, it still possesses the massive richness, opaque purple color, and sweet, earthy fruit that oozes over the palate with extraordinary intensity and purity. The change in the 1995's blend gives the wine a more spice-driven, animal character, with the distinctive aged beef/Asian spice/smoked duck characteristics more exaggerated. This wine needs 12–15 years of cellaring and should last 40–50 years. It is a modern-day classic.

DOMAINE DE BEAURENARD

1997	Châteauneuf du Pape Cuvée Boisrenard	E	(88–90)
1996	Châteauneuf du Pape Cuvée Boisrenard	E	90
1995	Châteauneuf du Pape Boisrenard	E	92
1997	Châteauneuf du Pape Cuvée Classique	D	(85–87)
1996	Châteauneuf du Pape Cuvée Classique	D	87
1995	Châteauneuf du Pape Cuvée Classique	D	89
1995	Côtes du Rhône	A	85
1995	Côtes du Rhône-Villages Rasteau	A	?

This 75-acre estate continues to be one of the leaders in Châteauneuf du Pape, offering both a cuvée classique and a luxury cuvée, the latter revealing evidence of exposure to new oak casks. There is also a round, generous Côtes du Rhône produced as well as a rustic Rasteau Côtes du Rhône-Villages.

Consistently one of the high-quality Châteauneuf du Pape estates, Domaine de Beaurenard has turned in four impressive efforts in the two lighter years of 1997 and 1996. The dark plum/garnet-colored 1997 Châteauneuf du Pape Cuvée Classique is an evolved, medium-bodied, richly fruity offering with dried herb, peppery, plum, black cherry, and berry aromas and flavors. This soft, fruit-driven, charming, delicious Châteauneuf should be consumed over the next 3–4 years. The 1997 Châteauneuf du Pape Cuvée Boisrenard (made from 70–90-year-old vines and aged 12 months in small casks and foudres) is a completely different animal. It displays a dark ruby/purple color, as well as an intense blackberry and raspberry-scented nose with some *pain grillé*. Dense, rich, and medium to full bodied, with a lush texture, good glycerin and alcohol, and a heady finish, this flamboyant, tasty, rich Châteauneuf du Pape should drink well for a decade.

The excellent 1996 Châteauneuf du Pape Cuvée Classique has admirably survived its bottling. The wine exhibits a medium deep ruby color, and an open-knit, expansive nose of pepper, fruitcake, spice, and black cherry fruit. In the mouth, a kirsch component emerges, and while not complex, the wine is richly fruity, generous, and ideal for drinking over the next 5–7 years. It is a shame restaurants do not serve more wines such as this. The saturated ruby/purple-colored 1996 Châteauneuf du Pape Cuvée Boisrenard possesses an excellent rich nose of black currants, complemented by pepper, toast, and earthy smells. Fat and medium to full bodied, with excellent depth, outstanding purity and equilibrium, and an exceptionally long finish, this supple-textured, showy, seductive Châteauneuf du Pape can be drunk now as well as over the next 7–9 years.

Beaurenard's 1995s possess more color, aromatics, flavor texture, and aging potential than the 1996s. The dense ruby/purple-colored 1995 Châteauneuf du Pape Cuvée Classique offers up a sweet nose of blackberries, cranberries, and cherries. The wine possesses beautiful pure fruit, medium to full body, a sweet, glycerin-imbued midpalate, and a lusty, heady, richly textured, silky finish. It is a classic Châteauneuf du Pape that can be drunk young, or cellared for a decade. The 1995 Châteauneuf du Pape Boisrenard is one of the finest of the modern-styled, new-oak-aged (20% is aged in new-oak casks) Châteauneufs. It reveals an opaque purple color, and a tight but backward nose that reluctantly gives up scents of flowers, licorice, and toasty new oak. The wine is full bodied, with plenty of grip, tannin, and concentration. It is a well-defined, rich, full-bodied Châteauneuf du Pape that could easily be mistaken for a grand cru red Burgundy. Anticipated maturity: 2000–2015.

The Côtes du Rhône offerings include an uncomplex, tasty, fruity (cherries and kirsch), slightly tannic, round, and generous 1995 Côtes du Rhône. It should drink well for several years. More tannic, rustic, and harder, with considerable power and body is the 1995 Côtes du Rhône-Villages Rasteau. Readers who prefer soft, fruity wines should stick with the Côtes du Rhône. Those masochists who enjoy astringent toughness should check out the 1995 Rasteau.

DOMAINE DE LA BECASSONNE

1997 Côtes du Rhône	B	87

If my memory is correct, this is among the finest dry white Côtes du Rhône André Brunel (the renowned proprietor of Les Cailloux in Châteauneuf du Pape) has made. Eight hundred cases of this dry white were imported to the United States. A blend of 40% Roussanne, 40% Grenache Blanc, and 20% Clairette, it offers up smoky, roasted nut, and honeyed scents, with considerable spice. Medium bodied, clean, and fresh, with surprising flavors on the attack, this is an excellent example of the progress Rhône Valley producers have made with their dry white wines.

ALBERT BELLE PÈRE ET FILS

1997 Crozes-Hermitage Cuvée Louis Belle	D	(87–88)
1996 Crozes-Hermitage Cuvée Louis Belle	D	86
1995 Crozes-Hermitage Cuvée Louis Belle	D	88
1997 Crozes-Hermitage Cuvée Louis Belle (White)	D	83
1996 Crozes-Hermitage Les Pierrelles	D	(84–86)
1996 Hermitage	E	88
1995 Hermitage	E	91
1996 Hermitage (White)	E	85

To my taste, Belle's wines continue to exhibit improvement, taking on more complexity and richness with each high-quality vintage. The 1995 Crozes-Hermitage Cuvée Louis Belle reveals a sweet fruitcake/incense/black fruit-scented nose. Smoke and pepper characteristics are meshed with this wine's spice-driven aromatics. Medium to full bodied, with excellent extraction, fine overall balance, and a sweet, medium-bodied finish, this attractively made Crozes-Hermitage should drink well during its first 8–10 years of life.

The beautifully impressive 1995 Hermitage displays a superripe (*sur-maturité*) black fruit character, with subtle notes of pepper, smoke, and herbs. The wine possesses a dark ruby/purple color, as well as powerfully rich, intense flavors on the attack, and striking equilibrium and finesse in the mouth. The sweet tannin is well integrated, and the wine refreshing yet authoritatively flavorful. This sweet, rich, outstanding Hermitage should be at its peak between 2002 and 2016.

The mineral, citrusy, light- to medium-bodied 1997 Crozes-Hermitage Cuvée Louis Belle blanc (80% Marsanne and 20% Roussanne) is correct and serviceable. It should be consumed over the next 2–3 years. The 1996 Hermitage blanc was closed when I tasted it. A blend of 70% Marsanne and 30% Roussanne, aged half in *barrique* and half in tank before being blended, it is a medium-bodied, fresh, citrusy white Hermitage with floral notes in the nose, and crisp, tangy acidity. It should drink well for 4–5 years. I would have enjoyed more flesh and fruit concentration.

As for the red wines, the 1997 Crozes-Hermitage Cuvée Louis Belle which was picked at high sugars, resulting in nearly 13% natural alcohol. This soft, sexy Crozes offers plenty of strawberry and jammy cherry fruit intermixed with aromas of smoked herbs, meats, and wood spice. There is excellent purity and ripeness, medium to full body, a supple texture, and a chewy finish. It should drink well for 5–7 years. The 1996s are slightly leaner wines, with more of the vintage's green pepper herbaceousness. The 1996 Crozes-Hermitage Les Pierrelles (it spent 12 months in *barrique* before bottling) is a supple, well-made, medium-bodied, lightweight example with herbaceous, tomato skin-scented aromas, green pepper, cherrylike flavors, and a clean, supple finish. I would have scored it higher had it not been for the vegetal characteristics. The very good, soft 1996 Crozes-Hermitage Cuvée Louis Belle (a selection from the oldest vines that was aged 12 months in *barrique*, of which 30% were new) reveals spicy oak, no evidence of herbaceousness, and toasty *pain grillé* notes to support its moderately rich red currant/black cherry flavors. Drink this medium-bodied, smoky Crozes-Hermitage over the next 4–5 years. Lastly, the 1996 Hermitage (all from the lower slopes in the *lieux-dit* Les Murets) is aged for 20 months in cask, of which 50% are new. This wine offers a saturated dark ruby/purple color, as well as attractive cassis aromas intermixed with toasty oak. In the mouth, it is rich and full bodied, with fine underlying acidity, excellent depth, and a spicy, pure, well-delineated finish. It will benefit from 2–3 years of cellaring and keep for 12–15 years.

GUY BERNARD

1995 Côte Rôtie		D	86

The dark ruby-colored 1995 Côte Rôtie has some spicy, sweet new oak in its modest black fruit-scented bouquet. This is an elegant, crisp, medium-bodied Côte Rôtie that can be drunk now and over the next 5–8 years.

BOIS DE BOURSAN

1995 Châteauneuf du Pape	C	90
1997 Châteauneuf du Pape Cuvée Classique	D	(87–89)
1996 Châteauneuf du Pape Cuvée Classique	D	88
1997 Châteauneuf du Pape Cuvée Prestige Felix	D	(87–90)
1996 Châteauneuf du Pape Cuvée Prestige Felix	D	90

Proprietor J. P. Versino is becoming one of the stars of Châteauneuf du Pape. He has turned in four impressive performances in the two lighter-styled vintages of 1996 and 1997. I can't imagine what he may achieve in the potentially great 1998 vintage. As for the 1997s, the 1997 Châteauneuf du Pape Cuvée Classique exhibits a dense ruby/purple color as well as stunning aromas of overripe blackberry fruit intermixed with cassis, cherries, and a touch of *pain grillé*. This medium- to full-bodied, topflight Châteauneuf du Pape displays terrific fruit intensity, and a layered, pure, concentrated finish. It should be one of the most concentrated and delicious wines of the vintage. Anticipated maturity: 2001–2012. The 1997 Châteauneuf du Pape Cuvée Prestige Felix possesses a more international style due to its new-oak (*barrique*) influence. The wine's opaque saturated purple color is accompanied by thick, juicy, full-bodied black currant, and blackberry flavors with explosive richness and depth. Atypical for a 1997, it is impressively endowed, and should age nicely for 12 or more years.

In 1996, Monsieur Versino also fashioned two stars of the vintage. The 1996 Châteauneuf du Pape Cuvée Classique is close to outstanding. This dark ruby/purple-colored wine's knockout aromatics include scents of clove, wood smoke, anise, licorice, and black cherries. It is deep, rich, and medium to full bodied, with a layered, concentrated mouth-feel. Succulent and jammy, with admirable concentration and length, it is already delicious to drink, yet promises to evolve for 10–12 years. The opaque saturated black/purple-colored 1996 Châteauneuf du Pape Cuvée Prestige Felix offers a toasty vanillin and new-oak-dominated bouquet, with cassis fruit and kirsch liqueur in the background. The wine is impressively built, with medium to full body, gobs of fruit, and a pure, layered, concentrated finish. The tannin is sweet, and the oak stands out only because so few Châteauneuf du Pape producers utilize new barrels. Everything is in balance, although I suspect some of Versino's critics will argue that the wine lacks typicity. However, it is unquestionably an impressively made, concentrated, outstanding wine that can be drunk now as well as over the next dozen years.

The 1995 Châteauneuf du Pape is an outstanding wine in this excellent vintage. The color is a dark ruby/purple with a slight garnet hue at the edge. The knockout nose offers up intense, jammy aromas of fruitcake, black cherries, prunes, smoke, minerals, and Asian spices. Full bodied, with outstanding concentration, and a seductive, expansive, succulent mouth-feel, this wine, while accessible, will benefit from another 2–3 years of cellaring and will keep for 12–15. Very impressive!

DOMAINE DE BOIS DAUPHIN

1995 Châteauneuf du Pape (J. Marchand)	C	86
1995 Châteauneuf du Pape Clos des Pontifes	E	90

This estate offers two totally different cuvées of red wine. The regular cuvée is a typical Châteauneuf du Pape, soft and peppery, with the salty, seaweed, iodine, *garrigue*, kirsch components that are so much a part of many of the wines from this Provençal village. The Clos des Pontifes sees some aging in small new-oak casks, and represents a more concentrated, internationally styled, but still authentic Châteauneuf du Pape. It is just bigger, richer, and more influenced by new oak.

Marchand's 1995 Châteauneuf du Pape is an iodine, seaweed, *garrigue*, kirsch, and peppery-scented wine with medium body, and more fruit and lushness than the 1996. With decent acidity and a plump mouth-feel, this ripe wine should be drunk over the next 5–6 years. The closed 1995 Châteauneuf du Pape Clos des Pontifes possesses an impressively saturated ruby/purple color, smoky *pain grillé* notes in the black cherry and cassis-scented nose, a lush texture, and a layered, medium-bodied, concentrated style, with surprising elegance and equilibrium. The effect of the new oak is measured, rather than aggressive, and the wine is purely made, with a sweet midpalate, and a rich, concentrated, long finish. Give it another 1–2 years of cellaring and drink it over the following decade.

HENRI BONNEAU

1996 Châteauneuf du Pape	D	89
1995 Châteauneuf du Pape	D	91
1994 Châteauneuf du Pape	D	91
1993 Châteauneuf du Pape	D	(78–81?)
1997 Châteauneuf du Pape Cuvée G	E	(90–91)
1996 Châteauneuf du Pape Cuvée G	E	(86–88)
1995 Châteauneuf du Pape Cuvée G	E	(91–93)
1992 Châteauneuf du Pape Cuvée Marie Beurrier	E	91
1997 Châteauneuf du Pape Cuvée P	EE	(92–94)
1996 Châteauneuf du Pape Cuvée P	EE	(90–92)

1995 Châteauneuf du Pape Cuvée P	EE	(93–97)
1992 Châteauneuf du Pape Réserve des Céléstins	EE	93

What a thrill it is to taste with Henri Bonneau. He is a great character, in addition to being an extraordinary wine producer. With the death of Jacques Reynaud, a persuasive argument can be made that Henri Bonneau remains the leading candidate to continue to protect the heart and soul of traditional Châteauneuf du Papes.

The great master of Châteauneuf du Pape, Bonneau was in an ebullient mood when I visited in the fall of 1998. He insisted that I taste the fermenting 1998, which he claimed is "undoubtedly as great as my 1990." Bonneau said that it was the first time in his career of making Châteauneuf du Pape (since 1957) that he finished the harvest before October. Certainly what I tasted was spectacularly dense and concentrated. While it is too soon to know whether it will be as profound as the 1990, the 1998 unquestionably appears to possess fabulously great potential.

Bonneau recently sold virtually all of his 1994 to a *négociant* for a handsome price. It would appear that he will end up liquidating most of his 1993 as well (there is no shortage of prospective buyers for his wine in bulk). This cellar, which has given me so many great memories, has become a bit more simple to traverse. Bonneau has begun a lettering system for the barrels, assigning his potential Cuvée Marie Beurrier with a "G," and his potential Cuvée Céléstins with a "P." However, I am sure Bonneau will change his mind numerous times as the wines evolve. Keep in mind that he just bottled his 1992 Cuvée Céléstins and 1992 Cuvée Marie Beurrier. Both of those wines, retasted in the cellars and stateside, are even more spectacular than I stated in earlier reports. Moreover, they are the wines of the vintage, possessing levels of concentration and complexity that exceed anything else produced in this difficult vintage for Châteauneuf du Pape.

I tasted Bonneau's 1993 Châteauneuf du Pape, a wine I have not enjoyed in the past (certain barrels appeared to be sweeter than others). The wine seems to be drying out, with a hardness, leanness, and toughness now evident. Henri Bonneau does not appear to be a fan of this cuvée, so I suspect it may not make it into the bottle. There is one remaining *foudre* of 1994 (85–88), which he said he might label Châteauneuf du Pape, perhaps elevate it to Marie Beurrier status, or even sell it off given the raw materials he has in 1995, 1996, 1997, and 1998.

Tasting Bonneau's Châteauneuf du Papes is an extraordinarily thrilling experience. Few wines reach such levels of concentrated meat essences intermixed with smoky aromas, and lofty, mind-numbing levels of extract and alcohol. These classic, old-style wines age as well as a first-growth Bordeaux. On my most recent visit, I participated in a splendid vertical following the barrel/*foudre* tastings. The wines included 1986 (95, and the Rhône's wine of the vintage), 1983 (90, and fully mature), 1957 (100 points of pure perfection and what I hope the 1990 will turn into with another 15–20 years of cellaring), and a vintage from the forties, either 1949 or 1947 (Bonneau was not sure since the label had completely disintegrated), rated 98 and pure nectar of Grenache!

As for the wines a handful of people will have a chance to purchase and taste, the 1997 Cuvée G exhibits a dark ruby/purple color, a big, smoky, grilled meat-scented nose, ripe, sweet, medium- to full-bodied flavors, excellent density, and surprising fat and glycerin. The 1997 Cuvée P possesses all of the above, in addition to more thickness, an unctuous texture, and huge levels of glycerin and extract. According to Bonneau, this wine surpasses 14% natural alcohol. It displays a remarkable palate presence and amazing richness.

The 1996 Cuvée G is nowhere near the quality of the 1997. It exhibits what the French call *griottes* (black cherry jam) in the nose, along with mineral, scorched earth, truffle, and roasted herb aromas. Although lush and round, it does not possess the depth and concentration normally found in Bonneau's cellars. The 1996 Cuvée P is another animal altogether. Fat, full bodied, and smoky, with roasted herbs, gobs of pepper, and jammy blackberry liqueur, it is an exotic, flamboyant, over-the-top style of Châteauneuf du Pape. It will make a splendid bottle of wine, having more in common with the 1992 than other vintages.

Both the 1995s offer profound levels of concentration, extract, power, and massiveness. The 1995 Cuvée G reveals blackberries intermixed with truffles, roasted meat, and a Côte de Boeuf-like essence to its flavors. Thick, juicy, and exotic, with plenty of tannin and power, it possesses plenty of structure and muscle, as well as 20+ years of longevity. The best young cuvée I tasted (not including the fermenting 1998) is the 1995 Cuvée P. Aromas of *sur-maturité*, apricots, prunes, and peaches combine with meat essences, black cherries, chocolate, truffles, and licorice to create a soaring aromatic profile. The wine exhibits fabulous concentration, unreal levels of glycerin, and a superb, chewy, mind-boggling finish. This is a classic, old-style Châteauneuf du Pape the likes of which are increasingly rare.

In late 1997, Bonneau released his 1992 Châteauneuf du Pape Réserve des Célestins, which I had followed since its origins. Like many of his wines, what appears in the bottle, either under the Réserve des Célestins or Marie Beurrier label, is significantly better than what is tasted in the hodgepodge of tiny rooms that make a tasting Chez Bonneau as memorable as any. The 1992 Châteauneuf du Pape Réserve des Célestins is the wine of the vintage (although Chapoutier's 1992 Barbe Rac is not far behind). It is a huge, massive, full-bodied, powerhouse Châteauneuf, with smoky aromas intermixed with scents of beef blood, aged beef, black fruits, prunes, and truffles. The wine boasts superb richness, mouth-coating, thick glycerin, extraordinary power and purity, and a long, peppery, spicy finish. The magic of Henri Bonneau's distinctive *élevage* strikes again, as this spectacular wine's intensity will blow tasters away. The 1992 Châteauneuf du Pape Marie Beurrier is just short of outstanding. This wine carries even higher alcohol than the Réserve des Célestins, as well as copious quantities of sweet, jammy, overripe black cherries intermingled with earth, truffles, pepper, and fruitcakelike aromas. Chewy, lush, and supple, this spice-driven Châteauneuf should drink well for at least a decade.

The following notes are based on my tastings of several barrels of each wine. Tasting through the 1994 Châteauneuf du Pape cuvées indicates there will be both a Marie Beurrier and Réserve de Célestins produced in this vintage. This wine continues to grow in stature and, like many wines in these cellars, puts on weight and fruit. It will probably merit a score in the low 90s when released, especially the top cuvées, which will go into the Réserve des Célestins. Henri Bonneau makes no bones about the fact that he prefers 1994 as a vintage to 1995 and 1996, but he is also the first to admit that it is too early to judge any of his wines. The 1994 cuvées all exhibit high tannins, as well as formidable concentrations of kirschlike fruit, amazing power, high alcohol, and mouth-coating levels of extract. This powerful, rich Châteauneuf du Pape will come close to rivaling Bonneau's superb 1988. The Réserve de Célestins cuvées appear capable of 20–30 years of evolution, and the Marie Beurrier Cuvées, 10–20 years.

In 1995, Henri Bonneau felt the quality level was the same as in 1996. In contrast, I thought the 1995 cuvées I tasted to be far richer than his 1996s. The lighter (a misnomer in these cellars) wines, which go into the Marie Beurrier, are peppery, powerful, earthy, sweet, and rich. The Réserve des Célestins cuvée is spectacular and, to my palate, slightly superior to the 1994. The density, richness, and naturalness of Bonneau's wines just have to be tasted to be believed. The 1995 cuvées possess even more tannin than the 1994s, and at the top level, there is an extra dimension of the sweet kirsch fruit and unctuous texture that is akin to drinking blood. It will be a tannic wine that will require 5–8 years of cellaring when released—which is whenever Bonneau decides the wine is ready to bottle. If his wine needs 5 years in cask, it will get just that; Bonneau makes no concessions to the marketplace.

The 1996s, at the lower end, appear soft with a late-harvest, prunelike character, somewhat disjointed, but sweet, round, ripe, and fruity. The better cuvées exhibit plenty of fat, high alcohol, and oustanding concentration and intensity. At this early stage, it appears readers will have both a Marie Beurrier and Réserve des Céléstins to look forward to in 1994, 1995, and 1996. However, for the next year or two, readers will have to be content with whatever quantities of the 1992 Marie Beurrier and 1992 Réserve des Céléstins are released. These remarkable wines are extremely limited in availability, but thanks to the persistent efforts of Alain Juguenet, they are imported to the United States.

It is impossible to know when the 1995, 1996, 1997, or 1998 will be available. Bonneau will often bottle whenever he decides a wine is showing particularly well. The fact that he bottled his 1992 in 1998 (a mere six years after the vintage), suggests to me we may not see the 1995s for another 2–3 years. Nevertheless, this gentleman marches to the beat of his own drummer, and what an uncompromising sound it makes.

LE BOSQUET DES PAPES

1995	Châteauneuf du Pape	D	88+
1995	Châteauneuf du Pape Cuvée Chantemerle	E	90+
1997	Châteauneuf du Pape Cuvée Classique	D	(84–86)
1996	Châteauneuf du Pape Cuvée Classique	D	87

The proprietors, the Boirons, produced a backward, medium- to full-bodied, tannic 1995 Châteauneuf du Pape with the textbook Châteauneuf du Pape nose of crushed black pepper, black cherries, smoke, herbs, and olives. Spicy, long, dense, and deep, this powerful 1995 needs 2–3 years of cellaring. Anticipated maturity: 2001–2016. The dense plum/garnet-colored 1995 Châteauneuf du Pape Cuvée Chantemerle, made from an 8.6-acre parcel of 90-year-old Grenache vines, initially seems closed aromatically, but with coaxing, copious amounts of overripe black cherry and kirsch aromas emerge, along with scents of roasted meats, smoke, and grilled herbs. The wine is extremely full bodied and moderately tannic, with layers of sweet, glycerin-imbued, jammy fruit, and high tannin. This powerhouse requires 2–3 years of cellaring. Anticipated maturity: 2002–2018.

Bosquet des Papes produced a peppery, herbal 1997 Châteauneuf du Pape with seductive cherry fruit intermixed with notes of licorice, coffee, and cedar. It is a pleasant, open-knit, round, slightly diluted but fruity wine to drink over the next 4–5 years. The deeper, richer 1996 Châteauneuf du Pape exhibits an evolved dark plum/garnet color, a peppery, *garrigue*, spicy, leathery, and black cherry-scented nose, medium body, luscious fruit purity and depth, and a rich, medium-bodied, soft finish. A fuller, more complete example than the 1997, it should drink well for 5–6 years.

DOMAINE LA BOUISSIÈRE

1997	Gigondas Cuvée Prestige La Font de Tonin	D	(88–90)
1996	Gigondas Cuvée Prestige La Font de Tonin	D	76

The impressive, black/purple-colored 1997 Gigondas Cuvée Prestige La Font de Tonin exhibits toasty new oak, gobs of cassis, blackberry fruit, and powerful, concentrated, medium- to full-bodied flavors. Its low acidity and plump, forward style suggest it should be drunk during its first 8–10 years of life. Hopefully, it will be bottled without excessive fining and filtration. In total contrast, the 1996 Gigondas Cuvée Prestige La Font de Tonin reveals an evolved garnet/plum color, earthy, *garrigue*, and green pepperlike aromatics, a lean, sharp, angular personality, and a hard finish. It has nowhere to go but down.

DANIEL BRUSSET - LES HAUTS DE MONTMIRAIL

1997	Gigondas	D	(89–92)
1995	Gigondas	D	92

This estate, with 68 parcels of terraced vineyards on the craggy slopes of the Dentelles, behind the village of Gigondas, continues to produce one of the appellation's most extraordinary wines. Daniel Brusset's estate celebrated its 50th birthday in 1997.

The 1995 Gigondas Les Hauts de Montmirail is performing even better from bottle than it did from cask. The color is a saturated black/purple. This unevolved wine offers a huge nose of sweet black raspberries, cherries, and blackberries, as well as subtle *pain grillé* notes from new oak. Extremely full bodied, ripe, and impressively layered, this graceful yet large-scaled Gigondas is crammed with fruit and, at the same time, well delineated, with moderate tannin in the heady finish. This large-scaled wine competes favorably with the profound wines Brusset produced in 1989 and 1990. Anticipated maturity: 2000–2015+.

Sadly, I was not able to taste the 1996, which had shown so well from barrel. Brusset's 1997 is a textbook Gigondas for him—oaky, with huge, jammy aromas of blackberries, cassis, and *pain grillé*. A highly extracted, formidably endowed Gigondas made in an international style, it should be a stunning wine, even better than the 1996. Additionally, it should drink well young given its low acidity and plump, forward fruit. Anticipated maturity: 2001–2010.

BERNARD BURGAUD

1997 Côte Rôtie	D	(86–88)
1996 Côte Rôtie	D	88?

Burgaud has turned out two fine Côte Rôties that may ultimately merit higher scores. The 1997 Côte Rôtie is one of the densest and biggest in my tastings but is slightly disjointed and out of balance. The wine possesses a dark ruby/purple color, an explosive licorice, incense, black fruit, and earth-scented nose, plenty of power and ripeness, and surprisingly high tannin for the vintage. A blend taken from both *foudre* and barrel, this offering reveals good power and richness, but needs to achieve better integration of its elements. It is one of the few 1997s that requires 1–3 years of cellaring when released; it will keep for a decade or more. Even though production of the saturated opaque purple-colored 1996 Côte Rôtie was only 30 hectoliters per hectare (2 tons per acre), the wine's acid is mouth-searingly high, which gives me pause for concern. However, it also possesses high extract levels and copious quantities of fruit. The knockout aromatics consist of freshly ground pepper, licorice, black truffles, and cassis intermixed with smoked herbs and roasted game birds. Rich and chewy, but tangy from its high acidity, this wine requires 2–3 years of cellaring; it should keep for 15. The acidity will keep it fresh for many years, but will it ever be seductive?

CHÂTEAU CABRIÈRES

1997 Châteauneuf du Pape Cuvée Prestige	D	(87–88)
1996 Châteauneuf du Pape Cuvée Prestige	D	86
1997 Châteauneuf du Pape Cuvée Tradition	D	(85–87)

Note: These are particular cuvées selected by French wine broker Alain Corcia, and bottled unfined and unfiltered for his clients in the United States and Japan. They are different, and superior wines to those sold elsewhere.

This famed property possesses spectacular potential (much of it still unrealized), as evidenced by these three supple, richly fruity wines. The dark ruby-colored 1997 Châteauneuf du Pape Cuvée Tradition exhibits copious quantities of black cherry and strawberry fruit intermixed with Provençal herbs, smoke, and spice. This medium-bodied, soft wine is ideal for current consumption. Made from a selection of the estate's oldest vines, the 1997 Châteauneuf du Pape Cuvée Prestige offers more glycerin, alcohol, fruit, and ripeness. It cuts a broader swath on the palate, and possesses more volume, but it remains a forward wine redolent with black cherry fruit intermixed with earth, pepper, and Provençal spices. Drink it over the next 4–5 years. The 1996 Châteauneuf du Pape Cuvée Prestige is similarly styled, but not as fat in the mouth. It displays black cherry fruit intermixed with olives, pepper, and earthy notes. It should be consumed over the next 2–3 years.

LES CAILLOUX

1995	Châteauneuf du Pape Cuvée Centenaire	E	96
1997	Châteauneuf du Pape Cuvée Classique	D	(87–90)
1996	Châteauneuf du Pape Cuvée Classique	D	88
1995	Châteauneuf du Pape Cuvée Classique	D	92

I was not surprised by the high quality of proprietor André Brunel's 1996 and 1997 Châteauneuf du Papes. As for the 1996 Châteauneuf du Pape Cuvée Classique, the vintage's hallmarks are evident in its open-knit, forward style. The wine exhibits a deep ruby color, and an expansive black raspberry, cherry, spicy nose of cedar, herbs, and smoked meats. In the mouth, it reveals copious amounts of pepper, plum, and cherry fruit, with a notion of underbrush. The wine possesses more tannin than many of its peers, but it is still an expansive Châteauneuf to drink during its first 7–8 years of life. The dark ruby-colored 1997 Châteauneuf du Pape Cuvée Classique offers a juicy, succulent, fruit-driven personality with less of the pepper and spice found in its 1996 sibling. The 1997 has a black raspberry/kirsch liqueur rich fruitiness with good glycerin in its medium- to full-bodied, lush, low-acid finish. It should drink well for 5–6 years.

Through hard work and an open mind concerning all facets of viticulture and vinification, André Brunel has become one of the stars of Châteauneuf du Pape. Remarkably consistent in difficult vintages, he hits the bull's eye in the great years. I would not classify 1995 as a great year for Châteauneuf du Pape, although it is certainly excellent, and overall the finest vintage since 1990, but you would never know that by tasting André Brunel's sumptuous 1995s.

The 1995 Châteauneuf du Pape is a precocious, medium- to full-bodied, lush, layered, complex wine offering up abundant quantities of sweet black cherry and kirsch fruit in a spicy, compelling bouquet. This multidimensional, low-acid wine displays plenty of earth, smoke, and truffle notes to accompany the kirsch, plum, and prunelike fruit. Sweet and rich in the mouth, with an explosive finish, it should drink well for 12–15 years. The mind-boggling 1995 Châteauneuf du Pape Cuvée Centenaire (500 cases produced) is a candidate for the wine of the vintage. Made from a 5.6-acre parcel of Grenache vines planted in 1889, it boasts a dense, opaque plum color. Initially the wine appears closed aromatically, especially when compared to the cuvée classique, but it blossoms in the glass, offering up sexy aromas of black truffles, blueberries, black raspberries, and kirsch. Explosive richness and an opulent, sumptuous texture come together in this silky, full-bodied, irresistible wine. It is so flamboyant and showy that it is impossible to resist, but it will age magnificently for 15–20 years. Bravo!

DOMAINE DE CASSAN

1997	Gigondas	D	(88–90)
1996	Gigondas	D	85

Another impressive 1997 Gigondas (this appellation appears to have benefitted from the superb weather at the end of the summer since it harvests much later than Châteauneuf du Pape), this wine offers an opaque ruby/purple color, and a big, thick, black cherry and blackberry nose, with pepper and *garrigue* notes. In the mouth, there is pure blackberry fruit, surprising power and tannin, and a full-bodied, lengthy finish. It is one of the biggest wines I tasted from Gigondas in this vintage. Anticipated maturity: 2001–2012. Domaine de Cassan's 1996 Gigondas is a competent effort in this difficult vintage. It offers tangy acidity, plenty of black raspberry and cherry fruit, a plump, ripe style, and straightforward flavors. Drink this cleanly made, charming wine over the next 4–5 years.

DOMAINE CAYRON

1997 Gigondas	D	(86–88)
1996 Gigondas	D	78?
1995 Gigondas	D	90+

The 1997 Gigondas's dark plum color is followed by a sweet nose of licorice, tar, incense, and cherry jam. The wine is medium to full bodied, with a spicy, rustic style and plenty of weight and richness. The wine's low acidity and plump, chewy, evolved fruit suggest it should be drunk during its first 7–8 years of life. I was unimpressed with the 1996 Gigondas both from barrel and bottle. This uninspiring effort reveals an evolved garnet color, stewed prune/plumlike fruit in the nose, a gentle, friendly attack, and earthy, rustic notes in the attenuated finish. Drink it over the next 3–4 years.

This has long been one of the most traditionally made wines of Gigondas. There is no doubting the quality of the exquisite 1995 Gigondas. It exhibits an impressively saturated, dark purple/dense plum color. The nose offers up intense aromas of wood fires, jammy black fruits, licorice, minerals, truffles, and roasted olives. This low-acid, full-bodied powerhouse is a Gigondas classic—layered, high extract yet remarkably harmonious, with well-integrated tannin and acidity. This beauty requires another 2–4 years of cellaring; it should keep for 15+.

DOMAINE CHANTE PERDRIX

1997 Châteauneuf du Pape	D	(86–88)
1996 Châteauneuf du Pape	D	87

I have always enjoyed this estate's wines and continue to liquidate what was once a considerable stock of the sumptuous 1989 (by the way, it is drinking fabulously well). The proprietors, the Nicolets, look for overripeness in their wines, thus producing one of the more flamboyant, exotically scented, Provençal-styled Châteauneuf du Papes. The 1997 Châteauneuf du Pape reveals a textbook olive, peppery, black cherry-scented nose intermixed with *garrigue*/earthy smells. There is plenty of thickness, surprising glycerin for the vintage, deep fruit, and a pruny ripeness and richness. The wine's low acidity and supple, up-front character suggest it will be delicious to drink during its first 5–6 years of life. The 1996 Châteauneuf du Pape smells like an old hippie haven with its incense, smoky, roasted herbs, and fleshy, overripe black cherry fruit. It is a rich, fruit-driven, lush, low-acid wine with copious quantities of glycerin, and a chewy, exotic fatness and fleshiness. It is difficult not to be charmed by such an appealing 1996. Drink it over the next 5–6 years.

CHAPOUTIER

1996 Banyuls	D	92
1995 Banyuls	D	93
1996 Banyuls Terra Vinya	D	92
1995 Banyuls Terra Vinya	D	91
1997 Les Béates Coteaux d'Aix en Provence	A	(84–87)
1997 Châteauneuf du Pape Barbe Rac	EE	(87–88)
1996 Châteauneuf du Pape Barbe Rac	EE	90
1995 Châteauneuf du Pape Barbe Rac	EE	93
1997 Châteauneuf du Pape La Bernadine	EE	(87–89)

1995	Châteauneuf du Pape La Bernadine	EE	91
1997	La Ciboise Coteaux du Tricastin	A	85
1997	Condrieu	E	85
1997	Cornas	D	(83–85)
1995	Cornas	D	90
1997	Côte du Rhône Belleruche (Red)	B	(80–83)
1997	Côte du Rhône Belleruche (White)	B	82
1997	Côte Rôtie	D	(87–89)
1996	Côte Rôtie	D	86
1995	Côte Rôtie	D	89
1997	Côte Rôtie La Mordorée	EEE	(92–94)
1996	Côte Rôtie La Mordorée	EEE	91+?
1995	Côte Rôtie La Mordorée	EEE	95+
1997	Crozes-Hermitage Les Meysonnières	C	86
1997	Crozes-Hermitage Les Meysonnières	C	85
1997	Crozes-Hermitage Petite Ruche (Red)	C	86
1997	Crozes-Hermitage Petite Ruche (White)	C	85
1997	Crozes-Hermitage Les Varonnières	E	(90–93)
1996	Crozes-Hermitage Les Varonnières	E	90+
1995	Crozes-Hermitage Les Varonnières	E	94
1997	Ermitage Le Pavillon	EEE	(96–98)
1996	Ermitage Le Pavillon	EEE	96+
1995	Ermitage Le Pavillon	EEE	99+
1997	Hermitage Chante Alouette	EE	90
1995	Hermitage Chante Alouette	EE	93
1997	Hermitage Cuvée de l'Orée	EE	(98–100)
1996	Hermitage Cuvée de l'Orée	EE	99
1995	Hermitage Cuvée de l'Orée	EE	97
1997	Hermitage l'Ermite	EE	(91–94)
1996	Hermitage l'Ermite	EE	99
1997	Hermitage Le Méal (Red)	EEE	(91–94)
1996	Hermitage Le Méal (Red)	EEE	92
1997	Hermitage Le Méal (White)	EEE	(96–100)
1997	Hermitage La Sizeranne	E	(87–88+?)
1996	Hermitage La Sizeranne	E	90+
1995	Hermitage La Sizeranne	E	92

1997	Hermitage Vin de Paille	EEE	(96–99)
1996	Hermitage Vin de Paille	EEE	(96–99)
1995	Hermitage Vin de Paille	EEE	97
1996	Les Matines Béates Coteaux d'Aix en Provence	D	89
1995	Les Matines Béates Coteaux d'Aix en Provence	D	85
1997	Les Matines Coteaux d'Aix en Provence	C	(78–81)
1996	Les Matines Coteaux d'Aix en Provence	C	87
1997	Muscat de Rivesaltes	C	90
1997	Muscat Sec VDP Côtes Catalans	A	89
1997	St.-Joseph Deschants (Red)	D	85
1997	St.-Joseph Deschants (White)	D	86
1997	St.-Joseph Les Granits (Red)	E	92
1996	St.-Joseph Les Granits (Red)	E	93
1995	St.-Joseph Les Granits (Red)	E	95
1997	St.-Joseph Les Granits (White)	E	(90–93)
1996	St.-Joseph Les Granits (White)	E	93
1995	St.-Joseph Les Granits (White)	E	94
1997	Terra d'Or Coteaux d'Aix en Provence	E	(90–93)
1996	Terra d'Or Coteaux d'Aix en Provence	E	92+
1996	Terra d'Or Coteaux d'Aix en Provence	E	91
1996	Viognier La Coufis VDP L'Ardeche	B	90
1995	Viognier La Coufis VDP L'Ardeche	B	93

The brilliant Michel Chapoutier was in a reflective mood when I spent a day tasting through this house's enormous portfolio in the fall of 1998. Chapoutier has been investing in southern France, adding impressive vineyard holdings in Coteaux d'Aix en Provence and Banyuls, while continuing to look for properties in the Languedoc-Roussillon. Michel Chapoutier is also involved in a major project in Australia, and continues to fine tune his bevy of Rhône wines. Tasting here is one of the highlights of my year, although sobered by the fact that the very best wines, the single-vineyard cuvées, are extremely limited in availability, not to mention frightfully expensive.

Chapoutier feels that 1998 may be the firm's finest vintage since 1990, with the potential for extremely high quality wines. I tasted through many cuvées that were still unsettled, having barely finished malolactic fermentation, and they do appear to be extremely promising. Chapoutier compares 1998 to 1947, saying the wines are extremely high in tannin, but low in acidity. As for 1997, this vintage possesses low acidity and supple tannin. On the other hand, 1996 possesses the highest level of natural acidity in more than 10 years.

Chapoutier firmly believes that wines should be made 100% from one varietal—the so-called *mono-cépage* philosophy. His attractive lower-level whites all lean toward the more mineral style of winemaking. A blend of Bourboulenc and Grenache, the 1997 Côtes du Rhône Belleruche is one of the few non-*mono-cépage* whites. It is a light-bodied, citrusy, fresh white to enjoy over the next year. The 1997 Crozes-Hermitage Les Meysonnières, from old Marsanne vines, exhibits a honeyed, white peach component as well as the telltale minerality. It is destined to be drunk over the next several years, as is the 1997 Crozes-Hermitage La Petite Ruche, a flinty, Chablis-styled wine with glycerin, freshness, and a citrusy, fruity component. The 1997 St.-Joseph Deschants displays the most mineral-like character, as well as more apricots, peaches, and honey. Bargain hunters should search out Chapoutier's 1997 Muscat Sec from the Côte Catalans. This wine, which achieved 13.5% alcohol naturally, is a perfumed, refreshing, fruit cocktail-flavored offering with a dry, austere finish. It is best consumed over the next 6–9 months.

Readers should be able to find the Burgundian-styled 1997 Hermitage Chante Alouette. It achieved 13.9% natural alcohol, and was aged in small *barriques,* of which one-third were new. It offers the telltale acacia flower, white peach, honeyed citrus character commonly found in top white Hermitage. Full bodied, with good fat and glycerin, it is ideal for drinking over the next decade (although it will undoubtedly keep much longer). The 1997 Condrieu is less successful, with a flabby, loosely knit character, and some minerality. While it offers an elegant, midweight style, there is no real shape or delineation. Drink it over the next 6–9 months.

The single-vineyard luxury cuvées are spectacular. Unfortunately, there are only 300–400 cases of each. The 1996 St.-Joseph Les Granits white was made from incredibly tiny yields of 10–15 hectoliters per hectare ($^{2}/_{3}$–1 ton per acre). The wine reveals a remarkable liquid mineral/orange marmalade character. This intense, medium- to full-bodied, beautifully pure wine should drink well for a decade. Cut from the same mold with slightly higher alcohol, the 1997 St.-Joseph Les Granits white offers an apricot/orange liqueurlike note, along with the pronounced mineral characteristic of the granitic soil in which this 80-year-old parcel of vines is planted. What is so amazing about all of these single-vineyard wines is that they are aged in 100% new oak, but there is very little evidence of wood in the wines, a testament to their extraordinary concentration and richness. Because of low acidity, look for the 1997 to have a faster evolutionary track than the 1996—7–10 years.

It is no secret that I adore Chapoutier's luxury cuvée of white Hermitage called Cuvée L'Orée. Made from 90-year-old vines and microscopic yields of less than a ton of fruit per acre, these wines flirt with perfection in top vintages. Both the 1996 and 1997 are compelling white Hermitages. Made from 100% Marsanne, they are as rich and multidimensional as the fullest, most massive Montrachet money can buy. They are unctuously textured, yet extraordinarily and beautifully balanced. I suspect they will drink well early in life, and then shut down for a few years. They should last for 4–5 decades. The 1996 possesses some of the most amazing glycerin levels I have ever seen in a dry white wine. The 1997 is also a huge, chewy, multidimensional wine with spectacular concentration and richness. Notes of white flowers, honey, minerals, and peaches are present in astronomical quantities. In short, these wines must be tasted to be believed. In 1997, Michel Chapoutier introduced another luxury cuvée of white Hermitage called Le Méal. As palate-staining as L'Orée, it displays, in addition to cherry notes, more of an orange Grand Marnier characteristic to its fruit. It is an immense, full-bodied, fabulously powerful and concentrated dry white with a steely finish. There are approximately 300 cases of this spectacular offering. Look for it to shut down in 3–4 years and last for 3–4 decades.

A sweet, reasonably priced wine is the 1997 Muscat de Rivesaltes. This exotic, tropical fruit-scented wine offers copious quantities of tangerine and orangelike fruit, great body, and a flamboyant, rich, moderately sweet finish. Although it will not make "old bones," it should offer decadently rich drinking for several years. The 1997 and 1996 Hermitage Vin de Paille are both huge, thick, unctuously textured, sweet wines that will last for 50 or more years. What I found striking about the 1996 Vin de Paille was that the nose was identical to white truffles, something I had had my share of a week earlier when I was in Piedmont.

As for the red wines from Chapoutier, I was not impressed with the 1997 cuvées of Entre Nous and Cigalas, which are VDP wines. However, I did enjoy the moderately priced cuvées of Coteaux d'Aix reds, the 1997 Les Matines and 1997 Les Béates. The 1997 Les Matines (a Syrah/Grenache dominated blend) is a straightforward, light- to medium-bodied wine meant to be consumed over the next several years. While neither complex nor rich, it is refreshing and vibrant, if somewhat simple. Far better is the 1997 Les Béates, a blend of equal portions of Cabernet Sauvignon, Syrah, and Grenache. The wine possesses cassis/blackberry fruit, medium body, good spice, and rustic, hard tannin in the finish. It should drink well for 3–4 years. The pleasant, fruity, soft but simple 1997 Côtes du Rhône Belleruche (100% Grenache) is best consumed over the next year. More interesting is the 1997 La Ciboise, a 100% Grenache cuvée from the Coteaux du Tricastin. This wine offers more cherry and kirsch notes presented in a medium-bodied, fruity, elegant, lush style. It should be enjoyed over the next 2–3 years.

Chapoutier did well with the 1997 Crozes-Hermitage La Petite Ruche, a peppery/cassis tank-fermented and -aged, seductive, medium-bodied, fruity wine. There is no evidence of wood, and the wine is better because of it. The more serious 1997 Crozes-Hermitage Les Meysonnières (about 30% of this cuvée was aged in *barrique* and the remainder in tank) exhibits a more mineral-dominated, herb-tinged cassis character, spicy, medium-bodied flavors, and an excellent finish with good ripeness, glycerin, and length. Like its less-expensive sibling, La Petite Ruche, it should be drunk over the next 3–4 years. The medium ruby-colored 1997 St.-Joseph Deschants offers toasty vanillin in the nose (50% of the cuvée is aged in cask), as well as copious quantities of black cherry and cassis fruit. Although not complex, it is a medium-bodied, spicy, ripe, fruity, satisfying wine for drinking over the next 3–4 years.

Other appellation wines include a straightforward, *barrique*-aged 1997 Cornas that reveals a dark ruby/purple color and ripe blackberry/cassis fruit in the nose. However, the wine narrows out and becomes attenuated in the lean, austere finish. The only surprises in the bottled 1996s were the 1996 Côte Rôtie and the 1996 Côte Rôtie La Mordorée, both of which were less impressive from bottle than they were in cask. The dark ruby/purple-colored 1996 Côte Rôtie offers attractive herb-tinged cassis, pepper, Asian spices, and bacon fat in the nose, but in the mouth, the wine is strikingly acidic with loads of tannin. It is extremely backward due to its searing acidity level. While I enjoyed many of this wine's characteristics, the acidity scares me—hence the lower rating. The 1997 Côte Rôtie is a sweeter, more flattering wine with a textbook black olive, bacon fat, black raspberry, and cherry-scented nose, medium body, a more accessible, softer style, and good density and ripeness. There is some tannin, but because of its lower acidity, it comes across as more user-friendly. The 1996 Hermitage La Sizeranne exhibits a saturated dense purple color, a classic, smoky, cassis-scented nose, and fresh acidity nicely meshed with the wine's rich, concentrated black fruit character and high tannin. This full-bodied, muscular, backward La Sizeranne requires patience. It is aged all in cask, of which 50% were new. Anticipated maturity: 2004–2020. The 1997 Hermitage La Sizeranne possesses huge amounts of tannin, some of which is vegetal and green. The wine is dry and structured, with a tough finish. Michel Chapoutier feels it is the finest La Sizeranne made since 1990, but my tasting notes are at odds with that position. The color is impressively saturated, but the wine is pinched and compressed, particularly in the finish. I would like to have another look at this wine after it has been bottled. The 1997 Châteauneuf du Pape La Bernadine (100% Grenache) exhibits a Provençal herb, kirsch, licorice, cherry, and spicy-scented nose. Medium to full bodied, soft, and round, with heady alcohol in the supple finish, it will drink well young and keep for 5–7 years.

Chapoutier's single-vineyard, old-vine cuvées are unquestionably among the world's greatest red wines. Even in difficult vintages these offerings possess remarkable character and volume. The 1996 Châteauneuf du Pape Barbe Rac displays an exotic nose of barbecue spices, burning wood, and sweet cherry fruit. The plum/cherry color reveals some lightening at the edge. The wine is full bodied and dense, with copious spice, tobacco, and earthy notes. This rich, chewy, outstanding Châteauneuf du Pape is one of the finest wines of the vintage. The deep ruby-colored 1997 Châteauneuf du Pape Barbe Rac exhibits plenty of kirsch, smoke, and herbs in its meaty, fragrant bouquet. Full bodied, dense, rich, and layered, with good volume and persistence (particularly for a 1997) but hard and tough in the finish, it should be consumed over the next 7–8 years.

Readers looking for a spectacular Provençal wine should taste Michel Chapoutier's 1996 and 1997 Terra d'Or from Coteaux d'Aix en Provence. These wines, made from 50% Cabernet Sauvignon and 50% Syrah, and aged in small oak casks, are immensely impressive. Made from tiny yields of 15 hectoliters per hectare (1 ton per acre) (it achieved 14.5% natural alcohol), the 1996 Terra d'Or Coteaux d'Aix en Provence is even more impressive from bottle than it was from barrel. It boasts an opaque black/purple color, as well as a knockout nose of cassis, kirsch, underbrush, truffles, and *pain grillé*. Rich and full bodied, with an unctuous texture, and intense, smoky, black currant flavors with a touch of licorice, this sensationally extracted, pure, well-built wine should be at its peak between 2001 and 2020. Remarkably, the 1997 Terra d'Or Coteaux d'Aix en Provence is richer and more concentrated. It may be the finest wine from this region that I have ever tasted. The color is a saturated black/purple. The wine offers jammy aromas of black raspberries, blackberries, incense, smoke, fennel, and toasty new oak. Extremely full bodied, chewy, and unctuously textured, it is a strikingly concentrated, compelling example of what can be achieved in this area of southern France. Anticipated maturity: 2003–2020.

It is hard to find a better Crozes-Hermitage than Chapoutier's single-vineyard Les Varonnières. Because of its high acidity, the 1996 Crozes-Hermitage Les Varonnières has gone into a closed, tightly knit stage. Nevertheless, the saturated dark ruby/purple color and gorgeous nose of smoked meats, blackberries, kirsch, and anise are impressive. The wine is medium to full bodied and highly extracted, but the vintage's high acidity causes it to be tight and firm. Anticipated maturity: 2003–2020. The 1997 Crozes-Hermitage Les Varonnières is a softer, fatter, less-acidic offering. It possesses a saturated dark ruby/purple color, as well as a pronounced cherry liqueur nose with smoke, roasted herbs, and underbrush notes in the background. Full bodied, dense, chewy, and made in a user-friendly, accessible style, this wine should be delicious when released and age well for 12–15 years.

No one is producing better old-vine cuvées of St.-Joseph than Michel Chapoutier. Both the 1996 and 1997 Les Granits are spectacular. I have a slight preference for the profound 1996 Les Granits. It is a fabulous expression of Syrah, and in a blind tasting could easily be confused with a top-class Hermitage. It offers up a saturated black/purple color, followed by smoky cassis with flinty notes in the background. There are huge amounts of fruit, gobs of tannin, and remarkable purity and palate presence. Anticipated maturity: 2002–2015. The 1997 St.-Joseph Les Granits is also massive and full bodied, with a floral component to go along with the blackberry/cassis fruit and flinty *terroir* characteristic. Superb ripeness, low acidity, and fleshy, ripe fruit result in an opulent, splendid wine. Anticipated maturity: 2001–2012.

As I indicated earlier, I was less impressed with the 1996 Côte Rôtie La Mordorée from bottle than I was from cask. Michel Chapoutier still believes it is one of the finest examples he has produced but agrees that the high acidity has left everything in the wine compressed. It is certainly an outstanding offering, but it will require 5–7 years of patience. Made from microscopic yields of 15 hectoliters per hectare (1 ton per acre), it exhibits a saturated purple color, and a reticent but promising nose of toasty new oak, cassis, black olives, and smoked game. In the mouth, the wine is medium to full bodied and dense, but the high acidity and compressed, tightly knit style make it difficult to penetrate. The finish is long, but the wine is backward and unyielding. Anticipated maturity: 2006–2025. The 1997 Côte Rôtie La Mordorée is an extremely expressive, open-knit, aromatic, and seductive example. Chapoutier believes it is the finest he has ever made, but I would still give that honor to the

1991. The 1997 is softer, more accessible, and easier to understand than the 1996 or 1995 La Mordorée. The saturated ruby/purple color is accompanied by telltale aromas of black raspberries, roasted herbs, smoke, and meat. The wine is medium to full bodied and moderately tannic, with lower acidity than the 1996, superb concentration, and an intense black cherry, camphorlike, olive component. This wine should be drinkable upon release and last for 2 decades.

Michel Chapoutier continues to offer a dizzying array of single-vineyard wines from the slopes of Hermitage. In addition to the firm's most widely distributed cuvée, La Sizeranne, there is the fabulous Le Pavillon, and, since 1996, Le Méal and L'Ermite. All of these wines are outstanding, and, save for Le Méal, close to perfection. The 1996 Hermitage Le Méal (Chapoutier calls it the Lafite-Rothschild of Hermitage) is a mineral-dominated, high-acid, medium- to full-bodied, high-strung, extremely intellectual wine. It exhibits a saturated ruby/purple color, as well as mineral-dominated aromatics with notes of cassis, kirsch, and underbrush. Made from 80-year-old vines, it requires 10–15 years of cellaring. Although not the most charming, opulent, or viscous style of Hermitage, it does possess the strongest *terroir* character of any of Chapoutier's wines. I might call it the Ausone of Hermitage! Anticipated maturity: 2012–2040. The 1997 Hermitage Le Méal displays more fat, plumpness, and richness, without losing the floral minerality so obvious in the 1996. It is a finesse-styled Hermitage, with more concentrated black fruits, and a high-toned, structured, well-delineated personality. Because of low acidity and a plump, plush texture, this wine will be approachable at an earlier age. Anticipated maturity: 2005–2035.

Both vintages of the famed Ermitage Le Pavillon flirt with perfection. The 1996 Ermitage Le Pavillon needs at least a decade of cellaring. The wine possesses a saturated black/purple color, in addition to fabulously sweet aromas of blackberries, framboise, blueberries, violets, roasted herbs, and meats. Massively concentrated and full bodied, with staggering levels of extract, this wine is superpure, with high tannin, good but not intrusive acidity, and a 45-second finish. This is one of the superstars of the vintage in France! Anticipated maturity: 2010–2050. The 1997 Ermitage Le Pavillon displays a similarly saturated purple color, and a fabulously intense nose of blackberry liqueur intermixed with floral scents, smoke, licorice, tar, and Chinese black tea aromas. There is wonderful concentration, massive body, and a monster finish in this decadently rich Hermitage. It possesses lower acidity than the 1996 but every bit as much concentration, extract, and length. Anticipated maturity: 2008–2035.

One of the candidates for France's wine of the vintage is unquestionably Chapoutier's 1996 Hermitage l'Ermite. In October 1997 I reported that this was a virtually perfect wine made from a small parcel of vines, believed to be over 100 years old, located close to the tiny white chapel owned by the Jaboulets on the highest part of the Hermitage Hill. Yields were a minuscule 9 hectoliters per hectare (slightly more than 1/2 ton per acre). Now that this wine is in bottle, it is unbelievable! Unfortunately, only 30 cases were exported to the United States. The wine boasts a saturated black/purple color, as well as a phenomenal nose of rose petals, violets, blackberries, cassis, and *pain grillé*. In the mouth, it is phenomenally rich, with a viscous texture, and a multidimensional, layered finish that lasts for over a minute. Its purity, perfect equilibrium, and unbelievable volume and richness are the stuff of legends. Anticipated maturity: 2010–2050. The fabulous 1997 Hermitage l'Ermite possesses the ripeness and exotic characteristics of a great Pomerol, but the structure, smoky minerality, and power of Hermitage. The color is a saturated black/ruby. The wine is rich, chewy, thick, and impeccably well balanced. This wine will be more approachable in its youth than the 1996 l'Ermite but is capable of lasting 30–40 years.

Michel Chapoutier has turned in some spectacular performances with limited production (around 4,000 500 ml bottles) Banyuls. The 1996 Banyuls, 1995 Banyuls Terra Vinya, and 1996 Banyuls Terra Vinya are rich, chocolatey wines that smell like cappuccinos infused with cherry liqueur. Rich and pure, but not the least bit heavy, it is good to see another top-quality producer emerge from Banyuls, one of the most spectacular appellations in southern France.

As I reported in my book on the Rhône Valley, Chapoutier has increasingly moved toward organic farming, even for those vineyards under contract. In the estate vineyards, he applies biodynamic farming principles with considerable passion and enthusiasm. Moreover, Michel Chapoutier has also become the king of the *mono-cépage* wines, preferring that all of his wines be made totally from one varietal so they can, as he says, "correctly translate the characteristics of the *terroir* and varietal into the aromas and flavors of the wine." This estate has become the most exciting house in the entire Rhône Valley—particularly when tasting through the entire portfolio. Chapoutier has also been aggressively seeking vineyard sites in Provence. As readers will note from the following tasting notes, there are now three cuvées of a Coteaux d'Aix en Provence of which Chapoutier is a co-proprietor, as well as small quantities of Muscat de Rivesaltes, Banyuls, and a handful of other wines. All of this is welcome news for consumers searching for high-quality wines. Although Michel Chapoutier may be outspoken and controversial, there is no question that his wines are extraordinary, especially the top luxury single-vineyard cuvées. The latter wines are designed for the long term, so readers seeking immediate gratification should look elsewhere.

The powerful 1995 Hermitage Chante Alouette is a honeyed peach/pear, intensely concentrated wine with terrific fruit, a chewy texture, long luscious flavors, and decent acidity for a wine of such power and intensity. Either drink it early or put it away for 10–15 years.

Among the luxury white wine cuvées, readers have a splendid portfolio from which to choose, assuming they can both find and afford the wines. The 1995 St.-Joseph Les Granits (made from the same 80-year-old parcel of vines as the 1996) is rich and full bodied, with loads of glycerin, and a distinct minerality combined with the apricot/peachlike fruit. It is a gloriously dense, powerful, yet elegant white St.-Joseph that, along with the 1996, should age for 10–15 years. These two St.-Josephs are reference point/breakthrough wines that establish a new level of quality for this appellation. Both wines are totally *barrique*-aged, of which one-third is new oak.

The extraordinary white Hermitage Cuvée de l'Orée is mind-boggling in both 1995 and 1996. Both wines represent the essence of white Hermitage. Made from 100% Marsanne from extremely old vines and microscopic yields of 12 hectoliters per hectare ($^3/_4$ ton per acre), the wines overwhelm any evidence of their *barrique* aging. Both possess extraordinary intensity, full body, the multilayered texture of a great Montrachet, and intense, honeyed, mineral-like fruit flavors that ooze over the palate with remarkable richness, yet no sense of heaviness. These are undoubtedly the greatest white Hermitages I have ever tasted. Both should drink fabulously for another 2–3 years and then shut down for 10–15 years. Both wines should easily last 40–50 years—assuming excellent storage.

The new estate that Michel Chapoutier co-owns in Coteaux d'Aix en Provence produces three levels of wine. The most commercial level is Les Matines, the richer second level is Béates, and the third level is the luxury cuvée from old vines called Terra d'Or, a wine with Domaine Trevallon-like richness and complexity. The 1996 Les Matines Coteaux d'Aix en Provence is a peppery, licorice, smoky-scented wine with a dark ruby color, copious quantities of black cherries and Provençal herbs in its flavors, light tannin, and good flesh. It is the perfect wine to serve with hamburgers, pizza, and barbecued foods. The 1996 Béates, which sees some aging in *barrique* as opposed to Les Matines' 100% tank-fermentation and aging, is made from 70% Cabernet Sauvignon and the rest Grenache and Syrah. An excellent, dense, medium-bodied wine, it offers black raspberry/cherry fruit in its earthy, licorice, and truffle-scented nose. The 1995 Béates (not vinified by Chapoutier) is a straightforward, medium-bodied wine with good fruit but a rustic personality and coarse tannin. As Chapoutier admits, the raw materials for the 1995 were superior to those in 1996, but since he controlled the vinification in 1996, a better wine was produced. The top cuvée, the 1996

Terra d'Or, is macerated for 8 weeks. The wine is 100% *barrique*-aged, and the grapes come from the finest section of the vineyard, with the lowest yields. The 1996 averaged 15 hecto-liters per hectare (about 1 ton of fruit per acre), and only 5,000 bottles were produced. A breakthrough effort for the Coteaux d'Aix en Provence, the wine boasts an opaque black/pur-ple color, as well as a supersweet nose of cassis, black raspberries, licorice, smoke, and vanillin. It possesses terrific concentration, full body, great precision and grip, and a long af-tertaste. This should be an amazing wine when it is bottled and released. It will drink well young and last for 15 years.

The 1995 Cornas, which I prefer to the 1996, offers a saturated dark purple color, a sweeter, more peppery and riper cassis aroma, less acidity, plenty of tannin, medium to full body, and a sweet, dense, very *sauvage* personality. It is a big, deep, chewy Cornas that will benefit from 2–5 years of cellaring and keep for 15 years.

Chapoutier makes no bones about the fact that he prefers his 1996 Côte Rôties to his 1995s. The 1995 Côte Rôtie is less expressive than the 1996, with high acidity, but excellent olive, Provençal herb, black raspberry, and cassis fruit. Medium bodied, dense, and back-ward, this wine requires at least 5–7 years of cellaring. Although good, it is closed. The 1995 Côte Rôtie La Mordorée is a superb wine. It possesses an intensely saturated black/purple color, and a smoky, black raspberry, coffee, and chocolate-scented nose with black olives thrown in for complexity. It is a medium- to full-bodied, rich, extraordinary example of Côte Rôtie that possesses power as well as finesse. I suspect the 1995 will need 4–5 years of cel-laring to reveal its personality. It should drink well from 2003–2020.

The 1995 Hermitage La Sizeranne is performing even better out of bottle than it did im-mediately prior to bottling. It is a full-bodied, dense ruby/purple-colored wine with a sweet, smoky, chocolate, cassis, and tar-scented nose, great fruit intensity, full body, a layered tex-ture, sweet tannin, and good grip. It should be cellared for a minimum of 4–5 years and will keep for 15–20.

The 1995 Châteauneuf du Pape La Bernadine is a delicious, open-knit, forward wine. The deep ruby color with purple hues is accompanied by a sweet nose of black raspberries, blackberries, cassis, prunes, and cherries. The wine is full bodied, with sweet, lush fruit, moderate tannin, and fine density and power. It can be drunk now but should be at its peak of maturity between 2002 and 2012. As for the luxury cuvée, the 1995 Châteauneuf du Pape Barbe Rac is a fragrant wine with a dense purple color, and a sensational Provençal nose of olives, jammy black cherries and raspberries, roasted herbs, and pepper. Extremely dense and huge in the mouth, with massive body, glycerin, and tannin, this powerful Châteauneuf du Pape requires cellaring. Anticipated maturity: 2000–2020.

Among the other luxury cuvées is the Crozes-Hermitage Les Varonnières. This is clearly the most spectacular wine made in the appellation, even richer and denser than Alain Grail-lot's La Giraude and Paul Jaboulet's Thalabert. As I reported in 1996, the 1995 Crozes-Hermitage Les Varonnières is the finest Crozes-Hermitage I have ever tasted. Now in bottle, it offers an opaque purple color, and a spectacular nose of black fruits, licorice, minerals, and smoke. Dense, with terrific fruit purity, and layers of concentration, this wine is loaded with extract and glycerin. The finish lasts for 30+ seconds. Amazing! Anticipated maturity: 2000–2015.

The 1995 St.-Joseph Les Granits possesses less acidity than the 1996, is more supple, and less massive, but it is an amazingly fabulous, sweet-tasting (from ripe fruit, not sugar) wine with layers of cassis fruit. Made from an 80-year-old 5-acre parcel situated behind the vil-lage of Mauves, the 1995 comes across as both elegant and powerful—the quintessential St.-Joseph—the likes of which I have never before tasted. Anticipated maturity: 2001–2010.

The 1995 Ermitage Le Pavillon is magnificent. The wine is more accessible than the 1996 (due to lower acidity and more immediately accessible glycerin and fruit), with a magnificent black/purple color, and layers of cassis fruit, smoky, roasted meat, and mineral characteristics that are the result of barrel fermentation and high extraction of fruit. It is huge but not heavy, gorgeously proportioned, and dazzlingly well defined. A monster Hermitage of immense proportions, it somehow manages to keep everything in balance. This backward Pavillon will require 10–12 years of cellaring. It should age well through the first half of the next century.

There are four after-dinner wines from Chapoutier in 1996, all of them outstanding. It is hard to believe a *vin de pays* from l'Ardeche could be as good as the 1995 and 1996 Coufis. The 1996 Viognier Coufis VDP l' Ardeche is a sweet, honeyed style of Viognier with copious quantities of peach and pearlike fruit presented in an unctuously thick style. Even better is the 1995 Viognier Coufis VDP l'Ardeche (only 1,000 bottles produced), which is extremely sweet but gorgeously ripe, concentrated, and focused. It is a nectarlike Viognier dessert wine to drink by itself or with fruit tarts. Chapoutier's 1995 Hermitage Vin de Paille (2,500 half-bottles were produced in the vintage) is also an extraordinary, nectarlike wine. It exhibits an orange marmalade, honeyed corn, supersweet richness that is almost too intense to have with dessert. While the 1996 possesses slightly better acidity, the 1995 is a heavier, fatter wine. This wine will last 50+ years.

Lastly, a good value in sweet wine is Chapoutier's 1995 Banyuls, a fruity, nonoxidized style of Banyuls with tons of chocolatey black cherry fruit, moderate sweetness, medium to full body, outstanding purity, and real vibrancy and freshness, something not usually associated with Banyuls. This wine will drink impeccably with chocolate desserts. It should last for a decade or more.

DOMAINE DE LA CHARBONNIÈRE

1995	Châteauneuf du Pape Cuvée Classique	D	86
1997	Châteauneuf du Pape Mourre des Perdrix	E	(86–88)
1996	Châteauneuf du Pape Mourre des Perdrix	E	87
1995	Châteauneuf du Pape Mourre des Perdrix	E	90
1995	Châteauneuf du Pape Les Hautes Brusquières	E	90+
1997	Châteauneuf du Pape Les Hautes Brusquières Cuvée Speciale	E	(87–88)
1996	Châteauneuf du Pape Les Hautes Brusquières Cuvée Speciale	E	89
1997	Châteauneuf du Pape Cuvée Tradition	D	(77–80)
1996	Châteauneuf du Pape Cuvée Tradition	D	85
1996	Châteauneuf du Pape Vieilles Vignes	E	88
1995	Châteauneuf du Pape Vieilles Vignes	E	90+

Proprietor Michel Mared is one of Châteauneuf du Pape's up-and-coming stars. Readers should see more of his wines in the marketplace since he secured Kermit Lynch as his importer, although the Les Hautes Brusquières Cuvée Speciale had been a selection made by Eric Solomon. I suspect that relationship will end given Lynch's exclusivity to sell this estate's wines. The 1996s and 1997s are generally well-made wines that take advantage of the forward, easygoing nature of these vintages. While the 1997 Châteauneuf du Pape Cuvée Tradition was austere, tart, and straightforward, the 1997 Châteauneuf du Pape Cuvée Mourre des Perdrix was an elegant, stylish wine with Burgundian-like black cherry fruit mixed with floral scents, pepper, and earth. With good depth, nice softness, some structure, but a forward and appealing, layered texture and richness, it should drink well for 7–8 years. The 1997 Châteauneuf du Pape Les Hautes Brusquières Cuvée Speciale exhibits more glycerin, with a forward, lusty, up-front personality. It should be consumed over the next 5–7 years.

The 1996s have turned out well. The dark ruby-colored 1996 Châteauneuf du Pape Cuvée Tradition offers a cedary, sandalwood, and black cherry-scented nose, medium to full body, fine softness, and a stylish combination of power and finesse. It will not age long but will provide fine drinking over the next 4–5 years. The 1996 Châteauneuf du Pape Mourre des Perdrix displays a distinctive earthy, strawberry/black raspberry and cherry, fruit-driven aromatic profile. In the mouth, it seems more closed than the bouquet suggests. The wine is medium bodied and slightly angular, with good structure, depth, and ripeness. This is one 1996 where 12–18 months of cellaring will be beneficial. It should age for 7–8 years. The 1996 Châteauneuf du Pape Vieilles Vignes is the most structured, tannic, and closed offering, as well as the richest and most concentrated. The wine is medium bodied, with a deeper, more saturated ruby color, and plenty of black fruits in its nose, along with pepper, wood smoke, and spice. A powerful, reserved, backward 1996, it will be at its finest between 2000 and 2010. The 1996 Châteauneuf du Pape Les Hautes Brusquières Cuvée Speciale again reveals more glycerin, sweetness, and chewiness than the other cuvées. It possesses copious quantities of black cherry fruit, medium body, excellent purity, and a spicy, ripe, long finish. It should drink well for 7–8 years.

Domaine de la Charbonnière's 1995s have a more saturated color than the 1996s, cut a deeper, fuller impression on the palate, and possess more character and aromatics. The 1995 Châteauneuf du Pape Cuvée Classique offers a medium ruby color, a soft, berry/cherry-scented nose, round, ripe flavors, nice sweetness from the glycerin, and light tannin in the medium-bodied finish. It is a wine to drink over the next 5–6 years. The 1995 Châteauneuf du Pape Mourre des Perdrix is textbook Châteauneuf, displaying pure kirsch liqueur, cherries, and herbes de Provence. The wine is ripe and sweet, with an expansive midpalate, medium to full body, excellent integration of acidity and tannin, and a long, jammy finish. It is a hedonistic, well-structured wine that should be at its best between 1999 and 2010. One of the two most backward 1995s is the 1995 Châteauneuf du Pape Cuvée Vieilles Vignes. Once again, kirsch, pepper, and spice are noticeable in the wine's aromatics. Fuller bodied, with a deep ruby color, this impressive, rich wine exhibits good acidity and structure. A classic, young Provençal wine made more in a *vin de garde* style, it needs 2–4 years of cellaring, and should age well for 12–15 years.

Last, the 1995 Châteauneuf du Pape Cuvée Hautes Brusquières is the most tannic of these offerings, with the densest, most saturated ruby/purple color. It is a big, muscular, unfiltered, full-bodied, impressively knit, powerful, closed offering that needs 3–4 years of cellaring; it should keep for 15–20 years.

G.A.E.C. CHARVIN

1997	Châteauneuf du Pape	D	(87–88)
1996	Châteauneuf du Pape	D	87
1995	Châteauneuf du Pape	D	91
1995	Côtes du Rhône	A	85

This small estate in the northern section of the appellation consists of only 20 acres, from which less than 3,000 cases of high-quality Châteauneuf du Pape emerge. The wine is often similar to Rayas because of its pure black raspberry/kirsch-scented nose and flavors, in addition to an impressive, expansive, chewy texture.

Although not totally identical, both the 1996 and 1997 Châteauneuf du Pape possess dark ruby colors, a distinctive raspberry/framboise fruitiness, medium body, good ripeness, excellent purity, and fruit-driven, open-knit, forward personalities. The 1996 Châteauneuf du Pape reveals more spice and pepper at the moment, but both characteristics may also emerge in the younger 1997. Both wines are forward, and should be consumed over the next 5–7 years.

The 1995 Châteauneuf du Pape exhibits a dense purple color, as well as a sweet nose of black raspberries, cherries, and subtle herbes de Provence. It is an aromatic, full-bodied wine with outstanding sweetness and layers of rich, spicy black fruits on the palate. Typical of the vintage, it reveals some tannin and relatively good acidity. I would suggest cellaring it for 2–3 years and consuming it over the following 12–15.

For value, Charvin also fashions a spicy, *garrigue*, peppery, cherry jam-scented and -flavored Côtes du Rhône, of which the 1995 is a fine example. Although it possesses some robust tannin in the finish that is unlikely to melt away, this is a solidly made, exuberant wine to drink over the next 3–4 years.

J. L. CHAVE

1997	Hermitage	E	(90–94)
1996	Hermitage	E	91
1995	Hermitage	E	95+
1995	Hermitage Cuvée Cathelin	EEE	97+
1997	Hermitage (White)	E	(90–94)
1996	Hermitage (White)	E	93
1995	Hermitage (White)	E	94
1997	St. Joseph	D	(86–87)
1995	St. Joseph Offerus	D	87
1997	Vin de Paille	EE	(96–98+)
1996	Vin de Paille	EE	98

The admirable father and son team of Gérard and Jean-Louis Chave were very pleased with the 1998 harvest. When I saw them several weeks after its conclusion, they told me they thought it would be, qualitatively, finer than 1996 or 1997 for both whites and reds. Certainly the Chaves did exceptionally well in both 1996 and 1997, so I can't wait to taste their 1998s. The 1997 Hermitage white had not been assembled at the time of my visit in the fall of 1998, so the tasting notes that follow represent the different *lieux-dits* (vineyards) that were waiting to be blended. Everything, Peléat (88–90), Rocoules (92–94), l'Hermite (94–97), and l'Hermite Roussanne (94–96), looked to be very concentrated, fat, and honeyed. Low acidity and high alcohol (13.5%–14%), in addition to a white flower/peachy succulence were present throughout these cuvées. There appears to be less minerality in the 1997 than in 1996 or 1995, and it should be one of the more luscious, opulently textured blends ever assembled by the Chaves. This wine will have been blended and bottled by the time this report is released. The bottled 1996 Hermitage white is sensational. While it is not as fat as the 1997, it is a powerful, heady, alcoholic, deep, chewy, superb white Hermitage offering notes of grilled nuts, sherry finolike scents, thick, juicy, honeyed citrus, and a touch of peach and roses. Structured and powerful, it should have 10–15 or more years of longevity.

Tasting through Chave's red wines is always immensely educational. It is fascinating to see the differences among each parcel of vines. While Les Dionnières and l'Hermite were the least impressive, they did exhibit good raspberry/cassis fruit, although Les Dionnières seemed to be mostly pepper and tough, hard tannin. The superb cuvées included Le Méal (pure cassis, full body, and gobs of fruit), Beaumes (explosive richness, very Burgundian, with black raspberry, earth, truffle, and spice), Peléat (extremely ripe, fleshy, voluptuously textured, low acid, yet dynamite crème de cassis richness), and the monster, full-bodied, profound Les Bessards (huge, chewy, thick, blackberry/cassis, roasted herb, and an ironlike mineral character that gives the wine great complexity). Les Bessards, which represents one-third of the blend, was the finest cuvée, although Peléat, Beaumes, and Le Méal were all exceptional, and l'Hermite will provide elegance. This will be a top-notch 1997 red Hermitage, more generous and user-friendly than the 1996 or 1995. The 1997's lower acidity and super-ripeness will be appreciated by readers who like to drink these wines at an earlier age. While it will last for 25 years, the 1997 will be more accessible than the 1996 and 1995. The 1996 red Hermitage possesses the vintage's tangy acidity, as well as a saturated ruby/purple color, and copious quantities of smoke, cassis, fennel, and minerals in the moderately intense, still young aromatics. The wine displays beautiful balance, outstanding purity, and a medium-bodied, rich, elegant personality. This is not the massive, thick, succulent style of the 1990, or the softer, more forward style of the 1985 and 1997, but rather a synthesis in style of the 1988 and 1991. Anticipated maturity: 2009–2030.

I had a chance to retaste both the 1995 Hermitage and 1995 Hermitage Cuvée Cathelin. Both are sensational wines, but they each require a decade of cellaring. I also tasted the 1990 Hermitage Cuvée Cathelin. Pure perfection, this spectacular Hermitage possesses everything one could ask for in a Syrah. Moreover, it will be drinkable within 2–3 years and will continue to develop for 25–35 more years.

Chave also produces an estate-bottled St.-Joseph. The 1997 is an excellent example of a lush, richly fruity, berry/cherry, elegant style. This fruity St.-Joseph will provide delicious drinking for the next 5–7 years.

Gérard and Jean-Louis Chave produced a Vin de Paille in both 1996 and 1997. Previously, the cuvée was made only in 1986, 1989, and 1990. Both the 1996 and 1997 are spectacular, extremely unctuous offerings with awesome flavors, with massive sweetness, glycerin, and extract, as well as amazing honeyed, earthy, spicy, jammy aromatics. The scent of Piedmontese white truffles is unmistakable, particularly in the 1996, which had just finished fermenting! The 1997 was still fermenting when I tasted it. After spitting, orange marmalade, apricot jam, and white trufflelike flavors continued to linger on the palate, even though there was no wine left in my mouth. These legendary wines will have 50–100 years of longevity.

Since son Jean-Louis Chaves joined father Gérard, there have been subtle refinements in the winemaking program. The white wine always went through full malolactic, but now there is *bâtonnage* (stirring the lees), as well as more barrel fermentation and a greater percentage of new oak. I have always loved Chave's white Hermitage, and have been buying it consistently since the 1978 vintage. However, I must say that if the 1994 signaled a new level of quality, the 1995 and 1996 continue that, with both vintages producing blockbuster white Hermitages that possess the texture of a great white Burgundy, in addition to extraordinary intensity and richness. Americans have never taken a liking to white Hermitage, but it ages as well as the red, and if you do not drink it during the first 2–3 years after the vintage, it is best to wait for 2 decades to consume it as it goes through a long, stubborn, dumb period. The 1995 white Hermitage had been assembled and was awaiting bottling when I tasted it. The wine is low in acidity but fabulously rich, with an extraordinary floral, honeysuckle, peachlike fruit character. With awesome intensity and an unctuous texture, this may be the finest white Hermitage Chave has ever produced. It is powerful and extremely showy at present. Given its equilibrium and overall density, this wine should last 20+ years. Chave said the yields were just over a ton of fruit per acre in 1995, versus 2 tons per acre in 1996 (about one-half the yield of most top white Burgundy producers' Chardonnay vineyards).

The magnificent 1995 Hermitage is one of the classic Rhônes of the vintage. The wine, which had just been bottled, was revealing no signs of fatigue. The color is opaque purple, and the wine is beautifully made, offering up scents of violets and black currants, along with the telltale aromas of tar, truffle, mineral, and earth. This wine could be called the Musigny of Hermitage. It is medium to full bodied (less massive than the 1990 and 1989), with good underlying acidity, and powerful but sweet tannin in the finish. Do not expect the 1995 to possess the power of the 1989 or 1990 as it is made along the lines of the 1991 but even more fragrant. Anticipated maturity: 2006–2030.

The 1995 Hermitage Cuvée Cathelin, only the third vintage of this offering, is less aromatic than the cuvée classique. Rich and powerful, with a formidable tannin level in the finish, it possesses a saturated purple color, great purity of fruit, and considerable mouth-feel and length, but what a full-bodied, awesomely endowed baby! Much less evolved than the 1990 and 1991 were at a similar stage, it will require a minimum of 10–12 years of patience and will last for 30–40+ years.

Jean-Louis Chave has started a *négociant* business to take advantage of the family's contacts with some of the better growers in the appellation of St.-Joseph. The wine being produced is called Offerus (named after the man who is believed to have planted the first Syrah vines in the Rhône). Chave's goal is to make a limited quantity of high-quality St.-Joseph from purchased grapes. The wine will be vinified at a new installation built several blocks from the family's cellars. The 1995 St.-Joseph Offerus is an impressive, ripe, richly fruity, supple wine with an excellent dark ruby/purple color, medium body, fine purity, and a sweet, rich finish. It should drink well for 5–6 years.

LOUIS CHÈZE

1997 St.-Joseph Cuvée des Anges	D	(88–90)
1996 St.-Joseph Cuvée des Anges	D	86
1997 St.-Joseph Cuvée Prestige Caroline	D	(86–87)
1996 St.-Joseph Cuvée Prestige Caroline	D	85
1997 St.-Joseph Cuvée Ro Rée	D	(85–86)
1996 St.-Joseph Cuvée Ro Rée	D	84

This estate turned out very good 1997s and competent 1996s. The 1997s possess more saturated purple colors, lower acidity, more accessible rich, concentrated fruit, medium body, and forward styles. The amount of new oak increases with each cuvée, from little oak in the Cuvée Ro Rée, more noticeable oak in the Cuvée Prestige Caroline, and 100% new oak casks for the Cuvée des Anges. The 1997 St.-Joseph Cuvée des Anges is a rich, chewy, full-bodied, impressively endowed wine that should drink well for a decade. The 1996s are leaner, with noticeable acidity, and more red than black fruits, with the Cuvée des Anges the finest of the group. I would opt for drinking the 1996s over the next 5–6 years.

AUGUSTE CLAPE

1997 Cornas	D	(88–90)
1996 Cornas	D	88
1995 Cornas	D	92

The great master of Cornas, Auguste Clape, and his son, Jean-Marie, have fashioned two excellent wines in 1996 and 1997. Clape's 1997 Cornas flirts with an outstanding rating. The wine boasts a saturated purple color, as well as a sweet, blackberry-scented nose with violets, tar, and trufflelike aromas. Medium to full bodied, with low acidity, excellent purity, and light to moderate tannin, this is an atypically soft, expansive, forward Cornas that should drink well when released and keep for a decade or more. The deep ruby/purple-colored 1996 Cornas offers beautiful aromatics of jammy plums, blackberries, and cassis. The wine is excellent in the mouth, spicy, and medium to full bodied, with exuberant, zesty acidity, and unobtrusive yet firm tannin. From a cooler year, this well-made wine is ideal for drinking now and over the next 12–15 years.

A candidate for the wine of the vintage, Clape's 1995 Cornas exhibits an opaque purple color, and a fabulously ripe, sweet nose of licorice, black plums, and cassis, followed by full-bodied, dense, concentrated, well-balanced flavors with nicely integrated acidity and tannin. This should be a 20-year wine.

LES CLEFS D'OR

1997 Châteauneuf du Pape	D	(85–87)
1996 Châteauneuf du Pape	D	87

Two similar wines, the bottled 1996 Châteauneuf du Pape reveals soft, raspberry, resinylike fruit, and a forward, evolved style. Medium bodied, expansive, spicy, and peppery, it should be consumed over the next 4–5 years. The 1997 Châteauneuf du Pape displays more green pepper and earthy *garrigue* aromas. With good color extraction and medium body, this is a straightforward Châteauneuf to drink over the next 3–4 years.

DOMAINE CLOS DU CAILLOU

1995 Châteauneuf du Pape	D	88
1997 Châteauneuf du Pape Non Filtré	D	(87–89)
1996 Châteauneuf du Pape Non Filtré	D	89
1995 Côtes du Rhône	A	75
1995 Côtes du Rhône Bouquet des Garrigues	A	84

Now run by Claude Pouizin and the Vacherons (a Loire Valley family), this estate is taking what was already a very good wine and increasing its richness and seductiveness. I thought the 1996 Châteauneuf du Pape Non Filtré was showing exceptionally well. It may merit an outstanding score, although it clearly has a limited longevity of 6–7 years. The color is dark ruby/purple. The wine has terrific fruit purity in its nose—raspberries and cherries galore. In the mouth, it is medium to full bodied and layered, with a voluptuous texture, resulting in a sexy, opulently styled wine with low acidity. It is difficult to resist this fruit-driven Châteauneuf. Enjoy it over the next 6–7 years. Cut from the same mold, the 1997 Châteauneuf du Pape Non Filtré may be slightly less intense, but remains a disarming black raspberry and cherry-scented and -flavored wine with medium to full body, low acidity, and pure, delicious fruit that may not possess the grip and complexity to merit a higher score, but it delivers plenty of pleasure and hedonistic appeal. Both of these Châteauneufs are undeniably hedonistic, delicious wines that score high on the pleasure meter.

This estate's wine bottle sports a new, more elegant label since proprietor Claude Pouizin is sharing winemaking responsibilities with Monsieur Vacheron. The 1995 Châteauneuf du Pape is similarly styled to the 1996, with slightly more structure. The wine possesses a dark plum/garnet color, and a sweet, Provençal herb, peppery, incenselike aroma that I found exotic. As the wine sat in the glass, aromas of ripe peaches and apricots, and jammy cherry fruit emerged. Toasty notes also made its way into this flamboyant, intensely fragrant wine. This medium-bodied Châteauneuf du Pape displays fine depth and considerable character. It should drink well for 7–8 years—at the minimum.

This estate also produces two cuvées of Côtes du Rhône. The superior cuvée is Bouquet des Garrigues. The garnet-colored, peppery 1995 displays abundant herbes de Provence, and copious quantities of fruit and spice. It is an up-front, fruity wine to drink over the next 2–3 years. For whatever reason, the similarly colored 1995 Côtes du Rhône was dried out and hollow on the midpalate.

DOMAINE LE CLOS DE CAZAUX

1996 Vacqueyras	C	87

This 100-case lot, made specifically for the American importer by proprietor Jean-Michel Vaché, is 100% Syrah. The wine exhibits a dense ruby/purple color, an explosive, berry-scented bouquet, excellent ripeness, a fleshy, soft texture, low acidity, and generous amounts of blackberry and cassis fruit. Although not complex, it is unquestionably mouth-filling and satisfying. If more complexity develops, it will merit an even higher score. This wine should age nicely for 5–6 years.

CLOS DU JONCUAS

1997 Gigondas	C	(87–90)
1996 Gigondas	C	87
1995 Gigondas	C	90+

The 1995 Gigondas had still not been bottled in the fall of 1997, but proprietor Chastan appears to have produced a blockbuster, amazingly concentrated 1995. The black inky color is followed by huge, charcoal-scented, meaty, beef blood, black raspberry/cherry flavors that are extraordinarily concentrated and pure. This dense, massive example of Gigondas is impeccably made, with outstanding purity and equilibrium. I have never tasted a wine this impressive from Clos du Joncuas. Let's hope it gets into the bottle without an oenologist's insisting on excessive fining and filtration. This could be one of the leading candidates for the wine of the vintage in this outstanding year in Gigondas.

Chastan continues to turn out impressively made, concentrated, opulent Gigondas. His spectacular 1995 has been followed by two noteworthy efforts in the more difficult 1996 and 1997 vintages. The saturated black/ruby/purple-colored 1997 Gigondas exhibits sweet, pure, jammy black raspberries and cassis in its spicy nose, opulently textured, fat, low-acid, velvety flavors, and a heady glycerin/alcoholic finish. This hedonistic, plump Gigondas should drink well for 7–8 years. The dark ruby/purple-colored 1996 Gigondas possesses more acidity, but it is well meshed with the wine's concentrated, complex, rich, black cherry and currant fruit. Medium to full bodied and pure, with pepper and framboise fruit, this structured, slightly tannic wine should be at its finest between 2001 and 2010. These are impressive wines for their vintages!

CLOS DU MONT OLIVET

1997 Châteauneuf du Pape	D	(85–87)
1996 Châteauneuf du Pape	D	88
1995 Châteauneuf du Pape	D	90

The 1996 and 1997 Châteauneuf du Pape are both very good yet forward, tasty efforts from Clos du Mont Olivet. The 1997 Châteauneuf du Pape exhibits a spicy, peppery, cherry-scented nose, a forward, evolved style, a plump, tasty midpalate, and good jammy fruit. Drink this evolved (note the ruby/garnet color), low-acid, elegant Châteauneuf over the next 4–5 years. The dark garnet-colored 1996 Châteauneuf du Pape is richer, fuller, and more generous, with surprising fat and richness in the midpalate. It is a very fine effort in this medium-weight vintage. The nose offers aromas of pepper, leather, spice, roasted herbs, and meat along with kirsch liqueurlike notes and flavors. Medium to full bodied and expansive, with a certain corpulence and lushness, this excellent Châteauneuf du Pape will be a crowd-pleaser for another 7–8 years. By the way, this 1996 performed better out of bottle than it did when I tasted it from *foudre* in 1997.

Clos du Mont Olivet's 1995 Châteauneuf du Pape reveals a deep ruby color with purple nuances. A sexy, ripe wine, it offers up aromas of kirsch, black raspberries, and pepper, along with fine glycerin and moderate tannin. It is not massive or huge, nor does it possess the rustic tannin that characterizes some years of Clos du Mont Olivet. Rather, it is lush, full bodied, forward, round, and concentrated. This delicious Châteauneuf will provide ideal drinking between 2002 and 2016.

CLOS DE L'ORATOIRE DES PAPES

1997	Châteauneuf du Pape	C	(84–86)
1996	Châteauneuf du Pape	C	87

This old, well-known estate produces modern-styled, richly fruity Châteauneuf du Pape. I am glad to see the 1996 has more substance than I have noticed in several earlier vintages where the raw materials were superior. Is the estate beginning to make more seriously endowed wines? The light 1997 Châteauneuf du Pape is a charming, framboise/pepper/kirsch-scented wine that is typical of this estate's offerings over the last 15–20 years. It is made in a mainstream, commercial manner, but I do not say that pejoratively as the wine is cleanly made, fruity, and typical of many efforts from this lighter-styled vintage. Drink it over the next 3–5 years. The 1996 Châteauneuf du Pape appears to have more to it. The color is an evolved plum/dark ruby. The nose offers up aromas of chocolate, spice cake, cedar, raspberries, and cherries. Medium bodied and soft, with excellent fruit depth, this seductive, hedonistically styled Châteauneuf du Pape should drink well for 5–6 years.

CLOS DES PAPES

1997	Châteauneuf du Pape	D	(87–89)
1996	Châteauneuf du Pape	D	89
1995	Châteauneuf du Pape	D	94

This extraordinary estate is enjoying an even higher level of quality now that proprietor Paul Avril has the full-time assistance of his son, Vincent. Most Clos des Papes require some aging as there has been a tendency over the last decade to increase the percentage of Mourvèdre (now about 20%) in the final blend.

Paul Avril, one of the stars of this appellation, performed well in the lighter-styled 1996 and 1997 vintages. Both are sexy examples with significantly more density and richness than the majority of the Châteauneuf du Papes from these two vintages. Even though the 1996 Châteauneuf du Pape requires consumption within its first 8 or so years of life, it is close to outstanding. From its exotic, gorgeously fragrant nose of pepper, crushed seashells, Provençal olives, and plum/cherry fruit, this dark garnet-colored wine is open knit, juicy, rich, fat, medium to full bodied, and expansive and succulent. It delivers its considerable quantity of fruit and spice in an easygoing, generous, precocious style. Yummy! The similarly styled 1997 Châteauneuf du Pape may be a touch lighter and shorter in the finish, although that is a difficult judgment to make at this time. The wine's deep ruby color is followed by aromas of cherry jam, intermixed with pepper, pine, and earth. In the mouth, cassis/blackberry fruit (no doubt from the Mourvèdre and Syrah components) makes an appearance. This soft, low-acid, medium-bodied, seductive offering should drink well for 5–8 years.

CLOS ST. JEAN

1995	Châteauneuf du Pape	D	87?

This is an old style, herbes de Provence, roasted pepper, olive, and meaty style of Châteauneuf du Pape with old, musty barrel smells that may or may not blow off with bottle age. The wine possesses plenty of body and guts, but it is probably too rustic and funky for many tasters. It should last for 10–12 years.

CLUSEL-ROCH

1996 Côte Rôtie	E	79
1996 Côte Rôtie Les Grandes Places	E	87

I did not taste Clusel-Roch's 1997s. The first bottle of 1996 Côte Rôtie was corked, but the second exhibited a medium ruby color, as well as a cool-year red currant and cranberry-scented nose intermixed with barrel aromas and roasted notes. Medium bodied with sappy acidity, this foursquare, one-dimensional Côte Rôtie should be consumed during its first 3–4 years of life. The 1996 Côte Rôtie Les Grandes Places is very good, possibly excellent. The color is medium ruby/plum. Sweet red currant aromas intermixed with plums and raspberries are followed by a medium- to full-bodied, deep, smoky wine with fine purity, spicy oak, and unobtrusive acid levels—particularly for a 1996. Anticipated maturity: 2001–2007.

JEAN-LUC COLOMBO

1997 Cornas La Louvée	D	(90–91+)
1996 Cornas La Louvée	D	89
1995 Cornas La Louvée	D	92
1997 Cornas Les Mejeans	D	(86–88)
1996 Cornas Les Mejeans	D	85
1997 Cornas Les Ruchets	D	(89–91)
1996 Cornas Les Ruchets	D	89
1995 Cornas Les Ruchets	D	91
1997 Cornas Les Terres Brûlées	D	(88–90)
1996 Cornas Les Terres Brûlées	D	79

Oenologist/consultant/vineyard owner, Jean-Luc Colombo, is making some of the finest Cornas produced. His wines, made in a completely different style than those of such superstars as Auguste Clape, are an intelligent blend of *barrique* and concentrated Syrah from this appellation's sun-baked hillsides. There are four cuvées offered, all packaged in a distinctive Bordeaux bottle (the only wines of the appellation not put in a Burgundy-shaped bottle). Colombo claims the three finest vintages for Cornas in the nineties are 1998, 1997, and 1991. He likes the 1997s, even though he says they are dangerously low in acidity, but the Syrah has such extract and tannin it often benefits from vintages such as 1997.

The 1997 Cornas Les Mejeans is a forward, low-acid, plush wine with uncommon accessibility. The wine exhibits a dark ruby color, a sweet nose of grilled meats, roasted herbs, and black fruits, excellent richness, and a sweet, round, surprisingly elegant palate feel. It should be drunk over the next 7–8 years. The saturated ruby/purple-colored 1997 Cornas Terres Brûlées reveals more blackberry fruit in the aromas and flavors, medium to full body, supple tannin, low acid, and a deeper, fuller, longer finish. It will benefit from 1–2 years of cellaring and keep for 12–14. The biggest, richest wines made by Jean-Luc Colombo are from his Les Ruchets and La Louvée vineyards. These hillside parcels tend to produce structured, concentrated wines that admirably soak up their oak cask aging. The 1997 Cornas Les Ruchets possesses a deep opaque ruby/purple color and a reserved, but impressively built personality with telltale cassis intermixed with licorice, minerals, and smoke. Dense and full bodied, with outstanding purity and length, the 1997 is more forward than most vintages but should spend 2–3 years in the cellar. It will keep for 12–15 years. The 1997 Cornas La Lou-vée is similarly styled, but fuller bodied, with more mineral characteristics, as well as a heavier, weightier feel in the mouth. Dense, concentrated, and powerful, with outstanding purity, it is accessible (because of the vintage's low acidity) but still a backward, formidably endowed Cornas to cellar for 3–4 years; it should keep for 15 or more.

The 1996 selections tend to be less saturated in color, with more new oak in their aromat-ics, and the vintage's higher acidity on display. In particular, I was struck by the leanness and acid personality of the 1996 Cornas Terres Brûlées. I enjoyed the softer, more commer-cial as well as friendlier style of the 1996 Cornas Les Mejeans. Both of these wines require consumption over the next 2–3 years. The saturated purple-colored, medium-bodied 1996 Cornas Les Ruchets offers spicy *pain grillé* intermixed with violets, tar, and sweet cranberry and black currant fruit. The acidity is better meshed than in the Terres Brûlées. The oak ap-pears to have sweetened Les Ruchets since I tasted it in late 1997. The finish is moderately long. Anticipated maturity: 2001–2010. The dark purple-colored 1996 Cornas La Louvée exhibits *pain grillé* intermixed with smoke, minerals, and black fruits. Unevolved, with a minty component in the background, this well-made, medium-bodied, rich, concentrated, excellent Cornas needs 3–4 years of cellaring; it should keep for 12–15 years. None of the 1996s possess the palate expansion or depth of fruit and extract found in the 1997s.

Jean-Luc Colombo has become one of the stars of Cornas. Well known as an oenologist for dozens of Rhône Valley clients, Colombo has had a positive influence in the Rhône, un-doubtedly improving the quality of many estate's wines. As for his own wines, there are usu-ally three cuvées of Cornas. In ascending order of quality they are: Les Terres Brûlées, Les Ruchets (from a specific vineyard), and La Louvée (formerly known as Cuvée JLC).

The 1995 Cornas La Louvée (formerly Cuvée JLC) is made from late-harvested Syrah grapes, aged in 100% new oak, and bottled with neither fining nor filtering. Seventy-five cases were made of this spectacular wine, which offers gobs of black fruits, a thick, unctuous texture, and a sweet, rich finish revealing well-integrated tannin. The wine possesses enough acidity to provide definition and focus. It should drink well for 2 decades. The outstanding 1995 Les Ruchets was aged in 70% new oak casks, put through a malolactic fermentation in cask, and fined but not filtered. The wine exhibits a black/purple color, followed by an excel-lent nose of wild blueberries, cassis, earth, and vanilla. Medium to full bodied, deep and rich, it is an impressive Cornas that requires 2–3 more years of cellaring; it should last for 15 years.

DOMAINE DE LA CÔTE DE L'ANGE

1997	Châteauneuf du Pape	D	(85–86)
1996	Châteauneuf du Pape	D	87
1995	Châteauneuf du Pape	D	89

Proprietor Jean-Claude Mestre fashions traditional, old-style Châteauneuf du Papes that have much in common with the wines of Pegau and Henri Bonneau. The 1997 Châteauneuf du Pape offers up an exotic nose of sausage, pepper, licorice, *garrigue,* and cherries. In the mouth, there is good fruit, medium body, and an evolved, soft, cedary, smoky, spicy style. The wine is ripe but slightly diluted. Drink it over the next 4–5 years. Exhibiting a darker plum color, the 1996 Châteauneuf du Pape reveals an intriguing nose of incense, pepper, licorice, and ripe black cherry fruit. Traditionally styled, with considerable muscle, rustic tannin, and medium to full body, this is an attractive, robust Châteauneuf to drink now and over the next 5–7 years.

The 1995 offering from Jean-Claude Mestre is not totally dissimilar from the big, block-buster style of Bonneau's Châteauneuf du Pape. Pepper, *garrigue,* truffles, and ripe, jammy black plum' and cherry fruit reluctantly emerge with coaxing from this dark ruby-colored wine. In the mouth, there are gobs of tannin, structure, and grip, but there is no hiding its fleshy, full-bodied, beef bloodlike taste. Not a Châteauneuf du Pape to sip casually, this large-scaled, traditionally styled, dense, concentrated wine needs 2–5 years of cellaring. It should keep for 15. Those who admire the wines of Henri Bonneau and Domaine de Pegau will undoubtedly appreciate this offering.

DOMAINE DES COTEAUX DES TRAVERS

1996 Côtes du Rhône	B	84
1996 Côtes du Rhône-Villages Cairanne	B	85
1996 Côtes du Rhône-Villages Rasteau	C	85
1996 Côtes du Rhône-Villages Rasteau Cuvée Prestige	C	86+

1996 is not a strong vintage in the southern Rhône, but this Rasteau vigneron has turned out four attractive wines. The light ruby-colored 1996 Côtes du Rhône possesses ripe kirsch scents in the nose, round, medium-bodied, graceful flavors, and an easygoing finish. Drink it over the next year. The light to medium ruby-colored 1996 Côtes du Rhône-Villages Cairanne reveals truffle, licorice, earth, and underripe peach and cherry fruit in its aromatic profile. The wine is denser and richer on the palate than the Côtes du Rhône cuvée, with more glycerin as well as more spice and structure. It should drink well for 1–2 years. The 1996 Côtes du Rhône-Villages Rasteau is more tightly knit and less expressive aromatically than the Cairanne. It offers attractive ripe herb and spice-tinged black cherry fruit, and a clean, spicy, tannic, and structured finish. This wine should improve for 6 more months and last for 2–3 years. Last, the 1996 Côtes du Rhône-Villages Rasteau Cuvée Prestige possesses the darkest ruby color of this quartet, spicy oak in the nose, and moderate quantities of black cherry fruit. Rich in the mouth, particularly for a 1996, this fleshy, medium-bodied, nicely structured wine reveals good levels of kirsch, pepper, and glycerin, giving it a fine rich, medium- to full-bodied finish. Drink it over the next 2–3 years.

DOMAINE CROS DE LA MURE

1996 Côtes du Rhône	B	85

Proprietor Eric Michel has fashioned an attractive Côtes du Rhône made from 50% Grenache and the balance Syrah and Mourvèdre. The wine is dark ruby-colored with purple nuances. An uncomplicated, intense, pure, blackberry nose is sweet and rich. This soft, medium-bodied, delicious Côtes du Rhône is meant to be drunk over the next 1–2 years.

DOMAINE COURBIS

1997 Cornas Champelrose	D	(83–85)
1997 Cornas Les Eyats	D	(87–88)
1997 Cornas La Saparotte	D	(88–90)

While the 1997 Cornas Champelrose possesses a dark ruby color, it is neither extracted nor rich. Medium bodied, with tar and black currant fruit, this spicy, straightforward, monolithic Cornas should be drunk during its first 5–6 years of life. The 1997 Cornas Les Eyats is a more serious effort. This ruby/purple-colored wine exhibits superb ripeness, medium to full body, excellent extraction of fruit, and copious quantities of mouth-searing tannin. Surprisingly, this wine has more acidity than I expected given the vintage. It will be at its finest between 2003 and 2012. The top wine of this trio is the 1997 Cornas La Sabarotte. It boasts an old vine intensity and midpalate, as well as gobs of sweet plum, black raspberry, and currant fruit, and notes of toasty new oak. I suspect this cuvée sees more new barrels than its two siblings. The wine is medium to full bodied, pure, moderately tannic, and impressively long. Anticipated maturity: 2003–2014.

YVES CUILLERON

1997	Condrieu Les Chaillets	E	92
1995	Condrieu Les Chaillets Vieilles Vignes	E	96
1995	Condrieu La Côte	E	90
1995	Condrieu Les Eguets Vendange Tardive	E	90+
1997	Condrieu La Petite Côte	E	89
1997	Côte Rôtie Coteau de Bastenon	EE/EEE	(85–86)
1996	Côte Rôtie Coteau de Bastenon	EE/EEE	74
1997	St.-Joseph Coteau St.-Pierre	D/E	90
1997	St.-Joseph Lyseras	D/E	90
1997	St.-Joseph Cuvée Prestige l'Amarybelle	D/E	(88–89)
1996	St.-Joseph Cuvée Prestige l'Amarybelle	D/E	82
1997	St.-Joseph Cuvée Prestige Le Lombarde	D/E	89
1997	St.-Joseph Les Serines	D/E	(90–92)
1996	St.-Joseph Les Serines	D/E	86

Yves Cuilleron, one of the northern Rhône's most brilliant white-winemakers, seems to be capturing some of his white wine magic with his newest red wine cuvées, particularly those from St.-Joseph. His Côte Rôtie still lags behind the quality of the other wines.

Cuilleron's 1997 whites are fat, low-acid wines that will provide sumptuous drinking provided they are consumed over the next several years. There is no denying their rich, ostentatious styles. The 1997 Condrieu La Petite Côte (13.5% alcohol) is an excellent, richly fragrant, perfumed, complex Viognier with honeysuckle and orange marmalade notes followed by a medium- to full-bodied personality. This delicious, open-knit, accessible Condrieu should be enjoyed over the next 1–2 years. Even more profound is the 1997 Condrieu Les Chaillets (also 13.5% alcohol). This wine possesses more definition, a pronounced mineral character, and lavish quantities of honeysuckle, apricot/peach, and tropical fruit. A superb Condrieu, it displays full body, outstanding purity, and a luscious mouth-feel. It offers everything one could want in a great Condrieu. However, it should be consumed over the next 1–2 years.

Cuilleron has also turned out three gorgeous whites from St.-Joseph. He works mainly with the Marsanne grape, although his cuvée from the Coteau St.-Pierre is 100% Roussanne! The 1997 St.-Joseph Lyseras exhibits a honeyed lemony/citrusy nose, copious quantities of ripe fruit, medium to full body, and low acidity. It is meant to be drunk now and over the next 12–18 months. The 1997 St.-Joseph Cuvée Prestige Le Lombarde offers *pain grillé* intermixed with tropical fruit, especially honeyed citrus, pineapple, and mango. It is a fullbodied, low-acid, exuberantly fruity, fresh wine to drink over the near term. The 1997 St.-Joseph Coteau St.-Pierre (100% Roussanne) reveals spicy new oak intermixed with honeyed/rose petal liqueurlike richness, extremely full body, copious quantities of cherry fruit, an unctuous texture, and a long, layered, dry finish. It is a sensational Roussanne from St.-Joseph that needs to be drunk over the next several years.

Among the reds, I thought Cuilleron's 1997 cuvées of St.-Joseph were the finest he has yet made. The 1997 St.-Joseph Cuvée Prestige l'Amarybelle exhibits a saturated purple color, and intense, jammy cassis aromas intermixed with *pain grillé*. Medium bodied, with low acidity, excellent purity, and a gutsy, exuberant richness, this wine should drink well for 7–8 years. The brilliant, opaque purple-colored 1997 St.-Joseph Les Serines boasts a dazzling, multilayered texture, ripe, concentrated, black cherry and cassis fruit, impeccable purity and balance, and a long, sweet, ripe finish. It should drink well for a decade. Both the 1996 St.-Joseph Cuvée Prestige l'Amarybelle and 1996 St.-Joseph Les Serines possess deep ruby colors, but are much crisper, with higher acidity, and more green pepper and red fruits than the black fruit characteristics of the 1997s. The 1996 l'Amarybelle was a bit oaky and short and lean in the finish. The 1996 Les Serines possesses more fruit, as well as spicy oak and green pepper, but it is a tasty, medium-bodied, elegant wine that should drink well for 7–8 years.

The 1996 Côte Rôtie Coteau de Bastenon is vegetal, with annoyingly high acidity, and an excessive green pepper/olive character. It is far inferior to the 1997 Côte Rôtie Coteau de Bastenon, which offers an impressively saturated purple color, a monolithic personality but riper fruit without the off-putting vegetal influence. It should drink well for a decade, but neither of these wines compares favorably with Cuilleron's efforts in St.-Joseph.

The profound 1995 Condrieu Les Chaillets Vieilles Vignes is about as remarkable as Condrieu can be. The huge, fruit cocktail, spring flower garden, apricot/peach, and mineral-scented nose is both ostentatious and fabulously compelling. This wine tastes like concentrated incense, with unbelievable thickness and richness, yet fine underlying structure. It is a sensational effort. While I am sure some observers will claim it can be cellared for 5 or more years, I would opt for drinking it over the next 2–3 years. The 1995 Condrieu La Côte is a textbook Condrieu, offering up honeyed peach/apricot aromas, exotic, rich, low-acid, plump flavors with a chewy texture, and admirable intensity and purity in the long, layered finish. It is a Condrieu to drink over the next 1–2 years. The 1995 Condrieu Les Eguets Vendange Tardive had just been bottled, and unfortunately, its personality has yet to emerge. Undoubtedly, it should be an outstanding effort given its superconcentrated, unctuous texture, and medium sweet style. However, it is not yet delineated. While impressively rich and full on the palate, this wine requires another 6–12 months of bottle age to take on more personality.

CUVÉE DU BOISDAUPHIN

1995 Châteauneuf du Pape	D 91

Pierre Jacumin's small estate produces one of my favorite Châteauneuf du Papes. Because he had sold his entire production as soon as it was bottled, he did not have a single bottle of his 1995 left for me to taste on my most recent trip. Consequently, the following tasting notes, from my book on the Rhône Valley, are reprinted here in lieu of a new review. The outstanding 1995 Châteauneuf du Pape exhibits an opaque ruby/purple color, accompanied by a sweet, heady nose of cedar, Provençal herbs, black and red fruits, and earth. With layers of ripe, chewy fruit, this rich, sumptuously textured yet structured, full-bodied Châteauneuf is a beauty. It will be flattering to drink young, yet will age impeccably for 12–15 years.

CUVÉE DU VATICAN

1995 Châteauneuf du Pape	D 90
1995 Côtes du Rhône	A 86

If my memory is correct, the first case of Châteauneuf du Pape I ever purchased was the 1970 Cuvée du Vatican (one bottle remains in my cellar). I am impressed by how well the 1995 Châteauneuf du Pape has turned out. It may be the finest wine Felicien Diffonty has produced in several decades, and my score may turn out to be conservative. This is a big, old-styled, classic, blockbuster Châteauneuf du Pape with a saturated garnet/plum color, a gorgeous display of roasted herbes de Provence, licorice, kirsch, truffles, and earth. Explosive on the palate, with full body, mouth-coating glycerin, and copious quantities of jammy fruit that cascade down the gullet with no hard edges, this is a luscious, flamboyant wine with a terrific personality. Anticipated maturity: now–2012.

For considerably less money, readers can purchase a deep, robust, exuberant 1995 Côtes du Rhône. Cut from the same cloth as the Châteauneuf du Pape, it is an attractive, supple, richly fruity wine. Drink it over the next 2–3 years.

DELAS FRÈRES

1995	Côtes du Rhône St. Esprit	A	78
1995	Crozes-Hermitage Les Launes	D	79
1995	Hermitage Cuvée Marquise de la Tourette	EE/EEE	85
1995	Viognier VDP de la Drôme	A	82
1995	Cornas Chante Perdrix	D	83?
1995	Côtes du Rhône St. Esprit	A	75
1995	Côtes du Ventoux Val Muzols	A	74
1995	Merlot VDP d'Oc	A	85

Noticeable improvements under the new ownership of the Louis Roederer firm will be especially dramatic with the 1997 and 1998 vintages, made under the brilliant administration of their new oenologist, Jacques Grange.

The 1995 Viognier VDP de la Drôme possesses some honeysuckle/apricot fruit, but its finish is acidic and short. The most interesting white wine is the very good 1995 Hermitage Cuvée Marquise de la Tourette. The light to medium straw color is followed by aromas of white flowers, honey, and a touch of *pain grillé* in the background. It is a dense, medium- to full-bodied wine with good chewiness and texture. The wine's low acidity and fleshy, up-front appeal should win friends over the next 4–5 years. The other two white wines, the Côtes du Rhône and Crozes-Hermitage were very bland and one dimensional.

Among the red wines, I was disappointed with the high acidity, leanness, and general lack of fruit and fat in the 1995 Côte du Ventoux and 1995 Côte du Rhône. The dark ruby-colored 1995 Merlot VDP d'Oc exhibits an attractive nose of sweet berry fruit, round, medium-bodied, plump flavors, and good purity and ripeness. This is a pleasant, nicely endowed wine to drink over the next several years. The 1995 Cornas Chante Perdrix reveals a pronounced pungent, earthy, peppery, black currant-scented nose, medium body, high tannin, good purity, but a certain austerity and leanness. Will the fruit dry out?

EDMUND & DAVID DUCLAUX

1997	Côte Rôtie	D	(85–86)
1996	Côte Rôtie	D	85

Duclaux's elegant, open-knit, easygoing style is displayed in both these offerings. The 1997 Côte Rôtie exhibits a lovely cherry, kirsch, and roasted herb-scented nose, and low-acid, fleshy, round, medium-bodied, moderately concentrated flavors. It will provide delicious drinking young and last for 5–7 years. The 1996 Côte Rôtie reveals lower acidity than many of its peers and thus can be drunk now and over the next 4–5 years. Although not concentrated, it offers an attractive, straightforward nose of wood spice, cherry liqueur, and herbs, with a touch of earth in the background. This tasty, medium-bodied, reasonably well endowed wine is soft for a 1996, and easy to drink and understand. It should be consumed over the next 5–6 years.

ERIC ET JOEL DURAND

1997 Cornas	D	(87–88)
1996 Cornas	D	87

Two fine efforts, the Durands' 1997 Cornas displays a dark ruby/purple color, an excellent floral, tar, and blackberry-scented nose, rich, medium- to full-bodied flavors, with low acidity, and sweet tannin. This will be a Cornas to drink early, but it has the necessary richness to keep 10–12 years. The 1996 Cornas reveals a less saturated, medium ruby color, pure black fruits in the nose, toasty new oak, an elegant, stylish personality, higher acidity, and a Burgundian-like black cherry and cassis aromas and flavors. Drink it over the next decade.

DOMAINE DES ENTREFAUX

1996 Crozes-Hermitage	B	86

Black raspberry, gamey, and licorice aromas emerge from this medium-bodied, lighter-styled, soft Crozes-Hermitage. Drink this fragrant, well-made wine over the next 2–3 years.

PHILIPPE FAURY

1997 Condrieu Cuvée Classique	E	87
1997 Condrieu Cuvée Prestige	E	89
1997 St.-Joseph	C	86

Philippe Faury produces fine whites but appears to be less sure with his reds (I did not enjoy his 1996 Côte Rôtie or 1996 St.-Joseph red, both vegetal, lean, attenuated wines). The excellent 1997 Condrieu Cuvée Classique exhibits mineral, spicy, floral, honeyed notes, medium body, and fine flesh and fruit. The 1997 Condrieu Cuvée Prestige is richer and more unctuously textured, with higher alcohol, and is a more complete wine both aromatically and on the palate. For good value, the 1997 St.-Joseph offers orange peel, citrusy, and flintylike aromas and flavors, medium body, and excellent purity. All three of these wines should be consumed over the next 1–2 years.

DOMAINE DE FERRAND

1997 Châteauneuf du Pape	D	(87–88+)
1996 Châteauneuf du Pape	D	(86–89?)
1995 Châteauneuf du Pape	D	86

I am impressed with the efforts made by Philippe Bravay. The 1996 Châteauneuf du Pape was one of the few wines of this vintage not yet in bottle when I visited the region in the fall of 1998. It possesses a dense ruby color, and a sweet nose of black cherries macerated in brandy, with mushroomy notes in the background. This is one of the more concentrated wines of the vintage, but notes of wet dog and a mushroomy character are cause for concern. It could be very good to excellent given its richness, but it will need to be retasted after bottling. The alcohol is a lofty 14.5%. The dark plum-colored 1997 Châteauneuf du Pape exhibits a sweet blackberry and raspberry-scented nose, with earth, truffles, and spice. Lighter than the 1996, this is a heady, hedonistic, well-made wine with an expansive finish.

Domaine de Ferrand may be an estate worth watching. The young vigneron, Philippe Bravay, has begun to estate-bottle the production from this 5 hectare (12+ acres) estate located in the northern sector of Châteauneuf du Pape, in what is known as the Quartier de Grès. Previously, the wines were sold to the *négociant* Bernard. The 1996 vintage is the first harvest to be controlled completely by the estate. Ferrand's 1996 Châteauneuf du Pape exhibits one of the most saturated black/purple colors of any wine of the vintage, with a surprising liqueurlike, cassis, black raspberry intensity that is atypical for such a lighter-styled vintage. The nose was somewhat reduced, suggesting the wine needed racking, but this could be an excellent, impressive wine. The dark ruby-colored 1995 Châteauneuf du Pape reveals a textbook spicy, peppery, herbes de Provence nose with sweet, jammy black cherry fruit. The wine is round, generous, fruity, and ideal for drinking over the next 5–6 years.

DOMAINE FONT DE MICHELLE

1997 Châteauneuf du Pape Cuvée Tradition	D	(86–87)
1996 Châteauneuf du Pape Cuvée Tradition	D	86
1995 Châteauneuf du Pape Cuvée Tradition	D	89
1997 Châteauneuf du Pape Cuvée Tradition (White)	D	87
1997 Châteauneuf du Pape Cuvée Étienne Gonnet	E	(87–89)
1996 Châteauneuf du Pape Cuvée Étienne Gonnet	E	89
1995 Châteauneuf du Pape Cuvée Étienne Gonnet	E	92
1997 Châteauneuf du Pape Cuvée Étienne Gonnet (White)	E	89
1997 Côtes du Rhône (100% Viognier)	C	87

I had a chance to taste through the brothers Gonnets' 1998 cuvées when I visited the estate in the fall of 1998. They claim the 1998s will possess the "concentration of 1990" and the "freshness and structure of 1978," and they are indeed impressive wines, but we will have to wait a year for the red wines. For now, there are attractive, supple, richly fruity 1997s and 1996s that beg for consumer attention. This is one of the best-run estates in Châteauneuf du Pape, making modern-styled, concentrated, character-filled wines. A terrific insider's wine is the Côtes du Rhône, made from a vineyard outside Châteauneuf du Pape planted with 100% Viognier. The 1997 Côtes du Rhône (Viognier) is a tasty, rich, fruity, honeysuckle-dominated wine with good flesh and purity. It should drink well for a year. The 1997 Châteauneuf du Pape Cuvée Tradition white possesses good fat, low acidity, excellent ripeness, and an intriguing nose of citrus and white flowers. It, too, should be drunk over the next year. More interesting is the 1997 Châteauneuf du Pape Cuvée Étienne Gonnet white. Made from 50% Roussanne, 25% Clairette, and 25% Grenache Blanc, this partially barrel-fermented wine is excellent. It possesses deep concentration of fruit, full body, and enough acidity to provide definition and uplift. Consume it over the next 2–3 years.

With respect to the red wines, Michel Gonnet says that the 1997 vintage was "very sanitary," but it was "difficult to achieve full maturity." The 1997 Châteauneuf du Pape Cuvée Tradition red (70% Grenache, 10% Syrah, 10% Cinsault, and 10% various grapes) exhibits a dark ruby color, and a big, peppery, Provençal nose of *garrigue* and olives. Tasty, with excellent ripeness, a soft, easygoing style, and a fleshy finish, it is ideal for drinking over the next 6–7 years. The 1997 Châteauneuf du Pape Cuvée Étienne Gonnet red (70% Grenache, 15% Syrah, and 15% Cinsault from the estate's oldest vines) is fuller bodied, with more ripeness, and offering more volume and concentration on the palate. This richly fruity 1997 appears closer in quality to the Cuvée Tradition than in most years. Drink it over the next 7–8 years.

The 1996 Châteauneuf du Pape Cuvée Tradition red is an elegant, medium-bodied, cherry-scented and -flavored wine with little concentration but sweet fruit, a touch of green peppers and olives, and a round, pleasant finish. It should drink well for 3–4 years. The dark ruby/purple-colored 1996 Châteauneuf du Pape Cuvée Étienne Gonnet red offers an attractive nose of licorice, black cherries, cassis, and cedar. With excellent richness, medium body, and fine purity, this lush, soft wine should provide lovely drinking over the next 6–7 years.

I had a chance to retaste the two cuvées of 1995, and both are well worth buying. The 1995 Châteauneuf du Pape Cuvée Tradition and 1995 Châteauneuf du Pape Cuvée Étienne Gonnet are impressively built, concentrated efforts that should drink well for 10–15 years. The 1995 Châteauneuf du Pape Cuvée Tradition offers a dark, plum/purple color. It shares with the 1996 a *garrigue* (Provençal herbs), spice box, tangy iodine, salty, peppery character, in addition to sweeter, richer fruit, and more glycerin. The 1995 also finishes with more alcoholic clout and extract. It is a forward, sexy style of Provençal red wine to drink over the next 7–8 years. The 1995 Châteauneuf du Pape Cuvée Étienne Gonnet reveals thrilling intensity. Aromatically, it offers up subdued aromas of black cherries, olives, *pain grillé*, and licorice. Unevolved and full bodied, with powerful, concentrated flavors, copious amounts of glycerin (note the thick legs that slowly ooze down the inside of the glass), outstanding concentration, and moderate tannin in the powerful finish, this wine requires several years of cellaring; drink it between 2000 and 2013.

DOMAINE DE FONTAVIN

1996	Châteauneuf du Pape	C	87
1997	Gigondas	C	(86–87)
1996	Gigondas	C	86
1996	Gigondas Cuvée Combe Sauvage	D	89
1995	Gigondas Cuvée Combe Sauvage	D	88

Proprietors Michel and Martine Schouvet have turned in very good efforts in these lighter vintages. The excellent 1996 Châteauneuf du Pape offers aromas of black cherries intermixed with cassis and smoke. A fruit-driven wine, with medium body, good purity, and a soft, gentle texture, it will drink well for 5–6 years. The evolved dark plum-colored 1997 Gigondas exhibits a sweet kirsch-scented nose with pepper and spice. This soft, sexy, evolved wine requires consumption over the next 4–5 years. The 1996 Gigondas reveals an unusually evolved garnet color, a cedary, strawberry, earthy-scented nose, sweet, medium-bodied, jammy flavors, and a round finish. It is a straightforward, tasty Gigondas to drink over the next 3–4 years.

Domaine de Fontavin's 1996 Gigondas Cuvée Combe Sauvage is a winner. The color is a dark ruby/purple, and the wine possesses a sweet inner core of ripe fruit suggestive of old vines and/or low yields. The dense purple color is followed by a medium- to full-bodied wine with sweet kirsch and framboiselike fruit intertwined with pepper, spice, and licorice. This purely made, dense, chewy Gigondas should age well for a decade, although it will be accessible young.

The 1995 Gigondas Cuvée Combe Sauvage is an intensely fragrant wine with loads of peppery spice, along with jammy cherry, kirsch, and blackberry flavors. Broadly flavored and expansive, with full body, a touch of *pain grillé*, and a generous palate, this is a soft, accessible yet well-endowed Gigondas to drink over the next 8–10 years.

CHÂTEAU FORTIA

1997	Châteauneuf du Pape	D	(87–88)
1996	Châteauneuf du Pape	D	88
1995	Châteauneuf du Pape	D	91

These wines are being made by the well-known Cornas oenologist, Jean-Luc Colombo. Because of pre-bottling tastings, I expected the 1996 Châteauneuf du Pape to be better. It is unquestionably a fine Fortia. This is one of the few Châteauneuf du Papes that contains a significant percentage of Syrah (usually about 40%). The 1996 exhibits a deep ruby color, as well as a sweet, black raspberry, and blackberry-scented nose with herb and spice notes. The wine possesses fine body and purity, in addition to moderate tannin in the finish. It will benefit from 1–2 years of cellaring and keep for a decade. Jean-Luc Colombo was unhappy with the Syrah in 1997, thus the 1997 Châteauneuf du Pape's final blend is 70% Grenache, 15% Mourvèdre, and 15% Syrah. The wine is already evolved and delicious. The color is a healthy dark ruby, and the wine reveals sweet black fruits in the nose, along with prune and blackberry scents. Round, with rich fruit, good spice, and medium body, its low acidity suggests it should be drunk over the next 5–6 years.

The 1994 was outstanding and the 1995 appears to be sensational. The 1995 Châteauneuf du Pape continues to put on weight and is even better than I predicted from barrel. The wine boasts a dense purple color, followed by a terrific set of aromatics (cassis and prunes). This concentrated, medium-bodied, broadly textured, low-acid, sexy wine has a finish that lasts for 25 seconds. It is deeper than the 1996, and possibly longer-lived because it carries more weight and length. Anticipated maturity: 1999–2015.

DOMAINE DE GACHON (PASCAL PERRIER)

1997 St.-Joseph	D	(89–91)
1996 St.-Joseph	D	90

Readers looking for spectacularly rich, brilliantly made wines from one of the less expensive northern Rhône appellations should check out the work Pascal Perrier is doing. These cuvées were put together by the American importer, so the tasting notes that follow relate only to those wines sold in the United States. The 1996 St.-Joseph exhibits an opaque ruby/purple color, and a knockout nose of nearly overripe prunes, black raspberries, and cherries. Made from 20-year-old vines and modest yields of 2 tons of fruit per acre, this wine is rich and full bodied, with tons of cassis fruit intermixed with pepper, and an almost vinous, sappy, refreshing yet not intrusive acidity. Drink this chewy, full-bodied Syrah now and over the next 7–8 years. The 1997 St.-Joseph has the potential to be even more explosive given its lower acidity and lusher, more flamboyant personality. Fifty percent of this cuvée is aged in new oak casks and is then blended with the balance, which has been aged in *cuve* (blend). It boasts a saturated ruby/purple color, as well as a sumptuous nose of Asian spices, black currants, blackberries, and toasty vanillin. Explosively rich, full bodied, and savory, with low acidity, this chewy, tasty, intense St.-Joseph can be drunk now as well as over the next 7–8 years. Excellent value.

DOMAINE DU GALET DES PAPES

1997 Châteauneuf du Pape Cuvée Tradition	D	(85–86)
1996 Châteauneuf du Pape Cuvée Tradition	D	87
1995 Châteauneuf du Pape Cuvée Tradition	D	87
1997 Châteauneuf du Pape Vieilles Vignes	E	(87–88)
1996 Châteauneuf du Pape Vieilles Vignes	E	88
1995 Châteauneuf du Pape Vieilles Vignes	E	90

Jean-Luc Mayard runs one of the finest estates in Châteauneuf du Pape. A modestly sized property of just over 31 acres, the wines are a synthesis in style between the old, traditionally made examples, and the more modern fruit-driven Châteauneufs. The 1997 Châteauneuf du Pape Cuvée Tradition exhibits an evolved medium plum color, and soft, lush, plum, dried cherry fruit intermixed with cedar, fruitcake, and spice aromas. Medium bodied, round, and forward, it should be consumed over the next 3–4 years. The 1997 Châteauneuf du Pape Vieilles Vignes (made from 60–100-year-old vines) reveals a deeper plum/ruby color, as well as more depth, glycerin, and sweetness, and peppery spice inter-mixed with blackberries, cherries, and minerals. It is an excellent, medium-bodied, forward, well-made example that will drink well upon release and will keep well for 7–8 years.

The excellent 1996 Châteauneuf du Pape Cuvée Tradition boasts a dark plum color, sweet, jammy cherry fruit, explosive ripeness on the palate, and a rich, nicely textured, low-acid finish. Drink it over the next 6–7 years. The dark ruby-colored 1996 Châteauneuf du Pape Vieilles Vignes is holding more in reserve. It reveals fine extract, and a spicy, cedary, cinna-mon, black cherrylike personality, but the aromatics have not yet fully emerged. While this offering possesses medium to full body, excellent depth, and good length, it is atypical for the vintage as it will benefit from 1–2 years of bottle age. Moreover, it will keep for 10–12 years.

The medium dark ruby-colored 1995 Châteauneuf du Pape Cuvée Tradition offers a fra-grant aromatic profile consisting of jammy cherries, smoke, Asian spices, and pepper. Fruity and round, with a kirsch liqueurlike flavor, this medium-bodied, generously endowed, cor-pulently styled Châteauneuf should drink well for 7–8 years, possibly longer. The 1995 Châteauneuf du Pape Vieilles Vignes exhibits a deep, dark plum color, a spicy, smoky, black cherry, raspberry, and *garrigue*-scented nose, explosive richness in the mouth, with copious quantities of spicy pepper, jammy red and black fruits, and abundant glycerin. This is a lay-ered, multidimensional, expansively flavored, sexy Châteauneuf du Pape. It can be drunk now and over the next 10–12 years.

YVES GANGLOFF

1996 Côte Rôtie	D 86
1996 Côte Rôtie La Barbarine	E 87

Sadly, the passionate producer Yves Gangloff owns only 5 acres of vines, located in Côte Rôtie and Condrieu. In 1996 he fashioned two very good Côte Rôties. The dark ruby-colored 1996 Côte Rôtie offers up aromas of black tea, coffee, pepper, spicy oak, and cherry fruit. It is a sexy, spicy, open-knit Côte Rôtie with slightly tart acidity but good freshness and ripeness, as well as a spice-driven, intriguing style. It should drink well for 7–10 years. The 1996 Côte Rôtie La Barbarine exhibits a dark garnet color, and an attractive nose of Provençal olives intermixed with cherry jam, smoky barbeque, and *pain grillé* scents. Ripe, dense, and spice driven, with noticeable new oak, this medium-bodied, tightly knit, well-structured and concentrated Côte Rôtie will be at its finest between 2001 and 2012.

CHÂTEAU DE LA GARDINE

1997 Châteauneuf du Pape Cuvée Tradition	D	(85–86)
1996 Châteauneuf du Pape Cuvée Tradition	D	86
1995 Châteauneuf du Pape Cuvée Tradition	D	88
1996 Châteauneuf du Pape Cuvée des Générations	E	88+
1995 Châteauneuf du Pape Cuvée des Générations	E	92

In both the 1996 and 1997 vintages, the Châteauneuf du Pape Cuvée Tradition is a dark ruby-colored wine with medium body, and attractive cassis fruit. The 1997 reveals more earth, cherry, and peppery fruit than the 1996. Both are soft, fruity wines meant for near-term consumption—over the next 3–5 years. In contrast, the opaque-colored, slightly inter-nationally styled 1996 Châteauneuf du Pape Cuvée des Générations exhibits toasty new oak and plenty of black currant fruit. The wine is surprisingly powerful and structured for a 1996, as well as dense and backward. This intense, impressively endowed Châteauneuf needs several years of cellaring. Anticipated maturity: 2001–2012.

The Brunel family has been making terrific Châteauneuf du Pape over the last decade, and both 1995 cuvées are very strong efforts. The 1995 Châteauneuf du Pape Cuvée Tradi-tion exhibits an impressively saturated dark purple color, and a classic, sweet nose of cassis, black cherries, truffles, olives, and pepper. Medium to full bodied, with considerable power and richness, this wine has shed some of its high tannin, and appears to be even better than I thought last year. This powerful, medium- to full-bodied, impressive Châteauneuf du Pape should be at its best between 1999 and 2010. The opaque purple-colored 1995 Châteauneuf du Pape Cuvée des Générations could, aromatically speaking, pass for a top first- or second-growth Médoc. Lead pencil, *pain grillé,* and cassis aromas jump from the glass. With airing more jammy black cherry and pepper notes emerge. The wine is fabulously rich and full bodied, and intentionally made in an international style that downplays the typicity of the appellation. This profound, layered wine possesses awesome richness and length, as well as 20+ years of aging potential. Anticipated maturity: 2000–2020.

DOMAINE DE LA GARRIGUE

1995 Gigondas	C	88+

For some reason, the Bernard family, which also owns the best restaurant in Gigondas, Les Florets (which I highly recommend), rarely want to include their wines in comparative tast-ings, but every time I have had one, I have marked it extremely well. The 1995 Domaine de la Garrigue's Gigondas, a classic powerhouse, reveals the herbes de Provence/earthy concoc-tion that the French call *garrigue.* Throw in copious quantities of black cherries, kirsch, olives, and truffles, and the result is a forceful, rich, full-bodied wine with a tannic finish. This muscular, large-scaled Gigondas could merit an outstanding score with another 2–3 years of cellaring. The 1995 Gigondas should be cellared for 3–5 years and drunk over the following 10–12.

JEAN-MICHEL GÉRIN

1995 Côte Rôtie Champin Junior	D	88
1997 Côte Rôtie Champin Le Seigneur	D	(87–90)
1996 Côte Rôtie Champin Le Seigneur	D	86?
1995 Côte Rôtie Champin Le Seigneur	D	86
1997 Côte Rôtie Les Grandes Places	EE	(90–91)
1996 Côte Rôtie Les Grandes Places	EE	90
1995 Côte Rôtie Les Grandes Places	EE	90
1997 Côte Rôtie La Landonne	EE	(90–93)
1996 Côte Rôtie La Landonne	EE	88+

In addition to these Côte Rôties, I also tasted Jean-Michel Gérin's Condrieu, but I have yet to find a vintage I have liked. It is simply too oaky for such a perfumed, fruit-driven varietal. However, Gérin is producing superb Côte Rôties, and his 1997s are extremely promising.

In contrast to the 1997s, Gérin's 1996s possess high acidity. The 1996 Côte Rôtie Champin Le Seigneur displays a dark ruby color, and an unevolved smoky, roasted nose. It is medium bodied, with attractive berry fruit, but the finish quickly becomes attenuated and compressed because of the wine's tart acidity. I am not sure the acidity will ever mesh fully with the other components. The 1996 Côte Rôtie La Landonne's deep ruby color is followed by a moderately intense nose of roasted herbs, black raspberry fruit, and toasty new oak. There is some acidity, but this example possesses more concentration and fruit, thus the acid is more tolerable. Nevertheless, it is worrisome for a wine to be this tangy and angular. More bottle age should result in a softer, more expansive fruitiness. Anticipated maturity:

2002–2010. The most concentrated and richest of these 1996s is the Côte Rôtie Les Grandes Places. The wine exhibits a dark ruby color with purple nuances, and plenty of toasty *pain grillé* notes intermixed with blackberry and raspberry fruit. The wine is medium to full bodied and fleshy, with good acidity, but it is tannin that gives a wine structure and grip as opposed to acidity. Anticipated maturity: now–2012.

Gérin produced super 1997s. Even the 1997 Côte Rôtie Champin Le Seigneur may merit an outstanding score. It is a low-acid, sexy, voluptuously textured wine with tons of smoky new oak, gobs of sweet black cherry and blackberry fruit, a sweet, rich, chewy attack, and a full-bodied mouth-feel. The display of fruit and wood is almost garish in this immensely enjoyable, hedonistic Côte Rôtie. Anticipated maturity: now–2007. The 1997 Côte Rôtie La Landonne boasts a saturated black/purple color, as well as seductive, sweet oak in the aromas that, with airing, becomes increasingly intermixed with plums, blackberries, licorice, and bacon fat. Surprisingly silky and more seductive than I would have expected from this Côte Brune vineyard, this rich, low-acid, concentrated Côte Rôtie should prove to be a head turner. Anticipated maturity: now–2012. The splendid 1997 Côte Rôtie Les Grandes Places reveals an impressively saturated opaque purple color. The nose offers up gorgeous quantities of superripe black raspberries, blackberries, toasty oak, smoke, and *pain grillé*. Expansive and full bodied, with fabulous concentration, outstanding purity, and low acidity, this is a hedonistic, lush, heady, decadently styled Côte Rôtie to consume over the next 12–15+ years.

Gérin is undoubtedly one of Côte Rôtie's finest winemakers, having produced a succession of very good vintages. Gérin produced two excellent and one outstanding 1995. The 1995 Côte Rôtie Champin Le Seigneur is a lavishly oaked, spicy, deep ruby-colored Côte Rôtie with copious quantities of black raspberry and cassis fruit intermingled with toasty components. The wine is medium bodied, accessible, and already performing well. Consume it over the next 8–10 years. The 1995 Côte Rôtie Champin Junior is not dissimilar from the Champin Le Seigneur. With slightly more acidity, it is a medium-bodied, richly fruity, generously wooded, open-knit, and attractive Côte Rôtie. The wine is purely made, with plenty of peppery black fruits to go along with its overt toasty vanillin character. It will age well for 10–12 years. The superb 1995 Côte Rôtie Les Grandes Places boasts a dense black/ruby/purple color, and a gorgeously fragrant nose of jammy cassis, intermixed with smoky, toasty oak, and layers of ripe, concentrated black fruit (primarily black raspberries and cassis). This medium-bodied, concentrated Côte Rôtie has not lost its sense of elegance and overall balance. Anticipated maturity: now–2015.

DOMAINE LES GOUBERT

1995 Gigondas Cuvée Classique	D	90
1995 Gigondas Cuvée Florence	D	92

Jean-Pierre Cartier, who did so much to bring attention to the high-quality wines of Gigondas in the eighties, seemed to slump at the end of that decade and the beginning of the nineties, but he has made a strong comeback with his current releases. Cartier produces more wines than just Gigondas, turning out one of the finest Viogniers of the southern Rhône, in addition to making very good wines in Beaumes de Venise and Sablet. His top wine is the Gigondas Cuvée Florence, a wine made from a selection of the best lots, and named after his fiery-haired daughter.

Both 1995 cuvées are outstanding wines. The 1995 Gigondas Cuvée Classique is one of the top regular cuvées Cartier has produced since the mid-eighties. It displays a dark ruby/purple color, as well as a wonderfully sweet nose of blackberries, kirsch, and floral scents. The wine is medium to full bodied, powerful, rich, and beautifully silky and accessible. It will drink well when released later this year and age well for 10–12 years. The superb

1995 Gigondas Cuvée Florence boasts a blockbuster nose of *pain grillé*, violets, flowers, blackberries, and kirsch. Full bodied, superconcentrated, extremely pure and unevolved, this opaque purple-colored wine is just hinting at its overall potential. The wine possesses brilliant balance, sweet tannin, enough acidity to provide vibrancy and uplift, and a finish that lasts for 30+ seconds. There is some tannin to be resolved, but this large-scaled, beautiful Cuvée Florence is the finest Jean-Pierre Cartier has made since his sensational 1985 (which I last drank in July 1997, and still rated it 91 points). The 1995 should be at its best between 2001 and 2017.

DOMAINE DU GOUR DE CHAULE* * *

1995 Gigondas	C	88

Proprietor Madame Bonfils owns 25 acres in Gigondas. Her 1995 is a medium- to full-bodied, generous, warm, concentrated style of Gigondas with an evolved medium plum color, good acidity, and loads of sweet, dusty, black cherry fruit intermingled with peppery, herbes de Provence aromas. A spice- and fruit-driven wine, this lusty Gigondas will drink well young, yet age nicely for a decade.

ALAIN GRAILLOT

1997 Crozes-Hermitage	C	(85–87)
1996 Crozes-Hermitage	C	84
1997 Crozes-Hermitage (White)	C	87
1996 Crozes-Hermitage La Guiraude	D	86
1997 Hermitage	D	(83–85)
1996 Hermitage	D	85
1997 St.-Joseph	C	86

One of my favorite Crozes-Hermitage producers has turned out lighter, more herbaceously styled wines in both the 1996 and 1997 vintages. The deep ruby/purple-colored 1997 Crozes-Hermitage possesses more up-front fruit, and is more appealing, with less noticeable acidity. It offers an attractive black cherry/spicy component with subtle toasty new oak. It should turn out to be a good midweight Crozes to drink during its first 3–4 years of life. Readers should note that because of the lightness of the vintage, there will be no Crozes-Hermitage La Guiraude produced in 1997. The 1996 Crozes-Hermitage exhibits a deep ruby color, and a smoky, dried herb, and spicy-scented nose that is slightly green. In the mouth, the wine is medium bodied, with moderate tannin, tangy, crisp acidity, a green pepper character, and an attenuated, lean finish. I tasted this wine twice, but could not work up much enthusiasm. Slightly better, but still revealing the herbaceous green pepper and high acidity of the vintage is the 1996 Crozes-Hermitage La Guiraude. This offering reveals tangy acidity and a pinched finish, but an attractive dark ruby/purple color, and smoky, red currant and cassis aromas intermixed with notes of Provençal herbs. Medium bodied and moderately tannic, it should be drunk earlier rather than later.

The dark ruby-colored, medium-bodied 1997 St.-Joseph reveals good fruit, a floral and cassis-scented nose, and an easygoing personality that suggests consumption over the next 5–6 years is warranted.

Graillot's Hermitage is never his best wine, and the 1997 and 1996 are both lightweight examples. The medium-bodied 1997 offers up jammy cherry aromas intermixed with tomato skin, pepper, minerals, and smoke. Drink this soft Hermitage during its first 5–6 years of life. Interestingly, I thought the St.-Joseph possessed more depth than the Hermitage. How can that be? The 1996 Hermitage reveals more cassis, and a deeper, richer palate-feel, as well as mouth-searing acidity levels. It should age nicely for a decade.

The 1997 Crozes-Hermitage white is one of the finest Graillot has produced. A blend of 80% Marsanne and 20% Roussanne, it is made in a honeyed, rich, chewy style with the vintage's ripeness and low acidity well evidenced. Fleshy, with juicy fruit, this tasty, attractive, medium-bodied Crozes offers both authoritative flavor and elegance. Drink it over the next 1–3 years.

DOMAINE GRAMENON

1996 Côtes du Rhône Les Laurentides	B	85

The 1996 Côtes du Rhône Les Laurentides possesses less concentration and ripeness than the 1995 or 1994. Exhibiting more acidity and tannin, as well as peppery, earthy, kirsch aromas and flavors, medium body, and a dry finish, it is a good rather than stunning Laurentides. Yet it remains a good value, and is very Provençal in its aromas and flavors. Drink it over the next 2 years.

CHÂTEAU DU GRAND MOULIS

1995 Côtes du Rhône-Villages Cuvée de l'Ecu	B	88

A gorgeous Côtes du Rhône-Villages, this deep ruby/purple-colored offering includes 95% Syrah in the blend. It offers aromas of sweet, jammy cassis, truffles, herbes de Provence, and chocolate. Medium to full bodied, with excellent concentration and purity, a savory, fleshy mouth-feel, and light tannin, this is a boldly styled, rich, flavorful Côtes du Rhône-Villages for consuming over the next 5–6 years.

DOMAINE DU GRAND PRIEUR

1996 Côtes du Rhône	B	86

Textbook kirsch, Provençal herb, smoky, earthy notes emerge in this medium-bodied, satisfying wine's aromatics. Cherry jam is the most obvious component on the palate. Soft and spicy, this 1996 Côtes du Rhône is ideal for drinking over the next year.

DOMAINE GRAND-ROMANE

1997 Gigondas	D	(86–89)
1996 Gigondas	D	86

Two very fine efforts from this estate, the 1997 Gigondas exhibits toasty new oak, a sexy, creamy texture, big, thick, blackberry and vanillin aromas, chewy, highly extracted flavors, and low acidity. This opulent, oaky Gigondas may merit a higher score if the wood becomes better integrated. The 1996 Gigondas is more austere and medium bodied, yet the wood is extremely well integrated. The wine possesses an evolved plum color, good ripeness, and a spicy, lean, short finish. Drink it over the next 3–4 years.

DOMAINE DU GRAND TINEL

1995 Châteauneuf du Pape	D	87
1997 Châteauneuf du Pape Cuvée Alexis Establet	D	(87–89)
1997 Châteauneuf du Pape Cuvée Classique	D	(86–87)
1996 Châteauneuf du Pape Cuvée Classique	D	87

This large estate (136 acres) produces classic Châteauneuf du Pape that is consistently successful. Given the good availability of Grand Tinel's wines, it is not surprising that this is a crowd-pleasing Châteauneuf. It never quite hits the lofty heights, but it is an immensely enjoyable wine. In 1997, the estate introduced an old vine cuvée called Alexis Establet. It will be interesting to see how spectacular this offering will be in a year such as 1998. The 1997 Châteauneuf du Pape Cuvée Classique exhibits an evolved garnet/ruby color, as well as a textbook Provençal nose of roasted nuts, pepper, herbs, peanut butter, and kirsch liqueur. There is luscious fruit, a robust, medium- to full-bodied character, and an open-knit, chewy, pleasant finish. It should drink well for 4–5 years. The 1997 Châteauneuf du Pape Cuvée Alexis Establet offers a medium dark ruby color, a sweet, expansive nose of *sur-maturité* (cherry liqueur/kirsch and apricots), a ripe personality, medium to full body, excellent purity, and a lusty, high alcohol finish. Drink it during its first 6–7 years of life.

The 1996 Châteauneuf du Pape Cuvée Classique has turned out very well. It possesses a dark ruby/garnet color, and a fruit-driven nose with notes of pepper and Provençal herbs in the background. Rich, fleshy, and soft, it will provide ideal drinking over the next 5–6 years.

The dark garnet-colored 1995 Châteauneuf du Pape offers up an intriguing spicy, peppery, seaweed, herbes de Provence, black cherry-scented nose. The wine is fat, with a heady alcohol content, excellent intensity, light to moderate tannin, and a fleshy, full-bodied personality. It has firmed up since I last tasted it and should keep for another 10–12 years. Readers should note that this estate bottles the wine as it is sold, so there can be multiple *mise en bouteille*, with some wines not being bottled for a number of years. The later the wine is bottled, the less fruity and fresh it will be. I believe that earlier bottlings of Grand Tinel offer the most potential for the wine to develop.

GRAND VENEUR

1997 Châteauneuf du Pape	C	(86–87)
1996 Châteauneuf du Pape	C	85
1997 Châteauneuf du Pape La Fontaine	D	90

Proprietor Alain Jaume makes one of the finest white Châteauneuf du Papes of the village. The luxury cuvée of 1997 Châteauneuf du Pape La Fontaine (100% Roussanne) is a dense, rich, honeyed wine with terrific fruit intensity. It is amazing that this offering, which is vinified in 100% new oak, does not reveal more toasty oak aromas. Drink it over the next 1–2 years.

Alain Jaume is moving toward more naturally bottled reds and hopes that his 1997 will be bottled with neither fining nor filtration. That was not the case with the 1996 Châteauneuf du Pape, which offers a dark plum color, and a nose of sweaty saddle leather intermixed with underbrush, *garrigue*, and plum/cherry aromas and flavors. An earthy, truffle, and spice-dominated Châteauneuf du Pape, it should be consumed over the next 3–4 years. Revealing more fruit, intensity, and texture, as well as greater color saturation, the 1997 Châteauneuf du Pape has good potential. The fact that Jaume intends to bottle it with no fining or filtration should preserve the wine's delicious character, and medium- to full-bodied, nicely layered, velvety style. With fine ripeness and low acidity, it requires consumption over the next 6–7 years.

DOMAINE LES GRANDS BOIS

1994 Côtes du Rhône	B	86
1997 Côtes du Rhône-Villages Cuvée Gabrielle	C	(85–87)

Proprietor Marc Besnardeau was a sommelier in Paris before he decided to become a grower/winemaker. The unfiltered 1994 Côtes du Rhône, made from low yields, was produced from a vineyard on the famed sun-drenched, Mistral battered *Plan de Dieu* in the Vaucluse. The wine reveals a spice box, cedary, fruitcake, roasted nut, and black cherry-scented nose with earth and truffles in the background. In the mouth, it is chewy, full bodied, rustic, dense, concentrated, and mouth-filling. This chunky, husky Côtes du Rhône is soft enough to be drunk now but promises to drink well for 3–4 years.

The soft, unfiltered 1997 Côtes du Rhône-Villages Cuvée Gabrielle is redolent with black cherry fruit and spicy pepper. Soft, round, and medium bodied, with no hard edges, its low acidity and ripe, plump style suggest it is best consumed over the next 1–2 years.

DOMAINE DU GRAPILLON D'OR

1997	Gigondas	C	(85–87)
1996	Gigondas	C	85

Two reasonably successful wines for their vintages, the 1997 Gigondas exhibits overripe notes of plums and cherries intermixed with fragrant, peppery, dried herb, roasted vegetable aromas. Fruity on the attack, with medium to full body, and an open-knit, evolved, precocious style, this wine will require consumption during its first 3–4 years of life. Let's hope the estate bottles it early to preserve its charm and fruit. The 1996 Gigondas is a medium-bodied wine with sweet black cherry fruit intermixed with pepper, licorice, and earth. There is some spiciness, but the finish is short and muted. It is good but not inspiring. Drink it over the next 3–4 years.

GUIGAL

1996	Châteauneuf du Pape	C/D	(86–88)
1995	Châteauneuf du Pape	C/D	88
1997	Condrieu	D/E	90
1997	Condrieu La Doriane	E	94
1997	Côte Rôtie Blonde et Brune	E	(88–91)
1996	Côte Rôtie Blonde et Brune	E	(85–87)
1995	Côte Rôtie Blonde et Brune	E	90
1994	Côte Rôtie Blonde et Brune	E	89
1997	Côte Rôtie Chateau d'Ampuis	EE	(90–92)
1996	Côte Rôtie Chateau d'Ampuis	EE	(89–91)
1995	Côte Rôtie Chateau d'Ampuis	EE	92
1997	Côte Rôtie La Landonne	EEE	(96–99)
1996	Côte Rôtie La Landonne	EEE	(90–93)
1995	Côte Rôtie La Landonne	EEE	(95–96+)
1994	Côte Rôtie La Landonne	EEE	98
1997	Côte Rôtie La Mouline	EEE	(94–96)
1996	Côte Rôtie La Mouline	EEE	(91–94)
1995	Côte Rôtie La Mouline	EEE	(96–98+)
1994	Côte Rôtie La Mouline	EEE	95
1997	Côte Rôtie La Turque	EEE	(96–99)
1996	Côte Rôtie La Turque	EEE	(93–95)
1995	Côte Rôtie La Turque	EEE	(98–100)

1994 Côte Rôtie La Turque	EEE	96
1996 Côtes du Rhône (Red)	A	(82–84)
1995 Côtes du Rhône (Red)	A	85
1997 Côtes du Rhône (Rosé)	A	87
1997 Côtes du Rhône (White)	A	85
1995 Gigondas	C	86
1997 Hermitage	E	(90–93)
1996 Hermitage	E	(87–89)
1995 Hermitage	E	(90–92)
1996 Hermitage Blanc	E	(90–92)
1995 Hermitage Blanc	E	90
1994 Hermitage Blanc	E	91

As difficult as it may be to find the limited production (400–800 cases each) of Côte Rôtie La Mouline, La Turque, and La Landonne, readers should have no problem securing Guigal's very good Côtes du Rhône and sumptuous Condrieu. I remember when this was just a tiny *négociant* firm, but today it seems like the entire underside of the village of Ampuis is a maze of Guigal cellars. Over 100,000 cases of red Côtes du Rhône are produced, and the white wine production has also grown. In addition, Guigal is the most significant producer of Condrieu, as well as the largest producer of Côte Rôtie. As I have stated many times over the last twenty years, Marcel Guigal is not only a brilliant winemaker, but perhaps even more of a genius *éléveur*. The practice of upbringing wines, knowing when to sulfur and when to rack, was learned from his father, who Marcel claims was the real genius behind this lost art. Who in his right mind would keep a wine for over 40 months in 100% new oak casks? Marcel Guigal routinely does that with his single-vineyard Côte Rôties. Having followed them for more than 2 decades, I can unequivocally say that their overt oakiness is completely absorbed by the wines within their first 5–7 years of life.

For value, readers can look forward to a tasty 1997 Côtes du Rhône blanc. This cuvée has become better as Guigal has bulked up the percentage of Viognier (now about 20% of the blend), and begun adding Roussanne from the nearby village of St.-Péray. The 1997 is a low-acid, fat, honeyed style of white Côtes du Rhône meant to be enjoyed during its first year of life. There are two vintages of red Côtes du Rhône in the marketplace. Reflective of Guigal's origins in the northern Rhône, this wine, while containing plenty of Grenache, is buttressed by increasing quantities of Syrah and Mourvèdre. The 1995 Côtes du Rhône red, which has been a winner since its release, is still available in the marketplace. Given the production of more than one million bottles, there are more than a dozen separate *mise en bouteilles,* but the blend is essentially the same for each bottling. The 1995 Côtes du Rhône, which I tasted from several different bottlings, all revealed deep ruby colors, plenty of peppery, cassis fruit, good spice, and a solid, rustic generosity. It is meant to be drunk during its first several years of life, although it will hold up for 4–5. The 1996 Côtes du Rhône red is a softer, fruitier wine with less spice and muscle, reflecting the fact that this is a lighter vintage in the Rhône Valley. These wines are aged in both *foudre* and tank, and then blended prior to bottling. One of the consistently fine wines that rarely receives the credit it deserves is Guigal's Côtes du Rhône rosé. The delicious 1997 Côtes du Rhône rosé is a strawberry and cherry-scented wine with surprising body, gobs of fruit, and excellent purity and character. It should drink well for another year.

Guigal has replaced Georges Vernay as "Monsieur Condrieu." Now the largest producer of

Condrieu, Guigal's 1997 Condrieu is the finest he has produced since 1994. Across the board the wines from Condrieu are luscious, fat, and tasty, although they are meant to be consumed during their first several years of life. Two-thirds of Guigal's regular bottling of Condrieu (more than 25,000 cases produced) are fermented and aged in tank, and one-third is fermented and aged in *barrique*. This offering is remarkable for its consistent quality. The 1997 Condrieu, which is a fatter, fleshier wine than the 1996, is redolent with floral aromas intermixed with apricot, grapefruit, peach, and honey scents. It is a powerfully styled Condrieu with low acidity and undeniable charm and seductiveness. However, I would not recommend aging of more than 2 years. The single-vineyard Condrieu La Doriane has become one of the three or four finest wines of the appellation. Made from a 4.5-acre parcel, this offering is spectacular in 1997. The 1997 Condrieu La Doriane achieved nearly 14% natural alcohol. Aged in 50% new oak and 50% stainless-steel tanks, the wine is put through a complete malolactic fermentation, giving it a creamy, unctuous texture, a trait especially evident in the 1997. While dry, the wine possesses a fabulous nose of tropical fruits intermixed with floral scents and an underlying minerality. Intensely aromatic, spicy, and superrich, this sensational La Doriane is the finest Guigal has produced from this hillside vineyard overlooking the famous Condrieu hotel/restaurant, Beau-Rivage.

Among Guigal's most notable *négociant* wines (for which he buys wines to blend) is his Hermitage. It is no secret that he has been seeking to purchase a top domaine from this hallowed appellation. At present he purchases wine from several small producers. The white Hermitage tends to begin life in a backward state, only to evolve and age nicely for 10–15 years. I felt both his 1994 and 1995 white Hermitages, which I had tasted in 1997, were even better in 1998. The 1994 Hermitage blanc (90% Marsanne and 10% Roussanne), which had put on weight, revealed the unmistakable mineral/honeyed rose petal and citrusy nose of young white Hermitage, intermixed with a notion of fino sherry. Grilled nuts make an appearance on the palate in this massive, ripe, full-bodied offering. This huge dry white is meant only for serious wine connoisseurs. Although drinkable now, I suspect it will shut down, not to reemerge for a decade. The 1995 Hermitage blanc is a more closed, less unctuously textured example, particularly when tasted after the 1994. The full-bodied 1995 exhibits a liquid minerality, a floral-scented nose, high alcohol, a powerful constitution, and a long, chewy, intense finish. The backward 1996 Hermitage blanc offers tremendously high extract, along with surprisingly crisp, tangy acidity. It reveals a liquefied pineapple/grapefruit/mineral aromatic profile, as well as flavor intensity. This full-bodied, monster-sized white Hermitage exhibits plenty of depth, richness, extract, and alcohol in the finish. It is somewhat of a paradoxical wine given its high extract and extraordinary power, yet tangy acidity. This wine will need time in the bottle after its release, but it should be one of the longest-lived white Hermitages Guigal has produced.

The 1995 red Hermitage, which primarily comes from Hermitage Hill's two top vineyards, Le Méal and Les Bessards, with some fruit from Les Dionniers, is a powerful, rich, dark ruby/purple-colored wine with plenty of smoky cassis fruit. The wine is kept in a combination of both *foudre* and barrel, with no SO_2 additions until bottling. Dense and chewy, with outstanding intensity and purity, this large-scaled Hermitage should age well for 15–20 years.

Guigal's other *négociant* wines emerge from two of his favorite southern Rhône appellations, Gigondas and Châteauneuf du Pape. He is trying to find estates to purchase in both of these appellations, but he was outbid by American importer Kermit Lynch for Domaine Les Pallières in Gigondas, and seems obsessed about finding an old vine estate in Châteauneuf du Pape, despite the fact that prices in that appellation have tripled in the last 12 months. Guigal is now buying juice which he blends. The 1995 Gigondas was bottled after spending 3 years in wood *foudres*. It is a peppery, spicy, heady, good bistro red. I did not find it to be significantly better than the fine 1995 Côtes du Rhône, but it does cut a broader swath across the palate, and it possesses more rustic tannin. Drink it over the next 5–6 years. The 1996

Gigondas (an extremely difficult vintage for this appellation) is almost as good as the 1995. It offers a dark ruby color, followed by a big, spicy, earthy, peppery nose with Provençal herbs and *garrigue* notes in the background. The wine is savory and generous, not complex, but warm and substantial. Drink it over the next 5–6 years.

Guigal's Châteauneuf du Papes are made primarily from Grenache, although he has begun to add about 20% Mourvèdre to the blend to give the wines more structure and ageability. The excellent 1995 Châteauneuf du Pape displays an intensely fragrant nose of kirsch, pepper, Provençal herbs, and earth. Medium to full bodied, round, generous, and supple, this meaty wine can be drunk now as well as over the next 7–10 years. Guigal did a fine job in the more difficult 1996 vintage. The 1996 Châteauneuf du Pape exhibits a more evolved dark garnet color, in addition to delicious black cherry fruit intermixed with roasted meat and pepper aromas. Although more evolved than the 1995, it is a very good effort for the vintage. Consume it over the next 5–6 years.

Guigal admits to producing in excess of 20,000 cases of Côte Rôtie Blonde et Brune. I suspect the amount is even higher given the fact that there is one master blend for each vintage, and 3–5 different *mise en bouteilles*. The fist *mise* of the 1995 Côte Rôtie Blonde et Brune was a mere 150,000 bottles! Having frequently conducted tastings of all his Côtes Rôtie Blonde et Brune from different *mise* within the same vintage, I have found subtle differences, but in general it is the same wine. Some may be more fragrant, but the level of richness and quality is uniform. As for recent vintages of the Blonde et Brune, the 1994 Côte Rôtie Blonde et Brune is an elegant, savory, complex wine with gamey, smoky notes, plenty of jammy black cherry and raspberry fruit, medium body, and dry tannin in the finish that is nicely balanced by the sweet oak and the vintage's opulent style. There were four separate bottlings of the 1994 Côte Rôtie Blonde et Brune, all of them consistently excellent, and possibly outstanding. Anticipated maturity: now–2010. The 1995 Côte Rôtie Blonde et Brune is a classic wine for the appellation. Its dark garnet/ruby/purple color is followed by a jammy nose of *pain grillé*, white flowers, black raspberries, olive, and pepper. Firmly structured with a rich, fleshy midsection, and plenty of tannin in the finish, this gorgeously seductive Côte Rôtie should be Marcel Guigal's finest Blonde et Brune since the 1991. Anticipated maturity: 2001–2014. The component parts of the 1996 Côte Rôtie Blonde et Brune ranged in numerical scores from the low 80s to 90. There are more herbaceous and green olive characteristics, as well as higher acidity, and a grilled meat, cherry fruit note in all the cuvées. It will undoubtedly be a very good Côte Rôtie, but I suspect it will not be as impressive as the 1995 or as seductive as the 1994. However, readers should remember that Guigal is one firm where the wines consistently taste better out of bottle than they do when tasting in the cellars. The 1997 Côte Rôtie Blonde et Brune seems to return to the charming, seductive, fleshy, elegant style of vintages such as 1991. All the component parts were deliciously ripe and fruity, with low acidity, good flesh, and outstanding ripe raspberry fruit intermixed with smoky oak. A seductive, flattering style, this should be an excellent Côte Rôtie that will be delicious upon its release in 3–4 years.

Marcel Guigal purchased the only château in Ampuis, the Château d'Ampuis, and is in the process of renovating this huge edifice. In 1995 he launched this cuvée of Côte Rôtie, which is made in limited quantities of approximately 28,000 bottles. It is a blend of some of Côte Rôtie's finest hillside vineyards, that is, La Garde, Le Clos, La Grande Plantée, La Pommière, Le Pavillon Rouge, and La Moulin. The 1995 Côte Rôtie Château d'Ampuis, which is released to the marketplace in early 1999, is a sensational offering. The bottled wine is even better than its individual component parts. It boasts a dense, saturated deep ruby color, as well as a flamboyant, intense bouquet of crushed pepper, Provençal herbs, black raspberry jam, and smoky sweet oak. The wine is medium to full bodied, with good underlying acidity, but much more voluptuous and unctuous than it appeared to be from cask. Long, concentrated, and explosively rich, this wine may merit an even higher score after it has had some time to mesh together in bottle. It is a terrific Côte Rôtie to drink over the next 10–15+ years. While tasting through all the elements of the 1996 Côte Rôtie Château d'Ampuis, I was struck by the diversity in quality of the different components. There are lighter, more herbaceous cuvées, such as La Moulin and La Grande Plantée, as well as sumptuously rich, substantial cuvées, such as La Pommière, Le Pavillon Rouge, and Le Clos. This wine may score anywhere between 88 and 91. It should age well for 10–12 years. The 1997 Côte Rôtie Château d'Ampuis will be forward, with plenty of lush, jammy black fruits intermixed with smoky oak (from aging in primarily *barrique,* although much of this cuvée will be brought up in *foudre*). It should be an easy-to-drink and -understand Château d'Ampuis, with more fat and succulence than the 1996, but not the structure or longevity of the 1995. However, it is still early to make that call.

The three single-vineyard 1995s will all be spectacular wines. Marcel Guigal continues to believe this is the vintage of the nineties for his wines. The 1995s possess the structure and power of such years as 1988 and 1983, but with the sweetness and opulence of fruit found in the 1985, 1989, 1990, and 1991. The 1995 Côte Rôtie La Mouline (11% Viognier included in the blend) was scheduled to be bottled (unfined and unfiltered of course) in February, after 42 months in 100% new oak. This is one of the most extraordinary wines made in the world. As I have said many times, if I were ever stranded on the proverbial desert island with only one wine to drink, it would have to be La Mouline. A compelling perfume of violets, black raspberries, coffee, pepper, and *pain grillé* soars from the glass. Medium to full bodied and lush, with a terrific multilayered texture and outstanding purity, this is a phenomenal example of La Mouline. It possesses enough structure and substance to last for 2 decades, although it will be delicious upon release. The 1995 Côte Rôtie La Turque (about 7% Viognier in the blend) is cut from the same mold, with a denser ruby/purple color, and more roasted herb, olive, and Asian spice characteristics. It exhibits exceptional concentration and is even more velvety and concentrated than La Mouline. The fabulous 1995 La Turque is a virtually perfect wine with flamboyance, harmony, and remarkable opulence and length. It should drink well when released and last for 2 decades. The brawny, black/purple-colored 1995 Côte Rôtie La Landonne reveals the more animal, *sauvage* side of the Syrah grape. Licorice, prune, iron, and vitaminlike aromas compete with copious quantities of black fruits and smoke in this complex, structured, muscular, massive Côte Rôtie. This will not be as enjoyable to drink young as La Mouline and La Turque. It will require 5–6 years of cellaring and should keep for 30+ years.

Perhaps it was their stage of development, but the 1996 single-vineyard Côte Rôties seemed less expansive and impressive when compared to my tasting notes of a year earlier. These are still profoundly complex wines that I would be thrilled to drink on any occasion, but they did not sing as loudly in 1998 as they did in 1997. Moreover, the vintage's tart acidity and cooler climate feel appears to be pushing its way through the wines' highly extracted, concentrated personalities. The 1996 Côte Rôtie La Mouline, which includes a whopping 18% Viognier in the blend, offers up an elegant, Musigny-like nose of black raspberries, bacon fat, spicy oak, and coconut/exotic fruit aromas. Silky and luscious, with no evidence of the vintage's tart acidity, it is one of the most opulent, exotic, and evolved La Moulines I have ever tasted. It should provide a profound drinking experience in another year. The 1996 Côte Rôtie La Turque exhibits a dark ruby/purple color, a pronounced grilled herb, black cherry, and incense-scented nose, good underlying acidity, the telltale black fruit, prune, raspberry, and *griotte* character Marcel Guigal refers to when talking about this vineyard, and a long, concentrated finish with moderate tannin and acidity. It is a Burgundian-styled, elegant wine that complements the Musigny-like style of the 1996 La Mouline. Look for it to drink well within 1–2 years after release and last for 15+ years. Consistent with previous tastings, the 1996 Côte Rôtie La Landonne is the most backward of this trio. It is extremely tannic and closed with the most saturated color, more noticeable acidity, and a subdued roasted herb, sausage and smoked meat character. None of the green pepper notes noticeable last year were present in this tasting. While this will be an impressive wine, it will require 5–7 years of cellaring upon release. It should keep for 25 years. All in all, the 1996 single-vineyard offerings look to be medium-weight wines with exceptional aromatic profiles, brilliant concentration, and some of the vintage's acidity, but that is meshed with the exceptional extract and ripeness Guigal achieved by harvesting so late in October 1996.

The 1997 single-vineyard offerings appear to be sumptuous, exotic, evolved, and luscious wines reminiscent of the 1991s and 1985s. They were showing exceptionally well when I tasted them in late fall 1998. All were more concentrated, riper, expansive, and layered than the 1996s. If not as muscular and powerful as the 1995s, they are more seductive and riper. The dark purple-colored 1997 Côte Rôtie La Mouline offers up a note of grilled cherries and cassis, spectacular, opulent, viscous flavors with gobs of fruit, low acidity, chewy, sweet tannin, and a 40+-second finish. The bacon fat, smoke, and black cherry/black raspberry jam characteristics of this exotic wine are all present. It should be irresistible when released in 2001. The 1997 Côte Rôtie La Turque is dazzling, displaying high extract, and a flamboyant, penetrating, exquisite nose of black fruits intermixed with smoke, violets, and pepper. Powerful and rich, with no hard edges, this layered, multidimensional, staggeringly concentrated and intense wine will turn heads when it is released. Moreover, if La Mouline is capable of drinking well for 12–15 years, La Turque should last for 2 decades or more. The virtually perfect 1997 Côte Rôtie La Landonne is another blockbuster effort. The fullest bodied of these three 1997s, this massive, concentrated, black/purple-colored wine offers more of the earth tones intermixed with meaty smells along with exaggerated levels of ripeness and concentrated prune/raspberry/cherry fruit. Enormous in weight and richness, yet not overbearing, this monument to Syrah should age well for 30 years, although it will be the least approachable and friendly of the 1997 single-vineyard Côte Rôties when released in several years.

The president of France decided to recognize what Marcel Guigal has meant not only to the Rhône Valley, but to all of France, as he received France's Legion of Honor in November 1997. Certainly he means plenty to American wine lovers, as this has been a remarkably consistent source for an array of amazing wines for decades.

PAUL JABOULET-AINÉ

1997	Châteauneuf du Pape Les Cèdres	D	(84–86)
1996	Châteauneuf du Pape Les Cèdres	D	84
1997	Châteauneuf du Pape Les Cèdres (White)	C	88
1996	Châteauneuf du Pape Les Cèdres (White)	C	87
1997	Condrieu	D	89
1997	Cornas	D	(90–92)
1996	Cornas	D	87
1997	Cornas Domaine St.-Pierre	D	(91–94+)
1996	Cornas Domaine St.-Pierre	D	88+
1997	Côte Rôtie Les Jumelles	E	(90–93)
1996	Côte Rôtie Les Jumelles	E	85?
1997	Côtes du Rhône Parallèle 45	A	82
1996	Côtes du Rhône Parallèle 45	A	84
1996	Côtes du Rhône-Villages	A	82

1995	Côtes du Rhône-Villages	A	87
1997	Côtes du Ventoux	A	82
1996	Côtes du Ventoux	A	77
1996	Crozes-Hermitage Cuvée Speciale	D	92
1997	Crozes-Hermitage Les Jalets	B	(84–86)
1996	Crozes-Hermitage Les Jalets	B	85
1995	Crozes-Hermitage Les Jalets	B	78
1997	Crozes-Hermitage La Mule Blanche	C	87
1996	Crozes-Hermitage La Mule Blanche	C	85
1997	Crozes-Hermitage Raymond Roure	D	(87–88)
1996	Crozes-Hermitage Raymond Roure	D	91
1997	Crozes-Hermitage Raymond Roure (White)	D	87
1997	Crozes-Hermitage Thalabert	C	(87–88)
1996	Crozes-Hermitage Thalabert	C	89
1995	Crozes-Hermitage Thalabert	C	87
1996	Gigondas	C	83
1995	Gigondas	C	84
1997	Hermitage La Chapelle	EE	(92)
1996	Hermitage La Chapelle	EE	92
1995	Hermitage La Chapelle	EE	91
1997	Hermitage Chevalier de Stérimberg (White)	EE	92
1996	Hermitage Chevalier de Stérimberg (White)	EE	91
1995	Hermitage Chevalier de Stérimberg (White)	EE	90
1997	Hermitage Pied de la Côte	D	(84–86)
1996	Hermitage Pied de la Côte	D	84
1995	Hermitage Pied de la Côte	D	82
1997	St.-Joseph Le Grand Pompée	C	(87–89)
1996	St.-Joseph Le Grand Pompée	C	86
1997	St.-Joseph Le Grand Pompée (White)	C	88
1997	Vacqueyras	C	86
1996	Vacqueyras	C	85
1995	Vacqueyras	C	85

When I arrived at Jaboulet's industrial looking building in the southern outskirts of Tain l'Hermitage in the fall of 1998, Jacques quickly made clear his views of the 1997 vintage by stating that it was "the greatest year in my 32 years of winemaking . . . the late harvest we did in mid-October has given us another 1961." This comment actually pertained to the Jaboulet northern Rhônes, which are indeed spectacular in 1997. In my opinion, they are among the stars of the vintage. However, the 1997 southern Rhônes as well as some of the lesser cuvées are competent but uninspiring.

My notes on some of the wines that will be of little interest to readers are intentionally abbreviated. Jacques Jaboulet predicts (and I agree with him) that quality will explode in the Côtes du Ventoux over the next 10–15 years. For now, there are a lot of pleasant wines, with a handful of star performers. Jaboulet's 1996 and 1997 Côtes du Ventoux are both supple, light- to medium-bodied wines with peppery, kirschlike fruit. The 1996 is tannic and lean, whereas the 1997 is softer, with more strawberry fruit and suppleness. As for the 1996 and 1997 Côtes du Rhône Parallèle 45, the 1996 possesses a dark plum color, kirschlike fruit, and a straightforward, medium-bodied, easygoing style that requires consumption over the next 2–3 years. The 1997 is even more evolved, exhibiting an evolved plum/garnet color, charming raspberry and cherry fruit, and a soft, low-acid, moderately endowed personality. The 1996 Côtes du Rhône-Villages (no 1997 was offered because the quality was so disappointing) is a soft, solid, bistro red with effusive fruit, no complexity, but medium body, and kirsch/strawberry notes.

Another appellation where the Jaboulets produced no 1997 is Gigondas. Jacques Jaboulet told me he found nothing of value to purchase in 1997, calling the vintage "undrinkable" in Gigondas. The 1996 Gigondas is soft and pretty, with medium body, some fruit, and an elegant, lightweight style that requires consumption over the next 2–3 years. The Jaboulets did produce a Vacqueyras in 1996 and 1997, and both were among my favorites of the less-expensive southern Rhônes in this portfolio. The ruby-colored 1996 Vacqueyras is a seductive, peppery, berry offering with a Grenache-like nose, good generosity, a certain elegance, and enough glycerin to cover the wine's framework. It should be drunk over the next 2–3 years. Although not complex, the 1997 Vacqueyras (90% Grenache) offers medium body, and pepper, spice, and cherry/strawberry fruit flavors. It should be drunk over the next year or two. The 1996 Châteauneuf du Pape Les Cèdres is an evolved, lightweight, medium ruby-colored offering revealing amber at the edge. With peppery, berry fruit, and a notion of kirsch, it should be drunk over the next 2–3 years. Cut from the same mold, the 1997 Châteauneuf du Pape Les Cèdres is riper, with low acidity, and round, tasty, cherry fruit presented in a medium-bodied, evolved 100% Grenache style. It, too, should be drunk over the next 2–3 years.

According to Jacques Jaboulet, 1997 was at its greatest in the northern Rhône. As the following tasting notes suggest, he has some impressive cuvées to back such boasting. At the lightest end of the northern Rhône spectrum is the Crozes-Hermitage Les Jalets and St.-Joseph Le Grand Pompée. The 1996 and 1997 Crozes-Hermitage Les Jalets are both bistro-styled reds offering medium body, and attractive gamey, cranberry, and black currant fruit flavors buttressed by tangy acidity in the case of the 1996, and soft tannin in the 1997. Both wines are meant to be drunk during their first 5–7 years of life. I had a slight preference for the 1997 as it is a softer, more open-knit style. While the acid levels in the 1996 are noteworthy, they are not excessive. The dark ruby/purple-colored 1996 St.-Joseph Le Grand Pompée exhibits an attractive, moderately intense nose of black raspberries and currants, medium body, crisp acidity, good ripeness, and a firm, moderately endowed finish. Far superior is the 1997 St.-Joseph Le Grand Pompée. After a maceration period that lasted over a month, this offering reveals an opaque ruby/purple color, and rich, chocolatey, smoky, blackberry flavors that suggest the superripeness the Jaboulets achieved in this vintage. The wine possesses excellent, nearly outstanding concentration, plenty of structure and tannin, and a sweet midpalate and length. An excellent, nearly outstanding St.-Joseph Le Grand Pompée, it is among the finest ever made at this estate.

Shrewd purchasers have no doubt long found the Crozes-Hermitage Thalabert to be one of the finest Jaboulet offerings in terms of its quality/price rapport. I have been buying the better vintages of this wine for twenty years, and it is always a solidly made, mini-Hermitage that drinks exceptionally well for 10–15 years. Both the 1996 and 1997 Crozes-Hermitage Thalabert are successful wines. The 1996 Crozes-Hermitage Thalabert may merit an outstanding score. The wine possesses a dense, saturated purple color, crisp, tangy, blackberry, prune, and cassis aromas buttressed by the vintage's telltale acidity, outstanding extract, purity, and richness, and a medium-bodied, long finish. It will be at its finest between 2000 and 2014. The 1997 Crozes-Hermitage Thalabert (a 32-day *cuvaison*) is made in a tannic, *vin du garde* style with a saturated ruby/purple color, copious cassis fruit, and notes of smoked herbs, Asian spices, and earth. Powerful and muscular, it requires 4–5 years of cellaring, and will last for 15+ years. Readers may want to note that the Jaboulets will be releasing 20,000 3-bottle cases of a 1996 Crozes-Hermitage Cuvée Speciale for the turn of the century. There also will be 1,000 magnums of this wine. It is a selection from the oldest Crozes-Hermitage vines owned by the Jaboulets (I assume most of it emerges from the Thalabert Vineyard). Explosive, rich, and immensely impressive, it is one of the finest Crozes-Hermitages I have ever tasted. The color is a saturated black/purple. The wine possesses considerable size and substance, with gobs of cassis fruit intermixed with roasted herbs, truffles, and smoked meat characteristics. It should reach its peak in 3–4 years and last for 15 or more. This terrific Crozes-Hermitage has more in common with a Hermitage than most wines from this appellation.

Another impressive offering from Crozes-Hermitage is Jaboulet's 1996 Crozes-Hermitage Raymond Roure. One thousand cases were produced of this fabulous wine, which was aged nearly 2 years in wood, and came in at a remarkably high 13.2% natural alcohol. It offers an opaque plum/ruby color, as well as a superrich, concentrated, weighty, full-bodied, monster personality with the vintage's acidity nearly buried by the wine's high extract and muscular, superconcentrated style. This immensely impressive, classic, old-style Crozes-Hermitage behaves like a topflight Cornas. Anticipated maturity: 2001–2016. Although the 1997 Crozes-Hermitage Raymond Roure does not possess the weight of the 1996, it exhibits a saturated purple color, and excellent ripe prune, plum, and blackberry fruit intermixed with roasted herbs, smoke, saddle leather, and truffles. Long and full bodied, with excellent fatness, moderate tannin, and the potential to merit a 90-point score, this impressively endowed wine will be at its finest in 2–3 years and will last for 14–15.

Cornas has never been one of Jaboulet's strong points, but they now produce two cuvées, the regular Cornas and Cornas St.-Pierre. The latter is indeed impressive, although I thought the regular bottling in 1997 justified the accolades bestowed upon this vintage by Jacques Jaboulet. The dark ruby/purple-colored 1996 Cornas offers up an earthy, iron, and black cherry-scented nose, medium to full body, an animal-like, *sauvage* character, and notes of tar and pepper. It should drink well for a decade. The 1997 Cornas reveals a dense black/ruby/purple color, as well as sweet, ripe fruit with an element of *sur-maturité*. The telltale cassis, licorice, mineral, animal, and meaty aromas are present, but the wine possesses a velvety texture, concentrated fruit, and a long, powerful, rich finish. It should drink well for 15 years. I was impressed with the 1996 Cornas Domaine St.-Pierre, but the 1997 is one of the most spectacular wines of Cornas I have tasted. Fortunately, there are about 2,000 cases of this cuvée. The 1996 Cornas Domaine St.-Pierre exhibits a saturated purple color, and rich, blackberry and mineral notes supported by tangy acidity, and dusty, firm, aggressive tannin. The wine is rustic, mouth-filling, and chewy, with considerable volume and depth, but the acidity and tannin keep my score low. Anticipated maturity: 2002–2014. The spectacular 1997 Cornas Domaine St.-Pierre is a massively endowed effort that has benefited from a 28-day maceration. The wine boasts an opaque purple color, followed by a stunning nose of blackberry and cassis liqueur intertwined with scents of minerals, violets, pepper, and tar. Huge and ponderous on the palate, with beautifully integrated tannin, acidity, and alcohol, this ripe, concentrated Cornas should develop at a glacial pace. Anticipated maturity: 2003–2018.

I have never been a great fan of Jaboulet's Côte Rôtie Les Jumelles. It can be very good, sometimes outstanding (1959 and 1961), but is generally a solid effort, with high acidity. The medium ruby-colored 1996 Côte Rôtie Les Jumelles is a serviceable, competent effort. While the wine offers up plum, cranberry, and cassis fruit, the high acidity is cause for concern. There does not appear to be enough flesh to balance out the wine's tartness. In complete contrast, the 1997 Côte Rôtie Les Jumelles is a spectacular effort. Jacques Jaboulet believes it is the finest made since 1961. The wine offers an opaque purple color, as well as a knockout nose of black olives, cassis, dried Provençal herbs, and pepper. There is medium to full body, superb concentration, moderate tannin, and a layered, sweet midpalate and finish. This excellent Côte Rôtie should age effortlessly for 20–25 years. Anticipated maturity: 2004–2023.

For a number of years, the Jaboulets have been bottling their younger vines and lighter cuvées of Hermitage under the label Hermitage Pied de la Côte. This wine generally has more in common with a Crozes-Hermitage than a serious Hermitage. Such is the case in both 1996 and 1997. The 1996 Hermitage Pied de la Côte reveals the vintage's high acids, whereas the 1997 is a softer, rounder, more red currant and raspberry-styled wine with low acidity. Neither wine is very concentrated, and for that reason they are both best consumed in their vigorous youth—5–6 years. Jaboulet has produced their two finest Hermitage La Chapelles since 1989 and 1990. Both the 1997 and 1996 are stunningly rich and concentrated, with 25–30+ years of longevity. Believe it or not, the profound 1996 Hermitage La Chapelle (production 8,100 cases) is surpassed by the blockbuster, monumental 1997. The saturated black/purple-colored 1996 exhibits a broodingly backward nose of minerals, cassis, and spices. Full bodied, with sweet tannin, black fruits galore, admirable structure, and considerable complexity, this backward, thick La Chapelle possesses good acidity (but not intrusive), and a style reminiscent of a brawny, tannic 1983 and powerful, backward, unevolved yet immensely promising 1989. Anticipated maturity: 2007–2030. The 1997 Hermitage La Chapelle competes with the monumental wines made in 1990, 1978, and 1961. The harvest was completed on October 14, with some cuvées achieving 14.5% natural alcohol (the alcohol level in the final blend is 13.5%). The wine looks impressive, with a viscosity and unctuous richness. There is amazing fat and chewiness, as well as spectacular aromatics of overripe black currants and blackberries intermingled with barbecue spices, soy, and jammy black fruits. The tannin seems lost in the wine's full-bodied, silky-textured, voluptuously rich, staggeringly concentrated style. The midpalate explodes with sweetness, glycerin, and extract. The finish lasts for 40+ seconds. The 1997 should be remarkably approachable given its opulence, although, like the 1990, it will firm up and close down. The wine was scheduled to be bottled without filtration in February 1998, and released in late 1999. It is undoubtedly a mind-blowing Hermitage La Chapelle. Anticipated maturity: 2004–2035.

The Jaboulet white wines have increased significantly in quality over the last decade. The finest whites include the 1996 and 1997 Châteauneuf du Pape Les Cèdres. These wines possess a Condrieu-like, honeyed, citrusy, apricot, floral fruitiness, medium to full body, and loads of fruit and intensity. However, they require drinking during their first several years of life. Other stars are the 1997 St.-Joseph Le Grand Pompée (100% Marsanne), with a rose petal, nutty richness, 1997 Crozes-Hermitage La Mule Blanche (50% Roussanne and 50% Marsanne), a serious, honeyed, concentrated wine, and 1997 Crozes-Hermitage Raymond Roure, a fat, sherrylike offering with a roasted nut character to its rich, concentrated fruit. The spectacular 1996 Hermitage Chevalier de Stérimberg (33% Roussanne and 67% Marsanne) has been 100% barrel fermented, put through 100% malolactic fermentation, and aged in 100% new oak. However, the oak is completely submerged beneath the wine's extraordinary rose petal, apricot, nutty, and peachlike richness. The wine displays huge quantities of glycerin, a sensational texture, and terrific purity and depth. This spectacular offering is capable of lasting for 10–20+ years. Even better is the 1997 Hermitage Chevalier de Stérimberg. Made in the same style as the 1996, it is a bigger, richer, fuller wine with massive honeyed characteristics, a white Burgundy-like texture, and an impressive 14% natural alcohol. Nevertheless, there is enough acidity to provide clarity and freshness in this superbly rendered, full-bodied, unctuously thick wine. The 1995 Hermitage Chevalier de Stérimberg offers a whiff of white flowers, honey, and cherry notes. This full-bodied, muscular, tightly knit wine is just hinting at its overall potential. It is still delicious, but if these wines are not drunk within 1–3 years of release, they are best cellared for 10–15 years. They have the potential to last for 2 decades or more.

Last, don't ignore Jaboulet's 1997 Condrieu, one of the finest made in many years. It exhibits an apricot jamlike nose, with an intriguing floral scent. Crammed with concentrated fruit, the wine is medium to full bodied, dry, lush, and pure. Drink it over the next 1–2 years.

One of the best buys in the Rhône Valley is the Jaboulet firm's Côtes du Rhône Parallèle 45. To the extent that any 1995s are still languishing on retailers' shelves, readers are advised to check it out, as it is a gutsy, deep, richly fruity wine that can handle 7–10 years of cellaring. More and more the Jaboulets have moved to the southern Rhône's Gard department for this wine's grapes. Additionally, they continue to increase the amount of Syrah in the blend (a not so obvious choice given their northern Rhône heritage). The 1995 Côtes du Rhône-Villages is a smoky, peppery, supple wine with dense blackberry and earthy fruit, medium body, a sweet, soft texture, and fine length. It should drink well for 5–6 years.

Jacques Jaboulet believes that 1996 was a better year for this firm than 1995. The 1995 Vacqueyras is a masculine, medium- to full-bodied, spicy, Provençal herb-scented and -flavored wine with good fruit, body, and spice. An attractive midweight wine, it should be consumed over the next 4–5 years. Both the 1995 and 1996 Gigondas are pleasant, although not terribly exciting. The 1995 Gigondas tastes peppery and lean, with floral, berry fruit, and a harsh, tough finish.

I was disappointed with the 1995 Crozes-Hermitage Les Jalets. It possesses high levels of acidity, meager flavor intensity, and a washed-out, nondescript finish. The 1995 Crozes-Hermitage Thalabert, made from small yields, is extremely closed. It exhibits a dark ruby/purple color, followed by dense, sweet, herb-tinged, cassis aromas, ripe, concentrated flavors, plenty of tannin, and excellent to outstanding density and richness. The wine clearly merits an upper 80s point score, but it needs 2–3 years of cellaring. It will age well for 10–15 years.

The cuvée of Hermitage called Pied de la Côte represents about 20%–25% of the estate's Hermitage production that is declassified or eliminated from their top cuvée, the famed Hermitage La Chapelle. The 1995 Pied de la Côte is a light- to medium-bodied, soft, herbaceous, peppery wine that is pretty, but straightforward and simple. Its bigger sibling, the renowned Hermitage La Chapelle, is a superb wine in 1995. The 1995 Hermitage La Chapelle is performing extremely well, although it needs 8–10 years of cellaring. It possesses a blackberry/blueberry component, lower acidity, an intense, full-bodied palate, a dense purple color, and a finish that lasts for 25–30 seconds. It is thick, rich, and promising, but it should not be consumed before 2005. Anticipated maturity: 2005–2025.

JEAN-PAUL ET JEAN-LUC JAMET

1997 Côte Rôtie	D/E	(91–94)
1996 Côte Rôtie	D/E	90
1995 Côte Rôtie	D	92+

This estate has been one of the most consistent small producers of Côte Rôtie over the last decade. Aside from a disappointing 1993, the Jamets have fashioned super wines in 1988, 1989, 1991, 1995, 1996, and 1997. Aged for nearly 2 years in a combination of small barrels and larger *foudres,* the wines are bottled without fining or filtration. I asked Jean-Luc Jamet when the best time to drink their wines was, and he surprised me by saying, "between 8 and 12 years of age." I have found Jamet's dense, powerful vintages only to begin to evolve and open at age 10 (that is, the 1988 and probably the 1991 as well). The 1997 Côte Rôtie, which was "an exceptional" year for the Jamets, was harvested between mid-September and October 10. The Jamets were the last to finish harvesting, a fact that shows in this wine, which possesses elements of *sur-maturité* and phenomenal ripeness. The color is an opaque saturated purple (one of the most intensely colored wines of the vintage). The spectacular aromatics consist of framboise, bacon fat, leather, coffee, pepper, and Asian spices. Full bodied, with massive fruit saturation, this monster Côte Rôtie is one of the most concentrated and richest wines of 1997. Its low acidity and explosive, flamboyant style argue in favor of early maturity, but it will unquestionably keep for 10–15+ years. Jamet's prices remain among the more reasonable of the appellation, particularly given the high quality.

The 1996 Côte Rôtie is more classic than the fleshy, flamboyant 1997. The dark ruby/purple color is followed by notes of overripeness (even in such a cool year). The wine is full bodied and dense, with copious tannin, roasted duck, bacon fat, animal, pepper, and cassis notes intermixed with apricots (about .5% of Viognier is included), and a chewy, well-structured, surprisingly long finish. It needs several years in the bottle, but possesses all the components necessary to age well for 12–15 years.

The spectacular 1995 Côte Rôtie reveals an even more opaque purple color. The wine exhibits fabulous concentration, massive body, and a finish that lasts for nearly 30 seconds. At present, it is more impressive for its potential than its current drinkability. The juicy, smoky Syrah character is well displayed in the tar, licorice, cassis-scented nose. Thick, viscous, highly extracted flavors are pure and mouth-coating. This large-scaled Côte Rôtie will be at its apogee between 2002 and 2018. These are impressive efforts!

DOMAINE DE LA JANASSE

1997	Châteauneuf du Pape Cuvée Chaupin	D	(88–90)
1996	Châteauneuf du Pape Cuvée Chaupin	D	87
1995	Châteauneuf du Pape Cuvée Chaupin	D	91
1997	Châteauneuf du Pape Cuvée Classique	D	(87–88)
1996	Châteauneuf du Pape Cuvée Classique	D	86
1995	Châteauneuf du Pape Cuvée Classique	D	88
1997	Châteauneuf du Pape Vieilles Vignes	D	(90–92)
1996	Châteauneuf du Pape Vieilles Vignes	D	89
1995	Châteauneuf du Pape Vieilles Vignes	D	93
1997	Côtes du Rhône	A	(84–85)
1996	Côtes du Rhône	A	86
1995	Côtes du Rhône	A	86
1997	Côtes du Rhône Les Garrigues	B	(85–87)
1996	Côtes du Rhône Les Garrigues	B	86
1995	Côtes du Rhône Les Garrigues	B	87

A well-run estate, Domaine de la Janasse rests in the capable hands of the youthful, ambitious, highly conscientious Aimé and Christophe Sabon. Just about everything that emerges from this domaine is of impeccably high quality. Now that they are bottled, the 1996s taste even better than they did previously. Both vintages of Côtes du Rhône offer easygoing, friendly, Grenache-based wines with plenty of pepper, kirsch, and spicy fruit. Both are low-acid, round, ripe, modestly concentrated wines with plenty of delicious fruit and heady alcohol. The Côtes du Rhône Les Garrigues is a 100% Grenache-based wine with more glycerin and body than the regular cuvée, but both are fine restaurant/bistro dry reds with immense crowd appeal. All four of these Côtes du Rhônes should be consumed over the next 1–3 years.

The 1996 Châteauneuf du Papes have turned out extremely well. In contrast to the more tannic 1995s, they offer immediate charm and appeal. They are meant to be drunk over the near term—5–7 years. The 1996 Châteauneuf du Pape Cuvée Classique's smoky, spicy, leathery, black cherry, and olive-scented nose jumps from the glass. It is a medium-bodied, lush, elegant wine with excellent richness, and a straightforward, spicy, moderately long finish. It needs to be drunk over the next 4–5 years. The 1996 Châteauneuf du Pape Cuvée Chaupin (made from 80-year-old Grenache vines) exhibits a medium ruby color, followed by a sweet, kirsch liqueur-scented nose with notes of raspberries, spice, and pepper. The wine reveals excellent sweetness and richness on the palate, with cedar and *garrigue* flavors. This complex, broadly flavored, medium- to full-bodied, soft Châteauneuf du Pape will offer ideal drinking over the next 5–6 years. The most serious and fullest bodied of the 1996s is the 1996 Châteauneuf du Pape Vieilles Vignes. It boasts a deep ruby color, and an explosive black cherry, raspberry, peppery-scented nose. Fat, rich, and intense, with low acidity, good glycerin, and generous levels of fruit extract and spice, this heady, full-flavored offering is top-notch, particularly for the vintage. Drink it over the next 7–8 years.

A late spring freeze as well as hail significantly reduced Domaine de la Janasse's 1997 production. Their strong, lush, forward 1997s are richer and more intense than the 1996s. The saturated dark ruby-colored 1997 Châteauneuf du Pape Cuvée Classique exhibits the telltale cherry, kirsch liqueur and peppery-scented nose, full body, admirable ripeness and purity, and low acid, heady, precocious style. It should drink well for 5–8 years. The 1997 Châteauneuf du Pape Cuvée Chaupin possesses greater color saturation (dark ruby/purple), as well as a heady, black raspberry and cherry jam-scented nose with pepper, allspice, and fruitcakelike aromas and flavors. Voluptuously textured and lush, with a marvelous combination of red and black fruits intermixed with Provençal herbs, this tasty, nicely layered, supple Châteauneuf du Pape should continue to drink well for 7–8 years. The outstanding 1997 Châteauneuf du Pape Vieilles Vignes displays an impressively saturated dark ruby/purple color. The wine is more reserved aromatically, with scents of incense, licorice, fennel, olives, and black raspberry liqueur. Notes of cherries and blackberries make an appearance in the mouth. This offering possesses the highest levels of extract and glycerin, the fullest body, and the most power, muscle, and tannin. Nevertheless, it is precociously styled, and thus best consumed in its vigorous youth—over the next 10–12 years.

As I indicated in my book on the Rhône, Janasse's 1995s are brilliant wines. The 1995 Châteauneuf du Pape Cuvée Classique is the least complex, with a dark ruby color, and a spicy, peppery, kirsch-scented nose with a touch of prunes. With moderate tannin and grip, this is a firm, medium- to full-bodied, attractively made style of Châteauneuf du Pape that will benefit from another 1–2 years of cellaring and last for a decade. The 1995 Châteauneuf du Pape Cuvée Chaupin exhibits a denser ruby/purple color, a black raspberry-scented nose, more restraint, and a closed, tannic style. Full bodied, with good flesh, this wine needs 1–2 years of cellaring. Long, textured, and well defined, it will have a plateau of maturity between 2000 and 2015. The exceptional 1995 Châteauneuf du Pape Vieilles Vignes offers a saturated plum/purple color, as well as fabulous quantities of fruit. It has a multifaceted nose of pepper, spice, black fruits (plums, cherries, and raspberries), and a touch of licorice and cedar. The wine is terrifically endowed, rich, and full-bodied but not overbearing or excessively alcoholic. It will provide fabulous drinking between 2000 and 2016.

Last, readers should always seek out the excellent Côtes du Rhône made by Domaine de la Janasse as well as their vin de pays. The 1995s are both fine offerings, with the regular Côtes du Rhône concentrated and fruity, with plenty of Bing cherry fruit, medium body, and light tannin in the dusty finish. It is a deep ruby-colored, robust Côtes du Rhône to drink over the next 4–5 years. The tannic, surprisingly serious, clove, pepper, spice, and truffle-scented 1995 Côtes du Rhône Les Garrigues boasts fine intensity and power. This big, muscular wine will benefit from 1–2 years of cellaring and keep for 7–8 years. These are impeccably made offerings from one of the finest estates in Châteauneuf du Pape.

DOMAINE DE LA JAUFRETTE

1997 Châteauneuf du Pape	C	(86–87)
1996 Châteauneuf du Pape	C	86

These are two good, fruity, sexy, cherry/raspberry-driven wines, with evolved dark ruby/plum colors. It is hard to choose a favorite, but both need to be drunk during their first 4–5 years of life. Proprietor Chastan has turned out generous, charming, hedonistic Châteauneuf du Papes with low acidity and plenty of character.

LAFFOY ET GASSE

1997 Côte Rôtie	D	(84–86)
1996 Côte Rôtie	D	83
1997 Côte Rôtie Vieilles Vignes	E	(86–88+)
1996 Côte Rôtie Vieilles Vignes	E	86

The wines from this estate, owned by Vincent Gasse and Marie-Claude Laffoy, are cultivated under the strict biological requirements of organic farming. I had a slight preference for the 1997s, which had a more open-knit appeal than the tart, narrowly constructed, acidic 1996s. The 1997 Côte Rôtie exhibits a dark ruby color, followed by sweet cherry/berry fruit in the nose, medium body, and surprisingly good acidity for the vintage. However, it comes across as one-dimensional and foursquare, at least at this stage of its development. Drink it over the next 5–6 years. The 1997 Côte Rôtie Vieilles Vignes possesses more flavor dimension and aromatic complexity than its sibling. Its deep ruby color is accompanied by an herb-tinged nose with blackberry fruit intermixed with allspice, cranberries, cherries, cassis, and earth. Good ripeness, excellent definition, and a medium-bodied, nicely textured mouth-feel make for a very good to excellent Côte Rôtie. Anticipated maturity: 2000–2008.

The 1996 Côte Rôtie displays a cool-year red fruit (currants) nose with little spice or additional complexity, although some pepper does emerge with airing. The wine's high acidity gives it a mouth-searing, narrow feel on the palate. While it will last for 10–12 years, not enough fat or fruit are present to provide charm. The 1996 Côte Rôtie Vieilles Vignes is similarly knit, but with more flesh and fat to balance out the wine's tart acid profile. It offers a sweet black currant nose intermixed with pepper, herbs, and a touch of violets. Vanillin from barrel aging is apparent in this medium-bodied, tightly-knit Côte Rôtie. It should be good, possibly very good if drunk between 2000–2008.

DOMAINE DES LAMBERTINS

1995 Vacqueyras	B	86

An impressive Vacqueyras, this dark ruby-colored wine exhibits a smoky, roasted herb, and dried cherry fruit-scented nose, sweet, rich flavors on the palate, good ripeness, and chocolatey overtones. This medium-bodied Vacqueyras can be drunk now or cellared for 3–4 years.

PATRICK LESEC RHÔNE VALLEY SELECTIONS

1997	Châteauneuf du Pape Les Galets Blondes	E	(88–90)
1996	Châteauneuf du Pape Les Galets Blondes	E	88
1995	Châteauneuf du Pape Les Galets Blondes	E	89+
1995	Châteauneuf du Pape Cuvée des Garrigues	E	89
1995	Côte Rôtie Les Dames Brunes	E	88
1997	Domaine Coursodon (Michel Perraud) Cornas Cuvée Sarah	D	(90–92)
1996	Domaine Coursodon (Michel Perraud) Cornas Cuvée Sarah	D	89
1997	Domaine Coursodon (Michel Perraud) Cornas Le Vignon	D	(90–92+?)
1997	Domaine Coursodon (Michel Perraud) St. Joseph Cuvée Sensonne	D	(92–94)
1997	Domaine Perillière Côtes du Rhône-Villages	A	87
1997	Domaine Pierredon Côtes du Rhône	A	(85–86)
1997	Domaine de Remizières (Desmeure) Crozes-Hermitage Cuvée Christophe	E	(90–93)
1996	Domaine de Remizières (Desmeure) Crozes-Hermitage Cuvée Christophe	E	90
1997	Domaine de Remizières (Desmeure) Crozes-Hermitage Cuvée Christophe (White)	E	(88–90)
1996	Domaine de Remizières (Desmeure) Crozes-Hermitage Cuvée Christophe (White)	E	85
1997	Domaine de Remizières (Desmeure) Hermitage Cuvée Emilie	EE	(87–90)
1996	Domaine de Remizières (Desmeure) Hermitage Cuvée Emilie	EE	93+
1997	Domaine de Remizières (Desmeure) Hermitage Cuvée Emilie (White)	EE	90?
1996	Domaine de Remizières (Desmeure) Hermitage Cuvée Emilie (White)	EE	88
1995	Château de Saint-Cosme Gigondas	D	87
1995	Château de Saint-Cosme Gigondas Cuvée Valbelle	D	90
1995	Domaine Saint-Jean de Bébian Coteaux de Languedoc	D	90

All of these wines are individual cuvées selected by the French-based broker, Patrick Lesec. His philosophy is to pick a particularly concentrated cuvée and have it brought up with minimal racking, virtually no sulfur additions, and bottled with neither fining nor filtration. These wines are both impressive and good values. I have also included the Domaine St.-Jean de Bébian Coteaux de Languedoc since it is represented in the United States by Patrick Lesec.

The two least expensive offerings are the 1997 Domaine Pierredon and 1997 Domaine Perillière. The 1997 Domaine Pierredon Côtes du Rhône is made of equal parts Grenache, Syrah, and Mourvèdre. It exhibits good ripeness for the vintage, a low-acid, fleshy personality, and coffee/peppery/berry fruit. Drink it over the next 1–2 years. The 1997 Domaine Perillière Côtes du Rhône-Villages is 50% Syrah and 50% Grenache. Like its counterpart, it is bottled unfiltered. Made from the Côtes du Rhône region known as the Garde, it displays an intense sweet berry fruitiness, an attractive kirsch, cassis, spicy, peppery character, and a fruit-driven personality that begs for consumption over the next several years.

In Châteauneuf du Pape, Patrick Lesec makes a selection of old-vine Grenache called Les Galets Blondes. The 1996 Les Galets Blondes Châteauneuf du Pape (14.7% alcohol) is an appealing, fleshy, plump Châteauneuf with a medium deep ruby color, and copious amounts of black cherry fruit intermixed with pepper, raspberry, and olive aromas. The wine's considerable glycerin and evolved style suggest it should be drunk over the next 3–4 years. The 1997 Les Galets Blondes Châteauneuf du Pape reveals more evidence of *sur-maturité* (the overripe cherry component), blackberry fruit, an opulent texture, excellent fatness, and a rich, full-bodied, low-acid, fleshy, succulent personality. It should have a longer aging curve of 7–8 years.

In the northern Rhône, Patrick Lesec works with Philippe Desmeure of Domaine de Remizières. All of these wines, which are the products of malolactic in barrel, extremely low SO$_2$ levels, and no fining or filtering, are limited production, impressive Rhône offerings. The 1996 Domaine de Remizières Crozes-Hermitage Cuvée Christophe boasts a dense ruby/purple color, as well as attractive sweet, new saddle leather aromas intertwined with roasted herbs and black currants. This full-bodied wine possesses terrific intensity and texture, and good rather than intrusive acidity. Anticipated maturity: 2002–2015. The terrific 1997 Domaine de Remizières Crozes-Hermitage Cuvée Christophe is one of the finest examples of Crozes I have tasted. The wine's saturated black/purple color is accompanied by superb aromatics of roasted coffee, blackberries, cassis, *pain grillé*, and smoke. Rich, with superb definition, full body, copious quantities of fruit and glycerin, and a long finish, this is about as good as Crozes-Hermitage can be. Production was just over 300 cases. Anticipated maturity: now–2015.

Domaine de Remizières Hermitage Cuvée Emilie is produced in 4,000-bottle lots. The 1996 (75% new oak is utilized) is a broad, powerful, backward yet impressively endowed wine. The color is a saturated purple, and the bouquet offers up youthful aromas of jammy black fruits intermixed with toasty new oak. Floral characteristics become apparent with airing. The wine has superpurity, full body, and moderate tannin in the long, concentrated finish. Anticipated maturity: 2003–2018. The fabulous 1997 Domaine de Remizières Hermitage Cuvée Emilie is an explosive example of Syrah from selected Hermitage vineyards. The opaque black color is followed by a flamboyant nose of bacon fat, smoky licorice, and cassis. Full bodied, superconcentrated, and massive in the finish, this low-acid, formidably endowed Hermitage should age effortlessly for 2 decades, although it will be more approachable in its youth than its 1996 sibling.

Patrick Lesec's white wine selections from the Domaine de Remizières include the Crozes-Hermitage Cuvée Christophe and Hermitage Cuvée Emilie. Both the 1997 and 1996 Crozes-Hermitage Cuvée Christophe blanc include 10% Roussanne, and are given partial malolactic fermentation. The 1997 is significantly better than the 1996, largely because it had more lees stirring and was bottled without filtration. It is an intense, powerful, richly honeyed wine with plenty of character. The 1996 reveals a citrusy, leaner style, and is shorter in the mouth. Its higher acidity gives it a more compressed personality. Consume it over the next 3–4 years. The Domaine de Remizières 1996 Hermitage Cuvée Emilie blanc (almost all of it comes from Les Rocoules *lieux-dit*) displays classy, refined fruit in its grapefruit/pineapple-scented nose. Mineral notes appear in the mouth. The wine is medium bodied and well made with crisp, tangy acidity. It should last for 5–10 years. The disjointed Domaine de Remizières 1997 Hermitage Cuvée Emilie blanc is revealing copious quantities of new oak. It is a more leesy, buttery, honeyed style of Hermitage with greater richness, more texture, and better length. This large-scaled offering should drink well young, yet last for a decade.

From Michel Perraud, Patrick Lesec has put together three impressive cuvées of Cornas. The Domaine Coursodon 1996 Cornas Cuvée Sarah exhibits a saturated dark purple color, good acidity, medium to full body, and excellent purity. This spicy, robust, toasty Cornas comes close to being outstanding. It should drink well for 10–15 years. The 1997 Domaine Coursodon Cornas Cuvée Sarah possesses more sweetness and richness in the mouth than its older sibling. The color is an impressively saturated black/ruby/purple. The nose offers up aromas of cassis, minerals, mint, and licorice, and the wine is rich, full bodied, dense, powerful, and muscular. Moderate tannin in the finish suggests 3–4 years of cellaring is warranted. Anticipated maturity: 2002–2015. The classically styled 1997 Domaine Coursodon Cornas Le Vignon is almost uncivilized with its powerful display of rustic tannin, full body, and large quantities of tar-flavored black currant fruit. This earthy, *sauvage*-styled Cornas should be at its finest between 2002 and 2015. Last, Patrick Lesec has produced 3,000 bottles (about 10 barrels) of a sensational 1997 St.-Joseph Sensonne from the Domaine Coursodon. This wine can compete with the luxury single-vineyard St.-Joseph Les Granite from Michel Chapoutier. Made from 60-year-old Syrah vines planted on the appellation's northern hillsides, it possesses an opaque black/purple color, and a super nose of jammy cassis and minerals. In the mouth, toasty new oak makes an appearance along with abundant quantities of black fruits. This full-bodied wine offers copious glycerin, low acidity, admirable power, and a terrifically long finish. It should drink well for 10–15+ years.

The 1995 Côte Rôtie Les Dames Brunes is an elegant, soft, attractive Côte Rôtie with licorice, pepper, and cassis scents, low acidity, supple, medium-bodied flavors, and surprising length and intensity. This impressive Côte Rôtie lingers on the palate longer than I initially expected. Drinkable now, this wine will age for 7–8 years.

Patrick Lesec directs/assists in the production of two cuvées of Châteauneuf du Pape, as well as Gigondas. The 1995 Châteauneuf du Pape Cuvée des Garrigues is very Provençal in its character. Peppery and spicy, with intense herbes de Provence aromatics, the wine exhibits meaty, smoky, grilled vegetablelike flavors with plenty of juicy, cherry fruit. Extremely evolved (it is already revealing some amber at the edge), this fragrant, smooth, round, medium- to full-bodied wine should be drunk over the next 5–6 years. The 1995 Châteauneuf du Pape Les Galets Blondes tips the scales at 14.7% natural alcohol. Made from primarily Grenache, with a small amount of Syrah and Mourvèdre, it is not racked until it is assembled for bottling, which is done with no fining or filtration. Fortunately, there are 500 cases of this powerful, rich, multilayered Châteauneuf du Pape that is bursting with black fruit. This sweet (from ripeness not sugar), full-bodied, concentrated wine should turn heads with its hedonistic display of fruit, glycerin, and alcohol. It is a big, rich, accessible style of Châteauneuf du Pape that should drink marvelously well for 12–15+ years.

In Gigondas, Patrick Lesec works with Château de Saint-Cosme to produce two wines, a cuvée classique, and an old-vine cuvée called Valbelle. The excellent 1995 Gigondas exhibits plenty of earthy, peppery, black fruits in its aromatics and flavors, good richness, medium to full body, and some tannin in the finish. This wine will benefit from another year or two of cellaring and will drink well for a decade. There is no doubting the quality of the 1995 Gigondas Valbelle. This outstanding, exotic wine exhibits seductive, toasty, sweet oak intertwined with gobs of peppery black cherry and plumlike fruit. The wine envelops the taster with copious quantities of glycerin, extract, and sweet fruit. Round, seductive, and fat, this expansive, ostentatiously styled Gigondas can be drunk now or cellared for 7–10 years.

Domaine St.-Jean de Bébian in the Coteaux du Languedoc is attempting to increase their quality level, particularly since it is now owned by the proprietor of France's top wine magazine, *Revue du Vin de France*. The 1995, which had just been bottled when I last tasted it, was tight, and, sadly, had been filtered (many French sommeliers still insist on sediment-free wines). While it is still an outstanding wine, the unfiltered barrel samples scored 2–4 points higher. It offers a deep ruby color, and a tight but reticent nose of blackberries, cherries, pepper, and earth intermingled with subtle notions of toasty oak and olives. The wine is tannic and medium bodied, with outstanding concentration, but some of the textural layers present in cask have been ripped out by the filter. Spicy, with a tendency toward austerity, this wine requires another 2–4 years of cellaring; it should keep for 15+.

DOMAINE DE MAROTTE

1996 Côtes du Ventoux	A	84
1995 Côtes du Ventoux	A	85
1995 Côtes du Ventoux Vieilles Vignes	B	85

The 1996 Côtes du Ventoux exhibits a medium ruby color, a peppery, cherry, earthy-scented nose, and a medium-bodied personality with kirschlike flavors. The finish is short, but the wine is well made and clean. The 1995 Côtes du Ventoux exhibits strawberry, cherry, and smoky aromas and flavors, fine ripeness, low acidity, ripe tannin, and an easygoing quaffing style. Drink it over the next 1–2 years. Last, the 1995 Côtes du Ventoux Vieilles Vignes has some tannin to shed, but I doubt it will melt away before the fruit fades. It is a nice cherry-scented, medium-bodied wine with an olive, pepper, and curranty nose. In the mouth, earth, spice, and fruit are presented in a moderately intense format. Drink it over the next 1–2 years.

MAS DE BOIS LAUZON

1996 Châteauneuf du Pape	D	90

A sleeper of the vintage, this tiny estate in northern Châteauneuf du Pape has produced one of the vintage's stars. It is on a fast evolutionary track, so readers lucky enough to latch on to a few bottles should plan to drink it over the next 5–7 years. Tasted twice, once in a peer group tasting and once drunk with a meal, this wine delivers everything expected of a hedonistic, spicy, fruit-driven Châteauneuf du Pape. The wine's saturated dark ruby color is accompanied by aromas of fruitcake, pepper, black cherries, and black currants. There is also a touch of olive, plenty of cedar, and gobs of fruit in this full-bodied, velvety-textured, hedonistic wine. The producers, Daniel and Monique Chaussy, do not make much wine, but this is one of the gems of the 1996 vintage.

CHATEAU MAUCOIL

1996 Châteauneuf du Pape Cuvée Privilege	D	86

Readers should note that this is a particular cuvée selected by French wine broker Alain Corcia and bottled unfined and unfiltered for the American and Japanese marketplaces. It is a different wine from the cuvée sold elsewhere. Skeptics who believe excessive fining and filtration do not have an impact on wine should taste the cuvée sold in Europe next to this. There is a striking difference, which I suspect is even more noticeable in lighter years such as 1996 than in more concentrated vintages such as 1990. This unfiltered cuvée exhibits a dark ruby color, and a heady, alcoholic, black cherry and kirsch liqueur-scented nose with cedar, spice cake, and pepper aromas. It is a tasty, richly fruity, elegant wine for consuming over the next 3–4 years.

DOMAINE DE MONTVAC

1997 Vacqueyras	C	86
1995 Vacqueyras Cuvée Vincila	C	87

Both of these wines are unfiltered selections made by the American importer. This property merits a close watch since the daughter, Cecile Dusserre, has taken over. The 1997 Vacqueyras (a blend of 70% Grenache, 20% Syrah, and 10% Mourvèdre) is a richly fruity wine with little complexity but plenty of spice, ripeness, and low acidity giving it a plush mouthfeel. Drink it over the next 4–5 years. The Vacqueyras Cuvée Vincila is produced from the property's oldest Grenache vines (65–70 years). The blend is generally 60% Grenache and 40% Syrah, although the importer told me the 1995 is primarily Grenache. It boasts a deep ruby color, followed by chewy black cherry fruit with jammy notes in the background. As the wine sat in the glass, pepper, earth, licorice, and smoke emerged. It is medium to full bodied, concentrated, and mouth-filling. Drink it over the next 4–5 years.

DOMAINE DE LA MORDORÉE

1995 Châteauneuf du Pape	D	90
1997 Châteauneuf du Pape Cuvée Classique	D	(88–91)
1996 Châteauneuf du Pape Cuvée de la Reine des Bois	E	94
1997 Côtes du Rhône	A	86
1997 Côtes du Rhône (Rosé)	A	85
1997 Lirac	B	87
1995 Lirac	B	88
1996 Lirac Cuvée de la Reine des Bois	C	90
1995 Lirac Cuvée de la Reine des Bois	C	89
1995 Lirac Cuvée de la Reine des Bois Blanc	C	87

Domaine de la Mordorée, the property of Christophe Delorme, has become one of the superstar estates of the southern Rhône, turning out exquisite Châteauneuf du Pape, as well as highclass Lirac, Côtes du Rhône, and Tavel rosé. Not all of the wines qualify as "best buys," but readers who have followed my Rhône Valley reports and adore these Provençal wines, would be foolish not to try the wines from this impeccably run estate. There are generally two cuvées of top wines from Lirac and Châteauneuf du Pape, a regular cuvée and the Cuvée de la Reine des Bois, the latter being produced from the estate's oldest vines and most concentrated juice. About 4,000 cases of the 15,000 case production are imported to the United States.

This estate is at the top of its game, producing some of the finest wines in the southern Rhône. The 1996 Châteauneuf du Pape Cuvée de la Reine des Bois is undoubtedly the wine of the vintage for Châteauneuf du Pape. From its youngest days this offering possessed a level of concentration and intensity far beyond anything else produced in the village. Now that it is in bottle, it is a sensational wine, having more in common with a great vintage such as 1990 or 1989 than 1996. In that sense, it could be called atypical for the year. It boasts a saturated black/purple color, as well as a knockout nose of blackberry fruit intermixed with licorice, roasted herbs, and kirsch. Full bodied, with a sweet, massive midpalate, fabulous harmony, and outstanding concentration and length, this Châteauneuf, which achieved 14% alcohol naturally, is a gorgeously textured, superb wine that should continue to evolve for 15+ years. Bravo!

I tasted only one 1997, the Châteauneuf du Pape Cuvée Classique. While it possesses impressive potential, it is not at the level of the 1996. The color is opaque ruby/purple. The wine displays a nose of blackberry/cherry liqueurlike fruit intermixed with wood smoke, allspice, and pepper. Full bodied, rich, and chewy, with outstanding purity and low acidity, this plump, fleshy, flamboyantly styled Châteauneuf du Pape should drink well young, yet evolve for a dozen or more years.

Domaine de la Mordorée's value-priced wines in the marketplace include a delicious 1997 Côtes du Rhône rosé, a candylike, kirsch, framboise-scented and -flavored wine that is dry, crisp, medium bodied, slightly austere, and classy. Drink it over the next 10–12 months. Mordorée's red wines possess considerable richness and are textbook examples of the heights southern Rhône reds can attain. The excellent 1997 Côtes du Rhône, a blend of 50% Grenache, 20% Syrah, 10% Mourvèdre, 5% Carignan, and 5% Counouise, reveals the vintage's low acidity, good fatness, ripe fruit, medium body, and plenty of peppery, herbes de Provence, kirsch, and plumlike flavors. Forward and showy, it is ideal for drinking over the next 2–3 years. The 1997 Lirac is even better, exhibiting a dark ruby/purple color, plenty of roasted herb, dried cherry, smoky, peppery, fruit flavors, excellent ripeness, and a delicious, medium-bodied, nicely layered, well-textured feel in the mouth. It should drink well for 4–5 years. At $15 a bottle, the outstanding 1997 Lirac Cuvée de la Reine des Bois is a brilliant wine that is capable of lasting a decade. It boasts an opaque purple color, as well as a knockout nose of cassis, kirsch, black raspberries, truffles, pepper, and spice. Fat and superbly concentrated, yet with well-integrated acidity and tannin, this exquisite Lirac could easily pass for a top Châteauneuf du Pape in a blind tasting. Anticipated maturity: now–2008.

Two other terrific bargains from Domaine de la Mordorée are the red wine cuvées of 1995 Lirac. The 1995 Lirac (40% Syrah and 60% Grenache) exhibits an opaque purple color, a sweet, black raspberry, peppery-scented nose, dazzling concentration and ripeness, fine opulence, and a heady, rich personality with plenty of black fruits in its chewy texture. Although not complicated, its good acidity and robust style will give this soft, well-endowed wine 4–5 years of drinkability. Slightly more complex aromatically, the 1995 Lirac Cuvée de la Reine des Bois (a blend of equal proportions of Syrah, Grenache, and Mourvèdre) reveals a deep purple color, a smoky, herbes de Provence, cassis, and licorice-scented nose, peppery, concentrated flavors, no hard edges, and a lush, ripe, nicely layered finish. Low acidity and sweet oak give this wine a precocious appeal; it should drink well for 4–6 years. Domaine de la Mordorée's 1995 Châteauneuf du Pape is one of the finest wines of this topflight vintage (the best since 1989 and 1990). Made from 70% old vine Grenache, 10% Mourvèdre, 10% Syrah, 5% Vaccarese, and 5% Cinsault, this is a large-scaled, rich, full-bodied wine that needs another 2–3 years of cellaring. It reveals a dense purple color, and a tight but promising nose of herbes de Provence, kirsch, smoke, and pepper. Full bodied, concentrated, and moderately tannic, this wine should be at its best between 2001 and 2012.

The immense progress this estate has achieved over the last few years is also noticeable in their white wine program. It is rare that I can recommend a white wine from Lirac, but Domaine de la Mordorée's 1995 Lirac Cuvée de la Reine des Bois, a blend of 35% Grenache Blanc, 20% Clairette, 15% Marsanne, 15% Roussanne, and 15% Viognier, is a serious, barrel-fermented white wine. It exhibits gobs of honeyed tropical fruit, a subtle touch of oak, and low acidity in its plump, plush texture. This wine should be drunk before the end of 1997.

MOULIN DE LA GARDETTE

1996	Gigondas Cuvée Classique	D	86
1997	Gigondas Cuvée Speciale	D	(88–91)
1995	Gigondas Cuvée Speciale	C/D	91

Proprietor Jean-Baptiste Meunier is fashioning impressive wines from this small 17.4-acre estate. The impressively endowed 1995 Gigondas Cuvée Speciale is made from 80% Grenache and 20% Syrah from vines averaging 70 years in age. This unfiltered powerhouse possesses a dark opaque purple color, and a gorgeous nose of sweet blackberry and kirsch fruit intermixed with pepper and earth. Extremely full bodied and hugely extracted, with jammy fruit and tangy acidity for its degree of ripeness, this classic example of Gigondas can be drunk young, or cellared for 15+ years.

The powerful, impressively built, rich, sweet, expansive, cherry liqueur/kirsch-dominated 1997 Gigondas Cuvée Speciale should turn out to be an excellent, possibly outstanding example. The wine is robust and slightly rustic, with low acidity, and copious layers of fruit, glycerin, and extract. It offers a savory, mouth-filling impression. Anticipated maturity: 2001–2012. The 1996 Gigondas Cuvée Classique exhibits a peppery, roasted herb, smoky nose, blackberry, roasted, medium-bodied flavors, and a soft midpalate. The finish is austere, with hard tannin. Drink it over the next 5–7 years.

MOULIN-TACUSSEL

1995 Châteauneuf du Pape	C/D	86

Moulin-Tacussel's 1995 Châteauneuf du Pape, which did not perform well when I first tasted it, has turned out to be an attractive, reasonably fine wine with subtle mint, a notion of herbes de Provence, and moderate quantities of black cherry fruit. It is an uncomplex, spice-driven, medium-bodied wine with some sweetness, and a clean, ripe, soft finish. It should be drunk over the next 3–5 years.

CHÂTEAU DU MOURRE DU TENDRE

1993 Châteauneuf du Pape	D	87
1988 Châteauneuf du Pape	E	93
1995 Côtes du Rhône-Villages	A/D	86

This small estate run by Pierre Paumel, whose family also owns the outstanding restaurant/hotel just outside the village of Châteauneuf du Pape called Le Sommellèrie, has fashioned three interesting wines. The 1995 Côtes du Rhône-Villages is a dense wine for its appellation, with plenty of peppery black cherry fruit intermixed with serious body and length. This mouth-filling, easy-to-drink wine should continue to offer uncomplicated, savory drinking over the next 2–3 years. The 1993 Châteauneuf du Pape reveals some of the vintage's austerity, but is well above the average. It exhibits black fruits intermixed with pepper, dried herbs, and spice. Medium bodied, with austerity in the finish but plenty of depth and structure, I do not think the tannin will ever become completely integrated, so drink it over the next 5–6 years. A tiny quantity of 1988 Châteauneuf du Pape ($60 a bottle) has been released by Paumel. This is a sumptuous, classic Châteauneuf du Pape with an explosive nose of kirsch liqueur intermixed with floral scents and spices. Full bodied, rich, and chewy, with outstanding concentration and purity, this wine, which is just achieving full maturity, should continue to drink well for 5–7 years.

GUY MOUSSET

1997 Châteauneuf du Pape Clos St. Michel Cuvée Classique	E/EE	(82–84)
1996 Châteauneuf du Pape Clos St. Michel Cuvée Classique	E/EE	79
1997 Châteauneuf du Pape Clos St. Michel Cuvée Réservée	E/EE	(86–88)
1996 Châteauneuf du Pape Clos St. Michel Cuvée Réservée	E/EE	87

There is a vast difference between Guy Mousset's generic cuvée and Cuvée Réservée. In both vintages, the latter offering is richer and denser as well as more concentrated and interesting. The 1996 Châteauneuf du Pape Cuvée Classique reveals some pepper and *garrigue* but an evolved personality. It offers little concentration and a soft, flaccid finish. Drink it over the next several years. The 1996 Châteauneuf du Pape Cuvée Réservée exhibits an impressive dark ruby color, in addition to sweet blackberry and cherry fruit notes, medium to full body, excellent ripeness, and a round, generous finish. Drink it over the next 5–7 years.

The 1997 Châteauneuf du Pape Cuvée Classique is slightly more interesting than its older sibling, displaying a spicy, herbaceous, peppery, pruny nose. In the mouth, black cherries become the dominant flavor component in this light- to medium-bodied, soft wine. It will require consumption over the next 2–3 years. The 1997 Châteauneuf du Pape Cuvée Réservée is a fatter, thicker, more unctuously textured wine offering copious quantities of black cherry fruit with a touch of new oak in the background (suggesting a small percentage of *barriques* are being used), a foursquare personality, and good glycerin and alcohol. It should drink well for 5–7 years.

CHÂTEAU DE LA NERTHE

1997	Châteauneuf du Pape Cuvée Beauvenir (White)	E	88
1995	Châteauneuf du Pape Cuvée Beauvenir (White)	E	89
1997	Châteauneuf du Pape Cuvée des Cadettes	E	(90–91)
1996	Châteauneuf du Pape Cuvée des Cadettes	E	89
1995	Châteauneuf du Pape Cuvée des Cadettes	E	93
1997	Châteauneuf du Pape Cuvée Classique	D	(87–90)
1996	Châteauneuf du Pape Cuvée Classique	D	87
1995	Châteauneuf du Pape Cuvée Classique	D	88
1997	Châteauneuf du Pape Cuvée Classique (White)	D	87

Under the meticulous administration of Alain Dugas, this estate is beginning to exploit its considerable potential. The wines have consistently been very good to excellent, but I get the impression they are pushing the envelope of quality even further. They have unquestionably done well in the tricky 1996 and 1997 vintages. Moreover, they had just finished the 1998 harvest when I visited, and Dugas was ecstatic over the 1998s, claiming their tiny yields were approximately 2 tons per acre and had produced wines with an average natural alcohol of 13.2%. As for the more forward, softer 1996s and 1997s, there are some very good cuvées to be sampled. In most vintages there are two cuvées of both red and white Châteauneuf du Pape, the cuvée classique and the limited production, old-vine Mourvèdre-based Cuvée des Cadettes. For the whites, there is the cuvée classique and a Roussanne-dominated Châteauneuf du Pape Clos de Beauvenir.

The 1996 Châteauneuf du Pape Cuvée Classique red (a blend of 56% Grenache, 18% Mourvèdre, 16% Syrah, and 10% various other varietals) exhibits a deep ruby color, as well as an excellent cherry, peppery, spicy nose, a sweet, fleshy midpalate, good softness and texture, and an expansive, easygoing, cherry-dominated personality. The wine's forward style suggests it should be drunk over the next 6–7 years. The 1997 Châteauneuf du Pape Cuvée Classique red (44% Grenache, 24% Syrah, 20% Mourvèdre, 7% Cinsault, and the balance tiny portions of other varietals) is a richer, more successful offering. The color is a deeper, more saturated ruby with purple nuances. The wine offers sweet, jammy plum/black cherry and raspberry aromas, deep, rich, full-bodied, fat flavors, some of the telltale pepper and spice, and a finish with substantial fruit and glycerin. This wine, which will be the first cuvée classique to be bottled without fining or filtration, appears to have the potential to drink well for a decade.

Limited quantities of the Cuvée des Cadettes are produced (400–1000 cases). There are only 7,000 bottles of the 1996 Châteauneuf du Pape Cuvée des Cadettes, which is made from a blend of 46% Mourvèdre, 32% Grenache, and 22% Syrah. A small portion of this wine spends time in *barrique*. The dark ruby/purple-colored 1996 possesses a spicy, new saddle leather, raspberry, peppery, earthy nose, medium body, plenty of tannin, a slightly austere finish, excellent purity, good richness, and a serious, muscular style with good grip and structure. Drink it over the next 10–12 years. The outstanding 1997 Châteauneuf du Pape Cuvée des Cadettes (36% Grenache, 32% Mourvèdre, and 32% Syrah; 11,000 bottles produced) is unquestionably one of the stars of this vintage. The color is a saturated ruby/purple. The nose offers up copious quantities of cassis, kirsch, new saddle leather, Asian spices, and earth. Rich and full bodied, with a creamy texture, low acidity, and a luscious, massive finish for the vintage, this is a superb example from a light year. It should drink well for 10–15 years. The 1995 Châteauneuf du Pape Cuvée des Cadettes (44% Grenache, 28% Mourvèdre, and 28% Syrah; 19,000 bottles produced) was not released until early 1998. It boasts a dark ruby/purple color as well as a super nose of new saddle leather, prunes, wood fire, spice, cassis, and kirsch. Full bodied and dense, with superb concentration and purity, this wine is approachable but should evolve and improve for another 7–8 years; it will last for 15 or more.

There are two 1997 cuvées of white wine (considered a top-notch vintage for the small production of Châteauneuf du Pape blanc). The 1997 Châteauneuf du Pape Cuvée Classique blanc (47% Grenache Blanc, 20% Roussanne, 17% Clairette, and 16% Bourboulenc is aged in both tank and *barrique*. In order to preserve its crisp acidity, the wine is not put through malolactic fermentation. An excellent white Châteauneuf, it offers a lemony, citrusy, honeyed personality, an exuberant, richly fruity style, medium to full body, fine purity, and nicely integrated, subtle wood notes. The 1997 Châteauneuf du Pape Clos de Beauvenir (53% Roussanne, 47% Clairette) was made in limited quantities of just over 400 cases. This 100% barrel-fermented wine has its malolactic fermentation blocked, resulting in a rich, full-bodied, spicy, oaky style. It is more Burgundian in orientation, with the oak influence more noticeable than in the cuvée classique. The Clos de Beauvenir should age nicely for 3–4 years.

The 1995 Châteauneuf du Pape Cuvée Beauvenir (59% Roussanne and 41% Clairette) reveals some of the toasty, *pain grillé*-like scents that are the result of barrel fermentation, good, ripe, honeysuckle and tropical fruit flavors, medium body, fine richness, average acidity, and a spicy, long finish. It is a classy, nearly outstanding example of white Châteauneuf du Pape that is intended to rival the splendid cuvée of old-vine Roussanne produced by Beaucastel.

The red 1995 Châteauneuf du Pape Cuvée Classique was bottled in March 1997, and was released in November 1997. An excellent wine, it offers up a stylish, lead pencil, vanillin, black currant-scented nose, medium to full body, admirable structure and tannin, spicy, rich fruit, and fine length. It is a classic, elegant, modern-styled Châteauneuf du Pape that should be cellared for 2–3 years and consumed over the following 15.

ROBERT NIERO

1997 Condrieu	D/E	87
1997 Condrieu Coteau du Cheri	E	88

These are two elegantly styled Condrieus with plenty of the vintage's alcohol, but more finesse and freshness than some of the fatter, riper cuvées. The 1997 Condrieu Coteau du Cheri reveals more minerality, and a longer finish. Both are floral, honeyed Condrieus with good definition and purity. Drink them over the next 1–2 years.

MICHEL OGIER

1997 Côte Rôtie	E	(88–90)
1996 Côte Rôtie	E	87
1997 Côte Rôtie Belle-Hélène Côte Brune	EE	(91–94)
1995 Côte Rôtie Côte Blonde	E	89+
1997 Syrah La Rosine Vin de Pays	B	(86–87)
1996 Syrah La Rosine Vin de Pays	B	87

Ogier, in addition to making one of the finest values in Côte Rôtie (La Rosine Syrah from a vineyard near Condrieu), also fashions one of the village's most elegant, stylish Côte Rôties, primarily from Côte Blonde fruit. In 1997 he produced a cuvée dedicated to his wife, Hélène. It is an impressive 100% new oak offering (125 cases in 1997) from 45-year-old vines on the Côte Rozier, next to La Landonne. Interestingly, he made three barrels of this wine in 1995 that turned out so well he decided to do it again in 1997. The wine spends 30 months in barrel before it is bottled unfiltered. The 1997 Côte Rôtie Belle-Hélène Côte Brune is a spectacular offering, revealing a saturated ruby/purple color, as well as a knock-out nose of toasty new oak intermixed with cassis, blackberries, and roasted spices. Full bodied, with the wood well absorbed, this masculine, massive Côte Rôtie possesses spectacular intensity and purity, but has lost neither its typicity nor elegance because of the extensive new oak treatment. It should drink well upon release and last for 10–15+ years. The 1997 Côte Rôtie may also turn out to be outstanding. It displays a deep purple color, a sweet nose of smoke, pine needles, blackberry/cassis fruit, and a floral note. The wine has medium body, outstanding purity, a low-acid, opulent texture, and admirable depth and length. Although some tannin is present, this beauty will drink well young and last for 12–15 years.

The 1996 Côte Rôtie reveals terrific color saturation (dark ruby/purple), and a more tannin/acid profile than either 1997 cuvée. Bottled in June 1998, the 1996 includes just under 1% Viognier added to the blend. Smoke, black currant, and earthy notes are followed by a dense, structured, moderately tannic example, with the acidity keeping the wine firm and austere. While not as extroverted and sexy as the 1997s, it is a very good Côte Rôtie in this angularly styled vintage. Give it 2–3 years of cellaring and enjoy it over the next 12+ years.

For value, Ogier's La Rosine Syrah is a wine to take seriously. Along with Auguste Clape's Côtes du Rhône (also made from 100% Syrah), it is one of the finest examples from the northern Rhône that can be purchased for a song. The 1997 La Rosine Syrah reveals terrific color, as well as jammy cassis fruit, a soft, easygoing, medium-bodied personality, and rustic tannin in the finish. It is an ideal gutsy bistro red to consume during its first 3–4 years of life. From a cooler year, the 1996 La Rosine Syrah exhibits a deep color with noticeable tannin, excellent purity, and gobs of red currant/cherry fruit. It should drink well for 3–4 years.

The 1995 Côte Rôtie Côte Blonde is a beautifully silky, delicate yet intensely flavored wine that should merit an outstanding rating with a few more years of age. The muscular, powerful, backward 1995 displays a slightly harder edge than the 1996, as well as Ogier's trademark sweetness of fruit, roundness, and undeniable finesse and elegance. The color is a healthy dark ruby/purple. It offers up that gorgeous Côte Rôtie perfume of black fruits, floral scents, roasted herbs, and spice. This medium-bodied, deliciously rich, yet still youthful wine should be at its finest in 2–3 years; it will last for 10–12 years.

DOMAINE DE L'ORATOIRE ST.-MARTIN

1996 Cairanne Cuvée Prestige	C	89
1996 Cairanne Haut Coustias (White)	C	88

1995 Cairanne Haut Coustias	C	91
1996 Cairanne Réserve des Seigneurs	B	88
1996 Côtes du Rhône	B	87

Even before my book on the Rhône Valley was published in 1997, I had been touting the wines from this exceptional estate in the Côtes du Rhône village of Cairanne. The newest releases are impressive wines that should be sought out by Rhône Valley enthusiasts, as well as readers looking for wines with considerable personality and flavor. The 1996 Haut Coustias white, a blend of 40% Marsanne, 40% Roussanne, and 20% Viognier, is an impressive southern Rhône white with high extract, elevated levels of glycerin, and copious quantities of full-bodied, glycerin-imbued, fleshy flavors suggestive of cloves, butter, roasted nuts, and peaches. Complex, thick, and juicy, it will provide ideal drinking over the next year.

Made from vines averaging 40 years in age, the 1996 Côtes du Rhône, an 80% Grenache/20% Syrah blend, exhibits a dark ruby color, excellent ripeness, and sweet, tarry, black cherry fruit intermixed with herbs and pepper. The 1996 Cairanne Réserve des Seigneurs, a 60% Grenache, 30% Mourvèdre, and 10% Syrah blend, boasts a dark ruby, nearly purple color, as well as beautifully pure, blackberry, kirsch, and smoky aromatics. In the mouth, this rich, fruit-driven wine reveals layers of flavor, good spice, and a supple, low-acid finish. It should drink well for 2–4 years. The 1996 Cairanne Cuvée Prestige, a blend of 60% Grenache and 40% Mourvèdre made from a meager 25 hectoliters per hectare (under 2 tons per acre), is produced from several parcels planted in 1905. The wine offers outstanding intensity, peppery, leathery, sweet black cherry, and berry aromas, a layered, nicely textured, medium- to full-bodied personality, moderate tannin, and outstanding purity. This effort may merit an even higher score with another six months of bottle age. It should drink well for 5–7 years. The compelling 1995 Cairanne Haut Coustias possesses an opaque purple color, followed by viscous, splendidly rich, blackberry and kirsch liqueurlike flavors. This is a dazzling example of what can be achieved in such less prestigious Côtes du Rhône appellations as Cairanne. A blend of 45% Mourvèdre, 45% Syrah, and 10% Grenache, and given some barrel treatment, this explosively rich, full-bodied, blockbuster Côtes du Rhône can be drunk now, or cellared for a decade. Wow!

ALAIN PARENT

1997 Condrieu Lys de Volan	E	93
1997 St.-Joseph "420 Nuits"	D/E	(89–91)

A producer to take seriously, Alain Parent is turning out spectacular Condrieu from his hillside vineyard. In 1997, yields were a little more than a ton of fruit per acre, and the wine was aged in *barrique*, of which 60% was new. Considerable lees contact and stirring were done, and the 1997 Condrieu Lys de Volan was bottled with only a light pad filtration. It is a rich, leesy, Burgundian-styled Condrieu with copious quantities of floral, white peach, and apricotlike fruit. In the mouth, there is a leesy, buttery complexity in addition to exquisite extract and richness. Marvelously well balanced with well-integrated wood, and enough acidity to provide definition, this sumptuously styled Condrieu should drink well for 1–2 years. Readers looking for a terrific, massive 100% Syrah made from low yields and bottled unfiltered should check out Alain Parent's 1997 St.-Joseph "420 Nuits". Made from 15-year-old Syrah vines, and aged in 100% new *demi-muids*, it is sensationally extracted and rich, with super-intense aromas of wood smoke, cassis, pepper, and a touch of dried tomatoes. Full bodied, and beautifully pure and rich, with the oak playing a subtle role, this large-scaled St.-Joseph should provide gorgeous drinking early (because of its low acidity and evolved style) but keep for 10–12 years.

DOMAINE DU PEGAU

1995	Châteauneuf du Pape	C	93+
1997	Châteauneuf du Pape Cuvée Réservée	D	(85–87)
1996	Châteauneuf du Pape Cuvée Réservée	D	88

Since most readers will never have access to a bottle of Henri Bonneau's phenomenal Châteauneuf du Pape, the Réserve des Céléstins, they should try a bottle of the wine that comes closest to that style. Paul Féraud produces blockbuster, chewy, old-style Châteauneuf du Pape in much the same manner as his mentor, Henri Bonneau. Féraud's offerings are uncompromising, high-alcohol, massive wines that hit the heights in the great vintages, yet do surprisingly well in lighter years. No doubt influenced by his daughter, Laurence, Féraud bottles much earlier than Bonneau, who often does not bottle a Céléstins until it has had at least 5 years of élevage in the dark, cramped cellars under his house. Féraud tends to bottle within 2 years, except for his limited production Cuvée Laurence, which is bottled after 5–6 years of barrel aging.

Producing traditionally made Châteauneuf du Papes, Domaine du Pegau has had an impressive track record for nearly 20 years. During the month of December 1998 (what I affectionately call the season of swallowing rather than spitting), I amused myself as well as my wife with a mini-vertical of Pegau, tasting the 1979, 1981, 1983, 1985, 1989, and 1990. I was pleased that all of these vintages were living up to my high expectations. However, owners of the 1979, 1981, and 1983 should make plans to consume them over the next few years (the 1981 is a phenomenal Châteauneuf du Pape). There is a tendency to call these wines rustic, but that is a pejorative I find objectionable. These are full-bodied, concentrated wines containing all the Provençal as well as Châteauneuf du Pape flavors and aromas. The wines are based on ripe, low-yielding, old-vine Grenache. Under the influence of Paul Feraud's daughter, Laurence, the wines are now bottled earlier, which is to their benefit, but these boldly styled, powerful Châteauneuf du Papes can handle plenty of aging in the estate's old *foudres*.

The 1997 Châteauneuf du Pape Cuvée Réservée is made in a firm, tannic style, with good black cherry fruit, and a dry, allspice, peppery character. In the mouth, the wine is spice driven, with medium body, a slight austerity, and a moderately long finish. Although it is not a star of the vintage, it is a very good 1997 Châteauneuf du Pape, but firmer and more backward than most wines of the vintage. The 1996 Châteauneuf du Pape Cuvée Réservée is one of the better wines of the vintage, exhibiting a dark plum color, and a sweet, expansive nose of black fruits, licorice, *garrigue*, olives, and roasted coffee. Ripe, dense, full bodied, and deliciously supple and generous, this mouth-filling, substantial, velvety-textured wine can be drunk over the next 7–10 years.

Domaine du Pegau's 1995 Châteauneuf du Pape, reminiscent of the 1985, should prove to be a classic. It boasts a deep ruby/purple color, followed by a gutsy, olive, sausage, peppery, and black cherry-scented nose, massive body, a layered texture, and rustic tannin in the blockbuster finish. It is a huge, concentrated, backward style that is the antithesis of the 1996. Remarkably, alcohol levels achieved in 1995 averaged between 14.5% and 15.5%— with no sugar additions! Buyers of this wine will need patience, as I do not see it being ready to drink for 4–5 years. Anticipated maturity: 2003–2020.

DOMAINE PELAQUIE

1995	Côtes du Rhône	A	86
1996	Laudun Côtes du Rhône-Villages	B	86
1995	Lirac	B	86+
1994	Lirac	B	86

The 1996 Laudun Côtes du Rhône-Villages is a crisp, well-made, dry white produced from a blend of Claret, Bourboulenc, Roussanne, and Grenache Blanc. A touch of Viognier is also included, which has resulted in a peachlike nose, with floral and mineral notes. It is a medium-bodied, clean, crisp, surprisingly elegant, dry white Rhône to drink over the next year.

The dark garnet-colored 1995 Côtes du Rhône, which is dominated by Syrah, is a tasty wine with peppery, herb, olive, tarlike, berry fruit. It has a northern Rhône feel and texture, despite the fact it is from the south. Its structure and cool climate characteristics suggest it should drink nicely for 2–3 years. Between the two Liracs, the 1994 is more dominated by pepper and herbes de Provence/*garrigue*, with round, fully mature flavors. This medium-bodied offering is made from a blend of Grenache and Mourvèdre. The 1995 Lirac exhibits a sweeter, riper, and denser personality, as well as more tannin, tar, and saddle leather notes, the latter component no doubt due to the 40% Mourvèdre in the blend. The wine displays good spice, plenty of red cherry fruit, and medium body. Drink it over the next 2–3 years.

DOMAINE DU PÈRE CABOCHE

1997	Châteauneuf du Pape	C	85
1995	Châteauneuf du Pape	C	86
1997	Châteauneuf du Pape Cuvée Elisabeth Chambellan	D	(86–88)
1995	Châteauneuf du Pape Cuvée Vieilles Vignes Elisabeth Chambellan	D	90

Jean-Pierre Boisson, the mayor of Châteauneuf du Pape, tends to bottle these wines early to preserve their fruit and charm. His wines are richly fruity, easily accessible, modern-styled classics. In the bigger, more muscular, structured, and concentrated vintages they possess extra dimensions of depth, but there is no denying the crowd-pleasing appeal of these two cuvées. The 1997 Châteauneuf du Pape's medium ruby color is followed by an expansive, sweet nose of black cherry candy with a touch of *sur-maturité* (orange/apricot scents). The tropical fruit character continues on the soft, round, medium-bodied palate. Drink this expansive, delicious, up-front Châteauneuf over the next 3–5 years. Made from older vines, the more expansive 1997 Châteauneuf du Pape Cuvée Elisabeth Chambellan possesses layers of fruit, with more glycerin and alcohol. There is virtually no tannin in this hedonistic, richly fruity, round, spicy, fruit-driven wine. Drink it over the next 3–5 years.

The 1995s are both delicious. The 1995 Châteauneuf du Pape is made in a lighter, modern-day style, with plenty of elegant berry fruit, a whiff of pepper, and smoky, roasted herbs. This medium-bodied, refreshingly fruity Châteauneuf du Pape will require drinking over the next 3–4 years. Surprisingly, it is not that different than the 1996, even though one would expect the 1995 to be more concentrated. The opulently textured, meaty 1995 Châteauneuf du Pape Cuvée Vieilles Vignes Elisabeth Chambellan is a succulent, hedonistic, aromatic, and flavorful wine. The medium to dark ruby color is deceptive in view of the wine's intensity and richness of fruit. It possesses layers of jammy cherry fruit, intermixed with flavors of plums, prunes, fruitcake, and the telltale pepper and roasted herb notes. Medium to full bodied, with high alcohol, this is a luxuriantly fruity style of Châteauneuf that is meant to seduce the taster. It will not make old bones, but for drinking over the next 5–7 years, this wine delivers the goods.

DOMAINE DU PÈRE PAPE

1996	Châteauneuf du Pape Clos du Calvaire	D	86
1996	Châteauneuf du Pape La Crau de la Mère	D	90
1996	Châteauneuf du Pape Domaine du Grand Coulet	D	88

These fine 1996s are among the more full flavored and robust Châteauneuf du Papes of this soft, commercially styled vintage. The dark ruby-colored 1996 Châteauneuf du Pape Clos du Calvaire offers excellent plum and black cherry fruit intermixed with pepper, Provençal herbs, and spice. A medium-bodied, round, tasty wine with good fruit and an easygoing finish, it will drink well during the next 4–5 years. The 1996 Châteauneuf du Pape Domaine du Grand Coulet exhibits more *garrigue*, pepper, and cedar in addition to copious black cherry and plumlike fruit. Medium to full bodied, with excellent richness, a sweet, expansive palate, and a jammy, lush finish, this excellent Châteauneuf du Pape possesses low acidity and a forward, hedonistic style. Drink it over the next 5–6 years. The outstanding 1997 Châteauneuf du Pape La Crau de la Mère is one of the vintage's stars. A beauty, it boasts a deep ruby color, followed by explosive jammy, blackberry, and cherry fruit intermixed with spice and pepper. Medium to full bodied and dense, with superb purity, and a multilayered, unctuously textured finish, this wine combines power and concentration with an aromatic, supple style. The deep ruby/purple color hints of the impressive extraction obtained in this vintage. Drink it over the next 6–8 years.

ANDRÉ PERRET

1997 Condrieu Clos Chanson	E	90
1997 Condrieu Coteau de Chèry	E	92
1997 Condrieu Vandange d'Automme	E	88?

André Perret makes brilliant Condrieu, as evidenced by the following wines. His 1997 Condrieu Clos Chanson (from a 1.25-acre parcel overlooking the village of Chavanay) exhibits the textbook peach/apricot/acacia flower scents of a top-quality Condrieu. It is full bodied, with terrific fruit intensity, a luscious, unctuous texture, and a powerful, long, ripe, exotic finish. It will not make "old bones," but for drinking over the next several years, this is a dazzling Condrieu. The spectacular 1997 Condrieu Coteau de Chèry (made from a whopping 6.2-acre parcel of 10- and 50-year-old vines) rivals Guigal's single-vineyard Condrieu La Doriane for complexity and richness. From its light green/gold color, to its exotic, leesy, mineral, peach/apricot aromatics that inundate the olfactory senses, to its full-bodied, exquisitely pure, well-delineated personality, this is an outstanding Condrieu that should drink well for several years. I had mixed emotions about Perret's 1997 Condrieu Vandange d'Automme. It seemed disjointed when I tasted it. Not terribly sweet, although certainly an after-dinner or aperitif-styled Condrieu, this medium- to full-bodied wine exhibited fine ripeness, but its component parts seemed jumbled. Perhaps it needs more time to pull itself together.

DOMAINE ROGER PERRIN

1995 Châteauneuf du Pape	C	87
1995 Châteauneuf du Pape Réserve des Vieilles Vignes	D	88

This modest estate of just under 30 acres produces about 2,200 cases of estate-bottled Châteauneuf du Pape with the balance sold off to leading *négociants*. Both 1995 cuvées are excellent, with the Réserve de Vieilles Vignes possibly meriting a higher score after some bottle age. The 1995 Châteauneuf du Pape exhibits a deep ruby/purple color, followed by an excellent nose of pepper, black fruits, and spice. Long, dense, and medium bodied, this is an excellent, structured, tannic style of Châteauneuf du Pape that will benefit from 2–3 years of cellaring; it will keep for 12–15. Composed of 80% Grenache and 20% Syrah, and aged in small oak casks, of which one-third were new, the 1995 Châteauneuf du Pape Réserve de Vieilles Vignes is reminiscent of the luxury Cuvée des Générations from Château de la Gardine. It possesses the potential to merit an outstanding rating. It exhibits an impressive dark ruby/purple color, and attractive vanillin/*pain grillé* scents to go along with plenty of ripe black cherry and curranty fruit. There is an underlying mineral character to this full-bodied, stylish, oaky wine. Anticipated maturity: now–2007.

DOMAINE DE PIAUGER

1996 Gigondas	C	85
1995 Gigondas	C	88

This well-run estate has turned out a clean, soft, fruity, medium-bodied 1996 Gigondas with a moderately dark plum color. It is a wine to drink over the next 4–5 years. The 1995 Gigondas is more concentrated, with intense black raspberry and cherry fruit, medium to full body, a peppery, spicy, herbes de Provence-scented nose, and layers of lush, jammy fruit. It is an elegant, authoritatively flavored Gigondas that can be drunk now or cellared for 7–8 years.

DOMAINE DE LA PRESIDENTE

1995 Cairanne Côtes du Rhône Villages	A	85

Proprietor Max Aubert, a well-known name in the southern Rhône Valley, has produced a textbook Côtes du Rhône, with plenty of cherry/kirsch and herbes de Provence-scented and -flavored fruit. The wine is medium bodied, soft, and attractive. Drink it over the next 1–2 years.

CHÂTEAU RASPAIL

1995 Gigondas	C	88

One of the largest estates in Gigondas (just under 100 acres), Château Raspail is owned by the well-known *négociant* firm of Gabriel Meffre. The 1995 Gigondas is one of the finest efforts I have ever tasted from Gabriel Meffre. It exhibits a saturated plum/purple color, sweet, ripe, peppery, black raspberry and cherry fruit, good, crisp underlying acidity, a backward, tart personality, full body, some spice, and moderate tannin in the long finish. The 1995 is best cellared for another 2–3 years and held for 15 years.

DOMAINE RASPAIL-AY

1997 Gigondas	C	(85–88)
1996 Gigondas	C	86
1995 Gigondas	C	89+

The 1997 Gigondas possesses a deep ruby/purple color, a sweet cassis/cherry-scented nose, and an opulent, soft, open-knit personality with low acidity and fine plumpness. Hopefully, it will be bottled early to preserve its fruit as it requires drinking over the next 4–5 years. The 1996 Gigondas exhibits an evolved plum/garnet color, as well as smoky, cherry fruit intermixed with dried herbs, and a silky, medium-bodied, accessible style. It should be consumed over the next 3–4 years.

The 1995 Gigondas requires 3–4 more years of cellaring as it is still monolithic, unevolved, and backward. The color is a dense purple, and the wine is lively, with high quality, rich fruit. At present, everything is compressed by the wine's firm acidity and high tannin. Although rich in the mouth, with copious black raspberry and cherry aromas and flavors, full body, and a long finish, patience is required. This wine appears to have closed down even more in the last year, making it a candidate for a cellaring of 15 or more years.

CHÂTEAU RAYAS

1997	Châteauneuf du Pape	E	(87–90)
1996	Châteauneuf du Pape	E	89
1995	Châteauneuf du Pape	E	99+
1997	Châteauneuf du Pape (White)	D	(86–87)
1997	Fonsalette Côtes du Rhône	D	(86–87)
1996	Fonsalette Côtes du Rhône	D	90
1995	Fonsalette Côtes du Rhône	D	90
1997	Fonsalette Côtes du Rhône (White)	D	(83–85)
1997	Fonsalette Côtes du Rhône Cuvée Syrah	E	(87–89)
1996	Fonsalette Côtes du Rhône Cuvée Syrah	E	90
1995	Fonsalette Cuvée Syrah	E	94+
1997	Pignan Châteauneuf du Pape	E	(87–89)
1995	Pignan Châteauneuf du Pape	E	87+?

Françoise Reynaud has been in charge of Rayas since the death of her brother in 1997. She is capably assisted by her nephew, Emmanuel Reynaud. I was pleased with the 1998 Rayas cuvées, which I was allowed to taste even though many were still fermenting. Some have the potential to achieve 15.6%–17% natural alcohol, so there will be no problem with ripeness. I will be anxious to revisit the winery and taste through the multiple cuvées after they have finished their malolactic fermentations. Both 1997 and 1996 are relatively light years, although the Fonsalette 1996 cuvées are surprisingly powerful, rich wines. Jacques Reynaud conducted the harvest and winemaking of the 1996s, but died before they were assembled and bottled.

The two white 1997s, which were put through 100% malolactic fermentation, are soft, round, fruity wines, with the 1997 Fonsalette Côtes du Rhône blanc crisp and fresh, with white peachlike fruit. It is a medium-bodied wine to consume over the next several years. The 1997 Rayas Châteauneuf du Pape blanc exhibits some of the same peachlike character, but there are more apricot liqueur notes in addition to sherrylike aspects. The wine possesses good fruit flavors, medium body, and a slightly eccentric personality.

It appears the 1997 Fonsalette Côtes du Rhône red will be open knit and attractive. All the cuvées taste in the 86–89 point range. The wine is medium ruby-colored, with cherry and raspberry fruit, a degree of elegance, and a richly fruity, round, generous style that should be pleasing. The 1997 Pignan Châteauneuf du Pape, made from 100% Grenache, reveals a deceptively unimpressive medium ruby color, but intense, sweet, raspberry and cherry fruit mixed with kirsch liqueur. Spicy, with pepper, roasted peanut, and fine ripeness, it will drink well early and last for 7–10 years. The 1997 Rayas Châteauneuf du Pape is similar to the 1996—a medium ruby-colored, moderately weighted wine with plenty of sweet raspberry and cherry fruit, excellent to outstanding aromatics, but neither the depth nor the concentration found in a great vintage. There is plenty of heady alcohol, and the wine reveals an unmistakable cherry liqueur component. Dry tannin can be detected in the wine's finish. Look for it to drink beautifully young and keep for 10–12 years. It reminds me of a better, fruitier version of the 1986. The 1997 Fonsalette Côtes du Rhône Cuvée Syrah exhibits an opaque black/purple color, and a sweet, blackberry and animal-scented nose. Although the wine is rich on the attack, it narrows out to reveal considerable tannin and a tough, rustic personality. If this wine fleshes out in the finish, it will merit a score in the upper 80s. If it doesn't, look for an impressive-looking wine, but one that is angular and coarse in the mouth. Undoubtedly it will last 10–20 years.

One of the surprises of the vintage is the power and richness of the Fonsalette cuvées. The 1996 Fonsalette Côtes du Rhône boasts a dense ruby/purple color, as well as a chocolatey, blackberry, superconcentrated palate impression, and considerable body. This wine is atypically massive for this vintage. Muscular and structured, with huge fruit and richness, it was made from fully ripened fruit and an extremely late harvest. While it has softened in the bottle, this offering is still dominated by its truffle and blackberry jam aspects. Anticipated maturity: 2001–2018. The dense 1996 Fonsalette Côtes du Rhône Cuvée Syrah is, surprisingly, sweeter and more supple than the regular Côtes du Rhône. It offers an intriguing nose of animal fur, blackberries, cassis, and earthy overtones. Medium to full bodied, concentrated, chewy, and thick, this is a mouth-filling, palate-staining Syrah that should age well for 15 or more years. The 1996 Rayas Châteauneuf du Pape exhibits a medium ruby color, and a fragrant bouquet of kirsch, raspberries, and dried, smoky herbs. This evolved, medium- to full-bodied, delicious, open-knit wine lacks the depth of top vintages. Nevertheless, it is seductive and ideal for drinking over the next 7–9 years.

The question everyone asks is, can the magic of Jacques Reynaud's winemaking and *élevage* be captured by his sister and nephew? It is still too early to say, but I certainly think the 1998, with its superb raw materials, will be a good judge of what Rayas is capable of producing under the new regime.

As expected, my visit to Château Rayas in July of 1997 was an emotional one given the fact that Jacques Reynaud passed away that January. While it is impossible to replace the legendary Jacques Reynaud, I left Château Rayas feeling confident that everything is in good hands at this estate. To the extent possible, Françoise Reynaud intends to maintain the quality of the wines to honor the legacy of her brother.

I have had the profound 1995 Rayas Châteauneuf du Pape four times since it was bottled, and can state unequivocally that it is the quintessential Rayas. The wine is extraordinarily concentrated, with an unbelievable concentration of ripe black raspberry, cherry, and kirsch flavors that are not dissimilar from a great vintage (such as 1947, 1950, 1982) of the famed Pomerol, Château Lafleur. It possesses an old-vine intensity, multiple layers of richness, and admirable structure, as well as surprisingly fine acidity. This is a phenomenally compelling but backward Rayas that is more concentrated than the 1990, and, yes, as ageworthy as the surreal 1978. Owners should resist drinking it for another 4–5 years; it will last for 20–30 years. This is among the most awesome young wines I have tasted this year.

The 1995 Château Fonsalette Côtes du Rhône is a 20-year wine that requires 4–5 years of cellaring. It exhibits a black/purple color, good acidity and tannin, a closed, dense, moderately tannic personality, exceptional richness, and a powerful, full-bodied finish. Yields of 2 tons per acre were slightly higher than the 1–1¹/₃ achieved in 1996. This is a wine for those who cannot find or afford to purchase Rayas.

The amazing 1995 Château Fonsalette Cuvée Syrah should be cellared for 10–15 years. The wine is ferociously tannic, but, wow, what extraordinary intensity of flavor it possesses. With its viscous texture, and peppery, smoky, sweet cassis, and truffle-scented nose and flavors, this wine offers a sensational mouthful of brutally savage and intense Syrah grown in the southern Rhône. I suspect this wine will evolve for 30–40+ years.

Last, I have opened two bottles of 1995 Pignan. It is quite backward, seemingly austere, but perplexing. The color is a healthy dark ruby. The closed nose eventually gives up jammy cherry notes, smoke, and earth. Medium bodied, unevolved, tannic, and rather compressed, this Pignan needs 2–3 years of bottle age. My instincts suggest there is more to this wine than I have been able to discern from tasting it. Time will tell. Anticipated maturity: 2001–2010.

CHÂTEAU REDORTIER

1997	Gigondas	D	(84–86)
1996	Gigondas	D	86
1995	Gigondas	D	89

This is one of the excellent, sometimes outstanding Gigondas estates, producing just under 2,000 cases from a small vineyard holding of 12.4 acres. The wines, which are all aged in vats, are bottled without filtration. The 1995 Gigondas may merit an outstanding score with another 1–2 years of bottle age. The wine exhibits a dark purple color, followed by an unmistakable nose of black raspberries, smoke, tar, and blueberries. Rich, with a multilayered texture, this medium- to full-bodied, impeccably made wine reveals sweet, expansive richness, and plenty of peppery, sweet black fruits. Already supple and accessible, it should hit its plateau of maturity in 4–5 years and last for 12–15.

The 1996 and 1997 Gigondas are more similar than dissimilar. They are sweet, open-knit, attractive, straightforward, mainstream wines lacking the power and richness of a great vintage but offering plenty of charm and hedonistic appeal, assuming they are consumed within their first 4–5 years of life. The 1997 Gigondas displays medium body, a peppery, cherry, *garrigue*-scented nose, and a soft, easygoing, low-acid finish. The 1996 Gigondas reveals a darker, more saturated color, tangier acidity, and a lush, richly fruity, peppery, Provençal herb, and cherry-scented and -flavored style.

DOMAINE DES RELAGNES

1997	Châteauneuf du Pape	C	(84–86)
1996	Châteauneuf du Pape	C	87
1997	Châteauneuf du Pape La Cuvée Vigneronne	D	(86–87)

Henri Boiron told me he thought 1996 was less homogeneous than 1997 for Châteauneuf du Pape. Certainly all three of these offerings are richly fruity, round, soft, easily understood wines that will provide delicious near-term pleasure. The 1997 Châteauneuf du Pape offers a medium deep ruby color, and a textbook nose of Provençal herbs intermixed with plum, brandy, and cherry notes. The wine reveals sweet fruit, medium body, and some dilution, but it is ripe and seductive. Drink it over the next 3–4 years. The 1997 Châteauneuf du Pape La Cuvée Vigneronne is denser, with a deep ruby color, plenty of jammy black cherry fruit in the nose, nice glycerin, light tannin in the finish, and a medium-bodied, nicely concentrated and textured style. While not a blockbuster, this seductive Châteauneuf is ideal for drinking over the next 6–7 years. The 1996 Châteauneuf du Pape is a similarly styled, elegant, pleasant, fruit-driven, medium-bodied offering with plenty of black cherry fruit intermixed with cedar, dried herbs, and spice. Even a touch of pepper emerges as the wine sits in the glass. Drink it over the next 3–4 years.

DOMAINE DE LA RÉMÉJEANNE

1997	Côtes du Rhône Les Arbousiers	B	85
1997	Côtes du Rhône Les Eglantiers	B	85
1996	Côtes du Rhône Les Eglantiers	B	86
1997	Côtes du Rhône Les Genevrières	D	85

One of the top Côtes du Rhône estates in the Gard, proprietor Rémy Klein turns out tasty, easygoing Côtes du Rhônes. The 1997s and 1996s are lighter than what he would achieved in vintages such as 1995 and 1990. With the exception of the 100% Syrah cuvée, Les

Eglantiers, these wines are meant to be consumed over the next 1–2 years. The 1997 Côtes du Rhône Les Arbousiers offers a cherry/kirsch component as well as soft, light- to medium-bodied flavors, good balance, and no hard edges. The medium ruby-colored 1997 Côtes du Rhône Les Genevrières exhibits sweet cherry fruit intermixed with lavender notes, and an attractive, soft, easygoing style. Both the 1996 and 1997 Côtes du Rhône Les Eglantiers have deeper colors, more tannin, size, and structure, but I am not sure the 1997 is any better for it. Certainly the 1996 includes more pepper, cassis, fruit, and succulence, but these wines must be drunk very early given their fragility and lightness.

DOMAINE DE LA ROQUETTE

1997	Châteauneuf du Pape	C	(85–87)
1996	Châteauneuf du Pape	C	87
1995	Châteauneuf du Pape	C	90

These wines are made by Daniel and Frederic Brunier, whose family acquired this estate in 1986. Although the wines were good in the past, quality under the Bruniers has improved immensely. The 1995 Châteauneuf du Pape is the finest wine I have tasted under the Brunier administration. It possesses a deep ruby/purple color, and an excellent black cherry, herbes de Provence, olive, and peppery-scented nose. The wine achieved 14.5% natural alcohol, and offers plenty of glycerin in its opulent, rich, full-bodied texture. Some tannin is present, but the wine's overall impression is one of lusciousness, generosity, and copious quantities of fruit and extract. It should drink well for 7–8 years.

Roquette's wines are being produced by the Brunier family at a completely new cuverie. The 1997 Châteauneuf du Pape is a soft, round, charming offering with seductive black cherry and kirschlike fruit. It possesses excellent equilibrium, low acidity, and a soft, fleshy, round finish. The medium ruby-colored 1996 Châteauneuf du Pape is fatter in the mouth, but with the same forward, evolved style with copious quantities of red fruits intermixed with spice, earth, and smoke. Both the 1996 and 1997 should be consumed over the next 4–5 years.

RENÉ ROSTAING

1997	Côte Rôtie Côte Blonde	EE	(90–91)
1996	Côte Rôtie Côte Blonde	EE	90+
1995	Côte Rôtie Côte Blonde	EE	95
1997	Côte Rôtie Cuvée Classique	EE	(86–88)
1996	Côte Rôtie Cuvée Classique	EE	87
1995	Côte Rôtie Cuvée Normale	EE	88
1997	Côte Rôtie La Landonne	EE	(88–91)
1996	Côte Rôtie La Landonne	EE	88+
1995	Côte Rôtie La Landonne	EE	92
1997	Côte Rôtie La Viaillère	EE	(87–89)
1996	Côte Rôtie La Viaillère	EE	87
1995	Côte Rôtie La Viaillère	EE	90

René Rostaing likes 1997 as a vintage, but he feels the wines are forward and precocious. All of his offerings possess 12.5%–12.8% natural alcohol. These low-acid Côte Rôties are already showing reasonably well, although they lack the concentration of great vintages such as 1991 and 1988. The softness of the 1997s is apparent across the board. For example, the dark ruby-colored 1997 Côte Rôtie Cuvée Classique is an evolved, forward, fat wine with cassis and raspberry fruit flavors, medium body, and an easygoing, succulent, luscious, straightforward appeal. Drink it over the next 7–8 years. The 1997 Côte Rôtie La Viaillère reveals a similar dark ruby color, plenty of pepper, herbs, and ripe black fruits in the nose, vanillin and toasty oak, and a medium-bodied, rich, layered finish. Rostaing told me 1997 will be the last vintage in which he will vineyard designate La Viaillère, as he prefers to blend it with his Cuvée Classique. Look for the 1997 to drink well when released next year and evolve for 7–8 years thereafter. The intensely peppery, more animal, leathery, roasted herb, and black currant-scented 1997 Côte Rôtie La Landonne is already enticing and exotic. Flattering and rich in the mouth despite its Côte Brune origins, this elegant, rich, concentrated, spicy, flamboyant Côte Rôtie should drink well upon release, yet last for a decade. Year in and year out, the finest offering from Rostaing is his limited production (usually 4,000+ bottles) Côte Rôtie Côte Blonde (which often includes 3%–4% Viognier in the blend). The 1997 exhibits a dark ruby color, followed by a sexy apricot, blackberry, raspberry, bacon fat, and toasty nose, and luscious, medium- to full-bodied, open-knit flavors that caress the palate with glycerin and fruit. The wine's low acidity, fleshy texture, and forward, evolved style are appealing. It should drink well for 8–10 years after its release.

The 1996s offer a contrasting style since their acids are slightly crisper, and the wines well endowed but more structured because of the acidity and more noticeable tannin. All the 1996s, which were bottled in July 1998, are fine examples of this very good, but irregular vintage in the northern Rhône. The 1996 Côte Rôtie Cuvée Classique displays a deep ruby color, as well as a textbook nose of cassis, pepper, flowers, toast, and bacon fat. Good acidity, excellent purity, medium body, and firm tannin give this wine a youthful, less evolved style than its 1997 counterpart. Although drinkable, it will benefit from several more years of cellaring and should last for a decade or more. The 1996 Côte Rôtie La Viaillère offers up a smoky, peppery, roasted herb, earthy, mineral/animal nose. While it is not for everybody, it is very Côte Rôtie-like. In the mouth it continues to reveal more complexity in addition to a more muscular, tannic, attenuated finish. Medium bodied, with noticeable acidity and plenty of minerals and earth, it should be at its finest between 2000 and 2008. The 1996 Côte Rôtie La Landonne may merit an outstanding score if the tannin melts away without a proportional loss of fruit. The wine was backward and closed when I tasted it in late fall 1998. The wine's dark ruby color with purple nuances is followed by reticent aromas of smoke, roasted meat, earthy iron, and herb notes. It is sweet on the attack, with excellent length, medium to full body, and a boatload of tannin. While the tannin gives the wine good grip, it also is cause for concern about the wine's equilibrium. My instincts suggest it will be fine, but it requires 3–4 years of cellaring. Anticipated maturity: 2003–2015. In contrast, the 1996 Côte Rôtie Côte Blonde is the epitome of elegance, finesse, and black raspberry fruit wrapped in smoky oak and pepper. Luscious, with an opulent texture, enough tangy acidity to provide delineation, and a fleshy, sweet finish, this well-structured wine is the most flashy of these offerings. Rostaing's Côte Blonde always performs well regardless of its evolutionary stage. The 1996 should drink well for 10–12 years.

The dense purple-colored 1995 Côte Rôtie Côte Blonde boasts an awesome, mind-boggling nose of violets, cassis, blueberries, and vanillin. Sumptuous and rich on the palate despite crisp acidity, this is a wine of exceptional intensity, a multilayered personality, and fabulous persistence and delineation. It is a tour de force for Côte Rôtie. Unfortunately, quantities are extremely limited as the yields of just over one ton of fruit per acre were well below normal. The 1995 Côte Rôtie Cuvée Classique possesses a black raspberry and violet-scented nose, a fabulous saturated ruby/purple color, excellent ripeness, and density, and a long, medium-bodied, crisp finish. The acidity gives the wine vibrancy. This wine should drink well for at least a decade. The 1995 Côte Rôtie La Landonne is another backward, tart, opaque purple-colored wine that is just beginning to reveal its character. Tannic and rich, with a chocolatey, smoky, black currant/cassis-scented nose, this powerful, impenetrable wine will require cellaring until the turn of the century; drink it over the following 10–12 years. The 1995 Côte Rôtie La Viaillère possesses surprisingly noticeable acidity, a fresh, pure nose of blackberries, blueberries, and currants. Deeply colored, ripe, dense, medium to full bodied, and tannic, this is a backward, tart, crisp style of Côte Rôtie that will age for 15–20 years.

DOMAINE ROGER SABON

1997 Châteauneuf du Pape Les Olivets	D	(86–88)
1997 Châteauneuf du Pape Cuvée Prestige	E	(90–91)
1996 Châteauneuf du Pape Cuvée Prestige	E	89
1995 Châteauneuf du Pape Cuvée Prestige	E	95
1997 Châteauneuf du Pape Cuvée Réservée	D	(88–90)
1996 Châteauneuf du Pape Cuvée Réservée	D	87
1995 Châteauneuf du Pape Cuvée Réservée	D	90
1996 Châteauneuf du Pape Le Secret de Sabon	E	90

The former mayor of Châteauneuf du Pape continues to turn out a very impressive portfolio of Châteauneuf du Pape. He succeeded in both the 1996 and 1997 vintages, producing wines that are similar in both quality and character—charming, richly fruity, expansive wines that are easy to drink and understand. The 1996 Châteauneuf du Pape Cuvée Réservée exhibits a dark plum color, and a sweet nose of white chocolate intertwined with cherry jam, olives, and pepper. Dense, round, and lush, with a silky texture and low acidity, this attractive, plump offering can be drunk now and over the next 4–5 years. Not surprisingly, the 1996 Châteauneuf du Pape Cuvée Prestige is a more complex, big, rich, and deep wine. The color is a dark plum/garnet. The nose offers up a symphony of *garrigue*, olive, cedar, earth, black cherries, and currants. This full-bodied, lush, richly fruity, spicy, peppery wine is already delicious, yet promises to drink well for 5–7 more years, possibly longer. In 1996, Roger Sabon vinified a small parcel of exceptionally old vines (over 70 years of age) and produced tiny quantities of a 1996 Châteauneuf du Pape Le Secret de Sabon. Made from a blend of 70% Grenache, 10% Syrah, 10% Mourvèdre, and 10% diverse varietals, there are only 1,000 bottles of this outstanding Châteauneuf du Pape. One of the vintage's most concentrated wines, this luscious offering reveals copious quantities of black fruits intermixed with herbs, pepper, and allspice. Impressive alcohol and glycerin give the wine a viscous, chewy texture—atypical for a 1996. It should drink well for a decade.

The 1997s appear to be richer, riper, and more expansive than the 1996s, but forward and evolved, in keeping with the character of this advanced vintage. The 1997 Châteauneuf du Pape Les Olivets displays a dark ruby color with purple nuances. The wine offers sweet plum, peppery, spicy, fruitcakelike aromas intermixed with cherry jam and spice box scents. Medium to full bodied and soft, it is ideal for consuming over the next 5–6 years. The impressively rich 1997 Châteauneuf du Pape Cuvée Réservée exhibits a dark ruby, slightly purple color. The wine offers elements of *sur-maturité* in its nose of overripe cherries and prunes intermixed with Asian spices, leather, meat, and smoky notes. Full bodied, with good glycerin, a hedonistic, fleshy mouth-feel, and impressive length, this expansive, full-bodied, soft Châteauneuf is ideal for drinking over the next 7–10 years. Slightly better is the 1997 Châteauneuf du Pape Cuvée Prestige. This wine is more powerful, with more elevated alcohol, and a fuller-bodied, weightier, more concentrated personality. The sweet rich fruit includes plums, cherries, and cassis intermixed with aromas of dried herbs, black pepper, and

Provençal *garrigue* scents. A decadently rich, superb 1997 offering, this pure, impressively rich, fruit-driven wine can be drunk upon release, or cellared for a decade or more. These are impressive offerings from one of the most conscientious growers/winemakers of the village.

Now that the 1995 Châteauneuf du Papes are in bottle, they are even better than I had predicted. The 1995 Châteauneuf du Pape Cuvée Réservée is an outstanding wine, with a dense, rich, saturated plum color, and a smoky, chocolatey, herb, and black fruit-scented nose. The wine is deep and spicy, with loads of personality, muscle, richness, and length. Decent acidity, soft tannin, and the wine's fruit-driven richness suggest it will be at its best between now and 2010. The explosively rich, full-bodied, macho-styled, deep ruby/purple-colored 1995 Châteauneuf du Pape Cuvée Prestige offers a smorgasbord of Provençal aromas including smoked herbs, freshly crushed black pepper, and black plum and kirschlike fruit. Deep, powerful, and superconcentrated, this is a classic, old style Châteauneuf du Pape that will require 1–3 years of cellaring; it will keep for 2 decades.

DOMAINE SAINT-BENOÎT

1996	Châteauneuf du Pape Elise	D	79
1997	Châteauneuf du Pape Grande Garde	D	(88–90)
1996	Châteauneuf du Pape Grande Garde	D	89
1997	Châteauneuf du Pape Onyx	D	(78–83)
1997	Châteauneuf du Pape Soleil et Festins	D	(84–86)
1996	Châteauneuf du Pape Soleil et Festins	D	80
1997	Châteauneuf du Pape La Truffière	D	(86–87)
1996	Châteauneuf du Pape La Truffière	D	88

This new estate, created in 1989, continues to turn out interesting, high-quality Châteauneuf du Pape from nearly four dozen vineyard parcels spread throughout the appellation. The 1997s are fruity, seductive wines that are typical of the vintage. I was not impressed with the 1997 Châteauneuf du Pape Onyx, which seemed thin and diluted, with no real core of fruit or character. However, the other cuvées are very good wines that should drink well for 4–6 years. For example, the 1997 Châteauneuf du Pape Soleil et Festins offers plenty of raspberries and cherries in its straightforward bouquet. It is an elegant, Burgundian-styled wine that could easily pass for a Côte de Beaune in a blind tasting. This fruit-driven, stylish, attractive offering is best drunk over the next 3–4 years. More serious and rugged is the 1997 Châteauneuf du Pape La Truffière. Made from 50% Grenache, 25% Mourvèdre, and 25% Syrah, it offers a medium ruby color, as well as an earthy, new saddle leather, spice box, and black cherry-scented nose and flavors. There is more glycerin, as well as tannin in the earthy, trufflelike finish. Despite its large size, I would opt for consuming it over the next 3–4 years given its fragile constitution and moderate concentration. The deep ruby-colored 1997 Châteauneuf du Pape Grande Garde (made from the oldest vines, averaging 70+ years of age, and usually 100% Grenache) exhibits surprising expansiveness and richness, making it one of the vintage's stars. It is made in a seductive, sexy, forward style for a St.-Benôit, with plenty of black raspberry and cherry fruit and a touch of kirsch liqueur. Medium bodied, with copious spice, it is primarily a fruit-driven wine with more glycerin and length than the other cuvées. Drink it over the next 5–6 years.

I tasted three 1996 cuvées, two of which were largely unimpressive. The 1996 Châteauneuf du Pape Elise reveals a green pepper, *garrigue*-dominated nose with too much earth. It is a medium-bodied, pinched/compressed wine that will not improve with age. The 1996 Châteauneuf du Pape Soleil et Festins is similar, but with more fruit, light body, and elegance. Both wines should be consumed over the next 2–3 years. More serious is the 1996

La Truffière and 1996 Grande Garde. The 1996 Châteauneuf du Pape La Truffière reveals a new saddle leather, earthy, meaty complexity due to the 25% Mourvèdre included in the blend. The wine exhibits a dark ruby color, as well as jammy plum and strawberry notes intermixed with cedar and smoke. There is excellent texture, good richness, medium body, and low acidity. Drink it over the next 5–7 years. The dark plum-colored 1996 Châteauneuf du Pape Grande Garde offers up a sweet nose of strawberries, kirsch liqueur, and pepper. Fleshy, with copious amounts of glycerin and fat, this wine possesses the best fruit and palate feel of this quartet. Medium to full bodied, with excellent purity, and a lusty, high alcohol finish, it should be consumed over the next 5–7 years.

SAINT-COSME

1997	Châteauneuf du Pape (White)	C	87
1997	Côte Rôtie Montsalier	E	(90–93)
1997	Côtes du Rhône	A	87
1997	Côtes du Rhône (White)	A	87
1997	Gigondas Cuvée Classique	D	(90–93)
1996	Gigondas Cuvée Classique	D	90
1996	Gigondas Cuvée Valbelle	D	93

One of the up-and-coming superstars of the southern Rhône, the young, intensely committed Louis Barruol, has turned around the fortunes of this well-placed Gigondas domaine. He has begun producing a small line of impressive *négociant* wines (the Côte Rôtie Montsalier is a splendid example), but most important, he is making blockbuster Gigondas that rivals the finest wines of the appellation. I was particularly blown away by the quality of the 1996s and 1997s. Moreover, his profound 1998s achieved an average of 14.5% natural alcohol, and have saturated black colors. Saint-Cosme is definitely a name to search out.

For starters, there is the 1997 Côtes du Rhône red (70% Syrah from the Valréas area and 30% Grenache from the terraces near Gigondas), part of the *négociant* line as it does not emerge from the estate's vineyards. It exhibits a dense ruby/purple color, as well as a gorgeously jammy cassis-scented nose, with licorice and earth in the background. It possesses considerable intensity and richness, low acidity, and medium to full body. Drink this pure offering over the next 2–3 years.

The estate cuvées of Gigondas come from the property's well-placed 37 acres surrounding the village. In top years, two cuvées are produced, the cuvée classique and a cuvée aged in *barrique* called Valbelle. In 1997 no Valbelle was produced. These wines are kept in contact with their lees for extensive periods and there are very few rackings. The SO$_2$ level is also extremely low by modern day standards. The 1996 Gigondas Cuvée Classique (80% Grenache, 15% Syrah, and 5% Cinsault) is a stunning wine for this appellation and vintage. As Louis Barruol said, most Gigondas vignerons got spooked by the dreary, overcast, drizzly weather and picked too soon. His harvest, which ended in mid-October, produced Gigondas cuvées that averaged between 14%–14.5% alcohol. Barruol is a philosophical as well as candid young man, saying that by waiting in 1996 and 1997, he was able to harvest fully mature fruit, whereas by waiting in 1994, he was ruined by the rain. The saturated ruby/purple-colored 1996 Gigondas Cuvée Classique exhibits a big, thick, juicy, plum/prune, and jammy kirsch-scented nose with pepper, licorice, and mineral scents. Full bodied, with low acidity and a voluptuous texture, this pure, gorgeously proportioned Gigondas is a star of the vintage. It should drink well for a decade. The 1996 Gigondas Cuvée Valbelle (90% Grenache and 10% Syrah, made from 100+ year-old vines planted just after the phylloxera epidemic) is aged 50% in new oak casks and 50% in 1-year-old casks. Like all of Saint-Cosme's offerings, it is bottled unfined and unfiltered, with extremely low levels (under 20 parts ppm) of SO_2. The wine is exceptionally fat, massive, and rich, but possesses no hard edges, with elements of *sur-maturité* (note the apricot/peachlike notes that compete with the fabulously sweet cassis, kirsch, and blackberries for the taster's attention). Full bodied and luscious with a velvety texture, great purity, and stunning richness, this may be the Gigondas of the vintage. It tastes like a wine from a great vintage, rather than one from an irregular year. It should drink well for 10–15 years.

As stated above, there is no Valbelle in 1997, but the 1997 Gigondas Cuvée Classique is remarkable. The dark saturated purple/black color is followed by aromas of sweet blackberry liqueur intermixed with pepper, floral scents, truffles, and Asian spices. Full bodied, with spectacular concentration, low acidity, and a blockbuster finish, this powerful yet beautifully harmonious Gigondas should drink well for 10–12 years.

Among the other *négociant* wines produced by Louis Barruol is the compelling 1997 Côte Rôtie Montsalier. As often as I asked, Barruol would not reveal the source for this extraordinary wine. It emerged from three separate Côte Rôtie *terroirs* and was aged in 100% new casks. Sadly, only 2,400 bottles of this outstanding wine were produced, so the following tasting note is mainly of academic interest. This black-colored wine, a syrup of Syrah, boasts a terrific cassis, bacon fat, and smoky-scented nose with grilled meat notes in the background. Rich and full bodied, with low acidity, spectacular concentration, and a finish that lasts for nearly a minute, this classic Côte Rôtie could compete with some of Marcel Guigal's great single-vineyard offerings. It should drink well for 15 or more years.

The other two *négociant* wines I tasted from Louis Barruol were the 1997 Côtes du Rhône blanc, and 1997 Châteauneuf du Pape blanc. The 1997 Côtes du Rhône blanc, made from equal parts Roussanne, Marsanne, and Grenache Blanc, has gorgeous fruit that seemingly jumps out of the glass with its apricot, fruit cocktail-scented nose. With excellent richness, this offering is a match for the more expensive 1997 Châteauneuf du Pape blanc. The latter wine, while ambitious, with more structure and definition, is not superior, hedonistically speaking, to the Côtes du Rhône. The Châteauneuf du Pape is a blend of 80% Grenache Blanc and 20% Clairette. Both wines should be consumed over the next 2–3 years because of their low acidity.

SAINT-DESIRAT CAVE COOPERATIVE

1995 Domaine de Rochevine	C	85+?
1995 St.-Joseph	C	85
1995 St.-Joseph Cuvée Côte Diane	C	88
1995 St.-Joseph Gold Medal	C	87

This excellent cooperative specializes in St.-Joseph. The following cuvées are all well-made wines available for modest prices. The 1995 St.-Joseph exhibits a dark ruby/purple color, followed by a clean, cassis-scented nose, elegant, medium-bodied flavors, and sweet tannin. It should be drunk over the next 3–5 years. The similarly colored 1995 St.-Joseph Gold Medal offers more intensity and sweet fruit in its lovely black fruit/floral/mineral-scented nose. It is a medium-bodied, harmonious, well-made northern Rhône to drink during its first 5–6 years of life. Saint-Desirat's 1995 Domaine de Rochevine, a more ambitiously styled wine, is more spice- than fruit-driven. It offers a boatload of tannin that is somewhat intrusive. If it does not completely melt away, this wine will taste austere and angular. There is good weight and a sweet attack, but the wine's overall equilibrium is a concern.

The finest wine of this quartet is the 1995 St.-Joseph Cuvée Côte Diane. It possesses a dense ruby/purple color, and a lovely sweet black fruit-scented nose with minerals and spice in the background. Medium bodied, with more concentration than the other cuvées, the Côte

Diane cuts a broader, more expansive mouth-feel, but it still reveals elegance and sweet fruit. This attractive St.-Joseph can be drunk now or cellared for 8–12 years.

DOMAINE DE SAINT-SIFFREIN

1995 Châteauneuf du Pape	C	89

This moderately sized estate of 42 acres, owned by the Chastan family, produces textbook, reliable Châteauneuf du Pape. The 1995 Châteauneuf du Pape is a denser, fuller-flavored wine than the 1996 with more flesh and concentration. Peppery spice can be found in its abundant quantities of jammy black cherry fruit and kirsch. Dense and full bodied, with an inner sweetness that can only come from low yields and old vines, this is a lush, impressively made Châteauneuf du Pape that will benefit from another 1–2 years of cellaring; it will keep through the first decade of the next century.

DOMAINE SAINTE-ANNE

1997 Gigondas	C	(89–92)
1996 Gigondas	C	86

One of the stars of the vintage, Domaine Sainte-Anne's 1997 Gigondas is a broodingly backward, powerful, formidably endowed, opaque purple-colored wine with gobs of fruit, glycerin, and extract. Its huge, rich flavors, outstanding purity and balance, and superb finish suggest an outstanding Gigondas will be forthcoming if it is not excessively processed at bottling. This wine is one of the best endowed, longest, and most complete wines of the vintage. Anticipated maturity: 2002–2015. The dark garnet-colored 1996 Gigondas offers a textbook southern Rhône bouquet of *garrigue*, pepper, spice, roasted herbs, and sweet black cherry fruit. The wine possesses fine ripeness and glycerin, and a plump, medium-bodied, open-knit accessible style. Drink it over the next 4–5 years.

DOMAINE SANTA DUC

1997 Côtes du Rhône	A	85
1997 Gigondas Cuvée Classique	D	86
1996 Gigondas Cuvée Classique	D	86
1995 Gigondas Cuvée Classique	D	90
1996 Gigondas Les Hautes Garrigues Cuvée Prestige	E	90
1995 Gigondas Les Hautes Garrigues Cuvée Prestige	E	95

Probably the leading estate in Gigondas, Yves Gras's Santa Duc continues to turn out some of the most complete, concentrated, and potentially complex wines of the southern Rhône. In the two difficult vintages of 1996 and 1997, the wines are solidly made, with the 1996 Gigondas Les Hautes Garrigues Cuvée Prestige stunning. As for the 1997s, they are soft, forward, open-knit, low-acid wines with good ripeness, but a touch of dilution. The 1997 Gigondas possesses a slightly more saturated color, as well as more pepper and a larger frame in the mouth. Both 1997s are easygoing, forward, bistro-style reds to drink over the next 3–5 years.

The 1996 Gigondas Cuvée Classique exhibits the vintage's higher acidity, in addition to more structure. It should last 7–8 years, but I do not believe it will surpass the 1997 Cuvée Classique in terms of enjoyment. The outstanding 1996 Gigondas Les Hautes Garrigues Cuvée Prestige boasts a knockout nose of floral scents intermixed with blackberry fruit, pepper, and licorice. Subtle *pain grillé* notes are present. The wine is medium to full bodied, expansive, rich, and beautifully textured, with a supple finish. It is a remarkable wine given the vintage conditions. Drink it over the next 5–7 years.

In my estimation, Yves Gras is the reigning superstar in Gigondas. The 1995 vintage is unequivocally a splendid success for Santa Duc. The wines, now in bottle, are even stronger and richer than they tasted in cask. The superb 1995 Gigondas Cuvée Classique exhibits a dense purple color, and a sensational nose of cassis, kirsch, tar, and smoke. The wine hits the palate with explosive ripeness and richness, and no evidence of oak. A gutsy, brilliant effort, this full-bodied, lusciously concentrated, textbook Gigondas should drink well for 10–12 years. The magnificent 1995 Gigondas Les Hautes Garrigues, a selection made only in the greatest years, is a powerhouse Gigondas with an alcohol percentage approaching the midteens. This opaque purple-colored wine offers a stunning nose of crushed minerals, black raspberries, blackberries, and vanillin. In spite of its huge extraction, marvelous concentration, and massive richness, this wine is brilliantly balanced by sweet tannin and tangy acidity. It possesses a viscosity and richness that make me think this may be among the half-dozen greatest bottles of Gigondas I have ever tasted. I own the 1989 and 1990 Les Hautes Garrigues, and the 1995 appears to be superior to those two classics! Made from a 50-year-old parcel of hillside vineyards planted with 70% Grenache, 15% Syrah, and 15% Mourvèdre, yields are as low as half a ton of fruit per acre. Bottled without filtration, this remarkable wine represents the essence of Gigondas. How long will it last? This wine will age beautifully for 2 decades!

CHÂTEAU DE SÉGRIES

1997 Côtes du Rhône	A	85
1997 Lirac	B	87
1996 Lirac	B	85

A new proprietor, Henri de Lanzac, has begun to make significant improvements to this well-known, but often underachieving estate. With the help of his cousin Christian Delorme, of the superbly run Domaine de la Mordorée (which produces top-notch Châteauneuf du Pape and Lirac), Lanzac has made Château de Ségries a property to follow. The 1997 Côtes du Rhône, a blend of 60% Grenache, 30% Syrah, and 10% Mourvèdre and Cinsault, exhibits a sappy, black fruit character with pepper and cherry notes in the background. The wine is undoubtedly an excellent value, with good spice, hints of Provençal olives, and a fruit-driven, medium-bodied personality. Drink this mouth-filling, palate-friendly wine over the next 1–2 years. The 1996 Lirac reveals deeper fruit, and more power, largely because it is a blend of 60% Grenache and 40% Syrah. There is tannin in the finish, but very good texture and ripeness, particularly for a 1996. Even better is the 1997 Lirac, a wine with copious quantities of sweet black cherry, peppery fruit, hints of cassis, good fat and depth, and a nicely textured, medium-bodied, low-acid finish. It should drink well for 2–3 years.

DOMAINE DES SÉNÉCHAUX

1995 Châteauneuf du Pape	C	87

This estate, now owned by Pascal Roux of Château de Trignon, has produced an intriguing, jammy, Provençal-tasting wine in 1995. The medium ruby-colored 1995 Châteauneuf du Pape reveals a peppery, roasted herb-scented nose with tar, licorice, and fruitcakelike smells. This is a well-made, elegant, richly fruity, medium- to full-bodied Châteauneuf with a smooth finish. I would opt for drinking it over the next 5–7 years as it is not going to make old bones, even in this excellent vintage.

CHÂTEAU SIMIAN

1997 Châteauneuf du Pape	C/D	(87–88)
1996 Châteauneuf du Pape	C/D	87
1995 Châteauneuf du Pape	C/D	88

This small 10-acre estate is well situated on Châteauneuf du Pape's plateau, behind the ruins of the Papal Palace. The cellars are further north in the village of Piolenc, the "Garlic Capital" of France. The dark ruby/purple-colored 1995 is medium bodied, with elegant, jammy cherry/kirschlike flavors that are sweet, round, and generous. There is no sense of heaviness or excessive alcohol in this well-made, savory, mouth-filling Châteauneuf du Pape that should continue to drink well for 10–12 years. This estate deserves more attention, but the tiny production of only 1,700 cases of red wine ensures that most of it is sold to private clients.

The 1996 and 1997 are two very good efforts from Proprietor Serguier et Fils. The 1996 Châteauneuf du Pape's evolved, dark plum/ruby color is followed by a spicy nose of black cherries, cedar, pine needles, and pepper. It is a fruit-driven wine with attractive levels of glycerin, low acidity, and an excellent long, lusty finish. Drink it over the next 4–5 years. The 1997 Châteauneuf du Pape may be even better if it is bottled without excessive fining/filtration. It possesses a dark ruby color, attractive roasted herb, black cherry, and raspberry notes, excellent concentration, low acidity, heady alcohol, and a rich, chewy, very good finish. This well-made Châteauneuf should drink well for 7–8 years. Both wines are blends of 80% Grenache, 15% Syrah, and 5% miscellaneous varietals.

JEAN-MICHEL SORREL

1997	Hermitage Vieilles Vignes Les Vignons	E	(85–87)
1996	Hermitage Vieilles Vignes Les Vignons	E	(82–85)

The 1996 Hermitage Vieilles Vignes Les Vignons' high acidity gives the wine a lean, compressed, attenuated style. Although there is attractive ripe cassis fruit and earth in the aromatics and on the attack, the wine quickly narrows in the mouth. Drink it over the next decade. The 1997 Hermitage Vieilles Vignes Les Vignons exhibits a dark ruby/purple color, a sweeter, cassis-dominated personality with medium body, good fat and ripeness, low acidity, and an attractive, lush, accessible style. It should drink well for a decade.

MARC SORREL

1997	Crozes-Hermitage	C	(84–86)
1996	Crozes-Hermitage	C	83
1995	Crozes-Hermitage	C	83
1997	Crozes-Hermitage Blanc	C	(79–82)
1996	Crozes-Hermitage Blanc	C	86
1995	Crozes-Hermitage Blanc	C	82
1997	Hermitage	D	(86–88)
1996	Hermitage	D	86
1995	Hermitage	D	85
1997	Hermitage Le Gréal	E	(90–92)
1996	Hermitage Le Gréal	E	90
1995	Hermitage Le Gréal	E	91
1997	Hermitage Les Rocoules	E	(88–90)
1996	Hermitage Les Rocoules	E	90
1995	Hermitage Les Rocoules	E	87
1997	Hermitage (White)	D	(85–87)

1996 Hermitage (White)	D 86
1995 Hermitage (White)	D 85

This small estate, making artisanal-styled wines, usually hits the high notes with their single-vineyard offerings of Les Rocoules Hermitage white and Le Gréal Hermitage red (actually a blend of Méal and Greffieux). Marc Sorrel has also been increasing his production of both red and white Crozes-Hermitage, wines that are meant for easy and quick consumption. He was able to bottle his white 1996 Crozes-Hermitage (made from under 2 tons per acre) without filtration, something he does routinely with his Hermitage wines. Made primarily from Marsanne, with 10%–15% Roussanne added (depending on the vintage), the Crozes-Hermitage offers an intriguing roasted nut, Fino Sherry-scented nose, medium body, and ripe fruit. Underlying acidity gives the wine good support. It should drink well for 5–6 years. The 1997 white Crozes-Hermitage is a lighter, fruitier wine without the complexity and intensity of the 1996. Its lower acidity and more open-knit style suggest drinking it over the next several years.

The red 1996 Crozes-Hermitage was 100% destemmed because of the cool year. It is a tangy Syrah, with an elegant, spicy, herbaceous, berry-scented nose, medium body, and a refreshing vigor and lightness. It should be drunk over the next year. Also destemmed, the 1997 red Crozes-Hermitage is fruitier and deeper, with a smoky, roasted herb, berry fruitiness, some herbaceousness, low acidity, and a medium-bodied style. It should be consumed over the next 2–3 years.

With respect to his Hermitage cuvées, Marc Sorrel was honest in saying that he thought 1997 was less successful for him than 1998, 1996, or 1995 . . . with one exception, his cuvée of Gréal 1997. As for the whites, the 1997 Hermitage (100% Marsanne) is surprisingly forward, and much lighter than this wine normally tends to be. It achieved 12.4% alcohol, and is refreshing with notions of white peachlike aromas intermixed with minerals. However, it lacks the body and power normally found in this cuvée. The 1997 Hermitage Les Rocoules exhibits a Californian-like, tropical fruit-scented nose with a surprising apricot/honeyed note reminiscent of Condrieu. This medium-bodied offering is atypical for Sorrel in its evolved style. Precocious and up-front, it will provide ideal drinking over the next 4–6 years. The 1996 Hermitage is elegant, stylish, and well made, with citrusy fruit, but not much power or depth. It is made from 100% Marsanne, primarily from Les Greffiers vineyard on Hermitage Hill. The 1996 Hermitage Les Rocoules (13.5% alcohol) includes 10%–15% Roussanne in the blend. A more honeyed, richer, fuller-bodied white Hermitage, it is more typical of what Sorrel routinely does with this cuvée. Notes of white flowers are apparent in this offering, which possesses decent acidity, but not the obtrusive acidity noticeable in some 1996 wines.

Of the four red 1996 and 1997 Hermitage cuvées, there is a vast difference between Sorrel's Gréal and his cuvée classique. The 1996 Hermitage Cuvée Classique (100% destemmed) is a tasty, attractive, open-knit wine with cassis and cranberry fruit intermixed with tar, earth, and spice. Medium bodied and elegant, it is ideal for drinking over the next 5–8 years. The delicious 1997 Hermitage Cuvée Classique is a sexier, lusher, fruitier wine than its older sibling (Sorrel prefers the 1996). A dark ruby-colored offering with low acidity, it will drink well over the next 5–9 years. The significantly more concentrated 1996 Hermitage Le Gréal is a powerful Syrah exhibiting a saturated ruby/purple color, crème de cassislike fruit, medium to full body, and good but not excessive acidity. Although not a powerhouse like such vintages as 1990 and 1989, relying more on finesse than muscle for its appeal, there is plenty of substance to this lovely wine. It should drink well now and over the next 15 years. The opaque purple-colored 1997 Hermitage Le Gréal is more evolved and flamboyant than the more reserved and elegant 1996. Sexy and rich, with copious quantities of crème de cassis fruit, medium body, low acidity, and good spicy meaty richness on the mid-palate, it is a showy Hermitage that should drink well young and last for a decade or more.

The 1995 Crozes-Hermitage blanc is a more elegant, lighter-styled wine than the 1996, with less alcohol, acidity, and extract. It is a pleasant, straightforward Crozes to drink over the next several years.

I retasted the 1995 Hermitage Cuvée Classique blanc and 1995 Hermitage Les Rocoules, and both are well-made wines, but not at the top level Sorrel achieved in vintages such as 1991, 1990, 1989, and 1988. The 1995 Hermitage Cuvée Classique blanc exhibits crisp acidity, a straightforward nose of white fruits, minerals, and spice, and medium body. It is ideal for drinking over the next 3–4 years. The 1995 Hermitage Les Rocoules displays an evolved light golden color, good power, low acidity, and a tendency toward flabbiness, with cherry, almond, and rubber cementlike scents and flavors. This is a spicy, disjointed, and awkward wine. I would opt for drinking it earlier rather than later.

The red wine cuvée of 1995 Crozes-Hermitage is a light, herbaceous wine. It offers good acidity, and some Provençal herbs along with notions of prunes, raspberries, and black currants. It is a medium-bodied, fruity wine to drink over the next 3–4 years.

The 1995 Hermitage Cuvée Classique displays a dark ruby color, but it tastes austere, tannic, and hard, with an excess of structure for its level of fruit. This wine may dry out before it ever fully blossoms. It needs 2–3 years of cellaring and should keep for a decade. The top cuvée of Hermitage, the dark ruby/purple-colored 1995 Hermitage Le Gréal possesses plenty of smoky, gamey aromas, along with a cassis and mineral component. Full bodied, powerful, and backward, this is an impressively endowed, rich but tannic Gréal that requires 5–8 years of cellaring. It should keep for 20–25 years, but patience is required.

TARDIEU-LAURENT

1995	Bandol Vieilles Vignes	D	92
1997	Châteauneuf du Pape	D	(91–94)
1996	Châteauneuf du Pape	D	92
1995	Châteauneuf du Pape Cuvée des Garrigues	D	89+
1997	Cornas Cuvée Coteaux	D	(90–92)
1996	Cornas Cuvée Coteaux	D	93
1995	Cornas Cuvée Coteaux	D	92
1997	Cornas Vieilles Vignes	D	(91–93)
1996	Cornas Vieilles Vignes	D	95+
1995	Cornas Vieilles Vignes	D	94
1995	Côte Rôtie	E	86
1997	Côte Rôtie Côte Brune	EE	(94–96)
1996	Côte Rôtie Côte Brune	EE	94
1997	Côtes du Rhône Guy Louis	B	(89–91)
1996	Côtes du Rhône Guy Louis	B	90
1995	Côtes du Rhône Guy Louis	B	89
1996	Côtes du Rhône-Villages Cairanne Vieilles Vignes	C	92
1995	Crozes-Hermitage	C	86
1997	Crozes-Hermitage Vieilles Vignes	D	(90–92)
1997	Gigondas	C	(90–92)

1996 Gigondas	C	90
1995 Gigondas	C	91
1997 Hermitage	EE	(94–96)
1996 Hermitage	EE	93+
1995 Hermitage	E	94+
1995 Hermitage L'Hermite	EE/EEE	93+
1997 Hermitage Vieilles Vignes	EE/EEE	(90–92)
1997 Vacqueyras Vieilles Vignes	C	(88–90)
1995 Vacqueyras Vieilles Vignes	C	90

In my 20th anniversary issue of *The Wine Advocate* (December 1998), I listed Michel Tardieu and his partner, Dominique Laurent, as two of the most influential people of the last 20 years. As the following tasting notes demonstrate, Michel Tardieu's work with his Rhône Valley *négociant* firm is spectacular. This superstar estate in the southern Rhône will have an impact for decades to come. It is mind-boggling that he is able to buy juice (not grapes) and fashion wines that are so extraordinarily faithful to their appellations, yet possess a level of richness and complexity that elevates them to the ranks of the finest wines of their respective appellations. All of these wines are the products of minimal intervention. No sulfur is used during the wines' *élevage* in small barrels, and bottling is accomplished with neither fining nor filtration, so the essence of each *terroir* has been preserved for you—the consumer. I was blown away by these wines and intend to purchase as many as my budget will allow.

There are some terrific buys in the Tardieu-Laurent portfolio. Readers looking to maximize their purchasing power should focus on such offerings from the southern Rhône as Vacqueyras, Côtes du Rhône Guy Louis, Gigondas, and Châteauneuf du Pape. The 1997 Vacqueyras Vieilles Vignes is a potentially superb wine with an opaque purple color, and sumptuous aromas of black cherries and raspberries intertwined with pepper and soil scents. Dense, full bodied, and remarkable for a Vacqueyras, it should drink well for 7–8 years. The 1997 Côtes du Rhône Guy Louis, a blend of equal parts Syrah and Grenache, is one of the most opulently textured, richest Côtes du Rhônes I have ever tasted. The wine's black ruby color is followed by gorgeously sweet aromas of black cherries and blackberries intermixed with raspberries and licorice. Meaty, with elements of *sur-maturité* and low acidity, this well-proportioned Côtes du Rhône will be delicious young, yet keep for a decade or more. The outstanding 1997 Gigondas possesses notes of *sur-maturité*, jammy blackberry liqueurlike notes in both its aromatics and flavors, a superb, full-bodied texture, spectacular concentration, and no evidence of wood from its *barrique* aging. This wine is sensationally long, luscious, and hedonistic. Speaking of decadently rich, full-throttle southern Rhône wines, the 1997 Châteauneuf du Pape satisfies those criteria. A star of the vintage for the appellation, it is a shapely, full-bodied, voluptuously textured wine bursting with black raspberry fruit intermixed with kirsch liqueur, pepper, cedar, and roasted herb scents and flavors. There is tremendous viscosity and length, as well as low acidity in this full-flavored, expansive, superconcentrated Châteauneuf. It should drink well for 10–15 years.

I tasted six wines from the northern Rhône, all of them potentially outstanding—and then some. The 1997 Crozes-Hermitage Vieilles Vignes comes from a well-known producer in l'Arnage. Michel Tardieu requested that I not reveal his sources for fear that other *négociants* would seek him out. The 1997 Crozes-Hermitage Vieilles Vignes boasts a dazzlingly thick black/purple color, and sweet, bacon fat, leathery, and cassis flavors. This full-bodied, beautifully rich Crozes-Hermitage reached 13.4%–13.6% alcohol naturally. It should drink well for a decade.

I have long admired the efforts Michel Tardieu has turned out in Cornas, Côte Rôtie, and Hermitage, and in both 1996 and 1997 he has produced fabulous wines. There are two cuvées of Cornas. The 1997 Cornas Cuvée Coteaux exhibits a saturated black color, as well as a fabulous nose of melted licorice, acacia flowers, jammy cassis, minerals, and smoke. In the mouth, roasted meat and *jus de viande* characteristics, as well as lush tannins emerge in this superb, full-bodied, succulent Cornas. The *barrique* aging undoubtedly helps tame some of the rustic, coarse tannin frequently found in the wines from this appellation. Look for this Cornas to age nicely for 10–15+ years. One of the greatest Cornas I have ever tasted is Tardieu-Laurent's 1997 Cornas Vieilles Vignes. This wine takes concentration, power, and body to an extreme limit, but it possesses remarkable balance and well-integrated acidity, tannin, and alcohol. Black-colored, with Cornas' telltale blackberry, cassis, and tar aromas, fabulous concentration, and a long, intense finish, this fabulous effort is more backward than the Cornas Cuvée Coteaux, and should be at its finest between 2001 and 2020. An amazing accomplishment!

My two favorite wines from this estate in 1997 are the Côte Rôtie Côte Brune and Hermitage. The 1997 Côte Rôtie Côte Brune emerges from such topflight vineyards as Rozier, La Landonne, and Les Grandes Places. It offers a spectacular, complex bouquet of roasted coffee, grilled meats, *jus de viande*, bacon fat, and gobs of black raspberry and cassis fruit. It also possesses the telltale roasted characteristic that gives Côte Rôtie its name. Full bodied, with modest alcohol (13.3%) for such a weighty, rich wine, it also has remarkable elegance and complexity for a wine so massive. A tour de force in winemaking, it can compete with even the single vineyard efforts from Marcel Guigal. It will drink well when released (because of low acidity) and last for 15–20 years. The 1997 Hermitage (13.7% alcohol) is a blend from such vineyards as Le Méal, Les Greffieux, Les Dionnières, and Beaumes. It is a candidate for the finest Hermitage of the vintage, possibly rivaling those of Jaboulet and Chapoutier. The color is a saturated black/purple. The wine reveals a Richebourg-like, floral, violet complexity intermixed with jammy cassis, blackberries, and cherries. Dense, exceptionally full bodied, massive, unctuous, and pure, this is a huge Hermitage with a blockbuster finish. Any evidence of tannin and new *barriques* are submerged behind the wine's texture and extraordinary fruit extraction. Amazing! Anticipated maturity: 2003–2020. The 1997 Hermitage Eremites is an impressively endowed dark ruby/purple-colored wine with copious quantities of sweet black currant fruit intermixed with notes of coffee, tar, and earth. Although dense, full bodied, and outstanding in all aspects, this wine is simply overwhelmed when tasted alongside the profound/compelling 1997 Côte Rôtie Côte Brune and 1997 Hermitage. Look for the 1997 Hermitage Eremites to age well for two decades.

Michel Tardieu was apologetic that the 1996s had been bottled less than two weeks before my visit. After tasting through them, I cannot imagine they could have performed any better. These wines are bottled with minimal SO_2 additions, and no fining or filtration. The transfer from wood to glass can often cause a wine to taste more compressed, but if these wines had any more in them, it would be hard to believe. As a group, these are the finest 1996s anyone has produced in the southern Rhône, and the northern 1996s rival the finest produced in the vintage. In fact, the southern Rhônes go beyond anything I tasted anywhere else in the valley, making Michel Tardieu's performance even more remarkable.

The 1996 Côtes du Rhône Guy Louis (90% Syrah and 10% Grenache) ranks alongside the greatest Fonsalettes I have ever tasted. The color is an amazingly saturated black/purple. The wine offers a super nose of crushed blackberry fruit intertwined with pepper, truffles, and flowers. Extremely youthful and full bodied, with huge quantities of glycerin (it boasts 14.4% alcohol), and a remarkable 35-second finish, this is great stuff! Moreover, it should drink well for 15 or more years. Every bit as impressive is the black-colored 1996 Côtes du Rhône-Villages Cairanne Old Vines. Produced from 100% old vine Grenache, and aged 15 months in 100% new oak casks, this wine reveals little evidence of wood! It exhibits a gorgeous, exotic nose of blackberries intermixed with Asian spices, smoked olives, roasted meats, and pure cherry jam. Rich, unctuously textured, thick, and full bodied, this opulent wine displays none of the telltale *pain grillé,* vanillin of new oak casks—that's how rich and concentrated it is. This low-acid, spectacularly layered wine is undoubtedly one of the finest Cairannes I have ever tasted. It should drink well for 10–15 years. Also super, the saturated purple-colored 1996 Gigondas offers thick, juicy aromas of *sur-maturité,* kirsch liqueur, and black raspberry jam. Full bodied and supple, with more elegance and less weight than the Cairanne or Côtes du Rhône, this spicy, pure, concentrated Gigondas is already drinking well and should age for 15 years.

In 1996 there are two cuvées of Châteauneuf du Pape, both outrageously rich, if not overwhelming, and possibly the finest Châteauneuf du Papes of the vintage. The 1996 Châteauneuf du Pape (13.6% natural alcohol) is mostly Grenache, but there is 5%–6% Mourvèdre and Syrah in the final blend. This wine spent time in both new oak and 1-year-old barrels. It is a full-bodied offering with huge amounts of glycerin, noticeable *pain grillé* scents, and terrific black cherry liqueurlike fruit intermixed with cedar, spicy nuts, roasted herbs, and pepper. Amazing texture and chewiness give this wine a surreal character for this vintage. It should drink well for 12+ years. Even better is the awesome 1996 Châteauneuf du Pape Vieilles Vignes. This wine was aged in 100% new oak casks, and never racked until it was assembled for bottling, which was done without fining or filtration. It achieved 14.5% natural alcohol. Made from 100% old-vine Grenache, it has an amazingly explosive bouquet of spring flowers, jammy cassis, overripe apricots, and floral scents. Magnificently textured, with gobs of fruit, huge quantities of glycerin, and awesome concentration and purity, this wine seems unreal in a vintage such as 1996 (1990 would make more sense for this style of wine). For its size, weight, and remarkable concentration, it possesses a level of complexity and harmony that is frightening. How did Michel Tardieu and Dominique Laurent produce something like this in 1996? Look for this wine to drink well for 15–16 years.

It should come as no surprise that both cuvées of 1996 Cornas are also spectacular, although perhaps not as hedonistic and voluptuous as the southern Rhône cuvées. The vintage's higher acidity is more noticeable in these wines, although the *barrique* treatment has toned down the vintage's tart and tangy personality. The 1996 Cornas Cuvée Coteaux displays a superb black/purple color, and a gorgeously ripe nose of smoked olives and grilled meats along with the telltale cassis. The wine possesses terrific richness, medium to full body, moderate acidity, and high tannin in the finish. It is among the most backward and noticeably structured wines Michel Tardieu has fashioned. Anticipated maturity: 2003–2015. The 1996 Cornas Vieilles Vignes boasts a saturated black/purple color, as well as a nose of liquid minerals and blackberry fruit. Massive in the mouth, with less acidity, meaty, leathery components, huge body, and moderate tannin, the acidity seems lower, but maybe the level of concentration is higher. This mammoth Cornas should be cellared for 3–4 years; it will keep for 2 decades.

The 1996 Côte Rôtie is a worthy rival to the extraordinary 1997. The color is an opaque purple. The spectacular nose of bacon fat, violets, roasted herbs, and black raspberry jam explodes upward from the glass. In the mouth, the wine reveals a plush texture, medium to full body, gorgeous purity, and thrilling levels of extract and fruit. The tannins are present, but the vintage's high acidity is obscured behind the wine's roasted elements and lavish fruit and glycerin. Drink it over the next 15+ years. The 1996 Hermitage is a wine of massive richness, extraordinary purity, and enormous potential. The saturated opaque purple color is followed by a youthful, unevolved bouquet of tar, cassis, blackberries, and stones. Superb in the mouth, with full body, fabulous richness, and a layered, multidimensional personality, it is another tour de force in winemaking, but it requires 7–10 years of cellaring. Anticipated maturity: 2010–2025.

The 1995 Bandol Vieilles Vignes (100% Mourvèdre aged in 1-year-old barrels) is phenomenal. In fact, other than Domaine Pradeaux's Cuvée Vieilles Vignes, I cannot think of a more monster-sized, massive, concentrated Bandol. The wine possesses mouth-searing levels of tannin, an opaque black color, an extraordinary combination of blueberry and blackberry flavors intermixed with leather, earth, and a steely component. Huge, frightfully backward, and in need of a minimum of 10–15 years of cellaring, this wine has the potential to last 40 or more years. It should only be purchased by readers with the requisite patience.

It was inspirational to taste wines of such majestic richness and complexity from two irregular vintages such as 1996 and 1997. There is true genius in these cellars.

This young *négociant* business, which is owned and energized by two talented men, Dominique Laurent of Nuits St.-Georges and Michel Tardieu of the Rhône Valley, is turning out some remarkable wines. Sadly, they are made in very limited quantities. These are all exquisite Rhône wines that are typical of their appellations. Their cold, underground cellars are located in the Château of Loumarin, which is about a forty-minute drive east of Avignon, in the foothills of the Ventoux Mountains.

By the way, in this tiny village is a restaurant that I think is turning out some of the world's most extraordinary cuisine. The Restaurant La Frenière blew me away when I first ate there in 1996. Having returned for a meal in mid-July 1997, I am convinced the chef, Madame Sammut, is a genius. Her exquisite cooking easily merits three Michelin stars, rather than the one star it receives. This lovely restaurant/auberge offers inspired quintessential Provençal cuisine that is not to be missed.

Readers looking for a terrific bargain should check out the Côtes du Rhône Guy Louis. Three vintages to date have all been very good, with the 1995 nearly outstanding. Now in bottle, it is a blend of equal parts Syrah and Grenache. The wine exhibits a deep ruby/purple color, followed by a wonderful nose of black currant fruit, pepper, spice, and subtle toasty oak. Loaded with fruit, medium to full bodied, with multiple layers of flavor, it should drink well for 10–12 years.

Readers should also check out the high-class Vacqueyras made by Tardieu-Laurent. The 1995 (only 100 cases produced) is performing even better out of bottle than it did from cask. One of the finest examples of Vacqueyras I have ever tasted, it possesses a deep ruby/purple color, accompanied by intense smoky, peppery, sweet, jammy aromas. It is a muscular, medium- to full-bodied wine with a subtle influence of new oak. Fleshy and tannic, this is a seriously endowed *vin de garde* that is best cellared for 1–3 years; it should keep for 12–15 years. What a Vacqueyras!

Michel Tardieu and Dominique Laurent's policy of extremely low levels of SO_2 at bottling, in addition to no racking (until assemblage prior to bottling), fining, or filtration, has worked wonders with these wines. The 1995 Gigondas (125 cases produced from extremely old vines) is a 70% Grenache/30% Mourvèdre blend that achieved 14.7% alcohol naturally. The wine, impressive from barrel, was singing from bottle in 1997! It is a classic example of a large-scaled, succulent, juicy, full-bodied Gigondas bursting with herb-tinged black cherry and plumlike fruit. Broad and intense, with impressive layers of extract, glycerin, and alcohol, this wine is about as hedonistic as Gigondas can be. The wine is relatively soft, but I am sure some formidable tannin is disguised by the wine's level of fruit and extract. This Gigondas will keep for 12–15 years, but I don't see how purchasers will resist it.

The closed 1995 Châteauneuf du Pape displays a dense ruby/purple color, and a tight set of aromatics that exhibit some new oak and jammy cherry/plum scents. This is the only Tardieu-Laurent offering where the wood still dominates the wine's personality. There is a good mouth-feel, with layers of fruit, full body, excellent purity as well as overall balance, but the wine is tannic and closed, with considerable structure. It offers accessibility (largely because of its 15% natural alcohol), but it should be purchased only by those who are willing to cellar it for 3–4 years. This wine has a minimum of 15 years of evolution ahead of it.

The 1995 Crozes-Hermitage reveals a dense purple color, followed by a sweet nose of cassis, olives, licorice, and incense. The wine is rich and dense, with lower acidity than the

1996, but is boldly flavored, powerful, and intense. The acidity and tannin suggest 2–3 years of cellaring is required. Look for this Crozes-Hermitage to be long-lived, aging well for 14–15 years.

There are two cuvées of Cornas produced by Tardieu-Laurent. The Cornas Coteaux is made from hillside vineyards that average 20 years in age. Most of the grapes emerge from a vineyard called Les Chaillots. The 1995 Cornas Cuvée Coteaux (only 75 cases) achieved 13% alcohol naturally. Aged in 100% new oak, the wine has soaked up the influence of new wood. It is a powerful, rich wine with a dense purple color, and an exceptionally intense nose of earthy black fruits, minerals, smoke, and grilled meats. It is a great Cornas that is showing even better out of bottle than it did from cask. The wine's layers of richness, sweet tannin, and awesome mouth-feel suggest it will be at its best between 2000 and 2020. Lovers of Cornas must try and find a few bottles of the extraordinary 1995 Cornas Vieilles Vignes. Seventy-five cases of this wine were produced from the same vineyard parcels as the 1996. No SO$_2$ was added to the wine, and it was bottled without fining or filtration. The Vieilles Vignes, which is slightly lower in alcohol (12.8%) than the Coteaux cuvée, is one of the most fabulous Cornas I have tasted. The color is a dense black/purple, and the nose offers up a fabulous array of sweet cassis aromas intermingled with tar, smoke, and floral scents. Amazingly rich, with multiple layers of concentrated flavors, this is a wine of extraordinary depth, ripeness, and intensity. While it possesses enough fat and sweetness to be accessible, it should drink well for 18–20 years. Fortunate buyers of this wine should have the discipline to cellar it for 4–5 years.

Two other wines that were performing better out of bottle than they did from cask include the two cuvées of 1995 Hermitage. The 1995 Hermitage Cuvée L'Hermite is made in microscopic amounts from old vines grown on the largest hill of Hermitage in a vineyard called L'Hermite. To that is added a small dollop of wine from a tiny old vine parcel in Rocoules. The wine boasts an opaque purple color, and a dense, sweet nose of cassis fruit. It reveals extraordinary finesse for its massive size, and great purity, ripeness, and overall equilibrium. A fabulously concentrated wine with well-integrated acidity and tannin, it will be at its best in 5–7 years, and keep for 20+. The 1995 Hermitage Cuvée Classique (125 cases) is made largely from two Hermitage vineyards called Les Beaumes and Les Diognières. The wine has taken on considerable weight and depth, and is now one of the vintage's great wines. It possesses extraordinary elegance and finesse for a Hermitage, yet marvelous intensity and richness. Full bodied, with layers of sweet cassis fruit, a multilayered texture, and plenty of ripe tannin in the 45-second finish, it is an awesome example of Hermitage that should be at its best between 2005 and 2020.

The 1995 Côte Rôtie exhibits good density, ripeness, and aromatics. This should turn out to be an excellent, medium-bodied, stylish Côte Rôtie with plenty of the appellation's smoky, peppery, black raspberry fruit. It can be drunk young or cellared for 10 years.

As a postscript, readers should be aware that all of these wines are very reasonably priced.

DOMAINE DE TERRE FERME

1997 Châteauneuf du Pape	C	(85–86)
1996 Châteauneuf du Pape	C	86

These two wines are more alike than dissimilar. Both vintages offer elegant, soft, fruity, round wines meant for early consumption. The plum-colored 1997 Châteauneuf du Pape exhibits ripe black cherry fruit intertwined with Provençal herbs, olives, and allspice. This medium-bodied offering requires drinking over the next 3–4 years. The surprisingly good, elegant 1996 Châteauneuf du Pape has survived its bottling without too much flavor-stripping filtration. It offers Bing cherry, Asian spice, incense, roasted herb, and earth notes. Medium bodied, soft, and round, it should drink well for 4–5 years.

CHÂTEAU DE LA TOUR

1996	Côtes du Rhône	A/D	81
1997	Côtes du Rhône (White)	A/D	86
1997	Vacqueyras	C	(78–81)
1996	Vacqueyras	C	86
1995	Vacqueyras	C	88
1996	Vin de Pays	B	84
1997	Vin de Pays (White)	B	83

To put it bluntly, I expected more from these wines produced by Emmanuel Reynaud. While I recognize the vintages were not the easiest years, many other Rhône producers were able to get more from their vineyards. The white wine offerings include a soft, flabby, unstructured 1997 Vin de Pays, and a much better 1997 Côtes du Rhône. The latter wine, though low in acidity, is fleshy, soft, and monolithic.

The red wines are pleasant. They include a good, easy-to-drink, cherry-scented and -flavored, soft, light- to medium-bodied 1996 Vin de Pays, and a strangely tannic, vegetal 1996 Côtes du Rhône. The 1997 Vacqueyras exhibits an evolved garnet/light ruby color, and some fat on the attack, but it became attenuated and lean in the mouth. The two finest wines are the 1996 and 1995 Vacqueyras. The 1996 Vacqueyras is a textbook, old style Côtes du Rhône with plenty of *garrigue*, pepper, and berry fruit (predominantly cherries and strawberries), and a medium-bodied, rustic finish. Even better, the deep ruby-colored 1995 Vacqueyras offers sweet, jammy strawberry/cherry aromas with hints of licorice, spice, and animal notes in the flavors, good ripeness, and a medium- to full-bodied, luscious finish. It should drink well for 5–7 years.

CHÂTEAU DU TRIGNON

1997	Côtes du Rhône	A	84
1996	Côtes du Rhône-Villages Rasteau	B	85
1997	Côtes du Rhône-Villages Sablet	B	85
1997	Gigondas	C	(86–87)
1996	Gigondas	C	86
1995	Gigondas	C	90

This estate is coming of age now that Pascal Roux is responsible for the winemaking. Château du Trignon's 1997 Gigondas exhibits an evolved dark plum color, and an open-knit, sexy style with copious quantities of sweet black cherries and berry fruit. This very good, soft, velvety-textured Gigondas will need to be drunk during its first 4–5 years of life. The 1996 Gigondas is one of the more successful wines of this difficult vintage. It possesses more acidity than the 1997, as well as a plump, richly fruity style with pepper, tar, and black cherry/kirsch notes in the boisterous aromatics. Medium bodied and soft, it is ideal for drinking over the next 5–6 years.

Château du Trignon's 1995 Gigondas is a knockout wine. It possesses a dense purple color, followed by an explosive peppery, blackberry, and *garrigue*-scented nose, medium- to full-bodied, powerful flavors with admirable thickness, and juicy, succulent, rich fruit. This sexy, spicy, deeply concentrated wine is smooth enough to be drunk now but forceful and rich enough to be cellared for 10–12+ years. Impressive!

This estate has been producing better and better wines over recent vintages, which is well evidenced by the two white cuvées of 1997. The 1997 Côtes du Rhône blanc is a soft wine with lemon and honey notes, a touch of pear, medium body, and a clean, round, dry finish. Drink it over the next 8 months. Even more aromatic, the 1997 Côtes du Rhône-Villages Sablet offers a honeyed citrus, light peach, and flowery-scented nose. The wine hits the palate with good texture and ripeness, then narrows out slightly. Drink this clean, dry wine over the next year.

The 1996 Côtes du Rhône-Villages Rasteau reveals an evolved, medium ruby color, followed by a spicy, peppery, *garrigue*, kirsch and cherry-scented and flavored personality. This soft, medium-bodied wine should be consumed over the next several years.

DOMAINE DU TUNNEL (STEPHANE ROBERT)

1996 Cornas	C	85
1996 Cornas Cuvée Prestige	D	89

The 1996 Cornas is a solidly made, elegant, spicy, dark ruby-colored wine with medium body and the vintage's tangy acidity. It is more compressed than the impressively endowed 1996 Cornas Cuvée Prestige. The latter wine exhibits a saturated purple color, as well as classic cassis aromas intermixed with tar and spice. Powerful, rich, and ripe, with good acidity, this pure, concentrated Cornas will be at its finest between 2001 and 2012.

PIERRE USSEGLIO

1997 Châteauneuf du Pape	C	(87–88)
1996 Châteauneuf du Pape	C	88
1995 Châteauneuf du Pape	C	90

There are three different Usseglios, all bottling wines under their name in Châteauneuf du Pape. My favorite wines generally are those of Pierre Usseglio, although making such a choice is often difficult. This is a small estate, and the wines usually sell out quickly. At first, the outstanding 1995 Châteauneuf du Pape is tightly knit and difficult to penetrate, but airing brings forth marvelous richness and intensity. The dark ruby color is accompanied by copious amounts of sweet black cherry and raspberry fruit, along with pepper, iodine, and earth. It is full bodied, powerful, and rich, with plenty of sweet fruit and glycerin on the attack, but then some of the wine's muscle and tannin kick in. This is a structured, intensely rich Châteauneuf du Pape that will benefit from another 2–3 years of cellaring. It should drink well for 12–15 years.

The 1997 Châteauneuf du Pape exhibits admirable depth for the vintage, as well as the year's easy-to-drink personality. There are cherries galore in this spicy, peppery, fragrant, expansively flavored, medium- to full-bodied wine. While it is an ideal Châteauneuf for beginners, it will satisfy even such diehard fans of the appellation as myself. Enjoy it over the next 3–4 years. Pierre Usseglio's richer, more expansive 1996 Châteauneuf du Pape is another charming surprise from this vintage. The dark ruby/garnet color is followed by jammy cherry aromas intermixed with smoked Provençal herbs, licorice, and fruitcake. The wine possesses excellent richness, a cherry/kirsch, peppery, richly fruity character, sweet glycerin, medium to full body, and no hard edges in the lusty, high alcohol finish. Drink it over the next 6–7 years.

RAYMOND USSEGLIO

1997 Châteauneuf du Pape Cuvée Classique	E/EE	(78–80)
1996 Châteauneuf du Pape Cuvée Classique	E/EE	87
1996 Châteauneuf du Pape Cuvée Impériale	E/EE	89

Readers should not confuse Raymond Usseglio with Pierre Usseglio. Raymond Usseglio has turned out a lightweight 1997 Châteauneuf du Pape Cuvée Classique with elegant, medium-bodied black cherry flavors intermixed with herbs, earth, and smoky notes. Simple and one-dimensional, it warrants consumption within the next 3–4 years. Usseglio was far more successful in 1996. His 1996 Châteauneuf du Pape Cuvée Classique offers textbook Provençal aromas and flavors. Notes of olives, *garrigue,* herbs, and black raspberry and cherry fruit soar from the glass of this expressive wine. In the mouth, it is lush, round, medium to full bodied, and pure, with gobs of jammy fruit and glycerin. It should drink well for 5–6 years. The 1996 Châteauneuf du Pape Cuvée Impériale may deserve an even higher rating. It exhibits a deep ruby/garnet color, as well as an expansive, seductive aromatic pro-file of black raspberry jam intermixed with incense, licorice, smoke, and pepper. Medium to full bodied, with sweet fruit, surprisingly intense extract and richness for a 1996, and an ex-pansive, chewy, long finish, this is a gorgeously opulent, hedonistic Châteauneuf du Pape to consume over the next 8–10 years.

CHÂTEAU VAUDIEU

1995 Châteauneuf du Pape	C/D	86+

This large estate, southeast of Rayas, produces nearly 23,000 cases of red wine from a blend of 80% Grenache, 10% Syrah, 5% Mourvèdre, and 5% Cinsault. There is an unwarranted tendency to criticize Château Vaudieu because it is owned by the omnipresent Meffre family, who has major holdings throughout the Rhône Valley. Although made in a modern, risk-free style, the wine is richly fruity, medium to full bodied, and certainly good. It will never be outstanding, but the wine is consistent and predictable. The 1995 Châteauneuf du Pape re-veals a dark garnet color, as well as an elegant, peppery, spicy nose with hints of fruitcake and red fruits. It is not complex, but it does possess fine density, medium to full body, and good richness in the finish. Lushness and overall generosity make for a modern-styled, pleasing, cleanly made Châteauneuf du Pape. Anticipated maturity: now–2005.

GEORGES VERNAY

1997 Condrieu	D/E	88
1997 Condrieu Les Chailées de l'Enfer	E	92
1996 Condrieu Coteaux du Vernon	E	88
1997 Viognier VDP Collines Rhodaniennes	C	85

Georges Vernay continues to fashion super Condrieu, but I was disappointed in his 1996 and 1997 St.-Joseph and Côte Rôtie. However, his impressive white wines include rich, full-bodied Condrieus that are among the finest of the appellation. The 1997 Condrieu offers a telltale orange skin, honeysuckle, and apricot-scented nose with floral notes in the back-ground. Ripe, honeyed, full bodied, and loaded with fruit, this soft, fleshy wine should be en-joyed over the next year. Among the two higher-priced cuvées, the 1997 Condrieu Les Chailées de l'Enfer is superb. It boasts spectacular aromatics, full body, layers of unctuously textured fruit, and a heady, long finish. It overwhelms the 1996 Condrieu Coteaux du Vernon. The latter wine is more structured, revealing the vintage's higher acidity, but with less fat, fruit, and hedonistic appeal. Nevertheless, it should age atypically well for a Condrieu—4–5 years. The 1997 Viognier VDP Collines Rhodaniennes is a low-key yet tasty, textbook Viog-nier with good ripeness and low acidity. It requires consumption over the next year.

NOËL VERSET

1997 Cornas	D	?
1996 Cornas	D	76
1995 Cornas	D	89

The 1996 and 1997 were each tasted twice, and I still cannot believe how badly they performed. For much of the seventies and eighties, Verset, along with Clape, produced reference point Cornas (I was an enthusiastic purchaser and drinker of his wines), but he appears to have lost the magic touch as we end the twentieth century. The 1997 Cornas was untastable given the bizarre, woody, musty aromas. The 1996 Cornas, tasted twice from bottle, revealed an acidic, old, musty oak component that dominated the wine's otherwise impressive fruit. The wine's funky, unclean wood character permeated what would have been an admirable flavor component. It is with considerable regret that I report on these wines given the many fine vintages I have purchased and consumed of Verset's Cornas. Notes such as this are among the most lamentable aspects of my job.

Verset's excellent, nearly outstanding 1995 Cornas offers a deep purple color, followed by a sweet, fragrant nose of jammy cassis fruit intermixed with minerals, licorice, and spice. Full bodied, with copious spice, as well as impressive extraction of ripe fruit, this medium- to full-bodied, surprisingly accessible Cornas can be drunk now as well as over the next 12–15 years.

J. VIDAL-FLEURY

1997 Côte Rôtie La Chatillonne	E	(87–89)
1996 Côte Rôtie La Chatillonne	E	(85–86)
1995 Côte Rôtie La Chatillonne	E	90
1994 Côte Rôtie La Chatillonne	E	89+
1995 Côtes du Rhône	A	84
1996 Côtes du Rhône-Villages Cairanne	B	84
1995 Côtes du Ventoux	B	84
1994 Crozes-Hermitage	B	86
1994 Hermitage	D	85

The outstanding 1995 Côte Rôtie La Chatillonne offers up thrilling aromatics consisting of bacon fat, raspberry jam, cedar, and spice. The wine is ripe, with low acidity, a lush, elegant, concentrated palate, medium body, and no hard edges. This is an evolved, complex, silky-textured Côte Rôtie to drink now and over the next 8–10 years. The 1994 Côte Rôtie La Chatillonne displays some dry tannin in the finish, which kept my score below the outstanding category, but I loved the wine's deep ruby color, and sweet black raspberry nose intermixed with scents of violets, grilled nuts, smoke, and toast. It is an excellent rich, medium- to full-bodied Côte Rôtie that will drink well for a decade. The 1996 Côte Rôtie La Chatillonne reveals a cool, cold climate, herbaceous, green pepper characteristic to its fruit. Although soft, pretty, medium bodied, and elegant, the subtle greenness kept my score low. It also exhibits the vintage's tangy/tart acidity in the moderately long finish. Lastly, the 1997 Côte Rôtie La Chatillonne appears to be very good, and may improve if it fleshes out. The dark ruby color is followed by a big, spicy, black raspberry-scented nose with hints of minerals, mint, and pepper. Medium bodied, with moderate acidity, and good definition, it should drink well for 7–8 years.

The 1994 Hermitage reveals ripe raspberry fruit, but the wine comes across as understated and restrained for this appellation. It offers good spice and berry fruit, but does not deliver the complexity or force one expects of a top-notch Hermitage. A reasonably good value from Vidal-Fleury is the 1996 Côtes du Rhône-Villages Cairanne, a spicy, cherry, peppery wine with medium body, notes of dried herbes de Provence, and a clean, spicy, quick finish. Drink it over the next 1–2 years.

The following three offerings are consistently good values from the Guigal-owned Vidal-Fleury firm in Ampuis. The light ruby-colored 1995 Côtes du Ventoux should be sought out by those looking for a light-bodied, soft, quaffable and friendly dry red wine. It offers light to medium body, soft strawberry and cherry fruit, not much complexity, but a silky, soft, clean style. Drink it over the next year. The 1995 Côtes du Rhône is deeper-colored, with more body and glycerin, as well as more spice, pepper, and a kirschlike quality. Although not concentrated, it is soft, round, and easy to understand and drink. Consume it over the next several years. The finest wine of this trio is the 1994 Crozes-Hermitage. This is an authentic, dark ruby/purple-colored Syrah with an attractive, wild berry and cassis-scented nose. Soft and gentle, with medium body, very good concentration, and the superfriendly style exhibited by all Vidal-Fleury's reds, this wine should drink well for 2–3 years.

The other wines from Vidal-Fleury were uninspiring. They included a pleasant 1996 Côtes de Ventoux and 1995 Châteauneuf du Pape, a good 1997 Crozes-Hermitage and 1995 St.-Joseph, a mediocre 1996 Côtes du Rhône, and a lean, hard, out of balance 1995 Cornas.

DOMAINE DE LA VIEILLE JULIENNE

1997	Châteauneuf du Pape Cuvée Classique	D	(83–85)
1996	Châteauneuf du Pape Cuvée Classique	D	85
1995	Châteauneuf du Pape Cuvée Classique	D	87
1996	Châteauneuf du Pape Cuvée Réservée Vieilles Vignes	E/EE	88
1995	Châteauneuf du Pape Cuvée Réservée Vieilles Vignes	E	91
1995	Côtes du Rhône	B	86
1996	Côtes du Rhône Vieilles Vignes	C	85
1995	Côtes du Rhône Vieilles Vignes	C	85

This estate, run by the Arnaud-Daumen family, has begun to produce serious Châteauneuf du Pape from their vineyards, primarily located in the northern sector of Châteauneuf du Pape. Readers looking for a good value should seek out the Côtes du Rhône Vieilles Vignes. It is a well-made, fruit-driven, medium-bodied, soft, easy-to-understand wine with excellent Grenache character (roasted peanuts, kirsch, and *garrigue*). I thought both the 1995 and 1996 to be equivalent in quality. Both are meant to be consumed over the next several years.

The 1997 Châteauneuf du Pape Cuvée Classique reflects the vintage's character in its soft, open-knit, ripe strawberry/cherry-scented and -flavored style. There is good ripeness, medium body, low acidity, and an evolved personality. I would opt for drinking it over the next 2–3 years. The 1996 Châteauneuf du Pape Cuvée Classique exhibits a light to medium ruby color, and a moderately intense, soft, black cherry, strawberry, and raspberry-scented nose. With a silky texture, medium body, and ripe flavors, with a touch of dilution in the finish, its open-knit, evolved style suggests it should be consumed over the next 3–4 years. The most impressive cuvée is the 1996 Châteauneuf du Pape Cuvée Réservée Vieilles Vignes. It boasts a dark ruby color, followed by a robust nose of black currants, kirsch, smoke, and cherry jam. There is excellent concentration, medium to full body, a supple texture, and a heady, lusty, alcoholic finish. This very good to excellent 1996 offering should continue to drink well for 5–6 years.

There are two 1995 Châteauneuf du Papes, with the Cuvée Réservée representing a selection from 70–100-year-old vines. This wine is made only in top vintages. The 1995 Châteauneuf du Pape Cuvée Classique is a textbook Provençal Châteauneuf du Pape with its sweet, gamey, meaty, roasted herb, black cherry, peppery aromas and flavors, rich, nicely textured, medium- to full-bodied flavors, and good depth, ripeness, and extract. Already approachable, it promises to last for 7–8 years. The outstanding, rich, dark ruby/purple-colored 1995 Châteauneuf du Pape Cuvée Réservée reveals evidence of exposure to new oak casks (check out the *pain grillé* notes). An impressive, full-bodied *vin de garde,* this classic, well-endowed wine offers plenty of smoke, black fruits, cherries, hickory, and barbecue-like scents, along with copious quantities of fruit and structure. Drink this rich, impressively endowed Châteauneuf du Pape between 1999 and 2015.

Another sign of the good things emerging from this estate is their very good 1995 Côtes du Rhône. An attractive dark ruby/garnet-colored wine with a peppery, spicy, fruitcake-scented nose, ripe berry fruit, medium body, and an overall sense of elegance, it will drink well over the next 3–4 years.

LE VIEUX DONJON

1997	Châteauneuf du Pape	C	(86–87)
1996	Châteauneuf du Pape	C	88
1995	Châteauneuf du Pape	C	91+

One of my favorite estates in Châteauneuf du Pape, Le Vieux Donjon is impeccably run by the Michel family. They produce traditionally made, classic Châteauneuf du Pape without any compromises. The 1997 Châteauneuf du Pape offers a big, peppery, iodine, iron, cherry/kirsch-scented nose that jumps from the glass. In the mouth, the wine is medium bodied, soft, round, and seductive, but it lacks the concentration and intensity of this estate's finest vintages (that is, 1995, 1990, 1989, and 1988). It should be consumed over the next 4–5 years as it is atypically evolved and forward for Le Vieux Donjon. It is a fine choice for restaurants. The same can be said for the 1996 Châteauneuf du Pape. It is the quintessential Provençal wine given its flashy display of pepper, licorice, and herbes de Provence scents intertwined with black cherries and salty ocean breeze notes. Generous, expansive, and fat for the vintage, it exhibits jammy cassis/cherry and olive flavors, medium to full body, and no hard edges. Drink this delicious, sumptuously styled Châteauneuf over the next 5–7+ years.

The classic 1995 Châteauneuf du Pape needs 3–4 years of cellaring. It displays a provocative, exotic nose of sausage, pepper, bacon fat, cassis, and kirsch. Superconcentrated, moderately tannic, full-bodied flavors offer additional nuances of truffles, licorice, and ripe black fruits. This is a gorgeously rich, full-bodied, backward 1995 with moderate tannin. It should keep for 15–18 years.

VIEUX TÉLÉGRAPHE

1997	Châteauneuf du Pape	C	(87–89)
1996	Châteauneuf du Pape	C	88
1995	Châteauneuf du Pape	C	93
1995	Châteauneuf du Pape Hippolyte Cuvée Speciale	E	93
1997	Châteauneuf du Pape Hippolyte Cuvée Speciale (White)	E	89
1995	Châteauneuf du Pape Vieux Mas des Papes	E	88
1997	Châteauneuf du Pape (White)	D	88
1997	Le Pigeoulet	A	85

Daniel Brunier told me that the problem in 1997 for Châteauneuf du Pape was the huge quantity of rain during July and August. In spite of the dry months of September and October, the soil was too saturated to shed the excess moisture, thus the ripe, but diluted style of many wines. Value seekers should search out Brunier's vin de pays, the 1997 Le Pigeoulet. A concoction of Grenache, Syrah, Cabernet Sauvignon, Cinsault, and a few other varietals, it is a round, fruity, medium ruby-colored wine revealing pepper, cherry fruit, a touch of cassis, and an elegant, soft personality. An ideal bistro selection, it is meant to be drunk during its first several years of life.

The 1997 and 1996 Châteauneuf du Papes are similarly styled, being evolved, forward, richly fruity wines with medium body, and plenty of smoke, pepper, allspice, black cherry and Provençal herb aromas. Both are seductive, round, charming, and sexy. The 1996 possesses slightly more depth, is fuller bodied, and with riper fruit concentration, but they are very close in quality. The 1997 reveals more pepper, spicy aromas. Because of its fragility, Daniel Brunier intends to bottle the 1997 early to preserve its attractive level of fruit. Neither wine will make old bones, but both will offer delicious drinking for 6–7 years.

1997 was an excellent vintage for white Rhônes. I enjoyed both the 1997 Châteauneuf du Pape blanc and 1997 Châteauneuf du Pape Cuvée Hippolyte Cuvée Speciale blanc. It is the first time they have made a white Cuvée Hippolyte (this bottling is destined to be drunk mostly with Brunier's friends). It is the same blend as the regular cuvée, but is put through 100% malolactic fermentation and then given an *élevage* in 40% small barrels, with the balance kept in tank. It is then blended together. The wines exhibit similar styles (surprising given the fact that the regular cuvée has its malolactic blocked), with citrusy, honeyed, rose petal-like scents, good fruit, and medium- to full-bodied personalities. I find these whites drink well with an assortment of grilled fish dishes. The regular cuvée will drink well for 1–2 years, and the Cuvée Hippolyte for 3–4 years.

I tasted the 1998 Vieux-Télégraphe (which marks the 100th anniversary of this domaine). Black-colored, with fabulous raspberry, kirsch, smoky, blackberry fruit, it should prove to be one of the finest wines produced at this estate in over a decade, although that is somewhat unfair given the consistency and excellence of this estate's wines. Stay tuned.

Vieux-Télégraphe's 1995 Châteauneuf du Pape offers the essence of black fruits. A blend of 65% Grenache, 15% Syrah, 15% Mourvèdre, and 5% miscellaneous grapes, the 1995 is undoubtedly the finest wine this estate has produced since the renowned 1978. The wine possesses a roasted herb, meaty character accompanied by a lavish display of jammy black fruits, as well as superb concentration, admirable fat and density, adequate acidity, and a lusty, full-bodied finish with some tannin. Already delicious, it will keep for another 15+ years. It is one of the top wines of the 1995 vintage.

Vieux-Télégraphe has begun to produce a second cuvée, keeping their oldest vines for the estate's grand vin. The second wine, Vieux Mas des Papes, is supple, rich, and ideal for drinking within the first 7–8 years of life. The excellent 1995 exhibits gobs of sweet licorice, Provençal herb, and jammy black cherry fruit. This ripe, plump, low-acid wine possesses a velvety texture as well as an alcoholic finish. Although not complex, it represents a delicious, jammy mouthful of pure fruit.

Limited quantities of the 1995 Hippolyte were produced from equal portions of Grenache, Mourvèdre, and Syrah. An interesting wine, but it will probably only be tasted by members of the wine trade who purchase Vieux-Télégraphe, or writers who visit the estate. The 1995 reveals huge tannin, but fabulous concentration, full body, and remarkable power and structure. In contrast to the regular cuvée, it is more backward and dominated by Mourvèdre and Syrah. For drinking over the next 10–15 years, I actually prefer the estate's classic cuvée of Châteauneuf du Pape. The Hippolyte will require 5–8 years of cellaring, as it is less flattering and precocious than Vieux-Télégraphe's classic Châteauneuf du Pape.

FRANÇOIS VILLARD

1997	Condrieu Coteaux de Poncin	E	91
1995	Condrieu Coteaux de Poncin	E	92
1997	Condrieu Le Grand Vallon	E	87
1997	Condrieu Les Terrasses du Palat	E	89
1995	Condrieu Les Terrasses du Palat	E	87
1995	Côte Rôtie	D	88
1996	Côte Rôtie La Brocarde	E	87?
1996	St.-Joseph Les Côtes du Mairlant	D	87
1997	St.-Joseph Les Côtes du Mairlant (White)	D	89
1996	St.-Joseph Les Côtes du Mairlant (White)	D	87
1997	St.-Joseph Reflet	D	(88–89)
1996	St.-Joseph Reflet	D	88
1995	St.-Joseph Reflet	D	87

One of the most talented young producers to emerge from the northern Rhône during the decade of the nineties, François Villard has quickly developed a reputation for very fine Condrieu, and increasingly good reds from both St.-Joseph and Côte Rôtie. His 1997 Condrieu include three vineyard-designated wines. The 1997 Condrieu Le Grand Vallon displays surprisingly good acidity for the vintage, as well as an apricot and honeysuckle-scented nose, good ripeness, and medium to full body. It should be consumed during its first year of life. The more mineral-dominated 1997 Condrieu Les Terrasses du Palat reveals peach, apricot, and honeysuckle aromas in the moderately intense nose, fine elegance allied to power, and surprisingly crisp acidity for its full-bodied, ripe style. Close to outstanding, it should be drunk over the next 2–3 years. The superb 1997 Condrieu Coteaux de Poncin offers a tropical fruit-scented nose of honeyed citrus and pineapple. There is gorgeous fruit, superb definition, an underlying mineral component, and a dry, full-bodied, pure finish. This gorgeous Condrieu will last well beyond its peak drinking years, 1999–2001.

From St.-Joseph, Villard has turned out two delicious white wines (blends of 80% Marsanne and 20% Roussanne). The 1997 St.-Joseph Côtes du Mairlant exhibits an orange marmalade/peachy, Condrieu-like nose, medium body, excellent rich fruit, adequate acidity, and a honeyed finish. It should drink well for 2 years. Revealing more oak in the nose, the 1996 St.-Joseph Côtes du Mairlant is a full-bodied, expansive, dry, ripe white wine. The higher acidity gives the wine more nerve than the plusher 1997.

Villard's red wine cuvées continue to improve. The opaque purple-colored 1997 St.-Joseph Reflet displays medium to full body, and plenty of toasty new oak nicely complemented by ripe cassis fruit. Although monolithic, this excellent wine offers good purity, richness, and palate appeal. The 1996 St.-Joseph Reflet possesses toasty new oak, black cherry liqueur and cassis aromas, medium body, excellent depth, unobtrusive acidity, and moderate tannin in the long finish. Both Reflet cuvées should drink well over the next 7–8 years. The 1996 St.-Joseph Côte du Mairlant (I did not taste the 1997) exhibits a dark plum color, followed by sweet aromatics of cassis and red currants. Sweet and rich in the mouth, with a seductive cranberry/cherry liqueurlike fruitiness, this medium-bodied wine possesses enough acidity to provide definition and freshness. It should drink well for 4–6 years. The saturated dark ruby/purple-colored 1996 Côtes Rôtie La Brocarde reveals the vintage's noticeably high acidity, along with smoky, raspberry/blackberry fruit presented in a medium-bodied, tart, crisp style. The high acidity gives the wine an angular, compressed feeling in the mouth. Anticipated maturity: 2001–2010.

Villard's impressive red wine portfolio includes excellent 1995s. The 1995 St.-Joseph Reflet is a beautifully made wine, revealing more evidence of *pain grillé*/vanillin from aging in toasty new oak. The wine is dark purple-colored, with a sweet, smoky, black fruit-scented nose, medium body, and is long, rich, and pure in the mouth. Give it 2–4 years of cellaring and drink it over the subsequent 15 years. This is a well-endowed, concentrated, classic St.-Joseph from one of the up-and-coming stars of the northern Rhône.

Villard also demonstrates a steady hand with Côte Rôtie, although I can't say these wines are significantly better than his exquisite St.-Joseph. The 1995 Côte Rôtie is a softer, more accessible wine than the 1996, with loads of smoky, jammy berry fruit, licorice, and roasted olives in its aromatics. Meaty, black cherry, and cassis flavors are soft, velvety-textured, and medium to full bodied. This excellent, mouth-filling, accessible Côte Rôtie should drink well for 10–12 years.

Readers should also check out the two cuvées of Condrieu that I tasted from bottle. Villard's 1995 Condrieu Les Terrasses du Palat is a ripe, soft, luscious Condrieu made to be consumed over the next 1–2 years. Slightly fuller and more honeyed, with full body and plenty of sweet honeysuckle and peachlike fruit is the 1995 Condrieu Coteaux de Poncin.

ALAIN VOGE

1996 Cornas Les Vieilles Fontaines	D	91+
1996 Cornas Vieilles Vignes	D	90
1995 Cornas Vieilles Vignes	D	90+

Alain Voge, who appears to have recovered well from a liver transplant, has produced two of the finest wines of the irregular 1996 vintage. The 1996 Cornas Vieilles Vignes exhibits supersweet blackberry fruit wrapped with earth, tar, and minerals. Full bodied and classic in its flavor profile, this wine has a sweet attack, and noticeable but not obtrusive acidity. This rustic, flavorful, pure, expansive Cornas should drink well during its first decade of life. Voge's 1996 Cornas Les Vieilles Fontaines possesses one of the most saturated black/purple colors of the 1996 northern Rhônes. This monster Cornas reveals evidence of new oak (Voge claims to use only 10%–15% new oak casks). Full bodied, deep, superextracted and concentrated, it represents the essence of Cornas. If it fully resolves its tannin and acidity, this wine could merit an even higher score. Only those with patience should invest in this limited production classic. Anticipated maturity: 2006–2020.

Voge's 1995 Cornas Vieilles Vignes boasts a dense ruby/purple color, and a knockout nose of smoked meats, black fruits, grilled herbs, and minerals. Full bodied, rich, and intense, with mouth-searing tannin as well as layers of jammy, concentrated fruit, this macho wine requires 5–7 years of cellaring. It should keep for 20 years.

BERGERAC AND THE SOUTHWEST

The Basics

TYPES OF WINE

This remote corner of France, while close to Bordeaux, remains an unexplored territory when it comes to wine. Some appellations have recognizable names such as Madiran, Bergerac, Cahors, and Monbazillac, but how many consumers can name one producer, good or bad, from the Côtes du Frontonnais, Gaillac, Pacherenc du Vic Bilh, Côtes de Duras, or Pécharmant? The best wines are serious, broodingly deep red wines from Madiran, Pécharmant, and Cahors; lighter, effusively fruity reds from Bergerac and the Côtes du Frontonnais; and some fine sweet white wines from Monbazillac and Jurançon. Remarkable dry white wine values are plentiful in the Côtes de Gascogne.

GRAPE VARIETIES

In addition to the well-known varieties such as Cabernet Sauvignon, Merlot, and Syrah, this vast area is home to a number of grape varieties that are little known and mysterious to the average consumer. In Madiran, there is the Tannat; in the Côtes du Frontonnais, the Mauzac and Negrette. For the white wines of Pacherenc du Vic Bilh and Jurançon, rare varieties such as the Gros Manseng, Petit Manseng, Courbu, and Arrufiac are planted.

FLAVORS

The red wines of Bergerac are light and fruity; those of Madiran and Cahors are dense, dark, rich, and often quite tannic. The red wines from the Côtes de Buzet, Côtes de Duras, and Côtes du Frontonnais, often vinified by the carbonic maceration method, are light, soft, and fruity. The best dry white wines are crisp, light, and zesty. Some surprisingly rich, sweet wines that resemble a fine Sauternes can emerge from Monbazillac and Jurançon.

AGING POTENTIAL

Except for the top red wines of Madiran, Pécharmant, and Cahors, all of the wines from France's southwest corner must be drunk within 5 years.

Bergerac: 2–5 years   Jurançon: 3–8 years
Cahors: 4–12 years   Madiran: 6–15 years
Côtes de Buzet: 1–5 years   Monbazillac: 3–8 years
Côtes de Duras: 1–4 years   Pécharmant: 3–10 years
Gaillac: 1–4 years

OVERALL QUALITY LEVEL

The overall quality level is extremely irregular. Improvements have been made, but most wines are sold for very low prices, so many producers have little incentive to increase quality. For the top estates listed below, the quality is good to excellent.

FRANCE'S GREATEST WHITE WINE VALUE?

Just about every shrewd importer has been making a trek to the area of Armagnac in search of crisp, fruity, deliciously light, dry white wines from a region not entitled to either appellation or VDQS status, the Côtes de Gascogne. Grapes such as Ugni Blanc, Colombard, Gros Manseng, and Sauvignon produce dry wines with crisp acidity, fragrant, lemony, fruity bouquets, zesty, lively flavors, and light- to medium-bodied, crisp finishes. Almost all sell for under $8 a bottle. They have proven exceptionally successful in the American marketplace. These are wines to buy by the case and drink within 12 months of the vintage. For example, the 1998s (released in spring 1999) should be consumed by spring 2000. If you are not already gulping these light, fruity wines, you are missing one of the most unlikely success stories in the wine world. The most successful, palate- and purse-pleasing dry white wines are those from Domaine de Pouy (my favorite), Domaine de Pomès, Domaine de Tariquet, Domaine de Rieux, Domaine de Tuilerie, Domaine Varet, Domaine Lasalle, Domaine de Joy, Domaine de Puits, and Domaine de Puts.

FRANCE'S LEAST-KNOWN AND RAREST SWEET WINE?

Adventurous readers looking for a fascinating sweet wine that is an insider's secret should check out the remarkable offerings of Domaine Cauhaupé, Domaine Guirouilh, Clos Uroulat, and Cru Lamouroux. These sweet white wines age for 15–20 years in top vintages such as 1989, 1990, 1996, and 1997 with flavors not dissimilar to a top Barsac/Sauternes, only with a more roasted nut character. Prices are moderate for wines of such quality. Another potential source of superb sweet wines is Monbazillac. Several estates, in particular Grande Maison and Tirecul La Grivière, are producing top cuvées with Yquem-like richness.

MOST IMPORTANT INFORMATION TO KNOW

Learn the top two or three estates for each of the better-known appellations and their styles of wine.

BUYING STRATEGY

The finest recent vintages have been 1995 and 1996 in Madiran, and 1998 in Cahors and the Jurançon. Most of these wines remain undervalued.

RATING BERGERAC AND THE SOUTHWEST'S BEST PRODUCERS

Dry Red Wines
* * * * *(OUTSTANDING)*

Chateau du Cedre Le Prestige (Cahors)	Moulin des Dames (Bergerac)
Château Montus Cuvée Prestige (Madiran)	

* * * *(EXCELLENT)*

Château d'Aydie-Laplace (Madiran)	Domaine de Barréjat (Madiran)
Domaine de Bachen (Tursan)	Domaine Bibian (Madiran)

Château Bouscassé Vieilles Vignes
  (Madiran)
Clos de Gamot (Cahors)
Clos de Triguedina Prince Phobus (Cahors)
Château de Lagrezette (Cahors)
Château Montus (Madiran)

Domaine Pichard (Madiran)
Domaine Pichard Cuvée Vigneau (Madiran)
Château Le Roc Cuvée Réservée (Côte du
  Frontonnais)
Tour des Gendres (Bergerac)

* * *(GOOD)

Domaine de l'Antenet (Cahors)
Château de Belingard (Bergerac)
Château Calabre (Bergerac)
Château de Cayrou (Cahors)
Château de Chambert (Cahors)
Château Champerel (Pécharmant)
Clos La Coutale (Cahors)
Clos de Triguedina (Cahors)
Château Court-Les-Mûts (Bergerac)
Domaine Jean Cros (Gaillac)
Domaine de Durand (Côtes de Duras)
Domaine du Haut-Pécharmant
  (Pécharmant)
Domaine de Haute-Serre (Cahors)

Château de la Jaubertie (Bergerac)
Château Michel de Montague (Bergerac)
Château de Padère (Buzet)
Château de Panisseau (Bergerac)
Château Le Payssel (Cahors)
Château Pech de Jammes (Cahors)
Château du Perron (Madiran)
Château de Peyros (Cahors)
Château Pineraie (Cahors)
Château Poulvère (Bergerac)
Château Saint-Didier Parnac (Cahors)
Domaine des Savarines (Cahors)***/****
Château Thénac (Cahors)
Château de Tiregand (Pécharmant)

Dry White Wines
* * * *(EXCELLENT)

Domaine de Bachen (Tursan)
Château Calabre (Bergerac)
Château Court-Les-Mûts (Bergerac)
Château Grinou (Bergerac)
Domaine de la Jaubertie (Bergerac)

Moulin des Dames (Bergerac)
Château de Panisseau (Bergerac)
Château Tiregard-Les Galinux (Bergerac)
Tour des Gendres Cuvée des Doges
  (Bergerac)

* * *(GOOD)

Château Belingard (Bergerac)
Château Haut-Peygonthier (Bergerac)
Domaine de Joy (Côtes de Gascogne)
Domaine Lasalle (Côtes de Gascogne)
Domaine de Pomès (Côtes de Gascogne)
Domaine de Pouy (Côtes de Gascogne)
Domaine de Puits (Côtes de Gascogne)

Domaine de Puts (Côtes de Gascogne)
Domaine de Rieux (Côtes de Gascogne)
Domaine de Saint-Lannes (Côtes de
  Gascogne)
Domaine Tariquet (Côtes de Gascogne)
Domaine de Tuilerie (Côtes de Gascogne)
Domaine Varet (Côtes de Gascogne)

Sweet White Wines
* * * * *(OUTSTANDING)

Domaine Cauhaupé Cuvée Quintessence
  (Jurançon)
Grande Maison Cuvée Madame
  (Monbazillac)

Tirecul La Gravière Cuvée Madame
  (Monbazillac)

* * * *(EXCELLENT)

Domaine Cauhaupe (Jurançon)
Clos Uroulat (Jurançon)
Cru Lamouroux (Jurançon)
Grande Maison Cuvée Monsieur
  (Monbazillac)

Domaine Guirouilh Cuvée Petit Cuyalaa
  (Jurançon)
Tirecul La Gravière (Monbazillac)

* * *(GOOD)

Domaine Bellegarde Sélection de Petit
  Marseng (Jurançon)
Château Le Fage (Monbazillac)

Château du Treuil-de-Nailhac
  (Monbazillac)

* *(AVERAGE)

Domaine Bru-Baché (Jurançon)
Henri Burgue (Jurançon)

Clos Lapeyre (Jurançon)
Château Rousse (Jurançon)

2. ITALY

The Basics

TYPES OF WINE

The glories of Piedmont (aside from the scenery and white truffles) are the robust, rich, multidimensional red wines made from the Nebbiolo grape. The top wines made from the Nebbiolo—Barbaresco, Barolo, Gattinara, and Spanna—are at their best between 6 and 15 years of age but can last up to 25 years. At the opposite extreme are the wines called Dolcetto d'Alba, which are wonderfully supple, rich, and fruity but are meant to be drunk within their first 4–5 years of life. Then there is Barbera. Historically these have been too acidic for non-Italian palates, but a new generation of winemakers has begun to turn out splendid and expensive examples. Last, there is Cabernet Sauvignon and a host of insipid, usually inferior red wines that are less likely to be seen in the international marketplace. I am referring to Freisa, Grignolino, and Brachetto. Piedmont's white wine production is growing, and while most of the wines are overpriced and bland, some potential is evident with the indigenous Arneis grape and Cortese di Gavi. Chardonnay is making its ubiquitous presence felt; Erbaluce di Caluso is underrated; and Moscato, the low-alcohol, fizzy, slightly sweet wine, is perhaps Piedmont's best value in white wine. Finally, there is the ocean of sweet, industrially produced Asti Spumante.

GRAPE VARIETIES

Nebbiolo, Barbera, and Dolcetto are the top red wine grapes in Piedmont, producing the finest wines. For the white wines, the Muscat, Arneis, Cortese di Gavi, and Erbaluce di Caluso are the most successful. Of course, there are many other grapes, but the wines made from these varietals are generally of little interest.

Flavors

RED WINES

Barolo Barolo is one of the world's most stern, tannic, austere, yet full-flavored wines; the aromas of road tar, leather, Bing cherries, tobacco, and dried herbs dominate. It is a massive yet intensely fragrant wine.
Barbaresco Often better balanced as well as lighter than Barolo (less tannin, more fruit),

MILES
0   60
KILOMETERS
0   50   100

Central Italy

LIGURIAN SEA

ADRIATIC SEA

• Lucca
• Pisa   • Firenze
• Livorno   Arrezo •
Siena •
8 •   • Pesaro
          • Ancona
          • Macerata
3   2
Perugia •   Ascoli Piceno
• Spoleto
Terni •   L'Aquila •   • Pescara
Viterbo •   • Chieti
5   4
• Roma   Isernia •
          6
• Latina

Grosseto •

CORSICA

TYRRHENIAN SEA

Olbia •
• Sassari
• Alghero
Nuoro •
• Bosa   7
Tortoli •
Oristano •

Cagliari •

N
W ✦ E
S

◼ WINE REGIONS

1 Tuscany   5 Lazio
2 Marche   6 Molise
3 Umbria   7 Sardinia
4 Abruzzo   8 San Marino

with the same aromas and flavors, Barbaresco frequently has more intense jammy fruit and sometimes more cedar and chocolate; it can be sublime.

Dolcetto   Purple in color and not at all sweet, as the name incorrectly implies, this dry, exuberant, effusively fruity and grapey wine tastes of blackberries, almonds, chocolate, and spices and is very soft and supple. It is a joyful wine.

Barbera   In the old days it was too acidic, harsh, and oxidized—and dirt cheap. The new-style Barberas, often aged in 100% new French oak, exhibit saturated purple color, great fruit, and superrichness that serve to balance out the naturally high acidity. The best Barberas will set consumers back $25–$50, so their potential market is microscopic. But a taste of the 1997s can be addictive.

Gattinara/Spanna   These wines come from Nebbiolo grown in the hills north of Barolo and Barbaresco. Intense tar and earthy aromas dominate, and there is a pronounced Oriental spice box character to the bouquet. The wines tend to be softer and fruitier than Barolo, but no less ageworthy.

Carema   The lightest of the Nebbiolo-based wines, Carema, made in a marginal mountainous climate near Valle d'Aosta, can be quite smooth, fruity, and elegant, but adequate ripeness is often a problem.

A CLOSER LOOK AT THE BAROLO AND BARBARESCO REGIONS

The Barolo region consists of over 3,000 acres of vineyards, most of them situated on the hillsides surrounding five villages—La Morra, Serralunga d'Alba, Monforte d'Alba, Barolo, and Castiglione Falletto.

Barolo   This old village is located south of La Morra. Barolo is said to combine the velvety, supple, easygoing, more feminine side of Nebbiolo with considerable structure and concentration. The word *classic* is frequently used to describe the wines of Barolo by the local cognoscenti. Barolo ranks fourth in importance among the five most significant wine-making communes of Barolo. Barolo has 375 acres of vineyards shared by 139 growers. By analogy to Bordeaux, Barolo might be considered the Margaux or St.-Julien of this viticultural zone.

Highly Regarded Barolo Vineyards: Bricco delle Viole, Brunate (this vineyard is shared with La Morra), Cannubi (often considered the most historic and among the finest of the Barolo vineyards), Cannubi Boschis, Castellero, Cerequio (also shared with La Morra), Costa di Rose, Sarmassa, and La Villa.

Castiglione Falletto   The smallest of the five principal Barolo communes in terms of acreage and growers, Castiglione Falletto is a picture-postcard-perfect hilltop village situated between Barolo and Serralunga d'Alba. The vineyards are all on steep hillsides ringing the village. Allowing for different styles of wines, Castiglione Falletto's reputation is for wines of boldness, richness, full body, power, and concentration—in brief, the Pauillac of Barolo. There are 255 acres of vines owned by 93 growers.

Highly Regarded Castiglione Falletto Vineyards: Bricco Boschis, Fiasc, Monprivato, Montanello, Rocche, and Villero.

Monforte d'Alba   The hilltop town of Monforte d'Alba is the third largest vineyard area in Barolo, consisting of 486 acres farmed by 185 growers. Once again, all the vineyards are situated on steep hillsides. Monforte d'Alba appears to be the St.-Estèphe of Barolo. The locals claim that Barolo's longest-lived, most concentrated, firmest wines are produced from the hillsides of this small town.

Highly Regarded Monforte d'Alba Vineyards: Bussia (there is a bevy of subvineyards within Bussia, such as Bricotto, Cicala, Colonella, Dardi, Gran Bussia, and Soprana) and Ginestra (another vineyard noted for its numerous subplots, such as Casa Mate, Ciabot, La Coste, Mentin, Pernot, Pian della Poldere, Sori Ginestra, and Vigne del Gris).

La Morra   La Morra, another picture-postcard-pretty hilltop village, is believed to produce the most supple, seductive Barolos. Keeping in mind that individual winemaking styles can easily transcend the historic generalities attributed to a particular area, La Morra's Barolos are believed to be the most velvety textured and easiest to drink when young. La Morra is to Barolo what the appellation of Pomerol is to Bordeaux. Of the five winemaking zones, La Morra is the largest, with 955 acres under vine and 372 registered producers.

Highly Regarded La Morra Vineyards: Arborina, Brunate, Cerequio, Fossati, Giachini, Marcenasco, Monfalletto, Rocche, Rocchette, La Serra, and Tettimorra.

Serralunga d'Alba   With just under 500 acres, this is the second largest zone in the Barolo area. There is more limestone to be found in Serralunga d'Alba's hillside vineyards than elsewhere. Interestingly, it was in this zone that Angelo Gaja purchased a 70-acre parcel to launch his Barolo estate, and it is in this commune that Bruno Giacosa makes his famed Rionda vineyard Barolo, often considered Barolo's most classic wine. The wines of Serralunga d'Alba are among the richest and fullest bodied, with great staying power. If we continue the comparison with appellations of Bordeaux, these wines might well be considered a synthesis in the style of Pauillac/St.-Estèphe, but, of course, with a Nebbiolo personality.

Highly Regarded Serralunga d'Alba Vineyards: Arione, Brea, Ceretta, La Delizia, Falletto, Francia, Gabutti, Lazzarito, Ornato, Parafada, Rionda, and Sperss.

Barbaresco   There are only three major production zones in the Barbaresco region— Neive (around the village of the same name), Barbaresco (around the picturesque old village), and Treiso (around the town of the same name). All of Barbaresco's vineyards are on hillsides.

Highly Regarded Barbaresco Vineyards: Barbaresco—Asili, Costa Russi, Montefico, Montestefano, Porra, Rabaja, Rio Sordo, Sori San Lorenzo, and Sori Tilden; Neive—Albesani, Basarin, and Gallina; Treiso—Marcarini and Pajore.

SOME THOUGHTS ON THE MODERN VERSUS TRADITIONAL STYLE OF BAROLO AND BARBARESCO

Today it is fashionable among wine journalists to argue about whether Barbaresco and Barolo are made in the so-called modern style or made by the "traditionalists" with a healthy respect for the customs of the past. The modernists are said to believe in producing supple wines from riper fruit and aging the wines in small new oak casks. Since they are produced from riper fruit, the wines tend to be lower in acidity and possess a more creamy-textured personality with sweeter tannin. Many of these wines are stunning and have deservedly won plaudits from wine critics throughout the world. The old- or traditional-style winemakers of Barolo usually eschew aging in new oak casks, preferring to age the wines in large old *foudres.* They make little concession to modern-day taste that demands up-front, forward wines. These wines can also be profound. The traditionally made Barolos and Barbarescos often taste more tannic. But when they are rich and concentrated (as many are), wines made by the modern style are compelling, since they rely entirely on the intensity of their fruit to express the personality of the vineyard. Great wines emerge from both schools. In fact, the finest Barolos or Barbarescos, whether they are made by a modernist or a traditionalist, share more common characteristics than differences. Both schools of thought believe in harvesting physiologically mature fruit. Both schools adhere to the belief that low yields and nonmanipulative winemaking result in wines that best express their *terroirs.* Both schools avoid the excessive use of clarification techniques such as fining and filtration.

Barolo and Barbaresco are produced in what must be one of the most pure, unspoiled, virgin countrysides of Europe. All of the finest vineyards are situated on steep hillsides. The locals all possess firmly held opinions as to the quality that emerges from vineyards throughout these two zones.

WHITE WINES

Arneis   The ancient wine of Piedmont, Arneis is a rich, gloriously fruity, mouth-filling wine that is soft, even unctuous. This may seem to imply a certain heaviness, but the best examples are light and a joy to drink.

Gavi or Cortese di Gavi   Often outrageously overpriced and frightfully bland, this supposedly prestigious wine is high in acidity, has a lemony, flinty, stony character, and, in the best examples, has good body.

Moscato d'Alba   One of the world's most seductive wines to smell and drink, Moscato d'Alba when well made, and when drunk within 18 months of the vintage is a gorgeously fragrant, apricot- and floral-scented, slightly sweet, crisp, vibrant wine that is ideal as an aperitif. It should not be confused with the cloyingly sweet Asti Spumanti.

AGING POTENTIAL

Arneis: 2–3 years	Dolcetto: 3–5 years
Barbaresco: 8–25 years	Gattinara/Spanna: 8–20 years
Barbera: 5–15 years	Gavi: 2–4 years
Barolo: 8–25 years	Moscato: 12–18 months
Carema: 6–12 years	

OVERALL QUALITY LEVEL

The best Piedmont wines are impeccably made, brilliant wines. Producers such as Bruno Giacosa, Angelo Gaja, Elio Altare, and Luciano Sandrone, to name just a few, fashion wines of great individuality and uncompromising quality. But despite the number of compelling Barolos, Barbarescos, and some *barrique*-aged Barberas, a considerable quantity of wine made in Piedmont is still technically defective, with shrill levels of acidity and a flawed, musty taste. Some of this is the result of inferior grapes still being utilized, but most of it is due to indifferent, as well as careless and primitive, winemaking methods. In short, Piedmont offers the best and worst in wine quality. If you are going to shop with confidence, you must know who are the finest producers.

MOST IMPORTANT INFORMATION TO KNOW

Learning the top producers for Barbaresco, Barolo, Nebbiolo d'Alba, Barbera, and Dolcetto is of utmost importance. However, since the early eighties more and more of the best producers have begun to make single-vineyard wines, so some understanding of the finest vineyards and who is successfully exploiting them is required. Following is a list of the major Piedmontese vineyards that consistently stand out in my tastings and the producers making the finest wine from these vineyards.

PIEDMONT'S BEST RED WINES

VINEYARD	WINE	BEST PRODUCER(S)
Alfiera	Barbera d'Asti	Marchesi Alfieri
Annunziata	Barolo	Lorenzo Accomasso, Silvio Grasso, the late Renato Ratti
Arborina	Barolo, Nebbiolo	Elio Altare

VINEYARD	WINE	BEST PRODUCER(S)
Arionda or Vigna Rionda	Barolo	Bruno Giacosa
Asili	Barbaresco	Bruno Ceretto, Produttori del Barbaresco, Bruno Giacosa
Baroco	Barbaresco	Roagna
Basarin	Barbaresco	Castello di Neive, Moccagatta
Batasiolo	Barolo	F.lli Dogliani
Bernadotti	Barbaresco	Giuseppe Mascarello
Bianca	Barolo	Fontenafredda
Big	Barolo	Poderi Rocche Manzoni Valentino
Bofini	Barolo	Batasiolo
Boscaretto	Barolo	F.lli Dogliani, Scarpa, Batasiolo
Boschis	Barolo	Cavalotto
Briacca	Barolo	Vietti
Bric Balin	Barbaresco	Moccagatta
Bric del Fiasc	Barolo	Paolo Scavino, Azelia
Bric in Pugnane	Barolo	Giuseppe Mascarello
Bricco Asili	Barbaresco	Bruno Ceretto
Bricco Asili Faset	Barbaresco	Bruno Ceretto
Bricco Cicala	Barolo	Aldo Conterno
Bricco Colonello	Barolo	Aldo Conterno
Bricco del Drago Vigna Le Mace	Dolcetto	Cascina Drago
Bricco Faset	Barbaresco	La Spinona
Bricco Fiasco	Barolo	Azelia
Bricco della Figotta	Barbera d'Asti	Giacomo Bologna
Bricco Marun	Barbera d'Alba	Matteo-Correggia
Bricco Punta	Barolo	Azelia
Bricco Rocche	Barolo	Bruno Ceretto
Bricco dell'Uccellone	Barbera	Giacomo Bologna
Bricco Viole	Barolo, Barbera d'Alba	G. D. Vajra
Bricco Visette	Barolo	Gian Marco Ghisolfi
Briccolina	Barolo	Batasiolo
Maria de Brun	Barbaresco	Ca Rome
Brunate	Barolo	Giuseppe Rinaldi, Elvio Cogno, Ceretto, Luigi Copo, Robert Voerzio, Vietti, Sebaste, Michele Chiarlo, Marcarini, Enzo Boglietti
Bussia	Barolo	Bruno Giacosa, Clerico, Fennochio, Giuseppe Mascarello, Michele Chiarlo, Sebaste, Prunotto, Parusso
Camp Gros	Barbaresco	Marchese di Gresy
Campo Quadro	Barbaresco	Punset-Marina Marcarino
Cannubi	Barolo	L. Sandrone, Luciano Rinaldi, Bartolo Mascarello, Marchesi di Barolo, Paolo Scavino, Enrico Scavino, E. Pora, Carretta, Giacomo e Figli Brezza, Alfredo Prunotto
Cannubi-Boschis	Barolo	L. Sandrone, Francesco Rinaldi

VINEYARD	WINE	BEST PRODUCER(S)
Casa Mate	Barolo	Elio Grasso
Cascina Alberta	Barbaresco	Contratto
Cascina Francia	Barolo, Dolcetto, Barbera	Giacomo Conterno
Cascina Nuova	Barolo	Elio Altare
Cascina Palazzo	Barolo	Francesco Rinaldi
Cascina Rocca	Barbaresco	Riccardo Cortese
Castelle	Gattinara	Antoniolo
Castiglione	Barolo	Vietti
Cere quio	Barolo	Michele Chiarlo, Cogno-Marcarini, F. Oddero, Roberto Voerzio, Marengo-Marenda
Ciabot Berton	Barolo	Luigi Oberto
Ciabot Mentin Genestra	Barolo	Clerico
Clara	Barbera d'Alba	Luigi Viberti
Codana	Barolo	Paolo Scavino, Vietti
Cole	Barbaresco	Moccagatta
Collina della Vedova	Barbera d'Asti	Alfiero Boffa
Conca	Barolo	Renato Ratti
Conca Tre Pile	Barbera d'Alba	Aldo Conterno
Costa Russi	Barbaresco	Angelo Gaja
Crichet Paje	Barbaresco	Roagna
Cua Longa	Barbera d'Asti	Alfiero Boffa
Darmagi	Cabernet Sauvignon	Angelo Gaja
Delizia	Barolo	Fontanafredda
DLA Roul	Barolo	Poderi Rocche Manzoni Valentino
Falletto	Barolo	Bruno Giacosa
Faset	Barbaresco	F.lli Oddero, Luigi Bianco, Bruno Ceretto
Francia Serralunga	Barolo	Giacomo Conterno
Gaiun	Barbaresco	Marchese di Gresy
Gallina	Barbaresco	Bruno Giacosa, Giuseppi Rivetti
La Ghiga	Barbaresco	La Spinona
Giachini	Barolo	Renato Corino
Giada	Barbera d'Alba	Andrea Oberto
Ginestra	Barolo	Clerico, Prunotto, Renzo Seghesio, Conterno Fantino
Gramolere	Barolo	Manzone
Gran Bussia	Barolo	Aldo Conterno
Gris	Barolo	Conterno Fantino
Il Crottino	Barbera d'Asti	Giorgio Carnevale
Il Fale	Barbera d'Asti	Viarengo e Figlio
Larigi	Barbera	Elio Altare
Lazzarito	Barolo	Fontanafredda, Vietti
Marcenasco	Barolo	Renato Ratti
Margaria	Barolo	Michele Chiarlo
Margheria	Barolo	Massolino-Vigna Rionda, Luigi Pira
Mariondino	Barolo	Parusso
Martinenga	Barbaresco	Marchese di Gresy
Masseria	Barbaresco	Vietti

VINEYARD	WINE	BEST PRODUCER(S)
Messoirano	Barbaresco, Barbera, Dolcetto	Castello di Neive
Moccagatta	Barbaresco	Produttori del Barbaresco
Monfalletto	Barolo	Cordero di Montezemolo
Monfortino	Barolo	Giacomo Conterno
Monprivato	Barolo	Giuseppe Mascarello, Brovia
Montanello	Barolo	Tenuta Montanello
Monte Stefano	Barbaresco	Produttori del Barbaresco, Alfredo Prunotto
Montefico	Barbaresco	Produttori del Barbaresco
Montetusa	Barbera	Poderi Bertelli
La Mora	Barolo	Renato Corino
Mugiot	Barbera d'Alba	Piazzo
Ornato	Nebbiolo, Barbera, Barolo	Pio Cesare
Osso San Grato	Gattinara	Antoniolo
Otinasso	Barolo	F.lli Brovia
Ottin Fiorin Collina Gabuti	Barolo	Cappellano
Ovello	Barbaresco	Produttori del Barbaresco
Pajana	Barolo	Clerico
Panirole	Barbera d'Alba	Giuseppe Mascarello
Pian della Polvere	Barolo	R. Fenocchio
Pian Romualdo	Barbera d'Alba	Alfredo Prunotto
Pomorosso	Barbera d'Asti	Coppo
Pora	Barbaresco	Produttori del Barbaresco
Pozzo	Barbera	Renato Corino
Prapo	Barolo	Bruno Ceretto
Rabaja	Barbaresco	Produttori del Barbaresco, Giuseppe Cortese, Bruno Rocca
Rabera	Barolo	G. E. Vagra, Giuseppe Rinaldi
Rapet	Barolo	Ca Rome
Rio Sordo	Barbaresco	Brovia, Produttori del Barbaresco
Rionda (same as Arionda)	Barolo	Bruno Giacosa, Michele Chiarlo, Giuseppe Mascarello, Massolino-Vigna Rionda, Luigi Pira
Rocche	Barolo	Brovio, Renato Corino, Andrea Oberto, Armando Parusso, Aurelio Settimo, Vietti
Rocche di Bussia	Barolo	F.lli Oddero, Parusso
Rocche di Castiglione Falletto	Barolo	Bruno Giacosa, Vietti, Parusso
Rocche de la Morra	Barolo, Barbera	Roche di Costamagna
Ronchi	Barbaresco	Albino Rocca
La Rosa	Barolo	Fontanafredda
Rosignolo	Barbera d'Alba	Cantine Sant'Evasio
San Pietro	Barolo	Fontanafredda
San Rocco	Barolo	Erevi Virginia Ferrero, Azelia
Santo Stefano	Barbaresco	Bruno Giacosa, Castello di Neive
La Serra	Barolo	Cogno-Marcarini, Roberto Voerzio, Marcarini

VINEYARD	WINE	BEST PRODUCER(S)
Serra Boella	Barbaresco	Cigliuti
Sori d'Paytin	Barbaresco	Pasquero-Secondo
Sori San Lorenzo	Barbaresco	Angelo Gaja
Sori Tilden	Barbaresco	Angelo Gaja
Sori Valgrande	Barbaresco	F.lli Grasso Cascina Valgrande
Sperss	Barolo	Angelo Gaja
Terlo Ravera	Barolo	Enrico e Marziano Abbona
Truchet	Barbera d'Asti	Giovine Riconda
Val dei Preti	Nebbiolo	Matteo-Correggia
Vecchie	Barbera d'Asti	Vinchio e Vaglio
Vignabajla	Dolcetto	Angelo Gaja
Vignarey	Barbera d'Alba	Angelo Gaja
Vignasse	Barbera d'Alba	Roberto Voerzio
Le Vigne	Barolo	Luciano Sandrone
La Villa	Nebbiolo, Barbera	Elio Altare, Aldo & Ricardo Seghesio
Villero	Barolo	Giuseppe Mascarello, Bruno Giacosa, Cordero di Montezemolo
La Volta	Barolo	Bartolomeo di Cabutto
Zonchera	Barolo	Bruno Ceretto

PIEDMONT'S BEST WHITE WINES

Americans have always had a fondness for the slightly sweet, sparkling Asti Spumantes of Italy. While "serious" wine enthusiasts have an attitude problem with Asti drinkers, the fact is that there is Asti Spumante in the market, even from such industrial-size producers as Cinzano, Martini and Rossi, and, on a smaller scale, Fontanafredda, that is fresh, clean, and yes . . . delicious!

The real jewel, however, among these slightly sweet, sparkling wines from northern Italy is not Asti Spumante, but Moscato d'Asti. While most Asti Spumantes possess an alcohol level similar to that of most of the world's dry wines (around 12%), Moscato d'Asti rarely has an alcohol level in excess of 5.5%. Although these sparkling wines are usually bottled with a regular cork rather than a champagne-style cork, they are effervescent, bubbly wines. Their low alcohol, combined with their extraordinary, fragrant, perfumed character, makes them the most underrated delicious aperitif or dessert wines produced in Europe. Most Moscato d'Asti is vintage-dated, and readers should be purchasing nothing older than 1997. The 1998 vintage, which has just been released and is appearing in the marketplace, is the vintage of choice. These wines are meant to be drunk within 7–8 months of release. They are among the most thrillingly light, exuberant, fresh, perfumed wines in the world. The lack of aggressive bubbles, in addition to the low alcohol, accentuates the freshness and liveliness of these wines. They are the perfect summer wine!

The following Moscato d'Asti producers make wines that have consistently stood out for their freshness, elegance, and wonderfully perfumed peach, apricot, and floral bouquets. Most Moscato d'Asti is attractively priced between $8 and $12 a bottle.

MOSCATO D'ASTI'S BEST PRODUCERS

Note: Buy only the freshest vintage.

Giuseppe Barbero Bricco Riella
Gian Lugi Bera

Giorgio Carnevale
Cascina Fonda

La Caudrina
La Caudrina-La Galeisa
Tenuta del Fant Il Falchetto
Marchesi di Gresy La Serra
Sergis Grimaldi
Icardi La Rosa Selvatica
La Morandina

Elio Perrone Clarté
Elio Perrone Sourgal
G. Rivetti La Spinetta (multiple cuvées)
Paolo Saracco
Paolo Saracco Moscato d'Autunno
Sator Arepo Tenet-Vigna Senza Nome
Gianni Voerzio Vigna Sergente

OTHER FINE WHITE WINES FROM PIEDMONT

For what one gets in the bottle, the top white wines of Piedmont are vastly overpriced (Gavi prices have fallen, but this neutral-tasting wine continues to be a rip-off). The exception is the aforementioned lovely flower blossom- and apricot-scented Moscato and the dry version of Erbaluce. Arneis, a perfumed dry white wine with loads of character, is my favorite white from Piedmont. However, at prices of $18–$30 it is expensive. Chardonnay and Sauvignon have arrived in Piedmont; Angelo Gaja produces the finest, but also the most expensive.

The best Piedmont white wines are listed below. Readers should look for the 1998s and 1997s—nothing older!

WINE	PRODUCER(S)
Arneis	Bruno Giacosa, Castello di Neive, Bruno Ceretto
Brut Spumante	Bruno Giacosa
Chardonnay Bussiador	Aldo Conterno
Chardonnay Gaia and Rey	Angelo Gaja
Chardonnay Giarone	Poderi Bertelli
Chardonnay Rossi-Bass	Angelo Gaja
Cortesi	Pio Cesare, Broglia Fasciola, Rocca Albino
Erbaluce di Caluso	Carretta, Boratto, Ferrando
Gavi	La Scolca, La Chiara
Roero Arneis	Carretta
Sauvignon	Angelo Gaja
Traminer	Poderi Bertelli

BUYING STRATEGY

Most of the greatest Piedmont wines are just beginning to arrive in the marketplace. While 1988, 1989, and 1990 were outstanding vintages in Piedmont, 1991, 1992, 1993, and 1994 were mixed years. However, 1995, although irregular, can be very good; 1996 is a classic vintage made along the style of such long-lived, muscular wines as the 1978s and 1971s; and 1997 is an eccentric year of extraordinarily high ripeness, alcohol, and richness. The 1997s are the most hedonistic young Barolos and Barbarescos, not to mention Barberas, that I have ever tasted from Piedmont. They are spectacular, albeit unusual wines. Moreover, 1998, which I had not tasted at the time this book went to press, is being billed as another great year, giving Piedmont four very high-quality vintages in succession. Prices are very high given the tiny quantities of the finest wines and the worldwide demand, which continues to be insatiable.

VINTAGE GUIDE

1998—I arrived in Piedmont to taste the 1995s, 1996s, and 1997s at the end of the 1998 harvest. Everybody was enthusiastic about the crop, with some of the old-timers, such as

Aldo Conterno, claiming they had never before seen four high-quality vintages in a row. While I have not tasted any of the wines, reports suggest 1998 is a textbook Piedmontese vintage that was successful for both Nebbiolo and Barbera. The style of the wines is believed to be classic, with considerable tannin, intense aromatics, and outstanding ripeness. In that sense, it is more similar to 1996 than the freakish 1997 vintage.

1997—An abundant vintage of overripe, low-acid, high alcohol, unctuously textured Nebbiolos and Barberas that are off the charts in terms of the hedonistic pleasures they deliver. There is nothing "classic" or "typical" about the vintage, but the wines, while often over the top, are among the most extraordinary Barolos, Barbarescos, and Barberas I have ever tasted. This is the type of vintage that only comes along every 30–40 years. The only comparison might be 1947, a year where the alcohol was extremely high and the acidity very low. Skeptics claim that in the Barolo villages of Barolo and Monforte d'Alba a number of growers harvested too soon, fearing a complete loss of grape acidity. However, this was not borne out in my tastings, although these are low-acid wines. Undoubtedly villages such as La Morra and, to a lesser extent, Castiglione Falletto hit the bull's eye. These wines will be superexpensive and magnificent young, and the finest will last longer than skeptics believe.

1996—A great classic vintage made in a style similar to 1978 and 1971, the 1996s are tannic, concentrated, structured, muscular wines that require time in the bottle. It was a cool year, with little sunshine, but the saving grace for this fabulous vintage was nearly 2 months of abnormally dry and warm weather in September and October. The finest wines were made by those producers who waited to harvest until October.

1995—Called by everybody a very good to excellent vintage, when the reality is that it is an irregular vintage with some highlights, as well as a bevy of uninspiring wines. The wines are evolved, forward, and not always well concentrated. Quality varies, so select with care.

OLDER VINTAGES

The early nineties were a disastrous time for Piedmont, with 1991 and 1992 poor years and 1993 and 1994 average quality years . . . despite hype to the contrary. The last great Piedmontese vintages were 1989 and 1990, with 1988 a close third. Prior to that, 1985 has turned out to be a good rather than an exceptional year, as has 1982. The 1978 vintage proved to be a fabulous one, with very long-lived wines that are just reaching their peak of maturity. Before that, the great classics are 1971 and 1964.

RATING PIEDMONT'S BEST PRODUCERS

* * * * * (OUTSTANDING)

Elio Altare Barbera Vigna Larigi	Brovia Barolo Rocche
Elio Altare Barolo Brunate	Bruno Ceretto Barbaresco Bricco Asili
Elio Altare Barolo Vigna Arborina	Bruno Ceretto Barolo Bricco Rocche
Azelia Barolo Bricco Fiasco	Bruno Ceretto Barolo Propo
Azelia Barolo San Rocco	Clerico Barolo Bricotto Bussia
Batasiolo Barolo Cru Bofani	Clerico Barolo Ciabot Mentin Ginestra
Giacomo Bologna Barbera d'Asti Bricco della Figotta	Clerico Barolo Mosconi Per Cristina Riserva
Giacomo Bologna Barbera dell'Uccellone	Clerico Barolo Pajana
Brovia Barolo Monprivato	Aldo Conterno Barolo Bussia Soprano

Aldo Conterno Barolo Gran Bussia Riserva
Aldo Conterno Barolo Vigna Cicala Bussia
Aldo Conterno Barolo Vigna Colonnello
  Bussia
Giacomo Conterno Barolo Cascina Francia
  Riserva
Giacomo Conterno Barolo Monfortino
Cascina Drago Bricco del Drago Vigna Le
  Mace
Angelo Gaja Barbaresco Costa Russi
Angelo Gaja Barbaresco Sori San Lorenzo
Angelo Gaja Barbaresco Sori Tilden
Angelo Gaja Barolo Conteisa
Angelo Gaja Barolo Sperss
Bruno Giacosa Barbaresco Asili
Bruno Giacosa Barbaresco Rabaja
Bruno Giacosa Barbaresco Santo Stefano
Bruno Giacosa Barolo Falletto
Bruno Giacosa Barolo Rionda
Bruno Giacosa Barolo Le Rocche
Bruno Giacosa Barolo Villero
Silvia Grasso Barolo Bricco Luciani
Marchese di Gresy Barbaresco Martinenga
  Camp Gros
Marchese di Gresy Barbaresco Martinenga
  Gaiun
Giuseppe Mascarello Barbera d'Alba
  Panirole
Giuseppe Mascarello Barolo Monprivato
Andrea Oberto Barolo Vigneto Rocche
Parusso Barolo Bussia Vigna Fiurin
Parusso Barolo Bussia Vigna Munie
Parusso Barolo Bussia Vigna Rocche

Parusso Barolo Mariondino
Luigi Pira Barolo Marenga
Luigi Pira Barolo Margheria
Luigi Pira Barolo Vigna Rionda
Alfredo Prunotto Barolo Bussia
Quorum Barbera d'Asti
Renato Ratti Barolo Marcenasco Conca
Renato Ratti Barolo Marcenasco Rocche
Fratelli Revello Barolo Conca
Fratelli Revello Barolo Vigna Giachini
Fratelli Revello Barolo Vigna Rocche
Albino Rocca Barbaresco Vigneto Brich
  Ronchi
Albino Rocca Barbaresco Vigneto Loreto
Poderi Rocche Manzoni Valentino Barolo
  Riserva Vigna Big
Luciano Sandrone Barolo Cannubi Boschis
Luciano Sandrone Barolo Le Vigne
Paolo Scavino Barolo Bric del Fiasc
Paolo Scavino Barolo Cannubi
Paolo Scavino Barolo Rocche dell
  Annunziata
Seghesio Barolo Vigneto La Villa
G. D. Vajra Barbera d'Alba Riserva Bricco
  della Viole
G. D. Vajra Barolo Bricco della Viole
Vietti Barolo Brunate
Vietti Barolo Rocche
Roberto Voerzio Barolo Brunate
Roberto Voerzio Barolo Capalot Riserva
Roberto Voerzio Barolo Cerequio
Roberto Voerzio Barolo La Serra

* * * * (EXCELLENT)

Enrico and Marziano Abbona Barbaresco
Enrico and Marziano Abbona Barbera
  d'Alba
Enrico and Marziano Abbona Barolo
Marchesi Alfieri Barbera d'Asti
Elio Altare Barolo
Elio Altare Dolcetto
Elio Altare La Villa****/*****
Antoniolo Gattinara Osso San Grato
Antoniolo Gattinara San Francesco
Antoniolo Gattinara Vigneto Castelle
Azelia Dolcetto d'Alba Bricco dell'Oriolo
Azelia Dolcetto d'Alba Vigneto Azelia
Bava Barbera d'Asti Superiore
Poderi Bertelli Barbera Giarone

Poderi Bertelli Barbera Montetusa
Boasso Barolo Gabutti
Alfiero Boffa Barbera d'Asti Collina della
  Vedova
Alfiero Boffa Barbera d'Asti Vigna Cua
  Longa
Alfiero Boffa Barbera d'Asti Vigna More
Enzo Boglietti Barolo Brunate
Enzo Boglietti Barolo Case Nere
Enzo Boglietti Barolo Fossati
Alessandro Brero Barolo
Giacomo e Figli Brezza Barolo Cannubi
Ca del Baio Barbaresco Asili
Ca Rome Barbaresco Maria di Brun
Ca Rome Barolo Vigna Rionda

Bartolomeo di Cabutto Barolo La Volta
Dott. G. Cappellano Barolo Ottin Fiorin Collina Gabuti
Giorgio Carnevale Barbera d'Asti Il Crottino
Tenuta Carretta Barbaresco
Tenuta Carretta Barolo Cannubi
Bruno Ceretto Barolo Brunate
Bruno Ceretto Barolo Zonchera
Cerutti Barbera d'Alba Ca' Du Ciuvin
Pio Cesare Barbaresco
Pio Cesare Barolo Ornato
Pio Cesare Dolcetto d'Alba
Michele Chiarlo Barbera d'Asti Valle del Sole
Michele Chiarlo Barolo Brunate
Michele Chiarlo Barolo Vigna Rionda
Cigliuti Barbaresco Serraboella
Cigliuti Barbera d'Alba Serraboella
Guasti Clemente Barbera d'Asti
Clerico Arté
Clerico Dolcetto
Codera di Montezemolo Barolo Monfalletto
Aldo Conterno Barbera d'Alba Conca Tre Pile
Paolo Conterno Barbera d'Alba Ginestra
Coppo Barbera d'Asti Camp du Rouss
Coppo Barbera d'Asti Pomorosso
Renato Corvino Barbera Vigna Pozzo
Renato Corvino Barolo
Renato Corvino Barolo Arborina
Renato Corvino Barolo Giachini
Renato Corvino Barolo La Mora
Renato Corvino Barolo Rocche
Renato Corvino Dolcetto
Giuseppe Cortese Barbaresco Rabaja
Alessandria Crissante Ruge
Cascina Drago Bricco del Drago
Cascina Drago Dolcetto d'Alba
Cascina Drago Nebbiolo
Luigi Einaudi Barolo
Luigi Einaudi Barolo Cannubi
Luigi Einaudi Barolo Costa Grimaldi
Stefano Farina Barbaresco
Stefano Farina Barolo
Giacomo Fenocchio Barolo Bussia
Giacomo Fenocchio Barolo Villero
F.lli Ferrero Barolo Annunziata
Fontanafredda Barolo Le Delizia
Fontanafredda Barolo Gallaretto Serralunga
Fontanafredda Barolo La Rosa

Conterno Fantino Barolo Sori Ginestra
Conterno Fantino Barolo Vigna del Gris
Gianni Gagliardo Barolo Preve
Angelo Gaja Barbaresco
Angelo Gaja Barbera d'Alba Vignarey
Angelo Gaja Darmaggi Cabernet Sauvignon
Gian Marco Ghisolfi Barolo Bricco Visette
Bruno Giacosa Barbaresco Gallina
Silvio Grasso Barolo
Silvio Grasso Barolo Ciabot Manzoni
Marchese di Gresy Barbaresco Martinenga
Marchese di Gresy Dolcetto Monte Aribaldo
Manzone Barbera d'Alba
Manzone Barolo Le Gramolere****/*****
Manzone Barolo Le Gramolere Bricat
Manzone Barolo San Stefano Perno
Marcarini Barolo Brunate****/*****
Marcarini Barolo La Serra****/*****
Marengo Barolo Bricco delle Viole
Marengo Barolo Brunate
Bartolo Mascarello Barolo
Bartolo Mascarello Dolcetto d'Alba
Massolino-Vigna Rionda Barolo Sori Vigna Rionda
Massolino-Vigna Rionda Barolo Sori Vigneto Margheria
Massolino-Vigna Rionda Barolo Vigna Rionda
Matteo-Correggia Barbera d'Alba Bricco Marun****/*****
Matteo-Correggia Nebbiolo d'Alba Val Preti
Moccagatta Barbaresco Basarin
Moccagatta Barbaresco Bric Balin
Moccagatta Barbaresco Cole
Mauro Molino Barolo Vigna Concha
Mauro Molino Barolo Vigna Gancia
Castello di Neive Barbaresco Santo Stefano
Andrea Oberto Barbera d'Alba Giada
Luigi Oberto Barolo Ciabot Berton****/*****
Palladino Barbaresco
Parusso Barolo
Parusso Dolcetto d'Alba Mariondino
Elia Pasquero Barbaresco Sori Paitin
Luigi Pellissero Barbaresco Vanotu
Luigi Pira Barolo
Poggio Petorcino Barolo
Produttori di Barbaresco Barbaresco Asili
Produttori di Barbaresco Barbaresco Moccagatta

Produttori di Barbaresco Barbaresco Monte
Stefano
Produttori di Barbaresco Barbaresco Ovello
Produttori di Barbaresco Barbaresco
Rabaja
Alfredo Prunotto Barbaresco Monte Stefano
Alfredo Prunotto Barbera d'Alba Pian
Romulado
Alfredo Prunotto Barolo
Cannubi****/*****
Renato Ratti Barolo Marcenasco
Fratelli Revello Barolo
Giovine Riconda Barbera d'Asti Superiore
Vigna del Truchet
Francesco Rinaldi Barolo****/*****
Giuseppe Rinaldi Barolo
Giuseppe Rinaldi Barolo Brunate
Riserva****/*****
Giuseppe Rivetti Barbaresco Valeirani
Giuseppe Rivetti Barbaresco Vigneto
Gallina
Giuseppe Rivetti Barbaresco Vigneto
Starderi
Giuseppe Rivetti La Spinetta Pin Vino da
Tavola
Roagna Barbaresco
Roagna Barbaresco Baroco
Bruno Rocca Barbaresco Coparossa
Bruno Rocca Barbaresco Rabaja
Rocche di Costamagna Barolo Rocche de
la Morra
Rocche di Costamagna Barolo Rocche de
la Morra Vigna Francesco
Poderi Rocche Manzoni Valentino Barolo
Riserva****/*****
Poderi Rocche Manzoni Valentino Barolo
Riserva DLA Roul
Luciano Sandrone Barolo
Luciano Sandrone Dolcetto****/*****
Cantine Sant'Evasio Barbera d'Alba
Rosignolo

Giancarlo Scaglione Le Grive Vino da
Tavola
Paolo Scavino Barbera Carati
Paolo Scavino Barolo
Mauro Sebaste Barolo Monvigliero
Mauro Sebaste Barolo Prapo
Mauro Sebaste Barolo La Serra
Aurelio Settimo Barolo Vigneti Rocche
Sottimano Barbaresco Cotta Vigna Brichet
****/*****
Sottimano Barbaresco Curra Vigna Masue
****/*****
Sottimano Barbaresco Gaia Principe Vigna
del Salto ****/*****
Sottimano Barbaresco Pajore Vigna
Liunetta ****/*****
Tenuta La Tenaglia Emozioni Vino da
Tavola
Tenuta La Tenaglia Giorgio Tenaglia Vino
da Tavola
Terra da Vino Barbera d'Asti La Luna e I
Falò
Traversa Barbaresco Sori Ciabot
Traversa Barbaresco Sori Stardari
Viarengo e Figlio Barbera d'Asti Il Fale
Superiore
Luigi Viberti Barbera d'Alba Vigna Clara
Luigi Viberti Barolo****/*****
Vietti Barbaresco Masseria
Vietti Barolo Castiglione
Vietti Barolo Lazzarito
Vietti Barolo Villero
Vinchio e Vaglio Barbera d'Asti Superiore
Vigne Vecchie
Giovanni Voerzio Barolo La
Serra****/*****
Roberto Voerzio Barbera d'Alba
Vignasse****/*****
Roberto Voerzio Dolcetto d'Alba Privino
Roberto Voerzio Vignaserra Vino da Tavola
Attilio Zunino Barolo Sori di Baudana

* * * (GOOD)

Cantina Anselma Barolo
Antoniolo Gattinara
Azelia Barolo Bricco Punta***/****
F.lli Barale Barbaresco Rabaja
F.lli Barale Barolo Castellero
Marchesi di Barolo Barbaresco
Marchesi di Barolo Barolo di Barolo

Marchesi di Barolo Barolo Cannubi
Marchesi di Barolo Barolo Sarmassa
Batasiolo Barbaresco
Batasiolo Barolo
Batasiolo Barolo Cru Boscareto
Batasiolo Barolo Cru Briccolina
Batasiolo Dolcetto d'Alba

Batasiolo Moscato d'Asti
Pietro Berruti Barbaresco La Spinona
Bersano Barbera d'Asti Cascina Cremosina
Poderi Bertelli Cabernet I Fossaretti
F.lli Serio & Battista Borgogno Barolo
    Cannubi
Giacomo e Figli Brezza Barbera d'Alba
    Cannubi***/****
Giacomo e Figli Brezza Barolo Bricco
    Sarmassa***/****
Brovia Barbaresco Rio Sordo
Brovia Barolo Ca Mia
Barolo Rocche dei Brovia
Barolo Villero
Ca Dei Gancia Barolo Cannubi
Ca Rome Barbaresco
Ca Rome Barolo Vigna Carpegna
Ca Rome Barolo Vigna Rapet
Bartolomeo di Cabutto Barbera d'Alba
    Bricco della Viole
Dott. G. Cappellano Barolo
Tenuta Carretta Barbera Bric Quercia
Tenuta Carretta Nebbiolo d'Alba Bric
    Paradiso***/****
Tenuta Carretta Nebbiolo d'Alba Bric
    Tavoleto***/****
F.lli Casetta Barbaresco Vigna Ausario
F.lli Casetta Barbera d'Alba Vigna
    Lazaretto
Cascina Castlet Barbera d'Asti
Cascina Castlet Barbera d'Asti Superiore
Cavallotto Barolo Bricco Boschis
Bruno Ceretto Barbaresco Asij
Bruno Ceretto Barbaresco Bricco Asili
    Faset***/****
Bruno Ceretto Barbera d'Alba Piana
Bruno Ceretto Dolcetto d'Alba Rossana
Bruno Ceretto Nebbiolo d'Alba Lantasco
Pio Cesare Barbera d'Alba
Pio Cesare Barolo
Michele Chiarlo Barbera d'Asti
Michele Chiarlo Barilot
Michele Chiarlo Countacc! Vino da Tavola
Aldo Conterno Il Favot
Giacomo Conterno Barbera d'Alba Cascina
    Francia
Cordero di Montezemolo Barbera d'Alba
Cordero di Montezemolo Barolo Enrico VI
Cordero di Montezemolo Dolcetto
    Monfalletto
Giuseppe Cortese Dolcetto d'Alba

Luigi Dessilani Gattinara
Luigi Dessilani Ghemme
Luigi Dessilani Spanna
Az. Agr. Dosio Barolo Vigna Fossati
Luigi Einaudi Dolcetto
Fantino-Conterno Barbera d'Alba Vignato
Fratelli Ferrero Barolo Manzoni
Tenuta Dei Fiori Barbera d'Asti
Fontanafredda Barbera d'Alba Vigna
    Raimondo
Fontanafredda Barolo
Gianni Gagliardo Barolo La Serra
Angelo Gaja Dolcetto d'Alba Vignaveja
Angelo Gaja Nebbiolo d'Alba
    Vignaveja***/****
Attilio Ghisolfi Barolo Bricco
    Visette***/****
F.lli Giacosa Barbaresco Rio Sordo
F.lli Giacosa Barolo Pira
F.lli Grasso Cascina Valgrande Barbaresco
    Bricco Spessa
F.lli Grasso Cascina Valgrande Barbaresco
    Riserva
Silvio Grasso Barbera d'Alba Fontanile
Icardi Barbera d'Alba Vigna dei Gelsi
Icardi Nebbiolo delle Langhe
Eredi Lodali Barbaresco Rocche dei Sette
    Fratelli
Manzone Dolcetto
Manzone Nebbiolo
Marengo-Marenda Barbaresco Le Terre
    Forti
Marengo-Marenda Barbera Le Terre Forti
Giuseppe Mascarello Barbera d'Alba
    Fasana
Giuseppe Mascarello Barolo
    Dardi***/****
Giuseppe Mascarello Dolcetto Gagliassi
Massolino-Vigna Rionda Barolo Parafada
A. A. Luigi Minuto Barbaresco Cacina
    Luisin Rabaja
A. A. Luigi Minuto Barbaresco Sori Paolin
Moccagatta Barbera Basarin
Mauro Molino Barolo
Castello di Neive Dolcetto d'Alba Basarin
Castello di Neive Dolcetto d'Alba
    Messoriano
Luigi Oberto Barbera d'Alba Ciabot Berton
Vittorio Ochetti e Alfonso Pierluigi Barbera
    d'Asti Superiore
F. lli. Oddero Barbaresco

F. lli. Oddero Barolo Mondoca di Bussia
Soprana

F. lli Oddero Barolo Rocche dei Rivera di `
Castiglione

F. lli Oddero Barolo Vigna Rionda

Armando Parusso Barbera
Pugnane***/****

Agostino Pavia e Figli Barbera d'Asti
Bricco Blina

Elio Perrone Barbera delle Langhe Vigna
Grivo

Piazzo Barbaresco Riserva

Piazzo Barbaresco Sori Fratin

Piazzo Barbera d'Alba Mugiot

Piazzo Barolo Poderi di Mugiot

Produttori di Barbaresco Barbaresco

Produttori di Barbaresco Barbaresco Pora

Alfredo Prunotto Barbaresco

Alfredo Prunotto Barbera d'Alba

Alfredo Prunotto Barbera d'Alba Fiulot

Punset-Marina Marcarino Barbaresco
Campo Quadro

Bruno Rocca Nebbiolo d'Alba

Rocche di Costamagna Barbera d'Alba
Rocche de la Morra

Rocche di Costamagna Rocche della
Rocche

Gigi Rosso Barbaresco Viglino

Gigi Rosso Barolo Cascina Arione

Il Milin Rovero Barbera d'Asti

Il Milin Rovero Barbera d'Asti Vigneto
Gustin

Scarpa Barbaresco

Scarpa Barbaresco Payore Barberis di
Treiso

Scarpa Barolo Boscaretti di Serralunga
d'Alba***/****

Scarpa Barolo I Tetti di Neive

Scarpa Rouchet Vino da Tavola

Enrico Scavino Dolcetto d'Alba

Mauro Sebaste Barolo Le Coste

Aldo & Ricardo Seghesio Barbera

Aldo & Ricardo Seghesio Dolcetto d'Alba

Sigilla dell'Abate Barolo Riserva

Emiliana Martini Sonvico Barbera d'Asti
Superiore Vigna dell'Angelo

Terricci Terricci Vino da Tavola

Azienda Trinchero Barbera d'Asti La
Barslina

Vaselli Santa Giulia Rosso

Mauro Veglio Barolo Arborina

Mauro Veglio Barolo Castillero

Mauro Veglio Barolo Gattera

Mauro Veglio Barolo Rocche

Viarengo e Figlio Barbera d'Asti Il Fale

Viarengo e Figlio Barbera d'Asti Morra

A. A. Viberti Eraldo Barolo

Vietti Barbera d'Alba Pian Romualdo

Vietti Barbera d'Alba Scarrone

Villa Monte Rico Vino da Tavola

GIANFRANCO ALESSANDRIA

1996	Barolo	E-EE	(87–89)
1995	Barolo	E-EE	87
1997	Barolo San Giovanni	EE-EEE	(92–93+)
1996	Barolo San Giovanni	EE-EEE	90
1995	Barolo San Giovanni	EE-EEE	88

From Monforte d'Alba, this producer believes in using open-top small fermenters and punching down as opposed to many of the Marc de Grazia school of Barolo/Barbaresco producers who use rotary fermenters. The generic Barolo is aged in *foudres* and the single-vineyard San Giovanni in *foudres* and *barriques* (approximately 30% new). These classic Barolos exhibit rose petal, tobacco leaf, tarlike fragrances with additional nuances. The traditionally styled 1995 Barolo possesses structure, tannin, and a masculine, austere personality. Although not as fruit driven as some offerings, it is well made and enjoyable. Drink it over the next 10–12 years. The dark ruby-colored 1995 Barolo San Giovanni offers a big, sweet nose of soy, seaweed, black cherry liqueur, and pepper. Exotic, medium to full bodied, and moderately tannic, it will be at its finest between 2000 and 2012.

The richer 1996s possess more formidable personalities. For example, the 1996 Barolo exhibits Nebbiolo's telltale tobacco, damp earth, black cherry, and melted road tar aromas. The wine is dense, rich, and full bodied, with considerable muscle, outstanding purity, and a deep, concentrated, moderately tannic finish. Anticipated maturity: 2001–2014. The text-book 1996 Barolo San Giovanni offers a classic tar and rose petal bouquet with notes of cherry liqueur, smoke, and dried herbs. This dark ruby-colored wine is full bodied, dense, and layered, with outstanding concentration and purity. There is moderate tannin as well as superb depth and muscle. Anticipated maturity: 2002–2015.

While I did not taste Alessandria's regular Barolo in 1997, I did taste the 1997 Barolo San Giovanni. It displays all the glycerin and huge extract and richness of this eccentric vintage. Dark ruby/purple colored, this sexy Barolo offers up powerful aromas of blackberries, jammy cherries, smoke, and dried herbs. There are huge quantities of glycerin, massive body, and a superb, concentrated, muscular, moderately tannic finish. The alcohol is in excess of 14%, and the acidity is low. Anticipated maturity: 2002–2018.

ELIO ALTARE

1997 Barolo	E-EE	(90–91)
1996 Barolo	E-EE	89+
1995 Barolo	E-EE	89
1997 Barolo Arborina	EE-EEE	(93–96)
1996 Barolo Arborina	EE-EEE	92
1995 Barolo Arborina	EE-EEE	91
1994 Barolo Arborina	E	90
1993 Barolo Arborina	D	95
1997 Barolo Brunate	EE-EEE	(92–94)
1996 Barolo Brunate	EE-EEE	90?
1995 Barolo Brunate	EE-EEE	90
1993 Barolo La Morra	D	91

Elio Altare, from La Morra, is another producer who uses rotary fermenters, large oak *foudres* for his regular Barolo, and small *barriques* for his two single-vineyard wines (50% new oak for the Arborina and 75% for the Brunate). Malolactic is done in barrel, and there is no fil-tration at bottling. These are among the most feminine, gloriously perfumed offerings from Piedmont. They represent beautiful examples of symmetry, complexity, and rich, ripe fruit.

I first raved about Elio Altare's brilliant wines nearly a dozen years ago, and I remember some old-timers in the wine business raising their eyebrows about such laudatory praise for a producer who was then totally unknown in Piedmont. Over a decade later Altare has turned out as many great wines as anybody in Piedmont. His two 1993 Barolos are brilliant wines. The 1993 Barolo La Morra possesses a medium dark ruby color, followed by a spicy, sweet, seductive nose of black fruits, cherries, smoke, spice, and tar. On the palate, the wine ex-hibits an expansive, lush, voluptuous texture, silky tannin, well-integrated acidity, and gobs of fruit and glycerin. Although it offers gorgeous drinking now, it will evolve well for a decade. The 1993 Barolo Arborina is one of the vintage's most profound wines, and not far off the mark of the spectacular 1990 and 1989 Arborinas. The wine boasts an opaque deep ruby color, a stunning concoction of aromas, ranging from melted tar, toast, and smoked herbs, to jammy black cherry fruit and roasted meats. Compelling in the mouth, with layers of opulence and sweet fruit presented in a medium- to full-bodied, authoritatively rich yet graceful style, this is an awesome, extremely rich, superbly balanced Barolo that should drink well now and over the next 12–15 years.

The 1994 Barolo Arborina reveals Musigny-like complexity and finesse. The deep ruby color exhibits amber at the edge, suggesting it is on a fast evolutionary track. The fragrant bouquet offers exceptionally sweet aromas of toasty new oak, ripe black raspberry and cherry fruit, flowers, licorice, and spice. The wine is layered, full bodied, and gorgeously rich, but it manages to avoid any notion of heaviness. Expansive and layered, with compelling richness and length, this is Barolo at its sexiest and most intellectually satisfying. However, it needs to be drunk quickly—over the next 4–6 years.

Among the regular Barolos, Altare has turned out a gorgeous 1995 Barolo with a medium ruby color and a sweet nose of high-quality tobacco intermixed with jammy cherry fruit. It is lush, with spice and oak in the background, a nicely layered, exotic mouth-feel, and no hard edges. This evolved Barolo requires consumption over the next 6–7 years. The 1996 Barolo exhibits a more saturated, less evolved dark ruby color. It reveals notes of *sur-maturité* in its ripe, fruity style. Not as sexy and forward as the 1995, the 1996 is broodingly backward, spicy, rich, and highly extracted. Anticipated maturity: 2001–2010. Typical of the vintage, the 1997 Barolo is opulently textured and fat, with low acidity and, as my notes read, "a whore, even in this vintage." It is an extremely sexy, rich, flattering wine that will have many fans. Drink it over the next decade.

Among the crus, Altare has turned in stunning efforts. The lush, voluptuously textured 1995 Barolo Arborina exhibits one of the most saturated dark ruby/garnet colors of this vintage. Full bodied, with great purity, it possesses a layered complexity that comes from low yields and ripe fruit and a bouquet of Asian spices, tobacco, smoke, and black cherries. This is a sweet, rich, forward, but hedonistically styled Barolo. Anticipated maturity: now–2008. In contrast, the outstanding 1995 Barolo Brunate is more muscular and backward, although it possesses good density, superb ripeness, and more tannin and body. Give it 2–3 years of cellaring and consume it over the following 10–15 years.

Altare's 1996 Barolo Arborina is reminiscent of a terrific grand cru from Burgundy's Côte d'Or. Intensely aromatic, with notes of black cherry jam, earth, *pain grillé*, and floral scents, this saturated dark ruby-colored offering reveals superb ripeness, substantial richness, a full-bodied, layered personality, adequate acidity, and sweet tannin in the finish. It is a stunning Barolo to drink now and over the next 15 years. The 1996 Barolo Brunate is the proverbial "iron fist in a velvet glove." It possesses a dark ruby color, closed personality, powerful, muscular flavors of cherries, incense, smoke, and dried herbs, and a tannic finish. Cellar it for 4–5 years and enjoy it over the following 2 decades.

The two 1997s are spectacular. The saturated dark ruby/purple-colored 1997 Barolo Arborina offers a stunning nose of smoky, sweet oak intertwined with jammy cassis, cherry liqueur, licorice, and truffles. Full bodied, with explosive fruit, terrific purity, and layers of glycerin and extract, this magnificent, mouth-filling, teeth-staining Barolo possesses extraordinary symmetry for its size, as well as low acidity and nearly overripe tannin. There is not a hard edge to be found. Anticipated maturity: 2002–2018. More muscular and backward, the 1997 Barolo Brunate displays extraordinary fruit concentration, excellent purity, and the classic tar, cherry, and rose petal fragrance with subtle notes of toasty new oak. It is muscular and tannic, with a finish lasting for more than 30 seconds. Anticipated maturity: 2004–2020.

ANSELMA

1994 Barbera d'Alba   **B   86**

The top offerings I tasted from Anselma included a delicious, dark ruby-colored, soft, effusively fruity, spicy 1994 Barbera d'Alba. The wine is round and cleanly made, with good glycerin, an appealing texture, and a soft, medium-bodied finish. Drink it over the next 3–4 years.

GIACOMO ASCHERI

1997 Barolo Sorano	EE-EEE	(76–78?)
1996 Barolo Sorano	EE-EEE	87+
1995 Barolo Sorano	EE-EEE	88

This small producer has turned out a 1995 and 1996 that are much more impressive than the herbaceous, slightly diluted, unusual 1997. The 1995 Barolo Sorano exhibits a rose petal-scented fragrance. This medium-bodied, elegant, finesse-style, racy wine offers a graceful combination of cherry fruit intermixed with cedar, leather, and dried herbs. This lovely, forward Barolo can be drunk now and over the next 8–10 years. The more tannic, structured, muscular 1996 Barolo Sorano offers an intriguing nose of melted asphalt, tomato skin, and jammy strawberry and cherry fruit. It exhibits some tannin, more muscle than the 1995, an understated, restrained style, and a longer finish than its older sibling. Give it 2–3 years of cellaring and drink it over the following decade. The 1997 Barolo Sorano is unimpressive, with hard, dry tannin, an element of dilution, and a vegetal character to the meager fruitiness. It did reveal such classic Nebbiolo characteristics as melted tar and a floral component, but it was compressed and lean.

AZELIA

1994 Barolo	D	87
1993 Barolo	D	90
1997 Barolo Bricco Fiasco	EE-EEE	(91–95)
1996 Barolo Bricco Fiasco	EE-EEE	(91–93+?)
1995 Barolo Bricco Fiasco	EE-EEE	90+
1994 Barolo Bricco Fiasco	D	90
1993 Barolo Bricco Fiasco	D	92
1997 Barolo San Rocco	EE-EEE	(91–96)
1996 Barolo San Rocco	EE-EEE	(91–93)
1995 Barolo San Rocco	EE-EEE	90

The 1993s of Luigi Scavino may even be more impressive than the dazzling 1989s and 1990s he produced. The 1993 Barolo is a terrific example of the vintage. It is elegant, with sweet tannin, a well-delineated personality, and an up-front, beautifully fragrant, surprisingly evolved set of aromatics. The wine possesses tremendous fruit and depth, gobs of ripe cherries, peachlike fruit, full body, outstanding purity, and a long, opulently textured, full-bodied finish. Drink it over the next decade. The 1993 Barolo Bricco Fiasco exhibits an impressively saturated dark ruby/purple color, followed by aromas of spicy, toasty new oak, lead pencil, black cherries, and tar. Rich and well focused, this large-framed, superconcentrated Barolo possesses nicely integrated tannin and acidity, giving it a forward, sweet, rich, flavorful personality, as well as considerable aging potential (10–15 years). The 1993 Bricco Fiasco is marginally superior to the outstanding 1989 and 1990.

The solidly made, medium ruby-colored 1994 Barolo reveals aromas of asphalt, cherry, and licorice in the nose. In the mouth, it is medium bodied and soft, with plenty of sweet berry fruit intermixed with spice, light tannin, and low acidity. Consume it over the next 3–5 years. The outstanding 1994 Barolo Bricco Fiasco is a surprisingly powerful wine that is crammed with concentrated strawberry/cherry fruit intermixed with cedar, Asian spices, cigar smoke, and dried herb aromas and flavors. Powerful and concentrated, particularly for a 1994, this luscious, multidimensional wine can be drunk now as well as over the next 4–6 years. It is very impressive!

Another believer in rotary fermenters to extract color and fruit, Azelia also uses approximately 40% new oak casks for aging his single-vineyard Barolos. He hit the bull's eye in all three of the most recent vintages. The 1995 Barolo San Rocco displays classic rose petal/melted tar aromas combined with exotic scents of soy and roasted meat-like smells. Intense, with full body, toasty oak, and black cherry fruit, this large-scale, concentrated wine is on a fast evolutionary track, already exhibiting compelling complexity and richness. Anticipated maturity: now–2008. The 1995 Barolo Bricco Fiasco offers a pronounced bouquet of tobacco smoke intermixed with melted asphalt/tar, truffles, and kirsch/cherry liqueur. This fragrant, dense, concentrated, full-bodied Barolo is powerful and long, but more backward than the San Rocco. Anticipated maturity: 2002–2016.

Azelia produced two compelling 1996s. The 1996 Barolo San Rocco possesses a spicy, cedar box, fruitcake, and cherry liqueur nose, a sweet, full-bodied personality with loads of glycerin, evidence of toasty oak, and a rich, multilayered, low-acid, structured/delineated finish. It is a big, mouth-filling Barolo with considerable complexity. Anticipated maturity: 2002–2020. The 1996 Barolo Bricco Fiasco explodes with notes of tobacco, balsam wood, cedar, tar, and the telltale cherry fruit. In the mouth, toasty oak makes an appearance. Full bodied, tannic, deep, and powerful, with a huge impact and density, this modern-style wine has the body and force of a more traditionally made Barolo. Anticipated maturity: 2004–2020.

The two 1997s are typical of the vintage—amazingly rich, frightfully low in acidity, with huge quantities of fruit, glycerin, and alcohol. The alcohol levels must surpass 14.5%, but it only adds to the wines' hedonistic, sensual appeal. The dark ruby/purple-colored 1997 Barolo San Rocco is an amazing wine. It boasts monstrous quantities of glycerin, fruit, concentration, body, and extract. There is not a hard edge to be found, and the finish lasts for 45+ seconds. I am sure plenty of tannin is lurking underneath the wine's massive fruit, but it is well concealed. Anticipated maturity: 2003–2018. The 1997 Barolo Bricco Fiasco is an unctuously textured, full-bodied, tannic yet dense, unformed Barolo that is far less evolved than the 1997 San Rocco. Dense and superconcentrated, with a deep ruby/purple color, it exhibits black fruits, smoke, toast, and tobacco aromas and flavors. Anticipated maturity: 2006–2019.

BERTELLI

1994 Barbera d'Asti	E	87
1993 St. Marsan Rosso	D	87

Bertelli is one of Italy's most interesting wine producers. He is willing to go out on a limb and challenge traditional notions about which varietals should be grown in Piedmont and how such wines should be made. Bertelli's portfolio is extensive, but his wines are made in limited quantities. His selections include many exciting wines, as well as some I find overoaked and out of balance.

One Bertelli red wine offering I can recommend is the 1993 St. Marsan Rosso, made from 100% Syrah and aged in small oak casks. The wine's deep ruby/purple color is followed by a peppery, spicy, herb, and cassis nose, medium body, an elegant, Crozes-Hermitage-like style, and a round, deliciously fruity finish. This wine should drink well for 4–6 years.

A complex nose of cedar, *pain grillé*, black fruits, grilled meats, and roasted herbs jumps from the glass of the fragrant 1994 Barbera d'Asti. The color is a medium ruby with lightening at the edge. In the mouth, the wine reveals good weight, hefty tannin, plenty of spice, and a sweet richness on the attack. This ruggedly constructed, tannic Barbera will never become totally harmonious, but there is enough fine flavor and complexity to merit such a high rating. Drink it over the next 3–4 years.

A. S. BIAGIO

1997 Barolo	E-EE	(88–90)
1996 Barolo	E-EE	(87–89)

This La Morra producer's 1996 Barolo is an opulent, dark ruby-colored effort with gobs of cherry fruit, earth, olive, Provençal herb, and cedary notes. Rich, with good ripeness and a medium-bodied, firm, but fleshy finish, it should be at its finest between 2002 and 2014. The 1997 Barolo exhibits that overripe fruit characteristic that the French refer to positively as *sur-maturité*. Its dark ruby color is followed by aromas of jammy cherry and blackberry fruit, and *garrigue* (that Provence mélange of earth and herbs), full-bodied, fat, succulent flavors, low acidity, and a chewy, high-alcohol finish. This full-throttle Barolo, while not complex, is impressive in a hedonistic sense. Anticipated maturity: 2002–2015.

BOASSO

1996 Barolo Gabutti	EE-EEE	(88–91+?)
1995 Barolo Gabutti	EE-EEE	90
1994 Barolo Gabutti	D	88
1993 Barolo Gabutti	D	90?

This producer from Serralunga d'Alba uses open-top fermenters with no new oak, preferring to age the wines in small *foudres*. I was not able to taste Boasso's 1997. The 1995 Barolo Gabutti reveals a Châteauneuf du Pape–like, kirsch liqueur, peppery nose with notes of licorice and dried herbs. I had expected a more muscular, old-style Barolo, but this is a fruit bomb with extraordinary ripeness and glycerin and a sexy, lush style. Anticipated maturity: now–2012. The dark plum/ruby-colored 1996 Barolo Gabutti offers a nose of overripe black cherries, incense, licorice, smoke, and earth. It is monolithic, dense, and concentrated, but slightly disjointed. Hence the question mark. There is huge potential, but this wine has not yet pulled itself together. Anticipated maturity: 2005–2015.

Boasso's 1994 Barolo Gabutti reveals the vineyard's telltale cherry liqueur, licorice, and new saddle leather aromas but comes across as more tightly knit, tannic, and fuller bodied than many 1994s. Unlike most wines from this open-knit vintage, this wine may improve for another 1–2 years and last for 6–10 years. It is one of the most structured, backward, and muscular Barolos of the vintage. Anticipated maturity: 2000–2010.

Based on the 1993's palate-satisfying qualities, gorgeous lush texture, and length, it would rate an even higher score, but the weedy, wet straw component in the otherwise sweet, black cherry-scented nose is questionable. Except for this component (flaw?), there is plenty about which to get excited, from the seamless richness to the explosive finish of this enticing, rich, opulently styled Barolo.

ENZO BOGLIETTI

1997 Barolo Brunate	EE-EEE	(90–93)
1996 Barolo Brunate	EE-EEE	(87–89)
1997 Barolo Case Nere	EE-EEE	(88–91)
1996 Barolo Case Nere	EE-EEE	(87–88)
1995 Barolo Case Nere	EE-EEE	85
1997 Barolo Fossati	EE-EEE	(87–89)
1996 Barolo Fossati	EE-EEE	(87–90)

This La Morra producer has fashioned attractive wines. American importers might want to take notice, since I was unable to locate an importer for this producer. The only 1995 I tasted was the Barolo Case Nere, a medium ruby-colored, elegant wine with smoked herb, cedar, tar, and cherry aromas. Spicy, with good ripeness, medium body, and an open-knit, evolved character, it can be drunk now and over the next 4–5 years.

The dark ruby-colored 1996 Barolo Case Nere was denser, with licorice, fennel, cedar, and black cherry aromas. Medium to full bodied, with moderate tannin and excellent purity, this traditionally made Barolo will be at its finest between 2003 and 2012. The 1996 Barolo Brunate offers a classic nose of melted tar, cherry and black raspberry fruit, weedy tobacco, herb, and leather scents. Rich, with medium body, moderate tannin, and a dusty, rustic finish, it will benefit from 1–3 years of cellaring and keep for 10–12 years. The 1996 Barolo Fossati's bouquet reveals the influence of new oak, along with cherry liqueur, spice, and licorice. Broad and expansive in the mouth, with full body and moderate tannin, it should prove to be Boglietti's longest-lived 1996. Anticipated maturity: 2002–2018.

The 1997s all possess saturated purple colors, lower acidity, and more open-knit textures with copious levels of glycerin and extract. Each appears to have more of the black fruit, cassis/black raspberry character than the more red fruit-dominated 1996s and 1995. The powerful, rich, deep 1997 Barolo Case Nere may turn out to be outstanding if it develops more delineation and complexity. Anticipated maturity: 2002–2016. The softest wine of this group is the lush, open-knit 1997 Barolo Fossati. Somewhat diffuse, although impressively ripe and hedonistic in its orientation, it should drink well for 10–15 years. The largest scaled and most complete 1997 is the Barolo Brunate. Revealing evidence of *barrique* aging with its subtle *pain grillé* scents, it is a massive Barolo with layers of concentrated fruit, low acidity, high alcohol, and outstanding richness and length. Anticipated maturity: 2005–2020.

GIACOMO BOLOGNA

1993 Barbera dell'Uccellone	D	87
1995 Brachetto d'Acqui	C	89
1995 Il Baciale Rosso Monferrato	C	85

Some spectacular Barberas have emerged from this winery, especially in ripe years such as 1990 and 1989. While this 1993 Barbera dell'Uccellone is very good, it will never be mistaken for a great vintage of this *barrique*-aged Barbera. The wine's dark ruby color is accompanied by lavish quantities of toasty new oak and plenty of sweet berry fruit on the attack, but it narrows out in the mouth. It is medium bodied, with good acidity and a compact finish. It should drink well for 4–5 years.

Readers looking for fun wines to taste and savor should consider the following two efforts. The 1995 Brachetto d'Acqui is a slightly sweet, bubbly, light salmon-colored wine offering plenty of effervescent strawberry/cherry fruit. A more bubbly, pinkish version of Piedmont's famous Moscato, it is a pleasant, low-alcohol (about 6%) wine for quaffing on a hot summer day. Drink it before the end of the year. The uncomplicated 1995 Il Baciale Rosso Monferrato is made in a Beaujolais style. Soft, round, and easygoing, it is meant to be drunk over the next 6–8 months.

BONGIOVANNI

1996 Dolcetto d'Alba	C	90

Proprietor Davide Mazzone, a disciple of Conterno Fantino, has turned out a blockbuster Dolcetto. Black/purple colored, with intense berry fruit, this full-bodied, gorgeously rich, multilayered Dolcetto is oozing with fruit and extract. It is unquestionably one of the most seductive and fruitiest Dolcettos I have ever tasted. The finish lasts 20+ seconds, which is unbelievable for Dolcetto. This wine is impossible to resist; readers should take advantage of its exuberance and vigor by consuming it over the next several years.

FRANCESCO BOSCHIS

1996 Dolcetto di Dogliani	B	85
1996 Dolcetto di Dogliani Sori San Martino	C	87
1996 Dolcetto di Dogliani Vigna dei Prey	C	89

These three enticing Dolcettos are all noteworthy for their intense strawberry jamminess, low acidity, perfumed personalities, and natural textures. The 1996 Dolcetto di Dogliani displays a medium dark ruby color, a sweet, ripe, strawberry-scented nose, soft, sexy, straightforward, medium-bodied flavors, and low acidity. Although not complex, it is a more delicious and satisfying wine than the point score suggests. Drink it over the next year. The 1996 Dolcetto di Dogliani Sori San Martino's saturated dark ruby color is followed by sweet, jammy strawberry/cherry liqueur aromas, a terrific texture, a sweet, fat, plush midpalate, and a pure, ripe, chewy finish. It should drink well for 2–3 years. The most tightly knit and structured wine of this trio is the 1996 Dolcetto di Dogliani Vigna dei Prey. Its ruby purple color is accompanied by restrained aromatics, as well as amazing ripeness and richness, with exceptional purity, copious quantities of blackberry and cherry aromas and flavors, medium to full body, and a sweet, chewy midpalate and finish. This offering may deserve an outstanding rating. Drink it over the next 2–3 years.

ALESSANDRO BRERO

1996 Barbera d'Alba Poderi Roset	C	87
1997 Barolo	E-EE	(88–91)
1996 Barolo	E-EE	(87–88)
1995 Barolo	E	89
1997 Dolcetto d'Alba Poderi Roset	B	87

The traditionally styled 1995 Barolo exhibits an evolved deep garnet color with amber at the edge. It offers a spicy, dried herb, earthy, foresty nose with hints of cherry cough syrup, smoke, and leather. Medium to full bodied and expansive, it is soft enough to be drunk now and over the next 7–8 years. Brero's dark ruby-colored 1996 Barolo displays a bouquet of black cherries and, atypically, cassis notes, along with *pain grillé* (the influence of new casks, I suspect). Ripe and medium to full bodied, it is made in a more modern style than the 1995. Anticipated maturity: 2002–2012. The potentially outstanding 1997 Barolo possesses a dark ruby/purple color, excellent ripeness, abundant black cherry fruit, and the vintage's hefty alcohol supported by considerable glycerin and extract. Its low acidity and plush, succulent style will have many admirers. Anticipated maturity: 2001–2015.

The 1997 Dolcetto d'Alba Poderi Roset boasts a deep ruby/purple color, a delicious, white chocolate, raspberry, and coffee nose, pure flavors, no hard tannin, and a fleshy, nicely textured mouth-feel. All 380 cases were bottled unfiltered. It should drink well for 1–3 years. The 1996 Barbera d'Alba Poderi Roset was aged in 100% French barrels, of which 50% were new, and bottled unfiltered. It displays a vibrant, black cherry, strawberry bouquet nicely supported by smoky, *pain grillé* notes. The wine is fleshy, with excellent purity, a chewy mouth-feel, and enough of Barbera's tangy acidity to provide definition. It should drink well for 3–4 years.

F. LLI BROVIA

1997 Barbaresco Rio Sordo	EE-EEE	(83–85)
1996 Barbaresco Rio Sordo	EE-EEE	86
1995 Barbaresco Rio Sordo	EE-EEE	86+
1997 Barolo Ca Mia	EE-EEE	(86–89)
1996 Barolo Ca Mia	EE-EEE	(86–87+?)
1995 Barolo Ca Mia	EE-EEE	88
1997 Barolo Rocche dei Brovia	EE-EEE	(84–86)
1996 Barolo Rocche dei Brovia	EE-EEE	(88–90)
1995 Barolo Rocche dei Brovia	EE-EEE	86
1997 Barolo Villero	EE-EEE	(86–88)
1996 Barolo Villero	EE-EEE	(90–91+)
1995 Barolo Villero	EE-EEE	89

Brovia, whose cellars are in Castiglione Falletto, produced sound 1995s, very good 1996s, and less impressive 1997s. The 1997s reveal less color saturation than the 1996s. This adds to the minority school of thought that 1997 was not as consistently superb a vintage as believed.

The 1995 Barbaresco Rio Sordo is a light- to medium-bodied effort for drinking over the next 4–5 years. Forward and evolved, with a medium garnet color already exhibiting considerable amber at the edge, it offers weedy tobacco, smoke, earth, and dried fruit aromas and flavors. Although soft, elegant, and medium bodied, it lacks depth. Anticipated maturity: now–2005. The 1995 Barolo Rocche dei Brovia is a darker plum-colored wine with notes of cherries, cranberries, and red currants in its slightly spicy nose. Made in a light- to medium-bodied, elegant style, it is soft and easy to drink. Anticipated maturity: now–2007. The more serious 1995 Barolo Ca Mia exhibits a darker garnet color in addition to more black raspberry and currant fruit in the nose along with notes of new saddle leather and cigar smoke. It possesses good purity, medium to full body, excellent richness, and a moderately long finish. Anticipated maturity: now–2009. The dark ruby/garnet-colored 1995 Barolo Villero is the most backward, youthful, concentrated, and complete of the 1995s. While closed, it does offer aromas of roasted herbs, minerals, tobacco, and leather. In the mouth, sweet black cherry fruit makes an appearance. Anticipated maturity: 2001–2012.

Brovia's 1996s are far denser, more complete, more tannic wines. The 1996 Barbaresco Rio Sordo is the most forward. Displaying a ruby color with purple nuances, it offers fresh, tangy black currant flavors with dried herbs in the background. It possesses good concentration but a compressed, narrowly constructed finish. Anticipated maturity: now–2007. The 1996 Barolo Rocche dei Brovia's opaque ruby color with purple nuances is followed by dense black cherry fruit intermixed with notes of raspberry liqueur, spice, and earth. This is a fuller-bodied, rich, potentially outstanding wine with moderate tannin and 2 decades of longevity. Anticipated maturity: 2005–2018. The dark ruby-colored 1996 Barolo Ca Mia is severe and austere, with high levels of tannin and sweet fruit that tastes like cherry cough syrup mixed with cedar and spice box notes. The tannin level is worrisome; thus the question mark. Anticipated maturity: 2004–2015. The outstanding, ruby/purple-colored 1996 Barolo Villero displays a nose of melted road tar, chocolate, earth, black cherries, dried herbs, and coffee. Rich, full bodied, and nearly massive, this is a classic Barolo that will last for 20–25 years. Anticipated maturity: 2007–2030.

The 1997s possess significantly less color and concentration than the 1996s. The 1997 Barbaresco Rio Sordo tastes similar to a light- to medium-bodied Pinot Noir. Its framboise and cherry flavors are alluring, but the wine is medium bodied, smoky, and light. Drink it over the next 4–5 years. The unevolved 1997 Barolo Rocche dei Brovia is neither concentrated nor deep. It reveals a moderate ruby color and some ripeness, but it seems shallow, particularly for a 1997. It is atypical for this vintage. The soft, opulent, medium- to full-bodied 1997 Barolo Ca Mia exhibits plenty of cherry and cranberry fruit intermixed with new saddle leather and smoke. A spicy, fruit-driven wine, it possesses fine body, some of the vintage's telltale glycerin, and high alcohol. Anticipated maturity: 2001–2012. Last, the 1997 Barolo Villero offers spicy, cinnamon, and cherry fruit in its moderately endowed nose. Elegant, medium to full bodied, and lush, it does not reveal any of the vintage's hallmark glycerin, high alcohol, and sweet fruit. Anticipated maturity: 2000–2012.

CAPPELLANO

1993 Barolo Classico	D	90
1993 Barolo Ottin Fiorin Collina Gabuti	D	90+

This traditional producer owns one of Barolo's smallest estates, with only 7.5 acres of vineyards in the Serralunga d'Alba area. The Cappellanos were among the first Piedmontese families to estate-bottle—in 1870. The 1993 Barolo Classico possesses a dense garnet color, as well as a spicy, fragrant, rose petal, earth, tar, and dried cherry fruit bouquet. Rich and full bodied, with lovely sweetness of fruit, this large-scale, traditionally made, smoky Barolo suggests aromas of *parmesano reggiano* and white truffles. It is an intriguing, complex, fragrant wine that is drinkable now yet promises to last for a decade. The 1993 Barolo Ottin Fiorin Collina Gabutti emerges from a 5-acre vineyard that yielded only 1.2–1.7 tons of fruit per acre. It exhibits a deep ruby/garnet color with amber at the edge. Sweet, rich, black cherry fruit intermingled with earth, smoke, rose petals, and tar offers the classic, old-style Barolo aromatic profile. Full bodied, muscular, and virile, with moderate tannin, high extract, and some rusticity, this fleshy, distinctive, singular style of Barolo is a wine to drink over the next 12–15 years.

CA'ROME

1993 Barbaresco	D	86
1993 Barbaresco Maria di Brun	D	87
1993 Barolo Rapet	D	88

I enjoyed the sweet tobacco/spicy fruitiness of the straightforward but tasty 1993 Barbaresco. The wine is neither concentrated nor potentially long-lived, but its elegant, lighter style will provide delicious drinking for another 3–4 years. The 1993 Barbaresco Maria di Brun is a fuller-bodied, denser, sweeter wine with copious quantities of jammy black cherry fruit intermixed with tobacco, cedar, and spice. The wine possesses terrific aromatics, medium to full body, and a velvety texture. If it puts on any weight, it will merit an even higher score. It is a gorgeous, chewy, elegant, yet authoritatively flavored Barbaresco for drinking now and over the next 7–8 years. Ca'Rome's 1993 Barolo Rapet needs another 2–4 years of cellaring. The wine reveals a deep ruby/garnet color, an old-style, spicy, tar, rose petal, cedar, and cherry nose, dense, medium-bodied, dusty, tannic flavors, and medium to full body. It exhibits some of the telltale, weedy tobacco, and tarlike aromas of the Nebbiolo grape. Although rustic and tannic, it possesses plenty of depth and richness. Readers who prefer the more modern style of Barolo that has been aged in small *barriques* and bottled earlier to preserve its fruit will find this wine somewhat old-fashioned. It should last for 10–12 years.

TENUTA CARRETTA

1997 Barbaresco Cascina Bordino	EE-EEE	(87–88)
1996 Barbaresco Cascina Bordino	EE-EEE	87
1995 Barbaresco Cascina Bordino	EE-EEE	86
1997 Barolo Cannubi	EE-EEE	(90–92+)
1996 Barolo Cannubi	EE-EEE	(87–88)
1995 Barolo Cannubi	EE-EEE	86
1997 Dolcetto d'Alba	B	86

Carretta's offerings tend to be firmly structured, masculine wines with considerable body and tannin. Yet his 1995 Barbaresco Cascina Bordino is surprisingly soft, with a plum/garnet color, smoky, soy, gamey, spicy, earthy, fruit flavors, and damp foresty scents. Medium bodied and round, it will provide ideal drinking over the next 5–6 years. The 1996 Barbaresco Cascina Bordino exhibits a dark ruby color, as well as attractive notes of jammy strawberries and cherries, roasted nuts, cedar, and spice box scents. Long, rich, and medium bodied with moderate tannin, it will be at its finest between 2001 and 2012. The most opulently textured and flamboyant of this trio is the dark ruby/purple-colored 1997 Barbaresco Cascina Bordino. It offers copious quantities of sweet black raspberry and cherry fruit meshed with earth, loamy soil scents, weedy tobacco, and spice. A medium-bodied example, with more glycerin, alcohol, and lower acidity than its siblings, it should drink well young and last for 10–12 years.

The 1995 and 1996 Barolo Cannubi could not be more different. The 1995 Barolo Cannubi is more open knit, with good power for the vintage, but is destined to be drunk over the next 5–8 years. It possesses attractive licorice and tar scents, medium body, and some tannin, but not enough depth to encourage aging for more than a decade. The 1996 Barolo Cannubi is a more powerful, masculine wine, with good tannin and dusty, earthy aromas intertwined with sour cherry notes. Tobacco and asphalt scents also make an appearance. This structured, muscular wine will be at its finest between 2002 and 2012. The outstanding, powerful 1997 Barolo Cannubi exhibits a dense ruby/purple color, in addition to intense aromas of jammy black fruits, spice, cedar, and dried herbs. Powerful and rich, with outstanding ripeness, it will drink well between 2005 and 2020.

Based on the 1997 Dolcettos I tasted, this vintage may be as great as the Piedmontese are claiming. The early-released Dolcettos possess dense purple colors, gobs of ripe fruit, and good freshness and underlying acidity. This effort from Carretta, whose other releases, particularly the 1995 and 1994 Barbarescos and Barolos, did not perform particularly well (too severe, diluted, and angular), is a velvety, medium-bodied, succulent 1997 Dolcetto d'Alba with plenty of chocolate and berry-tinged fruit. A delicious, fun wine, with a slight tanginess in the lush finish, it should be consumed over the next year.

BRUNO CERETTO

1997 Barbaresco Bricco Asili	EE-EEE	(91–94)
1996 Barbaresco Bricco Asili	EE-EEE	(91–93)
1995 Barbaresco Bricco Asili	EE-EEE	89
1997 Barbaresco Faset	EE-EEE	(90–93)
1996 Barbaresco Faset	EE-EEE	(89–91)
1995 Barbaresco Faset	EE-EEE	87

1997	Barolo Bricco Rocche	EE-EEE	(94–97)
1996	Barolo Bricco Rocche	EE-EEE	(92–96)
1995	Barolo Bricco Rocche	EE-EEE	90
1993	Barolo Bricco Rocche Brunate	E	87
1997	Barolo Brunate	EE-EEE	(92–94+)
1996	Barolo Brunate	EE-EEE	(91–93)
1995	Barolo Brunate	EE-EEE	88+
1997	Barolo Prapo	EE-EEE	(92–95)
1996	Barolo Prapo	EE-EEE	(92–94)
1995	Barolo Prapo	EE-EEE	89

The best of the 1993 Ceretto offerings, the Barolo Bricco Rocche Brunate is soft, supple, and Burgundian-like in its complex aromas of herbs, sweet dried cherry fruit, and underbrush. Medium bodied and expansive, with copious amounts of sweet fruit, this is a delicious, precocious, nearly mature Barolo for consuming over the next 3–4 years.

Ceretto has produced an impressive portfolio of 1995s, 1996s, and 1997s from his vineyards in and around the village of Castiglione Falletto. His 1995s are the most evolved of the three vintages, with garnet colors revealing amber at their edges. They are delicious wines that should drink well for 7–10 years. The 1995 Barbaresco Bricco Asili exhibits a beautifully etched nose of cherry jam, vanillin, and dried herbs. Elegantly styled, with medium body, sweet, smoke-tinged fruit, and soft tannin, this is a sexy, complex, easygoing Barbaresco to enjoy over the next 8–10 years. The 1995 Barbaresco Faset is less complex, with a dark ruby/garnet color, good lushness, medium body, a spicy, cedary, cigar box-scented nose, ripe fruit, and a supple finish. Drink it over the next 7–8 years.

The 1995 Barolo Prapo offers a dried herb, cedar, tomato, and red currant bouquet. In the mouth, cherries and plums make an appearance, along with smoked herb and toasty oak notes. Medium bodied, graceful, and layered, it can be drunk over the next 8–10 years. The 1995 Barolo Brunate is more of a fruit-driven wine, with gobs of cherry liqueur as well as notes of sandalwood, cedar, and flowers. Firmer, with more tannin and an earthier, more terroir-driven personality than the more open-knit Prapo, it is drinkable but may improve with a few years of bottle age. Anticipated maturity: now–2010. The most concentrated and fullest bodied of the Ceretto Barolos is the 1995 Barolo Bricco Rocche. It offers a classic nose of melted tar, Asian spice, incense, and cedar, as well as gobs of black fruits, a whiff of high-quality tobacco, full body, and a layered, moderately tannic, concentrated finish. Anticipated maturity: 2001–2015.

All of Ceretto's 1996s exhibit a more saturated ruby color with purple nuances. Additionally, they are richer, with more extract, tannin, and body. The seductive, dark ruby-colored 1996 Barbaresco Bricco Asili offers a classic bouquet of road tar, cherry liqueur, tobacco, and dried herbs. Medium to full bodied and surprisingly supple for the vintage, it exhibits firm tannin in the finish. Anticipated maturity: 2001–2014. The 1996 Barbaresco Faset is not as aromatically complex as the Bricco Asili. It reveals more oak, in addition to a raspberry/black cherry fruit component. Rich, medium bodied, and potentially outstanding, it will be at its finest between 2002 and 2014.

The opaque ruby/purple-colored 1996 Barolo Prapo offers a moderately intense nose of scorched earth, dried herbs, and sweet black fruits. Medium to full bodied, with an exciting level of fruit extract, superb purity, and a multidimensional, layered personality, this terrific Barolo will require 2–4 years of bottle age. Anticipated maturity: 2003–2018. The 1996 Barolo Brunate's dark ruby color is followed by aromas of Chinese black tea, pepper, earth, and cherries. Ripe, full bodied, and structured, with excellent depth, a sweet midpalate, and a firm finish, this wine requires moderate patience. Anticipated maturity: 2003–2016. Ceretto's opaque ruby/purple-colored 1996 Barolo Bricco Rocche is sensational stuff. The richest of these offerings, it combines explosive levels of fruit, glycerin, and extract with an uncanny sense of elegance and finesse. There are copious quantities of black cherry fruit, intermixed with raspberries, cedar, spicy oak, licorice, and tar. This terrific, complex, multidimensional Barolo should be at its finest between 2003 and 2018.

True to the vintage, Ceretto's 1997s possess more glycerin, lower acidity, and a forward, unreal, atypical lushness and opulence. The seductive 1997 Barbaresco Bricco Asili boasts a dark ruby color with purple nuances. Rich and full bodied, with a velvety texture, terrific fruit intensity, low acidity, and a candylike mouth-feel, this is an opulent, sexy Barbaresco to consume over the next 10–12 years. The exotic 1997 Barbaresco Faset offers an explosive nose of red and black fruits, dried herbs, roasted nuts, and toasty oak. Already delicious and impossible to resist, this voluptuously textured, dense, layered, fruit-driven offering is an undeniably compelling Barbaresco to enjoy during its first 10–15 years of life.

I was turned on by the 1997 Barolo Prapo. Its personality represents the essence of earth and white truffles. Opaque ruby/purple colored, with a dazzling display of jammy cherry fruit, mushrooms, new oak, smoke, and Asian spices, this full-bodied, fabulously concentrated wine reveals no hard edges. Anticipated maturity: 2001–2020. Readers looking for raspberries, assorted black fruits, smoke, cedar, and dried herbs should check out the 1997 Barolo Brunate. An opulently textured, silky, full-bodied wine with dazzling levels of glycerin, fruit, and 14+% alcohol, it is remarkably smooth for such a young wine, yet incredibly harmonious and magnetic in its attractions. Anticipated maturity: now–2016. The spectacular 1997 Barolo Bricco Rocche adds several layers of flavor and a plusher texture, with enough glycerin, fruit, and alcohol for the palate to get lost. The opaque purple color is followed by subtle new oak, fabulous purity, and a finish that lasts for nearly a minute. Full bodied, but marvelously rich and well balanced, it should be terrific when released early next year. Anticipated maturity: 2002–2020.

PIO CESARE

1997	Barbaresco	E-EE	(86–88)
1996	Barbaresco	E-EE	(90–91)
1995	Barbaresco	E-EE	88
1997	Barolo	E-EE	(86–88)
1996	Barolo	E-EE	(89–92)
1995	Barolo	E-EE	(88–89)
1993	Barolo	D	85
1993	Barolo Ornato	D	86

This traditional house continues to make subtle winemaking refinements that enhance the wines' fruit character without compromising their full-bodied, traditional, ageworthy style. I still have bottles of 1969 and 1970 Pio Cesare Barolos that are drinking beautifully at nearly 30 years of age. I did not taste this estate's more recent single-vineyard offerings (such as Ornato). The excellent 1995 Barbaresco is one of the vintage's most delicious wines. A smoky, black cherry- and leathery-scented nose is followed by excellent ripeness, medium to full body, moderate tannin, an excellent texture, and a long, spicy finish. Anticipated maturity: now–2011. The 1996 Barbaresco is more tannic, with a firmer, more muscular style, but not the charm of the 1995—at least not yet. The wine is concentrated, with dense fruit and plenty of black cherries, leather, smoke, and tobacco nuances. However, I would cellar it for

2–3 years. Anticipated maturity: 2002–2016. Interestingly, Pio Boffa claims his 1996s are clearly more successful than his 1997s. He believes that 1996, not 1997, will be considered the great classic vintage for the villages of Barolo and Monforte d'Alba. Boffa says that many growers in these two villages picked too early in 1997, fearing they would lose too much grape acidity. The 1997 Barbaresco is a very good wine with good lushness and intensity, low acidity, plenty of black cherry fruit, and some of the vintage's glycerin, but a slight greenness to the tannin. Drink it over the next 7–10 years.

The dark ruby/garnet-colored 1997 Barolo exhibits a spicy, aromatic nose with scents of earth, dried herbs, leather, and sweet black fruits. In the mouth, it is powerful, with excellent richness, moderate tannin, and a rustic but impressively endowed finish. The classic 1996 Barolo is potentially outstanding. Its dark ruby color is accompanied by a smoky, black cherry-scented nose with roasted herb, nuts, and mineral notes. Full bodied, spicy, and long, but needing 4–5 years of cellaring, this should prove uncommonly long-lived. Anticipated maturity: 2004–2022. Less impressive is the 1997 Barolo. It possesses full body and some lushness, but a slight astringency to the tannin gives the wine a compressed, austere finish. There are black fruits in its aromatic and flavor profiles, medium to full body, and fine size. Anticipated maturity: 2003–2014.

Two correct but uninspiring efforts, Pio Cesare's 1993 Barolo and 1993 Barolo Ornato are both dry, austere, and tannic wines, yet complex and pleasant enough to merit a recommendation. The 1993 Barolo exhibits an evolved light ruby color with amber at the edge. The nose (perhaps this wine's best feature) offers scents of cigar smoke, cedar, spice, and dried cherry fruit. The wine reveals sweetness on the attack, but it quickly becomes compressed and angular. It is a good, aromatic, spice-dominated Barolo for consuming over the next 2–3 years. The deeper garnet-colored 1993 Barolo Ornato is more restrained aromatically. In the mouth, there is more sweetness of fruit, as well as the telltale tar, rose petal, and cherry notes of the Nebbiolo grape, intermixed with smoke and roasted herb nuances. Medium bodied with dry tannin, this is an attractive effort for drinking over the next 2–3 years.

MICHELE CHIARLO

1993 Barolo Vigna Rionda	E	86

Light ruby colored, with amber at the edge, this 1993 Barolo Vigna Rionda offers an attractive combination of spice box, cherries, and earthy aromas. The tannin is elevated, but there is sweet fruit on the attack, as well as good spice. Drink it over the next 2–3 years.

CHIONETTI

1995 Dolcetto di Dogliani San Luigi	C	87

Based on my first introduction to the 1995 Dolcettos from Piedmont, Chionetti's 1995 Dolcetto di Dogliani San Luigi is head and shoulders above the firm's good 1994s. The color is a healthy dark purple, and the nose offers up plenty of ripe berry fruit. This soft, supple wine is ideal for drinking over the next several years.

CIGLIUTI

1997 Barbaresco	E-EE	93
1996 Barbaresco	E-EE	?
1993 Barbaresco Serraboella	E	89+

I had trouble with the only sample I tasted of the 1996 Barbaresco, which seemed to possess vegetal tannin and a hard, tough texture. The color is a healthy dark ruby/purple. While the wine exhibits sweet fruit on the attack, it becomes narrow, with greenness and astringency dominating its personality. Given the high quality of this producer, I look forward to tasting another bottle. There was no problem with the atypical but exotic, ostentatious, spectacularly rich 1997 Barbaresco. I suspect those oenologists who subscribe to the antileisure school of winemaking would argue the acidity is too low, but this wine reveals a soaring chocolatey, cedary, black cherry liqueur bouquet. With fabulous intensity and glycerin, this seductive, hedonistic offering possesses all the characteristics of a terrific Barbaresco (a rose petal, tar, and cherry liqueur-like fragrance), with unbelievable body and a voluptuous mouth-feel. Anticipated maturity: now–2008.

I recently consumed Cigliuti's prodigious 1990 Barbaresco Serraboella, and believe me, the wine demanded a score in the upper 90s. The 1993 is no 1990, but it offers a gorgeously perfumed nose of sweet cedar, spice, and gobs of cherry fruit, earth, and cheese rind. Full bodied, lush, and supple on the attack, this is a sexy, more earthy and rustic wine than most of Marc de Grazia's selections. Medium to full bodied, with nearly outstanding concentration, this is a distinctive, flamboyant Barbaresco to drink over the next 7–8 years.

ALARIO CLAUDIO

1997 Barolo Vigneto Riva	E-EE	(91–93)
1996 Barolo Vigneto Riva	E-EE	(91–92)
1995 Barolo Vigneto Riva	E-EE	91

A new estate from the village of Verduno, Alario Claudio produces small quantities of hedonistic, sumptuously styled Barolos that are fermented in open-top fermenters and aged in 60%–80% new French oak casks. The 1995 Barolo Vigneto Riva exhibits copious quantities of cedar, smoke, and cherry fruit in its evolved aromatics. With good fat and medium to full body, it is a hedonistic, evolved, lush Barolo to enjoy over the next 7–10 years. The saturated ruby/purple-colored 1996 Barolo Vigneto Riva reveals an intense cherry, coffee, cedar, smoky nose. There is great richness, full body, terrific purity, surprisingly low acidity for a 1996, and a lush, multidimensional personality. While tannin is present in the finish, this is a large-scale, gorgeously made Barolo that should be at its best between 2001 and 2015. Last, the dark ruby/purple-colored 1997 Barolo Vigneto Riva is reminiscent of a fruit cocktail, with a heady, intoxicating blend of spice, blackberry and cherry liqueur and toasty, smoky oak aromas. Full bodied and superconcentrated, with exceptional viscosity and dazzling purity and balance, this large-scale, massive, low-acid Barolo should drink well young yet last for 15–18 years.

DOMENICO CLERICO

1994 Barolo Bricotto Bussia	D	89
1997 Barolo Ciabot Mentin Ginestra	EE-EEE	(90–94)
1996 Barolo Ciabot Mentin Ginestra	EE-EEE	90
1995 Barolo Ciabot Mentin Ginestra	EE-EEE	91
1994 Barolo Ciabot Mentin Ginestra	D	91
1993 Barolo Ciabot Mentin Ginestra	D	90
1997 Barolo Mosconi Per Cristina Riserva	EE-EEE	(92–95)
1996 Barolo Mosconi Per Cristina Riserva	EE-EEE	95
1995 Barolo Mosconi Per Cristina Riserva	EE-EEE	92
1997 Barolo Pajana	EE-EEE	(92–95)
1996 Barolo Pajana	EE-EEE	94
1995 Barolo Pajana	EE-EEE	90+

| 1994 Barolo Pajana | D | 91 |
| 1993 Barolo Pajana | D | 94 |

One of the truly fun characters of Piedmont turned in superlative performances in 1993 and 1994. The 1993 Barolo Ciabot Mentin Ginestra offers up truffle, earthy, spicy aromas accompanied by copious quantities of sweet black cherry fruit. As the wine hits the palate, it has the telltale sweetness, ripeness, beautifully knit, well-etched, medium- to full-bodied character of the vintage. Neither the acidity, the tannin, nor the alcohol is obtrusive in this pure, expansive, tasty, and complex Barolo. It should drink well for 10–12 years. Readers may remember my laudatory praise for the debut vintage of Clerico's Barolo Pajana in 1990. As I was dictating my tasting notes for the 1993, my first two words were "kick ass." I realize that doesn't say everything readers want or need to know about a wine, so consider the following description. It is an opaque dark color, with a chocolate, black raspberry, cherry, and truffle nose, sweet, rich, concentrated fruit flavors, an expansive midpalate, and impressive opulence and richness in the nicely textured, long finish. Although unevolved, the wine is accessible. It should drink well for 10–15 years.

Clerico's three Barolo vineyards on the slopes of Monforte have served him well in the irregular 1994 vintage. The 1994 Barolo Bricotto Bussia exhibits a deep plum/ruby color with no lightening at the edge. The wine is a full-bodied example of the vintage, with copious quantities of jammy cherry fruit intertwined with new saddle leather, soy, cedar, and asphalt notes. Sultry and layered, with hedonistic levels of glycerin and fruit, this evolved yet luscious Barolo can be drunk now as well as over the next 3–5 years. The 1994 Barolo Pajana displays a Lafite-Rothschild-like lead pencil note in its fragrant bouquet of black cherries, currants, minerals, and *pain grillé*. This beautifully focused, well-delineated, dense, full-bodied wine possesses surprising depth and richness for a 1994, outstanding purity, and a multidimensional personality. It is one of the most complete and ageworthy 1994 Barolos I have tasted. Anticipated maturity: now–2005. Similar in quality but different in style, the 1994 Barolo Ciabot Mentin Ginestra is a sumptuous, medium- to full-bodied, multilayered, exceptionally complex Barolo (aromas of charcoal, smoke, tobacco, Asian spices, fruitcake, and framboise dominate). Deep, opulently textured, and full bodied, it, like its sibling, the Pajana, is a tour de force in winemaking. It should drink well for 5–8 years.

One of the most gifted winemakers in Piedmont, Domenico Clerico has fashioned nine riveting wines in 1995, 1996, and 1997 from the vineyards surrounding the village of Monforte d'Alba. Clerico utilizes rotary fermenters and 20% new oak for the Ciabot Mentin Ginestra, 50% for the Pajana, and 100% for the Mosconi Per Cristina Riserva. These are wines of extraordinary richness, amazing aromatics, and sensual personalities that satiate both the hedonistic and the intellectual senses. In general, the 1995s are the most forward and evolved, the 1996s the most muscular and structured, and the 1997s off the charts in terms of their thickness, exoticism, and sumptuousness.

The 1995 Barolo Ciabot Mentin Ginestra offers a knockout nose of tobacco, mint, dried red fruits, balsam wood, and cherry liqueur. There are tons of glycerin, low acidity, medium to full body, and striking richness and lushness. It is about as sexy a 1995 Barolo as readers will find. I would opt for drinking it over the next decade, as it is already irresistible. The 1995 Barolo Pajana is a synthesis in style between a grand cru burgundy and a first-growth Bordeaux. It is slightly less aromatic than the 1995 Ciabot Mentin Ginestra, with a saturated ruby/purple color, lush black raspberry and cherry fruit, and a touch of black currants. The medium- to full-bodied, fruit-driven, low-acid 1995 Pajana should be consumed over the next 10–12 years. The amazing 1995 Barolo Mosconi Per Cristina Riserva (aged in 100% new oak and lovingly named after Clerico's 7-year-old daughter, who died tragically) is the richest, most complete of these offerings. This debut vintage offers up notes of kirsch, Chinese black tea, flowers, licorice, and subtle spicy new oak. Amazingly rich and full bodied, with terrific purity, symmetry, and length, it can be drunk now but should be even better with 2–3 years of cellaring; it will keep for 12–15 years.

The 1996s are spectacularly powerful, rich, concentrated wines. The 1996 Barolo Ciabot Mentin Ginestra possesses a deep, dark purple color and a nose of overripe plums, cherries, and cassis. Rich and full bodied, with admirable glycerin, subtle oak, and licorice/floral notes, it is a large-scale yet beautifully balanced Barolo to drink between 2004 and 2018. The striking resemblance of the 1996 Barolo Pajana to a top-class Pomerol is unmistakable. Although huge and massive, it possesses fabulous purity of fruit and toasty, sweet *pain grillé* that complements the wine's highly concentrated black cherry/chocolatey personality. Dense and layered, with considerable viscosity, low acidity, and moderate tannin in the impressive, long finish, it will be at its best between 2006 and 2020. The profound 1996 Barolo Mosconi Per Cristina Riserva exhibits a black raspberry liqueur-like nose. As it sits in the glass, notes of cherries, cassis, *pain grillé*, and smoke emerge. Massive, powerful, chewy, unctuously textured, and long, with subtle oak and immense fruit concentration, this spectacular Barolo should age effortlessly for 2 decades.

¯Put your seat belts on . . . light the candles . . . and crank up the music when you taste through Domenico Clerico's 1997s. It is not so much that they are superior to the 1996s, it's just that they are so unbelievably hedonistic, fat, rich, and flamboyant that they are hard to ignore. I suspect a vintage such as this comes along in Piedmont once or twice a century. Enjoy these wines for their splendid ripeness and exotic, over-the-top personalities. The 1997 Barolo Ciabot Mentin Genestra is a massive, black/purple-colored wine offering notes of black raspberries, cherries, smoke, and floral scents. Superb, with considerable body, huge quantities of glycerin, and a monster finish, it manages to retain a sense of elegance and symmetry despite its gigantic size. The 1997 Barolo Pajana boasts a stunningly riveting nose of black raspberry liqueur, creamy ice cream, toasty oak, licorice, and truffle scents. There is terrific fruit intensity, great purity, and a full-bodied, unctuous texture; it is a whoppingly big and impeccably well-balanced and vinified wine that should be at its best in 2–3 years and last for 2 decades. There are sweet levels of glycerin and awesome concentration in the mammoth, multidimensional 1997 Barolo Mosconi Per Cristina Riserva. The most backward of the three 1997s, it requires 4–5 years of cellaring, although it is hard to resist because of its glycerin, alcohol, and fruit. Anticipated maturity: 2006–2025.

ALDO CONTERNO

1993	Barolo Bricco Bussia Vigna Cicala	EE	86
1993	Barolo Bricco Bussia Vigna Colonnello	EE	86
1997	Barolo Bussia Soprano	EE-EEE	(91–94)
1996	Barolo Bussia Soprano	EE-EEE	(90–92)
1995	Barolo Bussia Soprano	EE-EEE	88
1993	Barolo Bussia Soprano	EE	85
1997	Barolo Cicala	EE-EEE	(91–93)
1996	Barolo Cicala	EE-EEE	(90–92)
1995	Barolo Cicala	EE-EEE	87
1997	Barolo Colonnello	EE-EEE	(92–95)
1996	Barolo Colonnello	EE-EEE	(90–93)

Aldo Conterno is one of the great producers of Piedmont. His wines, which represent an enlightened traditional style, are among the most ageworthy Barolos, often needing 5–6 years to reveal their full character. Conterno, although successful in 1995, produced brilliant wines in both 1996 and 1997. The dark ruby-colored 1995 Barolo Cicala possesses a muted but promising nose of spice box, cedar, tobacco, and cherry fruit. It exhibits good ripeness, medium body, high tannin, and noticeable yet subtle oak. This very good 1995 can be drunk now as well as over the next 10–12 years. The denser 1995 Barolo Bussia Soprano displays a more saturated ruby color. The rich, cedary, smoky, tobacco, and tar nose is classic Nebbiolo. Excellent, with a layered texture and a rich, spicy, austere, moderately tannic finish, it is accessible enough to be drunk but should evolve nicely for a decade.

I tasted three single-vineyard Barolos in 1996. The outstanding 1996 Barolo Cicala offers a jammy, sweet cherry-scented nose with cranberry, tobacco, dried tomatoes, smoke, and white truffle notes. There is admirable purity, richness, and length, medium to full body, and considerable power and tannin. Give this mouth-filling Barolo 4–5 years of cellaring. Anticipated maturity: 2005–2020. The 1996 Barolo Colonnello is even more aromatic, offering scents of melted asphalt, cedar, tobacco, spice box, and assorted red and black fruits. Following a soft entry, the immense richness, fleshy, full-bodied power of this wine became apparent. The finish offers considerable tannic clout and power. Anticipated maturity: 2005–2022. The 1996 Barolo Bussia Soprano is the least evolved, although potentially finest of the 1996s. Its dark ruby color is accompanied by restrained but fabulous aromas of dried herbs, roasted nuts, tobacco, black fruits, and smoky oak. Dense, layered, and immense, with a rich, chewy, full-bodied, explosive ripeness, and fruit character, this massive, mouth-staining Barolo demands 5–6 years of cellaring. Anticipated maturity: 2006–2025.

Aldo Conterno's 1997s are freakishly fat, ripe, and extremely high in tannin. It is a bizarre vintage, but give me this kind of eccentricity every year and I would be set for life. The 1997 Barolo Cicala exhibits a saturated dark purple color and a superb, overripe nose of black cherry jam intermixed with leather, licorice, rose petal notes, and spice. Full bodied, with a juicy succulence that is atypical for a young Aldo Conterno, this wine displays dazzling fruit, seductive, compelling levels of glycerin and extract, and lofty alcohol. This spectacular offering will become more delineated and structured with further aging. Anticipated maturity: 2004–2020. The 1997 Barolo Colonnello offers up a raspberry/cherry jam-scented nose, huge, fat, full-bodied flavors, low acidity, and mind-boggling levels of glycerin, extract, tannin, and alcohol. Huge, immense, and eccentric by classic Barolo standards, this wine pushes the Nebbiolo characteristics to extreme levels of ripeness and richness. An unreal style of wine, it will become more classic as it ages. Anticipated maturity: 2004–2025. The gigantic dark ruby/purple-colored 1997 Barolo Bussia Soprano possesses the most structure, muscle, and tannin of this trio of single-vineyard 1997s. It came across as a traditionally made Barolo with mouth-searing tannin, as well as huge quantities of glycerin, black raspberry and cherry liqueur-like fruit, a skyscraperlike structure, and a finish that lasts for 15+ seconds. The wine's low acidity is counterbalanced by the monster structure. It will last for 2–3 decades, but when will it become drinkable? Anticipated maturity: 2006–2030.

Surprisingly uninspiring efforts in 1993 from Aldo Conterno, the trio of 1993 Barolos shares very evolved garnet colors with plenty of orange and amber at the edges. The wines exhibit hard, dry tannin, as well as a lack of sweet fruit, suggesting to me that they need to be drunk up. Moreover, the wines faded quickly after only 4–5 hours of aeration. The wines do offer some of Nebbiolo's dried cherry, faded rose petal, smoky, asphaltlike aromas, but they lack the flavor dimension, rich extract, and density found in the finest examples of this good vintage. The 1993 Bussia Soprano is the lightest wine, with the most tannic and astringent finish, making its overall balance suspect if it is aged for more than another 4–5 years. Both the 1993 Bricco Bussia Vigna Cicala and 1993 Bricco Bussia Vigna Colonnello possess sweeter fruit and more tobacco, cedar, fruitcake, and jammy cherries in their modest aromatic profiles. These are all medium-bodied, correctly made, but unexciting Barolos from one of the reference-point producers of Piedmont. I would opt for drinking them over the next 2–5 years.

GIACOMO CONTERNO

1996 Barbera d'Alba	C	85?
1993 Barolo Francia	EE	88+?
1990 Barolo Monfortino Riserva	EEE	96+
1996 Dolcetto d'Alba	C	87

The two most famous Conternos are Giacomo, who produces these wines, and his nearby neighbor, Aldo. Both are legends in Piedmont, with the wines of Giacomo Conterno about as traditional as can be found in our high-tech world. In contrast, Aldo Conterno's wines tend to be a synthesis in style between modern-day techniques and the more artisanal methods of the past.

Giacomo Conterno's current releases include the long-awaited yet surreal 1990 Barolo Monfortino Riserva, which spent 7 years in *foudre* before being bottled. (In the old days it was often kept 10 or more years before bottling.)

As for the two 1996s, the 1996 Dolcetto d'Alba, which had 28 days of skin contact, is an outsize, tannic, monster Dolcetto that needs time in the bottle. Most Dolcettos are meant to be drunk within the first 2–3 years of life, but Conterno's need 2–3 years of cellaring! While the 1996 possesses elegance and lovely berry fruit, the tannin level is excruciatingly high. It will last for 10–12 years. I am not as convinced by the 1996 Barbera d'Alba's balance. It reveals extremely high acidity (typical of Barbera), which translates into shrillness in the mouth. The moderately intense nose of strawberry fruit, rose petals, and spice is promising. The wine possesses weight and richness, but oh, the acidity. This wine should last easily for a decade.

The dark ruby/garnet-colored 1993 Barolo Francia offers a moderately intense aromatic profile consisting primarily of earthy, aged Parmesan cheese and trufflelike scents intermixed with leathery-scented fruit. In the mouth, the wine is austere, frightfully tannic, full bodied, and, for lack of a better word—a beast! It offers intense black cherry fruit, but it needs another 4–5 years of cellaring. Given my experience with Conterno Barolos (the first vintage I purchased was 1964), they never shed all their tannin, but they do become more compellingly fragrant and rich. The 1993 should age for 15 more years, but the tannin level will be admired by traditionalists and/or masochists more than those seeking to drink a Barolo within 20 minutes of purchase.

The profound 1990 Barolo Monfortino Riserva appears to be another exhilarating effort in a succession of great Monfortinos. (The 1985, 1982, 1978, 1971, 1967, and 1964 remain Piedmontese classics.) The 1990 displays a medium ruby color with amber at the edge. The intensely fragrant bouquet offers aromas of smoky tobacco, jammy cherries, aged Parmesan cheese, licorice, dried herbs, and truffles. In the mouth, the wine boasts awesome extract, full body, mouth-searing levels of tannin, and a massive, 40+-second finish. This old-style, monster Barolo still needs 5–6 years of cellaring, although it is hard not to be seduced by the wine's fabulous bouquet. Look for this Monfortino to age for another 2 or 3 decades!

CONTERNO-FANTINO

1997 Barolo Sori Ginestra	EE-EEE	(90–92)
1996 Barolo Sori Ginestra	EE-EEE	(90–92+)
1995 Barolo Sori Ginestra	EE-EEE	85?
1997 Barolo Vigna del Gris	EE-EEE	(89–90)
1996 Barolo Vigna del Gris	EE-EEE	(90–91)
1995 Barolo Vigna del Gris	EE-EEE	87?

1998 Dolcetto Bricco Bastia	C	90
1996 Monpra Vino da Tavola	D	89

Usually a reliable producer, Conterno-Fantino, located in the village of Monforte d'Alba, has a mixed portfolio in 1995, 1996, and 1997. Both 1995 Barolos are tannic, with austere personalities. The 1995 Barolo Sori Ginestra reveals cedar and plumlike fruit in the nose but is intensely vegetal, hard, and lacks length. The darker ruby-colored 1995 Barolo Vigna del Gris is astringently tannic, extremely compressed, and extremely earthy. With airing, cedar, dried herbs, spicy oak, and cherries emerge, but this wine is difficult to evaluate. Anticipated maturity: 2002–2012.

The 1996 vintage is very successful. The ruby/purple-colored, mineral-dominated 1996 Barolo Sori Ginestra offers spicy oak in the nose, as well as attractive black cherry fruit intertwined with prunes, and toasty oak. With moderate levels of glycerin, full body, high tannin, and excellent purity, as well as superb richness and extract, this layered wine requires cellaring. Anticipated maturity: 2005–2020. The opaque purple-colored 1996 Barolo Vigna del Gris is dense, with considerable evidence of new oak and powerful, muscular, black currant/cherry flavors, as well as less minerality and earth than in the Sori Ginestra. It is a huge wine of great intensity. Anticipated maturity: 2004–2020.

Both 1997s were noticeably oaky, and made in an international style that submerged some of the Nebbiolo character behind a veneer of heavy toasty wood. The lavishly oaked 1997 Vigna del Gris displays a dark ruby color with purple nuances. Low in acidity and corpulent, with plenty of fat and rich fruit, this wine possesses outstanding potential. Anticipated maturity: 2001–2015. The purple-colored 1997 Sori Ginestra exhibits a sweeter, more substantial attack, in addition to jammy cherry flavors, explosive fruit, tons of new oak, and a huge, 40-second finish. Less oak would make it even more exciting. Anticipated maturity: 2002–2018.

The sumptuous, opaque purple-colored 1998 Dolcetto Bricco Bastia possesses explosive fruit, exhilarating levels of glycerin and concentration, and a velvety-textured, hedonistic, nearly unctuous finish. Pure and thrilling, this sexy Dolcetto should drink well for 3–4 years. Although the 1996 Monpra *vino da tavola* (equal parts Barbera and Nebbiolo) is more tannic, it is an impressively endowed effort with notes of toasty vanillin, cherries, dried herbs, leather, and spice. Dense, huge, and full bodied, but closed, it requires 2–3 years of cellaring, and should drink well for a decade or more.

COPPO

1995 Barbera d'Asti Camp du Rouss	C	85
1994 Pomorosso	D	88

Two of Coppo's current releases did not impress me—the 1995 Barbera d'Asti L'Avocata and the 1994 Mondaccione, a curiosity made from 100% Freisa. However, two other wines were good, especially in view of the fact they are from the 1994 and 1995 vintages, both problematic years for Piedmont. The 1995 Barbera d'Asti Camp du Rouss is a 100% Barbera from 30–40-year-old vines, aged in small French oak barrels and bottled unfiltered. The wine reveals a medium ruby color, ripe, spicy, richly fruity aromas, and round, pretty, medium- to full-bodied flavors. Obvious new oak, combined with sweet fruit, and low acidity, particularly for a Barbera, has resulted in a delicious, up-front, midweight wine to drink over the next 1–2 years. I also enjoyed the forward, sweet cherry-scented 1994 Pomorosso. It is also a 100% Barbera aged in small *barriques*, of which 80% are new. The wine possesses a deep ruby color, a seductive, vanillin, and black cherry-scented nose, lush, round, deep flavors that exhibit excellent concentration, well-integrated acidity and wood, and a clean, succulent, lusty finish. Drink it over the next 2–4 years.

CORDERO DI MONTEZEMOLO

1997 Barolo	E-EE	(90–92)
1996 Barolo	E-EE	(90–92)
1995 Barolo	E-EE	86
1997 Barolo Monfalletto	EE-EEE	(92–96)
1996 Barolo Monfalletto	EE-EEE	(91–93)
1995 Barolo Monfalletto	EE-EEE	88

This La Morra producer has fashioned a bevy of very fine wines from this wonderful trilogy of Barolo vintages. The dark ruby-colored, evolved 1995 Barolo exhibits the telltale rose petal and melted road tar fragrance, along with sweet black fruit notes. Round, medium bodied, and delicious, it can be enjoyed over the next 7–8 years. The classic 1995 Barolo Monfalletto is an old-style *vin de garde*. It reveals a dark ruby/garnet color and an earthy nose of truffles, black cherries, tar, and dried herbs. Rich and full bodied, with excellent concentration, it needs 3–4 years of cellaring and should keep for 15 years. It will be uncommonly long-lived for a 1995.

The greatness of the 1996 vintage is obvious in the saturated ruby/purple colors of Codero's wines. The knockout 1996 Barolo will require patience. It possesses a black/ruby/purple color as well as superrich blackberry and cherry flavors combined with licorice, fennel, and subtle new *barrique* aromas. Long and dense, with mouth-searing tannin, it will be at its finest between 2007 and 2020. The 1996 Barolo Monfalletto reveals more mineral and new saddle leather notes in addition to black raspberries, cherries, tar, and rose petals. Extremely full bodied, with new oak coming through in the flavors, this powerful, multidimensional, sensational Barolo should offer thrilling drinking after a decade of cellaring. Anticipated maturity: 2008–2025.

The 1997 Barolo may not be better than the gorgeous 1996, but it is powerful and rich, with copious quantities of sweet black cherry and currant fruit, leather, spice, and tar. Dense and chewy, with the vintage's low acidity and extravagant ripeness well displayed, it will drink well between 2004 and 2018. The explosive fruit and viscosity of the 1997 Barolo Monfalletto sets it apart from Codero's other offerings. It stood out as one of the great wines in what is an exotic, atypical, but undeniably sensational vintage. The color is a saturated black/purple. The wine offers jammy notes of blackberries, tar, *barrique*, and earthy smells. Unctuously textured, with a massive midpalate and finish, this huge, nearly over-the-top Barolo will be controversial, but wow, what intensity of flavor it possesses. Given the wine's syrupy constitution, there is probably more tannin than it exhibited. My best guess is that this huge, massive Barolo will be in its prime between 2007 and 2020+.

CORINO

1997 Barolo	E-EE	(88–90)
1996 Barolo	E-EE	87
1995 Barolo	E-EE	88
1997 Barolo Arborina	EE-EEE	(89–91)
1996 Barolo Arborina	EE-EEE	(88–92)
1995 Barolo Arborina	EE-EEE	90
1997 Barolo Giachini	EE-EEE	(91–94)
1996 Barolo Giachini	EE-EEE	90

1995 Barolo Giachini	EE-EEE	89
1997 Barolo Rocche	EE-EEE	(90–92)
1996 Barolo Rocche	EE-EEE	(89–92)
1995 Barolo Rocche	EE-EEE	90

Corino is one of the increasing number of Piedmontese producers utilizing rotary fermenters. With respect to wood cooperage, no new oak is utilized for the generic Barolo, and approximately 40% new oak casks are employed for the single-vineyard wines. His offerings tend to be velvety and forward, even in the classic vintages, so readers can imagine the decadent level of richness Corino's wines achieved in 1997. Read on.

The surprisingly evolved 1995 Barolo displays a ruby/garnet color with amber at the edge. It offers abundant black cherry notes in the perfumed, woodsy aromatics. Succulent, round, and gentle, this is a delicious Barolo to enjoy over the next 4–6 years. The 1996 Barolo is also supple and velvety, but it is less complex aromatically. Perhaps additional nuances will emerge with further bottle age. Spicy, ripe, and attractive, it can be consumed now and over the next 8–9 years. The sexy, low-acid, voluptuously textured, plump 1997 Barolo is typical of this exotic vintage. It is already delicious and complex, with gobs of fruit. Drink it over the next 7–8 years.

Corino's 1995 single-vineyard offerings are complex, aromatic, developed, and forward wines. The medium ruby-colored 1995 Barolo Giachini exhibits a knockout nose of sweet cinnamon, allspice, coffee, black fruits, and toast. An expansive, ripe, medium- to full-bodied, seductive effort, it is not huge, but it is complex and disarming. Consume it over the next 5–6 years. The 1995 Barolo Arborina reveals a more deeply saturated ruby color in addition to an attractive nose of sweet black cherry liqueur, dried herbs, tobacco, and cedar scents. Lush and sexy, with medium to full body, an alluring texture, low acidity, and an evolved, complex style, it can be savored over the next 6–8 years. The 1995 Barolo Rocche possesses a dark ruby color, medium to full body, and spicy, roasted herb, tobacco, and cherry fruit aromas. As the wine sits in the glass, more of Nebbiolo's road tar and rose petal notes emerge. Deep and rich, this outstanding 1995 can be drunk over the next decade.

The 1996s, true to the vintage character, possess more color saturation, tannin, structure, and depth and are less evolved. The dark ruby-colored 1996 Barolo Giachini offers a big, smoky, Asian spice, seaweed, and cherry liqueur nose. Medium to full bodied, lush, and sexy with some tannin, this delicious wine should be at its finest with another 1–2 years of bottle age and keep for 10–12 years. The 1996 Barolo Arborina is a dense, severe, muscular effort with intriguing peppery, seaweedlike notes (or is it *garrigue?*) in the bouquet as well as rich, concentrated, black cherry fruit with subtle oak in the background. This powerful, structured, macho-style Barolo requires 2–3 years of cellaring. Anticipated maturity: 2002–2015. The 1996 Barolo Rocche also reveals a dried Provençal herb, peppery, smoky character reminiscent of some wines from southern France. The wine has plenty of tannin and sweet black cherry fruit intermixed with charcoal scents. Medium to full bodied, moderately tannic, and complex, it will benefit from 2–3 years of cellaring. Anticipated maturity: 2002–2012.

Corino's 1997s smell like Nebbiolo infused with overripe, gloriously fragrant Pinot Noir. The 1997 Barolo Giachini possesses explosive aromatics consisting of flowers, black fruits, coffee, and roast beef. Dense and chewy, with no hard edges, this expansive, seductive, fabulously complex, velvety-textured wine flows over the palate with no hard edges. Drink this extraordinary wine over the next 12–15 years. The more tannic, muscular, leaner 1997 Barolo Arborina exhibits admirable concentration, full body, low acidity, and a boatload of tannin (surprising, given how many wines obscure the tannin with their glycerin and rich fruit). In any event, it will be at least excellent, possibly outstanding, but it will require bottle time. Anticipated maturity: 2004–2015. The 1997 Barolo Rocche's dark ruby color is followed by a firm yet promising nose of smoked herbs, cherry liqueur, dried olives, and subtle new oak. Rich, pure, and dense, with stunning concentration, firm tannin, and a layered mouth-feel, this effort will also benefit from several years of bottle age. Anticipated maturity: 2002–2016.

CORTESE

1997 Barbaresco Rabaja	EE-EEE	(89–92)
1996 Barbaresco Rabaja	EE-EEE	86
1995 Barbaresco Rabaja	EE-EEE	76

Cortese's 1995 Barbaresco Rabaja is disappointing, even in this irregular vintage. Spicy tobacco and dried tomato notes dominate the nose. The wine is medium bodied, compressed, austere, and lean, with hard tannin in the finish. It will become increasingly attenuated as it ages. Drink it up. The 1996 Barbaresco Rabaja displays a saturated ruby color and a spicy, tobacco, licorice, and cherry nose. A traditionally styled Barbaresco, with dry tannin, medium body, and very good extract, it should handsomely repay 2–3 years of cellaring and keep for 12–15 years. The overripe style of the 1997 vintage is well displayed in the dense, purple-colored 1997 Barbaresco Rabaja. The alcohol level is high and the acid level low in this monster Barbaresco with gargantuan quantities of glycerin, fruit, extract, and alcohol. With a forward, plush texture, it will drink well young yet keep for 15+ years.

LUIGI EINAUDI

1997 Barolo	E-EE	(88–91)
1996 Barolo	E-EE	(83–84?)
1995 Barolo	E-EE	86
1997 Barolo Cannubi	EE-EEE	(90–92+)
1996 Barolo Cannubi	EE-EEE	(90–92)
1995 Barolo Cannubi	EE-EEE	79?
1997 Barolo Costa Grimaldi	EE-EEE	(88–91+)
1996 Barolo Costa Grimaldi	EE-EEE	(90–91)
1995 Barolo Costa Grimaldi	EE-EEE	87

This traditional producer has a mixed portfolio, but at the top level there are some exciting wines. The medium garnet/ruby-colored 1995 Barolo exhibits a soft, elegant style, as well as herb-tinged berry fruit meshed with foresty, truffle, and dried herb/smoky notes. Round and moderately endowed, it should be consumed over the next 5–7 years. The 1995 Barolo Costa Grimaldi is a stylish, graceful, easy-to-understand and -drink wine from this open-knit vintage. Medium bodied, with smoked herb, cherry, earth, and cedar notes, it possesses sweet fruit and a clean, lovely finish. Drink it over the next 6–7 years. The dark ruby/garnet-colored 1995 Barolo Cannubi offers aromas of cedar, tobacco, new saddle leather, cherries, and melted road tar. In the mouth, the tannin is astringent and the wine austere and angular, without the requisite fat and concentration to support such structure. I suspect it will dry out with further aging.

The backward 1996 Barolo offers a classic bouquet of licorice, tar, and black cherries. It is extremely austere, seriously endowed, but aggressively tannic, with bitterness in the finish. Perhaps cellaring will smooth it out, but it did not possess the concentration and depth to balance the tannin. Anticipated maturity: 2004–2010. I have no reservations about the outstanding scores given both the 1996 Barolo Costa Grimaldi and 1996 Barolo Cannubi.

Both are terrific, old-style, impressively endowed efforts. The saturated ruby-colored 1996 Barolo Costa Grimaldi is a full-bodied, husky, hefty wine with gorgeous aromas of roasted nuts, cherries, dried herbs, licorice, and flowers. This ripe, rich, huge Barolo will require 7–8 years of cellaring. Anticipated maturity: 2008–2020. The opaque ruby/purple-colored 1996 Barolo Cannubi is a powerfully built, uncompromising wine with huge extract, brawny flavors, and high levels of tannin. It is a traditionally made Barolo that requires a decade of cellaring. Everything is present for future brilliance, but patience will be essential. Anticipated maturity: 2010–2025.

Even in a vintage like 1997, with low acidity, overripe fruit, and its over-the-top style, Einaudi produced classic, backward, chewy, blockbuster Barolos that will require nearly as much cellaring as his 1996s. The dark ruby/purple-colored 1997 Barolo offers a sweet, smoky, foresty black fruit-scented nose as well as a chewy texture. It should be drinkable in 4–5 years and keep for 12–15. The 1997 Barolo Costa Grimaldi is, as the French would say, a classic *vin de garde*. It exhibits an opaque purple color and mouth-searing levels of tannin, but also mouth-filling levels of extract and richness in addition to a full-bodied, chewy personality. Flavors of dried herbs, licorice, asphalt, assorted black fruits, and gamey meat emerge with coaxing. This is a huge, stubbornly backward, brooding Barolo for traditionalists. Anticipated maturity: 2008–2020. Even more impressive, the 1997 Barolo Cannubi boasts a saturated ruby/purple color in addition to a sweet nose of black fruits intermixed with tar, rose petals, dried herbs, and earthy notes. Impressively built, with a skyscraperlike texture, with one level segueing to another, this nuanced, full-bodied Barolo is excruciatingly tannic. This massive effort requires 8–10 years of cellaring. Anticipated maturity: 2009–2025.

STEFANO FARINA

1997	Barbaresco	E-EE	(88–91)
1996	Barbaresco	E-EE	(87–89)
1995	Barbaresco	E-EE	87
1997	Barolo	E-EE	(90–93)
1996	Barolo	E-EE	(90–91)
1995	Barolo	E-EE	89

While unfamiliar with this La Morra producer, I was impressed by what he has achieved with the following six wines. All of Stefano Farina's wines are well balanced, with nicely integrated acidity, alcohol, and tannin. The saturated ruby/purple-colored 1995 Barbaresco offers a sweet, jammy nose of herb-tinged cherry liqueur intermixed with a touch of toasty new oak. The wine is evolved, fleshy, round, and made with a hedonist's mentality. Drink it over the next 7–8 years. The opaque purple-colored 1996 Barbaresco may merit an outstanding score if it develops more complexity. There is spicy new oak intertwined with black fruits in this modern-style effort, as well as good flesh, texture, and purity. The acidity provides vibrancy and buttresses the wine's weightiness. Drink it over the next 10–12 years. Not surprisingly, the 1997 Barbaresco exhibits an opaque purple color and overripe, cherry, blackberry, smoky, oaky aromas. The wine is fleshy, with excellent richness and a low-acid, succulently textured finish. Anticipated maturity: now–2010.

The Barolos offer more complex aromas and intense, rich, chewy flavors. If new oak was utilized, it has been integrated less intrusively than with the Barbarescos. The evolved plum/ruby-colored 1995 Barolo offers a sweet, fragrant bouquet of roses, black and red fruits, spice, and tar. It is a classic Barolo, with medium to full body, fine depth, and an intriguing *terroir* earthiness in the smooth finish. Anticipated maturity: now–2012. The superb

1996 Barolo exhibits purple nuances in its plum/ruby color. It possesses an opulent texture, super richness, copious sweet fruit and glycerin in the midpalate, and a long, nicely nuanced, layered finish. Still youthful, but impressively endowed, it will be at its peak between 2003 and 2014. The most gigantic of Farina's wines is the 1997 Barolo. It displays telltale aromas of roasted herbs, jammy cherries and blackberries, spice, and tar. Thick and viscous, with outstanding ripeness, the vintage's low-acid, fleshy/accessible personality, and a heady, high-alcohol finish, it will become more civilized as it ages. Anticipated maturity: 2002–2016.

GIACOMO FENOCCHIO

1997 Barolo Bussia	EE-EEE	(86–89)
1996 Barolo Bussia	EE-EEE	(85–87)
1995 Barolo Bussia	EE-EEE	84
1996 Barolo Villero	EE-EEE	(85–87)
1995 Barolo Villero	EE-EEE	85

These traditionally made, old-style Barolos are aged in big, old Slovenian oak casks. Fenocchio, whose cellars are in Monforte d'Alba, has turned out a competent but largely uninspiring group of wines from 1995 and 1996. Both the 1995 and 1996 Barolo Villero reveal textbook rose petal, melted tar, and cherry fruit flavors, but not much depth or length. Both wines need to be drunk over the next 4–5 years. I was surprised by how soft the 1996 was, as well as by its lack of intensity, although the wine is good to very good. The evolved 1995 Barolo Bussia exhibits an earthy, dried herb, smoky, *garrigue*-scented nose. Drink this soft Barolo over the next 4–5 years. The 1996 Barolo Bussia displays a more saturated color with amber at the edge. It is an elegant, lighter-style effort with attractive floral/berry fruit combined with herbs, leather, and spice. It should be consumed during the next 5–7 years. Last, the 1997 Barolo Bussia possesses the most richness and silkiness of these offerings. Dark ruby colored, with plenty of sweet, jammy cherry and strawberry fruit, licorice, and dried Provençal herbs, this lush, medium- to full-bodied Barolo will be ready to drink upon release. Anticipated maturity: 2001–2008.

FRATELLI FERRERO

1997 Barolo Manzoni	EE-EEE	(87–90)
1996 Barolo Manzoni	EE-EEE	(88–90)
1995 Barolo Manzoni	EE-EEE	86

All three of these wines from this La Morra producer are at least very good. The 1996 and 1997 may turn out to be outstanding. The dark ruby-colored 1995 Barolo Manzoni offers up a textbook nose of tar, roses, cherry fruit, and spice. The attack is sweet and the wine medium bodied, cleanly made, and soft. It lacks concentration and length but will provide attractive drinking over the next 3–4 years. The 1996 Barolo Manzoni possesses more power, body, tannin, and intensity. This traditionally made offering reveals earthy, leather, and dried herb-scented cherry fruit in both its bouquet and flavors, as well as dusty, astringent tannin in the finish, suggesting that 2–4 years of cellaring is essential. Anticipated maturity: 2004–2013. The opaque ruby/purple-colored 1997 Barolo Manzoni's bouquet reveals scents of cherry liqueur and cassis. There is low acidity, excellent density, a diffuse personality, and plenty of impact on the palate given its high level of glycerin, alcohol, and fruit. This wine should become more delineated with cellaring. Anticipated maturity: 2003–2015.

GIANNI GAGLIARDO

1997 Barolo Preve	EE-EEE	(87–89)
1996 Barolo Preve	EE-EEE	(88–89)
1993 Barolo Preve	D	87

This producer from the village of La Morra has fashioned a tasty, serious 1993 Barolo. The color is a healthy dark ruby, and the wine offers up copious quantities of sweet cherry fruit intermixed with cedar and spice box aromas. The wine possesses good flesh, medium body, sweet glycerin, and plenty of delineation and spice. Drink it over the next 4–5 years.

Two more excellent offerings from Gagliardo: The 1996 Barolo Preve is a full-bodied, classically textured and flavored wine with savory cedar, cigar box, and black cherry notes intertwined with melted road tar. Rich, fleshy, and purely made, it should drink well for 12–15+ years. The 1997 Barolo Preve is a fatter, more layered wine with low acidity and powerful cherry liqueur, spice box, fruitcake, and dried herb aromas and flavors. There is good purity in addition to a rich, fleshy mouth-feel. Anticipated maturity: 2002–2018.

ANGELO GAJA

1997 Barbaresco	E-EE	(91–93)
1996 Barbaresco	E-EE	91
1995 Barbaresco	E-EE	90
1993 Barbaresco	EE	85
1997 Barbaresco Costa Russi	EE-EEE	(94–96)
1996 Barbaresco Costa Russi	EE-EEE	94
1995 Barbaresco Costa Russi	EE-EEE	90
1993 Barbaresco Costa Russi	EEE	87?
1997 Barbaresco Sori San Lorenzo	EE-EEE	(95–97)
1996 Barbaresco Sori San Lorenzo	EE-EEE	95
1995 Barbaresco Sori San Lorenzo	EE-EEE	91+
1993 Barbaresco Sori San Lorenzo	EEE	87
1997 Barbaresco Sori Tilden	EE-EEE	(96–100)
1996 Barbaresco Sori Tilden	EE-EEE	95+
1995 Barbaresco Sori Tilden	EE-EEE	91+
1993 Barbaresco Sori Tilden	EEE	89
1997 Barolo Conteisa	EE-EEE	(91–93)
1996 Barolo Conteisa	EE-EEE	(93–95)
1997 Barolo Sperss	EE-EEE	(96–100)
1996 Barolo Sperss	EE-EEE	(94–96)
1997 Darmaggi Cabernet Sauvignon	EE-EEE	(92–94)
1996 Darmaggi Cabernet Sauvignon	EE-EEE	(90–91)
1995 Darmaggi Cabernet Sauvignon	EE-EEE	(88–89)

It seems cavalier if not ridiculous to suggest that Angelo Gaja may have produced some of the finest wines in his renowned career, but certainly the 1995s, 1996s, and 1997s are astonishing efforts. Moreover he was thrilled with the 1998s, so he may have four terrific vintages in a row!

The 1995 tends to be a good rather than great vintage in Piedmont, but Gaja's sensational 1995s are among the stars of the vintage. All of the following wines possess extremely saturated dark ruby/purple colors, almost atypical for Nebbiolo. The 1995 Barbaresco offers a superb nose of licorice, cherry fruit, strawberries, flowers, and toasty scents. Ripe, dense, and lush, with an alluring, sexy personality, it is one of the more forward, generic Barbarescos Gaja has produced. Anticipated maturity: now–2011. The three single-vineyard wines are qualitatively similar but represent different expressions of Nebbiolo. The 1995 Barbaresco Sori San Lorenzo offers telltale cigar tobacco, spice box, and cedar notes with black currant and cherry fruit in the background. The new oak plays a subtle role. Structured and more noticeably tannic than the regular cuvée, this is a dense wine with surprising levels of glycerin, a saturated plum color, and intriguing flavors of black fruits, soy, and cedar. Although accessible, it needs more bottle age. Anticipated maturity: 2002–2016. The 1995 Barbaresco Costa Russi reveals the most saturated purple color of any of Gaja's 1995 Barbarescos. A full-bodied, more fruit-driven, and powerful wine, it possesses copious quantities of black raspberry and cherry fruit, as well as toasty new oak. There is even an element of sur-maturité in this large-scale, expansively flavored effort. I would not be surprised to see it age for 20–25 years. Anticipated maturity: 2004–2020+. The 1995 Barbaresco Sori Tilden reveals a liqueurlike viscosity to its richness. It offers spicy, black raspberry fruit in addition to melted asphalt, smoke, truffle, and toast notes. This complex, expansive Barbaresco does not possess the saturated purple/plum color of the Costa Russi, but it is deeply colored for the vintage, with superb richness, full body, and beautifully integrated acidity, tannin, and alcohol. Anticipated maturity: 2004–2020+. The 1995 Darmaggi Cabernet Sauvignon is an elegant wine with medium body, classic weedy tobacco and cassis flavors, sweet, supple tannin, and excellent equilibrium. Anticipated maturity: 2003–2018.

Angelo Gaja likes his 1995 Barbarescos every bit as much as his 1996s. I tend to think the 1996s are more powerful and concentrated. Perhaps it is just a question of Gaja preferring the finesse and elegance of the 1995s to the structure, muscle, and potential of the more massive 1996s. The saturated ruby/purple-colored 1996 Barbaresco offers an intense nose of cassis, minerals, cherry liqueur, and earth. Powerful and muscular, with full body, moderate tannin, and a backward, impressively built, structured style, this large-scale Barbaresco should be at its finest between 2004 and 2018. The sensational black/purple-colored 1996 Barbaresco Sori San Lorenzo is mind-boggling. In addition to scents of minerals, dried herbs, and spice box, it exhibits fabulously concentrated black cherry and currant fruit and a hint of raspberries. It is an oversize wine with unreal richness, layers of concentration, and a full-bodied, powerful finish. Anticipated maturity: 2005–2025. The 1996 Barbaresco Costa Russi could pass for a terrific grand cru red burgundy given its undeniable fragrance of raspberries, violets, and toast. Full bodied, with sensational fruit intensity and purity, this large-scale, meaty, fleshy wine reveals considerable tannin in its stunning finish. Compellingly rich and more internationally styled, it is an impressive effort. Anticipated maturity: 2006–2025. The 1996 Barbaresco Sori Tilden represents the essence of its terroir and the Nebbiolo grape. From its nuanced smoky, mineral, black cherry, cedar, spice box aromas to its full-bodied, hugely extracted palate with no hard edges, this is a dense, superbly delineated, multidimensional Barbaresco that should prove to be one of the greatest Gaja has ever produced. Anticipated maturity: 2005–2030. The outstanding 1996 Darmaggi Cabernet Sauvignon is a structured, dense, black/purple-colored wine with excellent cassis fruit and an unevolved but promising personality. There are copious quantities of tannin, a massive midpalate, and a sweet, long finish. However, it will require considerable patience. Anticipated maturity: 2008–2025.

Readers may have difficulty imagining that after tasting the thrilling 1995s and 1996s, Angelo Gaja appears to have exceeded those brilliant wines in 1997. At this stage, the 1997s look to be the finest wines he has ever made. My enthusiasm is obviously due in part to the stylistic preference I have for more opulently textured wines with lower acidity and thus a broader window of drinkability. Undoubtedly the 1997 Barbaresco is the best generic Barbaresco I have ever tasted. It possesses opulence, glycerin, and extract that must be tasted to be believed. With explosive fruit, low acidity, high alcohol, and huge concentration and richness, it is a spectacular wine that should be drinkable when released and last for 15+ years. The full-bodied 1997 Barbaresco Sori San Lorenzo exhibits an intense nose of Asian spices, smoked meats, and black cherry liqueur. Low in acidity, fat, and plush, with unbelievable richness and glycerin as well as surprising forwardness, this large-scale, satiny-textured Barbaresco will be drinkable upon release and last for 2 decades. True to form, the 1997 Barbaresco Costa Russi is a more fruit-driven offering, with even more elements of *sur-maturité* than in 1995. This low-acid, fat, decadently rich, succulent example is extremely ripe with notes of black raspberries, blackberries, and spice. It, too, will be drinkable upon release and will last for 2 decades. The spectacular 1997 Barbaresco Sori Tilden may flirt with perfection given its unreal level of richness, gorgeous symmetry, and finish that lasts for nearly a minute. It boasts explosive richness symbolized by the essence of black cherry/berry fruit intermixed with earth, licorice, spice box, and subtle new oak. An extraordinary, mammoth, unctuous wine with no hard edges, it somehow manages to be neither heavy nor overbearing. Admittedly, Gaja's 1997s are shaped more by their vintage conditions than by their *terroir* or *cépage* characteristics, but these subtle nuances will emerge with further aging. The black/purple-colored 1997 Darmaggi Cabernet Sauvignon is the finest Gaja has yet made. It possesses fabulous extract, huge quantities of tannin, sensational unctuosity, thickness, and richness, and fabulously pure black fruits intertwined with *pain grillé* and earthy notes. The wine is totally unevolved but loaded with fabulous potential. Its low acidity suggests it will be drinkable before the 1995 or 1996. Anticipated maturity: 2005–2025.

Angelo Gaja is producing Barolo from Sperss and, beginning in 1996, a vineyard near the village of La Morra called Conteisa. One of the great wines of the vintage, the spectacular 1996 Barolo Sperss boasts an opaque ruby/purple color in addition to enormously ripe notes of black cherries, tar, flowers, and white truffles. Extremely full bodied, with compelling intensity and purity, this is a large-scale, massive Barolo with plenty of tannin and 2–3 decades of ageability. Anticipated maturity: 2005–2030. The opaque purple-colored 1996 Barolo Conteisa reveals a sweeter, riper nose with an element of *sur-maturité* given its overripe cassis, melted road tar, licorice, and spice-scented bouquet. More accessible than the Sperss, it exhibits a voluptuous texture, layers of concentrated fruit, and full body. Its tannin is largely concealed by the wine's glycerin, alcohol, and extract. Anticipated maturity: 2001–2020.

The 1997 Barolo Sperss is another candidate for perfection. The saturated purple/blue color is followed by a striking nose of truffles, licorice, black cherries, tar, and cassis. The wine is full bodied, with spectacular intensity, mind-blowing opulence, and a multilayered, sweet midpalate that is found only in the world's greatest wines. Soft because of its low acidity, with high glycerin, gorgeous fruit levels, and a finish that lasts for over a minute, this is an awesome Barolo! Anticipated maturity: now–2025. The 1997 Barolo Conteisa is outstanding in its own right but noticeably less profound than the 1997 Barolo Sperss. It is full bodied, with copious extract, a succulent, explosive richness, noticeable new oak, and tar-tinged, black cherry fruit presented in a layered, concentrated, velvety-textured format. Anticipated maturity: now–2018.

Gaja's 1993 Barbarescos (he declassified all his crus in 1991 and 1992) are good, but anyone expecting a level of quality matching what he obtained in 1988, 1989, and 1990 will be disappointed. The wines are more compact and downsized compared with the three afore-mentioned vintages. For example, the 1993 Barbaresco exhibits a medium ruby color, an attractive nose of cherries and spice, medium body, good acidity, moderate tannin, and a lean, compact feel on the palate. It lacks the aromatic and flavor dimension obtained in a great year. The 1993 Barbaresco Sori San Lorenzo reveals a more distinctive nose of cedar, tobacco, leather, and red cherry fruit. In the mouth, the wine quickly dries out and is slightly attenuated. Nevertheless this is a classy, elegant, medium-bodied, lighter than normal style of Sori San Lorenzo. It should drink well for 10–12 years. More perplexing and difficult to evaluate is the 1993 Barbaresco Costa Russi. The wine possesses a nice inner core of sweet cherry fruit, but its tannin is so high that it finishes with mouth-searing astringency as well as some bitterness. There is good purity of fruit and medium body, but the wine is tightly knit and may need more time in the bottle. It is a gamble as to whether the fruit will dry out before the tannin subsides. The most interesting of the Gaja 1993 Barbarescos is the medium ruby-colored 1993 Barbaresco Sori Tilden. It offers up a Burgundian-like, sweet cherry, earthy, smoky tobacco character. In the mouth, the wine reveals the most intensity, sweetest fruit, and greatest length of this quartet. Rich, medium to full bodied, and spicy, with some of the vintage's telltale dry tannin, the wine has plenty of fruit for balance. This is an excellent example of Sori Tilden that should drink well for 10–15 years, but it is not comparable to the 1988, 1989, or 1990.

Three wines I tasted from Gaja that did not make the recommended list include the vegetal, woody, tannic 1991 Darmaggi Cabernet Sauvignon ($90), the richer, riper, but still too oaky and tannic 1993 Darmaggi Cabernet Sauvignon ($90), and the good but uninspiring 1994 Barbera Sito Rey ($42).

GASTALDI

1994 Barbaresco	D	88
1989 Rosso Vino da Tavola	E	90

Gastaldi has hit the high notes in the irregular 1994 vintage. The intense yet delicate, somewhat fragile 1994 Barbaresco offers a classic expression of Nebbiolo in its gorgeously perfumed nose and sweet, round, richly fruity flavors. The color is medium ruby, with a hint of amber at the edge. The excellent aromatics offer scents of rose petals, cherry fruit, spice, smoke, and licorice. This soft, rich, medium-bodied Barbaresco possesses decent acidity, an evolved style, and a sweet, dry, long finish. Drink it over the next 2–3 years. The 1989 Rosso *vino da tavolo* (made from a clone of Nebbiolo) displays a singular personality, with a dark ruby color and a fabulous nose of cedar wood, smoke, chocolate, and jammy fruit. Full bodied, with copious quantities of glycerin and alcohol, gorgeous layers of fruit, and a heady, long, concentrated finish, this distinctive wine should continue to evolve effortlessly for a decade or more.

SERGIO GERMANO

1997 Dolcetto d'Alba Lorenzino	B	87
1997 Dolcetto Pra di Po	C	89

Two more gorgeous examples of what appears to be a fabulous vintage, Germano's 1997 Dolcettos are loaded. For example, the 1997 Dolcetto d'Alba Lorenzino possesses a saturated dark ruby/purple color and a big, roasted nut, chocolate, and black cherry/berry nose. Those aromas follow through in the lovely, expansive, succulent palate. Pure and fruity, this is a crowd pleaser. Even more concentrated, and nearly outstanding, is the 1997 Dolcetto Pra di Po. It offers a saturated opaque purple color, followed by a knockout nose of cherry liqueur, framboise, and white chocolate. Intense and full bodied, with stunning richness, this juicy, layered, concentrated Dolcetto should drink well for 4–5 years . . . but who can defer their gratification that long?

ATTILIO GHISOLFI

1997 Barolo Bricco Visette	EE-EEE	(88–90)
1996 Barolo Bricco Visette	EE-EEE	(86–87)
1995 Barolo Bricco Visette	EE-EEE	86

This small producer in Monforte d'Alba has fashioned a soft, evolved, already mature 1995 Barolo Bricco Visette. The color is already revealing amber and orange at the edge. This medium-bodied Barolo offers the hallmark tar, rose petal, and spicy nose. Medium bodied and not terribly concentrated, it is ideal for drinking over the next 5–6 years. The dense, more saturated ruby-colored 1996 Barolo Bricco Visette is fuller bodied and more extracted, with weedy tobacco intermixed with dried herbs, cherry liqueur, and copious notes of new saddle leather. The wine starts off impressively, but it becomes more compressed and short in the finish, which kept my score low. Anticipated maturity: 2002–2012. The viscous, low-acid, thick-textured 1997 Barolo Bricco Visette offers abundant aromas of black cherry and berry fruits, licorice, fennel, and smoked meats. Dense, full bodied, and rich, with a diffuse personality but impressive richness, this is the finest of these three vintages from Attilio Ghisolfi. Anticipated maturity: 2002–2016.

BRUNO GIACOSA

1995 Barbaresco	EE	87
1997 Barbaresco Bricco Asili	EE-EEE	(88–91)
1996 Barbaresco Bricco Asili	EE-EEE	(94–97)
1996 Barbaresco Bricco Asili	EE-EEE	90
1995 Barbaresco Gallina	EE	88
1996 Barbaresco Rabaja	EE-EEE	(93–95)
1997 Barbaresco Santo Stefano	EE-EEE	(87–90)
1996 Barbaresco Santo Stefano	EE-EEE	(92–94+)
1995 Barbaresco Santo Stefano	EE-EEE	91
1996 Barbera d'Alba	C	85
1995 Barbera d'Alba	C	86
1993 Barolo Collina Rionda	EE	91
1997 Barolo Falletto	EE-EEE	(91–93)
1996 Barolo Falletto	EE-EEE	(94–96+)
1995 Barolo Falletto	EE-EEE	90+
1993 Barolo Falletto	EE	90
1996 Barolo Villero	EE-EEE	(92–95+)
1995 Dolcetto d'Alba Falletto	C	87
1996 Nebbiolo d'Alba Valmaggiore	C	88
1995 Nebbiolo d'Alba Valmaggiore	C	86

It is always thrilling to visit Bruno Giacosa, Piedmont's undeniable guardian of the traditional school of winemaking. His Barolos and Barbarescos are among the most exhilarating wines of the world (for example, memories of his 1978s, 1971s, and 1964s). On my most recent visit, Giacosa was in a philosophical mood and surprised me by telling me that he thought both 1996 and 1998 were far better vintages than 1997. He was not the only producer to express such an opinion. Pio Boffa of Pio Cesare thought that while 1997 may have been spectacular in communes such as La Morra, it was less successful in Monforte d'Alba and Barolo than initially believed (because the harvest was too early). Giacosa has unquestionably produced wonderful 1997s and even more spectacular 1996s. That being said, readers should not forget what he achieved in 1995. Because of a disastrous flowering in 1996, Giacosa's crop size was 50% less than normal!

Bruno Giacosa now owns a parcel of the renowned Asili vineyard in Barbaresco, from which he has fashioned a gorgeously elegant 1995 Barbaresco Bricco Asili. The color is a deceptively light ruby with some amber at the edge. The nose offers redolent aromas of kirsch, dried Provençal herbs, new saddle leather, and smoke. In the mouth, Asian spice and soy notes make an appearance in the rich, jammy cherry flavors that also offer an intriguing tomatolike characteristic. This lush, open-knit, full-bodied Barbaresco will drink well between 2001 and 2014. One of the ironies when tasting Giacosa's wines is that he does not own any vines in the Santo Stefano vineyard, yet he consistently produces the finest wine from this hillside parcel. The 1995 Barbaresco Santo Stefano reveals an intensely fragrant nose of coffee, soy, tobacco, dried herbs, and cherry cough syrup. Full bodied, with moderate tannin in the finish, this is an expressive, rich, expansively flavored Barbaresco that can be drunk now as well as over the next 12–15 years.

I also enjoyed the outstanding 1995 Barolo Falletto. It possesses a medium dark ruby color with some lightening at the edge. The intense nose of cedar, spice box, soy, tar, rose petals, and black fruits is followed by a wine with a sweet attack, full body, and dense, layered, concentrated, spicy flavors. As this muscular, tannic wine sat in the glass, notes of allspice and dried herbs became increasingly apparent. Cellar it for 4–5 years and consume it over the following 12 years. Readers should note that all Bruno Giacosa's 1995s sport white labels, with none of the Riserva red labels having been produced.

Although they will be difficult to find upon their release in several years, Giacosa has produced spectacular 1996s. He believes they are the finest wines he has made since 1971 (even better than his glorious 1990s, 1989s, 1988s, and so on). Every 1996 he will release from Barbaresco and Barolo will be a red label Riserva! They will be released early in the next century and will require 5–10 years of cellaring by purchasers. For example, the 1996 Barbaresco Santo Stefano, a sensationally dark ruby/purple-colored wine, is the most backward example from this vineyard I have ever tasted from Bruno Giacosa. This superrich offering possesses an inner palate of sweet fruit, glycerin, and extract, as well as fabulous spice box, cedar, and black and red fruit notes in the nose, full body, and a finish that lasts for 35+ seconds. The tannin is high, and the wine is muscular and intense, but incredibly pure with fabulous equilibrium. Anticipated maturity: 2008–2030. The 1996 Barbaresco Rabaja (Giacosa's debut vintage from this noted vineyard) displays an intriguing nose of soy, dried Provençal herbs, new saddle leather, and red and black fruits. Tannic and full bodied, with an enormous impact on the palate, it is extremely concentrated, yet the fruit, alcohol, tannin, and acidity are all marvelously well integrated. Anticipated maturity: 2006–2025. The saturated deep ruby/purple-colored 1996 Barbaresco Bricco Asili boasts a fabulous, fruit-driven nose of black raspberries, cherry liqueur, dried herbs, tobacco, and cigar box notes. Extremely rich, with sensational fruit purity, full body, and an amazingly extracted, long finish, this is one of the most profound young Barbarescos I have ever tasted. Anticipated maturity: 2007–2025.

There are two red label Riserva Barolos in 1996. The 1996 Barolo Villero should be used to teach a course in what great Barolo smells like. It possesses a classic, rose petal, melted tar, and cherry liqueur nose that soars from the glass. In the mouth, it exhibits licorice, black cherry fruit, fruitcake, spice box, and other assorted nuances in its profoundly complex personality. Full bodied and marvelously concentrated with exquisite harmony, this appears to be a fabulously young Barolo that will age effortlessly for 3 decades. Anticipated maturity: 2010–2035. The saturated ruby/purple-colored 1996 Barolo Falletto exhibits an extraordinary nose of smoke, earth, white truffles, black fruits, licorice, and floral scents. Extremely massive, with layers of concentration, high tannin, a muscular personality, and a 40+-second finish, this classic, young Barolo will require patience. Why can't I turn my body clock back 20 years? Anticipated maturity: 2012–2035.

Bruno Giacosa told me that in 1996 his maceration lasted 30 days, whereas in 1997 it lasted 60 days. He is openly critical of the 1997 vintage, saying it was a difficult year—too hot and dry, with raisined grapes, low acidity, and excessive sugars and alcohol. That being said, his 1997s appear to be beauties, but not as potentially complex and profound as the 1996s. The 1997 Barbaresco Santo Stefano exhibits more glycerin and up-front fruit and character than the more backward 1996. The wine reveals good black cherry fruit, spice box, cedar, and tobacco leaf characteristics in its full-bodied, dense, expansive, rich, low-acid personality. Unlike most Giacosa wines, this effort will be ready to drink when released and will age nicely for 10–15 years. The 1997 Barbaresco Bricco Asili displays a more saturated ruby/purple color, as well as a heady alcoholic clout, low acidity, and more muscle and structure. Although expansive and rich, it is less evolved than the Santo Stefano. Full bodied, with gobs of sweet cherry and herb-tinged fruit, it should be at its best between 2002 and 2016.

The 1997 Barolo Falletto is typically full bodied, with a knockout nose of kirsch, cherry liqueur, fruitcake and cigar box smells. Expansive, lush, rich, and muscular, with the vintage's open-knit, forward character, it will mature more quickly than the 1996 and last for 15–20 years. As critical as Bruno Giacosa was of his 1997s, I thought the wines were all potentially outstanding and, while less successful than his monumental 1996s, brilliantly made wines.

The 1996 Barbera d'Alba is a soft, elegant, medium ruby/garnet-colored wine with berry fruit intertwined with cedar, weedy tobacco, and leathery scents. It should be consumed over the next 1–2 years. The 1996 Nebbiolo d'Alba Valmaggiore could easily be called "the poor person's Barolo." The vintage's excellence is reflected in the sweetness and richness of this offering. The color is dark ruby with lightening at the edge. The knockout aromatics offer up cedar, tobacco, dried herbs, cherry liqueur, smoke, and pepper scents. Beautifully rich in the mouth, with textbook Nebbiolo flavors, this medium- to full-bodied wine reveals a silky texture and a lush, concentrated finish. It should continue to drink well, perhaps improve, over the next 5–8 years.

All three of the 1995 Barbarescos are evolved, with more limited aging potential than Giacosa's wines from such great vintages as 1990, 1989, 1988, and 1978. The 1995 Barbaresco displays an amber edge to its evolved garnet/ruby color, as well as aromas of cedar, spice, weedy tobacco, dried herbs, and cherry fruit. In essence, it is similar to the 1996 Nebbiolo d'Alba Valmaggiore, but not as fragrant. In the mouth, there are licorice, floral, and berrylike flavors, backed by good acidity, medium body, and fine richness. It is a traditionally styled, unfiltered Barbaresco to drink over the next 5–6 years. The medium ruby-colored 1995 Barbaresco Gallina offers aromas of tobacco, kirsch liqueur, cedar wood, fruitcake, and spicy, rose petal-like notes. Medium to full bodied, with surprising intensity and richness for such a light-colored wine, it exhibits ripe fruit (cherries galore), a lush texture, and moderate tannin in the long finish. The alcohol tips the scales at 13.5%. This offering should be drunk over the next decade. Giacosa's 1995 Barbaresco Santo Stefano (only 540 cases produced) cuts a richer, fuller path on the palate. It possesses copious quantities of glycerin and sweet cherry liqueur-like notes, as well as more white pepper, dried herbs, and tobacco scents. Sweet, ripe, and luscious, with medium to full body and obvious complexity, this is a highbrow, hedonistically satisfying wine that should be at its best with another 1–2 years of cellaring and keep for 10–12 years.

Giacosa's 1993 Barolo from the famed Collina Rionda vineyard is an outstanding example of a traditionally made Barolo that never sees a day in new oak. Although it is *barrique*-aged, the emphasis is on Nebbiolo's varietal character. The wine reveals an amber edge to its garnet color. The nose offers up celestial aromas of ginger, cinnamon, spice, and sweet, black cherry fruit. Full bodied, exotic, and dense, with considerable opulence yet a firm underpinning of tannin, this old-style, impeccably made, mouth-coating Barolo requires 2–3 years of aging; it will drink well for 15–18 years.

Bruno Giacosa made virtually no wine in 1991 and 1992 because the grapes were below his qualitative standard. Moreover there are no Riservas in 1993, and little wine was produced in 1994. Readers thirsting for Giacosa's exquisite Piedmontese wines will eventually enjoy a moderate portfolio of 1995s and a full range of 1996s, the latter being the finest vintage in Piedmont since 1989 and 1990. Giacosa's masterful touch is associated primarily with Barbaresco and Barolo, but he also produces Dolcetto, Barbera, and Nebbiolo. The 1995 Dolcetto d'Alba Falletto is a deep ruby-colored wine with a spicy, tarry, chocolatey nose full of ripe berry flavors. The wine possesses excellent texture and purity, delicious fruit, medium body, and a clean, silky finish. It is meant to be drunk over the next 2–4 years. The 1995 Barbera d'Alba is a traditionally styled wine with a gamey, leathery, herb, and berry bouquet and long, lush, rustic flavors. The wine's medium body also offers copious amounts of tobacco and spice. It possesses underlying crisp acidity and surprising muscle. Drink it over the next 3–5 years. Copious quantities of cedar, tobacco, and sweet dried cherry fruit can be found in the medium-bodied, spicy 1995 Nebbiolo d'Alba Valmaggiore. It displays a deep garnet color, admirable complexity, and a sweet, long finish. Drink it over the next 3–4 years.

For decades Giacosa was content to buy his grapes only in the greatest vintages, but he has begun acquiring small parcels of some of Piedmont's top vineyards. He now owns a portion of the Asili vineyard in Barbaresco and recently purchased part of the Falletto vineyard in Barolo. The 1993 Barolo Falletto is the first wine made from his estate-grown vines. The wine exhibits a deep garnet color with some amber at the edge. A provocative, complex, compelling nose of dried fruits, cedar, spice, and roasted meat and herbs is followed by a deep, rich, outstandingly concentrated wine with bold, robust, deep flavors that exhibit abundant glycerin, as well as notes of white chocolate, figs, fruitcake, and sweet red and black fruits. This smoky, rich, nuance-filled, luscious, full-bodied Barolo should drink well for the next 10–12 years.

As a postscript, readers should check out what I consider to be the finest Arneis made in Piedmont. Giacosa's 1997 Arneis is a gorgeous, outstanding dry white with a wonderfully textured mouth-feel, plenty of tangerine, orange, and pear notes, and an herb/honeyed character. It is a delicious, unwooded, dry white to enjoy over the next year.

SILVIO GRASSO

1997	Barolo	E-EE	(90–92)
1996	Barolo	E-EE	88
1995	Barolo	E-EE	87
1994	Barolo	D	85
1993	Barolo	D	89
1997	Barolo Bricco Luciani	EE-EEE	(92–95)
1996	Barolo Bricco Luciani	EE-EEE	(91–93)
1995	Barolo Bricco Luciani	EE-EEE	88
1994	Barolo Bricco Luciani	D	89
1993	Barolo Bricco Luciani	D	89+
1997	Barolo Ciabot Manzoni	EE-EEE	(91–93)

1996 Barolo Ciabot Manzoni	EE-EEE	91
1995 Barolo Ciabot Manzoni	EE-EEE	87
1994 Barolo Ciabot Manzoni	D	86+
1993 Barolo Ciabot Manzoni	D	91

Silvio Grasso, from La Morra, does not employ any new oak for his standard Barolo and about 20% for his single-vineyard wines. Grasso has produced a bevy of sensational efforts over recent vintages.

The three 1993 Barolos represent a breakthrough in quality for Silvio Grasso. The 1993 Barolo exhibits a medium ruby color, soft, sweet, ripe, cherry- and rose petal-scented fruit, medium body, round, accessible flavors, low acidity, ripe tannin, and excellent depth. This forward wine is already delicious and complex. Drink it over the next 6–8 years. The exceptional 1993 Barolo Ciabot Manzoni is Pomerol-like in its sweet, coffee, chocolatey, black cherry richness and opulent texture. It is silky, layered, and compelling. The wine's gorgeous texture and velvety texture make for a lusty, rich, convincing glass of high-class Barolo. It should drink well for a decade. The 1993 Barolo Bricco Luciani is denser, less evolved, and in need of another 12 months of bottle age to blossom as fully as Grasso's other two offerings. It could turn out to be as good as, if not better than, the Barolo Ciabot Manzoni. Although closed, it was harmonious and concentrated when I tasted it in October of 1996.

Typical of the vintage, Grasso's 1994 Barolo exhibits an evolved medium garnet color with considerable amber at the edge. The nose offers up plenty of *pain grillé*, smoky, toasty notes, along with sweet, asphalt-tinged, cherry fruit. This aromatic, light- to medium-bodied, soft, lush Barolo requires consumption over the next 2–4 years.

As for the two 1994 single-vineyard offerings from Grasso, the 1994 Barolo Bricco Luciani offers toasty new oak aromas intermixed with scents of soy, kirsch, smoke, and tar. Heady, with excellent richness, good purity, and a nicely layered, silky texture, this luscious, evolved, medium ruby-colored Barolo should be drunk over the next 3–4 years. One of the tightest knit and most austere of the 1994 Barolos is Grasso's 1994 Barolo Ciabot Manzoni. This wine reveals toasty new oak aromas (according to Grasso, he utilizes 30%–50% new oak, depending on the vintage) as well as powerful, concentrated flavors. The new oak and elevated tannin give this offering atypical texture and personality for the easygoing 1994 vintage. It requires 1–2 years of cellaring, after which my point score may look conservative. If the fruit does not fade, this wine should drink well for 5–7 years.

The 1995 Barolo exhibits a medium ruby/garnet color in addition to a textbook nose of cherries, spice, balsam wood, and a touch of tar. Elegant, soft, and medium bodied, it will provide ideal drinking over the next 6–7 years. The fuller-bodied, lush 1996 Barolo offers a sexy display of glycerin and intense aromatics. It will drink well over the next decade. The uncommonly fat, overripe, opulent 1997 Barolo is low in acidity and bursting with jammy black cherry fruit. Its silky texture and high glycerin and alcohol provide a hedonistic mouthful of wine.

The dark ruby-colored 1995 Barolo Ciabot Manzoni exhibits a big, toasty nose with scents of ripe cherries, saddle leather, cedar, and tobacco. This medium-bodied, evolved Barolo requires consumption over the next 5–7 years. The 1995 Barolo Bricco Luciani displays a more saturated ruby/garnet color with no amber at the edge. It possesses spicy oak, a fresh, medium- to full-bodied feel, moderate tannin, and an excellent cherry-dominated nose as well as flavors with hints of Asian spices, leather, and tar. Anticipated maturity: 2001–2010.

The classic character of the 1996 vintage is well displayed in Silvio Grasso's two single-vineyard crus. The 1996 Barolo Ciabot Manzoni offers a saturated ruby/purple color in addition to a sumptuous bouquet of truffles, saddle leather, black cherries, and floral scents. This expansive, full-bodied, chewy blockbuster is soft enough to be drunk early but should age nicely for 15+ years. Even better is the 1996 Barolo Bricco Luciani. The classic Nebbiolo aromas of rose petals and melted road tar is intermixed with *pain grillé*, cherry liqueur, tobacco, and spice. With explosive richness, high levels of glycerin, and a powerful, muscular, concentrated finish, this superb example possesses high levels of tannin and extract. Anticipated maturity: 2002–2016.

Not surprisingly, Grasso's massive 1997s are sensational Barolos that taste like the essence of Nebbiolo. They boast a whopping 14.5% or higher alcohol. Their aromatics consist of brandied cherries intertwined with tar, rose petals, and spicy wood. The dark ruby/purple-colored 1997 Barolo Ciabot Manzoni offers exceptionally rich, jammy aromas that combine the aforementioned scents with subtle *pain grillé*. Sweet in the mouth because of the high glycerin and alcohol, this hefty wine has plenty of tannin but no hard edges, with everything well balanced. This is another example from this freakishly spectacular year. Anticipated maturity: 2002–2020. The Godzilla-like 1997 Barolo Bricco Luciani is a multidimensional, compelling/prodigious Barolo that is gigantic in its scope and stature. It boasts an opaque ruby/purple color and a phenomenal black cherry-scented nose intermixed with earth, road tar, spice, and fruitcake notes. The huge amounts of tannin are nearly concealed by the prodigious levels of glycerin, extract, and fruit. This wine is overwhelming in its richness. Anticipated maturity: 2003–2020.

MARCHESI DI GRESY

1996 Barbaresco Martinenga	EE-EEE	(86–88)
1995 Barbaresco Martinenga	EE-EEE	87
1996 Barbaresco Martinenga Camp Gros	EE-EEE	(88–90)
1995 Barbaresco Martinenga Camp Gros	EE-EEE	87
1996 Barbaresco Martinenga Gaiun	EE-EEE	(90–91)
1995 Barbaresco Martinenga Gaiun	EE-EEE	86

One of my favorite producers of high-class Barbaresco, Marchesi di Gresy employs a style of exceptional refinement and gracious elegance, without the weight of the region's biggest wines, but with considerable flavor authority. I did not taste any 1997s, but I am sure they must be special wines. The 1995s are very good, and the 1996s are outstanding.

The 1995 Barbaresco Martinenga Camp Gros reveals a Burgundian nose of black cherries, flowers, spice, and subtle toasty oak. In the mouth, notes of tobacco emerge in this graceful, medium-bodied, refined, supple-textured, lush wine. Drink it over the next 6–7 years. Similarly styled, the 1995 Barbaresco Martinenga Gaiun displays more tannin as well as a more structured personality. The 1995 Barbaresco Martinenga possesses the finest delineation, undeniable finesse, and copious quantities of beautifully etched black cherry fruit interspersed with scents of new oak, minerals, flowers, and spice. It is an attractively rendered, medium-bodied Barbaresco to consume over the next 7–8 years.

The 1996 Barbaresco Martinenga Camp Gros offers more black cherry and black raspberry notes with strawberry jam in the mouth. A fuller wine, with more fruit, extract, and structure, this potentially outstanding Barbaresco requires 2–3 years of cellaring. Anticipated maturity: 2002–2012. The superb 1996 Barbaresco Martinenga Gaiun boasts a dark ruby/purple color as well as a gorgeous, Musigny-like nose of flowers, minerals, and black fruits. It is impeccably made, with great elegance, medium body, terrific fruit intensity, and no sense of heaviness. Drink this stylish, harmonious Barbaresco over the next 10–12 years. For whatever reason, the 1996 Barbaresco Martinenga was backward, lean, austere, and impossible to evaluate. I am sure it has the same level of potential as the other single-vineyard offerings, but it was impossible to penetrate. I will wait until it has had another year of evolution to retaste it.

GIACOMO GRIMALDI

1997 Barolo Le Coste	EE-EEE	(90–94)
1996 Barolo Le Coste	EE-EEE	(87–88?)

A new producer for me, Giacomo Grimaldi is based in the village of Barolo. His 1996 Barolo Le Coste revealed a reduced character, and I did not have the opportunity to taste a second sample. Certainly there is a lot to like. This classic old-style Barolo exhibits aromas of melted road tar, rose petals, and petroleum. Although hard to evaluate, it is full bodied and at least excellent. I look forward to tasting it again. It appears to be a wine that will last for 12–15 years. The 1997 Barolo Le Coste is sensational. The superb ruby/purple color is followed by intense aromas of black cherry and orange fruit. Dense and fat, with low acidity, huge amounts of glycerin, and sensational fruit and length, this outstanding Barolo carries considerable extract and alcohol. Grimaldi is not a believer in new oak cask aging, preferring old *foudres*. The 1997 has 15 or more years of aging potential.

A. A. ICARDI

1997 Barolo	E-EE	(87–90)
1996 Barolo	E-EE	87
1995 Barolo	E-EE	86
1996 Dolcetto d'Alba Rousori	C	87

These modern-style Barolos are forward and fruit driven. For example, the 1995 Barolo possesses a dark plum color, plenty of glycerin, a rich, precocious, fleshy appeal, low acidity, and a mélange of tobacco, spice, dried herbs, and jammy cherry fruit. Drink this medium-bodied offering over the next 3–4 years. The 1996 Barolo exhibits a more briery, raspberry, Zinfandel-like personality, with pepper and dried herbs in the background. There is excellent extract, medium to full body, and moderate tannin. The slightly austere, astringent finish suggests 2–3 years of cellaring will be beneficial. It should keep for 10–12 years. The most intense wine of this trio, the 1997 Barolo reveals an exotic, black raspberry/cherry jam-like character, atypical fatness, high glycerin, full body, and a highly extracted, rich, chewy, succulently textured finish. The acidity is low, the alcohol high, and the pleasure factor undeniable. Drink it over the next 10–15 years.

The 1996 Dolcetto d'Alba Rousori is a deep purple-colored, exuberant Dolcetto bursting with fruit and exhibiting the superripeness and promising potential of the 1996 Piedmontese vintage. It is a supple, chewy-textured wine loaded with fruit and copious flavors of black plums, cherries, and chocolate. Drink it over the next 2–3 years.

MALVIRA

1994 Roero	C	87

This interesting wine tastes like a textbook Merlot. Gobs of kirsch and cherry fruit with a touch of white chocolate can be found in both the aromas and the ripe, sweet fruit. Supple and round, this sexy, lush wine should be consumed over the next 2–4 years.

MANZONE

1997 Barolo Le Gramolere	EE-EEE	(89–91+)
1996 Barolo Le Gramolere	EE-EEE	(88–90)
1995 Barolo Le Gramolere	EE-EEE	91
1993 Barolo Le Gramolere	D	91
1997 Barolo Le Gramolere Bricat	EE-EEE	(89–91+)

1996 Barolo Le Gramolere Bricat	EE-EEE	(86–88?)
1995 Barolo Le Gramolere Bricat	EE-EEE	89+
1997 Barolo San Stefano Perno	EE-EEE	(90–92)
1996 Barolo San Stefano Perno	EE-EEE	(87–89?)
1995 Barolo San Stefano Perno	EE-EEE	90

Manzone's cellars in Monforte d'Alba follow a quasi-modern school of winemaking. They use open-top tanks and practice considerable pumping-over. About 20% of the wine is aged in new oak and the remainder in *foudre*. Bottling is accomplished without filtration.

Another sweet, seductive, round, evolved, and fragrant 1993 Barolo, Manzone's Le Gramolere offers dazzling ripeness, rich, sweet, spicy, cherry, smoky fruit, medium to full body, an appealing lushness and generosity to its personality, and a sweet, easygoing, elegant finish. This disarmingly tasty wine is typical of how seductive and forward so many 1993 Barolos have turned out.

The 1995s are successful and may be as good as what Manzone produced in 1996 and 1997. The 1995 Barolo San Stefano-Perno exhibits a deceptively light medium ruby color, as well as knockout aromas of sweet berry fruit intermixed with spice box notes, floral scents, and subtle toast. Sweet, rich, and fruit driven, with a supple, lush texture, medium to full body, and gorgeous balance, this wine can be drunk now or over the next 10–12 years. The 1995 Barolo Le Gramolere reveals a candied cassis character, as well as black raspberry and cherry fruit on the palate. The sumptuous aromas and silky texture are reminiscent of a top-class, opulently styled grand cru red burgundy. Delicious and forward, it will provide ideal drinking over the next decade. The 1995 Barolo Le Gramolere-Bricat, from his parcel of Nebbiolo planted at the top of this hillside vineyard, is more structured and backward, without the expressive characteristics of the other cuvées. In 2–3 years this may be the better wine, but for now it is closed, less fruit driven, and more muscular and tannic. Anticipated maturity: 2002–2014.

Manzone's 1996s were tannic, austere examples that may have been going through a stubborn phase of their evolution. The ruby/purple-colored 1996 Barolo San Stefano-Perno displays an intriguing nose of licorice, cherry liqueur, oak, and earth. There is sweet fruit on the attack, but the tannin and structure take over, compressing the midpalate and finish. This Barolo has the potential for an outstanding rating . . . if the tannin becomes more integrated. I will be anxious to retaste it after bottling. Anticipated maturity: 2004–2015. The 1996 Barolo Le Gramolere is a dark ruby-colored, earthy, structured, medium- to full-bodied wine with a great deal of muscle and intensity, an herbaceous, tobacco, smoky, dried fruit-scented nose, and an old-style, traditional, astringent finish. This wine could turn out to be a classic, but it also could be slightly rustic and tannic. Time will tell. Anticipated maturity: 2005–2016. Even more tannic is the 1996 Barolo La Gramolere-Bricat. An impressive, powerful example, with cherry cough syrup notes meshed with dried herbs, roasted scents, a touch of tar and earth, this backward Barolo requires 5–6 years of cellaring. Anticipated maturity: 2006–2015.

Even though several Barolo producers argued that 1997 was more successful in La Morra than in Monforte d'Alba, that was not always borne out in my tastings. Manzone, whose vineyards are situated on the hillsides of Monforte d'Alba, produced three potentially outstanding 1997s. They display the vintage's equilibrium and velvety texture and an expansive, open-knit richness that conceals moderately high tannin. The dark ruby-colored 1997 Barolo San Stefano-Perno offers a smoky, *pain grillé* nose with notes of ripe black cherry fruit, melted asphalt, and dried herbs. Deep and full bodied, with the vintage's high glycerin, low acidity, and succulent, fat, fruitiness, it should be at its finest between 2002–2018. The 1997 Barolo La Gramolere is more stylish and complex, with the oak more subdued and vibrant, expressive, expansive sweet cherry fruit oozing from both the aromas and flavors. More tannin and less noticeable new oak are evident. The wine is structured, with a sweet midpalate and finish. Anticipated maturity: 2004–2020. Last, the 1997 Barolo La Gramolere-Bricat boasts cherry liqueur aromas intertwined with roasted coffee, smoke, rose petals, and licorice. Full bodied, dense, and powerful, with more dry tannin and austerity than the other crus, this impressive Barolo needs 4–5 years of aging and should last for 2 decades. Anticipated maturity: 2006–2025.

MARCARINI

1996 Barbera Ciabot	C	88+
1993 Barolo Brunate	D	87+
1993 Barolo La Serra	D	88
1996 Dolcetto d'Alba Boschi di Berri	C	88
1997 Dolcetto d'Alba Fontanazza	B	86
1996 Dolcetto d'Alba Fontanazza	B	87

Some of the early-released 1997 Dolcettos are revealing the saturated purple color achieved in this highly touted vintage, in addition to creamy textures and ripe, sweet fruit. Marcarini's 1997 Dolcetto d'Alba Fontanazza possesses a dark purple color, a ripe, blueberry/blackberry-scented nose, gobs of lush fruit, not much complexity, but undeniable charm and character. Drink it over the next 2 years. The dark purple-colored, exuberant 1996 Dolcetto d'Alba Boschi di Berri provides plump, tarry, black cherry, and berry flavors, a lush, expansive palate, no hard edges, and a generous finish. Although short on complexity, it is high on satisfying levels of glycerin and fruit. Drink it over the next 2–3 years.

A massive wine, the 1996 Barbera Ciabot boasts an opaque black/purple color, huge extract, gargantuan body, and layers of fruit and glycerin, which provide a formidable, intense, muscular impression. The wine is not revealing much complexity, but it does have immense size. If a few more nuances develop (and why shouldn't they?), this could be an outstanding Barbera. However, readers looking for restrained, undersize wines should steer clear of this monster. It should last for at least a decade.

After tasting an extremely disappointing, washed-out, virtually fruitless 1995 Dolcetto d'Alba from Marcarini, I was pleased by the impressive 1996 Dolcetto d'Alba Fontanazza— a good sign that this vintage may be the finest in Piedmont since 1989 and 1990. The wine exhibits a deep purple color, a tangy, delicious, chocolatey, berry fruitiness, and considerable vibrancy in addition to unbridled levels of fruit and purity. It is a textbook Dolcetto to drink over the next 2–3 years.

I also enjoyed Marcarini's two 1993 Barolo offerings. The 1993 Barolo La Serra reveals an evolved dark garnet color as well as a sweet, seductive nose of Bing cherries, fruitcake, tobacco, and herbs. Sweet and velvety textured on the palate with medium to full body, this is a luscious, low-acid, seductive style of Barolo for drinking over the next 7–8 years. The 1993 Barolo Brunate is equally sweet but comes across as denser, more structured, and tannic, even though it is relatively accessible. The wine possesses a deep garnet color with more ruby hues, an earthy, cherry-scented nose, and lush, medium- to full-bodied, spice-driven flavors. It should evolve and perhaps improve for up to a decade.

MARENGO

1997 Barolo Bricco delle Viole	EE-EEE	(87–89)
1997 Barolo Brunate	EE-EEE	(90–92)
1996 Barolo Brunate	EE-EEE	(91–93)

1995 Barolo Brunate	EE-EEE	91
1994 Barolo Brunate	D	90
1993 Barolo Brunate	D	89

This La Morra producer utilizes open-top fermenters (as opposed to the rotary fermenters so popular with many of the newer-style Piedmontese producers) and uses approximately 25% new oak casks for aging his Barolos.

A gorgeous perfume of sweet tea, allspice, and cinnamon is distinctive as well as intriguing in Mario Marengo's 1993 Brunate. Soft, round, seductive flavors support the personality of the 1993 vintage. This wine is medium bodied, plump, well balanced, and ideal for drinking over the next 5–8 years.

A top-notch example from the 1994 vintage, Marengo's Barolo Brunate exhibits the seamless, velvety texture typical of many Barolos from the vineyards surrounding La Morra. New saddle leather, flowers, tobacco smoke, cherry liqueur, and cedar are noticeable in the wine's aromatic and flavor profiles. Dense and lush, with outstanding intensity, this velvety-textured, multilayered, medium- to full-bodied Barolo is one of the stars of the vintage. Drink it over the next 4–5 years.

The 1995 Barolo Brunate is a beauty for the vintage. It is a wine of tenderness, voluptuous, silky fruit, medium body, and lovely cherry, strawberry, and tobacco flavors with toasty, smoky notes in the subtle finish. Rich, fleshy, and medium to full bodied, this beauty will drink well for a decade. The velvety-textured 1996 Barolo Brunate offers up a textbook bouquet of rose petals, cherry liqueur, and tobacco leaf scents. Melted tar notes also emerge with swirling. On the palate, there are gorgeous levels of black cherry and truffle flavors. Dense and full bodied, with lofty but not excessive alcohol (14%), this sensational Barolo has moderate tannin underlying the layers of glycerin-imbued, rich, chewy fruit. Anticipated maturity: 2002–2016.

In 1997 Marengo produced two Barolos. The excellent, soft, lush, exotic 1997 Barolo Bricco delle Viole displays distinctive strawberry liqueur-like notes intermixed with smoky oak, leafy tobacco, and dried herbs. Open, lush, and medium to full bodied, without much structure, this wine should drink well young and last for 10–12 years. The 1997 Barolo Brunate is a classic Barolo with telltale cigar box, cherry liqueur, tar, and rose petal scents. Heady, with plenty of alcohol and glycerin, low acidity, and a big, fat, rich, flavorful palate, it is an exotic, flamboyantly styled 1997 with considerable tannin underlying the glycerin and flesh. Anticipated maturity: 2003–2018.

BARTOLO MASCARELLO

1997 Barolo	E-EE	(89–91)
1996 Barolo	E-EE	(87–88+)
1995 Barolo	E-EE	86

One of my favorite traditional producers, Bartolo Mascarello appears to have been less successful than some of his peers in these three vintages. The 1995 Barolo displays a moderate cranberry color with a pink edge leading to amber. It is light to medium bodied, with intriguing spicy box notes intermixed with strawberry and cherry fruit. Moderate tannin in the finish suggests this wine will have limited longevity of 7–10 years. It is a light effort, even considering the vintage. The 1996 Barolo reveals surprisingly high acidity in its relatively backward, tannic profile. It was closed and tough textured when I saw it, with sour cherry, dried nut and kirsch liqueur notes. The wine did not develop in the glass, remaining austere and compressed. Anticipated maturity: 2003–2014. The dark ruby/plum-colored 1997 Barolo exhibits the sweetest fruit of this trio, with cherry and black raspberry fruit. In the mouth, it is elegant, dense, and medium bodied, with a nicely nuanced and layered personality. Sweet tannin and good glycerin give the wine plumpness and richness. Anticipated maturity: 2003–2020.

GIUSEPPI MASCARELLO

1997 Barolo Monprivato	EE-EEE	(90–93)
1996 Barolo Monprivato	EE-EEE	(87–89)
1995 Barolo Monprivato	EE-EEE	87

This traditional producer has turned out a 1995 Barolo Monprivato with earthy, truffle, licorice, and dusty black cherry fruit notes. Medium to full bodied, with good ripeness, excellent purity, and a nicely extracted, rustic, generous style, it is already accessible yet promises to last for 10–12 years. The 1996 Barolo Monprivato is more structured and muscular, but not as concentrated or powerful as I expected given this producer's track record. It exhibits a dark plum color with amber at the edge. The smoky, dried herb, cedary, tobacco leaf notes compete with cherries, leather, and licorice. Medium to full bodied, with a soft attack and moderate tannin in the finish, this is a very good to excellent Barolo that falls short of being outstanding. Anticipated maturity: 2003–2012. The 1997 Barolo Monprivato offers an explosive nose of overripe cherry fruit intermixed with spice box, smoke, cedar, and new saddle leather scents. Succulent, fat, and rich, with high levels of glycerin, this heady, lush, full-bodied, seductive Barolo can be drunk young but will keep for 15+ years.

A. A. LUIGI MINUTO

1996 Barbaresco Cascina Luisin Rabaja	EE-EEE	(90–92)
1996 Barbaresco Cascina Luisin Rabaja	EE-EEE	88
1995 Barbaresco Cascina Luisin Rabaja	EE-EEE	87
1997 Barbaresco Sori Paolin	EE-EEE	(86–87)
1996 Barbaresco Sori Paolin	EE-EEE	81?
1995 Barbaresco Sori Paolin	EE-EEE	86

Three very good efforts have emerged from this producer. The 1995 Barbaresco Sori Paolin reveals a dark ruby color as well as sweet, attractive cherry fruit blended with cedar, cigar box, and leathery notes. Medium bodied and supple, with decent acidity, this is a stylish, delicious Barbaresco to enjoy over the next 5–7 years. The more closed 1996 Barbaresco Sori Paolin possesses medium body, high acidity, more tannin, and a colder feel in the mouth than the more generous 1995. It is a bigger, more muscular wine with plenty of structure and excellent fruit and purity, but it is closed, firmly knit and austere. Anticipated maturity: 2002–2010. The velvety, supple, impressively extracted 1997 Barbaresco Sori Paolin's opaque ruby/purple color is followed by gobs of blackberry and cherry fruit aromas, a sweet midpalate, the vintage's telltale high glycerin and low acidity, and a thick, juicy finish. Drink it over the next 10–12 years.

Minuto's Barbarescos from the Cacina Luisin Rabaja vineyard were distinctly superior to his offerings from the Sori Paolin vineyard. The 1995 Barbaresco Cascina Luisin Rabaja reveals an open-knit, intensely spicy, cedar box and black fruit bouquet. It is fleshy, expansive, fully mature, and ideal for drinking over the next 4–5 years. The 1996 Barbaresco Cascina Luisin Rabaja is nearly outstanding. It possesses a distinctive cigar tobacco-scented nose with aromas of kirsch liqueur, spice, and earth. Medium to full bodied, with excellent richness and good spice and length, it displays more tannin than the 1995 but should be drunk over the next 7–8 years. The outstanding dark ruby/purple-colored 1997 Barbaresco Cascina Luisin Rabaja offers an intense nose of licorice, black cherry fruit, dried herbs, and wood, in addition to a velvety texture, full body, and an opulent, lush, low-acid finish. Already accessible, it should be delicious when released next year. Anticipated maturity: now–2010.

MOCCAGATTA

1997 Barbaresco Balin	EE-EEE	(88–90?)
1996 Barbaresco Balin	EE-EEE	90
1995 Barbaresco Balin	D	89
1997 Barbaresco Basarin	EE-EEE	(88–90)
1996 Barbaresco Basarin	EE-EEE	89
1995 Barbaresco Basarin	D	87
1993 Barbaresco Basarin	D	88
1993 Barbaresco Bric Balin	D	89+
1997 Barbaresco Cole	EE-EEE	(88–90?)
1996 Barbaresco Cole	EE-EEE	90+
1993 Barbaresco Cole	D	90
1995 Barbaresco Vigneto Cole	D	90

The elegant yet concentrated, beautifully delineated style of the 1993 vintage is well displayed in these offerings from Moccagatta. The 1993 Barbaresco Basarin exhibits a dark ruby color, a stylish, gamey, cherry, spice, and rose petal nose, a sweet attack, medium to full body, and broad, expansive flavors. It is the most supple, forward, and advanced of this trio. Drink it over the next 10–12 years. The 1993 Barbaresco Bric Balin reveals a deeper ruby color as well as more density in its midpalate. It offers a classic tobacco, Bing cherry, spice, and sweet jammy nose, excellent richness, sweet, supple tannin, medium to full body, and gorgeous focus and precision to its personality. As with its siblings, the wine's balance/equilibrium is nearly perfect. It was the last to open up in the glass, but after 15 minutes it was beautifully aromatic and rich. It, too, will drink well for 10–12 years. The 1993 Barbaresco Cole offers an intriguing nose of allspice, cinnamon, black cherries, and rose petals. Again, it is an evolved wine aromatically, as well as rich, medium to full bodied and seemingly restrained, but in actuality it is long, authoritatively deep and broad, but oh, so graceful and elegant. It will drink well for 12+ years.

Moccagatta's 1995s reflect the vintage's silky, evolved, soft, alcoholic style. They are userfriendly, charming, seductive Barbarescos that should be consumed over the near term. The 1995 Barbaresco Basarin exhibits a medium ruby color with amber at the edge, as well as an evolved nose of ripe cherry fruit intermixed with spice, weedy tobacco, and roasted herbs. This medium-bodied, heady, soft Barbaresco should be drunk over the next several years. The 1995 Barbaresco Balin is a richer, more layered example with an opulent texture. Aromas and flavors are suggestive of cherry liqueur intermixed with charcoal, *herbes de Provence*, rose petals, and licorice. Fruity, medium to full bodied, and satiny textured, this easygoing, lush Barbaresco should be consumed over the next 2–4 years. The 1995 Barbaresco Vigneto Cole reveals the most expansiveness, as well as the fattest, longest finish of this trio. It exhibits a textbook, cigar box, cedar, and cherry/kirsch bouquet, as well as undeniably seductive, expansive flavors that coat the mouth with glycerin and sweet fruit. Medium to full bodied, fat, and evolved, this sexy Barbaresco should be consumed over the next 2–4 years.

I had a definite preference for Moccagatta's 1996s over the 1997s, if only because the barrel samples of the 1997s were slightly reduced. The terrific 1996s, while not huge, are beautifully knit with fruit-driven personalities and considerable complexity. The dark ruby-colored 1996 Barbaresco Basarin offers a sexy bouquet of black cherry jam intermixed with spice and wood notes. The wine is dense and fat, with abundant glycerin and a hedonistic, up-front appeal. Drink it over the next 10–12 years. The sensational 1996 Barbaresco Balin displays a saturated ruby color and a provocative nose of black cherry liqueur, melted road tar, vanillin, and floral scents. Full bodied, with layers of glycerin and fruit, this is a mouth-coating, rich, surprisingly silky-textured Barbaresco to drink over the next 10–12 years. The 1996 Barbaresco Cole reveals more evidence of new oak in its smoky, toasty nose. There is also more extract, concentration, and tannin, as well as good purity and a 40-second finish. Full bodied and in need of 2–3 years of cellaring, it should keep for 15–16 years.

As stated, the 1997s, particularly the Balin and Cole cuvées, were slightly reduced with leesy characteristics. They are all full-bodied, fat, low-acid, atypically rich Barbarescos seemingly with the right component parts. The 1997 Barbaresco Basarin did not reveal any traces of reduction. It tasted like Nebbiolo jam, with an extraordinary amount of black cherry fruit and spice, low acidity, powerful fruit-laden flavors, and copious quantities of glycerin. This hedonistic wine and its two siblings should drink well for 10–12 years.

MAURO MOLINO

1997	Barolo	E-EE	(88–90)
1996	Barolo	E-EE	(84–86)
1994	Barolo	D	86
1997	Barolo Vigna Concha	EE-EEE	(89–92+)
1996	Barolo Vigna Concha	EE-EEE	(91–94)
1995	Barolo Vigna Concha	EE-EEE	90
1997	Barolo Vigna Gancia	EE-EEE	(90–91)
1996	Barolo Vigna Gancia	EE-EEE	92
1995	Barolo Vigna Gancia	EE-EEE	87

Light ruby colored, with some amber at the edge, the evolved, straightforward, medium-bodied 1994 Barolo from Mauro Molino reveals rose petal, licorice, and tobacco notes in addition to sweet, dried cherry flavors. Round and soft, with little depth in reserve, this is a Barolo to enjoy over the next 2–3 years.

Molino, from La Morra, has turned out an attractive, evolved, open-knit, medium-bodied 1995 Barolo Vigna Gancia with fine ripeness and a spice box/cherry-dominated personality. Although not a blockbuster, it is elegant, soft, and ideal for drinking over the next 4–5 years. The richer 1995 Barolo Vigna Concha possesses more depth than its medium ruby color suggests. Additionally it is pure, well delineated, and made in an elegant, suave, savory style with abundant sweet red fruits, cigar box spices, and a touch of new saddle leather. It should drink well for 7–10 years.

In 1996 Molino produced a generic Barolo in addition to his two single-vineyard cuvées. The 1996 Barolo is a pleasant, straightforward, soft, medium ruby-colored wine that needs to be drunk over the next 4–5 years. In contrast, the superb, saturated ruby/purple-colored 1996 Barolo Vigna Concha is a massive effort with oodles of black cherry fruit intertwined with licorice, smoke, and spicy notes. Full bodied and superconcentrated, with copious quantities of glycerin, it is soft and voluptuous. Enjoy it now and over the next 10–12 years. The opaque dark ruby/purple-colored 1996 Barolo Vigna Gancia offers a nose of *surmaturité*. This unevolved, backward wine possesses chewy plum/cherry fruit, terrific extraction, fine purity, and a full-bodied, moderately tannic, youthful finish. Anticipated maturity: 2002–2016.

Molino's 1997 Barolo is a lush, glycerin-imbued, heady wine with all the characteristics of this vintage—high alcohol, low acidity, and gobs of fruit—well displayed. This delicious, tasty fruit bomb offers plenty of pleasure. The 1997 Barolo Vigna Concha and 1997 Barolo Vigna Gancia are powerful, dark ruby/purple-colored offerings with smoky, toasty noses, intense black fruit characters, full body, and moderately high tannin. These huge efforts are the largest wines I tasted from Molino. Both are grapey, unformed, and in need of 4–5 years of cellaring. They have the potential to last for 2 decades.

ANDREA OBERTO

1997 Barolo Vigneto Rocche	EE-EEE	(91–94)
1996 Barolo Vigneto Rocche	EE-EEE	(90–92)
1995 Barolo Vigneto Rocche	EE-EEE	86

A consistently fine producer, these three examples are all fine for their respective vintages. The dark ruby-colored 1995 Barolo Vigneto Rocche exhibits a rich, modern style as well as a textbook nose of roses, tar, spicy black cherry fruit, and a touch of *barrique* and foresty aromas. Rich and medium bodied, with a short finish but excellent ripeness, this moderately sized Barolo can be drunk now as well as over the next 10–12 years. The black/purple-colored 1996 Barolo Vigneto Rocche is immensely impressive. Muscular and massive, this full-bodied, highly extracted wine displays an intense nose of licorice, black fruits, and roasted herbs. Powerful, with high extraction and tannin, this wine offers mouth-filling levels of extract and considerable structure. Readers will need to be patient. Anticipated maturity: 2005–2020. The 1997 Barolo Vigneto Rocche boasts huge quantities of glycerin, which, combined with high alcohol, low acidity, and jammy black cherry and blackberry fruit, makes for an opulent texture and viscous mouth-feel. It is a freak as far as classic Barolo goes, but a delicious one. Layered, thick, and almost over the top, it is a knockout, dramatic effort that will be immensely popular. Anticipated maturity: 2003–2020.

F. LLI ODDERO

1997 Barbaresco	E-EE	(85–87)
1996 Barbaresco	E-EE	85
1997 Barolo Mondoca di Bussia Soprano	EE-EEE	(89–91)
1996 Barolo Mondoca di Bussia Soprano	EE-EEE	(87–88+?)
1995 Barolo Mondoca di Bussia Soprano	EE-EEE	88
1997 Barolo Rocche dei Rivera di Castiglione	EE-EEE	(87–89)
1997 Barolo Vigna Rionda	EE-EEE	(87–89)
1995 Barolo Vigna Rionda	EE-EEE	87

Another producer from the village of La Morra, Oddero has released two 1995s that are similar in quality, although the Vigna Rionda is more tannic. The 1995 Barolo Mondoca di Bussia Soprano exhibits a smoky ashtraylike nose with notes of cedar, leather, and dried herbs and fruits. As the wine sat in the glass, the classic tar and rose petal concoction emerged. This is an old-style, rustic Barolo with an evolved plum/garnet color, hard tannin, and a lot of character and spice. It should drink well for 10–12 years. The 1995 Barolo Vigna Rionda possesses more rustic tannin, as well as good concentration and an old-style, tough, chewy character that may not appeal to readers who enjoy modern, supple-style wines. Nevertheless, it is a fine wine that can be drunk now or cellared for 10–15 years.

The 1996 Barbaresco is a good, elegant offering with spicy tobacco-tinged cherry fruit, medium body, and a lightly tannic finish. It is ideal for drinking over the next 7–8 years. Oddero's 1996 Barolo Mondoca di Bussia Soprano possesses a dark color, considerable concentration, huge body, and brutal tannin levels (thus the question mark). The wine is leathery, chunky, and rustic. If the tannin melts away without a proportional loss of fruit, this could be close to outstanding, but the astringency of the tannin is cause for concern. Anticipated maturity: 2003–2015.

Not surprisingly, the 1997s exhibit the vintage's attractive levels of glycerin, fat, low acidity, and overripe style. The 1997 Barbaresco displays a dark ruby color as well as chewy, exuberant, cherry liqueur fruit flavors intertwined with dried herb and spice notes. It is a luscious Barbaresco to enjoy over the next decade. The opaque ruby/purple-colored 1997 Barolo Mondoca di Bussia Soprano displays huge glycerin and extract, full body, copious fat, and the potential to be outstanding. Its low acidity and succulent texture suggest drinking over the next 10–15 years. The dark ruby/purple-colored 1997 Barolo Rocche dei Rivera di Castiglione is full bodied, fat, monolithic, and lacking complexity, but chewy and weighty. It is a husky Barolo to drink between 2002 and 2015. Last, the 1997 Barolo Vigna Rionda possesses high alcohol, copious quantities of cherry fruit, full body, and low acidity. While it does not reveal much complexity, it does offer gobs of fruit. More character will undoubtedly emerge after several years of bottle age. Anticipated maturity: 2001–2016.

PAITIN

1993 Barbaresco Sori Paitin	D	88

This is a modern-style Barbaresco, with clean, pure, coffee-flavored, black cherry fruit with a touch of cola. The wine's deep ruby color is followed by smoky, earthy scents as well as sweet, rich, pure, elegant cherry fruit. Drink this midweight, luscious, accessible Barbaresco over the next 6–8 years.

PARUSSO

1997 Barolo	E-EE	(89–91)
1996 Barolo	E-EE	(87–89)
1993 Barolo	D	90
1997 Barolo Bussia Vigna Fiurin	EE-EEE	(92–95)
1996 Barolo Bussia Vigna Fiurin	EE-EEE	(89–91)
1997 Barolo Bussia Vigna Munie	EE-EEE	(91–93+)
1996 Barolo Bussia Vigna Munie	EE-EEE	(91–93)
1995 Barolo Bussia Vigna Munie	EE-EEE	90
1994 Barolo Bussia Vigna Munie	D	89
1993 Barolo Bussia Vigna Munie	D	88+
1997 Barolo Bussia Vigna Rocche	EE-EEE	(91–95)
1996 Barolo Bussia Vigna Rocche	EE-EEE	(92–94)
1995 Barolo Bussia Vigna Rocche	EE-EEE	90
1994 Barolo Bussia Vigna Rocche	D	90
1993 Barolo Bussia Vigna Rocche	D	91
1997 Barolo Mariondino	EE-EEE	(91–94)

1996 Barolo Mariondino	EE–EEE	(90–92)
1995 Barolo Mariondino	EE–EEE	87
1993 Barolo Mariondino	D	89

My scores may turn out to be somewhat conservative for the quartet of yummy, succulent, gorgeously proportioned 1993 Barolos from Parusso. The 1993 Barolo offers a fragrant nose of jammy strawberry fruit intermixed with spice, fruitcake, and a Viognier-like peach/apricot note of overripeness. Cherrylike flavors are evident in this medium-bodied, intensely perfumed, sweet, quintessentially elegant and seductive wine. It is too delicious to resist, so consume it over the next 5–7 years. Made in a totally different style, the 1993 Barolo Mariondino displays a Burgundian-like, herb, cherry, and cinnamon nose, smoky, earthy notes, and round, ripe, seductive flavors. It is medium to full bodied, generous, and silky, with well-integrated acidity and tannin, a characteristic of the 1993 vintage, which has turned out far superior than I would have thought—at least for the top producers.

Parusso's excellent 1993 Barolo Bussia Munie is a denser, more closed, slightly tight wine with a deep ruby color and spicy, medium-bodied flavors that exhibit admirable ripeness and plenty of length. I recommend aging this Barolo for another 1–2 years; it should keep for 12–15. The 1993 Barolo Bussia Rocche is the biggest, richest, densest, and fullest bodied of this quartet. It is unevolved, but not as backward as the Bussia Munie. The wine reveals smoky, tar, black cherry, tobacco, trufflelike aromas, full body, outstanding concentration, and a sweet but unevolved personality and finish. This wine will offer topflight drinking between now and 2012.

Parusso produced two fine efforts in the irregular 1994 vintage. The 1994 Barolo Bussia Vigna Munie possesses a medium ruby color with lightening at the edge. It offers a fully evolved, complex nose of cedar, spice, tobacco smoke, dried herbs, and black cherry liqueur. Dense, rich, and complete, with medium body, the sweet, silky texture so prevalent in this vintage's finest examples, and heady alcohol in the finish, this is a Barolo to drink over the next 2–3 years. The 1994 Barolo Bussia Vigna Rocche is also soft but reveals more tannin and definition. Medium bodied, with more power and concentration than many 1994s, the wine offers an overall impression of charm and finesse as well as full maturity. This delicious tobacco- and cherry-scented and -flavored Barolo can be drunk now but should have a longer lifeline than most 1994s—say, 5–7 years.

Parusso told me that he thought the 1995, 1996, and 1997 vintages were all exceptional for his crus. The 1995 was shaped by excellent weather, although there was some unusual hail in August that gave some growers problems. The next year, 1996, was cooler with more moisture, but its greatness was achieved by fabulous climatic conditions at the end of September and throughout October, allowing a late harvest under virtually perfect conditions. Parusso compared 1997 with 1947 because of the extraordinary heat and the potential difficulties in fermenting grapes that were extremely high in sugar but low in acidity. Parusso, who has installed rotary fermenters, utilizes 25% new oak for his regular Barolo and 50%–70% new oak for his single-vineyard wines. As the following notes attest, these are exciting wines.

The 1995 Barolo Mariondino's medium ruby color is followed by a fragrant nose of dried herbs, tobacco, spice box, and cherry cola. Ripe, with subtle oak, medium to full body, and an expansive, fleshy, open-knit personality, this Barolo can be enjoyed over the next 7–8 years. The 1995 Barolo Bussia Vigna Munie is more opulent but just as evolved and tasty. It offers intriguing floral notes intertwined with melted tar and berry fruit. Exhibiting toasty oak and light tannin in the long finish, this lush, expansive wine can be drunk over the next decade. The 1995 Barolo Bussia Vigna Rocche is the fullest bodied, most powerful and tannic of the 1995s. In addition to the telltale dried herbs, cherry liqueur, leather, and floral scents, it offers layered, concentrated, full-bodied flavors, outstanding purity, admirable muscle and glycerin, and moderate tannin in the impressively endowed finish. Anticipated maturity: 2001–2012.

The 1996 Barolo exhibits the most new oak. Sexy, forward, and made in a lush, medium-to full-bodied style with gobs of red and black fruits, lavish wood, sweet tannin, and a concentrated, fleshy mouth-feel, it will be drinkable between 2000 and 2012. The dark ruby-colored 1996 Barolo Mariondino displays a distinctive almond, cherry liqueur, licorice, and smoky oak nose. Medium to full bodied, expansive, and pure, this classic, nicely structured, layered Barolo should be accessible young yet keep for 12–15 years. The terrific 1996 Barolo Vigna Munie is more exotic, with sweet scents of melted road tar, cherries, tobacco, and cigar box. Medium to full bodied, dense, and full of fruit, this intense wine will also be accessible young but keep for 15 or more years. Even better is the 1996 Barolo Vigna Rocche. In addition to the tar, smoke, dried herbs, leather, and cherry fruit aromas, it reveals a distinctive mineral/powdered rock character. A full-bodied, powerful Barolo that possesses superb richness, a multidimensional personality, and a boatload of tannin, this is Parusso's biggest, most concentrated 1996. There is moderate tannin in the finish, but the fruit and *terroir* characteristics dominate. Anticipated maturity: 2003–2020. While the full-bodied 1996 Barolo Bussia Vigna Fiurin is backward, tannic, and closed, it exhibits impressive potential. There is good spice, smoke, and intense fruit concentration in addition to high levels of tannin. This 1996 will require patience. Anticipated maturity: 2005–2020.

The 1997s reveal this terrific vintage's jammy, low-acid, exotic, flamboyant character. They all possess considerable tannin, but their ostentatious personalities are overwhelming. For example, tasting the dark ruby-colored, low-acid 1997 Barolo is akin to drinking strawberry jam. Ripe, fat, exotic, and hedonistic, this fruit bomb will be drinkable upon release and last until 2010. The 1997 Barolo Mariondino's opaque purple color is followed by redolent aromatics of cassis and cherry jam, smoke, earth, and dried herbs. Medium to full bodied, layered, and dense, with high levels of glycerin, extract, and a lofty degree of alcohol, this large-scale yet remarkably velvety-textured wine is nearly drinkable. Anticipated maturity: 2000–2015. In contrast, the 1997 Barolo Bussia Vigna Munie is closed, tannic, and exhibiting more oak, but what amazing concentration and intensity! This powerful Barolo behaved more like a structured, muscular 1996 than an exotic, overripe 1997. Long, pure, and in need of 5–6 years of cellaring, it should be at its finest between 2005 and 2020. The opaque purple-colored 1997 Barolo Vigna Rocche is a huge, massive, mouth-staining Barolo that should be spectacular in a decade. Sensationally rich, and oozing with glycerin, extract, alcohol, and tannin, it is phenomenally pure and amazingly well balanced. Anticipated maturity: 2006–2025. The 1997 Barolo Bussia Vigna Fiurin was closest in style to the Vigna Rocche. Extremely dense and powerful, with some noticeable new oak, the wine possesses an overwhelming level of richness, glycerin, alcohol, and tannin that leaves a hefty impression on the palate. Remarkably, this monster Barolo has no hard edges. Anticipated maturity: 2006–2025.

ELIA PASQUERO

1997 Barbaresco Sori Paitin	EE–EEE	89+
1996 Barbaresco Sori Paitin	EE–EEE	92
1995 Barbaresco Sori Paitin	D	90

A terrific 1995, the complex, fully mature, multidimensional 1995 Barbaresco from Elia Pasquero is a beautiful wine. The color is deep ruby with some lightening at the edge. The knockout nose consists of cherry liqueur intertwined with aromas of tobacco, wood fire, dried herbs, and roasted meat. Deep and lush, with no hard edges, a plump, succulent texture, medium to full body, and layers of glycerin and sweet, jammy fruit, this hedonistic, seductive Barbaresco should be drunk now and over the next 2–4 years.

At this estate, the 1996 was performing more like a 1997, and vice versa. The 1996 Barbaresco Sori Paitin exhibits terrific fruit intensity, along with toasty *pain grillé* notes in the flamboyant aromatics. In addition to oak, there is plenty of tobacco leaf, jammy cherries, and dried herbs. Full bodied, round, luscious, and accessible, this Barbaresco should drink well for a decade. The 1997 Barbaresco Sori Paitin reveals more structure and obvious tannin, as well as a dense, chocolatey, black cherry-scented nose with hints of rose petals and licorice. Spicy, deep, rich, and potentially outstanding, this wine needs 3–4 years of bottle age (atypical for a 1997). Anticipated maturity: 2003–2015. ·

LUIGI PELLISSERO

1997 Barbaresco Vanotu	EE-EEE	(86–88)
1996 Barbaresco Vanotu	EE-EEE	86?
1995 Barbaresco Vanotu	EE-EEE	85

These three mainstream Barbarescos are competent, well-made efforts. The elegant 1995 Barbaresco Vanotu exhibits dusty cherry fruit, spice, earth, and medium body. Drink it over the next 3–4 years. The 1996 Barbaresco Vanotu reveals a more stemmy, vegetal character, in addition to a lean, tannic, hard finish. I have reservations about it ever achieving full harmony. The finest of this trio is the 1997 Barbaresco Vanotu, a deep ruby-colored wine with ripe black cherry and cassis fruit, a cedary, spicy component, very good ripeness, and a moderately long finish. It should be drunk during its first 7–8 years of life.

LUIGI PIRA

1997 Barolo	E-EE	(90–91)
1996 Barolo	E-EE	91
1995 Barolo	E-EE	86
1993 Barolo Cannubi	E	90
1997 Barolo Marenga	EE-EEE	(92–95)
1996 Barolo Marenga	EE-EEE	(91–94)
1995 Barolo Marenga	EE-EEE	91+
1997 Barolo Margheria	EE-EEE	(92–95)
1996 Barolo Margheria	EE-EEE	(90–93)
1995 Barolo Margheria	EE-EEE	91
1997 Barolo Vigna Rionda	EE-EEE	(96–100)

There are so many exceptional winemakers in Barolo and Barbaresco that it is unfair to single out Luigi Pira as a star, but certainly his performances in 1995, 1996, and 1997 are remarkable. They qualify this estate as one of the leaders in Piedmont. These are wines of extraordinary complexity and breathtaking richness.

Each of Pira's wines is given a different *élevage*, although malolactic is done in either *foudre* or *barrique*. This cellar also employs rotary fermenters. The regular Barolo is kept in *foudre*, the Margheria 80% in *foudre* and 20% new cask, the Marenga 50% *foudre* and 50% new casks, and in 1997 the glorious Rionda was aged in 100% new 500-liter barrels.

Marc de Grazia is working with this estate in an attempt to resurrect the glory it attained in the late sixties and early seventies (the 1971 was legendary). The 1993 Barolo Cannubi is a more rustic, coarser style of Barolo than I suspect de Grazia prefers, but there is no doubting that there is room for this robust style as well as the more graceful, *barrique*-aged Barolos. The big, tarry, rose petal, cedar, and cherry nose jumps from the glass. In the mouth, some coarse tannin hits the palate, but it is overwhelmed by an abundance of sweet, chewy, rich, ripe fruit. This full-bodied, quasi-old-style Barolo is rustic but accessible as well as immensely satisfying. It should drink well for a dozen years.

The classic 1995s are among the superstars of that good vintage. The 1995 Barolo exhibits an evolved ruby color with some amber at the edge. It offers tobacco, licorice, and cherry fruit aromas, but the wine dries out a bit in the mouth. Fully mature, with a lean finish, it is ideal for drinking over the next 3–5 years. The 1995 Barolo Margheria reveals stunning aromas of smoky wood, truffles, cherry liqueur, cedar, and dried herbs. Evolved, with a soft, opulently-textured mouth-feel, full body, and outstanding ripeness and purity, it displays a forward, accessible style that suggests it should be drunk over the next 10–12 years. The 1995 Barolo Marenga displays rose petal notes in addition to melted asphalt, truffles, new saddle leather, and cherries. It is a layered wine with tea/coffee flavors that add nuances to the copious glycerin, rich black cherry fruit, and full-bodied, velvety texture. Anticipated maturity: 2001–2014.

In 1996 Pira appears to have hit all the sweet spots. His 1996 Barolo should prove to be an uncommon value for a sensational generic Barolo. It offers road tar, rose petal, tobacco, woodsy spices, and cherry fruit aromas that jump from the glass of this evolved, gorgeously proportioned, full-bodied effort. The dark ruby color is followed by a sweet, expansive, hedonistic wine that offers a lot of pleasure. Complex and mouth filling, it is ready to drink. Anticipated maturity: now–2012. The 1996 Barolo Margheria combines the best of the traditional style of Barolo with the more progressive modern winemaking style. The color is a saturated plum. Overripe aromas of black fruits are accompanied by scents of soy, coffee, smoke, licorice, and dried herbs. Dense and full bodied, with terrific fruit intensity, this multidimensional, layered wine is exceptionally rich yet sweet and forward. Anticipated maturity: now–2015. The 1996 Barolo Marenga is even more profound, with a dark ruby color and a sumptuous nose of jammy plum liqueur and black cherries. It is a sensual, full-bodied wine with an opulent texture, fabulous extract, and an explosive, 50-second finish. It coats the palate, is unbelievably rich in fruit, glycerin, and extract, and should prove to be a modern-day classic. Anticipated maturity: 2005–2020.

Another stunning regular Barolo, Luigi Pira's 1997 is a viscous, superbly etched, fat, juicy, succulent example with gobs of plum and black cherry fruit meshed with smoke, dried herbs, and roasted meat-like smells. Its superb ripeness, fruit-driven personality, and high glycerin and alcohol result in a sumptuous generic Barolo. Anticipated maturity: now–2012. The spectacular offerings from Pira's vineyards in and around Serralunga d'Alba are among the more riveting examples from this atypical but profoundly great year. The 1997 Barolo Margheria boasts a sensational bouquet of melted licorice, smoke, and cherry liqueur. It soars from the glass of this full-bodied, sensationally extracted, harmonious wine with no hard edges. The acidity is low, the alcohol high, and the fruit richness off the charts. This sumptuous, luxuriously rich, full-blast Barolo will become more delineated and civilized with further aging. Anticipated maturity: 2002–2020. The opaque ruby/purple colored as well as prodigious 1997 Barolo Marenga reveals massive concentration as well as more thickness and richness than the Margheria. The Marenga exhibits layers of unctuously textured fruit, extraordinary purity, low acidity, sweet tannin, and fabulous quantities of black fruit, dried herb, and cedar/leather notes. Already sumptuous, it will display more structure and tannin as some of its baby fat falls away. Anticipated maturity: 2003–2025. The 1997 Barolo Vigna Rionda is a candidate for perfection. Longtime readers may remember my ecstatic reviews of some of the Barolos produced from this vineyard by Bruno Giacosa (the 1978 is a staggering example). Pira's awesome 1997 Vigna Rionda expands the parameters that define greatness. The extraordinary nose seems more like the 1990 Cheval Blanc than a wine made from 100% Nebbiolo. Aromas of black currants, coconut, plums, dried herbs, new saddle leather, and smoke enthrall the olfactory senses. In the mouth, it is extremely full bodied and sensationally concentrated, with no hard edges and a finish that lasts for nearly a minute. While unctuous and fabulously concentrated, it does not come across as heavy-handed. The alcohol must be well above 14.5%. Given its level of glycerin, this is a Barolo for drinking over the next 20–25 years. A breathtaking wine from one of Piedmont's new superstars!

PODERI COLLA

1996 Barbera d'Alba	C 88
1993 Barolo Bussia Darda Le Rose	D 88+
1994 Bricco del Drago	C 88
1993 Bricco del Drago	C 87
1996 Nebbiolo d'Alba	C 86

I have always enjoyed these wines, and while the 1993 and 1994 are qualitatively equal, they are made in different styles. The 1993 Bricco del Drago offers an unmistakable nose of black raspberries and white chocolate scents, as well as tasty, ripe, savory, berry flavors with earth and spice. It is a medium-bodied, complex wine with a sweet personality. It is already drinking well and should continue to do so for at least a decade. The 1994 Bricco del Drago may be even better than the 1993. Although the color is similar, it appears slightly more saturated, with more purple in the middle. It possesses a chocolatey, black cherry, and raspberry nose with layers of sweet fruit. A blend of Dolcetto and Nebbiolo, it is a silky-textured, lush example of Bricco del Drago. The wine is layered, with an open-knit, exuberant, gutsy personality. It should drink well for 10–12 years. These are somewhat insiders' wines, but readers who love the wines of Piedmont should be sure to taste them.

I also tasted the 1993 Barolo Bussia Darda Le Rose. While impressive, it was extremely tannic and backward. It was one of the few Barolos I have tasted from the 1993 vintage that seems capable of lasting for at least 2 decades. A deep ruby/plum/garnet color is followed by sweet, flowery, cedary, dried cherry aromas, and ripe, medium- to full-bodied, tannic flavors with sweet fruit and glycerin, but tightly knit and backward. This is a powerful, old-style Barolo that is atypically concentrated for the vintage. Give it another 3–4 years of cellaring and drink it over the following 15–20.

Although I was unimpressed by this firm's 1995 Barbaresco Roncaglia, as well as by the 1993 and 1994 Barolo Bussia (I am sure the vintages are largely responsible), Poderi Colla produced two fine 1996s. The intriguing 1996 Barbera d'Alba is a sexy, oaky, root beer-, and white chocolate-scented wine. A medium-bodied, plum-colored wine with some amber at the edge, it is evolved, but lush, and ideal for drinking over the next 1–2 years. The 1996 Nebbiolo d'Alba also reveals some amber at the edge of its ruby/garnet color. The wine displays fine roundness, straightforward, sweet fruit, and a spicy, tobacco/cigar-scented and -flavored personality. Drink it over the next 1–2 years.

PODERI COLLA-TENUTA RONCAGLIA

1997 Barbaresco	E-EE	(80–83)
1996 Barbaresco	E-EE	(72–74)
1995 Barbaresco	E-EE	80

None of these offerings was particularly inspiring. The 1995 Barbaresco exhibits an evolved medium ruby color with considerable amber at the edge. It offers cherry syrup and roasted coffee notes presented in a medium-bodied, light, indifferent style. It should be drunk over the next 4–5 years. Surprisingly, the 1996 Barbaresco is even more evolved, already revealing considerable amber to its light ruby/garnet color. The spicy, tobacco leaf, cedary nose was more spice than fruit driven. Short in the mouth, with a compressed finish, this is an austere, attenuated Barbaresco to consume over the next 3–4 years. Sweeter, with a more open-knit texture, the 1997 Barbaresco reveals more glycerin and ripeness, but it is diluted, compressed, and narrowly constructed.

POGGIO PETORCHINO

1996 Barbera d'Alba Bricco del Merlo	D	90
1997 Dolcetto d'Alba Vigna del Mandorlo	C	87

Owned by Elvio Cogno and his son, Walter, this winery has fashioned two fine efforts. The 1997 Dolcetto d'Alba Vigna del Mandorlo is an excellent example of this underrated and satisfying dry red wine. The color is deep ruby/purple, and the wine is richly fruity, pure, medium bodied, and gushing with personality. Although not complex, it offers a significant mouthful of jammy fruit. Drink it over the next several years. The 1996 Barbera d'Alba Bricco del Merlo is sensational. The wine's dark ruby/purple color is accompanied by aromas of tomato jam, black cherries, and spice. Medium to full bodied, with no hard edges and superb fruit purity, this nicely layered Barbera should drink well for 5–6 years.

PRODUTTORI DEL BARBARESCO

1991 Barbaresco Torre	C	87
1990 Barbaresco Torre	D	89
1994 Nebbiolo delle Langhe	B	87

This is one of my favorite grower-run cooperatives in the world. Longtime readers know of the praise I have bestowed on this winery's single-vineyard Barbarescos since the 1978 vintage. There have been some superlative years for Produttori del Barbaresco, including the aforementioned 1978, but also 1979, 1982, 1985, and the great Piedmontese trilogy of 1988, 1989, and 1990. Current releases include a good value in Nebbiolo, the 1994 Nebbiolo delle Langhe. This is the type of red wine that can be served slightly chilled. It is deceptively rich and fruity, particularly after looking at the relatively feeble, light ruby color. The wine tastes of cherry jam, with a Burgundian-like sweetness, fleshiness, and spicy earthiness. Drink this delicious wine over the next 2 years.

The 1991 Barbaresco Torre is obviously not comparable to any of the wines produced by this co-op in 1990 or 1989. Nevertheless it is an attractive, fully mature, medium ruby/garnet-colored wine, with a textbook weedy, tobacco, tar, rose petal, and dried cherry fruit bouquet. Sweet on the attack, with elegant, medium-bodied, savory flavors with no hard edges, it should be consumed over the next 5–6 years. The 1990 Barbaresco Torre reveals a darker ruby color with some lightening at the edge. This ripe wine exhibits the vintage's more noteworthy maturity, as it sings with ripe, sweet, intensely jammy, cherry, gamey aromas intermingled with spice and fruitcake-like scents. Perfumed and luscious on the palate, with dry tannin in the finish, this medium- to full-bodied, concentrated, excellent Barbaresco can be drunk now as well as over the next 10–12 years. Given the stratospheric prices of high-quality Barbaresco and Barolo, these wines are very good values.

PRUNOTTO

1997 Barbaresco	E-EE	(86–88)
1996 Barbaresco	E-EE	87
1995 Barbaresco	E-EE	78
1995 Barbera d'Alba Pian Romulado	C	89

1994	Barbera d'Alba Pian Romulado	C	88
1996	Barbera d'Alba Fiulot	B	87
1997	Barolo	E–EE	(89–92)
1996	Barolo	E–EE	89+
1995	Barolo	E–EE	88
1994	Barolo	D	86
1994	Barolo Bussia	E	90
1993	Barolo Bussia	E	90
1996	Nebbiolo d'Alba Occhetti	C	89

This estate, acquired by the Antinori family of Tuscany, has had the benefit of Renzo Cotarella as its winemaker since 1991. One of the best buys from what is becoming an increasingly expensive wine region, Prunotto's 1996 Barbera d'Alba Fiulot is an unqualified success. Nearly 5,000 cases are made of this wine, which is aged briefly in stainless steel before being bottled. It is an exuberant, dark ruby/purple-colored wine with delicious notes of jammy black cherries and spices. It displays great color, a soft, luscious texture, and a tasty, medium-bodied, explosively fruity personality. It is a delicious, all-purpose wine to drink over the next 3–4 years. This is not the only fine Barbera Prunotto makes. Winemaker Renzo Cotarella reveals his allegiance to his brother Riccardo Cotarella's philosophy of extracting sweet rich fruit in the dark purple-colored, fruit-driven 1994 Barbera d'Alba Pian Romulado. Smoky, ripe, and luscious, with a sense of elegance, but also intense and layered, this is a beautifully pure, super wine from the 1994 vintage that is meant to be drunk now as well as over the next 3–4 years.

Prunotto's 1993 Barolo Bussia is one of the more outstanding wines from this above average to good Piedmontese vintage. Revealing a dark ruby color with garnet at the edge, it offers up a sweet, cherry, spice-driven, gamey, tobacco-scented nose, followed by a fleshy, medium- to full-bodied wine with low acidity and a smoky, long, heady finish. It should drink well for 5–7 years.

This winery has been producing better wines, particularly since its acquisition by Tuscany's Antinori family. While the wines have become more fruit driven, they have not lost any of their varietal or *terroir* characteristics. The impressive 1995 Barbera d'Alba Pian Romulado is a *barrique*-aged, single-vineyard Barbera. Made in a sexy, seductive style, it exhibits a saturated purple color, followed by a knockout nose of blackberries and spice. Velvety textured, with rich, chewy flavors, outstanding purity and ripeness, and a lusty finish, this offering should be consumed over the next 2–3 years. Equally fine is the 1996 Nebbiolo d'Alba Occhetti. This unfiltered, deep ruby/garnet-colored wine displays an elegant, spicy, smoky, dried herb, black cherry, and raspberry nose. In the mouth, hints of licorice, floral scents, and fruitcake combine with the wine's jammy fruit. This harmonious, medium- to full-bodied wine should continue to drink well for 5–7 years.

Prunotto's 1994 Barolos are among the more successful wines from that tricky vintage. The straightforward 1994 Barolo reveals scents of earth, tea, black cherries, leather, and spice. The wine is medium bodied, elegant, and soft. It should be drunk over the next 3–4 years. The outstanding 1994 Barolo Bussia could have emerged from a far better vintage given its ripeness, purity, and harmonious personality. It boasts a deep ruby/garnet color as well as a sweet, penetrating nose of black fruits, cherries, rose petals, and white truffles. The wine is almost sweet because of its high glycerin level and ripe tannin. Nicely textured, rich, full bodied, and gorgeous to drink, this unfiltered Barolo will offer hedonistic satisfaction for at least another 4–5 years.

Given how well Prunotto's wines have performed in vintages such as 1993 and 1994, I expected more from the following years. The 1995 Barbaresco reveals soft, tobacco-tinged cherry fruit, moderate concentration, and a lean, compressed, diluted, austere finish. Drink it over the next 5–6 years. The dark ruby-colored 1996 Barbaresco exhibits attractive cherry fruit in the nose along with notes of cedar, roasted almonds, and herbs. Well made, pure, and medium bodied, with moderate tannin in the angular finish, it should be at its finest between 2000 and 2008. The spicy, soft, richly fruity, dark ruby-colored 1997 Barbaresco offers copious quantities of cherry, strawberry, and cassis fruit, dried herbs, and new saddle leather characteristics, but not much depth or intensity. It is very good, but hardly inspiring, particularly in this vintage. Drink it over the next 7–8 years.

Two of the three Barolos are foursquare, monolithic, and lacking the character I have come to expect from Prunotto's wines. The 1995 Barolo is an elegant, lighter-style example with attractive, smoke-tinged, herbaceous, cherry fruit, medium body, and an earthy, *terroir*-driven personality. Moderate tannin in the finish suggests aging is necessary, but this wine does not have the stuffing for extended cellaring. Drink it over the next 5–6 years. The 1996 Barolo exhibits more minerality, along with black cherries and melted road tar notes. Medium to full bodied, spicy, rich, and potentially very good, it is foursquare and simple. Perhaps more complexity will emerge with bottle age. Anticipated maturity: 2003–2014. The exotic 1997 Barolo offers aromas of licorice, smoke, and overripe black cherries, powerful, concentrated, moderately tannic flavors, good glycerin and extraction, and a spicy, well-endowed, concentrated finish. Anticipated maturity: 2002–2014.

RENATO RATTI

1993	Barolo Marcenasco	E	86
1997	Barolo Marcenasco Rocche	EE-EEE	(90–93)
1996	Barolo Marcenasco Rocche	EE-EEE	(90–91)
1995	Barolo Marcenasco Rocche	EE-EEE	88
1993	Barolo Rocche	E	85

Cherry, tobacco, spice cake, earth, and herbs are all present in this medium- to full-bodied, dry, angular, yet complex 1993 Barolo Marcenasco. As with many 1993s, after the sweet attack, the wine becomes angular and compressed in the finish. It should be consumed over the next 2–3 years. The feeble-looking 1993 Barolo Rocche possesses a light ruby color with plenty of amber at the edge. (The color could be mistaken for a 20-year-old Barolo.) The nose offers up good quantities of tar, rose petals, and cherry fruit intertwined with cedar, tobacco, and spice. The wine is dry, medium bodied, and tannic but is clearly meant to be drunk over the next several years before more fruit fades.

The 1995 Barolo Marcenasco Rocche is a very good wine for the vintage, offering aromas of tobacco smoke, cedar, spice, and lively, sweet jammy cherry notes. There is excellent richness, an open-knit, round personality, a sweet midpalate, and ripe tannin in the moderately long, medium- to full-bodied finish. Drinkable already, this Barolo promises to evolve for 8–10 years. The 1996 Barolo Marcenasco Rocche exhibits a more impressively endowed ruby/purple color and an aggressive nose of roasted herbs, spices, and black cherry and berry fruit. Full bodied, with subtle oak in the background, this dense, concentrated, highly extracted wine is a classic. Anticipated maturity: 2004–2018. The blockbuster 1997 Barolo Marcenasco Rocche boasts a dense ruby/purple color in addition to an exotic blackberry and cherry jam/kirsch liqueur, dried herbs, cedar, and spicy vanillin bouquet. This deep, opulently textured, low-acid, full-bodied wine is oozing with extract and richness. While it is easy to drink, it will become more tannic and delineated as it evolves. Anticipated maturity: 2003–2020.

FRATELLI REVELLO

1997	Barolo	E-EE	(88–90)
1996	Barolo	E-EE	88
1995	Barolo	E-EE	90
1994	Barolo	D	88
1993	Barolo	D	90+
1997	Barolo Conca	EE-EEE	(90–92)
1997	Barolo Vigna Giachini	EE-EEE	(90–93)
1996	Barolo Vigna Giachini	EE-EEE	90
1995	Barolo Vigna Giachini	EE-EEE	89+
1994	Barolo Vigna Giachini	D	88
1997	Barolo Vigna Rocche	EE-EEE	(92–96)
1996	Barolo Vigna Rocche	EE-EEE	91+

This small winery in La Morra is owned by two brothers who have approximately 17 acres of vines. The brothers Revello were new to me when I first tasted their 1993 Barolo, but I was wowed by their deep, more backward, superbly concentrated Barolo. It is one of the few 1993s to require 2–3 years of cellaring. The wine boasts a dense garnet/ruby color, a smoky, tar, spice, underbrush, and sour cherry nose, full body, chewy, fleshy, corpulent flavors, considerable extract, and a spicy, tannic finish. It possesses the charm, equilibrium, and harmony characteristic of the 1993 vintage, as well as more muscle. Drink it between now and 2015.

The 1994 Barolo is a medium ruby-colored wine, with the vintage's telltale evolved personality. However, it is sexier than many of the 1994s I have tasted, with plenty of smoky, jammy cherry fruit, medium body, a voluptuous texture, and a low-acid, lush finish with heady alcohol. It requires near-term consumption. Slightly richer is the 1994 Barolo Vigna Giachini. This wine adds floral and spicy new oak aromas to those of cherry liqueur, tar, and cigar box scents. Bigger and richer than its sibling, it possesses full body, excellent fruit purity, fine length, and 3–5 years of drinkability. It, too, should be consumed over the near term.

Like the other generic Barolos from Revello, the 1995 Barolo was aged in 2–3-year-old oak casks. A successful wine for the vintage, it exhibits a sexy, explosive, Bing cherry-scented nose with notes of chocolate, black tea, and spicy oak. Lush and round, it is not dissimilar from some of the idiosyncratic, opulent 1997s. This evolved 1995 should be consumed over the next 5–6 years. The medium-bodied 1995 Barolo Vigna Giachini is a more tannic, restrained example, with a moderate ruby color revealing amber at the edge. The moderately scented bouquet reveals notes of tobacco, dried herbs, and cherry fruit. This closed Barolo needs another 1–2 years of bottle age. It should drink well for 10–12 years.

The 1996 Barolo offers a tangy, black cherry-scented nose with hints of smoke, earth, and leather. Spicy, medium bodied, and moderately tannic, it is more structured and muscular than its more evolved 1995 sibling. Anticipated maturity: 2002–2008. The dark ruby-colored 1997 Barolo exhibits a sweet nose of overripe cherry fruit, Asian spices, and, surprisingly, cassis. A heady, low-acid, silky-textured Barolo with plenty of fat and alcohol, it should drink well during its first 7–8 years of life.

Revello's single-vineyard crus in both 1996 and 1997 are exceptional. Readers who prefer more structure, muscle, and tannin will prefer the 1996s; those who like flamboyant, spectacularly rich, nearly overripe, jammy wines with huge quantities of glycerin and extract will enjoy the 1997s. The 1996 Barolo Vigna Giachini reveals a deep ruby color as well as a muscular, powerfully scented nose of cherry fruit, cedar, fruitcake, dried herbs, and licorice. In the mouth, tobacco flavors make an appearance. This wine is layered, full bodied, opulent, and dense, with most of the tannin concealed by high extraction and concentration. It is a wine of strength and symmetry with a superb inner core of fruit. Anticipated maturity: 2002–2020. The 1996 Barolo Vigna Rocche is extremely fragrant, offering dried herb, jammy cherry fruit, smoke, Asian spices, and new saddle leather aromas. In the mouth, there is superb purity, full body, and huge amounts of tannin. This backward, dense, monster-size Barolo will be at its finest between 2005 and 2020.

The dense, dark ruby-colored 1997 Barolo Vigna Giachini offers up toasty new oak, black fruit, kirsch, licorice, smoke, and roasted spice scents. Exceptionally lush, with great purity, full body, and oodles of glycerin, this intense, low-acid, plump wine coats the palate. Anticipated maturity: now–2015. The limited-production 1997 Barolo Conca is another flamboyantly sweet, toasty, powerful wine with abundant fruit, medium to full body, low acidity, and a layered, velvety texture. It should drink well for 12–15 years. My tasting notes say the 1997 Barolo Vigna Rocche is "out of sight!" The color is a saturated ruby/purple. The spectacular nose reveals kirsch liqueur intermixed with smoke, *pain grillé*, incense, new saddle leather, tobacco, and black tea. There is massive body, extraordinary symmetry and balance for a wine of such richness, and a blockbuster finish that lasts over 45 seconds. This sensational, multidimensional Barolo will give untold pleasure for at least 2 decades. An amazing wine!

GIUSEPPE RINALDI

1991 Barolo Brunate	D 85

In great vintages Giuseppe Rinaldi is capable of producing spectacular wines, but this 1991 Barolo is good rather than inspirational. The advanced medium garnet/ruby color is followed by fully mature aromas of tea, herbs, and sweet, dried cherry fruit. Medium bodied, and somewhat compressed and pinched on the palate, this spicy, fully mature Barolo should be drunk over the next 2–3 years.

GIUSEPPE RIVETTI

1995 Barbaresco La Spinetta	EE-EEE	87
1997 Barbaresco Valeirani	EE-EEE	(90–92)
1997 Barbaresco Vigneto Gallina	EE-EEE	(90–92)
1996 Barbaresco Vigneto Gallina	EE-EEE	90
1997 Barbaresco Vigneto Starderi	EE-EEE	90+
1996 Barbaresco Vigneto Starderi	EE-EEE	90

Rivetti's medium garnet/ruby-colored 1995 Barbaresco La Spinetta exhibits a sweet, evolved nose of spicy oak, cherry liqueur, tobacco, and vanillin. Expansive (13.5% alcohol), ripe, and long, with copious quantities of fruit, this medium- to full-bodied Barbaresco should drink well now and over the next 8–10 years.

The classic structure and power of the vintage is well displayed in both of Rivetti's 1996 Barbarescos. The 1996 Barbaresco Vigneto Starderi's deep ruby color is followed by an explosive nose of sweet cherry liqueur, vanillin, and wood smoke. This full-bodied, highly extracted, intense, sexy, moderately tannic wine is powerful yet well balanced. Despite its ability to improve for 10–15 years, it is easy to drink at present. The terrifically fruity, more flattering 1996 Barbaresco Vigneto Gallina is full bodied, with outstanding concentration, plenty of earthy, plum/cherry, smoky, spice notes, low acidity, and moderate tannin in the layered finish. It should drink well for a dozen or more years.

In 1997 Rivetti added another single-vineyard Barbaresco called Valeirani. The 1997 is a fat, seductive, supple, low-acid style of Barbaresco that will be ready to drink upon release. It possesses terrific fruit purity, gorgeous aromatics (black fruits, smoke, weedy tobacco, vanillin), mouth-coating levels of glycerin, and at least 14% alcohol. Drink this hedonistic offering during its first 10–12 years of life. The more backward 1997 Barbaresco Vigneto Starderi displays more tannin and structure, a deep saturated plum/ruby color, and earth, new wood spice, and black cherry liqueur notes in the restrained but impressively ripe and pure aromatics. With high alcohol, tannin, and a reserved, structured finish, this heady Barbaresco should be at its best between 2001 and 2012. The most muscular, full bodied, and heaviest of these three single-vineyard efforts is the 1997 Barbaresco Vigneto Gallina. It offers a knockout nose of cherry liqueur/kirsch intermixed with roasted nuts, cigar smoke, and dried herbs. Full bodied, masculine, and powerful, with high tannin and extraordinary extraction and richness, this multidimensional, compelling Barbaresco will drink well between 2002 and 2018.

There are two Rivetti wines that are worth seeking out. The 1997 Barbera Gallina (93) is an explosive blackberry-scented wine that is all glycerin, fruit, and alcohol. Only 5,000 bottles were produced, but it is one of the most decadently rich Barberas I have ever tasted. It should drink well for a decade. About 200 cases were made of the 1996 Pin (89+), a proprietary red wine blend of 50% Nebbiolo, 25% Cabernet Sauvignon, and 25% Barbera. The color is a saturated black/purple, and the wine is tannic and backward, made in a Médoc-like style. Although rich, it was closed and revealing too much oak to merit an outstanding score (it was brought up in 100% new oak casks).

These are all very well-made offerings from one of Piedmont's young stars.

ALBINO ROCCA

1997	Barbaresco Vigneto Brich Ronchi	EE-EEE	(94–97)
1996	Barbaresco Vigneto Brich Ronchi	EE-EEE	93
1995	Barbaresco Vigneto Brich Ronchi	EE-EEE	87
1993	Barbaresco Vigneto Brich Ronchi	D	94
1997	Barbaresco Vigneto Loreto	EE-EEE	(92–94)
1996	Barbaresco Vigneto Loreto	EE-EEE	91
1995	Barbaresco Vigneto Loreto	EE-EEE	89

On my last visit to Albino Rocca, one of my favorite Piedmontese producers, I was impressed with his 1995s but blown away by the quality of the 1996s and 1997s, two extraordinary vintages for both Piedmont and Albino Rocca. The 1995 Barbaresco Vigneto Loreto is a dark ruby/purple-colored offering with a sweet nose of cedar, Provençal herbs, chocolate, smoky, jammy, black cherry fruit, and new oak. The wine is full bodied, rich, round, and ideal for drinking now and over the next 7–8 years. The 1995 Barbaresco Vigneto Brich Ronchi is a more structured and noticeably tannic wine with a moderately intense nose of cedar, black cherries, and dried herbs. It has a long aftertaste but seems closed and is less seductive than the Vigneto Loreto. This is one 1995 that requires 1–2 years of cellaring; it should keep for a dozen years.

In contrast with the 100% barrique-aged Brich Ronchi, the 1996 Barbaresco Vigneto Loreto is aged in moderately large foudres. This dazzling, sexy offering possesses an opaque ruby/purple color, terrific fruit and purity, and enough glycerin and concentrated flavors to conceal moderate levels of tannin. The black cherry characteristic combined with smoke, cedar, and fruitcake smells is to die for. This full-bodied, intense Barbaresco will get even better over the next several years and will age for 14–15 years. The large-scale as well as compelling 1996 Barbaresco Vigneto Brich Ronchi reveals spectacular aromas of intense chocolate-covered cherry candy-like notes intermixed with smoky new wood. It is dense and full bodied, with layers of concentration and glycerin. This superb, mouth-filling Barbaresco can be drunk now or cellared for 10–15 years.

Just when I thought it couldn't get any better, Albino Rocca's 1997 Barbarescos broke new ground for wine quality. The saturated ruby/purple-colored 1997 Barbaresco Vigneto Loreto boasts huge, soaring aromatics of black fruits, spices, flowers, and dried herbs. Extremely full bodied, with silky tannin, phenomenal extract, great purity, and a seamless, velvety texture, this explosively rich fruit bomb will be impossible to resist young. A prodigious wine, it will last for 10–15 years. Like the 1996, the 1997 Barbaresco Vigneto Brich Ronchi reveals a chocolate-covered cherry candy-like nose. A classic effort, with some overripeness but beautifully balanced with low acidity and an expansive, plush mouth-feel, this full-bodied, fabulously concentrated wine represents the essence of the Nebbiolo grape. It is the kind of rarity that makes 1997 such an original vintage, combining atypicity with extraordinary hedonistic and intellectually compelling qualities. Anticipated maturity: now–2012.

The 1993 is an awesome Barbaresco! From the huge, fragrant, chocolate, cedar, allspice, tobacco, and black cherry nose to the wealth of sweet, jammy fruit packed into this full-bodied, seamless, velvety-textured wine, this is the kind of Barbaresco that makes me think Nebbiolo is Italy's answer to a prodigious Pinot Noir. Deeply colored, with an opaque ruby/garnet center, this gorgeously proportioned Barbaresco is drinking beautifully now, but it promises to age well for 10–15 years.

BRUNO ROCCA

1996	Barbaresco Coparossa	EE-EEE	(89–91)
1995	Barbaresco Coparossa	EE-EEE	89
1997	Barbaresco Rabaja	EE-EEE	(88–90)
1996	Barbaresco Rabaja	EE-EEE	87
1995	Barbaresco Rabaja	EE-EEE	88

These are all intelligently made, modern-style Barbarescos, with the new oak component well meshed with the wines' other elements. The 1995 Barbaresco Coparossa is a sexy, opulently styled wine with notes of *garrigue* (an earthy/herb mélange), cedar, coffee, smoke, and jammy fruit. Round and opulently styled, with a lush texture, a forward, evolved personality, and fine glycerin and depth, this alluring Barbaresco can be drunk now and over the next 6–7 years. The 1996 Barbaresco Coparossa is slightly higher in alcohol, more muscular, and, while not as sexy and forward as the 1995, potentially a better wine. Full bodied, with cherry cough syrup, tobacco, earth, and hints of white truffle aromas, this nicely layered wine possesses a muscular mouth-feel, no hard edges, and moderately sweet tannin in the long finish. Anticipated maturity: 2001–2012.

Because the oak was more obvious, and the wine less exotic and forward than its sibling, the 1995 Coparossa, the 1995 Barbaresco Rabaja was more subdued. It offered interesting balsam wood, cherry, *pain grillé*, and spice notes, as well as medium body, attractive sweet fruit, very good purity, and a well-endowed but tightly knit finish. Anticipated maturity: 2000–2009. The 1996 Barbaresco Rabaja exhibits toasty new oak, jammy cherry scents, dried herbs, and spice. Ripe and tightly structured, with medium body and a muscular, astringent, well-delineated finish, it should drink well between 2002 and 2012. The 1997 Barbaresco Rabaja is more structured and tannic than typical for this vintage. It displays sweet black cherry fruit in the nose, along with noticeable new oak. Powerful, tannic, and dense, this offering may merit an outstanding rating if it develops more complexity and the tannin becomes better integrated. This is unquestionably the most backward of the Bruno Rocca offerings. Anticipated maturity: 2004–2016.

SANDRONE

1997 Barolo Cannubi Boschis	EE-EEE	(94–96)
1996 Barolo Cannubi Boschis	EE-EEE	(94–96)
1995 Barolo Cannubi Boschis	EE-EEE	89
1994 Barolo Cannubi Boschis	E	90
1993 Barolo Cannubi Boschis	E	92
1997 Barolo Le Vigne	EE-EEE	(94–96)
1996 Barolo Le Vigne	EE-EEE	(90–92)
1995 Barolo Le Vigne	EE-EEE	90
1993 Barolo Le Vigne	E	92

Sandrone has been performing at a superstar level since the 1982 vintage, but in 1993 he had significantly more competition from—his best friends. Nevertheless, his two 1993s are near the top of the qualitative pyramid for the 1993 vintage. The dark ruby-colored 1993 Barolo Cannubi Boschis is reserved, but it reveals a sweet, elegant nose of roasted meats and nuts intermixed with scents of underbrush and black fruits. As the wine sits in the glass, notes of melted tar and rose petals emerge. More firmly structured than many 1993s, it is full bodied, with considerable character, outstanding concentration, and an expansive inner core of sweet fruit. Cellar it for 1–3 more years and drink it over the subsequent 15+. More precocious and exotic, Sandrone's 1993 Barolo Le Vigne is a blend of five separate parcels. It boasts a dark ruby color, a Pomerol-like sweet, chocolatey, coffee, and jammy black cherry bouquet, medium to full body, a lush, soft texture, and a heady, rich finish. It should reach its plateau of maturity in 2–3 years and last for 12–15.

Sandrone's 1994 is a feminine-style, elegant Barolo with a medium ruby color and an attractive, smoky, black cherry, and raspberry nose. Mineral and new oak notes are also apparent in the wine's fragrance. In the mouth, it is expansive and long, with considerable finesse and elegance. Not a blockbuster in the style of the 1990, it is an elegantly wrought wine with outstanding purity and harmony. Drink it over the next 4–5 years.

In more recent vintages, one of the great masters of Piedmont has again turned in exemplary efforts. For his wine's upbringing, Sandrone utilizes about 10% new oak, with the balance aged in *foudres*. He is not a member of the group that uses rotary fermenters, preferring open-top fermenters, and doing considerable pumping over and punching down to extract flavor and color (the Burgundian method). To my surprise, in the 1995 and 1997 vintages I enjoyed his Barolo Le Vigne as much as his renowned Cannubi Boschis. In 1995 I actually had a slight preference for the Barolo Le Vigne. The classic 1995 Barolo Le Vigne offers telltale aromas of tar, rose petals, and cherry liqueur, medium to full body, a silky, open, accessible style, sweet, expansive flavors, a gorgeous texture, and a classic finish with no hard edges. It is a beautifully made Barolo that can be drunk now or cellared for 10–15 years. The 1995 Barolo Cannubi Boschis is more backward but may turn out to be just as exciting, if not more so. Although full bodied, it was extremely closed and difficult to penetrate. It possesses a dark ruby color in addition to plenty of dried herb, balsam wood, and black cherry aromas and flavors. While it is unquestionably excellent, possibly outstanding, it needs 4–5 years of cellaring; it should keep for 15 or more years.

The dark ruby/purple-colored 1996 Barolo Le Vigne is an elegant, large-scale Barolo with everything in balance. There is sweet tannin and a measured yet powerful, rich style with copious amounts of black fruits intermixed with minerals, spice, and dried herbs. The wine is tight and in need of 3–4 years of cellaring. Anticipated maturity: 2004–2018. The spectacular 1996 Barolo Cannubi Boschis offers aromas of cassis, cherry liqueur, and flowers. In the mouth, it is dense, superb, and full bodied, with fabulous intensity and layers of extract. Muscular, concentrated, broad, and powerful, it demands 5–6 years of cellaring. Anticipated maturity: 2006–2020.

Both of Sandrone's 1997s are extraordinarily sumptuous, glycerin-imbued, fat, full-bodied wines with up-front appeal. But don't be fooled. Both are loaded with tannin and in need of cellaring. The 1997 Barolo Le Vigne's saturated ruby/purple color is accompanied by a terrific nose of blackberries and cherry fruit intertwined with minerals and spice. The wine possesses amazing levels of glycerin, low acidity, lofty alcohol, and good fatness. This powerful, concentrated Barolo should be at its finest between 2003 and 2018. The 1997 Barolo Cannubi Boschis is equally rich but even more backward. Massive in the mouth, oozing glycerin and extract, with blackberry and cherry fruit meshed with dried herb, mineral, and subtle oak notes, this huge, chewy, unctuously textured, powerful wine will drink well between 2003 and 2020.

SANT AGATA

1997 Na Vota Ruche di Castagnole Monferrato	**C**	**86**

This soft, cherry- and earth-scented and -flavored wine is produced from an obscure indigenous varietal, Ruche, which is grown in the Piedmont region. The wine is tasty, soft, and ideal for drinking over the next several years.

PAOLO SCAVINO

1997 Barolo	E-EE	(90–92)
1996 Barolo	E-EE	(89–90)
1995 Barolo	E-EE	90
1997 Barolo Bric del Fiasc	EE-EEE	(93–96)
1996 Barolo Bric del Fiasc	EE-EEE	(91–94)
1995 Barolo Bric del Fiasc	EE-EEE	91+
1994 Barolo Bric del Fiasc	E	91
1993 Barolo Bric del Fiasc	E	95
1997 Barolo Cannubi	EE-EEE	(95–96)
1996 Barolo Cannubi	EE-EEE	(90–93)
1995 Barolo Cannubi	EE-EEE	91
1994 Barolo Cannubi	E	90
1993 Barolo Cannubi	E	92+
1997 Barolo Rocche dell Annunziata	EE-EEE	(95–96)
1996 Barolo Rocche dell Annunziata	EE-EEE	(94–96)
1995 Barolo Rocche dell Annunziata	EE-EEE	92
1993 Barolo Rocche Annunziata Riserva	?	94

Paolo Scavino, his wife, and his two daughters run this 8-hectare (20 acres) estate, which has been producing extraordinary Barolos since the beginning of the decade. At this modern-style domaine, Scavino employs rotary fermenters with paddles, temperature-controlled fermentation, and malolactic in *barrique*. All the top Barolos spend time in *barrique* (approximately 30% new oak) and are bottled without filtration. If readers have not yet discovered Scavino's Barolos, they are fabulous wines.

While the 1993s may not possess the power, intensity, and extract of the great 1990s, qualitatively they are equals. For example, the 1993 Barolo Rocche Annunziata Riserva is one of the great Barolos of the vintage. The wine is deep, dark garnet/ruby colored, with a stunningly sweet nose of lead pencil, black currants, cherries, smoke, roasted meats, toast, and vanillin. Made from 56-year-old vines, it is broad, rich, and packed with fruit and extract. Full bodied and broodingly deep and intense, this compelling Barolo manages to marry power and richness with a sense of elegance, harmony, and finesse. It needs another 1–2 years of bottle age and should drink well for 15+ years. Sixty-six percent new oak casks were used for this vineyard.

The 1993 Barolo Cannubi (50% new oak casks) is the most backward wine of this trio. The dark ruby/purple color is followed by a nose that reluctantly gives up aromas of smoke, earth, and black cherries. The wine makes a beautiful impression with its display of richness and well-integrated tannin and acidity. The finish lasts for nearly a minute. This is a youthful as well as one of the least evolved Barolos I tasted. It will require 2–4 years of cellaring when released and will drink well for 15–20 years.

The awesome 1993 Barolo Bric del Fiasc (one-third new oak casks) is a candidate for the Barolo of the vintage. Made from 45-year-old vines, this full-bodied, blockbuster Barolo is amazingly rich, superbly balanced, and oh, so profound. The fragrant, penetrating bouquet of black cherries, new saddle leather, tar, and rose petals, intermixed with subtle spicy toast, is followed by an exceptionally rich, medium- to full-bodied wine with terrific delineation and focus, as well as gorgeously integrated acidity, tannin, and alcohol. This dazzling young Barolo should reach full maturity in 5–6 years and last for 15+.

Scavino's splendid 1993s have been followed by strong efforts in the more difficult vintage of 1994. The 1994 Barolo Cannubi boasts a deep ruby/garnet color as well as a fragrant bouquet of smoked herbs, sweet berry/cherry fruit, licorice, and spice box notes. Rich, concentrated, and layered, this medium- to full-bodied, pure, lush, silky smooth Barolo is ideal for drinking now and over the next 3–4 years. The 1994 Barolo Bric del Fiasc reveals a Château Margaux–like nose of violets, black currants, asphalt, and toasty new oak. In the mouth, it is deep, rich, and full bodied, with the vintage's telltale silky texture, low acidity, and up-front, evolved personality. This deep, concentrated, layered, yet voluptuously textured Barolo is already delicious. Anticipated maturity: now–2004.

The medium ruby-colored 1995 Barolo is an expansive, evolved, aromatic offering with notes of cedar and balsam wood, sweet cherry jam, and rose petals. The light color is deceptive given its intense bouquet and expansive, lush, concentrated style. It will not be long-lived, but for drinking over the next 7–8 years, this is a seductive, hedonistically styled Barolo. The 1995 Barolo Cannubi is one of the sexiest Scavino 1995s. The dark ruby color is accompanied by a sumptuous nose of tobacco smoke, coffee, black fruits, and *pain grillé*. The wine is dense, velvety textured, full bodied, and silky, with no hard edges. This is a voluptuous wine to enjoy over the next decade. The 1995 Barolo Bric del Fiasc is the most backward of the 1995s, with notes of smoke, tar, soy, jammy black cherry and blackberry fruit, and *pain grillé*. Full bodied, concentrated, expansive, soft, and seductive, with 13.5% alcohol and moderate tannin in the finish, I would opt for drinking it over the next 10–12 years. The superb 1995 Barolo Rocche dell Annunziata boasts a dark ruby color as well as terrific extract, full body, and copious quantities of glycerin. While it possesses the velvety, evolved personality of the other 1995s, there is more stuffing and richness, but fewer nuances. Give it another 1–2 years of bottle age and drink it over the next 12–14. Already complex and approachable, the 1995 Scavino Barolos are all sensual, Burgundian-like, fragrant, forward wines with fine balance.

Given the vintage differences, one might expect the 1996s to be fuller bodied, more powerful and concentrated wines with greater aging potential. Scavino produced one of the great wines of this classic year, the 1996 Barolo Rocche dell Annunziata. The color is a healthy dark ruby. The nose offers scents of smoky charcoal, licorice, *pain grillé*, black cherries, incense, tobacco, and leather. Full bodied and massive, with superb balance, nicely integrated acidity and tannin, and a finish that goes on for nearly a minute, this is a profound Barolo to drink now and over the next 2 decades. Nearly as spectacular is the 1996 Barolo Bric del Fiasc. It displays a saturated plum color, a smoky, black cherry-scented nose, explosive, fleshy flavors with plenty of glycerin, a more evolved and seductive character than the larger-scale Annunziata, extraordinary intensity, and impeccable balance. Exotic Asian spice and fruitcake aromas add to its complexity. Anticipated maturity: 2001–2018. The dark plum/ruby-colored 1996 Barolo Cannubi possesses exceptional extract and cherries galore intermixed with smoke, tobacco, and new saddle leather scents. This full-bodied, supple-textured, glorious Barolo can be drunk now or cellared for 15–16 years. With more of a fruit-driven personality, the generic 1996 Barolo is also outstanding. Sexy and forward, it does not possess the complexity and stature of the three single-vineyard offerings, but it is a wonderful introduction to the Scavino style. It should age nicely for 10–12 years.

Scavino calls his 1997 Barolos "big and fat." He is one of many Piedmontese producers who has had a hard time trying to understand these wines, which are aberrations in terms of their sumptuous richness, viscous personalities, and high-alcohol, low-acid styles. The 1997 Barolo offers an exotic nose of incense, Asian spices, cherry liqueur, and jam. Full bodied and overripe, with low acidity, spectacular fruit and glycerin, and high alcohol, it is a lusty, knockout Barolo to drink over the next 7–10 years. One of the vintage's most profound wines, the 1997 Barolo Cannubi boasts a dense ruby color with purple nuances, as well as an explosive nose of cedar, saddle leather, soy, and copious quantities of jammy black fruits. In the mouth, it is huge, chewy, and unctuously textured, with unreal levels of glycerin and fruit. Compared to the wine's blockbuster richness, the tannin in the finish seems incidental. This behemoth should drink well between 2001 and 2018. The fabulous, saturated ruby/purple-colored 1997 Barolo Bric del Fiasc displays a terrific bouquet of tobacco-tinged tar and black cherry fruit. It is a huge, massive, concentrated Barolo with multiple layers of richness. Like all of Scavino's 1997 Barolos, the alcohol level is a whopping 15%–15.6%, yet these dry wines are neither overripe nor heavy. Magnificently concentrated, they are likely to become more civilized and delineated with aging. While the 1997 is almost too sumptuous to resist, it is only hinting at its ultimate potential. Anticipated maturity: 2001–2017. The limited-production 1997 Barolo Rocche dell Annunziata exhibits a dark plum/purple color and a flamboyant nose of Asian spices, cedar, *pain grillé*, black fruits, and dried herbs. Powerful, with stunning levels of fruit, glycerin, extract, and alcohol, low acidity, and a finish that lasts nearly a minute, this awesome Barolo redefines this varietal's parameters. Anticipated maturity: 2001–2018.

As a postscript, I had the opportunity to taste a minivertical of Scavino's Barolo Bric del Fiasc, from the 1990, 1989, 1988, 1985, and 1982 vintages. All of these wines were made in the old style, without aging in small oak casks. The 1990 may be the wine with the greatest raw material. While it matches the complexity of the 1993, I do not believe Barolo can be any more concentrated than Scavino's 1990 Bric del Fiasc (rated 95+ in October 1996). The wine is a huge, youthful Barolo of massive proportions. It is gorgeous! The 1989 (rated 92+) was also spectacular, although more tannic, without the wealth of glycerin, extract, and massive fruit of the 1990. However, these two siblings should age effortlessly for 20–30+ years. How fortunate readers owning both vintages will be to have an opportunity to compare them as they evolve. The 1988 (rated 91+) was also dense, big, and tannic, as well as slightly more rustic and coarse. It is an impressive, muscular, rich Barolo. The 1985 (rated 89) reveals a certain flatness and, to my taste, was fully mature. It is not the first time I have tasted a 1985

Barolo or Barbaresco that has not lived up to expectations. Nevertheless it is one of the finest and most complex-tasting Barolos of that vintage—a year that appears to be on a fast evolutionary track. The 1982 (rated 92) was sensational. Clearly an old-style Barolo with gobs of cedar, herbs, tobacco, leather, and cherry fruit, this full-bodied, powerful, rustic, but immensely rich, chewy Barolo has reached its plateau of full maturity. However, I expect this wine to continue to drink splendidly well for another 10–15 years.

MAURO SEBASTE

1997 Barolo Monvigliero	EE-EEE	(88–91)
1996 Barolo Monvigliero	EE-EEE	(87–89)
1995 Barolo Monvigliero	EE-EEE	87
1997 Barolo Prapo	EE-EEE	(90–91+)
1996 Barolo Prapo	EE-EEE	(90–92)
1995 Barolo Prapo	EE-EEE	89
1997 Barolo La Serra	EE-EEE	(88–91)

This small producer tends to produce wines that reflect the finest aspects of both the traditional and more modern school of winemaking. Sebaste's total production is about 1,200 cases. The 1995 Barolo Monvigliero reveals an evolved garnet color with a pink/amber edge, in addition to expansive aromas of meats, dried herbs, spice, cedar, and cherries. There is excellent fruit in the mouth, medium to full body, a supple texture, and a fine finish. Drink this accessible Barolo over the next 5–7 years. The dense plum/ruby/purple-colored 1996 Barolo Monvigliero exhibits surprising softness and notes of sweet cherry jam, smoke, cigar box, cedar, and fennel in the fragrant bouquet. Lush, ripe, medium to full bodied, and a bit longer and more weighty than the 1995, it should be drinkable between now and 2011. The vintage's opulence is well displayed in the 1997 Barolo Monvigliero. The color is a dark ruby, and the wine is exotically rich, ripe, and obviously a creation of its vintage's condition more than its *terroir*. The creamy, fat, succulent texture, gorgeously ripe fruit, and long, glycerin-imbued finish are admirable. It is a candidate for an outstanding rating after bottling. Anticipated maturity: now–2012.

Sebaste's Barolos from the Prapo vineyard are fuller bodied, bigger structured, and more muscular offerings. The 1995 Barolo Prapo offers Nebbiolo's classic bouquet of melted road tar, rose petal, and cherry liqueur-like scents. Medium to full bodied, with a distinctive licorice/cherry fruitiness, as well as excellent richness and purity, it is an open-knit Barolo to enjoy over the next 15 years. The opaque purple-colored 1996 Barolo Prapo displays a fabulous nose of black fruits (cherries and raspberries galore) intertwined with earth, white truffle, and tarlike scents. Full bodied, huge, and massive, with spice, moderate tannin, and a blockbuster finish, this wine requires cellaring. Anticipated maturity: 2004–2020. The licorice, smoky cassis, overripe style of the 1997 Barolo Prapo defines this exotic, flamboyant vintage. Dark ruby/purple colored, it possesses abundant levels of glycerin, high alcohol, and low acidity. It should be delicious young yet keep for 15–18 years.

The 1997 Barolo La Serra is the debut vintage for this sexy, lush, ostentatiously styled wine. The color is a dark ruby, and the wine is viscous and open knit, with gobs of fruit, glycerin, alcohol, and extract. This heady, chewy Barolo needs more delineation, but it displays considerable promise. Anticipated maturity: 2001–2016.

SEGHESIO

1997 Barolo Vigneto La Villa	EE-EEE	(91–94)
1996 Barolo Vigneto La Villa	EE-EEE	(91–94)

1995 Barolo Vigneto La Villa	EE-EEE	90
1994 Barolo Vigneto La Villa	D	90

This exceptional producer from the village of Monforte fashioned the outstanding 1994 Barolo Vigneto La Villa from a superb, south-facing, hillside vineyard. This wine boasts a dark ruby/garnet color with no lightness at the edge. The nose offers truffle, ripe cherry, plum, and licorice aromas that intensify as the wine sits in the glass. Full bodied, powerful, and layered, this is among the most concentrated and complete 1994 Barolos I have tasted. Extremely rich, with some tannin, this already delicious wine promises to evolve and improve for 2–3 years and last for nearly a decade. Impressive!

Seghesio utilizes open-top fermenters and about 20% new oak, which is blended with the balance of the wine that has been aged in *foudres*. The deep ruby-colored 1995 Barolo Vigneto La Villa is a Burgundian-style wine with a nose of cherry liqueur, dried herbs, smoke, toasty oak, and seaweed scents. There is low acidity and a medium- to full-bodied, plush texture. I would opt for drinking it over the next 5–7 years. The explosive 1996 Barolo Vigneto La Villa offers redolent aromatics of kirsch liqueur, blackberries, soy, toasty new oak, licorice, and dried herbs. The wine is full bodied, with huge quantities of glycerin and fabulous concentration as well as richness. There is plenty of tannin and muscle in the finish, so it will benefit from 3–4 years of cellaring. Anticipated maturity: 2004–2018. The 1997 Barolo Vigneto La Villa is one of the more tannic 1997s I tasted. It possesses huge tannin, exhilarating levels of blackberry and cherry fruit, full body, and a tightly wound, muscular style that is at odds with the many exotic, flamboyant, ostentatiously styled wines of this vintage. Anticipated maturity: 2005–2020.

AURELIO SETTIMO

1997 Barolo Rocche	EE-EEE	(90–92)
1996 Barolo Rocche	EE-EEE	(90–92)
1995 Barolo Rocche	EE-EEE	(87–88)

This small producer in La Morra has turned out three fine efforts. Settimo's 1995 Barolo Rocche is a complex, evolved effort with notes of soy, roasted meats, dried herbs, and earthy fruits. The color is dark garnet with amber/orange at the edge. Complex, savory, fleshy, and ready to drink, this medium- to full-bodied Barolo should be at its best now and over the next decade. The old-style, traditionally made, impressively endowed 1996 Barolo Rocche exhibits a fragrant bouquet of chocolate, melted asphalt, soy, smoke, and white truffles. It is powerful, massive, moderately tannic, dense, and chewy, with considerable intensity. There are a few hard edges, and fans of the more modern-style Barolo will feel it is rustic, but it is loaded with flavor and personality. I adored it. Anticipated maturity: 2002–2015. The vintage's sweet glycerin, low acidity, and lofty alcohol are well displayed in the 1997 Barolo Rocche. It possesses a boatload of black cherry and berry fruit, as well as a voluptuous texture and a powerful, long, concentrated finish. This impressive old-style Barolo will be ready to drink upon release and should keep for 15 years.

SIGILLO DELL'ABATE

1990 Barolo Riserva	C	88+
1989 Barolo Riserva	C	88

It is rare to find Barolos from the extraordinary vintages of 1989 and 1990 being released 7 or so years following the vintage, but this traditional winery put these wines on the market in 1997. The 1989 Barolo Riserva exhibits a medium ruby color with mature-looking amber/orange hues at its edge. The nose offers up a classic combination of rose petals, tobacco, sweet dried cherry fruit, and spice aromas. The bouquet is followed by full-bodied, fleshy, expansive, silky flavors. This fully mature wine is made in the old, traditional style of long aging in large oak vessels. It is complex aromatically, as well as savory and full in the mouth. Do not be deceived by the advanced color, as this Barolo has another 7–8 years of life ahead of it. The 1990 Barolo Riserva is much less evolved. The color is a darker ruby/garnet with only a touch of amber at its edge. It is a broad, powerful style of Barolo, with dried fruits, herbs, cedar, and copious quantities of spice in its fragrant bouquet. Rich and medium to full bodied, with plenty of sweet cherry fruit, minerals, earth, and moderate tannin, this backward Barolo should be cellared for 3–4 years and drunk over the following 15.

SOTTIMANO

1995	Barbaresco Brichet	D	88
1997	Barbaresco Cotta Vigna Brichet	EE-EEE	(90–92)
1996	Barbaresco Cotta Vigna Brichet	EE-EEE	89+
1997	Barbaresco Curra Vigna Masué	EE-EEE	(92–93)
1996	Barbaresco Curra Vigna Masué	EE-EEE	(91–92)
1995	Barbaresco Curra Vigna Masué	D	89
1997	Barbaresco Gaia Principe Vigna del Salto	EE-EEE	(91–93)
1996	Barbaresco Gaia Principe Vigna del Salto	EE-EEE	89
1997	Barbaresco Pajoré Vigna Liunetta	EE-EEE	(90–91)
1995	Barbaresco Vigna Lunetta	D	86

Complex, forward, sexy 1995 Barbarescos have been produced by Sottimano. The 1995 Barbaresco Vigna Lunetta displays an evolved medium garnet color with considerable amber at the edge. The nose offers up sweet cherry fruit intermixed with cigar smoke, fruitcake, and tobacco notes. Evolved, sweet, round, straightforward, lush, medium-bodied flavors suggest this wine is ideal for drinking now and over the next 1–2 years. The 1995 Barbaresco Brichet possesses a deeper ruby color with less garnet and amber. The nose exhibits sweeter, more intense cedar, smoke, and black cherry fruit. In the mouth, the wine is medium bodied and riper and longer than the Vigna Lunetta, with a plush texture and round, evolved, attractive flavors. Drink it over the next 2–3 years. The finest wine of this group is the more multidimensional, richer, fuller-bodied 1995 Barbaresco Curra Vigna Masué. This example boasts outstanding aromatics (smoke, tobacco, fruitcake, cherry liqueur, rose petals, and a touch of asphalt). Lush, full bodied, round, and ready to drink, this excellent, nearly outstanding wine possesses admirable richness and a pure, textbook Barbaresco style. It will continue to drink well for 2–4 years.

All of Sottimano's vineyards are in the Neive area. The 1996s look classic in the style of 1989 and 1971. The 1997s are freaks of Mother Nature, with opulence and levels of glycerin, alcohol, and fruit that are largely unprecedented in Piedmont. The 1996 Barbaresco Gaia Principe Vigna del Salto is a wine of both richness and structure. Its dark ruby color is accompanied by an intriguing nose of spice box, tobacco smoke, cedar, and cherry liqueur. The wine is dense, medium to full bodied, and structured, with moderate tannin. It requires several years of bottle age. Anticipated maturity: 2001–2015. The 1996 Barbaresco Cotta Vigna Brichet is similarly styled, with more smoke and cherry liqueur notes intermixed with attractive scents of new saddle leather and spice. The wine is ripe and full bodied, with moderate tannin and outstanding purity. Anticipated maturity: 2001–2015. The 1996 Barbaresco Curra Vigna Masué is the most expansive, full bodied, and concentrated of the three 1996s. The wine displays a dark ruby color, as well as an explosive nose of cherry liqueur, incense, dried herbs, smoke, cedar, and soy. Full bodied, dense, and powerful, with fabulous concentration and a sweet, layered midpalate and finish, this large-scale, mouth-coating Barbaresco will be at its finest between 2002 and 2016.

I would not be surprised if all the 1996 Sottimano Barbarescos easily achieved 14% alcohol. I am sure the 1997s are even higher, although it is completely hidden by the wines' wealth of fruit, glycerin, and concentration. For example, the 1997 Barbaresco Pajoré Vigna Liunetta is a sexy, open-knit, lush, voluptuous effort with notes of cherries, dried herbs, Chinese black tea, and tar. Full bodied and ripe, with terrific fruit, this well-textured wine displays a seamless, velvety style. Drink it over the next 7–8 years. The dark ruby/plum-colored 1997 Barbaresco Cotta Vigna Brichet offers a fabulous nose of roasted coffee intermixed with melted asphalt, cherries, chocolate, and spicy wood. Full bodied, with dazzling fruit extraction, low acidity, and a layered, plump, opulently rich finish, it is typical of the hedonistic yet thrilling level of the 1997 Piedmontese Barbarescos and Barolos, not to mention Barberas. Drink it over the next 10–12 years. The 1997 Barbaresco Gaia Principe Vigna del Salto is even better. A full-bodied powerhouse, it exhibits teeth-staining extract, but there is not a hard edge to be found. The alcohol is close to 14.5%, and the wine is low in acidity with gobs of glycerin, fruit, and personality. It is a sumptuous, mouth-filling Barbaresco that is impossible to resist. Anticipated maturity: now–2012. Last, the 1997 Barbaresco Curra Vigna Masué is a powerful yet hedonistic, soft, supple-style wine with immense body, oodles of fruit (primarily cherries and kirsch), powerful, heady flavors, extremely low acidity, and a freakishly ripe, layered, concentrated finish. Anticipated maturity: now–2010.

LA SPINETTA

1995 Barbaresco Vursu-Vigneto Gallina	E	91

If the finest 1995 Barbarescos can be summarized with the words "soft, silky, low acid, hedonistic, and sexy, without much weight and structure, but plenty of fruit and charm," La Spinetta's offering is a classic of the vintage. This deep ruby-colored wine possesses superb fruit, not a great deal of power or volume, but gorgeously layered, soft flavors that offer up gobs of cherry fruit intermixed with cedar, tobacco, smoke, and dried herbs. It finishes with no hard edges. Drink it over the next several years.

LA SPINONA

1997 Barbaresco	E-EE	87
1996 Barbaresco	E-EE	82
1997 Barolo	E-EE	(87–90)

The lean, straightforward, medium-bodied 1996 Barbaresco offers attractive fruit, but it falls away in the mouth. Consume it over the next 5–6 years. The more interesting 1997 Barbaresco exhibits a layered texture and riper, sweeter black cherry fruit with dried herbs and spice in the background. It is medium to full bodied and ideal for drinking over the next decade. The dark ruby-colored 1997 Barolo reveals the vintage's jammy overripeness in its aromatics. Full bodied, low in acidity, and thick, but not complex, it will merit the higher score if more complexity emerges. Anticipated maturity: 2002–2014.

TRAVERSA

1996 Barbaresco Sori Ciabot	EE-EEE	(90–92)
1995 Barbaresco Sori Ciabot	EE-EEE	90
1996 Barbaresco Sori Stardari	EE-EEE	(90–91)

These outstanding, modern-style Barbarescos are *barrique*-aged and bottled in heavy, thick antique bottles. The 1995 Barbaresco Sori Ciabot possesses a deep ruby/plum color as well as stunning aromatics consisting of dried herbs, smoke, tobacco, red and black fruits, cedar, and Asian soy sauce. The wine is fleshy, rich, and full bodied, with subtle new oak, terrific extract, and a succulent texture. It will not be long-lived but should drink well for 5–7 years. The 1996 Barbaresco Sori Ciabot is even richer and fuller bodied, with huge extract and a terrific black cherry and raspberry fruitiness intermixed with *pain grillé*, smoke, new saddle leather, and jammy notes. Full bodied and massive, yet impeccably well balanced, this superb Barbaresco can be drunk now as well as over the next 10–12 years. Last, the 1996 Barbaresco Sori Stardari is an impressively endowed, modern-style effort with copious quantities of black cherry and cassis fruit intermixed with new oak, weedy tobacco, and cigar box notes. All are presented in a silky-textured format. Anticipated maturity: 2000–2012.

MAURO VEGLIO

1994 Barolo	D	87
1997 Barolo Arborina	EE-EEE	(88–90)
1996 Barolo Arborina	EE-EEE	(90–92+)
1995 Barolo Arborina	EE-EEE	89
1994 Barolo Arborina	D	87
1997 Barolo Castillero	EE-EEE	(90–92)
1996 Barolo Castillero	EE-EEE	(91–93)
1997 Barolo Gattera	EE-EEE	(87–89)
1996 Barolo Gattera	EE-EEE	(87–89)
1995 Barolo Gattera	EE-EEE	?
1997 Barolo Rocche	EE-EEE	(83–85?)
1996 Barolo Rocche	EE-EEE	(90–92)
1995 Barolo Rocche	EE-EEE	86
1994 Barolo Rocche	D	89

An elegantly styled Barolo with a light ruby color, Veglio's 1994 possesses sweet, spicy, cherry, and smoky notes, medium body, excellent purity, admirable harmony, and a soft, moderately endowed, silky finish. Drink it over the next 2–3 years.

Veglio's two single-vineyard 1994 Barolos are close to being outstanding—high praise for an average to slightly above average quality vintage. Veglio, a neighbor of Elio Altare, has turned out two sexy wines. The 1994 Barolo Arborina displays a garnet color with considerable amber at the edge. One would think the wine was a decade old based on the color. However, the nose offers up plenty of cedar, tobacco, spice box, rose petal, and cherry liqueur aromas that jump from the glass. In the mouth, the wine is medium to full bodied, with good grip and structure, as well as more tannin than most 1994s. It is a candidate for drinking over the next 1–4 years. The 1994 Barolo Rocche is a denser, more concentrated wine with an evolved ruby/garnet color. It has completely soaked up the evidence of its 100% new oak cask aging, offering only subtle *pain grillé* notes in its otherwise explosive nose of jammy cherry fruit, Asian spice, and cigar smoke. In the mouth, dried herbs are added to the flavors of this medium- to full-bodied, dense, surprisingly rich 1994. It displays a silky finish despite the presence of atypically high tannin. Drink it over the next 2–5 years.

I was struck by the inconsistency of Mauro Veglio's three most recent vintages. I did not understand the lemony, grassy, vegetal 1995 Barolo Gattera. It tastes more like a white wine than a red and is completely at odds with the other Veglio offerings. The 1995 Barolo Rocche is a middle-weight, elegant, finesse-style Barolo with good spice, some tannin, medium body, and attractive cherry fruit. Drink it over the next 7–8 years. The epitome of finesse, the medium ruby-colored 1995 Barolo Arborina is already revealing amber at the edge. Evolved and stylish, with sweet cherry fruit, medium body, and a heady finish, it will drink well for 6–7 years.

This producer has, atypically, produced better 1996s than 1997s. Three of the four Veglio 1996s appear to have outstanding potential. The 1996 Barolo Gattera is a more interesting example than the 1995. Medium bodied and soft, with an elegant, kirsch liqueur-scented and -flavored personality, it is ideal for consuming over the next 7–8 years. Full bodied and powerful, the 1996 Barolo Rocche possesses copious quantities of cherry liqueur/kirsch intermixed with leafy tobacco, roasted nuts, smoke, and spice. This full-bodied, moderately tannic, classic Barolo should be at its finest between 2002 and 2014. The 1996 Barolo Arborina reveals the telltale rose petal, melted road tar, and jammy cherry nose with notes of tobacco in the background. Made in a soft, forward style, it is medium to full bodied, with dazzling fruit intensity, outstanding purity, sweet tannin, and a soft, lush finish. Anticipated maturity: 2001–2015. The 1996 Barolo Castillero smells like an herb garden planted next to a roaring charcoal fire. There are copious amounts of cherry fruit, new saddle leather, and animal-like aromas. This is a more *sauvage* Barolo, with impeccable density, medium to full body, and gobs of fruit and spice. It should drink well for 10–15 years.

For whatever reason, Veglio's 1997s appear less successful, although certainly very good. The 1997 Barolo Gattera offers a smoky, dried herb fragrance, medium body, lush fruit, low acidity, and the vintage's telltale high alcohol. It should drink well for 7–8 years. The 1997 Barolo Rocche was closed and seemingly not as successful as the other offerings. It was astringent, hard, and foursquare, but perhaps it was not showing well when I tasted it. The dark ruby-colored 1997 Barolo Arborina is medium to full bodied, with good tannin, smoky tobacco, strawberry, and cherry fruit, and moderate tannin in the long finish. Anticipated maturity: 2002–2012. The finest wine of this quartet is the dark ruby/purple-colored 1997 Barolo Castillero. It exhibits wonderful sweetness, high levels of glycerin, a massive, full-bodied feel, outstanding purity, and a corpulent, sweet, chunky finish. Anticipated maturity: 2002–2015.

A. A. VIBERTI ERALDO

1997	Barolo	E-EE	(87–89)
1996	Barolo	E-EE	(86–88)
1995	Barolo	E-EE	87

These three attractive Barolos represent a synthesis in style between modern techniques and respect for tradition. The 1995 Barolo reveals a healthy, modern dark ruby/purple color, *pain grillé* notes in the nose, sweet fruit, medium to full body, moderate tannin, and a lush, accessible style. Drink it over the next 7–8 years. The saturated ruby/garnet-colored 1996 Barolo possesses a classic, structured, broodingly backward personality with plenty of dried herbs, leather, and cherrylike fruit. The wine is medium to full bodied and compressed in the finish, but if the tannin melts away without significant loss of fruit, it will merit a score in the upper 80s. Anticipated maturity: 2003–2015. The finest wine of this trio is the 1997 Barolo. It is opulent and full bodied, with dazzling levels of rich black cherry fruit blended with licorice, tar, and spicy wood. Powerful, thick, and viscous, with truffle notes in the background, this user-friendly, expansively flavored Barolo should be at its best between 2001 and 2015.

VIETTI

1997	Barbaresco	E-EE	(87–88)
1996	Barbaresco	E-EE	(85–86)

1995 Barbaresco	E-EE	86
1995 Barbaresco Masseria	EE-EEE	88
1997 Barolo	E-EE	(86–87)
1996 Barolo	E-EE	(85–87)
1995 Barolo	E-EE	83
1996 Barolo Brunate	EE-EEE	(88–90+)
1995 Barolo Brunate	EE-EEE	86+
1997 Barolo Lazzarito	EE-EEE	(91–93)
1995 Barolo Lazzarito	EE-EEE	85
1997 Barolo Rocche	EE-EEE	(90–91)
1996 Barolo Rocche	EE-EEE	(88–90+?)
1995 Barolo Rocche	EE-EEE	85?
1996 Barolo Villero Riserva	EE-EEE	(89–91)

This is not the entire lineup of Vietti offerings, but they performed unevenly in my tastings. Vietti adheres to a traditional style of winemaking, and I suspect these wines will perform even better with time in bottle. I have been purchasing Vietti's wines since the 1971 vintage, and they are classics in terms of their potential to age gracefully for 2 decades or more.

The 1995 Barbaresco exhibits an evolved garnet color, in addition to a spicy, tobacco-tinged nose with scents of cherry jam and cigar smoke. It is an easygoing, round, fruit/spice-driven wine to drink over the next 5–6 years. More substantial is the 1995 Barbaresco Masseria. The nose offers dried Provençal herbs intermixed with notes of seaweed, smoke, earth, and kirsch liqueur. Weighty, expansive, and lush, this medium- to full-bodied offering reveals some of the Nebbiolo's telltale tar characteristic with airing. Drink this beauty over the next 8–10 years. The dark ruby-colored 1996 Barbaresco reveals a spicy, cedary, sweet nose, excellent fruit, smoky oak, grilled herbs, and meat notes. The finish is short, but it should open with time. This will not be a blockbuster Barbaresco, but it is elegant and well made. Anticipated maturity: 2001–2010. The dark ruby-colored, fat, soft 1997 Barbaresco exhibits the vintage's succulence as well as gobs of tannin and black cherry fruit intertwined with smoke and damp foresty smells. With high glycerin and low acidity, it is an ideal candidate for consuming over the next 10–12 years.

I tasted four 1995 Barolos from Vietti. The regular 1995 Barolo's evolved garnet color is followed by a round, soft, fruity nose of dried herbs, red fruits, cedar, and spice box. The finish is slightly pinched, compressed, and austere. This fully mature Barolo is best consumed over the next 3–4 years. Frankly I expected more. I was not impressed by the three single-vineyard Barolos, although they are all good wines. The 1995 Barolo Lazzarito exhibits a moderately intense nose of cranberries, cherries, dried herbs, smoke, and earth. It is compressed in the mouth, displaying high levels of astringent tannin. Although it will drink well for 7–8 years, the wine lacks the concentration to stand up to its structure. The well-made 1995 Barolo Brunate offers a low-key, weedy, cedary, herb, and smoky personality with moderate levels of sweet cherry fruit and a short, tannic finish. Anticipated maturity: 2000–2007. The 1995 Barolo Rocche possesses the most saturated color of all the Vietti 1995s, but it is evolved, with high levels of tannin that scorch the back of the palate. This gives the wine an attenuated, compressed, tough-textured finish. I am not sure it has the proper balance to age gracefully.

In 1996 I tasted four Barolos, all significantly better than Vietti's 1995s. The 1996 Barolo exhibits good sweetness, in addition to a distinctive, cedary, herb, and spice box aromatic profile. It is medium bodied, with good concentration and moderate levels of astringent tannin. Anticipated maturity: 2001–2012.

The 1996 Barolo Villero Riserva reveals spicy oak intermixed with copious quantities of jammy cherries, *garrigue*, smoke, and earth. Sweet, deep, and full bodied, with a classic rose petal and tarlike fragrance, this bold, masculine, powerful Barolo possesses plenty of tannin. It should age easily for 2 decades. Anticipated maturity: 2006–2020. Exhibiting a more saturated color, the 1996 Barolo Brunate came across as more closed, but powerful, rich, and potentially outstanding. The wine has good depth but is broodingly backward and unevolved. Anticipated maturity: 2007–2020. The most saturated color and the sweetest, richest fruit are found in the 1996 Barolo Rocche. It is extremely full bodied and tannic, a bit hard, but impressively endowed. If the tannin becomes better meshed, it will be an outstanding wine, but it will require patience from prospective purchasers. Anticipated maturity: 2007–2015.

The 1997s I tasted appear to be spectacular wines. The 1997 Barolo is a medium-bodied, supple-textured wine with plenty of dried herbs, coffee, and cherry syrup notes. Drink this accessible Barolo during the first decade of the next century.

The 1997 Barolo Lazzarito offers explosive levels of glycerin, fruit, and extract, as well as the vintage's sweet, low-acid, chewy texture. With fabulous length, this full-bodied, powerful, concentrated wine's high tannin level is largely submerged beneath the glycerin and extract. Anticipated maturity: 2006–2025. The 1997 Barolo Rocche is cut from the same mold, only sweeter, more tannic, and fuller bodied, with immense levels of extract and richness. This powerful, mouth-filling wine will need a decade of cellaring. Anticipated maturity: 2009–2025.

GIOVANNI VOERZIO

1996 Barbera d'Alba Ciabot della Luna	D	88
1997 Barolo La Serra	EE–EEE	(91–94)
1996 Barolo La Serra	EE–EEE	(90–92)
1995 Barolo La Serra	EE–EEE	90
1994 Barolo La Serra	E	86
1997 Dolcetto Rochettevino	C	87

The 1997 Dolcetto Rochettevino is a dark ruby/purple-colored wine with an intensely fragrant nose of roasted nuts, blackberries, and a whiff of mocha. Supple, with a beautiful texture, soft acidity, and copious quantities of fruit, this is an excellent Dolcetto to drink over the next 1–2 years. The dark, dense, saturated purple-colored 1996 Barbera d'Alba Ciabot della Luna offers an intriguing nose of tomatoes, ripe plums, and *pain grillé* from being aged in French oak. This unfiltered cuvée's fleshy texture, medium body, excellent depth, and expansive mouth-feel are typical of a naturally bottled wine made from ripe fruit. This attractive, nearly outstanding Barbera should drink well for 5–6 years.

The 1994 Barolo La Serra should be the best wine of this trio, but because it is from a mediocre vintage, it ranks a distant third. However, it is well above many of the severe, austere, mediocre wines from this vintage. Evolved, and revealing a medium garnet/ruby color with some lightening at the edge, it is well balanced for the vintage, offering up a fragrant cedar, soy, weedy tobacco, dried herb, and cherry-scented nose. Spicy and round, this fully mature Barolo should be drunk over the next 1–3 years.

This small producer in the village of La Morra follows the new school of winemaking, utilizing a high percentage of *barriques* for aging his wine. However, these are not internationally styled Nebbiolos, as they all display the varietal's textbook characteristics.

The 1995 Barolo La Serra is unquestionably one of the vintage's most successful wines. Initially appealing spicy oak gets lost in a blast of black cherry fruit, tar, rose petals, dried herbs, and spices. Rich, full bodied, open knit, and chewy, with a noteworthy succulence and lushness, this beautifully knit, evolved, precociously styled, mouth-filling Barolo is ideal for drinking over the next decade. The 1996 Barolo La Serra exhibits a deeper, more saturated ruby color, as well as dried herb, tobacco, spice box, cherry liqueur, and coffee aromas, superb density, huge extract, and a long, full-bodied, moderately tannic finish. This classic Barolo possesses super purity and considerable glycerin. Anticipated maturity: 2004–2024. The exotic, tremendously extracted 1997 Barolo La Serra reveals the vintage's overripe characteristics of jammy cassis, black cherries, toasty new oak, and cigar smoke. Huge, massive, and thick, with considerable fatness and a boatload of glycerin, this wine seems more forward than I believe it will actually turn out to be. There is considerable tannin in the 45-second finish, but it is sweet and well integrated. I suspect by the time it is in bottle, the tannin will be more noticeable and give the wine the structure and backbone to last 20+ years.

ROBERTO VOERZIO

1997	Barolo Brunate	EE-EEE	(92–95)
1996	Barolo Brunate	EE-EEE	(92–95)
1991	Barolo Brunate	E	88+
1997	Barolo Capalot Riserva	EE-EEE	(93–96)
1996	Barolo Capalot Riserva	EE-EEE	(91–94+)
1995	Barolo Capalot Riserva	EE-EEE	91
1997	Barolo Cerequio	EE-EEE	(90–92)
1996	Barolo Cerequio	EE-EEE	(90–91)
1995	Barolo Cerequio	EE-EEE	86
1991	Barolo Cerequio	E	88
1997	Barolo La Serra	EE-EEE	(91–94)
1996	Barolo La Serra	EE-EEE	(90–93+)
1995	Barolo La Serra	EE-EEE	87
1991	Barolo La Serra	E	88

Roberto Voerzio is one of my favorite Piedmontese producers. His La Morra vineyards have some of the highest density of vines of the region (approximately 3,200 vines per acre). Voerzio's wines represent a synthesis in style between the modern *barrique*-aged and the traditional. While all his wines are *barrique*-aged (about 50% new), they possess enough structure and intensity to make such traditionalists as Giovanni Conterno or Bruno Giacosa proud.

The 1995 Barolo La Serra exhibits a textbook nose of melted road tar, rose petals, and cigar box aromas, moderate tannin, ripe fruit, medium body, and a dry, austere finish. It is a very good, classic Barolo, but the slight austerity kept my score more conservative. Drink it over the next decade. The superb 1996 Barolo La Serra's opaque ruby/purple color is followed by aromas of black fruits (blackberry, cherry, and a hint of raspberry), superb purity, highly extracted, powerful, monster-size flavors, mouth-searing levels of tannin, and an impressively endowed, 40+-second finish. This backward, pure, intensely concentrated Barolo will require patience. Anticipated maturity: 2008–2025. The 1997 Barolo La Serra boasts off-the-chart extraction levels, with huge power, glycerin, and alcohol. The acidity is low, and there is an element of *sur-maturité* to the wine's black fruit character. This opulently styled, viscously textured, opaque ruby/purple-colored wine is atypical, but wow, what an amazing drinking experience! My instincts suggest these wines will become more delineated and structured as they continue both their evolution in cask/*foudre* and in bottle. They are extremely high in tannin, even though most of it is hidden by the flamboyant display of glycerin, fruit, and alcohol. Anticipated maturity: 2004–2025.

I was surprised that Roberto Voerzio's 1995 Barolo Cerequio displayed such an evolved color. The amber, rusty edge suggested a wine that was far older than 4 years. The nose of tea, dried herbs, and cedar aromas makes this a spice- rather than fruit-driven wine. It is medium bodied, evolved, and fully mature. The finish is slightly compressed, but the wine possesses the textbook spice, melted road tar, and dried cherry-like flavors of an old-style Barolo. Drink it over the next 5–6 years. The opaque ruby/purple-colored 1996 Barolo Cerequio possesses extremely high tannin and extract, but it is very backward and even more closed and firm than Voerzio's 1996 Barolo La Serra. Full bodied, powerful, and rich, but broodingly backward and stubborn, it possesses all the correct component parts, but patience will be required by potential purchasers. Anticipated maturity: 2010–2025. The freakishly opulent, black raspberry liqueur-like 1997 Barolo Cerequio is another example of this unusual yet gorgeously eccentric vintage. Deep, huge, thick, and oozing with glycerin and fruit, this unformed Barolo is oh, so promising. There is frightfully low acidity and mind-boggling levels of alcohol and richness in this silky wine. No doubt there is plenty of tannin lurking beneath the surface, but this wine needs to develop more delineation. Anticipated maturity: 2005–2025.

In 1995 Roberto Voerzio did not produce a Barolo from his famed Brunate vineyard since it was devastated by a hailstorm. The following year he did fashion a fabulous, black/purple-colored 1996 Barolo Brunate, which is the most gigantic of all the Voerzio Barolos I tasted. Monstrously sized, with huge alcohol, high tannin, and spectacular extract, this layered, chewy wine is sensationally promising. Although stubbornly backward, it possesses wonderful ripeness, but this wine is so huge, it needs 5–6 years to evolve. Anticipated maturity: 2006–2030. My tasting notes for the 1997 Barolo Brunate begin with the word "wow." With a crème de cassis–like nose, as well as the soft, supple texture characteristic of the finest 1997s, this Barolo possesses extraordinary density, high glycerin, remarkable extract, an element of overripeness, and an exotic flamboyance. There is nothing "classic" or "typical" about many of the 1997 Barolos, but from a purely hedonistic perspective, they are sumptuous wines. Anticipated maturity: 2006–2020.

This is the first time I tasted Voerzio's single-vineyard Capalot Riserva wines. Made from a plot of the oldest vines in his Brunate vineyard, the wine, bottled only in magnums (approximately 1,000), is produced in only the top vintages. The following three offerings are remarkable efforts. The 1995 Barolo Capalot Riserva is a thick, chewy offering with a stunning display of aromatics (cigar smoke, Chinese black tea, new oak, cherry liqueur, and dried Provençal herbs). Extremely full bodied, rich, and surprisingly huge for a 1995, this Barolo possesses amazing extract as well as a finish that lasts for nearly a minute. Extremely rich and powerful, but accessible, it can be drunk now as well as over the next 15 years. The profound 1996 Barolo Capalot Riserva boasts a dense, ruby/purple color and a pure nose of black cherries, raspberries, and blackberries. Layered and multidimensional, with a sweet midpalate and a blockbuster finish, this is an immense, full-throttle Barolo that should age effortlessly for 15–25 years. Impressive! The dark ruby/purple-colored 1997 Barolo Capalot Riserva reveals more new oak than its siblings, in addition to the vintage's low acidity, thick, unctuous texture, and huge, massive body oozing with fruit and extract. It is a remarkably velvety-textured blockbuster that will be delicious young yet become more delineated and reveal more tannin as it ages. It should keep for 20–25 years. As indicated, the production of the Capalot Riserva is 1,000 magnums per vintage. Production for the Cerequio is 350–400 cases, the Serra 400 cases, and the Brunate 300 cases.

Roberto Voerzio turned out three very good 1991 Barolos from his vineyards surrounding the village of La Morra. All these single-vineyard Barolos share deep garnet colors that suggest full maturity, but the wines' flavors and structure indicate surprising longevity. The softest wine is the 1991 Barolo La Serra (although that may be splitting hairs), a wine with a textbook Nebbiolo nose of black cherries, tobacco, spice, cedar, dried fruits, and roses. The other wines reveal similar bouquets, but they are neither as open nor as fragrant as La Serra. All three are medium- to full-bodied, admirably concentrated wines that are soft enough to be drunk now, but they exhibited few signs of fruit deterioration or oxidation after 24 hours of aeration. The 1991 Barolo Brunate is the most backward offering, but it is still accessible. The 1991 Barolo Cerequio's personality is closer to La Serra. These three 1991 Barolos displayed less significant differences than usual. They are successful wines for what is considered a mediocre vintage for Barolo. Roberto Voerzio's offerings are well above that image of quality. Look for these wines to offer near-term drinking and age well for 10–15 years, with the potential to raise their scores by 1–3 points.

ATTILIO ZUNINO

1997 Barolo Sori di Baudana	EE-EEE	(88–89)
1996 Barolo Sori di Baudana	EE-EEE	(88–90)
1995 Barolo Sori di Baudana	EE-EEE	88

This small producer from the village of Serralunga has fashioned three very fine wines. The excellent 1995 Barolo Sori di Baudana offers up textbook Barolo aromas and flavors of tar, rose petals, cedar, and sour cherries. There is admirable concentration, a powerful structure, good sweetness in the midpalate, and a fine finish. It is made in a dense, traditional style. Anticipated maturity: 2001–2012. Although similarly styled, the backward 1996 Barolo Sori di Baudana is fuller bodied, with more muscle and chewy tannin. Anticipated maturity: 2003–2017. The potentially outstanding 1997 Barolo Sori di Baudana is the sweetest of these offerings, with the most viscosity and fullest body. It reveals low acidity as well as impressively chewy red and black fruit flavors intertwined with earth, soy, asphalt, and spice box characteristics. There is moderate tannin in the luscious, jammy finish. Anticipated maturity: 2002–2018.

TUSCANY

The Basics

TYPES OF WINE

Beautiful Tuscany is the home of Italy's most famous wine, Chianti, and one of Italy's most celebrated wines, Brunello di Montalcino. Both wines can be either horrendous or splendid. Quality is shockingly irregular. Yet it is in Tuscany that Italy's wine revolution is being fought, with adventurous and innovative producers cavalierly turning their backs on the archaic regulations that govern wine production. They are making wines, often based on Cabernet Sauvignon, Merlot, and Sangiovese, aged in small oak casks, filled with flavor and personality, and put in designer bottles. I disagree completely with those critics who have called them French look-alikes, and though entitled to be called only Vino da Tavola, they represent some of the most exciting red wines made in the world. The same cannot be said for Tuscany's white wines. Except for the light, tasty whites called Vernaccia from the medieval hill fortress of San Gimignano, Tuscan whites are ultraneutral, boring wines. Shame on those producers who package these wines in lavish-looking bottles that are appallingly overpriced.

GRAPE VARIETIES

The principal and greatest red wine grape of Tuscany is Sangiovese. The highest-yielding, most insipid wine from Sangiovese comes from the most widely planted clone called Sangiovese Romano. The better producers are using clones of Sangiovese with names such as Sangioveto, Prugnolo, and Brunello. These all produce a richer, deeper, more complex wine. Of course, Cabernet Sauvignon, Merlot, Cabernet Franc, and even Pinot Noir and Syrah are making their presence felt in Tuscany.

As for the white wines, there is the sharp, uninteresting Trebbiano, produced in ocean-size quantities. Trebbiano is an inferior grape, and the results are distressingly innocuous wines. Vernaccia has potential, and of course there are such international blue bloods as Chardonnay and Sauvignon Blanc. Tuscany, in my mind, means red not white wine, but if you are inclined to try a white wine, then take a look at my list of recommended producers for Vernaccia di San Gimignano.

FLAVORS

Chianti Classico   It is virtually impossible to provide specific information given the extraordinary range in quality—from musty, poorly vinified, washed-out wines to ones with soft, supple, raspberry, chestnut, and tobacco flavors, crisp acidity, medium body, and a fine finish. Stick to only the recommended producers that are listed subsequently. Remember, at least 50% of wines called Chianti, despite tighter regulations governing quality, are thin, acidic, and unpleasant.

Brunello di Montalcino   It should be rich, powerful, tannic, superbly concentrated, and heady, with a huge, spicy bouquet of smoky tobacco, meat, and dried red fruits. Only a few are. Most close encounters offer an alarming degree of tannin and musty old oak to the detriment of fruit. Selection is critical. Rosso di Montalcino is red wine made from the Brunello clone of Sangiovese that is not aged long enough to qualify as Brunello di Montalcino. It is often much less expensive and considerably fresher.

Carmignano   This is an underrated viticultural area wherein the wines show good fruit, balance, and character. The best of them behave like Chiantis with more character and structure. Not surprisingly, Carmignano is made from Sangiovese with 10%–15% Cabernet added.

Vernaccia di San Gimignano   Tuscany's best dry white table wine, this nutty, zesty, dry, fruity white is meant to be drunk within 2–3 years of the vintage. It is a satisfying rather than thrilling wine.

Vino Nobile di Montepulciano   A neighbor of Chianti with identical characteristics (the grape is the same), Vino Nobile di Montepulciano costs more but rarely provides more flavor or pleasure.

Morellino di Scansano   This is an emerging viticultural region south of Siena. I have tasted the wines from only a few estates, but it appears this is an area that requires more at-

tention. Made from Sangiovese, Morellino di Scansano may be the frugal consumer's alternative to Brunello di Montalcino. The wines are rich, expansive, and, for now, undervalued!
Other Tuscan Whites   The names Bianco di Pitigliano, Bianco Vergine della Valdichiana, Galestro, Montecarlo, Pomino, and any Tuscan producer's name plus the word *bianco* translate into wines that taste wretchedly neutral and bland and provide no more flavor than a glass of water. Sadly, most of them cost $20–$35, so the operative words are *caveat emptor!*
Vino da Tavolas   The most thrilling red wines of Tuscany are the designer show wines that are being made by Tuscany's most innovative growers. They can be 100% Cabernet Sauvignon, 100% Sangiovese, or a blend of these two grapes plus Cabernet Franc. Even some Merlot, Syrah, and Pinot Noir can now be found. They are usually aged in mostly new French oak casks. Top Tuscan vintages, such as 1982, 1985, 1988, 1990, 1995, and 1997, can offer sensational aromatic dimension and remarkable flavor breadth. Following are the best-known Vino da Tavolas, their top vintages, and grapes used.

GUIDE TO THE BEST-KNOWN VINO DA TAVOLAS

NAME	PRODUCER	TOP VINTAGES	PRIMARY GRAPE	RATING
Acciaiolo	Fattoria di Albola	1997, 1995, 1990, 1988	Sangiovese	***
Agricoltori del Geografico	Geografico	1997, 1995, 1990, 1988	Cabernet/Sangiovese	****
Alte d'Altesi	Altesino	1997, 1995, 1990, 1988	Sangiovese	****
Altero	Poggio Antico	1997, 1995, 1988	Sangiovese	****
Anagallis	Lilliano	1997, 1995, 1990, 1988	Sangiovese	****
Ania	Gabbiano	1997, 1995, 1990, 1988	Cabernet Sauvignon	***
Armonia	Querciavalle	1997, 1995, 1990, 1988	Sangiovese/Canaiolo	***
Balifico	Castello di Volpaia	1997, 1995, 1990, 1988	Sangiovese	****
Barco Reale	Capezzana	1997, 1995, 1990, 1988	Cabernet Sauvignon	***
Bel Convento	Del Roseti	1997, 1995, 1988	Sangiovese	**
Bianchi-V. Scanni	Monsanto	1997, 1995, 1990, 1988	Sangiovese	***/****
Predicatodi Biturica	Geografico	1997, 1995, 1990, 1988	Sangiovese	***
Boro Cepparello	Isole e Olena	1997, 1995, 1990, 1988	Sangiovese	***
Boscarelli	Boscarelli	1997, 1995, 1990, 1988	Sangiovese	****
Brancaia	Fonterutoli	1997, 1995, 1990	Sangiovese	***
Bru scone dei Barbi	Barbi	1997, 1995, 1990, 1988	Sangiovese	**
Buriano	Rocca di Castagnoli	1997, 1995, 1990	Cabernet Sauvignon	***

NAME	PRODUCER	TOP VINTAGES	PRIMARY GRAPE	RATING
Ca' del Pazzo	Caparzo	1997, 1995, 1990, 1988	Sangiovese	****
Cabernet Sauvignon	Altesino	1997, 1995, 1990, 1988	Cabernet Sauvignon	****
Cabernet Sauvignon	Avignonesi	1997, 1995, 1990, 1988	Cabernet Sauvignon	****
Cabreo Il Borgo	Ruffino	1997, 1995, 1988	Cabernet Sauvignon/ Sangiovese	***
Cabreo Vigneto	Ruffino	1997, 1995, 1990, 1988	Sangiovese	***
Campaccio Barrique	Terrabianca	1997, 1995, 1988	Sangiovese	*****
Cancelli	Badia a Coltibuono	1997, 1995, 1990	Sangiovese	***
Capannelle Barrique	Rossetti	1997, 1995, 1990, 1988	Sangiovese	***
Capannelle Rosso	Capannelle	1997, 1995, 1990, 1988	Sangiovese	***
Capannelle Rosso	Rossetti	1997, 1995, 1990, 1988	Sangiovese	***
Carmartina	Fattoria Querciabella	1997, 1995, 1990, 1988	Sangiovese	***
Carmerlengo	Pagliarese	1997, 1995, 1990, 1988	Sangiovese	**/***
Case Via	Fontodi	1997, 1995, 1990	Syrah	****
Castruccio	Castruccio	1997, 1995, 1990	Sangiovese	***
Cerviolo	San Fabiano Calcinaia	1997, 1995, 1988	Sangiovese	***/****
Cetinaia	San Polo	1997, 1995, 1990, 1988	Sangiovese	**
Cignale	Castello di Querceto	1997, 1995, 1990, 1988	Cabernet Sauvignon	****/*****
Cipresso	Terrabianco	?	Sangiovese	*****
Colle Picchioni-dVassallo	Paola di Mauro	1997, 1995, 1990, 1988	Sangiovese	**
Collezione de Marchi l'Ermo	Isole e Olena	1997, 1995, 1990, 1988	Syrah	****
Coltassala	Castello di Volpaia	1997, 1995, 1990, 1988	Sangiovese	****
Coltibuono Rosso	Badia a Coltibuono	1997, 1995, 1990, 1988	Sangiovese	***
I Coltri Rosso	Melini	1997, 1995, 1990, 1988	Cabernet Sauvignon/ Sangiovese	**
Colvecchio	Banfi	1997, 1995, 1990	Syrah	**
Concerto	Fonterutoli	1997, 1995, 1990, 1988	Sangiovese	***

NAME	PRODUCER	TOP VINTAGES	PRIMARY GRAPE	RATING
Coniale di Castellare	Castellare di Castellina	1997, 1995, 1990, 1988	Cabernet Sauvignon/ Sangiovese	****/****
Cortaccio	Villa Cafaggio	1997, 1995, 1990, 1988	Cabernet Sauvignon	*****
La Corte	Castello di Querceto	1997, 1995, 1990, 1988	Sangiovese	****
Donna Marzia	Giuseppe Zecca	1997, 1995, 1990, 1988	Sangiovese	**
Elegia	Poliziano	1997, 1995, 1990, 1988	Prugnolo	****
Etrusco	Cannatoio	1997, 1995, 1990	Sangiovese	**
Farnito	Capineto	1997, 1995, 1990	Cabernet Sauvignon	****
Flaccianello	Fontodi	1997, 1995, 1990, 1988	Sangiovese	****
Fontalloro	Felsina Berardenga	1997, 1995, 1990, 1988	Sangiovese	****
Gerardino	Vignamaggio	1997, 1995, 1988	Sangiovese	***
Geremia	Castello di Cacchiano	1997, 1995, 1990, 1988	Sangiovese	***
Geremia	E. Ricasoli-Firidolfi	1997, 1995, 1988	Sangioveto/Canaiolo	*****
Ghiaie della Furba	Cappezzana	1997, 1995, 1990, 1988	Cabernet Sauvignon	***/****
La Giola di Riecine	Riecine	1997, 1995, 1990, 1988	Sangiovese	****
Granchiaia	Le Macie	1997, 1995, 1990, 1988	Sangiovese	**
Grattamacco	Podere Grattamacco	1997, 1995, 1990, 1988	Sangiovese	**
Grifi	Avignonesi	1997, 1995, 1990, 1988	Sangiovese	****
Grosso Senese	Il Palazzino	1997, 1995, 1990, 1988	Sangiovese	****/*****
Isole e Olena Rosso	Isole e Olena	1997, 1995, 1990, 1988	Sangiovese	**
Liano	Umberto Cesari	1997, 1995, 1990, 1988	Sangiovese	**
Logaiolo	Fattoria dell'Aiola	1997, 1995, 1990, 1988	Sangiovese	**
Maestro Raro	Felsina	1997, 1995, 1990, 1988	Cabernet Sauvignon	****/*****
Magiolo	Castelli del Grevepesa	1997, 1995, 1990	Cabernet Sauvignon/ Sangiovese	***
Marzeno di Marzeno	Zerbina	1997, 1995, 1990, 1988	Sangiovese	**

NAME	PRODUCER	TOP VINTAGES	PRIMARY GRAPE	RATING
Masso Tondo	Le Corti	1997, 1995, 1990, 1988	Sangiovese	****
Merlot	Avignonesi	1997, 1995, 1990, 1988	Merlot	****
Merlot	Castelgiocondo	1997, 1995, 1990	Merlot	***/****
Monte Antico	Monte Antico	1997, 1995, 1990, 1988	Sangiovese	****
Monte Vertine	Monte Vertine	1997, 1995, 1990, 1988	Sangiovese	***
Mormoreto	Frescobaldi	1997, 1995, 1990, 1988	Cabernet Sauvignon/ Sangiovese	***
Nemo	Monsanto	1997, 1995, 1990, 1988	Cabernet Sauvignon	****
Nero del Tondo	Ruffino	1997, 1995, 1988	Pinot Noir	**
Niccolo da Uzzano	Castello di Uzzano	1997, 1995, 1990, 1988	Sangiovese	**
Ornellaia	L. Antinori	1997, 1995, 1990, 1988	Cabernet Sauvignon	*****
Ornellaia Masseto	L. Antinori	1997, 1995, 1988	Merlot	*****
Palazzo Altesi	Altesino	1997, 1995, 1990, 1988	Sangiovese	****/*****
Il Pareto	Nozzole	1997, 1995, 1990, 1988	Cabernet Sauvignon	****/*****
Parrina	DOC	1997, 1995, 1990, 1988	Sangiovese	**
Percarlo	San Giusto	1997, 1995, 1990, 1988	Sangiovese	*****
Le Pergole Torte	Monte Vertine	1997, 1995, 1990, 1988	Sangiovese	****
Piano del Cipresso	Terrabianca	1997, 1995, 1988	Sangiovese	****/*****
Poggio Brandi	Fattoria Baggiolino	1997, 1995, 1990, 1988	Sangioveto	****
Porta della Pietra	John Matta	1997, 1995, 1988	Sangiovese	****
Prunaio	Viticcio	1997, 1995, 1990, 1988	Sangiovese	****
Querciagrande	Podere Capaccia	1997, 1995, 1990	Sangiovese	****
Il Querciolaia	Castello di Querceto	1997, 1995, 1990, 1988	Cabernet Sauvignon/ Sangiovese	****
RF	Castello di Cacchiano	1997, 1995, 1990, 1988	Sangiovese	****
R and R	Castello di Gabbiano	1997, 1995, 1990, 1988	Cabernet Sauvignon/ Sangiovese	****
Ripa della More	Vicchiomaggio	1997, 1995, 1990, 1988	Cabernet Sauvignon/ Sangiovese	****

NAME	PRODUCER	TOP VINTAGES	PRIMARY GRAPE	RATING
Rocca di Montegrossi	Castello di Cacchiano	1997, 1995, 1990, 1988	Sangiovese	****
Roccato	Rocca delle Macie	1997, 1995, 1990, 1988	Cabernet Sauvignon/ Sangiovese	****
Rosso di Altesino	Altesino	1997, 1995, 1990	Cabernet Sauvignon/ Sangiovese	****
Rosso dell'Oca	Fattoria di Petriolo	1997, 1995, 1990, 1988	Merlot	****
Saffredi	Le Pupille	1997, 1995, 1990	Sangiovese/ Merlot/Alicante	*****
Sammarco	Castello di Rampolla	1997, 1995, 1990, 1988	Cabernet Sauvignon	*****
San Felice	Predicato di Biturica	1997, 1995, 1990, 1988	Sangiovese	**
San Martino	Villa Cafaggio	1997, 1995, 1990, 1988	Sangiovese	*****
Sangioveto di Coltibuono	Badia a Coltibuono	1997, 1995, 1990, 1988	Sangiovese	****
Sangioveto Grosso	Monsanto	1997, 1995, 1990, 1988	Sangiovese	****
Santa Cristina	Antinori	1997, 1995, 1990, 1988	Sangiovese	**
Santacroce	Castell'In Villa	1997, 1995, 1990, 1988	Sangiovese	****
Sassello	Castello di Verrazzano	1997, 1995, 1990, 1988	Sangiovese	**
Sassicaia	San Guido	1997, 1995, 1990, 1988	Cabernet Sauvignon	*****
Secentenario	P. Antinori	nonvintage	Cabernet Sauvignon/ Sangiovese	****
Ser Gioveto	Rocca delle Macie	1997, 1995, 1990, 1988	Sangiovese/ Cabernet Sauvignon	***/****
Ser Niccolo	Conti Serristori	1997, 1995, 1990, 1988	Sangiovese	**
Il Sodaccio	Monte Vertine	1997, 1995, 1990, 1988	Sangiovese	*****
I Sodi di San Niccolo	Castellare	1997, 1995, 1990, 1988	Sangiovese	***
Sodole	Guicciardini Strozzi	1997, 1995, 1990, 1988	Sangiovese	****/*****
Solaia	P. Antinori	1997, 1995, 1990, 1988	Cabernet Sauvignon	*****
Solatia Basilica	Villa Cafaggio	1997, 1995, 1990, 1988	Sangiovese	****/*****
Soldera Intistieri	Soldera	1997, 1995, 1988	Sangiovese	***/****
Sorbaiano Montescudaio	Geografico	1997, 1995, 1990	Sangiovese	***
Spargolo	Cecchi	1997, 1995, 1990	Sangiovese	**

NAME	PRODUCER	TOP VINTAGES	PRIMARY GRAPE	RATING
Le Stanze	Poliziano	1997, 1995, 1990, 1988	Cabernet Sauvignon	****
Stielle	Rocca di Castagnoli	1990	Cabernet Sauvignon/ Sangiovese	***/****
Summus	Banfi	1997, 1995, 1990	Sangiovese/ Pinot Noir/ Cabernet Sauvignon	**
Tavernelle	Villa Banfi	1997, 1995, 1988	Cabernet Sauvignon	**
Tignanello	Antinori	1997, 1995, 1990, 1988	Sangiovese	*****
Tinscvil	Castello di Monsanto	1997, 1995, 1990, 1988	Sangiovese	****
Tremalvo	Barone Ricasoli	1997, 1995, 1988	Cabernet Sauvignon	**
L'Unico	Petroio	1997, 1995, 1990	Cabernet Sauvignon/ Merlot/Pinot Noir	***
Vigna L'Apparita	Castello di Ama	1997, 1995, 1990, 1988	Merlot	****/*****
Vigna di Bugialla	Poggerino	1997, 1995, 1990, 1988	Cabernet Sauvignon/ Sangiovese	****
Vigna Il Chiuso	Fattoria di Ama	1997, 1995, 1990, 1988	Pinot Noir	***
Vigna di Fontevecchia	Agricola Camigliano	1997, 1995, 1990, 1988	Sangiovese	**
Vigna Pianacci	Castello di Luiano	1997, 1995, 1990, 1988	Sangiovese	**
Vigna Il Vallone	Santa Anna	1997, 1995, 1990, 1988	Cabernet Sauvignon/ Sangiovese	****
Le Vignacce	Villa Cilnia	1990, 1988	Sangiovese	***/****
Vigneto La Gavine	Villa Cerna	1997, 1995, 1990	Cabernet Sauvignon	****
Vigorello	San Felice	1997, 1995, 1988	Cabernet Sauvignon/ Sangiovese	***
Villa di Bagnolo	Marchesi Pancrazi	1997, 1995, 1990	Pinot Noir	***
Vinattieri Rosso II	M. Castelli	1997, 1995, 1990, 1988	Sangiovese	***
Vocato	Villa Cilnia	1997, 1995, 1988	Cabernet Sauvignon	***

AGING POTENTIAL

Brunello di Montalcino: 8–25 years

Carmignano: 5–8 years

Chianti Classico: 3–15 years*

Rosso di Montalcino: 5–8 years

Tuscan Whites: 1–2 years

Vino Nobile di Montepulciano: 5–10 years

Vino da Tavolas (red wine blends): 5–20 years

*Only a handful of Chianti producers make wines that age and last this long.

OVERALL QUALITY LEVEL

For one of the world's most famous wine regions, the quality, while on the upswing, is depressingly variable. Some famous estates in Brunello continue to live off their historic reputations while making poor wine, and there is an ocean of mediocre Chianti producers. The exciting new-breed Sangiovese/Cabernet, Cabernet Franc, and Merlot wines can be superb, but they are produced in limited quantities and are expensive. As for the white wines, the situation is intolerable, and the Italians need to wake up to the fact that high-tech, computerized, stainless-steel tanks, centrifuges, sterile bottling, and obsessive reliance on micropore filter machines are a fail-safe policy for making pleasureless wines.

MOST IMPORTANT INFORMATION TO KNOW

Forget the Italian wine regulations that are supposed to promote a better product. There are many disgustingly poor wines that carry the government's highest guarantee of quality, the DOCG, or Denominazione di Origine Controllata e Garantita. Many of the Vino de Tavolas are vastly superior wines, and this title is supposedly left for Italy's lowest level, the generic wines. The operative rule is, who are the top producers? Then and only then will you be able to make your way through the perilous selection process for Italian wines.

BUYING STRATEGY

A fundamental rule with respect to Tuscan wines is to buy all the 1997s that can be afforded. Unanimously called the "vintage of the century" for Tuscany, this is a vintage of extraordinary ripeness and richness that should rival the finest produced in such great years as 1990 and 1985. It is a consistently superb vintage throughout Tuscany's viticultural regions.

VINTAGE GUIDE

1997—The greatest vintage since 1985.

1996—A good to very good vintage, but irregular in quality.

1995—An excellent year that may not quite live up to the initial high hopes, 1995 is very good, and in many cases outstanding.

1994—An above average vintage with considerable irregularity. Where well chosen, there are some fine wines, but this is a model of inconsistency.

1993—This vintage, slightly above average in quality, has been overhyped. High-acid, tannic wines were produced.

1992—A difficult vintage with diluted wines produced.

1991—This was a very difficult year throughout Tuscany. Some light, agreeable, correct wines that should have been drunk in the first 3–5 years after the vintage were made. On paper, it is a below-average-quality vintage.

1990—This is the best year for Tuscany between 1985 and 1997. The wines exhibit terrific color, superripe aromas, wonderful richness, and surprisingly crisp acidity, something that is difficult to achieve in years of great ripeness. The bigger Chiantis and Chianti Classico Riservas will last for 10–15 years, and the Cabernet Sauvignon/Sangiovese–based Vino da Tavolas should last for 15 or more years. In Brunello di Montalcino, this is the greatest vintage in 3 decades!

1989—Tuscany was inundated by rain in 1989. Consequently the wines exhibit a certain hollowness and lightness. Some competent examples have emerged, but this is a below average vintage.

1988—Touted as a great year in Tuscany, 1988 is certainly a very good one. The wines display pronounced tannins and considerable structure. In some cases the green, astringent tannins suggest that not all the grapes reached full physiological maturity. Nevertheless there are enough good wines to rate this vintage as one of the best of the decade. It is eclipsed in quality by 1982, 1985, 1990, 1995, and 1997.

1987—Light, agreeable, pleasantly fruity wines were made in 1987, but most are now fading. Avoid.

1986—A good vintage that at present is lost in the hype surrounding 1985. The wines are well balanced and round. The Chianti Classico Riservas are recommended, but should be drunk up.

1985—A smashing, no-holds-barred, incredible year, with the wines bursting at the seams with a superripe, velvety, opulent, plummy fruitiness, full body, and a lushness and precociousness not seen since 1971. The wines are seductive, glamorous, voluptuous, and fabulously tasty. The lighter-style Chiantis should have been drunk up; the serious Chiantis and Vino da Tavolas will drink well until 2000–2005. The Brunellos will keep for another 10 years. The wines from the top producers are not to be missed.

1984—A dreadful year, much worse in Tuscany than in Piedmont to the north. Rain and a paucity of sunshine were the culprits. No doubt the trade will say the wines are light and commercial, but at this point this looks to be a vintage to pass up.

1983—Quite highly regarded. Tuscany had weather similar to that experienced in Bordeaux hundreds of miles to the west. A drought year of intense heat caused sugars and the consequent alcohol level to skyrocket in the grapes. The wines are ripe, alcoholic, fat, low in acidity, and jammy, with deep layers of fruit. All are in decline or fully mature.

1982—Considered more "classic" than 1983, which I suppose means less powerful and less opulently fruity and rich wines. Certainly it is a good vintage, with firm tannins, fine depth, and ripeness. The second-best year between 1975 and 1990, 1982 is a year to be taken seriously. For Brunello di Montalcino, it is the best vintage since 1970.

OLDER VINTAGES

Avoid 1978, 1977, 1976, 1974, 1973, and 1972; 1971 and 1970 are superb years if the wines have been well stored.

RATING TUSCANY'S BEST PRODUCERS

Note: Most producers make both a Chianti Classico and a Chianti Classico Riserva. In the following chart, for purposes of simplification, the star rating shown for each producer's Chianti Classico also pertains to their Chianti Classico Riserva, unless otherwise noted. I have treated Brunello di Montalcino and Brunello di Montalcino Riserva in the same manner. Single-vineyard Chiantis are treated as a separate qualitative item, as are the vast number of Vino da Tavolas. Production of the single vineyards and Vino da Tavolas is often extremely small, often not more than 500–1,000 cases. Thus, as with so many great wines of the world, availability is poor outside of a handful of the top Italian wine specialist shops.

* * * * *(OUTSTANDING)

Altesino Brunello di Montalcino Montosoli

Altesino Brunello di Montalcino Vigna
  Altesino

Ambra Carmignano Riserva Vigna Alta

L. Antinori Merlot Masseto Vino da Tavola

L. Antinori Ornellaia Vino da Tavola

P. Antinori Solaia Vino da Tavola

P. Antinori Tignanello Vino da Tavola

Argiano Solengo Vino da Tavola

Felsina Berardenga Chianti Classico
  Riserva Rancia

Casse Basse Brunello di Montalcino

Corelli Brunello di Montalcino

Costanti Brunello di Montalcino

Le Macchiole Messorio Merlot Vino da
  Tavola

Monte Vertine Il Sodaccio Vino da
  Tavola
Neukom Doris Nardo di Montepeloso Vino
  da Tavola
Ornellaia Merlot Masseto Vino da
  Tavola
Ornellaia Vino da Tavola
Pertimali Brunello di Montalcino
Ciacci Piccolomini d'Aragona Brunello di
  Montalcino
Poggio Scalette Il Carboniaone Vino da
  Tavola
Le Pupille Saffredi Vino da Tavola
Castello dei Rampolla Sammarco Vino da
  Tavola

E. Ricasoli-Firidolfi Rocca di Montegrossi
  Geremia Vino da Tavola
Ruffino Chianti Classico Riserva Ducale
  (gold label)
San Giusto a Rententano Percarlo Vino da
  Tavola
San Guido Sassicaia Vino da Tavola
Azienda Agricola La Torre (Luigi Anania)
  Brunello di Montalcino
Tua Rita Guisto dei Notri Vino da Tavola
Tua Rita Redigaffi Vino da Tavola
Castell'In Villa Chianti Classico Riserva
Villa Cafaggio Cortaccio Vino da Tavola
Villa Cafaggio San Martino Vino da Tavola

* * * * *(EXCELLENT)

Altesino Alte d'Altesi Vino da Tavola
Altesino Brunello di Montalcino
Altesino Cabernet Sauvignon Vino da
  Tavola
Altesino Palazzo Altesi Vino da
  Tavola****/*****
Castello di Ama Merlot Vigna L'Apparita
  Vino da Tavola
Ambra Carmignano
P. Antinori Chianti Classico Peppole
P. Antinori Chianti Classico Riserva Badia
  a Passignano
P. Antinori Chianti Classico Riserva
  Marchese
P. Antinori Secentenario Vino da Tavola
Avignonesi Merlot Vino da Tavola
Avignonesi Vino Nobile di Montepulciano
Badia a Coltibuono Chianti Classico
Badia a Coltibuono Sangioveto di
  Coltibuono Vino da Tavola
Barbi Brunello di Montalcino
Barbi Brunello di Montalcino Riserva
Barbi Brunello di Montalcino Vigna del
  Fiore
Felsina Berardenga Chianti Classico
Felsina Berardenga Fontalloro Vino da
  Tavola
Boscarelli Boscarelli Vino da Tavola
Boscarelli Vino Nobile di Montepulciano
La Braccesca Vino Nobile di
  Montepulciano
Caparzo Brunello di Montalcino La Casa
Caparzo Ca del Pazzo Vino da Tavola

Frederico Carletti Vino Nobile di
  Montepulciano
Castelgiocondo Brunello di Montalcino
  Riserva
Cerbaiona Brunello di
  Montalcino****/*****
Corrina I Cipressi
Costanti Rosso di Montalcino
Dei Vino Nobile di Montepulciano
Dei Vino Nobile di Montepulciano Riserva
Farneta Bentiboglio Vino da Tavola
Fattoria Poggio Piano Vino da Tavola
Fontodi La Case Via Syrah Vino da Tavola
Fontodi Chianti Classico
Fontodi Chianti Classico Riserva
Fontodi Chianti Classico Riserva Vigna
  del Sorbo
Fontodi Flaccianello Vino da Tavola
Castello di Gabbiano R and R Vino da
  Tavola
Geografico Agricoltori del Geografico Vino
  da Tavola
Gracciano Vino Nobile di Montepulciano
Isole e Olena Collezione de Marchi l'Ermo
  Vino da Tavola
Lilliano Anagallis Vino da Tavola
Lisini Brunello di Montalcino
Luce Vino da Tavola
Le Macchiole Paleo****/*****
Monsanto Chianti Classico Il
  Poggio****/*****
Monsanto Nemo Vino da Tavola
Monsanto Sangioveto Grosso Vino da Tavola

Monsanto Tinscvil Vino da Tavola
Monte Antico Rosso
Monte Vertine Le Pergole Torte Vino da
 Tavola
Monte Vertine Riserva Vino da Tavola
Moris Farms Morellino di Scansano
Nozzole Chianti Classico Riserva
Nozzole Il Pareto Vino da
 Tavola****/*****
Podere Il Palazzino Chianti Classico
Podere Il Palazzino Chianti Classico
 Riserva
Podere Il Palazzino Grosso Senese Vino da
 Tavola****/*****
Castello della Paneretta Chianti Classico
 Vigneto Torre a Destra
Pertimali Rosso di Montalcino
Ciacci Piccolomini d'Aragona Rosso di
 Montalcino
Pieve di Santa Restituta Brunello di
 Montalcino Rennina ****/*****
Pieve di Santa Restituta Brunello di
 Montalcino Sugarille ****/*****
Poggio Antico Altero Vino da Tavola
Poggio Antico Brunello di
 Montalcino****/*****
Poggio Brandi Vino da Tavola
Il Poggione (Roberto Franceschi) Brunello
 di Montalcino
Le Pupille Morellino di Scansano Riserva
Castello di Querceto Chianti Classico
Castello di Querceto Chianti Classico
 Riserva
Castello di Querceto Cignale Vino da
 Tavola****/*****
Castello di Querceto La Corte Vino da
 Tavola
Castello di Querceto Il Querciolaia Vino da
 Tavola

Castello dei Rampolla Chianti Classico
 Riserva
E. Ricasoli-Firidolfi Chianti Classico
E. Ricasoli-Firidolfi Chianti Classico
 Riserva
E. Ricasoli-Firidolfi Chianti Classico
 Riserva Rocca di Montegrossi
Ruffino Chianti Classico Riserva Ducale
 (tan label)
San Felice Brunello di Montalcino
 Campogiovanni
San Giusto a Rententano Chianti Classico
Fattori Santa Anna Vigna Il Vallone Vino
 da Tavola
Guicciardini Strozzi Sodole Vino da
 Tavola****/*****
Terrabianca Campaccio Vino da Tavola
Terrabianca Campaccio Riserva Vino da
 Tavola
Terrabianca Chianti Riserva Croce
Terrabianca Chianti Scassino
Terrabianca Cipresso Vino da Tavola
Tenuta di Trinoro Palazzi
Tenuta di Trinoro Vino da Tavola
Azienda Agricola La Torre (Luigi Anania)
 Rosso di Montalcino
Val di Suga Brunello di Montalcino
Val di Suga Brunello di Montalcino Vigna
 Spuntali
Castell'In Villa Chianti Classico
Castell'In Villa Santacroce Vino da Tavola
Villa Cafaggio Chianti Classico
Villa Cafaggio Solatio Basilica Vino da
 Tavola****/*****
Castello di Volpaia Balifico Vino da Tavola
Castello di Volpaia Chianti Classico
 Riserva
Castello di Volpaia Coltassala Vino da
 Tavola

* * * (GOOD)

Altesino Rosso di Altesino
Altesino Rosso di Montalcino
Castello di Ama Chianti Classico
Castello di Ama Chianti Classico single-
 vineyard cuvées***/****
Avignonesi Cabernet Sauvignon Vino da
 Tavola
Avignonesi Grifi Vino da Tavola
Badia a Coltibuono Chianti Cetamura

Badia a Coltibuono Coltibuono Rosso Vino
 da Tavola
Erik Banti Morellino di Scansano
Boscarelli Chianti Colli Senesi
Brolio Chianti Classico Riserva
Caparzo Brunello di Montalcino
Carpineto Chianti Classico Riserva
Castelgiocondo Merlot Vino da
 Tavola***/****

Castellare Chianti Classico

Castellare I Sodi di San Niccolo Vino da Tavola

Castruccio Vino da Tavola

Cennatoio Chianti Classico

Cennatoio Etrusco Vino da Tavola

Cennatoio Mammolo Vino da Tavola

Colognole Chianti Ruffina

Dievole Chianti Classico Novecento

Dievole Chianti Classico Riserva

Dievole Chianti Classico Vigna Dieuele

Dievole Chianti Classico Vigna Sessina

Castello di Farnetella Chianti Colli Senesi

Fonterutoli Brancaia Vino da Tavola

Fonterutoli Chianti Classico***/****

Fonterutoli Chianti Ser Lapo

Fonterutoli Concerto Vino da Tavola

Fossi Chianti

Frescobaldi Montesodi Chianti Ruffina

Frescobaldi Mormoreto Vino da Tavola

Castello di Gabbiano Ania Vino da Tavola

Castello di Gabbiano Chianti Classico Riserva***/****

Cantina Gattavecchi Chianti Colli Senesi

Cantina Gattavecchi Vino Nobile di Montepulciano

Geografico Brunello di Montalcino

Geografico Chianti Classico

Geografico Chianti Classico Castello di Fagnano

Geografico Chianti Classico Contessa di Radda

Geografico Sorbaiano Montescudaio Vino da Tavola

Isole e Olena Boro Cepparello Vino da Tavola

Isole e Olena Chianti Classico

Lanciola Chianti Fiorentini

Lanciola Chianti Le Masse di Greve

La Leccia Chianti Classico

Lilliano Chianti Classico

Lilliano Chianti Classico Riserva Eleanora

Le Masse di San Leolino Chianti Classico

Le Masse di San Leolino Chianti Classico Riserva

Monsanto Chianti Classico Riserva***/****

Castello della Paneretta Chianti Classico

Castello della Paneretta Quattro Centennario Vino da Tavola

Petroio Chianti Classico Montetondo

Petroio L'Unico Vino da Tavola

Poggio Antico Rosso di Montalcino

Poggio Bonelli Chianti Classico Riserva

Poggio Galiga Chianti Rufina

S. Quirico Chianti

Roccadoro Chianti Classico

Rodano Chianti Classico

Ruffino Cabreo Il Borgo Vino da Tavola

Ruffino Chianti Classico

Ruffino Chianti Classico Aziano

Ruffino Chianti Classico Nozzole

San Felice Vigorello Vino da Tavola

Fattori Santa Anna Rosso di Santa Anna

Talosa Chianti

Talosa Rosso di Montalcino

Talosa Vino Nobile di Montepulciano

Toscolo Chianti Classico

Toscolo Chianti Classico Riserva

Tenuta Trerose Vino Nobile di Montepulciano Riserva

Villa di Geggiano Chianti Classico Riserva

Villa La Selva Selvamaggio

Castello di Volpaia Chianti Classico

THE BEST OF THE REST

Following are wines and/or producers not to be missed from other viticultural regions of Italy.

***** *(OUTSTANDING)*

Dal Forno Romano Amarone della Valpolicella

Dal Forno Romano Recioto

Dal Forno Romano Valpolicella

Falesco Montiano Vino da Tavola

Fantasie del Cardeto Vino da Tavola

Maculan Acininobili (Sweet) Veneto

Maculan Torcolato (Sweet) Veneto

Miani Merlot

Miani Ronco Calvari

Montrevetrano

Pieve del Vescovo Lucciaio

Quintarelli Alzero Vino da Tavola
   Cabernet Franc
Regaleali Chardonnay Sicily

Rubino della Palazzola Vino da Tavola
Schiopetto Sauvignon
Terra di Lavoro Vino da Tavola

* * * * (EXCELLENT)

Allegrini La Poja ****/*****
Allegrini Valpolicella La Grola
Allegrini Valpolicella Palazzo della Torre
Anselmi Soave (various cuvées)
Argiolas Costera
Argiolas Turriga
Bellavista Cabernet Sauvignon Solesine
   Vino da Tavolo
Bellavista Chardonnay Annunciata
Bellavista Chardonnay Storica
Bellavista Chardonnay Uccellanda
Bellavista Franciacorta Grand Cuvée
Borgo del Tiglio Chardonnay
La Carraia Merlot Fobiano
Colli Amerini Carbio Rosso Superiore
Falesco Grechetto
Falesco Merlot d'Aprilia Doc
Foradori Pinot Bianco Sparzon
·Foradori Teroldego Sgarzon Trentino
Francesco Gravner Breg

Francesco Gravner Chardonnay
Francesco Gravner Ribolla Gialla
Francesco Gravner Sauvignon
Inama Soave (various cuvées)
Librandi Ciro Rosso Riserva Duca
   Sanfelice
Librandi Gravello
Elio Monti Montepulciano d'Abruzzo
Regaleali Cabernet Sauvignon
Schiopetto Pinot Bianco Collio
Schiopetto Tocai Friulano
Taurino Notarpanaro
Taurino Salice Salentino Rosso Riserva
Venegazzu Della Casa
Venegazzu Della Casa Capo di Sato
Villa Russiz Merlot Graf de la Tour Friuli-
   Collio
Villa Russiz Sauvignon de la Tour Friuli-
   Collio

CASTELLO D'ALBOLA

1993	Acciaiolo Vino da Tavola	D	87
1996	Chianti Classico	B	86
1994	Chianti Classico Riserva	C	85

The 1993 Acciaiolo, a blend of 65% Sangioveto and 35% Cabernet Sauvignon, aged in small oak casks, is a well-made, dark ruby-colored wine with copious quantities of spicy new oak. An internationally styled attractive wine, with new oak, black currant fruit, *pain grillé* nuances, medium body, moderate tannin, and good purity, it needs 1–2 years of aging and should keep for a decade.

The charming, light-bodied, fruity, soft 1996 Chianti Classico will be a crowd pleaser. Supple, with a medium ruby color, good cherry fruit, and an easygoing finish, it will drink well for 1–2 years. The 1994 Chianti Classico Riserva is a more ambitiously styled wine, with more wood, tannin, and body, but nowhere near the charm, suppleness, and overall pleasure of its younger sibling. The 1994 Riserva is a good wine, and perhaps more intensity will emerge as the wine evolves in the bottle, but for now it appears to be a more intellectually oriented Chianti designed for those who prefer to talk about wine rather than drink it. I'll stick with the 1996, although I admire the 1994 Riserva. The latter wine should last for 4–5 years.

ALTESINO

1994	Alte d'Altesi Vino da Tavola	D	90
1993	Alte d'Altesi Vino da Tavola	D	89
1993	Borgo d'Altesi	D	86

1990 Brunello di Montalcino	D	90
1990 Brunello di Montalcino Montosoli	D	94
1990 Brunello di Montalcino Riserva	E	91+
1994 Palazzo Altesi Vino da Tavola	D	88
1993 Palazzo Altesi Vino da Tavola	C	90
1995 Rosso di Altesino	B	87
1995 Rosso di Montalcino	C	88

One of the finer producers of Brunello di Montalcino, Altesino has had an impeccable track record of producing high-quality wine since their first vintage in the early seventies. The following releases are all noteworthy. The softest, lightest wine is the 1995 Rosso di Altesino, a 90% Sangiovese Grosso/10% Cabernet Sauvignon blend aged in tank and bottled early to preserve its ripe fruitiness and succulent texture. The wine is round and attractive, with a dark ruby/purple color, low acidity, and copious quantities of sweet strawberry/cherry fruit. It is a luscious restaurant-style wine to drink over the next several years. The impressive 1995 Rosso di Montalcino is fashioned from 100% Sangiovese Grosso and bottled after 7 months of aging in Slavonian barrels. It possesses an outstanding nose of superripe wild blueberry and cherry scents. Not complex, the wine is pure, with a fruit-driven personality, medium to full body, and luscious quantities of jammy fruit balanced by velvety tannin. It should continue to drink well for 5–6 years. It provides a glimpse of the outstanding raw materials that I suspect will be found in its bigger sibling, the unreleased Brunello di Montalcino.

I have always enjoyed Altesino's Vino da Tavolas, of which the 1994 Palazzo Altesi is another fine example. This is the most Burgundian-style wine made by Altesino. Aged in French oak barrels, of which one-third are new, this 100% Sangiovese Grosso is produced in limited quantities of approximately 1,000 cases. The 1994 initially exhibits a leesy, kinky nose, but that blows off to reveal sweet vanillin and gobs of ripe jammy cherry and plum fruit intermixed with weedy tobacco and spicy herbs. The wine is soft and round, as well as expansive and luscious on the palate, with low acidity. It should drink well for 5–6 years. The 1994 Alte d'Altesi Vino da Tavola is a bigger, denser, fuller, more tannic wine made from 70% Sangiovese Grosso and 30% Cabernet Sauvignon. It is more Bordeaux-like wine than the Palazzo Altesi, offering a dark purple color, and sweet tobacco and black currant aromas intertwined with smoky notes from new wood casks. Deep and dense, this medium- to full-bodied wine displays excellent winemaking, a spicy, ripe black fruit personality, admirable succulence, and even more depth than the Palazzo Altesi. It will last for a decade, although it will be hard to resist its current charms. It, too, is made in limited quantities of just over 1,000 cases.

The 1993 Palazzo Altesi (300 cases produced from 100% Sangiovese Grosso) is my favorite of the trio of 1993s. The wine possesses fabulous fruit, a Burgundian-like, expansive, chewy midpalate, and sexy, voluptuous, oak- and floral-tinged red and black fruit flavors. Soft tannin adds to the sumptuousness of this delicious wine. It is ideal for drinking now and over the next 5–7 years. The 1993 Borgo d'Altesi (200 cases made from 100% Cabernet Sauvignon) was the debut vintage. Although it exhibited an impressive dark ruby color as well as good weight and purity on the palate, it is closed, with a compressed, tannic, tough-textured personality. It should open with 1–2 years of cellaring, but at present it does not appear to be an exciting effort from Altesino. Last, the 1993 Alte d'Altesi (400 cases made from 70% Sangiovese Grosso and 30% Cabernet Sauvignon) offers a gorgeously perfumed, fragrant nose of fruitcake, tobacco, black currants, and new saddle leather. There is excellent richness, an attractive, multilayered texture, sweet, ripe fruit, and soft but noticeable tannin. Although accessible, it is capable of lasting for 7–8 years.

Altesino's two sensational 1990 Brunellos offer intense perfumes of jammy cherry fruit, tobacco, smoke, herbs, and licorice, immense richness and extraction of flavor, full body, and gobs of glycerin and alcohol. The single-vineyard Montosoli possesses a thicker, richer texture, more depth and length, and a slightly more focused personality. Both can be drunk today but promise to evolve for 10–20 years. The 1990 Riserva exhibits a broodingly deep garnet/plum color, sweet aromas of tobacco, chocolate, herbs, and dried cherries, full body, outstanding depth, and an impressive yet tannic finish. Give it 5–6 years of cellaring. Anticipated maturity: 2000–2015.

CASTELLO DI AMA

1992 L'Apparita Vino da Tavola	EE	90

A remarkable achievement in the so-so 1992 vintage for Tuscany, Castello di Ama's L'Apparita, a 100% Merlot that has been barrel-fermented and aged in new *barriques,* exhibits an opaque purple color, followed by an exceptionally rich, black cherry-scented nose with licorice, chocolate, and smoky new oak characteristics. Full bodied yet extravagantly smooth, rich, and luscious, this intense, beautifully made wine is already delicious to drink, although it is still unevolved. Based on how well past vintages have aged, the 1992 should last for 12–15+ years. The first vintage of this luxury-priced Merlot was 1985. In May 1997 I tasted a bottle of the 1985 from my cellar and found it to be still youthful and impressive.

FATTORIA AMBRA

1995 Barco Reale	B	87
1994 Carmignano Riserva Le Vigne Alte	D	91
1993 Carmignano Riserva Le Vigne Alte	C	90
1992 Carmignano Riserva Le Vigne Alte	C	87
1994 Carmignano San Cristina in Pilli	B	92

This has long been one of my favorite Marc de Grazia estates. The wines of Carmignano, a small hillside village northwest of Florence, are terribly underrated and thus underpriced. Sadly, too many of the growers still sell in bulk to larger firms, with only a handful of producers estate-bottling. Ambra has been a consistent top scorer in my tastings, producing primarily Sangiovese-based wines that include small percentages of Cabernet as well as Canaiolo and Mammolo. These are easy-to-understand, voluptuous, expansive, sexy wines. I was very impressed with the current offerings.

Ambra turned in a good performance with the 1992 Carmignano Riserva Le Vigne Alte. Although not quite as fat, ripe, and opulent as the 1994, this medium ruby wine reveals tobacco, strawberry, and smoky aromas, ripe, medium-bodied, soft flavors, and a classy finish. Drink it over the next 1–2 years. The outstanding 1993 Carmignano Riserva Le Vigne Alte exhibits the telltale cherry/strawberry fruit in its nose and flavors, as well as medium to full body, a touch of smoke, and a dense, concentrated finish. Soft, round, yet more structured than the 1994, this is a gorgeously complex, seductive wine that is hard to resist. It should drink well for another 4–6 years. The 1994 Carmignano Riserva Le Vigne Alte is a terrific wine. This is the first time I have seen the Vineyard Montalbiolo also designated on the label. The wine possesses a dark ruby color, followed by a penetrating, intense fragrance of berries, smoke, toast, and flowers. Soft, round, and opulently textured, this medium- to full-bodied, seamlessly constructed wine caresses the palate with gobs of fruit, but no sharp acid or hard tannin. It is a thrilling, sumptuously styled wine to drink over the next 4–5 years.

Ambra's 1994 Carmignano San Cristina in Pilli is a killer wine. Dark ruby colored, with a lusty, fragrant nose of red and black fruits, spice, and fruitcake, it is a lush, creamy-textured, silky wine with surprising concentration (in a vintage where dilution was supposed to be the rule of thumb). Its low acidity and amazing levels of ripe fruit suggest drinking this show-stopper over the next 3–4 years. I would love to see how this wine would fare in a blind tasting of top-notch grand cru red burgundies—just a thought. The 1995 Barco Reale offers a wonderful introduction to just how impressive Tuscany's 1995 vintage appears to be. The opaque purple color is followed by an uncomplicated wine that is loaded with gobs of smoky, ripe black cherry and currant fruit. Pure, with high extract and a somewhat monolithic, plump character, this tasty, mouth-filling, fleshy wine should drink well for another 4–5 years. Readers should note its excellent value.

LODOVICO ANTINORI

1994 Masseto Vino da Tavola	EE	91+
1995 Ornellaia Vino da Tavola	E	92

The "other" Antinori continues to turn out stunning wines from this small estate in Bolgheri on the Tuscan coast. The omnipresent Michel Rolland is the consultant, and that is evident in the rich texture and ripe, concentrated style of these wines. Is the 1995 Ornellaia better than previous vintages? It is too soon to know, but this is unquestionably another stunning wine in what has been a strong succession of top wines since 1988. The color is a saturated, thick-looking ruby/purple. The nose offers up aromas of roasted coffee, jammy black cherry liqueur, and cassis intermixed with spice. On the palate, the wine is rich and full bodied, with well-integrated wood, tannin, and acidity. Pure, youthful, and accessible, this impressively endowed wine should drink well for 10–15+ years. The rich 1994 Masseto is a Merlot-dominated cuvée with lavish quantities of spicy new oak. In addition to the obvious *pain grillé* notes, the Masseto exhibits less evolution than the 1995 Ornellaia. This full-bodied, spicy, rich wine cuts a broad swath on the palate. It requires another 12–18 months of bottle age, after which it should continue to improve for a decade. It will last for 15 or more years.

PIERO ANTINORI

1996 Chianti Classico Badia a Passignano	B	85
1995 Chianti Classico Badia a Passignano	C	87
1993 Chianti Classico Badia a Passignano Riserva	D	88
1990 Chianti Classico Riserva (Villa Antinori) ·	B	88
1990 Chianti Classico Riserva Badia a Passignano	D	91
1990 Chianti Classico Riserva Marchese Antinori	C	90
1995 Goado Al Tasso Bolgheri	E	89
1996 Sangiovese Santa Cristina	A	84

Made from Antinori's Belvedere estate along the Tuscan coast, the 1995 Goado Al Tasso Bolgheri, a blend of 60% Cabernet Sauvignon and 40% Merlot, was aged 14 months in oak casks. The wine boasts a knockout nose of *pain grillé*, black currants, licorice, and sweet, jammy cherry fruit. It is concentrated and medium bodied, with a thick, juicy, succulent personality and copious glycerin and sweet tannin in the long finish. Although accessible, it promises to evolve for 7–8 years.

The 1996 Sangiovese Santa Cristina exhibits a berry-scented nose with spice and leather. In the mouth, the wine is medium bodied, short, cleanly made, and pleasant. It should drink well for 1–2 years. The more serious and concentrated 1996 Chianti Classico Badia a Passignano reveals a dark ruby color and, initially, more restrained aromatics of attractive black cherry and leather-scented fruit. In the mouth, the wine is somewhat austere but cleanly made, with medium body, and a ripe, dusty, strawberry/cherry fruitiness. It should drink well for 3–4 years.

All the Chiantis from the reliable Antinori winery are excellent. The 1995 Chianti Classico Badia a Passignano exhibits a healthy dark ruby/garnet color, followed by an attractive smoky, earthy, spice, underbrush-scented nose, medium body, good flesh, and a rich, well-textured and -extracted finish. There is sweetness because of the wine's glycerin and suppleness. Drink it over the next 5 years. The 1993 Chianti Classico Badia a Passignano Riserva reveals a denser plum/garnet color, a grilled meat, smoky, animal, spicy-scented nose, medium to full body, high extract, and a supple, fleshy mouth-feel. Long in the mouth, with a more structured feel, this youthful Chianti is capable of lasting another 10–12 years. Very impressive!

Antinori's 1990 Badia a Passignano is a terrific single-vineyard Chianti Classico. Made from Sangiovese and aged for 15 months in small oak casks, it is a powerful, rich, intense, medium- to full-bodied Chianti with a healthy dark ruby/purple color, a big, spicy, black cherry- and leather-scented nose, rich, concentrated, moderately tannic flavors, and an authoritative finish. Young and exuberant, yet approachable, this large-scale, superimpressive Chianti should age effortlessly for 10 or more years. The 1990 Chianti Classico Riserva-Marchese Antinori is a classic, textbook Chianti, displaying a healthy garnet color, a big, spicy, cedary, tobacco, and berry nose, full body, excellent concentration, and moderate tannin in the finish. It should drink well for 10–12 years.

Slightly lighter, but more precocious and charming, the Villa Antinori 1990 Chianti Classico Riserva is fruity, soft, and ideal for drinking over the next 5–6 years. These are all excellent wines that remain reference points for Tuscany. Kudos to Piero Antinori.

ARGIANO

1993	Brunello di Montalcino	D	88+
1992	Brunello di Montalcino	D	86
1991	Brunello di Montalcino	D	85
1990	Brunello di Montalcino	D	87+?
1995	Rosso di Montalcino	C	86
1996	Solengo Vino da Tavola	E	94
1995	Solengo Vino da Tavola	E	92

This excellent producer has fashioned two very fine wines. The 1993 Brunello di Montelcino's dark ruby color is followed by an intriguing nose suggestive of almond extract, truffles, and black cherry fruit intertwined with incense and Asian spices. Complex, rich, and medium to full bodied, with tart acidity and moderate tannin, this youthful Brunello will benefit from several more years of cellaring. It should evolve for 10–15+ years. Argiano's 1996 Solengo, a blend of Cabernet Sauvignon, Sangiovese, Merlot, and Syrah (500 cases produced), is a blockbuster effort. The wine boasts a saturated ruby/purple color, as well as an excellent nose of jammy blackberries, cassis, *pain grillé*, and spice. Full bodied, with superb depth, a layered texture, low acidity, and a blockbuster finish, this is an impressively endowed, smoky, rich, exotic, accessible, dry red that should age nicely for 12–15 years. Bravo to Argiano!

Argiano produced a below-average-quality, thin, watery 1994 Rosso di Montalcino that was disappointing. The excellent, sweet, earthy, ripe berry-flavored 1995 Rosso di Montalcino is well made, with copious quantities of ripe fruit, a supple texture, and good richness and depth. Drink it over the next 3–4 years.

The other offerings include a lighter-style, medium ruby-colored, soft, stylish 1991 Brunello di Montalcino. It reveals good sweetness on the attack, not much color saturation or depth, but fine equilibrium and a pleasant personality. Drink it over the next 4–5 years. The dark, murky garnet-colored 1990 Brunello di Montalcino offers sweet, gamey, earthy fruit in the nose, along with a suggestion of smoked meats, hickory wood, and cedar/tobacco. The wine is ageworthy but austere, medium to full bodied, and ferociously tannic. The high tannin level is cause for concern, but if it melts away, this wine may merit an even higher score. Potential purchasers should recognize that it needs at least 3–4 years of cellaring; it should keep for 15+ years. The 1992 Brunello di Montalcino, from a lowly regarded vintage, is a soft, round, medium-bodied wine with plum and cherry-flavored fruit, a notion of underbrush, earth, and spice, moderate weight, and a soft finish. For a Brunello, it is forward, precocious, and flattering. Drink it over the next 5–6 years.

An exceptionally impressive wine, the 1995 Solengo (meaning, to go it alone) is a superb blend of Sangiovese and Syrah. The wine, which was aged in new French oak casks, boasts a dense, saturated ruby/purple color, as well as a stunning nose of black currants, chocolate, smoke, and an elusive floral scent. Long, dense, and extravagantly rich, with full body and exceptional purity, this low-acid yet fleshy, powerful, silky-textured wine impressively conceals some serious tannin. The wine is exceptionally rich and layered in the mouth, but unevolved, yet it possesses enormous potential. Approximately 1,500 cases were made of this wine, which was released in September 1997. It should improve for 5–10 years and last for 2 decades. This is a brilliant wine!

AVIGNONESI

1990	Campannelli Vino da Tavola	EE	90
1995	Grifi Vino da Tavola	D	90
1993	Grifi Vino da Tavola	D	89
1995	Merlot Vino da Tavola	E	88
1993	Merlot Toro Desiderio Vino da Tavola	E	87
1991	Merlot Toro Desiderio Vino da Tavola	D	85
1990	Merlot Toro Desiderio Vino da Tavola	E	88
1995	Vino Nobile de Montepulciano	D	89
1993	Vino Nobile de Montepulciano Riserva	D	86

All of these offerings performed exceptionally well. However, I was disappointed in Avignonesi's 1996 Pinot Nero (Pinot Noir) and a superexpensive 1993 Avignonesi/Capannelle blended proprietary wine called "50 & 50." The latter wine costs a whopping $120, yet I rated it 78 points.

There is no problem with the quality of the three 1995s. The 1995 Vino Nobile di Montepulciano is an evolved, complex wine to drink over the next 4–5 years. The nose of cedar, new saddle leather, sweet tobacco, and strawberry/cherry fruit is followed by a lush, medium-bodied, elegant, round, gentle wine that is all finesse and seductive charm. The opaque ruby/purple-colored 1995 Merlot offers a promising nose of unevolved, sweet black cherry fruit intermingled with scents of toasty oak and spice. Medium bodied, with excellent concentration, fine purity, and overall equilibrium, this flawless, juicy, symmetrical Merlot should be at its best after another 1–2 years of cellaring; it will keep for a decade. My favorite is the 1995 Grifi. A big, smoky, blackberry, cedary, lead pencil, and currant nose is followed by a ripe, medium-bodied wine with outstanding concentration, superb balance, and a marriage of finesse and power. Beautifully crafted, with sexy layers of lush fruit, it should be consumed over the next 5–7 years.

Avignonesi's 1993 Grifi possesses a healthy dark ruby/purple color, followed by sweet, attractive berry fruit intermixed with gobs of smoky, spicy new oak. Medium to full bodied, supple, round, and mouth filling, it is Burgundian-like in its opulent richness and chewy texture. Drink this fleshy, sexy wine over the next 5–6 years. The 1993 Vino Nobile de Montepulciano Riserva is a tightly knit wine, with plenty of tannin, good spice, and dark plummy fruit intermixed with earthy, spicy, wood aromas. This medium-bodied wine is unlikely to improve, but it should last for 5–6 years.

The 1993 Merlot Toro Desiderio exhibits copious, nearly excessive amounts of toasty new oak in its aromatic profile. The wine also possesses sweet currant and black cherry fruit. In the mouth, the oak is less intrusive, with the fruit giving this wine an excellent texture, and a savory palate feel that is enhanced by clean winemaking, and earlier enough bottling to preserve the wine's freshness. This is a medium-bodied, attractive Merlot for consuming over the next 5–6 years. Although the 1991 Merlot Toro Desiderio is a good wine, it lacks charm and fruit. A dark ruby color is followed by aromas of spicy new French oak and black cherries. The wine is medium bodied, cleanly made, and fresh and should offer serviceable drinking for 2–3 years. At $8–$10 it would be a reasonable bargain, but at its current price it is just a wine for label drinkers.

The 1990 Capannelli is outstanding. The price may be painful, but that is a problem with most limited-production wines of this quality. It offers sweet, rich, jammy black cherry fruit intermixed with aromas of white chocolate, mocha, and vanillin. Medium to full bodied, dense, smoky, and ostentatious, this lush, fat, exuberantly fleshy wine is delicious to drink and should continue to hold for 8–9 years. The 1990 Merlot Toro Desiderio will please Merlot lovers, some of whom may score it even higher. The wine is full bodied, with terrific fruit purity and ripeness. What kept it from receiving an outstanding score was its lack of complexity. Yes, it possesses plenty of jammy fruit, abundant sweet, toasty oak, and a soft, silky, seamless texture, but hard tannin in the finish, and the wine's one-dimensional quality and fruit/oak-driven personality make it excellent rather than exceptional. Already delicious, it should continue to drink well for 10–12 years.

BADIA A COLTIBUONO

1993	Chianti Cetamura	A	85
1995	Chianti Classico	C	86
1993	Chianti Classico	A	87
1994	Chianti Classico Riserva	D	86
1990	Chianti Classico Riserva	C	89+
1995	Sangioveto	E	86
1990	Sangioveto	D	94
1988	Sangioveto	D	89+
1985	Sangioveto	D	94

One of the more famous wineries in Chianti, this is a reliable name for solidly made, ageworthy Chiantis. I was disappointed in the 1995 Cetamura Chianti, their value-priced *négociant* wine, normally a candidate for one of my best buys. Lamentably the 1995 was shallow and thin. In contrast, the 1995 Chianti Classico exhibits good cherry, spicy, leathery scents in a medium-bodied, deep ruby-colored, supple format. It possesses 4–5 years of aging potential.

The 1994 Chianti Classico Riserva, from a difficult vintage, is a soft, elegant, strawberry-scented and -flavored wine with excellent red berry fruit (cherries), toast, and a peppery, spicy, tobacco-scented finish. It should drink well for 2–3 years. The 1995 Sangioveto, which can be an outstanding wine, is high in acidity and closed, without the concentration and extract I expected. It is medium bodied, crisp, and tart, with good ripeness and an attractive perfume of new oak, strawberries, cherries, and tobacco. Perhaps another 1–2 years of cellaring will result in more flesh and forwardness, but I am not convinced. I would opt to drink it over the next 3–4 years.

The least expensive Chianti offering from Badia a Coltibuono, Cetamura has regularly made the "Best Buy" recommendations of *The Wine Advocate*. The noteworthy 1993 exhibits a sweet, berry-scented nose with aromas of tobacco, dried flowers, and herbs. Elegant, with admirable fruit and ripeness, this is an attractive, supple, medium-bodied Chianti to drink over the next 2–3 years.

Tuscany's 1993 vintage has turned out to be better than expected. Although the vintage is not comparable to 1985 or 1990, it produced some good, solid wines. The 1993 Chianti Classico reveals a typical Chianti nose of cedar, saddle leather, and Bing cherry fruit. Medium bodied, with good spice, it is a wine to drink over the next 3–4 years.

The sweet, rich, medium- to full-bodied 1990 Chianti Classico Riserva (all the Riservas are made from 90% Sangiovese and 10% Canaiolo) exhibits a deep ruby/garnet color and a moderately intense, sweet nose of tobacco, red and black fruits, and toasty oak. Ripe, medium to full bodied, with excellent, possibly outstanding richness, this firmly structured yet accessible Chianti should reach full maturity in 2–3 years and last for 12–15. It is an impressive 1990.

A spectacular Sangioveto, the 1990 Badia a Coltibuono Sangioveto boasts an opaque dark plum/garnet color, as well as a huge nose of smoky, ripe black fruits, and truffles. Sweet and rich, with fabulous concentration, a multilayered, chewy texture, and an expansive, sweet, inner core of fruit, this is a spectacular, full-bodied, supple, yet marvelously concentrated wine that can be drunk now or aged for another 12–15+ years.

Badia a Coltibuono's 1988 Sangioveto is full bodied, dense, and concentrated, with considerable structure and tannin. A dark ruby/garnet color is followed by a nose of mushroomy, earthy, ripe fruit aromas intermingled with scents of spice and new saddle leather. Although the wine is less successful and less concentrated than the 1990, it offers a muscular, beefy mouthful of young Sangioveto. The wine can be drunk now, but it will benefit from 2–3 more years of cellaring. It should last through the first decade of the next century.

A spectacular, fully mature Sangioveto, the 1985 offers a huge nose of black fruits, Asian spices, leather, overripe, jammy plums, and other black fruits. Full bodied, with a huge, sweet entry, a supple, intensely concentrated palate, and a long, rich finish, with great fruit and overall balance, this beautiful wine should be drunk over the next 10–12 years.

FATTORIA BAGGIOLINO

1995 Poggio Brandi Vino da Tavola	D	88+?
1993 Poggio Brandi Vino da Tavola	D	86
1990 Poggio Brandi Vino da Tavola	D	89

The 1995 Poggio Brandi, an 80% Sangiovese/20% Ciliegiolo blend crafted by oenologist Franco Bernabei and bottled after 16–18 months of oak aging, reveals copious quantities of the two hallmarks that characterize Tuscany's finest 1995s—high extract and high tannin. This is a substantial, mouth-filling, full-bodied, muscular wine, but its rustic tannin is cause for concern. The color is deep ruby/purple, and the wine offers attractive chocolatey, cherry liqueur, smoky aromas. In the mouth, it is a big, ripe, muscular effort, but the finish contains mouth-searing levels of tannin. While the wine's overall balance merits caution, it is purely made, and the fruit extract is evident. Give it 2–3 years of cellaring and hope the tannin melts away faster than the fruit. Anticipated maturity: 2002–2010.

These wines, made primarily from Sangiovese and aged 18 months in casks, often remind me of an exotic, spicy Pomerol. The soft, midweight 1993 Poggio Brandi exhibits plenty of toasty, smoky oak and chocolate-filled, cherry candylike fruit. It is ideal for drinking over the next 3–4 years. The bigger, richer, more exotic 1990 Poggio Brandi reveals greater quantities of fruit and glycerin, as well as nearly outstanding richness. The wine possesses a big, smoky, tobacco, earthy, cedary, ripe, jammy cherry nose, low acidity, abundant glycerin, and a fleshy, expansive mouth-feel. It should be drunk over the next 4–5 years.

BARBI

1994 Brigante dei Barbi Proprietary Red	E	87
1988 Brunello di Montalcino	D	88+
1990 Brunello di Montalcino Vigna del Fiore	D	93
1988 Brunello di Montalcino Vigna del Fiore	D	90

Although Barbi fashioned some marvelous Brunellos throughout the sixties and early seventies, it has been a long time since I have tasted a Barbi Brunello as good as these three offerings. The big, tannic, backward 1988 Brunello di Montalcino exhibits a medium to dark ruby color and a moderately intense bouquet of cedar, herbs, and jammy fruit. Full bodied, powerful, tannic, and long, with excellent concentration and structure, this is a Brunello to lay away for 1–3 years and drink over the subsequent 15. The 1988 Brunello di Montalcino Vigna del Fiore exhibits a wonderful attractive, complex nose of new saddle leather, Asian spices, sweet red and black fruits, and cedar. Full bodied, with velvety texture and intense fruit that is beginning to mellow into a complex format, this rich, powerful Brunello can be drunk now or cellared for another 10–15 years. Impressive!

The 1990 Vigna del Fiore is a densely colored, rich, massive Brunello with juicy, succulent fruit, full body, layers of concentration, and a long, spicy, sweet, supple finish. Based on the handful of 1990 Brunello di Montalcinos I have seen, this may be a great vintage for this historic viticultural zone.

Dark ruby/plum colored, with a big, meaty, spicy, peppery, and herb nose, the 1994 Brigante dei Barbi Proprietary Red is a fleshy, robust wine that possesses fine depth, an open-knit texture, and dry tannin in the finish (which lowered my overall score). Drink it over the next 2–5 years.

BIONDI SANTI

1990 Brunello di Montalcino Tenuta Greppo	E	85

I tasted this wine as soon as I opened it, as well as 1 hour later, 8 hours later, and 18 hours later. The neck brochure suggests 8 hours of breathing is necessary to give the wine every opportunity to impress. The light ruby color is among the least saturated of all the 1990 Brunellos. As the neck label suggests, the wine opens with airing, offering up a subtle aromatic profile of dried roses, saddle leather, and earthy notes. With a transparent, watery color, this austere, medium-bodied, tart, high-acid wine lacks fruit, extract, and concentration. This is the most famous estate in Tuscany (perhaps Italy), and while this wine's high acidity and tannin will ensure 20–40 years of longevity, the wine will never provide much pleasure.

BOSCARELLI

1995 Boscarelli Vino da Tavola	D	87+
1994 Boscarelli Vino da Tavola	D	86
1990 Proprietary Red Wine	D	92
1994 Vino Nobile di Montepulciano	C	86
1990 Vino Nobile di Montepulciano Riserva	C	87+
1995 Vino Nobile di Montepulciano Riserva del Nocio	D	90
1993 Vino Nobile di Montepulciano Riserva del Nocio	D	88

The 1995 Boscarelli Vino da Tavola, a blend of 80% Sangiovese Grosso and 20% Cabernet Sauvignon, is typical of many of the better 1995 Tuscan wines. The color is dense ruby/purple, and the wine is ripe, but it is extremely tannic and backward. This is a structured, spicy, medium-bodied wine with excellent depth, but it requires cellaring. Readers will especially appreciate its earth-tinged berry fruit, licorice, smoke, and briery character. Anticipated maturity: 2001–2010. As for the 1995 Vino Nobile di Montepulciano Riserva del Nocio, this is an outstanding, dense, purple-colored wine offering a superb combination of fruit and structure. The fruit is dominant, giving the wine jammy cherry, smoky, dried herblike aromas and flavors. Medium bodied and spicy, with moderate tannin and impressive purity and depth, this stylish, well-endowed wine can be drunk now or cellared for 10–12 years.

Boscarelli's 1994 Vino da Tavola is a soft, plush, straightforward wine with a dark ruby color and gobs of black cherry fruit intermingled with scents of smoke, earth, and herbs. An accessible, medium-bodied, open-knit wine, it will provide ideal drinking over the next 2–3 years. The spicy, leathery, earthy-scented 1994 Vino Nobile di Montepulciano possesses moderate quantities of cherry fruit. Medium bodied, with hard tannin in the finish, this spicy, earthy, dusty-textured wine will please those who prefer their Italian wines somewhat rustic. It should drink well for 3–4 years.

In contrast, the excellent 1993 Vino Nobile di Montepulciano Riserva del Nocio is a sweeter, richer wine with a deep ruby/garnet color and loads of smoky, sweet, ripe, jammy black cherry fruit intermingled with whiffs of new saddle leather. In the mouth, the wine is medium bodied, with layers of juicy, succulent fruit, good spice, adequate acidity, and a dry, tannic, mineral-dominated finish. This wine can be drunk now as well as over the next 5–6 years.

In view of the disappointing 1991 and 1992 Vino Nobile di Montepulcianos, readers in search of a good Tuscan red should look for Boscarelli's 1990 Riserva. It possesses a deep garnet color, sweet ripe fruit, dusty tannin, medium to full body, good flavor extraction, and a backward, tannic personality. Give it several more years of cellaring. Boscarelli's 1990 Proprietary Red Wine, a blend of 90% Sangiovese and 10% Cabernet Sauvignon, hits the bull's-eye. It exhibits an opaque ruby/purple color and a sensational nose of smoky herbs, toasty new oak, and gobs of black cherry and currant fruit. Dense and full bodied, with gobs of flavor, this multidimensional and multilayered wine possesses a gorgeously succulent mid-palate as well as a finish that lasts for 20–30 seconds. It is a knockout example from this outstanding vintage in Tuscany.

LA BRACCESCA

1995 Rosso di Montalpulciano	B	85
1994 Rosso di Montepulciano	B	87
1993 Rosso di Montepulciano	B	87
1994 Vino Nobile di Montepulciano	C	87
1992 Vino Nobile di Montepulciano	C	88

This Tuscan estate, owned by the Antinori family, can claim Renzo Cotarella as its winemaker. A large estate of 179 acres, La Braccesca has been producing wines since 1900. The 1995 Rosso di Montepulciano is a medium-weight, fruity, grapey wine with little complexity but good elegance and moderate quantities of pure strawberry/cherry fruit. It is well balanced, with enough acidity to provide uplift. Drink it over the next 2–3 years. The deep ruby-colored 1994 Vino Nobile di Montepulciano is a richer, sweeter, fleshier wine, with more concentrated fruit and good spice. It is an elegant, pure, fruit-driven wine with low acidity and open charm, suggesting it should be drunk over the next 2–3 years.

Considering that 1994 and 1992 are both extremely difficult vintages in Tuscany, it is admirable that this estate fashioned such superlative efforts. The 1994 Rosso di Montepulciano is a vanillin-tinged, ripe, richly fruity, supple wine with a dark ruby color, a sweet nose, and round, generous flavors. It is not going to make old bones, but for drinking over the next 3–4 years, this is an attractive wine. The 1993 Rosso di Montepulciano is cut from a similar mold. It reveals more complexity in the nose, as some leathery, herbal, earthy elements have emerged to go along with the ripe fruit. The wine is medium bodied, with excellent definition and richness, a silky texture, and a soft finish. It is best drunk over the next 2–3 years.

Very few 1992 Tuscan wines have been recommended in these pages, but La Braccesca's 1992 Vino Nobile di Montepulciano is an exception to the rule. A surprisingly saturated dark ruby/purple color is followed by a sweet, rich, medium-bodied wine with fine concentration, moderate tannin, and good balance, ripeness, and purity. Although it may always possess a tough edge, it is a reasonably priced Vino Nobile that should age well for 7–8 years.

LE CALCINATE

1995 Chianti Colli Senese	A	86
1994 Gemignano	B	89
1994 Teodoro	C	89

In late fall 1994 I had a conversation with a few people in the trade, specialists in Italian wines, who were depressed about Tuscany's vintage conditions. The prevailing sentiment was that heavy September rains had washed away the 1994 vintage and that most wines would be thin and diluted. The early-released 1994 Tuscan wines I had seen, inexpensive Chiantis for the most part, appeared to confirm that assessment. However, one of the cardinal rules of wine tasting is that in every great vintage there are poor wines, and in every poor vintage there are great wines; thus vintages should not be pigeonholed in black-and-white terms. As I have stressed so many times, it is more important to learn the finest producers in each region. Wine broker Marc de Grazia has found an estate that was able to overcome a troublesome vintage and turn out wines that would appear to have come from a vintage such as 1990 or 1988, rather than 1994.

The impressive 1994 Teodoro, a wine made in a more international style (it is a blend of Cabernet Sauvignon, Merlot, and Sangiovese), offers a deep ruby color, a moderately intense nose of plums and smoke, sweet, velvety-textured flavors, and a low-acid, lush, layered finish. It provides a seductive, hedonistic mouthful of quality grape juice for drinking over the next 2–3 years.

This 1995 Chianti Colli Senese displays a pure, red and black fruit character (predominantly overripe cherries), good spice, medium body, soft tannin, and enough acidity to provide vibrancy. This is a worthwhile introduction to what appears to be a special vintage in Tuscany. The 1994 Gemignano, which spent 8 months in small oak casks, possesses a dark ruby color, a sweet, complex nose of toast, vanilla, and jammy strawberry, cherry, and currant fruit. Medium bodied, with an expansive, supple texture, this fully mature, delicious wine is a reasonably good bargain. Drink it over the next several years.

CASA EMMA

1996 Chianti Classico	C	87

This dark ruby-colored Chianti displays vivid cherry fruit intermixed with notes of new saddle leather and spice. A medium-bodied wine with good acidity and an attractive finish, this muscular, well-endowed Chianti is drinkable now and should age nicely for 3–4 years.

CASTELLO DI CAMIGLIANO

1990 Brunello di Montalcino   **E 80**

Castello di Camigliano's 1990 Brunello di Montalcino is made in a soft, light- to medium-bodied, forward style without much extraction or ageworthiness. It reveals some ripeness and a clean, fruity style, but it can easily be surpassed by many Rosso di Montalcinos. Drink it over the next 3–4 years.

I CAMPETTI

1995 Rosso Monteregio Castruccio   **A 87**

An excellent bargain, the 1995 Rosso Monteregio Castruccio, made primarily from San-giovese, reveals ripe berry fruit, spice, a touch of tobacco and smoke, and a tasty, medium-bodied, surprisingly concentrated personality. It provides plenty of wine for its modest price. To realize what a terrific bargain it is in Sangiovese, just compare it with any Sangiovese being produced in California (most of which sell for $15–$30). This wine should drink well for 2 years.

CAPARZO

1990 Brunello di Montalcino (Green Label)   **D 88**

1990 Brunello di Montalcino La Casa   **E 91**

This excellent estate has turned out two large-scale, tannic, backward Brunellos that appear to be among the more concentrated wines of the vintage. The dark ruby-colored 1990 Brunello di Montalcino (green label) displays a tight, backward nose of spice, leather, herbs, and dusty black cherry fruit. Full bodied, as well as excruciatingly tannic, this firm, back-ward wine needs 5–6 years of cellaring. It may not completely resolve its tannin (somewhat akin to my feeling on the 1975 Bordeaux vintage) as it evolves over the next 20 years. A surer bet (and much more expensive) is Caparzo's 1990 Brunello di Montalcino La Casa. This is one of the few opaque, saturated-colored Brunellos of the vintage. The nose offers up intense aromas of ripe berries, tobacco-tinged, leathery, smoky, roasted herbs, and grilled meat. There is huge flavor extraction, massive tannin, extraordinary density and richness, and a monster finish. This wine is considerably thicker and richer than the green label bot-tling and in need of 5–7 years of cellaring. This is an outstanding example of this excellent vintage, but do not expect the tannin to completely melt away.

CAPRILI

1990 Brunello Di Montalcino   **D 91**

Although this estate never receives the recognition it deserves, it has always produced one of my favorite Brunello di Montalcinos. The 1990 reveals a complex, multidimensional nose of roasted herbs, sweet, hickory smoke-scented fruit, tobacco, and earth. Full bodied, with a supple, velvety-textured, concentrated personality, this long, glycerin-endowed, powerful Brunello possesses enough fruit to balance the moderate tannin. Approachable now, it should drink well for 15+ years.

CARPINETO

1990 Chianti Classico Riserva   **C 87**

An excellent Chianti, this dark ruby/garnet-colored wine offers a spicy, earthy, black cherry-scented nose, medium to full body, muscular, austere, authoritative flavors, and a spicy, moderately tannic finish. It is just beginning to open and should age well for 7–8 years.

CASALOSTE

1995 Chianti Classico	C	86
1994 Chianti Classico Riserva	D	87

Two very good Chiantis, the medium ruby-colored 1995 Chianti Classico exhibits an earthy, chestnut, and cherry-scented nose, ripe, tasty, medium-bodied flavors, fine elegance, good acidity, and a sweet, smoky, berry-flavored finish. Drink it over the next 4–5 years. The 1994 Chianti Classico Riserva is a softer wine, with a dark ruby color, excellent leathery, licorice, and cherry scents and flavors, an easygoing personality, and a plump, fleshy finish. It should drink well for 2–4 years.

CASE BASSE (SOLDERA)

1993 Brunello di Montalcino	EEE	90
1993 Brunello di Montalcino Casse Basse	EEE	95?
1991 Brunello di Montalcino Riserva	EEE	94
1990 Brunello di Montalcino	EE	98

I have not yet met proprietor Gianfranco Soldera, but the reports about his uncompromising commitment to perfection are legendary. In fact, potential purchasers must meet Soldera's specifications before he will agree to sell them wine! These unfined, unfiltered, totally natural 1993 offerings are two of the most aromatic and expressionistic red wines made in Italy. They are obviously made from grapes taken to the limit of ripeness, as well as vinified with caution thrown to the wind. Both are spectacular wines, although readers who have been weaned on technically flawless examples should be warned that the 1993 Casse Basse possesses noticeable levels of volatile acidity. The dark plum/garnet-colored 1993 Brunello di Montalcino offers up a knockout nose of fruitcake, Asian spices, incense, flowers, red and black fruits, earth, and minerals. It is one of the most complex bouquets I have ever smelled in a wine. In the mouth, it is sweet, ripe, and round, with exceptional purity and ripeness, but, surprisingly, not the weight one would associate with such a provocative and persistent fragrance. Medium bodied, with a gorgeously layered, supple texture, it should drink well for a decade or more. The dark garnet 1993 Brunello di Montalcino Case Base exhibits an even more intensely perfumed nose with volatile acidity giving the wine an exotic, somewhat over-the-top style. Higher tannin cuts a bigger, more powerful path on the palate. This fuller-bodied wine is dense and rich, yet sweet and approachable. It should drink well for 12–15 years. Both of these fascinating wines are made in extremely limited quantities, as the estate's production is approximately 2,000 cases.

Everyone I know who has met proprietor Gian Franco Soldera has the same impression—the man is an uncompromising perfectionist who makes great wines but seems not to want to sell them to anybody on planet Earth unless they meet his "qualifications." From his 16-acre Case Basse vineyard (planted in 1973), Soldera produces three wines—a Vino da Tavola called Intistieti and two Brunellos, with the Riserva being made only in top years. The wines are aged in large Slavonian oak *foudres* for 4–5+ years, before being bottled without any fining or filtration. Readers may remember my enthusiastic notes on the two cuvées of 1990 Brunello. In 1991 only a Riserva was made. It is a magnificent Brunello that gets my nod as the wine of the vintage. The wine reveals a dark ruby color with some amber at the edge. An extraordinary nose offers up provocative aromas of grilled meats, sweet black cherries, Asian spices, balsamic vinegar, and smoke. The wine exhibits superb richness, incredibly sweet, pure fruit, full body, and layers of depth. The finish easily lasts for 35–40 seconds. This is a terrific, remarkable, compellingly complex, already delicious Brunello that promises to age well for 10–15+ years. Only the price is painful.

The 1990 Brunello di Montalcino from Case Basse is a modern-day classic, as well as one of the greatest Brunellos I have ever tasted. It exhibits a deep ruby color and a magnificent, rich, complex nose of roasted herbs, sweet, jammy, red and black fruits, cedar, spice, and oak. The wine is extremely powerful and full bodied, with layers of highly concentrated, ripe fruit. Despite its massive size, it retains a gracefulness and sense of elegance. The velvety texture and layers of fruit conceal the wine's high tannin. It is approachable young but should age effortlessly for 15–20 years. Kudos to proprietor Gianfranco Soldera.

CASTELGIOCONDO

1990 Brunello di Montalcino	D	85?

Although the color is a healthy dark ruby, this tightly knit, hard, tannic style of Brunello does not appear to possess sufficient fat and fruit extraction to balance out its astringent components. The wine's high acidity, hard tannin, and earthy rusticity result in a compressed, compact example of the vintage. It needs 7–8 more years of cellaring, but do not expect any miracles to occur.

CASTELLARE

1995 Chianti Classico	C	85
1994 Chianti Classico Riserva	C	86
1993 Chianti Classico Riserva	C	84
1990 Chianti Classico Riserva	C	89
1993 Chianti Classico Riserva Il Poggiale	D	87+
1993 Coniale Vino da Tavola	D	90
1991 Coniale Vino da Tavola	D	89+
1993 I Sodi di San Niccolo Vino da Tavola	D	88+

This estate, owned by Paolo Panerai, has made significant changes (cutting yields, eliminating fining, and curtailing the amount of filtration) since the 1993 vintage. The vineyards, which are managed with no pesticides, consist of 49 acres in Tuscany's heartland. The 1995 Chianti Classico displays a solid ruby color with garnet at the edge and a moderately intense, black cherry, smoky nose that opens after 10–12 minutes in the glass. It possesses chalky tannin in the finish but does offer elegant, textbook Chianti flavors in a medium-bodied, slightly rustic format. Drink it over the next 4–5 years. The more open-knit, flattering 1994 Chianti Classico Riserva exhibits aromas of cigar tobacco, roasted almonds, leather, and sweet strawberry and cherry fruit. This charming, medium-bodied wine possesses low acidity, no roughness around the edge, and a clean, soft, pleasant finish. Drink it over the next 3–4 years. It is another example of a charming 1994 Chianti, a vintage that was relatively difficult because of harvest rains.

Castellare's limited-production 1993 Chianti Classico Riserva Il Poggiale is a single-vineyard offering made primarily from Sangioveto (75%). The wine is closed and firm, reluctantly giving up whiffs of saddle leather, underbrush, soy, and red fruits. It hits the palate with excellent richness, solid tannin, medium body, and plenty of spice. Give it 2–3 more years of cellaring and consume it over the following 12 years.

Castellare produces two Vino da Tavolas, the most famous being their I Sodi di San Niccolo, an 85% Sangioveto and 15% Malvasia Nero blend. I liked the 1993 I Sodi di San Niccolo for its exotic, lush, jammy black cherry aromas intermingled with *pain grillé* and black currants. The wine is deep, with sweet, ripe fruit, good integration of acidity and tannin, and a spicy, medium-bodied, classically elegant and measured finish. It is an excellent wine to drink now and over the next 7–12 years. In contrast, the 1993 Coniale, a 100% Cabernet Sauvignon-based wine aged in French oak, of which one-third is new, is a more backward, youthful wine. It reveals a dense, dark ruby/purple color, as well as an extroverted, intensely spicy, oaky, black currant-scented nose with smoky tobacco in the background. Rich, medium to full bodied, and large-scale, this is a moderately tannic, unevolved, youthful wine that requires an additional 3–4 years of cellaring. It should keep through the first decade of the next century.

Castellare's spicy, leathery, medium-bodied 1993 Chianti Classico Riserva exhibits decent fruit, an earthy character, and a spicy finish. Although not concentrated or complex, it should offer serviceable drinking for another 1–2 years. I have had many good Chiantis and Vino da Tavolas from the 1991 vintage, making me wonder why this vintage has not received better press. While it is not nearly as profound as the 1990 vintage, and there is a problem with inconsistency, there are quantities of good wine available. The impressive 1991 Consiale (100% Cabernet Sauvignon aged in small oak casks for 12–14 months) offers an intense dark ruby color, a closed but spicy, leathery, vanillin and smoky-scented nose, dense, rich, muscular, concentrated flavors with considerable extraction, and a medium- to full-bodied, spicy finish. The wine needs 1–3 years of cellaring to shed its tannin, after which it will keep for 10–15 years.

I prefer the 1990 Chianti Classico Riserva to the proprietary red wine, I Sodi di San Niccolo. It exhibits a dark ruby/garnet color, a rich, intense nose of cedar, damp earth, leather, and jammy, black cherry fruit. Medium to full bodied and soft, it is a gorgeously rich, velvety-textured Chianti for drinking over the next 7–8 years.

CECCHI
1993 Chianti Classico Riserva Teuzzo   D 84

If this wine did not have an excess of oak, it would have merited a better review. The medium ruby/garnet color is followed by spicy, earthy aromas and excessive wood that overwhelms the earthy, cherry fruit. It is lean and austere, but pleasant. Drink it over the next 2–3 years.

CENSIO
1997 Chianti   A 85

A blend of 90% Sangiovese, 5% Canaiolo, and 5% Malvasia and Trebbiano (the latter two white grapes), this wine admirably displays what Tuscany can do so well, but California struggles with—make a tasty Sangiovese for a reasonable price! This 1997 Chianti exhibits good, clean winemaking, a medium ruby color, a berry, new saddle leather, spicy nose, light to medium body, and a soft texture. Some of Sangiovese's strawberry fruit is apparent in the finish. Drink it over the next year.

CERBAIONA
1993 Brunello di Montalcino   EE 90

This wine's intriguing aromatic complexity, which offers up scents of iodine, Asian spices, tobacco, dried herbs, smoke, and cherry fruit, is thought-provoking. Round, generous, and rich, with considerable complexity, this Brunello exhibits decent acidity, an expansive palate, and an evolved, complex personality. Consume it now and over the next 7–8 years.

CIACCI PICCOLOMINI D'ARGONA
1990 Brunello di Montalcino Vigne de Pianrosso (Bianchini)   E 94

This wine is a candidate for one of the finest Brunello di Montalcinos of the vintage. A thick-looking color suggests considerable intensity and extraction. The huge nose of black truffles, jammy black cherries, and toasty new oak is followed by a massively endowed, full-bodied, immensely concentrated wine that tastes almost sweet because of the exceptional ripeness and fruit density. No doubt there is significant tannin lurking beneath the layers of fat and glycerin. This is a terrific Brunello di Montalcino for drinking over the next 20 years. Unfortunately, as with so many great wines, quantities are minuscule.

CIGNALE

1994 Vino da Tavola	D 89

This wine may turn out to be outstanding. The color is dark purple, and the wine offers up plenty of sweet, tobacco-tinged, cassis fruit in a medium- to full-bodied, seductive, sexy format. Round, deep, succulent, and opulently textured, this luscious Vino da Tavola can be drunk now as well as over the next 7–8 years. Unfortunately, only 150 cases were imported.

LE CINCIOLE

1994 Chianti Classico	B 85
1993 Chianti Classico	B 86
1994 Chianti Classico Le Valle	D 88

This estate is a newcomer to the Tuscan scene, with 1993 its first vintage. The 1993 Chianti Classico exhibits an open, soft, slightly commercial, but pleasant strawberry fruitiness, light to medium body, and a clean, fresh finish. Drink it over the next 1–2 years. Interestingly, the 1994 Chianti Classico is less open and fruity when compared with other 1994 Tuscan Chiantis, with more of a compressed style. Nevertheless it possesses straightforward cherry and strawberry fruit and medium body, but a monolithic, monochromatic character. It is a good, chunky Chianti to drink over the next 2–3 years.

Typical of the vintage, the 1994 Chianti Classico Le Valle reveals spicy, toasty, new oak intertwined with jammy strawberry and cherry fruit. Sexy, round, supple, and delicious, this Chianti caresses the palate with no hard edges. However, it needs to be consumed over the next 1–2 years to take advantage of its flattering, up-front style.

CISPIANO

1996 Chianti Classico	B 86
1995 Chianti Classico Riserva	C 88

The soft, dark ruby/purple-colored 1996 Chianti Classico exhibits a fruit-driven personality. Although not complex, it possesses good ripeness, none of the hollowness or tannic ferocity exhibited by some 1996s, and a clean, rich, exuberant, surprisingly supple finish. Drink it over the next 2–3 years. The dark ruby/purple-colored 1995 Chianti Classico Riserva is powerful, as well as monolithic and heavy. It offers a tight but promising nose of loamy earth scents intermingled with saddle leather, roasted herbs, and black cherry fruit. It is dense, full bodied, and moderately tannic, with a long, muscular finish. Still youthful and unevolved, this offering requires another year of cellaring; it will last for 7–10 years.

COL D'ORCIA

1990 Brunello di Montalcino	E 77?

A severe, austere, tough-textured wine with little charm or obvious ripe fruit, this highly structured, tannic Brunello reveals vague scents of cedar, new saddle leather and earth, tough, spicy, compressed flavors, and a boatload of tannin in the astringent finish. At least 5–10 years of cellaring is recommended, but do not expect much fruit to be present at the end of that sojourn.

CORRINA

1996 Chianti Rufina	B	88
1995 Chianti Rufina	B	86
1996 Erte Proprietary Red	B	87
1996 I Cipressi Proprietary Red	C	88
1995 I Cipressi Proprietary Red	C	88+
1996 Sangiovese	A	86
1995 Vigna Spartigalla Vino da Tavola	C	89

One normally does not find Tuscan wines this good for such a low price. The 1996 Sangiovese exhibits a dark ruby color, followed by an excellent strawberry, leather, and cherry nose, soft, round, ripe flavors with medium body, and good purity. It is ideal for enjoying over the next 1–2 years. The 1996 Chianti Rufina, from the estate's vineyards, is a blend of 93% Sangiovese, 5% Canaiolo, and 2% Colrino. It possesses a dark ruby/purple color and an excellent black cherry, earth, and peppery nose. Spicy, with loads of fruit, admirable density, and a touch of new oak in the flavors, this excellent Chianti should drink well for 3–4 years. The medium ruby-colored 1995 Chianti Rufina is more smoky, with cherry fruit, herbs, and earth. While pure, it does not reveal the depth and intensity of the 1996. Drink it over the next 4–5 years.

Two fine proprietary red wines from Corrina include the 1995 Vigna Spartigalla. Its dark ruby/purple color is accompanied by loads of sweet black cherry fruit infused with attractive notes of new saddle leather, cedar, and weedy tobacco. In the mouth, there is superb ripeness and rich, medium-bodied flavors that coat the palate with good viscosity, purity, and extract. The wine displays slight tannin in its structured finish, making me believe it will be even better with 1–2 more years of bottle age. It will keep for a decade or more. The 1995 I Cipressi is a single-vineyard cuvée of 50% Sangiovese and 50% Cabernet Sauvignon aged in small oak casks, of which 25% was new. Although backward, this wine exhibits considerable promise, revealing an opaque ruby/purple color as well as a nose of *pain grillé*, black truffles, earth, and sweet black currant and cherry fruit. In the mouth, it is medium bodied, nicely structured, pure, and impeccably well made. Tight but accessible, it should be consumed between now and over the following 8–10 years.

This fine Tuscan estate has fashioned two interesting wines, both 55% Sangiovese and 45% Cabernet Sauvignon blends. The 1996 Erte is a surprisingly good value for a classy wine from this part of Italy. Its color is dense dark ruby with purple tints, and aromatically, the wine offers moderately intense aromas of strawberries, cherries, tobacco, leather, and spice. The wine possesses good texture, zesty acidity, and light tannin in the medium-bodied finish. Drink it over the next 3–4 years. The single-vineyard 1996 I Cipressi was aged in 25% new oak casks. The wine reveals a dark purple color and more black currant/cassis aromas intermixed with cigar and spice box scents. Medium to full bodied, this is a denser, more tannic wine, with excellent concentration and purity. It should be at its peak after another 1–2 years of bottle age and last for a decade or more.

E. ROBERTO COSIMI IL POGGIOLO

1990 Brunello di Montalcino (Black Label)	D	87?
1990 Brunello di Montalcino Sassello (Designer Bottle)	E	92

Of these two interesting wines, the designer-bottled, presumably single-vineyard-designated 1990 Brunello di Montalcino Sassello is the more fragrant, flattering, sweeter, and richer offering. It reveals a dark garnet color and an intensely fragrant, sweet nose of tobacco, sweet, jammy fruit, herbs, spices, and woodsy aromas. Explosively rich, ripe, and opulent (a description rarely applied to Brunello), this large-scale, delicious wine can be drunk now or cellared for another 10–15 years. The tightly knit 1990 Black Label Brunello di Montalcino possesses more of the damp, leafy, earthy components, along with more noticeable tannin and acidity and a closed, less impressive palate because of lower extract and intensity. A more iffy proposition, it should be cellared for 4–5 years.

COSTANTI

1990 Brunello di Montalcino	E	90+?

Costanti is unquestionably one of this appellation's most reliable producers. That being said, I have bestowed this outstanding rating more on potential than on how the wine is currently showing. It exhibits a dense dark ruby color, a nonexistent nose, and mouth-searing, astringent, bitterly hard tannin. Extremely backward, dense, and impenetrable, this wine possesses considerable weight and intensity on the palate, but I am worried about the rustic side of the tannin, as well as the fact that a more realistic assessment of the wine's direction cannot be made for at least 8–10 years. Overall, 1990 appears to have sweeter, riper fruit than the 1988 vintage, but this may be an example where Costanti's 1988s, as well as his glorious 1985s, surpass what he produced in 1990. Readers who love Costanti (as I do) may want to buy this wine on faith, but I wouldn't sell the farm for this particular effort. Don't touch a bottle before 2006.

DEI

1995 Rosso di Montepulciano	B	86
1994 Santa Catarina	D	90
1993 Vino Nobile di Montepulciano	C	88
1992 Vino Nobile di Montepulciano	C	85
1991 Vino Nobile di Montepulciano Riserva	C	88

Dei fashions tasty wines that need little aging to showcase their charms. For example, the 1995 Rosso di Montepulciano exhibits a deep ruby/purple color, a soft, generously endowed personality, and gobs of ripe plummy, cherry fruit with a touch of chocolate. Although it has not yet begun to display all its nuances, it is a soft, round, generous wine for drinking over the next 2–4 years. The dark ruby-colored 1993 Vino Nobile di Montepulciano offers up a gorgeous nose of smoke, roasted herbs, tobacco, and sweet, jammy black fruits. Round and copiously fruity, with full body and layers of concentration, this wine falls just short of being outstanding. It should be consumed over the next 5–6 years. The lightest wine in this group, the 1992 Vino Nobile di Montepulciano, reveals a soft, strawberry, cherry, and tobacco nose, elegant, supple, light- to medium-bodied flavors, and a short finish. Drink it up.

While Carmignano gets my vote as the most underrated Tuscan appellation, a close second is Vino Nobile di Montepulciano. These wines offer a refreshing contrast to the tannic, brawny, often irregular Brunello di Montelcinos, as they can be, in the finest vintages, voluptuously textured, soft, round, generous wines that drink deliciously young yet possess an uncanny ability to age. Not surprisingly, the local cognoscenti refer to Vino Nobile di Montepulciano as the Pomerols of Tuscany.

Dei fashions tasty wines that need no aging to show well. The excellent 1991 Vino Nobile di Montepulciano Riserva possesses a deep ruby color, spicy, tobacco, earthy, underbrush scents, and rich, medium- to full-bodied flavors that exhibit good structure, some tannin, and excellent concentration. This backward wine will age well for a decade. The 1994 Santa Catarina boasts a dark ruby/purple color followed by a gorgeously scented nose of ripe black cherries, cassis, and leather, terrific layers of fruit, powerful, concentrated, authoritative flavors, and supple, sweet, ripe tannin with well-integrated spice and wood. Interestingly, this is a blend of 50% Sangiovese, 25% Merlot, and 25% Cabernet Sauvignon. It is an impressive wine for drinking now and over the next 5–7 years.

DUE PORTINE (GORELLI)

1991 Brunello di Montalcino	D	89

It is interesting that the 1991 Brunello di Montalcinos taste softer than the 1990s, a vintage where the fruit was clearly riper and lower in acidity. This 1991 exhibits plenty of cedar, earth, licorice, and berry fruit aromas, full body, a soft underbelly, and copious quantities of black fruits, licorice, and trufflelike flavors. This medium- to full-bodied wine is very evolved and thus should be drunk over the next 7–8 years.

FANTI

1990 Brunello di Montalcino	D	88

Fanti is just beginning to estate bottle its production, having previously sold the grapes to other producers. The 1990 offers up an attractive, sweet, ripe, forward nose of cherries, earth, herbs, and a touch of cedar and licorice. Medium to full bodied, ripe, round, and richly fruity, this is a supple, forward style of Brunello di Montalcino that can be drunk now or cellared for another 10–15 years.

CASTELLO DI FARNETELLA

1995 Chianti Colli Senesi	B	85
1993 Nero di Nubi (Pinot Nero) Vino da Tavola	D	86

The understated, classy, light-bodied 1995 Chianti Colli Senesi exhibits clean, stylish, strawberry and cherry fruit, with a touch of earth, leather, and spice. A medium-bodied, fruit-driven wine, it is a lighter-style, well-crafted Chianti. The 1993 Nero di Nubi will remind few tasters of Pinot Noir, but it is an attractive, spicy wine with a strong nuances of new oak, soft, dark fruit characteristics, plenty of spice and vanillin, and a medium-bodied, supple finish with no tannin or astringency. I would opt for drinking it over the next 1–2 years.

FATTORIA DI FELSINA

1995 Chianti Classico Berardenga	C	86
1994 Chianti Classico Berardenga	C	87
1993 Chianti Classico Riserva	C	84
1993 Chianti Classico Riserva Rancia	D	89+
1993 Fontalloro Vino da Tavola	D	87+
1992 Maestro Raro Berardinga Cabernet Sauvignon	D	84
1990 Maestro Raro Berardinga Cabernet Sauvignon	D	86?
1988 Maestro Raro Berardinga Cabernet Sauvignon	D	86

The 1994 Chianti Classico Berardenga is a sexy, soft, silky-textured wine from this vintage that has produced a surprising number of wines with Burgundian-like textures as well as a charming precociousness. The wine possesses nice smoky oak to go along with ripe, low-acid, cherry, leather-tinged flavors. It is a spicy, soft, captivating Chianti to drink over the next 2–3 years. In contrast, the 1993 Chianti Classico Riserva is a more tannic, tough-textured, hard wine with ripe fruit but pronounced levels of earth, acidity, and tannin—will it ever come into balance? It may benefit from 1–2 more years of cellaring, but I am concerned about the overall harmony among its component parts. The 1993 Chianti Classico Riserva Rancia is a deeply colored, rich Chianti that promises to drink well for 10–12 years. This dark ruby-colored wine exhibits a rich, complex aromatic profile (primarily melons, spice, and black fruits), with medium to full body, sweet tannin, and an intense, concentrated red and black fruit character. This impressive offering is one of the finest 1993 Chiantis I have tasted.

Felsina's proprietary red wine called Maestro Raro, a Cabernet Sauvignon aged in small oak casks, is a deeply colored but excruciatingly tannic style of Cabernet that requires considerable patience. In tasting five vintages (1988, 1989, 1990, 1991, and 1992), I was struck by how backward, woody, and tannic these wines are. Although deeply colored, the 1992 is a lean, woody wine. More interesting are the 1990 and 1988. The 1990 exhibits earthy, ripe fruit, high tannin, plenty of wood, and a compact personality, but there is good depth present. The question mark next to the wine's rating is due to its high tannin. About 3–4 more years of bottle age will reveal whether this wine has any serious merit. The 1988 is a deep, dark, opaque ruby/garnet-colored wine with a pronounced nose of tar, new oak, and spice. It possesses the sweetest fruit, as well as excruciating levels of tannin. The wine is not far from reaching full maturity. Potential purchasers will have to confront the wine's brutal astringency along with the fruit. Two other vintages, 1989 and 1991, were palatable wines, but they were dominated by wood and tannin.

Felsina's excellent 1995 Chianti Classico Berardenga possesses a healthy dark ruby color, followed by an attractive sweet jammy nose of cherries and spice. The wine possesses medium body, tangy acidity, a nice texture, and a clean finish. The 1993 Fontalloro exhibits a deep ruby/purple color, lavish quantities of new oak, excellent density, medium body, and moderate tannin in the fine finish. The wine needs several more years of cellaring and should keep for 10–15 years.

FONTERUTOLI

1995	Brancaia Vino da Tavola	D	88
1994	Brancaia Vino da Tavola	D	87+
1991	Brancaia Vino da Tavola	D	90
1996	Chianti Classico	C	88
1995	Chianti Classico	B	88
1993	Chianti Classico	B	86
1995	Chianti Classico Riserva	D	92
1991	Chianti Classico Ser Lapo	C	89
1994	Chianti Classico Ser Lapo Riserva	D	84?
1994	Concerto Vino da Tavola	D	89+
1991	Concerto Proprietary Red Wine	D	87
1996	Poggio Alla Badiola Vino da Tavola	B	85?
1995	Poggio Alla Badiola Vino da Tavola	B	86
1995	Siepi Vino da Tavola	C	93
1994	Siepi Vino da Tavola	D	89+
1993	Siepi Vino da Tavola	D	88

Fonterutoli is one of Tuscany's most reliable producers of Chianti and proprietary red wines—the so-called Vino da Tavolas. The 1995 Chianti Classico exhibits an opaque purple color, excellent richness, copious quantities of dense black raspberry and cherry fruit, a touch of earth, medium body, admirable purity, and a layered texture. This is a gorgeous, richly fruity yet structured style of Chianti that should drink well for 4–5 years. The 1994 Chianti Classico Ser Lapo Riserva reveals an impressive opaque purple color, but it is closed aromatically. On the palate, the wine is hard textured, tough, lean, and austere—and in need of 1–3 years of cellaring. Toasty new oak dominates the wine's fruit. Currently this effort lacks charm, and its overall equilibrium and balance are questionable. Readers should give it more bottle age to see if it sheds its tannin and develops more sweetness of fruit and precociousness. The single-vineyard 1995 Sangiovese Poggio Alla Badiola offers a deep ruby color, followed by a pretty, low-key, cherry-scented nose with hints of new oak and spice. This round, elegant, subtle, and restrained wine possesses tender tannin and good fruit, but it is essentially one-dimensional and straightforward. It should continue to drink well for 3–4 years.

The 1994 Brancaia is relatively closed, despite the fact that it is a Sangiovese (85%) and Merlot (15%) blend. The wine possesses a deep purple color, oaky, compressed aromatics, excellent richness, a chewy texture, and plenty of vanillin, spice, and jammy strawberry/black cherry fruit. However, it is in need of another 1–2 years of cellaring, after which it should merit a score in the upper 80s. Anticipated maturity: 2000–2008.

The top wines from Fonterutoli are the Siepi (a 50% Sangiovese/50% Merlot blend) and the Concerto (a blend of 80% Cabernet Sauvignon and 20% Sangiovese). The opaque purple-colored 1994 Siepi displays a tight but promising nose of sweet black cherry fruit intertwined with new oak, earth, and mocha. Rich, with terrific fruit intensity, medium to full body, moderate tannin, and a long, impressively powerful finish, this wine is still tight and, for a 1994, surprisingly backward and ageworthy. Give it another 1–3 years of cellaring, after which it may merit an outstanding score. Anticipated maturity: now–2010. The 1994 Concerto exhibits an even more saturated opaque purple color and an intense yet youthful and unevolved cassis-dominated aroma interspersed with scents of vanillin, roasted nuts, cedar, and tobacco. Full bodied, and broodingly deep, rich, and powerful, this is a persuasive, young, unevolved, Cabernet Sauvignon–dominated wine that has been aged in a high percentage of new French oak. Given its high tannin level and grapey, unevolved personality, this wine needs another 3–4 years of cellaring. Anticipated maturity: 2002–2014.

This excellent producer turned out two very fine 1993s, including a supple, richly fruity, stylish 1993 Chianti Classico and a densely colored, nearly opaque 1993 Siepi. The latter wine possesses wonderfully ripe fruit, some new barrel influence, medium body, and a soft, fleshy, pure winemaking style. Both wines should be drunk over the next 4–5 years.

The real surprise was the excellent quality of Fonterutoli's 1991s. The 1991 Chianti Classico Ser Lapo is excellent, nearly outstanding. The wine displays a dark color, considerable concentration, medium to full body, intriguing, spicy, hickory smoke, and black cherry components, and a long, ripe, tannic finish. It should drink well for 7–8 years. The 1991 Concerto, a Cabernet Sauvignon/Sangiovese blend, exhibits a dark color, fine ripeness, medium body, and a fleshy, chunky, monolithic, but nicely endowed personality. It should drink well for 7–8 years. The best of this group is the outstanding 1991 Brancaia. A Merlot/Sangiovese blend, this is a terrific example of this underrated vintage (at least for some producers). The wine reveals great raw materials, with gobs of thick, unctuously textured, black cherry fruit wrapped in toasty new oak. Medium to full bodied, deep, and supple, this is a gorgeously proportioned, seductive wine for drinking over the next 6–7 years.

The 1996 Chianti Classico is a beautiful wine from an irregular Tuscan vintage. The color is an impressively saturated dark ruby/purple. The wine offers up copious amounts of blackberry and cherry fruit intermixed with scents of lead pencil, new saddle leather, and licorice. In the mouth, it is deep and medium bodied, with an excellent texture and fine length. Although this wine has some light tannin to resolve, it is accessible. It should drink well for 8–10 years. Even more impressive is the exceptional 1995 Chianti Classico Riserva. Its saturated dark purple color is followed by a superb nose of black raspberries and cherry liqueur, intermixed with new oak, earth, and leather. Full bodied, with superb concentration, exquisite harmony, and copious quantities of sweet tannin, this knockout Chianti Classico Riserva should drink well for 10–15 years. Moreover, production was 4,500 cases, of which nearly 2,000 were destined for the United States. Less impressive is the slightly lean, angular 1996 Poggio Alla Badiola (one of the so-called super Tuscan wines made primarily from Sangiovese). While the price is reasonable, this medium-bodied wine is one-dimensional/monochromatic. It displays a dark ruby color, along with earthy, light cherry notes in the restrained nose and a leathery, spicy, angular finish. Purchasers should consume it over the next 2–3 years.

Fonterutoli's other two super Tuscan blends were far superior. The 1995 Brancaia (a blend of 85% Sangiovese and 15% Merlot) boasts a dark ruby/purple color and a sweet nose of black cherry fruit, *pain grillé*, smoke, and roasted Provençal herbs. The wine is moderately tannic and medium bodied, with some of the vintage's hard tannin noticeable in the finish. There is excellent richness, fine purity, and good overall balance. If the tannin becomes completely integrated in the wine's personality, my numerical score will rise by a point or two. Anticipated maturity: 2000–2010. The explosively rich, superb, opaque purple-colored 1995 Siepi (a blend of equal parts Merlot and Sangiovese) is an exceptional effort. The splendid aromatics of strawberry liqueur, kirsch, blackberries, and toasty oak are followed by a rich, full-bodied wine with layers of intense flavors gently infused with high-quality French oak, giving the wine definition and subtle complexity. The finish lasts for 30+ seconds. The wine does possess the 1995 vintage's tannic clout, but there is enough sweet fruit for balance. Anticipated maturity: 2001–2016.

FONTODI

1995	Chianti Classico	C	85
1994	Chianti Classico •	C	83
1994	Chianti Classico Riserva	C	86
1993	Chianti Classico Riserva	C	86
1994	Chianti Classico Riserva Vigna del Sorbo	D	87
1993	Chianti Classico Riserva Vigna del Sorbo	D	88
1994	Flaccianello Vino da Tavola	D	87
1993	Flaccianello Vino da Tavola	D	90
1993	Syrah Case Via	D	85

The 1993 Chianti Classico Riserva offers a deep ruby color and an attractive earthy, tar, spicy nose. This medium-bodied, slightly compact wine possesses a stern personality, but it is well made. Drink this solid Chianti over the next 5–6 years. The dark ruby-colored 1993 Chianti Classico Riserva Vigna del Sorbo is more interesting. It possesses an intense raspberry/cherry and earthy-scented nose intermingled with scents of spicy vanillin from new oak casks. The wine is medium bodied and tannic, as well as rich, firmly structured, spicy, and long. It will benefit from another 1–2 years of cellaring and last for up to a decade.

Fontodi's lean, somewhat austere 1993 Syrah Case Via is muted aromatically, but it exhibits a dark ruby color, surprising acidity, and a firm, compact personality. It should last for 7–8 years. The outstanding 1993 Flaccianello boasts a dark ruby color as well as a super nose of red and black fruits, spice, and earth. Dense, rich, and well delineated, this medium-to full-bodied, tannic, youthful wine can be drunk, but it promises to be even better with 2–3 more years of cellaring. This impressive wine is impeccably made and well balanced. Anticipated maturity: now–2008.

The 1994 Chianti Classico's light strawberry and cherry fruit, intertwined with earth, spice, and wood aromas offers some pleasure. On the palate, this wine is high in acidity and somewhat sharp, but refreshing in a light- to medium-bodied style. Drink it over the next several years.

Fontodi's 1995 Chianti Classico is a tangy, berry, earthy, uncomplicated wine that offers gutsy fruit, medium body, and plenty of spice in its clean finish. Drink it over the next 2–3 years. It has more size and depth than the 1994. The 1994 Chianti Classico Riserva possesses a dark ruby color, an attractive, sweet, cedary, black cherry-scented nose, medium body, and some tannin and new oak, but excellent fruit ripeness. It should drink well for 2–5 years. I also immensely enjoyed the 1994 Chianti Classico Riserva Vigna del Sorbo. It is a fleshier, richer, more expansively flavored wine, with a healthy dark ruby color, sweet berry fruit, medium body, a generous, succulent mouth-feel, and plenty of spice in the long finish. It is a sexy Chianti to drink over the next 4–5 years.

Last, the deep berry-flavored 1994 Flaccianello offers hints of tar and smoky oak. This accessible wine possesses good extract, adequate acidity, and a ripe, lusty finish. It will drink well for 5–6 years. It reinforces the fact that Tuscan's finest estates turned out accessible, upfront, precocious tasting wines from the 1994 vintage.

FRESCOBALDI

1992 Brunello di Montalcino Castel Giocondo	D	86
1997 Chianti Remole	A	85

The earthy, sweet, round, forward 1992 Brunello is not concentrated, but it does offer immediate gratification. The wine is round and supple, with plenty of earthy, tar, smoky, black cherry fruit and spice. Drink it over the next 2–3 years. Medium ruby colored, with an attractive cherry candied nose of moderate intensity, the medium-bodied 1997 Chianti Remole displays good underlying acidity, unobtrusive alcohol, and a clean, fresh finish.

TENUTA FRIGGIALI

1990 Brunello di Montalcino Centolani	D	90

This is an impressive, rich, full-bodied, sweet, concentrated wine, with the fruit nearly masking what is clearly an elevated level of tannin. The wine boasts excellent length, a sweet, jammy, cherry, leather, and spicy fruitcake nose, and considerable power and authority. Although approachable, it will be at its best between 2000 and 2020.

FULIGNI

1993 Brunello di Montalcino	E	88+
1990 Brunello di Montalcino	D	90
1995 Rosso di Montalcino	E	86

The 1995 Rosso di Montalcino is a soft, richly fruity, medium-bodied wine with little complexity, but plenty of dusty black cherry fruit and tobacco scents. Round, easy to understand, and low in acidity, it should be consumed over the next 2–4 years. The 1993 Brunello di Montalcino is a good wine for the vintage. It possesses a deep ruby/garnet color, followed by a sweet, smoky, leathery, red and black currant-scented nose, long, dense, rich flavors, medium to full body, and moderate tannin in the impressively endowed finish. It is an excellent, possibly outstanding example of Brunello that will be at its finest between 2000 and 2015.

The 1990 Brunello di Montalcino was the first wine (an outstanding one at that) I tasted from this producer. It exhibits a forward, sweet, herb, toast, smoky, and ripe cherry nose, medium- to full-bodied, supple, fat flavors with good glycerin, and a highly extracted personality. Pure and well balanced, with gorgeous layers of sweet, jammy fruit and noticeable yet ripe tannin, this is about as sumptuous as Brunello di Montalcino gets. Approachable now, it should continue to evolve and drink well for 10–15 years.

GATTAVECCHI

1995 Chianti Colli Senesi	B	86
1995 Vino Nobile de Montepulciano	C	85

I had a slight preference for Gattavecchi's less expensive 1995 Chianti Colli Senesi. It offers a medium ruby color, followed by a spicy, leathery, earthy nose with a hint of cherries. The finish is austere, with some of the vintage's hard tannin evident, but this wine is medium bodied and cleanly made. It will probably never resolve all of its tannin, so readers are advised to drink it over the next 3–4 years. The 1995 Vino Nobile de Montepulciano is a lighter, softer wine, with a restrained, low-keyed personality. The bouquet reveals a whiff of jammy cherry fruit intermixed with roasted herbs and berry aromas. It is a spicy, medium-bodied, supple-style wine to drink over the next 1–2 years.

GEOGRAFICO

1988 Capitolare di Biturica Proprietary Red	C	89
1990 Chianti Classico Tenuta Montegiachi	C	87

This large, high-quality producer has turned out a very good 1990 Chianti Classico. It offers up cedary, spicy, tobacco, leathery scents, medium body, excellent flavor concentration, and a dusty, spicy finish. Drink it over the next 4–6 years. The 1988 Capitolare di Biturica is a Sangiovese/Cabernet Sauvignon blend with sweet, ripe, New World–ish fruit, a supple, round, generously endowed personality, and a silky smooth finish with no hard edges. Drink it over the next 7–8 years.

GRACCIANO

1993 Rosso di Montepulciano	A	87

An excellent bargain, this wine reveals copious quantities of rich, sweet, spicy, jammy fruit, a round, supple texture, admirable flavors of cherries, roasted nuts, and spices, and a clean, medium- to full-bodied, velvety-textured finish. It should drink well for 2–3 years.

GRATI (POGGIO CALIGA)

1990 Chianti Riserva	A	87

This 1990 Chianti Riserva exhibits a deep ruby color, a spicy, cherry, and tobacco nose, and round, ripe, medium-bodied flavors with loads of ripe fruit. A supple, mouth-filling wine, it should drink well for 5–7 more years.

IL GREPPONE MAZZI

1990 Brunello di Montalcino	D	78

A simple, one-dimensional Brunello di Montalcino, this medium-bodied, moderately concentrated wine exhibits hard tannin in the finish. There is not enough sweet, ripe fruit to balance out the wine's astringency. More intensity, fat, and fruit extraction is warranted if this wine is to carry its structure and tannin without drying out.

IL PRINCIPE

1990 Chianti Riserva Rufina	C	86

This rustic, husky, dark ruby-colored Chianti possesses scents of saddle leather, berry fruit, and spice. Medium bodied, with good acidity and enough depth to last for another 3–4 years, this one-dimensional wine would be a good accompaniment for grilled meats.

IL VIVAIO

1994 Il Latini Vino da Tavola	C	86

Named after the boisterous yet famous Florentine steakhouse/trattoria, this rugged, leathery, bistro-style red wine offers a deep ruby/purple color, copious amounts of spice and berry fruit, and a leathery toughness. Do not expect a lot of polish or silkiness in this gutsy, mouth-filling, uncomplicated red wine whose rusticity is part of its charm. Drink it over the next year.

LANCIOLA

1996 Chianti Classico Le Masse di Greve	C	85?
1994 Chianti Classico Le Masse di Greve	C	86
1995 Chianti Classico Le Masse di Greve Riserva	C	88+
1994 Chianti Classico Le Masse di Greve Riserva	B	84?
1995 Chianti Colli Fiorentini	B	86
1994 Chianti Colli Fiorentini Riserva	B	84?
1995 Terricci Vino da Tavola	D	88
1994 Terricci Vino da Tavola	D	88

These solidly made Chiantis are not the most opulent or hedonistic, but they will be admired by those who prefer Chiantis with grip and tannin. The softest wine, the 1994 Le Masse di Greve, possesses plenty of tannin but more flesh and obvious fruit than its siblings. There is an earthy, cherry fruitiness, whiffs of leather and tar, and a spicy, medium-bodied finish. Drink it over the next 2–3 years. The 1994 Fiorentini Riserva exhibits a dark plum color, cedar, asphalt, and smoky notes in the nose, coarse tannin in its rustic, medium-bodied personality, and an austere, hard finish. If it drops some of the tannin, it will be far better balanced. For now, this is a good but tough-textured Chianti to drink over the next 5–6 years. The 1994 Le Masse di Greve Riserva displays a medium dark garnet color, followed by sweet, soft, dried cherry fruit and leather aromas and tannic, hard, medium-bodied flavors dominated more by their tannin and leatherlike notes than by fruit. This wine should drink well for 2–4 years.

The 1995 Chianti Colli Fiorentini is softer, with more of a fruit-dominated personality. Yet the leather, earth, spice, and tangy acidity are present in this medium-bodied wine. It should be consumed over the next 3–4 years.

I may have slightly overrated the 1996 Chianti Classico Le Masse di Greve. Its austere, dry, leathery personality and tannic finish are cause for concern. Nevertheless there is attractive sweet strawberry/cherry fruit behind the wine's framework. If that component emerges, and the tannin and structure recede, this wine will be at least a mid-80-point effort. If not, my score may look exceptionally generous. This wine's painful level of tannin will be appreciated primarily by masochists. Drink it over the next 2–3 years. Better balanced is the 1995 Chianti Classico Le Masse di Greve Riserva. It exhibits an opaque purple color and a big, sweet, black cherry, spicy, peppery, herb, and earth nose. In the mouth, the wine is ripe, with medium body, moderate tannin, and a leathery, bing cherry, spicy finish. The wine is still unevolved and in need of another 1–2 years of cellaring. Anticipated maturity: 2000–2010.

The 1995 Terricci (a blend of Sangiovese and Cabernet Sauvignon, aged in French casks) displays a dark ruby/purple color as well as an excellent nose of black cherry fruit intermixed with spice, herbs, smoke, and earth. Rich and full bodied, with excellent depth, this spicy, moderately tannic wine is slightly restrained and backward. Anticipated maturity:

2001–2012. The 1994 Terricci, a blend of 80% Sangiovese and 20% Cabernet Sauvignon and Cabernet Franc, exhibits a dense purple color, a sweet, cassis, cedar, leathery, spicy nose, fat, opulently textured flavors, excellent, possibly outstanding, richness (gobs of jammy black cherry fruit), and a chewy, intense, long, silky-textured finish. Although it does reveal some tannin, the wine is open knit, expansive, and flattering.

LISINI

1993 Brunello di Montalcino	D	90
1990 Brunello di Montalcino	D	88+
1996 Rosso di Montalcino	C	87

Rosso di Montalcinos can be a good introduction to Brunello. Many readers actually prefer Rossos, because they are bottled quickly and tend to possess more exuberant, lively fruit than the Brunellos, which are kept significantly longer in cask. Lisini's 1996 Rosso di Montalcino exhibits a medium deep ruby color, an attractive tobacco leaf, tarry, leathery, berry bouquet with plenty of spice, exuberant fruit, decent acidity, and a quick but pleasant finish. Drink this wine over the next 3–4 years. The dark garnet/plum-colored 1993 Brunello di Montalcino is a more perfumed, complex, and complete wine. It offers a penetratingly intense nose of wood fire, sweet cherry jam, fruitcake, tobacco, and spice. Full bodied and rich, this evolved Brunello should be consumed over the next 7–8 years.

The tannic, dense, full-bodied, backward, earthy 1990 Brunello di Montalcino reveals plenty of roasted herbs and ripe fruit, but the elevated tannin level is of some concern. Give this muscular, large-scale Brunello another 7–8 years of cellaring. If fate is kind, the tannin will melt away long before the fruit fades.

FATTORIA DI LUCIGNANO

1994 Chianti Colli Fiorentini	A	87
1993 Chianti Colli Fiorentini	A	85

It has been many years since I first wrote about the excellent wine values produced by Italy's Fattoria di Lucignano. The 1994 vintage was a difficult year in Tuscany, but Lucignano's 1994 Chianti Colli Fiorentini is a noteworthy wine. Its medium ruby color is followed by sweet, jammy aromas of strawberries and spice. This round, smooth, sexy, velvety-textured 1994 Chianti should make plenty of friends for both its purse and palate-pleasing qualities. Drink it over the next 12–18 months. Don't hesitate to serve it slightly chilled. The 1993 (on paper a superior vintage for Chianti) Chianti Colli Fiorentini is deeper, but without the charm and up-front precociousness of the 1994. Nevertheless it is a fine bargain, with attractive, earthy, cherry fruit, good spice, and meaty flavors, as well as more structure and body. It should drink well for another 2 years.

MASTROIANNI

1990 Brunello di Montalcino Riserva	E	89?
1990 Brunello di Montalcino Schiena d'Asino	E	87+

The big, spicy, tannic, backward 1990 Brunello di Montalcino Schiena d'Asino exhibits a dark garnet/ruby color, closed aromatics (scents of earth, pepper, and underbrush can be found), plenty of muscle and power, but not much fruit. It is a cleanly made wine that cuts a full impression on the palate, but it finishes with excruciating tannin. If the tannin becomes more integrated, this wine will merit a score in the upper 80s, but it will not reach full maturity before the turn of the century. Look for it to last through 2010+. The 1990 Brunello di Montalcino Riserva is a big, earthy, smoky, tobacco, coffee, dark fruit-scented and -flavored wine that is medium to full bodied, tannic, rich, and intense. Impressively made, complex, and rich, it is capable of another 10–15 years of development.

MONSANTO

1993 Chianti Classico Riserva	C	86

From what is an average to above average vintage for Tuscany, Monsanto's 1993 Chianti Classico Riserva displays a medium garnet color, medium body, and a sweet, round, tobacco, dried fruit, and spicy personality. Drink it over the next 2–3 years.

MONTE ANTICO

1995 Vino da Tavola	B	87

This wine, always one of Tuscany's finest values, is made from Sangiovese by the famed Italian oenologist Franco Bernabei. A top-notch effort, the dark ruby-colored 1995 exhibits aromas of roasted nuts, black cherries, dried herbs, and smoke. The wine possesses excellent richness as well as sweet, ripe, berry, cherry, and strawberry fruit, excellent purity, and a soft, easygoing finish. It should drink well for 2–3 years. It is an excellent value.

MONTE BERNARDI

1994 Chianti Classico	D	87
1993 Chianti Classico	D	85
1994 Sa'etta	D	87

Readers should note the extravagant prices on these wines, which are well made but hardly proportional to the level of quality suggested by the producer's ego. The 1993 Chianti Classico is slightly lean and compact, but cleanly made and spicy. It is a solid, well-made wine that tastes like an $8–$12 Chianti. The 1994 Chianti Classico is far more interesting, with plenty of cedar, smoke, and ripe berry fruit in the nose, attractive strawberry/framboiselike flavors, a soft, round texture (another seductive 1994 from that "horrible" Tuscan vintage), and an easygoing, lush finish. It is a sexy Chianti to drink over the next 1–2 years. It would merit more attention if it were priced at $15–$20.

The 1994 Sa'etta possesses the firm, astringent edge I noted in the 1993 Chianti Classico. Other than that, however, the wine exhibits soft, round, ripe cherry and raspberry flavors, medium body, and a spicy, firm finish. These are good, oenologically correct wines, but the pricing policy is absurd.

MONTE VERTINE

1994 Le Pergole Torte	E	87

This well-known proprietary red wine made from Sergio Manetti's Sangioveto vineyards is an exceptionally elegant, medium ruby-colored wine with kirsch and cherry aromas intermixed with leathery, cigar boxlike spices. In the mouth, there is dry tannin, which is slightly intrusive, but the wine's fruit is clean. The overall impression is of a stylish, spicy, complex, medium-weight red for consuming over the next 4–5 years.

MONTECALVI DE BERNADETTE N RENZO BOLLI

1995 Proprietary Red Wine	D	90

About 600 cases of this full-bodied, rich, 100% Sangiovese were produced. Made from a particular clone of Sangiovese known as Rauscedor 23, this wine boasts a dense purple color, followed by a terrific nose of new saddle leather, chocolate, damp foresty scents, and rich berry fruit. Deep, powerful, moderately tannic, and well endowed, this youthful, impressive wine should hit its stride after another 2–3 years of bottle age and last for 10–15 years.

MONTELLORI

1993 Castelrapiti Rosso Vino da Tavola	C	86+
1993 Chianti Il Moro	A	86
1994 Chianti Vigne del Moro	B	86
1994 Salamartano Rosso Vino da Tavola	D	88+

Located 25 miles from Florence, this winery has been producing wines for nearly a century. Their current offerings include a dark plum-colored 1994 Chianti Vigne del Moro with spicy, ripe, gutsy flavors redolent with leather and cherries. The wine possesses adequate acidity, a tarry, tangy personality, medium body, and a fleshy finish. Drink it over the next 2–3 years. The dark garnet-colored 1993 Chianti Il Moro exhibits an elegant, cherry, leather, and spicy nose, rich, medium-bodied, fruity flavors, an overall sense of balance, and an easygoing, soft finish. Drink it over the next 1–2 years. It is uncomplicated, but savory and tasty. The 1993 Castelrapiti Rosso Vino da Tavola is a blend of 75% Sangiovese and 25% Cabernet Sauvignon aged in small *barriques,* of which one-third are new. The wine is tannic and overlaid with wood, but enough cedar, spicy, red currant, cherry, and smoky, weedy, tobaccolike fruit come through to give it appeal. This well-made, medium-bodied Vino da Tavola is capable of lasting another 3–4 years. The finest wine of this quartet is the 1994 Salamartano Rosso Vino da Tavola, a 50% Cabernet Sauvignon/50% Merlot blend aged completely in French oak casks. Although this tightly knit wine requires 2–3 more years of cellaring, it should turn out to be at least excellent. It exhibits an opaque ruby/purple color, high acidity, medium to full body, excellent concentration and purity, and a spicy, vanillin-flavored finish. It should last for 12–15 years—an ager.

MORIS ESTATE

1993 Morellino di Scansano	A	88
1994 Morellino di Scansano Riserva	B	88

Readers should think of these 100% Sangiovese wines as the frugal person's Brunello di Montalcino. The 1993 Morellino di Scansano exhibits a dark garnet color and a fragrant, spicy, cigar, tobacco, and red cherry bouquet with a whiff of saddle leather. This medium- to full-bodied wine possesses excellent concentration, some loamy, earthy notes, and plenty of fruit, richness, and length. This rustic but nicely textured wine should drink well for 3–4 years. It may be the finest Sangiovese available in the United States for under $10! An excellent bargain.

The 1994 Morellino di Scansano Riserva is a thick, rich, concentrated wine that may merit a higher score with additional bottle age. The color is a dense ruby/purple/plum. In the mouth, the wine exhibits that unfiltered taste and texture. Chewy, leathery, cherry, tobacco, and fruitcakelike aromas and flavors can be found in this medium- to full-bodied wine, as well as excellent, possibly outstanding, concentration. This is a robust, moderately tannic wine that is just beginning to be drinkable. It should continue to improve for another 3–4 years and will last for a decade. Impressive!

NEUKOM DORIS

1995 Montepeloso Rosso	C	89+
1994 Montepeloso Rosso	C	89
1995 Nardo di Montepeloso Vino da Tavola	D	92+
1994 Nardo di Montepeloso Vino da Tavola	D	93

This estate has been getting attention from the serious segments of the Italian press. Both vineyards (a total of 13.5 acres) are located on the Tuscan coast, not far from the famed wine-making estates of Sassicaia and Ornellaia. I was blown away by the intensity these wines possessed, particularly in the relatively difficult, lighter 1994 vintage. The Montepeloso Rosso is made from 100% Sangiovese, aged in large French and Italian oak *foudres,* and bottled without fining or filtration. The Nardo di Montepeloso is a blend of 70% Sangiovese and 30% Cabernet Sauvignon aged completely in new French barrels and bottled without fining or filtration.

The 1994 Montepeloso Rosso is excellent, nearly outstanding. It displays a dark ruby/purple color and a complex, sweet, smoky, chocolatey, jammy, red berry nose that could pass for a top-class Merlot. This expansive, medium- to full-bodied, meaty, chewy, silky-textured, layered wine is crammed with fruit and character. Accessible now, it should continue to drink well for 8–9 years. The 1995 Montepeloso Rosso is similarly styled—rich, full, and impressive, with the same smoky, chocolatey, black cherry and berry-scented nose. However, it is more tightly knit, larger scaled, backward, and less evolved. Greater ripeness is noticeable, as well as additional power and tannic ferocity. The 1995 should be cellared for 2–4 years and drunk over the following 10–12.

The Nardo di Montepeloso, a Sangiovese/Cabernet Sauvignon blend, is produced from low yields of under 2 tons of fruit per acre, but the production is a microscopic 350+ cases. The 1994 boasts spectacular aromatics of lead pencil, chocolate, cassis, jammy black cherries, and spicy oak. The wine possesses extraordinary intensity, gorgeous purity, a multilayered palate feel, and an explosive finish. The tannin is well integrated with the wine's acidity, alcohol, and new oak. Anticipated maturity: 2000–2020. The exquisite 1995 Nardo di Montepeloso reveals a saturated black/purple color as well as a huge, sweet, unformed nose of prunes, black currants, and smoky new oak. The wine is massive on the palate, with a full-bodied personality, viscous, intense layers, and a lush, pure finish. This is a winemaking tour de force! Give it 3–4 years of cellaring and drink it over the following 2 decades.

NOTTOLA

1994	Vino Nobile di Montepulciano	C	89
1995	Vino Nobile di Montepulciano Vigna del Fattore	B	86

The 1995 Vino Nobile di Montepulciano Vigna del Fattore is a wine of finesse and elegance. It displays medium dark ruby color, a sweet strawberry/cherry nose with roasted nut scents in the background, medium body, supple tannin, lively fruit, and well-integrated acidity. This wine should be drunk over the next 2–3 years.

The small *barrique*-aged Vino Nobile from the irregular but interesting 1994 vintage offers a dark ruby color and copious quantities of earthy, peppery, *terroir* characteristics to go along with some sweet dried cherry fruit. There is also a hint of almonds that brings to my mind several of the finest Valpolicellos from northeastern Italy. The wine possesses excellent ripeness, a nicely textured, elegant mouth-feel, good spice, and a silky personality. Made from 100% Prugnolo (a clone of Sangiovese), and bottled without fining or filtration after aging 2 years in barrel, it should be consumed over the next 5–6 years.

NOZZOLE

1994	Il Pareto Vino da Tavola	D	90
1993	Il Pareto Vino da Tavola	D	89

The internationally styled 1993 possesses a dark ruby/purple color, followed by a big, sweet, oaky nose with copious quantities of ripe black currant fruit. Medium to full bodied, purely made, and concentrated, it is ideal for drinking now and over the next 7–8 years. I would never guess that it emanated from Tuscany.

The 1994, 100% Cabernet Sauvignon aged in French casks, is a well-endowed, rich, boldly styled wine that offers a flamboyant display of new oak and jammy black cherry and currant fruit. Full bodied, spicy, and unevolved, but rich in glycerin and extract, this is an impressively textured, mouth-filling, teeth-staining red that should continue to improve for another 7–8 years and last for 15.

ORNELLAIA

1993	Masseto Vino da Tavola	EE	91
1992	Masseto Vino da Tavola	EE	89
1993	Vino da Tavola	D	88
1995	La Volte dell'Ornellaia	C	85

The Marchese Lodovico Antinori makes these luxuriously fruity, rich wines from his vineyards in Bolgheri, an area not far from the famed Sassicaia. With the help of Bordeaux's brilliant oenologist Michel Rolland, these wines seem to be going from strength to strength. The 1993 Ornellaia Vino da Tavola is a dense ruby/purple-colored wine with copious quantities of chocolatey, berry fruit, obvious evidence of toasty new oak, medium to full body, silky tannin, and a long, rich finish. Amazingly, it held up for 48 hours in a decanter without aeration. It can be drunk now as well as over the next 10–12 years. Barrel samples of the 1994 Ornellaia, tasted in Europe with the proprietor, exhibited a soft, supple, easygoing style. The 1995 Ornellaia looks to be sensational and appears to be a return to the exceptional quality of the 1990 and 1988.

The single-vineyard, 100% barrel-fermented Merlot Masseto is stunning in both the 1992 and 1993 vintages. The 1992 was not an easy vintage in Tuscany, but the 1992 Masseto possesses a saturated ruby/purple color as well as a big, sweet nose of vanillin, jammy black and red fruits, and spice. Fleshy, open knit and expansively rich and layered, this is an intriguing, luscious wine that can be drunk now or cellared for 7–8 years. The 1993 Masseto reveals a deeper, more saturated ruby/purple color, plenty of sweet, toasty oak, gobs of fruit, full body, plenty of suppleness, and gorgeously pure, sweet fruit. In a blind tasting, it would be easy to mistake for a top-notch, right bank Bordeaux. The 1993 is still youthful but accessible. It can be drunk now and over the next 10–12 years. It should come as no surprise that this wine is Italy's greatest Merlot and is in a class with the first-growths of Bordeaux.

The inexpensive 1995 La Volte is a straightforward, fruity, supple-style wine that offers honest cherry fruit in a medium-bodied format. The color is an attractive dark ruby/purple, and the wine is soft and refreshing. It is ideal for drinking over the next 2–3 years.

SIRO PACENTI

1990	Brunello di Montalcino	D	92

This exotic, superfragrant, pungently scented 1990 Brunello di Montalcino comes across as far more opulent and flattering than most wines of the vintage. It is somewhat similar to the extravagantly priced Soldera Case Basse—for one-fourth to one-third the price! This full-bodied, in-your-face Brunello offers an expansive, round palate with gobs of superripe, jammy fruit (black fruits, roasted herbs, and smoked meats dominate the wine's personality), gorgeous concentration, and an unmistakable personality. I am impressed! This wine can be drunk now as well as over the next 10–15 years.

P. PACENTI-CANALICCHIO DI SOPRA

1990	Brunello di Montalcino Campione	D	92+

This sensationally concentrated, huge, full-bodied wine possesses enough tannin to make it nearly impenetrable. The color is an opaque garnet/ruby, and the nose offers up significant evidence of superb ripeness and intensity. Extremely full bodied and tannic, with massive fruit extraction, this spicy yet tightly wound Brunello has awesome potential . . . if readers are willing to wait another 5–8 years for the magic to unfold. It should keep for 25–30+ years.

LA PALAZZA

1993 Magnificat	D	86?

Aside from some leesy, funky smells (mercaptins) in the nose, this nearly opaque dark ruby/purple-colored, Cabernet Sauvignon–based wine is dense, rich, and full bodied, with plenty of earthy, cassis fruit, layers of flavor, excellent richness and depth, and noticeable evidence of aging in toasty new oak. If this wine improves with airing, it will justify a slightly higher numerical score. It should drink well for another 5–7 years.

PODERE IL PALAZZINO

1993 Chianti Classico	B	86
1993 Chianti Classico Grosso Senese	D	90

The quality of these wines over the last decade has been virtually flawless. The two new releases are both from the good 1993 vintage. The 1993 Chianti Classico exhibits good raspberry and cherry fruit presented in a spicy, lean, elegant, understated style. It is not one of the most expressive 1993s, but it is attractive Chianti for drinking over the next 2–3 years. The dazzling 1993 Grosso Senese Chianti Classico (formerly a Vino da Tavola) is made from 100% Sangiovese aged completely in small French oak casks. To quote a friend of mine (who has never been enthralled with Italian wines) after he tasted it blind, "This is one of your kick-ass wines." It exhibits a deep ruby/purple color, an ostentatious set of aromatics (black raspberries, cherries, sweet vanillin, and toast), full body, and superb ripeness. The wine is round and opulent (much more so than either the 1985 or 1988), with outstanding richness and a layered, expansive, chewy feel on the palate. Elegant and flattering to drink, this wine will probably not go through a closed or difficult stage; it should drink well over the next 7–10 years.

PERTIMALI DI LIVIO SASSETTI

1991 Brunello di Montalcino	D	90
1990 Brunello di Montalcino	D	94
1990 Brunello di Montalcino Riserva	E	94+
1994 Rosso di Montalcino	C	87
1994 Vigna Fili di Seta	D	89

Some time ago I participated in a blind tasting of Rosso and Brunello di Montalcino where all twelve tasters preferred most of the Rosso di Montalcinos to the Brunellos. What is the lesson to be gleaned from that exercise? Brunello di Montalcinos are more serious wines, but Rosso di Montalcinos provide delicious, up-front, richly fruity drinking where patience is not required. A great Brunello needs 7–10 years in the cellar, whereas a Rosso is meant to be drunk during its first 5–7 years of life. Pertimali's dark ruby-colored 1994 Rosso di Montalcino is a soft, plump, richly fruity, velvety-textured wine. It is a simple but delicious, fruity, round wine for consuming over the next 2–3 years. The 1991 Brunello di Montalcino is no 1990, but it is still an outstanding wine. It exhibits a deep ruby/garnet color, a fragrant, licorice, smoky, roasted meat and herb nose, sweet, black cherry, tobacco, cedar, and animal-like flavors, dense concentration, and a long, surprisingly soft, velvety-textured finish. I was surprised by how forward, delicious, and complex this 1991 Brunello already is. It should drink well for at least 10–12 years.

I am beginning to think that if I had only one Brunello di Montalcino to drink, it would have to be Pertimali. This producer has been making spectacular wines since 1982. Unfortunately, quantities are microscopic, making availability a major roadblock. The 1990 Brunello di Montalcino Riserva is a wine of immense proportions and extraordinary complexity. I cannot say it is better than the regular cuvée, since in large measure both possess the same exuberance, personality, and depth of fruit. Both are full-bodied, expansive wines offering dark ruby colors, spicy, cedar, tobacco, and fruitcake aromatic profiles, and sensational attacks. Even more noteworthy is their length, which unfolds and expands impressively. Loads of tannin and alcohol infuse these Brunellos with a potential of 15–20 or more years of longevity. Both 1990s are stunning Brunello di Montalcinos that can be drunk now or cellared.

The 1994 Vigna Fili di Seta, a blend of 75% Sangiovese/25% Cabernet Sauvignon aged in small casks (of which 50% are new), reveals terrific aromas of black currants, leather, and spice, medium to full body, copious quantities of fruit with underlying tobacco notes, and a long, silky-smooth finish. It is a mouth-filling, generous wine to drink over the next 5–6 years.

FATTORIA DI PETROIO

1996 Chianti Classico	B 87

This elegant, stylish Chianti was fashioned from 95% Sangiovese, 4% Canaiolo, and 1% Colorino. Moreover it was bottled unfiltered. A smoky, charcoal, and kirsch nose also offers up notes of saddle leather and loamy soil with airing. In the mouth, this medium-bodied wine reveals plenty of spice, sweet fruit, good density, and a well-focused, neatly packaged, elegant personality. It should drink well for 3–4 years.

PETROLO

1996 Terre di Galatrona Vino da Tavola	C 85?
1994 Torrione Vino da Tavola	D 90

Although the 1996 Terre di Galatrona, a blend of 70% Sangiovese and 30% Merlot, is somewhat compact and compressed, it is a noteworthy, well-made, crisp, elegant wine, but it lacks soul and flavor depth and expansiveness. Drink it over the next 2–3 years. Far superior is the 1994 Torrione, a proprietary Vino da Tavola made from 100% Sangiovese. It displays a dark ruby/plum color and a sexy, smoky, extroverted personality with intense ripe cherry fruit nicely blended with new saddle leather and *pain grillé* notes. The wine is medium bodied and rich, with excellent fruit and fine overall harmony and length. An exceptionally stylish, highly successful wine, it manages to avoid the hollowness and austerity possessed by many 1994s. Anticipated maturity: now–2008.

FATTORIA DI PIAZZANO

1993 Chianti Rio Camerata	A 87
1994 Piazzano Piazzano	D 88

For neophytes, one of the most difficult things to comprehend in the fine wine market is that price is not always proportional to quality. It remains difficult for many consumers to fathom this reality when staring at a bottle marked $10 and one marked $25. Logic overwhelmingly suggests that the $10 wine cannot be as good as the $25 bottle. This winery has turned out a $10 1993 Chianti Rio Camerata that is excellent. It is a generous, supple, dark ruby-colored wine that possesses oodles of earthy, cherry fruit, surprising fragrance, and well-integrated acidity and tannin. Plump, rich, and delicious, it is capable of lasting for another 2–3 years.

The 1994 Piazzano Piazzano exhibits a deep color, fine body, and a suggestion of *barrique* aging. This is an excellent, complex, leathery, black cherry-scented and -flavored, medium- to full-bodied Chianti that should drink well for 5–6 years.

PIEVE SANTA RESTITUTA

1988 Brunello di Montalcino	D	88+
1990 Brunello di Montalcino Rennina	E	92
1990 Brunello di Montalcino Sugarille	E	91

This estate, now owned by Angelo Gaja, has turned out a medium ruby/garnet-colored 1990 Brunello di Montalcino Sugarille with some amber at the edge. It exhibits a complex nose of cedar, tobacco, spices, and ripe, earthy, red and black fruits. Full bodied and rich, with considerable tannic clout, this is a forceful, large-scale Brunello. Initially it appears accessible, but the wine quickly closes down as it sits in the glass. It requires another 4–5 years of cellaring and should keep for 15–20 years.

In contrast, the 1990 Brunello di Montalcino Rennina exhibits a mature ruby/garnet color and a remarkably open, sexy, lush, and opulent personality. Sweet, jammy aromas of red fruits, smoked nuts, roasted herbs, and spice soar from the glass of this expressive Brunello. Soft, expansive, and silky, this full-bodied wine reveals no hard edges and tastes great, but it is seemingly close to full maturity. There is no denying the seductive power and allure this Brunello possesses. Drink it over the next 7–10 years.

The dark garnet-colored 1988 Brunello exhibits a spicy, leathery, earthy nose with plenty of evidence of ripe, sweet, dried cherry fruit. Full bodied, with high tannin, excellent sweetness and richness, and a midpalate of considerable depth, this wine requires 5–6 years of cellaring, but it should keep for 2 decades.

PODERE POGGIO SCALETTE

1995 Il Carbonaione	E	94
1994 Il Carbonaione	E	91
1993 Il Carbonaione	D	91
1992 Il Carbonaione	D	90

This 30-acre estate owned by the renowned winemaker Vittori Fiore produces approximately 1,500 cases of a 100% Sangiovese di Lamole–based wine from a vineyard planted between 1920 and 1930. Yields are frightfully low (about 1.2 tons of fruit per acre), and the wine is aged in large *foudres* before bottling. This is one of the most exciting wines emerging from Tuscany.

This is the only outstanding 1992 wine I tasted from central Italy. If Podere Poggio Scalette can do this well in a difficult vintage, it is inspiring to think what might be produced in a top year. The wine reveals a dark, saturated garnet color with purple tints. The sweet, ripe nose of roasted herbs, nuts, chocolate, and earthy, berry fruit is followed by a wine of sensational richness and opulence, expansive, sweet, ripe fruit, and a smooth, supple texture because of well-integrated acidity. Drink it now and over the next 7–8 years. Only 150 cases of this 100% Sangiovese (aged in 100% new French oak casks) were made.

This wine made a huge impression on me when I tasted the 1992. The 1993 is just as ravishing, but, sadly, Fiori produced only 400 cases of this wine. In addition to possessing one of the most attractive labels I have seen, this opaque ruby/purple-colored wine offers lavish quantities of smoky, toasty oak and black cherry/cassis fruit. Generous, rich, and full bodied, with outstanding concentration and some tannin in the structured, long, glycerin-imbued, nicely textured finish, this is a brilliantly made wine that should drink well for 10–12 years.

The 1994 Il Carbonaione exhibits a dense, dark purple color, followed by a sweet nose of *pain grillé,* vanillin, and copious quantities of black cherry and black currant fruit. Rich, full bodied, pure, and long in the mouth, with outstanding harmony among its structural components (alcohol, acidity, and tannin), this is a beautifully made, classic Tuscan Sangiovese. Although approachable because of the sweet, rich fruit, this wine needs another 1–3 years of cellaring. It will drink well for 15 years. This wine would be a great match with *Bistecca alla Fiorentina* (grilled Porterhouse steak). The 1995 Il Carbonaione is an explosive blockbuster of a wine, with extraordinary density and massive flavor concentration. It displays an opaque purple color, fabulous aromatic purity (black currants, new oak, floral scents, and a touch of cedar), extraordinary ripeness, and great presence on the palate, but no sense of heaviness or astringency. The wine is formidably deep, powerful, and impressive. Anticipated maturity: 2000–2015. Wow!

LA PODERINA

1990 Brunello di Montalcino	E	88
1990 Brunello di Montalcino Riserva	E	89

An attractive, well made, modern-style wine, La Poderina's closed 1990 Brunello needs another 5–6 years of cellaring. It exhibits a healthy deep ruby color, a spicy, leathery, cedar, and black cherry nose, ripe, medium- to full-bodied flavors, and a rich, pure finish. The 1990 Riserva is slightly darker colored (plum/garnet), tannic, and spicy, with marginally more volume in the mouth. It, too, is made in a clear, measured, modern-day style. It should be at its peak in 4–5 years and keep for 10–12.

POGGIO ANTICO

1993 Altero Vino da Tavola	E	90
1993 Brunello di Montalcino	E	91
1990 Brunello di Montalcino	D	90
1996 Rosso di Montalcino	D	84

I was pleased but largely unmoved by Poggio Antico's 1996 Rosso di Montalcino. The attractive nose of spice, cigar smoke, and berries is followed by a tasty, medium-bodied wine with cherry/kirsch flavors. The finish quickly dissipated into acidity and tannin. Drink this over the near term—1–2 years. More impressive is the 1993 Altero, a 100% Sangiovese Grosso aged in *barrique.* It displays a deep plum color and a sweet tobacco, vanillin, smoky, underbrush, and jammy, berry bouquet. The flavors are lush and round, with medium to full body, outstanding purity, and a nicely layered, supple finish. This wine is already evolved, complex, and delicious. Drink it over the next 7–10 years. The 1993 Brunello di Montalcino is a full-bodied, powerful wine with surprisingly sweet tannin. The color is dark garnet with some amber at the edge. The nose offers up waves of smoke, roasted nuts, fruitcake, black cherries, Asian spices, and herbs. Rich, with no hard edges, plenty of glycerin, and a long finish, this evolved, complete wine can be drunk now or cellared for 10–12 years.

Although the outstanding 1990 Poggio Antico Brunello di Montalcino is ripe and dense, with medium to full body, it is not nearly as sexy and opulent as this estate's 1985. It exhibits plenty of density, but it seems less impressive than I would have thought given previous efforts from this winery. A weedy, tobacco component adds to the wine's complexity. This is not the most backward 1990 Brunello, but it does require 2–4 years of cellaring. It should drink well for 10–15 years.

POGGIO CHIARI

1995 Vino da Tavola   D   88+

Made from a tiny 5-acre estate, this wine is produced from 100% Sangiovese aged for 2 years in new French oak. Unfortunately only 300 cases were produced. The wine possesses a saturated dark purple color and a youthful, grapey, jammy, cassis nose with sweet oak in the background. Profoundly concentrated, deep, and medium to full bodied, with superb richness and a long finish with well-integrated acidity and tannin, this Vino da Tavola is extremely backward, tasting as if it had just been bottled. My numerical score may ultimately look conservative, as this wine displays all the component parts to merit an outstanding score with another 2–3 years of cellaring; it should keep for 15+ years.

IL POGGIONE (ROBERTO FRANCESCHI)

1993 Brunello di Montalcino   D   86

1990 Brunello di Montalcino   E   ?

1988 Brunello di Montalcino   D   89?

The medium ruby-colored 1993 Brunello di Montalcino reveals amber at the edge, followed by attractive earth, tobacco, and spice scents, with the fruit a secondary influence. In the mouth, it is medium bodied, with cedary, black cherry fruit, good spice, and a dry, compressed finish. Don't tempt fate by aging this wine more than another 2–3 years.

I certainly do not mind a little brett (a horsey, old saddle leather, aged beeflike aroma) in a wine, but the 1990 Brunello di Montalcino is dominated by that yeast, which inhabits many vineyards and wineries. The wine's fruit and some cedar and tobacco notes are, however, able to fight through the horsey aromas. On the palate, the wine exhibits a soft, ripe, medium-bodied style with noticeably hard tannin in the finish. I have had far better examples of Franceschi's Il Poggione than this uninspiring effort.

The impressive, large, full-bodied 1988 Brunello di Montalcino reveals some surprising amber at the edge, but it tastes youthful, with much of its potential ahead of it. The wine exhibits a big, spicy, leathery, earthy, berry nose, considerable body, and high tannin. Although the fruit is sweet, generous, and expansive, this wine may have a tendency to dry out before the tough tannin mellows. Drink it over the next 12–15 years.

POLIZIANO

1994 Elegia Vino da Tavola   D   86

1993 Le Stanze Vino da Tavola   D   85

1990 Vino Nobile di Montepulciano Vigna Asinone Riserva   D   88

1993 Vino Nobile di Montepulciano Vigneto Caggiole   D   84?

1990 Vino Nobile di Montepulciano Vigneto Caggiole Riserva   D   87

This excellent winery has fashioned spicy, sweet, round, rich wines that offer plenty of black cherry fruit intermixed with earth, leather, dried fruits, and spices. Approaching full maturity, the two 1990 Riservas are delicious to drink, but they can be kept for 5–7 more years. Both are full wines with plenty of glycerin, alcohol, and spice. The Vigna Asinone possesses slightly more aromatic dimension. Both reveal the vintage's sweet fruit, as well as plenty of spice, tobacco, and a chewy aftertaste. The supple, smoothly textured 1994 Elegia exhibits copious quantities of toasty new oak as well as jammy, red berry fruit. It is a medium-bodied, soft, elegant, lush wine for drinking over the next 4–5 years.

The medium dark ruby-colored 1993 Le Stanze reveals evidence of new oak in the nose, along with black cherry fruit and spice. Austere and tannic, but with enough ripeness and sweet vanillin to provide attraction, this medium-bodied wine will age well for 5–7 years, although it will have an angular, compressed personality. The light to medium ruby-colored 1993 Vino Nobile di Montepulciano Vigneto Caggiole displays plenty of acidity and tannin. It may ultimately turn out to be deficient in fruit. The wine exhibits earthy red fruit aromas in its shy aromatics, is lean and austere on the palate, but is cleanly made with good acidity and a compact finish. I don't expect it to improve, so drink it over the next several years.

LE PUPILLE

1997	Morellino di Scansano	B	88
1995	Morellino di Scansano	B	86
1992	Morellino di Scansano	B	85
1990	Morellino di Scansano Riserva	C	90
1989	Morellino di Scansano Riserva	C	86
1995	Saffredi	D	90
1991	Saffredi	D	89+
1990	Saffredi	D	94

This excellent 40-acre estate, owned by Elisabetta Geppetti, has produced a number of fine wines, including its value-priced Morellino di Scansano and its flagship wine, Saffredi. The latter offering, a blend of 75% Cabernet Sauvignon and the rest Merlot and Alicante, can reach sensational heights. I purchased the 1990 and have enjoyed every bottle I have opened. The 1995 Saffredi is not far behind the compelling 1990. Made from extremely low yields of less than 2 tons of fruit per acre and aged in small *barriques*, it is a medium- to full-bodied wine, with a moderate ruby color and sweet, cranberry/black cherry fruit intermixed with tobacco and *pain grillé* notes. Lush, with excellent concentration, sweet tannin, and a nicely textured feel, this elegant, concentrated wine should drink well for 7–10 years.

I have been impressed with the wines of this Tuscan estate. The small number of producers making Morellino di Scansano tend to turn out high-quality wines that merit more attention, especially in view of the fact that they might be the "poor person's Brunello di Montalcino."

For a reasonably good value in a non-wood-aged, tank-fermented, fruity wine, check out Le Pupille's 1995 Morellino di Scansano. The wine exhibits a ruby/purple color, a fruity, soft texture, excellent ripeness and richness, medium body, and good freshness. Made from 85% Sangiovese and 15% Alicante, it can be served slightly chilled, but it requires drinking over the next 2–3 years for its vibrancy and freshness. The 1997 Morellino di Scansano, made from 85% Sangiovese and 15% Alicante, Canaiolo, Malvasia, Nera, and Ciliegiolo, is a seductive, opulently textured, lush, fruit-driven wine with gobs of cranberry and black cherry liqueurlike aromas and flavors. Plump, fleshy, and gorgeous to drink because of the low acidity, ripe tannin, and good glycerin, it can be drunk over the next 3–4 years.

From the unexciting 1992 vintage, Le Pupille's Morellino di Scansano exhibits good, sweet fruit, fine ripeness, plenty of cherries in the wine's aromatics and flavors, and a supple, easygoing finish. Drink it over the next 2–3 years. It is a worthy effort in this rain-plagued vintage. The terrific 1990 Morellino di Scansano Riserva is a full-bodied wine that easily surpasses many of the more highly touted and luxury-priced Brunello di Montalcinos. It is dense and full bodied, with gobs of sweet hickory smoke and cherry-scented fruit, full body, outstanding extraction, and an overall sense of power allied with grace and balance. Drink it over the next decade. I adored the 1990 Saffredi (so much so that I purchased some), and the 1991 Saffredi is not far off the mark. Reminiscent of a Bordeaux Pauillac, it reveals an opaque dark ruby color as well as a wonderfully sweet nose of vanillin, cassis, and weedy tobacco. Dense, rich, and full bodied, with surprising glycerin and fat, this is a beautifully made wine from what has turned out to be an underrated vintage for Tuscany. Drink it over the next 7–10 years.

I bestowed an enthusiastic rating on this producer's 1988 Morellino di Scansano Riserva. In the difficult Tuscan vintage of 1989, Le Pupille turned out a ripe Sangiovese-based wine (with some Alicante added). The 1989 Morellino di Scansano Riserva reveals sweet, expansive, ripe fruit, light tannin, and a medium-bodied, spicy, supple finish. I have found few 1989 Tuscan wines that are so well balanced. Most have a tendency to be astringent and hollow, but this wine is an exception. Drink it over the next 4–5 years. The spectacular 1990 Saffredi (a blend of Sangiovese, Merlot, and Alicante) is a limited-production gem. Only 200 cases are available, so don't expect to find it easily. The wine boasts an opaque ruby/purple color, a huge, fabulously scented, penetrating bouquet of black and red fruits, smoky new oak, flowers, and spices. The wine is superconcentrated, with great purity and ripeness of fruit, high glycerin, a voluptuous texture, and a long, rich, concentrated finish. It is a beautifully balanced, powerful, yet elegant wine that can be drunk now or cellared for 10–15 years. Impressive!

CASTELLO DI QUERCETO

1993 Cignale Vino da Tavola		D	87?

This tightly knit, tannic, oaky, chocolatey-scented wine possesses a deep ruby/purple color and tannic, medium-bodied flavors that exhibit promise but are still compressed by the wine's acidity, wood, and tannin. There is good weight and volume in this Vino da Tavola, but it needs another 2–3 years of cellaring; it should keep for 10–15 years, but I do have some concerns about its drying out.

CASTELLO DEI RAMPOLLA

1995 Chianti Classico	C	86
1993 Chianti Classico	C	86
1994 Chianti Classico Riserva	D	87
1990 Chianti Classico Riserva	C	90
1994 Sammarco Vino da Tavola	E	87
1993 Sammarco Vino da Tavola	E	88
1991 Sammarco Vino da Tavola	E	86
1990 Sammarco Vino da Tavola	D	93
1996 Vigna d'Alceo Vino da Tavola	EE	92+

Castello dei Rampolla has long been one of my favorite Tuscan producers. I began purchasing their wines with the 1983 Sammarco. A recently drunk 1985 Sammarco was still in terrific shape, and it continues to behave like a top-class Graves from Bordeaux. The dark ruby/purple-colored 1994 Sammarco, a blend of 75% Cabernet Sauvignon and 25% Sangiovese, reveals aromas of lead pencil, charred leather, black cherries, and toasty oak. With moderately high tannin and a more angular, austere personality than is generally found in Sammarco, this very good to excellent effort will benefit from 1–2 years of cellaring. It should keep for 12 or more years. In 1996 Castello dei Rampolla produced an extremely limited-production (about 200 cases) Sangiovese/Cabernet Sauvignon/Petite Verdot blend called Vigna d'Alceo. This terrific wine bears more than a passing resemblance to a top-class Médoc. The opaque purple color is followed by gobs of toasty new oak and jammy cassis fruit intermixed with minerals, spice, and cedar. Medium bodied, with outstanding purity and concentration, exceptional harmony, and moderately high tannin, this is a promising, seriously endowed wine for readers with the patience to wait 4–5 years. It should keep for 2 decades.

The 1995 Chianti Classico is a dusty, leathery, berry-scented and -flavored wine with good body, a lusty, alcoholic punch, a supple texture, and admirable spice and fruit. It is one of the more earthy, spicy wines I have tasted from the 1995 vintage. Drink it over the next 2–3 years. The 1993 Chianti Classico, from a good rather than exciting vintage in Tuscany, offers a medium ruby color, followed by an attractive red currant-scented nose with hints of lead pencil and spice. Well made, elegant, and stylish, this wine is ready to drink, with clean, smoky, claretlike flavors. Consume it over the next 2–3 years.

The 1994 Chianti Classico Riserva exhibits copious quantities of lead pencil, tar, sweet, saddle leather, spicy, berry fruit in its medium-bodied format. It displays a healthy dark plum/garnet color and is expansive on the palate, with light tannin in the moderately long finish. Drink this excellent 1994 over the next 3–4 years.

The cedary, lead pencil, spicy-scented, medium-bodied 1991 Sammarco is the luxury cuvée of Sangiovese and Cabernet Sauvignon made by the well-known Chianti producer of the same name. I have had some extraordinary bottles of Sammarco (such as the 1982, 1983, 1985, and 1990). The 1991, while good, is low-key and compact. The wine reveals good density and richness, plenty of tannin, and fine underlying acidity, but the finish is abrupt and astringent. It is a candidate for 8–10 more years of aging, but I do not see it ever evolving into an exciting wine. The 1993 Sammarco is also a good rather than outstanding example of this wine. It exhibits a deep ruby color and a backward, unevolved nose of earth, new oak, spice, and Graves-like smoky, mineral character intertwined with black currants. In the mouth, the wine remains austere, but it possesses enough ripe, sweet fruit to coat the palate. Tannin dominates the finish. This wine will benefit from another 2–3 years of cellaring and keep for 10–12 years, but I suspect it is always going to be an austere, more compressed style of Sammarco.

This outstanding Tuscan producer has been exceptionally consistent over the last decade, so it is not surprising that the 1990s performed brilliantly. The 1990 Chianti Classico Riserva exhibits an impressively saturated dark ruby/garnet color and a spicy nose of ripe black cherries, earth, smoke, and roasted nuts. Very concentrated, medium to full bodied, with some moderate tannin still to be shed, this admirably endowed, rich, black cherry-flavored wine can be drunk now, but it promises to be even better in 2–3 years; it will last for 10–12 years. The 1990 Sammarco may prove to be a worthy rival to the glorious 1985. The saturated ruby/purple/garnet color is followed by an intense yet youthful fragrance of ripe black fruits, vanillin, and minerals. Full bodied, rich, and beautifully delineated and structured, it possesses considerable body, tannin, and extract. Although accessible, it is extremely young and ideally should have another 2–4 years of cellaring. It should age well for 15+ years. As I have said many times, Sammarco always reminds me of a top Graves because of the tobacco/mineral component it often displays.

RISECCOLI

1994 Chianti Classico Riserva	D	85
1994 Saeculum Vino da Tavola	D	88

Riseccoli's fully mature, medium garnet-colored 1994 Chianti Classico Riserva offers earthy, spicy, cherry fruit, as well as the telltale scent of new saddle leather. It should be consumed over the next 2–3 years. More complete, richer, and intriguing is the 1994 Saeculum, a Cabernet Sauvignon/Sangiovese blend aged in small *barriques*. Deep ruby/purple colored, with medium to full body and excellent, sweet, black currant, strawberry, and cherry fruit intermixed with smoke, leather, and peppery scents, this ripe, round Vino da Tavola possesses sweet tannin, fine concentration, and a nicely textured finish. Although it will not make old bones, it should drink well for 5–7 years.

ROCCA DI CASTAGNOLI

1990	Cabernet Sauvignon Buriano	D	89+
1993	Chianti Classico Riserva Capraia	C	?
1991	Chianti Classico Riserva Poggio a Frati	C	87
1990	Chianti Classico Riserva Poggio a Frati	D	88
1991	Stielle Vino da Tavola	D	86?
1990	Stielle Vino da Tavola	D	88?

I had little affection for this producer's 1991 or 1993 Chianti Classico Riservas, both of which were tart and excessively tannic and acidic—in short, deficient in fruit. The 1993 Chianti Classico Riserva Capraia may turn out to be a mid-80-point wine if it sheds enough of its tannin without losing its fruit. The question is, how will the fruit extract survive over the next 4–5 years? The wine exhibits a dark ruby/garnet color and attractive earthy, peppery, smoky, red berry fruit aromas, but it tastes compact, lean, and austere because of the brutal tannin level. It requires 2–3 years of cellaring. There should not be any problem with the muscular, full-bodied, tannic 1990 Chianti Classico Riserva Poggio a Frati. It reveals a dark garnet color with an amber edge, followed by sweet, earth, charcoal, gamey, cherrylike fruit interspersed with a whiff of cedar and tobacco. There is significant richness and extract in this old-style, somewhat tannic, dense, medium- to full-bodied wine, which could turn out to be outstanding if the tannin melts away and the fruit holds. It is a concentrated, traditionally made, serious, muscular, powerhouse Chianti designed to last 10–15+ years.

The 1990 Cabernet Sauvignon Buriano displays a St.-Julien-like lead pencil, cassis, and cedar nose, and medium-bodied, backward, tannic flavors with enough balancing, rich black currant fruit. The wine needs another 5–6 years of cellaring. Given its aging in new French *barriques*, it could easily be inserted as a ringer in a Bordeaux tasting. This wine should be close to full maturity in 5–6 years; it will keep for 15 or more. On first impression, the sweet 1990 Stielle Vino da Tavola is potentially outstanding. However, the tannin kicks in at the back of the palate, and in spite of delivering a blast of concentrated, oak-tinged cassis and red currant fruit, the wine finishes with an elevated level of astringency. It is another questionable candidate for attaining an ideal equilibrium between the fruit and the wine's structural components. This robust, forceful, powerful wine needs 4–6 years of cellaring. Anticipated maturity: 2002–2016.

The two 1991s were interesting to taste and compare with the riper, richer 1990 vintage. I thought the 1991 Chianti Classico Riserva Poggio a Frati to be excellent, offering a spicy, earthy, cedary, black cherry, and licorice nose, powerful cherry fruit flavors, and a medium-bodied finish. It also displays fine depth and moderate tannin and acidity. This wine, which is already drinkable, should age nicely for another 7–8 years. I am concerned that the 1991 Stielle Vino da Tavola (a blend of 60%–70% Cabernet Sauvignon and 30%–40% Sangiovese) may be too austere and tannic for its own good. The aging in new oak has sweetened some of the tannin, but this deep ruby-colored wine (with some amber at the edge), while dense and powerful, does display high tannin and a compressed personality. It is tightly knit and, despite the mature-looking color, seemingly unevolved and backward. Whether or not it comes together and gains more fruit at the expense of the tannin will be determined after a few more years of bottle age. I tend to believe the wine will dry out before it ever blossoms. Nevertheless it is certainly a good effort.

ROCCA DI MONTEGROSSI

1994 Chianti Classico	B 89
1993 Chianti Classico	B 88+
1990 Chianti Classico Riserva	D 92
1993 Geremia	D 91+

Over the last decade I have given some exceptional reviews to the wines from this Tuscan estate. The wines are terrific in top vintages, such as 1985, 1988, and 1990, but what is so impressive about Rocca di Montegrossi is the quality of the wines in difficult vintages. Take, for example, the 1994 Chianti Classico. If ever a Chianti were to taste like a grand cru red burgundy, it would be one of these soft, supple, expansively flavored, yet precocious and sexy 1994 Chiantis. Although the vintage was plagued by rain, the top producers were able to handle it well, attempting to go not for overly extracted, powerhouse wines, but, rather, for wines of suppleness, elegance, and gobs of up-front fruit. This 1994 Chianti Classico is a wine to drink over the next 1–2 years. Its smoky, strawberry-and-cherry-scented nose soars from the glass. Medium bodied and silky smooth, with sweet, ripe fruit, this is a delicious, dazzlingly pure wine that will make believers out of readers who previously felt this was a vintage to ignore. The bigger, richer 1993 Chianti Classico possesses a denser color, but it is less appealing (for the next year or so) than the 1994. It offers a deep, earthy, black cherry-scented nose, spicy, dense, well-endowed flavors, plenty of tannin, and crisp acidity. Still closed, this big-boned Chianti requires 1–2 years of cellaring; it will drink well for a decade or more.

The 1993 Geremia, the winery's 90% Sangiovese/10% Cannaiolo blend, is aged in small oak casks, of which one-third are new. It boasts a sweet, black cherry, toasty, earthy-scented nose, and medium- to full-bodied, concentrated flavors. Exhibiting density, thickness, and youthful tannin, this wine is firmly structured and closed yet promising. Give it 2–3 years of cellaring; it will evolve for 12–15 years. Looking for a profound example of Chianti? Check out Rocca di Montegrossi's 1990 Chianti Classico Riserva. From its smoky, tobacco, earth, and black cherry-scented nose to its dense, full-bodied, superbly concentrated flavors, this is a classic, intense Chianti that is just beginning to strut its stuff. Absolutely sensational, this wine should drink well for another 10–15 years.

SAN FELICE

1990 Brunello di Montalcino Campogiovanni	D 88
1988 Brunello di Montalcino Campogiovanni	D 89
1990 Vigorello Vino da Tavola	E 87

A dark plum/garnet color is followed by a 1990 VigorelloVino da Tavola with copious quantities of earth, new oak, and dusty, tannic-tinged fruit aromas. This is a rustic, medium- to full-bodied wine with high tannin as well as impressive extract. While it is not elegant, supple, or flattering, it is robust, large framed, and spicy. Give it 1–2 more years of cellaring and drink it over the next decade.

The medium- to full-bodied, highly structured 1990 Brunello di Montalcino Campogiovanni possesses fine ripeness, a spicy, forward, undeveloped nose, and the high acidity and tough tannin that mark so many wines of this vintage. After 5–6 more years of cellaring, it should turn out to be a very good but hardly inspirational example of Brunello di Montalcino.

San Felice produced a precocious, delicious, and complex 1988 Brunello di Montalcino from their 30-acre Campogiovanni Vineyard. The color is a healthy dark ruby, and the nose offers up expressive and intense aromas of sweet red and black fruits, roasted nuts, and cedar. Full bodied, rich, round, and generous, this large-scale, velvety-textured Brunello di Montalcino can be drunk now and over the next 10–12 years. This is unquestionably one of the most seductive and succulent 1988s I have tasted from Brunello di Montalcino.

SAN GIUSTO A RENTENTANO

1994 Chianti Classico	B	87
1993 Percarlo	D	92

San Giusto a Rentennano, the onetime ninth-century military fortress that was later a convent for nuns, has been one of my favorite producers ever since I extolled the virtues of the 1985 Percarlo, this estate's luxury, 100% Sangiovese, *barrique*-aged offering. Fans of that wine will be thrilled to know that the 1993 Percarlo is another terrific effort, ranking close to the sensational 1985 (which I had several months ago, when it was just beginning to reach full maturity). Aged in small oak casks, of which 33% are new, this wine exhibits a nearly opaque ruby/purple color, a sweet, fragrant, penetrating, black currant, vanillin, and smoky nose, full-bodied, concentrated flavors, copious quantities of glycerin and flesh, excellent purity, and enough acidity and tannin to buttress the wine's large proportions. The finish is 30+ seconds of extract, glycerin, and sweet tannin. This endearing wine is already beginning to drink well; it will last for another 10–15 years.

As for the 1994 Chianti Classico, it is a surprisingly delicious, hedonistic, up-front style of wine that should be consumed over the next year for its gaudy display of red fruits. Low in acidity, expansive, and supple, its charm is near-term. Once the fruit fades, there is not much depth to support aging, so take advantage of this gloriously fruity Chianti by drinking it over the next year.

SAN GUIDO

1995 Sassicaia Vino da Tavola	EE	92+
1993 Sassicaia Vino da Tavola	EE	86

One of the world's classic Cabernet Sauvignons, this wine has a phenomenal track record for being ageworthy and hitting some remarkable peaks of quality in great vintages (1985 is perfection in a bottle, and the unreleased 1997 may be an identical twin in the making). The exceptional 1995 has 2 decades of aging potential ahead of it. The wine boasts a nearly opaque ruby/purple color and a knockout nose of lead pencil, *pain grillé*, minerals, licorice, and black currants. As the wine sat in the glass, violet/floral notes began to emerge. In the mouth, it is tightly knit and tannic, but superbly concentrated as well as remarkably pure. It possesses that sweet, rich midpalate that often distinguishes great wines from merely good wines. The finish lasts for over 30 seconds. This wine should be purchased only by readers willing to wait the 5–6 years needed for it to shed its raw tannin and grapiness. The 1995 appears to be a Sassicaia to rival the estate's other top vintages. Anticipated maturity: 2004–2020.

A tannic, stern, austerely styled Sassicaia, the 1993 reveals a dark ruby/purple color followed by attractive cassis fruit with weedy tobacco and herbs in the background. New oak is present, but not intrusive. The wine is medium bodied, with high tannin, good acidity, and a firm, structured feel on the palate. Give it 2–3 more years of cellaring and drink it over the following 10–15+ years. The 1993 will never be remembered as one of the great Sassicaias.

SAN JACOPO DA VICCHIOMAGGIO

1995 Chianti Classico	C	84
1993 Chianti Classico	B	87

1993 Chianti Classico Riserva La Prima (Castello Vicchiomaggio)	D	87
1991 Chianti Classico Riserva La Prima	C	88+
1991 Chianti Classico Riserva Petri	B	87
1991 Ripa Delle More	C	88

The straightforward, medium-bodied, spicy, austere, earthy, cherry-flavored 1995 Chianti Classico is meant to be drunk over the next 1–2 years. It is well made but uncomplicated. The 1993 Chianti Classico Riserva La Prima is a richer, denser, medium- to full-bodied wine with a deep ruby color, leathery, black cherry fruit, and good spice, sweetness, and depth. A well-made, long Chianti, it is ideal for drinking over the next 2–3 years.

The 1993 Chianti Classico is a seductive, voluptuously textured, soft, supple Chianti revealing abundant quantities of gorgeously sweet cherry fruit in its aromatic profile, medium body, good glycerin, low acidity, and a round, generous, chewy, fleshy finish. Drink it over the next 3–4 years. Vicchiomaggio's 1991 Chianti Classico Riserva Petri is one of the finest 1991s I tasted from what is generally a disappointing vintage. The wine exhibits a deep, healthy, garnet/ruby color, an intriguing herb, berry, leather, and vanilla bouquet, sweet, ripe fruit, medium to full body, and light tannin in the heady finish. It has more in common with the 1990 than the 1991 vintage given its generosity and ripeness. Drink it over the next 4–5 years. Vicchiomaggio also produced a nearly outstanding 1991 Chianti Classico Riserva La Prima. From one of Tuscany's oldest vineyards, it is an atypically powerful, rich 1991, with evidence of new oak cask aging given its smoky, vanillin, toasty nose. Intense, ripe, and full bodied, with layers of chewy black cherry fruit, this wine is obviously made from low yields and old vines given its inner core of high extraction. Although impressive, it requires another 1–2 years of cellaring. It should keep for at least a decade.

The 1991 Ripa delle More, Vicchiomaggio's Vino da Tavola made from 100% Sangiovese aged in new French oak, offers a gorgeous, flattering nose of toasty, vanillin-scented new oak and plenty of jammy, red and black fruits. Well endowed, with medium to full body, excellent richness, and a chewy, fleshy, spicy, tannic finish, it can be drunk now and over the next 7–8 years.

SANTA MARIA DI AMBRA

1988 Casamurli	C	94
1993 Chianti Riserva Vigna Bigattiera	C	89
1993 Gavignano	C	87
1992 Gavignano	C	88

This has always been one of my favorite Marc de Grazia estates. The proprietors, the Zampi family, can trace winemaking at this domaine back to the sixteenth century. The excellent 1992 Gavignano and Casamurli, the spectacular barrel-fermented, *barrique*-aged Sangiovese (with a dollop of Malvasia Nera), are both impressive. The 1993 Gavignano, a blend of Sangiovese and Cabernet Sauvignon, is an elegant, Burgundian-like wine with black cherry fruit, nicely integrated, toasty French oak, and a spicy, expansive, medium- to full-bodied palate. Soft, round, and nearly fully mature, it should be drunk over the next 2–3 years. The 1992 Gavignano, from a more difficult vintage, tasted superior to the 1993. It revealed a smoky, earthy, toasty, black cherry-scented nose and dense, medium-bodied, concentrated flavors. The wine is fleshy and long, with no hard edges. Drink it over the next 1–2 years.

The 1993 Chianti Riserva Vigna Bigattiera, reminiscent of a top Pomerol, is another terrific effort. The wine reveals a medium dark ruby/garnet color, sweet, lush, black cherry, plum, and mocha-scented aromas, a sexy, silky, voluptuous texture, and a round, generous, fruit-and-glycerin-filled finish. This is about as lusty a Chianti as readers are likely to find.

Drink it over the next 2 years. Last, the 1988 Casamurli, which has been in the marketplace for several years, is performing splendidly, making me wonder just how profound the 1990 might be. The 1988, aged in small oak casks, is still a youthful, awesomely concentrated, deep ruby/purple-colored wine with a fabulous nose of smoke, licorice, black fruits, and cedar. Thick, rich, and full bodied, with layers of concentration, this is a sumptuous wine that coats the mouth with flavor without coming across as heavy or overbearing. It should drink well for another decade or more.

SCOPETONE

1991 Brunello di Montalcino	D	92
1994 Rosso di Montalcino	C	90

Don't expect to find truckloads of Scopetone's wines available at the local liquor store. This is only a 4-acre estate. The 1994 Rosso di Montalcino is a superb Rosso loaded with copious quantities of black cherry fruit. It reveals surprising glycerin and intensity, as well as a silky, opulent texture. This ostentatious, showy wine is ideal for drinking over the next 3–4 years. In contrast, the dark garnet-colored 1991 Brunello di Montalcino offers up a super, cedary, smoked duck, tobacco, and jammy cherry bouquet. This full-bodied wine possesses marvelous concentration, sweet tannin, and an explosively long finish. While it is hard to resist at present, it will evolve graciously for another 12–15 years.

SELVAPIANA

1993 Chianti Ruffina	B	87
1990 Chianti Ruffina Riserva Bucerchiale	C	90+
1993 Pomino	C	88

Selvapiana has fashioned three impressive wines. The 1993 Chianti Ruffina exhibits just how superior this Tuscan vintage is to 1991 and 1992. It displays a dark, garnet/plummy color and a rich, sweet nose of jammy fruit, new saddle leather, and spicy wood. Dense, medium to full bodied, with excellent concentration and fine overall balance, this is a forward, fleshy Chianti for drinking over the next 4–5 years. The outstanding 1990 Chianti Ruffina Riserva Bucerchiale is a backward but profound example of Chianti at its finest. The wine exhibits a dense, opaque, garnet/ruby color and a huge nose of roasted herbs, nuts, and sweet black cherries intertwined with scents of licorice and earth. Extremely full bodied with moderate tannin and layers of concentrated fruit, this superb Chianti requires 3–5 more years of cellaring. A classic! Anticipated maturity: 2000–2015.

The attractive 1993 Pomino, a blend of 80% Sangiovese and 20% Cabernet Sauvignon, offers gobs of ripe, sweet fruit (currants and black cherries), a youthful, exuberant, medium- to full-bodied palate, and a spicy, classy, slightly tannic finish. There is some evidence of new oak, but it is infused judiciously with the wine's other elements. This wine should drink well for 5–8 years.

GUICCIARDINI STROZZI

1993 Sodole Vino da Tavola	D	89

This dense, chocolatey, roasted coffee, and earthy, black cherry-scented wine is thick, intensely flavored, tannic, and rustic, as well as impressive and long. The wine is still youthful, but powerful and rich. Give it another 2–3 years of cellaring and drink it over the following decade.

TALOSA

1990 Vino Nobile di Montepulciano Riserva	B	87

A fragrant, cherry, spicy, new saddle leather, and earth nose is followed by a round, medium-bodied, pungently flavored wine with considerable spice and character. Drink it over the next 3–4 years.

TERRABIANCA

1994 Campaccio Vino da Tavola	D	86
1993 Campaccio Vino da Tavola	D	89
1991 Campaccio Vino da Tavola	C	89
1993 Campaccio Riserva Vino da Tavola	E	85
1991 Campaccio Riserva Vino da Tavola	D	90
1994 Chianti Classico Riserva Vigna della Croce	C	85
1993 Chianti Classico Riserva Vigna della Croce	D	88
1991 Chianti Classico Riserva Vigna della Croce	D	89
1993 Chianti Classico Scassino	B	87
1994 Cipresso Vino da Tavola	D	87
1993 Cipresso Vino da Tavola	D	87
1991 Cipresso Vino da Tavola	D	88
1996 La Fonte Vino da Tavola	C	86
1995 La Fonte Vino da Tavola	C	85+?
1996 Scassino Vino da Tavola	B	85
1995 Scassino Vino da Tavola	B	87

One of my favorite Tuscan wineries, Terrabianca has fashioned a bevy of pleasant wines, which, to my palate, fall short of previous efforts. As the scores suggest, there is nothing wrong with the quality of these examples, but they reflect the angular, tannic personalities of their respective vintages. The 1994 Chianti Classico Riserva Vigna della Croce exhibits a dark ruby color, followed by spicy, leathery, herb-tinged aromatics and flavors, good concentration, and a compressed, tannic, acidic, earthy finish. Drink it over the next 2–3 years. The dark ruby-colored 1996 La Fonte (a Sangiovese-dominated wine) offers a green pepper, dried herb, and black cherry nose. In the mouth, oak accompanies the herb-tinged, red currant, and cherry fruit. This spicy, medium-bodied, austere wine is flavorful and well made. Drink it over the next 2–3 years. The 1996 Scassino (also made from Sangiovese) is an austere, lean example, with an earthy, cedary, leathery nose, medium body, and a dry, severe, compressed finish. It is well made, but not a hedonistically styled wine. I would opt for drinking it over the next several years. More complex and interesting is Terrabianca's 1994 Cipresso. Another Sangiovese aged in oak, this intriguing wine displays a moderately intense nose of crushed seashells, iodine, pepper, roasted herbs, and sweet black cherry fruit. Evolved, and close to full maturity, this Rhône-like wine possesses good flesh, evidence of toasty new oak, and a spicy, peppery, round finish. Drink it over the next 1–2 years.

The 1994 Campaccio, a blend of Sangiovese and Cabernet Sauvignon, reveals the vintage's telltale austerity and leanness, as well as a good, sinewy, leathery style with moderate quantities of black cherry fruit intertwined with smoky oak and earthy notes. The short finish kept my score low. I do not believe this wine will develop or improve, so consume it in its muscular youthfulness over the next 2–4 years. The 1993 Campaccio Riserva (a San-giovese/Cabernet Sauvignon blend aged 16 months in oak casks) is the finest of this good but uninspiring group of new offerings from Vittorio Fiore's Terrabianca. It possesses a deep ruby color as well as a sweet black cherry and *pain grillé*–scented nose. In the mouth, it re-veals medium body and riper, sweeter fruit than is found in the other offerings, as well as less angularity and austerity. Drink it over the next 2–3 years.

This Tuscan firm made superb 1990s, but it has also demonstrated that high quality can be achieved in difficult vintages. These 1991 offerings are among the finest 1991s to emerge from Tuscany. But first, a comment on the 1993 Terrabianca Chianti Classico Scassino. This wine possesses good ripeness, an elegant, cherry- and earthy-scented nose, and fine preci-sion to its crisp, medium-bodied, moderately endowed flavors. It is a well-made, supple wine for consuming over the next 2–3 years.

As for the 1991 Chianti Classico Riserva Vigna della Croce, it offers a sweet, ripe, fruity nose that has more in common with a 1990 than a 1991. This is a silky wine, with excellent, nearly outstanding, richness, spice, and that intriguing toasty, tobacco, leather, cherry com-ponent often found in a top Chianti. The 1991 Cipresso reveals a similar sweet, ripe nose, excellent color saturation, and densely concentrated, medium- to full-bodied flavors with fine length and overall harmony. This wine should drink well for 5–7 years. The two cuvées of 1991 Campaccio are both beautifully made wines. The Riserva has the advantage of hav-ing more suppleness, as well as more ripe, sweet fruit in both its aromatics and flavors. Both wines exhibit impressive saturated, deep ruby colors, excellent purity, medium to full body, and extracted, rich personalities. I tasted them in a flight of top-notch 1990s, and believe me, they could not have been picked out as wines from the 1991 vintage.

The more current releases are all good, but more austere, leaner-style wines than the 1990s and not as concentrated as the 1991s. The 1993 Chianti Classico Riserva Vigna della Croce is one of the finest 1993 Chiantis I have tasted from this vintage. The healthy dark ruby color is followed by copious quantities of tobacco-tinged, sweet cherry, spicy fruit, with excellent richness. It offers admirable intensity, medium body, fine depth and suppleness, and impeccable balance. Drink this beautifully made, delicious Chianti over the next 3–4 years. The 1993 Campaccio, a proprietary red aged for 24 months in small barrels, reveals a Bordeaux-like lead pencil, vanillin, currant and cherry nose, medium to full body, excellent richness and depth, and good underlying acidity and tannin to give the wine delineation and balance. It is a purely made, spicy, rich wine for drinking over the next 6–7 years.

The 1995 La Fonte (primarily a Sangiovese wine) is a medium-bodied, well-made offering produced from the estate's younger vines. It possesses a rustic side, with coarse tannin and tart acidity, which gives the wine a compressed, pinched personality. It offers spicy, currant fruit intermingled with tobacco, dried flowers, and red currant scents and flavors. There are also notions of tar and smoke in the flavors. This wine might soften with another 1–2 years of cellaring, but it should be consumed over the next 3–4 years. A more promising wine, the 1995 Scassino possesses a deep ruby color and an elegant, clean, pure, black cherry-scented nose with whiffs of herbs, saddle leather, earth, and cigar smoke. It is spicy, with good fruit, medium body, softer tannin, and better integration of wood and acidity. A trifle richer is the 1993 Cipresso. It exhibits a deeper, more saturated ruby/plumlike color, spicy, vanillin, sweet red and black currant fruit, medium body, and a New World/international style with ripe fruit and lavish wood. This wine could have emerged from any of the world's wine-producing regions. Drink it over the next 5–6 years.

AZIENDA AGRICOLA LA TORRE (LUIGI ANANIA)
1990 Brunello di Montalcino   **E   93+**

This noteworthy estate's 1990 Brunello is a statuesque wine of immense power, richness, body, and alcohol. It exhibits a dark ruby/garnet color and an ostentatious bouquet of Asian spices, jammy black cherries, herbs, cedar, and leather. Dense and concentrated, with adequate acidity, this stunningly proportioned, massive Brunello should drink well young and hit its peak in 7–10 years; it will last for 20+ years.

TOSCOLO

1994 Chianti	A	85
1995 Chianti Classico	B	84
1993 Chianti Classico	B	86
1995 Chianti Classico Riserva	C	87

Made under the auspices of famed oenologist Franco Bernabei, the 1995 Chianti Classico Riserva is an attractive, round, flattering style of Chianti, with some of the vintage's dusty tannin, but primarily a fruit-driven personality. The color is deep ruby, and the nose offers up notes of new saddle leather, cherry liqueur, licorice, and herbs. This medium-bodied wine exhibits a ripe, rich, fruity attack that narrows slightly to reveal rustic tannin in the gutsy yet fleshy finish. It should drink well for 2–4 years.

I was unimpressed with Toscolo's 1995 Chianti DOCG, an innocuous, thin wine. The 1995 Chianti Classico is made in a light, commercial style, but it does offer a medium ruby color, crisp, tart, strawberry/cherry flavors, and a pure, easy-to-understand, uncomplicated format. Drink this elegant wine, with light to medium body and soft fruit, over the next 12–14 months.

The first 1994 Chianti I tasted, this soft, round, attractively scented and fruited, medium-bodied 1994 Chianti from Toscolo possesses no hard edges. It is easy to drink and understand. Restaurants should consider serving it by the glass. Drink it over the next 2–3 years. The 1993 Chianti Classico exhibits flinty, cherrylike fruit, good spice, medium body, and a well-made, ripe constitution with enough stuffing to drink well for another 2–3 years.

TRAVIGNOLI

1993 Chianti Ruffina	A	86

A good, spicy, leather, tobacco, and cherry-scented and -flavored Chianti, this wine has medium body, fine definition, adequate acidity, and attractive ripeness with no astringency or toughness. Drink it over the next several years.

TUA RITA

1996 Giusto Dei Notri Vino da Tavola	E	90
1994 Giusto Dei Notri Vino da Tavola	D	93
1996 Redigaffi Vino da Tavola	E	94
1994 Redigaffi Vino da Tavola	E	93

Tua Rita's 7.5-acre vineyard was a source for the Cabernet Sauvignon and Merlot used in the blend at Sassicaia until Tua Rita began to estate-bottle in 1992. Approximately 400 cases of the Giusto dei Notri are produced from a blend of 60% Cabernet Sauvignon and 40% Merlot. The wine is aged for 14 months in French oak barrels, of which 50% are new, and bottled without fining or filtration. Only 125 cases of the 100% Merlot, Redigaffi, are produced. It, too, is aged in 50% new French oak and is bottled without fining or filtration. Both wines are stunning . . . and keep in mind that the two I tasted were from a relatively difficult, rain-plagued vintage. Thus it is easy to imagine how extraordinary the 1995s might be.

The 1994 Giusto dei Notri Vino da Tavola exhibits a saturated opaque purple color (it looked like a barrel sample of a profound vintage of Mouton-Rothschild) as well as a knockout nose of black currants, sweet toasty oak, chocolate, smoke, and licorice. The wine is beautifully balanced, with superb purity, extraordinary concentration and length, medium to full body, and silky, sweet layers of flavor. It is both exceptionally intense and well balanced. Already accessible, it will continue to evolve gracefully for 10–12 years and last for 2 decades. The 100% Merlot 1994 Redigaffi is awesome. I suspect the likes of Christian Moueix and Michel Rolland from Pomerol would be thrilled to taste this wine, as it possesses the quintessential Merlot characteristics—chocolate, mocha, jammy black cherries, and toast, as well as subtle herbs. This wine is extraordinarily rich, full bodied, opulent, and, as my enthusiastic notes read, "great stuff." With full body, low acidity, luscious layers of chewy, jammy fruit, and a finish that lasts for over 30 seconds, this terrific Merlot rivals the sensational Merlot of Castella di Ama and Ornellaia's Masseto. It should drink well for 12–15+ years.

This tiny estate is turning out exceptional wines, the qualitative equals of the finest wines being produced at the nearby estates of Sassicaia and Ornellaia. Both cuvées are aged in French oak casks (50% new) for 12–15 months and are bottled without fining or filtration. The production of the 1996 Giusto dei Notri Vino da Tavola (a blend of 60% Cabernet Sauvignon and 40% Merlot) is a meager 450 cases. An outstanding wine, it boasts a black ruby/purple color as well as an intense nose of licorice, black currants, and a whiff of Provençal olives. Full bodied, thick, and layered, with moderately high tannin, a slight austerity in the finish, and a concentrated, complete, and powerful feel, this pure, harmonious wine requires 2–5 more years of cellaring. It should be at its finest between 2002 and 2012. The 1996 Redigaffi Vino da Tavola is a 100% Merlot made from yields of approximately 2 tons of fruit per acre. The first word in my tasting notes is "wow!" An explosive nose of cherry liqueur, smoke, coffee, vanillin, and other jammy black fruits is followed by a superbly delineated, rich, layered, multifaceted wine with full body, exceptional purity and concentration, a voluptuous texture, and a powerful, blockbuster finish. The high level of extract and richness conceals lofty tannin and alcohol. This wine can be drunk, but it promises to be even better in 4–5 years; it will last for 12–15 years.

UCCELLIERA

| 1994 Rosso di Montalcino | B 88 |

Another tasty, round, generously endowed, low-acid, plump 1994, this Rosso di Montalcino exhibits a dark ruby color, good fatness and glycerin, and a creamy texture. There are copious quantities of earthy, berry fruit in this silky-style wine that should be drunk over the next 2–3 years.

VAL DI SUGA

| 1990 Brunello di Montalcino | D 78 |

A simple, one-dimensional Brunello di Montalcino, this musty-scented, medium-bodied wine possesses some depth but little fruit, and it tastes muted and short. Do not expect additional cellaring to result in any pleasant surprises.

FATTORIA VARRAMISTA

| 1995 Vino da Tavola | D 90 |

An innovative blend dominated by Syrah, with small quantities of Merlot, this wine exhibits a textbook nose of bacon fat, smoked herbs, pepper, and black currants. Dense, rich, and medium to full bodied, with sweet tannin, an expansive mouth-feel, and an unevolved, grapey personality, this potentially outstanding wine should be at its best with another 1–2 years of cellaring, and it will keep for a decade or more.

FATTORIA DI VETRICE

1993 Chianti Ruffina	A	86

This solid Chianti displays attractive, earthy, black cherry fruit and spice, medium body, fine depth, and a soft, generous finish. Drink it over the next 2–3 years.

VILLA BANFI

1990 Brunello di Montalcino	D	84

One thing is certain about all the Villa Banfi wines—they are cleanly made, innocuous, and designed for the huge segment of the marketplace that prefers uncomplicated, easy-to-understand and -drink wines. This one-dimensional 1990 Brunello di Montalcino reveals a muted nose (some cherry and roasted herb notes eventually emerge), an undistinguished medium ruby color, a tart, tannic palate, and high acidity. The latter two characteristics give the wine a compact, compressed personality. This wine's motto should be "Sterile New World oenology meets and conquers Tuscany." From the largest estate in Brunello (373 acres), riper fruit and more risk taking in the winemaking process would be an encouraging development.

VILLA BOSCOROTONDO

1993 Chianti Classico	B	86

This 1993 Chianti Classico continues to confirm my pleasing tastings with this Tuscan vintage. Made in a powerful, rustic style with some tannin to shed, it possesses an attractive, spicy, smoky, richly fruity nose, plenty of body and spicy, earthy, ripe, black cherry and curranty fruit, and a moderately long finish. It can be drunk now or cellared for 5–6 years.

VILLA CAFAGGIO

1995 Chianti Classico	C	86
1993 Chianti Classico Riserva	D	85
1993 Chianti Classico Riserva Solatio Basilica	D	86+
1995 Cortaccio Vino da Tavola	E	89
1994 Cortaccio Vino da Tavola	D	86
1993 Cortaccio Vino da Tavola	D	86+
1993 San Martino Vino da Tavola	D	86

This Tuscan winery has turned out a bevy of attractive wines. The 1993 Chianti Classico Riserva offers a medium ruby color, an attractive strawberry-and-cherry-scented nose, sweet fruit, medium body, and a soft finish. It is a wine to drink over the next 2–3 years. The 1993 San Martino, a Tuscan Vino da Tavola, exhibits a dark ruby color, spicy oak and black cherries in its moderately endowed aromatics, good acidity, medium body, and a sinewy, austere, but elegant, firm personality. It will benefit from 6–12 more months of bottle age and drink well for 5–6 years. The 1993 Chianti Classico Riserva Solatio Basilica reveals sweet cherry/cedary fruit, good spice, medium body, and a tannic, high-acid, firm finish. The wine is pure but angular, suggesting further bottle aging is necessary to soften its edges. Cellar it for 6 more months and drink it over the following 6–7 years.

The 1993 and 1994 Cortaccio Vino da Tavola (Villa Cafaggio's proprietary Cabernet Sauvignon) possess deep ruby/purple colors as well as copious quantities of cassis fruit and toasty new oak. The 1993 is more unevolved and youthful than the 1994. The 1994 is more open, but both are tannic, youthful, grapey, one-dimensional, well-endowed wines that need another 2–4 years of bottle age. Both wines should last well for 12–15 years. The medium dark ruby-colored 1995 Chianti Classico is a delicious, forward, soft wine offering copious quantities of strawberry and cherry fruit, good spice, and a silky texture. It is an ideal restaurant Chianti, as well as a wine for consumers looking for a soft, medium-weight, ripe, fruity Chianti to consume over the next several years.

The 1995 Cortaccio, a Cabernet Sauvignon from the Tuscany commune of Greve, is impressive. The color is a healthy, thick-looking dark ruby/purple. The tight but promising nose offers up sweet toast, in addition to copious quantities of cassis. Secondary nuances should develop after a few years of bottle age. The wine is fleshy, rich, and medium to full bodied, with well-integrated wood, tannin, and acidity. Purity and equilibrium are the hallmarks of this rich, Bordeaux-like offering. Anticipated maturity: 2000–2010.

VILLA LA SELVA

1995	Felcaia Vino da Tavola	C	88
1994	Felcaia Vino da Tavola	D	89
1991	Felcaia Vino da Tavola	C	87
1994	Selvamaggio Vino da Tavola	D	90
1993	Selvamaggio Vino da Tavola	C	90
1991	Selvamaggio Vino da Tavola	C	90

The 1995 Felcaia, a *barrique*-aged Sangiovese, possesses a dark ruby color and a sweet, moderately intense nose of freshly plowed earth, new saddle leather, and strawberry/cherry fruit. Full bodied, ripe, and classy, this stylish, dark ruby/purple-colored wine has 10–12 years of good drinking ahead of it. The high tannin prevalent in other seriously endowed 1995s is there, but it is nicely balanced by the wine's glycerin and concentrated fruit. Anticipated maturity: now–2009. A Cabernet Sauvignon/Sangiovese blend aged in new oak, the 1994 Selvamaggio is an explosive, ostentatiously styled wine that should be consumed now and over the next 5–7 years. A nose of shiitake mushrooms and blackberry, currant, and cherry fruit, intermingled with enticing smoky oak, is sexy and intense. Full bodied and ripe, with layers of powerful, concentrated, jammy fruit, this is a knockout example of Vino da Tavola that can be drunk now or cellared for 5–7 years.

Villa La Selva's 1994 Felcaia, a Sangiovese aged in small French oak casks, is produced from vineyards situated between Arezzo and Siena. The wine exhibits a saturated dark ruby/purple color, sweet, ripe, cassis, vanillin, and toasty aromatics, and dense, rich, medium- to full-bodied flavors with layers of jammy fruit nicely buttressed by toasty new oak and ripe tannin. This impressively endowed, beautifully made wine is already accessible and flattering to drink. It should age well for a decade.

The superb 1993 Selvamaggio Vino da Tavola is a blend of 70% Cabernet Sauvignon and 30% Sangiovese, all aged in small French oak casks. The wine's opaque purple color is followed by an impressive vanillin, black currant, and licorice nose, sweet, full-bodied, concentrated flavors, low acidity, an expansive, chewy mouth-feel, and fine purity and depth. It cuts a broad and impressive richness on the palate. In spite of its flattering, up-front precociousness, this wine will benefit from 2–3 years of cellaring and keep for 15 years.

The two 1991 offerings prove that some producers were able to handle this difficult vintage with considerable competence. Villa La Selva's 1991 Felcaia is made from 100% Sangiovese and aged in new oak. The toasty, vanillin, berry aromas are followed by a medium-bodied, ripe, spicy, monolithic wine with excellent richness and a mouth-filling finish. Drink it over the next 4–5 years. The outstanding, opaque purple-colored 1991 Selvamaggio offers a super nose of smoky herbs, jammy cherries, underbrush, and chocolate. Full bodied and rich, with superb concentration, this is a muscular, well-balanced wine that should drink well for 7–8 years.

VILLA MONTE RICO

1993 Villa Monte Rico	C	87?
1992 Villa Monte Rico	D	88

The 1993 Villa Monte Rico is reminiscent of a highly extracted, large-bodied, tannic, back-ward Brunello. The wine is dense, powerful, and muscular, but not yet revealing much charm or friendliness. It needs another 2–3 years of cellaring to reveal whatever is lurking behind its body, structure, and imposing wall of tannin. The wine's purity, ripeness, and weight suggest good things will emerge, but will the tannin melt gracefully away? The 1992 Villa Monte Rico is a more supple, enticing, and user-friendly wine. The deep ruby color is followed by copious amounts of earthy, underbrush, and black cherry aromas, sweet, jammy fruit, medium body, and no hardness or toughness in the finish. It should be drunk over the next 3–4 years.

VILLA SANT' ANNA

1993 Chianti Colli Senesi	B	86
1988 Vin Santo	D	98

Believe it or not, I do taste Vin Santos every few years, but I have never had one quite as re-markable as this 1988 from Villa Sant' Anna. The dark amber color gives way to a penetrating smoked hazelnut/earthy-scented nose with aromas of truffles, soy, and leather. Offering an immense amount of flavor, this dry, sherrylike aperitif or dessert wine (whichever you pre-fer) is one of the most aromatic, complex, and provocative Vin Santos I have ever tasted. Like so many great wines, quantities are minuscule. The 1993 Chianti Colli Senesi reveals in-tense leathery, cherry fruit on the palate, good flesh, and an exuberant, ripe, medium-bodied style. It will provide uncomplicated but attractive drinking over the next 3–4 years.

CASTELLO DI VOLPAIA

1995 Chianti Classico	C	86
1994 Chianti Classico Riserva	C	85
1991 Chianti Classico Riserva	C	86

Both the 1994 and 1995 reveal a Burgundian-like laciness and perfumed cherry/raspberry fruitiness. The medium ruby-colored 1995 Chianti Classico, while simple, is endearing for its straightforward display of red and black fruits, spice, and light touch of oak. Round, soft, and seductive, it is ideal for consuming over the next 1–3 years. The light to medium ruby-colored 1994 Chianti Classico Riserva is already revealing considerable evolution. It pos-sesses more spice, tannin, and acidity, as well as a drier, more austere finish. It is a good but fragile Chianti that needs to be drunk over the next several years.

The attractive, mature 1991 Chianti Classico is revealing dried red fruits, dusty earth, and spice aromas in its moderately intense aromatics. The wine is medium bodied and elegant, with sweet cherry fruit accompanied by hints of tobacco and wood. The soft finish possesses some acidity and light tannin. Drink it over the next 3–4 years.

LE VOLTE

1996 Vino da Tavola	C	87

This excellent value from the winery responsible for Ornellaia is a blend of Sangiovese and Cabernet Sauvignon, aged in small oak casks and bottled unfiltered. The 1996 is a particu-larly successful example of this robust, fleshy, dry red wine. The color is dark ruby, and the wine offers up copious quantities of sweet jammy cherry and berry fruit. Mouth filling, rich, and expansive, with good flesh and a touch of wood, this uncomplicated but immensely satis-fying red wine can be drunk now and over the next 3–4 years.

OTHER SIGNIFICANT RED WINES OF ITALY

ACONE (CAMPANIA)

1997 Vin Giocondo	A	85

This biodynamically managed vineyard has produced an attractive wine from southern Italy. Acone's 1997 Vin Giocondo is made primarily from Aglianico. This pleasant, dark ruby-colored wine with crisp acidity, lively cranberry and cherry fruit, medium body, spice, and a refreshing, vibrant finish is a good bistro/trattoria red to drink over the next 1–2 years.

ALLEGRINI (VENETO)

1993 Amarone Classico	D	88
1991 Amarone Classico	D	85
1988 Amarone Classico	D	91
1993 La Poja Vino da Tavola	D	90
1992 La Poja Vino da Tavola	D	91
1991 La Poja Vino da Tavola	D	90
1990 La Poja Vino da Tavola	E	92
1997 Valpolicella Classico	B	86
1996 Valpolicella Classico	A	86
1995 Valpolicella Classico La Grola	C	90
1994 Valpolicella Classico La Grola	C	88
1993 Valpolicella Classico La Grola	B	87
1995 Valpolicella Classico Palazzo della Torre	C	90
1994 Valpolicella Classico Palazzo della Torre	C	90
1993 Valpolicella Classico Palazzo della Torre	B	90

This winery has made enormous qualitative progress over the last 3 or 4 years. The 1997 Valpolicella Classico is a fresh, earthy, cherry-scented wine with lively acidity, light to medium body, and a zesty, exuberant style. It is not a big wine, but rather a delicate Valpolicella with gobs of personality and liveliness. I would opt for drinking it over the next several years. The 1995 Valpolicella La Grola is a spectacular single-vineyard Valpolicella, exhibiting a deep ruby/purple color and a knockout nose of black cherries and blackberry fruit, along with underlying mineral scents. In the mouth, it is a medium- to full-bodied, layered wine, with a velvety texture, outstanding concentration and purity, admirable harmony, and a finish that lasts 25–30 seconds. Additionally, the wine's equilibrium is superb. This gorgeous, rich, opulent Valpolicella should drink well for 5–6 years.

Another outstanding effort from Allegrini is the 1995 Palazzo della Torre. Made by the *ripassa* method of running the unfermented Valpolicella juice across the pressings and pomace of the Amarone, this is a muscular, dense ruby/purple-colored wine with a robust, peppery, truffle, dried herb, earthy, blackberry aromatic profile. Full bodied yet sweet (from fruit extract, not sugar), with a velvety-textured attack, this large-scale, delicious, round, low-acid, mouth-filling dry red should drink well for 5–7 years. Don't miss it!

I am becoming increasingly fond of this estate's entire portfolio of Valpolicellas. The least expensive offering is the 1996 Valpolicella Classico, a spicy, cherry/strawberry-scented, elegant wine with medium body, good fruit, and a soft, round texture. This personality-filled Valpolicella is ideal for drinking over the next several years with seafood or veal dishes. The

1994 Valpolicella Classico La Grola, a single-vineyard offering, is close to outstanding. A deep ruby/purple color and sweet, black cherry, nutty, smoky aromas are followed by an intense, savory, supple-textured wine with excellent concentration, undeniable finesse, and admirable equilibrium. It is a tasty, fleshy Valpolicella for consuming over the next 5–6 years. Even better is the 1994 Valpolicella Classico Palazzo della Torre. This is a full-bodied, rich, dense style of Valpolicella made by the *ripassa* method of taking Valpolicella juice and running it through Amarone pressings. This intensifies the wine's earthiness and richness. This offering exhibits copious amounts of tar, licorice, hickory smoke, and luscious black cherry fruit. Powerful, full bodied, and rich, this dry, pure wine will provide an ideal accompaniment to grilled meats and vegetables. It should drink well for a decade.

Most Americans think of Valpolicella as an industrial product of northeast Italy with a faint ruby color, little fruit, and a thin, sharp personality. And why shouldn't they? The vast majority of Valpolicella available on these shores is textbook garbage. Tasting these Valpolicellas brings to mind one of the great producers of this region, Quintarelli. Allegrini's 1993 Valpolicella La Grola is a serious, ambitiously made, dark ruby-colored, dense wine with plenty of rich, berry fruit and crisp acidity. It would work beautifully with a rich pasta dish such as lasagne. Drink it over the next 3–4 years. The 1993 Valpolicella Palazzo della Torre is a beauty. It is a blend of 70% grapes that are harvested and vinified normally and 30% that were left on mats until December to dry and raisin. They were then vinified and blended back into the vat of the traditionally vinified wine. The blended wine was aged for 18 months in *barriques*. The wine offers up complex aromas of leather, spice, cedar, dried fruits, and berries. Rich and full bodied, with undeniable elegance and precision, this is one of the most provocative and persuasive Valpolicellas I have tasted. It should drink well for 3–5 years.

La Poja, made from a hilltop vineyard in Valpolicella planted exclusively with a relatively unknown grape called Corvia Veronese, is believed to be the first wine totally vinified with this varietal. The wine spends 18 months in small French oak casks. It possesses the structure of a Sangiovese and the sweetness and ripeness of Pinot Noir. It exhibits rich fruit, medium body, and admirable persistence and length on the palate, without being heavy. The 1991 and 1990 have more similarities than differences. The 1990 exhibits more intensity and ripeness, no doubt from the hotter, drier growing season. While I felt these wines tasted like a hypothetical blend of Sangiovese and Pinot Noir, importer Leonardo LoCascio claims they taste like a blend of Sangiovese and Syrah. However, the bottom line is that they are very fine, rich, complex wines that merit serious attention. Unfortunately, only 1,000 cases were produced in each vintage. The 1992 La Poja is an amazingly rich, powerful, spicy wine with gobs of concentration, a deep ruby/purple color, and loads of sweet cherry and strawberry fruit. With its smoky, nutty, spiciness, copious quantities of fruit, medium to full body, and outstanding purity and concentration, this is a breakthrough dry red wine for Allegrini. Sadly, only about 800 cases were made. The 1993 La Poja displays a dark plum color and an intriguing nose of sweet black cherries, earth, pepper, and spice. Medium bodied, fleshy, muscular, layered, with good underlying, tangy acidity and moderate tannin, this impeccably well-made wine should drink well for a decade or more.

Allegrini's 1991 Amarone is satisfying but somewhat coarsely textured, with dry, hard flavors, good, spicy, trufflelike aromas, and plenty of body, but not enough sweet fruit to balance out the wine's structural components. Although attractive, it is not at the same quality level as Allegrini's Valpolicellas and Vino da Tavolo La Poja.

Allegrini's current offerings of Amarone Classico include the tar/freshly laid asphalt-scented, medium- to full-bodied, opaque purple-colored 1993. This rich wine possesses loads of fruit as well as 14% alcohol. It should last for 2 decades or more. Even better, the saturated ruby/purple-colored 1988 Amarone Classico offers peppery, asphalt, and truffle aromas and thickly textured, powerful flavors that are just beginning to achieve harmony among the acidity, tannin, alcohol, and fruit. This is a big, dense, savory Amarone to drink over the next 15–20 years. These heavyweight wines are essentially dry, gutsy reds with plenty of character, but they must be matched with rich cheeses or grilled foods.

D'ANGELO (BASILICATA)

1994 Aglianico del Vulture	B	90
1991 Aglianico del Vulture Vigna Caselle Riserva	C	88+?
1993 Canneto	D	85?

The 1994 Aglianico del Vulture (made from 100% Aglianico) is my favorite of these three wines. It is a big, weighty, husky, full-bodied wine with a dark garnet/purple color. Explosive levels of black fruits, tar, glycerin, smoke, and alcohol jump from the glass of this hugely impressive, big, chunky, fleshy wine. It can be drunk now and over the next 6–7 years. Readers looking for finesse and elegance will want to bypass this blockbuster. The 1991 Aglianico del Vulture Vigna Caselle Riserva is also made from 100% Aglianico but is aged longer before its release. It is an ambitious, backward, more intellectual style of wine that is full bodied but tightly knit, with smoky, black cherry fruit and loads of truffle and earthlike aromas and flavors. I actually prefer its less expensive sibling, but this should turn out to be an interesting wine given another 1–2 years of cellaring. It should last for 12 years. I had mixed feelings about the 1993 Canneto, a 100% Aglianico wine aged in small French barrels, of which one-third were new. It is not particularly expressive and comes across as tannic and compressed, with a bland, international style. Nevertheless, it is a well-made, competent offering that should drink well for 5–6 years.

APOLLONIO (PUGLIA)

1997 Copertino Riserva "Divoto"	B	87
1997 Salice Salentino Riserva	B	87

This winery in Puglia has produced a dense ruby/garnet-colored 1997 Salice Salentino Riserva with a big, smoky, melted road tar, peppery, kirsch nose of moderate complexity. In the mouth, it is fleshy, with lively fruit, excellent ripeness, and a nicely textured and layered feel. It is a clean, modern-style offering from this rustic area of Italy. Drink it over the next 2–3 years. The 1997 Copertino Riserva "Divoto" possesses surprising elegance for a wine from this area of Italy. It reveals a deep ruby color, followed by an attractive black cherry and spice-scented nose, long, sweet, ripe flavors, medium body, good integration of acidity and tannin, and a charming, clean finish. It should drink well for several years.

ARGIOLAS (SARDINIA)

1996 Costera (Cannonau)	B	87
1994 Costera	B	87
1993 Costera	B	87
1992 Costera	B	87
1996 Perdera	A	85
1995 Perdera	A	84
1994 Perdera	A	86
1993 Perdera	A	85
1992 Perdera	A	86
1993 Turriga	D	90

1992 Turriga	D	89
1990 Turriga	C	90
1989 Turriga	C	90

Importer Leonardo LoCascio is thrilled about the prospects for high-quality wines from Sardinia, a place he claims is experiencing a profound winemaking revolution. Not only are the hillside vineyards being resurrected and replanted, but some of Italy's most influential oenologists (for example, Signor Tacchis, the winemaking architect behind Solaia and Sassicaia) are frequent visitors to this island.

Sardinia is receiving more attention from the wine community as the result of efforts such as these from the Argiolas winery, which first bottled wines in 1989. While they make a decent, albeit bland white wine, the real prizes are the reds, which are made from both the indigenous varietal of Sardinia, Monica, and from the Cannonau grape. The red wine offerings include the 1996 Perdera, which is made from the indigenous Monica. Fermented in tank and aged in French barrels, this excellent wine boasts a dark ruby/purple color, an evolved, cedary, cherry, fruitcake, and peppery nose, soft, berrylike flavors, a hint of chocolate, and an easygoing, graceful finish. This wine can be drunk now as well as over the next 3–4 years. The 1996 Costera, made from the Sardinian grape called Cannonau (Grenache), offers a dark plum color and earthy, smoked herb, pepper, and cherry jam aromas. In the mouth, this is a broadly textured wine with meaty, beef blood, smoky charcoal-like flavors, medium body, and a lusty, exuberant, heady finish. It is a hedonistic, delicious, full-flavored red to drink over the next 4–5 years.

The 1995 Perdera (100% Monica) is a dark ruby/garnet-colored wine with a spicy, peppery, Carignan-like, gamey, earthy nose. This well-made, exuberant, gutsy, rustic, straightforward, pleasant wine cuts a clean impression on the palate. The 1994 Costera (100% Cannonau) is a far more intriguing wine. It offers up aromas of animal fur, earth, kirsch, tar, and sweet black cherry fruit. There is a touch of overripeness, a medium- to full-bodied, lush palate, and a big, spicy, peppery, alcoholic finish. This is a gutsy wine to drink with full-flavored dishes over the next 3–4 years. Argiolas's luxury cuvée, the 1992 Turriga, is made primarily from Cannonau, with small quantities of Malvasia Rossa and Carignano in the blend. It is aged in 100% new French barrels for 18–24 months before being bottled unfiltered. The 1992 falls just short of being outstanding. The wine exhibits a dark ruby/purple color and a sweet, spicy, black cherry, and cassis nose with smoke and vanillin. Dense, rich, and fruity, with medium to full body, low acidity, and plenty of power and density, this luscious wine will benefit from another 1–2 years of cellaring and will keep for 12 years.

The 1994 Perdera (which spends 4 months in oak) is a soft, richly fruity, round wine with a peppery, earthy component and some rusticity. It is a mouth-filling, generous, robust, quaffing wine to drink over the next 2–3 years. The perfect pizza wine?

The 1993 Perdera, made from an indigenous grape, is reminiscent of a peppery, spicy, medium- to full-bodied, southern Côtes du Rhône. This deeply colored wine offers an attractive, earthy, leathery, ripe berry-scented nose, copious amounts of spicy, ripe fruit, and a supple texture with good glycerin and potent alcohol. Drink it now and over the next 4–5 years. The 1993 Costera could be Sicily's answer to Châteauneuf du Pape. Exhibiting gobs of black cherry and raspberry fruit, the wine is full bodied, rich, velvety smooth, and cleanly made. It should drink well for another 5–6 years. The impressive 1990 Turriga is aged in 100% new oak casks. The opaque purple color and sweet nose of toasty vanillin, black cherries and cassis are followed by a long, deep, medium- to full-bodied, pure, well-balanced wine with excellent extraction as well as nicely integrated acidity and tannin. An internationally styled wine, it should drink well now and over the next decade.

The 1992 Perdera reveals an excellent medium to dark ruby color, a black cherry and raspberry-scented nose, pure, ripe berry fruit, soft tannin, adequate acidity, and a generous mouth-feel and finish. This soft, well-made wine is ideal for consuming over the next 3–4 years. The 1992 Costera, made from a grape called Cannonau (indigenous to Sardinia and believed to be this island's clone of Grenache), exhibits a thick, smoky, peppery, spicy, black fruit nose, full body, an unctuous, chewy, fleshy texture, and fine purity and length in the heady finish. This boldly flavored, rich, meaty wine should drink well for 5–6 years. The most intriguing Argiolas wine is the 1989 Turriga. A dazzling nose of smoke, black cherries, damp earth, sweet oak, and cedar jumps from the glass. This dark ruby/garnet-colored wine is full bodied, wonderfully expansive, and chewy, with gobs of fruit, excellent purity, and a voluptuously textured finish. Even though it is already delicious, it possesses outstanding concentration and balance, so expect it to drink well for at least a decade. Very impressive!

The top cuvée produced by this Sardinian winery, the 1993 Turriga Vino da Tavola is made in a French style. The wine is aged in 100% new French oak casks for 18–24 months and bottled unfiltered. I have recommended this offering in previous vintages, and the 1993 appears to be the finest wine yet released. It offers up an exotic, jammy nose of black fruits and lavish quantities of sweet, toasty new oak. Medium to full bodied, with copious amounts of fruit, considerable glycerin, and a creamy, layered texture, this powerful, robust, chewy wine can be drunk now and over the next 5–6 years.

PAOLO BEA (UMBRIA)

1991 Rosso di Montefalco	C	88?
1990 Rosso Vino da Tavola	C	90?
1991 Sagrantino di Montefalco Passito	D	93?

I have had Paolo Bea's wines in the past, and they are both controversial and incredibly variable in quality and character. These wines elicit a similar reaction as those of the Coturri brothers in Sonoma. Readers will be divided between extraordinary admiration or outright condemnation. Their exaggerated, distinctive, and funky styles guarantee plenty of controversy. With that caveat in mind, the 1991 Rosso di Montefalco is an exotic, late-harvest, ripe, chewy, alcoholic wine with considerable thickness and texture. Its aromas and flavors range from herbs and melted road tar to overripe jammy black cherry fruit. It is a wine to drink with cheese at the end of a meal. The smoky, licorice and cherry liqueur-scented and flavored 1990 Rosso Vino da Tavola is a huge, ponderous wine with extraordinary flavor extraction. Smelling like a concoction whipped up by a deranged monk who spent too much time in solitary confinement, it pushes the olfactory senses into overdrive with its array of earthy, jammy fruit and herb scents. This provocative wine is remarkably intense and, dare I say . . . interesting. The most amazing wine of this trio is the after-dinner 1991 Sagrantino di Montefalco Passito. It offers a huge, smoky, bacon fat, raisiny nose that symbolizes the wine's unrestrained, almost excessive personality. Sweet, with pruny, raisiny flavors, amazing concentration, and 15.7% alcohol, it possesses a finish that explodes in the mouth. Italians consider this to be an important historical wine, as it has been made for centuries from Umbria's indigenous Sagrantino grape. Given its strength and uncontrollable exuberance, its ageability should be significant, but I have not had any experience with such wines. Only 25 cases were imported to the United States.

BELLA VISTA (FRANCIACORTA)

1994 Cabernet Sauvignon Solesine Vino da Tavola	D	87

Overwhelming quantities of sweet, vanillin-tinged new oak dominate what is otherwise a noteworthy nose of sweet cassis fruit. This wine is fat, opulent, and hedonistically made, but unformed, grapey, and monolithic. Nevertheless, all the right components appear to be present for this wine to develop into a more complex, silky-textured, seamless, lush, medium- to full-bodied Cabernet Sauvignon. However, new oak dominates at present. Give this wine 2–3 years of cellaring; it should keep for 15 years.

CANTELE (APULIA)

1995 Primitivo	C	84
1991 Salice Salentino	A	84

A berry/pepper-scented, light- to medium-bodied, fruit-driven wine, this 1995 Primitivo can be served chilled, but it requires consumption over the next 1–2 years. The briery, spicy, peppery, medium-bodied 1991 Salice Salentino exhibits dusty tannin as well as an attractive, earthy, berry fruit character. Medium bodied and uncomplex, it will offer pleasant drinking over the next 1–2 years.

CANTINA BOTROMAGNO (APULIA)

1993 Pier delle Vigne Rosso	B	86

There are 5,000 cases of this gutsy, robust Italian red wine made in the backwater "heel" of Italy. It reveals an amber edge to its evolved medium ruby color, as well as a spicy, tar, earthy nose, meaty, smoky, dried herblike flavors, and a robust finish. The wine is rustic but neither coarse nor astringent. It should be served with full-flavored grilled foods or with robust cheese. Drink it over the next 1–2 years. The wine is made from 60% Aglianico and 40% Montepulciano.

CANTINA TOLLO (ABRUZZO)

1995 Montepulciano d'Abruzzo Colle Secco	A	86
1997 Montepulciano d'Abruzzo Villa Diana	A	85

Both of these wines are meant to be consumed over the next year. The 1997 Montepulciano d'Abruzzo Villa Diana is a soft, lightweight red that is to be prized for its uncluttered personality, attractive strawberry, cherry, and cranberry fruit, silky texture, low acidity, and light-bodied finish. The wine is all tank-fermented and -aged and can be served slightly chilled. Nearly 100,000 cases of this wine are brought into the United States, so no complaints about availability . . . please! The 1995 Montepulciano d'Abruzzo Colle Secco is a more cherry-dominated wine with bigger, bolder flavors, medium body, and more depth. This offering sees some aging in old oak *foudres* before bottling.

CANTINA ZACCAGNINI (ABRUZZO)

1995 Montepulciano d'Abruzzo	B	86
1995 Myosotis Red Table Wine	B	85

Bottled by the Agricola Zaccagnini in Bolognano, the 1995 Myosotis (note, the vintage does not appear on the bottle, only on the case) exhibits a medium dark ruby color, a peppery, spicy, robust nose, and rustic, medium-bodied flavors with moderate tannin but plenty of guts and fruit. There is an element of overripeness, and the tannin intrudes in the finish, but the wine is round and generous. Drink it over the next 1–2 years. The 1995 Montepulciano d'Abruzzo is not as rustic, with less color saturation but more kirsch, peppery, black cherry fruit. On the attack, it offers good ripeness and purity, medium body, and a savory, uncomplicated, mouth-filling style. Drink it over the next 1–2 years.

LA CAPRENSE (CAMPANIA)

1996 Ventroso	D	86+

If this wine, which exhibits a certain austerity and a slight leanness (typical of many 1996s from central and southern Italy), fills out, it may merit a higher score. Made from a blend of

85% Aglianico and 15% Piedirosso, it offers a dark ruby color and a noteworthy sour/sweet cherry-scented nose intermingled with aromas of roasted nuts, earth, and herbs. The wine's angular personality begs for more flesh and ripeness, but there is good richness and a spicy, medium-bodied finish with light to moderate tannin. Consume this wine over the next 5–6 years.

LA CARRAIA (UMBRIA)

1995 Merlot Fobiano	D	91
1997 Sangiovese	B	89

Founded in 1976, this estate is co-owned by the famed Italian oenologist Riccardo Cotarella and Edoardo Gialletti. The real bargain from this estate is the 1997 Sangiovese, a 100% Sangiovese fermented in tank, aged in French *barriques,* and bottled unfined and unfiltered. For $11 this wine is a knockout selection. Moreover, nearly 5,000 cases of this wine are imported to the United States. My notes read, "makes most American Sangiovese look pathetic." Deep ruby/purple colored, with a fragrant nose of cherry liqueur, weedy tobacco, *pain grillé,* and spice, this dense wine exhibits plenty of Sangiovese's strawberry/cherry fruit, an opulent texture, low acidity, and fine purity. The wine's fleshiness is almost atypical for Sangiovese, yet there is no sense of heaviness, and the acidity and tannin are sweet and ripe. This is a hedonistic, gorgeous wine to consume over the next 3–4 years. A great value!

The outstanding 1995 Merlot Fobiano, made by the brilliant oenologist Riccardo Cotarella, is a blend of 90% Merlot and 10% Cabernet Sauvignon aged in 100% new French oak casks for 12 months and bottled unfined and unfiltered. It reveals an opaque purple color, followed by a gorgeously intense blackberry-and-cassis-scented nose with subtle smoky oak in the background. The wine's attack offers up ripe, multilayered flavors, full body, and a seamless, silky texture. Very pure, with Cotarella's multilayered, sumptuously endowed hallmarks and a lusty, succulent finish, it is hard to resist a wine such as this, but it will age well for a decade.

DUCHI DI CASTELLUCCIO ORO (ABRUZZI)

1993 Montepulciano d'Abruzzo	B	87

The area of Abruzzi is a treasure-trove for big, rustic, chewy, uncivilized, but mouth-filling, boisterous reds. This offering displays surprising class, elegance, and character for a wine from this area of southern Italy. The healthy dark plum/garnet color is accompanied by earthy, peppery, gamelike scents and plenty of sweet black cherry fruit. Medium bodied and lusciously rich, with good intensity and no hard edges, this is a wine to drink over the next 2–3 years.

CATALDI MADONNA (ABRUZZI)

1996 Montepulciano d'Abruzzo	A	84
1995 Montepulciano d'Abruzzo	B	86

The medium ruby-colored 1996 Montepulciano d'Abruzzo offers light-intensity cherry fruit, good spice, tangy acidity, and a clean aftertaste. Drink it over the next year. The delicious, richly fruity 1995 Montepulciano d'Abruzzo could pass for a midweight Zinfandel. Peppery, briery, spicy fruit jumps from a glass of this cleanly made, round, well-endowed wine. The color is a healthy dark ruby, there are no hard edges, and the wine is satisfying and savory. Drink it over the next several years.

COLLI AMERINI (UMBRIA)

1994 Carbio Rosso Superiore	B	91
1996 Carbio Vino da Tavola	C	86

1995 Carbio Vino da Tavola	C 87
1995 Sangiovese Torraccio	D 88

The 1995 Carbio, a red wine concoction made from Sangiovese, Canaiolo, Montepulciano, Merlot, Barbera, and Ciliegiolo, is aged in new French oak and bottled unfined and unfiltered. It is an intriguing, distinctive wine that is somewhat uncivilized and rustic. With soft, medium- to full-bodied, savory flavors that come across as peppery and earthy, in addition to gobs of cherry fruit, it is reminiscent of a rustic Côtes du Rhône from southern France. There is good flesh and ripeness in this spice-driven wine; drink it over the next 5–6 years. The 1995 Sangiovese Torraccio is a 100% Sangiovese aged in new French Allier barrels and bottled unfined and unfiltered by consulting oenologist, Riccardo Cotarella. The wine exhibits an attractive, earthy, strawberry, and black cherry nose with hints of new saddle leather. It is spicy and fruity, with excellent richness, low acidity, and a seamless, supple, lush mouthfeel. This hedonistic, flattering, dry red wine should be drunk over the next 4–5 years.

The dark plumlike color and sexy, smoky, licorice, roasted herb, and black fruit nose of the 1994 Carbio Rosso Superiore are enticing. Rich, jammy, medium to full bodied, with underlying complexity, this gloriously fruity, smooth-textured wine should be drunk over the next 5–6 years. It is made from an interesting blend of Cabernet Sauvignon, Merlot, Barbera, and other indigenous red wine varietals from Umbria.

The 1996 Carbio VDT, a blend of Sangiovese, Merlot, Barbera, Montepulciano, Gamay, Canaiolo, and Ciliegiolo, is a dark ruby-colored, older-style Italian red. The wine offers up meaty, spicy, new saddle leather, smoked meat, and herb scents; there may even be a touch of brett (a leathery, animal note) in the wine's aromatics. In the mouth, there is good sweetness and ripeness. The wine is spicy and meaty but will be controversial because of its animal notes. Drink it over the next 4–5 years.

CORNACCHIA (ABRUZZI)

1993 Montepulciano d'Abruzzo	A 89
1993 Montepulciano d'Abruzzo Poggio Varano	B 90
1993 Montepulciano d'Abruzzo Vigne Le Coste	B 92

For the moment, the wines of Montepulciano d'Abruzzo may be the best bargains of the wine world. (Italy's lira is in even worse shape than America's dollar.) These three wines from Cornacchia offer convincing evidence that this is the place to be—whether you are a consumer, retailer, wholesaler, or Italian wine importer. The 1993 Montepulciano d'Abruzzo (5,000 cases available) exhibits an opaque purple color that is reminiscent of a California Petite-Sirah, a huge, spicy, peppery, black cherry nose, gutsy, full-bodied, exuberant flavors, and a chewy, blockbuster finish. While it will never win any awards for finesse, it is a mouthfilling, explosively fruity, rich, pure, well-made wine. Drink it over the next 5–6 years. The 1993 Montepulciano d'Abruzzo Poggio Varano (500 cases available) is a black/purple-colored wine made from a specific vineyard site and aged in 50% new oak casks. Given the incredible fruit and richness being obtained from Montepulciano d'Abruzzo, new oak is an ideal vehicle for elevating the wine's complexity and structure. This is an amazingly rich, dense, massively constituted, full-bodied wine with great purity of fruit and a finish that lasts for nearly a minute. The sweetness and extraction of fruit almost suck up the oak, making the wine even more sexy and voluptuous. A great wine, as well as a terrific bargain, it should continue to drink well for 5–10 years. Cornacchia's 1993 Montepulciano d'Abruzzo Vigna le Coste (500 cases available) reveals an opaque black/purple color and a jammy, intense nose of licorice, cassis, and spice that is reminiscent of a top cuvée of Hermitage. The wine coats the palate with a viscous assemblage of juicy, succulent black fruits, wood, and a creamy texture that borders on being unctuous. This is a huge, superbly made wine with enough acidity for uplift and enough tannin for structure. If you have not already discovered the joys offered by the wines from this unheralded region of Italy, check out these three dazzling offerings from Cornacchia.

COVIO (UMBRIA)

1994 Fantasie del Cardeto Rosso	C	86

This medium dark ruby-colored, spicy wine is well made, with compact, berry/earth-driven, savory, well-balanced flavors. The wine is spicy and pleasing, but one-dimensional. It is a blend of 90% Sangiovese and 10% Merlot aged primarily in new French oak. Drink it over the next several years.

DAL FORMO ROMANO (VENETO)

1989 Amarone	EE	96
1990 Amarone della Valpolicella	EEE	95
1988 Recioto	E (375 ml)	96+
1992 Valpolicella	D	90
1991 Valpolicella	D	88

Readers who follow the Italian wine scene must argue incessantly over who makes the greatest wines of Veneto—Quintarelli or Dal Formo Romano? Both are at the top of their game, producing spectacular wines that are reference points for an area of northeast Italy that is beginning to show signs of awakening from a long period of moribund mediocrity. The 1992 Valpolicella boasts a huge, smoky, sweet, gamey, jammy nose. The wine is fabulously textured, rich, full bodied, and loaded with extract. Elements of tar and sweet, chocolatey, cedarlike berry fruit cascade over the palate with an unctuous texture and an amazing finish. Readers weaned on the ocean of industrial swill that parades under the name of Valpolicella will have their senses shocked by this wine's complexity and intensity. It should continue to drink well for 7–8 years. Dal Formo's 1991 Valpolicella is about as good as it gets (including the exquisite Valpolicellas produced by Quintarelli). A dark ruby/purple color is followed by gobs of sweet, chewy, black cherry, currant, and spicy fruit with that unmistakable smoky, almondlike extract in the aromas and flavors. Medium to full bodied, with sexy, voluptuously textured, luscious flavors, this gloriously fruity, exuberant, in-your-face style of Valpolicella is a marvel to drink. If it possessed a few additional nuances, this wine would be outstanding. Long and rich, it will drink well for 8–10 years.

I do not drink much Amarone (although I methodically taste them every year), as I find most of it to be too pruny, somewhat oxidized, and not fresh enough, even allowing for the particular style of these wines. Yet even I get excited by such spectacular Amarones. Quintarelli has made many great ones, and I have enough bottles in my cellar to prove my faithfulness to his wines. Dal Formo Romano's 1989 Amarone is one of the greatest I have ever tasted. The color is a dark, saturated, murky garnet/ruby/charcoal. Incredibly sweet, rich aromas of prunes, chocolate, overripe black fruits, intermixed with a touch of truffles, cedar, licorice, and spice, soar from a glass of this extraordinary wine. Thick and unctuous, but dry, this is a spectacularly endowed, multidimensional Amarone that can be drunk now and over the next 25 years. Sadly, only 50 cases were exported to the United States, most of which, I suspect, has been allocated to some of our country's finest Italian restaurants. It should be savored with cheese at the end of a meal. The profound 1990 Amarone della Valpolicella is a magnificent example of Amarone. Dry and massively proportioned, with a dark plum color, this wine offers up copious quantities of chocolate, smoke, tar, and sweet pruny fruit, with intriguing nuances. Full bodied, powerful, and rich, with no hard edges, this is a heady, sensationally endowed wine that should drink well for 15 years. Wow! An amazing wine.

Another mind-boggling effort from Dal Formo Romano is the 1988 Recioto. After the grapes were air-dried for 6 months on straw mats, this wine was aged 3 years in 100% new French oak casks. Although outrageously expensive, it represents the essence of this style of wine. It is off-dry rather than sweet, with a dark garnet color and a nose of smoke, prunes, overripe plums, hickory wood, and chocolate. Extremely full bodied and exceptionally rich, with some residual sugar, this wine has been blazingly well defined by its sojourn in new oak casks. Remarkably, the wine has soaked up its 18 months in new oak, as there is not a hint of vanillin or *pain grillé* notes in either its aromas or flavors. This legendary Recioto should drink well for 2–3 decades.

DUCHI (ABRUZZO)

1996	Montepulciano d'Abruzzo	A	84

Light to medium ruby colored, with a light-intensity, strawberry/cherry-scented nose, this forward, uncomplicated, cleanly made wine is soft and easy to understand and drink. Consume it over the next year.

FALESCO (UMBRIA)

1997	Merlot dell'Umbria	C	90
1996	Merlot dell'Umbria	B	89
1994	Merlot di Aprilia Doc	B	88
1993	Merlot d'Apulia	B	87
1996	Montiano Vino da Tavola	D	93
1995	Montiano Vino da Tavola	D	95
1994	Montiano Vino da Tavola	D	93
1993	Montiano Vino da Tavola	D	90
1997	Vitiano Vino da Tavola	B	89
1996	Vitiano Vino da Tavola	B	88
1995	Vitiano Vino da Tavola	B	89

Riccardo Cotarella is doing in Umbria and southern Italy what Michel Rolland and, before him, Professor Emile Peynaud and Professor Ribereau-Gayon did in Bordeaux—immensely improving quality through their winemaking philosophy. Just about everything Cotarella is associated with is of high quality. He is clearly the genius behind the renaissance going on in Umbria and Campania. His winemaking style emphasizes ripe fruit, soaring aromatics, natural textures, and no commercial manipulation and eviscerating clarification techniques. All of his wines are bottled without any filtration and, in most cases, no fining.

Two exceptional values are the 1997 Vitiano and the 1997 Merlot. A blend of equal parts Merlot, Cabernet Sauvignon, and Sangiovese, the 1997 Vitiano is an unfined/unfiltered red wine that is amazing for its price. It exhibits a deep ruby/purple color followed by a sweet nose of black currants, *pain grillé*, and dried herbs. In the mouth, there is a chewy texture, remarkable concentration (particularly for a wine in this price range), gorgeous levels of sweet black fruit, and low acidity. The wine is fleshy, flamboyant, and thrilling to drink. Moreover it will evolve and last for 3–5 years. Fifteen thousand cases of this beauty were imported into the United States, so many readers should be able to latch on to a few bottles or cases. The stunning 1997 Merlot (100% Merlot that has been barrel-fermented and aged in

French oak) is a sumptuous, thick, juicy, dark ruby/purple-colored wine with terrific fruit intensity and purity (gobs of black cherry, berry, and mocha notes), medium to full body, a silky texture, and a lush, heady finish that lasts for more than 30 seconds. This unfined, unfiltered Merlot, made from low yields, can be drunk now because of its succulent personality, but it will age well for 7–8 years. These are two dazzling wine values from one of Italy's genius winemakers/oenologists, Riccardo Cotarella.

The 1996 Vitiano (a 33% Merlot, 33% Cabernet Sauvignon, 34% Sangiovese blend) exhibits a dark purple color as well as sweet, jammy, black cherry fruit intermingled with scents of chocolate and *pain grillé*. Lush and medium to full bodied, with excellent depth and an explosive, smoky, rich finish, this hedonistic wine should drink well for 5–6 years. It is a super value. The 1996 Merlot dell'Umbria is a 100% Merlot fermented in stainless-steel tanks, aged in barrel, and bottled with neither fining nor filtration. It boasts a dense, saturated purple color, a sweet, black cherry, blackberry, toasty nose, beautiful ripeness, a gorgeous smoky, lavishly rich, medium- to full-bodied texture, and a fruit-bomblike personality. This sumptuous, savory wine is priced at least 50%–75% below wines of similar quality. I would not be surprised to see this wine merit an outstanding score with another 2–4 months of bottle age. It should drink well for 5–6 years.

A stunning wine is the 1995 Montiano (1,000 cases produced). Made from 100% Merlot from vineyards planted on the hillsides of Lazio (at a relatively high altitude of 980 feet), this unfined/unfiltered, profoundly rich red wine is a knockout. The color is a saturated purple, and the nose offers up glorious aromas of smoked meats, cassis, chocolate, and vanillin. Spectacular richness combined with beautifully integrated acidity, tannin, and wood make for an opulently textured, multilayered, stunningly proportioned wine of exceptional purity and richness. With marvelous intensity, but no sense of heaviness, this fabulous wine provides a strong case for the potential that exists in southern Italy. Yields from the 30-acre vineyard averaged 2.8 tons of fruit per acre. Drink it over the next 10–12 years.

Cotarella's highest achievements are to be found in his red wine portfolio. He has gone against the flow of modern-day commercial winemaking. For example, he has 1) fought for lower yields, 2) harvested physiologically mature fruit by hand, 3) utilized small *barriques*, and 4) bottled the wines with minimal clarification, frequently with no fining or filtration. The following wines, some of the most exciting reds of Italy, emerge from a largely unknown wine region for reds, Umbria. The nearly outstanding 1995 Vitiano (4,500 cases) is a sensational bargain. A blend of equal parts Cabernet Sauvignon, Merlot, and Sangiovese, it exhibits an opaque purple color, a subtle influence of toasty oak from aging in small *barriques*, wonderful purity, a lush, chewy texture, medium body, and gobs of rich, smoky, chocolatey, black currant, and cherry fruit. Drink this supple, explosively fruity, delicious wine over the next 3–4 years. The 1994 Merlot di Aprilia is a textbook Merlot (you don't often hear me say that). The chocolatey, black cherry, mocha nose is followed by a wine with attractive, smoky, sweet, rich, chewy flavors, medium to full body, excellent ripeness and purity, and a long, nicely layered, silky finish. This 100% Merlot was aged in 50% Allier and 50% Nevers small French oak casks. (In fact, malolactic fermentation took place in these casks.) It should drink well for 5–7 years. This is a terrific bargain in high-quality Merlot.

An impressive effort from Falesco, the 1993 Merlot d'Apulia reveals an opaque dark ruby color, ripe berry and herb-scented and -flavored fruit, a lush, chewy texture, and a soft finish. Drink it over the next 2–3 years.

Two wines of which Cotarella is especially proud are the 1993 and 1994 Montalciano (1,200 cases each), made from a tiny 10-acre Umbrian vineyard that produces about 2,000 bottles per acre. (That is a small yield!) The 1993 was the debut vintage of this 80% Merlot/20% Cabernet Sauvignon blend that was aged in 100% new French oak and bottled with no clarification. It exhibits a saturated deep purple color, an intense, smoky, spicy, vanillin, and cassis nose, rich, elegant, authoritatively powerful flavors, good backbone and structure, and a long finish. Although young and unevolved, it is a very promising wine of first-growth quality. The impressive 1994 Montiano is even richer. The opaque purple color is followed by sexy, smoky, toasty new oak aromas, a ripe, concentrated, black fruit character (black currants and cherries), a formidable flavor intensity and extract, medium to full body, great purity, and a layered yet structured, rich finish. This is a compelling wine! Both these wines should evolve effortlessly for 10–15+ years.

The 1996 Montiano is a tour de force in winemaking. This wine (100% Merlot) was bottled unfined and unfiltered after aging in French oak casks. Sadly, only 500 cases were produced. It boasts an opaque purple color followed by a knockout nose of blackberry liqueur intermingled with smoke, *pain grillé*, and chocolate. Full bodied and thick, with a voluptuous texture, layered richness, superb purity, and a finish that lasts over 30 seconds, this is a profoundly concentrated and complex Merlot to drink now and over the next 10–15 years. Kudos to Riccardo Cotarella.

FANTASIE DEL CARDETO (UMBRIA)

1995 Vino da Tavola	C	87
1993 Vino da Tavola	B	90

This exceptional, bargain-priced 1993, also produced by Ricardo Cotarella, has to be tasted to be believed. You can taste the Merlot in this smoky, chocolatey, fat, exuberant, full-bodied wine, which has just enough oak to add complexity and definition. Made from 90% Sangiovese and 10% Merlot, the wine is deliciously rich and supple, with gobs of fruit, glycerin, and length. Drink it over the next 5–7 years. It is hard to believe wines of this quality can still be found for $12. An outstanding bargain.

The complex, evolved nose of tobacco, herbs, ripe berry fruit, and *barrique* scents of the 1995 is followed by a structured, well-made Vino da Tavola (a blend of 90% Sangiovese and 10% Merlot). The wine was aged in French oak barrels (of which 85% were new) and bottled unfiltered. The slightly austere finish kept my score lower, but this is a well-crafted, attractive, fragrant, medium-bodied red to drink over the next decade.

FARNESE (ABRUZZI)

1993 Montepulciano d'Abruzzo	A	86

Another terrific bargain from Italy's Montepulciano d'Abruzzo area, this dark ruby-colored wine offers plenty of spicy, berry fruit, a touch of earth, and medium- to full-bodied, clean, mouth-filling flavors and finish. This is a wine to buy by the carload, as it can be purchased in 1.5-liter bottles for $7.50.

FEUDI DI SAN GREGORIO (CAMPANIA)

1993 Albente	A	86
1996 Rubrato	B	86
1996 Serpico	D	89
1995 Serpico	D	89
1994 Taurasi	C	86
1993 Taurasi	C	86

Produced from 100% Aglianico, the 1994 Taurasi is a solidly made, ruggedly constructed, chewy red with a medium ruby color and a sweet black cherry-scented nose intermingled with notes of earth, saddle leather, and roasted almonds. There is admirable depth, an exuberant personality, and a soft, lightly tannic finish. Drink it over the next 2–3 years. The outstanding 1996 Serpico Vino da Tavola, a blend of 60% Aglianico, 30% Piedirosso, and 10% Sangiovese, is aged in French oak casks and bottled without filtration. It boasts a deep ruby/purple color, a Bordeaux-like nose of lead pencil, black currants, weedy tobacco, and spice, outstanding richness, well-integrated wood, low acidity, and a spicy, deep, layered finish. This impressive proprietary red wine can be drunk now or cellared for a decade.

The 1993 Taurasi, made from 100% Aglianico and aged in French and Slavonian oak, displays a nearly opaque dark ruby/purple color. The nose offers aromas of melted road tar, earth, spice, and sweet black raspberry fruit. The wine possesses a leathery, rich, deep, red berry fruitiness that offers sweetness, softness, and an undeniable seductiveness. This medium-bodied, fleshy, round, low-acid wine can be drunk now and over the next 5–6 years. The nearly outstanding 1995 Serpico is a limited-production (about 160 cases) wine made from 60% Aglianico, 30% Piedirosso, and 10% Sangiovese, aged in 100% French oak for 12 months prior to being bottled without filtration. The wine exhibits a dark ruby/purple color and a spicy, black raspberry and black cherry nose with sweet vanillin aromas. Fleshy, generous, full bodied, lush, and heady, this low-acid, big, flattering, showy red wine will drink well for the next 5–7 years. Interestingly, the vineyard in Campania is located only about 25 miles from the superb vineyards of Montevetrano.

The 1993 Albente is a plum-and-cherry-scented, spicy, dry red wine with medium body, fine freshness, and a mouth-filling, chewy texture. Although not complex, it is a well-made, satisfying red wine for drinking over the next 3–4 years.

I also enjoyed the 1996 Rubrato, a dark ruby-colored, peppery, mouth-filling red made from the Aglianico grape. This wine was aged in old Slavonian oak for 6 months prior to bottling. Soft and peppery, with plenty of cherry/berry fruit, good spice, a suggestion of melted road tar, and a robust, savory finish, this is a chunky, husky red to drink over the next several years.

FORADORI (TRENTINO)

1996 Granato VDT	E	91+
1997 Teroldego Rotaliano	C	90
1996 Teroldego Rotaliano	C	86
1996 Teroldego Sgarzon	D	88+

This brilliantly run winery is pushing quality higher and higher. The 1997 Teroldego Rotaliano displays the vintage's spectacular potential. (Italians are calling 1997 one of the greatest vintages in the last 50 years.) Aged in old *barriques,* the wine possesses an amazingly saturated, thick purple color, as well as an extremely rich, intense nose of animal fur, blackberry liqueur, licorice, and a touch of violets. In the mouth, it is intense and full bodied, with exquisite ripeness and purity. This is a mouth-filling, well-endowed wine that should evolve easily for 10–15 years. Because of the extraordinary fruit ripeness, this low-acid wine is accessible and delicious. The deep ruby/purple-colored, mouth-staining 1996 Teroldego Sgarzon reveals evidence of new oak aging in its powerful, full-bodied personality. The predominant aromas in the nose are smoke, *pain grillé,* and jammy cassis. Thickly textured, full bodied, powerful, and macho, this intense, chewy wine lacks the potential complexity and silkiness of the 1997 Teroldego Rotaliano, but it is an impressive, full-flavored, dry red from northern Italy. It will age well for at least a decade.

Foradori's Vino da Tavola, the 1996 Granato, offers an opaque purple color, palate-saturating extract levels, and a powerful, rich, ripe, jammy finish. The wine is massive and impressive, but youthful and unevolved. Flavors of cherry liqueur, kirsch, blackberries, and new oak dominate the wine at present. Look for this monster to age for 10–15 years.

The tangy, Zinfandel-like, dry 1996 Teroldego Rotaliano possesses a dark ruby color, admirable berry fruit and spice, medium body, but little complexity. It is refreshing and mouth filling, with enough acidity to cut through a variety of pasta dishes. Drink it over the next 2–3 years.

GIROLAMO DORIGO (FRIULI)

1990 Montsclapade Vino da Tavola	D 88

This dense, plummy, cassis-scented wine exhibits excellent richness, full body, an earthy, tarry, spicy character, personality, and a soft texture. There are no hard edges in this expressionistic example of red wine that has not been overoaked. The dark purple/garnet color suggests the wine is still in a youthful state, so 10 more years of evolution is not improbable.

LIBRANDI (CALABRIA)

1991 Ciro Rosso	A 86
1994 Ciro Rosso Classico	A 86
1990 Ciro Rosso Classico	A 87
1987 Duca San Felice	B 87
1991 Gravello	C 87
1990 Gravello	C 89
1989 Gravello	C 89+

The Ciro Rossos are made from the Gaglioppo grape, which is believed to have been first planted in this area in the boot of Italy by the ancient Greeks. The 1994 Ciro Rosso Classico is a simple, earthy, mouth-filling, medium-bodied wine that has never seen any oak. Its garnet/plummy color and sound, round, mouth-filling flavors make it an ideal country-style wine that can be served without any pretense. Spicy, with a southern Rhône-like straightforwardness and satisfying quality, it should be drunk over the next several years. The 1990 Ciro Rosso Riserva Duca San Felice is a wine with an average bouquet but a smashing finish. Bordering on being raisiny, it possesses a late-harvest Zinfandel-like character with dense, rich, ripe fruit, an unctuous texture, thick, chewy flavors, full body, and plenty of alcohol. While it will never win awards for finesse or subtlety, it delivers plenty of gutsy, meaty, overripe berry fruit in a full-bodied format. Drink it over the next 4–5 years.

This winery also produced a pleasant 1995 Ciro Ross (83 points) and a 1991 Duca San Felice (84 points) that are distinctive, earthy, tomato-tasting wines with notes of leather and spice. The 1991 Gravello (a 60% Gaglioppo/40% Cabernet Sauvignon blend, aged in 100% new oak casks for at least 1 year) is a tannic, backward wine with sweet, earthy, peppery, rustic, black cherry and cassis fruit, fine density, medium to full body, and considerable power, as well as elevated tannin levels. I am not sure this wine will ever pull itself together, but it is mouth filling, large-scale, and impressive from an architectural standpoint. Drink it over the next decade.

The 1990 Gravello proprietary red wine spent nearly 3 years in oak barrels, resulting in a full-bodied, richly fruity, glycerin-endowed, well-made wine with plenty of power, punch, and extraction. Drink this cleanly made, spicy, jammy wine over the next 4–5 years.

These following three red wine offerings from southern Italy's so-called boot all possess rich, overripe, robust, intense personalities. The 1991 Ciro Rosso exhibits a big, spicy, melted road tar, earthy, rustic, peppery nose, chewy, thick, rich flavors of sweet, jammy cherries, and low acidity. This mouth-filling, alcoholic wine is filled with character. Drink it over the next 3–4 years. The 1987 Duca San Felice offers up a spicy, cedary, jammy, cherry-scented nose with a touch of chocolate and truffles. Stylistically it is reminiscent of a ripe, medium- to full-bodied Grenache-based wine from France's Languedoc-Roussillon, such as a Minervois. This mouth-filling, supple, dense wine is a candidate for 5–6 years of cellaring. The most impressive wine of this trio (also the most expensive) is the 1989 Gravello. Made from 60% Gaplioppo and 40% Cabernet Sauvignon, this is a rich, spicy, smoky, toasty wine (some new oak cask aging has obviously taken place), with great ripeness, wonderful richness, a full-bodied, layered personality, soft tannin, and chewy fruit in the finish. This wine is capable of 5–8 years of cellaring. These are all intriguing, distinctive wines with broad appeal.

LUNGAROTTI (UMBRIA)

1991 Rubesco Rosso di Torgiano	B	84
1985 San Giorgio Vino da Tavola Umbria	D	88

The well-known firm of Lungarotti has turned out a pleasant, medium ruby-colored, soft, earthy 1991 Rubesco that is ideal for uncritical drinking. With a nice spicy note, ripe fruit, and medium body, it should last for 2–3 years. More impressive, as well as more expensive and limited in availability, is the 1985 San Giorgio, a Cabernet Sauvignon–based wine. It reveals a mature ruby color with some lightening at the edges. The cedary, spicy, curranty nose is reminiscent of a very good St.-Julien or Pauillac. The wine exhibits medium to full body, an attractive suppleness, smoky, well-integrated oak, and sweet, round, expansive flavors. It is supple, delicious, complex, and ideal for drinking over the next 4–6 years.

MACULAN (VENETO)

1996 Cabernet Fratta	E	87

I have tasted many vintages of Maculan's red wines, including his Fratta Cabernet and Merlot Marchesante. Until recently his reds have been dominated by undesirable vegetal and overtly herbaceous characteristics. In fact, the 1995 Cabernet Fratta suffers from that problem, as well as a compressed, tight, lean style. However, in 1996 there was obviously a philosophical change in winemaking, as there is more glycerin and a creamier texture, and the blatant herbs have been replaced by a deep, jammy, black currant richness. According to Leonardo Locasio, Paul Pontallier, Château Margaux's winemaker, has been unofficially consulting with Maculan. I suspect this extended to the vineyard, where leaf pulling and crop thinning have been employed. A barrel sample of the 1997 looked to be outstanding. In any event, the 1996, made from a blend of 65% Cabernet Sauvignon and 35% Cabernet Franc, is rich, medium bodied, and elegant. It should age well for 5–12 years.

DI MAJO NORANTE (MOLISE)

1995 Aglianico	B	87
1995 Ramitello Rosso	B	88
1997 San Giorgio Sangiovese	A	87

In my search for the mightiest values on planet Earth, this winery distinguished itself with a bevy of distinctive, original, flavorful, tasty wines that are selling at bargain-basement prices.

Tired of being ripped off by overpriced mediocrities parading under the name of Sangiovese from California? Check out the 1997 San Giorgio Sangiovese from Di Majo Norante. Made from 100% Sangiovese, tank-fermented, and aged in old oak *foudres*, this is a terrific bargain. The medium ruby color is accompanied by a sweet nose of strawberry jam and black cherries. The wine is round and richly fruity, with a soft texture, fine balance, and a lush, velvety finish. It can be served slightly chilled and drunk over the next 12–18 months. It makes a mockery of many of the $20–$30 Sangioveses from California that, frankly, are overcropped, overpriced, and mediocre. Different in style is the slightly fuller, meatier, more aromatically complex 1995 Aglianico. This wine exhibits a deep ruby color and an earth, smoke, roasted herb, and dried fruit-scented bouquet. In the mouth, it is more complex and deep, with medium body, a spicy, berry, meaty-flavored personality, and a robust finish. It should continue to drink well for 2–3 years. The finest wine in this group is the 1995 Ramitello Rosso. It is a soft, forward, chewy red wine with saddle leather, black chocolate, cedar, and jammy cherry aromas and flavors. The wine cuts a weighty, expansive feel on the palate, with excellent length as well as fine purity and overall equilibrium. It is a muscular, exuberant, soft, dry red made from 70% Prugnolo and 30% Aglianico. Given the fact that this wine can probably be bought for several dollars less if purchased by the case, this is another excellent value from this winery tucked in the hinterlands of Molise.

MARTILDE (LOMBARDY)

1996 Barbera Unfiltered	C	90

A superb Barbera, this tank-fermented and -aged offering offers proof of how rich, succulent, and ripe this vintage is for northern Italy. The color is deep purple. The wine explodes from the glass with gobs of sweet black cherry, cranberry, and other ripe dark fruits. In the mouth, it is medium bodied, loaded with fruit, with no obvious tannin but with good tart acidity that brings everything into focus. Pure, explosively fruity, and rich, this Barbera should drink well for 2–4 years . . . what a fun wine to drink!

MAZZI (VENETO)

1990 Amarone Cru Punta di Villa	D	92
1993 Valpolicella Cru Poiega	C	88

I have praised these beautiful wines in the past, so I am pleased to see these releases perform so well. The 1993 Valpolicella Cru Poiega is the antithesis of the industrial-processed, mass-produced style of Valpolicella that is available in so many American wine and liquor shops. This wine reveals a deceptively light medium ruby color, but gorgeously ripe berry flavors, a round, medium-bodied, soft texture, with noticeably more weight and intensity than indicated by the wine's color. There is excellent purity, a gracious, elegant style, and a soft finish with enough acidity to give the wine zest and fragrance. Drink it over the next 2–3 years. The 1990 Amarone Cru Punta di Villa is a smoky, tar, roasted nut, and jammy-scented and -flavored wine with massive body, excellent delineation to its large-boned personality, and a spicy, medium-dry finish.

MONTEVETRANO (CAMPANIA)

1997 Vino da Tavola	EE	(93–95)
1996 Vino da Tavola	E	94
1995 Montevetrano	E	92+
1994 Montevetrano	D	93+

This winery has become one of the superstars of Italy. Sadly, the vineyard's small size (10 acres) and low yields (about 2 tons of fruit per acre) result in extremely small production. For example, only 280 six-bottle packs of the 1996 were imported to the United States. As for the 1997, which is still in barrel, proprietor Silvia Imparato and her oenologist, Riccardo Cotarella, have turned in a spectacular effort. A blend of 60% Cabernet Sauvignon, 30% Merlot, and 10% Aglianico that has been aged in 100% new French oak and bottled unfined and unfiltered, it is an explosively rich, black/purple-colored wine with aromas of black raspberries, blueberries, minerals, and vanillin. In the mouth, the wine is full bodied, with layers of extract, low acidity, sweet tannin, and a stunningly proportioned, opulently textured finish. It should turn out to be the finest wine this estate has yet produced.

Also terrific, the 1996 possesses a minimum of 2 decades of aging potential. It boasts an opaque purple color and dense, thick aromas of black raspberry ice cream intermingled with roasted herbs and grilled meats. In the mouth, the wine is rich and full bodied, with an unctuous texture, loads of blackberry fruit, sweet tannin, and a layered, thick, low-acid finish. The 1996 will benefit from 2–3 more years of cellaring and will drink well for 2 decades.

The 1995, like so many vintages of this wine, combines the elegance, richness, and intensity of a great Château Margaux with the lushness and succulence of a top Pomerol such as La Conseillante. Gorgeous levels of sweet blueberry and cassis fruit jump from the glass of this dense purple-colored wine. The aromatics and fruit are sweet, ripe, and pure. On the palate, there is superb concentration, layers of flavor, medium to full body, impeccable balance, and that rare combination of finesse and strength. The wine is supple enough to be drunk at present, but rich and well balanced enough to last for 12–15 years. This is a beautifully full, elegant wine that has to be tasted to be believed.

The 1994 Montevetrano is another fabulously concentrated, opaque purple-colored wine with a tight but promising nose of vanilla, chocolate, cassis, and wild blueberries. Full bodied, rich, and layered, with highly extracted, sweet flavors, this graceful yet powerfully rich and flavored wine admirably combines elegance with force. Ideally it should be given 4–5 more years of cellaring, but I expect those lucky enough to purchase a few bottles of the 400+ cases made each year will drink it long before it reaches full maturity. It should last for 15 years. Like its glorious predecessors, the 1994 was aged in 100% new French Allier oak and bottled without any fining or filtering. What a wine!

ELIO MONTI (ABRUZZI)

1995	Montepulciano d'Abruzzo	A	90
1994	Montepulciano d'Abruzzo	A	88
1993	Montepulciano d'Abruzzo	A	90
1992	Montepulciano d'Abruzzo	A	88

These wines, which I have recommended in the past, should come with warning labels boldly stating, "Not for Wimps." These 100% Sangiovese wines, bottled with no fining or filtration, possess amazingly saturated opaque black/purple colors, huge amounts of fruit and glycerin, and a gamey, earthy, trufflelike component. The wines are dense, full-bodied blockbusters that push flavor extraction and body to the maximum. Although they will undoubtedly last for 5–7 years, their appeal is their 1) gutsy exuberance, 2) copious quantities of fruit, and 3) uncomplicated, yet whoppingly rich, earthy personalities.

The 1992 is another terrific example of just how much good wine a consumer is capable of finding for under $10. The opaque, dense, purple/black color is followed by a huge but uncomplex nose of ripe cassis fruit, black cherries, and subtle licorice and earthy notes. Gorgeously rich and fruity, as well as deep and full bodied, this huge yet velvety-textured wine can be drunk now or cellared for 5–6 years. Since it was bottled unfiltered, expect this wine to throw a sediment given its saturated color and dense, chewy, rich style.

The 1993 is another huge, rich, ripe, full-bodied, superconcentrated wine from this sunbaked region of southern Italy. It has to be tasted to be believed! Do not expect a great deal of complexity, but for a wine that oozes extract, ripeness, and extraction, this is a large-scale, rich, chewy, cleanly made, cassis and earth-scented and -flavored wine that should drink well now and over the next 3–4 years.

Even though the 1994 has lost its baby fat, it remains a huge mouthful of fruit and body. The 1995's color is reminiscent of inky Welch's grape juice. It offers a huge, earthy, black cherry, licorice, cassis, and spicy nose and dense, broad, chewy flavors that resemble liquefied grilled steak. The wine possesses amazing glycerin and texture. These wines are not for everybody, but readers wanting to try a more adventurous lifestyle should seek them out.

CAMILLO MONTORI (ABRUZZI)

1995 Montepulciano d'Abruzzo	A	84
1994 Montepulciano d'Abruzzo Fonte Cupa	C	87

The chunky, full-flavored, rustic 1994 Montepulciano d'Abruzzo Fonte Cupa, from southern Italy, reveals a Zinfandel-like, briery, peppery fruitiness, medium to full body, good, clean winemaking, and an uncomplicated, but solidly fruity, spicy finish. Drink it over the next several years. The dark ruby-colored 1995 Montepulciano d'Abruzzo is a straightforward, foursquare wine with plenty of deep berry fruit and spice. Elegant, well made, medium bodied, and gutsy, it will provide uncritical quaffing. Like the 1994 Fonte Cupa, it possesses a briery, Zinfandel character. Drink it over the next 2–3 years.

LA PALAZZOLA (UMBRIA)

1995 Merlot	D	90
1996 Rubino	D	90
1995 Rubino	D	94+

Owned by Stefano Grilli, who brought in the well-known oenologist Riccardo Cotarella 5 years ago, this estate is poised to explode onto the worldwide arena given the quality of the wines. The 1995 Rubino, a blend of 80% Cabernet Sauvignon (from 12-year-old vines) and 20% Merlot (from 60-year-old vines?) fermented in tank, aged in 100% new French oak, and bottled unfined and unfiltered, is a sensational wine with a degree of richness and explosiveness that is matched by few wines made anywhere in the world. It has more in common with a great vintage of Sassicaia (the 1985, for example) than other Italian wines. The saturated black/purple color suggests a wine of extraordinary intensity, ripeness, and quality. The nose offers up striking aromas of lead pencil, vanillin, blueberries, cassis, roasted peanuts, and licorice. Every time I returned to my glass, more nuances had emerged. Intense on the palate, with a cascade of lavishly ripe fruit nicely buttressed by toasty oak and sweet tannin, this wine is extraordinarily long, still unevolved and backward, but remarkably well balanced. This is an exquisite, potentially profound Cabernet-based wine from Umbria that should be at its best between 2000 and 2020. Approximately 1,500 cases of the 1995 Rubino were produced.

La Palazzola's 1995 Merlot, which was vinified, aged, and bottled in the same manner as the Rubino, is extremely limited in quantity. Only 100 cases of this outstanding wine, made from 100% Merlot from a vineyard planted in 1990 were produced. A dense ruby/purple color is accompanied by closed aromatics. Scents of black cherry, earth, smoke, and spice do emerge with coaxing, but this wine needs 5–6 years of cellaring. As ironic as it sounds, it is more structured and backward than the Cabernet Sauvignon–based Rubino. In short, it takes no special talent to recognize the Merlot's intense richness, high extract, and overall depth and intensity. It is another brilliant but young wine (impeccably vinified and bottled by Riccardo Cotarella) that needs 4–6 years of cellaring, after which it should last for 2 decades. Wow!

The Rubino has been a huge hit in other vintages, so I was not surprised by its strong showing in the good rather than exceptional 1996 vintage. Sadly, only 600 cases of this unfined/unfiltered Vino da Tavola were produced. It boasts a dark ruby/purple color as well as a textbook, Bordeaux-like nose of *pain grillé*, cedar, cassis, and jammy cherry fruit. The wine's aromatics became more intense with airing. In the mouth, this sexy, surprisingly soft, full-bodied wine exhibits a multidimensional personality, layers of fruit, glycerin, and richness, and copious quantities of toasty new oak. It is an outstanding example of what can be done with low yields and impeccable winemaking. Not surprisingly, the oenologist is Riccardo Cotarella. Look for this wine to drink well for another 5–7 years.

PERVINI (PUGLIA)

1993	Bizantino Rosso del Salento	B	87
1994	Galante Rosso del Salento	A	85
1996	I Monilli Primitivo del Tarantino	A	86
1994	Primitivo	B	85

Four good values from southern Italy include Pervini's 1994 Galante Rosso del Salento, a blend of 80% Negro Amaro and 20% Primitivo. I should warn readers that this wine possesses that distinctive southern Italian cheesy, earthy, kinky nose that may not be admired by those who prefer their wines more fruit driven and grapey. This is the antithesis of many of today's sterile wines, but it displays considerable character, a medium ruby color, and plenty of tar-infused, earthy, black cherry fruit. The nose reminded me of the rind on a good Stilton, and that may not be to everyone's liking—especially in wine. It should drink well for several years. The 1993 Bizantino Rosso del Salento is a more mainstream effort, without the cheesy component, but with more tar, pepper, herbs, and sweet red and black fruits. The wine possesses an evolved medium ruby/garnet color as well as a velvety texture, a full-bodied, savory mouth-feel, and excellent purity. It should drink well for 3–4 years. The 1994 Primitivo is soft and earthy, with berry fruit, good ripeness on the attack, and a medium-bodied, low-acid, friendly finish. I would opt for drinking it over the next several years.

The intriguing southern red 1996 I Monilli Primitivo del Tarantino reveals a smoky, barbecue spice, smoldering coals sort of nose that dominates any evidence of fruit. In the mouth, ripe, zesty, berry fruit emerges, along with roasted herb, grilled meat, and earthy notes. Round, expansive, and filled with personality, this rugged, rustic Italian red should be drunk over the next year.

PIEVE DEL VESCOVO (UMBRIA)

1996	Colli Del Trasimeno Rosso	A	84
1996	Lucciaio Vino da Tavola	C	86
1995	Lucciaio Vino da Tavola	C	91
1994	Lucciaio Vino da Tavola	C	89
1997	Piovano	B	88
1994	Rosso	A	86

This estate has been receiving considerable attention from the Italian *Gambero Rosso* magazine. Located in Umbria, the estate has hired the renowned Riccardo Cotarella as winemaker. The 1996 Colli del Trasimeno Rosso is a good, inexpensive, leathery and berry-scented wine with a touch of brett, sweet fruit, a one-dimensional personality, and a clean, crisp finish. Produced from a blend of 80% Sangiovese and 20% Canaiolo and Gamay, it is a savory, easy-going wine to drink, slightly chilled if desired. The superb 1995 Lucciaio is an unfined/unfiltered, opaque purple-colored wine made from a blend of Canaiolo, Gamay, Sangiovese, and a dollop of Merlot. Aged in French barrels for 12 months prior to bottling, this wine offers a stunning nose of flowers, black currants, and vanillin scents. An explosively fruity, sumptuously textured wine, with layers of fruit, full body, and expansive flavors (primarily black cherries and cassis) and a low-acid, lush, juicy finish, this is a classy, intense, impeccably balanced wine that should continue to drink well for 5–7 years.

The 1994 Lucciaio displays a dark purple color, an expressive, smoky and black fruit nose (the malolactic fermentation was done in small oak casks), a soft, fat midpalate, and a long, lush, velvety finish. Drink this rich, flattering wine over the next 5–7 years.

Looking for an even greater bargain? The 1994 Rosso, a blend of Sangiovese, Canaiolo, and Gamay, is a dark ruby-colored wine with abundant quantities of easygoing, soft, ripe fruit tinged with herbs, earth, and spices. It is a round, uncomplicated, delicious wine for drinking over the next 2–3 years.

The 1997 Piovano, a blend of 80% Sangiovese and 20% Canaiolo, is aged in 3-year-old French oak casks before bottling. The wine exhibits a deep ruby/purple color and an excellent briery, blackberry-scented nose that is ripe but uncomplicated. In the mouth, this is a full-bodied, soft, round, delicious wine that is best drunk over the next 2–3 years. Fruit driven, with good levels of glycerin, sweet tannin, and low acidity, this is another wine made by the famed Umbrian oenologist Riccardo Cotarella.

Typical of the vintage, 1996 Lucciaio displays good structure, moderate tannin, and a leaner, less generously endowed personality than the 1995. Aged 12 months in French *barriques*, and bottled unfined and unfiltered, the 1996 exhibits a dark purple color, sweet, toasty new oak in the nose, medium body, and excellent, concentrated flavors that are one-dimensional but clean and spicy. In the mouth, this blend, primarily Canaiolo, Gamay, and Sangiovese, cuts an attractive, stylish, midweight feel. Drink it over the next 4–5 years.

REGALEALI (SICILY)

1995 Cabernet Sauvignon	D	89
1994 Cabernet Sauvignon	D	91
1993 Cabernet Sauvignon	D	91+
1990 Cabernet Sauvignon	D	91+
1997 Rosato	B	86
1995 Rosato	B	87
1994 Rosso	B	86
1991 Rosso	B	86
1993 Rosso del Conte	D	90
1989 Rosso del Conte	C	88

This winery is producing some highly extracted, powerful, rich reds that deserve considerable attention. The lightest wine of the trio of 1994s is the 1994 Rosso, a wine made from 90% Nero d'Avola, a native varietal of Sicily, and 10% Perricone. Over 30,000 cases are produced of this wine, which is aged in large Slavonian oak barrels. It exhibits a deep ruby color as well as a sweet, tarry, earthy, peppery, fruit character with surprising complexity. More elegant than one might expect from the bouquet, this juicy, black plum-flavored wine possesses good underlying acidity and a smoky, peppery quality that matches well with grilled foods. It should drink well for 2–3 years. I was knocked out by the 1993 Rosso del Conte. Made from tiny yields of under 1.8 tons of fruit per acre, from a vineyard planted in 1959, 1965, and 1972, this wine could easily pass as the Italian version of the black-colored Cornas wines from the northern Rhône Valley. It boasts an opaque purple color and comes on like a huge locomotive running across the palate, offering up highly extracted, dense, full-bodied, muscular flavors of cassis, blackberries, and spice. Surprisingly smooth textured for such a massive wine, this pure, intensely concentrated Rosso del Conte is accessible now but promises to drink well for another 10–15+ years. Impressive! Regaleali continues to build on the progress this winery has made with Cabernet Sauvignon. The 1994 Cabernet

Sauvignon (about 3,000 cases produced) is a large-scale, full-bodied, black/purple-colored wine that was aged 12 months in French oak casks, of which 50% were new. It is an extroverted, complex, unevolved, grapey (blueberries/blackberries galore), full-bodied, powerful wine. There is no doubting the impressive raw materials this wine contains. Readers who prefer their wines grapey will enjoy it already, but those who like their Cabernet more civilized should cellar it for 2–3 years. It will last for 15, possibly 20, years. Very impressive!

The 1995 Cabernet Sauvignon may ultimately merit an outstanding score, as it remains exceptionally youthful. Still dominated by its 12-month aging in 50% new French oak casks, this dark, dense purple-colored wine displays jammy cassis aromas intermingled with toasty oak, tar, cassis, and spice. There is juicy, thick, highly concentrated fruit on the attack, as well as low acidity, medium to full body, and lofty alcohol. While the wine possesses plenty of tannin, it is sweet because of the grapes' exceptional ripeness. If the oakiness becomes better integrated, this Cabernet is a candidate for an outstanding score. Anticipated maturity: now–2012.

The impressive 1993 Cabernet Sauvignon is made from an 8-year-old vineyard with extremely low yields. Unfortunately, only 300 cases of this unfined, unfiltered black beauty have been produced. This Cabernet pushes concentration to the limit, but with another 5–10 years of aging, something truly profound should emerge. A thick, viscous black/purple color is followed by subtle, olive/cassis, smoky, roast meat aromas. The flavors are massive, thick, and juicy, with abundant amounts of oak-tinged, wood smoke-flavored black fruits. Thick, chewy, and ripe, this large-scale, hulking Cabernet is surprisingly soft, with huge amounts of tannin lurking behind all the fat, glycerin, and fruit. Yields were under 2 tons per acre. This wine should hit its peak in 7–8 years and last for 2 decades.

The Regaleali 1990 Cabernet Sauvignon is one of the finest Italian Cabernet Sauvignons I have tasted. Made from 8-year-old vines, it is a massive example of Cabernet. It exhibits a black/purple color, phenomenal extract and richness, and a big, chewy, cassis, cherry, licorice, and chocolatey nose with hints of saddle leather in the background. Full bodied and moderately tannic, this extremely young, unevolved wine should continue to improve for up to a decade and last for 20 years. Bravo!

The 1991 Rosso is a reasonably good value in a plumply styled, chewy, black cherry-scented and -flavored wine. While it may lack complexity, it offers good body and fruit. Drink it over the next 2–3 years. The 1989 Rosso del Conte exhibits plenty of black cherry and cassis fruit in the nose, as well as notes of toasty new oak and herbs. This well-defined, structured wine is deep, long, and crammed with ripe fruit and has light tannin and decent acidity. Already delicious, this impressive wine should age well for up to a decade.

Fine rosé deserves more respect, and the medium salmon-colored, dry, austere 1995 Rosato is fresh and lively, with good body and precision. It is an excellent rosé for drinking over the next 12–18 months. The 1997 Rosato offers up a strawberry jam-scented nose, crisp, flavorful, medium-bodied flavors, and a zesty finish. It should drink well over the next year.

RIO GRANDE (UMBRIA)

1995 Casa Pastore Rosso dell'Umbria	D	86
1996 Casa Pastore Vino da Tavola	C	87

Made from a blend of 80% Cabernet Sauvignon and 20% Merlot, the spicy, elegant, clean 1996 Casa Pastore VDT errs only in the sense that it is somewhat monolithic. Aged in French casks and bottled unfined and unfiltered, it exhibits a dark ruby color with purple nuances as well as aromas of new oak, cassis, and cherry fruit. The wine's finesse-style personality follows through on the palate. The finish is medium bodied, clean, and refreshing. More personality and intensity would have resulted in a higher score, but this is a very good effort that should drink well for 5–6 years.

A blend of 80% Cabernet Sauvignon and 20% Merlot, fermented in tank, aged in new French oak, and bottled unfined and unfiltered, the 1995 Casa Pastore exhibits an elegant, cedary, Bordeaux-like character to its aromatics, soft, spicy, medium-bodied flavors with good richness, and a smooth texture. Its finish is short, but the vines are still young, having been planted only in 1988. This wine is reminiscent of a midlevel Médoc. Drink it over the next 4–5 years.

RIVERA TERRA AL MONTE (SOUTHERN ITALY)

1991 Aglianico Rosso	A	86

This dark ruby-colored wine offers an attractive, peppery, ripe cherry nose, forward, precocious-tasting fruit, good cleanliness and richness, and medium body. There is no evidence of intrusive acidity or tannin. Drink it over the next 1–2 years.

RUBINA DELLA PAZZOLA (UMBRIA)

1994 Vino da Tavola	C	93
1993 Vino da Tavola	C	91

Made from 80% Cabernet Sauvignon and 20% Merlot, both of these wines possess sensational fruit extraction, full body, first-growthlike complexity and stature, and an amazing degree of richness. Produced under the tutelage of Riccardo Cotarella, both wines were bottled unfined and unfiltered. The 1994 is sweeter and more expansive in the mouth, with superlative levels of fruit and richness. It is a gorgeously made, seamless wine with no hard edges. Given its extract and overall balance, it will drink beautifully young, but it will develop even more complexity over the next 10–15 years. The opaque purple-colored 1993 exhibits a similar density, as well as an inner core of ripe black currant fruit nicely wrapped with smoky, toasty oak, low acidity, and layers of chewy, concentrated fruit. Too delicious to resist at present, it will age for 15+ years. There are 2,000 cases of each of these wines made by Riccardo Cotarella from the La Palazzola estate in southern Umbria. They are exquisite wines by any standard of measurement.

SAN LEONARDO (TRENTINO)

1995 Vino da Tavola	D	89
1990 Vino da Tavola	D	88
1993 Vino da Tavola di Vallagarina	D	87

The 1993 Bordeaux blend (Vallagrina) of Cabernet Sauvignon, Cabernet Franc, and Merlot exhibits a healthy dark ruby/purple color, followed by a big, spicy, cigar box, weedy tobacco, cassis nose and flavors, medium to full body, soft tannin, and a good finish. It is still youthful but promises to develop nicely over the next 7–8 years. The 1990 possesses a dark, thick-looking garnet color and intensely chocolatey, smoky, prune, and plum scents. Although tannic, it exhibits copious quantities of sweet fruit and aromas of earth, animal fur, grilled meat, and black fruits. Exuberant, savory, big, and husky, this is a large-scale, rustic wine that will benefit from 2–3 years of cellaring; it will last for 2 decades. It is impressive, if somewhat uncivilized.

These wines have a tendency to be too herbaceous for my taste, but after enjoying the 1994, I thought the 1995 was the best wine I have yet tasted from San Leonardo. Although it retains some herbaceousness, that component is much more subtle. This is a dense ruby/purple-colored wine with a smoky, tobacco, spice, and earthy red and black fruit bouquet, medium to full body, and a chewy, rustic personality. It will last for a decade, but I would opt for drinking it over the next 5–7 years.

SANTA ANASTASIA (SICILY)

1996 Litra Cabernet Sauvignon	C	88
1997 Passomaggio	B	85

The famed Italian oenologist Giacomo Tachis is the consultant for this project in Sicily. The 1997 Passomaggio is a straightforward, nicely textured, medium-bodied, ripe, fruity wine with notes of cherries, earth, and spice. There is some herbaceousness and leathery qualities in the finish, which kept my score low, but this is a solid, modestly priced effort. Drink it over the next 1–2 years. More interesting is the 1996 Litra Cabernet Sauvignon, which offers a California-like, eucalyptus/cassis-scented nose. Once past the saturated ruby/purple color and moderately intense aromatics, this is a fleshy, medium- to full-bodied wine with plenty of black cherry fruit, excellent ripeness, and a deep, spicy, New World–like personality. There are copious quantities of new oak *(pain grillé*–like notes) and moderate tannin in the chewy finish. Anticipated maturity: 2000–2008.

SANTA BARBARA (PUGLIA)

1995 Brindisi	A	86
1996 Salice Salentino	A	85

Two fine values from this backwater region of southern Italy, the 1996 Salice Salentino and 1995 Brindisi are both made from a blend of Malvasia Nera and Negroamaro. The 1996 Salice Salentino exhibits a light ruby color as well as a soft, berry fruitiness, not much body or length, but delicious fruit that has been presented in an easily quaffable style. It should be drunk over the next year. The deeper-colored 1995 Brindisi reveals more tar/melted asphalt and earthy notes, as well as more body and spice. It is a solidly made red that should be drunk uncritically in bistros or trattorias.

CANTINA SANTADI (SARDINIA)

1994 Carignano	A	86
1993 Carignano	B	87
1994 Rocca Rubia	C	85
1993 Rocca Rubia	B	85?
1991 Rocco Rubia	B	86
1994 Terre Brune	D	87
1993 Terre Brune	D	88

The evolved medium ruby-colored 1994 Rocca Rubia reveals some amber at the edge. A complex nose offers up cedar, *garrigue,* earthy, dusty cherry fruit and peppery notes. In the mouth, this savory, surprisingly mature, medium-bodied wine is round and gutsy. It is a good bistro/trattoria-style red to consume over the next year. The 1994 Terre Brune, made primarily from old-vine Carignan, is a surprisingly strong effort from a grape that can make good but rarely excellent wines. The color is dark ruby, and the bouquet is filled with scents of earth, black fruits (primarily plums and cherries), and smoky, herbal notes. In the mouth, there is an exuberant rich fruitiness, a surprisingly good texture and midpalate (unusual for Carignan), and a dense, full-bodied, powerful finish. Although not complex, it is a seriously endowed, impressively extracted wine to consume over the next 2–5 years.

Both the 1993 Carignano and 1991 Rocco Rubia are opulent, round, richly fruity, supple reds for drinking over the next 2–3 years. They reveal good winemaking as well as plenty of ripe, jammy fruit, not much complexity, but mouth-filling, savory personalities that should make them popular with readers looking for good wine values.

Of the other three attractive offerings from the sun-bleached *terroirs* of Sardinia, the 1994 Carignano (made from old-vine Carignan) offers uncomplicated but deliciously attractive cherry, strawberry, and earthy scents. This open-knit, fleshy, supple wine is meant to be drunk over the next 1–2 years. I found it to be generous, mouth filling, medium bodied, and attractive, but designed for its hedonistic rather than its intellectual value. Although closed and muted when I tasted it, the 1993 Rocca Rubia offers plenty of body, high-volume flavors, and a big, fleshy, spicy, earthy, peppery style. It possesses a deep garnet/ruby color and should last another 4–5 years, although it offered virtually no interest aromatically. If the nose develops more interest, this wine could merit a score in the mid- to upper 80s. The most impressive of these wines is the 1993 Terre Brune. Made from nineteenth-century vines of unknown origin, but believed to be old, head-pruned Carignan, this dark plum-colored wine offers smoky, licorice, pepper, and blackberry and cherry aromas and flavors in a full-bodied, rich, rustic format. The wine is deep, concentrated, and intriguing, but intensely smoky and earthy. Its loaded with personality, so be prepared for a distinctive tasting experience. Given the wine's concentration and youthful feel, as well as overall balance, it should evolve well for another 5–7 years.

SELLA & MOSCA (SARDINIA)

1992 Marchese di Villamarina	B	86
1992 Riserva Cannonau di Sardegna	B	85

Both of these wines possess a southern, hot-climate, roasted character with intriguing noses of asphalt, black fruits, spice, and animal fur. The 1992 Marchese di Villamarina exhibits a dark plum/garnet color, a roasted coffee, chocolatey, overripe plum and cherry bouquet, and rich, round, savory flavors. It is a husky, robust wine loaded with character. Drink it over the next 4–5 years. The medium garnet-colored 1992 Riserva Cannonau di Sardegna offers sweet fruit and spice, glycerin, and alcohol in the finish. Medium bodied, rustic, but mouth filling and pleasing, it should be drunk over the next 2–3 years.

SPERI (VENETO)

1993 Valpolicella Classico Saint Urbano	C	87

This delicious Valpolicella offers generous quantities of earthy, almond-flavored, black cherry fruit in a medium-bodied, soft, spicy format. The wine is light in the mouth, but bursting with fruit and personality. A delicious, complex Valpolicella to drink over the next 2–3 years, it is the antithesis of so many industrially processed wines with virtually no personality or character.

STELLA (UMBRIA)

1997 Merlot	A	85
1995 Merlot	A	86

Made from 100% Merlot, with a telltale authentic black cherry-scented nose, the dark purple-colored 1995 reveals surprising fruit and ripeness, medium body, and a round, engaging flavor profile. It should drink well for 2 or so years.

The 1997 Merlot is a tank-fermented and -aged wine with a medium ruby color, soft berry/cherry fruit, low acidity, a graceful, easily understood style, and a clean, delightful finish. This soft, tasty Merlot is ideal for drinking over the next 1–2 years. It is another excellent value!

DR. COSIMI TAURINO (APULIA)

1990	Notarpanaro	B	87
1988	Notarpanaro	B	90
1986	Notarpanaro	B	90
1990	Patriglione	D	90
1988	Patriglione	D	88
1995	Salice Salentino	A	86
1990	Salice Salentino	A	87
1994	Salice Salentino Riserva	A	86
1993	Salice Salentino Rosso Riserva	A	87

These wines from Apulia, in the heel of Italy's "boot," have been longtime favorites of mine. They are distinctive, earthy, spicy, and in many ways, the southern Italian version of a rustic California Zinfandel. The medium- to full-bodied 1995 Salice Salentino exhibits rustic tannin in the finish but offers plenty of meaty, smoky, dried herb, and beef bloodlike flavors. It is not for everybody, and may even be called kinky by some, but it is loaded with personality, and when served with grilled foods, it is an ideal mate. It should drink well for 3–4 years. The 1994 Salice Salentino Riserva reveals plenty of this wine's spicy, smoky, earthy character, as well as copious quantities of ripe berry fruit. It exhibits more sharpness in the flavors than usual, but it finishes with good, spicy, peppery, dusty, black cherry fruit. A well-made wine, it should drink well for 3–4 years. The 1990 Notarpanaro (which also tastes like the Italian version of Zinfandel) possesses dry almondlike flavors to go along with the weedy tobacco, licorice, and berry fruit. Spicy, round, and generously endowed, with a late-harvest, Amarone-like character, it should be drunk over the next several years.

Dr. Cosimo Taurino's Salice Salentino has become one of the best-known wine bargains in the United States. It is a rich, supple, mouth-filling wine from Apulia. The old head-pruned vines produce a wine that invites comparisons to the peppery, rustic, savory, mouth-filling wines of France's southern Rhône Valley. The 1993 is filled with scents of ripe fruit, dried meats, and herbs. Gutsy, rich, and soft, this is a delicious, fairly priced wine for drinking over the next 3–4 years. Readers who want something richer, thicker, and more viscous should check out Taurino's 1988 Notarpanaro. It is hard to believe $12 can purchase a wine with this much intensity. This single-vineyard offering exhibits plenty of jammy, black cherry fruit aromas and flavors intermixed with tobacco, leather, and licorice. It boasts full body, admirable intensity, and a supple, silky smooth, spicy, earthy finish. The wine's power suggests it should drink well for 4–5 years. The kinky 1990 Patriglione reveals a mature, garnet/ruby color and an earthy, late-harvest, Amarone-style nose of coffee, cedar, dried fruits, and roasted nuts. There is evidence of wood, plenty of earthy, dusty-textured flavors, and a spicy finish. Unlike the Salice Salentino and Notarpanaro, the Patriglione is best served after the meal, by itself, or with hearty Italian cheese. Both the Salice Salentino and Notarpanaro are excellent values.

Taurino's Salice Salentino has long been one of the world's best wine bargains. The 1990 continues to offer huge appeal as well as value. It may be even better than previous examples. Some of the tar/earth notes that are disliked by some consumers have disappeared in favor of a wonderfully pure, smoky, black cherry, curranty nose. The wine is medium to full bodied, with a multilayered, rich, fleshy texture, gobs of fruit, and a smooth-as-silk finish. A delicious bargain, it will offer a robust, gutsy, chewy glass of dry red wine over the next 5–10 years. It is a wine worth buying by the case. The 1986 Notarpanaro increases the levels of concentration, glycerin, body, and alcohol and adds an element of rusticity and tannin. The wine is full bodied, chewy, thick, and rich. It is a winter-weight wine that is best consumed with a hearty soup, a cassoulet, or a stew. Despite its fullness and richness, it is extremely easy to drink. Consider it Italy's answer to a blockbuster, heavyweight Châteauneuf du Pape from France or a California late-harvested Zinfandel, but without any residual sugar. Last, sugar addicts should check out the extremely ripe, raisiny, chewy 1988 Patriglione. It provides an almost overwhelming glass of wine and is meant to be served at the end of a meal, with a cheese course, or by itself. Its viscous texture and intense, earthy, tar, and jammy black cherry aromas and flavors ooze across the palate. This distinctive wine is clearly the most controversial of these offerings. The Notarpanaro and Patriglione are both such rich, alcoholic wines that they will have no difficulty holding their fruit and aging well for 10 or more years.

TERRA DI LAVORO (CAMPANIA)

1995 Terra di Lavoro Vino da Tavola	D	90?
1994 Terra di Lavoro Vino da Tavola	D	91

This is a tiny estate of 5 acres with extremely low yields (under 2 tons of fruit per acre). Not surprisingly, particularly in view of the quality, the consulting oenologist is Riccardo Cotarella. The wines, from grapes grown on hillside slopes just north of Naples, are produced from a blend of 80% Aglianico and 20% Piedirosso, the latter an indigenous Campania grape. I was blown away by the distinctiveness and individuality of these wines. Made from a vineyard planted at an elevation of 1,300 feet, on a volcanic, gravelly soil base, the wines are aged in 100% new French Allier and Nevers oak and bottled without any fining or filtration. The 1994 is my favorite, largely because it has had several years of bottle age. A striking blueberry, licorice, and black olive-scented nose blasts upward from the glass. In the mouth, this wine could pass for a hypothetical blend of Chapoutier's Hermitage Le Pavillon and Madame Ducasse's renowned Pomerol Évangile. I kept asking myself, Is it Merlot or Syrah that I was smelling? Of course it was neither. This wine reveals extraordinary purity, fully body, remarkable richness, and a layered, complex, powerful presence, yet it never hints at being overweight or too big for its own good. It offers a beautiful combination of black fruits, minerals, spices, and olives in a compelling format. Already delicious, it promises to age well for 12 years. This wine must be tasted to be believed.

The 1995 exhibits a similar blueberry component, but the wine is likely to be more controversial. Although I expect it to settle down with bottle age, at present it is somewhat uncivilized, with exotic floral aromas intertwined with scents of leather, animal fur, and copious amounts of black and blue fruits. This chocolatey, fruity, expansively flavored wine is medium to full bodied, with brilliant concentration and excellent purity, but it is somewhat kinky at present. If it evolves along the lines of the 1994, it will be another knockout wine from this tiny vineyard in southern Italy.

CANTINA TOLLO (ABRUZZI)

1993 Cagiolo	C	85
1995 Montepulciano d'Abruzzo Colle Secco	A	86
1994 Montepulciano d'Abruzzo Colle Seco	A	86
1996 Montepulciano d'Abruzzo Valle d'Oro	A	85

1995 Montepulciano d'Abruzzo Valle d'Oro	A	85
1996 Montepulciano d'Abruzzo Villa Diana	A	82

As I have pointed out for a number of years, top-class bargains can be found in Abruzzi, a region situated in the southern Italy, along the Adriatic coast. The wines produced are named after the grape of the same name—Montepulciano d'Abruzzo. Cantina Tollo's wines are pleasant, well-made, clean offerings that represent bargains given today's superhigh wine prices. The 1996 Montepulciano d'Abruzzo Villa Diana exhibits a light ruby color, a straightforward, strawberry and cherry nose of light to moderate intensity, elegant, clean, fresh flavors, and a short, compact finish. It requires consumption over the next 12 months. The bigger 1996 Montepulciano d'Abruzzo Valle d'Oro could easily be mistaken for a Valpolicella. It possess earthy, spicy, dried almondlike flavors, medium body, crisp freshness, and a certain softness. Drink this pleasant wine over the next 1–2 years. The 1995 Montepulciano d'Abruzzo Colle Secco is the most peppery, spicy, and fruitiest of these Montepulcianos, with more of a gamey, black cherry fruitiness, light to medium body, and a soft texture. It should be drunk over the next 2–3 years.

Neither the 1994 Montepulciano d'Abruzzo Colle Secco nor 1995 Montepulciano d'Abruzzo Valle d'Oro is complicated or complex, but both offer relief from the absurd wine pricing that seems to be the norm. Both wines offer deep ruby colors, elegant ripeness in their straightforward berry aromas, medium body (the 1994 Colle Secco is slightly more powerful and higher in alcohol), and smooth textures with no hard edges. Both wines can be served slightly chilled, provide considerable flexibility with an assortment of dishes, and are ideal quaffing wines.

The 1993 Cagiolo, a single-vineyard-designated wine, reveals cherry fruit and almond extract in its nose, medium body, and a light but refreshing, zesty, tangy character.

GIUSEPPI TRABBUCCHI (VENETO)

1995 Amarone	D	90
1995 Valpolicella Terre di S. Colombano	C	88

Another high-quality Valpolicella, the 1995 Terre di S. Colombano possesses a spicy, strawberry/cherry-scented nose and nicely etched, medium-bodied flavors with a touch of roasted herbs and red fruits. There is excellent depth, good purity, and plenty of character, with no hard edges. Drink it over the next 2–3 years. The powerful, dry 1995 Amarone exhibits a dark plum/garnet color, followed by a big, smoky, licorice, truffle, roasted herb, and berry bouquet. In the mouth, melted road tar, smoked meats, Asian spices, and dark fruits are presented in a full-bodied, powerful, heady style. This is a mouth-filling, alcoholic (15%) wine to consume with cheese or intensely flavored dishes.

VILLA DEL BORGO (FRIULI)

1997 Merlot	A	85

Readers seeking a lighter-style Merlot should check out Villa del Borgo's 1997. Although its light ruby color is unimpressive, the wine offers clean, alluring strawberry and cherry notes in its moderately intense nose. With finesse, lightness, and considerable charm, it could be served slightly chilled over the next 1–2 years.

VILLA DIANA (ABRUZZI)

1993 Montepulciano d'Abruzzo	A	85
1992 Montepulciano d'Abruzzo	A	85

Consumers and retailers are intelligently stockpiling just about any Montepulciano they can find. These big, dense, chewy wines, which are sold for a song, are Italy's potential gold mine. The 1992 Villa Diana is a terrific wine for the price, offering a dark ruby/purple color, tart, crisp, richly fruity flavors, medium body, excellent purity, and a nicely textured mouthfeel. It should drink well for another 3–4 years. A super value!

Villa Diana's soft, round, richly fruity, medium-bodied 1993 Montepulciano does not possess the extraordinary extract and intensity of the Monti offering recommended elsewhere in this chapter, but it is a fine wine bargain. It is designed to be drunk now and over the next 1–3 years.

VILLA RUSSIZ (FRIULI-COLLIO)

1995 Merlot Graf de la Tour	D	91
1994 Merlot Graf de la Tour	D	90

I was impressed by these two vintages of Merlot. Both are made in extremely limited quantities (approximately 250 cases produced in each vintage). The opaque purple-colored 1994 Merlot Graf de la Tour offers a big nose of cocoa, coffee, jammy black cherries, and earth. In the mouth, it is a revelation for Merlot from Friuli-Collio. Plump, deep, and full bodied, with terrific richness and a multilayered personality, this chewy, blockbuster Merlot can be drunk now or cellared for a decade. The 1995 appears to be even better. Its explosive nose reveals a Pomerol-like, black raspberry, coffee, mocha, chocolatey/cherry profile, splendidly fullbodied and concentrated flavors, good power, and an unctuous texture. It should drink well for a decade or more. Admittedly, very little of this wine will make it to the United States, but efforts such as this need to be commended in order to encourage other producers to strive for similar results. Bravo!

VIVIANI (VENETO)

1993 Valpolicella Classico Superiore	C	86

This is an attractive, light- to medium-bodied Valpolicella with copious quantities of strawberry and cherry fruit and a smooth, silky-textured, accessible personality. With no heaviness, hard tannin, or high acidity, it offers delicious drinking now and over the next 1–3 years.

ZENATO (VENETO)

1990 Amarone	D	90
1994 Ripassa	C	88
1995 Valpolicella Classico	A	87
1994 Valpolicella Classico	A	86
1995 Valpolicella Ripassa	C	88

Most knowledgeable observers of the Italian wine scene claim the next revolution in Italian winemaking, similar to what took place in Tuscany and Piedmont in the eighties, will be in Veneto, the lovely area tucked in the northeast corner of Italy, not far from the borders of Austria and Croatia. Zenato's wines certainly seem to be on the rebound.

Zenato's 1995 is a gorgeous example of Valpolicella Classico! The deep ruby color is followed by aromas of jammy strawberries and cherries, dried fruits, and herbs. The wine possesses an excellent texture, soft tannin, medium body, and a ripe, velvety finish. Most Valpolicella tends to be thin, acidic, and diluted, but this offering is the antithesis of such plonk. It should continue to drink well for 2–3 years. The 1995 Valpolicella Ripassa is so named because it is made by the Italian method called *ripassa*. This means the wine is passed over the pressings, or so-called pomace, that are left over from making the fullbodied Amarone, to give the wine more strength, body, and complexity. The 1995 Valpolicella Ripassa exhibits a deep, opaque purple color and a super nose of blackberries and raspberry liqueur, with tar, prune, and truffle notes in the background. In the mouth, it is full bodied, not terribly complex, but full flavored, gutsy, and chewy. This is a mouth-filling, robust, fleshy, dry red that should drink well for 5–7 years.

The 1994 Valpolicella Classico (about 20,000 cases produced) is aged mostly in stainless steel, spending approximately 6 months in barrel. The wine is a very good value, offering ripe, tasty, almond-scented cherry/strawberry fruit. Soft and delicious, this is a medium-bodied, pretty, easy-to-drink and -understand wine that should be consumed over the next 2 years. Zenato's Ripassa is made in a style that is unique to this area of Italy. The wine is passed through the pressings of their Amarone, thus giving it more guts, body, and earthiness. The 1994 is excellent. It boasts a dark ruby/garnet color, followed by big, peppery, earthy, dried cherry fruit aromas, full body, and a chewy texture. A macho, robust wine, it would be terrific with a good *parmesano reggialo* cheese. Consume it over the next 5–6 years. Zenato's 1990 Amarone is a heavy, winter-weight wine. The color is a dark murky garnet/ruby/purple. The wine possesses copious quantities of spicy, earthy fruit, as well as aromas and flavors of prunes, raisins, and truffles. Full bodied, with super concentration, excellent purity, and a mouth-filling, chewy, muscular personality, this dry, smoky, earthy wine should drink well for 15+ years.

ZENI (TRENTINO)

1992 Teroldego Rotaliano	C	87

This dark garnet-colored wine possess copious quantities of earthy, black cherry fruit, good body and spice, and a hearty, robust personality. The wine should drink well for at least a decade.

ZERBINA (MARZENO FANZA)

1990 Marzeno di Marzeno Vino da Tavola Romagna	D	91
1990 Pietramora Sangiovese di Romagna	D	89

I was very impressed with the high quality of these two offerings, a new discovery for me. The 1990 Pietramora (100% Sangiovese) is a dark ruby/purple-colored wine with gobs of rich, black currant and black cherry fruit nicely touched by subtle oak. Medium to full bodied, pure, rich, and supple, this delicious, well-knit wine should drink well for 5–6 years. The 1990 Marzeno di Marzeno is a 50% Sangiovese/50% Cabernet Sauvignon blend aged in small oak casks, of which 30% are new. It possesses a nearly opaque ruby/purple color and a big, spicy nose1 of vanilla, black currants, and flowers. Medium to full bodied, with considerable flavor, purity, and extraction, as well as exceptional balance, this rich, supple, lightly tannic, impressive wine could easily be mistaken for a top Tuscan Vino da Tavola. The finish lasts for nearly 45 seconds. It should drink well for at least a decade.

3. GERMANY AND AUSTRIA

GERMANY

The Basics

Germany's winedom is controlled by the 1971 law that divided German wines into seven grades, all based on ascending levels of ripeness and sweetness, as well as price:

1. Tafelwein
2. Qualitatswein (QbA)
3. Kabinett
4. Spätlese
5. Auslese
6. Beerenauslese
7. Trockenbeerenauslese

In addition to these, there are other categories of German wines. The Trocken and Halbtrocken wines are the two generic types of dry German wine. The Trockens tend to be drier but also boring, thin wines with little body or flavor. Halbtrockens also taste dry but are permitted to have slightly more residual sugar and are marginally more interesting. I rarely recommend either because they are not very good; they are commercial creations made to take advantage of the public's demand for "dry" wine. A third type of wine is called Eiswein, Germany's rarest and most expensive wine. It is made from frozen grapes, generally picked in December or January or even February. It is quite rare, and a very, very sweet wine, but it has remarkably high acidity and can last and improve in the bottle for decades. It does have great character, but one must usually pay unbelievably steep prices to experience it.

There are also the sparkling wines of Germany called Deutscher Sekt, which should be drunk only by certified masochists, as they are a ghastly lot of overly sulfured wines. Last, there is the German wine that everyone knows about, the ubiquitous Liebfraumilch. This sugary, grapey drink is to quality German wine what California wine coolers are to that state's serious producers' wines.

GRAPE VARIETIES

Müller-Thurgau   Representing 25% of Germany's vineyards, Müller-Thurgau has become the most widely planted grape because of its predilection to give prolific yields of juice (6–6²/₃ tons of fruit per acre is not uncommon). Ignore all of the self-serving promotion from German wine importers about Müller-Thurgau, because it is not a great wine grape, and the Germans have planted it for quantity, not quality.

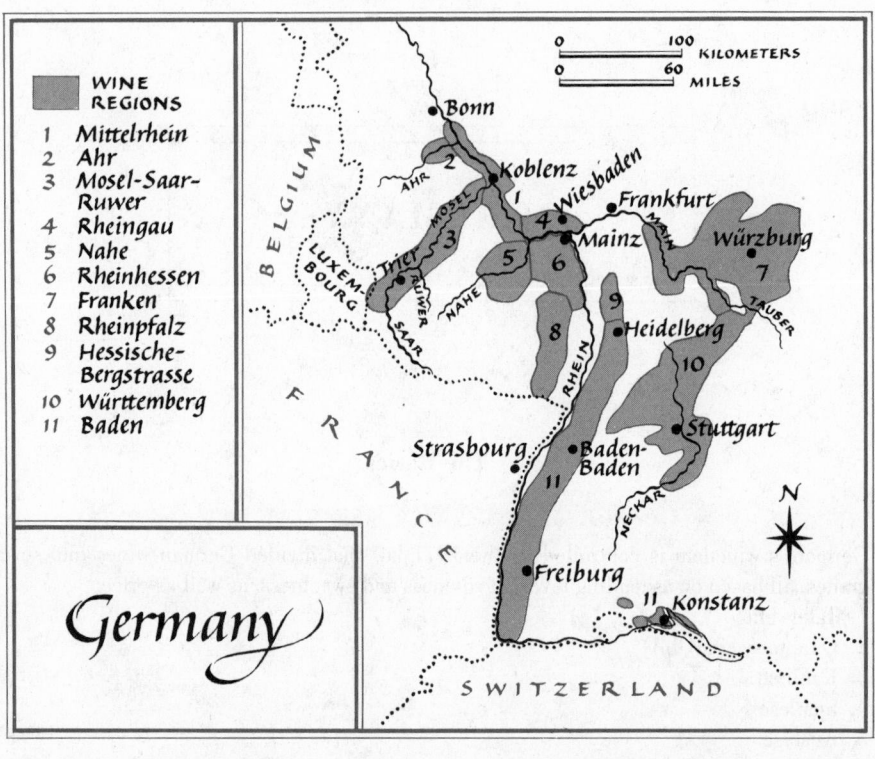

WINE
REGIONS

1 Mittelrhein
2 Ahr
3 Mosel-Saar-Ruwer
4 Rheingau
5 Nahe
6 Rheinhessen
7 Franken
8 Rheinpfalz
9 Hessische-Bergstrasse
10 Württemberg
11 Baden

Germany

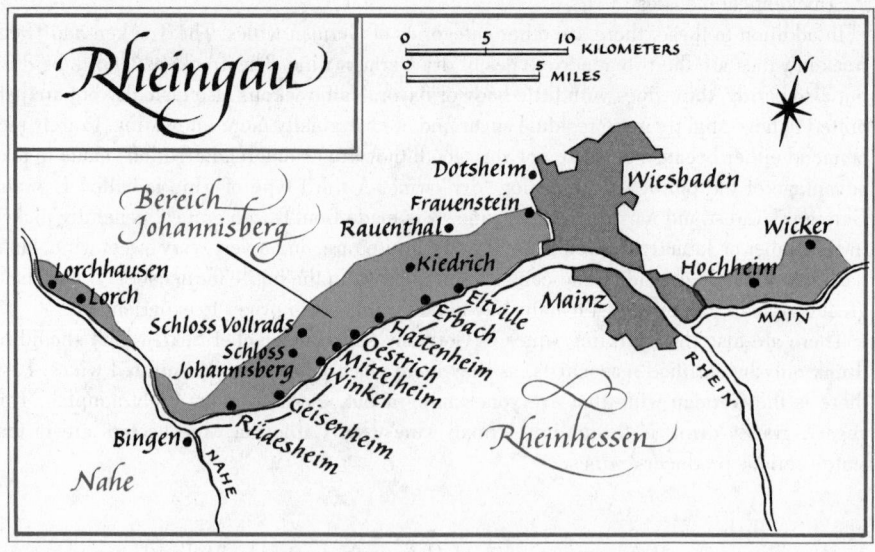

Rheingau

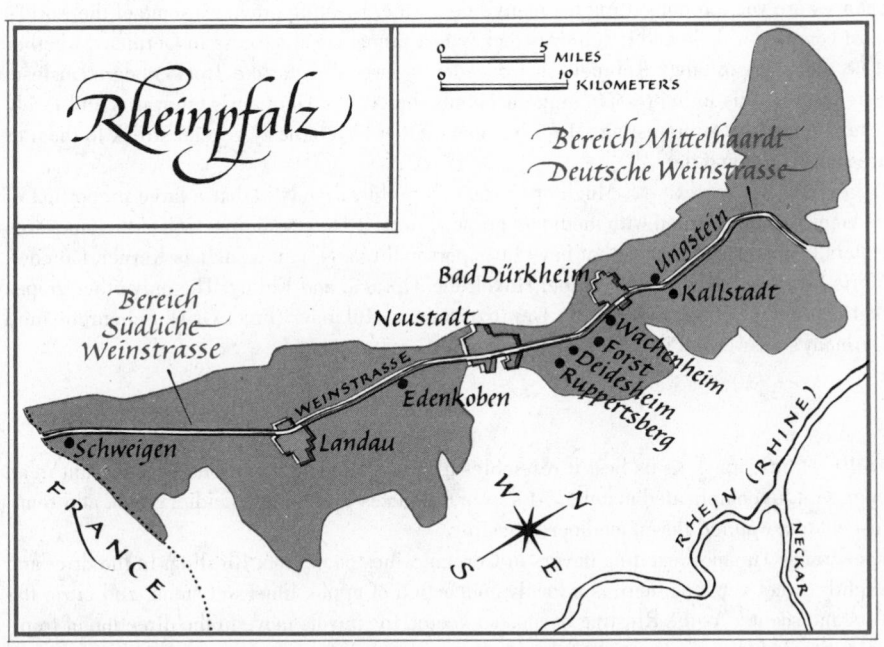

Rheinpfalz

5 MILES
10 KILOMETERS

Bereich Mittelhaardt
Deutsche Weinstrasse

Ungstein

Bad Dürkheim

Kallstadt

Bereich
Südliche
Weinstrasse

Neustadt

Wachenheim
Forst
Deidesheim
Ruppertsberg

WEINSTRASSE

Edenkoben

Schweigen

Landau

FRANCE

RHEIN (RHINE)

NECKAR

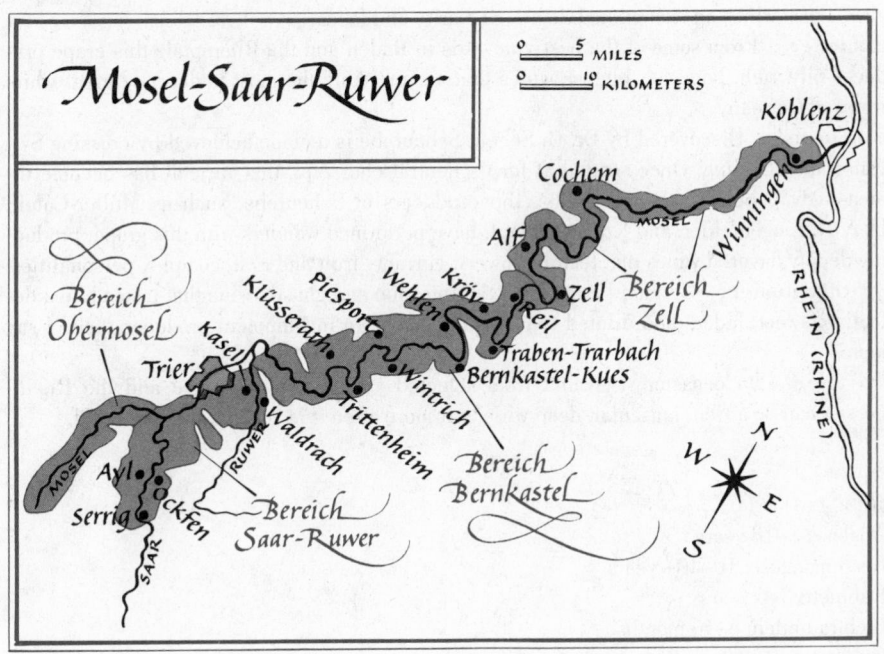

Mosel-Saar-Ruwer

5 MILES
10 KILOMETERS

Koblenz

Cochem

MOSEL

Winningen

Alf

Bereich
Zell

Zell

Kröv

Reil

Wehlen

Piesport

Klüsserath

Traben-Trarbach

Bereich
Obermosel

Kasel

Bernkastel-Kues

Trier

Wintrich

Trittenheim

RHEIN (RHINE)

MOSEL

Waldrach

RUWER

Ayl

Bereich
Bernkastel

OCKFEN

Serrig

SAAR

Bereich
Saar-Ruwer

Riesling While Riesling accounts for only 20% of the vineyards in Germany, it produces about 95% of that country's finest wines. If the bottle does not say Riesling on it, then chances are you are not getting Germany's best wine. Riesling produces some of the world's most complex whites, and it achieves its greatest pinnacles of success in Germany, whether it be a dry, crisp, tangy Kabinett or a decadently sweet, nectarlike Trockenbeerenauslese.

Sylvaner This unimpressive grape accounts for 10% of Germany's vineyards and rarely results in anything interesting. Most Sylvaners either have a nasty vegetal streak to them or are simply dull and flat.

Other Grape Varieties Much of Germany's problem today is that a large proportion of its vineyards are planted with mediocre grape varieties. The remaining 45% of the vineyards generally consists of grapes that have little personality and names such as Kerner, Gutedel, Morio-Muskat, Bacchus, Faberrebe, Huxelrebe, Optima, and Ebling. The only other grapes that can do something special are Gewürztraminer, Rulander (Pinot Gris), Scheurebe, and Germany's answer to Pinot Noir, Spätburgunder.

FLAVORS

Müller-Thurgau At its best it resembles a can of fruit salad, obvious but pleasant in an open-knit, uncomplicated manner. At its worst it tastes washed out, acidic, green, and reminiscent of a watered-down, mediocre Riesling.

Riesling The most exciting flavors in German wines come from Riesling. In the drier and slightly sweet versions there is a lovely concoction of apple, lime, wet stone, and citric flavors and scents. As the Riesling becomes sweeter, the flavors move in the direction of tropical fruits such as mangoes and pineapples, as well as honeyed apples, peaches, and apricots. Behind all the flavor (in the top Rieslings) is a steely, zesty, vibrant natural fruit acidity that gives those wines an exceptional degree of clarity and focus.

Rulander From some of the best vineyards in Baden and the Rheinpfalz this grape produces oily, rich, honeyed, intense wines that are probably the most underrated great white wines of Germany.

Scheurebe Discovered by Dr. G. Scheu, Scheurebe is a clone achieved by crossing Sylvaner and Riesling. Once scoffed at for its neutral character, this varietal has become increasingly popular with consumers. Top producers of Scheurebe, such as Müller-Catoir, H. & R. Lingenfelder, and Kruger-Rumpf, have performed wonders with this grape, producing deeply flavored wines that feature flowery, curranty fruit and rich, complex personalities.

Spätburgunder German Pinot Noir is a grotesque and ghastly wine that tastes like a defective, sweet, faded, and diluted red burgundy from an incompetent producer. Need I say more?

Sylvaner On occasion, Sylvaner from selected vineyards in Franken and the Rheinhessen can be a rich, muscular, deep wine, but more often it is vegetal, thin, and dull.

AGING POTENTIAL

Auslese: 3–18 years
Beerenauslese: 10–40+ years
Kabinett: 3–6 years
Liebfraumilch: 8–16 months
Qualitatswein (QbA): 2–4 years
Spätlese: 3–12 years
Tafelwein: 8–16 months
Trockenbeerenauslese: 10–40+ years

OVERALL QUALITY LEVEL

The top level of quality is impeccably high and dominated by small estates that usually produce Riesling. However, the German government has been inexcusably remiss over recent decades in allowing too many high-yielding, low-quality grapes to be planted (the 1987 average yield per acre was an incredible 6½ tons of fruit), which has encouraged consumers to become increasingly skeptical about the seriousness of German wine quality. For example, in the mediocre year of 1987, 77% of the wine produced was allowed to be called QbA, and only 2% was declassified as simple table wine (Tafelwein). That's ridiculous. A campaign to promote the top-quality German estates that are making the finest German wines is long overdue. Until the consumer begins to believe that Germany is serious about quality, sales of these wines will remain difficult.

THE MOST IMPORTANT INFORMATION TO KNOW

For American readers, while a number of importers have small portfolios of German wines, there are three major players who dominate the German wine business in America. From a consumer's perspective, the most important is Terry Theise Selections, whose wines are imported by Michael Skurnik Imports in New York City. By ignoring many of the overrated, more famous German wine names, and by beating the back roads of less renowned viticultural regions, Theise has put together a portfolio of producers who turn out individualistic wines of astonishing quality, often at modest prices. Theise keeps his profit margins low so the wines can be represented effectively in the marketplace. The result is a bevy of phenomenal wines and extraordinary wine bargains. If you are going to seriously buy German wines, look for the words "Terry Theise Selection" on the label. You are unlikely to be disappointed.

Between the other two major players in the German wine market, the most visible and promotion-conscious is Rudy Weist of ILNA Selections in Santa Barbara, California. Weist's portfolio is concentrated on the more renowned and prestigious domaines that are all members of an elite association of winemaking estates referred to collectively as the VDP. Each of these estates sports a neck or back label that identifies its members. There are over 200 members. In theory, all of them are dedicated to producing the highest-quality wines, usually from Riesling. There are a number of fabulous producers in this group, as well as an appalling number of underachievers who charge exceptionally high prices because their wines are produced from renowned vineyards.

The third major importer of German wines is Romaine C. "Bob" Rice of Chapin Cellars in Virginia Beach, Virginia. Rice is a low-profile importer who is content to have most of his German producers represented regionally, so you are not likely to see him promoting his name as much as that of his producers. His reasonably priced portfolio includes numerous excellent wines. In addition to becoming familiar with these German wine importers, there are other facts to keep in mind when buying German wines:

• There are eleven major wine-producing zones in Germany. Within these zones there are three subdistricts, the most general of which is called a Bereich. This is used to describe a wine from anywhere within the boundaries of that particular Bereich. An analogy that may help facilitate this distinction would be the closest French equivalent, a wine entitled to appellation Bordeaux Contrôlée or Appellation Bourgogne Contrôlée. Within the Bereich there are more specific boundaries called Grosslagen, to which the closest French equivalent would be the generic Appellation St.-Julien Contrôlée or Appellation Morey-St.-Denis Contrôlée. These would be wines that are not from a specific château or specific vineyard, but from a specific region or collection of sites for vineyards. There are 152 different Grosslagen in Germany. The most specific zone in Germany is called an Einzellagen, which is a specific site or vineyard. There are 2,600 of them in Germany, and again, by analogy, the closest French equivalent would be a specific St.-Julien château such as Ducru-Beaucaillou, or a specific premier cru or grand cru burgundy vineyard in Morey-St.-Denis such as Clos des Lambrays. Perhaps this will help one to understand the breakdown of the German wine zones. However, few people have the patience to memorize the best Einzellagens or Grosslagens, so it is much more important to try to remember the names of some of the best producers.

• The majority of the best producers in Germany are located in the following nine wine zones.

OVERALL CHARACTERISTICS OF THE NINE MAJOR GERMAN WINE ZONES

Middle Mosel   For German wine lovers, as well as tourists to Germany's wine regions, the Middle Mosel is the most beloved and scenic. The frightfully steep, slate-based slopes are so forbidding, it seems impossible vineyards could be planted on such dangerously precipitous hills. With its plethora of high-profile producers, such as J. J. Prüm, Willi Haag, Ernest Loosen, and Dr. Thanisch, this region has no shortage of admirers and potential buyers. The fact is that while Riesling grown on these slopes has unlimited potential, this is also an area filled with overpriced, underachieving producers who have long lived off their reputations. Nevertheless, anybody who has tasted a great Wehlener Sonnenuhr, Brauneberger Juffer, Erdener Treppchen, Zeltinger Sonnenuhr, or Graacher Himmelreich knows that this area's soils can produce magical Rieslings. By analogy, the Middle Mosel is to Germany what Puligny-Montrachet is to Burgundy. Although there are a number of great producers, prices are high, and the quality is frightfully irregular.

Lower Mosel   This obscure vineyard area with supersteep slopes is located at the junction of the Mosel and the Rhine. The wines from the Lower Mosel are underestimated, a fact that consumers should put to good use. Try some recent vintages from two of this area's most spectacular producers, von Schleinitz and von Heddesdorff, and experience the high quality available at reasonable prices. Although the vineyard sites are not considered to be as ideal as those in the Middle Mosel, top Lower Mosel producers can produce wines equal in quality to those from the Middle Mosel.

Saar   Also referred to as the Upper Mosel, this cool region is able to maintain the steely, razor-blade sharpness of the Riesling grape. Many authorities consider the Saar vineyards to be among the greatest in Germany, but as in the Middle Mosel, fame has its price. Some fabulous producers are located in this area. However, some well-known Saar producers have a tendency to overcrop, making relatively hollow, flabby wines that lack definition. Superlative producers include the likes of Egon Müller, Dr. Wagner, von Kesselstatt, and, from time to time, Zilliken.

Ruwer   Trier is the spiritual and commercial center for the Ruwer wines. Textbook, quintessential Rieslings emerge from this area from producers such as Friedrich-Wilhelm-Gymnasium, Geltz Zilliken, Karthäuserhof, von Kesselstatt, Karlsmuhle, and von Schubert's Maximin Grunhaus.

Rheingau   Many of the most famous producers of German wine are located in this highly renowned region. However, it is not unusual for many of the unknown overachievers to outperform their more celebrated neighbors. Three of the most prominent underachievers are Schloss Groenesteyn, Schloss Vollrads, and Schloss Johannisberg. If you want to taste what many consider to be some of the finest Rieslings made in Germany, check out producers such as H. H. Eser, Freiherr zu Knyphausen, Deinhard's Konigin Victoria Berg, Dr. Heinrich Nagler, and the best cuvées of Schloss Schonborn.

Rheinhessen   All of the German wine zones offer considerable diversity in quality, but none more than the Rheinhessen, which has Nierstein as its commercial center. Müller-Thurgau and Sylvaner are the two most popular grape varieties of this region. Additionally, such odd grapes as Scheurebe, Huxelrebe, and Kerner have found an enthusiastic reception among this region's producers. This is also the region where most of Germany's Liebfraumilch is produced. Consumers often make major errors in buying wines from this region.

Over recent years some of the best producers have included Freiherr Heyl zu Herrnsheim, J.U.H.A. Strub, and Merz.

Rheinpfalz   The Rheinpfalz is the warmest of the major German wine zones. Although Müller-Thurgau is widely planted, it is Riesling, Rulander, and Scheurebe that produce the most stunning wines. If you think German wines are too understated, light, and wimpish, check out the powerful, meaty, fleshy, supergenerous wines from the Rheinpfalz. The quality level appears to be hitting new heights with every vintage. This is the home of the producer Müller-Catoir, who is making some of the most riveting wines of Germany. It is also the base for supertalented producers such as H. & R. Lingenfelder, Kurt Darting, Klaus Neckerauer, Koehler-Ruprecht, Kimich, Werleaa, and perhaps one of the best-known Rheinpfalz estates, Dr. Burklin-Wolf.

Nahe   This is another underrated source of high-class Riesling, as well as a wine zone with a competitive group of producers who, for now, lack the one superstar needed to draw worldwide attention to this region's virtues. A Nahe wine is considered to possess some of the character of a Saar wine and the spice, meatiness, and flesh of a Rheingau. The curranty, smoky aromas of a Nahe is reminiscent of that found in a red wine, making it among the most distinctive of all German wines. None of the Nahe producers are well-known, so prices tend to be low, except for those producers who are members of the prestigious VDP group (like Hans Crusius). Top producers include von Plettenberg, Hehner-Kiltz, Kruger-Rumpf, Adolph Lotzbeyer, and perhaps the finest, Helmuth Donnhoff and Prince zu Salm.

Franken   With the wonderful city of Würzburg as its commercial center, the wines of Franken have developed a considerable cult following. Although these wines fetch high prices and are put in unattractive squat bottles that are impossible to bin, Franken wines can be bold, dramatic, and heady. Moreover, they enjoy remarkable loyalty from their admirers. This is one region where the Sylvaner grape hits heights that exist nowhere else on earth. The two best estates are Burgerspital and Hans Wirsching. I have also been increasingly impressed (especially by the 1990s) with wines from Schloss Sommerhausen. Once past the quality of these superlative producers, it is caveat emptor.

• The best German wines are those produced at the Kabinett, Spätlese, Auslese, Beerenauslese, and Trockenbeerenauslese levels of ripeness and sweetness. Most consumers tasting a Kabinett would not find it particularly sweet, although there is residual sugar in the wine. Because of a high natural acidity found in German wines, to most palates a Kabinett generally tastes fresh, fruity, but not sweet. However, most tasters will detect a small amount of sweetness in a Spätlese, and even more with an Auslese. All three of these types of wines are ideal for having as an aperitif or with food, whereas the wines entitled to Beerenauslese and Trockenbeerenauslese designations are clearly dessert wines that are very rich and quite sweet. One should keep in mind that the alcohol level in most German wines averages between 7% and 9%, so one can drink much more of this wine without feeling its effects. One of the naive criticisms of German wines is that they do not go well with food. However, anyone who has tried a fine Kabinett, Spätlese, or Auslese with Oriental cuisine, with roast pork, or even with certain types of fowl such as pheasant or turkey can tell you that these wines work particularly well, especially Spätlese and Auslese.

• The best German wines age like a fine Bordeaux. In great vintages, such as 1990 or 1971, one can expect a Kabinett, Spätlese, or Auslese from a top producer to evolve and improve in the bottle for 3–20 years. Beerenauslese and Trockenbeerenauslese have the ability in a great vintage to improve for 2, 3, or 4 decades. This is a fact, not a myth, to which those who have recently tasted some of the great Ausleses from 1959 can easily attest. German wines at the top levels, from the top producers, do indeed improve remarkably in the bottle, although the trend among consumers is to drink them when they are young, fresh, and crisp.

VINTAGE GUIDE

1997—After the tooth-shattering acidity of the 1996s, Mother Nature reversed gears for the 1997 vintage. As opposed to the 1996s, the 1997s are forward, lush, low-acid offerings for near-term drinking. In this vintage consumers should concentrate on wines from the Spätlese and below levels; the Ausleses rarely have the complexity to match their higher prices, nor do they have the balance for extended cellaring. This is an excellent vintage for consumers who want to discover German wines, as there are multitudes of delicious Kabinetts at reasonable prices.

1996—This is an atypical vintage. High levels of maturity are combined with exceedingly high levels of acidity. In fact, the 1996 Germans may be the most acidic wines I have ever tasted. At the Spätlese level and above (Auslese and above for those fearing searing acidity), a multitude of incredibly pure wines were fashioned. These efforts will require patience for their richness to cover some of the acid. Below the Spätlese level the vast majority of wines are to be avoided; they simply don't have the stuffing to face the record acidity levels. Consumers searching for extraordinary wines at the Auslese level and above for extended cellaring are well advised to search out 1996s crafted by Germany's finest producers.

1995—The 1995 vintage is extremely uneven, with some concentrated, profound, and exceptionally balanced wines having been produced, as well as many that are plagued by negative characteristics of rot (as opposed to the positive effects of botrytis). The Mosel fared best, and the Rheinpfalz suffered immensely (even outstanding producers like Lingenfelder were unable to escape the vintage's rot in the Pfalz).

1994—The superb weather in October resulted in an abundant crop of sweeter-style wines. Quality is uneven, but some outstanding wines were produced. In complete contrast with the stylish, elegant, high-acid 1993s, the 1994s are relatively powerful, rich, and made for near-term drinking.

1993—Delicate, crisp, light-bodied wines were produced in bountiful quantities. The vintage favors Kabinett, Spätlese, and Auslese producers.

1992—This is a good vintage, with some superlative, drier-style wines coming from the Ruwer and Middle Mosel. Most estates reported it was very difficult to produce sweet wines in these areas. Therefore this is a vintage of mostly Kabinetts and Spätleses—a good sign for consumers looking for wines from the drier end of the German wine spectrum. All things considered, 1992 is a good to very fine year throughout the Mosel, Saar, Ruwer regions, with less superrich dessert wines than in years such as 1990 and 1989. In the Rheingau, Rheinpfalz, and Rheinhessen, the vintage looks to be very good to excellent, with plenty of rich wines, as well as sweet late-harvest wines, particularly in the Rheinhessen.

1991—This has turned out to be a surprisingly good vintage, far better than many of the doom-and-gloom reports suggested. Although not of the level of 1990 or 1989 in terms of rich, intense, sweet Spätlese and Auslese wines, it is a very appealing vintage, particularly for the top estates in the drier Kabinett styles. The downside of the 1991 vintage is that some wines have shrill levels of acidity, raising questions as to whether their fruit will hold up. Most German-wine specialists suggest this was a year of the winemaker rather than of Mother Nature, and those producers who were able to keep yields down and who picked physiologically ripe fruit made wines with crisp acidity and good depth and character. Those who didn't made hollow, high-acid wines that merit little attention.

1990—This is an outstanding, perhaps even great, vintage. The wines have fabulous ripeness, surprisingly crisp acidity, and an intense perfume and midpalate. In addition to many outstanding Kabinetts and Spätleses, this is another vintage, much like 1989, where there were spectacular sweet Ausleses and even more decadently rich Beerenauslese and Trockenbeerenauslese wines produced. If you are a German-wine enthusiast, this vintage is a must-buy.

1989—This is another top-notch vintage that has been compared with 1976, 1971, and 1959. The late harvest and the extraordinary amount of sweet wine made at the Auslese, Beerenauslese, and Trockenbeerenauslese levels garner considerable enthusiasm. Unlike 1990, where every wine zone enjoyed success, or 1991, where it was a question of the wine-maker's ability, in 1989 the Saar, Rheinpfalz, Ruwer, and Rheinhessen produced top wines. This was not a rain-free harvest, production yields were high, and acidity levels in many cases remain suspiciously low, suggesting most consumers would be well advised to drink the wines below the Auslese level over the next 3–4 years. One area of good but somewhat disappointing wines in the context of the vintage is the Middle Mosel, where a number of the most famous domaines overcropped and have produced somewhat fluid, loosely knit, fragile wines.

1988—The strength of this vintage is the Middle Mosel. Based on my tastings, the drier Kabinetts and Spätlese offerings look to be the best wines made. This vintage has now been largely forgotten in all the hype over 1989 and 1990.

1987—A mediocre vintage followed an unusual growing season that was characterized by a poor, wet, cold summer but a glorious September and a mixed bag of weather in October. The quality is expected to be better than either 1980 or 1984, and many growers reported harvests close in size to those in 1986. The average production was a whopping 6.3 tons of fruit per acre, which is excessive. Interestingly, this appears to be a good year for the rare nectar-like Eisweins. Consumers should be drinking their wines that are below the Auslese level, as they are fading.

1986—A copious crop of grapes has resulted in pleasant, agreeable, soft, fruity wines that will have broad commercial appeal. Because of the size of the crop, prices dropped after the smaller-than-normal crop in 1985. All in all, this vintage will be regarded by the trade as a useful, practical year of good rather than great wines. Wines below the Auslese level should already be drunk up.

1985—The German wine trade has touted this year rather highly, but except for a handful of areas, it is not comparable to the outstanding 1983 vintage. Nevertheless, it is a very good year, with a moderate production of wines with good acidity and more typical textures and characteristics than the opulent, richly fruity 1983s. Like 1983, the dryness during the summer and fall prevented the formation of *Botrytis cinerea*. The Rieslings in many cases can be very good but will be firmer and slower to evolve and less open than the more precocious, overt, fruity 1983s. Overall, the 1985s should be at their best between now and 1998. The top successes are in the Middle Mosel, with potentially great wines from villages such as Urzig and Erden. Wines below the Auslese level should already have been drunk, and the Ausleses are at their peak.

1984—Fresh, light, very pleasant, straightforward wines that are neither green nor too acidic were produced in this vintage of average quality and below average quantity. They will not keep, so drink up the 1984s. The Mosel estate of Dr. F. Weins-Prüm Erben made excellent wines in 1984, as did Monchhof.

1983—This vintage has received the most publicity between the 1976 and 1990 vintages. Most growers seem to feel that it is certainly the best since the 1976. It was a very large crop throughout all viticultural areas of Germany, but it was especially large and exceptional in quality in the Mosel-Saar-Ruwer region. The wines have excellent concentration, very fine levels of tartaric rather than green malic acidity, and a degree of precocious ripeness and harmonious roundness that gives the wines wonderful appeal now. However, because of their depth and overall balance, Ausleses should age well for another 4–5 years. The vintage seemed strongest at the Spätlese level, as very little Auslese, Beerenauslese, and Trockenbeerenauslese wines were produced. In addition, 1983 is a great year for Eiswein, where, as a result of an early freeze, above-normal quantities of this nectarlike, opulent wine were produced. However, despite larger quantities than normal, the prices are outrageously high for the Eisweins but very realistic and reasonable for the rest of the wines.

OLDER VINTAGES

The great sweet wine vintage that can sometimes still be found in the marketplace is 1976, a vintage that, by German standards, produced incredibly ripe, intense, opulent wines, with a significant amount of wine produced at the Auslese and Beerenauslese levels. The top wines should continue to last for another 2–12 years. Some critics have disputed the greatness of this vintage, saying that the 1976s are low in acidity; but that is a minority point of view. The wines remain reasonably priced at the Auslese level, but the Beerenausleses and Trockenbeerenausleses from this vintage are absurdly expensive. The 1977 vintage should be avoided, and 1978, unlike in France, was not a particularly successful year in Germany. Well-kept 1975s can provide great enjoyment, as can the wines from another great vintage, 1971. I would avoid the wines from 1972, and the once good 1973s are now in serious decline!

RATING GERMANY'S BEST PRODUCERS

* * * * * (OUTSTANDING)

J. J. Christoffel (Mosel)

Kurt Darting (Rheinpfalz)

Fritz Haag (Mosel)

Heribert Kerpen (Mosel)

J. F. Kimich (Rheinpfalz)

H. & R. Lingenfelder (Rheinpfalz)

Egon Müller (Saar)

Müller-Catoir (Rheinpfalz)

Klaus Neckerauer (Rheinpfalz)

J. J. Prüm (Mosel)

Willi Schaefer (Mosel)

von Schubert-Maximin Grunhaus (Ruwer)

Selbach-Oster (Mosel)

Werlé (Rheinpfalz)

* * * * (EXCELLENT)

Christian-Wilhelm Bernard (Rheinhessen)

von Bretano (Rheingau)

Burgerspital (Franken)

Dr. Burklin-Wolf (Rheinpfalz)

Schlossgut Diel (Nahe)

Hermann Donnhoff (Nahe)****/*****

August Eser (Rheingau)

H. H. Eser-Johannishof (Rheingau)

F. W. Gymnasium (Mosel)

Willi Haag (Mosel)

Freiherr von Heddesdorff (Mosel)

Hehner-Kiltz (Nahe)

Weingut-Weinhaus Henninger (Rheinpfalz)

Freiherr Heyl zu Herrensheim
   (Rheinhessen)

von Hoauvel (Saar)

Immich-Batterieberg (Mosel)

E. Jakoby-Mathy (Mosel)

Weingut Karlsmuhle (Mosel-Ruwer)

Christian Karp-Schreiber (Mosel)

Karthauserhof (Christophe Tyrell) (Ruwer)

von Kesselstatt (Mosel-Saar)

Freiherr zu Knyphausen (Rheingau)

Koehler-Ruprecht (Rheinpfalz)

Konigin Victoria Berg-Deinhard (Rheingau)

Kruger-Rumpf (Nahe)

Kuhling-Gillot (Rheinhessen)

Franz (Gunter) Kunstler (Rheingau)

Dr. Loosen-St.-Johannishof (Mosel)

Alfred Merkelbach (Mosel)

Meulenhof/Erben Justen/Erlen (Mosel)

Monchhof (Mosel)

Nahe Staatsdomaine (Nahe)

Pfeffingen (Rheinpfalz)

von Plettenberg (Nahe)

Jochen Ratzenberger (Mittelrhein)

Jakob Schneider (Nahe)

von Simmern (Rheingau)****/*****

J.U.H.A. Strub (Rheinhessen)

Dr. Heinz Wagner (Saar)

* * * (GOOD)

Paul Anheuser (Nahe)

Basserman-Jordan (Rheinpfalz)

Erich Bender (Rheinpfalz)

Josef Biffar (Rheinpfalz)***/****

Bischoflisch Weinguter (Mosel)
Bruder Dr. Becker (Rheinhessen)
Christoffel-Berres (Mosel)
Conrad-Bartz (Mosel)
Hans Crusius (Nahe)
Josef Deinhart (Mosel-Saar)
Epenschild (Rheinhessen)
Dr. Fischer (Saar)
Four Seasons Co-op (Rheinpfalz)
Hans Ganz (Nahe)
Gebruder Grimm (Rheingau)
Gernot Gysler (Rheinhessen)
Grans-Fassian (Mosel)
Gunderloch-Usinger (Rheinhessen)
J. Hart (Mosel)
Dr. Heger (Baden)
von Hoauvel (Mosel)
Toni Jost (Mittelrhein)***/****
Klaus Klemmer (Mittelrhein)
Johann Koch (Mosel)
Gebruder Kramp (Mosel)
Lehnert-Matteus (Mosel)
Josef Leitz (Rheingau)
Licht-Bergweiler (Mosel)
Lieschied-Rollauer (Mittelrhein)
Schloss Lieser (Mosel)
Weingut Benedict Loosen Erben (Mosel)
Adolf Lotzbeyer (Nahe)
Mathern (Nahe)***/****
Weingut Merz (Rheinhessen)
Herbert Messmer (Rheinpfalz)
Theo Minges (Rheinpfalz)
Eugen Muller (Rheinpfalz)
Dr. Heinrich Nagler (Rheingau)

Peter Nicolay (Mosel)
von Ohler'sches (Rheinhessen)
Dr. Pauly Bergweiler (Mosel)
Petri-Essling (Nahe)
Okonomierat Piedmont (Mosel-Saar-Ruwer)
S. A. Prüm (Mosel)
S. A. Prüm-Erben (Mosel)
Erich Wilhelm Rapp (Nahe)
Reuscher-Haart (Mosel)
Max Ferdinand Richter (Mosel)
Salm (Nahe)
Prinz zu Salm (Nahe)
Peter Scherf (Ruwer)
von Schleinitz (Mosel)
Georg Albrecht Schneider (Rheinhessen)
Schloss Schonborn (Rheingau)
Schumann-Nagler (Rheingau)
Wolfgang Schwaab (Mosel)
Seidel-Dudenhofer (Rheinhessen)
Bert Simon (Saar)
Schloss Sommerhausen (Franken)
Sturm (Rheinhessen)
Dr. Thanisch (Mosel)
Unckrich (Rheinpfalz)
Christophe Vereinigte Hospitien (Mosel)
Wegeler-Deinhard (Mosel, Rheinpfalz,
   Rheingau)
Adolf Weingart (Mittelrhein)
Dr. F. Weins-Prüm (Mosel)
Domdechant Werner (Rheingau)
Winzer Vier Jahreszeiten (Pfalz)
Gunter Wittman (Rheinhessen)
Wolff-Metternich (Rheinhessen)
G. Zilliken (Mosel)

* * (AVERAGE)

Baumann (Rheinhessen)
Bollig-Lehnert (Mosel)
von Buhl (Rheinpfalz)
Stephan Ehlen (Mosel)
Alexandre Freimuth (Rheingau)
Le Gallais (Mosel)
Siegfried Gerhard (Rheingau)
Martin Gobel (Franken)
Schloss Groenestegn (Rheingau)
Louis Guntrum (Rheinhessen)
Schloss Johannishoff (Rheingau)
Burgermeister Carl Koch (Rheinhessen)
Lucashof (Rheinpfalz)

Milz-Laurentiushof (Mosel)
Claus Odernheimer/Abteihof St.-Nicolaus
   (Rheingau)
Geh. Rat Aschrott'sche (Rheingau)
J. Peter Reinert (Mosel-Saar)
Schloss Reinhartshausen (Rheingau)
Schloss Saarstein (Saar)
Schmidt-Wagner (Mosel)
Henrich Seebrich (Rheinhessen)
Staatsweingüter Eltville (Rheingau)
Studert-Prüm/Maximinhof (Mosel)
Schloss Vollrads (Rheingau)

AUSTRIA

Thanks to the enormous talents of some of its winemakers as well as the dedication and hard work of two high-quality U.S. importers (Terry Theise and Vin Divino), Austria is bursting on the American scene as a source of superb white wines. From vineyards located in eastern Austria (west, north, and southeast of Vienna), Austria's top Rieslings and Grüner Veltliners can compete qualitatively with many of the finest whites fashioned in the world's most famous wine regions. Certainly the best dry Rieslings of the Wachau (on the Danube west of Vienna) and the sweet wines of Burgenland (near the shores of the Neusiedlersee on the Hungarian border) are some of the finest white wines made.

Consumers should know that the 1995, 1996, and 1997 vintages are first rate, with 1997 being stellar. The top producers of the Wachau, Austria's finest wine growing region, include the Weingartner cooperative, Franz Hirtzberger, Emmerich Knoll, Nikolaihof, F. X. Pichler, Rudi Pichler, and Prager. Readers who crave sweet wines should not miss the mind-boggling Beerenausleses and Trockenbeerenausleses crafted by the Burgenland's Alois Kracher.

Austrian Rieslings are extremely distinctive from those produced in Alsace or Germany. They have the harmony between acidity and fruit found in French Rieslings, as well as the sharp focus found in the Germans. The finest Grüner Veltliners are fresh, peppery whites with considerable complexity, flavors reminiscent of smoked bell peppers, white/yellow fruits, rhubarb, and flowers.

A Spotlight on Alois Kracher's Extraordinary Sweet Wines

A few years ago, Alois Kracher burst into my life like an air-raid siren during a peaceful nap. His 1991s shattered all my preconceptions about sweet wines. There are not one but two Alois Krachers. This father and son team (Austrians do not use the "junior" or "senior" suffixes) have a range of varietals (including Welschriesling, Scheurebe, Chardonnay, Muskat-Ottonel, Traminer and Zweigelt) planted along the banks of the Neusiedlersee in eastern Austria near Hungary. The elder Kracher is responsible for the viticulture (in this region one of the most difficult aspects of vineyard work is devising ways to prevent birds from devouring the ripe grapes. The Krachers have each row of vines encased in netting), and Kracher-*fils* handles all the cellar work.

The 1995 vintage is the finest year for sweet wines that both Krachers have ever witnessed in the Neusiedlersee, permitting the younger Kracher to fashion an unprecedented number of trockenbeerenausleses—the highest/sweetest level in the Germanic ranking of wines with residual sugar. I tasted all fifteen of Kracher's mind-boggling 1995 trockenbeerenausleses not once but twice, before and after bottling. Overall, the 1996s are not at the quality level of the otherworldly 1995s, yet are superb, world-class sweet wines.

The wines were fermented in wood, with Alois Kracher deciding on a case-by-case basis whether they should be placed in new barrels or traditional older casks, how much time each should spend on its lees, whether they should be racked into more new oak or stainless steel tanks, and so on—no recipe winemaking here!

Kracher divides his wines into three basic categories: 1) "Zwischen den Seen" (between the lakes), the more traditional cuvée vinified in previously used casks, 2) "Nouvelle Vague" (new wave), a modern, nontraditional approach using new oak barrels (the Zwischen den Seen and Nouvelle Vague wines are, with one exception, single varietal wines), and 3) "Grande Cuvée," a multivarietal blend. Kracher said, "In the best vintages, I try to make the Grande Cuvée a very individual wine with the greatest possible finesse by highest possible concentration and potential." These wines are available only in 375 ml bottles (half-bottles) and carry the name of the varietals (except in the case of the "Grande Cuvée") and a number from 1 to 15, since Kracher wanted to indicate what he perceived to be their relative level of concentration (#15 is, in his opinion, the most concentrated). While each wine is distinctly different, they are all opulent, luscious, unctuous, thick, highly concentrated, extracted, fullbodied, extremely botrytised, and amazingly long. Most important, each wine is outstanding in its own right.

Because of a lack of space, abbreviated notes follow. I have included the residual sugar (g/rs), alcohol (alc.) and acidity (g/a) data to assist readers in their selection. Also, I have provided basic vinification information so that readers may see how Kracher adapts his vinification techniques and timetable to each wine. His goal is to get the most concentration, extraction, and finesse while maintaining "freshness and life, which is wine in Austria."

1997 Cuvée Beerenauslese   D 87

84 grams of residual sugar per liter (g/rs), 14.1% alcohol (alc.), 6.7 grams acidity per liter (g/a), 15,000 bottles. Produced from an assortment of varietals, the 1997 Cuvée Beerenauslese offers aromas of smoky grass clippings amid ripe apricots and peaches. On the palate, it is medium bodied, well structured, and offers considerable quantities of botrytis-dusted yellow fruits. Drink it over the next 6–7 years.

1996 Beerenauslese #1, Traminer "Nouvelle Vague"   D 89

88 g/rs, 13.8% alc., 8.6 g/a, 5,400 bottles. This wine's lively aromas reveal spicy white fruit and new oak. Apple, herbal and stony flavors are found in its well-concentrated, flavorful, oily textured, and medium-bodied core. Anticipated maturity: now–2008.

1996 Trockenbeerenauslese #2, Bouvier & Muskat-Ottonel "Zwischen Den Seen"   D 90

146 g/rs, 12.2% alc., 9.4 g/a, 2700 bottles. My apologies to Alois Kracher for this analogy, but this wine's nose reminded me of floral-scented, jellied room deodorants. It is a lovely offering, crammed with guava paste, dried apricots, and lemons. Medium to full bodied, extremely well balanced, and impressively persistent in the finish, this outstanding Trockenbeerenauslese can be drunk over the next 15 years.

1996 Trockenbeerenauslese #3, Scheurebe "Zwischen Den Seen"   E 92

176 g/rs, 9.6% alc., 11.6 g/a, 5,400 bottles. Smoky tropical fruits laced with botrytis are found in this TBAs aromatics. The wine has superb focus, an oily texture, as well as an expressive flavor profile crammed with intricate layers of sweet peaches, apricots, raspberries, and lemon. Drink it over the next 20 years.

1996 Trockenbeerenauslese #4, Chardonnay/Welschriesling "Nouvelle Vague"   E 94+

182 g/rs, 11.5% alc., 9.3 g/a, 1,600 bottles. This stunning blend of superripe Chardonnay and Welschriesling offers coconut, mangoes, papayas, and candied citrus fruit aromatics. Resembling a topflight effort from Barsac's famous Château Climens, this impeccably bal-

anced wine is medium to full bodied, silky textured, elegant, and redolent with sweet/spicy yellow fruits. It is gorgeously pure, highly delineated, and amazingly long in the finish. Anticipated maturity: now–2020.

1996 Trockenbeerenauslese #5, Zweigelt Rosé "Nouvelle Vague"   E   88

258 g/rs, 8.8% alc., 9.3 g/a, 1,100 bottles. This amber/bronze TBA Zweigelt Rosé reveals raspberry and sweet brambleberry aromas. It is fat (verging on flabby), medium bodied, and filled with botrytis-dusted candied red fruits. While it may last longer, I would suggest drinking it over the next 5–6 years.

1996 Trockenbeerenauslese #6, Muskat-Ottonel "Zwischen Den Seen"   E   88

139 g/rs, 12.5% alc., 8.9 g/a, 1,100 bottles. This rose, candied tangerine peel, blood orange, and botrytis-scented wine is medium bodied, silky textured, and concentrated. Its personality is crammed with sugar-coated grapefruits and is exceptionally long. A certain bitterness found in its midpalate and finish prevented it from meriting a more exalted review. Anticipated maturity: now–2006.

1996 Trockenbeerenauslese #7, Grande Cuvée "Nouvelle Vague"   E   90+

158 g/rs, 12.5% alc., 9.2 g/a, 4,800 bottles. Kracher's 1996 Grande Cuvée may ultimately deserve a higher score. It displays awesome apricot jam and botrytis aromas followed by a medium- to full-bodied, well-focused character. This raisin and peach-flavored, intense wine is highly concentrated as well as extremely persistent. It is at present slightly disjointed, yet cellaring may bring harmony to its personality. Anticipated maturity: 2002–2020.

1996 Trockenbeerenauslese #8, Chardonnay "Nouvelle Vague"   EE   95

168 g/rs, 11.8% alc., 9.6 g/a, 400 bottles. Coconut-laced, overripe apricots and peaches are intermingled with botrytis scents in this fabulous TBA. It is Sauternes-like in its flavor profile, yet fresher and livelier. This refined wine has superb delineation, breadth, and a creamy texture packed with toasty yellow fruits. Medium to full bodied and impeccably focused, its finish reveals candied lemon flavors that seemingly last forever. Drink it over the next 15 years.

1996 Trockenbeerenauslese #9, Welschriesling "Zwischen Den Seen"   EE   97

231 g/rs, 9.8% alc., 8.5 g/a, 700 bottles. The mind-boggling TBA #9 exhibits mouth-watering aromas of bergamots (a pear-shaped citrus fruit that is the primary flavoring in Earl Grey tea), raspberries, cherries, currants, and botrytis. Its satin-textured, medium- to full-bodied character is superconcentrated, highly complex, and powerful. Layers of red fruits, mangoes, pineapples, papayas, and pink grapefruits can be found in its expressive personality and awesomely long finish. This magnificent wine can be drunk now or over the next 25 years.

1995 Trockenbeerenauslese #1, Welschriesling "Zwischen Den Seen"   E   93

195 grams of residual sugar per liter (g/rs), 11% alcohol (alc.), 8.5 grams acidity per liter (g/a), 5,000 bottles. Fermented in used casks and then racked into stainless steel to preserve the wine's freshness and bottled after 10 months. Flower and spice aromas are found in this sweet, earthy, apricot-jammed and well-balanced nectar. It will be at its best between now and 2015+.

1995 Trockenbeerenauslese #2, Welschriesling "Zwischen Den Seen"   EE   95

236 g/rs, 8.5% alc., 10 g/a, 900 bottles. Fermented and aged in used casks and bottled after 10 months. Aromatically revealing candied pineapples, this wine's superthick core is packed with mineral, herbal, spicy, earthy, metallic, floral, apricot, peach, apple compote, and red berry flavors. Its striking, highly focused acidity perfectly balances the unctuous sweetness. A 40+-second finish! Drink it between 2005 and 2020+.

1995 Trockenbeerenauslese #3, Scheurebe "Zwischen Den Seen"   E   94+

174 g/rs, 12% alc., 9 g/a, 2,600 bottles. Fermented in used casks, then racked into stainless steel and bottled after 10 months. Mango, kiwi, and pink grapefruit aromas followed by oily layers of lychee nut, minerals, steel, and crisp white grapes in a beguiling, superbly balanced, and elegant character. Anticipated maturity: now–2018+.

1995 Trockenbeerenauslese #4, Scheurebe "Zwischen Den Seen"   EE   96

197 g/rs, 11.5% alc., 10.5 g/a, 1,000 bottles. Fermented and aged in used casks and bottled after 10 months. Lychee, candied pink grapefruit, kiwi, and spicy smoke scents and a massive, powerful core of hugely rich floral, caramel-covered apricots, flowers, candied apples, and fresh herbs. Drink it between 2003 and Armageddon (or when the cork disintegrates, whichever comes first).

**1995 Trockenbeerenauslese #5, Muskat-Ottonel
"Zwischen Den Seen"**   EE   92+

171 g/rs, 11% alc., 8.5 g/a, 1,100 bottles. Fermented and aged in used casks and bottled after 12 months. Kracher feels this wine (like #s 2, 4, 6, 11, and 14) will be at its best after 15 years of cellaring. Aromatically displaying orange blossoms, candied tangerines, minerals and earth, this intensely rich wine is packed with sweet raspberry candy, lychee, sugar-coated oranges, and papaya flavors. Anticipated maturity: 2005–2020.

**1995 Trockenbeerenauslese #6,
Scheurebe "Zwischen Den Seen"**   EE   (94–96)

130 g/rs, 12.5% alc., 9.5 g/a, 2,000 bottles. Fermented and aged in used casks and bottled after 18 months (this note is from a barrel sample as the bottled sample I tasted was corked). Candied pink grapefruit, white pepper and spicy red berry (raspberries, cherries, and strawberries) scents are found in the oily, mango, papaya, banana, apricot, and sweet herbal tea-flavored wine. Drink it between 2003 and 2020+.

**1995 Trockenbeerenauslese #7, Chardonnay/Welschriesling
"Nouvelle Vague"**   EE   94

164 g/rs, 12.5% alc., 9.5 g/a, 4,200 bottles (80% Chardonnay and 20% Welschriesling). Fermented and aged in new oak, then bottled after 16 months. Sweet oak, coconut, vanilla, cardamom, nutmeg, and smoky aromas are followed by a magnificently complex and focused core of candied cherries, tropical fruits, and smoky/sweet oak flavors. Somewhat like a Helen Turley Chardonnay gone mad. Anticipated maturity: 2005–2025.

1995 Trockenbeerenauslese #8, Traminer "Nouvelle Vague"   EE   93

167 g/rs, 13% alc., 8.9 g/a, 1,600 bottles. Fermented and aged in new oak, then bottled after 16 months. Aromatically, this wine exhibits coconut (from the new oak), roses, sweet Earl Grey tea, mango and kiwi. In the mouth its incredibly thick personality is jam-packed with concentrated vanilla, cardamom, tropical fruits, and perfumed red berries. Anticipated maturity: 2005–2020+.

1995 Trockenbeerenauslese #9, Zweigelt Rosé "Nouvelle Vague"   EE   93

189 g/rs, 11.5% alc., 10 g/a, 3,300 bottles. Fermented in new oak, then racked into more new oak (the Dominique Laurent 200% new oak treatment) and aged 16 months before bottling. Kracher says he used the 200% new oak because he lost most of the red wine color (it displays a pink/orange brick robe) and flavors due to the high levels of botrytis. He feels the oak has replaced much of the lost tannins and red wine character turning it into what he calls a "cigar wine." Violets, oak spice, red cherries and currants are found in the aromas, followed by a caramel, raspberry, potpourri, rose petal-laced character. Drink it between 2005 and 2025+.

1995 Trockenbeerenauslese #10, Zweigelt Rosé "Nouvelle Vague"   EE 95+

245 g/rs, 8.5% alc., 10 g/a, 1,800 bottles. Fermented and aged in the oak used to ferment #9 and bottled after 15 months. Sporting a copper/hot pink/orange color and revealing a nose reminiscent of the fruit-flavored candies found on the checkout counters of every *épicerie* in France (cherry, raspberry, strawberry, red currant, etc.), this spectacular wine tastes like sugar-coated cherries intermingled with fresh raspberries and roses in a perfumed, refined, elegant, and focused syrup. Anticipated maturity: 2005–2025+.

1995 Trockenbeerenauslese #11, Muskat-Ottonel
"Zwischen Den Seen"   EE 98+

230 g/rs, 8% alc., 10 g/a, 400 bottles. Fermented and aged in used casks and bottled after 16 months. A floral, smoky, mineral-infused nose is followed by an amazingly elegant yet thick as Jell-O wine crammed with candied citrus zests, orange blossoms, apricot, lavender, ginger, cherries, currants, peaches, and apricots. A sublime wine, Kracher correctly describes it as "soft and feminine." Drink this gem between 2007 and 2025+.

1995 Trockenbeerenauslese #12, Grande Cuvée   EE (96–98)

210 g/rs, 12% alc., 10 g/a, 15,000 bottles. A blend of 40% Chardonnay, 30% Welschriesling, and 10% Traminer fermented in new oak barrels as well as 20% Scheurebe fermented in cask (this note is based on a barrel sample as the bottled wine I was to receive broke in transit). Smoky, spicy, mineral, and tropical fruit-infused aromas are followed by stunning layers of lively, fresh red berry and mangoes in a focused, precise, and sublimely balanced core. Anticipated maturity: 2002–2025+.

1995 Trockenbeerenauslese #13, Chardonnay "Nouvelle Vague"   EE 96+

250 g/rs, 8.5% alc., 11 g/a, 800 bottles. Fermented and aged in new oak barrels, then bottled after 16 months (the bottled wine was markedly better than the barrel sample I tasted on this wine). The finest late-harvest Chardonnay I have ever tasted! This wine has pink grapefruit, white pepper, smoky scents and a divine personality filled with baked papaya, mango, apricots, and peaches so thick that a knife and fork are almost required to consume this masterpiece. Awesome balancing acidity and length! Drink it between 2002 and 2030+.

1995 Trockenbeerenauslese #14, Scheurebe
"Zwischen Den Seen"   EE 96

310 g/rs, 7% alc., 12 g/a, 2,300 bottles. Fermented and aged in used casks and bottled after 18 months. Smoke, spice, thyme, rosemary, roasted herbs, candied apples, white pepper, and red currants aromas are followed by a massive silky core of sweet herbal teas, cherries, minerals, and spicy red fruits (I find that highly concentrated white wines often exhibit red fruit aromas and flavors when they are young). Unbelievably unctuous yet exquisitely refined due to its perfectly balanced acidity. This wine will still be drinking spectacularly when the theory behind *The Planet of the Apes* is unraveled.

1995 Trockenbeerenauslese #15, Welschriesling
"Zwischen Den Seen"   EE 95+

370 g/rs, 5.5% alc., 13 g/a, 900 bottles. Fermented (for 12 months!) in used casks, then racked into stainless steel and bottled after 16 months. If my math is correct, there is almost a third of a pound of pure sugar per half-bottle of this wine! Yet, amazingly, it is well balanced due to its humongous level of acidity. Of course, it's as thick as Jell-O and may be better suited to pancakes than a glass, but . . . Revealing intense cherry-flavored cough medicine, white pepper, thyme, chrysanthemum tea, and floral scents, this syrup is as concentrated, extracted, and rich as any wine I have ever tasted. Baked tropical fruits (bananas, mangoes, papayas, etc.) and candied red berries can be discerned among the waves of oily viscosity that ooze across the palate. I recommend cellaring this wine for *at least* 10 years

before opening it, but readers may find it wise to invest in cryogenics if they intend to drink it at its apogee. Anticipated maturity: 2010–2030+.

1996	Chardonnay/Welschriesling "Days of Wines and Roses" Burgenland	B	86
1997	Chardonnay/Welschriesling "Days of Wines and Roses" Burgenland	B	89
1998	Chardonnay/Welschriesling "Days of Wines and Roses" Burgenland	B	89

Yes, the same Alois Kracher who fashions mind-blowing sweet wines also produces a delicious dry white. The 1996 Chardonnay/Welschriesling "Days of Wines and Roses" offers Earl Grey tea aromas and an extremely well-made, light- to medium-bodied, and precise character with flavors reminiscent of potpourri and red currants. It should be drunk over the next year while it still possesses its floral freshness. The brilliance of Kracher's winemaking skills is evident in his 1997 Chardonnay/Welschriesling "Days of Wines and Roses." This wine displays an expressive, exciting, lively, and beguiling nose of white flowers, sea shells, and buttercream cake icing. On the palate, this highly concentrated, well-extracted, rich, medium- to full-bodied, and intense offering boasts layers of spiced pears, white peaches, anise, stones, red berries, and a medley of perfumes. Its lingering finish is pure, precise, and redolent with potpourri flavors. Drink it over the next 3 years. Interestingly, the lively aromatics of the 1998 Chardonnay/Welschriesling "Days of Wines and Roses" are reminiscent of a rich, deeply ripe Sauvignon Blanc. Its scents of freshly cut grass, flowers, and sweet yellow fruits lead to its medium-bodied, complex character. This wine is gorgeously pure, well balanced, and has a seamless flavor profile composed of pears, red candies, minerals, tangy lemons, and traces of cinnamon. Anticipated maturity: now–2003.

4. SPAIN AND PORTUGAL

SPAIN

The Basics

TYPES OF WINE

Aside from the glories of sherry, which is synonymous with Spain, this beautiful sun-drenched country is best known as a treasure trove for red wine values. The majority of white wines, which once tasted musty and oxidized, are, thanks to high technology, usually innocuous, with sterile personalities and no real flavor. There are a few exceptions, such as the fragrant, crisp, tasty whites made from the Albarino grape, especially those from the Bodegas de Vilarino. Other refreshing, inexpensive white wines have emerged from Albet I Noya Sat, Angel Lorenzo's Martivilli, Sat Godeval, Vitivinicola Del Ribeiro, and the Sauvignon Blanc of the Marquis de Grinon. And while the booming Spanish sparkling wine business stays in the headlines, few makers of sparkling wine actually produce exceptional wine; most of it is reliably pleasant, relatively innocuous, and very cheap—under $15—hence the appeal.

Red wine is king in Spain, but unfortunately this country is still one of unrealized potential rather than existing achievement. The best red wines all come from northern Spain. The areas that stand out for quality are the famous Rioja region, the generally well-known Penedès viticultural area in Catalonia near the Mediterranean coast, the Ribera del Duero region, and several emerging areas such as Navarra and Toro. To understand Spanish red wines, one must first realize that the Spanish want their red wines supple, with an aged taste of maturity, as well as a healthy (many would say excessive) dosage of oak. Once you realize this, you will understand why many Spanish wineries, called *bodegas,* age their wines in huge oak or concrete vats for 7 or 8 years before they are released. While tastes are changing, the Spanish are not fond of grapey, tannic, young wines, so expect the wineries to mature the wines for the Spanish consumer. Consequently most Spanish wines have a more advanced color and are smooth and supple, with the sweet vanillin taste of strong oak (usually American) well displayed. Many wineries actually hold back their best lots for a decade or more before releasing them, enabling the consumer to purchase a mature, fully drinkable wine.

GRAPE VARIETIES

RED WINES

Cabernet Sauvignon   An important part of Spain's most expensive and prestigious red wine, the Vega Sicilia, Cabernet Sauvignon has flourished where it has been planted in Spain.

Carinena   In English this is the Carignan grape, and in Spain this workhorse grape offers the muscle of Arnold Schwarzenegger. Big and brawny, the tannic, densely colored wine made from this grape varietal is frequently used as a blending agent, particularly with Grenache.

Fogoneu   This varietal is believed to be related to the French Gamay. It produces light, fruity wines that are meant to be drunk young. Most Fogoneu is planted on the island of Majorca.

Garnacha   The Spanish spelling of Grenache, Garnacha is widely planted in Spain. Three types of Garnacha are utilized. The Garnacha Blanc, which produces white wines, is relatively limited, although it is especially noticeable in Tarragona. The Garnacha Tinto, which is similar to the Grenache known in France, is one of the most widely planted red wine grapes in Spain. There is also the Garnacha Tintorera, which is actually Alicante, the grape that produces black-colored, tannic, dense wines. It is used primarily for blending.

Merlot   This relatively new varietal for Spain has performed well. It is planted primarily in the Ribera del Duero.

Monastrell   This varietal produces sweet, alcoholic wines. Although widely planted, it is most frequently found in hotter microclimates.

Tempranillo   The finest indigenous red wine grape of Spain, Tempranillo travels under a number of names. In Penedès it is called Ull de Llebre, and in the Ribera del Duero it is called Tinto. It provides rich, well-structured wines with good acidity and plenty of tannin and color. The bouquet often exhibits an intense black raspberry character. It makes an ideal blending mate with Garnacha but is complex enough to stand on its own.

WHITE WINES

The white wine grapes parade under names such as Albarino, Chardonnay, Macallo, Malvasia, Palomina (utilized for sherry), Parellada (the principal component of most sparkling wine cuvées), Pedro-Ximenez, Riesling, Sauvignon, Torrontes, Verdejo, Xarello, and Moscatel. Few of these varietals have proven to be capable of making anything more than neutral-tasting wines, but in the mid-1990s several appear to have potential, as yields have been kept low and the wines have been impeccably vinified, not eviscerated by food-processor techniques. The best is the Albarino, which, when produced by a top winery in Galicia, has a stunning perfume similar to that of a French Condrieu. However, in the mouth the wine is much lighter, with less body and intensity. At its best it is light, refreshing, and fragrant. Several wineries consistently produce fresh, lively, tasty dry white wines. Readers should look for the splendid values from Marqués de Gelida (sparkling), Vega Sindoa (good Chardonnays), Bodegas Godeval, and Bodgeas Martin Codax (for delicious Albarinos).

Other white wines that have shown potential include some of the Chardonnays, and Torrontes, which, when made in Galicia, has a perfumed personality, lovely fruit salad-like flavors, and a pleasant finish.

FLAVORS

Penedès   The dominant winery here is Torres, which produces a bevy of excellent red wines from the typical Spanish varietals. Yet the top wine is the 100% Cabernet Sauvignon Black Label Gran Coronas, which has a rich, open-knit bouquet of plums, sweet oak, and often licorice and violets. Its chief rival is the Cabernet Sauvignon from Jean Leon, another concentrated, blackberry-scented and -flavored, full-throttle wine with a whopping influence from sweet, toasty oak. The best vintages are 1995, 1994, 1990, 1989, 1987, 1984, 1981, and 1978.

Ribera del Duero   Two of Spain's greatest red wines are produced in this broad river valley: Pesquera, which comes primarily from the Tempranillo grape; and Vega Sicilia, primarily a Cabernet Sauvignon/Merlot/Malbec wine. What is noticeable about these wines is the

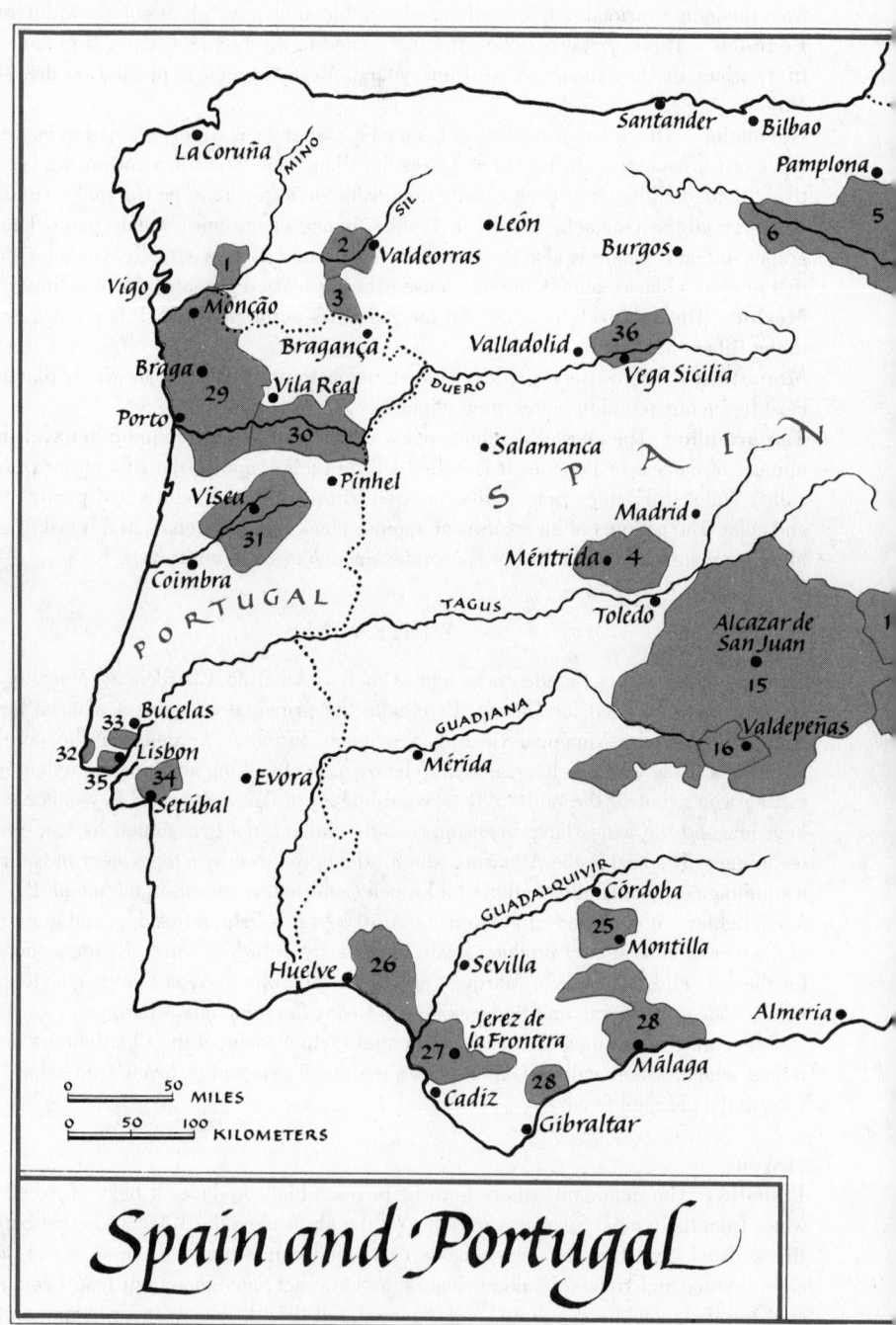

Spain and Portugal

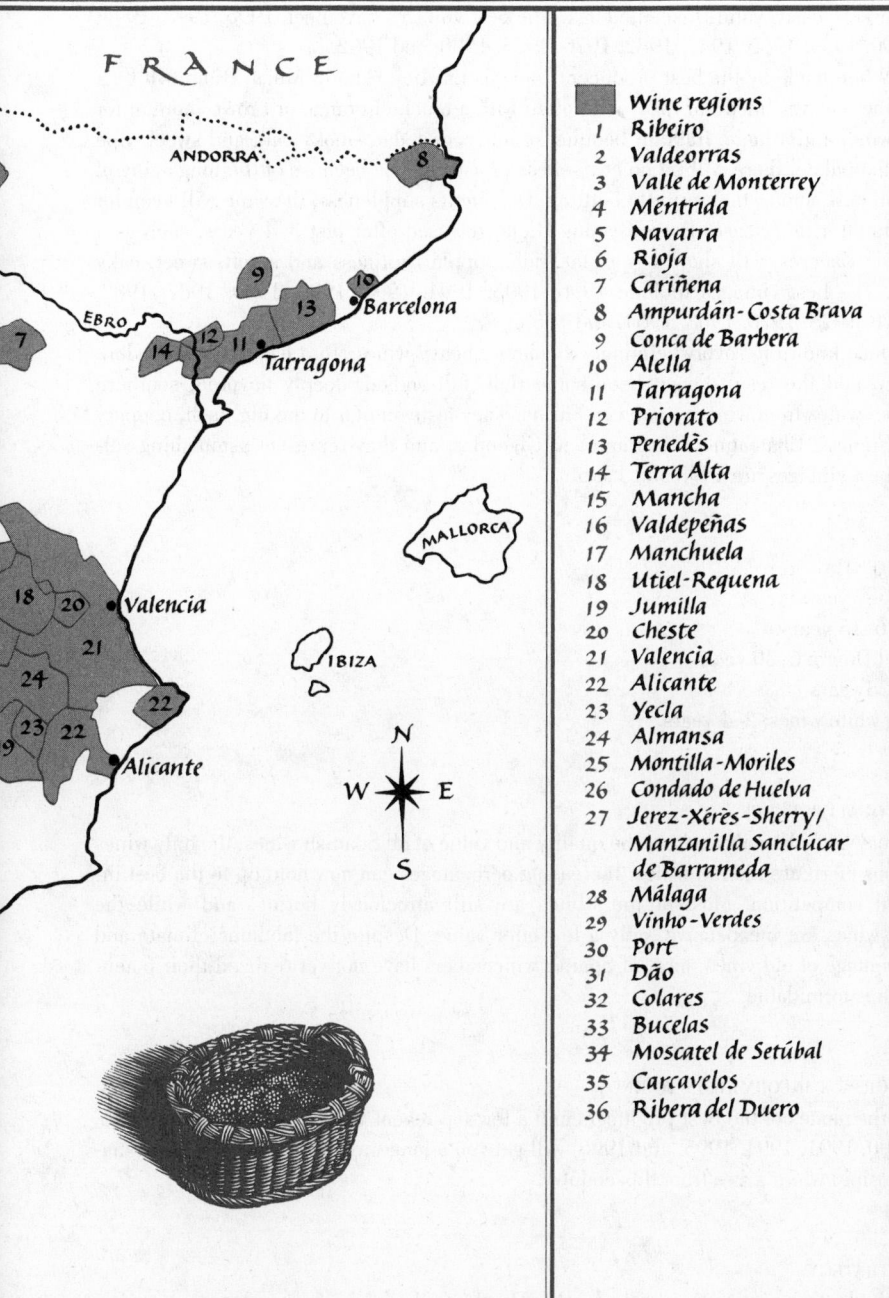

FRANCE

ANDORRA

8

EBRO

9

13 •Barcelona

7

14 12 11

Tarragona

MALLORCA

18 20 •Valencia

21

24

23 22

9

22

•Alicante

IBIZA

N
W ✳ E
S

	Wine regions
1	Ribeiro
2	Valdeorras
3	Valle de Monterrey
4	Méntrida
5	Navarra
6	Rioja
7	Cariñena
8	Ampurdán-Costa Brava
9	Conca de Barbera
10	Alella
11	Tarragona
12	Priorato
13	Penedès
14	Terra Alta
15	Mancha
16	Valdepeñas
17	Manchuela
18	Utiel-Requena
19	Jumilla
20	Cheste
21	Valencia
22	Alicante
23	Yecla
24	Almansa
25	Montilla-Moriles
26	Condado de Huelva
27	Jerez-Xérès-Sherry/ Manzanilla Sanlúcar de Barrameda
28	Málaga
29	Vinho-Verdes
30	Port
31	Dão
32	Colares
33	Bucelas
34	Moscatel de Setúbal
35	Carcavelos
36	Ribera del Duero

remarkable purity of berry fruit that can be found in the top vintages. Take superripe fruit and combine it with a minimum of 3 years (in the case of Vega Sicilia, 8–12 years) in oak casks, and you have powerfully heady, supple, explosively rich wines that offer a great deal of spicy, sweet, toasty, vanillin-scented oak. The best vintages have been 1996, 1995, 1994, 1991, 1990, 1989, 1986, 1983, 1982, 1976, 1975, 1968, and 1962.

Rioja   When made by the best producers, such as La Rioja Alta or Muga, Rioja will be a mature wine having a medium ruby color often with a touch of orange or brown (normal for an older wine) and a huge, fragrant bouquet of tobacco, cedar, smoky oak, and sweet, ripe fruit. On the palate, there will be no coarseness or astringence because of the long aging of the wine in cask and/or tank prior to bottling. Despite its suppleness, the wine will keep for 5–10 years after its release. Even a young Rioja, released after just 3–4 years, such as a Marqués de Cáceres, will show a ripe, fat, rich, supple fruitiness and a soft, sweet, oaky character. The best vintages include 1996, 1995, 1994, 1991, 1990, 1989, 1987, 1982, 1981, 1978, 1973, 1970, 1968, 1964, and 1958.

Toro   Once known for overwhelmingly alcoholic, heavy wines, Toro has adopted modern technology, and the results have been some rich, full-bodied, deeply flavored, southern Rhône–like wines from wineries such as Farina. They taste similar to the big, lush, peppery wines of France's Châteauneuf du Pape and Gigondas, and they represent astonishing values. The best vintages are 1998 and 1996.

AGING POTENTIAL
Navarra: 5–7 years
Penedès: 6–15 years
Ribera del Duero: 6–30 years
Rioja: 6–25 years
Sparkling white wines: 2–4 years

OVERALL QUALITY LEVEL
While it may be fashionable to tout the quality and value of all Spanish wines, the only wines with serious merit are the red wines. Increasing percentages can now hold up to the best international competition. Most of the whites are still atrociously boring, and while the sparkling wines are inexpensive, only a few offer value. Despite the fabulous climate and high percentage of old vines, most of Spain's winemakers have not yet realized their potential, which is formidable.

MOST IMPORTANT INFORMATION TO KNOW
Knowing the names of the best producers and a few top recent vintages (1982, 1985, 1986, 1987, 1990, 1991, 1994, 1995, and 1996) will get you a long way if you avoid the great majority of insipid white wines from this country.

BUYING STRATEGY
Spain is the hottest wine region in the world. Thanks to the work of several innovative importers, particularly Jorge Ordonez and Eric Solomon, this country is securing a bigger and bigger share of the fine wine market, as well as continuing to provide a bevy of exceptional bargains. There are some stormclouds on the horizon due to the fact that much of Spain had less than stellar vintages in 1997 and 1998. However, there are abundant quantities of high-

quality 1994s, 1995s, and 1996s in the marketplace, as well as others scheduled to be released over the next several years. Given the terrific climate, the multitude of fabulous *terroirs*, and the requisite financial incentive to produce world-class wine, look for more and more unknown names to become overnight stars.

VINTAGE GUIDE

1997—Because this was a difficult vintage throughout Spain, the quality in 1997 is significantly below the levels achieved in 1994, 1995, and 1996.

1996—This is a spectacular vintage in Ribera del Duero and good to very good in Priorato and Rioja.

1995—In many areas of Spain this vintage will turn out to be as stunning as 1994. Everyone from Rioja, Ribera del Duero, and Priorato was thrilled with the ripeness and richness. As my early tastings have indicated, these wines can often be as stunning as the 1994s. It appears to be a great vintage for Spain's top producers.

1994—Spanish wine producers are beating their breasts with considerable enthusiasm, claiming 1994 is Spain's vintage of the century. It was one of the hottest years on record, and unlike France, Spain was not troubled by September rain. Reports from such great wine regions as Rioja and Ribera del Duero are nothing short of spectacular. Such lesser-known regions as Toro, Priorato, Navarra, and Penedès are also raving about their wines' quality.

1993—A more homogeneous and successful vintage in Spain than in other Western European wine regions, 1993, while very good, will undoubtedly be overshadowed by the greatness of 1994.

1992—This is a mixed vintage because of the heavy rains that hit most of northern Spain. In Rioja producers talked about a great vintage until the harvest was picked in a soaking downpour. Good—rather than outstanding—quality wines have emerged. At least one great wine was produced: the 1992 Cabernet Sauvignon of Marqués de Griñon from his Dominio de Valdepusa.

1991—This was a better vintage for most of Spain than it was in France. Many top viticultural areas, such as Ribera del Duero and Rioja, have produced high-quality wines. Spain is one of Europe's surprising success stories in this vintage.

1990—Overall an abundant, high-quality crop was produced throughout Spain, but the quality is less consistent than in France or Italy.

1989—Another generous, abundant crop of good-quality wine was produced.

1988—A cooler but certainly good year for Spain, with most areas reporting good rather than excellent or outstanding quality.

1987—Rioja is considered to be of very high quality and not far off the mark of wines produced in Rioja's two best vintages of the decade of the eighties, 1981 and 1982. Elsewhere the vintage is mixed, although it is generally considered to be above average in quality.

1986—Considered to be spectacular in the Duero, the crop size was down from 1985. In Rioja it is a good year.

1985—Virtually every wine-producing region of Spain reported 1985 to be a very successful, high-quality vintage. In Rioja it was a record-setting crop in size.

1984—This vintage has a terrible reputation because of a poor, cool European summer, but the better red wines of Spain have turned out to be among the best made in Europe.

1983—A hot, dry year caused some problems, but the wines range from good to very good.

1982—For Rioja and Ribera del Duero this was the finest vintage since 1970 and largely regarded as a great year, superior to 1985 and equal to 1986 in the Duero.

1981—Spain enjoyed a very good vintage in 1981, but as time has passed it has become apparent that Rioja had an exceptional year, in many cases equal to 1982.

1980—An average-quality year.

1979—A good year in the Penedès area, but only average in Rioja.

1978—For Rioja, Penedès, and the Ribera del Duero, the best overall vintage between 1970 and 1981.

OLDER VINTAGES

For most of northern Spain, 1970 was a great vintage. Prior to that, 1964 was another superb vintage. Well-kept bottles of 1970 and 1964 red wines from Rioja and the Ribera del Duero are still excellent.

RATING SPAIN'S BEST PRODUCERS OF DRY RED TABLE WINES

* * * * * (OUTSTANDING)

Abadia Retuerta Cuvée Campanario (Sardon del Duero)

Abadia Retuerta Cuvée Palomar (Sardon del Duero)

Abadia Retuerta Pago Negralato (Sardon del Duero)

Abadia Retuerta Valdebon (Sardon del Duero)

Bodegas Ismael Arroyo Valsotillo Reserva (Ribera del Duero)

Artadi Rioja Grandes Anadas Reserva Especial (Rioja)

Artadi Rioja Pagos Viejos Reserva (Rioja)

Artadi Rioja Vina El Pison Reserva (Rioja)

Clos Dofi (Priorato)

Rene Barbier Clos Mogador (Priorato)

Clos Erasmus (Priorato)

CVNE Contino (Rioja)

L'Ermita (Priorato)

Muga Prado Enea Reserva (Rioja)

Marqués de Murrieta Castillo Ygay Gran Reserva (Rioja)

Pesquera Ribera del Duero (Castilla-León)

Dominico de Pingus (Duero)

Remelluri (Rioja)

Fernando Remirez de Ganuza Rioja Old Vines Unfiltered (Rioja)

Bodegas Reyes Teofilo Reyes (Ribera del Duero)

La Rioja Alta Reserva 890 (Rioja)

La Rioja Alta Reserva 904 (Rioja)

Senoria de San Vicente (Rioja)

Sierra Cantabria Rioja Coleccion Privada (Rioja)

Vega Sicilia N.V. Gran Reserva Especial (Ribera del Duero)

Vega Sicilia Unico Reserva (Ribera del Duero)

* * * * (EXCELLENT)

Abadia Retuerta (Sardon del Duero)

Abadia Retuerta Rivola (Sardon del Duero)

Albet I Noya Sat (Penedès)

Bodegas Ismael Arroyo Valsotillo (Ribera del Duero)

Artadi Rioja Vina de Gain Crianza (Rioja)

Bodegas Arzuaga Reserva (Ribera del Duero)

René Barbier (Cataluna)

Can Rafols dels Caus Penedès (Cataluna)

Capcanes Garnacha Especial (Tarragona)

Bodegas Julian Chivite 125 Anniversario Reserva (Navarra)

Clos Martinet (Priorato)

Costers del Siurdana—Clos de l'Obac (Priorato)

CVNE Imperial (Rioja)

CVNE Viña Real (Rioja)

Domecq-Marqués de Arienzo Reserva (Rioja)

Enate Crianza (Somontano)

Faustino Martinez Faustino I (Rioja)

J. M. Fuentes Gran Clos (Priorato)

Fra Fulco Carignan Vinyes Velles (Cataluna)

Grandes Bodegas Marqués de Velilla Reserva (Ribera del Duero)

Mas Igneus FA 112 (Priorato)

Jean Léon Penedès (Cataluna)
Martinez Bujanda Conde de Valdemar
(Rioja)
Martinez Bujanda Conde de Valdemar
Gran Reserva (Rioja)
Bodegas Mauro
Bodegas Muga (Rioja)****/*****
Marqués de Murrieta Coleccion 2100
(Rioja)
Marqués de Murrieta Reserva (Rioja)
Baron de Ona Rioja Reserva (Rioja)
La Rioja Alta Viña Alberdi (Rioja)
La Rioja Alta Arana (Rioja)
La Rioja Alta Ardanza (Rioja)

Marqués de Riscal Baron de Chirel (Rioja)
Bodegas Rodero S. L. Val Ribeno Crianza
(Ribera del Duero)
Bodegas Telmo Rodriguez Alma (Navarra)
Scala dei Priorato Cartoixa Priorat
(Cataluna)
Sierra Cantabria (Rioja)
Vega Sauco Reserva (Toro)
Vega Sicilia Valbuena (Ribera del Duero)
Bodegas de Vilarino-Cambados (Rias
Baixas)
Vinicola del Priorat (Priorato)
Bodegas y Vinedos Alion (Ribera del
Duero)

* * * (GOOD)

Agricola de Borja (Campo de Borja)
Señorío de Almansa (Castillo-La Mancha)
Amezola de la Mora (Rioja)
Arboles de Castillejo (La Mancha)
Palacio de Arganza Bierzo (Castilla-León)
Bodegas Ismael Arroyo (Ribera del
Duero)***/****
Pablo Barrigon Tovar (Castilla-León)
Pablo Barrigon Tovar San Pablo (Castilla-
León)
Pablo Barrigon Tovar Viña Cigalena
Reserva (Castilla-León)
Pablo Barrigon Tovar Viña Solona (Castilla-
León)
Masia Barril Priorato (Cataluna)
Bilbainas Viña Pomal (Rioja)
Marqués de Cáceres (Rioja)
Marqués de Cáceres Reserva (Rioja)
Campo Viejo (Rioja)
Julian Chivite Gran Feudo (Navarra)
Martin Codax Albarino white wine (Galicia)
CVNE Cune (Rioja)
Estola (Castillo-La Mancha)
Farina Colegiata Toro (Castilla-León)
Farina Gran Colegiata Toro (Castilla-León)
Faustino Martinez Faustino V (Rioja)
Faustino Martinez Faustino VII (Rioja)
Franco Españolas Bordon (Rioja)
Marqués de Griñon (Ribera del Duero)
Marqués de Griñon (Rioja)
Marqués de Griñon Cabernet Sauvignon
(Dominio de Valdepusa)
Inviosa Lar de Barros (Extremadura)
Baron de Ley El Coto (Rioja)

Lan Viña Lanciano Reserva (Rioja)
Los Llanos Valdepeñas (Castillo-
La Mancha)
Lopez de Heredia Bosconia Reserva (Rioja)
Lopez de Heredia Tondonia Reserva (Rioja)
Bodegas Magana (Navarra)
Mauro Ribera del Duero (Castilla-León)
Montecillo Viña Monty Reserva (Rioja)
Bodegas Hermanos Morales (La Mancha)
Bodegas Nekeas Vega Sindoa El Chaparral
Old Vine (Navarra)
Ochoa Reserva (Navarra)
Parxet Alella white wine (Cataluna)
Perez Pascuas Viña Pedrosa Ribera del
Duero (Castilla-León)
Pazo de Señorans Rias Baixas white wine
(Galicia)
Piqueras Castilla de Almansa (Castillo-
La Mancha)
Salvador Poveda (Alicante)
Raimat Costers del Segre (Cataluna)
Rioja Santiago Gran Condal (Rioja)
Riojanas Monte Real Reserva (Rioja)
Santiago Ruiz Rias Baixas Albarino white
wine (Galicia)
Bodegas de Sarria Gran Viño del Señorío
Reserva (Navarra)
Bodegas de Sarria Viña del Perdon
(Navarra)
Scala dei Priorato Negre (Cataluna)
Miguel Torres Coronas Penedès
(Cataluna)
Miguel Torres Gran Coronas Penedès
(Cataluna)

Miguel Torres Gran Coronas Black Label
    Penedès (Cataluna); since 1981, for
    vintages prior to and including
    1981*****
Torres Gran Sangre de Toro Penedès
    (Cataluna)
Miguel Torres Gran Viña Sol Green Label
    Penedès (Cataluna)

Miguel Torres Viña Sol Penedès (Cataluna)
Viñas del Vero Compania Somontano
    (Aragon)
Castilla de Vinicole Grand Verdad
    (Castillo-La Mancha)
Castilla de Vinicole Señorío de Duadianeja
    (Castillo-La Mancha)

* * (AVERAGE)

Alavesas Solar de Samaniego (Rioja)
Los Arcos Bierzo (Castilla-León)
Masia Bach Penedès (Cataluna)
Berberana Berberana Reserva (Rioja)
Berberana Carta de Plata (Rioja)
Berceo (Rioja)
Beronia (Rioja)
Bilbainas Viña Paceta (Rioja)
Bilbainas Viña Zaco (Rioja)
Bleda Jumilla (Murcia)
Bordejé (Aragon)
Borruel (Aragon)
Campo Viejo (Rioja)
Carricas (Navarra)
Casa de la Viña (Castillo-La Mancha)
Castano Yecla (Murcia)
Corral Don Jacobo (Rioja)
Cueva del Granero (Castillo-La Mancha)
Augusto Egli (Valencia)
Eval (Alicante)
Freixenet Penedès (Cataluna)
Frutos Villar Cigales (Castilla-León)
Poveda Garcia (Alicante)
Irache Gran Irache (Navarra)
Lagunilla Viña Herminia (Rioja)
Lan Lander (Rioja)
Lopez de Heredia Cubillo (Rioja)

Louis Megia Duque de Estrada (Castillo-
    La Mancha)
Marqués de Monistrol Penedès (Cataluna)
Montecillo Cumbrero (Rioja)
Olarra Anares (Rioja)
Olarra Anares Gran Reserva (Rioja)
Olarra Cerro Añon Gran Reserva (Rioja)
Olarra Cerro Añon Reserva (Rioja)
Frederico Paternina Banda Azul (Rioja)
Frederico Paternina Conde de los Andes
    Gran Reserva (Rioja)
Frederico Paternina Viña Vial (Rioja)
Penalba Lopez Ribera del Duero (Castilla-
    León)
Pulido Romero (Medellin)
Raimat (Costers del Segre)
Castell del Remei (Cataluna)
Ribero Duero Ribera del Duero (Castilla-
    León)
Marqués de Riscal Gran Reserva (Rioja)
Marqués de Riscal Reserva (Rioja)
Ruiz (Canamero)
Miguel Torres Pinot Noir Penedès
    (Cataluna)
Unidas Age Marqués de Romeral (Rioja)
Unidas Age Siglo (Rioja)
Viños de León (Castilla-León)

RATING SPAIN'S BEST PRODUCERS OF SPARKLING WINE

* * * * (EXCELLENT)

Marqués de Gelida

Leopardi Llopart

* * * (GOOD)

Bilbainas
Cadiz
Cavas Ferret
Chandon
Gran Cordornieu Brut

Freixenet Cuvée DS
Freixenet Reserva Real
Juvé y Champs Gran Cru
Juvé y Champs Gran Reserva
Juvé y Champs Reserva de la Familia

Mont Marcal Brut
Josep-Maria Raventos Blanc Brut
Segura Viudas Aria

Segura Viudas Brut Vintage
Segura Viudas Reserva Heredad

* (AVERAGE)

Castellblanch
Conde de Caralt
Paul Cheneau
Cordornieu Extra Dry
Cordornieu Non-Plus-Ultra
Cordornieu Rosé Brut
Freixenet Brut Nature
Freixenet Carta Nevada

Freixenet Cordon Negro
Lembey
Marqués de Monistrol
Muga Conde de Haro
Castello de Perelada
Segura Viudas Brut
Segura Viudas Rosé

SPAIN'S GREATEST RED WINE BARGAINS

Agricola de Borja (Campo de Borja)
Albet I Noya Sat (Penedès)
Señorío de Almansa (Castillo-La Mancha)
Arboles de Castillejo (La Mancha)
Ismael Arroyo (Ribera del Duero)
Berberana d'Avalos Tempranillo (Rioja)
Berberana d'Avalos Tempranillo Tinto
   (Rioja)
Dominio Eguren Protocolo (Manchuela)
Farina Colegiata Toro (Castilla-León)
Farina Gran Colegiata Toro (Castilla-León)
Marqués de Griñon (Rioja)
Marqués de Griñon Durius (Rioja)
Jean León Penedès (Cataluna)

Los Llanos Valdepeñas (Castillo-
   La Mancha)
Bodegas Magana (Navarra)
Bodegas Nekeas (Navarra)
Martinez Bujanda Conde Valdemar Viño
   Tinto (Rioja)
Bodegas Hermanos Morales (La Mancha)
Marqués de Murrieta Tinto Crianza (Rioja)
La Rioja Alta Viña Arana (Rioja)
La Rioja Alta Viña Ardanza (Rioja)
Bodegas de Sarria Gran Viño del Señoría
   Reserva (Navarra)
Bodegas Sierra Cantabria (Rioja)
Vinicola del Priorato (Priorato)

ABADIA RETUERTA (SARDON DEL DUERO)

1996	Cuvée Campanario	D	93+
1996	Cuvée Palomar	D	92+
1996	Pago Negralato	EE	(93–96)
1997	Rivola	B	87
1996	Rivola	B	89
1996	Valdebelon	EE	(96–97)

This is one of the most exciting projects in all of Europe. With over 500 acres planted in vines, just outside the appellation of Ribera del Duero, this large, impeccably run enterprise seems set to become a dominant player at the top of the Spanish wine hierarchy. All of the vineyards, planted at elevations of between 2,100 to 2,700 feet, are hand-harvested. The state-of-the-art winery, designed with the assistance of Bordeaux's Pascal Delbeck, contains over 80 fermentation tanks and a design that allows everything to be accomplished by gravity, as opposed to pumps, which can bruise a wine. All of the following wines are aged in small oak casks, primarily French (some American oak is utilized), and the wines are bottled without filtration. This high-quality winery will turn many a skeptical head now that the following offerings have been released.

A good introduction to this estate's wines is the 1997 Rivola, one of the finest values in the wine market. Made from 60% Tempranillo and 40% Cabernet Sauvignon, it is a pretty, round, richly fruity offering with plenty of charm, as well as sexy, smoky oak in the background. The wine spent only 3 months in oak casks, resulting in a fruit- rather than wood-driven personality. Medium ruby colored, with forthcoming aromatics and seductive fruit flavors (cherries and currants), it should be consumed over the next year.

One of the best values I discovered in 1997 was Abadia Retuerta's debut vintage (7,000 cases) of 1996 Rivola. Made from 60% Tempranillo and 40% Cabernet Sauvignon that is aged for 3 months in new French and American oak casks, it tastes like a $30 bottle of red wine. A knockout nose of smoke, charcoal, and cassis is intense and pure. The wine hits the palate with a blast of dense, creamy-textured, rich, black currant, and cherry fruit. Medium to full bodied, with an opulent texture and plenty of sweet, spicy *pain grillé* notes, this is a sexy, lush, gorgeously made wine. Already drinking splendidly well, it possesses the necessary stuffing to last for 5–7 years. Think of it as a blend of a first-class Pomerol and Vega Sicilia Unico. Don't miss this one!

There are 5,000 cases of the dark ruby/purple-colored 1996 Abadia Retuerta. A blend of 65% Tempranillo, 30% Cabernet Sauvignon, and 5% Merlot, this offering is aged in an assortment of French and American oak, of which 50% is new, and is bottled unfiltered. The 1996 exhibits a Médoc-like personality, with notes of black currants, cherries, lead pencil, and *pain grillé*. In the mouth, it is medium bodied, elegant, and complex, with hints of tobacco leaf, fruitcake, and cedar. This savory, spicy, well-endowed wine should drink well now and over the next decade.

The following wines are produced in more limited quantities (between 100- and 1,500-case lots) and are meant to exploit the microclimates of particular vineyard sites. The 1996 Cuvée Palomar is a 50% Cabernet Sauvignon/50% Tempranillo blend. The latter varietal comes from a chalky hillside, and the Cabernet Sauvignon comes from a gravelly vineyard that was once a riverbed. The 1996 was aged in 100% new French oak and bottled without filtration after 16 months of aging. It boasts an impressively saturated dark ruby/purple color, as well as complex aromas of cedar, new saddle leather, roasted herbs, and black currants. Rich, full bodied, and harmonious, this elegant yet authoritatively flavorful wine exhibits impressive purity and overall equilibrium. Moderate tannin in the finish suggests 2–3 years of bottle age will be beneficial. The wine is capable of lasting for 15 or more years. The 100% Tempranillo 1996 Cuvée Campanario represents a blend of the finest parcels of Tempranillo. The wine was aged in 100% new French Limousin oak for 16 months, then bottled without filtration. It reveals a saturated purple color and is more backward both aromatically and on the palate, as well as more impressive. The wine's bouquet falls in the black fruit spectrum of aromas—blackberries, black raspberries, and overripe cherries. Full bodied and tightly knit, with intriguing mineral notes, this powerful, rich, layered wine could easily pass for a top-class Bordeaux in a blind tasting. As a result of 28 days of maceration, the high tannin is sweet and well integrated in the wine's framework. However, I would not recommend drinking this offering for a few more years. Anticipated maturity: 2001–2020.

The 1996 Pago Negralato was to be bottled approximately 1 month after I tasted it. Made from a single Tempranillo vineyard planted more than 2,100 feet above sea level, the wine exhibits a distinctive character thanks to the alluvial and clay soil mixture. This is unquestionably a spectacular effort, displaying a saturated purple color and knockout aromas of blackberry, chocolate, licorice, and earthy. Exquisitely balanced, this full-bodied wine is crammed with fruit, yet it does not come across as heavy or overbearing. Along with its single-vineyard sibling, the Valdebelon, this wine has benefited from having its malolactic take place in barrel (which tends to integrate the wood into the wine earlier and, some say, more effectively than when it is done in tank). The layers of fruit are ripe, the wine's purity impeccable, and the overall balance impressive. This stunningly rich, potentially brilliant wine will admirably showcase the heights that Tempranillo can achieve. Anticipated maturity: 2002–2018.

Last, the 1996 Valdebelon is made from a parcel of 100% Cabernet Sauvignon planted in the estate's highest vineyard (at an altitude of over 2,400 feet). With yields of under 1½ tons of fruit per acre, this wine is reminiscent of an exotic, hypothetical blend of Mouton-Rothschild and Latour. The color is opaque purple, and the nose offers up aromas of black currants, lead pencil, minerals, walnuts, and crème de cassis. Structured, dense, and full bodied, with an exotic, flamboyant personality, this superb, concentrated Cabernet Sauvignon is ostentatious at present but will undoubtedly shut down after several years in the bottle, unfolding slowly over the next 2 decades.

Congratulations are in order for this impressive new winery that is already turning out wines of exceptional quality.

BODEGAS ALBET I NOYA (PENEDÈS)

1996 Cabernet	C	85
1994 Cabernet Sauvignon	C	88
1993 Cabernet Sauvignon	C	88
1995 Cabernet Sauvignon Estate	C	86
1995 Reserva Marti	C	86+
1995 Tempranillo	C	84?
1994 Tempranillo	C	85
1993 Tempranillo	C	89

These are modern-style reds from the appellation of Penedès in Spain's Catalonia region. The 1996 Cabernet exhibits an opaque purple color, followed by green pepper, spicy, licorice, and red currant aromas. In the mouth, there is some leanness, and the flavors are more red than black currants. Moderate tannin in the finish gives the wine a certain angularity/austerity. This is a good, well-structured, cleanly made wine for consuming over the next 4–5 years. The 1995 Reserva Marti (a 60% Tempranillo, 30% Cabernet Sauvignon, 10% Syrah blend) reveals more noticeable new oak in the cherry-scented, moderately intense aromatics. The wine possesses good roundness and richness, but the oak is intrusive. There is moderate tannin and fine volume, purity, and overall balance, but the threshold of wood flavoring is too elevated. This wine should drink decently for 5–6 years.

The two 1993s offer serious levels of intensity and plenty of sweet, toasty new oak. They exhibit a more international style than most Spanish red wines. I have a slight preference for the saturated ruby/purple-colored 1993 Tempranillo because of its more intense fragrance and sweeter, more up-front, jammy, black cherry and cassis fruit. It is voluptuously textured, with low acidity, light tannin, and a rich, fleshy, medium- to full-bodied finish. This impressively made wine will drink well over the next 7–8 years. The 1993 Cabernet Sauvignon displays medium to full body, an excellent, precise nose of spicy new oak, tobacco, and subtly herbaceous cassis fruit, excellent concentration, good spice, moderate tannin, and fine cleanliness and balance. A little more soul would have propelled both of these wines into the outstanding category. Although the Cabernet Sauvignon is more structured, it can be drunk now and over the next decade.

These designer-packaged wines (note the heavy, tall glass bottles and fancy labels) are well made in an international/California-like style. The 1994 Tempranillo exhibits ripe, curranty fruit, tart acidity, medium body, and clean, oenologically correct and measured winemaking. Drink it over the next 2–3 years. The 1994 Cabernet Sauvignon reveals a more impressively saturated, dark ruby/purple color, a moderately endowed, black currant- and toast-scented nose, medium body, good ripeness, tart acidity (added?), fine purity, and an attractive international style of new oak, ripe fruit, and religiously clean winemaking. It offers more depth and personality than the Tempranillo. For the price it is a good value, given what is happening in the wine market today. Drink it over the next 7–8 years.

I have mixed emotions concerning the 1995 Tempranillo. It was hard to find much to like about the overtly herbaceous, vegetal, coffee-scented nose. However, once past the greenness, the wine exhibits an excellent ripe berry fruitiness, medium body, and fine spiciness. More interesting is the 1995 Cabernet Sauvignon Estate. It exhibits a dense ruby/purple color, followed by uncomplicated, spicy, black currant flavors that are ripe, grapey, and cleanly presented. This foursquare, rich, chunky wine is a reasonably good value in Cabernet that should drink well for 5–8 years.

BODEGAS ANTANO (VALLADOLID)

1995 Vina Cobranza	C	86
1994 Vina Cobranza Reserva	C	85

Both of these wines are produced from Tempranillo grown in the Valladolid area of Spain. The 1995 Vina Cobranza exhibits a healthy dark ruby color, as well as sweet black cherry fruit, medium body, good cleanliness, and a spicy, light- to medium-bodied finish. Drink it over the next year. The 1994 Vina Cobranza is denser and kinkier, with saddle leather, flowers, spice, and blackberry aromas and flavors. Medium bodied, with surprising acidity, good punch and depth, and a sour cherry-like finish, it should be consumed over the next 1–2 years.

BODEGAS ISMAEL ARROYO (RIBERA DEL DUERO)

1991 Mesoneros de Castilla Crianza	B	88
1996 Valsotillo	C	92+
1995 Valsotillo	C	90+
1994 Valsotillo	C	90+?
1991 Valsotillo	D	87
1990 Valsotillo Gran Reserva	E	93+
1989 Valsotillo Gran Reserva	E	95
1994 Valsotillo Reserva	D	92
1990 Valsotillo Reserva	D	92+

The Ribera del Duero is one of the hotbeds of high-quality Spanish wines, as investors and new producers emerge with each new vintage. While the 1991 Valsotillo will not make anyone forget the marvelous 1990, it is an excellent wine, with a dark ruby/purple color, a rich, spicy, smoky, black raspberry-scented nose, dense, concentrated, low-acid, firmly structured flavors, and intense length. The wine is still closed and thus will benefit from 1 hour of decanting. It should easily last for 15–20 years. As so often happens with such profound wines, only small quantities (80 cases) of the 1989 Valsotillo Gran Reserva are available in the United States. The wine possesses an opaque ruby/purple color and a fabulous nose of minerals, sweet, rich, black cherry and black raspberry fruit intermingled with a subtle hint of wood. Remarkably concentrated, with formidable flavor extract, great intensity and purity, and impressive levels of extract, glycerin, and alcohol, this is a full-bodied, rather huge wine that should drink well for 20–30 years. It is even more concentrated than some of the greatest vintages of its nearby neighbor—Vega Sicilia. Although approachable because of its extraordinary ripeness, it will hit its prime at the turn of the century and last for 2 decades.

I have been putting my money where my mouth is with this wine, having purchased the 1989 and waiting patiently for it to reach full maturity. These are uncompromising wines of extraordinary power and richness that are hugely extracted but ferociously tannic. They are aged in some of Spain's coldest cellars (located 90 feet below the surface with a constant temperature of 52 degrees Fahrenheit). As a result, they tend to be extremely backward and unevolved when released. The 1994 Valsotillo, from one of Spain's greatest vintages this century, is made from 100% Tinta del Pais and spends 14 months in barrels, of which 90% are American oak. The production is approximately 8,000 cases and the Gran Reserva only 500 cases. The 1994 Valsotillo should be purchased only by readers with 20–25 years of drinking life left in their throats and livers. This opaque saturated purple-colored wine is totally closed. The nose reluctantly offers up sweet, earthy, blueberry/blackberry fruit, along with aromas of underbrush, *garrigue,* and minerals. Although massive and awesomely extracted, the wine is painfully tannic. Undoubtedly it is a blockbuster, but when will it reach maturity . . . 5, 10, or 15 years? The raw materials are present for a promising future.

The 1990 Valsotillo Gran Reserva could easily be put in a tasting next to Henri Bonneau's Réserve des Célestins Châteauneuf du Pape. It boasts an opaque garnet color, followed by earthy, smoked beef, blood, and black fruit aromas with a whiff of jammy cherries. Extremely full bodied, dense, muscular, virile, and almost excessive in its extract and power, this is a huge, leviathan of a wine that will require an additional 5–6 years of cellaring. It has at least 25–30 years of aging potential, but I am not convinced all the tannin will ever fully melt away. However, no one may care, as this wine offers a smorgasbord of aromas and flavors.

Both the 1991 Mesoneros de Castilla Crianza and the 1990 Valsotillo Reserva are made from an old clone of the Tempranillo grape, called the Tinta del Pais. They are impressive wines from an up-and-coming star of this undiscovered viticultural region. The 1991 Mesoneros de Castilla Crianza exhibits an opaque ruby/purple color and a tight but promising nose of black fruits, damp earth, and spices. Muscular and concentrated, with moderate tannin, and a full-bodied, highly extracted, backward, pure, rich style, this *bodega*'s cellars are among the coldest of Spain, thus the unevolved state of this wine. It is an impressive, potentially 20-year wine that can be purchased for a song. Although accessible, it will not reach full maturity for another 2–3 years.

Even more impressive is the top cuvée, the 1990 Valsotillo Reserva. Also made from 100% Tinta del Pais, it is a classic, superrich, full-bodied, marvelously concentrated wine that should age effortlessly for 20–25+ years. Made from extremely old vines, the wine reveals a saturated, opaque purple color and a huge, intense nose of black fruits, minerals, licorice, and spice. Full bodied, with sweeter tannin than its sibling, this is a youthful, awesomely rich wine, whose tannin level is concealed by a remarkable quantity of concentrated fruit. It will evolve slowly over the next 20+ years. It is a great bargain since this estate is known only by a handful of insiders.

The 1996 Valsotillo, made from 100% Tinta del Pais, spent 14 months in barrel and was bottled with no fining yet a light filtration. Its opaque purple color promises more potential than such top vintages as 1989 and 1994. The wine offers a barrage of blackberry fruit intermixed with smoke, licorice, truffle, and mineral scents. There is sensational purity, full body, and a blueberry/blackberry fruitiness that lingers on the palate for over 30 seconds. There is loads of sweet tannin in this full-bodied, massively endowed wine, but it is extremely ripe and well integrated. This should prove to be one of the more dazzling regular bottlings that the Bodegas Ismael Arroyo has yet produced. Sadly, there are only 250 cases for the United States. Anticipated maturity: 2000–2015. The 1995 Valsotillo has closed down since I first tasted it. The wine still reveals an opaque purple color, as well as thick, chewy, highly extracted flavors of black cherries, blackberries, and roasted herbs. Intense, thick, and viscous, yet restrained when compared with the more ostentatious 1996 and ultraconcentrated 1994 Reserva, this outstanding wine should drink well between 2000 and 2015.

The 1994 Valsotillo Reserva (made from 100% Tinta del Pais that spent 24 months in oak) reveals a similar personality but is more powerful, evolved, and intoxicating in terms of its brash display of blackberry liqueur intermixed with licorice, mineral, and floral scents. This opaque purple-colored, full-bodied wine is brawny, expansive, rich, and brilliantly well balanced. Anticipated maturity: 2000–2015.

ARTADI (RIOJA)

1994 Rioja Grandes Anadas Reserva Especial	EE	96
1994 Rioja Pagos Viejos Reserva	D	92
1994 Rioja Viña El Pison Reserva	D	93+
1995 Rioja Viña de Gain Crianza	C	90

This estate qualifies as a fabulous discovery. A relatively new enterprise dedicated to producing wines at the top of the qualitative hierarchy, Artadi has turned out four spectacular Riojas. Founded in 1989, this winery possesses vineyards that are all planted at cool, high altitude (around 1,500 feet) *terroirs*. These are brilliant wines that merit considerable attention. The 1995 Rioja Viña de Gain Crianza is made from 40–50-year-old Tempranillo vines. The grapes were destemmed, fermented for a lengthy 30 days, and then aged for 24 months in equal portions of American and French oak casks. It is a beautiful, aromatic, elegant, savory, mouth-filling, well-nuanced, and textured Rioja. The lead pencil and berry fruit (blackberries and cherries), medium body, gorgeous layers of supple fruit, and lush, heady finish are alluring as well as pure and satisfying. The wine is already delicious, complex, and seamless, but it is capable of lasting for another decade. The 1994 Rioja Pagos Viejos Reserve is made from 100% Tempranillo (50-year-old vines) grown in a vineyard planted at 2,000 feet. The wine is given a lengthy fermentation/maceration and aged for 32 months in 100% new French oak casks. What I find so exceptional about this wine is that the oak is a very subtle component, which should give readers an idea of how rich and concentrated the wine's fruit is. The color is a saturated dark ruby/purple. The sweet nose of lead pencil, cassis, blackberries, minerals, and vanillin is followed by a full-bodied wine with opulent richness, a terrific texture, and sexy, open-knit, candied fruit flavors that gush across the palate with no hard edges. The finish exceeds 30 seconds. This is an immensely impressive, complex, compelling Rioja from a terrific vintage. Anticipated maturity: now–2014.

The tightest-knit, in addition to being the most backward, of this quartet of Artadi Riojas is the 1994 Rioja Viña El Pison Reserva. This dazzling wine is made in limited quantities (about 450 cases). Made from a Tempranillo vineyard planted in 1945 on pure limestone soil, and aged 24 months in 100% French oak casks, this tight, backward wine should be cellared for 5–6 years. The color is saturated opaque ruby/purple. The nose is tight but promising, with blackberry, cigar box, mineral, and *pain grillé* notes. Well delineated, full bodied, and well textured, this wine displays explosive richness and intensity at the back of the palate—always an encouraging sign for longevity. Outstanding purity and layers of fruit are buttressed by good acidity and sweet tannin. This superb Rioja has at least 2 decades of aging potential. Wow!

Despite my excitement over those three wines, consider the following. The 1994 Rioja Grandes Anadas Reserva Especial (made from a single Tempranillo vineyard planted 80–100 years ago) was aged for 40 months in 100% new French oak casks. Approximately 100 six-bottle cases were imported to the United States. This intellectually and hedonistically satisfying wine is one of the most compelling and prodigious Riojas I have ever tasted. It possesses amazing richness and a fabulous smoky, black fruit-scented nose that soars from the glass. Full bodied, with extraordinary richness, layers of fruit, beautifully integrated acidity, tannin, and wood, and a whoppingly long 45+-second finish, this wine must be tasted to be believed. It is also one of the most expensive Riojas I have ever tasted, but this wine has a 20-year upside potential. It is a tour de force in winemaking. Kudos to Artadi! Anticipated maturity: 2000–2020.

ARZUAGA (RIBERA DEL DUERO)

1995 Arzuaga Crianza	C	87
1994 Arzuaga Crianza	D	87
1994 Arzuaga Reserva	D	90

The 1994 Arzuaga Reserva's medium ruby color does not suggest the fragrance and flavor intensity possessed by this silky-textured wine. The knockout nose of spicy oak and jammy cherry/raspberry fruit is followed by a round, medium- to full-bodied wine with low acidity, lavish oak, gobs of fruit, and a velvety finish. Over the next 5–6 years, this crowd pleaser will provide opulent drinking.

Although the 1995 Arzuaga Crianza reveals a deeper saturated ruby color, less aromatic intensity, and a firmer palate, it merits enthusiasm for its cascade of berry fruit nicely wrapped in toasty oak. Medium bodied, firmer, and more woody, it is a hedonistically styled wine to drink over the next 4–5 years.

The modern-style (or is it international?) 1994 Crianza exhibits a dark ruby color and a sweet, lead pencil, *pain grillé*, toasty oak-scented nose with some attractive cola/black cherry and plumlike fruit flavors. Round, fleshy, and up-front, this is an attractive, medium-bodied red wine to drink over the next 5 years.

RENÉ BARBIER (CATALUNA)

1995 Clos Mogador	D	90+
1994 Clos Mogador	D	92
1992 Clos Mogador	D	90+

This luxury cuvée is from Priorato, an area in northern Spain that is eliciting considerable interest from the international wine crowd. The finest wines from Priorato are phenomenally concentrated and intense and generally need 8–10 years of cellaring. The 1992 from René Barbier could easily be inserted in a tasting with young, tannic, concentrated Bordeaux. It will require 10 years of cellaring before it sheds enough of its tannin to be attractive. The wine exhibits a dense, opaque ruby/purple color and plenty of sweet, spicy vanillin, and new oak in the nose, along with black currants and toast. Extremely youthful and backward, this full-bodied, concentrated wine tastes more like a barrel sample than a finished wine. However, it exhibits undeniable potential.

Proprietor René Barbier is a pioneer in the potentially superstar Tarragona region of Priorato. The 1994 is an old-vine Grenache-dominated wine (about 40%), with approximately 35% Cabernet Sauvignon, 20% Syrah, and the rest Pinot Noir and Merlot. Yields were frightfully low. While backward and tannic, the wine is dense, powerful, and rich, with an opaque black/plum color and aggressive levels of toasty new oak. If the oak was not so lavish, the wine might merit an even higher rating, because it is superextracted and pure, with remarkable balance for its massive size and weight. The 1994 requires 5–6 years of cellaring; it should age for 25 years or more. The 1995 exhibits sweeter fruit and aggressive oak, but better integration of the wood than its older sibling. Full bodied, with a blackberry, raspberry, peppery component to its aromas, along with the telltale *pain grillé* notes from new oak, an unctuous texture, and a whoppingly long, intense finish, it is almost too intense to drink at present. Anticipated maturity: 2003–2020.

AGRICOLA DE BORGIA (BORJA)

1997 Vina Borgia	A	87

One of the world's great wine values, this wine, made from 100% Grenache, is tank-fermented and aged. It offers something virtually no other region in the world seems capable of producing—an exuberant, gutsy, pure, rich, flavorful, dry, thrillingly priced red wine that can be drunk over the next 2 years. The color is dark ruby with purple nuances. This fruit-driven example offers up copious quantities of berry fruit in an uncomplicated, but nicely layered, medium-bodied, pure format. It is a savory red that I would be delighted to find in any bistro or trattoria. Fortunately it is widely available, as nearly 20,000 cases were brought into the United States. Drink it over the next year.

AGRICOLA DE BORJA (CAMPO DE BORJA)

1996 Borsao	A	86
1995 Borsao	A	88
1994 Borsao	A	89
1997 Viña Borja	A	87
1996 Viña Borgia	A	85
1995 Viña Borgia	A	87
1994 Viña Borgia	A	87

The two 1994s from the obscure viticultural region of Campo de Borja are, fortunately, not too limited in quantity. There are nearly 4,000 cases of the 1994 Viña Borgia and 10,000 cases of the 1994 Borsao Tinto. They are colossal values with prices from another era—the 1960s! The 1994 Viña Borgia Tinto exhibits a saturated dark ruby/purple color, a big, peppery, black cherry and curranty nose, medium-bodied, supple flavors, wonderful purity, an inner core of surprising richness and sweet fruit, and a long, heady, mouth-filling finish. Made from 100% Grenache (or, as the Spanish call it, Garnacha), it is unbelievably similar to a top-notch Côtes du Rhône that can be drunk now or cellared for 2–3 years. It is remarkable that a wine of this quality can be made for $4 a bottle. Even better is the 1994 Borsao Tinto, an 80% Grenache/20% Tempranillo blend that has seen no aging in oak. It possesses an amazingly saturated dark ruby/purple color, an intense, sweet nose of pepper, black cherries, and framboise, medium to full body, layers of concentrated fruit, low acidity, and a spicy, earthy, heady, glycerin-imbued finish. It appears to be Spain's answer to a good, fleshy, meaty Gigondas. Drink it over the next 5–6 years. These are amazing values!

Two remarkable bargains, both of the 1995s are primarily Grenache-based wines. They are Spain's answer to a luscious, peppery, ripe, smoky, medium- to full-bodied, supple Côtes du Rhône from France. The 1995 Viña Borgia (100% Garnacha; 10,000 cases for America) is an awesome value. The wine exhibits a deep ruby/purple color, a smoky, black cherry, peppery nose, wonderful texture, creamy, ripe, chewy fruit, excellent definition and richness, and a spicy, long finish. It is amazing that a wine of this quality, and mouth-filling levels of extract, ripeness, and purity, can be found for under $5 a bottle! The 1995 Borsao (80% Garnacha and 20% Tempranillo; 30,000 cases) emphasizes superb levels of ripe black cherry and raspberry fruit, with a roasted, smoky, peppery character, velvety texture, low acid, and a plush, medium-bodied, soft, surprisingly long finish. Both of these wines should drink well for 2–3 years. I asked the importer if there was one bottling or multiple bottlings based on demand, and I was told that only one bottling is done for his cuvée; thus the only bottle variation that might occur should be from bottles that have been mistreated in the distribution system. For the record, importer Jorge Ordonez ships everything to this country in temperature-controlled reefer containers.

Two more excellent bargains, the 1996s from the Agricola de Borja are not as fat and richly fruity as their 1995 and 1994 counterparts, but they are still among the better wine values available in the marketplace. The 1996 Viña Borgia (100% Grenache) is a medium to dark ruby-colored wine with a spicy, peppery, cherry-scented nose, robust, easygoing, medium-bodied flavors, and no hardness or angularity. Think of it as Spain's version of a Côtes du Rhône; consume it over the next 1–2 years. Revealing slightly more character, the 1996 Borsao (80% Grenache and 20% Tempranillo) is a distinctive, Rhône-like wine with earthy, peppery, cherrylike fruit. It is medium bodied and soft, with more smoke and black cherry characteristics than found in its sibling, good glycerin, fine, clean winemaking, and a spicy finish. It should drink well for 1–2 years.

A blend of 80% Grenache and 20% Tempranillo, the 1997 Camp de Borja displays a Côtes du Rhône-like character. Dark ruby colored, with peppery, black cherry, earthy, kirsch liqueur aromas, it provides uncomplicated, exuberant, zesty, fleshy fruit and good fat and length. The wine is both mouth filling and delicious—what else can readers ask for $5.50? It is all tank-fermented, and bottled early to preserve its freshness and lively fruit. Drink it over the next 12 months.

BODEGAS BRETON Y CIA (RIOJA)

1994 Dominico de Conté	D	87
1991 Dominico de Conté	D	89
1990 Dominico de Conté	E	91
1989 Dominico de Conté	E	87
1994 Lorinon Rioja Crianza	B	85
1994 Lorinon Rioja Reserva	C	88
1991 Rioja Reserva	D	86

Under the Lorinon label, some aromatic, soft, elegant, medium-bodied Riojas are produced. The 1994 Lorinon exhibits a medium ruby color, as well as fragrant, berry, mineral, and smoky aromatics, light-bodied, elegant flavors, and a supple finish. It is a delicate, finesse-style Rioja to drink over the next 2–3 years. The 1994 Lorinon Rioja Reserva possesses a deep ruby color, and pure, black cherry fruit nicely complemented by spicy oak. However, it appears less expressive than some of its siblings. I suspect this wine will merit a higher rating after another 5–6 months of bottle age. The dark ruby/garnet-colored 1991 Rioja Reserva offers a sweeter nose, with more smoke, lead pencil, tobacco, herbs, and red fruit scents. The wine possesses lively acidity, medium body, and an attractive, plush palate. It should drink well for 3–4 years.

The top cuvées, from a single vineyard, appear under the Dominico de Conté label. These wines are aged for 30 months in oak. The 1991 Dominico de Conté Rioja possesses a dark ruby color and an excellent, sweet, smoky, spicy, red fruit-scented nose. This well-crafted, medium-bodied, elegant Rioja offers excellent richness and length, moderate tannin, and a nicely textured finish. It should improve for another 2–3 years and last for 15 years. The fuller-bodied, dark plum-colored 1990 Dominico de Conté Rioja exhibits lower acidity and is fleshier and more concentrated in the mouth. This expansive, broad-shouldered wine displays the wonderful sweetness that is an undeniable characteristic of great vintages. Dense and rich, it provides superb aromatics as well as a medium- to full-bodied, concentrated finish with no hard edges. Already delicious, this compelling Rioja should continue to drink well for 10–15 years. The 1989 Dominico de Conté Rioja is similar to the 1991's style, with slightly less intensity and more elegance. The most mature of these offerings, it possesses an advanced deep garnet color. Although close to full maturity, it is capable of lasting another 10–12 years given the wine's jammy fruit, richness, and freshness. It offers up an excellent nose of smoke, roasted herbs, sweet cherry currant-like fruit, tobacco, and minerals. Rich and round, with no hard edges, this is an opulently textured, luscious style of Rioja to drink over the next decade.

I expected great things from the 1994 Dominico de Conté Rioja given the vintage's reputation and the high quality of so many wines. For whatever reason, the wine comes across as muted. Although very good, with sweet, jammy strawberry and cherry fruit infused with plenty of toasty oak, it lacks depth, complexity, and intensity in the finish. Drink it over the next 5–6 years.

CAPCANES (TARRAGONA)

1996 Garnacha Especial	D	92
1996 Capcanes Costers Del Gravet Les Vinyasses	C	90
1996 Capcanes Mas Donis Garnacha/Syrah Vinyes Velles	A	87

What a decadent, intense wine the 1996 Garnacha Especial has turned out to be. Made from 105-year-old Grenache vines, this could easily be a Spanish Châteauneuf du Pape . . . if there were such a thing. One major difference between this effort and most Châteauneuf du Papes is that 50% of the oak barrels in which this wine was aged were new. Nevertheless, the oak is only a smoky nuance in what is mainly a fruit, glycerin, and body-driven wine. This dark ruby/purple-colored, complex wine offers a penetrating fragrance of black cherries (kirsch liqueur), roasted herbs, black berries, and pepper. Intense and full bodied, with exciting levels of extract and terrific purity, this hedonistic, decadent, mouth-filling, velvety-textured wine can be drunk now or cellared for a decade or more. Very impressive!

The Capcanes Mas Conis 1996 is primarily a Grenache cuvée with a hefty amount of old-vine Syrah in the blend. Bottled without fining or filtration, the wine reveals an opaque purple color, a straightforward, gorgeously pure, ripe, black currant-and-kirsch-scented nose, a sweet, ripe, fleshy entry, abundant fruit, glycerin, and extract, and a soft, low-acid, ripe, fleshy finish. This hedonistic, deliciously rich, red wine should be consumed over the next 2–3 years. Two thousand cases were released in April of 1997. Even more serious is the Capcanes Costers del Gravet 1996 Les Vinyasses. Five hundred cases of this unfiltered wine were released in September 1997. This dense purple-colored wine boasts a big, smoky, toasty, rich, jammy, strawberry, cherry, and curranty nose. Medium to full bodied, still youthful, but outrageously fruity, ripe, and pure, it is reminiscent of a grapier young Pesquera. However, Pesquera now sells for twice the price. Les Vinyasses should drink well for 7–8 years. These are remarkable values from Spain!

CARCHELO (JUMILLA)

1997 Monastrell	A	86

This 75% Mourvèdre, 25% Merlot blend exhibits a dark ruby/purple color, loads of juicy, sweet, blackberry and cherry fruit, some tannin and structure, medium body, and excellent purity. It should drink well for 1–3 years.

BODEGAS CASA CASTILLO (JUMILLA)

1997 Jumilla	A	87

Made from 90% Monastrell (Mourvèdre) and 10% Cabernet Sauvignon, this dense purple-colored offering exhibits closed aromatics, but impressive richness and a northern Rhône-like character in the mouth. There is moderate tannin, full body, and gobs of blackberry and kirschlike fruit, but this example tastes more like a barrel sample than a bottled wine. It spent 4 months in wood, with the malolactics done in barrel, yet the oak's influence seems restrained, if virtually nonexistent. There is considerable depth to this wine, which is still monolithic but impressive. It requires 6–7 months of additional bottle age, but given its composition of Mourvèdre and Cabernet, it should age well for 7–8 years, with more aromatics likely to develop.

CAUS LUBIO (PENEDÈS)

1994	Caus Lubio	A	88
1993	Caus Lubio	A	86

These wines, blends of Cabernet Sauvignon, Cabernet Franc, and Merlot, yearn to taste like a good Bordeaux. The 1993 is a medium-bodied, dark ruby/garnet-colored wine with a spicy, cedary, curranty nose. It offers ripe fruit and some spice but finishes with an angular austerity. Consume this very good wine over the next several years. The 1994 exhibits sweeter fruit, more richness and flavor dimension, copious quantities of jammy black fruits, along with fruitcake, smoked herb, and toasty aromas and flavors. The wine is lush, round, medium bodied, and ideal for drinking over the next 2–3 years.

CAVAS MURVIEDRO (VALENCIA)

1994	Las Monteros	A	86
1994	Tempranillo Crianza	A	85
1994	Vino Noble	A	84

This winery, situated in the sun-drenched province of Valencia, has fashioned three very good values. The dark ruby-colored 1994 Tempranillo Crianza offers attractive strawberry and cherry, spicy, earthy scents, medium body, good acidity, and light tannin. It should drink well for 1–2 years. The 1994 Vino Noble displays a lighter ruby color, as well as a fragrant, floral, and berry-scented nose, good acidity, light to medium body, strawberry/cranberry flavors, and a crisp, tart finish. I would opt for drinking it over the next year. The most impressive wine of this trio is the 1994 Las Monteros, which is packaged in a heavy, antique bottle. The color is a dark ruby/garnet, and the nose offers more earth, underbrush, and sweet and sour cherry fruit. The wine possesses good depth, medium body, and copious fruit in the midpalate and finish. Underlying acidity gives freshness and vibrancy to this wine, which should also be drunk over the next 1–2 years.

CLOS ERASMUS (PRIORATO)

1994	Priorat Unfiltered	D	99
1993	Priorat Unfiltered	D	94
1992	Priorat Unfiltered	D	93
1990	Priorat Unfiltered	D	91

This 5-acre vineyard produces only 250 cases, but the story is not unlike that of the young Italian photographer, Silvia Imparato, whose wines are called Montevetrano. The Clos Erasmus vineyard, which is planted in 45% Cabernet Sauvignon, 45% Grenache (80-year-old vines), and 10% Syrah, with yields averaging between 1–1⅓ tons of fruit per acre, is a steeply terraced, sun-drenched parcel in the Priorato region of Spain. In the past I have highly recommended other wines from this area—such as Clos Mogador and Clos d'Orlac—which are made from vineyards adjacent to those of Clos Erasmus. These wines exhibit an old-vine intensity, as well as sweet, roasted, tarlike, black cherry, and cassis scents that are reminiscent of some of the great Vega Sicilia vintages.

The 1990 boasts a terrific color, adds a chocolate note to the aforementioned aromatics, great richness and ripeness, a dense, opulent palate, and a lush, viscous, full-bodied personality. There is undoubtedly tannin concealed beneath all the fruit, but this wine can be drunk now or cellared for 12–15+ years. The brilliant 1992 was macerated for more than 5 weeks (talk about extended *cuvaisons*). This prodigious wine exhibits a dense color and superrich, jammy, black cherry, and cassis fruit intertwined with toasty new oak (100% new oak casks are used). The wine is full bodied, with layers of flavor, a sweet midpalate, and a long, rich, well-defined finish. Approachable now, it promises to be even better in 4–5 years and will last for up to 2 decades. The 1993 is even more spectacular. The opaque ruby/purple color is followed by a stunningly fragrant nose of black fruits, melted road tar, toasty new oak, and truffle/licorice scents. Extremely full bodied, with layers of flavor, this immense but well-balanced wine is a winemaking tour de force. Given the fact that three of Spain's hottest new wines have emanated from the steep, terraced hillsides of Priorato—Clos Mogador, Clos d'Orlac, and now Clos Erasmus—it is only a matter of time before the world's wine connoisseurs begin beating a path to this remote, rugged region of northeastern Spain.

The 1994, made from a blend of very old-vine Grenache and younger-vine Syrah and Cabernet Sauvignon grown on terraced vineyards, is among the most exciting wines I have tasted. Unfortunately only 300 cases are produced, all of which is exported to the United States. It is aged in 100% new French oak casks and bottled without fining or filtration. The 1994 is considered to be one of Spain's all-time great vintages, so it is not surprising that this wine possesses more potential than the exceptional 1993 and 1992. Try to imagine a hypothetical blend of Pétrus, l'Évangile, Rayas (the Châteauneuf du Pape), and Napa's 1993 Colgin Cabernet Sauvignon. The color is an opaque black/purple. The nose offers up spectacularly rich, pure aromas of blackberries, minerals, and subtle vanillin from new oak barrels. Extremely rich and dense, with unbelievable levels of concentration and extract, this amazing wine is a strong candidate for a 3-digit rating when it develops more maturity in 5–8 years. Since it is a newly created wine, there is no track record established for ageability, but a wine such as this should keep for 20–25 years. This is one of the most exciting young wines anyone could possibly taste. Awesome!

CLOS MARTINET (PRIORATO)

1994 Clos Martinet	E	90+
1994 Martinet Bru	D	87

Another extraordinary black-colored, concentrated, blockbuster wine from Priorato, Clos Martinet is produced by the Perez y Ovejero family. Made from a 15-acre vineyard planted with old-vine Grenache and Carignan, and more recent additions of Cabernet Sauvignon, Merlot, and Syrah, the wine is aged completely in new French oak. Only the finest grapes are utilized in Clos Martinet, with the balance going into a wine called Martinet Bru. The objective is to produce about 500 cases of the Clos Martinet in top years, such as 1994 and 1995. The opaque ruby/purple-colored 1994 appears potentially less complex than the l'Ermita, Clos Erasmus, or Clos de l'Obac, which are made in nearby vineyards. Nevertheless, the Clos Martinet 1994 is a strikingly rich, full-bodied, tannic, structured style of Priorat with full body, outstanding richness and density, and a long finish, with surprising acidity. The flavors include plums, black cherries, and black currants. The aromatics are tightly restrained, but with 15–20 minutes of coaxing the wine begins to strut its sweet fruit and purity. The oak is noticeable but not intrusive. This powerful, muscular, dense, full-throttle, dry red wine needs 3–4 years of cellaring; it should keep for 15+ years. The 1995 Martinet Bru has a dark purple/cranberry color, a sweet cherry and mineral-scented nose, and medium- to full-bodied flavors. After 30 hours of aeration, this wine improved dramatically. Fleshy but elegant, this excellent wine will drink well for 8–10 years.

BODEGAS CONTADO DE HAZA (ROA DEL DUERO/BURGOS)

1995	Contado de Haza	C	90
1994	Contado de Haza	C	87

This winery, owned by Pesquera's Alejandro Fernandez, is doing whole-cluster fermentation and aging the wines for 15 months in American oak barrels. The 100% Tempranillo vineyard was planted by Fernandez in the 1980s on a south-facing slope. The first two vintages of this wine to be shipped internationally, 1994 and 1995, are extraordinarily impressive. The 1995 Contado de Haza exhibits an opaque ruby/purple color, followed by an expressive, sweet, jammy, toasty nose of black cherries, plums, and prunes. Generous and full-bodied fruit flavors ooze across the palate with a certain viscosity. Strikingly silky with low acidity, this marvelously concentrated, voluptuously textured, sexy wine can be drunk now or aged for 12–15 years. The 1994 Contado de Haza reveals a nose of melted chocolate, smoke, jammy red and black fruits, and vanillin. Full bodied, with no sense of heaviness, this rich wine possesses rustic tannin in the finish. Overall, the 1995 is more harmonious than the earthier, more tannic 1994. Excellent value.

COOP DEL CAMPO SAN ISIDRO (CALATAYUD)

1997	Viña Alarba	A	86
1995	Viña Alarba	A	87

Four thousand cases of the chunky, fleshy 1997 Viña Alarba, made from 90% old-vine Grenache and 10% Syrah, are available. Produced from a high-altitude vineyard, the wine is not complex aromatically, but it does offer husky blackberry, peppery, cassis flavors tinged with smoke, tar, and coffee nuances. The wine makes a good impact on the palate, but readers should think of it as a monolithic, uncomplicated, mouth-filling, well-made red wine to drink over the next several years.

The 1995 is worth buying by the case given its quality/price rapport. The medium to dark ruby/purple color is followed by an excellent set of aromatics consisting of uncomplicated sweet black cherry fruit. The rich, round, cleanly made wine is a delicious fruit bowl of the Garnacha and Tempranillo grapes. Supple, medium bodied, and tasty, it can be served slightly chilled or at room temperature. Fortunately there are 8,000 cases of this wine for the American market. It should drink well for several years. Excellent value.

COOP NRTA. SRA. DE LA CABEZA (LA MANCHA)

1994	Casa Gualda	A	87
1995	Casa Gualda	A	86

These wines, made from various blends of Cabernet Sauvignon and Cencibel (the latter grape is the local clone of Tempranillo), are from one of the finest small coops in Spain. Both are soft, fat, ripe, fruity wines displaying a southern Rhône-like combination of pepper, medium to full body, smooth, low-acid flavors, and fine ripeness. The 1995 (it possesses only 10% Cabernet) exhibits additional notes of tar, spice, and roasted ripeness. The mouth-filling, fuller 1994 (40% Cabernet in the blend) is more rustic, with more glycerin and higher alcohol. Both wines are outstanding bargains that will last for 3–4 years.

COSTERS DEL SIURDANA (PRIORATO)

1996	Clos de l'Obac	D	?
1995	Clos de l'Obac	D	96

1994 Clos de l'Obac	D	90
1993 Clos de l'Obac	D	92+
1995 Dol'c de l'Obac (Sweet Red)	EE	96
1994 Dol'c de l'Obac (Sweet Red)	EE	95
1993 Dol'c de l'Obac (Sweet Red)	EE	91
1996 Miserere	D	85
1995 Miserere	D	89+
1994 Miserere	D	88
1993 Miserere	D	90

One of the superstar wineries of Priorato, Costers del Siurana is a 30-acre estate owned by the Pastrana family. The Miserere, which emerges from a separate estate owned by the Pastranas, is aged 12 months in French oak casks and bottled unfiltered. It is a blend of Cabernet Sauvignon, Garnacha, Tempranillo, Merlot, and Carignan. The 1996 reveals a Burgundian, almost Volnay-like nose of black cherries intermixed with toasty new oak. In the mouth, the wine is medium bodied and refreshing, with a snappy, zesty acidity and the subtle influence of French oak. This stylish, elegant, charming wine should be consumed over the next 6–7 years.

Three separate tastings of the 1996 Clos de l'Obac reinforced my initial impression that this is the most backward and tannic wine this estate has yet produced. A blend of Cabernet Sauvignon, Grenache, Syrah, Merlot, and Carignan, it spent 14 months in 100% new French oak and was bottled unfiltered. While the average age of the Cabernet Sauvignon, Syrah, and Merlot is 10 years, the Grenache and Carignan date from vineyards planted in 1945, 1950, and the early 1900s. The wine may merit an outstanding score with another 2–3 years of bottle age. At present it is lighter and more acidic and tannic than either the 1995 or 1994. The color is a medium deep ruby. The tight nose offers scents of kirsch, minerals, smoke, and *pain grillé*. In the mouth, both the acidity and tannin are high, and the wine elegant and restrained, with impressive purity and richness, but very closed and difficult to assess (thus the question mark). Although it gives the impression of weight and richness, the mouth-searing tannin combined with its tart acids keep the finish compressed and tightly wound. Give this effort 4–5 years of cellaring; it has the potential to last for 2 decades.

I hope readers have been taking my advice and searching out the spectacular, limited-quantity wines produced on the sun-drenched, steep terraced vineyards of Priorato, usually produced from blends of extremely old-vine Grenache and young-vine Cabernet Sauvignon and, on occasion, Syrah and Merlot. Make no mistake about it, this region has become one of the hottest areas for rare, limited-production, great wines. One of the finest practitioners in Priorato is Costers del Siurana, who makes limited quantities of three outstanding wines. There are several hundred cases of the 1995 Miserere, an estate-bottled blend of Cabernet Sauvignon, Grenache, Tempranillo, Merlot, and Carignan. This wine may merit a 90-point score after a few more months in bottle. It exhibits a dense ruby/purple color and a pure, earthy, peppery, blackberry, and cassis nose with nicely integrated toasty oak. The wine is powerful and full bodied on the palate, with a lot of guts, glycerin, and extract. Although still unformed, grapey, and raw, this is an impressively made wine that needs another 2–3 years of cellaring; it should keep for 12–15 years. The profound 1995 Clos de l'Obac, with a total production of 150 cases, is an unfiltered wine that pushes extraction and intensity to the limit. Aged in 100% new French oak casks, it offers an opaque purple color and huge, intense, unevolved, but impressive aromas of kirsch, cassis, and blackberries intermingled with smoky, toasty oak. The wine possesses awesome concentration, phenomenal fruit extraction, and an explosive, tannic, glycerin-endowed, long finish. Compared with previous vintages of this wine, the 1995 is a backward, tannic *vin de garde* that needs a minimum of 8–10 years of cellaring! This is a wine with 30–40 years of longevity, but readers unwilling to invest in a decade of patience will be disappointed in its performance. It is an exquisite, classic, uncompromising wine! Anticipated maturity: 2007–2030.

There are a whopping 75 cases of the late harvest 1995 Dol'c de l'Obac. A pruny, rich curiosity, it is reminiscent of a hypothetical blend of top Italian Amarone and luxurious French Banyuls. It is extremely full bodied and oozing with glycerin, fruit, and extraction. The alcohol is not as high as I suspected (15.5%), and the wine is clearly meant to be drunk at the end of a meal or with cheese. While the tiny quantities produced make this review somewhat academic, this is an amazing effort that should age beautifully for 25–30 years.

These well-made wines from one of Spain's most exciting viticultural areas, Priorato, are worth a search of the marketplace. The 1994 Miserere, a Cabernet Sauvignon, Grenache, Tempranillo, Merlot, and Carinena blend, exhibits the modern international style that is so popular in Italy's Tuscany and Piedmont sections, as well as in Spain. Plenty of sweet, spicy, new French oak and black currant notes are followed by a dark ruby/purple-colored, elegant wine with excellent richness, fine purity and balance, and a clean, stylish, sculptured winemaking style. It should drink well for 5–7 years. More interesting and complex is the 1994 Clos de l'Obac, produced from old-vine Grenache grown on steep terraced vineyards and blended with young-vine Cabernet Sauvignon and Merlot. The wine boasts an impressive dark ruby/purple color and a pure black raspberry-scented nose intertwined with aromas of slate and new oak. The attack offers ripe, sweet fruit buttressed by tannin and an underlying mineral component. Rich but very young, this full-bodied wine is more like a barrel sample than a bottled wine. Give it 2–3 years of cellaring and drink it over the following 10–15. The 1994 Dol'c de l'Obac is largely of academic interest, since there are only 50 cases of this 16% alcohol wine. The style resembles a blend of a late-harvest Zinfandel and a vintage port. This dense, viscous, full-bodied, overripe, beautifully flowery, sweet-smelling wine gushes with black fruits and toasty aromas. At present the fruit easily covers the lofty alcohol level. Drink this young, grapey, slightly sweet wine with heavy-duty cheese. Given the alcohol level as well as its intensity, this wine should age for 20+ years.

The wines from this up-and-coming Priorato estate are noteworthy for 1) impeccable high quality, 2) designer labels, and 3) heavy bottles. The 1993 Miserere, a Cabernet Sauvignon/Grenache/Tempranillo/Merlot/Carignane blend exhibits a saturated dark ruby/purple color and a sweet, flattering, precocious nose of jammy black fruits intertwined with scents of vanilla and spice. It is rich and full bodied, with a voluptuous texture, low acidity and tannin, and an overall impression of rich, concentrated black fruit. Drinkable now, it promises to last for 10–15 years. The 1993 Clos de l'Obac is one of Spain's greatest red wines. I have tasted only a few vintages, but this is an immensely impressive, gorgeously rich, well-proportioned wine that can easily compete with the world's finest wines. The 1993 is a blend of Cabernet Sauvignon, Grenache, Syrah, Merlot, and Carignane that was bottled unfiltered after spending 2 years in 100% new French oak casks. In a blind tasting it would be hard to pick this out as a Spanish wine. The 1993 exhibits an opaque purple color and a huge nose of sweet black cherries and raspberries intertwined with smoky toasty oak scents. The wine is extremely full bodied, rich, and pure, with adequate acidity and good underlying tannin, all of which support the full-bodied, rich style. Supple and opulent enough to be drunk now, it promises to age well for 20 years.

Of more limited interest is the expensive 1993 Dol'c de l'Obac late-harvest wine. Despite its almost 18% alcohol, it tastes remarkably well balanced for its size, thickness, and intense flavors. Although it contains a lot of residual sweetness, it is extremely well made in a late harvest, portlike style. It should last for 25+ years.

DOMINICO EGUREN (MANCHUELA)

1997 Protocolo	A	87
1996 Protocolo	A	85

The 1997 Protocolo comes across as a classy, Médoc-like Cabernet Sauvignon, which makes no sense given the fact that it is made from 100% Tempranillo and tank-aged and fermented, with no exposure to oak! The cedary, herb-tinged, peppery, chocolatey, black cherry nose is alluring. In the mouth, the wine is surprisingly deep and rich, with medium to full body, a velvety texture, and a nicely delineated style. It is a wine to buy by the case.

An inexpensive yet excellent bargain for its quality, the 1996 Protocolo, made from 100% Tempranillo, is a pleasant red table wine with a medium ruby color, a spicy, robust, peppery, strawberry and cherry nose, and good fruit. Although one-dimensional, it is soft, round, and pleasing. Drink this serviceable, quaffing red wine slightly chilled over the next 6–12 months.

DOMINICO DE PINGUS (DUERO)

1996 Dominico de Pingus	EEE	97
1995 Dominico de Pingus	EEE	98
1996 Fleur de Pingus	D	90
1995 Fleur de Pingus	D	90

In the summer of 1996 I broke the story about the extraordinary Dominico de Pingus produced by the young Danish winemaker Peter Sisseck (Pingus is Danish slang for Peter, as well as the name of a well-known European cartoon). I tasted the 1995 Dominico de Pingus immediately before bottling (it will not be filtered), and it is an extraordinary wine. Sadly, only 325 cases were produced, and only 350 cases in 1996. Made from 60+-year-old Tempranillo vines planted in the heart of Ribera del Duero, these wines are produced from yields of under ½ ton of fruit per acre, or about 1.1 pounds of fruit per vine. Malolactic fermentation is done in new oak, and the wine is then aged in 100% new oak casks, with the white wine technique of *bâtonnage* (lees stirring) utilized. *Bâtonnage* is rarely used for red wine. All of these wines, tasted in September 1997, are spectacular.

The 1995 Dominico de Pingus exhibits an opaque purple color, an extraordinary sweet nose of black fruits, truffles, and nicely integrated, subtle *pain grillé*. The wine is massive, huge, and full bodied, with layers of concentrated, pure fruit, loads of glycerin, and beautifully sweet tannin. Although one would think it would taste Bordeaux-like, both the 1995 and 1996 have their own style that falls somewhere between St.-Émilion's Valandraud, Pesquera's Janus, and Vega Sicilia's Unico! The 1995 will age effortlessly for 25–30+ years. The lucky few who are able to latch on to a bottle or two should be prepared to cellar it for 4–6 years. The 1996 Dominico de Pingus is cut from the same mold. Yields are slightly higher but still microscopic. The color is an opaque black/purple, and the exotic nose offers copious quantities of sweet cedar, smoke, and jammy blackberry and cassis fruit. New oak is present, but it is pushed largely to the background by the wine's massive concentration. The tannin is sweet and well integrated, and the wine is full bodied and harmonious. Although more forward than the 1995, the 1996 is still a candidate for 25–30 years of aging. These are brilliant winemaking efforts!

For readers not fortunate enough to latch on to Dominico de Pingus, there is Fleur de Pingus, made in far more abundant quantities. Both the 1995 and 1996 are outstanding wines. One thousand cases were made of the 1995 Fleur de Pingus, a sweet, rich, open-knit, black currant-scented wine that offers lavish new oak and ripe, opulently textured fruit flavors of blackberries and cassis. A full-bodied, rich, expansively flavored wine, it should drink well for 10–15+ years. The 1996 Fleur de Pingus exhibits more structure, grip, and spice, as well as intensely concentrated fruit, full body, and outstanding purity and harmony. Bravo to proprietor Peter Sisseck for these extraordinary Spanish wines!

BODEGAS DURON (RIBERA DEL DUERO)

1990 Gran Reserva	C	85
1991 Reserva	C	86

Both of these wines are more earth and spice driven than fruit driven, although the 1991 Reserva's fruit is purer and fresher than the 1990 Gran Reserva's. Both wines possess an earthy overlay of black cherry fruit with a subtle dosage of new oak. Drink both of these medium-bodied wines over the next 3–4 years.

ENATE (SOMONTANO)

1995 Crianza (Tempranillo/Cabernet)	A	88
1995 Reserva (Cabernet)	C	87
1994 Reserva (Cabernet)	C	86
1995 Tinto (Cabernet/Merlot)	A	86

These are well-made, clean, medium-weight wines. The less expensive cuvées were aged in American oak and the more expensive in new French oak. Made in a more elegant, supple, less weighty style than some of the newer-breed Spanish wines, all four can be drunk over the next 4–5 years. The dark plum/garnet-colored 1995 Tinto (Cabernet and Merlot), which spent 6 months in old oak, offers round, soft, peppery, sweet berry flavors with a touch of vanillin, as well as good body and length. The 1995 Crianza (a blend of Tempranillo and Cabernet) was aged for 9 months in new American oak. Because of that it reveals more sweet vanillin and sexy spice in the nose. It also possesses a deep ruby/purple color, jammy, ripe berry fruit, excellent texture, and a clean, pure finish. A fine value, it is my favorite offering of this quartet.

The 1994 Reserva (Cabernet) spent 14 months in new French oak. It reveals a tarry, vanillin, spice box, and curranty nose and elegant, refined, restrained, medium-bodied flavors with good depth and spice. Although the finish is slightly short, the wine is well made in an international style. Last, the 1995 Reserva (Cabernet) was given the same treatment as the 1994 but appears to possess slightly sweeter fruit. It is an elegant, finesse-style Spanish red that should drink well between now and 2004.

BODEGAS FARINA (ZAMORA)

1990 Grand Peromato Tinto	A	85
1992 Peromato Tinto	A	84

The Bodegas Farina in Zamora has produced two solidly made red wine values. The 1992 Peromato (made from 100% Tinto del Pais) is a moderately ruby-colored, straightforward, fruity, medium-bodied wine with good spice, pepper, and length. Drink it over the next year. The 1990 Grand Peromato (100% Tinto del Pais aged 6 months in American oak) reveals more spice, as well as vanilla and red berry fruit, low acidity, light tannin, and a medium-bodied, heady finish. It should be drunk over the next 1–2 years.

FINCA ALLENDE (RIOJA)

1995 Allende	C	90

A small (45 acres) estate for Rioja, Finca Allende's modern-style, *barrique*-aged Rioja exhibits impressive credentials. The opaque purple color suggests a wine to be taken seriously.

The nose offers up subtle nuances of both French and American oak intertwined with black-berry and cherry fruit, as well as cedar and tobacco scents. Bottled unfiltered (a rarity in Rioja), the wine is full bodied and rich, with moderate tannin and a nicely structured, impressively endowed finish. It will benefit from another 1–2 years of bottle age. Anticipated maturity: 2000–2012.

J. M. FUENTES (PRIORATO)

1995 Gran Clos	D	89+

This is the debut vintage for the 5-acre J. M. Fuentes estate, located in the promising appellation of Priorato. Just under 400 cases of this wine were made. A blend of 80% Grenache, 10% Cabernet Sauvignon, and 10% Carignan, the wine possesses a dark ruby/purple color, dense kirsch, jammy cherry, toasty aromas, rich, medium- to full-bodied flavors, and wonderful glycerin and sweetness in the long finish. Still an infant in terms of development, it should last for 10–15 years.

FRA FULCO (CATALUNA)

1996 Carignan Vinyes Velles	D	92
1995 Carignan Vinyes Velles	D	90

Carignan is not expected to produce wines at this level of quality. It is a good blending grape and from time to time can stand as a major component of southern Rhône, Spanish, and California cuvées, offering a good, monolithic, savory, rustic personality. Both of these offerings take Carignan to new heights of quality. Both are from a new estate run by a well-known Spanish professor of oenology. Made from a blend of 20% Cabernet Sauvignon and 80% Carignan from 100-year-old vines, they are aged in 100% new oak and are bottled without any filtration. The 1995 Carignan boasts an opaque purple color, followed by peppery, spicy, meaty aromas that jump from the glass. In the mouth, there is a certain rusticity to the wine's tannin, but it is gorgeously pure, with layers of rich fruit that conceal the use of 100% new oak barrels. The wine is full bodied, dense, and corpulent. I have no idea how it will age, but its accessibility and wonderful perfume indicate it is best drunk over the next 7–8 years for its exuberance and slightly uncivilized, but immensely satisfying personality-filled style. The 1996 Carignan exhibits an inky purple color. Even more muscular and richer than the 1995, it possesses sweeter tannin and a more velvety finish. This massive, large-scale wine makes a huge impact on the palate. Both wines should be drunk with grilled meats. The 1996 will drink well for 10–12 years. It is not for the shy.

GRANDES BODEGAS (RIBERA DEL DUERO)

1997 Marqués de Velilla	A	87
1996 Marqués de Velilla	B	88
1996 Marqués de Velilla Monte Villalobon	B	87+
1994 Marqués de Velilla Reserva	D	91

All of these wines, which are made from 100% Tinta del Pais and estate-bottled, are amazing values from this Spanish appellation. There are 2,000 cases of the 1997 Marqués de Velilla, a soft, sexy, charming, delicious, fruit-driven wine with gobs of fat, glycerin, and appeal. This pure example offers up plenty of black cherry and berry fruit, medium body, excellent balance, and a fleshy, chewy finish. It should drink well for 4–5 years. The 1996 Monte Villalobon is cut from a similar mold but comes across as more tannic and structured, with more earth intermixed with copious quantities of black fruits. This wine requires another 1–2 years of bottle age; it should last for a decade.

Two impressive wines from Ribera del Duero, the 1996 Marqués de Velilla is a blend of 85% Tinta del Pais and 15% Cabernet Sauvignon, aged in some new American oak. Produced from the vineyard's youngest vines (approximately 10 years old), it possesses a dark ruby color, as well as copious quantities of black cherry and berry fruit, medium to full body, a soft, charming, seductive texture, and enough spice for complexity. This round, mouth-filling, fleshy, satisfying Spanish red will drink well for 4–5 years. The dark plum/garnet-colored 1994 Marqués de Velilla Reserva is 100% Tinta del Pais from older vines. The explosive aromatics offer cigar smoke, cedar, fruitcake, black cherries, licorice, and smoke. The wine is rich, with outstanding concentration, a multilayered, opulent texture, full body, and a chewy, dense, heady finish. This is a sumptuous, rich wine to drink now and over the next decade.

MARQUÉS DE GRIÑON (LA MANCHA)

1992 Cabernet Sauvignon Dominio de Valdepusa	C	92
1992 Rioja	B	87
1988 Rioja Reserva Coleccion Personal	C	89
1992 Tinto Durius	A	87

Carlos Falcon, the Marqués de Griñon, produces high-quality wines in three viticultural areas. The least expensive wines, the Durius offerings, include a well-made 1992 Tinto. An outstanding bargain, the 1992 Durius Tinto is a blend composed primarily of Grenache. Although not complex, the wine is rich and mouth filling, with a Côtes du Rhône–like, peppery, spicy, black cherry-scented nose, excellent, pure, rich, chewy flavors, and plenty of glycerin, alcohol, and fruit. Drink it over the next 4–5 years.

The Marqués de Griñon produces 40,000 cases of a modestly priced, delicious Rioja. The 1992 Rioja exhibits a medium dark ruby color and a soft, spicy, sweet American oak-scented nose intertwined with scents of black and red fruits. Supple and velvety textured, it possesses excellent purity, gobs of fruit, and a long, silky finish. Drink it over the next 4–5 years. There are only 6,000 cases of the 1988 Rioja Reserva Coleccion Personal. This is a broader, more complex wine with scents and flavors of tobacco, minerals, vanillin, and currants, layers of rich, opulently textured fruit, medium to full body, a wonderful, expansive sweetness from ripe grapes (not sugar), and a lush finish. It should drink well for 5–7 years.

While the Marqués de Griñon has always made very good wines, his finest offering to date is the 1992 Cabernet Sauvignon Dominio de Valdepusa from his vineyards in La Mancha. There are 6,000 cases of this 100% French oak-aged wine, whose vinification and upbringing are overseen by none other than Michel Rolland, Pomerol's omnipresent, world-class oenologist. The wine is splendidly rich, with an opaque ruby/purple color, a huge nose of black currants, lead pencil, and sweet yet subtle oak, layers of flavor, great extraction and richness, sweet tannin, and a long, complex finish that is bursting with jammy black currant fruit. This terrific Cabernet Sauvignon is unquestionably the finest the Marqués de Griñon has ever produced. Approachable already, it promises to last for 15–20 years.

The Marqués de Griñon is not content to rest on his laurels. Barrel samples of the 1994 Syrah suggest this is going to be a blockbuster Syrah that should make some of the Rhône Valley's top producers nervous. Approximately 4,000 cases will be made. The outstanding barrel samples were smoky and rich, with that wonderful bacon fat and cassis character. Readers should also be on the lookout for a new offering from the Marqués de Griñon produced from a vineyard in the Ribera del Duero, not far from Pesquera. The 1994, which was aged in new oak casks, was spectacular when tasted from barrel. It was to be released in 1996.

CASA GUALDA (LA MANCHA)

1996 Crianza	A	84

From a cooperative, this blend of 40% Cabernet Sauvignon and 60% Tempranillo is a medium dark ruby-colored, straightforward, fruit-driven wine with good cleanliness, a velvety texture, and fresh, lively, berry flavors. Approximately 1,000 cases are available. It is a good value.

BODEGAS GUELBENZU (NAVARRA)

1994 EVO	C	87
1996 Jardin Garnacha	A	85
1995 Tinto	A	87

I enjoyed the 1996 Jardin Garnacha (100% Grenache) from this *bodegas*. The wine offers an unmistakable nose of black raspberries and roasted nuts. This somewhat kinky, dark ruby/purple-colored wine's only negative is rustic tannin in the finish. Overall it is a fleshy wine with sweet fruit and an attractive peppery, spicy character. Drink it over the next 1–2 years. The 1995 Tinto, a Cabernet Sauvignon, Merlot, and Grenache blend from vines planted in 1980, displays a dark plum/purple color and a peppery, spicy, earthy, black fruit-scented nose. It is a dense, country-style, medium-bodied, robust wine that is attractive and well endowed. Consume it over the next 2–3 years.

Bodegas Guelbenzu's top-of-the-line, dark ruby-colored 1994 EVO (a blend of 60% Cabernet Sauvignon, 24% Tempranillo, and 16% Merlot) spent time in new oak barrels. It is obviously made from even riper fruit, as noted by the touch of prunes in the wine's aromatics. Offering plenty of richness, slightly coarse tannin, and a powerful, rugged personality with admirable depth, this is a chunky, robust wine that will drink well for 3–4 years.

BODEGAS INVIOSA (RIBERA DEL GUADIANA)

1994 Lar de Barros	A	88

I have always had a soft spot in my heart for this Pomerol look-alike. A big, thick, sweet, chocolatey, jammy black cherry-scented nose is an attention grabber. The wine (a blend of 75% Tempranillo, 15% Grenache, and 10% Graciano) exhibits luscious jammy cherry fruit, a touch of spicy new oak, good smoke, ripeness, and plenty of intensity. A fun wine to drink, it should improve over the next 12–18 months and last for 4–5 years. Great value.

JEAN LEON (PENEDÈS)

1991 Cabernet Sauvignon Reserva	D	87

I have been following Jean Leon's Cabernet Sauvignons for over 20 years, and the new vintages are far softer and less massively extracted than those from the mid- and late 1970s (the 1974 I have cellared is still not ready for prime-time drinking). This 1991 exhibits a medium ruby color with some lightening at the edge. The wine reveals a sweet, cedary, cassis-scented nose, soft, open-knit, tobacco and curranty flavors, medium body, light tannin, and a round finish. Drink it over the next 3–4 years.

BARON DE LEY (RIOJA)

1994 Rioja Reserva	C	87

This modern-style Rioja exhibits a medium ruby color followed by a sweet, toasty, jammy, plum, cherry, and currant nose. The wine possesses good expansiveness, round, generous flavors, no hard edges, and a lush finish. It should drink well for 3–4 years.

BODEGAS V. MAGANA (NAVARRA)

1996 Baron de Magana Finca La Sarda	D	87
1991 Eventum	B	87
1991 Eventum Crianza	A	87
1989 Merlot Reserva	C	86?

Readers are advised to seek out the Bodegas Magana's wines, as they have only scratched the surface of their potential. There are not many Merlots better than the 1991 Eventum Crianza, a 70% Merlot/30% Tempranillo blend. Bottled unfiltered, it is not one of those vegetal, washed-out Merlots lacking flavor and fruit. This dark ruby/purple-colored wine offers a provocatively striking nose of coffee and jammy black cherries. It exhibits excellent ripeness, a rich, medium- to full-bodied, supple palate, super purity and fruit, and a velvety-textured, medium-bodied finish. Drink it over the next 4–5 years. The 1989 Merlot Reserva would have been even more impressive had not a slight musty element in the nose lowered the score. It reveals a saturated color, sweet, ripe, black cherries, almonds, and roasted herbs and nutlike flavors, with a touch of overripeness (a positive rather than negative trait), and a medium- to full-bodied, velvety finish. However, the winery needs to invest in more new oak, as the mustiness is no doubt from old barrels. It's a shame, given this wine's outstanding potential save for this minor detracting component. This Merlot should drink well for 5–6 years.

The 1991 Eventum was showing better in 1996 than it did in 1995. Made from the oldest Merlot plantings in Navarra (28 years), it exhibits wet forest, black cherry, earthy aromas, medium body, plenty of jammy, cherry-tinged fruit flavors, a supple texture, and an easygoing finish. Drink it over the next 2–3 years. Good value.

I tasted three other wines from Magana, including a 1994 Dignus, 1994 Reserva, and 1989 Merlot Reserva, that, while not badly made, were just not interesting. The finest wine I tasted from this estate was the Rhône Valley-like, dense plum/purple-colored 1996 Baron de Magana Finca La Sarda. This wine has spicy oak, peppery, gutsy, black cherry and kirsch-like fruit, a robust, medium- to full-bodied character, and fine texture and length. The wine is also a very good value.

BODEGAS MARTINEZ BUJANDA

1994 Conde de Valdemar	A	85
1990 Conde de Valdemar Gran Reserva	C	85
1992 Conde de Valdemar Reserva	C	84
1995 Rioja Conde de Valdemar	B	85

The straightforward, fruity, cherry- and strawberry-scented and -flavored 1995 Rioja Conde de Valdemar reveals spicy oak, medium body, and a one-dimensional but pleasing, user-friendly personality. It should be consumed over the next 2–3 years.

The other three efforts are up-front, fruity, lavishly wooded wines, yet all lack serious concentration. They should also be drunk over the next 1–3 years. The 1994 Rioja possesses a medium ruby color, as well as sweet fruit (black cherries), briery, berrylike flavors, medium body, and a soft, woody finish. It is meant to be drunk over the next several years. The light ruby-colored 1992 Reserva reveals more depth as well as a compressed finish. In spite of the weaker color, it possesses more fruit than the 1994, surprising in view of the many outstanding wines produced in the 1994 vintage. The light ruby-colored 1990 Gran Reserva is already displaying considerable amber at the edge. The enticing nose offers aromas of sweet tobacco, lavish toasty new oak, and dried red fruits. Although somewhat attenuated in the mouth, it represents a good glass of Rioja if consumed over the next 1–2 years.

MAS IGNEUS (PRIORATO)

1997 Barranc dels Closos	B	85
1997 FA 112	D	88
1997 FA 206	E	86

A relatively new operation, Mas Igneus is the collaboration of several wineries. These three efforts from the Priorato appellation are good rather than inspiring. The 1997 Barranc dels Closos is a blend of 75% Garnacha, 23% Carinena, and 2% Cabernet Sauvignon that has been aged 3 months in oak casks. A medium to dark ruby-colored, soft, fruity, round wine that tastes as if it were made via the carbonic maceration method (as in Beaujolais), it will provide ideal drinking over the next 6–18 months. While there is not much complexity or depth, it is a fruity, one-dimensional yet pleasing, cleanly made effort.

The 1997 FA 206 (signifying that it was aged in 2-year-old French Allier barriques for 6 months) is a blend of 50% Carinena (Carignan), 39.4% Garnacha (Grenache), and 10.6% Cabernet Sauvignon. The wine reveals a dark ruby color, but somewhat one-dimensional, straightforward flavors presented in a medium-bodied, cleanly made format. Subtle spice and wood notes emerge, and the fruit is fresh and lively, but the wine is monochromatic, although pleasing. Drink it over the next 1–2 years. The more expensive 1997 FA 112 (aged for 12 months in new French Allier oak) is a 67.5% Garnacha, 16% Syrah, 9% Carinena, 5% Cabernet Sauvignon, and 2.5% Merlot blend. This wine reveals a Châteauneuf du Pape–like kirsch- and peppery-scented nose, medium body, obvious new oak, good ripeness and fleshiness, and a medium- to full-bodied finish. It is the finest wine of this trio, but does the quality support the lofty price tag? It should drink well for 3–4 years.

BODEGAS MAURO (RIBERA DEL DUERO)

1994 Ribera del Duero	D	90
1993 Ribera del Duero	D	86
1991 Seleccion Especial	D	86?
1990 Tinto Reserva	D	89
1992 Tinto	C	89
1996 Tudela del Duero	D	94
1995 Tudela del Duero	D	89
1994 Tudela del Duero	D	90

The deep ruby-colored, earthy 1993 Ribero del Duero exhibits licorice, pepper, spice, and plum/cherry-like fruit, all presented in a well-made, medium-bodied, close-to-the-vest style. It should continue to drink well for 3–5 years. The 1994 Ribero del Duero has a lot more to it than its older sibling. Of course, the 1994 vintage is now somewhat legendary, which may explain why the wine possesses more intensity and richness. The deep ruby/purple color is accompanied by a sweet, toasty nose with black fruit, chocolate, and *pain grillé* scents. Plump, round, fleshy, and Pomerol-like in its succulence and lushness, this jammy wine possesses enough acidity to provide grip and delineation. Drink it now and over the next decade.

The Tudela del Dueros, a blend of primarily Tempranillo and old-vine Grenache, are produced just outside the Ribera del Duero region. The 1996 Tudela del Duero appears to be the finest Mauro I have ever tasted. A fabulously rich, unctuously textured, thick, juicy wine with plenty of new oak, it offers jammy, black cherry, berry aromas and flavors with a touch of smoke, tar, and coffee. Huge, thick, and bursting with extraction and promise, it can be drunk now but will be even better in 5–6 years. The opaque plum-colored 1995 Tudela del Duero displays a moderately intense nose of fruitcake, cedar, black fruits, and earth. In the mouth, the wine is sweet, round, and rich, with copious amounts of glycerin, medium body, and spicy new oak. Although obvious, it is attractive and mouth filling in a savory fashion and should drink well for 7–10 years. The outstanding 1994 Tudela del Duero does not appear to be as thick and unctuous as the 1996, but it is more complete than the 1995. The wine possesses a dark ruby/purple color and a smoky, *pain grillé*-scented nose with aromas of black cherries, kirsch, and currants. Medium bodied, with copious quantities of smoky, ripe, roasted flavors, this fruit-driven wine provides plenty of glycerin as well as a long, velvety-textured finish. It should drink well for 7–8 years.

The 1991 Seleccion Especial's longer aging in wood is obvious given the heavy overlay of toast, smoke, and *pain grillé* notes. In the mouth, the wood has provided leanness and tannin, without the fruit and charm of this estate's other offerings. It is an ambitious, serious effort, but I suspect it will dry out and never achieve the charm of the other wines.

The two Tintos were made by Mariano Garcia, the winemaker at Vega Sicilia who consults at Mauro. The 1992 Tinto possesses a dark saturated ruby/purple color, excellent aromatics (wonderfully sweet, jammy, black cherry and currant fruit and a good use of toasty new oak), medium to full body, supple, sweet fruit flavors, light tannin, and a medium- to full-bodied, long finish. It should drink well for 10–15 years. Although sweeter, more expansive, peppery, spicy, oaky, and fuller bodied, the 1990 Tinto Reserva is cut from the same cloth. It does not exhibit as much intensity as the more grapey 1992. The 1990 should drink well for 10–12+ years.

BODEGAS MONTECILLO (RIOJA)

1995 Cumbrero	A	86
1994 Cumbrero	A	87
1991 Reserva	C	87
1991 Rioja Viña Cumbrero	A	88
1988 Rioja Reserva	A	90

Looking for a delicious, soft, slightly spicy Rioja that is selling for a song? The medium ruby-colored 1995 Cumbrero, which has been so attractive in previous vintages, continues its success as a top value. The wine offers generous amounts of pure cherry fruit infused with toast and spice. In the mouth, it is round and medium bodied, with no hard edges. Drink it over the next 1–2 years. The richly fruity, modern-style 1994 Cumbrero offers loads of cherry/berry fruit, moderate quantities of spicy oak, and a supple texture. A medium-bodied wine to drink over the next 2–3 years, it is also an excellent value. The 1991 Reserva reveals a medium ruby/garnet color with amber at the edge. The full-blown nose offers up smoked herbs, dried fruits, tobacco, cedar, and an aged, attractive, smoky, curranty smell. In the mouth, the wine is soft, with ripe fruit, generosity, and ampleness, excellent purity, and plenty of toasty oak in a smooth-as-silk, mature Rioja flavor profile. It should drink well for 3–4 years.

Two other bottlings from Bodegas Montecillo also offer amazing amounts of character, fruit, complexity, and richness for bargain-basement prices. The 1991 Viña Cumbrero has a deep ruby color and a fragrant, intense nose of cedar, spicy vanillin, and sweet, jammy red and black fruits. The wine is velvety textured, rich, and medium bodied and caresses the palate with a cascade of sweet fruit. It is a gorgeously made, delicious Rioja to drink over the next 2–3 years. The 1988 Rioja Reserva is another astonishing wine for the price. The huge, sweet, smoky, toasty-scented nose is intermingled with scents of jammy red and black fruits.

The wine hits the palate with a gush of fruit, has a layered, multidimensional personality, medium to full body, and no hard edges. It is an opulent, lusty Rioja that should drink well for 3–4 years, possibly longer. These are both wines to buy by the case.

BODEGAS HERMANOS MORALES (LA MANCHA)

1994 Gran Creacion	A	87
1993 Gran Creacion	A	87
1992 Gran Creacion	A	87

The 1994 Gran Creacion is an evolved red wine that requires drinking over the next several years. Some aggressive smoky, spicy oak is interwoven with copious quantities of ripe, black currant/cherry fruit in this excellent, silky-textured, mature wine. Made from a blend of 40% Cabernet Sauvignon and 60% Tempranillo, it is an excellent value.

Tons of sweet, toasty new oak might offend those who do not enjoy this component in copious proportions, but once past the veneer of aggressive oak, the 1993 Gran Creacion exhibits a sweet, rich, ripe, black fruit character, a flamboyant personality, a rustic, medium- to full-bodied style, and good length. It is not the most elegant or subtle wine, but it is mouth filling and well made, in addition to being amazingly low priced! Is this wine, a blend of 60% Tempranillo and 40% Cabernet Sauvignon, Spain's Caymus Special Selection look-alike? An excellent bargain.

The 1992 Gran Creacion red is a 40% Cabernet Sauvignon/60% Tempranillo blend that offers amazing flavor intensity and character for a bargain-basement price. The wine possesses a saturated dark ruby color, a sweet, earthy, underbrush, and curranty fruit-scented nose, round, medium- to full-bodied, soft, generous flavors, and a supple finish with fleshy, glycerin-imbued alcohol giving it body and weight. This is a mouth-filling, cleanly made, delicious wine that can be drunk now or over the next 3–4 years. Don't miss it!

BODEGAS EMILIO MORO (RIBERA DEL DUERO)

1996 Ribera del Duero	C	87

A richly fruity, chocolatey wine, Moro's 1996 Ribera del Duero exhibits medium body, good depth, plenty of toasty oak (from its aging in 100% new American wood casks), and a pure, fruit-driven finish. It should drink well for 5–6 years.

BODEGAS MUGA (RIOJA)

1987 Gran Reserva	D	88
1989 Prado Enea Rioja Gran Reserva	D	91
1994 Reserva Unfiltered	B	90
1992 Reserva Unfiltered	B	88
1991 Reserva Unfiltered	B	90
1990 Reserva Unfiltered	B	90
1994 Torre Muga Reserva Especial	D	94
1991 Torre Muga Reserva Especial	E	90+

The Bodegas Muga is one of the most traditionally run wineries in Spain, believing in long wood aging for their red wines and releasing the wines only when they are close to full maturity.

One of the most exceptional wine bargains in the marketplace is the 1990 Muga Unfiltered Reserva. Made from 70% Tempranillo, 20% Garnacha, and 10% Graciano and

Mazuel, this wine spent 2 years in oak and was bottled unfiltered. Although fully mature, it will last for another 10–15 years. The color is dark ruby, with no amber at the edge. The gorgeously sweet, vanillin, jammy, red and black currant nose offers up scents of cedar and spice. Expansive on the palate, with full body and sensationally layered, succulent fruit, this complex, complete, flavorful wine offers intensity as well as a voluptuous texture at a quality level suggestive of a $35–$50 bottle. Drink it over the next 15+ years. This is a Rioja to buy by the case.

The 1991 Unfiltered Reserva (70% Tempranillo, 20% Garnacha, and 10% Graciano and Mazuelo) offers a dark garnet/ruby color and a fragrant, persuasive nose of sweet, jammy, cherry, and currant fruit intermixed with scents of stones, herbs, and vanillin. The wine's wonderful texture reveals layers of fruit, low acidity, and a round, generous mouth-feel. There is not a hard edge to this wine, which was bottled unfiltered to preserve all of its character. Drink it over the next 5–7 years. The 1987 Gran Reserva is typical of the traditional style of Spanish Rioja. Very light in color, with aromas of wood, currants, tobacco, and smoke, this graceful, elegant, silky-textured wine should continue to drink well for 5–7 years.

Muga's 1994 Reserva Unfiltered is a terrific bargain in high-class red wine. A blend of 70% Tempranillo, 20% Garnacha, and 10% Mazuelo and Graciano, this wine (4,500 cases imported into the United States), is the essence of chocolate, truffles, tobacco, and cherries in its nose and flavors. Dense and ripe, with a full-bodied personality, this is a deep, rich, round, compelling Rioja for drinking now as well as over the next decade. Readers should seriously contemplate purchasing this wine by the case.

Another fine value from Spain is Muga's 1992 Rioja Reserva Unfiltered. The wine exhibits a plum color, followed by a sweet, fragrant nose of ripe fruit, tobacco, smoke, and vanillin. Dense and medium to full bodied, with layers of spicy, ripe berry fruit, it is an expressive, youthful, yet authoritatively powerful and flavorful Rioja to drink over the next 5–6 years.

A new offering, and another of the supercuvées to emerge from this region, is the 1991 Torre Muga Reserva Especial. The concept behind this wine is to produce a luxury cuvée of Rioja based on a selection of the finest lots of wine. Aging for 22 months in large American oak vats was followed by 16 months in small new French oak casks. While the price may be high, it is not out of line with the quality of the wine. A blend of 75% Tempranillo, 15% Mazuelo, and 10% Graciano, the wine boasts a dark garnet color and an intense, fragrant nose of spicy, toasty, new oak, smoke, black fruits, and minerals. Full bodied, rich, and powerful, as well as elegant and harmonious, this wine is still youthful despite the fact it is over 6 years old. Give it another 2–3 years of bottle age and drink it over the following 15–18 years. It is an unevolved wine, yet quite impressive!

Another dazzling effort from this traditionally run bodegas, the 1989 Prado Enea (a new release) is a blend of 80% Tempranillo and the rest Garnacha, Mazuelo, and Graciano. The moderate ruby/garnet color reveals some amber at the edge. The stunning aromatics offer penetrating scents of Asian spices (primarily soy), intermixed with iodine, crushed seashells, cedar, fruitcake, new saddle leather, and black fruits. In the mouth, this expansive, full-bodied wine displays both richness and elegance. This superb, old-style Rioja offers intense flavors, as well as extraordinary complexity and precision. Readers used to grapey, oak-dominated wines will need to recalibrate their palates when drinking this intensely scented yet subtle, stylish, profoundly complex wine. Anticipated maturity: now–2011. For statisticians, this wine was aged 1 year in vat, 4 years in barrel, and 3 years in the bottle.

The 1994 Torre Muga is a terrific Rioja. A blend of 75% Tempranillo, 15% Mazuelo, and 10% Graciano, this wine emerges from the estate's oldest vines and is aged in small barriques. A breakthrough in what will undoubtedly be a bevy of cult Riojas, made from old vines and aged in small casks, this is a full-bodied, superbly concentrated, fragrant, multidimensional wine. The color is a deep dark ruby, with some lightening at the edge. The nose offers up sweet scents of black cherry liqueur, raspberries, licorice, smoke, lead pencil, and *pain grillé*. In the mouth, there are lush layers of fruit that cascade over the palate, as well as full body and gobs of glycerin. This Rioja possesses gorgeous sweetness of fruit (from extract, not sugar), as well as impeccable purity and overall harmony. Anticipated maturity: now–2015. In contrast with the barrel, vat, and bottle aging experienced by the Prado Enea, the 1994 Torre Muga spent 22 months in American oak vats, followed by 16 months in 100% new Allier oak casks!

BODEGAS MURIEL (RIOJA)

1985 Rioja Gran Reserva	C	87
1994 Viña Muriel Crianza	A	87

Another outstanding bargain from Spain is Bodegas Muriel's 100% Tempranillo 1994 Viña Muriel Crianza. From a great vintage, this wine offers plenty of smoky, sweet, toasty oak, medium to full body, and no hard edges. The color is a deep ruby/garnet. Drink this seductive, jammy, richly fruity wine over the next 3–4 years. Looking for a wine with more aromatic complexity and an even softer edge? Check out Bodegas Muriel's 1985 Rioja Gran Reserva. The wine possesses a deep garnet color and a provocative cedary, smoky, fruitcake, and lush tobacco-scented nose. Round, rich, overripe fruit is abundantly displayed in this medium-bodied, elegant, fragrant, and supple-textured wine.

MARQUÉS DE MURRIETA (RIOJA)

1996 Coleccion 2100 (Red)	A	88
1989 Rioja Gran Reserva Especial Castillo Y Gay	D	92
1994 Rioja Reserva	C	90
1991 Rioja Reserva Especial	C	86

This traditionally run *bodegas* estate-bottles all of its wines. The wines have been, and will continue to be, made in a traditional style, but to Murrieta's credit, they have introduced a new, richly fruity style of wine under the Coleccion 2100 label. The quality of the red 1996 Coleccion 2100 Rioja is stunning. At $10 a bottle, this is a wine to purchase by the case. It is a rare bargain that actually has wide availability (300,000 bottles were produced). Made from a ripe vintage of Tempranillo, the wine reveals a natural alcohol of 13.5% and was aged for 6 months in 100% American oak. It is a delicious, supple, expansively flavored, medium-bodied, gorgeously fruity Rioja with plenty of black cherry and berry fruit soaring from the glass. Toasty vanillin oaks add an additional nuance. The wine's low acidity, plump, fleshy fruitiness, and lush texture are hedonistic. Already delicious, it should age well for 3–4 years, perhaps longer.

Murrieta's other wines are essentially all the same blends that spend differing amounts of time in wood. The Reservas tend to spend 2½ years in 15-year-old American oak barrels, and the Reserva Especiales spend 3½ years in old American wood, followed by an additional 3 years of bottle age. Readers should keep an eye out for the 1994 Rioja Reserva. The first of a trilogy of exceptional vintages for Rioja, the wine exhibits a dark ruby/purple color, followed by aromas of sweet black cherry and berry fruit intermixed with vanillin and spice. Medium bodied and rich, with gobs of glycerin, a fleshy, fat texture, outstanding purity, and a long, lush finish, this Rioja is already displaying complexity, accessibility, and suppleness, yet it can be cellared for a decade or more. The 1991 Reserva Especial is an austere, more evolved wine with a medium ruby/garnet color and earthy, tobacco, berry, and cherry aromas. In the mouth, there is good ripeness on the attack and medium body, as well as dry tannin and austerity in the finish. This good to very good effort is overwhelmed by the 1994 Reserva and the 1989 Castillo y Gay Grand Reserva Especial. The latter wine, which represents 25%

of the estate's production and is produced only in top vintages, is the flagship wine of Marqués de Murrieta. The deep ruby/purple-colored 1989 offers up smoky, sweet, jammy black cherry fruit aromas intertwined with scents of minerals, tobacco, and vanillin. Medium bodied and ripe, with outstanding levels of fruit, glycerin, and extract, low acidity, and ripe tannin, this hedonistic, luscious Rioja can be drunk now and over the next 15+ years.

BODEGAS NEKEAS (NAVARRA)

1996	Vega Sindoa Cabernet/Tempranillo	A	87
1995	Vega Sindoa Cabernet/Tempranillo	A	90
1994	Vega Sindoa Cabernet/Tempranillo	A	88
1993	Vega Sindoa Cabernet/Tempranillo	A	87
1997	Vega Sindoa El Chaparral Old Vine	A	89
1996	Vega Sindoa Merlot	A	86
1995	Vega Sindoa Merlot	A	87
1993	Vega Sindoa Merlot	A	87
1996	Vega Sindoa Tempranillo	A	87
1995	Vega Sindoa Tempranillo	A	89
1997	Vega Sindoa Tempranillo/Merlot	A	86

This family-owned (eight separate families) winery in Navarra, in the foothills of the Pyrenees, has become one of the leading sources of terrific wine values. The production from all estate-grown fruit is about 66,000 cases, of which half is sold in America. These wines are must-purchases for readers seeking to maximize their purchasing power. This *bodegas* draws its estate-bottled grapes from relatively young vines planted on an estate of nearly 500 acres. All of the vineyards are situated at altitudes of 1,350–1,500 feet.

Bodegas Nekeas's red wines were very promising, especially given the fact that these wines are priced low and made from young vines. These red wine offerings include the 1997 Tempranillo/Merlot. It is hard to believe how much flavor this $6 wine offers. It displays a Zinfandel-like peppery, berry character, light to medium body, sweet, ripe fruit, not much complexity, but plenty of savory, mouth-filling fruit, glycerin, and purity. This wine can be drunk over the next 1–2 years, and I would not hesitate to serve it slightly chilled on a warm day. One of my favorite Vega Sindoa wines is the 1996 Cabernet/Tempranillo. Made from a blend of 60% Cabernet Sauvignon and 40% Tempranillo that spent 9 months in oak, this dark ruby-colored wine reveals purple nuances and gorgeous toasty oak in a bouquet dominated by blackberry and cherry liqueur-like fruit notes. Lush, with Cabernet's cassis character dominating the wine on the palate, this medium-bodied, subtly oaked example displays excellent purity, a nicely textured, plump feel, and a surprisingly long, rich, succulent finish. Although it tastes as though it costs $25 or more, this Cabernet/Tempranillo blend is available for a song—$7. Over 7,000 cases were brought into the United States, so this is one of those rare gems where availability should not be a problem. Drink it over the next several years. The 1996 Merlot (100% Merlot) is more restrained, but there is no doubting its Merlot personality. Aromas of coffee, melted chocolate, smoke, and herb-tinged black cherry fruit are present in both the wine's aromatics and flavors. There is good fatness in the mouth, a judicious dosage of toasty oak, and a plump, round, nicely textured finish. My instincts suggest this wine will get even better over the next 4–6 months; it should last for 2–4 years.

If you are looking for even more richness, the 1995 Merlot is a better wine, no doubt because 1995 was a far superior vintage for Navarra. It is an amazingly opulent, fat, chewy-textured wine bursting with smoky, jammy black cherry fruit. Pure and fleshy, with low acidity, it offers a lusty, exuberant mouthful of Merlot fruit that falls just short of being outstanding. If the 1995 Merlot must be tasted to be believed, so must the 1995 Cabernet/Tempranillo. This wine's opaque purple color and spectacular 92–93-point nose (cassis, toasty oak, and chocolate) are followed by a low-acid wine with terrific fruit purity and intensity. Aged for 9 months in 40% French Allier oak and 60% American oak casks, it offers copious quantities of cassis fruit in a full-bodied, rich, fleshy style. It is easy to complain about the huge prices now fetched by top French and California wines, so readers should seriously look at wines such as this, which offer amazing quality for the price. All of these wines are at least excellent values, but the 1995 Merlot and 1995 Cabernet/Tempranillo are two of the greatest wine bargains I tasted in 1997.

The 1996 Tempranillo is a super value. It exhibits an opaque purple color as well as a beautiful yet uncomplicated bouquet of jammy cassis and cherries. There are gobs of fruit, high extraction, a pure, one-dimensional, but concentrated palate, enough acidity for uplift, surprising fat and flesh, and a fresh finish. Drink it over the next 3–4 years.

The 1995 Vega Sindoa Tempranillo is a terrific wine for the price. The dark ruby/purple color and sweet, peppery, spicy, black cherry-scented nose are again reminiscent of a top-notch French Côtes du Rhône. The attack exhibits sweet, ripe fruit, surprising layers of flavor and a smooth, velvety, heady finish. This is a gutsy, rich, well-balanced, mouth-filling wine for drinking over the next 3–4 years. The 1994 Vega Sindoa Cabernet/Tempranillo is another exceptional bargain. Made from a blend of 60% Cabernet Sauvignon and 40% Tempranillo, this dark ruby/purple-colored wine displays an excellent, spicy, oaky nose with jammy black cherry and raspberry fruit scents. Dense, with the oak largely soaked up by the wine's ripeness and viscosity, this is a more structured and delineated wine than the 100% Tempranillo, as well as more elegant, stylish, and convincingly flavorful. It is smooth enough to be drunk now, but it promises to age well for 5–6 years.

The 1993 Vega Sindoa Cabernet/Tempranillo exhibits a dark ruby/purple color, a sweet, cassis, and oaky-scented nose, ripe, surprisingly fleshy, medium- to full-bodied, corpulent flavors, and an excellent finish. The wine possesses light tannin and adequate acidity, as well as fine purity and balance. Drink this honey-textured wine over the next 4–5 years. An outstanding bargain!

The 1993 Vega Sindoa Merlot is a refreshing rarity in a marketplace awash with pathetically vegetal, thin, acidic, suspicious New World Merlots. This offering exhibits a dark ruby color, an attractive display of varietal character (cherry, mocha, spice), ripe fruit, medium body, admirable purity and cleanliness, and a spicy, medium-bodied finish. Soft and round, it is ideal for drinking over the next 2–4 years.

The star of Bodegas Nekeas is the 1997 El Chaparral Old Vine. There are 2,000 cases of this wine, which is made from 25 parcels of old-vine Grenache. Readers can be sure I will be purchasing several cases for enjoying over the next several years. It tastes like an excellent Châteauneuf du Pape, and even though they can be terrific values, a Châteauneuf du Pape of this quality would sell for $20–$30 a bottle. The dark ruby/purple-colored El Chaparral Old Vine boasts a knockout nose of black raspberries, kirsch, spice, and pepper. In the mouth, the wine is expansive, round, and lush, with a slight *pain grillé* note in the background. It is an authoritatively flavored, rich, chewy, velvety-textured, old-vine Grenache that should drink well for 5–7 years. The youngest Grenache vines for this cuvée were 60 years old, the oldest in excess of 100 years. The wine was macerated for 25 days and then put directly into Allier French oak and American oak, where it remained on its lees for 5 months. Readers should be buying this wine by the truckful—it's that good! In fact, readers should taste every wine in this lineup, as they are terrific wine values!

BODEGAS OCHOA (NAVARRA)

1994 Merlot Crianza	B 86
1994 Tempranillo Crianza	B 87

This Navarra winery has been producing wines since the fifteenth century. The dark ruby/purple-colored 1994 Merlot Crianza offers an attractive nose of sweet, chocolatey, jammy, black cherry fruit, excellent texture, an expansive, fleshy character, and a clean, ripe finish with a touch of spice from aging in wood. Drink this well-made Merlot over the next 2–3 years. The 1994 Tempranillo Crianza is more elegant and not as fat, but beautifully delineated with a dark ruby/purple color, sweet, blackberry and cherry fruit, medium body, some spice, and a subtle earthiness in the background. It is a medium-bodied, fleshy, well-structured wine that should drink well for 3–4 years.

BARÓN DE ONA (RIOJA)

1990 Rioja	C 90
1994 Rioja Reserva	C 89
1992 Rioja Reserva	C 86
1991 Rioja Reserva	C 87
1990 Rioja Reserva	C 89

This estate in the Rioja Alta is owned by the Bodegas La Rioja Alta. The 1990 Rioja, which is aged in once used casks that are purchased from Château Margaux, is an elegant, impressive, concentrated, new style of Rioja with copious amounts of toasty vanillin from new oak, as well as sweet, black currant and cherry flavors presented in a silky-textured, medium-bodied format. This impeccably made wine lingers on the palate, with excellent purity and equilibrium. Already attractive, it promises to last for another decade.

Among these suave, lush, Pomerol-like Riojas, the 1991 Rioja Reserva exhibits a dark garnet color, sweet plum, tobacco, and toasty oak notes in the nose, round, gentle, graceful flavors, a silky texture, and a heady, seamless finish. Drink this very good Rioja over the next 4–5 years. The 1990 Rioja Reserva reveals more cedar and tobacco notes in addition to *pain grillé* and jammy kirsch and plumlike fruit. This dark garnet-colored wine is medium bodied, silky, hedonistic, and generous, with no hard edges. These stylish Riojas are meant for near-term consumption.

Along with the 1990, the 1994 Rioja Reserva is one of the best wines I have tasted from Barón de Ona. The color is a dark ruby/purple, and the wine offers up sweet berry fruit intermixed with toasty oak and spice. Lush yet elegant, with medium body, low acidity, and an up-front, juicy, succulent appeal, it should be consumed over the next 7–8 years. The 1992 Rioja Reserva exhibits a dark ruby color, followed by spicy, smoky, lead pencil, and oaky scents and elegant, pure flavors of cherries, strawberries, and currants. Medium bodied, slightly shorter than the 1994, but well made, this is a wine to drink over the next 3–4 years.

ALVARO PALACIOS (PRIORATO)

1996 Clos Dofi	EE	91
1995 Clos Dofi	EE	95
1994 Clos Dofi	EE	95
1996 L'Ermita	EEE	95

| 1995 L'Ermita | EEE | 96 |
| 1994 L'Ermita | EEE | 97+ |

This remarkable estate is the creation of Señor Alvaro Palacios, a young, passionate wine-maker who was impressed enough by the potential in the northeast corner of Spain's Catalonia to purchase a property in Priorato. Palacios studied and worked in Bordeaux with the firm of Jean-Pierre Moueix. His two Priorato vineyards include L'Ermita, which is an organically cultivated 25-acre vineyard, of which 5 acres are planted in extremely old vines, and Clos Dofi, a 17-acre vineyard. At L'Ermita, 80% of the plantings are Grenache, followed by Cabernet Sauvignon and small quantities of Carignan. At Clos Dofi, 60% is planted in Grenache, with the remainder Cabernet Sauvignon, Merlot, and Syrah. The stressed vines, which are planted on the terraces of Priorato, yield extraordinarily tiny quantities of wine, L'Ermita often producing less than a ton of fruit per acre. They are aged in 100% new French oak and bottled without filtration. The first vintage for Clos Dofi was 1989, and the first for L'Ermita was 1993. Having recently done a vertical tasting of both wines, I can unequivocally state they are spectacular wines, but they should be purchased only by connoisseurs with patience.

The superb, backward 1994 Clos Dofi requires 3–5 years of cellaring. The color is a dense saturated purple, and the nose offers up black currant, raspberry, and kirsch aromas intermixed with vanillin and minerals. Tannic and medium bodied, with exquisite ripeness and overall equilibrium, this powerful wine should be at its best between 2002 and 2016. The 1995 Clos Dofi was singing when I recently tasted it. The color is a saturated opaque purple, and the nose offers up explosive levels of cherry liqueur, crème de cassis, and *pain grillé*. Full bodied, with lower acidity and sweeter tannin than the 1994, this is a dense, massive, beautifully proportioned wine with exquisite equilibrium. While it will be more approachable than the 1994, it should age just as long—15–20 years. Still in cask, the 1996 Clos Dofi appears to be a less massive, more elegant, finesse-style wine, with a dense ruby/plum color and sweet red and black currant aromas intermixed with smoke, spice, fruitcake, and earth. In the mouth, it is medium bodied, well delineated, and long in the finish, without the weight or opulence of the 1995 and 1994. Anticipated maturity: 2002–2016.

As for L'Ermita, the 1994 is the current vintage in the marketplace; quantities are absurdly small. The color is a saturated inky/purple, and the soaring nose provides thrilling levels of sweet blackberry and cherry liqueur-like fruit. In spite of being full bodied, massive, and huge, it manages to not taste heavy despite its gargantuan proportions of fruit, glycerin, tannin, and extract. This chewy, glycerin-imbued, phenomenally intense wine possesses all the component parts necessary to become a modern-day legend. Anticipated maturity: 2003–2020. A clone of the 1994, the 1995 L'Ermita does not reveal quite the power and density of its older sibling, but that is a tough call . . . especially at this age. The color is an opaque purple, and the wine displays more *pain grillé*, grilled *jus de viande*, blackberry, and floral notes in its aromatics, which seem slightly more evolved than the 1994s. In the mouth, the 1995 is deep, powerful, and rich, with low acidity, better sweetness and integration of tannin (only when compared with the massive 1994), layers of extract and flavor, and a 40-second finish. It is a remarkable wine with formidable style, intensity, and flavor. Anticipated maturity: 2002–2020. The 1996 L'Ermita appears to be another blockbuster effort from Alvaro Palacios. The color is a saturated purple. The expressive nose boasts aromas of *pain grillé*, roasted coffee, chocolate-covered, jammy cherry candy, minerals, and new oak. Full bodied, dense, and thick, with an unctuous texture, lower acidity, and higher alcohol than the 1995 and 1994, this is a meaty, chewy, masculine wine with a flamboyant personality, in addition to a monster finish. It is superintense but exceptionally well balanced, especially in view of its proportions. Anticipated maturity: 2003–2020.

PESQUERA (RIBERO DEL DUERO)

1994 Janus	EE	97
1995 Tinto Crianza	C	93
1994 Tinto Crianza	C	95+

I first wrote laudatory comments about Pesquera over a decade ago, so I am thrilled to see proprietor Alejandro Fernandez continue to build on his noteworthy track record. His new releases are splendid. The superb 1995 Tinto Crianza was released in January 1998. It exhibits an opaque ruby/purple color, as well as a wonderfully sweet, jammy black cherry and cassis nose with hints of roasted herbs, vanillin, and spice. Thick, juicy, and full bodied, this low-acid, huge, accessible, and flamboyantly fruity Pesquera should drink well now yet age well for 10–12 years.

It is no secret that 1994 is one of the greatest vintages in the last 30 years for northern Spain. Pesquera's 1994 Tinto Crianza is undoubtedly representative of the fabulous ripeness and intensity the grapes achieved. From its opaque purple color to its extraordinary aromatics, which consist of melted chocolate, roasted meats, jammy black fruits, and spice, this is an extraordinary, well-endowed, full-bodied wine of remarkable richness and intensity. There are impressive levels of glycerin and extract, but no hard edges or sense of heaviness in this blockbuster effort. Drink it now as well as over the next 12–15 years. What a joy it is to write about the 1994 Janus. Fernandez has made this superluxury cuvée only in 1982, 1986, and 1991. The 1994 Janus may be the greatest Pesquera ever made. This wine is awesome in its richness, intensity, and potential complexity. It is a gentle giant, with no hard edges and profound levels of rich, concentrated black fruits nicely meshed with smoky, spicy new oak. It is an opulent, accessible, yet still unformed wine that should provide fabulous drinking for 12–15 years. Given its sweetness and lush personality, no one will be committing infanticide by drinking this marvelous wine in its youth.

BODEGAS PROTOS S.A. (RIBERA DEL DUERO)

1994 Crianza	C	87+
1996 Protos	A	86
1995 Protos	A	87

The deep ruby-colored 1996 Protos is a richly fruity wine without much complexity but plenty of sweet berry fruit. It is reminiscent of a Spanish-style Zinfandel. Soft and medium bodied, it will be a treat to drink over the next 2–3 years. The 1995 Protos reveals a similar deep ruby color, more complexity and sweetness of fruit, medium body, excellent purity, and a ripe, moderately long finish. Drink this round, generous wine over the next 2–3 years. The 1994 Crianza is the most interesting and complex wine of this trio, with more tannin, intensity, and richness. Offering sweet fruit, medium body, fine purity, and a moderately long finish, it should drink well for 5–6 years. All three wines represent very good values.

BODEGAS RAMIREZ (RIOJA)

1994 Ramirez de La Pascina Crianza	A	86
1995 Rioja	A	87

Another outstanding value from Spain, the 1995 Rioja (100% Tempranillo, aged in American oak barrels) displays a dark ruby color and moderately intense, spicy, cedary, cherry, and berry aromas, with pepper in the background (reminiscent of Zinfandel?). It is an elegantly styled Rioja, with medium body, pure fruit, subtle oak, and fine ripeness, as well as impressive equilibrium and harmony among its elements. This round, appealing wine should be drunk over the next 2–4 years.

An excellent value, the 1994 Ramirez de La Pascina Crianza, also made from 100% Tempranillo and aged in small American oak barrels, offers an attractive smoky, gravelly, red currant-scented nose, sweet, ripe fruit, medium body, and a clean, vibrant, refreshing finish. It is not a big wine, but it is a soft, fruit-driven offering for drinking over the next 2–3 years.

BODEGAS REAL SITIO DE VENTOSILLA (RIBERA DEL DUERO)

1996 Prado Rey	A	87

This large vineyard holder in Ribera del Duero has traditionally sold much of his production to Pesquera. The 1996 is the first estate-bottled offering from Bodegas Real Sitio de Ventosilla. The wine, which spent 3 months in 100% new oak, mostly American, is a top-notch value, especially for a wine with such richness and intensity of fruit. The dark ruby purple color is followed by earthy, sweet blackberry, raspberry, and currant aromas, lush, medium-bodied flavors, excellent purity, and a sexy dollop of vanillin/*pain grillé* new oak, and spice. This soft, round, delicious 100% Tempranillo will drink beautifully for 3–4 years. Excellent value.

REMELLURI (RIOJA)

1989 Gran Reserva	D	93
1996 Rioja	C	(90–91)
1995 Rioja	C	92
1994 Rioja	C	93
1993 Rioja	C	90

This relatively young winery is one of the showcase producers for the newer style of Spanish reds—earlier bottling, small *barrique* aging, and an unmanipulated, artisanal style. I enjoyed Remelluri's debut releases, and the recent offerings have taken the intensity level to greater heights as the estate's vineyards have matured. The 1994 Rioja is believed by the winery and their highly talented winemaker, Telmo Rodriguez, to be the greatest wine they have ever made (borrowing a page from France's marketing experts, 1994 is widely heralded as Spain's vintage of the century). The wine exhibits an opaque purple color, an exotic combination of smoky, black currant, Asian spices, roasted herbs, and tar scents vaguely reminiscent of an imaginary blend of La Mission-Haut-Brion and Mouton-Rothschild. The wine possesses a thick, unctuous texture, fabulous concentration and richness, and a long, lush, sweet, 40-second finish with amazing extract. Aged in 100% new oak and bottled unfiltered, this wine should be one of the great Spanish reds in the 1994 vintage. Be sure and keep an eye out for it . . . I'm certainly buying it.

The outstanding, smoky, tobacco-scented, complex 1993 Rioja is a rich, full-bodied, dark ruby/purple-colored, supple wine ideal for drinking over the next decade. It does not possess the thick viscosity of the 1994, but it is an outstanding example of this producer's Rioja. It is made primarily from Tempranillo, with small amounts of Graciano, Mazuelo, and Garnacha.

The barrel sample of 1996 Rioja is a full-bodied, tannic, backward style of Remelluri with an opaque purple color and copious quantities of toasty new oak aromas intermixed with blackberries, cassis, and raspberry fruit. Although rich, structured, and impressive, it is very tannic. This wine will be less accessible than vintages such as 1995 and 1994. Anticipated maturity: 2002–2018. The 1995 Rioja is more evolved, flamboyant, and delicious. If a Rioja could be said to be made in the style of St.-Julien/Pauillac, this wine meets such criteria. A blend of 80% Tempranillo and the rest Garnacha, Mazuelo, and Graciano, this offering reveals a dense, opaque purple color, as well as a superb bouquet of blackberry, cassis, and cherry liqueur notes intermixed with toasty new oak, smoke, dried herb, and grilled meat-like aromas. In the mouth, the wine is full bodied, with layers of concentration, surprisingly high levels of glycerin, low acidity, and a plush, multilayered, textured, supple mouth-feel. Drink this superb, modern-style Rioja now and over the next 12–15 years. Very impressive! Interestingly, winemaker Telmo Rodriguez obtained a degree in oenology from the University of Bordeaux and lists on his résumé experience at such blue-blood estates as France's Cos d'Estournel, Domaine du Trevallon, Domaine J. L. Chave, Pétrus, and California's Dominus.

Last, only 250 cases of the 1989 Rioja Gran Reserva have been released. The last vintage that Remelluri declared a Gran Reserva was 1985. The 1989 exhibits an opaque garnet color and a huge, provocative fragrance of hickory smoke, barbecue spices, chocolate, jammy black fruits, truffles, and herbs. The bouquet's immense complexity is followed by a wine of extraordinary power, richness, and body. Imagine a top Brunello di Montalcino aged in 100% new oak given an injection of steroids, and readers might have an image of just how rich and boldly styled this Rioja has turned out. The wine boasts remarkable length, an unctuous texture, and plenty of tannin lurking beneath the layers of creamy, sweet (from ripeness, not sugar) fruit. Already stunning, this wine should drink well for a decade.

FERNANDO REMIREZ DE GANUZA (RIOJA)

1994 Rioja Old Vines Unfiltered	E	92

With this debut release, this estate's proprietor is already being declared a rising star by the Spanish wine press. The 1994 Rioja Old Vines Unfiltered (7,000 cases produced) is a blend of 85% Tempranillo, 10% Graciano, 3% Garnacha, and 2% miscellaneous varietals, made from vines ranging between 31 and 96 years in age. Bottled unfined and unfiltered, this wine spent 1 year in fermentation tanks before being moved to 225-liter French and American oak barrels for 2 years of aging. Known for his severe selection, this producer has fashioned a wine that will cause considerable excitement. The dense, opaque dark ruby/purple color is accompanied by a full-bodied, fruit-driven wine that should develop into a splendid Rioja. It possesses a moderately intense nose of black raspberries, toast, licorice, and minerals. Concentrated, expansive, and crammed with fruit, this layered, multidimensional, spicy wine only hints at its considerable complexity. The finish is long (20 seconds or more), and the wine reveals flawless balance among its structural components (acidity, alcohol, and tannin). While it has a degree of accessibility, 2–5 years of cellaring will be beneficial. It should age well for 15–20 years.

BODEGAS TEOFILO REYES (RIBERA DEL DUERO)

1995 Bodegas Reyes	C	92
1996 Teofilo Reyes	D	92
1994 Teofilo Reyes	C	91

By most accounts, Teofilo Reyes is the most legendary winemaker in Ribera del Duero. He certainly has had plenty of experience, having made his first wine in 1950 at the age of 28. He was the winemaker for Pesquera from 1974 to 1993. In 1994, with the help of his two sons, he decided to begin his own winery. Made from 100% Tinta del Pais, his wine emerges from relatively old vines (about 40 years in age) and is aged for 14 months in American oak before being bottled unfiltered. Each vintage has been a success, and certainly the 1996 is among the most concentrated, explosively fruity, and intense to date. Fortunately nearly 2,500 cases are being imported to the United States. The wine boasts an opaque purple color, followed by exquisite blackberry liqueur notes intermixed with smoke, licorice, and new oak scents. It displays a brilliantly focused, ripe, concentrated style with full body, gobs of fruit, a viscous, creamy texture, and a lusty finish with beautifully integrated acidity and tannin. This is a knockout, ostentatiously styled Ribera del Duero to drink now and over the next 10–12 years.

Only 1,000 cases are available of the exceptionally concentrated 1994 debut vintage from Reyes. It is a dark purple-colored wine, with a nose of wonderfully pure scents of black raspberries, truffles, minerals, smoke, and licorice. The wine, aged in 100% new oak, seems to have soaked up the wood, as it plays a very minor part in the background of this lavishly rich, silky-textured, full-bodied wine made from 100% Tinta del Pais. A marvelous example of a Ribera del Duero, it can be drunk when released and should last for 15–20 years. Bravo!

The 1995 Bodegas Reyes is another highly promising wine. Reyes, who practices malolactic fermentation in small casks, uses 100% Tinta del Pais grapes (from 40-year-old vines), and aims for maximum extraction and little or no manipulation (this wine is bottled unfiltered). The 1995 exhibits an opaque ruby/purple color, followed by a terrific nose of black fruits, licorice, spice, and smoke. The wine is dense, rich, and full bodied, with no heaviness or overbearing, astringent tannin. Everything is seamless in this beautifully made, pure, full-bodied, intense Ribera del Duero. It should drink well young and last for 10–15+ years.

LA RIOJA ALTA (RIOJA)

1989	Gran Reserva 904	D	90
1987	Gran Reserva 904	D	89
1985	Gran Reserva 904	E	90
1982	Gran Reserva 890	E	92
1981	Gran Reserva 890	D	92
1978	Gran Reserva 890	E	93
1991	Viña Alberdi	B	87
1994	Viña Alberdi Reserva	B	87
1989	Viña Alberdi Reserva	B	88
1989	Viña Arana Reserva	C	87
1988	Viña Arana Reserva	C	88
1987	Viña Arana Reserva	C	86
1990	Viña Ardanza Reserva	C	87
1989	Viña Ardanza Reserva	C	87
1987	Viña Ardanza Reserva	C	87

Readers must recognize that this traditionally run firm tends to make wines that have spent considerable time in oak and are much lighter colored, more mature, and clearly ready to drink when released. The antithesis of modern-day fruit and oak-driven wines, they are all characterized by soft, tobacco, cedary, cigar box-scented noses, with sweet fruit and light garnet/ruby colors with amber edges. However, do not judge these offerings by their feeble colors, as they are very aromatic and their flavors are nuanced and complex. For example, both the 1989 and 1988 Viña Arana Reservas are light to medium ruby-colored, amber-tinged wines with aromatic fruitcake, cedar, smoky, cherry/strawberry noses, lush, round, silky-textured flavors, and considerable complexity. They are fragrant, pungent, soft, complex, nuanced wines that offer immediate drinkability. Although fully mature, they will age well for 5–6 years.

The 1987 Viña Arana Reserva exhibits a subtle lead pencil, fruity nose, with scents of tobacco and minerals, that is reminiscent of a fine Graves. New oak is apparent, but this wine's overall style emphasizes ripe fruit, a sense of elegance, suppleness, and clean, friendly, generous scents and flavors. Drink it over the next 3–4 years. The 1987 Viña Ardanza Reserva offers sweet, curranty, cedar, vanillin, and spice scents, medium body, and a plush, mature, rich, savory personality. Drink it over the next 3–5 years.

There is a touch of Grenache in the 1989 Viña Ardanza Reserva. The wine's medium garnet color reveals an amber edge. A sweet, caramel, smoky, strawberry, tobacco, and tar-scented nose is followed by an elegant, round, medium-bodied wine with good richness, refreshing but soft acidity, and a heady, nicely nuanced, layered finish.

The less expensive offerings include the 1989 Viña Alberdi Reserva, which is packaged in an embossed bottle. It offers a rich, sweet, jammy nose complemented by the generous use of toasty new oak. This round, fresh, lively, medium-bodied wine is a delight to drink. The wine's suppleness and seductive character are its hallmarks. Drink it over the next 4–5 years.

I was somewhat disappointed in the 1991 and 1993 Viña Arana Reserva. The 1994 Viña Alberdi Reserva is a medium ruby-colored, sweet, smoky, complex wine with copious quantities of vanillin, strawberry, raspberry fruit in both its aromas and flavors. A graceful, stylish, expansively flavored wine, it is lusciously fruity, elegant, and satisfying. It should drink well for 4–5 years. The dark garnet-colored 1990 Viña Ardanza Reserva offers up sweet plum, cherry, tar, and lead pencil notes in the complex bouquet. In the mouth, it is all finesse and elegance, with medium body, no hard edges, and a soft, round finish.

These traditionally made Spanish wines are successful. However, readers looking for more internationally styled Spanish reds that have saturated ruby/purple colors and grapey personalities are advised that this *bodegas* emphasizes the more mature, aged character of Spanish Rioja, with mature garnet colors with rust at the edge and fragrant, intense, evolved aromatic profiles. Even the younger wines, such as the 1991 Viña Alberdi, display plenty of complexity in their bouquets. The medium ruby-colored 1991 Viña Alberdi exhibits some amber at the edge, as well as a sweet, curranty, tobacco-scented nose and smoky, silky-textured, medium-bodied flavors with some American oak in evidence. It is a seductive, midweight Rioja for drinking over the next 3–4 years.

The flagship wines of this *bodegas* are their 904 and 890 Gran Reservas. These wines spend 8–10 years in cask and are then bottle-aged even longer. They are beautifully made wines with a complexity not unlike a mature vintage of a top-class Bordeaux Graves. The 1987 Gran Reserva 904 possesses a phenomenal set of aromatics (it merits a score in the mid-90s on the bouquet), but there is a certain shortness in the mouth. Nevertheless, I can enthusiastically recommend this medium garnet-colored wine. It offers up a beautiful cedary, tobacco, smoky, leathery, jammy cherry-scented nose, as well as elegant, medium-bodied, round flavors that are surprisingly fresh and youthful for an 11-year-old wine. Although it requires some introspection, it is an extremely finesse-styled Rioja that should continue to drink well for 7–8 years. I was turned on by the classy 1982 Gran Reserva 890. It exhibits an "Haut-Brion-ish" cigar box, mineral, roasted tobacco, and jammy berry nose that soars from the glass. In the mouth, the wine is expansive, lush, medium bodied, and far richer and more complete than its weak medium ruby/amber-like color suggests. This is a textbook, classic, old-style Rioja with gobs of character, fruit, and complexity. Drink it over the next 7–8 years.

The two newest releases of the flagship, traditionally made Riojas are the 1989 Gran Reserva 904 and 1982 Gran Reserva 890. These examples are the antithesis of modern-day, deep purple-colored, grapey, fat, rich wines. They are the epitome of old-style Riojas that achieve their complexity from delicacy, subtlety, and exceptional aromatics. Neither of these offerings will cut a weighty impression on the palate, but aromatically, both are knockouts. Moreover, their flavors are beautifully balanced, with no aggressiveness. The 1989 Gran Reserva 904 exhibits a dark garnet color, as well as a wood smoke, burning embers, charcoal, lead pencil, sweet strawberry and cherry nose with cedar, tobacco, and a remarkable Graves-like character. Complex, elegant, savory, subtle, yet layered flavors never achieve much weight, but they deliver considerable intensity and complexity. This wine should continue to drink well for another decade. Except for its strong vanillin component, the 1982

Gran Reserva 890 could easily be mistaken for a 25-year-old Haut-Brion. The 1982 Gran Reserva 890 reveals lead pencil, charcoal smoke, hot brick, cedar, strawberry, cherry, and fruitcake scents in one of the most complex aromatic profiles anyone could suck in past their olfactory senses. In the mouth, the wine is medium bodied and elegant, with delicate, intense, but light flavors. This is a gorgeous, complex, old-style Rioja the likes of which are impossible to find from other producers in this renowned Spanish appellation.

The 1985 Gran Reserva 904 exhibits a medium deep ruby color with considerable garnet and rust at the edge. The aromatics are extremely intense and compelling, offering up scents of plumlike fruit intermixed with smoke, minerals, tobacco, cherries, earth, and licorice. There is a sweet, rich impression on the palate, without any sense of heaviness or austere tannin. The wine is fresh and lively but possesses the mature, sweet, smoky, Graves-like style of a top Rioja. Medium bodied, beautifully concentrated and layered, and fully mature, it should keep for another decade. The 1981 Gran Reserva 890 boasts a knockout nose of smoke, charcoal, vanillin, black fruits, and cigar smoke. The wine's terrific fruit seemingly belies the relatively advanced medium ruby color with significant amber at the edge. There is tannin in the background, but the wine is broad and expansive, with considerable sweet fruit, glycerin, and length. The 1981 was considered one of the great vintages for Rioja, and this wine is at its peak of maturity, although it will last for another 15–20 years. These are exceptional examples of old-school Spanish Riojas that were aged in different-size oak vessels and not released until they had reached full maturity. If readers think these prices are high, consider the fact that this *bodegas* has aged the wine for the consumer, rather than asking you to buy it as a "future" in 1982 and hold it for 15 years before drinking it.

The 1978 Rioja Gran Reserva 890 reveals a light ruby color with orange at the edge. In contrast with the weak color, there is an exceptionally perfumed bouquet and rich, sweet fruit that cascades across the palate. The wine exhibits a mature, classic nose of gravel, lead pencil, sweet oak, and gobs of ripe black cherry and currant fruit that blossoms after 10–15 minutes in the glass. Expansive, with medium to full body, this penetratingly fragrant, concentrated wine is never heavy or tannic. It is a gentle, exceptionally complex, harmonious wine that is one of the finest mature Riojas I have ever drunk. While at its apogee, it should hold, where well cellared, for another 10+ years. Impressive!

BODEGAS RODERO S.L. (RIBERA DEL DUERO)

1995 Reserva	D	92
1994 Reserva	D	89
1995 Val Ribeno Crianza	D	90
1994 Val Ribeno Crianza	D	88

This estate is typical of what is happening in many of Europe's top viticultural areas. The grandfather was a founding member of the coop in Ribera del Duero, and his grandson, Carmelo Rodero, decided to leave the coop in 1987 after having sold grapes to many top Ribera del Duero wineries, including Vega Sicilia. This estate has grown to 60 hectares (approximately 150 acres), and a state-of-the-art winery was built in 1991. Despite the large acreage, production has been limited to 12,000 cases, with yields averaging a remarkable 1.8 tons of fruit per acre for the Tinto del Pais. The wines are aged in a combination of French and American oak, with slightly more of the latter. The Crianza is aged 12 months in oak, the Reserva 20 months, and the Gran Reserva 24 months. These impressive wines represent a noteworthy addition to the high-quality Spanish wine sweepstakes.

Of the two Crianzas, I marginally preferred the 1995. It exhibits an opaque purple color, as well as sweet, dense, black cherry and blackberry aromas intermingled with well-integrated toasty, smoky oak. Ripe, with a low-acid, seamless texture, layered flavors, and nicely integrated tannin and acidity, this is an opulently styled wine for drinking over the next 10–12 years. Fortunately about 4,000 cases were produced. The 1994 Crianza reveals a similar opulence, a plum/purple color, and a forward blackberry and cherry aromatic profile, but not quite the complexity or length of the 1995. This lovely wine should drink well for the next 7–8 years.

I had a preference for the 1995 Reserva, which offers an opaque deep color and a nose of roasted nuts, herbs, jammy cherries, kirsch liqueur, and blackberry fruit. This sweet (from glycerin and extract, not sugar), stunningly proportioned, full-bodied, gorgeously made wine possesses outstanding purity and layers of fruit in a supple texture. It should drink well for at least 10–12+ years. The soft, spicy 1994 Reserva (about 400 cases) reveals significantly more evolution in its aromatics. Cedar, herbs, earth, and red and black fruits are plentiful in this medium-bodied, elegant, cleanly made wine. There is moderate complexity, but the 1994 is far more evolved than the 1995. Carmelo Rodero rates 1994, 1995, and 1996 as top-notch vintages, with 1992, 1993, and 1997 mediocre.

BODEGAS TELMO RODRIGUEZ (NAVARRA)

1996 Alma (100% Old Vine Garnacha)	A	89
1995 Alma	A	86
1994 Alma	A	87

Telmo Rodriguez, the winemaker for the fine Remelluri estate, has produced a Grenache-based wine made from vines 40 years of age or older. The 1994 tastes like a mini-Rayas, with a sweet, raspberry, roasted nut, and kirsch bouquet, sweet, rich, fleshy, voluptuously textured flavors, obvious ripeness, purity of fruit, and a heady, high alcohol, lusty finish. It is a wine to drink during its first 4–5 years of life. A super value!

Rodriguez produces 4,000 cases of this 100% Garnacha (Grenache) wine that is akin to a gutsy, meaty French Côtes du Rhône. The 1995 Alma offers gobs of sweet black raspberry fruit, clean winemaking, medium body, and a real personality in addition to a mouth-filling, savory quality. It is not complicated or complex, but it is certainly satisfying. Drink it over the next 2 years. Excellent value.

The 1996 Alma is a very special wine. I am not sure it doesn't deserve a slightly higher rating. At $7, it is unquestionably a remarkable bargain. Made from 100% old-vine Grenache (minimum age is 40 years), it is akin to drinking a Châteauneuf du Pape. The wine boasts a dense, opaque ruby/purple color, as well as an intense nose of kirsch, pepper, and jammy raspberries. Round, expansive, and sweet, with high glycerin and gorgeous layers of fruit, this wine gushes with an abundance of intensity. With its medium to full body and outstanding purity, this terrific expression of Grenache must be tasted to be believed! Normally, Grenache of this quality costs $20–$30 a bottle! It should drink well for 4–5 years.

SENORIO DE SAN VICENTE (RIOJA)

1994 Rioja	D	93+
1991 Rioja	D	92
1995 Rioja	D	92

This single-vineyard, luxury Rioja is the brainchild of the Eguren family. The 45-acre vineyard possesses much denser vine spacing than most Rioja vineyards (about 4,500 vines per 2½ acres) and is planted at a high altitude of nearly 1,600 feet. Although made from young vines (12 years), the wine is given at least 30 days of maceration, aged for 20 months in American oak barrels, and bottled without filtration. Fewer than 1,000 cases were made of the 1991, but in 1994 the winery was in full production and produced just over 6,000 cases. This looks to be one of the more stunning, newer-style Riojas to emerge from Spain. Readers should take note, as I suspect prices will only go up.

The 1991 Rioja (made from 100% Tempranillo) displays a rich, garnet, mature-looking color. The intensely complex bouquet combines finesse with power. The wine offers sweet aromas of tobacco, black and red fruits, spice, and herbs. Smooth, with a lush, opulent texture and medium to full body, this perfumed wine is deliciously opulent, round, and complex. It is a seductive, hedonistic Rioja for drinking over the next 5–7 years. The dense garnet-colored 1994 Rioja appears to have a 10–12-year plateau of drinkability. Once again, the extraordinary aromatics consist of ripe, jammy fruits intermixed with smoke, cedar, tobacco, and spice. Admirable lushness and elegance that are suave and refined, supple tannin, and layers of richness, yet an overall restraint make me wonder if this is not a Rioja made in the image of a Château Margaux, where richness is combined with elegance. Interestingly, the owners refused to declare any wine in the difficult Rioja vintages of 1992 and 1993. This winery should be followed closely, as these seamless, complex, enthralling wines evidence.

The 1995 Rioja is one of the most hedonistic red wines being made in Spain, with a dark purple color and exotic, ostentatious aromatics reminiscent of a sexy, lavishly oaked Pomerol. Drinking this full-bodied, voluptuously textured, silky smooth red wine is akin to drinking cherry/framboise liqueur. Made from 100% Tempranillo, from a single vineyard, it is not likely to make "old bones," but for drinking over the next 5–9 years, it will prove outstanding.

SCALA DEI PRIORATO (CATALUNA)

1996	Cartoixa	C	91
1992	Crianza	A	86
1995	El Cipres	A	85
1994	El Cipres Unfiltered	A	89
1987	Gran Reserva Cartoixa	C	90
1995	Negre	B	86
1991	Negre Scala Dei	B	87
1993	Priorato	B	86

These Grenache-based wines have consistently placed well in my tastings. They are rich, peppery, medium- to full-bodied, supple, mouth-filling, satisfying wines. Readers should think of them as Spain's answer to Châteauneuf du Pape. The 1993 Priorato exhibits a deep ruby color, a peppery, earthy, spicy nose, ripe fruit, medium to full body, and a lush, delicious, uncomplicated, mouth-filling personality. Drink it over the next 4–5 years, as you would a top-class French Côtes du Rhone. The soft, richer 1991 Negre Scala Dei reveals more intense, jammy, red and black fruits in both the nose and flavors. The wine is full bodied, peppery, and spicy, with low acidity and a lush, velvety-textured, alcoholic finish. The finest wine in this trio is the 1987 Gran Reserva Cartoixa. Its dark ruby color with a touch of garnet and excellent nose of roasted herbs, black cherries, meat, and smoke are followed by a concentrated, full-bodied wine with layers of flavor, plenty of glycerin, a chewy texture, low acidity, and a forceful, rich, provocative finish. Although the alcohol level is high, it is well concealed by the wine's jammy fruit. Already delicious, it should age well for a decade.

Many knowledgeable insiders have long believed that this little-known region in eastern Spain, called Priorato, a rugged area with steep terraced vineyards of old Grenache vines, has unlimited potential for producing great wine. The 1994 El Cipres Unfiltered is a special bottling done for importer Eric Solomon. Readers should think of it as Spain's answer to a lusty, black raspberry, and jammy cherry-scented and -flavored Châteauneuf du Pape. The wine displays terrific purity, a peppery, spicy ripeness, full body, and a knockout, lusty, rich finish. Châteauneuf du Pape is a great value at $18–$20, but this wine's $7 price tag makes it a steal! Drink it over the next 4–5 years, although my instincts suggest it should still be going strong at age 10.

The soft, berry-scented and -flavored, cleanly made 1995 El Cipres reveals copious quantities of fruit, medium body, and a dry, spicy, austere finish. Drink it over the next 1–2 years.

The two value-priced wines, the 1992 Crianza and 1995 Negre, are similar in quality but slightly different in style. The fruitier, softer, lusher wine is the 1995 Negre, a silky-textured, medium-bodied wine with plenty of peppery, black cherry fruit, good glycerin, and an easygoing finish. It is meant to be drunk over the next several years. The 1992 Crianza possesses more structure, some tannin, medium body, and a similar emphasis on a red cherry fruit character. It should be consumed over the next 2–3 years for its uncomplicated fruit and suppleness. By the way, a more expensive 1991 Cartoixa Gran Reserva was pleasant but less fresh and fruity.

The 1996 Cartoixa appears to be a turning point for this winery, which has always produced good wines, although many cuvées were left too long in wood. Produced from 70-year-old Grenache wines, this special cuvée was made to the specifications of the American importer; thus it is available only here. Fifty barrels, of which 50% were new, were produced of this wine, which enjoyed a 25-day maceration, 1 racking, and no fining or filtration. It is Grenache at its most luxuriously rich. The wine's opaque ruby/purple color is accompanied by a knockout nose of jammy kirsch liqueur, roasted peanuts, smoked olives, chocolate, and *jus de viande*. Huge, dense, and massive, with rustic tannin in the finish, this wine possesses extraordinary concentration and richness and massive body yet is neither oversize nor undrinkable. It is reminiscent of a top-class Châteauneuf du Pape from the likes of Henri Bonneau or Vieux-Donjon. While Bonneau and Vieux-Donjon do not use new oak, the utilization of new oak by Scala Dei has been, remarkably, obliterated by the wine's extraordinary depth and richness of fruit. Anticipated maturity: now–2012.

BODEGAS SIERRA CANTABRIA (RIOJA)

1996	Codice	A	86
1995	Codice	A	89
1993	Codice	A	90
1992	Codice	A	87
1991	Crianza	A	87
1990	Crianza	A	90
1995	Crianza Unfiltered	A	87
1994	Crianza Unfiltered	A	90
1987	Gran Reserva	C	90
1985	Gran Reserva	C	88
1994	Reserva	B	90
1991	Reserva	B	86
1990	Reserva	B	89+
1996	Rioja	A	87
1996	Rioja Coleccion Privada	C	91

| 1995 Tinto | A | 88 |
| 1994 Tinto | A | 89 |

This estate vineyard, owned by the Eguren family, is considered to possess some of the finest Rioja vineyards, situated in an area called San Vicente de la Sonsierra. What is so remarkable about the wines of Sierra Cantabria, which have consistently made my best buy reports, is their continuing reasonable prices despite the immense popularity they enjoy, both in Spain and abroad. Year in and year out this winery produces as many top wine values as anyone, save for such large French *négociants* as Georges Duboeuf or La Val d'Orbieu. Here is another noteworthy lineup for readers seeking to maximize their purchasing power. Thirty-five percent of Sierra Cantabria's production comes from their own 267 acres of vineyards. To their credit, the vineyards are farmed in a nearly organic fashion, minimizing pesticides, herbicides, and so on.

The 1996 Codice (a blend of 90% Tempranillo and 10% Grenache) reveals loads of fruit, a medium-bodied, berry, earthy, spicy midpalate, good glycerin, and a supple-textured, lush finish. This wine should drink well for 2–3 years, and if more aromatics develop, it may merit a score 1–2 points higher. Already displaying intriguing cedar, chocolate, weedy tobacco, and black cherry fruit, the 1995 Crianza offers sweet aromatics, ripe fruit in the attack, medium body, excellent equilibrium, no hard edges, and a succulent, fleshy finish. This wine should continue to drink well for 3–4 years.

Made from 100% Tempranillo, the 1994 Reserva spent 16 months in American oak barrels. It is an outstanding example of what can be found in the marketplace for $15 a bottle. The wine exhibits a deep ruby color, followed by an impressive, open-knit bouquet of melted chocolate, cherry jam, pepper, herbs, and spices. Thick, with low acidity, excellent density and extract, medium to full body, and a pure, rich, toasty finish, this delicious, round, juicy, yet well-delineated Rioja should continue to evolve for 3–4 years and last for a decade.

Another terrific wine is the 100% Tempranillo 1996 Rioja. This dark ruby/purple-colored fruit bomb is medium bodied and fleshy, with excellent purity, plenty of cherry and raspberry fruit, a sweet, ripe personality, and a lush, low-acid, delicious finish. It should be drunk over the next 1–2 years. The 1995 red Codice, a blend of 90% Tempranillo and 10% Garnache aged 6–8 months in new oak, is an amazing wine for the price. A dark ruby/purple color is followed by a complex display of sweet, toasty oak and jammy black cherries. This hedonistic wine possesses lush ripeness, a silky, seamless texture, medium body, and a lavish richness that borders on opulence. This is an amazing, fruit-driven wine to drink over the next several years.

Another outstanding bargain from this *bodegas* is the 1994 Crianza Rioja. According to the importer, it took him 3 years of hard negotiating to get the winery to bottle this wine without filtration. Made from 100% Tempranillo, it is a sensational bargain. It displays a complex, spice box, tobacco, sweet black cherry, and curranty nose, with a whiff of lead pencil and smoke. Dense, with terrific fruit ripeness, a soft, velvety texture, medium body, and a flamboyant finish, this layered wine reminds me of a Spanish red Graves with its smoky tobacco-like fruit character. This beautifully supple-textured wine should be drunk over the next 4–5 years. An astonishing value!

Readers seeking less grapey, exuberantly fruity wines should check out the two Reserva offerings from Sierra Cantabria. The 1991 Rioja Reserva exhibits a mature garnet color, as well as a sweet, plum, fruitcake, tobacco, herb, and berry nose, satiny-textured, supple, fruity flavors, and a medium-bodied, moderately long finish. It is a well-made, textbook Rioja for consuming over the next 3–4 years. The 1987 Gran Reserva offers up expressive, complex, tobacco, smoke, charcoal, plum, and cherry aromas with a touch of prunes. Sweet, round, and soft, with medium body, and expansive, lush flavors, this complex Rioja can be drunk now as well as over the next 7–8 years.

This winery's red wine selections are nearly too good to believe! The 1995 Tinto is a supple, deep ruby-colored wine with purple nuances. A surprisingly sweet, spicy, blackberry-and-currant-scented nose is followed by a ripe, velvety-textured, low-acid, deliciously plump, nicely textured wine that is bursting with ripe aromas and fruit flavors. Wines such as this normally sell for three times the price. Drink it over the next 2–3 years. The knockout 1993 Codice red exhibits a dark ruby/purple nose and toasty, sweet new oak in its lavishly ripe, uncomplicated, but richly fruity nose. The wine offers a spicy, lead pencil-flavored, lush, medium- to full-bodied palate with gobs of fruit. There is glycerin, intensity, and surprising length to this wine, which could easily pass for a $30 bottle of luxury-priced Rioja. It should drink well for another 3–4 years—if readers can exhibit restraint. The 1991 Crianza is a medium ruby-colored wine displaying mature aromas of tobacco, cedar, and a Graves-like mineral, lead pencil-like note to go along with the sweet, curranty fruit. Although closed at first, it opens in the mouth to reveal plenty of supple ripe fruit, medium body, and a sense of elegance. It should drink well for 3–4 years.

The 1990 Rioja Reserva (100% Tempranillo) is a classy, more complex, rich, medium-bodied wine that again exhibits a character not unlike a fine Graves, with lead pencil, roasted red and black fruits, and toasty oak notes. It needs time to develop in the glass, but this supple, nicely textured, concentrated wine could merit an outstanding rating with another 1–2 years of bottle age and will last for 5–8 years. It is an ambitiously built "serious" wine that tastes as though it should cost $25 or more. As for the oldest offering, the 1985 Gran Reserva reveals a medium ruby/garnet color, followed by a classic, old-style Rioja nose of roasted herbs, sweet oak, minerals, and jammy, mature fruit. Round and velvety textured, with considerable complexity, this is a fully mature, finesse-style Rioja for drinking over the next 4–5 years. Remarkable values.

In Rioja, as in most of Spain's viticultural regions, 1994 is considered to be a legitimate candidate for "vintage of the century." Certainly the 1994s I have tasted indicate the fruit was exceptionally ripe and the yields not excessive. The 1994 Tinto is almost too good to be true. The wine is aged in tank and bottled early. A dark ruby/purple-colored wine, it boasts a gorgeously scented nose of sweet, jammy, black currants and spice, terrific concentration, a heady, opulently textured feel on the palate, pure, sweet fruit, and a long, lush finish. It is rich, full, and seductive, without any hard edges. Drink it over the next 2–3 years; it may last longer. I cannot think of a red wine from anywhere in the world that has given me so much flavor and joy for $5 a bottle! The 1990 Rioja Crianza, made from 100% Tempranillo, is another sensational bargain. Its dark ruby color is followed by a splendid nose of overripe black cherries, cedar, and herbs. Bottled without filtration, this delicious, voluptuously textured, jammy, richly fruity, expansively flavored wine reveals a burgundianlike sweetness and roundness. Full but not heavy, with subtle rather than overwhelming oak, this is another knockout bargain that is worth buying by the trunkful. Drink it over the next 7–8 years.

A special project wine pioneered by importer Jorge Ordonez, Sierra Cantabria's 1996 Rioja Coleccion Privada is the result of extremely late-harvested Tempranillo. Approximately 300 cases were produced from 50-year-old vines, and the wine was aged in 100% new American oak casks. It offers a spectacularly fragrant nose of cherry liqueur, weedy tobacco, and toasty, smoky oak. In the mouth, this full-bodied Rioja displays layers of concentrated, opulently textured cherry and berry fruit. With low acidity, but plenty of heady glycerin and alcohol (14.5%), this satiny-textured, stunning wine should drink well for 7–12 years. Impressive!

The lavishly oaked 1992 Codice, a blend of 59% Tempranillo and 5% Vieura, reveals a saturated ruby/purple color, a big, vanillin, smoky, and black currant nose, soft, fleshy, oak-imbued flavors, medium to full body, and a velvety finish. Although not the most subtle or intellectual wine, for $6 this wine delivers $15–$20 worth of flavor and intensity. Drink it over the next 2–3 years. A terrific value!

BODEGAS SOLABAL (RIOJA)

1995 Solabal Crianza   **B   86**

This unfiltered wine, made from 100% Tempranillo, possesses a dark garnet ruby color and a moderately intense nose of tobacco smoke, cherry fruit, and herbs. In the mouth, lead pencil notes make their appearance in this jammy, richly fruity wine that also reveals a degree of elegance. It is a medium-bodied, soft, easy-to-understand, and -consume wine. Drink it over the next 1–2 years. Approximately 1,500 cases were imported to the United States.

BODEGAS SOLAR DE URBEZO (CARINENA)

1997 Vina Urbezo   **A   87**

A dark ruby/purple-colored wine, this attractive blend of 70% Cabernet Sauvignon and 30% Tempranillo offers up smoky, toasty, black cherry aromas intermixed with *pain grillé*–like scents. Ripe, with good fatness and a fleshy, fruit-driven personality, this low-acid, hedonistic, plump red will provide ideal drinking over the next 1–2 years. Approximately 1,000 cases were imported.

TORRES (PENEDÈS)

1990 Gran Coronas Mas La Plana Estate Black Label   **D   86**

Made from 100% Cabernet Sauvignon, and aged in French oak for 8 months before bottling, this wine displays a distinctive New World–ish ripeness and oakiness. The dark ruby color is followed by uncomplicated aromas of jammy fruit. The wine is sweet, round, pleasant, and expansive, but easygoing and simple. It should be consumed over the next 3–4 years. It has been a long time since I tasted a Black Label Gran Coronas that recalls the great 1978 and 1981.

BODEGAS TORRES FILOSO

1996 Arboles   **A   86**

Dark ruby colored, with a distinctive nose of chocolate, beets, root beer, and spice, this medium-bodied, fleshy, Côtes du Rhône–styled wine offers an alluring peppery, berry fruitiness, clean winemaking, and a ripe, straightforward finish. A blend of equal parts Cabernet Sauvignon and Tempranillo, this soft wine should be consumed over the next 1–2 years.

VEGA SAUCO (TORO)

1995 Crianza	**B**	**87**
1994 Crianza	**B**	**90**
1996 Joven	**A**	**87**
1994 Reserva	**B**	**89**

These are amazing values from Spain. The 1996 Joven, a barrel-fermented cuvée made from 70-year-old Tempranillo vines, exhibits a dark purple color followed by a beautifully expressive, sweet, floral, and black fruit-scented nose, with vague notions of mocha and chocolate. Copious quantities of rich berry fruit hit the palate in a succulent style, with an opulent texture as well as gorgeous purity and ripeness. This is a dazzling, deliciously fruity, medium-bodied wine to drink over the next 3–4 years. It can be served slightly chilled. Fortunately 1,500 cases of this wine were available when it was released in April 1997. The 1994 Crianza (500 cases) is a remarkable $10 bottle of wine. The opaque purple color is accompanied by lavish quantities of sweet, smoky, toasty oak and equally formidable quantities of jammy black currant, strawberry, and cherry fruit. Rich, dense, medium to full bodied, with layers of concentration, this stunning, dry red wine tastes as if it should cost $30–$40 a bottle! Might this be the Caymus Special Selection of Spain? It should drink well for 5–7 years. This is a wine to stockpile!

Two other dynamite bargains, the 1995 Crianza, aged in 100% new American oak barrels, is a lusty, in-your-face, pure Tempranillo wine with plenty of black cherry and berry fruit, lavish quantities of smoky new oak, a plush, succulent texture, low acidity, and heady alcohol as well as extract and glycerin in the macho finish. There is some rusticity to the wine's tannin, but this is one heck of a wine for the price. It should drink well for 5–6 years. The 1994 Reserva, also aged in 100% new American oak for 22–24 months, is an old-vine Tempranillo selection from selected vineyards. This is a richer, fuller-bodied wine with grilled meat, smoked herb, and jammy black cherry aromas and flavors. Powerful, rich, and full bodied, with nearly outstanding density, this delicious wine is a best buy. It should be consumed over the next 5–6 years.

VEGA SICILIA (RIBERA DEL DUERO)

N.V.	Reserva Especial (004)	EEE	96
N.V.	Reserva Especial Lot 020/96	EEE	96
N.V.	Reserva Especial Unico (Lot 0196)	EEE	96
1986	Unico Reserva	EEE	92
1985	Unico Reserva	EEE	93
1982	Unico Reserva	EEE	95
1981	Unico Reserva	EEE	95
1980	Unico Reserva	EEE	90
1993	Valbuena	E	86
1992	Valbuena	E	89
1991	Valbuena	E	90
1990	Valbuena	E	91

Spain's most consistently great winery continues to turn out exciting wines. The 1991 Valbuena is a rich, opulent, fleshy, jammy wine with a deep ruby/purple color, full body, and gobs of sweet black cherry fruit intertwined with toasty new oak and spice. The wine is ripe, fleshy, expansive, and ideal for drinking now and over the next decade. The less expensive 1992 Valbuena exhibits an evolved dark plum color and a delightfully smoky, tarry, charcoal, and caramel-scented nose with plenty of jammy black cherry and currant fruit. Ripe, fruity, round, and velvety textured, this is an opulent, lush, soft wine to drink now and over the next decade. The 1993 Valbuena, from a difficult vintage, possesses plenty of sweet oak, a meaty, grilled herb-scented nose, moderately good concentration, and a soft, short finish. It is a good but hardly exciting effort.

The 1986 Unico Reserva tastes as if it were only 4–5 years old, evidence of just how youthful these wines tend to be. The color is an opaque plum/garnet. A harmonious wine that appears to have much of its development ahead of it, there is good glycerin, full body, copious tannin, and a backward yet promising style. This wine is less accessible than the 1985, 1983, or 1981 and may merit an even higher score. It is one of the few Vega Sicilia wines that will require cellaring at its release. The 1985 Unico Reserva is already revealing considerable complexity and low-acid, plump, round, rich flavors. There is no amber to be found in the wine's deep ruby/purple color. The nose offers tobacco, smoke, tar, and gobs of sweet black cherry fruit aromas. Full bodied, with a layered, nuanced character, high glycerin (hence the sweetness in the flavors), and a lush, round, generously endowed finish, this is a substantial as well as elegant, savory style of Unico Reserva that can be drunk now and over the next 15+ years. The 1982 Unico Reserva is fatter and richer than the 1985, displaying a dark plum/garnet color and a complex set of aromatics consisting of sweet tobacco, roasted herbs, tar, jammy kirsch, and caramel. Full bodied, with a viscous texture, forward, fat, ripe flavors, low acidity, and a knockout finish with copious amounts of glycerin, this is a succulent, hedonistic, luxuriously rich Unico that can be drunk now as well as over the next 15+ years. In contrast, the 1981 Unico Reserva is more restrained, with a personality similar to a classic Médoc (for example, Lafite-Rothschild). Lead pencil, tar, smoke, black currant, and weedy tobacco notes are followed by a medium-bodied wine with beautiful fruit, a supple texture, and a long finish. While not as flamboyant or expansive as either the 1982 or 1985, it is a classy, complex offering with an intriguing lead pencil/smoky note in its aromatics, flavor, and finish. It should drink well for 10–15 years. Although the 1980 Unico Reserva is an outstanding wine, it does not compare with the extraordinary 1970 and 1968. The 1980 is a spice- and earth-driven example of Unico, with noteworthy black truffle, cherry, currant, and oaky aromas that are followed by elegant, medium-bodied, spicy, mineral-like flavors with admirable levels of curranty fruit. This rich, long wine is ideal for drinking now and over the next 12–15 years.

The nonvintage Reserva Especial Lot 020/96, which was bottled in 1996, can be identified by the numbers 020/96 on the label. This terrific wine is made from a blend of top vintages of the Vega Sicilia Unico. This offering reveals an evolved, precocious character that suggests it may attain 25 years of age. The magic of many Vega Sicilia wines is their remarkable freshness despite their vintage. The wine possesses a deep, opaque garnet color and a sweet, roasted herb, oak, licorice, and black fruit aromatic profile. Lush, unctuously textured flavors possess terrific fruit and purity. Smooth, supple, and luscious, this beauty can be drunk now and over the next decade.

I thought the profound nonvintage Reserva Especial Unico (Lot 0196) (which appears on the label), to be outrageously complex and rich. A knockout nose jumps from the glass, offering aromas of kirsch, black cherries, currants, toast, spice, licorice, and intriguing floral scents. Full bodied, with fabulous concentration and ripeness, as well as a multilayered, hedonistic display of fruit and glycerin, this is a terrific wine that has obviously been made from a blend of fabulous raw materials. It should drink beautifully for another 2 decades.

In April 1995 I reported in *The Wine Advocate* on the release (after 25 years) of the 1970 Vega Sicilia Unico Reserva, which is another classic from this extraordinary winery. That wine will set readers back at least $150, provided you can find it! For less than half that price, consumers can purchase the 1990 Valbuena, a gloriously rich, opulently textured, super concentrated wine that is loaded with jammy black cherry and curranty fruit. The nose soars from the glass, offering up telltale aromas of toasty new oak and intense, concentrated fruit. Velvety textured, full bodied, and concentrated, with gobs of glycerin and a long, heady, layered finish, this wine can be drunk now or cellared for 15+ years. Each year Vega Sicilia releases 11 casks (approximately 275 cases) of a nonvintage blend of its wine. The offering, identified by the code 004 on the label, is a blend of the 1953, 1964, 1970, and 1974 Unico Reservas. Only vintages of at least 20–40 years of age are included in the blend. This release is a sensational effort. It is remarkably youthful and fresh but also reveals penetratingly mature aromas of cedar, minerals, tobacco, and celestial quantities of curranty and cherry fruit. Full bodied, velvety textured, sweet, and voluptuous, this massive, impeccably well balanced, rich wine can be drunk now and over the next 20+ years. Unfortunately it is extremely limited in availability.

Unico Reserva past glories: 1983 (93), 1976 (93), 1975 (96+), 1974 (90+?), 1970 (96), 1968 (98+), 1966 (95), 1964 (94), 1962 (95), 1953 (94), 1942 (90).

VILLA CRECES (RIBERA DEL DUERO)
1995 Crianza   **D 89**

I am sad to report that not much of this wine was produced, but for readers lucky enough to latch on to a few bottles, it is delicious. Made from a blend of 75% old-vine Tempranillo and 25% Cabernet Sauvignon, it exhibits an opaque purple color and an extraordinary nose of grilled beef intermixed with black berry fruit, roasted herbs, and iron. The wine possesses a viscous texture, excellent concentration and purity, superb intensity, no hard edges, and a long finish of 30+ seconds. It offers gorgeous drinking now and will last for 5–8 years.

BODEGAS VINEGRA (RIOJA)

1994 Don Teofilo I	C	86
1994 Don Teofilo I Reserva	D	86

Both of these modern-style Riojas are fruit-driven wines with dark ruby/purple colors. The 1994 Don Teofilo I exhibits copious amounts of black cherry fruit intermixed with spicy oak, and a supple texture. The 1994 Don Teofilo I Reserva reveals more oak and loamy, earthy notes in the nose, good spice, and more depth on the palate, as well as more grip and tannin (not necessarily a positive in a lighter-style Rioja). Both are cleanly made, attractive, mainstream, user-friendly wines to consume over the next 2–3 years.

VINICOLA DEL PRIORAT (PRIORATO)

1997 Onix	A	87
1996 Onix	A	90
1995 Onix	A	86

Most wines from Priorato fetch prices from $50 to $300 a bottle, so this inexpensive 1997 Onix from this increasingly esteemed appellation is a welcome relief. Made from a blend of Grenache and Carignan, this dense, thick, uncomplicated, chewy, medium- to full-bodied wine exhibits excellent ripeness, plenty of blackberry and cherry liqueur-like fruit, intriguing mineral, pepper, and spice notes, and a chunky, husky finish. Readers should not expect much aromatic complexity or finesse, but there is plenty of purity, fruit, glycerin, and mouth-staining richness in this inexpensive, robust, bistro red. Drink it over the next 3–5 years.

Wow! What an exceptional buy the 1996 Onix represents. Readers should consider this as the Spanish version of Cornas. Made from old-vine Grenache and Carignan, it displays a saturated black/purple color, followed by a beautifully ripe nose of sweet black fruits, along with a touch of prunes, licorice, and truffles. Although not complex, the wine is exceptionally powerful, rich, and layered, with extraordinary length and intensity. The tannin is well integrated, and the wine is full and fleshy. If more complexity emerges with additional bottle age, look for my numerical score to rise by several points. Buy this one by the case, and consume it over the next 5–6 years. Great value.

Made from a 5-year-old vineyard planted with Garnacha and Carinena, the 1995 Onix displays a deep ruby/purple color, crisp acidity, good freshness and vivaciousness, and a pleasing, up-front charm and appeal that, despite the wine's intensity, is Beaujolais-like. It is a delicious summertime, picnic wine that is best served chilled over the next 1–2 years.

BODEGAS Y VINEDOS (RIBERA DEL DUERO)

1994 Alion	D	91
1993 Alion	D	89

Alion is the branded name of this wine from Ribera del Duero. The wine is bottled after 14 months in French oak casks and 2 years in bottle. The 1994 Alion is an immensely impressive ruby/purple-colored wine with a knockout nose of toast, black fruits, roasted herbs, and meat (steak au poivre?). The wine reveals full-bodied, rich, intensely fruity, pure, and harmonious flavors as well as impressive integration of tannin, acidity, and alcohol and good length. Although accessible, it promises to evolve for another 10–15 years. The 1993 Alion possesses more aggressive tannin, in addition to a deep, dense, dark plum color and a sweet vanillin, black cherry, kirsch, and smoky-scented nose with a hint of coffee. Spicy and rich, with youthful, unevolved, grapey flavors, this is another attractive, excellent offering from this up-and-coming Ribera del Duero winery. It should drink well for 10–12 years.

PORTUGAL

Americans have finally begun to realize the great pleasures of a mature vintage port after a meal. For years, this sumptuous and mellow fortified red wine was seriously undervalued, as most of it was drunk in the private homes and clubs of the United Kingdom. Prices, which soared in the early and mid-eighties, collapsed in the early nineties. Although there is not much vintage port produced (there are rarely more than four declared vintages a decade), the international recession and bloated marketplace have resulted in stable prices.

WHAT TO BUY

The new vintage Port declaration is for 1997, with most of the top houses having declared that an excellent vintage. These wines will be available for sale at the end of the century. Other outstanding vintage years were 1994 and 1992. As with many fine wines, prices for the newest vintages are higher than older Ports that can be purchased through auction houses. Shrewd consumers should consider buying at auction such vintages as 1992 (where it was declared), 1991, 1985, 1983, and 1980. These are very fine rather than great years, but the top houses have turned in impeccable efforts, and the wines are closer to full maturity.

An obvious trend has been the explosion of single quinta offerings, most of which are very good to excellent, although not as compelling as the greatest vintage Ports. Most of the single quinta Ports are offered in years not declared as vintages.

VARIOUS PORT STYLES

Crusted Port   Rarely seen today, crusted port is usually a blend of several vintages that is bottled early and handled in the same manner as a vintage port. Significant sediment will form in the bottle and a crusted port will have to be decanted prior to drinking.

Tawny Port   One of the least expensive ways of securing a mature port is to buy the best shippers' tawny ports. Tawny ports are aged in wood by the top houses for 10, 20, 30, 40, or even 50 years. Tawny port represents a blend of vintages. Tawnys can have exceptional complexity and refinement. I highly recommend some of the best tawnys from firms such as Taylor Fladgate, Fonseca, and Graham's.

Ruby and Branded Ports   Ruby ports are relatively straightforward, deeply colored, young ports that are cherished for their sweet, grapey aromas and supple, exuberant, yet monolithic taste. Most of these ports are meant to be drunk when released. Each house has its own style. Four of the most popular include Fonseca's Bin No. 27, Taylor's 4XX, Cockburn's Special Reserve, and Graham's Six Grapes. Stylistically, all four of these ruby or branded ports are different. The richest and fullest is the Fonseca Bin No. 27; the most complex is usually the Taylor 4XX; the sweetest and fruitiest is the Graham Six Grapes; and the most mature and evolved, as well as the least distinguished, the Cockburn Special Reserve.

White Port   I have never understood the purpose of white port, but the French find it appealing. However, the market for these eccentricities is dead.

Late Bottled Vintage Port (L.B.V.P.)   Certain vintages are held back in cask longer than 2 years (the time required for vintage port) and bottled 5–7 years following the vintage. These ports tend to throw less sediment, as much of it has already been deposited in cask. In general, late-bottled ports are ready to drink when released. I often find them less interesting and complex than the best tawnys and vintage ports.

Single Quinta Vintage Port   This has become an increasingly important area, especially since the late eighties, when a number of vintages, particularly 1987, 1990, 1991, and 1992, could have been declared vintage years but were not because of the saturated marketplace. Many of the best single quintas, or vineyards, have been offered as vintage-dated single quinta ports. These are vintage ports from a single vineyard. Most port authorities feel it is the blending from various vineyards that gives vintage port its greatest character. Others will argue that in a top year, the finest single quinta ports can be as good as a top vintage port. I tend to believe that a great vintage port is superior to a single quinta port; yet the finest single quintas from 1987, 1990, 1991, and 1992 are stunning. Star ratings of the different single quinta port producers are provided where I have had sufficient tasting experience (more than two vintages) to offer a qualitative ranking.

SINGLE QUINTA VINTAGE PORTS

Quinta Agua Alta (Churchill)

Quinta Boa Vista (Offley)

Quinta do Bomfim (Dow)

Quinta do Cachao (Messias)

Quinta da Cavadinha (Warre)

Quinta do Confradeiro (Sandeman)

Quinta da Corte (Delaforce)

Quinta do Crasto (a consortium)

Quinta da Eira Velha (R. Newan)

Quinta Fojo (Churchill)

Quinta do Forte (Delaforee)

Quinta da Foz (Calem)

Quinta Guimaraenssd (Fonseca)

Quinta do Infantado (Roseira)

Quinta Malvedossd (Graham's)

Quinta da Roeda (Croft)

Quinta de la Rosa (Bergquist)

Quinta do Seixo (Ferreira)

Quinta do Tua (Cockburn)

Quinta de Val da Figueira (Calem)

Quinta de Vargellas (Taylor Fladgate)

Quinta do Vau (Sandeman)

Quinta do Vesuvio (Symington)

Vintage Port   Potentially the finest and most complex, and the subject of most of this chapter, are the vintage ports. Vintage ports are declared by the port shippers the second spring after the harvest. The 1991 was declared a vintage year by most of the top port shippers. For example, Graham's, Dow, Quinta do Noval, and Warre had declared it a vintage, but Fonseca and Taylor did not, preferring to declare 1992 instead. Vintage port, which is a blend of the very best cuvées from various vineyards, is bottled unfiltered 2 years after the harvest. It can improve and last for 50 or more years. To be a vintage port there must be exceptional ripeness, a great deal of tannin, and plenty of rich fruit and body. In fact, the quality of a shipper's vintage port is the benchmark by which a shipper is evaluated in the international marketplace. Each top house has a distinctive style, which I have tried to capture in the tasting notes.

These ports tend to be blends made from various vineyards rather than products of a single vineyard.

VINTAGE GUIDE
The greatest port vintages in this century have been 1912, 1927, 1931, 1935, 1945, 1948, 1955, 1963, 1970, 1977, 1983, 1985, 1992, 1994, and 1997.

VINTAGE YEARS FOR MAJOR FIRMS
Cockburn   1947, 1950, 1955, 1960, 1963, 1967, 1970, 1975, 1983, 1985, 1991, 1994, 1997

Croft   1945, 1950, 1955, 1960, 1963, 1966, 1970, 1975, 1977, 1982, 1985, 1991

Dow   1945, 1947, 1950, 1955, 1960, 1963, 1966, 1970, 1972, 1975, 1977, 1980, 1983, 1985, 1991, 1994, 1997

Fonseca   1945, 1948, 1955, 1960, 1963, 1966, 1970, 1975, 1977, 1980, 1983, 1985, 1992, 1994, 1997

Graham's   1945, 1948, 1955, 1960, 1963, 1966, 1970, 1975, 1977, 1980, 1983, 1985, 1991, 1994, 1997

Quinta do Noval   1945, 1947, 1950, 1955, 1958, 1960, 1963, 1966, 1967, 1970, 1975, 1978, 1982, 1985, 1991, 1994, 1995, 1997

Quinta do Noval Nacional   1931, 1950, 1960, 1962, 1963, 1964, 1966, 1967, 1970, 1975, 1978, 1980, 1982, 1985, 1987, 1994

Sandeman   1945, 1947, 1950, 1955, 1957, 1958, 1960, 1962, 1963, 1966, 1967, 1970, 1975, 1977, 1980, 1982, 1985

Taylor   1945, 1948, 1955, 1960, 1963, 1966, 1970, 1975, 1977, 1980, 1983, 1985, 1992, 1994, 1997

Warre   1945, 1947, 1950, 1955, 1958, 1960, 1963, 1966, 1970, 1975, 1977, 1980, 1983, 1985, 1991, 1994, 1997

RATING PORTUGAL'S BEST PRODUCERS OF PORT

* * * * * (OUTSTANDING)

Dow	Quinta do Noval Nacional
Fonseca	Taylor
Graham's	

* * * * (EXCELLENT)

Churchill	Graham's Malvedos
Churchill Quinta Agua Alta	Quinta do Infantado Touriga Nacional
Cockburn	Quinta do Noval
Croft	Symington Quinta do Vesuvio
Dow Quinta do Bomfim	Taylor Quinta de Vargellas
Ferreira Quinta do Seixo	Warre
Fonseca Guimaraens	

* * * (GOOD)

Calem Quinta da Foz

Croft Quinta do Roed

Delaforce

Delaforce Quinta do Forte

Ferreira

Gould Campbell

Quarles Harris

Martinez

Niepoort

Offley Forrester

Pocalas Junior

Quinta do Crasto

Quinta do Passadouro***/****

Quinta de la Rosa***/****

Quinta do Roriz

Ramos-Pinto

Sandeman

Sandeman Quinta do Vau

Smith-Woodhouse

Warre Quinta da Cavadinha

* * (AVERAGE)

Almeida Barros

Borges & Irmao

J. W. Burmester

C. da Silva

Calem

H. & C. J. Feist

Feuerheerd

Hooper

C. N. Kopke

Messias

Osborne

Pintos dos Santos

Quinta do Panascal

Quinta do Romaneira

Vasconcellos

Wiese & Krohn

Van Zellers

CHURCHILL

1994 Vintage Port   **D 89+**

Although Churchill's 1994 is a rich, full-bodied, powerful port, it does not possess quite the complexity, richness, and overall dimension of the top wines of the vintage. It is made in a slightly drier style, with plenty of guts and tannin. Give it at least a decade of cellaring. It will be one of the more austere (I do not mean that in a pejorative sense) examples of the vintage. Anticipated maturity: 2004–2025.

Other Wines Rated: Agua Alta—1992 (93), 1990 (92), 1987 (93); Vintage Port—1991 (89)

COCKBURN

1994 Vintage Port   **D 91**

An attractive, smoky, tarry, roasted black fruit character dominates this opaque ruby/purple-colored wine's aromatic profile. Low acidity, sweet, rich fruit, and a forward, expansive feel suggest this full-bodied wine will mature quickly, but it will last for at least 2 decades. Like a few other 1994s, it almost seems too easy to drink at this stage. Anticipated maturity: 2004–2020.

Other Wines Rated: Quinta do Tua—1987 (94); Vintage Port—1991 (88), 1985 (90), 1983 (95), 1955 (92)

CROFT

1994 Vintage Port   **D 90**

The 1994 Croft exhibits an impressive dark ruby/purple color, and a developed, forward, more evolved style than expected. It is moderately sweet, full bodied, expansive, pure, and rich, but made in an up-front, flattering style. Although outstanding, it is not one of the superstars of the vintage. It will keep for 20 years. Anticipated maturity: 2000–2020.

Other Wines Rated: 1991 (93), 1963 (90)

DELAFORCE

1994 Vintage Port	D 87

Less complex than many of the 1994 vintage ports, this one-dimensional port is full, rich, and concentrated. Although there is some bitterness in the back, this should turn out to be a very good to excellent 1994. Anticipated maturity: 2000–2018.

DOW

1994 Vintage Port	D 96

The massive 1994 is unquestionably the finest Dow I have tasted since the 1977. This opaque purple-colored wine is not as developed or flamboyant as Fonseca, but it is super-concentrated and multilayered, with huge masses of fruit and some tannin in the finish. This is a slightly drier style than Fonseca or Graham's, but it appears to be a classic, majestic, enormously constituted 1994 that should age effortlessly for 3 decades or more. It is one of the stars of the vintage. Anticipated maturity: 2004–2030.

Other Wines Rated: Quinta do Bomfim—1992 (93), 1990 (95); Vintage Port—1991 (90), 1983 (93), 1977 (95), 1970 (90), 1966 (91), 1963 (93), 1945 (93)

FERREIRA

N.V.	Dona Antonia Personal Reserve Porto	C 82
1991	Late Bottled Vintage Port	C 86
1983	Quinta do Seixo Vintage Port	D 87
N.V.	Ruby Port	C 85
N.V.	Tawny Port	C 83
N.V.	Vintage Character	B 85
1994	Vintage Port	D 87?
1991	Vintage Port	D 89
1987	Vintage Port	D 81
1985	Vintage Port	D 84
N.V.	White Port	C 82
N.V.	20 Year Old Port Duque de Braganca	C 86

Although the color is impressive, the 1994 vintage port tastes one-dimensional and awkward. The tannin and alcohol dominate the wine's personality, but there is good weight, depth, and length. At present, it is unknit and not yet harmonious. It should keep for 20 years, but I wonder about its balance. The rich, concentrated, young but accessible 1991 vintage port exhibits a dark ruby/garnet color, good glycerin, full body, and excellent purity. It should drink well for 10–15 years. The 1987 vintage port is a weak example of vintage port. It possesses a medium garnet color, some fruit, sweetness, and personality, but not much depth, complexity, or interest. More pruney and ripe, the old style 1985 vintage port is already threatening to dry out. The 1983 Quinta do Seixo vintage port is very good, but one would expect a lot more stuffing and intensity, given the 1983 vintage in Portugal. This fully mature port should be drunk over the next 5–10 years.

The late bottled 1991 vintage port offers a good, sweet, jammy glass of port with spice and ripeness but not a lot of complexity. The light amber-colored 20 year old Duque de Braganca reveals an attractive, spicy nose, sweet, ripe, full-bodied fruit, and copious amounts of alcohol. It is one of the better 20-year-old ports I have tasted. Light ruby with considerable amber and orange at the edge, the Dona Antonia Personal Reserve Porto is attenuated, short, and simple.

The N.V. white port is a heavy-handed, alcoholic, coarse wine that provides little other than an alcoholic high. The light ruby, almost orange-colored N.V. tawny port does not reveal much fruit, body, or flesh. It is nearly dried out. The medium ruby-colored N.V. ruby port offers attractive, moderately sweet fruit, and good body and freshness. The vintage character is a more tannic, structured wine with a deeper ruby/garnet color but not much fruit or personality. This is an uninspiring group of ports.

FONSECA

1994 Vintage Port	E 97

One of the most spectacular 1994s, this opaque purple-colored wine is an exotic, flamboyant, ostentatious port. Extremely fragrant and pungent, with a flashy display of jammy cassis, pepper, licorice, and truffles, this port is an attention grabber. Awesomely rich and full bodied, with superb length, richness, and overall balance, it possesses a huge midpalate, layers of flavor, an unctuous texture, and a blockbuster finish. Everything is in place, with the brandy and tannin well integrated, even concealed by the masses of fruit and glycerin. This wine will drink fabulously well at age 10, but will keep for up to 30 years. Anticipated maturity: 2002–2035.

Other Wines Rated: Guimaraens—1991 (93); Late Bottled Vintage Port—1988 (88); Twenty-Year-Old Tawny Port (86); Thirty-Year-Old Tawny Port (91); Vintage Port—1992 (97), 1985 (96), 1983 (92), 1977 (94), 1970 (97), 1966 (92), 1963 (97), 1955 (96), 1948 (100), 1945 (92)

GRAHAM'S

1994 Vintage Port	D 96

In a port tasting, tasting Graham's is almost like tasting a big, rich, succulent Merlot after a group of blockbuster, tannic Cabernets. Sweeter and more obvious than many ports, the opaque purple-colored 1994 is fruity, powerful, and rich, with an addictive hedonistic quality. It will be ready to drink in 8–10 years and will keep for up to 30. As always, this is a showy, flamboyant port that has the advantage of being slightly sweeter than other 1994s. A great Graham's. Anticipated maturity: 2002–2035.

Other Wines Rated: Malvedos Centenary—1990 (92), 1987 (92), 1986 (92), 1976 (90), 1958 (90); Malvedos Vintage Port—1993 (92); Vintage Port—1991 (94), 1985 (97), 1983 (94), 1980 (90), 1977 (95), 1970 (95), 1966 (92), 1963 (96), 1955 (95), 1948 (99), 1945 (96)

OFFLEY

N.V.	Boa Vista Special Reserve	C 85
1985	Boa Vista Vintage Port	D 77
1983	Boa Vista Vintage Port	D 72
1980	Boa Vista Vintage Port	C 75
1990	Late Bottled Vintage Port	C 84
1994	Vintage Port	D 89
N.V.	20 Year Tawny Baron de Forrester	D 78

The dark ruby-colored 1994 vintage port with purple hues is made in a lighter, more advanced and early to mature style. Slightly sweet, with well-integrated brandy showing in the nose, it is a full-bodied, rich, and impressive port, but not one of the stars of the vintage. It will require 10–20 years of cellaring. The 1990 late bottled vintage port (bottled in 1994) is a simple, grapey, one-dimensional fruity port. This full-bodied, chunky wine is pleasant, but it lacks character. A thin 1985, the Boa Vista vintage port displays vegetal and spicy characteristics. It is not my style. The 1983 Boa Vista vintage port is a rustic, fertilizer-smelling, earthy, very old, oxidized style of port that is too unusual and bizarre to merit a recommendation. Do not expect much improvement from the 1980 Boa Vista vintage port; it is a grapey, pruney, simple, and one-dimensional wine.

The straightforward, mouth-filling Boa Vista special reserve possesses alcohol but not much else. It is a pleasant, one-dimensional, foursquare wine. The 20-year tawny Baron de Forrester's light amber color appears unsubstantial. The wine does possess some fruit, as well as an aged, slightly oxidized character. I prefer more fruit in my port, but readers who like this desiccated, spicy, old style will enjoy it.

OSBORNE

1994 Vintage Port	D	90

Very dark ruby/purple-colored (not opaque), this is a rich, full-bodied, sweet port reminiscent of Graham's. Thick, viscous, rich, and full, this impressive port needs 5–10 years of cellaring. A sleeper. Anticipated maturity: 2002–2020.

QUINTA DO CRASTO

1990 Late Bottled Vintage Port	C	85
1994 Vintage Port	D	91
1985 Vintage Port	E	?

The opaque ruby/purple-colored, single quinta 1994 vintage port reveals plenty of smoky, jammy black fruits, licorice, and a touch of tar. Slightly sweet, rich, expansive, and full on the palate, with well-integrated alcohol and tannin, this 1994 should be ready to drink early in life, and will last for 20 years. The 1985 vintage port was flawed from a mercaptan/lees smell but otherwise displayed good sweetness and ripeness. However, the unclean nose is off-putting.

The 1990 late bottled vintage port exhibits good sweetness, a nice smoky, round, ripeness, but not much complexity or character. Drink it over the next 10 years.

QUINTA DO NOVAL

1984	Colheita	C	90
1981	Colheita	D	90
1976	Colheita	E	84
1974	Colheita	E	90
1971	Colheita	EE	92
1964	Colheita	EE	90
1937	Colheita	EEE	92
N.V.	Late Bottled House Reserve	C	82
N.V.	Late Bottled (Vintage Character)	B	91
1994	Nacional	EEE	99+
1970	Nacional	EEE	96
1963	Nacional	EEE	99+
1962	Nacional	EEE	98

N.V.	Ruby Old Coronation	B	89
1994	Vintage Port	D	95
N.V.	10 Year Old Tawny	D	88
N.V.	20 Year Old Tawny	E	91
N.V.	40 Year Old Tawny	EE	86

This famous estate, which is known for producing one of the world's most extraordinary wines, the Nacional (made from ungrafted 19th-century vines), was purchased in 1993 by the huge French insurance conglomerate collectively known as AXA. The vintage ports from Quinta do Noval have been irregular, but that is likely to change under the new owners, who are sparing no expense in building Quinta do Noval into a port lodge whose vintage ports and other offerings are as respected and esteemed as the microscopic quantity of Nacional. At a recent tasting of all the current releases being offered by the new American importer for Quinta do Noval, including some rare Colheitas, the quality was impressive.

The Ruby Old Coronation port is a good value at $11 a bottle. It is ideal for restaurants and consumers looking for a big, grapey, smoky, high-alcohol, lusty glass of fleshy fortified red wine. Soft with well-integrated alcohol, it reveals surprising character for so young a wine. Even more impressive is the nonvintage Late Bottled (vintage character) port, which is sweeter than the Old Coronation, with fabulous fruit, and that wonderful spice and smoky chocolate character found in quality port. Dense, rich, and showy, this is another excellent value in high-quality port.

Tawny ports are aged in wood from essentially a solera system for the number of years indicated on the bottle. In most cases I prefer the younger 10 or 20 year tawnys to the ancient 40 to 50 year old wines, but it is really a matter of taste. I tend to like more fruit rather than the oxidized and aged characteristics of the very old tawnys. Quinta do Noval's 10 Year Old Tawny exhibits a light ruby/garnet color, sweet jammy fruit, nice spice, cedar and smoke in the nose, and good concentration. My favorite of these three tawnys is the 20 Year Old Tawny. It offers an amber color, a spicy, tobacco, cedary, smoky, complex nose, dense, rich flavors that belie the color's aged, feeble look, and an expansive personality. It is a classic example of how delicious and complex a 20 year old tawny port can be. The 40 Year Old Tawny was a tad too old for my tastes. The wine was spicy, with an old cellar, stale, nutty aroma that seems to have greater appeal in the United Kingdom than elsewhere in the world.

One of the wines Quinta do Noval produces that was never exploited by previous importers are their Colheitas, which are essentially single-vintage Tawny ports that are kept in barrel until the winery is ready to sell them. These impressive wines are 100% from the vintage shown on the bottle. Considering their ages, they are reasonably priced. Among the younger vintages that are available, the 1984 Colheita possessed a medium amber color, with no remaining ruby to its hue, a sweet, jammy, dense, spice and cedar-scented nose, full body, and a silky texture. The similarly colored 1981 Colheita offered more cedar, earth, tobacco, and smoke in its nose, excellent richness, complex, sweet, spicy flavors, full body, and a lingering fragrance that made it one of my favorites among the younger Colheitas. The 1976 Colheita revealed a rust/amber color of considerable age, with the alcohol showing through and the fruit drying out. It was my least favorite of the entire Colheita selections. The 1974 Colheita exhibited a medium ruby/garnet color with significant amber at the edge. The nose revealed sweet, fruitcakelike aromas intermixed with tobacco, smoke, and roasted nuts. Spicy, round, rich, and full bodied, this is a sweet, surprisingly rich, beautiful, single-vintage, old Tawny that will provide impressive drinking for years to come.

The older Colheitas included the medium amber-colored 1971, an impressively rich, full-bodied, smoky, charcoal and sweet cherry-scented wine with a large, expansive, plump, succulent texture, moderate sweetness, and a smashingly long finish. It should continue to age well for another decade. The 1964 Colheita possessed a ruby/amber color, excellent richness, but perhaps not quite the fragrance, complexity, or richness of the 1971. Nevertheless, it is a top-notch example of a single-vintage, mature tawny port. The 1937 Colheita was superb, with its high alcohol amazingly well covered by the wine's flesh and richness. The medium amber color was representative of its age. The huge nose of orange marmalade, jammy cherries, tobacco, smoke, and white chocolate was followed by a dense, rich, drier style of single-vintage tawny that was full bodied, rich, and spicy. This wine was a thrill to drink.

I do not know what Quinta do Noval's opinion might be, but it seems to me that these single-vintage old tawnys, once bottled, are unlikely to change since the wine's evolution has taken place in barrel prior to bottling. I would think vintages such as these could easily last 15, 20, or even 30 years, but I am not sure since this type of port has rarely been exploited in the international marketplace.

Amazingly, the importer still has tiny stocks of such legendary ports as the 1970, 1963, and 1962 Nacionals. In most vintages the production of Quinta do Noval Nacional is no more than 250–275 cases. All three of these wines are candidates to achieve perfect scores. The 1970 Nacional remains a young, unevolved wine, as well as the lightest and least intense of this trio. That is not to suggest it is a wimpish wine as it is a powerful vintage port, but it is unbelievably graceful, youthful, and complex. The huge nose of licorice, smoke, jammy black cherry and cassis fruit is followed by a wine of seamless components, all superpacked with gorgeously pure fruit; yet the wine is not heavy or overbearing. There is a real sense of elegance to this spectacular, young Quinta do Noval Nacional. My best guess is that it might be worth opening a bottle to celebrate the new century, but this wine will not hit its peak until around 2010; it will last until 2030. Remarkably, the 1962 Nacional exhibited an even more opaque color than the 1970, as well as exquisite richness and concentration. Massive (but not in the Taylor style), this phenomenally concentrated, complex, still youthful vintage port is a tour de force in winemaking, and one of the greatest, can you believe this, young vintage ports I have ever tasted. This wine needs another 5–10 years to reach full maturity as neither the color nor aromatics reveal much development. It could easily have 100 years of longevity. Even more remarkable is the 1963 Nacional's opaque purple color, which looks more like a 1992 than a 33-year-old port. The wine possessed a fabulously smoky, cassis, black cherry, peppery nose. After 30 minutes in the glass, fruitcake notes and more evolved aromas emerged. This port is so concentrated it defies belief, with extraordinary balance and, like its two siblings, well-integrated alcohol and tannin. Again, the impression is one of a silky, succulent, voluptuously textured mouthful of exceptionally extracted port. This is a legend in the making. In 30–40 years it may well be considered, along with the 1931, as one of the greatest ports ever produced. Those lucky few with a bottle or two should plan to hold on to them for another decade before pulling the cork. It, too, is a hundred-year port.

The 1994 Vintage Port may be the finest regular vintage port I have tasted from this house in decades. Sadly, the production was absurdly small (approximately 800 cases) as the new owners, France's AXA, want to make a qualitative statement—immediately. It is opaque ruby/purple colored, with fabulous purity and richness, full body, moderate sweetness, layers of jammy fruit, and well-integrated alcohol. There is some tannin in the finish, but this is a large-scaled, authoritatively flavored as well as elegant example of port that needs cellaring. Anticipated maturity: 2004–2035. With respect to the 1994 Nacional, this is an incredibly rich, massive wine, yet at the same time, well balanced and amazingly well delineated. The color is an opaque purple. In addition to the abundant peppery, floral, cassis fruit, there is an ethereal character to this superrich, pure wine that is not the least bit heavy. A compelling Nacional, it possesses even more stuffing than the regular bottling (as one might suspect), and at least 30–40 years of longevity. Anticipated maturity: 2010–2050.

Other Wines Rated: Nacional—1987 (92), 1985 (96), 1966 (92), 1931 (100); Vintage Port—1991 (89)

QUINTA DO RORIZ

1988 Late Bottled Vintage Port	C	87
1991 Vintage Port	D	90

This single quinta is owned by the Quinta do Noval, which is just beginning to fully exploit the quality of these single-quinta ports. The late-bottled 1988 reveals plenty of lusty, high alcohol, gobs of ripe fruit, and a full-bodied, moderately sweet, intense style. I am not a great fan of late-bottled vintage port, but this effort is high class. The 1991 vintage port is even more impressive. It is a young, husky, muscular, opaque purple-colored wine with copious quantities of licorice, peppery, smoky, cassis fruit, a heady alcohol content that is not totally integrated, and layers of sweet, rich, jammy fruit that caress the palate with a lush texture. This impressive single quinta needs another 5–7 years of cellaring; it should keep through the first 2 decades of the next century.

RAMOS PINTO

1994 Vintage Port	D	91
1994 Ervamoira	D	91+

The 1994 Vintage Port exhibits an opaque ruby/purple color, a big, rich, smoky, licorice, cassis-scented nose, well-integrated alcohol, full body, outstanding purity and length, and layers of flavor. This is a superb 1994. Anticipated maturity: 2006–2030. The opaque purple-colored single-quinta 1994 Ervamoira is equally impressive. Although more backward, and perhaps not as sweet and expressive, it is superconcentrated, full bodied, exceptionally dense, and very tannic. This wine will mature at least 5 years later than the 1994 vintage port. Anticipated maturity: 2010–2030. Two sleepers of the vintage.

SMITH-WOODHOUSE

1994 Vintage Port	D	90

An underrated producer, Smith-Woodhouse has turned out a port with an impressively saturated dark ruby/purple color. This powerful port is moderately sweet, forward, rich, and full bodied, with nicely integrated alcohol and tannin. While it is not one of the vintage's blockbusters, it should be ready to drink in 3–5 years and keep for 15–20. Anticipated maturity: 1999–2018.
Other Wines Rated: 1992 (87), 1991 (88)

SYMINGTON QUINTA DO VESUVIO

1994 Vintage Port	D	92

This impressive wine, with an opaque ruby/purple color, reveals excellent richness, layers of flavor, well-integrated alcohol and tannin, moderate sweetness, and a long, heady finish. Pure and impressively built, it should drink well in 5–7 years. Anticipated maturity: 2002–2025.
Other Wines Rated: 1992 (90), 1991 (89+)

TAYLOR FLADGATE

1994 Vintage Port	E	97

When tasting young vintage ports, Taylor is always the most backward. Yet potentially, it has the capability to be the most majestic. This classically made, opaque purple-colored wine is crammed with black fruits (blueberries and cassis). It reveals high tannin and a reserved style, but it is enormously constituted with massive body, a formidable midpalate, and exceptional length. It is a young, rich, powerful Taylor that will require 10–15 years of aging.

Compared to the more flashy, forward style of the 1992, the 1994 has more in common with such vintages as 1977 and 1970. Anticipated maturity: 2008–2045.

Other Wines Rated: Late Bottled Vintage Port—1988 (89); Quinta de Vargellas—1991 (95), 1987 (90); Vintage Ports—1992 (100), 1985 (90), 1983 (94), 1980 (90), 1977 (96), 1970 (96), 1966 (91), 1963 (96), 1955 (96), 1948 (100), 1945 (96); Ten Year Tawny Port (93); Twenty Year Tawny Port (92); Thirty Year Tawny Port (87)

WARRE

1994 Vintage Port   D   94+

One of the finest Warres I have ever tasted, this opaque purple-colored wine is made in a drier style (à la Dow), yet it is expressive, extremely full bodied, with superb richness, purity, and well-integrated alcohol and tannin. It possesses a great midpalate as well as impressive length. Tasters should take note of the wealth of peppery, licorice-scented and -flavored raspberry and black currant fruit. Look for it to be ready to drink in 10–12 years and keep for 30+. This is a profound example of Warre vintage port. Anticipated maturity: 2008–2040. *Other Wines Rated:* Quinta da Cavadinha—1992 (91); Vintage Port—1991 (90), 1985 (90), 1983 (90), 1977 (92), 1963 (90)

TABLE WINES

Except for the unctuous, rich, almost decadent joys of vintage port and Madeira, one of the greatest nectars of all is Muscatel de Setubal. The Setubal from J. M. da Fonseca is legendary. The 1966 (rated 91) and 1962 Roxo (rated 98) are sensational wines with which to conclude a meal. The potential for fine wine from Portugal has yet to be discovered by most wine enthusiasts. Of course, the ubiquitous, spritzy, rather sweet Portuguese rosés are known the world over and are what many consumers first drink when they deem themselves too old or too sophisticated for soda pop. But Portugal produces some good red wines (that could even be superb if winemaking were not still adhering to 19th-century practices), as well as a few lively, crisp, tart white wines, the best of which are the *vinho verdes*. The best of the dry red wines are from such regions as Daato, Bairrada, and the Douro; the most reliable whites are from Palacio de Brejoeira, Antonio de Pires da Silva, and Casal Mendes.

VINTAGE GUIDE

Vintages in Portugal seem to have relevance only to the port trade. However, vintages do make a difference. Most of the best dry red wines emerge from Alentejo, Douro, and Dão. The best producers are listed below.

RATING PORTUGAL'S BEST PRODUCERS OF TABLE WINES

* * * * *(GOOD)*

Quinta do Carmo (Alentejo)

Quinto do Crasto (Douro)

Quinta do Cotto (Douro)

Ferreira (Douro)

J. M. da Fonseca (Dao Terras Altas)

J. M. da Fonseca (Garrafeira TE)

J. M. da Fonseca (Morgado do Reguengo-
  Portalegre)

J. M. da Fonseca (Quinta da Camarate)

J. M. da Fonseca (Rosado Fernandes)

Quinta de Foz de Arouce (Beiras)

Quinto da Gaivosa (Douro)

Quinta da Ponte Pedrinha (Dão)

Luis Pato (Bairrada)

João Portugal Ramos Trincadeira (Alentejo)

João Portugal Ramos Marques de Borba
  (Alentejo)

Quinta de la Rosa (Douro)

THE WINES OF NORTH AMERICA

California
Oregon
Washington State

5. CALIFORNIA

The Basics

TYPES OF WINE

Virtually every type of wine seen elsewhere in the wine world is made in California. Fortified port-style wines, decadently sweet, late-harvest Rieslings, sparkling wines, and major red and white dry table wines from such super grapes as Chardonnay and Cabernet Sauvignon are all to be found in California.

GRAPE VARIETIES

The fine wines of California are dominated by Cabernet Sauvignon and Chardonnay, as much of the attention of that state's winemakers is directed at these two grapes. California, however, makes wonderful red Zinfandel and increasing amounts of world-class Merlot and Syrah, plus some Petite Sirah. Despite improved quality, Pinot Noir is still a questionable wine in the hands of all but several dozen or so California wine producers. Two notable trends in the late eighties have proven popular with consumers. These include the proliferation of proprietary red wine blends (usually Cabernet Sauvignon–dominated and super-expensive), and the development of authoritatively flavored, robust, supple red wines made from blends of Syrah, Carignane, Grenache, Mourvèdre, and Alicante, collectively referred to as the "Rhône Rangers." As for the white wines, Sauvignon Blanc and Semillon, and blends thereof, can be wonderfully complex and fragrant, but the great majority remain nondescript wines. It is a shame that Chenin Blanc has so little sex appeal among consumers, because it can be a very inexpensive, delicious drink. Colombard and Muscat suffer from the same image problems as Chenin Blanc, but shrewd consumers know the good ones and seek them out. Gewürztraminer and dry Rieslings have been dismal wines, although a handful of wineries have broken through the wall of mediocrity. For years California has made it simple for the consumer, naming its wines after the varietal from which it is made. By law a Chardonnay or Cabernet Sauvignon must contain 75% of that grape in the wine. The recent trend, accompanied by very high prices, has been to produce luxury-priced proprietary wines with awe-inspiring, often silly names such as Dominus, Opus, Rubicon, Trilogy, Legacy, Affinity, Icon, and Insignia. These wines are supposed to be the winery's very best lots of wine blended together for harmony. Some of them are marvelous. But remember: All of them are expensive and most of them are overpriced.

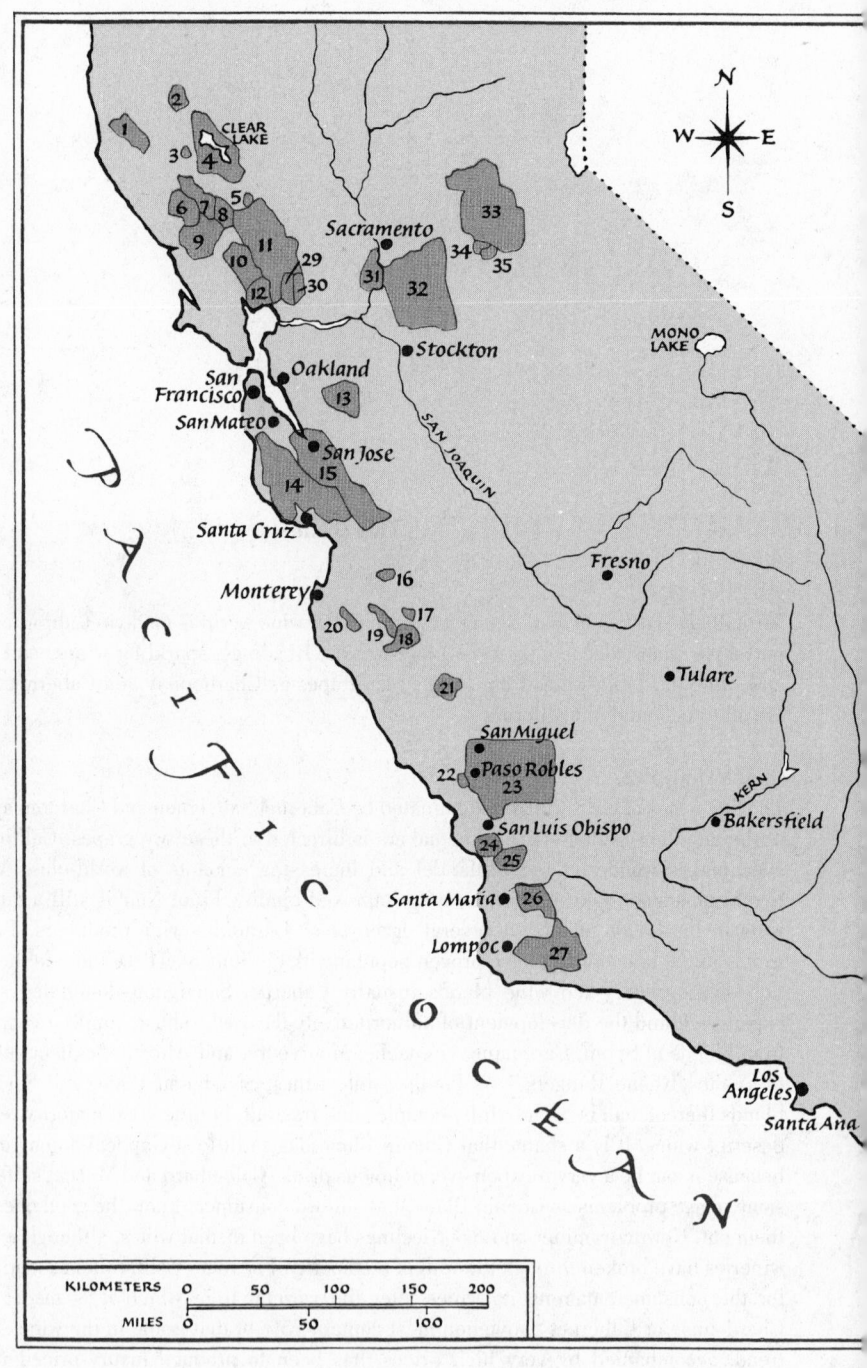

CLEAR LAKE

2

1

3

4

5

6 7 8

9

10 11

12

29

30

Sacramento

31

32

33

34

35

Stockton

San
Francisco

Oakland

San Mateo

13

San Joaquin

San Jose

14 15

Santa Cruz

Monterey

16

20

17

19 18

Fresno

21

Tulare

San Miguel

22

Paso Robles

23

Kern

San Luis Obispo

Bakersfield

24

25

Santa Maria

26

Lompoc

27

Los
Angeles

Santa Ana

N
W E
S

MONO
LAKE

PACIFIC

OCEAN

KILOMETERS   0   50   100   150   200

MILES   0   50   100

California

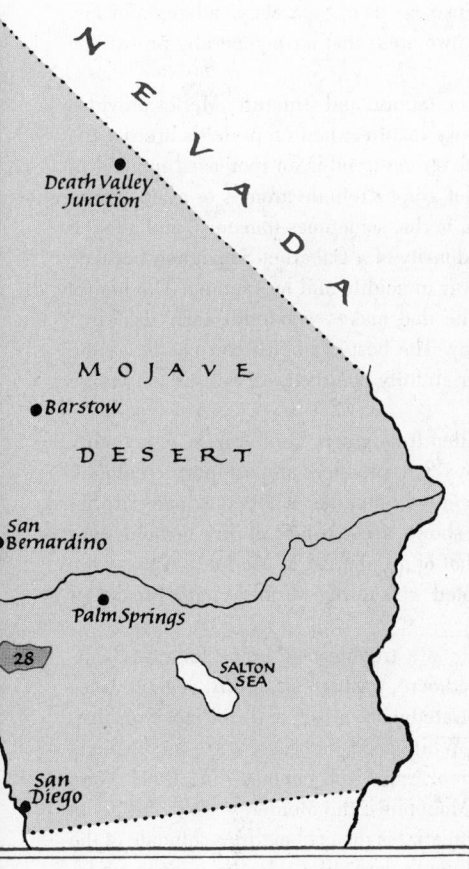

NORTH COAST

1 Anderson Valley
2 Potter Valley
3 McDowell Valley
4 Clear Lake
5 Guenoc Valley
6 Dry Creek Valley
7 Alexander Valley
8 Knights Valley
9 Russian River Valley
10 Sonoma Valley
11 Napa Valley
12 Los Carneros

CENTRAL COAST

13 Livermore Valley
14 Santa Cruz Mountains
15 Santa Clara Valley
16 Mount Harlan
17 Chalone
18 Arroyo Seco
19 Santa Lucia Highlands
20 Carmel Valley
21 San Lucas
22 York Mountain
23 Paso Robles
24 Edna Valley
25 Arroyo Grande
26 Santa Maria Valley
27 Santa Ynez Valley
28 Temecula

INTERIOR

29 Solano County Green Valley
30 Suisun Valley
31 Clarksburg
32 Lodi
33 El Dorado
34 Shenandoah Valley
35 Fiddletown

Flavors

RED WINE VARIETALS

Cabernet Franc Now being used by more and more wineries to give complexity to a wine's bouquet, Cabernet Franc is a cedary, herbaceous-scented wine that is usually lighter in color and body than either Cabernet Sauvignon or Merlot. It rarely can stand by itself, but used judiciously in a blend, it can provide an extra dimension. Reference-point California wines with significant proportions of Cabernet Franc that have stood the test of time include the 1971 Robert Mondavi Reserve Cabernet, the 1977 Joseph Phelps Insignia red wine, La Jota's 1986, 1990, 1991, 1992, and 1993 Cabernet Franc, Dalla Valle's 1990, 1992, 1993, and 1994 Maya (an exquisite wine with nearly 50% Cabernet Franc in the blend), and the Havens Bourriquot (two-thirds Cabernet Franc).

Cabernet Sauvignon The king of California's red wine grapes, Cabernet Sauvignon produces densely colored wine with aromas that can include black currants, chocolate, cedar, leather, ground meat, minerals, herbs, tobacco, and tar. Cabernet Sauvignon reaches its pinnacle of success in Napa, Sonoma, and the Santa Cruz Mountains, although a few excellent examples have emanated, infrequently, from Paso Robles, Santa Ynez, and Monterey. The more vegetal side of Cabernet Sauvignon, with intense smells of asparagus and green beans, is found in wines from Monterey or Santa Barbara, two areas that have generally proven too cool for this varietal.

Merlot If Cabernet Sauvignon provides the power, tannin, and structure, Merlot provides opulence, fatness, higher alcohol, and a lush, chewy texture when crop yields are not too high. It has grown in importance in California. One strong trend is an increased number of wines that are made predominantly from the Merlot grape. Telltale aromas of a top Merlot include scents of plums, black cherries, toffee, tea, herbs, sometimes tomatoes, and a touch of orange. Merlot wines will never have the color density of a Cabernet Sauvignon because the Merlot grape's skin is thinner, but they are lower in acidity and less tannic. The higher alcohol and ripeness result in a fleshy, chewy wine that makes wonderful early drinking. Wines made primarily from Merlot are here to stay. The best examples can challenge the best of France, but far too many remain hollow, frightfully acidified, as well as too tannic and vegetal.

Petite Sirah Unfortunately, this varietal has fallen from grace. Petite Sirah, in actuality the Duriff grape, is unrelated to the true Syrah, yet it produces almost purple-colored, very tannic, intense wines with peppery, cassis-scented bouquets. The wines age surprisingly well, as 15- to 20-year-old examples have shown a consistent ability to hold their fruit. The complexity and bouquet will rarely be that of a Cabernet or Merlot, but these are important wines. The Petite Sirah grape has adapted well to the warmer microclimates of California.

Pinot Noir The thin-skinned, fickle Pinot Noir is a troublesome grape for everybody. While California continues to produce too many mediocre, washed-out, pruny, vegetal wines from this varietal, no American region has demonstrated more progress with Pinot Noir than California. Major breakthroughs have been made. While good Pinot Noirs are increasingly noticeable from the North Coast areas of Mendocino, Napa, and Sonoma, fine Pinot Noirs also emanate from farther south—the Santa Cruz Mountains, the Monterey area, and Santa Barbara. Yet the area that has shown the greatest potential is the cool maritime climate of the Sonoma Coast. A good Pinot Noir will exhibit medium to dark ruby color, an intense explosion of aromatics, including red and black fruits, herbs, earth, and floral aromas. Pinot Noir tends to drop what tannin it possesses quickly, so some acidity is important to give it focus and depth. Most Pinot Noirs are drinkable when released. Few evolve and improve beyond

7–8 years in the bottle. Consumers should be particularly apprehensive of any Pinot Noir that tastes too tannic.

Sangiovese The Italian ancestry of many northern California grape growers and producers is increasingly evident with the number of wineries making Sangiovese. There are significant new plantations of this varietal, which is the most important red wine grape in the pastoral countryside of Tuscany, Italy. It is the predominant grape of most Chiantis and Vino da Tavolas. In California's fertile soils it achieves mind-boggling crop levels: 8–12 tons of fruit per acre. Without effective pruning practices or severe crop thinnings, the wines produced are diluted, thin, acidic, and of little interest. However, when the vines are crop-thinned by 40%–50%, the result can be fruity, strawberry/cherry/leather-scented and -flavored wines with medium body and penetrating acidity that is ideal for cutting through tomato-based sauces and working with the fusion Mediterranean/Pacific Rim cuisines found in California and elsewhere. To date, impressive Sangiovese has emerged from such wineries as Staglin Family Vineyards, Swanson, and Ferrari-Carano. The largest plantations are found in the Atlas Peak Vineyard, whose wines have been disappointing to date. Many producers are beginning to add some Cabernet Sauvignon to the blend in order to give the wine more color, body, and depth, as the higher crop yields tend to produce a lighter wine than desired.

Syrah Syrah is the great red grape varietal of France's Rhône Valley. An increasing number of California wineries have begun to bottle 100% Syrah wines, and some have been exquisite. The style ranges from light, fruity, almost Beaujolais-like wines, to black/purple-colored, thick, rich, ageworthy, highly extracted wines bursting with potential. A great Syrah will possess a hickory-, smoky-, tar-, and cassis-scented nose, rich, full-bodied, occasionally massive flavors, and considerable tannin. Like Cabernet Sauvignon, a Syrah-based wine is a thoroughbred when it comes to aging, easily lasting for 10–20 or more years. Neyers, Edmunds St. John, Dehlinger, Sine Que Non, Havens, and Thackrey have made the most compelling examples.

Zinfandel Seemingly against all odds, Zinfandel, the red, full-bodied type, is making a fashion comeback. Its reasonable price, combined with its gorgeous, up-front, peppery, berry (cherries, blackberries, and raspberries) nose, spicy fruit, and lush, supple texture have helped to boost its image. Additionally, Zinfandel's burgeoning popularity might be explained by a growing, and may I say healthy, trend away from excessively priced glamour wines, particularly the chocolate and vanilla flavors of California's Chardonnay and Cabernet Sauvignon. Zinfandel is grown throughout California, but the best clearly comes from relatively old vines grown on hillside vineyards. Selected vineyards (especially head-pruned old vines) from Napa, the Dry Creek Valley, Sonoma, Sierra Foothills, Paso Robles, and Amador have consistently produced the most interesting Zinfandels. While soil certainly plays an important role (gravelly loam is probably the best), low yields, old vines, and harvesting fully mature, physiologically rather than analytically ripe fruit are even more important. Today, most Zinfandels are made in a medium- to full-bodied, spicy, richly fruity style, somewhat in the image of Cabernet Sauvignon. While there is some backbone and structure, it is usually a wine that consumers can take immediate advantage of for its luscious, rich fruit, and can drink during the first decade of its life. While many Zinfandels can last longer, my experience suggests the wines rarely improve after 7–8 years and are best drunk within that time.

Carignan A somewhat lowly regarded grape that deserves more attention, some of California's oldest vineyards are planted with Carignan. As wineries such as Trentadue and Cline have proven, where there are old vines, low yields, and full ripeness, the wines can have surprising intensity and richness in a Rhône-like style. There is a dusty earthiness to most Carignan-based wines that goes along with its big, rich, black fruit and spicy flavors.

Alicante Bouchet Another grape that has fallen out of favor because of its low prestige, its standing remains revered by those who know it well. It yields a black/purple-colored wine with considerable body and richness. It needs time in the bottle to shed its hardness, but when treated respectfully, as the two Sonoma wineries Trentadue and Topolos do, this can be an overachieving grape that handsomely repays cellaring. When mature, the wine offers a Châteauneuf du Pape-like array of spicy, earthy flavors, and significant body and alcohol. Coturri has made some monster wines from this grape.

Mourvèdre/Mataro This variety is making a comeback. Some wineries, such as Edmunds St. John, Cline Cellars, and Sean Thackrey, have turned out fascinating wines from this varietal. Mataro produces a moderately dark-colored wine with a mushroomy-, earthy-, raspberry-scented nose, surprising acidity and tannin, and considerable aging potential.

WHITE WINE VARIETALS

Chardonnay The great superstar of the white wines, Chardonnay at its best can produce majestically rich, buttery wines with, seemingly, layers of flavors suggesting tropical fruits (pineapples and tangerines), apples, peaches, and even buttered popcorn when the wine has been barrel-fermented. It flourishes in all of California's viticultural districts, with no area having superiority over another. Great examples can be found from Mendocino, Sonoma, Napa, Carneros, Monterey, Santa Cruz, and Santa Barbara. The problem is that of the 800+ California wineries producing Chardonnay, fewer than 100 make an interesting wine. Crop yields are too high, the wines are manufactured rather than made, and are excessively acidified, making them technically flawless but lacking bouquet, flavor intensity, and character. The results are tart, vapid wines of no interest. Moreover, the wines have to be drunk within 12 months of the vintage. Another popular trend has been to intentionally leave sizable amounts of residual sugar in the wine while trying to hide part of it with additions of acidity. This cosmetically gives the wine a superficial feel of more richness and roundness, but these wines also crack up within a year of the vintage. Most Chardonnays are mediocre and overpriced, with very dubious aging potentials. Yet they remain the most popular "dry" white wine produced in California.

Chenin Blanc This maligned, generally misunderstood grape can produce lovely aperitif wines that are both dry and slightly sweet. Most wineries lean toward a fruity, delicate, perfumed, light- to medium-bodied style that pleases increasing numbers of consumers who are looking for delicious wines at reasonable prices. This varietal deserves more attention from consumers.

French Colombard Like Chenin Blanc, Colombard is a varietal that is rarely accorded much respect. Its charm is its aromatic character and crisp, light-bodied style.

Gewurztraminer Anyone who has tasted a fine French Gewurztraminer must be appalled by what is sold under this name in California. A handful of wineries, such as Navarro, Martinelli, and Babcock, have produced some attractive, although subdued Gewurztraminers. The bald truth remains that most California Gewurztraminers are made in a slightly sweet, watery, shallow, washed-out style.

Muscat There are several Muscat grapes used in California. This is an underrated and underappreciated varietal that produces remarkably fragrant and perfumed wines that are loaded with tropical fruit flavors. They are ideal as an aperitif wine or with desserts.

Pinot Blanc This grape, a staple of Alsace, France, where it is used to produce richly fruity, but generally straightforward, satisfying wines, has had mixed success in California. Some producers have barrel-fermented it, attempting to produce a large-scale, Chardonnay-style wine, with little success. Chalone is one of the few wineries to have succeeded with this style. In my opinion, Pinot Blanc is best vinified in a manner that emphasizes its intense fruity characteristics, which range from honeyed tangerines and oranges, to a more floral, applelike fruitiness. Pinot Blancs do not typically age well, but they provide immediate appeal and satisfaction in an exuberant yet uncomplicated manner. The finest Pinot Blancs have emerged from Arrowood, Chalone, Murphy-Goode, Wild Horse, Benziger, and Beringer. Most Pinot Blancs should be drunk within 2–3 years of the vintage, the only exception being those made in a full-bodied, structured style such as Chalone.

Sauvignon Blanc   California winemaking has failed miserably to take advantage of this grape. Overcropping, excessive acidification, and a philosophy of manufacturing the wines have resulted in hundreds of neutral, bland, empty wines with no bouquet or flavor. This is unfortunate, because Sauvignon is one of the most food-friendly and flexible wines produced in the world. It can also adapt itself to many different styles of fermentation and upbringing. At its best, the nonoaked examples of this wine possess vivid, perfumed noses of figs, melons, herbs, and minerals, crisp fruit, wonderful zesty flavors, and a dry finish. More ambitious barrel-fermented styles that often have some Semillon added can have a honeyed, melony character, and rich, medium- to full-bodied, grassy, melon and figlike flavors that offer considerable authority. Unfortunately, too few examples of either type are found in California. No viticultural region can claim a monopoly on either the successes or the failures.

Semillon   One of the up-and-coming California varietals, on its own, Semillon produces wines with considerable body and creamy richness. It can often be left on the vine, and has a tendency to develop botrytis, which lends itself to making sweet, honeyed, dessert wines. But Semillon's best use is when it is added to Sauvignon, where the two make the perfect marriage, producing wines with considerable richness and complexity.

White Riesling or Johannisberg Riesling   Occasionally some great late-harvest Rieslings have been made in California, but attempts at making a dry Kabinett- or Trocken-style Riesling as produced in Germany most frequently result in dull, lifeless, empty wines with no personality or flavor. Most Riesling is planted in soils that are too rich and in climates that are too hot. This is a shame. Riesling is another varietal that could prove immensely popular to the masses.

AGING POTENTIAL

Cabernet Franc: 5–15 years	Pinot Blanc: 1–3 years
Cabernet Sauvignon: 5–25 years	Pinot Noir: 4–7 years
Chardonnay: 1–3 years	Riesling (dry): 1–2 years
Chenin Blanc: 1–2 years	Riesling (sweet): 2–8 years
Colombard: 1–2 years	Sauvignon Blanc: 1–2 years
Gamay: 2–4 years	Semillon: 1–4 years
Merlot: 5–10 years	Sparkling Wines: 2–7 years
Muscat: 1–3 years	Syrah: 5–20 years
Petite Sirah: 5–15 years	Zinfandel: 3–10 years

OVERALL QUALITY LEVEL

The top 4 or 5 dozen producers of Cabernet Sauvignon, Merlot, or proprietary red wines, as well as the 4 or 5 dozen or so who produce Chardonnay, make wines that are as fine and as multidimensional as anywhere in the world. However, for well over 20 years my tastings have consistently revealed far too many California wines that are not made, but manufactured. Excessively acidified by cautious oenologists, and sterile-filtered to the point where there is no perceptible aroma, many wines possess little flavor except for the textural abrasiveness caused by shrill levels of acidity and high alcohol, and in the case of the red wines, excessive levels of green, astringent tannins. Producers have tried to hide their excessive crop yields by leaving residual sugar in the finished wine hoping to give the impression of more body. This practice is only a quick fix, as the white wines tend to fall apart 6–9 months after bottling and the red wines taste cloying.

The time-honored philosophy of California winemaking, which includes the obsession with the vineyard as a manufacturing plant; the industrial winemaking in the cellars; and the pre-occupation with monolithic, simplistic, squeaky-clean wines that suffer from such strictly con-trolled technical parameters, is weakening. It is no secret that the principal objective of most California wineries has been to produce sediment-free, spit-polished, stable wines. The means used to attain this goal too frequently eviscerate the wines of their flavor, aromas, personality, and pleasure-giving qualities. But significant changes (especially noticeable in vintages of the nineties) are underfoot. Only a fool could ignore the fact that California is now producing many of the greatest wines in the world. While most retailers legitimately carp about the microscopic allocations they receive of the limited-production gems from the most fashionable wineries, it is obvious that California wine quality is surging to greater and greater heights.

Why am I so bullish on California wines? Consider the following:

1. California has had 8 consecutive vintages of largely dazzling quality. Starting with 1990, every vintage has provided that state's growers with enough high-quality fruit to turn out numerous sensational wines. The 1991 vintage is unquestionably a great one for red wines, less so for the whites. The 1992 vintage produced rich, opulently styled red and white wines. The most perplexingly irregular of the last 8 vintages are 1993 and 1996. However, the top reds and whites can be sensational in a more restrained and classic fashion than 1997, 1995, 1994, 1992, 1991, and 1990.

What does a reasonably intelligent person make of this? California is in a position to dom-inate the American fine wine scene for the next 3–4 years. The 1997 vintage looks to be an especially exceptional one, with some Cabernet producers, borrowing a little hyperbole from the French, calling it the vintage of the century.

2. Even more important than the 8 consecutive vintages of outstanding quality is the shift in mind-set of many top wine producers. I have had little help from my colleagues in at-tempting to change the industrial/food-processor mentality espoused by the University of California at Davis. For as long as I can remember, this school of thought resulted in sterile, frightfully acidic, nearly undrinkable harsh and hollow wines that, amazingly, garnered raves from segments of the West Coast wine press. Large, highly influential wineries such as Robert Mondavi, Beringer, Newton, and now Sterling are fully cognizant of how much dam-age was wrought by such an antiwine philosophy, designed largely for the standardization of bulk wine production. Handcrafted wines that reflected the *terroir*, vintage, and varietal, in addition to providing immense pleasure, have had an enormous influence on others. A decade ago it was distressing to see the number of wineries that automatically, without any thought whatsoever, compromised and in many cases destroyed a wine by blind faith in the following techniques: a) by harvesting grapes based on analytical rather than physiological ripeness; b) by adding frightfully high levels of tartaric acid to the fermenting juice because it was the "risk-free" thing to do; c) by processing the youthful grape juice utilizing cen-trifuges and filters that eviscerated and purified the wine before it had a chance to develop any personality; d) by prefiltering wine intensely before it was allowed to go to barrel; and e) by fining and sterile-filtering everything as a rule of thumb so that a wine had no aromatics and nothing but a monolithic personality. The adoption of a less-traumatic and less-interventionist wine philosophy, emphasizing the importance of the vineyard's fruit and pre-serving its characteristics, is increasingly widespread. The results are increasing quantities of compellingly rich, natural-tasting, unprocessed wines that should be causing French wine producers to shudder. And while many wineries continue to fight this trend toward higher-quality, more-natural wines, often with considerable support from a gullible wine press, the fact is that you, the wine consumer, are the beneficiary!

3. As financially devastating as the phylloxera epidemic has been for California viticul-ture, the silver lining is that the replanting of vineyards over the last decade has addressed important issues that key industry personnel refused to acknowledge as being important prior to this epidemic. Many new vineyards have been planted with tighter spacing, thus

making the vines struggle. The result is deeper root systems and vines that produce smaller quantities of higher-quality grapes. Additionally, the problem of varietals planted in the wrong soils and/or microclimates can be rectified by these new plantations. Superior root-stocks and less productive clones that produce smaller crops with more individual character are other positive results of the phylloxera epidemic. As time passes, it will become evident that the mistakes made in the forties, fifties, and sixties have been largely corrected, ironi-cally because of phylloxera. If the grapes from these new vineyards are markedly superior, as they should be, it takes no genius to realize that wine quality will also improve.

4. The influence of the French, combined with a new generation of well-traveled, open-minded, revisionist California winemakers, must also be given credit for the remarkable progress in quality. California wines are as rich as they have ever been, but they no longer possess the heaviness of those great vintages of the sixties and seventies. Do readers realize why the finest French cuisine and French wines are cherished throughout the world as stan-dards of reference? Because France, in both her cooking and her wines, achieves, at the highest level of quality, extraordinary intensity of flavor without weight or heaviness. Call this elegance, harmony, finesse, or whatever, but it is what I now detect in increasing num-bers of California's finest wines.

BUYING STRATEGY

After erratic, so-so years in 1988 and 1989, California is on a roll, with excellent to terrific vintages every year this decade. There are an unprecedented 8 years in a row (1990–1997) where most of the state's producers have turned out wines that were made from ripe fruit. Only the top producers who keep crop yields to a minimum and refuse to excessively manip-ulate and process their wines will turn out the best wines, but it is clearly a time to be buying California wines.

The best California buys continue to be the Rhône Ranger blends and Zinfandels for red wines, and when you can find them, the good Chenin Blancs, Sauvignon Blancs, and Colom-bards for white wines.

VINTAGE GUIDE

1998—An unusually cool and wet summer caused difficulty in vineyards that were not properly pruned and maintained. The finest wines were produced by harvesters who waited out the unusual rains of early September. Although 1998 is the most irregular vintage of the decade, late harvesters are thrilled with the quality, even if the quantity is much lower than expected. Some sensational wines were produced by late pickers in just about every region, but overall, this is the most inconsistent vintage during the decade of the nineties.

1997—A long, cool year resulted in excellent potential for fabulous quality . . . provided producers did not pick too soon. Unexpected rain at the end of August and the beginning of September in the North Coast caused some Zinfandel producers to harvest too early. Overall, producers who waited until October to harvest their Cabernet Sauvignon tended to produce stunning wines with brilliant aromatics, gorgeous richness, and excellent potential for com-plexity. The finest examples of North Coast Cabernet Sauvignon, Merlot, and proprietary red wine blends will rival the greatest 1995s, 1994s, and 1991s. The Chardonnays possess more natural acidity than usual and therefore seem slightly more compressed. However, there are many fine, long-lived examples. Most California Chardonnays require consumption within several years of the vintage, but the finest 1997s should evolve nicely for 4–5 years, perhaps longer. Pinot Noir also benefited from the long, cool growing season, provided producers did not panic and pick too soon. The 1997 was the best overall vintage for the Santa Cruz Moun-tain region since 1994. Farther south, the vintage was irregular, but the potential for high quality exists.

1996—The year 1996 was hotter than either 1994 or 1995 but troublesome, with spikes of extremely torrid heat spells that stressed many vineyards throughout California. Overall, the vintage is excellent, with many outstanding wines. The Chardonnays, however, lack the aromatic nuances and complexity found in 1994, 1995, and 1997. The red wines can possess rugged, tannic constitutions, but the finest examples are impeccably well balanced, concentrated, and intense. The full-bodied Zinfandels tend to be extremely high in alcohol, yet they are consistently gutsy and exuberant. The Pinot Noirs also turned out well in this tricky vintage. South of San Francisco, in the Santa Cruz Mountains as well as in Paso Robles and Santa Barbara, 1996 was more mixed.

1995—While 1994 will continue to garner extraordinary press for the greatness of many red wines, 1995 is a worthy rival. A long, cool growing season provided fabulous hang time, and virtually the identical potential as 1994 for ripeness and richness. My tastings have consistently confirmed that the 1995 Chardonnay vintage was superior to 1994. However, most 1995 California Chardonnays should have been consumed by 1999. For the North Coast red wines, it is a superb vintage, one of the three or four finest of this star-studded decade. The year 1995 was also consistently excellent for Zinfandel and very fine for Pinot Noir. The Santa Cruz Mountain area enjoyed a very good vintage, as did Paso Robles and Santa Barbara.

1994—Many Cabernet Sauvignon, Zinfandel, and Syrah producers are calling this the vintage of the century. September rains caused a few problems in Santa Barbara, the Central Coast, and Carneros, but the cool, extremely long growing season was ideal for all red wine varietals. This should be an exceptional year, especially in Napa, Sonoma, and Mendocino. My tastings have confirmed the high promise, especially for the North Coast Cabernets.

1993—If the 1993s are not as dramatic as the finest 1994s, 1992s, 1991s, and 1990s, they are by no means inferior. This is another rich, velvety-textured vintage for red wines, and a beautifully balanced year for whites. This vintage has been criticized for reasons I am unable to understand, but there are many great wines.

1992—An abundant crop was harvested that ranged from very good to superb in quality. When Mother Nature is as generous as she was in most viticultural regions in 1992, the potential high quality can be diluted by excessive crop yields and harvesting grapes that are not physiologically mature. However, the top producers have turned out fat, rich, opulent, low-acid, dramatic wines. The white wines need to be drunk up. The finest reds are flattering and richly fruity, and will keep for 10–20 years.

1991—A cool, surprisingly long growing season resulted in potentially excessive crop yields. However, those producers who had the patience to wait out the cool weather and harvest fully mature fruit, as well as to keep their yields down, made some superb red wines that will compete with the finest 1994s, 1993s, 1992s, 1990s, 1987s, 1986s, 1985s, and 1984s. For all the red wine varietals it is a splendid year, with many producers expressing a preference for their 1991s because of the incredibly long hang-time on the vine. The 1991 vintage produced an enormous crop of good white wines that should be consumed by the end of 1995.

1990—For Cabernet Sauvignon, Zinfandel, and other major red wine varietals, 1990 was a mild growing season. The crop was moderate in size, particularly when compared with 1991 and 1992. The wines are concentrated, rich, and well made. It was a banner year for California's top red wines. For Chardonnay, it was a super year, but most of these wines should have been consumed by mid-1994.

1989—What started off as a promising vintage was spoiled by significant September rains that arrived before most producers were able to harvest. There is no question that the better drained hillside vineyards suffered less dilution than the vineyards on the valley floors. In addition, those producers who had the foresight to wait out the bad weather were awarded with some beautifully hot, Indian summer weather that lasted through much of October. Virtually everything, both white and red, was harvested during or immediately after the rains, resulting in diluted and problematic wines. Those wines 1) from well-drained hillside vineyards; 2) from producers who waited for the rains to stop; 3) from producers who gave their vineyards a chance to throw off the excess moisture; and 4) from those who waited sufficient time for the grapes to replenish their acids and sugars, made fine wines that will suffer only because of the general mediocre reputation of this vintage. Certainly all of the white wines from 1989 should have been consumed by now. Some excellent to outstanding red wines were produced, but selection is critical.

1988—A cooler-than-normal summer had an impact on the concentration levels of most of the red wines. However, the top Cabernet Sauvignons and Zinfandels, as well as other red wine varietals, were not without some charm and pleasure. They are soft, up-front, consistent wines that lack depth and aging potential. Most California 1988 red wines should be drunk by 1998. The 1988 vintage was a better one for Chardonnay and Sauvignon, but if you have any stocks languishing in your wine cellar, their time may already have passed.

1987—This has turned out to be more mixed than I initially believed, but there is no question that even at the bottom level of the quality hierarchy the wines are at least good. At the top level, there are many outstanding red wines, particularly Zinfandel and Cabernet-based wines that show superb color, wonderful richness, and considerable aromatic dimension. While some wines resemble the soft, forward, precocious 1984s, others have the structure and depth of the finest 1985s. The best producers have made wines with considerable richness and the potential for 10–15 more years of aging. Along with 1990 and 1991, 1987 is one of the finest Zinfandel vintages in the last 2 decades.

1986—Overshadowed by the resounding acclaim for 1985, 1986 has produced rich, buttery, opulent Chardonnays that have lower acidities than the 1985s, but frequently more fruit and plumpness. The best examples should have been drunk up (Mount Eden, Chalone, and Stony Hill being three exceptions). The red wines follow a similar pattern, exhibiting a rich, ripe, full-bodied character with generally lower acids than the nearly perfect 1985s, but also more tannins and body. It appears to be an excellent year for red wines that should age quite well.

1985—On balance, this should still turn out to be the finest vintage for California Cabernet Sauvignon between 1974 and 1990. An ideal growing season preceded near-perfect conditions for harvesting, especially in Napa and Sonoma, followed by Santa Cruz and Mendocino. While less extroverted and opulent in their youth than the 1984s, the Cabernets are certainly longer-lived. Revisionists have begun to question the relatively high acidity and lean, compact, evolutionary stage many of the wines are going through in 1995/1996, but this should be temporary. The finest wines are superrich, but less showy and dramatic than most people expect from California Cabernet. It is a slow-developing year for sure!

1984—An excellent year, somewhat overshadowed by 1985, 1984 was one of the hottest years on record, with temperatures frequently soaring over 100 degrees F during the summer. An early flowering and early harvest did create problems, as many grape varietals ripened at the same time. The style of the Chardonnays and Cabernets is one of very good to excellent concentration, an engaging, opulent, forward fruitiness that gives the wines appeal in their infancy, but good overall balance. Mendocino is less successful than elsewhere, but the ripe, rich, forward character of the wines of this vintage gives them undeniable charm and character. The majority of winemakers call 1985 a more classic year, 1984 a more hedonistic and obvious year. Recent tastings of the top 1984 Cabernets have shown wines that are all drinking splendidly now and should continue to hold their fruit for at least another decade. The top red wines are splendidly rich and dramatic, and more impressive in 1995 than the more ballyhooed 1985s. Only a handful of the white wines still retain their fruit.

1983—An average year for most of California's viticultural regions, although the Chardonnays from Napa were very good—but most are now too old. The Cabernets are medium bodied, rather austere, and lack the flesh and richness found in top years. Nevertheless, some stars are to be found (such as the Hess Collection Reserve, Opus One, Château Montelena, and Dunn). The red wines will keep for at least another 2–4 years.

1982—The growing season was plagued by heavy rains, then high temperatures. The press seemed to take a cautionary approach to the vintage, and as it turns out, justifiably so. Sonoma is more consistent than Napa, and Santa Cruz is surprisingly weak in 1982. The Sonoma red wines are ripe, rich, very forward, and much more interesting than those of Napa, which range in quality from outstanding to out of balance. The Chardonnays were mediocre, diluted, and lacking depth and acidity.

1981—Like 1984, it was a torridly hot growing season that had all varietals ripening at once. The harvest commenced early. Many fine, ripe, rich, dramatic Chardonnays were produced, but they should have been drunk up by 1987. The Cabernets are good rather than exciting, with the best of them having another 2–4 years of life. Most 1981 Cabernets, because of their forward character, should have been drunk.

1980—A relatively long, cool growing season had wineries predicting a classic, great vintage. The Cabernets are very good, but hardly great. The Cabernets do, however, have good acidity levels and seem by California standards to be evolving rather slowly. This is a vintage that has a top-notch reputation, but in reality appears to be a very fine rather than a monumental year.

OLDER VINTAGES

Since I fervently believe California's Chardonnays and Sauvignon Blancs rarely hold their fruit or improve after 3 years, older vintages are of interest only with respect to California red wines, principally Cabernet Sauvignon.

1979—This year produced a good vintage of tannic, well-endowed wines that are now fully mature.

1978—An outstanding vintage (and a very hot year) that produced concentrated, rich, plummy, dense wines that have aged well. The best examples should continue to offer splendid drinking for at least another 10–15 years. This has turned out to be a great year for California Cabernet.

1977—An above-average vintage that rendered elegant, fruity, supple wines that are now just beginning to tire a bit.

1976—A hot, drought year in which production yields per acre were very small. The wines are very concentrated and tannic, sometimes out of balance. Nevertheless, the great examples from this vintage (where the level of fruit extract matches the ferocity of the tannins) should prove to be among the longest-lived Cabernets of this generation. Despite irregularity here, there are some truly splendid Cabernets.

1975—A cool year, most authorities consider the wines rather hollow and short-lived. However, some magnificent examples have emerged from this vintage that should last for another 10–15 years. As a general rule, most 1975 California Cabernets should be consumed over the next 4–5 years.

1974—One of the great blockbuster years for California Cabernet, as well as a year that introduced many American consumers to the potential for full-bodied, rich, complex wines from the best wineries. While many have criticized the wines for aging erratically and quickly, the best 1974s exhibit a richness, voluptuousness, and intensity that recalls such vintages as 1984, 1987, and 1990. Some of the top 1974s are not yet ready for prime-time drinking. However, this is a vintage that must be approached with caution on the auction market because of the potential for badly stored, abused bottles. Additionally, there are some major disappointments from big names.

1973—A large crop was harvested after a moderately warm, but not hot summer. The quality is uneven, but the wines are well balanced, with many having the potential for long aging.

1972—A rain-plagued vintage, much like 1989, it is almost impossible to find any successes that have survived 20 years of cellaring.

1970, 1969, 1968, 1958, 1951—All great vintages.

WHERE TO FIND CALIFORNIA'S BEST WINE VALUES

(Wineries That Can Be Counted On for Value)

Alderbrook (Sauvignon Blanc, Chardonnay)

Amador Foothill Winery (white Zinfandel)

Arrowood Domaine du Grand Archer (Chardonnay, Cabernet Sauvignon)

Belvedere (Chardonnay cuvées)

Beringer (Knight's Valley Chardonnay, Sauvignon Blanc, Gamay Beaujolais)

Bonny Doon (Clos de Gilroy, Ca' Del Solo cuvées, Pacific Rim Riesling)

Buehler (Zinfandel)

Carmenet (Colombard)

Cartlidge and Browne (Chardonnay, Pinot Noir, Zinfandel, Cabernet Sauvignon)

Cline (Côtes d'Oakley)

Duxoup (Gamay, Charbono)

Edmunds St. John (New World and Port o' Call reds, Pinot Grigio and El Niño whites)

Ehler's Grove (Sauvignon Blanc)

Estancia (Chardonnay cuvées, Meritage red)

Fetzer (Sundial Chardonnay)

Franciscan (Merlot, Chardonnay)

Guenoc (Petite Sirah, Zinfandel)

Hacienda (Chenin Blanc)

Hess Collection (Hess Select Chardonnay, Cabernet Sauvignon)

Husch Vineyard (Chenin Blanc, Gewürztraminer, La Ribera Red)

Kendall-Jackson (Vintner's Reserve Chardonnay, Fumé Blanc, Vintner's Reserve Zinfandel)

Kenwood (Sauvignon Blanc)

Konocti (Fumé Blanc)

Laurel Glen (Counterpoint and Terra Rosa proprietary red wines)

Liberty School—Caymus (Cabernet Sauvignon, Sauvignon Blanc, Chardonnay)

J. Lohr (Gamay, Cypress Chardonnay)

Marietta Cellars (Old Vine Red, Zinfandel, Cabernet Sauvignon)

Mirassou (white burgundy—Pinot Blanc)

Robert Mondavi (the Woodbridge wines are fine bargains)

Monterey Vineyard (Classic cuvées of Merlot, Cabernet Sauvignon, Chardonnay, Sauvignon Blanc, and Zinfandel, generic Classic White and Classic Red)

Moro Bay Vineyards (Chardonnay)

Mountain View Winery (Sauvignon Blanc, Chardonnay, Pinot Noir, Zinfandel)

Murphy-Goode (Fumé Blanc)

Napa Ridge (Chardonnay, Cabernet Sauvignon, Sauvignon Blanc)

Newton (Claret Proprietary Red Wine)

Parducci (Sauvignon Blanc)

Robert Pecota (Gamay)

J. Pedroncelli (Sauvignon Blanc, Zinfandel, Cabernet Sauvignon)

Joseph Phelps (Vins du Mistral cuvées)

R. H. Phillips (Night Harvest cuvées of Chardonnay and Sauvignon Blanc)

Preston (Cuvée du Fumé)

Ravenswood (Zinfandel and Merlot Vintner's blends)

Château Souverain (Chardonnay, Merlot, Cabernet Sauvignon, Sauvignon Blanc)

Stratford (the Chardonnay and Canterbury line of wines, particularly Chardonnay and Sauvignon Blanc)

Ivan Tamas (Trebbiano, Fumé Blanc, and Chardonnay)

Trentadue (Old Patch Red, Zinfandel, Carignan, Sangiovese, Petite Sirah, Merlot, Salute Proprietary Red Wine)

Westwood (Barbera)

RATING CALIFORNIA'S BEST PRODUCERS OF CABERNET SAUVIGNON, MERLOT, OR BLENDS THEREOF

* * * * * *(OUTSTANDING)

Abreu Vineyards Madrona Ranch (Napa)

Araujo Estate Eisele Vineyard (Napa)

Arrowood Reserve Speciale (Sonoma)

Arrowood Reserve Speciale Merlot (Sonoma)

Bacio Divino Proprietary Red Wine (California)

Behrens and Hitchcock Kenefick Ranch (Napa)

Behrens and Hitchcock TLK Ranch (Napa)

Beringer Chabot Vineyard (Napa)

Beringer Merlot Bancroft Vineyard (Napa)

Beringer Private Reserve (Napa)

Bryant Family Vineyard (Napa)

Cardinale Proprietary Red Wine (California)

Caymus Special Selection (Napa)

Colgin Lamb Vineyard (Napa)

Dalla Valle (Napa)

Dalla Valle Maya Proprietary Red Wine (Napa)

Dominus (Napa)

Dunn (Napa)

Dunn Howell Mountain (Napa)

Etude (Napa)

Fisher Lamb Vineyard (Napa)

Fisher Merlot RCF Vineyard (Napa)

Fisher Wedding Vineyard (Sonoma)

Flora Springs Hillside Reserve (Napa)

Flora Springs Trilogy Proprietary Red Wine (Napa)

Grace Family Vineyard (Napa)

Harlan Estate Proprietary Red Wine (Napa)

La Jota Anniversary Cuvée (Napa)

Laurel Glen (Sonoma)

Peter Michael Les Pavots Proprietary Red Wine (California)

Robert Mondavi Reserve (Napa)

Robert Mondavi To-Kalon Estate Reserve (Napa)

Château Montelena Estate (Napa)

Mount Eden Old Vine Reserve (Santa Cruz)

Newton Cabernet Sauvignon (Napa)

Newton Merlot (Napa)

Pahlmeyer Proprietary Red Wine (Napa)

Pahlmeyer Merlot (Napa)

Joseph Phelps Insignia Proprietary Red Wine (Napa)

Plumpjack Reserve (Napa)

Pride Mountain Claret (Napa)

Pride Mountain Reserve (Napa)

Ridge Monte Bello (Santa Cruz Mountain)

Screaming Eagle (Napa)

Shafer Hillside Select (Napa)

Silver Oak (Alexander Valley)

Silver Oak (Napa)

Simi Reserve (Sonoma) (since 1986)

Spottswoode (Napa)

Philip Togni (Napa)

* * * * *(EXCELLENT)

Anderson's Conn Valley Vineyard (Napa)

Arrowood (Sonoma)

Barnett Spring Mountain Rattlesnake Hill (Napa)

Beaulieu Cabernet Sauvignon Private Reserve (Napa)

Behrens and Hitchcock Cuvée Lola Proprietary Red Wine (Napa)

Bellerose Merlot (Sonoma)

Beringer St. Helena Vineyard (Napa)

Beringer State Lane Vineyard (Napa)

Beringer Tre Colline Vineyard (Napa)

Blackjack Ranch (Santa Barbara)

Cakebread Cellars Benchland Select (Napa)

Cakebread Cellars Three Sisters (Napa)

Carmenet Moon Mountain Estate Reserve Proprietary Red Wine (Sonoma)

Clark-Claudon (Napa)****/*****

Clos Pegase Hommage Proprietary Red Wine (Napa)

B. R. Cohn Olive Hill Vineyard (Sonoma)

Coturri Jessandre Vineyard (Sonoma)

Coturri Merlot Feingold Vineyard (Sonoma)

Robert Craig Affinity Proprietary Red Wine (Napa)

Robert Craig Mount Veeder (Napa)

Cuvaison ATS Selection (Carneros)

Dehlinger Bordeaux Blend (Sonoma)

Diamond Creek Gravelly Meadow (Napa)

Diamond Creek Lake (Napa)

Diamond Creek Red Rock Terrace (Napa)

Diamond Creek Volcanic Hill (Napa)

Durney Reserve (Monterey)

Elyse Morisoli Vineyard (Napa)

Far Niente (Napa)

Gallo Frei Ranch (Sonoma)

Gary Farrell Ladi's Vineyard (Sonoma)

Gary Farrell Merlot Ladi's Vineyard (Sonoma)

Ferrari-Carano (Sonoma) (since 1991)

Ferrari-Carano Merlot (Sonoma) (since 1991)

Ferrari-Carano Reserve Red Proprietary Wine (Sonoma)

Fisher Coach Insignia (Sonoma) (since 1991)

Flora Springs Cypress Ranch (Pope Valley)

Forman (Napa)

Forman Merlot (Napa)

Foxen (Santa Barbara)

Franciscan Meritage Oakville Estate (Napa)

Frazier (Napa)

Gainey Cabernet Franc Limited Selection (Santa Ynez)

Geyser Peak Estate Reserve (Sonoma)

Geyser Peak Reserve Alexandre Proprietary Red Wine (Sonoma)

Girard (Napa)

Girard Reserve (Napa)

Harrison Winery (Napa)

Hartwell Stag's Leap (Napa)

Havens Bourriquot (Napa)****/*****

Havens Merlot Reserve (Napa)

Heitz Bella Oaks (Napa)

Heitz Martha's Vineyard (Napa) (prior to 1986 a 5-star wine)

Hess Collection (Napa)

Hess Collection Reserve (Napa)

Paul Hobbs Hyde Vineyard (Sonoma)

Jones Family Vineyard (Napa)

JSJ Signature Series Buckeye Vineyard (Alexander Valley)

JSJ Signature Series Veeder Peak Vineyard (Napa)

Judd's Hill (Napa)

Justin Cabernet Franc (Paso Robles)

Justin Cabernet Sauvignon (Paso Robles)

Justin Isosceles Proprietary Red Wine (Paso Robles)

Justin Merlot (Paso Robles)

Kenwood Artists Series (Sonoma)

Kenwood Jack London Vineyard (Sonoma)

Kunde Estate Reserve (Sonoma)

La Jota (Napa)

La Jota Cabernet Franc (Napa)****/*****

Lail Vineyards J. Daniel Cuvée Proprietary Red Wine (Napa)

Lancaster Reserve Proprietary Red Wine (Alexander Valley)

Laurel Glen Terra Rosa (Sonoma)

Lokoya Diamond Mountain (Napa)

Lokoya Howell Mountain (Napa)

Lokoya Mount Veeder (Napa)

Lokoya Rutherford (Napa)

Marietta (Sonoma)

Matanzas Creek Merlot (Sonoma)

Philip Melka Metisse Proprietary Red Wine (Napa)

Merryvale Profile Proprietary Red Wine (Napa)

Robert Mondavi Oakville Unfiltered (Napa)

Monticello Corley Reserve (Napa)

Opus One (Napa)

Page Mill Volker Eisele Vineyard (Napa)

Paoletti (Napa)

Joseph Phelps Backus Vineyard (Napa)

Pine Ridge Andrus Reserve (Napa)

Pine Ridge Howell Mountain (Napa)

Plumpjack Estate (Napa)

Pride Mountain Cabernet Franc (Napa)

Pride Mountain Vineyards (Napa)

Rancho Sisquoc Cellar Select Red Estate (Santa Maria)

Ravenswood Merlot Sangiacomo (Sonoma)

Ravenswood Pickberry Proprietary Red Wine (Sonoma)

Reverie Diamond Mountain (Napa)

Reverie Special Reserve Proprietary Red Wine (Napa)

Rochioli Reserve Neoma's Vineyard (Sonoma)

Rockland (Napa)****/*****

Rubicon Proprietary Red Wine (Napa)

Saddleback Cellars (Napa)

Saddleback Cellars Venge Family Reserve (Napa)****/*****

Saddleback Cellars Venge Family Reserve Merlot (Napa)****/*****

St. Francis Reserve (Sonoma)
St. Francis Merlot Reserve (Sonoma)
St. Jean Cinq Cépages Proprietary Red
   Wine (Sonoma)****/*****
Santa Cruz Mountain Merlot (Santa Ynez)
Seavey (Napa)****/*****
Selene Merlot (Napa)
Shafer Merlot (Napa)
Signorello Founder's Reserve (Napa)
Silverado Limited Reserve (Napa)
Château Souverain Winemaker's Reserve
   (Sonoma)
Spring Mountain Estate (Napa)
Spring Mountain Mirabelle Alba Chevalier
   Proprietary Red Wine (Napa)
Spring Mountain La Perla Chevalier
   Proprietary Red Wine (Napa)
Stag's Leap Cask 23 Proprietary Red Wine
   (Napa)
Stag's Leap Fay Vineyard (Napa)
Stag's Leap Wine Cellars Stag's Leap
   Vineyard (Napa)
Staglin (Napa)

Stonefly Cabernet Franc (Napa)
Stonestreet Christopher's Vineyard
   (Sonoma)
Stonestreet Legacy Proprietary Red Wine
   (Alexander Valley)
Stonestreet Three Block Vineyard (Sonoma)
Tudal (Napa)
Tulocay Cliff Vineyard (Napa)
Viader Proprietary Red Wine (Napa)
Villa Mt. Eden Signature Series
   (Mendocino)
Vineyard 29 (Napa)
Vine Cliff Cellars (Napa)
Von Strasser Diamond Mountain (Napa)
Von Strasser Diamond Mountain
   Reserve****/***** (Napa)
White Rock Claret Proprietary Red Wine
   (Napa)
Whitehall Lane Leonardi Vineyard (Napa)
Whitehall Lane Morisoli (Napa)
Whitehall Lane Reserve (Napa)
ZD Estate (Napa)

*** (GOOD)

Ahlgren Bates Ranch (Santa Cruz)
Ahlgren Besson Vineyard (Santa Cruz)
Alexander Valley (Sonoma)
Amizetta Vineyards (Napa)
S. Anderson (Napa)
Arrowood Merlot (Sonoma)
Barnett Spring Mountain (Napa)
Bellerose Cuvée Bellerose (Sonoma)
Benziger (Glen Ellen)
Benziger Tribute (Glen Ellen)
Beringer Knight's Valley (Napa)
Boeger (El Dorado)
Boeger Merlot (El Dorado)
Brutocao Albert Vineyard (Mendocino)
Brutocao Merlot (Mendocino)
Buehler (Napa)***/****
Burgess Cellars Vintage Selection (Napa)
Cain Cellars Cain Five Proprietary Red
   Wine (Napa)
Cain Cellars Merlot (Napa)
Carmenet Proprietary Red Wines
   (Sonoma)
Caymus (Napa)
Chalk Hill (Sonoma)
Chimney Rock (Napa)

Cinnabar (Santa Cruz)
Clos du Bois (Sonoma)
Clos du Bois Briarcrest (Sonoma)
Clos du Bois Marlstone (Sonoma)
Clos du Bois Merlot (Sonoma)
Clos Pegase (Napa)
Clos Pegase Merlot (Napa)
Clos du Val Merlot (Napa)
Clos du Val Reserve (Napa)
Cloverdale Ranch Estate (Alexander
   Valley)
Cooper-Garrod Cabernet Franc (Santa Cruz)
Cooper-Garrod Cabernet Sauvignon (Santa
   Cruz)
Corison (Napa)
Cosentino (Napa)
Coturri Remick Ridge Vineyard (Sonoma)
Coturri View's Land Vineyard (Sonoma)
Cuvaison (Napa)
Cuvaison Merlot (Napa)
Dry Creek Meritage (Sonoma)
Duckhorn (Napa)
Duckhorn Merlot (Napa)
Duckhorn Merlot 3 Palms Vineyard (Napa)
Durney (Monterey)

Eberle (Paso Robles)

Estancia (Alexander Valley)

Estancia Meritage Proprietary Red Wine (Alexander Valley)

Estancia Merlot (Alexander Valley)

Far Niente (Napa)

Gary Farrell (Sonoma)

Fetzer Barrel Select (California)

Field Stone Alexander Valley (Sonoma)

Field Stone Reserve (Sonoma)

Louis Foppiano Fox Mountain Reserve (Sonoma)

Franciscan Oakville Estate (Napa)

Franciscan Merlot (Napa)

Frog's Leap (Napa)

Frog's Leap Merlot (Napa)

Gainey Cabernet Franc (Santa Barbara)

Gainey Merlot Limited Selection (Santa Barbara)

E. & J. Gallo Estate (Sonoma)

Grgich Hills Merlot (Napa)

Groth Merlot (Napa)

Groth Reserve (Napa) (***** before 1987)

Gundlach-Bundschu Cabernet Franc (Sonoma)

Havens Wine Cellar Merlot (Napa)

Heitz (Napa)

Husch (Mendocino)

Husch Estate La Ribera (Mendocino)

Iron Horse Cabernets Proprietary Red Wine (Sonoma)

Johnson-Turnbull (Napa)

Johnson-Turnbull Vineyard Selection 67***/****

Jordan (Sonoma)

Kalin Cellars Reserve (Marin)

Robert Keenan (Napa)

Robert Keenan Merlot (Napa)

Kendall-Jackson Grand Reserve (California) (since 1991)

Kathryn Kennedy (Santa Clara)

Kenwood (Sonoma)

Klein Vineyards (Santa Cruz)

Liberty School (California)

Livingston Moffett Vineyard (Napa)

Long (Napa)

Longoria (Santa Ynez)

Longoria Cabernet Franc (Santa Ynez)

Longoria Merlot (Santa Ynez)

Maacama Creek Melim Vineyard (Sonoma)

Madrone (El Dorado)

Madrone Cabernet Franc (El Dorado)

Madrone Quintet Reserve Red Table Wine (El Dorado)

Michel-Schlumberger (Dry Creek)

Robert Mondavi Napa (Napa)

Château Montelena Calistoga Cuvée (Napa)

Monterey Vineyards Classic Cabernet Sauvignon (California)

Monterey Vineyards Classic Merlot (California)

Monterey Vineyards Classic Red (California)

Monticello Cellars Jefferson Cuvée (Napa)

Monticello Cellars Merlot (Napa)

Mount Eden (Santa Clara)

Murphy-Goode Merlot (Sonoma)

Murrieta's Well Vendimia Proprietary Red Wine (Livermore)

Napa Ridge (Napa)

Nelson Estate Cabernet Franc (Napa)

Newton Claret (Napa)

Oakville Ranch (Napa)

Peachy Canyon (Paso Robles)

Peachy Canyon Merlot (Paso Robles)

J. Pedroncelli Reserved (Sonoma)

Robert Pepi Vine Hill Ranch (Napa)

Joseph Phelps (Napa)***/****

Joseph Phelps Merlot (Napa)

Pine Ridge Merlot (Napa)

Pine Ridge Rutherford Cuvée (Napa)

Pine Ridge Stag's Leap District (Napa)

A. Rafanelli (Sonoma)

Rancho Sisquoc Cabernet Franc (Santa Barbara)

Rancho Sisquoc Estate (Santa Barbara)

Rancho Sisquoc Merlot Estate (Santa Barbara)

Ravenswood (Sonoma)

Ravenswood Merlot Vintner's Blend (North Coast)

Raymond Private Reserve (Napa)

Renaissance (Yuba)

Ridge Santa Cruz (Santa Clara)

Ritchie Creek (Napa)

J. Rochioli (Sonoma)

Rocking Horse (Napa)

St. Clement (Napa) (since 1991)

St. Clement Oroppas (Napa)

St. Francis Merlot (Sonoma)

Santa Cruz Mountain Bates Ranch (Santa
  Cruz)***/****
Sebastiani single-vineyard cuvées
  (Sonoma)
Signorello Unfined/Unfiltered
  (Napa)***/****
Silverado (Napa)
Silverado Merlot (Napa)
Simi (Sonoma)
Château Souverain (Sonoma) (since
  1990)
Château Souverain Merlot (Sonoma)
Spring Mountain Estate Miravalle Vineyard
  (Napa)
Stag's Leap Wine Cellars (Napa)

Sterling Diamond Mountain Ranch (Napa)
  (since 1992)
Stratford Merlot (Napa)
Swanson (Napa)
Swanson Merlot (Napa)
Tantalus (Sonoma)
The Terraces (Napa)
Trefethen Reserve (Napa)
Trentadue (Sonoma)
Trentadue Merlot (Sonoma)***/****
Truchard Merlot (Napa)
Whitehall Lane (Napa)
Whitehall Lane Merlot Summer's Ranch
  (Alexander Valley)

* * *(AVERAGE)*

Alexander Valley Vineyard Merlot
  (Sonoma)**/***
Bargetto (Santa Cruz)
Beaulieu Beau Tour (Napa)**/***
Beaulieu Rutherford (Napa)**/***
Bel Arbors (California)
Bel Arbors Merlot (California)
Belvedere Wine Co. (Sonoma)
Belvedere Wine Co. Merlot (Sonoma)
Benziger Merlot (Glen Ellen)
Brander Bouchet Proprietary Red Wine
  (Santa Ynez)
Buena Vista Carneros (Sonoma)
Buena Vista Private Reserve (Sonoma)
Buttonwood Farm Merlot (Santa Ynez)
Cafaro (Napa)
Cafaro Merlot (Napa)
Chappellet (Napa)
Chappellet Merlot (Napa)
Clos Pegase Merlot (Napa)
Clos du Val (Napa)
B. R. Cohn Merlot (Sonoma)
Congress Springs Noblesse Proprietary Red
  Wine (Santa Clara)
Conn Creek (Napa)
Creston Manor (San Luis Obispo)
Cronin (Santa Cruz)
Cutler Cellar (Sonoma)
De Loach (Sonoma)
De Moor (Napa)
Dry Creek (Sonoma)**/***
Firestone (Santa Ynez)
Firestone Merlot (Santa Barbara)
Firestone Reserve (Santa Ynez)

Firestone Vintage Reserve Proprietary Red
  Wine (Santa Ynez)
Folie à Deux (Napa)
Louis Foppiano (Sonoma)
Freemark Abbey Bosché (Napa)
Freemark Abbey Sycamore (Napa)
Gainey Merlot (Santa Ynez)
Gan Eden (Sonoma)
Glen Ellen (Sonoma)
Grand Cru Vineyards (Sonoma)
Greenwood Ridge (Sonoma)
Groth (Napa)
Guenoc Beckstoffer Vineyard (Carneros)
Gundlach-Bundschu (Sonoma)
Gundlach-Bundschu Rhinefarm Vineyard
  (Sonoma)
Hacienda (Sonoma)
Hacienda Antares Proprietary Red Wine
  (Sonoma)
Hagafen (Napa)
Hanna (Sonoma)
Hanzell (Sonoma)
Haywood (Sonoma)
William Hill Gold Label Reserve (Napa)
Indian Springs Merlot (Sierra Foothills)
Jekel Home Vineyard (Monterey)
Jekel Symmetry Proprietary Red Wine
  (Monterey)
Château Julien (Monterey)
Château Julien Merlot (Monterey)
Kendall-Jackson Vintner's Reserve
  (California)
Konocti (Lake)
Konocti Merlot (Lake)

Charles Krug Vintage Selection (Napa)

Lakespring (Napa)

Lakespring Reserve (Napa)

Leeward (Ventura)

J. Lohr Reserve (Santa Clara)

Markham (Napa)

Markham Merlot (Napa)

Louis Martini (Sonoma)

Mayacamas (Napa) (***** before 1976)

McDowell Valley Vineyards (California)

Meridian Vineyards (San Luis Obispo)

Mirassou (Santa Clara)

Montevina (Amador)

Morgan Winery (Monterey)

J. W. Morris Fat Cat (Sonoma)

Mount Veeder (Napa)

Mount Veeder Meritage Proprietary Red
   Wine (Napa)

Mountain View Winery (Santa Clara)

Murphy-Goode (Sonoma)**/***

Nalle (Sonoma)

Domaine Napa (Napa)

Nevada City (Nevada County)

Newlan (Napa)

Parducci (Mendocino)

Parducci Merlot (Mendocino)

Robert Pecota (Napa)

J. Pedroncelli (Sonoma)

Peju Province (Napa)

R. H. Phillips (Yolo)

Château Potelle (Napa)

Preston Vineyards (Sonoma)

Quail Ridge (Napa)

Rabbit Ridge (Sonoma)

Raymond Napa (Napa)

Raymond Private Reserve

Rocking Horse Claret (Napa)

Rombauer (Napa)

Roudon-Smith (Santa Cruz)

Round Hill (Napa)

Round Hill Reserve (Napa)

Rubissow-Sargent (Napa)

Rubissow-Sargent Merlot (Napa)

Rutherford Hill (Napa)

Château St. Jean (Sonoma)

St. Supery (Napa)

Santa Barbara Winery (Santa Barbara)

Santa Ynez Cabernet Sauvignon Port
   (Santa Ynez)

Sarah's Vineyard Merlot (Santa Clara)

V. Sattui (Napa)

Sebastiani regular cuvées (Sonoma)

Seghesio (Sonoma)

Sequoia Grove (Napa)

Sequoia Grove Estate (Napa)

Shenandoah Vineyards Amador (Amador)

Sierra Vista (El Dorado)

Silverado (Napa)

Robert Sinsky Claret (Sonoma)

Smith and Hook Merlot (Santa Lucia)

Stag's Leap Winery Napa (Napa)

Steltzner (Napa)

Steltzner Merlot (Napa)

Sterling Merlot (Napa)

Sterling Napa (Napa)

Sterling Reserve Proprietary Red Wine
   (Napa)

Stevenot (Calaveras)

Stone Creek (Napa)

Stonegate (Napa)

Stonegate Merlot (Napa)

Stratford (California)

Straus Merlot (Napa)

Rodney Strong Alexander's Crown
   (Sonoma)

Rombauer Merlot (Napa)

Sullivan (Napa)

Sullivan Merlot (Napa)

Sutter Home (Napa)

Ivan Tamas (Livermore)

Tobin James (Paso Robles)

Villa Mt. Eden California (Napa)

Villa Mt. Eden Cellar Select (Napa)

Villa Zapu (Napa)

Weinstock Cellars (Sonoma)

Wellington Vineyards (Sonoma)

Wild Horse (San Luis Obispo)

J. Wile and Sons (California)

RATING CALIFORNIA'S BEST PRODUCERS OF CHARDONNAY

* * * * * (OUTSTANDING)

Arrowood Reserve Speciale Michel
   Berthoud (Sonoma)

Beringer Private Reserve (Napa)

Beringer Sbragia Select (Napa)

Cuvaison ATS Selection (Carneros)

Ferrari-Carano Reserve (Sonoma)

Fisher Whitney's Vineyard (Sonoma)

Gainey Limited Selection (Santa Ynez)

Hanzell Vineyards (Sonoma)

JSJ Signature Series Cambria Vineyard (Santa Barbara)

JSJ Signature Series Camelot Vineyard (Santa Maria)

JSJ Signature Series Upper Barn Vineyard (Sonoma)

JSJ Signature Series Verité (Santa Maria)

Kalin Cellars Cuvée LD (Sonoma)

Kalin Cellars Cuvée W (Livermore)

Kistler Vineyards Camp Meeting Ridge (Sonoma)

Kistler Vineyards Cuvée Cathleen (Sonoma)

Kistler Vineyards Durell Vineyard (Sonoma)

Kistler Vineyards Dutton Ranch (Sonoma)

Kistler Vineyards Hudson Vineyard (Sonoma)

Kistler Vineyards Kistler Estate (Sonoma)

Kistler Vineyards McCrea Vineyard (Sonoma)

Kistler Vineyards Vine Hill Road (Sonoma)

Landmark Demaris Reserve (Sonoma)

Landmark Lorenzo Vineyard (Sonoma)

Marcassin Hudson Vineyard (Carneros)

Marcassin Lorenzo Vineyard (Sonoma)

Marcassin Marcassin Vineyard (Sonoma)

Marcassin Upper Barn Gauer Vineyard (Sonoma)

Martinelli Charles Ranch (Sonoma Coast)

Martinelli Martinelli Road (Sonoma Coast)

Martinelli Woolsey Road (Sonoma Coast)

Merryvale Silhouette (Napa)

Peter Michael Belle Côte (Sonoma)

Peter Michael Clos du Ciel (Sonoma)

Peter Michael Cuvée Indigene (Sonoma)

Peter Michael Mon Plaisir (Sonoma)

Peter Michael Point Rouge (Sonoma)

Robert Mondavi Reserve (Napa)

Mount Eden Vineyards Santa Cruz Estate (Santa Clara)

Newton Unfiltered (Napa)

Neyers El Novillero (Carneros)

Neyers Thieriot (Sonoma Coast)

Pahlmeyer Unfiltered (Napa)

Patz and Hall Alder Springs (Mendocino)

Patz and Hall Carr Vineyard (Napa)

Patz and Hall Hyde Vineyard (Carneros)

Joseph Phelps Ovation (Napa)

J. Rochioli Allen Vineyard (Sonoma)

J. Rochioli River Block (Sonoma)

J. Rochioli South River (Sonoma)

Shafer Red Shoulder Ranch (Napa)

Silverado Limited Reserve (Napa)

Robert Talbott Estate (Monterey)

Robert Talbott Diamond T Estate (Monterey)

* * * * (EXCELLENT)

Anderson's Conn Valley Fournier Vineyard (Carneros)

Arrowood (Sonoma)

Au Bon Climat Bien Nacido (Santa Barbara)

Au Bon Climat Sanford & Benedict Vineyard (Santa Barbara)

Au Bon Climat Talley Vineyard (Santa Barbara)

Bancroft (Napa)

Bannister Allen Vineyard (Russian River)

Bannister Porter-Bass Vineyard (Russian River)

Brewer-Clifton Sweeney Canyon (Santa Ynez)

Byron Estate (Santa Barbara)

Byron Reserve (Santa Barbara)

Cain Cellars (Napa)

Calera Mt. Harlan (San Benito)

Cambria Katherine's Vineyard (Santa Maria)

Cambria Reserve (Santa Maria)

Chalone Estate (Monterey)

Chimère (Santa Barbara)

Cinnabar (Santa Clara)

Crichton Hall (Napa)

Cronin cuvées (San Mateo)

De Loach O.F.S. (Sonoma)

Dehlinger (Russian River)

Dehlinger Selection (Russian River)

Durney Estate (Monterey)

Edna Valley (San Luis Obispo)

El Molino (Napa)

Ferrari-Carano (Sonoma)

Forman (Napa)

Foxen (Santa Barbara)

Franciscan (Napa)

Gallo Estate (Sonoma)

Green and Red Catacula Vineyard (Napa)

Harrison (Napa)

Hess Collection (Napa)

Paul Hobbs Dinner Vineyard (Sonoma)

Kalin Cellars Cuvée CH (Sonoma)

Kalin Cellars Cuvée DD (Marin)

Kendall-Jackson Camelot Vineyard (Lake)

Kunde Estate Kinneybrook Vineyard
(Sonoma)

Kunde Estate Wildwood Vineyard (Sonoma)

Landmark Overlook (California)

Long Vineyards (Napa)

Longoria (Santa Barbara)

Matanzas Creek (Sonoma)

Peter McCoy Clos des Pierres Vineyard
(Sonoma)****/*****

Merryvale Reserve (Napa)

Château Montelena (Napa)****/*****

Mount Eden MacGregor Vineyard (Edna
Valley)

Murphy-Goode Reserve Island Block
(Alexander Valley)

Napa Ridge Frisinger Vineyard (Napa)

Napa Ridge Reserve (North Coast)

Newton (Napa)

Neyers (Carneros)

Neyers (Napa)

Fess Parker Marcella's Vineyard (Santa
Barbara)

Patz and Hall (Napa)

Pine Ridge Dijon Clones (Napa)

Château Potelle VGS Mount Veeder (Napa)

Rabbit Ridge (Sonoma)

Rabbit Ridge Russian River Valley
(Sonoma)

Ramey Hyde Vineyard
(Carneros)****/*****

Rancho Sisquoc Estate (Santa Barbara)

Kent Rasmussen (Carneros)

Ravenswood Sangiacomo (Sonoma)

Ridge Santa Cruz Mountain (Santa Cruz)

St. Francis Reserve (Sonoma)

Château St. Jean Belle Terre Vineyard
(Sonoma)

Château St. Jean Robert Young Vineyard
(Alexander Valley)

Saintsbury Reserve (Carneros)

Salmon Creek (Napa)

Sanford (Santa Barbara)

Sanford Barrel Select (Santa Barbara)

Sanford Sanford & Benedict Vineyard
(Santa Barbara)

Shafer (Napa)

Signorello Vineyards (Napa)

Signorello Vineyards Founder's Reserve
(Napa)****/*****

Simi Winery Reserve (Sonoma)

Sonoma-Loeb Private Reserve (Sonoma)

Château Souverain single-vineyard cuvées
(Sonoma)

Steele California (Sonoma)

Steele Durell Vineyard (Sonoma)

Steele Goodchild Vineyard (Santa Barbara)

Steele Lolonis Vineyard (Mendocino)

Steele Du Pratt Vineyard (Mendocino)

Steele Sangiacomo Vineyard (Carneros)

Stonestreet (Sonoma)

Stony Hill (Napa)

Swanson (Napa)

Robert Talbott Logan (Monterey)

Talley Vineyards (Arroyo Grande)

Marimar Torres (Sonoma)

Trefethen (Napa)

Williams-Selyem Allen Vineyard (Sonoma)

Château Woltner St. Thomas Vineyard
(Napa)

Château Woltner Titus Vineyard (Napa)

ZD (Napa)

* * * (GOOD)

Acacia (Napa)

Adler Fels (Sonoma)

Alderbrook (Sonoma)

Alderbrook Reserve (Sonoma)

S. Anderson (Napa)

Arrowood Domaine de Grand Archer
(Sonoma)

Au Bon Climat (Santa Barbara)

Babcock (Santa Barbara)

Bargetto Cyprus (Central Coast)

Beaulieu Carneros Reserve (Napa)

Belvedere Wine Company (Sonoma)

Benziger (Sonoma)

Beringer (Napa)

Bernardus (Monterey)

Brutocao (Mendocino)

Burgess Cellars Triere Vineyard (Napa)
Calera Central Coast (California)
Canepa (Alexander Valley)
Chalk Hill (Sonoma)
Christophe (Napa)
Clos du Bois Barrel-Fermented (Sonoma)
Clos du Bois Calcaire (Sonoma)
Clos du Bois Flintwood (Sonoma)
Clos Pegase (Napa)
B. R. Cohn Olive Hill Vineyard (Sonoma)
Cooper-Garrod (Santa Cruz)
Cuvaison (Napa)
De Loach (Sonoma)
Edmeades (Mendocino)
Far Niente (Napa)
Gary Farrell (Sonoma)
Fetzer Barrel Select (Mendocino)
Fetzer Sundial (California)
Thomas Fogarty (Monterey)
Folie à Deux (Napa)
Frog's Leap (Napa)
Gainey (Santa Barbara)
Geyser Peak (Sonoma)
Grgich Hills (Napa)
Guenoc Estate (Lake County)
Guenoc Genevieve Magoon Vineyard
    (Guenoc Valley)
Hacienda Clair de Lune (Sonoma)
Handley (Dry Creek)
Hanna (Sonoma)
Hess Collection Hess Select (Napa)
Hidden Cellars (Mendocino)
Husch Vineyards (Mendocino)
Iron Horse Vineyards (Sonoma)
Jekel Vineyard (Monterey)
Kendall-Jackson Proprietor's Grand
    Reserve (California)
Kendall-Jackson Vintner's Reserve
    (California)
Kenwood Vineyards Beltane Ranch
    (Sonoma)
Kistler (Sonoma)
Konocti (Lake)
Charles Krug Carneros Reserve (Napa)
Kunde Estate (Sonoma)
La Crema (California)
J. Lohr Riverstone (Monterey)
Lolonis (Mendocino)
MacRostie (Carneros)
Meridian Vineyards (San Luis Obispo)

Michel-Schlumberger (Dry Creek)
Robert Mondavi (Napa)
Monterey Vineyards Classic Chardonnay
    (Monterey)
Monticello Cellars Corley Reserve (Napa)
Monticello Cellars Jefferson Cuvée (Napa)
Morgan (Monterey)
Morro Bay (Central Coast)
Murphy-Goode (Sonoma)
Murphy-Goode Reserve (Sonoma)
Napa Ridge (Napa)
Navarro Vineyards (Mendocino)
Fess Parker (Santa Barbara)
Philippe-Lorraine (Napa)
R. H. Phillips Vineyard (Yolo)
Pine Ridge Knollside Cuvée (Napa)
Pine Ridge Stag's Leap District (Napa)
Rombauer (Napa)
St. Francis (Sonoma)
Saintsbury (Carneros)
Santa Barbara (Santa Ynez)
Santa Barbara Winery Lafond Vineyard
    (Santa Ynez)
Sarah's Estate (Santa Clara)
Sarah's Ventana Vineyard (Santa Clara)
Sausal Winery (Sonoma)
Seavey (Napa)
Sebastiani single-vineyard cuvées
    (Sonoma)
Silverado Vineyards (Napa)
Simi Winery (Sonoma)
Robert Sinsky (Sonoma)
Sonoma-Cutrer Cutrer (Sonoma)
Sonoma-Cutrer Les Pierres (Sonoma)
Sonoma-Cutrer Russian River Ranches
    (Sonoma)
Sonoma-Loeb (Sonoma)
Château Souverain (Sonoma) (since 1990)
Stag's Leap Wine Cellars Reserve (Napa)
Sterling Diamond Mountain Ranch (Napa)
Sterling Winery Lake (Napa)
Storrs (Santa Cruz)
Stratford (Napa)
Stratford Partner's Reserve (Napa)
Rodney Strong Chalk Hill (Sonoma)
Ivan Tamas (Livermore)
Thomas-Hsi (Napa)
Truchard (Carneros/Napa)
Vine Cliff Cellars Proprietress Reserve
    (Napa)

Vita Nova (Santa Barbara)
Wente Brothers Reserve (Alameda) (since 1988)
Wente Brothers Wente Vineyard (Alameda) (since 1988)
William Wheeler (Sonoma)

Whitehall Lane Reserve (Napa)
Wild Horse (Central Coast)
Château Woltner Estate Reserve (Napa)
Château Woltner Frederique Vineyard (Napa)

* * (AVERAGE)

Alexander Valley (Sonoma)
Beaulieu Napa Beaufort (Napa)**/***
Bel Arbors (California)
Boeger (El Dorado)
Bonny Doon (Santa Cruz)
Bouchaine (Los Carneros)
Bouchaine (Napa)
David Bruce (Santa Cruz)
Buena Vista Carneros (Sonoma)
Buena Vista Private Reserve (Sonoma)
Davis Bynum (Sonoma)
Cakebread Cellars (Napa)
Calloway Calla-Lees (Temecula)
Carey Cellars Barrel Select (Santa Barbara)
Chalone Gavilan (Monterey)
Chamisal (San Luis Obispo)
Chappellet (Napa)
Chimney Rock (Napa)
Clos du Val (Napa)
Congress Springs (Santa Clara)
Conn Creek (Napa)
Cosentino (Napa)
Cottonwood Canyon (San Luis Obispo)
De Moor (Napa)
Dry Creek (Sonoma)
Eberle (Paso Robles)
Fetzer Bonterra
Firestone (Santa Barbara)
Louis Foppiano (Sonoma)
Fox Mountain Reserve (Sonoma)
Freemark Abbey (Napa)
Freemont Creek (California)
Glen Ellen (Sonoma)
Groth Vineyards (Napa)
Gundlach-Bundschu (Sonoma)
Hagafen (Napa)
Hagafen Reserve (Napa)
Havens (Napa)
Haywood Winery (Sonoma)
William Hill Gold Label Reserve (Napa)
William Hill Silver Label (Napa)
Indian Springs (Sierra Foothills)

Jordan Vineyard (Sonoma)
Château Julien Barrel Fermented (Monterey)
Karly (Amador)
Robert Keenan (Napa)
Lakespring (Napa)
Leeward (Central Coast)
J. Lohr Cypress (Santa Clara)
Markham Vineyards (Napa)
Louis Martini (Napa)
Mayacamas (Napa)
McDowell Valley Vineyards (Mendocino)
The Meeker Vineyard (Sonoma)
Meridian (San Luis Obispo)
Merryvale Vineyards (Napa)
Mirassou (Monterey)
Morgan Reserve (Monterey)
Mount Veeder (Napa)
Mountain View Winery (Santa Clara)
Napa Creek Winery (Napa)
Newlan (Napa)
Obester Winery Barrel Fermented (Mendocino)
Page Mill (Santa Clara) .
Parducci (Mendocino)
J. Pedroncelli (Sonoma)
Robert Pepi (Napa)
Château Potelle (Napa)
Quail Ridge (Napa)
Qupé (Santa Barbara)
Raymond (Napa)
Raymond Private Reserve (Napa)
Richardson (Sonoma)
Round Hill (Napa)
Rutherford Hill Jaeger Vineyard (Napa)
St. Clement (Napa)
St. Supery (Napa)
Santa Barbara Winery Reserve (Santa Ynez)
Schug Cellars Beckstoffer Vineyard (Carneros)

Sea Ridge (Sonoma)
Sebastiani regular cuvées (Sonoma)
Seghesio Winery (Sonoma)
Sequoia Grove Carneros (Napa)
Sequoia Grove Estate (Napa)
Sierra Vista (El Dorado)
Stag's Leap Wine Cellars (Napa)
Stearns Wharf (Santa Barbara)
Sterling (Napa)
Stevenot (Calaveras)
Stone Creek (all cuvées) (Napa)
Taft Street Winery (Sonoma)
Tulocay (Napa)

Vichon Coastal Selection (California)
Villa Mt. Eden Grand Reserve (Napa)
Villa Zapu (Napa)
Weinstock Cellars (Sonoma)
Mark West Vineyards (Sonoma)
Westwood (El Dorado)
William Wheeler (Sonoma)
White Oak (Sonoma)
White Oak Limited Reserve (Sonoma)
Whitehall Lane Le Petit (Napa)
Windemere (Sonoma)
Zaca Mesa (Santa Barbara)

RATING CALIFORNIA'S BEST PRODUCERS OF PINOT NOIR

* * * * * (OUTSTANDING)

Calera Jensen Vineyard (San Benito)
Calera Mills Vineyard (San Benito)
Calera Reed Vineyard (San Benito)
Calera Selleck Vineyard (San Benito)
Dehlinger Goldridge Vineyard (Russian River)
Dehlinger Octagon Vineyard (Russian River)
Dehlinger Reserve (Russian River)
Hartford Court (Sonoma Coast)
Kistler Cuvée Catherine (Sonoma)
Kistler Hirsch Vineyard (Sonoma Coast)
Kistler Vine Hill Vineyard (Sonoma)
Marcassin Marcassin Vineyard (Sonoma Coast)

Martinelli Reserve (Russian River)
Robert Mondavi Reserve (Napa)
Ojai Pisoni Vineyard (Monterey)
J. Rochioli Reserve East Block (Russian River)
J. Rochioli Reserve Three Corner Vineyard (Sonoma)
J. Rochioli Reserve Estate West Block (Sonoma)
Saintsbury Reserve (Carneros)
Talley Vineyards Rincon Estate (Arroyo Grande)
Talley Vineyards Rosemary's Vineyard (Arroyo Grande)

* * * * (EXCELLENT)

Bannister (Russian River)
David Bruce Reserve (Santa Cruz)
Cambria Julia's Vineyard (Santa Maria) (since 1991)
Chimère (Santa Maria)
Conn Valley Vineyards Valhalla Vineyard (Napa)
El Molino (Napa)
Étude (Carneros)
Gary Farrell Bien Nacido Vineyard (Santa Barbara)
Gary Farrell Howard Allen Vineyard (Sonoma)
Foxen Sanford & Benedict Vineyard (Santa Barbara)
Franus-Havens Beau Terroir Vineyard (Carneros)

Gainey Sanford & Benedict Vineyard (Santa Barbara)
Handley Reserve (Anderson Valley)
Hansel Family Vineyard (Russian River)
Kalin Cellars Cuvée DD (Sonoma)
Kalin Cellars Cuvée JL (Sonoma)
Kistler Camp Meeting Ridge (Sonoma)
Landmark Kastania Vineyard (Sonoma Coast)
Littorai One Acre Vineyard (Anderson Valley)
Littorai Savoy Vineyard (Anderson Valley)
Longoria (Santa Ynez)
Mount Eden Vineyards Estate (Santa Cruz)
Ojai Bien Nacido (Santa Barbara)
Patz and Hall Alder Springs Vineyard (Mendocino)

Patz and Hall Pisoni Vineyard (Monterey)

Kent Rasmussen (Carneros)

J. Rochioli Estate (Sonoma)

Château St. Jean Durell (Sonoma)

Saintsbury (Carneros)

Sanford (Santa Barbara)

Sanford Barrel Select (Santa Barbara)

Sanford Sanford & Benedict Vineyard
(Santa Barbara)

Siduri Hirsch Vineyard (Sonoma Coast)

Siduri Pisoni Vineyard (Monterey)

Siduri Rose Vineyard (Anderson Valley)

Signorello (Napa)

W. H. Smith Hellenthal Vineyard (Sonoma
Coast)

Solitude Sangiacomo Vineyard (Napa)

Stonestreet (Sonoma)

Talley Vineyards (San Luis Obispo)

Lane Tanner Sanford & Benedict Vineyard
(Santa Barbara)

Williams-Selyem Allen Vineyard (Sonoma)

Williams-Selyem Cohn Vineyard (Sonoma)

Williams-Selyem Olivet Lane Vineyard
(Russian River)

Williams-Selyem Rochioli Vineyard
(Sonoma)

* * * (GOOD)

Au Bon Climat La Bauge Au Dessus Bien
Nacido Vineyard (Santa Barbara)

Au Bon Climat Sanford & Benedict
Vineyard (Santa Barbara)

Au Bon Climat Talley Vineyard (Arroyo
Grande)

Bernardus (Santa Barbara)

Byron (Santa Barbara)

Byron Reserve (Santa Barbara)

Carneros Creek (Napa)

Chalone Estate (Monterey)

Château de Baun (Sonoma)

Coturri Horn Vineyard (Sonoma)

Dehlinger (Sonoma)

Edna Valley Vineyards (San Luis Obispo)

Ferrari-Carano (Napa)

Foxen (Santa Maria)

The Hitching Post High Liner (Santa
Barbara)***/****

The Hitching Post (Santa Maria)

The Hitching Post Sanford & Benedict
Vineyard (Santa Barbara)

Kendall-Jackson Grand Reserve
(California)

Meridian Reserve (Santa Barbara)

Robert Mondavi (Napa)

Monticello Estate (Napa)

Morgan (Monterey)

Navarro (Mendocino)***/****

Page Mill Bien Nacido Vineyard (Santa
Barbara)

Saintsbury Garnet (Napa)

Santa Barbara (Santa Barbara) (since 1989)

Santa Barbara Reserve (Santa Barbara)
(since 1989)

Santa Cruz Mountain (Santa Cruz)

Robert Sinsky (Sonoma)

Steele Carneros (Sonoma)

Steele Sangiacomo Vineyard (Sonoma)

Robert Stemmler (Sonoma)

Stonestreet (Sonoma)

Lane Tanner (Santa Barbara)

Westwood (El Dorado)

Wild Horse Cheval Sauvage (Santa Barbara)

**(AVERAGE)

Adler Fels (Sonoma)

Alexander Valley (Sonoma)

Austin Cellars Reserve (Santa Barbara)

Beaulieu Carneros Reserve (Napa)

Bon Marché (Napa)

Bouchaine (Napa)

David Bruce (Santa Cruz)

Buena Vista (Sonoma)

Davis Bynum (Sonoma)

Calera (Central Coast)

Cambria (Santa Maria)

Clos du Val (Napa)

Cottonwood Canyon (Santa Barbara)

Cronin (Santa Cruz)

Thomas Fogarty (Santa Cruz)

Gainey (Santa Barbara)

Gundlach-Bundschu (Sonoma)

Hacienda (Sonoma)

Hanzell Vineyards (Sonoma)

Husch (Mendocino)

Charles Krug Carneros Reserve (Napa)

Meridian (Santa Barbara)

Mountain View Winery (California)

Parducci (Mendocino)

Pepperwood Springs (Mendocino)
Richardson (Sonoma)**/***
Roudon-Smith (Santa Cruz)
Santa Ynez Rancho Vineda Vineyard
   (Santa Maria)
Schug Cellars Beckstoffer Vineyard
   (Carneros)
Schug Cellars Heinemann Vineyard (Napa)
Sterling (Napa)
Rodney Strong River East Vineyard
   (Sonoma)

Joseph Swan (Sonoma)
Truchard (Napa)
Tulocay (Napa)
Tulocay Haynes Vineyard (Napa)
Mark West (Sonoma)
Whitcraft Bien Nacido Vineyard (Santa
   Barbara)**/***
Whitcraft Olivet Lane Vineyard (Russian
   River)**/***
Whitehall Lane (Napa)
ZD (Napa)

RATING CALIFORNIA'S RHÔNE RANGERS

* * * * * (OUTSTANDING)

Araujo Estate Syrah Eisele Vineyard
Arrowood Syrah Saralee's Vineyard
Behrens and Hitchcock Petite Sirah
Calera Viognier
Clos Mimi Syrah
Roger Craig Syrah
Dehlinger Syrah Estate
Edmunds St. John Syrah Durell Vineyard
Jade Mountain Syrah Paras Vineyard
La Jota Petite Sirah
Neyers Syrah Hudson Vineyard
Ojai Vineyard Bien Nacido
Ojai Vineyard Roll Ranch
Ojai Vineyard Stolpman Vineyard
Paloma Syrah

Pride Mountain Viognier
Ridge Grenache Lytton Estate
Ridge York Creek Petite Sirah
Rockland Petite Sirah
Sean Thackrey Orion (Syrah)
Sean Thackrey Sirius (Petite Sirah)
Sean Thackrey Taurus (Mourvèdre)
Sine Qua Non Roussanne and Chardonnay
   Blend
Sine Qua Non Syrah (and other cuvées)
Turley Cellars Petite Syrah Aida Vineyard
Turley Cellars Petite Syrah Hayne Vineyard
Turley Cellars Petite Syrah Rattlesnake
   Acres

* * * * (EXCELLENT)

Alban Vineyards Grenache
Alban Vineyards Syrah Lorraine Estate
Alban Vineyards Syrah Reva
Arrowood Viognier Saralee's Vineyard
Beringer Viognier Hudson Ranch
Bonny Doon Clos de Gilroy (Grenache)
Bonny Doon Le Sophiste (Blend)
Bonny Doon Vin Gris de Cigare Rosé
Cambria Syrah Tepusquet Vineyard
Cline Cellars Côtes d'Oakley (Blend)
Cline Cellars Mourvèdre
Coturri Alicante Bouchet Ubaldi Vineyard
Coturri Petite Sirah Ubaldi Vineyard
Dehlinger Syrah Goldridge Vineyard
Dover Canyon Rhône Reserve
L'Ecosse Syrah
Edmeades Sirah Eaglepoint
Edmunds St. John Les Côtes Sauvage
Edmunds St. John El Niño

Edmunds St. John Mourvèdre
Edmunds St. John Port o' Call (Blend)
Edmunds St. John Syrah Grand Heritage
Ferrari-Carano Syrah
Field Stone Petite Sirah
Folie à Deux Syrah
Franys Mourvèdre Brandlin Vineyard
Frey (Syrah)
Havens Syrah
Jade Mountain Les Jumeaux (Blend)
Jade Mountain Marsanne
Jade Mountain Mourvèdre
Jade Mountain La Provençale (Blend)
Jade Mountain Syrah
Jade Mountain Syrah Paras Vineyard
Jaffurs Syrah Bien Nacido Vineyard
Jaffurs Syrah Thompson Vineyard
Kendall-Jackson Syrah Durell Vineyard
Marietta Old Vine Red

Marietta Petite Sirah
Andrew Murray Hillside Reserve
Andrew Murray Les Coteaux
Andrew Murray Roussanne
Andrew Murray Viognier
Ojai Syrah California
Ojai Viognier Roll Ranch
Fess Parker Mélange du Rhône
Fess Parker Syrah
Preston Syrah
Qupé Marsanne
Qupé Syrah Bien Nacido Vineyard
Qupé Viognier
Qupé Viognier Ibarra-Young Vineyard
Ravenswood Icon (Blend)

Renard Syrah Timbervine Ranch
Renard Syrah Arroyo Vineyard Cuvée
   Jacques
Ridge Mataro Bridgehead
Ridge Mataro Evangelo Vineyard
Swanson Syrah
Trentadue Old Patch Red (Blend)
Trentadue Petite Sirah
Trentadue Salute
Truchard Syrah
Wellington Vineyards Côtes de Sonoma
   Old Vines
Wellington Vineyards Syrah Alegrai
   Vineyards

*** (GOOD)

Benziger
Bonny Doon Le Cigare Volant (Blend)
Bonny Doon Cinsault
Bonny Doon Old Telegram (Mourvèdre)
Bonny Doon Pinot Meunier
Bonny Doon Syrah
David Bruce Petite Sirah
Edmunds St. John Viognier
Elyse Coeur de Val
Elyse Nero Misto Proprietary Red Wine
Fetzer Petite Sirah Reserve
Field Stone Petite Sirah
Field Stone Viognier Staten Family
   Reserve
Guenoc Petite Sirah
Hop Kiln Petite Sirah
Marietta Cellars Petite Sirah
McDowell Valley Vineyards Les Vieux
   Cépages
Joseph Phelps Syrah

Joseph Phelps Vin du Mistral cuvées
R. H. Phillips Mourvèdre EXP
R. H. Phillips Viognier EXP
Preston Faux Proprietary Red Wine
Preston Marsanne
Qupé Bien Nacido Cuvée
Qupé Los Olivos Cuvée
Qupé Syrah
Ritchie Creek Viognier
Santino Satyricon (Blend)
Shenandoah Serene (Blend)
Sierra Vista Fleur de Montagne (Blend)
Sierra Vista Lynelle (Blend)
Stag's Leap Winery Petite Sirah
Joseph Swan Côtes du Rosa Unfiltered
Joseph Swan Vin du Mystère
Trentadue Carignan
Unalii Syrah
Voss Shiraz
Zaca Mesa Syrah

** (AVERAGE)

Alban Viognier
Alderbrook Syrah Shiloh Hill Vineyard
Christopher Creek Petite Sirah
Christopher Creek Syrah
Duxoup Syrah
Louis Foppiano Petite Sirah
Jory (various cuvées)
Karly Petite Sirah
Meridian Syrah
J. W. Morris Petite Sirah Bosun Crest
Parducci Bono Syrah
Parducci Petite Sirah

Preston Viognier
Roudon-Smith Petite Sirah
Sierra-Vista Syrah
Domaine de la Terre Rouge
Topolos Alicante Bouschet
Topolos Grand Noir
Topolos Petite Sirah
William Wheeler Quintet (Blend)
Zaca Mesa Alamo Cuvée (Blend)
Zaca Mesa Malbec
Zaca Mesa Mourvèdre
Zaca Mesa Syrah

RATING CALIFORNIA'S BEST PRODUCERS OF ITALIAN-INSPIRED VARIETALS—SANGIOVESE, BARBERA, NEBBIOLO

***** (OUTSTANDING)

Flora Springs Sangiovese
Il Podere Dell'Olivos Barbera
Il Podere Dell'Olivos Teroldego
Jessandre Vineyard (Sangiovese/Cabernet)

Pride Mountain Sangiovese
Saddleback Cellars Venge Family Reserve
   Sangiovese Penny Lane
Wild Horse Malvasia Bianca Barrel
   Fermented

**** (EXCELLENT)

Au Bon Climat Barbera
Beringer Sangiovese
Edmunds St. John Pinot Grigio
Edmunds St. John Pallini Rosso
Ferrari-Carano Siena
Robert Mondavi Barbera
Robert Pepi Colline di Sassi
Kent Rasmussen Dolcetto

Kent Rasmussen Sangiovese
Shafer Firebreak (Sangiovese/Cabernet)
Staglin Family Vineyard Stagliano
   Sangiovese
Swanson Sangiovese L'Ecosse Dolcetto
Ivan Tamas Trebbiano Noel Barbera
L'Uvaggio di Giacomo La Pantera Barbera
Wildhorse Tocai Fruilano

*** (GOOD)

Bonny Doon Ca do Solo Il Fiasco
Brindiamo Gioveto
Brindiamo Nebbiolo
Brindiamo Rosso Vecchio
Dalla Valle Pietre Rosso
Konrad Barbera
Robert Mondavi Sangiovese
Robert Mondavi Malvasia

Mosby Dolcetto di Fior
Mosby Primitivo
Preston Barbera
Sterling Pinot Grigio
Sterling Sangiovese
Sean Thackrey Pleiades
Trentadue Sangiovese
Westwood Barbera

** (AVERAGE)

Atlas Peak Sangiovese
Mosby Brunello di Santa Barbara Carrari
   Vineyard

Sebastiani Barbera

RATING CALIFORNIA'S BEST PRODUCERS OF SAUVIGNON BLANC AND SEMILLON AND BLENDS THEREOF

***** (OUTSTANDING)

Araujo Estate Eisele Vineyard (Napa)
Ferrari-Carano Fumé Blanc Reserve
   (Sonoma)
Gainey Sauvignon Blanc Limited Selection
   (Santa Ynez)
Kalin Cellars Sauvignon Blanc Reserve
   (Potter Valley)
Mason Cellars (Napa)
Peter Michael Sauvignon Blanc l'Apres-
   Midi (California)

Robert Mondavi Fumé Blanc Reserve
   (Napa)
Robert Mondavi To-Kalon Estate Reserve
   (Napa)
J. Rochioli Old Vine Block (Russian River)
Selene Sauvignon Blanc (Napa)
Simi Sendal Proprietary White Wine
   (Sonoma)

* * * * (EXCELLENT)

Babcock Sauvignon Blanc (Santa Barbara)
Babcock Sauvignon Blanc 11 Oaks Ranch
  (Santa Barbara)
Byron Sauvignon Blanc (Santa Barbara)
Caymus Conundrum Proprietary White
  Wine (Napa)
Chalk Hill Sauvignon Blanc (Sonoma)
Chimney Rock Fumé Blanc
Clos du Bois Sauvignon Blanc (Alexander
  Valley)
Cronin Sauvignon Blanc (Napa)
Dry Creek Fumé Blanc (Sonoma)
Ehler's Grove Sauvignon Blanc Reserve
  (Napa)
Gary Farrell Sauvignon Blanc Rochioli
  Vineyard (Russian River)
Handley Cellars Sauvignon Blanc (Dry
  Creek)
Hidden Cellars Alchemy Proprietary White
  Wine (Mendocino)
Hidden Cellars Sauvignon Blanc
  (Mendocino)
Kalin Cellars Sauvignon Blanc (Potter
  Valley)
Kalin Cellars Semillon (Livermore)
Karly Sauvignon Blanc (Amador)
Kendall-Jackson Sauvignon Blanc Grand
  Reserve (California)
Kenwood Vineyards Sauvignon Blanc
  (Sonoma)

Kunde Estate Winery Sauvignon Blanc
  Magnolia Lane (Sonoma)
Matanzas Creek Sauvignon Blanc (Sonoma)
Robert Mondavi Fumé Blanc (Napa)
Murphy-Goode Fumé Blanc Reserve
  (Sonoma)
Navarro Sauvignon Blanc (Mendocino)
Ojai Cuvée Speciale Ste. Helene
  (California)
Page Mill Sauvignon Blanc French Camp
  Vineyard (Napa)
Robert Pepi Sauvignon Blanc Reserve
  (Napa)
Preston Cuvée de Fumé (Sonoma)
Rancho Sisquoc Sauvignon Blanc (Santa
  Barbara)
J. Rochioli Sauvignon Blanc (Russian
  River)
Château St. Jean Fumé Blanc La Petite
  Étoile (Sonoma)
Sanford Sauvignon Blanc (Santa Barbara)
Signorello Sauvignon Blanc (Napa)
Signorello Semillon Barrel Fermented
  (Napa)
Spottswoode Sauvignon Blanc (Napa)
Stonestreet Sauvignon Blanc (Alexander
  Valley)
Rodney Strong Sauvignon Blanc Charlotte's
  Home Vineyard (Sonoma)

* * * (GOOD)

Adler Fels Fumé Blanc (Sonoma)
Ahlgren Semillon (Santa Cruz)
Alderbrook Sauvignon Blanc (Sonoma)
Babcock Fathom Proprietary White Wine
  (Santa Barbara)
Beaulieu Fumé Blanc (Napa)
Bel Arbors Sauvignon Blanc (California)
Bellerose Sauvignon Blanc (Sonoma)
Benziger Fumé Blanc (Sonoma)
Beringer Alluvium (Napa)
Beringer Sauvignon Blanc (Napa)
Bernardus Sauvignon Blanc (Monterey)
Brander (Santa Ynez)
Brutocao Sauvignon Blanc (Mendocino)
Buena Vista Fumé Blanc (Lake)
Buttonwood Farm Sauvignon Blanc (Santa
  Ynez)
Cain Cellars Sauvignon Musqué (Napa)

Carmenet Meritage Proprietary White
  Wine (Sonoma)
De Loach Fumé Blanc (Sonoma)
De Lorimer Spectrum Estate (Alexander
  Valley)
Duckhorn Sauvignon Blanc (Napa)
Ferrari-Carano Fumé Blanc (Sonoma)
Fetzer Fumé Blanc (Mendocino)
Fetzer Sauvignon Blanc Barrel Select
  (Mendocino)
Field Stone Sauvignon Blanc (Sonoma)
Gabrielli Ascenza White Table Wine
  (Mendocino)
Gainey Sauvignon Blanc (Santa
  Ynez)
Geyser Peak Sauvignon Blanc (Sonoma)
Geyser Peak Semchard
Grgich Hills Fumé Blanc (Napa)

Guenoc Winery Langtry Meritage (Lake County)

Louis Honig Cellars Sauvignon Blanc (Napa)

Husch Vineyards Sauvignon Blanc (Mendocino)

Iron Horse Fumé Blanc (Sonoma)

Karly Sauvignon Blanc (Amador)

Konocti Fumé Blanc (Lake County)

Lakewood Sauvignon Blanc (Clear Lake)

Lakewood Semillon (Clear Lake)

Liberty School California White Wine (Caymus—Napa)

Lolonis Fumé Blanc (Mendocino)

Monterey Vineyards Classic Sauvignon Blanc (California)

Morgan Sauvignon Blanc (Monterey)

Mt. Konocti Semillon/Chardonnay (Lake County)

Murphy-Goode Fumé Blanc (Sonoma)

Napa Ridge Sauvignon Blanc (Napa)

Page Mill Sauvignon Blanc (San Luis Obispo)

R. H. Phillips Sauvignon Blanc (Yolo)

Preston Vineyards Cuvée de Fumé (Dry Creek)

Rabbit Ridge Proprietary White Wine (Sonoma)

Rabbit Ridge Sauvignon Blanc (Sonoma)

Stag's Leap Sauvignon Blanc Rancho Chimiles (Napa)

Ivan Tamas Fumé Blanc (Livermore)***/****

William Wheeler Fumé Blanc (Sonoma)

* * (AVERAGE)

Austin Sauvignon Blanc (Santa Barbara)

Austin Sauvignon Blanc Reserve (Santa Barbara)

Davis Bynum Fumé Blanc (Sonoma)

Calloway Fumé Blanc/Sauvignon Blanc (Temecula)

Christophe Sauvignon Blanc (Napa)

Clos Pegase Sauvignon Blanc (Napa)

Clos du Val Semillon (Napa)

Louis Foppiano Sauvignon Blanc (Sonoma)

E. & J. Gallo Sauvignon Blanc (California)

Glen Ellen Sauvignon Blanc (Sonoma)

Grand Cru Sauvignon Blanc (Sonoma)

Groth Sauvignon Blanc (Napa)

Hanna Sauvignon Blanc (Sonoma)

Jekel Scepter Proprietary White Wine (Monterey)

Château Julien Sauvignon Blanc (Monterey)

Lakespring Sauvignon Blanc (Napa)

Liberty School Sauvignon Blanc (California)

Louis Martini Sauvignon Blanc (Napa)

Mayacamas Sauvignon Blanc (Napa)

Obester Sauvignon Blanc (Mendocino)

J. Pedroncelli Primavera Mista Proprietary White Wine (California)

Joseph Phelps Sauvignon Blanc (Napa)

Château Potelle Sauvignon Blanc (Napa)

St. Clement Sauvignon Blanc (Napa)

Château St. Jean Fumé Blanc (all cuvées) (Sonoma)

St. Supery Sauvignon Blanc (Napa)

Santa Ynez Semillon (Santa Ynez)

Seghesio Sauvignon Blanc (Sonoma)

Shenandoah Sauvignon Blanc (Amador)

Silverado Sauvignon Blanc (Napa)

Simi Semillon (Napa)

Steltzner Sauvignon Blanc (Napa)

Sterling Sauvignon Blanc (Napa)

Stratford Sauvignon Blanc (California)

Weinstock Sauvignon Blanc (Sonoma)

RATING CALIFORNIA'S BEST PRODUCERS OF ZINFANDEL

* * * * * (OUTSTANDING)

Behrens and Hitchcock (Napa)

Robert Bialé Aldo's Vineyard (Napa)

Robert Bialé Monte Rosso (Sonoma)

Robert Bialé Old Crane Ranch (Napa)

De Loach O.F.S. (Russian River)

Franus Brandlin Ranch (Napa)

Hartford Court Hartford Vineyard (Russian River)

Hartford Court Fanucchi-Wood Road (Russian River)

Marietta Angeli Cuvée (Alexander Valley)

Martinelli Jackass Hill (Russian River)

Martinelli Jackass Vineyard (Russian River)
A. Rafanelli (Sonoma)
Ravenswood Belloni/Wood Road Vineyard (Sonoma)
Ravenswood Cooke Vineyard (Sonoma)
Ravenswood Dickerson Vineyard (Napa)
Ravenswood Old Hill Vineyard (Sonoma)
Ravenswood Monte Rosso Vineyard (Sonoma)
Ridge Geyserville Proprietary Red Wine (primarily Zinfandel) (Sonoma)
Ridge Lytton Springs (Sonoma)
Ridge Pagani Ranch (Sonoma)

Rosenblum Cellars Marston Vineyard (Napa)
Rosenblum Cellars Samsel Vineyard (Sonoma)
Turley Cellars Aida Vineyard (Napa)
Turley Cellars Black-Sears Vineyard (Napa)
Turley Cellars Hayne Vineyard (Napa)
Turley Cellars Moore Vineyard (Napa)
Turley Cellars Tofanelli Vineyard (Napa)
Turley Cellars Vineyard 101 (Alexander Valley)
Turley Cellars Whitney Vineyard (Napa)

＊＊＊＊(EXCELLENT)

Bannister (Dry Creek)
Caldwell Aida Vineyard (Napa)
Cline (Contra Costa)
Cline Reserve (Contra Costa)
Coturri Chauvet Vineyard (Sonoma)
Coturri Philip Coturri Estate (Sonoma)
De Loach single-vineyard cuvées (Sonoma)
Dover Canyon Templeton Gap Reserve (Paso Robles)
Dry Creek Old Vines (Sonoma)
Eberle (Paso Robles)
Edmeades Ciapusci (Mendocino)
Edmeades Zeni (Mendocino)
Edmunds St. John (Napa)
Elyse Howell Mountain (Napa)
Elyse Morisoli Vineyard (Napa)
Gary Farrell (Russian River)
Ferrari-Carano (Dry Creek)
Folie à Deux Old Vine Eschen Vineyard (Amador)
Franciscan (Napa)
Frey (Mendocino)
Gallo-Sonoma Chiotti Vineyard (Dry Creek)
Gallo-Sonoma Frei Ranch Vineyard (Dry Creek)
Gallo-Sonoma Stefani Vineyard (Dry Creek)
Green and Red Chiles Mill Vineyard (Napa)
Hartford Court Dina's Vineyard (Russian River)
Hartford Court Highwire Vineyard (Russian River)
Hop Kiln Winery Primativo (Sonoma)
Howell Mountain Beatty Ranch (Howell Mountain)

Howell Mountain Black-Sears (Howell Mountain)
Howell Mountain Old Vine (Howell Mountain)
Jacuzzi Family Vineyard (Contra Costa)
Lamborn Family Vineyard (Napa)
Limerick Lane Cellars (Sonoma)
Lytton Springs Reserve (Sonoma)
Marietta Cellars (Sonoma)
Robert Mondavi (Napa)
Norman (Paso Robles)
Peachy Canyon Reserve (Paso Robles)
Peachy Canyon West Side (Paso Robles)
Château Potelle Mount Veeder (Napa)
Preston (Sonoma)
Rabbit Ridge (Sonoma)
Rabbit Ridge OVZ (Sonoma)
Ravenswood Old Vines (Sonoma)
Renwood (Amador)
Ridge (Paso Robles)
Ridge Dusi Ranch (Paso Robles)
Rosenblum Cellars (Contra Costa)
Rosenblum Cellars (Paso Robles)
Rosenblum Cellars (Sonoma)
Rosenblum Cellars Richard Sauret Vineyard (Paso Robles)
Rosenblum Cellars George Hendry Vineyard (Napa)
Rosenblum Cellars Brandlin Ranch (Napa)
Eric Ross Occidental Vineyard (Russian River)
Ross Valley (Sonoma)
St. Francis Old Vines (Sonoma)
Saddleback Cellar Old Vines (Napa)

Saucelito Canyon Vineyard (Arroyo Grande)
Sausal Winery (Sonoma)
Sausal Winery Private Reserve (Sonoma)
Scherrer Old Vines (Alexander Valley)
Scherrer Shale Terrace (Alexander Valley)
Seghesio Old Vine (Sonoma)
Seghesio Home Ranch (Alexander Valley)
Seghesio San Lorenzo (Alexander Valley)
Storybook Mountain Eastern Exposure
   (Napa)
Storybook Mountain Estate (Napa)
Storybook Mountain Howell Mountain
   (Napa)

Storybook Mountain Reserve (Napa)
Joseph Swan cuvées (Sonoma)
The Terraces (Napa)
Turley Cellars Dogtown (California)
Turley Cellars Duerte Vineyard (Contra
   Costa)
Turley Cellars Spenker Vineyard (Lodi)
Wellington Old Vine (Sonoma)
Whaler Vineyard Estate Flagship
   (Mendocino)
Zoom (Contra Costa)

* * * *(GOOD)*

Amador Foothill Grand Père Vineyard
   (Amador)
Benziger (Sonoma)
Beringer (Napa)
Boeger (El Dorado)
David Bruce (Santa Cruz)
Brutocao Cellars (Mendocino)
Buehler (Napa)
Cakebread Cellars (Napa)
Caymus (Napa)
Clos du Bois (Sonoma)
Clos du Val (Napa)
Cosentino The Zin (Sonoma)
D'Annco Old Vines
Deer Park (Napa)
Deux Amis (Sonoma)
De Loach Estate (Sonoma)
De Moor (Napa)
Dry Creek (Sonoma)
Edizione Pennino (Niebaum-Coppola—
   Napa)
Edmeades Estate (Mendocino)
Fetzer Barrel Select (Mendocino)
Fetzer Reserve (Mendocino)
Frick (Santa Cruz)
Fritz (Sonoma) (since 1988)
Frog's Leap Winery (Napa)
Greenwood Ridge Vineyards (Sonoma)
Grgich Hills (Sonoma)
Guenoc (Lake County)
Gundlach-Bundschu (Sonoma)
Gundlach-Bundschu Rhinefarm Vineyard
   (Sonoma)
Hidden Cellars (Mendocino)
Hop Kiln (Sonoma)

Kendall Jackson Vintner's Reserve
   (California)
Kenwood Jack London Vineyard (Sonoma)
Lake Sonoma Old Vine Reserve (Dry Creek)
Mariah Vineyards (Mendocino)
Meeker Vineyard (Sonoma)
Monterey Peninsula Ferrero Ranch
   (Amador)
Mountain View Winery (Amador)
Nalle (Sonoma)
J. Pedroncelli (Sonoma)
Joseph Phelps (Alexander Valley)
Quivira (Sonoma)
Ravenswood Vintner's Blend (Sonoma)
Ridge Howell Mountain (Napa)
Ridge Sonoma (Santa Clara)
Rocking Horse Lamborn Vineyard (Napa)
Schuetz-Oles-Korte Ranch (Napa)
Seghesio Winery (Sonoma)
Shenandoah Sobon Estate (Amador)
Sierra Vista (El Dorado)
Signorello (Napa)
Sky Vineyards (Napa)
Sonora TC Vineyard (Amador)
Château Souverain (Dry Creek)
Steele
Sterling (Napa)
Rodney Strong Old Vines River West
   Vineyard (Russian River)
Summit Lake (Napa)
Sutter Home Reserve (Amador)
Tobin James (Paso Robles)
Topolos Rossi Ranch (Sonoma)
Topolos Russian River Valley (Russian
   River)

Topolos Ultimo (Sonoma)

Trentadue (Sonoma)

Wellington Vineyards Old Vines (Sonoma)

Mark West Robert Rue Vineyard (Sonoma)

Whaler Vineyard Estate (Mendocino)

Wild Horse (San Luis Obispo)

* * (AVERAGE)

Bel Arbors (California)

Burgess Cellars (Napa)

Duxoup Wineworks (Sonoma)

Eagle Ridge Fiddletown (Amador)

Louis Foppiano Reserve (Sonoma)

Haywood Winery (Sonoma)

Karly (Amador)

Charles Krug (Napa)

Lolonis (Mendocino)

Louis Martini (Sonoma)

Mazzocco (Sonoma)

Montevina (Amador)

Obester (San Mateo)

Parducci (Mendocino)

Roudon-Smith (Santa Cruz)

Round Hill (Napa)

St. Supery Vineyards (Napa)

Santa Barbara Beaujour (Santa Ynez)

Santino Wines (Amador)

V. Sattui Suzanne's Vineyard (Napa)

Sebastiani (Sonoma)

Shenandoah Special Reserve (Amador)

Stevenot (Calaveras)**/***

Sutter Home (California)

Teldeschi (Sonoma)

Twin Hills Ranch (Paso Robles)

Villa Mt. Eden Cellar Select (California)

White Oak (Sonoma)

RATING CALIFORNIA'S BEST SPARKLING WINE PRODUCERS

* * * * * (OUTSTANDING)

None

* * * * (EXCELLENT)

Domaine Chandon Reserve Brut (Napa)

Maison Deutz Blanc de Noir (San Luis
   Obispo)

Iron Horse cuvées (Sonoma)

Mumm Blanc de Noir Rosé (Napa)

Roederer L'Ermitage (Anderson Valley)

Roederer Estate (Anderson Valley)

* * * (GOOD)

Domaine Carneros (Napa)

Domaine Chandon Blanc de Noir (Napa)

Domaine Chandon Brut (Napa)

Domaine Chandon Etoile (Napa)

Maison Deutz (San Luis Obispo)

Handley (Mendocino)

Robert Mondavi Brut (Napa)

Monticello Domaine Montreaux (Napa)

Domaine Mumm Brut Prestige Cuvée
   (Napa)

Domaine Mumm Brut Winery Lake Cuvée
   (Napa)

Schramsberg J. Schram (Napa)

Tribault Brut (Monterey)

Tribault Brut Rosé (Monterey)

* * (AVERAGE)

Anderson cuvées (Napa)**/***

Beaulieu Brut (Napa)

Domaine Carneros (Napa)

Culbertson Blanc de Noir (Riverside)

Culbertson Brut (Riverside)

Culbertson Brut Rosé (Riverside)

Richard Cuneo (Sonoma)

Gloria Ferrer cuvées (Sonoma)**/***

Jordan J Cuvée (Sonoma)

Mirassou (Monterey)

Piper Sonoma (Sonoma)**/***

Santa Ynez Brut (Santa Ynez)

Scharffenberger Cellars cuvées
   (Mendocino)

Schramsberg Vineyards cuvées (Napa)

Shadow Creek Champagne Cellars Brut
   (San Luis Obispo)

ABREU VINEYARDS (NAPA)

1997 Cabernet Sauvignon Madrona Ranch	Napa	E	(96–99)
1996 Cabernet Sauvignon Madrona Ranch	Napa	E	96
1995 Cabernet Sauvignon Madrona Ranch	Napa	E	95
1994 Cabernet Sauvignon Madrona Ranch	Napa	E	94
1993 Cabernet Sauvignon Madrona Ranch	Napa	E	95

When someone writes the history of Napa Valley and of the golden age that California's North Coast has been enjoying since the 1990 vintage, David Abreu's name is likely to receive considerable mention. Why? While the production of his exquisite wines from the old Madrona Ranch in St. Helena is so small that it is all sold via a mailing list (about 600 cases), his importance as Northern California's most demanding vineyard manager is even more significant. Abreu's clients include the likes of Araujo, Bryant, Colgin, Harlan, Spottswoode, Viader, Neyers, and Helen Turley and John Wetlaufer. If David Abreau handles the job, you can be assured no compromises will be permitted in the vineyard, and frankly, 90% of a wine's quality is determined by the fruit. All of his own production is unfined and unfiltered, and his wines are worth every arm-twisting, brow-beating effort necessary to procure.

For many years I have heard glowing praise bestowed on David Abreu, the Michael Jordan of vineyard management in northern California. I finally had a chance to spend some time with him and tour two of the vineyards he manages, the Bryant Family Vineyard as well as Ann Colgin and Fred Schrader's new vineyard on Highway 29, just across from Freemark Abbey. Abreu began producing a tiny quantity of Cabernet Sauvignon from the Madrona Ranch (400 cases) in northern Napa Valley in 1986. He sold the 1988 through 1990 vintages in bulk as the wine did not meet his high standards. Starting in 1991, the small production was sold to California restaurants and via a mailing list, so readers wanting to secure a few bottles of Abreu's superb Cabernets should be sure to leave their names and addresses on his answering machine. His wine spends 2 years in 100% new small French oak barrels. He also does malolactic fermentation in barrel, a trendy, new technique being practiced by some of the world's most fashionable Merlot and Cabernet Sauvignon producers. In tasting through all of Abreu's commercially available wines, I was struck by how consistent in quality they are. The exceptional 1991 and 1992 have been followed by phenomenal wines in 1993, 1994, 1995, 1996, and 1997. Most of these wines are 95% Cabernet Sauvignon, with the balance Cabernet Franc. The only exception is the 1995, which is a blend of 90% Cabernet Sauvignon, 5% Merlot, and 5% Cabernet Franc. The wines are worth owning; I am putting my money where my mouth is.

Abreu has recently leased six acres off Spring Street in St. Helena that are being planted in equal parts Merlot and Cabernet Sauvignon, so more wine is in the works. These unfiltered wines are produced from extremely ripe fruit and are aged in 100% new oak (the malolactic fermentation is also done in barrel). They are among the great Cabernets of Napa Valley.

The 1995 Cabernet Sauvignon Madrona Ranch is a strikingly superb Cabernet Sauvignon. Although it includes 5% Cabernet Franc and 5% Merlot in the blend, I would never have guessed it. Aged in 100% new Taransaud barrels (as are all his wines), the 1995 boasts an opaque purple color, in addition to a fabulous bouquet of blueberries, blackberries, cassis, licorice, minerals, and smoky, toasty oak. The wine's aromatics soar from the glass, and in the mouth, the bouquet's promise is fulfilled. A thick, juicy, black-fruit character comes across in cascades of fruit, glycerin, and extract. All of this has been buttressed by sweet tannin and good acidity. A voluptuously textured, blockbuster yet remarkably harmonious wine, it is one of the finest efforts of the vintage. Anticipated maturity: 2001–2025. I know it's splitting hairs, but the 1996 Cabernet Sauvignon Madrona Ranch may be a touch better. The alcohol level (14.2%) is higher, and the pH ranks alongside that attained by the great

Bordeaux vintages (3.8 and above in years such as 1982 and 1990). Perhaps that is why a taster's palate can get lost in the wine's midpalate and length. The color is opaque black/purple. The wine possesses a nose of crème de cassis and blackberry/blueberry liqueur. The oak has been soaked up completely by the wine's extraction and richness. The finish lasts for 40+ seconds. This is an extremely multidimensional, profoundly concentrated, awesome Cabernet Sauvignon that should deliver untold levels of pleasure, complexity, and most important, joy, for at least 25–30 years. After tasting the 1995 and 1996, it is unbelievable to pick up a glass of the 1997 Cabernet Sauvignon Madrona Ranch and realize it is even longer, silkier, and possibly more complete and complex than its two predecessors. I actually dislike writing tasting notes of wines that flirt with perfection, simply because they leave even someone as verbose as I am speechless. The 1997 possesses everything found in the 1995 and 1996, but it is more evolved, with all of its component parts even more integrated and silky; the finish lasts nearly a minute. The wine is opaque purple-colored, phenomenally concentrated, with that crème de cassislike richness that comes only from strikingly low yields. These are riveting wines produced by a former *Wine Advocate* "Hero of the Year." Once again, readers' only chance of ever sampling one of these sumptuous Cabernet Sauvignons is to get on David Abreu's mailing list.

The impressively rich, dense purple-colored 1994 Cabernet Sauvignon Madrona Vineyard exhibits a blueberry/blackberry/cassis-scented nose, with a touch of violets and subtle new oak. In the mouth, the wine has disguised its tannic clout with extraordinary extraction of fruit, medium to full body, and a silky yet powerful personality. It, too, is a 20–25 year wine that can be drunk now or cellared.

The 1993 Cabernet Sauvignon, another great wine from an often "maligned" vintage, boasts a fabulous dark purple color, as well as sweet, jammy, toasty black fruits, fruitcake, cedar, and black trufflelike smells. Packed with extract and glycerin, this is an expansive, chewy, pure Cabernet that should be cellared for another 2–3 years after its release in 1997; it will easily last until 2025. This is great stuff!

All of these wines possess fabulous purity and an undeniable sweet, rich, crème de cassis-like fruit character. David Abreu's mailing list should be a high priority for readers who love California Cabernet.

ACACIA (NAPA)

1996	Chardonnay	Carneros	C	87
1995	Chardonnay Reserve	Carneros	D	87
1996	Pinot Noir	Carneros	C	85
1994	Pinot Noir	Carneros	C	88
1994	Pinot Noir Reserve	Carneros	D	82
1993	Pinot Noir Reserve	Carneros	C	85
1994	Pinot Noir St. Clair Reserve	Carneros	D	87
1993	Pinot Noir St. Clair Reserve	Carneros	C	89
1996	Viognier Caviste	Carneros	D	87
1995	Zinfandel Old Vines	Carneros	C	88
1993	Zinfandel Old Vines	Napa	B	88

This is a group of soundly made wines, with my favorites being the creamy-textured, fruity, exuberant 1996 Chardonnay, the excellent apricot and honeysuckle-scented and -flavored, medium- to full-bodied 1996 Viognier Caviste, and the delicious, briery, peppery, robust 1995 Zinfandel Old Vines. The Chardonnay and Viognier both need to be drunk over the next year. I suspect the Zinfandel, which is produced from grapes grown on Howell Mountain and Mt. Veeder, will hold nicely in the bottle for 3–4 years.

The 1993 Zinfandel Old Vines (much of the fruit came from the Papani Vineyard made famous by Ridge, as well as the Beatty Vineyard on Howell Mountain) tastes more like a southern Rhône than many Châteauneuf du Papes. It offers up a peppery, roasted herb, jammy black cherry-scented nose, followed by excellent ripeness, and medium- to full-bodied, smooth, silky flavors and finish. Drink it over the next 3–4 years.

The 1995 Chardonnay Reserve is also good, with sweetness evident in a leesy, Burgundian-like, ripe, fruity style. The wine reveals both purity and a sense of elegance.

I have had mixed emotions about Acacia's Pinot Noirs, as they are often too stylized, sculptured, and acidified. Based on these Pinots, it appears several positive refinements in style have been implemented, to the benefit of the wines and, of course, the consumer. The 1994 Pinot Noir Carneros exhibits a medium to deep ruby color, followed by a sweet nose of red fruits, smoke, and vanillin. Round, pure, and beautifully concentrated, this supple, sexy Pinot can be drunk over the next 2–3 years. The 1993 Pinot Noir Reserve is a bit lean and tart, without the depth or intensity of the 1994, but it is pleasant and well proportioned. The 1993 Pinot Noir Reserve St. Clair (only 100 cases produced) is a better example of what this winery can achieve. The wine reveals a deep ruby color, and a complex nose of smoke, toast, berry fruit, and underlying floral and roasted herb scents. Ripe, sweet, and expansive, it combines power with elegance in a velvety-textured, rich format. Drink it over the next 2–3 years.

As for the other Pinot Noirs, they are straightforward, red fruit-driven wines with medium body, tart acidity, and subtle doses of smoky, toasty oak. The best of the remaining group is the 1994 Pinot Noir St. Clair Reserve, which possesses more aromatic and flavor dimensions. All of these Pinots should be consumed over the next 2–3 years. In essence, these seem to be safely made, middle of the road, generally uninspiring wines.

ADELAIDA CELLARS (SAN LUIS OBISPO)

1993	Cabernet Sauvignon	San Luis Obispo	C	86+?
1994	Sangiovese	San Luis Obispo	C	87
1993	Sangiovese	San Luis Obispo	B	88
1994	Zinfandel	Paso Robles	C	87

The 1993 Sangiovese (in a designer bottle) is an impressive example of what is too frequently a diluted demonstration of this varietal's suitability for California. However, Adelaida's Sangiovese exhibits a dense color, an attractive strawberry/cherry/saddle leather-scented nose, medium body, excellent fruit and purity, and a soft, spicy, refreshing finish. An impressive example of this varietal, it should drink well for 4–5 years. The attractive 1994 Sangiovese possesses plenty of jammy strawberry/cherry scents and flavors, an evolved garnet/medium-ruby color, good spice, sweet fruit, and a round, attractive palate. It is ideal for drinking over the next several years.

I am not totally convinced by the 1993 Cabernet Sauvignon. The color is a healthy, dark saturated plum, and the wine offers up weedy, dill pickle, toasty new oak, smoky aromas, along with ripe black currant fruit. In the mouth, there is good thickness, intensity, and depth, as well as a spicy, rich finish. If the weediness ages into a cedary component, this wine could merit 2–3 more points. In any event, it should last for 10–15 years.

The classy, red berry, curranty, dusty nose of the 1994 Zinfandel is followed by a wine with medium to full body, pure fruit, and plenty of ripeness and glycerin. It is ideal for drinking now and over the next 5–6 years.

AETNA SPRINGS CELLARS (NAPA)

1996 Merlot Hoatzin Vineyard	Napa	C	87

A textbook Merlot, this deep ruby-colored wine displays an evolved, spicy nose including scents of jammy black cherries, chocolate, mocha, and wood. Layered in the mouth, with medium body, excellent richness, fine purity, and enough acidity to provide definition, this stylish, flavorful Merlot can be drunk over the next 5–6 years.

ALBAN VINEYARDS (EDNA VALLEY)

1995 Grenache Alban Estate Vineyard	Edna Valley	D	87
1995 Syrah Lorraine Estate	Edna Valley	D	90
1995 Syrah Reva Alban Estate Vineyard	Edna Valley	C	87+

All three of these intriguing Rhône Ranger wines from Alban Vineyards merit interest. The 1995 Grenache Alban Estate Vineyard exhibits a murky dark ruby color, a peppery, kirsch, and earthy-scented nose, and robust, muscular, concentrated flavors that possess an underlying coarseness, as well as plenty of depth, power, and richness. Six to twelve months of bottle age will help this ruggedly constructed Grenache. It should drink well for 10–12 years. The superb 1995 Syrah Lorraine Estate displays a saturated dark ruby/purple color, and knockout aromatics consisting of hickory smoke, bacon, and cassis fruit. Opulent on the palate, this full-bodied, concentrated, lush, chewy Syrah has low enough acidity and sweet enough fruit to be drunk now, but it promises to develop nicely for 10–15 years. Slightly less impressive (or is it just too closed?), the 1995 Syrah Reva reveals more tannin, and is far less impressive aromatically and on the palate. Nevertheless, it offers a mouth-filling, full-bodied, muscular style of wine that should unfold gracefully with another 2–3 years of bottle age. It is solidly made, with plenty of earthy black fruits (primarily cassis), and a long, spicy, concentrated finish. It should keep for 10–12 years. These are impressive wines from the "first American winery and vineyard established exclusively for Rhône varieties."

ALDERBROOK VINEYARDS (SONOMA)

1994 Pinot Noir	Russian River	C	87
1994 Zinfandel	Sonoma	B	90
1993 Zinfandel	Dry Creek	B	88
1996 Zinfandel George's Vineyard Estate	Dry Creek	C	82
1996 Zinfandel OVC	Sonoma	C	86
1995 Zinfandel Old Vines/Old Clones	Sonoma	C	83

A light to medium ruby color is hardly illustrative of just how tasty the soft, smoky 1994 Pinot Noir is. An attractive gamey, sweet, jammy cherry, Burgundy-like nose jumps from the glass. The wine reveals smoky wood, copious quantities of cherry fruit, good expansiveness, and a soft, velvety finish. It is a tasty, round Pinot Noir for drinking over the next 1–2 years. Made from a vineyard planted in 1912, the ruby-colored 1996 Zinfandel George's Vineyard exhibits high acidity. It attempts to be elegant and lighter in style, but comes across as attenuated, although pleasant and cleanly made. Drink it over the next year. A tangy cranberry and sweet/sour cherry-scented and -flavored wine, the medium- to full-bodied, spicy, straightforward 1996 Zinfandel OVC is well-made, but foursquare and obvious. Nevertheless, if you are looking for a solidly made, gutsy (14.1% alcohol), bistro-styled, ruby-colored Zinfandel to drink over the next several years, this wine is not unreasonably priced.
The 1995 Zinfandel is spice-driven—ginger, allspice, pepper, and leafy notes dominate

the wine's fruit component. On the palate, it is somewhat hard and acidic, but it does exhibit enough fruit to provide appeal as well as pleasure to its medium-bodied, crisp, cleanly made style. It is significantly less concentrated and impressive than the 1994. Anticipated maturity: now–2001.

I have never tasted such an impressive Zinfandel from Alderbrook as the 1994. This opaque purple-colored, highly extracted wine exhibits surprising force and richness, beautiful balance, outstanding purity, and a wonderful, sweet inner core of luscious fruit. Long and rich, this knockout Zinfandel is available for a very reasonable price. Drink it over the next 4–5 years. Excellent value.

The big, rich, muscular, smooth 1993 Zinfandel offers copious quantities of peppery, raspberry and cherry fruit, as well as power and body. The "force" will be with you when drinking this lush, heady, generously endowed Zinfandel. Consume it over the next 4–5 years.

ALTAMURA WINERY (NAPA)

1994 Cabernet Sauvignon	Napa	D	86
1993 Cabernet Sauvignon	Napa	D	86
1993 Sangiovese	Napa	C	87

A graceful, stylish, elegant Cabernet Sauvignon, Altamura's 1994 offers a medium-ruby color. Cedar, spice, vanillin, and red currant fruit in the nose and flavors are complemented by medium body, and a supple-textured finish. I would opt for drinking it over the next 5–7 years.

The deep ruby-colored, cassis- and cherry-scented 1993 Cabernet Sauvignon reveals lavish quantities of toasty new oak, medium body, and an attractive spiciness. Although blatantly oaky, it leans toward the elegant, stylish family of California Cabernets, and is youthful as well as accessible. It should drink well for 7–10 years.

Inside the tall, flashy, designer bottle is a very good example of Sangiovese. The color is a healthy dark ruby, and the wine offers up scents of cherries, new saddle leather, and spice. Medium bodied, crisp, and refreshing, with fine depth and ripeness, this is a wine to drink over the next 2–4 years.

AMADOR FOOTHILL WINERY (AMADOR)

1995 Zinfandel Clockspring Vineyard	Amador	C	81
1995 Zinfandel Ferrero Vineyard	Shenandoah	C	75
1994 Zinfandel Ferrero Vineyard	Shenandoah	B	87

The 1995 Zinfandel Clockspring Vineyard (14.3% alcohol) is a medium-bodied, simple, straightforward offering with adequate quantities of ripe fruit, some spice and pepper, but little depth or length. It should be drunk over the next several years. The 1995 Zinfandel Ferrero Vineyard (14.5% alcohol) exhibits a dark plum color, but, like so many 1995 Zinfandels, it is a hollow, tannic, excessively acidic, fruitless wine. Even with additional cellaring, this wine will lack charm and flesh. The dark ruby/purple-colored 1994 Zinfandel possesses a sweet, seductive, ripe nose of jammy berry fruit and spices. Round, generous, and easy to understand, this user-friendly wine should drink well for 5–7 years.

ANDERSON'S CONN VALLEY VINEYARD (NAPA)

1995 Cabernet Sauvignon	Napa	E	91
1994 Cabernet Sauvignon	Napa	E	90?
1993 Cabernet Sauvignon	Napa	E	90+
1997 Cabernet Sauvignon Reserve	Napa	D	(87–90)

1996	Cabernet Sauvignon Reserve	Napa	D	86?
1995	Cabernet Sauvignon Reserve	Napa	D	87
1995	Chardonnay	Napa	D	90
1997	Chardonnay Fournier Vineyard	Carneros	D	(90–91)
1996	Chardonnay Fournier Vineyard	Carneros	D	89
1995	Chardonnay Fournier Vineyard	Carneros	D	85
1997	Eloge Proprietary Red Wine	Napa	E	(90–92)
1993	Eloge Proprietary Red Wine	Napa	E	90
1995	Pinot Noir	Napa	D	90
1994	Pinot Noir	Napa	D	86?
1996	Pinot Noir Dutton Ranch	Russian River	D	88
1996	Pinot Noir Valhalla Vineyard	Napa	D	86
1995	Pinot Noir Valhalla Vineyard	Napa	D	85
1994	Pinot Noir Valhalla Vineyard	Napa	D	92
1993	Pinot Noir Valhalla Vineyard	Napa	D	89
1997	Pinot Noir Valhalla/Dutton	California	D	(87–90)

Total production for Anderson's Conn Valley Vineyards in 1997 will approach 8,000 cases. The bulk of the production is Cabernet Sauvignon, but there are increasing quantities of interesting Chardonnay (about 1,000–1,500 cases). The 1995 Chardonnay Fournier Vineyard is extremely tight, with high acidity, and a structured, backward feel. There is good underlying minerality and vague notions of honeyed, ripe fruit in this solidly made Chardonnay. The question is, will it develop? The winemaking philosophy employed by Gus and Todd Anderson includes extensive lees stirring, no malolactic fermentation, and bottling after 18 months with no filtration. (This is a tricky proposition when the wine has not gone through malolactic.) Fermentations are done by indigenous yeasts, and the wine is aged in a combination of barrels from François Frères and Demptos. Hopefully this 1995 will open with bottle age. The 1996 Chardonnay Fournier Vineyard is an improvement. More expansive and fuller bodied, with a smoky, mineral, white fruit-scented nose, and stony, crisp, leesy flavors, it is French in style, powerful, complex, and more open and richer than the 1995. The finest wine of this trio appears to be the 1997 Chardonnay Fournier Vineyard. It possesses the full body of the 1996, but even more aromatics. Notes of minerals, white fruits, and nicely integrated toasty oak are followed by a rich wine, with high glycerin and alcohol (14.1%), yet it is well balanced because of good acidity and extract. These wines should all age nicely for 4–5 years.

I have enjoyed the Pinot Noirs from Conn Valley. The 1995 Pinot Noir Valhalla Vineyard exhibits a stemmy, cinnamon, intense herbaceousness to its aromatics, plus dry, hard tannin in the finish. A well-made, medium ruby-colored Pinot Noir, it leans toward that varietal's vegetal side. It should drink well for 3–4 years. The 1996 Pinot Noir Valhalla Vineyard displays a deceptively light ruby color, followed by a complex, smoky, cherry, dried herb, spicy-scented nose, nicely concentrated fruit, medium body, and a clean, refreshing, lightly tannic finish. Overall, the 1996 is more open-knit and less herbaceous than the 1995. The two finest Pinot Noirs are the 1996 Dutton Ranch and 1997 Valhalla/Dutton. The 1996 Pinot Noir Dutton Ranch exhibits a light to medium ruby color, a complex nose, and a sweet inner-palate of berry fruit/cherry with a slight notion of chocolate, strawberries, and Asian spices. This attractive Pinot is best consumed over the next 3–4 years. The medium ruby-colored, sweet 1997 Pinot Noir Valhalla/Dutton Vineyard blend (50% from each vineyard) offers plenty of strawberry and cherry fruit aromas, along with high quality, smoky, toasty oak. There is good spice, medium body, and nicely integrated acidity and tannin in this broodingly backward wine. It requires another year of cellaring and should last for 5–6 years.

I have admired and purchased a number of Anderson's Cabernet Sauvignons. This Bordeaux-styled California Cabernet is aged in barrel, of which 40%–50% is new. Some vintages in the early and mid-nineties have displayed a chalky, astringent tannin level, which may not completely age out of the wines. This chalky tannin character is noticeable in the 1995, 1996, and 1997 but, curiously, not as much in the proprietary red wine, Eloge. Nevertheless, there is a lot to like in these Cabernets. The 1995 Cabernet Sauvignon Reserve (4,400 cases) could easily pass for a classy Bordeaux in a blind tasting. The nose offers up earth, minerals, black currants, and cigar box/tobacco aromas. This dark ruby/purple-colored wine is lean and tannic, with sweet black currant fruit on the attack, but a dry, angular, tannic finish. There is a sense of weight and ripeness, but this 1995 still needs 4–5 years of cellaring; it will keep for two decades. The dark ruby-colored 1996 Cabernet Sauvignon Reserve (2,200 cases) reveals damp forest aromas, a notion of mint, black currant fruit, and a touch of blackberries. The wine possesses high tannin, medium body, and some austerity. It requires 5–6 years of cellaring, and will last for 20 years, but I am not sure the tannin will completely melt away. While the 1997 Cabernet Sauvignon Reserve possesses the sweetest fruit, it again exhibits extremely dry tannin in the finish. The wine's fragrance is typical of the vintage—evolved, seductive, and showing plenty of sweetness and charm. This medium-bodied Cabernet needs 5–7 years of cellaring, after which it will last for 15+ years.

Conn Valley has introduced a luxury-priced proprietary wine, called Eloge. The goal is to produce about 1,000 cases, although there are only 250 cases of the 1993 Eloge. No 1994, 1995, or 1996 was produced, but there was another Eloge in 1997 (800 cases). The 1993 Eloge is a blend of 68% Cabernet Sauvignon, and the remainder Cabernet Franc and Merlot. The wine leans toward a St.-Emilion in its tobacco leaf, cedary, black cherry, and currant-scented nose. A classy, rich, finesse-styled wine, it would be hard to pick out as a Napa Cabernet. The wine has good grip and delineation, as well as a medium-bodied, excellent finish. There is some hard tannin, but it is less noticeable in the Eloge than in the Reserve Cabernet Sauvignon. Anticipated maturity: 2002–2020. The 1997 Eloge (a blend of 65% Cabernet Sauvignon, 25% Cabernet Franc, and 20% Merlot) exhibits a smoky, earthy, black currant-scented nose with intriguing scents of coffee, cherries, Asian spices, and cigar box. Rich and full bodied, with sweet, jammy fruit, soft tannin, and an opulent texture, this luscious, concentrated, impressively endowed wine should prove to be outstanding. Anticipated maturity: 2004–2020.

The debut 1995 Chardonnay produced by Todd and Gus Anderson is a powerful, viscous, superrich wine that should make additional friends for this high quality producer in Napa's scenic Conn Valley. The wine was not put through malolactic, but it was given extensive sur-lees aging, as well as fermented in barrel. It possesses marvelous intensity and richness, but it must still survive a sterile filtration (this is obligatory when malolactic fermentation is blocked), so it remains to be known how much intensity is lost. However, this wine could lose 10% of its flavor and still turn out to be exceptional.

The Cabernet Sauvignons produced at Anderson's Conn Valley Vineyard represent a synthesis in style between the extravagant ripeness so frequently achieved in top California vintages and the more elegant, restrained style produced in Bordeaux. Recent vintages are all consistently good, although the 1994 Cabernet may not be the hugely successful wine that so many other estates produced in this benchmark vintage. I would have expected it to be much better than the 1993. Admittedly, I saw the wine immediately after bottling (no fining or filtration takes place at Conn Valley), but the wine tasted reticent, although impressive, and possibly meriting an outstanding score. The 1994 Cabernet Sauvignon exhibits a dark ruby/purple color, a tight but burgeoning nose of black fruits, white flowers, and earth. On the palate, it reveals a sweet, spicy, black currant-flavored attack, medium to full body, and strong tannin in the finish. The middle needs to fill out a bit more. Give this wine 2–4 years of cellaring and drink it over the next 2 decades. The 1993 Cabernet Sauvignon is currently in a dormant stage of development. The wine's dark ruby/purple color is followed by aromas of sweet, earthy, black currants, but it then retreats into a shell. Full bodied, but noticeably tannic, it possesses the extract and fruit to balance out the tannin, but it is currently closed and in need of 1–3 years of cellaring. This is another candidate for 15–20 years of aging. The 1995 Cabernet Sauvignon may turn out to be the finest Conn Valley Cabernet since 1990. The wine is the sweetest and richest of recent vintages, with nicely integrated tannin, a dense, deep, ruby/purple color, velvety texture, and the seamless quality possessed by many 1994s. It should drink well for 20 years.

Word is finally getting out about the exquisite Cabernet Sauvignons produced by the father and son team of Gus and Todd Anderson from their vineyard tucked in the Conn Valley hills behind the Meadowwood Country Club and Resort. Not as well known are the tiny quantities of sumptuous Pinot Noir that emerge from their Valhalla Vineyard. This wine is atypical for a Napa Pinot Noir as it reveals a black cherry, raspberry, blackberry fruitiness that has more in common with an Oregon Pinot Noir than the cherry/strawberry/herbal notes that tend to be the hallmarks of California Pinots. The 1993 Valhalla Pinot Noir, which was largely sold to the winery's mailing list clients, is loaded with black fruit. It offers up a sweet, vanilla, smoky, oaky, black raspberry-scented nose, generous, medium- to full-bodied, velvety-textured flavors, and plenty of intensity and length. It should be drunk over the next 3–4 years. Although the 1994 Pinot Noir Valhalla was still in barrel when I tasted it in 1995, since this property neither fines nor filters, I would not expect the bottled wine to lose any of its exceptional quality. Only 150 cases are made of this wine, which is aged in 100% new French oak. The nose blasts upward from the glass, revealing intense, jammy, black fruits intertwined with smoky new oak. Full bodied and sweet (from fruit extraction, not sugar), this elegant, authoritatively flavored Pinot Noir reveals layers of ripe fruit, and a long, lush, chocolate/cherrylike finish. It is a dead ringer for a top-notch Côte de Nuits from the Domaine Méo-Camuzet. Drink it over the next 4–5 years.

The Anderson family has considerable interest in Pinot Noir, which is evidenced by their numerous trips to Burgundy. Their Pinot Noir production is now up to a whopping 150 cases. They produce a naturally made, unfined, unfiltered Pinot that can be one of the pleasant surprises of Napa Valley. The 1994 Pinot Noir was in an awkward stage when I tasted it, revealing strong animal, tomato, leafy aromas, and a muddled personality. There is plenty of flavor, but the wine was disjointed and funky. Another evaluation following 6–12 months of additional bottle age should prove more accurate. The 1995 Pinot Noir looks to be superb, with a dark ruby/purple color, copious quantities of sweet, Richebourg-like black cherries intertwined with flowery aromas, and high-quality toasty new oak. Sweet, round, and full bodied, this is a seductive, layered, succulently textured Pinot Noir for drinking during its first 5–6 years of life.

ARAUJO ESTATE WINES (NAPA)

1997 Cabernet Sauvignon Eisele Vineyard	Napa	EE	(91–94)
1996 Cabernet Sauvignon Eisele Vineyard	Napa	EE	94
1995 Cabernet Sauvignon Eisele Vineyard	Napa	EE	98
1994 Cabernet Sauvignon Eisele Vineyard	Napa	E	95
1993 Cabernet Sauvignon Eisele Vineyard	Napa	D	96
1995 Sauvignon Blanc	Napa	C	90

1997 Sauvignon Blanc Eisele Vineyard	Napa	C	89
1996 Sauvignon Blanc Eisele Vineyard	Napa	C	88
1997 Syrah Eisele Vineyard	Napa	E	(90–91)
1996 Syrah Eisele Vineyard	Napa	E	92
1995 Syrah Eisele Vineyard	Napa	E	97
1994 Syrah Eisele Vineyard	Napa	E	98+
1997 Viognier Eisele Vineyard	Napa	D	85

This reference point winery is always one of my favorite stops in northern California. I have been an admirer of the Eisele Vineyard Cabernet Sauvignons since I first tasted the 1974 Conn Creek Eisele. It has been inspiring to see how proprietors Daphne and Bart Araujo have taken this superb *terroir* and built it into a world-class winery and vineyard operation, producing not only spectacular Cabernet Sauvignon but also fabulous Syrah and excellent Sauvignon Blanc. The 1997 Sauvignon Blanc Eisele Vineyard (about 1,200 cases produced) is a refreshing, straw-colored wine that has had 10% Viognier added. Primarily made from the most fragrant Sauvignon Blanc clone, Musqué, it reveals a Muscat-like bouquet with plenty of melon, figs, and honey. There is excellent freshness, and a zesty, snappy personality with good underlying minerality. It is a beautifully knit, complex Sauvignon to drink over the next 1–2 years. A small quantity of 1997 Viognier Eisele Vineyard was produced. It is a lighter-styled, refreshing, elegant example, but somewhat uninspiring, particularly when compared to the other Araujo offerings.

Thankfully, more and more Syrah is being produced at Araujo, but quantities remain tiny. The 1997 Syrah Eisele Vineyard enjoyed a 38 to 40-day maceration, and has had 7% Viognier added to the blend. The wine is aged in Taransaud oak barrels, of which 60% were new. The 1997 is a sexy, surprisingly evolved, extremely fragrant wine that typifies the 1997 vintage with its expansive aromatics and seductive personality. The wine's saturated dark purple color is followed by a textbook smoky, bacon fat, toasty, tropical fruit, blackberry, honeysuckle, pepper, and spicy-scented nose. Evolved, juicy, rich, and concentrated, but surprisingly refined for a wine of such intensity, this beautifully made Syrah should be ready to drink when released, and age nicely for 10–15 years. Bottled with no fining or filtration, the 1996 Syrah Eisele Vineyard (350 cases) displays an intense, peppery, blackberry jam/crème de cassis nose that soars from the glass. Rich, full bodied, and impeccably pure, with rugged tannin in the finish, this beauty possesses 20 years of aging potential, although I suspect it will be accessible when released. The spectacular 1995 Syrah Eisele Vineyard is one of the greatest New World Syrahs I have ever tasted. Approximately 300 cases were made, and it is even better out of bottle than it was in barrel. The color is an opaque purple. The bouquet offers explosive notes of wood fire, licorice, jammy blackberries and cassis, in addition to the unmistakable scent of black truffles/licorice. Full bodied and rich, with sensational flavor extraction, remarkable harmony, and a 35+-second finish, this is profoundly great Syrah. While it is approachable, it will not reach full maturity for another 7–8 years; it will keep for 3 decades. Wow!

Araujo's Cabernet Sauvignon Eisele Vineyard has become a benchmark. I believe the 1995 Cabernet Sauvignon Eisele Vineyard is the finest produced under the Araujo regime. It is close to perfection. The wine combines extraordinary power and richness with remarkable complexity and finesse. The saturated purple/black color is followed by aromas of sweet vanillin intermixed with riveting scents of black currants, minerals, exotic spices, coffee, and toast. There is nothing garish about this subtle yet powerful giant of a wine. A Napa Valley classic, it is full bodied and extremely rich, yet retains its sense of balance and symmetry. This fabulous Cabernet Sauvignon should age effortlessly for 30 or more years.

Anticipated maturity: 2001–2030. The 1996 Cabernet Sauvignon Eisele Vineyard had been bottled several months before my visit in the fall of 1998. A blend of 91% Cabernet Sauvignon, 6% Cabernet Franc, and 3% Petit Verdot, there are 2,200 cases. A superb example, it suffers only because it follows what appears to be a modern-day legend—the 1995. The 1996 boasts a saturated purple color, and a moderately intense nose of black fruits intermixed with blueberries, spice, iron, and earthy notes. Dense and structured, with more noticeable tannin than the 1995 or 1994 possesses, it is a brooding, massive Cabernet Sauvignon with outstanding long-term potential. However, it is less capable of providing the near-term joys found in such vintages as 1994 and 1995. Powerful and closed, but promising, the 1996 was in a brooding, brawny state when I tasted it. Anticipated maturity: 2005–2025. The aromatically forward 1997 Cabernet Sauvignon Eisele Vineyard will be among the more seductive and sexy Cabernet Sauvignons produced in the nineties. It possesses all the ingredients necessary for greatness—concentration, purity, and richness—but what sets it apart from other vintages is its evolved aromatic personality. The wine tastes as if it is 6–12 months older than it actually is (something I found with many 1997 North Coast reds). The color is a healthy saturated dark purple. The wine is elegant, rich in fruit, medium to full bodied, and extremely expressive, even flamboyant. This should prove to be a sexy, ostentatiously styled Eisele Vineyard Cabernet Sauvignon that will drink beautifully upon release, yet its balance suggests at least two decades of longevity.

The 1994 Cabernet Sauvignon Eisele Vineyard is just beginning to emerge from a period of post-bottling dormancy. Like its siblings, it exhibits an impressively saturated dark purple color. This wine is intent on revealing its charms at a relatively early age given its knockout aromatics. Although slightly less powerful than the 1993 and marginally less concentrated than the 1995, the 1994 is still a profoundly rich, silky-textured wine with an uncanny balance between its smooth tannin and layers of cassis and blackberry/mineral-tinged fruit. This wine is particularly impressive if it is first decanted for 45 or so minutes. It will age well for 15–20 years.

The Eisele Vineyard 1993 Cabernet Sauvignon is one of the half dozen or so candidates for wine of the vintage. I have tasted it three times out of bottle, once rating it as high as 98 but never less than 96. It is a mind-boggling Cabernet Sauvignon that is remarkably well balanced for its size and intensity. The color is an opaque purple, and the nose offers up smoky, chocolatey, black currant, licorice, and mineral scents. On the palate, the wine reveals fabulous density, concentration, sweetness of fruit as well as tannin, and a 30–40-second finish. Although there is a high percentage of new oak, this wine has completely soaked it up, a testament to its extract and concentration of fruit. While the wine displays a certain precociousness, unusual for a 1993, there is plenty of tannin lurking in the finish, but it is well concealed by the wine's exceptional richness. This beauty is destined to age effortlessly for 20–25 years.

The 1994 Syrah Eisele Vineyard (which is blended with 8% Viognier) may be the single greatest Syrah yet produced in California. The wine exhibits an opaque purple color, followed by a fabulous nose of black fruits, pepper, minerals, and a subtle whiff of Viognier's honeysuckle fruit. It is magnificent on the palate, with massive richness yet, remarkably, no heaviness or coarseness. It is a tour de force in winemaking.

With such masterful reds, it is easy to overlook Araujo's Sauvignon Blanc Eisele Vineyard. Don't make that mistake. The 1996, which includes 10% Viognier, as well as a large portion of the Musqué clone of Sauvignon, is an extremely aromatic, barrel-aged Sauvignon with convincingly intense honeysuckle, ripe melon, and apricot scents. Medium bodied, with a plush texture, and loads of vibrant fruit, this wine is best drunk over the next year.

The Sauvignon has evolved nicely over the last several vintages. An intelligent decision was made to add 8%–10% Viognier to the blend, giving the wine a more aromatic personality. At present, the melony/fig fragrance of the Sauvignon is nicely complemented by the subtle honeysuckle/apricotlike component of Viognier. The 1995 exhibits excellent purity, medium body, intense fruit, and a dry, crisp, surprisingly long finish. This is one of the best Sauvignons readers will find from California. It will not be long-lived, but 12–18 months of enjoyment is forecast.

Araujo Estate Wines is another estate where readers should try and get on the mailing list, or at least on the waiting list for the mailing list!

ARROWOOD (SONOMA)

1997 Cabernet Sauvignon	Sonoma	D	(88–90)
1996 Cabernet Sauvignon	Sonoma	D	89
1995 Cabernet Sauvignon	Sonoma	D	91
1994 Cabernet Sauvignon	Sonoma	D	91
1993 Cabernet Sauvignon	Sonoma	C	90
1995 Cabernet Sauvignon Reserve Speciale	Sonoma	E	94
1994 Cabernet Sauvignon Reserve Speciale	Sonoma	E	95
1997 Chardonnay	Sonoma	C	88
1996 Chardonnay	Sonoma	C	90
1995 Chardonnay	Sonoma	C	91
1996 Chardonnay Reserve Cuvée Michel Berthoud	Sonoma	D	92
1995 Chardonnay Reserve Cuvée Michel Berthoud	Sonoma	D	93
1994 Chardonnay Reserve Cuvée Michel Berthoud	Sonoma	D	93
1996 Chardonnay Reserve Cuvée Michel Berthoud	Sonoma	D	91
1997 Domaine du Grand Archer Cabernet Sauvignon	Sonoma	D	87
1996 Domaine du Grand Archer Cabernet Sauvignon	Sonoma	C	87
1995 Domaine du Grand Archer Cabernet Sauvignon	Sonoma	C	87
1994 Domaine du Grand Archer Cabernet Sauvignon	Sonoma	B	87
1993 Domaine du Grand Archer Cabernet Sauvignon	Sonoma	B	87
1997 Domaine du Grand Archer Chardonnay	Sonoma	B	87
1996 Domaine du Grand Archer Chardonnay	Sonoma	B	87

1995	Domaine du Grand Archer Chardonnay	Sonoma	B	87
1997	Domaine du Grand Archer Merlot	Sonoma	B	84
1996	Domaine du Grand Archer Merlot	Sonoma	C	84
1995	Domaine du Grand Archer Merlot	Sonoma	C	87
1994	Domaine du Grand Archer Merlot	Sonoma	B	87
1997	Malbec	Sonoma	D	(89–90)
1996	Malbec	Sonoma	D	90
1995	Malbec	Sonoma	D	90
1994	Malbec	Sonoma	D	92
1993	Malbec	Sonoma	D	93
1997	Merlot	Sonoma	D	(84–86)
1996	Merlot	Sonoma	D	88
1995	Merlot	Sonoma	D	89
1994	Merlot	Sonoma	D	90
1993	Merlot	Sonoma	D	89+
1995	Merlot Reserve Speciale	Sonoma	E	90
1994	Merlot Reserve Speciale	Sonoma	E	92
1997	Pinot Blanc Saralee's Vineyard	Russian River	D	91
1995	Pinot Blanc Saralee's Vineyard	Russian River	D	92
1997	Syrah Saralee's Vineyard	Russian River	D	(90–92)
1996	Syrah Saralee's Vineyard	Russian River	D	95
1995	Syrah Saralee's Vineyard	Russian River	D	95
1994	Syrah Saralee's Vineyard	Russian River	D	96+
1997	Viognier Estate	Sonoma	D	90
1997	Viognier Saralee's Vineyard	Russian River	D	88
1996	Viognier Saralee's Vineyard	Russian River	D	91
1995	Viognier Saralee's Vineyard	Russian River	C	93
1997	Viognier Saralee's Vineyard Selected Late Harvest	Russian River	D	91
1997	White Riesling Hoot Owl Vineyard Special Select Late Harvest	Alexander Valley	D	95
1995	White Riesling Select Late Harvest Preston Ranch	Sonoma	D (375 ml)	96

1997 White Riesling Preston Ranch Special
     Select Late Harvest   **Russian River   D   97**

It is ironic that in the 1970s, when Dick Arrowood was one of the darlings of the wine media during his sojourn at Château St. Jean, I was rarely as enamored with his wines as some of my peers. However, since he began his own operation in Sonoma, he has become one of my favorite producers and unquestionably a reference point for world-class wine. Just about everything he touches is noteworthy, including some delicious, value-priced wines offered under the Domaine du Grand Archer label. Frugal consumers should be looking for the 1997 Domaine du Grand Archer Chardonnay, a delicious, richly fruity (apricots and pineapples), lush wine that is also an attractive value, the 1997 Domaine du Grand Archer Cabernet Sauvignon, a deep cassis-scented and -flavored, medium-bodied wine, with sweet tannin and plenty of fruit character, and the 1996 Domaine du Grand Archer Cabernet Sauvignon, which is similar to the 1997, with plenty of punch, muscle, and cassis fruit, as well as a vel-vety-textured, up-front, user-friendly style. The Chardonnay needs to be consumed over the next 1–2 years, the Cabernets over the next 5–7 years. I was less impressed with the Do-maine du Grand Archer Merlots. The 1997 is a tarry, chocolatey, berry-scented, straightfor-ward wine with pleasant fruit. The 1996 Domaine du Grand Archer Merlot is cut from the same mold. Both should be consumed over the next 2–3 years.

There are two Viogniers in the portfolio, both among the finest examples of this varietal in California. The 1997 Viognier Saralee's Vineyard (700 cases) is a powerful, medium-bodied, honeysuckle/tropical fruit/apricot-scented wine with lively freshness, and heady levels of al-cohol (14.5%) and glycerin. It should be consumed over the next 12–18 months. Even better is the 1997 Viognier Estate (260 cases). Less alcoholic (14.2%), this example offers an in-triguing bouquet of honeysuckle, orange marmalade, tangerines, and honeyed citrus. Full bodied, with excellent definition and richness, as well as gorgeous purity of fruit, this is a knockout Viognier to drink over the next 1–2 years.

Another dazzling offering from this portfolio is Pinot Blanc. Although relatively unher-alded, this has been a perennial winner. The 1997 Pinot Blanc Saralee's Vineyard (900 cases) boasts a gorgeously ripe nose of orange blossoms, pineapples, and other tropical fruits. Medium to full bodied, with terrific fruit presence, good underlying acidity, and an ex-uberant freshness, it will be flexible with an assortment of culinary dishes. Although it will not be long-lived, it will drink well for 2–3 years.

I have consistently extolled the virtues of Arrowood's Chardonnays. These wines are given full malolactic, 100% barrel fermentation and are bottled with no filtration. The 1997 Chardonnay Sonoma reveals a smoky, leesy, Burgundian nose of ripe pears, honey, buttered citrus, and subtle toasty oak. Richly fruity, with medium to full body, and admirable fresh-ness and vigor, this is a tasty, attractive Chardonnay for consuming over the next 4–5 years. The winery's flagship Chardonnay is the Reserve Speciale Cuvée Michel Berthoud. While the 1996 is lighter than the fabulous 1995, it is undeniably an outstanding effort, revealing full body, and a textbook nose of subtle *pain grillé*, white peaches, tropical fruit, and hazel-nuts. The oak regime of 25% new oak, 25% one-year-old barrels, and 50% two- and three-year-old barrels lets the fruit dominate the wine's other characteristics. The oak is beautifully integrated in this full-bodied effort. Crammed with extract and richness, this wine should drink well for 3–4 years.

No one in California is making better Malbec. Arrowood manages to take this little-respected grape and turn it into a sexy, gorgeously scented, seductive wine that deserves far more attention. Not a blockbuster heavyweight, it offers extraordinary aromatic fragrance, gorgeous levels of intense black raspberry and strawberry fruit, but no sense of heaviness. The 1997 Malbec possesses all these components, medium body, a vivid fruit character, and fine purity. It should drink well upon release, and last for a decade. Among the other 1997 reds, Arrowood has turned out a competent 1997 Merlot with a plush texture but green tannin in the finish. It reveals some of Merlot's coffee bean/berry fruit but seems a bit austere and angular. Both the 1997 Cabernet Sauvignon and 1997 Syrah Saralee's Vineyard display outstanding potential. The dark ruby/purple-colored 1997 Cabernet Sauvignon exhibits classic cassis aromas, a spicy, medium-bodied personality, sweet tannin, fine extract, and a silky style. The evolved, rich 1997 Syrah Saralee's Vineyard has 7% Viognier fermented in the vats with the Syrah. While not the blockbuster à la the 1995 and 1996, it is still a sexy, succulent, exotic Syrah with loads of blackberry and cassis fruit intermingled with a touch of honeysuckle. This fruit-driven wine should provide delicious as well as charming drinking at an early age, and last for 7–10 years.

All the 1996s and 1995s had been bottled and were performing exceptionally well. The dark ruby-colored 1996 Merlot Sonoma exhibits an attractive nose of black cherries intermixed with chocolate, spice, and subtle new oak (about a third new oak is utilized). Revealing some tannin, this wine is made in the lush, forward, fleshy style admired by Merlot enthusiasts. It should drink well for 5–7 years. The 1996 Malbec displays a knockout nose of strawberry/raspberry/blackberry jam, as well as a creamy texture, medium body, copious amounts of pure fruit, and a soft, sexy, lush personality. It should drink well for 7–10 years. The saturated ruby/purple-colored 1996 Cabernet Sauvignon offers a moderately intense nose of cedar, spice box, cassis, licorice, and subtle oak. Full bodied, with terrific fruit, plenty of spice, and outstanding purity and richness, this is a fine, impressively endowed, accessible effort that promises to drink well for 12–15 years. The 1996 Syrah Saralee's Vineyard (made from tiny yields of one ton of fruit per acre) offers up a phenomenal blackberry liqueur-scented bouquet, with a touch of apricot/orange marmalade jam thrown in for additional complexity. Some Viognier was obviously fermented with this offering. Bacon fat, smoky oak, melted road tar, and pepper also emerge in this profoundly complex, superconcentrated, full-bodied classic. This wine is revealing more forwardness than it did previously, but wow, what a stunning Syrah! Anticipated maturity: 2000–2015. The 1995 Syrah Saralee's Vineyard may be even better. It has the advantage of an extra year of bottle age, so the wine's perfume is more evolved, but both of these cuvées are extraordinary. Like all of Arrowood's top red wines, it was bottled with neither fining nor filtration. A similar blackberry jam/cassis-scented nose is followed by a sweet, unctuous texture, and explosive fruit, glycerin, and extract levels. Soft tannin can be found in the silky 30-second finish. Crammed with fruit, this classic Syrah satisfies both the hedonistic and intellectual senses. It should age effortlessly for 15 or more years.

The Reserve Speciale wines spend just under two years in oak casks, and are bottled unfined and unfiltered. These stunning offerings are among the finest of their type. Production is minuscule for the Reserve Speciale Merlot (108 cases), and modest for the Cabernet Sauvignon Reserve Speciale (1,700 cases for the 1995). The 1995 Merlot Reserve Speciale possesses a dense purple color, in addition to a big, smoky, toasty, oaky nose with notes of black currant and cherry fruit. The wine exhibits coffee/chocolate notes in the flavors, an unctuous texture, full body, and outstanding purity and length. Already accessible, this 1995 promises to evolve for 15+ years. The spectacular 1995 Cabernet Sauvignon Reserve Speciale is a worthy rival to the monumental 1994. It offers an opaque purple color and a knockout nose of tobacco, jammy cassis, *pain grillé,* and floral scents. This wine has superb extract and purity, full body, multiple layers of richness, and a ripe, seamless, palate-staining finish. Although approachable, it is not quite as accessible as the glorious 1994. Anticipated maturity: 2001–2020.

Dick Arrowood has a stunning résumé with respect to his nectarlike dessert wines. I tasted three offerings in 1997, all of which merit enthusiastic recommendations. The 1997 Viognier Saralee's Vineyard Selected Late Harvest was harvested at 32% sugar, and has 8% residual sugar and 11.7% alcohol. The wine has lost some of Viognier's honeysuckle/apricotlike notes, but it is extremely rich, unctuously textured, and sweet. While it is unquestionably outstanding, it was blown off the tasting table by the following two wines. The prodigious 1997 White Riesling Preston Ranch Special Select Late Harvest was picked at 34.7% sugar, and at bottling retained 17.8% residual sugar with a lowly 9% alcohol. It offers a phenomenal nose of honeyed tropical fruits and spring flower garden scents. The wine is thick and juicy, with unbelievable balance and zesty underlying acidity. When I asked what the HSS on the label meant, Arrowood said it was an abbreviation for a ZZ Top song called "Hot, Sweet, and Sticky." This is a terrific late-harvest Riesling that can easily compete with some of the finest Trockenbeerenauslese Rieslings produced in Germany. The 1997 White Riesling Hoot Owl Special Select Late Harvest was picked at even higher sugar levels—39% at harvest, with 22.8% residual sugar and 9.4% alcohol. It is a heavier, thicker, more oily example, with fabulously pure, refreshing fruit, a mélange of tropical fruit aromas and flavors, and extraordinary richness and viscosity. These two white Rieslings are so concentrated they can be drunk with a spoon. Both will age for at least a decade.

The Domaine du Grand Archer wines offer true quality, flavor, and personality. For example, the 1996 Domaine du Grand Archer Chardonnay (a blend of 93.5% Chardonnay, 3.5% Viognier, and 3% Pinot Blanc) does not reveal any influence of new oak. It offers abundant quantities of vibrant, buttery fruit that jumps from the glass, covering the palate with a succulent personality. While it is not the most complex style of Chardonnay, it is loaded with fruit and flavor, is medium bodied, pure, and ripe. The rich 1995 Chardonnay exhibits a buttery, tropical fruit component, a touch of wood, surprising depth and complexity, and a surprisingly long finish. It is hard to believe $10 can buy a Chardonnay of this quality.

The 1995 Domaine du Grand Archer Merlot is more evolved, exhibiting a dark garnet/plum color, a smoky, coffee, chocolatey, jammy black-cherry nose, and spicy, dense, fleshy flavors with well-integrated acidity and tannin. A very good Merlot, it will drink well for 5–8 years. The 1994 Domaine du Grand Archer Merlot is superior to about 85% of its peers. Moreover, it is priced 30%–50% less. It offers a deep ruby/purple color, and a big, spicy, mocha, black-cherry-scented nose with subtle oak in the background. Round and generous, with a creamy texture and luscious fruit, this delicious Merlot can be consumed for 3–4 years after its release. Like the other Arrowood red wines, it was bottled with no fining or filtration.

Domaine du Grand Archer's 1994 Cabernet Sauvignon exhibits a thick color, and rich, spicy, weedy, black currant aromas with a judicious touch of toasty oak. This medium- to full-bodied wine reveals adequate acidity, a natural, plush, succulent mouthfeel, and plenty of sweet fruit and length. It possesses the concentration found in Cabernets costing $20–$30 a bottle.

Readers should also look for the 1993 Domaine du Grand Archer Cabernet Sauvignon, a sweet, ripe, supple Cabernet for drinking over the next 4–5 years. Unfortunately, there are only 1,100 cases, but it is a terrific bargain in user-friendly Cabernet Sauvignon.

Arrowood's Chardonnays are vibrantly pure wines with plenty of leesy, Burgundian-like complexity, plush, opulently textured palates, and loads of fruit. The most fruit-dominated cuvée is the 1996 Chardonnay. It possesses a light, buttery, smoky character, but fruit is its primary characteristic, with both tropical fruit and a honeyed apple component abundantly displayed. This medium- to full-bodied wine exhibits outstanding delineation as well as impeccable winemaking—a hallmark of all the Arrowood offerings. It should drink well for 2–3 years. The 1995 Chardonnay has a terrific, smoky, roasted hazelnut, richly fruity nose, followed by a full-bodied wine with a thick texture oozing with juicy Chardonnay fruit. Those characteristics, along with crisp acidity and subtle oak combine to make this a dazzling, full-flavored, elegant Chardonnay for drinking during its first 2–3 years of life.

Readers seeking a roasted hazelnut, smoky, creamy-textured, fuller-bodied, and more concentrated Chardonnay should try the 1996 Chardonnay Reserve Speciale. This wine may be slightly less intense than the magnificent 1995, but it is a dead ringer for a top-notch Burgundy. Extremely concentrated and full bodied, it will provide sumptuous drinking over the next 2–4 years. The grape sources are primarily from the Russian River, with about 20% of the grapes coming from Alexander Valley and 17% from Sonoma Valley. Another terrific white from the Arrowood portfolio is the 1996 Viognier Saralee's Vineyard. Arrowood's Viognier may be the finest Viognier made in California, and the 1996 is another convincing example of what heights this grape can but rarely does attain in the New World. This luscious wine boasts an apricot/peach/honeysucklelike fragrance that jumps from the glass. On the palate, the wine is full bodied, with good fatness, ripe fruit, and enough acidity to provide vibrancy and delineation. Drink it over the next several years. Among California's Viogniers, only Calera's and Pride Mountain's come close to matching the breadth of flavor and accurate varietal character displayed by Dick Arrowood's offering.

There are 1,000 cases of the spectacular, full-bodied, Burgundian-styled 1994 Chardonnay Reserve Cuvée Michel Berthoud. Aged in 100% new Louis Latour barrels, the wine's subtle notes of smoky, vanillin-tinged new oak take a backseat to the huge amount of ripe, full-bodied, exuberant, ostentatious Chardonnay fruit. This unfiltered wine possesses a superb texture, a great midpalate, and a long, pure, ripe finish. It is a tour de force in Chardonnay winemaking, with layers of knockout flavors and superb length. Just beginning to open, this wine should last for another 3–4 years. The 1995 Chardonnay Reserve Cuvée Michel Berthoud is another formidably endowed, leesy, smoky, hazelnut, ripe fruit-scented and -flavored wine that cuts a full swath on the palate. Complex, with good structure, enough acidity to provide focus, and a whoppingly rich finish, this wine should drink well young, yet keep for 2–3 years.

Arrowood's 1995 Pinot Blanc Saralee's Vineyard is among the finest Pinot Blancs made in California. Unfortunately, only small quantities are available. Aged in 100% Louis Latour *barriques,* and put through full malolactic fermentation, this dense, honeyed tangerine/orange-scented wine is bursting with fruit. Exhibiting little evidence of its oak aging despite the new barrel regime, it offers a sumptuous texture, layers of fruit, and a long, dry, rich finish. The wine's hallmarks are its pure, layered flavors, subtle oaky notes, and gorgeously rich midpalate and texture. The fabulous 1995 Viognier Saralee's Vineyard is one of the finest I have tasted from California. Yields were extremely tiny, and the spectacular honeyed peach/apricot-scented nose and wonderfully pure, ripe, unctuously textured, thick flavors coat the palate with the essence of the Viognier grape. Admirable acidity provides delineation to the wine's component parts. This should prove to be one of California's reference point Viogniers, but it is very limited in availability. Drink it over the first 1–3 years after its release.

The 1995 White Riesling boasts an amazing deep golden color, a fabulous honeyed nose, syrupy, viscous, pineapple and apricotlike flavors, fine acidity, only 8.8% alcohol, and a rich, pure TBA-like finish. This wine will last for a decade or more. For sweet wine lovers, this is another winemaking tour de force.

When asked about comparing the 1994, 1995, and 1996 Merlot and Cabernet Sauvignon vintages, Dick Arrowood felt that 1994 produced the richest, most opulent wines, with the roundest tannin. He went on to say that 1995 was slightly more forward, with attractive aromatics, but the wines possessed more jagged edges and aggressive tannin, yet impressive extract in addition to a firmer character. As for the 1996s, Arrowood did not feel they were as fleshy and round as the 1994s, but they were relatively supple, and usually possessed excellent aromatics and density. In essence, they are firmer, but not as tough as some 1995s. As the following tasting notes attest, all of the reds from Arrowood were exceptionally successful.

Arrowood's 1995 Merlot seems slightly more backward than the 1996, exhibiting some of the tannic muscle Dick Arrowood ascribes to this vintage. The wine possesses an opaque purple color, a tight but interesting nose of black cherries and currants intermixed with coffee and smoky notes. Sweet, juicy, intensely ripe fruit hits the palate, yet the wine's tannin gives it definition, and a more backward personality than the 1996. While this Merlot can be drunk early, it will be better following 1–2 years of cellaring. It should keep for 12–15 years.

The 1994 Merlot's saturated, inky black color is followed by a sweet, jammy nose of black fruits, licorice, vanilla, and smoke. Full bodied, with a voluptuous palate, as well as a layered texture, this low-acid, plump, fleshy Merlot should drink well for a decade after its release next year. Yummy!

The opaque purple-colored, unfiltered 1993 Merlot (there is 16% Cabernet Franc in the blend) offers up a sweet, chocolatey, rich, berry-scented nose, soft, medium-bodied flavors with a creamy texture, and tannin in the finish. The wine exhibits fine purity and an authentic Merlot varietal character. It may merit an outstanding score with 4–6 months of bottle age.

No one is making better Malbec in California than Dick Arrowood. It's a shame that this grape is held in such low esteem because it can be marvelous when treated with the same respect as Merlot and Cabernet Sauvignon. The 1995 Malbec has a slight edge over the 1996, perhaps because it happens to be a year older. It appears to possess more body and intensity. There is no doubting this saturated purple-colored wine's knockout nose of black raspberries, jammy strawberries, and crème fraiche. Extremely opulent and lush, with berry fruit gushing across the palate, this wine possesses a palate feel and texture totally unlike Merlot and Cabernet Sauvignon. It reveals the precision of Cabernet, the body of Merlot, and an indescribable but not unbearable "lightness of being." Pure, with light tannin in the finish, this expressive, personality-filled wine should drink well for 12–15 years.

The 1994 Malbec exhibits raspberry jam, vanilla ice cream, cream puff-scented aromas and flavors. A gush of wild black fruits is allied to a silky texture, medium to full body, and superb purity. Arrowood has been intelligent in not overoaking these Malbecs, building in just enough new oak to provide delineation. Arrowood made 500 six-bottle cases of exquisite 1993 Malbec. Aromatically and texturally, the wine reminds me of a top vintage of the famed Pomerol château, l'Évangile (a wine made from 71% Merlot and 29% Cabernet Franc). The wine offers intense aromas of black raspberries, great fruit, a rich, layered, concentrated palate, and admirable sweetness and texture. This is a profound, complex, gorgeously made wine that may turn out to be historic, as it displays just what heights Malbec can achieve in selected soils and climates. Bottled unfined and unfiltered, and brought up in one-third new oak, one-third 1-year old oak, and one-third 2-year-old oak, this wine is not to be missed. All of these Malbecs can be drunk upon release, yet they promise to last for at least 10–12 years.

There are few Sonoma County Cabernet Sauvignons better than those produced by Dick Arrowood. Arrowood's success with Cabernet Sauvignon, so obvious in the decade of the nineties, continues unabated, with a succession of top quality wines. The outstanding 1995 Cabernet Sauvignon boasts an opaque purple color, followed by a rich, black currant-dominated bouquet with background aromas of new oak, earth, and spice. Extremely full bodied, with admirable fruit purity, and a layered, multidimensional personality, this wine is intensely rich, with formidable levels of glycerin and extract. The wine's tannin is largely concealed by the wealth of fruit. While this Cabernet will be drinkable young, it promises to evolve for 15+ years.

A blend of 82% Cabernet Sauvignon, 6% Cabernet Franc, 5% Petit Verdot, 4% Malbec, and 3% Merlot, the unfiltered 1993 Cabernet Sauvignon possesses an unformed nose of cassis fruit and subtle wood and licorice. The opaque purple color suggests terrific ripeness and richness. And guess what the wine offers? Deep, full bodied, with gorgeous purity, a natural mouth-feel, and no hard tannin or tart acidity, this is a wine of considerable sumptuousness. Although approachable, it will not achieve full maturity for 3–5 years; it will keep for 15 years. Another sensational, opulent, rich, extremely aromatic and concentrated red wine from Arrowood, the 1994 Cabernet Sauvignon possesses stunning concentration and intensity, impressive balance and purity, and copious quantities of sweet tannin in the long finish. It should eclipse even the super 1993.

Arrowood's two 1994 Reserve Speciale wines, a 1994 Merlot and 1994 Cabernet Sauvignon, were made in limited quantities, but, wow, what dazzling wines they are! The 1994 Merlot Reserve Speciale (100 cases) includes about 3.7% Cabernet Franc in the blend. With 13.8% alcohol, it is a sexy, rich, full-bodied Merlot with terrific layers of fruit, glycerin, and extract. The wine spent 22 months in oak casks, but reveals little evidence of new wood given its extraordinary concentration, power, and depth. It possesses a knockout nose of ripe berry fruit intertwined with Asian spices, subtle toast, and a whiff of coffee and chocolate. Powerful, yet round and harmonious, this is a blockbuster Merlot that should drink well for 15 or more years. Arrowood's 1994 Cabernet Sauvignon Reserve Speciale is an exquisite wine made from a blend of vineyards (Wildwood, Smothers, Balbi, Belle Terre, and others). The largest percentage of fruit is from Sonoma Valley, although a small quantity comes from Alexander Valley and Dry Creek. The wine exhibits an opaque purple color, and a spectacular nose of jammy cassis, lead pencil, vanillin, and spice. Thick, unctuously textured flavors ooze over the palate with extraordinary purity, ripeness, and richness. In spite of its size, the wine somehow manages not to taste heavy or overdone. This sensational Cabernet Sauvignon is one of the finest I have tasted from Sonoma. It is a candidate for 25–30 years of cellaring, although it is soft enough to be drunk young. Production was 1,200 cases, and the wine, like all of the top Arrowood reds, was bottled with neither fining nor filtration.

Increasingly, there is a bevy of exceptional Syrahs emerging from California. One of the finest is Arrowood's Syrah from the Saralee Vineyard off Slusser Road in the Russian River basin. The 1994 Syrah Saralee's Vineyard, made from yields of one ton per acre, is available in extremely limited quantities. It is one of the most riveting Syrahs I have tasted from California or anywhere for that matter. The color is an opaque inky black, and the nose offers up copious quantities of smoky chocolate, cassis, and bacon fat aromas. The wine is unbelievably rich, yet amazingly well delineated on the palate, with full body, layers of superconcentrated, unctuously textured fruit, and a finish that must be tasted to be believed. It is an exquisite Syrah that even such Rhône Valley icons as Marcel Guigal or Michel Chapoutier would be thrilled to taste. Rhône Ranger fans are advised to get in line for a bottle or two of this Syrah nectar. It should drink well for 15+ years. Everything Dick Arrowood and winemaker Michel Berthoud produce these days merits significant attention.

DAVID ARTHUR (NAPA)

1995 Meritaggio		Napa	D	90

This impressive proprietary blend (75% Cabernet Sauvignon, 8% Cabernet Franc, 7% Merlot, 5% Petit Verdot, and 5% Sangiovese) displays an opaque purple color and a sweet nose of earth, vanillin, and truffle-scented jammy black fruits. Full bodied, with low acidity, a viscous texture, and impressive purity and length, this is an exceptionally well endowed, accessible wine that can be drunk now as well as cellared for a decade. Impressive!

AU BON CLIMAT (SANTA BARBARA)

1996 Chardonnay Alban Vineyard	Edna Valley	D	87
1996 Chardonnay Estate Nuits Blanches	Santa Barbara	D	87
1996 Chardonnay Talley Vineyard Reserve	Arroya Grande Valley	D	86
1997 Pinot Noir La Bauge Au Dessus	Santa Barbara	D	(86–87)
1993 Pinot Noir Estate La Bauge au Dessus	Santa Barbara	D	88
1995 Pinot Noir La Bauge Bien Nacido Vineyard	Santa Barbara	D	85

1995	Pinot Noir Isabelle	California	E	89+
1994	Pinot Noir Isabelle	California	E	87
1994	Pinot Noir Rincon and Rosemary's	Arroyo Grande Valley	D	87
1997	Pinot Noir Rosemary's Vineyard	Santa Barbara	E	(87–90)
1993	Pinot Noir Sanford & Benedict Vineyard	Santa Ynez	D	89
1993	Pinot Noir Talley Vineyard Rosemary's	Arroyo Grande	D	93
1996	Il Podere dell Olivos Barbera Riserva Bon Natale	Santa Barbara	C	87
1995	Il Podere dell Olivos Barbera Riserva Bon Natale	Santa Barbara	C	89
1997	Il Podere dell Olivos Fiano	Central Coast	C	87
1996	Il Podere dell Olivos Refosco	Santa Barbara	C	87
1996	Il Podere dell Olivos Teroldego	Santa Barbara	C	88
1997	Il Podere dell Olivos Tocai Friulano	Central Coast	C	87

Major changes are planned for Jim Clendenen's Au Bon Climat. Clendenen, one of the most colorful winemakers in California, has purchased 70 acres and has begun to plant a tightly spaced Pinot Noir vineyard from Dijon clones. This will ensure that Clendenen is not dependent on purchased fruit.

This winery produces a numbing assortment of offerings, both under the Au Bon Climat label and the funky, quasi-Italian designation, Il Podere dell Olivos label. Given his long-standing image as being in the forefront of Pinot Noir and Chardonnay, I was surprised that Clendenen's efforts with Italian varietals seemed to taste more complete than his recent Chardonnay and Pinot Noir efforts.

Readers looking for delightfully fresh, tank-fermented and aged whites will have fun with the 1997 Tocai Friulano and 1997 Fiano. Both wines are accurate interpretations of their varietals. They are ripe, fruity, dry, exuberant offerings with plenty of character and purity. However, they require consumption over the next year or so. The freshness and liveliness of the two white wines were matched by the exuberance, richness, and impressive dimensions of the 1995 and 1996 Barbera, 1996 Refosco, and 1996 Teroldego (an unbottled sample of the 1997 Teroldego also looked immensely impressive). Both Barberas were opaquely colored, revealed spicy oak, rich, concentrated fruit, and tangy acidity that was balanced by considerable extract and richness. The 1995 Barbera is slightly more evolved and interesting, undoubtedly because of its additional year of bottle age. The black/purple-colored, full-bodied 1996 Refosco is a huge wine, with earth and black fruit aromas, a palate-staining extract level, and a chewy, robust finish. While it will not provide much elegance or finesse, it is loaded with fruit. The massive, opaque black-colored 1996 Teroldego boasts an outstanding nose of licorice, tar, prune and plumlike fruit. Dense, full bodied, and concentrated, this hulking wine fills the mouth. The unreleased 1997 Teroldego should be even bigger if the sample I tasted was an accurate indication. It is hard to predict how long any of these quasi-Italian reds will last, but 4–5 years is a conservative guess, with the Teroldego lasting longer.

For the second consecutive vintage I had mixed emotions about Au Bon Climat's Chardonnays and Pinot Noirs. I enjoyed the 1996 Chardonnay Alban Vineyard, a wine with plenty of acidity but equal proportions of tropical fruit, toast, and spice. Drink this very good to excellent Chardonnay over the next 2–3 years. The monolithic 1996 Chardonnay Reserve Talley Vineyard exhibits white peach and tropical fruit scents intermixed with vanillin, spice, and earth. Medium bodied, with crisp acidity, and a short but sufficient finish, it should drink well for 2–3 years.

Au Bon Climat's 1996 Pinot Noirs were too high in acidity and insufficiently deep to merit recommendations. The 1997s possess sweeter fruit, more ripeness, and less annoying acidity. The finest is the 1997 Pinot Noir Rosemary's Vineyard. Revealing outstanding potential, it possesses a super ruby/purple color, as well as excellent black raspberry and cherry aromatics intermixed with *pain grillé*. Medium bodied, extremely pure, and well knit, this Pinot Noir should reach full maturity in 1–2 years, and last for 8–10.

Jim Clendenen, who labels his wines "mind behind," has turned out an exquisite 1993 Talley Vineyard Rosemary's Pinot Noir that should send chills up the spines of even the most quality-conscious Burgundians. The color is a healthy dark ruby, with a smashingly intense aromatic profile that blasts from the glass. Jammy, sweet red and black fruits, spice, and smoke saturate the olfactory senses. In the mouth, the wine is all satiny smooth, velvety-textured, voluptuous richness with layers of sweet, expansive, ripe fruit, full body, beautifully integrated acidity, and no hard edges. The finish lasts for at least 30–45 seconds. This is a gorgeous Pinot Noir for drinking over the next 5–7 years. Bravo!

The 1993 Pinot Noir La Bauge au-Dessus is more compact and structured, offering a good ruby/garnet color, a spicy, animal, herb, smoky, gamelike element in the nose, juicy red fruit, and a medium- to full-bodied personality. Although fully mature, the wine's structure indicates it will age for another 4–6 years. I do not believe the 1993 equals the quality of the 1990 or 1991. Nevertheless, the 1993 is a fine wine that most Pinot powermongers would be pleased to own and drink.

The 1993 Pinot Noir Sanford & Benedict Vineyard displays a medium to dark ruby color, a vivid, herbal, sweet, berry-scented nose, a good attack with plenty of soft, ripe, velvety fruit, and a narrow finish with moderate tannin and noticeable acidity. It is an excellent Pinot Noir that should be consumed over the next 4–5 years.

In 1997, I tasted through a dozen Pinot Noir releases from Au Bon Climat, a winery I admire immensely. To put it candidly, eight of the wines were unimpressive. They were correct and generally well made, but lacking the intensity, complexity, and sumptuous expansiveness one expects from the finest Pinot Noirs. The good news is there are four wines I thought were quite good. For starters, the 1995 Pinot Noir La Bauge Bien Nacido Vineyard exhibits a healthy dark ruby color, followed by a spicy, weedy, toasty, oak-dominated nose, and medium body. There is adequate ripe fruit on the attack, after which the wine narrows out with high tannin dominating the wine's extract. This wine should improve over the next 1–2 years and, hopefully, exhibit more equilibrium between its component parts. It will last for a decade, but I do not foresee considerable complexity or charm emerging. The 1994 Rincon and Rosemary's Pinot Noir reveals a less saturated dark ruby color. The wine offers an animal, smoked meatlike nose with underbrush, black fruits, and gobs of spicy new oak. On the palate, the tannin level is surprisingly elevated, and not particularly well integrated. It possesses more expansiveness and chewiness than La Bauge (is that because it is a year older?), medium body, good fruit concentration, and a spicy, moderately tannic, short finish. It is a very good Pinot Noir that can be drunk now as well as over the next 5–7 years.

The deep ruby-colored 1994 Pinot Noir Isabelle (which comes in one of the heaviest bottles I have ever picked up) displays a sweet, smoky, round, spicy nose, plenty of new oak, as well as sweet cherry fruit, medium body, a velvety texture, some tannin, and an appealing roundness and ripeness. This is an attractive, complex, delicious Pinot for drinking over the next 5–7 years. The finest wine among these releases is the 1995 Pinot Noir Isabelle. It possesses a dark ruby color with purple hues. The nose offers up complex, sweet, black cherry and raspberry fruit intermixed with toasty, smoky oak. The wine is richer than the 1994, with medium to full body, excellent extract and purity, and a long finish. It is the sweetest, richest, and potentially most complex and long-lived of what is undeniably an uninspiring showing from one of my favorite Pinot Noir producers.

For readers' information, the other wines I tasted included wines that were too tannic, with high levels of tart, shrill acidity, and in some cases, intensely vegetal/weedy characteristics. These included the 1995 Pinot Noir Mistral Vineyard Central Coast (good aromatics, but tart, light-bodied flavors), the 1994 Pinot Noir La Bauge au-Dessus (relatively thin, weedy, vegetal, and extremely high in acidity), the 1994 Pinot Noir Central Coast (a green, vegetal-tasting wine dominated by new oak), the 1994 Pinot Noir Santa Maria (it possessed fine, smoky, herbal, animal-like aromatics marred by a tart, lean, compressed, austere personality), the 1994 Pinot Noir Paragon Vineyard (a thin, sinewy, tough-textured wine), the 1994 Pinot Noir Sanford & Benedict Vineyard (a frail, light ruby color and excessive oak dominated this fragilely constructed, malnourished wine), the 1995 Pinot Noir Sanford & Benedict Reserve (green oak and vegetal flavors, with high acidity make for an unattractive, lean style of Pinot Noir), and, lastly, the 1995 Ici-La-Bas Les Révèles (an Oregon Pinot Noir that typifies all the problems of this vintage—hollow, thin, diluted, and generally charmless).

Speaking of disappointing news concerning Au Bon Climat, four Chardonnays and one Pinot Blanc were also tasted. All of them were extremely acidic wines lacking concentration and depth. These included the 1995 Chardonnay Alban Vineyard, 1995 Chardonnay Reserve Talley, 1995 Chardonnay Le Bouge Bien Nacido, 1995 Chardonnay Sanford & Benedict Reserve, and 1995 Pinot Blanc Bien Nacido Reserve. I do not know whether it is a vintage aberration for this winery, but these offerings lack the depth, richness, and high quality I have come to expect from Au Bon Climat.

BABCOCK VINEYARDS (SANTA BARBARA)

1995 Chardonnay Grand Cuvée	Santa Barbara	D	86
1996 Sangiovese Eleven Oaks	Santa Ynez	D	86
1995 Sauvignon Blanc Eleven Oaks	Santa Ynez	C	87

Given the glut of mediocre and overpriced Sangioveses emerging from California, it is encouraging to find a Sangiovese with substance and depth. This dark ruby-colored 1996 Sangiovese exhibits a tight but promising nose of new saddle leather, strawberries, and cherries, and raspberry-flavored fruit. Structured in the mouth, but dense, medium bodied, and pure, this is a well-made, tannic wine that should improve with 1–2 years of bottle age, and last for 4–5.

The 1995 Sauvignon Blanc Eleven Oaks Vineyard is a stylish, complex, nicely extracted wine with crisp, melony fruit, medium body, subtle, well-integrated oak, and a dry, flinty, austere finish. Drink this classy, distinctive-styled Sauvignon over the next several years. The 1995 Grand Cuvée (Chardonnay) is made in a high-toned, mineral style with delicate oak, a Chablis-like austerity, crisp, lemony/orangelike fruit, and zesty acidity. It is a subtle style of Chardonnay.

BACIO DIVINO (NAPA)

1995 Proprietary Red Wine	Napa	E	94
1993 Proprietary Red Wine	Napa	D	93+

Made by the export manager for Caymus Vineyards, Klaus Janzen, the 1993, a 65% Cabernet Sauvignon, 25% Sangiovese, 10% Petite Sirah blend, is smashing! With an opaque purple color, a sweet, classy nose of well-integrated spicy new oak, and black currant, cherry, and plum fruit, this layered, full-bodied wine is loaded with extract, pure, large scaled, and lavishly wooded, but gorgeously knit together as all of its component parts are in balance. The wine remains youthfully grapey, but another 2–3 years of bottle age should bring forth an original masterpiece. Drink it over the next 15 years.

The second awesome release from this tiny winery dedicated to producing intriguing wines, the 1995 Bacio Divino (a blend of 66% Cabernet Sauvignon, 22% Sangiovese, and 12% Petite Sirah) is a formidable wine of exceptional richness, layers of flavor, and a multi-dimensional personality. The color is a deep saturated ruby/purple. The nose offers up juicy/jammy strawberry, black currant, and blackberry notes wrapped with subtle toasty oak. Full bodied, with outstanding ripeness and purity, a silky texture, and an explosive finish, this is a sumptuous example of what can be done with three grapes rarely blended together in such proportions. By the way, sentimentalists will be moved by the government warning label that reads, "contains sulphites and also some of the winemaker's heart and soul." This wine should continue to drink well for a decade.

BANNISTER (SONOMA)

1996 Chardonnay Allen Vineyard	Russian River	D	89
1995 Chardonnay Allen Vineyard	Russian River	D	90
1995 Chardonnay Porter-Bass Vineyard	Russian River	C	88
1995 Pinot Noir	Russian River	D	87
1996 Pinot Noir Floodgate Vineyard	Anderson Valley	D	90
1995 Pinot Noir Floodgate Vineyard	Anderson Valley	C	86
1996 Zinfandel	Dry Creek	C	89
1994 Zinfandel	Dry Creek	C	88
1995 Zinfandel Bradford Mountain Vineyard	Russian River	C	90
1993 Zinfandel Bradford Mountain Vineyard	Dry Creek	B	89
1994 Zinfandel Rochioli Vineyard	Russian River	C	90

This winery continues to turn out a parade of exceptional wines that emphasize excellent varietal character, outstanding purity, and vibrant personalities. The 1996 Pinot Noir Floodgate Vineyard is another example of the high potential for complex Pinot that exists in northern California's Anderson Valley. Other top California Pinot Noir specialists, for example, Siduri, Handley, and Littorai, have also exploited this up-and-coming region. Bannister's 1996 Pinot Noir Floodgate exhibits a dark ruby color, as well as a terrific nose of black fruits, earth, spice, and sweet toast. In the mouth, the wine is ripe, with a nicely layered palate, adequate acidity, exceptional purity and ripeness, and a long, silky-textured, opulent finish. This outstanding Pinot Noir is already delicious, yet promises to last for 4–5 years.

The 1996 Chardonnay Allen Vineyard (a well-known Russian River *terroir*) possesses a big, full-bodied personality that exhibits some restraint, but an overall chunky style. The wine's aromatics are reticent for a Bannister offering, but reveal notes of citrus, honey, and butter. In the mouth, there is a deep, densely packed constitution, excellent ripeness, decent acidity, and a robust mouth-feel. If more complexity emerges, this will be a candidate for an outstanding rating. It should drink well for several years.

I continue to be enthralled with the wines from Bannister. They are well-endowed, fruit-filled examples that are well balanced, pure, and surprisingly lively and elegant for their size and richness. For example, the 1995 Chardonnay Allen Vineyard (370 cases) is a full-bodied, backward wine that can be drunk now, but promises to be even better with an additional 2–6 months of bottle age. Vague hints of pineapple, vanillin, and tangerines are present in the wine's aromatics. It has considerable power and intensity, as well as remarkably fresh acidity and liveliness. The buttery, creamy texture typical of Chardonnays that have undergone full malolactic fermentation is present, but it is more subtle and restrained in this offering. The oak and tannin are also beautifully integrated.

The 1995 Pinot Noir exhibits a dark ruby color with purple nuances. Black fruits, all-spice, soy, and a touch of aged beeflike aromas intertwined with sweet oak gush from the nose of this long, deep, nicely extracted, supple wine. It remains extremely youthful, and in need of another 6–8 months of bottle age. A well-made, medium-bodied Pinot with excellent concentration, and an ethereal Pinot Noir perfume, it should be drunk over the next 5–6 years. The 1995 Zinfandel Bradford Mountain Vineyard displays a dark ruby/purple color, followed by a sexy, up-front, lush, briery, blueberry, raspberry, root beer sort of nose. The wine's attack offers sweet, round flavors with good purity, a hallmark of all the Bannister wines. Sweet glycerin, a lush texture, and a silky-smooth, alcoholic finish make for a sump-tuous, mouthfilling, yet elegant Zinfandel to drink over the next 3–4 years. The full-flavored, rich, briery, spicy 1993 Zinfandel Bradford Mountain Vineyard possesses good body, excel-lent purity, and, despite its size, a fine sense of balance. A sleeper, drink it over the next 5–6 years.

There is an alluring purity and equilibrium to everything I have tasted from Bannister. These are classic examples of what one expects of a particular varietal, without being over-weight, flabby, or excessively wooded. For example, the 1994 Zinfandel may not be the rich-est, fullest, or most extroverted, but it offers a deep ruby color, clean, pure, briery, peppery, black raspberry fruit, medium body, a sense of elegance and balance, and nicely integrated acidity. It is soft, but delineated. Drink it over the next 2–3 years.

Sadly, only 169 cases were produced of the textbook 1994 Zinfandel Rochioli Vineyard. This deep ruby-colored wine offers up an explosive nose of briery, bramblelike, wild berry fruit. The soaring aromatics are followed by a wine with no hard edges. Medium bodied, and crammed with fruit, this silky-textured, beautifully pure, luscious Zinfandel should be drunk over the next 2–3 years for its glorious display of charm and character. Delicious!

The delectable 1996 Zinfandel exhibits a dark ruby color, as well as an elegant, berry-scented nose, and lush, low-acid, medium- to full-bodied flavors with no hard edges. This is a full-flavored yet harmonious and well-balanced wine to consume over the next several years. Kudos to Marty Bannister.

A rich, ripe, tropical fruit-scented and -flavored wine, Bannister's 1995 Chardonnay from the Porter-Bass Vineyard is full bodied, with a good underpinning of acidity, layers of fruit, fine texture, and excellent purity. The high quality, spicy oak is subtle and well integrated. Drink it over the next 2 years. The delicate, light ruby-colored 1995 Pinot Noir Floodgate Vineyard exhibits moderate quantities of ripe cherry fruit, spicy oak, and earth. Made in a Côte de Beaune-like style, it offers good purity, ripeness, and overall balance. It should drink well for 3–4 years.

BARNETT VINEYARDS (NAPA)

1994 Cabernet Sauvignon Estate	Spring Mountain	D	87
1993 Cabernet Sauvignon Spring Mountain	Napa	D	87+
1994 Cabernet Sauvignon Rattlesnake Hill Estate	Spring Mountain	E	93+
1993 Cabernet Sauvignon Spring Mountain Rattlesnake Hill	Napa	E	89

The 1994 Cabernet Sauvignon Rattlesnake Hill Estate is undeniably the finest Cabernet Barnett Vineyards has produced since their marvelous 1991. The wine has an opaque purple color, as well as an earthy, raspberry liqueur-scented nose that is vibrant and intense. The wild mountain black fruit quality so common in the top wines of Spring Mountain comes across on the palate of this immensely impressive, explosively rich, superextracted wine. Patience, however, is required as the tannin is high, and most of the wine's character and richness are in the explosive finish as opposed to its attack. This should turn out to be an exquisite Cabernet Sauvignon, but only for the true connoisseur who is willing to invest in 5–7 years of cellaring. Anticipated maturity: 2003–2030. Wow! The 1994 Cabernet Sauvignon Estate offers up an enticing wild berry, currantly, and raspberry-scented nose, intertwined with aromas of smoky oak. On the palate, there is good acidity, mouth searing tannin, medium body, and excellent flavor, purity, and richness. The high tannin precludes current enjoyment, so readers should give this wine 3–4 years of cellaring. It should keep for 15–16 years.

Barnett's 1993 Cabernet Sauvignon Spring Mountain reveals the intense fragrance and perfume this vineyard routinely achieves. Copious aromas of raspberries, violets, and cranberries leap from the glass. The wine is medium bodied, pure, and elegant with less concentration than the terrific wines made in 1991 and 1992; drink it over the next 10–15 years. The 1993 Cabernet Sauvignon Spring Mountain Rattlesnake Hill offers a sweet, currantly nose, an exquisite elegance, and wonderfully rich, ripe fruit with moderate tannin in the finish. Neither as intense nor as muscular as the 1991s or 1992s, it is a stylish, complex Cabernet Sauvignon that should drink well during its first 10–15 years of life. As good as Barnett's 1993s are, I thought them to be less concentrated as well as lighter than the same wines from the 1992 and 1991 vintages.

BEAULIEU (NAPA)

1994 Cabernet Sauvignon Beau Tour	Napa	B	86
1994 Cabernet Sauvignon Clone Six Signet Collection	Napa	EE	91
1994 Cabernet Sauvignon Private Reserve Georges de Latour	Napa	E	91
1994 Cabernet Sauvignon Rutherford	Napa	C	87
1995 Zinfandel	Napa	C	88
1994 Zinfandel Signet Collection	Napa	C	82

The 1994 Cabernet Sauvignon Clone Six, a limited bottling from BV's new Signet Collection series of wines (all expensive and made in small quantities) is an immensely impressive offering. The color is a saturated dark ruby/purple. The wine, from an old clone of Cabernet Sauvignon, is a rich, full-bodied, powerful yet harmonious Cabernet with gobs of black currant fruit, a nice touch of oak, and outstanding ripeness and purity. It is also long in the mouth, with a youthful, unevolved personality. This should prove to be an impressive, long-lived Cabernet Sauvignon. Anticipated maturity: 2001–2015.

Beaulieu's dense, saturated ruby-colored 1995 Zinfandel offers up textbook aromas of jammy black fruits, pepper, and spice. Lush, with loads of glycerin and alcohol (14.5%), this medium- to full-bodied, extremely well made Zin is a treat to drink. The wine's low acidity and luscious abundance of ripe berry fruit suggests near-term drinking (over the next 3–4 years). Kudos to BV for this excellent wine. Beaulieu's 1994 Signet Collection Zinfandel reveals an underlying vegetal character, light flavor intensity, and an easygoing, medium-bodied finish. It is a good but uninspiring example of Zinfandel. Drink it over the next 3–4 years.

The 1994 Cabernet Sauvignon Beau Tour and 1994 Cabernet Sauvignon Rutherford both reveal good, rich, sweet black currant fruit, supple tannin, and medium body. The 1994 Cabernet Sauvignon Beau Tour is the finest regular Napa offering Beaulieu has made in nearly a decade. It possesses excellent fruit and ripeness, a chewy texture, and a lush mouthfeel. It should drink well for 4–6 years. The 1994 Cabernet Sauvignon Rutherford exhibits a deeper ruby/purple color, a larger-framed personality, an expansive texture, fine ripeness, and a moderately long finish. Cleanly made, with sweet fruit and ripe tannin, it should drink well for a decade. How good it is to see this renowned winery get its feet back on the ground. These are good values.

The 1994 Cabernet Sauvignon Private Reserve Georges de Latour is one of the finest efforts from Beaulieu in some time. Not since the mid-eighties has BV made a Private Reserve Cabernet with such richness and potential. The wine boasts a dark ruby/purple color, an attractive nose of sweet, toasty new oak, and ripe red and black fruits. In the mouth, there is a layered texture, full-bodied richness, excellent purity, and sweet tannin in the long finish. This wine can be drunk now as well as over the next 15–20 years. Bravo to BV!

BEHRENS AND HITCHCOCK (NAPA)

1994	Cabernet Sauvignon Cuvée Lola Unfiltered Reserve	Napa Valley	D	93
1996	Cabernet Sauvignon Inkgrade	Napa	D	92
1995	Cabernet Sauvignon Inkgrade	Napa	D	92+?
1994	Cabernet Sauvignon Inkgrade Vineyard Lot 2	Napa Valley	D	91+
1996	Cabernet Sauvignon Kenefick Ranch	Napa	D	93
1994	Cabernet Sauvignon Lot 2 Hyampom Vineyard	Trinity County	C	88
1994	Cabernet Sauvignon Staglin Vineyard	Napa Valley	D	90+
1995	Cabernet Sauvignon TLK Ranch	Napa	D	96
1997	Cuvée Lola Proprietary Red Wine	Napa	D	(90–93)
1996	Cuvée Lola Proprietary Red Wine	Napa	D	92
1997	Merlot	Napa	D	(89–92)
1997	Merlot	Oakville	D	(90–93)
1996	Merlot	Oakville	D	94
1995	Merlot Oakville	Napa Valley	D	91
1997	Ode to Picasso Proprietary Red Wine	Napa	D	(91–93)
1996	Ode to Picasso Proprietary Red Wine	Napa	E	87
1997	Petite Sirah	Napa	D	(91–93)
1995	Petite Sirah	Dry Creek Valley	D	92
1997	Zinfandel	Napa	D	(90–92)
1996	Zinfandel	Dry Creek	D	89
1995	Zinfandel	Napa	D	94

Les Behrens, a former restaurant owner, and Bob Hitchcock, a former corporate tax consultant, are quickly making a name for themselves. The reasons for their success are obvious— they produce sumptuously rich, complex red wines that are bottled with virtually no fining or filtration. Their debut vintage was 1993, and their small production has climbed from 2,500 in 1997 to 3,000 cases in 1998. Another garage winery, neither Behrens nor Hitchcock has any formal schooling in winemaking, yet they are turning out fabulous wines. After having given positive reviews to several of their offerings, I made a point of visiting the winery on my last trip to Napa. I was not unimpressed. Most of the wines see about 25% new oak, with the balance 1-year-old barrels. This winery does extremely hot fermentations to extract as much color and flavor as possible, considerable racking, and natural bottlings so the wine's character is not eviscerated.

There are several 1996s yet to be released, including two outstanding efforts, the 1996 Cabernet Sauvignon Inkgrade and 1996 Cabernet Sauvignon TLK Ranch. The 1996 Cabernet Sauvignon Inkgrade exhibits a saturated purple color, followed by a fragrant nose of exotic black fruits (blueberries and cassis). In the mouth, subtle doses of attractive floral notes, spice, and vanillin emerge. This multilayered wine possesses sweet tannin, a voluptuous texture, and superb concentration and purity. It is a sexy, opulently styled Cabernet Sauvignon to drink when released and over the next 15 years. As the wine sat in the glass, the blueberry/blackberry liqueur aspect became even more pronounced, making this wine totally disarming. The 1996 Cabernet Sauvignon Kenefick Ranch, a dense, black/purple-colored wine, is full bodied and extremely rich, with a sweet, black fruit-scented nose, intertwined with licorice and floral notes. Concentrated, full bodied, and powerful, yet beautifully balanced, this 1996 has managed to tame the vintage's rustic tannin, resulting in a wine of uncommon silkiness and equilibrium. Anticipated maturity: now–2015.

The dark plum-colored 1997 Merlot Oakville, from a parcel of vines close to Dalla Valle, Screaming Eagle, and the new Rudd Cellars, is a jammy offering with gobs of ostentatiously rich black cherry fruit intermixed with smoke and spicy oak. It hits the palate with generous amounts of glycerin, and thick, juicy fruit. This succulently textured wine is a thrill to drink. It should provide Merlot lovers with plenty of excitement. Moreover, it should continue to drink well for a decade. Named after a long deceased cat, the 1997 Ode to Picasso (a blend of 80% Syrah and 20% Merlot) is far superior to the very good 1996. It reveals the winery's telltale aromas of blackberries, blueberries, and cassis, as well as terrific fruit intensity, a layered texture, and huge flavors. Although built like a fortress, it possesses glorious levels of fruit and plenty of power. Accessible enough to be drunk young, it will keep for 12–15+ years. The 1997 Cuvée Lola (a blend of 75% Cabernet Franc and 25% Cabernet Sauvignon and Merlot) is one of the finest Cabernet Franc-dominated wines I have tasted from northern California, ranking alongside the superb efforts turned in by Dalla Valle, La Jota, and Pride Mountain. The wine exhibits a cedary, cigar box, black currant, and raspberry-scented nose, superb ripeness, rich, fleshy, low-acid flavors, and a rich but not weighty midpalate and finish. This wine will be drinkable upon release, and keep for 12+ years.

Readers looking for blockbuster-sized, bigger than life wines should check out Behrens and Hitchcock's 1997 Petite Sirah. It boasts a thick, purple color, as well as a huge nose of minerals, Asian spices, smoke, and black fruits. Extremely powerful, full bodied, and ripe, with a jammy yet well-delineated personality, this monster Petite Sirah will benefit from 4–5 years of cellaring and keep for 2 decades or more. Readers may remember that I immensely enjoyed the Zinfandels produced by Behrens and Hitchcock (the 1995 was fabulous). Their fruit comes from a 30-year-old, head-pruned vineyard. The fine 1997 Zinfandel offers copious quantities of black cherry, briery, raspberry, and peppery fruit. The wine displays loads of glycerin, medium to full body, a lush, round, generous mouthfeel, and heady alcohol in the lusty finish. It is a wine to drink over the next 3–4 years.

My notes also indicate I tasted a 1997 Merlot Napa, which will probably be bottled separately rather than blended with Oakville Merlot. This example revealed a more chocolatey, coffee, crème brûlée character than the Oakville cuvée, in addition to full body, outstanding richness of fruit, and a spicy, dense, concentrated finish. More monolithic than the Oakville but potentially outstanding, it is another superb offering from this small winery. Readers are well advised to get on Behrens and Hitchcock's mailing list as a large percentage of their small production is sold via this route.

The fabulously rich 1995 Zinfandel Napa (a blend of 85% Zinfandel, 12% Petite Sirah, and, lo and behold, 3% Viognier) is one of the finest I have tasted. The saturated opaque purple color is followed by a knockout nose of blackberry liqueur intermingled with raspberries, pepper, and spice. The wine is explosively rich, with loads of glycerin, layers of concentrated, jammy fruit, full body, and a heady finish. This is a hedonistic, gloriously perfumed, and decadently concentrated wine to drink over the next 3–4 years.

The most expensive wine in the Behrens and Hitchcock portfolio performed the least well. The dark ruby/purple-colored 1996 Ode to Picasso is a blend of Syrah, Cabernet Sauvignon, Merlot, and Viognier. The wine's bouquet is dominated by the Viognier. In fact, that component is not yet integrated into the wine's overall personality, which kept my score lower than it may eventually become. The honeysuckle, apricot, blackberry, and currant-scented nose is followed by a wine with good ripeness, a round, gentle, graceful entry, sweet ripe fruit, and a spicy, moderately long finish. Even in the flavor profile, the Viognier appears to have the upper hand, dominating the varietal characteristics of Merlot, Cabernet Sauvignon, and Syrah. Although very good, the question is, will it become better, and will the Viognier become more meshed in the wine's overall composition? In any event, this wine should drink well for 7–8 years.

What a sumptuous, knockout, gloriously rich, layered, and juicy Merlot Behrens and Hitchcock have produced. The 1996 Merlot Oakville possesses a dark ruby/purple color, dazzling, sweet, black cherry liqueur-like notes in its aromatics, and judicious notes of spicy oak. The wine's purity and multiple layers of texture that combine thrilling levels of fruit, glycerin, and extract into a seamless, voluptuously endowed wine are to be both enjoyed and admired. Diaphanous, this wine can be peeled one layer at a time given its thick, rich, high-rise effect on the palate. The fruit is superripe and well balanced with copious sweet tannin and low acidity. This is a full-bodied, sensationally endowed Merlot to drink over the next decade. Nearly as impressive is the 1996 Cuvée Lola, a proprietary red wine made from a Bordeaux-like blend of Cabernet Sauvignon, Merlot, and Cabernet Franc. This wine is characterized by a saturated ruby/purple color, layers of flavor, outstanding purity, and black currant, plum, and cassis flavors. The wine is rich but avoids any sense of heaviness or roughness. The wine's structural components—tannin, acidity, and alcohol—are all meshed together into a silky format. This offering can be drunk now or cellared for 12–15 years.

The two formidable Cabernet Sauvignons are among the superstars of the 1995 vintage. I do have one reservation with respect to the 1995 Cabernet Sauvignon Inkgrade—some leesy, mercaptan notes in the nose are at first disconcerting. However, they quickly blow off as the wine is exposed to air. Once past that, the wine's opaque purple color and blueberry and exotic floral notes (orchids) are impressive. Ripe and dense, with fabulous flavor concentration, and a long, multilayered, textured personality that caresses and saturates the palate with copious quantities of fruit, glycerin, and richness, this is a large-scaled but beautifully balanced Cabernet Sauvignon that should be at its best with another 2–3 years of cellaring, and last for 15 or more years. The 1995 Cabernet Sauvignon TLK Ranch is a powerhouse but exhibits remarkable symmetry for its massive size. The color is saturated purple, and the wine possesses fabulously sweet blackberry, blueberry, and cassis aromas nicely dosed with subtle, toasty oak. Thick, juicy, and full bodied, with outstanding purity, and admirably integrated acidity, tannin, and alcohol, this stunningly proportioned Cabernet Sauvignon possesses sweet tannin and low acidity, giving it up-front appeal. However, all the component parts are present for 15–20 years of cellaring.

The opaque black/purple-colored 1995 Merlot Oakville (100 cases) possesses an expressive blueberry-scented nose that is a perfect match for its sumptuous personality. The wine exhibits superb richness, medium to full body, a natural texture, with sensual levels of fruit, glycerin, and extract. It is a full-bodied, seamlessly styled Merlot that should drink well for a decade. This exquisite wine merits the attention of serious wine drinkers.

Except for the Trinity County Cabernet Sauvignon, the differences between the Cabernet Sauvignon cuvées are negligible. In fact, the wines could be blended together with no loss of character (I actually did such a blending). Nevertheless, I would be happy to own any of these wines. If Behrens and Hitchcock want to continue to offer small quantities of each cuvée, so be it—they are superb Cabernets. The only nonoutstanding example is the excellent 1994 Cabernet Sauvignon Lot 2 Hyampom Vineyard from northern Trinity County, not far from the Oregon border. I do not believe I have ever tasted a Cabernet Sauvignon from this region. The wine possesses a dark purple color, a spicy, sweet, black currant and blueberry-scented nose, medium body, a multiple-layered texture, and a round, generous finish. It should drink well for 12 or more years. The 1994 Cabernet Sauvignon Inkgrade Vineyard Lot 2 offers explosive levels of black fruits. The wine is full bodied, powerful, and flawlessly made, with sensational concentration, and a character not unlike the other Cabernets but seemingly more evolved aromatically. Anticipated maturity: 2000–2020. The 1994 Cabernet Sauvignon Cuvée Lola Unfiltered Reserve is singing slightly louder than its siblings. The blueberries, cassis, vanillin/*pain grillé*, high extract, full body, and silky texture are all present. This cuvée possesses even more weight and presence on the palate. If the Cuvée Lola is the most dramatic among this group of impressive wines, the 1994 Cabernet Sauvignon Staglin Vineyard is the most backward. This wine displays all the potential to be superb—natural texture, great ripeness, impeccable purity, full body, and layers of blueberry and cassis fruit. The tannin is more pronounced, however; thus this is a wine to lay away for 5–6 years, and drink over the following 10–15.

Lovers of the underrated Petite Sirah varietal will adore Behrens and Hitchcock's 1995, which is close in quality to the extraordinary Petite Sirahs from Ridge's York Creek and Turley's Hayne Vineyard. Boasting 15.2% alcohol, this dense black/purple-colored wine is very full bodied, extremely powerful, has low acidity, a blackberry, blueberry, cassis character, some pepper, and extraordinary viscosity and intensity. This huge, mouth-coating style of Petite Sirah is not for everybody, but for fans of this wine, it is a knockout. It should drink well for 2 decades.

Made from 85% Zinfandel, 10% Petite Sirah, and 5% Carignan, the dark ruby-colored, medium- to full-bodied 1996 Dry Creek Zinfandel reveals copious quantities of sweet black cherry fruit intermingled with spice, pepper, and dusty notes. The wine is classy and powerful yet elegant, particularly for a Dry Creek Zinfandel. Purely made and stylish, it is ideal for consuming over the next 3–4 years.

BELVEDERE WINE COMPANY (SONOMA)

1996	Chardonnay	Alexander Valley	B	87
1995	Chardonnay	Alexander Valley	B	86
1996	Chardonnay	Russian River Valley	C	87
1995	Chardonnay	Russian River Valley	B	88
1994	Zinfandel	Dry Creek	B	85+

This winery has turned out an attractive, tropical fruit, roasted nut, smoky-scented 1996 Sonoma Chardonnay with copious quantities of fruit, medium body, and a good texture. Drink it over the next year. The 1996 Chardonnay Russian River is a more buttery wine, with toasty notes in the background. Possessing rich tropical fruit, medium to full body, and a long, well-delineated finish, it is more ambitious, but no more tasty than the Sonoma cuvée.

Another fine effort from this winery, the well-priced, fleshy, layered 1995 Russian River Chardonnay displays plenty of honeyed pineapple and other tropical fruits, medium to full body, excellent cleanliness, and a chewy, pure, attractive finish. Drink it over the next year. The 1995 Alexander Valley Chardonnay is a fleshy, copiously fruity wine without much complexity, but with a satisfying, mouth-filling exuberance and ripeness. Drink it over the next year.

The barrel sample I tasted of Belvedere's 1994 Zinfandel appeared to be made in an easy-going, straightforward, richly fruity style that will have many fans. Neither complicated nor showy, it will offer good purity and ripeness if drunk over the next several years.

BENZIGER WINERY (SONOMA)

1994 Cabernet Sauvignon Reserve	Sonoma Mountain	D	86
1996 Chardonnay Reserve	Carneros	D	87
1996 Chardonnay Reserve Yamakawa Vineyard	Carneros	D	86
1995 Fumé Blanc	Sonoma	B	88
1995 Imagery Series Cabernet Franc	Alexander Valley	D	90
1994 Imagery Series Cabernet Franc	Alexander Valley	C	88
1993 Imagery Series Cabernet Franc	Alexander Valley	C	88
1995 Imagery Series Malbec	Alexander Valley	D	85
1995 Imagery Series Malbec Blue Rock Vineyard	Alexander Valley	C	88
1993 Imagery Series Petit Verdot	Alexander Valley	C	88+
1994 Imagery Series Petite Sirah	Paso Robles	C	90
1993 Imagery Series Petite Syrah Shell Creek Vineyard	Paso Robles	C	89+
1995 Imagery Series Pinot Blanc	North Coast	C	87
1993 Imagery Series Sangiovese	Dry Creek Valley	C	87
1994 Imagery Series Syrah	Central Coast	C	88
1996 Imagery Series Viognier	Alexander Valley	D	88
1995 Imagery Series White Burgundy	North Coast	C	90
1995 Merlot Reserve	Sonoma County	D	86
1994 Tribute Proprietary Red Wine	Sonoma Mountain	D	87
1993 Tribute Red Table Wine	Sonoma Mountain	C	87
1996 Zinfandel	Sonoma	C	78
1995 Zinfandel	Sonoma	C	88
1994 Zinfandel	Sonoma	C	88+
1993 Zinfandel	Sonoma	C	89

This family-owned winery continues to turn out an attractive portfolio of well-made wines. Moreover, given the unbelievable pricing strategy being employed by many other California wineries, they remain sensibly priced. The 1995 Fumé Blanc is a delicious melon and honey-scented and -flavored wine with a soft, round, succulent, medium-bodied texture, and ripe, pure fruit. It should drink well for another year.

Benziger's 1995 Pinot Blanc Imagery Series is a tangerine and honey-scented and -flavored wine with an opulent texture, and plenty of flesh, ripeness, and fruit. This is an uncomplicated but gloriously fruity wine to drink over the next year. Even better is the 1995 White Burgundy Imagery Series, a blend of Chardonnay, Pinot Blanc, and Pinot Meunier. Honeysuckle and ripe tropical fruit aromas jump from the glass of this medium- to full-bodied, luscious, in-your-face wine. Low acidity, a viscous texture, and outstanding purity, along with copious quantities of fruit make for a hedonistic glassful of white wine. However, do not push your luck and cellar it; this wine requires drinking over the next 8–12 months.

The 1994 Imagery Series red wine offerings scored well in my peer group tastings. The 1994 Syrah reveals a healthy dark ruby/purple color, plenty of toasty new oak in its peppery nose, and abundant quantities of sweet black currant flavors. This medium- to full-bodied, lush Syrah is ideal for drinking over the next 5–8 years. While I did not detect its presence, the wine includes 4% Viognier in the blend. Benziger's black/purple-colored 1994 Petite Sirah Imagery Series is a monstrous-sized wine displaying huge, roasted herb, smoky black currant fruit with a touch of tar. Full bodied, moderately tannic, and extremely concentrated, this wine is best aged for 1–3 years, and drunk over the subsequent 10–15. Another attractive wine, the 1994 Cabernet Franc Imagery Series exhibits a dark ruby color, followed by sweet, complex, red and black currant aromas nicely infused with oak and a whiff of menthol. Spicy, medium bodied, with excellent depth, adequate acidity, but little tannin, this stylish, well-made Cabernet Franc should drink well for the next 5–7 years.

The 1993 Imagery Series red wine offerings include a 1993 Cabernet Franc from the Blue Rock Vineyard in Alexander Valley. It displays the elegant, red and black fruit/menthol character of this complex varietal. The wine is not heavy, tannic, or full bodied, but it does offer intense fruit, a wonderful sweet midpalate, and a soft, lingering finish. It is ideal for drinking over the next 7–8 years. The 1993 Sangiovese, from the Larga Vista Vineyard in Dry Creek, is one of the finest Sangiovese wines made in California. It reveals attractive new saddle leather and strawberry/cherrylike aromas, excellent richness, medium body, and a ripe, long finish with no intrusive acidity or tannin. Benziger is especially proud of its Petit Verdot. The 1993, from the Blue Rock Vineyard in Alexander Valley, possesses an intense, sweet vanillin, blueberry/cassis-scented nose, a fabulous, saturated, purple color, great fruit and ripeness, medium to full body, and plenty of muscle, extract, and intensity, without the excessive tannin of this varietal. It should drink well for 15–20 years. Another wine that merits consideration is the 1993 Petite Sirah from the Shell Creek Vineyard in Paso Robles. It exhibits an opaque black/purple color, and a sweet nose of ripe black fruits intermixed with scents of earth and pepper. Full bodied, rich, and chewy, this lusty, big, backward Petite Sirah will age well for 15+ years.

The 1993 Tribute (a blend of Cabernet Sauvignon, Cabernet Franc, Merlot, and Petit Verdot) possesses sufficient amounts of toasty, spicy oak, fine richness, a Bordeaux-like austerity, medium body, and moderate tannin in the finish. This wine will benefit from another 1–2 years of cellaring; it will last for 10–12 years.

An excellent Viognier, Benziger's 1996 Imagery Series possesses gobs of citrusy, peach, and apricot aromas and flavors, medium body, beautiful fruit and purity, and has enough acidity to provide definition. Made from Alexander Valley's River Ranch and Blue Rock vineyards, this delicious Viognier is ideal for drinking over the next year.

Produced from grapes grown in the Blue Rock Vineyard in Alexander Valley, Benziger's 1995 Imagery Series Cabernet Franc provides a seductive, silky mouthful of wine. This deep ruby-colored Cabernet Franc offers up an intense, provocative nose of spice, fruit cake, cedar, and black fruits. On the palate, the wine is round, sweet, elegant, and soft. If it's possible for Cabernet Franc to behave as a sumptuous Pinot Noir, this one does. The wine is not likely to make old bones, nor will it please those who like the feel of rough tannin grinding across the palate, but this is a delicious, stylish, complex, silky-smooth Cabernet Franc to drink over the next 3–4 years. The 1995 Imagery Series Malbec, which is also produced from Alexander Valley's Blue Rock Vineyard, will not make California's premier Malbec producer (Dick Arrowood of Arrowood Winery) jealous, but it is a good effort. The nose possesses sweet red currant and raspberry scents, as well as a touch of herbs and earth. This soft, grapey Malbec is a pleasant, plump yet refreshing wine that should drink well for 3–4 years. In contrast to the precociousness of the Malbec and Cabernet Franc, the dark ruby/purple-colored 1994 A Tribute is dense, tannic, and backward. There is plenty of wood tannin, spice, and vanilla, along with attractively ripe black currant fruit. Medium to full bodied but tight, this is a wine to lay away for another 1–2 years. It should evolve for a decade, possibly longer.

The medium ruby-colored 1996 Zinfandel offers up modest berry fruit, pepper, and spice aromas. In the mouth, the wine narrows, exhibiting shrill acidity, and a hard, austere, angular finish. It should be drunk up.

An excellent Zinfandel, Benziger's dark ruby/purple-colored 1995 displays textbook aromas of pepper, spice, and black cherries. Deeply etched, full-bodied flavors possess excellent purity, and plenty of varietal character. This low-acid, plush, fleshy wine boasts 14.5% alcohol; it can be drunk now and over the next 4–5 years. Benziger's 1994 Zinfandel had not been bottled when I tasted it, hence the range of scores. It exhibits a dark ruby/purple color, as well as a deep, spicy, lavishly oaked nose. The attack offers gobs of ripe fruit, noticeable American oak notes, and a rich, medium-bodied, spicy style. There is plenty of Zinfandel varietal character displayed in this in-your-face Zin. Drink it over the next 5–6 years. Benziger's 1993 Zinfandel is a delicious, full-bodied, exuberantly fruity Zinfandel for drinking over the next 7–8 years. This multilayered, concentrated wine exhibits up-front, precocious, peppery, and berry fruit, medium to full body, a nice touch of American oak, and a heady, velvety-textured finish. Don't miss this gorgeous Zinfandel!

I enjoyed Benziger's 1996 Chardonnay Reserve. Packaged in a heavy, thick bottle, this fruit-driven wine exhibits copious quantities of citrusy, tropical fruit characteristics nicely framed by toasty oak. The medium-bodied, pure finish adds to the wine's broad appeal. Drink it over the next year. The 1996 Chardonnay Reserve Yamakawa Vineyard reveals a more evolved color, as well as more honeyed, buttery, roasted nutlike aromatics, crisp acidity, and a chunky, fleshy feel in the mouth. Although not as defined or as complex as the previous wine, it is a flavorful Chardonnay that should drink well for the next 12 months.

While I was somewhat disappointed with the 1995 Tribute and 1995 Cabernet Sauvignon Reserve Ash Creek Vineyard, I was pleased with the following two wines. Benziger's 1995 Merlot Reserve exhibits a deep, saturated ruby/purple color, a big, sweet, chocolatey, cherry-scented nose, tart acidity, fresh, lively fruit, medium body, and a clipped finish. It should drink well for 4–5 years. The 1994 Cabernet Sauvignon Reserve displays a more saturated dark ruby/purple color. More closed, tannic, and obviously oaky, this structured, deep wine will benefit from another 1–3 years of cellaring. It should keep for a decade.

Another attractive Malbec from California, the medium-bodied 1995 Imagery Series Blue Rock Vineyard offers a captivating nose of black raspberry fruit, cream, and spicy new oak. In the mouth, there is intense fruit and excellent purity, yet modest weight and soft tannin. An elegant, finesse-styled Malbec, the wine's charm and pleasure is imparted largely by the lovely fruit character.

BERINGER (NAPA)

1997	Alluvium Proprietary Red	Knight's Valley	C	(85–87)
1996	Alluvium Proprietary Red	Knight's Valley	D	88+
1995	Alluvium Proprietary Red	Knight's Valley	D	89
1994	Alluvium Proprietary Red	Knight's Valley	D	89
1993	Alluvium Proprietary Red	Knight's Valley	D	90
1997	Alluvium Proprietary White	Knight's Valley	C	88
1996	Alluvium White	Knight's Valley	C	89

1995	Alluvium White	Knight's Valley	C	88
1997	Cabernet Franc	Howell Mountain	C	(87–90)
1996	Cabernet Franc	Howell Mountain	C	89
1995	Cabernet Franc	Howell Mountain	C	90
1995	Cabernet Franc Terre Rouge	Howell Mountain	C	91
1994	Cabernet Franc Terre Rouge	Howell Mountain	C	91
1997	Cabernet Sauvignon	Knight's Valley	C	(86–87)
1996	Cabernet Sauvignon	Knight's Valley	C	88
1995	Cabernet Sauvignon	Knight's Valley	D	87
1994	Cabernet Sauvignon	Knight's Valley	C	89
1993	Cabernet Sauvignon	Knight's Valley	C	90
1997	Cabernet Sauvignon Bancroft Ranch	Howell Mountain	D	(92–95)
1996	Cabernet Sauvignon Bancroft Ranch	Howell Mountain	D	92+
1995	Cabernet Sauvignon Bancroft Ranch	Howell Mountain	EE	94
1994	Cabernet Sauvignon Bancroft Ranch	Howell Mountain	EE	92
1997	Cabernet Sauvignon Chabot Vineyard	Napa	EE	(91–94)
1996	Cabernet Sauvignon Chabot Vineyard	Napa	EE	93+
1995	Cabernet Sauvignon Chabot Vineyard	Napa	E	92+
1994	Cabernet Sauvignon Chabot Vineyard	Napa	E	93+
1993	Cabernet Sauvignon Chabot Vineyard	Napa	E	90?
1997	Cabernet Sauvignon Marston Vineyard	Spring Mountain	E	(90–92)
1996	Cabernet Sauvignon Marston Vineyard	Spring Mountain	E	89
1994	Cabernet Sauvignon Marston Vineyard	Spring Mountain	EE	95
1997	Cabernet Sauvignon Private Reserve	Napa	E	(92–94)
1996	Cabernet Sauvignon Private Reserve	Napa	E	91+
1995	Cabernet Sauvignon Private Reserve	Napa	E	93
1994	Cabernet Sauvignon Private Reserve	Napa	E	94
1993	Cabernet Sauvignon Private Reserve	Napa	E	92+
1997	Cabernet Sauvignon St. Helena Vineyard	St. Helena	E	(90–94)
1996	Cabernet Sauvignon St. Helena Vineyard	St. Helena	E	88
1995	Cabernet Sauvignon St. Helena Vineyard	St. Helena	E	93
1997	Cabernet Sauvignon State Lane Vineyard	Napa	E	(90–92)
1996	Cabernet Sauvignon State Lane Vineyard	Napa	E	90

1995 Cabernet Sauvignon State Lane Vineyard	Napa	E	90
1996 Cabernet Sauvignon Terre Rouge	Howell Mountain	E	90
1995 Cabernet Sauvignon Terre Rouge	Howell Mountain	EE	90
1994 Cabernet Sauvignon Terre Rouge	Howell Mountain	EE	88
1997 Cabernet Sauvignon Tré Colline Vineyard	Howell Mountain	EE	(90–93)
1996 Cabernet Sauvignon Tré Colline Vineyard	Howell Mountain	EE	88+
1995 Cabernet Sauvignon Tré Colline Vineyard	Howell Mountain	EE	90
1997 Chardonnay	Napa	C	87
1996 Chardonnay	Napa	C	87
1995 Chardonnay	Napa	C	88
1997 Chardonnay Private Reserve	Napa	D	91
1996 Chardonnay Private Reserve	Napa	D	92
1995 Chardonnay Private Reserve	Napa	D	92
1994 Chardonnay Private Reserve	Napa	C	93
1997 Chardonnay Sbragia Limited Release	Napa	D	95
1996 Chardonnay Sbragia Limited Release	Napa	D	93
1995 Chardonnay Sbragia Limited Release	Napa	D	96
1994 Chardonnay Sbragia Limited Release	Napa	D	96
1994 Meritage Red	Knight's Valley	D	91
1993 Meritage Red	Knight's Valley	D	90
1997 Merlot Bancroft Ranch	Howell Mountain	D	(93–96)
1996 Merlot Bancroft Ranch	Howell Mountain	D	93
1995 Merlot Bancroft Ranch	Howell Mountain	E	91
1994 Merlot Bancroft Ranch	Howell Mountain	D	92+
1993 Merlot Bancroft Ranch	Howell Mountain	D	93+
1995 Nightingale	Napa	D	92
1996 Petite Syrah Hayne Vineyard	Napa	D	93
1997 Petite Syrah Marston Vineyard	Napa	D	(92–94)
1996 Pinot Noir	North Coast	C	87
1996 Pinot Noir Stanly Vineyard	Napa	D	90+
1995 Pinot Noir Stanly Vineyard	Napa	D	90
1994 Pinot Noir Stanly Vineyard	Napa	D	85
1993 Pinot Noir Stanly Ranch	Carneros	D	81?

1994 Riesling Special Select Late Harvest	Napa	D	94
1997 Sangiovese	North Coast	C	85
1995 Sangiovese	Knight's Valley	D	87
1994 Sangiovese	Knight's Valley	C	87
1997 Sauvignon Blanc	Napa	B	85
1995 Sauvignon Blanc	Napa	B	85
1995 Syrah	Napa	C	91
1997 Syrah Marston Vineyard	Spring Mountain	D	(90–92)
1997 Viognier	Napa	C	86
1996 Viognier	Napa	D	90
1995 Viognier	Carneros	C	90

Beringer is an extraordinarily well run winery that continues, in spite of its huge size, to behave as if it were a tiny boutique operation bent on producing the world's finest wines. Much can be gleaned about a company and its products from the people working behind the scenes. In the case of Beringer, everyone with whom I have ever had any contact has been the consummate professional, from their team of talented winemakers, led by Ed Sbragia, to their knowledgeable public relations team, spearheaded by Tor Kenward. Personal accolades aside, tasting is always the final arbiter of quality, and on that basis, let me proceed with some exciting notes.

The white wine releases include the 1997 Sauvignon Blanc, a textbook Sauvignon (20% Semillon is added to the blend) that sees a touch of new oak. A weighty, rich example, it offers plenty of buttery, melony fruit, and a spicy finish. It should drink well for several years. The 1997 Alluvium Proprietary White is an intriguing blend of 50% Semillon, 40% Sauvignon Blanc, 8% Chardonnay, and 2% Viognier. It is 100% barrel-fermented, and put completely through malolactic. A Burgundian-styled white, it possesses a leesy, smoky, honeysuckle-scented nose, an excellent, rich, creamy texture, and roasted nut flavors intermixed with fruit and glycerin. It should drink well for 2–3 years.

Beringer's Chardonnays are all good, including their value-priced 1997 Chardonnay Napa. This cuvée sees about 20% new oak and is completely barrel-fermented. Most of the fruit comes from southern portions of Napa, including Yountville and Carneros. The 1997 exhibits citrusy tropical fruit, a fleshy texture, good underlying acidity, and a fragrant bouquet. More aromatic than other vintages, it is also elegant and flavorful. Enjoy it over the next several years. The flagship Beringer Chardonnays are the Private Reserve and Sbragia Limited Release. The 1997 Chardonnay Private Reserve (20,000 cases) was given complete barrel fermentation as well as malolactic, and aged in small barrels, of which 85% were new. One of California's finest Chardonnays, this effort has consistently been an outstanding wine. The fact that Beringer is able to make such a high quantity at this quality level is admirable. The 1997 tips the scales at 13.4% alcohol, which is buried beneath the smoky, toasty, rich, buttery, tropical fruit. The wine displays leesy, roasted nut characteristics, as well as a boatload of glycerin in its long finish. It should drink well for 2–4 years. There are 1,000 cases of the 1997 Chardonnay Sbragia Limited Release. Given 100% new French oak aging, it represents Chardonnay at its richest and most intense. When I recently served my last bottle of 1994 Sbragia Limited Release, my guests went ga-ga over the wine's intensity and hedonistic qualities. The 1997 offers a knockout nose of buttered corn, and ripe citrus fruit intermixed with roasted nuts and toast scents. Unctuously textured, full bodied, and powerful, this is a smashingly rich, lavishly endowed, exotic, ostentatious Chardonnay during its first 4–5 years of life.

Another dry white I tasted from Beringer, the 1997 Viognier, is a competent but uninspiring effort. It reveals leafy, honeysucklelike fruit, medium body, but not much complexity or delineation. It should be consumed over the next 6–12 months.

I was impressed with the 1996 Viognier. There are not many outstanding Viogniers produced in California, but Beringer's 1996, which was put through full malolactic fermentation, is produced from grapes grown in Hudson Ranch, the well-known Carneros vineyard. This wine, fermented in used oak casks, reveals an extravagant apricot and tropical fruit-scented nose, followed by fat, ripe, expansive flavors with barely enough acidity to provide vibrancy. It is undoubtedly a wine to drink over the next year for its ostentatious display of fruit and its succulent, lush texture.

The exotic 1996 Alluvium is an intriguing blend of 45% Semillon, 45% Sauvignon, 9% Chardonnay, and 1% Viognier. The wine is completely barrel fermented, followed by aging in 50% new oak casks. The oak appears to frame this sizeable, but surprisingly subtle, rich, well-defined wine. Put through malolactic fermentation to give the wine a creamier texture, the 1996 exhibits copious amounts of honeyed melon, fig, and smoky flavors accompanied by excellent richness and length. This complex wine should drink well for 1–2 years. The 1995 Alluvium white wine (a blend of Sauvignon Blanc and Semillon) has been barrel fermented and dosed with a tiny percentage of Viognier (4%). It is an excellent, rich, elegant, spicy wine displaying creamy-textured ripe fruit, medium body, and a judicious touch of toasty oak (50% new French oak barrels were used for the aging of this wine). A wine of personality and character, it will offer ideal drinking over the next several years. A small quantity of pure Sauvignon is produced. The crisp, melony 1995 Sauvignon Blanc is made in a dry, austere, medium-bodied style, with adequate quantities of melony fruit. Drink it over the next year. In 1995, Beringer's production of Viognier was increased to 600 cases, made largely from fruit grown in the highly esteemed Hudson Ranch Vineyard in Carneros. The 1995 Viognier is a medium- to full-bodied, honeysuckle and apricot-scented wine with rich fruit, an unctuous texture, and enough acidity to provide vibrancy and freshness. Given its fragrant, penetrating bouquet, fatness, and richness, this is a wine to drink over the next 1–2 years.

The 1995 Chardonnay Napa, aged 8 months in small oak casks, possesses ripe, buttery, tropical fruit, good acidity, medium to full body, surprising opulence and intensity for a wine in this price range, and a clean, refreshing finish. It should drink well for several years. Both the 1995 Chardonnay Private Reserve and 1995 Chardonnay Sbragia Limited Release are wines that take the intensity of Chardonnay to the maximum. The 1995 Chardonnay Private Reserve, coming on the heels of a succession of wonderful wines produced under this label, is a 100% malolactic Chardonnay that is aged in 85% new French oak casks for 9 months. Although, 10,000 cases are made, the entire production seems to disappear from the marketplace within 24 hours of its release—an amazing testament to the wine's quality and popularity. While it does not pretend to be a French white Burgundy, it offers a big, smoky, hazelnut, buttery bouquet, gorgeous up-front flavors, superb concentration, and admirable glycerin and extract. This is a meaty, mouth-filling, lush, and lusty Chardonnay to drink during its first 1–2 years of life. The 1,500 cases of 1994 Chardonnay Private Reserve will not last long on retailers' shelves as they are destined to disappear into the mouths of serious Chardonnay freaks. Beringer has fine-tuned this wine, which ten years ago was among the most oaky California Chardonnays, without compromising its intensity and unctuous texture. The 1994 possesses good underlying acidity and structure, but its finest attributes are the ripeness and thick, honeyed, viscous, mouthfilling, spring flower blossom, honeyed apple, and peach/apricotlike flavors presented in a full-bodied style. It should drink well for 2–3 years.

It is going to be the rare case where a 1996 Napa Chardonnay turns out to be better than its 1995 counterpart. The latter vintage is undoubtedly one of the classic vintages for California Chardonnay, while 1996 is merely good. Beringer's three cuvées of 1996 Chardonnay are all extremely well made. For a reasonably good value, the 1996 Chardonnay Napa, aged 8 months in small oak casks and put through a 100% malolactic fermentation, is a lush, tasty, buttery, tropical fruit-driven wine with medium body, round, generous fruit, and excellent purity and ripeness. Keep in mind that Beringer produces over 100,000 cases, so it is widely available. The 1996 Chardonnay Private Reserve follows the extraordinary 1995 and 1994. Production has doubled to nearly 20,000 cases of this lush, full-bodied wine. The 1996 is more structured than previous vintages, but I do not think it will last any longer. The wine is given a full malolactic fermentation, with 85% of the cuvée aged in new oak casks. The result is a smoky, medium- to full-bodied, honeyed Chardonnay with copious quantities of ripe, buttery tropical fruit. The *sur-lie* aging, as well as the stirring of the lees gives this wine a Burgundian-like, smoky, hazelnut complexity. This deep, well-endowed Chardonnay should drink well for 2–3 years.

The most lavishly rich Beringer Chardonnay is always the Sbragia Limited Release. The 1996 (production is inching up to nearly 2,000 cases) is the most tightly knit wine yet produced by Beringer's multigifted winemaker, Ed Sbragia. This 100% new French oak-aged, full malolactic, blockbuster Chardonnay takes hedonism to a rarely encountered level. While the 1996 is extremely substantial and full bodied, it does appear to possess more delineation and finesse than some of the overwhelming examples of the past. This is a buttery, tropical fruit, smoky style of Chardonnay reminiscent of the old-style Chalone Chardonnays from the late seventies and early eighties. The 1996 displays good acidity, plenty of power and punch, and lavish richness and length. While it offers a mouthful of unbridled Chardonnay fruit, the wine displays a surprising number of nuances.

The Chardonnay Sbragia Limited Release is essentially a selection of the best barrels of Chardonnay in the Beringer cellars. In 1995, just over 500 cases were produced, most of which was sold directly at the winery. This 100% new French oak, full malolactic, blockbuster style of Chardonnay takes hedonism to the maximum. It exemplifies the definition of "opulence, lavish richness, and ostentatiousness." Despite its huge, rich, viscous style, and massive body and extract, the wine has remarkable balance and purity. It appears this wine requires immediate drinking, but vintages back through 1991 have aged far better than I would have guessed. The 1994 Chardonnay Sbragia Limited Release is an extraordinary success. The wine's primary vineyard source is the Gamble Ranch. It is aged in 100% new oak, which would dominate most Chardonnays, but not this massively endowed, oily, honeyed wine that offers huge amounts of flavor. It is about as concentrated as any Chardonnay in the world, and although more consistent, it is reminiscent of the old-style Chalone Chardonnays, such as the monumental 1980 and 1981, the likes of which Chalone has not made since. The 1994 Sbragia Limited Release should drink well for 2–3 years. The last bottle of 1991 I had (in November 1994) made me look like a stooge for my initial comment that it should be drunk immediately. It had not lost a bit of fruit and was going strong after three years. If you have never tasted the intensity of a great Domaine de la Romanée-Conti Montrachet, check out the Sbragia Limited Release, for about $33 a bottle as opposed to about $600 for a bottle of the DRC Montrachet.

As for the red wines, I am largely unconvinced by Beringer's Pinot Noirs. Progress has been made (the 1996s are very good), but this is one varietal that appears to be the Achilles' Heel in what is otherwise a superb portfolio. There are now two cuvées, a Stanly Ranch and a North Coast offering. Beringer occasionally produces merely mortal wines, as evidenced by the structured, lean, tannic, aggressively oaky 1993 Pinot Noir Stanly Ranch. The 1994 Pinot Noir Stanly Ranch is one-dimensional, but round, light-bodied, and pleasant. However, both the 1995 and 1996 Pinot Noir Stanly Ranch are major improvements. The 1995 Pinot Noir Stanly Ranch actually requires a year or two in the bottle. This black/purple-colored wine exhibits a sweet nose of plum and black cherry fruit, followed by subtle spicy, toasty, oaky notes. In the mouth, it is medium bodied and rich, with plenty of length and light to moderate tannin. It should age well for 7–8 years. The deep ruby/purple-colored 1996 Pinot Noir Stanly Ranch reveals a blueberry/raspberry-scented nose. The wine is dense and chewy, with excellent purity and light tannin in the finish. Lower in acidity, with softer tannin than the 1995, the 1996 and 1995 are significantly more concentrated than the 1994. There are 10,000 cases of the medium ruby-colored 1996 Pinot Noir North Coast, an attractive wine made in the style of Saintsbury's successful "Garnet" Pinot Noir. It is a soft, fruit-driven example with hedonistic levels of black cherry fruit. Low acidity, subtle toasty notes, and jammy fruit make for a luscious style of Pinot. Drink it over the next 2–3 years.

I was impressed with the Sangiovese offerings I tasted. No new oak is utilized as Beringer has decided to emphasize the medium-bodied, aromatic side of Sangiovese, thus enhancing its flexibility with an assortment of foods. The medium dark ruby-colored 1995 Sangiovese (10% Cabernet Sauvignon was added to the blend) exhibits the loamy soil, strawberry jam, new saddle leather-scented nose associated with this varietal. The wine possesses excellent richness, good underlying acidity, and some tannin, but it is essentially a fruit-driven wine to consume over the next 2–3 years. Lighter in color, body, and flavor than either the 1995 or 1996, the 1997 Sangiovese is soft, easygoing, straightforward, and not up to the quality of the two previous vintages.

Beringer produced a very good 1994 Sangiovese. The medium ruby-colored 1994 Sangiovese reveals a textbook, strawberry, cherry, new saddle leather-scented nose, medium body, crisp underlying acidity, and a dry, refreshing finish, with Chianti-like sour cherry notes. Drink this midweight Sangiovese over the next 3–4 years.

To my surprise, Beringer is making Syrah and Petite Sirah—and doing an impressive job with both. Only several hundred cases are made of each, and these wines are likely to be sold only at the winery. The 1997 Syrah Marston Vineyard is an unevolved offering with an opaque purple color, and a lovely bouquet of grilled meats, blueberries, *pain grillé*, and licorice. The wine possesses outstanding extract, beautiful harmony among its structural components, and a long, smoky, rich finish. Anticipated maturity: 2001–2015. Two wines of compelling concentration and attention-getting power are the 1996 Petite Sirah Hayne Vineyard and 1997 Petite Sirah Marston Vineyard. Both of these wines see 100% new oak (50% American and 50% French). They are hugely extracted, black purple-colored, totally unevolved wines. The 1996 Petite Sirah Hayne Vineyard is beginning to reveal secondary aromas of smoke, Asian spices, and cigar box, in addition to classic cassis, blackberry flavors. A monster wine, it needs at least 5–7 years of cellaring; it will keep for 2–3 decades. The 1997 Petite Sirah Marston Vineyard has a small amount of fruit (25%) from the Hayne Vineyard added to the blend. This wine boasts phenomenal intensity, massive body, and a boatload of tannin and glycerin. A huge example, it will not become civilized for another 5–6 years. It should keep for 20–25 years.

Beringer does a superb job with its production from the Bancroft Ranch on Howell Mountain. About 8,000 cases of their single vineyard Merlot are produced. This wine spends 20 months in French oak coopered by the well-known house of Seguin-Moreau. The 1995 Merlot Bancroft Ranch exhibits an opaque ruby/purple color, followed by a stunning nose of chocolate, minerals, black cherries, and toast. A serious, mountain-styled Merlot, it displays full body, outstanding concentration and purity, and moderate tannin. It needs to be cellared for another 2–3 years, but will last 15 years. The 1996 Merlot Bancroft Ranch was showing much better when I tasted it in 1998 than it did eleven months earlier. The wine boasts a saturated purple color, as well as an exquisite nose of brandy-infused black cherries intermixed with melted chocolate. Dense and full bodied, with striking sweetness and purity, this multi-layered Merlot has developed beautifully. Although it will benefit from another 4–5 years of bottle age, it can be drunk now, or cellared. It, too, will keep for 15 years. The 1997 Merlot

Bancroft Ranch is an explosive example. It reveals a similar opaque purple color, and a penetrating sweet nose of vanillin, lead pencil, minerals, and textbook black cherry and currant fruit. Less chocolate is noticeable, but that will undoubtedly emerge after more time in barrel. An enormously endowed, yet remarkably evolved and seamless young wine, it should be accessible when released, and last for two decades.

The 1993 and 1994 Bancroft Vineyard Merlots are two of the greatest Merlots that have been produced in California. Both are huge, massive, exceptionally concentrated Merlots with opaque purple colors, marvelous, concentrated flavors, lush, viscous textures, an expansive inner core of fruit, and well-integrated tannin. Beringer is not afraid to let the pH get as high as 3.7 (à la a Bordeaux from a great vintage such as 1990, 1989, and 1982), and thus the full textural aspects of the wine are well displayed. It is exceedingly difficult to pick a favorite among recent vintages of Bancroft Merlot, as they are all extraordinary wines. Capable of delicious drinking upon release, these Merlots are so concentrated and well balanced that they will last for 15+ years. The 1994 Merlot Bancroft Vineyard is one of the most dazzling Merlots they have yet produced. While closed initially, the wine opens quickly in the glass. The dark ruby/purple color is followed by smoky, chocolatey, and black cherry aromas with new oak in the background. In the mouth, this wine is full bodied, with explosive levels of glycerin and richness on the back of the palate. Dense, concentrated, tannic, and angular, it is capable of lasting 15+ years. In fact, I recommend 3–4 years of cellaring before serious consumption begins.

Beringer's Alluvium Proprietary Red is a Merlot-dominated wine, with quantities of Cabernet Sauvignon and dollops of Cabernet Franc, Petit Verdot, and, occasionally, Malbec. The following vintages all include a minimum of 75% Merlot, with 10%–20% Cabernet Sauvignon. These wines are made in a claret style, with less power and extraction but more finesse and accessibility. They appear to contain enough tannin for 10–12 years of aging potential. The 1995 Alluvium Proprietary Red reveals a dark ruby color, an elegant, berry, earth, and cherry-scented nose, medium to full body, and admirable complexity and accessibility. Last year I thought the wine was outstanding. While I rated it slightly lower this year, it is nevertheless an excellent offering. I would opt for drinking it over the next 7–10 years. The 1996 Alluvium Proprietary Red is a lusher, riper wine with nicely displayed sweet black currant and cherry fruit. Although there is some tannin at the back of the mouth, the wine's appeal is its savory, fleshy, up-front style and purity of fruit, with an absence of aggressive acidity, tannin, or alcohol. It should drink well for a decade. The 1997 Alluvium Proprietary Red is lighter than its two predecessors. Soft, with good berry fruit, spice, and a medium-bodied finish, it should drink well for 5–7 years.

The 1993 Alluvium's dark ruby/purple color is followed by a sweet, jammy nose of smoke, licorice, black cherries, and cassis, along with underlying mocha nuances. The wine exhibits terrific fruit, a soft, expansive velvety texture, and a surprising degree of succulence. It is another outstanding red wine from the underrated 1993 vintage. It should drink well for 10–15+ years. The 1994 Alluvium is a textbook proprietary wine. It displays a dark ruby color, followed by an attractive black fruit-scented nose with subtle toasty oak intertwined with herbs, earth, and chocolatey notes. In the mouth, black cherry fruit and toast are presented in a medium- to full-bodied, silky-smooth, delicious format. Very accessible, it should continue to drink well for a decade.

The single-vineyard Cabernet Francs from Howell Mountain are aged in 100% new French oak, which has been soaked up nicely. These are charming, softer, less extracted offerings than the single-vineyard Merlots or Cabernet Sauvignons. Nevertheless, they are not wimpish wines. The dark ruby/purple-colored 1995 Cabernet Franc Howell Mountain offers a complex nose of herbs, earth, black fruits, and spicy wood. Medium bodied, round, and velvety textured, this attractive wine needs to be consumed during its first decade of life. The same finesse, elegance, spice, and fruit character can be found in the medium-bodied 1996

Cabernet Franc Howell Mountain. However, its aromatics include a slight touch of menthol/mint. Drink this stylish wine over the next 7–8 years. The 1997 Cabernet Franc Howell Mountain is cut from the same mold. Spicy, with ripe fruit and intelligently put together, it is not quite as extracted or as flavorful as the 1995 or 1996. However, it should put on more weight after additional cask aging.

Because of space limitations, I will keep my notes on Beringer's limited production, single-vineyard Cabernet Sauvignon series short. All of the latter Cabernet Sauvignons are part of what Beringer calls their "Vineyard Collection." Produced in 200 case lots, readers expecting to find them sitting on a shelf in their local retail shops will be disappointed, as they are destined to be sold via Beringer's mailing list, or directly from the winery. That is not the case with the Knight's Valley Cabernet Sauvignon or Private Reserve Cabernet Sauvignon, both of which are made in abundant quantities. One of the safest choices a consumer can make, both have been consistently fine and accurate representations of Cabernet's varietal characteristics. The 1995 Cabernet Sauvignon Knight's Valley reveals a deep ruby color, followed by copious quantities of sweet black currant fruit, good acidity, light tannin, and a round, lush, seductive finish. Enjoy it over the next 7–8 years. The 1996 Cabernet Sauvignon Knight's Valley offers more smokiness intertwined with jammy black currant fruit. The wine's excellent richness, plush, user-friendly style, and fruit-driven personality have resulted in a crowd-pleasing, modestly priced Cabernet Sauvignon that should last for a decade or more. The 1997 Cabernet Sauvignon Knight's Valley exhibits the vintage's forward, evolved aromatics, sweet tannin, and grapey, ripe fruit. Although it appears to be as concentrated as the 1995 and 1996, it is still youthful. It should last for 7–8 years.

Beringer is now producing 50,000 cases of Knight's Valley Cabernet Sauvignon. All of it is aged in small oak casks, of which 35% are new. Wines to look for include the gorgeously rich, lush, cassis-scented and -flavored 1993 Cabernet Sauvignon Knight's Valley. This soft, loaded wine will provide beautiful drinking over the next 5–7 years. Not a wimpish wine, it contains nearly 14% alcohol. The excellent, nearly outstanding 1994 Cabernet Sauvignon Knight's Valley exhibits a dark ruby/purple color, and a sweet black currant-scented nose with smoky oak, and earthy, chocolatey notes. I thought this medium-bodied, richly fruity, delicious wine was outstanding in 1996, but slightly less prodigious in 1997. It should drink well for a decade, and possibly earn an even higher score.

I cannot recall a disappointing vintage of Beringer's Private Reserve Cabernet Sauvignon. A production of 10,000–15,000 cases makes the wine's outstanding quality even more enviable. The 1995 Cabernet Sauvignon Private Reserve is a full-bodied, explosively rich, deep purple-colored wine bursting with ripe fruit. It displays smoky oak, gobs of cassis, a touch of cigar box and cedar, and a layered, multidimensional feel. This voluptuous, seductive offering is already drinking well, yet should age effortlessly for 15–20 years. The 1996 Cabernet Sauvignon Private Reserve reveals more concentration as well as higher tannin. I know it is a trade-off, but I suspect this vintage will not be as sexy in its youthfulness as the 1995. The black ruby/purple-colored 1996 offers more licorice, in addition to the obvious levels of *pain grillé*, jammy black currant fruit, and spice notes. Structured, full bodied, and powerful, this may be a Private Reserve to cellar for several years, and consume over the subsequent 15–18. The 1997 Cabernet Sauvignon Private Reserve is still a baby in terms of its development, but it does display terrific fruit intensity, outstanding ripeness and purity, the vintage's telltale sweet, velvety tannin, and a blossoming perfume of blackberries, cassis, and floral scents. It should be an outstanding Private Reserve, but it is hard to say if it will surpass the top vintages of the nineties. By the way, statisticians should note that the Private Reserve is always at least 97% Cabernet Sauvignon, and aged for 22–24 months in 100% new French oak. One of the common threads I find in the Private Reserve Cabernet Sauvignon is a smoky, chocolatey, licorice character that works well with the lavish quantities of fruit and glycerin these wines possess.

Beringer's Private Reserve has always been one of my favorite California Cabernets, particularly since the late seventies. They can be drunk young but age exceptionally well, giving every indication of holding their fruit and evolving nicely for 2 decades. The 1993 Cabernet Sauvignon Private Reserve has begun to close down, revealing more of the vintage's strong, tannic personality than other top 1993s. The wine's opaque purple color is followed by a promising sweet, smoky, chocolatey, licorice, and black currant-scented nose, and deep, powerful, full-bodied flavors. Abundant tannin in the finish suggests this is a Private Reserve to lay away for 2–3 years. Normally these Private Reserves possess a precociousness and silky, up-front richness. Aromatically, the 1993 Private Reserve is rewarding, but after the initial attack of sweet fruit, the wine's tannin takes precedence. It is an outstanding wine, but more of a long-term prospect. Compared with the flattering precociousness of the 1994, 1992, 1991, and 1990, the 1993 will offer less immediate appeal. Anticipated maturity: 2000–2015. The terrific 1994 Cabernet Sauvignon Private Reserve offers an opaque purple color, a gorgeous nose of toasty oak, and a silky, concentrated texture with unobtrusive acidity or tannin. The wine possesses layered richness, remarkable balance, sweet, pure fruit, and a finish that lasts for nearly 30 seconds. These wines are aged in 100% new oak, and tend to possess at least 97% Cabernet Sauvignon, with the balance Cabernet Franc. Amazingly, the oak is not a pronounced component in the final wine, a testament to excellent winemaking and the concentration these wines possess. Like so many top 1994s from Napa and Sonoma, this wine was accessible when released in early 1998, but will age well for 2 decades.

The following notes are intentionally abbreviated given the limited quantities available. As previously mentioned, these offerings fall under the umbrella "Beringer Vineyard Collection." Production is about 200 cases of each wine. The State Lane Vineyard is situated on extremely rocky soil in the Yountville area. Beringer's 1995 Cabernet Sauvignon State Lane Vineyard possesses a St.-Emilion-like cherry, tobacco, and sweet currant-scented nose, and soft, round, ripe, berry flavors. A seductively styled, medium- to full-bodied, accessible Cabernet, it is ideal for consuming now and over the next 15 years. The same silky tannins can be found in the 1996 Cabernet Sauvignon State Lane Vineyard. This vintage tended to produce harder, more tannic and rustic wines, but that is not the case with this cuvée. The wine possesses plenty of sweet, jammy, plum and black currant fruit, cigar box and spice aromas, some cedar, and a silky, layered, lush, medium- to full-bodied personality. It can be drunk during its first 15–18 years of life. The 1997 Cabernet Sauvignon State Lane Vineyard reveals a more elegant, finesse style. The wine's sweet red and black currant fruit is intermixed with spicy oak, minerals, and cigar box notes. Soft, lush, and fragrant, this graceful, stylistic Cabernet Sauvignon will provide delicious near-term drinking but will last for a decade or more. The Marston Vineyard is situated on Spring Mountain. Both the 1996 and 1997 Cabernet Sauvignon Marston Vineyard are qualitatively similar, although the 1997 exhibits sweeter fruit, a more seamless texture, and emphasizes the black fruit spectrum, whereas the 1996 reveals more red currant notes. Both wines are medium to full bodied, with the 1996 slightly less concentrated than the 1997. Both are impressively constructed, rich wines that are not quite as seductive and forward as the State Lane offerings. I envision both Marston Vineyard cuveés lasting for 2 decades.

Two hundred cases were produced of the 1994 Cabernet Sauvignon Marston Vineyard. This stunning Cabernet boasts a dense black/purple color, jammy blueberry and cassis aromas, and a fruit-driven style. Despite being aged in 100% new oak, little wood is noticeable in this sexy, voluptuously textured, dazzlingly concentrated, richly fruity wine. Its low acidity and purity make for a compellingly drinkable Cabernet Sauvignon. Anticipated maturity: now–2012.

A new offering from Beringer is the Cabernet Sauvignon Tré Colline from Howell Mountain. These are tannic, backward, full-bodied wines with considerable punch and depth. The

1995 is a multidimensional, full-bodied, spicy wine with copious quantities of black currant fruit intermixed with cedar and weedy tobacco. Full bodied, pure, and nicely textured, it should be at its best with another 2–3 years of cellaring, and keep for 2 decades. The dense purple-colored 1996 Cabernet Sauvignon Tré Colline is backward, tannic, and in need of 5–6 years of bottle age. All the component parts are present, but this wine requires patience. The 1997 Cabernet Sauvignon Tré Colline appears to be a sensational effort. It is full bodied, concentrated, and explosively rich, with gobs of black currant fruit intermixed with minerals, *pain grillé*, and spice box aromas. With the vintage's sweet tannin well integrated in the wine's plush, fleshy personality, look for it to drink well young, and last for 20 years.

The St. Helena Vineyard Cabernet Sauvignon series offers another interesting style. The 1995 Cabernet Sauvignon St. Helena Vineyard exhibits a fragrant, smoky nose of loamy soil scents, underbrush, and ripe, brandy-infused black currants and cherries. This rich wine is full bodied, with superb density and a lush texture. A beautifully made, complex wine with a terrific midpalate and length (always signs of high quality), it can be drunk now or cellared for 15+ years. The 1996 Cabernet Sauvignon St. Helena Vineyard is the antithesis of the 1995—stern, tannic, and backward. While broodingly powerful and brawny, its tannin dominates at present. It was closed when I tasted it, so I will be anxious to retaste it prior to release. The 1997 Cabernet Sauvignon St. Helena Vineyard appears to be a return to a more flamboyant and concentrated style. It reveals intense blackberry and cassis fruit intermixed with roasted coffee and weedy tobacco scents. There is great persistency, a fabulous midpalate, and a blockbuster finish, with good fruit, glycerin, and equilibrium.

Undoubtedly the best-known Beringer single vineyard Cabernet is from their Chabot Vineyard. Like the other offerings in this series, this is a 100% Cabernet Sauvignon aged in 100% new oak casks. The accessible 1995 Cabernet Sauvignon Chabot Vineyard reveals medium to full body, and a knockout nose of roasted herbs, grilled meats, coffee, cassis, and cherry fruit. In the mouth, it is viscous and full bodied, with a chewy midsection, and a spicy, long, rich finish. It will last for 2 decades. The 1996 Cabernet Sauvignon Chabot Vineyard offers aromas and flavors of chocolate liqueur infused with brandy as well as loamy soil intermixed with damp forest, underbrush scents. Full bodied, with massive power, and chewy, thick, structured, chocolatey fruit flavors, this is a complex yet backward, formidably endowed Cabernet Sauvignon with palate-staining levels of extract and tannin. Give it 3–4 years of bottle age, and consume it over the following 2 decades. The 1997 Cabernet Sauvignon Chabot Vineyard reveals more smoke, chocolate, and black currant fruit in its nose. Surprisingly, none of the foresty, underbrush aromas found in the 1996 have yet made an appearance. Extremely full bodied, huge, chewy, thick, and viscous, it is a blockbuster Cabernet that will last for 20+ years.

The 1993 Chabot Vineyard Cabernet Sauvignon is very good, but it gets lost when tasted in the company of the 1994, 1992, and 1991. Although it is a big wine, it is not as concentrated or impressive as those other three vintages. The 1994 Cabernet Sauvignon Chabot Vineyard is a backward, full-bodied, muscular wine that is 5–7 years away from drinkability. With airing, the wine reluctantly gives up scents of pepper, iodine, cassis, mint, and earth. This full-bodied, large-scaled Cabernet begs for more bottle time. This wine should only be purchased by those willing to invest patience, as it will not provide enjoyable drinking when young.

The limited production Cabernet Sauvignon Bancroft Ranch offerings are also outstanding. Previously I had a slight preference for the 1996 over the 1995, but an extra year of bottle age has caused the 1995 to leap-frog over the 1996. For now, the 1995 looks to be slightly more complete and multidimensional than the 1996, but readers should look out for the phenomenal 1997. The 1995 Cabernet Sauvignon Bancroft Ranch exhibits an opaque black/purple color, and stunning aromatics consisting of minerals, blueberries, blackberries, and cassis. Terrific in the mouth, it offers full body, a racy, chewy texture, high tannin, but wonderful sweetness and balance. It was impressive and flamboyant when I tasted it in September of 1998. Anticipated maturity: 2000–2025. The 1996 Cabernet Sauvignon Bancroft Ranch may possess an even more saturated, thicker, black/purple color. Some tannin has emerged since I tasted it last year, when it was far more velvety. This is a powerhouse, extremely full bodied, palate-staining wine. Its enormous extract, richness, and elevated tannin seem to suggest this wine is about ready to settle down for a long period of dormancy. Anticipated maturity: 2005–2025. The 1997 Cabernet Sauvignon Bancroft Ranch is behaving much like the 1996 did last year, revealing an extroverted, ostentatious, and flamboyant personality. Aromas of blueberry/blackberry liqueur intermixed with toasty new oak, licorice, and meat smells are followed by a dazzlingly rich, explosive, full-bodied wine that coats the palate with enormous concentration. This wine possesses exceptional purity, multiple layers of extract and glycerin, and a finish that lasts for 30+ seconds. A seamless, surprisingly evolved, showy wine, it should be accessible when released. Yet don't be surprised if this wine shuts down. Anticipated maturity: 2001–2025.

Also look for the 1994 Cabernet Sauvignon Bancroft Vineyard. This opaque purple-colored wine offers toasty, smoky oak in its nose, as well as the telltale cassis and mineral aromas that emerge from Howell Mountain wines. Rich, powerful, full-bodied flavors, and excellent purity and sweetness of fruit further characterize this broad-shouldered wine. There is also plenty of tannin, suggesting it will require 3–4 years of cellaring after its release. It will keep for 2 decades.

Beringer is also turning out some excellent to outstanding Meritage blends, which are mostly Merlot-based wines. Both the 1993 and 1994 are composed of 80% Merlot and 20% Cabernet Sauvignon from grapes grown in Knight's Valley. The 1993 exhibits a dark, impressive purple color, a coffee, chocolate, jammy, berry-scented nose, soft, fat, succulent flavors, outstanding ripeness, and a thick, rich, low-acid finish. It is a seductive wine for drinking during its first decade of life. Even fatter, richer, and riper, the 1994 Meritage should ensure that Merlot fans have a steady fix of high quality Merlot for the next several years.

A Cabernet Sauvignon Terre Rouge was produced in 1994, 1995, and 1996. These are among the more backward, austere, and angular of these single-vineyard wines. The 1994 Cabernet Sauvignon Terre Rouge reveals a dark ruby color, spice, leafy tobacco, and earthy aromas, sweet black cherry and cassis fruit, medium body, and moderate tannin. It will need 2–4 years of cellaring and will keep for 15 or more. The 1995 Cabernet Sauvignon Terre Rouge offers a dense, dark purple color, more fatness and fleshiness to its texture, fuller body, and concentrated, rich flavors. More forward than the 1994, with less austerity, it should drink well for 12–15 years. I found the 1996 Cabernet Sauvignon Terre Rouge to be more fruit than structure driven. It exhibits copious quantities of red and black fruit in its nose, low acidity, obvious glycerin, a thick, chewy texture, and a spicy, medium- to full-bodied finish. Although the 1996 will not be as backward as the 1994, neither will it be as fleshy as the 1995.

Beringer's 1995 Cabernet Franc Terre Rouge possesses sweet fruit, along with a structured feel. Medium bodied, with an attractive red and black currant, mineral, spicy-scented nose, this wine displays a moderately intense personality, as well as spice and sweet tannin in the finish. It should drink well young, yet keep for 10–12 years. The 1994 Cabernet Franc Terre Rouge exhibits a dense ruby/purple color, a spicy, fragrant, black fruit, mineral, and chocolatey-scented nose, rich flavors, and a moderately weighty feel on the palate. The wine's tannin and acidity are soft and well integrated. Although it is easy to understand and drink, this Cabernet Franc promises to evolve gracefully for a decade. Given the generally modest pricing of this estate's wines, this might be less of a value if the price of the 1993 Terre Rouge ($40) is similar for the 1994 and 1995 vintages.

The 1995 Syrah (only 50 cases produced) will probably be sold at Beringer's famed Rhine House at the winery in St. Helena. This debut effort looks to be a terrific Syrah. The wine contains a small amount of Grenache (7%). It is an opaque purple-colored wine with a force-ful, peppery, chocolatey, cassis-scented nose, and thick, dense, full-bodied flavors, the latter component oozing with extract and glycerin. With a sweet, long, lavishly rich finish, this wine should drink beautifully for 10–15 years.

Two outrageously rich, sweet nectars are Beringer's 1995 Nightingale, an 80% Semil-lon/20% Sauvignon Blanc, barrel-fermented, decadently rich, honeyed wine that should age well for 15+ years, and the 1994 Special Select Late Harvest Riesling. The latter wine was made from grapes harvested at an amazing 47% sugar. With a finished alcohol of 7.4%, and an unctuous, thick texture, this is the type of sweet wine that will throw sugar lovers into a frenzy. My experience has shown that the Nightingale offerings age gracefully, holding their fruit and sweetness for 10 or more years. I have less experience with Beringer's Late Harvest Rieslings, thus I would opt for drinking them over the next 5–7 years.

BETTINELLI (NAPA)

1995 Cabernet Sauvignon	Napa	C	88
1993 Cabernet Sauvignon	Napa	C	87+
1995 Merlot	Napa	D	86+?

Made from vineyards situated on Spring Mountain, above St. Helena, these are well-made, full-bodied wines with various levels of tart acidity. The dark purple-colored 1995 Merlot ex-hibits rich, toasty oak, along with black cherry and berrylike flavors. The wine's tangy acidity keeps everything tightly knit, but despite the wine's acidic edge, it is rich and well made, with a moderately long, medium-bodied finish. Once the fruit fades, the high acid will make the wine shrill, so consume it over the next 5–6 years.

The 1993 Cabernet Sauvignon is an excellent, full-bodied Cabernet with deep, earthy, black currant flavors intermingled with smoky oak. With tart acidity, and a low PH texture (compressed), this moderately tannic, dense wine possesses excellent raw materials. It would merit a higher score if the wine had not been so acidic. Nevertheless, there remains much to like about it. Drink it over the next 8–10 years. The finest wine of this trio is the 1995 Caber-net Sauvignon (325 cases produced). It reveals good fruit, a sweet, ripe, black currant rich-ness, high quality, toasty new oak, and less noticeable acidity (or is there just more depth and fruit?). The wine is long, full bodied, and in need of another 1–2 years of cellaring. It should keep for 10–12 years.

ROBERT BIALÉ VINEYARDS (NAPA)

1996 Zinfandel Aldo's Vineyard	Napa	D	90
1996 Zinfandel Monte Rosso Vineyard	Sonoma	D	92
1996 Zinfandel Old Crane Ranch	Napa	D	90

As expensive as these wines appear, they are all outstanding Zinfandels. The 1996 Zinfandel Aldo's Vineyard (875 cases) is an unfiltered, sexy wine with considerable personality. This dark plum-colored effort offers up earthy, jammy, sweet cranberry and raspberry notes along with pepper, incense, and spice. Generous, with a robust constitution, and gobs of glycerin (14.6% alcohol), this supple, full-bodied, concentrated, hedonistic, opulently textured Zin-fandel should be consumed over the next 3–4 years. While it is difficult to pick a favorite from this exceptional trio of '96s, I had a slight preference for the unfiltered 1996 Zinfandel Monte Rosso Vineyard (675 cases produced). It possesses the most saturated plum/purple color, and displays its personality in a flamboyant, full-bodied manner. This gorgeous Zin boasts copious quantities of pepper, spice, and rich cherry/black raspberry jamlike notes. The subtle oak influence adds to the creamy texture of this concentrated, dramatically styled, full-bodied wine. Drink this sinfully rich Zinfandel now and over the next 5–6 years.

Lastly, the 1996 Zinfandel Old Crane Ranch (800 cases bottled without filtration) is another hedonistic, fat, layered, ostentatious Zinfandel with copious quantities of berry fruit, glycerin, extract, and alcohol (15.4%). The wine's low acidity, lavish richness, and attention-getting style will be immensely pleasing to Zinfandel enthusiasts over the next 4–5 years.

BLACKJACK RANCH (SANTA BARBARA)

1997 Cabernet Sauvignon	Santa Barbara	D	(87–90)
1997 Chardonnay Reserve	Santa Barbara	D	90

This new operation is run by the passionate and seemingly sure-handed Roger Wisted. Wisted has always had a love for wine, and finally decided that just buying and drinking it was not enough. So he planted his own vineyard, and while waiting for it to mature, bought grapes to produce his own wines. I am very impressed with his first two efforts. The 1997 Chardonnay Reserve (14.4% alcohol) reveals copious quantities of tropical fruit (primarily pineapple), as well as toasty new oak, honeysuckle, and vanilla. This intense, full-blown and -bodied, layered, pure, ripe, lusty, hedonistic Chardonnay should drink well for 2–3 years. The 1997 Cabernet Sauvignon (under 500 cases) is made from purchased fruit grown in a 17-year-old vineyard in Los Olivos. Aged in equal parts American and French oak, it will be released in another year. While still grapey, unevolved, and backward, it reveals outstanding potential. The vegetal character often found in Cabernets from this area is not present in this offering. Made from extremely ripe fruit, Blackjack Ranch's 1997 Cabernet Sauvignon is an opaque black/purple-colored wine with moderately intense aromatics consisting of cassis, blackberries, licorice, and cigar box scents. The oak is well integrated, and the tannin high, but the wine possesses a sweet, rich midpalate, excellent to outstanding texture, and fine length. It should be an impressive debut release for Roger Wisted's Blackjack Ranch. Anticipated maturity: 2002–2020.

BONNY DOON VINEYARD (SANTA CRUZ)

1996 Ca' del Solo Barbera	Monterey	C	86
1996 Ca' del Solo Il Fiasco Proprietary Red Wine	California	C	85
1996 Cardinal Zin	California	C	83
1995 Le Cigare Volant Proprietary Red Wine	California	C	87
1994 Le Cigare Volant	California	C	88
1995 Old Telegram (Mourvèdre)	California	D	90

The irrepressible Randall Grahm has produced some intriguing red wines. His Ca' del Solo offerings (amusingly labeled "Vino Non Filtrato") include a robust 1996 Il Fiasco and a delicious 1996 Barbera. The 1996 Il Fiasco possesses a healthy saturated dark ruby color, a sweet/bitter black cherry-scented nose, ripe, uncomplicated cherry and almondlike flavors, crisp acidity, and good flesh and ripeness. This is a straightforward, refreshingly fruity, vibrant wine to drink over the next several years. Roberto Parkero from the Castello di Mongo calls it the perfect pizza wine. The saturated ruby/purple-colored 1996 Ca' del Solo Barbera exhibits a textbook Barbera nose of strawberries and other red and black fruits. The wine reveals good acidity, plenty of ripeness, medium body, and a clean finish. I would opt for drinking this exuberant, robust Barbera over the next several years.

I believe the 1995 Old Telegram is Grahm's finest effort under this label in a decade. The color is a dark ruby/purple, and the wine displays an intensely fragrant nose of jammy black raspberries and spice. In the mouth, it is rich, medium to full bodied, and gorgeously pure, with admirable layers of flavor and extract. This is a high class, young, expansively flavored Mourvèdre that should age effortlessly for a decade or more. Impressive!

The one-dimensional, clean, fruity, somewhat acidic 1996 Cardinal Zin reveals Zinfandel's textbook cherry/raspberry fruit intermixed with spice and pepper. A medium-bodied, decently made, but simple wine, it should be drunk over the next 1–2 years.

Lastly, the 1994 Le Cigare Volant, a Grenache, Mourvèdre, Cinsault, Syrah blend, is Grahm's interpretation of a California-styled Châteauneuf du Pape. The 1994 celebrates this wine's tenth year. Surprisingly, the best vintage Grahm made was the first one, 1984. The 1994 is, nevertheless, a strong effort, exhibiting a deep ruby color, plenty of jammy, raspberry, and cherry fruit, medium body, good spice, fine purity, and a long finish. It is ideal for drinking over the next 4–5 years. Think of it as a Côtes du Rhône/St. Joseph blend, rather than a Châteauneuf du Pape. The 1995 Le Cigare Volant (a 45.5% Syrah, 36% Mourvèdre, 17.6% Grenache, and .9% Roussanne blend) exhibits a dark ruby color, followed by aromas of sweet berry fruit, earth, and spice. It is not a complex wine, nor does it possess the concentration and impressive personality of the 1995 Old Telegram. Nevertheless, it is an attractive, fleshy, medium-bodied, mouth-filling, savory wine for consuming over the next 5–6 years.

BREWER-CLIFTON (SANTA BARBARA)

1996	Chardonnay Marcella's Sierra Madre Vineyard	Santa Maria	D	87
1997	Chardonnay Sweeney Canyon	Santa Ynez	D	89
1997	Pinot Noir	Santa Maria Hills	D	90
1997	Pinot Noir Julia's Vineyard	Santa Barbara	D	88

As is often the case, these hand-crafted wines are available only in small quantities. Nevertheless, they are worth knowing about. Hopefully, Brewer-Clifton will begin to produce more wine as it is all top-notch. The two Chardonnays, made from low yields, are both unfined and unfiltered, with well-integrated acidity. There are less than 100 cases of the 1997 Chardonnay Sweeney Canyon (15.1% alcohol). It offers spicy oak, honeyed citrus, buttery fruit, an alluring texture, and admirable richness. The 1996 Chardonnay Marcella's (named after Fess Parker's wife) offers an intriguing nose of roasted hazelnuts, and smoky, lemony, tropical fruit. Medium to full bodied, ripe, and rich, it, like the 1997 Sweeney Canyon, should drink well for several more years.

The Brewer-Clifton team has also demonstrated a sure hand with Pinot Noir. The 1997 Pinot Noir Julia's Vineyard (72 cases) exhibits an attractive, plump, earthy, smoky, Pommard-like nose with notes of apple skins and black cherries. This deep ruby/colored wine displays ripe fruit, medium body, and a friendly, open-knit texture. The outstanding 1997 Pinot Noir (72 cases) offers dried herbs, smoked meats, and black fruits in its complex aromatics. Rich, medium to full bodied, long, ripe, and nicely layered, it should drink well for 4–5 years.

BRYANT FAMILY VINEYARD (NAPA)

1997	Cabernet Sauvignon	Napa	EEE	(98–100)
1996	Cabernet Sauvignon	Napa	EEE	99
1995	Cabernet Sauvignon	Napa	EEE	99
1994	Cabernet Sauvignon	Napa	EEE	98
1993	Cabernet Sauvignon	Napa	EEE	97+

The wine from this hillside vineyard near Napa's Pritchard Hill, has already become mythical (1992 was the debut vintage). Winemaker Helen Turley will have more production with which to work in upcoming vintages as the new vineyard plantations come of age. This is a wine of world-class quality, and is certainly as complete and potentially complex as any first-growth Bordeaux. To date, it has been characterized by extraordinary richness, complexity, and harmony, as well as the potential to evolve and improve for 20 or more years. The 1997 Cabernet Sauvignon displays an impressively saturated black/purple color, and fabulously fragrant aromatics consisting of licorice, toast, asphalt, violets, blackberries, and cassis. Full bodied, staggeringly concentrated, yet velvety textured, with perfect integration of acidity, tannin, and alcohol, this is another prodigious Cabernet Sauvignon from Bryant. The 1997 is slightly more evolved than the 1996 and 1995 were at a similar stage, and appears to possess even more glycerin and length. Although the alcohol level reached 15%, there is not a trace of heat in the finish. This is an astonishing achievement. When I tasted this wine in September of 1998, it was one of the few times that year (while tasting professionally) that I swallowed instead of spit. Anticipated maturity: now–2020. The opaque purple-colored 1996 Cabernet Sauvignon offers a spectacular, exotic bouquet of Peking duck skins, blackberry and cassis liqueur, roasted herbs, and burning charcoal. It is phenomenally intense, with record levels of dry extract and glycerin. This hedonistic blockbuster is crammed with jammy fruits nicely buttressed and framed by adequate acidity and tannin. Drink this marvelous Cabernet Sauvignon now or cellar it for 2 decades. This is mind-boggling stuff!

Don't I wish there were tens of thousands of cases of wine such as this! Believe me, it is frustrating to write about limited production wines with such distinctive characters. I realize that only a handful of readers will be fortunate enough to obtain a bottle. It is also distressing to see these wines fetch museum prices at auctions, bid up to levels that only multimillionaires can afford. Nevertheless, twenty years of writing has proven time and time again that glowing reviews on these wines motivate other producers to attain a similar level of quality.

Bryant Family Vineyard's extraordinary Cabernet Sauvignon is made from their stunningly beautiful hillside vineyard on Napa's Pritchard Hill. This is a wine of not only Bordeaux first-growth quality, but of such compelling personality, individuality, and stature that it may be one of the single greatest Cabernet Sauvignons. Think about it . . . this winery has produced only five Cabernet Sauvignons, and four of them have been virtually perfect. This wine is made by the extraordinary Helen Turley, who has almost single-handedly (her husband, John Wetlaufer, should be included in this equation) redefined what it takes to produce California wines of exceptional purity, richness, complexity, and longevity. Certainly if I were the owner of a first-growth Bordeaux estate, I would not want to have my wine served in the company of a Bryant Cabernet Sauvignon!

The 1995 Cabernet Sauvignon is cut from the same mold as the 1996, displaying astonishing levels of black fruits (the usual suspects—blueberries, blackberries, raspberries, and cassis), phenomenal concentration, and virtually perfect balance and equilibrium.

Another potentially perfect wine, the 1994 Cabernet Sauvignon boasts a fabulous nose of cassis, cream, blueberries, violets, minerals, and spice. It smells like a hypothetical blend of a great vintage of L'Évangile, Clinet, and Mouton-Rothschild. The opaque purple/black color is followed by a full-bodied wine stacked and packed with fruit, glycerin, and extract. No component part is out of place in this formidably endowed, remarkably well balanced wine. The purity, richness, sweetness and depth of fruit suggest that the wine's potential is limitless. Much like its cellarmate, the 1994 Colgin Cabernet Sauvignon (also made by Helen Turley), the Bryant Family Vineyard's 1994 should evolve into one of California's legendary Cabernets. It will age effortlessly for 25–30 years.

The 1993 Cabernet Sauvignon has turned out even better than I first predicted (and I thought it was an amazing wine from barrel). It exhibits an opaque purple/black color, and a huge, fragrant, penetrating bouquet of minerals, licorice, toast, and remarkable layers of black fruits. Although extremely full bodied, the wine's hugeness and massive concentration come across as beautifully poised, balanced, and delineated. The tannin is not as sweet as in the 1994, but it is ripe. The quantity of tannin should ensure this wine's graceful evolution for another 20–25 years, although it will be easy to drink within 2–3 years.

I wrote an article in *Food and Wine* magazine itemizing the characteristics of a great wine. They are: 1) the ability to please both the palate and the intellect, 2) the ability to hold the taster's interest, 3) the ability to offer intense aromas and flavors without heaviness, 4) the ability to taste better with each sip, 5) the ability to improve with age, and 6) the ability to offer a singular personality. These wines satisfy every one of those requirements.

I often wonder if I get too excited about wines such as this. Yet time is on their side. I truly believe that in 20, 40, or 60 years, when the history of what appears to be a golden age for California wines is analyzed, these wines, and the work of their winemaker, will be even more admired and appreciated by future generations than they are today.

BYRON VINEYARD (SANTA BARBARA)

1996 Chardonnay Estate	Santa Maria Valley	D	90
1996 Chardonnay Reserve	Santa Maria Valley	C	89
1996 Pinot Noir Reserve	Santa Maria Valley	C	88
1995 Pinot Noir Reserve	Santa Barbara	D	86

Both of Byron's 1996 Chardonnays are extroverted, tropical fruit-dominated wines. The 1996 Chardonnay Reserve is more restrained, with the obvious oak balanced by the wine's rich, concentrated fruit, and lusty, spicy personality. There are pineapples and mangoes galore in this seductively styled offering. Consume it over the next several years. The 1996 Chardonnay Estate exhibits a more evolved light gold color, as well as a knockout nose of pineapples, tangerines, and orange blossoms. This hedonistic, fleshy, medium- to full-bodied Chardonnay possesses excellent purity, and an attractive finish. It should drink well for 1–2 years.

This winery also fashioned a soft, supple, big, smoky 1996 Pinot Noir Reserve with abundant quantities of white pepper, strawberry and cherry fruit aromas, rich, glycerin-endowed, medium-bodied flavors, and a spicy finish with subtle toasty oak. Already delicious, it will continue to drink well for 3–4 years.

The herb and sweet cherry-scented and -flavored, boldly oaked 1995 Pinot Noir Reserve reveals a medium plum color, plenty of new oak (almost excessive amounts) in the nose, sweet, ripe fruit on the entry, good purity, and that unmistakable tomatolike herbaceousness that Santa Barbara Pinot Noirs tend to possess. Drink it over the next 2–3 years.

CAIN CELLARS (NAPA)

1995 Cain Five Proprietary Red Wine	Napa	D	87
1994 Cain Five Proprietary Red Wine	Napa	E	91
1993 Cain Five Proprietary Red Wine	Napa	D	85+?

Although the 1993 possesses attractive ripe, dense, black cherry and curranty fruit, it is extremely herbaceous, with strong scents of herbs, accompanied by aromas of black olives, toasty new oak, and moderate fruit. Its vegetal character is more powerful than I prefer. Otherwise, it is medium bodied, with light tannin, and an adequate finish. It should last for a decade.

The 1994, a blend of 62% Cabernet Sauvignon, 25% Merlot, 6% Cabernet Franc, 4% Malbec, and 3% Petit Verdot, is one of the finest efforts Cain Cellars has yet made. Fortunately, there were 5,500 cases produced. The wine reveals an opaque purple color, followed by a smoky, sweet cassis, subtle vanillin-scented nose, rich, medium- to full-bodied, supple flavors, and beautifully integrated acidity, tannin, alcohol, and wood. This outstanding effort is accessible, but should age effortlessly for 15 years. Shame on me for underrating this wine from cask!

The mid-sized, dark ruby-colored 1995 offers spicy, sweet black cherry fruit in the nose and flavors, a polished, nicely textured, restrained style, and a spicy, medium-bodied finish. It should drink well young, yet last for 8–12 years.

CAKEBREAD CELLARS (NAPA)

1994 Cabernet Sauvignon	Napa	D	86
1995 Cabernet Sauvignon Benchland Select	Napa	E	89+
1993 Cabernet Sauvignon Reserve	Napa	E	86
1995 Cabernet Sauvignon Three Sisters	Napa	E	90
1996 Chardonnay	Napa	D	87
1995 Chardonnay	Napa	D	87
1995 Chardonnay Reserve	Napa	D	88
1995 Merlot	Napa	D	87
1997 Sauvignon Blanc	Napa	B	87
1995 Sauvignon Blanc	Napa	C	87
1994 Zinfandel Howell Mountain	Napa	C	88+

Cakebread Cellars' 1997 Sauvignon Blanc displays further evidence of this winery's new-found level of quality. It possesses admirable melony/citrusy fruit, medium body, fine texture, and surprising length for a Sauvignon. Dry and cleanly made, it is ideal for consuming over the next year.

The two 1995 Cabernet Sauvignons are the most impressive I have tasted from Cakebread Cellars. The 1995 Cabernet Sauvignon Three Sisters comes from hillside vineyards planted on the eastern side of Napa Valley. The wine exhibits a saturated dark ruby/purple color, followed by a pure nose of cassis, minerals, and subtle new oak. Rich and expansive in the mouth, with power and concentration nicely allied to finesse and elegance, this wine possesses a soft texture, as well as enough tannin and acidity for delineation. Charming and intense, this is a beautifully rendered Cabernet Sauvignon that can be drunk now, or cellared for 10–15 years. Also dark ruby/purple-colored, the 1995 Cabernet Sauvignon Benchland Select offers restrained aromatics, more tannin, and a closed personality. The predominant flavor characteristics are black currants intermixed with tobacco and cedar. The finish is long, with moderate tannin. Anticipated maturity: 2000–2014.

I have noted that recent releases from Cakebread have been significantly higher in quality. The 1995 Chardonnay Reserve is an expansive, broad-shouldered Chardonnay with a light gold color, a rich, honeyed, tropical fruit-scented and -flavored personality, and a subtle hint of new oak. Considerable glycerin coats the palate, yet the wine possesses enough acidity to provide balance and uplift. Drink this generously endowed, full-flavored Chardonnay over the next 1–2 years. Readers looking for a pure Chardonnay without much wood influence would be well-advised to check out Cakebread's 1996 Chardonnay. This wine exhibits a lemony, ripe apple, citrusy nose, medium body, outstanding purity, and delicious fruit flavors that highlight gobs of glycerin and freshness. Drink it over the next year.

A restrained, deep ruby-colored Cabernet Sauvignon, the 1993 Reserve offers up an earthy, loamy, berry/cassis-scented nose with oak in the background. On the palate, the wine is medium bodied with astringent tannin, adequate acidity, and good depth. I suspect it will always display a certain austerity and severity to its tannin, but it is generally well made, and capable of lasting for another 10–12 years. The dark ruby/purple-colored 1995 Merlot exhibits a moderately intense nose of black cherries and spice. It is a fruit-driven wine with a plump, rich personality, adequate acidity, and a fleshy, juicy mouth-feel. Drink it over the next 2–3 years.

The attractive, medium dark ruby-colored 1994 Cabernet Sauvignon, while not one of the stars of the vintage, offers clean, pure cassis fruit that has been subtly oaked. It possesses good flesh, overall elegance, sweet tannin, and a restrained style. Drink it over the next 7–8 years.

Attractive citrusy, mineral, flint, and herbal aromas emerge from the delicately made, medium-bodied, nicely textured, dry 1995 Sauvignon Blanc. Crisp and refreshing, it should be drunk over the next year. Perhaps the finest Cakebread Chardonnay I have ever tasted, the medium- to full-bodied 1995 exhibits a light medium straw color, followed by a tight but promising nose of smoky ripe fruit and subtle vanillin, and excellent richness and delineation. This wine possesses a Burgundian-like structure. Drink it over the next 2–4 years. Improvement in wine quality is a reality at this Napa Valley winery.

A tightly knit, more restrained and firmer-styled Zinfandel, much of this 1994's appeal comes at the back of the mouth. There is a mineral and black raspberry-scented nose, rich, dense, black cherry and raspberry flavors, medium to full body, excellent purity, and a spicy, long, structured, stony finish. This classy, potentially complex Zinfandel should be given 6–12 months of bottle age and drunk over the next 7–8 years. Has anyone else noticed that Cakebread is making better and better wines?

CALDWELL (NAPA)

1996 Cabernet Sauvignon Aida Vineyard	Napa	D	87+
1996 Zinfandel Aida Vineyard	Napa	D	87

This wine is made by Tom Eddy, who also has his own label. The wine is produced from the vineyard originally made famous by Turley Cellars' powerhouse Zinfandels and Petite Sirahs. However, the vineyard has a new owner, and 1998 will be the last vintage for an Aida-designated Turley wine. The 1996 Caldwell Zinfandel Aida is similar to the Turley offerings. It possesses a dark ruby color, plenty of spicy oak in the nose, and a sophisticated, elegant, polished personality. The wine is well balanced, with its 14.8% alcohol amazingly well hidden by the wine's excellent richness. Tasty and forward, it is capable of lasting 5–7 years.

The 1996 Cabernet Sauvignon Aida Vineyard needs a minimum of 3–4 years of cellaring to permit some of the tannin to melt away. Tightly knit, with an opaque purple color, restrained aromatics (consisting primarily of *pain grillé*, earth, underbrush, and blackberry and cherry fruit), this powerful, full-bodied, expansive, thick wine is unevolved and monochromatic. If it evolves as I expect, look for the score to rise, but patience is required. Anticipated maturity: 2001–2017.

CAMBRIA WINERY (SANTA MARIA)

1996 Chardonnay Katherine's Vineyard	Santa Barbara	C	89
1996 Chardonnay Reserve	Santa Barbara	D	90
1995 Chardonnay Reserve	Santa Barbara	D	88
1997 Pinot Noir Julia's Vineyard	Santa Maria	C	87
1996 Pinot Noir Julia's Vineyard	Santa Maria	C	84
1995 Pinot Noir Julia's Vineyard	Santa Maria	C	86
1994 Pinot Noir Julia's Vineyard	Santa Barbara	C	85
1996 Pinot Noir Reserve	Santa Maria	D	89
1994 Pinot Noir Reserve	Santa Barbara	D	89
1996 Sangiovese Tepusquet Vineyard	Santa Maria	C	87

1997	Syrah Tepusquet Vineyard	Santa Maria	C	(86–87)
1996	Syrah Tepusquet Vineyard	Santa Barbara	C	87
1995	Syrah Tepusquet Vineyard	Santa Barbara	C	87
1997	Viognier Tepusquet Vineyard	Santa Maria	C	86
1996	Viognier Tepusquet Vineyard	Santa Maria	C	84

This Santa Barbara winery holds a well-deserved reputation for its rich, tropical fruit-dominated Chardonnays, and tasty, supple Pinot Noirs. Additionally, Sangiovese, Syrah, and Viognier are produced. The 1997 Viognier Tepusquet Vineyard is a crisp, elegant, fruit-driven wine with adequate varietal character, melony, honeyed fruit, good purity, and a flavorful, crisp finish. While not the biggest Viognier, it will be popular with consumers. Drink it over the next year. The 1996 Chardonnay Katherine's Vineyard, from a vineyard named after Jess Jackson's daughter, possesses tangy underlying acidity, and a broad, tropical fruit-dominated personality with a degree of delicacy. A crowd-pleasing style of Chardonnay (33% new French oak barrels are used), with everything in the correct place, it will provide noteworthy drinking during its first 1–2 years of life. The 1996 Chardonnay Reserve is a 100% barrel-fermented cuvée given extensive lees contact. Sixty percent new French oak is used in the wine's upbringing. It is a rich, tropical fruit-dominated wine with good acidity, excellent definition, and a medium- to full-bodied, spicy finish. The wood adds a complex element without dominating this wine's disarming fruit qualities. Drink it over the next several years; 1,000 cases were produced.

Although not profound, Cambria's Pinot Noirs offer plenty of sex appeal. The 1997 Pinot Noir Julia's Vineyard displays a medium ruby color, followed by smoky, berry, and herb aromas with toasty oak in the background (40% new oak is utilized). The wine possesses good ripeness and light tannin. It is meant to be an expansive, broad-flavored Pinot Noir for consuming over the next 2–3 years. The 1996 Pinot Noir Reserve (a selection made both in the vineyard and cellar) is a richer, deeper offering that is given 18 months of barrel aging. Production is limited to less than 700 cases. The wine exhibits a dark plum color, and a seductive black cherry/plumlike perfume with hints of Asian spices, *pain grillé,* and roasted herbs. Savory, round, and disarming, this is a delicious, easy-to-understand and -drink Pinot that should be consumed over the next 2–4 years.

I am generally unimpressed with most California Sangiovese, but Cambria has fashioned a fine 1996 Sangiovese Tepusquet Vineyard. Interestingly, 15% Syrah was added to the blend. This wine has a medium ruby color, and a pronounced cherry/strawberry jam-scented nose with some spice in the background. A fruity, tasty wine with balancing acidity, this popularly styled wine needs to be consumed during its first 1–3 years of life. Both of Cambria's Syrahs are made in a softer, more fruit-driven style. They are medium weight, charming, and drinkable upon release. The dark ruby-colored 1996 Syrah Tepusquet Vineyard reveals attractive sweet cassis and black raspberries in its aromatics. Spice and pepper are present in this medium-bodied, pleasant, cleanly made Syrah. About 2% Viognier was added to the blend. Produced from 100% Syrah, 1997 Syrah Tepusquet Vineyard is a deeper, richer wine with more color, body, and glycerin. Both of these Syrahs are made in a soft, round style meant to be drunk over the next 3–5 years.

I found Cambria's 1996 Viognier Tepusquet Vineyard to be a light, crisp, medium-bodied wine that faded in the finish. Nevertheless, there is enough up-front honeysuckle-scented and -flavored fruit to provide pleasant drinking over the next year. The 1995 Chardonnay Reserve offers a light golden color, an excellent, toasty, smoky, tropical fruit-scented nose, bold, rich, nicely textured flavors, medium to full body, and a longer finish than the regular bottling. Nevertheless, I would also opt for drinking this wine over the next year.

Cambria's Pinot Noir offerings are well made, with the telltale tomato/herbaceousness that seems to be a characteristic of Santa Barbara. The 1995 Pinot Noir Julia's Vineyard exhibits a deep ruby color, followed by a spicy, roasted vegetable, meaty nose with cherry and cranberry fruit lurking in the background. The wine is soft and round, but leans toward the vegetal side of Pinot Noir. I suggest drinking it over the next 2–3 years, before it begins to taste like V-8 juice. The 1996 Pinot Noir Julia's Vineyard is similarly styled, with less herbaceousness, as well as less flavor intensity. Soft and round, it will provide competent drinking over the next several years.

The 1994 Pinot Noir Julia's Vineyard exhibits a dark ruby color, followed by a peppery, spicy, herbal-scented nose, intermixed with aromas of jammy cherries. This medium-bodied wine should be drunk over the next 1–2 years. It is a midweight, soft, straightforward style of Pinot Noir. More enticing and seductive is the 1994 Pinot Noir Reserve. This wine reveals a strawberry, black cherry, earthy, slightly tomato-scented nose, a seductive, creamy texture, ripe fruit on the palate, medium to full body, considerable toasty oak, and a soft, layered finish. A delicious Pinot Noir, it falls just short of being exceptional. It should drink well for 2–3 years.

The more Syrah I taste from Santa Barbara, the more I think this varietal should be planted at the expense of further Pinot Noir. Santa Barbara Syrahs appear to possess a natural richness and classic varietal character that is not always apparent in the region's Pinot Noirs. The 1995 Syrah Tepusquet Vineyard displays a dense ruby/purple color, followed by an alluring blackberry and cassis-scented nose with notes of smoke, tar, and pepper. In the mouth, it is medium bodied and round, with a lush texture and an easy-to-understand personality. The finish is all silky tannin and ripe fruit. This forward-styled Syrah should be consumed over the next 7–8 years.

CARDINALE (NAPA)

1997	Proprietary Red Wine	California	EEE	(94–96)
1996	Proprietary Red Wine	California	EE	94
1995	Proprietary Red Wine	California	EE	91
1996	Royale Proprietary White Wine	Napa	E	90

Cardinale is the jewel in the Kendall-Jackson portfolio. The wine, which draws its fruit from the finest vineyards owned by Jess Jackson (the Alexander Mountain Estate, Liparita Vineyard on Howell Mountain, Veeder Peak, and the winery's Napa Vineyard), is a luxury-priced cuvée aged for 20–22 months in 100% new French oak, and bottled without filtration. Malolactic fermentation is done in barrel, and the production is modest, averaging 2,800–4,000 cases. I was blown away by both the 1997 and 1996. Cardinale's winemaker is Charles Thomas, an articulate, brilliant young man who was a star winemaker at Mondavi before he was lured away by Jess Jackson. The 1997 (92% Cabernet Sauvignon and 8% Merlot) boasts an impressively saturated black/purple color, as well as sensational aromas of blackberries, violets, minerals, cassis, and cherry liqueur. There is fabulous concentration and purity, an endless midpalate, and a terrific 45-second finish. This is an exquisite, gorgeously pure, seamless classic that should be accessible when released but will age for 2–3 decades. The 1996 is no weak sister. A blend of 89% Cabernet Sauvignon and 11% Merlot (3,200 cases), this opaque purple-colored wine offers up a fabulous nose of black fruits (cassis, cherries, and blackberries), subtle new oak, marvelously full body, more aggressive tannin than the 1997, and an impressively layered midpalate and finish. The wine is extraordinarily well endowed, impeccably well balanced, and brilliantly well delineated for its massive size. Anticipated maturity: 2002–2022. The outstanding 1995 (2,800 cases made from a blend of 77% Cabernet Sauvignon and 23% Merlot) is somewhat overwhelmed when tasted next to the extraordinary 1996 and 1997. The wine's opaque purple color is followed by copious quantities of toast, cassis, tobacco, earth, and spice in a full-blown bouquet. Full bodied, with superb purity, and a gorgeous marriage of power and elegance, this classic offering should age effortlessly for 20–25+ years. Kudos to winemaker Charles Thomas!

I thought Cardinale's 1996 Royale to be a promising white Graves lookalike. It is primarily Sauvignon Blanc, but there is a healthy dose of Semillon added to fatten the wine, and give it a creamier texture. It is a boldly styled, pure, lush, medium- to full-bodied dry white with a subtle influence of toasty oak. Top-notch waxy, citrusy flavors build in the mouth of this medium-bodied wine, which also has a long, clean finish with substantial fruit and overall equilibrium. This wine will continue to improve for another year and will last for 3–4.

CARMENET VINEYARD (SONOMA)

1995	Cabernet Franc	Sonoma	C	86
1994	Cabernet Franc	Sonoma	C	86
1994	Cabernet Franc Moon Mountain Estate	Sonoma Mountain	B	87
1993	Cabernet Franc Moon Mountain Estate	Sonoma	B	89
1993	Cabernet Sauvignon Moon Mountain Estate Dynamite	Sonoma	C	86
1997	Chardonnay Sangiacomo Vineyard	Carneros	C	87
1996	Chardonnay Sangiacomo Vineyard	Carneros	C	84
1997	Colombard Saviez Vineyard Old Vines	Napa	B	86
1996	Colombard Saviez Vineyard Old Vines	Napa	B	85
1995	Dynamite Cabernet	Sonoma	C	83
1994	Meritage Moon Mountain Estate	Sonoma	C	90
1993	Meritage Moon Mountain Estate	Sonoma	B	89
1996	Merlot Sangiacomo Vineyard	Carneros	D	88
1993	Moon Mountain Proprietary Red Wine	Sonoma	D	87
1995	Moon Mountain Proprietary Red Wine Estate Reserve	Sonoma	D	90
1995	Moon Mountain Proprietary Red Wine Estate Reserve	Sonoma	C	88
1997	Reserve Proprietary White (70% Semillon/30% Sauvignon)	Edna Valley	C	90
1995	Sauvignon Blanc Reserve Paragon Vineyard	Edna Valley	C	87
1994	Vin de Garde Moon Mountain Estate	Sonoma	C	91
1993	Vin de Garde Moon Mountain Estate	Sonoma	C	89+?

I have long been an admirer of Carmenet's Colombard. The 1997 Colombard Saviez Vineyard Old Vines is a medium-bodied, grassy, herb- and fruit-dominated wine with notes of hay, fennel, and melony fruit. Fresh and exuberant, it is a fun, bistro white to enjoy over the next year. The outstanding 1997 Reserve Proprietary White is a delicious, Graves-like, opulently textured blend of Sauvignon Blanc and Semillon. It reveals good oak, plenty of luscious honeyed, citrusy fruit, fine purity, and a chewy, fleshy finish. Although intense, good underlying acidity buttresses the wine's weight. Drink it over the next 3–4 years. The attractive, fleshy, tropical fruit-scented and -flavored 1997 Chardonnay Sangiacomo Vineyard carries its 13.8% alcohol well. With excellent fruit, this is an easy to understand and consume Chardonnay with the oak present but not overdone.

I was impressed with the outstanding 1995 Moon Mountain Estate, a blend of 79% Cabernet Sauvignon, 19% Cabernet Franc, and 2% Petit Verdot. This wine could easily pass for a top-class Bordeaux in a blind tasting. It reveals a saturated ruby/purple color as well as a classy black currant, lead pencil, licorice, and vanillin-scented nose. Medium bodied and elegant, with excellent purity, and a Graves-like roasted herb/mineral component, it is young but accessible. Anticipated maturity: 2002–2016. Far more accessible is the plump, hedonistic 1996 Merlot Sangiacomo Vineyard. It reveals a dark ruby color, and a big, smoky, berry, chocolatey nose. Fleshy and medium bodied, with excellent richness and depth, it is meant to be drunk over the next 5–7 years.

I am perplexed by the Carmenet wines. On the positive side, they possess elegance and finesse, but on the negative side, they are extremely tannic and too high in acidity. Their leanness and austerity are at odds with the notion that wine is a beverage of pleasure. There is quality to be found, and I especially liked the 1995 Sauvignon Blanc Reserve Paragon Vineyard. It possesses a honeyed, herbal, fruity character, medium body, and excellent richness and length. One of my all-time favorites in terms of value and drinkability has been the Old Vine Colombard. The 1996 Saviez Vineyard offering, while not as richly fruity and savory as previous vintages, is soft, with nice fruit in its aromatics and flavors. It requires consumption over the next year. I also thought the 1996 Chardonnay Sangiacomo was an attractive, well-made, straightforward Chardonnay presented in a medium-bodied, easygoing format.

To reiterate, Carmenet's red wines are tannic and lean. The 1993 Moon Mountain Proprietary Red Wine reveals the most richness, character, and length, as well as a red currant, tart personality. The red wines should last for 10–12 years; the whites need to be drunk over the next year.

Although the 1993 Cabernet Franc will not make anyone forget La Jota's Cabernet Franc, it is an attractive, complex, rich wine with a smoky, black currant, herbal nose, surprisingly fat, sweet, ripe, expansive fruit, and a medium-bodied, soft, silky finish. It should drink well for a decade. The supple 1993 Meritage (83% Cabernet Sauvignon and 17% Cabernet Franc) possesses a smoky, spicy, oaky, black cherry and currant-scented nose, medium body, fine ripeness and purity, and an overall sense of grace and balance. It should be drinkable early in its life and last for 10–15 years. The 1993 Vin de Garde (76% Cabernet Sauvignon and 24% Cabernet Franc) is (presumably because of its name) meant to be Carmenet's longest-lived red wine. It reveals gobs of intensity, concentration, and richness, as well as velvety sweet tannin, medium to full body, and an excellent to outstanding ripeness, extraction, and potential. Its spicy, herbal side is less pronounced than in the other two offerings. It should drink well for 15+ years after its release.

Carmenet's 1995 Cabernet Franc exhibits a dark ruby color, followed by a tart, restrained, medium-bodied, red currant-scented nose with hints of raspberries. It is moderately endowed, pleasant and clean, although slightly firm with intrusive acid. This wine should drink well after 2–3 more years of aging; it should last for 10–12 years. The more substantially endowed 1995 Moon Mountain Estate Reserve, reveals a dark ruby/purple color with a textbook cedary, tobacco, weedy, black currant-scented nose. It exhibits good sweetness and ripeness of fruit on the attack, medium body, obvious spicy new oak (almost too much), and a moderately tannic, narrowly focused, spicy finish. This is a very good, potentially excellent wine that should provide restrained yet elegant drinking for 10–14 years.

The 1993 Moon Mountain Dynamite Cabernet Sauvignon (from young vines) is a crisp, medium-bodied, streamlined Cabernet that technocrats will undoubtedly like more than I did. It is a good, reasonably priced wine revealing fine cherry and cassis fruit with a touch of herbs, a borderline high level of acidity, good spice, and a clean, fresh finish. Drink it over the next 6–7 years.

The medium-bodied 1994 Cabernet Franc Moon Mountain Estate is not yet that expressive for this fragrant varietal. The healthy dark ruby/purple color is followed by emerging aromas of cherries and spice. Soft, forward, and elegant, this appears to be a precocious 1994 that will require drinking during its first decade of life. In total contrast, the 1994 Vin de Garde Moon Mountain Estate exhibits an opaque ruby/purple color, as well as a huge, exotic nose of cassis, herbs, ginger, and coconut. Sweet tannin and an underlying mineral component are present in this fabulously extracted, rich, full-bodied, spicy wine. This large-scaled, structured wine clearly lives up to its name. It will undoubtedly require 5–7 years of cellaring after its release; it displays the potential to last for 20+ years. Lastly, the 1994 Meritage Moon Mountain Estate stood out for its well-focused personality, which exhibited sensational elegance, and, for the vintage, a soft, supple style that came across as less aggressive and extracted than many other 1994s. Deeply colored, with loads of red and black fruits, this will not be one of the biggest wines of the vintage, but it has the potential to be an outstanding effort in a stylish, measured, but authoritatively flavored manner. Because of its softness, it should drink well when released, and keep for up to 15 years.

CARTLIDGE AND BROWNE (CALIFORNIA)

1997 Chardonnay	California	A	88
1996 Chardonnay	California	A	87
1997 Pinot Noir	California	B	86
1994 Pinot Noir	California	A	86
1997 Zinfandel	California	A	87
1996 Zinfandel	California	A	86
1995 Zinfandel	California	A	86

A strong argument can be made that some of the finest wine values in California emerge under the Cartlidge and Browne label. Their Chardonnay is an astonishing bargain! The 1997 Chardonnay (20,000 cases) offers copious quantities of honeyed tropical fruit, outstanding purity, medium body, and a ripe apricot- and pineapple-flavored personality. The wine reveals a subtle touch of oak, which tends to both delineate and add complexity to this lush, richly fruity Chardonnay. Drink it over the next 8–12 months. A great value.

The 1997 Pinot Noir is another terrific bargain, particularly for this high-priced varietal. This wine could easily compete with Pinots selling for twice the price. The color is medium ruby, and the wine offers copious amounts of soft berry/cherry fruit in a nicely layered and textured, medium-bodied format. The acidity is low, and the wine charming and seductive. It is all a Pinot Noir should be. Consume it over the next 1–2 years. The 1997 Zinfandel offers textbook peppery, berry notes in its provocatively fragrant bouquet. While the color is not dense, the wine reveals abundant ripe, jammy fruit, low acidity, and a fleshy, fat mouth-feel. It is a delicious, medium-bodied, fruit-driven Zinfandel to enjoy over the next 1–2 years. All three of these offerings are astonishing values!

This winery, known for its excellent bargains, turned out another knockout Chardonnay in 1996 that provides plenty of high quality flavors for an unbeatable price. The 1996 California Chardonnay exhibits a clean, fruit-driven personality with subtle, buttery, smoky, hazelnut aromas that suggest a large quantity of this wine was barrel fermented. Refreshing yet perfumed, concentrated, medium bodied, and impeccably pure, this is a bright, richly fruity, well-crafted Chardonnay for consuming over the next 12–18 months. The 1996 Zinfandel is the ideal restaurant Zinfandel, with a medium ruby color, soft, delicious, spicy, berry fruit, medium body, and savory, silky-textured finish. It should be drunk over the next several years. Both wines are exceptional values. The 1995 Zinfandel is not a big, blockbuster, high alcohol Zin, but rather, a medium-bodied, exuberantly fruity, delicious, peppery, and berry-scented wine that comes across as elegant. Tasters will not have to wade through masses of tannin, alcohol, and glycerin to enjoy this wine, which can be served slightly chilled. Drink it over the next 1–2 years.

The 1994 Pinot Noir shocked me with its complexity and richness. The wine's shy nose is not indicative of the impressive flavors. It boasts a medium deep ruby color, good cherry fruit backed up by subtle herbs in the nose, and a smoky, jammy, cherry, smoked herb, meaty, Gevrey-Chambertin/Côte de Nuits-like character. This velvety-textured Pinot Noir with an expansive midsection is an amazing wine for the price. Drink it over the next 1–2 years.

CAYMUS VINEYARD (NAPA)

1994	Cabernet Sauvignon	Napa	E	91
1993	Cabernet Sauvignon	Napa	C	89
1994	Cabernet Sauvignon Special Selection	Napa	EE	95
1995	Sauvignon Blanc	California	B	87

Caymus is one of a handful of Napa Valley wineries that has enjoyed an enviable success record since the early 1970s. The winery continues to focus on three wines—Sauvignon Blanc, their exotic white proprietary wine called Conundrum (usually a blend of Viognier, Sauvignon Blanc, Chardonnay, and Semillon), and Cabernet Sauvignon. Chuck Wagner and his father, Charlie, have begun to look south to develop vineyards as there is not enough Caymus to fulfill the marketplace's needs. Their Monterey vineyard Chardonnay Mer et Soleil is a good example of this direction. The current and upcoming releases include the 1995 Sauvignon Blanc, another noteworthy, elegant, ripe, tasty, melony style of Sauvignon that is long on fruit and deliciousness. Although not as opulent as the 1994, it is very good. This 100% barrel-fermented Sauvignon is best drunk within its first year of life.

Cabernet is king at Caymus. During the decade of the nineties, there has been a succession of sumptuous, rich, concentrated, lavishly wooded, cassis-flavored Caymus Cabernet Sauvignons. The 1993 Cabernet Sauvignon has closed down since bottling, but it is still a deep, dark ruby/purple-colored wine with a tight but promising nose of black currants and sweet vanillin, toasty oak. This backward wine is full bodied, dense, powerful, as well as tannic. It will benefit from 2–3 more years of cellaring, and keep for 12–15 years. The sumptuous 1994 Cabernet Sauvignon appears to be one of the best Napa Cabernets Caymus has produced. Remarkably, there is plenty to go around—25,000 cases, approximately the same production as Lafite-Rothschild and Margaux. The wine exhibits a dark purple color, and a sweet, jammy black currant-scented nose. The lush, juicy, succulent texture is crammed with glycerin and extract. Surprisingly soft (a hallmark of this vintage), with a smooth texture, this full-bodied, oaky Cabernet should drink well for 10–12+ years. I have followed the Special Selection Cabernet Sauvignon since the debut 1975 vintage, and the 1994 appears to be one of the finest yet made at Caymus. Its saturated purple color is accompanied by an exuberant, sweet, enveloping fragrance of smoky new oak, and jammy blackberry and cassis fruit. In the mouth, this lavishly wooded, black fruit-filled Cabernet is extremely full bodied, with superb levels of fruit, glycerin, and extract. Like many 1994 Cabernet Sauvignons, it possesses extraordinary equilibrium, with the sweet tannin giving the wine considerable accessibility. The finish lasts for nearly 30 seconds. This will be a fun wine to drink young, but do not discount its aging ability as it should last for two decades.

I tasted a number of different component parts of the 1995 Cabernet Sauvignon, all of which—at least from an aromatic, flavor, and textural perspective—resembled the 1994

Napa. Interestingly, when I saw Chuck Wagner in late October of 1996, he was not yet sure whether there would be a Special Selection in 1995, which is surprising in view of the vintage's high quality.

CHALK HILL WINERY (SONOMA)

1994 Cabernet Sauvignon Estate	Sonoma	D	89
1993 Cabernet Sauvignon Estate	Sonoma	C	88

Chalk Hill has been fashioning very fine wines, so let's hope the departure of winemaker David Ramey to Dominus does not change things. The 1993 Cabernet Sauvignon Estate exhibits a healthy dark ruby/purple color, followed by an attractive, moderately intense nose of chocolate, smoke, and rich cassis fruit. Medium to full bodied, with a tannic edge, this wine reveals excellent richness, fine purity, and an appealing texture. Although young and unevolved, it is accessible. It should drink well for 10–12 years. The 1994 is an intriguing Rhône-like Cabernet Sauvignon with a Provençal nose of olives, iodine, black cherries, tobacco, and weedy cassis. Medium to full bodied and lush, with plenty of spice, this is an exotic, delicious wine (although not exactly what I think of as North Coast Cabernet) that should drink well for 12–15 years.

CHALONE WINE GROUP (MONTEREY)

1997 Chardonnay	California	D	90
1996 Chardonnay	California	D	89
1995 Chardonnay	California	D	89+
1997 Chardonnay Reserve	California	D	91
1996 Chardonnay Reserve	California	D	91
1994 Chardonnay Reserve	California	D	91+
1996 Pinot Blanc Reserve	California	D	90
1994 Pinot Blanc Reserve	California	D	90
1994 Pinot Noir Estate	California	C	88
1993 Pinot Noir Estate	California	C	86
1993 Pinot Noir Estate Gavilan	California	B	88
1994 Pinot Noir Reserve	California	D	78
1993 Pinot Noir Reserve	California	D	87?

This winery has been producing amazingly long-lived Pinot Blancs for over two decades. The 1996 Pinot Blanc Reserve boasts a rich, custard, honeyed orange/lemony nose and flavors, medium to full body, terrific fruit intensity, and the structure and overall personality of a serious white Burgundy. It will age for 7–8 years. All of the Chardonnays are noteworthy efforts. The fragrant, flamboyant yet charming 1997 Chardonnay exhibits an attractive buttery, vanillin, and earthy-scented nose, chewy fruit, and considerable power, ripeness, and structure. This pure wine should age well for 6–7 years. The full-bodied 1997 Chardonnay Reserve reveals well-integrated wood, acidity, and alcohol. The wine is Burgundian in style, with smoky, leesy fruit flavors, good spice, and fine purity. Although large scaled, it is elegant and accessible. Drink it now and over the next decade.

The medium-bodied, spicy, oaky 1996 Chardonnay reveals notes of buttery pears and honey in its moderately intense bouquet. The wine is well built, with good complexity, and a finesse-styled personality. It should drink well for 7–8 years. The powerful, full-bodied, concentrated 1996 Chardonnay Reserve is significantly richer than the regular bottling, exhibiting a long, layered, impressively endowed personality. Although more backward than the 1997 Reserve, it promises to last a decade or more.

Chalone has been gradually refining the style of its Pinot Noir, utilizing more new oak, and beginning (correctly in my view) to destem much of the fruit. This has resulted in softer, less herbaceous wines that may not be as long-lived, but are more charming. Chalone's 1994 Pinot Noir Estate exhibits a light ruby color, as well as wonderfully sweet, succulent, cherry and berry fruit intermingled with scents of smoke, earth, and wood. Excellent richness, and a long, lush finish make for a glass of sexy Pinot Noir that is far more forward than the old style Chalone Pinots. I found Chalone's 1994 Pinot Noir Reserve too vegetal, with an annoyingly tart, shrill acid level, in addition to being an earthy, spice-driven wine without sufficient fruit.

The two 1993 Pinot Noir offerings are also noteworthy, although not as open knit, sweet, and ripe as the 1994s. The 1993 Pinot Noir Estate exhibits black olive, cherry, and spicy scents, medium to full body, slight tannin, and good acidity. It should drink well for 5–6 years. The good 1993 Pinot Noir Reserve is more tightly knit and closed than the regular bottling. It should ultimately turn out to be the better wine.

The impressive Pinot Blanc and Chardonnay offerings need cellaring, as they are built in a medium- to full-bodied, backward style. The powerful 1995 Chardonnay can be drunk, but it is still dominated by its structure. The wine is full bodied, with stony, mineral, citrusy fruit also displaying notions of honey, white flowers, and smoky oak. There is undoubtedly a *terroir* character, which is expressed in the wine's minerality. Give it another year of cellaring, and drink it over the following 7–8. The superb 1995 Chardonnay Reserve is extremely youthful, backward, and full bodied, with a smoky, earthy, buttery, and mineral-scented nose, huge, chewy flavors, crisp acidity, and outstanding extraction. An enjoyable wine of restraint and impeccable equilibrium, it is 1–3 years away from full maturity. It is a candidate for a decade's worth of aging.

Chalone's 1994 Pinot Blanc Reserve requires 2–4 years of cellaring. Fortunately, a disturbing mustiness in the aromatics blows off to reveal citrusy, mineral, and orange blossom-like scents, followed by backward, rich, medium- to full-bodied flavors with tangy acidity, and imposing structure. The wine is impressively weighty in the mouth, without "feeling" heavy. It is about as large-scaled a Pinot Blanc as anyone will find in California. I would not be surprised if this wine lasted for 10–12 years.

Lastly, the Gavilan wines, made from Chalone's youngest vineyards, have turned out extremely well. Readers looking for fine Chardonnay and Pinot Noir in the under $14 range are well advised to check them out. The soft Gavilan 1993 Pinot Noir displays plenty of red and black fruits, good spice, and a supple, easygoing finish. It should drink well for 1–2 years.

CHIMNEY ROCK (NAPA)

1995 Cabernet Sauvignon Reserve Stag's Leap	Napa	E	88
1995 Chardonnay	Carneros	C	87
1995 Fumé Blanc	Napa	B	87

A finesse-styled, character-filled Cabernet Sauvignon, this rich, intense 1995 offering from Chimney Rock exhibits a dark ruby/purple color and a stylish nose of tobacco, cassis, herbs, and minerals. Medium bodied, with outstanding purity, impressive overall equilibrium, and an excellent finish, this is a delicious, complex, suave Cabernet that can be drunk now or cellared for 10–12 years.

An elegant, smoky, Burgundian-styled Chardonnay, Chimney Rock's 1995 possesses sweet, leesy fruit, subtle oak, medium body, and very good concentration. It is a stylish, finesse-styled Chardonnay, yet there is no shortage of flavor. The only negative is the wine's short finish.

The 100% Sauvignon 1995 Fumé Blanc exhibits attractive melony flavors, crisp acidity, an enticing texture, and fine purity—all presented in a medium-bodied, elegant format. How encouraging it is to see Chimney Rock begin to achieve more aromatics, flavor, and texture in their wines. Drink this 1995 Fumé Blanc over the next year.

CLARK-CLAUDON VINEYARDS (NAPA)

1995 Cabernet Sauvignon	Napa	D	93+

Another limited production (300 cases) wine made from a vineyard on the eastern side of Howell Mountain, this brilliantly made Cabernet suggests this winery knows what to do with top-quality fruit. While the 1995 will be hard to find, readers who are interested in profound California Cabernet Sauvignons should seek out future releases. This opaque purple-colored wine boasts knockout aromatics of smoke, charcoal, black currants, lead pencil, minerals, and high-quality French oak. Impressive on the palate, with a classy richness married to well-integrated wood, acidity, and tannin, this is a full-bodied, fabulously rich, expressive, impeccably balanced Cabernet Sauvignon. Anticipated maturity: now–2015.

CLINE CELLARS (SONOMA)

1996 Zinfandel	California	A	85
1995 Zinfandel	California	B	86
1994 Zinfandel	Contra Costa	B	88
1993 Zinfandel	Contra Costa	B	89
1996 Zinfandel Ancient Vines	Contra Costa	C	90
1995 Zinfandel Ancient Vines	Contra Costa	B	86
1996 Zinfandel Big Break Vineyard	Contra Costa	C	87
1995 Zinfandel Big Break Vineyard	Contra Costa	B	89
1994 Zinfandel Big Break Vineyard	Contra Costa	C	91
1993 Zinfandel Big Break Vineyard	Contra Costa	C	91
1996 Zinfandel Bridgehead Vineyard	Contra Costa	C	87
1995 Zinfandel Bridgehead Vineyard	Contra Costa	B	88
1994 Zinfandel Bridgehead Vineyard	Contra Costa	C	91
1993 Zinfandel Bridgehead Vineyard	Contra Costa	C	90+
1996 Zinfandel Live Oak Vineyard	Contra Costa	C	88
1994 Zinfandel Reserve	Contra Costa	C	89+
1993 Zinfandel Reserve	Contra Costa	C	91

Over recent years, Cline Cellars has emerged as one of California's most reliable Zinfandel producers. Moreover, this winery has unquestionably raised the image of Zinfandel from Contra Costa. And finally, it has kept prices moderate, which is to be applauded.

This reliable winery has produced four fine 1996 Zinfandels. They possess some of the most saturated ruby/purple colors of the vintage, as well as big, muscular, full-bodied personalities. For example, the 1996 Zinfandel Big Break Vineyard displays a dense ruby/purple color, a rich, briery, earthy, black cherry and raspberry-scented nose with licorice and underbrush in the background, full body, excellent depth, and good ripeness. It finishes with plenty of power and extract. It should drink well for 5–6 years. The full-bodied, dense 1996 Zinfandel Live Oak Vineyard reveals a more saturated purple color, a bold, expansive flavor profile, admirable weight, and an undeniably macho style. It might be short on finesse, but it does not cheat the taster in terms of flavor depth and mouth-filling capacity. Drink it over the next 5–6 years.

The medium- to full-bodied, tannic 1996 Zinfandel Bridgehead is more backward and slightly more angular than its three siblings. It exhibits a dense color, excellent purity, and gobs of earthy black cherry and berry fruit, but it comes across as more compressed. The outstanding 1996 Zinfandel Ancient Vines (made from a 110-year-old vineyard) offers an impressively pigmented ruby/purple color, and sweet, intense black cherry liqueurlike notes in the penetrating bouquet. As the wine sits in the glass, minerals, pepper, spice, and coffee scents emerge. Rich, with sensational purity and flavor intensity, this full-bodied, multilayered wine coats the palate, and has a 30+-second finish. Drink it over the next 5–7 years.

There is a certain overripeness to Cline's 1996 Zinfandel in addition to the plummy fruit. The color is dark ruby, and the wine is soft, not complex, but straightforward and exuberant. Drink it over the next 1–2 years. The 1995 California Zinfandel is a well-made, deep ruby-colored wine with moderate levels of black cherry fruit intertwined with dusty, earthy scents. It is an attractive, cleanly made wine for drinking over the next 2 years. The 1995 Zinfandel Ancient Vines (6,692 cases produced) exhibits a dark plum color, and an intriguing nose of olives, iodine, pepper, and plumlike fruit. Soft and round, with medium body, and a short but pleasant finish, it requires consumption over the next several years.

Two of the more concentrated wines of the vintage are Cline's single vineyard Zinfandels. Each vineyard produced just under 1,500 cases. The 1995 Zinfandel Bridgehead Vineyard is a high-toned, deep ruby/purple-colored wine with a peppery, black cherry-scented nose, ripe, medium-bodied, concentrated flavors, good acidity, plenty of length, and a layered, concentrated personality—rare for this vintage. There is a deep midpalate, as well as plenty of sweet fruit in the finish. This wine is already drinking well, but it will keep for 5–6 years. The densest, richest, and most powerful of the 1995 Cline Zinfandels is the 1995 Zinfandel Big Break Vineyard. The wine boasts a saturated ruby/purple color, followed by a big, smoky, chocolatey, briery, peppery nose with American oak in the background. Still tightly knit, this pure, medium- to full-bodied wine offers black cherrylike flavors intermingled with minerals and spice. Although neither viscous nor voluptuous, it is a classic, well-structured, concentrated Zinfandel to drink now and over the next 6–7 years.

The 1994 Zinfandels are beautifully made, pure wines that are a must purchase for Zinfandel enthusiasts. It is splitting hairs to try and pick a favorite, but this is what my palate recorded. The 1994 Zinfandel possesses a healthy, saturated dark ruby/purple color, a lovely nose of straightforward, ripe, jammy, black raspberry fruit, medium to full body, excellent purity, and a soft, heady, well-focused finish. Drink it over the next 3–4 years. The 1994 Zinfandel Reserve (with a gold rather than bluish/green capsule) exhibits a more saturated, denser, ruby/purple color, and a tighter but more intense set of aromatics, consisting of black raspberries, licorice, and spicy oak. Rich and full bodied, with significantly more structure and definition than the 1994 regular cuvée, this is an impressively endowed wine for drinking over the next 6–7 years. It should easily merit an outstanding rating with 6 more months of cellaring, but it is the least flattering of this quartet.

Both the 1994 Big Break and 1994 Bridgehead Zinfandels are knockout examples of this varietal. Just over 800 cases of each are produced from century-old, head-pruned vineyards. Readers can take their pick as to which one they prefer. . . . I couldn't make that choice. The 1994 Bridgehead Zinfandel seems softer and more forward, but both are enormously endowed, wonderfully pure, rich, sumptuous wines bursting with blackberry, raspberry, and jammy blueberry fruit. Extremely full bodied and powerful, yet surprisingly well balanced and harmonious, these lusty wines should age well for 6–7 years. Both wines possess a finish that lasts for 30+ seconds. Bravo to Cline Cellars, a perennial source of extremely well made wines!

The 1993 Zinfandels may be the most impressive group of wines Cline Cellars has yet produced. The 1993 Zinfandel Contra Costa exhibits a healthy dark ruby/purple color, a big, berry and loamy earth-scented nose, full body, adequate tannin, and an abundance of wild berry fruit. Drink it over the next 5–8 years. The opaque purple-colored 1993 Zinfandel Big Break reveals a huge nose of sweet berry fruit and earth. Massive, rich, and totally dry, this high alcohol, seriously concentrated wine can be drunk now or cellared for 10–15 years. It is a rich, mouth-filling wine crammed with black cherry and black raspberry fruit. The 1993 Zinfandel Bridgehead Vineyard displays considerable structure and tannin, but there is no doubting the excellent concentration of ripe berry fruit. It is spicy and intense but more closed than the other offerings. Lastly, the 1993 Zinfandel Reserve is the best-balanced of these large, full-throttle wines. It offers an opaque ruby/purple color, a big, spicy, berry-scented nose, full body, light to moderate tannin, adequate acidity, and superb purity and richness. The regular cuvée should last for a decade, and the Bridgehead, Reserve, and Big Break for 20 years.

CLOS PEGASE (NAPA)

1997	Cabernet Sauvignon	Carneros/Napa	D	(88–90)
1996	Cabernet Sauvignon	Carneros/Napa	D	88
1995	Cabernet Sauvignon	Napa	C	88
1994	Cabernet Sauvignon	Napa	C	91
1993	Cabernet Sauvignon	Napa	C	87+
1997	Chardonnay Mitsuko's Vineyard	Carneros/Napa	C	87
1996	Chardonnay Mitsuko's Vineyard	Carneros/Napa	C	86
1996	Hommage Proprietary Red Wine	Carneros/Napa	E	87
1995	Hommage Proprietary Red Wine	Carneros/Napa	E	85?
1994	Hommage	Napa	E	?
1993	Hommage	Napa	D	89
1997	Merlot	Carneros/Napa	D	(86–87)
1996	Merlot	Carneros/Napa	D	84?
1994	Merlot	Napa	C	90
1993	Merlot	Napa	C	88

After a dismal beginning, Clos Pegase appears to be getting more serious about wine quality, as evidenced by the following releases. The owners have wisely brought in Burgundian-trained Ted Lemon to consult, and he appears to be in the process of fleshing out the wines' midpalates, giving them more length, ripeness, and natural textures. The 1996 Chardonnay Mitsuko's Vineyard reveals toasty oak in the nose, as well as lemony, citrusy, honeyed notes. It is medium bodied, well made, and pleasant, although uninspiring. Slightly better is the 1997 Chardonnay Mitsuko's Vineyard, which possesses more of the lemony, honeyed, white flower dimension, ripe fruit on the attack, some spice, and a foursquare but substantial personality. It should drink well for 2–3 years.

The Merlots include about 10% Cabernet Sauvignon. The dark ruby-colored 1996 Merlot reveals minty notes along with spice, chocolate, and berry fruit, clipped, compressed flavors, tart acidity, and an abrupt, compressed finish. The wine has good flavors, but tastes too acidified. The dark ruby-colored 1997 Merlot is far better. One can see Ted Lemon's hand in the fatter, richer, more textured and layered midpalate. This plump wine reveals berry fruit intermixed with chocolate and notes of underbrush. The wine's excellent finish exhibits well-integrated wood and lower acidity than the tart 1996. The 1997 should drink well for 5–7 years.

The 1996 Cabernet Sauvignon reveals a complex, spice box, cedar, olive, and black currant-scented bouquet, medium-bodied flavors, and moderate tannin in the finish. A well-made Cabernet that has not been excessively manipulated or acidified, it should drink well for a decade. Even better is the 1997 Cabernet Sauvignon, which possesses a dark ruby/purple color, and a firm underpinning of tannin, sweet, creamy, black currant flavors intertwined with cedar, Provençal herbs, and new oak. Medium to full bodied, with a relatively long finish, it should be an excellent, possibly outstanding Cabernet Sauvignon that will be drinkable young, yet keep for 10–12 years.

The luxury cuvée of 1995 Hommage was produced from 100% Cabernet Sauvignon. I am not particularly enthusiastic about this offering as it is austere, tannic, and a bit punchless, with lean, dried-out flavors. There are some attractive cedar and black currant notes in the bouquet and on the attack, but the wine quickly narrows in the mouth. Perhaps 2–3 years of cellaring will help, but I am not convinced. The 1996 Hommage appears vastly superior to the 1995, with more chocolate, cassis, and riper fruit (or is it a case of less manipulated and eviscerated fruit?). This medium- to full-bodied effort still has dry tannin in the finish to resolve, but there is more flesh and richness to balance out the wine's tannic structure. Anticipated maturity: 2000–2012.

Clos Pegase's 1993 Merlot exhibits plenty of sweet, chocolatey, berry fruit intermingled with a subtle dose of herbs. The wine is medium to full bodied, with excellent purity, and an attractive, sweet, creamy texture. Drink it over the next 4–5 years. The medium- to full-bodied, well-structured 1993 Cabernet Sauvignon reveals moderately intense, ripe aromas of cassis, oak, and olives. The emphasis is on fruit, extract, and balance. It should drink well for a decade. The 1993 Hommage has begun to close up, revealing more tannin than I remember. It is a spicy, cedary, rich, cassis-scented, full-bodied wine with the tannin beginning to assume a more prominent position in the wine's flavor profile. It is a concentrated, potentially outstanding wine.

The question mark attached to the proprietary red wine, the 1994 Hommage, may ultimately turn out to be unfair, but at present, this wine is totally muted and monolithic. Although rich and intense, it does not display much personality. I also noticed a touch of mustiness in the barrel sample, but I was unable to retaste it. Everything else about the wine looked fine, but I'll report on it again before it is in the bottle.

The 1994 Merlot offers a dark purple color, and a big, chocolatey, black raspberry/cherry-scented nose bordering on overripeness. Dense and chewy, with surprisingly tough tannin in the finish, this is a fleshy, boldly styled Merlot for drinking during the first dozen years after its release. The 1994 Cabernet Sauvignon exhibits gorgeous ripe blueberry and raspberry fruit in its flamboyant nose. Deep and velvety textured, with impressive extraction, this full-bodied, sweet-tasting (from ripe fruit, not sugar), sexy Cabernet should drink well when released and keep for 12–15 years.

This winery continues to exhibit to progress in quality. The 1995 Cabernet Sauvignon is a medium-weight, nicely made wine with a dark ruby/purple color, and sweet plum, jammy cassis, and cherrylike aromas with lavish toasty oak in the background. On the palate, the wine reveals adequate acidity, an attractive, fleshy, corpulent mouth-feel, good glycerin and extract, and an easy-to-understand, plump, chewy style. It should drink well when released and last for a decade.

B. R. COHN WINERY (SONOMA)

1994 Cabernet Sauvignon 10th Anniversary
    Olive Hill Vineyard   Sonoma   D   86+

An impressively saturated dark purple color is followed by a wine with copious quantities of *pain grillé*, vanillin, and black currant fruit. The wine offers medium body and good ripeness on entry, but it quickly closes down to a medium-bodied, tannic, backward, lean style. There is high tannin holding everything tightly in place. Will it unfold? Anticipated maturity: 2003–2015.

COLGIN CELLARS (NAPA)

1997 Cabernet Sauvignon Herb Lamb Vineyard	Napa	EE	(96–99)
1996 Cabernet Sauvignon Herb Lamb Vineyard	Napa	EE	97
1995 Cabernet Sauvignon Herb Lamb Vineyard	Napa	EE	98
1994 Cabernet Sauvignon Herb Lamb Vineyard	Napa	EE	96
1993 Cabernet Sauvignon Herb Lamb Vineyard	Napa	EE	95

What more can I say about Colgin Cellars' offerings? The proprietor is Ann Colgin and the winemaker is . . . yes, the wine goddess herself, Helen Turley. Since the debut vintage in 1992, these wines have knocked on perfection's door. Wines that are a privilege to taste, they are incredibly harmonious, extraordinarily concentrated, and aromatically provocative. Yet rhetoric aside, most important is the fact that they are immensely satisfying. The Colgin Cabernets are aged in 100% new Taransaud barrels for 18 months, and bottled with no fining or filtration. The 1997 Cabernet Sauvignon Herb Lamb Vineyard boasts an opaque black/blue/purple color, as well as a fabulous nose of wild blueberries, orchids, acacia flowers, smoky new oak, and crème de cassis liqueur. The wine reveals the vintage's telltale seamlessness, precociousness, and evolved style. Full bodied, with extraordinary intensity, and perfect harmony among all its structural components—tannin, acidity, and alcohol—this wine possesses terrific fruit purity in addition to a prodigious finish. It is a spectacular, velvety-textured wine that should be the most evolved Colgin Cabernet yet produced. Anticipated maturity: 2000–2018. The saturated black/purple-colored 1996 Cabernet Sauvignon Herb Lamb Vineyard displays this winery's hallmark—a provocative nose of blueberry jam, orchid flowers, and smoky new oak intertwined with cassis. Additional aromas of licorice and exotic Asian spices emerge as the wine sits in the glass. Extremely full bodied and rich, with more noticeable tannin than the 1997, this large-scaled yet extraordinarily rich wine is like drinking cassis/blueberry liqueur. Its sweet tannin and remarkable 40+-second finish are amazing. Anticipated maturity: now–2022.

The 1996 and 1995 could be mistaken for identical twins, although close examination reveals that the 1995 has a slightly firmer tannic edge, and the 1996 slightly lower acidity. However, both possess Colgin's telltale opaque black/purple color, phenomenal aromatics consisting of blackberries, raspberries, blueberries, cassis, subtle new oak, and a notion of floral scents (is it acacia or lilac?). In the mouth, both wines are full bodied, remarkably supple and opulent, with a purity and presence of fruit that must be tasted to be believed. Their finishes last for 45+ seconds. I suspect each of these wines will get even better over the next 5–10 years before reaching their full plateau of maturity, where they should remain for 2 decades or more. They are the quintessential examples of Cabernet Sauvignons that marry power with elegance. As a friend said after tasting a Colgin Cabernet Sauvignon, "They float like a butterfly, but sting like a bee." I am not sure Muhammad Ali or Ann Colgin would agree with that, but it paints another picture of these extraordinary wines. These wines are made by Helen Turley, the prodigiously talented winemaker/consultant.

The potentially perfect 1994 Cabernet Sauvignon is a totally dry wine, but the sweetness and taste of this wine's fruit is akin to a savory blend of a chocolate-covered, blueberry/cassis-filled candy bar and vanilla ice cream melting in the mouth. This full-bodied wine is silky, seductive, opulent, voluptuously textured, and extraordinarily fragrant, expansive, and rich. In spite of this, the wine remains graceful and well balanced, without any sense of heaviness or obtrusive tannin or acidity. I clearly underrated the 1994 from my earliest barrel tastings, but the last two times I have had it, from barrel immediately prior to bottling and in bottle, have persuaded me that this wine is one of the most exciting and remarkable young Cabernet Sauvignons I have tasted! It should drink well for another 25–30 years. Damn, I adore this wine!

The 1993 Cabernet Sauvignon Herb Lamb Vineyard should turn out to be one of the most exceptional wines of the vintage. The color is an opaque purple. The nose offers up cassis, blueberry, black raspberry, and toasty scents, followed by gorgeously rich, sweet (from extract, not sugar) flavors, full body, gobs of glycerin, and wonderfully ripe tannin in the intense finish that must last for 40+ seconds. It is an exceptional Cabernet Sauvignon that will be approachable upon release; it will age for 20+ years. It is a tour de force in winemaking.

Once again, the only way to purchase these wines is via the winery's mailing list. As a postscript, Ann Colgin has acquired a new vineyard called Tychson Hill, which is superbly situated near the Grace Family Vineyard adjacent to Route 29 north of St. Helena, so additional Cabernet will be forthcoming in several years.

CORISON WINES (NAPA)

1995 Cabernet Sauvignon	Napa	D	88+
1994 Cabernet Sauvignon	Napa	D	88
1993 Cabernet Sauvignon	Napa	D	90+

The dark purple-colored 1995 Cabernet Sauvignon displays a tight but promising nose of spice, vanilla, and black currants. Straightforward on the palate, with medium body, as well as excellent concentration and ripeness, this tightly knit 1995 should turn out to be a very good, possibly outstanding Cabernet Sauvignon made in a stylish, suave, savory manner. I especially admired the balance between the wine's tannin and fruit.

The opaque ruby/purple color and muted nose of the 1994 Cabernet Sauvignon are followed by a harmonious blend of fruit, acidity, body, tannin, and alcohol. There is fine length and purity, as well as medium to full body. Although undoubtedly excellent, the wine is closed, monolithic, and unyielding. It has 10–15 years of potential ageability.

A very impressive effort from Corison, the 1993 Cabernet's dark ruby/purple color is followed by a smoky, sweet, jammy, black currant-scented nose, beautiful, ripe, cassis flavors, attractive suppleness, and a medium- to full-bodied, lush finish. It should drink well for 15 years.

COSENTINO WINERY (NAPA)

1994 Cabernet Sauvignon Reserve	Napa	D	81
1995 Chardonnay	Napa	B	?
1994 M. Coz Proprietary Red Wine	Napa	E	83
1993 Merlot Estate Oakville	Napa	D	90
1995 Merlot Reserve	Napa	D	86
1994 Pinot Noir Unfined/Unfiltered	Carneros	C	88
1994 Pinot Noir Unfined/Unfiltered	Napa	C	86
1994 Pinot Noir Unfined/Unfiltered	Russian River	D	88
1994 The Poet Proprietary Red Wine	Napa	D	83

1995 The Zin	California	C	86
1993 The Zin	Sonoma	C	87

The problem I have with Cosentino's wines is that they are so blatantly woody. One could accuse this winery of attempting to make a Spanish Rioja wine out of Napa Cabernet, but for whatever reason, the oak aromas and flavors that come through in these wines are aggressive rather than savory and subtle. In all three of the examples from 1994, the oak obliterates the fruit, giving these wines a one-dimensional, woody personality. Otherwise, I have no complaints, as the fruit is ripe, the wines are bottled without fining or filtration, and they possess good glycerin and punch. However, I do not think the oak will dissipate with aging, or at least not enough of it.

Damp, woodsy aromas compete with vivacious berry fruit in the attractive, round, supple-textured 1995 Zinfandel. The color is medium deep ruby. The wine is medium to full bodied, cleanly made, and ideal for drinking over the next 2–3 years. Two positives for the 1993 Zinfandel—Mitch Cosentino has bottled his Zinfandel without fining or filtration, and his penchant for the unbridled use of oak has been restrained. The result is a plump, seductive, voluptuously textured, fleshy Zinfandel with a dark ruby color, gobs of cherry and raspberry fruit, medium to full body, and a smoky, rich, heady finish. This wine should have immense appeal if drunk over the next 5–6 years.

High quality, smoky, spicy oak jumps from the glass of the light straw-colored 1995 Chardonnay. Roasted nut, earthy, oaky flavors are well infused with wood, but this medium-bodied wine possesses the requisite extract to stand up to the wood. Drink it over the next year.

The 1994 Pinot Noir Unfined/Unfiltered displays a Burgundian-like, gamey, sweet black cherry and smoky-scented nose, medium to full body, a lovely softness, and good structure from high-quality oak barrels. The medium ruby/garnet color suggests it is evolving quickly, but the flavors are fresh, vigorous, and exuberant. Drink this luscious Pinot Noir over the next 2–3 years.

The other two attractive Pinot Noirs from Cosentino are both deceptively light ruby-colored (the Carneros is even slightly cloudy). Both are fragrant, spicy, sweetly fruity wines that are authentic examples of high-class Pinot Noir. The 1994 Napa bottling is more straightforward, with plenty of cherry fruit, toast, smoke, and herb notes. The more complex 1994 Carneros displays a Burgundian/Côte de Beaune-like bouquet. Flavorful, expansive, and soft, it is a delicious, high-quality Pinot. Both wines beg to be drunk over the next 3–4 years.

The 1993 Merlot Oakville is one of the finest red wines I have tasted from this winery. The oak is well integrated (which is not always the case here), and the wine offers up gorgeous levels of sweet, jammy, berry fruit with notes of coffee and herbs, as well as plenty of unctuously textured thickness and richness on the palate. This soft wine is ideal for drinking now and over the next 5–6 years.

Cosentino's user-friendly 1995 Merlot Reserve possesses a medium ruby color, and plenty of smoky, toasty oak in the nose to complement the ripe cherry fruit. Soft, smoky, and round, with low acidity, and a plump, alluring texture, this is a Merlot to drink over the next 2–4 years.

H. COTURRI & SONS (SONOMA)

1994 Merlot Feingold Vineyard	Sonoma Mountain	C	86
1993 Merlot Feingold Vineyard	Sonoma	C	90
1994 Pinot Noir Horn Vineyards	Sonoma	C	88
1993 Pinot Noir Horn Vineyards	Sonoma	C	88

1993 Sangiovese Jessandre Vineyard	Sonoma	C	92
1995 Zinfandel Estate	Sonoma Mountain	C	89
1994 Zinfandel Estate	Sonoma Mountain	C	88
1993 Zinfandel Estate	Sonoma Mountain	C	90
1996 Zinfandel Philip Coturri Family Vineyard	Sonoma Valley	B	87
1995 Zinfandel Philip Coturri Family Vineyard	Sonoma Valley	D	90
1994 Zinfandel Philip Coturri Estate	Sonoma Mountain	C	89
1993 Zinfandel Philip Coturri Estate	Sonoma Mountain	C	92
1994 Jessandra Vittoria Santa Vittoria (70% Cabernet Sauvignon/30% Sangiovese)	Sonoma Mountain	D	90+

I am a fan of the best bottles Coturri produces, but I feel obligated to provide the following notice: None of my reviews provoke more controversy than those of Coturri. For every reader who writes to thank me for turning them on to these organically made, unfined, unfiltered, unsulfured wines, there are others who have accused me of consuming excessive amounts of illegal substances before tasting Coturri's wines, or, even worse, just incompetence. The debate over Coturri's wines is due to the fact that some Coturri offerings (which I do not recommend) are flawed by excessive amounts of volatile acidity, off aromas, etc. Coturri's adherence to a puristic approach of bottling barrel by barrel, refusing to assemble all of the barrels into a master blend, should be discontinued. This practice, also used by numerous Burgundians, results in notoriously frustrating bottle variation. Nevertheless, the following wines were superrich, pure examples of their varietals. They are too interesting and provocative not to recommend. However, readers who prefer wines that fall within strictly defined parameters are forewarned. Those who possess adventurous spirits and are interested in different winemaking styles should try one of Coturri's offerings before investing in a case. These are some of the most intriguing, albeit controversial, wines I have ever reviewed. Readers who find these wines to their liking tend to be obsessed by the positive qualities of the Coturri winemaking philosophy.

I have written in detail about the idiosyncratic wines from this small winery tucked on the Sonoma Mountain hillside. Some offerings can be problematic, but when everything goes right, Coturri makes some of the richest, most distinctive, personality-filled wines, particularly the Zinfandels, available in California. For example, the 1995 Zinfandel Sonoma Mountain (15.8% alcohol) is a dense purple-colored wine, with a gorgeous nose of jammy cherries and raspberries. The wine is highly extracted and rich, with loads of glycerin, full body, and considerable purity. Drink this thick, nearly unctuous Zinfandel over the next 5–6 years. This winery bottles its offerings in small lots, so let's hope all the bottles taste as excellent as this. The 1995 Zinfandel Philip Coturri Family Vineyard (15.8% alcohol) is another huge, rich, full-bodied wine loaded with jammy, briery, raspberry fruit. Hedonistic, with gorgeous texture, layers of flavor, full body, and beautifully integrated acidity, tannin, and alcohol, this back-strapping, large-scaled Zin should drink well for 5–7 years.

Think of the 1996 Zinfandel Philip Coturri Family Vineyard as the equivalent of an Amarone made from Zinfandel! The cheesy, smoky nose of freshly laid asphalt intermixed with jammy black fruits recalls both a Piedmont wine and an Amarone from Veneto. Although powerful, full bodied, and cleanly made, the wine is big, coarse, and rustic. Nevertheless, it possesses considerable flavor authority and a chewy, long texture. It should drink well for 5–6 years.

The first two 1994 Zinfandels released by Coturri are mammoth, late-harvest Zinfandels with high alcohol contents. The 1994 Zinfandel Sonoma Mountain offers a jammy, pruny, black raspberry and cherry-scented nose, thick, low acid, fleshy flavors, an unctuous texture, some sweetness, and a long, clean, rich, fleshy finish. It has not yet taken on much complexity, but it is a huge mouthful of Zinfandel. Drink it òver the next 4–5 years. Although the 1994 Zinfandel Philip Coturri Estate possesses even higher alcohol (15.2%), it comes across as completely dry, with classic Zinfandel aromatic and flavor profiles. There are gobs of spice, pepper, and jammy black cherries in this full-bodied, powerful, concentrated wine. The color is not as saturated as the Sonoma Mountain cuvée, but the wine cuts an equally broad path across the palate. Drink it over the next 5–7 years.

Zinfandel fanatics should try a bottle of Coturri's 1993 Zinfandel Estate and 1993 Zinfandel Philip Coturri Estate Vineyard. Although the 1993 Zinfandel Estate possesses some residual sugar, it is extremely rich with a huge, black fruit, spice, and roasted herb-scented nose, gigantic body, glycerin, and flavor extraction, and a low-acid, off-dry finish. It should drink well for 5–6 years. Even more impressive is the exceptionally rich 1993 Zinfandel Philip Coturri Estate. One of the richest, most intense, well-balanced Zinfandels I have ever tasted, this 15.3% alcohol wine does not taste alcoholic because of the tremendous amounts of fruit and concentration. It should drink well for 5–7 years or longer. The aging curve suggested for these wines is conservative in view of the fact that no SO$_2$ is used, so Coturri must rely on the wine's high alcohol content for ageability. Intriguing, controversial, but frequently riveting wines are the rule of thumb from this idiosyncratic producer.

Coturri's 1994 Merlot Feingold Vineyards is a rich, medium- to full-bodied, surprisingly structured Merlot that will benefit from a few more months of bottle age. There is no evidence of volatile acidity (thankfully). The wine exhibits a deep ruby/purple color, and good black cherry fruit with an underlying loamy/mineral character. It is spicy and rich, as well as structured, suggesting it will last for 5–7 years.

The 1993 Merlot from the Feingold Vineyard was Coturri's debut Merlot release. I did not find anything controversial about this superconcentrated, rich wine. Because Coturri utilizes no SO$_2$ my instincts suggest the wine may evolve quickly, although I have not found that to be the case with several older bottlings I have in my cellar. The 1993 Merlot offers a saturated black/purple color, and a huge, rich nose of spices, earth, and black cherry fruit. Amazingly full bodied and unctuous, with low acidity and magnificent fruit and richness, this thick, chewy Merlot should drink well for 5–7 years, possibly longer.

The 1993 Santa Vittoria (made at H. Coturri but displaying a different black and gold label with the words Jessandra Vittoria) is a limited production proprietary red wine made from 70% Cabernet Sauvignon and 30% Sangiovese. While this is often the most impressive wine in the Coturri portfolio, it is extremely difficult to find given its microproduction. The 1994 exhibits an opaque purple color, a reluctant set of aromatics that gradually emerge to reveal scents of new saddle leather, black fruits, earth, and spice. Structured and tannic, as well as impressively endowed and concentrated, this is less flattering and up-front when compared to the 1993, but potentially a 12–15-year wine. It is always difficult to estimate the longevity of the Coturri wines. Why? Because they are superconcentrated, but the fact that no sulfur is used at bottling often precludes as much cellaring potential as the raw materials suggest. The Jessandra Vittoria is a wine of considerable richness, length, complexity, and aging potential. Lucky purchasers of it should cellar it for 1–2 years and drink it over the following 10–12.

Coturri's 1994 Horn Vineyards Pinot Noir is a big, rich, intense, full-bodied wine with a dark purple color, meaty, animal-like Pinot flavors, soft, silky tannin, and plenty of muscle and punch in the finish. Approachable now, the wine should drink well for a decade. While it is not the most elegant style of Pinot, it is large scaled and impressively endowed. The 1993 Pinot Noir Horn Vineyard reveals a deep, dark, garnet/ruby/purple color, gobs of rich, jammy, sweet, plum and raspberry fruit, full body, outstanding concentration, low acidity, and considerable power and density. This is a chewy, opulent, spicy, intense Pinot Noir that should drink well for 5–8 years.

ROBERT CRAIG (NAPA)

1995 Affinity Proprietary Red Wine	Napa	D	90
1994 Affinity Proprietary Red Wine	Napa	D	87
1993 Affinity Proprietary Red Wine	Napa	D	87
1995 Cabernet Sauvignon Howell Mountain	Napa	D	91
1994 Cabernet Sauvignon Howell Mountain	Napa	D	90+
1993 Cabernet Sauvignon Howell Mountain	Napa	D	91
1995 Cabernet Sauvignon Mt. Veeder	Napa	D	90
1994 Cabernet Sauvignon Mt. Veeder	Napa	D	88
1993 Cabernet Sauvignon Mt. Veeder	Napa	D	90

All three of the 1995 offerings are exceptionally symmetrical, well-balanced wines of elegance, finesse, and purity. They are ideal models of what a Bordeaux-styled red from California should taste like. Although not blockbusters, they offer plenty of flavor depth and complexity. A classic wine, the dark ruby/purple-colored 1995 Affinity reveals a lead pencil, black currant, and vanillin-scented nose that could easily pass for a classy Médoc. It displays good richness and purity on the entry, medium to full body, outstanding concentration, and exceptional harmony. This is a beauty. Anticipated maturity: 2000–2012. The 1995 Cabernet Sauvignon Mt. Veeder is a fuller-bodied wine more dominated by black currant and cherry fruit. Riper, with more weight, it is still a finesse-styled wine by California standards. Its exceptional purity, subtle oak, complexity, and overall balance suggest it will drink well now, as well as over the next 12–15 years. Not surprisingly, the 1995 Cabernet Sauvignon Howell Mountain possesses the most tannin but also the richest constitution. The wine exhibits a deep ruby/purple color (similar to its two siblings), a classic, mineral, black currant, and *pain grillé*-scented nose, deep, rich, powerful flavors with outstanding concentration, considerable finesse, well-integrated tannin, and a structured, well-delineated, austere, but impressively long finish. This wine will benefit from 2–3 years of cellaring, and keep for 15–20 years.

The 1994 Cabernet Sauvignon Mt. Veeder is a full-bodied, dense, ruby/purple-colored, elegant wine with earthy, cassis fruit. It is a well-structured, medium-weight Cabernet with excellent ripeness, a graceful personality, and attractive layers of fruit. Although tight, it is accessible, and should drink well for 10–12+ years. Another enticing offering from Robert Craig is the 1994 Cabernet Sauvignon Howell Mountain. The wine, with a saturated dark purple color, offers up attractive, youthful aromas of lead pencil, vanillin, minerals, spice, and black currant fruit. A typical mountain Cabernet with copious quantities of tannin, this medium- to full-bodied, concentrated, impressively endowed wine is well crafted, yet backward and in need of 4–5 years of cellaring. Patience will be a virtue. Anticipated maturity: 2002–2012.

The Bordeaux-styled 1994 Affinity has a dark ruby/purple color, followed by a tight but promising nose of lead pencil, vanillin, minerals, and black currants. Restrained on the palate, with excellent ripeness, medium body, and austere tannin (but sweet ripe fruit underneath), this elegant, stylized wine requires another 1–3 years of cellaring; it will drink well for 8–10 years. The 1993 Affinity (a blend of 76% Cabernet Sauvignon, 21% Merlot, and 3% Cabernet Franc) reveals a less saturated purple color, a ripe berry-scented nose with less cassis and wood notes. The wine is sweet, soft, and round on the attack, finishing with medium body and moderate tannin. Drink it over the next 10–12 years. It is a pure, well-made wine.

The two 1993 Cabernet Sauvignons are beautifully built, authoritatively flavored and dense wines with an undeniable sense of finesse and elegance. There is good purity, well-integrated toasty oak, and fine acidity. While both wines are accessible, each is in need of some time in the cellar. The 1993 Cabernet Sauvignon Mt. Veeder exhibits a Bordeaux-like gracefulness and firm tannin, as well as superb black currant aromas and flavors intertwined with high-quality oak, minerals, and spice. It should age well for 10–15 years. The 1993 Cabernet Sauvignon Howell Mountain reveals more smoky, sweet French oak, and gorgeously rich black currant fruit infused with minerals and floral notes. Rich, full bodied, and moderately tannic, this is a powerful yet classy wine for drinking over the next 15 years. Impressive winemaking is evident in all of these efforts from Robert Craig.

CUVAISON WINERY (NAPA)

1994	Cabernet Sauvignon	Napa	D	87
1993	Cabernet Sauvignon	Napa	C	85
1994	Cabernet Sauvignon ATS Selection	Carneros	D	90
1996	Chardonnay	Napa/Carneros	C	86
1995	Chardonnay ATS Selection	Carneros	D	90
1994	Chardonnay ATS Selection	Carneros/Napa	D	87
1995	Chardonnay Reserve	Carneros	D	89
1994	Merlot	Napa	C	88

Cuvaison's impressive 1994 Cabernet Sauvignon ATS Selection (by the way, the packaging is extraordinary) is one of the more backward, tannic, and less accessible North Coast Cabernet Sauvignons from this vintage. However, it boasts plenty of potential. The color is a healthy dark ruby/purple. The wine reveals gobs of pure black currant fruit nicely wrapped by attractive smoky, toasty oak. Medium bodied, well delineated, and impressively concentrated, this well-endowed, cleanly made, classically styled Cabernet Sauvignon should be at its best between 2002 and 2012.

The Burgundian-styled 1995 Chardonnay ATS Selection possesses big, leesy, honeyed, toasty aromas and flavors. Impressively rich, with medium to full body, nicely integrated acidity and oak, and an attractive layered, complex finish, this youthful wine will drink well for another 1–3 years. The 1995 Chardonnay Carneros Reserve exhibits a lovely ripe tropical fruit character with honeyed pineapple fruit. Acidity gives the wine vibrancy, but is not too aggressive. In the mouth, this medium- to full-bodied wine offers layers of flavors, as well as excellent purity. This is a big (14.1% alcohol), satisfying, full-flavored Chardonnay that should drink well for another year.

The 1996 Chardonnay Napa/Carneros is an attractive, buttery, toasty, smoky wine with medium body, good force and power, yet little finesse or elegance. Its solid Chardonnay flavors are presented in a medium-bodied format. Drink it over the next year.

The rich, honeyed pear, buttery-styled 1994 Chardonnay is restrained, yet possesses intensity without aggressive components. It is a medium-bodied, stylish Chardonnay with well-integrated wood, acidity, and alcohol. The wine's creamy texture is nicely buttressed by tangy acidity. Drink this rich, measured, subtle Chardonnay over the next 2–3 years. An excellent Cabernet Sauvignon, the dark ruby/purple-colored 1994 exhibits loads of cassis fruit, medium body, good sweetness, and a long finish. The tannin is well integrated, and the wine is soft and accessible, although there is fine grip and structure. It should drink well for 12–15 years.

The opaque ruby/purple-colored 1993 Merlot exhibits more richness, intensity, and character than the surprisingly soft, medium-bodied, moderately concentrated Cabernet Sauvignon. The Merlot offers terrific fruit, plenty of chocolatey, mocha, herb, and black cherry flavors, an expansive, round, generous palate, and a medium-bodied, velvety finish. It should drink well for 10–12 years. The pleasant, above average quality 1993 Cabernet Sauvignon is soft, with pleasing cassis aromas framed by subtle oak. Spicy, round, and low in acidity, it is a wine to drink during its first 5–7 years of life.

By the way, at auctions, value seekers should keep an eye out for the 1975 Cuvaison Cabernet Sauvignon with Philip Togni's signature on the side of the label, and the back label that reads, "Grapes from vineyards at the summit of Spring Mountain, St. Helena." This wine, the last Cuvaison made by Philip Togni, represented a special cuvée that was extremely concentrated. I had not tasted the wine until recently, but had heard of its reputation, and knew that Togni considered it the finest wine he had made at Cuvaison. Having just tasted it, I can say it is a stunningly rich, complex Napa Cabernet Sauvignon that has still not reached its apogee. The wine exhibits a dense, murky purple color with no amber, rust, or brown. It reveals classic notes of mineral and cassis, along with scents of underbrush. Extremely full bodied, dense, and powerful, with extraordinary freshness and vibrancy, it will last another two decades. I suspect bottles of it that show up at auction could be purchased for a song given the vintage and the fact that this winery has never been considered among the California superstars. I scored it 93 points.

DALLA VALLE (NAPA)

1996	Cabernet Sauvignon	Napa	E	94
1995	Cabernet Sauvignon	Napa	D	93
1994	Cabernet Sauvignon	Napa	D	94
1993	Cabernet Sauvignon	Napa	D	93
1996	Maya Proprietary Red Wine	Napa	EE	96+
1995	Maya Proprietary Red Wine	Napa	EE	97+
1994	Maya Proprietary Red Wine	Napa	EE	99
1993	Maya Proprietary Red Wine	Napa	EE	98

Dalla Valle has turned out two stunning 1996s. The 1996 Cabernet Sauvignon reveals surprising sweetness and accessibility for a wine from this vintage. The opaque purple color is followed by a full-bodied wine with outstanding richness and depth. Cabernet Sauvignon's blackberry/cassis character is well represented, and the oak has been completely submerged beneath the wine's mass of fruit, glycerin, and extract. There are no hard edges, and the tannin does not suffer from any of the rusticity this vintage is capable of producing. While it can be drunk, this wine promises to age effortlessly for 15–20 years. The 1996 Maya (a blend of 55% Cabernet Sauvignon and 45% Cabernet Franc) offers stunning aromatics of black currants, intermixed with loamy soil scents, new saddle leather, underbrush, and vanillin. Full bodied and flavorful, with superb purity, this is another exquisite of a provocative and compelling blend of Cabernet Sauvignon and Cabernet Franc. While there is noticeable tannin, it is sweet. Already delicious, this offering will continue to improve for 10–15 years, and last for three decades.

The 1995 Cabernet Sauvignon exhibits an opaque blue/black/purple color, followed by sweet cassis aromas intermingled with scents of earth, spice, smoke, and grilled meats. This dense, powerful, muscular, concentrated wine provides an enormous mouth-feel. Wineries need more than luck to produce multidimensional wines with this concentration, ripeness, sweetness of fruit, and overall intensity and complexity. The terrific 1995 Maya is cut from the same mold as all the great Mayas of this decade. Its tannin may be even riper than in the 1994, but the wine is still an unevolved, massive, and unformed giant, although it is obvious that this will be another legendary effort. Do readers ever wonder why wines such as these are never made in 100,000 case lots?

The 1994 Cabernet Sauvignon, which I have drunk with great pleasure despite its back-wardness, possesses a full-bodied, multilayered personality, with plenty of tannin, but suffi-cient earthy, black currant/plumlike fruit to balance out the wine's structure. With an opaque purple color, a high tannin level, and gorgeous layers of fruit and intensity, it will be at its peak after 4–6 years of cellaring, and will last for 20–25 years. The 1994 Maya is prodigious. The color is saturated opaque purple. The wine offers up restrained but gorgeously sweet earth, oak, mineral, and black fruit aromas. Full bodied, with substantial quantities of glyc-erin and extract, this wine's large-scaled tannin seems to be well submerged beneath the wine's fabulous layers of fruit. Although more accessible than I would have thought prior to bottling, it is a candidate for 20–30 years of evolution.

Although closed, the 1993 Cabernet Sauvignon is crammed with so much sweet, black currant fruit that it does not take a genius to figure out what this wine is all about. It offers an opaque garnet/purple color, a moderately intense, cassis, smoky, herb, and earthy nose, fab-ulous concentration, good muscle, and a boatload of sweet tannin. While drinkable, it needs another 4–5 years of cellaring. It will easily last for 20 years. The 1993 Maya is awesome. The opaque purple color accompanies a bouquet of stony, jammy cassis, roasted herbs, and smoky, meaty scents that are just beginning to unfold and soar from the glass. The wine pos-sesses unbelievable concentration, powerful tannin, and a finish that lasts for 45+ seconds. It is an extraordinarily well endowed and well balanced wine that requires 5–7 years of cel-laring. It will age effortlessly through the first 25 years of the next century.

I don't think I need to reinforce the fact that these offerings are extremely difficult to find, but isn't that the way it always is with such extraordinary wines?

DE LOACH VINEYARDS (SONOMA)

1993 Cabernet Sauvignon Estate	Russian River	C	86+
1995 Chardonnay	Russian River	C	86
1995 Chardonnay O.F.S.	Russian River	D	88
1994 Zinfandel Estate	Russian River	B	87
1995 Zinfandel Barbieri Ranch	Russian River	C	87
1994 Zinfandel Barbieri Ranch	Russian River	C	88
1995 Zinfandel Estate	Russian River	C	88
1995 Zinfandel Gambogi Ranch	Russian River	C	88
1994 Zinfandel Gambogi Ranch	Russian River	C	90
1993 Zinfandel Gambogi Ranch	Russian River	B	86
1995 Zinfandel O.F.S.	Russian River	D	90
1994 Zinfandel O.F.S.	Russian River	C	91
1995 Zinfandel Papera Ranch	Russian River	C	90
1994 Zinfandel Papera Ranch	Russian River	C	89
1995 Zinfandel Pelletti Ranch	Russian River	C	92
1994 Zinfandel Pelletti Ranch	Russian River	C	85

1993 Zinfandel Pelletti Ranch	Russian River	B	87
1995 Zinfandel Saitone Ranch	Russian River	C	91

These are seriously made as well as delicious wines. The white wine offerings include a tasty, medium-bodied, fruity 1995 Chardonnay revealing attractive honeyed apple, peach, and pearlike fruit. The fruit rather than wood and structure is emphasized in this cleanly made wine. Drink it over the next year. The 1995 Chardonnay O.F.S. (meaning Our Finest Selection) is a more lavishly wooded, honeyed, rich, concentrated wine with medium to full body, and copious quantities of toasty oak and thick, honeyed fruit. While it is not the finest O.F.S. Chardonnay I have tasted, it is an excellent wine for drinking over the next 1–2 years.

One of the surprises in my tastings was the fine performance of De Loach's 1993 Cabernet Sauvignon O.F.S. Although De Loach is not known as a Cabernet producer, this is a solidly built, lean but well-made, ripe, concentrated wine with good body, plenty of pure, earthy, black currant fruit, and spice. Still young, it should age well for another 5–7 years. While it is not profound, most readers will enjoy this chunky, mouth-filling Cabernet Sauvignon.

De Loach produced seven Zinfandels in 1995, all of which merit considerable interest. They are powerful yet accessible Zinfandels with alcohols ranging from 15% to 17.5%. Remarkably, they possess the concentration and ripe fruit necessary to conceal the alcohol—at least for the next several years. The 1995 Zinfandel Estate is an attractive, deep ruby-colored, briery, spicy, richly fruity wine with medium body and plenty of punch. Drink it over the next 2–3 years. The dark ruby-colored 1995 Zinfandel Barbieri Ranch (15% alcohol and produced from vines planted in 1905) is one of the least powerful wines. Made in a similar style to the regular cuvée, it reveals medium body, ripe fruit, attractive spice and purity, and 3–4 years of drinkability. The 1995 Zinfandel Gambogi Ranch (15% alcohol and produced from vines planted in 1909) exhibits a darker ruby/purple color, more intense, ripe, jammy black cherry and raspberry fruit in the vivid nose, medium to full body, crisp underlying acidity that buttresses the wine's high alcohol, and a powerful, surprisingly lively style. Drink it over the next 3–4 years. From vines planted in 1934, the 1995 Zinfandel Papera Ranch (16.5% alcohol) is a dense, muscular-looking, deep ruby-colored wine with more viscosity, glycerin, and obvious alcohol. Powerful, rich, and dry, with no late-harvest character, and, surprisingly, much of the alcohol well concealed, this lusty Zinfandel will drink well for 4–5 years.

De Loach's 1995 Zinfandel Saitone Ranch, produced from vines planted in 1895, contains 16.5% alcohol. Dark ruby-colored, with a sweet, expansive, blackberry, raspberry, cherry, pepper, and spice-scented nose, full body, and gobs of glycerin and extract, this chewy, large-scaled but well-balanced Zinfandel should drink well for 5–6 years. The 1995 Zinfandel Pelletti Ranch (a 17.5% alcohol monster produced from vines planted in 1928) boasts an opaque dark purple color, followed by jammy, late-harvest aromas of overripe black fruits, pepper, and spice. Dry, thick, full bodied, and massively endowed with gobs of glycerin, this viscous Zinfandel offers maximum intensity and power. Although huge, it is neither overwhelming nor too heavy. I would, however, prefer to imbibe this wine after dinner, with an intensely flavored cheese. Look for it to last for 7–8 years. Lastly, the dry, full-bodied 1995 Zinfandel O.F.S. (16.5% alcohol) possesses layers of briery, rich berry fruit, excellent purity, fine spice, and a lusty, high alcohol, rich, layered finish. Already delicious, this is a textbook Zinfandel made in a big, bold, ostentatious style. It should drink well for 5–6 years. Kudos to De Loach for turning out such an impressive portfolio of 1995s!

De Loach's 1994 Zinfandels are far more impressive than the winery's hit or miss 1993s. For starters, there is a delicious estate-bottled 1994 Zinfandel that is bursting with spicy berry fruit. Medium to full bodied, with a good midpalate, and plenty of fruit in the soft finish, this supple wine should be drunk over the next 2–4 years.

Among the single vineyard Zinfandels, the 1994 Barbieri Ranch (from vines planted in

1905) exhibits a dark ruby color, medium to full body, gobs of briery, rich, cherry Zinfandel fruit, excellent purity, and a moderately long, rich finish. The 1994 Papera Ranch (from a vineyard planted in 1934) reveals a sweet, smoky, roasted, berrylike fruitiness, soft, expansive, chewy flavors, more fat and glycerin than the Barbieri, and a heady, lush finish. Like the Barbieri, it is a candidate for 5–6 years of superb drinking, although it will last 10+ years. The 1994 Pelletti Ranch (from a vineyard planted in 1928) is the most muted and least expressive of the De Loach 1994s. Perhaps it was going through a closed stage of development, but it does not appear to have the fatness, richness, or aromatics of the other offerings. It is certainly good, but not nearly as impressive.

The superb 1994 Gambogi Ranch (from a vineyard planted in 1909) is a textbook Zinfandel. The wine is full bodied and rich (15.2% alcohol), with layers of jammy, briery, berry fruit, and considerable spice, glycerin, extract, and richness, without any intrusive tannin. There is enough acidity to provide clarity to the wine's large-scaled components. Drink it over the next 5–8 years. Lastly, the 1994 O.F.S. is a dazzling Zinfandel, getting my nod as the best of this sextet. Extremely full bodied, rich, and velvety textured, this large-scaled, highly extracted Zinfandel delivers a boatload of flavor and intensity. Drink it over the next 5–6 years.

The only two 1993 De Loach Zinfandels I can recommend are the Pelletti Ranch and Gambogi Ranch. The other three offerings—the Estate, Papera Ranch, and Barbieri Ranch—merited scores of 80–84. The 1993 Gambogi and Pelletti Ranch offerings are lighter than followers of these wines may have anticipated. They possess good varietal characters (briery red fruits and spice), peppery, medium-bodied palates, and easygoing, supple personalities. Both should be drunk over the next 2–4 years.

DEER PARK WINERY (NAPA)

1995 Zinfandel Beatty Ranch	Napa	D	83
1995 Zinfandel Estate	Napa	D	?
1993 Zinfandel Howell Mountain	Napa	C	87

These are two unusual and somewhat perplexing 1995 Zinfandels. Deer Park's 1995 Zinfandel Estate reveals a dense, nearly opaque, plum center to its color, as well as a provocative, earthy, iodinelike, marshy-scented nose lacking fruit and varietal character. The peculiar aromatics are followed by a medium- to full-bodied wine with considerable concentration, as well as astringent tannin and sharp acid. Will this wine ever pull itself together? The 1995 Zinfandel Beatty Ranch possesses a deep plum color, a spicy (allspice and cinnamon), straightforward, peppery nose, an absence of ripe fruit, and plenty of structure, acidity, and tannin, as well as medium body. This wine appears to lack ripe fruit, glycerin, and charm.

The barrel sample of unbottled 1993 Zinfandel revealed an opaque purple color, an intense, powerful nose of jammy black cherries, earth, and oak, long, rich, medium- to full-bodied flavors with impressive extraction, and a firm, noticeably tannic finish that suggests 3–4 years of cellaring would be beneficial. This could be a 10–15-year Zinfandel if the fruit holds up. On the other hand, it could easily turn out to be too tough and austere.

DEHLINGER (SONOMA)

1993 Bordeaux Blend Proprietary Red Wine	Russian River	C	91
1996 Cabernet/Merlot Blend	Russian River	D	91
1995 Cabernet/Merlot Blend	Russian River	D	91
1994 Cabernet/Merlot Blend	Russian River	D	91
1993 Cabernet/Merlot Blend	Russian River	C	91

1996 Cabernet Sauvignon	Russian River	D	90
1995 Cabernet Sauvignon	Russian River	D	91
1994 Cabernet Sauvignon	Russian River	D	92
1993 Cabernet Sauvignon	Russian River	C	90
1997 Cabernet Sauvignon Estate	Russian River	D	(92–95)
1996 Cabernet Sauvignon Estate	Russian River	D	92
1995 Cabernet Sauvignon Estate	Russian River	D	91
1995 Chardonnay	Russian River	C	87
1997 Chardonnay Estate	Russian River	D	89+
1996 Chardonnay Estate Unfiltered	Russian River	D	86+
1995 Chardonnay Estate Unfiltered	Russian River	C	87
1997 Chardonnay Selection	Russian River	D	90
1997 Pinot Noir Estate	Russian River	D	(90–92)
1996 Pinot Noir Estate	Russian River	D	91
1995 Pinot Noir Estate	Russian River	D	89
1994 Pinot Noir Estate	Russian River	C	91
1993 Pinot Noir Estate	Russian River	C	89
1997 Pinot Noir Goldridge Vineyard Estate	Russian River	D	(89–91)
1996 Pinot Noir Goldridge Vineyard Estate	Russian River	D	89
1995 Pinot Noir Goldridge Vineyard Estate	Russian River	C	88
1994 Pinot Noir Goldridge Vineyard Estate	Russian River	C	90
1993 Pinot Noir Goldridge Vineyard Estate	Russian River	C	88
1994 Pinot Noir Goldridge Vineyard 20 Year Old Vines	Russian River	D	91
1997 Pinot Noir Octagon Vineyard	Russian River	D	(91–93)
1996 Pinot Noir Octagon Vineyard	Russian River	D	90
1995 Pinot Noir Octagon Vineyard	Russian River	D	90
1994 Pinot Noir Octagon Vineyard	Russian River	D	93
1997 Pinot Noir Reserve	Russian River	D	(91–93)
1994 Pinot Noir Reserve Estate	Russian River	D	92+
1994 Syrah	Russian River	C	92
1993 Syrah	Russian River	C	89
1997 Syrah Estate	Russian River	D	(90–92)
1996 Syrah Estate	Russian River	D	94
1995 Syrah Estate	Russian River	D	93
1994 Syrah Estate	Russian River	C	91

1997 Syrah Goldridge Vineyard	Russian River	D	(88–90)
1996 Syrah Goldridge Vineyard	Russian River	D	90
1995 Syrah Goldridge Vineyard	Russian River	C	90
1994 Syrah Goldridge Vineyard	Russian River	C	89

Wine lovers have finally caught on to the impressive quality of Tom Dehlinger's portfolio. His tasting room, which was used to generate direct sales, has been shut down because the demand for his wines from his mailing list has increased significantly. Yet the soft-spoken, self-assured Tom Dehlinger remains one of the most humble winemakers/owners in northern California, preferring to let his wines speak for themselves—all 7,000–8,000 cases.

This is a top-notch, albeit somewhat unheralded, source for delicious Pinot Noir. While some of the new Dijon clones have been planted (particularly Clone 777), Dehlinger's Pinots are all from such old California clones (which originally came from Burgundy) as Martini, Swan, and Pommard. There can be as many as four separate Pinot Noirs if Dehlinger decides to produce a Reserve bottling, as he did in 1994 and 1997. In 1996, there are three efforts, Goldridge Vineyard (1,150 cases), Estate (990 cases), and Octagon Vineyard (140 cases). What is so likable about the Dehlinger Pinot Noirs is that they are made in a richly fruity, chocolatey style with plenty of spice, plush textures, and copious quantities of glycerin and alcohol. They are both user-friendly and faithful to the varietal's trademark. For example, the 1996 Pinot Noir Goldridge Vineyard exhibits an impressive dark ruby/purple color, and a superb bouquet of jammy plums/cherries intermixed with earthy underbrush and melted chocolate. With airing, Asian spices enter the mélange. This is a chewy, medium- to full-bodied, plump, hedonistic Pinot (14.5% alcohol) that can be drunk now as well as over the next 5–6 years. The outstanding 1996 Pinot Noir Estate is similar, with more glycerin, a sweeter black cherry/kirsch component, roasted herb characteristics, full body, 14.5% alcohol, superb purity, and a nicely layered, chewy texture. This wine should drink well for 5–7 years. The 1996 Pinot Noir Octagon Vineyard is the most limited in availability. It offers up a fabulous nose of jammy strawberries, cherries, a touch of prunes, roasted meat smells, and spicy oak. Full bodied, with considerable glycerin and extract, and a dense, lush, voluptuously textured finish, it should drink well for 5–6 years. Visitors should note that the Octagon Vineyard is the vineyard that surrounds the spooky-looking house that is a dead ringer for the Bates Motel in Alfred Hitchcock's classic movie *Psycho*.

Tom Dehlinger believes 1997 is the finest Pinot Noir vintage since 1994. The 1997 Pinot Noir Goldridge Vineyard offers a lovely, evolved berry fragrance intermixed with earth and spicy oak, smoke, and black cherry fruit presented in a full-bodied, heady style. This soft, seamless wine should drink well young, yet last for 4–5 years. The superb 1997 Pinot Noir Estate provides gorgeous levels of pure black fruits intermixed with chocolate, smoke, subtle new oak, and allspice/cinnamon notes. Beautifully rendered in the mouth, this full-bodied, superbly extracted, velvety-textured wine is as hedonistic as Pinot Noir can be. The wine's dark saturated plum color and admirable length auger well for 5–7 years of enjoyment. The 1997 Pinot Noir Octagon Vineyard continues the succession of sexy wines from this source. The black cherry/chocolatey component is accompanied by black raspberry, meaty fruit flavors. The wine possesses a deep midpalate, as well as an unctuously textured, long, lush finish. Like so many 1997 Pinots, this young wine displays a velvety, seductive quality, suggesting it will be delicious when released. Tom Dehlinger also has produced a 1997 Reserve Pinot Noir (450 cases). Made from the Pommard clone, this offering is one of the few Dehlinger wines to reveal noticeable evidence of *pain grillé* or smoky new oak. (Only 35%–40% new oak is utilized for Dehlinger's Pinot Noirs.) The most sumptuous of these offerings, the Reserve exhibits a concentrated style, no hard edges, low acidity, fabulous fruit, full body, and enviable levels of glycerin and extract. It will be drinkable upon release, and should last for a decade. Dehlinger told me his alcohol levels were near record highs in 1997, with all of these Pinot Noirs averaging between 14.2% and 14.4%.

Tom Dehlinger's modesty is best exemplified by the fact that he calls his proprietary red wine a Cabernet/Merlot Blend. Production for this outstanding wine is limited to 400 cases. The 1996 reveals a saturated opaque purple color, followed by a gorgeous nose of blackberries, vanillin, licorice, and floral notes. Chewy and full bodied, with a viscous texture, low acidity, sensational fruit extraction, and a mouth-coating finish, this is a large-scaled yet sexy wine that can be drunk now or cellared for 15 or more years. It tips the scales at 14.5% alcohol.

While most people consider Dehlinger to be a Pinot Noir producer, his Cabernet Sauvignon deserves more attention. Tom Dehlinger told me that approximately 70% of his Cabernet Sauvignon crop is sold to other wineries, but he keeps the finest lots from his ridgetop vineyards for his Cabernet Sauvignon, which is produced in 400–650 case lots. The 1997 Cabernet Sauvignon may develop into the finest example produced at this winery, but both the 1995 and 1996 are outstanding. The 1995 Cabernet Sauvignon (460 cases) is a pure Cabernet with an opaque purple color, and telltale aromas of cassis, asphalt, loamy soil notes, and smoky, toasty oak. The wine is full bodied and layered, with a chewy texture, and impressive purity and length. There is good tannin in the finish, but this remains a grapey, unevolved Cabernet Sauvignon with considerable potential. Anticipated maturity: 2001–2020. The 1996 Cabernet Sauvignon (375 cases) includes 11% Merlot in the blend. The wine is topflight, from its saturated purple color to its brooding flavors of licorice, black currants, roasted herbs, charcoal, and spice. Amazingly rich and extracted, with moderate tannin in the 30-second finish, this Cabernet's structural components are secondary to its extraordinary amount of fruit, glycerin, and alcohol. Cellar it for 2–3 more years, and consume it over the next 2 decades. The remarkable 1997 Cabernet Sauvignon appears to be the finest Tom Dehlinger has yet produced. There are 650 cases of this wine, which includes 7% Merlot. It boasts an opaque black/purple color, in addition to a seductive nose of violets, blackberries, blueberries, and chocolate. Immense, but so velvety textured it tastes seamless, this full-bodied classic offering inundates the palate with fruit. Wow! What a sensational Cabernet Sauvignon!

This winery is also producing very fine Syrah. Tom Dehlinger believes Syrah is a natural in California, setting a crop that can yield an astonishing ten tons of fruit per acre. He prunes and crop-thins to get his yields down to 3–4 tons per acre. That still seems high, but I cannot argue with the extraordinary flavors and richness these wines possess. The 1996 Syrah Goldridge Vineyard (230 cases) is a hedonistic, fat, succulently textured Syrah with gobs of peppery, crème de cassis fruit, a notion of burning wood fires, and pepper, full body, outstanding purity, and no hard edges. Despite its size, it is a Syrah to consume over the next 15 years. The smoky 1996 Estate Syrah (360 cases) reveals an opaque black/purple color in addition to a terrific blackberry liqueur-scented nose. This viscous example possesses massive body and fabulous flavor extraction. While it is remains unevolved and grapey, it reveals remarkable potential. The wine's silky texture suggests early drinkability, but it still tastes like a barrel sample. Look for it to do wonders in the bottle over the next 15+ years.

The 1997 was a relatively difficult year for Syrah. Dehlinger has turned in two fine efforts, but neither wine possesses the extraordinary intensity, power, or richness of the 1996s. The dark purple-colored 1997 Syrah Goldridge Vineyard is a medium-bodied, clean, pure, richly fruity, smoky and cassis-scented and -flavored wine that will require consumption during its first 7–8 years of life. While the 1997 Estate Syrah is not a blockbuster/powerhouse like the 1996, it is an outstanding effort. It exhibits an opaque purple color, and intense blackberry/cassis aromas intermixed with bacon and peppery smells. In the mouth, the wine is full bodied and rich, with sweet tannin, and a precocious, evolved style . . . in total contrast to the 1996. This wine should drink well when released and last for a decade.

A small amount of white wine is produced at Dehlinger. In 1997 there are two offerings, including the first full malolactic Chardonnay he has produced. The 1997 Chardonnay Estate (3,300 cases), which has been bottled unfiltered, is made in a crisp, Chablis-like style with the emphasis on fresh pear, citrus, and mineral-like aromas and flavors. This is no wimpish wine (14.2% alcohol), but a clean, fresh, steely Chardonnay that is increasingly rare in California. The 1997 Chardonnay Selection (400 cases) comes from a 3-acre vineyard planted with the Kistler Clone. It is put through full malolactic, and is aged in a higher percentage of new oak (50%). This offering displays a lemony, honeyed character, with less noticeable minerality. There is more glycerin, fuller body, and a deep, concentrated midpalate. It should drink well for 4–5 years.

Looking at the equation of points for value, Tom Dehlinger's wines still represent some of the best bargains in California. I can imagine there must be immense pressure on him to increase prices given both the quality of his wines, and the fact that he is dead center in the Russian River, a viticultural region that is as hot as a firecracker when it comes to popularity. His lineup includes many enticing entities. I suspect the overall level of Pinot Noir is slightly below the splendid 1994s, but that may be because the 1994s are so open and showy, in contrast to the 1995s, which are slightly more retarded in their development.

Tom Dehlinger's commitment to excellence is in part exemplified by the fact that he served me two 1995 Chardonnays from his Russian River vineyard. The regular commercial cuvée, which I rated 87 points, was a steely, excellent, richly fruity, fresh, lively wine with good body, and an attractive, mineral, citrusy, ripe fruit character. It was bottled with no fining and a light filtration. Dehlinger served me the same wine bottled unfined and unfiltered, which I rated 2 points higher. The unfiltered Chardonnay had a chewier, richer midpalate, and more intense aromatics and flavors. It was Tom Dehlinger's way of pointing out what effect filtration can have. Where circumstances warrant, Dehlinger may begin to bottle his Chardonnays unfiltered, as he does with his red wines. What is interesting about the issue of filtration versus nonfiltration is that the differences in complexity, texture, and flavor become even more apparent with aging.

Dehlinger produced a crisp, Chablis-like, mineral-laden 1996 Chardonnay Estate. It offers lemony, pear, citruslike aromas and flavors, medium body, a vivacious personality, and a clean finish. The 1995 Chardonnay Estate is beginning to reveal more orange blossom and pearlike notes in its steely, medium-bodied personality. These are authoritatively flavorful Chardonnays made in an attractive, steely style that is refreshing in view of all the bold, heavyweight Chardonnays so common in the marketplace.

It is easy to pigeonhole Dehlinger as a Pinot Noir winery, but that ignores the fact that this winery turns out top-notch Cabernet Sauvignon and an innocuously named proprietary blend, in addition to several superb Syrahs. However, it is their Pinot Noir that most excites consumers. Dehlinger produces as many as four cuvées of Pinot Noir—the Estate, Goldridge Vineyard Estate, Octagon Vineyard (from a hilltop parcel of vines near an old, spooky house in which the Addams family would feel comfortable), and, from time to time, Goldridge Vineyard 20 Year Old Vines. The latter wine was last produced in 1994. The 1994 Pinot Noirs are all available in the marketplace, or through the winery's mailing list. They are gorgeous Pinots that have a high quality/value ratio. The dark ruby-colored 1994 Pinot Noir Goldridge Vineyard offers a spicy, gamey, smoky, complex set of aromatics, outstanding richness, a long, round, full-bodied palate with a silky texture, and plenty of spice, jammy black cherries, and underbrushlike flavors. Already drinking well, it should continue to evolve for 4–5 years. The gorgeous, flamboyant 1994 Pinot Noir Estate possesses sweet, ripe, layered flavors, and a knockout nose of spices, red and black fruits, earth, and smoke. At 14.5% alcohol, the wine has gobs of glycerin and a sweet midpalate (from extract and glycerin, not sugar). Full, rich, and loaded with personality and flavor, it is a classic Russian River Pinot Noir . . . and a bargain at $24 a bottle. Drink it over the next 5–6 years. The 1994 Pinot Noir Octagon Vineyard (10% stems are retained in this cuvée during the fermentation) is slightly more expensive as only 100 cases were produced from Dehlinger's minuscule hilltop vineyard. The wine reveals the telltale Dehlinger intense fragrance of allspice, sweet black fruits, toast, and smoke. On the palate, a cascade of raspberry, cherry flavors are accompanied by power, full body, a silky texture, and ripe tannin in the finish. This bold, lusty Pinot Noir is already difficult to resist. The 1994 Pinot Noir Reserve (500 cases produced), the most structured and closed of these offerings, had only been in bottle for a month when I tasted it. It appears to be another exceptional ripe, rich, concentrated, dense, complex, and expansively flavored Pinot Noir that needs 2–6 months of bottle age. It has a 30–35-second finish, as well as exceptional purity and personality.

Dehlinger's 1993 Pinot Noir Estate is medium dark ruby-colored, with a lovely, intense, earthy, black cherry-scented nose, lush, silky-textured flavors that exhibit full body, enticing fat and roundness, and a generous, copiously fruity finish. This wine is fully mature, but capable of lasting another 3–4 years. The 1993 Pinot Noir Goldridge Vineyard is a terrific bargain in high-class, complex, rich, savory Pinot Noir. The dark plum color is followed by a bouquet of sweet black cherries, chocolate, spice, and smoke. Dense, rich, soft, and silky, this is a delicious Pinot Noir for drinking over the next 2–4 years.

The 1995 Pinot Noirs reveal a more meaty, animal, plant material side to their aromatics and flavors than the flamboyantly fruit-driven 1994s. For example, the 1995 Pinot Noir Goldridge Vineyard Estate is a medium ruby-colored wine with a big, spicy, earthy, cinnamon, smoky-scented nose, rich, jammy, silky-textured fruit, medium body, and a lush finish. It should drink well for 5 years. The 1995 Pinot Noir Estate exhibits more intensity, a marginally deeper ruby color, and a satiny texture with plenty of ripe black cherry and berry fruit. Medium bodied and soft, it is ideal for drinking over the next 5–6 years. The most interesting wine is the 1995 Pinot Noir Octagon Vineyard. The deepest and richest of these Pinots, it boasts a ripe strawberry, cherry, chocolatey, earthy character. Medium to full bodied, hedonistic and lush, it possesses savory, expansive flavors, low acidity, and gorgeous ripeness. It should drink well for 5–6 years.

Dehlinger's proprietary red wine, Bordeaux Blend, deserves a more substantial name. The 1993 is a blend of 55% Cabernet Sauvignon and 45% Merlot. It is a rich, full-bodied, concentrated wine with considerable intensity and sweet, black currant fruit intermingled with hints of chocolate, vanilla, smoke, and black cherries. Opulent, rich, and mouth-filling, they are ideal for drinking over the next 10–15 years. For whatever reason, they tend to be overlooked in the Dehlinger portfolio.

It is symbolic of Tom Dehlinger's low profile that his top of the line proprietary red wine is called a "Cabernet/Merlot Blend." The huge, thick, chocolatey aromas of the 1993 combined with scents of black and red currants and smoky oak tease the olfactory senses. Dense, full bodied, and concentrated, yet still very young, this large scaled, impressively endowed wine should drink well for 15+ years. Approximately 300 cases were produced of this 40% Cabernet/60% Merlot blend. This is not a wine to be ignored, its humble name notwithstanding. The 1994 Cabernet/Merlot Blend contains equal proportions of these varietals. The opaque purple/black color is followed by sweet, powerful aromas of black currants, licorice, chocolate, and sweet vanilla. The wine is full bodied, dense, powerful, yet seamless and silky. The tannin is gorgeously well integrated, a characteristic of the 1994 vintage. This wine can be drunk now or cellared for 15–20 years. The opaque purple-colored 1995 Cabernet/Merlot Blend (70% Cabernet Sauvignon/30% Merlot) displays a sweet, rich nose of melted road tar, black currants, earth, minerals, and toast. Rich, with great fruit and ripeness, this full-bodied wine will be at its best after 2–4 years of cellaring; it will keep for 15+ years.

The 1994 Cabernet Sauvignon is another top-notch effort from this classic vintage. This opaque purple-colored, sexy wine reveals the vintage's precocious, flattering style. It offers up plenty of jammy black fruits intermingled with smoke, spice, licorice, and charcoal. Full bodied, with low acidity, outstanding ripeness, and a fleshy, multilayered feel, this wine can be drunk now or cellared for 15+ years. In 1996 I thought the 1995 Cabernet Sauvignon might turn out to be even better, and it still may, but the 1994 was singing when I saw it in October of 1997. As for the 1995 Cabernet Sauvignon, it is the qualitative equivalent of the 1994, perhaps slightly more structured and tannic, but sweet, rich, and loaded with fruit. Like its siblings, it is a 100% Cabernet Sauvignon that spends 30 months in oak casks (of which 40%–50% are new). It will be fascinating to follow both the 1994 and 1995 over the next decade to see which wine eventually comes out on top, but both are worth owning. The opaque purple-colored, dense, chewy, full-bodied 1993 Cabernet Sauvignon is more tannic and structured when tasted next to the 1994 and 1995. Although lacking some of the 1994's and 1995's velvety texture, it remains a well-made, large-scaled, well-endowed Cabernet Sauvignon to drink over the next two decades. The 1996 Cabernet Sauvignon appears slightly below the quality of the 1994 and 1995. Although deeply colored and supple, it seems to lack the exceptional concentration and intensity of its two predecessors. Nevertheless, it is no wimpy wine, and it may justify an outstanding rating after bottling.

The smoky, black raspberry, cassis-scented and -flavored 1993 Syrah is full bodied, round, and surprisingly soft and generous. There is gorgeous extract and low acidity, as well as ripe fruit. The Dehlinger vinification has resulted in an elegant, sensual Syrah for drinking over the next 7–8 years. The 1994 Syrah has an opaque ruby/purple color and a huge nose of smoky black raspberry and blackberry fruit, followed by a wine with large, powerful flavors, admirable body and glycerin, and amazing length and richness. Its purity and intense Syrah character are beautiful to behold. While very approachable and silky, it is capable of lasting for 12–15+ years.

Syrah continues to go from strength to strength at Dehlinger. The 1994 Syrah Estate has shut down in the bottle, and will require 4–5 years of cellaring, after which it will age well for 15–20 years. The color is an impressive opaque purple, and the wine reluctantly offers up sweet cassis, pepper, tar, and earthy scents. Full bodied and chewy, with excellent purity, this is an impressively endowed yet moderately tannic Syrah for laying down for a few years. The 1994 Syrah Goldridge Vineyard is a richly fruity, medium-weight Syrah with a dark purple color, gobs of sweet black currants in the nose, round, generous flavors, and some tannin in the finish. The wine should drink well for up to a decade. The 1995 Syrah Goldridge Vineyard (aged in 20% new oak) reveals an attractive peppery, bacony, sweet blackberry-scented nose, and ripe, rich, full-bodied flavors with plenty of sweet fruit. With an impressive chewy texture and excellent purity, it is a candidate for 10–18 years of cellaring, although it can be drunk now if matched with rich foods. My notes for the 1995 Syrah Estate said, "amazing Syrah." The wine possesses an opaque black/purple color, outstanding smoky, tarlike, blackberry flavors, immense body, admirable purity, and a long, deep, explosively rich finish with the tannin nearly concealed by the wine's wealth of fruit, glycerin, and extract. This terrific Syrah should age effortlessly for 15 or more years.

DEL DOTTO (NAPA)

1997 Cabernet Sauvignon	Napa	E	(88–90+)
1996 Cabernet Sauvignon	Napa	E	89

1995 Cabernet Sauvignon	Napa	D	89+
1995 Giovanni's Tuscan Reserve	Napa	D	88

This small 7-acre vineyard just north of St. Helena is primarily planted with Cabernet Sauvignon, with a tiny amount of Sangiovese. Production has been limited, as part of the crop was sold to Whitehall Lane, but that changed with the 1997 vintage. Consequently, Del Dotto's production will soar from just under 500 to 4,000 cases. The wines are aged in both American and French oak, and the proprietary red, Giovanni's Tuscan Reserve, is available only in 500 ml bottles. The delicious 1995 Giovanni's Tuscan Reserve, a blend of 70% Cabernet Sauvignon and 30% Sangiovese, displays a dark plum color, full body, gorgeous, jammy strawberry fruit intermixed with raspberries and cassis with a subtle touch of spicy oak, and a fleshy, chewy texture. I would opt for drinking it over the next 3–4 years.

The Cabernet Sauvignons (500 cases of both the 1995 and 1996) are aged in 100% new oak, of which 50% is American oak coopered by French barrelmakers. The exotic, opaque purple-colored 1995 Cabernet Sauvignon offers exceptionally ripe, jammy black cherry and currant flavors intermixed with lavish quantities of toasty new oak. Full bodied and obvious, but undeniably appealing in an ostentatious manner, this brassy, big, thick, juicy wine is already drinking well, but promises to evolve for 10–12 years. Like the 1995, the 1996 Cabernet Sauvignon is scheduled to be bottled with no fining or filtration. Even richer than its older sibling, it displays more of Cabernet Sauvignon's classic cassis character, as well as an opaque purple color, layers of fatness, full body, outstanding purity, and an explosive, long finish. Neither the 1995 nor 1996 could be called elegant or finesse-styled wines, but they are gorgeously made and opulent, with undeniable crowd appeal. The 1997 Cabernet Sauvignon exhibits the vintage's fragrant, forward, expressive style. Although not as fat or concentrated as the 1996 and 1995, it is made in a more restrained style. Is it the vintage, or a subtle shift in winemaking? All of these wines are made by hippie/cowboy, Nils Venge.

DIAMOND CREEK VINEYARDS (NAPA)

1994 Cabernet Sauvignon Gravelly Meadow	Napa	D	92
1993 Cabernet Sauvignon Gravelly Meadow	Napa	D	87?
1994 Cabernet Sauvignon Red Rock Terrace	Napa	D	91?
1994 Cabernet Sauvignon Volcanic Hill	Napa	D	94
1993 Cabernet Sauvignon Volcanic Hill	Napa	D	90?

As a fan of Diamond Creek Cabernet Sauvignons in the seventies and early eighties, I have frequently detailed my lack of enthusiasm for vintages after 1984. For that reason, I am happy to report that barrel samples of Diamond Creek's 1994s look to be the most reassuringly fine examples of this estate's Cabernets that I have tasted since 1984. Let's hope they put the wines into the bottle naturally, without excessive fining or filtering. Certainly the raw materials are very impressive.

All three of the 1994 wines are backward, well-built, tannic wines meant to last for 2 decades or more. I suspect they will be among the least flattering wines to taste when released. The dark ruby/purple-colored 1994 Gravelly Meadow Cabernet Sauvignon exhibits a nose of loamy, dusty earth intermingled with scents of jammy, ripe black fruits and oak, full body, and layers of flavor. Although young and unevolved, it displays exceptional promise if cellared for 7–8 years. Even more tannic, but still impressively endowed, is the 1994 Cabernet Sauvignon Red Rock Terrace. The color is a murky ruby/purple, and the nose reluctantly offers up jammy red and black currant scents, along with mineral and vanillin notes. Sweet, ripe, full bodied, but ferociously tannic, this is a wine to lay away for at least a decade. The most impressively endowed wine of this trio is the 1994 Volcanic Hill Cabernet Sauvignon.

The color is opaque purple. The wine offers a glorious display of black currant, plum, and blueberry fruit gently infused with toasty oak. The roasted, smoky, richness of this wine is immediately apparent when it hits the palate. There are layers of ripe, unctuously textured fruit, full body, and hard-hitting tannin in the finish. It is backward, rich, and extremely impressive. The barrel tasting notes of Diamond Creek's 1994s offer promise of great raw materials. I hope that is translated into superb wines in the bottle.

The two 1993s appear to be very good, but they are not made in the style of the great Diamond Creek Cabernets made in 1978, 1977, 1976, and 1974. Admirers of those wines would not recognize the still tannic but far less concentrated, tough, austere style of wine now being produced. The 1993 Gravelly Meadow possesses good fruit, extremely high tannin (excessive?), and a medium-bodied, spicy finish. It needs 5–6 years of cellaring as it is atypically backward for a 1993. The 1993 Volcanic Hill exhibits smoky, black cherry fruit, is medium to full bodied, and excruciatingly tannic. Is there enough fat, flesh, and flavor extraction to stand up to the tannin? Does anyone have an explanation why a winery that became legendary among California Cabernet Sauvignon enthusiasts would completely change the style of its wines after having enjoyed such remarkable success and loyalty from its fans?

DOMINUS (NAPA)

1997	Dominus Napanook Vineyard	Napa	EE	(91–94)
1996	Dominus Napanook Vineyard	Napa	EE	95
1995	Dominus Napanook Vineyard	Napa	E	93
1994	Dominus Napanook Vineyard	Napa	E	99
1997	Napanook Proprietary Red Wine	Napa	D	(87–89)
1996	Napanook Proprietary Red Wine	Napa	D	90

In 1997, Dominus's production has grown to approximately 5,000 cases of their second wine, Napanook, and 8,000 cases of their flagship wine, Dominus. The 1997 Napanook (a blend of 61% Cabernet Sauvignon, 22% Cabernet Franc, and 17% Merlot, all aged in *barriques*, of which 20% is new) is a low-acid, lush, hedonistic wine with both elegance and flavor richness. There is plenty of weedy, black currant fruit in the nose and flavors, a silky texture, and a user-friendly, deliciously endowed finish. This seductive, immediately accessible wine should be consumed during its first decade of life. Although the 1997 Dominus (87% Cabernet Sauvignon, 9% Cabernet Franc, and 4% Merlot) tips the scales at 14% alcohol, it is well hidden by the wine's sweet, rich, concentrated style. The wine's deep ruby/garnet color is accompanied by beautiful aromatics of licorice, Asian spices, black cherries, and cassis. An elegant, complex, medium- to full-bodied wine, it has a long, silky-textured finish. This is one of the most accessible wines produced by Dominus, as well as its most graceful offering to date. The wine should be ready to drink upon release and will evolve nicely for 12–15 years.

There are 2,000 cases of the 1996 Napanook, a blend of 74% Cabernet Sauvignon, 13% Cabernet Franc, and 13% Petit Verdot. Made in a peppery, spicy, herbaceous, earthy style, it exhibits a dark plum color, an intensely aromatic cassis and pepper-scented nose, a lush entry on the palate, and succulent, low-acid, rich, concentrated flavors with more tannin than the 1997. Already drinkable, the 1996 is appealing for its intense fragrance and rich flavors. It should age well for 10–12 years. The 1996 Dominus, a blend of 82% Cabernet Sauvignon, 10% Cabernet Franc, 4% Merlot, and 4% Petit Verdot, tips the scales at 14.2% alcohol. Although this offering lacks the power, intensity, and compelling characteristics of the 1991 and 1994, it is not far off the pace of those two monumental wines. A super nose of roasted coffee, chocolate, dried herbs, black fruits and kirsch is both intense and persuasive. The wine displays terrific richness, medium to full body, low acidity, a succulent, opulent texture, and superb purity. This beautifully made 1996 is one of the few wines that has successfully tamed the vintage's elevated tannin level. It should be relatively drinkable upon its release, yet evolve nicely for 2 decades. Impressive!

The 1995 Dominus (6,000 cases produced from a blend of 80% Cabernet Sauvignon, 10% Cabernet Franc, 6% Petit Verdot, and 4% Merlot) is a ripe, plummy, supple, expansively flavored wine with copious quantities of black currant fruit. Full bodied and low in acidity, it possesses exceptional concentration and purity. Qualitatively, it is built along the lines of the 1992 and 1990. While it is not as powerful or intense as the 1996 or 1994, the 1995 is a large-scaled, rich, concentrated wine that should provide splendid drinking for 2 decades.

I have had a difficult time keeping the corks in my bottles of 1994 Dominus. Eight thousand cases were produced from a blend of 70% Cabernet Sauvignon, 14% Cabernet Franc, 12% Merlot, and 4% Petit Verdot. In this vintage, 174 days passed between bud break and the harvest, a remarkable period of time for any wine region in the world. The 1994 is a strikingly thick, compellingly rich wine with the texture of a great Pomerol, despite being made primarily from Cabernet Sauvignon. The wine exhibits a dense purple color, and an incredibly fragrant nose of jammy black fruits, spice, smoke, and loamy, trufflelike scents. In the mouth, it is full bodied, with thrilling levels of extract and richness, but no sense of heaviness or harshness. This seamless Dominus possesses no hard edges, as its acidity, tannin, and alcohol are beautifully meshed with copious quantities of ripe fruit. This wine offers early drinking, yet has the potential to last for 30+ years.

On what I suppose is a distressing note, I have noticed huge demand for Dominus in recent auction activity. At a Sotheby's auction on October 25, Dominus fetched prices of $23,150 for one imperial of 1991, and $10,450 for two 1991 double magnums. Although none of this is the fault of anybody at Dominus (blame Christian Moueix and his team for producing profound wine) if this trend continues, I wonder how any true admirers will be able to afford the wine.

DOVER CANYON (PASO ROBLES)

1996 Cabernet Sauvignon	Paso Robles	C	87
1996 Merlot Reserve	Paso Robles	C	87
1997 Rhône Reserve	Central Coast	C	88
1995 Zinfandel	Paso Robles	C	87
1996 Zinfandel Templeton Gap Reserve	Paso Robles	C	90

Dog enthusiasts will no doubt want to bark at the label, but these wines, while not exquisite enough to howl about, are very, very good. Dover Canyon has turned out an attractive 1997 Rhône Reserve from a blend of 75% Viognier and 25% Roussanne. This honeyed wine is richly fruity, thickly textured, and offers a mouthful of fruit. Serve it with strongly flavored fish or chicken dishes, or grilled vegetables, etc. The wine's low acidity and forward style suggest consumption is warranted over the next year.

The 1996 Merlot Reserve, an unfiltered blend of 85% Merlot and 15% Cabernet Sauvignon, exhibits a dark ruby/purple color, followed by a spicy, highly extracted, black raspberry and mocha-scented and -flavored personality. It is a lovely, fleshy, fat wine with good definition and uplift. It should drink well for 5–7 years. Although the 1996 Cabernet Sauvignon is more monolithic, it offers plenty of promise. This dense purple-colored, full-bodied wine is tight and closed, but rich in the mouth, with copious quantities of chewy, cassis and black cherry flavors interspersed with a dusty, mineral component. The finish is long, sweet (from ripe tannin and extract, not sugar), and clean. Give this Cabernet another 8–12 months of bottle age, and drink it over the following 7–8 years.

What a wonderful surprise! The excellent dark ruby/plum-colored 1995 Zinfandel offers up a briery, peppery, wild berry-scented nose, medium body, and classic, pure, sweet, ripe, black cherry flavors that are nicely balanced with the wine's glycerin, acid, alcohol (14.8%), and tannin. This forward, lush, flattering-styled Zinfandel will have many admirers. Drink it over the next 5–6 years. Readers should note the cute back label with the winemaker's tasting notes—"Dog-gone good."

My favorite wine from this estate is the 1996 Zinfandel Templeton Gap Reserve. It tips the scales at 14.8% alcohol, but holds everything in balance with a daring and heady display of copious black cherry and raspberry fruit, gobs of pepper and earth, abundant glycerin, and a full-bodied, silky-textured finish. By any standard, this wine is dog-gone good! Drink it over the next 3–4 years.

DRY CREEK VINEYARD (SONOMA)

1994	Cabernet Sauvignon	Dry Creek Valley	C 87
1994	Cabernet Sauvignon 25th Anniversary	Dry Creek Valley	D 89
1995	Chardonnay Barrel Fermented	Sonoma	C 87
1995	Chardonnay Reserve	Dry Creek Valley	C 88
1995	Fumé Blanc	Sonoma	B 87
1996	Fumé Blanc Reserve	Dry Creek Valley	C 88
1995	Fumé Blanc Reserve	Dry Creek Valley	B 88
1995	Meritage	Dry Creek Valley	D 86
1994	Merlot Reserve	Dry Creek Valley	C 87
1994	Zinfandel	Dry Creek Valley	C 87
1993	Zinfandel Old Vines	Dry Creek Valley	C 87
1995	Zinfandel Old Vines 25th Anniversary	Dry Creek	D 88
1995	Zinfandel Reserve	Dry Creek	C 87
1994	Zinfandel Reserve	Dry Creek Valley	C 89+

Three good efforts from David Stare, the 1995 Meritage (a blend of 75% Cabernet Sauvignon, 19% Cabernet Franc, and 6% Petit Verdot) exhibits a medium dark ruby color, followed by an earthy, loamy, berry, herb, and oak-scented nose, medium body, attractive sweet fruit, a supple texture, and a round, accessible finish. This wine will provide delicious drinking for 4–6 years. The dark ruby-colored 1994 Cabernet Sauvignon 25th Anniversary reveals a tight but promising nose of sweet kirsch, black currants, and high quality French oak. In the mouth, the wine is fleshy, medium to full bodied, and well knit, with good tannin and a well-delineated, focused style. There is excellent purity, a graceful, elegant, complex, Bordeaux-like character to the wine, and moderately long aging potential. Anticipated maturity: 2000–2010. The 1996 Fumé Blanc Reserve is an excellent Sauvignon Blanc offering with copious quantities of melony fruit, a notion of figs, and subtle spice. A medium-bodied, deliciously fruity, and intense wine without much weight, this exceptionally well made Sauvignon can be drunk over the next 12–18 months.

Dry Creek has always made delicious Sauvignons, and their 1995 Fumé Blanc Reserve is a gorgeously textured, plump, succulent style of Sauvignon with gobs of honeyed melonlike fruit. With fine length and richness, as well as plenty of guts, it is an ostentatious, brilliantly fruity, complex wine with just enough oak to give it complexity. Drink it over the next year. The 1995 Fumé Blanc exhibits a light straw color with a greenish hue. The nose offers scents of spice, vanillin, subtle herbs, and minerals. Medium bodied, crisp, and surprisingly well textured, with dry, well-delineated fruit flavors, and a spicy finish, this wine should be consumed over the next 1–2 years.

Dry Creek's 1995 Barrel Fermented Chardonnay is one of the better efforts from this winery, which is more widely known for its Sauvignon Blanc. The wine exhibits buttery apple fruit with a subtle hint of toasty oak. Medium bodied and fresh, with good but not excessive acidity, this well-endowed, mouth-filling wine should drink well for 1–2 years. The 1995 Chardonnay Reserve offers a creamy, citrusy, custardlike richness, and plenty of vanillin and spicy ripe fruit. Consume this rich, round, opulent, nicely textured Chardonnay over the next year.

This estate's 1994 Cabernet Sauvignon is the ideal restaurant Cabernet. It possesses a healthy dark ruby color, and a big, open-knit, sexy, vanillin and black currant-scented nose that is easy to understand and admire. Soft and supple, with a silky texture, and plenty of berry fruit, this is a delicious, medium-bodied Cabernet Sauvignon to drink over the next 7–8 years. Attractive herb-tinged, mocha, chocolatey, sweet fruit with spicy new oak is the hallmark of the medium-bodied, silky-textured, plush 1994 Merlot Reserve. It should continue to drink well for 5–6 years.

The excellent 1995 Zinfandel Old Vines 25th Anniversary is one of the most noteworthy efforts from this vintage. It possesses a dense ruby/purple color, followed by a big, fragrant, spicy, pungent nose of pepper, jammy red and black fruits, and earth. Rich, medium to full bodied, and harmonious, this wine exhibits a pleasing midsection and fine length. It should drink well for 5–6 years. The 1995 Zinfandel Reserve reveals the stemmy, gingery, allspice character found in many 1995 Zinfandels. In contrast to the 25th Anniversary cuvée, it is more spice than fruit driven. Nevertheless, it provides some dusty, earthy, chewy fruit, medium body, and a nicely layered, well-balanced, harmonious personality. Drink it over the next 4–5 years.

The 1994 Sonoma Zinfandel is a ripe, jammy, fat wine with loads of fruit, enough acidity to provide vibrancy and delineation, medium to full body, and an earthy, smoky finish. It should provide delicious drinking during its first 5–6 years of life. The sweeter, richer 1994 Zinfandel Reserve offers more pepper, alcohol, glycerin, and extract. Full bodied and fleshy, with loads of briery, black raspberry fruit and spice, it will drink well for 7+ years.

The fruity, medium-bodied 1993 Zinfandel exhibits good concentration, a fragrant, cherry, dusty, spicy-scented nose, more elegance than usual, and a crisp, medium-bodied finish. The wine does not display the power and intensity of previous vintages. It should drink well for 5–6 years.

DUNN VINEYARDS (NAPA)

1996 Cabernet Sauvignon	Howell Mountain	E	96
1995 Cabernet Sauvignon	Howell Mountain	E	96
1994 Cabernet Sauvignon	Howell Mountain	E	96+
1993 Cabernet Sauvignon	Howell Mountain	E	95+
1995 Cabernet Sauvignon	Napa	D	94
1994 Cabernet Sauvignon	Napa	D	94
1993 Cabernet Sauvignon	Napa	D	93

I have been buying Randy Dunn's wines since he first began producing them in 1979. I have worried about whether they ever become drinkable given their massive personalities and huge tannic structures. I am not sure I know the answer, but a blind tasting with my wine group in late September was a revelation since one of the group served over a dozen vintages of Dunn's Cabernet Sauvignons. What was so striking was that in the first flight, which included vintages from the early eighties, the wines were thought to be from the early nineties! Undoubtedly, these wines age at a glacial pace. While I have been consistently advising readers that they will last for 25–30 years, they may be 40–50 year wines, possibly needing 25–30 years just to reach their plateau of maturity! No vintage from the eighties or nineties was revealing much age. All the wines were relatively stunning in quality, with some of the lighter years, such as 1983 and 1988, surprisingly impressive, but not as phenomenal as Randy Dunn's greatest vintages (1982, 1984, 1985, 1990, 1991, 1992, 1993, 1994, 1995, and 1996). One of the interesting findings from this vertical tasting is that the fruit levels remain incredibly fresh and concentrated, yet the tannin levels do soften. Because the wines are sterile filtered, I am not sure they will ever develop aromatic complexity, but who really knows? The remarkable aspect is that at 15–18 years of age, Dunn's Cabernet Sauvignons taste as if they are only 3–5 years old. Furthermore, there are no signs of fruit degradation or oxidation, always positive attributes when measuring a wine's ageability.

As for the 1995s, this appears to be a fabulous vintage. I doubt there will be much difference in quality between the 1995s and Randy Dunn's spectacular 1994s. The saturated black/purple-colored 1995 Cabernet Sauvignon possesses a promising yet backward nose of minerals, lead pencil, and blackberries/cassis. The wine was bottled in June, but it is showing no ill effects. This mammoth offering displays extraordinary concentration and purity, as well as a thick, unctuous texture with high tannin levels. It will evolve for 30–50 years. When will it reach its plateau of maturity? My best guess is 10–15 years—minimum. The 1995 Cabernet Sauvignon Howell Mountain is similar in all respects to the Napa Valley, but somewhat heavier in the mouth, with an aggressive tannic bite, and more length. It possesses mineral-tinged blackberry and cassis fruit, massive body, and extraordinary purity and length. It should not be touched for 12–15 years. Again, it will undoubtedly live through the first half of the next century. The 1996 Cabernet Sauvignon Howell Mountain boasts phenomenal richness, along with the blackberry/blueberry purity of fruit that is such a hallmark of these mountain wines, humongous body, amazing extract of fruit (it oozes across the palate) that suggests crème de cassis, and a blockbuster finish with well-integrated acidity and tannin. A leviathan of a wine, it is every bit as big and rich as the 1995 and 1994.

I saw a composite blend that will represent 75% of the 1997 Cabernet Sauvignon Howell Mountain. It also appears to be a terrific wine from Dunn. Randy Dunn feels 1997 is one of the most successful vintages of the nineties, so fasten your seatbelts!

One of the issues about which Randy Dunn is sensitive is the fact that his wines are so remarkably consistent that it is often difficult to tell vintages apart. I think the vintage character will become more apparent when the wines are 15–20 years of age. Even the most professional palate will be inundated with a furious blast of tannin and concentrated cassis and blackberry fruit when these wines are young. With that in mind, the following notes do sound similar, but I feel 1994 may turn out to be Dunn's finest of the three most recent vintages. At present, 1995 looks to be the most tannic, and 1996, similar to, but softer than 1994. Given the fact that both of Dunn's debut vintages of 1979 and 1980 are still relative infants in terms of development, in all likelihood, the 1994s, 1995s, and 1996s possess a minimum of 25–30 years of aging potential!

The 1994s might be ready to drink within 10–15 years. It is hard to believe these wines spend 30 months in oak casks before bottling as they are incredibly unevolved and backward when released. The 1994 Cabernet Sauvignon Napa reveals an opaque purple color, followed by a sweet, rich, black currant and crème de cassis-scented nose with no evidence of oak. This fruit bomb displays considerable breadth and expansiveness on the palate, in essence revealing only two dimensions—fruit and tannin. It is slightly softer and more precocious than the 1995 and 1996, so perhaps it will only need 10, rather than 15 years of cellaring. This immensely impressive Cabernet is a candidate for 20–30 years of cellaring. Look out for the behemoth 1994 Cabernet Sauvignon Howell Mountain. This black/purple-colored wine adds a few more nuances (minerals, licorice, and floral scents) to the lavish display of crème de cassis. Full bodied, with a blockbuster level of extract and density, this is an outstanding Cabernet Sauvignon for readers with patience, good genes for longevity, or the foresight to purchase it for their children. Anticipated maturity: 2006–2030.

This is also another producer who turned out outstanding 1993s, a vintage that has received some unjustifiably tough press from West Coast wine critics. The 1993 Cabernet Sauvignon Napa exhibits a black/purple color, and a sweet nose of cassis, vanillin, and violet/mineral character. Sweet on the attack, with superb concentration and purity, this formidably endowed, full-bodied wine needs at least 8–10 years of cellaring; it is a 30–year wine. The 1993 Cabernet Sauvignon Howell Mountain reveals an opaque black color, huge tannin, terrific purity, and density, a broad, heavyweight mouth-feel, and gobs of ripe tannin. It is a massive Cabernet Sauvignon that requires a decade of cellaring—at the minimum.

EBERLE WINERY (PASO ROBLES)

1995 Zinfandel Sauret Vineyard	Paso Robles	C	87
1994 Zinfandel Sauret Vineyard	Paso Robles	C	87+
1993 Zinfandel Sauret Vineyard	Paso Robles	C	90

The 1995 Zinfandel Sauret Vineyard is a muscular, full-bodied, structured style of Zinfandel that should turn out to be well balanced as well as impressively fruity and rich. The dense, saturated ruby/purple color is followed by reticent earthy, black cherry aromas that emerge with airing. The wine offers excellent richness and concentration, plenty of spice, medium to full body, and no shortage of acidity or tannin. Give it another year of bottle age, and drink it over the following 5–6.

Although the dark, opaque ruby/purple-colored 1994 Zinfandel Sauret Vineyard is closed and compressed, it exhibits plenty of ripe fruit, a muscular, husky, broad-shouldered style, considerable acidity, and a thick, robust, coarse finish. This wine needs 6–12 more months of bottle age. If the acidity becomes more integrated, it will merit a score in the upper eighties. It should keep for 6–7 years.

Eberle's full throttle 1993 Sauret Vineyard Zinfandel exhibits an opaque purple color, and a huge, lavishly oaked, berry-scented nose. Thick, full-bodied, massively endowed flavors contain considerable alcohol (14.8%), and the wine's mouth-filling, glycerin-imbued, superb finish lasts for nearly a minute. This extroverted, muscular, well-balanced Zinfandel should drink well for a decade. Readers are forewarned—this is not a wimpy wine!

ECHELON (CENTRAL COAST)

1997 Chardonnay	Central Coast	B	86
1997 Pinot Noir	Central Coast	C	87

Two terrific bargains, Echelon's 1997 Chardonnay (60,000 cases) offers plenty of honeyed pear fruit with toasty oak in the background. Medium bodied, pure, exuberant and fruity, it is meant to be drunk over the next year. The 1997 Pinot Noir (25,000 cases) is a good bargain. The wine reveals a light to medium ruby color, and a moderately intense nose of berry fruit intermixed with smoke. Round, easygoing, graceful, and richly fruity, this wine should be consumed over the next year.

EDMEADES ESTATE (MENDOCINO)

1996 Chardonnay	Mendocino	C	87
1996 Gewürztraminer	Mendocino	C	89
1996 Petite Sirah Eaglepoint	Mendocino	C	89
1996 Pinot Noir	Anderson Valley	C	87
1995 Pinot Noir	Anderson Valley	C	87
1993 Pinot Noir Denison Vineyard	Anderson Valley	C	76
1996 Zinfandel	Mendocino	C	87
1995 Zinfandel	Mendocino	C	86
1996 Zinfandel Ciapusci Vineyard	Mendocino	C	88
1993 Zinfandel Ciapusci Vineyard	Mendocino	C	86
1994 Zinfandel Estate Ciapusci Vineyard	Mendocino	D	89
1995 Zinfandel Estate Eaglepoint Vineyard	Mendocino	D	90
1996 Zinfandel Zeni Vineyard	Mendocino	D	90
1995 Zinfandel Estate Zeni Vineyard	Mendocino	D	90
1994 Zinfandel Estate Zeni Vineyard	Mendocino	D	88
1993 Zinfandel Zeni Vineyard	Mendocino	C	89

This is an unheralded source for surprisingly user-friendly, well-made wines. Only indigenous yeasts are used for fermentation, in addition to a light filtration, resulting in wines with natural textures and intriguing aromatics. California rarely produces successful Gewürztraminer, but Edmeades' 1996 Gewürztraminer is a bone dry, excellent example of this varietal. Unmistakable Gewürztraminer aromas of rose petals and spicy grapefruit are present in the wine's bouquet. In the mouth, it is medium to full bodied, with some tannin, and a dry, richly fruity finish. This nearly outstanding example should be drunk over the next 1–2 years. The 1996 Chardonnay displays a crisp, elegant, medium-bodied style, earthiness, tangy acidity, and a ripe pear, white peach, and citrusy nose and flavors. Consume it over the next year.

The best buy among the red wines is the 1996 Pinot Noir from Anderson Valley. It exhibits a medium ruby/garnet color, followed by a moderately intense nose of plums, black cherries, earth, and spice. Soft, round, and well made, this open-knit Pinot Noir can be enjoyed over the next several years. Edmeades is best known for its Zinfandels. The two fine 1996s include the 1996 Zinfandel Zeni Vineyard, which possesses plenty of this varietal's peppery, briery, raspberry fruit, good freshness, and loads of glycerin and concentration. This lush, supple-textured Zinfandel should be consumed over the next several years. The evolved dark plum-colored 1996 Zinfandel Ciapusci Vineyard offers a spicy, peppery, fruity nose, lush, medium-bodied flavors, and good fat and depth. Although not as deep and rich as the Zeni cuvée, it is an excellent Zinfandel for drinking over the next 2–3 years.

Readers looking for muscular, brawny, full-bodied, tannic reds need search no further than Edmeades' 1996 Petite Sirah Eaglepoint. This wine reveals an opaque black/purple color, as well as a boldly styled nose of jammy blackberry fruit intertwined with cassis and earth. It is a broodingly dense, chewy, uncomplex wine with intense flavors, full body, and excellent, nearly outstanding purity and length. Consume it now, or cellar it for 10–15 years.

Edmeades Vineyards is another northern California estate that was purchased by Jess Jackson and is part of his portfolio of high-quality, small winemaking estates known as *Artisans and Estates*. Edmeades is known for its delicious, fruity Zinfandels from Mendocino.

Chardonnay and Pinot Noir are recent additions to its lineup. While I have not tasted the new or upcoming releases of Chardonnay, the 1995 Pinot Noir Anderson Valley, one of the hotbeds for promising Pinot Noir in northern California (along with the Sonoma Coast and Russian River), is a tasty, soft, delicious, dark ruby-colored Pinot Noir with copious amounts of strawberry and cherry fruit, a nice dollop of spicy oak, and a round, medium-bodied, silky texture. Although not the most profound Pinot, it is a user-friendly, delicious, reasonably priced wine.

The lightweight, fruity, one-dimensional 1993 Pinot Noir Dennison Vineyard exhibits tart acidity, average flavor concentration, and a clean, crisp, short finish. Drink it up.

The Zinfandels tend to reflect the philosophy of winemaker Van Williamson who says, "I want to make wines that can be enjoyed by everyday folks as well as the wine connoisseur." I certainly enjoyed Edmeades' 1994 Zinfandels. The 1994 Zinfandel Zeni Vineyard offers up a moderately intense nose of red and black fruits, minerals, spice, and a whiff of pepper, super purity to its fruit, medium body, good density, ripe concentration, a round, generous midpalate, and a soft finish. Already delicious, it should be consumed over the next 4–5 years. The 1994 Zinfandel Ciapusa Vineyard is less accessible, more structured, and richer, with an underlying tart character adding a different textural dimension to this rich, red curranty/cranberry/raspberry-flavored wine. Elegant and pure, with fine density and a delicious, surprisingly long finish, this textbook, medium-weight, impeccably made Zinfandel is crammed with fruit. Like its sibling, it will drink well for 4–5 years.

I am pleased to see the consistently high quality of the 1995s. Edmeades produced two of the finest Zinfandels of the vintage, as well as a very good regular cuvée. The 1995 Zinfandel is lighter and less well-endowed than the two single vineyard wines, but it offers a wonderful introduction to the seductive qualities of a well-made Zinfandel. In a vintage that produced many hollow, acidic wines, Edmeades' 1995 Zinfandel exhibits plenty of ripe, tasty, berry fruit, medium body, an elegant overall personality, and excellent balance and length. The wine's 13.9% alcohol is well hidden behind the gush of berry fruit. It is a delicious, straightforward, fleshy Zinfandel that should drink well for 2–3 years.

I adored the 1995 Zinfandel Eaglepoint Vineyard. The wine's saturated opaque purple color is accompanied by intense aromas of black raspberries, cherries, minerals, and spice. Opulently textured and rich, with layers of fruit, this wine is atypical of the vintage given its wealth of fruit, surprising level of glycerin, and gorgeously proportioned, layered finish. This is a beautifully made, pure, medium- to full-bodied Zinfandel that has managed to hide its lofty alcohol (15.2%) content. Drink it over the next 5 years. Another outstanding wine is the 1995 Zinfandel Zeni Vineyard. Tasters would never guess it boasts 15.2% alcohol. It exhibits a saturated plum color, and an exotic, spicy, sweet, jammy, black cherry, strawberry, and currant-scented nose with a subtle suggestion of toasty new oak. This wine possesses terrific fruit and richness, more structure and tannin than the Eaglepoint Vineyard, and plenty of spice, body, and length. Drink this well-defined, very pure, textbook Zinfandel over the next 5–7 years.

The Zinfandel-dominated 1996 Zinfandel (there is 17% Petite Sirah and 5% Pinot Noir in the blend) reveals a dark ruby color, followed by a fragrant, smoky, oaky, raspberry and cherry-scented nose. Supple and medium to full bodied, with easygoing fruit, this is a friendly, open-knit, expansive wine to consume over the next 1–2 years.

If you can find any of the 1993 Zinfandel offerings from the Edmeades Vineyard, the 1993 Zinfandel Ciapusci Vineyard exhibits a nearly opaque dark ruby color, and a moderately intense nose of berry fruit and earth. Closed, with moderate tannin, this is a structured, tightly knit wine that will benefit from 1–2 years of cellaring. The tannin level is cause for worry, but there is good ripeness and richness. Drink it between 1997 and 2007. The 1993 Zinfandel Zeni Vineyard (from 70-year-old vines) reveals a similar dark ruby color, as well as a more promising and open nose of red and black fruits and spice, highly extracted, black raspberry and cherry flavors, full body, and light tannin in the structured finish. The wine is young, exuberant, fresh, and pure. Drink it over the next decade.

EDMUNDS ST. JOHN (ALAMEDA)

1995 Les Côtes Sauvages	California	C	87+
1993 Les Côtes Sauvages	California	B	86
1993 Pallini Rosso (Zinfandel/Grenache)	California	C	89
1996 Pinot Grigio	El Dorado County	C	85
1995 Syrah	California	C	88
1994 Syrah	California	B	89
1993 Syrah	California	C	88+
1995 Syrah Durell Vineyard	Sonoma	D	90+
1993 Syrah Durell Vineyard	Sonoma	D	93
1993 Syrah Grand Heritage	California	D	92
1994 Zinfandel	Amador	C	78
1993 Zinfandel	Amador	C	?

One of my favorite small California wineries, Edmunds St. John continues to turn out artisanal, non-oaked (all the wines are aged in barrel, but no new wood is used) wines that are filled with personality and flavor. The 1995 Pinot Grigio is a straightforward, creamy-textured, spicy wine with honeyed fruit, nice glycerin and body, and a clean, fresh mouthfeel. My instincts suggest this wine will reveal far more character when matched with food. My score may be a bit stingy as this wine possesses fine length, but I still think it should be drunk over the next year.

The 1995 Les Côtes Sauvages, a Rhône Ranger blend of Grenache, Syrah and Mourvèdre, exhibits a murky dark plum color, and a wild berry, earthy, plant, and animal-scented nose that is dominated by its Mourvèdre component. In the mouth, it is firm, but rich and medium to full bodied, with plenty of black fruits, attractive glycerin, and moderate tannin in the long, spicy finish. This meaty, firmly knit wine should continue to open and expand over the next 2–5 years and last for 10–12, at the minimum. Looking for a robust Syrah for only $15 a bottle? Edmunds St. John's 1995 Syrah offers textbook varietal character—tar, smoke, cassis, pepper, and loads of spice and meaty components. A dense, rustic style of Syrah with good tannin, full body, and considerable depth, it is a gutsy, mouth-filling wine with undeniable character. This wine should drink well for a dozen or more years. The opaque purple-colored 1995 Syrah Durell Vineyard displays a provocative bacon fat, smoky, earthy nose filled with suggestions of overripe plums, black currants, and prunes. Extremely full bodied, with layers of sweet black fruits, moderate tannin, and outstanding purity and depth, this exceptional Syrah offers only a hint of its ultimate potential. It should evolve effortlessly for the next 15+ years, and merit an even loftier score. Another terrific Syrah from one of my favorite wineries, the opaque purple-colored 1993 Durell Vineyard displays a big, smoky, cassis, and bacon fat-scented nose, full body, outstanding concentration, considerable richness, and impressive length. The tannin is largely concealed by the wine's copious fruit. Although approachable, it will not hit its peak for 2–5 years; it will age well for 15 years.

Tasting the 1994 Zinfandel, a stemmy, vegetal, spicy, cinnamon-scented nose is at odds with previous experiences. Impressive Zinfandels usually emerge from Edmunds St. John, and although this wine reveals softness and ripeness, it lacks size and extract. Given the talent and track record here, this is a disappointment.

Edmunds St. John's 1994 Syrah is a gorgeously smoky, cassis-scented and -flavored wine that reveals delicious up-front fruit, no noticeable tannin, and enough acidity for delineation and vibrance. It is pure and rich, as well as a supervalue. It should drink well for 4–5 years. The 1993 Syrah Grand Heritage is a blend from Sonoma's Durell Vineyard (58%) and the Fenaughty Vineyard (42%) in El Dorado. It reveals scents of toasty new oak, lavishly rich Syrah fruit (primarily cassis), full body, sweet, ripe tannin, and a long, layered, concentrated finish. This wine has traditionally been the flagship wine of the Edmunds St. John portfolio, and once again, it is a terrific example of Syrah that can be drunk now or cellared for 12+ years. The 1993 Les Côtes Sauvages is lighter than past vintages, but it could easily be mistaken for a juicy, savory, spicy, red and black fruit-scented and -flavored Côtes du Rhône. Supple and medium bodied, with an easygoing, Mediterranean/Provençal character, it should be drunk over the next 1–3 years.

For over a decade winemaker Steve Edmunds has turned out one thrilling wine after another. However, two bottles tasted of the 1993 Zinfandel displayed old, stale hay and pine aromas, as if the barrels were of an unusual origin or type of wood. Once past the awkward, musty hay scents, the wine exhibited splendidly rich, sweet fruit, full body, and the hallmark of all the Edmunds St. John wines—great concentration and balance. However, the unusual and eccentric aromatics are off-putting. On the other hand, if you are looking for a succulent, gorgeously opulent, smooth as silk wine made from 79% Zinfandel and 21% Grenache, the 1993 Pallini Rosso will more than satisfy any reader's hedonistic needs. It is a medium to dark ruby-colored wine bursting with ripe berry, peppery, spicy fruit. Medium to full bodied, this soft wine will offer ideal drinking over the next 3–4 years.

The 1993 Syrah is a dark ruby/purple-colored wine with a tight but promising nose of smoke, black currants, and earth. Although full bodied, moderately tannic, rich, and full, it is a tamer, more subtle and restrained Syrah than the blockbuster Syrahs Edmunds St. John produced in 1992 and 1991. It is a 10–15 year wine that should reach its apogee in 4–5 years.

EDNA VALLEY VINEYARD (EDNA VALLEY)

1993 Pinot Noir Estate	Edna Valley	C	?
1993 Pinot Noir Paragon Vineyard Estate	Edna Valley	C	86

The soft, fruity, elegant, medium-bodied 1993 Pinot Noir Paragon Vineyard reveals an undercurrent of fresh tomato and basil, accompanied by straightforward, rich, cherry fruit nicely framed by toasty oak. Drink it over the next several years.

The two bottles of 1993 Pinot Noir Estate I tasted both exhibited what at first appeared to be a musty cork component in the aromas and flavors. As the wine sat in the glass, however, I began to think the problem was in the wine, not the cork. Several readers have also written me with questions about the wine's distracting mustiness. This can be an herbaceous, beefy, robust, mouth-filling style of Pinot Noir, but the 1993 is disappointing.

EHLER'S GROVE (NAPA)

1997 Chardonnay Winery Reserve	Napa	D	89
1996 Dolcetto	Napa	B	87
1994 Dolcetto	Napa	B	85
1994 Merlot Winery Reserve	Napa	C	87
1997 Sauvignon Blanc	Napa	B	85
1997 Sauvignon Blanc Reserve	Napa	C	87

This winery makes reliably good wines thanks to the efforts of owner/winemaker Paul Moser. The two 1997 Sauvignon Blancs are crisp, tasty, fruit-driven, flinty wines with plenty of varietal character. The 1997 is lighter bodied but refreshing, with subtle herb, melon, and citrusy fruit. The crisp, fresh, vivacious 1997 Reserve (8%–10% Chardonnay is included in the blend) reveals more definition, a richer, more honeyed character, and deeper fruit. Both wines should be drunk over the next year. The flamboyant 1997 Chardonnay Winery Reserve may be outstanding. Most of the fruit from this wine came from the excellent Hyde Vineyard in Carneros. The wine exhibits a gorgeously rich, honeyed, orange peel, and tropical fruit-scented nose with a Muscat-like fragrance and intensity. Ripe, with beautifully pure flavors, medium body, and excellent length and purity, it should drink well for 12–18 months.

Ehler's Grove has fashioned an authentic-tasting 1996 Dolcetto that recalls some of Piedmont's finest examples. Offering a hedonistic mouthful of plush berry fruit, it is soft, nicely textured, medium bodied, and exuberantly fruity and refreshing. Drink it over the next 1–2 years.

The following are the most impressive wines I have tasted from Ehler's Grove, a winery that appears to be improving quality, while keeping prices very fair. The 1994 Dolcetto actually tastes like a Dolcetto, with a strawberry, chocolatey, red fruit-scented nose, and easygoing, light- to medium-bodied, Starbuck coffeehouselike flavors. Drink this spicy, fresh wine over the next year. The 1994 Merlot Winery Reserve is not as great a bargain as some of southern France's Merlots, but considering what one gets in the bottle, it is fairly priced for a California Merlot. The wine exhibits a deep ruby color, a spicy, coffee, chocolatey, berry, mocha-scented nose, a fresh, lively, flavorful personality, medium body, and fine elegance, depth, and character. Drink it over the next 2–3 years.

EL MOLINO (NAPA)

1995 Chardonnay	Napa	D	87

While not up to previous efforts, El Molino's 1995 is a fine example of California Chardonnay. The complex, leesy, oaky nose is slightly dominated by wood, but in the mouth, the wine's fruit is more forthcoming. Medium to full bodied, tightly knit, and more muted than I expected, this is a very good wine to consume over the next 2 years.

ELYSE (NAPA)

1995 Cabernet Sauvignon Morisoli Vineyard	Napa	C	90+
1994 Cabernet Sauvignon Morisoli Vineyard	Napa	C	91
1995 Cabernet Sauvignon Tietjen Vineyard	Napa	C	87+?
1993 Nero Misto	Napa	C	88
1994 Petite Syrah Barrel Select	Napa	C	87
1996 Zinfandel Coeur du Val	Napa	C	79
1994 Zinfandel Coeur du Val	Napa	C	87
1993 Zinfandel Coeur du Val	Napa	C	87
1994 Zinfandel Howell Mountain	Napa	C	88
1993 Zinfandel Howell Mountain	Napa	C	88
1993 Zinfandel Morisoli Vineyard	Napa	C	86

These Cabernet Sauvignons offer contrasting styles. The 1995 Cabernet Sauvignon Tietjen Vineyard will undoubtedly be a controversial wine. It offers an unusual wild, savage, earthy, berry-scented aroma, with a touch of the ubiquitous brett yeast making its leathery, animal-like appearance. Although rich, with sweet, ripe fruit, and medium body, the wine is rustic with coarse tannin in the finish. This wine needs to be retasted after bottling to see what emerges. Certainly the 1995 Cabernet Sauvignon Morisoli Vineyard had no such problem. This impressive wine exhibits a lavishly oaky nose, along with copious quantities of spring flowers, blueberries, and black currants. A complex, elegantly styled Cabernet Sauvignon, it possesses medium body and outstanding concentration, as well as a distinctive, ethereal style that has more in common with a grand cru red Burgundy than a Napa Cabernet Sauvignon. This intriguing, provocative wine should drink well for 10–15 years. The hallmarks of the admirably made 1994 Cabernet Sauvignon Morisoli Vineyard include an unmistakably sweet, blueberry, cassis, and mineral-scented bouquet, and dense, concentrated flavors that build to a full-bodied, layered finish. The wine reveals nicely integrated acidity, ripe but noticeable tannin, and a long aftertaste. This youthful, impeccably made Cabernet should drink marvelously well for 15–20 years after its release.

The dense, tannic, dark purple-colored 1994 Petite Syrah Barrel Select reveals copious amounts of pure, peppery, black fruits, and medium to full body, but it is backward, tight, and in need of 2–3 years of cellaring. It is capable of 10+ years of evolution.

A healthy, saturated dark ruby/purple color of the 1996 Zinfandel Coeur du Val is followed by a light intensity nose of oak, sour cherries, and cranberry liqueur. One-dimensional in the mouth, with an almost hybrid, funky fruitiness, this medium-bodied, slightly innocuous Zinfandel provides pleasant, uncritical quaffing. Drink it over the next year.

Two high-quality 1994 Zinfandels, the 1994 Elyse Coeur du Val exhibits an attractive dark purple color, a briary, ripe berry-scented nose, soft, round, plump flavors, excellent intensity, a generous amount of glycerin and plushness, and an easygoing finish. This is a hedonistic, up-front, flattering style of Zinfandel for drinking over the next 3–4 years. The 1994 Zinfandel Howell Mountain reveals an opaque purple color, and an unevolved but promising, sweet nose of overripe black cherries with a subtle whiff of pepper. Medium to full bodied, with surprising elegance, this wine manages to avoid some of the hard tannins that often emerge from grapes grown in the Howell Mountain appellation. It possesses a suppleness and elegance reminiscent of a fine classified growth from the Margaux appellation of Bordeaux—believe it or not! This stylish wine should drink well for 6–7 years.

The 1993 Zinfandel Coeur du Val reveals the telltale briery, spicy, peppery nose of a good Zinfandel. The color is dark ruby, and the wine offers up-front, spicy, rich black raspberry fruit in a medium-bodied format. Drink it over the next 2–3 years. The 1993 Zinfandel Howell Mountain possesses less color saturation, but it contains copious quantities of earthy, raspberry fruit, a sumptuous midpalate, and a spicy, long finish. Drink it over the next 2–4 years as it is forward and accessible, particularly for a Zinfandel from Howell Mountain. Lastly, the 1993 Zinfandel Morisoli Vineyard is the least distinguished of this trio of Zinfandels, although this vineyard normally turns out striking wines. It exhibits a light ruby color, good spice and fruit, medium body, and a sweet, rich, ripe finish, making me think I may be too Grinchlike in my score. Drink it over the next 4–5 years.

The 1993 Nero Misto (mixed black) is a blend of 44% Petite Sirah, 30% Zinfandel, and 26% unknown field blend grapes. The wine exhibits a dark ruby color, gobs of ripe jammy fruit in the nose, and a supple, round texture. Somewhat Rhône Ranger-ish, with plenty of spice and ripe fruit, it will provide delightful drinking over the next 2–3 years.

ESTANCIA (FRANCISCAN VINEYARDS) (NAPA)

1995 Cabernet Sauvignon	Alexander Valley	B	85
1994 Cabernet Sauvignon	Sonoma/Napa	C	88
1996 Chardonnay	Monterey	B	86

1996 Chardonnay Reserve	Monterey	C	87
1995 Duo	Alexander Valley	D	86
1996 Fumé Blanc Pinnacles	Monterey	B	86
1994 Meritage	Alexander Valley	C	88
1994 Merlot	Alexander Valley	B	88

Estancia has turned out a delicious, spicy, honeyed, nicely textured 1996 Fumé Blanc that offers plenty of flavor, excellent purity, and very good richness. Drink it over the next year. The difference between the two 1996 Chardonnay cuvées is that the Reserve possesses more obvious smoky oak, and a toasty, hazelnut, buttery aromatic profile. Both wines reveal an attractive, creamy texture, medium body, and excellent purity. Both are soft and accessible, and appear to have been bottled without excessive processing. Consume both wines over the next 12 months.

The attractive, elegant 1995 Duo, a blend of 70% Cabernet Sauvignon and 30% Sangiovese, displays a dark ruby color, a sweet cherry and new saddle leather-scented nose, medium body, soft tannin, and a clean finish. Not large scaled, this wine relies on its pretty fruit, and charming, easygoing personality. The 1995 Cabernet Sauvignon is a straightforward, simple, fruity Cabernet with herb-tinged cherry and cassis fruit, medium body, low acidity, and light tannin. It is ideal for drinking over the next 2–3 years. The dark ruby-colored 1994 Merlot Alexander Valley is a plump, luscious, opulently textured, juicy Merlot with berry fruit, a luscious texture, and a long, coffee-infused, plump, chewy finish. Drink this hedonistic, delicious Merlot over the next 3–4 years. The 1994 Cabernet Sauvignon (a blend of 55% Sonoma and 45% Napa grapes) is not a huge wine, but it does offer copious amounts of cassis fruit, nicely integrated toasty oak, smoke, herbs, and cedar. This medium-bodied, soft, pure Cabernet should drink well for 7–8 years.

The dark ruby/purple-colored 1994 Meritage is a blend of 66% Cabernet Sauvignon, 27% Cabernet Franc, and 7% Merlot. Although lavishly wooded, the wine's high concentration of ripe fruit, admirable purity, and excellent richness counterbalance the oak. The wine is fleshy and full bodied, with plenty of character, low acidity, and a precocious style. It will age well for 5–7 years. This is one of the finest, most seriously endowed wines yet produced by Estancia.

ÉTUDE (NAPA)

1997 Cabernet Sauvignon	Napa	E	(91–94)
1996 Cabernet Sauvignon	Napa	E	92
1995 Cabernet Sauvignon	Napa	D	94
1994 Cabernet Sauvignon	Napa	D	95+
1993 Cabernet Sauvignon	Napa	D	92+
1997 Cabernet Sauvignon Eden Rock	Napa	D	(87–90)
1997 Pinot Blanc	Carneros	C	88
1997 Pinot Gris	Carneros	C	87
1996 Pinot Noir	Carneros	D	88
1996 Pinot Noir Heirloom	Carneros	D	91

Tony Soter, one of California's finest and most influential wine consultants, has an impressive portfolio of new offerings. Some of his least-known (quantities tend to be under 500 cases per vintage) wines are his tank-fermented and aged, crisp, vibrant, dry whites. The 1997 Pinot

Gris is a steely, honeyed, round, refreshing wine with hints of tropical fruits. This delightful offering does not go through malolactic fermentation (in order to preserve its freshness), so it should be consumed within its first year of life. Even better is the 1997 Pinot Blanc, a fresh, vibrant, citrusy wine with fruity tangerine and nectarine notes, excellent richness, lively acidity, and a steely, exuberant finish. Both of these impeccably made whites are better for the fact that they are 100% tank fermented and aged, and bottled early to capture their freshness.

Among the more tasty Pinot Noirs in the marketplace is Étude's 5,000 case production. Aged in 60% new French oak and bottled without filtration, the deep ruby-colored 1996 Pinot Noir Carneros exhibits a smoky, spicy, intense nose. The wine possesses fine ripeness, plenty of cherry/berry fruit with vague underbrush notes, and silky, round flavors. While this is not a huge Pinot Noir, it is both silky smooth and complex. The finest Pinot Noir I have yet tasted from Étude is the 1996 Heirloom, a 275-case lot of the best barrels (in this vintage, a selection of 12 separate barrels). Bottled with no fining or filtration, this dark, saturated ruby-colored offering reveals knockout aromatics of smoke, *pain grillé*, and black fruits. The wine's texture is rich, multilayered, and plush. There is real depth in the midpalate, and the finish is long, round, and generous. I should note that Tony Soter has a vineyard in Oregon's Willamette Valley, so readers can look forward to what should be some superlative Pinot Noirs starting with the 1998 vintage.

The current Cabernet Sauvignon release is the 1995, a wine which has performed consistently well since I first tasted it. It is one of those 1995s that easily rivals the 1994, adding evidence to my belief that these two years in Napa and Sonoma might turn out to be the finest back-to-back vintages California has ever enjoyed. Étude's 1995 Cabernet Sauvignon boasts a saturated black/purple color, as well as a terrific nose of licorice, cassis, and subtle toasty oak. Full bodied, and crammed with extract, and rich, ripe black fruits, this dense, symmetrical Cabernet will require several years of cellaring when released, but it should age effortlessly for 15–20 years. It is every bit as good as the terrific 1994, and may ultimately prove to be better, as well as longer lived. The 1996 Cabernet Sauvignon displays an impressively saturated ruby/purple color, and a tight but promising bouquet of licorice, black currants, and toasty oak. There is more tannin than in the 1995 or 1997, but it is not intrusive. Fleshy, with fine purity, medium to full body, and a sweet midpalate and finish, this wine should be cellared for 3–4 years, and consumed over the following 15–20 years.

The 1997 Cabernet Sauvignon Eden Rock is a soft, supple, forward style of Cabernet Sauvignon with plenty of black currant fruit, nicely integrated wood, soft acidity, and a medium-bodied, silky finish. It should be showy upon release, and evolve nicely for 12 or more years. Étude's 1997 Cabernet Sauvignon is a richer, more expansive example with an opaque purple color, graceful, creamy-textured black currant flavors, and subtle notes of toasty oak. Expressive aromatically (black fruits galore) and full bodied, it possesses the vintage's telltale silkiness and depth. Because of its low acidity and ripe personality, it should drink well upon release and last for 2 decades.

The awesomely rich 1994 Cabernet Sauvignon is another spectacular example of this splendid vintage. It possesses an opaque purple color, a wonderful sweetness, full body, and layers of cedary, mineral, and spice-tinged blackberry and cassis fruit. Although there is a boatload of tannin, it is sweet and well integrated. The finish lasts for nearly 30 seconds. This dazzling Cabernet Sauvignon gets my vote as the finest Cabernet Sauvignon Tony Soter has yet made at Étude.

The 1993 Cabernet Sauvignon is an opaque purple-colored wine with full-bodied, super-concentrated richness. A hallmark of the Tony Soter-made wines is their purity and delineation. Not surprisingly, this dense, concentrated wine possesses such characteristics. There are gobs of sweet black fruits, a touch of licorice, vanilla, and spice, and formidable concentration and intensity. The tannins are moderate, but persistent, so I suspect this wine will benefit from another 2–4 years of cellaring. It should age well for 20 years.

By the way, I had a chance to do a mini-vertical of the Étude Cabernet Sauvignons, and all of them performed extremely well. Most of them appeared to need additional cellaring, and each of them suggested to me that they have another 2 decades of life. I rated the 1993, 92+ (it needs 2–4 years of cellaring), 1992, 91 (fascinating), 1991, 95 (an awesome wine), and the 1990, 90 (outstanding but dwarfed by more recent efforts).

FANUCCHI VINEYARDS (SONOMA)

1996 Zinfandel	Sonoma	C	86
1995 Zinfandel Old Vines	Sonoma	C	86
1994 Zinfandel Old Vines	Russian River	C	87

The 1996 is a mainstream, powerful, but foursquare Zinfandel that is too monolithic to merit a higher score. Nevertheless, it possesses a dark ruby color, fine ripeness, and spicy, briery fruit backed up by tangy, tart acidity. Drink it over the next 3–4 years.

The 1995 Zinfandel Old Vines may develop into something more special than my rating suggests. It is impressive from a concentration and purity standpoint, but it tasted straightforward and monolithic. The color is an impressively saturated ruby/purple, and its nose offers moderately intense aromas of red currants and cherries. The fruit is pure and ripe in this medium- to full-bodied, supple, slightly tannic Zinfandel. Although simple, it is delicious, well made, and admirably expresses the fruit characteristic of Zinfandel more than many other wines from this vintage. The 1994 is a richly fruity, ripe, jammy Zinfandel with a dark ruby color, straightforward aromatics, and a pure, ripe palate. Drink it over the next 2–3 years.

FAR NIENTE (NAPA)

1994 Cabernet Sauvignon Estate	Napa	E	88

Dark ruby/purple-colored, with a classy vanillin, black currant-scented nose that has not yet begun to unfold and reveal further nuances, this medium- to full-bodied wine is very expressive, with rich, concentrated, curranty flavors, and moderate tannin. There is good sweetness and lushness on the attack, adequate acidity, and a long, tight but promising finish. This wine should improve for another 5 years, and last for 15.

FERRARI-CARANO WINERY (SONOMA)

1996 Chardonnay	Alexander Valley	C	85
1995 Chardonnay Reserve	Napa/Sonoma	D	87
1997 Fumé Blanc	Sonoma	B	85
1993 Merlot	Sonoma	C	90
1993 Siena (Sangiovese/Cabernet Sauvignon/Merlot)	California	C	90
1994 Syrah	Sonoma	D	92
1993 Syrah	Sonoma	D	87
1994 Zinfandel	Sonoma	C	85
1993 Zinfandel	Sonoma	C	90

The two Chardonnays and the 1997 Fumé Blanc are not up to previous Ferrari-Carano efforts, but they are still noteworthy enough to be recommended. The 1997 Fumé Blanc is a medium-bodied, graceful, citrus/melony-scented and -flavored wine with good intensity, fine definition, and an abrupt finish. Drink it over the next year. The 1996 Chardonnay is more foursquare and monolithic than in the past, but it offers lemony custard and honeysuckle notes in a medium-bodied, subtle style. It is pleasant, cleanly made, and ideal for drinking over the next year. More interesting is the 1995 Chardonnay Reserve, a blend of Napa (87%) and Sonoma (13%) grapes. This wine exhibits honeyed pineapple and other tropical fruits, admirable richness, medium to full body, tart acidity, and a moderately long finish. Drink this cleanly made Chardonnay over the next year.

This high class winery turned out a surprisingly simple 1994 Zinfandel with a dark garnet color, and a light intensity nose of pepper, herbs, and red cherry fruit. The wine offers attractive roundness, moderate concentration, medium body, and astringent tannin in the finish. It is neither dense nor concentrated, so readers are well advised to drink it over the next 1–3 years.

The 1993 Zinfandel is so limited in quantity that virtually all of it is sold directly from this showcase property's salesroom in northern Alexander Valley. The 1993 Zinfandel (it boasts 14.4% alcohol) reveals an impressive, saturated, ruby/purple color, a powerful nose of brandy/macerated black cherries, and smoky oak, rich, ripe, full-bodied flavors, admirable purity, and a plush, satiny smooth, alcoholic finish. Drink it over the next 6–8 years.

The proprietary wine called Siena (usually a blend of Sangiovese, Cabernet Sauvignon, and Merlot) evolved from a two-thirds Cabernet Sauvignon-based wine in 1991, to a 70% Sangiovese wine in 1994. The 1991 Siena was a good beginning effort, and the 1992 Siena built on it with attractive cherry fruit, good ripeness, medium body, and a spicy finish. But it is the 1993 Siena that jumps significantly in quality, with more of a cedary, cherry nose, excellent flavor richness and definition, and a spicy, easygoing finish with just enough acidity to provide focus.

Recent Ferrari-Carano Merlots have not exhibited the herbal, vegetal character that plagued this winery's first Merlot releases. The 1993 is a larger-scaled wine than the 1992, made from 89% Merlot and the rest Malbec, Cabernet Sauvignon, and Cabernet Franc. The wine offers a purple/ruby color, great fruit and intensity, plenty of alcohol and glycerin, full body, and a decadent, lavishly rich, seductive style that is hard to ignore. It should drink well for at least a decade.

Lastly, there will be tiny quantities of Syrah released from Ferrari-Carano's 20-acre Syrah vineyard. The 1993 Syrah (150 cases) is certainly a competent first effort, although it lacks the depth and intensity I noticed in the barrel sample of the stunningly rich, full-bodied 1994 Syrah.

One of the bright shining success stories of California, Ferrari-Carano has a brilliant future.

FETZER VINEYARD (MENDOCINO)

1996 Chardonnay Sundial	California	A	86
1995 Chardonnay Sundial	North Coast	A	86

A consistent winner in the under $10 Chardonnay sweepstakes, the well-made 1996 Chardonnay Sundial displays plenty of tropical fruit (oranges and pineapples), medium body, excellent freshness, no evidence of oak, and a crisp, dry, lusciously fruity finish. Drink it over the next year for its exuberant, straightforward, but satisfying style. The tank-fermented, deliciously fruity, crisp 1995 Chardonnay offers citrusy, apple, and tropical fruit aromas and flavors. Drink this medium-bodied, fresh, lively wine over the next year.

FIELD STONE (SONOMA)

1993 Cabernet Sauvignon Staten Family Reserve	Alexander Valley	D	86+
1996 Sauvignon Blanc	Sonoma	B	87

This winery has fashioned a crisp, mineral, flinty, subtle 1996 Sauvignon Blanc that is medium bodied, dry, fresh, and vibrant. Spicy, with good underlying acidity, and considerable complexity, it could pass for an attractive, midlevel white Graves from Bordeaux. Drink it over the next 2 years. The grapey, youthfully styled 1994 Cabernet Sauvignon Staten Family Reserve exhibits a dark ruby color, good acidity, and plenty of tannin and spice. It possesses character, medium body, and a certain austerity. Cellar it for 3–4 years, and drink it over the following decade.

FIFE (NAPA)

1994 Cabernet Sauvignon Reserve	Spring Mountain	D	86?
1995 Max Cuvée Proprietary Red Wine	Napa	C	90
1994 Max Cuvée Proprietary Red Wine	Napa Valley	C	91+
1995 Merlot	Napa	C	86
1994 Petite Syrah	Napa Valley	C	86
1995 Petite Syrah Redhead Vineyard	Mendocino	C	89
1995 Zinfandel Old Vines	Napa	C	86+?
1994 Zinfandel Redhead Vineyard	Mendocino	C	90
1994 Zinfandel Spring Mountain District	Napa	C	90
1994 Zinfandel Les Vieilles Vignes	Napa	C	90

A relatively new winery, Fife continues to produce an impressive array of concentrated, well-balanced, ageworthy wines. The 1994 Max Cuvée, a proprietary blend, boasts an inky black/purple color, as well as an exceptionally ripe, pure nose of black fruits, licorice, and spice. Full bodied, with layers of concentration, a corpulent, thick texture, yet no sense of heaviness, this is an exceptionally rich wine with soft tannin. Although approachable, it will be at its best between 2000 and 2015. I am pleased to report that the 1994 Zinfandel Redhead Vineyard (14.6% alcohol) is another textbook Zin from Fife. It offers a dark ruby/purple color, followed by a spicy blast of briery, black raspberry, peppery fruit. This pure, luscious, soft, mouth-filling wine is meant to be drunk over the next 2–3 years. The 1994 Zinfandel Les Vieilles Vignes displays an opulent personality, with a deep ruby/purple color, and a gorgeous display of sweet, toasty, smoky new oak, and jammy, pure, ripe berry fruit. Luscious in the mouth, with low acidity, copious quantities of fruit, chewy glycerin, and heady alcohol, this is a lusty, full-bodied, rich Zinfandel for drinking over the next 5–6 years. The 1994 Spring Mountain District Zinfandel is also a beauty, offering more of a black raspberry-scented nose, exquisite ripeness and purity, and a more elegant, less bulky style than the Vieilles Vignes. The Spring Mountain cuvée is all finesse, fruit, and delicacy. These wines are beautifully made Zinfandels.

While it is not at the same level as the previously reviewed wines, the 1994 Petite Syrah is an interesting wine. The color is a healthy dark garnet/purple. The wine is muscular and structured, with pure fruit, but at present its personality is buried behind a wall of high, relatively unintegrated tannin. The conservative score reflects the fact that I am not confident that the tannin will fully melt away. Nevertheless, this is a big, rustic mouthful of red wine that should last for 10–15 years.

Initial releases from this winery have all been interesting and well-made wines. Newer offerings include a tannic, tough-textured, dark ruby-colored 1995 Merlot. The wine is tightly knit and unexpressive. Nevertheless, there is good glycerin, ripeness, and richness, but the tannin level may be too elevated for the wine's fruit extraction. Dusty, sweet berry fruit is intermixed with wood and earth in this medium-bodied wine. It should keep for a decade, but whether it will achieve perfect harmony remains to be seen. The 1995 Max Cuvée exhibits an impressively saturated deep purple color, and a closed but promising nose of sweet black currant fruit intertwined with high-quality *pain grillé*/vanillin notes. The wine is dense, closed, tannic, and medium to full bodied, as well as impressively pure and rich. Most of the wine's sweetness and intensity are at the back of the mouth, indicating this offering needs 4–5 years of cellaring. Anticipated maturity: 2002–2015. In contrast, the 1995 Zinfandel Old Vines is more open and one-dimensional. This medium deep ruby-colored wine offers uncomplicated berry fruit in a medium-bodied, spicy, slightly rustic format. As in the Merlot, the tannin may be too elevated for the amount of sweet fruit. I would opt for drinking this wine over the near term (2–3 years).

Fife's dark plum-colored 1994 Cabernet Sauvignon Reserve displays muted aromatics that include vague notions of ripe plums and blackberries. Sweet oak as well as excruciatingly high tannin levels (which give cause for concern) are both apparent in the flavors. If the tannin melts away and the fruit holds, this wine should be good. Give it 2–3 years of bottle age, and drink it over the following decade. Petite Sirah (at this estate spelled Syrah) lovers will enjoy Fife's 1995 Petite Syrah Redhead Vineyard. The color is a dense ruby/plum. This wine is as ferociously tannic as the Cabernet Sauvignon Reserve, but it manages to integrate the tannin better because of its high extraction of fruit. There is plenty of blackberry, earthy, peppery, sweet fruit in this dense, full-bodied wine. Only masochists will enjoy it at present, but my instincts suggest this wine will be excellent with another 2–5 years of bottle age.

FISHER VINEYARDS (SONOMA)

1995	Cabernet Sauvignon Coach Insignia	Napa	D	88
1994	Cabernet Sauvignon Coach Insignia	Napa	C	89
1993	Cabernet Sauvignon Coach Insignia	Napa	C	90+
1997	Cabernet Sauvignon Lamb Vineyard	Napa	E	(94–96)
1996	Cabernet Sauvignon Lamb Vineyard	Napa	E	91
1995	Cabernet Sauvignon Lamb Vineyard	Napa	E	88
1994	Cabernet Sauvignon Lamb Vineyard	Napa	D	90
1993	Cabernet Sauvignon Lamb Vineyard	Napa	D	95
1997	Cabernet Sauvignon Wedding Vineyard	Sonoma	E	(92–96+)
1996	Cabernet Sauvignon Wedding Vineyard	Sonoma	E	94
1995	Cabernet Sauvignon Wedding Vineyard	Sonoma	E	92
1994	Cabernet Sauvignon Wedding Vineyard	Sonoma	E	92
1993	Cabernet Sauvignon Wedding Vineyard	Sonoma	D	93
1997	Chardonnay Coach Insignia	Sonoma	D	90
1996	Chardonnay Coach Insignia	Sonoma	C	88
1995	Chardonnay Coach Insignia	Sonoma	C	91
1997	Chardonnay Whitney's Vineyard	Sonoma	D	91
1996	Chardonnay Whitney's Vineyard	Sonoma	D	89
1995	Chardonnay Whitney's Vineyard	Sonoma	D	92
1997	Coach Insignia Cabernet Sauvignon Proprietary Red Wine	Napa	D	(90–93)
1996	Coach Insignia Cabernet Sauvignon Proprietary Red Wine	Napa	D	90+

1997 Merlot RCF Vineyard	Napa	D	(89–91)
1996 Merlot RCF Vineyard	Napa	D	88
1995 Merlot RCF Vineyard	Napa	D	87
1994 Merlot RCF Vineyard	Napa	D	89
1993 Merlot RCF Vineyard	Napa	D	89

This impeccably run winery is isolated in the mountains near the Napa/Sonoma border. It is hard to believe, but in 1999, proprietors Jumelle and Fred Fisher will be celebrating their 20th anniversary as wine producers. I was impressed with all the following wines. Readers should note that the Coach Insignia offerings are some of the finest values in the marketplace. The 1997 Chardonnay Coach Insignia (3,800 cases) combines California's opulence, ripeness, and richness with finesse and personality. The color is light to medium straw, and there are copious amounts of melons, tangerines, and mangoes in the aromas and flavors. This buttery Chardonnay, which reveals subtle notes of oak, is a beautifully knit, surprisingly heady (14.1% alcohol) wine that should drink well for 2–3 years. The 1997 Chardonnay Whitney's Vineyard (400 cases) is 100% barrel fermented and aged, of which 45% are new. Primarily made from an old Wente clone, it possesses more minerality than the Coach Insignia. The backward, full-bodied 1997 is intensely rich with wet stone/cold steel notes nicely etched in the spicy, leesy, smoky fruit flavors. The wine is highly extracted yet displays good underlying structure and acidity. It should drink well for 5–6 years.

1996 and 1997 were both strong vintages for Fisher Vineyards. The 1997 reds are extremely high in alcohol (most of the wines came in around 14.5%) which is well hidden by the rich fruit and extract. The 1996s are undoubtedly lower in alcoholic power. The Merlot from Fisher's RCF Vineyard in northern Napa Valley is one of California's high quality Merlots. The 1996 Merlot RCF Vineyard's dark ruby color is followed by a sweet nose of black cherries, cranberries, and a touch of cherry liqueur. There is excellent richness, medium body, tangy acidity, and an elegant, overall impression. This is a flavorful, moderately weighted Merlot to enjoy over the next 10–12 years. The 1997 Merlot RCF Vineyard possesses an unusually dense, saturated ruby/purple color. As usual, Fisher added 20% Cabernet Franc to the blend in 1997, giving the wine more aromatic dimension, and lightening it in the mouth. The wine's fruit is sweet and ripe, with an element of *sur-maturité* not evident in the 1996. Pure, with gobs of black cherries, chocolate, smoky oak, and weedy tobacco, this potentially outstanding Merlot should be at its peak between 2000 and 2012.

Beginning with the 1996 vintage, the Coach Insignia is now a Proprietary Red Wine. In most vintages it is dominated by Cabernet Sauvignon, but the Fishers wanted the flexibility to put together a blend that might fall below the legally required 75% Cabernet Sauvignon needed to label the wine with a varietal name. The 1996 Coach Insignia Proprietary Red Wine, a blend of 69% Cabernet Sauvignon, 20% Merlot, and 11% Cabernet Franc, tips the scales at 14.1% alcohol. An outstanding wine, it is one of the better values in the luxury category. The nose offers up telltale aromas of sweet toasty oak intermixed with black currants and white chocolate. There are medium to full bodied flavors, as well as a layered, velvety palate, outstanding purity, and plenty of black fruits in the moderately tannic finish. Anticipated maturity: 1999–2015. The 1997 Coach Insignia Proprietary Red Wine is a blend of 80% Cabernet Sauvignon, 11% Merlot, and 9% Cabernet Franc. Powerful yet gracious, it boasts a saturated dark purple color, and copious quantities of black fruits intermixed with smoke, vanillin, and subtle weedy scents. The wine is sweet in the mouth (from ripe tannin and fruit), with medium to full body, a seamless, silky texture, and an intense finish. Common characteristics of the 1997s are their evolved aromatics, sweet tannin, and seductive personalities, even at such young ages. The 1997 Coach Insignia possesses those attributes. Anticipated maturity: now–2012.

There are two single vineyard Cabernet Sauvignons offered by Fisher. The Lamb Vineyard emerges from a Napa parcel on Pickett Lane, near the Araujo estate. The Wedding Vineyard comes from a Sonoma vineyard planted in 1974, situated directly adjacent to the winery. These are limited production offerings, with only 100–500 cases of the Lamb Vineyard produced, and about 400–500 cases per year of the Wedding Vineyard. The powerful (14.1% alcohol) 1996 Cabernet Sauvignon Lamb Vineyard has been aged in barrel, of which 50% is new. Like all of Fisher's reds, it is bottled without filtration. The color is an opaque purple, and the wine is closed, offering hints of licorice, blueberries, black currants, and spicy oak. In the mouth, it is long, rich, restrained, with the tannin still making a noticeable impression, outstanding purity, a full-bodied mouth-feel, and superb potential. This wine requires another 4–5 years of cellaring. Anticipated maturity: 2003–2020. The saturated black/purple-colored 1997 Cabernet Sauvignon Lamb Vineyard reveals a more expressive nose of violets, blueberries, and blackberry jam. Spectacular, with smoky, rich, unctuously textured flavors, beautifully sweet, well-integrated tannin, low acidity, and a 25–30-second finish, this should prove to be a terrific Lamb Vineyard offering. It will be more accessible upon release than its older sibling, yet it will age for 20+ years.

The 1995 Cabernet Sauvignon Wedding Vineyard is a massive, full-bodied, black/purple-colored wine with gobs of fruit, as well as high tannin. It offers up mineral, black cherry, spicy, and charcoal-like notes in the nose and flavors. Extremely dense and powerful, yet needing 4–5 years of cellaring, this wine may evolve for two decades or more. Anticipated maturity: 2003–2025. Although backward, the 1996 Cabernet Sauvignon Wedding Vineyard is a potentially dazzling example of this single-vineyard offering. The color is an opaque saturated purple. The nose reveals superb blueberry, coffee, roasted herb, and blackberry aromas similar to those found in a top-class Graves. The wine possesses superb richness, a distinctive loamy soil/mineral hint to the black fruit flavors, high glycerin, and well-concealed alcohol (14.1%). The tannin is high, but sweet and well integrated. This appears to be a classic, but patience will be required. Anticipated maturity: 2004–2025. The 1997 Cabernet Sauvignon Wedding Vineyard possesses palate-staining thickness, an unctuous texture, and the sweet, ripe tannin that makes this vintage similar to 1994. Soaring aromatics consist of jammy blackberries, blueberries, cassis, and violets. The mineral/Graves-like character has not yet emerged from the jammy fruit, but no doubt will after another 1–2 years of cellaring. This explosively rich, amazingly concentrated, massive Cabernet Sauvignon will require 4–5 years of cellaring, and will keep for 30–40 years. While it may not be better than the 1996, the tannin is sweeter, yet the extract level, despite higher yields in 1997, is as impressive as any Wedding Vineyard Cabernet Sauvignon I have yet tasted. Stay tuned!

The mountain vineyards of Jumelle and Fred Fisher are strikingly beautiful, and well worth a visit for readers traveling in northern California. The Chardonnay releases include the 1996 Chardonnay Coach Insignia (1,300 cases). This floral, beeswax-scented Chardonnay possesses attractive citrusy fruit, medium to full body, excellent purity, and a fresh, lively personality. While not as stunning as the 1995, it is an attractive, well-made Chardonnay that should drink well for several years. The 1996 Chardonnay Whitney's Vineyard is a 100% barrel-fermented wine made from a 20-year-old vineyard. Previous vintages of this wine have been extraordinary (such as 1995), whereas the 1996 is a mere mortal. Slightly higher acidity gives the wine more compactness, but it is still a rich, medium-bodied, smoky, leesy, honeyed Chardonnay with refreshing vibrancy, and a clean, precise winemaking style. The influence of wood is subtle. It should drink well for 2–3 years.

Readers should stock up on the 1995 Chardonnay Coach Insignia, a great Chardonnay selling at what is a modest price in today's marketplace. Bottled unfiltered, this wine smells and tastes great. The big, smoky, honeyed, leesy nose is followed by a powerful, rich, full-bodied, creamy-textured wine with hints of oranges and buttery tropical fruits. Drink it over the next 1–2 years. The 1995 Chardonnay Whitney's Vineyard is even more intense, with a smoky, orange peel and ripe pineapple-scented nose, layers of chewy, unctuously textured fruit, and a mouth-feel not dissimilar from a top vintage of Burgundy's Coche-Dury Meursault. This fat, ripe Chardonnay is ideal for drinking over the next 1–2 years.

In tasting through the 1995 and 1996 red wines from Fisher, it is obvious that the 1995s are more jagged, with rougher, harder tannin. The wines possess good stuffing, but it will take a few more years of aging for that to become obvious. The 1996s are all noteworthy successes, with rich, striking personalities.

As for the Merlots, the 1995 Merlot RCF Vineyard (1,300 cases) is a medium-bodied, chocolatey, coffee-scented and -flavored wine with slight astringency to its tannin, good black cherry fruit, and a tight, crisp finish. This wine, which has 20% Cabernet Franc in the blend, needs another 1–2 years to be fully expressive. It should keep for 10–12. The dark ruby-colored 1994 Merlot RCF offers medium-bodied, elegant, vanillin-tinged, black cherry aromas and flavors. Still tightly knit, this wine will benefit from another year of cellaring; it will drink well for a decade. I initially thought it had the potential to be outstanding, but at present it appears it will fall a point or two short. The 1993 Merlot RCF Vineyard exhibits a sweet, cherry/curranty nose, a good, vibrant feel from natural acidity, medium to full body, excellent depth, and a fresh, lively, crisp finish. It should drink well for 10–12 years.

The 1993 Cabernet Sauvignon Coach Insignia is marked by an intense, chocolatey, black currant-scented nose intermingled with aromas of toasty oak. The attack is all sweet, ripe, fresh fruit that is tannic, unevolved, and extremely young. This rich, powerful wine requires 2–4 years of cellaring; it will keep for 2 decades or more. The 1994 Cabernet Sauvignon Coach Insignia reveals a medium dark color, a Bordeaux-like, austere, spicy, oaky, earthy, cassis-scented nose, plenty of tannin, medium body, and a firm, closed personality. This wine needs another 1–3 years of cellaring; it will keep for 12–15 years. The 1995 Cabernet Sauvignon Coach Insignia exhibits a deep, rich ruby/purple color, a loamy, red currant-scented, elegant bouquet, medium-bodied, structured, restrained flavors, high acidity, and a grapey, rich finish. This wine continues to close down, and should be cellared for 3–4 years upon its release. It should keep for 2 decades, but I suspect it will be a more angular, structured, tannic Coach Insignia than other vintages. The extremely impressive 1996 Cabernet Sauvignon Coach Insignia offers an ostentatious chocolatey, smoky, red and black currant-scented nose, lush, dense, medium-to full-bodied flavors, sweeter tannin than the 1995, and a more layered impression on the palate, with splendid quantities of glycerin, fruit, and extract. It is a plump, layered wine that should be at its best in several years and last for 15 or more.

Napa's Lamb Vineyard has turned out some marvelous Cabernets. The 1993 Cabernet Sauvignon Lamb Vineyard is an intense, concentrated, opaque purple-colored wine with gobs of black raspberry and chocolatelike fruit. Extremely young, it requires 5–7 years of cellaring. Impressive and pure, it is one of Fisher's most concentrated Cabernet Sauvignons. My experience has been that this wine explodes in the glass with 4–6 hours of decanting! The 1994 Cabernet Sauvignon Lamb Vineyard exhibits a dark ruby/purple color, and a sweet nose of cassis fruit, lead pencil, and spice. While the wine may have been slightly tired when I saw it a few months after bottling, it still revealed plenty of intensity, sweet berry fruit nicely wrapped in oak, medium to full body, and moderate tannin in the long finish. Sadly, there are only 595 cases of this 100% Cabernet Sauvignon. These wines are made in limited quantities (about 300 cases in 1995 and only 100 cases in 1996). The 1995 Cabernet Sauvignon Lamb Vineyard is a leaner, tighter, more angular and astringent wine, with a dark purple color, leafy, tobacco, smoky flavors, a backward, unformed personality, and plenty of tannin in the finish. It is certainly excellent, and probably will unfold over the next decade, but the wine still plays it tight to the vest. Anticipated maturity: 2003–2012.

The Wedding Vineyard cuvée is the flagship Cabernet of the Fisher winery. Made from a vineyard planted in 1974, this wine possesses a striking aromatic profile consisting of cedar, cigar smoke, tobacco, and minerals. In that sense, it resembles California's version of Bordeaux's famed Château Haut-Brion or Château La Mission-Haut-Brion. This wine can also test the patience of readers, as it is rarely accessible when released, but it does possess 20–30 years of aging potential. The 1993 Cabernet Sauvignon Wedding Vineyard is a rich, authoritatively flavored, gorgeously pure, intense wine with plenty of smoky, toasty oak married to ripe, superintense fruit. This full-bodied, tannic, large-scaled Cabernet Sauvignon should drink well now and last for 20 years. The 1994 Cabernet Sauvignon Wedding Vineyard (500 cases) displays a knockout Graves-like nose of sweet, medium- to full-bodied, rich, concentrated flavors, good acidity, high tannin, and profound concentration and length. It comes across like a race horse ready to burst from the starting gate. This wine needs 4–5 years of cellaring and should keep for 2 or more decades.

FLORA SPRINGS WINE CO. (NAPA)

1997	Cabernet Sauvignon Cypress Ranch	Pope Valley	D	(89–90+?)
1995	Cabernet Sauvignon Cypress Ranch	Pope Valley	D	88
1994	Cabernet Sauvignon Estate	Napa	C	90
1997	Cabernet Sauvignon Hillside Reserve	Rutherford	E	(92–93)
1996	Cabernet Sauvignon Hillside Reserve	Rutherford	E	92+
1995	Cabernet Sauvignon Hillside Reserve	Rutherford	E	92
1994	Cabernet Sauvignon Hillside Reserve	Napa	E	94+
1993	Cabernet Sauvignon Hillside Reserve	Napa	D	91+
1996	Cabernet Sauvignon St. Rutherford Vyd.	Napa	D	88
1997	Cabernet Sauvignon 20th Anniversary Reserve	Napa	EE	(94–96)
1995	Chardonnay	Carneros	C	91
1996	Chardonnay Barrel Fermented	Napa	C	88
1997	Chardonnay Barrel Fermented Reserve	Napa	C	89
1996	Chardonnay Lavender Hill Vineyard	Carneros	D	90
1995	Chardonnay Reserve	Napa	D	89
1997	Merlot Windfall Vineyard	Napa	D	(90–92)
1996	Merlot Windfall Vineyard	Napa	D	91
1995	Merlot Windfall Vineyard	Napa	D	90
1997	Pinot Grigio	Napa	B	84
1995	Pinot Noir	Carneros	C	89
1996	Pinot Noir Lavender Hill Vineyard	Carneros	D	86
1997	Sangiovese	Napa	C	89
1996	Sangiovese	Napa	C	87
1997	Sauvignon Blanc Reserve	Napa	C	85
1997	Trilogy Proprietary Red Wine	Napa	E	(92–95)
1996	Trilogy Proprietary Red Wine	Napa	E	91

1995 Trilogy Proprietary Red Wine	Napa	E	90
1994 Trilogy Proprietary Red Wine	Napa	E	93+
1993 Trilogy Proprietary Red Wine	Napa	E	91

Flora Springs' 1997 Sauvignon Blanc Reserve comes from a 35-year-old vineyard that is in the process of being replanted. Given *sur-lies* aging and stirring, it is a fragrant, melony, medium-bodied, clean, straightforward Sauvignon to drink over the next 1–2 years. The 1997 Chardonnay Barrel Fermented Reserve is a heady wine (14% alcohol), with copious amounts of ripe tropical fruit (primarily pineapple intermixed with peach, pear, and apple). Luscious, with subtle oak, and a fruit-driven personality, this hedonistic Chardonnay will drink well for several years. Flora Springs' Italian-inspired offerings include a 1997 Pinot Grigio. The 1997 Pinot Grigio is a tank-fermented, round, fresh, lively wine with good fruit. Although not complex, it is unquestionably a fair value. It should be drunk over the next year.

Winemaker Ken Deiss produces one of the finest Sangioveses in Napa Valley. The 1997 Sangiovese is the richest effort I have yet tasted from Flora Springs (their first vintage of Sangiovese was 1992). Although the 1997 reveals dry tannin in the finish, it represents the essence of strawberry and framboiselike fruit. This exuberant, youthful, lovely wine is meant to be drunk in its medium-bodied, vigorous youth. It will last for 3–4 years, but is best consumed on the earlier side.

Beginning in 1996, what used to be called the Cabernet Sauvignon Estate is now known as the Cabernet Sauvignon St. Rutherford Vineyard. The 1996 is 100% Cabernet Sauvignon, aged in *barriques*, of which 15% was American. The wine reveals gobs of spicy new oak and tobacco-tinged, weedy, black currant fruit intermixed with cedar, dried herbs, and licorice, high tannin, and medium to full body. This chunky, fleshy, robust Cabernet Sauvignon should be at its best with another 2–3 years of bottle age and keep for 14–15 years.

Flora Springs is making a serious jump into the Merlot sweepstakes, and their effort deserves accolades. Their limited production Merlot (about 400 cases) comes from a vineyard at the corner of Highway 29 and Bella Oaks Lane. The outstanding 1996 Merlot Windfall Vineyard possesses a dark purple color, as well as a sweet, expressive, smoky, chocolatey nose with coffee and berry fruit in the background. The wine is succulent, fleshy, full bodied, and hedonistic. This superb, ripe, mouth-filling Merlot can be drunk over the next 10–12+ years. Bravo! While it is cut from the same mold, the 1997 Merlot Windfall Vineyard displays more tangy acidity, but it shares its predecessor's smoky, roasted coffee, chocolatey, black cherry scents and flavors. There is sweet richness in the mouth, soft tannin, plenty of glycerin, and an evolved style. Once again, the 1997 appears to be on a slightly faster evolutionary track than its older sibling. The 1997 should drink well during its first decade of life.

Flora Springs owns a large vineyard (175 acres planted and another 100 purchased) in Pope Valley. Their Pope Valley offering, the 1997 Cabernet Sauvignon Cypress Ranch, is a foursquare, concentrated, spicy wine with copious quantities of black fruits, excellent density, significant muscle, and moderate tannin. Leafy tobacco, spice, and dusty sandlewood notes emerge with airing. This chunky, robust Cabernet should age well for 15 or more years. If the tannin becomes completely integrated, look for the question mark to be deleted.

All the recent vintages of Flora Springs' proprietary red wine, Trilogy, have been stunning. The turnaround in quality began in the early nineties, and continues unabated. The 1996 Trilogy, a blend of 44% Cabernet Sauvignon, 40% Merlot, and 16% Cabernet Franc, reveals a saturated dark ruby/purple color, and a gorgeous nose of violets, black currants, *pain grillé*, and minerals. Deep and rich, yet remarkably polished, this medium- to full-bodied, beautifully symmetrical wine has everything in the proper place. Although accessible enough to be drunk early in life, its balance suggests a graceful evolution for 15–20 years. It is a distinctive, beautiful wine! The proposed blend for the 1997 Trilogy is 40% Cabernet Sauvignon, 40% Merlot, and 20% Cabernet Franc. A terrific wine, it may turn out to be the most dazzling Trilogy I have yet tasted. It boasts a wonderfully sweet aromatic profile of black fruits, floral scents, licorice, and damp forest scents. Smoky, toasty new oak is nicely integrated into the wine's full-bodied, rich, multilayered palate. Impeccably balanced, with palate-staining flavors, this looks to be a sensational Trilogy that will be more accessible young than the 1996, and will age for 2 decades.

The unfiltered Hillside Reserve Cabernet Sauvignons, which are made in limited quantities of about 800 cases per vintage, are special wines that deserve readers' attention. The dark ruby/purple-colored, stunningly rich 1996 Cabernet Sauvignon Hillside Reserve is still in need of bottle age. The wine reveals a saturated color, as well as a promising but restrained nose of toasty new oak, jammy blackberries, cassis, licorice, and spice. It is extremely rich and spicy in the mouth, with moderate tannin, full body, superb purity of flavor, and outstanding potential. Anticipated maturity: 2003–2022. The 1997 Cabernet Sauvignon Hillside Reserve appears to be just as wonderful as the 1996, but with slightly sweeter fruit, softer tannin, and more near-term appeal, yet 15–20 years of ageability. It reveals the same rich black currant fruit intermixed with spicy tobacco, new oak, immense body, and well-integrated acidity and tannin. Readers lucky enough to find any should be on the lookout for the 1997 Cabernet Sauvignon 20th Anniversary Reserve, which was made from the richest dozen barrels of the Hillside Reserve. At present, this wine is similar to the Hillside Reserve but is richer, sweeter, longer, and more explosively concentrated. A fabulous Cabernet, it should merit a rating in the mid to upper nineties when bottled in several years. The Flora Springs Reserve Cabernet Sauvignons spend 12 months in old oak barrels, and are then moved to 100% new oak for 10 months, after which they are racked into tanks and bottled unfiltered. As my tasting notes have consistently revealed, the wines are usually better from bottle than they were from barrel. The Cabernet Sauvignon 20th Anniversary Reserve is a spectacular wine, but production will be only 250–275 cases.

The 1996 Chardonnay Barrel Fermented, which is not put through malolactic, is aged 100% sur-lie, and in 50% new oak casks. The grapes emerge from both Oakville and Rutherford. The result is a richly fruity, smoky, opulent, buttery wine with good fat, plump flavors. While not complicated, it offers gobs of Chardonnay fruit in a lusty format, and should drink well for 1–2 years. The 1996 Chardonnay Lavender Hill Vineyard (1,000 cases) is an unfiltered, 100% malolactic Chardonnay which has as its hallmark copious quantities of honeyed tropical fruit, and toasty, smoky oak. The wine displays a lush texture, medium to full body, plenty of spice, and lavish quantities of fruit. It should drink well for 2–3 years.

All of Flora Springs' Chardonnays are now completely barrel fermented, and if circumstances permit, bottled unfiltered. The 1995 Chardonnay Reserve has benefitted from extensive lees contact. It is an opulent, smoky, butterscotch, Burgundian-styled Chardonnay with an unctuous texture, considerable body, and outstanding richness and fruit. It will not make old bones, but for drinking over the next 1–2 years, it represents a juicy mouthful of lavishly wooded Chardonnay. The 1995 Chardonnay Carneros is superior; it is 100% barrel fermented in 50% new oak, with 100% malolactic fermentation, and reveals a leesy, smoky, complex, grilled hazelnut-scented nose, gobs of tropical fruit on the palate, full body, and a layered, fleshy texture with enough acidity to provide delineation to its component parts. Large scaled and concentrated, this is a wine to drink over the next 1–2 years.

Flora Springs continues to fashion a competent Pinot Noir. The 1996 Pinot Noir Lavender Hill Vineyard (about 600 cases) is bottled with neither fining nor filtration. About 25% of the grape stems are utilized in the vinification. The wine offers a meaty, cinnamon, and allspice-scented, Gevrey-Chambertin-like nose. In the mouth, there are soft, inviting, ripe, earthy, berry and plumlike flavors. This is an attractive, primarily spice-driven Pinot Noir to consume over the next 3–4 years.

One of the pleasant surprises for me at Flora Springs was the quality of their 1995 Pinot Noir Carneros. This dark garnet-colored wine exhibits a spicy, animal, Côtes de Nuits-scented nose, and ripe, tangy, fleshy, black cherry and plum fruit nicely knit with toasty oak. This young, seductive, flavorful Pinot Noir should drink well for another 5–6 years. Approximately 600 cases were produced. The Flora Springs Sangiovese can also be very good. Along with the Sangiovese from Swanson and Shafer's Firebreak, it is one of the three best I have tasted from California. The 1995 Sangiovese (3,000 cases) possesses a deep ruby color, sweet, jammy, strawberry and cherrylike aromas, medium to full body, an expansive, fleshy texture, and fine length and intensity. The wine is aged in old barrels, which brings the fruit and quality of this varietal to the forefront. It is meant to be drunk young, so don't let it dry out—drink it over the next 3–4 years.

Given the plethora of ripoff Sangioveses produced in California, it is nice to see the job Flora Springs does with this varietal. Their offering is a 100% Sangiovese. While the 1996 does not quite match the 1995 for intensity and richness, it is an attractive strawberry/cranberry-scented and -flavored wine with excellent acidity. Earthy, mushroomy flavors add to the wine's character, and, I suspect, its ability to stand up to tomato-based sauces. This wine's medium garnet/ruby color and forwardness suggest it should be drunk over the next several years.

The 1995 Merlot Windfall Vineyard (300 cases) possesses a dense ruby/purple color, as well as a gaudy nose of *pain grillé*, melted chocolate, and jammy cherry flavors. Soft, ripe, medium to full bodied, chewy, and fat, this is a delicious, decadent style of Merlot that will drink well for a decade.

The 1995 Cabernet Sauvignon Hillside Reserve is a backward, tannic wine with an opaque purple color, and copious quantities of sweet black currant fruit, cedar, and spice. Muscular, rich, and full bodied, with sweet tannin, this is a layered, concentrated, unevolved and youthful Cabernet Sauvignon that requires 4–5 years of cellaring. All the necessary "goodies" are present in this formidably endowed wine. While it will not provide seductive drinking at an early age, it will last 20 years.

Ken Deiss, the winemaker at Flora Springs, thinks that the 1994 and 1995 Cabernet Sauvignon vintages have more in common than differences. This was borne out in my tastings, as both vintages possess that rare quality of producing very concentrated, ripe Cabernets with sweet, well-integrated tannin. Flora Springs' Hillside Reserve Cabernet Sauvignons have soared in quality in the nineties. This 100% Cabernet Sauvignon is aged in 2–3-year-old barrels, then moved to 1-year-old barrels, and then into 60% new oak casks for no longer than 8–10 months. The 1993 Cabernet Sauvignon Hillside Reserve displays a dense purple color, followed by a sweet, jammy, black plum, and cassis-scented nose, no obvious oak, full-bodied, spicy flavors with moderate tannin, and exceptional concentration. The wine reveals a youthful appearance and personality. There is enough fruit to cover the strong tannin in the finish. It should be cellared for 3–5 years and consumed over the next two decades. The 1994 Cabernet Sauvignon Hillside Reserve exhibits an opaque purple color, a classic, cedar, black currant, and earthy-scented nose, and rich, full-bodied flavors that ooze jammy black currants. The wood influence is subtle, although some spicy vanillin can be detected. This wine possesses terrific fruit purity, an opulent texture, and an impressively long, harmonious finish. When released next year, the 1994 Reserve should be more accessible young than the 1993 Reserve, yet as long lived (20–30 years). The 1995 Cabernet Sauvignon Hillside Reserve offers up a chocolatey, cassis, and earthy-scented nose, followed by sweet, jammy flavors, sensational depth, ripeness, and balance, and a sweet finish with well-integrated, silky tannin. It is similar in style to the 1994.

Trilogy, Flora Springs' proprietary red table wine, is generally a blend of equal proportions of Cabernet Sauvignon and Merlot, with approximately 15%–17% Cabernet Franc included. With its curranty, cedary, tobaccolike sweetness and ripeness, Trilogy may be the Napa Valley wine that most recalls certain St.-Emilions. Approximately 3,500–4,000 cases of this wine are made in a top vintage. The 1993 Trilogy has tougher tannin than the 1994 and 1995, but the dark purple color, and promising nose of black fruits, spicy oak, and floral aromas, in addition to the wine's full-bodied richness and long finish, suggest exciting things will emerge. Given the rustic tannin in the finish, this wine needs 4–5 years of cellaring, but it should age well for 25 years. The 1994 Trilogy (2,000 cases) exhibits rich, ripe fruit, along with some toasty vanillin and sweet, jammy black fruit scents. Fleshy, harmonious, full-bodied flavors reveal admirable extract and cleanliness. Despite its softness, this impressive wine is unformed, so give it 2–3 years of cellaring; it will age for 2 decades or more. The 1995 Trilogy (44% Merlot, 39% Cabernet Sauvignon, and 17% Cabernet Franc) is a spicy, Médoc-styled wine with medium to full body, excellent spice and richness, as well as an overall sense of elegance and equilibrium. It is a delicious wine to drink now and over the next 15+ years.

One of the best bargains in the Flora Springs portfolio is the 1994 Cabernet Sauvignon Estate (unfortunately, only 1,600 cases are available). It is bursting with ripe, jammy black fruits. This full-bodied, fleshy, fat, in your face, 100% Cabernet Sauvignon was bottled unfiltered, revealing a chewy, open-knit texture. It exhibits excellent purity, as well as spicy oak. Drink it over the next 7–10 years.

Lastly, Flora Springs produced a 1995 Cabernet Sauvignon Cypress Ranch. There are only 375 cases of this wine, which is aged in 25% new oak. Like Flora Springs' other wines, with the exception of the barrel-fermented Chardonnay and Sangiovese, it will be bottled without fining or filtration. A textbook, unformed Cabernet Sauvignon, the Cypress Ranch's pronounced spiciness, and weedy, tobacco-tinged black currant fruitiness make for a solid first impression. This lusty, muscular Cabernet possesses aggressive tannin, which should melt away after some time in the bottle. It should age well for 12–15 years.

FOLIE À DEUX (NAPA)

1996 Cabernet Sauvignon	Napa	D	86
1995 Cabernet Sauvignon	Napa	C	86
1995 Cabernet Sauvignon Reserve	Napa	D	90
1995 Merlot Reserve	Napa	D	87
1995 Sangiovese	Napa	C	85
1996 Syrah	Amador	D	88
1996 Zinfandel Old Vine	Amador	C	88
1995 Zinfandel Old Vine	Amador	C	87
1996 Zinfandel Old Vine Eschen Vineyard Fiddletown	Amador	D	89

This winery, with Scott Harvey (formerly of Amador's Renwood) making the wine, seems to be on the right track. While I was not impressed with two straightforward 1996 Chardonnays, Folie à Deux's reds acquitted themselves well. The least complex and impressive red is the 1996 Cabernet Sauvignon. It is soft, ripe, one-dimensional, rich, and fruity, but not terribly complex. Although well made, savory, and mouth-filling, it will not improve much in the bottle. Consume it over the next 4–6 years. The winery has added a Syrah to the portfolio. Less than 600 cases were made of the 1996, but it is a promising, satisfying, big, chewy, cassis, and tar-scented and -flavored wine with a dark ruby/purple color, medium to full body, and no hard edges. It should drink well for 7–8 years.

The 1995 Sangiovese is an attractive, midweight, strawberry-scented, creamy-textured wine with abundant berry fruit, excellent purity, and a lush, round finish. Although not complicated or rich, it is elegant, charming, and ideal for drinking over the next several years.

The Merlot and Cabernet Sauvignon cuvées are all lavishly wooded, which I suspect is the result of the new administrator having to invest in a high percentage of new barrels. The 1995 Merlot Reserve is a fleshy, seductive, plum-colored wine with gobs of jammy black cherry fruit, luxuriant quantities of toast, smoke, and chocolate, low acidity, and a plush texture. Drink this medium- to full-bodied, delicious Merlot over the next 3–4 years, but you must love oak in order to appreciate it. The same thing is true for the 1995 Cabernet Sauvignon, a blatantly woody, yet fleshy, uncomplicated, spicy, toasty wine with black currant fruit, medium body, low acidity, and an aggressive, exuberant, All-American style. It is sure to be a crowd pleaser, although I suspect those who want their oak in more restrained doses will find it bordering on vulgar. Drink it over the next 5–6 years. The outstanding 1995 Cabernet Sauvignon Reserve also possesses the sweet, toasty oak component, as well as more glycerin, higher fruit extraction, and layers of jammy black currant fruit. It reminds me of the style of Cabernet Sauvignon fashioned by Silver Oak, but I suspect there is some French oak utilized in addition to American wood. The wine is ripe, chewy, and crammed with glycerin, wood, fruit, and alcohol. Plenty of tannin can be detected, so I would opt for holding this wine for 2–3 years, and drinking it over the following 12–15.

The highly extracted, fat, full-bodied, smoky, toasty, peppery 1995 Old Vine Zinfandel shares a similar lusty, flamboyantly scented style. The oak is toned down, but this is not a subtle wine. It is a ripe, high alcohol, succulent Zinfandel to drink over the next 2–4 years.

Scott Harvey made some fabulous Zinfandels when he was employed by Amador's Renwood Winery. He has obviously kept many of those contacts. The two 1996 Folie à Deux Zins I tasted included the 1996 Zinfandel Old Vine (1,544 cases made from 76-year-old vines). This dark ruby-colored Zinfandel exhibits lush, peppery, berry, jammy-scented aromas and flavors, loads of glycerin, low acidity, and a soft, forward, seductive style. It should be drunk over the next 2–3 years. The wine's alcohol level is a modest 13.5%. The dark ruby-colored 1996 Zinfandel Old Vine Eschen Vineyard (472 cases produced) is a jammier style of Zinfandel, with fuller body, more layers of fruit, and a broad, expansive mouth-feel. This wine, which is dominated by a peppery, berry, earthy component, should drink well for 3–4 years.

FORMAN VINEYARDS (NAPA)

1997	Cabernet Sauvignon	Napa	E	(90–92)
1996	Cabernet Sauvignon	Napa	E	92
1995	Cabernet Sauvignon	Napa	E	88+
1994	Cabernet Sauvignon	Napa	E	91
1993	Cabernet Sauvignon	Napa	E	92
1997	Chardonnay	Napa	D	88
1996	Chardonnay	Napa	D	89
1995	Chardonnay	Napa	D	89
1997	Merlot	Napa	D	(87–90)
1996	Merlot	Napa	D	89

1995 Merlot	Napa	D	88
1994 Merlot	Napa	D	89

Ric Forman's nonmalolactic 1997 Chardonnay, which was bottled in July, is unquestionably a successful wine. Very aromatic, with scents of cold steel, citrus, minerals, and flower blossoms, it is an elegant yet concentrated Chardonnay, with honey notes, good fruit extraction and richness, all buttressed by zesty acidity. One of the finest of the nonmalolactic Chardonnays, it should drink well for 4–5 years. The 2,000 case production sells out immediately, which tells you how successful it is.

The 1997 Merlot reveals more lushness and accessibility than Forman's wines sometimes do. Made from 100% Merlot grown in the estate's vineyard, it boasts a dark ruby color, followed by an attractive nose of black cherries and berries intermingled with soil notes, subtle oak, and floral scents. Medium bodied and delicious, it should be accessible when bottled. Moreover, it should last for at least a decade. The 1997 Cabernet Sauvignon (about 75% Cabernet Sauvignon with the rest Cabernet Franc and Merlot) displays a saturated ruby/purple color, and an exceptional bouquet of blackberry and cassis fruit intermingled with cedar, herbs, and wood spice. The wine is deep, medium to full bodied, and richly fruity with firm tannin in the moderately long, ripe finish. Like many 1997s, it will be enjoyable in its youth, yet will last for 15 or more years.

The 1996 Merlot (80% Merlot and 20% Cabernet Franc) is made in a Bordeaux-like style. The nose offers up aromas of coffee and berry-tinged fruit intermixed with herbaceous, spicy oak. The wine possesses excellent texture, medium body, and an intriguing black tea flavor in the fruit character. A sexy Merlot made in Ric Forman's telltale polished, refined, and graceful manner, it should drink well for 10–15 years. One of the most impressive recent Cabernet Sauvignons from Forman is their 1996. I was amazed how well it was showing despite having been bottled only a month earlier. The saturated ruby/purple color is followed by gorgeous jammy black currant fruit aromas, along with spicy oak and licorice. There is good acidity, but the wine appears to possess more viscosity than most Rick Forman offerings, as well as a chewy fleshiness, enough acidity for delineation, and moderate tannin in the convincingly long finish. This classic Bordeaux-styled wine should be at its finest between 2001 and 2020.

It is hard to believe that Ric Forman has been making wine in Napa Valley for over 30 years, and he's still a young guy. To say that he is one of the most experienced winemakers in northern California is an understatement. His opinion on recent California vintages is that 1994, 1995, and 1996 are remarkably similar in quality, and it is not always easy to tell them apart. Forman's winemaking style produces lean, elegant, exceptionally ageworthy wines. His 1996 Chardonnay offers pear and lemon blossom scents and flavors in a crisp, medium-bodied style. There is more power and weight in this wine than might be expected given the fact that it is not put through malolactic fermentation. Underlying acidity gives the wine vibrancy and lift in the mouth. Drink this pure, well-delineated Chardonnay over the next 2–3 years. Forman's 1995 Chardonnay is one of the most interesting nonmalolactic-styled wines being produced in California. Crisp acidity buttresses a wine of admirable purity and delineation. Subtly oaked, with power, richness, good underlying acidity, and a creamy, ripe texture, this wine should drink well for 3–4 years.

Forman's 1994 Merlot, the debut vintage for this varietal, is a deep ruby-colored, open, seductive Merlot with berry/mocha fruit in the nose, medium to full body, and round, generous, nicely oaked flavors. This soft, open-knit, rich, excellent, nearly outstanding Merlot should drink well for 7–8 years. The 1994 Cabernet Sauvignon exhibits a dense, ruby/purple color, an unevolved but promising sweet, cedar, black currant, vanillin-scented nose, medium to full body, fine elegance, underlying acidity, ripe tannin, and a Graves-like, tobacco component that provides complexity. This wine should be accessible young, but will not hit its stride for 5–6 years; it will last for 2 decades. The 1993 Cabernet Sauvignon is a more muscular wine, with considerable tannin (sweet rather than astringent), full body, outstanding ripeness, admirable purity, and a long, textured, structured finish. Although approachable, 3–4 years of cellaring are warranted. It, too, is a 20-year wine.

The 1995 red wines were revealing a more closed character than they possessed previously. For example, the 1995 Merlot was softer than the Cabernet Sauvignon, with a deep ruby/purple color, and a cherry- and raspberry-scented nose with judicious toasty oak in the background. This is a pretty, elegant, attractive style of Merlot with enough acidity for vibrancy, as well as excellent purity and tasty cherrylike flavors. It should drink well for 10–15 years. The tighter, more tannic 1995 Cabernet Sauvignon exhibits a deep ruby/purple color, followed by an elegant cassis-scented nose with graceful, restrained and measured fruit flavors. Medium to full bodied, with moderate tannin and an overall impression of tightness, this is a harmonious, well-made wine that is not nearly as expressive this year as it was in 1996. Ideally, this Cabernet needs 3–4 years of cellaring, and should keep for 20 years.

FOXEN VINEYARDS (SANTA BARBARA)

Year	Wine	Region		Score
1996	Cabernet Sauvignon	Santa Barbara	D	88
1997	Chardonnay	Santa Maria Valley	D	88
1996	Chardonnay Tinaquaic Vineyard	Santa Barbara	D	88
1997	Chenin Blanc	Santa Barbara	C	89
1996	Merlot	Santa Barbara	D	86
1996	Pinot Noir Sanford & Benedict Vineyard	Santa Ynez	D	86
1997	Syrah	Santa Barbara	D	87
1996	Syrah Morehouse Vineyard	Santa Ynez	D	90
1997	Viognier Rothberg Vineyard	Santa Barbara	D	86

One of the most noteworthy achievers in Santa Barbara, Foxen produces a range of wines. One of their unheralded successes (not commercially, but critically) is their Chenin Blanc. The 1997 is a serious, full-bodied, dry Chenin Blanc with luscious quantities of honeyed fruit. Made in a meaty, chewy style reminiscent of a beefed-up Chardonnay, it offers plenty of floral, tropical fruit, and undeniable Chenin Blanc character. Any evidence of oak is well submerged beneath the wine's copious quantities of fruit and glycerin. Drink this mouth-filling example over the next year. I tasted two Chardonnays from Foxen, both full-bodied, tropical fruit-driven wines. The 1997 Chardonnay Santa Maria exhibits well-integrated, toasty oak, admirable body, loads of sexy, honeyed orange and pineapple fruit, crisp acidity, and a pure, clean, easy-to-understand style. I would opt for drinking it over the next 1–2 years. The full-bodied 1997 Chardonnay Tinaquaic Vineyard is more honeyed, with a chewy, denser style, and more noticeable toasty oak, although in both wines, fruit dominates. Although the Tinaquaic cuvée is more structured, it is not better than the regular cuvée, only more restrained. It, too, should be drunk over the next 1–2 years. Tipping the scales at 15% alcohol, the monolithic 1997 Viognier Rothberg Vineyard is tasty and chewy, but I did not find enough varietal character to give it higher marks. It is a juicy, succulent, pleasant tasting wine, but where's the Viognier? Consume it over the next year.

The 1996 Pinot Noir Sanford & Benedict Vineyard is typical of many Santa Barbara Pinot Noirs. The nose reveals a V-8 vegetable juice component intermixed with smoke and cherry fruit. Good acidity gives the wine a tart, tangy feel. This medium-bodied, fruity, easy-to-understand Pinot Noir should be drunk over the next 2–3 years. Foxen's 1996 Merlot is a tasty, fleshy, lush wine on the attack, but tart acidity and light tannin strike a discordant note in the wine's finish. It offers Merlot's chocolatey, cherry, herb-tinged side in an uncompli-cated, medium-bodied format. Drink it over the next several years. More impressive is the dark ruby/purple-colored 1996 Cabernet Sauvignon, which offers up a dense, black cherry, curranty, weedy, tobacco-tinged nose with plenty of smoke and jammy fruit. This medium- to full-bodied, nicely textured, attractive wine displays better balance between its component parts—alcohol, acidity, tannin, and extract. Although accessible, it promises to age nicely for 10–14 years.

The 1997 Syrah is a smoky, bacon fat and black currant-scented wine with an underlying vegetal characteristic reminiscent of a good, middle-weight Crozes-Hermitage. Fruity and soft, with a peppery, spicy, weedy component, it is a Syrah meant for drinking now and over the next 3–4 years. The most impressive offering in the Foxen portfolio is the 1996 Syrah Morehouse Vineyard. This dark ruby/purple-colored wine possesses a textbook bacon fat, fried meat, and smoky-scented nose intermixed with superripe black raspberry and cassis fruit, full body, outstanding concentration and purity, and a luscious, silky finish. Drink this seductive, intensely flavored Syrah now and over the next 7–10 years.

FRANCISCAN ESTATE (NAPA)

1995 Cabernet Sauvignon Oakville Estate	Napa	C	89
1994 Cabernet Sauvignon Oakville Estate	Napa	C	86
1995 Chardonnay Cuvée Sauvage Oakville Estate	Napa	D	86
1996 Chardonnay Oakville Estate	Napa	C	89
1994 Magnificat Proprietary Red Wine	Napa	D	87

Many of Franciscan's top cuvées have been blatantly woody, but the 1996 Chardonnay Oakville lowers the oak intensity while retaining the vibrant burst of varietal fruit. The color is light straw. The wine exhibits a leesy, Burgundian-like character with notes of melted but-ter, roasted nuts, and honeyed flavors. Full bodied, subtly wooded, luscious, and nicely tex-tured, this concentrated Chardonnay should drink well for several years. In contrast, the 1995 Chardonnay Cuvée Sauvage, a wine fermented with indigenous yeasts, and bottled un-filtered, cuts a broader feel in the mouth, but is more muted aromatically as well as slightly monolithic. Ironically, using indigenous yeast, bottling the wine naturally, and eschewing fil-tration, is supposed to achieve just the opposite! The Cuvée Sauvage is more closed than its flamboyant sibling.

The dark ruby-colored 1995 Cabernet Sauvignon Oakville Estate exhibits a toasty, smoky, weedy, black currant-scented nose, medium body, soft, rich, chewy flavors, nicely integrated tannin and wood, and low acidity. Accessible and fleshy, it will offer ideal drinking over the next 7–8 years.

Franciscan's 1994 Cabernet Sauvignon Oakville Estate is an unpretentious wine with a dark plum color, sweet, spicy, red and black fruits, and abundant toasty oak. Medium bod-ied, soft, and round, it is ideal for drinking over the next 7–8 years. The dark plum-colored 1994 Magnificat is more tightly knit, revealing abundant toasty, smoky oak in the nose, along with jammy prune and black currant fruit intermixed with weedy tobacco and cedar. The wine is medium bodied, with moderately high tannin, new wood (perhaps excessive), and a sweet, rich, long finish. A blend of 75% Cabernet Sauvignon, 24% Merlot, and 1% Cabernet Franc, this wine will benefit from another 1–2 years of cellaring and keep for 12–15 years.

FRANUS (NAPA)

1995 Cabernet Sauvignon	Napa	D	86+
1996 Zinfandel	Napa	C	87

1995 Zinfandel	Napa	C	89
1996 Zinfandel Blanchon Vineyard	Contra Costa	C	88
1996 Zinfandel Brandlin Ranch	Mt. Veeder	C	90
1995 Zinfandel Brandlin Ranch	Mt. Veeder	C	90
1994 Zinfandel Brandlin Ranch	Mt. Veeder/Napa	C	91
1993 Zinfandel Brandlin Ranch	Napa	C	90
1994 Zinfandel Hendry Vineyard	Napa	C	91
1993 Zinfandel George Hendry Vineyard	Napa	C	90

The three 1996 Zinfandels are all high-quality wines from Peter Franus, a small, emerging producer of Zinfandel and Pinot Noir. Well made with surprising complexity, these Zinfandels will provide lovely drinking over the next 3–4 years. The 1996 Zinfandel Napa is an aromatic, harmonious, impeccably made wine with smoky, spicy, berry fruit, some pepper, soft acidity, ripe tannin, and plenty of fruit. It is a medium-bodied, supple Zinfandel to drink over the near term. The 1996 Zinfandel Blanchon Vineyard tips the scales at 14.3% alcohol, yet there is no hint of overripeness or raisiny/pruny notes. The wine offers up a kirsch liqueur/plum-scented nose, with pepper and spice. Ripe and medium to full bodied, with low acidity, a chewy, fleshy texture, and good glycerin, this plump, hedonistic Zinfandel should drink well for 2–3 years. The intensely spicy, black fruit, and mineral-dominated 1996 Zinfandel Brandlin Ranch emerges from the slopes of Mt. Veeder. It possesses the darkest, most saturated ruby color of these three Zinfandels. While medium to full bodied, it is structured and possibly more age-worthy (I believe in drinking most Zinfandels during their first 4–7 years of life). This wine reveals some spice, but black fruits and minerals dominate the nose and flavors. It is medium to full bodied, with an inner core of rich fruit. Additionally, there is more delineation and structure in the finish, although I would still opt for drinking this wine over the next 3–4 years.

The 1995 Zinfandel Napa reveals a textbook, briary (the French would call it *sauvage*) nose with aromas of wild berry fruits. The color is an evolved dark garnet, and the wine is dense, medium to full bodied, with crisp, tangy acidity, excellent richness, and a spicy, peppery, earthy personality reminiscent of a Rhône Valley wine. Somewhat tight and structured, it should be consumed over the next 5–6 years. The beautiful, plum-colored 1995 Zinfandel Brandlin Ranch displays a knockout nose of black cherries, raspberries, cola, and peppery fruit. Loads of yummy, glycerin-endowed, chewy fruit hit the palate with medium to full body, and excellent purity. Drink this dense, chewy, mouth-filling, savory Zinfandel over the next 3–4 years.

The dark plum/purple-colored 1994 Hendry Vineyard Zinfandel reveals sweet black fruit in the nose. It explodes on the palate, offering full body, layers of rich, creamy fruit, well-hidden, high alcohol (14.2%), and a clean, succulent, fleshy, large-scaled finish. This beautifully made, lush Zinfandel should drink well for 6–8 years. The 1994 Zinfandel Brandlin Ranch displays a similar dark plummy color, a spicy, mineral, peppery nose, sweet, ripe, full-bodied flavors, an inner core of fruit and expansive chewiness, and a long, ripe finish. These wines are pure and rich, with natural, multilayered textures. The Brandlin Ranch will also drink superbly for 6–8 years. This is high-quality winemaking!

The Franus 1993 George Hendry Zinfandel (850 cases) offers an attractive, complex nose of smoky vanillin and red and black raspberry scents. The wine is dense, powerful, and rich, with great fruit and purity, and a nicely structured, highly extracted, full-bodied finish. This is an impressive, large-scaled yet graceful Zinfandel for drinking over the next 7–8 years. The 1993 Zinfandel Brandlin Ranch (900 cases from a head-pruned, 70-year-old vineyard on Mt. Veeder) exhibits an opaque ruby/purple color, a wonderfully sweet oak and vanillin-scented, rich, concentrated, cherry and raspberry fruit nose, an expansive, full-bodied, deeply etched, flavorful personality, good spice and purity, and a heady, long finish. These are impressive Zinfandels!

Lastly, Franus's dark purple-colored 1995 Cabernet Sauvignon exhibits beautiful black currant fruit in its nose intermingled with high quality, smoky, spicy, toasty new oak. While unevolved and young, this wine is deep, medium to full bodied, classy, and stylish. It is certainly very good, even excellent, but I did not detect the extra layers of richness, length, and overall potential to rate it outstanding. Give it 2–3 years of cellaring, and drink it over the following 10–12.

FRAZIER (NAPA)

1995 Cabernet Sauvignon	Napa	D	89
1995 Merlot Lupine Hill Vineyard	Napa	D	90

From an unfamiliar winery, Frazier's impressive 1995 Merlot Lupine Hill will have me searching out subsequent vintages. This is a textbook, plump, rich Merlot with a dark ruby/purple color, as well as fragrant aromas of white chocolate and cherry jam. Thick, with a soft, unctuously textured, full-bodied personality, this rich, plush, hedonistically satisfying Merlot is a fruit- and body-driven wine with a subtle dosage of oak. It should drink well for 7–8 years.

The deep, chocolatey and blackberry-scented, full-bodied, extroverted, fleshy 1995 Cabernet Sauvignon possesses plenty of character. Although it lacks complexity, finesse, and elegance, it offers substantial flavors in a robust, exuberant format. It should drink well for a decade.

J. FRITZ WINERY (SONOMA)

1996 Chardonnay Dutton Ranch	Russian River	C	88
1996 Chardonnay Dutton Vineyard Ruxton Ranch	Russian River	D	89
1996 Chardonnay Shop Block	Russian River	D	89
1996 Sauvignon Blanc Estate Jenner Vineyard	Dry Creek Valley	B	87
1993 Zinfandel	Dry Creek	B	76
1996 Zinfandel Old Vines	Dry Creek Valley	C	84
1996 Zinfandel Rogers' Reserve Unfined/Unfiltered	Dry Creek Valley	D	88
1994 Zinfandel Rogers' Reserve	Dry Creek	C	89
1995 Zinfandel 80-Year-Old Vines	Dry Creek	C	90

Keep a close eye on this winery as the entire winemaking team has been changed, as evidenced by the higher quality of wines that are emerging. A young, enthusiastic winemaker, Rob Lawson, is in charge. Furthermore, the winery's new consultant is genius/wine goddess Helen Turley. Production is approximately 12,000 cases, with an ultimate goal of 18,000 cases. Another objective is to bottle the 1997s without filtration. The following wines, which I thought were all very good, are made in a newly evolving style now that the Lawson/Turley team is in place. Prices are fair, and the wines have already begun to reveal some of the natural expansive textures and aromatics consistent with Helen Turley-influenced wines.

The 1996 Sauvignon Blanc Jenner Vineyard is from a 15-year-old Dry Creek vineyard owned by J. Fritz. Ten percent of the wine was put through malolactic, resulting in a crisp, medium-bodied, richly fruity Sauvignon offering plenty of ripe fig and melon aromas and flavors, as well as a creamy, soft texture. This wine should be drunk over the next year.

The three Chardonnays are made from whole-cluster pressed grapes, given a full malolactic fermentation, and aged in both French and American oak. There are 4,000 cases of the

1996 Chardonnay Dutton Ranch. Given today's marketplace, this is a reasonably good value. It is a big, lusty, in-your-face style of Chardonnay with 14.2% alcohol. The wine exhibits loads of honeyed pineapple and buttery fruit, full body, and a clean, pure, heady finish. It should be drunk over the next 1–2 years. The 1996 Chardonnay Shop Block is produced from a 70-year-old Chardonnay vineyard that Rob Lawson claims is the oldest in California. The wine is medium to full bodied, with smoky, earthy, nut-scented aromatics, ripe, chewy fruit, zesty acidity, and an excellent finish. I am not sure this wine, which is tighter than the 1996 Dutton Ranch, might not deserve an even higher ranking with another 2–3 months of bottle age. The 1996 Chardonnay Dutton Vineyard Ruxton Ranch's high alcohol (14.2%) is nearly concealed by the wine's orange, tangerine, tropical fruit, mineral, and buttery-scented nose and flavors. Long, with medium to full body, and excellent purity and ripeness, this wine should drink well for several years.

The restrained, medium dark plum-colored 1996 Zinfandel Old Vines possesses light intensity aromas of sweet berry fruit intermixed with vanillin and herbs. On the palate, the wine exhibits tangy acidity, and a compressed flavor profile that tails off in the finish. The wine is cleanly made, with good varietal character in the nose and on the attack, but it could be deeper in the mouth. Drink it over the next 2–3 years. More substantial is the 1996 Zinfandel Rogers' Reserve. Made from an 80-year-old Dry Creek vineyard, and bottled without fining or filtration, this exceptionally perfumed Zinfandel provides a gush of sweet, peppery, berry fruit. In the mouth, this medium- to full-bodied wine hides its alcohol with layers of cherry and raspberry fruit, and plenty of glycerin. It is a tasty, hedonistic, lush wine to drink over the next 4–5 years.

A strong argument can be made that the 1995 Zinfandel 80-Year-Old Vines is one of the three or four most delicious and hedonistic Zinfandels of the vintage. Bottled unfined and unfiltered, Fritz's 1995 is undoubtedly the finest wine I have tasted from this winery. The deep ruby color is appealing, but the wine's aromas and flavors are what provide a real turn-on. Intensely fragrant aromas of jammy strawberries and cherries soar from the glass of this full-bodied, luscious wine. With its layers of glycerin-imbued fruit, low acidity, and head-spinning level of alcohol (15.4%), this is a lush, layered, voluptuously textured Zinfandel to drink over the next 2–3 years.

The unfined and unfiltered 1994 Rogers' Reserve Zinfandel, made from an 80-year-old vineyard in the Dry Creek Valley, displays fabulous ripeness, and a rich, fragrant black fruit-scented (raspberries and cherries) nose with nicely integrated oak. Excellent to outstanding concentration, a plush, natural mouth-feel, without exaggerated acidity, and a medium- to full-bodied, long finish, all combine to make this an exciting, potentially outstanding Zinfandel. It should keep for 6–7 years.

Made from an 80-year-old Dry Creek vineyard, the dark ruby-colored 1993 Zinfandel is acidic, compact, and lean, with a low pH, tart style. I am not sure if the grapes were harvested too soon, or if there was an excessive amount of acidity added to the wine, but it is a narrowly constructed Zinfandel lacking charm and fruit.

THE GAINEY VINEYARD (SANTA YNEZ)

1997	Chardonnay Limited Selection	Santa Barbara	D	89
1996	Chardonnay Limited Selection	Santa Barbara	D	88
1996	Merlot Limited Selection	Santa Barbara	D	88+
1997	Pinot Noir Limited Selection Bien Nacido Vineyard	Santa Barbara	D	88
1996	Sauvignon Blanc Limited Selection	Santa Barbara	C	87
1995	Sauvignon Blanc Limited Selection	Santa Barbara	C	87

One of Santa Barbara's finest wineries, Gainey's Limited Selection cuvées represent their top wines. The 1996 Chardonnay Limited Selection offers a big, smoky, lusty, tropical fruit-scented nose with toasty oak, lush, deep, concentrated fruit, medium to full body, and a user-friendly, fleshy style. Drink it over the next year. The 1997 Chardonnay Limited Selection exhibits attractive mineral, tropical fruit, and buttery scents, followed by leesy, smoky complexity, excellent richness, medium to full body, and fine purity. This wine possesses better aromatics than the 1996, as well as more length. Drink it over the next 1–2 years. The 1996 Sauvignon Blanc Limited Selection reveals an attractive, melony and herb-scented nose, with some oak, but copious quantities of fruit. In the mouth there is admirable richness, medium body, excellent purity, and waxy fig and melony flavors. Drink it over the next year.

The deep ruby-colored 1997 Pinot Noir Limited Selection Bien Nacido Vineyard displays a moderately intense nose of strawberry jam intermixed with smoke, roasted herbs, and *pain grillé*. Tasty, round, and charming, it possesses good power and depth, but no hard edges. This Pinot should drink well for 3–4 years. The potentially outstanding 1996 Merlot Limited Selection offers an opaque ruby/purple color, pure cassis and black cherry fruit, smoky oak, medium to full body, sweet tannin, and excellent, possibly outstanding concentration. There is no hint of the "veggies" that often appear in Santa Barbara reds. If this wine is bottled without too much processing, it will be a fine example of Santa Barbara Merlot. Anticipated maturity: 2000–2007.

Approximately 1,900 cases of the 1995 Sauvignon Blanc Limited Selection were produced. It is an ambitiously styled, oaky, medium- to full-bodied Sauvignon that is meant to imitate a high-class dry white Graves. Aromas of sweet vanillin intermixed with ripe, honeyed fruit can be found in this exuberantly styled Sauvignon that should be drunk over the next year.

GALLO-SONOMA (SONOMA)

1994	Cabernet Sauvignon Barrelli Creek Vineyard	Alexander Valley	C	86?
1994	Cabernet Sauvignon Frei Ranch	Dry Creek Valley	C	88
1994	Cabernet Sauvignon Stefani Vineyard	Dry Creek	C	86
1995	Chardonnay Estate	Northern Sonoma	D	88
1995	Zinfandel	Sonoma	B	85
1995	Zinfandel Barrelli Creek	Alexander Valley	B	89
1997	Zinfandel Chiotti Vineyard	Dry Creek	B	89
1995	Zinfandel Chiotti Vineyard	Dry Creek	C	88
1995	Zinfandel Frei Ranch Vineyard	Dry Creek	B	90
1994	Zinfandel Frei Ranch Vineyard	Dry Creek	C	91
1993	Zinfandel Frei Ranch Vineyard	Dry Creek	C	88
1996	Zinfandel Stefani Vineyard	Dry Creek	C	90

Loamy soil, tar, roasted herb, and black currant aromas and flavors are pleasing in the medium-bodied, rustic, well-made 1994 Cabernet Sauvignon Stefani Vineyard. The tannin is unobtrusive, and the wine soft and easy to drink, if somewhat monolithic. Consume it over the next 4–5 years.

The well-made 1995 Chardonnay offers attractive, buttery, honeyed floral and citruslike fruit in its moderately intense aromatics. The wine is medium to full bodied, fresh, pure, and impeccably well made. It possesses considerable power, alcohol, and weight. Yet my instincts suggest it could have been even better without the heavy-handed acid additions. Drink it over the next 2–3 years.

The saturated dark ruby-colored 1994 Cabernet Sauvignon Frei Ranch displays a moderately intense bouquet of black currants, coffee, crème de cassis, and spice. Pure and rich, this medium- to full-bodied Cabernet possesses well-integrated, unobtrusive acidity and tannin. The finish possesses some dusty tannin, but this spicy, rich Cabernet Sauvignon should continue to improve for 7–8 years and last for 12–15. The 1994 Cabernet Sauvignon Barrelli Creek reveals less earthiness in the mélange of flavors. Additionally, the color is slightly less saturated than the Frei Ranch. Nevertheless, it possesses a healthy dark ruby color, a moderately intense nose of black currants, tobacco, and herbs, and dry, medium-bodied, tannic flavors that are leaner and more austere. Whether it will come into total harmony is debatable. This is a good, spicy, earth- and tannin-driven Cabernet Sauvignon that should benefit from 1–3 years of cellaring and last for a decade.

All of these Zinfandels are fine examples, with the early-released 1997 Zinfandel Chiotti Vineyard revealing what appears to be the high promise of this exciting vintage. It possesses explosive fruit, knockout purity, admirable opulence, and a sexy, hedonistic, exotic character. Soft, round, and pure, its gush of black raspberry, smoke-infused, cherry fruit hides the 14.9% alcohol remarkably well. Drink this seductive Zinfandel over the next 4–5 years. As for the 1995s, the herbaceous, peppery, straightforward, soft, easygoing 1995 Zinfandel Sonoma is appealing in a mainstream, commercial sense. The nearly 14% alcohol gives a nice glycerol impact on the palate. Drink it over the next year. The saturated ruby/purple-colored 1995 Zinfandel Frei Ranch continues to perform exceptionally well. It is a full-bodied, powerful, concentrated wine with no hard edges, well-integrated acidity, and copious quantities of earthy blackberry and cherry fruit. Drink it over the next 4–5 years. Although similar in character, the 1995 Zinfandel Barrelli Creek comes across as more late harvest in style, with an Amarone/asphalt note in the nose. Also present are aromas and flavors of black cherries, full body, and loads of glycerin. This powerhouse, concentrated, exotic Zinfandel should be consumed over the next 3–4 years.

The 1996 Zinfandel Stefani Vineyard (14.9% alcohol) exhibits a dark ruby/purple color, followed by highly extracted, chewy, viscous, full-bodied flavors, lavish quantities of toasty oak, and a juicy, succulent finish. Along with the other Gallo-Sonoma Zinfandels, this offering reveals a hedonistic, up-front quality. Drink it over the next 5 years.

In spite of what appears to be a concentrated, impressively endowed wine, the 1995 Zinfandel Chiotti Vineyard offers leesy, mercaptan aromas that detracted from the otherwise impressive components. Two bottles revealed the same defect. In total contrast, the 1994 Zinfandel Frei Ranch Vineyard is a marvelously concentrated, complex, rich, beautifully made wine. Much has been written about Gallo's efforts to compete at the high end of the quality pyramid. This offering is a textbook, full-bodied, gorgeously pure, complex Zinfandel that should drink well for 5–7 years. The big, sweet, smoky nose offers copious quantities of earthy, black cherry fruit with a subtle touch of wood. Rich, full bodied, and dense, with well-integrated acidity and tannin, this seamlessly styled Zinfandel is sure to please most readers.

The 1993 Zinfandel's impressively saturated dark ruby color and textbook Zinfandel nose of pepper, black cherries, and raspberry fruit is followed by an excellent, medium- to full-bodied, deep, spicy wine with a firm underpinning of acidity and tannin. This refreshing, zesty Zinfandel is ideal for consuming over the next 5–8 years.

Readers not yet familiar with the improved quality of the Gallo estate wines should check out these attractive Zinfandels.

DAN GEHRS (SANTA BARBARA)

1997	Chenin Blanc Le Chenière	Monterey	B	88
1997	Pinot Blanc	Monterey	B	89
1997	Viognier	Santa Barbara	C	88

While I was unimpressed with the red wine offerings from Gehrs, a Cabernet Sauvignon, Pinot Noir, and Syrah, his three white wines are the finest he has produced over recent years. Readers/restaurants looking for delicious, fruit-driven whites need look no further than the following three offerings—all terrific values. The 1997 Chenin Blanc Le Chenière is a beautifully poised wine with intense aromas of flowers, pineapples, and other fruits. The dazzling nose is followed by a pure, medium-bodied, fruit-dominated wine that has obviously been tank fermented and aged. There is a touch of honey in the finish, but the overall impression is one of exuberant fruit, with slight minerality. It should be consumed over the next year for its aromatics and refreshing style. The 1997 Pinot Blanc exhibits a textbook mineral and orange blossom-scented nose, terrific clarity, gorgeous fruit flavors, and an excellent, medium-bodied, crisp, dry finish. This is a sexy, charming Pinot Blanc with beautifully displayed fruit. Drink it over the next year. Lastly, the 1997 Viognier offers that varietal's telltale apricot and honeysuckle-scented nose, copious quantities of fruit, medium body, and a modest 13.5% alcohol (lower than many Viogniers). It has been vinified to emphasize the fruit characteristics, and, thankfully, has not been given any exposure to oak. It should drink well for another 8–12 months.

GRACE FAMILY VINEYARD (NAPA)

1995	Cabernet Sauvignon	Napa	EEE	94
1994	Cabernet Sauvignon	Napa	EEE	94+
1993	Cabernet Sauvignon	Napa	EEE	91

This wine is only available via the winery's mailing list, and I am sure there are more potential suitors than wine to be sold. Current production has dwindled, largely because much of the vineyard is in the process of being replanted due to the phylloxera scourge. For example, in 1995 only the upper block of the vineyard was in production. Only 75 cases will emerge from this vintage, further ensuring a preposterously high price. In 1994 there are 175 cases. These beautifully made wines are among the finest Cabernets in California. I rarely report on them because they are, for all intents and purposes, unobtainable. Yet there is no doubting the high quality aspirations of the owner, and the skills exhibited by winemaking consultant Heidi Barrett in the production, aging, and bottling of these 100% Cabernet Sauvignon wines.

The 1993 Cabernet Sauvignon is a topflight example of this high class vintage. Deep purple-colored, with well-integrated, spicy, toasty oak competing with gobs of sweet black currant fruit and spice, this full-bodied, well-endowed, concentrated Cabernet is powerful yet well balanced. It needs another 2–3 years of cellaring to resolve some tannin, but it will easily last 15–20 years. The 1994 Cabernet Sauvignon is the last wine made from the original vineyard plantings. The opaque purple color is accompanied by an explosive bouquet of black currants and cherries, intermingled with toasty, new oak. Full bodied, with a lead pencil, cedary, cassislike characteristic not dissimilar from a high class Pauillac, this tightly knit yet formidably endowed Cabernet Sauvignon should last for 20–25 years. I hope the handful of multimillionaires who latch onto a bottle or two will have enough patience to cellar it for 5–6 years before pulling a cork.

The 1995 is a magnificent Cabernet Sauvignon, but, lamentably, only 3 barrels (425 magnums) were produced as the vineyard is in the process of being replanted. The wine is powerful for a 1995, with an opaque purple color, and intensely ripe black currant aromas intermingled with smoke, *pain grillé*, licorice, and chocolate. This deep, full-bodied, multilayered wine is the essence of Napa Cabernet Sauvignon. Although it reveals plenty of tannin, it is well meshed in the wine's impressive richness and layered texture. Still youthful and grapey, this Cabernet will develop well for another 15–20+ years.

GREEN AND RED VINEYARD (NAPA)

1995 Zinfandel Chiles Mill Vineyard Unfiltered	Napa	C	86
1996 Zinfandel Chiles Mill Vineyard Unfiltered	Napa	C	89
1994 Zinfandel Chiles Mill Vineyard Unfiltered	Napa	C	89
1993 Zinfandel Chiles Mill Vineyard Unfiltered	Napa	C	90

The most Burgundian of all the 1996 Zinfandels I tasted, this medium ruby-colored wine possesses a gorgeously fragrant nose of black cherries, floral scents, minerals, pepper, and spice. It is medium bodied, lush, and sexy, in the style of a premier cru Beaune or Volnay. There is a nicely textured finish with lively acidity, sweet fruit, and glycerin. This Zinfandel is ready to drink, so readers should take advantage of its considerable charms.

The 1995 is a good example of a restrained, subtle Zinfandel that offers enough sweet fruit to give the wine appeal and attractiveness. The medium ruby color is followed by pure, dusty, black cherry aromas that drift from the glass. Dry and elegant, yet concentrated and harmonious, this is a lighter-styled, pretty, delicious Zinfandel to drink over the next 3–4 years.

I am not sure I haven't underrated the 1994. It exhibits a dark ruby color, a pure, ripe, cherry/raspberry fruitiness, a seamless, silky texture, medium to full body, and a luscious finish. It is all fruit, beautifully captured without any excesses. Drink this soft, smooth Zinfandel over the next 3–4 years.

Typical for this winery, the 1993 Zinfandel Chiles Mill Vineyard is a fragrant, intensely flavored, gracefully balanced wine that will drink well young, yet age for a decade. Burgundy enthusiasts will admire the intense, briery, black raspberry-scented nose, as well as the sweet (from ripe grapes, not sugar), expansive, fleshy palate. This wine combines earthy *terroir* characteristics with its rich, berry fruitiness. It is a concentrated, medium- to full-bodied, seductive, velvety-textured Zinfandel. Impressive!

GRGICH HILLS CELLARS (NAPA)

1995 Zinfandel	Sonoma	C	74
1993 Zinfandel	Sonoma	C	(76–79)

It is obvious from the last several years of wine releases from Grgich Hills that at least four or five dozen wineries in northern California have bypassed this producer. Grgich's 1995 Zinfandel is typical of the old-style California winemaking—overly manipulated, acidified, denuded wines that win high marks from the techno-wizards, but provide little interest or pleasure for those who actually consume wine. There are correct, albeit vague, aromas of cherries in this dusty, medium-bodied wine. Austere, with high acidity, and an attenuated personality, this Zinfandel already has one foot in the grave. Disappointing.

Grgich Hills had not yet bottled the 1993 Zinfandel when I tasted it, hence the estimated rating. This wine, while possessing an impressive opaque purple color exhibits a slight earthy, barnyard character to its bouquet, as well as a lack of flesh in its austere, high-acid flavors. Perhaps it will soften and display more charm and flesh with further aging, but the high acidity is cause for concern.

GROTH VINEYARDS AND WINERY (NAPA)

1995 Cabernet Sauvignon	Napa	C	86
1994 Cabernet Sauvignon	Napa	D	84
1994 Cabernet Sauvignon Reserve	Napa	EE	89
1997 Sauvignon Blanc	Napa	B	87

The 1997 Sauvignon Blanc is an aromatic, medium-bodied wine with fresh fruit (primarily melons), good ripeness, and a clean, rich finish. It should be drunk over the next year.

The 1995 Cabernet Sauvignon is a straightforward, gutsy Cabernet with plenty of black currant fruit, subtle oak, nice spice, a one-dimensional personality, but good depth and texture. It should drink well for 7–10 years. The luxury-priced 1994 Cabernet Sauvignon Reserve reveals a dark plum/purple color, and lavish quantities of toasty new oak in the smoky, vanillin, and cassis-scented nose. This forward, soft, medium- to full-bodied wine possesses very good to excellent concentration, but the abundant wood flavors push the taster's tolerance to the limit. While this Reserve offering is undoubtedly excellent, I did not detect the depth or concentration necessary to support aging beyond a decade.

What begins as an attractively dark ruby/purple-colored 1994 Cabernet Sauvignon with a spicy, peppery, vanillin, and black currant-scented nose quickly sags in the middle, with a hollowness and lack of extract. The finish offers tannin, without the necessary glycerin and extract. The 1994 Groth Cabernet Sauvignon will last for 7–8 years.

GUENOC WINERY (LAKE COUNTY)

1994 Cabernet Sauvignon Reserve Bella Vista Vineyard	Napa	D	86
1995 Chardonnay Genevieve Magoon Vineyard Unfiltered Reserve		C	87
1994 Langtry Meritage	Napa	D	86

This winery has a tendency to over-oak just about every one of its red wines. The 1994 Langtry Meritage reveals such boisterous levels of smoky oak in its aromatics that they nearly submerge what appears to be very good ripe red and black currant fruit. The wine is sweet on the entry with medium body, but the heavy dosage of oak gives the wine a more one-dimensional character than I suspect it possesses. Although it is soft, round, and generous, it is clearly designed for those who like plenty of wood in their wines. Anticipated maturity: now–2010.

Guenoc's 1995 Chardonnay Genevieve Magoon Unfiltered Reserve pushes oak to the limit, but there is no doubting the flamboyant, in-your-face style of this chewy, medium- to full-bodied, richly fruity Chardonnay. Its honeyed, opulent style and lavish wood are not for everybody, but for those who like dramatic Chardonnays, this wine will fit the bill. However, it requires consumption over the next 8–9 months. Why? Once the fruit begins to fade, the wood will become obtrusive.

Although straightforward, the 1994 Cabernet Sauvignon Reserve Bella Vista Vineyard is an attractive, plump, black cherry and plum-tasting Cabernet Sauvignon with deep fruit, medium body, and well-integrated tannin. Soft enough to be drunk now, it promises to keep for 5–7 years.

HANDLEY CELLARS (MENDOCINO)

1996 Chardonnay	Dry Creek Valley	C	87
1995 Chardonnay	Dry Creek Valley	C	87
1996 Chardonnay Estate	Anderson Valley	C	87
1995 Chardonnay Estate	Anderson Valley	C	86
1996 Pinot Noir	Alexander Valley	C	87
1995 Pinot Noir	Alexander Valley	C	87
1993 Pinot Noir	Anderson Valley	C	87
1995 Pinot Noir Reserve	Anderson Valley	D	90
1994 Pinot Noir Reserve	Anderson Valley	D	87

1997	Sauvignon Blanc	Dry Creek Valley	C	86
1996	Sauvignon Blanc	Dry Creek Valley	B	86
1995	Sauvignon Blanc	Dry Creek Valley	B	87

This winery continues to turn out impressive wines at reasonable prices. Winemaker Milla Handley produces fruit-driven wines of excellent ripeness, purity, and overall symmetry. For example, the 1997 Sauvignon Blanc is a textbook Sauvignon from the hot Dry Creek Valley, but it does not reveal any of the cooked characteristics possessed by some whites from that region. Handley Cellars' offering exhibits a moderately intense nose of figs, melon, earth, and herbaceous fruit. The wine provides a lovely combination of medium body, good glycerin, and pure, crisp, elegant, lingering flavors. This delicious mid-weight Sauvignon should drink nicely for 12–18 months. The two 1996 Chardonnays are similar in quality, although different in style. The more elegant and fruit-driven is the 1996 Estate Chardonnay from Anderson Valley. It reveals copious quantities of pear and citrus fruit, with a subtle touch of toast. Medium bodied, with admirable purity, refreshing yet not excessive acidity, and a moderately weighty feel in the mouth, this is a bright, vivacious Chardonnay to drink over the next 1–2 years. The 1996 Chardonnay Dry Creek Valley possesses more density, a fuller body, and more weight, as well as some of the dusty earthiness that characterizes Dry Creek. It is a solidly made, more muscular style that should drink well for 12–18 months.

This winery has slowly but surely been building a reputation for high-class Pinot Noir. The 1996 Alexander Valley Pinot Noir offers loads of delicious jammy strawberry and cherry fruit that jumps from this medium ruby-colored wine in a forthright manner. In the mouth, there is a long, layered, textured feel, excellent ripeness, and a medium-bodied, pure finish. It should drink well for 3–4 years. The 1995 Pinot Noir Reserve is undoubtedly the finest Pinot Noir Handley has yet produced. Bottled with neither fining nor filtration, this outstanding Pinot offers additional evidence for the quality of wines from this varietal in the Anderson Valley. Handley's 1995 Reserve exhibits a saturated deep ruby/purple color, as well as a knockout nose of black cherries and blackberries. In the mouth, it is medium to full bodied with gobs of fruit, an opulent texture, enough acidity for definition and vibrancy, and a long, 30+-second finish. This is an exquisite, complex Pinot Noir to consume over the next 3–4 years.

The seductive 1995 Pinot Noir possesses a sweet, cherry, Côte de Beaune-like character, with an added touch of chocolate. The wine is lush and round, with excellent fruit, light tannin, and enough acidity to provide lift and balance. Drink it over the next 2–3 years. The 1994 Pinot Noir Reserve (the debut Pinot Noir from the estate) exhibits a deep ruby color, a big, spicy, sweet, cranberry/strawberry/cherry-scented aroma, nice fat and flesh, and moderate tannin in the clean finish. Fruity, ripe, and accessible, it will be even better with another 12 months of aging, after which it should drink well for 4–5 years. The 1993 Pinot Noir's frail, watery, light ruby color offers a deceptive initial impression of this fragrant, elegant, supple Pinot Noir. The wine's nose reveals berry fruit aromas intermingled with scents of smoke and wood. Soft, round, and medium bodied, it offers delicate flavors that linger on the palate. It is a classic example of just how much flavor exists in such a light-colored wine made from Pinot Noir. Drink this delicious example over the next 1–3 years.

Handley's Sauvignon and Chardonnay are consistently good, if rarely outstanding. Furthermore, they are modestly priced in an era when big ticket prices seem to be the rule. The 1996 Sauvignon Blanc exhibits a flinty, light, smoky, melony-scented nose, elegant, light- to medium-bodied flavors, spice, crisp acidity, and nice fruit in the moderately long finish. It is a wine to drink over the next year. The 1995 Sauvignon Blanc reveals good fig/melony fruit, crisp acidity for freshness, medium body, and fine balance. Drink it over the next year.

I tasted two cuvées of 1995 Chardonnay, of which my favorite was the 1995 Estate

Chardonnay from Anderson Valley. A citrusy nose with a touch of orange peel is followed by a lusciously fruity, medium-bodied, stylish, cleanly made wine that is neither heavy-handed nor over-oaked. It will be admired for its fresh, lively display of fruit. Drink it over the next 1–2 years.

The well-made, medium-bodied 1995 Chardonnay possesses good freshness, plenty of fruit, fine depth, and no evidence of oak, although I suspect some may be lurking in the background. Drink this satisfying, mouth-filling wine over the next year.

HANSEL FAMILY VINEYARD (RUSSIAN RIVER)

1997 Chardonnay	Russian River	D	89
1996 Pinot Noir	Russian River	D	89

These two offerings from a small winery in the Russian River are made with considerable guidance from proprietor Walter Hansel's friend Tom Rochioli. Readers should note quantities of these impressive wines are limited, and the entire production is sold via a mailing list. The 1997 Chardonnay reveals a Meursault-like roasted hazelnut aroma intertwined with the tropical fruit aspects of California (primarily pineapples). The wine possesses a lush, fleshy texture, outstanding purity, and plenty of extract and richness. This Chardonnay may merit an outstanding score with a few more months of bottle age; it should drink well for 3–4 years.

The complex 1996 Pinot Noir exhibits a Pommard-like earthy/spicy character. Some of Pinot's sweet, apple skin personality comes through in the black cherry flavors. A broad, dense, medium- to full-bodied Pinot Noir with considerable personality and flavor authority, it should drink well for 5–6 years.

HARLAN ESTATE (NAPA)

1997 Proprietary Red Wine	Napa	EEE	(92–96)
1996 Proprietary Red Wine	Napa	EEE	98
1995 Proprietary Red Wine	Napa	EEE	99
1994 Proprietary Red Wine	Napa	EEE	100
1993 Proprietary Red Wine	Napa	EEE	95
1995 The Maiden	Napa	E	90

The Harlan Estate (a mountainside vineyard looking down on Martha's Vineyard) is now approaching 35 acres in size (with 26 acres in production). It produces singular wines of prodigious intensity, complexity, and majestic richness. Production has been averaging under 2 tons per acre, save for the abundant 1997 vintage, where it crept up to a modest 2.75 tons per acre. Case production to date has been extremely small, and my enthusiasm for the 1994 may have created a logjam for that wine when the 1,500 cases were released in the spring of 1998. Bob Levy is the winemaker, and France's renowned oenologist, Michel Rolland, the consultant. Proprietor Bill Harlan is a perfectionist (as anyone who has stayed at his impeccably run Meadowwood Country Club and Resort knows). In pursuit of the best, Harlan Estate may be one of the few wines made in the world that is produced by sorting grape by grape rather than bunch by bunch! The brutal selection and labor-intensive triage consists of eliminating every tiny stem and leaf morsel that make it past the first inspection team. Michel Rolland told me that never in his experience (which is worldwide) has he witnessed the meticulous attention to every detail that characterizes the harvest at Harlan. The results are wines that are among the finest I have ever tasted—from anywhere. The style of these wines is seemingly a synthesis between the extraordinary fruit and ripeness that Napa Valley can achieve, and the complexity of the greatest Bordeaux. Depending on the vintage,

I find Harlan Estate's wines reminiscent of a hypothetical blend of a profound California Cabernet and La Mission-Haut-Brion, or Mouton-Rothschild, or Cheval Blanc!

Proprietor Bill Harlan, his winemaker, Bob Levy, and consultant, Frenchman Michel Rolland continue to produce what may be the single most profound wine in California. These wines possess all the elements of greatness—individuality, power combined with elegance, extraordinary complexity, remarkable aging potential, and compelling richness without ponderousness. All the vintages produced to date give signs of improving in the bottle for 20–30+ years. In 1995, a second wine, which has not yet been named, has been produced, which allows the selection process to be even more severe once the 35-acre vineyard is in full production. Recent production has been 1,500 cases for the 1994, 1,200 cases for the 1995, 1,500 for the 1996, and approximately 2,500 cases for the 1997.

As for the two cuvées of 1995, the second wine is an outstanding offering (300 cases made from 100% Cabernet Franc). It possesses a dense, murky ruby/purple color, and an expressive, cedary, leathery, spicy nose with plenty of black fruits. Some minerality comes through, but this complex, evolved yet structured, full-bodied wine is an amazing second wine. It should drink well for 10–15 years. The 1995 Proprietary Red Wine is almost as perfect as the 1994. It has gotten even better in the bottle, and remains one of the most remarkable young Cabernet Sauvignons I have tasted. The wine, a blend of 85% Cabernet Sauvignon and 15% Merlot, was aged in 100% new oak, which adds subtle *pain grillé*/toasty scents. This opaque purple-colored Cabernet offers up a nose of smoke, coffee beans, black and blue fruits, minerals, and roasted herbs. It is extremely full bodied, with spectacular purity, exquisite equilibrium, and a seamless personality with everything in total harmony. The finish lasts for more than 40 seconds. This extravagantly rich, profoundly complex 1995 will give its 1994 sibling a run for its money. Anticipated maturity: 2001–2027.

The 1996 Proprietary Red Wine appears to be one of the vintage's most noteworthy offerings. Some 1996s tend to be rustic, with more obtrusive tannin than their 1995 and 1994 counterparts, but that charge cannot be made against the Harlan Estate. The 1996 exhibits a telltale opaque purple/plum color, as well as a spectacular soaring nose of wood fire, roasted herbs, black currants, tobacco, minerals, and allspice. The wine is full bodied and multilayered, with terrific flavor concentration, well-integrated tannin, and a blockbuster finish. This is another candidate for perfection. As accolades spilled from my mouth like a baby dribbling milk, I was told the wine had been bottled the day before my visit! Anticipated maturity: 2004–2035. Many readers who have been on the waiting list for Harlan Estate may finally receive an allocation in 1997. This year produced the highest yields to date (a still modest 2.7 tons per acre) at this hillside vineyard. I tasted through the component parts of the 1997 Proprietary Red Wine, and everything fell within the 92–96 category. This wine reveals the more evolved aromatics typical of the 1997 vintage. The sensational fragrance (coffee, smoked herbs, nuts, crème de cassis, plum liqueur, and *pain grillé*) is more intense and forthcoming than any previous Harlan Estate vintage. The tannin is silky, and the wine is stunningly concentrated and proportioned, but on a faster evolutionary track than its siblings. I will have another look at the 1997 after the wine has had time to mesh together. It should be another candidate for 20+ years of cellaring.

What can I say about the 1994? I tasted the wine for three consecutive years, and each time it satisfied all of my requirements for perfection. The opaque purple color is followed by spectacular aromatics that soar from the glass, offering up celestial levels of black currants, minerals, smoked herbs, cedar wood, coffee, and *pain grillé*. In the mouth, this seamless legend reveals full body, and exquisite layers of phenomenally pure and rich fruit, followed by a 40+-second finish. While accessible, the 1994 begs for another 5–7 years of cellaring. It should easily last for 30+ years. Every possible jagged edge—acidity, alcohol, tannin, and wood—is brilliantly intertwined in what seems like a diaphanous format. What is so extraordinary about this large-scaled wine, with its dazzling display of aromatics and prodigious flavors and depth, is that it offers no hint of heaviness or coarseness. Harlan's 1994 comes close to immortality in the glass.

The 1993 should be as prodigious as the 1992. It is an opaque purple-colored wine with spectacular ripeness, purity, and potential. Dense, full bodied, with a chocolatey, toasty, mineral, and black currant-scented nose, this wine has a rich, full-bodied, chewy texture nicely buttressed by ripe tannin. In addition, the wine reveals more noticeable tannin in the finish, particularly when it is compared to the 1992 or 1994. This is another 20–25-year wine.

Much of this wine will be sold to the winery's mailing list customers. If you miss out on the 1994, try and get on the waiting list for future vintages. While perfect wines are few and far between, history has taught me that wineries with such lofty aspirations as Harlan Estate will continue to push the envelope of quality.

HARRISON WINERY (NAPA)

1995 Cabernet Sauvignon	Napa	C	85
1994 Cabernet Sauvignon	Napa	C	89
1993 Cabernet Sauvignon	Napa	C	89

The 1995 Cabernet Sauvignon has a moderately endowed nose of spicy new oak and sweet, ripe red currant fruit, followed by a straightforward, monolithic style of Cabernet Sauvignon that displays some appealing softness but not a great deal of depth or length. It is correctly as well as cleanly made but neither concentrated nor long. Drink it over the next 7–8 years.

The 1994 Cabernet Sauvignon has a dense, saturated ruby/purple color, followed by a wine that requires coaxing to reveal its aromatic development. Aromas of blackberries, cassis, earth, and a touch of herbs are followed by a deep, rustic, tannic wine with considerable power and structure. If the tannin and acidity become better integrated, this wine will merit an outstanding score, but it is too soon to know if that will be the case. It will require 5–6 years of cellaring and has the potential for 20 years of evolution.

Made from a vineyard on Pritchard Hill, Harrison's 1993 Cabernet Sauvignon reveals some aggressive oak that bordered on being excessive. Otherwise, it possesses impressively extracted, rich, black cherry and cassis flavors intertwined with hints of Provençal herbs. The wine is medium to full bodied, spicy, rich, moderately tannic, and well made. If it develops more complexity and the oak becomes better integrated, it may rate an outstanding rating.

HARTFORD COURT (SONOMA)

1995 Chardonnay Arrendell Vineyard	Green Valley	D	94
1996 Chardonnay Seascape Vineyard Unfiltered	Sonoma Coast	D	91
1996 Pinot Noir	Sonoma Coast	D	88
1997 Pinot Noir Arrendell Vineyard	Green Valley	D	(88–90)
1996 Pinot Noir Arrendell Vineyard	Green Valley	D	87
1995 Pinot Noir Arrendell Vineyard	Green Valley	D	91
1997 Pinot Noir Dutton-Sanchietti Vineyard	Russian River	D	86
1996 Pinot Noir Sanchietti Vineyard	Russian River	D	87
1995 Pinot Noir Sanchietti Vineyard	Russian River	D	89
1995 Zinfandel	Russian River	D	89
1997 Zinfandel Dina's Vineyard	Russian River	D	90

1997 Zinfandel Fanucchi Vineyard	Russian River	D	87
1996 Zinfandel Fanucchi Vineyard	Russian River	D	91
1996 Zinfandel Fanucchi-Wood Road Vineyard	Russian River	D	91
1997 Zinfandel Hartford Vineyard	Russian River	D	89
1996 Zinfandel Hartford Vineyard	Russian River	D	90
1995 Zinfandel Hartford Vineyard	Russian River	D	90
1994 Zinfandel Hartford Vineyard	Russian River	D	92
1997 Zinfandel Highwire Vineyard	Russian River	D	90

One of the star estates in the Kendall-Jackson group known as *Artisans and Estates,* Hartford Court is a "showcase château" in the Russian River Valley, just off Martinelli Road. I have enjoyed everything this winery has released to date.

The 1997 Pinot Noir Arrendell Vineyard is a beautifully fruity, dark ruby-colored wine with loads of apple skin, cherry jam, and spice in its aromatics and flavors. There is tangy underlying acidity, fine ripeness, and a fleshy mouth-feel with just enough acidity and tannin to buttress the wine and give it delineation. This effort should age nicely for 5–6 years. The dark ruby-colored 1997 Pinot Noir Dutton-Sanchietti Vineyard is tightly knit, with more acidity, leanness, and toughness in the finish. There are attractive, earthy red fruits intermixed with dried herbs, spice, and a note of pepper. This structured, less generously styled Pinot Noir should evolve nicely and expand over the next year. Anticipated maturity: 2000–2005.

Hartford Court produced four fine 1997 Zinfandels. All were aged in 100% French oak and achieved natural alcohol levels between 14.7% and 15.2%. Production ranged from 300 cases for Dina's Vineyard to 700 cases for the Highwire Vineyard. Exhibiting a dark ruby/purple color, the 1997 Zinfandel Hartford Vineyard offers up an attractive nose of jammy, briery, and raspberry fruit, medium to full body, tangy acidity, and a spicy, exuberant personality. This wine should drink well for 4–5 years. The 1997 Zinfandel Highwire Vineyard reveals a saturated dark purple color, as well as more pepper and black raspberries in its moderately intense aromatics. This lovely, rich, medium- to full-bodied wine balances power with finesse. Drink this stylish, flavorful Zinfandel over the next 5–6 years. The outstanding dark ruby/purple-colored 1997 Zinfandel Dina's Vineyard is close in quality to the Highwire. There are abundant quantities of jammy black cherries and raspberries, intermixed with pepper and toasty oak in this medium- to full-bodied yet elegant wine. It should drink well for 5–7 years given its good underlying acidity and extract. The 1997 Zinfandel Fanucchi Vineyard is a fruit bomb, but the underlying tart acidity is somewhat intrusive. Although the wine exhibits a fine berry/briery character, good ripeness, and plenty of purity, the acid level is unintegrated at this stage. It should drink well for 5–6 years.

Hartford Court's 1996 Chardonnay Seascape from Sonoma Coast is a dead ringer for a high-class white Burgundy. This wine exhibits a smoky, honeyed citrus, orange rind, lusciously fruity personality with underlying minerals. Add to that impressive delineation that is rare for a wine of this richness and size. Still youthful and backward, it promises to evolve gracefully for 2–5 years.

The first Chardonnay to be released under the Hartford Court label was the 1995 Chardonnay Arrendell Vineyard, of which, sadly, there are only 300 cases. It is a spectacular Chardonnay, offering a complex, smoky, hazelnut, honeyed, citrus blossom-scented nose, followed by layers of creamy-textured, concentrated fruit nicely buttressed by adequate acidity. New oak barrels have provided a subtle notion of smoke and toast, but the fruit dominates the wine's personality. This full-bodied, rich, elegant Chardonnay is undoubtedly going to make heads turn. It should drink well for 2–3 years.

The 1996 Pinot Noir Sonoma Coast (about 70% comes from the Hirsch Vineyard) reveals a beautiful premier cru Beaune-like nose of kirsch, sour cherries, and spice. The wine possesses excellent concentration, medium body, and crystal clear focus and purity. This fresh, vivacious Pinot should drink well for 3–5 years. There are two single vineyard Pinot Noir offerings, one from the Arrendell Vineyard in Green Valley, and the other from the Russian River vineyard called Sanchietti. I have a slight preference for the Arrendell cuvée because of its richer, more complex nose. However, both are expressive and fragrant, with excellent levels of black cherry and smoke intertwined with meat, herb, and spice notes. The 1995 Pinot Noir Arrendell gets my nod over the 1996, simply because it is a richer, more multidimensional wine with excellent vibrancy to its smoky, cherry fruit flavors. The 1996 Pinot Noir Arrendell is more marked by new oak. While very good to excellent, it does not possess the flavor, length, and overall equilibrium of the 1995. The 1995 Pinot Noir Sanchietti appears to be marginally superior to its 1996 counterpart. The medium ruby-colored 1995 displays a Burgundy-like black cherry, earth, herb, and smoky-scented nose, excellent richness, good texture, and a clean, refreshing finish. The 1996 Pinot Noir Sanchietti is shorter, but lush, hedonistic, and well made.

Readers know of my affection for the Zinfandels produced by Hartford Court. They come from an 80-year-old, head-pruned, Russian River vineyard owned by Don Hartford. The 1995 Zinfandel Hartford Vineyard is a terrific example of this varietal. Tipping the scales at 14.6% alcohol, it is no shy wine. It offers up copious quantities of raspberry, black cherry, briery fruit with smoky, toasty new oak in the background. Dense and full bodied, with wonderful exuberance and lushness, it should drink well for 3–4 years. The 1996 Zinfandel Fanucchi Vineyard is potentially even more spectacular. Although unevolved and grapey, it reveals enormous density of fruit, richness, and concentration. A real powerhouse, with no hard edges, it possesses low acidity and layers of fleshy, glycerin-imbued Zinfandel fruit. It should drink well for 7–8 years.

As evidenced by the following two impeccably well made, medium- to full-bodied offerings, Hartford Court's magic with Pinot Noir and Chardonnay is also applicable to Zinfandel. The 1996 Zinfandel Hartford Vineyard displays a thick-textured, dark purple color, and moderately intense cranberry/cherry liqueurlike aromatics nicely dosed with spicy new oak. Pepper and subtle herbs are also noticeable. While it does not possess the necessary length to merit an exceptional score, this is a rich, harmonious, pure, concentrated Zinfandel with considerable character. Moreover, it is capable of drinking well for 5–6 years. Like its sibling, the 1996 Zinfandel Fanucchi-Wood Road Vineyard carries a powerful 14.7% alcohol. It is denser, with a black raspberry/blackberry character, fuller body, and a less evolved personality. Intense, with beautifully ripe fruit, outstanding purity and equilibrium, this wine is already delicious to drink, but my instincts suggest it will be even better with another 3–6 months of cellaring; it will last for 5–7 years.

Zinfandel fanatics should take note of the 1994 Zinfandel Hartford Vineyard. Made from an old, head-pruned, low-yielding 80-year-old vineyard, this wine reveals an opaque purple color, and that sexy Zin perfume of crushed black raspberries, cherries, pepper, and spice. It is a wine of exceptional purity, with full body, high alcohol (14.2%), good, crisp acidity, and a knockout, blockbuster finish. Drink this Zinfandel over the next 5–6 years. Tasted several times in the summer of 1996, this exquisite wine just got more profound. One of the few 1995 Zinfandels with a saturated dark purple color, the excellent, nearly outstanding 1995 Zinfandel from Hartford Court exhibits pure, ripe black cherry and raspberry fruit gently infused with toasty, spicy oak. Well balanced without annoyingly high acidity or harsh tannin, it is a concentrated, medium-bodied, backward, rich, flavorful, intense wine. Cellar it for another year, and drink it over the subsequent 7–8. Like the 1994 Hartford Court Zinfandel, this wine is made from 81-year-old, head-pruned, Russian River vines.

HARTLEY OSTINI HITCHING POST (SANTA BARBARA)

1996	Pinot Noir Bien Nacido Vineyard	Santa Maria	D 88
1993	Pinot Noir	Santa Maria	C 84?
1993	Pinot Noir Bien Nacido Vineyard	Santa Maria	D 87
1993	Pinot Noir Sanford & Benedict Vineyard	Santa Ynez	D 87

I have had mixed results with my tastings of the Hartley-Ostini Hitching Post Pinots. They have a tendency to be overtly herbaceous, and/or kinky. Such is not the case with the 1996, which is a meaty, spicy, smoky, herb-tinged Pinot Noir. This deep ruby-colored wine reveals gobs of grilled vegetable, jammy cherry, plum, and smoky scents in its complex aromatics. In the mouth, it is medium bodied and ripe, with excellent concentration, good overall balance, and a distinctive Pinot Noir character. Drink it over the next 4–5 years.

The other three Pinot Noirs, available from the Hitching Post Restaurant, are fragrant, spicy, meaty wines with good depth and richness. The straightforward 1993 Pinot Noir Santa Maria exhibits an herb, earth, and berry-scented nose, a good attack, but high acidity in the finish. It is a pleasant yet tart medium-bodied Pinot for drinking over the next several years. The 1993 Pinot Noir Bien Nacido Vineyard reveals a deeper color, a lovely texture with a layered, rich berry fruit and spice personality, lush glycerin, and heady alcohol in the finish. Drink it over the next 4–5 years. The 1993 Pinot Noir Sanford & Benedict Vineyard offers a sweet nose, wonderfully expansive, ripe, earthy flavors, medium to full body, and a supple texture. It should drink well for 4–5 years.

HARTWELL VINEYARD (NAPA)

1994	Cabernet Sauvignon Stag's Leap District	Napa	EE 90
1993	Cabernet Sauvignon Stag's Leap District	Napa	EE 89

Hartwell's Cabernet Sauvignon is produced in very limited quantities (175 cases in 1993, 225 cases in 1994, and nothing in 1995 because the vineyard was replanted because of the phylloxera epidemic). This estate's Cabernets have become somewhat of a cult wine, largely because the vineyard is planted with the same clones of Cabernet that are on the Grace Family Vineyard. Moreover, the wine is made by one of Napa Valley's most fashionable consultants, Heidi Barrett. The 1993 exhibits an elegant, more laid back style than several previous vintages. The deep ruby/purple color is followed by copious amounts of toasty, smoky new oak, and attractive currant aromas. The wine possesses sweet, ripe fruit, medium body, moderate tannin, and a long, nicely textured, spicy finish. It may develop into an outstanding wine with another 2–4 years of cellaring. It should age well for 15+ years.

The 1994 reveals that vintage's sweeter fruit, and harmonious personality. It has a dark ruby/purple color, followed by plenty of blackberry and black currantlike fruit in the nose, complemented by some subtle toasty oak. The wine displays a richer, riper personality, medium to full body, more layers of fruit, and finer integration of wood, tannin, and acidity. It is an impressively endowed, outstanding, well-balanced Cabernet that admirably reflects its Stag's Leap origin. Anticipated maturity: 1999–2017.

HAVENS WINE CELLARS (NAPA)

1996	Bourriquot	Napa	D 91
1995	Bourriquot Proprietary Red Wine	Napa	D 89
1994	Bourriquot Proprietary Red Wine	Napa	D 88+
1993	Bourriquot Proprietary Red Wine	Napa	D 89

1995 Merlot	Napa	D	85+
1993 Merlot	Napa	C	86
1996 Merlot Reserve	Napa	D	90
1995 Merlot Reserve	Napa	D	87
1993 Merlot Reserve	Napa	D	90
1996 Syrah	Carneros	D	89
1994 Syrah	Carneros	D	90
1993 Syrah	Carneros	C	91

Mike Havens, working out of a warehouse in the city of Napa, appears to have settled into an admirable pattern, producing richer and richer Merlots, complemented by a fine Syrah, and a Cheval Blanc-inspired proprietary red wine called Bourriquot. There is also a small quantity of Sauvignon Blanc. Havens supplements his Carneros vineyard with purchased grapes.

There are two cuvées of Merlot, a softer cuvée designed for early consumption, and a more concentrated, larger-scaled Reserve offering. Recent vintages have moved toward less acidification and riper fruit, resulting in wines with significantly more charm, flesh, and succulence. The 1993 Merlot exhibits a deep ruby color, a spicy, coffee, smoky, black cherry-scented nose, medium body, good suppleness, and a fine finish. Drink it before the end of the century. The 1993 Merlot Reserve exhibits fat, curranty, cherry fruit, medium to full body, excellent purity, and a succulent texture. The 1993 Reserve should drink well for at least a decade.

This Merlot specialist has fashioned a 1995 Merlot that is medium bodied, supple, and round, with a pleasant chocolatey, berry fruitiness, soft tannin, decent acidity, and subtle French oak. It is a mid-weight Merlot to drink over the next 5–6 years. Deeper and richer, the 1995 Merlot Reserve reveals a textbook black cherry, coffee, tobacco-scented nose, attractive new oak, medium body, and round, generous, plush flavors. A blend of 89% Merlot and 11% Cabernet Franc, it should drink well for 7–8 years.

The finest wine of the Bourriquots is the 1995. This 66% Cabernet Franc/34% Merlot blend is winemaker Havens' Napa Valley imitation of Bordeaux's famed Cheval Blanc. It reveals a deep ruby/purple color, followed by big, spicy, mineral, licorice, floral-tinged, black currant aromas, medium body, excellent to outstanding fruit concentration, a soft, layered palate, and a rich, moderately tannic finish. The wine needs 2–3 years of cellaring, but it should keep for 15–18 years, possibly meriting an outstanding rating. The 1994 Bourriquot is also a blend of two-thirds Cabernet Franc and one-third Merlot. It reveals a deep color, some attractive, leafy, currantylike scents, medium body, plenty of tannin, excellent richness, and a firm, structured finish. Cellar it for 2–3 years and drink it over the subsequent 15 years. The 1993 Bourriquot reveals loads of sweet black currant fruit gently touched by toast oak and herbs, as well as a juicy, voluptuous texture, moderately sweet tannin, an expansive midpalate, and a fine finish. It should drink well for 15+ years.

The distinctive dark purple-colored 1994 Syrah exhibits an exaggerated, flamboyant set of aromatics (minty, black raspberry, and cassis scents). The wine is soft and medium to full bodied, with excellent richness, well-integrated tannin and acidity, and spicy wood. Already delicious, this wine should drink well for another decade. The 1993 Syrah offers up a big, smoky, bacon fat, and cassis-scented nose with Hermitage-like aromas and texture. Its sweet, overripe jammy fruit and excellent density and full body must conceal the wine's tannin, although not much is evident when tasting the wine. This will be a forward, flattering, mouth-filling Syrah for drinking during its first 10–12 years of life.

Aside from a straightforward, rough-textured 1996 Merlot Havens' other offerings performed exceptionally well. The 1996 Merlot Reserve should satisfy Merlot lovers given its deep ruby color, and rich, chocolatey, weedy, intensely smoky and seductive aromatics. Lushly textured, with impressive black cherry, chocolate, and berry flavors, this full-bodied, elegant, stylish Merlot reveals plenty of depth and richness, but no hard edges. Drink it over the next 7–8 years. The 1996 Bourriquot, Napa's answer to Cheval Blanc (each is made from a blend of two-thirds Cabernet Franc and one-third Merlot), offers an exotic, complex, evolved, coffee bean and berry-scented nose. In the mouth, this rich, full-bodied wine exhibits sweet tannin, low acidity, a lush texture, and a moderately long finish. With its gobs of fruit, expansive palate, and distinctive personality, it is more than a good imitation of Cheval Blanc. Drink it over the next 10–15 years. Lastly, the 1996 Syrah, while not a blockbuster, is an attractive tar, cassis, bacon, and smoky-scented wine with medium to full body, excellent concentration, soft tannin, and a round, generous, expansive mouth-feel. This delectable, elegantly styled Syrah is ideal for drinking over the next 5–9 years.

HAYWOOD WINERY (SONOMA)

1994 Zinfandel Los Chamizal Vineyard	Sonoma	C	85
1993 Zinfandel Los Chamizal Vineyard Rocky Terrace	Sonoma	C	89
1994 Zinfandel Rocky Terrace	Sonoma	C	86

The 1993 Zinfandel Los Chamizal Rocky Terrace is the finest Haywood Estate offering I have tasted. With its designer label and heavy, tall, Italian glass bottle, something special inside is to be expected. Readers are not likely to be disappointed. This is a rich, full-bodied, intensely flavored, well-focused, muscular, impressively endowed Zinfandel. Supple and lusty, with a long finish, it should drink well for 7–8 years. By the way, a Haywood 1993 Zinfandel from the Los Chamizal Vineyard packaged in a standard bottle, without the Rocky Terrace designation, tasted mediocre next to this impressive bottling.

I had tasted the 1994 Los Chamizal prior to bottling and thought very highly of it, but I worried about this winery's tendency to process their wines excessively. Now in the bottle, the 1994 Zinfandel Los Chamizal is a ripe, elegant, soft, richly fruity wine with adequate acidity, medium body, and good length. It requires drinking over the next several years. It lacks the multilayered feel and richness it had prior to bottling. The 1994 Zinfandel Rocky Terrace is cut from the same mold, but richer, with riper fruit, and more glycerin and length. Consume it over the next 2–3 years.

HENDRY RANCH (NAPA)

1995 Zinfandel Block 7	Napa	C	80
1994 Zinfandel Block 7	Napa	C	88

The 1995 is an evolved, medium ruby-colored, intensely spicy Zinfandel that is light, open knit, soft, and one-dimensional. It requires drinking over the next 1–2 years. The 1994 is a sexy, succulent, hedonistic style of Zinfandel with a medium deep ruby color, moderate body, a Pomerol-like lushness and roundness, copious quantities of black cherry and cranberry fruit, and a low-acid, lush texture. Drinking this voluptuously styled, medium-weight wine is fun! It should be consumed over the next 3–4 years.

HESS COLLECTION WINERY (NAPA)

1995 Cabernet Sauvignon	Napa	C	89
1994 Cabernet Sauvignon	Napa	B	86
1993 Cabernet Sauvignon	Napa	C	85
1993 Cabernet Sauvignon Reserve	Napa	D	86

1995 Chardonnay	Napa	C	86
1993 Hess Select Cabernet Sauvignon	California	B	85
1993 Hess Select Pinot Noir Unfiltered	California	B	86

The smoky, oaky-styled 1995 Chardonnay possesses buttery, applelike fruit, a notion of roasted nuts, medium body, and a quick finish. It is a straightforward, mouth-filling, savory wine for drinking over the next year.

The 1995 Cabernet Sauvignon possesses admirable potential, yet the high level of hard tannin in the finish raises reservations about its overall balance. Nevertheless, there are plenty of positive characteristics to be found in this opaque purple-colored wine. Exhibiting sweet, earthy, cassis-scented fruit, the wine is medium to full bodied and dense, with potentially outstanding raw materials. Let's hope the winery does not strip the aromas, fruit, and body out of the wine by too much processing prior to bottling. If this wine remains intact, it should be one of the finest regular Cabernets Hess Collection has yet produced.

The polite, understated 1993 Cabernet Sauvignon is cut from a similar mold to the 1992, with more red than black currant fruit, medium body, a delicate personality, and immediate accessibility. Drink it over the next 3–4 years.

The Hess Select 1993 Pinot Noir, priced under $10, offers plenty of flavor. It exhibits a light to medium ruby color, attractive cherry and raspberry fruit, medium body, and a velvety texture. If it had a Côte d'Or appellation on it, no one would quibble about paying $25, but at $10, this is an authentic Pinot Noir for drinking over the next 3–4 years. The Hess Select 1993 Cabernet Sauvignon is also a noteworthy value, offering up plenty of fleshy cassis fruit in an uncomplicated, drinkable, supple style. It is a cleanly made, perfumed, mouth-filling wine for drinking over the next 4–6 years.

The 1994 Cabernet Sauvignon was disappointing considering both the winery and the vintage. The wine exhibits a dark ruby color, followed by a moderately intense nose of vanillin and red/black currant fruit. In the mouth, it is medium bodied, with good depth, a heavy overlay of wood, light to moderate tannin, and a short finish. This 1994 Cabernet should be drunk over the next 5–7 years. The dark ruby-colored 1993 Cabernet Sauvignon Reserve reveals a similar heavy vanillin/toasty oak character. Although dominated by wood, this wine offers compact, ripe black currant fruit in a medium-bodied format. Like its younger sibling, the muscular, tannic 1993 Reserve is technically flawless, but hedonistically, it is uninspiring. It should be consumed between now and 2005.

HIDDEN CELLARS (MENDOCINO)

1995 Alchemy	Mendocino	C	84
1995 Petite Sirah Eagle Point Ranch	Mendocino	C	87
1996 Zinfandel Heritage Eagle Point Ranch	Mendocino	D	86?
1996 Zinfandel Heritage Ft. Hitzman	Mendocino	D	86
1996 Zinfandel Heritage The Sorcery	Mendocino	D	87
1994 Zinfandel McAdams Vineyard	Mendocino	C	86
1993 Zinfandel McAdams Vineyard	Mendocino	C	87
1996 Zinfandel Old Vines	Mendocino	C	86
1994 Zinfandel Old Vines	Mendocino	C	87

The style of Zinfandel produced by Hidden Cellars emphasizes the naked expression of Zinfandel fruit, without any makeup, particularly new oak. For that reason, fruit lovers will find these wines to be authentic, textbook examples of Zinfandel. The 1994 Zinfandel Old Vines is deeper colored than the McAdams Vineyard offering. It possesses a briery, raspberry-scented nose, a deep ruby color, crisp acidity, a fresh, lively mouth-feel, medium body, and a surprising 14.2% alcohol, a component I found remarkably well concealed. This fruity, well-structured Zinfandel can be drunk slightly chilled over the next 3–4 years. The light ruby-colored 1994 Zinfandel McAdams Vineyard offers up a seductive, spicy, raspberry-scented nose, followed by a medium-bodied wine exhibiting clean winemaking, tart acidity, and a fresh, lively finish. Both of these wines would make ideal accompaniments to pasta or grilled dishes.

The medium ruby-colored, spicy, richly fruity 1993 McAdams Vineyard Zinfandel displays medium to full body, a soft, velvety texture, and a heady, lush finish. Already delicious, it will offer ideal drinking over the next 4–5 years.

The 1995 Alchemy (a 67% Sauvignon/33% Semillon blend) offers a vegetal, green, spicy nose, ripe fruit, medium body, and an attractive texture. I subtracted points for the greenness in the nose, but otherwise this is a competent Sauvignon. Petite Sirah lovers should seek out Hidden Cellars' 1995 Eaglepoint Ranch. This dense, purple-colored, thick, rich wine may be short on complexity, but it is big on intense flavors and extract. There is still plenty of tannin to be shed, but I would not be surprised to see this wine merit an even higher score after 5–6 years of cellaring. It is purely made and highly extracted, with copious amounts of black currant fruit intertwined with spice. Full bodied, tannic, and tough in the mouth, this impeccably pure wine should keep for 15+ years.

The 1996s make an interesting group of wines, although the Eagle Point and Ft. Hitzman Heritage cuvées border on being excessively alcoholic for the amount of extract they contain. They are large-scaled wines without as much complexity as is found in such high alcohol Zinfandels as those from Turley or Martinelli. Readers will be impressed with their size, saturated colors, and massive feel in the mouth. For example, the 1996 Zinfandel Heritage (59% from the Forrer Vineyard and 41% from the Hitzman Vineyard) is a monolithic, high-alcohol, thick, chewy, tough-textured wine with good depth and richness, but it comes across as rustic and ponderous. The same can be said for the 1996 Zinfandel Eagle Point Ranch Heritage. With 16% alcohol, it is a big, impressively extracted, profoundly concentrated, but essentially one-dimensional wine that is short on charm and complexity. I should note that these two wines could gain more complexity, and merit higher scores as they will certainly last 8–10 years given their high extract and alcohol.

The 1996 Zinfandel Old Vines is an elegant, briery wine displaying the varietal's classic sour cherry, peppery, and raspberry character. Medium bodied and clean, it will provide ideal drinking over the next 2–3 years. Lastly, the 1996 Zinfandel The Sorcery exhibits a smoky, American oak, and cherry-scented nose, supple, round, low-acid flavors, good depth, and more charm and finesse than the other three offerings. However, it should be drunk over the next 1–2 years.

PAUL HOBBS (SONOMA)

1994 Cabernet Sauvignon Hyde Vineyard	Carneros	D	84
1994 Cabernet Sauvignon Liparita Vineyard	Howell Mountain	D	85

The absence of any real texture in these wines, combined with their high acidity, and cool climate taste (red currants and strawberries), make for a compressed style of Cabernet. The 1994 Cabernet Sauvignon Liparita Vineyard is made in a pure, yet linear, extremely subdued and restrained style that comes across as too tart for my palate, but perhaps others will find it more alluring. It will keep well given its high-acid profile. Anticipated maturity: 1999–2010. The 1994 Cabernet Sauvignon Hyde Vineyard reveals a plummy/purple color, intriguing cranberry and other red fruit aromas and flavors, high acidity (especially for this vintage), medium body, and a one-dimensional personality. It should age well for 10–12 years.

HOP KILN WINERY (SONOMA)

1996 Zinfandel	Sonoma	C	86
1994 Zinfandel Estate M. Griffin Vineyard	Russian River	C	89
1996 Zinfandel Primitivo	Sonoma	C	87
1994 Zinfandel Primitivo	Sonoma	C	90
1993 Zinfandel Primitivo	Sonoma	C	87

Two highly competent 1996 offerings from Hop Kiln, the dark ruby/purple-colored 1996 Zinfandel exhibits tangy, briery, red cherry fruit, medium body, and a spicy, clean, zesty finish. It should drink well over the next 1–2 years. The 1996 Zinfandel Primitivo displays a more saturated dark ruby/purple color, as well as peppery, spicy, black raspberry and cherry fruit intermingled with subtle oak. Medium to full bodied, with dryness in the finish, this robust, flavorful, mouth-filling Zinfandel should drink well for 3–4 years. Both of these wines were bottled unfined and unfiltered.

Two fine 1994 Zinfandels from a producer who consistently turns out fine wines, the Hop Kiln 1994 Zinfandel M. Griffin Vineyard offers up a sweet, peppery, spicy, exuberant set of aromatics, medium to full body, good density, moderately high alcohol (14.5%), fine ripeness, and a muscular, chewy, rich finish. This excellent, cleanly made, rich, gorgeously fruity, chewy Zinfandel should be drunk over the next 5–6 years. I have a slight preference for the 1994 Primitivo, a wine with outstanding ripeness and richness, full body, a real mid-palate, and a spicy, sumptuous finish. It is a knockout Zinfandel for drinking over the next 5–7 years.

The medium dark ruby-colored 1993 Zinfandel displays a briery, wild berry-scented nose, full-bodied, dense, concentrated flavors, a broad, expansive palate, clean winemaking, and moderate tannin in the finish. It will benefit from 1–2 years of cellaring and should keep for a decade. It is a full-throttle Zinfandel, coming in at 14.7% alcohol.

HOWELL MOUNTAIN VINEYARDS (HOWELL MOUNTAIN)

1997 Cabernet Sauvignon	Howell Mountain	D	?
1996 Cabernet Sauvignon	Howell Mountain	D	?
1997 Zinfandel Beatty Ranch	Howell Mountain	D	90+
1996 Zinfandel Beatty Ranch	Howell Mountain	D	90
1997 Zinfandel Black-Sears Vineyard	Howell Mountain	D	(90–92)
1996 Zinfandel Black-Sears Vineyard	Howell Mountain	D	87
1997 Zinfandel Old Vine	Howell Mountain	D	90
1996 Zinfandel Old Vine	Howell Mountain	C	89+?

I have my doubts about these two Cabernet Sauvignons. This new winery, which tends to make wines from a blend of two Howell Mountain vineyards, Black-Sears and Beatty Ranch, has produced structured, tannic, hard, astringent Cabernets that seem somewhat clipped and compressed. There is plenty of depth and ripe fruit, as well as an unmistakable minerality, but their tannin level scares me. I will reserve judgment until these wines have had several years in bottle.

Far more interesting and better balanced are three beautiful 1997 Zinfandels, made from extremely old vines. The 1997 Zinfandel Old Vine (from 25- and 80-year-old vines) exhibits a deep ruby/purple color, a fragrant, black cherry, mineral, peppery nose, explosive fruit, low acidity, and a rich, glycerin-endowed, fleshy, hedonistic mouth-feel. It will provide ideal drinking over the next 4–5 years. It tips the scales at 15.5% alcohol, so be forewarned. The 1997 Zinfandel Beatty Ranch (from 80-year-old vines) is more structured and tannic. The nose offers up black raspberry fruit intertwined with dusty soil, pepper, and mineral scents. Medium to full bodied, moderately tannic yet gorgeously pure and layered, this Zinfandel may be even better with another 6–12 months of bottle age. It should keep for 7–8 years. Lastly, the 1997 Zinfandel Black-Sears Vineyard (made from 25-year-old vines) is a fat, chewy, full-bodied, beautifully etched offering with gobs of black cherry, raspberry, and blackberry fruit. It reveals more glycerin and a chewier mouth-feel than its two siblings, as well as a plump, hedonistic, opulently textured finish. I would opt for consuming this brawny (16% alcohol) yet seductive Zinfandel over the next 4–5 years.

These wines are made by Littorai's Ted Lemon. As the numbers attest, they are exceptionally fine Zinfandels. The least impressive is the 1996 Zinfandel Black-Sears Vineyard. While it admirably conceals its 15% alcohol, this dark ruby/purple-colored wine possesses a berry, briery nose, firm, austere flavors with deep cherry fruit, and a structured, tightly knit personality. Although very good to excellent, it comes across as too structured. Time will tell, but this is a big, well-delineated Zinfandel with considerable power, as well as aging potential of 7–8 years. The outstanding 1996 Zinfandel Beatty Ranch received a "wow" in my tasting notes. At 15.5% alcohol, one would suspect it would be hot, but this wine is super-concentrated and beautifully balanced. It boasts a deep ruby/purple color, followed by knockout aromatics of black raspberries, minerals, and spice. Deep, full bodied, and concentrated, with the alcohol well concealed, this large-scaled, intricately detailed, intensely flavored wine can be drunk now, or cellared for 7–10 years (atypically long for Zinfandel). Nearly as superb is the 1996 Zinfandel Old Vine. It delivers a similar alcoholic clout (15.5%), but in this case, some heat shows up at the back of the palate. The wine displays a dark plum color, and sweet blackberry, raspberry, and cherry notes dosed with subtle oak and spice. Full bodied, rich, and slightly hot in the heady, dense finish, it should drink well for 5–6 years.

JADE MOUNTAIN (NAPA)

1996	Côtes du Soleil	California	B	85
1994	Côtes du Soleil	California	B	86
1994	Les Jumeaux	California	C	88
1996	Marsanne et Viognier	Napa	C	85
1993	Merlot	Napa Valley	C	86
1995	Merlot Caldwell Vineyard	Napa	D	82?
1996	Mourvèdre	California	C	85
1996	La Provençal	California	C	85
1994	La Provençal	California	C	87
1995	Syrah	Carneros/Napa	C	80?
1994	Syrah	Napa	C	87
1996	Syrah Hudson Vineyard	Napa	C	86
1995	Syrah Mt. Veeder	Napa	D	88+
1996	Syrah Paras Vineyard	Napa	D	90
1997	Vin Gris de Mourvèdre	California	B	88
1997	Viognier Paras Vineyard	Napa	D	90

The 1997 Viognier Paras Vineyard (from a hillside vineyard on Mt. Veeder) is a full-bodied, honeyed, floral style of Viognier with good texture, chewy richness, and a lush, pure finish. Consume it over the next year. Another underrated wine, the 1997 Vin Gris de Mourvèdre (95% Mourvèdre and 5% Viognier) is a serious dry rosé offering copious aromas of raspberry and strawberry fruit. The wine's fleshy, full-bodied style is undoubtedly due to the addition of Viognier. Drink this gloriously fruity rosé with spicy food.

The two 1996 Syrahs offer contrasting styles. The more serious 1996 Syrah Paras Vineyard, reveals smoky bacon fat and cassis aromas. The wine is medium to full bodied, lush, nicely textured, expansive, and rich with no hard edges. Drink this seductive Syrah over the next 7–8 years. The 1996 Syrah Hudson Vineyard, while supple and easy to drink, does not possess the concentration of the Paras Vineyard offering. There is more structure and the same smoky, black currant fruit, but the wine is monolithic and foursquare. It should be drunk over the next 5–6 years.

Overall, the following releases from Jade Mountain tasted far less impressive than previous efforts, but there are some enticing wines in this portfolio. The 1996 Marsanne et Viognier possesses an uncomplex, fruit cocktail-like nose, medium body, good purity, but not a great deal of aromatic dimension or flavor complexity. It is a nice, chunky, straightforward wine to drink over the next year.

The dark ruby-colored 1996 Mourvèdre exhibits a spicy, earthy nose with a moderate level of sweet red berry fruit. In the mouth, this is a lighter-styled Mourvèdre, without much body or tannin, a superficial ripe fruitiness, and a pleasant, charming finish. I do not generally consider Mourvèdre to be a casual sipping wine, but this one might qualify. Drink it over the next several years. Jade Mountain's 1996 La Provençal, a Mourvèdre/Syrah blend, displays a medium ruby color, and a smoky, raspberrylike nose with a vague notion of spice. More black fruits (primarily cassis) make an appearance in this soft, round, medium-bodied, straightforward, easy-to-drink wine. It should be consumed over the next 2–3 years. The medium ruby-colored 1996 Côtes du Soleil exhibits a monochromatic aromatic profile consisting of red berries. Medium bodied, fruity, soft, and pleasant yet lacking character, this wine should drink well for 2–3 years. The 1995 Merlot Caldwell Vineyard possesses a medium dark ruby color, and a tight bouquet consisting primarily of earth and toasty oak. There is some ripe, chocolatey, berry fruit on the attack, but that quickly dissipates to an attenuated, compact, compressed style. I am not sure this wine will ever fully blossom.

The two 1995 Syrahs offer contrasting personalities. The 1995 Syrah Carneros/Napa displays a healthy dark ruby color, a muted nose of earth, spice, and black fruits, an ungenerous mouth-feel (some might call it elegant), and a lean, austere finish. It is unimpressive by the standards of this winery's previous efforts. In total contrast, the 1995 Syrah Mt. Veeder is excellent. It possesses a dense, deep ruby/purple color, followed by a provocative nose of sweet black plums, currants, smoke, and licorice. In the mouth, the wine is ripe, tannic, backward, dense, full bodied, and pure. This is an excellent, possibly outstanding Syrah that requires 3–4 years of bottle age; it should keep for 15 years.

The 1994 Côtes du Soleil (a Grenache/Mourvèdre blend) exhibits an attractive, medium dark ruby color, good ripe berry fruit, pepper, herbs, and spice, medium body, fine purity, and a soft, round finish. It will provide uncomplicated, tasty drinking over the next 3–4 years. The 1994 La Provençal (a Syrah, Mourvèdre, and Grenache blend) is cut from the same mold—soft and round, with spicy, herb, olive, and peppery fruit, medium body, adequate acidity, and a clean, forthright personality. Drink it over the next 2–3 years. The 1994 Syrah is a lighter-styled Syrah offering gushing levels of sweet, jammy, berry fruit and cassis. It is made in a low-acid, flattering, soft style with good ripeness. Drink this easy, accessible-styled Syrah over the next 4–5 years. The 1994 Les Jumeaux (a Cabernet Sauvignon/Mourvèdre/Syrah blend) remains one of my favorite wines from Jade Mountain. It offers an intriguing black cherry, cassis, herb, pepper, spicy component, medium to full body, some tannin, good grip, a savory mouth-feel, and a well-delineated, spicy finish. This wine will continue to improve for another 12–18 months and will keep for 7–8+ years. The 1993 Merlot, made from fruit grown in Napa Valley's Caldwell Vineyard, initially exhibits tart acidity, but it opens to reveal soft, coffee, berry scents and flavors in a medium-bodied, compact but cleanly made, attractive style. Drink it over the next 3–4 years.

JAFFURS (SANTA BARBARA)

1997 Roussanne Stolpman Family Vineyard	Santa Barbara	C	86
1996 Syrah	Santa Barbara	C	84?
1995 Syrah	Santa Barbara	D	86
1994 Syrah	Santa Barbara	D	90
1996 Syrah Thompson Vineyard	Santa Barbara	D	87
1997 Viognier	Santa Barbara	C	88

Stolpman Family Vineyard is one of the large new vineyards coming on line (a percentage of the production will be estate bottled under its name). This has been a source for high-quality Rhône Ranger grapes such as Roussanne and Syrah, as well as other varietals. The 1997 Roussanne Stolpman Family Vineyard exhibits an intriguing orange skin/rose petal-scented nose, as well as grapey, concentrated flavors, medium body, elegance and glycerin, and enough acidity to provide delineation. It should drink well for 12–18 months. More interesting, the 1997 Viognier offers aromas of orange marmalade, honeysuckle, lemon butter, and apricots, as well as full body, zesty acidity, and a pure, refreshing, long finish. Viognier's appeal lies in its aromatics, so enjoy this offering over the next year before the aromas deteriorate.

The 1996 Syrah would have been better if it had not had such tart acidity, making me wonder if much of it was added. The wine exhibits a dark ruby color, attractive blackberry and smoky notes, a compressed texture, but good Syrah character. Less acidity would have made the wine taste more expansive as well as given it more flesh and charm. Drink it over the next 2–4 years. The 1996 Syrah Thompson Vineyard offers blackberry liqueur aromas intermixed with melted asphalt, smoke, and pepper. There is excellent richness, fine purity, and a chewy, medium-bodied personality. The acidity is well balanced with the wine's fruit and structural components. It should drink well for 5–6 years.

The 1995 Jaffurs Syrah possesses a medium ruby color, followed by a sweet nose of red and black fruits. In the mouth, the wine is medium bodied and soft, with some tannin, low acidity, and attractive ripeness. Drink this medium-weight, forward-styled Syrah over the next 4–5 years.

Wow! The big, plum, cassis, smoke, bacon fat, and toasty new oak-scented 1994 Syrah offers a gorgeous mouthful of rich fruit. It possesses full body, sweet tannin, excellent purity, and an exceptionally long finish. It should drink well for 7–8 years. Who are these folks?

JARVIS VINEYARDS (NAPA)

1994 Cabernet Franc Estate Grown	Napa	D	87
1993 Cabernet Sauvignon Estate Grown	Napa	E	87
1995 Chardonnay Estate	Napa	D	86
1993 Lake William Proprietary Red Wine Estate Grown	Napa	D	90
1994 Merlot Estate Grown	Napa	D	88

The 1995 Chardonnay Estate is an attractive, spicy, woody, medium- to full-bodied Chardonnay with creamy, Burgundian, leesy notes, good depth, and a pleasant finish. It should drink well for 12–18 months.

The 1994 Cabernet Franc possesses a deep ruby color, a fragrant, cedary, spicy, red currant nose, sweet fruit, medium body, and a sense of elegance and class. Already drinking well, this wine should continue to evolve for 7–8 years. The dark ruby/purple-colored 1994 Merlot Estate Grown offers plenty of sweet berry fruit, with a touch of chocolate, spice, and oak in the nose, medium to full body, excellent concentration, and well-integrated tannin and acidity. Drink it over the next 5–6 years. The 1993 Cabernet Sauvignon Estate Grown displays a dark ruby/purple color, followed by a straightforward but well-endowed nose of cassis fruit, vanilla, and earth. Medium bodied and moderately tannic, with rich, sweet fruit, but not a great deal of complexity, this wine will benefit from another year of cellaring; it should drink well for 7–8 years. Lastly, the 1993 Lake William Proprietary Red Wine (a blend of 64% Cabernet Sauvignon and 36% Cabernet Franc) is still young and unevolved, but sweet, pure, and rich, with gobs of red and black currant fruit, a nice touch of spicy oak, and a medium- to full-bodied, concentrated finish. It requires another 2–3 years of cellaring. Overall, these are nicely crafted, stylized, Bordeaux-like red wines.

JSJ SIGNATURE SERIES (CALIFORNIA)

1996	Cabernet Sauvignon Veeder Peak Vineyard	Napa	E	91+
1996	Cabernet Sauvignon Buckeye Vineyard	Alexander Valley	D	90
1997	Chardonnay Cambria Vineyard	Santa Barbara	E	94
1997	Chardonnay Camelot Vineyard	Santa Maria	C	89
1997	Chardonnay Paradise Vineyard	Arroyo Secco	C	87
1997	Chardonnay Upper Barn Vineyard	Sonoma	E	93
1997	Chardonnay Verité	Santa Maria	E	93
1996	Merlot Alexander Valley Estate	Alexander Valley	D	89
1996	Merlot Buckeye Vineyard	Alexander Valley	D	88+
1997	Pinot Noir Arrendell Vineyard	Russian River	E	91
1995	Zinfandel Veeder Peak	Napa	D	90

This series of wines has been inaugurated by Kendall-Jackson's owner, Jess Jackson, to highlight the particular characteristics of his finest vineyards. All of these offerings are meant to compete at the pinnacle of the quality hierarchy. Quantities are small (250–500 cases), and they are packaged in heavy, expensive bottles. There is a bevy of impressive Chardonnays, all barrel fermented, aged in 100% new French oak, and given considerable lees stirring. For example, the 1997 Chardonnay Camelot Vineyard offers a layered, honeyed, tropical fruit-scented nose with notes of smoky oak. Full-bodied, hedonistic, sexy, and ostentatious, it should drink well for several years. The 1997 Chardonnay Paradise Vineyard is more structured and backward, exhibiting gravelly/stony scents in the nose, an unmistakable minerality, medium body, and more acidity. This Chablis-styled Chardonnay should drink well for 2–4 years. Even more impressive is the profound 1997 Chardonnay Cambria Vineyard. Sensational tropical fruit aromas soar from a glass of this spectacularly endowed, full-bodied, concentrated wine. There is terrific stuffing, lush texture, and a formidable finish revealing copious amounts of glycerin and extract. Oak adds nice spice, but does not dominate this flamboyant Chardonnay, which should drink well for 3–4 years. The powerful 1997 Chardonnay Upper Barn (the vineyard made famous by Marcassin's Helen Turley and John Wetlaufer) is not as dramatic as the Cambria Vineyard, but it displays more structure and liquid stone notes, as well as a lemony, buttery, spicy personality. Impressively concentrated, with considerable power and length, this wine may turn out to be the longest lived of these top-flight Chardonnays, lasting for 4–5 or more years.

The red wines include a terrific dark ruby-colored 1997 Pinot Noir Arrendell Vineyard. This offering reveals notes of spice, jammy plums, and dried cherry fruit intertwined with toasty oak. A concentrated, medium- to full-bodied, complete, savory, delicious Pinot Noir, it promises to evolve nicely for 5–6 years. There are two single-vineyard Merlots in the JSJ Signature Series. The 1996 Merlot Buckeye Vineyard possesses a dark ruby/purple color, as well as a tightly knit, lavishly oaked nose with black cherry fruit, herbs, white chocolate, and spice scents. Medium to full bodied, with good flesh and high tannin, it requires 2–3 more years of cellaring and should keep for 12–15. The dark ruby/purple-colored 1996 Merlot Alexander Valley Estate offers up a moderately intense, restrained nose of cranberry liqueur intermixed with vanillin and spice. It is a rich, medium- to full-bodied, tannic, backward wine in need of 2–4 years of cellaring. It should age well for 15 years or longer. While it is an impressive offering, it was closed when I tasted it in late September.

The outstanding 1996 Cabernet Sauvignon Buckeye Vineyard is destined to last for two decades. The wine boasts an opaque purple color, and a rich nose of minerals, black currants, and spicy oak. A dense, full-bodied powerhouse, with nicely integrated wood, acidity, and tannin, this firm Cabernet is loaded with extract and richness. The blend contains small quantities of Cabernet Franc and Merlot. Anticipated maturity: 2001–2020. The opaque purple-colored 1996 Cabernet Sauvignon Veeder Peak offers a Margaux-like nose of spring flower garden scents intermixed with black currants, smoky new oak, and spice. Dense and full bodied, with outstanding purity and richness, this brawny, muscular, concentrated wine should be at its best between 2003 and 2022. Another topflight offering is the outstanding 1995 Zinfandel Veeder Peak. It reveals surprising elegance, along with jammy raspberry and blackberry fruit. Medium to full bodied, with good overall balance and freshness, and pepper and briery fruit in the long, glycerin-endowed finish, it should drink well for 3–5 years.

Within this JSJ Signature Series will be a wine made by a former winemaker from Kendall-Jackson. In 1997, John Hawley produced a special cuvée called Verité. This is Jess Jackson's acknowledgment of the contribution made by the topflight winemakers who have worked at Kendall-Jackson. It is an admirable goal. John Hawley has turned out 200 cases of superb Chardonnay. The 1997 (from the Santa Maria Valley) offers flamboyant tropical fruit intermixed with toast, smoke, and buttered citrus. With a honeyed texture, admirable underlying acidity, and heady, lusty finish, this sexy, corpulent Chardonnay will offer sumptuous drinking over the next 2–3 years.

JUDD'S HILL (NAPA)

1995 Cabernet Sauvignon	Napa	C	87
1994 Cabernet Sauvignon	Napa	C	90

This 2,000 case winery located in the Conn Valley, behind the Seavey Winery, has turned out an outstanding 1994 Cabernet Sauvignon. The wine exhibits a saturated dark ruby/purple color, sweet, ripe, black currant fruit, low acidity, mature tannin, and a well-balanced, flamboyant, succulent, opulent texture with layers of rich fruit nicely married with smoky oak. This hedonistic, forward, Pomerol-styled Cabernet can be drunk now as well as over the next 12–15 years.

The medium-bodied 1995 Cabernet displays an unmistakable minty, red/black currant-scented nose, medium body, an elegant, restrained style, very good concentration, and fine length. It bears a striking resemblance to some of the Cabernet Sauvignons produced by Napa Valley's Johnson-Turnbull winery. This very good, possibly excellent Cabernet Sauvignon will age well for 10–12 years.

ROBERT KEENAN (NAPA)

1996	Cabernet Sauvignon	Napa	D	88
1995	Cabernet Sauvignon	Napa	D	87
1995	Cabernet Sauvignon Hillside Estate	Napa	D	88
1994	Cabernet Sauvignon Hillside Estate	Napa	D	88
1996	Chardonnay	Napa	C	86
1995	Chardonnay	Napa	C	85
1996	Merlot	Napa	D	88
1995	Merlot	Napa	D	85
1994	Merlot	Napa	D	86

After years of producing compressed, high-acid wines, Keenan (Nils Venge is their consultant) has begun turning out fleshy, attractive, and by today's standards reasonably priced products. The 1996 Chardonnay is a richly fruity (ripe pears) wine with medium body, and excellent purity. It should be drunk over the next 1–2 years. The 1995 Chardonnay, made from purchased grapes, is a lighter, more elegant, clean, straightforward style of Chardonnay to drink over the next 1–2 years.

I had a slight preference for the 1996 red wines over the 1995s, but they are all very good to excellent efforts. The 1995 Cabernet Sauvignon exhibits a dense ruby color, full body, plenty of deep, uncomplicated, exuberant black currant fruit, spice from new oak, and a fleshy finish. This wine should drink well for 7–8 years. The dark ruby/purple-colored 1995 Merlot is more astringent, with rough, more jagged tannin, and lacking richness in the midpalate. Nevertheless, it is a spicy, well-made wine with good density, but a monolithic personality. It should drink well for 5–6 years.

The 1995 Cabernet Sauvignon Hillside Estate displays the winery's softer, more velvety-textured style of wine without the tough overlay of tannin and compact midpalate. The 1995 possesses a deep ruby/purple color, spicy, ripe fruit, power and intensity, and moderate tannin in the finish. While it may never merit an exceptional rating, the wine should score in the upper eighties after bottling.

The dense purple-colored 1996 Cabernet Sauvignon possesses copious quantities of jammy black currant fruit, earth, and smoke in its moderately intense aromatics. Medium to full bodied, concentrated, spicy, and mouth-filling, I would not be surprised to see more nuances emerge as this wine evolves. It will be accessible when released, and capable of lasting for 10–15 years. The 1996 Merlot is much sweeter and richer than the 1995, with smoky, chocolatey, black cherry fruit, good density, and a clean, long, tannic finish. It should drink well for 10 years.

The 1994 Merlot is well made, with ripe, black cherry and berry fruit, some spice, medium body, and a clean finish with light to moderate tannin. It should drink well for 7–8 years. The 1994 Cabernet Sauvignon Hillside Estate exhibits a dark ruby/purple color, followed by a sweet, black cherry, earthy, mineral-scented nose, and a fleshy midpalate with depth and ripe fruit. Some rough tannin springs up in the finish. This wine will benefit from 4–5 years of cellaring and keep for up to 15.

KENDALL-JACKSON (CALIFORNIA)

1995	Cabernet Franc Grand Reserve	California	C	84
1994	Cabernet Franc Grand Reserve	California	C	82
1995	Cabernet Sauvignon Grand Reserve	California	D	83+

1994 Cabernet Sauvignon Grand Reserve	California	D	87
1995 Cabernet Sauvignon Vintner's Reserve	California	C	84
1997 Chardonnay Grand Reserve	California	D	88
1996 Chardonnay Grand Reserve	California	C	85
1997 Chardonnay Vintner's Reserve	California	C	86
1997 Fumé Blanc Vintner's Reserve	California	B	86
1995 Merlot Grand Reserve	California	D	85
1994 Merlot Grand Reserve	California	D	86+
1995 Merlot Vintner's Reserve	California	B	82
1997 Pinot Noir Grand Reserve	Sonoma/Carneros	D	85
1996 Pinot Noir Grand Reserve	California	D	78
1997 Pinot Noir Vintner's Reserve	California	C	86
1997 Sauvignon Blanc Grand Reserve	California	C	87
1996 Sauvignon Blanc Grand Reserve	California	C	87
1997 Sauvignon Blanc Vintner's Reserve	California	B	85
1996 Semillon Vintner's Reserve	California	B	86
1997 Syrah Grand Reserve	California	C	(86–88)
1995 Syrah Grand Reserve	California	C	86
1997 Syrah Vintner's Reserve	California	C	85
1997 Viognier Vintner's Reserve	California	C	87
1996 Zinfandel Grand Reserve	California	D	76
1996 Zinfandel Vintner's Reserve	California	B	79

The reasonably priced Vintner's Reserve series of Kendall-Jackson's wines are noteworthy for their faithfulness to their varietal personalities, and their reasonable prices. The Chardonnay is a revelation given the fact that 65% of it is barrel fermented, and in 1997, 100% of the multiple cuvées were put through malolactic fermentation. But the most amazing statistic is the production—two million cases! Obviously there must be some bottle variation, but major efforts are made to guarantee uniformity and consistency. The 1997 Chardonnay Vintner's Reserve is one of the finest I have tasted in recent vintages. The bouquet offers up pear and tropical fruit notes in addition to applelike aromas. This fruit-driven, medium-bodied, fresh, lively, tasty Chardonnay should be consumed during its first year of life. The 1997 Sauvignon Blanc Vintner's Reserve (5% barrel fermented) is a crisp, soft, light-bodied, fruity wine with a melony character. Drink it over the next 12 months. I enjoyed the 1997 Fumé Blanc slightly more because of its riper, plusher texture. A tiny amount of Semillon is added for fatness. It exhibits good, waxy, melony fruit, and like many of these wines, good purity and a fruit-driven personality. The surprisingly fine 1997 Viognier Vintner's Reserve is made primarily from Santa Clara/Contra Costa fruit. It exhibits this varietal's honeysuckle and apricotlike notes, medium body, good underlying acidity, no noticeable oak, and a touch of residual sugar. It is a tasty, medium-bodied, textbook Viognier to drink over the next year.

Among the reds, the quality of the 1997 Pinot Noir's Vintner's Reserve was impressive. The wine possesses a light ruby color, and a red currant, cherry, and blackberry-scented nose with spicy oak in the background. This medium-bodied, savory Pinot presents an accurate portrait of this varietal's character. There are many luxury-priced Pinot Noirs from both the New World and the Old World that are not as pleasurable as this offering. The 1997 Syrah Vintner's Reserve (made primarily from Paso Robles fruit) displays blackberry and cassis notes intermixed with dusty earth tones and pepper. It is soft, fruit driven, and well made. This is the finest series of Vintner's Reserve wines I have yet tasted from Kendall-Jackson. They are obviously fine values.

The Grand Reserve wines are more expensively made offerings from better fruit sources. All are aged in French oak, given considerable lees contact, and enjoy 100% malolactic fermentation. There is a significant difference between these cuvées and the Vintner's Reserves. The Grand Reserves, in addition to being oak aged, are unquestionably deeper, broader, and richer. The 1997 Sauvignon Blanc Grand Reserve (made primarily from Lake County fruit) is a lush, melony, honeyed, full-bodied Sauvignon with considerable appeal. Broad, expansive, rich, and leesy, this personality-filled example should drink well for 12–18 months. The 1997 Chardonnay Grand Reserve (65,000 cases, aged in 50% new oak) exhibits a creamy, honeysuckle, ripe tropical fruit-scented nose with smoky oak in the background. It is a medium- to full-bodied, ripe, lush, pure Chardonnay with a succulent, fat texture. Enjoy it over the next 1–2 years.

For the difference in price, I was unimpressed with the 1997 Pinot Noir Grand Reserve, especially when compared to the less expensive Vintner's Reserve. The 1997 Grand Reserve is a smokier, more herbaceous-scented wine, with more depth, body, and tannin, but I preferred the lighter-styled Vintner's Reserve. The 1997 Syrah Grand Reserve could turn out to be excellent given its saturated ruby/purple color, attractive, moderately intense crème de cassis and blackberry-scented nose, and fruity, medium-bodied flavors. Soft, with low acidity, and spicy, peppery notes in the background, it should age nicely for 4–5 years.

The overall quality level of KJ's 1996 Vintner's Reserve and Grand Reserve offerings was less impressive than in previous vintages. There is no doubt that 1996's short crop (and consequently higher prices) may have made access to the large quantities of high quality white wine juice more problematic, but I also noticed that the red wines tasted more tart, with less expansive textures, and higher acidity. After all, these are price point wines. In any event, the most attractive wines from the least expensive sector of the Kendall-Jackson lineup are the Vintner's Reserve cuvées. I enjoyed the waxy, pungent, light-bodied, citrusy 1996 Semillon Vintner's Reserve.

Although I did not enjoy the crisp, tart, spicy, peppery, light- to medium-bodied 1996 Zinfandel Vintner's Reserve, this wine may be ideal for neophytes who are just being introduced to wine. The 1995 Merlot Vintner's Reserve (200,000 cases produced) is largely made from North Coast fruit. It reveals tart acidity (too high for my palate), as well as attractive berry, cherry, cola, and herblike flavors in its light to medium-bodied style. It is a fresh, lively Merlot that lacks richness. The 1995 Cabernet Sauvignon Vintner's Reserve (about 250,000 cases) exhibits a more saturated ruby color, and a pleasing red currant, "Petit Bordeaux"-like personality with some ripeness, medium body, and a soft style.

I generally felt the Grand Reserve series to be one of the most successful groups of wines from Kendall-Jackson. All of the following offerings tend to be above average in quality, but they did not possess the breadth of flavor and aromatic dimension I had anticipated. My favorites include the excellent 1996 Sauvignon Blanc Grand Reserve, which offers a floral, honey, melony-scented nose, medium body, excellent flavor concentration, and a dry, rich finish. I also thought the 1996 Chardonnay Grand Reserve was a well-made, lighter-styled wine. I particularly admired its citrusy, tangerine, tropical fruit flavors that are presented in a pure, crisp, medium-bodied style. However, both of these wines should be drunk over the next 1–2 years.

The 1996 Pinot Noir Grand Reserve smells similar to my wife's tomato garden with its blatant herbaceousness. The wine is also generously oaky. Some atypical varietal flavors of chocolate are picked up on the palate. This is a straightforward, unusual Pinot Noir to consume over the next 3–4 years. The straightforward, medium-bodied, berry-scented and flavored, spicy 1996 Zinfandel Grand Reserve also lacks intensity and richness. The 1995 Syrah Grand Reserve is well made, but it exhibits entirely too much new oak, although I did detect some smoky bacon fat once the aggressive oak aromas faded into the background. Some sexy black plum and cassis fruit are present in both the aromatics and flavors of this flashy wine that comes across as oak driven. The 1995 Cabernet Franc Grand Reserve exhibits a strawberry and berry-scented nose, medium body, and an elegant, light style. It is very perfumed and attractive in a low-key sort of way. It should drink well for 4–5 years. The 1995 Merlot Grand Reserve displays a dark ruby color, a spicy, oak-dominated, berry-scented nose, ripe, medium-bodied flavors, and is overall a good, straightforward, competent effort. It should last for 2–3 years. The densest wine following the Grand Reserve Syrah is the 1995 Cabernet Sauvignon Grand Reserve, but it finishes with shrill acidity, and comes across as compressed and lean. It will undoubtedly dry out before it ever blossoms.

Two other very good efforts in the Grand Reserve program are the 1994 Grand Reserve Merlot and 1994 Grand Reserve Cabernet Sauvignon. The Merlot exhibits medium body, plenty of ripe mocha/coffee, berry fruit, a soft texture, and fine finish. At $40 a bottle, this wine hardly qualifies as a good value, but it should drink well for 6–8 years. The 1994 Grand Reserve Cabernet Sauvignon is richer, with sweeter fruit, as well as an attractive black currant/chocolatey character, good acidity, medium to full body, and a slightly tannic finish. It should age well for a decade, but it will not develop into anything exceptional.

The 1994 Cabernet Franc Grand Reserve is uninteresting, compact and compressed, with little fruit, flesh, or character.

J. KIRKWOOD (NAPA)

1996 Merlot		Napa D	91

This is the first release from a 3-acre hillside vineyard west of Napa in what is known as Brown's Valley. The 1996 was aged in 100% new French oak, fermented with indigenous yeasts, and bottled with neither fining nor filtration after 20 months of aging. Sadly, there are only 280 cases of this knockout Merlot. The proprietor, a well-known Napa doctor, was so quality conscious, he decided the 1997 did not match the quality of the 1996, so this offering will be the only one for the next twenty-four months or so. The wine possesses a dense ruby/purple color, as well as striking aromatics, consisting of black chocolate, jammy berries, and *pain grillé*, beautifully integrated new oak, low acidity, and a plump, full-bodied, rich, concentrated style. The extraordinary fruit ripeness of California's best North Coast microclimates is accompanied by the complexity and multidimensional personality found in a top-quality Pomerol. This beauty should easily drink well for 10–12 years.

KISTLER VINEYARDS (SONOMA)

1996 Chardonnay	Sonoma Coast	D	90
1995 Chardonnay	Sonoma Coast	D	90
1997 Chardonnay Camp Meeting Ridge Vineyard	Sonoma Coast	E	(94–96)
1996 Chardonnay Camp Meeting Ridge Vineyard	Sonoma Coast	E	91
1995 Chardonnay Camp Meeting Ridge Vineyard	Sonoma Coast	E	92+

1997	Chardonnay Cuvée Cathleen	Sonoma County	E	(94–96)
1996	Chardonnay Cuvée Cathleen	Sonoma County	E	95
1995	Chardonnay Cuvée Cathleen	Sonoma County	E	94+
1997	Chardonnay Durell Vineyard	Sonoma Valley	E	(90–92)
1996	Chardonnay Durell Vineyard	Sonoma Valley	E	90
1995	Chardonnay Durell Vineyard	Sonoma Valley	E	90
1997	Chardonnay Dutton Ranch	Russian River	E	(93–95)
1996	Chardonnay Dutton Ranch	Russian River	E	91
1995	Chardonnay Dutton Ranch	Russian River	E	93
1996	Chardonnay Hudson Vineyard	Carneros	E	93
1995	Chardonnay Hudson Vineyard	Carneros	E	95
1997	Chardonnay Hudson Vineyard E Block	Carneros	E	(94–96)
1996	Chardonnay Hyde Vineyard	Carneros	E	93
1997	Chardonnay Kistler Vineyard	Sonoma	E	(92–94)
1996	Chardonnay Kistler Vineyard	Sonoma	E	91
1995	Chardonnay Kistler Vineyard	Sonoma	E	94
1997	Chardonnay McCrea Vineyard	Sonoma Mountain	E	(92–94)
1996	Chardonnay McCrea Vineyard	Sonoma Mountain	E	91
1995	Chardonnay McCrea Vineyard	Sonoma Mountain	E	90
1997	Chardonnay Vine Hill Road Vineyard	Russian River	E	(91–92)
1996	Chardonnay Vine Hill Road Vineyard	Russian River	E	89
1995	Chardonnay Vine Hill Road Vineyard	Russian River	E	93
1997	Pinot Noir Camp Meeting Ridge Vineyard	Sonoma Coast	E	(91–94)
1996	Pinot Noir Camp Meeting Ridge Vineyard	Sonoma Coast	E	92
1995	Pinot Noir Camp Meeting Ridge Vineyard	Sonoma Coast	E	93+
1994	Pinot Noir Camp Meeting Ridge Vineyard	Sonoma Coast	E	88
1997	Pinot Noir Cuvée Catherine	Russian River	E	(95–97)
1996	Pinot Noir Cuvée Catherine	Russian River	E	96
1995	Pinot Noir Cuvée Catherine	Russian River	E	94
1994	Pinot Noir Cuvée Catherine	Russian River Valley	E	92
1993	Pinot Noir Cuvée Catherine	Sonoma	E	94
1997	Pinot Noir Hirsch Vineyard	Sonoma Coast	E	(90–93)
1996	Pinot Noir Hirsch Vineyard	Sonoma Coast	E	89

1995 Pinot Noir Hirsch Vineyard	Sonoma Coast	E	92+
1994 Pinot Noir Hirsch Vineyard	Sonoma Coast	E	92
1997 Pinot Noir Kistler Vineyard	Russian River	E	(94–96)
1996 Pinot Noir Kistler Vineyard	Russian River	E	94
1994 Pinot Noir Vine Hill Vineyard	Russian River	E	91

After each visit to Kistler I am moved to write one accolade after another because of the extraordinary efforts and quality of the wines produced by owner/winemaker Steve Kistler and his assistant, Mark Bixler. It begins to sound like a broken record, but this winery is turning out prodigious wines. While everyone knows about Kistler's remarkable Chardonnays, I believe their Pinot Noirs will ultimately prove even more historic.

Steve Kistler believes the 1997 Chardonnays are among the finest he has ever produced. The vintage's high yields do not appear to have had an impact on the wines' level of concentration and intensity. Moreover, the 1997s possess an atypical level of tangy, underlying acidity, giving the wines a wonderful vibrancy. Additionally, the 1997's splendid aromatics are matched only by the 1995's. I tasted eight Chardonnays. While they share a certain similarity, they possess distinctive attributes that justify the winery's decision to differentiate them. All are fermented with both indigenous and commercial yeasts, given extensive stirring during prolonged contact with the lees, and bottled unfiltered after full malolactic fermentation. The percentage of new French oak varies, with higher percentages for the Camp Meeting Ridge, Hudson, and Cuvée Cathleen offerings. The 1997 Chardonnay McCrea Vineyard, made from an old Wente clone, personifies this varietal's lemony, buttery, citrusy, mineral style. It offers medium to full body, splendid concentration, considerable richness and texture on the midpalate, and gorgeous elegance, purity, and overall balance. Tangy acidity gives the wine admirable freshness. It should age well for 5–7 years. The 1997 Chardonnay Vine Hill Road Vineyard (from both Hyde and Dijon Burgundy clones) is a more restrained wine with noticeably higher acidity. It reveals suggestions of cold steel, wet stones, and that liquid minerality found in certain Chardonnays. Medium to full bodied, with excellent depth, and more austerity and backwardness than its siblings, it will benefit from another year of cellaring, and keep for 6–7 years. Readers looking for a Chardonnay that possesses the tropical fruit spectrum, without completely abandoning the complex mineral character, will be pleased with the 1997 Chardonnay Durell Vineyard. The poor vigor of these rocky soils, combined with such clones as Hyde, has resulted in a wine with zesty acidity, medium to full body, outstanding ripeness and purity, and loads of orange blossom/lemony fruit in addition to hints of peach and pineapple. This 1997 requires 1–2 years of cellaring, and should have an unusually long life of 8–10 years. The more flamboyant, Burgundian-styled 1997 Chardonnay Dutton Ranch displays a roasted hazelnut, sweet, rich, tropical fruit-scented nose, full body, and laserlike clarity to its component parts. Rich and intense, it is similar to a tightly knit Burgundian grand cru. With less minerality yet more of the smoky, leesy, roasted nut characteristics, this wine combines abundant tropical fruit and honeyed citrus. It should be delicious upon release, and keep for 5–7 years.

The 1997 Chardonnay Kistler Vineyard (made from the Mt. Eden clone, which is alleged to be a suitcase clone from Burgundy's Corton-Charlemagne vineyard) is a multidimensional wine with a rich, full-bodied, creamy texture, superb buttery, honeyed fruit, subtle *pain grillé*, gorgeously rich fruit, white flowers, buttered popcorn, and liquid gravel-like notes. Combining power with finesse, it should drink well young, and age for 5–7 years. The dazzling 1997 Chardonnay Camp Meeting Ridge Vineyard is the most explosive, viscous, powerful, and mineral laden of the Kistler Chardonnays. Like its siblings, it surpasses 14% alcohol, but that is well hidden by the wine's outstanding extract and layered personality. A lush, leesy complexity emerges, but this is an extremely rich, highly concentrated, stunning

Chardonnay with prodigious fruit extraction in addition to astonishing length. This is the finest Camp Meeting Ridge Chardonnay to date. Another leesy, smoky, Burgundian-styled, exotic offering is the 1997 Chardonnay Hudson Vineyard, whose fruit comes from the same E Block that Helen Turley and John Wetlaufer made famous with their Marcassin Hudson Vineyard Chardonnay. Kistler's effort possesses a Meursault-like, buttery character with gobs of tropical fruit and glycerin, yet firm buttressing acidity. My instincts suggest it will be the most forward of these Chardonnays, as well as the shortest-lived (4–5 years). After being blown away by so many sensational Chardonnays, it is difficult to find the adjectives and superlatives to describe the 1997 Chardonnay Cuvée Cathleen. This offering is produced from a selection of barrels that Steve Kistler and Mark Bixler believe to be the richest and most complete. Negligibly better than the other brilliant cuvées, it possesses exceptional richness, length, and intensity. Layers of fruit, smoky, buttery popcorn, tropical fruit and mineral scents soar from the glass, and are exceptionally intense and well balanced. This terrific, full-bodied effort should age for 8–10 years.

It is also easy to get excited about Kistler's Pinot Noirs. All are aged in 100% new oak, made in small lots (250–500 cases), and bottled with neither fining nor filtration. They are trying to keep the levels of SO_2 to minimal dosages so the wines can be as expressive as possible. These Pinot Noirs can easily hold their own in blind tastings with the finest red Burgundies. The opaque black/purple-colored 1997 Pinot Noir Hirsch Vineyard looks more like Syrah than Pinot Noir. However, the nose offers up aromas of blackberries, cherries, and smoke intermixed with *pain grillé*, roasted herbs, and meat. Medium to full bodied, with light to moderate tannin, and an exuberant style with firm acidity, this is a classic. Anticipated maturity: 2000–2014. The 1997 Pinot Noir Camp Meeting Ridge Vineyard exhibits a dark ruby/purple color, and a more feminine, less muscular personality with plenty of sweet black raspberry and cherry fruit. A softer, more luscious style of Pinot Noir, it will provide more flattering drinking than the Hirsch. The wine is extremely expansive, with sweet tannin, adequate acidity, and admirable staying power. Anticipated maturity: now–2010.

Two of the most spectacular Pinot Noirs I have ever tasted are Kistler's 1997 Kistler Vineyard and 1997 Cuvée Catherine. The 1997 Pinot Noir Kistler Vineyard (500 cases) is made from the Dijon clone 777, and two California clones, Pommard and Calera. It boasts a dense, saturated dark ruby/purple color, as well as an exceptionally sweet nose of roasted herbs and black cherry jam intermixed with raspberries, truffles, and toasty oak. Sweet and expansive, this full-bodied wine possesses fabulous concentration and purity, a grand cru-like level of potential complexity, and a 30+-second finish. It must be tasted to be believed. Look for this wine to be drinkable upon release, and last for at least a decade. There are approximately 250 cases of the 1997 Pinot Noir Cuvée Catherine. Like its siblings, it has over 14% alcohol, but that is totally obscured by the wine's sensational concentration, extract, and overall equilibrium. A dense ruby/purple-colored, full-bodied Pinot Noir, it offers up aromas of blackberries, raspberries, and cherry liqueur intermixed with licorice, smoke, and meat. Chewy yet not heavy, this wine does reveal some tannin, but it is largely hidden by the wine's fruit, glycerin, and extract. Wow, what an amazing performance!

The two 1996 Pinot Noirs I tasted are remarkable wines. The 1996 Pinot Noir Kistler Vineyard exhibits a Vosne-Romaneé/Richebourg-like violet, black cherry, and smoky-scented nose of considerable intensity. Full bodied, with superb richness, admirable delineation, a lush, concentrated midpalate, and black cherry, earthy notes in the spicy finish, this is another impressive, superconcentrated Pinot Noir with both complexity and equilibrium. It should drink well for a decade. The 1996 Pinot Noir Cuvée Catherine, a blend of fruit from the Sonoma Coast and Kistler Vineyard, is another thrilling, sumptuously styled Pinot. The color is a healthy saturated ruby/purple. The wine is rich and full bodied, with floral (violets and lilacs) scents intertwined with cherry jam, overripe strawberries, and smoke.

Extremely full bodied, with spectacular richness, terrific purity, and a multilayered texture, this, like the other Kistler Pinot Noirs, is a tour de force! Anticipated maturity: now–2010.

While the 1996 vintage was a more difficult year because the hang-time was shorter, and growing conditions were hotter, with particularly torrid weather in August, owner/winemaker Steve Kistler and his trusty assistant, Mark Bixler, turned in exemplary efforts with their Chardonnay portfolio. Moreover, Kistler Vineyards, along with Marcassin, Martinelli, Rochioli, Dehlinger, and Williams-Selyem, in addition to a handful of other wineries, are rewriting the book when it comes to California Pinot Noir. Read on.

All the Kistler Chardonnays are made in a Burgundian manner. They are barrel fermented, given full malolactic fermentation, extensive lees stirring, racked out of their barrels following a year's cask aging, and allowed to settle in tank until bottling, which usually occurs without any fining or filtration. All of the following wines were tasted from tank as they were awaiting bottling. The 1996 Chardonnay McCrea Vineyard is a smoky, crisp, light golden-colored wine, with medium to full body, and a leesy, bread doughlike aroma, with plenty of honeyed citruslike fruit intermixed with spice and smoke. Produced from one of Sonoma's coolest microclimates, it possesses tart acidity for a 1996, and merits 5–7 years of cellaring. The 1996 Chardonnay Vine Hill Road Vineyard has the highest acidity of the Kistler offerings, and is normally a tight, restrained wine. The 1996, while revealing fine elegance, and a lemony, citrusy, applelike fruitiness, also exhibited crisp, tart acidity, medium body, and a subtle personality. I suspect there are some minerals lurking in the background of this tightly knit Chardonnay that should age well for 5–6 years. Typically, the 1996 Chardonnay Dutton Ranch is a more flamboyant wine, offering the telltale concoction of tropical fruit intertwined with smoky, meaty aromas. The wine possesses tangy acidity for a 1996, as well as provocative, rich, intense flavors that have obviously enjoyed plenty of lees stirring, and high quality French oak. This is a tasty, excellent, possibly outstanding wine that is more tightly knit than usual. It is a candidate for 3–5 years of cellaring. Kistler's light golden-colored 1996 Chardonnay Kistler Vineyard reveals outstanding aromatics of white peaches, acacia flowers, popcorn, and spice. On the palate, it offers layers of flavor, a layered texture, and a well-balanced, long aftertaste. It should drink well for 4–6 years.

A new offering in the Kistler lineup is the stunning 1996 Chardonnay Hyde Vineyard (500 cases produced), which is made from an old Wente clone of Chardonnay that produces extremely low yields and tiny berries. This wine offers a roasted hazelnut, creamy, lemon custard, smoky nose. In the mouth, this medium- to full-bodied wine exhibits terrific layers of rich fruit, a roasted, exotic character, full body, high acidity, and underlying minerality. A compelling Chardonnay, it should drink well for 4–5 years. The 1996 Chardonnay Sonoma Coast, which is actually an assemblage of many different small lots, has a light golden color, followed by a buttery, white peach, and popcorn-scented nose, with excellent layers of fruit. The wine is well made and clean, with gravelly, stony scents and copious quantities of fruit. Again, it reveals good acidity for a 1996, medium to full body, and 4–5 years of aging potential. I have always been a fan of the flamboyant, gaudy Chardonnay from the Hudson Vineyard, and Kistler's 1996 Chardonnay Hudson Vineyard is one of the more opulently styled wines in this portfolio, with a smoky, buttery, tropical fruit-scented nose, thick, juicy, succulent flavors, adequate acidity, and a lusty, pure, plump, layered finish. It is one of the more forward Kistler Chardonnays, yet should age well for 3–4 years. In total contrast is the 1996 Chardonnay Camp Meeting Ridge Vineyard. One of the least expressive, more backward wines of this group, it rivals the Vine Hill cuvée for high acidity and restraint. However, at the back of the mouth, tropical fruit flavors of peaches, corn, and wet stones compete for attention. All of this is held together by crisp acidity, and subtle toasty oak from high quality French oak barrels. This wine reminds me of some of the more backward grand crus from Burgundy's Côte d'Or.

The 1996 Chardonnay Durell offers citrusy, tropical fruit, and mineral aromas, medium body, excellent richness, and a long, tangy, tight but promising finish. It should unfold with another 1–2 years of bottle age and last for 5–6 years. Lastly, the 1995 Chardonnay Cuvée Cathleen, a selection made from the finest barrels, is spectacular. Given the overall thrilling quality at this winery, one can imagine just how extraordinary this wine is. The Cuvée Cathleen possesses a light golden color, followed by a ripe, honeyed, leesy nose filled with fruit, roasted nuts, minerals, and spice. Extremely full bodied, with superrichness, purity, and multiple dimensions, this fabulously rich, explosively fruity, ripe, Burgundian-styled Chardonnay will benefit from 1–2 years of cellaring and keep for 7–8 years.

With respect to the Pinot Noirs, they are among my favorites being made in the New World. The wines are 100% destemmed, the fermentations are 100% natural (indigenous yeasts), they are put through a complete malolactic fermentation, and totally aged in new oak. Bottling is accomplished with neither fining nor filtration. Sadly, the wines are made in small lots. The dense ruby-colored 1996 Pinot Noir Camp Meeting Ridge Vineyard (150 cases) is a fruit bomb, offering copious quantities of lush black fruits intermixed with underbrush, minerals, and spice. Gorgeously proportioned, medium to full bodied, with well-integrated tannin and acidity, its vibrancy, purity, and liveliness are commendable. This wine should drink well young and keep for a decade. The 1996 Pinot Noir Hirsch Vineyard (150 cases) requires 3–5 years of cellaring. It is a macho, muscular, tannic wine with meaty, beefy aromas and flavors, and black cherry fruit intertwined with an earthy *terroir* characteristic. However, the tannins are elevated, and the wine in need of cellaring. Because of that, it is more angular and austere than the other cuvées.

The 1995 Chardonnay Dutton Ranch is the most forward, evolved, open knit, and complex. The wine possesses a bright, medium straw/gold color, suggesting more advanced maturity. The flamboyant nose offers up plenty of sweet, rich, honeyed pear/pineapple, and smoky aromas. This full-bodied Chardonnay possesses exceptional fruit purity, a layered texture, and a sweet midpalate. This was the only 1995 Kistler Chardonnay that seemed close to offering immediate drinkability, although I suspect this wine has a minimum of 4–5 years of life. The 1995 Chardonnay McCrea Vineyard (from Sonoma Mountain's cooler microclimate) was difficult to evaluate coming after the up-front, full-bodied, showy Dutton Ranch. The wine was less open, had higher acidity, and a lemony custard pielike subtlety to its fruit. Ripe, full bodied, powerful, restrained, and buttressed by significant acidity, it will benefit from 1–2 years of cellaring and last for 6–7. The 1995 Chardonnay Vine Hill Road Vineyard was also tight, but unlike the McCrea Vineyard Chardonnay, 5–10 minutes of swirling and breathing caused the wine to blossom beautifully. It offers an Acacia flower, sweet, honey-suckle-scented nose, with plenty of concentrated fruit. Full bodied and well delineated, this appears to be a dazzling, complex, unfined, unfiltered Chardonnay with a provocative stony minerality that provides additional complexity. It should improve for at least a decade.

The 1995 Chardonnay Kistler Vineyard possesses a complex set of aromatics, exhibiting a buttery, hazelnut character that I often find in the Marcassin and Peter Michael Chardonnays, as well as in a bevy of top-class white Burgundies. The Kistler Vineyard offers terrific tropical fruit flavors, along with a more subtle, complex aromatic profile. Full bodied and concentrated, with plenty of fresh acidity, this is a well-endowed, rich, broadly flavored Chardonnay that should drink well for 7–8 years. The 1995 Chardonnay Cuvée Cathleen, a selection of the best barrels made by Steve Kistler and Mark Bixler, was tightly knit when I tasted it. Nevertheless, the wine revealed spectacular concentration and potential. The wonderful balance between its power, acidity, alcohol, and extract is flawless. Fortunate tasters will appreciate how the wine cascades over the palate with superconcentrated fruit, infused with some high quality French oak. On the back of the palate, the wine reveals explosive richness and length. The finish lasts for 30–35 seconds. This is another large-scaled, tightly knit, Burgundian-styled Chardonnay that needs 1–2 years of cellaring; it should keep for a decade or more. It was bottled without fining or filtration.

The ostentatious 1995 Chardonnay Hudson Vineyard is produced from a Carneros vineyard well known as a source of grapes for Kistler and Marcassin's Chardonnay. Several other wineries produce terrific Pinot Noir and Syrah from the Hudson Vineyard. I could have mistaken the 1995 Hudson Vineyard Chardonnay for a Bâtard-Montrachet from the likes of Louis Latour. The wine possesses an open-knit, lemon custard, honeyed, tropical fruit, buttery-scented nose, and stunningly rich, ostentatious flavors that tease the palate with remarkable purity and intensity. Low in acidity, but fabulously rich, full flavored, and mouth-filling, this is a profound California Chardonnay. Drink it over the next 4–7 years.

The 1995 Chardonnay Camp Meeting Ridge Vineyard tastes as if someone added liquefied wet stones to the blend. The wine possesses creamy, citrusy, rich fruit flavors buttressed by tart acidity. It is a backward, flinty, powerful yet elegant style of Chardonnay that is Kistler's Corton-Charlemagne lookalike. Beneath all the minerals and crisp acidity is a wine with intense concentration, as well as a powerful style. Give it 1–2 years of cellaring and drink it over the following decade. Although the 1995 Chardonnay Durell Vineyard is excellent, it was overwhelmed by its stablemates. While closed, it exhibits attractive, citrusy, pineapple, and mineral components, along with spicy wood. Full bodied, but leaner, with some austerity, this wine needs to be reevaluated after an additional 6 months of bottle age. It may have the potential to be outstanding, but it was closed and tight. Lastly, the 1995 Chardonnay Sonoma Coast offers a creamy, mineral, lemon custardlike nose, impressive, ripe flavors, and a medium-bodied, graceful, suave personality. This attractive wine should be drunk during its first 5–7 years of life.

Kistler's impressive Pinot Noir portfolio was launched with the 1994s. The 1995 Pinot Noirs appear to be as good as the impressive 1994s. The 1995 Pinot Noir Hirsch Vineyard exhibits an opaque ruby color, a beefy, black fruit, spicy, earthy-scented nose, full body, plenty of tannin, and admirable intensity and richness. The wine needs 1–2 years of cellaring, but it promises to keep for a decade. Only 250 cases were produced from this Sonoma Coast vineyard. The 1995 Pinot Noir Camp Meeting Ridge Vineyard (also 250 cases) is a dense, full-bodied, Côte de Nuits-like wine with gobs of sweet black fruits, earth, and underbrush. Full bodied and powerful, with more tannin and structure than the Hirsch cuvée, this is another impressive Sonoma Coast Pinot Noir. Lastly, the 1995 Pinot Noir Estate Cuvée Catherine is one of the most remarkable Pinot Noirs I have tasted from California. The opaque ruby/purple color and sweet nose of black fruits, smoked meat, and minerals are followed by a wine of exceptional richness, purity, and delineation. It is still backward and closed, but wow, what concentration, intensity, and overall balance. Might not this wine prove to be an historical effort?

By the way, the 1994 Hirsch Vineyard Pinot Noir is another California Pinot that seemingly breaks new ground. It boasts a deep ruby/purple color, with a nose of earth, meat, and ripe black fruits. Full bodied and powerful, this wine could easily be mistaken for a top grand cru from the Côte de Nuits given its richness, aromatic complexity, and flavor dimension.

The medium to dark ruby-colored 1994 Camp Meeting Ridge Vineyard Pinot Noir reveals a meaty, cinnamon, cherry-scented bouquet, round, ripe, medium-bodied flavors, and a long, soft, richly fruity finish. The 1994 Pinot Noir Vine Hill Vineyard exhibits a deeper color, a riper, more intense fragrance, superb richness and depth, full body, lovely integrated oak and acidity, and an opulent, silky-textured finish. It could easily pass as a top grand cru from Burgundy's Côte d'Or. It should drink and age well for 5–6 years. The 1994 Pinot Noir Estate Cuvée Catherine exhibits a dense color, and gorgeous wild berry aromas ranging from cherries to raspberries. Rich and full bodied, with layers of creamy fruit and a super texture, this superb Pinot Noir should drink well young yet keep for 7–8 years.

The sensational 1993 Cuvée Catherine possesses a smoky, sweet, earthy, black fruit character reminiscent of a top premier or grand cru from Vosne-Romanée. In the mouth the wine displays exquisite richness and ripeness, a fleshy, voluptuous texture, and a stunning finish. It should drink well for 7–8 years. It is clearly one of the finest Pinot Noirs I have tasted from California.

Kistler Vineyards is at the pinnacle of the California qualitative pyramid. Particularly admirable is the fact that they got there the hard way—they earned it.

KUNDE (SONOMA)

1994	Cabernet Sauvignon Estate	Sonoma	C	87
1993	Cabernet Sauvignon Estate	Sonoma	C	87
1993	Cabernet Sauvignon Estate Reserve	Sonoma	C	90
1995	Chardonnay Estate Kinneybrook Vineyard Unfiltered	Sonoma	C	91
1995	Chardonnay Estate Reserve Unfiltered	Sonoma	C	88
1995	Chardonnay Estate Wildwood Vineyard Unfiltered	Sonoma	C	90
1995	Merlot Estate	Sonoma	C	86+
1994	Merlot Estate	Sonoma	C	87
1995	Sauvignon Blanc Magnolia Lane	Sonoma	C	87
1995	Syrah Estate	Sonoma	C	88
1994	Syrah Estate	Sonoma	C	89
1993	Vallée de la Lune	Sonoma	B	89
1995	Viognier Estate	Sonoma	C	90
1995	Zinfandel Estate Century Vines	Sonoma	C	88
1994	Zinfandel Estate Century Vines	Sonoma	B	89
1993	Zinfandel Estate Century Vines Shaw Vineyard	Sonoma	B	89
1995	Zinfandel Robusto	Sonoma	C	89

The Kunde family has been growing grapes in Sonoma since 1904. With over 700 acres of gorgeously situated vineyards, primarily on Sonoma's rust-colored hillsides, this winery is in a position to become a powerful qualitative leader in northern California. Much of the vineyard production is sold to other wineries, but Kunde has continued to increase its estate-bottled production, now over 70,000 cases, approximately one-third of the total vineyard yield. Because of the talents of their winemaker, David Noyes, the hallmark of the Kunde wines has been pure, rich, concentrated fruit that is presented in a soft, expansive, user-friendly style. The Reserve wines are exposed to more oak, but there is not a wine in the Kunde portfolio, even the Reserve Cabernets, that cannot be drunk when released. The entire portfolio of offerings is consistently very good to excellent. Yet I suspect they could (and perhaps should) produce some limited production, superpremium cuvées of Chardonnay and Cabernet Sauvignon. Obviously they possess the vineyard sources to do so. All the following wines can be recommended with considerable enthusiasm. Moreover, this is one winery where prices are among the fairest in northern California.

The 1995 Sauvignon Blanc Magnolia Lane (76% Sauvignon Blanc, 15% Semillon, and 9% Viognier) is a fragrant, richly fruity, medium-bodied wine bursting with lemony, melony fruit, exceptional purity, and a dry, crisp, moderately weighty feel in the mouth. Drink this fruit- and character-filled Sauvignon over the next year.

There are four Chardonnay cuvées, but I did not taste the Sonoma Estate Chardonnay on my most recent visit. If possible, winemaker David Noyes bottles the single-vineyard wines without any filtration. This is a winery that intentionally avoids as much processing and manipulation of the juice as possible. The 1995 Chardonnay Reserve offers up ripe pineapple, orange, and apple-scented fruit, medium to full body, uncomplicated, fleshy flavors, and a delicious, forward personality. Drink it over the next 1–2 years.

The single-vineyard wines see more oak (about 30%–35%), but the emphasis is placed on the vineyard character. Together with their ripe, rich fruit, these are fun and exciting wines. The full-bodied 1995 Chardonnay Wildwood Vineyard Unfiltered (14.4% alcohol) displays obvious tropical fruits in its aroma (oranges and pineapples), rich, fleshy, ripe flavors, admirable depth, and a soft, opulent finish. The 1995 Chardonnay Kinneybrook Vineyard Unfiltered may be even richer than the 1994. The dense 1995 possesses terrific purity and ripeness, full body, and excellent extract. It will be interesting to compare these two wines over the next several years.

Another dry white wine readers should not miss is Kunde's 1995 Viognier. This wine exhibits a textbook, honeysuckle, peach/apricot-scented nose, a medium- to full-bodied, dry finish, and enough acidity to provide vibrancy and focus to the wine's power and richness. Drink it over the next year.

The red wines possess the same up-front, forward charms as the whites. What is so admirable about Kunde's red wines is that they have great flavor intensity, yet they are supple and velvety textured. The 1994 Merlot exhibits a dark ruby/purple color, copious quantities of jammy black cherry fruit in the uncomplicated bouquet, soft, fat, fleshy flavors, low acidity, and a smooth, coffee/berry-flavored finish. Drink it over the next 5–7 years. The similarly styled, dark ruby/purple-colored 1995 Merlot offers sweet, black cherry, smoky aromas, and plenty of flesh and fatness in its straightforward, juicy, succulent personality. Similarly, it should be drunk over the next 5–7 years.

As I have said before, this winery should do more with Rhône Ranger blends given their access to top quality fruit. For example, the 1995 Syrah (only 1,500 cases produced), which has been blended with 16% Viognier, reveals a deep purple color, as well as sweet, rich, cassis flavors with pepper and spicy notes. I did not detect any oak in this round, generously endowed, lusty Syrah. With its low acidity, this Syrah needs to be drunk up while young—say over the next 5–7 years. The 1994 Syrah Estate is made in a Côte Rôtie-like style. The addition of 22% Viognier has resulted in a captivating, intense, honeysuckle, peach, cassis, and black pepper-scented nose. Ripe, with sweet tannin, a soft, velvety texture, and a long, full-bodied finish, this is an ideal Syrah for drinking over the next 5–6 years. Unfortunately, only 300 cases were produced.

Another Rhône Ranger-styled wine is the modestly priced 1993 Vallée de la Lune, a blend of 20% Petite Sirah, 25% Syrah, 50% Grenache, and 5% Zinfandel. This could be a big seller. Only 600 cases were made in 1993, and none was produced in 1994. Winemaker David Noyes did produce a 1995. Readers can compare this wine with a high class Côtes du Rhône. It is a mouth-filling, exuberant, richly fruity wine offering scents of pepper, black cherries, spice, and a whiff of Provençal herbs. This succulent, hedonistic, oh, so pure and delicious wine is a joy to drink. Moreover, it will age for 4–5 years.

Not surprisingly, the 1994 Cabernet Sauvignon Estate is a juicy, forward, plump, black currant-scented and -flavored wine with no evidence of oak, but gobs of chewy, fleshy fruit. This delicious, low-acid Cabernet should be drunk over the next 5–7 years. The 1993 Cabernet Sauvignon Estate exhibits a healthy dark ruby/purple color, a sweet, cassis nose, nicely textured, corpulent flavors, low acidity, and a satiny smooth finish. It should drink well for 7–8 years. Lastly, the 1993 Cabernet Sauvignon Reserve, which was released in 1997, possesses a dark ruby/purple color, attractive, spicy, subtly vanillin, sweet, jammy, black fruit aromas, full body, outstanding richness, and a nicely textured, chewy finish. There are approximately 1,000 cases of this outstanding Cabernet Sauvignon. It will drink well now, yet age for 12–15 years.

Kunde's 1995 Zinfandel Century Vines (6,000 cases from the Shaw Vineyard, planted in 1882) is an outstanding, seductive, briery, richly fruity, full-bodied Zinfandel with no hard edges. Lush and flavorful, it will be a real crowd pleaser. This wine needs to be drunk over the next several years to take advantage of its gushing, rich black cherry fruitiness. The 1995 Zinfandel Robusto, a dry, late-harvest-styled wine that tips the scales at 16.1% alcohol, is not as lush as the Century Vines. It reveals a deeper, more extracted, dense ruby/purple color, an earthier, more peppery-scented nose, and large-scaled, dry, full-bodied flavors bursting with extract, glycerin, and richness. Although tightly knit, it is full-flavored and rich, with layers of Zinfandel fruit presented in an uncomplicated but gutsy, bold format. It should drink well for 4–5 years.

The 1994 Zinfandel Estate Century Vines possesses a silky texture, berries galore, and dense, medium- to full-bodied, super-smooth flavors and finish. It should be drunk over the next 5–6 years. Interestingly, the Kunde Winery adds tiny quantities of Grenache and Petite Sirah to their Zinfandel. Excellent value.

The 1993 Zinfandel Estate Century Vines is a round, generous, richly fruity, briery, spicy Zinfandel with no hard edges. It is destined to be gulped down by fans of this varietal over the next 4–5 years. Although not complex, for pure, rich fruit and a savory character, it is hard to resist.

LA CREMA (SONOMA)

1996 Chardonnay	Sonoma Coast	D	85
1996 Chardonnay Durell Vineyard Unfiltered	Sonoma	D	86
1996 Chardonnay Reserve	Sonoma Coast	D	86
1994 Pinot Noir	Sonoma	C	78
1996 Pinot Noir Reserve	Sonoma Coast	D	85
1994 Pinot Noir Reserve	Russian River	C	84
1996 Syrah Reserve	Sonoma Coast	D	85
1996 Zinfandel Reserve	Sonoma Coast	C	85
1995 Zinfandel Reserve	Sonoma Coast	C	85

All of these wines appear to be made in a cookie-cutter fashion. The Chardonnays possess good tropical fruit, including some lemon zest and orange rind, medium body, and moderate amounts of new oak. They are well made, clean, competent wines that require consumption over the next 1–2 years. The red wines are essentially cut from the same mold as the whites—medium bodied, moderately concentrated, with obvious new oak. The 1996 Pinot Noir Reserve exhibits a medium garnet/ruby color, attractive sour cherry fruit that is sweet on the attack, and straightforward ripeness and roundness. The soft, picnic-styled 1996 Syrah Reserve displays a dark ruby color, attractive, peppery, cassis aromas, and a light- to medium-bodied personality. It is ideal for drinking over the next several years. The best of the three reds is the 1996 Zinfandel Reserve, a berry-laden wine with good aromatics, a supple texture, medium body, and adequate acidity. None of these offerings will provide exciting drinking, but they are all well made and ideal for present consumption.

The Sonoma Coast possesses extraordinary potential for Chardonnay and Pinot Noir, but I do not recall tasting many Zinfandels from this cool, coastal area. La Crema's 1995 Zinfandel Reserve comes across as somewhat one-dimensional and simple, but it does possess good fruit, a medium deep ruby color, moderate body, vibrancy, elegance, and overall, decent equilibrium among its component parts. It will not make old bones, so consume it over the next 1–2 years.

The two 1994 Pinot Noirs were not impressive. They are correct, cleanly made wines with plenty of new wood, and vague, soft, earthy, cherry fruit. Lacking sufficient depth and richness to merit a recommendation, both wines should be drunk over the next 1–3 years. The 1994 Pinot Noir Reserve from the Russian River reveals more stuffing, but it is one-dimensional.

LA JOTA VINEYARD (NAPA)

1994	Cabernet Franc	Napa	D	93
1993	Cabernet Franc	Napa	D	92
1997	Cabernet Franc Howell Mountain	Napa	D	(92–95)
1996	Cabernet Franc Howell Mountain	Napa	D	93
1995	Cabernet Franc Howell Mountain	Napa	D	93
1994	Cabernet Sauvignon	Napa	C	92
1993	Cabernet Sauvignon	Napa	C	92
1997	Cabernet Sauvignon Howell Mountain Select	Napa	D	(90–92)
1996	Cabernet Sauvignon Howell Mountain Select	Napa	D	92
1995	Cabernet Sauvignon Howell Mountain Select	Napa	D	91
1994	Cabernet Sauvignon Howell Mountain Select	Napa	C	93
1995	Cabernet Sauvignon Howell Mountain 14th Anniversary	Napa	E	94
1994	Cabernet Sauvignon Howell Mountain 13th Anniversary	Napa	E	96
1993	Cabernet Sauvignon Howell Mountain 12th Anniversary	Napa	E	96
1997	Petite Sirah Howell Mountain	Napa	D	(90–93)
1996	Petite Sirah Howell Mountain	Napa	D	94
1995	Petite Sirah Howell Mountain	Napa	D	92
1994	Petite Sirah Howell Mountain	Napa	D	97
1993	Petite Sirah Howell Mountain	Napa	C	91

This is simply one of the best damn wineries in California. Quality since the 1991 vintage has soared, mainly because of two very nice people, owners Bill and Joan Smith. The total production is a modest 4,500–5,000 cases, primarily from their own vineyards on Howell Mountain, with some supplemental fruit from neighboring parcels owned by other growers. The 1997 vintage produced an abundant crop of extremely high quality fruit. The 1997 Cabernet Sauvignon Howell Mountain Select exhibits the vintage's precocious, evolved aromatics that are already striking and seductive. From the black currants, Asian spices, toasty oak, and smoke, the wine offers up sweet, expansive, jammy black fruits, full body, and ripe tannin. For growers who kept their yields modest, this will be one of the most seductive vintages of California Cabernet Sauvignon in the nineties. This wine will drink well for 15 or more years, but it will be uncommonly evolved and delicious upon release. In keeping with the vintage character, the 1997 Cabernet Sauvignon 16th Anniversary Release (about 1,400 cases produced) is far more accessible than other vintages from the nineties. The color is an opaque black plum, and the nose offers classic cassis intermixed with licorice, foresty scents, and minerals. Full bodied and powerful, with a 45–50-second finish, it is the most developed and evolved Anniversary Release I have tasted in the nineties. While it will not be mature when released, it should hit its plateau of maturity in 4–5 years, and keep for two decades or more. It is a seductive, voluptuously textured style of Anniversary Release.

I have been reporting for some time that no one makes better Cabernet Franc in North America than La Jota, and they continue to reveal an uncommon ability to capture the complex elements of this varietal, yet give it far more intensity and richness than their peers. The 1997 Cabernet Franc is awesome. Aromas of burning embers intermixed with cedar, cigar box, *jus de viande,* and black currants, with a touch of minerals, all soar from the glass of this decadently rich wine. In the mouth, its superb ripeness, soft, almost undiscernible tannin, medium to full body, and layers of richness make for a profoundly interesting drinking experience. Like the other 1997s in La Jota's portfolio, this wine will be drop dead beautiful to drink at release, and will age well for 12–15 years. The 1997 Petite Sirah, which has been blended with 10%–12% Viognier, is another highly successful wine. Most of the grapes for this cuvée come from the old Park Muscatine Vineyard owned by Randy Dunn. Unlike some of the massive, backward, hugely tannic and extracted Petite Sirahs from the likes of Turley, this is an unusually silky-styled effort that does not compromise the extraordinary fruit intensity and richness achieved by this varietal in California. The opaque purple-colored 1997 is fleshy and exotic, with gobs of blackberry and plum fruit intermixed with honeysuckle and spice. A sensational Petite Sirah, with low acidity, sweet tannin, and a stunning finish, it should drink well for 15–18 years, if not longer.

The bottled 1996s are even more impressive than they were last year. The 1996 Cabernet Sauvignon Howell Mountain Select is a beautifully rendered wine with an opaque plum color, and knockout aromatics of cedarwood, cassis, cigar box, and roasted Provençal herbs. With more structure than the 1997, it is a jammy, rich, concentrated, full-bodied wine that can be drunk now or cellared for two decades. This beauty remains one of the better values in great California Cabernet Sauvignon. The 1996 Cabernet Sauvignon 15th Anniversary Release (1,050 cases produced) boasts an opaque purple color, as well as beautiful aromas of smoke, blackberries, Asian spices, charcoal, and subtle trufflelike scents. Huge, massive, and full bodied, with phenomenal flavor extraction, and beautifully integrated tannin and acidity, this flamboyant, exceptionally well endowed Cabernet Sauvignon continues the succession of titanic wines made under this label. Anticipated maturity: 2002–2027. The unfined and unfiltered 1996 Cabernet Franc reveals a smoky, meaty, beef blood and black fruit-scented nose with loamy soil scents providing additional aromatic dimension. The wine possesses exceptional richness of fruit, thrilling quantities of glycerin, an impressive midpalate, and an admirably long finish. Fruit ripeness, texture, and richness are important in any wine, but La Jota manages to cram all of these components into the difficult to grow and make Cabernet Franc varietal. This effort is another benchmark Cabernet Franc that should drink well for 12–15+ years. The 1996 Petite Sirah also stands out as a reference point for its type. It offers a saturated black/purple color, followed by a stunning nose of roasted meats, saddle leather, beef juices, and spicy wood. There is compelling richness, super intensity, and gobs of black fruits in this surprisingly supple, chewy, exciting offering. It should drink well for 20 years.

I am convinced La Jota is making the finest Cabernet Franc produced in California. I love this wine, and I am consistently reminded of how well it ages whenever I taste the 1986, superb since its birth. This is not one of the more delicate styles of Cabernet Franc, but it does have compelling complexity, as well as a rich, intense, concentrated character. The 1995 Cabernet Franc is another knockout effort that may be even better than the 1996. It boasts a black/ruby/purple color, as well as more structured aromatics with smoke, beef juices, saddle leather, and black fruits soaring out of the glass. On the palate, the wine reveals earthy, roasted meat, blackberry, and cassis flavors, with good glycerin, more noticeable tannin than the 1996, and a well-delineated, spicy, intense finish. The wine may take more time to round out when it is released, but their Cabernet Franc redefines the quality standards for this varietal. The spectacular 1994 Cabernet Franc offers a pronounced sweet, smoky, earthy, roasted meat, black cherry, and cassis-scented nose. Dense, with fabulous concentration, a chewy texture, and a full-bodied, long, layered finish, this wine is already difficult to resist, but it should keep for 12–15 years. The 1993 Cabernet Franc (350 cases) displays a gorgeously scented, aromatic nose of black currants, herbs, and spices, as well as a velvety, decadent richness, smooth as silk tannin, and a long, lusty, low acid finish. Drink it over the next 12–15 years.

The 1995 Petite Sirah is a huge, monolithic wine with an opaque blue/black color, huge body, copious amounts of thick, juicy fruit, and a lashing of tannin at the back of the palate. It is a touch more angular and backward than either the 1994 is, or the 1996 promises to be, but it has exceptional potential. Anticipated maturity: 2005-2020. La Jota's 1994 Petite Sirah Howell Mountain (aged in 90% new French oak) is an awesome wine. It exhibits one of the most extraordinary jammy blueberry-scented noses I have ever encountered. Unbelievably rich and full bodied, yet remarkably soft, this multilayered, fabulously concentrated wine will be approachable young (rare for Petite Sirah), yet age for 20 or more years. Petite Sirah can be the most underrated wine made in California. Put this one on your shopping list—it is great! The 1993 Petite Sirah is a worthy successor to the terrific 1991 and excellent 1992. The deep ruby/purple color is followed by intense aromas of pepper, jammy black currants, spicy oak, and earth. Rich and full bodied, with a viscous texture, this wine oozes with ripe, concentrated fruit. It is enormous, but neither heavy-handed nor out of balance. The ripe tannin is remarkably well integrated. This terrific Petite Sirah can be drunk now or cellared for 20 years.

The two Cabernet Sauvignon cuvées are similar in quality. The Howell Mountain Select and Anniversary Release share dense, concentrated, full-bodied personalities with superlative levels of fruit and extract. The Anniversary cuvée usually has a bit more depth, ripeness, and overall potential, but that is not always easily discernible when they are young. Each wine will last—at the minimum—20 years. Readers can decide whether they prefer the more open-knit opulence of the 1994, the more austere, jagged tannins of the big 1995, or the forceful power of the 1996. As for the 1994 Cabernet Sauvignon Howell Mountain Select, this wine performed exceptionally well in a large tasting of 1994 California Cabernets I conducted. The wine is full bodied, with an opaque purple color, as well as potentially sweeter, more up-front fruit than the Anniversary Release. It is opulent, aromatic (black fruits, truffles, earth, and spice galore), and fleshy, but it boasts plenty of tannin. Look for it to close down in another year or two, not to reemerge for 7–8. It will last 2 decades. The formidable 1994 Cabernet Sauvignon 13th Anniversary may be the finest Cabernet Sauvignon Joan and Bill Smith have yet made. It boasts an opaque purple color, followed by a smoky, toasty, mineral, and cassis-scented nose, great persistence in the mouth, massive body, and an expansive, chewy, blockbuster finish, without coming across as excessively heavy or overweight. Give it 5–6 years of cellaring and drink it over the following 20–25 years. It is a Cabernet legend in the making!

The 1995 Cabernet Sauvignon Howell Mountain Select revealed some rough tannin when I tasted it in October of 1997. While none of these wines is filtered, the Smiths did do a light egg-white fining in an attempt to produce a more civilized style. The 1995 is deep, muscular, rich, and impressive, but it is in need of 5–6 years of cellaring. I suspect this wine will age effortlessly for another 2 decades. Also a monster, the tannic 1995 Cabernet Sauvignon 14th

Anniversary Release is unquestionably a huge, mountain-styled Cabernet. It exhibits a black/purple color and a reticent but promising nose of minerals, smoke, black currants, and underbrush. Although full bodied and excruciatingly tannic, there is enough fruit to balance out the wine's structure. It may be as backward as the Cabernet Sauvignon made by Dunn on another Howell Mountain slope; this wine needs 5–8 years of cellaring.

The 1993 Cabernet Sauvignon 12th Anniversary is nearly as profound as the 1992. A compelling wine, it possesses an opaque black color, and a fabulous nose of chocolate, smoke, and cassis. Extremely full bodied, with sweet tannin, low acidity, and fantastic concentration, this is a spectacular Cabernet Sauvignon for drinking now and over the next 25 years.

There are 1,250 cases of the 1993 Cabernet Sauvignon Howell Mountain. Approximately half the price of the Anniversary Selection, it is certainly not a mere half the wine. In fact, it is a great Cabernet Sauvignon, offering an opaque purple color, a rich nose of black fruits, earth, and toast, and a sweet, immensely generous, full-bodied, glycerin-infused finish. Considerable tannin is undoubtedly lurking behind the exceptional quantities of fruit, but it is impossible to taste given this wine's impressive concentration, ripeness, and length. Approachable now, it should glide through the next 15–20 years with nary a problem. The stunning 1994 Cabernet Sauvignon Howell Mountain reveals an opaque black color, gobs of sweet cassis and licorice scents, remarkable fat and opulence, and a chewy, long finish.

LAIL VINEYARDS (NAPA)

1995 J. Daniel Cuvée		Napa E	91

Robin Lail is a veteran Napa Valley resident who was raised in a winemaking family (her father was the legendary John Daniel who fashioned many of Inglenook's greatest Cabernet Sauvignons). A former partner of Christian Moueix in the Dominus operation, Robin Lail has branched out on her own to produce limited quantities (about 450 cases) of a graceful, elegant, proprietary red wine from vineyards in Yountville, Vine Hill Road, and Howell Mountain. The 1995 J. Daniel Cuvée is the debut release from Lail Vineyards. An outstanding effort, it is a blend of 56% Merlot and 44% Cabernet Sauvignon made by Philip Melka (the winemaker at Seavey). The wine is a beautifully rendered, Médoc-like California red with a dense, saturated ruby/purple color, and stylish, complex aromatics consisting of tobacco, black currants, crème de cassis, and subtle toasty oak (approximately 33% new oak casks are utilized). The wine is medium to full bodied, with sweet tannin, a graceful, long mid-palate and finish, and 15 or more years of potential evolution. From the finesse/elegant school of California proprietary reds, this wine is rich and layered, with everything in impeccable balance. Anticipated maturity: now–2015. Given the small quantities produced, this wine will undoubtedly be sold largely via a mailing list.

LANCASTER RESERVE (ALEXANDER VALLEY)

1995 Proprietary Red Estate	Alexander Valley E	90

Only 8,600 bottles were produced of this proprietary wine (a blend of 82% Cabernet Sauvignon and 18% Cabernet Franc). It is extremely backward and unevolved, with an opaque purple color, and a promising nose of blackberries, raspberries, and copious quantities of toasty new oak. This massive, tightly knit, full-bodied, tannic wine exhibits impressive depth and purity, but it requires 3–4 years of cellaring. Patience will be necessary for those who latch onto this limited production gem. Anticipated maturity: 2002–2018.

LANDMARK VINEYARDS (SONOMA)

1997 Chardonnay Demaris Reserve	Sonoma	E	(90–91)
1996 Chardonnay Demaris Reserve	Sonoma	D	92

1995	Chardonnay Demaris Reserve	Sonoma	C	90
1997	Chardonnay Lorenzo Vineyard	Russian River	E	(91–92)
1996	Chardonnay Lorenzo Vineyard	Russian River	D	92
1997	Chardonnay Overlook	California	E	(88–89)
1996	Chardonnay Overlook	Sonoma	C	89
1995	Chardonnay Overlook	Sonoma	C	88
1995	Pinot Noir	Sonoma	C	89
1994	Pinot Noir	Sonoma	C	89
1997	Pinot Noir Grand Detour Van der Kamp Vineyard	Sonoma Mountain	D	(90–92)
1996	Pinot Noir Grand Detour Van der Kamp Vineyard	Sonoma Mountain	D	90
1997	Pinot Noir Kastania Vineyard	Sonoma Coast	E	(91–93)

Winemaker Eric Stern deserves accolades for the high quality work he is doing at Landmark. These are naturally made wines from top vineyard sources. Everything is fermented with indigenous yeasts, and all the wines, except for the Overlook Chardonnay, are bottled with neither fining nor filtration. The complex, Burgundian-styled Chardonnays have soared in quality. The winery also produces serious Pinot Noir. The most abundantly produced wine is the Overlook Chardonnay (15,000 cases in 1997). The 1996 Chardonnay Overlook possesses excellent viscosity, an elegant, rich, leesy, lemon butter, honeysuckle, smoky, concentrated, medium- to full-bodied personality. This well-made Chardonnay enjoyed 25% new oak. It should continue to drink well for 2–3 years. The unfined/unfiltered 1996 Chardonnay Demaris Reserve is fermented in 90% new oak, and spends 12 months in contact with its lees, with considerable stirring. This is a profoundly complex offering, with liquid minerals, roasted hazelnuts, buttered citrus, and orange blossomlike aromas and flavors. It is a full-bodied yet beautifully textured wine with good underlying acidity, and impressive length. I'm still drinking my 1995 Demaris Reserve, which continues to evolve and improve. The 1996 should continue to evolve for another 3–5 years. In 1996, Landmark began purchasing fruit from the well-known Lorenzo Vineyard. This has been a source for Helen Turley and Terry Leighton (Kalin Cellars). Landmark's 1996 Chardonnay Lorenzo Vineyard is another lovely unfined/unfiltered Chardonnay bursting with potential. It exhibits a light straw color, a distinctive nose of liquid minerals, lime/lemon, and smoky, roasted nut scents, and rich, full-bodied flavors with notes of white flowers, peaches, and citrus. A classic, powerful yet elegant Chardonnay, it should drink well for 4–5 years.

In 1997 yields were higher, but quality was stunning. The 1997 Chardonnay Overlook will include fruit from both Monterey and Santa Barbara, as production has grown to 15,000 cases. There is no drop in quality, as this offering will be bottled without filtration. It possesses more tropical fruit in the nose (Santa Barbara's influence?), with copious amounts of honeyed citrus and lemon butter notes. The oak's influence is subtle in this fruit-driven, elegant, rich, complex, nicely textured wine. It should drink well for 2–3 years. The stunning 1997 Chardonnay Demaris Reserve (2,500 cases) displays a smoky, concentrated style, tangy acidity (slightly higher than in 1996), excellent aromatics (leesy, buttery tropical fruits), and a full-bodied, concentrated finish with a zesty vibrancy and purity. Although less evolved than the 1996, it promises to last for 4–5 years. Once again the 1997 Chardonnay Lorenzo Vineyard exhibits the intense minerality of this vineyard's fruit. Additionally, notes of tangerines, orange blossoms, ripe apples, and citrus fruit make an appearance in this medium- to full-bodied, gorgeously proportioned wine. Moreover, it has the finest length. The Lorenzo is capable of lasting 5 or more years.

The 1995 Chardonnay Overlook is a rich, medium- to full-bodied wine with an enticing blend of lemony/citrusy fruit, a whiff of honey, and subtle oak in the background. With excellent ripeness, good underlying acidity, and a fresh, vibrant personality, it should drink well for several years. The bigger, richer 1995 Chardonnay Demaris Reserve was aged in a higher percentage of new oak barrels. With more body and intensity, this spicy, well-defined, full-bodied, powerful Chardonnay's bouquet is reminiscent of lemon meringue pie. It offers up leesy, yeasty, breadlike aromas, along with honeyed, lemony, citrus notes. This rich, dense, promising wine should drink well for 2–3 years.

As delicious and complex as Landmark's Chardonnays are, the Pinot Noirs are getting better with each vintage. These unfined/unfiltered, Burgundian-styled offerings are given 60% new oak. There are 1,000 cases of the Grand Detour, but only 125 cases of the new Kastania Vineyard Pinot Noir from the Sonoma Coast. The 1996 Pinot Noir Grand Detour Van der Kamp Vineyard offers a big, smoky, complex nose filled with aromas of black cherries, *jus de viande*, clove, and allspice. It is a meaty, full-bodied, richly spicy yet supple-textured, expansive, delicious Pinot Noir. The wine's provocative aromatics and earthy, smoky style will serve it well over the next 5–6 years. The 1997 Pinot Noir Grand Detour Van der Kamp Vineyard possesses even sweeter fruit. Eric Stern told me the alcohol is higher, coming in above 14%. The 1997 displays more viscosity than the 1996, as well as a sumptuous mouthfeel, and copious quantities of black cherry and currant fruit intermixed with underbrush, smoke, and *pain grillé* notes. It is a full-bodied, hedonistic, yet intellectually satisfying Pinot Noir to enjoy over the next 5–6 years. Sadly, the 1997 Pinot Noir Kastania Vineyard's limited production ensures that few consumers will have a chance to taste it. From a 5-acre vineyard, this spectacular example boasts a saturated opaque ruby/purple color, followed by telltale aromas of black raspberries, black cherries, and cassis. Medium to full bodied and rich, with a silky texture, and superb purity, it has soaked up its aging in 100% new French oak casks, leaving only a subtle hint of wood. Simply stated, this is one more persuasive example of what heights Pinot Noir can achieve from the Sonoma Coast's hillside vineyards.

The 1995 Pinot Noir, from a Sonoma Mountain vineyard, reveals a Burgundian, earthy, smoked meat, black cherry-scented nose, sweet, round, expansive flavors, a medium- to full-bodied weightiness in the mouth, and an expansive texture. Already delicious, this wine will continue to drink well for another 5–6 years. In 1994, an unfined/unfiltered Pinot Noir was produced from a vineyard on Sonoma Mountain. Only 450 cases were made of this excellent wine. It exhibits a sweet, intense nose of black cherries, earth, and spice, full body, good fatness, an expansive, chewy, soft texture, and a sweet, ripe, heady finish. It is reminiscent of a bigger-styled, fleshy wine from Beaune. Drink this seductive Pinot Noir over the next 4–5 years.

LAUREL GLEN (SONOMA)

1994 Cabernet Sauvignon	Sonoma Mountain	D	93
1993 Cabernet Sauvignon	Sonoma Mountain	D	95

Laurel Glen is one of California's most admirable operations, and its estate Cabernet Sauvignon is at the top of the qualitative hierarchy. The 1994 reveals an opaque purple color, and a tight but promising nose of jammy black fruits, spice, earth, and a whiff of Provençal herbs. Full bodied, with layers of chewy, fleshy, ripe fruit, this highly extracted, moderately tannic, blockbuster Cabernet should prove to be accessible when released. That being said, this wine should be cellared for 4–5 years and drunk over the following 15–20.

Laurel Glen has been producing one dazzling effort after another, especially since 1990. The wines are agonizingly difficult to find in the marketplace. The blockbuster, backward

1993 Cabernet Sauvignon rivals Girard's Reserve as one of the most powerful, tannic wines of the vintage, but there is more sweetness and a higher level of concentration and ripe fruit in the Laurel Glen offering, making its aging potential less risky. This is a huge, massive, herb, black currant/black cherry, smoky, chocolatey wine with gobs of fruit, eye-popping extract levels, and mouth-searing tannin. Based on this barrel sample, my best guess for the wine's anticipated maturity is between 2002 and 2025. Impressive! But patience is definitely required.

LIMERICK LANE VINEYARDS (SONOMA)

1994 Zinfandel Collins Vineyard	Russian River	C	87
1993 Zinfandel Collins Vineyard	Russian River	C	82

The tasty, medium-bodied 1994 Zinfandel reveals a soft underbelly, a plush texture, and pure fruit. It is not especially concentrated or big, but it is elegant and delicious. Drink it over the next 3–4 years. The vinous, spicy, lightly fruity, medium-bodied 1993 Zinfandel is made in a pleasant, straightforward style. There is some acidity, but not enough concentration to merit a more enthusiastic review. A clean, correct wine for drinking over the next 4–5 years, it appears significantly different in style than its predecessors, especially the 1992, one of the stars of that vintage.

LITTORAI (NAPA)

1997 Chardonnay Mays Canyon	Russian River	D	(89–92)
1996 Chardonnay Mays Canyon	Russian River	D	91
1995 Chardonnay Mays Canyon	Russian River	D	91
1996 Chardonnay Occidental	Sonoma Coast	D	91
1995 Chardonnay Occidental	Sonoma Coast	D	89+
1995 Pinot Noir	Anderson Valley	D	88
1997 Pinot Noir Hirsch Vineyard	Sonoma Coast	D	(86–87?)
1996 Pinot Noir Hirsch Vineyard	Sonoma Coast	D	87+
1995 Pinot Noir Hirsch Vineyard	Sonoma Coast	D	88+
1994 Pinot Noir Hirsch Vineyard	Sonoma Coast	D	90
1997 Pinot Noir One Acre	Anderson Valley	D	(90–94)
1996 Pinot Noir One Acre	Anderson Valley	D	87
1995 Pinot Noir One Acre	Anderson Valley	D	88
1997 Pinot Noir Savoy Vineyard	Anderson Valley	D	(88–89+)
1996 Pinot Noir Savoy Vineyard	Anderson Valley	D	89
1995 Pinot Noir Savoy Vineyard	Anderson Valley	D	89
1994 Pinot Noir Savoy Vineyard	Anderson Valley	D	90
1997 Pinot Noir Thieriot Vineyard	Sonoma Coast	D	(86–87)

This small artisanal producer has moved to a barn/winery high on Howell Mountain, adjacent to the Black Sears Vineyard. Proprietors Heidi and Ted Lemon continue to turn out some of California's most elegant, flavorful, subtle wines.

Littorai's 1997 Chardonnays were still finishing their malolactic fermentation when I visited, so I was not able to taste the new offerings. Moreover, there will no longer be a Chardonnay offered from the Occidental Vineyard on the Sonoma Coast. The only Chardonnay I tasted is the 1997 Chardonnay Mays Canyon, which appears to be an elegant, Burgundian-styled wine with excellent richness, an attractive, leesy, gravelly nose intertwined with tropical fruits, mango, and tangerine notes. The oak was barely discernible in this medium- to full-bodied, complex, potentially outstanding Chardonnay that should age well for 4–5 years.

In 1997 there are four Pinot Noir offerings. Ted Lemon told me that he did a *saignée* of all his 1997 Pinots because of high yields, and that all of these wines were scheduled to be bottled with neither fining nor filtration. The 1997 Pinot Noir Thieriot Vineyard comes from both the Pommard and Joseph Swan clones. The vineyard is across from the Summa Vineyard, a site where Williams-Selyem produced a handful of terrific Pinots. The Thieriot Vineyard offering reminds me of a good premier cru Beaune with its bing cherry, earthy, loamy soil scents. Medium bodied and elegant, with crisp, tangy acidity, and a fresh, vibrant appeal, it should age nicely for 4–5 years. More interesting and complex is the stylish 1997 Pinot Noir Savoy Vineyard. Made from the Dijon clone 115 and the Pommard clone, it possesses a medium ruby color, attractive, deeper, richer, black cherry and cassis aromas, excellent ripeness on the attack, medium body, firm tannin, and a pure style with a subtle influence of wood. This wine will benefit from 1–2 years of cellaring and keep for nearly a decade.

Many of the Pinot Noirs I have tasted from the Sonoma Coast's Hirsch Vineyard tend to be powerhouse Pinots that push tannin levels to the limit—at least for my palate. That seems to be the case even with the subtle touch of winemaker Ted Lemon. The 1997 Pinot Noir Hirsch Vineyard (made primarily from such clones as Mount Eden and Pommard) is the densest of these first three wines, but the tannin level is scary, and I am not sure it will ever become completely integrated. It gives the wine an angular personality, and adds to the austere finish. It is potentially a very fine Pinot Noir given its earthy black fruit character and meaty, mineral, peppery notes. The wine is medium bodied and purely made, but the tannin is a legitimate cause for concern. There are 200 cases of the spectacular 1997 Pinot Noir One Acre Vineyard from Anderson Valley. This wine could easily pass for a top-notch premier cru from the Côte de Nuits. Made from modest yields, it reveals a deep ruby color with purple nuances. The aromatics include black cherries, cassis, spice, herb, and flower blossoms. Medium to full bodied, with terrific fruit purity, and a lush, open-knit texture, this complex Pinot Noir possesses sensational potential. The wine will be approachable when released, yet should age nicely for 7–8 years.

In 1996, I saw many Chardonnays with less flavor, complexity and length than their 1995 counterparts, but that is not the case at Littorai. The 1996 Chardonnay Occidental will be bottled unfiltered after having spent its entire barrel life on its lees. It is an exceptional Chardonnay, with a mineral, honeyed citrus, medium- to full-bodied personality. With its intense but subtle flavors that unfold in the glass and on the palate, this poised, luscious, layered Chardonnay gives every indication of developing nicely for another 3–4 years. The 1996 Chardonnay Mays Canyon, from a gravelly hillside vineyard surrounded on three sides by the Russian River, reveals scents of tropical fruits intertwined with subtle *pain grillé* and orange rind notes. A thicker, richer wine buttressed by surprisingly fine acidity for a 1996, this is an exceptional, interesting, complex Chardonnay that should age nicely for 2–4 years.

The 1995 Chardonnays, which are largely sold out, include the 1995 Chardonnay Mays Canyon, a deep, rich, honeysuckle-scented, flavorful wine with a wonderful texture and length. The wine is full bodied, with a more obvious California personality than the mineral-laden, peach, orange, and citrusy 1995 Chardonnay Occidental. Both wines possess tangy underlying acidity, as well as the hallmarks of all the Littorai wines—purity, equilibrium, and subtlety.

Ted Lemon is not the first to exploit Pinot Noir in the Anderson Valley, but he is one of the best. His 1996 Pinot Noir One Acre is a delicious, cherry-scented and -flavored Pinot that reminds me of a premier cru from the Côte de Beaune. Forward and ripe, it possesses a silky texture, and finishes with nice length and the judicious use of new oak (about 50% new oak barrels were employed). Drinkable now, it should be consumed over the next 2–3 years. The 1996 Pinot Noir Savoy Vineyard is a deeper, richer wine with medium body, a deep ruby color, and an attractive nose of cherries, blackberries, and a touch of plum. There is firm tannin in the wine's medium-bodied, attractive finish. While it can be consumed now, it promises to improve over the next 1–2 years, although I think drinking it within its first 5–7 years of life makes sense. The most structured of the 1996 Pinot Noirs is the Hirsch Vineyard. I have tasted Hirsch Vineyard offerings from Littorai, Kistler, Siduri, and Whitcraft, and an imposing structure is a characteristic of this vineyard's wines. Littorai's Hirsch Vineyard exhibits a deep ruby/purple color, followed by a distinctive earthy, *terroir* character with the blackberry/cherry fruit pushed to the background. This is an intellectual rather than pleasure-oriented style of Pinot Noir. It is easy to admire the winemaking and quality of the wine, but it is a spartan style of Pinot. Give it a minimum of 1–2 years of cellaring.

In retasting the 1995 Pinot Noirs, the 1995 Pinot Noir One Acre is a delicate, delicious, soft, round, berry-laden, hedonistic Pinot. It is ideal for drinking now and over the next 3–4 years. The 1995 Pinot Noir Savoy has begun to close down, but it does reveal a Volnay premier cru purity of berry fruit, elegant, moderately intense aromatics, a subtle influence of toasty oak, and firm tannin. It fills out beautifully in the midpalate, and is destined to evolve for another 4–6 years. Lastly, the 1995 Pinot Noir Hirsch Vineyard is the most austere, with the firmest tannin, and the toughest texture. It needs another 1–2 years of cellaring, but it promises to offer a gutsy, meaty, mineral, and peppery personality. Although it does not possess the finesse of either the One Acre or Savoy Vineyard cuvée, it is an intriguing, larger-scaled Pinot Noir that should evolve for up to a decade.

The 1995 Pinot Noir Anderson Valley is a dead ringer for a high class premier cru from Beaune. The wine exhibits a deep ruby color, a Volnay-like, black cherry sweetness, a supple texture, and an attractive floral note combined with subtle toasty oak. Although tight, it reveals a soft, velvety texture, and a gentle tactile impression. Bottled unfined and unfiltered, it needs another 6–12 months of bottle age, after which it will drink well for 5–7 years.

A longer time in bottle has permitted the 1994s to begin exhibiting more character. The 1994 Pinot Noir Savoy Vineyard in Anderson Valley offers a sweet, black fruit and sour cherry-scented nose with aromas of earth and spicy oak. The wine is ripe and fleshy, as well as elegant and well balanced. It should drink well for 5–6 years. Similar to the 1995, the 1994 Pinot Noir Hirsch Vineyard displays a medium ruby color, followed by a tight, sour cherry and vanilla-scented nose, complete, rich, medium- to full-bodied flavors, superb purity, and a long finish. Much of the wine's personality comes through at the back of the palate, suggesting that this wine still needs 1–2 years of cellaring. It will age gracefully for 10–12 years.

LOKOYA (NAPA)

1995	Cabernet Sauvignon Diamond Mountain	Napa	EE	93
1995	Cabernet Sauvignon Howell Mountain	Napa	EE	90
1995	Cabernet Sauvignon Mt. Veeder	Napa	EE	91
1994	Cabernet Sauvignon Mt. Veeder	Napa	D	94
1994	Cabernet Sauvignon Oakville District	Napa	D	89
1995	Cabernet Sauvignon Rutherford	Napa	EE	94
1996	Chardonnay	Napa	D	88
1995	Chardonnay	Napa	D	90

Another luxury operation in the Kendall-Jackson portfolio, this winery appears to be doing everything right. The wines are 100% Cabernet Sauvignons made in limited quantities of

250–350 cases. The wines are aged in 100% French oak casks (45%–75% new), malolactic fermentation is done in barrel, and the wines are bottled with no filtration. All of these wines revealed outstanding aromatics, natural, chewy, expansive textures, and exceptionally ripe, concentrated fruit. Moreover, they are candidates for 20 or more years of cellaring. In short, I am very enthusiastic about this project.

The 1995 Cabernet Sauvignon Mt. Veeder (1,600 cases) reveals an opaque purple color, and a sumptuous, Médoc-like nose of lead pencil, minerals, black currants, and smoky oak. It is extremely full bodied and massive in the mouth, with sweet tannin, a layered, plushly textured midpalate, and a firm, exceptionally long, pure finish. This classic mountain-styled Cabernet Sauvignon can be drunk now, but it will be even better with 5–7 years of cellaring. It will keep for 2 decades. The limited production 1995 Cabernet Sauvignon Howell Mountain (25 cases) is dominated by minerals and wet stones intertwined with blackberry and cassis flavors. More structured and tannic, as well as less extroverted than the Mt. Veeder, the Howell Mountain cuvée is not for readers seeking immediate gratification. Anticipated maturity: 2005–2018. The sensational 1995 Cabernet Sauvignon Diamond Mountain (330 cases) boasts an opaque blue/black color, followed by outstanding aromatics of jammy blackberry and currant fruit intertwined with roasted herbs, cold steel, minerals, and spicy new oak. There is fabulous intensity, terrific levels of glycerin and extract, full body, and sweet tannin in the long, low-acid finish. This superb, dazzling Cabernet Sauvignon reveals tremendous upside potential. Anticipated maturity: 2000–2020. The 1995 Cabernet Sauvignon Rutherford (300 cases) possesses the most developed aromatics, consisting of black currants, cherries, loamy soil scents, and *pain grillé*. It is the most expansive and fullest bodied, with stunningly concentrated flavors that exhibit no angularity or sharpness. The acidity, tannin, alcohol, and wood are all gorgeously integrated into this fleshy, succulent, voluptuously textured wine. The finish lasts for 40+ seconds. Despite its accessibility, this Cabernet will be even better with another 5 years of cellaring and will keep for 20–25 years.

It appears that the Kendall-Jackson group known as *Artisans and Estates* is positioning Lokoya as their superluxury wine estate, along with Cardinale, Hartford Court, Kristone, and Stonestreet. There are other estates in this group, but these appear to be the most expensive wines in the portfolio. I have been impressed with the initial releases from Lokoya, which produces intense wines largely from mountainside vineyards. The 1996 Chardonnay, made from grape sources on Veeder Peak, Carneros, and the Liparita Vineyard on Howell Mountain, is not quite as impressive as the 1995 (a common thread in contrasting the two vintages for Chardonnay), but it reveals high-toned, ripe, buttery, mineral-laden flavors with good body, fine underlying acidity, and a pure, moderately long finish. The wine is not as expressive as it will be after another 6 months of bottle age. It should keep for 2–3 years. The 1995 Chardonnay offers a Burgundian-like earthy, mineral personality, with smoked hazelnut, rich, buttery popcorn, and tropical fruit scents. The wine is medium to full bodied, rich, and well delineated by zesty acidity in addition to the influence of high quality French barrels. It should drink well for 2–4 years.

The 1994 Cabernet Sauvignon Oakville District (800 cases) is made from 100% Cabernet Sauvignon, of which 90% came from the Vine Hill Ranch and 10% from Mt. Veeder. The wine was aged for 22 months in small barrels, of which 40% were new. It exhibits an opaque purple color, a sweet, ripe, olive, chocolate, smoky, cassis-scented nose, dense, full-bodied flavors, moderate tannin, potentially exceptional extract, fine purity, and a long, spicy finish. The wine admirably combines the purity and ripeness of California fruit with a slight degree of the austerity and restraint exhibited by a top Bordeaux. Even more impressive is the 1994 Cabernet Sauvignon Mt. Veeder (700 cases). This wine is an immense, monster-styled Cabernet Sauvignon that is vaguely reminiscent of the pre-1976 vintages of Mayacamas, but with more complexity and finesse. It is a mountain Cabernet with an opaque black/purple color, followed by a tight, backward, but promising nose of licorice, minerals, and black fruits. The inky color suggests a formidably endowed wine, and that is just what this huge, superconcentrated, impressively endowed Cabernet Sauvignon represents. The wine is not just a ponderous heavyweight, as anyone who examines its equilibrium, harmony, and potential for 20–30 years of aging should notice. Remarkably, this wine was kept in 60% new French oak barrels, but the oak has been soaked up by the wine's intense fruit level. Patience will be a virtue required by prospective purchasers of this wine. Anticipated maturity: 2003–2020.

LOLONIS WINE CELLARS (MENDOCINO)

1994 Cabernet Sauvignon Estate	Mendocino County	B	87+
1994 Zinfandel Organic	Mendocino	C	84+
1994 Zinfandel Private Reserve Organic	Mendocino	C	85
1996 Zinfandel Redwood Valley	Mendocino	C	87

A fairly priced, high quality Zinfandel, this 1996 offering, from an organically cultivated vineyard, exhibits a dark ruby color, and delicious, up-front raspberry/cherry and assorted berrylike fruit intermixed with copious quantities of spice and pepper. On the palate, the wine is supple, round, medium to full bodied, and graceful. With a charming, seductive personality, this middle-weight Zin (the alcohol is a reasonable 13.5%) is symmetrical, harmonious, and a good value. Drink it over the next 2–3 years.

The attractive dark ruby/purple-colored 1994 Cabernet Sauvignon Estate possesses aromas of sweet, toasty, black currant fruit nicely dosed with wood. The earthy, medium-bodied flavors display fine ripeness, sweet fruit, and a monolithic but copious, generously endowed personality. Drink this soft, mouth-filling Cabernet over the next 8–9 years.

Both of the 1994 Zinfandels are earthy, loamy, peppery-styled Zinfandels with medium to full body and attractive fruit, as well as aggressive, coarse tannin. The dark ruby-colored 1994 Zinfandel possesses higher acidity than the deeply saturated, purple-colored 1994 Private Reserve. Both are well made, straightforward, generally unexciting wines that will age for 4–5 years.

LONG VINEYARDS (NAPA)

1995 Cabernet Sauvignon	Napa	D	86+
1994 Cabernet Sauvignon	Napa	C	89?
1993 Cabernet Sauvignon	Napa	C	84?

The 1995 Cabernet is more reminiscent of a briary, peppery Zinfandel than a Cabernet Sauvignon. Elegant, soft, round, and made in an up-front style, this easygoing, fruity, midweight, moderately endowed wine is well made, but there is not a lot to it. Drink it over the next 6–7 years.

The full-bodied, muscular, backward 1994 Cabernet Sauvignon offers up a moderately intense, smoky, chocolatey, black cherry, and cassis-scented nose, rich, tightly wound flavors, moderate acidity, high tannin, and a firm, structured, austere finish. Although it should turn out to be an excellent Cabernet, it is formidably tannic and backward, and will require 5–7 years of cellaring after its release. It's a keeper.

Although it exhibits an impressively saturated color, the lean, compact 1993 Cabernet Sauvignon reveals an excess of tannin, a slight deficiency in ripeness, and an overall sense of toughness and rusticity without enough fat, fruit, or charm. At present, the tannin dominates what appears to be a meager expression of Cabernet Sauvignon fruit.

LONGORIA WINE CELLARS (SANTA BARBARA)

1996 Chardonnay Santa Rita	Santa Ynez	D	87
1994 Pinot Noir Bien Nacido Vineyard	Santa Maria Valley	D	86
1993 Pinot Noir Bien Nacido Vineyard	Santa Ynez	D	86

The oak may be a bit excessive, but the medium- to full-bodied 1996 Chardonnay Santa Rita provides attractive buttery, pear, pineapple, and honey aromas and flavors. It offers a chunky, fleshy personality, but less perfume and complexity than exhibited by previous examples.

Medium dark garnet-colored, with an herbal, toasty new oak, spicy, woody nose, the medium-bodied, sweet, jammy-styled 1994 Pinot Noir has been heavily wooded, but the fruit has managed to survive. While it is living dangerously, at present it is satisfying, spicy, and ideal for drinking over the next several years. The spicy, rich, medium- to full-bodied 1993 Pinot Noir possesses very good berry flavors, a subtle herbaceousness, and good length. Drink it over the next 5–6 years.

MacROSTIE (CARNEROS)

1996 Chardonnay	Carneros	C	86

Vibrant tropical fruit dosed with moderate levels of wood dominate the personality of this medium-bodied, cleanly made Chardonnay. Although not complex, it is mouth-filling, fruity, and attractive in an unpretentious way. Drink it over the next year.

MARCASSIN VINEYARD (SONOMA)

1997 Chardonnay Gauer Ranch Upper Barn	Sonoma	E	96
1996 Chardonnay Gauer Ranch Upper Barn	Sonoma	E	94
1995 Chardonnay Gauer Ranch Upper Barn	Sonoma	E	96
1997 Chardonnay Hudson Vineyard	Carneros	E	94
1996 Chardonnay Hudson Vineyard	Carneros	E	92
1995 Chardonnay Hudson Vineyard	Carneros	E	97
1997 Chardonnay Lorenzo Vineyard	Carneros	E	93+
1996 Chardonnay Lorenzo Vineyard	Carneros	E	96
1995 Chardonnay Lorenzo Vineyard	Carneros	E	95
1997 Chardonnay Marcassin Vineyard	Sonoma Coast	E	(99–100)
1996 Chardonnay Marcassin Vineyard	Sonoma Coast	E	97
1995 Chardonnay Marcassin Vineyard	Sonoma Coast	E	90+
1997 Pinot Noir Marcassin Vineyard	Sonoma Coast	E	(94–98)
1996 Pinot Noir Marcassin Vineyard	Sonoma Coast	E	98
1995 Pinot Noir Marcassin Vineyard	Sonoma Coast	E	93

I cannot think of any other winemakers whom I respect and admire more than Helen Turley and her husband, John Wetlaufer. Their contributions to California viticulture and wine-making are rewriting the book on how to achieve world-class quality. In their case, the formula is fundamentally simple: 1) go back to nature, asking the vineyard to produce conservatively, 2) vinify the wine with indigenous yeasts, 3) treat the wine in barrel as if it were an infant (which it is), and 4) bottle it with tender loving care (no fining or filtration). One after another compelling wines have emerged under the Marcassin label. That alone would suffice as a noteworthy achievement, but consider the range of extraordinary wines (Gewürztraminer, Chardonnay, Zinfandel, Pinot Noir, Merlot, and Cabernet Sauvignon) that Helen Turley has produced for Pahlmeyer, Colgin, Bryant Family Vineyards, and Martinelli, all her clients. Has anybody ever produced such a diverse array of wines with such singular artistic greatness?

Marcassin continues to purchase fruit from the Hudson, Lorenzo, and Gauer Ranch vineyards (now renamed by its owner, Kendall-Jackson, the Alexander Mountain Vineyard), but fortunately their 9-acre Sonoma Coast vineyard has come into production, giving consumers a taste of this Montrachet-like, steely/mineral-laden Chardonnay and their earthy, Clos de la Roche-inspired Pinot Noir. Tasting Marcassin can be challenging from a critic's perspective—the wines are almost beyond critique!

Although quantities are still minute, the total production has risen, as the 1997 vintage was a generous one. The 1997 Chardonnay Gauer Ranch Upper Barn (approximately 360 cases) exhibits a light gold color, and a blossoming nose of tropical fruits intermixed with leesy, buttery notes, roasted nuts, citrus, and floral scents. The potential complexity of this wine's bouquet is awesome. It is medium to full bodied (14.1% alcohol), with a multilayered, honeyed richness and fabulous concentration, yet no sense of heaviness. The wine hits every sweet spot on the palate, overloading the olfactory senses. It is one of the finest Gauer Ranch cuvées to be released. I would recommend 1–2 years of bottle age before consuming this wine over the following 7–8 years. The 1997 Chardonnay Hudson Vineyard (about 275 cases) tips the scales at a lofty 14.4% alcohol, but you would never know that when tasting the wine since there is not a trace of hotness. Sadly, the Turley/Wetlaufer team has decided to no longer purchase fruit from this vineyard, preferring to deal only with vineyard sources that they can totally control. The wine's exotic nose of jammy orange marmalade, pineapple, and loamy soil notes is brilliant. Complex, rich, and expansive on the palate, with medium to full body, and a slightly closed personality, it offers an exotic, spicy, earthy, mineral-dominated finish. This is a superb, complex, Burgundian-styled Chardonnay that should be at its best between late 1999 and 2006. It displays an eerie resemblance to a Chassagne-Montrachet grand cru. As usual, the 1997 Chardonnay Lorenzo Vineyard is the most steely, mineral-dominated cuvée. Just prior to dictating the tasting note for this wine I had the privilege of drinking the 1995 Lorenzo, and it performed even better than my original evaluation suggested. I could not have asked for a greater Chardonnay. The 1997 Lorenzo offers a light to moderate gold color, followed by a citrusy, mineral, cold steel-like nose, a characteristic of its *terroir*. The wine exhibits fabulous texture in the mouth, along with a certain tightness, but very good acidity, exceptional purity and concentration, and a layered, extremely long finish. Tasting wines immediately after bottling is hardly ideal, but my instincts suggest this wine will be the least forthcoming of these three Marcassin Chardonnays. Anticipated maturity: 2000–2007.

I'm going out on the proverbial limb and state that I do not believe I have ever tasted a greater Chardonnay made in the New World (for that matter I have rarely tasted a white Burgundy this extraordinary) as Marcassin's 1997 Chardonnay Marcassin Vineyard. All 200+ cases would find a home in my cellar, but like most mailing list customers, I will be lucky to get 2 or 3 bottles. It is an astonishing wine/work of art. What makes it even more compelling than its siblings? Aromatically it offers all the leesy, Burgundian-styled complexity one could want—roasted nuts, honeyed citrus, minerals, etc., etc. Layers of flavor in this exceptionally full-bodied wine totally hide its powerful alcohol (14.5%), yet its most provocative character is its liquid minerality, something I have only tasted in Comte Lafon's Meursault-Perrières and a handful of Chevalier-Montrachets and Montrachets. There is a liquid petrol note similar to that found in the most concentrated Montrachets and Rieslings, in this spectacular, mind-boggling, prodigious Chardonnay that must be tasted to be believed. Anticipated maturity: 2001–2010.

After tasting the 1997, I expected to be let down by the 1996 Chardonnay Marcassin. No such chance—it is also an expressionistic, brilliant, multilayered wine possessing everything one could desire in a Chardonnay. The 1996 is slightly more powerful than the 1997 (14.7% alcohol), and in addition to high glycerin, it has extraordinarily high extract, with its liquid minerality character also prominent. There is slightly more of a honeyed nature to the fruit, yet this is a powerful wine that juxtaposes intensity with finesse and complexity. There is superb definition and phenomenal flavor purity. It should drink well for 5–10 years.

The good news does not stop with the Chardonnay portfolio. The 1996 Marcassin Vineyard Pinot Noir (275 cases) has just been released. Made from a Sonoma Coast vineyard, it represents a synthesis in style between a profound grand cru Burgundy (Clos de la Roche and Clos St.-Denis come to mind) and a pure, ripe, rich, unmistakably California offering. The dark plum-colored 1996 exhibits an explosive nose of kirsch liqueur, jammy cherry fruit, prunes, Asian spices, smoke, minerals, and vague damp foresty scents. Exceptionally rich and full bodied, with enough acidity, tannin, and wood to frame its copiously endowed personality, this is a riveting Pinot Noir that proves just how special Sonoma Coast hillside *terroirs* can be. Although it will be approachable in its youth, it will evolve gracefully for a decade or more. The 1997 Pinot Noir Marcassin Vineyard (only 7 tons of fruit were harvested from 6 tightly spaced acres of vines) does not yet reveal the 1996's nuances, but it boasts a saturated ruby/purple color, superb, pure, ripe aromas of black fruits intermixed with smoke, earth, truffles, and exotic spices. The juicy, succulent, black cherry fruit character noticeable in the 1996 is also present in the 1997. The wine is full bodied, with spectacular richness, awesome complexity, and remarkable length. For their size, richness, and intensity, both of these Pinot Noirs are impeccably balanced, with no component part out of sync. The only way to describe these wines is to quote the Beatles—"ubladi, ublada."

The prodigious 1995 Chardonnay Lorenzo Vineyard (8 barrels or 200 cases) exhibits a light gold color, a huge, sexy, smoky, citrusy, mineral, and hazelnut-scented nose, crisp, tart acidity, and an unevolved, backward style. The wine is powerful and rich, with layers of intensity, outstanding purity, and a firm underpinning of acidity. This will be a closed, potentially long-lived Chardonnay that will age for 5–7 years, assuming anybody has the discipline to lay away a few bottles. The profound 1995 Chardonnay Hudson Vineyard (14 barrels or 350 cases) should turn out to be one of the all-time wonders from the Turley/Wetlaufer vinous treasure trove. The huge, smoky, hazelnut, citrusy, honey-scented nose is to die for. In the mouth, the wine reveals awesome richness, an underlying mineral component, layers of concentrated fruit, full body, and marvelous length and balance. It is an unctuously textured, mouth-filling Chardonnay that should provide thrilling drinking for 5–7 years. And guess what? The 1995 Chardonnay Gauer Ranch Upper Barn is equally riveting. Perhaps even more flamboyant (to the point of decadence), this full-bodied Chardonnay immensely satisfies both the intellectual and hedonistic senses. Reminiscent of a rich, buttery, honeyed Bâtard-Montrachet from Michel Niellon (but purer and more complete), this is an explosively intense, complex, multidimensional wine that is utterly amazing. Drink it over the next 4–6 years. 1995 was more generous for Marcassin than 1994, producing 650 cases of Chardonnay.

There are magnums as well as 750 ml bottles produced of the 1995 Marcassin Vineyard Chardonnay and 1995 Marcassin Vineyard Pinot Noir. There is only one barrel of each wine (roughly 25 cases of each). Allocation by lottery may resolve the distribution problem for those customers on the winery's mailing list. When I tasted the 1995 Marcassin Vineyard Chardonnay, the first thought that went through my head was the same as when I tasted the 1982 Comte Lafon Montrachet. It is a backward wine with a liquid stony, mineral essence to its character. On the palate, the honey and citrus character of the Chardonnay grape begins to be apparent, but the wine's unmistakable liquid minerality is the hallmark of this formidably endowed, full-bodied Chardonnay. Relatively high acidity buttresses all the components, so it will be fascinating to follow this wine's evolution. It needs 2–3 years of cellaring, after which it will evolve for 10–15 more years.

The 1996 Chardonnays may not quite attain the level of the 1995s, but keep in mind, 1995 was a magical vintage for most northern California white wine producers. 1996's short growing season and overbearingly hot temperatures resulted in most 1996 Chardonnays tasting slightly less complex, but Marcassin's offerings are prodigious efforts in what is a very good rather than exceptional vintage for Chardonnay. The light golden-colored 1996 Chardonnay Gauer Ranch Upper Barn exhibits a superb, ostentatious nose of rich, buttery, leesy tropical fruit, and subtle, smoky, *pain grillé* notes. The wine is full bodied, gaudy in its display of lavish fruit and ripeness, yet remarkably well delineated, as well as exceptionally long and fresh in the mouth. Since I have a difficult time keeping my hands off of my tiny stock of Marcassin Chardonnay, I am sure I will be gluttonous when it comes to drinking this wine. To the extent anybody has the discipline to resist drinking this wine, it will age well for 3–5 years. For pure complexity in a more restrained, less flamboyant style, the 1996 Chardonnay Lorenzo Vineyard is *hors classe*. It possesses crisp acidity, an extraordinarily youthful, honeyed citruslike set of aromatics, full body, admirable concentration, and smoky, roasted hazelnut, mineral-laden flavors that coat the palate, enduring suspended animation for 40+ seconds. These wines are so pure, complex, and irresistible young, it is tempting to think they will not age. A bottle of 1991 Chardonnay (from my cellar) was drunk in 1997, and to the ecstasy of my guests, there was no evidence that it had lost anything from the magical peak it had attained 3 or 4 years before! This is just additional evidence that Marcassin's Chardonnays possess more longevity than suspected.

The 1996 Chardonnay Hudson Vineyard is a mere mortal among Marcassin wines. It is unquestionably an exceptional wine, but it seemingly possesses less dimension and complexity than the Upper Barn, Lorenzo, and the estate bottled Marcassin Vineyard. Rich and fat, with copious quantities of spice and buttery fruit, intriguing leesy, tangerine, and mineral-like scents in the background, and a thick, unctuous finish, this is a Chardonnay to consume over the next 2–3 years.

The 1995 Pinot Noir Marcassin Vineyard (only 25 cases for the world) is the debut vintage for this wine. It possesses one of the most enthralling and exquisite Burgundian-like Pinot noses I have ever smelled in a young American Pinot Noir. The color is a healthy medium dark ruby, and the sweet nose of jammy red and black fruits, truffles, smoked duck, and earth reminded this taster of a grand cru from Flagey-Echèzeaux or Vosne-Romanée. The wine reveals a delicacy and sweetness on the palate, without the weight one expects from such intense aromas and flavors. A remarkably complex wine, it will be a dazzling, full-bodied, perfumed style of Pinot Noir that should drink well during its first 5–7 years of life. I doubt it will be long-lived, but all the Marcassin wines have held their fruit and character longer than I would have expected.

P.S. In all likelihood there will be two other single vineyard Pinot Noirs emerging under the Marcassin label. Both are from Sonoma Coast vineyards situated close to the Marcassin Vineyard. One is the 1997 Searidge Meadow Pinot Noir (92–93) and the other the 1997 Blueslide Ridge Pinot Noir (92–94). Both of these wines appear to be terrific offerings. These vineyards were planted and are owned by the Martinelli family, and the fruit is being divided between Martinelli (who will also produce single vineyard Pinot Noirs under their label) and Marcassin.

MARIETTA CELLARS (SONOMA)

1995 Angeli Cuvée	Alexander Valley	D	92
1994 Angeli Cuvée	Alexander Valley	C	86
1996 Cabernet Sauvignon	Sonoma	C	90+

1995 Cabernet Sauvignon	California	C	85?
1994 Cabernet Sauvignon	Sonoma	C	88
1993 Cabernet Sauvignon	Sonoma	B	88+
N.V. Old Vine Red Lot 22	California	B	88
N.V. Old Vine Red Lot 15	California	B	90
N.V. Old Vine Red Lot 18	California	B	89
N.V. Old Vine Red Lot 21	California	B	86
1996 Syrah	California	C	88
1995 Syrah	California	C	88
1994 Syrah	California	C	89
1993 Syrah	California	B	90
1996 Zinfandel	Sonoma	C	90
1995 Zinfandel	Sonoma	C	87
1994 Zinfandel	Sonoma	B	87

The 1995 Angeli Cuvée, 1996 Cabernet Sauvignon, Syrah, and Zinfandel, and Old Vine Red Lot 22 make up the strongest group of Marietta wines I have tasted in recent vintages. There are some terrific buys, including the 20,000 cases of nonvintage Old Vine Red Lot 22. This wine has become a darling of intelligent consumers, as evidenced by the fact that the entire production is allocated. The Lot 22 offering, primarily from the 1996 and 1997 vintages, is a blend of Zinfandel, Petite Sirah, Carignane, Gamay, and Cabernet Sauvignon, from vineyard sources in Napa, Sonoma, and Mendocino. It is a weighty, seriously endowed wine with a dark purple color, as well as a supernose of cherries, black currants, pepper, spice, and loamy soil notes. Full bodied and richly extracted, with copious quantities of berry fruit, excellent purity, and an expansive, silky-textured finish, this wine can be drunk now as well as cellared for 2–3 years. Marietta's Old Vine Red is consistently one of the best bargains in exuberant, dry reds.

Marietta has also hit the bull's eye with a succulent, full-bodied, heady, powerful 1996 Zinfandel. Ruby-colored, with a fragrant nose consisting of briery fruit intermixed with spice and raspberries, it is a luscious, high alcohol (14.4%), chewy, fruit-driven wine with enough glycerin in the finish to satisfy hedonists. Drink it over the next 3–4 years. I suspect one has to go back to the 1990 vintage to find a Marietta Cabernet Sauvignon with as much quality and potential as the 1996. It is a full-bodied, tannic yet promising, opaque purple-colored Cabernet loaded with potential. Some of the rustic tannin should melt away over the next 2–5 years. At present, it is concentrated, with textbook cedary and black currant fruit displayed in a dramatic, rich, full-bodied style. There is good thickness and richness, as well as plenty of lusty alcohol (14.6%) in this large-scaled Cabernet Sauvignon that should age nicely for 10–12 years. In today's inflated marketplace, Cabernet Sauvignons of this quality usually sell for $30 and up a bottle. Readers take note.

The 1996 Syrah, which emerges from Sonoma and Mendocino vineyards, is a full-bodied, blackberry-scented wine with pepper, sweet licorice, and weedy, underbrush notes. With excellent ripeness, good spice, and a robust, muscular personality, this Syrah offers gutsy, mouth-filling flavors that should continue to develop for 5–7 years. Lastly, the 1995 Cuvée Angeli, a blended proprietary wine dominated by Zinfandel (80%), with additions of Petite Sirah/Syrah (10%) and Carignan (10%), is far superior to the 1994. It boasts an opaque purple color, followed by spectacular aromatics of jammy blackberry/raspberry/cherry fruit intermixed with pepper and spice. Deep, full bodied, and chewy, with copious glycerin and 14.5% alcohol, this dry, large-scaled Zinfandel-tasting wine is not to be missed. Moreover, it should continue to drink well for 5–6 years. Winemaker Chris Bilbro has turned out a superb portfolio of red wines.

The Lot 21 exhibits a medium dark ruby color, attractive blackberry and currant fruit, medium body, good spice and pepper, and a firm, compact finish. Although not as impressive an effort as previous examples, this wine remains a very fine value in terms of a full-flavored, mouth-filling, gutsy, exuberant, dry red wine. Drink it over the next 2–3 years.

Proprietor/winemaker Chris Bilbro should receive an award from wine consumers for making such tasty wines while maintaining realistic prices. One of the finest values in the wine world is Marietta's Old Vine Red, a recent rendition being Lot 18. This wine, usually a blend of Petite Sirah, Cabernet Sauvignon, Zinfandel, Carignan, and who knows what else, is always a deep ruby/purple-colored wine with copious quantities of peppery black fruits intertwined with scents of earth. A chewy, fleshy, full-bodied, mouth-filling wine, this juicy, burly effort disappears as quickly as Marietta releases the 10,000+ cases produced. While most of the Old Vine Red is consumed within the first 1–2 months of purchase, it gives every indication of lasting for 5 or more years.

The Lot 15 is made from 25% Petite Sirah, 20% Cabernet Sauvignon, 5% Carignan, and the rest Zinfandel and other red wine grapes. This opaque purple-colored wine offers up huge quantities of sweet black cherries and cassis, intermixed with scents of pepper, truffles, and spices. Full bodied, with a kirschlike flavor, this dense, chewy, fleshy wine is California's answer to a topnotch Châteauneuf du Pape. There may be 10,000 cases of this superb wine, but it disappears quickly from the shelves of retailers.

This winery also does a fine job with Cabernet Sauvignon. Marietta's 1993 Cabernet Sauvignon is an opaque, richly extracted, full-bodied wine with considerable intensity, an excellent mouth-feel, and outstanding length and richness. This wine is consistently one of the best Cabernet Sauvignons money can buy—anywhere in the world—for $14 or less a bottle. It should drink well for 10–12 years. Although the 1994 Cabernet Sauvignon is not as brilliant as the 1992, it tastes as good as most Cabernets costing $10–$15 more a bottle. The wine's deep, dense, ruby/purple color is followed by moderately intense aromas of ripe black fruits with toasty wood notes in the background. Full bodied, tannic, dense, and chewy, this wine will benefit from 1–2 years of cellaring; it should age well for a decade.

The dark ruby-colored, forward 1995 Zinfandel offers spicy, raspberrylike flavors, a juicy, medium- to full-bodied personality, excellent chewiness, and light tannin in the moderately long finish. It should drink well for 3–4 years. The 1994 Zinfandel reveals an attractive tarry, berry-scented nose, medium- to full-bodied flavors, a soft texture, and a peppery, spicy personality. It should drink well for 3–4 years.

Another winner is the 1993 Syrah. It exhibits an opaque purple/black color, and an unformed but potentially outstanding set of aromatics that include plenty of thick, juicy black fruits, pepper, and spice. Full bodied yet surprisingly soft, this mouth-filling Syrah possesses an excellent texture, tremendous length, and fine purity. It is a large-scaled, remarkably approachable wine that can be drunk now or held for 12–15 years. The 1994 Syrah reveals an opaque purple/black color, and a youthful, unformed but impressive nose of black fruits and pepper. Full bodied, concentrated, and cleanly made, this wine is accessible, but ideally needs another 2–3 years of cellaring. It should last for 12–15 years. Lastly, the 1995 Syrah reveals a deep ruby/purple color, as well as a nose of blackberry and cassis fruit, medium to full body, moderate tannin, and a structured, earthly, spicy finish. This wine will benefit from another six months of bottle age, and will drink well for 5–6 years.

To my surprise, neither the 1994 Angeli Cuvée nor the 1995 Cabernet Sauvignon performed as admirably as I would have expected. The 1994 Angeli Cuvée, a blend of Zinfandel, Petite-Sirah, and Carignan, displays a saturated ruby/purple color, tight aromatics (mostly black fruits, earth, and wood), and a lean, tannic, austere personality with moderately sweet fruit. There is good purity, but this is a tannin-dominated wine that will probably not come into total harmony. Drink it over the next 5–6 years. The 1995 Cabernet Sauvignon reveals a moderately intense, simple, oaky, blackberry, and currant-scented nose. In the mouth, the wine is structured, spicy, and tannic. There is good ripeness and purity, but the tannin gives the wine a compressed feel, and accentuates its astringency. While this wine will last for a decade, its overall balance is suspect.

MARTINELLI (SONOMA)

1997	Chardonnay Charles Ranch	Sonoma Coast	D	90
1996	Chardonnay Charles Ranch	Sonoma Coast	D	90
1995	Chardonnay Charles Ranch	Sonoma Coast	D	91
1995	Chardonnay Goldridge Vineyard	Russian River	D	89
1997	Chardonnay Martinelli Road Vineyard	Russian River	D	93
1996	Chardonnay Martinelli Road Vineyard	Russian River	D	92
1997	Chardonnay Woolsey Road Vineyard	Russian River	D	91
1996	Gewürztraminer Dry Select	Russian River	D	90
1994	Pinot Noir Estate	Russian River	D	90
1996	Pinot Noir Martinelli Vineyard	Russian River	D	92
1995	Pinot Noir Martinelli Vineyard	Russian River	D	90
1997	Pinot Noir Martinelli Vineyard Reserve	Russian River	D	(90–92)
1996	Pinot Noir Martinelli Vineyard Reserve	Russian River	D	94
1995	Pinot Noir Martinelli Vineyard Reserve	Russian River	D	92
1996	Zinfandel Jackass Hill Vineyard	Russian River	E	96
1995	Zinfandel Jackass Hill Vineyard	Russian River	E	97
1994	Zinfandel Jackass Hill Vineyard	Russian River	E	97
1993	Zinfandel Jackass Hill Vineyard	Russian River	E	94
1997	Zinfandel Jackass Vineyard	Russian River	E	(95–97)
1996	Zinfandel Jackass Vineyard	Russian River	E	93
1995	Zinfandel Jackass Vineyard	Russian River	E	93
1994	Zinfandel Jackass Vineyard	Russian River	E	93
1993	Zinfandel Jackass Vineyard	Russian River	E	90

The Russian River is exploding with interest from serious wine consumers. And why not? This area is an extraordinary source for Chardonnay, Pinot Noir, and Zinfandel. Additionally, there are a number of wineries intent on turning out exquisite wines, most notably Kistler, Dehlinger, Hartford Court, Rochioli, Rabbit Ridge, Williams-Selyem, and of course, Martinelli. This winery's emergence is in large part due to the hiring of winemaking consultant Helen Turley. The Martinelli family has always had superb vineyards, but when Turley found a family willing to estate-bottle more and more of its top juice, it did not take long for their wines to soar to the top of California's qualitative pyramid. Readers should take note that this is a remarkable source for not only Chardonnay and Pinot Noir, but for the finest Gewürztraminer made in California, in addition to the outrageously rich, kick-ass Jackass Zinfandel. While everyone wants Martinelli's Zinfandel, it is just one of several superb wines produced at this winery.

With an existing treasure-trove of fine vineyards in the Russian River region, the Martinelli's are planting some tightly spaced Pinot Noir vineyards on the Sonoma Coast. Martinelli's new releases are all unfiltered cuvées, with three Chardonnays worthy of excitement. The 1997 Chardonnay Woolsey Road is a smoky, buttery wine with copious quantities of toasty new oak, a leesy complexity, chewy, fleshy texture, and good acidity. Like many of the better 1997 Chardonnays, it is extremely aromatic. I would opt for drinking it over the next 2–3 years. The 1997 Chardonnay Charles Ranch (14.5% alcohol) is more golden colored, as well as full bodied, with viscous richness, a high glycerin level, and a roasted nut, honeyed tropical fruit and mineral character. Although the wine's color is surprisingly evolved, its flavors are fresh, exuberant, and rich. It should continue to drink well for 1–2 years. My favorite of the Martinelli Chardonnays is the 1997 Chardonnay Martinelli Road, from a relatively new 6-acre vineyard planted with Dijon (Burgundy) clones. It offers a super, Meursault-like nose of hazelnuts, *pain grillé*, smoke, and buttered citrus fruits. The wine is full bodied, with an unctuous texture, terrific fruit purity, and a layered, long, lusty finish. All of these are hedonistically styled, naturally made Chardonnays that should drink well for 2–3 years.

The 1997 Pinot Noir Reserve is a decadently styled, sweet, ripe wine with a deep ruby color, and a pronounced jammy plum/cherry-scented nose with toasty oak in the background. Spicy, rich, and flavorful, with an expansive, open-knit texture, enough acidity and tannin to provide definition, and a long finish, this offering will be a crowd-pleaser when released, yet promises to evolve and perhaps improve for 3–4 years. It will last for 7–8 years. The 1997 Zinfandel Jackass Vineyard appears to be another winner. This offering, which was given a 3–5 day cold soak, boasts a "modest" 16% alcohol. It possesses a saturated deep ruby/garnet color and spectacular aromas of jammy cherries, plum liqueur, kirsch, spice box, cedar, and pepper. This full-bodied, complete, rich, palate-staining Zinfandel represents the essence of this varietal. It should age well for 7–10 years, or longer. While I did not taste the 1997 Jackass Hill Vineyard (it was still fermenting), I can only imagine how spectacular it might be.

Martinelli's top Chardonnays emerge from either the Goldridge Vineyard (Russian River) or the Charles Ranch (Sonoma Coast). There were 600 cases of each in 1995, with the Goldridge scheduled for release in March 1997, and the Charles Ranch in September 1997. Both wines had just been bottled when I tasted them. The light to medium straw-colored 1995 Chardonnay Goldridge Vineyard exhibits a penetrating fragrance of ripe tropical fruit and spice. There is excellent to outstanding ripeness, full body, impressive richness, and a layered texture. This offering may merit a higher score with more bottle age. The 1995 Chardonnay Charles Ranch displays a creamy, complex, custard pie, lemony, honeyed fruit-scented nose, and long, dense, full-bodied flavors that possess exceptional concentration, delineation, and freshness. *Pain grillé* notes give the wine a Chassagne-Montrachet-like smokiness. This wine, which should be enjoyed for its layers of fruit and complexity, is as thrilling as the 1994.

I tasted two 1996 Chardonnays. The 1996 Chardonnay Charles Ranch is produced from a vineyard on the Sonoma Coast, not far from the Marcassin vineyard. The wine sees about 40% new oak casks, is barrel fermented, given extensive lees contact and stirring (*bâtonnage*), and bottled without filtration. Its light gold color is accompanied by copious quantities of honeysuckle, citrus, smoke, ripe peach and pearlike aromas and flavors. Full bodied with a chewy texture, this exquisite Chardonnay will drink well for several years. The 1996 Chardonnay Martinelli Road Vineyard is made from France's Dijon clone of Chardonnay. It is a lavishly rich, opulent, fat wine oozing with buttery fruit complemented by mineral nuances and lemony overtones. Full bodied, with an unctuous texture, this is a thrilling

Chardonnay from a cool climate vineyard that was harvested at full physiological maturity. It should drink well for several years.

The best Gewürztraminer I had ever tasted from California came from Z. Moore. Ironically, I later learned that the fruit for that fine Gewürztraminer came from the Martinelli vineyards. This fruit makes up the composition of Martinelli's Gewürztraminer. The 1996 Gewürztraminer Dry Select offers provocative aromas of rose petals, lychee nuts, and honeyed grapefruit. It displays a strikingly intense nose, full body, and massive quantities of pure fruit. The glycerin coats the mouth, giving the taster the impression of sucking on a marrow bone made from Gewürztraminer! With 14.8% alcohol, this is the quintessential expression of Gewürztraminer in California. For those who love Gewürztraminer's gaudy, over-the-top personality, this wine will provide thrilling drinking over the next several years.

Admittedly, Martinelli's Jackass Zinfandel is one of California's most famous wines, but readers should not ignore the extraordinary progress they have made with Russian River and Sonoma Coast Pinot Noir. When I tasted their two cuvées of 1996 Pinot Noir, they immediately took me back to the late sixties when I was a student living outside Washington, D.C., making frequent buying trips to what was then called plain old Pearson's Liquor Shop. At that time, Pearson's had an extraordinary collection of 1961, 1962, 1964, and 1966 red Burgundies that could be purchased for a song. I cut my teeth on many a Domaine Parent Pommard Les Grandes Epenottes and Pommard Les Rugiens from those vintages. They were marvelously full-bodied, meaty, fragrant Pinots the likes of which I have never tasted again from either Domaine Parent or any other Pommard producer. When I tasted Martinelli's 1996 Pinot Noir Martinelli Vineyard and 1996 Pinot Noir Martinelli Vineyard Reserve, I was reminded of my student days of Parent's gloriously decadent, rich Pinots. These are fascinating wines, offering gorgeous levels of smoky, meaty, earthy, black cherry fruit in a full-bodied, glycerin-imbued, lusty style that is about as hedonistic as Pinot Noir can be. While I was blown away by the 1996 Pinot Noir Martinelli Vineyard, the Reserve Pinot Noir was even more spectacular and amazingly concentrated. They have it all! Bottled unfined and unfiltered, they represent the essence of the Pinot Noir grape as translated by the Martinellis and their consultant winemaker, Helen Turley. Both wines should drink well for 5–6 years, perhaps longer, but I can't imagine anyone having enough discipline to hold on to these wines as long as they continue to drink as well as they do today.

Martinelli's 1994 Pinot Noir Estate, also bottled without fining or filtration, is an outstanding example of this varietal. Unfortunately, only 200 cases are produced of this sumptuously styled, meaty, black cherry and smoke-scented wine. It exhibits a dark garnet color, sweet, chewy, fleshy, Burgundian-like fruit, high alcohol (14.3%), and a soft, gorgeously proportioned, lusty finish. This is what Burgundy should be—pure, expansive, succulent, and loaded with gobs of fruit—but so rarely is. The 1994 Pinot Noir Estate was the first outstanding Martinelli Pinot Noir. This was followed by two superlative 1995s. The 1995 Pinot Noir Martinelli Vineyard exhibits a Domaine Dujac-like complexity with its cinnamon, black cherry, spicy, smoky nose. It offers sweet, gamey, plum and black cherrylike flavors, excellent richness and purity, and a long, lusty finish. Drink this round, generous Pinot Noir over the next 6–7 years. Remarkably, there is a 1995 Pinot Noir Martinelli Vineyard Reserve, also a terrific example of this varietal. It possesses a deep ruby color, a big, spicy, smoky, earth, and black fruit-scented nose, and layers of ripe, jammy flavors buttressed by new oak, acidity, and sweet tannin. The finish is long and authoritative. These Pinot Noirs offer further evidence of just how exciting California Pinot Noir has become. The Reserve was released in September 1997; it will drink well for 7–8 years, possibly longer.

Let's not forget the 1996 Zinfandel Jackass Vineyard (15.6% alcohol) and the 1996 Zinfandel Jackass Hill Vineyard. It's a toss-up as to who is making better Zinfandel—Napa's Turley Cellars, or Martinelli. These 1996s are both exceptional Zinfandels, with the Jackass Hill a candidate for the Zinfandel of the vintage. The 1996 Zinfandel Jackass Vineyard reveals a murky plum/purple color. Outstanding aromatics soar from the glass, offering aromas of licorice, blackberry liqueur, truffles, underbrush, smoke, and meat. The wine's unctuousness, full body, and supple texture result in a decadently rich, lavishly endowed Zinfandel to drink over the next 5–7 years. The 1996 Zinfandel Jackass Hill Vineyard displays a similar plum/purple color. The nose offers a smorgasbord of aromas, including cherry, blackberry, and strawberry liqueur intermingled with smoky, toasty oak, roasted Provençal herbs, Asian spice, and chocolatey, meaty overtones. Exceptionally full bodied, with gobs of glycerin, remarkable purity, and profound balance for such a large Zinfandel, this is a true work of art. It should drink well for 7–8+ years.

Are the Jackass 1996s better than the 1995s and 1994s? In my estimation, the 1995 and 1994 Jackass and Jackass Hill Zinfandels are among the most amazing wines I have ever tasted. I cannot say the 1996s are superior, but no one who loves Zinfandel should be without them. They are artistic creations.

The 1995 Zinfandel Jackass Vineyard exhibits a superintense, jammy, blackberry, cherry, strawberry-scented nose and flavors. Full bodied, with gorgeous purity and ripeness, this juicy, succulent, unfiltered Zinfandel is a quintessential example of how intense and impressive Zinfandel can be. I had the 1994 Jackass Vineyard Zinfandel (93 points) with Thanksgiving dinner a few years ago, and it was akin to having liquefied strawberry shortcake, only dry, intoxicating, and incredibly perfumed. These wines are best drunk young, despite their lofty alcohol levels and extract. My recommendation is to consume them during their first 5–8 years of life.

The 1995 Jackass Hill Zinfandel is among the greatest Zinfandels I have ever tasted. Winemaker Steve Ryan spent many a night next to the fermenting tanks coaxing this wine to dryness. It boasts the most amazing extract, purity, and mouth-feel I have ever tasted in a Zinfandel, and believe me, California has produced a bevy of prodigious Zinfandels during the last six years. The opaque black/ruby-colored, dry 1995 Jackass Hill exhibits awesome richness and massive body, with an astonishing inner core of sweet, ripe fruit. I once said the 1994 Jackass Hill (97 points) would become my benchmark Zinfandel, but the 1995 has equaled that wine. When I was asked how much alcohol I thought the wine contained, I said 14.5%–15%, largely because I did not detect any hotness because of the wine's concentration. When I was told that this dry wine was closer to 18%, I was dumbfounded. Anticipated maturity: now–2004.

The two Martinelli 1993 Zinfandels, of which there are 400 cases of the Jackass Vineyard and 375 cases of the Jackass Hill, are sensational wines by any standard of measurement. The 1993 Zinfandel Jackass Vineyard displays an opaque ruby/purple color, a huge, dramatic, fragrant nose of Asian spices, black and red fruits, minerals, and oak. It possesses great richness, full body, a velvety-textured, rich, inner core of fruit, and a long, heady finish that lasts more than a minute. Not a light, innocuous Zinfandel (the alcohol is 15.3%), it is dry, pure, and amazingly well balanced. Drink it over the next 8–10 years. Remarkably, the 1993 Zinfandel Jackass Hill, from an 85-year-old parcel of vines in the Russian River Valley, is a leading candidate for "Zinfandel of the Vintage." The opaque black/purple color is followed by a sensational nose of raspberry ice cream/candy that envelops the taster. The wine hits the palate with a glorious cascade of red and black fruits, an unctuous texture, and layer upon layer of rich, well-balanced, ripe fruit. This full-bodied, astonishingly concentrated Zinfandel should drink well for 10–12 years. Both wines were bottled unfined and unfiltered. This plot of vines was planted by the current owner's grandfather, Giuseppe Martinelli, and named Jackass Hill by his family because "only a jackass would plant vines on such an impossibly steep 45-degree slope."

More and more wines made from small high-quality producers such as Martinelli are being sold via a mailing list. Readers wishing to secure a bottle or two of their most limited production offerings should know what to do. These wines are best drunk young, despite their lofty alcohol levels and extract. My recommendation is to consume them during their first 5–8 years of life.

MATANZAS CREEK (SONOMA)

1996 Chardonnay	Sonoma	D	85
1995 Merlot	Sonoma	D	86
1994 Merlot	Sonoma	D	94
1993 Merlot	Sonoma	D	91
1995 Chardonnay Matanzas Creek Journey	Sonoma Valley	EE	90
1994 Merlot Matanzas Creek Journey	Sonoma Valley	EEE	84

So what's new? Matanzas Creek continues to turn out rich, concentrated Merlots that provide a reference point for what heights this grape can achieve in California. The 1993 Merlot exhibits a deep, saturated purple color, a smoky, black cherry, and vanillin-scented nose, a wonderfully sweet entry on the palate, and a rich, full-bodied, tarry, well-balanced finish. No, it is not as exotic or concentrated as the 1992, but it has nothing to be ashamed of either. It should drink well for 12–15 years. The 1994 possesses a saturated ruby/purple color, a flashy display of aromatics (chocolate, jammy red and black fruits, and vanilla), full body, loads of dense, thick, unctuously textured flavors, low acidity, and a long, spicy, powerful finish. For its size, this wine keeps everything in perspective. It should drink well for 10–12 years. It is a worthy rival to the stunning 1992 and 1993.

An oaky/earthy-scented wine, with just enough fruit for balance, this medium-bodied, straightforward 1996 Chardonnay does not seem up to the level of quality of previous Matanzas Creek efforts. It is a solidly made, rustic wine that should be drunk over the next year. The 1995 Merlot was more impressive prior to bottling. The color is dark plum, and the nose is restrained and straightforward. The wine does offer some coffee, underbrush, dried herb, and cherry fruit in a medium-bodied, attractive, but uninspiring style. Less concentrated than previous efforts, it is a good Merlot that should continue to drink well for 5–7 years.

I had mixed feelings about the luxury Journey cuvées from Matanzas Creek. The 1995 Chardonnay Journey is top class, offering buttery fruit, fine underlying acidity, and well-integrated, toasty new oak. It is full bodied, with outstanding concentration and richness, and exceptionally Californian in its expansive, open-throttle style. I do not understand the 1994 Merlot Journey. The color is a dark ruby/purple, but the wine's aromas are monochromatic, consisting of new oak and grapey, berry fruit. It is tough textured, with medium body and good concentration. But may I ask—where is the complexity and profound depth one expects from a $150 wine! I also opened a 1992 Matanzas Creek Merlot from my cellar, and left the bottle open for several days to see if I had missed something. The 1994 Journey did not develop, and the 1992 was unquestionably superior.

PHILIP MELKA (NAPA)

1996 Metisse Proprietary Red Wine	Diamond Mountain	D	90

Philip Melka is the winemaker for Seavey in Conn Valley. This small project, about 240 cases, is a blend of 40% Cabernet Sauvignon, 30% Cabernet Franc, and 30% Merlot. A Bordeaux-styled red (Melka was trained under Christian Moueix), this 1996 is a stylish, complex, elegant wine. It boasts a dark ruby/purple color, followed by attractive aromatics consisting of black currants, lead pencil, cedar, spice box, and *pain grillé*. Medium bodied, with graceful, ripe fruit, and nicely integrated tannin and acidity, this is an exceptionally harmonious, graceful wine that opens beautifully in the glass. It will not knock tasters over with its power or extract, but there is plenty going on in this stylish, complete wine. Enjoy it now and over the next 12–14 years.

MERIDIAN VINEYARDS (SAN LUIS OBISPO)

1996 Chardonnay	Edna Valley	B	88
1996 Chardonnay	Santa Barbara	B	84
1995 Chardonnay	Santa Barbara	B	87
1996 Chardonnay Limited Release	Santa Barbara	D	91
1995 Chardonnay Limited Release	Santa Barbara	C	91
1995 Chardonnay Reserve	Edna Valley	C	90
1996 Gewurztraminer Limited Release	Santa Barbara	B	89
1996 Pinot Noir	North Coast	C	79
1995 Pinot Noir Bien Nacido Free Run	Santa Barbara	C	79
1996 Pinot Noir Reserve	Santa Barbara	D	86
1995 Pinot Noir Reserve	Santa Barbara	C	85
1995 Pinot Noir Riverbench Free Run	Santa Barbara	C	87
1995 Pinot Noir Sierra Madre Free Run	Santa Barbara	C	84
1995 Pinot Noir White Hills Free Run	Santa Barbara	C	87
1996 Sauvignon Blanc	California	A	85
1995 Sauvignon Blanc	California	A	86
1996 Syrah	Paso Robles	C	90

The 1995 Sauvignon Blanc exhibits a fresh, ripe, citrusy, fruity character, medium body, and more length and texture than is generally found in an under $10 Sauvignon. Drink it over the next year. Meridian produced three Chardonnays in 1995. The 1995 Chardonnay Santa Barbara was put through full malolactic and has benefitted from 100% barrel fermentation. The wine reveals tropical fruit aromas and flavors, medium to full body, crisp, underlying acidity, and a refreshing mouth-feel. It is not the most complex or concentrated style of Chardonnay, but it is well made, and ideal for drinking over the next 1–2 years. Both the 1995 Chardonnay Reserve Edna Valley and the 1995 Chardonnay Limited Release Santa Barbara are outstanding wines. Moreover, they sell for prices 20%–50% below most other Chardonnays of this quality. The 1995 Chardonnay Reserve Edna Valley is a broad, full-bodied, husky wine that is just beginning to open and reveal its full character. It possesses copious quantities of tropical fruit, subtle oaky notes, good acidity, and admirable intensity and power in the finish. It will be even better with another 3–6 months of bottle age; it will keep for 2–3 years. The 1995 Chardonnay Limited Release (primarily from Beringer's Riverbench Vineyard) was aged in 100% new oak casks, but the oak is largely concealed by the wine's huge, massive extraction of buttery, rich Chardonnay fruit. Powerful, full, and intense, it is vaguely reminiscent of Beringer's Sbragia Select Chardonnay. Look for this impressive wine to turn some heads at blind tastings. It should drink well for 2–3 years.

In the past, I have found Meridian's Pinot Noirs to be vegetal, with a pronounced tomato skinline aroma. All of the following Pinot Noirs represent a major improvement. No, they are not at the level of the top efforts being produced in Sonoma or Napa, but progress is evident. The least impressive of this group is the 1995 Pinot Noir Bien Nacido, which exhibits good density and a dark ruby color, but lean, compact, tart flavors, and a herbaceousness that was not concealed by the wine's toasty oak. The 1995 Pinot Noir Sierra Madre possesses a deep ruby color, as well as a damp, mossy, herb, earthy character, spice, and medium body. The

1995 Pinot Noir Riverbench reveals a monolithic, muted, slightly cranberry/raspberrylike nose, a fine palate, medium body, ripe berry fruit, and nice texture and length. It should drink well for 4–5 years. The 1995 Pinot Noir White Hills appears to be the most complete wine of this group. It possesses more black fruit, an expansive, chewy texture, fragrant berry aromas, and a silky texture. Lastly, the 1995 Reserve Pinot Noir reveals wild, gamy, berry, spicy, subtly herbaceous raspberry fruit and minerals on the palate, and a medium-bodied, tart, but pleasant texture and finish. All of these Pinots are best drunk within their first 2–4 years of life.

The textbook 1996 Sauvignon Blanc may not be the biggest or most complex, but it does offer exuberant melony, citrusy fruit with enough acidity for focus and balance. It, too, should be consumed over the next year. I drink plenty of Alsatian Gewurztraminer, and find most California versions hopelessly innocuous, but I was superimpressed with Meridian's 1996 Gewürztraminer Limited Release. It is a dry Gewurztraminer with surprising power and intensity (14% natural alcohol). There is no doubting that the Gewurztraminer produced by Martinelli from their Russian River vineyard is the finest being made in California, but Meridian's offering may be the second best. Offering a classic Gewurztraminer nose of rose petals, spice, grapefruit, and lychee nuts, excellent richness, and plenty of punch, this is a heady, intoxicatingly perfumed wine that readers will adore—provided they like this varietal's gaudy personality. Drink it over the next year.

Meridian's Chardonnay program gets more interesting with each passing year. While the 1996 Chardonnay Santa Barbara is a tropical fruit-laden wine with crisp acidity and medium body, it is somewhat one-dimensional when compared to some of California's other Chardonnays. However, it is also reasonably priced. More interesting is the 1996 Chardonnay Edna Valley. Burgundian-like aromas of roasted nuts, and smoky, leesy fruit intertwined with exotic coconut scents has resulted in a rich, medium-bodied, honeyed, hedonistic style of Chardonnay. This is an attractive, in-your-face Chardonnay to drink over the next year. The outstanding 1996 Chardonnay Limited Release is a full-bodied, superconcentrated, smoky, voluptuously styled wine with gobs of tropical fruits laced with *pain grillé*, mineral, and smoky notes. There is no denying the outrageous level of glycerin and fruit in this showy Chardonnay. A fun wine made in a big, flamboyant style, it should be consumed over the next 1–2 years.

I am not totally persuaded by Meridian's Pinot Noir program, but I see some promise, especially with the Reserve wines. The dark-colored 1996 Pinot Noir North Coast is compressed, lean, and attenuated in the mouth. The 1995 Pinot Noir Reserve is performing slightly better than it did previously. It reveals a Pommard-like, apple skin, sweet blackberry, rustic side, medium body, and a spicy finish. The deep purple-colored 1996 Pinot Noir Reserve possesses more chocolate than spice in its flavors, adequate concentration, medium body, and smoky, berry fruit in the finish. These are competent rather than exciting efforts.

A wine I did find fascinating is the 1996 Syrah. A textbook effort, it exhibits an opaque purple color, and an intensely aromatic bacon fat, blackberry, and cassis-scented nose. Full bodied, with dense, superconcentrated flavors, and no hard edges, this is a succulent, hedonistic style of Syrah to consume during its first 10–12 years of life. Impressive!

MERRYVALE VINEYARDS (NAPA)

1995 Cabernet Sauvignon Reserve	Napa	D	89+
1996 Chardonnay Reserve	Napa	D	86
1995 Chardonnay Reserve	Napa	D	91
1996 Chardonnay Silhouette	Napa	E	91

1995 Chardonnay Silhouette	Napa	D	94
1996 Chardonnay Starmont	Napa	C	86
1993 Merlot	Napa	D	86
1995 Merlot Beckstoffer IV Vineyard	Napa	D	88
1995 Merlot Reserve	Napa	D	89
1995 Profile Proprietary Red Wine	Napa	E	90
1994 Profile Proprietary Red Wine	Napa	E	92
1993 Profile Proprietary Red Wine	Napa	?	90
1995 Vignette Proprietary White Wine	Napa	C	87
1994 Vignette Proprietary White Wine	Napa	C	87

Given the quality of Merryvale's wines, I am surprised this winery does not receive more attention. Their Profile Proprietary Red Wine ranks among the top three or four dozen red wines of northern California, and their Silhouette Chardonnay is a brilliant Burgundian-styled wine with extraordinary richness and complexity. The wines I tasted in October of 1997 included an attractive 1996 Chardonnay Starmont. It possesses a crisp, mineral, Chablis-like character, zesty acidity, an elegant, medium-bodied style, and an emphasis on the fruit rather than oak. The 1996 Chardonnay Reserve is an ambitious wine, with more butter and honey. In spite of that, I liked the mineral-laden, crisp, less oaky style of the Starmont just as much. Both wines should drink well for 2 years. The fascinating 1996 Chardonnay Silhouette boasts a fabulous nose of smoke, butter, and toast, followed by full-bodied leesy, orange, mineral, and honeyed citruslike flavors, a layered concentration, and excellent equilibrium and length. Fortunately, 1,000 cases of this large-scaled wine were produced. This wine could be inserted as a ringer in a grand cru white Burgundy tasting; it would be difficult to pick it out as a California Chardonnay.

Even more impressive is the 1995 Chardonnay Silhouette. The light to medium straw color is accompanied by an explosive, sweet, fragrant bouquet of ripe peaches, pineapple, and buttery popcorn. Full bodied, with a thick, chewy texture, this superconcentrated, powerful yet harmoniously constructed wine will drink well for 4–5 years. Think of it as Merryvale's answer to the exquisite Bâtard-Montrachet from Chassagne-Montrachet's Michel Niellon.

The 1995 Chardonnay Reserve offers elegant, ripe, honeyed fruit notes combined with high class, smoky wood that tantalizes the olfactory senses. The wine displays fine ripeness, deeper, richer, more extracted flavors than the 1993 or 1994, some lusty alcohol, and a long, medium- to full-bodied finish. It should drink well for another 3–4 years.

The 1994 and 1995 Vignettes represent the first two vintages of Merryvale's proprietary white wine. Primarily a Sauvignon Blanc-based wine (70%–75%) with the balance Semillon, the wine is barrel fermented and bottled early to preserve its freshness. The first two vintages are very good wines, with the 1995 Vignette revealing a more honeyed, riper, melony character, dry, medium-bodied flavors, good purity, and plenty of length. It is a classy, judiciously wooded wine with fine elegance. Drink it over the next 2–3 years. The 1994 Vignette possesses slightly higher acidity, as well as some of the melony ripeness of the 1995, but it is more restrained and subtle. The finish is reassuringly crisp and pure. It should drink well for 1–3 years.

Among the red wines, the 1995 Merlot Reserve may turn out to be an outstanding wine with another 1–2 years of bottle age. The wine reveals a dense purple color, and a tight but promising nose of melted chocolate, and jammy blackberry and cherry fruit. It hits the palate with good richness, an attractive spicy, cinnamon component, excellent equilibrium, and a long, lush, concentrated finish. It should drink well over the next 10–12 years. The opaque purple-colored 1995 Merlot Beckstoffer IV Vineyard (250 cases) reveals toasty new oak in the nose, as well as impressive richness, purity, and body, but it was closed and unevolved when I tasted it. My numerical rating may turn out to be somewhat stingy once this wine has a chance to open and expand. This is the type of wine that I wish could have been given 4–5 hours in a decanter to see what is behind its imposing structure. It will last for 12–15+ years.

Initially, the dark ruby-colored 1993 Merlot is dominated by earthy, loamy notes. With ten minutes of airing, the chocolatey, ripe black cherry fruit makes a subtle appearance. The wine is tight, medium bodied, and muscular, with surprising tannin in the finish. It is a good Merlot that will improve for 1–2 years and keep for 7–8.

Another impressive wine that needs time in the cellar is the 1995 Cabernet Sauvignon Reserve. It boasts a dense dark ruby/purple color, as well as a sweet, cedary, vanilla, and black currant-scented nose with hints of weedy tobacco and olives. Full bodied and highly extracted but tannic, this wine may merit an outstanding score after 5–6 years of bottle age. It will last for 20+ years.

The exceptional Profile cuvées should receive more attention from wine consumers. The outstanding 1995 Profile (14.5% alcohol) is made from 50% Cabernet Sauvignon, 39% Merlot, and the balance Cabernet Franc. It needs 4–5 years of cellaring, so readers looking for Cabernet-based wines with immediate accessibility should be forewarned. The wine exhibits an opaque purple color, followed by copious amounts of toasty, smoky, high quality new oak in the nose, along with equally impressive quantities of black currants, plums, and cherries. Deep and full bodied, with high tannin but outstanding concentration, this is an impressively built, Bordeaux-like wine. Anticipated maturity: 2002–2020. Even better is the 1994 Profile (a blend of 60% Cabernet Sauvignon, 30% Merlot, and 10% Cabernet Franc). It possesses an opaque purple color, and seems to hit every sweet spot on the taster's palate, offering loads of cassis, roasted herbs, toast, and licorice. This multilayered, rich, concentrated wine also reveals impeccable balance and elegance. There is restraint, power, and concentration—a rare combination in such a big wine. The 1994 is more accessible than the 1995, and thus can be drunk young or cellared for 15–20+ years. The 1993 Profile (approximately 30% Merlot in the blend) reveals high quality, toasty, vanillin-scented, new French oak intertwined with black currant fruit aromas. The wine is rich and full bodied, with excellent definition, and a powerful, chewy finish. The tannin is present, but it is riper and better integrated than in the 1992. This wine will be accessible young, but capable of lasting for 15 years.

PETER MICHAEL WINERY (SONOMA)

1997 Chardonnay Belle Côte	Knight's Valley	E	93
1996 Chardonnay Belle Côte	Knight's Valley	E	93
1995 Chardonnay Belle Côte	Knight's Valley	E	92
1997 Chardonnay La Carrière	Knight's Valley	E	94
1996 Chardonnay Clos du Ciel	Napa	E	92
1995 Chardonnay Clos du Ciel	Napa	E	94
1997 Chardonnay Cuvée Indigène	Sonoma	E	95
1996 Chardonnay Cuvée Indigène	Sonoma	E	93
1995 Chardonnay Cuvée Indigène	Sonoma	E	95
1997 Chardonnay Mon Plaisir	Sonoma	E	94
1996 Chardonnay Mon Plaisir	Sonoma	E	92

1995 Chardonnay Mon Plaisir	Sonoma	E	92+
1997 Chardonnay Point Rouge	Sonoma	E	95+
1996 Chardonnay Point Rouge	Sonoma	E	94
1995 Chardonnay Point Rouge	Sonoma	E	98
1997 Les Pavots Proprietary Red Wine	Knight's Valley	E	(96–98)
1996 Les Pavots Proprietary Red Wine	Knight's Valley	E	96
1995 Les Pavots Proprietary Red Wine	Knight's Valley	E	91
1994 Les Pavots Proprietary Red Wine	Knight's Valley	E	94
1993 Les Pavots Proprietary Red Wine	Sonoma	E	92
1997 Pinot Noir Pisoni Ranch	Santa Lucia Highlands	E	(88–90)
1997 Sauvignon Blanc L'Après Midi	Sonoma	E	88
1996 Sauvignon Blanc L'Après Midi	Sonoma	E	87
1995 Sauvignon Blanc L'Après Midi	Sonoma	C	91

This brilliantly run winery continues to push the quality of their wines to even more remarkable heights. The light straw-colored 1997 Sauvignon Blanc l'Après Midi possesses terrific acidity (much more than usual), as well as wonderfully intense, mineral-laden, melony, citrusy fruit. Crisp and medium bodied, it is ideal for consuming over the next several years. In 1998, the source for this fruit will change from the Liparita Vineyard on Howell Mountain, to Peter Michael's own estate vineyards.

There are five cuvées of leesy, complex, full-bodied, unfiltered Chardonnays. There are 3,000 cases of the exquisite 1997 Chardonnay Belle Côte, which is made primarily from such old California Chardonnay clones as Wente, fermented with indigenous yeasts, aged in French barrels (50% new), and bottled unfiltered. The light straw/gold color is followed by sumptuous leesy, toasty, and honeyed pineapple scents with a touch of mineral. The wine is medium to full bodied, with exquisite texture, a sexy, rich aftertaste, and superb purity—a hallmark of every Peter Michael wine. All of the Chardonnays save for the unbottled Point Rouge had been bottled in August of 1998, yet were singing at high volume when I tasted them in September. A new offering, the light gold-colored 1997 Chardonnay La Carrière (only 125 cases produced), comes from a hillside situated below the Belle Côte Vineyard. It is planted with Dijon Burgundy Chardonnay clones, in addition to the Hyde clone. Aged in 30% new oak, this offering reveals a distinctive mineral character not dissimilar from certain Corton-Charlemagnes. Liquid stonelike flavors are pronounced in the mouth, in addition to citrus and subtle oak notes. This distinctive, high-toned, *terroir*-driven, concentrated wine is more subtle than some of Peter Michael's efforts. It should drink well for 3–4 years.

The dazzling 1997 Chardonnay Mon Plaisir (1,200 cases) displays a light to medium straw color, and expressive aromatics consisting of tangerine/orange and other tropical fruits. In the mouth, notes of lemon butter make an appearance in this full-bodied, expansive, rich, fleshy Chardonnay that tips the scales at 14.1% alcohol. With fabulous fruit, the Mon Plaisir appears to be the qualitative equal of the more expensive Cuvée Indigène and Point Rouge. It should drink well for 4–5 years. The 1997 Chardonnay Cuvée Indigène (named so because it is fermented completely with indigenous vineyard yeasts) exhibits a light gold color, and a complex nose of smoky, leesy Chardonnay fruit intermixed with smoky, roasted hazelnuts, orange blossoms, and citrus. Full bodied, with excellent underlying acidity, and more minerality to its flavors than Mon Plaisir, this profoundly concentrated, complex Chardonnay is a prodigious offering. Production was 550 cases, with the alcohol a boisterous 14.1%. Look for this wine to drink well for 5–7 years. In 1997 there are 150 cases of the Point Rouge. It was the only Chardonnay that had not yet been bottled. This offering, which emerges from the famed Upper Barn parcel of the Gauer Ranch (renamed by Kendall-Jackson to Alexander Mountain Estate), is aged in 100% new oak, and was to be bottled by year's end. It is slightly richer, but at this stage of development, did not seem more complex than Peter Michael's other top cuvées. The Point Rouge's complex bouquet consists of toasty oak, flowers, apples, orange blossoms, buttered lemons, and honey. Full bodied, marvelously pure, multilayered, and exceptionally long (44 seconds by my stopwatch), the 1997 appears to be superior to the outstanding 1996, but perhaps a notch below the monumental 1995. In any event, it is a compelling Chardonnay in what is a superb portfolio of great Burgundian-styled Chardonnays made by winemaker Mark Aubert. Like most of the 1997 Peter Michael Chardonnays (which seem to have crisp acidity for their weight and richness), this offering will age well for 4–6 years.

This is another winery that is cognizant of the exquisite Pinot Noir fruit emerging from the Pisoni Vineyard in the Santa Lucia Highlands. This vineyard, believed to be planted with cuttings from La Tâche in Vosne Romanée, is a source of some remarkable Pinot Noirs. Peter Michael's dark ruby-colored 1997 Pinot Noir Pisoni Ranch reveals purple nuances, as well as the telltale black raspberry and cassis notes with spicy oak in the background. Medium to full bodied and expansive, with excellent purity, and a lush, seductive palate, this heady (14.1% alcohol) wine should be consumed over the next 5–6 years.

I have been buying Les Pavots for a number of years, and I must say that the 1996 and 1997 are the two finest efforts I have ever tasted. The 1996 Les Pavots (a blend of 74% Cabernet Sauvignon, 20% Merlot, and 6% Cabernet Franc) tips the scales at 14.2% alcohol. The saturated black/purple color is accompanied by a knockout nose of violets, blackberries, licorice, and *pain grillé*. Full body and high extract levels are buttressed by sweet tannin as well as adequate acidity. About 2,800 cases were produced of this provocative, rich, distinctive proprietary red wine, which was aged in 50%–60% new Taransaud barrels, and bottled unfined and unfiltered. This is a must purchase! Anticipated maturity: 2003–2025. Remarkably, the 1997 Les Pavots (80% Cabernet Sauvignon, 10% Merlot, and 10% Cabernet Franc) may be superior! Production was more abundant, yet the wine is even more concentrated than previous vintages. Mark Aubert believes he will produce 4,000 cases—at this quality level! This terrific offering boasts a saturated black/purple color, as well as fabulously sweet black raspberry and crème de cassislike fruit intermixed with truffle, Asian spice, and floral scents. The wine possesses a seamless, velvety-textured, opulent personality. With its phenomenal concentration and purity, the wine's tannin is virtually concealed by the depth of fruit, glycerin, and overall richness. Totally dry, it almost tastes sweet because of its high alcohol (14.8%) and fabulous extract. Wow! Anticipated maturity: 2002–2030.

The 1995 Chardonnay vintage undoubtedly rivals the 1994, with several cuvées possibly superior. The 1995s possess remarkably complex, multidimensional aromas and flavors, as well as strikingly expansive, compelling textural profiles. All are bottled unfiltered. For example, it would be hard to surpass the 1992, 1993, and 1994 Chardonnay Clos du Ciel, but believe it or not, the 1995 is an even richer, more complex wine. Fortunately, there are 1,800 cases of this Bâtard-Montrachet lookalike. The 1995 Chardonnay Clos du Ciel offers crisp acidity, which is essential for a wine of this intensity, weight, and richness. The subtle, smoky oak intermingles with scents of honey, hazelnuts, lemon custard, and butter, creating a lavishly rich, assertive yet remarkably complex, full-bodied Chardonnay that caresses the palate with gobs of fruit, glycerin, and personality. The acidity gives it a vibrant finish, and ensures at least 4–5 years of longevity—assuming purchasers have such discipline. The 1995 Chardonnay Mon Plaisir was tighter and more backward and unevolved when I tasted it in late October. This Chardonnay, made from volcanic soils, has relatively high acidity, yet tremendous richness, length, and presence in the mouth. There is a strong liquid stone, Chablis-like character to the wine, but this is a bigger and bolder wine than most Chablis. It should drink well when released early next year, but I am not sure it will possess the exotic, lavish opulence and richness of the Clos du Ciel.

One of the most glorious Chardonnays made in California over the last few years has been Peter Michael's Cuvée Indigène. The terrific 1995 (700 cases produced) is a worthy rival to the profound 1994. The 1995 exhibits a light lemony/gold color, and sweet, exotic, custard pie, ripe pineapple, smoky beer nut, *pain grillé*-like aromas. Full bodied, fabulously rich, and unctuously textured, it is not just a big, thick, well-extracted Chardonnay. The wine's balance is perfect, as good acidity provides the necessary delineation to this wine's large-scaled personality; it should drink well for 5–6 years. The Point Rouge is the most extracted and concentrated Chardonnay made by Peter Michael. In 1993, 1994, and 1995 it has possessed Montrachet-like credentials. The 1995 Point Rouge (225 cases) is a remarkably powerful, awesomely endowed, thick, stunning Chardonnay that exhibits aromas of grilled nuts, liquefied minerals/stones, and fabulous buttery, smoky fruit. Full bodied, yet impeccably well defined and balanced, this is a winemaking tour de force, as well as one of the finest Chardonnays I have tasted—from anywhere in the world!

A new entry into the Peter Michael Chardonnay portfolio is the outstanding 1995 Chardonnay Belle Côte. Made from 4-year-old vines, this wine (900 cases) reveals a floral component as well as a honeysuckle, Viognier-like element. It has great fruit, superb richness, and crisp acidity—essential to buttress its impressively endowed flavors.

The 1995 Sauvignon Blanc l'Après Midi should not be forgotten in the rush for Peter Michael's Chardonnays. This wine is unquestionably one of the three or four finest Sauvignons in California. It has become so popular that the 700 cases produced are immediately sold out upon release. The wine offers up a Muscat/Viognier-like fragrance because of the clone used by Peter Michael to make this 100% Sauvignon Blanc. The lemony, tropical fruit-scented, intensely fragrant bouquet is supported by rich, medium-bodied flavors that possess balance, crisp acidity, and personality. This barrel-fermented, complex Sauvignon Blanc must be tasted to be believed. Drink it over the next year.

1996 was a much hotter year than 1997, 1995, and 1994. While the 1996s are outstanding wines, in some cases the aromatics are more muted because of 1996's high heat. This was most noticeable in Peter Michael's 1996 Sauvignon Blanc l'Après Midi. Year in and year out this is one of the two or three finest Sauvignons made in California, but in 1996 the wine seems very good to excellent, rather than stunning. Although crisp and medium bodied, it does not reveal the knockout nose it possessed in previous vintages. Barrel fermented, and made from the Sauvignon clone called Musqué, there are honeyed melon, floral, and tropical fruit scents in the wine's bouquet. While the 1996 is a more subdued example of l'Après Midi, it is still a very good wine. Drink it over the next year.

As the following tasting notes and ratings evidence, the Chardonnays are slightly more bunched in scores and quality than in vintages such as 1995 and 1994. Sadly, I learned that 1996 will be the last vintage for the Clos du Ciel. The estate was not sure whether the name Clos du Ciel would continue, but the source for these grapes has been lost. As for the 1996 Chardonnay Clos du Ciel, it is a beautifully made wine with an exotic honeysuckle, orange rind, and tropical fruit-scented nose infused with a subtle dose of toasty oak. The wine possesses a lush, round texture, considerable complexity, and a medium- to full-bodied, lusty finish. I would opt for drinking it over the next several years. Two thousand cases were produced of the 1996 Chardonnay Belle Côte from Peter Michael's 15-acre vineyard in Knight's Valley. This is the finest example of Belle Côte I have yet tasted. A beautifully aromatic wine, with leesy, Burgundian-like aromas, in addition to those of white peaches, citrus, and honey, this full-bodied, well-endowed Chardonnay possesses low acidity, a lush, open-knit, expansive texture, and mouth-filling levels of extract. This is an opulent, flamboyant, exceptionally complex Chardonnay that should drink well for 1–3 years. There are 1,800 cases of the 1996 Chardonnay Mon Plaisir. This wine always comes across as more backward and closed than the other cuvées. The moderately intense bouquet of honeyed apples and citrus is followed by a wine with hints of minerals, rich fruit, medium to full body, and a well-delineated, structured, nicely textured finish. It is a classy Chardonnay. Made from volcanic soils, this wine usually possesses more acidity and a more intensely mineral character than Peter Michael's other cuvées. I have always been a fan of the Chardonnay Cuvée Indigène, so named because it is made from 100% indigenous yeasts and is what the professionals call a "naturally fermented" wine. It always possesses exuberant, intense ripe fruit and richness, along with smoky, beer nut, *pain grillé*-like aromas. The 1996 is a full-bodied, gorgeously proportioned, exotic Chardonnay that leans toward Burgundy in its aromatics, but clearly comes down on the California side with its ostentatious display of ripe fruit. As much as I love the Cuvée Indigène, I have found that recent vintages have gotten even better after a year or so in the bottle. I have never believed these wines should be cellared for more than four or five years, but I am beginning to wonder if that advice might be a bit conservative. Moreover, I suggest decanting this wine 30–45 minutes prior to serving as aeration always seems to enhance the wine's perfume. In any event, this is a stunningly rich, intense Chardonnay that is among the finest being made in California. The 1996 Chardonnay Point Rouge may not equal the near perfection of the 1995, but it is an extremely powerful, fabulously concentrated, compelling wine by any standard of measure. In 1996, the acidity seems slightly lower, and the wine perhaps more evolved than recent examples, but this is a classically rendered Chardonnay, as well as a lesson in what can be achieved in California. A wine to satisfy both the intellect and palate, the rich 1996 Point Rouge provides plenty of honeyed citrus, buttery tropical fruits, full body, and exceptional purity and presence in the mouth. Aromatically complex (intensely fragrant) and extremely long, this thrilling Chardonnay should age for 2–4 years. By the way, the 1995 Chardonnay Point Rouge, which I referenced above, is unquestionably one of the two or three greatest Chardonnays I have ever tasted!

The Chardonnays from Peter Michael are easy to understand, but I am not sure Les Pavots is as fathomable. First of all, Les Pavots is made in a backward, Bordeaux-like style that does not offer the gush of jammy fruit so noticeable in many California Cabernets. However, this is an authoritatively rich wine overlaid with a structural profile that suggests the wine needs 4–5 years of cellaring—at least in top vintages such as California has experienced in the nineties. The black/ruby/purple-colored 1995 Les Pavots (a 73% Cabernet Sauvignon, 14% Merlot, and 13% Cabernet Franc blend), which achieved 13.9% alcohol naturally, reveals a sweet, tobacco, lavender, and cassis-scented nose, medium-bodied, tannic, elegant flavors, outstanding purity, ripeness, and length, yet a measured, restrained style. Less forthcoming than either the 1996 or 1994, this rich, nicely proportioned proprietary red is California's answer to a graceful Médoc. Anticipated maturity: 2001–2020. The superb 1994 Les Pavots is, to my palate, the finest example of this wine Peter Michael has yet made. Since its bottling, this deep, saturated purple-colored wine has taken on a gorgeous nose of cassis intermixed with violets, licorice, and attractive spicy oak. Sweet, rich, and surprisingly showy for a Les Pavots, this medium- to full-bodied wine possesses a luscious, multilayered texture, outstanding depth, and attractively integrated tannin and acidity. When I tasted it, it was more evolved and delicious than I had anticipated given its recent bottling. The 1993 Les Pavots, another impressive wine from a vintage that has plenty of skeptics in the West Coast press, reveals a dense, ruby/purple color, and a complex nose of smoke, spice, toast, and black fruits. Medium to full bodied, with an inner core of sweet, rich fruit, outstanding purity, and a powerful yet elegant personality, this layered, multidimensional wine should drink well young, but keep for 20+ years.

All of Peter Michael's top wines, including the Chardonnays, are bottled without filtration.

Readers should make it a point to visit this winery situated in Knights Valley, not far from the Napa/Sonoma county line. The quality is extraordinary, and the commitment and talent of the winery staff laudatory. Moreover, the winery seems committed to achieving even greater quality.

MICHEL-SCHLUMBERGER (SONOMA)

1993 Cabernet Sauvignon	Dry Creek Valley	C	88
1995 Cabernet Sauvignon Reserve	Dry Creek	C	85?
1994 Cabernet Sauvignon Reserve	Dry Creek Valley	D	88+
1993 Cabernet Sauvignon Reserve Estate	Sonoma	C	88
1993 Merlot Estate	Sonoma	B	87

Winemaker Fred Payne has turned out a supple, round, smoky, herbal, curranty, and cherry-scented and -flavored 1993 Merlot. Easygoing, with good concentration, it will be ready to drink when released. It should last for 5–8 years. The 1993 Cabernet Sauvignon Reserve reveals generous (excessive?) aromas of aggressive new oak, medium ruby color, fine density, ripeness, and richness, and moderate tannin in the long finish. It will be approachable and easy to drink and understand when released. It should last for a decade.

The dark ruby/purple-colored 1993 Cabernet Sauvignon offers pure black currant scents and flavors nicely complemented by cedar, spice, vanillin, and lead pencil. Although exceptionally well made, it reveals high tannin and appears to require another 2–3 years of bottle age. If the tannin melts away sufficiently to reveal the wine's admirably concentrated fruit characteristics, this 1993 Cabernet Sauvignon will merit an even higher score. There is a long finish in this wine, which appears to be a synthesis in style between an austere Bordeaux and a grapey California Cabernet. Anticipated maturity: 2000–2012.

The 1994 Cabernet Sauvignon Reserve's dense opaque purple color is followed by a concentrated wine that emphasizes the pure cassis side of Cabernet Sauvignon. It is still one-dimensional, unevolved, and grapey, but it is a well-layered, serious, backward wine that should express more with another 5–6 years of cellaring. It will last for two decades, and it will be more nuanced and complex once the tannin begins to melt away. Anticipated maturity: 2003–2020.

There was not enough extract, richness, or ripeness of fruit in the 1995 Cabernet Sauvignon Reserve to counterbalance the astringent tannin and pronounced blatantly oaky character. It is a medium-bodied, spicy, harder style of Cabernet without sufficient depth to stand up to the structural components.

ROBERT MONDAVI (NAPA)

1994 Barbera	California	C	88
1996 Cabernet Sauvignon	Napa	D	88
1995 Cabernet Sauvignon	Napa	C	89
1994 Cabernet Sauvignon	Napa	C	88
1997 Cabernet Sauvignon	Oakville District	D	(90–93)
1996 Cabernet Sauvignon	Oakville District	D	92
1995 Cabernet Sauvignon	Oakville District	D	91
1994 Cabernet Sauvignon	Oakville District	D	90
1993 Cabernet Sauvignon	Oakville District	D	90
1997 Cabernet Sauvignon	Stag's Leap	D	(90–92)

1996 Cabernet Sauvignon	Stag's Leap	D	88
1997 Cabernet Sauvignon Reserve	Napa	EE	(94–97)
1996 Cabernet Sauvignon Reserve	Napa	EE	92
1995 Cabernet Sauvignon Reserve	Napa	EE	93
1994 Cabernet Sauvignon Reserve	Napa	EE	98
1993 Cabernet Sauvignon Reserve	Napa	EE	93
1995 Cabernet Sauvignon Stag's Leap District	Napa	D	89
1996 Cabernet Sauvignon 30th Anniversary Reserve	Napa	EE	95
1997 Cabernet Sauvignon To-Kalon Estate Reserve	Napa	EE	(98–100)
1996 Cabernet Sauvignon To-Kalon Vineyard	Napa	EE	94
1997 Chardonnay	Carneros	C	88
1996 Chardonnay	Carneros	C	88
1995 Chardonnay	Carneros	C	87
1997 Chardonnay	Napa	C	87
1996 Chardonnay	Napa	C	86
1995 Chardonnay	Napa	C	87
1997 Chardonnay Reserve	Napa	D	92
1996 Chardonnay Reserve	Napa	D	91
1995 Chardonnay Reserve	Napa	D	91+
1997 Fumé Blanc	Napa	C	86
1996 Fumé Blanc	Napa	B	86
1995 Fumé Blanc	Napa	B	86
1996 Fumé Blanc Reserve	Napa	D	90
1995 Fumé Blanc Reserve To-Kalon Estate	Napa	C	90
1997 Fumé Blanc To-Kahon Estate Reserve	Napa	D	90
1997 Fumé Blanc To-Kalon I Block	Napa	E	94
1996 Fumé Blanc To-Kahon I Block	Napa	E	90
1995 Fumé Blanc To-Kahon I Block	Napa	E	90
1997 Merlot	Carneros	D	(88–91)
1996 Merlot	Carneros	D	89
1996 Merlot	Napa	C	88
1995 Merlot	Napa	C	87
1994 Merlot	Napa	C	86
1993 Merlot	Napa	C	89

1997	Pinot Noir	Napa	C	90
1997	Pinot Noir	Carneros	D	90
1996	Pinot Noir	Carneros	D	87
1995	Pinot Noir	Carneros	D	84
1994	Pinot Noir	Carneros	B	87
1993	Pinot Noir	Carneros	B	89
1996	Pinot Noir	Napa	C	86
1995	Pinot Noir	Napa	C	82
1993	Pinot Noir	Napa	B	89
1997	Pinot Noir Reserve	Napa	D	92
1996	Pinot Noir Reserve	Napa	D	89
1995	Pinot Noir Reserve	Napa	D	89
1994	Pinot Noir Reserve	Napa	D	89
1993	Pinot Noir Reserve	Napa	D	87
1994	Sangiovese	California	C	85
1995	Sangiovese Reserva La Famiglia	Napa	C	79
1997	Sauvignon Blanc	Stag's Leap	C	87
1996	Sauvignon Blanc Stag's Leap District	Napa	C	87
1995	Sauvignon Blanc Stag's Leap District	Napa	C	86
1997	Zinfandel	Napa	C	(89–90)
1995	Zinfandel	Napa	C	89
1994	Zinfandel	Napa	C	86
1993	Zinfandel	Napa	C	93

If there is one brilliant example of a winery never content with resting on its laurels and/or maintaining the status quo, it is Robert Mondavi. Constant experimentation in addition to the challenging of existing beliefs, result in better and more complete wines from this venerable producer. I spent time with Robert Mondavi during my trip to Napa in September 1998, and what a remarkable man he is—a youthful, exuberant, 85-year-old with a long-term view of the future. When is the President of the United States going to give this man our highest civilian honor for the profound and positive influence he has had on wine, food, and American culture?

I think it is safe to say that no white wine at Robert Mondavi goes through 100% malolactic fermentation given winemaker Tim Mondavi's belief in trying to produce wines with flavor, vibrancy, and as he says, "nerve." There are four Sauvignon/Fumé Blancs produced, all bottled without filtration. The most abundant production is the 1997 Fumé Blanc. Mondavi was one of the first to label Sauvignon Blanc as Fumé, and this is a tasty, fresh, light- to medium-bodied, crisp, melony, subtly smoky wine with zesty underlying acidity. It should drink well for several years. The 1997 Sauvignon Blanc Stag's Leap displays a more mineral/gravelly quality in its citrusy, crisp fruitiness. A delicate, fresh, lively, light-bodied Sauvignon, it sees about 33% fermentation in old oak barrels, with the balance of the cuvée fermented in tank. The 1997 should drink well for 2–3 years. The two most impressive Fumés are the 1997 To-Kalon Estate Reserve and 1997 To-Kalon Estate I Block. Both these wines possess terrific fruit character, with the 1997 Fumé Blanc To-Kalon Estate Reserve slightly more delicate but beautifully delineated, with a leesy, citrusy, grapefruit, melony character intertwined with smoke, minerals, and spice. A medium-bodied, enthralling style of Fumé Blanc, it should drink well for 3–4 years. The 1997 Fumé Blanc To-Kalon Estate I Block is produced from the oldest Sauvignon Blanc vines of the estate vineyard. It offers a subtle, honeyed, citrusy nose, followed by rich, medium-bodied, elegant, exceptionally long, and remarkably concentrated flavors. The overall impression remains one of delicacy and finesse. It should drink well for 4–5 years.

Mondavi's Chardonnays are given partial malolactic, although the percentage is less and less, with Tim Mondavi pushing for more precision and vibrancy. Yields continue to be lowered, resulting in concentrated, refreshing, food-friendly wines. The 1997 Chardonnay Napa exhibits an elegant pear, honey, lemon butter-scented nose, with subtle wood in the background. In the mouth, it is lush, ripe, and round, as well as extremely well delineated and zesty. It should drink well for 3–4 years. The subtle, mineral-imbued 1997 Chardonnay Carneros offers a spring flower blossom, white peach, moderately intense bouquet. Medium bodied and pure, with a hint of toasty oak, this restrained example is reminiscent of a high-class Graves. A Chardonnay for white Graves lovers, it should drink well for 3–4 years. The flagship Chardonnay, the 1997 Chardonnay Reserve, is a beautifully rich, expansive, complex offering that reminds me of some grand cru whites produced by the Burgundian *négociant* Joseph Drouhin. Everything is in balance in this delicate, extremely long wine. It unfolds as it sits in the glass, revealing subtle buttery popcorn, orange blossom, lemon zest, and restrained toasty new oak. A medium- to full-bodied Chardonnay, with good underlying acidity, it should be uncommonly long-lived for a California Chardonnay, 5–10 years.

At Mondavi, no varietal has been studied as intensely as Pinot Noir. Farming has moved toward organic, and the wines are being made as naturally as possible. Mondavi's 1997 Pinot Noirs, which are the finest they have yet produced, are indicative of such qualitative efforts. Much of the new production of California North Coast Pinot Noir is emerging from Dijon plant material (clones such as 667, 777, and 115). Robert Mondavi also utilizes such old California clones (which were brought from Burgundy years ago) as Calera and Swan. Readers looking for an easy-to-find, gorgeous Pinot Noir need search no further than Mondavi's 1997 Pinot Noir Napa. A remarkable 33,000 cases were produced, mostly from their Carneros vineyard. An outstanding example, it exhibits a deep ruby color, in addition to superb aromatics of black cherry fruit intertwined with spicy oak, loamy soil scents, and forest aromas. A beautifully textured, medium- to full-bodied palate is soft, pure, and bursting with black cherry fruit. The alcohol is a lofty 13.8%, which gives the wine plenty of glycerin and flesh. This Pinot should drink easily for 4–5 years. The denser, dark ruby-colored 1997 Pinot Noir Carneros reveals more noticeable new oak in the aromatics, as well as high-strung cherry/raspberry aromas, and a creamy texture. The fruit is beautifully pure in this medium-bodied, elegant, vibrant wine. It is a more finesse-styled Pinot, and perhaps less obvious than the crowd-pleasing Napa Valley bottling. Like its siblings, the 1997 Pinot Noir Reserve (which sees 70% new oak) is bottled with neither fining nor filtration. It boasts the deepest ruby/purple color, a terrific texture, and copious quantities of sweet cherry/kirsch fruit intermixed with cassis and raspberries. While the oak is noticeable, the wine's greater concentration, body, and power have soaked most of it up. This is an opulently textured Pinot Noir with superb potential. It should be at its best after another 1–2 years of cellaring and will keep for a decade. Bravo to the Mondavi winery for these efforts.

Robert Mondavi has joined the Merlot sweepstakes, producing some excellent wines, but not yet hitting the bull's eye with this varietal. As Tim Mondavi says, "What is Merlot?" The problem may be that California has fewer clones to choose from, and there is a tendency to give this wine less attention because it seems to be such an easy sell in spite of the ocean of insipid Merlots that inhabit the marketplace. Mondavi's efforts are unquestionably fine, and come close to being outstanding. The 1996 Merlot Napa exhibits a dark ruby/purple color, as well as berry aromas and flavors intermixed with loamy soil, coffee bean, and spicy oak notes. The wine is medium bodied, with good richness, yet it has a slightly monolithic personality. A very good effort, it should evolve nicely over the next 7–8 years. The 1996 Merlot Carneros is a better effort. There is more clay in Mondavi's Carneros vineyard. This example reveals a deeper, more saturated ruby/purple color, in addition to a more intriguing fragrance of black cherry jam intermixed with loamy soil and new oak scents. Beautifully rendered in the mouth, with medium body, excellent intensity, and well-integrated tannin and acidity, this impressively endowed Merlot comes close to meriting an outstanding evaluation. It should drink well for a decade or more. The 1997 Merlot Carneros offers up more of the roasted coffee notes intermixed with jammy, berry fruit. The oak has been nicely disguised by the wine's concentration. Like many 1997s, it is evolved aromatically, and already delicious to drink. This Merlot should be sexy and forthcoming upon release, and age nicely for a decade.

Cabernet Sauvignon is still king at Robert Mondavi, as evidenced by the following releases. The 1996 Cabernet Sauvignon Napa is an elegant, medium-bodied example with more tannin than most regular bottlings (a characteristic of the vintage). This structured wine offers weedy black currant fruit, subtle oak, and a well-built, concentrated finish. About 8% Cabernet Franc was added to the blend. The 1996 is approachable, but it promises to be even better with several more years of bottle age, and will last 12–15+ years. The 1996 Cabernet Sauvignon Stag's Leap possesses the crisp, restrained, lighter-bodied style of wines from that region. Sweet black cherries intermixed with floral scents are present in the wine's aromatics. In the mouth, tar and floral characteristics combine with black fruit to give this Cabernet an enthralling, supple, approachable style. There is some tannin in the finish, and the wine is more austere than the Napa bottling, but it should drink well for 12–15 years. The outstanding 1996 Cabernet Sauvignon Oakville offers an opaque purple color, and knockout aromas of crème de cassis, vanillin, and weedy tobacco. Full bodied, rich, and muscular, as well as complex, this fleshy, deep wine is immensely impressive. As it sits in the glass, blueberry/blackberry aromas emerge, adding to its overall appeal. Anticipated maturity: 2001–2020. The 1996 Cabernet Sauvignon Reserve may be no better than the Oakville, but it is made in a slightly different style. The color is opaque purple, and the wine reveals more vanillin, a touch of mint, and plenty of black currant fruit in its moderately intense aromatics. Some of the vintage's dry tannin (from this year's stressed vineyard conditions) are present in the wine's finish. A more stylish, restrained, less exuberant example than the 1996 Oakville, it is an outstanding offering that should be consumed between 2002 and 2025. None of the above 1996 Cabernet Sauvignons match the majesty, richness, and breadth of the 1996 Cabernet Sauvignon 30th Anniversary Reserve. This special bottling (about 1,000 cases) is a fabulous wine. From its opaque purple color and stunning aromatics of blackberries, cassis, *pain grillé*, licorice, and Asian spices, to its full-bodied, concentrated, superbly extracted style, this wine possesses virtually everything. Layers of fruit, glycerin, extract, and sweet tannin are presented in a flamboyant format. The tannin level is high, but so is the wine's richness and length. It is a sensational effort. Anticipated maturity: 2005–2030.

While I did not taste the 1997 Napa Cabernet Sauvignon, the 1997 Cabernet Sauvignon Stag's Leap is a beauty, displaying this area's polished style, along with more intensity and richness than previous vintages. The color is opaque ruby/purple. The bouquet offers up gobs of licorice, spicy oak, and rich black cherry and currant fruit. In the mouth, there is a slight orange rind touch to the black currant fruit in addition to copious amounts of well-integrated, sweet tannin. The vintage's forward, evolved nature is evident in this medium-bodied, floral, Margaux-styled Cabernet. It should drink well upon release, and evolve for 10–15+ years. The 1997 Cabernet Sauvignon Oakville is fabulous, even more sexy, richer, and opulent than the 1996. The wine's opaque purple color is followed by soaring aromatics of toasty new oak, black currants, spice box, and *pain grillé*. Full bodied, with gorgeously sweet, well-integrated tannin (a noticeable hallmark of the top 1997 Cabernets), and an opulent, voluptuous texture, this superconcentrated, seamless Cabernet Sauvignon should be thrilling to drink. Anticipated maturity: 2002–2030. The 1997 Cabernet Sauvignon Reserve (15,000–18,000 cases) is considered by Tim Mondavi to rival the great Reserves made in 1987, 1990, 1991, and 1994. I can't say I disagree. The wine boasts a saturated, thick-looking black/purple color, as well as fabulously unevolved, but beautiful aromas of crème de cassis that soak up the 100% new oak aging. The wine has a fabulous palate presence, explosive richness, gobs of glycerin, marvelous extract, and superb purity. The moderately high tannin in the finish is barely discernible at this stage in the wine's development. Weighty yet impeccably well balanced and defined, this appears to be a sumptuous Cabernet Sauvignon that will be relatively drinkible upon release.

Is it possible that the greatest Cabernet Sauvignon yet produced by Robert Mondavi will be 1,000 cases of the 1997 Cabernet Sauvignon To-Kalon Estate Reserve? Made from 100% Cabernet Sauvignon from the oldest vines on the estate (averaging 35 years), this profound offering exhibits a saturated black/purple color, and a celestial bouquet of intense aromas of cassis, subtle spicy oak, *pain grillé*, exotic spices, and floral scents, with a touch of licorice thrown in for additional complexity. Full bodied and seamless, with a silky, multilayered texture, a fabulously rich midpalate, and a 45+-second finish, this is a staggeringly rich, compelling Cabernet Sauvignon. Anticipated maturity: 2005–2040.

Lest I forget, the Mondavis also make a Zinfandel. They are trying to keep the alcohol level down as they are adamantly against the powerhouse, high alcohol Zinfandels so common in California. The outstanding, full-bodied 1997 Zinfandel Napa contains rich fruit, plenty of intensity and glycerin, and, it seems to me, high alcohol. It is a delicious, briery, peppery, intensely fruity Zinfandel to drink over the next 4–5 years.

For a number of years I have had the privilege of tasting the nearly 50-year-old block of Sauvignon Blanc grapes, referred to as the I Block, from Mondavi's To-Kalon Vineyard. Until 1995, this wine was blended with the Fumé Blanc Reserve, but in 1995 it was bottled separately. Unfortunately, there are only 200 cases of this zesty Sauvignon. It possesses intense fruit, crisp acidity, and plenty of that honey, melony, figlike Sauvignon character. With airing, the texture opens to reveal multiple layers of delicate flavors. This wine should age effortlessly for 5 or more years.

Because the Mondavi family has always believed this varietal offers considerable flexibility with an assortment of culinary dishes, they produce three other Sauvignon Blanc cuvées. Their 1995 Fumé Blanc is a crisp, light- to medium-bodied, delicately herbed wine that relies more on subtlety than a flashy display of fruit or oak. It should drink well for 1–3 years. The 1995 Fumé Blanc Reserve is a more intense, pungent, earthy, honeyed, buttery style of Sauvignon, with fuller body and gorgeously ripe, rich fruit, that manages to retain its delicacy and elegance. This 100% barrel-fermented wine is medium bodied and flavorful, yet not overpowering. It should drink well for 2–3 years. Lastly, the most crisp, dry, and austere of the Robert Mondavi Sauvignons is the 1995 Sauvignon Blanc Stag's Leap District. This wine begs for food, as it is too tart to stand alone and be drunk as an aperitif. Spicy and pure, with a floral component, in addition to less body, it should drink well for 1–2 years.

Mondavi's Chardonnays continue to aim for full-bodied flavor, but with increasing degrees of subtlety and elegance. The Reserve Chardonnays of the late seventies and eighties were often excessively woody. Today, these Reserve wines have more in common with a top-class Domaine Leflaive Bâtard-Montrachet than many of their California counterparts. There are three Chardonnay cuvées—Napa Valley, Carneros, and the limited production Reserve. The tasty, crisp 1995 Napa Chardonnay offers copious amounts of unadulterated, ripe, citrusy, buttery, apple-flavored fruit. Medium bodied, pure, and fresh, it is a Chardonnay to drink over the next 1–2 years. The 1995 Carneros Chardonnay reveals more floral, ripe tropical fruit aromas, medium body, a softer, creamier texture, as well as crisp, underlying acidity. It, too, should be drunk over the next several years.

The 1995 Chardonnay Reserve is initially reticent given its tightly wound first impression. As the wine sits in the glass, it continues to unfold and blossom, providing a top-class example of Mondavi's finest Chardonnay. A smoky, *pain grillé*, flowery, buttery, citrusy nose is followed by a full-bodied, rich wine with excellent length. This exceptional, young and unevolved Chardonnay is immensely impressive; it will drink well for 4–6 years.

The 1996 Fumé Blanc exhibits a light straw color, followed by tart, fresh, melony flavors, and flinty, mineral and figlike fruit on the palate. It is fresh, subtle, medium bodied and stylish. At the same time, it captures the varietal's personality. Drink it over the next several years. Even more vibrant and acidic is the 1996 Sauvignon Blanc Stag's Leap District. This is a vivacious, grapefruit-scented and -flavored wine with spicy, medium-bodied fruit, a strong underlying mineral character (as if it wanted to be a white Graves), and a dry finish. Based on how well the 1995 is showing at present, the 1996 should have two years of life. Both of the previous wines had their malolactic fermentations blocked, but that was not the case with the 1996 Fumé Blanc Reserve. Barrel fermented and put through 100% malolactic fermentation, this wine possesses a creamier, more honeyed texture, excellent ripe, rich aromatics, and medium to full body. It is a more pungent, intensely flavored, weightier wine than its two predecessors. Readers looking for something rare in Sauvignon Blanc should try to latch on to a bottle or two of the 1996 Sauvignon Blanc To-Kalon I Block. Made from extremely old vines planted just south of the Mondavi winery, it boasts a citrusy, melony, grapefruitlike nose, followed by dry, medium-bodied flavors with surprising length and intensity. It is a subtle, restrained wine that should age easily for 4–5 years.

The Mondavi Chardonnays have moved from a full malolactic style to something that Burgundy's Jacques Lardière (the oenologist for Louis Jadot) has perfected—partial malolactic fermentation for dry, rich, full-bodied whites. This is done in order to maintain a level of natural acidity and enhance the wine's stability. Tim Mondavi has increasingly advocated this position, particularly for the house's big whites. To do so, and also get the wine into the bottle unfiltered is no easy task, but the Mondavis have succeeded. The 1996 Chardonnay Napa is a medium-bodied, graceful, citrusy, buttery, fresh, pure wine that is ideal for drinking over the next several years. The 1996 Chardonnay Carneros is a more layered, richer, smokier, spicier wine with softer, richer flavors, and a more expansive texture. It can even be called "luscious," which may be the antithesis of Tim Mondavi's notion of a wine that is "bright, with plenty of nerve." There are 7,000 cases of the 1996 Chardonnay Reserve. This wine started off in the glass as monolithic, but it developed magnificently, revealing medium to full body, and a spicy, saddle leather, smoked hazelnut, honeysuckle, and buttery-scented nose. This seemingly shy wine comes alive with airing, displaying layers of rich fruit, as well as excellent purity and equilibrium. In addition, it possesses surprising structure for a California Chardonnay. The wood influence is there, but very restrained. This wine should age well for 2–3 years.

Mondavi's Pinot Noirs are all well made, with the Reserve the finest. The dark ruby-colored 1995 Pinot Noir Napa offers spicy, sweet, cranberry, and red currant fruit, subtle oak, and meaty flavors suggestive of plant material, herbs, and cherries. It is an attractive, straightforward Pinot Noir to drink over the next 4–5 years. The 1996 Pinot Noir Carneros offers a dark plum color, followed by a richer, more generous jammy cherry nose with spice and minerals in the background. The wine is medium bodied and crisp, with good balance. The most impressive of this trio of Pinots is the 1996 Pinot Noir Napa Reserve. It displays a dark plum color, and moderately intense, herbaceous, animal, black plum, and cherry aromas. Restrained but rich, with crisp acidity, and clean winemaking, this medium-bodied, tightly knit Pinot Noir will benefit from another 1–2 years of bottle age and last for 4–8 years.

The 1995 Pinot Noir is a spicy, soft, deep ruby-colored wine that is crisp and tart, with a notion of tar and berry fruit, but its compact personality could have been more fleshy and seductive. The 1995 Pinot Noir Carneros exhibits a deep, dark garnet color, an attractive, moderately intense, cinnamon, spicy, red fruit-scented nose, and pleasant but straightforward flavors, with noticeable acidity. It should drink well for 3–4 years. The 1995 Pinot Noir Reserve is excellent, possibly outstanding. It does not display the sweet, expansive texture and layers of fruit found in the finest Pinot Noirs, but it is a well-crafted, deep ruby-colored, medium-bodied wine with good spice, smoke, earth, and berrylike flavors. Only the slightly clipped and compact texture is a letdown. It will drink well for 5–6 years.

The 1994 Pinot Noir Reserve is a lusher, more open-knit, seductive, and voluptuously textured Pinot Noir, with sweeter fruit, a round, generous mouth-feel, medium to full body, low acidity, and a soft, silky finish. It should drink well for 3–4 years. The 1993 Pinot Noir Reserve is beginning to reveal some lightening at the edge. It possesses a user-friendly, herb, berry, and vanillin-scented nose, and medium- to full-bodied, ripe, spicy flavors. Some alcohol is noticeable in the finish. Overall, these are very good to excellent Pinot Noirs that will provide readers with considerable enjoyment. All of them should be drunk younger rather than older.

The 1994 Pinot Noir Carneros displays an attractive spicy, cinnamon-scented nose, sweet cherry fruit, a soft, velvety texture, and a fruity finish. Drink it over the next 4–5 years as it is not likely to be long-lived. The 1993 Pinot Noir Carneros exhibits more extract and richness. It offers a broad, attractive nose of red and black fruits, vanilla, and herbs. Seductive, round, and generous, this mouth-filling, savory Pinot Noir will offer fine drinking for another 3–4 years. The 1993 Pinot Noir Napa is nearly outstanding. It exhibits considerable fatness, a sweet, intense nose of black fruits, earth, toast, and flowers, medium body, and a velvety texture. This is a Volnay-like Pinot Noir with 4–5 years of drinkability.

The only wine I tasted under the La Famiglia designation was the 1995 Sangiovese Reserva. The wine is light bodied, with tart acidity, and a distinctive earthy, strawberry/cranberrylike character moving in the direction of mushrooms on the palate. As my score and tasting notes suggest, I was not particularly moved by this effort. I did, however, enjoy the 1995 Zinfandel, a textbook wine with briery, peppery aromatics, and dense, chewy, heady flavors of black fruits (raspberries and cherries). Some spice is added to the mix in this full-bodied, mouth-filling Zinfandel.

The medium-bodied, straightforward 1994 Zinfandel offers a spicy, peppery, black cherry-scented nose, ripe fruit, an easygoing personality, and an elegant, uncomplicated finish. Although ready to drink, it lacks a focal point of interest. Consume it over the next several years.

The 1993 Zinfandel is a knockout! A decadent, ripe, full-bodied, blockbuster Zinfandel (14.7% alcohol), this dry wine is loaded with spicy, peppery, earthy, berry aromas and unctuously rich, full-bodied, crunchy flavors. It will drink well for at least a decade.

The 1994 Sangiovese exhibits a textbook strawberry, cherry, and new saddle leather-scented nose, crisp, elegant, tart flavors, medium body, and a fine finish. It is good, but incapable of challenging the finest Sangioveses being produced by the likes of Swanson, Coturri, Ferrari-Carano, Staglin, and Shafer. The unfined and unfiltered 1994 Barbera is the best bet among Mondavi's Italian-inspired reds. Although not complex, it reveals a dense color, rich berry fruit, medium body, and crisp acidity to hold all the ripeness and fruit extraction together. It should drink well for 4–5 years.

Mondavi's Merlot seems to be getting better and better, not surprising in view of the extraordinary efforts this winery makes to increase the quality of its offerings. The 1993 Merlot reveals more of a chocolatey, black cherry component than the 1992, and a more complete mouth-feel without the 1992's tough, tannic finish. The fruit is sweeter, more concentrated, and, as a result, more interesting. Drink the 1993 Merlot over the next 7–8 years. The 1994 Merlot exhibits an impressively saturated ruby/purple color, followed by a light intensity nose of roasted coffee and sweet cola/cherrylike fruit. The wine reveals dry tannin in the finish, which lowered what would have been a higher score. This spicy, medium-bodied, attractive Merlot possesses 5–8 years of aging potential. The dark ruby-colored 1995 Merlot Napa offers up a dense, black cherry, fruit-driven nose. In the mouth, it is medium to full bodied, somewhat foursquare, but fleshy with good acidity, followed by an attractively long finish.

The 1993 Cabernet Sauvignon Oakville is a noteworthy successor to the impressive 1992. The wine's dark ruby/purple color is followed by a sweet, ripe nose of black currants, floral scents, licorice, and vanillin. Exhibiting plenty of cassis fruit, this pure, dense, concentrated, full-bodied yet undeniably elegant wine should drink well for 12–15 years. The 1993 Cabernet Sauvignon Reserve outperformed the 1992 at the winery, revealing a concentrated, splendidly saturated dark purple color, wonderfully sweet, intense aromas of chocolate, smoke, vanilla beans, and rich black currant fruit. The wine tastes more extracted than the 1992, with a sweeter, more expansive, glycerin-imbued midsection and finish. Although it carries as much tannin as the 1992, the tannin is riper as well as better integrated. The 1993 is a 25–30-year wine that ideally needs another 4–5 years of cellaring.

The 1994 is unquestionably a great vintage for North Coast Cabernet Sauvignon and stands above 1990, 1991, 1992, and 1993—all outstanding vintages with no shortage of heroic performances. Remarkably, 1995 may turn out to be as profound as 1994, giving California its two greatest back to back vintages of Cabernet Sauvignon—ever! The quality of the 1994 vintage is well displayed at Robert Mondavi. The 1994 Cabernet Sauvignon Napa (about 80,000 cases produced) is one of the finest regular Cabernets Mondavi has made. It exhibits a deep ruby color, and sweet, rich, black currant aromas intertwined with scents of vanilla and spice. Soft, round, medium to full bodied, and harmonious, the wine is accessible, yet capable of lasting for 10–15 years. The youthful 1994 Cabernet Sauvignon Oakville District (6,900 cases) could be mistaken for a Mondavi Reserve Cabernet. The color is a saturated ruby/purple, and the nose offers up attractive, complex scents of lead pencil, vanillin, *pain grillé*, and ripe cassis fruit. Dense, rich, and medium to full bodied, with moderate tannin, this young, impressively endowed Cabernet Sauvignon should be at its best between the turn of the century and 2010.

I have drunk some memorable Reserve Cabernet Sauvignons from Robert Mondavi, including the gloriously fragrant, elegant 1971, the powerful, dense 1974, the seductive 1978, the mammothly endowed, tannic blockbuster 1987, the silky, opulent, superconcentrated 1990, and the compellingly rich, layered 1991. However, if I were to select the Reserve Cabernet Sauvignon that may turn out to be the greatest Mondavi has yet made, the 1994 might edge out the 1991 and 1987. It may not appear to be the case, but I am often at a loss for words when it comes to writing about truly profound wines. They seem to have their own stature, presence, and character that transcend the significance of mere words. That being said, Mondavi's 1994 Cabernet Sauvignon Reserve is an exquisite wine, as well as a Cabernet that may turn out to be one of the wines of the vintage. The deep opaque purple color, and tightly wound nose and flavors still reveal enough profound aromas and flavors to mark this as one of Mondavi's most sensational efforts. The nose possesses a Margaux/Mouton-like cassis, lead pencil, floral aroma, backed up by copious quantities of black currant fruit. In the mouth, my notes said, "great stuff." The wine is full bodied, layered, multidimensional, and astonishingly well balanced, with an inner depth and core of exceptional richness and intensity. All of this has been accomplished without any notion of obtrusive weight, tannin, or alcohol. The finish lasts for 35+ seconds. Because of its luxurious quantity of fruit, this wine will be accessible young, thus much of it will be drunk long before it ever reaches full maturity. However, for those able to buy more than a bottle or two, and who possess the discipline to wait 10–15 years, this wine should prove to be a formidable California Cabernet with a rare complexity, elegance, and richness. It should be at its best between 2002 and 2025.

Mondavi have added a number of new regionally labeled Cabernet Sauvignons to their portfolio. In addition to their Oakville cuvée, they have a Stag's Leap District Cabernet, and a single vineyard wine from their famed To-Kalon plantation. The 1995 Cabernet Sauvignon Napa is a beautifully made wine that comes close to being outstanding. It boasts a textbook cassis and eucalyptus-scented nose with oak in the background. On the palate, the wine is medium to full bodied, with excellent ripeness, clean fruit, and a long, spicy finish. It avoids some of the vintage's hard tannins. The debut release of 1995 Cabernet Sauvignon Stag's Leap District is an uncommonly elegant, Margaux-styled wine with medium body, and sweet black currants in the nose with a notion of toasty oak. Good acidity and a soft underbelly make for a pleasant, seductive wine that should drink well young but keep for 15 years. In 1995, the Cabernet Sauvignon Oakville District is again outstanding. The wine reveals textbook cedar, cassis, and *pain grillé* notes in the nose, terrific fruit intensity and purity, medium to full body, and excellent harmony among its elements. This has resulted in an authoritatively flavored yet graceful Cabernet Sauvignon that will benefit from 2–5 years of cellaring, and keep for 2 decades. The 1995 Cabernet Sauvignon Reserve is slightly less impressive than when I tasted it last year, although still an outstanding wine. I may have caught it at a closed stage following bottling. There are 15,000–20,000 cases of Reserve Cabernet made, and in 1995, a quintessentially elegant style has been produced. The wine is less weighty than the 1994, 1991, or 1990. It has great promise and raw materials, with superb fruit and richness, medium body, and subtle lead pencil notes to go along with black currant, mineral, and *pain grillé* scents and flavors. Based on this tasting, I would lower my overall rating, but it is still an exceptional California Cabernet Sauvignon made in a compellingly elegant, graceful style. Anticipated maturity: 2000–2018.

CHÂTEAU MONTELENA (NAPA)

1997	Cabernet Sauvignon Calistoga Cuvée	Napa	C	(87–88)
1996	Cabernet Sauvignon Calistoga Cuvée	Napa	C	86
1995	Cabernet Sauvignon Calistoga Cuvée	Calistoga	C	85
1993	Cabernet Sauvignon Calistoga Cuvée	Calistoga	C	88
1997	Cabernet Sauvignon Estate	Napa	EE	(92–96)
1996	Cabernet Sauvignon Estate	Napa	EE	94
1995	Cabernet Sauvignon Estate	Napa	EE	94
1994	Cabernet Sauvignon Estate	Napa	EE	95
1993	Cabernet Sauvignon Estate	Napa	EE	91+
1997	Chardonnay	Napa	D	88
1996	Chardonnay	Napa	D	90
1995	Chardonnay	Napa	D	89
1997	Johannisberg Riesling	Potter Valley	C	89
1997	St. Vincent (Zinfandel/Sangiovese)	Napa	D	(88–90)
1996	St. Vincent (Zinfandel/Sangiovese)	Napa	D	87

1995 St. Vincent (Zinfandel/Sangiovese)	Napa	D	87
1994 Zinfandel Estate	Napa	C	89
1993 Zinfandel Estate	Napa	C	88

I once made the statement that Château Montelena is the "Cal Ripken of California Cabernet producers." Of course I was referring to the fact that no other winery in California has such a consistent record of excellence over the last 25 years. That point was brought home to me at a blind tasting on October 8, 1998, where a vertical of Château Montelena was served, including every vintage from 1978 through 1995. Not only was the consistency of the wines mind-boggling (virtually every wine was extolled for the same reasons—great fruit, richness, texture, vigor, and youthfulness), but even the so-called difficult vintages for Napa were hugely successful at Château Montelena. The other striking fact was that among the twelve tasters, when the first flight of 1978 through 1983 Montelenas was served, every taster thought the wines were from vintages in the early nineties! I have always thought these wines had 20–25 years of aging potential, but after the tasting I would argue that Montelena's Cabernet Sauvignon have the potential to evolve for 30–40 years. All of the wines were unbelievably youthful, including the oldest! Space precludes tasting notes, but following are the scores I gave the wines: 1978 (92), 1979 (93), 1980 (88+), 1981 (88), 1982 (96), 1983 (92), 1984 (94), 1985 (91+), 1986 (96), 1987 (96+), 1988 (90), 1989 (92), 1990 (93), 1991 (94+), 1992 (93), 1993 (95), 1994 (95), 1995 (95).

Montelena's Chardonnays are made in the nonmalolactic style, from what is known as Clone 4 (large clustered grapes, about four times the size of the new Dijon clones of Chardonnay). The wines possess a crisp minerality, and tend to be flexible with food. While they rarely achieve the complexity of a Marcassin, Peter Michael, or Mt. Eden, they are among the finest nonmalolactic Chardonnays made in California (only Shafer's Red Shoulder Ranch is better). The 1997 Chardonnay exhibits textbook apple and pineapple fruit, fresh, lively, medium- to full-bodied flavors with excellent purity, and a vibrant, exuberant finish. Bo Barrett feels these wines are best at five years of age. Even better than when I tasted it last year, the 1996 Chardonnay reveals mineral and peachlike scents in the nose, superb ripeness, long, fresh, concentrated fruit flavors, and good underlying acidity. It should drink well for 4–5 years. The only other white wine made by Château Montelena, a dry Johannisberg Riesling, is only sold at the winery, as production is limited to 1,000 cases. The 1997 Johannisberg Riesling possesses 0.67% residual sugar, as well as a knockout nose of apples, apricots, and peaches, and light- to medium-bodied, pure, exuberant, fresh fruit flavors. This is a delicious, dry Riesling to consume over the next 1–2 years.

Montelena was among the first estates to blend Zinfandel and Sangiovese. Their 1997 St. Vincent (90% Zinfandel and 10% Sangiovese) may be the finest they have yet produced. It possesses more color than most vintages (dark ruby/purple), good fatness, and abundant cherry and strawberry fruit intermixed with pepper, spice and notes of new saddle leather. This forward, delicious wine should be consumed over the next 3–4 years. The lighter-styled, more feeble looking 1996 St. Vincent (70% Zinfandel and 30% Sangiovese) exhibits a light ruby color, followed by plenty of glycerin, alcohol, and strawberry jam/kirsch aromas and flavors. There is far more richness and power than the surprisingly light color suggests.

Bo Barrett wants to push the Calistoga Cuvée of Cabernet Sauvignon to a higher quality level. In short, he desires sweeter tannin, more fat, and a fleshier texture. The 1997 Cabernet Sauvignon Calistoga Cuvée is the first of the "new and improved" Calistoga cuvées. It offers a saturated ruby/purple color, and plenty of blackberry and cassis fruit presented in an uncomplicated, medium- to full-bodied, chewy style. Ten percent Cabernet Franc and 10% Merlot have been added to provide softness and aromatic dimension. The wine should drink well for 7–10 years. The 1996 Cabernet Sauvignon Calistoga Cuvée reveals some of the vintage's dry, mouth-searing tannin. Although structured and elegant, it does not possess the fat, ripeness, and beauty of the 1997. The wine is very California-like in its display of brash cassis fruit, but it lacks the midpalate and length found in the 1997.

Montelena's Estate Cabernet Sauvignons are equivalent to buying blue chip stock. They get better and better with age, and as the vertical tastings I have attended so persuasively attest, they are still relatively young wines at 20 years of age! Bo Barrett feels the 1997 Cabernet Sauvignon Estate is one of the greatest wines Montelena has made. It does appear to be a remarkable offering, with over 14% alcohol, an opaque black/purple color, a sensational crème de cassislike richness, extraordinary purity, remarkable fruit intensity, and gobs of glycerin and extract. Like many of the finest 1997s, it will be sexy to drink at a young age, and while it does possess a high tannin level, they are extremely ripe and well integrated. The 1997 should prove uncommonly accessible when released, but will easily last 20–30 years. The 1996 Cabernet Sauvignon Estate is a powerful, black ruby/purple-colored wine with cherry liqueurlike flavors, full body, loamy, earthy scents, and a terrific, long finish that suggests 20–30 years of ageability. At the winery, I rated the 1995 Cabernet Sauvignon Estate one point below what I gave it in the blind tasting. Nevertheless, my notes on both tastings are nearly identical. This is another winery where the 1995 may be as strong as the 1994. The color is an opaque purple. The wine is full bodied and powerful, with classic notes of cassis intermixed with loamy soil scents, underbrush, and spice. There is massive body and elevated, but sweet tannin that is well integrated with the wine's other components, a blockbuster midpalate, and a finish that lasts for 30+ seconds. Anticipated maturity: 2000–2025. The 1994 Cabernet Sauvignon Estate, which has been closed since bottling, has just begun to open and display its enormous potential. The saturated black/purple color is followed by aromas of gorgeously pure blackberry and cassis scents. Toasty oak notes are barely discernible given the wine's bombastic display of black fruits, huge, chewy glycerin level, and sensational finish. It will be exciting to follow the evolution of the 1994 and 1995.

Modern-day society seems to always be in search of new stars, but this winery has been a super hero for great California Cabernet Sauvignon for nearly 25 years!

Montelena produces two cuvées of Cabernet. The lighter, fruitier Calistoga offering is designed for restaurants and consumers looking for a taste of the Montelena style without as much power, density, and tannin. The 1995 Cabernet Sauvignon Calistoga Cuvée is leaner than the 1996, with a dark ruby color, a cassis-scented nose, a good attack with spice and black fruit, but a dry finish. While attractive, it possesses less fat and flesh than the 1996. However, I should note I tasted this wine immediately after bottling, which can be a particularly difficult time to taste some young wines. The 1993 Cabernet Sauvignon Calistoga Cuvée is one of the finest examples of this wine yet made, offering an attractively deep, dark ruby color, plenty of sweet cassis in the moderately intense nose, and a medium- to full-bodied, ripe, supple style that is ideal for consumers looking for immediate gratification and restaurants desiring a delicious glass of Cabernet where the tannin will not strip the enamel from their clients' teeth. The 1993 Calistoga Cuvée should drink well for 5–7 years.

Some Montelena Zinfandels have carried lofty levels of alcohol, but the 1994 Zinfandel Estate possesses a civilized 14%. The wine reveals a medium ruby color, followed by expansive, silky flavors, and low acidity. It is a Zinfandel to drink over the next 3–4 years. The 1993 Zinfandel Estate is a fat, heady, soft, lush wine with a peppery, berry-scented nose, a silky texture, and gobs of fruit and alcohol in the lusty finish. Drink it over the next 4–5 years.

I enjoyed the 1995 St. Vincent, which tips the scales at 14.1% alcohol. Sadly, only 700 cases will be available. A fleshy, medium ruby-colored wine with abundant quantities of strawberry and berry fruit, it is slightly fuller than the 1996, with better color saturation, as well as a smooth, silky texture. It should drink well for 4–5 years.

Montelena's 1995 Chardonnay exhibits the classic pineapple, pear, citrusy scents that are so prominent in this offering. Picked very ripe, with its malolactic fermentation blocked, these wines can often age well for 5–10 years. Not every vintage is a candidate for cellaring, but my instincts tell me the crisp, mineral-scented, well-delineated, full-bodied 1995 is going to be an ager. It is more backward than the 1994 or 1993 at a similar stage of development. As much as I love a full-blown, malolactic, Burgundian-styled Chardonnay, I also admire and appreciate this type of California Chardonnay.

The Estate Cabernet Sauvignons, Montelena's flagship wines, have been remarkably consistent. From fruit grown in their Calistoga vineyards, which are dry farmed (nonirrigated), approximately 10,000 cases of this wine are estate-bottled each year. It is hard to find less than a stellar vintage. The 1993 Cabernet Sauvignon Estate possesses the most aggressive tannin of the Estate Cabernets. It is a weighty, hefty, powerful wine, with a dense purple color, ripe, sweet black fruit flavors, considerable muscle and depth, and a spicy, full-bodied, tannic finish. This wine has all the necessary components to age effortlessly for 20+ years. However, it will require 3–4 years of cellaring in order to shed some of its tannin.

MORAGA VINEYARDS (BEL AIR)

1996 Cabernet Sauvignon	Bel Air	E	89
1995 Cabernet Sauvignon	Bel Air	E	89
1994 Cabernet Sauvignon	Bel Air	E	89
1993 Cabernet Sauvignon	Bel Air	E	89+

One of California's most interesting vineyards, Moraga is a 7-acre parcel located in the wealthy Los Angeles suburb of Bel Air. Think it over—I bet an acre of land in this high rent district probably sells for as much as an acre of grand cru Chambertin or Montrachet in Burgundy! These wines are intriguing, offering a Bordeaux-like austerity as well as Médoc-like aromatics of weedy tobacco, cedar, and currants. They give every indication of being ageworthy wines with 15–20 years of possible evolution. The vineyard, which I once walked with the proprietor, is made from decomposed fossils, limestone, and sandstone. Recent vintages have been aged in 100% new French oak casks. The 1996 Cabernet Sauvignon displays a dense purple color, a striking *pain grillé*, black cherry, and cassis-scented nose, and rich, spicy, medium- to full-bodied flavors with good acidity and moderately high tannin. The wine is tightly knit, and in need of 4–5 years of cellaring. It should keep for 15+ years. The 1995 Cabernet Sauvignon (450 cases produced) is another Bordeaux lookalike, at least aromatically. It exhibits a tobacco leaf, smoky, cedar, and black currant-scented nose, followed by crisp, tart acidity, some austerity, but flavorful, youthful, rich red and black currant fruit. Medium bodied and spicy, with moderately aggressive tannin in the finish, it needs 4–5 years of cellaring, and should age for 2 decades. The 1994 Cabernet Sauvignon (545 cases) reveals evolved fruitcake, cedary, tobacco, roasted herb, and cassis aromas, as well as rich, concentrated flavors. It is impressively rich, with an herb-tinged, black currant personality, medium to full body, sweet but noticeable tannin, and excellent purity, all framed by toasty new oak. The wine gives every indication of being ready to drink with another 2–3 years of cellaring. It should last for 15–20 years. The 1993 Moraga reveals a classic St.-Julien/Pauillac nose of tobacco, cedar, and cassis, as well as new oak. More tannic than the 1994, the full-bodied 1993 exhibits excellent ripeness, a chewy texture, and good spice. This is an impressive Cabernet with 12–15 years of aging potential.

MOUNT EDEN VINEYARDS (SANTA CLARA)

1996 Cabernet Sauvignon Estate	Santa Cruz	D	90
1995 Cabernet Sauvignon Estate	Santa Cruz	D	88

1993	Cabernet Sauvignon Estate	Santa Cruz	D	88
1996	Cabernet Sauvignon Old Vine Reserve	Santa Cruz	E	92+
1995	Cabernet Sauvignon Old Vine Reserve	Santa Cruz	E	90+
1996	Chardonnay Estate	Santa Cruz	E	95
1997	Chardonnay Estate 25th Anniversary	Santa Cruz	E	(91–92+)
1996	Chardonnay MacGregor Vineyard	Edna Valley	C	88
1995	Chardonnay MacGregor Vineyard	Edna Valley	C	88
1996	Pinot Noir Estate	Santa Cruz	D	90
1995	Pinot Noir Estate	Santa Cruz	D	87
1993	Pinot Noir Estate	Santa Cruz	D	89

Very few vineyard sites can match the extraordinary view from the top of Mount Eden. Overlooking the Santa Clara Valley, this vineyard, at 2,000 feet, was planted by the legendary Martin Ray. In many respects, Mount Eden was the birthplace of the boutique/garage winery. There are five wines produced, two cuvées of Cabernet Sauvignon, a Pinot Noir, and two Chardonnays, the estate offering and one from Edna Valley. The 1997 Chardonnay 25th Anniversary, which is given full malolactic fermentation and aged in all French oak, of which 50% is new, is bottled without fining or filtration. While I do not believe this wine possesses the intensity, richness, or longevity of the 1996, it is nevertheless an outstanding wine. It possesses a complex, honeysuckle, and citrusy-scented nose with subtle oak and a pronounced mineral component. Full bodied, with superb fruit purity, fine underlying acidity, and a long finish, it should last for a decade. The profound 1996 Chardonnay Estate is the finest Chardonnay Mount Eden has produced since their riveting 1992. This wine possesses the grandeur and volume, in addition to complexity, of a grand cru white Burgundy. The nose offers up subtle scents of smoke, roasted nuts, and honeyed, citrusy fruit. The wine cuts a full-bodied path on the palate, yet it possesses sufficient balancing acidity to give it striking delineation. The level of concentration is awesome, as is the 41-second finish. This spectacular, complex, leesy, multidimensional Chardonnay is more evolved than the 1992 was at a similar state. However, given how beautifully that wine has aged, this Chardonnay should improve for another 5–7 years, and last more than a decade. It is a tour de force in winemaking.

Mt. Eden's Pinot Noirs are elegant, Côte de Beaune-styled examples, with surprising longevity. I had my last bottle of 1985 this fall, and was extremely pleased to see how fresh, lively, and complex it had remained. The 1995 Pinot Noir offers a medium ruby color, as well as an excellent, sweet, black cherry nose intermixed with smoke, dried herbs, and minerals. There is lovely ripeness, medium body, and a quick finish. Drinkable now, it promises to evolve for another 4–5 years. The 1996 Pinot Noir is reminiscent of a good Beaune or Volnay premier cru. Bright, jammy, strawberry, and fruit flavors are intertwined with spicy oak and minerals. Elegant and medium bodied, with total harmony, this beautifully rendered Pinot Noir should drink well for 5–7 years.

There have been some legendary Cabernet Sauvignons produced at Mount Eden, with some of the older vintages requiring 2–3 decades of cellaring (such as 1974). I asked winemaker/proprietor Jeffrey Patterson what he thought were the top recent vintages of his estate Cabernet Sauvignon. He felt the finest five vintages in the last two decades have been 1994, 1989, 1988, 1987, and 1985. There are two cuvées of Cabernet Sauvignon. The 1995 regular cuvée of Cabernet Sauvignon, a blend of 75% Cabernet Sauvignon, 22% Merlot, and 3% Cabernet Franc, sees 30% new American oak and 70% used French barrels. The dark ruby/purple-colored 1995 offers a firm, restrained nose of black currants, minerals, earth, and spicy oak. Medium bodied, moderately tannic, and firmly structured, it requires 2–3 years of cellaring, and should keep for 15+ years. The outstanding 1996 Cabernet Sauvignon possesses greater thickness and richness, medium to full body, fine purity, and a black cherry/cassis component, intermixed with minerals and spice. Although more accessible than the 1995, it promises to be as long-lived.

Mount Eden's flagship Cabernet Sauvignon Old Vines is a 100% Cabernet Sauvignon from two parcels planted in 1955 and 1958. Winemaker Jeffrey Patterson feels the greatest vintages for this cuvée have been 1973, 1974, 1975, 1976, 1986, 1990, 1992, and 1994. I was impressed with both the 1995 and 1996. The 1995 Cabernet Sauvignon Old Vine Reserve was bottled unfiltered, but was given a slight egg white fining. It is a backward, concentrated example in need of a decade of cellaring. Medium to full bodied, with a deep ruby/purple color, and plenty of ripe cassis in the nose, it displays an unevolved, austere, formidably dense and muscular personality. Anticipated maturity: 2005–2025. The 1996 Cabernet Sauvignon Old Vine Reserve is more highly extracted, as well as full bodied, with a saturated ruby/purple color, and a restrained but blossoming nose of minerals, licorice, spicy oak, black cherries, and cassis. Pure, rich, dense, and promising, but destined for considerable longevity, this is another wine that should be cellared for 8–10 years. Anticipated maturity: 2007–2035.

Mount Eden's 1993 Estate Cabernet Sauvignon is made from grapes grown in parcels of their vineyard not included in their Old Vine cuvée. I found it to be a very strong effort. It is tannic and dense, with earthy, black currant, and licorice scents and flavors, and considerable body and richness. However, it is backward and almost formidably tannic. The wine possesses a good inner core of sweet fruit, as well as admirable length, but I would recommend cellaring it for 7–8 years; it will keep for 15–20 years. Made from 75% Cabernet Sauvignon, 22% Merlot, and 3% Cabernet Franc, it is an undervalued wine that should be high on readers' "must purchase" lists.

The stylish, medium ruby-colored 1993 Pinot Noir Estate reveals an excellent nose of red and black fruits, vanillin, spice, and minerals. Medium to full bodied, with sweet ripeness, an expansive texture, and a generously endowed finish, this wine will improve for 1–4 years and keep for a decade.

The Mount Eden 1995 Chardonnay MacGregor Vineyard's unusually evolved medium gold color is striking. The nose offers up copious quantities of tropical fruit intermixed with gobs of smoky, spicy oak. Good acidity, as well as abundant fruit and glycerin has resulted in a tantalizing mouthful of Chardonnay. Drink it over the next year.

This superlative producer has turned out a very good Chardonnay from Edna Valley. The 1996 Chardonnay MacGregor Vineyard offers a smoky, hazelnut personality reminiscent of a top quality Meursault or Chassagne-Montrachet premier cru. The wine is rich, lusty, and obvious in its flavor profile, yet undeniably delicious and sumptuous in texture and personality. It should be drunk over the next 1–2 years.

MURPHY-GOODE (SONOMA)

1994	Cabernet Sauvignon Murphy Ranches	Alexander Valley	C	86
1993	Cabernet Sauvignon Murphy Ranches	Alexander Valley	C	88
1994	Cabernet Sauvignon Reserve Brenda Block	Alexander Valley	D	89
1995	Chardonnay Barrel Fermented	Alexander Valley	B	87
1996	Chardonnay Reserve Island Block	Alexander Valley	C	89
1995	Chardonnay Reserve Island Block	Russian River	C	88
1995	Chardonnay Reserve J and K Murphy Vineyard	Russian River	C	90

1996 Fumé Blanc	Sonoma	B	86
1995 Merlot Murphy Ranches	Alexander Valley	C	86
1994 Merlot Murphy Ranches	Alexander Valley	C	88
1996 Fumé Blanc Fumé II The Deuce	Sonoma	C	89
1996 Zinfandel	Sonoma	C	85
1995 Zinfandel	Sonoma	C	89
1994 Zinfandel	Sonoma	C	89

The flamboyant, intensely aromatic 1996 Fumé Blanc Fumé II The Deuce possesses admirable flavor intensity, a creamy texture, medium body, excellent concentration, and gobs of ripe, herb-tinged, honeyed melon, and figlike fruit. Drink this beauty over the next year. The deliciously fruity, medium- to full-bodied 1996 Chardonnay Reserve Island Block displays subtle oak, copious quantities of tropical fruit, and good length. It will not make old bones, but will offer delicious drinking over the next 1–2 years.

Readers looking for exuberantly fruity, rich, pure Fumé Blancs have plenty to choose from at Murphy-Goode. There are 35,000 cases of the delicious 1996 Sonoma Fumé Blanc. It exhibits ripe, melony, lemony custardlike aromas, tasty, medium-bodied, spicy, silky-textured flavors, and enough acidity to provide vibrancy and freshness. This medium-bodied, rich, flavorful Fumé Blanc should drink well for 12 months.

Among the Chardonnays, the 1995 Alexander Valley Chardonnay possesses copious quantities of pear, lemony, citrusy notes, ripe fruit, and low acidity that emphasizes the wine's fruit and soft texture. Drink it over the next 1–2 years. The 1995 Chardonnay Reserve Island Block is rich, medium to full bodied, with high quality smoky oak, crisp acidity and a restrained style suggesting it will be even better with another 4–6 months of bottle age. It is rich, ripe, and nicely dosed with high quality toasty oak. Drink it over the next 2–3 years. The 1995 Chardonnay Reserve J and K Murphy Vineyard reveals a more honeyed tropical fruit, and toasty personality, with a more exotic, ostentatious personality. It is creamy, rich, full bodied, and loaded with fruit. Once again, excellent winemaking, and a judicious use of toasty new oak barrels have produced a spicy, impressively endowed wine. It should drink well for 2–4 years.

Murphy-Goode's Zinfandels emerge primarily from two vineyard sources, Sonoma's Cuneo and Saini Vineyards. Production is modest, with only 650 cases produced. The 1994 Zinfandel displays a deep ruby color, followed by Zinfandel's appealing spicy, ripe, pure, peppery, berry fruit character, and a soft, lush, medium- to full-bodied finish. Delicious now, it promises to drink well for another 2–3 years. The intensely fragrant (jammy blackberries and spices) 1995 Zinfandel offers a deep, saturated ruby/purple color, sweet, spicy oak, plenty of round, soft, rich, berry flavors, admirable opulence, and a lush, silky texture. Drink it over the next 2–3 years.

A lively, strawberry, tart sour cherry-scented and -flavored wine, the medium-bodied 1996 Zinfandel is commercial in style, but pleasant and accurate from a varietal perspective. Drink it over the next 1–2 years.

Progress is clearly evident with Murphy-Goode's newer releases of Merlot and Cabernet Sauvignon. The dark ruby-colored 1994 Merlot Murphy Ranches (83% Merlot and 17% Cabernet Sauvignon) offers up a moderately intense nose of coffee beans, smoke, and ripe berry fruit. Although not complicated, it provides plenty of lush, silky, low-acid flavors with good ripeness, fruit, and glycerin. Slightly more complexity and delineation could have elevated this wine to an even higher qualitative category. Drink it over the next 3–5 years. The 1994 Cabernet Sauvignon Murphy Ranches (5,000 cases) is a dark plum/garnet-colored wine with a spicy, sweet, overripe nose of black fruits intertwined with scents of earth and spice. It is not complex, but it does offer mouth-filling, rich, tarry flavors that taste as if the harvest occurred under torridly hot conditions. There is a warm climate taste to this chunky, robust Cabernet Sauvignon that should drink well for 5–7 years. The 1994 Cabernet Sauvignon Reserve Brenda Block (1,700 cases) is a dark garnet/purple-tinged color. The wine exhibits superripeness, and a jammy, black cherry, cassis character nicely dosed with spicy oak. This vanillin-scented, medium- to full-bodied, dense, layered, low-acid Cabernet Sauvignon possesses plenty of sweet tannin, but the wine's hallmark is its purity and luscious, rich fruit. It should drink well young and age for 10–12 years. It would appear to be the finest Cabernet Sauvignon Murphy-Goode has yet produced.

The medium- to full-bodied, pure, rich, black currant-scented and -flavored 1993 Cabernet Sauvignon Murphy Ranches exhibits a sense of elegance and zesty, fresh exuberance. It is a delicious, supple wine for drinking now and over the next 7–8 years.

ANDREW MURRAY VINEYARDS

1996 Roussanne	Santa Barbara	D	89
1996 Syrah Hillside Reserve	Santa Barbara	D	90+
1996 Syrah Les Coteaux	Santa Barbara	C	90
1997 Viognier	Santa Barbara	D	87

This relatively new producer is an emerging star in Santa Barbara. The hillside vineyards are dedicated to Rhône varietals, and early efforts are impressive. Roussanne appears to have found a promising home in Santa Barbara's various microclimates and soils. A number of impressive efforts, from Alban, Fess Parker, Sine Qua Non, Ojai, Qupé, and Andrew Murray, have shown that this varietal offers plenty of flavor, complexity, and elegance. Andrew Murray's 1996 Roussanne reveals the varietal's telltale rose petal aromatics intermixed with scents of ripe apricots and citrus. This medium- to full-bodied wine possesses a terrific texture, in addition to a layered, chewy palate with fine ripeness and impressive length. Consume this Roussanne over the next 2 years. The 1997 Viognier exhibits an evolved color with a hint of copper. The nose offers up uncomplicated, but intense smells of honeysuckle and ripe tropical fruit. While concentrated and dry, with a fine texture, this cleanly made, attractive wine is a bit clunky, bordering on heavy. Given its fragile construction and delicate aromatics, it requires drinking over the next year.

I tasted two Syrah cuvées. The 1996 Syrah Les Coteaux is more rustic, or as the French would say, *sauvage*. Its robust, exuberant, kinky character is hard to ignore. The color is saturated purple. The bouquet offers leesy, peppery, black currant, and berry aromas intermixed with tar and loamy soil scents. This full-bodied wine exhibits explosive fruit, Syrah's telltale smokiness, and a rich, moderately tannic, spicy finish with copious quantities of glycerin. The tannin is not totally integrated, but the wine is impressively large and aromatic. It would provide an ideal accompaniment to grilled steak or game birds. Moreover, it should continue to improve for 5–7 years and last for 12 or more. The impressive 1996 Syrah Hillside Reserve is more restrained, elegant, tannic, and backward. I admired its saturated purple color, as well as its pure blackberry/cassis aromas intermixed with spicy new oak. There is a touch of minerality and good spice, but it is a more polite, suave, and gracefully constructed wine than its sibling. Nevertheless, it should unleash more of its personality with another 1–2 years of bottle age and will keep for a decade or more.

NALLE WINERY (SONOMA)

1996 Zinfandel	Dry Creek	C	85
1994 Zinfandel	Dry Creek	C	86

I had hoped for a bit more depth and richness from this producer. With airing, the intriguing cinnamon, spice, red currant, and cherry-scented nose of the 1994 Zinfandel offers up notes of herbs and coffee. Medium bodied, charming, soft, and meant to be drunk within the next 2–3 years, this stemmy, spicy, distinctive Zinfandel is enjoyable and satisfying.

The 1996 is a vibrant, pretty Zinfandel with weedy, underbrush, and berry/raspberry aromas. On the palate, there is tart acidity, an elegant, midweight style, and a straightforward, crisp, compressed finish. A good quaffing, fruit-driven Zinfandel with above normal acidity, it should be consumed over the next 2–3 years for its exuberance and freshness.

NAPA RIDGE (NAPA)

1996 Cabernet Sauvignon	Central Coast	B	85
1995 Cabernet Sauvignon	Central Coast	A	85
1994 Cabernet Sauvignon Oak Barrel	Central Coast	A	87
1993 Cabernet Sauvignon Oak Barrel	Central Coast	B	87
1995 Cabernet Sauvignon Reserve	Napa	C	88
1993 Cabernet Sauvignon Reserve	Napa	C	88
1997 Chardonnay	North Coast	A	86
1996 Chardonnay	North Coast	A	86
1995 Chardonnay	Central Coast	A	85
1995 Chardonnay Coastal Vines	North Coast	A	86
1995 Chardonnay Frisinger Vineyard	Napa	C	89
1996 Chardonnay Reserve	Napa	C	90
1995 Chardonnay Reserve	Napa	C	90
1993 Merlot	North Coast	B	85
1997 Pinot Noir	North Coast	B	86
1996 Pinot Noir	North Coast	A	87
1995 Pinot Noir	North Coast	A	86
1994 Pinot Noir	North Coast	B	86
1995 Pinot Noir Reserve	Carneros	C	87
1996 Sauvignon Blanc	North Coast	A	86
1995 Sauvignon Blanc	North Coast	A	85
1997 Triad	North Coast	A	86

Readers punch-drunk over rising wine prices know that the words "Napa Ridge" and "value" are synonymous. The current releases, which are all in that magical $9–$11 range, are well worth the price of admission. The 1997 Triad (it is not a wine for Chinese gangsters) is an intriguing blend of three grapes—60% Chardonnay, 21% Sauvignon Blanc, and 19% Semillon. It is a fruity, spicy, smoky wine with good richness, and an exuberant, fresh, lively style. Drink it over the next year. The 1997 Chardonnay (a consistently good value) is a honeyed, richly fruity, medium-bodied wine that provides plenty of pleasure for a modest price—if it is consumed over the next year.

Napa Ridge turns out delicious Pinot Noir for a song. There are 40,000 cases of the 1997. While it is not quite as successful as several previous vintages, there is still a lot to like in this light ruby-colored offering. It reveals more acidity than usual, as well as ripe strawberry/cherry fruit, and a round, medium-bodied palate, with a touch of wood spice and herbs. It is a tasty, fruity Pinot Noir to drink over the next 1–2 years. The 1996 Cabernet Sauvignon offers a dark ruby color, followed by a soft, herb-tinged, cedary, berry-scented nose, lovely, supple flavors, and dusty, light tannin in the silky-smooth finish. Most of the fruit comes from Paso Robles, and has been vinified to make it an easygoing, user-friendly Cabernet Sauvignon. Drink it over the next 2–3 years.

The tasty 1996 Sauvignon Blanc, of which 50% is barrel fermented and put through malolactic, includes 25% Semillon in the blend. It exhibits toasty smoky oak, gobs of citrusy, honeyed fruit, and an attractive, fresh, medium-bodied personality. Drink it over the next year.

I also enjoyed the two 1996 Chardonnays. The inexpensive 1996 Chardonnay North Coast reveals an excellent butterscotch-scented nose, as well as plenty of fruit, an uncomplicated, exuberant character, and a rich, medium-bodied personality. It is a Chardonnay to drink over the next year. The 1996 Chardonnay Reserve, from a selection of Napa Valley grapes, is an exotic, sumptuous, fleshy Chardonnay that is 100% barrel fermented, a fact displayed in its smoky, hazelnut, leesy aromas. This wine possesses copious quantities of buttery fruit, medium to full body, and a decadent texture and lushness. It is not meant to make old bones, but it will provide a thrill a sip over the next year.

Napa Ridge's 1995 Chardonnay displays less intensity and richness than in prior vintages, but it is a pleasant, fruity, medium-bodied wine that is comparable to the richly fruity, mineral Chardonnays made in France's Maconnais region.

The 1995 Sauvignon Blanc is a crisp, fresh, light-bodied Sauvignon with plenty of citrusy fruit, and a dry finish. It should be drunk over the next year. There are three Napa Ridge Chardonnays produced. The least expensive is the 1995 Chardonnay Coastal Vines, of which 85% is put through malolactic, and 80% is barrel fermented. It packs plenty of punch for under $10, offering loads of tropical fruit, as well as a nice dosage of buttery flavors. While not the most complex or perfumed Chardonnay, it is fleshy and fruity. This is a wine to buy by the case; it should drink well for 12–18 months. Toasty oak lovers will think I have underrated the 1995 Chardonnay Frisinger Vineyard. This wine is blatantly oaky, but it displays a wonderful leesy, complex, Burgundian-like, smoky, hazelnut, buttery-scented nose. Despite the oak-dominated aromatics, the wine's palate impression offers outstanding fruit, extract, purity, and ripeness. In fact, if the wine's bouquet had been less oaky, it would have merited a 90-point score. In the mouth, the wine possesses plenty of tropical fruit flavors, as well as a mouth-filling, lusciously fruity style. It should drink well for 1–2 years. The 1995 Reserve Chardonnay is made from a selection of Napa Ridge's finest lots. It is 100% barrel fermented and aged in 100% new oak, something that I found interesting in view of the fact that this wine exhibited far less toasty new oak than the Frisinger Vineyard. The Reserve is a tighter, more structured Chardonnay, with plenty of power and intensity. It offers subtle vanillin to go along with its honeysuckle, buttery, citruslike character. Drink it over the next 2–3 years.

In my opinion, winemaker David Schlottman fashions the best value in Pinot Noir not only in America but in the world. The 1996 Pinot Noir North Coast reveals a light to medium ruby color, followed by a textbook Pinot nose of earth, plants, and sweet black cherry fruit. A silky, seductive, medium-bodied wine with no hard edges, this round, supple Pinot is fun to drink. When is the last time anyone drank an excellent Pinot Noir that was also a terrific value? Consume it over the next 1–2 years. The 1995 Pinot Noir Reserve is made primarily from the Sangiacomo Vineyard in Carneros. It is a more ambitious wine, with more obvious wood, but I do not like it any better than the North Coast Pinot. It may last longer, but I am not sure it will ever deliver as much pleasure as its less expensive sibling. In any event, it is an excellent earthy, cherry cola-scented and -flavored Pinot Noir with good aromatics, and a pure style. Drink it over the next 2–3 years.

Readers looking for a top-notch value in Pinot Noir should also seek out Napa Ridge's

1995 Pinot Noir North Coast. At $8, it is an outstanding bargain. Behind the medium ruby color is a wine that offers up copious amounts of berry/cherry fruit, a soft texture, a suggestion of toast, and a fruity, medium-bodied personality. It is an ideal Pinot Noir to serve slightly chilled over the next 1–2 years. Napa Ridge's 1994 Pinot Noir is a tasty, soft, berry-scented and -flavored wine with surprising fat and lusciousness for its modest price. It is not a Pinot Noir for laying away as it should be consumed over the next 3–4 years.

There are not many Cabernet Sauvignons available for under $10 a bottle, but Napa Ridge's 1995 Cabernet Sauvignon Central Coast avoids the vegetal spice (call it the V-8 juice syndrome), and offers plenty of red and black currants in a tasty, elegant, soft, richly fruity style. It is low in acidity, the tannin is unobtrusive, and the wine cleanly made. It should drink well for 2–3 years. The more ambitious 1995 Cabernet Sauvignon Reserve reveals good smoky cassis fruit in its nose, a lush, medium- to full-bodied texture, a fleshy midsection, and a round, generous finish. Only $15 a bottle, it tastes like a $25–$30 bottle of Cabernet Sauvignon. Drink it over the next 5–7 years.

The 1994 Cabernet Sauvignon Oak Barrel exhibits a sweet red and black curranty nose, with a touch of sour cherry fruit. Spicy, medium to full bodied, soft, and round, with no hard edges, this is a Cabernet Sauvignon to drink over the next 3–4 years. The 1993 Cabernet Sauvignon Oak Barrel Central Coast could easily pass for a midlevel St.-Julien/Pauillac. The attractive, moderately intense nose of tobacco and weedy, black currant fruit is followed by a ripe, silky-textured wine with plenty of fruit. Its dark color and overall balance suggest it should be drunk over the next 4–5 years. The medium dark ruby-colored 1993 Cabernet Sauvignon Reserve offers up a sweet nose of black currants, licorice, earth, and oak. The wine reveals some of the 1993 vintage's aggressive tannin, but there is enough fruit to balance the tannin. Medium to full bodied and approachable, it is capable of lasting for 5–10 years.

The 1993 Merlot exhibits a sweet cherry and spicy nose intermingled with some coffee notes. This medium dark ruby-colored wine is soft and round on the palate, with a good dosage of wood. Drink it over the next 2–3 years.

NEWTON VINEYARDS (NAPA)

1993 Cabernet Sauvignon	Napa	D	92
1996 Cabernet Sauvignon Unfiltered	Napa	D	93+
1995 Cabernet Sauvignon Unfiltered	Napa	D	92
1997 Chardonnay Unfiltered	Napa	D	(90–92)
1996 Chardonnay Unfiltered	Napa	D	93
1993 Claret	Napa	C	86
1997 Claret Unfiltered	Napa	C	(84–85)
1993 Merlot	Napa	D	91
1997 Merlot Unfiltered	Napa	D	(90–92)
1996 Merlot Unfiltered	Napa	D	90
1997 Pinot Noir Unfiltered	Napa	C	87
1997 Viognier Unfiltered	Napa	D	90

Newton has one of the most spectacular settings of any winery on California's North Coast. Situated high in the mountains above St. Helena, with gorgeous terraces and flower gardens, this estate has a distinctly French orientation. Much of the winery's staff appears to be French students trying to improve their English skills. Moreover, proprietress Su Hua Newton makes no secret of the fact that she looks for inspiration from France's finest winemakers.

Her wines are unquestionably made with this philosophy in place. Not surprisingly, France's talented Michel Rolland is the consulting oenologist. Newton exports 30% of their production, with Switzerland the largest foreign buyer. All of the Newton wines are fermented with natural yeasts in order to obtain more complex aromatics. The malolactic fermentations take place in barrel to promote greater integration of wood, and to encourage more textural richness in the wines. All of the wines, including the Chardonnay, are bottled without filtration.

I have been buying Newton's unfiltered Chardonnay (to the extent I can find any) since the 1992 vintage. I recently polished off my last bottle of the 1992, which was still fabulous. This is a barrel-fermented, unfiltered Chardonnay with lees stirring. Su Hua Newton's reference is undoubtedly Burgundy's Coche-Dury, as she tries to replicate the extraordinary complexity and texture he routinely achieves. The 1997 Chardonnay Unfiltered is a sexy, voluptuously textured, enormously rich wine that is aged in 1-year-old oak barrels. The wine exhibits gobs of honeyed fruit, with an ocean of pear and pineapple scents to go along with the citrus and subtle minerality. Rich, full bodied, and beautifully textured, this wine should age nicely for 4–5 years. Many 1996 Chardonnays are impressive, but often reveal a muted aromatic profile. One of the vintage's most stunningly aromatic wines, Newton's 1996 Chardonnay Unfiltered offers up notes of pineapples, bananas, roasted nuts, and honeysuckle. Rich and full bodied, with creamy texture and a spectacular finish, it should continue to drink well for 2–3 years. I am not a fan of most California Viogniers, but Newton's 1997 Viognier Unfiltered (only 150 cases) is a flamboyant, intensely rich, opulently styled example that will make believers out of skeptics. However, I would opt for consuming it over the next year to take advantage of its ostentatious aromatics.

The least expensive red wine in the Newton portfolio is Claret, a selection made from younger vines and/or barrels that are deemed not rich enough for the Merlot or Cabernet Sauvignon program. The 1997 Claret reveals some herbaceousness (mostly green peppercorn scents), sweet red currant fruit, and a spicy, medium-bodied, lush texture. It is ideal for drinking over the next 2–3 years. The 1997 Pinot Noir Unfiltered was made from only 2 tons of fruit from a 4-acre vineyard. Aromatically, the wine scores higher than my overall rating. Copious aromas of spice, herbs, sweet red fruits, and flowers, intermixed with smoky oak provide an attractive initial impression. There is good ripeness and complexity on the attack, but the wine then narrows out. Nevertheless, this is a fine debut release.

Newton was one of the first California wineries to produce high quality, ageworthy Merlot made in an elegant style, with admirable character, richness, and depth. The 1997 Merlot Unfiltered (produced from a severely thinned crop) possesses a saturated ruby color, and a lovely nose of sweet black cherry fruit intermixed with herbs, minerals, and spice. Lush, ripe, and fragrant, this forward Merlot should be accessible when released, and last for 12 or more years. The dense ruby/purple-colored 1996 Merlot Unfiltered is a fuller-bodied example, with more of the varietal's chocolate, coffee, roasted herb, and damp foresty characteristics. The wine is spicy, lightly oaky, tightly knit, rich, pure, and structured. It requires 2–4 more years of cellaring and should keep for 12–15.

Newton's Cabernet Sauvignons cut a broader, more textured mouth-feel. The 1996 Cabernet Sauvignon Unfiltered exhibits an opaque purple color, as well as a robust, nearly massive constitution, a boatload of tannin, and considerable power, depth, and muscle. Atypically rugged and brawny for a Newton Cabernet Sauvignon, it should age effortlessly for 2–3 decades. Prospective purchasers should be aware that this vintage will require 4–6 years of cellaring for some of the tannin to melt away. Also tannic, but more classically constructed, the 1995 Cabernet Sauvignon Unfiltered offers rich cassis fruit intermixed with loamy soil scents, *pain grillé*, and floral notes. Long in the mouth, with an expansive texture, impeccable symmetry, and fine overall balance, this wine finishes with a tannic clout, as well as outstanding ripeness and presence in the mouth. Like the 1996, it should be long-lived, but will be ready to drink at an earlier age. Anticipated maturity: 2002–2020.

Newton's Claret is a cuvée created from wines deemed not sufficiently rich or structured enough to go into the estate-bottled Merlot and Cabernet Sauvignon. This wine, of which there are approximately 3,000 cases, is a good value. The 1993 Claret exhibits straightforward, ripe, red and black currant fruit, more structure and tannin than the 1992, as well as medium body, and a spicy finish. The 1993 Merlot, which is bottled without fining or filtration, includes 5% Cabernet Sauvignon and 15% Cabernet Franc. It reveals a more saturated color than the 1992 Merlot, intense, black cherry, earth, and oak aromas, full-bodied, concentrated flavors, and moderate tannin. The wine will benefit from 2–3 years of cellaring and keep for 15+ years.

The unfined and unfiltered 1993 Cabernet Sauvignon is more precocious and flattering than the 1992, with seemingly lower acidity, a more velvety texture, wonderful richness, and an opulent, forward, cassis fruitiness that is easy to understand. Highly extracted, rich and full, with no hard edges, the 1993 will be drinkable upon release and age effortlessly for 20–25 years.

NEYERS VINEYARD (NAPA)

1995	Cabernet Sauvignon	Napa	D	90
1997	Chardonnay	Carneros	D	89
1996	Chardonnay	Carneros	D	87
1997	Chardonnay	Napa	D	91
1996	Chardonnay	Napa	D	90
1997	Chardonnay El Novillero Vineyard	Carneros	D	91
1997	Chardonnay Thieriot Vineyard	Sonoma Coast	D	93
1996	Chardonnay Thieriot Vineyard	Sonoma Coast	D	90
1997	Merlot Neyers Ranch	Conn Valley	D	89
1997	Syrah Hudson Vineyard	Napa	D	94
1996	Syrah Hudson Vineyard	Napa	D	92
1995	Syrah Hudson Vineyard	Napa	D	91
1997	Zinfandel Pato Ranch	Paso Robles	D	(88–90)
1996	Zinfandel Pato Ranch	Contra Costa	D	89
1995	Zinfandel Pato Ranch	Contra Costa	C	90

Bruce Neyers, the national sales representative for Kermit Lynch Wine Merchants, and his multitalented winemaker, Ehren Jordan, have turned this operation around, making it another cherished source for high class wines. In 1997, Neyers produced four lovely, distinctively different Chardonnays. The 1997 Chardonnay Napa (14.1% alcohol) is a full-bodied, rich, leesy, Burgundian-styled wine with notes of roasted almonds, cloves, honeysuckle, and smoky, buttery fruit. It possesses a terrific texture, a long, lush finish, and could easily pass for a top premier cru (Verger) from Chassagne-Montrachet. The 1997 Chardonnay Carneros (14.2% alcohol) is made from a blend of the Hudson and Sangiacomo vineyards. It reveals less of the Burgundian, leesy, smoky roasted character, and more of California's tropical fruit character. Despite the higher alcohol, it comes across as more elegant and fruit-driven, with an evolved medium light gold color, moderate weight, good density, and a tasty, luscious, in-your-face style. It should drink well for 1–3 years. The 1997 Chardonnay El Novillero Vineyard (350 cases) was bottled without filtration. The wine exhibits a toasty, pineapple, and tangerine-scented nose, beautifully pure flavors, a creamy texture, full body, and outstanding presence, length, and richness. It is a stunningly rich, complex Chardonnay that should evolve nicely for 3–4 years, perhaps longer. The 1997 Chardonnay Thieriot Vineyard (350 cases) is less evolved than its three siblings, with more zesty acidity. It is a full-bodied, powerful, rich Chardonnay, with the most potential for aging. This chewy wine's acidity buttresses its enormously concentrated fruit. Mineral notes give it a more tightly knit, complex style. A sensational Chardonnay, it will be at its best by summer/fall, 1999 and last for 3–4 years.

The 1997 Merlot Neyers Ranch (from a vineyard in the Conn Valley) exhibits the telltale black chocolate and cherry liqueur fruit components typical of a fine Merlot. The color is a dark plum. In the mouth, this full-bodied, fleshy, seductive Merlot provides gobs of glycerin, a lush texture, and copious fruit. With a bit more complexity, it would have merited an outstanding score. On a purely hedonistic level, this wine may score higher with many readers. Drink it now and over the next 7–8 years. Another decadently styled offering is the 1997 Zinfandel Pato Ranch. It possesses lofty alcohol, a briery, peppery, berry nose with a touch of prunes, and dusty, earthy flavors heavily dosed with exceptionally ripe fruit (cherries and raspberries). Long, lusty, and heady, this Zinfandel requires consumption over the next 3–4 years. The Neyers/Jordan team has consistently done stunning work with Syrah from the Hudson Vineyard. The 1997 Syrah, which will be bottled without fining or filtration in February 1999, will benefit from another 1–2 years of bottle age and should keep for 10–15. A knockout Syrah, it offers up huge bacon fat, *jus de viande*, pepper, and smoky notes intermixed with blackberry and cassis fruit. Dense, full bodied, and powerful, with exceptional richness, outstanding purity, and nicely integrated new oak (50%–60% new French oak barrels were utilized), this terrific Syrah is a must purchase for Rhône wine enthusiasts.

Neyers' 1995 Zinfandel Pato Ranch is one of the stars of this decidedly irregular vintage. The wine possesses a knockout nose of jammy black cherry and raspberry fruit intermixed with smoke, spice, and toast. Medium to full bodied, lush, and opulently textured, this compellingly rich, lusty, seductive Zinfandel needs to be drunk over the next 2–3 years—but who can wait that long?

The dark ruby-colored 1996 Zinfandel Pato Vineyard is a broadly flavored, intensely spicy Zinfandel with a roasted character. With its sweet plum, berry, and raspberry fruit, this full-bodied wine weighs in at 15.1% alcohol. A dry, expansive, expressive wine, its low acidity and evolved style suggest consuming it over the next 1–2 years.

Bruce Neyers and his talented winemaker, Ehren Jordan (also the winemaker for Turley Cellars), have turned out three beautiful 1996 Chardonnays. The 1996 Chardonnay Napa exhibits a light, gold/green color, followed by rich, buttery, ripe fruit, with a touch of clove, apricot, and honeysuckle, medium to full body, refreshing acidity, and a nicely layered finish. It is an elegant yet authoritatively flavored Chardonnay that should drink well for several years. Made in a lighter, fruitier style, the 1996 Chardonnay Carneros does not possess as much weight as the other bottlings. It offers attractive tropical fruit, a subtle dosage of wood, medium body, and enough acidity for balance. Drink this well-made, complex, finesse-styled Chardonnay over the next year. Lastly, the 1996 Chardonnay Thieriot Vineyard reveals a light golden color with a slight greenish hue. The most tightly knit and backward wine of this trio, it is rich and full bodied, with a leesy, creamy texture, and good underlying acidity. This beauty should be even better with another 4–6 months of bottle age and will drink well for 3–4 years. At present, most of the impressive fruit flavors, extract, and glycerin are in the wine's long finish.

Neyers' black/purple-colored 1995 Syrah Hudson Vineyard needs 2–4 years of bottle age. The nose offers up copious quantities of classic pepper and cassis, with a hint of mint in the background. Some attractive new oak frames a well-constituted, full-bodied, rich, pure, smoky, cassis-flavored wine that is bursting with promise. Purchasers should be patient and hold several bottles for 2–4 years. This wine should drink well through the first decade of the next century.

A sensational Syrah from the Neyers winery, the 1996 Hudson Vineyard has it all. The color is opaque ruby/purple. The nose offers up creamy blackberry and cassis aromas complemented by spicy wood. In the mouth, the wine is full bodied, tightly knit, and youthful, with expansive, chewy flavors, as well as outstanding purity and length. It will benefit from another 1–2 years of bottle age, and will keep for 10–15 years. Bravo!

I was impressed by the 1995 Cabernet Sauvignon, which combines both power and elegance in a medium- to full-bodied style. The color is a dense, dark ruby/purple. The wine offers up copious quantities of black currant, berry fruit nicely dosed with smoky oak. Purely made, with a flattering texture (a characteristic of the Neyers wines), this luscious, soft, well-endowed Cabernet Sauvignon can be drunk now as well as over the next 7–8 years.

NIEBAUM-COPPOLA ESTATE WINERY (NAPA)

1994	Edizione Pennino Zinfandel Estate	Napa	C	87
1994	Francis Coppola Family Wines Cabernet Franc	Napa	C	82
1995	Francis Coppola Family Wines Chardonnay	Napa	C	86
1994	Francis Coppola Family Wines Merlot	Napa	C	86
1994	Rubicon Proprietary Red Wine	Napa	E	86+?
1993	Rubicon Proprietary Red Wine	Napa	D	89

With Francis Ford Coppola fully in charge of the old Inglenook estate, this property is well positioned to assume a higher profile for its wine quality. The flagship wine remains the Rubicon Proprietary Red, but there is also a lineup of varietal wines released under the Francis Coppola Family Wines label. These are relatively straightforward and commercial, well-made wines that reflect their varietal character. In addition, there is the Edizione Pennino Zinfandel label.

Current releases include the 1995 Francis Coppola Family Wines Chardonnay. This wine has been given full barrel malolactic fermentation, and has had 5% Viognier added to the blend to juice up the aromatics. The wine offers fine fruit, an elegant, crisp, subtle personality, medium body, and good concentration. Drink it over the next 1–3 years.

The 1994 Francis Coppola Family Cabernet Franc exhibits a weedy, green pepper, herbal nose, medium body, spicy, red currant flavors, and a measured, tart, restrained personality. It is well made, but not exciting. The 1994 Francis Coppola Family Wines Merlot is a good, midweight, soft, berry, coffee-flavored wine with a pleasing texture, fine purity, and a tart, short finish. Drink it over the next 3–4 years.

Zinfandel fans will be pleased with the 1994 Edizione Pennino Zinfandel. The ripe berry, peppery-scented nose is textbook Zinfandel. Medium dark ruby, this estate-bottled wine is made in a velvety, midweight style that should offer considerable flexibility with an assortment of culinary dishes. Already delicious, it promises to keep for another 4–5 years.

There have been numerous changes and refinements to the style of Niebaum-Coppola's proprietary red wine, Rubicon. Over a decade ago I wrote that this wine, with its rustic tannin and abrasive flavor profile, behaved as if it wanted to be an old-fashioned Barolo. That has all changed in the nineties, as the wine has begun to take on a more supple texture, with less aggressive tannin, and a flavorful but more complete and elegant personality. The blend has gradually increased to over 90% Cabernet Sauvignon. The wine is aged in small French oak casks for two years, of which approximately 50% is new. There is no fining, but the wine is sterile filtered at bottling.

An impressive effort from Niebaum-Coppola, the 1993 Rubicon exhibits a thick-looking, ruby/purple color, as well as herb-tinged, peppery, earthy, black currant fruit intermixed with spice and foresty, loamy scents. In the mouth, the wine is slightly rustic, with medium to full body, outstanding concentration, good spice, and moderately astringent tannin in the long finish. This very good effort is approachable, but still requires several more years of cellaring; it should keep for 15 or more years. The 1994 Rubicon displays some promising characteristics, such as a saturated dark ruby color, and a restrained but promising nose of earth, black fruits, spice, and a whiff of licorice. However, in the mouth, the wine takes on a tannic structure, coming across as austere and high in tannin. Is the wine's tannin too much for its depth and fruit? Time will tell, but at present, this wine seems less of a sure thing than it did before bottling. There is plenty of grip, structure, and tannin, but these structural components currently dominate the wine's ripe fruit. There is quality, but is there balance? This wine will last for 15 or more years.

NORMAN VINEYARDS (PASO ROBLES)

1994 Zinfandel The Classic	Paso Robles	B	84
1996 Zinfandel The Monster Estate	Paso Robles	C	86
1994 Zinfandel The Monster	Paso Robles	C	87

While it is hardly a monster, Norman's 1996 Zinfandel is a robust, full-bodied, quasi-late-harvest style of wine. The saturated dark ruby color is followed by heady scents of earth and black fruits, as well as a whiff of volatile acidity (vinegar). In the mouth, the wine is jammy, with 14.5% alcohol, and fresh, tart acidity. A chunky, slight, coarse, but extremely flavorful Zinfandel, it should be drunk over the next 2–3 years.

The dark ruby/purple-tinted 1994 Zinfandel The Classic is a foursquare, straightforward Zinfandel with a monolithic personality, muted aromatics, and enough tasty, medium-bodied fruit to carry it for 2–3 years. The 1994 Zinfandel The Monster's name is an overstatement vis à vis some of the massive, blockbuster Zinfandels made in California. The wine's subdued aromatics consist of peppery-tinged, cherry fruit. The taste suggests an elegant, medium-bodied, well-balanced, cleanly made Zinfandel that is clearly among the mainstream of easygoing, supple Zinfandels designed for near-term drinking.

OAKFORD CELLARS (NAPA)

1995 Cabernet Sauvignon Estate	Napa	D	90
1994 Cabernet Sauvignon Estate	Napa	D	91
1993 Cabernet Sauvignon Estate	Napa	D	91

Oakford Cellars is a tiny Cabernet Sauvignon producer with an 8-acre vineyard strategically located above the Oakville Grade near the Harlan Estate Vineyard and Heitz's Martha's Vineyard. Proprietor Charles Ball first produced a wine in 1987. In 1994 he hired the immensely fashionable, in demand Heidi Barrett, to assist in the winemaking. The wine is aged in 50% French oak casks and 50% American oak casks (one-third of each type is new) for 18–20 months and is bottled with minor clarification. These are tannic, large-scaled, dense, mountain Cabernet Sauvignons that are not flattering in their youth, but possess considerable promise and aging potential. This is another winery where readers are advised to get on the mailing list if they want an opportunity to purchase the wines as only 1,000 cases are produced.

The 1993 Cabernet Sauvignon exhibits a beautiful saturated purple color, and tight but intense, jammy aromas of cassis, earth, and spicy, aggressive wood. Full bodied and powerful, with exceptional intensity, this large-scaled, muscular wine will require 2–4 years of cellaring and will keep for 20 or more years.

The 1994 Cabernet Sauvignon, somewhat of a sleeper, is a medium- to full-bodied, rich, smoky, mineral and black currant-laden Cabernet. It reveals a classic structure, but the austerity it once possessed has been shed in favor of a well-structured, undeniably rich, well-delineated, pure Cabernet Sauvignon that should handsomely repay 5–6 years of cellaring; it will keep for 20+ years. Also impressive, the 1995 Cabernet Sauvignon reveals sweeter tannin than the 1994 (an anomaly in comparing these two vintages), rich, ripe, full-bodied fruit, admirable density and extract, fine overall equilibrium, and a long, heady, concentrated finish. Whether it develops as much intensity as the 1994 remains to be seen, but these wines have lived up to, and even surpassed, my earlier reviews.

OJAI VINEYARD (SANTA BARBARA)

1997	Chardonnay Bien Nacido Vineyard	Santa Barbara	D	88
1996	Chardonnay Reserve	Arroyo Grande	D	86
1996	Chardonnay Sanford and Benedict	Santa Barbara	D	90
1997	Chardonnay Talley Vineyard	Arroyo Grande	D	87
1996	Chardonnay Talley Vineyard	Arroyo Grande	C	88
1997	Chardonnay Talley Vineyard Reserve	Santa Barbara	D	90
1996	Chardonnay Talley Vineyard Reserve	Arroyo Grande	D	89+
1997	Pinot Noir Bien Nacido Vineyard	Santa Barbara	D	(87–88)
1996	Pinot Noir Bien Nacido Vineyard	Santa Barbara	D	90
1997	Pinot Noir Pisoni Vineyard	Santa Lucia Highlands	D	(90–93)
1996	Pinot Noir Pisoni Vineyard	Santa Lucia Highlands	D	93
1997	Sauvignon Blanc	Santa Barbara	C	87
1996	Sauvignon Blanc/Semillon	Santa Barbara	B	88
1995	St. Helene Reserve Proprietary White Wine	Santa Barbara	C	90
1997	Syrah	California	C	(87–89)
1996	Syrah	California	C	90
1995	Syrah	California	C	88
1994	Syrah	California	C	89
1994	Syrah	Santa Barbara	C	93
1993	Syrah	California	C	87
1997	Syrah Bien Nacido Vineyard	Santa Barbara	D	(91–93)
1996	Syrah Bien Nacido Vineyard	Santa Barbara	D	94
1995	Syrah Bien Nacido Vineyard	Santa Barbara	D	92+
1997	Syrah Cuvée Henry Daniel	Santa Barbara	D	(92–95)
1997	Syrah Roll Ranch	California	D	(91–93)
1996	Syrah Roll Ranch	California	D	95+
1995	Syrah Roll Ranch	Santa Barbara	C	90
1997	Syrah Stolpman Vineyard	Santa Barbara	D	(90–92)
1996	Syrah Stolpman Vineyard	Santa Barbara	D	95

1996 Viognier Late Harvest	Santa Barbara	C	92
1997 Viognier Roll Ranch	Santa Barbara	C	85
1996 Viognier Roll Ranch	Santa Barbara	C	90
1995 Viognier Roll Ranch Vineyard	California	D	90

This small producer (about 6,000 cases total production) continues to turn out a sensational portfolio of wines. Working from a small barn/warehouse on the hillside below a high-priced residential development, Adam Tolmach's wines are reference points for what can be done with Santa Barbara fruit. Ojai's Syrahs and Pinot Noirs are their strong suit, but the winery's Chardonnays seem to get better with each vintage. I tasted three 1997 Chardonnays on my visit to the winery in September. Like all the wines made at Ojai, the 1997 Chardonnay Talley Vineyard is a naturally made product—no fining or filtration, barrel fermentation, malolactic in barrel, aggressive lees stirring, virtually no racking until assembling for bottling, and no acid additions. The Talley Vineyard exhibits a distinctive crisp, mineral, citrusy nose, and rich, medium-bodied flavors with the citrus/wet stone component well displayed. There is good acidity, an open-knit texture, and fine structure. It should drink well for 2–3 years. The 1997 Chardonnay Bien Nacido Vineyard offers a variety of tropical fruit flavors, with less minerality than the Talley Vineyard. It is medium to full bodied, with a fruit-driven personality, well-integrated acidity and toasty oak, and a clean, glycerin-imbued finish. It should drink well for 2 years. My favorite of this trio is the 1997 Chardonnay Bien Nacido Vineyard Reserve. This wine is made exactly as the other offerings, except for the fact it was fermented with indigenous rather than commercial yeasts. Three hundred cases of this rich, complex Chardonnay have been produced. The nose offers aromas of smoky oak, ripe fruit, and minerals. The wine possesses a layered texture and leesy, complex, concentrated finish (which are not found in its two siblings). The style of this brilliant Chardonnay is more French-like, with the purity and ripe fruit so easily obtainable in California. It should drink well for 2–4 years.

Pinot Noir yields were higher in 1997 than in 1996. While neither of the 1997s equal their 1996 counterparts, both are well made and merit attention. Ojai's Pinot Noirs are destemmed, fermented at relatively hot temperatures, and kept in barrel, on their lees, until assembled prior to bottling. As with all the winery's reds, there is no fining or filtration. The 1997 Pinot Noir Bien Nacido Vineyard reveals an attractive ruby/purple color, and a sweet nose of cherry/plum fruit intermixed with a whiff of green pepper, allspice, and *pain grillé* notes. The wine is rich and fleshy, with good body, and an elegant, Côte de Beaune-like finish, with the cherry fruit component dominating its personality. It should drink well for 3–5 years. The 1997 Pinot Noir Pisoni Vineyard may not be as thick or massively extracted as it was in 1996, but it is a beautifully made Pinot with this varietal's black fruit character offering a complete contrast to the Bien Nacido. The wine's saturated ruby/purple color is followed by a seductive nose of blackberries and raspberries. Full bodied, with rich fruit, more power, viscosity, and body than Bien Nacido, and a long, silky-textured finish, the Pisoni Vineyard Pinot Noir should drink well for 7–10 years.

Syrah is king at the Ojai Vineyards. Even though the 1997s were made from higher yields than the 1996s, they are among the most concentrated and finest wines I tasted from Santa Barbara. The deep ruby/purple-colored 1997 Syrah California (10% Grenache and 10% Mourvèdre have been added to the blend) offers a peppery, leathery, mineral, kirsch, and blackberry-scented nose, good depth, not as much complexity (as the other cuvées), but full body, and a luscious, accessible, low-acid profile that will give it considerable charm and seductiveness during its first 7–10 years of life. The 1997 Syrah Stolpman Vineyard reveals a saturated purple color, as well as a gorgeous nose of jammy blackberries intermixed with spice, smoke, and pepper. Full bodied, yet neither as massive nor as intense as the extraordinary 1996, this chewy, outstanding Syrah should age effortlessly for a decade. However, it will be on a faster evolutionary track than the 1996. The 1997 Syrah Bien Nacido Vineyard is more intense in the mouth. It boasts an opaque purple color, and a knockout nose of blackberries, cassis, cedar, minerals, and a hint of flowers. Full bodied, accessible (because of low acidity), it exhibits copious quantities of fruit, glycerin, and extract, with no hard edges. A silky-styled, hedonistic Syrah, it should drink well young yet age for 10–15 years. The most backward of these Syrahs is the 1997 Syrah Roll Ranch. Interestingly, 2.5% Viognier was added to the blend. It is a powerful, tannic wine with a saturated ruby/purple color, superb richness, and a boatload of tannin in the structured, formidable finish. This Syrah should be cellared for 2–3 years, and consumed over the following 12–15.

Named after Adam Tolmach's recently born son, the full-bodied, blockbuster 1997 Syrah Cuvée Henry Daniel is made from exceptionally low yields (primarily from the Bedford Thompson Vineyard). There are approximately 360 cases of this sensational Syrah that has been blended with 5% Viognier. The thick, oozing, black/purple color is accompanied by a fabulous nose that combines Syrah's blackberry/cassis component with Viognier's floral and honey notes. Already complex, this rich, chewy, exceptionally well balanced, stunningly proportioned, superrich Syrah should age effortlessly for 15–20 years.

Over the last several years, there has been considerable evidence that Adam Tolmach's Ojai Vineyard is among the leading candidates for Santa Barbara's top winery. The brilliance of these wines over the last several vintages has been uncontestable. Ojai's new releases include many stunning wines, particularly the Pinot Noir and Syrah offerings. This is not to say the whites are uninteresting. The 1997 Sauvignon Blanc is the first time this offering has been made from 100% Sauvignon. The wine possesses a light straw color, and a delicate nose of minerals, figs, and melony fruit. It offers medium body, an alluring, textured mouthfeel, vibrant acidity, and a clean, refreshing yet flavorful finish. Drink it over the next year.

When comparing the two Talley Vineyard Chardonnays, the 1996 Chardonnay Talley Vineyard regular bottling reveals more up-front flavors and a broad-shouldered personality. The wine displays excellent purity, ripe, citrus, pear, and honeylike flavors, medium to full body, good acidity, and a judicious touch of toasty oak. It should drink well for several years. The 1996 Chardonnay Talley Reserve is a bigger, denser, longer, more concentrated wine with the same characteristics as its sibling. Yet it cuts a fuller, heavier mouth-feel. I do not see it having greater aging potential than the regular bottling, but it is undoubtedly a bigger, richer wine. I had a slight preference for the 1996 Chardonnay Sanford and Benedict Vineyard. This offering reveals more overt tropical fruit, plenty of spice, a fleshy, glycerin-imbued, chewy mouth-feel, adequate acidity, and a medium- to full-bodied, long finish. It is a gutsy, full-flavored yet elegant, symmetrical Chardonnay that should drink well for 1–2 years.

The 1997 Viognier Roll Ranch is a good rather than stunning effort from Ojai. A subdued style of Viognier, it exhibits that varietal's telltale honeysuckle and peach-scented nose. In the mouth, the wine is medium bodied and dry, with good depth but a surprisingly restrained personality. It should be consumed over the next year.

Adam Tolmach has fashioned two exceptional Pinot Noirs. The deep ruby/purple-colored 1996 Pinot Noir Bien Nacido Vineyard reveals some of the telltale herb (V-8 vegetable juice) character (a hallmark of Santa Barbara Pinot), combined with copious quantities of full-bodied black cherry and berry fruit. The wine is dense, concentrated, exceptionally pure, and creamy textured. It is a sumptuous, herb-tinged, full-throttle Pinot Noir with no hard edges. It should drink well for at least 2–4 years. I have been impressed by the quality of Pinot Noirs emerging from the Pisoni Vineyard in the Santa Lucia Highlands (readers may recall that Peter Michael produces a Pinot from this vineyard). Ojai's 1996 Pinot Noir Pisoni Vineyard represents the essence of Pinot Noir. It is one of the most concentrated and well-balanced Pinots I have ever tasted. This wine possesses the extract level one expects from a

Domaine Leroy Richebourg or Romanée St.-Vivant. Obviously produced from extremely ripe fruit and low yields, this is a mammoth yet unbelievably harmonious Pinot Noir. The opaque ruby purple color is followed by scents of kirsch, jammy cherries, and spice that are unmistakably Pinot, but leaning toward the black fruit side of this varietal (Côte de Nuits). The wine is full bodied and saturates the palate with layers of glycerin, ripe fruit, and a sumptuous texture. Beautifully balanced, awesomely rich, and dazzlingly pure, this is one of the most extraordinary expressions of New World Pinot Noir I have ever tasted. I would not be surprised to see this wine evolve magnificently for a decade. Moreover, my score may look stingy with another several years of bottle age.

If I were to invest in vineyard land in California, I would consider three spots—northern California's Anderson Valley and Sonoma Coast for Pinot Noir and Chardonnay, and Santa Barbara for Syrah. The basic offering, the 1996 Syrah California, is an outstanding wine that could easily pass for a dazzling Rhône. It possesses a beautiful ruby/purple color, as well as a terrific nose of cassis and pepper intermingled with a whiff of tar and herbs. Rich, with luscious smoky fruit, this medium- to full-bodied, ripe, low-acid yet gorgeously knit Syrah can be drunk now and over the next 6–7 years. The 1996 Syrah Bien Nacido is a wine of exceptional extraction, richness, and depth. The color is an opaque black/purple, and the wine offers up classic tar, cassis, and bacon fat aromas. Full bodied, with no hard edges, this profoundly concentrated, mouth-filling, voluptuously textured Syrah possesses all the necessary components to age beautifully for a decade or more. However, the wine's explosive richness and enticing aromatics will ensure that much of it is drunk within hours of purchase. The 1996 Syrah Stolpman Vineyard comes across as a classic Hermitage with less earth, but with the blackberry liqueur/crème de cassislike trademarks. It boasts an opaque black/purple color, as well as an extraordinary nose of black fruits, blackberries, and cassis, fullbodied, awesomely concentrated flavors, gobs of glycerin, low acidity, and a 40+-second finish. This is a thrilling, thick, juicy, succulent, formidably endowed Syrah that should age effortlessly for 10–15 years. Lastly, the most backward of this quartet is the 1996 Syrah Roll Ranch Vineyard. Cut from the same mold as its siblings, it is a black/purple-colored, fullbodied blockbuster with gobs of cassis and blackberry liqueurlike flavors, but more tannin and earth in the flavors, as well as a more structured, backward feel in the mouth. The wine has huge extract, fabulous purity, and is another tour de force in Syrah winemaking.

This winery has always done a super job with its Sauvignon Blanc/Semillon blends. The two current releases are both scrumptious wines. The 1996 Sauvignon Blanc/Semillon (40% of the former and 60% of the latter) displays a honeyed, melony, waxy nose, medium body, terrific freshness and liveliness, adequate underlying acidity that tastes totally natural, and a ripe, long finish. It is a boldly fruity, extroverted wine that should drink well for several years. The 1995 St. Helene Reserve (67% Sauvignon Blanc/33% Semillon) is a beautifully crafted, intense, delicate yet powerful style of dry white wine. It possesses a fig, melony, honey, and subtle herb character, medium body, a chewy texture, and vibrant acidity that gives the wine vivaciousness and freshness. It should drink well for 2–3 years.

The 1995 Chardonnay Arroyo Grande Reserve (all from the Talley Vineyard) is a technically flawless Chardonnay with lovely apple/buttery fruit, crisp acidity, medium body, and nice flavors, but it is monochromatic compared to the winery's other offerings. It should drink well for 2–3 years.

Rhône Ranger enthusiasts will go bonkers over the three splendid Syrahs from the 1995 vintage. The ruby/purple-colored, uncomplicated 1995 Syrah possesses striking levels of sweet cassis fruit in the nose, along with a touch of licorice and pepper. This dense, mediumbodied wine offers delicious levels of jammy fruit, and plenty of glycerin and punch. It should drink well for another 5–7 years. The 1995 Syrah Roll Ranch is an explosively rich wine with terrific intensity, a black/purple color, super purity, no hard edges, full body, high glycerin, and moderate tannin, the latter component largely concealed behind the wine's impressive fruit extraction. This is a young, grapey Syrah that should evolve beautifully for the next 10–12 years. The profound 1995 Syrah Bien Nacido Vineyard makes me think that Syrah may do better in selected Santa Barbara microclimates than Pinot Noir. This killer Syrah boasts an opaque black/purple color, and an awesome nose of smoke, licorice, Asian spices, and black fruits. Some *pain grillé* notes are present, but they play an accessory role to the wine's cassislike jamminess. Full bodied, with superb delineation, this layered, textured, thick yet beautifully balanced, dense Syrah should be at its best by the turn of the century and last for 15 years. The 1993 Syrah is a lighter-styled but typical cassis-scented and flavored, medium- to full-bodied wine with light tannin, admirable depth, and a vibrant feel. If you are not up to handling some of the massive Syrahs in the marketplace, this wine can be drunk now and over the next 6–7 years.

The 1994 Syrah exhibits a deep ruby/purple color, a telltale, smoky, bacon fat, and cassis-scented nose, a succulent, soft, opulent texture, great fruit, and a classic, open-knit Syrah character. The wine almost tastes sweet because of the grape ripeness. This is a hedonistic, lush Syrah to drink over the next 4–5 years. The 1994 Syrah Santa Barbara smells like a terrific Hermitage. A huge, dramatic nose of bacon fat, smoke, and jammy black fruits is followed by a dense, full-bodied, layered wine crammed with ripe fruit. Its creamy texture, sumptuous thickness, lushness, and admirable purity combine to give this flamboyant Syrah a compelling character. I suspect there is more tannin than the wine is currently revealing. This is a mouth-filling, gorgeously proportioned, well-endowed Syrah to drink over the next 10–12 years.

Ojai also produced two outstanding Viogniers. The drier wine, the 1996 Viognier Roll Ranch, exhibits a honeysuckle and apricot-scented nose, medium to full body, crisp, underlying acidity that keeps the wine from tasting flabby and out of focus, and a long, heady finish. I would opt for drinking it over the next 12–18 months. The nectarlike, sweet 1996 Late Harvest Viognier exhibits an unctuous texture, and copious quantities of uncomplicated, chewy, sweet, honeysuckle fruit. It is a super late harvest Viognier to drink by itself at the conclusion of a meal.

Ojai's 1995 Viognier Roll Ranch Vineyard is one of the finest Viogniers I have tasted from the south central coast of California. The wine reveals textbook honeysuckle, peach, and apricotlike flavors that soar from the glass. Medium to full bodied, with underlying crisp acidity for vibrancy and delineation, this is a luscious, purely made, sexy Viognier that should drink well for the next 12–18 months.

OPUS ONE (NAPA)

1994 Proprietary Red Wine	Napa	EE	92

This is an impressive effort from Opus One. The wine, a blend of 95% Cabernet Sauvignon, 2% Cabernet Franc, 2% Merlot, and 1% Malbec, possesses a dark ruby/purple color, followed by a generous, complex nose of lead pencil, toasty oak, violets, and black currants. In the mouth, there is a beautiful texture, soft, generous, low-acid, full-bodied richness, and a stunningly proportioned, rich, intense finish. The influence of 18 months in new French oak casks gives the wine a subtle oaky note in addition to giving it excellent delineation. Because of the wine's softness and generosity, it can be drunk now as well as over the next 18–20 years.

PAHLMEYER (NAPA)

1997 Chardonnay	Napa	E	(93–95)
1996 Chardonnay	Napa	E	95
1995 Chardonnay	Napa	E	94
1996 Malbec	Napa	E	91

1997	Merlot	Napa	E	(94–96)
1996	Merlot	Napa	E	97
1995	Merlot	Napa	E	94
1994	Merlot	Napa	E	95
1993	Merlot	Napa	E	90
1997	Proprietary Red Wine	Napa	E	(96–100)
1996	Proprietary Red Wine	Napa	E	95
1995	Proprietary Red Wine	Napa	E	96
1994	Proprietary Red Wine	Napa	E	96
1993	Proprietary Red Wine	Napa	C	96

In 1997 I was "blown away" by Pahlmeyer's 1995s and 1996s, but after retasting the 1996s and seeing the 1997s, I must say that Jason Pahlmeyer is on fire, thanks primarily to terrific grape sources and the winemaking genius of Helen Turley. The 1997 Chardonnay (which comes from a vineyard in the Coombsville area of Napa Valley) was bottled without filtration. A spectacular Chardonnay, with relatively good availability in the marketplace (2,500 cases produced), it is slightly lighter than the blockbuster 1996, as well as more aromatically intense. There are gorgeously complex aromas of tropical fruits, leesy, smoky notes, and *pain grillé*. Full bodied, with superb purity, it is a terrific Burgundian-styled Chardonnay that should age nicely for 5–6 years. The awesome 1996 Chardonnay is one of the finest made at Pahlmeyer. A massive yet remarkably well balanced example, it boasts a leesy complexity, rich, honeysuckle, buttered citrus, and roasted hazelnut characteristics. Since it was bottled unfiltered, it is throwing some sediment, so don't have a coronary if you see what professionals call "floaters." The wine's spectacular length and richness suggest another 4–5 years of longevity. This is undoubtedly one of the 1996 vintage's superstar Chardonnays.

Tasting through the cuvées of 1997 red wines was fascinating. The 1997 Merlot (15% Cabernet Sauvignon was included in the blend) is about as chocolatey-styled a wine as I have ever tasted. My notes read, "liquid Snickers." The opaque black/purple color is followed by a fabulously intense, exotic nose of melted chocolate, plum/cherry liqueur, and high quality toasty oak. Hugely extracted, marvelously full bodied, and unctuously textured, this amazingly complex, rich, palate-staining Merlot is one of the finest examples of this varietal I have ever tasted—from California. There is plenty of power and tannin, so it should drink well for 2 decades. The 1996 Merlot (3,000 cases) is a worthy rival. Bottled unfined and unfiltered, this blend of 93% Merlot and 7% Cabernet Franc tips the scales at a heady 14.6% alcohol. Could it be better than the 1997? The wine is opaque black/purple-colored, with a knockout nose of plums, black cherries, chocolate, raspberries, licorice, and toasty new oak. Viscous in the mouth, with superb purity, this is a riveting, mind-boggling Merlot that sets a new reference point for this varietal in California. It can be drunk now but has the potential to last for 15 or more years.

The 1997 Proprietary Red Wine (a blend in progress, presently composed of 65% Cabernet Sauvignon, 10% Merlot, 10% Cabernet Franc, and the rest Petit Verdot) flirts with perfection. This wine shares some of the chocolatey characteristics of the two Merlot vintages, but there is more cassis liqueur, blackberries, blueberries, and *pain grillé* notes in this lavishly rich, flamboyant proprietary red. The wine's flavors lingered for 42 seconds on the palate. Full bodied, marvelously concentrated, and extremely well balanced, this wine's acidity, tannin, and high alcohol are completely buried beneath the complex fruit and extract of this profound offering. I remember shaking my head in disbelief at the quality of these wines. Like all the Pahlmeyer reds, they are bottled unfined and unfiltered, so what you see is what you get. The 1996 Proprietary Red Wine (a blend of 73% Cabernet Sauvignon, with the rest Cabernet Franc, Merlot, Petit Verdot, and Malbec) possesses a modest 14.3% alcohol. While it is a great wine, it is somewhat overshadowed by its more flashy siblings. It exhibits an opaque purple color, and a stunning nose of cherry liqueur intertwined with prunes, black currants, coffee, smoke, and blackberries. Fabulously rich and lush, with a midpalate so deep and concentrated that it overloads the sensory organs, this multidimensional, gloriously extracted wine provides superb richness allied to extraordinary complexity and symmetry. It should drink well for 2 decades.

There are small quantities of 1996 Malbec. Produced from fruit grown in the Napanook Vineyard owned by Christian Moueix, this exotic, wild wine is not for everybody, but it ranks with the finest California Malbecs I have ever tasted (only Dick Arrowood's offering rivals it). The dark saturated ruby/purple color is accompanied by aromas of vanilla ice cream drenched with raspberry jam. Smoky *pain grillé* notes (from aging in new Taransaud barrels) also make an appearance. In the mouth, the wine's display of fruit is so ostentatious as to be gaudy. It does not possess the body or length of Pahlmeyer's Merlots or Proprietary Reds, but it is an enormously fat, fruity, and undeniably sexy and disarming wine. It should drink well for 10–15 years.

Pahlmeyer's 1995 Chardonnay appears to be a return to the style of the 1993. This unfiltered gem offers up fabulously sweet, ripe, honeyed pineapple and citrusy fruit aromas, intermingled with hazelnut and toasty oak scents. The wine is extremely full bodied and rich, with a layered texture, outstanding purity, and a lusty finish. This superb California Chardonnay should drink well for 5–6 years.

I do not believe it is an exaggeration to say that Pahlmeyer's Merlot is now the finest being produced in California. One might quibble over other styles of Merlot, but no producer achieves more complexity, flavor, and thrills per sip than Pahlmeyer. The 1995 Merlot is an awesomely endowed, full-bodied, pedal to the metal style of Merlot with great richness in addition to a knockout nose of blackberry, raspberry, mocha, and smoky aromas that soar from the glass. The wine has a sweet attack (from its formidable glycerin and extract level, not sugar), full body, extraordinary layers of concentrated fruit, and a blockbuster finish. Amazingly, the wine, like its 1996 counterpart, possesses gorgeously integrated acidity, tannin, and alcohol. Can California Merlot get any better than this? Both Merlots will drink well when released, and last for 15–20 years.

The 1994 Merlot is a terrific example of this varietal, and one of the finest I have ever tasted from California. The wine reveals a dense purple color, followed by a superfragrant nose of chocolate, mocha, toast, and black cherry fruit. Full bodied, but not heavy, this expansive, chewy, opulently textured wine should drink well for 15 or more years. The 1993 Merlot displays plenty of toasty, vanillin-scented new oak, ripe, concentrated berry fruit, medium to full body, an intriguing, nicely textured, expansive palate, and a round, generous finish. It is a delicious, succulent Merlot with enough structure to carry it over the next 7–8 years, perhaps longer.

Pahlmeyer's proprietary red table wine tends to be Cabernet Sauvignon-dominated (usually 80%–85%) with small portions of Malbec, Petit Verdot, Cabernet Franc, and Merlot. The 1995 Proprietary Red Wine may be even better than the 96-point score I bestowed on it. It is unquestionably among the top dozen 1995s. The wine boasts an explosive blackberry/blueberry/cassis-scented nose that has completely soaked up all the new oak in which it has been aged for the last 22 months. Purple/black in color, it exhibits fabulously extracted, layered black fruit flavors that coat the palate, offering a seamless texture and voluptuous impression. The 1994 Proprietary Red Wine exhibits a similar purple/black color, as well as sweet, integrated tannin, a gorgeous black currant, toast, tar, and licorice-scented nose, fabulous texture, and a 35–45-second finish. The 1994 may be slightly sweeter in the midpalate than the 1995, but the differences are negligible. The abundant tannin is mostly concealed by the wine's wealth of fruit, glycerin, and alcohol. This wine should drink well from the late nineties through the first 2 decades of the next century. Very impressive!

Pahlmeyer's 1993 has an unbelievable resemblance to a fine vintage of Bordeaux's renowned Château Léoville-Las Cases. The saturated dark ruby/purple color is followed by a pristine nose of black currants, minerals, and spicy, high-quality oak. Medium to full bodied, rich and elegant, this well-endowed, beautifully concentrated, graceful Cabernet Sauvignon will need 5–7 years of cellaring and will keep for 20+ years. This fascinating wine could easily be confused with a top class Médoc if tasted blind.

If great wine satisfies both the palate and the intellect, these Pahlmeyer offerings are prodigious. Despite the forward drinkability of these reds, all of them will last for 20-25 years. These are mind-boggling efforts. This is another winery where getting on the mailing list is essential to securing a few bottles of these liquid gems.

PALOMA (NAPA)

1996 Merlot	Napa Valley	D	94
1995 Merlot	Napa Valley	D	92+
1994 Merlot	Napa Valley	D	91+

What a discovery! This fabulous 1994 Merlot was made from an estate on Spring Mountain. Only 625 cases were produced of this blockbuster, inky/purple-colored wine. It is obviously the result of talented winemaking given its purity and wonderful integration of toasty French oak with gobs of black cherry and raspberry fruit. The wine reveals full body, marvelous extraction and richness, terrific equilibrium, and a layered, textured, expansively flavored personality. This impressive wine still needs 2–3 years of cellaring, but it should prove to be uncommonly long-lived for a Merlot, say 15–20 years. This is an exceptionally impressive wine made in a large-scaled, boldly styled, massively endowed format!

The 1995 Merlot is another terrific effort from this small winery owned by Barbara and Jim Richards. A blend of 80% Merlot and 20% Cabernet Sauvignon, the wine was fined with egg whites but not filtered prior to bottling. Its opaque purple color suggests a wine of extraordinary intensity. The nose is subdued, but swirling brings forth scents of jammy cassis, licorice, *pain grillé,* and sweet cherry fruit. It possesses an inner core of intense fruit, a lush texture, and flavors of fruit and chocolate, with a subtle overlay of smoky oak. Full bodied, moderately tannic, and exceptionally intense with a lingering finish, this is a Merlot to cellar for 2–3 years and drink over the following 2 decades. Very impressive!

Bob Foley, the winemaker at Pride Mountain, produces this Merlot from Spring Mountain fruit. The 1996 is about as concentrated, thick, and promising a Merlot as readers are likely to find from either the New or Old World. The color is an impressive opaque purple. The nose merely hints at what should emerge with another 2–3 years of cellaring. At present, readers will have to be content with *pain grillé* notes intermingled with plums, prunes, and black cherry liqueur. Full bodied, deep, and exceptionally well balanced, with beautifully integrated acidity and tannin, this massive, rich, ageworthy Merlot should be at its best between 2000 and 2015.

GIANNI PAOLETTI (NAPA)

1995 Cabernet Sauvignon	Napa	D	90

Approximately 300 cases of this exceptionally well made, promising Cabernet Sauvignon were produced. The wine possesses a saturated black/ruby/purple color, as well as a subtle yet impressive nose of ripe cassis, licorice, vanilla, and spice. Although restrained and unevolved, it exhibits a nicely layered, multidimensional personality with deep, full-bodied flavors, and a sense of elegance and symmetry. This wine is accessible, but it promises to be better with another 2–3 years of aging and will last for 15–16 years.

PARADIGM WINERY (NAPA)

1995 Cabernet Sauvignon Oakville Estate	Napa	D	90
1994 Cabernet Sauvignon Oakville Estate	Napa	D	87+
1993 Cabernet Sauvignon Oakville Estate	Napa	D	87
1995 Merlot Oakville Estate	Napa	D	87
1994 Merlot Oakville Estate	Napa	D	88
1995 Zinfandel Oakville Estate	Napa	C	88
1994 Zinfandel Oakville Estate	Napa	C	86

These wines are made by one of Napa's most talented wine consultants, Heidi Barrett (the wife of Bo Barrett of Château Montelena), who is also the consultant to such Napa blue bloods as Grace Family Vineyards, Screaming Eagle, Vineyard 29, Hartwell, and, until 1996, Dalla Valle. Paradigm's offerings are elegant wines that marry Bordeaux-like restraint with California's ripe fruit flavors. Made in a claretlike, medium-bodied style, the 1994 Zinfandel Oakville Estate reveals excellent berry fruit, modest alcohol, and a clean, refreshing, briery finish. It will appeal to readers who find the Zinfandels such as those made by Turley and Martinelli too concentrated and intense. The 1995 Zinfandel Oakville Estate raises the level of concentration, offering peppery, briery fruit, along with a classy sweet raspberry richness. The wine is medium bodied, with more length and flavor dimension than the 1994, a sweet, soft midpalate and texture, and a succulent, classy, spicy finish. It should drink well for 4–5 years.

The 1994 Merlot Oakville Estate is an excellent, medium-bodied, elegant wine offering attractive berry fruit and spice, as well as a subtle dosage of toasty new oak. It is a wine to drink over the next 5–7 years. The soft, round 1995 Merlot Oakville Estate is cut from the same cloth, emphasizing restrained yet pure, harmonious flavors presented in a medium-bodied, nicely concentrated, impeccably well balanced style.

With respect to the Cabernet Sauvignons, this is one winery where the 1995 out-classes the 1994. While the 1994 Cabernet Sauvignon Oakville Estate is certainly very good, it is tightly knit, although some tobacco and cassis aromas do emerge from this deep ruby-colored wine. It is sweet and pure on the palate, with medium body, pleasing olive and black currant flavors, and light to moderate tannin in the finish. I suspect 1–2 years of cellaring will enhance this wine's personality. It should keep for 12–15 years. The 1995 Cabernet Sauvignon Oakville Estate cuts a deeper impression on the palate, offering up copious quantities of black cherry, currant, and herb-tinged flavors in a medium- to full-bodied, plush style. The wine possesses more layers of flavor, excellent purity, and a spicy, long finish. It should drink well upon release and last for 15 or more years. The 1993 Cabernet Sauvignon Estate could easily pass for a stylish, high quality Médoc. The color is a medium dark ruby, and the wine offers a curranty, earth, herbaceous nose, some austerity on the palate, but fine ripe flavors, good texture and ripeness, and a medium-bodied, slightly tannic finish. Although it has some aggressive tannin to shed, it is well balanced, and a candidate for 10–15 years of cellaring.

FESS PARKER (SANTA BARBARA)

1996 Chardonnay Marcella's Vineyard	Santa Barbara	C	89
1997 Mélange du Rhône	Santa Barbara	C	90
1997 Muscat Canelli	Central Coast	B	89
1996 Pinot Noir American Tradition Reserve	Santa Barbara	D	87
1994 Pinot Noir American Tradition Reserve	Santa Barbara	D	87

1993 Pinot Noir American Tradition Reserve	Santa Barbara	C	85
1995 Syrah	Santa Barbara	C	88
1994 Syrah	Santa Barbara	C	88
1993 Syrah	Santa Barbara	C	87
1993 Syrah American Tradition Reserve	Santa Barbara	D	89

Delicious offerings from Fess Parker, the 1996 Chardonnay Marcella's Vineyard (named after his wife) is an excellent, nearly outstanding wine with wonderful purity, copious amounts of buttery tropical fruit, nicely integrated toasty oak, adequate acidity, and lemon butter/orange blossom notes for additional complexity. The texture is succulent, and the wine delicious. It should drink well for several more years. I was thrilled by the 1997 Mélange du Rhône. I hope Fess Parker and his winemaker son, Eli, continue to pursue this style of wine. Made from a blend of 58% Marsanne, 34% Viognier, and 8% Roussanne, this full-bodied (13.5% alcohol), fruit-driven wine offers an alluring bouquet of lemon blossoms, apricot jam, orange skin, and honeysuckle. There is admirable purity, a nicely textured feel, and a dry, long, rich finish with noticeable glycerin. There are 1,300 cases of this beautifully made wine; it is selling for a song! Consume it over the next year.

The 1996 Pinot Noir American Tradition Reserve is a silky, sexy, medium ruby-colored Pinot Noir with abundant jammy black cherry fruit nicely dosed with smoky oak. Soft, round, and elegant, it will provide ideal drinking over the next 2–3 years.

These fine offerings from Fess Parker include a jammy, leafy, herb, and cherry-scented and -flavored 1994 Pinot Noir American Tradition Reserve that is a textbook example of Pinot from California's south central coast. The overall impression is one of up-front, flattering fruit. A succulent, round, delicious Pinot, with good weight, glycerin, and body, it is meant to be drunk over the next several years, before the herbal component dominates the wine's fruit.

Fess Parker's 1993 Pinot Noir American Tradition Reserve reveals a medium ruby color, a sweet, berry-scented nose, medium body, clean, pure fruit, tart acidity, and a moderately long, crisp finish. Drink it over the next 2–3 years.

The serious, dark ruby/purple-colored 1993 Syrah American Tradition Reserve reveals an intense, cassis, smoky, peppery character, full body, a backward personality, admirable length, and gobs of sweet Syrah fruit. Although wrapped in a cloak of tannin, formidably structured, and built for the long haul, this wine opens beautifully in the glass. As it opens, a smoky, bacon fat character reminiscent of Côte Rôtie gradually emerges. Give it 12 more months in the bottle and drink it over the following 10–12 years. It is a candidate for an outstanding score after more aging. The 1994 Syrah is made in a nonaggressive, supple, medium- to full-bodied style that emphasizes plenty of peppery, black currant, and plum fruit. Spicy and rich, with no hard edges, this plump, savory, deliciously fruity Syrah should drink well over the next 7–9 years. Although not as strong as his 1992, Fess Parker's 1993 Syrah is a lovely, rich, supple wine with gobs of black fruits, medium to full body, and a velvety finish. It should drink well for 5–8 years.

Earthy, peppery, black currant, and berry aromas emerge from the dark ruby-colored 1995 Syrah. An accessible style of Syrah with good spice, it is medium bodied, soft, and plump. Drink this crowd-pleasing Syrah over the next 4–5 years.

The delectable, tropical fruit salad-scented 1997 Muscat Canelli is sure to be a big hit with the masses. With slight residual sugar, zesty acidity for balance, and a glorious concoction of tropical fruits (apricots and peaches galore), this intensely scented, fruity, cleanly made wine is a joy to drink, both as an aperitif and with fruit desserts. Given its flamboyant aromatics, it is best consumed during its first year after release. For what it's worth, my parents have an addiction to this wine!

PATZ AND HALL WINE CO. (NAPA)

1997 Chardonnay	Napa	D	89
1996 Chardonnay	Napa	D	88
1995 Chardonnay	Napa	D	90
1996 Chardonnay	Russian River	D	90
1995 Chardonnay	Russian River	D	91
1997 Chardonnay	Sonoma Coast	D	91
1997 Chardonnay Alder Springs	Mendocino	E	94
1997 Chardonnay Carr Vineyard	Mt. Veeder	D	92
1996 Chardonnay Carr Vineyard	Mt. Veeder	D	91
1995 Chardonnay Carr Vineyard	Mt. Veeder	D	90
1997 Chardonnay Hyde Vineyard	Carneros	D	92
1996 Chardonnay Hyde Vineyard	Carneros	D	91
1997 Pinot Noir	Russian River	D	87
1997 Pinot Noir	Sonoma	D	85?
1997 Pinot Noir Alder Springs	Mendocino	E	90
1997 Pinot Noir Hyde Vineyard	Carneros	D	87
1997 Pinot Noir Pisoni Vineyard	Santa Lucia Highlands	D	90

This high-quality producer owns no vineyards but is obviously exploiting some of the finest sources for fruit on California's North Coast. There are 7,200 cases of sumptuous, Burgundian-styled Chardonnays that will be big hits with consumers. Moreover, the bevy of Pinot Noirs offered by Patz and Hall will quickly place this winery among the upper hierarchy of California Pinot producers. All of these wines are bottled unfiltered.

I was thrilled with the five 1997 Chardonnays I tasted, all of them outstanding, complex, subtle, rich, and distinctively different. The 1997 Chardonnay Sonoma Coast displays a smoky, leesy, orange peel, citrusy nose as well as flavors, a terrific texture, rich, pure fruit, full body, plenty of glycerin and alcohol (14.2%), and a lusty, heady finish with mouth-cleansing, tangy acidity. This wine (120 cases) went through full malolactic fermentation, and was aged in French oak, of which 80% was new. It should continue to drink well for 3–4 years. The 1997 Chardonnay Napa (3,300 cases) comes from three vineyard sources—Atlas Peak, Hyde Vineyard, and Caldwell Vineyard. Less Burgundian than the more mineral-dominated Sonoma Coast offering, the Napa Chardonnay exhibits copious quantities of tropical fruit, full body, rich fruit, and a more direct, less complex but satisfying, impeccably made style. It is best consumed over the next 1–2 years. The 1997 Chardonnay Hyde Vineyard (1,100 cases) offers Mediterranean, orange blossom, exotic, cointreau-like aromatics. Call this wine "Parkerized," as it has gobs of fruit, terrific purity, and a flamboyant, full-bodied personality. Much of the Chardonnay planted in the Hyde Vineyard is the Musqué clone, which gives an extra dimension to the wine's fragrance. This offering tips the scales at 14.2% alcohol, but it is very sexy juice. Drink it over the next several years.

The limited production 1997 Chardonnay Alder Springs is made from Dijon Clone 76 (a clone known for extremely small berries and tiny clusters). This hillside vineyard (at an elevation of 1,400 feet) has produced just two barrels of wine for Patz and Hall, which was aged in 100% new oak. A spectacular Chardonnay (my notes read "profound stuff"), it offers a striking liquid minerality in its citrusy, honeyed nose, as well as notes of flower blossoms, verveine, and smoky new oak. This is a blockbuster, complex, thrilling Chardonnay for enjoying over the next 2–3 years. Bravo! Lastly, the 1997 Chardonnay Carr Vineyard is another full-bodied powerhouse, loaded with rich fruit, leesy, smoky minerals, a touch of butter, and a pure, concentrated, beautifully layered mouth-feel. Large-scaled (14.2% alcohol) and extremely rich, yet impeccably well balanced, it should last for 2–3 years.

Patz and Hall's Pinot Noirs may not quite reach the thrilling level attained by their Chardonnays, but this estate is gaining ground with each new vintage. All these wines are bottled with no filtration, and most without fining, although some fining agents are added to the Russian River and Alder Springs Pinots. The 1997 Pinot Noir Russian River (13.8% alcohol) exhibits a medium ruby color, a smoky, herb-tinged, cherry/kirsch-scented nose, round, delicious, fresh flavors, and a clean, tasty mouth-feel. While it is not a large-scaled Pinot, it offers jammy fruit as well as an agreeable personality. Drink it over the next several years. The 1997 Pinot Noir Hyde Vineyard (13.8% alcohol) is a medium-bodied, lush, attractive wine with black cherries dominating its aromatics and flavors. It possesses a character similar to a Beaune premier cru. As the wine sits in the glass, the perfume becomes more intense, revealing notes of black raspberries. A beautifully made wine from Dijon Clone 113, it should drink well for 3–5 years. The 1997 Pinot Noir Sonoma County was closed when I tasted it. More tannic and dominated by earth, it possessed a harder edge than the other four Pinots. A muscular, herbaceous, peppery, more earthy-scented Pinot, it should be good, although not as special as the other examples.

It is amazing how many outstanding Pinot Noirs have already emanated from the Pisoni Vineyard in the Santa Lucia Highlands. Add Patz and Hall's 1997 Pinot Noir Pisoni Vineyard to the list. This effort exhibits a deep ruby/purple color, as well as sweet black fruits (currants and raspberries), and complex, rich, medium- to full-bodied flavors with surprising fat, glycerin and lushness. This is an exceptionally pure, lengthy, concentrated, seductive Pinot Noir for drinking now, and over the next 5–6 years. Very impressive! Even more exciting is the 1997 Pinot Noir Alder Springs, which is a breakthrough Pinot Noir for Mendocino. Sadly, there are only two barrels (about 46 cases). The wine boasts a saturated dark ruby/purple color, and a knockout nose of smoky, toasty oak intermixed with brandied cherries, mocha, and black raspberries. Rich, concentrated, and full bodied, this is a hedonistic, decadently rich Pinot Noir to consume over the next 5–6 years. Kudos to Patz and Hall for a brilliant portfolio of wines in 1997.

In 1996, this winery's production climbed to 4,500 cases, much of it full flavored, wonderfully decadent and hedonistic Chardonnay that should be sought out by those looking for high-quality wine from this varietal. The 1996 Chardonnay Russian River is a barrel- and malolactic-fermented wine that spent 11 months on its lees before bottling. It is a dense, full-bodied, ripe Chardonnay with considerable quantities of tropical fruit, minerals, citrus, and a honeyed lemon nuance to its flashy flavors. The acidity and alcohol are beautifully meshed with the wine's lush texture. Drink this exceptional Chardonnay over the next several years. The excellent, medium-bodied 1996 Napa Chardonnay exhibits admirable purity and plenty of ripe fruit, but not the follow-through and length of Patz and Hall's other Chardonnays. This wine is made from a number of Napa vineyard sources, including Hyde, Caldwell, Carr, and Atlas Peak. A super Chardonnay, the 1996 Hyde Vineyard, is made from both a Musqué clone of Chardonnay, as well as the old Wente clone. It is a medium- to full-bodied, exotic wine with an intense fragrance of tangerines, honeysuckle, and ripe tropical fruit. The wine reveals outstanding purity (a hallmark of all the Patz and Hall wines), enough acidity to provide vibrancy, and a lusty, heady finish. These wines see a healthy percentage of new oak, but the fruit is so strongly presented that the oak plays a secondary role. The

1996 Chardonnay Carr Vineyard possesses the most complex set of aromatics, offering up scents of melted butter, cloves, apples, and bread dough. The wine's spicy character nicely complements the medium- to full-bodied, richly fruity, mineral-laden style. With plenty of glycerin, this is an intensely concentrated, ripe, and well-balanced wine. It may evolve beyond 2–3 years.

The outstanding 1995 Napa Chardonnay exhibits a light greenish gold color, a big, spicy, bold, excellent purity and ripeness (honeyed orange/lemonlike flavors), zesty underlying acidity, and a firm, well-structured finish. The 1995 Russian River Chardonnay reveals more intense tropical fruit, a well-integrated, smoky, toasty barrel component, crisp acidity, gobs of flesh and body, excellent purity, and a well-knit finish. Both of these full-flavored, assertively styled yet delicious wines possess 14.2% alcohol; they should drink well for 2–3 years. From its lavishly oaked nose, to its exotic tropical fruits, high-quality spicy oak, and layered impression, the 1995 Chardonnay Carr Vineyard is a boldly styled, robust, full-throttle wine to drink over the next year. What an exuberant, gutsy, rich, ostentatious style of Chardonnay! It is definitely not for wimps!

PEACHY CANYON WINERY (PASO ROBLES)

1995 Para Siempre	Paso Robles	D	85
1994 Para Siempre	Central Coast	D	86
1996 Zinfandel Dusi Ranch	Paso Robles	D	89
1995 Zinfandel Dusi Ranch	Paso Robles	C	85
1994 Zinfandel Dusi Ranch	Paso Robles	C	89
1993 Zinfandel Dusi Ranch	Paso Robles	C	93
1996 Zinfandel Eastside	Paso Robles	C	88
1995 Zinfandel Eastside	Paso Robles	C	85
1994 Zinfandel Eastside	Paso Robles	C	87
1993 Zinfandel Eastside	Paso Robles	C	90
1996 Zinfandel Especiale	Paso Robles	C	87?
1995 Zinfandel Especiale	Paso Robles	C	85
1996 Zinfandel Estate	Paso Robles	D	87
1995 Zinfandel Estate	Paso Robles	C	86
1994 Zinfandel Leona's Vineyard Second Crop	Paso Robles	C	89+
1995 Zinfandel Old Bailey Ranch	Paso Robles	C	88
1996 Zinfandel Westside	Paso Robles	D	86
1995 Zinfandel Westside	Paso Robles	C	87
1994 Zinfandel Westside	Paso Robles	C	88
1993 Zinfandel Westside	Paso Robles	C	90+

The 1993s are impressive Zinfandels with three totally different personalities. Readers who are familiar with the decadent, overripe cherry fruitiness of a great Pomerol, such as Lafleur, will see a resemblance in Peachy Canyon's 1993 Zinfandels from their Eastside and Westside vineyards. The 1993 Zinfandel Eastside (13.8% alcohol) exhibits an old vine, intense, cherry-scented nose that borders on overripeness. It is full bodied, wonderfully expansive and chewy, with light tannin, low acidity, and a gorgeously layered, unctuously textured finish. This is a terrific Zinfandel for drinking over the next 7–8 years. The 1993 Zinfandel Westside adds exotic spices to the essence of cherry fruit. The wine is extremely full bodied and rich, with gobs of alcohol, exceptional concentration, and a late-harvest, dry, full-bodied, heady finish. This is a superb Zinfandel for drinking over the next decade. Amazingly, the extroverted 1993 Zinfandel Dusi Ranch is even richer. Sensationally ripe and rich, it offers awesome flavor intensity, amazing balance for its size, and a viscous, rich, full-bodied finish that lasts 45 seconds. It does not possess the intense cherriness of the other wines given its massive composition, but it is a huge, winter-weight Zinfandel to cuddle alongside during a cold, damp day. Its alcohol is listed as a dizzyingly high 15.1%.

Following the blockbuster, powerful, concentrated Peachy Canyon Zinfandel from previous vintages, the 1994s are more restrained and elegant. The 1994 Eastside Zinfandel (12.8% alcohol) exhibits wild cherry, blueberry, and raspberry fruit, medium body, lovely purity, and a supple, smooth style. Drink it over the next 3–5 years. The medium dark ruby-colored 1994 Zinfandel Dusi Ranch (13.6% alcohol) displays a spicy, earthy, peppery, smoky red and black fruit character, medium to full body, fine purity, and a supple, smooth texture. While it does not possess the weight of previous vintages, it is a delicious, nearly outstanding Zinfandel for drinking over the next 4–5 years. The 1994 Zinfandel Westside reveals a textbook, briery, spicy, peppery nose, well-hidden alcohol (14.6%), excellent ripeness, a rich, medium- to full-bodied style, and a spicy, clean finish. Like its siblings, it is more subtle than usual. The late-harvest 1994 Zinfandel Leona's Vineyard Second Crop (15.2% alcohol) possesses an opaque, dense garnet/purple color, a jammy, cherry-scented nose, and amazingly well concealed alcohol. Rich, dry, full bodied, with no raisiny or pruny notes, this is an impressive, excellent, nearly exceptional example of full-throttle Zinfandel that should drink well for 6–7 years.

Made from a blend of Cabernet Sauvignon, Cabernet Franc, and Merlot, the 1994 Para Siempre offers an uncomplicated, but richly fruity nose of red and black currants, earth, and spice. On the palate, the wine reveals medium body, harsh tannin, good ripeness, and a solid, one-dimensional but pleasing personality. Drink it over the next 3–4 years.

A blend of Cabernet Sauvignon, Cabernet Franc, and Merlot, the medium ruby-colored 1995 Para Siempre reveals some amber at the edge. The nose offers up gobs of dusty, sweet, jammy, berry fruit, and loamy, earthy scents. Medium bodied and supple, with charm and appeal, this attractive, easygoing, uncomplex red wine offers immediate pleasure. Drink it over the next 2–4 years.

Peachy Canyon turned in a bevy of wines in 1995 that are good but well below the high quality of previous vintages. However, the wines, with their angular personalities, are typical for the vintage, with less glycerin and extraction, yet more acidity. In spite of the high alcohol, the wines are not comparable to the intense richness of fruit found in such vintages as 1994, 1993, 1992, 1991, and 1990.

The 1995 Zinfandel Estate is a dark ruby-colored wine with an excellent sweet, dusty, blackberry and cherry-scented nose, vibrant, medium-bodied flavors with tart acidity, and a soft, open-knit personality. This wine requires consumption over the next 2–3 years. My favorite 1995 Peachy Canyon Zinfandel is the 1995 Zinfandel Old Bailey Ranch (14.6% alcohol). It possesses a deep ruby color, as well as a gorgeously seductive nose of pepper, sweet black cherry fruit, and spice. The wine's excellent richness, chewy fruit and glycerin on the midpalate, in addition to its spicy, smoky finish, all make for an excellent mouth-filling, savory style of Zinfandel. Drink it over the next 2–3 years. The 1995 Zinfandel Especiale (14.6% alcohol) is a distinctively spicy, peppery Zin without the sweet fruit of its two predecessors. It reveals an evolved medium ruby/garnet color, a soft, straightforward palate, adequate acidity, and moderate weight. It is the least concentrated and color saturated Peachy Canyon Zinfandel I have tasted over recent years. Drink it over the next 2–3 years. The similarly styled 1995 Zinfandel Dusi Ranch (14.6% alcohol), normally a blockbuster Zinfandel, is a light- to medium-bodied wine with straightforward fruit, and little intensity or depth. It is easygoing and flattering, with moderate ripeness, and no flaws. Drink it over the next several years.

The other very good to excellent wine in this portfolio is the 1995 Zinfandel Westside. Soft, with a moderately deep ruby color, medium body, an attractive, easygoing, low-acid style, and round, tasty, attractive, berrylike flavors, this wine usually superrich, is forward and commercial in its open-knit, immediately drinkable style. Moreover, it needs to be drunk up over the next several years because of its lack of extract and length. The same can be said for the 1995 Zinfandel Eastside. Displaying a more weedy, tobacco, green pepper, and tar-scented nose, the Eastside Zin possesses a medium ruby color, with obvious lightening at the edge. It is an elegant, understated, restrained style of Zinfandel—much in keeping with the majority of Zinfandels produced in 1995.

The 1996 Zinfandel Dusi Ranch reveals a hint of a late-harvest character (freshly laid asphalt in the nose). It is a powerful, fragrant, dense, ruby/purple-colored, full-bodied wine with gorgeous layers of extract, fine purity, and a deep, chewy, exuberant finish. Intense, rich, and mouth-filling, it should drink well for 5–6 years. The more elegant 1996 Zinfandel Estate offers sweet black cherry fruit intermixed with dusty earth and peppery notes. In the mouth, it is medium to full bodied, with a classic briery flavor profile, fine purity, and a clean, fleshy, moderately long finish. Consume it over the next 2–3 years.

The 1996 Zinfandel Eastside boasts nearly 14.8% alcohol. A gorgeous nose is reminiscent of a top Châteauneuf du Pape in its pepper, kirsch, and spicy, smoky-dominated aromatic profile. It is rich, full bodied, and slightly heavy (which kept me from giving it 90 points). With its lush, heady, opulently textured finish, this is a powerful, authoritatively rich Zinfandel to drink over the next 4–5 years. For whatever reason, the 1996 Zinfandel Westside is more restrained, medium bodied, and measured when compared to the other Peachy Canyon offerings. Although it possesses a dark ruby color, and jammy cherry and strawberry fruit in the nose, it is more monolithic. Perhaps I caught it during a dormant stage. Lastly, the late-harvest-styled 1996 Zinfandel Especiale contains over 15% alcohol, in addition to big, thick, tarry, cherrylike flavors oozing with glycerin and richness. It is a heavyweight Zinfandel that is likely to be fatiguing after a glass or two. Nevertheless, it should age well for 5–8 years.

J. PEDRONCELLI WINERY (SONOMA)

1994	Zinfandel	Dry Creek	A	85
1994	Zinfandel Bushnell Vineyard	Dry Creek	B	89+
1996	Zinfandel Mother Clone	Dry Creek	C	86
1995	Zinfandel Mother Clone	Dry Creek	B	86
1994	Zinfandel Mother Clone	Dry Creek	B	88+
1993	Zinfandel Mother Clone Special Vineyard Select	Dry Creek	C	88
1996	Zinfandel Pedroni-Bushnell	Dry Creek	C	83
1995	Zinfandel Pedroni-Bushnell	Dry Creek	B	84
1993	Zinfandel Pedroni-Bushnell	Dry Creek	C	85

Both of the 1996 wines performed well, but they are somewhat lean and austere. The 1996 Zinfandel Mother Clone boasts 14.5% alcohol, in addition to good berry/cherry fruit, as well as pepper and spice notes in the nose. This well-made wine possesses an elegant attack and stylish, graceful flavors, but it is not exciting. Drink it over the next 2–3 years. The 1996

Zinfandel Pedroni-Bushnell lacks the stuffing, extract, and richness to balance out the wine's high alcohol (14.7%), and attenuated, rough-hewn style. The finish is short, and the acid is high, especially for such a modestly endowed wine.

Both of the 1995 offerings from Pedroncelli exhibit medium ruby colors, suggesting wines of moderate concentration and weight. The slightly superior 1995 Zinfandel Mother Clone was riper, with a more endearing, supple texture. It reveals a bramble bush/wild berry-scented nose, tasty, soft, medium-bodied flavors, crisp acidity, and an elegant, short finish. It should be drunk over the next several years. The 1995 Zinfandel Pedroni-Bushnell possesses a similar personality, but it is more dominated by minerals, coming across on the palate as tightly knit, with a leaner flavor profile. It also needs to be consumed over the near term as neither of these wines possess sufficient depth of fruit to age longer than 2–3 years.

The straightforward, soft, elegant, medium-bodied 1994 Zinfandel possesses enough briery fruit to please most Zinfandel fans. A pleasant restaurant-styled, fairly priced Zinfandel, it is meant to be drunk over the next 2–3 years. The 1994 Zinfandel Bushnell Vineyard and 1994 Zinfandel Mother Clone, in addition to being excellent values, are nearly outstanding. Both offer excellent varietal character, medium to full body, considerable richness and intensity, and admirable winemaking. They are somewhat unevolved and backward, with the Bushnell Vineyard the more supple and open of the two efforts. They are surprisingly strong, impressive efforts from Pedroncelli, and I would not be surprised to see both wines merit a few more points to their already lofty scores with another 3–4 months of bottle age. Both should drink well for 6–7 years. Kudos to Pedroncelli for these fine efforts.

Pedroncelli's 1993 Mother Clone Special Vineyard Selection is the finest, richest Zinfandel I have tasted from this reliable Sonoma winery. The color is a healthy dark ruby. The nose exhibits glorious levels of sweet, jammy, berry fruit, spice, and earth. The wine already offers attractive drinking, with medium to full body, well-integrated acidity, and no obvious tannin. This is a well-balanced, graceful, flavorful Zinfandel for drinking over the next 5–6 years. The 1993 Zinfandel Pedroni-Bushnell possesses good fruit but not the depth, ripeness, or body of the Special Selection. It is a straightforward, flavorful wine that is ideal for near-term drinking (4–5 years).

ROBERT PEPI WINERY (NAPA)

1996	Arneis	Central Coast	C	84
1997	Barbera	Sonoma	B	86
1996	Barbera	Sonoma	C	87
1995	Colline di Sassi (Sangiovese)	Napa	C	88
1994	Colline di Sassi (85% Sangiovese/ 15% Cabernet Sauvignon)	Napa Valley	C	87+
1995	Due Baci (Cabernet Sauvignon/Sangiovese)	Napa	D	89
1994	Due Baci	Napa Valley	D	90
1996	Malvasia Bianca	Central Coast	C	86
1996	Pinot Grigio	Central Coast	C	78
1996	Sangiovese Two Heart Canopy	California	C	84
1995	Sangiovese Two Heart Canopy	California	C	85
1997	Sauvignon Blanc Howell Mountain	Napa Valley	C	87
1997	Sauvignon Blanc Two Heart Canopy	Napa Valley	B	84

1997 Teroldego	Central Coast	B	86
1996 Tocai Friulano	Central Coast	C	81

This interesting winery produces between 25,000 and 30,000 cases, of which 18,000 are Sauvignon Blanc and nearly 10,000 Sangiovese. The 1997 Sauvignon Blanc Two Heart Canopy (there is 9% Semillon) is two-thirds barrel fermented, and has its malolactic fermentation blocked in order to retain the natural crisp, tart, tangy acids. A pleasant, melon-scented wine with good freshness, light body, and a clean, vibrant finish, it should drink well for 1–2 years. More substantial, complex, and complete is the 1997 Sauvignon Blanc Howell Mountain, which receives 100% barrel fermentation, and considerable lees stirring. This excellent wine offers copious quantities of smoky, herb-tinged, ripe, melony fruit, medium body, excellent freshness, and a creamy texture and length. Drink this well-made Sauvignon over the next several years.

The red wines are also well made. The 1997 Barbera (which sees 40% new oak) is made from a 25-year-old Sonoma vineyard. Although not complex, it possesses gobs of red fruits intermixed with smoke and earth, and tangy, but not annoying acidity. This one-dimensional, richly fruity, pleasant Barbera will drink well over the next few years. The evolved 1996 Sangiovese Two Heart Canopy is a light ruby-colored offering with spice, saddle leather, and strawberry fruit in the easygoing, light-intensity bouquet. Medium bodied, fresh, and one-dimensional, this clean wine will provide uncritical quaffing over the next 2–3 years. One of the finest reds in the Pepi portfolio is the 1995 Colline di Sassi Sangiovese. Made from a blend of Sangiovese and Cabernet Sauvignon that is 100% *barrique* aged (California's version of a Tuscan *vino da tavola*), this wine exhibits a deep ruby color, and a plum, cranberry, and leathery-scented nose with hints of tobacco, spice, and vanillin. A complex, round example with excellent depth, and an undeniable Tuscan character, it should drink well for 5–7 years. It is hard to speculate how well the 1997 Teroldego will age. Production is tiny, but this wine boasts a black/purple color, gobs of fruit, and a thick, chunky, rustic style. While not complex, it is a mouth-filling, chewy, big red.

Arneis is an indigenous grape of Piedmont, and one of the finest examples of a wine made from this varietal is that of Bruno Giacosa. Pepi's 1996 Arneis is a light-bodied, nicely perfumed wine with good fruit, and a dry finish. While it does not possess much character, it offers a refreshing nut and fruit personality allied with zesty crispness. It will be more attractive to drink with food than on its own merits. However, it needs to be consumed over the next year.

Among the three 1996 offerings of Pinot Grigio, Tocai Friulano, and Malvasia Bianca, the first two were straightforward, pleasant, but essentially one-dimensional wines (no different from 99% of their Italian counterparts). However, the 1996 Malvasia Bianca is a fragrant, fruit cocktail-scented wine with medium body, loads of exuberant fruit, and considerable lemony/apricot/peach flavors, and crisp acidity. Drink it over the next year.

Robert Pepi did a fine job with the 1996 Barbera. Made from a 20-year-old vineyard in Sonoma (owned by the Kunde family), this is a soft, chewy, friendly wine with plenty of black cherry fruit dosed with a subtle, spicy, oaky component. Smooth, round, and accessible, with no hard edges, this is a nice plump pasta wine to drink over the next 2–3 years. In the increasingly crowded field of Sangiovese mediocrities, I thought Pepi's 1995 Sangiovese Two Heart Canopy was a well-made wine. It possesses a medium ruby color, followed by an attractive nose of sour cherry and strawberry fruit. Refreshing acidity provides zest to this medium-bodied wine. It has just enough bite to balance out tomato-based pasta dishes. Even better is the 1995 Colline di Sassi (hill of stones). According to the winery, this vineyard was planted from cuttings of Sangiovese Grosso that were obtained from the famed Brunello di Montalcino estate of Biondi-Santi. A 75% Sangiovese/25% Cabernet Sauvignon blend, the wine reveals attractive new saddle leather, smoky cherry and strawberry fruit in the nose, medium body, excellent denseness, and a sweet, sexy, forward style with toasty oak notes.

This wine could easily pass for a *vino da tavola* from Tuscany. The 1995 Due Baci, a blend of equal parts Cabernet Sauvignon and Sangiovese aged in small oak casks, exhibits a dark ruby/purple color, a smoky, rich, chocolatey, roasted coffee, and black cherry-scented nose, and rich, medium-bodied flavors that include spice, hints of new saddle leather, roasted herb, and olives. This rich, attractive wine is excellent. Drink this beauty over the next 7–8 years.

The 1994 Colline di Sassi is a blend of 85% Sangiovese and 15% Cabernet Sauvignon aged for 14 months in used French oak barrels. It offers up a moderately intense, cherry, earthy, new saddle leather-scented nose, followed by soft, ripe, medium-bodied flavors with an open-knit character, as well as good structure and wood influence. This spicy, richly fruity wine is ideal for drinking over the next 3–4 years. The 1994 Due Baci (a 65% Cabernet Sauvignon and 35% Sangiovese blend) was aged for 16 months in small French oak barrels and bottled unfiltered. The wine displays an opaque ruby/purple color, and a sweet, jammy, black fruit-scented nose with noticeable aromas of oak and earth. This is a deep, medium- to full-bodied, tightly knit wine with outstanding richness, and a long, spicy, well-structured finish. It should drink reasonably well young yet age for a decade.

PER SEMPRE (NAPA)

1994 Cabernet Sauvignon	Napa	D	89
1994 Cabernet Sauvignon Select Reserve	Napa	D	88

These wines, made by Di Loreto Cellars, performed in an admirable fashion. The 1994 Cabernet Sauvignon exhibits an attractive dark ruby color, and a complex, evolved, cedary, spicy, black currant, toasty nose. In the mouth, the wine reveals a savory, ripe style, generous amounts of oak and spice, good extraction, and rich fruit. This pure, attractive Cabernet Sauvignon can be drunk now as well as cellared for 10–15 years. The 1994 Cabernet Sauvignon Select Reserve is a more ambitious wine, with a higher level of toasty new oak, and, presumably, riper fruit. However, the wine is less accessible, closed, and more noticeably oaky than its less expensive sibling. Nevertheless, it is a fine Cabernet Sauvignon that requires 2–3 years of bottle age. If the oak becomes better integrated, look for this wine to merit a higher score. It is a medium- to full-bodied Cabernet with plenty of black currant fruit, lavish quantities of toasty new oak, sweet, well-integrated tannin, and sound acidity.

PETERSON (SONOMA)

1995 Cabernet Sauvignon Bradford Mountain Vineyard	Dry Creek	C	88
1995 Merlot	Dry Creek Valley	C	88
1994 Merlot	Dry Creek Valley	C	87
1996 Pinot Noir	Anderson Valley	C	88
1995 Zinfandel	Dry Creek Valley	C	84
1994 Zinfandel	Dry Creek Valley	C	89
1993 Zinfandel	Dry Creek Valley	C	87
1995 Zinfandel Bradford Mountain	Dry Creek Valley	C	88
1994 Zinfandel Bradford Mountain	Dry Creek Valley	C	88

Ironically, even though Peterson's newest releases (the 1995 Cabernet Sauvignon Bradford Mountain, the 1995 Merlot, the 1996 Pinot Noir, and the 1995 Zinfandel Bradford Mountain Vineyard) were tasted in four separate peer groups, they ended up with identical numerical ratings. Should I label Peterson the "88 Point Winery"? I have had mixed emotions about this winery's offerings in the past, some being very good, and others somewhat kinky, but these new releases have all achieved a high level of consistency and quality. The 1996 Pinot Noir Anderson Valley is a fat, chocolatey, deep ruby-colored wine with copious quantities of smoke, berry fruit, and spice in both its nose and flavors. In the mouth, this low-acid, chunky, fleshy, full-throttle Pinot Noir saturates the palate with plenty of flavor and character. Although not the most complex Pinot, it is immensely satisfying and hedonistic. The wine's low acidity and forward personality suggest it should be drunk over the next 2–3 years. Peterson's 1995 Zinfandel Bradford Mountain Vineyard is a big, tannic, muscular Zin that has been bottled unfined and unfiltered. It should have a lifeline of 6–8 years, if not longer. I increasingly subscribe to the theory that most Zinfandels should be prized for their exuberance and drunk in their gutsy youth. This offering displays a dense ruby color, and a big, spicy, peppery, briery nose. In the mouth, it is ripe and full bodied, with flavors oozing extract, glycerin, and richness. This is a hefty, full-throttle Zinfandel that may improve over the next 12–18 months, and merit a slightly higher score.

Peterson's 1995 Merlot reveals a plump, highly extracted style. A blend of 84% Merlot, 10% Cabernet Franc, and 6% Petit Verdot, it offers Merlot's telltale mocha/coffee bean character, but the emphasis is on tons of juicy, ripe, succulently textured fruit. This extracted wine possesses sweet tannin, admirable intensity, and cuts a bold, flavorful, chewy mouthfeel. It should drink well for 7–10 years. Lastly, the excellent, nearly outstanding 1995 Cabernet Sauvignon Bradford Mountain Vineyard offers earth, melted chocolate, and black currant flavors in its moderately intense aromatics. A saturated ruby/purple color is followed by a tannic wine with excellent richness, good overall balance, clean winemaking, and a deep, highly extracted, chewy, full-bodied style. This Cabernet will benefit from another 1–2 years in the bottle and keep for 10–15.

Readers seeking finesse-styled, understated, measured wines need not read any further. Peterson makes big, chunky, husky, full-bodied, forceful wines that are loaded with flavor. In some cases, the tannin is not as well integrated as one might like, but there is no doubting the boatload of flavor found in these wines. Peterson's soft 1995 Zinfandel (14.2% alcohol) is a spicy, solid, chunky-styled wine without much complexity. It reveals a medium dark garnet color, good peppery, earthy fruit on the attack, medium body, and some muscle but not much complexity or length. It should drink well for 2–3 years.

The deep ruby/purple-colored 1994 Zinfandel Bradford Mountain offers up a cherry, earthy, peppery-scented nose, as well as full-bodied, muscular flavors that seem quite tannic, but impressively endowed and ripe. This wine will never shed all its tannin, so tasters should expect a bold, rustic mouthful of wine. The 1994 Merlot displays a chocolatey, tarlike nose with cherry notes in the background. Sweet, ripe fruit, light tannin, and plenty of body, glycerin, and alcohol make for a meaty mouthful of wine. Drink it over the next 4–5 years.

Looking for a California Zinfandel that tastes similar to a Barolo/Amarone blend? The tarry, earthy, smoky, meaty-scented, sweet, exotic 1994 Zinfandel reveals tons of flavor, as well as a flamboyant personality. Peterson's winemaking style is reminiscent of some of Coturri's wines, as well as those of Joseph Swan. This is undoubtedly a controversial wine, and I have no doubt that many readers will admire its rustic, chocolatey, smoked meat character, while others will find it bizarre. This is a big, rich, chewy Zinfandel that tastes as if it were made in southern Italy. It should drink well for 5–6 years.

Made from Norton Ranch grapes, the 1993 is a muscular, full-bodied, rich Zinfandel revealing excellent color saturation, plenty of berry fruit, a spicy nose, and a sweet (from ripeness, not added sugar), full-bodied palate. The emphasis is on the Zinfandel fruit rather than the new oak or this varietal's stemmy, earthy side. This wine should drink well for 7–9 years.

JOSEPH PHELPS VINEYARD (NAPA)

1997	Cabernet Sauvignon	Napa	D	(87–90)
1996	Cabernet Sauvignon	Napa	D	88+
1995	Cabernet Sauvignon	Napa	D	90
1994	Cabernet Sauvignon	Napa	C	89
1993	Cabernet Sauvignon	Napa	C	89
1997	Cabernet Sauvignon Backus Vineyard	Napa	EE	(94–96)
1996	Cabernet Sauvignon Backus Vineyard	Napa	EE	92+
1995	Cabernet Sauvignon Backus Vineyard	Napa	EE	93
1994	Cabernet Sauvignon Backus Vineyard	Napa	E	94+
1993	Cabernet Sauvignon Backus Vineyard	Napa	D	93
1997	Chardonnay	Carneros	C	87
1996	Chardonnay	Carneros	C	87
1997	Chardonnay Ovation	Napa	E	(90–93)
1996	Chardonnay Ovation	Napa	E	91
1995	Chardonnay Ovation	Napa	E	92
1997	Delice du Semillon	Napa	D (375 ml)	94
1995	Delice du Semillon	Napa	D	91
1995	Eisrebe-Scheurebe Select Late Harvest	Napa	C	90
1997	Insignia Proprietary Red Wine	Napa	EE	(94–96)
1996	Insignia Proprietary Red Wine	Napa	EE	92
1995	Insignia Proprietary Red Wine	Napa	EE	97
1994	Insignia Proprietary Red Wine	Napa	EE	96
1993	Insignia Proprietary Red Wine	Napa	EE	96
1997	Johannisberg Riesling Select Late Harvest	Anderson Valley	D (375 ml)	94
1995	Le Mistral	Napa	C	90
1994	Le Mistral	Napa	C	90
1993	Le Mistral	Napa	C	88
1997	Merlot	Napa	D	(88–90)
1996	Merlot	Napa	D	87
1995	Merlot	Napa	D	88

1994 Merlot	Napa	C	88
1993 Merlot	Napa	C	89
1997 Sauvignon Blanc	Napa	C	85
1997 Vin de Mistral Le Mistral	Napa	D	87
1996 Vin de Mistral Le Mistral	Napa	D	88
1996 Vin de Mistral Muscat	Napa	C	90
1997 Vin de Mistral Syrah	Napa	D	(88–90)
1996 Vin de Mistral Syrah	Napa	D	90
1995 Vin de Mistral Syrah	Napa	D	86?
1994 Vin de Mistral Syrah	Napa	C	89+
1993 Vin de Mistral Syrah	Napa	C	90
1997 Vin de Mistral Viognier	Napa	D	87

The 1997 Sauvignon Blanc, which sees a touch of barrel fermentation, and little malolactic, is a straightforward, clean, light-bodied, round Sauvignon with vague notions of figs and melons. Drink it over the next year. Both the 1997 Delice du Semillon and 1997 Johannisberg Riesling Select Late Harvest are decadently rich, unctuous, exceptionally pure and sweet wines that will thrill nectar lovers. The 1997 Delice du Semillon resembles a full-bodied Sauternes, whereas the 1997 Johannisburg Riesling recalls a trockenbeerenauslese. Both wines should drink well for another decade.

The 1997 Vin de Mistral Viognier (100% Viognier) comes from vineyard sources in Carneros, Yountville, and St. Helena. It is a light- to medium-bodied Viognier, with honeysuckle and peachlike notes in the aromatics and flavors, good fruit, but little complexity. Consume it over the next year.

The Vin de Mistral Le Mistral is a Côtes du Rhône-like blend of Grenache, Syrah, Mourvèdre, Carignane, Petite Sirah, Alicante, and Syrah. The dark ruby-colored 1996 Le Mistral is a gutsy, bistro red with an exotic nose of incense, peppers, red and black fruits, and perfume. While it is not complex, and is displaying less fat than when I tasted it in 1997, it remains a fun, delicious wine to enjoy over the next 7–8 years. The more alcoholic 1997 Le Mistral is red and black fruit-driven, with less spice than the 1996. The 1997 possesses excellent glycerin and ripeness, and a gutsy, exuberant, cherry/strawberry and cassis fruit character. Soft and generous, it is ideal for drinking over the next 5–6 years. About 700–800 cases of both the 1996 and 1997 Vin de Mistral Syrah were produced. The 1996 Vin de Mistral Syrah is a sexy, lush, opulently styled wine revealing more precociousness and early charm than I predicted a year ago. Aged in both American and French oak, it possesses a dark ruby/purple color, a spicy, bacon fat, cassis, and blackberry-scented nose, soft, lush flavors, and a heady, concentrated finish. It is best drunk during its first 10–12 years of life. The full-bodied, powerful 1997 Vin de Mistral Syrah is more alcoholic, with a peppery, black currant-scented nose. While there is more tannin and glycerin in the 1997, it does not possess the 1996's forward charms. Given the way the 1996 evolved over the last 12 months, I would not be surprised to see the 1997 put on additional weight, in addition to becoming more supple. It is a candidate for drinking during its first 10–12 years of life.

All three vintages of Merlot were more similar than different. The 1997 Merlot offers the most expressive aromatics, sweetest fruit, and the lushest, most generous personality, with plenty of chocolate and berry fruit, as well as the highest degree of alcohol (about 14.1%). The 1996 Merlot (which includes 5%–10% Cabernet Sauvignon in the blend) is the most tannic, revealing mint and a more masculine, structured style. Dense and chewy, it will pro-

vide excellent drinking during its first 7–10 years of life. In contrast, the 1995 Merlot is neither as fat or ripe as the 1997, nor as structured as the 1996. It exhibits a saturated dark
ruby color, followed by a soft, friendly personality with copious quantities of chocolate,
licorice, and smoky, berry fruit intermixed with tobacco and dried herbs. Lush, full bodied,
and chewy, this wine should drink well for another decade.

Among the three Cabernet Sauvignon vintages, I preferred the 1995. Although the 1996
matches the former wine in terms of intensity, it had just been bottled when I tasted it, and
seemed muted and closed. The 1997 looks very fine, but more forward and round. The 1995
Cabernet Sauvignon spent 16 months in cask (primarily French oak), and was bottled with
minimal filtration. It exhibits a dark ruby/purple color, as well as an attractive black cherry,
cassis, and dried herb-scented nose with spicy oak. Rich, full bodied, and concentrated, it
offers plenty of cassis fruit and a chewy style. It can be drunk or cellared for 15+ years. More
structured, tannic, and dense, the 1996 Cabernet Sauvignon requires patience. Most readers
will prefer to drink the 1995 or 1997 than the more backward 1996. The 1996 reveals a saturated ruby/purple color, low acidity, and plenty of tannin and muscle in the brawny finish.
Anticipated maturity: 2000–2015. The plump, rich, round, evolved 1997 Cabernet Sauvignon is a treat to drink. Whether it develops more complexity remains to be seen, but there
is no doubting this vintage has produced wines with splendid fruit, evolved aromatics, and
silky, seductive personalities. This 1997 should drink well when released and last for 10–12
years.

Readers should be paying particular attention to Phelps' Backus Vineyard Cabernet
Sauvignon. This is a 100% Cabernet, aged completely in French oak for 18–22 months. It
comes from a 6.75-acre vineyard situated adjacent to some of the great Napa Valley vineyards of Dalla Valle, Plumpjack, Groth, the Venge Family Reserve, and Screaming Eagle.
This vineyard is being expanded to 22 acres, so the production (about 600 cases) will be increasing in 4–5 years. As for current and upcoming vintages, the 1995 Cabernet Sauvignon
Backus Vineyard is a wine of great intensity. A massive, saturated black/purple-colored example, it offers an intriguing bouquet and flavors of prunes, black currants, roasted herbs,
chocolate, and coffee, huge amounts of glycerin and body, and a gigantic, oversized finish
with considerable tannin. This is one wine where the extract level matches the tannin's ferocity, but readers looking for something to cuddle up with over the near-term should be advised that it needs 5–6 years of cellaring. Anticipated maturity: 2003–2025. The 1996
Cabernet Sauvignon Backus Vineyard is a tremendous wine, but it suffers in contrast to its
older and younger siblings. The saturated ruby/purple color is accompanied by aromas of
vanillin, minerals, kirsch, and cassis. The wine is full bodied, with impressive, palate-
staining richness. Yet compared to the 1995 or 1997, it comes across as monolithic. With a
30+-second finish, the 1996 is a macho, weighty wine with considerable tannin. It requires
another 5–7 years in the cellar, and should easily last for 3 decades. The creamier-textured,
more opulent and seductive 1997 Cabernet Sauvignon Backus Vineyard will be far more delicious in its youth than any of this vineyard's previous vintages. The fruit is sweeter and
more developed, and the aromatics more evolved than in either the 1996 or 1995. The 1997
displays a saturated purple color, gobs of creamy-textured blackberry and black currant
fruit, superb purity, good structure, and a voluptuously textured, long finish lasting for more
than 35 seconds. Unless it closes down in the aging process, it will be the most seductive
Backus Vineyard Cabernet Sauvignon I have yet tasted. It should drink well for 20–25 years.

Joseph Phelps is doing a phenomenal job with their Insignia. The winery produces
10,000–12,000 cases of this proprietary red wine, all of it aged in 100% new oak. Vintages
since 1991 have been superb. Perhaps the best back-to-back vintages ever produced of Insignia are the 1994 and 1995, which rival the great Insignias made in 1974 and 1976. The
1994 Insignia (a blend of 88% Cabernet Sauvignon, 10% Merlot, and 2% Cabernet Franc) is
spectacular. I have had the wine a half-dozen or more times, and it is unquestionably opu-

lent, sexy, flamboyant, explosively rich, concentrated, and a thrill to drink. Already gorgeous, it promises to evolve gracefully for 2 decades or more. The color is a healthy saturated dark purple. The spicy nose offers aromas of black currants, allspice, *pain grillé*, and soy, with scents of a burning wood fire thrown in for additional complexity. This full-bodied, opulent, dazzling wine is exhilarating to drink. The 1995 Insignia may be slightly better—as hard as that is to believe. The final blend is 90% Cabernet Sauvignon, 7% Merlot, and 3% Petit Verdot. The 1995 exhibits a character similar to the 1994—cassis, fruitcake, cedar, herbs, coffee, and black fruits intermixed with smoke—but the 1995 is slightly longer in the mouth. It is a wine of extraordinary extraction, full body, and marvelously pure fruit. Moreover, it has managed to soak up the 100% new oak aging, leaving only subtle *pain grillé* notes. The tannin may be slightly more noticeable in the 1994, but my instincts suggest the 1995 is even richer and longer than the 1994—as amazing as that sounds. This prodigious Insignia should be at its best over the next 20–25 years. Only 7,000 cases were produced of the 1996 Insignia (a blend of 83% Cabernet Sauvignon and 17% Merlot). Although it is a notch below the 1995 and 1994, it is a topflight effort. With a saturated ruby/purple color, and a monolithic, structured personality, it possesses aromas and flavors of Asian spices, coffee, fruitcake, cedar, and crème de cassis. The wine's structure, tannin, and weightier feel suggest a brawnier, more muscular wine without the explosive personality and seductive charms of its two predecessors. A terrific, highly extracted effort, the 1996 should be at its finest between 2000–2020. Lastly, I tasted all the component parts that will compose the 1997 Insignia. And guess what—it looks to be on a par with both the 1994 and 1995. Its alcohol level is slightly high (exceeding 14%), and the pH is in the 3.7 range (much like a great vintage of Bordeaux). This should be a sensational, seductive Insignia with many of the same characteristics exhibited by the 1994 and 1995, but my instincts suggest it has more glycerin, lower acidity, and a creamier mouth-feel. Stay tuned.

While Phelps has a well-deserved reputation for their Vin de Mistral series, and a splendid portfolio of red wines, this winery has made significant progress with their Chardonnay program. I remember the days when the Chardonnays were rather bland and insipid, but that has all changed. For example, the 1997 Chardonnay Carneros exhibits a Burgundian, smoky, lees character with copious quantities of honeyed citrus and tangerine notes. It is a medium-bodied, deliciously fruity wine for consuming during its first 1–2 years of life. The flagship Chardonnay, called Ovation, is a serious wine made in the style of a grand cru white Burgundy. It is given full lees stirring, 14 months of aging in Louis Latour barrels, and is bottled without filtration. Limited quantities of 1,500 cases are produced. The 1996 Chardonnay Ovation is a viscous, full-bodied, concentrated wine with aromas of smoked nuts, white peaches, and honeyed citrus fruit. Ripe, multidimensional, chewy, and exceptionally complex, this could easily pass for a top grand cru from Puligny- or Chassagne-Montrachet. It should drink well for 2–3 years. The 1997 Chardonnay Ovation is a large-scaled, smoky, leesy, Burgundian-styled wine with copious quantities of toasty oak, and honeyed white peach and citrus fruit. Rich in glycerin, high in alcohol, and mouth-filling, it should drink well for 2–3 years.

The 1994 Le Mistral is a 30% Mourvèdre, 20% Syrah, 30% Grenache, and 20% Petite Sirah blend that should prove to be outstanding. The wine offers up a knockout, peppery, sweet, jammy, black raspberry-scented nose followed by a luscious, viscous texture, full body, and outstanding ripeness with no hard tannin or astringency. It will provide a savory, large-scaled, fleshy glassful of wine. Readers should think of it as California's answer to Châteauneuf du Pape. The 1995 Le Mistral exhibits a deep opaque purple color, a wonderfully expressive, sweet, peppery, raspberry-scented nose, full body, sweet tannin, and excellent layered richness and length. The wine is already accessible but promises to be even better with 2–3 years of cellaring. It should keep for a decade or more. Le Mistral is Joseph Phelps' answer to Bonny Doon's Le Cigare Volant, but is, in my opinion, slightly superior.

Another top-notch, reasonably priced Vin du Mistral is the 1993 Le Mistral, mostly Grenache, but with some Petite Sirah, Mourvèdre, Syrah, and Carignan in the blend. California's answer to a big, rich, fleshy Rhône wine, it exhibits a deep ruby color, a lot of pepper, black cherry, and raspberry fruitiness, full body, some fatness and chewiness, and a lusty, heady finish. It is a mouth-filling, rich wine for drinking over the next 4–5 years.

There is no doubt in my mind that Phelps' Vin de Mistral Syrah has lagged behind Le Mistral. The 1995 Vin de Mistral Syrah (700 cases produced from vineyards in Carneros and Yountville) appears to be the second consecutive high-quality wine produced from this grape. Although not as expressive as the 1994 or 1996, the 1995 is a structured, closed wine that I may have caught during a difficult period. The wine reveals an opaque purple color, peppery, sweet blackberry fruit, and considerable tannin, but it sags a bit in the midpalate, and possesses an aggressive finish. While it will age well, whether it will fill out remains debatable. Certainly it is a very good wine, but it requires 3–4 years of cellaring; it should keep for 15 years. The dark purple-colored 1994 Vin de Mistral Syrah is fatter and richer than the 1995. It offers up a smoky, cassis, spicy, peppery-scented nose, dense, full-bodied flavors, excellent sweetness of fruit, and a rich, expansive, chewy texture. The tannin is well concealed by the wine's fruit. This Syrah should improve for 2–6 years and drink well for 10–12.

The 1993 appears to be the finest Syrah Joseph Phelps has made under their Vin du Mistral series. It reveals a deep, thick-looking, purple color, a superripe, jammy nose of red and black fruits and spice. Gorgeously rich and opulent, with a layered texture, high glycerin, and extract, this silky, voluptuously textured wine should drink well for 7–8 years.

The 1996 Chardonnay Carneros is an elegant, attractive, medium-bodied, Burgundian-styled wine with smoky, honeyed citrus, and hazelnutlike flavors, fine spice, crisp, delineating acidity, and an attractive finish. It will drink well for 2–3 years.

Approximately 800 cases of the 1995 Chardonnay Ovation were made. This lavishly rich, barrel-fermented, 100% malolactic style of Chardonnay offers a fine imitation of a grand cru white Burgundy. Bottled without filtration, this impressively built, powerful, concentrated wine exhibits that leesy, smoky, hazelnut, ripe, buttery fruit component found in a top Côte d'Or Chardonnay, adequate acidity, plenty of glycerin and richness, and a long finish. The purity and underlying acidity give the wine freshness and balance. It should drink well for 4–5 years, perhaps longer.

Nectar maniacs can get a fix with two wines from the Phelps portfolio. The 1995 Delice du Semillon is a powerful Sauternes-like wine with gobs of buttery pineapplelike fruit intermixed with toasty new oak. Unctuously textured, thick, and sweet, it possesses enough acidity to bring everything into focus. These wines have a tendency to age well, and this offering should easily last for a decade. Readers who prefer sweet wines with no new oak, extremely low alcohol, as well as high levels of residual sugar, should check out the 1995 Eisrebe-Scheurebe, a trockenbeerenauslese-styled wine with 23% residual sugar and 7.5% alcohol. This is a syrupy wine that should offer extraordinary drinking for 5–8 years. Very viscous, with refreshing levels of acidity, this is an impressive effort.

In spite of Phelps' worthy efforts with respect to its Mistral portfolio and excellent Chardonnays and sweet wines, this winery's international reputation is built on their Merlot and Cabernet Sauvignon. The 1993 Insignia Proprietary Red Wine is made from 80% Cabernet Sauvignon and 20% Merlot. The wine continues to exhibit spectacular richness, and is even stronger from bottle than it was from cask. It boasts an opaque purple/black color, and a fabulous nose of Asian spices, sweet, toasty oak, black fruits, and minerals. This highly extracted, huge, full-bodied wine possesses great sweetness and ripeness of fruit, an expansiveness to its flavors, and a blockbuster finish. A great Insignia, it rated even higher than the 1992.

A wine not to be forgotten in all the hoopla over the Insignia is the Backus Vineyard Cabernet Sauvignon, situated in a high-rent neighborhood. Sadly, only 600 cases are produced. With several years in the bottle, the 1993 Cabernet Sauvignon Backus Vineyard has become an extraordinary wine. It boasts an opaque purple color, followed by a fabulous nose of licorice, jammy black cherry, cassis fruit, minerals, and smoke. Powerful, full bodied, moderately tannic yet exceptionally well endowed, this wine needs another 2–4 years of cellaring; it will keep for 20+ years. I believe the 1994 Cabernet Sauvignon Backus Vineyard is the finest wine this vineyard has yet produced. Phelps' 1994 Backus exhibits an opaque black/purple color, and huge, sweet aromatics consisting of jammy black cherry and cassis fruit, minerals, smoke, and a hickorylike barbecue spice. The wine is thick and super-extracted, with huge proportions of fruit, extract, and tannin. A gargantuan Cabernet Sauvignon, it demands 5–6 years of cellaring and should last for 20–25 years.

Another wine that readers should not forget is Joseph Phelps' Merlot. This wine has improved significantly in quality, and is now one of the stars of Napa. The 1993 Merlot is a thick, lush, nicely textured, dark purple-colored wine with attractive smoky, chocolatey, berry fruit, and a soft, husky, richly fruity finish. Drink it over the next 7–8 years. An excellent Merlot, the dark ruby/purple-colored 1994 offers plenty of sweet, jammy, chocolatey, black cherry fruit in its moderately intense aromatics. The wine is medium bodied, soft, and succulent, with low acidity, copious amounts of fruit, and good ripeness. Drink this delicious, lush Merlot over the next 2–4 years.

The 1994 Cabernet Sauvignon Napa (a blend of 95% Cabernet Sauvignon, 4% Cabernet Franc, and 1% Merlot) appears to be one of the finest regular Cabernet Sauvignon cuvées Phelps has produced since the terrific 1975. It will be interesting to see if the 1994 outperforms Phelps' beautiful 1993 Cabernet Sauvignon Napa. For now, I give a one-point edge to the 1993, but perhaps that is only because the wine has had an additional year in bottle. The 1994 is a deep ruby/purple-colored wine with a sweet, ripe, black fruit, vanillin, and underbrush-scented nose, medium to full body, a layered texture, adequate acidity, and sweet tannin in the finish. The wine is mouth-filling, pure, and impressive.

R. H. PHILLIPS VINEYARD (YOLO)

1996 Chardonnay Barrel Cuvée Dunnigan Hills	Yolo County	A	86
1997 Sauvignon Blanc Night Harvest	Dunnigan Hills	A	86

A consistently delicious wine from R. H. Phillips, this light-bodied, citrusy, melony, fresh, lively 1997 Sauvignon Blanc is dry, richly fruity, and a delight to drink. It should be consumed over the next year. This is an attractive, tropical fruit-based, medium-bodied 1996 Chardonnay with good purity, and a lively style. Although not complex, it is well made, with enough Chardonnay flavor to satisfy most readers. Drink it over the next 8–12 months.

PINE RIDGE WINERY (NAPA)

1995 Andrus Reserve	Napa	EE	90
1994 Andrus Reserve Proprietary Red Wine	Napa	EE	90+
1993 Cabernet Franc Trois Cuvées	Napa	D	87
1995 Cabernet Sauvignon	Howell Mountain	D	87
1994 Cabernet Sauvignon	Howell Mountain	D	90
1993 Cabernet Sauvignon	Howell Mountain	D	92
1995 Cabernet Sauvignon	Rutherford	C	85
1994 Cabernet Sauvignon	Rutherford	C	88
1995 Cabernet Sauvignon	Stag's Leap District	D	84
1994 Cabernet Sauvignon	Stag's Leap District	D	89

1993 Cabernet Sauvignon	Stag's Leap District	D	90+
1996 Chardonnay Dijon Clones Stag's Leap District	Napa	D	90
1995 Merlot	Carneros	D	86
1995 Merlot	Carneros	D	82+?
1994 Merlot	Carneros	D	88

Winemaker/proprietor Gary Andrus is frequently hitting the bull's-eye. If readers have not followed Pine Ridge's recent releases, they should give these wines a try, as just about everything has increased significantly in quality. Most of the following wines were bottled without fining or filtration.

The 1993 Cabernet Sauvignon Stag's Leap District displays black olive, spice, herb, and cherry/cassis fruit, wonderful richness allied to considerable elegance, outstanding intensity, and overall grace and balance. It is an attractive wine for drinking over the next 15+ years. For those with considerable patience, the 1993 Cabernet Sauvignon Howell Mountain is the most backward, formidably tannic wine of this trio. It exhibits an opaque ruby/purple color, a tight but promising nose of minerals and black fruits, dense, full-bodied flavors, and significant tannic clout in the finish. It requires cellaring until the turn of the century and should last for 20 years thereafter.

All of the following Pine Ridge Cabernets will benefit from 2–3 years of cellaring. They are made in a medium-weight, somewhat austere Bordeaux style. The excellent 1994 Cabernet Sauvignon Rutherford reveals a classic black currant, *pain grillé* nose, medium body, high tannin, wonderful elegance, and a measured, rich fruit character that is pronounced, but never excessive. The wine finishes with a bite of tannin. While accessible, 2–4 years of cellaring will be beneficial. This wine should age well for 15 or more years. The refined 1994 Cabernet Sauvignon Stag's Leap District boasts a dark ruby/purple color, followed by a spicy, vanillin, herb, mineral, and black currant-scented nose. In the mouth, there are more red than black currants, as well as rich, pure, long, medium-bodied flavors that exhibit exceptional purity and equilibrium. The tannin should gradually fall away to reveal a quintessentially elegant style of Napa Cabernet Sauvignon. Anticipated maturity: 2001–2016. Pine Ridge's 1994 Cabernet Sauvignon Howell Mountain needs at least 5–6 years of cellaring. It possesses a saturated purple color, and a Bordeaux-like nose of black fruits, licorice, minerals, and cedar. Tannic and reserved, with intense richness and concentration, this is a medium- to full-bodied, large-scaled, unevolved 1994 Cabernet that should prove to be outstanding for those with enough discipline to wait it out. Anticipated maturity: 2003–2020. Cut from a similar cloth, the 1994 Andrus Reserve exhibits a dark saturated plum/purple color, followed by a tight nose of cedar, vanillin, and praline-tinged cassis fruit. Extremely dense and rich, with a more backward and tannic personality than even the Howell Mountain cuvée, this well-delineated, full-bodied wine will need—yes—a full decade of cellaring. It is a 25–30-year wine, but patience is essential. Anticipated maturity: 2006–2030.

Pine Ridge's 1994 Merlot exhibits a good dark ruby color, attractive spicy notes, a monolithic aromatic dimension, and admirable weight, brightness, and purity. My instincts suggest the wine is closed, but I liked its purity of fruit, depth, and ripeness. I would not be surprised to see this Merlot merit a higher score after it receives some bottle age. It should drink well for a decade. The 1995 Merlot needs to flesh out and develop more richness to merit a higher score. At present, it offers an appealing vanilla, chocolate, berry fruitiness, but it is hollow in the mouth with tart acids, and a crisp, lean finish. Although pleasant and correctly made, it is essentially a one-dimensional wine to drink over the next 5–7 years.

The high level of harsh tannin in the 1995 Cabernet Sauvignon Stag's Leap dominates what appears to be good but uninspiring levels of ripe curranty fruit intermixed with spicy, toasty oak. The wine is medium bodied and elegant, but astringent and potentially austere. Perhaps more bottle age will add flesh to this wine, but I am suspicious. The finest wine of this trio is the 1995 Cabernet Sauvignon Howell Mountain. It possesses the deepest purple color, as well as the sweetest nose (aromas of *pain grillé,* smoke, black currants, herbs, and earth), medium to full body, excellent, possibly outstanding concentration, and the potential to evolve for 12–15+ years. This wine will, however, require patience as its tannin level suggests 3–5 years of cellaring will be necessary.

Made in an austere Bordeaux-like style, Pine Ridge's 1993 Cabernet Franc Trois Cuvées possesses good spice, a menthol, curranty fruitiness, medium body, not much weight, but considerable finesse and elegance. Although soft enough to be drunk now, the wine's balance augurs for another 7–8 years of drinkability. Quite classy!

The attractive 1995 Merlot (a blend of 95% Merlot, 3% Malbec, and 2% Cabernet Sauvignon) is an elegant, Bordeaux-inspired wine with well-integrated toasty oak, sweet cherry/kirschlike fruit, medium body, soft, ripe tannin, and nicely integrated acidity. Its elegance and suppleness will be best appreciated over the following 5–6 years. A blend of 84% Cabernet Sauvignon, 8% Merlot, 6% Petit Verdot, and 2% Malbec, the 1995 Cabernet Sauvignon Rutherford is a more compact, tannic wine that has not yet begun to open. The moderate dark ruby color is followed by aromas of cedar, herbs, black currants and spice. There is good texture, moderate tannin, and a plump sweetness in the finish. Although not complex, it will offer attractive drinking over the next 4–5 years. A classic Bordeaux-(Médoc) styled wine, the 1995 Andrus Reserve exhibits a dark ruby/purple color, followed by attractive aromas and flavors of lead pencil, spice, cedar, and black currants. While it is moderately tannic, medium bodied, with outstanding concentration and purity, the wine remains tight and backward. It requires 3–4 years of cellaring and should keep for at least 15. It is an impressively elegant, finesse-styled proprietary red wine from Pine Ridge.

The limited-bottling (7,800 bottles) 1996 Chardonnay Dijon Clones is made from Chardonnay clones from France's Côte d'Or. The wine is tightly knit, but oh, so promising. The light to medium straw color is followed by scents of butter, hazelnuts, smoke, and leesy notes. Medium to full bodied with well-integrated acidity, this complex, pure, well-endowed Chardonnay can only get better over the next 6–12 months. It should keep for 3–4 years.

PLUMPJACK (NAPA)

1997 Cabernet Sauvignon Estate	Oakville	E	(90–92)
1996 Cabernet Sauvignon Estate	Oakville	E	87
1995 Cabernet Sauvignon Estate	Oakville	D	91
1997 Cabernet Sauvignon Reserve	Oakville	E	(92–95)
1995 Cabernet Sauvignon Reserve	Oakville	E	95+
1997 Chardonnay Reserve	Oakville	D	85

The goal of this winery, which sits on the premises of the former Villa Mt. Eden, is to gradually build its production to 10,000 cases. Production in 1998 is projected to be about 7,500 cases. The principal wine is Cabernet Sauvignon, but there is also Chardonnay and a small quantity of so-so Sangiovese. The wines are made by Nils Venge, who is located down the street. The 1997 Chardonnay Reserve (made from purchased fruit) is put through partial malolactic fermentation, then aged in 100% new oak. It is a good, straightforward Chardonnay with tropical fruit notes (primarily pineapple), fine purity, medium body, and a moderately intense bouquet. Although it will not win any prizes for being supercomplex or profoundly rich, it is a well-made Chardonnay.

In 1996, there is no Reserve Cabernet Sauvignon. As the winery explained, all the grapes came in at the same time and were equally fine, so nothing needed to be culled out. Aged in

100% new oak, the 1996 Cabernet Sauvignon is an elegant, stylish, black currant-scented wine with good flavor and richness, medium body, and an attractive spiciness. Offering black fruits and plenty of *pain grillé*, it is a good effort. Anticipated maturity: 2001–2015. In 1997, there are two cuvées, a regular Cabernet and Reserve. I thought both wines were far more fragrant, seamless, and complete than the beefy but angular 1996. The 1997 Cabernet Sauvignon exhibits a saturated, dense ruby/purple color, and impressive aromatics consisting of crème de cassis, *pain grillé*, and soil scents. The wine is full bodied, with outstanding fruit richness, fine purity, and a long, spicy, well-balanced finish. Already more accessible than the more noticeably tannic 1996, the 1997 should age nicely for 15+ years. The blockbuster 1997 Cabernet Sauvignon Reserve (approximately 250 cases) is a powerful, ultraconcentrated wine that should have 20–25 years of aging potential. The wine boasts an opaque purple color, followed by a stunning bouquet of flowers, black currants, minerals, and toasty oak. Rich and powerful, but neither heavy-handed nor overdone, this full-bodied wine reveals exceptional fruit purity and flavor extraction, sweet tannin, and enough acidity to give it vibrancy and delineation. Anticipated maturity: 2002–2022.

The 1995 Cabernet Sauvignon Estate, made by winemaker Tuck Beckstoffer with backup consulting from nearby neighbor Nils Venge of Saddleback Cellars, is a highly extracted, extremely rich, full-bodied Cabernet that will win many fans. Approximately 1,000 cases were produced of this dense purple-colored wine that reveals a ripe prune and cassis-scented nose with lavish smoky oak. Full bodied, deep, and chewy, with sweet tannin and plenty of extract and glycerin, this is an impressively endowed, supple style of Cabernet Sauvignon that should drink well for 10–15+ years. The 1995 Cabernet Sauvignon Reserve (approximately 500 cases produced) is an awesome wine that tastes like a synthesis in style of some of the richest, most powerful Cabernets from the Oakville district. It may come closest in style to resembling the profound Cabernets of Harlan Estate. This spectacular Cabernet Sauvignon is a worthy candidate for 20–30 years of cellaring. The opaque black/purple color is followed by intense aromatics offering smoke, coffee, roasted meats, and copious quantities of blackberry and cassis fruit. Extremely dense, full bodied, and crammed with extract, this persuasively rich, authoritative Cabernet Sauvignon is among the most noteworthy wines of the 1995 vintage. While it can be drunk young, this wine begs for 5–6 years of cellaring. It will be a long-distance runner, although I am not sure how many readers will be able to ignore its lavish display of decadent levels of ripe fruit and toasty oak.

PRESTON VINEYARDS (SONOMA)

1996 Cuvée de Fumé (Sauvignon Blanc)	Dry Creek Valley	B	85
1995 Cuvée de Fumé	Dry Creek	B	86
1993 Faux Proprietary Red Wine	Dry Creek	B	87
1994 Gamay Beaujolais	Dry Creek	B	86
1994 Zinfandel Estate	Dry Creek	B	88
1993 Zinfandel Estate Old Vines/Old Clones	Dry Creek Valley	B	88
1995 Zinfandel Old Vines/Old Clones	Dry Creek Valley	C	87

It is refreshing to see a winery that believes wine is synonymous with fun. From the colorful labels and capsules, to the wine's themselves, there is an obvious conviction at Preston Vineyards that wine is a beverage of pleasure. These releases from Preston will deliver some inexpensive thrills. The dark-colored 1994 Gamay Beaujolais is loaded with rich, strawberry and cherry fruit. Medium bodied, crisp, and fresh, it will offer delightful drinking over the next year with anything from pizza and hamburgers, to steak au poivre. The 1993 Faux is a Rhone Valley-inspired, fleshy, smooth-as-silk, smoky, berry, herb, and peppery-scented red wine with gobs of fruit, medium body, and a satiny-textured finish. It is best drunk over the next 12 months. Don't hesitate to serve either of these wines slightly chilled.

The 1996 Cuvée de Fumé, an attractive blend of Sauvignon Blanc (83%) and Semillon (17%), exhibits an herbaceous, flinty, spicy nose, good fruit, and a chewy, round texture. Effusively fruity and soft, it can be drunk over the next year. The well-priced 1995 Cuvée de Fumé (also an 83% Sauvignon Blanc/17% Semillon blend) is a deliciously fruity, exuberant, dry wine with fig, melony, and herb-flavored fruit, good flesh and ripeness, and a medium-bodied, crisp finish. Drink it over the next year.

The attractive, dark plum-colored 1995 Zinfandel is soft and ripe, with a sweet, fragrant nose of jammy fruit and underbrush, heady alcohol, and an easygoing, lush, up-front style. Unlike many 1995s, the wine's delicious fruitiness is not marred by sharp acid or astringent tannin. Drink it over the next 2–3 years.

An authentic-tasting Zinfandel from Dry Creek, Preston's 1994 exhibits peppery, briery, berry fruit, medium to full body, attractive sweetness on the attack, and an excellent mid-palate and finish. Drink it over the next 5–6 years. Excellent value.

The 1993 Zinfandel Estate Old Vines/Old Clones is one of the vintage's most sexy, lush, and velvety-textured Zinfandels. It reveals a healthy, medium to dark ruby color, and a forceful, enticing, sweet, berry-scented nose with evidence of wood and spice. Round, deep, full bodied, and supple, this well-proportioned, brawny Zinfandel should be drunk over the next 6–7 years.

PRIDE MOUNTAIN VINEYARD (NAPA)

1996	Cabernet Franc	Sonoma	D	91
1995	Cabernet Franc	Sonoma	C	92
1993	Cabernet Franc	Sonoma	C	88
1995	Cabernet Sauvignon	Napa	C	84
1995	Cabernet Sauvignon Reserve	Napa	E	98
1994	Cabernet Sauvignon Reserve	Napa	E	95+
1996	Merlot	Napa	C	90+
1995	Merlot	Napa	C	82
1993	Merlot	Napa	C	86
1995	Reserve Claret	Napa	E	96
1994	Reserve Claret	Napa	E	95
1993	Reserve Claret	Napa	E	93
1997	Viognier	Sonoma	D	89

This Spring Mountain winery continues to push the envelope of quality as evidenced by the current releases—the finest wines they have yet produced. Moreover, these wines catapult Pride Mountain into the top echelon of California's quality wineries. The 1995 Cabernet Franc is one of the greatest Cabernet Francs I have tasted from California. A blend of 75% Cabernet Franc and 25% Cabernet Sauvignon (400 cases produced), this wine reminded me of the unblended cuvée of Cabernet Franc that usually goes into Dalla Valle's extraordinary proprietary red wine called Maya. For a Cabernet Franc, the wine possesses an uncommonly dense black/purple color, and a sweet nose of licorice, underbrush, red as well as black currants, and toast. Amazingly extracted, yet somehow retaining its elegance, this wine offers the essence of black fruits in its long, rich, medium- to full-bodied flavors. There is enough acidity and some tannin, but the wine's extraordinary purity and equilibrium are hallmarks of this smashing effort. Anticipated maturity: 2000–2016.

Pride Mountain's first Reserve wine, the 1993 Reserve Claret (102 cases produced) is a blend of essentially 50% Cabernet Sauvignon and 50% Merlot, with tiny dollops of Cabernet Franc and Petit Verdot. An awesome wine, it exhibits an opaque plum/purple color, as well as a sweet, rich nose of minerals, smoke, spice, and jammy black currants and plum. Deep, full bodied, and chewy, yet strikingly well defined, this is a fabulous effort that should drink well for 15–20 years. Even better is the 1994 Reserve Claret (98 cases produced). It possesses an opaque purple color, followed by a less-evolved nose with similar underbrush, cassis, smoke, and *pain grillé* notes. Full bodied, superextracted, with layers of ripe fruit, and well-integrated tannin and acidity, this is an enormously endowed, layered wine that unfolds magnificently in the glass and on the palate. Anticipated maturity: 2001–2020.

The 1994 Cabernet Sauvignon Reserve (the first Reserve Cabernet Sauvignon they made) is produced from 100% Cabernet Sauvignon and aged completely in French oak casks. It is another profound Cabernet from the exceptional 1994 vintage. The wine's opaque purple color and huge, massive richness do not come across as heavy, despite the wine's extraordinary intensity and thickness. There is enough acidity for freshness, and plenty of sweet, well-integrated tannin. This large-scaled, magnificently endowed Cabernet Sauvignon needs 5–6 years of cellaring, but it should keep for 25+ years.

I thought the 1995 Merlot and 1995 Cabernet Sauvignon to be more narrowly constructed wines than the other offerings in this impressive portfolio. The 1995 Merlot exhibits a dark ruby/purple color, medium body, and a crisp, high-acid personality with good fruit, but an attenuated finish. It should drink well for 6–7 years. The 1995 Cabernet Sauvignon is tightly knit and dense, with surprisingly high acidity, attractive black currant fruit and minerals, medium body, and moderately high tannin in the tightly compressed finish. This wine will need 2–3 years of cellaring.

The 1996 Cabernet Franc (a blend of 75% Cabernet Franc and 25% Cabernet Sauvignon) has filled out considerably, exhibiting a dense ruby/purple color, followed by a knockout nose of black cherries, herbs, and spice. In the mouth, the wine is rich, with more layers of flavor than I originally noted when I tasted it at the winery. This superb, medium- to full-bodied example is the quintessential Cabernet Franc, offering elegance along with plenty of power and richness. It should drink well for 10–15 years. Another wine that tasted better in mid-July of 1998 than it did at the winery nine months earlier is the 1996 Merlot. A blend of 95% Merlot and 5% Cabernet Sauvignon, it boasts a dense purple color, as well as a beautiful nose of black fruits, smoke, herbs, and underbrush. Thick and full bodied, with terrific fruit, purity, and extraction, this is a deeper, richer, more complete wine than I originally predicted. It should age well for 10–12 years.

The two limited production offerings from Pride Mountain Vineyards are the 1995 Claret Reserve and 1995 Cabernet Sauvignon Reserve. There are 230 cases of the former, and 330 cases of the latter. The fabulous 1995 Claret Reserve (a blend of 64% Cabernet Sauvignon, 33% Merlot, and 3% Petit Verdot) offers an opaque ruby/purple color, and a classic crème de cassis nose intermixed with toasty new oak and minerals. Full bodied, with superb texture, dense, massively rich flavors, and a 40+-second finish, this is a gorgeously made, Bordeaux-styled wine with dazzling levels of fruit and extract. Anticipated maturity: 2000–2015. The 1995 Cabernet Sauvignon Reserve has come of age now that it is in the bottle. This is the essence of North Coast Cabernet Sauvignon, offering portlike thickness and richness, a superb black currant, mineral, cedar, and *pain grillé*-scented nose, full-bodied flavors of extraordinary intensity and overall balance, and a long, moderately tannic, multidimensional finish. Anticipated maturity: 2003–2025. Shame on me for underestimating these beauties!

The 1993 Merlot and 1993 Cabernet Franc from Pride Mountain are classy, well-made wines with considerable character. The medium/dark ruby-colored 1993 Merlot offers an attractive nose of curranty/cherry fruit and spices. Medium bodied and well balanced, with good purity, ripeness, and length, this supple wine should drink well for 5–6 years. Pride's 1993 Cabernet Franc is slightly superior, displaying more elegance as well as a more complex nose of black currants, herbs, and spicy oak. The wine is medium to full bodied, graceful, and rich, but not heavy or noticeably tannic. It should drink well for 7–10 years.

Sadly, Pride Mountain makes little Viognier, but what they do produce is excellent to outstanding. The 1997 may be slightly shorter in the mouth than previous efforts, but it reveals a textbook apricot, honeysuckle, and peach-scented nose, good underlying acidity, lively, fruit-driven, medium- to full-bodied flavors, and considerable volume in the mouth. Drink it over the next year.

QUINTESSA (NAPA)

1995 Proprietary Red Wine	Rutherford	E	87
1994 Proprietary Red Wine	Rutherford	E	89

This luxury cuvée produced from a single vineyard is primarily Cabernet Sauvignon. The 1995 is made in an exceptionally restrained, polite style that is meant to emulate a Bordeaux, but may go too far in terms of delicacy and subtlety. It is an attractive wine, with a dark ruby color, and a moderately intense nose of red/black currants, and spicy new oak. In the mouth, it is elegant and medium bodied, with good richness, moderate tannin, and a pure finish. Subtlety is a worthy goal in winemaking, but this example may err too far in that direction. Already supple and velvety textured enough to drink now, it should age nicely for 7–10 years.

A blend of 39% Cabernet Sauvignon, 31% Merlot, and 30% Cabernet Franc, the dark ruby/purple-colored 1994 possesses an elegant, graceful bouquet (sweet cherries and kirsch) that has been subtly influenced by toasty new oak. The medium-bodied, subtle yet rich, red currant/black currant flavors unfold nicely in the mouth. This is an understated, measured, impeccably well made, claret-styled Cabernet Sauvignon that offers beautiful richness and layers of harmonious flavors. Impressive. Drink it over the next 10–14 years.

QUIVIRA VINEYARDS (SONOMA)

1996 Dry Creek Cuvée	Dry Creek Valley	B	84
1996 Zinfandel	Dry Creek	C	87
1995 Zinfandel	Dry Creek	C	85
1994 Zinfandel	Sonoma	C	88

The 1996 Dry Creek Cuvée, a Rhône-like blend of 62% Grenache, 19% Mourvèdre, 11% Syrah, and 8% Zinfandel, offers peppery, berry fruit, rustic tannin, medium body, and straightforward cherry/berry flavors. A good value, it is ideal for drinking over the next 1–2 years.

Readers looking for lower alcohol, finesse and elegantly styled Zinfandels will find the charming, medium-bodied, midweight 1996 Zinfandel from Quivira appealing. It possesses a moderately saturated ruby color, as well as an elegant nose of sour cherries, spice, and raspberries. A pretty wine with good balance, tangy acidity, and a pure, moderately long finish, it should be drunk in its zesty youth—over the next 2 years.

Quivira's 1995 Zinfandel begins as a textbook tangy, ripe berry and peppery-scented Zinfandel. Yet the wine's sharp acids make their presence known, and the result is a wine that comes across as lean, medium bodied, and compressed. Lamentably, the wine's meagerly endowed flavors are a letdown after the dazzlingly perfumed, textbook bouquet. Drink it over the next 2–3 years. A classically styled Zinfandel, Quivira's 1994 is rich and pure, with plenty of the varietal's briery, peppery, black and red fruit character. There is moderate body, plenty of purity, and a clean, crisp, long finish. It is an attractive, medium-weight Zinfandel for drinking over the next 5–6 years.

QUPÉ WINE CELLARS (SANTA BARBARA)

1996	Chardonnay Reserve Bien Nacido Vineyard	Santa Barbara	D	85
1996	Los Olivos Cuvée (Syrah, Mourvèdre, Grenache)	Santa Barbara	C	87
1997	Marsanne Ibarra-Young Vineyard	Santa Barbara	B	85
1997	Proprietary White Bien Nacido Vineyard	Santa Barbara	C	87
1996	Roussanne Alban Vineyard	Edna Valley	D	89
1993	Syrah	Central Coast	C	87
1997	Syrah Hillside Estate Bien Nacido Vineyard	Santa Barbara	D	(90–92)
1996	Syrah Hillside Estate Bien Nacido Vineyard	Santa Barbara	D	86
1997	Syrah Reserve Bien Nacido Vineyard	Santa Barbara	D	(87–90)
1996	Syrah Reserve Bien Nacido Vineyard	Santa Barbara	D	86
1997	Viognier Ibarra-Young Vineyard	Santa Barbara	D	90

Qupé, one of the original Rhône Rangers, continues to do a fine job with an assortment of varietals. Among the whites, the 1997 Marsanne Ibarra-Young Vineyard is a crisp, fruity, slightly neutral, but refreshingly vibrant, medium-bodied wine with citrusy fruit presented in a straightforward manner. I would opt for drinking it over the near term. More interesting is the 1997 Proprietary White, a blend of 67% Chardonnay and 33% Viognier. It possesses copious quantities of fruit, a floral, honeyed, tropical fruit-dominated personality, excellent freshness, a good palate feel, and a lusty finish. It is amazing how well these two grapes blend, resulting in a hedonistically styled wine. Even better are the 1996 Roussanne Alban Vineyard and 1997 Viognier Ibarra-Young Vineyard. The 1996 Roussanne Alban Vineyard is not a shy wine, tipping the scales at 14.3% alcohol. However, the wine's pure richness, considerable glycerin, and honeyed grapefruit/rose petal-like liqueur hide any notion of hotness. This powerful, deep, concentrated, chewy, dry white will admirably complement poultry and fish dishes. It should drink well for 1–2 years. One of the finest California Viogniers I have tasted is Qupé's 1997 Viognier Ibarra-Young Vineyard (13.5% alcohol). A splendid nose of apricots and peaches is followed by a full-bodied, dry, ripe wine with refreshing acidity, as well as a lively, fruit-driven personality. It should be consumed over the next year.

With respect to the reds, I was unimpressed by the herbaceous, lean, tart 1997 Syrah Central Coast. Far better is the 1996 Syrah Hillside Estate Bien Nacido Vineyard. Medium bodied, richly fruity, and uncomplex, it offers an attractive berry and cassis flavor profile. Made in an accessible, easy-to-understand style, it should drink well for 3–4 years. Another tasty red is the 1996 Los Olivos Cuvée, a blend of Syrah (44%), Mourvèdre (44%), and Grenache (12%). Behaving like a Côtes du Rhône, with plenty of leather and black currant fruit, this dark ruby-colored wine offers pepper, spice, and copious quantities of black fruits in its uncomplicated yet tasty flavor profile. It is a wine to enjoy over the next 4–5 years. Qupé's dark ruby-colored 1996 Syrah Reserve Bien Nacido Vineyard is a good, rich, blackberry, peppery, herb-tinged wine with straightforward berry fruit displayed in a medium-bodied, spicy format. It is a user-friendly Syrah for consuming over the next 4–5 years.

The two 1997 Syrahs are more serious efforts. The 1997 Syrah Reserve Bien Nacido Vineyard possesses a deep ruby/purple color, and plenty of smoky, blackberry fruit intermixed with toast, damp foresty scents, and pepper. The wine exhibits excellent richness, sweet tannin, and a medium- to full-bodied, long finish. It should drink well during its first 7–10 years of life. The most concentrated Syrah in this estate's portfolio is the 1997 Syrah Hillside Estate Bien Nacido Vineyard. It boasts an opaque ruby/purple color, as well as thick, juicy fruit, full body, adequate acidity and tannin, and a powerful, gutsy, earthy finish. Unquestionably the most complete wine among these offerings, this impressively endowed Syrah should hit its stride with 2–3 years of bottle age and last for 10–15.

Qupé's 1993 Central Coast Syrah is not one of those blockbuster, inky-colored, thick monsters but rather, a wine that tastes like it came from a cool climate. It possesses ripe, sweet cherry/cassis flavors that are authentically varietal. Medium bodied, soft, and elegant, this wine comes across a supple style of Syrah, vaguely reminiscent of some St. Josephs from the Rhône Valley. Drink it over the next 3–4 years.

RABBIT RIDGE VINEYARDS WINERY (SONOMA)

1996 Zinfandel	Sonoma	C	86
1994 Zinfandel Olsen Vineyard	Dry Creek	C	89
1996 Zinfandel OVZ Reserve	Sonoma	D	88
1995 Zinfandel OVZ Reserve	Sonoma	D	90
1994 Zinfandel San Lorenzo Reserve	Sonoma	D	91

This noteworthy Zinfandel producer turned out two lavishly wooded, smoky, full-bodied 1996s that should have broad popular appeal. The 1996 Zinfandel is a good value given today's wine pricing. It reveals loads of American oak in the nose, along with smoke, black cherries, and a briery, raspberrylike fragrance. On the palate, the wine exhibits some wood, but the fruit dominates the finish. This is a well-made, straightforward, chunky, robust Zinfandel to drink over the next several years. The 1996 Zinfandel OVZ Reserve is made from over 100-year-old vines. The color is saturated dark purple. The nose offers plenty of toasty, smoky American wood, in addition to jammy kirsch and raspberry fruit. Full bodied (14.9% alcohol), with a lofty glycerin level, this wine has retained its balance and freshness despite its massive size. However, as with many 1996s, there is not much length, so I would opt for consuming it over the next 2–4 years.

One of the vintage's most impressive wines, the dense purple-colored 1995 Zinfandel OVZ Reserve exhibits a glorious nose of jammy black fruits, pepper, and spice. Full bodied, with sufficient fruit, glycerin, and extract to back up the lavish quantities of toasty new oak, this is a lush, plump, rich wine that cascades over the palate with no hard edges. Drink this beauty over the next 3–4 years.

Made from 100-year-old benchland vines in Sonoma County, the 1994 Zinfandel San Lorenzo Reserve is a stunningly rich, deep purple-colored Zinfandel with lavish quantities of toasty new oak, full body, great extract and purity, and a luscious, multilayered finish. It should drink well for 7–8 years. The purple-colored 1994 Zinfandel Olsen Vineyard offers gobs of red and black fruits in a full-bodied, succulent, vanillin, toasty (from new oak barrels) style. Dense and rich, this is a lusty, gutsy, juicy Zinfandel for drinking over the next 3–4 years.

A. RAFANELLI WINERY (SONOMA)

1995 Zinfandel	Dry Creek	C	92
1994 Zinfandel	Dry Creek	C	89
1993 Zinfandel	Dry Creek	C	91

Rafanelli has made so many gorgeous Zinfandels it is hard to say the 1995 Zinfandel Unfiltered is one of their finest, but, wow, I was knocked out by the opaque purple color, as well as the gorgeously pure display of blackberry, raspberry, and cherry fruit. Full bodied, with no hard edges, a voluptuous texture, and layers of fruit, this is a delicious, full-throttle, impeccably well balanced wine that should drink well for another 6–7 years. Kudos to Rafanelli.

Not the superconcentrated heavyweight I would have expected from this vintage, Rafanelli's 1994 is, however, a textbook, richly fruity, peppery, soft, generous, medium-bodied wine with excellent depth and balance. Plenty of sweet black cherry/raspberry, vanillin-tinged fruit slides over the palate with no bumps or bruises. Drink this beauty over the next 3–5 years.

A classic Rafanelli Zinfandel, the 1993 displays a splendid ruby/purple color and an intense fragrance of jammy black raspberries and cherries. With fruit that seemingly explodes, this full-bodied, pure, classy Zinfandel fills the mouth. It should drink well for 5–8 years.

RAMEY (NAPA)

1996 Chardonnay Hyde Vineyard	Carneros/Napa	D	89

This offering is made by David Ramey, formerly at Dominus and Chalk Hill and currently the winemaker at the new Rudd Cellars on Napa's Silverado Trail. Ramey's 1996 Chardonnay Hyde Vineyard is still tight, and I would not be surprised to see it gain an extra point or two with a few more months of bottle age. The wine is fermented with native yeasts, given 14 months *sur-lie* aging for 21 months in barrel, and bottled unfiltered. This is a medium- to full-bodied, expressive, light gold-colored Chardonnay that offers attractive lemony, pear, citrus, and honeyed notes along with plenty of smoky oak. Purely made, with a good texture and a spicy finish, it will improve for another year and last for 2–3, possibly longer.

RAVENSWOOD WINERY (SONOMA)

1995 Merlot Sangiacomo	Sonoma	C	86
1994 Merlot Sangiacomo	Sonoma	B	88?
1993 Merlot Sangiacomo	Sonoma	B	90
1995 Pickberry Proprietary Red Wine	Sonoma	D	86?
1994 Pickberry Proprietary Red Wine	Sonoma	D	81
1993 Pickberry Proprietary Red Wine	Sonoma	D	93
1996 Zinfandel	Lodi	B	88
1995 Zinfandel	Napa	C	85
1994 Zinfandel	Napa	C	83
1996 Zinfandel	Sonoma	C	87
1995 Zinfandel	Sonoma	C	88
1994 Zinfandel	Sonoma	C	86
1993 Zinfandel Belloni/Wood Vineyard	Sonoma	C	92+
1996 Zinfandel Cooke Vineyard	Sonoma	C	90
1995 Zinfandel Cooke Vineyard	Sonoma	D	92
1994 Zinfandel Cooke Vineyard	Sonoma	D	89
1993 Zinfandel Cooke Vineyard	Sonoma	D	90
1996 Zinfandel Dickerson Vineyard	Napa	D	85
1995 Zinfandel Dickerson Vineyard	Napa	D	87

1994 Zinfandel Dickerson Vineyard	Napa	D	88
1993 Zinfandel Dickerson Vineyard	Napa	C	87
1996 Zinfandel Monte Rosso Vineyard	Sonoma	D	92
1995 Zinfandel Monte Rosso Vineyard	Sonoma	D	92
1994 Zinfandel Monte Rosso Vineyard	Sonoma	D	87+
1993 Zinfandel Monte Rosso Vineyard	Sonoma	D	91
1995 Zinfandel Old Hill Ranch	Sonoma	D	91+
1994 Zinfandel Old Hill Ranch	Sonoma	D	91+
1993 Zinfandel Old Hill Ranch	Sonoma	D	90+
1996 Zinfandel Old Hill Ranch Limited Edition	Sonoma	D	90
1993 Zinfandel Old Vines	Sonoma	D	87
1996 Zinfandel Vintner's Blend	California	B	85
1994 Zinfandel Wood Road Vineyard	Sonoma	D	90+
1996 Zinfandel Wood Road-Belloni Vineyard	Russian River	D	90
1995 Zinfandel Wood Road-Belloni Vineyard	Russian River	D	90

With Ravenswood's production soaring to nearly 100,000 cases (60% of which is Vintner's Blend Zinfandel and Merlot), it is amazing that proprietor/winemaker Joel Peterson can continue to turn out such intense wines, particularly in view of the cramped cellars in which he must work. The small quantities (only 500–600 cases) of single vineyard Zinfandel he produces continue to be among the most enticing, flavorful and distinctive in California. The 1993s are all excellent to outstanding wines, save for the Dickerson Vineyard, which was not as rich as prior efforts.

Readers are most likely to come across a bottle of the 1993 Old Vines Zinfandel, as there is much more of it than the other cuvées. It exhibits a healthy dark ruby/purple color, a sweet, black cherry, earth and spicy-scented nose, layered, opulent flavors, full body, adequate acidity, and a gutsy, robust finish. It can be drunk now or cellared for 5–6 years. I continue to admire the wines that emerge from the Cooke Vineyard. The 1993 reveals a saturated, plummy/purple color, rich, black raspberry aromas with hints of licorice, truffle, and earth scents, gobs of chewy, unctuously textured fruit that suggests old vines, and a full-bodied, expansive, highly extracted finish. This complex Zinfandel can be drunk over the next 10–12 years. The 1993 Zinfandel Dickerson Vineyard (apparently being replanted) has less color saturation, and less concentration and extract than found in the 1990 and 1991. Typical for this vineyard, the nose offers up a touch of mint, along with other, more Cabernet-oriented aromatics. Delicate and classy, with medium body and good concentration, this is a stylish, compact wine by Ravenswood's standards. Drink it over the next decade.

It must be a sign of the difficult times that the Louis Martini winery is selling Zinfandel grapes from their renowned Monte Rosso vineyard, but it is a bonus for consumers. Ravenswood's 1993 Zinfandel Monte Rosso is a knockout example of what this vineyard can produce. The wine exhibits an opaque purple color, sweet, mineral and black fruit aromas, and adequate acidity. It is a rich, classically structured, powerful, authoritatively flavored wine with layers of fruit, and a moderately tannic, spicy finish. Although delicious, it only hints at what will emerge with 12–18 additional months of cellaring. This silky, structured, well-focused Zinfandel will have many admirers. Drink it over the next 10–12 years. The opaque black/purple-colored 1993 Zinfandel Belloni/Wood Road is the quintessential California Zinfandel with its full-bodied, opulent richness, layers of highly extracted black cherry, black raspberry, and peppery fruit, and noticeably high alcohol accompanying the wine's deep, thick, richness. Because of the vintage's low acidity it is forward, yet enormously rich and intense. Zinfandel does not get much better than this! Drink it over the next decade. Lastly, the 1993 Zinfandel Old Hill offers up a dusty, earthy, spicy nose, followed by rustic, full-bodied, broad-shouldered flavors, a massive, heady, slightly tannic finish, and an uncivilized personality. This rich wine possesses an intriguing texture, but the earthy components, combined with more tannin than the other offerings, make it less flattering to drink. Give it 8–12 months of cellaring and drink it over the following 12+ years.

Ravenswood fashioned an impressive array of distinctive 1994 Zinfandels. Only the Sonoma and Napa offerings were in bottle when I tasted them, although the single vineyard wines were about to be bottled. The 1994 Napa Zinfandel possesses ripe, briery fruit, medium body, a tannic, tart edge, and a good, clean, straightforward style with moderately high alcohol (13.8%). Drink it over the next 2–3 years. The 1994 Sonoma Zinfandel is a fuller-bodied, riper, more alcoholic wine with an additional layer of sweet fruit, an interesting texture, less aggressive acidity, and a longer finish. It should drink well for 4–5 years.

The dark ruby-colored 1994 Zinfandel Dickerson Vineyard exhibits attractive mint and black cherry fruit aromas along with a touch of spice, medium body, a certain austerity and leanness, and good purity. Moderately endowed, this is a restrained yet elegant Zinfandel for drinking over the next 5–6 years. The 1994 Cooke Vineyard Zinfandel reveals an opaque purple color followed by a peppery, smoked meat-scented, dense, rich, concentrated nose, dusty, rich, tannic flavors, surprisingly tart acidity, and admirable depth, fat, and richness in the long finish. This wine is still unresolved and disjointed, but save for the high acidity, all the component parts are impressive, so it should be only a matter of time until this wine develops into an outstanding Zinfandel for consuming over 6–7 years. The opaque purple color of the 1994 Zinfandel Wood Road is more reminiscent of a young Hermitage than Zinfandel. The unformed nose offers some smoky, meaty, peppery, black fruit, and earth characteristics. Crisp acidity (again) suggests a lower pH than one might suspect given the wine's color and richness. Although closed, full-bodied, and cloaked in a tough, tannic structure, the wine is impressively weighty, rich, and pure on the palate. If this were made from another varietal I would recommend 2–3 years of cellaring, but since it is a Zinfandel, it will be much more approachable after bottling, and be ready to drink within a year. It should last for 7–8+ years. The dark ruby/purple-tinted 1994 Monte Rosso Vineyard Zinfandel exhibits good spice, pepper, and rich fruit, as well as a more diffuse palate without the inner core of depth, richness, and delineation of the Wood Road or Cooke Vineyard. It is a lusty, round, generously endowed, well-made Zinfandel for drinking over the next 5–6 years. The opaque purple color of the 1994 Old Hill Zinfandel is followed by a reluctant nose of wonderfully rich, jammy black cherries and loamy, soil-like notes. Sweet and rich on the entry (not from sugar, but grape ripeness), this full-bodied, opulently styled, unctuously textured, dense, concentrated wine should drink well for a decade.

While the 1995 Zinfandel Napa may be the least distinguished of the 1995 Zinfandel offerings from Ravenswood, it is still a delicious, dark ruby-colored, medium-bodied, heady Zinfandel that needs to be drunk over the next 2–3 years. Some dusty tannin lowered my overall score, but this is a well-balanced, clean, peppery, gutsy Zinfandel that fills the mouth with berry fruit, and is faithful to this varietal's characteristics. The 1995 Zinfandel Dickerson Vineyard has more in common with a Cabernet Sauvignon than a Zinfandel. The healthy dark ruby/purple color is followed by a tight but spicy nose that suggests an exciting combination of sweet, ripe, peppery, black cherry fruit intertwined with minerals, spice, and a vague notion of herbs. Classy, stylish, and gracefully built, this authoritatively flavored, medium-bodied Zinfandel needs another 1–2 years of cellaring; it should keep for a decade.

The 1995 Zinfandel Sonoma (14.5% alcohol) is a broadly flavored, mouth-filling, savory wine with Zinfandel's telltale, earthy, peppery, sweet, jammy black cherry-scented aromas, medium to full body, an expansive, chewy texture, and a lusty, high alcohol finish. Already delicious, it should continue to drink well for 6 years.

Zinfandel lovers will be pleased to know there were 3,045 cases produced of the 1995 Zinfandel Wood Road-Belloni, a wine produced from four separate Russian River vineyards (Arata, Belloni, Chelli, and Rue). This nearly opaque purple-colored wine is a powerful, tight, full-bodied, well-structured Zinfandel that is loaded with earthy, dark fruits. Its broodingly backward, yet formidably endowed personality offers spice, jammy black fruits, and plenty of glycerin and alcohol (14.9%). This is a classic, rich, ageworthy Zinfandel that should provide marvelous drinking over the next decade. The 1995 Zinfandel Cooke Vineyard from Sonoma Valley is made in much more limited quantities (435 cases). It offers an explosive nose of licorice, pepper, allspice, black plum and cherry fruit. A great Zinfandel with fabulous concentration, the wine's wealth of fruit and glycerin conceal the lofty alcohol level of 15.2%. Totally dry, this superconcentrated wine reveals none of the late harvest characteristics suggested by its high alcohol and huge size. This is a tour de force in Zinfandel winemaking! Drink it over the next 10–12 years. I also thought the 1995 Zinfandel Old Hill Ranch (865 cases produced from 110-year-old vines) to be an outstanding Zinfandel. Although it is the tightest knit of the Ravenswood offerings, the opaque ruby/purple color, exquisite briery and wild berry-scented nose, full-bodied, powerful flavors, and exceptional purity, texture, and length, all point to a lustrous future for this massive Zin. Give it another 1–2 years of cellaring and drink it between 1999 and 2008.

I was knocked out by the 1995 Zinfandel Monte Rosso Vineyard. This Arnold Schwarzenegger-like Zinfandel (15.4% alcohol; 1,650 cases) screams from the glass with peppery, loamy, black fruitlike scents. On the palate, the wine is huge, with mouth-coating layers of highly extracted fruit allied with chewy glycerin. This opaque purple-colored wine appears to possess 10–15 years of aging potential. It is one of the great wines of the vintage. Kudos to proprietor Joel Peterson for producing a bevy of Zinfandels that are particularly brilliant in view of the overall quality level that has emerged from this vintage.

Not surprisingly, Ravenswood turned out a portfolio of powerful, full-throttle 1996 Zinfandels that live up to the winery's motto, "No Wimpy Wines." The least expensive offering is the 1996 Zinfandel Vintner's Blend. For an introductory Zinfandel with muscle, but not much charm, this medium-bodied, earth and spice-driven wine cuts a broad path on the palate. Although good, it could use a bit more lively fruit. Drink it over the next several years. The hedonistic 1996 Zinfandel Lodi (14.3% alcohol) reveals a southern Rhône-like, peppery, *herbes de Provence, garrigue*-scented nose intermixed with iodine and cherry liqueur. This is an immensely satisfying, rich, expansively flavored wine for consuming over the next 3–4 years. It should blend beautifully with grilled foods. For whatever reason, I have been uninspired by a succession of Dickerson Vineyard offerings. The 1996 Zinfandel Dickerson Vineyard exhibits a vivid ruby color, eucalyptus, pepper, and spice in its light intensity nose, dry, medium-bodied, lean, austere flavors, and a metallic, short finish. New wood is obvious, but this is a high-strung, angular Zinfandel that could use more fat and charm. It should age well for 5–7 years. The attractive, medium- to full-bodied 1996 Zinfandel Sonoma possesses a spicy, licorice, earth, and peppery-scented nose, with cranberry/cherry liqueurlike flavors, some herbaceousness, but plenty of fruit, spice, and robust, exuberant personality. It is a hearty, mouth-filling Zin that boasts 14.5% alcohol. Drink it over the next 3–4 years.

Ravenswood fashioned four exceptional Zinfandels in 1996. The 1996 Zinfandel Old Hill Ranch Limited Edition offers a saturated ruby/purple color, followed by a knockout nose of briery fruit, charcoal, chocolate, and peppery spice. In the mouth, there is some rusticity to the wine's structure, but it provides a full-bodied, exciting combination of blackberry and cherry fruit supported by copious quantities of glycerin, as well as decent acidity. It will offer a compelling mouthful of Zinfandel over the next 5–6 years. The 1996 Zinfandel Cooke Vineyard (14.8% alcohol) exhibits a dense, dark ruby/purple color, a big, dusty, pepper-tinged, cherry liqueur-scented nose, and full-bodied, multilayered flavors with plenty of muscle and length. This viscous wine saturates the palate, and finishes with notes of earth and jammy fruit. Drink it over the next 4–5 years for its exuberance and fiery character. (Readers should note that the 1996 Cooke Vineyard is sold only at the winery's tasting room.) The highly extracted, saturated purple-colored 1996 Zinfandel Wood Road/Belloni Vineyard is a macho Zin in every sense of the word. Not only does it boast nearly 15% alcohol, it possesses explosive richness, and layers of grilled meat, blackberry and cherry liqueurlike flavors that have been heavily spiced, not to mention crammed with glycerin and extract. This knockout Zinfandel is almost *sauvage* (as the French would say), but it is oh, so rich and gutsy. It should drink well for 5–7 years. My favorite of this noteworthy group is the 1996 Zinfandel Monte Rosso. Another powerhouse with 15% natural alcohol, this exquisite example offers a dark saturated plum/purple color. Sweet cedar, iodine, pepper, fruitcake, Rhône-like notes soar from the glass of this fleshy, massive Zin. Huge and rich in the mouth, yet neither coarse nor ponderous, it boasts layers of flavor, outstanding purity and harmony, and a whoppingly long finish. Already delicious, it should be consumed over the next 6–7 years.

Given this winery's history of past performances, neither the 1995 Merlot Sangiacomo or the 1995 Pickberry performed as well as I expected. The medium-bodied 1995 Merlot Sangiacomo offers up-front, sweet, chocolatey, toasty, smoky, berry aromas and flavors. It provides sweet fruit on the attack, but then falls off, revealing less than stellar extraction, depth, and overall harmony. The wine offers pleasure on the front of the palate, but there is little follow-through. I would opt for drinking it over the next 5–7 years. I have enjoyed some brilliant examples of Ravenswood's Pickberry, but the 1995 does not appear to be one of them. Although it is a very good wine, the tart, high acid level makes me suspicious of an overzealous acid adjustment, and the raw new oak, which has not yet meshed with the fruit, is off-putting. Nevertheless, the wine exhibits a deep ruby/purple color, attractive sweet, smoky, herb-tinged, black cherry, and black currant aromas and flavors, medium body, and an elegant, polished style. Neither of these wines appear to be of the same high quality as previous releases from top vintages.

The 1994 Merlot Sangiacomo exhibits a deep, plummy color, and a pruny nose, suggesting considerable overripeness, intermingled with strong aromas of new oak. Although disjointed and clumsy at present, this wine possesses plenty of extract, body, and length, but it is not yet fully knitted together. Hard tannin in the finish is also unintegrated. Wines go through different stages, so this is hardly a definitive look at this Merlot from one of California's most accomplished wineries.

I had severe reservations about the 1994 Pickberry in barrel, and those concerns have become magnified after tasting it from bottle. The wine, a blend of 63% Merlot, 21% Cabernet Sauvignon, and 16% Cabernet Franc, was tough as nails, lean, backward, and tannic from barrel. Now that it has been bottled, it possesses similar characteristics, with an even bigger hole in the midpalate. It tastes attenuated in the finish, and has a dull, muted nose. In fact, my rating may prove to be generous. This is a disappointing performance from one of my favorite wineries.

Ravenswood's wines are not for those tasters seeking subtle, lighter-styled offerings. The 1993 Merlot Sangiacomo exhibits an opaque purple color, a big, smoky, herb, coffee, and black cherry-scented nose, dense, medium- to full-bodied flavor, crisp, underlying acidity, attractive sweetness and succulence to its flavors and texture, and moderate tannin in the finish. This wine will benefit from 1–3 years of cellaring and will last for 12–15. The impressively built, opaque purple-colored 1993 Pickberry is an extremely powerful, chewy wine with considerable fruit extraction, huge body, high tannin, and superb purity and richness. It requires 5–6 years of cellaring and will drink well for 20+ years. It may turn out to be as good as the glorious 1992.

RENWOOD WINERY (AMADOR)

1996	Barbera	Amador	C	85
1995	Barbera	Amador	C	89
1995	Nebbiolo	Amador	C	87
1996	Sangiovese Clockspring Vineyard	Amador	C	87
1995	Sangiovese Clockspring Vineyard	Amador	C	88
1995	Zin Old Vine	Amador	D	88
1994	Zinfandel Fiddletown	Amador	D	90+
1995	Zinfandel Fiddletown-Eschen Vineyard	Amador	D	89+
1995	Zinfandel Grandmère Vineyard	Amador	D	89
1994	Zinfandel Grandmère Vineyard	Amador	D	91
1995	Zinfandel Grandpère Vineyard	Amador	D	88+
1994	Zinfandel Grandpère Vineyard	Amador	D	92
1993	Zinfandel Grandpère Vineyard	Amador	C	90
1995	Zinfandel Jack Rabbit Flat-Fox Creek Vineyard	Amador	D	88+
1994	Zinfandel Old Vine	Amador	D	90
1993	Zinfandel Old Vine	Amador	C	90
1993	Zinfandel Old Vine Eschen Vineyard Fiddletown	Amador	C	92

This winery, which does such a superlative job with old vine Zinfandel, has fashioned two of the finest Italian-inspired varietal wines I have tasted from California (when is that bubble going to break?). Longtime readers know of my disappointment with the majority of Sangiovese offerings, but Renwood's 1995 Sangiovese Clockspring Vineyard is a classic example of what can be obtained with this varietal in selected California *terroirs*. The wine possesses a dark ruby color, followed by a big, spicy, leathery, and cherry-scented nose, medium-bodied flavors, dusty tannin, excellent extract, and an overall voluminous, rich palate with the telltale tangy acidity that allows Sangiovese to work so well with various dishes. The wine cuts a fresh, vibrant feel at the back of the palate despite its lofty 14.3% alcohol. It is a delicious Sangiovese to drink over the next 2–3 years.

Barbera is an even more problematic grape in terms of making high-quality wine in California, but Renwood's 1995 Barbera is one of the finest I have tasted from the New World. Sweet, plummy, cherry fruit bursts from this medium- to full-bodied wine. It also boasts plenty of alcoholic clout (14.3%), excellent purity, and gobs of tangy red and black fruits. There is little tannin to be found, but the wine does reveal firm acidity, and a long finish. It should drink well for 2–3 years.

Also excellent, the 1995 Nebbiolo displays a medium dark ruby/garnet color, and an expressive nose of spicy, jammy black cherry fruit. Medium bodied, soft, and round, yet bursting with fruit, it possesses a relatively evolved, complex character. This Nebbiolo should drink well for 3–4 years. Impressive!

New oak and ripe fruit are presented in an uncomplicated, gutsy, exuberant style of the 1996 Barbera. This wine is clean, woody, and mouth-filling, but simple and monolithic.

Drink it over the next 3–4 years. In contrast, the 1996 Sangiovese Clockspring Vineyard is one of the better efforts from this often disappointing California varietal. The wine exhibits good spice, a whiff of new saddle leather, and strawberry and cherry jamlike notes. Medium ruby colored, luscious, round, richly fruity, and well balanced, this pure Sangiovese will drink well for 2–3 years.

Winemaker Scott Harvey turns out limited production, exceptionally high quality Zinfandels from some of Amador's most renowned vineyards. The Old Vine cuvée comes from a 54-year-old plot, a youngster when compared to the 83-year-old Eschen Vineyard and 125-year-old Grandpère Vineyard. The 1993 Zinfandel Old Vine reveals a saturated black/ruby color, a late harvest nose of prunes, overripe black cherries, spices and earth. Full bodied, with sweet, expansive, opulently textured fruit, this wine finishes dry despite what appears to be a late harvest style. Massive and rich, it is reminiscent of a pre-1978 Montevina Zinfandel from the same region. Drink it over the next 8–10 years as its high alcohol will unquestionably hold it together. The 1993 Zinfandel Old Vine Eschen Vineyard Fiddletown exhibits the most saturated black/purple color of this trio, and an enormously promising black cherry and raspberry-scented nose that soars from the glass. This highly extracted, full-bodied, velvety-textured, mouth-filling, in-your-face, alcoholic, dry Zinfandel is remarkably well balanced given its size. Drink it over the next 10–15 years. Most readers will enjoy this wine more if they do not take notice of the alcohol content listed on the label.

The 1993 Zinfandel Grandpère Vineyard offers a dark garnet/ruby purple color, decadent, sweet, earthy, cherry scents, a heavyweight, huge, full-bodied impact on the palate, an unctuous texture, and thick, viscous flavors that flow slowly across the palate. It is a dead ringer for the 1975 Montevina Late Bottled, an Amador Zinfandel that remains remarkably fresh, fruity, and delicious at age 20. I would opt for drinking the Grandpère over the next 12–15 years. By the way, the 125-year-old Grandpère Vineyard is reputed to be the oldest vineyard in California. These are impressive wines!

This winery produced fabulous 1994 Zinfandels. The thick, rich, highly concentrated fruit and high alcohol of Amador County's Zinfandel fruit is translated into large, full-bodied, muscular wines with noteworthy purity, balance, and sumptuousness. The only wine that had been bottled was the 1994 Old Vine Zinfandel, a 14.2% alcoholic bruiser. It is a beautifully fat, ripe wine with well-integrated alcohol, no hard edges, a velvety texture, and lavish quantities of succulent, earthy, black raspberry and cherry fruit. Drink it over the next 3–4 years. The opaque garnet/black/ruby-colored 1994 Zinfandel Fiddletown's shy aromatics explode on the palate with huge fruit, massive levels of glycerin and extract, and an unctuous, decadent, thick finish. This silky-textured wine is, as they say, a double whopper—it takes two hands to hold a glass of this heavyweight. Drink this thrilling, rich Zinfandel over the next 7–10 years.

The 1994 Zinfandel Grandmère Vineyard tastes sweet, even though it possesses no residual sugar. In addition to the sweet toasty oak, fabulous ripeness, and purity, there are layers of black cherry fruit, picked at high sugar levels, and vinified dry. This is a viscous, blockbuster Zinfandel for drinking over the next 6–9 years. The 1994 Zinfandel Grandpère Vineyard offers an opaque purple color that resembles black ink. A fabulous nose of old vine black cherries, black raspberries, earth, licorice, and pepper is an attention grabber. This is an unctuously textured, low-acid, extremely rich, ripe, dry Zinfandel that coats the mouth with amazing flavor extraction as well as silky richness. The finish lasts for 40–45 seconds. If readers admire huge, rich, yet well-balanced Zinfandels, these wines represent a tour de force in winemaking.

Undoubtedly, the 1995 Zinfandels are among the most promising, concentrated, and interesting wines of the vintage. However, a few caveats need to be stated. All of these wines are extremely rich and full bodied, but also excruciatingly tannic. At present, it appears they possess the requisite concentration to stand up to the tannin. Certainly there are few 1995 Zinfandels with the dense, saturated, opaque purple color exhibited by all of these wines.

In addition to its dense purple color, the 1995 Zin Old Vine (14.7% alcohol) possesses loads of earth, licorice, and blackberry and cherry fruit. Ripe and sweet, with medium to full body, and a long, rich texture, this wine is the only Renwood offering that is close to full maturity. It should keep for 7–8 years. The 1995 Zinfandel Fiddletown-Eschen Vineyard (a 15.3% alcohol monster made from 85-year-old vines) boasts an opaque purple color, and a strikingly sweet, rich nose of jammy blackberry and cherry fruit intermingled with smoke and chocolatelike scents. Extremely full bodied, powerful, and tannic, this should be an outstanding Zinfandel . . . but when will it reach maturity? I suspect 1–2 years of cellaring should result in enough tannin melting away to make this wine appealing. There are not abundant quantities of this wine as only 1,525 cases were produced. The 1995 Zinfandel Grandmère (15.5% alcohol; 2,521 cases) reveals a compelling nose of blueberry jam, black raspberries, smoky oak, and scorched earth. Roasted herb and tarlike scents emerge with coaxing. If aromatics alone justified a numerical rating, this wine would be rated in the low 90s, but the excruciating tannin level gives it a coarse, hard finish. Although powerful and promising, the aggressive tannin may prove worrisome. Potential suitors are advised to cellar it for 1–2 years; it should keep for a decade or more. The 1995 Zinfandel from the renowned Grandpère Vineyard (15.7% alcohol; 1,225 cases) is similar to the Grandmère with its tarry, peppery, smoky, earthy nose intermingled with copious amounts of jammy black fruit (cherries and raspberries) aromas. Long, dense, and powerful, with a sweet attack and highly extracted flavors, this full-bodied, ferociously tannic Zinfandel is extremely backward, and in need of 1–3 years of cellaring. It should keep for over a decade, but will sufficient tannin melt away before the fruit begins to fade?

Lastly, the 1995 Zinfandel Jack Rabbit Flat-Fox Creek Vineyard is another opaque purple-colored, impressively built wine with gorgeously sweet aromas of earth and black fruits. Medium to full bodied and deep, with a powerful, hulklike presence on the palate, this spicy, well-endowed Zinfandel is aggressively tannic and backward. In general, I'm an optimist regarding the future development of these wines, but the tannin is not nearly as well integrated as it was in this estate's 1994s.

REVERIE (NAPA)

1996 Cabernet Franc Diamond Mountain	Napa	D	86
1995 Cabernet Franc Diamond Mountain	Napa	D	89
1996 Cabernet Sauvignon Diamond Mountain	Napa	D	89
1995 Cabernet Sauvignon Diamond Mountain	Napa	D	88
1996 Special Reserve Diamond Mountain	Napa	E	90
1995 Special Reserve Diamond Mountain	Napa	E	90

This winery is experimenting with Tempranillo (the 1995, 1996, and 1997 were all pleasant, but uninspiring efforts), as well as Barbera (the 1997 may turn out to be surprisingly good, but this varietal's naturally high acidity needs to be tamed). So far, Reverie's finest efforts have been with Cabernet Sauvignon. For example, the 1996 Cabernet Sauvignon Diamond Mountain (75% Cabernet Sauvignon and 25% Cabernet Franc) is a complex, Bordeaux-styled offering with tobacco, spice box, cedar, and black currant fruit. This dark ruby-colored wine displays a layered midpalate, and excellent length. While some tannin is noticeable, the wine's overall style is elegant and pure. The 1996 Cabernet Franc (85% Cabernet Franc and 15% Cabernet Sauvignon) is a leaner, more restrained and subtle wine, with intriguing aromatics of cigar box, menthol, mineral, and currants. In the mouth, the wine borders on austere, but does come through nicely in the finish.

Reverie's one outstanding offering is the 1996 Special Reserve proprietary red (87% Cabernet Sauvignon and 13% Cabernet Franc). Only 252 cases of this beauty were produced. Bottled unfiltered, this is a Bordeaux-styled wine with a Médoc-like, mineral, lead pencil, and black currant fruitiness intertwined with weedy tobacco and spice box scents. Dense, with high tannin as well as beautiful, rich, ripe fruit, this stylish, graceful, potentially complex wine would be difficult to pick out as a California Cabernet in a blind tasting. Anticipated maturity: 2002–2020.

The medium dark ruby-colored 1995 Cabernet Franc possesses a 92-point nose and an 88-point palate. It offers a terrific raspberry, floral, and vanillin-scented nose that leaps from the glass. The wine possesses excellent richness, medium body, and fine purity and equilibrium. It should drink well for a decade or more. The classic, elegant, restrained and closed, medium-bodied 1995 Cabernet Sauvignon displays fine density, but extremely high tannin. Enough black currant fruit emerges for optimism, but patience is required. Give this wine 3–5 years of cellaring, and consume it over the following 15 years. The outstanding 1995 Special Reserve makes me think that its 1996 sibling will certainly come around with more time in barrel. The 1995 Special Reserve, a blend of 90% Cabernet Sauvignon, 5% Cabernet Franc, and 5% Petit Verdot, possesses a deep ruby/purple color, a spicy, ripe, concentrated character, tight aromatics, but enticing quantities of red and black fruits, minerals, and *pain grillé* notes. This elegant wine should repay readers willing to cellar it for 5–6 years. It appears to have all the necessary raw materials to last for 2 decades or more.

RIDGE VINEYARDS (SANTA CLARA)

1997	Cabernet Sauvignon Monte Bello	Santa Cruz	EE	(90–91+)
1996	Cabernet Sauvignon Monte Bello	Santa Cruz	EE	95+
1995	Cabernet Sauvignon Monte Bello	Santa Cruz	EE	91+
1994	Cabernet Sauvignon Monte Bello	Santa Cruz	EE	91
1993	Cabernet Sauvignon Monte Bello	Santa Cruz	EE	93+
1997	Chardonnay	Santa Cruz	D	87
1996	Chardonnay	Santa Cruz	D	87
1997	Geyserville Proprietary Red Wine	Sonoma	D	(90–93)
1996	Geyserville Proprietary Red Wine	Sonoma	D	89
1995	Geyserville Proprietary Red Wine	Sonoma	C	90
1994	Geyserville Proprietary Red Wine	Sonoma	C	92
1993	Geyserville Proprietary Red Wine	Sonoma	C	89
1996	Grenache Lytton Estate	Sonoma	C	88
1996	Lytton Springs Proprietary Red Wine	Sonoma	D	90
1993	Lytton Springs Proprietary Red Wine	California	C	88
1997	Mataro	Bridgehead-Contra Costa	D	89
1993	Mataro (Mourvèdre) Bridgehead Vineyard	Contra Costa	C	90+
1996	Syrah Lytton Estate	Sonoma	C	88
1997	Zinfandel	Paso Robles	D	(90–92)
1994	Zinfandel	Sonoma	C	89
1993	Zinfandel	Sonoma	C	90

1997 Zinfandel	York Creek	C	(88–90)
1996 Zinfandel Dusi Ranch	Paso Robles	D	88
1995 Zinfandel Dusi Ranch	Paso Robles	C	89
1994 Zinfandel Dusi Ranch	Paso Robles	C	90
1993 Zinfandel Dusi Ranch	Paso Robles	C	91
1997 Zinfandel Lytton Springs	Sonoma	C	91
1995 Zinfandel Lytton Springs	Sonoma	C	91
1994 Zinfandel Lytton Springs	Sonoma	C	91
1993 Zinfandel Lytton Springs	Sonoma	C	92
1997 Zinfandel Pagani Ranch	Sonoma	C	(90–92)
1996 Zinfandel Pagani Ranch	Sonoma	D	88
1995 Zinfandel Pagani Ranch	Sonoma	C	89
1994 Zinfandel Pagani Ranch	Sonoma	C	91
1993 Zinfandel Pagani Ranch	Sonoma	C	91
1996 Zinfandel Sonoma Station	California	D	89
1995 Zinfandel Sonoma Station	Sonoma	C	87
1996 Zinfandel York Creek-Spring Mtn.	Napa	D	89
1995 Zinfandel York Creek	Napa	C	88

Nestled high in the Santa Cruz Mountains, with a precipitous view of the San Andreas fault, Ridge Vineyards has long been one of the classic reference points for high-quality California wines. While the winery now has a Japanese owner, longtime winemaker Paul Draper continues to have complete control of vineyard management and winemaking. Production has inched up to 60,000 cases, with the potential for 8,000 cases of the famed Monte Bello Cabernet Sauvignon. However, most vintages tend to produce between 3,000–4,000 cases. On my recent visit, I had a chance to take a look at some works in progress. Chardonnay has never been one of Ridge's strong efforts, even though neighboring Mount Eden does a superlative job. Ridge's Chardonnays, which are put through full malolactic fermentation, are beefy, chewy wines with tropical fruit and citrusy, applelike notes. Although elegant, they are monolithic and foursquare. Both the 1996 and 1997 Chardonnays are good to very good efforts, but not complex. Both wines should drink well for several more years.

The 1997 Cabernet Sauvignon Monte Bello exhibits an opaque purple color, as well as an elegant, black currant, mineral, and smoky oak-scented nose. The wine is medium to full bodied, tannic, and in need of 10 years of cellaring. Not a blockbuster, this offering is more elegant and finesse-styled than usual. However, as with previous Monte Bellos, it will take a long time to come around, yet it will keep for 2–3 decades. The 1996 Cabernet Sauvignon Monte Bello (80% Cabernet Sauvignon, 11% Merlot, and 9% Petit Verdot that reached 13.4% alcohol) represents a severe selection of only 40% of the vineyard's crop. A blockbuster, powerful, concentrated Monte Bello, it possesses an opaque purple color, plenty of spicy oak in the nose (100% American oak has always been used for aging Monte Bello), and a deep, layered, concentrated style. There is plenty of tannin, but it is sweeter than that found in the 1997, and the wine is more concentrated and extracted. There is a touch of oak in the flavors, which are otherwise dominated by minerals and jammy black fruits. This is a terrific Monte Bello that will have 30+ years of life. The 1995 Monte Bello is actually a Proprietary Red Wine as the blend is 69% Cabernet Sauvignon, 18% Merlot, 10% Petit Verdot, and 3% Cabernet Franc. It was made from an extremely severe selection of only 25% of the harvest. Paul Draper feels it is the biggest, brawniest, and most muscular Monte Bello of the 1990s, and in need of 10–15 more years of cellaring. This saturated ruby/purple-colored effort is still backward, with a closed nose of minerals, oak, and subtle black fruits. In the mouth, it is large scaled, tannic, rich, and long, but nearly abrasive because of the wine's high tannin level. This youthful, muscular, monster Monte Bello will require significant cellaring. Anticipated maturity: 2010–2035.

Ridge owns the Lytton Springs estate, from which it has produced two interesting Rhône Ranger wines. The 1996 Syrah Lytton Springs was blended with 5% Viognier, and tips the scales at 14.2% alcohol. The Viognier was vinified with the Syrah, resulting in a richly fruity (blackberries and currants), lush, round, hedonistically styled wine with low acidity, and a plump, savory character. It should drink well for 4–5 years. Also intriguing is the 1996 Grenache Lytton Springs (made from 92% Grenache, 6% Zinfandel, and 2% Petite Sirah). This wine's deep ruby color is followed by a gorgeous nose of jammy strawberries, kirsch liqueur, and dried cherries. Fruity, with good glycerin, medium to full body, and loads of fruit, this textbook, very yummy Grenache should be consumed over the next 4–5 years.

The 1997 Zinfandels are all high in alcohol, largely because of vintage conditions. All are slightly more successful than Ridge's very fine 1996s. For example, the 1997 Zinfandel Paso Robles offers overripe prunes, plums, and cherries in the nose, explosive fruit, copious glycerin, and a full-bodied, chewy, seductive character. It should be drunk over the next 4–5 years. The 1997 Geyserville Proprietary Red Wine (primarily Zinfandel) is a riveting example of this popular wine. The color is dark ruby/purple, and the wine is crammed with blackberries and cherry fruit intermixed with pepper, spice, and smoky oak. Full bodied and dense, it should drink well for 7–8 years. The more structured, tannic, dark ruby/purple-colored 1997 Zinfandel York Creek possesses outstanding potential, although it was backward and restrained when I tasted it in September. It is a candidate for 5–8 years of cellaring. I immensely enjoyed the 1997 Zinfandel Pagani Ranch, which offers copious quantities of glycerin, fat, and raspberry fruit intermixed with cherries, pepper, and smoky oak. This outstanding, ripe wine should provide delicious drinking during its first 5–6 years of life. Lastly, the 1997 Zinfandel Lytton Springs is an effusively fruity, full-bodied wine emphasizing Zinfandel's black cherry/raspberry character. With loads of glycerin, high alcohol, and outstanding purity and finish, this will be a hedonistic, luscious wine to enjoy during its first 5–6 years of life. Interestingly, Paul Draper told me the alcohol levels for all these 1997 Zinfandels were well above 15%.

An impressive lineup of 1993 Zinfandels was released by one of California's leading Zinfandel producers. For starters, there was the 1993 Geyserville (now officially a proprietary wine), which contains large quantities of Zinfandel. The wine is rich and fat, with excellent concentration, a seductive, earthy, black cherry component, good glycerin, low acidity, and a plump, heady, chewy style that already provides considerable pleasure and joy. Drink it over the next 7–8 years. The 1993 Sonoma Zinfandel possesses more richness and ripeness than the Geyserville. Dense, with a muscular, full-bodied personality, great fruit and ripeness, and a long finish, it is soft enough to be drunk now, but promises to keep for 6–7 years. The explosively rich 1993 Zinfandel Lytton Springs (an 86% Zinfandel, 8% Sirah, 3% Carignan, 2% Alicante, and 2% Grenache blend) offers a knockout nose of black fruits, wood, minerals, and licorice. Full bodied, with a sweet, expansive, superconcentrated personality, low acidity, 14.5% alcohol, and a powerful, authoritatively flavored finish, it offers a mouthful of juicy, succulent Zinfandel that should last for 7–8 years.

Once again Ridge turned out a blockbuster, massive Zinfandel from the Pagani Ranch vineyard. The 1993 is made from 82% Zinfandel, 12% Mourvèdre, 4% Alicante, and 2% Petite Sirah. The label indicates it contains a wimpish 14.9% alcohol! Amazingly, the wine does not taste hot or alcoholic, a tribute not only to fine winemaking, but to the massive level of fruit extraction that covers virtually all the tannin and alcohol in this gigantically constructed, chewy, rich Zinfandel. Full bodied, with a nearly opaque color, as well as gobs of earthy, black fruits, this is a classic Zinfandel for drinking over the next 7–8 years. Still not enough power for diehard Zin addicts? Check out the 1993 Zinfandel Dusi Ranch, with its "conservative" 15.9% alcohol level. One would expect some fire and heat in the mouth, as well as late harvest character, but neither is present in this enormously extracted, full-bodied, unctuously textured, spicy wine that lays on the fruit as if it were icing on a cake. A skyscraper of a wine, it is a tremendously rich, fun Zinfandel that will provide a thrill a second for at least the next 7–8 years. Kudos to Paul Draper for this marvelous array of expressive, full-throttle Zinfandels.

In 1994, winemaker Paul Draper produced five beautifully made, rich, distinctive Zinfandels. The 1994 Zinfandel Dusi Ranch (14.4% alcohol) is a fat, hugely extracted, opulent, luscious, full-bodied Zinfandel that coats the mouth with wonderful creamy, pure, jammy Zinfandel fruit. As in all five of these offerings, the high alcohol is well concealed behind admirable levels of physiologically ripe, concentrated fruit. Drink this fleshy wine over the next 4–5 years. A blend of 78% Zinfandel, 10% Mataro (Mourvèdre), 6% Petite Sirah, 3% Carignan, and 3% Alicante, the 1994 Zinfandel Sonoma possesses the lowest alcohol (13.6%) of this quintet. It reveals an attractive dark ruby/purple color, a sweet, overripe cherry/peppery nose, subtle earthy, *terroir* characteristics, full body, a broad, expansive feel on the palate, and a soft, low-acid, clean, rich finish. It, too, should drink well for 4–5 years.

The exceptional 1994 Lytton Springs Zinfandel (an 80% Zinfandel, 13% Petite Sirah, 4% Carignan, 2% Grenache, 1% Alicante blend that achieved 14.3% alcohol) is a big, smoky, ripe, full-bodied wine with outstanding fruit density (oodles of black cherries and raspberries with a hint of pepper and spice), an unctuous texture, well-hidden alcohol, and a forceful, brawny, velvety-textured finish. It should drink well for 5–7 years. With 14.3% alcohol, the 1994 Geyserville, which cannot legally be labeled a Zinfandel because it contains 28% Carignan, 8% Petite Sirah, and 4% Mataro, is the most classy and complex wine of this group. It is made in a Mediterranean/Provençal style reminiscent of what Zinfandel might taste like if it were planted in the rocky soils of Domaine Trevallon's vineyards just outside the hillside ghost village of Les Baux. The wine displays a deep purple color, a big, earthy, peppery, smoky, black and red fruit-scented nose, and gobs of sweet fruit. Profoundly rich and full bodied, this multidimensional wine possesses a layered, chewy palate, some tannin, good acidity, and a spicy, long, satisfying finish. Already delicious and complex, it should be drunk over the next 7–9 years.

The outstanding 1994 Zinfandel Pagani Ranch (75% Zinfandel, 18% Mataro, 4% Alicante, 3% Petite Sirah) is the most forceful Ridge Zinfandel as it achieved 14.7% natural alcohol. It is a rich, dense, full-bodied, sweet (from grape maturity, not sugar), jammy Zinfandel with gobs of ostentatiously styled, in-your-face characteristics. This bold, flashy wine is sure to win many a blind tasting. I believe Paul Draper's decision to add a healthy dose of Mataro has given this wine more delineation and structure than it has possessed in past vintages. For that reason, it may evolve beyond 5–7 years, but my instincts suggest its greatest pleasures will be revealed over the next 5–6 years. As usual, this is another terrific lineup of Zinfandels from Ridge.

It's hard to believe, but the 1995 Geyserville Proprietary Red Wine is winemaker Paul Draper's thirtieth consecutive vintage of this wine. Although outstanding, the backward 1995 (a blend of 62% Zinfandel, 18% Petite Sirah, 15% Carignan, and 5% Mataro) needs 1–2 years of cellaring. It is a deep ruby/purple-colored wine with an earthy, spicy, black currant, and plum-scented nose with pepper in the background. Full bodied, powerful, and muscular, with a broodingly unevolved style, this is a generous, well-made, exceptionally long Zinfandel-dominated wine that should evolve into one of the most interesting wines of the vintage. It is not for those seeking understated wines given its 14.2% alcoholic strength. Anticipated maturity: 1999–2010.

The 1995 Zinfandel Lytton Springs (84% Zinfandel, 14% Petite Sirah, and 2% Carignan) is a beautifully made, full-bodied, muscular wine exhibiting some overripe plum and prune-like characteristics of a late-harvest wine. It is dry and pure, with a tight but promising nose of pepper, black fruits, and spicy oak. Well textured, full bodied, and concentrated, this is a highly extracted wine to drink over the next 8–10 years. The 1995 Zinfandel Sonoma Station, 75% Zinfandel, with the balance Alicante and Petite Sirah, is a medium- to full-bodied, currently unexpressive Zinfandel that still merits high marks because of its large size, excellent purity, and mouth-filling richness. While it appears to lack complexity, it is long, chewy, and well made, but chunky and monochromatic. It should drink well for 5–7 years. I also enjoyed immensely the earthy, peppery, licorice, and black cherry-scented 1995 Zinfandel Dusi Ranch. At 14.7% alcohol, no one can accuse it of being undernourished, but the wine does not come across as a late-harvest Zinfandel, nor does it taste over the top, or overweight. It is a deep, ripe, full-bodied wine with copious quantities of fruit, low acidity, moderate tannin, and a fleshy, nicely textured mouth-feel. It should drink well for 7–8 years.

The 1995 Zinfandel York Creek (90% Zinfandel, 6% Petite Sirah, 4% Alicante) is an elegant, reserved, slightly austere wine with ripe, tarry, smoky, berry fruit, high tannin, medium body, and an abrupt finish. It will benefit from another year of cellaring and drink well for 5–7 years. Lastly, the 1995 Zinfandel Pagani Ranch (a concoction of 82% Zinfandel, 13% Mataro, and 5% Alicante made from 100-year-old vines) boasts 15.2% alcohol, as well as a distinctive tarry, melted asphalt, peppery nose with the fruit dominated by the other components. Dense and inaccessible, this formidably built wine may dry out before the tannin fades away. It is completely different in style than either the exquisite 1994 or 1993.

These Ridge Zinfandels are made in a backward, austere style, and, with the exception of the Geyserville, Lytton Springs, and Paso Robles, they are wines that may not develop as much character as previous vintages.

Ridge has produced a fine series of 1996 Zinfandels. They reveal the vintage's rich, high alcohol personality, and forward, immediately drinkable style. I do not believe the 1996 vintage will age more than 5–6 years, despite the high alcohol. The tiny Zinfandel crop resulted in concentrated wines, but they are not as exceptionally deep as one might have expected given the small yields.

Ridge's 1996 Zinfandel Sonoma Station (an 80% Zinfandel, 8% Petite Sirah, 8% Alicante, and 4% Carignan blend that achieved 14.4% alcohol) displays a dark ruby color, and a rich, briery, raspberry-scented nose with gobs of spice and pepper. Medium bodied, with excellent concentration, and subtle new oak in the background, this delicious, broadly flavored Zinfandel is best drunk over the next 4–5 years. Ridge has consistently done a fine job with their Zinfandel from the Dusi Ranch in Paso Robles. The 1996 (95% Zinfandel and 5% Petite Sirah with 14.6% alcohol) boasts a deep saturated ruby/purple color (among the darkest of the Ridge offerings), and subtle aromatics (primarily earth intermixed with black raspberries, pepper, and licorice). This medium- to full-bodied, spicy Zinfandel appears to possess a firm structure and ageability, but it does not have the underlying depth to warrant cellaring beyond 4–5 years. The 1996 Geyserville Proprietary Red Wine (a blend of 75% Zinfandel, 17% Carignan, 6% Petite Sirah, and 2% Mataro) tips the scales at 14.9% alcohol. In spite of the hefty alcohol content, it is an exceptionally elegant wine, with sweet, black raspberry and cherry fruit, medium body, and a dry, crisp, lightly tannic finish. This wine could easily pass for a high-class, midweight 1995 red Burgundy. As the wine sits in the mouth, its glycerin and multilayered texture are very appealing. It should drink well for 5–6 years.

The 1996 Zinfandel York Creek-Spring Mountain (91% Zinfandel and 9% Petite Sirah) reveals a Bordeaux-like austerity to its flavor profile. There is plenty of tannin, but that does not mean this offering can be cellared for any length of time. The blackberry/cherry notes combine with spicy oak, pepper, and minerals for a moderately intense, enticing bouquet. In the mouth, the wine exhibits firmness, some American oak, as well as good spice and sweet fruit. Consume this classy, complex Zinfandel over the next 5–6 years. The 1996 Lytton Springs Proprietary Red Wine (78% Zinfandel, 19% Petite Sirah, 2% Carignan, and 1% Grenache) possesses 14.5% alcohol. It boasts the sweetest, jammiest nose, as well as a healthy dark ruby/purple color, full body, robust, chewy flavors, and the best length of these offerings. This expansively flavored wine should drink well for 5–6 years. Lastly, the dark ruby-colored 1996 Zinfandel Pagani Ranch (82% Zinfandel, 11% Mataro, 4% Petite Sirah, and 3% Alicante) offers up aromas of earth, prunes, and ripe black fruits (almost Amarone in style). In the mouth, the wine is dry, medium to full bodied, rustic, less concentrated, and more civilized and restrained than several previous Pagani Ranch Zinfandels, which were blockbusters. This cleanly made wine should drink well for 4–5 years.

These are all excellent, nearly outstanding Zinfandels that share a certain firmness and structured feel (particularly when compared to the 1995s, 1994s, and 1993s). Because of the definition and angularity, it would be natural for readers to think these wines require cellaring. My instincts and experience suggest these Zinfandels need to be drunk in their exuberant youth—over the next 4–5 years.

When young, the Ridge Cabernet Sauvignon Monte Bello rarely reveals its full potential. Having said that, the 1993 and 1994 vintages of the Monte Bello Cabernet Sauvignon are immensely impressive, with perhaps the 1994 less expressive. The 1993 Ridge Monte Bello is a tightly wrapped, densely colored, pure, rich, full-bodied Cabernet with moderately intense aromas of vanilla, black raspberries, currants, and minerals. This rich wine cuts a deep path on the palate, with high tannin, adequate acidity, and a long, muscular, formidably endowed finish. Extremely unevolved and young, it needs 7–10 years of cellaring. The 1994 Cabernet Sauvignon Monte Bello was one of the most backward Cabernets in the March 1996 tasting. It almost defies inspection given its austere, extremely tannic, hard style. The opaque purple color is accompanied by a wine that smells and tastes ripe, rich, and brilliantly made, but it will require a minimum of 10–12 years of cellaring to shed enough tannin to become civilized. Although it should be a winner, it may not be as sure a bet as such vintages as 1991, 1992, and 1995.

The 1993 may be the most impressive Mataro (Mourvèdre) yet produced by Ridge. The 100-year-old vines from the Bridgehead Vineyard have turned out a full-bodied, rich, earthy, black fruit-scented wine crammed with dense, chewy fruit buttressed by considerable tannin. It also displays an alluring, underlying, smoky, cassis component. This impressive wine promises to age well for 10–12 years. The 1993 Lytton Springs Proprietary Red Wine is an 85% Zinfandel, 8% Petite Sirah, 3% Carignan, 2% Alicante and 2% Grenache blend. Its earthy, undistinguished nose does not do justice to the rich, full-bodied, ripe, complex palate. Perhaps I caught the wine in a shy state—aromatically speaking. Boasting 14.5% alcohol, it possesses plenty of chewy, earthy, berry fruit and spice. Although it does not appear to be as complex as the sumptuous 1992, 1991, or 1990, it is a well-made, excellent, broad-shouldered wine that should age well for a decade.

ROCHIOLI VINEYARD (SONOMA)

1997 Cabernet Sauvignon Neoma's Vineyard	Russian River	D	(90–92)
1996 Cabernet Sauvignon Neoma's Vineyard	Russian River	D	93
1993 Cabernet Sauvignon Neoma's Vineyard	Russian River	D	88+
1997 Chardonnay	Russian River	D	89
1996 Chardonnay	Russian River	C	87
1997 Chardonnay Allen Vineyard	Russian River	E	92

1996 Chardonnay Allen Vineyard	Russian River	E	91
1995 Chardonnay Allen Vineyard	Russian River	E	92
1996 Chardonnay Estate	Russian River	C	86
1995 Chardonnay Estate	Russian River	D	90
1997 Chardonnay River Block	Russian River	E	92
1996 Chardonnay River Block	Russian River	E	89
1997 Chardonnay South River Vineyard	Russian River	E	93
1996 Chardonnay South River Vineyard	Russian River	E	92
1997 Pinot Noir East Block	Russian River	E	(91–93)
1995 Pinot Noir East Block	Russian River	E	91
1997 Pinot Noir Estate	Russian River	D	87
1996 Pinot Noir Estate	Russian River	D	88
1995 Pinot Noir Estate	Russian River	D	89
1997 Pinot Noir Little Hill Block	Russian River	E	(92–95)
1996 Pinot Noir Little Hill Block	Russian River	E	91
1995 Pinot Noir Little Hill Block	Russian River	E	90
1997 Pinot Noir Three Corner Vineyard	Russian River	E	(90–92)
1996 Pinot Noir Three Corner Vineyard	Russian River	E	93
1995 Pinot Noir Three Corner Vineyard	Russian River	E	90
1993 Pinot Noir Reserve Three Corner Vineyard	Russian River	E	90
1997 Pinot Noir West Block	Russian River	E	(88–90+)
1996 Pinot Noir West Block	Russian River	E	93
1995 Pinot Noir West Block	Russian River	E	93
1993 Pinot Noir West Block	Russian River	E	93
1997 Sauvignon Blanc	Russian River	B	88
1997 Sauvignon Blanc Old Vine Block	Russian River	C	91
1996 Zinfandel Sodini Vineyard	Russian River	C	93

Virtually all the producers I visit in California are candid and direct about vintage conditions and how their wines are made. That being said, there is probably no more of a "straight-shooter" in the wine world than Tom Rochioli. His refreshing honesty and self-deprecating style are hard to resist. In fact, I often wonder if he realizes the superb quality of his wines! About the only way readers will be able to obtain the limited production single-vineyard Rochioli wines is to get their names on the winery's mailing list, something I highly recommend.

There are four Chardonnays, all delicious wines. The basic cuvée, the 1997 Chardonnay Russian River, is bottled without filtration. It contains mostly old California clonal material, but some Dijon clones are being added to the blend. The 1997, which reached 14.9% alcohol naturally, is a full-bodied, vibrant Chardonnay with notes of lemon custard, flower blossoms, and minerals. The oak is well submerged beneath the wine's pure fruit. This lovely, lush, powerful yet elegant Chardonnay should drink well for 2–3 years, perhaps longer.

Readers have three gorgeous 1997 single-vineyard Chardonnays to savor. Sadly, only about 250 cases of each wine has been produced. All three are fermented with whole clusters, indigenous yeasts, and aged in a high percentage of new French oak. Finally, they are bottled with no filtration. Moreover, my instincts suggest these Chardonnays will evolve for 3–4 years, and last for nearly a decade. The 1997 Chardonnay South River Vineyard (14.2% alcohol) comes from a vineyard planted on an old riverbed, and is made from the Hanzell Chardonnay clone. It is a full-bodied, smoky, roasted nut-scented wine with plenty of honeyed pineapple and other tropical fruit flavors, huge quantities of glycerin, and a chewy, substantial, oversized finish. This is not a Chardonnay for readers looking for light-bodied, restrained, subtle wines. Still young, and only hinting at its ultimate potential, it should be cellared for 1–2 years, and enjoyed over the following decade. The 1997 Chardonnay Allen Vineyard (made from Clone 108) exhibits a distinctive mineral/gravelly nose reminiscent of a white Graves. Additionally, there is extraordinary richness and honeyed intensity in the mouth, full body, *pain grillé* intermixed with tropical fruits. The size, alcoholic clout, and fruit quality of this chewy offering clearly point to a blockbuster California wine, but the minerality suggests France. This youthful wine requires another 6–8 months of bottle age, but it should keep for 7–8 years. The 1997 Chardonnay River Block displays a pronounced roasted hazelnut, smoky, leesy nose that soars from the glass. This wine took a long time to ferment dry, and it may turn out to be the most complex (at least aromatically) of Tom Rochioli's 1997 Chardonnays. Rich and multilayered, with hints of minerals, smoky notes, and gobs of ripe tropical fruit, it should be at its peak between 1999 and 2006.

There are two Sauvignon Blancs, the finest one virtually impossible to obtain except from the mailing list. The 1997 Sauvignon Blanc (30% barrel and 70% tank-fermented) offers an excellent citrusy, melony, and mineral-scented nose. Medium bodied, fresh, concentrated, and crisp, it reveals little evidence of oak. With a citrusy, zesty personality, and a dry, stylish finish, it should be consumed over the next 2–3 years. The superb 1997 Sauvignon Blanc Old Vine Block comes from a vineyard block planted in 1959, and believed to be the oldest Sauvignon Blanc vines in Sonoma. The wine offers a terrific Pouilly-Fumé-like, liquid stone, smoky-scented nose intertwined with aromas of ripe, honeyed citrus fruit. Surprisingly full bodied, with an exuberance, richness, and intensity rarely encountered in Sauvignon Blanc, this impressive offering should drink well for 4–5 years.

Tom Rochioli's four cuvées of Pinot Noir are among the most thrilling being produced in northern California. They represent the amazing progress the state has made with this fickle, easily bruised varietal. The 1997 Pinot Noir Estate offers a dark ruby color, and, as my notes stated, "cherries galore." Medium bodied, with copious quantities of fruit, not a great deal of complexity, and a satisfying, hedonistic personality, this plump, round wine can be drunk now and over the next 4–5 years. The 1997 Pinot Noir Three Corners Vineyard exhibits a dark ruby/purple color, a sweet plum, black currant, and cherry-scented nose, silky-textured, medium- to full-bodied flavors, and a smoky, toasty finish. The wine presents a seamless style and wonderful sweet fruit, without tasting overbearing or weighty. The alcohol level must be close to 14%, but the taster will never sense that given the wine's concentration and depth. Look for this Pinot Noir to evolve nicely for 5–7 years. My favorite Pinot Noir in the Rochioli stable is the 1997 Pinot Noir Little Hill Block. It boasts a saturated purple color, followed by a spectacular nose that could easily pass for the crème de cassis/black raspberry liqueur found in a top-notch Richebourg. The vineyard, which is planted in extremely rocky soil, achieved sugars that produced a wine with 13.8% alcohol. Aged in 50% new François Frères barrels, with the balance 1-year-old, this wine's silky texture is crammed with glycerin as well as concentrated red and black fruits. Floral scents and smoky *pain grillé* notes add to the wine's appeal and complexity. This full-bodied, gorgeously complete and concentrated Pinot Noir should be drunk over the next 5–6 years. Classic black cherry aromatics intermixed with smoky new oak jump from a glass of the 1997 Pinot Noir

West Block. This dark ruby/purple-colored wine, aged in 100% new François Frères oak, is full bodied, tighter than its predecessors, but nicely layered, with sweet kirsch and black cherrylike flavors, good glycerin, and fine purity. The slightly angular and tannic finish in this compressed example kept my score conservative. Lastly, the 1997 Pinot Noir East Block is made in the mold of the Little Hill cuvée. It is a full-throttle effort that, despite its wonderful richness and density, has retained its elegance and lushness. The color is a healthy dark ruby/purple. In the mouth, the wine displays medium to full body, outstanding flavor extraction, and a long, 30-second finish. The wine possesses adequate acidity and moderate tannin, but these components are virtually buried by the precocious fruit and ripeness. This spicy, black fruit-scented and -flavored Pinot should be at its best with another 6–12 months of aging and will evolve nicely for 5–7 years.

I know Tom Rochioli does not get the same thrill from making Cabernet Sauvignon as he does from Pinot Noir, Chardonnay, and Sauvignon Blanc, but that is no reason to ignore his outstanding 1997 Cabernet Sauvignon Neoma's Vineyard, a black/purple-colored wine with superb aromatics of new oak, black raspberries, olives, tar, and smoke. Full bodied, rich, and chewy, with impressive viscosity and extract, this large-scaled, silky-textured wine should evolve nicely for 15–20 years. Production was approximately 225 cases.

By the way Tom Rochioli also produced a 1997 Zinfandel Sodini Vineyard, but it had not finished malolactic fermentation when I tasted it 12 months following the harvest! Based on what I saw in cask, it seems to be loaded, but whether he can get it totally dry remains to be seen.

The 1996 Chardonnay River Block (150 cases) is the product of an old Wente clone of Chardonnay. The wine reveals an orange blossom and honey-scented nose, creamy, medium- to full-bodied, concentrated flavors, and a judicious touch of spicy oak. Its elegant, mineral, pineapple character adds to the wine's intriguing personality. It should drink well for 3–4 years. The 1996 Chardonnay Allen Vineyard is an explosively rich, viscous, full-bodied, in-your-face Chardonnay with a Burgundian-like, leesy, smoked hazelnut-scented character. A flamboyant, mouth-filling, buttery apple, thick, juicy Chardonnay, it needs to be matched with equally intense food. It will drink well for 4–5 years. The 1996 Chardonnay South River Vineyard (made from a Hanzell clone) is even more impressive. Made from extremely small yields, the wine possesses phenomenal ripeness and intensity, and a finish that lasts for more than 30 seconds. This full-bodied, high-octane Chardonnay offers plenty of buttery, honeyed tropical fruits, as well as the smoky *sur lie* complexity so common in top-class white Burgundy. Despite its tightness, this is a sensational effort that should age well for 3–4 years. Undoubtedly, the 1996 Estate Chardonnay is a toned-down wine compared to the three single vineyard offerings. Nevertheless, this is an excellent pear/pineapple-scented and -flavored wine with medium to full body, crisp acidity, and an enticing elegance. It should drink well for 2–3 years.

Sweet, buttery, honeyed, judiciously oaked fruit is present in the elegant, stylish 1996 Chardonnay. The wine unfolds on the palate with attractive fruit, and glycerin. It is a cleanly made, complex Chardonnay to drink over the next 2–3 years.

J. Rochioli's 1995 Allen Vineyard Chardonnay Reserve is a dead ringer for a grand cru white Burgundy. Attractive aromas of high quality French oak, smoke, and hazelnut emerge, along with copious quantities of sweet, rich, honeyed fruit. The wine displays a pronounced liquefied mineral content, medium to full body, plenty of structure, and an explosive finish, with most of the fruit detectable on the back of the palate. Although still young and tightly knit, it should be fascinating to follow this Chardonnay's evolution. The 1995 Chardonnay Estate Reserve offers up a smoky, citrusy, ripe apple, and lemon-scented nose intertwined with aromas of new oak barrels. Rich, full bodied, and pure, this attractive wine should drink well for 3–4 years.

The 1996 Pinot Noir Estate exhibits a sweet, smoky, black plum and cherry-scented nose, medium body, excellent ripeness and purity of fruit, enough acidity for definition, and a moderately long, easygoing finish with toasty new oak notes. It should drink well for 4–5 years. The 1996 Pinot Noir Little Hill Block offers up a knockout nose of raspberries, cherries, smoky, toasty oak, and floral scents. The wine is full bodied, with intense flavors, a layered, silky texture, and a lush, heady finish. It is a hedonistic as well as intellectually pleasing Pinot Noir to drink over the next 4–5 years. Remarkably, both the 1996 Pinot Noir Three Corner Block and 1996 Pinot Noir West Block appear to be even more complex and multidimensional. The dense, deep ruby/purple-colored 1996 Pinot Noir Three Corner Vineyard (125 cases) reveals a sweet black raspberry-scented nose with high quality *pain grillé* notes, and intriguing Asian spice scents. Sweet and ripe on the attack (from fruit maturity, not sugar), this full-bodied, dense, lushly textured Pinot Noir is an infant in terms of development, but it promises to drink well young and last for 7–8 years. Each year I seem to have a slight preference for the West Block Pinot Noir and the 1996 is again my favorite. Texturally, as well as from a perspective of concentration and length, this wine could easily pass for a great 1990 Grand Cru red Burgundy. Aromatically, it remains to be seen whether it will offer the same level of complexity, but my instincts suggest this is a profound Pinot Noir that should rival the finest Pinots made in America over recent years. The color is a deep ruby/purple. The exotic nose offers a mélange of black fruits intertwined with *pain grillé*, spice, and meaty nuances. Full bodied, dense, superbly concentrated, and pure, yet surprisingly fresh and lively, this is a glorious example of the extraordinary progress being made by a handful of American vintners with the fickle Pinot Noir grape. I would not be surprised to see this wine last for a decade.

In 1995 there were five separate cuvées of Pinot Noir. The 1995 Pinot Noir Estate exhibits a deep ruby color, a sweet, blackberry-scented nose, evidence of smoky wood, and round, generous, medium- to full-bodied flavors. This supple Pinot is ideal for drinking over the next 4–5 years. There are four limited production single vineyard 1995 Pinot Noirs. The 1995 Pinot Noir Little Hill Block displays an open-knit, sweet, jammy, black fruit-scented nose, ripe, medium- to full-bodied flavors, and a forward, soft style with excellent purity and plenty of Pinot Noir's unmistakable perfumed silkiness and character. Drink it over the next 4–5 years. The 1995 Pinot Noir Three Corner Vineyard exhibits a deeper color, copious quantities of up-front, sweet, smoky, black cherry fruit, medium to full body, outstanding purity, and no hard edges. This wine should drink for 5–6 years.

The impressive 1995 Pinot Noir West Block offers a nose of raspberries and black cherries, wonderful sweetness and richness, and that layered, soft, opulently textured feel of serious Pinot. Round, concentrated, and full bodied, this is a lush, silky wine to drink over the next 5–6 years. The 1995 Pinot Noir East Block is cut from the same mold, perhaps more earthy, but opulent and flashy, with gobs of rich fruit. It is hard to imagine many wineries turning out five Pinot Noirs of this quality from one vintage.

The 1993 Pinot Noir Three Corner Vineyard (from a small parcel of vines planted in 1970) offers a gorgeous, deep ruby/purple color, and a fragrant, intense nose of black raspberries, cherries, vanillin, and smoke. This sweet-tasting (from ripe fruit, not added sugar) wine possesses superb richness, full body, wonderful freshness and purity, and a layered, voluptuously textured, long, lusty finish. This Pinot Noir could easily be mistaken for a grand cru from the Côte de Nuits. Remarkably, the 1993 Pinot Noir West Block is even better. There are usually less than 200 cases of this wine. It offers sensational color, a knockout aromatic profile consisting of gobs of red and black fruits, smoky oak, minerals, and spice. Full bodied, sensationally rich, with an unctuous texture, and loads of sweet jammy fruit in the finish, the wine's components are well buttressed by adequate acidity and aging in 100% new French oak. This glorious Pinot Noir (an American Richebourg?) will drink beautifully over the next 7–8 years.

Two limited rarities include the superb 1996 Zinfandel Sodoni Vineyard (from vines planted in 1905). There are 400 cases of this fabulously intense, rich, black/purple-colored Zinfandel that must contain 15% alcohol. This full-bodied, voluptuously textured Zinfandel will provide sensational drinking for 5–7 years. Another noteworthy wine is the 1996 Cabernet Sauvignon Neoma's Vineyard (150 cases). Made from 38-year-old vines with yields of under 2 tons per acre, this wine exhibits a saturated black/purple color, and textbook jammy cassis aromas intermingled with minerals, tobacco, and licorice scents. Extremely full bodied, with phenomenal concentration, this wine reveals the telltale characteristics of the finest 1996s—low acidity, ripe tannin, and drop-dead levels of extract and nearly overripe fruit. Anticipated maturity: 2002–2025.

Still closed and tight, the hallmarks of the well-made 1993 Cabernet Sauvignon Neoma's Vineyard are its purity, gorgeous display of ripe black currant and cherry fruit, subtle dosage of new oak, and long, well-balanced finish. Youthful and unevolved, its full potential will not be realized for another 5–7 years, after which it should keep for 15 years.

ROCKING HORSE WINERY (NAPA)

1994	Cabernet Sauvignon Garvey Family Vineyard	Rutherford	D	91
1993	Cabernet Sauvignon Garvey Family Vineyard	Rutherford	C	90
1994	Cabernet Sauvignon Robinson Vineyard	Stag's Leap	D	87
1993	Cabernet Sauvignon Robinson Vineyard	Stag's Leap	D	88
1995	Zinfandel Lamborn Vineyard	Howell Mountain	C	88
1994	Zinfandel Lamborn Vineyard	Howell Mountain	C	90
1993	Zinfandel Old Paint	Napa	C	90+

I have had mixed emotions about Rocking Horse's wines in the past, but certainly these wines acquitted themselves well. The 1994 Zinfandel Lamborn Vineyard displays a dark ruby/purple color, followed by plenty of black cherry and raspberry fruit in the dense, peppery, earthy nose. Accessible, but still needing more time in the cellar, this is a full-bodied, powerful, muscular style of Zinfandel revealing evidence of spicy, American oak. It should drink well for 7–8 years. The 1993 Zinfandel Old Paint (from a 90-year-old vineyard that was ripped out following this vintage) exhibits a deep ruby/purple color, and a bouquet of earth, minerals, spice, pepper, plums, and raspberries. Spicy, deep, full bodied, and tannic, this is a forceful, well-knit, structured Zinfandel that should keep for a decade. I would be in no hurry to drink it since it still appears backward. This small winery has produced a delicious, but tannic, backward, mountain-styled 1995 Zinfandel from the Lamborn Vineyard. It offers pepper, spice, minerals, earth, and this varietal's telltale raspberry fruit. A deep ruby/purple-colored, well-structured, powerful Zinfandel, it has yet to reveal all of its charm. Nevertheless, it takes no special ability to recognize that this wine offers impressive depth, ripeness, purity, and intensity. It is impeccably made, but do not expect a lush, forward style of Zinfandel. Drink this rustic, macho Zin over the next 8–9 years.

The two 1994 Cabernet Sauvignons, made from different microclimates and soils, offer contrasting styles. I had an unequivocal preference for the 1994 Cabernet Sauvignon Garvey Family Vineyard. Eight hundred and fifty cases of this outstanding wine are produced from 100% Cabernet Sauvignon. The wine boasts an opaque purple color, full body, an explosively rich midpalate, and a 20–25-second finish. It is loaded with black currant, cedar, chocolatelike fruit, has a glorious texture, superb richness and chewiness, and that telltale, earthy, spicy, "Rutherford dust" characteristic. There are gobs of sweet tannin in the finish, but readers should not conclude that this wine is ready to drink. Purchasers of it should be prepared to give it 3–5 years of cellaring as it is a 20-year wine that could turn out to be even better than my numerical rating suggests. In contrast, the 1994 Cabernet Sauvignon Robinson Vineyard from the Stag's Leap area, south of Rutherford, is a lighter-styled (some would say more elegant), leaner wine with less body, more pronounced acidity, and a crisp, red currant character that offers an alternative style of Cabernet when compared with the black fruits of the Garvey Family Vineyard cuvée. It is well made, restrained, and understated, as well as polished and graceful. While it will drink well at an earlier age, 2–3 years of cellaring will be beneficial; it should keep for 15 years.

Rocking Horse has also turned in two noteworthy 1993 Cabernet Sauvignon efforts. I have a slight preference for the 1993 Cabernet Sauvignon Garvey Family Vineyard. The color is an opaque black/purple, and the wine is full bodied, with a sweet black currant nose, good richness, dusty tannin, and outstanding extract and length. It requires 3–4 years of cellaring, and should keep for 15+. The 1993 Cabernet Sauvignon Robinson Vineyard reveals that stylish, graceful, Stag's Leap elegance, attractive sweetness, medium body, zesty acidity, and finesse. This is an elegant, stylish Cabernet Sauvignon to drink over the next 10 or more years.

ROSENBLUM CELLARS (ALAMEDA)

1996	Zinfandel	Contra Costa	C	87
1995	Zinfandel	Contra Costa	C	86
1996	Zinfandel Annette's Reserve Rhodes Vineyard	Redwood Valley	C	86?
1995	Zinfandel Annette's Reserve Rhodes Vineyard	Redwood Valley	C	87+
1996	Zinfandel Ballentine Vineyard	Napa	C	88
1995	Zinfandel Brandlin Ranch Mount Veeder	Napa	C	86+?
1996	Zinfandel Continente Vineyard Old, Old Vines	Contra Costa	C	87
1995	Zinfandel Continente Vineyard Old Vines	Contra Costa	C	87
1995	Zinfandel Cullinane Vineyard	Sonoma	C	88
N.V.	Zinfandel Cuvée XVI	California	B	86
1996	Zinfandel George Hendry Vineyard Reserve	Napa	D	89
1995	Zinfandel George Hendry Vineyard Reserve	Napa	C	90
1996	Zinfandel Harris Kratka Vineyard	Alexander Valley	C	89
1995	Zinfandel Harris Kratka Vineyard	Alexander Valley	C	88
1995	Zinfandel Old Vines	Sonoma	C	87
1996	Zinfandel Pato Vineyard	Contra Costa	C	87
1995	Zinfandel Pato Vineyard	Contra Costa	C	89
1996	Zinfandel Richard Sauret Vineyard	Paso Robles	C	87
1995	Zinfandel Richard Sauret Vineyard	Paso Robles	C	78
1996	Zinfandel Rockpile Vineyard	Dry Creek	D	81
1996	Zinfandel Samsel Vineyard Maggie's Reserve	Sonoma	D	87

1995 Zinfandel Samsel Vineyard Maggie's Reserve	Sonoma	C	90
1996 Zinfandel 20th Anniversary Series Brandlin Ranch	Mt. Veeder	D	88
1996 Zinfandel 20th Anniversary Series Cullinane Vineyard	Sonoma	D	89
1996 Zinfandel 20th Anniversary Series St. Peter's Church Vineyard	Sonoma	C	90
1996 Zinfandel White Cottage Vineyard	Howell Mountain	C	88

Dr. Rosenblum, one of California's most noteworthy practitioners of Zinfandel winemaking, again turned out a bevy of fine wines in 1995. There seems to be less difference between the individual Zinfandels than in previous years, but certainly the overall level of quality, with the exception of the Richard Sauret Vineyard offering, is reassuringly high.

For starters, the 1995 Zinfandel Contra Costa is a peppery, earthy, medium-bodied wine with plenty of spice, a soft, easygoing style, and attractively plump, ripe fruit. With 13.8% alcohol and low acidity, this is a round, tasty Zinfandel to drink over the next several years. The dark ruby-colored 1995 Zinfandel Continente Old Vines (14.4% alcohol) is a more full-bodied, later-harvested style of Zinfandel with attractive sweet, ripe, black cherry fruit, medium to full body, a layered texture, and a seductive, low-acid, lush mouth-feel. I would opt for drinking it over the next 5–6 years. The 1995 Zinfandel Pato Vineyard is nearly out-standing. I felt as if I were in an Indonesian restaurant ordering a bevy of their small dishes that are part of the *Rijstaffel* tradition given the exotic nose of cumin, earth, pepper, cinna-mon, and soy. Rich, with excellent, deep, medium- to full-bodied flavors, this fleshy, low-acid, open-knit Zinfandel exhibits excellent ripeness, a gorgeous mouth-feel, and a lusty, heady finish. Surprisingly, it is one of the lower alcohol offerings from Rosenblum in 1995, containing 13.7%.

As suggested earlier, Rosenblum's 1995 Zinfandel Richard Sauret Vineyard (13.9% alco-hol) reveals a ruby/garnet color, tight, spice and earth-driven aromatics, and medium body. But the wine's lean palate and attenuated personality are reasons for concern about its over-all balance. The wine does not appear to have the requisite fruit, glycerin, and extract to stand up to its distinctively earthy, structured personality.

The 1995 Zinfandel Old Vines Sonoma is a far more interesting wine. It offers a medium dark ruby color, as well as a seductive, big, spicy, oaky nose with copious quantities of jammy cherry fruit. This is a medium-bodied, soft, attractive Zinfandel to drink over the next several years. Another offering from Sonoma, the 1995 Zinfandel Cullinane Vineyard (14.8% alcohol), is one of the more powerful wines in the Rosenblum portfolio. It possesses an evolved dark ruby/garnet color, gorgeously sweet, rich, black cherry and strawberry fruit in the nose, and an opulently textured, pure, fleshy mouth-feel. Although powerful, the alco-hol is well concealed behind the wine's abundant richness and layered fruit. Drink it over the next 5–6 years. I also admired the 1995 Zinfandel Harris Kratka Vineyard. While it is not a blockbuster Zin, this wine offers spicy new oak and sweet curranty fruit presented in a medium- to full-bodied, lush, well-etched style with fine ripeness, and good overall balance. It admirably carries its lofty level of 14.9% alcohol, as there is no sense of hotness or fire in the wine's finish. This Zinfandel begs to be drunk over the next 5–7 years.

The 1995 Zinfandel Annette's Reserve Rhodes Vineyard reveals an opaque center to its dark ruby/purple color. Toasty new oak notes vie with black cherry fruit for the taster's atten-tion. The wine is a more structured, medium-bodied style of Zinfandel with more noticeable tannin, and slightly higher acidity. Moreover, there is good depth of fruit. This wine requires 1–3 years of cellaring, but it should age well for 6–7 years. I also thought the 1995 Zinfandel

Brandlin Ranch to be a "close to the vest," earthy, spice-dominated Zinfandel, without the luscious fruit found in this wine in previous vintages. It is a very good Zinfandel, with a toasty oak-dominated nose. In the mouth, the wine offers red and black currants, cherries, underbrush and minerals in its medium-bodied, slightly sculptured, lean finish. Drink it over the next 5–6 years.

Two of the best Zinfandels from Rosenblum Cellars are the 1995 Samsel Vineyard Maggie's Reserve from Sonoma, and the 1995 Reserve George Hendry Vineyard. The 1995 Zinfandel Samsel Vineyard Maggie's Reserve offers a dark, nearly opaque ruby/purple color, and a toasty, spicy nose of vanillin, black cherries, underbrush, and pepper. Lusciously rich, ripe fruit hits the palate in layers in this multidimensional, full-bodied, well-balanced Zinfandel. It reveals none of the austerity, high acidity, or annoyingly sharp tannin found in so many wines from this vintage. Admirers of sweet black cherry aromas and flavors will be especially turned on by this offering. Drink it over the next 5–6 years. The outstanding 1995 Zinfandel Reserve George Hendry Vineyard exhibits a pure, mineral, currant, black cherry-scented nose intermixed with a subtle dose of oak. Medium to full bodied, deep, and leaning toward a more late-harvest style given the high alcohol and slight touch of pruniness in the wine's flavors, this broad, expansively flavored, cleanly made Zinfandel should drink well for 5–6 years.

Rosenblum's 1996s are consistently successful. They reflect the short, hot growing season as they do not possess the length of the two previous vintages. Therefore, no matter how big they might be, they are best consumed over the next 2–3 years.

Year in and year out one of the finest Zinfandel values is Rosenblum's nonvintage cuvée. The 1995 Cuvée XVI is a midweight, spicy, peppery, cranberry/raspberry-scented, fresh wine with an earthy/berry flavor profile, and a tart, clean finish. Drink it over the next year or two. Rosenblum offers three cuvées from Contra Costa. The 1996 Zinfandel Contra Costa exhibits a dark ruby color with purple nuances, as well as dusty, earthy notes in a moderately intense, peppery, berry-scented nose. In the mouth, there is good roundness, ripe fruit, and medium body. While there is not a great deal of depth behind the initial attack, there is an attractive, expansive, superficial mouth-feel. It should drink well over the next 2–3 years. The 1996 Zinfandel Continente Vineyard Old, Old Vines is a more powerful effort that does a relatively good job of supporting its lofty 15.4% alcohol. The wine has more late-harvest notes than the other Rosenblum Zinfandels, with a suggestion of raisined fruit and a touch of prune. The nose reveals the dusty earthiness that emerges from many Contra Costa wines, an underbrush, garrigue-like smell, and ripe, jammy, cherry fruit. In the mouth, the wine is expansive and fat, but more fragile than its siblings. Despite the presence of enough alcohol to stabilize the wine, I would prefer to drink this Zinfandel for its exuberance and mouth-filling qualities over the next 2–3 years. Rosenblum's third Contra Costa offering is the 1996 Zinfandel Pato Vineyard. This has been an increasingly fine source of Zinfandel (readers should also check out the Pato Vineyard Zinfandel from Neyers Winery). Rosenblum's offering carries over 14% alcohol, but it is exceptionally well hidden. This wine displays a Châteauneuf du Pape-like nose of iodine, crushed sea shells, and powerful black cherry, and pepper-tinged fruit. It is a deep, chewy, full-bodied, forceful, muscularly styled Zin with punch to its flavors. This powerhouse should age well, but it can be consumed in its fiery youth—say over the next 4–5 years.

The 1996 Zinfandel Richard Sauret Vineyard contains a relatively tame 13.6% alcohol. Reminiscent of a southern Rhône, it offers a peppery, kirsch, and earthy-scented nose, as well as tart acidity in the finish, which kept my score more conservative. It is a medium-bodied, very good, purely made, but slightly tart Zinfandel that should drink well for 2–3 years. The 1996 Zinfandel White Cottage Vineyard located on Howell Mountain is a new offering. This example offers more minerals, black cherry/black raspberry fruit notes, medium body, surprising elegance, and excellent purity. Additionally, a violetlike aroma emerges with breathing. A stylish, restrained Zinfandel boasting 13.7% alcohol, it should age well for

4–6 years. Another Rosenblum Napa Valley offering is the 1996 Zinfandel Ballentine Vineyard. This is a lush, richly fruity, medium- to full-bodied, ripe, well-made Zinfandel exhibiting more black than red fruits, subtle peppery notes, and a clean, spicy finish. It should drink well for 3–4 years. The 1996 Zinfandel George Hendry Vineyard Reserve is one of the stars of this consistently fine portfolio. The color is a saturated dark ruby/purple, and the bouquet offers up floral, blueberry/raspberry, and mineral notes. Ripe and full bodied, with a layered texture, it easily hides its lofty 14.9% alcohol. One of my favorite Rosenblum offerings, it should be consumed over the next 5–6 years.

The outstanding 1996 Zinfandel St. Peter's Church Vineyard (20th anniversary bottling) is produced from nearly 100-year-old vines. It is a superextracted, dark purple-colored Zinfandel with copious quantities of blackberry, raspberry, and spicy fruit intermingled with smoky *pain grillé* notes. A full-throttle, muscular wine that manages to retain its elegance (13.9% alcohol), this beautifully made Zinfandel will drink well for 4–6 years. From the Redwood Valley, Rosenblum has fashioned a very good 1996 Zinfandel Annette's Reserve Rhodes Vineyard. This example displays a briery, cranberry, red fruit character, as well as intrusive tart acidity. Medium bodied and crisp, with nice flavors, it is best drunk over the next several years. One of the more perfumed Rosenblum examples is the 1996 Zinfandel Harris Kratka Vineyard. This dark plum/cherry-colored wine is extremely aromatic, with plenty of spice, cherry liqueur, pepper, and underbrush notes. In the mouth, it is fresh, medium to full bodied, with excellent, nearly outstanding concentration. The wine's 14.6% alcohol is slightly noticeable in the finish, but well balanced vis à vis the wine's other components. It should be consumed over the next 3–4 years. One of the least distinctive of the Rosenblum 1996 Zinfandels is the 1996 Zinfandel Rockpile Vineyard. A narrowly focused wine with medium body, searing acid levels, extremely high alcohol (15.2%), and a compressed finish, it lacks charm, character, and flavor depth. It is not up to the level of the other Rosenblum offerings.

Just short of outstanding is the 1996 Zinfandel Cullinane Vineyard (20th anniversary bottling). Made from 97-year-old vines, this wine exhibits a claretlike nose of red currants and raspberries intermixed with earth and spicy notes. In the mouth, this saturated dark ruby/purple-colored wine is dominated by its raspberry fruit character. Powerful, deep, and layered, this rich, concentrated, multidimensional Zinfandel should evolve nicely for 5–6 years.

Finally, the 1996 Zinfandel Brandlin Ranch (20th anniversary series), from 91-year-old vines, is slightly tannic and more backward, but the wine opens in the mouth, exhibiting abundant black raspberry/briery fruit with an undercurrent of earth, mineral, and spicy notes. Medium to full bodied as well as expansive, this is an excellent, nearly outstanding Zinfandel that should evolve for 5–6 years. The 1996 Zinfandel Maggie's Reserve Samsel Vineyard, from Sonoma Valley, reveals a dark ruby/purple color, ripe berry fruit, spicy wood, and full body, as well as tangy, high acidity. The wine possesses an excellent finish, but the zesty acidity makes me think some of it may have been added. This long, mouth-filling, high alcohol (14.9%) Zinfandel should be consumed over the next 4–5 years.

SADDLEBACK CELLARS (NAPA)

1996	Cabernet Sauvignon	Napa	D	87+
1996	Cabernet Sauvignon	Napa	D	(88–90)
1995	Cabernet Sauvignon	Napa	D	90
1994	Cabernet Sauvignon	Napa	C	90
1993	Cabernet Sauvignon	Napa	C	90
1993	Cabernet Sauvignon Venge Family Reserve	Oakville	E	90
1997	Chardonnay	Napa	C	86

1996 Chardonnay	Napa	C	85
1995 Chardonnay	Napa	C	87
1997 Pinot Blanc	Napa	C	86
1996 Pinot Blanc	Napa	C	87
1995 Pinot Blanc	Napa	B	85
1994 Sangiovese	Napa	C	87
1996 Venge Family Reserve Cabernet Sauvignon	Oakville	E	(96–98)
1995 Venge Family Reserve Cabernet Sauvignon	Oakville	E	95
1994 Venge Family Reserve Cabernet Sauvignon	Oakville	E	95
1996 Venge Family Reserve Merlot	Oakville	D	90
1995 Venge Family Reserve Merlot	Oakville	D	91
1994 Venge Family Reserve Merlot	Oakville	D	90
1996 Venge Family Reserve Sangiovese Penny Lane Vineyard	Oakville	C	90
1995 Venge Family Reserve Sangiovese Penny Lane Vineyard	Oakville	C	86
1996 Venge Family Reserve Scout's Honor (Zinfandel/Sangiovese)	Oakville	C	89
1994 Zinfandel	Napa	C	91
1993 Zinfandel	Napa	C	91
1996 Zinfandel Old Vines	Napa	D	90
1995 Zinfandel Old Vines	Napa	C	92

Saddleback Cellars is a classic garage winery, and its owner, Nils Venge, a blend of cowboy and hippie. The man has an unbelievable track record of producing spectacular red wines, dating back to his early days at Villa Mt. Eden, followed by a sojourn at Groth, and today, at his own Saddleback Cellars. Venge is also the consulting winemaker for Plumpjack, Del Dotto, and Keenan—all wines that merit attention. Saddleback Cellars' white wines never hit the high notes, but they are refreshing, attractive, well-made offerings. For example, the 1997 Pinot Blanc exhibits a straightforward, fruity, orange peel, and honey-scented nose. This medium-bodied, fresh, lively wine will score well with consumers looking for a refreshing white to enjoy over the next year. The 1997 Chardonnay is made in Venge's nonmalolactic style. The wine possesses bracing acidity, a Chablis-like, zesty, tangy tartness, good fruit, excellent ripeness, and a clean, pure finish. As one who tends to prefer the more Burgundian-styled, malolactic fermented Chardonnays, I appreciate it, but tend to prefer another style. It should drink well for several years.

The delicacy and restrained nature of the white wines contrasts sharply with the blockbuster, in-your-face, unctuously textured, bombastic reds. As massive as these wines can be, they stand the test of time, as evidenced by some of Venge's classics that still remain in my cellar (the 1974 and 1978 Villa Mt. Eden, and the 1985 Groth Reserve). The thrilling levels of viscously textured fruit in the 1995 Cabernet Sauvignon Estate will impress most Cabernet fans. Still backward and unevolved, it offers juicy, jammy black fruits intermixed with toast. A huge, dense, chewy wine, with a plethora of fruit and glycerin, it should be cellared for 3–4 more years and consumed over the following 10–15. The similarly styled 1996

Cabernet Sauvignon Estate is chewy, full bodied, and thick. Not yet complex, it is superconcentrated, with gobs of toasty oak (about 40% American oak is utilized in the wine's upbringing), and a low-acid, chunky, heavyweight style. If the 1996 develops more complexity, it will merit a score in the low nineties. Anticipated maturity: 2001–2015.

The limited production wines from Nils Venge are labeled Venge Family Reserve. These special lots are made in quantities of less than 300 cases. The wines are aged for two years in small oak casks, 50% of which are new. The superb 1994 Venge Family Reserve Cabernet Sauvignon may well be matched in quality by the spectacular 1995 Venge Family Reserve Cabernet Sauvignon. Its opaque purple color, and nose of blackberries, cassis, licorice, coffee, and tar scents are outstanding. Concentrated, thick, and unctuous, with outstanding purity, and layers of extract, this large-scaled, beautifully made, all-American-styled Cabernet approaches "bigger than life" status. Anticipated maturity: 2001–2020. The saturated opaque purple-colored 1996 Venge Family Reserve Cabernet Sauvignon may turn out to be one of the greatest wines of the vintage. The vintage's elevated tannin has been tamed. The nose offers formidable quantities of black fruits, smoky oak, licorice, and coffee scents. Dense, with superb purity, layers of extract, and a finish that lasts for 40+ seconds, this awesome Cabernet Sauvignon appears to be even weightier than the blockbuster 1995 and 1994. Anticipated maturity: 2003–2025.

Nils Venge produces two Sangiovese cuvées. The 1996 Venge Family Reserve Sangiovese Penny Lane Vineyard (5% Cabernet Sauvignon is added to the blend) is one of California's finest. The fruit is picked very ripe (14% alcohol), and the wine is aged in Burgundy barrels. There is plenty of sweet, jammy strawberry/cherry/raspberry fruit in the nose, thick, juicy flavors, and soft tannin. Drink this offering over the next 3–4 years for its gutsy, exuberant style. The 1996 Venge Family Reserve Scout's Honor is a blend of 88% Zinfandel and 12% Sangiovese. (Château Montelena produces a similarly styled wine under the St. Vincent label.) Aged in 100% American oak, this offering is spicy and toasty, with briery, black raspberry, peppery notes in its sweet, jammy fragrance. Full bodied, hedonistic, and fun to drink, it should continue to offer immense pleasure for 2–4 years.

The outstanding 1996 Venge Family Reserve Merlot is a match for the fabulous 1994. The 1996 was made from Clone 7 and aged in 100% new French oak. By Venge standards the alcohol is relatively modest (13.5%) in this full-bodied, chewy, thick, highly extracted Merlot, which also possesses toasty, chocolatey, cherrylike flavors. Viscous and succulent, it is impossible to resist. This wine should be drinkable upon release, and last for 12–15 years. Readers weaned on sterile, insipid, wimpish Merlots will need to have their palates recalibrated after tasting this blockbuster.

The white wine offerings from Venge have always been pleasant, but generally uninteresting. However, that is changing. The 1995 Pinot Blanc may not be as richly fruity as the 1994, but it reveals plenty of crisp, elegant, orange peel-tinged aromas and flavors. It is light bodied, with good freshness and a midweight style. Venge's Chardonnays can be somewhat innocuous, but the 1995 Chardonnay appears to be one of the better examples he has made. The wine reveals excellent ripe pear and honeyed fruit, medium to full body, good length, a creamy texture, and a nice touch of toasty wood.

Although a longtime critic of Venge's white wines, I have gradually been moving toward more favorable reviews. His nonmalolactic style of Chardonnay produces wines with vivid fruit, citrusy acidity, and pear/orangelike flavors. The 1996 Chardonnay reveals those characteristics, plus medium body, and a one-dimensional but attractive, fruity, straightforward style. Drink it over the next 1–2 years. I enjoyed the 1996 Pinot Blanc a bit more, largely because it is a lusher, medium- to full-bodied wine with expressive, soft, orange, and buttery applelike flavors. With excellent purity as well as copious quantities of fruit, it should be drunk over the next year.

The 1995 Venge Family Reserve Sangiovese Penny Lane Vineyard includes 15% Cabernet Sauvignon in the blend. It is a lush, strawberry-scented wine with a medium garnet color, and an evolved style. Its Asian spice, jammy berry, lush personality suggests it should be consumed over the next 1–2 years.

As a critic of the insipid, vegetal, often appallingly overpriced Merlots that inundate the marketplace, it is a pleasure to taste the real thing. Venge has produced a number of terrific wines that will please both Merlot and Cabernet Sauvignon lovers. The first Merlot I tasted from Nils Venge was the 1994 Merlot Venge Family Reserve, a wine aged 18 months in 100% new oak casks. Unfortunately, only 120 cases were made of this lusty, decadent, chewy, intensely flavored Merlot. Gobs of smoke, vanillin-tinged, black cherry, and choco-latey flavors tumble out of a glass of this mouth-filling, creamy-textured wine. Full bodied, powerful, and dense, it will drink exceptionally well young but last for 12–15 years. I sus-pect anyone not on the winery's mailing list will have little chance of tracking down a bottle or two. The 1995 Venge Family Reserve Merlot has also been aged in 100% new oak, but it is so extraordinarily extracted and rich that the oak plays only a minor role in the wine's aro-matics and flavors. There are only 200 cases of this thick, black/purple-colored wine. The acidity is low, and the flavor and concentration extraordinarily high. This is a blockbuster, full-bodied, superconcentrated Merlot with a viscous personality and sensational extract. A pure, full-blooded heavyweight, it is even more impressive than the 1994. The 1995 will drink well for 15 or more years.

The Venge Family Reserve Cabernet Sauvignons are also splendidly rich, dense, full-bodied, superintense wines that possess 2 decades of aging potential. They are aged 2 years in small oak casks. Again, the production is tiny—120 cases of the 1993, and 240 cases of the 1994. The 1993 Cabernet Sauvignon Venge Family Reserve exhibits an opaque purple color, a promising, expressive, toasty, smoky, black fruit-scented nose, full body, as well as exceptional concentration and length. The wine possesses plenty of tannin beneath its im-pressive quantities of glycerin and rich fruit. Give it 2–3 years of cellaring and drink it over the following 2 decades. Another fabulous wine I tasted was the 1994 Venge Family Reserve Cabernet Sauvignon. An exquisite Cabernet Sauvignon aged for 18 months in oak casks (about 70% of which were new), it boasts an opaque black/purple color, as well as a nose of cassis, prunes, smoke, licorice, and earth. Exceptionally full bodied with jammy flavors, low acidity, and awesome levels of glycerin, extract, and fruit, this is a wild, unrestrained, super-concentrated Cabernet Sauvignon that should become increasingly civilized as it ages effort-lessly over the next 15–20 years.

The outstanding, opaque purple-colored 1993 Cabernet Sauvignon Estate offers a flashy nose of toasty oak, *pain grillé*, and copious quantities of sweet, thick cassis. This wine may not win points from those in search of lightness and finesse, but it will win accolades from powermongers looking for full-throttle, wonderfully pure, intense Cabernet Sauvignon with low acidity and great fruit. It should drink well for 12–15 years. The 1994 Cabernet Sauvi-gnon Estate is reminiscent of the Groth Cabernets produced in the mid-eighties. The wine exhibits plenty of chocolatey, cassis fruit, a nice touch of toasty oak, a thick, chewy texture, and mouth-filling extract and richness. The tannin is obscured by the wine's ripe fruit. The 1994 should drink well for 12–15 years. The 1995 Cabernet Sauvignon Estate is potentially a point or two superior to the 1994. The wine reveals a superb cassis and blueberrylike nose, round, soft tannin, outstanding purity and ripeness, and a long, silky-textured finish. It is an impressive example of California Cabernet Sauvignon.

The 1996 Cabernet Sauvignon under the Saddleback Cellars label is an attractive, tannic, beefy, meaty Cabernet that relies more on power and weight than finesse. The color is a healthy opaque purple, and the wine chewy, thick, burly, and muscular. Give it 3–4 years of cellaring, and consume it over the following 15 years.

Proprietor Nils Venge produces Zinfandel with unbridled power and richness. Some crit-ics suggest it is over the top, but I suspect they would have said the same thing about the

1947 Cheval Blanc or 1947 Pétrus if they had tasted those wines at a young age. That being said, readers looking for wimpish, subtle, innocuous wines (this is usually referred to as elegance) are advised to keep their distance.

If you are considering serving roasted boar at your next dinner party, the monstrous, yet immensely impressive, black/purple-colored, portlike 1993 Zinfandel is the wine to drink. It possesses an element of *sur-maturité,* offering up a huge, jammy, black cherry, licorice, peppery, and herb-scented nose. Exceptionally rich and full bodied, with no residual sugar, but a very ripe, blockbuster, chewy style, this enormous Zinfandel must carry at least 14+% alcohol. Fortunately, the wine has balance. Drink this Zinfandel over the next decade.

Another monster Zinfandel, the 1994 boasts an opaque dark ruby/purple color, a huge, toasty, oaky, smoky, jammy, black raspberry-scented nose, and unctuously thick, fat flavors that taste more like Zin gravy than wine. This thick, brawny, massive Zinfandel works in spite of its weight and intensity because everything is in proportion. Serve it with cheese or serious grilled food over the next 6–7 years.

Nils Venge fashioned one of the richest and most intense Zinfandels of the 1995 vintage. The color is an opaque black/plum. The nose offers smashingly lavish aromas of toasty oak and black fruits. Extremely rich and full bodied, but without any evidence of a late-harvest wine (a pruny, raisiny character), this pure, beautifully textured wine possesses layers of black raspberry fruit as well as copious quantities of glycerin, all nicely buttressed by adequate acidity. It is a compellingly rich, blockbuster-styled Zinfandel to drink over the next decade.

No one expects proprietor/winemaker Nils Venge to produce anything other than blockbuster, in-your-face, thick, gutsy, macho, and in this case, exotic Zinfandels. The 1996 Zinfandel Old Vines gracefully carries its 14.5% alcohol. It is a big, chocolatey, lavishly oaked, boldly styled wine with powerful, concentrated flavors that coat the mouth with glycerin, extract, and smoky black cherry and berry flavors. This is a low-acid, viscous, noticeably oaky Zinfandel. It is not for everybody, but it does make a huge impression in the mouth without numbing the palate. Drink it over the next 3–4 years.

Venge has always been a magician when it comes to red wines. Although it is sold only to mailing list customers, the 1994 Sangiovese is a noteworthy effort. The wine exhibits an attractive, cherry/strawberry/red currant-scented nose, surprisingly good color for this varietal, a plummy, overripe, richly fruity taste, and a soft, layered, plush texture. Many California Sangioveses are excessively acidic and lack concentration, but not this example. Drink it over the next 2–3 years.

ST. FRANCIS WINERY (SONOMA)

1995 Cabernet Sauvignon	Sonoma	C	86
1994 Cabernet Sauvignon	Sonoma	B	86
1993 Cabernet Sauvignon	Sonoma	C	87
1994 Cabernet Sauvignon King's Ridge Ranch	Sonoma	EE	92
1994 Cabernet Sauvignon Reserve	Sonoma	D	91
1993 Cabernet Sauvignon Reserve	Sonoma	D	88
1996 Chardonnay Reserve	Sonoma	C	86
1994 Merlot Estate Reserve	Sonoma	D	90
1993 Merlot Estate Reserve	Sonoma	D	88
1996 Zinfandel Old Vines	Sonoma	D	86
1995 Zinfandel Old Vines	Sonoma	C	87+?

1994 Zinfandel Old Vines	Sonoma	C	93
1993 Zinfandel Old Vines	Sonoma	C	92
1996 Zinfandel Reserve Pagani Vineyard	Sonoma	D	89
1995 Zinfandel Reserve Pagani Vineyard	Sonoma	C	90
1994 Zinfandel Reserve Pagani Vineyard	Sonoma	C	92

St. Francis' big, oaky, chocolatey style is evident in both the Cabernet Sauvignon and the Merlot. The 1994 Merlot Estate Reserve exhibits a saturated dark ruby color, followed by intensely smoky, oaky, jammy black cherry and chocolate aromas and flavors. This full-bodied, chewy, fleshy, soft, opulently styled wine should drink well for 7–8 years. A big, spicy, vanillin, ripe berry, chocolatey-scented wine, St. Francis' 1993 Merlot Estate Reserve possesses a sweet midpalate and fine texture. Drink this well-made Merlot over the next 5–6 years.

The medium- to full-bodied, supple 1993 Sonoma Cabernet Sauvignon is richly fruity and slightly herbaceous, without any hard edges. It is ideal for drinking over the next 5–6 years. It is ideal for restaurants. The 1993 Cabernet Sauvignon Reserve exhibits more cassis, weedy, new oak notes. Full bodied, with sweet fruit, good flesh, and fine length, it will drink well over the next 10–12 years.

Another outstanding effort from St. Francis is the 1994 Cabernet Sauvignon Reserve. It exhibits an opaque purple color, followed by a big, gaudy, ostentatious nose of cedar, Asian spices, jammy black fruits, prunes, and toasty new oak. This intense, ripe, full-bodied wine possesses explosive richness, lavish *pain grillé* notes, low acidity, and a heady, lusty, superlong finish. Yes, the new oak is high, but so is the wine's extract and fruit concentration. This is a Cabernet Sauvignon to be drunk with the stereo at high volume. As massive and rich as it is now, it should become more civilized with 3–5 years of cellaring. Anticipated maturity: now–2015. Even more impressive is St. Francis' 1994 Cabernet Sauvignon King's Ridge Vineyard. This wine, with its opaque purple color, and strikingly compelling nose of licorice, tobacco leaf, cassis, and smoke, is a full-bodied, heavyweight Cabernet with layers of flavor, a boatload of glycerin and extract, and copious quantities of sweet tannin in the monster finish. It is a dense, superconcentrated Cabernet Sauvignon that should have heads turning in amazement. Anticipated maturity: 2001–2020.

Readers looking for well-made Cabernet Sauvignon that is not too tannic and requiring cellaring should take a look at the attractive, elegant, richly fruity 1995 Cabernet Sauvignon from St. Francis. The color is a deep ruby, and the wine offers up copious amounts of cedar, spice, and red and black currants nicely buttressed by toasty oak. Medium bodied and supple, this is a forward, midweight style of Cabernet to drink over the next 5–7 years. The 1994 Cabernet Sauvignon's deep ruby color is followed by a moderately intense, herbal, black curranty nose with spicy wood and dusty tannin. This open-knit, soft, well-flavored Cabernet is not as lavishly wooded as the Reserve, but it will offer easygoing quaffing over the next 3–4 years.

St. Francis is making monster, pedal to the metal, full-throttle Zinfandels that are likely to score last in terms of subtlety, but who can ignore these opulent, lavishly rich, thrilling wines? I am not sure I could sit down and knock off a bottle of either of these wines, but a glass or two sure is enjoyable. These flamboyant, ostentatious Zinfandels succeed in pushing richness and new oak to the limit. If actors Robin Williams and Jim Carrey were winemakers, is this the type of Zinfandel they would produce? The 1994 Old Vines Zinfandel screams from the glass, in a reassuring rather than frightening manner. The wine boasts an opaque purple color, followed by a phenomenal nose of overripe black cherries and raspberries doused with high quantities of sweet, toasty, smoky oak, with plenty of licorice and pepper in the background. Superbly rich, smoky, hedonistic, and decadent, this wine is supple and velvety—like eating your favorite candy in liquid form (with plenty of alcohol). This spectacular blockbuster Zinfandel will last for 7–8 years, but it is best drunk in its first 4–5 years to take full advantage of its exuberance. The 1994 Zinfandel Pagani Ranch is cut from the same mold, with more structure and alcohol. It, too, is fabulously opulent and rich, with the same unctuous texture, thickness, and density of fruit as the Old Vine cuvée. These are amazing Zinfandels. There are other 1994 Zinfandels that are just as rich and full bodied, but there are none as ostentatious as this duo.

Produced from the Pagani vineyard's 101-year-old vines and 69-year-old vines from the Franciscus vineyard, the 1993 Zinfandel Old Vines is a huge, unctuously textured, block-buster Zinfandel with 15.4% alcohol. St. Francis's 1993 rivals the similarly styled, highly concentrated 1992. While the opaque purple-colored 1993 is rich and full bodied, the most remarkable thing about this wine is its brilliant display of peppery black cherry and rasp-berry fruit. It is huge and remarkably concentrated, but it is neither sweet nor overbearing—an amazing achievement given the wine's hefty alcohol. St. Francis has once again produced an extraordinary, decadently styled Zinfandel for drinking over the next 6–8 years.

Both of the massive 1995 Zinfandels were bottled without fining or filtration. The 1995 Zinfandel Old Vines may turn out to be outstanding, but at present it is controversial be-cause of the wine's overwhelming woodiness. It exhibits an opaque black/purple color, fol-lowed by an exotic nose dominated by raw wood. With breathing, some coconut and black cherry fruit scents emerge. Dense, full bodied, and exceptionally rich, but excessively toasty, this wine will benefit from another 6–12 months of bottle age. If the wood becomes more in-tegrated, this will be an outstanding example of a blockbuster, hugely concentrated, mas-sively thick Zinfandel that is atypical of the 1995 vintage. Certainly there was no problem with excessive wood in the 1995 Zinfandel Reserve Pagani Vineyard. Tipping the scales at 15.1% alcohol, it is amazing how well this wine's strength is hidden behind the layers of chewy, massively extracted, thick Zinfandel fruit. It boasts a saturated black/purple color, and a big, sweet nose of licorice, earth, vanillin, and raisiny black plums. Lush, full bodied, and huge, with exceptional concentration, this Zinfandel is sure to turn heads. Readers should not consider buying a bottle unless they enjoy mouth-staining, teeth-coating, full-bodied, behemoth Zinfandels. This wine should age well for at least a decade.

St. Francis fashions some of the most lavishly wooded, full-throttle, blockbuster Zinfan-dels in California, but readers will find the 1996s surprisingly civilized. The 1996 Zinfandel Old Vines carries only 14% alcohol! The wine reveals this estate's telltale woody spice, creamy texture, and dark ruby/purple color, but it does not measure up in terms of extrac-tion, richness, and completeness. Nevertheless, this is a soft, round, nicely made Zin to con-sume over the next 2–3 years. The dark ruby/purple-colored 1996 Zinfandel Reserve Pagani Vineyard (from 100-year-old vines) offers plenty of smoky, toasty new oak aromas along with jammy blackberry and raspberry, tar, licorice, and pepper notes. Although powerful, rich, and full bodied, it is not as concentrated as preceding vintages. While it is among the most fruit-driven and glycerin-endowed wines of the vintage, it falls just short of being outstand-ing. Drink it over the next 3–4 years.

An oaky, spicy style of Chardonnay, St. Francis's 1996 Reserve is medium bodied with a chewy texture and fine purity. Although fleshy and fruity, the wine lacks complexity and in-tensity in its aromatics. Drink it over the next 8–12 months.

CHÂTEAU ST. JEAN (SONOMA)

1996	Cabernet Sauvignon Reserve	Sonoma	E	92
1995	Cabernet Sauvignon Reserve	Sonoma	E	90+
1994	Cabernet Sauvignon Reserve	Sonoma	E	92
1993	Cabernet Sauvignon Reserve	Sonoma	E	91

1997 Chardonnay	Sonoma	B	87
1996 Chardonnay	Sonoma	B	87
1995 Chardonnay	Sonoma	B	87
1996 Chardonnay Belle Terre Vineyard	Alexander Valley	C	89
1995 Chardonnay Belle Terre Vineyard	Alexander Valley	C	89
1996 Chardonnay Durell Vineyard	Sonoma	D	88
1996 Chardonnay Robert Young Vineyard	Alexander Valley	D	90
1995 Chardonnay Robert Young Vineyard	Alexander Valley	D	88
1995 Chardonnay Robert Young Vineyard Reserve	Alexander Valley	D	89
1996 Cinq Cépages Proprietary Red Wine	Sonoma	D	93
1995 Cinq Cépages Proprietary Red Wine	Sonoma	D	92
1994 Cinq Cépages Proprietary Red Wine	Sonoma	D	87
1993 Cinq Cépages Proprietary Red Wine	Sonoma	D	88
1997 Fumé Blanc	Sonoma	A	86
1996 Fumé Blanc	Sonoma	A	85
1997 Fumé Blanc La Petite Étoile	Russian River	B	89
1996 Fumé Blanc La Petite Étoile	Russian River	B	89
1997 Gewürztraminer	Sonoma	A	87
1995 La Petite Étoile Proprietary White Wine	Sonoma	B	87
1996 Merlot	Sonoma	C	87
1995 Merlot	Sonoma	C	85
1994 Merlot	Sonoma	C	83
1996 Merlot Reserve	Sonoma	E	?
1995 Merlot Reserve	Sonoma	E	90+
1994 Merlot Reserve	Sonoma	E	91
1993 Merlot Reserve	Sonoma	D	90
1994 Pinot Noir	Sonoma	C	86
1996 Pinot Noir Durell Vineyard	Sonoma	D	88
1995 Pinot Noir Durell Vineyard	Sonoma	D	87
1997 Viognier Estate	Sonoma	D	89

Château St. Jean, one of the picture postcard photogenic sites in Sonoma Valley, is making the best wines of its 20-year history. This winery has made a 180-degree turn from the highly sculptured, excessively manipulated, industrial mindset of the seventies and eighties. Today, St. Jean's winemaking is based on a philosophy of nonmanipulation and natural bottling. The results are obvious, with wines that possess more aromatics and creamier textures. Most importantly, they provide more pleasure.

This is another winery that appears to be flourishing under Beringer's empire. Château St. Jean's offerings have been consistently fine over recent vintages. This estate was one of the first California wineries (along with Robert Mondavi) to establish a high-quality reputation for Fumé Blanc. That tradition continues with the nonmalolactic, crisp, minerally 1997 Fumés. The 1997 Fumé Blanc is a subtle, medium-bodied wine with a distinctive Loire Valley personality. There is plenty of minerality and herbaceousness, but the emphasis is primarily on melony, citrusy fruit. About 13% Semillon was added to the blend. It should drink well for 1–2 years. The terrific 1997 Fumé Blanc La Petite Étoile (100% Sauvignon Blanc) has been completely barrel fermented, and aged in casks, of which 50% are new. Although its malolactic fermentation has been blocked (to preserve its freshness and acidity), this wine boasts a sumptuous nose of honeydew melons, figs, lemon, butter, and minerals. Medium to full bodied, with a beautiful texture, good underlying acidity, and a heady alcoholic clout (14.5%), this is an elegant yet authoritatively flavored wine to drink over the next several years.

All Château St. Jean's Chardonnays are barrel fermented. Among the best buys in the marketplace is their Chardonnay Sonoma. The 1997 (which saw 25% new oak) is a fruit-driven, crisp wine exhibiting the buttery apple/flower blossom characteristics of this varietal. Medium bodied, pure, fresh, and lively, it is a wine to enjoy over the next several years. Two more ambitious, larger-scaled Chardonnays are the 1996 Belle Terre Vineyard and 1996 Robert Young Vineyard. The 1996 Chardonnay Belle Terre Vineyard exhibits a buttery apple-scented nose with subtle oak, tropical fruit, flowers, and wood notes. Full bodied, with a lush, nicely textured mouth-feel, this rich, excellent Chardonnay should drink well for 2–3 years. The 1996 Chardonnay Robert Young Vineyard is more intensely concentrated, with larger body, gorgeously ripe, buttery, honeyed fruit, complex peach/pear, citrusy notes, outstanding purity, and a long finish. Only 20% of this cuvée was put through malolactic in order to preserve its freshness. This wine should drink well for 2–3 years.

The 1997 Viognier, from a tiny 1-acre parcel owned by Château St. Jean, was given 100% barrel fermentation and 100% malolactic. Only 200 cases were produced of this outstanding wine. It exhibits a textbook bouquet of apricots, honeysuckle, and fruit cocktail with added smokiness for complexity, in addition to full body, and remarkably well hidden alcohol (15.7%). Most California Viognier is neutral and uninteresting, but this one is screaming at full volume. Drink it over the next year. I thought Château St. Jean's 1997 Gewürztraminer came close to hitting the bull's eye. It offers a crisp, grapefruit-scented nose, and dry, white corn and peachlike fruit. An attractively made, medium-bodied wine, it should be consumed over the next year.

The 1996 Merlot is a good value for this overcrowded, overpriced, often mediocre quality category. Ten percent Cabernet Franc has been added to the blend, resulting in a creamy-textured, ripe, mocha, berry, chocolatey-styled Merlot with good softness, excellent ripeness, and a pleasing, medium- to full-bodied, savory finish. It should drink well for 4–5 years. I was perplexed by the 1996 Merlot Reserve because of its herbaceous characteristics, dry, hard tannin, and austere, lean personality. In this case, the oak may have obliterated much of the wine's fruit, or I simply caught it at an unflattering stage of development. I will reserve judgment until I have had a chance to retaste it.

Château St. Jean produces one of California's most reasonably priced proprietary red wines. Moreover, its quality has soared dramatically in the nineties. The 1995 and 1996 are the two finest Cinq Cépages blends I have tasted. The 1995 Cinq Cépages is tasting even better than it was prior to bottling. The wine, which spends 2 years in 50% new oak barrels, is dominated by Cabernet Sauvignon (77%), with the other four varietals making up this blend. The 1995 offers a combination of finesse, complexity, richness, and accessibility. It possesses a saturated ruby color, and a flamboyant nose of cedar, licorice, tobacco-tinged black currant fruit, and sweet vanillin. Concentrated, full bodied, and loaded with fruit, this high-quality, impressively endowed wine can be drunk now as well as over the next 15–20 years. The 1996 Cinq Cépages is a bigger, more structured and muscular version of the

1995. It displays less charm, but more concentration. In my tasting notes, I called it "a California St.-Émilion." Cedar, fruitcake, and Provençal herbs are intertwined with chocolate, black currants, and toasty oak in this full-bodied, powerful, moderately tannic wine. Unlike the 1995, this vintage will require several years of cellaring; it should keep for 20 years.

The 1996 Cabernet Sauvignon Reserve is a powerful, rich, concentrated wine that will spend a total of 3 years in barrel before bottling. Full bodied, with a cocoa, vanillin, plum, prune, and black currant-scented nose, rich, chewy, full-bodied flavors, plenty of tannin, and copious amounts of glycerin and extract, it will last for 2 decades after its release at the turn of the century.

The straightforward 1996 Fumé Blanc is a medium-bodied, round, fruity wine that is meant to be drunk within its first year or two of release. Although straightforward, it is well made and attractive. The more ambitious 1996 Fumé Blanc La Petite Étoile is a nonmalolactic, 100% barrel-fermented offering with a creamier texture. This wine also benefits from more exposure to new oak casks (about 30%). It exhibits a smoky, clean, melony character with subtle honey and herbaceous notes. The barrel fermentation gives it a rounder texture, as well as good richness and a layered feel in the mouth. This is an attractive, nearly outstanding example of Fumé Blanc that should drink well for 2–3 years.

Château St. Jean has always enjoyed considerable success with their 100% Sauvignon Blanc, nonmalolactic La Petite Étoile. These are wines to drink within 1–2 years of release. The 1995 displays clean, crisp, melony fruit nicely touched by a honey note. This elegant, crisp, dry, tartly styled Sauvignon Blanc offers good flexibility with numerous culinary dishes. The 1995 reveals more grapefruit in its flavors, with less of the tropical fruit and fat of the 1994.

The Chardonnay offerings are led by Château St. Jean's flagship wine, the single vineyard Robert Young Chardonnay. The percentage of new oak casks is being increased to approximately 50%, and the utilization of new Chardonnay clones, such as Burgundy's well-known Dijon clone, will result in wines possessing more fruit extract. Since 1990 there have been two cuvées of Robert Young Chardonnay. Those barrels with extra ripeness and intensity are set aside for a reserve cuvée, and the others are blended together for the regular bottling. The 1995 Robert Young Chardonnay is an attractive, elegant, restrained, nicely executed Chardonnay. The elegant, crisp 1995 is not dissimilar from the 1993. This nonmalolactic wine possesses a crisp acid profile, and should keep for 2–4 years, although I do not expect any further development since it must be sterile filtered. The 1995 Chardonnay Robert Young Reserve is a nonmalolactic, barrel-fermented, intensely concentrated wine with loads of butterscotch and ripe fruit flavors. The wine's natural acidity gives delineation to this medium- to full-bodied, intensely flavored wine. As the wine sat in the glass, the unmistakable smell and taste of overripe pears emerged. This attractive wine should drink well for 2–3 years.

The 1995 Chardonnay Belle Terre Vineyard (from the Alexander Valley) was given full malolactic fermentation and aged entirely in small oak casks, of which 50% were new. This wine possesses a great deal more complexity and richness, as well as a creamier texture than the Robert Young offerings. The wine is rich, with loads of fruit, a lovely buttery, honeyed, citrusy component, and excellent purity.

Readers looking for one of the best Chardonnay values in the marketplace should check out St. Jean's 1996 Chardonnay Sonoma. About 80% of this wine goes through malolactic fermentation, and it includes a dollop of Robert Young Vineyard Chardonnay in the blend (about 20%). Remarkably, 100,000 cases of this wine are made (and there is only one bottling). It is a lush, fruit-driven, judiciously oaked, medium-bodied wine with loads of tropical fruit and excellent purity. It should drink well for 2 years. Chardonnay lovers should consider buying this one by the case!

An attractive, fairly priced, citrusy, cream custard-tasting Chardonnay, the fleshy, richly fruity, medium- to full-bodied 1995 Chardonnay exhibits plenty of ripe fruit, subtle oak, good depth, richness, and acidity, and a corpulent, pure mouth-feel. Drink it over the next year.

St. Jean also offers a 1996 Chardonnay Durell Vineyard, which is a mineral, flowery, medium- to full-bodied wine with attractive buttery fruit, excellent lushness, enough acidity for balance, and a clean, well-endowed finish. The influence of wood is subtle, and the quality of fruit is pure and ripe. This wine should drink well for 2–3 years.

The 1994 Pinot Noir is a soft, chocolatey, herbal, pleasant, midweight wine. I do not think the 1995 Pinot Noir Durell Vineyard has turned out as well from bottle as it suggested from cask. The wine is very good, but I was hoping it might even be better. An intriguing style of dark garnet-colored Pinot, it possesses obvious new oak, a chocolatey, meaty character to the wine's aromatics, and dense, ripe, round flavors that are concentrated but not well focused. The 1996 Pinot Noir Durell Vineyard reveals more complexity and richness. This dark ruby-colored wine offers meaty, plant, and berry fruit aromas in an exotic, lush, medium- to full-bodied style. It possesses adequate acidity, and a supple texture. Both of these Pinots should be drunk over the next 3–4 years.

The most noticeable improvements at St. Jean can be seen in the Merlot and Cabernet Sauvignon programs. The one-dimensional 1994 Merlot (86% Merlot and 14% Cabernet Franc) displays a dark ruby color, as well as vague cinnamon/chocolatey notes in the nose, and a compressed, lean, medium-bodied palate. The regular bottling of 1995 Merlot is a solid, straightforward, attractive, one-dimensional wine. Far more impressive were the Reserve bottlings. They spend 36 months in barrel, of which 50% are new. I thought all the vintages I tasted of the Merlot Reserve were potentially outstanding wines. The 1993 Merlot Reserve is a full-bodied, lush, opulent, dense, chocolate/black cherry fruit-driven wine that is both mouth-filling and concentrated. It will have 10–15 years of aging potential. The 1994 Merlot Reserve reveals a similar character, with copious quantities of chocolate-flavored, jammy black cherry fruit intertwined with lavish quantities of toasty new oak. It cuts a larger, more expansive feel on the palate, and displays impressive length and richness. The 1995 Merlot Reserve exhibits less aromatic and flavor dimension when compared to the 1994, but it is still a superbly concentrated, thick, juicy wine that may end up having slightly more tannin. With more of a monolithic personality, it tastes slightly muted and more backward in its development than the other vintages. These Reserve Merlots are all made in limited quantities of about 400 cases.

To my mind, the Cinq Cépages proprietary red wine offerings are not as exciting as the Reserve Merlots or Reserve Cabernet Sauvignons. The chocolatey, smoky, slightly herbal, spicy, tannic 1993 Cinq Cépages appears less impressive than the Reserve Cabernet Sauvignon and Reserve Merlot. Nevertheless, it offers elegance, some hard tannin, and a midweight, medium-bodied style. This wine has less aging potential than the Reserve Cabernet; I would opt for drinking it over the next 3–12+ years. The 1994 Cinq Cépages (a blend of 76% Cabernet Sauvignon, 10% Merlot, 9% Cabernet Franc, 3% Malbec, and 2% Petit Verdot) is a very good, elegant, spicy, tasty, medium-bodied wine that just misses the bull's eye in terms of being exciting. It should drink well for 10–15 years.

There are approximately 1,000 cases produced of St. Jean's Reserve Cabernet Sauvignon. This wine spends 36 months in oak casks, of which 50% are new. The wine is primarily Cabernet Sauvignon, although small portions of Cabernet Franc and Merlot are part of the blend. The 1993 Cabernet Sauvignon Reserve is a terrific wine from a vintage that has fewer weaknesses than some of my colleagues have suggested. In short, 1993 is a topflight vintage that has been lost in all the justifiable hype over 1994. The wine reveals an opaque purple color, and a tight but promising nose of loamy earth, black cherries, cassis, and smoke. Full bodied, dense, and tannic, with impressive levels of richness, this youthful, unevolved, exceptional Cabernet Sauvignon should be at its best between 2000 and 2015. The 1994 Cabernet Sauvignon Reserve should prove to be slightly superior, although from a perspective of richness and intensity, it does not eclipse the 1993. It possesses an open-knit, complex aromatic profile consisting of black fruits, cedar, tobacco, fruitcake, and new oak. Full bodied, with sweeter tannin than the 1993, this multidimensional, large-scaled Cabernet Sauvignon has impeccable balance, as well as a finish that lasts for nearly 35 seconds. Although accessible, 3–4 years of cellaring is recommended; it should keep for 2 decades. The 1995 Cabernet Sauvignon Reserve exhibits less aromatic and flavor dimension, but superb depth, ripeness, and richness. As with many 1995s, there is a muted character to the wine, but my instincts suggest that all the right stuff is present to develop into an outstanding wine. Patience is required as this wine will need at least 4–5 years of cellaring. It is another 20-year wine. No, I do not believe it will achieve the complexity and richness of the 1994, and perhaps not even the 1993, but it is an exceptional wine that could turn out to be a sleeper in 5–10 years.

ST. SUPERY (NAPA)

1994 Cabernet Sauvignon Dollarhide Ranches	Napa	C	86
1994 Meritage Proprietary Red Wine	Napa	D	87

These are the two finest efforts I have ever tasted from St. Supery, a winery of which I have been highly critical in the past for its one-dimensional, innocuous offerings. Things appear to have changed given the approachable style of these wines, as well as their more natural textures that have not been excessively acidified and manipulated. For example, the 1994 Cabernet Sauvignon Dollarhide Ranches is a round, fruity, deep ruby-colored wine with attractive plum and black currant fruit, medium body, a nice dosage of *pain grillé* notes, and a low-acid, soft, seductive finish. It will drink well for another 5–7 years. The 1994 Meritage displays a dark ruby/purple color, an aggressive overlay of vanillin-tinged new oak, a Spanish Rioja-like style with plenty of sexy, ripe berry fruit, but also outrageous levels of new oak. The oak may be too blatant for many readers, but I am giving the wine the benefit of the doubt because of the high-quality, rich berry fruit. This wine is soft, round, and ideal for drinking over the next 7–10 years.

SAUCELITO CANYON VINEYARD (ARROYO GRANDE)

1996 Zinfandel Estate	Arroyo Grande Valley	C	89
1995 Zinfandel Estate	Arroyo Grande Valley	C	84
1994 Zinfandel Estate	Arroyo Grande Valley	C	89
1993 Zinfandel Arroyo Grande Valley Estate	Arroyo Grande	C	90

The textbook 1996 Zinfandel offers copious quantities of black cherry, raspberry, and spicy fruit that soar from the glass. The color is a deep ruby/purple, and the wine is rich, layered, full bodied, and pure. Tasting it brought to mind a hypothetical blend of a top quality Châteauneuf du Pape and Zinfandel. The wine admirably conceals its 15% alcohol, but it is best drunk over the next 3–4 years to take advantage of its exuberant, fiery youth.

One of the deceptive characteristics of the 1995 Zinfandel vintage is that many wines possess impressive alcohol levels (suggesting ripe, concentrated wines), but they do not deliver much in terms of flavor except acidity and tannin. Saucelito Canyon's 1995 boasts an alcohol content of 14.7%, but it is a structured, somewhat tough-textured and restrained Zinfandel with more spice than fruit. While I enjoyed the wine's pronounced earthiness and distinctive style, it is completely different from previous efforts from this winery, which has produced Zinfandels that emphasized fruit rather than spice. The 1995 should be drunk over the next 2–3 years.

The 1994 is a seductive, voluptuously textured, delicious Zinfandel that may deserve an outstanding rating. I was unable to give it that extra point because it is not profoundly concentrated, but perhaps I am being too tough. Medium to full bodied, with an easygoing, jammy, overripe style, as well as luscious levels of succulent red and black fruit, this exuberant, delicious Zinfandel should be drunk over the next several years for its unabashed, obvious pleasures!

The 1993 is a whoppingly big, rich Zinfandel (14.5% alcohol), with a deep ruby/purple color, supersweet, ripe, briary, black cherry and currant scents to its flamboyant aromatic profile, great ripeness and richness, medium to full body, a velvety, voluptuous texture, and layers of jammy red and black fruits. Pure and seductive, this wine is ideal for drinking over the next 7–8 years.

SAUSAL WINERY (SONOMA)

1995 Zinfandel	Alexander Valley	C	77
1994 Zinfandel	Alexander Valley	C	88
1993 Zinfandel	Alexander Valley	C	90

Typical of the 1995 vintage, the dark ruby-colored 1995 Zinfandel possesses plenty of oak in the nose, as well as green, herbaceous, peppery, spicy aromas, austere, lean, tough-textured flavors, medium body, and a lack of glycerin, extract, and ripe fruit. It is unlikely to ever come into balance. The dark-colored, oaky, sweet, jammy 1994 Zinfandel exhibits loads of flavor, but it has not yet knitted together. There is good power and considerable character, but it needs 6–12 months of cellaring to bring all the component parts into focus. It should last for 7–8 years.

Always one of the top Zinfandel producers, Sausal's 1993 carries 14% alcohol in a full-bodied format. The wine offers a saturated dark ruby/purple color, and a fragrant, intense nose of black cherries, underbrush, pepper, and spice. Full bodied, well balanced, and admirably concentrated, it possesses just enough oak and acidity to give the wine structure and definition. It will offer delicious drinking over the next decade.

SCHERRER (ALEXANDER VALLEY)

1996 Zinfandel Old and Mature Vines	Alexander Valley	D	91
1995 Zinfandel Old and Mature Vines	Alexander Valley	D	90
1994 Zinfandel Old and Mature Vines	Russian River	C	90
1993 Zinfandel Old and Mature Vines	Alexander Valley	C	89+
1996 Zinfandel Shale Terrace	Alexander Valley	D	90

Fred Scherrer's grandfather planted these old Zinfandel vines in Alexander Valley, from which Scherrer has consistently made a textbook Zinfandel.

In 1996, Fred Scherrer made two cuvées, separating part of the vineyard planted on a bed of shale and claylike soil. The 1996 Zinfandel Shale Terrace reveals a dark ruby color, pleasing, gravelly, briery, peppery aromatics, medium to full body, and a complete, concentrated, supple mouth-feel. The dark ruby/purple-colored 1996 Zinfandel Old and Mature Vines possesses an extra flavor dimension with copious quantities of sweet berry fruit, plenty of glycerin, full body, excellent spice and purity, and a peppery, long, heady finish. The high alcohol (over 14%) is well hidden by the level of fruit and richness. Both should be consumed over the next 4–5 years.

The 1995 Old and Mature Vines Zinfandel exhibits a deep ruby/purple color, followed by a rich, briery, peppery nose, excellent purity, full body, and layers of concentrated Zinfandel fruit. It should age well for 7–8 years, but I recommend drinking it during its first 5–6 years of life.

Fortunately, there are 1,000 cases of the impressively endowed 1994 Zinfandel made from old vines. It is a big, beefy wine that has been aged in small oak casks, of which 20% were French. The wine exhibits an excellent dense ruby/purple color, a sweet, ripe, peppery, black cherry, loamy-scented nose, bold, forceful, full-bodied, well-balanced flavors with out-standing extract, excellent purity, and a spicy, closed, structured finish. This impeccably well made, complex, spicy, more austerely styled Zinfandel will drink well for 7–8 years.

The 1993 Zinfandel exhibits a healthy, dark ruby/purple color, a big, undeveloped but promising nose of peppery, black raspberry and cherry fruit, full body, excellent to outstand-ing concentration, decent acidity, and light tannin. Bottled without fining or filtration, this is a pure, young, immensely impressive Zinfandel that should drink well for a decade.

SCHUETZ OLES (NAPA)

1996 Zinfandel	California	C	76
1995 Zinfandel	California	C	86
1996 Zinfandel Korte Ranch	Napa	C	78
1995 Zinfandel Korte Ranch	Napa	C	87
1994 Zinfandel Korte Ranch	Napa	B	88

I was unmoved by the two 1996 offerings from Schuetz Oles. The 1996 Napa Zinfandel ex-hibits a pinched, narrowly constructed personality with an attractive saturated dark ruby color, little fruit, lean, angular flavors, and a hard, astringent finish. Sadly, it will not im-prove. The 1996 Zinfandel Korte Ranch reveals a similar style, although slightly riper, sweeter fruit can be discerned in both the nose and attack. However, the wine is compressed and one dimensional, with a tight, dry, severe finish. Both wines should be consumed sooner rather than later.

The 1995 California Zinfandel exhibits an evolved dark plum color, and a vivid, roasted peanut-scented nose that is reminiscent of a Grenache-based wine. The wine's attack offers sweet, plummy/berry fruit, good spice, medium body, and moderate weight. Crisp acidity vies with the fruit for the taster's attention. This is a straightforward, moderately endowed, well-made, uncomplicated style of Zinfandel to drink over the next 3–4 years. The dark plum-colored 1995 Zinfandel Korte Ranch offers an intriguing nose of black cherries, un-derbrush, allspice, and earth. It possesses more density and sweetness of fruit than the Cali-fornia bottling, as well as a tasty, vanillin-tinged oak character. This is a larger, medium-bodied, well-endowed, straightforward Zinfandel to drink over the next 5–7 years.

The 1994 Zinfandel Korte Ranch is another decadent, exotic, intensely spicy, peppery, richly fruity Zinfandel that keeps everything in harmony. The wine exhibits a deep ruby color, gobs of tasty, dense Zinfandel fruit, medium to full body, and a supple, velvety-textured finish with copious amounts of glycerin and alcohol. Drink it over the next 5–6 years. Very good value.

SCREAMING EAGLE (NAPA)

1997 Cabernet Sauvignon	Napa	EE	(97–100)
1996 Cabernet Sauvignon	Napa	EE	97+
1995 Cabernet Sauvignon	Napa	EE	99
1994 Cabernet Sauvignon	Napa	EE	94
1993 Cabernet Sauvignon	Napa	EE	97

This microscopic winery located near the Oakville Crossroads, below the hillside vineyards of Dalla Valle and Vine Hill, is a remarkable story. The creation of a single-minded propri-etor, Jean Phillips, Screaming Eagle became California's leading cult wine when the first vintage, the nearly perfect 1992, was released. Production is distressingly small—135 cases of the 1993, 175 cases of the 1994, and 225 cases of the 1995. However, with the vineyard coming into full production, there were 500 cases of the 1996 and 1997. The wines are made by the well-known Napa Valley oenologist, Heidi Barrett (a *Wine Advocate* heroine of the year in 1995). What makes Screaming Eagle such an extraordinary wine is its remarkably sweet, lavishly rich, opulently textured, superextracted black currant and black cherry fruitiness. Moreover, they are admirably pure, layered, velvety, and accessible. As delicious as these wines are young, they should age for 20 or more years, because of their extraordinary equilibrium.

As a wine consumer, I always have mixed emotions when writing about wineries with a microscopic production. Yet it is important to send a message about the extraordinary quality level of these reference point Cabernets produced by Screaming Eagle. This, I believe, counterbalances the sobering thought that few readers will ever get a chance to see the wine, much less taste it. Production doubled to 500 cases in 1996, but most important, Screaming Eagle's small production is never a reason to ignore what proprietor Jean Phillips has achieved at this tiny winery. What makes these wines so stunning is their black currant/cassis fruit. Screaming Eagle may be the most extravagantly pure and rich expression of cassis one can find— short of drinking cassis liqueur. There is an unbelievable purity to these wines, as well as phenomenal concentration and richness, yet in no sense are they heavy, ponderous, or out of balance. The 1992 Screaming Eagle is perfection in a bottle, the 1993 not far behind. In 1994, widely considered to be Napa Valley's greatest vintage for Cabernet Sauvignon in the nineties, Screaming Eagle made a marvelous wine, as opposed to one that flirts with immortality. The three vintages I tasted on my visit in September 1998 were awe inspiring.

The 1995 Cabernet Sauvignon is as close to a perfect wine as I could hope to taste. This opaque purple-colored wine exhibits a sensational purity of black currant fruit, intermixed with a notion of raspberries, violets, and well-disguised sweet vanillin. Full bodied, with remarkable intensity, exquisite symmetry, and a midpalate and finish to die for, this is a compelling, astonishingly seductive Cabernet Sauvignon that can be drunk now or cellared for 20–25 years. I may have done this wine a disservice by not giving it the big 3-digit score. The 1996 Cabernet Sauvignon (500 cases) reveals more noticeable tannin than the 1995, as well as a similarly opaque purple color, and a telltale crème de cassis-scented nose intermixed with subtle toasty oak, licorice, and flower blossoms. The 1996 may be a bit brawnier, but that is a tough call to make at this stage. This enormously concentrated, yet strikingly elegant Cabernet Sauvignon will require bottle aging when released. Anticipated maturity: 2002–2020. The 1997 Cabernet Sauvignon (500 cases) has more in common with the 1995 and 1992 than the 1996 or 1994. The opaque purple/black color is followed by intense, soaring aromas of crème de cassis, in addition to blueberry and blackberry fruit. The wine's extraordinary purity, great depth, and fabulously seamless, full-bodied, multilayered texture are something to behold, particularly in a wine so young. However, everything is in balance. This is another work of art from an extraordinary *terroir*. Like the 1992 and 1995, the 1997 should be uncommonly approachable at release given its voluptuous texture, but it possesses the richness and overall equilibrium to age well for 20–25 years.

The 1993 Cabernet Sauvignon is a remarkable wine, not dissimilar from the 1992. The 1993 reveals an opaque purple color, as well as a rich, jammy, pure nose of black currant/cassis fruit intertwined with scents of minerals and high-quality, spicy oak. The wine offers a cascade of lavishly rich, opulently textured, superextracted fruit that is beautifully buttressed by oak and sweet tannin. Remarkably long, pure, and rich, this is a compelling Cabernet Sauvignon with no hard edges. Perfectly balanced, marvelously concentrated, and exciting, look for this wine to drink well young but keep for 25 years.

The 1994 Cabernet Sauvignon was performing even better in 1997 than it was the year before. I still believe the 1995 has a slight edge, but that may be more noticeable 8–10 years from now than at present. The opaque purple-colored 1994's forward, gorgeously scented nose offers up a smorgasbord of black fruits, along with a subtle dosage of toasty oak and minerals. Full bodied, with a seamless, lush texture, this is a profoundly generous wine with everything going for it. The finish lasts for 35 seconds. As gorgeous as it is, this wine can be drunk young or cellared for 20–25 years.

I keep asking Jean Phillips what she does in order to achieve such purity of fruit. There are no secrets—yields are modest, grapes are harvested at 24 brix (which is normal), the wine is aged in Seguin-Moreau French barrels (about 60%–65% are new) for 18–20 months, and the wine is bottled with no filtration. Considerable punching down is done at Screaming Eagle, and the small, one-half-ton fermenters may hold the secret to the extraordinary fruit quality Jean Phillips achieves. On the other hand, it may simply be the *terroir* combined with the owner's obsession for brilliant wines. And let's not forget the consulting oenologist, Napa Valley's Heidi Barrett. Getting on the winery's mailing list is the only way to latch on to a bottle, unless you get lucky and find a bottle at one of Napa Valley's wine shops or restaurants.

SEAVEY (NAPA)

1997 Cabernet Sauvignon	Napa	D	(94–96)
1996 Cabernet Sauvignon	Napa	D	91
1995 Cabernet Sauvignon	Napa	D	94+
1994 Cabernet Sauvignon	Napa	D	91+
1993 Cabernet Sauvignon	Napa	D	91
1997 Chardonnay	Napa	C	87
1996 Chardonnay	Napa	C	87
1995 Chardonnay	Napa	C	87
1997 Merlot	Napa	D	(88–91)
1996 Merlot	Napa	D	87
1995 Merlot	Napa	C	87
1994 Merlot	Napa	C	89

Located in the pastoral, tranquil Conn Valley, Seavey Vineyards remains an unheralded source of high-quality wine. While the Chardonnay and Merlot are excellent, the Cabernet Sauvignon can be sensational. Even though it is expensive, given its quality it seems under-priced in the finest vintages. As for the Chardonnay, winemaker Frenchman Philippe Melka, believes in picking very ripe, but blocking malolactic fermentation. His aim is to produce a Chablis-like Chardonnay that is crisp and tangy, but has plenty of body and intense fruit. That appears to have been achieved with the 1997 Chardonnay, an attractive honeyed pear-scented wine with subtle toasty notes. Medium to full bodied, pure, and made in a style reminiscent of Sauvignon Blanc, it possesses good richness, and citrus notes that emerge as the wine sits in the glass. It should drink well for 4–5 years.

Approximately 200–300 cases of Merlot are produced by proprietors Mary and Bill Seavey. The malolactics for the reds are done in barrel. The deep ruby-colored 1997 Merlot offers a moderately intense nose of white chocolate, black cherries, currants, and cedar. The wine is fleshy, spicy, ripe, and foursquare. It should drink well for another decade. I thought the 1996 Merlot was even more impressive. The color is a saturated ruby purple, and the wine smoky, with plenty of thick, juicy black cherries, earth, and chocolate on display in abundant quantities. Full bodied and rich, with an opulent texture, this immensely attractive Merlot can be drunk now or cellared for 12–15 years.

Seavey has produced some exceptional Cabernet Sauvignons, and I predict the 1995 (950 cases) will be an unexpected winner in many blind tastings. It is performing even better this year than it did last, hence my elevated score. The color is an opaque purple. The wine displays a fantastic nose of classic black currants intermixed with cigar box and cedar scents. In the mouth, it is full bodied and backward, but persuasively rich, layered, and marvelously well balanced. There is a deep, sweet midpalate and explosive ripeness and richness in the long, heady finish. A sleeper pick in this outstanding vintage, it should evolve effortlessly for 20–30 years. Anticipated maturity: 2002–2028. The 1996 Cabernet Sauvignon (1,200 cases) was bottled in May 1998. It is slightly higher in alcohol than the 1995 (14.3% for the 1996 and 13.9% for the 1995), with allspice, black currants, loamy soil and toasty scents. In the mouth, this is a powerful, muscular, concentrated Cabernet with more noticeable (and slightly rougher) tannin than either the 1994 or 1995. The backward, outstanding 1996 will be a wine to put away for at least 5–6 years. Anticipated maturity: 2004–2025.

I am going to step out on the proverbial limb and state that I believe Seavey's 1997 Cabernet Sauvignon will be their finest Cabernet since the monumental 1991. There were 1,800 cases of this offering, which reveals that element of *sur-maturité* often found in the greatest wines. The opaque purple color is accompanied by fabulous sweet black fruits and promising floral, spice box scents complemented by the judicious use of oak barrels (35% new). Phenomenally deep, layered, and textured, with full body, and well-concealed high alcohol (14.5%), this is a terrific, unctuously textured, concentrated, and evolved Cabernet Sauvignon that should be accessible when released, but age for 20–25 years. Seavey does not sell wine futures, but this will certainly be a vintage to remember.

The 1996 Chardonnay is a nonmalolactic, barrel-fermented Chardonnay with an excellent honeyed citrus/ripe pear-scented nose, crisp acidity, and plenty of primary fruit aromas. While it will undoubtedly age well, I would suggest drinking it over the next 1–2 years. The 1995 Chardonnay (275 cases), a nonmalolactic, barrel-fermented California Chardonnay, offers crisp acidity, medium to full body, attractive honeyed pear and buttery fruit, and fine richness and length. It should drink well for 1–3 years.

As for the red wines, the Merlots are softer and more plush than the muscular, concentrated Cabernets. The 1994 Merlot (350 cases) is aged in 35%–45% new oak casks. The opaque purple color is followed by a wine with an impressively rich nose of black currants and spice. Still young, this ripe, rich, sweet, medium- to full-bodied 100% Merlot should last longer than I suggested in my review last year. It now appears it will evolve effortlessly for another 7–8 years and hold at that plateau for 5–6 years. The 1995 Merlot, which is more closed, with less concentration, offers a dark ruby/purple color, a sweet nose of black cherries, earth, and a whiff of smoke and chocolate. This medium-bodied, moderately tannic wine requires 1–2 years of bottle age. I do not see it ever offering quite the level of richness and intensity of the 1994, but certainly the raw materials are present.

The glories of this estate remain its Cabernet Sauvignons. The 1993 Cabernet Sauvignon has developed well. It is performing far stronger than it did when I first tasted it. The wine possesses a dark saturated purple color, a sweet, truffle, cassis-scented nose, and dense, powerful, full-bodied flavors with considerable glycerin, extract, and tannin. It reveals more sweetness of fruit, as well as a more expansive, chewy texture than it displayed immediately after bottling. For the 1993 vintage, this is a top-notch effort. Anticipated maturity: 2000–2020. After retasting the 1994 Cabernet Sauvignon, I was even more impressed. Made from low yields of approximately 2 tons of fruit per acre, from Seavey's east-facing hillside vineyards in the Conn Valley, the 1994 exhibits an opaque purple color, and an exuberant yet still young and unformed nose of spice, black fruits, and cedar. Full bodied, with layers of dense, ripe fruit, this rich, moderately tannic wine should be at its best in 3–5 years. It will keep for 2 decades or more.

This is another property where getting on the mailing list makes good sense.

SEGHESIO WINERY (SONOMA)

1993 Pinot Noir	Sonoma	B	68
1993 Zinfandel	Sonoma	B	85
1996 Zinfandel	Sonoma	B	87
1995 Zinfandel	Sonoma	A	86
1994 Zinfandel	Sonoma	A	86
1993 Zinfandel	Sonoma	B	86
1996 Zinfandel Home Ranch	Alexander Valley	D	88
1996 Zinfandel Old Vines	Sonoma	C	91
1995 Zinfandel Old Vines	Sonoma	C	87+
1994 Zinfandel Old Vines	Sonoma	B	90
1996 Zinfandel San Lorenzo	Alexander Valley	D	91
1995 Zinfandel San Lorenzo	Alexander Valley	C	89

Seghesio, which possesses well-located vineyards in both Alexander Valley and Sonoma, is producing better and better wines. The 1996 Zinfandel Sonoma reveals a healthy dark ruby/purple color, followed by an attractive tar, berry, earth, and peppery-scented nose, and elegant, vibrant, medium-bodied, crisp, cherry flavors. Although it is not complex, it is a well-crafted Zinfandel for drinking over the next 2–3 years. The dark ruby/purple-colored 1996 Zinfandel Old Vine (14.2% alcohol) exhibits a more intense framboise, kirsch liqueur, and jammy-scented nose. As the wine sits in the glass a toasty vanillin/flowery character emerges. There is excellent density, some tannin, tart acidity, gobs of black cherry and raspberry fruit, and a pure, layered, intense, well-balanced personality. Medium bodied and cleanly made, this super, classic Zinfandel can be drunk now and over the next 5–6 years.

The 1996 Zinfandel Home Ranch, from a vineyard first planted by the Seghesios in 1895, offers a dense ruby/purple color, and a broodingly backward but promising nose of earth, pepper, jammy black raspberries, and spice. There is a structured tightness to this medium-to full-bodied Zinfandel (typical of the 1996 Zins I tasted), but it possesses plenty of tarry, earthy, loamy flavors with good spice, body, and tannin. The wine cuts a deep impression on the palate, but it appears to need another 3–6 months in the bottle to fully open. It should last for 3–5 years. Lastly, the 1996 Zinfandel San Lorenzo (14.3% alcohol) is an effusively fruity, dark ruby/purple-colored, tightly knit wine with a wealth of black raspberry fruit, spice, tar and peppery notes. Full bodied, pure, and broodingly expansive and complex, this profoundly rich and interesting Zinfandel should drink well for 5–6 years.

Seghesio is to be applauded for the high-quality efforts emerging from their cellars. Readers are not likely to find a better Zinfandel value than Seghesio's 1995 Zinfandel Sonoma. This dark ruby-colored, delicious wine offers excellent cherry fruit presented in a lush, medium-bodied, fruity style with moderate weight, and no hard edges. It will provide an excellent introduction to Zinfandel's varietal characteristics if drunk during its first 2–3 years of life.

The 1995 Zinfandel Old Vines is more ambitious. Toasty new oak makes its presence known in the wine's aromatics, which also offer generous quantities of pure, ripe, black cherry fruit. This is a surprisingly elegant, pure, medium-bodied, somewhat tightly knit yet well-endowed Zinfandel that should drink well over the next 5–6 years. It is almost claret-like in its stylishness and restraint, yet it possesses good power, ripeness, and length. Even better is the nearly outstanding 1995 Zinfandel San Lorenzo. This dark ruby/purple-colored wine offers a vibrantly fragrant, moderately intense nose of black fruits, toast, and minerals. Medium bodied, with excellent purity, as well as Zinfandel's classic peppery/wild berrylike flavors, this suave, cleanly made, admirably knit, and well-balanced Zinfandel can be drunk over the next 5–6 years.

The two 1994 Zinfandels are noteworthy offerings from a winery long associated with reasonably good, low-priced wines. The 1994 Zinfandel is sure to be one of the bargain hunter's best buys in the increasingly expensive category of Zinfandel. The wine reveals medium body, lovely, ripe berry, peppery fruit, a soft, briery personality, and an easygoing finish. It is an uncomplicated but delicious Zinfandel offering plenty of fruit and character. One of the surprises in my tastings was Seghesio's 1994 Zinfandel Old Vines. Bottled unfined and unfiltered, and aged 15 months in American and French oak barrels, this is an ambitiously styled, serious, formidably endowed Zinfandel with just the right amount of wood. A big, rich, jammy, black cherry and raspberry-scented nose with a touch of spice is followed by a full-bodied wine with layers of flavor, and a smooth-as-silk, heady, lush finish. It should drink well for 5–6 years. This gorgeous Zinfandel is unquestionably a breakthrough in quality for Seghesio. It is an excellent value. Bravo!

A worthy example of this varietal, Seghesio's 1993 Sonoma Zinfandel is worth buying by the case. The wine offers a dark ruby color, a spicy, peppery, earthy, cherry-scented nose, ripe, medium-bodied flavors, good concentration, a sense of elegance, and a clean, fresh, lively finish. It is hard to beat for the price. Drink it over the next 4–5 years. The 1993 Dry Creek Valley Zinfandel exhibits smoky toasty oak, a pleasant, fruity, medium-bodied personality, good roundness, fine ripeness, and a crisp, adequate finish. Drink it over the next 2–3 years.

The 1993 Pinot Noir has washed-out, thin, high strung flavors that are too acidic and lack extraction.

SELENE (NAPA)

1996	Merlot	Napa	D	91+
1995	Merlot	Napa	D	92
1994	Merlot	Napa	D	90
1993	Merlot	Napa	D	89
1996	Merlot Hyde Vineyard	Carneros	D	90+
1995	Merlot Hyde Vineyard	Carneros	D	89
1996	Sauvignon Blanc Hyde Vineyard	Carneros	C	89

Mia Klein seems to improve the quality of her wines with each vintage. She is renowned for producing a fragrant, personality-filled Sauvignon Blanc made from 100% of the Musqué clone of this varietal. The 1996 Sauvignon Blanc Hyde Vineyard reveals that clone's intoxicating fragrance of honey, melon, and tropical fruits. Medium bodied and ripe, with loads of pure, fresh fruit, this dry wine is as delicious as Sauvignon Blanc can be. It should drink well for a year.

Beginning in 1995, the Merlot has been divided between two cuvées—a Hyde Vineyard offering made from a 1-acre parcel in one of the warmer sections of Carneros, and a Napa bottling. Based on the two vintages I have tasted, the latter wine appears to be the richer, fuller-bodied effort. The 1996 Merlot Hyde Vineyard reveals an attractive purple color, a sweet, licorice, and black cherry-scented nose with medium body, a hint of herbs and coffee, and enough acidity to provide balance. Long, rich, and plump, it will age well for 10 years. Even more impressive is the dense black/purple-colored 1996 Merlot Napa, which is a fatter, richer wine with lower acidity (a higher pH style), an expansive, savory texture, and a long, lush, medium- to full-bodied finish. The wine unfolds beautifully in the glass, and will be a hedonistic Merlot to consume over its first decade of life.

The 1995 Merlot Hyde Vineyard offers a dense purple color, followed by a bouquet of black cherries, smoke, and chocolate. Expressive and rich, with abundant black cherry fruit, this tasty, medium-bodied, spicy Merlot should drink well for 5–8 years. The 1995 Merlot Napa is a decadent, luxuriously endowed wine. From its opaque purple color, to its knockout nose of roasted coffee, smoky black cherry fruit, and chocolate, this rich, superbly concentrated wine possesses terrific intensity, and enough acidity and oak to provide a framework. The silky finish complements the intensely fragrant personality of this gorgeous Merlot. Drink it over the next 7–8 years.

With so many stripped, vegetal, herbal tea-scented Merlots, it is reassuring to taste such yummy stuff as this 1994 Merlot. When it is good, Merlot is a wonderfully soft, silky-textured, medium-weight, aromatically expressive wine with plenty of ripe berry fruit, often intermingled with scents of white chocolate, coffee, and spices. This luscious 1994 possesses plenty of those traits, plus the richness and plumpness to go along with its voluptuous texture. It is already drinking splendidly well—so why wait? I would opt for consuming this beauty over the next 5–6 years. Drinking the 1993 Merlot is akin to eating chocolate-covered, sweet cherry candy. Of course the wine is dry, but I am referring to the wine's beautiful extract, ripe style, smoky, intense fragrance, and chewy texture. Aged in small barrels, (50% new French oak), this is a soft, velvety-textured, seductive Merlot for drinking during its first 7–8 years of life. These are impressive wines.

SHAFER VINEYARDS (NAPA)

1997	Cabernet Sauvignon	Stag's Leap	E	(90–92)
1996	Cabernet Sauvignon	Stag's Leap	E	89
1995	Cabernet Sauvignon	Stag's Leap	E	91
1994	Cabernet Sauvignon	Stag's Leap	E	90
1993	Cabernet Sauvignon	Stag's Leap	E	89
1997	Cabernet Sauvignon Hillside Select	Stag's Leap	EE	(98–100)
1996	Cabernet Sauvignon Hillside Select	Stag's Leap	EE	(98–100)
1995	Cabernet Sauvignon Hillside Select	Stag's Leap	EE	98
1994	Cabernet Sauvignon Hillside Select	Stag's Leap	EE	99
1993	Cabernet Sauvignon Hillside Select	Stag's Leap	D	94
1997	Chardonnay Red Shoulder Ranch	Napa/Carneros	D	(90–92)
1996	Chardonnay Red Shoulder Ranch	Napa/Carneros	D	90
1997	Firebreak (Sangiovese/Cabernet Sauvignon)	Napa	C	(90–91)
1996	Firebreak (Sangiovese/Cabernet Sauvignon)	Napa	D	88
1997	Merlot	Stag's Leap	D	(88–90)
1996	Merlot	Stag's Leap	D	88
1995	Merlot	Stag's Leap	D	90

1994 Merlot	Stag's Leap	D	89
1993 Merlot	Stag's Leap	C	89

Shafer Vineyards, long one of Napa Valley's finest wineries, continues to build on its enviable track record. Each year I am more impressed with their winemaking. A tasting at the winery in September 1998 was one of the finest I have experienced—anywhere! Production is currently around 30,000 cases, which makes the superlative quality of their Red Shoulder Ranch Chardonnay (about 6,000 cases) and Hillside Select Cabernet Sauvignon (about 2,000 cases) remarkable. An argument could be made that Shafer is turning out the finest nonmalolactic Chardonnay in California. This sumptuous wine is fermented with indigenous yeast, given extensive lees stirring, and bottled after 14 months of aging in 50% new oak (some of which is American). The 1997 Chardonnay Red Shoulder Ranch combines finesse and power in a complex, smoky, pineapple-scented wine with copious quantities of fruit. Full bodied and rich, with no sign of heaviness, it is extremely well endowed, yet possesses plenty of acidity for structural strength and vibrancy. It should drink well for 3–4 years. The 1996 Chardonnay Red Shoulder Ranch may be slightly less complex than both the 1997 and 1995, but it is still an outstanding offering. Full bodied and complex, with aromas of roasted nuts, honeyed tropical fruits, and minerals, it is a chewy wine with decent acidity, and plenty of power, richness, and class. It should be enjoyed over the next 1–2 years.

Many a California Sangiovese is unimpressive, so the noteworthy efforts stand out. Shafer's is one of the handful of exceptions. Admittedly, they blend 15%–20% Cabernet Sauvignon with their Sangiovese. The outstanding 1997 Firebreak (85% Sangiovese and 15% Cabernet Sauvignon) does what Sangiovese should do—offer an easily understood, complex, drinkable, richly fruity wine with an absence of weight and tannin. The wonderful aromas of licorice, strawberry jam, saddle leather, spice, and dried herbs are followed by a medium-bodied, exuberant wine with sweet berry fruit, and a ripe, multilayered texture. This wine sees 30% new oak, which gives it spice and complexity but does not overwhelm the delicate fruit. It should be drunk over the next 4–5 years. The 1996 Firebreak (80% Sangiovese and 20% Cabernet Sauvignon) exhibits a dark ruby color, as well as a textbook Sangiovese nose of strawberries, leather, cherries, and damp forest scents. The wine possesses excellent richness, medium body, and an elegant, more restrained and subdued style than the richer, more fragrant 1997. It should drink well for 5–7 years.

Another varietal with which Shafer does superlative things is Merlot. This estate's Merlot, which increasingly comes from their Carneros vineyard, reveals true varietal character. Shafer often includes 15% Cabernet Franc in the blend, as well as a small dollop of Cabernet Sauvignon. The 1997 Merlot (80% Merlot, 15% Cabernet Franc, and 5% Cabernet Sauvignon) could merit an outstanding rating. While it may not possess the weight and rustic fullness of the 1996, it offers vivid fruit, soaring aromatics, and a soft, medium-bodied, well-textured personality with the emphasis on rich berry fruit, a seamless texture, and enough oak to provide additional nuances. It should drink well for a decade. The medium- to full-bodied 1996 Merlot (77% Merlot, 16% Cabernet Franc, and 7% Cabernet Sauvignon) is more exotic, with some of Merlot's chocolate overtones emerging in the black cherry fruit. While the 1996 may be fuller and heavier than the 1997, it is also an excellent effort. I would opt for consuming it over the next decade.

The excellent 1996 Cabernet Sauvignon (13.5% alcohol, and made from a blend of 94% Cabernet Sauvignon and 6% Cabernet Franc) is more sternly constructed, and possesses rougher tannin than the 1997. The wine's saturated ruby color is followed by a big, spicy, black currant, loamy soil, and smoky-scented bouquet. The midpalate is rich, pure, and well endowed, and there is noticeable tannin in the moderately long finish (a characteristic of many 1996 North Coast reds). This wine will benefit from 1–3 years of cellaring, and will keep for 12–15. The 1997 Cabernet Sauvignon (86% Cabernet Sauvignon, 7% Merlot, and 7% Cabernet Franc) is produced from sweeter, jammier fruit. On my visit to the winery, Doug Shafer told me they place 1997 on a par with the greatest vintages of the nineties, 1991, 1994, and 1995. This sentiment was echoed by many Napa Cabernet Sauvignon producers. This offering, which is 100% barrel aged (50% of which is American oak), displays a saturated ruby/purple color, and a jammy nose of black currants, tobacco leaf, earth, and vanillin. Dense, rich, and medium to full bodied, with sweet tannin and soft acidity, this sexy, opulently styled Cabernet should drink well when released and age for 12–15 years.

Since the 1991 vintage, one of the stars of the Cabernet Sauvignon sweepstakes has been Shafer's Hillside Select. Approximately 2,000–2,200 cases of this 100% Cabernet Sauvignon are produced. The wine is aged in 100% new oak for 30 months. Recent vintages have all been spectacular. In short, attempting to decipher qualitative differences between them is akin to splitting hairs. Certainly the 1994, 1995, and 1997 offerings flirt with perfection, and the 1996, while more ruggedly tannic, is a profound wine. I just hope that Cabernet lovers have the discretionary income and accessibility to cellar a few bottles. The current release, the 1994 Cabernet Sauvignon Hillside Select, is a prodigious Cabernet. I had it at a tasting in Japan, and the Japanese were as enthusiastic about it as my rating suggested they should be. They were crestfallen when informed they probably would not be able to buy multiple cases of the wine! The 1994 combines the vintage's spectacularly ripe, luscious fruit with a rarely seen degree of elegance and finesse. The wine is extremely rich, as well as gorgeously poised and graceful. The saturated ruby/purple color is accompanied by Médoc-like, lead pencil aromas intermixed with cassis, cedar, minerals, and spice. I wrote the word "great" four different times in my most recent tasting note, which mirrored every other tasting note I have. It is full bodied and seamless, with a silky texture, voluptuous richness, and fabulous purity. The finish lasts for over 40 seconds. Anticipated maturity: 2000–2025. Remarkably, the 1995, 1996, and 1997 may well be just as enticing. The 1995 Cabernet Sauvignon Hillside Select is a fabulous Cabernet Sauvignon. I initially rated this wine (92–94), but out of bottle, it is awesome! It reveals a saturated color similar to the 1994. While the aromatics are more restrained, the wine boasts plenty of black currants, lead pencil, mineral, and *pain grillé* scents. Deep, with spectacular purity, ripeness, and richness, and far more expansiveness and depth than it possessed a year ago, this wine offers a classic juxtaposition of power and elegance. It will take a few years to come around, but wow, what a wine! Anticipated maturity: 2003–2025. The immense 1996 Cabernet Sauvignon Hillside Select, which reveals the most structure and tannin, is one of the biggest, brawniest Hillside Selects to date. This 100% Cabernet Sauvignon is extremely full bodied, with fabulous concentration. Cascades of ripe black fruits roll over the palate, dispensing chewy glycerin, purity, and power. While it may never possess the symmetry of the 1994 and 1995, the 1996 is a fabulous Cabernet Sauvignon. Anticipated maturity: 2004–2030. The 1997 Cabernet Sauvignon Hillside Select appears to be a clone of the 1994. Like many of the finest wines of this vintage, it is already very expressive (much like the 1994), with an intense, explosive fragrance of flowers, licorice, and crème de cassis. It is medium to full bodied, with copious quantities of blackberry and black currant fruit that have masked any hint of the 100% new oak barrels in which it is aging. The 1997 is unquestionably another compelling Hillside Select Cabernet Sauvignon.

The complex, smoky, coffee, berry, and white chocolate-scented and -flavored 1993 Merlot reveals gorgeous levels of fruit, a lush, velvety texture, medium to full body, and a heady finish. There is not an astringent element to this wine. Drink it over the next 7–8 years.

Shafer's Merlot program has also increased in quality, as evidenced by the 1994 and 1995. The 1994 Merlot is one of the best Merlots on the market—soft, velvety-textured, with gobs of ripe cherry/cranberry fruit nicely dosed with smoky oak. The wine is medium to full bodied, yet elegant and expansive, with no hard edges. It should drink well and gracefully evolve over the next 7–8 years. The 1995 Merlot appears to be the qualitative equivalent, perhaps slightly superior, to the 1994. Certainly the 1995 is more fragrant and aromatic. Jammy black cherries, toast, and subtle herbaceous notes are followed by a wine with gorgeous layers of rich, glycerin-endowed, creamy-textured fruit. Deeper colored than the 1994, but as structured, the 1995 possesses more extract and length. It should drink well for 10–12 years.

The 1995 Cabernet Sauvignon Stag's Leap District is elegant, yet authoritatively flavored, with copious amounts of cassis fruit, spicy, smoky oak, medium body, and an excellent, restrained but well-balanced personality. It is a nicely extracted, fleshy, complex wine for drinking during its first 10–15 years of life.

A gorgeous Cabernet Sauvignon, Shafer's 1994 displays a dark purple color, as well as sweet, floral-scented, cassis fruit intermixed with subtle new oak and minerals. Medium to full bodied, spicy, and exceptionally pure, with a nicely layered texture, and outstanding equilibrium and depth, this is a classic, elegant, authoritatively flavored Cabernet Sauvignon that is impeccably made. It is still youthful, but given the penchant for most Americans (this author included) to enjoy the youthfulness of wines such as this, I would opt for drinking it now and over the next 12–15+ years. Very impressive!

The 1993 Cabernet Sauvignon Hillside Select is another outstanding wine that is close in quality to the 1992 and 1991. The 1993 boasts an opaque purple color, as well as a sweet, smoky nose of licorice, black currants, minerals, and vanillin. Huge, rich, and full bodied, with fabulous concentration and extract, but harder tannin than the 1992 or 1994, this is a large-scaled, well-balanced, powerful Cabernet Sauvignon to drink between 2000 and 2020.

The 1993 Cabernet Sauvignon Stag's Leap District is another fine example of Shafer's winemaking skill. The color is a healthy dark ruby/purple. The nose offers up cedar, spice, black currant, and vanillin scents. The wine is still young, structured, and backward, as well as sweet, round, and pure. Accessible now, this wine should continue to evolve and drink well for 7–10 years.

P.S. Rhône wine enthusiasts will be thrilled to learn that the Shafers have planted Syrah at their Oak Knoll Vineyard in Stag's Leap and will produce a crop of approximately 1,500 cases in 1999.

SHOOTING STAR (MENDOCINO)

1996 Cabernet Sauvignon	Clear Lake	C	87
1993 Cabernet Sauvignon	Clear Lake	A	84
1996 Carignane Forets Diverses Lolonis Vineyard	Mendocino	B	86
1996 Chardonnay	California	B	87
1996 Cote de Columbia Grenache	Washington	B	86
1995 Cote de Columbia Grenache	Washington	A	85
1996 Merlot	Clear Lake	B	86
1997 Sauvignon Blanc	Lake County	B	85
1996 Syrah	Lake County	B	86
1997 Zin Gris Pacini Vineyard	Mendocino	A	87
1996 Zinfandel	Lake County	B	87
1995 Zinfandel	Mendocino	A	87

Jed Steele is unquestionably one of California's most accomplished winemakers, and there is no doubting his Midas touch with wines. His second label, called Shooting Star, offers much needed relief for consumers trying to find good California wines at reasonable prices. The only Shooting Star offering I tasted that did not possess the character of the others was the 1996 Cabernet Franc, a competent wine that merits a score in the low 80s. The wines I enjoyed for their combination of pure fruit and attractive varietal character include the 1997 Sauvignon Blanc, a crisp, dry, melony wine without any of the vegetal "cat's pee" characteristics that Sauvignon can sometimes possess. A small amount of Semillon was utilized in the blend, which has fleshed the wine out. This tank-fermented and aged, lively, light-bodied example offers plenty of citrusy and melony flavors. Drink it over the next year. The delicious, richly fruity, uncomplicated 1996 Chardonnay is satisfying and tasty. It offers plenty of tropical fruit, medium body, and a vibrant, refreshing mouthful of wine for consuming over the next year.

I predict rosé wines will make a comeback, in large part because of efforts such as Shooting Star's 1997 Zin Gris. Made from fermenting Zinfandel must that is pulled out of tank with just the right amount of color saturation, this single-vineyard rosé (is that a first for California?) exhibits a light ruby color more akin to a lighter-styled Pinot Noir or red Burgundy. A robust Zinfandel, with surprising weight and flesh in the mouth with gobs of cranberry, strawberry, and cherry fruit, this comes close to being a full-bodied wine that tastes dry, although I suspect there is a touch of residual sugar hidden in the wine's gorgeous fruit. Sadly, only 300 cases were produced. Drink it over the next year.

Most readers who know my tastes would expect me to be well disposed toward a kirsch-dominated, peppery Grenache. The medium ruby-colored 1996 Côte de Columbia does not reveal any evidence of oak aging. Loaded with jammy cherry fruit, it is velvety textured, round, and hedonistic with some spice in the background that suggests exposure to oak. Drink this round, enjoyable Grenache over the next 1–2 years. If readers want to do something fascinating, slip a bottle of this wine into a premier cru or grand cru red Burgundy tasting and see what happens. An uncomplicated, but exuberantly rich, fruity Syrah, Shooting Star's 1996 exhibits a dark ruby/purple color, good spice, pure fruit, and a round, generous, medium-bodied finish. Drink it over the next 3–4 years. It is an excellent value. Is there a better value in Zinfandel than the Shooting Star cuvée produced by Jed Steele? This has been a consistent winner. The 1996 Zinfandel possesses a textbook Zinfandel character, with a medium ruby color, and expressive berry fruit and spice. In the mouth, the wine is richly fruity, soft, round, and delicious to drink. It will not be long-lived, but for drinking over the next 12–16 months, this is a winner. Readers should consider buying it by the case, and I would not hesitate to serve it slightly chilled. The intriguing, dark ruby-colored 1996 Carignane Forets Diverses Lolonis Vineyard exhibits a peppery, berry nose with spicy wood notes. In the mouth, it is a chunky, smoky, berry, fruit-driven dry red wine with plenty of hedonistic appeal. Pure, with a soft texture, this amply endowed Carignane should provide considerable pleasure over the next 2–4 years. Sadly, only 400 cases were produced from this organically cultivated vineyard.

I do not expect much from most New World Merlots, but I must say I was taken aback by the quality and richness of Shooting Star's 1996 Merlot. A dark ruby-colored wine with textbook black cherry and chocolatey notes in the nose, good flesh and depth, plenty of purity, and a nicely extracted, well-delineated finish, this example could easily pass for a Merlot costing $25–$35 a bottle. Merlot enthusiasts should put that information to good use. Drink it over the next 2–3 years. The 1996 Cabernet Sauvignon exhibits a healthy dark ruby/purple color, followed by sweet black currant fruit with loamy, earthy undertones. It is a purely made, fruit-driven wine with medium body, no hard edges, and good structure and definition. This wine should continue to drink well for 4–6 years.

The fruity, spicy 1995 Shooting Star Zinfandel is an excellent value. The wine's deep ruby color is followed by textbook, briery, richly fruity flavors presented in a supple, medium-bodied, pure format. Drink it over the next 1–2 years. The lighter-styled, ruby-colored 1995 Côte de Columbia Grenache reveals luscious cherry and raspberry (possibly strawberry) fruit that is unabashedly presented in a gushing, uncomplicated style. Fine underlying acidity gives vibrancy to this delicious, tasty wine. Drink it over the next 6–12 months.

The 1993 Cabernet Sauvignon is not quite as attractive or succulent as Shooting Star's 1993 Merlot. Nevertheless, it is a competent, above average quality Cabernet with lovely cassis fruit, spice, and light tannin.

SIDURI (California)

1996 Pinot Noir	Carneros	D	90
1996 Pinot Noir	Oregon	D	85
1995 Pinot Noir	Oregon	C	87
1994 Pinot Noir	Anderson Valley	D	90+
1997 Pinot Noir Archery Summit	Willamette Valley, OR	D	90
1997 Pinot Noir Hirsch Vineyard	Sonoma Coast	D	88+
1996 Pinot Noir Hirsch Vineyard	Sonoma Coast	D	89+
1995 Pinot Noir Hirsch Vineyard	Sonoma Coast	D	90+
1997 Pinot Noir Pisoni Vineyard	Santa Lucia Highlands	D	92
1995 Pinot Noir Rose Vineyard	Anderson Valley	D	90
1997 Pinot Noir Van Der Kamp Vineyard Old Vines	Sonoma Mountain	D	88
1996 Pinot Noir Van Der Kamp Vineyard Old Vines	Sonoma Mountain	D	88

This winery continues to specialize in high-quality Pinot Noir from some of the best vineyard sites in California and Oregon. I tasted four impressive 1997 offerings, all of which are bottled with minimal intervention (no filtration). The medium ruby-colored 1997 Pinot Noir Van Der Kamp Vineyard Old Vines offers a moderately intense nose of black raspberries, cherries, and spicy, roasted herbs. The wine is fleshy and open knit, with nicely integrated toasty new oak, and a lush, heady (14.1% alcohol) finish. This supple, hedonistic example will offer delicious and complex drinking for 3–4 years. The outstanding 1997 Pinot Noir Archery Summit exhibits a darker ruby color, and a firmer, more austere personality, but has beautifully pure black raspberry and cassis notes intermixed with earthy and vanilla scents. This is a classy, structured, exceptionally pure, backward, medium- to full-bodied Pinot Noir that should be at its best in 12 months and keep for 6–7 years.

The 1997 Pinot Noir Hirsch Vineyard is the most Burgundian of this quartet, exhibiting smoky, gamey, meaty notes in the aromatics, as well as sweet black cherry and berry fruit. There is good firmness, a lean, moderately tannic finish, and medium body. Although closed and angular, it is an intriguing Pinot Noir that appears to be more driven by its *terroir* than its siblings. Anticipated maturity: 2000–2007. It seems like no one can fail with the fruit emerging from the Santa Lucia Highlands' Pisoni Vineyard. Siduri's 1997 Pinot Noir Pisoni Vineyard is a sumptuously rich, dark ruby/purple-colored wine with soaring aromas of blackberry/framboise and cherry jam. One of the more hedonistic, lushly textured, and sumptuous Pinot Noirs I have tasted from Siduri, it will be a huge success with readers lucky enough to latch onto a few bottles. It should drink well for 3–5 years.

The 1996 offerings represent four different styles of Pinot Noir. The 1996 Pinot Noir Carneros (unfiltered) exhibits a medium plum/cherry color. The nose offers smoke, dried herbs, and sweet red and black fruits. In the mouth, the wine is charming, round, succulent, and generous. Its silky texture, gamey, cinnamon-tinged, kirschlike fruit, and roasted herb and meaty characteristics are complex and attractive. Although this Pinot will not make old bones, it will continue to offer hedonistic drinking for 4–5 years. The 1996 Pinot Noir Van Der Kamp Vineyard (Landmark also produces a fine Pinot Noir from this mountain vineyard) reveals a medium ruby color, less complexity than the Carneros, and sweeter, more jammy fruit. There is good body, nice glycerin, and an appealing tactile impression. The fleshy finish displays this varietal's renowned hedonistic lushness. Drink it over the next 4–5 years.

The 1996 Pinot Noir Hirsch Vineyard (unfiltered) comes from the Sonoma Coast, a hotbed for high-quality California Pinot Noir (Marcassin, Kistler, and La Jota are well established in this area). The Hirsch Vineyard's medium ruby/garnet color is similar to the other Siduri Pinots. The wine is more reticent aromatically, with dark berry fruit and earth emerging from the glass. On the palate, however, there is explosive fruit, more structure, and noticeable tannin. This is a more masculine style of Pinot Noir, with less of the forward charm of the Carneros and Van Der Kamp bottlings, yet more aging potential. Cellar it for another 6–12 months, and consume it over the following 6–7 years. Lastly, Siduri's 1996 Oregon Pinot Noir (unfiltered) is the least distinctive wine of this quartet. It is a light, more angular, austere wine, as well as more reserved aromatically. Some fine blueberry/cherry fruit and spice eventually emerge, but the angularity of the 1996 Oregon vintage is well displayed. There is structure, but I would not recommend cellaring given the fact that the fruit is less intense. Drink it over the next 2–3 years before it dries out.

The 1995 Oregon Pinot Noir (147 cases) exhibits a medium ruby color, a sweet, fragrant nose of black cherries, soft, silky, sexy flavors, medium to full body, low acidity, and a lush texture. Drink it over the next 3–4 years. The 1995 Pinot Noir Rose Vineyard (75 cases) is more closed than its older sibling, revealing a dark deep ruby color, and a reticent but promising nose of sweet black cherries, earth, and spice. The wine possesses excellent to outstanding depth, good structure, and a spicy, long, concentrated finish. It should drink well for 6–7 years. The 1995 Pinot Noir Hirsch Vineyard (50 cases) is another exceptionally promising wine from this vineyard, which has produced some splendid Pinot Noirs for the likes of Kistler. The wine's deep ruby/purple color is followed by spicy, thick aromas of earthy black fruits, truffles, and toasty new oak. Full bodied and powerful, with some tannin to shed, this is a backward yet pure, rich, authoritatively flavored Pinot Noir that needs another 1–2 years in the bottle; it should keep for a decade.

The terrific unfined, unfiltered 1994 Pinot Noir boasts an intense dark ruby/purple color, a fragrant, provocative nose of smoky, toasty vanillin from new oak intermingled with intense scents of jammy black cherries and black raspberries. Full bodied, rich, velvety textured, and concentrated, this is a natural tasting wine that blossoms beautifully as it sits in the glass. It is explosive on the back of the palate. It should drink well for 7–8 years. This appears to be an ambitious operation aiming for high quality.

SIERRA VISTA (EL DORADO)

1995 Fleur de Montagne	El Dorado	C	86
1996 Zinfandel	El Dorado	C	86
1995 Zinfandel	El Dorado	B	76+?
1994 Zinfandel	El Dorado	B	89
1993 Zinfandel Estate	El Dorado	B	78
1995 Zinfandel Estate Reserve	El Dorado	C	?
1996 Zinfandel Herbert Vineyard	El Dorado	C	87
1996 Zinfandel Reeves Vineyard	El Dorado	C	88

Think of the Fleur de Montagne as a California version of a good Côtes du Rhône. A blend of Grenache, Syrah, Mourvèdre, and Cinsault, the wine exhibits a dark ruby/purple color, an attractive black raspberry and cherry-scented nose, rich, medium-bodied, sweet flavors, excellent purity, and a long, spicy finish. It is a tasty, mouth-filling Côtes du Rhône lookalike for drinking over the next 1–3 years.

The 1996 Zinfandels are among the finest red wines I have tasted from Sierra Vista. All three are pure, rich, and concentrated. The tasty 1996 Zinfandel is a solidly constructed, medium- to full-bodied wine with a nicely layered texture, as well as plenty of briary, brambleberry/cherry fruit. Drink it over the next 1–2 years. The fuller-bodied, richer 1996 Zinfandel Herbert Vineyard possesses more spice, pepper, glycerin, and alcohol (14.2%). There is excellent depth, well-integrated acidity, and a good finish, with plenty of stuffing. Drink it over the next 3–4 years. The 1996 Zinfandel Reeves Vineyard is a big, rich, full-throttle offering with a deep ruby/purple color, and copious quantities of briary, sweet, jammy black raspberry and cherry fruit intertwined with dusty, earthy notes. In the mouth, it is full bodied, with excellent ripeness, admirable purity, and a fine, lusty, muscular finish. It should drink well for 5–6 years.

I am not sure what to write about either of the 1995 Zinfandels. Certainly the 1995 Zinfandel possesses an excess of acidity, tannin, and oak, obliterating any fruit that was captured from the vineyard. It is an example of a wine with little charm, flesh, or fruit. The 1995 Zinfandel Estate Reserve reveals an impressively saturated purple color, and lavish quantities of spicy, toasty oak. The wood (liquefied oak) is intrusive, dominating what little fruit exists on the palate. I have generally enjoyed the wines of Sierra Vista, so these performances are puzzling.

If the bottled wine turns out to be as good as the barrel sample I tasted, the 1994 Zinfandel could be the finest Zinfandel the underrated Sierra Vista Winery has yet produced. The wine exhibits an explosive nose of chocolate, briery, smoky, jammy berry fruit, exotic, full-bodied, concentrated flavors, adequate acidity, and a blockbuster, heady, alcoholic finish. It should drink well for 6–7 years. If the wine makes it through the bottling process in this condition, this will be an excellent value.

Despite some attractive, low-keyed, briary, cherry fruit in the nose, the medium-bodied 1993 Zinfandel suffers from excessive tannin, and a coarse, rustic personality that offers more structure and earthiness than fruit or charm.

SILVER OAK CELLARS (NAPA)

1997	Cabernet Sauvignon	Alexander Valley	E	(92–94)
1996	Cabernet Sauvignon	Alexander Valley	E	92
1995	Cabernet Sauvignon	Alexander Valley	E	94
1994	Cabernet Sauvignon	Alexander Valley	E	93
1993	Cabernet Sauvignon	Alexander Valley	E	90
1997	Cabernet Sauvignon	Napa	EE	(92–95)
1996	Cabernet Sauvignon	Napa	EE	92+
1995	Cabernet Sauvignon	Napa	EE	95
1994	Cabernet Sauvignon	Napa	EE	93
1993	Cabernet Sauvignon	Napa	EE	90?

This is one of America's favorite Cabernet Sauvignons. It is a wine that is virtually impossible to find in the marketplace, despite the fact that there are 40,000 cases of the Alexander Valley Cabernet, and 10,000 cases of the Napa Valley Cabernet. Readers would think such production would ensure widespread visibility in the marketplace, but that has not been the case. These ostentatious, flamboyant, lavishly oaked Silver Oak Cabernets are just too popular! The two cuvées are made in essentially the same manner, with the Alexander Valley always 100% Cabernet Sauvignon, but aged in slightly less new oak (about 50% new American oak). The Napa Valley bottling is a Cabernet Sauvignon-driven wine, but does include small percentages of Cabernet Franc and Petit Verdot. For example, the 1994 Napa is 89% Cabernet Sauvignon, 10% Cabernet Franc, and 1% Petit Verdot. The 1995 Napa is 96% Cabernet Sauvignon, 3% Cabernet Franc, and 1% Petit Verdot. The 1996 Napa is 91% Cabernet Sauvignon, 7% Cabernet Franc, 1.2% Petit Verdot, and .8% Merlot. In contrast to the Alexander Valley, the Napa is aged in 100% new American oak casks.

Owner/winemaker Justin Meyer has a simple winemaking philosophy—to make Cabernets that are soft and approachable upon release. Silver Oak is a lavishly oaked, extroverted, user-friendly Cabernet Sauvignon that is wildly popular . . . and why shouldn't it be? The wine is supple, explosively fruity, and delivers copious quantities of glycerin, extract, and richness wrapped in generous quantities of American oak. Critics have argued that the wines do not age particularly well, but that has largely been proven a myth. I doubt they will last as long as Château Montelena, Dunn, or other Napa Cabernets with a 30–40-year aging potential, but these wines have a broad window of drinkability, being delicious at release, and able to sustain their fruit and character for 15 or more years. Current and upcoming releases are all sexy, appealing wines.

The 1995 Cabernet Sauvignon Alexander Valley is performing far better after a year of bottle age. This dark ruby/purple-colored, seductive wine offers blazingly intense aromas of cigar box, smoky oak, and jammy black currants with a hint of Provençal herbs. Ripe and full bodied, with low acidity, and a fleshy, succulent texture, it is a wine to drink over the next 14–15 years. The 1996 Cabernet Sauvignon Alexander Valley is the most herbaceous of the Alexander Valleys. It reveals more tannin in the finish, as well as an atypical note of eucalyptus. It displays a huge nose of cigar box, spice, and jammy red and black currant fruit scents. This is a large-scaled, full-bodied, dense wine with a terrific midpalate impression. The 1997 Cabernet Sauvignon Alexander Valley displays an impressive saturated purple color (keep in mind it is the most youthful), followed by admirable levels of overripe black currant and blackberry fruit intermixed with Asian spices, cedar, and toasty oak. Deep and full bodied, with low acidity, and an evolved personality, this may be the most sumptuous and expressive of these offerings. It should drink well during its first 12–15 years of life.

The Napa offerings from Silver Oak tend to be less herbaceous and more oriented toward Cabernet Sauvignon's black fruit spectrum. They are every bit as exotic and ostentatious as the Alexander Valley cuvées, but more classic, tannic, perhaps longer-lived, and slightly less approachable. The 1994 Cabernet Sauvignon Napa (89% Cabernet Sauvignon and 11% Cabernet Franc) reveals toasty sweet oak in the nose, bombastic levels of black currant fruit and spice along with a hint of mint in the background. Supple and full bodied, with delirious levels of cedar and unctuously textured fruit, this fleshy, gorgeously made Cabernet Sauvignon should drink well for 14–15 years. A blend of 96% Cabernet Sauvignon and 4% Cabernet Franc, the 1995 Cabernet Sauvignon Napa has turned out even better than the 1994. It possesses a more saturated ruby/purple color, as well as a more flamboyant and exotic bouquet. Moreover, it seems less evolved. Full bodied and pure, with layer upon layer of concentrated black fruits, smoke, cedar, and toast, it should drink well for 16–17 years. The 1996 Cabernet Sauvignon Napa (91% Cabernet Sauvignon, 7% Cabernet Franc, 1.5% Petit Verdot, and .5% Merlot) is the most closed. Full bodied, with noticeable tannin, and a muscular, brawny personality, it is less sweet and viscous than the 1994, 1995, or 1997. The 1996 displays an atypically firm edge, but all the characteristics that make this wine so popular are present—black fruits, spice box, fruitcake, cedar aromas, and a chewy thickness. However, it appears to be backward, although it will not be released for at least 2 years. The 1997 Cabernet Sauvignon Napa (93% Cabernet Sauvignon, 5% Cabernet Franc, and 2% Petit Verdot) exhibits the vintage's telltale gorgeous, up-front aromatics (black fruits galore), and a dense, full-bodied, open-knit, expansive personality with gobs of fruit and a chewy, lush texture. It should provide hedonistic drinking when released, and keep for 15+ years.

The 1993 Cabernet Sauvignon Alexander Valley offers up a whiff of herbs in its tight nose, followed by chocolatey, spicy, black cherry, and cassis flavors, an exotic, medium- to full-bodied, concentrated palate, and moderate tannin in the lusty finish. It does not possess the definition and structure of the Napa cuvée, but it is more forward and fleshy. The 1993 Cabernet Sauvignon Napa Valley is one of the more tannic and backward wines I have tasted from Silver Oak. Now that it has been bottled, it has closed down, displaying far less lushness and obvious concentration than it did last year. The color remains a healthy dark ruby/purple, and the nose offers earthy, toasty new oak, and sweet black fruit aromas. Tight, yet powerful and rich, this full-bodied, dense, atypically backward Cabernet Sauvignon does not possess Silver Oak's usual approachability and precociousness. Nevertheless, this wine has plenty of merit. It should drink well after 3–5 years of cellaring, and last for 15+ years.

The 1994 Cabernet Sauvignon Alexander Valley reveals a provocative nose of tobacco, black cherries, cloves, fruitcake, and spice. Some plum and raspberry fruit also emerges on the palate. This is a hedonistic, sexy, seductive, full-bodied Cabernet Sauvignon with low acidity, and loads of toasty oak. It will be a huge crowd pleaser when released next year. It should show well for at least 12–15 years.

SILVERADO VINEYARDS (NAPA)

1995	Cabernet Sauvignon	Napa	C	85+
1994	Cabernet Sauvignon	Napa	C	86
1994	Cabernet Sauvignon Limited Reserve	Napa	E	78
1993	Cabernet Sauvignon Limited Reserve	Napa	E	88
1995	Chardonnay	Napa	C	80
1995	Chardonnay Limited Reserve	Napa	E	93
1995	Merlot	Napa	C	83
1994	Merlot	Napa	C	78
1995	Sangiovese	Napa	C	79
1994	Sangiovese	Napa	C	83

I realize these wines are commercially successful, but to my mind, this winery still practices the lamentable technique of adding too much acidity to their wines, particularly the reds. The wines too often possess a compact, compressed, tart character, simply because the added acidity lowers the wine's pH, obstructing and shielding the wine's texture, expansiveness, and flavors behind an abrasive wall of acid.

The 1995 Chardonnay is too lean and acidified for my taste, but there is obviously a market for such wines. The spectacular 1995 Chardonnay Limited Reserve boasts sensational aromatics consisting of smoked, citrusy, honeyed fruit, and subtle, high-quality new oak. In the mouth, it is full bodied, with superb purity and equilibrium, and layers of rich fruit. The finish lasts for nearly 30 seconds. This is brilliant!

I have been critical of the red wines from Silverado, which often taste frightfully austere with sharp levels of acidity. I did not taste their entire lineup of reds, but the 1995 Sangiovese is a soft, medium-bodied, tart, strawberry and cherry-scented and -flavored wine that is pleasant, but uninteresting—no different from the majority of California Sangioveses. What troubled me more was the extremely lean, painful, sharp personality of the 1994 Cabernet Sauvignon Limited Reserve. An austere wine, with high acidity, a disappointing medium ruby color, and minty, underripe red currant flavors, it has an astringent personality. To me, it is an inexplicable Cabernet Sauvignon from a vintage that has probably produced more profound Cabernets than any to date.

The beautifully packaged 1994 Sangiovese exhibits a medium ruby color, followed by a light intensity nose of strawberry jam and cherries. Although crisp and elegant, it is also too acidic. The tartness works better in Sangiovese since this grape does not produce much tannin. Drink this wine over the next 1–3 years. Both the 1994 and 1995 Merlots display medium deep ruby colors, lean personalities, high acidity, yet no real texture or expansiveness in the mouth. My guess is that their pHs are well below 3.5, which would be considered unacceptable in Bordeaux, except in poor vintages when the fruit never achieves maturity. I cannot comprehend this philosophy of winemaking—especially if the goal is to produce a wine of pleasure.

The 1994 and 1995 Cabernet Sauvignons possess similar tart acidic profiles, but they also exhibit more fruit, intensity, and character. They reveal aromas of nicely smoked, toasty barrels, ripe cherry and red currant fruit, and medium-bodied, moderately tannic personalities. The 1995 contains sweeter fruit than the more streamlined, compressed 1994. Both wines should age well for 10–15 years. The dense ruby/purple-colored 1995 Cabernet Sauvignon offers a smoky, toasty, currant-scented nose, medium body, fine richness, tart acidity, excellent purity, and a graceful, yet compressed finish. It should turn out to be a midweight, stylish, but perhaps too sculptured style of Cabernet Sauvignon. Lastly, the 1993 Cabernet Sauvignon Limited Reserve offers up a moderately intense nose of sour cherries, toasty, smoky new oak, and vanillin. Although crisp, with high acidity, the wine's more intense flavor profile helps to push the acidity to the background. This is a medium-bodied, fresh, and vibrant wine, but the acidic edge will always subdue and restrain the wine's richness, as well as conceal its flavors and texture. It will age for 15+ years.

SIMI WINERY (SONOMA)

1994	Cabernet Sauvignon	Alexander Valley	C	87
1993	Cabernet Sauvignon	Alexander Valley	C	87
1995	Cabernet Sauvignon Reserve	Sonoma	D	89
1994	Cabernet Sauvignon Reserve	Sonoma	D	89+
1993	Cabernet Sauvignon Reserve	Alexander Valley	D	87+
1996	Chardonnay	Carneros	C	87
1996	Chardonnay	Sonoma	C	86
1995	Chardonnay	Sonoma	C	86
1995	Chardonnay Reserve	Sonoma	D	87
1995	Shiraz	Sonoma	C	87

These are very good Chardonnays from Simi, although the Reserve does not hit the heights one would expect. The 1996 Chardonnay Sonoma is a straightforward, pleasant, tropical fruit, apple and pear-flavored wine with some spice, good structure, tart acidity, and a medium-bodied finish. Drink it over the next year. The more complex, intriguing 1996 Chardonnay Carneros reveals alluring aromatics, consisting of smoke, rich, ripe fruit, and a roasted nut character, in addition to a medium- to full-bodied, fleshy palate. There is good acidity, but it is more integrated and balanced than in the Sonoma bottling. The Carneros should drink well for 1–2 years. I liked it just as much as the 1995 Chardonnay Reserve. While the Reserve is a deeper, fuller-bodied wine, it is more tightly knit and overtly woody. It offers a deep, rich, full-bodied feel in the mouth, but seems more weighty than complex. The wine is well made, but a certain chunkiness kept my score from going higher. It should drink well for 1–2 years.

Some nice pear, apple, and orangelike flavors are present in the medium-bodied, uncomplicated, attractive, pleasant 1995 Chardonnay. Consume it over the next 1–2 years.

In my barrel tastings, the 1995 Simi Cabernet Sauvignon Reserve was among the more forward, opulently styled 1995s. This attractive wine, which has the potential to be outstanding, exhibits a deep ruby/purple color, and a friendly, open-knit, spicy, sweet black currant nose that borders on jamminess. Pure, with a multilayered texture, excellent concentration, sweet, plush, fat fruit, decent acidity, and a long, lusty finish, this Cabernet is reminiscent of a deep, rich, Right Bank Bordeaux made primarily from Merlot rather than Cabernet Sauvignon. It is capable of lasting for 10–15+ years.

Although closed, the 1994 Cabernet Sauvignon Reserve displays plenty of potential, and may merit an outstanding score with another 12–18 months of bottle age. The saturated ruby/purple color is accompanied by a tight but promising nose of black fruits, damp earth, wood, and spice. Impressive in the mouth for its purity, elegance, and balance, this well-structured, medium-weight Cabernet Sauvignon has plenty going for it, but patience is required. Anticipated maturity: 2001–2015.

The 1993 Cabernet Sauvignon Reserve is a restrained, French-styled Cabernet with an attractive black currant nose with subtle oak and earth overtones. On the palate, this lighter-styled wine is medium bodied and soft, with dry tannin in the finish. It should improve for 3–4 years, and it requires drinking during its first 10–12 years of life. I like the wine, but it tries too hard to taste like an austerely styled Bordeaux.

Another excellent Cabernet from Simi, the dark ruby/purple-colored 1994 exhibits copious quantities of black currant fruit nicely integrated with smoky, toasty oak. The wine is supple, medium to full bodied, fleshy, and ready to drink. Additionally, it will age well for 6–10 years. The 1993 Cabernet Sauvignon possesses gobs of black fruits, licorice, and herbs in the nose, medium to full body, and good ripeness. Although not complex, it is a mouth-filling, savory, enjoyable Cabernet Sauvignon with a decade's worth of aging potential.

Simi's 1995 debut vintage of Shiraz is an open-knit, fruity wine with a medium ruby color, as well as a lovely nose of crushed black fruits intertwined with floral, pepper, and vanilla scents. This medium-bodied, soft, round, effusively fruity Shiraz is meant to be drunk over the next 2–3 years.

SINE QUA NON (SANTA BARBARA)

1996 Against the Wall (Syrah)	Santa Barbara	D	94
1996 Left Field Shea Vineyard (Pinot Noir)	Oregon	D	87
1996 Omadhaun Poltroon (Roussanne and Chardonnay)	California	D	94
1995 The Other Hand (Syrah)	California	D	92+
1995 Red Handed Proprietary Red Wine	California	D	93+
1997 Roussanne and Chardonnay (no name yet given)	California	D	(91–93)
1997 Syrah	Santa Barbara	D	(91–94)

The total production from this garage winery in Ojai is sold via a mailing list. The wines, produced by Manfred and Elaine Krankl, are among the most dramatic and individualistic being fashioned in California. The packaging (amazingly heavy antique-looking glass bottles and artsy labels) alone invites consumption, but the quality in the bottle is the real reason to get your name on their mailing list. Almost all the Santa Barbara wines come from vineyards such as Bien Nacido, Alban, and Stolpman. In 1996, 1997, and 1998, a Pinot Noir from Oregon's Shea Vineyard has also been produced.

All of these wines are bottled with virtually no fining, and rarely any filtration. The blockbuster whites Sine Qua Non is now producing are a blend of Roussanne and Chardonnay, with the former varietal dominating the blend in both 1996 and 1997. The massive, dry 1996 Omadhaun Poltroon's 15.2% alcohol is well concealed beneath this full-bodied wine's glycerin and unctuous texture. The knockout nose of honeyed citrus and rose petals is followed by a chewy, remarkably pure, dry wine oozing with extract. I suspect it will become even more civilized with 12–18 months of bottle age, but I would opt for drinking it over the next 2–3 years. The 1997 Roussanne/Chardonnay (60% of the former and 40% of the latter, all from the Alban Vineyard) has not yet been named. It is similar to the 1996, with perhaps the spicy, honeyed, rose petal-scented nose even more intensely fragrant. This is another classic, full-bodied, whoppingly big white that demonstrates the heights Roussanne can achieve in selected microclimates. While I suspect its power, intensity, alcohol, and extract will serve it well for a relatively long ride, I will be drinking my tiny allocation within 2–3 years of the vintage.

The 1996 Pinot Noir from Oregon's Shea Vineyard called Left Field is the first wine from Sine Qua Non that has not received an outstanding rating. The color is medium ruby/garnet, and the nose complex, with plenty of smoky new oak intermixed with plum, damp forest aromas, and berry fruit. Like many 1996 Oregon Pinot Noirs, there is a slight austerity and hollowness in the midpalate. This elegant offering could easily pass for a classy Burgundy in a blind tasting. Given the moderate tannin in the finish, it should improve in the bottle, but the midpalate deficiency worries me. Drink it over the next 3–5 years.

Sine Qua Non has produced some spectacular Syrahs, buying fruit from the best sources in Santa Barbara—the Alban, Stolpman, and Bien Nacido vineyards. The 1997 Syrah exhibits a thick, saturated black/purple color, as well as a knockout nose of blackberry jam, spice, and floral notes. It is a full-bodied, stunningly rich and concentrated wine with nicely integrated acidity and sweet tannin. The new oak and the wine's structure barely contain the blockbuster level of extract and fruit. The likes of this thrilling Syrah are rarely found in California (although the potential in Santa Barbara, and the coastal areas of Russian River and the Sonoma Coast look exceptionally promising). It will be accessible young and keep for 15–20 years, although the wine's hedonistic qualities will ensure that much of it is consumed long before it ever hits its peak. Anticipated maturity: 2000–2020.

The 1996 Against the Wall Syrah is cut from the same mold as the 1997. The color is opaque black/purple, and the nose offers a combination of cassis/blackberry jamminess intermixed with tar, pepper, and spice. Thick, massively full, yet wonderfully rich and expansive, with admirable purity and mouth-staining levels of glycerin and extract, this full-bodied, silky-smooth Syrah is deceptively easy to drink, but I suspect it will age effortlessly for 15–20 years.

The 1995 The Other Hand is made from 100% Syrah grown in the Alban, Bien Nacido, and Stolpman vineyards, situated respectively in Edna Valley, Santa Maria, and Los Olivos. Aged 18 months in oak, of which 70% is new, this blockbuster, opaque purple-colored wine offers glorious notes of black fruits (primarily blackberry and cassis), subtle smoke, toast, and licorice, and a whiff of plant material and spice. Full bodied, yet gorgeously layered and nearly seamless in its flamboyant display of fruit, glycerin, and extract, this large-scaled, yet drinkable Syrah will benefit from another 5–6 years in the bottle, but it is already accessible. It is another example of why I think wineries in this region should be ripping out their Pinot Noir vines and replanting with Syrah! Look for this super Syrah to age effortlessly for 15 or more years.

The limited production 1995 Red Handed is a blend of 43% Grenache, 40% Syrah, and 17% Mourvèdre blend also aged 18 months in oak, of which 50% was new. This wine wants to be a southern California Châteauneuf du Pape, and comes close to duplicating the character of a hedonistic southern Rhône. Sadly, only eighty 6-bottle cases were produced. The color is an impressively saturated red/black/purple. The wine offers up aromas of cigar box, fruitcake, cedar, pepper, Provençal herb, and glorious levels of kirsch and other black fruits. The influence of oak frames the wine rather than adding much to the aromas or flavors. Extremely full bodied, rich, chewy, and loaded with personality (another wine that reflects its makers), with a multidimensional palate, and beautifully integrated alcohol, acidity, and tannin, this wine has a singular personality and stupendous quality. Anticipated maturity: now–2014.

Oh how I wish there were more small producers such as Elaine and Manfred Krankl. Take my advice—get on their mailing list!

W. H. SMITH WINES (SONOMA COAST)

1997 Pinot Noir	Sonoma Coast	D	88
1997 Pinot Noir Hellenthal Vineyard	Sonoma Coast	D	90
1997 Pinot Noir Little Billy	Sonoma Coast	C	87

These wines, made by Joan and Bill Smith of La Jota, are getting closer and closer to capturing the magic of this varietal. The 1997 Pinot Noir Little Billy is a reasonably priced offering made to be drunk over the next 2 years. The wine's feeble light ruby/garnet color is deceptive given the wine's sweet kirsch, earthy, and underbrush-scented nose. An elegant, stylish Pinot Noir, with a soft personality and easygoing finish, it should be drunk soon. The more complex 1997 Pinot Noir Sonoma Coast exhibits a distinctive nose of cinnamon, cloves, plums, *garrigue*, and red fruits. In the mouth, it is lush, with cherry/plum fruit notes, medium body, low acidity, and a sweet, ripe, glycerin-endowed finish. Its color is an evolved ruby/garnet, but the wine is tasty, ripe, and expansive. It should drink well for 2–3 years. The outstanding medium ruby-colored 1997 Pinot Noir Hellenthal Vineyard offers a provocative nose of cherry liqueur intermixed with Asian spices and *pain grillé*. It has more body, length, and depth, in addition to the rich, velvety-textured palate also shared by its two less expensive siblings. Harmonious and complex, this wine will not make "old bones," but will provide considerable silky-textured pleasure if consumed over the next 3–4 years.

SOBON ESTATE (AMADOR)

1995 Syrah	Shenandoah Valley	C	88
1994 Zinfandel Estate Cougar Hill	Shenandoah	C	88
1995 Zinfandel Fiddletown Lubenko Vineyards	Amador	C	86+?
1994 Zinfandel Lubenko/Fiddletown	Shenandoah	C	88+
1995 Zinfandel Rocky Top	Shenandoah Valley	C	86
1995 Zinfandel Vintner's Selection	Amador	C	85

Sobon Estate's deep purple-colored 1995 Syrah possesses copious aromas of sweet, spicy, peppery, cassis fruit, plenty of glycerin, full body, outstanding purity and ripeness, and sweet tannin in the finish. Still young and promising, it will be at its finest between 1998 and 2007.

The 1995 Fiddletown Lubenko Vineyards Zinfandel exhibits an impressive dark purple color, a tight but intense, jammy black cherry, raspberry, earthy-scented nose, medium to full body, good acidity, and a compressed but spicy, long, heady finish. It should drink well for 5–6 years. The 1995 Zinfandel Rocky Top displays a dense, plumlike color, followed by sweet vanillin and black fruit flavors intertwined with pepper, roasted peanuts, and spice. Full bodied, lush, and opulently textured, this rich, well-endowed Zinfandel should drink well for 5–6 years. The 1995 Sobon Family Vineyard Zinfandel Vintner's Selection is a blend of three Amador vineyards, Eschen, Fiddletown, and Paul's. The wine exhibits a dark ruby/purple color, and copious quantities of spicy new oak in the nose. It is a smooth, ripe, medium-bodied wine with attractive richness, a supple texture, and a moderately long finish. Despite all its oak and fruit, this is essentially a one-dimensional wine for drinking over the next 2–4 years.

Two impressive 1994 examples from Sobon Estate, the 1994 Zinfandel Cougar Hill exhibits a dark ruby/purple/garnet color, ripe, earthy, foresty aromas, burly, concentrated, rustic flavors, and a mouth-filling intensity and richness. It had just been bottled a few days before I tasted it, but it was revealing plenty of potential. It should drink well for 5–7 years. The 1994 Zinfandel Lubenko/Fiddletown reveals a denser ruby/purple color, a more muscular, fuller-bodied, beefier style as if it had an extra dosage of steroids, some austerity and toughness in the finish, as well as wonderfully rich, ripe fruit, a sweet midsection, and a long, spicy, slightly tough finish. Once again, it had been bottled less than a week when I tasted it, so this wine may turn out to merit an even higher score.

SONOMA-LOEB (SONOMA)

1996 Chardonnay Private Reserve	Sonoma	D	88
1995 Chardonnay Private Reserve	Sonoma	D	88

Notes of *pain grillé*, roasted nuts, and spice soar from the glass of the exotic, extroverted 1996 Chardonnay. Fleshy, with gobs of smoky oak, and a Meursault-like character, this medium- to full-bodied, flavorful, buttery wine should be consumed over the next year. The generously endowed, opulently textured, leesy, buttery, oak-tinged 1995 Chardonnay possesses a light gold color, a rich, creamy texture, excellent fruit purity and extract, and an impressive finish. It is a seductive, hedonistic style of Chardonnay to drink over the next several years.

SONORA WINERY (AMADOR)

1996 Zinfandel Old Vine Story Vineyard	Amador	C	86?
1996 Zinfandel Old Vine TC Vineyard	Amador	C	86

Sonora's 1996 Zinfandel TC Vineyard (made from 90-year-old vines) displays a raisiny, overripe, prunelike character to its jammy cherry fruit. Otherwise, this is a full-bodied, textbook Amador Zinfandel with plenty of guts, not a great deal of finesse, and a late-harvest, Amarone-like style. Drink it over the next 2–4 years. The 1996 Zinfandel Story Vineyard carries its nearly 15% alcohol with considerable grace. It does possess noticeable acidity and tannin, a slightly roasted/prunelike character, big, spicy, jammy, cherry/coffeelike fruit, full body, and a rustic, aggressive finish. It is an old style, uncivilized Zin that should drink well for 3–4 years.

CHÂTEAU SOUVERAIN (SONOMA)

1996 Cabernet Sauvignon	Alexander Valley	C	87
1995 Cabernet Sauvignon	Alexander Valley	C	87
1994 Cabernet Sauvignon	Alexander Valley	C	89
1993 Cabernet Sauvignon	Alexander Valley	B	88
1996 Cabernet Sauvignon Library Reserve	Alexander Valley	D	91
1994 Cabernet Sauvignon Library Reserve	Alexander Valley	D	92
1993 Cabernet Sauvignon Library Selection	Alexander Valley	D	93

1997 Cabernet Sauvignon Winemaker's Reserve	Alexander Valley	D	(90–92)
1996 Cabernet Sauvignon Winemaker's Reserve	Alexander Valley	D	90
1995 Cabernet Sauvignon Winemaker's Reserve	Alexander Valley	D	91
1994 Cabernet Sauvignon Winemaker's Reserve	Alexander Valley	D	90
1993 Cabernet Sauvignon Winemaker's Reserve	Alexander Valley	D	90+
1997 Chardonnay	Sonoma	B	88
1996 Chardonnay	Sonoma	B	85
1995 Chardonnay	Sonoma	C	88
1997 Chardonnay Winemaker's Reserve	Russian River	D	89
1996 Chardonnay Winemaker's Reserve (Rochioli Vineyard)	Russian River	D	90
1995 Chardonnay Winemaker's Reserve	Russian River	C	90
1997 Merlot	Alexander Valley	C	(86–88)
1996 Merlot	Sonoma	C	87
1995 Merlot	Alexander Valley	C	89
1994 Merlot	Alexander Valley	B	88
1997 Merlot Winemaker's Reserve	Alexander Valley	D	(89–91)
1996 Rhône Blend	Sonoma	C	88
1997 Sauvignon Blanc	Alexander Valley	A	86
1996 Sauvignon Blanc	Alexander Valley	A	87
1995 Sauvignon Blanc	Alexander Valley	A	86
1997 Viognier	Alexander Valley	C	86
1996 Viognier	Alexander Valley	C	(85–87)
1997 Zinfandel	Alexander Valley	C	(86–87)
1997 Zinfandel	Dry Creek Valley	C	(85–87)
1996 Zinfandel	Dry Creek Valley	B	87
1995 Zinfandel	Dry Creek Valley	B	86
1994 Zinfandel	Dry Creek Valley	B	88
1993 Zinfandel	Dry Creek Valley	B	86

Owned by the Beringer group, this winery has become one of consumers' best friends—offering reliably high quality wines for extremely fair prices. Readers who have not yet benefited from Souverain's excellent quality/price rapport should move quickly, as this is no longer a secret address for maximizing the power of your wine dollar. The 1997 Sauvignon Blanc (100% Sauvignon) had its malolactic fermentation blocked, resulting in a citrusy, melony, subtle, nicely fruited, clean, pure, light- to medium-bodied wine that is faithful to this varietal. Drink it over the next year. Souverain does an excellent job turning out high-quality Chardonnay. For example, not many Chardonnays offer as much flavor and character for the price as Souverain's 1997 Chardonnay. This wine receives 100% barrel fermentation and 9% lees stirring. The result is a creamy-textured, expansively flavored, big, smoky, Burgundian-styled Chardonnay with plenty of tropical fruit. With good texture and subtle oaky notes (25%–35% new is utilized), this tasty wine should be drunk over the next year. The 1997 Chardonnay Winemaker's Reserve (1,000 cases, primarily from the Allen Ranch and Westside Vineyards in the Russian River) reveals a Meursault premier crulike quality. The roasted hazelnut, smoky, leesy nose is followed by a full-bodied, buttery wine with admirable glycerin, richness, and length. It should drink well for 1–2 years, and possibly merit an outstanding score if the oak becomes slightly better integrated. Souverain's 1997 Viognier is an elegant, lighter-styled, fresh Viognier exhibiting honeysuckle/apricotlike fruit, medium body, and a clean finish. It should be consumed over the next year.

In 1997, two Zinfandels were produced. The 1997 Zinfandel Dry Creek possesses the varietal's textbook briery, berry, peppery nose, with spicy American oak in the background, medium body, and a sophisticated, soft, fruit-driven personality. It is meant to be consumed over the next 2–4 years. The 1997 Zinfandel Alexander Valley shares a similar elegance, as well as delightful freshness, a peppery, dusty, raspberry/cherry fruitiness, and more depth. Overall, it is a fruit-driven wine with softness and immense crowd appeal. It should drink well for 3–4 years.

Château Souverain launched a Merlot program in 1996. Based on the following three tasting notes, it is very successful. The dark ruby-colored 1996 Merlot Sonoma exhibits aromas of coffee beans, herbaceous black cherries, smoke, and toasty oak. Medium bodied, round, and user-friendly, it should drink well for 4–5 years. The deep ruby-colored 1997 Merlot Alexander Valley is denser and fatter, with excellent berry fruit, mocha/coffee notes, and a touch of herbaceousness. Made in a richer, more evolved style, with plenty of glycerin and fleshiness, this wine should drink well for 5–7 years. In 1997 there will be a Merlot Winemaker's Reserve, which may turn out to be outstanding. Approximately 200 cases were produced. The wine boasts an opaque purple color, and a knockout nose of black and red fruits, plus spicy oak and coffee. A deep, exotic, expansively flavored Merlot, it will provide hedonistic drinking for 7–8 years.

This winery's track record with Cabernet Sauvignon has been consistently impressive. One of the finest values in high class Cabernet Sauvignon each year is their Cabernet Sauvignon Alexander Valley. The 1996 is a sexy, fleshy wine with a bouquet of cigar box, smoke, cedar, and black currants that has been intermixed with lavish new oak. Hedonistic and lush, with ripe fruit, low acidity, and a plush texture, it will drink well for 7–8 years. All three vintages of Cabernet Sauvignon Winemaker's Reserve (approximately 1,000 cases in 1995, and 2,000 cases in both 1996 and 1997) are outstanding. The 1995 Cabernet Sauvignon Winemaker's Reserve offers a knockout nose of smoked herbs, black currants, and toasty oak. It is medium to full bodied, with terrific fruit purity, outstanding richness, and a deep, nicely layered texture. The wine's low acidity and plump, fleshy style suggest drinking now and over the next 12 years. The deep ruby/purple-colored 1996 Cabernet Sauvignon Winemaker's Reserve displays plenty of spice box, fruitcake, and black currant fruit intermixed with allspice, toasty oak, and weedy tobacco. Sweet (from extract, not sugar) on the attack, this full-bodied wine reveals copious quantities of glycerin, fruit, and extract. A beauty, it has managed to avoid the hard tannin exhibited by some 1996s. Drink it over the next decade. In 1996 there is also a limited production Cabernet Sauvignon Library Reserve. While it is no better than the Winemaker's Reserve, the oak is more noticeable, and the wine slightly more powerful. The Library Reserve is unquestionably an outstanding Cabernet, with new oak and slightly higher alcohol. It should drink well upon release and last for 10–12 years.

The 1997 Cabernet Sauvignon Winemaker's Reserve exhibits the vintage's forward, fragrant aromatics, sweet tannin, a velvety, seamless personality, and loads of black currant fruit that have been complemented by a nice dosage of vanillin, smoke, dried herbs, and spices. This beauty should be seductive when released and last for 10–14 years.

The 1996 Viognier was just about to be bottled when I tasted it, hence the projected range in scores. Aromatic, but not as intensely varietal as I expected, this medium-bodied, fruity, straightforward Viognier offers a tasty glass of wine, but it does not possess enough of the Viognier character to merit a higher rating. Drink it over the next year.

The 1995 Chardonnay Sonoma County is a 100% barrel-fermented wine that exhibits a smoky, vanillin, tropical fruit-scented nose, medium- to full-bodied, fleshy flavors, good richness, a soft texture, and a moderately long finish. It will provide delicious drinking over the next year. Even more impressive is the 1995 Chardonnay Winemaker's Reserve. This wine emerges from Rochioli's famed Allen Ranch and Westside Vineyard. It is a full-bodied, powerful Chardonnay that has been aged in 100% new French oak casks and put through a full malolactic fermentation. The exotic, honeyed pineapple/spiced apple-scented nose is followed by a ripe, creamy-textured wine loaded with fruit, glycerin, and extract. Drink it over the next 1–2 years. Impressive!

Souverain's 1996 Sauvignon Blanc is a midweight, tropical fruit and melon-scented and -flavored wine that appears to have been made from the aromatic clone of Sauvignon called Musqué. This pure, ripe Sauvignon is best drunk over the next 12–18 months. The exuberantly fruity, honeyed melon, herb, and fig-scented, medium-bodied 1995 Sauvignon Blanc is pure and delicious. It will provide ideal drinking over the next year.

This estate consistently produces fine Chardonnays, and their two 1996 offerings include a medium-bodied, soft, fruity, oaky 1996 Chardonnay Sonoma, and a Burgundian-like, complex, leesy, fuller-bodied 1996 Chardonnay Winemaker's Reserve. The latter wine was still tight and unevolved when I tasted it in October of 1997. The fruit comes from the renowned Rochioli Vineyard in Russian River, and the wine has been given both barrel fermentation and lees stirring. It offers a honeyed lemon, smoky-scented nose, rich, fleshy, muscular flavors, and an excellent to outstanding finish. This wine should last for 2 years.

Readers looking for attractive, mouth-filling, savory wines that are not burdened by considerable new oak or tannin, should taste Souverain's 1996 Zinfandel Dry Creek and 1996 Rhône Blend. The 1996 Zinfandel Dry Creek is not a weighty, high alcohol blockbuster, but rather, a suave, gracefully styled wine with fine ripeness, attractive berry/briery fruit, medium body, and a supple, smooth-textured finish. It is meant to be drunk over the next several years. I hope Souverain continues to produce their Rhône Ranger-inspired wine. Certainly their 1996 Rhône Blend (60% Syrah, 30% Mourvèdre, 10% Zinfandel) is an impressive debut offering. Blueberry, floral, peppery, and cassis aromas and flavors are packed into a medium- to full-bodied wine with good length, and attractive sweet, ripe fruit and spice. It should provide delicious drinking for 7–8+ years.

Obviously label design and packaging do not count when it comes to evaluating a wine. Nevertheless, good-quality wine deserves something better than the appalling, cheap-looking bottle and silly label with opening instructions ("turn the corkscrew clockwise") of the 1995 Zinfandel. Inside the distressingly designed bottle is a delicious, tasty, open-knit, exuberantly fruity Zinfandel that is meant to be drunk over the next 2–3 years. The wine is soft and round, with plenty of berry fruit. If you don't get indigestion from looking at the bottle or reading the prose on the back label, readers may even enjoy the wine more than I did.

The 1994 Zinfandel offers up an explosive, overripe berry-scented nose, gobs of lush, briery, peppery Zinfandel fruit, noticeable viscosity and thickness, and a long, heady, alcoholic finish. It is an up-front, in-your-face style of Zinfandel for drinking during its first 5–6 years of life. The 1993 Zinfandel exhibits plenty of toasty, smoky oak, wonderfully soft, ripe fruit, a velvety texture, and a plump, lush finish. Drink it over the next 3–4 years. A good value.

The Cabernet Sauvignons are all best buys, even the more expensive yet still reasonably priced Winemaker's Reserve. These are excellent wines that recall the glory days of Souverain in the late sixties and early seventies. I recently drank the 1974 Souverain Vintage Selection (an early *Wine Advocate* Best Buy pick which I highly recommended, but suggested drinking within 5–7 years of release). That wine is still holding onto all of its fruit, an example of how a wine that was never a blockbuster, but concentrated and impeccably well balanced can age so well. The following wines all appear to have at least 10–15 years of cellaring potential. The 1995 Cabernet Sauvignon Alexander Valley is loaded with black currant fruit and cassis, and is made in a silky-textured, rich, full-bodied style. Some smoky oak rests in the background, and the finish is nicely layered with no hard edges. This excellent Cabernet Sauvignon could easily sell for a much higher price.

The 1994 Cabernet Sauvignon Winemaker's Reserve is nearly as impressive as its younger sibling. Although cut from the same mold, it may have less concentration and length than the amazing 1995. The supple and precocious 1994 is already complex and evolved. It can be drunk now or over the next 12–15 years. The 1994 Cabernet Sauvignon Alexander Valley tastes similar to a Cabernet costing $20–$30. This beauty offers a deep ruby/purple color, a spicy, black currant, tobacco, cedar, and toasty-scented nose, lush, low-acid, ripe flavors, the silkiness that is a hallmark of the 1994 vintage, and a clean, ripe finish. It should drink well for 5–7 years, perhaps longer. The 1994 Cabernet Sauvignon Library Reserve (only 200 cases, and likely to be priced in the $30 range) boasts an opaque ruby/purple color, as well as a sweet, jammy nose of blue and blackberry fruit intertwined with subtle herbs, toast, Asian spices, and licorice. Full bodied, powerful, and rich, this wine, although loaded with extract, is accessible. Sweet tannin gives the wine a precocious, up-front appeal. It should age gracefully for 12–15+ years.

The 1993 Cabernet Sauvignon Winemaker's Reserve is a young, purple-colored wine with wonderfully smoky, cassis fruit intermingled with scents of oak. Rich, unctuously textured, thick, and pure, this is a soft yet persuasively flavored Cabernet Sauvignon for drinking now and over the next 10–12 years. This may be one of the best buys in serious, long-lived Cabernet Sauvignon. No price has yet been established for the 200 cases of 1993 Cabernet Sauvignon Library Selection. A great Cabernet, it is a worthy competitor for some of the finest Cabernet Sauvignons made in California. The wine possesses an opaque purple color, and a fabulously pure, rich nose of cassis fruit intermingled with scents of smoky oak. Full bodied, fat, and rich, with great presence on the palate, this opulent, layered Cabernet Sauvignon will be drinkable young, but keep for 15+ years. There is also an even less expensive Cabernet Sauvignon Alexander Valley. The 1993 is an excellent wine that should not be overlooked. It is a dense, rich, herb and black currant-scented wine with terrific fruit, a lush, velvety-textured personality, fine depth, and copious quantities of sweet cassis fruit and glycerin in the long, lusty finish. Drink it over the next 7–8 years.

I tasted a very exciting barrel sample of a 1995 Merlot from the Alexander Valley. Not much industrial wine processing is practiced at Souverain, so the range of scores should be relatively accurate. This deep ruby/purple-colored wine reveals a raspberry and blueberry-scented nose, and concentrated, ripe fruit infused with toasty, smoky, new oak that nicely complements the wine's black fruit-dominated personality. Supple and expansive, it is a candidate for 5–7 years of delicious drinking.

Château Souverain produced a fine 1994 Merlot, with more noticeable oak in its smoky, vanillin, jammy, cherry-scented nose. The wine exhibits admirable ripe fruit, the attractive, fat, supple side of Merlot, and finishes with plenty of fruit and character. It should drink well for 6–8 years.

These are underrated, high-quality wines that merit considerable attention.

SPOTTSWOODE WINERY (NAPA)

1996	Cabernet Sauvignon	Napa	E	94
1995	Cabernet Sauvignon	Napa	D	94
1994	Cabernet Sauvignon	Napa	D	93
1993	Cabernet Sauvignon	Napa	D	92
1996	Sauvignon Blanc	Napa	C	88
1995	Sauvignon Blanc	Napa	C	89

One of California's finest Sauvignons is consistently produced by Spottswoode Winery. Few readers ever get to taste Spottswoode's Sauvignon Blanc as much of it is sold to restaurants. It has become one of California's more interesting Sauvignons. The 1995 displays a white Graves-like personality, good aromatics, excellent freshness, plenty of oaky, waxy, melony fruit, and an underpinning of crisp acidity. It should be consumed during its first several years of life. Their 1996 Sauvignon Blanc is an attractive, ripe pineapple, honey, herbs, and melon-scented wine with medium body, excellent flavor richness, an alluring texture, enough acidity for definition, and a long finish. Drink this enticing Sauvignon Blanc over the next year.

Spottswoode's 5,000-case production of Cabernet Sauvignon is the winery's bread-and-butter wine. I have followed this wine since the debut release, and even vintages that seemed somewhat monolithic now appear to be evolving more gracefully. I have often made reference to the fact that while no California wine tastes like Château Margaux, the Spottswoode Cabernet possesses an aromatic profile, weight, and textural dimension that is vaguely reminiscent of that first-growth Bordeaux estate. This pure, fragrant wine depends on its beautifully layered fruit, ripeness, and balance to impress tasters, in contrast to those Cabernets that offer a blast of wood, glycerin, and alcohol. Recent vintages have been exceptionally successful.

If Napa's and Sonoma's 1993 Cabernet Sauvignons have a problem, I have yet to unearth it. Spottswoode's 1993 Cabernet Sauvignon is another outstanding wine from a vintage that has been roughly treated by the press. The wine offers a gorgeously deep purple color, a sweet, fragrant nose with a subtle floral component and plenty of black currant/cassis fruit. The oak influence is restrained. Medium to full bodied, with well-integrated acidity and tannin, this is a well-proportioned, intense, graceful style of Cabernet Sauvignon that will benefit from 3–4 years of cellaring. I don't doubt for an instant that it will evolve for 2 decades.

With respect to the 1994 Cabernet Sauvignon, a beautifully scented nose of cassis, lead pencil, high-quality new oak, and spice is followed by a wine with striking richness and balance. This dark ruby/purple-colored Cabernet possesses fabulous concentration, yet it never comes across as heavy or out of sync. A gloriously made, elegant yet powerfully flavored wine, it is accessible, yet capable of lasting for another 12–20 years. This sensational Cabernet Sauvignon exhibits the more complex, elegant side of California winemaking. Bravo!

Another outstanding example from this consistently high quality performer, Spottswoode's 1995 Cabernet Sauvignon stood out in my barrel tasting as one of the strongest efforts of the vintage. Although tightly wound, it exhibits an opaque purple color, and a tight but gorgeous nose of black currants, vanilla, minerals, and a touch of smoke and blueberries. Medium to full bodied and impeccably well balanced, this wine's structural components (acidity, alcohol, and tannin) are beautifully meshed together with the lavishly rich fruit that is presented in a medium- to full-bodied format. This should turn out to be a textbook, classic Napa Cabernet Sauvignon that admirably balances elegance and power. Anticipated maturity: 2000–2015.

A beautifully made Cabernet Sauvignon, the 1996 continues to offer a Château Margaux-like elegance allied with plenty of black currant fruit, and nicely integrated toasty oak. The wine is medium to full bodied and pure, with a layered mouth-feel. There is no sense of heaviness to this beautifully knit Cabernet Sauvignon. It should be at its peak in 5–6 years and last for 2 decades.

SPRING MOUNTAIN VINEYARDS (NAPA)

Year	Wine	Region		Rating
1993	Cabernet Sauvignon Estate	Napa	D	89
1993	Cabernet Sauvignon Estate Chevalier Vineyard	Napa	D	91
1995	Miravalle Alba Chevalier Proprietary Red Wine	Spring Mountain	D	90
1994	Miravalle Alba Chevalier Proprietary Red Wine	Spring Mountain	D	88
1993	Miravalle Alba Chevalier Proprietary Red Wine	Spring Mountain	C	89+
1996	Miravalle Alba Chevalier Proprietary White Wine	Spring Mountain	D	87
1996	Miravalle La Perla Chevalier Proprietary Red Wine	Spring Mountain	D	90
1997	Miravalle La Perla Chevalier Proprietary White Wine	Spring Mountain	D	90
1996	Premier Reserve (not yet named) Proprietary Red Wine	Spring Mountain	E	(91–93)
1996	White Wine Miravalle Alba Chevalier Vineyard	Napa	C	86

This operation, headed by veteran winemaker Tom Farrell (who assisted in the winemaking of the monumental 1968 Heitz Martha's Vineyard), is one of the most extraordinary vineyard developments in northern Napa. Over 240 acres, spread over the Spring Mountain hillsides, are being developed. Amazingly, there are 130 separate vineyard blocks. The origins of this vineyard site can be traced back to 1882. More recently, such estates as Château Chevalier produced fruit from these hillsides. Tom Farrell and his assistant, Bill Wren, sell about 20% of the production each year. Currently, they are making a proprietary red wine (primarily Cabernet Sauvignon) and a proprietary white wine, as well as some experimental wines. They have produced some Syrah (the 1997 is promising), and have planted Mourvèdre, Pinot Gris, and a small amount of Pinot Noir. The ultimate goal is to produce 20,000 cases of luxury-priced wines. The debut and upcoming releases are all impressive, French-styled wines with considerable character.

The 1997 Miravalle La Perla Chevalier Proprietary White Wine (a blend of 50% Sauvignon Blanc, 43% Chardonnay, and 7% Muscat Blanc) is outstanding. Sadly, only 14,000 bottles have been produced. The wine's floral, honeyed nose soars from the glass. Tasty and medium bodied, with crisp, tangy acidity yet excellent flavor depth and precision, it is a complex, dry white to enjoy over the next 2–3 years. About 1,000 cases were produced of the 1996 Miravalle Alba Chevalier Proprietary White Wine, a blend of 65% Sauvignon Blanc, 21% Chenin Blanc, 12% Chardonnay, and 2% Muscat Blanc. Like the 1997, it is all barrel fermented, but only the Chardonnay was put through malolactic fermentation. The goal is to produce a white similar to a fine white Graves. The 1996, while not possessing the soaring aromatics of the 1997, is an elegant, fresh, melony-scented ripe wine. Light bodied, complex, and very French-like in its aromatics and flavors, it should be consumed over the next 1–2 years.

The red wines, which are given extended macerations of between 14–45 days, tend to be primarily Cabernet Sauvignon-based wines, aged in 100% new oak. The 1993 Miravalle Alba Chevalier Proprietary Red could easily pass for a second- or third-growth Médoc. A blend of 76% Cabernet Sauvignon, 13% Merlot, and 11% Cabernet Franc, it exhibits an impressive dark ruby/purple color, fine ripeness, attractive black currants and minerals, well-integrated wood, and a tannic finish. Anticipated maturity: 2001–2016. The 1994 Miravalle Alba Chevalier Proprietary Red Wine (for Spring Mountain, a large production of 6,250 cases) is a blend of 93% Cabernet Sauvignon, 3% Merlot, and 4% Cabernet Franc. While it is less tannic than the 1993, more elegant and California-like, it retains a certain austerity, but does unfold nicely on the palate to reveal stylish, rich black currant fruit intermixed with subtle herbaceous notes, minerals, and wood spices. It requires 3–4 more years of cellaring, and should keep for a minimum of 10–15 years. The 1995 Miravalle Alba Chevalier Proprietary Red Wine (3,044 cases) is made from 100% Cabernet Sauvignon. This wine was performing impressively at a recent tasting, displaying an opaque purple color, and sweet black currant/crème de cassis notes intermixed with lead pencil and *pain grillé*. Margaux-like in its deep, rich, full-bodied, palate-staining personality, it is loaded with black fruits and silky tannin, and possesses the most length and deepest midpalate of these Cabernet-dominated proprietary reds. Anticipated maturity: 2002–2020.

The 1996 Miravalle La Perla Chevalier Proprietary Red Wine (4,231 cases, made from a blend of 87% Cabernet Sauvignon, 8% Merlot, and 5% Cabernet Franc) is as good as the 1995. It is a medium- to full-bodied, sweet, rich, chocolatey, black currant-scented and -flavored wine with a slight Médoc-like austerity, but sweet fruit, excellent balance, in addition to purity and depth. Although less massive than the 1995, it is as concentrated and long. Anticipated maturity: 2002–2020. In 1996, a reserve cuvée has been produced, although it had not been named when I visited the winery in September of 1998. The 1996 Premier Reserve/Cellar Selection (850 cases from a blend of 81% Cabernet Sauvignon, 16% Merlot, and 3% Petit Verdot) boasts an opaque purple color, followed by a textbook California Cabernet nose of mint, black currants, tobacco leaf, and spice. Dense, with dazzling fruit extract, full body, layers of concentration, moderate tannin, and a hefty, long but well-balanced finish, this appears to be slightly superior to the regular bottling, but it is in need of 4–5 years of cellaring. It should keep for 20–25 years.

The debut vintage of Cabernet Sauvignon was 1992. The 1993 Spring Mountain Estate Cabernet Sauvignon (7,000 cases) exhibits the same elegance and the subtle use of toasty new oak, excellent cassis fruit, a touch of minerals, and fine purity and length as the 1992. There is also a tiny quantity (300 cases) of the 1993 Spring Mountain Estate Cabernet Sauvignon Chevalier Vineyard, which is the richer, more concentrated wine of this duo. This wine exhibits black currant fruit, a spicy, licorice, mineral-scented bouquet, full body, and a sense of balance and grace without astringent tannin or high alcohol/heaviness. It is a classic, concentrated Cabernet Sauvignon that should drink well for 15+ years.

The 1996 White Miravalle-Alba-Chevalier, a 65% Sauvignon Blanc, 21% Chenin Blanc, 12% Chardonnay, and 2% Muscat blend, is a delightful, crisp, effusively fruity and refreshing white wine. While not complex, it is satisfying, as well as an ideal accompaniment to trattoria or bistro fish or fowl courses. Drink it over the next 8–10 months.

This impressive new operation appears to have only begun to exploit its full potential. Readers take note!

STAGLIN FAMILY VINEYARDS (NAPA)

1996	Cabernet Sauvignon	Rutherford/Napa	E	90
1995	Cabernet Sauvignon	Rutherford/Napa	E	90+
1994	Cabernet Sauvignon	Rutherford/Napa	D	88

| 1996 Sangiovese | Rutherford | D | 86 |
| 1995 Sangiovese | Rutherford | D | 84 |

This 50-acre estate features Sangiovese and Cabernet Sauvignon. Their Sangiovese is blended with about 18%–22% Cabernet Sauvignon. The medium ruby-colored 1995 Sangiovese offers a moderately endowed, strawberry and leather-scented nose, elegant, leafy, cranberry and berry flavors, and medium body. The finish contains excessive dry tannin, and comes across as austere. It requires immediate consumption. The sweeter 1996 Sangiovese reveals softer tannin, medium body, and an elegant personality. The wine offers sweet berry fruit and sour cherries in its attractive nose, and round, ripe, medium-bodied flavors with more flesh and intensity than in the 1995. Drink it over the next several years.

I find these Cabernet Sauvignons to be graceful, elegant, and undeniably stylish. The 1996 Cabernet Sauvignon exhibits a healthy dark ruby/purple color, and a sweet, restrained nose of lead pencil, toasty new oak, red and black currants, and sweet raspberries. Already approachable, the wine is medium to full bodied, with outstanding purity, and nicely integrated wood, acidity, alcohol, and tannin. Anticipated maturity: 2002–2018. The 1995 Cabernet Sauvignon is richer and more intense in the midpalate, as well as more backward. The wine is high in tannin, extract, and richness, yet the overall elegance, symmetry, and harmony among its elements are present. This pure, black fruit-dominated wine should be at its finest between 2003 and 2020.

There are approximately 4,000 cases of Cabernet Sauvignon made by Staglin. The 1994 Cabernet Sauvignon is a graceful, vanillin-scented, medium- to full-bodied wine that emphasizes Cabernet's red fruit character. It is pure and well balanced, with moderate tannin in the attractive, Bordeaux-like finish. Anticipated maturity: 2001–2016.

STAG'S LEAP WINE CELLARS (NAPA)

1995 Cabernet Sauvignon	Napa	C	85
1994 Cabernet Sauvignon	Napa	C	85
1993 Cabernet Sauvignon	Napa	C	90
1995 Cabernet Sauvignon Fay Vineyard	Napa	D	86
1994 Cabernet Sauvignon Fay Vineyard	Napa	D	89
1993 Cabernet Sauvignon Fay Vineyard	Napa	D	88
1995 Cabernet Sauvignon Stag's Leap Vineyard	Napa	D	87?
1994 Cabernet Sauvignon Stag's Leap Vineyard	Napa	D	89?
1993 Cabernet Sauvignon Stag's Leap Vineyard	Napa	D	89
1995 Cask 23 Proprietary Red Wine	Napa	EE	89?
1994 Cask 23 Proprietary Red Wine	Napa	EE	86?
1993 Cask 23 Proprietary Red Wine	Napa	EE	91
1995 Chardonnay	Napa	C	87
1995 Chardonnay Beckstoffer Ranch	Napa	D	88
1995 Chardonnay Reserve	Napa	D	90
1995 Hawk Crest Chardonnay	California	B	80
1995 Hawk Crest Sauvignon Blanc	California	A	85
1993 Merlot	Napa	C	87

1993	Petite Syrah	Napa	D	88
1995	Sauvignon Blanc	Napa	B	86
1995	White Riesling	Napa	A	85

The 1995 Stag's Leap White Riesling exhibits a tart, fresh, green apple character, light body, and a dry finish. It will provide a fine accompaniment to many Asian dishes if drunk over the next year. One of the better secondary labels in the marketplace is the inexpensive line of Hawk Crest wines produced by Stag's Leap Wine Cellars. The 1995 Hawk Crest Sauvignon Blanc is crisp, with light intensity, melony fruit, light body, and a dry finish. Drink it over the next 12 months. While not as fruity and deep as the 1994, the 1995 Hawk Crest Chardonnay offers fresh, one-dimensional, slightly herbal, light-bodied flavors in a clean format. It is best drunk over the next 6–12 months.

Stag's Leap Wine Cellars has produced better and better Chardonnays over the last few years, obtaining more flavor without compromising the wine's subtle, restrained, and elegant style. The 1995 Chardonnay Beckstoffer Ranch was aged in 100% new oak, with 15% of the blend put through malolactic. A more layered wine, with a peach, cream custard sort of nose, and citrusy flavors, it is suave, medium bodied, and subtle. Drink it over the next 2–3 years. The 1995 Chardonnay Napa is a 100% barrel-fermented wine exhibiting a judicious touch of oak, spicy, fresh, lemony, applelike flavors, medium body, moderate weight, and a delicate tactile impression. It is best drunk with politely seasoned/flavored dishes. The 1995 Chardonnay Reserve reminded me of a Domaine Leflaive Premier Cru. Elegant yet rich, with lemony, honeysucklelike aromas, restrained wood, medium body, zesty acidity, and fine richness and length, it is an impressive, crisp, subtle yet flavorful Chardonnay that should age well for 1–3 years, perhaps longer.

Stag's Leap Wine Cellars red wines have always been among my favorites, but I was surprised by the pronounced level of tart acidity found in the 1994s and 1995s. High acidity, together with a low pH, causes a wine's texture to become compressed. The result is a wine that tastes too compact and lean. The 1994s and 1995s possess excellent to outstanding raw materials, but can these two vintages signal a change in the winemaking philosophy at Stag's Leap? I hope not. The 1995 Cabernet Sauvignon exhibits a red currant nose, tart acidity, light to medium body, and a soft, pure finish. It should drink well for 7–8 years. The dark ruby-colored 1995 Cabernet Sauvignon Fay Vineyard offers elegant, subtle, restrained aromas, fresh, tart, acidic flavors, some cedar, tobacco, and spice, and a medium-bodied finish. It should drink well for 5–7 years. The 1995 Cabernet Sauvignon Stag's Leap Vineyard reveals more fruit and depth, but it comes across as a restrained, excessively subtle, round, crisp, edgy sort of wine with fine fruit, but overbearing acidity. Surprisingly, the 1995 Cask 23 Proprietary Red Wine is light, acidic, and excessively polite. The tart acid that is so much an annoying component of these 1995s is present in the Cask 23, giving it a lean, clipped and compact feel on the palate. I do not believe this is what fans of Stag's Leap Wine Cellars have come to expect. Nevertheless, the spicy, coffee, herb, cedary, red currant nose offers promise. There is good depth, but much of it is shielded by the wine's tart veneer. This wine should turn out to be graceful and elegant, but I am concerned about the textural deficiencies.

As for the 1994s, they were much more impressive when tasted previously. At present, they reveal similar degrees of tart acidity, although this component is not quite as pronounced. Surprisingly, the pH levels must be in the 3.4 range, which is very low by the standards of the world's greatest Merlots and Cabernets. The 1994 Cabernet Sauvignon displays lean, tart, red currant aromas that are straightforward and simple. In the mouth, the wine is fresh and pleasant, but sharp and lacking textural intensity and dimension. The 1994 Cabernet Sauvignon Fay Vineyard offers up a sweet, tobacco, coffee, spicy, herbal nose, followed by elegant, fruitcake, medium-bodied red currant flavors with a subtle hint of black fruits. The wine is round, with tangy acidity, but not the abrasive levels of tartness found in some of the other reds. The finish reveals good structure, purity, and tannin. This wine should drink well for 10–12 years. The 1994 Cabernet Sauvignon Stag's Leap Vineyard is a medium-bodied, midweight, sweet, ripe, smoky, vanillin, spicy (allspice?) wine with red and black fruits in the nose. On the palate, it is subtle and flavorful, with good acidity, medium body, and firm tannin. This Cabernet will benefit from several years of cellaring and last for 10–12 years.

In 1996 I reported on what is clearly a dramatic change in the winemaking style at this winery. The 1996s, 1995s, and 1994s are all much higher in acidity, with lean, sinewy, tart personalities. Now that the 1994 Cask 23 Proprietary Red Wine has been bottled, it is totally devoid of any of the Cask 23 characteristics shared by some of the marvelous vintages of the past (such as 1991, 1990, 1987, 1985, 1984, 1978, and 1974). The color is a dark ruby/purple, and the wine's closed aromatics reveal earth and red currant/cranberry fruit. On the attack, the wine exhibits shrill acidity, medium body, and a cursory finish, which serves to only make the tannin seem more astringent. This narrowly built, compressed, light- to medium-bodied Cask 23 is a total departure from previous efforts. What a shame!

The medium-bodied 1993 Merlot exhibits sour cherry and currant notes, intermixed with a cinnamon character. Drink it over the next 3–4 years. The 1993 Cabernet Sauvignon Fay Vineyard exhibits attractive toasty oak, sweet red currant fruit, medium body, tart acidity, and herbal, red currant flavors. This wine should keep for 10–12 years, but I am not sure it possesses the flesh and intensity to age beyond that, nor does it have the complexity or character exhibited by the 1992. The 1993 Cabernet Sauvignon Stag's Leap Vineyard reveals an earthy, spicy, curranty-scented, light intensity nose, medium body, considerable tannin and structure, above normal acid, and some sharp tannin in the finish. This wine has good depth, but I suspect it will always be somewhat austere and hard. Give it 2–3 years of cellaring and drink it over the following 10–12. Even the 1993 Cabernet Sauvignon Napa is revealing considerable complexity. It is deeply colored, with a cigar box, spicy, sweet black cherry and curranty nose, medium to full body, and superb harmony in the amazingly long finish.

The outstanding 1993 Cask 23 Proprietary Red Wine exhibits a dark ruby/garnet color, sweet, coffee, chocolate, cherrylike aromas, medium to full body, an alluring sweetness on the attack, but dry tannin in the finish. This effort possesses more expansiveness and richness, but the wine is well below the profound Cask 23's made in 1992, 1991, 1990, 1985, 1978, and 1974.

The opaque purple-colored 1993 Petite Syrah reveals licorice, pepper, earth, and underbrush in its modest aromatics. Full bodied, dense, and tannic, with good extract and muscle, but not yet silky smooth, it requires another 4–5 years of cellaring. It is one of the finest Petite Syrahs Stag's Leap has produced in the last decade.

STEELE (LAKE COUNTY)

1996 Chardonnay Bien Nacido Vineyard	Santa Barbara	D	88
1995 Chardonnay Bien Nacido Vineyard	Santa Barbara	C	88
1995 Chardonnay Dennison Vineyard	Mendocino	C	88
1996 Chardonnay du Pratt Vineyard	Mendocino	D	86
1995 Chardonnay du Pratt Vineyard	Mendocino	C	90
1996 Chardonnay Durell Vineyard	Carneros	D	87
1995 Chardonnay Durell Vineyard	Sonoma	C	88
1996 Chardonnay Goodchild Vineyard	Santa Barbara	D	88

1995	Chardonnay Goodchild Vineyard	Santa Barbara	C	85
1996	Chardonnay Lolonis Vineyard	Mendocino	D	87
1995	Chardonnay Lolonis Vineyard	Mendocino	D	88
1996	Chardonnay Parmelee Hill Vineyard	Sonoma Valley	D	85
1996	Chardonnay Sangiacomo Vineyard	Carneros	D	89
1995	Chardonnay Sangiacomo Vineyard	Carneros	C	89
1996	Chardonnay Steele Cuvée	California	C	87
1995	Chardonnay Steele Cuvée	California	C	87
1996	Pinot Gris Romani Family Vineyard	Anderson Valley	C	86
1995	Pinot Noir	Anderson Valley	C	85
1996	Pinot Noir	Carneros	C	87
1995	Pinot Noir	Carneros	C	86
1996	Pinot Noir Bien Nacido Vineyard	Santa Barbara	D	85
1995	Pinot Noir Bien Nacido Vineyard	Santa Barbara	D	87+
1994	Pinot Noir Bien Nacido Vineyard	Santa Barbara	C	88
1995	Pinot Noir du Pratt Vineyard	Mendocino	D	87
1994	Pinot Noir du Pratt Vineyard	Mendocino	D	89
1995	Pinot Noir Durell Vineyard	Carneros	C	86
1996	Pinot Noir Sangiacomo Vineyard	Carneros	D	85
1995	Zinfandel Catfish Vineyard	Clear Lake	D	86
1994	Zinfandel Catfish Vineyard	Mendocino	C	90
1995	Zinfandel du Pratt Vineyard	Mendocino	D	88
1995	Zinfandel Pacini Vineyard	Mendocino	D	87
1994	Zinfandel Pacini Vineyard	Mendocino	C	89+

One of our country's premier winemakers once again turned out a bevy of gorgeous Chardonnays. The 1996 Chardonnay Sangiacomo Vineyard displays a leesy, Burgundian-like, creamy-textured complexity, medium to full body, outstanding purity, and a light gold color. It is a smoky, roasted nut, rich, honeyed style of Chardonnay with sufficient acidity for delineation and balance. Drink it over the next 1–2 years. While it possesses a light gold color, the 1996 Chardonnay Bien Nacido Vineyard is more exotic, with an abundance of tropical fruit, well-integrated oak, medium body, and a clean, lively mouth-feel. There is zesty acidity in this fruity, well-made wine. Drink it over the next 1–2 years. Another Santa Barbara Chardonnay, the 1996 Chardonnay Goodchild Vineyard offers a more reserved nose, with less tropical fruit, and more butterscotch and roasted nut characteristics. This tightly knit, restrained, pure wine exhibits a Meursault-like buttery nuttiness. It should improve over the next 6–12 months and last for several years. The 1996 Chardonnay Steele Cuvée reveals a metallic, mineral-like character, as well as well-delineated flavors, medium body, and a judicious touch of smoky oak. This wine is built along the lines of the Goodchild cuvée, and should drink nicely for 1–2 years.

Steele's attractively made, medium-bodied 1996 Chardonnay Lolonis Vineyard offers clean, crisp fruit, tropical/citrus notes, decent acidity, and a fruit-driven personality. I would opt for drinking it over the next 12–16 months. From the well-known Durell Vineyard, Steele's 1996 Chardonnay exhibits a more *terroir*-driven personality, with more buttery, roasted nut, leesy, and Burgundian-like characteristics. It possesses good acidity, and appears more structural, mineral, and spicy than the more fruit-dominated Lolonis. This wine should drink well for 1–2 years. The light to medium straw-colored 1996 Chardonnay du Pratt Vineyard is restrained aromatically, and lighter, with a tightly knit personality, crisp, honeyed citrus, floral-like notes, medium body, vibrant acidity, and a lively yet restrained personality. Consume it over the next 12–18 months. The 1996 Chardonnay Parmelee-Hill Vineyard is the least concentrated and most acidic. Although tart and one dimensional, its crispness, freshness, and light-bodied appeal are admirable. Drink it over the next 6–9 months.

Although made in the light- to medium-bodied style popular in Oregon, the 1996 Pinot Gris Romani Family Vineyard possesses more richness and intensity than most Oregon wines made from this varietal. It is a fruity, plush, buttery wine without any noticeable oak. Drink this cleanly made wine over the next year.

The talented Jed Steele has produced three good, but hardly inspiring Pinot Noirs. The 1996 Pinot Noir Bien Nacido Vineyard exhibits a medium ruby color, followed by a leafy, vegetal nose with red cherry fruit in the background. In the mouth, the wine reveals tart acidity, a clipped, medium-bodied palate, and a good finish. It is a competent, albeit unexciting Pinot to drink over the next 1–2 years. The 1996 Pinot Noir Sangiacomo Vineyard displays a similar medium to dark ruby color, herbs and earth in the nose, as well as vague notes of candied cherry fruit. A spicier wine than the Bien Nacido, it possesses medium body, good fruit, and a short, compact finish. The finest wine of this trio is the 1996 Pinot Noir Carneros. It boasts a Burgundian-like, earth and black cherry-scented nose in addition to considerable sweetness and fragrance. In the mouth, the wine cuts a more expansive feel on the palate, with more texture, length, ripeness, and charm. It is an attractive, complex, elegant, rich, medium ruby-colored wine for consuming over the next 1–2 years.

My favorite of the trio of 1995 Zinfandels is the 1995 Zinfandel du Pratt Vineyard. The healthy dark purple color is accompanied by a wine that is loaded with rich blueberry and blackberry fruit. Lush, opulent, and pure, with good extract and richness, this wine manages to avoid any heaviness or hotness (the alcohol is only 13%). This lush, round, generously endowed Zinfandel should drink well for 2–4 years. The 1995 Zinfandel Pacini Vineyard exhibits a less saturated purple color, and more of a jammy cranberry-scented nose. Lighter than the du Pratt cuvée, it is nicely textured, rich, and supple, providing a delicious mouthful of explosive Zinfandel fruit. Drink it over the next 1–2 years. Lastly, the 1995 Zinfandel Catfish Vineyard from Clear Lake has a color similar to the Pacini offering. The Catfish Vineyard cuvée reveals more new oak than its siblings, as well as loads of berry fruit, medium body, and surprising elegance and finesse for a Zinfandel. Drink it over the next year.

The 1994 Zinfandel Pacini Vineyard offers a more brooding perspective on this popular varietal. The dark, thick ruby color reveals some purple hues. The wine is more closed (it is less flattering and charming than the Shooting Star Zin), but it cuts a wide swath on the palate with gobs of fruit, glycerin, alcohol, and richness. Give it 2–4 more months of cellaring and consume it over the following 5–6 years. The dark ruby/purple-colored 1994 Zinfandel Catfish Vineyard is similarly rich, yet even broader and more expansive, with layers of sweet rich black cherry and black raspberry fruit. Full bodied, exuberant, and fleshy, this is a hedonistic Zinfandel for drinking over the next 2–3 years.

Jed Steele again produced a bevy of good Chardonnays in 1995, but I have to admit that the following four 1995s I tasted did not possess the depth and richness of previous vintages. Acidity is higher, and while the wines are obviously well made, fresh, and lively, they are not as concentrated as previous vintages. The 1995 Chardonnay Dennison Vineyard exhibits an attractive, pear liqueurlike personality, with copious quantities of ripe fruit, a good underpinning of crisp acidity, enticing tangerine notes, mineral-like flavors, medium body, and the hallmark of all Steele's wines—freshness, purity, and balance. This delicious Chardonnay should drink well for 1–2 years. I also immensely enjoyed the 1995 Chardonnay Lolonis Vineyard. This crisp, citrusy, well-flavored wine displays medium body, a well-defined personality, a short finish, and plenty of fruit in the aromatics and flavors. Drink it over the next 1–2 years.

Less impressive is the 1995 Chardonnay Goodchild Vineyard (from Santa Barbara). The wine exhibits higher acidity and is less well endowed. It is fresh and lively, and for readers looking for an aperitif-styled, lighter Chardonnay with zesty acidity, this tropical fruit-scented and -flavored wine will prove to be adequate. I would opt for drinking it over the next year. The 1995 Chardonnay Durell is an elegant, restrained, exceptionally well made wine that marries finesse with sound fruit intensity. Medium bodied, with a light straw color, and attractive, lemon custardlike aromatics intermingled with honeyed apple/pear/pineapple notes, this crisp, refreshing, moderately endowed Chardonnay should drink well for 1–2 years.

I tasted four other 1995 Chardonnays under the Steele label, all impeccably made and deliciously fruity. The 1995 Chardonnay Steele Cuvée exhibits a tangerine, mineral, and honey-scented nose. Medium bodied, clean, pure, supple, and delicious, it should be drunk over the next year. The 1995 Chardonnay du Pratt Vineyard possesses some unreleased CO_2 that gives the wine attractive vibrancy. Boasting gobs of honeyed tropical fruit, this medium-to full-bodied, purely made wine is delicious to smell and taste. The long finish reveals plenty of tropical fruit. Drink this hedonistically-styled Chardonnay over the next year. The 1995 Chardonnay Sangiacomo Vineyard displays a smoky, buttery popcorn character, but the emphasis remains on unabashed, ripe, concentrated fruit. This medium-bodied, soft wine will be a treat to drink over the next 12 months. Although the 1995 Chardonnay Bien Nacido Vineyard offers an outstanding nose, the wine's flavor does not quite attain the same level of intensity. It possesses rich tropical fruit displayed in an exuberant, medium- to full-bodied, soft, luscious format. It should drink well for a year.

Although none of Steele's Pinot Noirs were outstanding, they are all well made, juicy, straightforward wines that need to be drunk over the next 4–5 years. The 1995 Pinot Noir Anderson Valley reveals a healthy dark ruby color, as well as an attractive, sweet, herbal and black fruit-scented nose with some oak in the background. This spicy, oaky wine is medium bodied, with a tannic toughness and quick finish. It should soften with another year of bottle age, but do not expect it to last longer than 3–4 years. The medium ruby-colored 1995 Pinot Noir Durell Vineyard exhibits dusty tannin in its flavors, a spicy, earthy bouquet, a northern Côte de Nuits-like earthiness, and less fruit than the other offerings. It reveals plenty of character, but, again, the tannin is elevated in the finish. This wine will benefit from another 6–12 months of bottle age; it should drink well for 4–5 years.

The 1995 Pinot Noir du Pratt Vineyard possesses the most saturated dark ruby/purple color of this group. The nose offers up copious quantities of black fruits and new oak. While not complicated, it is satisfying, rich, and round. Drink this generously endowed, medium- to full-bodied, spice/fruit-styled wine over the next 4–5 years. The 1994 Pinot Noir du Pratt Vineyard is nearly outstanding. The wine reveals a dark ruby/purple color, as well as a broad, penetrating, sweet nose of black raspberries with gentle oak in the background. Medium to full bodied, supple, and lush, with low acidity and gobs of ripe fruit, this is a hedonistic Pinot Noir to drink over the next 2–4 years.

The 1995 Pinot Noir Carneros displays a light ruby color that appears frail. The nose offers up attractive tomato, cherry, and toasty aromas. The wine reveals far more fruit and style than suggested by the weak color. There is plenty of soft berry fruit, herbs, smoke, and spice. This is the most forward and tannic of the Steele Pinot Noirs, and because of that, it is best drunk over the next 2–3 years.

The saturated ruby/purple-colored 1995 Pinot Noir Bien Nacido Vineyard could easily pass for a Syrah-based wine given its dense purple color. Still closed aromatically, it may be the most promising of the Steele Pinot Noirs—if drunk in 3–4 years. The tight aromatics unfold to reveal scents of earth, smoky new wood, and black cherry fruit intermixed with grilled vegetables. Concentrated, medium to full bodied, with moderate acidity, and tannin, this is a dense, youthful, backward Pinot Noir that requires another 1–2 years of bottle age. It should keep for a decade. Impressive!

Steele's 1994 Pinot Noir Bien Nacido Vineyard reveals a healthy dark ruby color, a super-expressive nose of jammy black cherries with a hint of pepper, herbs, and spices. Supple, rich, velvety, black cherry caress the palate, and Pinot Noir's expansive, lush fruitiness and texture are well displayed. If readers wonder why Pinot Noir is enjoyable, it is because it provides high alcohol, a velvety texture, and gobs of fruit, but never comes across as heavy or astringent (as a young Cabernet does). Drink this beauty over the next 2–3 years.

STELTZNER VINEYARDS (NAPA)

1995 Cabernet Sauvignon	Stag's Leap	C	88
1994 Cabernet Sauvignon	Stag's Leap	C	85
1993 Cabernet Sauvignon	Stag's Leap	B	84
1994 Cabernet Sauvignon Barrel Select Reserve	Stag's Leap	D	87
1994 Claret	Stag's Leap	B	85

Perhaps the finest young Steltzner Cabernet Sauvignon I have tasted, the 1995 reveals a dark ruby/purple color, and a moderately intense nose of pure black currants intermixed with blueberries and floral (violets) aromas. Rich, with medium to full body, as well as nicely integrated new oak, acidity, and tannin, this is an impressive, well-endowed Cabernet. It is soft enough to be accessible young but will keep for 12–15 years.

Steltzner's dark ruby/purple-colored 1994 Cabernet Sauvignon is a fruit-driven, supple, seductive, if somewhat one-dimensional Cabernet that is easy to understand and consume. It is a grapey, well-balanced wine with light tannin in the finish. I would not be surprised to see this wine develop more nuances and merit a higher score. Anticipated maturity: now–2008. The 1994 Claret, a blend of 50% Cabernet Sauvignon, 48% Cabernet Franc, and 2% Merlot, exhibits a dark ruby color, as well as moderate quantities of sweet black currant fruit with smoky oak in the background. Once again, its monolithic personality keeps the score lower than it may merit after 2–4 years of bottle age. I do like the wine's overall equilibrium and elegant style. Anticipated maturity: now–2008. The 1994 Cabernet Sauvignon Barrel Select Reserve possesses the most fat and intensity of flavor of this trio. It exhibits a deep plum color, and toasty *pain grillé* notes intermixed with prune, ripe plum, and cassis scents. The wine is medium bodied, elegant, and graceful. Soft tannin in the finish adds to the wine's harmonious impression.

I recognize that this winery prefers a light- to medium-bodied, polished, subtle style of Cabernet Sauvignon, but I would like to see more intensity, ripeness, and most of all, character. Steltzner's 1993 Cabernet Sauvignon is a straightforward, attractive, easygoing Cabernet that will be drinkable upon release and will last for a decade.

STERLING VINEYARDS (NAPA)

1996 Chardonnay	Napa	C	86
1995 Chardonnay	Napa	B	88
1993 Pinot Noir Winery Lake Vineyard	Carneros	C	86
1997 Sauvignon Blanc	North Coast	B	87

A well-made Chardonnay from Sterling (one of California's perennial underachievers), the smoky, Burgundian-styled 1996 provides excellent fresh fruit, high-class, unobtrusive toasty oak, adequate acidity (thankfully, not too acidified), medium body, and a notion of honey and white flowers. Drink it over the next year. The attractive 1997 Sauvignon Blanc exhibits an aromatic personality (figs, melons, and citrus), medium body, and a crisp, mineral-like character. This dry, refreshing, light- to medium-bodied Sauvignon should be drunk over the next year.

The 1995 is one of the finest regular bottlings of Sterling's Chardonnay that I have tasted in over 2 decades. The wine also sports an attractive new bottle design and label. The nose offers attractive, lingering, complex, Burgundian-like, smoky, roasted nut, and sweet fruit aromas. The wine is medium bodied, elegant, and flavorful, with a gentle, soft texture, and fine length. It is not a blockbuster, bold, ostentatious, oaky wine, but rather, a harmonious, silky, nicely crafted Chardonnay to drink over the next year.

With respect to the 1993 Pinot Noir Winery Lake Vineyard, a classy, smoked herb, and ripe cherry-scented nose is followed by a medium-bodied, soft, gracefully constructed Pinot that is meant to be drunk over the next 1–2 years.

STONEFLY VINEYARD (NAPA)

1996 Cabernet Franc	Napa	D	89

This is the first Cabernet Franc I have tasted from California that resembles a high-quality Loire Valley red from a ripe year (thoughts of Joguet's 1990 Chinons came to mind). The wine exhibits a raspberry and red currant-scented bouquet with faint notes of tobacco and cedar. Rich and smoky, this medium-bodied, intense yet elegant wine saw no new oak and is better because of it. A beautifully crafted, luscious, Loire-styled Cabernet Franc, it is a breakthrough for this varietal in California. It should drink well for 6–7 years.

STONESTREET (SONOMA)

1997 Cabernet Sauvignon	Alexander Valley	D	(89–91)
1996 Cabernet Sauvignon	Alexander Valley	D	88
1995 Cabernet Sauvignon	Alexander Valley	D	89
1994 Cabernet Sauvignon	Alexander Valley	D	92
1993 Cabernet Sauvignon	Alexander Valley	D	90
1996 Cabernet Sauvignon Christopher's Vineyard	Alexander Mountain	D	92+
1995 Cabernet Sauvignon Three Block Vineyard	Alexander Mountain	E	92+
1996 Chardonnay	Alexander Valley	C	87
1996 Chardonnay Upper Barn	Alexander Valley	D	90
1997 Gewürztraminer	Anderson Valley	C	84
1997 Legacy Proprietary Red Wine	Alexander Valley	EE	(92–94)
1996 Legacy Proprietary Red Wine	Alexander Valley	EE	93
1995 Legacy Proprietary Red Wine	Alexander Valley	EE	91
1994 Legacy Proprietary Red Wine	Alexander Valley	EE	91+
1993 Legacy Proprietary Red Wine	Alexander Valley	D	91
1996 Merlot	Alexander Valley	D	89

1995	Merlot	Alexander Valley	D	90
1994	Merlot	Alexander Valley	D	87
1993	Merlot	Alexander Valley	D	90
1996	Pinot Noir	Russian River	D	87
1995	Pinot Noir	Russian River	D	85
1994	Pinot Noir	Russian River	D	88
1997	Sauvignon Blanc Pinnacle Block	Alexander Mountain	C	87

One of the shining stars in the Kendall-Jackson empire is Stonestreet Winery, which has already established an excellent reputation for big, spicy, lavishly oaked Chardonnays, Merlots, and Cabernet Sauvignons. As the following tasting notes suggest, even better wines will soon be emerging. Stonestreet has produced a barrel-fermented, pleasant, crisp, elegant 1997 Gewürztraminer. Much better is the 1997 Sauvignon Blanc Pinnacle Block, a 100% Sauvignon Blanc cuvée that is completely barrel fermented and aged in 20% new *barriques*. It is a big, full-bodied Sauvignon (14.2% alcohol), with plenty of honeyed melon and figlike fruit, smoky oak, rich, chewy flavors, and a long, lusty finish. If you like Sauvignon Blanc made in a Chardonnay style, this will be immensely pleasing. Moreover, it should drink well for 1–2 years. In 1996 there are two Chardonnays, both aged in French oak. The 1996 Chardonnay (30,000 cases) is a naturally fermented offering with lavish quantities of toasty new oak, smoky, buttery fruit, a leesy complexity, and a chewy, medium- to full-bodied, lusty finish. While it is not complex or elegant, it delivers copious fruit, wood, and mouth-filling flavors. It should drink well for 1–2 years. The 1996 Chardonnay Upper Barn (500 cases) was aged 14 months in 50% new French oak, and given considerable lees stirring. The wine possesses an evolved light gold color, a powerful pineapple, buttery, toasty, smoky nose, excellent full-bodied flavors, loads of fruit, a chewy texture, and a heady, alcoholic (14.2%) finish. It will not make anyone forget the extraordinary Upper Barn Chardonnays produced by Helen Turley and John Wetlaufer, but it is a topflight effort that should drink well for 1–2 years.

The 1996 Pinot Noir (1,800 cases) is an aggressively wooded, cassis, black cherry, and smoky-scented and -flavored wine with outstanding ripeness, lush cherry flavors, and a heady (14.2% alcohol) finish. It should drink well for 3–5 years.

Stonestreet's Merlot program is hugely successful. About 20,000 cases of these in-your-face, extroverted, chocolatey, oaky Merlots are produced. The 1996 Merlot (a blend of 76% Merlot, 19% Cabernet Sauvignon, and 5% Cabernet Franc) exhibits a deep plum color, followed by knockout aromatics of roasted coffee, chocolate, and berry/cherry liqueur. Rich, smoky, exotic, and hedonistic, it should drink well for a decade. Like the Merlot, the 1996 Cabernet Sauvignon (a blend of 88% Cabernet Sauvignon and 12% Cabernet Franc) is an unfiltered, richly fruity, smoky, oaky, full-bodied wine with fine depth, an easy, open-knit, expansive chewiness, a supple personality, and sweet tannin in the finish. Accessible now, it promises to be even better over the next 4–12 years. The 1997 Cabernet Sauvignon exhibits the vintage's up-front, flattering, evolved style. The tannin is sweeter than in the 1996, and the wine offers copious amounts of prune, black currant, roasted herb and smoky fruit. Dense and fleshy, this appealing Cabernet should drink well for 12–15 years.

The 1995 Cabernet Sauvignon Three Block Vineyard from the Alexander Valley is made from 96% Cabernet Sauvignon and 4% Cabernet Franc. It is an unfiltered, dense, full-bodied wine with considerable power and richness. Aged in 50% new French oak, with more than 14% alcohol, it exhibits plenty of tannin, as well as impressively endowed flavors of roasted herbs, black currants, chocolate, and blackberries. Anticipated maturity: 2002–2020. The 1996 Cabernet Sauvignon Christopher's Vineyard (previously called the

Three Block Vineyard) is cut from the same mold. It is a hedonistic, opaque purple-colored wine with gobs of toasty new oak, thrilling levels of extract, rich, chewy, black currant and blackberry fruit, impressive glycerin, sweet tannin, and a knockout finish that must contain over 14% alcohol. Over 80% new French oak was utilized in this wine's upbringing. There are 500 cases of this unfiltered beauty. There are 5,000 cases of Legacy, Stonestreet's proprietary red wine. The 1996 Legacy Proprietary Red Wine (57% Cabernet Sauvignon, 26% Merlot, and 17% Cabernet Franc) reveals an opaque purple color, in addition to a sexy, chocolatey, jammy cassis, spicy, *pain grillé*-scented nose. Full bodied and chewy, with impressive levels of extract, lavish, smoky wood, and a juicy, succulent, glycerin-endowed personality, this wine will be at its peak between 2001 and 2020. The 1997 Legacy Proprietary Red Wine (56% Cabernet Sauvignon, 27% Merlot, and 17% Cabernet Franc) is even sweeter and richer than the marvelous 1996. There is more jammy black currant/cassis fruit, the oak is slightly more subtle, and the wine reveals exquisite texture, power, and richness. This offering will be showy when released, yet keep for 20–25 years—a seamless classic! Lest anyone think Stonestreet is a tiny winery, production has risen to 75,000 cases, and every bottle is on allocation!

The soft 1995 Pinot Noir exhibits a smoky, gamey, animal-scented nose with jammy black cherry fruit in the background. Elegant, with good spice, and lush, sexy, overripe plumlike flavors, this medium-bodied wine is ideal for drinking now and over the next 3 years.

Stonestreet's medium ruby-colored, unfined and unfiltered 1994 Pinot Noir exhibits a lusty, smoky, sweet berry-scented nose that reveals copious quantities of both ripe fruit and oak. This medium-bodied, softly textured, delicious Pinot is not the most concentrated or profoundly complex wine, but it offers a sexy glass of Pinot Noir for drinking over the next several years. Stonestreet does exceptionally well with its "big reds," such as Merlot, Cabernet Sauvignon, and their proprietary red wine called Legacy. The 1993 Merlot exhibits an opaque ruby color, a big, exotic, chocolatey, smoky, jammy black cherry-scented nose, rich, full-bodied, supple flavors, low acidity, and a lush, chewy finish. It is all a Merlot should be. Given its depth and richness, it should age well for 7–8 years. The chocolatey, smoky, lavishly wooded 1994 Merlot is a flamboyantly styled wine. The color is a healthy dark plum. The nose offers up plenty of vanillin, smoke, and spice. On the palate, the wine is full bodied, with noticeable wood tannin and spice. It needs another 1–2 years of cellaring, but should drink well for a decade. Those readers without the patience to wait several years are advised to decant this Merlot 45 minutes before drinking. The opaque plum-colored 1995 Merlot is a thick wine with compelling scents of roasted coffee, chocolate cake, smoky oak, and rich, jammy fruit. A blend of 84% Merlot, 15% Cabernet Sauvignon, and 1% Cabernet Franc, this wine is exceptional, seductive, rich, medium to full bodied, and ideal for drinking now and over the next dozen years.

Made from 100% Cabernet Sauvignon and aged for 20 months in oak barrels, of which 40%–50% are new, all three wines are exceptional. The wines, which are fined with egg whites, are never filtered. The 1993 Cabernet Sauvignon is a smoky, cassis, herb, and licorice-scented and -flavored wine with full body, outstanding richness, good ripeness, and an impressively long finish. Although accessible, this wine should continue to drink well for 12–15 years. The 1994 Cabernet Sauvignon appears to be even more intense and powerful, with an opaque purple color, and gobs of lavishly oaked, smoky, cassis fruit intertwined with aromas of roasted herbs and high quality toasty oak. This powerful Cabernet reveals plenty of tannin, low acidity, and outstanding concentration and purity. This large-scaled, remarkably well balanced wine should drink well young yet last for 2 decades.

The 1995 Cabernet Sauvignon is no shy wine, coming in at 14.2% alcohol. The wine reveals the ripe fruit their Alexander Valley vineyard achieves. The use of heavily toasted Demptos barrels and indigenous yeasts for fermentation give these wines provocative aromatics. The Cabernet Sauvignon is built along the line of the Merlot, offering a hedonistic mouthful of fleshy, rich, briery, dense, berry, smoky, and herb-tinged fruit. Full-bodied, with a lashing of sweet tannin, this lusty, decadently rich, flamboyant Cabernet Sauvignon should drink well for 12–15 years.

Stonestreet's proprietary red wine called Legacy has proven to be not only a wine of exceptional quality, but one of remarkable consistency. The blend can vary (the 1993 is a blend of 70% Cabernet Sauvignon, 20% Merlot, 10% Cabernet Franc), to one less marked by Cabernet Sauvignon (the 1994 is a blend of 51% Cabernet Sauvignon, 39% Merlot, 9% Cabernet Franc, 1% Petit Verdot). The 1995 is composed of 59% Cabernet Sauvignon, 23% Cabernet Franc, 17% Merlot, and 1% Petit Verdot. All of these wines are aged for 20–23 months in 100% new French oak barrels, and are bottled unfined and unfiltered. I found them to be flamboyant, opulently textured, rich, expressive, and dramatic proprietary reds that are loaded with character. Moreover, they possess 10–20 years of aging potential. The 1994 and 1995 may merit higher scores with more aging. The 1993 Legacy is an impressively constructed, rich, full-bodied wine from a vintage that is often overlooked in the justifiable hype for 1994 and 1995. The 1993, the most Cabernet-dominated wine of this trio, exhibits a dark purple color, and a sweet nose of smoky vanilla, toast, and gobs of black raspberry and cassis fruit. Like its two younger siblings, the wine reveals a smoky richness, a lush, full-bodied, chewy texture, outstanding purity, low acidity, and plenty of grip in the finish. The most powerful of these three Legacies, it also possesses the highest level of sweet tannin in the finish. It can be drunk now and over the next 15 years. The 1994 and 1995 vintages are similar in character, as both were years with exceptionally long hang times for the grapes (always a positive sign). Both wines possess a chocolatey, smoky, cassis, lavishly wooded character, juicy, succulent, full-bodied personalities, and plenty of length, extract, and fruit. Both are also remarkably seamless wines with immense potential. Because of their low acidity and ostentatious personalities, these wines will be flattering to drink young but will easily last for 12–15 years. The 1995 Legacy (a blend of 59% Cabernet Sauvignon, 22% Cabernet Franc, and the balance Merlot and Petit Verdot) has been aged for nearly 2 years in 100% new French oak barrels, and bottled unfined and unfiltered. It is an accessible, multilayered wine with tons of licorice and black fruit flavors, a voluptuous texture, and an expressive, flamboyant personality that offers even more rich fruit than it does toasty oak. At 14.2% alcohol, this is a boldly styled, fleshy, full-bodied wine that can be drunk or cellared for 15 years.

STORYBOOK MOUNTAIN VINEYARDS (NAPA)

1995 Zinfandel	Howell Mountain	D	84
1996 Zinfandel Eastern Exposures	Napa	C	87
1995 Zinfandel Eastern Exposures	Napa	C	87
1994 Zinfandel Eastern Exposures	Napa	C	88
1995 Zinfandel Estate Mayacamas	Napa	C	86
1996 Zinfandel Estate Reserve	Napa	D	90
1995 Zinfandel Estate Reserve	Napa	D	88+
1994 Zinfandel Estate Reserve	Napa	D	90+
1996 Zinfandel Howell Mountain	Napa	D	87
1996 Zinfandel Mayacamas Range	Napa	D	88
1994 Zinfandel Mayacamas Range	Napa	C	88+

Storybook Mountain Vineyard has been one of the consistent practitioners of the elegant, age-worthy style of Zinfandel. Recently, the wines have taken on more accessibility without compromising their ability to age; the top cuvées can easily last ten or more years. The 1996

Zinfandel Howell Mountain is a surprisingly soft, charming, seductive, Burgundian-styled wine with good lushness, and copious quantities of sweet black cherry fruit intermixed with smoke, minerals, and spice. Drink this friendly, seductive Zinfandel over the next 3–4 years. Made in the same elegant style, but more mineral-dominated is the medium-bodied, dark ruby/purple-colored 1996 Zinfandel Mayacamas Range. It exhibits excellent purity, fine equilibrium, sweet black cherry and raspberry fruit, and enough acidity for delineation and balance. Although young and unevolved, it is very promising. Drink it over the next 5–8 years.

The 1996 Zinfandel Eastern Exposures offers up an intriguing nose of berry fruit and powdered stones. Medium bodied, with crisp acidity, a sense of elegance, and a tangy, lean, clean, zesty finish, this elegant Zin can be drunk now and over the next 5–7 years. Lastly, the outstanding 1996 Zinfandel Estate Reserve boasts a whopping (for this producer) 14.5% alcohol, but you would never suspect that based on the wine's outstanding balance and concentration. Deep ruby/purple-colored, with a classy nose of spice, vanillin, black fruits, minerals, and a hint of flowers, this medium- to full-bodied effort reveals more approachability and sweetness on the attack than most Storybook Reserve Zinfandels possess at such a youthful age. Beautifully concentrated, pure, and long, the wine can be drunk now, but 2 more years of cellaring will be beneficial. Moreover, I predict this will be one of the few Zinfandels from 1996 to reach age 10 or 12 in a graceful, fresh condition.

Readers who have followed the evolution of the Storybook Mountain Zinfandels must realize that these wines, which emanate from steep hillside vineyards north of Calistoga, are among the longest-lived Zinfandels produced. In fact, some vintages of the Estate Reserves give every indication of evolving and improving for 10–15 years, a distinct rarity among Zinfandels. The 1995s are made in a restrained, but classic style.

The tightest, most backward and austere wine, the 1995 Howell Mountain Zinfandel, exhibits a dark ruby color, and reticent aromatics. With coaxing, the wine offers up powdered minerals and vibrant berry fruit. It possesses medium body, a restrained, subtle style, and excellent purity, but it tastes low-key and tannic. While it will improve, the question must be posed—is there sufficient fruit to outlast the wine's structure? Give it 1–2 years of cellaring and drink it over the following 4–6. The 1995 Zinfandel Estate Mayacamas reveals a dark ruby/purple color, and a tight but more obviously ripe nose of black-cherry fruit intermixed with minerals and spice. Crisp acidity, moderate tannin, and an elegant, medium-bodied personality result in an attractive, although intensely subtle style of Zinfandel. This wine needs 1–2 years of cellaring; it should age well for 8–10 years. The 1995 Zinfandel Eastern Exposures is a more concentrated wine. Its finesse is allied to attractively ripe, rich fruit. The healthy dark ruby/purple color is accompanied by an open-knit nose offering aromas of black currants, cherries, and minerals. The wine provides more sweetness on the attack, as well as a medium-bodied, slightly tannic yet nicely layered personality. It will benefit from 1–2 years of cellaring and will keep for a decade. The 1995 Zinfandel Estate Reserve reveals the ripest nose of this quartet. Although shy, the wine reveals a dark purple color, as well as an attractive floral, black cherry, and mineral-scented nose with hints of pepper and spice. It tends to behave more like a young Cabernet Sauvignon than a Zinfandel, but there is no doubting its sweet, ripe fruit and excellent purity. Medium bodied, with a layered texture, this well-built wine should prove to be uncommonly long-lived. It will benefit from another 1–2 years of cellaring and last for 10–15 years.

The 1994 Zinfandel Eastern Exposures continues the supple, deliciously fruity, black raspberry and peppery style. It offers a healthy dark ruby color, crisp acidity, medium body, and a refreshing, ripe, round, generous palate. It should drink well for 5–7 years. Although the 1994 Zinfandel Mayacamas Range is not as forthcoming aromatically, it does open with airing. It possesses a healthy dark ruby/purple color, and plenty of peppery, black cherry and raspberry fruit, with a firm mineral underpinning. The initially reserved attack yields rich, lovely, pure, full-bodied, deep, powerful yet elegant flavors. This wine requires 1–3 years of cellaring; it will keep for 10–12+ years. The flagship wine of Storybook Mountain Vineyards is their Reserve Estate. This wine has such aging potential that it was released late (the 1993 was released in the fall of 1996, and the 1994 in the fall of 1997). It is the most powerful and concentrated of these offerings, but in spite of its intensity and additional extract, alcohol, and fruit, the wine does not lose any finesse or elegance—a hallmark of this cuvée. The 1994 exhibits a dark ruby/purple color, a tight but promising nose of black fruits, full body, admirable richness, and a measure of restraint and tightness that suggest it needs 1–3 years of cellaring. This is one Zinfandel that can be cellared for more than a decade with little fear of disappointment. It should hit its stride in 3–5 years and keep for 15—atypically long by Zinfandel standards.

RODNEY STRONG VINEYARDS (SONOMA)

1994	Cabernet Sauvignon Alexander's Crown Vineyard Estate	Sonoma	C	86
1995	Chardonnay Chalk Hill Vineyard Estate	Sonoma	C	86
1996	Merlot	Sonoma	C	87
1993	Pinot Noir River East Vineyard Estate	Russian River	C	86
1997	Sauvignon Blanc Charlotte's Home	Northern Sonoma	B	86

A reasonably good value in the overheated wine market, the 1996 Merlot is a tasty Merlot with gobs of black cherry and currant fruit intermixed with sweet, toasty oak. The color is a saturated dark ruby purple. The wine possesses medium body, excellent richness, fine ripeness, and complete harmony among its structural elements. It offers delicious drinking, yet promises to last for 5–7 years.

A crisp, melony wine with a soft underbelly, light to medium body, and a fruit-driven personality, the 1997 Sauvignon should be drunk over the next 8–12 months. Citrusy, fruity notes are present in the light-intensity nose of the medium-bodied, somewhat commercial but flavorful, pleasant, cleanly made 1995 Chardonnay. It is ideal for drinking over the next year.

An overt, obvious, but tasty Pinot Noir, the 1993 River East Vineyard offering from Rodney Strong displays a light ruby color, plenty of herb and cherrylike fruit in the nose and flavors, and a soft midpalate. It is ideal for drinking over the next 1–3 years.

The friendly 1994 Cabernet Sauvignon displays a dark ruby color, and a sweet black currant-scented nose with subtle spice and earth in the background. The wine is supple and medium bodied, with excellent purity and a crowd-pleasing, open-knit personality. Drink it over the next 5–6 years.

JOSEPH SWAN VINEYARDS (SONOMA)

1994	Pinot Noir Estate	Russian River	D	86+
1993	Pinot Noir Steiner Vineyard	Sonoma	B	87
1995	Pinot Noir Wolf's Pierre Vineyard	Sonoma Mountain	D	85?
1993	Zinfandel Craighead Vineyard Laguna Ridge	Russian River	C	86
1995	Zinfandel Frati Ranch	Russian River	C	90
1993	Zinfandel Frati Ranch	Russian River	C	89
1995	Zinfandel Lone Redwood	Russian River	C	89
1995	Zinfandel Stellwagen Vineyard	Sonoma	C	87
1994	Zinfandel Stellwagen Vineyard	Sonoma	C	89
1993	Zinfandel Stellwagen Vineyard	Sonoma	C	87

1993 Zinfandel V.H.S.R. Bohn Vineyard	**Russian River**	C	78
1995 Zinfandel Zeigler Vineyard	**Sonoma**	C	87+
1994 Zinfandel Zeigler Vineyard	**Russian River**	C	86
1993 Zinfandel Zeigler Vineyard	**Russian River**	C	85

The 1993 Pinot Noir Steiner Vineyard possesses a deceptively light ruby color for the amount of flavor and intensity that follow. The wine is aromatic, with a sweet, berry fragrance, less herbaceousness than the 1992, round, corpulent, fruity flavors, adequate acidity, and a moderately intense, medium-bodied finish. It should drink well for 5–6 years, perhaps longer. The 1994 Estate Pinot Noir exhibits a Côte de Beaune-like cherry, earthy, spicy nose, medium body, chalky tannin in the finish, and a textbook Pinot Noir character. If the tannin softens, this wine will merit an even higher score. It will benefit from another 6–18 months of bottle age and last for a decade. The 1995 Pinot Noir Wolf's Pierre Vineyard reveals a more evolved color, in spite of the fact that it is a year younger. It is also slightly higher in acidity, and more dominated by earthy/herbal notes. More spice-driven than the 1994 Estate, it exhibits animal, gamey, fruit characteristics, as well as plenty of earth and tannin. I recommend a year of cellaring, followed by consumption over the subsequent 5–6 years.

Swan's style of Zinfandel appears to change with each new vintage. The 1993s are lighter than some of the blockbuster examples produced in the past. However, these five 1993 Zinfandels offer plenty of diversity. The medium-bodied 1993 Zeigler Vineyard Zinfandel possesses soft, peppery, herb, and cherry flavors, a pleasant, straightforward style, ripe fruit, and light tannin in the finish. Drink it over the next 5–6 years. The 1993 Zinfandel V.H.S.R. Bohn Vineyard exhibits an earthy, spicy nose, medium ruby/garnet color (more typical of Pinot Noir than Zinfandel), and compressed, angular, tart, high acid flavors and finish. It should be drunk up before the fruit fades. The 1993 Zinfandel Stellwagen Vineyard displays a medium ruby/garnet color, a sweet, peppery, berry-scented nose, seductive, ripe, lush flavors, heady alcohol, low acidity, and a plush, easygoing, user-friendly finish. Drink it over the next 5–7 years.

The 1993 Craighead Vineyard (from 123-year-old vines) displays a medium to dark ruby color, and a spicy, nicely extracted nose of cedar, cherry and strawberry fruit, as well as spice and earth. The wine is medium bodied, ripe, and low in acidity, with a heady, chunky finish. Although not complex, this well-made wine is ideal for drinking over the next 3–4 years. The richest, most concentrated, and potentially longest-lived of the 1993 Joseph Swan Zinfandels is the 1993 Frati Ranch Zinfandel. It possesses a saturated dark ruby/purple color, and a dense, expansive nose of red and black fruits, earth, spice, and herbs. Full bodied, with layers of rich cherry fruit nicely touched by subtle, earthy influences, this chewy, fleshy Zinfandel will benefit from another year of cellaring; it will last for 10–12 years.

Readers should be aware that the Joseph Swan Zinfandels are made in a divergent style. They are more earthy and spicy, with the *terroir* components being emphasized more than the unbridled, pure fruit of the Zinfandel grape. The dark ruby-colored 1994 Zinfandel Zeigler Vineyard exhibits a spicy, leafy, peppery nose, a sweet entry on the palate, medium to full body, and a round, soft, generous mouth-feel. It is forward for a Joseph Swan Zin, without the kinky, earthy components possessed by some of this estate's wines. Drink it over the next 5–6 years. Made in an exotic, Asian spice, gingery, truffle, and black fruit-scented style, the 1994 Stellwagen Vineyard Zinfandel is full bodied, dense, and rich. It is not a Zinfandel made in the commercial, mainstream manner. I find it provocative, interesting, and pleasurable, but it is not for everybody. Significantly more concentrated than the Zeigler Vineyard, the Stellwagen cuvée will last for 5–8 years.

Joseph Swan turned in four laudable performances in the 1995 vintage of Zinfandel. In ascending level of alcohol, the reviews are as follows. The dark garnet-colored, exotic 1995

Zinfandel Stellwagen (14.3% alcohol) offers up an intriguing gingery, spicy-scented bouquet. The fruit appears to be buried behind the multiple spices found in the wine's aromas and flavors. It is a medium-bodied, forward Zinfandel that should be drunk now and over the next 3–4 years. The opaque purple-colored 1995 Zinfandel Zeigler Vineyard (14.9% alcohol) is made in a totally different style. It offers gobs of ripe, earthy, spicy fruit, more tannin, higher acidity, and a more backward, unevolved style. While more dense, earthy fruit is present, this wine still needs 1–2 years of cellaring; it will age for a decade.

The 1995 Zinfandel Frati Ranch (15.6% alcohol) exhibits an opaque black/purple color, followed by a huge, intense, blackberry, cherry, Asian spice, earthy-scented nose. This massive, formidably endowed, tannic yet potentially outstanding Zinfandel could turn out to be the longest-lived Zinfandel of the vintage. The high alcohol is remarkably well concealed behind the wealth of fruit, glycerin, and structure. This is an impressive, dry Zinfandel with none of the late-harvest, raisiny/pruny characteristics readers might expect from a wine with this degree of alcohol. Anticipated maturity: 2000–2012+. Lastly, the 1995 Zinfandel Lone Redwood (15.9% alcohol) is obviously made in a late-harvest, more raisiny style. In fact, it comes across as slightly off-dry, although it possesses plenty of earthy, pruny, black plumlike fruit intermixed with spicy, herb, and licorice aromas. Thick, but not viscous, this full-bodied, rich, concentrated Zinfandel should drink well for a decade.

A 1995 Pinot Noir from the Steiner Vineyard was also tasted. I found it to be light and insipid.

SWANSON VINEYARDS AND WINERY (NAPA)

1996 Chardonnay	Carneros	D	86
1994 Sangiovese	Napa	C	87
1995 Syrah	Napa	D	87
1993 Syrah	Napa	D	92

For my tastes, Swanson's Sangiovese has been the most consistent and finest of the California Etruscan Ranger wines. The 1994 exhibits an attractive strawberry/cherry/spice-scented nose, soft, savory flavors, adequate acidity, and a lush finish. It should be drunk over the next 2–3 years. Don't hesitate to serve this wine slightly chilled.

What this winery has done with Syrah is well evidenced by the spectacular 1992. That wine has been followed by 400 cases of stunning 1993 Syrah. It exhibits a smoky, bacon fat, cassis-scented nose, and rich, full-bodied, dense, powerful flavors with moderate tannin. Give it 4–5 years of cellaring and drink it over the subsequent 15–20.

The 1996 Chardonnay is a robust, oaky, roasted nut, smoky-scented and flavored Chardonnay with good fruit, but it is lacking texture and length. There is plenty of wood and fruit on the attack, but the wine narrows out in the mouth. Although it is a good effort, I wonder if it could not have been better? Drink it over the next year. While the 1995 Syrah is not comparable to the compelling Syrahs made at Swanson in 1992 and 1993, it is a very good wine, if somewhat tannic and rustic, as well as frightfully expensive. The murky dark ruby/purple color is followed by classic Syrah aromas of bacon fat, tar, smoke, and crème de cassis. Tannic and ruggedly constructed, with medium to full body, meaty flavors, but not the texture or depth of fruit one would expect from the wine's size, this is a very good, muscular Syrah that should improve over the next 4–5 years and last for 10–15.

ROBERT TALBOTT VINEYARDS (MONTEREY)

1995 Chardonnay Cynthia's Cuvée	Monterey	D	88
1995 Chardonnay Sleepy Hollow Vineyard	Monterey	D	89
1996 Chardonnay (Logan)	Monterey	C	87

This high-quality Chardonnay producer has three fine offerings. My favorite, the 1995 Chardonnay Sleepy Hollow Vineyard, exhibits a light gold color, and moderate aromas of tropical fruit (primarily pineapple) intermixed with subtle wood, honey, and steely, mineral-like notes. There is good acidity, medium to full body, and a well-delineated, slightly austere finish. Still youthful, this wine should open, and possibly merit an outstanding score with another year of bottle age. I do not believe most California Chardonnays age gracefully, but this offering should last for 4–5 years. Far more evolved, and requiring consumption over the next 1–2 years is the 1995 Chardonnay Cynthia's Cuvée. It offers an explosively fruity nose of smoke, tropical fruit, and new wood. The color suggests an older wine than the flavors indicate. This full-bodied, ripe, chewy Chardonnay does not possess the complexity and potential ageability of the Sleepy Hollow offering. It should drink well for 1–2 years.

Lastly, the 1996 Logan Chardonnay is a surprisingly opulent, fruit-driven wine with less oak than its two bigger siblings. It possesses pure fruit, medium body, and a refreshing, lively style with some of the same minerality found in the Sleepy Hollow cuvée. Drink it over the next year.

TALLEY VINEYARDS (SAN LUIS OBISPO)

1996	Chardonnay Oliver's Vineyard	Edna Valley	C	89
1993	Pinot Noir Estate	Arroyo Grande Valley	C	86
1995	Pinot Noir Rincon Vineyard	Arroyo Grande Valley	D	90
1993	Pinot Noir Rincon Vineyard	Arroyo Grande Valley	D	86+?
1993	Pinot Noir Rosemary's Vineyard	Arroyo Grande Valley	D	87+

The complex, medium- to full-bodied, Burgundian-styled 1996 Chardonnay Oliver's Vineyard offers an intriguing nose of roasted nuts, honeyed pears, and spice. Rich, elegant, and nicely layered, with good equilibrium, this high-class Chardonnay will provide ideal drinking over the next 1–2 years. Another exceptional Pinot Noir from Talley Vineyards, the 1995 Rincon Vineyard (3,879 bottles produced) possesses a dark ruby color, and sweet black plum and cherry fruit nicely dosed with high-quality spicy new oak. Medium bodied, flavorful, and intense, yet not heavy, this beautifully made, elegant, and flavorful Pinot Noir should continue to improve for 3–4 years and last for a decade.

I admired all three of the 1993 Pinot Noirs, particularly their aromatics. If my judgment were based on smell alone, these wines would merit 90+ ratings. Even the regular cuvée of 1993 Pinot Noir Estate exhibits a complex, earthy, black cherry and floral-scented nose in a Burgundian-styled bouquet. The healthy dark ruby color is followed by a compact wine with medium body, fine flavor definition and richness, and a linear personality. Drink it over the next 5–6 years. Similar comments can be attributed to both the 1993 Rincon Vineyard (726 bottles produced) and 1993 Rosemary's Vineyard (786 bottles produced) Pinot Noirs. Both wines possess outstanding bouquets. Although firm, structured, and tannic, with good concentration, they are less exciting than the flashy display of intriguing Pinot scents suggests. Perhaps 1–2 years of cellaring will reveal more depth and richness. Both are impressive, well-made wines. Readers may want to insert these tannic, structured 1993 Talley Pinot Noirs in a blind tasting with some of the most tannic and acidic 1993 red Burgundies. The results would be interesting.

TESTAROSSA (MONTEREY)

1996	Chardonnay Bien Nacido Vineyard	Santa Barbara	D	87
1995	Chardonnay Bien Nacido Vineyard	Santa Barbara	D	90
1996	Chardonnay Chalone Appellation	Monterey	D	88

1995 Chardonnay Chalone	Monterey	D	89
1995 Chardonnay George Troquato Signature Reserve	California	D	89
1995 Chardonnay Reserve Michaud Vineyard-Chalone	California	D	90+
1996 Chardonnay Santa Maria	Santa Barbara	C	87
1996 Pinot Blanc Chalone Appellation	Monterey	C	86
1995 Pinot Blanc Chalone	Monterey	C	90

This winery, which made fine 1995s, has again turned in a fine performance with its 1996s. The big, brawny 1996 Pinot Blanc Chalone Appellation exhibits a light gold color, as well as honeyed apple and citruslike fruit, medium to full body, and a husky finish. Although not complex, it is a mouth-filling Pinot Blanc to enjoy over the next 1–2 years. The evolved, light gold-colored 1996 Chardonnay Santa Maria possesses a luscious, fragrant nose of honeyed fruit. There are copious quantities of glycerin, full body, and spicy new oak. While these 1996s do not display the complexity of their 1995 counterparts, they are flavorful, rich, and mouth-filling. Drink the 1996 Santa Maria Chardonnay over the next 1–2 years. The 1996 Chardonnay Chalone Appellation reveals a less evolved light gold color, as well as a more mineral-dominated nose intermixed with *pain grillé* and smoky scents. On the palate, the wine is more expressive, displaying rich fruit, a layered, full-bodied personality, fine purity, adequate acidity, and an intense finish. This wine should improve for 6 months and last for 2–3 years. Lastly, the 1996 Chardonnay Bien Nacido Vineyard offers aromas of high quality toasty oak intermixed with butter, pineapple, and smoke. Generously endowed, but monolithic, this full-flavored, attractively fleshy, meaty Chardonnay should be consumed over the next 1–2 years.

The 1995 Pinot Blanc Chalone reveals honeyed fruit, surprising levels of glycerin and extract, and beautiful balance and delineation. Pure and crisp, with considerable intensity, it is one of the finest California Pinot Blancs I have tasted. Moreover, it should drink well for 2–4 years. The 1995 Chardonnay Bien Nacido Vineyard is an exuberantly fruity (plenty of the tropical variety), medium- to full-bodied wine with considerable freshness. Everything is lively in this chewy, full-bodied, refreshing Chardonnay. I would opt for drinking it over the next year. The 1995 Chardonnay Chalone is a more mineral-laden wine with creamy custard, yeasty aromas and flavors. Medium to full bodied, pure, ripe, and long, it cuts a Burgundian-like swath on the palate but boasts fresher, more lively fruit. It should drink well for 1–2 years. The 1995 George Troquato Signature Reserve Chardonnay (named after the winery's winemaker) may ultimately merit a higher score as it is the most tightly knit of this group. It displays ripe tropical fruits and mineral notes in the restrained aromatics. In the mouth, the wine is full bodied, with high-quality toasty oak, good acidity, and fine length. Give it another 4–6 months of bottle age and consume it over the following 2–3 years. Also tightly knit, the 1995 Reserve Chardonnay Michaud Vineyard is an elegantly wrought, rich, mineral-laden wine with attractive layers of honeyed, buttery, yeasty fruit. Full bodied, with outstanding purity and ripeness, this superb Chardonnay should drink well for 4–6 years.

SEAN THACKREY & CO. (MARIN)

1995 Orion Old Vines Rossi Vineyard	California	D	91
1993 Orion Old Vines Syrah Rossi Vineyard	Napa	D	90+
N.V. Pleiades VI Old Vines	California	C	87

Sean Thackrey continues to fashion compellingly extracted, rich, concentrated wines from old vineyards in Napa Valley. The 1993 Orion is made from a vineyard planted in 1905 and believed to be Syrah. This wine exhibits intense, blackberry/cassis character. A touch of mint is thrown in for complexity. It is a full-bodied, gorgeous, highly extracted wine with sweet tannin. This 1993 possesses formidable potential and should keep for 12–15 years.

The dark ruby/purple-colored 1995 Orion Old Vines Rossi Vineyard reveals intense aromas of licorice, peppery black cherry and currants, with smoky, earthy notes in the background. On the palate, the wine is seamlessly textured, with medium to full body, outstanding concentration, and oodles of personality. Thick, rich, full bodied, and impressive, it should drink well for 10–12 years. The Pleiades VI Old Vines, a nonvintage blend of Syrah, Zinfandel, Carignane, Petite Sirah, Sangiovese, Nebbiolo, Grenache, Mourvèdre, and Merlot, displays a light to medium ruby color, followed by a spicy, cherry, earthy-scented nose, medium body, a lush texture, and a soft, fruity finish. It is a tasty bistro-styled red to drink over the next 1–2 years.

PHILIP TOGNI VINEYARDS (NAPA)

1995	Ca Togni	Napa	D (375 ml)	93
1994	Ca Togni	Napa	D (375 ml)	93
1997	Cabernet Sauvignon	Napa	E	(92–94)
1996	Cabernet Sauvignon	Napa	E	96
1995	Cabernet Sauvignon	Napa	D	95
1994	Cabernet Sauvignon	Napa	D	96
1993	Cabernet Sauvignon	Napa	D	92
1993	Cabernet Sauvignon Tanbark Hill Vineyard	Napa	D	88

Philip Togni, who bears a striking resemblance to the actor George C. Scott, and is probably both tough and contrary enough to have played the title role in the movie *Patton,* has finally produced an abundant quantity of his spectacular Cabernet Sauvignon. The 1997 Cabernet Sauvignon (approximately 2,350 cases) is the highest production he has been able to achieve since 1993 and 1991. The 1997 is one of the silkier, more evolved Togni Cabernets, which should be good news for all of us who have been squirreling away these massive monsters from the upper slopes of Spring Mountain. The 1997 exhibits a saturated black/purple color, and a sweet, evolved aromatic profile consisting of Provençal olives, crème de cassis, blackberries, and spice. Surprisingly easy to assess, with silky tannin, gorgeously pure fruit, full body, and layers of lavishly rich, creamy-textured fruit, this wine should be drinkable young (by Togni's standards), yet age effortlessly for 15–25 years. This may be the sexiest, most seductive Cabernet Sauvignon I have tasted from Philip Togni.

In contrast, the opaque purple-colored 1996 Cabernet Sauvignon is a blockbuster monster crammed with phenomenal potential. It offers up a sensational nose of licorice, chocolate, cassis, Provençal herbs, and *pain grillé.* The wine is succulent and full bodied, as well as extraordinarily powerful and backward. It should be drinkable within 5–7 years, and age beautifully for 3 decades. All of Philip Togni's wines are bottled with neither fining nor filtration, and, as Togni likes to say, "made as Bordeaux was . . . a long, long time ago."

Part mountain goat, part man, Philip Togni continues to fight vineyard diseases such as Pierce's, and frightfully low yields from his formidably steep Spring Mountain vineyards to produce some of California's most exciting wines. Togni turns out tiny quantities of a sweet, jammy dessert wine made from the black Muscat grape. The 1995 Ca Togni (50 cases—one barrel—of 375 ml bottles produced) is a decadently rich, sweet wine offering marvelous aromas of jammy berries, a silky texture, and a powerful, lusty finish. It is a wine of singular personality in addition to being great fun to drink. The 1994 Ca Togni is a marvelous, dark purple-colored, sweet, jammy wine made from black Muscat. The wine is full bodied, silky, moderately sweet, and ideal to drink by itself, or with an assortment of flavorful cheeses. It is available only in half bottles.

Cabernet Sauvignon is king at Togni, and they are wines of extraordinary concentration, flavor dimension, and aging potential. The 1995 Cabernet Sauvignon, a vintage that produced a number of top-notch wines (as well as some with rough tannin and muted personalities), is one of the year's bright shining successes. The wine displays an opaque purple color, as well as a lavishly intense nose of blackberry/blueberry/cassis fruit intermingled with chocolate and olive nuances. Dense and fruit-driven, with awesome levels of glycerin and extract, this formidably endowed, moderately tannic wine should be at its best with another 7–8 years of cellaring. Once again, Philip Togni has produced a wine with 25 or more years of aging potential.

The 1994 Cabernet Sauvignon is a remarkably rich, multidimensional wine. Extremely full bodied, with extraordinary fruit purity, this wine is, aromatically and texturally, compelling stuff. Unfortunately, the 1994 is already sold out, but those lucky enough to have purchased a few bottles own a monumental mountainside Cabernet Sauvignon that should age gracefully for 25–30 years. Incredibly, in an open bottle, this wine held up without oxidation an amazing six days! In 1993, the herbaceousness I noted appears to be translating into an attractive, cedary, spicy, cigar box character. Like all Togni Cabernets, the 1993 is an opaque purple with intense, jammy, black currant, mineral, and vanillin scents. Extremely full bodied, this is a wine with outstanding richness, an unctuous texture, and a huge, sweet, ripe finish. Although it is an exceptional example of Cabernet Sauvignon, it is sandwiched between the formidable 1992 and 1994. In 1993, Togni declassified 100 cases (4 barrels) of Cabernet Sauvignon that was more herbaceous and softer. The 1993 Cabernet Sauvignon Tanbark Hill Vineyard should elicit considerable interest from restaurants seeking a complex, concentrated, viscous-textured wine that is soft, delicious, and as Philip Togni says, "the only Cabernet I make that you can see through the wine's color." I would add the word "barely." This full-bodied, rich wine provides a big, chunky, muscular yet silky-textured mouthful of Cabernet fruit.

Since nearly 70% of Togni's wines are sold directly to wine consumers, it is incumbent upon readers wanting an opportunity to buy this wine to get their names on the winery's mailing list.

TRUCHARD VINEYARDS (NAPA)

1994	Cabernet Sauvignon Reserve	Napa	D	85+
1996	Chardonnay	Carneros/Napa	C	85
1995	Chardonnay	Carneros	C	85
1993	Merlot	Carneros	C	87
1994	Syrah	Carneros	C	90
1993	Syrah	Carneros/Napa	C	90
1994	Zinfandel	Napa/Carneros	C	88

The 1996 Chardonnay is an attractive, crisp, tropical fruit-scented and -flavored Chardonnay, with medium body and good purity. It should be drunk over the next year. The dense, earthy, dark ruby/purple-colored 1994 Cabernet Sauvignon Reserve reveals plenty of spice and tannin. I am not optimistic that the tannin will ever be fully resolved, but the wine offers good ripeness and purity, a nice attack, and a medium-bodied, structured, austere style. Give it 1–2 years of bottle age; if it improves, it should evolve gracefully for 10–15 years. If not, drink it over the near term.

Truchard's 1993 Merlot exhibits an attractive, black cherry and currant-scented nose with a whiff of mint and wood. Medium to full bodied, with admirable fruit and ripeness, this is a fleshy, well-made, nicely textured Merlot that should drink well for 4–5 years. The impressively endowed, dark ruby/purple-colored 1994 Syrah reveals that varietal's telltale, smoky, earthy, jammy cassis aromas, full body, outstanding fruit, ripeness, purity, and extraction, plenty of power, and a glycerin and fruit-dominated finish. It should drink well for 10–15 years. The 1995 Chardonnay is a solidly made, correct, medium-bodied wine with attractive citrusy fruit, a notion of smoke and wood, and tangerinelike flavors in the lemony, fleshy, medium-bodied finish. Drink it over the next 1–2 years.

Truchard's 1994 Zinfandel displays a pungent, intensely spicy, wild blueberry/peppery nose, round, generous, jammy flavors, excellent ripeness, and a silky smooth texture and finish. This classy, forward Zinfandel should be consumed over the next 5 years.

A textbook Syrah, Truchard's 1993 exhibits a classic nose of smoky bacon fat and cassis. The dark ruby/purple color is accompanied by a flattering, up-front nose that jumps from the glass. There is no astringent tannin to be found in this velvety-textured, rich, full-bodied, gorgeously opulent Syrah. Deep and soft, this is a top-class effort from this Napa winery. Drink it over the next 10–12 years.

TULOCAY (NAPA)

1994 Cabernet Sauvignon Cliff Vineyard	Napa	C	90+
1993 Cabernet Sauvignon Cliff Vineyard	Napa	C	88
1994 Pinot Noir Haynes Vineyard	Napa	C	87
1994 Zinfandel Cassanova Vineyard	Napa	C	90

Bill Cadman is an old-timer in Napa Valley, having made wines for over 20 years. His style of Cabernet Sauvignon, Pinot Noir, and Zinfandel has changed considerably over the last few years. Today the wines are more naturally textured, as well as richer and more complete than some of his earlier vintages. Cadman's Pinot Noirs, which he began producing in 1975, have gradually evolved in style until today they are made from completely destemmed fruit, all from vines planted in 1968 in the Haynes Vineyard in Napa. The wines are bottled after 2 years in oak casks without any fining or filtration. They have always been good wines with surprising longevity despite their flattering, up-front appeal. The 1994 Pinot Noir Haynes Vineyard displays a spicy, cinnamon, ripe black cherry-scented nose, medium body, a creamy texture, good purity, and a round, generous, promising, attractive finish. It should drink well for 3–5 years, although a vertical tasting of Tulocay Pinot Noirs held last year proved that even some of the older vintages (such as 1986 and 1987) were in remarkably fine condition.

The underrated Cabernet Sauvignons deserve far more attention, particularly since Cadman changed vineyard sources following the 1988 vintage from the Egan Vineyard near the Yountville crossroads, and moved to the Cliff Vineyard in the Stag's Leap District on a terraced hillside above the Silverado Country Club. These vintages should still be available in select marketplaces. The 1993 Cabernet Sauvignon Cliff Vineyard is less concentrated than the 1991, 1992, or 1994. It displays good black currant fruit, a chalky, tannic astringency not seen in those other vintages, excellent richness, and medium to full body. The wine's hardness kept my score from going higher. Give it 3–4 years of cellaring and drink it over the subsequent 2 decades. The unbottled 1994 Cabernet Sauvignon Cliff Vineyard exhibits the well-integrated, sweet tannin of this fabulous vintage, pure, ripe, cassis, black currant and black cherry fruit, well-integrated new oak (only about 10% new oak is utilized), adequate acidity, and a long, impressively endowed finish. It should last for 15+ years.

Only 125 cases of the large-scaled, black cherry-scented 1994 Zinfandel Cassanova Vineyard were produced. A thick purple color is accompanied by a rich, portlike style of Zinfandel. This multilayered, brawny, unfined and unfiltered wine boasts super flavor extraction, as well as 15.5% alcohol. Drink it over the next 5–7 years.

TURLEY CELLARS (NAPA)

1997 Charbono Tofanelli Vineyard	Napa	D	(89–91)
1997 Petite Syrah	Napa	D	(90–91)
1996 Petite Syrah Aida Vineyard	Napa	D	93
1995 Petite Syrah Aida Vineyard	Napa	D	94
1994 Petite Syrah Aida Vineyard	Napa	D	97
1993 Petite Syrah Aida Vineyard	Napa	D	95
1997 Petite Syrah Hayne Vineyard	Napa	D	(96–98)
1996 Petite Syrah Hayne Vineyard	Napa	D	98
1995 Petite Syrah Hayne Vineyard	Napa	D	95
1994 Petite Syrah Hayne Vineyard	Napa	D	98
1993 Petite Syrah Hayne Vineyard	Napa	D	91
1997 Petite Syrah Rattlesnake Acres	Napa	D	(91–93)
1997 Zinfandel Aida Vineyard	Napa	D	(93–95)
1996 Zinfandel Aida Vineyard	Napa	D	96
1995 Zinfandel Aida Vineyard	Napa	D	95
1994 Zinfandel Aida Vineyard	Napa	D	87
1993 Zinfandel Aida Vineyard	Napa	D	92
1997 Zinfandel Black-Sears Vineyard	Howell Mountain	D	(96–98)
1996 Zinfandel Black-Sears Vineyard	Howell Mountain	D	94
1995 Zinfandel Black-Sears Vineyard	Howell Mountain	D	94
1994 Zinfandel Black-Sears Vineyard	Napa	D	93
1997 Zinfandel Dogtown	California	D	(89–91)
1997 Zinfandel Duarte Vineyard	Contra Costa	D	(90–92)
1996 Zinfandel Duarte Vineyard	Contra Costa	D	89
1995 Zinfandel Duarte Vineyard	Contra Costa	D	88
1997 Zinfandel Grist Vineyard	Dry Creek	D	(92–95)
1996 Zinfandel Grist Vineyard	Dry Creek	D	91
1995 Zinfandel Grist Vineyard	Dry Creek	D	90
1997 Zinfandel Hayne Vineyard	Napa	D	(95–97)
1996 Zinfandel Hayne Vineyard	Napa	D	97
1995 Zinfandel Hayne Vineyard	Napa	D	96
1994 Zinfandel Hayne Vineyard	Napa	D	96
1993 Zinfandel Hayne Vineyard	Napa	D	95
1997 Zinfandel Moore (Earthquake) Vineyard	Napa	D	(94–96)

1996 Zinfandel Moore (Earthquake) Vineyard	Napa	D	94
1995 Zinfandel Moore (Earthquake) Vineyard	Napa	D	92
1994 Zinfandel Moore Vineyard	Napa	D	94+
1993 Zinfandel Moore Vineyard	Napa	C	89+
1997 Zinfandel Old Vines	California	C	(92–94)
1996 Zinfandel Old Vines	California	C	89+
1994 Zinfandel Sears Vineyard	Napa	?	88+
1997 Zinfandel Spenker Vineyard	Lodi	D	(87–88)
1996 Zinfandel Spenker Vineyard	Lodi	D	92
1997 Zinfandel Tofanelli Vineyard	Napa	D	(91–93)
1996 Zinfandel Tofanelli Vineyard	Napa	D	94
1997 Zinfandel Vineyard 101	Alexander Valley	D	(89–91)
1996 Zinfandel Vineyard 101 Alexander Estate	Alexander Valley	D	94
1996 Zinfandel Whitney/Tennessee Vineyard	Napa	D	94
1995 Zinfandel Whitney/Tennessee Vineyard	Napa	D	94
1994 Zinfandel Whitney Vineyard	Napa	D	88

Turley Cellars' offerings have become the reference point for Zinfandel, as they are the most complex, concentrated, hedonistic wines ever produced from this varietal. Critics claim the alcohol levels are too high, but proprietor Larry Turley and his winemaker, Ehren Jordan, would argue that the alcohol levels are high only because they picked ripe, not underripe fruit. Turley and Jordan have also taken the art of winemaking to a higher playing field. At the same time, they have resurrected a bevy of old head-pruned Zinfandel vineyards that had largely been ignored, or had their crops sold off to be unceremoniously blended into white Zinfandel. Turley Cellars' goal is to produce 10,000 cases of unfiltered, hand-crafted Zinfandel. As for the 1997 Zinfandels, Larry Turley feels they "are the best wines we have yet made." The wines are amazingly good, and as the following tasting notes suggest, readers could buy blind here and always end up with a juicy, complex, mouth-filling Zinfandel.

For starters, the 1997 Zinfandel Spenker Vineyard (from 105-year-old vines, with 15.1% alcohol) is a full-bodied, berry-scented and -flavored, lush wine with intriguing pepper, tar, and spicy notes. With excellent depth and purity, it is a candidate for 7–8 years of drinkability. The 1997 Zinfandel Dogtown (15.3% alcohol) is from a 65-year-old vineyard situated on the border of Amador. Its dark ruby/purple/garnet color is followed by copious quantities of briery, berry fruit intermixed with loamy soil, underbrush, and spicy notes. Full bodied and chewy, with excellent ripeness, this tasty, fleshy, full-throttle Zinfandel should drink well for 5–7 years. From tiny parcels of 55- to 104-year-old, head-pruned vineyards, the Turley team put together a blend called Zinfandel Old Vines. The dark ruby/purple-colored 1997 (15.3% alcohol) is the finest example of this cuvée they have produced. It offers a stunning nose of blackberry, raspberry and cherry fruit intermixed with Asian spices, pepper, and balsam wood. Explosively rich in the mouth, with high glycerin, and a smooth, concentrated finish, this wine should drink well for 7–8 years.

The 1997 Zinfandel Duarte Vineyard (from 102-year-old vines; 15.4% alcohol) is the finest wine I have tasted from this source. Duarte is one of the few remaining California vineyards where the vines are planted on their own roots, rather than being grafted, as the region's sandy soils have proved to be resistant to the phylloxera disease. This wine always seems to have a dusty, balsam wood, Provençal herb, peppery note, but the 1997 reveals more cherry liqueur and black raspberries. Additionally, the color is a saturated dark ruby/purple. Full bodied and concentrated, with deep layers of flavor that inundate the palate, it should drink well for 5–7 years. The 1997 Zinfandel Tofanelli Vineyard (from a 65-year-old vineyard; 15.8% alcohol) is a broodingly backward, expansive yet undeniably hedonistically oriented Zinfandel. The dark ruby/purple color is accompanied by notes of blackberries, *jus de viande*, pepper, roasted herbs, and truffles. Full bodied, with dazzling fruit extract, a voluptuous texture, and a spectacular finish, this is a superb Zinfandel to enjoy over the next 5–7 years. Slightly superior is the 1997 Zinfandel Grist Vineyard (16.3% alcohol). This is a perfumed, aromatic wine with a glorious display of cherry fruit. Think of a terrific red Burgundy with an element of *sur-maturité* and an unprecedented alcohol level, and readers may get a sense of what this blockbuster tastes like. The wine exhibits a dense ruby/purple color, fabulous purity, copious amounts of glycerin, and layers of kirsch/cherry fruit. This head-turning, knockout Zinfandel will be especially admired by both lovers of Burgundy and those who admire the famed Châteauneuf du Pape, Rayas. It should drink well for 7–8 years. The 1997 Zinfandel Vineyard 101 (from 85-year-old vines; 16% alcohol) is another Burgundian-styled wine, but more alcoholic and viscous. Full bodied, with surprising elegance for its weight and size, it displays a strong sense of minerality intertwined with notes of barbecue spices. With thrilling levels of black cherry and raspberry fruit, it should drink well now, and over the next 7 years.

Some of Turley's old stand-bys are once again compelling wines. The 1997 Zinfandel Aida Vineyard (from 30-year-old vines; 16.8% alcohol) is once again the Châteauneuf du Pape of northern California. This wine boasts an *herbes de Provence, garrigue,* peppery, black raspberry-scented, exotic nose that is eerily similar to a top-class Châteauneuf. The color is a saturated dark ruby/purple, and the wine unleashes its full power with layers of roasted meats, pepper, and jammy fruit flavors. This stunning Zinfandel will overload most tasters' olfactory sensors. Moreover, it should drink well for 7–8 years. The 1997 Zinfandel Black-Sears Vineyard (81-year-old vines; 17% alcohol) is the finest Black-Sears Turley has yet produced. Flirting with perfection, it is one of the most extraordinary Zinfandels I have ever tasted. This vineyard, located high on Howell Mountain, in a wilderness area inhabited by mountain lions, bobcats, and wild pigs, has turned out a saturated black/purple-colored wine with fabulous aromas of crème de cassis, minerals, cold steel, Asian spices, violets, and licorice. The wine possesses unbelievable fruit richness, layers of extract and glycerin, phenomenal purity, and a 40+-second finish. Somehow, some way, the 17% alcohol has been concealed beneath the wine's extraordinary richness. Is it any wonder that so many other Zinfandel producers are jealous of Turley Cellars? This offering should drink beautifully for 7–8 years. The 1997 Zinfandel Moore (Earthquake) Vineyard (from 91-year-old vines; 17.1% alcohol) is also spectacular. From its saturated black purple color, to its knockout aromatics of framboise, raspberries, kirsch (essentially the entire spectrum of red and black fruits seems to be present in this wine), this gorgeous, massively endowed, jammy yet structured Zinfandel easily disguises its 17.1% alcohol under its remarkable concentration and intensity. It should drink well for another decade.

My favorite Zinfandel in the Turley portfolio is usually the Hayne Vineyard. Along with Martinelli's Jackass Hill Zinfandel, it has tended to represent the be-all and end-all Zinfandel. The 1997 Zinfandel Hayne Vineyard is unquestionably a remarkable wine, but I am not sure it is better than the Black-Sears or Moore Vineyard. However, it will be the most backward and potentially longest-lived of these 1997s. It was the least evolved when I tasted it in September of 1998, displaying an opaque, saturated, thick-looking purple color, and unevolved but promising notes of black raspberry liqueur intermixed with minerals, spice, and cherry fruit. Massive yet phenomenally rich, admirably pure, and representing the essence of this varietal, this wine requires 12–18 months of bottle age; it should drink well for 10–15 years. An extraordinary Zinfandel, with 17.2% alcohol, it is the most powerful offering in the Turley portfolio. Anticipated maturity: 1999–2010.

Turley Cellars has added a curiosity in 1997. Readers will want to try what is the finest Charbono I have ever tasted. The opaque purple-colored 1997 Charbono Tofanelli Vineyard (from a 25-year-old vineyard) will be a revelation for readers who have tasted Charbonos made by other producers. The wine offers provocative aromas of earthy, blueberry jam, and lush, superripe, rich, round, concentrated flavors that must be tasted to be believed. No one would ever suspect that Charbono is capable of producing a wine of such richness and interest, but Larry Turley and Ehren Jordan have done just that. This is a powerhouse Charbono to drink over the next 7–8 years.

Turley Cellars' Petite Syrahs are the most amazing wines ever produced from this varietal. Petite Sirah tends to be disparaged, but when it is made from low yields and extremely ripe fruit, it possesses 2–3 decades of aging potential, and can reach astonishing levels of complexity. I have often used the 1971 Ridge Petite Sirah York Creek as an example of the heights these wines can achieve. That wine is just beginning to fade after lasting nearly 30 years. Turley's 1997 Petite Syrah Aida Vineyard (from 80-year-old vines) assaults the palate with such an overload of fruit, tannin, and extract that the taster's first impression is that this is something more than table wine. It is a massive, almost uncivilized, wildly out of control Petite Syrah that will require 10–15 years of cellaring and last for 30 or more. I have been conservative in my judgment because the tannin nearly melted the fillings in my teeth, but this is an amazing, astonishing wine that will be fascinating to follow over the next 3–4 decades. Lamentably, it will certainly outlive me. Anticipated maturity: 2008–2040. A new offering, the 1997 Petite Syrah Rattlesnake Acres is from a 50-year-old plantation of Petite Sirah. The wine's notes suggested I needed to return to my hotel to grab my floss after tasting this wine. The color is a saturated, thick black/purple. The wine reveals surprising amounts of toasty new oak in the nose (Turley only uses 25%–30% new oak). In the mouth, it is "beyond immense, massive, and gargantuan," and should be purchased only by those seeking an adventurous wine experience. Anticipated maturity: 2005–2040.

I do not believe I have ever tasted a more concentrated, essencelike wine than Turley's 1997 Petite Syrah Hayne Vineyard. Made from 55-year-old vines that yielded only 9.8 tons of fruit for five acres, this opaque black-colored wine is the biggest, richest, most concentrated, tannic wine I have ever tasted. It will need at least a decade to shed some of its ferocious tannin, and will undoubtedly last for 40–50 years. Even more remarkable is its purity and overall equilibrium. Despite its Godzilla-like size, this is an astonishingly concentrated, gorgeously made wine. The 1996 Petite Syrah Hayne Vineyard is indeed an historical effort, but the 1997 is even richer, despite the fact that yields were higher. As I said in my review of the 1996, I have never, ever, seen a wine like this!

The winery's debut Zinfandel vintage, 1993, quickly established that Turley Cellars was deadly serious about making blockbuster Zinfandels from some of California's oldest, pre-prohibition, head-pruned vineyards. The wines, aged in small oak casks (both American and French) of which 25% are new each year, are made from grapes that express the essence of Zinfandel. These wines, while hugely successful with knowledgeable wine consumers, have met with some controversy because of their enormous power, richness, weight, and lofty alcohol levels. The wines are extraordinarily rich, and clearly the most concentrated and powerful Zinfandels ever made. How they age remains subject to debate, but given the history of some of the powerhouse Zinfandels produced by Ridge in the early seventies (with similar alcohol levels), I suspect these wines will last longer than most Zinfandels. Let's not forget that alcohol is an important structural element. Combined with the concentration and extract of these wines, it is unlikely they will lose much fruit before they are 7–10 years old. These may be the most provocative and profound Zinfandels ever made. That being said, readers looking for a lighter-styled, Beaujolais-like Zinfandel need not read any further.

The 1993 Hayne Vineyard is one of the greatest Zinfandels I have ever tasted. Produced from a tiny, head-pruned vineyard planted in 1910 near the town of St. Helena, it exhibits the most saturated color, as well as a huge, fragrant nose of licorice, black fruits, spicy oak, and pepper. The wine is superrich, with layers of full-bodied flavors that reveal ripe fruit, well-integrated tannin, and a dry, heady, blockbuster finish. Velvety textured, massive but not overbearing or heavy, it is an extraordinary Zinfandel that should drink well for 10–15+ years. My second favorite wine is the 1993 Aida Vineyard, from a vineyard planted in 1970. The nose offers up smoky, herb, earthy, red and black fruits. The wine possesses full body, great concentration and richness, and a *terroir* component that dominates the Zinfandel varietal character. It is an immense, beautifully proportioned, dry wine with wonderfully sweet, ripe fruit. Drink it over the next 12–15 years. The 1993 Zinfandel Moore Vineyard (from a vineyard planted in the year of the great California earthquake, 1906) reveals the least saturated color, although it is a dark ruby with some purple tints. The nose is classic Zinfandel— briery, peppery, intense, and wonderfully pure. Once the wine hits the palate, the acidity seems higher, the wine more restrained, full bodied, with excellent concentration, but a more subtle and proportioned style. It should drink well for 10–12 years.

While Turley Cellars produced an extraordinary lineup of Zinfandels in 1994, the 1994 Aida and 1994 Whitney are the least concentrated, but are full bodied, robust, intense Zinfandels, with the Aida supporting 14.1% alcohol and the Whitney coming in at 15.9%. The soft, round 1994 Aida Zinfandel exhibits a peppery, robust personality with rustic acidity and a touch of tannin. It should be drunk during its first 5–6 years of life. Although very good, it is outclassed by the other wines. The 1994 Whitney Zinfandel (from the coolest vineyard the Turleys farm) is an intensely spicy wine with medium to dark ruby color, an attractive texture, some fat and considerably high alcohol (15.9%). This is a rich, excellent wine, but compared to the other Turley offerings, it is a lightweight—if readers can believe that.

The 1994 Zinfandel from the Black-Sears Vineyard (only 250 cases produced), is a gorgeously made, opulent, decadent Zinfandel. Totally dry, yet sporting 15.4% alcohol, this wine boasts an impressively saturated dark purple color, huge quantities of briery, spicy, black raspberry and cherry fruit, and a heady, high-octane finish. It should drink well for 8–10 years. This is the smallest lot of all the wines produced at Turley Cellars, with only 250 cases. The fabulous 1994 Zinfandel Moore Vineyard is one of the greatest Zinfandels I have ever tasted. The wine reveals a saturated black/ruby color, a set of aromatics offering up unprecedented levels of jammy black cherries, spices, and minerals scents. This supple, decadent, massively constituted (16.1% alcohol), dry, succulent, chewy Zinfandel should drink well for 10–15+ years. It is a tour de force in Zinfandel winemaking! A truly colossal Zinfandel is Turley Cellars' 1994 Zinfandel Hayne Vineyard. Frankly, Zinfandel does not get much richer than this. Its only rivals are the two enormously rich, unctuously textured wines from the Martinelli Family's Jackass Vineyard and Jackass Hill Vineyard. The 1994 Hayne possesses a dense purple color, and a huge nose of fabulously pure black fruits, pepper, and spices. The texture is akin to syrup, with a thickness and richness that must be tasted to be believed. With all this power and flavor authority, it is easy to think this wine is too heavy. But it is dry, well focused, and thrilling to drink. The alcohol is an unbelievable 17.2%, yet there is no hotness in the finish—which tells readers about the extraordinary concentration of fruit this wine possesses. Likely to be controversial because of its size and extremely concentrated style, the 1994 Hayne is an historical Zinfandel! Drink it during its first 15–20+ years of life.

The 1994 Zinfandel Sears Vineyard offers a big, peppery, black and red fruit-scented nose, plenty of spice, a chewy texture, and a long, heady, full-bodied finish.

One of the new vineyard sources for Turley Cellars is the Duarte Vineyard (planted between 1895 and 1898) near Oakley in Contra Costa County. The dark-colored 1995 Zinfandel Duarte Vineyard (15.2% alcohol) reveals rich, spicy, red and black fruits, along with notes of loamy earth, minerals, and herbs. The wine possesses admirable ripeness, sweet fruit, and medium to full body, but tasted alongside the other Turley Zinfandels, it is more monolithic with less aromatic and flavor dimension. Nevertheless, it will offer delicious, plump drinking for the next 4–6 years. The 1995 Zinfandel Black-Sears Vineyard, which has a northeasterly orientation on Howell Mountain, weighs in at 16.1% alcohol. Harvested on November 15 (because of the vineyard's cool climate elevation of 2400 feet), this is a fabulously rich, full-bodied, powerful Zinfandel. The deep saturated purple color and gorgeous, fragrant nose of black raspberries, pepper, and spice are suggestive of a top vintage of Pomerol from Bordeaux's right bank. This wine is enormously rich, full bodied, superconcentrated, with a creamy texture, and layers of glycerin-imbued, rich fruit. Its seductive power makes it one of the most hedonistic, dry, full-bodied Zinfandels I have ever drunk. It should continue to drink well for at least a decade, but who has the discipline to squirrel away a few bottles for that long? The 1995 Zinfandel Whitney Tennessee Vineyard (16.5% alcohol, from a vineyard planted in 1898) exhibits a dense black/ruby color, followed by a sensational, sweet, pure, black cherry, raspberry, mineral, and peppery-scented nose. Full bodied, with copious quantities of fruit, glycerin, and extract, this wine is a blockbuster Zinfandel that manages to conceal its exceptionally high alcohol. Mouth-filling, with multiple layers, and a sensationally complex, four-dimensional personality. The finish, which lasts for over 30 seconds, is explosive. I would opt for drinking this Zinfandel over the next 5–8 years, as one of the Turley's 1995s are more forward than the 1994s. Amazing!

The 1995 Zinfandel Aida Vineyard (16.2% alcohol) is the finest Zinfandel Turley has yet produced from this terroir. More than any other Turley Zinfandel, this wine possesses a southern Rhône/Provençal/*garrigue* (that *herbes de Provence*, earthy concoction) personality that jumps from the glass. The color is a deep, dense, murky garnet. Jammy black cherries, kirsch, strawberries, pepper, and earth make for one of the most complex smelling Zinfandels I have ever experienced. In the mouth, the wine is phenomenally rich, with no sense of flabbiness, high alcohol, or pruniness. It is an extraordinary, full-throttle Zinfandel that should be a benchmark for future Aida Vineyard Zinfandels. The wine's sumptuousness and low acidity suggest immediate drinkability, but this wine's massive richness indicates it will keep for 8 or more years.

If readers are not totally persuaded that Zinfandel is not a serious wine, keep reading. The 1995 Zinfandel Moore "Earthquake" Vineyard (16.9% alcohol, from a vineyard planted in 1906) is an off-dry, mind-boggling Zinfandel with a deep ruby/garnet color, huge quantities of sweet, jammy fruit, plenty of pepper, earth, cinnamon, and spice in the nose, and formidable quantities of glycerin and extract. It is an amazing Zinfandel, and perhaps the only wine aside from the Grist Vineyard Zinfandel that is best drunk with cheese rather than table fare. Again, one of its amazing hallmarks is its purity and overall balance, with no hotness in spite of the extraordinary alcohol level. Perhaps my favorite Turley vineyard of all is the Hayne Vineyard, as it produces both superstar Zinfandels and Petite Sirahs. The 1995 Zinfandel Hayne Vineyard is again the superstar in a noteworthy portfolio. The harvest, six tons of fruit (from a 6-acre vineyard), produced a wine that appears to be as powerful and rich as the 1994. I am tempted to say that Zinfandel does not get any better than this, but I could probably say that most red wines do not get much better than this. The opaque purple color is followed by gloriously levels of extraordinarily pure, sweet, cassis, kirsch, and pepper. The wine possesses an astonishing level of extract and ripe fruit. Despite its massiveness, full body, and loads of glycerin, it displays no sense of hotness or weightiness. It is a winemaking tour de force . . . marvelously concentrated, gorgeously perfumed, and sensational in all respects. The finish lasts for 30 seconds. The 1995, which is more flattering and precocious than the 1994, is best drunk over the next decade. As all these offerings demonstrate, this is extraordinary winemaking! Along with its predecessors, this is undoubtedly one of the greatest Zinfandels I have ever tasted.

The 1995 Zinfandel Grist Vineyard (17.3% alcohol) is a late harvest, slightly sweet style of Zinfandel that should be served after dinner or with strongly flavored cheese dishes. Although full bodied and rich, it does not possess the complexity of most other Turley Zinfandels. It is hugely extracted, superrich, and indeed impressive, yet not as flexible with an assortment of culinary dishes as the other wines. It should drink well for a decade.

Turley Cellars' 1996s are remarkable wines, and readers will be thrilled to know there are some intriguing new offerings. Those lots of Zinfandel from tiny parcels that are not large enough to be bottled on their own have been assembled together in a new release called 1996 Zinfandel Old Vines. This wine exhibits a terrific nose of sweet berry fruit, underbrush, and spice. Dense, chewy, and full bodied, this is a rich, concentrated, dry, lusty Zinfandel with 14.6% alcohol. It should drink well for 4–7 years, possibly longer. Another new offering is the 1996 Zinfandel Spenker Vineyard from Lodi. With its wild blueberry-scented nose interspersed with aromas of spice, this full-bodied, nicely layered, rich Zinfandel is dense and concentrated, with explosive berry fruit. The glycerin and alcohol (14.9%) are meshed together in a silky-textured format. This wine should drink well for 5–10 years.

The 1996 Zinfandel Grist Vineyard, which emerges from Dry Creek, tips the scales at a blockbuster 16.3% alcohol. This wine offers lusty levels of lavishly jammy black cherry fruit intermixed with raspberries, pepper, earth, and spice. Wow, what an astonishing level of pleasure this huge, massive Zin provides! It is a wine to drink over the next 5–8 years.

The following eight wines are the Zinfandels of the 1996 vintage. Critics will whine that they are the most alcoholic wines of the vintage, and yes, they are among the most potent. Yet they are unequivocally the most complex, concentrated, and complete wines of the vintage— offering layers of flavor, extraordinary textures, and unbelievable balance. Readers must certainly be aware of the fact that they have become almost impossible to obtain because of their huge popularity. Zinfandels such as Turley's set the standards for other producers, and encourage people to search out old, head-pruned parcels of Zinfandel vines and treat them as they would Cabernet Sauvignon or Pinot Noir—with tender, loving care.

Tasting these Zinfandels from bottle is a treat. For starters, the 1996 Zinfandel Vineyard 101 (from a 2.2-acre parcel of 80-year-old Alexander Valley vines) exhibits a dark ruby/purple color, followed by sweet berry fruit aromas intermixed with herbs and minerals, and gobs of chewy blackberry and cherry fruit. A thick, viscous, full-bodied, yet impeccably well balanced Zinfandel, it should drink well for 5–8 years. The 1996 Zinfandel Tofanelli Vineyard (15.9% alcohol) emerges from a head-pruned vineyard near Calistoga planted in 1933. This wine offers up smoky, roasted herb, prune, blackberry and raspberry scents with a touch of caramel. In the mouth, it is a substantial, full-bodied, superconcentrated, layered Zinfandel with beautifully integrated acidity, alcohol, and tannin. Already stunning, it promises to last for 7–8 years. I was blown away by several bottles of the 1996 Zinfandel Aida Vineyard drunk on vacation in Maui. After spending three weeks in Asia tasting primarily French wines and Saké, they hit all the sweet spots on my palate. The finest effort yet from this vineyard, the 1996 is reminiscent of a phenomenal Châteauneuf du Pape. This wine continues to remind me of California's version of Henri Bonneau's Châteauneuf du Pape Réserve des Célestins. With an alcohol content just above 15.5%, this full-bodied, meaty, dark ruby/purple-colored wine reveals celestial aromas of smoked duck, Provençal herbs, and pepper. On the palate, intense layers of glycerin-imbued, superrich, chewy levels of extract are sensational. It is a blockbuster, decadently rich Zinfandel to drink over the next 7–8 years. In contrast, the 1996 Zinfandel Whitney-Tennessee Vineyard (planted in 1898) seems almost claretlike in its civilized, less weighty style. There is gorgeous sweet black cherry and raspberry fruit in the nose, intertwined with earth, licorice, and pepper. Full bodied and wonderfully concentrated, with a seamless texture and a sensual, smooth as silk finish, it will drink well for 7–8 years.

The 1996 Zinfandel Duarte Vineyard, which offered a dusty, earthy, balsam wood character prior to bottling, has retained much of that in its flavors. There are copious quantities of black cherry/raspberry fruit in this dry, full-bodied wine. Although the Duarte does not possess the complexity and length of Turley's other offerings, it exhibits excellent richness and quality. Drink it over the next 5–6 years. The deep ruby/purple-colored 1996 Zinfandel Black-Sears Vineyard (planted high on Howell Mountain) reveals a sweet nose of black raspberries, truffles, smoke, and spice. This full-bodied wine is rich in glycerin and extract, with beautifully integrated alcohol (about 15%). It is a stylish, more restrained, impeccably clean, long Zinfandel that should drink well for 5–6 years. A more elegantly styled Turley offering is the 1996 Zinfandel Moore Vineyard (from a vineyard planted in 1906). It displays a telltale jammy raspberry, kirsch, peppery nose, as well as rich, nicely textured, full-bodied flavors, and outstanding balance and purity. Look for this example to age well for 7 or more years.

My favorite among this impressive portfolio is the 1996 Zinfandel Hayne Vineyard. Representing the essence of Zinfandel, it boasts a dark saturated purple color, mind-boggling fruit extract and concentration levels, compelling harmony and overall balance, particularly for a wine of such massive size, and a whoppingly long finish. The dominant characteristics are its blackberry/black raspberry/cherry liqueurlike flavors, voluptuous texture, and seamless integration of wood, alcohol, and acidity. I am not a great believer in the capability of Zinfandels to age, but this wine, although accessible now, should last well beyond a decade.

Kudos to Turley! These Zinfandels are the products of extraordinary vineyards and genius winemaking—no doubt about it. They sell out quickly, so readers should try to get their names on the winery's mailing list.

Turley continues to offer two of the blackest, densest, richest Petite Syrahs ever produced in California. The opaque black/purple-colored 1995 Petite Syrah Aida Vineyard offers up a licorice, smoke, earth, and cassis-scented nose, extraordinary sweetness of fruit, and monstrous-sized proportions of glycerin and tannin. This huge, massive Petite Syrah needs a decade of cellaring. Given the potent alcohol levels of Turley's Zinfandels, readers will be interested to learn this offering has only 13.5% alcohol. It should easily last for 25–30 years. The 1995 Petite Syrah Hayne Vineyard is absolutely enthralling, and as extraordinary as the 1994. It is still in an infantile state, but my notes suggested I was tasting a runaway, high speed train. An opaque purple color, massive richness, and huge thickness and extract should produce a phenomenal bottle of wine in 15–20 years. Not many of us have the patience to wait on such uncompromisingly made wines, but I suspect the time invested will be well worth it.

Alongside its siblings, the 1996 Petite Syrah Aida Vineyard looks like a wimp with only 13.8% alcohol, but what concentration and intensity this wine offers. From a 4.5-acre vineyard, only 3 tons of fruit were harvested in 1996. The result is an opaque purple-colored wine with a dense, mineral, earthy, peppery, blackberry-scented nose, huge, ripe, thick flavors, gobs of glycerin and fruit, and a long, moderately tannic finish. My guess is that this wine requires 5–6 years of cellaring and will keep for 2–3 decades. Perhaps the greatest Petite Syrah I have ever tasted is Turley's 1996 Petite Syrah Hayne Vineyard. From a 5-acre parcel of vines, only 6 tons of fruit were harvested. For a Turley offering, this wine possesses a conservative 15% alcohol. This full-bodied monster exhibits remarkable equilibrium, unprecedented purity and richness of fruit for a Petite Syrah, and a finish that lasts for nearly a minute. It is a compellingly rich, multidimensional wine the likes of which I have never seen from a Petite Syrah. It will undoubtedly need 10–15 years to reveal all of its nuances, but the wait will be worth it. This is an historical effort!

There is no doubt about it—as a fan of the underrated Petite Syrah, I have never tasted greater Petite Syrahs than the 1994 Aida or 1994 Hayne. Some of the extraordinary Petite Syrah produced by La Jota from the old Park-Muscatine Vineyard on Howell Mountain, and the now-discontinued Ridge Petite Syrahs from the Devil's Hill portion of York Creek Vineyard were previous benchmarks, but Turley Cellars' Petite Syrahs have set a new reference point for this varietal. The thick, opaque, black-colored 1994 Petite Syrah Aida Vineyard possesses 14.1% alcohol. Remarkably, the tannin is barely noticeable because of the enormous, thick layers of concentrated fruit that carries vast quantities of glycerin and fantastic extract. This wine was relatively flattering to drink in 1996. It should last for 20–25+ years. The 1994 Petite Syrah Hayne Vineyard is the new reference point for Petite Syrah. At 14.9% alcohol, this dry, awesomely endowed wine is not shy about displaying its virtues. The opaque purple/black color is followed by a nose of extraordinary intensity offering jammy smells of black raspberries and crème de cassis. Amazingly rich, with extraordinary purity (a hallmark of all the Turley wines), this full-bodied, blockbuster, Arnold Schwarzenegger-like wine is surprisingly flattering because of its soft tannin. This is an example of carrying extraction to the maximum, but the wine is amazingly well balanced. It should drink well for 30+ years.

Petite Sirah lovers will go ballistic when they taste the two 1993 offerings from Turley Cellars. The 1993 Petite Syrah Hayne Vineyard (from a vineyard planted in 1950) reveals a dense purple color, full body, an earth, pepper, and black fruit-scented nose, concentrated flavors, and a muscular, tannic finish. The black/purple-colored 1993 Petite Syrah Aida Vineyard (from a vineyard planted in 1911) is massively rich, with wonderfully integrated, sweet, ripe tannin, a huge, black fruit, licorice, earth, and peppery-scented nose, exceptional length, and moderately high, sweet tannin. It is an exceptional Petite Sirah that should last for 20–30+ years.

VIADER VINEYARDS (NAPA)

1996 Proprietary Red Wine	Napa	E	88
1995 Proprietary Red Wine	Napa	E	91
1994 Proprietary Red Wine	Napa	E	92
1993 Proprietary Red Wine	Napa	E	90

The wines from this superbly situated hillside vineyard on the lower slopes of Howell Mountain are going from strength to strength. Proprietor Delia Viader believes in blending these wines with a relatively high percentage of Cabernet Franc. In most vintages, the proportion of Cabernet Franc is close to 50%, with the balance Cabernet Sauvignon. Improvements noticeable in both the 1995 and 1996 (and for that matter the 1994) have included richer mid-palates, and less aggressive oak and acidity. A blend of 59% Cabernet Sauvignon and 41% Cabernet Franc, from Viader's beautiful hillside vineyards, this 1996 is made in a polished, graceful style. Medium bodied, with lush, herb-tinged, raspberry and black currant fruit intermixed with mineral and lead pencil notes, this lovely, stylish, restrained offering already provides pleasant drinking, yet should keep for 10–12 years. The similarly styled 1995 reveals an opaque purple color, remarkably sweet tannin for a wine from this vintage, and gorgeous levels of black currant fruit nicely complemented by toast, smoke, and floral scents. This rich, medium- to full-bodied wine fills the mouth without any sense of heaviness or harshness. It is a beautifully knit, lush, complex, elegant red wine that should drink well for 12–15 years.

Smoky, sweet, black and red currant aromas jump from the glass of the intriguing, saturated purple-colored 1994. Some new oak is noticeable in the background. The wine's attack exhibits terrific purity of fruit, more acidity than many 1994s, and sweet, ripe tannin, all packed into a tightly wound, medium- to full-bodied wine that only hints at its ultimate potential. This is not a large-scaled 1994, but it is a beautifully etched wine with considerable personality. It will benefit from 4–5 years of cellaring. It is unquestionably another 20-year effort from this vintage.

The 1993 Estate possesses gobs of sweet fruit, with the Cabernet Franc dominating the wine's personality at present. It has the potential to develop into an extremely complex, aromatic wine of considerable stature. In a blind tasting, it would be difficult to pick this wine out as a California Cabernet Sauvignon.

VILLA MT. EDEN WINERY (NAPA)

1994 Cabernet Sauvignon Signature Series	Mendocino	D	87
1993 Pinot Noir Cellar Select	California	C	77
1993 Pinot Noir Grand Reserve Bien Nacido	Santa Maria	C	85
1994 Zinfandel Cellar Select	California	B	84
1993 Zinfandel Cellar Select	California	B	87
1995 Zinfandel Grand Reserve Monte Rosso Vineyard	Sonoma	C	89
1995 Zinfandel Select	California	B	86

The intriguing dark purple-colored 1994 Cabernet Sauvignon offers up a peppery, iodine, herbaceous underbrush, and red currant-scented nose. In the mouth, more black fruits (primarily cassis) make an appearance, and the wine is medium bodied, with moderate tannin, but hints at a soft, lush personality emerging with another 1–3 years of bottle age. Anticipated maturity: now–2010.

The two 1995 Villa Mt. Eden Zinfandels represent a significant improvement in quality. The 1995 Zinfandel California is an attractive, soft, open-knit, seductive wine with copious amounts of lush, spicy cinnamon and pepperylike fruit. Evolved, with medium body, low acidity, and a tasty, fleshy mouth-feel, this is a delicious Zinfandel to drink over the next several years. Moreover, in these days of stratospherically priced wines, this is an excellent value. Villa Mt. Eden has never made a Zinfandel as fine as the 1995 Grand Reserve Monte Rosso Vineyard. The wine exhibits a dark ruby/purple color, followed by a lavishly oaked, gorgeously ripe nose of jammy black cherries, strawberries, and plums. Full bodied, with layers of corpulently textured fruit, this unctuously textured wine offers a lusty, mouth-filling style of Zinfandel that will have many admirers. It should drink well for 5–6 years.

A commercially styled Zinfandel with aggressive levels of toasty, spicy oak dominating the moderate quantities of berry fruit, the medium-bodied, soft, effusively fruity, easygoing 1994 Zinfandel is designed to be drunk now and over the next 3–4 years. I would not hesitate to serve it slightly chilled.

If you are searching for a user-friendly, supple, ripe, deliciously fruity, medium- to full-bodied Zinfandel that is pure, well balanced, and oozing with cherry and raspberry fruit, check out the satiny-textured 1993 Zinfandel Cellar Select from Villa Mt. Eden. It is medium to full bodied, round, generous, and ideal for drinking over the next 4–5 years.

The tasty, foursquare, forward 1993 Pinot Noir Grand reserve Bien Nacido offers plenty of ripe berry fruit, a nice touch of oak, and a soft, supple, silky, medium- to full-bodied finish. It is ideal for drinking over the next 2–3 years. The 1993 Cellar Select Pinot Noir is a lighter-bodied, more one-dimensional version of the Grand Reserve. It is soft and fruity, with barely enough concentration to provide pleasure. It should be drunk over the next year.

VINE CLIFF CELLARS (NAPA)

1995 Cabernet Sauvignon Oakville Estate	Napa	D	85
1994 Cabernet Sauvignon Oakville Estate	Napa	D	88
1996 Chardonnay	Napa	D	87

The 1995 Cabernet Sauvignon Oakville Estate plays it close to the vest. The color is a healthy dark ruby. The tight nose offers high quality new oak intermixed with laid-back black currant fruit. In the mouth, tart acidity competes for the taster's attention with attractive currant fruit and smoky oak. Drink it over the next 5–6 years.

The stylish, elegant 1994 Cabernet Sauvignon reveals plenty of toasty new oak, medium body, and an uncomplicated black fruit character. The wine has no hard edges, but the oak is slightly intrusive. This finesse-styled Cabernet is cleanly made, but not terribly complex or concentrated. Drink it over the next 5–8 years.

Vine Cliff's 1996 is a typical, modern-styled California Chardonnay with an emphasis on copious quantities of tropical fruit, plenty of acidity, and moderate toasty oak. In spite of that, the wine possesses some personality, an attractive, butterscotch and honeyed nose, fleshy richness, and a tart finish. Drink it over the next year.

VINEYARD 29 (NAPA)

1994 Cabernet Sauvignon	Napa	EE	90
1993 Cabernet Sauvignon	Napa	EE	89

This vineyard's innovative name, and beautiful presentation in a heavy, tall Italian bottle make for a grandiose impression. Based on the two vintages I tasted, the wine is excellent. Aged in 100% new French oak casks for 22 months before bottling, the 1993 Cabernet Sauvignon offers a dark ruby color, followed by a sweet, aggressively woody nose. The pungent wood dominated the wine's fruit, which lowered my score. Nevertheless, once past the oaky overlay, the wine exhibits fine ripeness, copious quantities of rich, chewy fruit, medium to full body, and wood tannin in the finish. I am not sure if everything will ultimately come together, but this is a flamboyant, oaky, spicy Cabernet Sauvignon that requires 2–4 more years of cellaring; it should keep for 15–20 years.

From a 3-acre vineyard, 400 cases were produced of the 1994 Cabernet Sauvignon. Aged for 22 months in 100% new French oak casks, it is a tightly knit, black currant-scented wine with plenty of sweet oak, as well as powerful, rich flavors that have been melded into a restrained, elegant, authoritatively flavorful wine. Patience is mandatory as this black beauty needs 4–5 more years of cellaring; it should keep for 2 decades.

VON STRASSER (NAPA)

1995 Cabernet Sauvignon Diamond Mountain	Napa	D	90
1994 Cabernet Sauvignon Diamond Mountain	Napa	D	91
1993 Cabernet Sauvignon Diamond Mountain	Napa	D	91
1995 Cabernet Sauvignon Diamond Mountain	Napa	D	92+
1996 Chardonnay Diamond Mountain	Napa	D	89
1995 Chardonnay Diamond Mountain	Napa	D	89

This winery is doing many things right, as evidenced by these releases. The 1996 Chardonnay exhibits a moderately intense nose of buttery, honeyed tropical fruit nicely intertwined with high quality French oak. Fleshy, medium- to full-bodied flavors reveal excellent purity, a chewy, lush texture, and plenty of hedonistic fruit. Drink this luscious Chardonnay over the next year.

Both 1995 Cabernet Sauvignons are outstanding. For starters, the 1995 Cabernet Sauvignon Diamond Mountain possesses a dense ruby/purple color, followed by a promising nose of cassis intertwined with earth, flowers, and spice. In the mouth, there is good grip and tannin, but the overall impression is one of a medium- to full-bodied wine where the fruit characteristics dominate the *terroir* and oak. Subtle vanillin and spice are present in this pure, black currant-flavored, long, impressive wine. Accessible now, it promises to get even better over the next decade and last for 15+ years. The 1995 Cabernet Sauvignon Reserve is prodigious. The color is nearly opaque purple. The nose offers up intense aromas of blackberries and cassis, intermingled with earth and vanillin. On the palate, the wine is formidably endowed, backward and tannic, but exceptionally dense, layered, and extremely rich. Yet there is no sense of heaviness, and the tannin is sweet rather than overbearing or astringent. This superb Cabernet Sauvignon has a long, promising future. Anticipated maturity: 2001–2020.

The 1995 Chardonnay is a full-blown, buttery, toasty, husky wine nicely dosed with oak. It fills the mouth with savory quantities of glycerin-laden, fleshy, buttery, tropical fruit. This well-made Chardonnay is a worthy candidate for drinking over the next year.

The 1994 is a beautifully made Cabernet Sauvignon. The healthy dark purple color is followed by a forward, sexy, up-front nose of jammy plums, black currants, vanilla ice cream, and cassis. On the palate, this full-bodied Cabernet reveals silky tannin, an opulent texture, and a full-bodied, concentrated finish. It manages to offer intensity without heaviness— something that is not easy to obtain. Drink this seductive Cabernet Sauvignon young as well as old, as I suspect it will have a very large window of drinkability—say 15 or more years.

Von Strasser fashioned an impressively made, well-balanced 1993 Cabernet Sauvignon that is a noteworthy successor to the outstanding 1992. It exhibits a black/purple color, and an attractive nose of sweet cassis fruit complemented by vanillin and herbs. It is medium to full bodied, and oozing with extract and ripeness, buttressed by adequate acidity and firm, moderately intense tannin. Put it away for 3–4 years and drink it over the following 15+.

VOSS VINEYARDS (SONOMA)

1993	Merlot	Napa	C	87
1997	Sauvignon Blanc	Napa	B	87
1994	Shiraz	Napa	C	87+?
1994	Zinfandel	Alexander Valley	C	?
1993	Zinfandel	Alexander Valley	C	85?

The delicious 1997 Sauvignon Blanc is dominated by its distinctive mango/melony, guava-like fruit character. Crisp and medium bodied, with a textured feel on the palate, this is a wine to drink over the next 12–18 months. The 1994 Shiraz reveals an unmistakable Australian character (more than just the spelling of Syrah as Shiraz). The color is a healthy dark ruby/purple, and the nose offers up scents of blackberries, tar, and smoky, woodsy notes. In the mouth, the wine seems less promising than the sensational aromatics suggest. There is a roughness (too much added acidity?) to the wine's texture, but there is no doubting this wine has been well endowed with plenty of jammy, concentrated black fruit. The finish is sweet, with loads of wood. Drink this Shiraz now and over the next 7–8 years.

The 1993 Merlot reveals a healthy, dark ruby/purple color, and an attractive nose of spice and black cherries with a touch of mint. Medium to full bodied, flavorful, and ripe, this is a broad, solidly made Merlot for drinking over the next 4–5 years. The dark garnet color of the 1994 Zinfandel is followed by a peppery, lavishly wooded nose that tends to obliterate much of this wine's fruit. In the mouth, there are dry, aggressive tannins and medium body, but frightful levels of oak. Although the unbottled, earthy, oaky 1993 Zinfandel is full of flavor, its huge, abrasive tannin dominates what appears to be generous fruit and good concentration. It is a dusty, hard, muscular Zinfandel with little charm or finesse. Perhaps it will pull itself together over the next several years, but I am doubtful.

WHITEHALL LANE (NAPA)

1996 Cabernet Sauvignon	Napa	C	87
1995 Cabernet Sauvignon	Napa	C	88
1994 Cabernet Sauvignon	Napa	C	88
1995 Cabernet Sauvignon Leonardini Vineyard	Napa	E	90
1994 Cabernet Sauvignon Morisoli Vineyard	Napa	E	92
1993 Cabernet Sauvignon Morisoli Vineyard	Napa	E	90
1995 Cabernet Sauvignon Reserve	Napa	D	91
1994 Cabernet Sauvignon Reserve Morisoli Vineyard	Napa	D	90
1996 Merlot	Napa	C	88
1995 Merlot	Napa	C	87
1994 Merlot	Napa	C	87
1996 Merlot Leonardini Vineyard	Napa	D	86
1994 Merlot Leonardini Vineyard	Napa	D	91
1993 Merlot Leonardini Vineyard	Napa	D	87
1995 Merlot Reserve Leonardini Vineyard	Napa	D	88
1994 Merlot Reserve Leonardini Vineyard	Napa	D	90
1993 Merlot Reserve Leonardini Vineyard	Napa	D	90

Whitehall Lane's 1995 Cabernet Sauvignon Reserve (2,400 cases) dominated a flight that included fourteen of its peers. It exhibits a saturated purple color, as well as a youthful yet promising nose of toasty new oak, briery fruit, cassis, and licorice. The wine is concentrated and pure, with sweet tannin, adequate acidity, and medium to full body. A seamless, beautifully proportioned Cabernet Sauvignon, it should be at its peak with another 2–3 years of bottle age, and keep for 15 or more. The 1996 Merlot is a round, user-friendly, plump wine with significantly more character than most Merlots possess. The color is a dark ruby/purple. The wine offers copious amounts of berry fruit intermixed with smoke, herb, and earthy notes. Fruity and succulent, with medium body, and a generous, crowd-pleasing, glycerin-imbued finish, it should be consumed over the next 5–6 years.

The 1996 Cabernet Sauvignon is a reasonably good value given today's frightfully high wine prices. The color is dark ruby, and the nose offers up earthy black currant fruit. The wine displays good richness, a corpulent, chunky mouth-feel, and fine purity. It is already drinking nicely, and should continue to do so for 6–7 years. The dark plum-colored 1996 Merlot Leonardini Vineyard offers chocolate, vanillin, and spice in its moderately intense bouquet. The wine's dominant chocolatey flavors continue on the palate of this medium-bodied, straightforward, pleasant but uninspiring Merlot. Drink it over the next 5–6 years. The opaque-colored 1995 Cabernet Sauvignon Leonardini Vineyard reveals more new oak, extract, richness, and intensity. There are copious quantities of cassis and vanillin flavors that border on overripeness. Rich, with soft tannin, this larger-scaled, more expansive wine can be drunk now as well as over the next 15 years.

The 1995 Merlot exhibits a healthy dark ruby color, followed by a big, sweet nose of toasty oak and jammy berry fruit. Silky smooth, with a nicely layered texture, this pure, ripe, concentrated wine should be consumed over the next 5–6 years. The more ambitiously styled 1995 Merlot Reserve Leonardini Vineyard reveals an opaque ruby/purple color, less expressiveness aromatically (it's more closed), and more toasty new oak. In the mouth, this wine possesses an extra dimension of richness and concentration. It is not as accessible as the regular Merlot, and over the next several years most readers will probably prefer the latter wine. Nevertheless, the Reserve Merlot is an excellent effort that should age well for 7–8 years.

The 1994 Merlot reveals smoky, toasty, black cherry flavors in a medium-bodied, plush, accessible style. There is enough structure to insure another 5–6 years of pleasure. The 1994 Merlot Reserve Leonardini Vineyard is a more extracted, richer, earthier, more aggressively oaked wine with full body, admirable intensity, richness, and length, and a long, spicy finish. Although still youthful and unevolved, it promises to provide considerable enjoyment between now and 2010.

Whitehall Lane hit the bull's eye with their dark ruby/purple-colored 1993 Merlot Reserve Leonardini Vineyard. It offers up intense scents of jammy, berry fruit, mocha, tobacco, cedar, and herbs. Full bodied and supple, with moderate tannin, this is a large-scaled, compellingly rich, nicely textured Merlot for drinking over the next 5–6 years.

The 1993 and 1994 Merlot Leonardini Vineyard are both impressive Merlots. Although the 1993 is lighter, it remains a rich, medium- to full-bodied, spicy, ready to drink Merlot with plenty of berry fruit and nicely integrated oak. It should drink well for 5–7 years. The blockbuster 1994 exhibits a black/purple color, fabulously ripe, rich, concentrated fruit, full body, and a great purity and balance. This is an immensely impressive Merlot that should age well for a decade or more.

An excellent, nearly outstanding Cabernet Sauvignon, Whitehall Lane's 1995 possesses a dark ruby/purple color, as well as sweet, jammy, cassis fruit, an appealingly thick texture, and no hard edges. The acidity, tannin, and alcohol are all well integrated in this seamless, opulently styled Cabernet Sauvignon. It should drink well for a decade or more.

The 1994 Cabernet Sauvignon exhibits a deep ruby/purple color followed by attractive spicy, weedy, cassis aromas, backed up by vanillin and oaky scents. Medium to full bodied, with excellent concentration, well-integrated tannin and acidity, and a vibrant, lively feel on the palate, this midweight Cabernet Sauvignon should drink well for 7–10 years.

The outstanding 1994 Cabernet Sauvignon Reserve Morisoli Vineyard is not quite ready for prime time drinking. It possesses a healthy dark ruby/purple color, enticing, sweet cassis, cedar, and vanillin components, medium to full body, high tannin, and some of the elusive lead pencil aromas often found in St.-Julien and Pauillac offerings. The wine needs another 2–3 years of cellaring, but it should evolve gracefully for 10–15 years. It is a fine example of this impressive vintage.

The terrific 1994 Morisoli Vineyard Cabernet Sauvignon exhibits a black/purple color, fabulous sweetness and ripeness of fruit, full body, layers of extract and richness, and a stunning finish. The tannin is sweet and long. This gorgeous Cabernet appears to be a terrific effort from what looks to be a sensational vintage for North Coast Cabernet Sauvignon. The 1993 Cabernet Sauvignon Morisoli Vineyard reveals an impressive saturated purple color, excellent purity, ripe cassis fruit, medium to full body, good tannin, adequate acidity, and a long, rich finish. It should be drinkable upon release and age well for 10–15 years.

WILD HORSE WINERY (SAN LUIS OBISPO)

1994 Cabernet Sauvignon	San Luis Obispo	C	86
1995 Chardonnay	Central Coast	C	86
1995 Malvasia Bianca	Monterey	B	89
1994 Merlot	Central Coast	C	86

1995	Pinot Blanc	Monterey	B	87
1994	Pinot Noir	Central Coast	C	85
1995	Zinfandel	Paso Robles	C	74
1994	Zinfandel Cienga Valley	Paso Robles	C	76

These wines rarely deserve the highest scores, but on a value/pleasure quotient, they have merit. I have always enjoyed the whites more than the reds. For example, the 1995 Malvasia Bianca offers an exciting fruit cocktail, apricot/peach-scented nose. Excellent ripeness, lush, richly fruity flavors, and pure, well-balanced winemaking have resulted in a delicious aperitif white for drinking over the next year. The dry, medium-bodied 1995 Pinot Blanc exhibits this varietal's typical crisp, tangerine and orange peel-scented nose, as well as attractive fruit, an elegant personality, and a clean, refreshing, vibrant finish. It needs to be drunk over the next year. The 1995 Chardonnay possesses the honeyed, lemony, citrusy fruit character found in Central Coast Chardonnays, freshness and vibrancy, and fine purity. Drink it over the next 12 months.

As for the red wines, the 1994 Pinot Noir resembles a good Gamay more than a Pinot Noir, but it offers grapey, cherry flavors, light to medium body, freshness, and spice. Serve it chilled, and do not age it for more than 1–2 years. The medium deep ruby-colored 1994 Merlot possesses a fleshy, one-dimensional personality, attractive berry fruit, and a soft texture. The 1994 Cabernet Sauvignon is made as if it were a Merlot—soft, round, fruity, yet reasonably well endowed. Medium bodied, with no hard edges, it is ideal for drinking over the next 3–4 years.

I am a fan of most of this winery's products, but these two Zinfandels are mediocre. The disappointing 1994 Zinfandel Cienga Valley is leafy and lean with abundant green pepper in the nose, but a shortage of ripe fruit. The high acidity and lack of glycerin only exacerbate the wine's fruit deficiency. Even worse is the 1995 Zinfandel Paso Robles. It offers a more distinctive earthy *terroir* character, but is frightfully hard, attenuated, and high in acidity. For a winery known for its ability to extract beautiful fruit from so many different varietals, Wild Horse somehow missed that objective with these two efforts.

WILLIAMS-SELYEM (SONOMA)

1996	Chardonnay	Russian River	E	87
1997	Pinot Noir	Sonoma Coastlands	E	(88–90)
1993	Pinot Noir	Sonoma	D	85
1997	Pinot Noir Allen Vineyard	Russian River	E	(87–89)
1996	Pinot Noir Allen Vineyard	Russian River	E	86
1993	Pinot Noir Cohn Vineyard	Sonoma	E	86
1996	Pinot Noir Ferrington Vineyard	Anderson Valley	E	91
1997	Pinot Noir Hirsch Vineyard	Sonoma Coast	E	(87–89)
1996	Pinot Noir Hirsch Vineyard	Sonoma Coast	E	86+?
1993	Pinot Noir Olivet Lane	Russian River	E	87
1997	Pinot Noir Precious Mountain	Sonoma Coast	E	(88–91)

Williams-Selyem has a near mythical reputation for their wines, which are sold exclusively via a mailing list. This winery was sold in 1997, but Burt Williams has been retained as a consultant to train former Hartford Court winemaker, Bob Cabral. When the history of California wines is written, Williams-Selyem will hold an important place. Not only was it one of the first wineries to exploit the potential of the Sonoma Coast and Russian River, particularly with vineyard-designated Pinot Noir and Chardonnay, but this is the ultimate "garage" winery. It will be interesting to see what direction the new owner follows, as production is scheduled to be increased. Hopefully, the quality can be maintained. All of the following offerings revealed high levels of tangy acidity, a style that allows the winery to utilize extremely low levels of sulfur, a worthy objective.

The 1997 Pinot Noirs possess light ruby colors, aggressive acidity, and copious quantities of the red fruit mélange—kirsch liqueur, strawberries, cherries, and red currants. The 1997 Pinot Noir Allen Vineyard (planted in 1972) exhibits a light ruby color, followed by an attractive, jammy strawberry and toasty oak-scented nose. Medium bodied, with zesty acidity, and a crisp, tart finish, it should drink well for 5–6 years. The 1997 Pinot Noir Sonoma Coastlands exhibits sweeter fruit, intermixed with smoke and *pain grillé*. This wine possesses a lush, Volnay-like personality with considerable seductiveness and intensity. The acidity is noticeable, but not overbearing. Typical of many wines from this area, the well-made 1997 Pinot Noir Hirsch Vineyard displays a forceful structure, and copious spice, earth, and tannin to go along with its black cherry fruit. It is a candidate for several years of cellaring before consumption. It should keep for 7–8 years, but the tannin may be problematic. The medium ruby-colored 1997 Pinot Noir Precious Mountain reveals a sweet, expansive, black cherry nose intermixed with floral notes, smoky, toasty oak, and herbs. Expansive in the mouth, with fine richness, less intrusive acidity than some cuvées, and light tannin in the finish, it should drink well for 5–7 years.

I tasted four 1996 Pinot Noirs on my last visit (all of which have been sold out). Like all Williams-Selyem's Pinots, they are bottled with no fining or filtration after only two rackings. These wines tend to be aged in François Frères Burgundy cooperage, with a high percentage of new oak. The 1996 Pinot Noir Allen Vineyard (13.7% alcohol) is a soft, light ruby-colored wine with good freshness, a stylish, understated, restrained personality, and pleasant berry fruit intermixed with cherries and strawberries. The color is deceptively light for the amount of flavor, but this is reminiscent of a good Côte de Beaune-Villages or premier cru. Drink it over the next 5–6 years. The 1996 Pinot Noir Hirsch Vineyard again reveals the vineyard's high tannin, as well as high acidity, raspberry and cherry fruit, and an intriguing earthy/*terroir*-driven, compressed personality. I found it somewhat austere and acidic, so I am reserving judgment until I can see another bottle in several years. It appears to be a keeper, but the high acidity combined with the high tannin causes me to worry about the wine's balance.

I was extremely impressed by the 1996 Pinot Noir Ferrington Vineyard. It boasts the most concentration, richness, and intensity of any Williams-Selyem Pinot Noirs, with enough extract and richness to balance out the tart acidity. The wine's dark ruby/purple color is followed by sweet black cherry, framboise, and raspberry aromas, with nicely integrated smoky oak. Sweet, floral, and rich, with medium to full body, vibrant acidity and tannin, this beautifully made, hedonistic, rich, fleshy wine will drink well for 5–6 years. Anderson Valley continues to be an intriguing venue for high quality Pinot Noir, as evidenced by such other wineries as Littorai and Siduri. Lastly, the 1996 Pinot Noir Rochioli Vineyard is close to outstanding. The wine possesses a medium ruby color, some of the tart acidity found in most of this winery's 1997 and 1996 Pinots, and good cherry fruit intermixed with earth and spicy new oak. The wine is rich on the attack (primarily jammy strawberries and cherries), but slightly compressed in the finish because of its crisp acids. This youthful wine promises to evolve nicely for 3–5 years.

I also tasted the 1996 Chardonnay Russian River (a whoppingly big wine that tips the scales at an amazing 15.6% alcohol). With some residual sugar (or were the glycerin levels so high as to give the impression of sweetness?), this monolithic, full-bodied, mouth-staining Chardonnay will merit a higher score if it develops more complexity. At present, it is all glycerin and alcohol. It should drink well for 5–6 years.

The Williams-Selyem Winery has long been a reference point for complex, sumptuous Pinot Noir. That being said, I thought the 1993s possessed a degree of herbaceousness and higher acidity than previous releases. The 1993 Olivet Lane Pinot Noir displays an evolved, medium ruby color with garnet and amber at the edge. It offers a fragrant, smoked game, spicy, berry, and herb-scented nose, medium body, good rather than excellent/outstanding concentration, and surprisingly high, tart acidity in the finish. The wine will age well for 3–4 years, but it is not as concentrated or layered as most Williams-Selyem Pinots. The 1993 Sonoma Coast Pinot Noir is made in a cool-climate style with a light to medium ruby color already revealing some lightening at the edge. The nose is spicy and herbaceous, with sweet oak but not as much fruit as one expects from this winery. The wine is medium bodied, slightly tart, with earthy, herb, and cherry flavors presented in a restrained, elegant format. Drink it over the next 3–5 years. Lastly, the 1993 Cohn Vineyard Pinot Noir reveals a similar medium ruby color with some lightening at the edge. The nose offers up moderately intense aromas of earth, herbs, berry fruit, and new oak. With an attractive supple texture, good concentration, adequate acidity, and noticeable alcohol and oak in the finish, this round Pinot should drink well for 3–4 years. As an unabashed fan of this winery's Pinot Noir, I must admit to being uninspired by the 1993s.

CHÂTEAU WOLTNER (NAPA)

1995 Private Reserve Red Howell Mountain	Napa	D	90

Château Woltner has been dedicated to producing Chardonnay from its Howell Mountain vineyard, and their track record with this varietal has been decidedly uninspiring. As many observers will attest, the finest results from Howell Mountain have been Cabernet-based wines. Therefore, it is ironic, but not surprising that Woltner's first red wine release, a proprietary blend of 63% Cabernet Sauvignon and 37% Merlot, may be the best wine this estate has produced. Only 300 cases were made of this complex, classy red made in the style of a topflight Bordeaux. The aromatics consist of cedarwood, earth, black currants, weedy tobacco, and spice. The wine is rich, full bodied, and tannic, with a sweet, concentrated mid-palate, and a long, structured, classy finish. Although not yet ready for prime-time drinking, it is an immensely impressive, outstanding example of a Bordeaux-styled red from the lofty altitudes of Howell Mountain. It was made from grapes harvested in late November, and given a 60-day skin maceration! Anticipated maturity: 2003–2016.

ZACA MESA WINERY (SANTA BARBARA)

1995 Chardonnay Chapel Vineyard	Santa Barbara	C	87
1995 Chardonnay Zaca Vineyard	Santa Barbara	B	87
1993 Cuvée Z	Santa Barbara	B	87
1995 Cuvée Z Proprietary Red Wine	Santa Barbara	C	87
1993 Pinot Noir Winemaker Series-Lane Tanner	Santa Barbara	C	70?
1995 Roussanne Zaca Vineyard	Santa Barbara	C	86
1994 Syrah	Santa Barbara	C	92
1993 Syrah	Santa Barbara	B	90
1995 Syrah Zaca Vineyard	Santa Barbara	C	86

Consumers suffering sticker shock from the marketplace's high prices should take a serious look at the recent offerings from Zaca Mesa. These are all well made, fruity, tasty wines that are meant to provide immediate charm and drinkability. The 1995 Roussanne Zaca Vineyard is an admirable first effort with this varietal. Although it does not remind me of any Roussanne I have tasted in France, I did enjoy the wine's flowery, honeysucklelike fruit, excellent body, and rich, crisp, clean style that does not appear to have seen any time in oak. Drink it over the next year. The 1995 Chardonnay Zaca Vineyard is a tropical fruit-scented and -flavored wine with medium body, lusty fruit, and an easygoing, uncomplicated, mouth-filling style. The 1995 Chardonnay Chapel Vineyard reveals more spicy, vanillin-tinged oak to accompany the copious amounts of tropical fruit. It is a soft, opulently textured wine that needs to be drunk over the next 12 months.

One of the breakthroughs for Zaca Mesa has been their work in the Rhône Ranger field. The 1993 Cuvée Z (a 49% Grenache/43% Mourvèdre/8% Syrah blend from vineyards in Santa Barbara) reveals plenty of tasty, peppery, berry fruit, medium to full body, a soft, lush, opulent palate, and a fleshy, funky but delicious finish. Drink it over the next 3–4 years. Zaca Mesa's efforts with Syrah are even more impressive as they are blending in Viognier in an attempt, I suspect, to make a Guigal La Mouline-like wine (which is a blend of 10% Viognier/90% Syrah). However, La Mouline sells for $150–$250 a bottle, whereas Zaca Mesa's Syrah retails for $14–$16. The 1993 Syrah (95% Syrah/5% Viognier) is a marvelous wine. The dark ruby/purple color is followed by a knockout nose of honeysuckle, apricots, and gobs of rich, sweet, black raspberry and cassis fruit. The wine offers a creamy texture, full body, and a long, lusty finish. This wine is far too delectable to ignore. But there is even better news! The 1994 Syrah, blended with 10% Viognier, is significantly better! Readers are advised to be on the lookout for it. Discounters will probably sell it for $12–$13 a bottle, making it unquestionably one of the richest, most hedonistic wines per penny spent that I have tasted and reviewed. The wine offers an opaque purple color, an exceptional nose of sweet berry fruit (jammy cassis, tropical fruits, and overripe peaches), a full-bodied, viscous, satiny smooth texture, and outstanding flavor extraction. This is a harmonious, gorgeously rich Syrah that may ultimately turn out to be Santa Barbara's answer to Côte Rôtie. Don't dare miss it!

The reds also include the 1995 Cuvée Z, a blend of 47% Mourvèdre, 31% Grenache, 15% Syrah, and 7% Cinsault. It offers up gobs of strawberry and cassis fruit in a medium-bodied, richly fruity, exuberant style. With its gushingly fruity style and bold personality, this wine provides plenty of punch and enjoyment. It does not knock me over to the extent the 1993 did, but this is the ideal bistro/café wine. The 1995 Syrah Zaca Vineyard is a blend of 90% Syrah and 10% Viognier. It offers up a spicy, exotic, bacon fat, black currant-scented nose, ripe, round, medium-bodied, juicy fruit flavors, and a surprisingly soft, succulent texture for a Syrah. Drink it over the next 5–6 years.

I do not understand Pinot Noirs made in such a low pH, high-acid (how much of it added?), vegetal style. Zaca Mesa's tart 1993 Winemaker Series-Lane Tanner possesses high acidity that keeps the taster from appreciating any of the sweet fruit component the wine may possess. The vegetal nose and lean, hard, tart flavors are unexciting.

ZD WINERY (NAPA)

1995 Cabernet Sauvignon	Napa	D	88
1994 Cabernet Sauvignon	Napa	D	90
1993 Cabernet Sauvignon	Napa	C	88+
1993 Cabernet Sauvignon Reserve	Napa	D	89+
1996 Chardonnay	California	D	87
1995 Chardonnay	California	C	86

The 1993 Cabernet Sauvignon is a muscular, heavyweight style of Cabernet Sauvignon. It possesses a dense, black/purple color, lavish quantities of toasty oak, plenty of glycerin and alcohol, and chewy, thick texture. Although somewhat monolithic, it is so impressively endowed that it deserves enthusiastic notes. While it will never be the most complex, fragrant, or suave Cabernet, it should age effortlessly for 2 decades.

The dark purple-colored, lavishly oaked 1993 Cabernet Sauvignon Reserve is spicy, ripe, full bodied, dense, and chewy. Readers should appreciate the abundant cassis, currant, earthy flavors of this grapey wine. Cellar it for 4–5 more years and drink it over the subsequent 20 years. The opaque purple-colored, exotic 1994 Cabernet Sauvignon is also generously wooded, with smoky black raspberry and cassis aromas. Medium to full bodied, with copious amounts of fruit, and soft tannin, this luscious, youthful, grapey Cabernet can be drunk now, but it promises to be better with 2–3 years of cellaring; it should keep for 12–15 years.

Based on previous vintages, the 1995 Chardonnay is not as rich or exuberant as I had expected. It exhibits ripe pineapple/pearlike fruit in its boldly oaked nose. After a good attack with medium body and fine fruit, the wine quickly dissipates on the palate. I would opt for drinking it over the next 8–12 months.

A big, toasty, butterscotch, lavishly oaked wine, the light gold-colored 1996 Chardonnay offers gobs of glycerin, a thick, juicy personality, and medium to full body. It is an old style, heavily wooded, bold Chardonnay that should be consumed over the next year. The "American-styled" 1995 Cabernet Sauvignon has plenty of macho power, lavish quantities of toasty new oak, and straightforward, pleasing, ripe black currant fruit. Attractive, savory, and mouth-filling, the wine is medium to full bodied, monolithic, and cleanly made, with 10–15 years of evolution ahead of it.

6. OREGON

The Basics

TYPES OF WINE
Oregon makes wine from most of the same grapes as California, although the cooler, more marginal climate in Oregon's best viticultural area, the Willamette Valley, has meant more success with cool-climate varietals such as Pinot Noir, than with hotter-climate varietals such as Cabernet Sauvignon, Merlot, Syrah, and Grenache. Chardonnay, Riesling, and Sauvignon Blanc have done well in Oregon, but the great white hope here is Pinot Gris, which has shown fine potential and a knack for being the perfect partner for the salmon of the Pacific Northwest. There is also believed to be good potential for high-quality sparkling wine in Oregon. Oregon's wines are distinctive, with a kinship to European wines. The higher natural acidities, lower alcohol content, and more subtle nature of Oregon's wines bode well for this area's future.

GRAPE VARIETIES
Chardonnay   Oregon can make some wonderful Chardonnay, but far too many winemakers have let it spend too much time in oak and have not chosen the best clones for their vineyards. The Chardonnay grape is naturally high in acidity in Oregon, and therein lies the principal difference between Chardonnay grown in Oregon and that grown in California. In California the majority of Chardonnays must have tartaric acid added to them for balance. In Oregon the wines must be put through a secondary or malolactic fermentation, à la Burgundy, in order to lower their acids. The high quality of Chardonnays produced from recent plantings of Dijon clones indicate that Oregon may have found the answer to its clonal problems with this varietal.

Pinot Gris   This is the hardest wine to find, as virtually all of it is sold and drunk before it has a chance to leave Oregon. However, winery owners, knowing a hot item, are planting as much of it as they can get their hands on. Fruitier and creamier than Chardonnay, Pinot Gris, from the world's most underrated great white wine grape, can be a delicious, opulent, smoky wine with every bit as much character and even more aging potential than Chardonnay. While it is a specialty of Oregon, much of it is mediocre and diluted.

Note: Robert M. Parker Jr. has a one-third interest in an Oregon vineyard that was commercially bonded in 1992 and began selling wine in 1993. Because of an obvious conflict of interest, this wine will never be mentioned or reviewed in anything written by me.

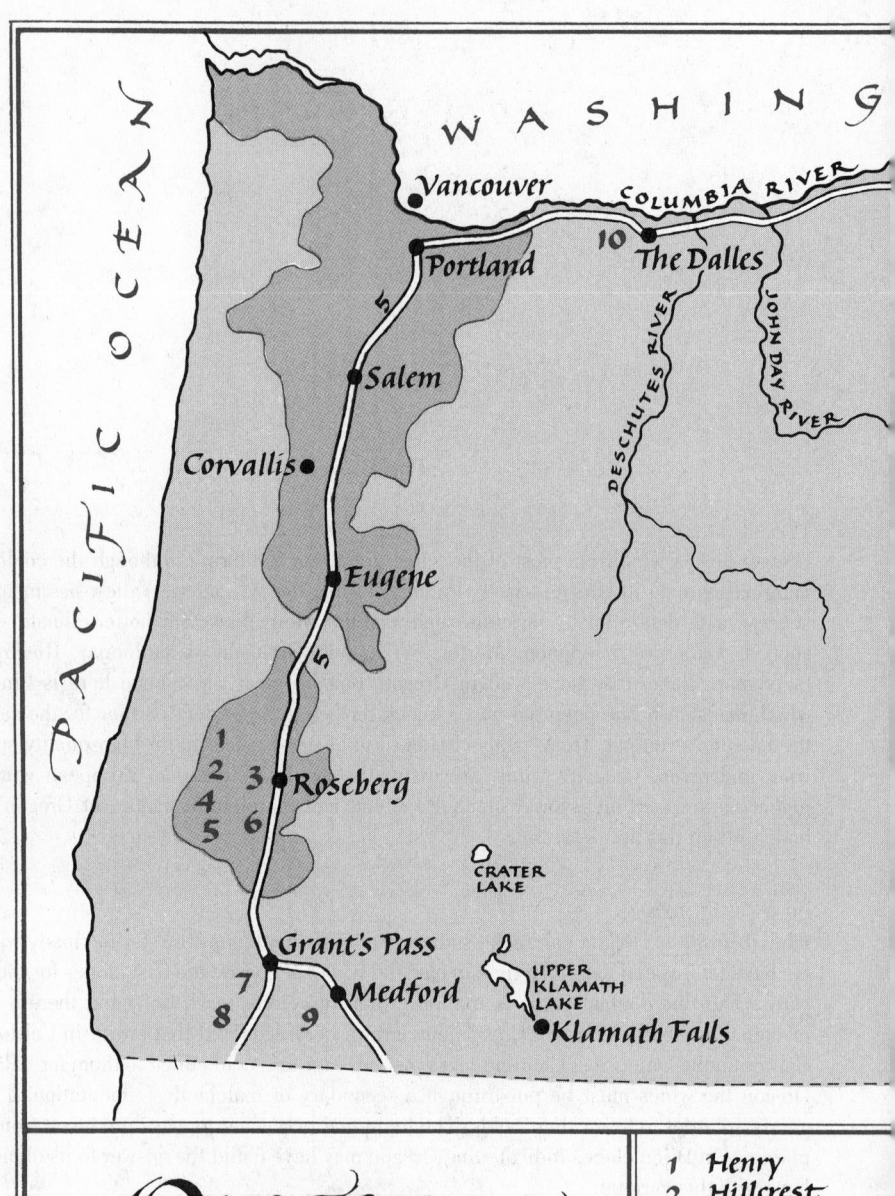

Oregon

1	Henry
2	Hillcrest
3	Garden Valley
4	Bjelland
5	Giradet

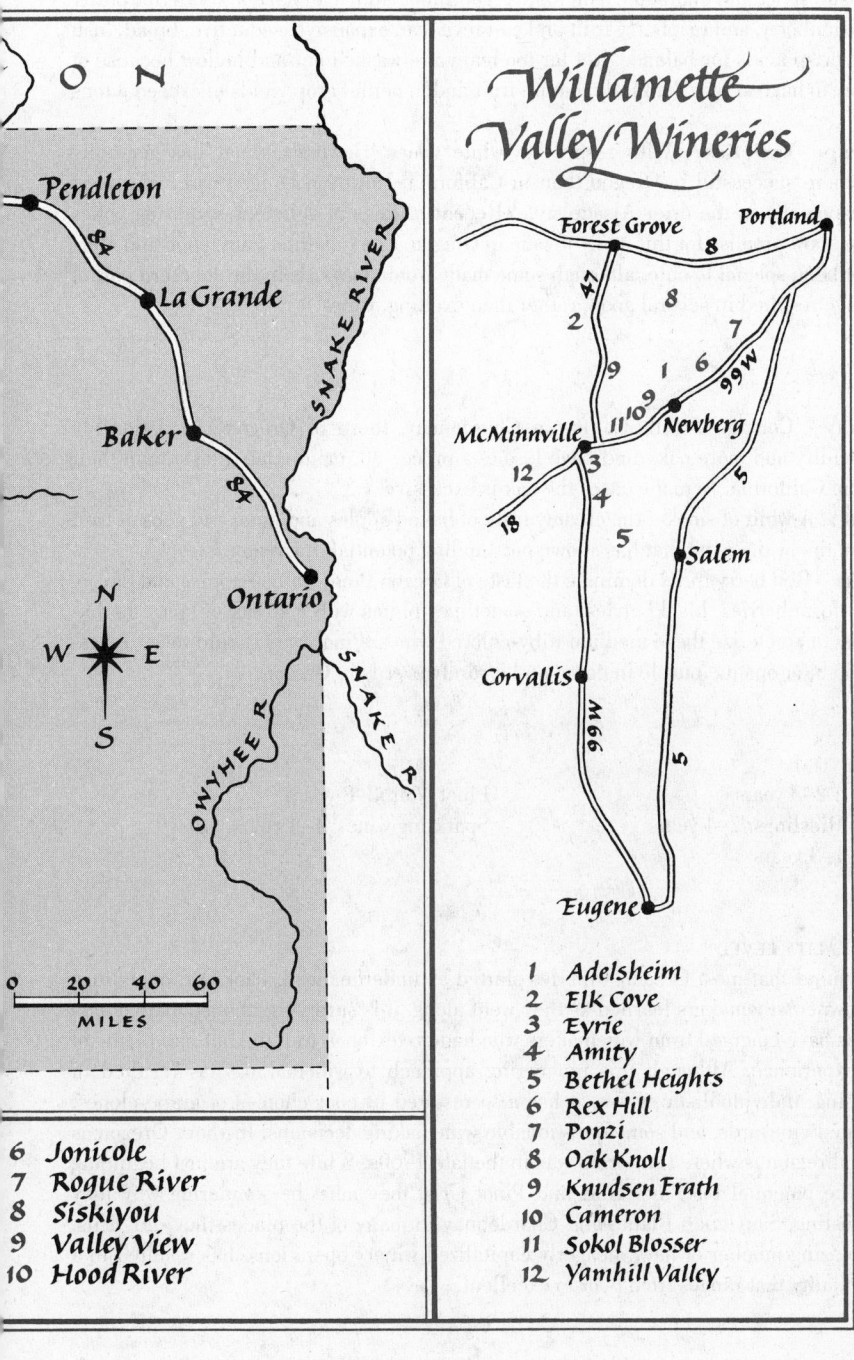

Willamette Valley Wineries

ON

Pendleton

84

La Grande

84

Baker

Ontario

SNAKE RIVER

OWYHEER R.

SNAKE R.

N
W   E
S

0   20   40   60
MILES

Forest Grove   Portland
47   8
            8
2
9   1   6   7
11 10 9   99W
McMinnville   Newberg
12   3
        4   5
18   5
            Salem

Corvallis

99W

5

Eugene

1   Adelsheim
2   Elk Cove
3   Eyrie
4   Amity
5   Bethel Heights
6   Rex Hill
7   Ponzi
8   Oak Knoll
9   Knudsen Erath
10   Cameron
11   Sokol Blosser
12   Yamhill Valley

6   Jonicole
7   Rogue River
8   Siskiyou
9   Valley View
10   Hood River

Pinot Noir   As in Burgundy, the soil, yield per acre, choice of fermentation yeasts, competence of the winemaker, and type of oak barrel in which this wine is aged profoundly influences its taste, style, and character. The top Oregon Pinot Noirs can have a wonderful purity of cherry, loganberry, and raspberry fruit and can reveal an expansive, seductive, broad, lush palate, and crisp acids for balance. Yet far too many are washed out and hollow because of the tendency to harvest less than fully mature fruit and to permit crop yields to exceed 3 tons per acre.

Other Grape Varieties   With respect to white wines, Gewürztraminer has generally proven no more successful in Oregon than in California. However, Oregon can make good Riesling, especially in the drier Alsace style. Recent tastings of delicious sparkling wines from Argyle show promise for this style of wine in Oregon. The Cabernet Sauvignon and Merlot have not been special to date, although some made from vineyards in the southern part of the state have resulted in several good, rather than exciting, wines.

FLAVORS

Chardonnay   Compared with California Chardonnay, those of Oregon are noticeably higher in acidity and more oaky and have less of a processed, manipulated taste than their siblings from California. In many cases the oak is excessive.

Pinot Gris   A whiff of smoke, the creamy taste of baked apples and nuts, and gobs of fruit characterize this white wine that has shown outstanding potential in Oregon.

Pinot Noir   Red berry fruits dominate the taste of Oregon Pinot Noirs. Aromas and flavors of cherries, loganberries, blackberries, and sometimes plums with a streak of spicy, herbaceous scents characterize these medium ruby-colored wines. Pinot Noir should never be astringent, harsh, or opaque purple in color, and it rarely ever is in Oregon.

AGING POTENTIAL

Chardonnay: 2–5 years   Pinot Noir: 3–8 years
Dry/off-dry Rieslings: 2–4 years   Sparkling wines: 1–4 years
Pinot Gris: 1–3 years

OVERALL QUALITY LEVEL

Bearing in mind that most Oregon wineries started as underfinanced, backyard operations where the owner/winemakers learned as they went along, it is surprising that so many interesting wines have emerged from winemakers who had no textbook training but had plenty of hands-on experience. Although this pioneering approach to winemaking has resulted in some stunning, individualistic wines, it has also resulted in poor choices of grape clones, poorly planted vineyards, and some questionable winemaking decisions. In short, Oregon as a viticultural region is where California was in the late 1960s. While they are just beginning to realize the potential for Pinot Noir and Pinot Gris, they must be wondering why they planted Riesling, Sauvignon Blanc, and Chardonnay in many of the places they did. This, plus the amazing number of new, meagerly capitalized winery operations, has resulted in a pattern of quality that ranges from poor to excellent.

MOST IMPORTANT INFORMATION TO KNOW

To purchase good wine, know the best wineries and their best wines. However, some additional information worth knowing is that the finest Pinot Noirs generally come from a stretch of vineyards in the Willamette Valley southwest of Portland. For Cabernet Sauvignon and

Merlot, the warmer Umpqua Valley to the south, and the Grant's Pass area farther south are better regions for those varietals.

VINTAGE GUIDE

1997—Initial reports out of Oregon were guarded but good; however, it appears that the producers were voicing hopes more than reality. Preliminary tastings of the vintage indicates that many wineries were caught with unripened fruit still on the vines when the rains appeared. Tannins are rough, and only on rare occasions does the fruit rarely appear likely to take the upper hand. As it happens, 1998 may be—from initial reports—a great vintage reminiscent of 1994.

1996—Oregon wineries deserved a reprieve from Mother Nature after what she did to them in 1995. However, that was not to be. While 1996 is a slightly better vintage than 1995, it is far from good. Rains were again the bane of producers, particularly those with high-yielding vineyards. The 1996s are austere, with firm tannins, and offer darker fruit flavors than is usually found in Oregon Pinots. In time, the tannins in the finest 1996s may melt away, allowing the fruit to blossom. However, this vintage will never be mistaken for a great year. The 1996 whites appear to be of good quality, yet their profiles suggest they will need to be drunk in the near term.

1995—After a string of good to outstanding vintages (1988–1994), things were bound to change. And change they did. Overall, 1995 is a poor vintage for Oregon, with only a handful of excellent to outstanding Pinot Noirs being crafted. Rain, rot, and poor winemaking were the culprits.

1994—This is Oregon's best vintage of the nineties, and certainly one of its very best ever. Low yields (the results of poor weather during the flowering season) and a warm summer resulted in the most concentrated and fruit-packed Oregon Pinot Noirs in memory. In fact, 1994, as with all great vintages, was such a wonderful year for Pinot Noir that even some underachieving estates crafted fine wines. Recent tastings indicate that the 1994 Pinot Noirs are quite ageworthy, as the finest have the fruit and tannic structure to last another 5–8 years. However, this is an irregular vintage for Pinot Gris and Chardonnay, with their quality ranging from excellent to mediocre, depending on the harvest date.

1993—A cool summer followed by warm weather in September and October resulted in a vintage that appears to have eclipsed 1992. The top Pinot Noirs reveal voluptuous textures, fragrant personalities, and a suppleness and richness that suggest this may be a breakthrough vintage for Oregon Pinot Noir. The limited quantities produced by the finest producers will make the top wines hard to find.

1992—This could have been the finest vintage for Oregon Pinot Noirs in decades. The weather was almost too hot and dry. However, beneficial rains arrived toward the end of the growing season and alleviated what was considerable stress in many of the hillside vineyards. Unfortunately, too many producers, worried about low acidity, used a heavy hand when adding acidity, resulting in many wines with incongruous personalities—very ripe flavors and tart, lean-textured personalities. Nevertheless, some terrific Pinot Noirs and big, dramatic, ostentatious Chardonnays have emerged. The Chardonnays must be drunk up, but the finest Pinot Noirs will keep for a decade.

1991—This is a very good, potentially excellent, vintage of wines that does not have the power or drama of the 1992s or the intensity of the 1990s. Nevertheless, rain at the end of the harvest caught those growers who had excessive crop yields and were waiting for further maturity. For that reason this is a tricky vintage to handicap, but certainly the Pinot Noirs look richly fruity, although softer and less structured than the 1992s and less tannic than the 1990s. It has good potential for high-quality wine—both red and white.

1990—A top vintage if yields were kept to a minimum, 1990 had plenty of heat and adequate rain, and the harvest occurred under ideal conditions. In fact, if it were not for 1992, this would be the best Oregon vintage in several decades. From the top producers, the Pinot Noirs are rich and full, as are some of the Chardonnays. If there is a disappointment, it is that many of the Pinot Gris wines lack concentration because yields were too high.

1989—This is a good vintage for Pinot Noir, Chardonnay, and Pinot Gris. The wines may not have the intensity of the 1990s, but they are generally rich, soft, elegant wines. In many respects it is a more typical, classic vintage for Oregon's best producers than 1990 or 1992.

1988—The first of an amazing succession of good years for the Oregon wine business. Fine weather, an abundant crop, and a trouble-free harvest have resulted in a number of excellent Pinot Noirs and Chardonnays.

1987—An excessively hot year resulted in most growers harvesting too soon because they were afraid of losing acidity in their grapes. However, the stress of the summer's heat caused many vineyards not to reach physiological maturity. As a consequence, many 1987s are lean, too acidic, and disappointing. Six years after the vintage the best wines still have a hard edge. It is unlikely they will ever fully blossom. If only the growers had waited!

OLDER VINTAGES

As a general rule, most Oregon Pinot Noirs must be consumed within 7–8 years of the vintage. There are always a few exceptions, as anyone who has tasted the 1975 Eyrie or 1975 Knudsen Erath Pinot Noirs can attest. But in general, aging Oregon Pinot Noir for longer than 7–8 years is a dangerous gamble.

Oregon's white wines should be drunk within several years of the vintage, even though they tend to have better natural acidity than their California counterparts. Yields are frequently too high and the extract levels questionable, so whether it is Pinot Gris, Chardonnay, or dry Riesling, if you are not drinking these wines within 3–4 years of the vintage, you are more likely to be disappointed than pleasantly surprised.

RATING OREGON'S BEST PRODUCERS OF PINOT NOIR

* * * * * (OUTSTANDING)

Domaine Serene	Ken Wright

* * * * (EXCELLENT)

Adelsheim	Domaine Drouhin
Archery Summit	Evesham Wood
Brickhouse	Panther Creek****/*****
Cristom****/*****	St. Innocent

* * * (GOOD)

Argyle***/****	Rex Hill***/****
Bethel Heights***/****	Torii Mor
Foris	WillaKenzie Estate***/****
Ponzi	

* * (AVERAGE)

The Academy**/***	Château Bianca
Amity**/***	Bridgeview
Autumn Wind	Broadley
Château Benoit	Callahan Ridge
Benton Lane	Chehalem**/***

Cooper Mountain

Duck Pond Cellars

Edgefield**/***

Elk Cove

Eola Hills

Erath Vineyards**/***

Firesteed

Fisher Family Vineyards

Flynn Vineyards

Girardet Cellars**/***

Golden Valley Vineyards**/***

Henry Estate Winery

High Pass Winery

Hinman Vineyards**/***

King Estate

Krist Hill

Medici Vineyards

Montinore Vineyards

Sokol Blosser**/***

Stag's Hollow Vineyards

Stangeland

Starr**/***

Tualatin Vineyards

Valley View Vineyard**/***

Westrey

Willamette Valley Vineyard**/***

Wine Country Farm Cellars

ADELSHEIM VINEYARD

1995 Elizabeth's Reserve Pinot Noir	D	86
1996 Oregon Pinot Noir	C	86*
1995 Polk County Seven Springs Vineyard Pinot Noir	D	85
1996 Ridge Crest Vineyards Willamette Valley Pinot Noir	D	86+*

The ruby-colored 1996 Oregon Pinot Noir has cherry and herbal aromas followed by a medium-bodied, silky-textured, and well-balanced character. Powerful flavors of black cherries are intertwined with hints of plums and minerals in this delicious wine. Anticipated maturity: 2000–2003. The darker-colored 1996 Ridgecrest Vineyards Willamette Valley Pinot Noir reveals cassis and blackberry aromas. This juicy, firm wine offers flavors of blueberry, black cherry, and road tar, is medium bodied and ripe, and finishes on a slightly tannic note. It is riper, denser, and more extracted than Adelsheim's Oregon Pinot but is not as generous. If this offering softens, it will merit a better rating. Anticipated maturity: 2001–2004.

According to Don Kautezner, 1995 was the second most difficult vintage he has faced in his 15 years as Adelsheim's winemaker (the worst was 1984, where rot, combined with unripened grapes, made Oregon winemakers feel as if they were participants in a Stephen King horror novel). There was so much rot on the grapes in 1995 that sorting was carried out in the vineyards by hand prior to destemming. Carrying the harvest back to the winery was not an option for Kautezner, as the rot-infested grapes would infect the few healthy ones. The sorting paid off, as both the Seven Springs and Elizabeth's Reserve bottlings show no signs of off flavors (the regular bottling does have some disturbing scents and flavors).

Produced from about 2 tons of fruit per acre, and aged in 18%–20% new oak, the medium ruby-colored 1995 Polk County Seven Springs Vineyard Pinot Noir is made from 15-year-old vines. It displays blackberry, currant, and stone aromas as well as a medium-bodied, oily-textured, mineral, and black cherry-filled character. Its finish is a little hard and dry at this stage, but it should soften over the coming year. Drink it between 1998 and 2000. Adelsheim's top cuvée, the Elizabeth's Reserve Pinot Noir is crafted from one of Oregon's oldest vineyards (planted in 1973). Aged in 33% new oak barrels, the 1995 displays a bril-

---

*When I tasted these offerings they were reductive (the opposite of oxidative). Aeration dramatically helped them shed the rubber and raw meat aromas associated with this condition. Cellaring them for 2–3 years should also resolve this problem. Readers who wish to consume them in the near term should decant them before serving. The notes offered here are from bottles that were allowed to breathe for a number of hours.

liant ruby color as well as a perfumed and red berry-laced nose. It possesses a medium to full body and a tightly wound core of dark fruit, smoky bacon, and herbs that is hidden behind a shell of hard tannin. Drink it between 2000 and 2004.

ARCHERY SUMMIT

1996 Oregon Pinot Noir Premier Cuvée	D	86
1995 Pinot Noir	D	85
1996 Pinot Noir Arcus Estate	E	88
1995 Pinot Noir Arcus Estate	E	88
1996 Pinot Noir Red Hills Estate	E	88+
1995 Pinot Noir Red Hills Estate	E	88
1997 Vireton (Blanc des Collines Rouges)	D	87

Gary Andrus, the managing director of this estate, is an accomplished winemaker and a certified bon vivant. A former Olympic downhill skier, Andrus is known primarily for his Cabernet- and Chardonnay-producing Pine Ridge Estate in California. He is, however, a devoted lover of Pinot Noir, traveling to Burgundy frequently to taste and purchase wines for his cellar. His tastes seem to have been shaped by his frequent travels to France, because his wines are quite Burgundian in nature—graceful, complex, and with darker fruit than many of his neighbors. There is no doubt that he is crafting some of Oregon's finest wines.

It is obvious, as one visits Archery Summit's new state-of-the-art winery, that Andrus and his business partners spared no expense in building a dream workplace. From the moment grapes arrive at harvest they are moved only via gravity. No pumping of wines is ever necessary. The facility is so large, in fact, that other wineries are using it to craft their wines at the same time as Andrus makes Archery Summit's many cuvées. Long tunnels have been dug into the hillside to provide plenty of storage space for their barrel-aging regime.

The medium ruby-colored 1995 Pinot Noir (2,000 case production) aromatically displays warm cinnamon and black currants and an oily-textured, medium-bodied personality with strawberry, cassis, and smoked salt pork flavors. Its vast quantities of fruit make up for this wine's relatively hard finish. Drink it between 1999 and 2002. Andrus produces microscopic quantities of two "reserve" bottlings. The medium to dark ruby-colored 1995 Arcus Estate Pinot Noir (1,000 bottles) has elegant red fruit and perfumed aromatics as well as a silky, medium- to full-bodied mouthful of graceful red and black fruits and flowers. The Arcus is feminine, floral, and delicate when compared with the more masculine, brawny, and powerful medium to dark ruby-colored 1995 Red Hills Estate Pinot Noir (1,000 bottles). Revealing intense blackberries and cassis aromatically, this medium- to full-bodied and oily-textured wine is jam-packed with chewy dark fruits and judicious quantities of new oak. Its long finish ends on strong tannin and notes of kirsch. Both of these wines should be drunk between now and 2004.

As Gary Andrus, Archery Summit's owner, served his 1997 Vireton (Blanc des Collines Rouges), I asked what we were about to taste. "It's only white wine," came the smiling response. It is crafted from a blend of varietals that are vinified separately and then blended together into the final *assemblage* (Andrus admits only to a high percentage of Pinot Gris). This wine has a lively, smoky, floral, and white fruit-scented nose. It is satin textured and medium bodied, has excellent balance, and reveals ripe pears intertwined with toasted hazelnut flavors. It may be only a white wine, but it is refreshing, delicious, and intriguingly different. Drink it over the next 2–3 years.

According to Andrus, Archery Summit's tightly spaced Pinot Noir vineyards yielded 1.46

tons per acre in 1996, with the harvest starting on September 26 and ending as the rains began on October 2. This estate's 1996s are extremely good, expressing the vintage's dark fruit character but not suffering from 1996's firm tannins.

The medium to dark ruby-colored 1996 Pinot Noir Premier Cuvée is reminiscent of a well-made Savigny. It offers metallic, brambleberry, and sweet red berry aromas as well as a gorgeously silky texture and medium body. Juicy red cherries, blueberries, and oak spices can be found in its lovely flavor profile. It will be at its best if drunk over the next 3–4 years. The slightly darker-colored 1996 Arcus Estate Pinot Noir exhibits a fresh, spicy, floral, candle wax-scented nose. On the palate, this juicy, medium- to full-bodied, and silky-textured wine has loads of blueberry and black raspberry flavors that last throughout its long and oak-spiced finish. Anticipated maturity: now–2003+. The 1996 Red Hills Estate Pinot Noir is dark ruby colored and displays a wild (verging on gamey) nose of cinnamon, clove, and juniper berry-laced black fruits. This powerful wine is broad shouldered, masculine, medium to full bodied, and packed with sweet cherry, blackberry, and metallic flavors. Anticipated maturity: 2000–2005.

ARGYLE

1995 Knudsen Vineyards Brut	D	86
1996 Reserve Pinot Noir	D	86
1996 Reserve Chardonnay	C	87

By Oregon standards, Argyle is a large winery, having produced 16,000 cases of wine in 1997. Its owner, the Dundee Wine Company (a partnership between Carl Knudsen and an Australian corporation), also operates a large vineyard management company (run by Allen Holstein) that is responsible for 350 acres of land (including Domaine Drouhin's property).

Rollin Soles, Argyle's winemaker, says that he gets "chill bones" from sparkling wines. Whether this means he fears the intricate process necessary for their production or whether it is because he loves drinking them escapes me. However, one thing is certain: Soles's sparklers are delicious and rank among the best being fashioned in the New World. Soles believes that Oregon's climate, particularly on the hillsides, is very much like Champagne's (unlike California and Australia, which are much warmer). He therefore obtains the requisite natural acidity and ripeness of fruit to make dry yet flavorful sparkling wines.

The 1995 Knudsen Vineyards Brut has aromas of pears and toasted nuts that also follow through in the wine's flavor profile. This well-crafted, refreshing, and dry sparkling wine is light to medium bodied and very flavorful and should be drunk over the next 2–3 years.

While Argyle is known primarily for its sparklers, still wines constitute 45%–50% of its production. The Chardonnays are produced from the vineyards of Carl Knudsen (formerly a principal at Knudsen-Erath). As with many Oregon producers, the team at Argyle believes the Dijon clone of Chardonnay produces a riper, more balanced, and more ageworthy wine than the California clones (primarily UCD4). Since 1990 this winery's in-house nursery has been propagating, growing, and grafting Knudsen's original vines with the Dijon clone. At present Argyle's series of Reserve Chardonnays are produced entirely from Dijon clonal material.

Superripe aromas of bananas with sweet vanilla icing and hints of minerals can be found in the nose of the 1996 Reserve Chardonnay. This rich, thick, oily-textured, and medium- to full-bodied wine offers candied pears, anise, tropical fruit, and toasted oak flavors. It should be drunk over the next 3–4 years.

The medium ruby-colored 1996 Reserve Pinot Noir has cinnamon, black cherry, and oak spice aromas. This medium- to full-bodied wine offers blackberry and sage flavors in its highly structured and firm personality. Drink it between 2000 and 2003.

BETHEL HEIGHTS VINEYARD

1996 Chardonnay	C	85
1996 Chardonnay Reserve	C	87
1996 Flat Block Reserve Pinot Noir	D	87
1996 Southeast Block Reserve Pinot Noir	D	87+

While most people seem to derive pleasure in the commonalities they find between Burgundy and Oregon, I love the differences. As I approached Bethel Heights, climbing the gravel road that leads up a steep hill, I was overjoyed to see a field with grazing sheep and llamas adjacent to the winery. While Côte d'Or *vignerons* of Henri Jayer's generation can remember grazing farm animals, the younger ones have no such memories. Certainly no living Burgundian can remember having to devise innovative techniques to protect livestock from wolves (the reason for the llamas) and vineyard trellises from elk, as Oregonians must.

Bethel Heights, like many Oregon wineries, has to confront the grim reaper of vineyards—phylloxera. While this vine-killing louse has not yet attacked this estate's vineyards, it is firmly entrenched in those of Bethel Height's neighbors. Sadly, this region's oldest Pinot Noir vines, dating back to the mid- to late seventies, are vulnerable to phylloxera because they were not planted on resistant root stock. Ted Casteel, responsible for this estate's viticulture, is presently replacing many of the estate's oldest vines with new plantings.

The 1996 Chardonnay displays aromas reminiscent of toasted bread, pears, and hazelnuts. This silky-textured, well-balanced, and floral wine has nut-laden flavors, good grip, and medium body. Ideally it should be drunk over the next 2 years. The 1996 Chardonnay Reserve is lovely. Anise, white flowers, and almond scents give way to a spiced apple, hazelnut cream, butterscotch-flavored core. This well-defined yet mouth-filling, medium- to full-bodied beauty has excellent depth. Anticipated maturity: now–2002.

Unlike with the whites, Terry Casteel (Ted's brother as well as the estate's winemaker) uses only indigenous yeasts when crafting his Pinot Noirs. While I found two of his 1996 reds (the Estate and Eola Hills Cuvée) to be just below the recommended range for these notes, I was impressed with both reserve offerings. The 1996 Pinot Noir Flat Block Reserve is ruby colored, and sweet blackberry scented and offers an attractive medium-bodied and velvety-textured character. This well-endowed wine coats the palate with intense blueberry, blackberry, and plum flavors. Anticipated maturity: now–2003. The slightly darker-colored Pinot Noir Southeast Block Reserve is more austere, backward, and tannic, yet it may ultimately be the more complete wine. It reveals deep-dish cherry pie aromas and a highly structured flavor profile crammed with blackberries and cassis. This medium- to full-bodied offering will never have a silky-soft finish, yet its beautifully ripened fruit will provide pleasure to drinkers between 2002 and 2005.

BRICK HOUSE

1995 Pinot Noir	C	87
1996 Cuvée du Tonnelier Pinot Noir	D	88+
1995 Cuvée du Tonnelier Pinot Noir	D	88?
1996 Willamette Valley Chardonnay	C	87
1996 Willamette Valley Pinot Noir	D	87+

Former television newsman Doug Tunnell abandoned the klieg lights and fame of network news to live in a small brick house (hence the name) and produce some of Oregon's finest wines. Employing organic viticulture and inquisitive winemaking (Tunnell loves to experiment), he has in a few short years rocketed to the top echelon of the area's producers.

Tunnell, a former CBS foreign correspondent, and currently Brick House's owner and head laborer, was in the vineyards on his tractor when I arrived to taste the 1996s. Watching him make his way to the winery on a perfect spring day made it easy to understand why in 1990 he made a sudden career change.

The 1996 Willamette Valley Chardonnay, produced from vines planted in 1992, has lovely aromas of toasted hazelnuts and an oily-textured, medium-bodied personality. This seductive, dense, and flavorful wine excites the palate with its spiced pear, anise, butterscotch, and vanilla-infused oak flavors. Drink it over the next 3 years.

In 1996 the difference between Brick House's regular Pinot Noir and its Cuvée du Tonnelier is the harvest date. The former was harvested on October 11 and the latter 1 week later. This extra week of hang time (and rain) resulted in softer tannins in the reserve bottling. The Willamette Valley Pinot Noir is ruby colored and has a warm and embracing nose of blackberries with traces of mocha. This creamed cherry-flavored wine is medium bodied, thick, and rich and has excellent palate presence yet finishes on a slightly rough and tannic note. Tunnell lightly fined it with 1 egg white per barrel to soften its tannins. No fining was performed on the softer Cuvée du Tonnelier. Both wines are eerily similar in their profiles. For example, the Tonnelier offers additional aromatic touches of cinnamon and possibly a silkier texture on the midpalate, with more intense blueberry flavors. The finish, however, is ripe, soft, and verging on plush. Both of these beauties have the potential to get better with cellaring. Drink them between now and 2004.

Harvested at 1.75 tons per acre, the 1995 Pinot Noir reveals rich and sweet aromas reminiscent of strawberries and root beer. A highly defined and structured, well-delineated, medium- to full-bodied core of ripe cherries, stones, and minerals further characterizes this delicious wine. Its long finish possesses a strong tannic backbone that will require a few years of cellaring. Anticipated maturity: now–2003. Shockingly, the aromas of the medium ruby-colored 1995 Cuvée du Tonnelier Pinot Noir (the name means "the Cooper's Cuvée") brought back memories of eating bananas Foster back when it was a popular dessert in the seventies. Cream, chocolate, caramel, banana, sweetness, and a spicy alcoholic warmth—it was all there in my glass! The wonderfully complex nose is followed by an intense blackberry, dark cherry, earth-tinged, thick, medium- to full-bodied character with excellent staying power. The question mark is due to the dominating wood flavors and slightly hot alcoholic finish. Anticipated maturity: now–2002.

CHEHALEM

1996 NYSA Vineyard Pinot Noir	D	86+?

Chehalem is the talk of Oregon. It seemed that everywhere I went people were extolling the qualities of this estate's wines. My tastings of their wines (both the 1995s and 1996s) left me as the odd man out. Generally I found the wines to be disjointed, dominated by oak, too tannic, and lacking in fruit. Only one Chehalem, the 1996 NYSA Vineyard Pinot Noir, merited a rating above the 85-point cutoff. It has a black cherry, cassis, oak spice-laden nose, followed by a dense and full-flavored core of blackberries and cherries. This medium- to full-bodied wine exhibits impressive layers of well-ripened fruit that might one day make this review appear excessively conservative. Only time will tell if its hard tannins will continue to dominate the wine or melt away.

CRISTOM

1996 Celilo Vineyard Chardonnay (Wash. State)	C	87
1996 Louise Vineyard Pinot Noir	D	88
1996 Marjorie Vineyard Pinot Noir	D	90
1996 Mt. Jefferson Cuvée Pinot Noir	C	87

1996 Reserve Pinot Noir	D 90
1995 Reserve Pinot Noir	D 87

Cristom was operating on all cylinders in 1996. I tasted the estate's four Pinots three times (once at the winery and twice in Washington, D.C.). Paul Gerrie, Cristom's owner, and Steve Doerner, its winemaker, are committed to crafting Burgundian-style wines with finesse and sweet, well-ripened fruit. Neither is a fan of what they referred to as "the overpowering burgundies now in vogue," preferring to make their wines in what they define as a classical style. They tend to utilize 50% whole clusters for their indigenous yeast-driven alcoholic fermentations. If it is a particularly cool vintage in which the stems are unripe, the percentage of stems is reduced to 30%.

The estate's oldest parcel, the Marjorie vineyard, was planted in 1983 and 1984, when this property was called Mirassou Cellars. Interestingly, it has 605 vines per acre, while the more recently planted parcels (such as the Louise vineyard) boast 2,300 vines per acre. This dramatic difference in the number of vines per acre illustrates the fact that the ubiquitous "tons per acre" measurement of yields is all but useless as a comparative tool in a wine-growing region that has such radical differences in vine density and viticulture. While it means something to compare vigneron's yields in Burgundy (where everyone has basically the same vine density), in Oregon it means little.

That being said, Gerrie and Doerner appear convinced that the superlow yields practiced by some of their Burgundian colleagues is a mistake. They feel that it leads to wines with too much power and too little balance or finesse. Yet they also agree that high yields make poor wine. In short, their opinion is that each vineyard has an optimal load for making the best wine and that any yield formula is meaningless.

The light to medium ruby-colored 1996 Mt. Jefferson Cuvée Pinot Noir (this is a proprietary name, not the name of a vineyard) has a delightful nose of violets, candied strawberries, and traces of cookie dough. On the palate, this medium-bodied, harmonious, and silky-textured wine is crammed with sweet cherries and floral notes. Drink it between 1999 and 2003. The 1996 Louise Vineyard Pinot Noir (1996 is this parcel's second crop) is ruby colored and has sweet aromas reminiscent of cherry-flavored Kool-Aid and perfume. This seductively ripe and velvety offering is crammed with sugar-coated red fruits, oak spices, and traces of cinnamon. It will also be at its best between now and 2003. The slightly darker-colored and highly impressive 1996 Reserve Pinot Noir (made from the estate's vineyards as well as from grapes purchased from the Canary Hill, Seven Springs, and Arcus vineyards) has a blackberry-and-cassis-scented nose. This concentrated, medium- to full-bodied, silky, and deeply flavorful offering is packed with sweet black fruits and loads of wood spices. The use of new oak is masterful! It is an outstanding wine that is delicious yet should only get better over the next few years. Drink it between now and 2005. Aromatically, the medium to dark ruby-colored 1996 Marjorie Vineyard Pinot Noir reveals earth, cherries, and blueberries. Its satiny texture, medium to full body, and wonderful combination of power and elegance make this one of the finest wines crafted in 1996. Soft candied cherries, roses, and strawberries can be found in its lovely flavor profile and in its structured yet smooth lingering finish. It should be at its best between now and 2005.

Cristom also produces four white wines, a Pinot Gris and three Chardonnays. My favorite is crafted from grapes purchased from one of Washington State's finest Chardonnay vineyards. The 1996 Celilo Vineyard Chardonnay (Columbia Valley) displays mineral, ripe white fruit, and toasted oak aromas. This well-balanced, well-endowed, medium- to full-bodied wine is rich and silky textured and has delicious anise, butterscotch, and sweet vanillin flavors. Anticipated maturity: now–2003. Bravo!

I've long been a fan of Cristom's wines. Paul Gerrie and Steve Doerner produce lush, forward Pinots that provide enormous pleasure from the day they are released. In the 1995 vintage, however, their Marjorie and Mt. Jefferson cuvées cannot be recommended, and the Reserve Pinot Noir, while very good to excellent, lacks the generous, luscious personality that I look for in Cristom's wines. Nevertheless it is a very good, medium to dark ruby-colored wine offering aromas of currants, raspberries, and truffles, an oily texture, and a deep, medium- to full-bodied core of blueberries and blackberries. Last, warm whiskey notes can be discerned in its long, dry finish. Drink it between now and 2001.

DOMAINE DROUHIN

1996 Chardonnay	D	85
1996 Cuvée Laurène Pinot Noir	D	89
1995 Cuvée Laurène Pinot Noir	D	89+
1996 Pinot Noir	D	87

One of the most compelling aspects of this job is the opportunity to meet the fascinating characters who inhabit the wine world. The passion and intensity found in the men and women responsible for the world's most extraordinary bottles is moving. Bill Hatcher, the person responsible for the day-to-day operations of Domaine Drouhin (he works hand-in-hand with Véronique Drouhin of Burgundy's famed Joseph Drouhin *négociant* house), is one of the most interesting people I have met. His huge, barnlike, cavernous office has the vast majority of the floor space dedicated to his basketball hoop, with the necessary space allotted for intense one-on-one games. Behind Hatcher's desk is a full-size refrigerator plastered with comic strips, jokes, bumper stickers, and posters (for example: "When I die, I want to go peacefully like my grandfather did, in his sleep . . . not screaming like the passengers in his car").

Armed with a BA in art history, a master's in English poetry, and an MBA in finance, Hatcher abandoned his career in the "real" world, sold his house and cars, and spent the fall of 1985 doing the harvest in Oregon. When he met Robert Drouhin, the scion of Burgundy's Drouhin *négociant* house, in September 1987 there was an immediate affinity. "Our ethos is the same, even though he is more Newtonian and I'm more realistic," he says. Hatcher has become, in his own words, a member of the Drouhin family, not an employee.

Domaine Drouhin, or DDO, as it's known in Oregon, produced 400 cases of 1996 Chardonnay. This anise-, mineral-, and butterscotch-scented wine has a silky texture, is well balanced and offers dried honey flavors. It is medium bodied, fresh, and dry yet finishes hollow. Drink it over the next 2 years.

The ruby-colored 1996 Pinot Noir has dark plums and black cherries on the nose and a silky, elegant, medium-bodied personality. This well-crafted, cherry-laced, appealing wine will provide excellent drinking over the next 4–5 years. The medium to dark ruby-colored 1996 Cuvée Laurène Pinot Noir offers toasty oak, spice, and floral aromas. This beautifully textured wine has excellent concentration, medium to full body, and well-defined yet dense flavors of cherries, blackberries, and blueberries. Typical of the vintage, it has a rather firm, astringent finish, yet it appears to possess the requisite fruit to outlast the tannins. Drink it between 2000 and 2004. The 1995 Cuvée Laurène Pinot Noir has a bright medium to dark ruby color and delightful aromas of sweet red berries intermingled with traces of underbrush. This lovely wine reveals excellent richness of fruit, extract, and balance. It is an elegant, velvety-textured, medium- to full-bodied, and feminine wine filled with plums, raspberries, and candied strawberries. Anticipated maturity: now–2004.

EVESHAM WOOD

1996 Seven Springs Vineyard Unfiltered Willamette Valley Pinot Noir	D	88

1996 Temperance Hill Vineyard Cuvée J Unfiltered Willamette Valley Pinot Noir	D	88+

1995 Unfiltered Cuvée J Pinot Noir	D	88+

1996 Unfiltered Willamette Valley Pinot Noir	B	86

While many well-known Oregon wineries have dramatically raised their prices (despite two consecutive less-than-stellar vintages), Evesham Wood has maintained its reasonable prices. Kudos!

To honor one of the finest Pinot Noir producers of our time, Burgundy's now retired Henri Jayer, Evesham Wood's top cuvée is named Cuvée J. The 1995 offering is excellent, revealing a medium to dark ruby color and sweet cassis and cherry aromas. It is medium to full bodied, rich, thick, complex, and oily textured, with loads of ripe strawberries, cherries, and a hint of sautéed mushrooms in its personality. Anticipated maturity: now–2003.

The 1996 Unfiltered Willamette Valley Pinot Noir is ruby colored and exhibits superb ripeness in its black cherry-scented nose. This medium-bodied, firm, and fruit-filled wine has black raspberry, cassis, and blueberry flavors that become somewhat compressed in the wine's tannic finish. This is an excellent value. Anticipated maturity: 2000–2003. The darker-colored Seven Springs Vineyard Unfiltered Willamette Valley Pinot Noir has a delightful nose of sweet black cherries that is followed by a deep, well-crafted, and exciting flavor profile. Ripe berries, currants, and blueberries saturate the palate in this surprisingly generous (for the vintage), medium- to full-bodied and velvety wine. Some cellaring will be required to soften this beauty's tannins. Drink it between 2001 and 2004. The medium to dark ruby-colored 1996 Temperance Hill Vineyard Cuvée J Unfiltered Willamette Valley Pinot Noir reveals sweet black fruits and toasted oak aromas. Silky textured and full flavored, it is densely packed with blueberries, currants, and black cherries that linger in its long finish. Oak flavors and tannins were highly present when I tasted it, but my instincts suggest the fruit will maintain its upper hand. Drink it between 2001 and 2005.

FORIS

1996 Rogue Valley Pinot Noir	B	85

While most of the wines appearing in this section hail from the Willamette Valley, southern Oregon's Rogue Valley, near the California border, is also home to a number of wineries. Foris's ruby-colored 1996 Rogue Valley Pinot Noir has a strawberry- and sage-scented nose. On the palate, this simple yet delicious wine impresses with its cherry, black raspberry, and strawberry flavors and its medium-bodied personality. It should be drunk over the next 2 years. This is an excellent value.

GIRARDET

1996 Barrel Select Umpqua Valley Pinot Noir	C	85

The Umpqua Valley, just north of the Rogue Valley, is also little known outside Oregon but does produce wines meriting attention. Girardet's 1996 Barrel Select Umpqua Valley Pinot Noir is medium to dark ruby colored and offers black cherry and raspberry aromas. This medium-bodied, cassis- and blackberry-flavored wine is dense, sweet, and soft. It will be a delight to drink over the next 2–3 years. This is a very good value.

PANTHER CREEK

1996 Bednarik Vineyard Pinot Noir	D	89
1996 Freedom Hill Pinot Noir	D	90?
1996 Reserve Pinot Noir	D	87
1996 Shea Vineyard Pinot Noir	D	?
1996 Willamette Valley Pinot Noir	C	86
1996 Winemaker's Cuvée Pinot Noir	D	89

Panther Creek's 1996s were sampled twice, once at the winery and later at a blind tasting in Washington, D.C. (I retasted the Freedom Hill a third and fourth time at home). At my winery tasting, serious rock and roll was being played in the background. Unbeknownst to Michael Stevenson, Panther Creek's assistant winemaker and head disc jockey, he had selected music from my favorite rock group, the Band. As I contemplated the wines I could hear Levon Helm belting out "Don't do it." Want to know what goes great with Pinot Noir? Great rock and roll!

The harvest began on October 9 and finished as heavy rains began at 2 P.M. on Saturday, October 12—"We were luckier than smart," was owner Ron Kaplan's comment. Yields averaged 2+ tons with a low of 2.01 tons per acre in Freedom Hill and a high of 2.4 tons in Shea (even though the latter vineyard was thinned three times). Kaplan says he is pleased with the vintage and that "the grapes came in clean, without any traces of rot." He went on to say that the wines had "very pronounced aromatics, atypical for newborn wine."

The ruby-colored 1996 Willamette Valley Pinot Noir has dark fruit, strawberry, and underbrush aromas that give way to a black raspberry and tangy currant-laced core of fruit. Medium bodied and silky textured, this delicious offering has a lovely note of oak spices on the finish. This is a very good value. Drink it between now and 2002. The slightly darker-colored 1996 Reserve Pinot Noir has a richer and riper nose as well as a silky personality filled with black cherries and cassis. With aeration, this well-delineated, tightly wound, and medium- to full-bodied wine offers flavors of dark raspberries, minerals, and stones. It will require some cellaring and should be at its best between 2000 and 2003. The medium to dark ruby-colored 1996 Winemaker's Cuvée has intriguing cherry syrup, cookie dough, dark plum, floral, and perfume aromas. This well-balanced, medium- to full-bodied, lively, and velvety-textured offering has flavors reminiscent of Dr. Brown's black cherry cola blended with fresh strawberries and blueberries. It is concentrated and well extracted and has a tannic finish. Anticipated maturity: 2000–2005.

Panther Creek's 1996 Shea Vineyard is very reduced. At the winery it offered aromas of rubber and gamey meats that slowly transformed into stewed plums, cherries, and strawberries following aeration. It displayed excellent concentration, intensity, and a flavor profile dominated by reduced flavors (rubber, raw beef, and game) as well as spicy oak. Kaplan informed me that he and his team (including winemaker Mark Vlossak) had been confounded by this wine since fermentation. I have tasted it twice since. The first time it displayed spicy cherry yogurt aromas, as well as a creamy, complex, cinnamon-tinged, and sweet cherry-filled character. It was absolutely delicious. However, at a subsequent showing it appeared more reduced than ever. Readers willing to cellar this wine for 5–6 years, or those who are willing to decant it for a number of hours, will be impressed by the wine's fruit (putting a few pennies in the wine will hasten the dissipation of the reductive notes). However, since I cannot expect readers to have loose change on hand at all times, I am reserving judgment.

The 1996 Bednarik Vineyard reveals a medium to dark ruby color and aromas of black cherries, pumpkin, and red currants. It is a medium- to full-bodied, silky-textured, and well-delineated wine with loads of forward red and black cherry fruit. When first tasted, it appeared to be one of the most backward of Panther Creek's 1996s. In my second tasting it was the most forward of the single vineyard wines, ending on a soft, long, and satiny finish. Anticipated maturity: now–2004.

Just to add to the inconsistent showings of this winery's 1996s, the Freedom Hill has perplexed me. I fell in love with this medium to dark ruby-colored wine's aromatics at the winery. It revealed perfumed layers of superripe cherries, plums, and violets with just a touch of spicy oak. On the palate, its seductive personality offered chewy-textured, mouth-coating, and concentrated waves of gorgeously sweet red and black fruits. Revisited three times since, it twice smelled of spicy apple cider, was completely disjointed, and had a hard tannic finish. However, the third time was the charm. It was back to its original state, seducing me with its fresh, sweet, and complex aromatics and flavors. I purchased a case of this wine after my original tasting and still have high hopes for it.

PONZI

1996 Chardonnay	C	85
1996 Pinot Gris	C	85
1995 Reserve Pinot Noir	D	86

Portland's suburban sprawl has all but reached Ponzi, the first estate (established in 1970) to put Oregon on the map of the world's best Pinot Noir-producing regions. As I drove down the dirt road that leads to the estate I was pleased to notice a handwritten sign advertising "Walnuts 70¢/Pound," proof that Portland had not yet completely taken over the area. When I met Dick Ponzi (I was speaking with the "founding father"), I was struck by the fact that Oregon is such a youthful wine region. In Burgundy they speak of certain vineyards first being planted over 1,300 years ago!

Ponzi produces, year in and year out, some of Oregon's finest Pinot Noirs. I was disappointed by some off flavors in his otherwise rich and berry fruit-filled regular cuvée but enjoyed the 1995 Reserve Pinot Noir offering. It is a medium ruby-colored wine with red and black berry aromas and a deeply sweet medium-bodied character filled with cherries and strawberries. A touch of dryness on the finish prevented it from meriting a higher rating. Drink it between now and 2002. Ponzi's 1995 Pinot Noir 25th Anniversary was disappointingly light and diluted . . . a far cry from the superb 1990 20th Anniversary bottling.

Ponzi's 1996 Pinot Noir also disappointed me. Having enjoyed many of this estate's offerings in the past, I was surprised to find it prematurely aging and lacking in fruit. Readers who have purchased it are well advised to drink up.

Revealing smoky mineral aromas, the 1996 Pinot Gris offers a light- to medium-bodied character with sweet pear, wood, and traces of red currant flavors. This fresh and fun wine will provide satisfying quaffing over the next year. The 1996 Chardonnay has mature aromas of butterscotch and buttery almonds. This medium-bodied, fat, and silky-textured wine is already offering deliciously evolved flavors, so I recommend consuming it in the near term.

REX HILL VINEYARDS

1996 Maresh Vineyard Oregon Pinot Noir	D	87
1996 Reserve Oregon Pinot Noir	D	87+?
1996 Willamette Valley Pinot Noir	C	86
1995 Willamette Valley Pinot Noir	C	86

Rex Hill's 1995 Willamette Valley offering is significantly better than their good but simple Kings Ridge Pinot Noir. This bright ruby-colored wine displays appealing aromas of plums, black cherry, and smoke as well as a medium-bodied, oily-textured character filled with strawberries, raspberries, and earthy undertones. Anticipated maturity: now–2001.

The ruby-colored 1996 Willamette Valley Pinot Noir has cherry, spice, and dark plummy aromas. This well-crafted, silky-textured, medium-bodied, and juicy Pinot has delightfully fresh black cherry flavors. A very good value, it should be consumed over the next 2–3 years. My instincts suggest that the 1996 Maresh Vineyard Pinot Noir will be a more complete wine with a year of bottle age. This medium to dark ruby-colored wine needs to soak up its presently oak-dominated aromas and flavors. If that occurs, it will blossom into an excellent Pinot Noir. Looking past the oak, I detected aromas of cassis and blackberries, as well as black currants and cherries in this wine's medium- to full-bodied flavor profile. Anticipated maturity: now–2004. The slightly darker-colored 1996 Reserve Oregon Pinot Noir offers aromas of cola, black raspberries, dried cherries, and currants. This medium- to full-bodied, silky-textured, thick, and chewy wine is well extracted and packed with enough fruit to stand up to its aggressive oakiness. It has excellent potential, but the oak needs to become better integrated. Anticipated maturity: now–2005.

ST. INNOCENT WINERY

1995 Seven Springs Vineyard Pinot Noir	D	90

Regrettably, I have been unable to visit St. Innocent. My schedules appear to conflict with those of Mark Vlossak, the highly talented winemaker at this outstanding winery as well as at Panther Creek. A recently purchased bottle of his 1995 Seven Springs Vineyard Pinot Noir once again drove home the point that Vlossak is crafting some of Oregon's finest Pinots. It is dark ruby colored and has intense and compelling aromas of black cherries, spices, and stones. This concentrated, medium- to full-bodied wine offers a mouthful of beautifully ripened and extracted red and black fruits as well as traces of metallic flavors. It is well structured but neither astringent nor tannic, and it should age effortlessly. Had I not been the one with the corkscrew, I could have been convinced that it had been crafted by Maurice Ecard of Savigny-Lès-Beaune fame! This superb wine, particularly in light of the difficulties faced by Oregon producers in 1995, is a testimony to Vlossak's tremendous skills.

DOMAINE SERENE

1995 Evenstad Reserve Pinot Noir	D	88+
1996 Evenstad Reserve Pinot Noir	D	89
1996 Mark Bradford Vineyard Pinot Noir	D	90+

Grace and Ken Evenstad are wine lovers from Minnesota. They share the passion, commitment, desire, and financial means to produce first-rate Pinot Noirs. These self-described red burgundy fanatics were convinced by some Oregon wines they tasted (including the 1975 Eyrie, Ken Wright's 1986s, and older offerings from Rex Hill) that the Willamette Valley is capable of producing world-class Pinot Noir. Currently Domaine Serene comprises 142 acres on the southernmost slopes of the Red Hills. The winery now produces 5,000 cases and should increase their output to 10,000 as they complete their planting plans.

Ken Wright, Evenstad's winemaker, uses 100% new French oak barrels (Seguin Moreau and François Frères) that have been steamed to remove the more aggressive wood flavors.

The 1995 Evenstad Reserve Pinot Noir is a resounding success for the vintage. This delicious ruby-colored wine offers clean and pure aromatics of cherries and oak spices. It is medium bodied and silky textured and filled with candied red cherries, assorted red fruits, and stones. Drink it between now and 2003.

The medium to dark ruby-colored 1996 Evenstad Reserve Pinot Noir is scheduled for release in early spring 1999. Aromas reminiscent of a cigar box filled with red and black cherries as well as potpourri are followed by a deliciously sweet personality. This medium- to full-bodied wine is velvety textured and filled with layers of black raspberries and cherries and has excellent purity of flavors, delineation, and focus. It should be at its best between 2002 and 2006. The 1996 Mark Bradford Vineyard, produced from an east-facing parcel at an elevation of 620 to 760 feet (planted with the Pommard clone), is certainly one of Oregon's wines of the vintage. This dark ruby-colored beauty reveals scrumptious flavors suggestive of cookie dough laced with cherry syrup aromas. With its dense, intense, and concentrated flavor profile, this wine exhibits a medium- to full-bodied character that coats the palate with velvety blueberries and black cherries. It possesses the vintage's telltale firmness but is buffered by superb ripeness, fat, and richness—qualities more associated with 1994 Oregon Pinot Noirs! It will not be released before spring 1999. Drink it between 2002 and 2006. Bravo!

SILVAN RIDGE—HINMAN VINEYARDS
| 1996 Eola Springs Vineyard Willamette Valley Pinot Noir | D | 85 |

The ruby-colored 1996 Eola Springs Vineyard Pinot Noir offers up blueberry, blackberry, and cola-tinged aromatics. This well-crafted, medium-bodied, juicy, and vibrant Pinot has spicy currant and blueberry flavors. It is delicious to drink yet will last through 2002.

SOKOL BLOSSER
| 1996 Yamhill County Pinot Gris | B | 86 |

Aromatically, this pleasing wine displays fresh, floral, spicy, and green apple scents. A touch of effervescence combined with its fruit cocktail, mandarin orange, and slightly toasty flavors make this a fun and easygoing, medium-bodied offering to drink over the next 2–3 years.

STARR
| 1996 Bert's Blend Reserve Willamette Valley Pinot Noir | D | 86 |

The impressive 1996 Bert's Blend Reserve Pinot Noir (120 cases) is a selection of Starr's finest barrels from the Fox Ridge Vineyard. It possesses a bright ruby color, floral, cherry, and spiced oak aromas, and a delightfully silky personality. This well-made wine is medium bodied and displays lively cherry and blackberry flavors that linger in its finish. Drink it over the next 2–3 years.

WILLAKENZIE ESTATE
1996 Gamay Noir	C	86
1996 Oregon Pinot Noir	C	86
1996 Pierre Léon Pinot Noir	C	89
1996 Pinot Gris	C	87

The résumé of WillaKenzie Estate's majority owner, Bernard Lacroute, reads like a *Who's Who* of the high-tech world (Digital Equipment, Intel, Sun Microsystems . . .). Originally from the Charollais region of France, a part of Burgundy known for its excellent beef, Lacroute and his wife, Ronni, purchased the estate's land in 1991 with Laurent Monthelieu, the winemaker. This former farm (numerous cows still graze the land) comprises 420 acres, 86 acres of which are now planted with vines (65 acres are in production). Ultimately Lacroute plans to have 120 acres of Pinot Noir, Pinot Gris, Pinot Meunier, Gamay Noir, and Chardonnay, with a total production of 20,000–25,000 cases.

WillaKenzie's Pinot Gris is produced in a fresh, vibrant style. The 1996 had its malolactic fermentation blocked to maintain its zesty malic acid and was crafted in 100% stainless steel. It reveals smoky, earthy, floral, and minerally aromas and an extremely appealing character of almonds, toasted hazelnuts, dried honey, and white flowers. This delicious, medium-bodied, and silky wine should be consumed over the next 2 years. It is an excellent value.

Readers who believe Gamay is for wimps should taste WillaKenzie's dark ruby/purple-colored 1996 Gamay Noir. Produced from 3–3.5 tons of fruit per acre, and aged in 35% new oak barrels for 11 months, it possesses a fresh, inviting nose of black fruits and violets. This silky, chewy, and medium- to full-bodied wine is masculine, structured, and crammed with blackberries and cassis. Anticipated maturity: now–2003. The medium to dark ruby-colored 1996 Oregon Pinot Noir has candle wax and red fruits aromas and a medium- to full-bodied core of intense black cherry fruit. This well-ripened wine is velvety and forward and offers satisfying near-term drinking. The 1996 Pierre Léon Pinot Noir, named after Bernard Lacroute's father (his portrait can be found in the winery's tasting room), is a serious, firm, but monolithic wine. Blackberry, blueberry, and metallic scents are followed by sweet black cherry flavors in this fresh, concentrated, medium- to full-bodied, structured, and impressively long wine. It should be at its best between 2001 and 2004.

KEN WRIGHT CELLARS

1996 Abbey Ridge Vineyard Pinot Noir	D	86+
1996 Canary Hill Vineyard Pinot Noir	D	89
1995 Canary Hill Vineyard Pinot Noir	D	89+
1996 Carter Vineyard Pinot Noir	D	88+
1995 Carter Vineyard Pinot Noir	D	88
1995 Freedom Hill Vineyard Pinot Noir	D	88
1996 Guadalupe Vineyard Pinot Noir	D	89+
1995 Guadalupe Vineyard Pinot Noir	D	90+
1996 McCrone Vineyard Pinot Noir	D	88
1995 Shea Vineyard Pinot Noir	D	86

From the confines of a former glove factory he converted into a winery, Ken Wright fashioned a remarkable quintet of 1995 Pinot Noirs. In order to accomplish this amazing feat (given the huge difficulties associated with this vintage), Wright eliminated a whopping 20% of his harvest. He does not own any vineyards but has long-term contracts that specify the yields he demands (less than 2 tons of fruit per acre). Furthermore, owing to his fear of autumn rains, Wright wants specific viticultural techniques (crop thinning and so on) employed to promote early ripening. The bunches are 100% destemmed and are put through a 4–5-day prefermentation cold soak. Surprisingly, considering the fact that Wright is a "terroir-ist," he uses commercial/artificial yeasts for his fermentations. The vineyard designated offerings are aged in 50% new oak barrels, while the regular Pinot Noir is aged in 25% new oak. The resulting wines are lush, forward, pure, succulent, and stylistically reminiscent of those produced by Claude Dugat, one of Burgundy's stars.

Like his fellow Pinot Noir producers in Burgundy, Ken Wright is a believer in the concept of terroir. He is convinced that each vineyard has a "signature" taste derived from that particular site's microclimate, geology, angle to the sun, and the like. Wright is at the forefront of a movement in Oregon to have terroir appellations officially recognized. If he has his way, names like Ribbon Ridge, Eola Hills, Dundee, WillaKenzie, Red Hills and others would appear on wine labels in the same way appellations such as Howell Mountain, Stag's Leap, and so on are recognized on California offerings. However, others in the Willamette Valley (including Dick Ponzi, one of the region's "founding fathers") are completely opposed to such terroir considerations and feel that the winemakers of the area should produce the best wines they can and leave it at that.

The elegant, ruby-colored 1995 Freedom Hill Vineyard Pinot Noir exhibits a pretty nose with scents reminiscent of cherries, roses, and violets. It is a well-crafted, silky, medium- to full-bodied succulent wine infused with the flavors of blackberries and plums. Drink it between now and 2003. The brilliant ruby-colored 1995 Shea Vineyard Pinot Noir reveals creamy red berry aromas and a velvety, medium-bodied character with blackberry and cherry flavors. This delicious but simple offering is Wright's weakest single vineyard wine in 1995 yet is spectacular when compared with what others produced. Anticipated maturity: now–2001. The impressive 1995 Canary Hill Vineyard Pinot Noir is ruby/purple colored and possesses a beguiling sweet and perfumed cherry and oak-spiced nose. It explodes on the palate with lively, candied red and black berries, a smooth-as-silk texture, and a full body. Well delineated and admirably persistent, it will almost certainly merit an outstanding score with 1–2 years of cellaring. Drink it between now and 2003. The darker-colored 1995 Carter Vineyard Pinot Noir offers intense aromatics of fresh blueberries and herbs. On the palate, jammy cherries and Asian spices are found in this medium- to full-bodied, thick wine. It could potentially merit a higher score if its slightly hard tannic finish softens out. Anticipated maturity: now–2003. Wright's fabulous Guadalupe Vineyard Pinot Noir is one of the two finest Pinot Noirs I tasted from Oregon's 1995 vintage (the other is Domaine Drouhin's Cuvée Laurène). Dark ruby colored and displaying a mouthwatering nose of milk chocolate-covered cherries, this intense, expansive, velvety, and gorgeously focused wine offers layer upon layer of superripe black raspberries, cassis, and cherries. Its admirable finish reveals soft, ripe tannins and a kaleidoscope of pure red fruit flavors. The very fact that this wine was produced in such a dreadful vintage is proof that Wright is in a class with the world's finest Pinot Noir producers. Anticipated maturity: now–2005. Bravo!

The ruby-colored 1996 Abbey Ridge Vineyard Pinot Noir has an oak-tinged, dried cherry, and candle wax-scented nose. Its structured and firm character reveals tangy black raspberry and underbrush flavors, a medium body, and a dry finish. With some cellaring this wine may ultimately deserve a more generous review if its fruit blossoms. Drink it between 2001 and 2004. Produced from a parcel located in the Eola Hills, the slightly darker-colored 1996 Carter Vineyard Pinot Noir has plum and charred oak aromas in addition to a juicy, toasty, and feminine personality filled with blueberries and cherries. This well-defined and medium-bodied offering was lip-smackingly good the day of my tasting, but it will most likely tighten up before roaring back to life. Anticipated maturity: 2001–2005. The 1996 Canary Hill Vineyard is planted with 100% Wädenswil—a clone of Pinot Noir. It is presently leased to Ken Wright and his partners, but they informed me that they plan to purchase it. Harvested at 2½ tons of fruit per acre, this medium to dark ruby-colored wine offers aromatics reminiscent of dark cherries immersed in toasty oak. This well-structured offering is packed with loads of sweet strawberries, juicy cherries, and hints of raspberries. It is medium to full bodied, with a soft, silky texture. It should be at its best between 2000 and 2005. My favorite is the 1996 Guadalupe Vineyard Pinot Noir. This medium- to dark ruby-colored wine displays a gorgeous richness of fruit in its cherry-infused scents. It is opulent, seductive, medium to full bodied and velvety textured and possesses copious quantities of sweet red fruit intermingled with spicy new oak flavors. It appears to be more structured than its 1995 counterpart but reveals equal portions of luscious red fruits. Anticipated maturity: 2000–2005. The 1996 McCrone Vineyard Pinot Noir was produced from a 4-year-old Dijon clone (#115) vineyard. This Burgundy clone is expected to produce very high-quality wine in Oregon (it's also widely planted in California, particularly in the Russian River and Sonoma Coast). It is ruby colored and offers wild game, beef blood, and spicy oak aromas. This medium-bodied, mouth-coating, seductive wine is densely packed with black cherries, strawberries, and dark raspberries. With aeration, traces of metallic flavors can be detected. It is reminiscent in style of the Guadalupe, but it lacks that wine's impressively long finish. Drink it between 2000 and 2004.

7. WASHINGTON STATE

Washington State is primed to become an increasingly important factor in the fine wine marketplace. At present, with the absurdly high prices charged by the top California wineries and Bordeaux châteaux, Washington's finest offerings (often of equal quality) are downright cheap in comparison. Furthermore, the state's largest wineries, such as Château Ste. Michelle, offer a bevy of reasonably priced wines for budget conscious consumers. If Washington State's producers resist the temptation to raise their prices, they should be able to gain significant market share in the coming three to four years.

Washington State produces some extraordinary wines and many poor ones. There is no doubt that Washington can produce wines as compelling, intense, flavorful, and elegant as any viticultural region in the world. The fact that the majority of the state's wines are average, or simply bad, should not detract consumers' attention from the glories crafted by those producers who are fulfilling Washington's enormous potential.

Outside of the Northwest, Washington's wines are not well known. As a former retailer, I know how rare it was to hear a customer say, "Tonight I would love to have something from Washington with dinner, what do you recommend?" Bearing this in mind, I am providing some information that is aimed at providing readers with a basic understanding of the region's geography, climate, winemakers and growers, as well as the multitude of wine styles.

A Geography Primer

Admittedly, I had a misconceived notion of Washington State prior to traveling there twice since joining *The Wine Advocate* three years ago. I had tasted numerous wines from there, knew that it was the home of Microsoft and numerous other high-tech companies, and that rain was plentiful. My trips have shown me that my middle-school geography teachers were not completely daft (mountains do stop rain, and microclimates really do exist). To begin to understand Washington State wines it is important to know a little about its geography.

Virtually all the wines described here are from the Columbia Valley Appellation (which includes the Yakima and Walla Walla Valleys). Primarily a desert, it is located in southeastern Washington, and overlaps into Oregon. As Pacific Ocean depressions approach the Washington coastline, they are often trapped by the coastal Olympic Mountains, dropping much of their precipitation on the rain forests located on the range's western slopes. When a weather front is powerful enough to remain intact after traversing the Olympic Mountains, it then faces the even higher elevations of the Cascade Mountains. Exceedingly few depressions are capable of clearing both these ranges, and as a consequence, eastern Washington

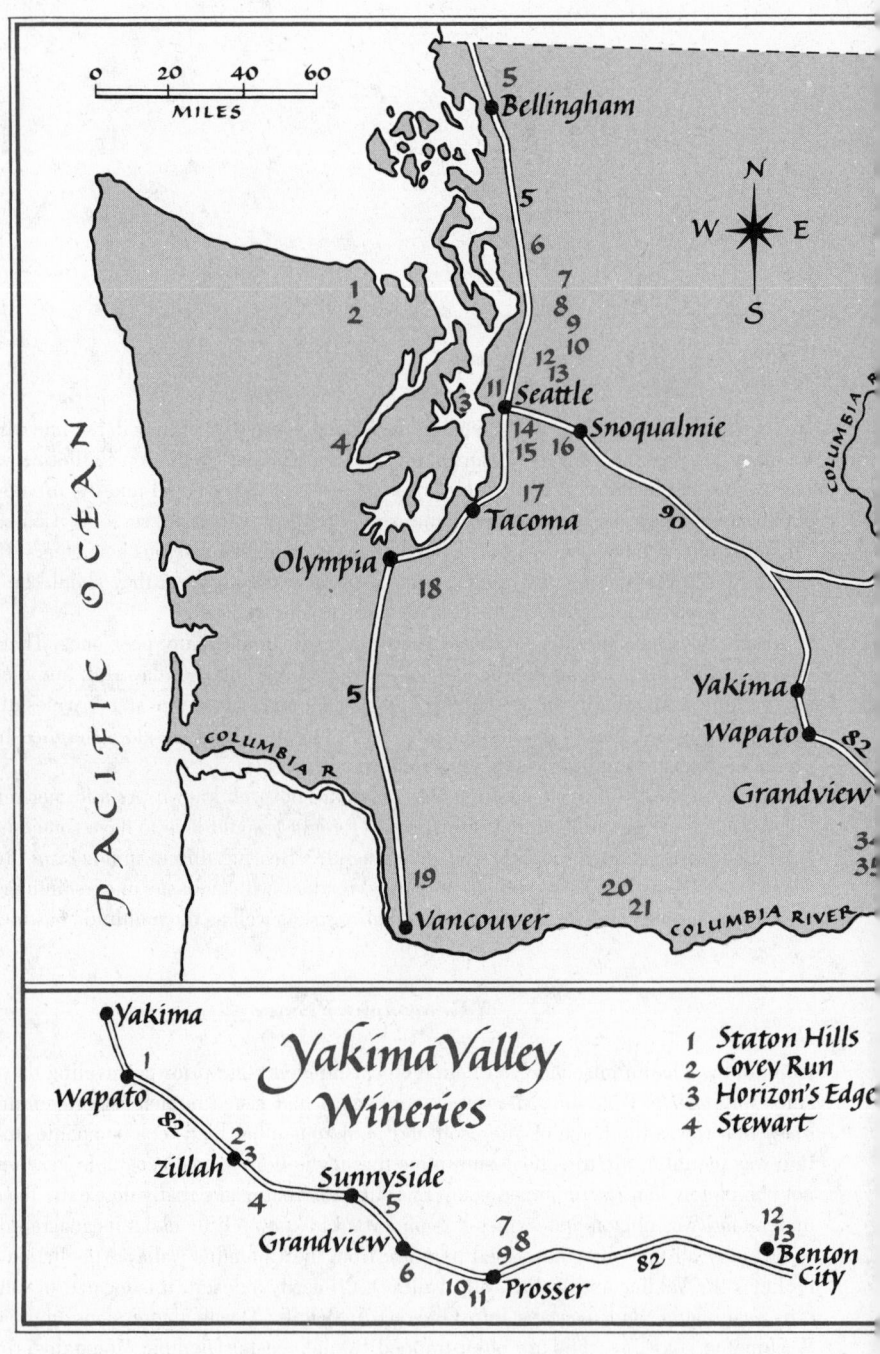

WASHINGTON STATE

PACIFIC OCEAN

0 20 40 60
MILES

5 Bellingham

N
W E
S

1
2

5

6

7
8
9
10

12
13

3 11 Seattle

14
15 16 Snoqualmie

4

17

Tacoma

90

Olympia

18

Yakima

Wapato 82

Grandview

3-4
35

5

COLUMBIA R

19

20
21

Vancouver

COLUMBIA RIVER

COLUMBIA R

Yakima

Yakima Valley
Wineries

1 Staton Hills
2 Covey Run
3 Horizon's Edge
4 Stewart

1

Wapato

82

2 3

Zillah

Sunnyside

4

5

12
13

Grandview

7
9 8

Benton
City

6

10 11 Prosser

82

Washington

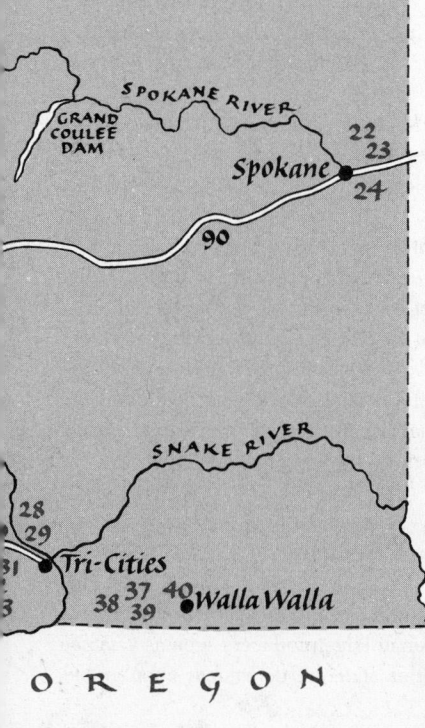

experiences desertlike conditions (as a matter of fact, soldiers of the U.S. Army undergo desert training in Yakima).

As I flew from Seattle to Walla Walla on my first tasting trip, I was amazed to see the contrast between the lush, green western slopes of the Cascades and the barren eastern side. From the tips of the Cascades all the way to Walla Walla, the only signs of vegetation were the trees bordering rivers and irrigated farms. One statistic dramatizes this weather pattern—within the town of Walla Walla, on the eastern edge of the Columbia Valley Appellation, annual rainfall increases by 1 inch per mile as one travels eastward. On the parched western edge of Walla Walla, abutting the l'Ecole No. 41 and Woodward Canyon wineries, are dusty asparagus fields. On the eastern edge, where Walla Walla Vintners and Glen Fiona are located, the rolling hills are lush and green. Rain, the bane of wine producers the world over is rarely a nuisance for Washington's main grape-growing region. Because Washington State vineyards are irrigated, viticulturalists can control the quantity of water each row of vines gets.

Readers should not assume that because Washington State borders Canada it has a cold climate. Once spring arrives, the Columbia Valley enjoys a grape-growing season that winemakers the world over would envy. Sun and heat are plentiful, evenings are cool—excellent for maintaining natural acidity levels.

This is not, however, a viticultural paradise. The winters and early springs can be a grape-grower's nightmare. Why? The region is prone, on average once every six years, to "killer freezes" (as they are known in these parts), the last of which descended from the arctic in late January and early February 1996, devastating the vineyards. Countless vines were destroyed, their trunks exploding because of the Arctic Express's extreme temperature. Most of the vines that survived produced exceedingly little. Interestingly, Merlot and Semillon were the most susceptible to the freeze, with Cabernet, Chardonnay, and Rhône varietals faring better. Depending on the varietal, yields in 1996 were down between 25% and 80%.

The Winemakers and Grape Growers

Unlike those in California, Oregon, Bordeaux, and Burgundy, the majority of Washington State wineries do not own vineyards. With the exception of large producers such as Château Ste. Michelle and Columbia Winery, winemakers in this state are dependent upon grapes purchased from growers.

For the most part, Washington State's producers are converted home-winemakers. Prior to going into wine full time Gary Figgins (Leonetti) was a machinist at the local Walla Walla cannery, Alexander Golitzen (Quilceda Creek) was an engineer for Scott Paper, Chris Camarda (Andrew Will) was a waiter as was Matthew Loso (Matthews Cellars), etc. It's the same story—they fell in love with wine, decided to try their hand at it, acquired grapes, and the rest is history. The grape growers, on the other hand, are farmers. Some are incredibly wealthy, others less so. One grower whose primary business is producing Washington's famed and delicious Fuji apples told me that he can earn four times as much money per acre with apple trees than with grape vines. So why the financial sacrifice, I asked. Ego gratification, came the reply. As his apples go to market they are mixed in with everyone else's. He earns his money by producing the most possible apples by acre, using ingenious systems to ensure that the apples will be evenly colored and unscarred. He has no contact with the people who buy them and laments the fact that there is no market for apples that taste good, just for those that are the most aesthetically pleasing. Growing grapes allows him to compete on a different level. Also, when he drinks wines crafted from his grapes, or sees someone order a bottle in a restaurant, he feels he has a strong connection to that wine.

As a wine lover, I respected the answer to my question. His reason for giving up potential earnings lead him to have moderate yields (he is immensely respected by winemakers) in order to compete qualitatively. Regrettably, however, few growers are as well-off as this gentleman and are not prepared to make the same sacrifice. This leads us to one of Washington winemakers' biggest problems: yields.

Farmers are paid by the ton, regardless of the type of crop they grow, and grapes are no different. The more you produce, the more you earn. Numerous winemakers in Washington State fight constant battles with their grape growers (as I have stated, very few wineries own their own vineyards) to reduce yields, but the incentives are just not there. In California, Burgundy, Oregon, and elsewhere, quality wineries purchase their fruit by the acre, not by the ton. The grower, who will be paid the same amount whether 2 tons per acre or 10 tons per acre are produced, has the financial incentive to follow the winemaker's directives. The killer freezes that cause severe damage in the Columbia River Appellation every 6 or so years prevent wineries from instituting this system in Washington State, however. They either do not have or do not wish to risk the financial resources. In a vintage like 1996, a winery with this type of arrangement would have had to pay growers their normal rates for exceedingly few grapes.

There is, however, a light at the end of the tunnel. Recently, some of the state's top producers, including Golitzen, Camarda, Figgins, and others, have begun purchasing land and planting vineyards. They are reinvesting earnings brought on by their wineries' successes to allow them to control the quality and quantity of the grapes that go into their wines. I predict that, as this becomes more prevalent in Washington State, the overall quality of wines will dramatically improve.

Wine Styles

We all have notions of what a Bordeaux, Burgundy, California, Tuscan, or Piedmontese wine tastes like. Granted, there are exceptions to every rule and even the greatest palates in the world can easily be tricked in a blind tasting. However, there are certain basic flavor profiles and styles that characterize all of the great wine-producing regions of the world—except Washington State. Having tasted hundreds of wines from the Columbia, Yakima, and Walla Walla Valleys, I was incapable of finding a regional signature.

The vast majority of the wines I tasted (those whose notes do *not* appear in the following pages), are disjointed, fruitless, vegetal, and immensely tannic. Furthermore, a large number of Washington winemakers have yet to learn what California's top 5–6 dozen producers discovered over the past 15 years—excessive acid adjustments make a wine undrinkable! On both my trips to Washington I have conducted large tastings as well as numerous estate visits. The group tastings have the enormous benefit of gathering wines from little-known producers, in addition to saving on travel time (Washington's wineries are spread out over hundreds of miles). The number of appallingly acidified wines I tasted on both trips is mind-boggling. More important, it is out and out bad winemaking.

Thankfully, the state's leading producers eschew acidification—winemakers such as Alexander Golitzen (Quilceda Creek), Chris Camarda (Andrew Will), Gary Figgins (Leonetti), and Mike Januik (Château Ste. Michelle) are crafting wines each year that will, hopefully, serve as a reference point for others in the industry.

Even though candied, superripe fruit immersed in loads of oak has brought fame and fortune to such wineries as Leonetti, many other producers craft subtle, elegant, and focused wines (DeLille and Quilceda Creek for example). Their polar opposites, dense, hyperextracted, and alcoholic wines can also be found in Washington.

Washington State as a wine region is still in its infancy, and that's the beauty of it. These

converted home-winemakers are defining the future of Washington wines before our eyes—
and palates. There are no traditions nor any parameters. Any style is acceptable. Anything
goes. It truly is a frontier.

Types of Wine

Virtually all the varietals seen in California are grown in Washington. However, Washington
has added to this mix Lemberger, a fruity, red vinifera grape that is capable of being made
into a Beaujolais-style, nonoak-aged wine, or more infrequently into a serious, cellarworthy
wine. A few producers are dabbling with Pinot Noir, and not surprisingly, most have failed.
Recent releases of Rhône Rangers (wines produced from the traditional Rhône varietals)
show promise. Washington's wineries, however, are banking on Chardonnay, Cabernet Sauvignon, and especially Merlot to bring them to prominence. There is also some hope for Sauvignon Blanc and Semillon. A relatively large percentage of the state's vineyards are planted
with Riesling, but this is diminishing as newly planted vineyards rarely include this varietal.
Fortunately, Washington's consumers appear to enjoy Riesling, which is usually bargain
priced ($8–$12), and producers continue to crank it out because it is easy and inexpensive
to make—the perfect cash-flow wine. For Riesling aficionados, these wines represent fine
values. Washington also produces this country's best Chenin Blancs and Muscats. Their
crisp natural acidity, easily obtained due to Washington's northern latitude, makes these
wines, finished in an off-dry to slightly sweet style, the ideal summer sipping and picnic
wines. Sadly, the market for these wines is limited. For better or worse, the state's future rests
with the superstar grapes—Cabernet Sauvignon, Merlot, and Chardonnay. The good news is
that these are the wines the marketing people claim consumers desire and Washington
State's main rival, California, is pricing itself out of the competition.

RED WINE VARIETALS

Cabernet Sauvignon   This is Washington's most successful grape variety. In capable
hands, it renders an almost opaque purple wine. Cabernet Sauvignon usually ripens fully in
eastern Washington, resulting in wines with curranty, plummy, cedary aromas, excellent extract, medium to full body, and good depth and concentration. Overwhelming aromas and flavors of herbs and vegetables are rarely as intrusive in Washington Cabernet Sauvignons as
they can be in California.

Merlot   Washington producers are hoping that Merlot will bring the state fame. Because of
the young age of the vineyards and the inexperience of the winemakers, the quality of Washington's Cabernet Sauvignon is clearly superior to its Merlot. However, some wineries
(Leonetti and Andrew Will, and Château Ste. Michelle, for example) are crafting some of the
finest Merlots ever made in the United States.

To no one's surprise, Washington Merlot yields a wine that is more supple than Cabernet.
The acids are lower and the tannins less aggressive. However, a number of Merlots continue
to exhibit an herbaceous character, and frequently lack the depth of flavor and concentration
of the state's best Cabernets.

Pinot Noir   This fickle grape variety is no easier to tame in Washington than in California. Nothing tasted to date remotely resembles what Pinot Noir can achieve in Burgundy or
in selected California and Oregon vineyards.

Lemberger   Originally grown in Germany, this grape, like Zinfandel, is highly adaptable
and can be successfully made in a variety of styles. Just a handful of wineries make Lem-

berger (vineyard acreage is less than 1% of the total in the state). This is lamentable, because the wine can be tasty, fruity, and quite quaffable when not oak aged and when served lightly chilled. Sadly, much of the Lemberger produced is dull and overcropped.

WHITE WINE VARIETALS

Chardonnay   Washington Chardonnay occupies more than 15% of vineyard acreage and can ripen fully while retaining excellent natural acidity. This has caused increasing numbers of producers to barrel-ferment it, and to encourage their Chardonnay to complete malolactic fermentation. Extended lees contact, in vogue in California, is also favored by many Washington producers. A number of wineries have invested heavily in new French oak barrels and are trying to make a wine in the Côte de Beaune style. Others are going after a fruitier style (à la Fetzer's Sundial), while others are aiming for something in between. In short, there is a wide range of styles, but the potential for making excellent Washington State Chardonnay exists, although much of it remains unrealized.

Chenin Blanc   Washington is capable of making wonderful Chenin Blanc in a slightly sweet style due to the naturally crisp acidity. Yet most wineries seemed surprised that anyone would be interested in tasting this ignored, often maligned varietal. However, at $9 a bottle from producers such as Hogue or Snoqualmie, Chenin Blanc can be a true delight, especially on a hot summer's day.

Gewürztraminer   Fortunately, plantings of this varietal are rapidly decreasing in Washington. It has proven no more successful in Washington than in California.

Muscat   Like Chenin Blanc, Muscat grown in Washington can render delicious, crisp, aromatic, perfumed wines that are incredibly refreshing on hot summer days. Latah Creek, Covey Run, Stewart, and Snoqualmie are particularly successful with Muscat. In addition, the price is right.

Sauvignon Blanc   When vinified in Washington, the potentially extroverted, herbal, grassy qualities of this grape are held in check. Many wineries also give the wines some exposure to oak barrels. As in California, most wineries strive for a safe, middle-of-the-road style that too often results in bland, insipid wines. Washington State Sauvignons are, however, priced to sell in the $8–$12 range, which makes them attractive to consumers.

Semillon   This is a grape with excellent potential in Washington. It yields a wine with plenty of body and richness combined with the lively acidity typically found in Washington grapes.

White (Johannisberg) Riesling   Washington's Rieslings are good, but they are often simple and one-dimensional when compared to the slatey, mineral-scented, aromatic complexity and incredible lightness and zestiness attainable in the best German Rieslings. However, Washington's abundant quantities of Rieslings are practically given away, usually selling for less than $9.

RECENT VINTAGES

1996—The 1996 vintage produced exceedingly low yields because of the killer frost that struck many vineyards in January. Some wines are terrific, due to the low yields and a warm summer. It is not a great year across the board, however, as some growers tried to make up for vine losses by having the surviving ones overproduce.

1995—From the top producers, the 1995 vintage is extremely impressive, in both reds and whites. The reds are not quite as powerful as the 1994s but in most cases appear to have riper, softer tannins. Those Cabernet Sauvignon producers capable of harnessing '94's power made greater wines in that year; however the 1995s are generally more classically structured and elegant. 1995 was a significantly cooler year than 1994, allowing for long hang times and late harvests.

1994—A small crop of powerful and highly concentrated wines rendered this a fabulous Washington State vintage. With the exception of the wineries that overly acidify, as well as those that overly extracted, this is a magnificent vintage for the state's reds and an excellent one for its whites.

1993—This is certainly a very good vintage, but more irregular in quality than either 1994 or 1992 which had the benefit of warmer growing seasons. The white wines are aromatic and ideal for drinking early in their lives. At their finest, the red wines are intense and rich but less consistent than either 1992 or 1994.

1992—A hot, dry year resulted in fine overall ripeness and considerable optimism. This is a year of opulent, fruity white wines and rich, powerful Cabernet Sauvignons.

1991—This is a good to very good, somewhat irregular year because of the relatively high crop yields and irregular growing season. For producers who kept yields moderate and picked physiologically ripe fruit, it has turned out to be a high-quality year.

1990—Initially believed to be less successful than either 1988 or 1989, producers are now exhibiting far greater enthusiasm for their red wines. Generalizations concerning such a vast, diverse viticultural region are fraught with the potential for error. With that caveat in mind, the 1990 red wines tend to be supple, rich, and forward. The hot summer and ideal harvest conditions produced fully ripe fruit for producers who harvested at the last moment. The red wines have exceeded the quality of the whites. In many cases the red wines have proven to be as good as the highly acclaimed 1988s and 1989s.

1989—Moderate temperatures allowed full ripening of the grapes. The red varietals were deeply colored, perfumed, and richly flavored. The white varietals had full fruit and good sugar levels balanced by excellent acidity. Washington producers appear unanimous that this is a great vintage.

1988—An excellent vintage for both reds and whites, but without the depth and concentration of 1989. The reds will, however, be long-lived and stylish. The white wines should have been consumed several years ago.

OLDER VINTAGES

Red Wines

1987—This is a vintage of correct, attractive wines without the flesh of 1988 and 1989.

1986—This has turned out to be a mediocre vintage. Most of the reds lack concentration.

1985—This is a tannic vintage in which only the most skilled winemakers made balanced wines. The finest wines are muscular, big, and long-lived.

1984—This was a poor vintage for Washington and is best ignored.

1983—The top red-wine producers consider 1983 to be a superb vintage and, along with 1989 and 1994, one of the best years in memory. The finest wines are only now beginning to open up and will need another 5 to 10 years to reach their apogee. The wines have depth, flavor, flesh, balance, and excellent structure. The 1983 Château Ste. Michelle Cold Creek Reserve Cabernet Sauvignon is a dazzling example from this vintage.

RATING WASHINGTON'S BEST PRODUCERS

* * * * * *(OUTSTANDING)*

DeLille Cellars	Quilceda Creek
Leonetti Cellars	Andrew Will

* * * * (EXCELLENT)

Château Ste. Michelle   Seven Hills

* * * (GOOD)

Columbia Winery   Matthews Cellars
L'Ecole No. 41   McCrea Cellars
Glen Fiona   Waterbrook Winery
Hedges   Woodward Canyon***/****
Hogue Cellars

* * (AVERAGE)

Apex Cellars**/***   Kiona**/***
Arbor Crest   Latah Creek
Barnard Griffin   Mountain Dome
Blackwood Canyon   Patrick M. Paul**/***
Bookwalter   Preston
W. B. Bridgman   Soos Creek
Canoe Ridge**/***   Staton Hills**/***
Cascade Estates   Stewart
Caterina   Tagaris
Columbia Crest**/***   Teft Cellars
Coventry Vale   Paul Thomas
Covey Run**/***   Tucker
Facelli**/***   Walla Walla Vintners**/***
French Creek   Washington Hills
Gordon Brothers Family Vineyards   Wilridge Cellars
Hyatt

APEX CELLARS

1994 Cabernet Sauvignon	D	85
1995 Chardonnay	C	86
1997 Chardonnay "Ne Plus Ultra" Outlook Vineyard	D	86

Revealing sweet butterscotch and baking spice aromas, this rich, oily Chardonnay displays excellent ripeness and an appealing tropical fruit intensity, intermingled with oaky-vanilla tones. Drink it before 2000. The strangely named 1997 Chardonnay "Ne Plus Ultra" Outlook Vineyard has subtle hazelnut, malt, and almond aromas that are followed by a silky-textured and medium-bodied personality. Its mineral and nut flavors (and price!) are reminiscent of a Meursault, but its heat and relatively high alcohol are purely New World. It should be drunk over the next 2 years.

The medium ruby-colored 1994 Cabernet Sauvignon exhibits cassis and candle wax aromas. This well-balanced, medium- to full-bodied, and juicy wine has loads of blackberries, currants, and black cherries in its simple yet delicious character. Anticipated maturity: now–2002.

BOOKWALTER

1994 Cabernet Sauvignon Vintner's Select	D	86

The summer of 1994 brought record temperatures to Washington State and drove grapes to unprecedented ripeness levels. This significantly helped little-known wineries like Bookwalter to craft excellent wines. The Cabernet Sauvignon Vintner's Select has mint, cassis, and blackberry aromas as well as a thick, full-bodied, and deeply flavorful core. Eucalyptus, supersweet cherries, and blackberries can be found in this highly structured, chewy-textured, and tannic wine. It will require cellaring to soften out. Projected maturity: 2000–2006.

CHATEAU STE. MICHELLE

1996	Canoe Ridge Estate Vineyard Chardonnay	D	89
1995	Canoe Ridge Estate Vineyard Chardonnay	D	89
1995	Canoe Ridge Estate Vineyard Merlot	D	87
1995	Cold Creek Vineyard Cabernet Franc	D	86+
1995	Cold Creek Vineyard Cabernet Sauvignon	D	86?
1994	Cold Creek Vineyard Cabernet Sauvignon	D	87?
1993	Cold Creek Vineyard Cabernet Sauvignon	D	88+
1996	Cold Creek Vineyard Chardonnay	D	89+
1995	Cold Creek Vineyard Chardonnay	D	88
1994	Cold Creek Vineyard Merlot	D	86
1995	Ethos	D	88+
1995	Horse Heaven Vineyard Cabernet Sauvignon	D	89+
1994	Horse Heaven Vineyard Cabernet Sauvignon	D	89+
1995	Horse Heaven Vineyard Merlot	D	87+
1996	Horse Heaven Vineyard Sauvignon Blanc	C	86
1996	Indian Wells Vineyard Chardonnay	D	88
1995	Indian Wells Vineyard Chardonnay	D	88
1995	Indian Wells Vineyard Merlot	D	87
1995	Late Harvest Semillon	C (375ml)	89
1994	Meritage	E	88
1995	Meritage	D	89
1996	Reserve Chardonnay	D	89+
1995	Reserve Chardonnay	D	88+
1994	Reserve Merlot	D	86?
1995	Reserve Merlot	D	88
1995	Reserve Syrah	D	85

Château Ste. Michelle's wines are for the most part beautifully made, well structured and well defined. While not all of its offerings can be recommended, it amazes me that a large operation can maintain such high standards. Furthermore, I was surprised to find, while talking with winemakers throughout the state, that the Château Ste. Michelle staff (including its president, Allen Shoup) enjoys a terrific reputation. Human nature being what it is, presidents of mammoth-sized wineries are regarded with envy, jealousy, and disdain by their smaller competitors. Yet Shoup, a class act, is held in high esteem by everyone. When times are tough for smaller producers this conglomerate often comes to their assistance by providing both advice and grapes. After the 1996 killer freeze, this winery supported numerous smaller outfits by sharing its significantly reduced, yet still large, harvest. Château Ste.

Michelle's philosophy (which is right on the money) is that it is in their interest that Washington gain the reputation as a topflight wine producing area.

It was refreshing to learn that Mike Januik, Château Ste. Michelle's talented winemaker, believes that one of the most important things a winemaker can do is "forget the U.C. Davis shtick and unlearn its fascination with a wine's pH." His goal for the last 8 years has been to eschew acidification, preferring to let nature express itself.

The 1996 Horse Heaven Vineyard Sauvignon Blanc (made with 23% Semillon) has a crème brûlée, vanilla, and lemon-laced nose. This fresh, rich, silky-textured, and medium-bodied wine is filled with tangy and bright citrus fruits. It should be drunk over the next year.

The 1995 Indian Wells Vineyard Chardonnay offers enticing aromas of pastry dough as well as an oily-textured, rich, medium-bodied and ripe personality with toast, smoke, and tropical fruit flavors. Well delineated and defined, yet possessing notes of banana and mango, this and the other single-vineyard Château Ste. Michelle Chardonnays could easily be perceived as a synthesis between traditional white Burgundy and California Chardonnay. Drink it between now and 2000. My favorite white wine from Château Ste. Michelle's impressive 1995 lineup is the Canoe Ridge Estate Vineyard Chardonnay. It reveals smoky mineral scents on the nose and a creamy, intensely ripe, thick, yet well-balanced, medium- to full-bodied flavor profile packed with white flowers, pears, and crisp peaches. I tasted this wine twice, once in Washington State and four months later in Washington, D.C., and it appeared to have gained in weight *and* delineation over that time span. Anticipated maturity: now–2002. The 1995 Cold Creek Vineyard Chardonnay displays a straw color with touches of gold and a lively honeysuckle-infused nose. This wine offers a well-concentrated, silky, medium- to full-bodied and superbly balanced core of minerals, stones, and ripe white fruits. Could it be the New World's version of a Chassagne-Montrachet from a warm vintage such as 1989? Anticipated maturity: now–2001. Château Ste. Michelle's Reserve Chardonnay may ultimately be their strongest effort in 1995 if its tightly wound core of warm, concentrated fruit opens to reveal additional complexity. Both times I tasted it, I was impressed by its ripe, crisp (almost citrusy) scents and its medium- to full bodied, racy and stone-filled character. Drink it between now and 2004.

I also enjoyed Château Ste. Michelle's 1996 Chardonnays. The 1996 Indian Wells Vineyard Chardonnay has a ripe, vanilla cream-scented nose and an oily-textured and well-balanced character. This elegant, medium-bodied, and soft wine reveals lovely pear, anise, and toasted oak flavors. Drink this beauty between now and 2003. The 1996 Canoe Ridge Estate Vineyard Chardonnay has an apricot and spice-laden nose. On the palate, this medium- to full-bodied, thick, and gorgeously defined wine offers butterscotch, hazelnuts, and candied lemon peel flavors. It should age effortlessly. Anticipated maturity: now–2004. Exhibiting malt, anise, and spiced apple aromas, the 1996 Cold Creek Vineyard Chardonnay is a mouth-coating, glycerin-packed wine. This rich, oily, and sultry offering, so wonderfully balanced, also offers mineral and pear flavors. Anticipated maturity: now–2003. The 1996 Reserve Chardonnay is quite Burgundian in style. It offers buttered anise and toast aromas followed by a medium- to full-bodied core of minerals, pears, white flowers, and sweet, creamy oak. This exquisitely balanced wine is oily textured, well defined, and possesses a long finish. Drink it between now and 2004.

The ruby-colored 1995 Cold Creek Vineyard Cabernet Franc reveals blackberry, herbal, and leather aromas. It is a medium-bodied, juicy, and firm wine with blueberry, cherry, and grilled oak flavors. Somewhat dry and hard, this wine may ultimately merit a higher rating if time is kind to it. Drink it between 2000 and 2004. The 1995 Reserve Syrah is dark ruby/purple-colored and has a pepper, blackberry, and blueberry-filled nose. Its lean and hollow palate does offer lovely leather, red and black fruit, and oak flavors. This medium-bodied wine is well made but lacks the density essential for a more exalted review. Drink it over the next 2–3 years.

It's a sign of the times that Château Ste. Michelle's Merlots are the winery's most expensive wines. Throughout the wine industry, consumer demand has driven up Merlot prices but not quality. Bulk prices for Merlot are exceedingly high so new vineyards are planted regardless of whether the sight is appropriate. Many of these young vineyards are incapable of producing wines with complexity and depth, yet consumer demand for simple, soft Merlots continues.

The medium to dark garnet-colored 1994 Cold Creek Vineyard Merlot offers a fresh, black cherry-scented nose and a medium- to full-bodied, thick and uncomplicated core of well-ripened red and black fruits. Drink it between now and 2002. The 1994 Reserve Merlot reveals a dark, almost black color and a tightly wound nose of blackberries with notes of green peppers. Its intense and concentrated personality is filled with cassis and black cherries. I am concerned by this wine's lean finish, hard tannins and (overly?) abundant oak. It may ultimately deserve the rating I have given it, but I have my doubts. Anticipated maturity: 2000–2004?

In general, I preferred Château Ste. Michelle's 1995 Merlots more than those from the riper 1994 vintage. The medium to dark ruby-colored 1995 Horse Heaven Vineyard Merlot has white pepper dusted blackberries and cassis, as well as stonelike aromas. This well-crafted, structured, delicious wine has tomato, black/red cherry, mocha, and violet flavors in its silky-textured and medium- to full-bodied personality. Anticipated maturity: now–2004. The darker-colored 1995 Canoe Ridge Estate Vineyard Merlot offers candied blackberry and blueberry aromas. Its red cherry, currant, and fresh herb-laden flavor profile reveals excellent ripeness of fruit. This medium- to full-bodied wine has a velvety-textured attack and midpalate, yet the severe and dusty finish suggests cellaring. Anticipated maturity: 2000–2005. I loved the similarly colored 1995 Indian Wells Vineyard Merlot's deeply ripe cherry-packed nose, yet found its personality to be austere and ungiving. It is a well-crafted wine, with loads of blackberry, blueberry, and black cherry flavors all held hostage by its firm and dusty tannins. Drink this wine between 2000 and 2005. The dark ruby-colored 1995 Reserve Merlot is packed with fruit and new oak. Aromatically revealing a host of sweet black fruits ensconced in wood spices, this is a medium- to full-bodied, juicy, and velvety-textured offering. Black currants, brambleberries, blackberries, vanilla, coffee, and toast all vied for my palate's attention. Readers who love candied fruit and oak should consume this wine over the next 4–5 years.

I am concerned about the tannin level in both the 1994 and 1995 Cold Creek Vineyard Cabernet Sauvignons. The 1995 reveals traces of vegetal scents to its otherwise blackberry and cookie dough-laced nose. It offers a chewy, medium- to full-bodied, and well-concentrated character with well-ripened currant and blueberry fruit. However, its finish, like that of the next wine is exceptionally tannic. Will the fruit hold up? Anticipated maturity: 2002–2009? Exhibiting a dark ruby color and minty blackberries on the nose, the 1994 Cold Creek Vineyard Cabernet Sauvignon has a powerful and intense personality. Layer upon layer of eucalyptus-tinged black fruits can be found in this superstructured and brooding wine. If the fruit outlasts the tannin my score will appear very conservative. Anticipated maturity: 2002–2009? The 1993 Cold Creek Vineyard Cabernet Sauvignon possesses a gorgeous dark garnet color and an intensely ripe, refined and elegant nose of cassis and blackberries. On the palate this is a well-defined, deep, powerful, full-bodied wine packed with black fruits and hints of eucalyptus. Anticipated maturity: 2001–2007.

Both the 1994 and 1995 Horse Heaven Vineyard Cabernet Sauvignons are potentially outstanding. The 1994 reveals a dark blue/purple color and black cherry-infused nose. This wine's light entry is followed by an expansive, powerful, thick, chewy and persistent core of jammy boysenberries and blueberries. Tannic and backward, it will require 4–5 years of cellaring. It should be at its peak between 2002 and 2009. The 1995 is medium to dark ruby-colored, and exhibits a nose of almond candies, juicy blackberries, and cassis liqueur. On the palate, this deep and intense wine is well concentrated, beautifully structured, and crammed with tangy and lively black currants and raspberries. I was also impressed by its long, well-focused, and fruit-filled finish. Anticipated maturity: 2002–2008.

The medium to dark ruby-colored 1994 Meritage, a blend of Cabernet Sauvignon, Merlot, and Cabernet Franc, exhibits a slightly muted dark berry, oak and Asian spice nose as well as a sweet cassis and vanilla-flavored character. This refined, somewhat crafted and "international-styled" wine has pasty tannins that did not appeal to me, yet the quality of its beautifully ripe fruit is undeniable. Drink it between 2001 and 2007. The dark ruby-colored 1995 Meritage reveals blackberry and fresh herb aromas. This precise, well-made, and concentrated wine has excellent concentration, intensity, and balance, as well as a silky-smooth texture. Its flavor profile, dominated by cassis and black cherries, is less oaky and it has a longer finish. Anticipated maturity: 2000–2008. The 1995 Ethos, another meritage wine, has a perfumed, sweet cherry-laced nose. This gorgeously defined, elegant, and extremely appealing wine has a medium to full body that offers loads of juicy blueberries and cassis. It is silky-textured, judiciously spiced by new oak, and should age gracefully. This is the last vintage for Ethos as Château Ste. Michelle has determined that offering two meritages is confusing to consumers. Drink it between now and 2007.

Of the 650,000 cases produced by Château Ste. Michelle, there are 600 of the 1995 Late Harvest Semillon. Aromatically revealing candied oranges, sweet white flowers, papaya, and nutmeg, this well-made and gorgeously balanced wine has a honeyed, strawberry, and cayenne pepper-flavored personality. Over the years I've gleefully drunk a number of late-harvest wines made by Mike Januik and have found them to always be delicious and ageworthy. This is no exception. Anticipated maturity: now–2009+.

Recently tasted older releases: 1994 Cold Creek Vineyard Chardonnay (88), 1993 Cold Creek Vineyard Chardonnay (89).

COLUMBIA CREST

1994 Cabernet Sauvignon	B	86+
1995 Estate Series Chardonnay	B	86
1994 Merlot	C	86

The straw-colored 1995 Estate Series Chardonnay reveals sweet oak aromas with touches of butterscotch followed by a thick, oily, medium- to full-bodied core of ripe fruit with strong vanilla flavors. This is a wine to drink young, over the next 2 years, while it still has the hedonistic sweetness of primary fruit balancing out the strong oak. Columbia Crest's 1994 Merlot offers a medium garnet color and a nose of sweet dark fruits. This well-made, medium-bodied, softly textured offering is filled with supple cherries as well as red and black currants. Drink it between now and 2001. The medium to dark garnet-colored 1994 Cabernet Sauvignon (*not* the Estate Series which is too tannic and oak-laden) possesses green pepper, cedar, and cassis scents and a lively, thick, medium- to full-bodied and uncomplicated black currant and boysenberry-infused flavor profile. Anticipated maturity: now–2002.

COLUMBIA WINERY

1995 Cabernet Franc Red Willow Vineyard	C	87
1994 Cabernet Sauvignon Otis Vineyard	C	88+
1994 Cabernet Sauvignon Red Willow Vineyard Signature Series	C	88
1994 Cabernet Sauvignon Sagemoor Vineyard Signature Series	C	89+
1996 Chardonnay Otis Vineyard Signature Series	C	87+
1996 Chardonnay Woodburne Cuvée	B	86

1996 Chardonnay Wyckoff Vineyard Signature Series	C	87
1996 Milestone Merlot Red Willow Vineyard	C	87+
1996 Pinot Gris	B	85
1996 Syrah	B	85
1995 Syrah Red Willow Vineyard	B	86

I have tasted numerous wines from Columbia Winery and have often found them to be vegetal and lean. However, in recent tastings I was impressed with a number of the estate's offerings, particularly their trio of delicious 1994 single-vineyard Cabernet Sauvignons.

The 1996 Pinot Gris, crafted entirely in stainless steel from Otis Vineyard grapes, reveals rich smoky and mineral-laced aromas. This dry, earthy, fresh, and well-balanced wine is soft and light to medium bodied. It should be consumed over the next 2 years. The 1996 Chardonnay Woodeburne Cuvée displays floral and sweet toasty oak scents followed by a delightfully ripe, medium-bodied, and silky-textured character. Flavors of candied almonds, hazelnuts, white flowers, and oak notes can be found in this well-made wine. It should be consumed over the next 2 years. Due to the 1996 freeze, yields for Columbia's Chardonnay Wyckoff Vineyard were down to 3.8 tons an acre (normal production is a whopping 6 tons per acre). It offers a floral and pear-scented nose and a medium- to full-bodied, glycerin-packed core of white flowers, butterscotch, and oak spices. This rich, thick, and oily-textured wine should be drunk over the next 3 years. Potentially better, the 1996 Otis Vineyard Chardonnay has mineral and stonelike aromas reminiscent of a white Burgundy. On the palate, this elegant, well-delineated, and medium- to full-bodied wine reveals apricot, mineral, anise, and grilled oak flavors. If given a year or more of cellaring, its powerful oak component should become better integrated. Anticipated maturity: now–2003.

The garnet-colored 1995 Cabernet Franc Red Willow Vineyard has a fresh herb and blackberry-scented nose as well as a soft, ripe, and medium-bodied core of blueberries and assorted black fruits. This wine has a powerful personality, excellent depth, lovely balance. It would have merited a higher rating if its finish had been more supple. Anticipated maturity: 1999–2003. The 1995 Milestone Merlot is ruby-colored and has a nutty, oaky, and almond paste-laced nose. This dense, thick, jammy, and medium- to full-bodied wine is crammed with candied red and black currants that linger throughout its plush finish. Drink it over the next 4–5 years.

While I was not enamored with either the 1992 or 1993 Columbia Valley Cabernet Sauvignons, all three of this winery's single-vineyard 1994s are super. The medium to dark ruby-colored Cabernet Sauvignon Red Willow Vineyard has a delightful nose made up of deeply ripe blackberries, blueberries, and violets. It offers a fresh mouthful of chewy and sweet cassis, assorted dark fruits, and traces of road tar. This medium- to full-bodied wine is powerful, well focused, and reveals gorgeously ripe tannins in the finish. Anticipated maturity: now–2005. The potentially outstanding Cabernet Sauvignon Sagemoor Vineyard is dark colored and exhibits an impressive aromatic profile of red cherries, black fruits, fresh herbs and grilled oak. Powerful candied blueberry flavors are intermingled with underbrush, spices, stones, and tar. This wine, the finest I have tasted from Columbia, is extremely concentrated, has superb depth, admirably harmonious equilibrium, and should develop beautifully with cellaring. Anticipated maturity: 2000–2007. The Cabernet Sauvignon Otis Vineyard is the most backward of this trio. Lighter in color than the Sagemoor, it possesses an austere nose of minerals, herbs, and black fruits. Supersweet blackberries, blueberries, plums, and stones can be discerned in this tightly wound and medium- to full-bodied wine's warm personality. This highly structured wine will require patience. Anticipated maturity: 2002–2009.

The 1996 Syrah exhibits a kinky nose of saddle leather, sweet black raspberries, and tobacco, vaguely reminiscent of northern Rhône reds. Its flavors are as beguiling as its aromas, revealing black fruits, cedar, and currants. Regrettably, this wine is painfully short with dry tannins. However, I was so taken by its nose and attack that it deserves to be recommended. It should be drunk within the next year or two. Interestingly, the 1995 Syrah Red Willow Vineyard behaved more like a new world Syrah. It has a medium to dark ruby color and a spicy, herbal, and sweet cassis-scented nose. This is a denser, riper, more concentrated, and longer wine than the 1996 Syrah, yet it lacks that offering's interesting particularities. Drink over the course of the next 3 years.

COVEY RUN

1993 Cabernet Sauvignon Whiskey Canyon	C	86
1996 Chardonnay Celilo Vineyard	B	86
1995 Chardonnay Celilo Vineyard	B	87

The medium to dark-colored 1993 Cabernet Sauvignon Whiskey Canyon has a beautiful nose of black currants, cedar, and tobacco. Its ripe and mouth-coating flavors of roasted green peppers intermingled with sweet black fruits are reminiscent of some California Cabernet Sauvignons from the seventies. While its alcohol renders it a touch warm and will particularly appeal only to those who like this style of wine, it is well made. Drink it over the next 3–4 years. Covey Run's two offerings from one of Washington State's finest Chardonnay vineyards are delicious. The 1996 Chardonnay Celilo Vineyard has an elegant nose of toasted oak, white fruits, and nuts. On the palate it offers pears, apples, stones, and tangy white currants. This medium- to full-bodied wine is also a little hot, but it delivers abundant flavor and depth. It should be drunk over the next 2–3 years. The 1995 Chardonnay Celilo Vineyard tastes like a younger wine. Its aromas of candied almond and vanilla malt shake, as well as its thick, creamy-textured, and butter-flavored personality are characteristics of fine young Chardonnays. This extremely well balanced and medium- to full-bodied wine should develop nicely with cellaring. Anticipated maturity: now–2003.

DELILLE CELLARS

1995 Chaleur Estate (Red)	D	90
1996 Chaleur Estate (White)	C	87
1995 D2	D	88
1995 Harrison Hill Vineyard	D	90

"We are francophiles." This was stated repeatedly during my visits to DeLille Cellars. The four partners, Chris Upchurch (the winemaker), Jay Soloff, Charles Lill (on whose land the winery is built), and Greg Lill (his son) created this winery with the intention of making Bordeaux-styled wines. The reds are blends of Cabernet Sauvignon, Merlot, and Cabernet Franc, with the white a mélange of Semillon and Sauvignon Blanc.

DeLille Cellars is located north of Seattle in the town of Woodinville, where such well-known wineries as Château Ste. Michelle and Columbia are also located. Readers who have a chance to visit DeLille and its beautiful grounds may enjoy Charles Lill's collection of sheep, geese, ducks, chickens, and peacocks.

DeLille produces four wines. The "Estate bottling," called Chaleur Estate ("We wanted a French name that was easily pronounceable in English and that's all we came up with," said Greg Lill), is crafted by Upchurch to express the winery's finest possible expression of the vintage—much like with a Bordeaux château's first wine. D2, named after the road (la départementale 2) that traverses Bordeaux's famous Médoc region, is their second wine. It is culled from barrels that are deemed not excellent enough for the first wine (there is no white D2). The barrels that are not considered worthy of D2 are sold off in bulk. Harrison Hill Vineyard, produced from Washington State's second oldest vines (the Otis Vineyard contains the oldest) is a single-vineyard wine made to express the site's sandy loam, gravel, and rock *terroir*.

DeLille Cellars' offerings are atypical for Washington State. They are not crammed with overpowering candied fruit, nor are they awash in loads of oak. These are wines that impress because of their balance, precision, and subtlety.

The 1996 Chaleur Estate (white) is two-thirds Sauvignon Blanc and one-third Semillon. Its alcoholic and malolactic fermentations were both done in Haut Brion barrels. It has an expressive nose of stones, minerals, and citrus/tropical fruits as well as a rich core of super-ripe white fruits, freshly cut grass, and lemons. This lovely and flavorful wine is reminiscent of a dry white Bordeaux, particularly from a warm vintage like 1990. It should evolve grace-fully. Anticipated maturity: now–2004.

The ruby-colored 1995 D2 has an enthralling nose of violets, fresh black currants, and black cherries. This feminine, elegant, exquisitely balanced, and harmonious wine has a silky texture as well as red cherry and blueberry flavors. It is medium bodied, charming, and should age gracefully. Anticipated maturity: now–2005. The dark ruby-colored 1995 Chaleur Estate (red) offers embracing aromatics of roses, cassis, cedar, and blackberries. This medium- to full-bodied, complex, refined, well-delineated wine was hitting on all cylin-ders when I tasted it. Layers of black fruits, blueberries, and cherries immersed in sweet oak spices can be found in this structured yet highly expressive wine. Anticipated maturity: 2000–2006. The medium to dark-colored 1995 Harrison Hill Vineyard reveals tobacco, cas-sis, black cherry, and smoky oak aromas. So typical of these wines, each element is in place, creating an elegant and harmonious tasting experience. Loads of sweet black cherries, vio-lets, roses, and cinnamon can be found in its medium- to full-bodied flavor profile. This well-defined yet plump wine should be at its apogee between 2000 and 2005.

Recently tasted older releases: 1992 Chaleur Estate (red) (89), 1993 Chaleur Estate (red) (87), 1994 Chaleur Estate (red) (88), 1995 Chaleur Estate (white) (86), 1994 D2 (86), 1994 Harrison Hill Vineyard (87).

L'ECOLE NO. 41

1995	Apogee Pepperbridge Vineyard	D	87
1995	Cabernet Sauvignon	D	87
1995	Seven Hills Vineyard Cabernet Sauvignon	D	86
1994	Seven Hills Vineyard Merlot	D	86

In the past I've been a fan of l'Ecole No. 41's whites, feeling they were often excellent values, but when I visited the estate, I was disappointed by the lack of ripeness and depth in the 1995 Semillon and 1995 and 1996 Chardonnays. However, Martin Clubb has fashioned some beautiful red wines, combining abundant sweet cassis and new oak.

The ruby-colored 1994 Seven Hills Vineyard Merlot reveals a pine and blackberry-scented nose as well as sweet and intense cassis, boysenberry, and eucalyptus flavors in its medium- to full-bodied, oily-textured character. Anticipated maturity: now–2003. Display-ing a ruby color and a wheat, blueberry, and herbal nose reminiscent of a Loire Valley Chi-non from a warm vintage, the 1995 Seven Hills Cabernet Sauvignon has an attractively sweet, creamy, and lush character. This medium-bodied and silky-textured wine is crammed with candied cassis that belies its vegetal aromatics. Anticipated maturity: now–2003. I've tasted the 1995 Apogee Pepperbridge Vineyard twice with consistent notes. Produced from 5-year-old vines, this blend of 67% Cabernet Sauvignon and 33% Merlot has a darker color and a sweet black currant and oak-laced nose. This wine is thick, dense, and rich, offering lively and spicy cassis flavors. It is well concentrated, medium to full bodied, and plush. Drink it between now and 2004. The ruby-colored, seductive 1995 Cabernet Sauvignon has a sweet red cherry and mocha-scented nose as well as a flavor profile reminiscent of cookie dough topped with mint chocolate and cherry ice cream. This medium-bodied wine will provide excellent near-term drinking. Anticipated maturity: now–2002.

FACELLI WINERY

1995 Cabernet Sauvignon	D	86
1995 Merlot	C	85

The ruby-colored 1995 Merlot has black raspberry and smoky oak aromas in addition to a juicy core of sweet cherry fruit. It is a well-made, light-bodied and pure wine crafted for near-term drinking. Anticipated maturity: now–2001. The slightly darker-colored 1994 Cabernet Sauvignon has lively blackberry aromas and a fresh core of tangy cherries and assorted dark fruits. This medium-bodied and concentrated wine will be at its best if drunk before 2002.

GLEN FIONA

1995 Grenache Noir	C	86

Rusty Figgins, the younger brother of Gary Figgins of Leonetti fame, is the owner and winemaker of this small start-up winery. A smart, vivacious, and joyful man, Figgins sets himself apart from other Walla Walla (and indeed, Washington) wineries by concentrating on Rhône varietals. His 1995 Syrah (76% Syrah, 19% Cinsault, and 5% Grenache) recently won an important award in Washington State. Tasting on two separate occasions, I found it to have superb aromas and fruit but an overly oaky, dry finish. I look forward to following Glen Fiona's efforts because I believe Figgins has the desire and ability to produce excellent Rhône-styled wines.

The ruby-colored 1995 Grenache Noir (it includes 6% Syrah) exhibits deep, black pepper-laced cassis aromas and a thick, chewy red and black raspberry-filled core. Only 167 cases of this delicious, thirst-quenching wine were produced (all sold in Seattle, Tacoma, and Walla Walla) so most readers will find it impossible to find. Drink it between now and 2002.

HEDGES

N.V. Cabernet/Merlot	B	87
1996 Cabernet/Merlot	B	85
1997 Fumé Chardonnay	A	85
1994 Red Mountain Reserve	D	88
1995 Red Mountain Reserve	D	87?
1994 Three Vineyards Red	C	86?
1995 Three Vineyards Red	C	87+

Hedges, owned by Tom and Anne-Marie Hedges and a consortium of Swedish shareholders, is one of the rare wineries in Washington State to offer quality wines at $10 or less. The 1997 Fumé Chardonnay, a blend of 55% Sauvignon Blanc and 45% Chardonnay, was vinified, save for a small percentage of the Chardonnay, in stainless-steel tanks. Its fresh smoky aromas are followed by a tangy, light- to medium-bodied core of white fruits, apples, flowers, and smoke. This lively and pleasing wine should be drunk over the next 12 months.

Washington suffered a terrible freeze in early 1996 that tremendously reduced the yields of certain varietals (some vineyards lost up to 80% of their Merlot). Since Hedges' Cabernet/Merlot blend is their "flagship" wine, they were confronted with a major supply problem. Hedges made two wines—a 1996 Cabernet/Merlot and a nonvintage Cabernet/Merlot composed of reserve wines from the 1995 vintage blended with wines from 1996—sold for the same price. The ruby-colored nonvintage Cabernet/Merlot (made of equal portions of each varietal) offers pure, fresh, and mouth-watering aromas of herb-tinged blackberries and cherries. This medium-bodied, silky-textured, well-crafted wine is jam packed with black raspberries and sweet cherries. A simple yet lip-smackingly good fruit-driven wine, it will be at its best if drunk over the next 3 years even though it has the capacity to hold on for years. The 1996 Cabernet/Merlot (51% Cabernet Sauvignon and 49% Merlot) displays a ruby color, aromas of plums, black raspberries, and cherries as well as a light- to medium-bodied core of tangy black currants. A warm and dry finish prevented this wine from meriting a higher rating, yet its vibrant fruit and fair price warrant a recommendation. Anticipated maturity: now–2001.

The backward and rustic 1994 Red Mountain Reserve (a blend of 56% Merlot and 44% Cabernet Sauvignon) was tasted twice with consistent notes. It possesses a deep nose filled with currant, blackberry, plum, and cigar box scents. On the palate, this thick, full-bodied and tannic wine displays mocha, superripe black cherries, eucalyptus and mint flavors. It is a mouth-coating and powerful wine that demands a grilled porterhouse steak. It requires 5+ years of cellaring, and should be at its best between 2003 and 2009. The ruby/purple-colored 1995 Red Mountain Reserve (a blend of 67% Cabernet Sauvignon and 33% Merlot) has an inviting and sultry nose of black cherries and raspberries. If the taster tends to believe a plush and soft wine has been made, the shock of its superstructure, tannin, and hardness will be unsettling. It possesses plenty of tangy blackberry fruit (discernible only after considerable effort). I am willing to give Cabernet Sauvignons the benefit of the doubt when it comes to tannic structure, but this wine is a gamble. Anticipated maturity: 2003–2009.

The ruby-colored 1994 Three Vineyards Red (100% Cabernet Sauvignon) offers sweet blackberry aromas, followed by a superripe, powerful and intensely extracted core of dark berries and eucalyptus. This admirably long wine would have merited a higher rating if its attack had matched the intensity of its midpalate and finish. Anticipated maturity: now–2004. The similarly colored 1995 Three Vineyards Red (2,600 cases produced) has a tobacco, cedar, and blueberry-scented nose. This gorgeously textured wine, a combination of silk and oil on the attack and midpalate, is crammed with blackberries, cherries, and oak spices. It is much more feminine and graceful than the 1994, yet it is medium to full bodied, concentrated, and firm. Anticipated maturity: now–2006.

Recently tasted older releases: 1993 Red Mountain Reserve (87), 1991 Red Mountain Reserve (90).

THE HOGUE CELLARS

1994 Cabernet Sauvignon Barrel Select	B	86
1995 Cabernet Sauvignon Reserve	C	88
1994 Genesis Merlot	C	86
1994 North Star Merlot	C	87
1994 Semillon	A	87
1997 Fumé Blanc	A	85

The Hogue Cellars consistently produces a delicious and fairly priced Fumé Blanc. The 1997 offers a fresh, floral, white peach and crisp apricot nose (more reminiscent of Viognier than Sauvignon Blanc) as well as a dry, clean, pure, refreshing, light-bodied, and slightly spritzy core of minerals, chalk, and white flowers. It should be drunk within the next 12 months.

The 1994 Semillon is an excellent example of this underappreciated varietal. Enticing aromas of honey intermingled with notes of candied pink grapefruit are followed by a light-to medium-bodied, thirst-quenching wine filled with loads of spices, citrus fruits and honey. Made for immediate consumption, it is not complex, but this Semillon delivers loads of near-term pleasure. A wonderful aperitif wine. Drink it over the next year.

The dark ruby-colored 1994 North Star Merlot reveals sweet cassis and blueberry aromas as well as a juicy, silky, medium- to full-bodied core of blackberries, cassis and Asian spices. Its long finish displays plenty of soft tannins. Anticipated maturity: now–2005. The 1994 Genesis Merlot has a warm and inviting nose of ripe black currants and milk chocolate. On the palate, this medium- to full-bodied, gorgeously ripe wine offers layers of black cherries and blackberries, fresh herbs, and vanilla-infused oak flavors. It should be at its best between now and 2003. The medium to dark ruby-colored 1994 Cabernet Sauvignon Barrel Select exhibits a coffee/malt and red cherry-scented nose. Its concentrated, extracted, and medium- to full-bodied core of fruit is densely packed with blackberries and currants. This thick and rich wine will require cellaring patience to allow its highly structured and tannic personality to soften. Anticipated maturity: 2001–2006. I was impressed with Hogue's 1995 Cabernet Sauvignon Reserve. This medium to dark ruby-colored wine has a beguiling black raspberry-infused nose that is followed by a powerful, well-delineated, and concentrated character. Dark cherries, cassis, and sweet oak flavors can be found in this expressive, deeply flavorful wine. It would have merited a higher score if it had not displayed an alcoholic finish. Anticipated maturity: now–2004.

KIONA VINEYARDS

1997 Chardonnay	C	85

Kiona's 1997 Chardonnay neither smells nor tastes like Chardonnay but is a delight to drink. Its potpourri, perfume, candied orange peel, and apricot nose smells like a hypothetical blend of Viognier and Muscat-Beaumes de Venise. On the palate, this light- to medium-bodied and slightly hot wine reveals fresh peach and floral flavors I tend to associate with Condrieu. My instincts suggest drinking this wine over the next year while its exuberant fruit has the upper hand in the component war between alcohol and acid.

LEONETTI CELLARS

1995 Cabernet Sauvignon	D	89
1994 Cabernet Sauvignon	D	91
1995 Merlot	D	90
1994 Merlot	D	92

Gary Figgins, Leonetti's owner and winemaker, is a gregarious and fun-loving man. He has one goal—to craft hedonistic and sultry wines. Leonetti is certainly Washington State's most famous winery, and as a consequence, its wines have drawn the most attention from the press and collectors. Figgins is in such demand from his legions of fans that he has instituted a once-a-year open house where customers can harvest their purchases, barrel taste, and talk to the man. I was in Washington State for a recent open house, and witnessed the private jets at the small Walla Walla airport, as well as the spillover business it generated at the wineries of Figgins' Eastern Washington colleagues. This phenomenon would generate envy and jealousy in every other viticultural region I can think of. In Walla Walla, Leonetti's neighbors are glad for the business and excited to have visitors.

Figgins, a former cannery machinist, bonded his winery in 1978, and built his cellars 5 years later. New oak barrels from the far reaches of the earth (and from numerous coopers) jam the underground aging cellar. I jokingly asked Figgins if he would purchase barrels from Botswana if they were available, and he laughed and said, "Sure, bring'em on, they could add a new African spice." He adores the spicy sweetness of oak and finds that even using

100% new barrels is not enough. Figgins therefore uses new wood staves (oak bars that criss-cross inside the barrel) to achieve the desired flavor profile. His fame and reputation permit him to obtain the quality of grapes he craves—superripe sweet fruit that will mesh admirably with the lavish use of new oak.

I love drinking Leonetti's wines, especially when they are young. Figgins' offerings consistently qualify as some of the world's best-drinking reds. They are candied oak bombs that satisfy my cravings for uninhibited pleasure. However, having tasted through a number of older releases, I do not believe these wines can be considered ageworthy. With time the explosive sultriness of the fruit and copious oak spices lose their exuberant youthful qualities. The wines, while still extremely pleasurable to drink, do taste more subtle, but this restraint makes them less interesting and fun. For example, when young the 1989 Cabernet Sauvignon Seven Hills Reserve was the sexiest, sultriest, and most hedonistically pleasurable Cabernet I had ever put to my lips. My score at the time was in the upper 90s; today, after time has tamed the wine, I rate it a 90—still outstanding and immensely pleasurable but no longer mind-boggling. This is not a knock at Leonetti's wines. I believe the most important factor is how much pleasure a wine gives, not how long it gives it. Figgins' wines tend to be superb the day they are purchased, so why defer your gratification?

The dark ruby/purple-colored 1995 Merlot offers aromas reminiscent of a deep-dish cherry pie dusted with Asian spices, grated vanilla bean, and then topped off with a healthy scoop of coffee ice cream. This thick, silky-textured, and intensely sweet (from glycerin not sugar) wine is lively, tangy, and immensely pleasurable. Layers of candied red fruits awash in toasted oak spices bathe the palate. This offering's long and oily finish does not reveal any of the dryness one would expect from oak tannins. Drink it over the next 5 years. The 1994 Merlot is even better. It offers an extremely dark color and a magnificently expressive nose of jammy blackberries and cassis soaked in a myriad of oak spices. This powerful, full-bodied, concentrated, and intensely thick wine is crammed with candied red and black cherries, Asian spices, chocolate, and vanilla cream. A testimony to his considerable winemaking skills, this massive wine is not ponderous. Anticipated maturity: now–2004.

Aromatically, the ruby-colored 1995 Cabernet Sauvignon reveals a blast of chocolate syrup-covered cherry ice cream, caramel, coconut, cassis liqueur, and mint julep. This medium- to full-bodied, silky-textured, rich, and candied wine offers loads of superripe red and black berry fruit as well as boatloads of pepper and Asian spices. Drink it over the next 4–5 years. The bright ruby-colored 1994 Cabernet Sauvignon has beguiling aromas of cassis jam and vanilla cream. This beautifully ripe wine is explosive, chewy, medium to full bodied, and hedonistic. Its flavor profile, filled with candied black raspberries, cherries, coconut, and caramel, represents liquid decadence. More decadent than intellectual, it will take tasters to levels of pleasure rarely attained. Anticipated maturity: now–2004.

Recently tasted older releases: 1993 Cabernet Sauvignon (87), 1992 Cabernet Sauvignon (87), 1991 Cabernet Sauvignon (88), 1990 Cabernet Sauvignon (88), 1989 Cabernet Sauvignon (87), 1988 Cabernet Sauvignon (90), 1990 Cabernet Sauvignon Reserve Seven Hills Vineyard (90), 1989 Cabernet Sauvignon Reserve Seven Hills Vineyard (90), 1987 Cabernet Sauvignon Reserve Seven Hills Vineyard (92).

MATTHEWS CELLARS

1996 Cabernet Sauvignon Reserve Elerding Vineyard	D	87+
1995 Red Wine	D	85
1996 Red Wine	D	86

How hot is the wine market? Well, Matthew Loso, the 27-year-old who started Matthew Cellars 4 years ago, sells all his wines on futures. According to him, Loso had never even tasted a sip of wine when he was promoted from waiter to wine steward at an airport restaurant 8 years ago. Shortly thereafter, he went to work for a large Washington winery, and was paid in grapes and barrels. Today he receives letters, faxes, and phone calls begging him to increase allocations.

Located in rented space in a Woodinville industrial park, Matthews Cellars produces two offerings, a Bordeaux-blend red and a Cabernet Sauvignon from Elerding Vineyard, one of Washington State's premier sites.

The ruby-colored 1995 Red Wine (a blend of 50% Cabernet Sauvignon, 40% Merlot, and 10% Cabernet Franc) has a candied blackberry-scented nose and a tangy, fresh, and medium-bodied personality. It reveals plenty of well-ripened fruit, but suffers from a surprisingly high level of unintegrated acidity. It is presently delicious and thirst quenching, but I question its ability to cope with its acid with increased bottle age. Drink up. The medium- to dark ruby-colored 1996 Red Wine (850 cases were produced of this 43% Cabernet Sauvignon, 37% Cabernet Franc, and 20% Merlot blend) has a gorgeously pure nose of red fruits, mint leaves, and blackberries. This feminine, medium-bodied rather plush wine also has a high level of acidity, but has more red cherry/raspberry fruit. Its finish is clipped (by acid?), but it is nonetheless a delicious wine for near-term drinking. Anticipated maturity: now–2001. The similarly colored 1996 Cabernet Sauvignon Reserve Elerding Vineyard was aged, like the previous offerings, in 100% new French oak. Aromatically revealing kirsch, black raspberry and mint notes, this medium- to full-bodied highly extracted wine is dense, thick, and rich. Its concentrated and powerful flavor profile is composed of cassis liqueur, violets, and vanilla bean. This wine will merit higher praise if its considerable fruit is capable of assimilating its whopping 14.6% alcohol content. Anticipated maturity: 2000–2006.

McCREA CELLARS

1994 Chardonnay	C	86
1996 Chardonnay	C	85?
1995 Chardonnay Elerding Vineyard	D	88
1994 Chardonnay Reserve	D	87
1996 Chardonnay Reserve	D	87
1996 Viognier Ciel du Cheval Vineyard	C	87

Doug McCrea, a former woodwind instrument teacher, is a gifted winemaker. He has crafted fine Chardonnays, Rhône-styled reds, and now a scrumptious Viognier. Three hundred cases of 1996 Viognier, a white peach, apricot, lily, and fresh scented wine, were produced. It reveals excellent vibrancy, balance, as well as flavors reminiscent of both Alsatian Gewürztraminer and Condrieu (rose water, lychee, pineapple, and peaches). A delightful apéritif wine, it should be consumed over the next year.

Regrettably, McCrea has decided that his Chardonnays must be artificially acidified in order to age well. Given my dislike of wines with unintegrated mouth-searing acidity, it is not surprising that I prefer his older releases to recent ones. Furthermore, my experience with the overacidified Chardonnays, so prevalent in California during the seventies and eighties, leads me to believe that these recent releases may last longer, but they will not improve.

Revealing lively white fruit scents, the 1996 Chardonnay is a tangy, floral, silky-textured, and medium-bodied wine. It possesses lovely pear and hazelnut flavors that are marred by a high level of unintegrated acid. The 1996 Chardonnay Reserve (100 cases produced from a barrel selection) has a mineral-laced, sweet oak, and white raisin-scented nose. While its acid is high, this wine is more harmonious and better balanced. It offers silky layers of candied almonds and spiced pears immersed in oak, yet the finish is marred by excessive acidity. Drink it over the next 2 years.

Sporting the straw and gold color of a mature wine, the 1995 Chardonnay Elerding Vineyard is delicious. Evolved aromas of butterscotch, anise, and candied almonds are followed by a lush, dense, silky, and immensely flavorful core of dried honey, apple compote, and minerals. This medium-bodied wine requires immediate consumption. Drink it over the next year.

The 1994 Chardonnay is a sweet, oak-scented, rich, polished, silky, and well-defined offering. On the palate it is mineral and white fruit-packed, medium bodied with an adequate length, while the '94 Chardonnay Reserve is more intense aromatically. It also displays orange marmalade and vanilla scents as well as a thick, chewy, full-bodied personality crammed with leesy, honeyed tea, and tropical fruit flavors. Both these wines should be drunk before 2001.

QUILCEDA CREEK

1995 Cabernet Sauvignon	D	92
1994 Cabernet Sauvignon	D	94+

Alexander Golitzen, known to everyone as either Al or Alex, is actually His Royal Highness, Prince Alexander. A former engineer for Scott Paper, an important member of Russian royalty, he is also one of the world's finest winemakers. His Cabernet Sauvignons are the most complex and ageworthy wines I have encountered from Washington State, often reminiscent of those from Château Margaux. They combine power with elegance, depth with finesse, and concentration with focus.

Since the founding fathers of Washington State's fine wine industry are still hard at work, we have few examples of generational transitions. Golitzen's son, Paul, however, is extremely bright, dedicated, and appears to have learned well at his father's side. Alexander Golitzen credits his son with much of the recent progress at Quilceda Creek and seems convinced that the winery will reach new heights under Paul's guidance.

The dark ruby-colored 1994 Quilceda Creek is an extraordinary wine that deserves to be mentioned in the same breath as California's top offerings. I recently served a bottle of it blind to Robert Parker amid wines from Dominus, Harlan Estate, Colgin, and others. While it did stand out as being different (it is much more Bordeaux-like than its California brethren), it was their qualitative equal. It offers deep and compelling aromas of red and black fruits, lead pencil, and traces of oak spices. This full-bodied, concentrated, and chewy wine is thick, dense, and gorgeously defined for such a massive wine. Its combination of power and elegance brought to mind the 1986 Margaux, one of the finest wines ever produced by that illustrious estate. When I first tasted the '94 Quilceda Creek at the estate in Snohomish, Golitzen was worried that it was too big and powerful. I found myself in the all-too-rare position of defending a wine's qualities to the person who had made it! At a subsequent tasting, the wine had lost some of its youthful exuberance and Golitzen was enthused to see that it was gaining focus and elegance. This is a truly magnificent wine, and it will age remarkably well. Drink it between 2004 and 2015+.

The dark ruby-colored 1995 Quilceda Creek contains 12% Merlot, a high figure for this Cabernet Sauvignon-dominated wine. It reveals an expressive, ripe, and violet-laced nose as well as wonderful layers of blackberry, red currant, cassis, and floral flavors. This medium-to full-bodied, elegant and refined wine is intensely concentrated and flavorful but certainly not on the level of the blockbuster 1994. In its youth this silky-textured wine is quintessential Golitzen, polished, precise, focused, and gracefully exhibiting highly defined sweet fruit. It is certainly ageworthy, but I predict it will attain its peak of maturity earlier than its older sibling. Anticipated maturity: 2003–2010+. Bravo!

Recently tasted older releases: 1993 Cabernet Sauvignon (89+), 1992 Cabernet Sauvignon (88), 1991 Cabernet Sauvignon (86), 1990 Cabernet Sauvignon (92), 1989 Cabernet Sauvignon (91), 1992 Cabernet Sauvignon Reserve (92), 1988 Cabernet Sauvignon Reserve (93).

SEVEN HILLS WINERY

1995 Klipsun Vineyard Merlot	C	89
1994 Seven Hills Vineyard Cabernet Sauvignon	C	88
1994 Seven Hills Vineyard Cabernet Sauvignon Reserve	D	89
1995 Seven Hills Vineyard Merlot	C	88

The Seven Hills Winery is actually located in Oregon (as is a substantial part of the Walla Walla Valley Appellation).

Owned by the Hendricks and McClellan families, the winery takes its name from one of the finest vineyards in Walla Walla. The Seven Hills vineyard (I spent considerable time walking this site and was unable to find the seven hills) is, ironically, primarily located in Oregon (yes, Washington State's most famous wine, Leonetti's Seven Hills Cabernet Sauvignon, is produced from Oregon grapes!).

The 1995 Merlot Seven Hills Vineyard is medium to dark ruby-colored and has dense aromas of sweet blackberries and cherries. This extremely well made wine (Casey McClellan is the winemaker) is chewy, thick, medium to full bodied, and offers loads of intense and ripe red and black fruits. It is a concentrated, velvety, and long finishing beauty. Drink it over the next 6 years. Produced from what certainly is one of the finest vineyards in the Columbia Valley Appellation, the dark ruby-colored 1995 Merlot Klipsun Vineyard reveals cassis liqueur and Asian spice aromas. This layered, massively ripe, and broad-shouldered wine is densely packed with candied black currants, blackberries, and cherries. It is rich, velvety-textured, and admirably spiced by the judicious use of new oak barrels. Also impressive is its long finish that reveals supple tannins. Anticipated maturity: now–2004.

The 1994 Cabernet Sauvignon Seven Hills Vineyard was aged in half American and half French oak barrels (30% new). Aromatically it reveals spiced corn and cherry aromas. This full-bodied, deep, thick wine is rich, chewy textured, and crammed with gorgeously ripe blackberries and cassis. Drink it over the next 5–6 years. Produced from what in Washington State passes for old vines (14 years), the dark-colored 1994 Cabernet Sauvignon Seven Hills Vineyard Reserve (140 cases were made) has intense aromas of cassis, leather, and Asian spices. This oily-textured, powerful, and dense wine is jam packed with sugarcoated red and black berry fruit and traces of eucalyptus. It is admirably concentrated and spicy (imagine a downsized Leonetti) and will provide considerable pleasure over the next 5–6 years.

STATON HILLS

1994 Chardonnay	B	86

The Staton Hills winery was purchased in 1992 by a Japanese family whose business interests include a wide variety of different companies in Japan and elsewhere. They installed Peter Ansdell as the winery's president. Ansdell, of British birth, was well schooled by August Sebastiani in the business of American winemaking, yet has some distinctly noncommercial aspirations for Staton Hills. For example, Ansdell wants to produce a European-styled Cabernet, not at all in the international style that is so commercially viable. He also plans wine releases when *he* feels they are ready to drink, not on a bottom-line-driven schedule. This means that it is quite possible that the Cabernets will not be released in chronological order as some vintages are accessible earlier than others.

Located at the top of Washington's Yakima Valley, only 80 miles from the Canadian border, most of the grapes used by Staton Hills are purchased from outside sources (a mere 15% are estate grown). As newly purchased acreage is planted with vines, 40% of the winery's grapes will be estate grown. At present, the winery produces 35,000 cases of wine (10% of which are Chardonnay, 10% Sauvignon Blanc, with the balance Cabernet), and has plans to eventually increase production to 50,000 cases. Ansdell's long-term goal is to be Washington State's finest nationally recognized winery for Cabernet. Paul Hobbs, well known for the wines he produces under his own name, is Staton Hill's consultant winemaker.

The 1994 Chardonnay offers almond cookie scents and an oily, medium-bodied personality with mineral, stone, walnut and light butter flavors. Oak was used judiciously in the crafting of this wine, with slight hints of toast being discernible on the nose and in its flavor profile. Drink it between now and 2002.

WALLA WALLA VINTNERS

1995 Cabernet Sauvignon	C	(84–88)

When I arrived at the new Walla Walla Vintners winery the owners informed me that I was the first wine journalist to visit them, which is not an amazing feat since they had opened only a week earlier. This winery, owned by a psychology professor, a hamburger and coffee stand franchise owner, and a CPA/insurance salesman, was bonded in 1995 and is located in a red barn on the western edge of Walla Walla. It is just below new vineyard land planted by Gary Figgins and his son. The 1995 Cabernet Sauvignon contained fruit from a number of well-known (in Washington!) vineyards, including Windrow, Canoe Ridge and Porteus. Medium to dark ruby-colored, it offers an attractive nose of red and black fruits as well as a medium- to full-bodied, silky, flavor profile packed with ripe black cherries and cassis. A judicious use of oak can be discerned on its long finish.

WATERBROOK WINERY

1994 Cabernet Sauvignon	C	88
1996 Sauvignon Blanc	B	86

I have consistently been impressed with Waterbrook Winery's Sauvignon Blancs, much more so than with their Chardonnays that taste excessively manipulated and lean. The 1996 Sauvignon Blanc has a lovely Sancerre-like nose of freshly squeezed ripe citrus fruits and a rich, beautifully ripe character reminiscent of candied lemon peels laced with traces of dried honey and pineapple. Drink it over the next year or 2.

The dark ruby-colored 1994 Cabernet Sauvignon displays highly expressive cassis liqueur aromas and a thick, mouth-filling, medium- to full-bodied character crammed with candied black fruits. This velvety textured, intense, flavorful, and explosive wine will provide considerable drinking pleasure over the next 5–6 years.

ANDREW WILL

1995 Cabernet Franc	D	89
1995 Cabernet Sauvignon	D	88
1995 Cabernet Sauvignon Boushey	D	90
1995 Cabernet Sauvignon Pepper Bridge	D	91+
1996 Merlot	D	88
1995 Merlot	D	89
1996 Merlot Ciel du Cheval	D	91
1995 Merlot Ciel du Cheval	D	91+
1995 Merlot Klipsun	D	91
1996 Merlot Klipsun	D	93+
1995 Merlot Pepper Bridge	D	87

1995 Merlot Reserve	D	90+
1994 Sorella	D	91
1995 Sorella	D	93
1996 Sorella	D	89+

In the introduction to his comments on Andrew Will in Issue #110 of *The Wine Advocate*, Robert Parker wrote that "No winery in America has made a series of Merlots as sumptuous and delicious as these 1995s." Well, the 1996s are just as good, if not better.

I have visited the home/estate (on Vashon Island and accessible by ferry from downtown Seattle) of owner/winemaker Chris Camarda twice in the last 18 months and found him to be an intensely passionate wine and food lover (his home-baked bread is to die for). A former waiter in Seattle's restaurants, Camarda felt he could make better wines than those he was serving, so he set out to prove it. The name Andrew Will was later created by combining the first names of his son and nephew, much to the chagrin of consumers who telephone (in an attempt to acquire these rare wines) and say they are a good friend of Mr. Will!

Camarda has not been able to drink wine for a number of years, but he continues to smell and taste it assiduously. An intelligent and thoughtful man, Camarda ponders each step of the winemaking process, debating with himself and others the pros and cons of every decision. When I visited the estate, he served me a bottle of his 1989 Ciel du Cheval "R" Merlot so that we could analyze his wine's potential ageworthiness, and it was over this bottle that I understood why Camarda is a great winemaker. His passionate, artistic side is buttressed and guided by a strong analytical and detail-oriented personality. The resulting wines are lush, opulent, packed with ripe sweet fruit, yet elegantly defined and structured.

Camarda produced 3,000 bottles in 1995, 2,000 in 1996 (due to the crop destroying freeze) and plans to produce 4,200 bottles in 1997. He purchases his grapes from some of Washington's top vineyards, Klipsun, Ciel du Cheval and Pepper Bridge), performs a one-third whole-berry fermentation using the indigenous yeasts, and then promotes rapid malo-lactic fermentations.

Alexander Golitzen of Quilceda Creek has told me a few times that tannin management is the key to being a great winemaker. Andrew Will Winery's 1996s have virtually perfect tannins. They are present but buffered by the loads of dominating sweet fruit. Furthermore, what is amazing about Camarda's wines is that they are concentrated yet graceful. Many highly extracted and powerful wines I taste impress me by their strength, yet seem heavy and ponderous. Camarda's blend power with elegance, concentration with finesse, and super-sweet fruit with definition. Chris Camarda is a brilliant winemaker.

The 1996 Merlot is medium to dark ruby-colored and offers a Pomerol-like nose of red cherries and stewed tomatoes. Raspberries, cherries, and blueberries can be found in this awesomely textured and chewy wine. It does not offer much complexity, but its luscious fruit and silky tannins are admirable. Drink it over the next 5 years. The dark-colored 1996 Merlot Ciel du Cheval was dominated by oak aromas. However, its extraordinary personality, crammed with concentrated and candied cherries and blackberries, is more than a match for the oak. This supple, powerful, and dense wine has a prodigious finish that is as smooth as it is long. Anticipated maturity: 2000–2008.

The opaque purple-colored 1995 Merlot Ciel du Cheval's aromas are reminiscent of a young, unbottled, right bank Pomerol from Bordeaux, with its black raspberry/cherry sweetness, and toasty vanillin. More closed than the regular cuvée and Klipsun Vineyard Merlot, it possesses superb potential as well as a rare richness allied to considerable elegance and complexity. Give this wine 1–2 years of cellaring and drink it over the following 12–15. It is an amazing Merlot from Washington State! The 1995 Merlot Pepper Bridge Vineyard displays a spicy, green pepper, herbal note to its black cherry, earth, and spicelike flavors.

Medium bodied, with more tannin, and less flesh and fruit, this is a very good bottle of wine, but in comparison to the other offerings, a less prodigious effort. It should drink well for 7–8 years. The 1995 Merlot Reserve (indicated by a red R on the label) exhibits a thick, dense, opaque ruby/purple color, followed by tight but promising aromas of pure black fruits, medium to full body, light to moderate tannin, and outstanding purity and richness. Once again, Andrew Will has managed to cram a considerable amount of flavor and intensity into a wine without its becoming flabby or overbearing. The 1995 Merlot Reserve requires 1–2 years of cellaring; it should age well for 10–12 years. The 1995 Merlot reveals a healthy dark plum color, a big, spicy, chocolatey, blackberry-scented nose, lush, chocolate, caramel, and black cherry flavors, medium body, admirable lushness and complexity, and a clean, pure, rich finish. It is a delicious Merlot to drink over the next 5–6 years. The dark ruby/purple-colored 1995 Klipsun Vineyard Merlot displays sweet, jammy black currant, cherry, and spicy new oak scents. On the palate, this hedonistically creamy, chewy, thick, and full-bodied Merlot explodes with powerful and highly concentrated, yet refined cassis, boysenberry and black cherry flavors. The superb finish reveals perfectly ripe tannins and sweet toasty oak notes. Anticipated maturity: now–2008. The 1996 Klipsun Merlot is superior and one of the finest Merlots I have ever tasted. It has a penetrating candied tomato and fresh herb-laden nose as well as a medium- to full-bodied, concentrated, well-structured, and velvety-textured character. Its unbelievably deep flavor profile offers layer upon layer of sweet cassis, cherries, mocha, and touches of toffee. It also possesses an unbelievably long finish that reveals Camarda's trademark silky tannins. Anticipated maturity: now–2008.

Andrew Will's medium to dark ruby-colored 1996 Cabernet Franc is a lovely wine. Its aromas of stewed tomatoes, wheat, mineral, herbal, and candied blueberries are reminiscent of a Chinon from an extremely hot and ripe vintage. On the palate, any similarities with a wine from the Loire ends abruptly. This magnificently balanced wine is crammed with jammy red, blue, and black fruits that reveal a level of ripeness unheard of in red Loire wines. It is medium to full bodied, highly focused, and well defined. Drink it over the next 7–8 years.

Exhibiting a fresh blackberry, thyme, and cassis-scented nose, the 1995 Cabernet Sauvignon is tightly wound, thick, medium bodied, and well focused. Well-ripened black currants and blueberries can be found in its tangy flavor profile as well as in its long finish. Drink it between 1999 and 2005. The 1995 Cabernet Sauvignon Boushey is dark ruby-colored and has an herbal, sweet blueberry and candied raspberry-laced nose. This gorgeously soft Cabernet is silky-textured, deep, concentrated, and has flavors reminiscent of cassis liqueur spiked with sugarcoated oranges. Anticipated maturity: now–2007. The similarly colored 1995 Cabernet Sauvignon Pepper Bridge has a compelling *garrigue* (the smell of Provence's sun-roasted wild herbs) and black cherry-scented nose. It is a fat, thick, luscious, superbly focused, and powerful wine. Camarda's deft use of new oak is to be admired. This Merlot's flavor profile is so crammed with cherries and blueberries that the touch of toast goes virtually unnoticed. It is more structured, complex, and longer than the Boushey, but shares that wine's extraordinarily supple tannins. Anticipated maturity: now–2009.

Chris Camarda named his meritage, or proprietary red, Sorella (which means sister in Italian) in honor of his recently departed sister (her portrait graces the label). The outstanding dark purple-colored 1994 Sorella (a Cabernet/Merlot blend) offers lovely aromas of sweet mocha, Asian spices, candied dark berries, violets and traces of sweet vanilla and mint. Its thick, full-bodied personality is packed with explosively jammy, yet delineated cassis fruit. When I served it blind to my tasting group, a friend commented that it had to be a topflight Pahlmeyer because of the huge amounts of glycerin, chewy fruit and supple tannins. Anticipated maturity: now–2010. The dark ruby-colored 1995 Sorella is also a superb wine. Its complex aromas, combining blackberries, gravel, sweat, led pencil, peanut oil, and salt, is reminiscent of a hypothetical cross between a Pauillac and Graves. It reveals a velvety mouthful of sweet blueberries, cassis, fresh herbs, and dark cherries. A medium- to full-bodied wine, it also boasts magnificent concentration and power. Even though it is forward and highly expressive, this wine also possesses a firm Bordeaux-like structure, yet with silky tannins. Anticipated maturity: now–2010. Produced from 10% Cabernet Franc, 25% Merlot (both from the Ciel du Cheval vineyard), and 65% Cabernet Sauvignon (from the Mercer Ranch vineyard), the medium to dark ruby-colored 1996 Sorella offers supersweet red fruit and Asian spice aromas. This gorgeously deep wine is crammed with cherries, raspberries, blackberries, brambleberries, and fresh herbs. Fruit driven, it is concentrated and extracted and the most tannic and backward wine I've tasted from Chris Camarda. Unlike his other offerings, this wine will require cellaring. Drink it between 2002 and 2010+. Bravo!

Note: The Andrew Will Winery is located in a residential neighborhood on Vashon Island. An ordinance prevents Anne and Chris Camarda from receiving visitors to the winery as it would impede on their neighbor's privacy.

Recently tasted older releases: 1995 Merlot Ciel du Cheval (92), 1994 Merlot Ciel du Cheval (89+), 1993 Merlot Ciel du Cheval (87), 1989 Merlot Ciel du Cheval (89), 1995 Merlot Pepper Bridge (91+), 1994 Merlot Pepper Bridge (90), 1993 Merlot Pepper Bridge (90), 1995 Merlot Klipsun (91).

WOODWARD CANYON

1996 Merlot	D	87
1995 Merlot	D	88
1993 Red Wine Special Selection	EE	87

The ruby-colored 1996 Merlot displays lovely aromatics of roses, cherries, and blackberries. This attractively sweet, well-balanced, and medium-bodied wine packs an enormous quantity of red and black fruit in its charming, silky, and lush character. It may be ageworthy, but why wait? Anticipated maturity: now–2004. The exuberant, dark ruby/purple-colored, lusciously fruity, supple 1995 Merlot reveals jammy berries, black fruits, herbs, smoke, chocolate, and spice. This medium-bodied, luscious wine can be drunk over the next 1–2 years.

The luxury priced 1993 Red Wine Special Selection (a blend of 73.7% Cabernet Sauvignon, 21% Merlot, and 5.3% Cabernet Franc) is black/purple-colored and reveals a warm eucalyptus, and cassis liqueur-scented nose. This medium- to full-bodied, verging on alcoholic, and superconcentrated wine is crammed with black currants, blackberries, mint, and licorice. While its structure, power, and hugely extracted fruit are impressive, it lacks the harmony I had expected. Anticipated maturity: 2002–2010+.

THE BEST OF THE REST

Australia and New Zealand
Argentina and Chile

8. AUSTRALIA AND NEW ZEALAND

AUSTRALIA

TYPES OF WINE

You name it and the Australians no doubt grow it, make it into wine, blend it with something else, and give it an unusual name. Australian wines have been hot, and not just in America. The combination of quality and value that many of them offer is the hottest thing in town from London to New York. Australia, like California in America, and Alsace in France, labels its wine after the grape (or grapes) that it is made from. All the major grape varietals are used here, and amazingly, great wines are turned out from all the varietals. The major viticultural districts (listed alphabetically) are as follows:

Adelaide Hills (South Australia) Located in southern Australia, this is a high-altitude, cooler-climate region. Chardonnay and Sauvignon Blanc are very promising.

Barossa Valley (South Australia) In southern Australia, this huge, well-known viticultural area north of Adelaide is the home of some of the titans of Australia's wine industry (such as Penfolds, Henschke, Seppelt, Wolf Blass, Orlando, and Hill Smith). It is also a source for some spectacular old-vine Shiraz wines.

Bendigo (Victoria) Bendigo is an up-and-coming area, although it has a long history as a wine-producing region. Cabernet Sauvignon holds the highest promise.

Central Victoria (Victoria) The traditionally styled wines of Château Tahbilk are the best that come from central Victoria and the Goulburn Valley. The wines are powerful, full bodied, and fruity from this area.

Clare Valley (South Australia) Located north of Adelaide and the Barossa Valley, this area is known for its white rather than red wines. Several superb Rieslings have emerged from this cool area.

Coonawarra (South Australia) Coonawarra is perhaps the most famous and, according to some, the best red wine–growing area of Australia. Situated in south Australia, west of the Goulburn Valley, top wineries such as Lindemans (their Limestone Ridge and St. George Vineyards are there), Petaluma, Penfolds, Rosemount, Orlando, Reynella, and Mildara pull their grapes from Coonawarra. Most observers consider this prime Shiraz and Cabernet territory.

Geelong (Victoria) Southwest of Melbourne near the coast is the small area of Geelong. It is a source for very good Cabernet.

Glenrowan (Victoria) Located in northeastern Victoria, this hot area is famous for its inky, rich, chewy red wines, especially the full-throttle Shiraz from one of Australia's historic

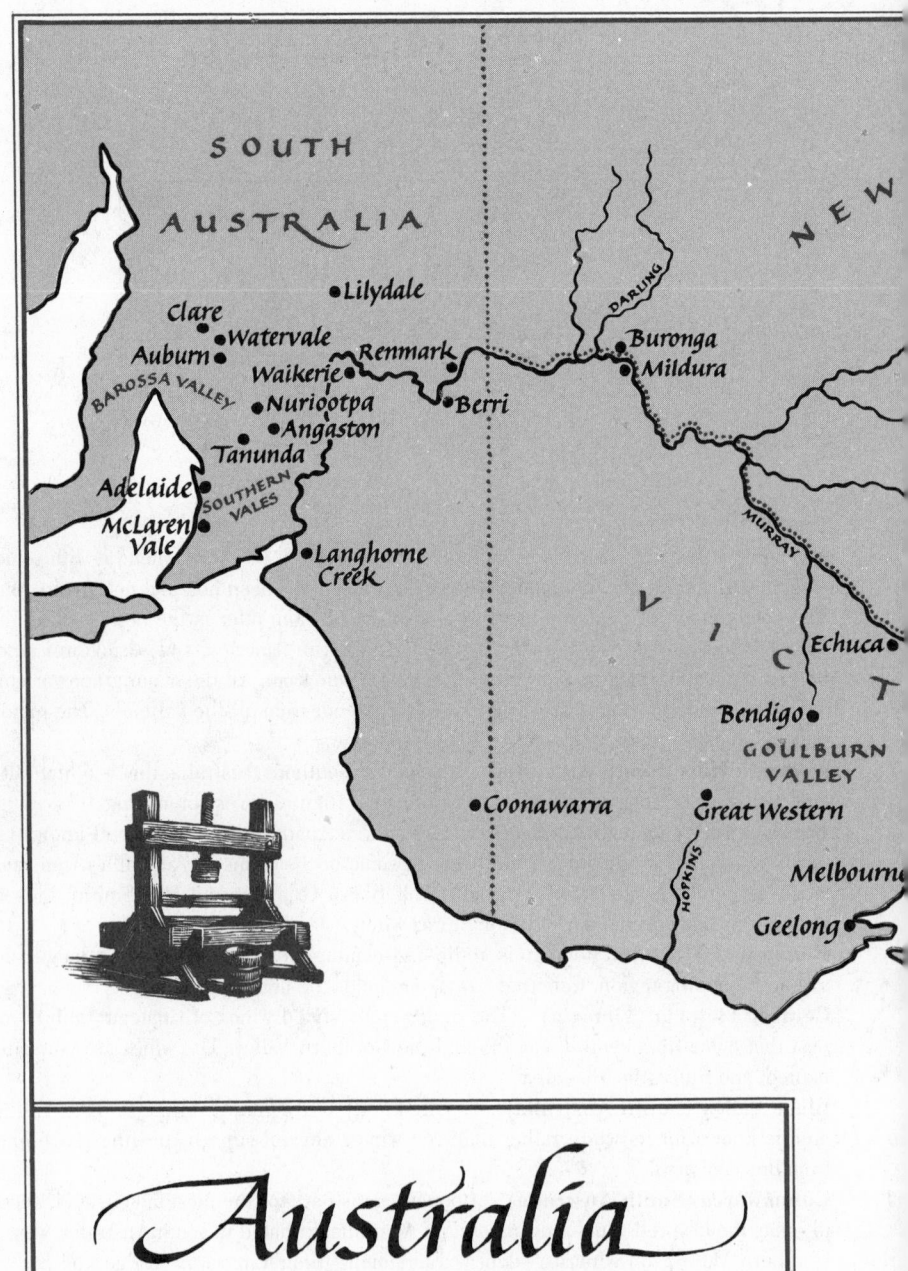

SOUTH
AUSTRALIA

NEW

DARLING

Lilydale
Clare
Watervale
Auburn
Renmark
Buronga
Mildura
Waikerie
BAROSSA VALLEY
Nuriootpa
Berri
Angaston
Tanunda
Adelaide
SOUTHERN
VALES
McLaren
Vale
MURRAY
Langhorne
Creek
V
I
Echuca
C
T
Bendigo
GOULBURN
VALLEY
Coonawarra
Great Western
HOPKINS
Melbourne
Geelong

Australia

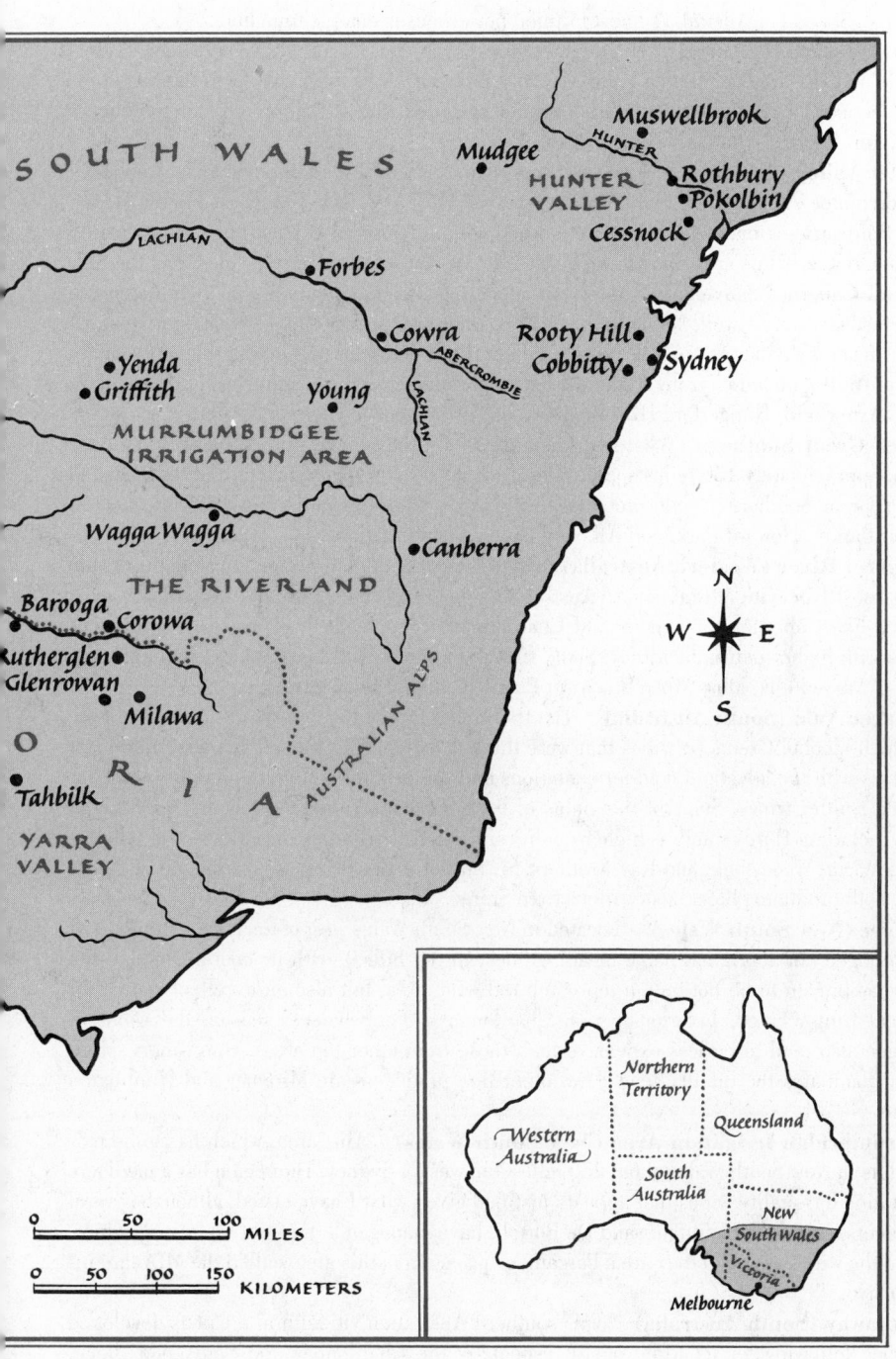

SOUTH WALES

Muswellbrook
Mudgee
HUNTER
HUNTER Rothbury
VALLEY Pokolbin
Cessnock

LACHLAN
Forbes
Cowra
ABERCROMBIE
Rooty Hill
Yenda Cobbitty Sydney
Griffith Young
LACHLAN

MURRUMBIDGEE
IRRIGATION AREA

Wagga Wagga
Canberra

THE RIVERLAND
Barooga
Corowa
Rutherglen
Glenrowan
Milawa

AUSTRALIAN ALPS

ORIA

Tahbilk

YARRA
VALLEY

N
W   E
S

0   50   100
————————————————— MILES

0   50   100   150
————————————————— KILOMETERS

Northern
Territory
Western   Queensland
Australia
South
Australia
New
South Wales
Victoria
Melbourne

producers, Bailey's. A more commercial Cabernet and Shiraz is made by Wynns. At nearby Milawa, Brown Brothers, one of the most successful high-quality Australian wineries, makes its home. Several of Australia's finest fortified powerhouses emerge from here.

Great Western (Victoria)   Situated between Ararat and Stawell, to the northwest of Melbourne and Geelong, is an area known for its sparkling wines (primarily from the huge producer Seppelt) and for its smooth, fat, low-acid, tasty red wines. The top red-wine producers are Mount Langi Ghiran and Cathcart Ridge.

Hunter Valley (New South Wales)   Less than a 3-hour drive from Sydney is Australia's famed Hunter Valley. It is to Sydney what the Napa Valley is to San Francisco and the Médoc is to Bordeaux—a major tourist attraction and source for some of Australia's most desired wines. Originally this area was known for its rich, exotic, full-bodied red wines from the Shiraz and Cabernet Sauvignon grapes, but more recently Chardonnay and Semillon have proven successful as well. No doubt because of their size and the intense competitive spirit here, this area's wineries are well represented in the export market. Familiar names from the Hunter Valley include Tyrell, Rothbury Estate, Lindemans, Rosemount, Saxonvale, Lake's Folly, Arrowfield, Hungerford Hill, Brokenwood, Evans, and Wyndham Estate.

Lower Great Southern (Western Australia)   In the remote southwestern tip of Australia, approximately 150 miles south of Perth, is a vast, burgeoning viticultural area called Lower Great Southern. Apple orchards thrive more than vineyards, but wineries such as Mount Barker, Howard Park, and Alkoomi have good reputations.

Margaret River (Western Australia)   In the very southwestern tip of this country is the Margaret River viticultural zone. Australian wine experts claim that Australia's most French-like Cabernet Sauvignons and Chardonnays come from this area, which produces wines with higher natural acidities. Some superb producers are located here, including the likes of Vasse Felix, Moss Wood, Leeuwin Estate, Cullens, and Pierro.

McLaren Vale (South Australia)   The traditional fare of this hot area south of Adelaide was high-alcohol Grenache wines that were thick and rich. This has all changed in the last 10 years with the advent of cold fermentations and the perception that the public yearns for lighter, fruitier wines. Some of the giants of the Australian wine business are in McLaren Vale, including Hardy's and its higher-quality sibling, Reynella. Smaller wineries of note are Wirra Wirra, Woodstock, and Kay Brothers. Several of my favorites are Coriole and d'Arenberg, both producing blockbuster wines from Shiraz.

Mudgee (New South Wales)   Located in New South Wales west of the famed Hunter Valley, Mudgee (an aboriginal name meaning "nest in the hills"), with its cool nights and hot days has proven to be not only a top-notch red wine area, but also an excellent source for tropical fruit-scented, luxuriously rich Chardonnays. For whatever reason, the wines of Mudgee also tend to be less expensive than those from other top areas. One winery, Montrose, dominates the quality scene; two other fine producers are Miramar and Huntington Estate.

Murrumbridge Irrigation Area (New South Wales)   This area, which has to be irrigated, is in New South Wales about 250 miles due west of Sydney. The region has a mediocre reputation for quality wines that appears justified given what I have tasted, although several producers, such as McWilliams and De Bortoli, have managed to turn out interesting wines. When the wines are good they are a bargain, as prices from this area, called the MIA, are inexpensive.

Padthaway (South Australia)   This southern Australian viticultural area has developed a strong following for its white wines, especially the Chardonnay and Sauvignon Blanc. Padthaway is one of Australia's newest "hot" areas, and two of Australia's largest producers, Lindemans and Seppelt, have shown just how tasty the white wines can be from this region.

Pyrenees (Victoria)   The attractive, rolling hill countryside of the Pyrenees, northwest of Melbourne, forms a triangle between Redbank, Moonambel, and Avoca. The top wines are the reds from the Cabernet Sauvignon and Shiraz grapes. The best white wines are from the Sauvignon grape. Wineries of note include Redbank, Taltarni, Mount Avoca, and Château Remy.

Riverland (South Australia)   Located in South Australia, Riverland is to Australia what the San Joaquin Valley is to California. This vast source of grapes of mediocre quality is dominated by huge cooperatives and producers who turn out Australia's jug wines and bag-in-the-box generic wines. Some big enterprises have their jug wine business centered here, including Penfolds, Kaiserstuhl, Angove, Berri, and Renmano. While most of the wines from this area are decidedly insipid, some good-value, fresh whites at bargain-basement prices can be found.

Rutherglen (Victoria)   Rutherglen is synonymous with Australia's fortified sweet wines, many of which are extraordinary. The famous sweet, nectarlike, ageless ports and fortified undeniably sublime Muscats and Tokays of William Chambers, Campbells, and Seppelt are made from Rutherglen grapes.

Swan Valley (Western Australia)   This hot, arid area in Western Australia, just northeast of the coastal city of Perth, produces large-framed, muscular red wines and increasingly better white wines. Houghton is the area's most famous winery, but good wines are made by Evans and Tate, as well as Moondah Brook.

Yarra Valley (Victoria)   This is the viticultural area most in fashion in Australia, and its proponents argue that the climate and resulting wines come closest in spirit to those of Bordeaux and Burgundy in France. I am not yet convinced. Located in Victoria, this is a cool-climate area outside Melbourne, and every major red and white glamour varietal is planted, from Cabernet Sauvignon, Merlot, and Pinot Noir to Chardonnay, Riesling, and Gewürztraminer. The best wineries are Lillydale, Yarra Yering, Coldstream Hills, and St. Huberts.

GRAPE VARIETIES

Red Wines

Cabernet Sauvignon   This varietal excels in Australia and generally produces a very fruity, often jammy, intensely curranty, fat wine, sometimes low in acidity, but round, generous, and surprisingly ageworthy in spite of an acid deficiency.

Pinot Noir   There are those who claim to have made successful wines from this infinitely fickle varietal, but the great majority of Australian Pinot Noirs to date have either been raisiny, unusual, often repugnant, or watery, pale, and innocuous. Three wineries that are likely candidates to produce fine Pinot Noir are Bass Phillip, Barratt, and Ashton Hills. Except for these three producers, anyone who suggests Australia is making good Pinot Noir does not have the consumer's best interests at heart.

Shiraz   Despite the Aussies' present-day infatuation with Cabernet Sauvignon, Merlot, and Pinot Noir, this is the grape that makes their greatest wines. The problem is that there is an enormous amount of it, and only a handful of producers treat Shiraz (Syrah) with the respect and care that is accorded Cabernet. It can produce Australia's greatest red wine when left to stand on its own, as Penfolds Grange convincingly proves, or it can offer more dimension and character to a red wine when blended with Cabernet Sauvignon, as Penfolds and Petaluma have proven time and time again.

White Wines

Chardonnay   The shrewd Aussies, taking full advantage of the wine consumer's thirst for Chardonnay wines, have consistently offered plump, fat wines filled with the flavors of apples, pears, oranges, and ripe melons. Although the wines still tend to be overoaked or, worse, artificially oaked, more and more Australian Chardonnays are fresh and exuberant and bottled early to preserve their youthful grapey qualities. With the advent of centrifuges and micropore filters, many Chardonnays have no bouquet or flavor. The one major disappointment is the aging potential of these naturally low-acid wines, but most consumers are drinking them within several months of purchase, so this is probably a moot issue.

Gewürztraminer   Regardless of the pronouncements of the local salespeople, who hype the quality of Gewürztraminer, this grape produces insipid, pale, watery wines that are a far cry from what Gewürztraminer does in France.

Marsanne   Château Tahbilk and Michelton are proponents of this grape, which tends to turn out one-dimensional, bland wines.

Muscat   This hot-climate grape excels in Australia and is at its best in the decadently rich, sweet, fortified Muscats that can age for decades. It is also made into a medium sweet table wine with which Brown Brothers does a particularly admirable job.

Riesling   Australia has proven to be the New World's best alternative to German-made Rieslings. This grape has done extremely well with Kabinett- and Spatlese-style drier Rieslings in the Barossa Valley and Adelaide Hills. Wineries such as Petaluma, Pewsey Vale, Rosemount, and Hill Smith have turned out some spectacular Beerenauslese- and Trockenbeerenauslese-style sweet wines. Overall, this grape gets good marks from me in Australia.

Sauvignon Blanc   The results have been mixed, as the hot climate causes this grape to overripen and take on a grotesque, vegetal, oily, thick fruitiness. Some fresh, tasty, dry Sauvignons are coming from Australia, but for now, New Zealand consistently beats Australia when it comes to quality Sauvignon-based wines.

Semillon   Semillon can be delicious, whether it is blended with Chardonnay or Sauvignon or allowed to stand by itself. It produces big, creamy, rich wines loaded with flavor. Wineries such as Rothbury, Rosemount, Montrose, Peter Lehmann, Henschke, and Evans and Tate have done better with Semillon than anyone. Some great sweet wines have been made from Semillon affected by the botrytis fungus. Look for those from Rothbury, Rosemount, and Peter Lehmann, which are world class.

FLAVORS

Red Wines

Cabernet Sauvignon   These wines can be very ripe, often overripe, with sweet, intense black currant flavors, supple, fat textures, and oodles of fruit. When poorly made or overly acidified, the wines are musty, dirty, and tart.

Pinot Noir   Raisiny, pruny fruit flavors with no finesse or complexity represent appallingly bad examples of Pinot Noir.

Shiraz   Intense aromas of cassis, leather, licorice, blackberries, cedar, tar, and pepper are found in wines that have a healthy dosage of Shiraz. Quite full bodied and rich, with softer tannins than Cabernet Sauvignon, these wines are drinkable young but frequently age better than the more glamorous Cabernet Sauvignons.

White Wines

Chardonnay   Tropical fruit flavors predominate in this creamy-textured, voluptuous wine. Oak is sometimes too noticeable, but better-balanced wines with the fruit in the forefront have been the rule in recent vintages.

Gewürztraminer   Where's the spice and exotic lychee nut character found in the great Gewürztraminers of Alsace? These are generally watery, thin wines that are usually disappointing.

Marsanne Marsanne can be described as usually neutral or, as Jancis Robinson says, "reminiscent of glue." It usually tastes much better old than young, but because it tastes so uninteresting young, no one ages it.

Muscat Huge aromas of brown sugar, fruit cake, crème brûlée, buttered and baked apricots, and oranges with honey and nuts give this varietal its appeal.

Riesling The classic Riesling aromas of spring flowers, green apples, and wet stones are present in the drier versions of this wine. As the wines get sweeter, aromas and flavors of oranges, peaches, apricots, butter, baked apples, and honeyed nuts arise.

Sauvignon Blanc Unfortunately, these wines seem to either be feeble, bland, and tasteless or oily, vegetal, and grotesque.

Semillon In the drier versions, lemon-lime aromas intertwined with honey and toasty oak are often the most interesting. With the sweet versions, buttery nuts and honey-coated raisin flavors take over.

AGING POTENTIAL

Cabernet Sauvignon:
  5–10 years
Pinot Noir: 4–6 years
Shiraz: 5–20 years
Chardonnay: 1–2 years
Gewürztraminer: 1–2 years
Marsanne: 4–12 years

Muscat (dry): 1–3 years
  (fortified): 5–50+ years
Riesling (dry): 1–4 years
  (sweet): 4–10 years
Sauvignon Blanc: 1–3 years
Semillon (dry): 2–8 years
  (sweet): 4–12 years

OVERALL QUALITY LEVEL

At the top level, wines such as the Penfolds Grange or Bin 707 Cabernet Sauvignon, in addition to some of the old-vine Shiraz cuvées from relatively small producers, are as fine as any red wine made in the world. Sadly, most of Australia's greatest wines are made in minuscule quantities, but readers lucky enough to latch on to any of the production of my 5-star wineries are sure to be impressed. Australia's overall wine quality is barely average, with oceans of mediocre and poorly made wines. There are, however, plenty of good, agreeable wines at attractive prices, and therein lies the reason for the success of Australia's wines. Australia is among the leaders in offering tasty, user-friendly wines at low prices. In that area Australian wines have very little competition.

MOST IMPORTANT INFORMATION TO KNOW

Given the remarkable diversity, the best thing for a consumer to do is to memorize the names of some of the better producers and restrict initial purchases to the surefire successes from that particular winery—usually Chardonnay, Cabernet, and Shiraz. Use the producer's chart for each varietal as a guideline until you have decided which wines and producers you prefer.

BUYING STRATEGY

For 95% of Australia's wines, buy only what you intend to drink over the next 12–16 months. The white wines have a particularly short shelf life, and the great majority of the reds are meant to be consumed within 2–4 years of the vintage. Thus, for dry white wines, only the 1999s, 1998s, and 1997s should be purchased. For inexpensive red wines, readers can safely purchase vintages back to 1994 without worrying about the wine's senility. Australia does produce sensational world-class red wines, but they are often offered in minute quantities. Readers should try to buy their Australian wines from some of the most creative importers, who have done a fabulous job in ferreting out some of the limited-production yet prodigious Australian wines. Those carrying the import labels of Dan Phillips-The Grateful Palate, Oxnard CA; John Larchet-The Australian Premium Wine Collection, whose importers at the time of writing were USA Wine West, San Rafael, CA, and Chicago Brands, Chicago, IL; Peter Weygandt-Weygandt Metzler, Unionville, PA; Ted Schrauth-Old Vines Australia, whose importers are Epic Wines, Santa Cruz, CA, and C. Daniele, New York, NY; and Rob McDonald-Old Bridge Cellars, San Francisco, CA, can offer immense joy and character. These importers do not have an exclusive on every great wine from Australia, but they are dealing with some of the smaller estates whose approach to winemaking is artisinal and oriented to the true connoisseur. Readers should also remember that Australia produces spectacular late-harvested fortified wines at a fraction of the price one pays for vintage ports and the sweet wines of France and Germany. These decadently rich wines are well worth seeking out.

VINTAGE GUIDE

As in California, constant sunny weather virtually guarantees at least good-quality wines in Australia, but each year is different as a result of drought, heat or cold waves, and hail. However, the extremes in quality that one often sees in Europe do not exist in Australia.

1998—Most of the top producers claim this may turn out to be the finest vintage in Western Australia, South Australia, Victoria, and the Hunter Valley in the decade of the nineties. All the elements came together for a superb year. Full physiological maturity with adequate acidity and an absence of rain should produce great wines in South Australia, Victoria, and possibly Hunter Valley. The only area of concern is Western Australia, where late summer rains ruined what would have been a great year. Producers who survived the rains and picked later are very pleased with what they have achieved. This will be an exciting vintage.

1997—Overall, this vintage does not match the quality of either 1996 or 1998. However, there are pockets of outstanding success. In the Hunter Valley, the red wines should be very good to excellent, but the whites suffered from overripeness. In Victoria, the vintage produced wines of extraordinary ripeness. Producers who kept their yields down made big, forceful, blockbuster wines. The 1997 Victoria offerings could easily rival their 1998 counterparts. In South Australia, rain affected some of the cooler-climate areas (such as Clare Valley), but producers who waited and harvested ripe grapes in Barossa and McLaren Vale should produce very good wines. One varietal that did fantastically well in the cooler areas is Riesling. In Western Australia, the high heat and rainfall before the harvest will make this a good rather than a great year.

1996—This has turned out to be a great year in Western Australia, producing fabulously concentrated, powerful wines, an excellent to great year in South Australia, with abundant high-quality, thick, rich, juicy offerings, and a very good year in Victoria. The latter region experienced more rain, but the grapes were superripe in every area save the Yarre Valley. In the Hunter Valley, 1996 is a very good vintage, although irregular.

1995—In South Australia and Western Australia, 1995 is a very good to excellent vintage. While some of the Coonawarra wines are light, and irregularity surfaced in McLaren Vale, Barossa Valley and Clare Valley both produced excellent wines. The examples from Western Australia possess extraordinary concentration and power. They may turn out to be as good as some of the more highly renowned vintages such as 1998. In Victoria, drought conditions produced tiny berries, as well as stressed fermentations and wines. It is a mixed, irregular vintage. In the Hunter Valley, 1995 is considered close to a disaster. Some of the white wines turned out fine, but the red wines are mixed, revealing the effects of the heavy rain that fell during the harvest.

OTHER VINTAGES

Among the other vintages of the nineties, 1994 was sensational in South Australia, particularly in the Barossa and Clare Valleys. It was excellent in Coonawarra, terrific in Victoria, and very great in Western Australia. Throughout Australia 1993 was a generally good year, although it never hit the fabulous peaks of 1994. The 1992 was also a sound vintage of very good quality, with the highlight being the Cabernet Sauvignon produced in Western Australia. Both 1991 and 1990 were generally great vintages throughout Australia. Top 1991 wines emerged from the Hunter Valley, Barossa Valley, Coonawarra, Victoria, and Western Australia. The one soft spot in the 1991 vintage was Clare Valley. In 1990 the Hunter Valley was a weak link in what was otherwise a great vintage, particularly in South Australia. The 1990 vintage was excellent in Victoria and Western Australia.

RATING AUSTRALIA'S BEST PRODUCERS OF
CABERNET SAUVIGNON AND SHIRAZ

* * * * * *(OUTSTANDING)*

Tim Adams Shiraz Aberfeldy (Clare Valley)

D'Arenberg The Dead-Arm (Shiraz) (McLaren Vale)

Brokenwood Shiraz Graveyard Vineyard (Hunter Valley)

Brokenwood Shiraz Rayner Vineyard (McLaren Vale)

Burge Family Shiraz Draycott (Barossa)

Burge Family Shiraz Draycott Reserve (Barossa)

Clarendon Hills Astralis (Shiraz) (Clarendon)

Coriole Cabernet Sauvignon (McLaren Vale)

Coriole Lloyd Shiraz (McLaren Vale)

Cullen Cabernet Sauvignon/Merlot Reserve (Margaret River)

Elderton Shiraz Command (Barossa)

Fox Creek Cabernet Sauvignon Reserve (McLaren Vale)

Fox Creek Shiraz Reserve (McLaren Vale)

Greenock Creek Shiraz Creek Block (Barossa)

Greenock Creek Shiraz Seven Acres (Barossa)

Henschke Shiraz Hill of Grace (Barossa)

Henschke Shiraz Mount Edelstone (Barossa)

Hewitson Shiraz L'Oizeau (McLaren Vale)

Highbank Proprietary Red Wine (Coonawarra)

Howard Park Cabernet Sauvignon/Merlot (Western Australia)

Killibinbin Shiraz (Langhorn Creek)

Peter Lehmann Stonewell Shiraz (Barossa)

The Magpie Estate Shiraz The Malcolm (Barossa)

Charles Melton Shiraz (Barossa)

Moss Wood Cabernet Sauvignon (Margaret River)

Mount Langi Ghiran Shiraz (Victoria)

Noon Eclipse Proprietary Red (McLaren Vale/Langhorn Creek)

Noon Shiraz Reserve (Langhorn Creek)

Parker Estate Cabernet Sauvignon Terra Rossa First Growth (Coonawarra)

Penfolds Cabernet Sauvignon Bin 707 (South Australia)

Penfolds Grange (South Australia)

Pikes Shiraz Reserve (Clare Valley)

Primo Estate Cabernet Sauvignon/Merlot "Joseph" Moda Amarone (Coonawarra)

Rosabrook Estate Shiraz Abattoir Block (Margaret River)

Rudsen Cabernet Sauvignon (Barossa)

Summerfield Cabernet Reserve (Pyrenees)

Summerfield Shiraz Reserve (Pyrenees)

Tait Cabernet Sauvignon (Barossa)

Three Rivers Shiraz (Barossa)

Torbreck Run Rig (Barossa)

Veritas Shiraz Hanisch (Barossa)

Veritas Shiraz Heysen (Barossa)

Warrenmang Shiraz Moonambel (Victoria)

Wild Duck Creek Estate Springflat Shiraz Reserve (Heathcote)

**** *(EXCELLENT)*

Tim Adams Shiraz (Clare Valley)

D'Arenberg Cabernet Sauvignon Copper
Mine Road (McLaren Vale)

D'Arenberg Ironstone Pressings
Grenache/Shiraz (McLaren Vale)

Ashton Hills Oblique Proprietary Red
(Adelaide Hills)

Ashton Hills Oblique Reserve (Adelaide
Hills)

Bannockburn Shiraz (Victoria)

Bowen Estate Cabernet Sauvignon (South
Australia)

Branson Wines Shiraz Coach House
(Barossa)

Brokenwood Shiraz (Hunter
Valley/McLaren Vale)

Canonolas Smith Alchemy (Mount
Canobolas)

Charles Cimicky Shiraz Signature (Barossa)

Clarendon Shiraz (Clarendon)

Clarendon Hills Shiraz (Clarendon)

Coriole Mary Kathleen Proprietary Red
Wine (McLaren Vale)

Coriole Redstone Cabernet Sauvignon
(McLaren Vale)

Coriole Redstone Proprietary Red Wine
(McLaren Vale)

Dromana Estate Cabernet/Merlot
(Mornington Peninsula)

Ebenezer Shiraz (Barossa)

Elderton Cabernet Sauvignon/Shiraz/Merlot
(Barossa)

Elderton Shiraz (Barossa)

Frankland Estate Shiraz Isolation Ridge
(Western Australia)

Galah Shiraz (Clare Valley)

Gnadenfrei Shiraz/Pinot Noir (Barossa)

Greenock Creek Cabernet Sauvignon
(Barossa)

Grosset Gaia Proprietary Red Wine (Clare
Valley)

Richard Hamilton Cabernet Sauvignon
Coonawarra Reserve (McLaren Vale)

Richard Hamilton Old Vine Shiraz Reserve
(McLaren Vale)

Huntington Estate Cabernet Sauvignon Bin
FB (Mudgee)

Jenke Shiraz (Barossa)

Stephen John Shiraz (Clare Valley)

Trevor Jones Shiraz (Barossa)

Katnook Estate Cabernet Sauvignon
(Coonawarra)

Katnook Estate Cabernet Sauvignon
Odyssey (Coonawarra)

Kilikanoon Cabernet Sauvignon (Clare
Valley)

Kilikanoon Shiraz (Clare Valley)

Château Leamon Shiraz Reserve (Bendigo)

Peter Lehmann Cabernet Sauvignon
(Barossa)

Lillydale Cabernet Sauvignon (Yarra Valley)

Lindemans Shiraz/Cabernet Limestone
Ridge (New South Wales)

Lindemans Pyrus Proprietary Red Wine
(New South Wales)

Lindemans Cabernet Sauvignon St. George
(New South Wales)

Majella Cabernet Sauvignon (Coonawarra)

Majella Cabernet Sauvignon/Shiraz Maleea
(Coonawarra)

Majella Shiraz (Coonawarra)

Maxwell Wines Cabernet Sauvignon Lime
Cave (McLaren Vale)

Maxwell Wines Shiraz Reserve (McLaren
Vale)

Charles Melton Cabernet Sauvignon
(Barossa)

Mount Langi Ghiran Cabernet
Sauvignon/Merlot (Victoria)

Noon Cabernet Sauvignon Reserve
(Langhorn Creek)

Oak Ridge Estate Cabernet Sauvignon
(Yarra Valley)

Orlando Cabernet Sauvignon Jacaranda
Ridge Coonawarra (South Australia)

Parker Cabernet Sauvignon Coonawarra
First Growth (Terra Rosa)

Penfolds Cabernet/Shiraz Bin 389 (South
Australia)

Penfolds Shiraz Bin 128 (South Australia)

Penfolds Shiraz Magill Estate (South
Australia)

Penfolds Shiraz/Cabernet Koonunga Hill
(South Australia)

Penley Estate Cabernet Sauvignon
(Coonawarra)

Petaluma Cabernet Sauvignon Coonawarra
(South Australia)

Pierro Cabernets (Margaret River)
Pikes Cabernet/Merlot (Clare Valley)
Pikes Shiraz (Clare Valley)
Primo Estate Shiraz (Adelaide)
Redbank Cabernet Sauvignon Long
    Paddock (Victoria)
Redbank Sally's Paddock (Victoria)
Riverside Meritage (Barossa)
Robertson's Well Cabernet Sauvignon
    (Coonawarra)
Rockford Shiraz Basket Press (Barossa)
Rothbury Estate Shiraz (Hunter Valley)
Rymill Merlot/Cabernet Franc/Cabernet
    Sauvignon
Rymill Shiraz
St. Hurbert's Cabernet Sauvignon (Yarra
    Valley)
Charles Sturt University Shiraz Reserve
    (New South Wales)
Summerfield Shiraz (Pyrenees)
Château Tahbilk Cabernet Sauvignon
    (Goulburn)
Château Tahbilk Shiraz (Goulburn)
Thistle Hill Cabernet Sauvignon (Goulburn)
Thistle Hill Cabernet Sauvignon (Mudgee)
Torbreck The Steading (Barossa)

Veritas Cabernet/Merlot
Veritas Cabernet Sauvignon
Veritas Shiraz/Mourvèdre
Viking Wines Cabernet Sauvignon
    (Barossa)
Viking Wines Shiraz (Barossa)
Virgin Hills Cabernet Sauvignon (Victoria)
Waninga Shiraz (Clare Valley)
Waninga Shiraz Reserve (Clare Valley)
Wild Duck Creek Estate Alan's Cabernets
    Pressings
Wild Duck Creek Estate Alan's Cabernets
    Vat 1
Wild Duck Creek Estate Springflat Shiraz
Wolf Blass Cabernet Sauvignon President's
    Selection Black Label (Victoria)
Wolf Blass Cabernet Sauvignon Yellow
    Label (Victoria)
Woody Nook Cabernet Sauvignon (Margaret
    River)
Wynns Cabernet Sauvignon John Riddoch
    (Coonawarra)
Yarra Yering Cabernet Sauvignon Dry Red
    #1 (Yarra Valley)
Yarra Yering Shiraz Dry Red #2 (Yarra
    Valley)

*** *(GOOD)*

Abbey Vale Merlot/Shiraz (Margaret River)
Tim Adams Cabernet (Clare Valley)
Alkoomie Cabernet Sauvignon (Western
    Australia)
Ashbrook Estate Cabernet Sauvignon
    (Western Australia)
Bailey's Cabernet Sauvignon (Glenrowan)
Balgownie Cabernet Sauvignon (Bendigo)
Jim Barry Shiraz McCrae Wood (Clare
    Valley)
Brand's Laira Cabernet Sauvignon
    (Coonawarra)
Brokenwood Cabernet Sauvignon (New
    South Wales)
Brown Bros. Cabernet Sauvignon (Victoria)
Capel'Vale Cabernet Sauvignon (Western
    Australia)
The Clairault (Margaret River)
Cullens Cabernet Sauvignon (Margaret
    River)
Deakin Estate Shiraz (Victoria)

Fern Hill Cabernet Sauvignon (McLaren
    Vale)
Geoff Hardy Kuitpo Cabernet (Adelaide
    Hills)
Hickinbotham Cabernet Sauvignon
    (Geelong)
Katherine Hills Cabernet Sauvignon (South
    Australia)
Hungerford Hill Cabernet Sauvignon
    (Hunter Valley)
Jindalee Shiraz (Murrays/Darling)
Tim Knappstein Cabernet Sauvignon (Clare
    Valley)
Lake Breeze Shiraz/Cabernet Bernoota
    (Langhorn Creek)
Lake Breeze Shiraz Winemaker Selection
    (Langhorn Creek)
Château Leamon Cabernets/Merlot
    (Bendigo)
Château Leamon Shiraz (Bendigo)
Peter Lehmann Shiraz (Barossa)

Leeuwin Estate Cabernet Sauvignon (Margaret River)

Lindemans Cabernet Sauvignon (Coonawarra)

Goeff Merrill Cabernet Sauvignon (South Australia)

Mildara Cabernet Sauvignon (Coonawarra)

Montrose Cabernet Sauvignon (Mudgee)

Orlando RF Cabernet Sauvignon (South Australia)

Passing Clouds Cabernet Sauvignon (Bendigo–Victoria)

Passing Clouds Cabernet/Shiraz (Bendigo–Victoria)

Passing Clouds Shiraz/Cabernet (Bendigo–Victoria)

Penfolds Shiraz Kalimna Bin 28 (South Australia)

Penfolds Shiraz St. Henri (South Australia)

Redman Cabernet Sauvignon (Coonawarra)

Rosemount Cabernet Sauvignon Show Reserve (Coonawarra)

Saxonvale Cabernet Sauvignon (Hunter Valley)

Seaview Shiraz Edwards and Chaffey (McLaren Vale)

Seppelt Cabernet Sauvignon (Barossa)

Sevenhill Cellars Cabernet Sauvignon (Clare Valley)

Seville Estate Cabernet Sauvignon (Victoria)

Taltarni Cabernet Sauvignon (Victoria)

Taltarni Shiraz (Victoria)

Vasse Felix Cabernet Sauvignon (Western Australia)

Wright's Cabernet Sauvignon (Western Australia)

Wyndham Estates Cabernet Sauvignon (South Australia)

Wyndham Estates Shiraz (South Australia)

Wynns Shiraz (Coonawarra)

RATING AUSTRALIA'S BEST PRODUCERS OF OTHER RED WINES

* * * * * (OUTSTANDING)

Barratt Pinot Noir (Adelaide Hills)

Bass Phillip Pinot Noir (Victoria)

Burge Family Grenache Old Vines (Barossa)

Clarendon Hills Merlot (Clarendon)

Clarendon Hills Old Vine Grenache Blewitt Springs Vineyard (Clarendon)

Clarendon Hills Old Vine Grenache Kangarilla Vineyard Clarendon

Greenock Creek Grenache Cornerstone Vineyard

Noon Eclipse (Grenache and Shiraz)

Rudsen Grenache (Barossa)

* * * * (EXCELLENT)

Tim Adams Grenache The Fergus (Clare Valley)

D'Arenberg The Custodian Grenache (McLaren Vale)

Ashton Hills Pinot Noir (Adelaide Hills)

Cherise Sangiovese (McLaren Vale)

Frankland Estate Olmo's Reward (Western Australia)

Richard Hamilton Burton's Vineyard (McLaren Vale)

Richard Hamilton Merlot Reserve (McLaren Vale)

Jenke Merlot (Barossa)

Kilikanoon Grenache Prodigal (Clare Valley)

The Magpie Estate Grenache The Faker (Barossa)

Maxwell Wines Merlot Reserve (McLaren Vale)

Charles Melton Nine Popes (Barossa)

The RBJ Mourvèdre/Grenache Theologicum (Barossa)

Rosemount Estate GSM (McLaren Vale)

Veritas Mourvèdre/Grenache (Barossa)

Woodstock Winery Grenache (McLaren Vale)

* * * *(GOOD)*

Ata Rangi Pino Noir (Martinborough, New
  Zealand)
Lenswood Vineyards (Knappstein) Pinot
  Noir (South Australia)

Woody Nook Merlot Gallagher's Choice
  (Margaret River)

RATING AUSTRALIA'S BEST PRODUCERS OF CHARDONNAY

* * * * **(OUTSTANDING)*

Barratt (Adelaide Hills)

Nicholson River (Gippsland)

* * * * *(EXCELLENT)*

Bannockburn (Geelong)
Canobolas Smith (Mount Canobolas)
Clyde Park (Geelong)
Cullen (Margaret River)
Dromana Estate Chardonnay Reserve
  (Mornington Peninsula)
Giaconda (Beechworth)
Grosset Chardonnay Piccadilly (Adelaide
  Hills)
Howard Park (Western Australia)
Trevor Jones Virgin Chardonnay (South
  Australia)
Leeuwin Artists Series (Margaret River)
Leeuwin Estate Chardonnay Estate
  (Margaret River)

Moorooduc Estate (Mornington Peninsula)
Mountadam (Adelaide Hills)
Pierro (Margaret River)
Rosemount Roxburgh (Hunter Valley)
Rosemount Show Reserve (Coonawarra)
Rothbury Estate Broken Back Vineyard
  (Hunter Valley)
Salitage (Pemberton)
Geoff Weaver (Lenswood)
Wise Vineyards Aquercus Unwooded
  Chardonnay (Western Australia)
Wise Vineyards (Western Australia)
Wise Vineyards Chardonnay Coat Door
  (Western Australia)

* * * *(GOOD)*

Cassegrain (New South Wales)
Cold Stream Hills (Yarra Valley)
Craigmoor (Mudgee)
Dalwhinnie (Victoria)
Katherine Hills (Southeastern Australia)
Hungerford Hill (Hunter Valley)
Jindalee (Murrays/Darling)
Katnook Estate (Coonawarra)
Krondorf (Barossa)
Lake's Folly (New South Wales)
Lindemans Bin 65 (New South Wales)
Maxwell Wines (McLaren Vale)
Michelton (Goulburn)
Miramar (Mudgee)
Moss Wood (Western Australia)

Orlando RF (South Australia)
Penley Estate (Coonawarra)
Petaluma (South Australia)
Reynella (Southern Vales)
Rothbury Estate Broken Back Vineyard
  Reserve (Hunter Valley)
Seaview Chardonnay Edwards and Chaffey
  (McLaren Vale)
Seppelt (Barossa)
Mark Swann (South Australia)
Tarra Warra (Victoria)
Tyrells Vat 47 (New South Wales)
Wynn's (Coonawarra)
Yarra Yering (Yarra Valley)
Yeringsberg (Yarra Valley)

* * *(AVERAGE)*

Balgownie (Victoria)
Brown Brothers (Victoria)
Capel Vale (Western Australia)
Cold Stream Hills Four Vineyards (Yarra
  Valley)

Cold Stream Hills Lillydale (Yarra Valley)
Mildara (Coonawarra)
Orlando (South Australia)

RATING AUSTRALIA'S BEST PRODUCERS OF RIESLING

***** (OUTSTANDING)

Clos Clare Riesling (Clare Valley)

**** (EXCELLENT)

Tim Adams Riesling (Clare Valley)
Ashton Hills Riesling (Adelaide Hills)
Grosset Riesling Polish Hill (Clare
  Valley)

Kilikanoon Riesling Blocks Road (Clare
  Valley)
Kilikanoon Riesling Morts Block (Clare
  Valley)

*** (GOOD)

Petaluma Riesling (South Australia)

Viking Wines Riesling (Barossa)

RATING AUSTRALIA'S BEST PRODUCERS OF DRY SAUVIGNON BLANC AND SEMILLON

***** (OUTSTANDING)

Nicholson River Semillon (Gippsland)

**** (EXCELLENT)

Branson Wines Semillon (Barossa)
Brokenwood Semillon (Hunter Valley)
Burge Family Semillon (Barossa)
Henschke (Barossa)
Leland Estate Sauvignon Blanc
  (Lenswood)
Lenswood Vineyards (Knappstein)
  Sauvignon Blanc (South Australia)
Maxwell Wines Semillon Old Vines
  (McLaren Vale)

Neudorf Sauvignon Blanc (Nelson, New
  Zealand)
Pierro Semillon/Sauvignon Blanc LTC
  (Margaret River)
Rothbury Estate (Hunter Valley)
Shaw and Smith Sauvignon Blanc
  (Adelaide Hills)
Stanley Brothers Semillon Full Sister
  (Barossa)
Geoff Weaver Sauvignon Blanc (Lenswood)

*** (GOOD)

Berri Estates (South Australia)
Evans and Tate (Margaret River)
Tim Knappstein (Clare Valley)
Krondorf (Barossa)
Peter Lehmann (Barossa)

Lindemans (Padthaway)
Mildara (Coonawarra)
Rosabrook Estate Sauvignon Blanc
  (Margaret River)
Rosemount (Hunter Valley)

RATING AUSTRALIA'S BEST PRODUCERS OF SWEET SAUVIGNON BLANC AND SEMILLON

***** (OUTSTANDING)

Peter Lehmann (Barossa)
Rosemount (Hunter Valley)

Rothbury Estate (Hunter Valley)

RATING AUSTRALIA'S BEST PRODUCERS OF FORTIFIED WINES

***** (OUTSTANDING)

Wm. Chambers Rosewood Tokay and
  Muscat
Morris Muscat and Tokay Liquor

Seppelt Para Port
Seppelt Show Wines
Yalumba Port

AUSTRALIA'S GREATEST WINE BARGAINS FOR LESS THAN $10

Berry Estates Semillon
Brown Brothers Cabernet Sauvignon
Brown Brothers Chardonnay King Valley
Brown Brothers Muscat Lexia
Coldridge Chardonnay
Coldridge Semillon/Chardonnay
Peter Lehmann Cabernet Sauvignon
Peter Lehmann Shiraz
Lindemans Chardonnay Bin 65
Michelton Semillon/Chardonnay
Montrose Cabernet Sauvignon
Montrose Chardonnay
Montrose Shiraz
Orlando Cabernet Sauvignon Jacob's Creek
Orlando Chardonnay Jacob's Creek
Orlando Sauvignon Blanc Jacob's Creek
Oxford Landing Cabernet Sauvignon
Oxford Landing Chardonnay
Penfolds Cabernet/Shiraz Koonunga Hill
Penfolds Chardonnay
Roo's Leap Chardonnay
Roo's Leap Fumé Blanc
Rosemount Cabernet Sauvignon/Shiraz
  Diamond Reserve
Rosemount Diamond Reserve Red
Rosemount Diamond Reserve White
Rosemount Semillon/Chardonnay Diamond
  Reserve
Rosemount Shiraz Diamond Reserve
Rothbury Estate Chardonnay Broken Back
  Vineyard
Rothbury Estate Shiraz
Seppelt Cabernet Sauvignon Black Label
Seppelt Cabernet Sauvignon Reserve Bin
Seppelt Chardonnay Black Label
Seppelt Chardonnay Reserve Bin
Seppelt Semillon/Chardonnay
Seppelt Shiraz Black Label
Seppelt Shiraz Reserve Bin
Seppelt Tawny Strafford Port
Tyrells Long Flat Red
Wolf Blass Cabernet Sauvignon Yellow
  Label
Wolf Blass Shiraz President's Selection
Wyndham Estates Cabernet Sauvignon Bin
  444
Wyndham Estates Chardonnay Bin 222
Yalumba Clocktower Port

ABBEY VALE (MARGARET RIVER)

1996 Merlot/Shiraz	C	86
1997 Sauvignon Blanc	C	87

The fleshy, chunky, dark ruby-colored 1996 Merlot/Shiraz possesses copious quantities of black cherry fruit intermixed with spice, pepper, and smoke. Medium bodied, pure, and exuberant, this is a mouth-filling, savory blend to drink over the next 3–4 years. By the way, the blend is 60% Merlot and 40% Shiraz.

A delicious, richly fruity, tank-fermented Sauvignon Blanc, Abbey Vale's 1997 is bursting with herb and melon aromas with floral notes in the background. Vivid ripe fruit is presented in a refreshing, primary fermentation style. This captivating, light-bodied Sauvignon should be drunk over the next year for its freshness and exuberant, fruity style.

TIM ADAMS (CLARE VALLEY)

1996 Cabernet	C	88
1997 The Fergus (Old Vine Grenache)	C	90
1996 The Fergus (Old Vine Grenache)	C	89
1998 Riesling	C	90
1997 Semillon	C	85
1996 Shiraz	C	89
1995 Shiraz	C	90
1996 Shiraz Aberfeldy	D	91

1995 Shiraz Aberfeldy	D 93
1994 Shiraz Aberfeldy	D 94

Tim Adams continues to provide an impressive array of wine from old, dry-farmed vineyards in the Clare Valley, about 65 miles from Adelaide. The 1998 Riesling is a 100% tank-fermented, dry, explosively fruity, flinty, citrusy wine with gorgeous freshness, loads of min-erality, and amazing length and purity. It is a tour de force for a down under Riesling. Some may claim it will drink well for 5–7 years, but this exuberant Riesling is best consumed over the next 12–18 months, before Riesling's telltale mothball/paraffinlike aromas begin to de-velop. The pure 1997 Semillon is fermented in both American and French oak casks. It is a full-bodied, crisp wine with an eccentric nose of green tea, clover, spice, and waxy, honeyed fruit. Spicy and perfumed, but a trifle kinky for my palate, this Semillon could work wonders with certain fish and Asian dishes. Drink it over the next 3–4 years.

Tim Adams's red wines are all boldly styled, fleshy, large-scale offerings that are best pur-chased by those who desire plenty of flavor. The 1997 The Fergus, a 100% old-vine Grenache cuvée, reveals a distinctive minty, kirsch, black cherry-scented nose that explodes upward from the glass. Hedonistic and full bodied, it does not possess a great deal of struc-ture, but it does provide waves of jammy fruit. Abundant quantities of pepper, spice, and al-cohol (14.5%) are present in the knockout finish. This example should drink well for 5–6 years. The opaque purple-colored 1996 Shiraz displays a distinctive blackberry, cassis, and minty nose with tar, licorice, and spicy notes. Medium to full bodied, and undeniably Aus-tralian in its exuberance and flamboyant style, this rich, chunky Shiraz should drink well for a decade or more. If it had possessed slightly more complexity and breadth of flavor, it would have merited an outstanding rating. The 1996 The Aberfeldy, a blockbuster 100% Shiraz made from a vineyard planted in 1904, has been aged for nearly a year in 1-year-old Ameri-can casks and then transferred to 100% new oak for 12 months. The wine has soaked up this treatment, which is also utilized by such wineries as Caymus in Napa Valley in order to im-part a more oaky profile upon release. Tim Adams seems to have used it to civilize this large-scale, monster wine. The alcohol is at least 14%. The wine boasts a dense purple color, as well as rich, subtle, eucalyptus, blackberry/mulberry, tar, and spicy aromas. Full bodied, powerful, rich, and oozing with glycerin and extract, this superb, uncompromisingly Aus-tralian Shiraz is accessible but should age nicely for 10–15 years. Last, the 1996 Cabernet (a blend of 90% Cabernet Sauvignon and 10% Cabernet Franc) is aged in both French and American oak. This full-bodied, pure effort offers herb-tinged black currant fruit intermixed with vanillin and floral scents. Although it does not display the breadth of flavor or complex-ity of the other Adams reds, this is a noteworthy, concentrated, excellent effort that should unfold with 1–2 years of bottle age and last for 12–15 years.

Rhône Ranger fans and lovers of Rhône Valley wines will be immensely impressed with what Tim Adams has accomplished with these releases. The 1996 Grenache-The Fergus of-fers an exotic, minty, black pepper, cassis, and kirsch nose, a dense purple color, copious quantities of sweet, ripe, low-acid, luscious fruit, medium to full body, and an excellent fin-ish. The minty, eucalyptus aromas and flavors make for a distinctive style of Grenache. This medium- to full-bodied wine is loaded with up-front fruit; it should drink well over the next 7–8 years.

Tim Adams produced three other superb examples of Shiraz from the Clare Valley. The 1995 Shiraz possesses a dense, murky, purple color, a beautiful, forward, blackberry/cassis-scented nose, full body, terrific richness, low acidity, and an expansive, chewy, fleshy mouth-feel. This attractive, up-front, supple, mouth-filling Shiraz will age well for 8–10 years. The limited-production Shiraz Aberfeldy (under 100 cases produced) emerges from an ancient, head-pruned vineyard planted in 1904. The wine is aged for 22 months in 100% new Amer-ican oak casks before bottling. It is a wine of enormous richness, power, glycerin, and impact. The 1995 coats the palate with a viscous display of minty eucalyptus and cassislike flavors. This opaque purple-colored, thick, heavy, unevolved, full-bodied, sumo wrestler of a wine is splendidly concentrated and dense. In spite of being aged in 100% new oak, the wine gives little evidence of toasty new wood, a tribute to the extraordinary concentration of fruit, which has soaked up the wood. The 1994 Shiraz Aberfeldy received a slightly higher score, only because it is a year older and has developed some attractive roasted aromas along with licorice, truffle, and cassis scents. It is an amazingly rich, thick, viscously textured wine that rolls over the palate, offering up layers of jammy blackberry and black currant fruit. This full-bodied, sumptuously textured wine possesses a finish that lasts for 30+ seconds. Both the 1994 and 1995 Shiraz Aberfeldys should drink well for 15 years. Sadly, only 50 cases of these wines made it to America's shores, but that is slightly over half the winery's total production!

D'ARENBERG (McLAREN VALE)

1995 D'Arry's Original (Shiraz/Grenache)	C	87
1994 D'Arry's Original (Shiraz/Grenache)	C	86
1995 Cabernet Sauvignon Copper Mine Road	C	90
1994 Cabernet Sauvignon The High Trellis	C	86
1996 Chardonnay The Olive Grove	C	86
1995 Chardonnay The Olive Grove	C	87
1995 Ironstone Pressings (Grenache/Shiraz)	D	90
1994 Ironstone Pressings (Grenache/Shiraz)	D	86
Nostalgia 12-year-old Tawny Port	D	91
1995 Peppermint Paddock Chambourcin	C	85+
1995 Shiraz Old Vines	C	86
1996 The Custodian (Grenache)	C	87
1995 The Custodian (Grenache)	C	88
1995 The Dead-Arm Shiraz	D	91
1994 The Dead-Arm Shiraz	D	90
1995 The Twenty Eight (Mourvèdre)	C	86
1995 Vintage Fortified Shiraz	D	90

Readers looking for reliable, reasonably priced Australian wines should check out these offerings from d'Arenberg. All of the wines are made from family-owned vineyards, many of which were planted in the early part of this century. While the overall style offers little complexity or nuances, they are, nevertheless, savory, well-made, fruit-driven wines that, with only a handful of exceptions, are meant to be drunk within several years of their release.

Both the 1996 and 1995 Chardonnay The Olive Grove are cleanly made, medium-weight, barrel-fermented wines that possess moderate levels of tropical fruit, good fat and lushness, and tasty, soft, pure styles. Both wines should be consumed within 2–3 years of the vintage. The only other white wine I tasted from d'Arenberg was a disappointing 1996 dry Dam Riesling.

The red wines are all exuberantly fruity, cleanly made rich wines. For example, the 1995 d'Arry's Original, a 50% Shiraz/50% Grenache blend aged in large old wooden *foudres,* is a dark ruby/purple-colored, expansive, straightforward, peppery, kirsch and black cherry-scented and -flavored wine. This husky, hedonistic offering is of surprisingly high quality for its price level. It could easily pass for a gutsy southern Rhône wine. Drink it over the next 2–3 years. The 1994 d'Arry's Original, although not as fleshy as its younger sibling, is made in the same mold. I also enjoyed the 1995 Shiraz Old Vine. Made from 80–100-year-old vines this is a fat, chunky, uncomplex, deliciously round, peppery, black currant-scented and -flavored wine with admirable depth, glycerin, and power. It will age well for 4–5 years.

The 1994 Cabernet Sauvignon The High Trellis is a straightforward, plummy-scented and -flavored, medium-bodied Cabernet Sauvignon with broad commercial appeal. Soft and fruity, with copious amounts of black currant fruit offered in a straightforward style, it should be drunk over the next 3–4 years. Readers looking for something interesting, as well as those who enjoy experimenting with French/American hybrids, should take a serious look at d'Arenberg's 1995 Chambourcin called Peppermint Paddock. It is an animal/barnyardlike wine with an impressively saturated dark purple color, an earthy, peppery, ripe nose, and excellent depth, but a one-dimensional personality and fruit flavors. It is the first Chambourcin I have tasted outside the mid-Atlantic states.

The 1995 The Twenty Eight is a old-vine cuvée of Mourvèdre, with one parcel of vines planted in the 1880s and the other in the 1920s. It reveals all the Mourvèdre characteristics—leathery, mushroomy, tree barklike scents compete with, if not dominate, those of black raspberries and plums. The wine is elegant, with a sweet attack and loads of fruit, but it comes across as a bit foursquare and one-dimensional. Drink it over the next 4–5 years. I also enjoyed the 100% Grenache wine called The Custodian. Both the 1996 and 1995 are textbook examples of Grenache. Peppery, kirsch, black cherry, and roasted peanut aromas are followed by medium- to full-bodied, fruit-filled wines with excellent berry richness and soft, fat, lush personalities. Both wines are meant to be drunk within the first 3–4 years of life.

Among the more limited-edition offerings are several wines that represent some of d'Arenberg's finest parcels, all of which are basket-pressed. For example, most readers will love the 1995 Ironstone Pressings, a Grenache/Shiraz blend that is a terrific, fruity, interesting wine of very high quality. It is medium to full bodied, with loads of black fruits (plums, blackberries, and cherries) in its aromas and flavors. Viscous and massive in the mouth, the wine is long and pure. Because of the wine's low acidity and voluptuous style, it is a wine to drink now and over the next 8–9 years. The medium- to full-bodied 1994 Ironstone Pressings is much less explosively rich, with low acid and a lush, straightforward, pruny/blackberry fruitiness. The Dead-Arm Shiraz is an old-vine Shiraz cuvée that is fermented in oak barrels and raised in mostly new American oak. It is a sexy, flashy, flamboyant Shiraz that is short on restraint but big on screaming fruit. The 1995 Dead-Arm Shiraz exhibits an opaque purple color as well as a fabulous nose of ripe, late-harvest-like, plummy, blackberry fruit and cassis. Viscous, thick, and rich, with layers of flavor, low acidity, and sexy new oak, this lusty-style Shiraz should drink well for at least a decade. The similarly styled 1994 Dead-Arm Shiraz is just beginning to reveal licorice and tarlike scents from the additional year of bottle age. It, too, should last for a decade.

The 1995 Cabernet Sauvignon Copper Mine Road is the debut vintage for what looks to be an exceptional example of McLaren Vale Cabernet Sauvignon. This black/purple-colored Cabernet offers ripe aromas of cassis fruit intermingled with smoke, vanilla, and earth. Dense, full bodied, and powerful, as well as silky smooth, this is a lush, fruit-driven wine with gobs of glycerin and impact on the palate. It should drink well for 10–12 years.

D'Arenberg's two after-dinner cuvées include a 12-year-old Tawny Port called Nostalgia. Medium amber colored, with copious quantities of sweet, raisiny, prune, and berrylike fruit, this rich, full-bodied, purely made, lusty-style Tawny Port is delicious, as well as reasonably priced. Readers looking for licorice, truffle, and cassislike flavors in a heavyweight, full-bodied style should check out the 1995 Vintage Fortified Shiraz. This wine is almost too much of a good thing. If you don't like to drink it, a tablespoon or two poured over vanilla ice cream would be marvelous. It is a huge, chocolatey, smoky, blackberry-scented and -flavored wine that oozes over the palate with copious quantities of glycerin and alcohol. I have no idea how it will age, but it should keep for 10–15 years and, hopefully, improve.

ASHTON HILLS (PICCADILLY)

1996 Chardonnay	C	86
1996 Oblique Proprietary Red	D	89
1997 Oblique Reserve	D	90
1997 Pinot Noir	D	88
1997 Riesling	C	90

Ashton Hills' winemaker, Steven George, is also the winemaker for the A. P. Birkes Wendouree winery. The latter winery is considered to be a national treasure of Australia, but I have never tasted or even seen a bottle of their wine offered for sale in this country. Apparently George is a great believer in Pinot Noir. His small 7-acre Pinot Noir vineyard is planted at a lofty elevation in Adelaide Hills.

With respect to Ashton Hills' white wines, I loved the 1997 tank-fermented Riesling. This delicate, stony, mineral-driven wine is dry, with exotic fruit flavors, excellent ripeness, superb equilibrium among its component parts, and surprisingly high alcohol (13.1%). The alcohol is well hidden by the wine's rich fruit- and mineral-dominated personality. Look for this Riesling to evolve for another 12–18 months. The 1996 Chardonnay is good but less expressive than the Riesling. It possesses a smoky, oaky nose but was muted and monolithic when I tasted it, particularly in the context of other Dan Phillips's selections. The Chardonnay reveals good body, purity, and richness, but it is shy and surprisingly restrained.

An impressive effort, Ashton Hills' 1997 Pinot Noir is a full-bodied, chocolatey wine with oodles of cherry fruit and spicy oak. It is reminiscent of some of Carneros's more flavorful Pinots in California. Round and generous, it clearly tastes as if it were produced from Pinot Noir—no small achievement. Drink it over the next 3–4 years.

The two proprietary red wine offerings are both classic, stylish wines. The fruit-driven 1996 Oblique (a blend of 44% Cabernet Sauvignon, 33% Cabernet Franc, and 23% Merlot) exhibits minty black currant aromas and flavors, medium body, excellent purity, and tobacco, fruitcake, and spice notes in the supple finish. Drink it over the next decade. The 1997 Oblique Reserve (46% Merlot, 36% Cabernet Sauvignon, and 18% Cabernet Franc) reveals a more saturated ruby/purple color as well as riper, more intense cassis aromas intermixed with *pain grillé*, dried herbs, and tobacco. Dense, full bodied, and pure, with a nicely layered finish, this wine offers richness and elegance married to substantial extract. Anticipated maturity: 2001–2015.

BANNOCKBURN (VICTORIA)

1996 Chardonnay	D	87
1996 Shiraz	D	88

Two very fine efforts have resulted from this estate's 1996 vintage. Bannockburn's 1996 Chardonnay is a medium-bodied, tart, high-acid example of this varietal. Pear, mineral, and citrus notes give it a fresh, crisp personality. Drink it over the next year. The 1996 Shiraz's intensely smoky, bacon fat-and-sausage-scented nose is attractive. As the wine sits in the glass, more toasty French oak scents emerge. Rich and seductive, with an expansive, flavorful attack and midpalate, the wine possesses a finish dominated by black fruits, pepper, and smoke. This delicious, forward-style Shiraz is meant to be enjoyed over the next 5–6 years.

BANROCK STATION (S.E. AUSTRALIA)

1997 Shiraz	C	86

Made by either partial carbonic or whole berry fermentation, this is an exuberantly fruity, charming, *nouveau*-style wine. With good weight and excellent purity, this is a fine bistro-style red to drink over the next 12–18 months.

BARRATT (PICCADILLY VALLEY, ADELAIDE HILLS)

1997 Chardonnay	D	91
1997 Pinot Noir	D	91

An amazing Australian Pinot Noir, this 1997, made with the assistance of consulting wine-maker Geoffrey Grosset, is one of the finest I have ever tasted from Australia. If I had had it blind, I would have mistaken it for a grand cru from the northern Côte de Nuits, particularly Morey-St.-Denis. Bottled unfined and unfiltered, the wine reveals a dark plum color, followed by a sensuous nose of smoky, foresty, sweet cherry, and Asian spice aromas with a subtle note of oak. On its aromatics alone this wine would score in the mid-90s. In the mouth, it is lush, with low acidity, a fleshy, open-knit texture, and classic Burgundian flavors of jammy cherries intermixed with earth and spice. The sad news is that the total production was 200 cases, only 25 of which were imported to America. Drink it over the next 3–4 years. Those lucky enough to latch on to a bottle should include it in a tasting against the finest red burgundies—it's that impressive! For statisticians, the wine was fermented in small half-ton fermenters and aged for 11 months in French oak *barriques*, of which 50% were new.

Barratt's 1997 Chardonnay is also immensely impressive, as well as extremely Burgundian in style. It is no shy wine, with 14.5% natural alcohol and exuberant smoky, hazelnut, honeyed fruit complexity. This offering, which could pass for a Meursault premier cru, possesses complex aromatics, rich, dense, full-bodied flavors, outstanding purity, and well integrated French oak. This gorgeous Chardonnay should age nicely for 5–6 years. Sadly, only 60+ cases were exported to the United States.

JIM BARRY (CLARE VALLEY)

1995 Shiraz McCrae Wood	D	85

This medium- to full-bodied, smoky, blackberry and cassis-scented and -flavored displays a touch of wood, plenty of pepper, and soft, expansive, fleshy flavors. Drink it over the next 3–4 years.

BRANSON WINES (BAROSSA VALLEY)

1998 Semillon	C	87
1997 Shiraz Coach House	D	90

Another wine made by famed Veritas winemaker Rolf Binder, the 1997 Shiraz Coach House is a mouth-filling, slightly complex, gorgeously made wine with intense blackberry and cherry fruit intermixed with pepper and spicy wood. In the mouth, new leather notes combine with spice. Its full-bodied, savory constitution gives the wine plenty of impact and length. The natural alcohol of 14.5% translates into loads of glycerin on the palate. Drink it over the next 7–8 years. The 1998 Semillon is a dry, crisp wine with this varietal's telltale fig, leafy vegetable, citruslike fruit character. Rich, concentrated, and medium bodied, it is best drunk with intensely flavored poultry and fish dishes. Drink it over the next 3–4 years.

BROKENWOOD (HUNTER VALLEY/McLAREN VALE)

1998 Semillon	C	?
1992 Semillon ILR Aged Reserve	D	86

1996 Shiraz	C 87
1996 Shiraz Graveyard Vineyard	E 95
1996 Shiraz Rayner Vineyard	D 92

Australians appear to have a fetish for Semillon that places it on a far higher pedestal of quality than I do. In addition, I am skeptical about how well Semillon ages, unlike the Aussies, who prize it at a much older age than I do. For example, Brokenwood's 1998 Semillon is a leafy, vegetal, medium-bodied wine that is too earthy and green for my taste. The 1992 Aged Reserve Semillon ILR is a good wine, with an intriguing, leafy, fino sherry, roasted nut, vegetal-scented nose, good citrus fruit, and a medium-bodied, spicy finish. Although attractive, has it really improved since it was first made? In any event, it is a curiosity that some readers may want to try, especially with rich fish dishes.

I tasted three Shiraz offerings, two of which were outstanding and the other very good. The 1996 Shiraz exhibits an impressively saturated ruby/purple color, a sweet, black currant and chocolatey nose, and chunky, dense, monochromatic flavors. It possesses good size and depth but lacks the additional dimensions of complexity and length required to receive high marks. Drink it over the next 5–7 years. The other two single-vineyard Shiraz offerings are spectacular efforts. The black/purple-colored 1996 Shiraz Rayner Vineyard offers a stunning nose of jammy blackberries, licorice, pepper, and toast. It is exceptionally full bodied, with massive levels of glycerin and extract, yet cleverly well balanced without any sense of heaviness or flabbiness. This opulently textured, unctuous Shiraz can be drunk now or cellared for 2 decades. Even better is the spectacular 1996 Shiraz Graveyard Vineyard, a well-known vineyard in the Hunter Valley whose vines average 28 years of age. When I put my nose in the glass of this wine, three wines came to mind—the famed Châteauneuf du Pape, Rayas, the renowned Pomerol microestate of Lafleur, and the grand cru burgundy Musigny. Incredible scents of black raspberry liqueur intermixed with flowers, kirsch, and spice soar from the glass of this profound, concentrated, multidimensional effort. Amazingly, the wine has been aged in American oak but reveals none of the aggressive whiskey barrel scents that American oak sometimes imparts. Although not as weighty in the mouth as the 1996 Rayner Vineyard, the Graveyard Vineyard is even more multidimensional and complex, with extraordinary concentration and an ethereal sense of richness and length. The finish lasts for nearly 50 seconds. This fabulously suave, yet remarkably concentrated and well-delineated wine is a wine-making tour de force as well as one of the most exceptional old-vine Shiraz I have tasted from Australia. Anticipated maturity: now—2015.

BURGE FAMILY (BAROSSA VALLEY)

1995 Grenache Old Vines	D 90
1998 Semillon	D 89
1996 Shiraz Draycott	D 92
1996 Shiraz Draycott Reserve	D 95

All of these wines emerge from the estate's vineyards, and the well-known Rolf Binder (of Veritas fame) is the consulting winemaker. This is a superb source for highly flavorful, intense wines. The 1998 Semillon, from the family's Alicot Vineyard, is a powerful (13.8% alcohol), lanolin, waxy, citrusy Semillon with medium to full body, nearly outstanding depth, and fine purity and overall balance. It begs for fish as an accompaniment to its chewy flavors. I realize Australian Semillons are alleged to possess uncommonly long lives, but my palate prefers them in their exuberantly fruity youth—2–3 years.

When I smelled the 1995 Grenache Old Vine, I thought, Now, this is a fun wine. Its dark ruby color is followed by a glorious nose of crushed black cherries and raspberries intermixed with pepper and tar that leaps from the glass. It is a hedonistic, succulent fruit bomb with low acidity and excellent purity. About 15% Shiraz was added to the blend. According to the importer, the Grenache vines average 73 years in age. Drink this hedonistic wine over the next 4–5 years. Readers looking for superextracted, blockbuster old-vine Shiraz should check out Burge's 1996 Shiraz Draycott and 1996 Shiraz Draycott Reserve. The 1996 Shiraz Draycott exhibits a saturated purple color and a terrific nose of raspberry jam intermixed with crushed pepper, tar, and earth. Sweet and unctuously textured, with full body, outstanding purity, and impressive levels of glycerin and extract, this large-scale Shiraz can be drunk now or cellared for 15+ years. Even more flamboyant, the 1996 Shiraz Draycott Reserve offers an opaque purple color, followed by aromas of toasty new oak intermixed with blackberry jam, prune liqueur, and pepper. Deep, with monstrous levels of extract and viscousness, this superb, multilayered, fabulously concentrated Shiraz has managed to retain its harmony and balance. It is velvety textured enough to be drunk now but should evolve and develop more complexity with another 5–7 years of cellaring. It will keep for 2 decades or more.

CANOBOLAS SMITH (MOUNT CANOBOLAS)

1996 Alchemy	D	90
1996 Chardonnay	D	90

These are two outstanding efforts from this winery on the slopes of Mount Canobolas in New South Wales. The opaque purple-colored 1996 Alchemy, a blend of 20% Shiraz and the balance Cabernet Sauvignon and Cabernet Franc, exhibits spicy, peppery, leathery, dried herb, and raspberry scents. Aromatically, this wine is reminiscent of a ripe vintage of the famed Châteauneuf du Pape Beaucastel. The complex bouquet is followed by a layered, restrained, yet rich wine with a distinctive personality and copious quantities of black raspberry and berry fruit intermixed with new saddle leather, earthy, spicy, peppery components. This medium- to full-bodied wine can be drunk now as well as over the next 7–8 years. I was also impressed with the gorgeous, medium- to full-bodied 1996 Chardonnay. The wine displays a honeyed, buttery, floral nose, rich, concentrated flavors, zesty underlying acidity, and outstanding purity. It is a beautifully made wine that could easily pass for a premier cru from Burgundy's Côte d'Or.

CAPEL'VALE (WESTERN AUSTRALIA)

1996 Chardonnay Frederick	D	89

This big, buttery, leesy Chardonnay reveals plenty of oak and complexity. The color is an evolved light gold. In the mouth, this serious, well-endowed, medium- to full-bodied wine offers earth, spicy oak, and buttery fruit. This is not a "sip by the pool" Chardonnay, but one to drink with full-flavored dishes. It should continue to improve for another year and last for 3–4 years.

CHAMBERS ROSEWOOD VINEYARDS (RUTHERGLEN)

N.V. Rare Muscat Liqueur	EEE	99
N.V. Rare Tokay Liqueur	EEE	99
N.V. Shiraz Port	C	92
N.V. Tawny Port	C	90

William Chambers is the undisputed king of the fortified wine business in Australia. They produce a bevy of fortified products, the finest of which are the Rare Muscat and Rare Tokay Liqueurs. The latter two offerings are simply mind-boggling. I have served them frequently to guests at charity dinners (with obvious awestruck appreciation), and they are explosively perfumed, unctuously textured, sweet wines that almost defy description. They are undoubtedly among the greatest after-dinner, fortified wines made in the world and can age for 40–50 years after they are bottled. According to Chambers, their average age is between 60 and 80+ years. If readers think they are superexpensive, keep in mind they are so extraordinarily rich and intense that a half bottle will easily serve 12 or so guests.

As for the two more reasonably priced offerings, the nonvintage Tawny Port exhibits a light amber color, followed by a sweet, fragrant, tar, fig, jammy strawberry and cherry nose, explosive richness, a lively, fresh bite to its flavors, and a long, lusty, full-bodied finish. It should drink well for a decade. Even more impressive is the nonvintage Shiraz Port. The color is an opaque black/purple. The wine is extremely unevolved and grapey and needs 4–5 more years in the bottle to settle down. It is an amazingly thick, chewy, tar, overripe blackberry and cassis-scented and -flavored wine that oozes across the palate with extraordinary purity, glycerin, extract, and alcohol. These are the products of one of Australia's true legends and are "must taste" efforts.

CHERISE (McLAREN VALE)

1996 Sangiovese	D	90
1995 Sangiovese	D	88

I am not sure many readers will be prepared to shell out $40 for an Australian Sangiovese, but those who do will find more character and authenticity to these two efforts than much of what emerges from California. The 1996 Sangiovese possesses better extract as well as more volume and richness. It also has a more complete feel in the mouth and finish. Both wines exhibit Sangiovese's telltale aromas of saddle leather, strawberry, and cherry fruit jam. These medium-bodied offerings are ideal food wines, but both need to be drunk over the next 3–4 years.

CHARLES CIMICKY (BAROSSA)

1997 Gnarled Vine Grenache	C	87
1995 Shiraz Signature	D	90

Made from century-old Grenache vines, the dark ruby-colored 1997 Gnarled Vine Grenache exhibits a sweet nose of cherries/raspberries and intense spice. Medium to full bodied, with tangy acidity, it is a vibrant, fruit-driven wine to enjoy over the next 2–3 years.

The impressive 1995 Shiraz boasts a saturated dense plum color, oaky, blackberry, peppery aromas, thick, concentrated, full-bodied flavors, outstanding purity, and a long, chewy, oaky finish. A potentially outstanding offering, the wine is accessible but will be even better after 2–4 years of cellaring; it will keep for 15 years.

THE CLAIRAULT (MARGARET RIVER)

1996 The Clairault	D	86

This dark ruby/plum-colored blend of 75% Cabernet Sauvignon, 15% Cabernet Franc, and 10% Merlot exhibits a Bordeaux-like nose of cedar, tobacco, sweet black currant fruit, and spicy oak. Medium bodied, elegant, and surprisingly stylish, particularly for an Australian red, it will appeal more to French wine lovers than those looking for the grapier, bigger, bolder styles that emerge from Australia. Drink it over the next 5–6 years.

CLARENDON (CLARENDON HILLS)

1995 Shiraz	D	90

Readers should not confuse this winery with Clarendon Hills. The Clarendon winery has produced an exuberant, explosively ripe, powerful Shiraz with an opaque purple color and a sweet, American oak-dominated nose with blackberry jamlike notes in the background. Unctuously textured, full bodied, and chewy, this is a muscular, macho-style wine that delivers plenty of fruit, alcohol, and glycerin. Drink it over the next 5–7 years.

CLARENDON HILLS (CLARENDON)

1997	Astralis (Shiraz)	EEE	98+
1996	Astralis (Shiraz)	EE	96+
1995	Astralis (Shiraz)	EE	96+
1994	Astralis (Shiraz)	EE	97
1997	Cabernet Sauvignon	D	90
1997	Chardonnay Kangarilla Vineyard	D	85
1997	Chardonnay Norton Summit Vineyard	D	85?
1997	Merlot	D	92
1996	Merlot	D	91
1995	Merlot	D	93
1994	Merlot	D	90
1994	Old Vine Grenache	D	93
1997	Old Vine Grenache Blewitt Springs Vineyard	D	90
1996	Old Vine Grenache Blewitt Springs Vineyard	D	92+?
1995	Old Vine Grenache Blewitt Springs Vineyard	D	97
1997	Old Vine Grenache Clarendon Vineyard	D	89
1995	Old Vine Grenache Clarendon Vineyard	D	95
1997	Old Vine Grenache Kangarilla Vineyard	D	90
1996	Old Vine Grenache Kangarilla Vineyard	D	95
1997	Semillon	D	?
1996	Shiraz	D	92
1995	Shiraz	D	89+?
1994	Shiraz	D	91
1997	Shiraz Brookmans Vineyard	EE	95
1997	Shiraz Liandra	E	92
1997	Shiraz Piggott Range Vineyard	EE	96

I have severe reservations about the white wines made at Clarendon Hills, but this winery produces some of the world's most sumptuous, explosively rich, blockbuster reds money can buy.

As for the whites, the 1997 Semillon is a monolithic, rustic wine with an evolved, Sauternes-like color. Revealing mushroomy aromas intermixed with paraffin, citrus, and nutty scents, it is extremely full bodied but heavy and awkward. I am no fan of Clarendon Hills' Chardonnays, as they are often oxidized and bizarre. The 1997 Chardonnay Kangarilla Vineyard displays an evolved light gold color and a heavy feel in the mouth, with some sweet, buttery fruit but little charm or complexity. There is good length and depth, but the wine comes across as heavy-handed and eccentric. The 1997 Chardonnay Norton Summit

Vineyard exhibits a distinctive butterscotchlike nose with minerals and spice in the background. The wine is dense but lacks definition and elegance. It is a curious Chardonnay.

Although the white wines are unusual, the red wines are crowd-pleasing, exotic offerings that take the level of richness and hedonism to sensational heights. All of these wines are worth trying if only because of their compelling purity, opulence, and explosive richness. For example, the 1997 Cabernet Sauvignon exhibits an overripe, flamboyant nose of jammy black currants intermixed with licorice, spice, and floral scents. The wine is fat and opulently textured with gobs of fruit. Its low acidity and big, chewy constitution suggest it can be drunk now as well as over the next 7–8 years. The terrific 1997 Merlot is a worthy successor to this estate's other blockbuster Merlots. The 1997 is more tannic than previous vintages, but superconcentrated with amazing purity. The dense ruby/purple color is followed by copious aromas of jammy black fruits, chocolate, kirsch, and spice. In the mouth, the wine is backward, with noticeable tannin and high alcohol, but the layers of glycerin, extract, and richness are awesome. This exotic, blockbuster Merlot should be at its finest between 2000 and 2012.

I have never tasted an Australian Merlot that was more concentrated than Penfold's Grange, a Shiraz-based wine. Clarendon Hills' 1995 Merlot (250 cases available for America) is an opaque purple-colored wine with a knockout nose of raspberry liqueur, chocolate, smoke, and spice. The wine is enormously extracted, with a density and texture reminiscent of pre-1976 vintages of Pétrus. Sumptuous and almost over the top in its richness and density, this unctuously thick, full-bodied wine is fabulous to smell, taste, and consume. This is great stuff! As youthful as this Merlot is, I have no doubt it will last for 15 or more years. The gratifying, opaque purple-colored 1994 Merlot boasts a huge, smoky, black cherry-scented nose, succulent, chewy flavors, massive body, and a juicy, nicely layered, long finish. It is all silk and fruit, but with more alcohol and intensity than one might expect. Drink it over the next decade. The 1996 Merlot offers a thick, juicy, full-bodied blast of black cherry fruit intertwined with notes of chocolate and earth. Unctuously textured and pure, not overdone, yet clearly massive, this soft, opulently styled Merlot can be drunk now or cellared for a decade.

The most provocative of the Clarendon Hills offerings is the Shiraz. The 1995 may be controversial. It possesses a liquefied pepper nose and flavors that push the flavor of Shiraz to the limit. Its huge, fragrant nose is followed by a dense, full-bodied, smoky, extremely rich wine that has a certain weediness to its flavors that kept my score from going higher. This pure, heavyweight should drink well young yet last for 15–20 years. While impressive, it is the least remarkable red wine in the Clarendon Hills portfolio. The 1994 Shiraz from vineyards near Clarendon, not far from Adelaide, is a dense purple-colored wine with an exotic nose of roasted meats, blueberries, tomatoes, chocolate, and smoke. Quite provocative, rich, massively endowed, but still young and generally unformed, this is another blockbuster Shiraz that can easily compete with such Australian superstars as Henschke Hill of Grace and Penfold's Grange. As the wine sat for about 10 minutes in the glass, it developed a more pronounced black pepper/black raspberry aroma, with the tomato character moving into the background. Since I became more and more impressed with this wine as it sat in the glass, I would suggest decanting it 30–45 minutes in advance. The husky, dense ruby/purple-colored 1996 Shiraz reveals a knockout nose of pepper, raspberry liqueur, blackberries, and spice. The wine possesses terrific fruit, full body, an unctuous texture, and a whoppingly long finish that lasts for over 30 seconds. Although soft and approachable, it will keep for a decade or more.

I tasted four spectacular 1997 Shiraz offerings from Clarendon Hills, the first single-vineyard designations I have seen aside from the Astralis. All four are fabulous wines that should be sought out by readers who cherish the Syrah grape at its most exuberant. The 1997 Shiraz Liandra (14.5% natural alcohol) is a blend of the Clarendon and Kangarilla vineyards. It has an opaque purple color, as well as black cherry and blackberry-scented aromatics with tarry pepper notes. The wine is enormous, with extraordinary fatness and succulence, an unctuous texture, and a long, 35-second finish. Drink it over the next 12–15 years. Even better is the 1997 Shiraz Brookmans Vineyard. Its saturated opaque purple color gives way to a peppery, dried herb, tar, asphalt, and blackberry liqueur nose. As the wine sits in the glass, intense aromas of allspice also emerge. Huge, massive, chewy, and full bodied, it is packed with fruit, glycerin, and character. Drink it over the next 12–15+ years. The massive 1997 Shiraz Piggott Range Vineyard (14.5% natural alcohol) is less spicy than its two predecessors but is a classic in the sense of its fabulous display of cassis and blackberry fruit. Extremely full bodied, with surreal levels of extract and richness, this powerful, mouth-staining Shiraz should be at its peak between 2000 and 2015. Nearly perfect, the 1997 Astralis (100% new French oak) is another explosive wine that represents the essence of Shiraz. The opaque purple color resembles a young vintage port. The nose offers up blackberry fruit intermixed with freshly melted asphalt and pepper. My notes read, "Beyond wine." The wine is dry but possesses unreal unctuosity and richness. This superendowed offering will be at its finest between 2001 and 2020. These are awesome Shiraz!

There are only 150 cases (100 came to the United States) of the debut vintage of 1994 Astralis. This is the hottest wine in Australian wine circles, as it came out ahead of two great vintages of Henschke's and Penfold's Grange in a recent tasting. If readers can believe it, it is a bigger, denser, more concentrated wine than the Grange! The Astralis boasts an opaque black/purple color and a fabulously pure nose of jammy black raspberry and blackberry fruit, with chocolate, smoke, and licorice notes in the background. Huge, massive, and bigger than life, this is the essence of the Syrah grape presented in an unbridled, enormously formatted style that will blow away most tasters. The wine's voluptuous texture allows it to be drunk now, although I suspect it will keep on going, à la the Energizer bunny, for another 20–25+ years.

The 1995 Astralis is a candidate for a perfect score. About 450 cases of this luxury cuvée are made (100 of which are imported into the United States). This single-vineyard, old-vine Shiraz made from 50–60-year-old vines is aged in 100% new French oak and is bottled with no fining or filtration. The saturated opaque black/purple color is followed by a huge yet tight nose of crushed black raspberries, cassis, bacon fat, violets, and toasty oak. The aromatics offer only a glimpse of what will emerge with another 5–10 years of cellaring. In the mouth, this wine reveals phenomenal richness and purity, huge body, but no sense of flabbiness. The oak is remarkably well integrated, which suggests to readers just how concentrated this wine is. It is a winemaking tour de force and unquestionably one of the greatest young red wines I have tasted. Since I have tasted only a few vintages of Astralis, I have been very conservative scoring it, but this wine should prove to be uncommonly rich and complex after another 3–5 years of cellaring; it should keep for 25–30 years—a legend!

The 1996 Astralis (550 cases) is softer than its 1995 counterpart. Aged in 100% new oak, the wood is soaked up by the wine's extraordinary flavor concentration and massive fruit extraction. The nose offers aromas of pure cassis intermixed with pepper and spice. This blockbuster wine exhibits remarkable richness, compelling layers of flavor, brilliant purity and overall equilibrium, and a fabulously nuanced finish. The 1996, which is slightly more accessible than the more backward 1995, can be drunk now, although this flamboyant effort will evolve for another 15–20 years. Frankly, along with Penfold's Grange, this may be the greatest Shiraz being made in Australia.

Normally my favorite wines from Clarendon Hills are the old-vine Grenache cuvées. While these wines are excellent, even outstanding, in 1997, they do not compete qualitatively with the spectacular Shiraz efforts. Nevertheless, these are all interesting old-vine Grenache 1997s that taste lighter and more evolved than vintages such as 1996 and 1995. The 1997 Old Vine Grenache Clarendon Vineyard (14.5% alcohol) is nearly elegant by the standards of previous mouth-staining examples. It does not possess the weight or richness of the 1995 and 1996, but it is a delicious wine with notes of peaches, kirsch, pepper, and spice in its supercharged aromatics. It is round, rich, medium to full bodied, and ideal for drinking now and over the next 4–5 years. The 1997 Old Vine Grenache Kangarilla Vineyard (14.5% alcohol) is more complex, with aromas of tobacco, dried herbs, pepper, and sweet black cherry fruit. A bigger, richer, and fuller-bodied wine than the Clarendon Vineyard, it reveals more significant depth and length. Anticipated maturity: now–2006. Last, the 1997 Old Vine Grenache Blewitt Springs Vineyard is the most concentrated, complex, and balanced of this trio. Deep, full, and rich, with low acidity, high alcohol (14.5%), and gobs of sweet black cherry/kirsch fruit, it should be drunk over the next 5–6 years.

Clarendon Hills' 1994 Old Vine Grenache is one of the few wines I have ever tasted that possesses that intense, black raspberry richness and purity that is reminiscent of the late Jacques Reynaud's beloved Château Rayas. Additionally, there is a Martha's Vineyard mint/eucalyptus component in this superconcentrated, full-bodied, flamboyant, unctuously textured wine. The mountains of fruit in this Grenache defy belief. Everything is held together by adequate acidity and the wine's inner structure. It should drink well for 10–15 years. These are amazing wines.

It's quite simple—the two cuvées of 1995 Old Vine Grenache from Clarendon Hills are even more mind-boggling than the 1994 Old Vine Grenache (which was a blend of these two vineyards). The 1995 Old Vine Grenache Blewitt Springs (made from 90-year-old vines) is one of the greatest Grenache wines I have ever tasted—from anywhere! Opaque purple colored, with a sensational nose of pure kirsch, black cherries, and spice, this exquisitely well-balanced, magnificently pure, rich wine coats the palate with layers of fruit in addition to abundant quantities of glycerin and extract. There are no hard edges, and given its enormous richness and exceptional balance, this opulent Grenache can be drunk now as well as over the next 15–20 years—an amazing achievement! The 1995 Old Vine Grenache Clarendon Vineyard is more developed and, at present, more fragrant, with a less saturated purple color (although it possesses an impressive hue). A huge, peppery, truffle, earth, cinnamon, and kirsch nose soars from the glass. Pungent, peppery flavors offer copious quantities of jammy black raspberry and black cherry fruit. More approachable than the 1995 Blewitt Springs, this full-bodied, luscious Grenache should drink well now and over the next 12–15 years. Wow! These wines are breakthrough efforts for this varietal in Australia.

Two of the most decadent wines made on planet Earth are the limited production (about 900 cases of each) of Old Vine Grenache. In 1996 there are three offerings, but I tasted only two, the Blewitt Springs and Kangarilla Vineyard. The 1996 Blewitt Springs is the first wine I have ever tasted that may be almost too rich to drink. Consequently I have a slight preference for the 1996 Kangarilla Vineyard (15% alcohol). The latter wine offers an opaque purple color and a smashingly intense, decadent nose of black raspberries, blueberries, and pepper, followed by equally impressive thick, viscous, superconcentrated, remarkably pure, and well-balanced flavors. There are no hard edges to this huge, old-vine Grenache. The wine's glycerin level (because of the high alcohol) gives it a sweet impression on the palate, and thus it can be drunk now. However, I predict this wine will last for 15 or more years. The opaque blue/black-colored 1996 Old Vine Grenache Blewitt Springs offers a nose of blackberry, cassis, and peppery aromas. Explosively sweet black fruit hits the palate with considerable weight and unctuosity. There may be some residual sugar, although I tend to think the high alcohol (15.5%) and the extremely elevated glycerin level give this wine its slightly sweet palate impression. Huge, and almost too rich and thick to drink with food, this wine might be best served at the end of the meal with well-flavored cheese or simply sipped by itself. The wine is remarkably impressive and powerful, but, wow, what weight and intensity it possesses! Is this too much of a good thing? Both the 1996 Old Vine Grenache cuvées were aged in 3–4-year-old barrels. No new oak is used, and the wines are better for it. Look for the 1996 Blewitt Springs to become more civilized with 3–4 years of bottle age and keep for 2 decades.

CLOS CLARE (CLARE VALLEY)

1997 Riesling	D	91
1997 Shiraz	D	86

I immensely enjoyed Clos Clare's 1997 Riesling, which competes with the finest of Alsace and Germany. Made by Geoffrey Grosset, of the winery of the same name, it emerges from a vineyard considered to produce many of Australia's finest Rieslings in the fifties, sixties, and seventies. The vineyard's limestone soil may explain why this Riesling has such an extraordinary character. It exhibits a petrol-like aroma also found in some of Alsace's legendary Rieslings (Trimbach's Clos St. Hune, for example), combined with tremendous intensity of lime and citrus that transforms into orange, tangerine, and flower blossoms as the wine sits in the glass. With the austerity of a great Riesling, medium body, and dazzling extract, this is a noteworthy New World Riesling. Clos Clare's 1997 Shiraz is an understated, soft, restaurant-style wine that is meant to be consumed over the next 2–3 years. It was not an easy vintage in the Clare Valley because of rain during the harvest, but this wine exhibits good berry fruit, medium body, and a velvety texture. It will appeal to readers seeking a lighter-style Shiraz made in the Rosemount style.

COLDSTREAM HILLS (VICTORIA/YARRA VALLEY)

1994 Chardonnay Reserve	D	88
1994 Pinot Noir	C	86

The 1994 Chardonnay Reserve, made from a hillside vineyard above the Yarra Valley, offers a buttery, ripe, smoky nose, well-integrated acidity, medium body, and classy, smoky, vanillin, Chassagne-Montrachet-like fruit. This cleanly made wine is ideal for drinking over the next several years. The 1994 Pinot Noir reveals a surprisingly evolved light to medium ruby color with some garnet at the edge. Spicy oak along with gamey, herbal aromas and tart cherry fruit are pleasant in the straightforward aromatics. Although the wine possesses high acid (no doubt from added acidity) and a tannic palate, it offers good cleanliness and a refreshing, lighter style. It is a competent, correct Pinot Noir for drinking over the next 2–3 years.

CORIOLE (McLAREN VALE)

1994 Cabernet Sauvignon	C	92
1996 Chardonnay	B	86
1994 Mary Kathleen Proprietary Red Wine	D	89+
1994 Lloyd Shiraz	C	90+?
1995 Redstone Proprietary Red Wine	C	88
1994 Sangiovese	B	86
1996 Semillon/Sauvignon Blanc	B	85

My first exposure to these wines has resulted in enthusiastic tasting notes. The 1996 Semillon/Sauvignon Blanc (60% of the former and 40% of the latter) is an attractively made, medium-bodied, waxy-style wine with plenty of meat, suppressed aromatics, but nice flesh and texture for this style of wine. There is little evidence of oak. Fresh and tasty, with surprising power (13.5% alcohol), it should be consumed over the next 12 months. The 1996

Chardonnay reveals some oak in its buttery, spicy, freshly scented bouquet. Although not very expressive, the wine is medium bodied, clean, plump, chewy, and substantial. This is a mouth-filling Chardonnay without a great deal of complexity, but its monolithic personality should not be dismissed because of the fruit and weight it possesses. Drink it over the next year.

With respect to the red wine cuvées, the 1995 Redstone, a 45% Shiraz, 20% Grenache, 35% Cabernet Sauvignon blend, displays an opaque purple color, followed by a sweet nose of black currant and blackberry fruit. Dense and medium to full bodied, with admirable power and richness, low acidity, and a monolithic yet expansive, generous mouth-feel, this is a well-endowed, big red to drink over the next 5–6 years. The attractive leathery, sweet cherry-scented and -flavored 1994 Sangiovese is a nice rendition of Australian Chianti. Better than many Sangioveses made in California, it exhibits medium body, good, fresh, lightness in the mouth, and enough tangy acidity to work well with Italian dishes. Drink it over the next several years. The most impressive of the Coriole wines is the 1994 Cabernet Sauvignon. A tight, backward, opaque purple-colored wine, it possesses a potentially knockout nose of black currants, licorice, earth, and vanillin. Full bodied, with sweet tannin, high fruit extraction, and superb ripeness and overall harmony, this large-scale Cabernet Sauvignon can be drunk now but is best cellared for 2–3 years. Anticipated maturity: 2000–2012.

The top-of-the-line cuvées from Coriole are a proprietary red called Mary Kathleen and a blockbuster Shiraz called Lloyd. The 1994 Mary Kathleen, a blend of 46% Merlot, 40% Cabernet Sauvignon, and 14% Cabernet Franc, boasts an opaque purple color as well as a tightly knit, reticent nose of black cherry fruit, earth, *pain grillé,* and spice. Full bodied, dense, and huge, this pure, thick wine with a chocolatey richness is impressive, but it needs 2–3 years of cellaring. It is well worth buying despite its lofty price tag. Potentially even more impressive, the 1994 Lloyd is a huge, monolithic, blockbuster. This wine exhibits a sweet, black fruit (blackberries and prunes), hickory smoke-scented nose, extraordinary ripeness, and mouth-coating levels of glycerin and extract. Massive, deep, rich, and still unformed, this wine should age effortlessly for 12–20 years. If more complexity develops, it will merit an even higher rating. Don't touch a bottle for 3–4 years.

GARRY CRITTENDEN (VICTORIA)

1997 Barbera	C	85
1996 Barbera	C	87
1997 Sangiovese	C	88
1996 Sangiovese	C	86

These limited-production wines are authentic examples of Sangiovese and Barbera (California wineries producing wines from these two varietals should take note). The 1997 Sangiovese possesses a hefty degree of alcohol (13.7%) but is made from tiny yields. The color is a medium dark ruby, and the bouquet offers up copious amounts of strawberry and cherry jamlike notes in addition to scents of new saddle leather. Medium bodied, with excellent purity, this flavorful, soft Sangiovese should be consumed over the next 1–2 years. The 1997 Barbera exhibits a denser ruby/purple color as well as a pronounced nose of red and black fruits intermixed with melted road tar and tomato skins.

The 1996 Sangiovese is an impressive effort for this varietal, which has rarely exhibited much character from vineyards in the New World. Crittenden's offering exhibits a dark color, round, sweet, leathery, Bing cherry fruit, and a medium-bodied, soft, plush personality. Fruity, with the sweet and sour cherry/leathery component found in a good Tuscan Chianti, this fresh Sangiovese is ideal for drinking over the next 2–3 years. The 1996 Barbera is a more tightly knit, more concentrated wine with copious quantities of wild berry fruit dis-

played in an exuberant, medium-bodied style. This refreshing wine emphasizes Barbera's
fruit and earth character, with no obvious oak in evidence—and it's all the better for it.
Spicy, with tangy acidity, this is an attractive, concentrated Barbera to consume over the next
3–4 years.

CULLEN (MARGARET RIVER)

1994 Cabernet Sauvignon/Merlot Reserve	E	91+
1995 Chardonnay	D	87

Cullen's 1995 Chardonnay, aged 7 months in 100% new oak, is a subtly wooded wine, with a
long, layered personality. Although youthful and unevolved, it offers measured levels of tangerine and citrus fruit in a medium-bodied, crisp, tart, but elegant style. This wine should
age nicely for another 1–2 years.

   While I tasted a pleasant but uninspiring 1994 Cabernet Sauvignon/Merlot, the 1994 Reserve offering of this wine is spectacular. The inky, saturated black/purple color is concentrated, full bodied, and reminiscent of a young barrel sample. Offering loads of cassis fruit
intermingled with scents of minerals, toasts, and flowers, this prodigious, superconcentrated
Cabernet Sauvignon/Merlot Reserve requires another 4–5 years of cellaring given its high
tannin level. The wine should last for 2 decades.

DALWHINNIE (VICTORIA)

1996 Cabernet Moonambel	D	86+?
1994 Cabernet Sauvignon	D	90
1996 Chardonnay	D	89
1994 Chardonnay	D	87
1996 Shiraz Moonambel	D	87+?
1994 Shiraz	D	88

I was impressed with Dalwhinnie's 1996 Chardonnay, a wine with an unmistakable minerality as well as tangy integrated acidity. With its racy, mineral-dominated character and
smoky, hazelnut, lemony, citrusy notes, it could easily pass for a top-class premier or grand
cru Chablis. A portion of the wine was put through malolactic fermentation, and it was aged
in 100% French oak casks. It is a serious, vibrant Chardonnay that should drink well for 4–5
years.

   Both the 1996 Shiraz Moonambel and 1996 Cabernet Moonambel were wrapped tight,
making evaluation very difficult. Both revealed saturated colors, good purity, surprisingly
high acidity, and considerable tannin. I don't see them developing into hedonistic examples
of Australian wine. In contrast, these are structure-dominated, backward, restrained, and intellectually oriented wines. Will these wines open and provide the richness of fruit they suggest they possess? Only time will tell, but both are unquestionably well made, and their
respective varietal characteristics are presented accurately. However, both wines are frightfully backward and unevolved.

   This highly respected winery's 1994 Chardonnay Moonambel exhibits a richly fruity, orange marmalade-scented nose, excellent ripeness, well-integrated acidity, and a clean,
medium- to full-bodied finish. Drink it over the next year.

   Dalwhinnie's outstanding 1994 Cabernet Sauvignon Moonambel displays an opaque purple color, as well as a minty, cassis-scented nose reminiscent of the Heitz Martha's Vineyard
Cabernet. Although the wine is still tightly knit, it possesses great fruit, purity, and a rich,
full feel in the mouth without tasting heavy or flabby. Give it another 2–3 years of cellaring
and drink it over the subsequent 2 decades. The 1994 Shiraz Moonambel (from a vineyard

planted in 1976) offers a medium dark ruby/purple color, good spice, chocolatey, cassis fruit, as well as mint notes, medium to full body, and good density. It does not possess the presence, stature, or focus of the Cabernet Sauvignon, but it is a young, backward, yet promising Shiraz. Anticipated maturity: now–2008.

DEAKIN ESTATE (VICTORIA)

1997	Chardonnay	B	85
1996	Chardonnay	A	86
1996	Chardonnay Alfred	A	87
1997	Merlot	B	85
1997	Shiraz	B	88
1996	Shiraz	B	86

The three 1997 wines offer reasonably good value, with the Shiraz a must-purchase. While the 1997 Chardonnay spent time in oak, it is primarily a fruit-driven wine with a creamy texture, uncomplicated tropical fruit characteristics, medium body, and an easygoing finish. Drink it over the next year. Although a good effort, the 1997 Merlot is typical of most Merlots—one-dimensional, fruity, and soft. Superior to the ocean of innocuous examples that inundate the market, it does offer a coffee bean and berry-scented and -flavored personality. Drink this low-acid Merlot over the next 1–2 years.

The real gem from this trio is the 1997 Shiraz. With a dark ruby/purple color and a knockout nose of lard/bacon fat intermixed with framboise and blackberries, this offering could easily pass for a classic Côte Rôtie. The wine has spent a limited amount of time in American oak casks (about 6 months), which has added a smoky, spicy note to its exuberant fruit. Ripe, rich, medium bodied, supple, and lush, this user-friendly Shiraz should be consumed over the next 3–4 years.

Deakin Estate's 1996 Shiraz should be at the top of every reader's bargain-priced wines shopping list. This seamless, elegant, cassis-scented and -flavored wine displays a dark ruby/purple color, an explosive, berrylike perfume, medium body, low acidity, and an extroverted personality. Although not complex, it is a savory, mouth-filling Shiraz to drink over the next 2–3 years.

The 1996 Chardonnay offers a combination of New World tropical fruit, along with crisp, floral notes and freshness reminiscent of a good Chardonnay from France's Mâcon region. Subtle, peachlike fruit and subtle oak also make their appearance in this wine's flavors. It is a straightforward, attractive, cleanly made Chardonnay to drink over the next 1–2 years. The reserve 1996 Chardonnay Alfred reveals more spicy oak in the nose, fuller body, and more density. It is a more serious and more concentrated wine, but frankly, for pure Chardonnay flavors, I enjoyed drinking the regular cuvée more than the reserve. The Alfred will last for another 2 years.

DROMANA ESTATE (MORNINGTON PENINSULA)

1995	Cabernet/Merlot	C	89
1997	Chardonnay	D	88
1996	Chardonnay Reserve	D	91
1997	Shiraz	C	89

Both of the 1997 offerings reveal a cool-climate character (meaning fresh acidity and no indication of *sur-maturité*, or overripeness). The 1997 Chardonnay offers aromas of white peaches, wet stones, and minerals, zesty acidity, excellent richness on the attack and midpalate, and subdued wood in the finish. Drink it over the next 3–4 years. The 1997 Shiraz exhibits a plum/purple color, as well as a nose of mocha, raspberry, plum, and cherry aromas and low-acid flavors with an evolved style. This fruit-driven wine reveals subtle notes of toasty oak and mineral components in the moderately long finish. Elegant and complex, it should be consumed over the next 7–8 years.

The 1996 Chardonnay Reserve (unfiltered) is an exceptionally impressive wine that spent 12 months on its lees. This has no doubt contributed to its complex, layered texture that is just beginning to open and reveal explosive richness. The wine is full bodied, with a big, spicy, complex, leesy, roasted nut, honeyed nose, and chewy, intense, complete flavors. Butter, citrus, honey, and roasted nut flavors give this wine considerable appeal and intensity. This looks to be a super Australian Chardonnay that should age for 2–3 years, perhaps longer. Slightly less impressive, but still close to outstanding, is Dromana Estate's 1995 Cabernet/Merlot (90% of the former and 10% of the latter). A spicy vanillin, internationally styled nose offers cassis fruit. Medium to full bodied, with toasty oak, excellent density, good purity, and copious tannin and depth characterize this well-made wine, which possesses plenty of everything except personality . . . and that may emerge with another 2–3 years of bottle age. Anticipated maturity: 2000–2015.

E AND E

1994 Shiraz Black Pepper	D 90

This gloriously sweet (from ripeness, not sugar) Shiraz boasts a dense dark purple plum color and an exotic, spicy nose of coconut, pepper, and blackberry fruit. There are no hard edges to this voluptuously textured, opulent, thick, rich, exuberant, mouth-filling Shiraz. Medium to full bodied and pure, it is ideal for drinking over the next 5–7 years.

EBENEZER (BAROSSA)

1996 Chardonnay	C 87
1994 Shiraz	D 88

An excellent Shiraz, the dark garnet/plum-colored 1994 reveals a big, oaky, spicy nose filled with jammy black fruits. In the mouth, the wine offers jammy sweet fruit, not a great deal of complexity, but a mouth-filling, hedonistic style filled with fruit and wood. Drink it over the next 5–6 years. Ebenezer's 1996 Chardonnay is a nicely presented, oak-tinged, citrusy, medium-bodied offering with good purity and ripeness. It possesses a tight texture, but plenty of weight, ripeness, and purity. With another 4–6 months of bottle age, it may merit an even higher score. The wine should age well for 2–3 years.

ELDERTON (BAROSSA VALLEY)

1996 Cabernet Sauvignon	C	91
1995 Cabernet Sauvignon/Shiraz/Merlot	D	90
1995 Command Shiraz	E	94
1994 Command Shiraz	E	92
1992 Command Shiraz	D	94
1996 Golden Semillon (White Dessert)	C	92
1996 Merlot	D	85
1994 Semillon Wood Matured	C	86?

1996 Shiraz	D	90
1995 Shiraz	B	91
1993 Shiraz Command	E	90

The 1996 Golden Semillon is a sweet dessert wine meant to compete with France's Barsac/Sauternes wines. It boasts a knockout nose of melted butter, tangerines, and orange liqueur. Exceptional acidity (much of it undoubtedly added) gives the wine orange marmaladelike flavors, yet the texture is nearly unctuous. There is outstanding purity and sweet, thick, juicy fruit. I suspect a good crème brûlée would work wonders with this dessert wine. It should last for 15 or more years.

The only other white wine I tasted from Elderton was a controversial, incense/mothball-scented 1994 Semillon. Its distinctive nose may put off as many readers as those it charms. However, once past the aromatics, the wine is a rich, full-bodied, exotic, flashy, chewy Semillon that boasts plenty of sweet, smoky American oak. It is not for everybody, but I suspect this wine could work wonders with rich fish and heavily sauced poultry dishes. It should drink well for 1–2 years.

Elderton's wines are not for tasters seeking subtlety and elegance. These are outrageously oaky, flamboyantly styled offerings with immense hedonistic appeal. For example, the 1996 Cabernet Sauvignon is a sumptuous, thick, oaky wine with an opaque ruby/purple color and a sweet, vanillin-scented nose with aromas of overripe black currants and licorice. With low acidity and a plump, fleshy mouth-feel, this heady, succulent Cabernet Sauvignon should be drunk over the next 7–8 years. The 1996 Merlot tastes tame in comparison with other efforts. Monolithic and foursquare, it reveals a dark ruby color, some oak and fruit, but no depth or length. It is a chunky, berry fruit-driven wine to be consumed over the next 2–3 years. The explosive richness and sweet American oak style of the 1996 Shiraz will also have immense crowd appeal. The wine is low in acidity, with stunning layers of blackberry fruit intermixed with pepper and copious new wood. It is plump, round, and hedonistic. Drink it over the next 5–7 years.

Elderton's top cuvée, the Command Shiraz, is the most concentrated and wooded wine of the portfolio. The opaque purple-colored 1995 Command Shiraz boasts huge toasty American oak aromas intermixed with thrilling levels of jammy black raspberry and berry fruit. The wine is explosively rich, with low acidity and spectacular concentration and purity. Although not complex, it is mouth filling, teeth staining, and ostentatious. Drink it over the next 7–10+ years. The 1994 Command Shiraz is cut from the same cloth, although slightly higher in alcohol (14.5% as opposed to the 1995's 14%). It possesses all of the same characteristics—massive fruit extraction, tons of new American oak, low acidity, and layers of chewy, glycerin-imbued, concentrated fruit. It should drink well for another decade. I suspect both wines will become more civilized and less exuberant with bottle age.

Elderton's 1995 Shiraz will be a big hit with anyone lucky enough to run across any of the several hundred cases that were imported to the United States. Dark ruby/purple colored, with a seductive, sweet, vanillin, and jammy black fruit-scented nose, this wine is crammed with copious quantities of extract, fruit, glycerin, and concentration. As hedonistic a Shiraz as readers are likely to find, this voluptuously textured, round, expansively flavored wine is deliciously pure and dramatic. Its low acidity and glorious levels of fruit should insure an enthusiastic reception. Drink it over the next 7–8 years.

Might the 1992 Command Shiraz be the Caymus Special Selection "Shiraz" of Australia? With its nearly 15% natural alcohol, lavish quantities of smoky, toasty wood, and oodles of thick, jammy cassis, blueberries, blackberries, and raspberries, this is a decadent, hedonistic, opulently textured fruit bomb that coats the mouth with thrilling levels of extract, glycerin, and alcohol. Its huge aromatics and bold flavors make a dramatic statement. Do not expect any subtlety in this blockbuster. Look for this opaque purple-colored Shiraz to drink well for another 15+ years.

The flamboyantly styled, lavishly oaked, exotic, opaque purple-colored 1993 Command Shiraz possesses an intense, smoky, jammy prune and blackberry nose, followed by dense, full-bodied, gorgeously silky-textured flavors that are bursting with fruit, glycerin, and alcohol. It is a mouth-filling, viscous style of Shiraz that makes an immediate impression. This wine should become more civilized over the next few years and drink well for a decade or more. The 1995 Cabernet Sauvignon/Shiraz/Merlot (60%, 30%, and 10%, respectively) spent 18 months in French and American oak casks. The wine exhibits a dark ruby color, followed by a straightforward nose of black fruits and spicy wood. In the mouth, it is a naturally textured wine (not excessively acidified) with good flesh, medium to full body, and copious quantities of blackberry and cassis fruit presented in a plump, lush style. Drink it over the next 5–7 years.

Kudos to proprietor Neil Ashmead, who is turning out some marvelously hedonistic, full-flavored wines from his estate vineyards in the warm Barossa Valley (50 miles northeast of Adelaide).

FOUR SISTERS (GOULBURN/McLAREN VALE)

1997 Sauvignon Blanc/Semillon	B	87
1996 Sauvignon Blanc/Semillon	B	87

Made by Mount Langi's winemaker/proprietor, Trevor Mast, the 1996 is a blend of equal parts Sauvignon Blanc and Semillon, all of which is stainless steel–fermented. The Semillon dominates the wine's character, with its waxy, citrusy, honeyed aromas and flavors combining with the Sauvignon's lime, fig, melony character. Crisp, fresh, pure, and lively, this light-bodied wine is all fruit and purity. Drink it over the next year.

The 1997 is a blend of 73% Sauvignon Blanc and 27% Semillon, from vineyards in Goulburn Valley and McLaren Vale. The wine is an exuberant, fleshy, elegant dry white that tastes like liquefied Key lime pie. Drink this fresh wine over the next year.

FOX CREEK (McLAREN VALE)

1996 Cabernet Sauvignon Reserve	D	93
1997 Merlot	D	89+
1997 Shiraz/Cabernets JSM	D	95
1997 Shiraz Reserve	E	96
1996 Shiraz Reserve	D	95
N.V. Vixen Sparkling Shiraz	D	89

This is one of Australia's hottest new wineries, winning plaudits for their superintense, blockbuster-style Shiraz and Cabernet Sauvignon. The vineyards are planted in distinctive black clay soils, and the yields are limited to 3 tons of fruit per acre. As my point scores suggest, I was very impressed with the Cabernet Sauvignon and Shiraz Reserves and, surprisingly, with the sparkling Shiraz.

One of the superstars of Australia, Fox Creek produces wines that almost go off the charts in terms of extract and richness. The first effort with Merlot, the 1997 (3-year-old vines and yields of only 1.6 tons of fruit per acre), did not receive an outstanding score simply because it was not complex. I suspect more complexity will emerge as the vineyard matures. The wine exhibits a saturated ruby/purple color, as well as copious quantities of toasty new oak in the nose and mocha-infused, jammy cherrylike fruit. It is medium to full bodied, rich, and monolithic, but impressively balanced and pure, with mouth-staining levels of extract. Low acidity and an up-front, flamboyant style suggest it can be drunk now and over the next 10–12 years. Merlot fanatics may rate it even higher than I did.

Celestial black currants intermixed with coffee, licorice, Asian spices, and *pain grillé* notes are more reminiscent of a blockbuster vintage of Mouton-Rothschild than what I would expect from a Shiraz/Cabernets blend. The profound 1997 Shiraz/Cabernets JSM, made from 61% Shiraz, 24% Cabernet Franc, and 15% Cabernet Sauvignon (14.5% alcohol and 2,500 cases produced), is a massive, complex, yet elegant and incredibly harmonious wine. The color is a saturated black/purple. This full-bodied wine is bursting with richness and the complex, savory elements that will make wine lovers go ga-ga. A thrilling, full-flavored offering, this wine is just beginning to strut its stuff. Anticipated maturity: 2001–2015. Every bit as impressive is the 1997 Shiraz Reserve. It conceals its nearly 15% alcohol behind a cascade of incredibly rich, concentrated fruit. This wine sees only new American oak, in contrast with the Cabernet Sauvignon, which is aged in 100% French oak. It boasts an opaque black/purple color in addition to knockout aromas of melted asphalt, blackberries, truffles, and licorice. Cherry jam notes also emerge in the flavors. Unctuously textured, incredibly ripe, pure, and full bodied, this wine would make even Australia's Grange look wimpish if tasted side by side. Anticipated maturity: 2003–2025.

The 1996 Cabernet Sauvignon Reserve (1,500 cases produced from 14-year-old vines) had an amazing 52-day maceration and spent 2 years in French oak. It is an opaque purple-colored wine, with a thick-looking, highly extracted personality. This is great stuff! The classic jammy cassis intermixed with vanillin has yet to take on secondary nuances. In the mouth, the wine is extremely dense and unevolved, still tasting like a barrel sample. Full bodied and superrich, with a 35+-second finish, this should evolve into a spectacular Cabernet Sauvignon over the next 2–3 years; it will last for 15 or more. The 1996 Shiraz Reserve (only the third vintage of this wine) is made from 14-year-old vines that average 3 tons of fruit per acre. I am pleased to report that 2,000 cases were produced. Typical of many of Australia's great reds, it boasts an opaque purple color followed by spectacular aromatics (cassis, pepper, blackberry jam, and tar) and viscous, chewy-textured, full-bodied, highly endowed flavors that coat the palate with glycerin, extract, and alcohol (14.5%). This superb, extremely concentrated, blockbuster Shiraz should drink well for 15–20 years.

The kinky, nonvintage Vixin, a sparkling Shiraz, tips the scales at 13.8% alcohol. Since I usually do not enjoy dark purple-colored bubblies, I did not think I would like this wine. However, I was turned on by this sparkling wine's burst of black cherry, cassis, and bubble gumlike fruit, medium to full body, and dry, well-chiseled personality. I am not sure where it belongs in a meal, but I suspect it could make an interesting partner for many Asian dishes. In any event, it is fun as well as different. Production was 2,000 cases. This is one wine from Fox Creek that is probably best drunk during its first year of life.

FRANKLAND ESTATE (WESTERN AUSTRALIA)

1997	Chardonnay	C	88
1995	Chardonnay	C	88
1995	Olmo's Reward	C	90
1994	Olmo's Reward	C	89
1993	Olmo's Reward	C	90+
1997	Riesling	C	89
1996	Shiraz Isolation Ridge	C	91+

1995 Shiraz Isolation Ridge	C 88
1994 Shiraz Isolation Ridge	C 91

This estate vineyard, located in the remote southwestern tip of Australia, a 4½-hour drive southeast of Perth, proved to be a major surprise in my recent tastings of Australian wines. These are among the most distinctive wines made in Western Australia. The 1997 Riesling exhibits a Germanic nose of earth, cinnamon, and red currants, and as it sits in the glass, notes of paraffin emerge. Drink this rich, dry, medium-bodied style Riesling over the next 1–2 years. The full-bodied 1997 Chardonnay (14.2% alcohol) reveals the telltale *terroir*-driven earthiness that seems to be a component part of all the Frankland Estate wines. Broodingly backward, with citrus notes intermixed with earth overtones and spice, it is a chewy, full-bodied, powerful example of Chardonnay. It should drink well for 2–3 years.

Frankland Estates' 1995 Chardonnay reveals a toasty, lavishly oaked nose, bold, butter-scotchlike flavors, and a dense, chunky, powerful palate with plenty of ripe fruit. This spicy, earthy, muscularly styled Chardonnay should age well for 2–3 years.

The 1995 Olmo's Reward Proprietary Red is a blend of Cabernet Franc, Merlot, Cabernet Sauvignon, Malbec, and Petit Verdot, with Cabernet Franc (40%) representing the highest percentage of the component parts. The wine reveals a Rutherford, dusty character in the nose not dissimilar from some of the older BV Private Reserves. With its opaque purple color and sweet currant-scented nose intermixed with tobacco, dried herbs, and earth, this rich, medium-bodied, firmly structured, yet well-delineated wine is impressive for its ele-gance and richness. It can be drunk now as well as over the next 10–12 years. I expect the aromatics to become even more impressive as the wine ages in bottle. The opaque, full-bodied, backward, impressively endowed 1996 Shiraz Isolation Ridge (14.2% alcohol) is in need of 1–3 years of cellaring. The nose offers up earthy notes intertwined with crushed black pepper, blackberry jam, and spice. It is full bodied and firmly knit, with noticeable tannin and a tight structure. The wine is weighty, rich, and pure, but in need of cellaring. Anticipated maturity: 2002–2015.

Also impressive is the Cabernet Sauvignon–dominated 1993 Olmo's Reward. It exhibits the textbook Rutherford dust nose that I associate with some of the great older vintages of Beaulieu Private Reserve Georges de Latour Napa Valley Cabernet Sauvignon. Opaque gar-net/ruby/purple colored, with a sweet cassis, cedary, earthy nose, this wine possesses full body, outstanding ripeness and concentration, and moderate tannin in the long, powerful fin-ish. Although accessible, it will benefit from another 1–2 years of cellaring and will keep for 12–15 years. I would be interested to know if other readers detect the classic BV style of winemaking (of the fifties, sixties, and seventies) in this wine.

The Cabernet Sauvignon–dominated 1994 Olmo's Reward also has an intriguing, BV Pri-vate Reserve Rutherford style to it. The wine possesses a dark ruby/plum color and sweet black currant/cassis fruit intermixed with spicy oak and loamy soil-like notes. Tannic, long, rich, and medium bodied, this youthful, slightly aggressive wine needs 2–3 years of bottle age. It should keep for 12–15 years.

Frankland Estates' 1994 Shiraz Isolation Ridge displays a dusty, earthy character similar to that in the Cabernet Sauvignon. Additionally, the jammy, black raspberry fruit is inter-twined with pepper and vanilla notes. Explosive on the palate, this full-bodied wine is rich and chewy, with plenty of glycerin giving it a fleshy, expansive mouth-feel. While drinkable, it is capable of improving for another 10–15 years.

A distinctively styled Shiraz, the dark plum-colored 1995 Isolation Ridge reveals a smoky, gamey, berry, and peppery nose, dense, chocolatey flavors, medium to full body, and moderate tannin. Pure, with the chocolate characteristic at present dominating the wine's personality, this mouth-filling Shiraz is already accessible, but it should age nicely for 7–8 years.

GALAH (CLARE VALLEY)

1994 Cabernet Sauvignon/Malbec	D	86
1996 Shiraz	D	89
1992 Sparkling Shiraz	D	89

The bird on this wine's label, an unusual-looking parakeet, is called a galah in Australia. These three offerings are among the more restrained wines I tasted from importer Dan Phillips, although they are certainly very good. The 1994 Cabernet Sauvignon/Malbec (250 cases produced) is an attractive, dark ruby/purple-colored wine with sweet black raspberry fruit, medium body, good focus, and a clipped finish. Perhaps more complexity will emerge, but this unevolved wine did not possess the personality of so many other selections from the Grateful Palate. The 1996 Shiraz (500 cases from 88-year-old vines) reveals a Martha's Vineyard-like, minty, eucalyptus, black currant nose with spice and pepper in the background. In the mouth, it was bursting at the seams, with an overall tannic structure and plenty of ripe, mint-infused, cassis fruit. Medium to full bodied, pure, and rich, yet tightly knit, this wine may merit an outstanding score with another 1–2 years in the bottle. It should keep for 10–12 years.

The intriguing 1992 Sparkling Shiraz smelled like a well-aged wine with its tar, pepper, and black fruit-scented nose. In the mouth, the wine reveals tiny pinpoint bubbles, very good effervescence, dry, rich flavors, and a bold, striking personality. It's not for everybody, and I must admit, drinking black/ruby-colored sparkling wines takes some getting used to, but this example was more interesting every time I returned to it.

GNADENFREI (BAROSSA VALLEY)

1998 Shiraz/Pinot Noir	D	91

I must admit that the idea of blending Pinot Noir with Shiraz seemed not only stupid, but appalling. Both wines have plenty of character on their own merits, so why blend them? That being said, I was knocked out by this wine's quality. Thus the tasting note and evaluation are based on what is in the bottle, not my reservations about the eccentric choice of blending grapes. Interestingly, Rolf Binder, the brilliant winemaker of Veritas, produced this offering. Amazingly, it is 70% Pinot Noir and 30% Shiraz, yet the Shiraz dominates. This superb wine, which has 15% natural alcohol, exhibits an opaque purple color, thick, juicy, black cherry, currant, and blackberry aromas, explosive richness, a viscous, thick, juicy texture, full body, and a spectacular finish. Only in the finish does some of the Pinot Noir character seem to reveal itself. Forget the blend, which is hard to understand; this wine is stunning! Anticipated maturity: now–2010.

GREENOCK CREEK (BAROSSA)

1996 Cabernet Sauvignon	D	94
1995 Cabernet Sauvignon	D	90
1997 Grenache	D	92
1996 Grenache Cornerstone Vineyard	D	93
1996 Shiraz Creek Block	E	96
1995 Shiraz Creek Block	D	95+
1996 Shiraz Seven Acres	E	97
1995 Shiraz Seven Acres	D	98

I was absolutely astounded by the quality of these wines, particularly the Grenache and two Shiraz cuvées. Owned by Annabelle and Michael Waugh, this winery, whose winemaker is Chris Ringland, is, according to importer Dan Phillips, one of the most amazing in Australia. Certainly one taste of these wines will make a believer out of anybody. Sadly, much of the production is already sold in Australia. All of these cuvées were made from yields of less than 1.75 tons of fruit per acre. Although alcohol levels are as high as 15% for the Grenache, they are not discernible given the wines' extraordinary wealth of fruit and intensity. The Greenock Creek vineyards are all situated in the northern Barossa Valley, the same area in which some of the finest sources for Penfold's Grange are located. These are massive, opulently textured, extraordinary wines. I kept the 1995 Shiraz Seven Acres open for a whopping 5 days without a trace of oxidation. I finally asked myself what in the world I was doing and drank the rest of the bottle.

Because of the extraordinary Grenache and Shiraz cuvées, it is easy to overlook the outstanding 1995 Cabernet Sauvignon, but that would be a mistake. Made from 10-year-old vines that yielded only 1.75 tons of fruit per acre (350 cases produced), this wine exhibits an opaque plum/purple color. The nose offers up moderately intense aromas of truffles, blackberries, cassis, and oak. In the mouth, the wine is massive, with extraordinary extraction, huge body, and a continuation of the earthy, truffle, blackberry jamlike fruitiness. The 14.6% alcohol is remarkably well concealed in this rich wine. While accessible, it is capable of lasting 15–17 years.

The 1996 Cabernet Sauvignon (from 10-year-old vines) may have only a "modest" 13.9% alcohol, yet it is a sensational wine. Its opaque saturated purple color is followed by copious amounts of cassis, earth, and spice aromas. There is superb concentration, huge body, outstanding purity, and a multidimensional, thick, viscous, concentrated finish. It is a blockbuster Cabernet Sauvignon that will be drinkable young because of low acidity but will evolve for 2 decades.

Sadly, the total production of the 1996 Grenache Cornerstone Vineyard was only 200 cases. Made from low yields and 60-year-old vines, this is a massive, huge, explosively rich, old-vine Grenache that manages to hide its whopping 15.6% alcohol. In fact, the only other old-vine Grenache I have tasted in the New World that can match this offering are the single-vineyard wines from Clarendon Hills. Extremely full bodied, unctuously textured, and succulent, yet not tasting overbearing or heavy, this dazzling Grenache offers copious quantities of kirsch liqueur and jammy cherry and black raspberry fruit, intermixed with roasted nut and peppery smells. It is a fabulous Grenache that should continue to drink well for 10–15 years.

The 1997 Grenache (15.8% alcohol from 60-year-old vines) exhibits a Château Rayas-like flamboyant, kirsch liqueur and raspberry-scented nose that saturates the olfactory sense. Explosive in the mouth, with full body, terrific purity, and a spectacularly layered, long, lusty finish, it deserves a "Wow!" Drink it over the next 5–7 years.

I felt I needed a seat belt when I tasted the two cuvées of 1995 Shiraz. My favorite was the 1995 Shiraz Seven Acre Vineyard. Made from only 8-year-old vines, and remarkably civilized at 14.8% alcohol, this wine, which held up for almost a week without any traces of oxidation, boasts an opaque purple color and a splendidly sweet, rich nose of blackberry liqueur, cherries, cassis, tar, and pepper. Only 25% new oak was utilized in the aging process, but that is not even discernible given the wine's extraordinary richness and purity of fruit. Layers of viscously textured fruit cascade over the palate with precision and purity. This is a fabulous, nearly perfect Shiraz that should age effortlessly for 2 decades or more. The 1995 Shiraz Creek Block (100 cases produced) was made from 60-year-old Shiraz vines and possesses a modest 14.1% alcohol. This wine is more akin to blackberry jam or dry port than wine, but it does not taste as heavy as one might initially suspect given the thickness and richness of fruit. One noticeable difference between it and the Seven Acre is that there is more of a mineral character underlying the full-bodied, massive concentration of this splendid wine. It is also slightly more tannic and closed, although still accessible as well as capable of turning heads at any wine tasting. Look for this monster Shiraz to become even more civilized over the following 15–20 years.

I rated the 1996 Shiraz Seven Acres slightly higher than the 1996 Shiraz Creek Block, but I would not be surprised to see these scores reversed at any given tasting. Both are amazing wines, representing the essence of old-vine Shiraz from the Barossa Valley. There are 500 cases of the Seven Acres and 100 cases of the Creek Block. The Seven Acres is made from 9-year-old Shiraz vines and the Creek Block from 60-year-old Shiraz, with the latter having 15.8% alcohol and the former 14.6%. The 1996 Shiraz Creek Block exhibits a dense purple color and a spectacular nose of roasted coffee intermixed with cassis, blackberries, licorice, and spice. The wine displays amazing ripeness, an unctuous texture, full-bodied palate, and a finish that lasts for 45+ seconds. Its high alcohol and tannin are nearly concealed by the wine's amazing concentration. Anticipated maturity: 2000–2020. The 1996 Shiraz Seven Acres possesses all of the above, in addition to more complexity in the nose (violets?), as well as a more delineated palate. It is an enormous, massive, fabulously concentrated, yet symmetrical wine. Although few readers will have a chance to try these wines, their names are worth knowing, as they are among the world's finest Shiraz.

These are amazing wines!

GREENPOINT

1992 Blanc de Blancs	D	89
1994 Brut Sparkling Wine	D	87
1994 Rosé Brut	D	90

Greenpoint is the Australian branch of France's Möet-Chandon sparkling wine empire. Production averages about 90,000 cases, and the wines have just begun to be exported. I found these three examples to be well made, and as longtime readers know, I am generally not a fan of New World sparkling wines. Thirty percent of the 1994 Brut (a 50-50 Chardonnay/Pinot Noir blend) was put through full malolactic fermentation. The wine is light and frothy, with soft, creamy-textured, fruity flavors, medium body, and lingering effervescence. This is a stylish, attractive, sparkling wine to drink over the next several years. The 1992 Blanc de Blancs, a 100% Chardonnay aged for 4 years on its lees, possesses both finesse and elegance. This fresh wine possesses a creamy-textured, Wheat Thins-like nose, excellent ripeness, light to medium body, and well-defined, tiny pinpoint bubbles. Dry, refreshing, and impressively made, it should be drunk over the next several years. Even better is the 1994 Rosé Brut. This is a soft, medium- to full-bodied, pure, strawberry/framboise-scented sparkling rosé, with excellent ripeness, a long, clean palate impression, and a dry, crisp finish. It is a delectable rosé sparkling wine for drinking over the next 1–2 years.

GROSSET (CLARE VALLEY)

1997 Chardonnay Piccadilly	D	90
1996 Chardonnay Piccadilly	D	89
1996 Gaia Proprietary Red Wine	D	90+
1995 Gaia Proprietary Red Wine	D	88+
1998 Riesling Polish Hill	C	92
1997 Riesling Polish Hill	C	88
1996 Riesling Polish Hill	C	90

All of these brilliantly packaged, impressively made wines are faithful to their varietal compositions. The 1998 Riesling Polish Hill is a medium- to full-bodied, multidimensional, ripe, dry Riesling with exceptional precision, length, and complexity and a knockout nose of petroleum, sweet sausage, citrus, and minerals. In the mouth, some of Riesling's tropical fruit characteristics are present, along with earthy, mineral notes. With tremendous purity, medium to full body, and a long, surprisingly intense finish, this powerful, dry Riesling (13.5% alcohol) is the finest Riesling I have ever tasted from Australia. This reasonably priced wine competes with the best wines from Alsace and Germany. It should last for 4–5 years, but I recommend enjoying it over the next 1–2 years. Grosset's 1997 Chardonnay Piccadilly is another well-delineated, impeccably vinified offering. About 45% of this cuvée is given malolactic fermentation. The wine is young but potentially complex, with full body, a smoky, buttery, roasted hazelnut nose, and tight yet impressively rich, structured flavors that open as the wine sits in the glass. This wine should be better with another 6–12 months of bottle age and last for 3–5 years.

The 1996 Gaia (75% Cabernet Sauvignon, 20% Cabernet Franc, and 5% Merlot) is a layered, well-focused, backward wine. Deep ruby/purple colored, it offers a moderately intense nose of sweet toasty oak and cassis. Layered, with the emphasis on elegance and finesse as opposed to pure weight and power, this rich, deep, Bordeaux-like blend should be at its finest between 2001 and 2014.

Not terribly complex, but satisfying, the fleshy, medium-bodied 1996 Chardonnay Piccadilly reveals small quantities of spicy oak, good body, and a clean, rich, nicely textured finish. It should drink well for 1–2 years. Grosset's 1997 Polish Hill Riesling is a classic, dry Riesling with copious quantities of lemony, citrusy, mineral-like flavors presented in a zesty, vibrant, well-delineated format. The wine is medium bodied, with excellent length and plenty of nervous energy and tension. Drink it over the next 1–3 years. While tasting this wine, I thought of a number of Asian dishes with which it would work splendidly well.

The finest dry Riesling I have ever tasted from Australia, the full-bodied, surprisingly intense, concentrated 1996 Riesling Polish Hill (13.5% alcohol) reveals gobs of citrusy, lemony, honeyed fruit in its floral-scented aromatics. The wine is 100% tank-fermented with lees stirring, thus displaying a degree of complexity, richness, and body that is atypical for a Riesling. However, all the Riesling varietal character is well displayed in this cleanly made, fleshy style of dry Riesling. It should drink well for 2–3 years, perhaps longer.

The 1995 Gaia, a blend of 75% Cabernet Sauvignon, 20% Cabernet Franc, and 5% Merlot, reveals an unmistakable Bordeaux-like style. This deep ruby/purple-colored wine is tightly wound in the nose, but it does offer up some high-class oak along with black currants and other berry fruit. In the mouth, the wine displays a linear, Bordeaux style, plenty of tannin, and a dry, hard finish. It needs time in the bottle. Anticipated maturity: 2002–2012. In a blind tasting, I would be hard-pressed to guess this wine was from Australia.

RICHARD HAMILTON (McLAREN VALE)

1995 Burton's Vineyard (70% Grenache/30% Shiraz)	C	91
1996 Cabernet Sauvignon Reserve	C	85
1995 Cabernet Sauvignon Coonawarra Reserve	C	89
1997 Chardonnay	C	85
1996 Merlot Reserve	C	90
1996 Old Vine Shiraz Reserve	D	90

Richard Hamilton's 1997 Chardonnay is apparently made from the oldest vines in McLaren Vale. I found the wine to be somewhat oaky and monochromatic, but crisp, with good tropical fruit as well as adequate depth. It may have been in a dormant state when I tasted it, but the level of oak seemed elevated for the amount of fruit and extract. Drink it over the next year.

The 1996 Cabernet Sauvignon Reserve is also a good rather than exciting wine. Medium to dark ruby colored, with an herb-tinged, berry- and red currant-scented nose, it is well made but does not possess the depth, richness, or flavor dimension of Hamilton's other two red wine cuvées. The opaque ruby/purple-colored 1996 Merlot Reserve exhibits a smoky, chocolatey, toasty nose intermingled with copious quantities of berry fruit. Full bodied, chewy, and opulently textured, it is a textbook, lavishly endowed Merlot to drink over the next 7–9 years. Readers should also note that it weighs in at 14% alcohol. Another outstanding offering from Richard Hamilton is the 1996 Old Vine Shiraz Reserve (made from 105-year-old vines). The wine offers explosive richness, a big, thick, melted tar, blackberry, peppery nose, thick, dense, viscously textured, full-bodied flavors, and a juicy, intense finish. It should continue to drink well for 5–10 years.

While the 1995 Burton's Vineyard does not quite compete with the extraordinary old-vine Grenache cuvées from Clarendon Hills, it is a noteworthy effort. Made from 50–80-year-old Grenache vines blended with younger-vine Shiraz, and aged in old American oak, it possesses a black/ruby color as well as a stunningly intense nose of kirsch, black raspberries, pepper, and a touch of prunes. The wine is dense, with terrific fruit intensity, spicy, smoky wood, and copious amounts of glycerin and alcohol in the lusty finish. Along with the wine's purity, large size, and gobs of fruit is a surprisingly vibrant acidity level. It should drink well for 5–8 years. The 1995 Cabernet Sauvignon Coonawarra Reserve is an explosively fruity wine, with weedy, tobacco-tinged, black currant aromatics. Sexy in the mouth, with plenty of oak and copious quantities of jammy black currant fruit, this low-acid, full-bodied, silky-textured, lusty Cabernet will provide delicious drinking now and over the next decade.

HANGING ROCK (VICTORIA)

1995 Sauvignon Blanc	C	88
1997 Sauvignon Blanc "The Jim Jim"	C	86

The Loire Valley Pouilly-Fumé look-alike 1995 Sauvignon Blanc demonstrates what high levels can be reached with this varietal by Australia's dedicated producers. It possesses textbook honeyed, melony nose, crisp, elegant, light- to medium-bodied flavors, surprising intensity in its well-textured personality, and a ripe, brilliantly well-delineated finish. It is an excellent, nearly outstanding Sauvignon Blanc to drink over the next several years.

A subtle, restrained style of Sauvignon Blanc, the delicately, nicely subdued 1997 Sauvignon Blanc "The Jim Jim" reveals herbs, spice, and herbaceousness in its nose, medium body, crisp acidity, and a clean, fresh, lively finish. It should be consumed over the next year.

GEOFF HARDY (ADELAIDE HILLS)

1996 Kuitpo Cabernet	C	85

This 100% Cabernet Sauvignon features a dark ruby color and a sweet nose of cedar, cassis, and spicy new oak. Although somewhat compressed in the mouth because of high acidity, it is medium bodied and clean, with elegant, stylish flavors. Drink it over the next 5–6 years.

HARDYS (COONAWARRA/PADTHAWAY/McLAREN VALE)

1991 Cabernet Sauvignon Thomas Hardy	C	87
1995 Chardonnay Eileen Hardy	C	86
1994 Shiraz Eileen Hardy	D	87
1993 Shiraz Eileen Hardy	C	90

The boldly wooded 1995 Chardonnay Eileen Hardy reveals plenty of vanillin and citrus fruit in a medium- to full-bodied, powerful format. Drink it over the next year before the fruit fades and the wood obliterates any noticeable varietal character. The 1994 Shiraz Eileen Hardy, which represents the winery's finest Shiraz cuvées, exhibits a murky, saturated dark plum color, as well as distinctive earth, American oak, and blackberry liqueur-like aromas and unctuously textured, thick, full-bodied, uncomplex, but rich, chewy, long flavors. Moderate tannin is present in this wine, which appears to have been boosted by an addition of tartaric/citric acidity. Chunky, mouth filling, and rustic, it should drink well for a decade.

The 1993 Shiraz Eileen Hardy is a large-boned, broad-shouldered wine with a dark opaque garnet color. Full bodied, with high flavor extraction, copious quantities of hickory smoked, blackberry, and cassis fruit, glycerin, and spice (pepper and American oak), and a lusty, full-bodied finjsh. The wine's tannin and acidity are sweet and well integrated. This bold, full-flavored Shiraz is the finest Shiraz produced by this winery; thus it receives the Eileen Hardy designation. The deep ruby-colored 1991 Cabernet Sauvignon Thomas Hardy exhibits a leafy, earthy, tobacco-scented nose, less body and richness than the Shiraz, but plenty of power and intensity. There is good glycerin, high extract, and that aggressive, unmistakable American oak character. It should drink well for 7–8 years.

HENSCHKE (BAROSSA)

1991 Shiraz Hill of Grace Keyneton Vineyard	EE	95+
1993 Shiraz Mount Edelstone Keyneton Vineyard	D	94
1993 Shiraz/Cabernet Sauvignon/Malbec Keyneton Estate	D	91

Other than the top cuvées of Penfold's Grange, and the old-vine Grenache and Astralis from Clarendon Hills, few other Australian wines are as rich as these offerings from Henschke—a winery that gets my nod as one of Australia's two or three finest producers. Each of these wines coats the mouth with glorious levels of jammy fruit, extract, glycerin, and silky tannin. They are all dense ruby/purple colored, full bodied, and capable of lasting at least a decade and, in the case of the 1991 Shiraz Hill of Grace, possibly 20+ years.

The 1993 Shiraz/Cabernet Sauvignon/Malbec (80%, 15%, and 5%, respectively) Keyneton Estate is the most forward of this trio. It exhibits mouthwatering levels of sweet black raspberry, blueberrylike fruit in a smoky, vanillin, earthy style. Medium to full bodied and lush, with acidity and tannin lurking underneath the fruit, this hedonistic, flamboyantly styled wine can be drunk over the next 10–12 years. The ostentatious 1993 Shiraz Mount Edelstone Keyneton Vineyard reveals a thicker-looking color and hits the palate with even more explosive richness and ripeness than the previous wine. It boasts a phenomenal sweet, rich, dense middle, as well as a huge, unctuous texture and finish. While approachable, it is capable of lasting for 10–15 years. The 1991 Shiraz Hill of Grace Keyneton Vineyard is the most backward wine, with an earthy minerality and explosive black fruits the likes of which are often seen in northern Rhône Valley wines made from ancient vines. This huge, broodingly backward, muscular, brawny, immensely concentrated, yet formidably endowed wine requires another 4–5 years of cellaring; it should keep for 15–20 years. These are awesome examples of what Australia is capable of producing.

HEWITSON (McLAREN VALE)

1996 Shiraz L'Oizeau	C	91

Made from an obscure area called the Fleurieu Peninsula, this impressive, opaque purple-colored wine reveals subtle notes of French oak intermixed with blackberries and cassis. Full bodied, rich, highly extracted, deep, and long, this classy wine is both stylish and complex. Another year or two of bottle age will only add to its enjoyment. Anticipated maturity: 2001–2015.

HIGHBANK (COONAWARRA)

1997 Proprietary Red Wine	D	92
1996 Proprietary Red Wine	D	91+

The impressively made 1997 Highbank Proprietary Red, a Bordeaux-inspired blend of 65% Cabernet Sauvignon, 23% Merlot, and 12% Cabernet Franc, tips the scales at 13.5% alcohol. It offers sweet French oak in the nose along with scents of black cherries and currants, a sweet, concentrated, full-bodied midpalate, and a long, rich, concentrated finish. The wine possesses adequate acidity, sweet tannin, and a pleasant dose of high-quality wood. Drink it over the next 10–15 years.

Another very impressive wine (only 100 cases were produced), the 1996, a Bordeaux blend of 66% Cabernet Sauvignon, 22% Merlot, and 12% Cabernet Franc, could easily pass for a classic Médoc in a blind tasting. The organically farmed vineyard has produced a deep opaque purple-colored wine that has been aged in French oak (as evidenced in the high-class cedar, spice, and vanillin scents). Full bodied, with outstanding richness, a chewy, multilayered texture, admirable purity, and superb overall equilibrium and palate presence, this is a beautifully knit, restrained, yet intensely flavorful Cabernet Sauvignon-based wine that is only hinting at its ultimate potential. Anticipated maturity: 2001–2015.

HILL OF CONTENT (McLAREN VALE/CLARE VALLEY)

1996 Cabernet Sauvignon	B	88
1997 Chardonnay	B	86
1996 Chardonnay	A	87
1996 Grenache/Shiraz	B	87
1997 Old Vines (Grenache/Shiraz)	B	87

This is the *négociant* label of John Larchet, one of the finest brokers of high-quality Australian wines. These reasonably priced offerings are exceptionally well-made, fruit-driven wines that will have broad appeal among consumers and restaurants. The 1997 Chardonnay reveals some spicy oak but primarily citrusy and pearlike fruit offered in a creamy, ripe, luscious style. It is meant to be drunk over the next 12–18 months. According to the importer, about 5% new oak casks were utilized in the wine's upbringing. The 1996 Chardonnay is made from a blend of nine separate vinifications, but do not let that dissuade you from giving this a try. In the overheated wine marketplace, this reasonably priced Chardonnay offers attractive ripe peach and apricot scents, a very good-textured feel on the palate, excellent freshness, a touch of honey, and a clean, lusty finish. It is meant to be drunk over the next year, but I am sure it will keep for several.

The 1996 Cabernet Sauvignon (8% Shiraz and 3% Grenache were added to the blend) offers copious quantities of blackberry and cassis fruit intermixed with a touch of mint. Medium bodied, with a supple texture, good fatness, and a fleshy, exuberant, nicely textured mouth-feel, it should be drunk over the next 4–5 years. The 1997 Old Vines (63% Grenache and 37% Shiraz) tips the scales at 14.5% alcohol. Readers should think of it as a high-class Côte du Rhône. Cherries, kirsch liqueur, pepper, and spice jump from the glass of this medium-bodied, soft, fruit-driven wine. It is meant to be enjoyed now and over the next 2–3 years.

The 1996 Grenache/Shiraz (63% Grenache from a vineyard planted in 1926 and 37% Shiraz) is a hefty (13.9% alcohol), peppery, kirsch and raspberry-scented and -flavored wine with excellent aromatics and richness. Fleshy, soft, and round, the wine is dominated by its red fruit character. Think of it as a very good Australian Côtes du Rhône. It should drink well for 3–4 years.

KATHERINE HILLS (SOUTH/SOUTHEASTERN AUSTRALIA)

1997 Cabernet Sauvignon	B	85
1998 Chardonnay	B	86

This light-bodied, refreshing 1998 Chardonnay (packaged in a Bordeaux-shaped bottle) offers citrusy, buttery fruit, medium body, and well-concealed alcohol (14%). It should be enjoyed over the next year for its freshness and exuberance. The light, fruity 1997 Cabernet Sauvignon possesses attractive black currant fruit, medium body, and a soft, short finish. However, it is to be appreciated for its unencumbered display of fruit and spice. Drink it over the next 1–2 years.

HOUGHTON (WESTERN AUSTRALIA)

1994 Shiraz Wildflower Ridge	A	86

A flowery, spicy, richly fruit wine, this 1994 Shiraz is not complex, but it will offer a generous, soft mouthful of red wine over the next 3–4 years.

HOWARD PARK (WESTERN AUSTRALIA)

1995 Cabernet Sauvignon/Merlot	D	91
1994 Cabernet Sauvignon/Merlot	D	91
1996 Chardonnay	D	89
1997 Chardonnay Mad Fish	C	87
1997 Riesling	C	87

Another impressive Riesling from Australia, Howard Park's 1997 exhibits an unmistakable citrusy/lime-scented nose. Light bodied and dry, it offers an exuberant, fresh, crisp style that is endearing. Doubters who think Riesling can reach such heights only in Alsace, Austria, or Germany need to take a look at some of Australia's finer efforts. The 1997 Chardonnay Mad Fish, which has been 100% tank-fermented and aged, is a treat to drink, offering copious quantities of crisp, orange blossom, apple, and tropical fruits in a straightforward, medium-bodied format. The wine's purity, freshness, and lively character are charming. Consume this easy-to-drink wine over the next 6–12 months. The antithesis of the Mad Fish Chardonnay is the 1996 Chardonnay, a 100% barrel-fermented effort that has been aged in new French oak. This wine has obviously had the full Burgundian treatment of lees stirring and the like. It might be outstanding, but I knocked off a point or two because the oak seemed a trifle elevated. Everything else was impressive. The moderately intense aromatics offer up smoke, roasted hazelnuts, and plenty of leesy, buttery fruit. In the mouth, the wine is powerful, rich, and full bodied, with admirable glycerin and length (it tips the scales at 14% alcohol). It should drink well for another year.

The most impressive of these wines is the 1995 Cabernet Sauvignon/Merlot (70% of the former and 30% of the latter). Possessing over 14% alcohol, this is an Australian-style/size, hugely extracted, chewy, rich, viscous wine with full body and copious quantities of glycerin. It offers plenty of chocolate and black currant fruit notes intermixed with *pain grillé* and damp forestlike aromas. With low acid, sweet tannin, and a huge, chocolatey, roasted coffee-flavored finish, this terrific, big, rich, heavyweight wine should drink well for 10 or more years.

Two hundred cases of the opaque purple-colored, classic 1994 Cabernet/Merlot have been produced. The wine reveals an opaque saturated purple color and sweet, jammy, black currant scents intermixed with toasty oak, vanilla, earth, and spice. There are weedy black currant flavors on the palate, gorgeous sweetness, low acidity, and plenty of tannin. This classic Australian Cabernet Sauvignon should drink well for 12–15 years.

HUGO ESTATE (McLAREN VALE)

1997 Chardonnay Unoaked	C	88
1997 Shiraz	C	86
1995 Shiraz	C	87

I think the Australians are on to something with these richly fruity, exuberant, muscular Chardonnays that can stand on their own without any assistance from oak. This 1997 Unoaked Chardonnay offers abundant lemony/citrus notes with a touch of a spring flower garden. Medium to full bodied, with excellent purity and a hint of minerals in the flavors, this tasty, refreshing Chardonnay should be drunk over the next 12–18 months. The 1997 Shiraz offers attractive kirsch and black cherry notes in its nose and flavors. However, its intrusive acidity and lavish oak kept my score conservative. It is a medium- to full-bodied wine boasting 13.9% alcohol. Cleanly made in an accessible style, it should be consumed over the next 1–2 years before the fruit fades and the acidity takes over. The full-bodied, ripe, jammy 1995 Shiraz exhibits a dark ruby/purple color, gobs of sweet cassis fruit, and not much complexity, but enough glycerin to give it an expansive, chewy mouth-feel. Soft, round, and generous, it should be consumed over the next 5–7 years.

JENKE VINEYARDS (BAROSSA VALLEY)

1996 Merlot	C	86
1996 Shiraz	C	89

I was not impressed with Jenke Vineyards' 1996 Mourvèdre and thought the 1996 Cabernet Sauvignon was foursquare and simple. However, there is no doubting the soft, sexy appeal of the Shiraz and Merlot. The 1996 Merlot is a medium ruby-colored, supple, evolved offering with a textbook nose of smoky, toasty oak intermixed with roasted coffee, herb, chocolate, and cherry aromas. Enjoy this lush, easy-to-drink Merlot over the next 1–2 years. More concentrated and serious is the black/purple-colored 1996 Shiraz, which spent 18 months in American oak casks. Its copious toasty notes work well with this varietal's flashy display of cassis and blackberry fruit. Low acidity and an opulent, seductive mouth-feel will provide a seductive glass of Shiraz over the next 3–4 years.

JINDALEE (MURRAYS/DARLING)

1997 Chardonnay	B	86
1997 Shiraz	B	85

The 1997 Shiraz is a medium dark ruby-colored wine with an herbaceous, berry-scented nose with wood smoke and spice in the background. On the palate, bacon fat flavors complement the round, light, fruity style. Not a blockbuster, this is a good, easygoing restaurant Shiraz that could be served slightly chilled. Drink it over the next year. A low-acid wine with abundant tropical fruit in its aromas and flavors, this fun, uncomplicated 1997 Chardonnay will offer pleasurable drinking over the next year.

STEPHEN JOHN (CLARE VALLEY)

1996 Shiraz	C	87

A reasonably good value in Shiraz, this wine, which spent 18 months in a combination of American and French oak, offers up an aromatic, peppery, spicy nose with black cherry and berry fruit. Not complex, this fruit-driven, foursquare, yet plump, mouth-filling wine is satisfying in a low-key manner. Drink it over the next 4–5 years.

TREVOR JONES (BAROSSA/SOUTH AUSTRALIA)

1994	Cabernet/Merlot	D	90
1997	Chardonnay Mergen	C	90
1995	Shiraz	D	91
1994	Shiraz	C	88
1996	Virgin Chardonnay	C	90

Trevor Jones is an up-and-coming star in the Barossa Valley. For my taste, he produces the finest nonwooded Chardonnay in Australia. The full-bodied 1997 Mergen Chardonnay offers copious quantities of orange/lemony, honeyed fruit, gorgeous freshness, plenty of muscle, excellent purity, and a fine finish. It sees about 20% malolactic fermentation and is to be admired for its vivacious display of fruit. Drink it over the next year to take advantage of its freshness and exuberance.

The unwooded, hence the title Virgin, 1996 Chardonnay blooms in the glass. This wine is given considerable lees contact, but no exposure to wood. The result is a layered, textured, expansively rich, lusty style of Chardonnay that emphasizes this varietal's honeyed, citrusy fruit. At first the wine appears rich and layered but somewhat simple. As it sits in the glass, more and more nuances emerge. I found myself enjoying this wine more with each additional sip. Many unwooded Chardonnays are also underfruited, but this example possesses the richness to make a believer out of anybody. Is this Australia's answer to a grand cru Louis Michel Chablis? It should age well for several years.

The exotic 1994 Cabernet/Merlot (85% Cabernet Sauvignon and 15% Merlot) exhibits a dense ruby/purple color, as well as an intriguing nose of peanut butter, toasty oak, chocolate, cedar, and cassis. It offers low acidity, outstanding fruit purity, and surprising elegance/finesse. As the wine sits in the glass, tobacco/mineral notes enhance the complex personality of this medium- to full-bodied, fruit-driven wine. It should drink well for 5–10 years. Readers looking for a huge fruit fix should check out the perfumed, black raspberry and blackberry-scented 1995 Shiraz. This medium- to full-bodied wine is loaded with fruit. Soft, with low acidity and a luscious, fleshy finish, it is a hedonistically styled wine to enjoy over the next 5–6 years.

Made from 30–100-year-old vines, the gutsy, medium ruby-colored 1994 Shiraz has flamboyant aromatics. When it hits the palate, it reveals more fat, pepper, tar, and cassis flavors, low acidity, excellent richness, and a chewy, fleshy finish. More aromatic complexity and intensity would have resulted in a higher score, but this is an attractive, easygoing Shiraz to drink over the next 5–6 years.

KATNOOK ESTATE (COONAWARRA)

1996	Cabernet Sauvignon	D	90
1994	Cabernet Sauvignon	D	87
1992	Cabernet Sauvignon Odyssey	E	91
1991	Cabernet Sauvignon Odyssey	D	89
1996	Merlot	D	87
1997	Sauvignon Blanc	C	87?

Katnook Estate's 1997 Sauvignon Blanc is no doubt impressive, but the question mark is due to its controversial personality. The wine is extremely intense and almost overwhelmingly vegetal, with an evolved light gold color. This full-bodied, thick, juicy Sauvignon also reveals telltale herb, flint, melony, and citrusy flavors, but the intense herbaceousness will be offputting to some tasters. Nevertheless, for extravagant intensity and richness, this Sauvignon Blanc has few rivals.

The elegant, minty 1996 Merlot is made in a lush, berry-scented manner, with attractive new oak. The wine displays good ripeness, but it leans toward the minty/eucalyptus style of this varietal. It should drink well for 5–6 years. The 1996 Cabernet Sauvignon is one of the finest red wines I have yet tasted from Katnook Estate. It reveals textbook weedy/black currant aromas intermixed with high-quality toasty wood, followed by rich, medium- to full-bodied flavors that unfold on the palate with considerable precision and purity. Although not a blockbuster, it is a concentrated, authoritatively flavored, finesse-style Cabernet that should drink well for 10–12 years. The luxury 1992 Odyssey (100% Cabernet Sauvignon) is Katnook Estate's top cuvée. The wine spends 30 months in French oak and comes across as a serious Bordeaux look-alike. The dark ruby/purple color is saturated to the rim. The nose offers up reticent but promising aromas of cigar box, cedar, fruit cake, black currant, and toasty notes. In the mouth, black cherry/black currant flavors are impressive and full bodied, with nicely integrated acidity and tannin. Is this Australia's answer to a top-class Pauillac? This wine is just beginning to open and promises to last for 15–20 years.

The impressive 1994 Cabernet Sauvignon has been aged 20 months in French oak casks. It is one of the more elegant, stylish Australian Cabernets, without the thickness and heaviness often found in many of that country's wines. It exhibits a red currant/cassis-scented nose, medium body, good acidity, fine purity, and a sense of elegance and restraint. The subtle note of French oak adds class to this noteworthy effort, which should be consumed over the next 7–8 years. The high-class, limited-production 1991 Cabernet Sauvignon Odyssey reveals a dark plum color with amber creeping in at the edge. The evolved color is not reflected in the wine's youthful, fresh personality. Still revealing dry wood tannins, this full-bodied, classy, cedary, spicy, black currant-scented and -flavored wine possesses layers of depth and a long finish. The elevated tannin level suggests another 2–3 years of cellaring is required. The wine should evolve nicely for another 10–15 years. Impressive!

KILIKANOON (CLARE VALLEY)

1997 Cabernet Sauvignon	D	88+
1997 Grenache Prodigal	C	89
1998 Riesling Blocks Road	C	87
1998 Riesling Morts Block	C	90
1997 Shiraz	D	89

This serious new estate, whose debut vintage is 1997, appears to be off to a roaring start. The 1997 Grenache Prodigal (made from moderately old Grenache vines) possesses 15% natural alcohol (all of it unbelievably well hidden) and was aged 14 months in old French *barriques*. It exhibits a gorgeous, intense, cherry/raspberry, slightly oaky nose. In the mouth, the wine displays more elegance than its whopping degree of alcohol suggests. It is a well-delineated, medium- to full-bodied, forward, impeccably made wine with abundant ripe, pure fruit. It can be drunk now and over the next 7–8 years. The younger 1997 Cabernet Sauvignon (aged 15 months in one-third new French *barriques*) requires another year of bottle age. The saturated dark ruby purple color is followed by a clean, structured wine with a youthful tobacco leaf and black currant-scented nose that will likely develop a more cedary character with cellaring. In the mouth, it is zesty and youthful, with lively fruit, nicely integrated new oak, adequate acidity, and a long, restrained finish. Stylish yet rich, it should be drunk between 2000 and 2010. The 1997 Shiraz may be outstanding, and my rating could be conservative. Aged in both American and French oak, the wine exhibits a dark ruby/purple color and a creamy, lusty, oaky nose intermixed with blackberry and cassis fruit. Ripe, with low acidity, a plush texture, full body, and a fruity personality, it should be consumed over the next 7–8 years.

I am more and more amazed by the high-quality Riesling emerging from some of Australia's finest producers. Kilikanoon has turned out two very good cuvées, one of which is exceptional. The 1998 Riesling Blocks Road is a dry, medium-bodied, lemony, citrusy Riesling with considerable elegance, purity, and fruit. It is an excellent wine to drink over the next several years. The outstanding 1998 Riesling Morts Block possesses a more intense minerality, along with notes of lemon, lime, peach, and pineapple. The wine is medium bodied and beautifully concentrated and focused, with a steely, crisp, dry, honeyed finish. This superb dry Riesling should drink well for 4–5 years.

KILLIBINBIN (LANGHORN CREEK)

1997 Shiraz	D	92

The name of this winery is the Aboriginal word for "to shine," and this succulent blackberry-scented and -flavored Shiraz certainly does that. It possesses an opaque purple color, full body, layers of juicy, succulent fruit, and a velvety texture. The wine reveals notes of pepper, licorice, and toasty oak as it sits in the glass. Production was 440 cases, and the alcohol is a relatively hefty 14.2%. Drink it over the next decade.

LAKE BREEZE (LANGHORN CREEK)

1996 Shiraz/Cabernet Bernoota	B	86
1996 Shiraz Winemaker Selection	C	90?

The 1996 Shiraz/Cabernet (55% of the former and 45% of the latter) exhibits copious quantities of vanillin oak in its berry-scented nose. Ripe, easygoing, soft, and user-friendly, given its direct, open-knit style, it should be consumed over the next 2–4 years. The late-harvest-style 1996 Shiraz Winemaker Selection possesses a lofty 14.7% alcohol. Amarone-like notes of melted asphalt and tar are the reason for the question mark. Nevertheless, there are positives, especially for readers who want something that will stain their palate and teeth. This wine exhibits a thick-looking plum/purple color, as well as an intense, smoky, melted road tar and earthy nose with jammy blackberry and cherry fruit. Full bodied and chewy, with considerable viscosity, low acidity, and a long finish, this wine should drink well for 10–12 years.

CHÂTEAU LEAMON (BENDIGO)

1997 Cabernets/Merlot	C	89
1997 Shiraz	C	85
1997 Shiraz Reserve	D	90

This central Victoria property's vineyards are known for their high percentage of granite. The 1997 Cabernets/Merlot (85% Cabernet Sauvignon and Cabernet Franc and 15% Merlot) is an earthy, peppery, opaque plum-colored wine with notes of mint, dried herbs, and black currant and cherry fruit. It is medium to full bodied, with good extraction, excellent ripeness, and a distinctive, earthy style. Surprisingly, the wine's 100% new oak aging is not detectable in either its aromatics or flavors. Drink this enjoyable blend over the next 10–12 years. The 1997 Shiraz (aged in equal parts new oak, 1-year-old, and 2-year-old *barriques*) reveals a minty, earthy nose with pepper and black currants playing second fiddle to the mint/eucalyptus. Medium bodied and slightly compressed in the finish, it is a solidly made, spicy wine, but it is too minty for my taste. Far superior is Château Leamon's 1997 Shiraz Reserve. Made from the estate's oldest vines, this wine was aged in 100% new oak and achieved a whopping 14.5% alcohol. It exhibits a deep plum/purple color, as well as sweet, jammy, blackberry aromas and flavors intertwined with smoky new oak. Some pepper is noticeable, but this is an unevolved, harmonious, exuberant, richly fruity, powerhouse wine that also displays considerable finesse and elegance. Anticipated maturity: now–2012.

LEASINGHAM (CLARE VALLEY)

1996 Riesling	A	85
1995 Shiraz	B	87

The 1995 Shiraz is a plump, fruity, concentrated wine with plenty of pepper and black-berry/cassis fruit. It does not pretend to be complex, with the oak playing a background role to the wine's fruit and body. Consume it over the next 5–7 years. The dry, citrusy, lime-tasting 1996 Riesling reveals high acidity, light body, and a floral, fresh style. Drink it over the next year.

LEEUWIN ESTATE (MARGARET RIVER)

1994 Chardonnay Estate	E	90
1993 Chardonnay Estate	E	90
1996 Riesling Estate	C	90
1995 Riesling Estate	C	87

This is one of the more heralded estates in Australia, selling their wines at high prices because of insatiable demand. I was impressed by the white wines from Leeuwin Estate, particularly the Rieslings and Chardonnays, but I found the Cabernet Sauvignons to be extremely vegetal and green, with plenty of body, but unintegrated acidity and an extremely austere style. The 1993, 1992, 1991, and 1987 Cabernet Sauvignons all tasted unusual to my palate and were rated between 65 and 82, the highest score going to the 1993. I also thought the Pinot Noirs I tasted were one-dimensional, herbaceous, unusual wines that merited scores in the low to mid-70s.

That being said, high praise is in order for the two vintages of Riesling I tasted. Both the 1995 and 1996 Rieslings from Margaret River are impressively made, dry, full-bodied Rieslings. Both vintages exhibit citrusy, crisp fruit, with the 1995 revealing medium body and the 1996 slightly fuller body. There is admirable layered intensity to the citrusy fruit, with good acidity and dry, long finishes. Both wines are marvelously clean, pure, well balanced, and ideal for drinking over the next several years.

I also enjoyed the 1993 and 1994 Chardonnay from Margaret River. These wines, always aged in 100% new French oak and made from low yields, are dense, full-bodied, dry, lush Chardonnays with well-integrated wood, natural tasting acidity, and powerful, long finishes. They are mouth filling, husky, and weighty. A tasting of several of the older vintages (1990, 1989, and 1988) left me wondering why they are renowned for their aging potential, but it could be because my palate prefers white wines fresh and lively as opposed to oxidized and stale. Both Chardonnays possess some New World–ish tropical fruit, as well as plenty of backbone and weight. They are best drunk with full-flavored dishes.

PETER LEHMANN (BAROSSA)

1995 Botrytis Semillon	C (375 ml)	90
1995 Cabernet Sauvignon	C	88
1994 Cabernet Sauvignon	C	88
1992 Cabernet Sauvignon Clancy's-Gold Preference	C	87
1995 Shiraz	B	87
1994 Shiraz	B	87

Peter Lehmann has once again produced fine wines at realistic prices. Readers seeking an under $20, heavily oaked (American wood) Cabernet Sauvignon will like the 1995, a Silver Oak look-alike. The 1995 Cabernet Sauvignon exhibits a dark ruby/purple color, a heavy overlay of charred, smoky *pain grillé*, full body, excellent richness and depth, good purity, and plenty of sweet, jammy fruit. It will never be a complex Cabernet, but it is mouth filling, generous, and well made—assuming readers enjoy a lot of wood. Drink it over the next 4–5 years. The 1995 Shiraz offers up a smoky, peppery, blackberry-scented nose with less new oak than its sibling. The wine possesses excellent ripeness, a one-dimensional, sweet, jammy midpalate, good length, and no hard edges. It should drink well for 3–4 years.

The current releases include a delicious dark ruby/purple-hued 1994 Shiraz. With its peppery, spicy, jammy black fruit, slightly herbaceous nose, this round, generous, sweet-tasting Shiraz offers a plush, succulently textured mouthful of wine. Already delicious, it is capable of lasting another 5–6 years. The 1994 Cabernet Sauvignon exhibits smoky oak along with copious quantities of jammy black fruits in its moderately fragrant aromatics. Rich, spicy, and juicy, with a broad, expansive flavor profile, this straightforward, in-your-face style of Cabernet Sauvignon should drink well for 4–5 years. The 1992 Cabernet Sauvignon Clancy's-Gold Preference is meant to be a more ambitious style of Cabernet Sauvignon. While it is well made, it errs on the side of being too restrained and elegant and not doing what Australian reds do best—offer a blast of jammy red and black fruits nicely dosed with high-quality wood. It is a very good wine, with more tannin, weight, and body than the regular cuvée. Drink it over the next 7–8 years.

One of the finest sweet wine values in the world has always been Peter Lehmann's Botrytis Semillon. The 1995 continues the winery's Midas touch with this wine. An enticing honeyed, woody, sweet tangerine/ripe pineapple-scented nose is followed by a full-bodied wine with gobs of acidified, rich, chewy fruit, excellent purity, and fine glycerin and length. It should drink well for 5–7 years, possibly longer.

LELAND ESTATE (LENSWOOD)

1998 Sauvignon Blanc	D	87
1997 Sauvignon Blanc	C	90

Importer Dan Phillips told me that winemaker Rob Coots is totally obsessed with producing world-class Sauvignon Blanc from his tightly spaced vineyard (4,000 vines per 2.47 acres). The 700 cases of 1997 were made from 12-year-old vines that produced about 3 kilos of fruit per vine (that's low). No oak was introduced in the wine's upbringing, and it is all the better for it. This Sauvignon begins subtly in its nose but blossoms impressively in the glass. Rich, tropical fruit aromas intertwined with scents of spice, melon, and gooseberry are present in this expansive, superbly crafted wine. It combines intensity and power with a sense of elegance and precision. This dazzling Sauvignon should drink well for 12–16 months. An intensely aromatic style of Sauvignon, the 1998 is light bodied, with well-integrated acidity, plenty of melony and grassy fruit, excellent purity, and a zesty finish. Drink it over the next 12 months for its freshness and purity.

LENGS AND COOTER (CLARE VALLEY)

1997 Shiraz	D	89
1996 Shiraz	D	90
1996 Swinton	D	87

These two home winemakers turned commercial a few years ago. The opaque purple-colored 1996 Shiraz, a blend of old-vine Shiraz from selected Clare Valley vineyards, offers an explosive blackberry and peppery-scented nose. As the wine sat in the glass, loamy soil, jammy cherry, and herb scents emerged. Full bodied, thick, and juicy, with gobs of fruit, this is not quite the size of some of the blockbusters the Grateful Palate represents, but it is no wimpish wine by any means. This thick, juicy, succulent Shiraz is soft enough to provide delicious drinking now and over the next decade.

The 1997s are also two very fine efforts from this winery. The 1997 Swinton (an 85% Cabernet Sauvignon and 15% Shiraz blend) displays a dark ruby/purple color, copious amounts of spicy new oak, and an international, somewhat monolithic style. Nevertheless, this is an excellent, flavorful, obviously wooded wine to consume over the next 5–7 years. The 1997 Shiraz offers up-front blackberry fruit, less obvious oak, a lush, medium- to full-bodied palate, excellent purity, and a soft, open-knit personality. It, too, should be drunk over the next 5–7 years.

LENSWOOD VINEYARDS (KNAPPSTEIN) - (ADELAIDE HILLS)

1994	Cabernets	D	90+
1996	Chardonnay	D	88
1995	Chardonnay	D	91
1997	Pinot Noir	D	84?
1996	Pinot Noir	D	88
1995	Pinot Noir	D	88
1998	Sauvignon Blanc	C	89
1997	Sauvignon Blanc	C	89
1996	Sauvignon Blanc	C	89
1997	Semillon	C	90

This winery is owned by Tim Knappstein, a well-known figure in Australian wine circles. Knappstein sold the rights to the use of his name and formed this winery dedicated to exploiting vineyards in the Adelaide Hills, 20 miles east of that city. These cool-climate vineyards are planted at an altitude of 1,700 feet. All of the following wines were impressively made.

The 1996 Sauvignon Blanc is one of the finest Sauvignons I have ever tasted from Australia. Its gorgeous, pungent, melony, peapod, honey, and figlike nose offers intense aromatics. The wine displays terrific delicacy on the palate, with great precision, medium body, and plenty of rich, concentrated fruit. It is a serious, well-endowed Sauvignon Blanc with intense fruitiness buttressed by crisp acidity. It should drink well for 1–3 years. Lenswood's 1995 Chardonnay is barrel-fermented, with 30% of the wine put through malolactic fermentation. It is a full-bodied, fleshy, Bâtard-Montrachet-like wine with a superb, complex, butterscotch, honeyed nose. Powerful, rich, dense, and chewy, with a creamy texture and outstanding purity, this is a knockout Chardonnay to drink over the next several years.

The 1997 Sauvignon Blanc offers a gorgeously pure, exuberant, expressive aromatic profile consisting of melons, honeyed citrus, and floral scents. Totally tank-fermented and -aged, this wine screams Sauvignon Blanc. There is excellent, nearly outstanding, richness, enough acidity to provide delineation and uplift, and a refreshing, lively, dry palate. It should drink well for another year.

Lenswood's 1998 Sauvignon Blanc is a classy, mineral-dominated wine with very good acidity, excellent freshness, and a vibrant personality. The moderately intense nose offers up scents of wet stones, dried herbs, flint, and ripe melony fruit. Medium bodied, with superb purity, this gorgeously scented and flavored Sauvignon Blanc should be consumed over the next year. I thought Lenswood's 1997 Semillon was outstanding. Seventy-eight percent of this cuvée was barrel-fermented, and it tastes as if considerable lees stirring were employed.

In contrast with the Sauvignon, the Semillon reveals toasty new oak in addition to Burgundy-like, leesy aromatics. Full bodied, with loads of personality, a slight degree of honey to its exceptional richness, and an almost over-the-top style, this wine offers terrific fruit, a thick, rich texture, and a dry finish. The principal characteristics of Semillon (waxy, citrusy notes) along with roasted nut components are present. Drink it over the next 3–4 years. The nicely textured, rich, full-bodied 1996 Chardonnay reveals attractive citrusy notes intertwined with minerality. The oak is spicy but generally well disguised. Full bodied and powerful, yet beautifully buttressed by well-integrated acidity, this fresh, lively, impressively built Chardonnay should drink well for 3–4 years.

Few Pinot Noirs the quality of Lenswood's 1996 Pinot Noir emerge from Australia. Wine-maker Tim Knappstein fashioned a dense ruby/purple-colored, tannic Pinot with intriguing chocolate and cherry scents as well as a hint of truffles. This medium-bodied, impressively built, structured wine is still young, requiring bottle age to soften some of its angularity, but it offers authentic varietal character and smoky Pinot fruit. Drink it over the next 5–6 years.

The 1997 Pinot Noir was not as fine as the 1996. This dark ruby/purple-colored wine was aged in 100% French oak and is somewhat dominated by wood. The subdued nose opens with airing to reveal notes of cherries, but the oak component is excessive. This wine is medium bodied and compressed, with a short finish. It is a correct, reasonably good Pinot Noir for consuming over the next 2–3 years.

Excellent Australian Pinot Noirs are nearly nonexistent, but Lenswood's 1995 Pinot Noir exhibits a Burgundian, Côte de Beaune-like, smoky, cherry/raspberry-scented nose, stemmy, sweet, round flavors, medium body, good spice, and notions of high-quality, new French oak casks. This medium-bodied, elegant Pinot should be drunk over the next several years. The 1994 Cabernets (made from a blend of 81% Cabernet Sauvignon and 19% Merlot; 220 cases imported) is an opaque purple-colored wine with wild blueberry/cassis-like aromas. Tasting more akin to a barrel sample than a finished wine, this hugely extracted, remarkably pure, well-balanced wine is still unevolved, backward, and tight. Two to five years of cellaring will prove beneficial. Over the next 12–15 years, this wine should develop into a classy, complex, concentrated Cabernet Sauvignon.

LINDEMANS (SOUTHEAST AUSTRALIA/PADTHAWAY)

1998 Chardonnay Bin 65	A	86
1997 Chardonnay Bin 65	A	84
1996 Chardonnay Bin 65	A	87
1994 Shiraz	C	86

One of the ironies in wine tasting is that virtually all the more expensive wines from Linde-mans that I tasted recently did not fare particularly well and, from my perspective, were not good enough to recommend. Too many of them, such as their 1992 Pyrus Coonawarra, 1992 Limestone Ridge Coonawarra, and 1992 Cabernet Sauvignon St. George, came across as frightfully acidified wines made by an oenologist playing it close to the vest. However, there is some good news, as the 1996 Chardonnay Bin 65 remains one of the world's most delicious Chardonnays in the under $10 category. The wine offers gobs of honeyed tropical fruit, enough acidity for definition, medium body, and a lush, richly fruity finish. This fresh, well-made wine will drink well for another year.

One of my all-time favorites when it comes to value picks, the light straw-colored 1997 Chardonnay Bin 65 offers more citrus and acid than previous examples, ripe pineapple and other tropical fruits, light to medium body, and a crisp finish. While it may not be quite as good as previous renditions, it is still a fine value.

A perennial "best buy," the 1998 Bin 65 Chardonnay is meritorious. The wine's light to medium straw color is accompanied by a delightful bouquet of citrusy, honeyed Chardonnay fruit with no oak in evidence. Crisp, medium bodied, fresh, and lively, it should be enjoyed over the next 12 months.

I also enjoyed Lindemans's 1994 Shiraz Padthaway, an opaque plum/purple-colored wine with an intense, smoky, vanillin, blackberry-scented nose. Although not complex, the wine is dense and chewy, offering a medium- to full-bodied mouthful of uncomplicated Shiraz. Drink it over the next 4–5 years.

THE MAGPIE ESTATE (BAROSSA)

1997 Grenache The Faker	C	90
1997 Grenache/Mourvèdre	C	87
1996 Shiraz The Malcolm	EE	99

An Austrian winemaker named Rolf Binder, who is also the winemaker for Veritas, has produced three intriguing wines, including an unreal Shiraz called The Malcolm. The latter wine takes winemaking to the extreme yet manages to pull it off without producing a total freak. However, for value, there are two interesting wines to consider. The 1997 Grenache The Faker (called that because it is extremely high in alcohol—14.5%—but tastes richly fruity and friendly) is a deep ruby-colored wine with textbook Grenache aromas of pepper, roasted peanuts, cherries, kirsch liqueur, and spice. Stunningly rich, it boasts a Châteauneuf du Pape-like sumptuousness, thickness, and full-bodied personality loaded with glycerin and fruit. While it will not make old bones, for drinking over the next 5–6 years, this wine delivers the goods. Slightly more lean, leathery, and tannic is the 1997 Grenache/Mourvèdre. Although it boasts 14% alcohol, the wine's Mourvèdre component (about one-half of the assemblage) provides telltale tree bark and leathery characteristics to the aromatics. Dark ruby/purple colored, with good density and soft underlying cherry fruit and spiciness, this austerely styled wine should drink well for 4–5 years.

How do you describe a wine such as the Magpie Estate's 1996 Shiraz The Malcolm? Yields were a minuscule 1 ton of fruit per acre from 60-year-old vines, production was 100 cases, and the wine's alcohol content is a mammoth 16.5%. This wine, which lasted 4 days in the bottle before I decided to pass the balance through my bowels, displays an opaque black/purple color and exotic, coffee, chocolate, Asian spice, roast duck, and blackberry and prune liqueur-like aromas. To say the wine is unctuously textured is an understatement. This wine looks like 10-W-40 motor oil. Very thick and dry, yet remarkably balanced, with fabulous purity and a finish that goes on for nearly a minute, this spectacular Shiraz will become more civilized with each year of aging. It is the type of wine some Pomerol estates produced in such vintages as 1947, 1949, and 1950 but would not dare to fashion today because modern oenologists refuse to let the grapes become this ripe. A winemaking tour de force, The Malcolm Shiraz should age effortlessly for 40 or more years.

MAJELLA (COONAWARRA)

1996 Cabernet Sauvignon	D	88
1996 Cabernet Sauvignon/Shiraz Maleea	D	91+
1996 Shiraz	D	88+

The Lynn brothers, who for years supplied grapes to some of the top cuvées of Winn and John Ridoch, have begun to estate-bottle their production. These are well-made, tightly knit wines that were extremely youthful and unevolved when I tasted them. All three possess the potential to improve in the bottle, so my ratings may turn out conservative. The 1996 Cabernet Sauvignon exhibits an opaque purple color, followed by a Médoc-like, herb, *pain grillé*, cassis, gravelly nose. Medium bodied and firm, with moderately high tannin and outstanding purity, this wine requires 2–3 years of cellaring and should keep for 10–15 years. The 1996 Maleea Cabernet Sauvignon/Shiraz is a blend of nearly equal parts of these two varietals. Aged in 100% new French oak, it comes across as backward, youthful, and unevolved. It reveals a classic nose of black currant, vanillin, weedy tobacco, and peppery scents, medium-to full-bodied, powerful flavors, high tannin, and an unevolved, youthful taste and texture. This wine requires 2–4 years of cellaring; it should keep for 15 or more years. Last, the 1996 Shiraz was backward and tightly knit when I tasted it. Perhaps it is Majella's winemaking style, but this deep ruby/purple colored, full-bodied wine needed coaxing in order to reveal some spice and sweet black fruits in its nose. In the mouth, it cuts an expansive, medium- to full-bodied feel, but the flavors are restrained, tightly knit, and still bound by the wine's oak, tannin, and acidity. Give this Shiraz 2–3 years of cellaring; it should keep for 12–15.

MAXWELL WINES (McLAREN VALE)

1996	Cabernet Sauvignon Lime Cave	C	91
1998	Chardonnay	C	85
1997	Merlot Reserve	D	90+
1998	Semillon Old Vines	C	87
1995	Shiraz Reserve	D	90

Except for the mainstream, straightforward Chardonnay and a muted bottle of 1997 Shiraz Ellen Street (probably just beginning to show some corkiness and, sadly, not available to retaste), this winery's McLaren Vale products were impressive. It is not easy to find world-class Australian Merlot, but this 1997 Reserve (aged 16 months in French and American oak) is a classic, Bordeaux-style wine with an opaque purple color and a thick, juicy nose of cherry liqueur intermixed with blueberries and spicy new oak. It is ripe, medium to full bodied, youthful, pure, and well structured. This is a more delineated, concentrated, and ageworthy Merlot than most New World examples of this varietal. Although young, it can be drunk now or cellared for 15 years. The 1996 Cabernet Sauvignon Lime Cave is an outstanding value. A California Cabernet of this quality would cost $50–$100. This offering boasts an opaque purple color, followed by a big, exuberant, ostentatious aromatic profile of smoke, herbs, earth, black currants, and spicy wood. Rich, full bodied, and layered, with a terrific texture, outstanding purity, and massive extract, this well-balanced, large-scale, mouth-filling Cabernet is soft enough to be drunk now but promises to evolve for at least a decade. The opaque ruby/purple-colored 1995 Shiraz Reserve reveals plenty of extract, some noteworthy peppery, cassis, and blackberry fruit in the nose, low acidity, good depth, and a pure, plush, open-knit, concentrated personality. This silky wine achieved over 14% natural alcohol and was aged both in French and American oak. Drink it over the next 8–10 years.

Among the white wines, the 1998 Semillon Old Vines exhibits a creamy, lanolin, citrusy, lime liqueur-like nose. This excellent, tasty, herb-tinged wine possesses surprising weight and length. Semillon is a good food wine, but drunk on their own, they often come across as clunky and controversial. Last, the 1998 Chardonnay, which was barrel-fermented in both French and American wood, is a solidly made, spicy, richly fruity wine that comes across with notes of honeyed citrus fruit in addition to buttered nuts. However, it is straightforward, medium bodied, and good, but uninspiring.

CHARLES MELTON (SOUTH AUSTRALIA/BAROSSA)

1996	Cabernet Sauvignon	D	92
1996	Nine Popes	D	91
1995	Nine Popes	C	89
1998	Rose of Virginia	C	89
1996	Shiraz	D	91
1995	Shiraz	D	93

I have noted in my tastings of high-quality Australian wines that those from Charles Melton consistently merit accolades. If I were to design a dry, full-bodied rosé, I would make it along the lines of Melton's 1998 Rose of Virginia, which falls somewhere between a full-bodied rosé and a medium-bodied dry red. It is made by bleeding the cuvées of old-vine Grenache and then is tank-fermented and bottled quickly to preserve its exuberance and freshness. The wine's aroma is similar to that of a terrific Beaujolais—jammy strawberries, framboise, and cherry fruit. In the mouth, this boldly flavored rosé offers a wallop of glycerin and alcohol. This hedonistic wine should be consumed over the next 6 months, but what a dramatic effort!

The 1996 Nine Popes, a satirically named wine that pokes fun at France's Châteauneuf du Pape, is made from dry-farmed vineyards, ranging in age from 30–130 years, planted with Grenache, Shiraz, and Mourvèdre. The deep ruby/purple-colored 1996 is a blend of 68% Grenache, 30% Shiraz, and 2% Mourvèdre. This big wine (14.5% alcohol) should offer immensely pleasing and mouth-filling drinking for a decade or more. It offers a knockout nose of black fruits intermixed with new saddle leather, spice, and earth. Expressive, with gobs of fruit, this intense, chewy, yet impeccably balanced and pure wine is a thrill to drink. Think of it as Australia's Châteauneuf du Pape, but fruitier. The 1996 Shiraz (14% alcohol) spent 15 months in French and American oak. It exhibits a dense ruby/purple color and a moderately intense nose of crème de cassis and blackberries. Stunning in the mouth, with outstanding purity, depth, and balance, this chewy, fruit-driven wine should develop even more complexity with 2–5 years of bottle age. It should keep for 10–12 years. My favorite wine among this all-star lineup is the 1996 Cabernet Sauvignon. Considered to be the Barossa Valley's finest vintage during this golden decade, the 1996's confirms its reputation by its extraordinary richness and depth. Aged in French oak for 15 months, and eclipsing 15% natural alcohol, this is a full-bodied, massive Cabernet with beautifully integrated wood, acidity, and tannin. Gorgeous aromas of Provençal herbs intermixed with black currant jam, fruitcake, cigar box, and cedar are terrific. The wine possesses fabulous depth, considerably viscosity, and a 40+-second finish. Already accessible, it promises to evolve for 10–15 years.

The 1995 Shiraz is a fabulous wine! Made from a vineyard whose vines range in age from 35 to 100 years, it spends 15 months in a mélange of American and French oak. The wine boasts a saturated purple color, followed by explosive aromatics with pronounced, intensely sweet, jammy cassis, licorice, and spice notes that soar from the glass. On the palate, the wine is full bodied, with marvelous concentration, fabulous purity, low acidity, and a seamless, mouth-coating personality. This is a dramatically styled, squealing Shiraz to drink over the next decade.

The 1995 Nine Popes, an intriguing blend of Grenache, Shiraz, and Mourvèdre, may be Australia's answer to a Rhône Valley Châteauneuf du Pape, although the wine's minty component is not likely to show up in most Châteauneuf du Papes. In addition to the mint, there is a wealth of kirsch, cassis, and black cherry fruit in this deeply saturated ruby/purple-colored wine. It exhibits medium to full body, outstanding purity, a nicely textured finish, and no hard edges. With more complexity and length, this wine would have merited an outstanding rating. Drink it over the next 5–7 years.

MOSS WOOD (MARGARET RIVER)

1996 Cabernet Sauvignon	E	91+
1995 Cabernet Sauvignon	D	92
1994 Cabernet Sauvignon	D	92

This serious producer has fashioned a 100% Cabernet Sauvignon from a dry-farmed vineyard in Margaret River. The 1996 is considered to be the decade's greatest vintage to date in Margaret River, and this wine is indeed impressive. Aged in French oak casks for 24 months before it was egg white–fined and lightly filtered, this tightly knit but gorgeously proportioned Cabernet Sauvignon exhibits a saturated ruby/purple color and a reticent but promising nose of violets, black currants, licorice, and truffles. Full bodied, deep, and crammed with extract, this pure, well-delineated Cabernet Sauvignon needs another 2–3 years of cellaring. It should be uncommonly long-lived for an Australian Cabernet, aging for at least 18–20 years.

One of the original Margaret River wineries, these Cabernet Sauvignons come from a vineyard planted in 1969. The wines are made from small yields of approximately 2 tons of fruit per acre. They are explosive, rich, opulently textured wines that represent the essence of Margaret River Cabernet Sauvignon. The dense purple-colored 1995 exhibits a classic black current, cedar, and spicy nose, full body, outstanding richness and power, and brilliant definition and length. Although still grapey and unevolved, it should age effortlessly for the next 12–15 years. The similarly styled 1994 is very dense and may have been produced from riper fruit given its lower acidity and more roasted, inky, jammy character. It is a large-scale, full-bodied, beautifully balanced Cabernet Sauvignon that is impressive to smell and taste. Both of these wines will benefit from 2–3 more years of bottle age and last for 15+ years. These are very impressive Cabernet Sauvignons.

MOUNT HORROCKS (WATERVALE)

1997 Chardonnay Unwooded	C	89
1996 Chardonnay Unwooded	C	87
1996 Riesling Corden Cut	C (375 ml)	90
1996 Shiraz	D	92

The exceptional 1996 Shiraz reveals a black/purple color and sumptuous aromatics consisting of eucalyptus, black raspberry liqueur, and pepper. The wine offers superb richness and full body in a fruit-driven, soft, lusciously textured, low-acid format. Drink this hedonistic Shiraz over the next 10–12 years. The steel-fermented, tank-aged 1997 Chardonnay Unwooded is a wonderfully vibrant, naked expression of fruit. Having been put through partial malolactic, this wine appears to be an Australian imitation of a top-class Chablis. The wine exhibits citrus in the nose in addition to white peach and floral scents. It possesses good body, lusty alcohol (13%), and terrific fruit intensity and purity. Drink it over the next 1–2 years for its exuberance and freshness.

I immensely enjoyed the clean, racy 1996 Chardonnay, which represents a naked expression of the grape unencumbered by wood aging. It exhibits a peppery, minty, honeyed nose and flavors, excellent delineation, medium body, fine depth, and gorgeous purity. There is also good flesh and plenty of fruit. Readers looking for an expressive Chardonnay that has never seen a second of wood will enjoy this wine as much as I. Drink it over the next year.

With its 11% alcohol, the 1996 Riesling Corden Cut is made in a Beerenauslese style (there are a hefty 112 grams per liter of residual sugar). The bouquet offers up beautiful honeyed nectarine and orange aromas, followed by an unctuous texture and thick, juicy flavors suggestive of buttery tropical fruits. With refreshing, well-integrated acidity, this exuberant as well as vivacious wine will drink well for 4–5 years.

MOUNT LANGI GHIRAN (VICTORIA)

1996	Billi Billi Creek	C	86
1995	Cabernet Sauvignon (57%)/Merlot (43%)	D	91
1993	Merlot	C·	92
1996	Shiraz	D	90
1995	Shiraz	D	95
1994	Shiraz	C	94

Trevor Mast, proprietor of this boutique Australian winery, believes in tiny yields, very ripe fruit, and no fining or filtration prior to bottling. The results speak for themselves. The blockbuster 1993 Merlot (68% Merlot, 25% Cabernet Sauvignon, and 7% Cabernet Franc) pushes the envelope of intensity and richness to extremes. A sweet, jammy nose of blackberries, earth, oak, and cherry extract soars from a glass of this opaque purple-colored wine. In the mouth, there are layers of lavishly rich fruit, awesome concentration, and a silky, high-alcohol, chewy finish. This wine will overwhelm just about any food other than extremely strongly flavored dishes. Imagine Pomerol's famed Château l'Évangile made in a Vendange Tardive style—that should give readers a glimpse of just how intense this wine is. Made from yields of 2 tons of fruit per acre, aged 18 months in 100% new oak casks, and bottled naturally, this is another head-turning, ostentatious red wine from Australia.

Unbelievably, the 1994 Shiraz tasted superior. It exhibits an opaque black/purple color, followed by an aromatic profile offering up head-spinning levels of smoke, bacon fat, over-ripe cassis, licorice, plum, and black pepper aromas. Those scents can also be found in the flavors of this huge, intensely concentrated Gorgonian Shiraz. It is silky enough to drink, but it should age effortlessly for 2 decades.

The organically cultivated vineyards of winemaker/proprietor Mast are planted at an altitude of 1,400 feet. The grapes are consistently harvested at high maturity levels, resulting in wines that are exceptionally rich and concentrated. The 1995 Cabernet/Merlot blend exhibits an opaque purple color and a wonderful nose of cassis and blueberry fruit that has not yet developed any secondary nuances. The wine is full bodied, with outstanding concentration and extract, as well as an unevolved personality. It is bursting with potential and should evolve effortlessly for 10–15+ years. Although forward enough to be drunk, it requires another 1–3 years to develop in the bottle. Impressive! Even more exceptional is the 1995 Shiraz. In 1995 yields were off 25%–30% according to Mast. He considers this wine to be reminiscent of the 1990, but perhaps richer. The wine possesses a saturated dense purple color, followed by a smoky, hickory, blueberry/cassis nose, great intensity and richness on the palate, and oodles of cassis fruit presented in a full-bodied, low-acid, moderately tannic style. This massive but well-balanced wine should drink well for 15–18 years.

I have always wondered what Mount Langi Ghiran meant in aboriginese, and I was told it means "home of the yellow-tailed black cockatoo." Too bad, I had hoped for something salacious. This vineyard is spectacularly situated 1,400 feet above sea level, on the slopes of the great dividing range in southwest Victoria. Although I have never visited the vineyard, I have met winemaker/owner Trevor Mast, who has proved his credentials over and over by making terrific Shiraz and Cabernet Sauvignon. He has now added a Billi Billi Creek cuvée. Named after King Billi Billi, a long-dead aboriginal chief, the wine is a blend of Shiraz, Cabernet Sauvignon, and Grenache. The 1996 possesses tangy acidity, plenty of pepper and black raspberry and cherry fruit, medium body, and a clean, crisp, bistro style. Although not deep or complex, it is mouth filling, rich, and well made. Moreover, it should provide plenty of pleasure over the next 4–5 years. The 1996 Shiraz won't make readers forget the spectacular 1995 and 1994. While outstanding, it is not made in the blockbuster mold of several previous efforts. The wine possesses a dark ruby/purple color, as well as peppery, licorice, and black fruit scents with loamy soil tones in the background, medium to full body, and blackberry/blueberry fruit and spicy wood notes (from its maturation in a combination of American and French barrels). It should drink well for a decade or more.

NICHOLSON RIVER (GIPPSLAND)

1997 Chardonnay	E	93?
1997 Semillon	D	92

Before I try to describe these wines, which take flavor, extraction, ripeness, and individuality to the limit, a word of warning: Some tasters will find them excessive, over the top, intense, botrytised wines, but they will undoubtedly excite flavor fanatics. The 1997 Semillon could easily pass as a more unctuous example of a dry Château d'Yquem. It boasts a deep golden color, as well as waxy, knockout aromatics, honeyed, full-bodied, extremely rich flavors, a dry finish, and a viscosity and flavor intensity that might well be unprecedented. The 1997 Chardonnay possesses unreal levels of ripeness, extract, and intensity. This massively concentrated wine oozes extract in its sweet corn, peach, mineral, and fruitcake-scented nose, extraordinarily massive flavors, exotic, eccentric personality, and 40+ seconds of palate-staining extract. It is huge, but balanced and unbelievably rich. Lobster and *foie gras* dishes should work with such a heavyweight wine. Since I have no experience with how these wines age, I am not comfortable making predictions, but certainly they possess the alcohol and extract to live beyond a few years.

NOON (LANGHORN CREEK)

1997 Cabernet Sauvignon Reserve	E	95
1997 Eclipse Proprietary Red	D	94
1997 Shiraz Reserve	E	98

The following three wines are among the most riveting new releases I have tasted from Australia (and I've had quite a few over the last year). A name to watch for is Drew Noon, who has taken over his father's winery and apparently hit the bull's-eye with everything I tasted in 1997. Noon's wines taste like the essence of their respective varietals, pushing concentration and extract to the limit, although I did not sense that they were over the top. These are wines of extraordinary depth and richness, with amazing upside potential in the bottle. All three were made from low yields and bottled unfiltered. For starters, the opaque purple-colored 1997 Eclipse (900 cases of a 65% Grenache, 35% Shiraz blend, from 35–60-year-old vines) somehow manages to hide its 16.3% alcohol. The wine offers up cherry/blackberry liqueur-like aromas and flavors and an unctuous texture, and despite its ripeness, size, and richness, it does not taste like a heavyweight, late-harvest, pruny wine. It seems to me that vineyards in this viticultural area (Langhorn Creek) can achieve an extraordinarily high degree of alcohol without the pruny flavors often associated with less alcoholic wines. This unfiltered beauty is extremely intense yet should evolve into a civilized, spectacular Shiraz/Grenache blend that will age well for 10–15+ years. The Noon 1997 Cabernet Sauvignon Reserve (made from 35-year-old vines with 15.3% alcohol) is more limited in availability. Approximately 250 cases were produced of this amazing wine. Although it displays a portlike viscosity, it is dry, with none of the late-harvest, pruny, Amarone characteristics often found in wines of such massive ripeness. Extremely full bodied, pure, and well balanced, this Cabernet is still unevolved and youthful, but it appears to possess all the potential required to develop into something profound. Anticipated maturity: 2005–2025.

The 1997 Shiraz Reserve comes close to resembling a dry vintage port. This is one of the most concentrated wines I have ever tasted (reminiscent of the Clarendon Hills Astralis); yields were not low at 3.5 tons per acre, but the 35-year-old vine age and *sur-maturité* of this wine have resulted in something special. It boasts an opaque black/purple color, followed by a sumptuous nose of licorice, Asian spices, tar, and concentrated blackberry fruit. This wine is thick in the mouth, with remarkably full body and surprising balance; the alcohol (15.8%), tannin, and acidity are lost in the cascades of fruit. Anticipated maturity: 2003–2025.

OXFORD LANDING (S.E. AUSTRALIA)

1997 Chardonnay	A	85
1997 Sauvignon Blanc	A	84

The 1997 Sauvignon Blanc is made in a light-bodied, crisp, refreshing, restrained style that requires consumption over the next 6–12 months. It is not expressive enought in its varietal composition to turn off readers who do not enjoy the pronounced Sauvignon Blanc character. The wine is also light enough to be drunk as an aperitif. Slightly better, the 1997 Chardonnay is a light- to medium-bodied, peachy, fruity wine with refreshing acidity, good purity, and a crisp, tart finish. Although straightforward, it is well made.

PARKER (COONAWARRA/TERRA ROSA)

1995 Cabernet Sauvignon Coonawarra Estate	C	?
1994 Cabernet Sauvignon Coonawarra Estate First Growth	D	90
1993 Terra Rosa First Growth	D	87?

If it were not for the pronounced bell pepper, vegetal note in both the aromas and flavors, the 1993 Terra Rosa First Growth might merit an outstanding rating. Full bodied, with gorgeously rich, sweet, black currant, and cedar-flavored fruit, it is lush and pure and coats the palate with a multitextured feel. The acidity, wood, and tannin are well integrated, but the vegetal character is a distraction. It should drink well for 10–15 years. Readers may remember that previous vintages of this wine were far less marked by such greenness.

The 1995 Cabernet Sauvignon Coonawarra Estate possesses marvelous texture and plenty of richness, but its pronounced bell pepper/asparagus, vegetal nose is a turnoff. Although it is not my style, some readers may be fond of this component, which can age into an attractive, cedary fragrance (remember the 1985 Smith and Hook Cabernet Sauvignon from California's Monterey County?). This wine is loaded with richness and fruit, has an excellent chewy texture, and possesses fine purity, but the aggressive bell pepper character makes me want to hold my nose when I drink this wine. Far more impressive is Parker's 1994 Cabernet Sauvignon Coonawarra Estate First Growth. This wine avoids the outright vegetal character, replacing it with a cigar box, cedary, cassis-scented nose. There is superb richness, an impressive, multilayered texture, full body, and outstanding purity and balance. It is a rich, complex Cabernet Sauvignon that should age well for 15 years.

PASSING CLOUDS (BENDIGO–VICTORIA)

1996 Cabernet Sauvignon	D	87
1996 Cabernet/Shiraz	D	87
1996 Shiraz/Cabernet	D	86

No, I am not going to comment on the winery's name. These are nicely made, medium-weight wines that incorporate medium body and relatively ripe fruit with a combination of American and French oak for aging. The 1996 Shiraz/Cabernet (66% of the former and 34% of the latter) exhibits a medium deep ruby color, followed by soft berry fruit intermixed with toasty new oak. Open knit and friendly, this wine should drink well for 2–3 years. The 1996 Cabernet/Shiraz (66% Cabernet and 34% Shiraz) reveals more blackberry and cassis fruit aromas, as well as a more saturated ruby color, excellent purity, soft, tarry, berrylike flavors, and an easygoing finish. It, too, should be consumed over the next 2–3 years. Passing Clouds' dark ruby/purple-colored 1996 Cabernet Sauvignon is a fruit-driven wine with tobacco and smoky black currant notes, fine purity and ripeness, and a soft, accessible finish. It should drink well for 3–4 years.

PENFOLDS (SOUTH AUSTRALIA)

1994	Cabernet Sauvignon Bin 407	C	86
1993	Cabernet Sauvignon Bin 407	C	90
1994	Cabernet Sauvignon Bin 707	E	90+?
1993	Cabernet Sauvignon Bin 707	D	94
1994	Cabernet/Shiraz Bin 389	C	88
1993	Cabernet/Shiraz Bin 389	C	91
1990	Cabernet/Shiraz Bin 90A	EE	91+
1995	Cabernet/Shiraz Koonunga Hill	C	86
1994	Chardonnay Reserve Bin 94A	D	87
1997	Chardonnay The Valleys	B	84
1995	Chardonnay Yattarna	E	87?
1992	Grange	EEE	93
1991	Grange	EE	95
1990	Grange	EE	95+
1989	Grange Hermitage	EE	91+
1988	Grange Hermitage	EE	91
1987	Grange Hermitage	EE	92
1986	Grange Hermitage	EE	99
1985	Grange Hermitage	EE	90
1984	Grange Hermitage	EE	90
1983	Grange Hermitage	EE	90+?
1982	Grange Hermitage	EE	95+
1981	Grange Hermitage	EE	96+
1980	Grange Hermitage	EE	96
1979	Grange Hermitage	EE	92+
1978	Grange Hermitage	EE	90
1977	Grange Hermitage	EE	94
1976	Grange Hermitage	EE	98
1974	Grange Hermitage	EE	87

1971	Grange Hermitage	EE	96
1970	Grange Hermitage	EE	87
1968	Grange Hermitage	EE	81
1967	Grange Hermitage	EE	90
1966	Grange Hermitage	EE	88
1965	Grange Hermitage	EE	87
1955	Grange Hermitage	EE	86
1994	Shiraz Kalimna Bin 28	D	88
1993	Shiraz Kalimna Bin 28	C	90
1993	Shiraz Magill Estate	D	84
1995	Shiraz/Mourvèdre Bin 2	A	87
1993	Shiraz St. Henri	C	88
1992	Shiraz St. Henri	C	90

I was disappointed in a number of Penfolds wines in recent tastings, including, surprisingly, a number of excessively acidified reds (such as the 1995 Bin 128 Shiraz, 1995 Bin 407 Cabernet Sauvignon, 1995 Old Vine Shiraz/Mourvèdre, 1995 Kalinna Bin 28 Shiraz, and 1995 Bin 389 Cabernet/Shiraz). The following three whites performed well. The 1997 Chardonnay The Valleys is a reasonably priced, citrusy, fresh, lively, medium-bodied wine with no evidence of oak and a clean finish. More serious is the 1994 Chardonnay Reserve Bin 94A. This wine possesses the nose of an old-style, robust California Chardonnay with plenty of butterscotch, toasty oak, and spice. Fully mature, fleshy, and medium to full bodied, with a high-acid profile (much of it added, I suspect), this wine should be consumed over the next 1–2 years. The luxury-priced 1995 Chardonnay Yattarna (an Aborigine word meaning "little by little—gradually") is meant to be the finest white wine in Penfolds's portfolio. It appears to me that the winemakers/oenologists would be well advised to cut back on their acid adjustments, something that also plagues too many of their reds. This wine is impressively built, but it possesses extremely high acidity, which keeps the wine more compressed than it would be with less artificial additions. The light gold color is followed by excellent honeyed citrus/buttery flavors, searing acidity, medium to full body, and a short finish, much of it induced by the extremely high acidity. I do not understand this style of winemaking and can imagine many Francophiles recoiling at a wine with such a high-acid profile. The wonderful raw materials have been suppressed by the wine's high acidity. It should continue to drink well for 4–5 years.

This winery continues to turn out an insipid selection of white wines, but the reds listed here are all noteworthy, and some are reasonably good values. The 1994 Cabernet Sauvignon Bin 407 exhibits a dense, dark plum/purple color, a sweet, chocolately, cassis-scented nose, medium to full body, tart acidity, moderate tannin, and plenty of depth and richness. The wine is slightly rustic, as well as mouth filling and savory. It should drink well for 6–7 years. I preferred the 1994 Cabernet/Shiraz Bin 389. A blend of 54% Cabernet Sauvignon and 46% Shiraz, it possesses a dense purple color and a big, sweet nose of blackberries, earth, and a touch of asphalt and smoke. Full bodied, with copious quantities of sweet, chewy fruit, this is a large-scale, dense wine that can be drunk now or cellared for up to a decade. More subtle and restrained is the 1995 Cabernet/Shiraz Koonunga Hill (a blend of 63% Cabernet Sauvignon and 37% Shiraz). Although it has some youthful tannin to resolve, it offers a dark ruby color, cedar, black currant, and spicy aromas, medium body, moderate tannin, and a clean finish. The wine is understated and possesses an excess of tannin, but it should round out to provide good drinking over the next 5–7 years. The most impressive of these Cabernet Sauvignons is the 1994 Bin 707. This murky plum-colored, blockbuster, backward, exceptionally tannic Cabernet displays abundant quantities of blackberry and cassis fruit, a heavy overlay of toasty vanillin from new oak casks, and mouth-searing levels of tannin. Although the wine is closed, it is firmly structured and enormously endowed in the mouth. Cellar this offering for 2–4 years and consume it over the following 15+.

The fleshy, sweet, peppery 1994 Shiraz Kalimna Bin 28 is a full-bodied wine revealing moderately intense blackberry fruit along with licorice, smoke, and pepper in the nose. There is not a great deal of complexity in this chewy, dense Shiraz, but it does display plenty of guts and a robust personality. This wine will benefit from another year of cellaring and last for a decade. The 1993 Shiraz Magill Estate reveals an evolved plum color, followed by a smoky, earthy, curranty nose with plenty of pepper in the background and sweet, gamey flavors on the attack. High acidity and tannin pinch the wine's finish. Overall, this is a pleasant, but narrowly constructed, uninspiring effort that is considerably overpriced. Far superior is the 1993 Shiraz St. Henri. It offers a smoky, hickory, spicy nose with hints of pepper and black fruits. More opulent and layered, with better flesh and fat than the Magill Estate, this chewy, concentrated, lusty Shiraz should drink well for 5–6 years.

Penfolds's 1993 Cabernet/Shiraz Bin 389 might be one of the finest under $20 wine currently available. The wine exhibits an opaque ruby/purple color, as well as a sweet, spicy nose of black fruits, cedar, pepper, and fruitcakelike aromas. Full bodied, fleshy, rich, long, and supple, with low acidity, this boldly flavored wine should continue to drink well for a decade. The 1993 Cabernet Sauvignon Bin 407 does not possess as much pepper and spice as the Cabernet/Shiraz blend. It offers copious quantities of jammy black currant fruit, full body, a chewy, lush texture, and a powerful finish with nicely integrated tannin. This wine will also drink well for a decade.

Another knockout value from Penfolds is the 1993 Kalimna Shiraz Bin 28. The dark ruby/purple color is followed by copious aromas of toasty American oak intermingled with jammy black fruits (particularly raspberries). Subtle green pepper notes are detectable in this flavorful, well-crafted, rich, medium-bodied, stylish Shiraz. Drink it over the next 5–6 years. The 1992 St. Henri Shiraz is a terrific example of the jammy, late-harvest, portlike style that is displayed by some of Australia's biggest red wines. A viscous, deep-looking, dark ruby/purple color is accompanied by plenty of sweet, black currant and jammy raspberry fruit. Medium to full bodied, the wine reveals good acidity (no doubt added), well-integrated toasty wood, and a thick, rich, chunky finish. It is an outstanding, albeit monolithic, Shiraz that should age well for 10–12 years and, I suspect, improve in the bottle. The leaner, tougher-style 1995 Shiraz/Mourvèdre Bin 2 is a reasonable value given its earthy, ripe, black fruit, spicy nose and medium body. It reveals a surprisingly dense color, as well as more sweetness (due to the Mourvèdre in the blend) than expected. There are not many wines that will provide more flavor, punch, and power than this $9 beauty. Drink it over the next 4–5 years.

The luxury-priced offerings from Penfolds include a spectacular 1993 Cabernet Sauvignon Bin 707. This opaque purple-colored wine exhibits a huge, jammy, black currant, vanilla, licorice, and earthy aromatic profiles as well as massive concentration of fruit, glycerin, and body. Readers will find plenty of sweet tannin in the awesomely endowed finish. This blockbuster, monster-size Cabernet Sauvignon is accessible because of its low acidity and ripe tannin. The formidable extract suggests it will drink well for 10–15+ years. A new wine for me, the 1990 Cabernet/Shiraz Bin 90A is another impressive offering, although I did not think it justified the lofty $100+ price tag. While I preferred the Bin 707, the Bin

90A is an outstanding wine with a deep, saturated ruby/purple color and a smoky, roasted herb, black currant, jammy nose. Thick, rich, and full bodied, with elevated tannin, this spicy, boldly styled wine will drink well for 15–20 years.

The opaque purple-colored 1992 Grange exhibits an unevolved, grapcy nose of sweet toasty oak, ripe prunes, black raspberries, and cassis. Full bodied, with lavishly displayed oaky notes, this formidably endowed, large-scale wine should develop into an impressive example of Grange, although my instincts suggest it will not be quite as good as the 1990, 1986, or 1982. The wine was kept open for 3 days without any traces of oxidation. Give it 2–4 years of cellaring and consume it over the following 20 years.

The 1991 Grange shocked me with its sweet, forward display of jammy black fruits, smoke, roasted coffee, and copious toasty oak scents and flavors. It is seemingly more forward than other recent vintages, but that could be because this viscous, low-acid, massively endowed wine's structural components (acidity and tannin) are buried beneath a cascade of sweet, unctuously textured fruit. This mouth-filling Grange, a humongous example of a dry red wine, is nearly impossible to match with food, but these wines inevitably become more complex and civilized with 10 or more years of cellaring. Look for the 1991 Grange to compete with, but never eclipse, the great 1990, 1986, and 1982. It will last and evolve for 20–25 years.

Penfolds's Grange, as it is now legally known, is the greatest red wine of Australia. (It was originally called Grange Hermitage, but the word "Hermitage" has been dropped by the Penfolds firm because of complaints from the renowed Hermitage appellation in France's Rhône Valley.) It is a created wine, having been "designed" by the late Max Schubert. The debut vintage, 1955, was considered a freak in its day and was criticized for being too powerful, too rich, and, in essence, out of control. I doubt much has changed over the years, as this wine is a leading candidate for the richest, most concentrated dry red table wine on planet Earth. It is often better tasted and admired by itself than actually drunk with a meal, as there are not many foods that can stand up to this thick, unctuous, powerful wine. Grange is made from selected dry-farmed vineyards that yield extremely small quantities of fruit, almost always Syrah (or as the Australians call it, Shiraz). Yields are rarely more than 1 to 1½ tons per acre. All of the wine is aged in small oak casks, all of them American oak barrels. The wine is not fined, but it is filtered at bottling. Given its immense size, this is one example where filtration may not cause much harm. Penfolds's Grange takes opulence and decadence to the limits, and for that reason it has replaced Bordeaux's Pétrus as the world's most exotic and concentrated wine. Consequently Grange's price has soared from $35–$50 to $100–125 a bottle, assuming you can find any of the 8,000–10,000 cases produced each vintage.

I recently participated in a comprehensive tasting of Penfolds's Grange through 1989. I added the 1990 tasting note from a purchased bottle. It is interesting to note that as massive, extracted, and overwhelming as this wine can be in its youth, with 10–15 years of age it takes on a more civilized character, resembling a great Pomerol or older Hermitage. To Penfolds's credit, the wine has been remarkably consistent since the mid-seventies. At $125 a bottle, it had better be!

The 1990 is the greatest, most complete, richest Grange since the monumental 1986. It rivals the 1986, 1982, 1981, and 1980 as the finest "young" Grange. The wine's opaque purple color is followed by a sweet nose of jammy black raspberry and cassis fruit intermingled with scents of minerals, licorice, and toasty oak. Extremely full bodied, with that layered, multidimensional feel that sets a truly profound Grange apart from just an outstanding one, the wine is fabulously concentrated and unctuous with a finish that lasts over 50 seconds. It is oh, so young, and in need of 5–10 years of cellaring. It should last through the first 2 decades of the twenty-first century.

A full-bodied, youthful, smoky, overripe cassis-scented wine with massive body and copious quantities of smoky, vanillin-scented new oak, the moderately tannic, juicy, opulent, muscular 1989 Grange Hermitage requires 5–7 years of cellaring. It should last for 20+ years.

Still monolithic, the opaque purple-colored 1988 Grange Hermitage possesses an earthy, cassis-scented nose that has not begun to reveal any complexity or nuances. Full bodied, with high tannin, this closed, thick, unctuous, typical Grange will reward those with patience. Give it 5–6 more years of cellaring.

As for the 1987, a youthful opaque purple color and a tight but promising nose of jammy cassis with a touch of prunes and smoky oak are followed by a backward, full-bodied, typical Grange that requires 5–6 more years of cellaring. This huge, lavishly oaked, unevolved wine is an outstanding effort with 20 years of aging potential.

The 1986 is my candidate for the finest Grange Hermitage yet produced. The wine has been phenomenal since its release in 1991. It exhibits an opaque black/purple color, followed by an extraordinary, compelling, sweet bouquet of black raspberries, cassis, minerals, smoky oak, and vanilla. This multidimensional wine's huge extraction of fruit, profound flavor concentration, astonishing balance, and layers of fruit make it the greatest of the modern-day Granges. Although still youthful, the wine's sweetness, ripeness of tannin, and extraordinary balance make it delicious today. It is capable of lasting another 20–25 years. This may turn out to be superior to the 1971 and 1976—imagine that!

The 1985 Grange is a rich, full-bodied, huge, chewy, fleshy wine with high tannin (although not as high as the 1983). Although still young and unevolved, it is accessible owing to its thick juiciness and massive fruit. While it will not be a legendary wine, it is an exceptional offering that continues to demonstrate the remarkable consistency of Penfolds's Grange Hermitage since the 1976 vintage.

The 1984 has always been one of the softer, more civilized, and subtle examples of Grange Hermitage. It does not possess the structure or tannin of the 1983, the concentration, extraction, or class of the 1982, or the massiveness of the 1981. Nevertheless, it is an outstanding wine, with good fatness, a clean, cassis- and oak-scented nose, a rich, full-bodied personality, a velvety texture, and light tannin in the finish. Although drinkable, it is not yet fully mature from a complexity perspective. This satiny-style Grange should drink well for another 10–15 years.

The 1983 was a difficult vintage in Australia, as many viticultural areas were plagued by drought, followed by brush fires and then floods. However, Penfolds has always been pleased with their 1983 Grange. It is an opaque, densely colored wine, but it has consistently tasted tannic and backward. From a pleasure standpoint, it is the youngest and most structured recent vintage of Grange Hermitage. Although the wine is full bodied, with huge reserves of black fruits, it is impossible to predict whether or not the austere tannin will melt away. I choose to be optimistic and believe that with 5–6 years of cellaring the wine will exhibit a more harmonious blend of fruit and tannin. It is capable of lasting another 20 years.

Although huge, phenomenally rich, and pure, the 1982 appeared less concentrated than the monster 1981. Nevertheless, this is no shy wine. Its weight and richness rival anything from California. However, the 1982 possesses more poise and—dare I say it?—elegance than other Grange vintages. The color remains an opaque ruby/purple, and the nose offers up sweet aromas of berries, vanilla, toast, and herbs. Intense, full bodied, unctuously textured, and moderately tannic, this youthful-tasting Grange Hermitage will benefit from another 3–4 years of cellaring; it should keep for at least 15 more years.

My tastings of the 1981 Grange have always revealed an exceptional wine, although there has been some variation in quality, with scores ranging from the low to the mid-90s. It has always exhibited phenomenal quantities of ripe fruit, an opulent, sweet palate, a dark purple color, and gobs of glycerin and alcohol in the lusty finish. At some tastings it appeared to be cut from the same cloth as the glorious 1971 and 1976. At other times it revealed a rustic side. In this tasting, it ranked as one of the great wines of the eighties, rivaling the 1982 and being eclipsed only by the nearly perfect 1986. The powerful 1981 remains youthful and un-evolved and in need of another 3–5 years of cellarings. (I know I recommended the same thing 5 years ago, but the wine has not budged in evolution.) It should keep for another 15+ years.

Potentially the greatest Grange after the 1976, the opaque purple-colored 1980 reveals lit-tle evolution in its color. The huge nose of peppery black currants, roasted herbs, tar, sweet oak, and lavish quantities of fruit is followed by a full-bodied, expansive, thick, chewy wine with that extraordinary flavor density exhibited by great vintages of Grange. The finish lasts for 40+ seconds, revealing Olympic-size quantities of glycerin and fruit, as well as consider-able ripe, sweet tannin. The low acidity and extraordinary ripeness and voluptuousness make this youthful wine deceptively easy to drink. However, it requires another 3–4 years of cellaring to develop more complexity.

The 1979's black/purple color is followed by a subdued nose revealing scents of mint, black currant, licorice, and earth. This huge, full-bodied, moderately tannic Grange is ex-tremely youthful and backward. Although not as thick or massive as either the 1978 or 1980, this is a large-scale, mouth-filling heavyweight from down under. It can be drunk now, but 2–4 more years of cellaring will result in more complexity.

Another blockbuster Grange, the opaque garnet-colored 1978 is the first Grange to exhibit obvious spicy new oak in its aromatics. Full bodied, with layers of highly extracted, overripe fruit, this muscular, thick wine is almost too rich. Although large-scale, it is accessible and impressive in an uncomplicated manner, thanks to its low acidity and voluptuous texture. Look for it to develop further complexity with another 5–6 years of cellaring.

Still extremely youthful, with an opque black/ruby color as well as undeveloped aromas of licorice, earth, overripe black fruits and prunes, the huge, lavishly rich, thick, full-bodied 1977 Grange is just beginning to open and reveal its potential. It is a heavyweight wine that can be drunk now but promises to last for 10–15 more years.

A legendary vintage, the massive, powerhouse 1976 is a reference point for what great Grange Hermitage is all about. The color remains a thick, opaque ruby/garnet with no signs of amber or brown. The wine is beginning to reveal some evolution in its huge, fragrant nose of coffee, cedar, chocolate, prunes, and overripe black cherries and currants. With massive richness and body, flavors that coat the palate in a viscous, pure, mind-boggling manner, and a finish that lasts for nearly a minute, this huge Grange Hermitage may one day resemble in its decadent richness and thick, unctuous texture such Bordeaux legends as the 1947 Pétrus, 1947 Cheval Blanc, and 1947 Lafleur. This wine can be drunk now or cellared for another 10–15 years. A natural-born legend!

The 1974 was considered an average-quality vintage for Penfolds's Grange Hermitage. The wine reveals considerable amber and orange in the color, a nose of chocolate, mocha, sweet berry, earth, and cedar scents, medium to full body, fatness, and sweetness, and high, coarse tannin in the finish. It requires drinking up, as the fruit fades quickly once the wine is in the glass.

I have had the 1971 on five separate occasions, and on each occasion it has been a prodi-gious example of Grange Hermitage. The wine has consistently revealed the fruit levels, in-tensity, and complexity that are the hallmarks of a classic Grange. In fact, it is the first great Grange Hermitage since the debut vintage of 1955. The color is a mature garnet with consid-erable amber/orange at the edge. The magnificent aromatic profile includes scents of cedar, caramel, coffee, toffee, chocolate, and gobs of jammy black cherry and currant fruit. It could easily be mistaken for an old, magnificent Pomerol given its voluptuous texture, glorious richness, unctuosity, and phenomenal concentration, fat, and length. The wine has been fully mature since I first tasted it in 1990, yet it is capable of lasting for another decade. This is the real thing!

The attractive, chocolate, mocha, coffeelike nose exhibits more spice than fruit in the 1970 Grange Hermitage. While this is a full-bodied, tannic, round, generous wine, it is also rustic and coarse, with noticeable alcohol. It will keep for another decade, but do not expect any miracles to occur.

Although the 1968 was considered to be one of the lightest Grange Hermitages, the wine spent more time in oak casks (20 rather than 16–18 months) than in any other vintage in an effort by the late Max Schubert to fatten it. Apparently his gamble did not pay off, as this is the most mediocre wine in the Grange Hermitage portfolio. The wine is clumsy from beginning to end, with dusty, coarse tannin, fading fruit, a hole in the middle, and an austere finish. The great opulence, flesh, lavishly rich fruit, and thick texture for which Grange is famous is nowhere to be found.

Of the oldest vintages, the 1967 possessed the richest, sweetest, most seductive fruit. The nose offered up intensely fragrant, candied, sweet berry/cedar/spicy aromas. Opulently textured, with gobs of red and black fruits, low acidity, and no tannin, this fully mature, richly fruity, medium- to full-bodied Grange Hermitage is a less muscular example of the early years.

Interestingly, the 1966 displays a more youthful, dark ruby/garnet color than its younger siblings, the 1967, 1968, and 1970. Some tannin remains in the alcoholic finish. The nose is completely open, revealing scents of cedar, jammy fruit, chocolate, and herbs. There is medium to full body, astringent, hard tannin, and enough fruit to stand up to the wine's high alcohol and structure. This very good to excellent wine should continue to drink well for another 5–10 years. Two other tastings of this vintage revealed similar results.

The 1965 Grange Hermitage's dull color reveals considerable amber and orange at the edge. It exhibits a pronounced nose of roasted coffee, sweet herbs, mocha, and cedar. There is some fruit in the attack, but it fades quickly to display a wine with more hot alcohol and structure than sweetness and extraction. Although it remains full bodied and is drinking reasonably well, this wine is decline.

The 1955 Grange Hermitage, which I have tasted twice and given approximately the same rating, is drying out, with the astringent tannin taking the upper hand. The color is a garnet/ruby with considerable orange/brown at the edge. The wine exhibits an attractive spicy, herbal sweetness and some jammy fruit, but the acidity and tannin dominate. While still alive, the 1955 Grange Hermitage is largely of academic interest, although there is enough joy and complexity in its aromatics to merit its very good rating.

PENLEY ESTATE (COONAWARRA)

1994 Cabernet Sauvignon	D	90
1994 Shiraz/Cabernet Sauvignon	C	87

A third wine I tasted from Penley Estate, the 1995 Phoenix, a 100% Cabernet Sauvignon, was lean and austere, with high acidity and an awkward, unknit style. The same cannot be said for either the 1994 Shiraz/Cabernet Sauvignon or the 1994 Cabernet Sauvignon. The deep saturated ruby/purple-colored 1994 Shiraz/Cabernet Sauvignon possesses a peppery, sweet, cassis, ripe cherry, and blackberry nose. Fine density and a vanillin, spicy, smoky personality make for a mouth-filling, young, but promising wine that can be drunk now or cellared for another 8–10 years. The outstanding 1994 Cabernet Sauvignon reveals an opaque purple color, gobs of *pain grillé*-like notes, and black currant, cherry, dusty, Cabernet-like fruitiness. The wine is full bodied and pure, with a multifaceted, medium- to full-bodied style and moderate tannin, which is largely concealed by high extract and rich, sweet fruit. This is an example of a young Australian Cabernet Sauvignon that should age well for 12–15 years.

PETALUMA (SOUTH AUSTRALIA)

1997 Chardonnay	D 86
1998 Riesling	C 86

The fresh, lively 1997 Chardonnay reveals floral scents intermixed with lemon blossoms, orange skin, and melony fruit in its moderately intense aromatics. The acidity is high, and the wine is medium bodied and refreshing, but it seems it would have been more interesting texturally and flavor-wise had there been less added acidity. Drink it over the next 2–3 years. Petaluma has always done a fine job with Riesling, and the 1998, their twentieth vintage of this wine, is made in a Kabinett/Spätlese style with attractive peach, apricot, and orange blossom aromas in the delightful bouquet. The wine is dry, with good acidity, fresh, lively flavors, and a medium-bodied finish. Drink it over the next several years.

PIERRO (MARGARET RIVER)

1996 Cabernets	D 91
1995 Cabernets	D 89
1994 Cabernets	D 91
1996 Chardonnay	D 90
1997 Semillon/Sauvignon Blanc LTC	C 89

The fruity 1997 Semillon/Sauvignon Blanc LTC (meaning Little Touch of Chardonnay) exhibits a soft, fleshy style, as well as copious quantities of toasty oak. The wine displays excellent flavor richness and plenty of honeyed, melony, and citrusy fruit presented in a medium-bodied, nicely layered style. Pure, with the wood adding a degree of complexity, this flamboyant wine should be drunk over the next year. The evolved light golden-colored 1996 Chardonnay (14.5% alcohol) reveals a dramatic, roasted cashew, honeyed, smoky nose. On the palate, the wine displays a Burgundian, leesy character, with tropical fruit intermixed with tangerine and citrus. This sexy, fleshy, juicy, succulent Chardonnay should be drunk over the next year.

The 1996 Cabernets is the third release of this cuvée, which is a blend of Bordeaux's five principal varietals—Cabernet Sauvignon, Cabernet Franc, Merlot, Petit Verdot, and Malbec. The wine, which spends 40 days (and nights) in contact with the skins, followed by 18 months in French oak, is impressive. It should be purchased only by those who are not seeking immediate gratification, as it is more backward than most Australian selections. It boasts a saturated ruby/purple color followed by textbook aromas of *pain grillé*, cigar box, cedar, and black currants that offer an admirable imitation of a high-class Bordeaux. In the mouth, there is full body, a layered texture, sweet tannin, and copious spice-tinged black currant fruit. This well-delineated offering should hit its peak in 4–5 years and last at least another decade.

The 1995 Cabernets is one of the most elegant and well-defined Cabernet-based wines I have ever tasted from Australia. It does not possess the blockbuster power of some of Australia's heavyweights, but, rather, offers a measured, intensely flavorful style. The wine exhibits a dark ruby/purple color, followed by a complex nose of weedy cassis, spice, toast, and floral scents. Medium bodied, with beautifully integrated tannin and acidity, this is an impeccably made, pure, still youthful style of Cabernet that should age effortlessly for 10–12 years. The 1994 Cabernets possesses riper, sweeter fruit and is a denser, richer, fuller-bodied wine. The wine reveals a deep ruby/purple color and an attractive nose of cedar, black currants, spicy oak, and minerals. It resembles a New World imitation of a top-notch St.-Julien in the Médoc. Medium bodied and richly concentrated, with an attractively layered style, this well-made, harmonious, Cabernet-based wine should drink well for another decade.

PIKES (CLARE VALLEY)

1997 Cabernet/Merlot	C	88+
1996 Cabernet/Merlot	C	90
1995 Cabernet Sauvignon	C	87+
1994 Merlot Reserve	D	86
1997 Proprietary Red	C	87
1998 Riesling	B	87
1997 Riesling	B	86
1996 Riesling	B	87
1995 Riesling	B	88
1997 Riesling Reserve	C	90
1996 Riesling Reserve	C	86
1997 Shiraz	C	90+
1996 Shiraz	C	90
1995 Shiraz	C	89
1994 Shiraz	C	90
1996 Shiraz Reserve	D	93
1994 Shiraz Reserve	D	91

This winery, named after its proprietor/winemaker Neil Pikes, is located 60 miles north of Adelaide in Clare Valley. The winery is well known in Australia for its Riesling, but the reds are also successful, richly fruity wines.

Readers seeking alternatives to Alsace and German Rieslings should give Pikes's offerings a try. The 1998 Riesling is a dry, lime/peach/apricot-scented wine with medium body, excellent freshness and purity, some apple notes in the mouth, and a textbook Riesling character. It should drink well for 1–2 years. The superb 1997 Riesling Reserve is made in a steely Alsatian style, with notes of white peaches, petroleum, minerals, and floral scents. The wine is medium bodied, with terrific fruit, a rich midpalate, and a long, dry finish with an oilier texture than the regular cuvée. Drink it over the next 2–3 years. Of the other four Rieslings, I had a slight preference for the 1995. This dry Riesling exhibits lemony, citrusy, waxy aromas with peach and apricot nuances. It is a ripe, medium-bodied, intense, crisp, vibrantly clean and focused Riesling that should last for 2 years. The 1996 Riesling is more austere and dry, but elegant, with attractive lemony, honeyed, citrusy notes, light to medium body, and an excellent finish. Drink it over the next several years. The 1997 Riesling is open-knit, fruity, and an obviously styled wine. A light straw color is followed by a wine with a moderately intense tropical fruit-scented nose, light to medium body, crisp, tart acidity, and a dry finish. It is a refreshing, vibrant Riesling to drink over the next 1–2 years. The drier 1996 Riesling Reserve is made in a restrained style, with more of this varietal's petroleum character expressed. Deeper, richer, and more concentrated, it is obviously a more serious effort, but whether or not it is more pleasurable is a matter of personal taste. This pure, crisp wine should drink well for 1–2 years, perhaps longer.

The red wine offerings range from very good to excellent. The 1997 Cabernet/Merlot (75% of the former and 25% of the latter) seemed to get better each time I tasted it, and my score may be at the conservative end of the spectrum. The saturated dark ruby/purple color is followed by lavish quantities of vanillin, mint, and cassis aromas. Black currant fruit is present in the mouth, along with noticeable wood and moderate tannin. This medium- to full-bodied, youthful wine requires 2–3 years of bottle age for all of its component parts to become integrated. It should keep for 12–15+ years. Readers who enjoy an oaky, minty style of Cabernet will rate this wine even higher. The 1997 Proprietary Red (primarily Shiraz with some Mourèdre and Grenache) exhibits a dark ruby color and an accessible, open-knit style with plenty of berry fruit, medium body, and a soft, elegant finish. Drink this good bistro-style red over the next 4–5 years.

Pikes's 1997 Shiraz is outstanding. It offers a saturated ruby/purple color, a sweet, peppery, blackberry-scented nose with a suggestion of eucalyptus in the background, medium to full body, adequate acidity, a fleshy, flamboyant style, and a lush, heady finish. It can be drunk now and over the next 7–8 years. The blockbuster, opaque purple-colored 1996 Shiraz Reserve offers spectacular aromatics (cassis, blackberries, cherry liqueur, pepper, new oak), as well as an intense, unctuously textured, full-bodied wine with stunning purity and concentration. This enormously rich Shiraz coats the palate yet is remarkably well balanced with an explosive finish. It can be drunk now as well as over the next 12–15 years.

At first, the red wines taste like big, rich, ripe, fruit balls, without much complexity being displayed. However, 15–20 minutes in the glass reveals additional nuances and flavor dimensions. The 1995 Cabernet Sauvignon Clarendon exhibits a dark ruby color, followed by a textbook nose of sweet black currants, a natural texture, smoky, black currant fruit and spice, medium body, and soft, ripe tannin. Everything is in harmony in this medium-weight, attractive, rich Cabernet Sauvignon that can be drunk now as well as over the next decade. The dark ruby/purple-colored 1995 Shiraz displays a fragrant, intense, peppery, berry-scented nose, with eucalyptus aromas that develop after 10–15 minutes. The wine has a sweet, medium- to full-bodied entry on the palate, good spice, admirable purity, and a soft, low-acid, lush finish. This is a plump, succulently textured Shiraz to drink over the next 7–8 years. Because of its additional year of bottle age, the 1994 Shiraz is revealing more of a peppery, blackberry, and cassis character than the more grapey 1995. The wine reveals an opaque purple color, followed by intriguing aromas of licorice, gobs of sweet black fruits, silky tannin, medium to full body, and an opulent finish. It will drink well for 10–12 years. In plain-speak, this wine is just out and out . . . yummy!

The grapey/purple-colored 1996 Cabernet/Merlot exhibits a minty, eucalyptus, black currant-scented nose reminiscent of some older vintages of Heitz's famed Martha's Vineyard Cabernet Sauvignon. Round, generous, and plump, with medium body, velvety texture, and a lush personality, this is a hedonistic wine (assuming you like mint). Rich, with low acidity, it should be consumed over the next 5–6 years. The 1994 Merlot Reserve reveals more oak influence, along with an attractive black cherry, spicy personality, medium body, and a soft, round palate. It is purely made, but not as complex or personality filled as the 1996 blend. Drink the 1994 Merlot Reserve over the next 5–6 years. The opaque purple-colored 1996 Shiraz reveals a eucalyptus and crème de cassis-scented nose with an additional component of spicy pepper. Dense and full bodied, with good fruit and flavor extraction, this is a fruit-driven, lusty, mouth-filling, savory wine that can be drunk now or cellared for a decade. The most concentrated and densest colored of these red wines is the 1994 Shiraz Reserve. Mint, pepper, black fruits and oak scents jump from the nose of this expressive wine. It is a medium- to full-bodied, thick, rich Shiraz, with plenty of oak and jammy fruit. Low acidity gives the wine immediate appeal, but there is enough stuffing to warrant 7–8 years of cellaring. Impressive!

PREECE (VICTORIA)

1996 Chardonnay	C	85
1996 Sauvignon Blanc	B	86

Preece's 1996 Sauvignon Blanc is a textbook herb, fig, and melon-scented and -flavored wine with medium body, outstanding purity, and a crisp, tangy acidity that provides uplift and zest to this wine. Drink it over the next year. This is a richly fruity, minimally wooded (I did not detect any spicy oak), medium-bodied, light straw-colored 1996 Chardonnay revealing ripe citrus, apple, and honeylike fruit presented in a straightforward, medium-bodied style. It should drink well for 1–2 years.

PRIMO ESTATE (COONAWARRA/ADELAIDE)

1996 Cabernet Sauvignon/Merlot "Joseph" Moda Amarone	D	94
1995 Cabernet Sauvignon/Merlot "Joseph" Moda Amarone	D	92
1996 Shiraz	C	88?

The 1996 Shiraz would have received a higher score if it had not been so blatantly woody. The wine offers a smoky, toasty oak-scented nose, but hiding behind the wood is plenty of thick, black cherry and currant fruit. It is corpulent, fat, dense, and appealing, but the wood seems to get in the way of this hedonistic, forward, precociously styled wine. If the wood becomes better integrated, this wine will merit a higher score. Drink it over the next decade.

The two wines called Joseph are Cabernet Sauvignon (90%) and Merlot (10%) blends. These wines, produced in limited quantities of 500–700 cases, are made by Joseph Grilli, who crafts them using the Amarone method, leaving the grapes to raisin before fermentation is commenced. However, unlike Amarone, these wine's possess no raisiny, pruny characteristics. The spectacular, opaque purple-colored 1996 Joseph is an individualistic expression of Cabernet Sauvignon. With no oxidation, this powerful, rich, full-bodied wine (14.5% alcohol) is oozing with extract and has a thick, unctuously textured midpalate and a 45-second finish. The wine is low in acidity and hugely concentrated, with Cabernet's telltale black currant fruit intermixed with tobacco, earth, and spice. Drink it over the next 10–20 years. The similarly styled 1995 Joseph is younger and revealing less complexity because of its youth. It is a wine of great intensity, with a saturated opaque ruby/purple color and a full-bodied, monster finish. It will be interesting to follow these intriguing wines over the next 10–15 years.

THE RBJ THEOLOGICUM (BAROSSA)

1996 Mourvèdre/Grenache Theologicum	D	88
1997 Proprietary Red Wine	D	91

The Proprietary Red tastes like a perfect synthesis in style between a Bandol and a southern Rhône. It is made from 45% Grenache and 55% Mourvèdre, with the average age of the vines being 50–100 years. It is the brainchild of winemakers Rolf Binder, Chris Ringland, and Russell Johnson and the Grateful Palate's Dan Phillips. The 1997 boasts an intense ruby/purple color, as well as a gorgeous nose of new saddle leather, blackberry jam, tree bark, and cherries. Elegant and French-like in its texture and well-balanced feel, this wine is supple yet promises to age well for at least a decade. This intriguing offering is well worth seeking out.

A collective effort from winemakers Chris Ringland, Rolf Binder, and Russell Johnstone, this trio has turned out 500 cases of a 50% Mourvèdre, 50% Grenache blend. The wine is peppery, with plenty of kirsch, raspberry, and *herbes de Provence*-scented fruit in its nose and flavors. Spicy and lush, it is reminiscent of a New World-style Côtes du Rhône. Drink this high-class offering over the next 4–5 years.

CHÂTEAU REYNELLA (McLAREN VALE)

1993 Cabernet Sauvignon Basket Pressed	B	88
1994 Shiraz Basket Pressed	B	89

Two big, rich, spicy wines, Château Reynella's 1994 Shiraz and 1993 Cabernet Sauvignon are boldly flavored, big, oaky offerings that are supple, full flavored, and well balanced. Both rely on considerable quantities of aggressive, toasty American oak for providing spice to their otherwise richly fruity personalities. The 1994 Shiraz reveals gobs of blackberry fruit in its full-bodied, silky-textured style. The 1993 Cabernet Sauvignon exhibits more depth, richness, and intensity, as well as a more youthful color, despite the fact that it is a year older. Both wines are approachable and capable of lasting 7–8 years.

RIVERSIDE (BAROSSA VALLEY)

1997 Meritage	D	91

This impressive, gorgeously fruity, medium- to full-bodied, dark ruby/purple-colored wine is made from equal parts Cabernet Sauvignon, Merlot, and Cabernet Franc. Polished, with elegance allied with muscle and power, and moderate tannin in the finish, this well-made offering could pass for a young Bordeaux in a blind tasting. Anticipated maturity: now–2012.

ROBERTSON'S WELL (COONAWARRA/VICTORIA)

1994 Cabernet Sauvignon	C	88
1996 Chardonnay	C	86

An extremely well-made Cabernet Sauvignon from Coonawarra, Robertson's Well's 1994 exhibits sweet black currant and berry aromas in its complex nose, which also reveals subtle toasty oak and spice. Rich and medium to full bodied, combining power and elegance, this is a classy, stylish, authoritatively rich Cabernet that is accessible enough to drink now but promises to age well for a decade or more. If an Australian wine can resemble a ripe Médoc from Bordeaux, this wine comes close. Drink it over the next 10–15 years.

Exhibiting ripe, honeyed pear aromas and flavors, the 1996 Chardonnay is uncomplicated but savory and fleshy. Fortunately it is one of the few Australian Chardonnays that has not had absurd levels of acidity added, leaving it shrill, tart, and unpalatable.

ROCKFORD (BAROSSA)

N.V. PS Marion Tawny Port	D	89+
1995 Shiraz Basket Press	E	91

Australia's resident wine expert (and prolific writer) James Halliday says that Rockford wines are "some of the most individual, spectacularly flavored wines made in the Barossa Valley, with an emphasis on old, low-yielding, dry-land vineyards." Certainly the 1995 Basket Press Shiraz, although a softer style than I expected from its inky purple color, is a sexy, rich, flamboyantly styled Shiraz, although not as outrageously thick and unctuous as several other Grateful Palate offerings. Nevertheless it is a beautiful wine, with low acidity, extremely ripe fruit, and plenty of the cassis, pepper, and tar that make these old-vine Shiraz (this one is made from 30–100-year-old vines) so special. It should drink well for 10–12 years. The nonvintage Tawny Port reveals a slight amber to its mature-looking color, as well as an elegant, spicy, peppery, sweet nose, rich, full-bodied flavors, and excellent ripeness, but not quite enough complexity to merit a higher score. It is a mouth-filling tawny that should continue to drink well for 5–10 years.

ROSABROOK ESTATE (MARGARET RIVER)

1998 Sauvignon Blanc	C	86
1998 Shiraz Abattoir Block	D	93

A spectacular Shiraz, the 1998 Abattoir Block is a massive, opaque purple-colored wine that was aged primarily in American oak. It displays hints of bacon fat in addition to copious pepper, blackberry, and cassis aromas as well as flavors. With 15% alcohol, it is not a shy wine, but neither does it possess any of the late-harvest characteristics one might expect in a wine with such a lofty alcoholic clout. It offers terrific richness, an unctuous texture, full body, and a spectacularly long finish filled with earthy, peppery, black fruit characteristics. This wine should drink well for 12–15 years. In contrast, the 1998 Sauvignon Blanc offers restraint and subtlety in its fig, mineral, and citrusy nose. It is a fresh, light- to medium-bodied, restrained, civilized wine to consume over the next several years.

ROSEMOUNT ESTATE (SOUTH AUSTRALIA/HUNTER VALLEY/ McLAREN VALE)

1996 Chardonnay	B	86
1996 Chardonnay Show Reserve	C	88
1998 Grenache/Shiraz	A	86
1997 Grenache/Shiraz	A	86
1996 GSM	D	87
1995 GSM	C	89
1994 GSM	C	88
1997 Sauvignon Blanc	B	85
1996 Sauvignon Blanc	A	86
1998 Semillon/Chardonnay	A	86
1997 Semillon/Chardonnay	A	85
1996 Semillon/Chardonnay	A	86
1998 Shiraz Estate	B	87
1996 Shiraz Show Reserve	B	87
1998 Shiraz/Cabernet	A	87
1997 Shiraz/Cabernet	A	87
1996 Shiraz/Cabernet	A	87
1996 Shiraz/Cabernet Sauvignon Mountain Blue	D	90
1995 Syrah Balmoral	D	88?
1993 Syrah Balmoral	D	88?
1996 Traditional	C	88
1997 Traminer/Riesling	A	87
1996 Traminer/Riesling	A	86

Rosemount Estate must be one of the world's leading wineries for producing a bevy of delicious wines at fair prices. Ironically, the most expensive white wine, their Roxburgh Chardonnay, was my least favorite. I tasted the 1993 in January 1997, and it was an excessively oaky, unfocused, flabby Chardonnay that had already dropped much of its fruit. In complete contrast, the other white wine offerings exhibit freshness, vibrancy, purity, and outstanding value. The fresh, light-bodied 1996 Sauvignon Blanc reveals melony, crisp, herbal fruit. It is ideal for drinking over the next year. The 1996 Traminer (60%)/Riesling (40%) is an aromatic, refreshing, vibrant wine offering gobs of citrusy fruit, a touch of green apple, good purity, and a light-bodied, crisp, dry, refreshing finish. Drink this delicious bargain over the next year. The waxy, citrusy, richly fruity 1996 Semillon (65%)/Chardonnay (35%) emphasizes the fruit character of these two varietals. The Chardonnay provides tropical fruit notes, and the Semillon adds weight and bulk to this medium-bodied, fleshy wine that is designed to stand up to a multitude of spicy, rich dishes. It, too, requires drinking over the next year. Another 1996, the South Australian Chardonnay, is medium bodied, and fruity, with hints of pineapple and ripe apples. Like all these lighter-style, fruity, cleanly made whites, it is best drunk over the next year. The richest of the white wine offerings is the 1995 Chardonnay Show Reserve. It exhibits the creaminess that comes from exposure to wood, plenty of buttery, pineapple, tropical fruit flavors, medium to full body, good freshness, and a spicy, long finish. It should drink well for 12–14 months.

The light- to medium-bodied, tangy 1997 Sauvignon Blanc offers a crisp, melony aromatic style, with very good fruit, freshness, and a dry, zesty finish. Drink it over the next year. The 1997 Traminer/Riesling is a floral, ostentatiously perfumed wine with light body, some sweetness, and an off-dry personality. The wine exhibits citrusy fruit, excellent purity, and a refreshing mouth-feel. However, don't push your luck, as this is a wine to consume over the next 8–12 months. The dry, medium-bodied 1997 Semillon/Chardonnay offers citrus/lemon aromas and flavors, good purity, a straightforward personality, and a crisp finish. Drink it over the next year.

Rosemount's humbly priced 1998 Semillon/Chardonnay is a richly fruity, citrusy wine with light body, excellent purity, and a refreshing, vivacious style. It is ideal for drinking over the next 8–12 months.

Few wineries are able to capture the light, exuberant, pure fruit in a whole berry/carbonic style as Rosemount Estate does with its fruity, open-knit blends. Readers looking for a Beaujolais-style wine with plenty of character and fruit should check out the 1998 Shiraz/Cabernet Sauvignon (65% of the former and 35% of the latter). Medium ruby colored, with copious aromas of berry fruit and pepper, this fleshy, medium-bodied, fruit-driven red can be served slightly chilled over the next year. More serious, the estate-bottled 1995 Syrah Balmoral exhibits nearly excessive oak, but there is no doubting its sweet blackberry-and-cherry-scented nose with aromas of licorice and spicy new oak. As the wine sits in the glass, notes of bacon fat emerge. Fleshy, medium to full bodied, and smoky, with excellent purity, this wine can be drunk now or cellared for 7–8 years.

The 1998 Grenache/Shiraz (65% Grenache and 35% Shiraz) reveals a Côtes du Rhône, kirsch, peppery character to its medium ruby-colored personality. Soft, refreshing, and easy to understand and consume, it is an ideal bistro red. Drink it over the next 1–2 years. The blackberry-scented and -flavored 1998 Shiraz Estate is a more seriously endowed wine, with more fat and glycerin. It possesses excellent purity, medium body, and a silky, lush, heady finish. It should drink well for 3–4 years. The exceptional 1996 Shiraz/Cabernet Sauvignon Mountain Blue (90% Shiraz and 10% Cabernet Sauvignon) exhibits a thick-looking opaque purple color. The nose reveals toasty vanilla scents intermixed with blackberry jam and crème de cassis. Low acidity and a rich, glycerin-imbued, lush texture are hedonistic and alluring. This jammy, thick, juicy, succulent wine should drink well for 7–8 years. An innovative blend of 50% Grenache, 40% Syrah, and 10% Mourvèdre, the 1996 GSM is an elegant, medium-bodied wine with the Mourvèdre buttressing and delineating the other two varietals. Spicy American oak makes an appearance, but this wine is stylish, refined, and interesting. Anticipated maturity: now–2006.

Rosemount's dark garnet/ruby-colored 1996 Shiraz Show Reserve is more evolved than the other 1996s, revealing considerable earthy, oaky overtones. The wine is smoky and spicy, with the Shiraz varietal character somewhat hidden behind the wood, leather, and earthy characters. Medium bodied, with excellent concentration, it is close to full maturity. Drink it over the next 5–6 years. The 1996 Traditional, a blend of 80% Cabernet Sauvignon, 10% Merlot, and 10% Petit Verdot, is a tannic, cedary, cassis-scented and -flavored wine with medium to full body, good guts and structure, and a moderately hard, youthful finish. This wine should improve with another 1–2 years of bottle age and keep for a decade.

The red wines I tasted include a vibrant, delicious 1996 Shiraz (65%)/Cabernet Sauvignon (35%). Bursting with plum, red berry, and blackberry flavors, this soft, medium-bodied, gorgeously fruity, round, personality-filled dry red wine can be served slightly chilled or at room temperature. One of the best red wine values in the marketplace, it is meant to be drunk young, so readers should not buy more than they plan to drink over the next 1–2 years. The 1994 GSM—the initials stand for Grenache (60%), Syrah (20%), and Mourvèdre (20%)—is a more ambitiously styled red that has been aged for 18 months in American oak barrels. This deep ruby/purple-colored wine is spicy, oaky, and peppery, with medium to full body, tart underlying acid, and a spicy, fleshy finish. Still youthful and unevolved, this attractive wine should drink well for 5–6 years. The 1993 Syrah Balmoral is a wine made from extremely old vines (the winery claims many are nearly 100 years of age). It is a deep ruby/purple-colored, tannic, backward wine that is not yet ready for prime-time consumption. It possess good weight, excellent purity, a surprisingly high (and, for me, somewhat annoying) acid profile, moderate tannin, and loads of peppery, black plum and cassis fruit. Give it another 1–2 years of cellaring and drink it over the following decade. Will the acidity mesh with the wine's fruit?

The 1997 Grenache/Shiraz, made from 65% of the former and 35% of the latter, is a lighter-style, almost Beaujolais-like red wine with a light ruby color, gobs of black cherry and framboiselike fruit, an alluring level of glycerin, and soft, easygoing flavors that flow across the palate with considerable suppleness. Drink it over the next year. The 1997 Shiraz/Cabernet reveals a deeper color, as well as minty, black currant aromas in the fragrant bouquet. It is also bigger in the mouth, with more structure and tannin and plenty of fruit. This is a delicious blend (65% Shiraz and 35% Cabernet Sauvignon) that should drink well for 1–2 years. Last, the 1995 GSM, a blend of 50% Grenache, 40% Syrah, and 10% Mourvèdre, is a seriously endowed, rich, concentrated dry red wine. The nose offers copious quantities of jammy black currant fruit intermixed with leather, smoke, and spice. Medium bodied and nicely structured, with a layered texture and a rich, moderately long finish, this wine should age nicely for 4–6 years.

Those wines priced less than $10 are excellent values.

ROTHBURY ESTATE (SOUTHEAST AUSTRALIA)

1994 Cabernet Sauvignon	C 86

This dark garnet-colored, robust wine offers spicy, peppery, earthy scents and flavors. There is a slight coarseness in the finish, but this wine is well made, generous, and ideal for drinking over the next 4–5 years.

RUSDEN (BAROSSA VALLEY)

1996 Cabernet Sauvignon	D 92
1997 Grenache	D 92

Importer Dan Phillips feels 21-year-old Christian Canute is a name to be reckoned with in the future. The assistant winemaker at Torbreck (according to Phillips, a younger version of Brad Pitt), Canute has turned in two impressive performances that justify excitement over his new releases, which will include an Australian Zinfandel! Production was minuscule for both wines, so the tasting notes are largely academic, but given the quality of the wines, this is a winery to search out. The 1997 Grenache (14.2% alcohol, from 40-year-old vines) tastes like an old-vine, sumptuous Châteauneuf du Pape. The wine's dark ruby color is followed by a super nose of black raspberries, kirsch liqueur, roasted herbs, and smoke. Although rustic, its full-bodied, glorious levels of fruit, extract, and glycerin take over, providing a dazzling and flamboyant display of Grenache's most hedonistic qualities. Its low acidity and evolved, plump style suggest drinking it over the next 3–4 years. The 1996 Cabernet Sauvignon exhibits a Pichon-Lalande-like style. A dense ruby/purple color is accompanied by rich, sweet, plum, and black currant fruit with well-integrated toasty oak. The wine possesses low acidity, a sexy, plush, velvety-textured style, medium to full body, and excellent purity. I would opt for drinking it over the next decade.

RYMILL (COONAWARRA)

1995	Cabernet Sauvignon	C	86+
1996	Chardonnay	B	86
1995	Merlot/Cabernet Franc/Cabernet Sauvignon	B	89
1995	Shiraz	C	89

These are well-made, substantial wines offering good value in the beefy, highly extracted Australian style. The evolved, plump, fat, light golden-colored 1996 Chardonnay requires consumption over the next 6–9 months. It offers up buttery pineapple and other tropical fruit aromas, along with toasty oak, low acidity, and a chunky, medium-bodied personality.

The more interesting reds include the 1995 proprietary blend of 40% Merlot, 30% Cabernet Franc, and 30% Cabernet Sauvignon. The wine possesses a nearly outstanding nose of spice, jammy cassis, licorice, and smoke. This dark ruby/purple-colored wine is fleshy, with excellent richness, a nicely layered texture, and copious amounts of plum and black currant fruit nicely touched with smoky wood. Drink this smoothly textured wine over the next 3–4 years. The dark ruby/purple-colored 1995 Cabernet Sauvignon exhibits a moderately intense nose of cassis, licorice, and spice. In the mouth, the wine is more structured and less successful than the blended cuvée, with moderate to high tannin, more evidence of oak, and a more structured, closed personality. This Cabernet will benefit from another 6–12 months of bottle age and should evolve nicely for 5–7 years. The 1995 Shiraz reveals an attractive dark purple color, as well as an uncomplicated but sweet, jammy, blackberry and cassis-scented nose. Opulently textured, with a certain viscosity, this medium- to full-bodied, peppery, spicy, black fruit-driven offers a mouthful of nearly overripe Shiraz. Succulent and juicy, it should take on more complexity and age nicely for 7–8 years.

SALISBURY (VICTORIA)

1997	Chardonnay	A	86
1997	Sauvignon Blanc	A	86

Two fine bargains from Victoria, both of these offerings are fruit-driven wines with plenty of flavor and punch for the price. The 1997 Sauvignon Blanc's citrusy, melony aromas are followed by a soft, medium-bodied, cleanly made wine. Drink it over the next year. The 1997 Chardonnay reveals ripe tropical fruit in addition to pear notes, adequate acidity, a plump, fleshy taste, a straightforward personality, and a pleasant mouth-feel and texture. It, too, will drink well over the next year.

SALITAGE (PEMBERTON)

1996 Chardonnay	D 90
1995 Chardonnay	D 88

This winery is better known for its Pinot Noirs, which I thought were intriguing, smoky, tomato-tasting Pinots with a heavy overlay of chocolate. I thought they were average to above average in quality, but not sufficiently interesting or complex enough to merit a recommendation. On the other hand, both vintages of Salitage's Chardonnay were impressive. My preference goes to the 1996 Chardonnay, a seriously endowed, creamy-textured, big, lusty, tropical fruit-scented and -flavored wine with a honeyed pear and tangerinelike personality. One hundred percent of the malolactic fermentation was blocked in order to preserve enough acidity to give the wine vibrancy and definition. Concentrated, rich, and long, with a New World-like personality, it should be consumed over the next 1–2 years. The 1995 Chardonnay is similar, but the 1 year of additional age has permitted some of the wine's baby fat to fall away, and it tastes less endowed and fruity than its younger sibling. It, too, should be drunk within 1–2 years.

SCOTCHMAN'S HILL (GEELONG)

1997 Chardonnay	C 89
1995 Chardonnay	C 90

Scotchman's Hill's 1997 Chardonnay exhibits an evolved light gold color in addition to a noteworthy butterscotch and smoky nose similar to that of a classic Meursault. Underlying the complex, mature aromatics are tangy acidity, medium body, and a ripe, buttery wine. It can be enjoyed now and over the next year.

The 1995 Chardonnay exhibits a distinctive honeyed pineapple nose, full body, and plenty of butterscotch notes. Given the wine's underlying crisp acidity, it has fine freshness. This chewy, big, boldly styled Chardonnay possesses the overall balance and depth to drink well for several years.

I also tasted two bottles of Scotchman's Hill's 1995 Pinot Noir. Although I thought it resembled Gamay rather than Pinot Noir, it was pleasant in its silky style (I rated it 84 points).

SEAVIEW (McLAREN VALE)

1996 Chardonnay Edwards and Chaffey	B 85
1995 Shiraz Edwards and Chaffey	C 85

The 1996 Chardonnay offers up a moderately intense nose of pear and citrus. Medium bodied, straightforward, but well made, with a touch of wood, this crisp, pretty wine should be drunk over the next year. The 1995 Shiraz exhibits an earthy, tar, peppery nose with black fruits in the background. It is a chunky, monolithic wine with good fruit, a mouth-filling personality, and nice pepper and spice. Drink it over the next 2–3 years.

SEPPELT (BAROSSA VALLEY)

1993 Cabernet Sauvignon Dorrien Vineyard	D 87+?

An impressively packaged wine (expensive designer glass and label), Seppelt's 1993 Cabernet Sauvignon Dorrien Vineyard reveals a dark plum color, followed by a tight, earthy nose with plenty of new oak and cedary cassis fruit. In the mouth, the wine is full bodied, with high acidity (I suspect much of it added), a low-pH compressed palate, and excellent ripeness, depth, and purity. Tight and backward, this wine requires 4–5 years of cellaring. Since the acidity is high, the wine will never be as expansive as it would have been had it not been acidified by an overly zealous oenologist—a major problem for many Australian wineries.

SEVENHILL CELLARS (CLARE VALLEY)

1997 Cabernet Sauvignon	C 86

A fruit-driven wine, this dark ruby-colored Cabernet Sauvignon displays pure, plump cassis fruit, no evidence of wood, average acidity, and a savory, mouth-filling finish. It is not a complicated wine, but it is attractive and cleanly made. Drink it over the next 4–5 years.

SHAW AND SMITH (ADELAIDE HILLS)

1998 Sauvignon Blanc	C 87

This 100% Sauvignon Blanc, which smells and tastes as if it has been completely tank-fermented and -aged, is an intensely fruit-driven wine with gobs of melony, honeyed citrus (limes) fruit. It is medium bodied, extremely pure, and delicious. Drink it over the next year.

STANLEY BROTHERS (BAROSSA VALLEY)

1996 Semillon Full Sister	C 89

Although dry, this offering smells like a sweet wine from France's Sauternes region. The waxy, honeyed nose is followed by a medium- to full-bodied Semillon with plenty of citrus and spicy oak, as well as intense power and muscle in its glycerin-imbued, ripe finish. I would match this large-scale wine with powerful fish or poultry dishes.

STANTON AND KALLEEN (RUTHERFORD GLEN)

20 Year Old Muscat	D 94
40 Year Old Collector's Muscat	D 92
N.V. Tokay Liqueur Gold Rutherford Glen	D 89

This winery, founded in 1878 and dedicated to producing fortified wines, is now being represented in the United States. I do not think anyone would disagree that the greatest fortified Muscats and Tokays from Australia emerge from William Chambers. However, this small winery has turned out some very realistically priced efforts. The Non Vintage Tokay Liqueur Gold possesses an amber color, as well as a grapey, pruny, honeyed character with moderate sweetness, plenty of viscosity, and full body. It is a fine after-dinner Tokay that should drink well for a decade. The fabulous 20 Year Old Muscat exhibits a dark amber color, admirable sweetness, and a fragrant, intense nose of pruny fruit, figs, honey, chocolate, and coffee. Fresh and filled with fruit, this is a spectacularly sweet, full-bodied, unctuously textured sweet wine that should drink well for another 10–15 years. Last, the Stanton and Kalleen 40 Year Old Collector's Muscat is unquestionably outstanding, but I am not sure its significantly higher price is justified, especially in view of how stunning the 20 Year Old Fortified Muscat performed. In any event, the chewy, decadent 40 Year Old Collector's Muscat reveals a dark amber color, copious quantities of fruit, extraordinary sweetness, and a mature, earthy, cheesy, honeyed nose of figs, prunes, and berry fruit.

CHARLES STURT UNIVERSITY (NEW SOUTH WALES)

1997 Shiraz Reserve	D 90
1996 Shiraz Reserve	D 90

Charles Sturt University, the principal viticulture and oenological school in Australia, has its own vineyards as well as winemakers, growers, and the like. These two offerings are impressive examples from the university and far more complex and interesting than I would have expected. The 1996 Shiraz Reserve reveals an impressively saturated black/purple color, tightly wound, reserved aromatics, excellent fruit and richness on the palate, medium to full body, and subtle earthy, new oak smells. While layered, pure, and fruit driven, it is not as open knit and expansive as the 1997 Shiraz Reserve. The latter wine was aged completely in French oak, rather than a combination of French and American, and achieved 14% natural alcohol. This is a dark purple-colored, heady wine with sweet black raspberry and cherry fruit intermixed with spice, nicely integrated oak, and earth. With ripe cassis and blackberry flavors, low acidity, and a layered, opulent texture, it may not possess the weight and structure of the 1996, but it is a more complete and balanced wine. Drink it over the next 7–8 years.

SUMMERFIELD (PYRENEES)

1997 Cabernet Reserve	E	92
1997 Shiraz	D	89
1996 Shiraz	D	89
1997 Shiraz Reserve	E	92

Two of these wines reveal a considerable amount of eucalyptus/mint in their aromatics and flavors. The black/purple-colored 1997 Cabernet Reserve offers a tremendously expressive bouquet of mint, black currants, crème brûlée, dried herbs, and spice. Full bodied, with terrific fruit extraction and purity, this layered, impressively endowed wine is capable of lasting 15–20 years. Anticipated maturity: 2002–2020. I detected plenty of mint in the 1997 Shiraz Reserve, as well as exceptional quantities of jammy black cherry, raspberry, and blackberry fruit. Full bodied, dense, and nicely framed by oak, this is a powerful, muscular, intensely concentrated wine that needs 2–3 years of bottle age. Anticipated maturity: 2002–2018.

The fruit-driven 1997 Shiraz does not possess enough complexity to merit an outstanding score, although many readers will rate it higher than I did. It possesses blackberry fruit, medium to full body, a succulent texture, low acidity, and a heady finish. Drink it over the next 7–8 years. The 1996 Shiraz is an accessible, soft, explosively fruity, black/purple-colored, hedonistic, powerful, and rich Shiraz. Although not complex, it is loaded with fruit and glycerin and possesses a mouth-filling, velvety texture. It should drink well for 5–6 years.

TAIT (BAROSSA VALLEY)

1996 Cabernet Sauvignon	D	90+

A backward but impressively endowed wine, this opaque black/purple-colored Cabernet offers cassis and black cherry fruit in its moderately intense nose. Fruit driven, with medium to full body and an outstanding midpalate, it reveals noticeable tannin in the unevolved, youthful finish. This exuberant, stylish Cabernet Sauvignon will be even better with 2–3 years of cellaring. Anticipated maturity: 2002–2012.

THREE RIVERS (BAROSSA)

1994 Shiraz	EE	95
1993 Shiraz	EE	99+

I kept wondering if the only reason I was not giving the 1993 Shiraz a perfect score was that only 50 cases were produced. Made from yields of under 1 ton of fruit per acre, from 100+-year-old vines, my first impression on tasting this Shiraz was, "My God, this smells like a pristine example of 1947 Cheval Blanc." It possesses a similar unctuosity, thickness, over-ripeness, and dry vintage port-like character. Moreover, I could not believe how complex the wine's aromatics were for its age. In addition to the telltale bacon fat, there were aromas of toast, smoke, cassis, cedar, and blackberry jam. Viscous, full bodied, extremely thick and heavy (no finesse to be found in this monster), this wine represents the maximum or, some would say, the extreme expression of its *terroir* and varietal composition. Yet the wine is focused and not heavy to drink. After keeping the wine open 4 days without any trace of oxidation but, rather, with further development and evolution, I decided there was no further reason to delay its destiny and drank it up. The wine achieved 15% alcohol naturally and spent 3 years in 100% new French oak. While it is lamentable that only 50 cases were produced, I feel readers should know about wines such as this. Moreover, they stand as a beacon for other winemakers who want to achieve something as special as what winemaker Chris Ringland has accomplished. This wine should evolve and continue to drink well for at least 15–20 years.

As for the 1994 Shiraz, it represents a downsized version of the 1993. It possesses many of the same characteristics but displays a less saturated color, slightly less viscosity, and lower alcohol. Nevertheless, it remains a blockbuster, sumptuous Shiraz that should drink well for 15–25 years.

TORBRECK (BAROSSA)

1996 **Run Rig**	E	96
1995 **Run Rig**	E	95
1997 **The Steading**	D	90
1996 **The Steading**	D	88

This new Australian winery is run by the young David Powell, who named the winery after a forest in Scotland where he met his wife. It is quickly becoming one of my favorite Australian wineries. Winemaker Powell seems to be doing everything right, fashioning wines of extraordinary complexity and richness. The 1997 The Steading, an Aussie-inspired Châteauneuf du Pape–like blend of 60% Grenache, 20% Shiraz, and 20% Mourvèdre, offers up complex notes of *pain grillé*, coffee, black raspberries, cranberries, and kirsch. Intense in the mouth, with a creamy texture, full body, and low acidity, this is a hedonistic, lush, lusty wine to drink over the next 7–10 years. The spectacular 1996 Run Rig reminds me of some of Marcel Guigal's single-vineyard Côte Rôties. Made from 40–120-year-old Shiraz vines with 3% Viognier added to the blend, this wine, which is aged for 30 months primarily in new French oak, with a touch of American wood, is spectacular in every sense of the word. Sensational aromatics leap from the glass, offering up cherry liqueur, smoke, *pain grillé*, roasted herbs, and blackberry fruit. It is full bodied, with exquisite concentration, an unctuous texture, low acidity, and beautifully integrated tannin and alcohol (14.5%). Yields were only 1.5 tons of fruit per acre, and production was a minuscule 150 cases. This staggering wine can be drunk now or cellared for 10–12 years.

The 1996 The Steading, a Mourvèdre, Grenache, Shiraz blend made from 50–120-year-old vines, is a serious Côtes du Rhône-like wine with copious amounts of peppery, raspberry, cherry, and earthy fruit. It cuts a medium-bodied, forward, and attractive feel on the palate but lacks a multidimensional personality. Savory, mouth filling, and enjoyable it is—complex it is not. Drink it over the next 2–4 years. The exquisite 1995 Run Rig, a blend of 95% Shiraz (70–100-year-old vines) and 5% Viognier, is Australia's answer to Marcel Guigal's Côte Rôtie La Mouline. Aged in new French oak, the wine has achieved 14.5% natural alcohol. It is a lavishly rich, compelling effort with spectacular aromatics as well as flavors. From the toasty vanillin, bacon fat, black raspberry, blackberry, and cassis aromas, to its stunningly proportioned, thick, medium- to full-bodied flavors, this seamless, silky-textured, juicy, succulent wine is a total turn-on. With airing, some tannin emerges, and the wine still tastes youthful. This is another wine I kept for 4 days in the bottle without any traces of oxidation. It, too, found its way down my gullet after I became bored with experimenting to see how much airing these wines could handle. The Run Rig can be drunk now, but it promises to evolve effortlessly for another 12–18 years.

TURKEY FLAT VINEYARDS (BAROSSA VALLEY)

1996 Cabernet Sauvignon	D	88
1997 Grenache Noir	C	90
1996 Shiraz	D	90
1994 Shiraz	D	89+

One of the most savory wines I tasted over the last several months is the Turkey Flat Vineyard 1997 Grenache Noir. This is textbook Grenache, with a hedonistic display of kirsch, cherry jam, and roasted peanuts. Seductive, with glorious levels of fruit, glycerin, and no hard edges, this full-bodied, velvety-textured wine is undoubtedly a crowd pleaser. Readers should be aware of its numbing level of alcohol—15.2%. Drink it over the next 4–5 years. Also outstanding is the 1996 Shiraz. It boasts a saturated opaque purple color and a classic blackberry/cassis nose with nicely integrated toasty oak. The wine is rich and full bodied with moderate tannin, a sweet midcore, and a layered, chewy finish. Accessible now, it promises to last a decade or more. It possesses a moderate 14.9% alcohol. Excellent but less impressive than its two siblings is the 1996 Cabernet Sauvignon. After spending 2 years in American and French oak casks, this wine exhibits a dark ruby color in addition to a sweet blackberry-scented nose with aggressive toasty oak aromas. It is medium bodied and finishes with less persuasive fruit and completeness when compared with the Shiraz and Grenache. Nevertheless it is an impeccably made, fine wine. Anticipated maturity: 2000–2010.

The dark ruby/purple-colored 1994 Shiraz offers up a big, earthy, peppery, sweet cassis nose with attractive oak in the background. Tightly knit, medium to full bodied, moderately tannic, youthful, and exuberant, it possesses outstanding purity and balance. Give it 1–2 more years of cellaring to shed some of its tannin, and drink it over the following 10 years. Remarkably, the Shiraz vines utilized for this cuvée were planted in 1847!

VASSE FELIX (MARGARET RIVER)

1994 Cabernet Sauvignon	D	87+
1995 Chardonnay	C	88
1996 Classic Dry White	C	88
1996 Semillon	C	88
1995 Shiraz	D	86

Unlike most of my Australian tastings, my tasting at this winery left me with a slight preference for its white wines over its reds. The 1996 Classic Dry White, a blend of Sauvignon Blanc, Chardonnay, and Semillon, is an interesting wine. Although I did not detect any oak, this fresh, citrusy, lemon blossom-scented wine displays loads of fruit. Pure, dry, elegant, and beautifully focused, it would be an ideal match with numerous fish and poultry dishes. Drink it over the next 1–2 years. The 1996 Semillon reveals a strongly oaked nose to go along with its lime/lemonlike nose and rich, medium- to full-bodied, intensely concentrated flavors. This is a waxy, creamy-textured wine with enough acidity to provide focus. It should be drunk over the next several years—preferably with heavily sauced and/or intensely flavored fish dishes. The light straw-colored 1995 Chardonnay exhibits an apple/citrusy-like nose, tart acidity, and beautifully rich, medium-bodied flavors revealing admirable concentration and subtle new oak. The wine does not taste Burgundian, Californian, and perhaps not even Australian. What it does taste like is a high-quality Chardonnay. Drink it over the next several years.

I enjoyed two restrained, elegant red wines that are not hedonistic, but, rather, admirably measured wines that emphasize subtlety. The 1994 Cabernet Sauvignon offers reticent, subtle, cedary, cassis scents, medium body, attractive, suave flavors, impressive purity, and good structure. It should drink well for 10–12 years. Slightly too polite for my tastes, the 1995 Shiraz possesses purity, ripe, peppery black currant fruit, elegance, and a medium-bodied, sculptured character. It will not turn heads, but it is a respectable, correctly made Shiraz.

VERITAS (BAROSSA)

1996 Cabernet Sauvignon	D	91
1997 Cabernet/Merlot	C	89
1997 Mourvèdre/Grenache	C	90
1996 Shiraz "Hanisch"	D	97
1996 Shiraz "Heysen"	D	91
1996 Shiraz/Mourvèdre	D	90
N.V. Tawny Port	C	91

Rolf Binder, who also makes the wines for the Magpie Estate, produces this astonishing array of full-flavored, maximum-extraction, ultraripe wines. The 1997 Cabernet/Merlot is a fine bargain in today's marketplace. It possesses an opaque purple color, followed by ripe (nearly overripe), jammy cherry and cassis aromas that have been presented in an uncomplicated but rich, low-acid, medium- to full-bodied format. There is explosively rich fruit as well as a viscous texture. I suspect more character and complexity will emerge from this wine, which may ultimately merit an outstanding score. Crammed with fruit and glycerin, it will provide plenty of hedonistic appeal over the next 10–12 years. The opaque purple-colored 1996 Cabernet Sauvignon possesses a similar viscous texture but is even more opulent, with thicker, richer, more concentrated fruit, as well as additional nuances to its personality. The wine offers pure aromas of blueberries, cassis, vanillin, and spice. It hits the palate with considerable power, thickness, and impeccable balance. This wine is made from 28-year-old Cabernet Sauvignon vines that average 3 tons of fruit per acre. The finish is youthful and sweet (from high extraction, not sugar). Because of its low acidity and thick, juicy style, this Cabernet can be drunk, but it promises to be even better over the next 10–15 years.

I am rarely impressed with Australian Mourvèdre, or Grenache, Mourvèdre, and Shiraz blends, but Veritas got it right with the following two offerings. The 1997 Mourvèdre/Grenache is a dense purple-colored, full-bodied, powerful, lusty wine with explosive black cherry and raspberry fruit intermixed with scents of loamy soil, herbs, spices, and smoke. Nicely textured, full bodied, thick, and accessible, this knockout wine should drink well for 10–15 years. Production was 3 tons of fruit per acre from 25–50-year-old vines. The alcohol is 14%. Although made in a totally different style, the 1996 Shiraz/Mourvèdre is of similar quality. More pepper, a touch of spicy, aggressive, American oak, and more tannin are noticeable in this full-bodied, well-structured, more austere example. Long, tightly knit, and restrained, it requires 1–2 more years of bottle age and should drink well over the following 10–12.

A strong argument can be made that the two Shiraz cuvées, Heysen and Hanisch, are the top wines from Veritas. The 1996 Shiraz "Heysen," made from 30-year-old vines that average 2.5 tons of fruit per acre, tips the scales at a whopping 15.1% alcohol, although you would never know it when tasting this superconcentrated wine. It is a killer Shiraz, with an opaque purple color, peppery, tar, sweet, layered, jammy blackberry fruit, hints of subtle new oak, and a massive, powerful, full-bodied finish that goes on and on. Still youthful, it promises to age easily for 12–15 years. I was blown away by the 1996 Shiraz "Hanisch." Yields were slightly lower for the Hanisch than for the Heysen, but the alcohol is the same at 15.1%. The Hanisch cuvée boasts copious quantities of jammy blueberry and blackberry fruit intermixed with truffle, tar, licorice, and chocolatey aromas. This is a spectacularly intense, massive, old-vine Shiraz that comes across more as a dry port than a dry table wine. With an unctuous texture as well as a finish that lasts for 40+ seconds, this terrific wine should last for 25–30+ years. Wow!

The Versitas Tawny Port is a terrific value for readers looking for an evolved, complex tawny port look-alike. This wine, made from Shiraz, Mourvèdre, Grenache, Frontinac, and Pedro Ximenez, is excellent, spicy, sweet, and attractive, with copious quantities of berry fruit, licorice, roasted nuts, and complex smoky scents. Rich, but evolved and supple, it is ideal for drinking over the next 3–4 years. Normally, tawny ports of this quality cost twice as much as this excellent value.

VIKING WINES (BAROSSA VALLEY)

1997 Cabernet Sauvignon	D	89
1998 Riesling	C	84
1997 Shiraz	E	91
1996 Shiraz	E	90

Made by a native of Sweden, Thor Soderstrom, the two Shiraz come from relatively old vines. I was told that the grapes from one plot of 40-year-old vines used to be purchased by Penfolds to be incorporated into their Grange. In 1996 this is another winery that hired Rolf Binder to oversee the wine making. The 1997 Shiraz (200 cases for the United States) is an unfiltered, jammy blackberry-scented, unbelievably sexy wine that some would call a "Parker hedonistic fruit bomb." Pure, rich, and full bodied, with considerable viscosity, purity, and length, it is less portlike than the 1996 Shiraz, a thick, fat, corpulently styled, outstanding wine that is slightly less structured and delineated than the 1997. Both wines are big, mouth-filling, highly extracted examples to drink over the next 10–12+ years. The dense ruby/purple-colored 1997 Cabernet Sauvignon possesses sweet blackberry and raspberry fruit, as well as cherries that emerge with breathing. With good glycerin and a big, chunky fruit character, this wine should drink well for 10–12 years.

Although well made, the 1998 Riesling is uninspiring. It displays steely, citrusy, lemon/limelike fruit flavors, but not much length. However, it is fresh and lively. Drink it over the next 2 years.

WANINGA (SKILLY HILLS, CLARE VALLEY)

1997 Shiraz	D	90
1996 Shiraz Reserve	D	92

Two of Australia's finest winemakers, Tim Adams and Geoffrey Grosset, are the forces behind these high-quality wines. Both wines are bottled unfiltered for the estate's American importer. The 1997 Shiraz is an immensely hedonistic, open-knit, exuberant, expressive offering with a full-throttle bouquet of pepper and jammy black fruits. If the soaring aromatics do not seduce the taster, the flavors will. This consumer-friendly fruit cocktail is rich and fleshy, with low acidity and an opulent, long texture. It should drink well for 5–6 years, assuming purchasers can resist its charms that long. Even though it is a year older, the 1996 Shiraz Reserve is less evolved and far more powerful, concentrated, and ageworthy. Its opaque purple color and unctuous texture suggest an impressively constituted wine . . . and it is. While I would not term it a fruit bomb like its younger sibling, it is a layered, rich, full-bodied, sexy, voluptuously textured, powerful wine crammed with black fruits, pepper, and toasty new oak. It can be consumed now but should be even better with 2–3 more years of bottle age; it will keep for 15 years.

WARRENMANG (VICTORIA)

1997 Shiraz Moonambel	D	96

A wine of awesome extraction and richness, this powerful behemoth was aged in 100% new American oak for 12 months and bottled unfiltered. The natural alcohol is a whopping 15.7%, but it is totally hidden by the wine's extraordinary concentration and intensity. The opaque inky purple color is followed by the blackberry/blueberry fruit spectrum intermixed with pepper, spice, and licorice. Extremely full bodied, with remarkable symmetry for its size and concentration, this wine coats the palate and has a finish of well over 40 seconds. The bad news—sadly, only 25 cases made it to the United States.

GEOFF WEAVER (LENSWOOD)

1995 Chardonnay	D	90
1997 Riesling	C	87
1998 Sauvignon Blanc	C	89
1997 Sauvignon Blanc	C	91

The former white wine maker for one of Australia's huge enterprises, BRL Hardy, Geoff Weaver is producing his own wines. These four beautiful dry white wines are made from relatively modest yields of 3 tons of fruit per acre. The 1997 Riesling (12.2% alcohol) is a well-delineated, tank-fermented, steely, citrusy, crisp, delicious Riesling that is dry, lively, and full of character. It possesses well-integrated acidity, in addition to admirable vibrancy and purity. The terrific 1997 Sauvignon Blanc is one of the finest examples of this varietal I have ever tasted from Australia. In addition to being explosively fruity, it offers up a textbook honeyed/melony nose and intense, flashy fruit flavors that do not evidence any exposure to oak. The wine reveals a mineral component under all the fruit, medium body, and a long, zesty finish. This dazzling Sauvignon Blanc should drink well for 12–18 months. When I remarked that the 1995 Chardonnay reminded me of a premier cru from Puligny-Montrachet, importer Dan Phillips was quick to tell me that Geoff Weaver had spent hours walking around the vineyards of Puligny-Montrachet, trying to memorize the flavors in the grapes. The wine reveals a green/gold color and a Leflaive-like nose of honey, citrus, mango, and oranges. Intense and beautifully focused, with a judicious touch of toasty oak, this is a medium-bodied, flavorful, stylish, and concentrated Chardonnay. I am not a great believer in aging Australian Chardonnays, but this one may evolve for 2–3 years.

I was unimpressed by an excessively woody, evolved 1996 Chardonnay, but the 1998 Sauvignon Blanc is close to outstanding. Loire Valley-like, with its flinty, big, steely nose and flavors of dried herbs, melon, and honey, this medium-bodied, gorgeously pure, well-delineated, bone dry Sauvignon possesses terrific fruit and character. Drink it over the next year.

WILD DUCK CREEK (HEATHCOTE)

1997 Alan's Cabernet	D	92+
1995 Alan's Cabernets Pressings	EEE (magnum)	90+
1996 Alan's Cabernets Vat 1	D	89+
1997 Springflat Shiraz	D	93+

1996 Springflat Shiraz	D	88+
1994 Springflat Shiraz Reserve	EE	91

Heathcote is a subregion of the larger appellation of Bendigo in Victoria. These extremely well-made wines are somewhat tightly knit but impressive for their purity and richness. The 1996 Alan's Cabernets Vat 1 offers an intriguing cranberry liqueur and cassis-scented nose with spicy wood in the background. Made from 65% Cabernet Sauvignon, 14% Cabernet Franc, 12% Merlot, and 9% Malbec and Petit Verdot, this tightly knit wine displays beautiful purity, medium to full body, and moderate tannin. I believe it will benefit from 2–3 more years of cellaring and will keep for a decade. The 1995 Alan's Cabernets Pressings, available only in magnum, tips the scales at 14.2% alcohol and is made from yields of 2 tons of fruit per acre. Sadly, only 150 magnums were produced—for the world. This is Australia's version of the classic Heitz Cabernet Sauvignon from Martha's Vineyard. Intense eucalyptus, minty, cassis aromas jump from a glass of this opaque purple-colored wine. It is beautifully made, intense, unevolved, and crammed with fruit, glycerin, and tannin. Extremely backward, it promises to be even better over the next decade and should keep for 20 years.

No matter how much I coaxed, the opaque purple-colored, tightly knit 1996 Springflat Shiraz revealed only toasty new oak in its nose. More nuances were noticeable in the wine's flavors, including minty cassis, black currants, and blackberries. The wine is medium bodied, oaky, unevolved, and in need for 2–3 years of cellaring. It should keep for 12–15 years. The 1994 Springflat Shiraz Reserve (only 50 cases produced) is an oaky, highly extracted, massive, full-bodied wine that has not yet begun to reveal much complexity or nuances. Thick and pure, with explosive length and moderately high tannin, it will also benefit from 2–3 years of cellaring.

The 1997 Alan's Cabernet (a 65% Cabernet Sauvignon, 12% Merlot, 14% Cabernet Franc, 8% Malbec, and 1% Petit Verdot blend) displays a saturated black/purple color, a minty, Heitz Martha's Vineyard-like nose, and a full-bodied palate redolent with eucalyptus, blackberry, and cassis flavors. This intense, moderately tannic wine will benefit from 2–3 years of bottle age. Anticipated maturity: 2002–2020. The spectacular, opaque purple-colored 1997 Springflat Shiraz is unevolved but possesses great intensity and promise. Tasting akin to a barrel sample with its flashy display of youthful cassis and blackberry fruit, this thick, rich offering possesses definition that is rare in a wine of such size and extract. Anticipated maturity: 2002–2018.

WISE VINEYARDS (WESTERN AUSTRALIA)

1997 Aquercus Unwooded Chardonnay	C	87
1997 Chardonnay	C	88
1998 Chardonnay Coat Door	C	88

Three fine offerings, the 1997 Aquercus Unwooded Chardonnay, from the Margaret River region of western Australia, exhibits a light straw color and ripe, honeyed pear, mango, and citrus flavors presented in a medium-bodied pure format. It should drink well for 1–2 years. The 1997 Chardonnay, which was aged in American oak in addition to lees aging, displays an attractive toasty, caramel note to its ripe, honeyed, rich fruit flavors. Medium to full bodied, with attractive tropical fruit flavors, it should drink well for 1–2 years. Last, the 1998 Chardonnay Coat Door does a masterful job of concealing its nearly 15% alcohol. The wine is young and unevolved, but it reveals honeyed tropical fruit, subtle spice, and a nicely textured, rich, fleshy finish. It too, should drink well for 1–2 years.

WOLFBLASS (SOUTH AUSTRALIA)

1994 Cabernet Sauvignon President's Selection	C	85

All of the other wines I tasted from this winery (the 1993 Cabernet Sauvignon/Shiraz Black Label, 1995 Cabernet Sauvignon/Shiraz Red Label, and 1995 Cabernet Sauvignon Yellow Label) were extremely acidified, processed wines that I found unpalatable. When are some Australian wineries going to wake up to the fact that they are dumping too much acidity into their wines, thus suppressing the aromatics and giving the wines an excessively tart, pinched character on the palate? California's Helen Turley and Tony Soter could make small fortunes doing consulting work with some of Australia's better wineries.

The only Wolfblass offering I found accessible was the 1994 Cabernet Sauvignon President's Selection. Although it is acidic, it possesses enough ripe cassis fruit, smoke, earth, and wood to give it appeal. Tartness is a problem, but the wine offers attractive ripeness and fruit. Drink it over the next 4–5 years.

WOODSTOCK WINERY (McLAREN VALE)

1997 Grenache	C	88

This sexy, voluptuously textured Grenache is made from 80-year-old vines and aged in large French oak *foudres*. It is a luscious, low-acid, fruit-driven Grenache with copious quantities of cherry/kirsch notes intermixed with pepper and leafy vegetable spices. The plump, full-bodied style with provide delicious drinking now and over the next 5–6 years.

WOODY NOOK (MARGARET RIVER)

1997 Cabernet Sauvignon	D	91
1997 Merlot Gallagher's Choice	D	89

The French *barrique*-aged 1997 Merlot Gallagher's Choice exhibits a dark ruby/purple color and a distinctive minty, chocolatey nose with abundant quantities of jammy black cherry fruit. In the mouth, it is fat, ripe, and exuberant, with plenty of depth and a chewy, lush texture. This hedonistically styled Merlot possesses both complexity and intensity. It should drink well for 7–8 years. The 1997 Cabernet Sauvignon is an impressively built wine with a saturated ruby/purple color and boldly etched aromas of black currants intermixed with spice, vanillin, tobacco, cedar, and black currants. It is full bodied and smooth, with well-integrated tannin and symmetry. The finish is explosive, with outstanding purity, depth, and intensity. This superb, youthful Cabernet Sauvignon can be drunk now or cellared for another 10–15 years.

DAVID WYNN/MOUNTADAM (EDEN VALLEY/BAROSSA VALLEY/ SOUTH AUSTRALIA)

1996 David Wynn Chardonnay Unwooded	B	87
1995 David Wynn Sauvignon Blanc	B	87
1996 David Wynn Shiraz Unwooded	B	86
1994 David Wynn Shiraz Patriarch	C	87
1994 Mountadam Chardonnay	C	90
1990 Mountadam Chardonnay/Pinot Noir Sparkling Wine	D	88
1994 Mountadam Pinot Noir	C	88

There are two levels of wine quality made by proprietor David Wynn. His less expensive cuvées appear under his name, and the top cuvées appear under the Mountadam label. Readers looking for good Australian values should check out David Wynn's 1995 Sauvignon Blanc, 1996 Unwooded Chardonnay, and 1996 Unwooded Shiraz. Wynn, taking advantage of the fact that not everyone wants a mouthful of toasty *pain grillé* flavors, has produced delicious wines that emphasize the honest, uncomplicated character of each varietal. The 1995 David Wynn Sauvignon Blanc is crisp and fresh, with a honeyed melon fragrance, lush, delicious fruit, good underlying acidity, and an excellent dry, mineral/herblike finish. It is a medium-weight Sauvignon to drink over the next year. The 1996 David Wynn Unwooded Chardonnay reveals a delightful, moderately intense, floral, honeyed orange, and melony nose, lively, ripe, medium-bodied flavors, good acidity, and copious quantities of fruit presented in a medium-weight, vivacious style. It should drink well for 1–2 years.

The 1994 Mountadam Chardonnay is another animal. The evolved light gold color is followed by a more Burgundian-like nose of smoky melted butter/popcorn as well as honeysucklelike aromas. The wine possesses an excellent texture, fine richness, medium to full body, plenty of ripe fruit, good underlying acidity, and moderate quantities of toasty oak. It is a delicious, robust Chardonnay to drink over the next 4–5 years.

While I tasted a 1995 David Wynn Pinot Noir and a 1995 David Wynn Cabernet Sauvignon, I could not recommend them. However, I did enjoy three of David Wynn's reds. The dark ruby/purple-colored 1996 David Wynn Unwooded Shiraz exhibits a beautiful nose of cassis fruit with a hint of pepper. Soft and lush, with a succulent texture and excellent purity, this is a textbook Shiraz without the weight and high alcohol of some of its siblings. Drink it over the next 3–4 years. The 1994 David Wynn Patriarch Shiraz displays an opaque blue/purple color, followed by jammy kirsch, blueberry, and cassis aromas and flavors. A medium- to full-bodied wine, with a hint of mint, it provides a lush, straightforward, ripe, chewy finish. Although it will not make old bones, this is a delicious, up-front, precociously styled Shiraz to drink now and over the next 5–6 years.

Australia is not known for making interesting Pinot Noir, but Wynn's 1994 Mountadam Pinot Noir boasts an evolved dark garnet color, wonderful sweet black raspberry and cherry fruit, good acidity, a layered texture, and a medium-bodied, elegant, lush finish. Although it possesses an unusual minty, chocolatey character, this is nearly an outstanding Pinot Noir— a rarity from Australia. Drink it over the next 3–4 years.

Last, the 1990 Mountadam Chardonnay/Pinot Noir Sparkling Wine is a bubbly rosé with an orange/salmon color, elegant, pinpoint, uniformly sized bubbles, good effervescence, terrific fruit, elegant, medium-bodied, dry flavors, and a crisp finish. It provides more flavor depth than most California sparkling wines, but not the complexity of great French Champagne.

WYNNS (COONAWARRA)

1997 Chardonnay	B	86
1996 Shiraz	B	85

Two fine values, Wynns's 1997 Chardonnay exhibits a creamy, lemony nose with scents of subtle oak and spice. Medium bodied, with good acidity, excellent purity, and a steely richness, this offering can be drunk over the next several years. The dark plum-colored 1996 Shiraz is an excellent bargain in the chunky red wine category. It offers attractive, moderately intense, smoky, blackberry, and earthy aromas. Although there is a bit too much acidity, it is difficult to suppress Shiraz's attractive red and black fruits, spice, and peppery characteristics. Drink it over the next 2–3 years.

NEW ZEALAND

An enormous amount of hype is associated with New Zealand's wines. The world's media appears to be enamored with this nation and its vinous products. Having tasted countless numbers, I can say that the following is clear. New Zealand has a number of dedicated producers who craft excellent Sauvignon Blancs and Chardonnays and a small handful who have made reds capable of competing on the world stage. However, the majority of this nation's wines are overly processed and too expensive for the quality they deliver.

The Sauvignon Blancs elicit the most excitement. They can be surprisingly rich, varying from mildly herbaceous to overwhelmingly green. What makes them stand out is that the well-integrated acidity tastes natural, and the best examples possess a stunning midpalate and length. All you have to do is taste the likes of a Sauvignon Blanc from Cloudy Bay, Goldwater, Grove Mill, Kumeu River, Montana, Morton Estate, Selaks, and Stoneleigh to see that special wines can emerge from this varietal. However, once you go past these wineries, the Sauvignons are often vegetal and washed out.

As for Chardonnay, New Zealanders have learned to handle the cool-climate acidity by putting their wines through full malolactic fermentation and giving them less contact and plenty of exposure to French oak. However, when yields are not kept low, the Chardonnays taste like a two-by-four, with enough oak to turn off a wine-loving lumberjack. The finest Chardonnays, showing balance between oak and fruit, have emerged from Babich's Irongate, Cloudy Bay, Corbins, Delegats, Kumeu River, Matua Valley, Morton Estate's Hawke's Bay, Selaks, Te Mata, Vidal Reserve, and the Villa Maria (*barrique*-fermented).

New Zealand's attempts with Cabernet Sauvignon, Merlot, and Pinot Noir continue to be annoyingly herbaceous and/or atrociously vegetal, with few exceptions. It is appalling that anyone can find something to praise in these offerings. If you like wines that taste like liquefied asparagus made by the Jolly Green Giant, you will find some merit in them. Although recent vintages suggest New Zealand's wineries are coming closer to purging some of this grotesque character, these wines still possess a nasty vegetal streak.

That being said, however, wines recently tasted from Felton Road (Pinot Noirs), Goldwater (Cabernet/Merlot blends), Stonyridge (Cabernet), and Te Mata (Cabernet and Merlot) have demonstrated that New Zealand has potential as a red wine producer—if it lowers yields, goes for optimal ripeness, and does not overprocess. For the other red wines, there are only two words to keep fixed in your mind—caveat emptor!

9. ARGENTINA AND CHILE

ARGENTINA

RATING ARGENTINA'S BEST PRODUCERS

* * * * * (OUTSTANDING)

Catena Cabernet Sauvignon Agrelo
  Vineyard
Catena Malbec Lunlunta Vineyard

Bodega Weinert Cabernet Sauvignon
Bodega Weinert Cavas de Weinert
Bodega Weinert Malbec

* * * * (EXCELLENT)

Altos de Madrano Malbec
Luigi Bosca Malbec
Caballero de la Cepa Cabernet Sauvignon
Catena Chardonnay Agrelo Vineyard
Arnaldo B. Etchart Cafayete
Arnaldo B. Etchart Cabernet Sauvignon
  (since 1991)
Arnaldo B. Etchart Malbec (since 1991)
Nicolas Fazio Malbec
Fabre Montmayou Grand Vin
Navarro Correas Coleccion Privada
  Cabernet Sauvignon

Navarro Correas Malbec
Nieto y Sentiner Cadus Malbec
Norton Privada
San Telmo Malbec
Pascual Toso Cabernet Sauvignon
Trapiche Fond de Cave Cabernet
  Sauvignon
Trapiche Iscay (Merlot/Malbec blend)
Bodega Weinert Carrascal
Bodega Weinert Merlot

* * * (GOOD)

Bianchi Cabernet Sauvignon Particular
Bianchi Chenin Blanc (a white wine)
Bianchi Malbec
Humberto Canale Cabernet Sauvignon
  Reserva
Humberto Canale Merlot Reserva
Etchart Torrontes (a white wine)
Flichman Cabernet Sauvignon
Nicolas Fazio Cabernet Sauvignon

Château Mendoza Cabernet Sauvignon
Château Mendoza Merlot
Mendoza Peaks Cabernet Sauvignon
San Telmo Cuesta del Madero (Cabernet
  Sauvignon/Malbec)
Trapiche Cabernet Sauvignon Oak Cask
Trapiche Merlot Médalla
Leon Unzue Malbec

* * (AVERAGE)

Andean Cabernet Sauvignon
Clos du Moulin Cabernet Sauvignon

Goyenechea (Aberdeen Angus) Cabernet
Sauvignon
Comte de Valmont Cabernet Sauvignon

CHILE

RATING CHILE'S BEST PRODUCERS

* * * * * (OUTSTANDING)

Almaviva (a Cabernet-based wine made by
the partnership of Mouton-Rothschild
and Concho y Toro)
Casa Lapostolle Cuvée Alexandre

Casa Lapostolle Merlot Clos Apalta
Sena (a Cabernet-based wine made by the
partnership of Robert Mondavi and Vina
Errazuriz)

* * * * (EXCELLENT)

Casa Lapostolle Cabernet Sauvignon Cuvée
Alexandre
Casa Lapostolle Chardonnay Cuvée
Alexandre
Casa Lapostolle Sauvignon Blanc
Concho y Toro Cabernet Sauvignon Don
Melchor Private Reserve
Concho y Toro Cabernet Sauvignon
Marques de Casa Concho

Cousino Macul Cabernet/Merlot Finis
Terrae
Cousino Macul Cabernet Sauvignon
Antiguas Reserva
Bruno Paul
Santa Rita Cabernet Sauvignon Casa Real
Los Vascos Cabernet Sauvignon Reserva

* * * (GOOD)

Concho y Toro Cabernet Sauvignon
Castillero del Diablo
Concho y Toro Chardonnay Castillero del
Diablo
Cousino Macul Cabernet Sauvignon

Errazuriz Panquehue Cabernet Sauvignon
Don Maximiano
Santa Monica Cabernet Sauvignon
Los Vascos Cabernet Sauvignon
Los Vascos Sauvignon Blanc

* * (AVERAGE)

Caliterra Cabernet Sauvignon
Caliterra Chardonnay
Canepa Sauvignon Blanc
Carta Vieja (all cuvées)
Cousino Macul Chardonnay
Cousino Macul Sauvignon Blanc
Sage Estate (all cuvées)
Saint Morillon Cabernet Sauvignon
Santa Carolina Cabernet Sauvignon
Santa Carolina Chardonnay
Santa Carolina Merlot
Santa Rita Cabernet Sauvignon 120 Estate

Santa Rita Cabernet Sauvignon Medalla
Real
Santa Rita Sauvignon Blanc 120 Estate
Tolva Cabernet Sauvignon
Tolva Sauvignon Blanc
Miguel Torres (all cuvées)
Traverso Cabernet Sauvignon
Traverso Merlot
Undurraga Cabernet Sauvignon
Undurraga Sauvignon Blanc
Valdivieso Sparkling N.V. Brut

INDEX